EDUCATIONAL PSYCHOLOGY

TWELFTH EDITION

ANITA WOOLFOLK

THE OHIO STATE UNIVERSITY

Boston Columbus Indianapolis New York San Francisco Upper Saddle River
Amsterdam Cape Town Dubai London Madrid Milan Munich Paris Montreal Toronto
Delhi Mexico City Sao Paulo Sydney Hong Kong Seoul Singapore Taipei Tokyo

Vice President and Editorial Director:
  Jeffery W. Johnston
Vice President and Publisher: Kevin Davis
Development Editor: Alicia Reilly
Editorial Assistant: Lauren Carlson
Vice President, Director of Marketing:
  Margaret Waples
Marketing Manager: Joanna Sabella
Senior Managing Editor: Pamela D. Bennett
Senior Project Manager: Mary M. Irvin
Senior Operations Supervisor: Matt Ottenweller
Senior Art Director: Diane Lorenzo

Text Designer: Candace Rowley
Cover Designer: Candace Rowley
Cover Art: Corbis Images
Photo Coordinator: Carol Sykes
Permissions Administrator: Rebecca Savage
Media Producer: Autumn Benson
Media Project Manager: Becky Norsic
Full-Service Project Management: Kathy Smith
Composition: Element LLC
Printer/Binder: Courier/Kendallville
Cover Printer: Lehigh-Phoenix Color Corp.
Text Font: Garamond Book

Credits and acknowledgments for materials borrowed from other sources and reproduced, with permission, in this textbook appear on appropriate page within text (or on the photo credits page).

Every effort has been made to provide accurate and current Internet information in this book. However, the Internet and information posted on it are constantly changing, so it is inevitable that some of the Internet addresses listed in this textbook will change.

Library of Congress Cataloging-in-Publication Data

Hoy, Anita Woolfolk
  Educational psychology / Anita Woolfolk.—12th ed.
    p. cm.
  Includes bibliographical references and index.
  ISBN 978-0-13-261316-3
  1. Educational psychology—Textbooks. I. Title.
  LB1051.W74 2013
                        370.15—dc23

2011045325

10 9 8 7 6 5 4 3 2 1

PEARSON

ISBN-10:   0-13-261316-6
ISBN-13: 978-0-13-261316-3

To William James, who wisely said in *Talks to Teachers* (1899),

"Psychology is a science, and teaching is an art;
and sciences never generate arts directly out
of themselves. An intermediary inventive mind must
make the application, by using its originality."

and also

To all the inventive minds reading this book
whose originality will prove James right.

ABOUT THE AUTHOR

So you will know your author a bit better, here is some information.

Anita Woolfolk Hoy was born in Fort Worth, Texas, where her mother taught child development at TCU and her father was an early worker in the computer industry. She is a Texas Longhorn—all her degrees are from the University of Texas, Austin, the last one a Ph.D. After graduating, she was a psychologist working with children in elementary and secondary schools in 15 counties of central Texas. She began her career in higher education as a professor of educational psychology at Rutgers University, and then moved to The Ohio State University in 1994. Anita's research focuses on motivation and cognition, specifically students' and teachers' sense of efficacy and teachers' beliefs about education. She is the editor of *Theory Into Practice,* a journal that brings the best ideas from research to practicing educators. With students and colleagues, she has published over 80 books, book chapters, and research articles. Anita has served as Vice-President for Division K (Teaching & Teacher Education) of the American Educational Research Association and President of Division 15 (Educational Psychology) of the American Psychological Association. Just before completing this 12th edition of *Educational Psychology,* she collaborated with Nancy Perry, University of British Columbia, to write the first edition of *Child Development* (Pearson, 2012), a book for all those who work with and love children. Her next project is the 4th edition of *Instructional Leadership: A Research-Based Guide to Learning in School* (Pearson), written with her husband, Wayne K. Hoy, the Novice Fawcett Chair of Educational Administration at The Ohio State University.

PREFACE

Many of you reading this book are enrolled in an educational psychology course as part of your professional preparation for teaching, counseling, speech therapy, nursing, or psychology. The material in this text should be of interest to everyone who is concerned about education and learning, from the nursery school volunteer to the instructor in a community program for adults with disabilities. No background in psychology or education is necessary to understand this material. It is as free of jargon and technical language as possible, and many people have worked to make this edition clear, relevant, and interesting.

Since the first edition of *Educational Psychology* appeared, there have been many exciting developments in the field. The Twelfth Edition continues to emphasize the educational implications and applications of research on child development, cognitive science, learning, motivation, teaching, and assessment. Theory and practice are not separated in the text, but are considered together. The book is written to show how information and ideas drawn from research in educational psychology can be applied to solve the everyday problems of teaching. To help you explore the connections between research and practice, you will find in these pages a wealth of examples, lesson segments, case studies, guidelines, and even practical tips from experienced teachers. As you read this book, I believe you will see the immense value and usefulness of educational psychology. The field offers unique and crucial knowledge to any who dare to teach and to all who love to learn.

NEW CONTENT IN THE TWELFTH EDITION

Across the book, there is increased coverage of a number of important topics. Some of these include:

- Increased coverage of the **brain, neuroscience, and teaching** emphasized in Chapter 2 and also integrated into several other chapters.
- Increased coverage of **the impact of technology on the lives of students and teachers today**.
- Increased emphasis on **diversity in today's classrooms** (see Chapters 1–6). Portraits of students in educational settings make diversity real and human for readers.
- An emphasis on **integrating across theories** to understand teaching and learning. Examples include:
  Chapter 2: Three questions across the theories.
  Chapter 6: Creating culturally compatible classrooms.
  Chapter 11: Looking across theories of learning.
  Chapter 12: Key concepts in motivation.

Key content changes in each chapter include:

- Chapter 1: Three **new themes** for the text: a discussion of the **context of teaching today**, a focus on **teachers' sense of efficacy**, and an explanation of **differentiated instruction**. My goal is that this text will provide the knowledge and skills that will enable you to build a solid foundation for an authentic sense of efficacy teaching in every context and for every student. Also, there is new information on the reauthorization efforts for the ***Elementary and Secondary Education Act*** and on a model that links personal and contextual factors in school to students' learning.
- Chapter 2: New information on the **brain and cognitive development**.

- Chapter 3: New sections on how **digital media** is affecting the lives and identities of students today.
- Chapter 4: New sections on **biases in the application of labels, multiple intelligences, learning styles cautions, ADHD,** and **student drug use**.
- Chapter 5: NEW CHAPTER *Language Development, Language Diversity, and Immigrant Education*, including discussions of diversity in language development and bilingualism, dialects in the classroom, teaching immigrant students, and the special challenges in teaching English Language Learners who have learning disabilities or special gifts.
- Chapter 6: Expanded coverage of **opportunity gaps** in education and a new section on **gender development** and **gender differences.**
- Chapter 7: New information about **behavioral interventions for students with autism** and **Bandura's challenge to behaviorism**.
- Chapter 8: New coverage of **cognitive science,** view of learning and memory, attention and multitasking, **cognitive load** and working memory, **imagery,** and **concept formation**.
- Chapter 9: New sections on **metacognition** and **learning strategies, cultural differences** in problem solving and in creativity, and **argumentation**.
- Chapter 10: *The Learning Sciences and Constructivism:* New material on **embodied cognition** and learning in a **digital world**.
- Chapter 11: *Social Cognitive Views of Learning and Motivation:* Significantly expanded coverage of observational learning and developing self-regulation.
- Chapter 12: Expanded section on **self-determination theory** and **goal theory**.
- Chapter 13: New section on **teaching self-management, creating caring communities,** and **cyber-bullying**.
- Chapter 14: New section on **teacher knowledge,** recent **research on teaching, adaptive** and **differentiated teaching, mentoring,** and **technology**.
- Chapter 15: Updates on **NCLB** and more on **authentic** assessment.

A CRYSTAL CLEAR PICTURE OF THE FIELD AND WHERE IT IS HEADED

The Twelfth Edition maintains the lucid writing style for which the book is renowned. The text provides accurate, up-to-date coverage of the foundational areas within educational psychology: learning, development, motivation, teaching, and assessment, combined with intelligent examination of emerging trends in the field and society that affect student learning, such as student diversity, inclusion of students with special learning needs, education and neuroscience, and technology.

Important New Content in Learning and Development

Some of the most significant changes in the new edition involve a reorganization and expansion of the learning and development content.

- The new edition includes expanded coverage of Cognitive Science, Self-Regulated Learning, and Argumentation as well as a new chapter devoted to *Language Development, Language Diversity, and Immigrant Education* (Chapter 5).
- Significantly increased coverage of the brain and neuroscience in Chapter 2 and integrated into five chapters—Chapters 3, 6, 7, 8, and 12.
- Increased coverage of technology can be found in Chapters 3, 4, 10, and 13.

TEXT FEATURES

With an unswerving emphasis on educational psychology's practical relevance for teachers and students in classrooms, the text is replete with current issues and debates, examples, lesson segments, case studies, and practical ideas from experienced teachers.

"Point/Counterpoint" sections in each chapter present two perspectives on a controversial question related to the field; topics include debates on the kinds of research that should guide education (p. 19), brain-based education (p. 40), the self-esteem movement (p. 98), pills or skills for students with ADHD (p. 141), the best way to teach English language learners (p. 190), tracking (p. 215), using rewards to encourage student learning (p. 274), what's wrong with memorization (p. 310), teaching critical thinking and problem solving (p. 345), problem-based education (p. 370), teacher efficacy (p. 409), the value of trying to make learning entertaining (p. 450), zero tolerance (p. 493), homework (p. 525), and holding children back (p. 569).

"Guidelines" appear throughout each chapter, providing concrete applications of theories or principles discussed.

"Guidelines/Family and Community Partnerships" sections offer specific guidelines for involving families—especially relevant now, when demand for parental involvement is at an all-time high—in the various aspects of children's learning.

---

454 CHAPTER TWELVE

POINT/COUNTERPOINT Does Making Learning Fun Make for Good Learning?

WHEN MANY BEGINNING teachers are asked about how to motivate students, they often mention making learning fun. But is it necessary for learning to be fun?

POINT

▶ **Teachers should make learning fun.** When I searched "making learning fun" on Google.com, I found 10 pages of resources and references. Clearly, there is interest in making learning fun. Research shows that passages in texts that are more interesting are remembered better (Schunk, Pintrich, & Meece, 2008). For example, students who read books that interested them spent more time reading, read more words in the books, and felt more positively about reading (Guthrie & Alao, 1997). Games and simulations can make learning more fun, too.

For example, when my daughter was in the 8th grade, all the students in her grade spent three days playing a game her teachers had designed called ULTRA. Students were divided into groups and formed their own "countries." Each country had to choose a name, symbol, national flower, and bird. They wrote and sang a national anthem and elected government officials. The teachers allocated different resources to the countries. To get all the materials needed for the completion of assigned projects, the countries had to establish trade with one another. There was a monetary system and a stock market. Students had to work with their fellow citizens to complete cooperative learning assignments. Some countries "cheated" in their trades with other nations, and this allowed debate about international relations, trust, and war. Liz says she had fun—but she also learned how to work in a group without the teacher's supervision and gained a deeper understanding of world economics and international conflicts.

A highly motivating 3rd grade teacher in another study had her class set up a post office for the whole school. Each classroom in the school had an address and zip code. Students had jobs in the post office, and everyone in the school used the post office to deliver letters to students and teachers. Students designed their own stamps and set postal rates. The teacher said that the system "improves their creative writing without them knowing it" (Dolezal, Welsh, Pressley, & Vincent, 2003, p. 254).

COUNTERPOINT

▶ **Fun can get in the way of learning.** As far back as the early 1900s, educators warned about the dangers of focusing on fun in learning. None other than John Dewey, who wrote extensively about the role of interest in learning, cautioned that you can't make boring lessons interesting by mixing in fun like you can make bad chili good by adding some spicy hot sauce. Dewey wrote, "When things have to be made interesting, it is because interest itself is wanting. Moreover, the phrase itself is a misnomer. The thing, the object, is no more interesting than it was before" (Dewey, 1913, pp. 11–12).

There is a good deal of research now indicating that adding interest by incorporating fascinating but irrelevant details actually gets in the way of learning the important information. These "seductive details," as they have been called, divert the readers' attention from the less interesting main ideas (Harp & Mayer, 1998). For example, students who read biographies of historical figures remembered more very interesting—but unimportant—information compared to interesting main ideas (Wade, Schraw, Buxton, & Hayes, 1993).

Shannon Harp and Richard Mayer (1998) found similar results with high school science texts. These texts added emotional interest and seductive details about swimmers and golfers who are injured by lightning to a lesson on the process of lightning. They concluded that, "in the case of emotional interest versus cognitive interest, the verdict is clear. Adjuncts aimed at increasing emotional interest failed to improve understanding of scientific explanations" (p. 100). The seductive details may have disrupted students' attempts to follow the logic of the explanations and thus interfered with their comprehending the text. Harp and Mayer conclude that "the best way to help students enjoy a passage is to help them understand it" (p. 100).

LANGUAGE DEVELOPMENT, LANGUAGE DIVERSITY, AND IMMIGRANT EDUCATION **195**

GUIDELINES

Providing Emotional Support and Increasing Self-Esteem for English Language Learners

Create learning activities that promote success in reading and writing.
Examples
1. Have weekly individual conferences with younger students and record their retelling of a story. Let students edit and revise the dictation and read it to a partner.
2. Do interactive journals with older students—collect each week and write back.

Make sure students have plenty of time to practice and get careful, targeted corrections.
Examples
1. Point out privately what is correct, almost correct, and wrong in written work.
2. Be sensitive about public oral corrections and build on what is correct, but do not accept clearly incorrect answers.

Connect teaching to relevant knowledge from students' lives.
Examples
1. Ask students to survey family members about favorite films—use film characters to discuss elements of literature—plot, point of view, etc.
2. Have students create construction firms and plan projects to learn math concepts.

Actively involve learners.
Examples
1. Use timelines in history compared to personal timelines based on family history.
2. Do projects in science based on animals or farming for rural students.

Use different grouping strategies.
Examples
1. Try pairs for writing stories and practicing oral presentations.
2. Create small teams to research recent immigrant groups' culture and language.

Provide native language support.
Examples
1. Learn and use as much of the students' language as possible—if they can learn, so can you.
2. Find Internet translation sources and local native speaking volunteers.
3. Bring native language magazines and books into the classroom.

Involve family and community members.
Examples
1. Bring in storytellers, local business owners, artists, craftspeople.
2. Create a Welcome Center for your class.

Hold high expectations for all students, and communicate these expectations clearly.
Examples
1. Keep scrapbooks of previous students who have gone on to careers or college.
2. Don't accept mediocre work.
3. Be a model of respect for diversity and an enemy of bigotry.

Source: Adapted from Echevarria, J., & Graves, A. (2011). Sheltered content instruction: Teaching English learners with diverse abilities (4th ed.). Columbus, OH: Pearson, pp. 67–77.

LANGUAGE DEVELOPMENT, LANGUAGE DIVERSITY, AND IMMIGRANT EDUCATION **197**

GUIDELINES —— FAMILY AND COMMUNITY PARTNERSHIPS ——

Welcoming All Families

Make sure communication with families is understandable.
Examples
1. Use the families' home languages wherever possible.
2. Use oral forms of communication—phone calls or home visits—whenever possible.

Balance positive and negative messages.
Examples
1. Send home notes or descriptions about their child's accomplishments or acts of kindness.
2. Explain disciplinary actions as ways of helping children succeed.

Establish systems for welcoming new families.
Examples
1. Assign more experienced "buddy" parents to communicate with new families.
2. Connect with multilingual media in your community to make announcements about school.

Make sure messages get through.
Examples
1. Establish telephone trees or texting networks.
2. Set the expectation that there will be a weekly note sent home so parents can ask their children about it.
3. Establish a class newsletter or Web site and incorporate multiple languages.

WHAT WOULD YOU DO?

TEACHERS' CASEBOOK: Reaching and Teaching Every Student

You have started a new job in a high school in your hometown. When you were in school, the students were fairly homogeneous—White, working to middle class, and English speaking. There was a "special education" class for students who had serious learning or developmental problems. But in the classes you are teaching, you find a wide range of reading levels, family incomes, and learning problems. Two of your students are virtually ready for college, whereas several others can barely read the texts—and their writing is impossible to decipher. Reading English texts is a challenge for some of your ELL students, although they seem to speak English with little trouble.

CRITICAL THINKING

- How would you differentiate instruction for these very dissimilar students?
- Do different philosophies of teaching provide different answers to this question?
- How will you grade work if you have successfully differentiated instruction?

"Teachers' Casebook" sections present students with realistic classroom scenarios at the beginning of each chapter and ask "What Would You Do?"—giving students the opportunity to apply all the important topics of the chapter to these scenarios via application questions. Students may then compare their responses to those of veteran teachers appearing at the end of each chapter.

Reaching Every Student: Severe Behavior Problems

Students with severe behavior problems provide some of the most difficult challenges for teachers. Two studies show how applied behavioral principles can be useful in helping these students.

Lea Theodore and her colleagues (2001) worked with the teacher of five adolescent males who were diagnosed as having severe emotional disorders. A short list of clear rules was established (e.g., use no obscene words, comply with the teacher's requests within five seconds, make no verbal putdowns). The rules were written on index cards taped to each student's desk. The teacher had a checklist on his desk with each student's name to note any rule breaking. This checklist was easily observable, so students could monitor their own and each other's performance. At the end of the 45-minute period, a student chose a "criterion" from a jar. The possible criteria were: performance of the whole group, student with the highest score, student with the lowest score, the average of all students, or a random single student. If the student or students selected to be the criterion had five checks or fewer for rule-breaking, then the whole class got a reward, also chosen randomly from a jar. The possible rewards were things like a power drink, a bag of chips, a candy bar, or a late-to-class pass. An ABAB design was used—baseline, two-week intervention, two-week withdrawal of intervention, and two-week return to group consequences. All students showed clear improvement in following the rules when the reward system was in place. Students liked the approach and the teacher found it easy to implement.

"Reaching Every Student" sections present ideas for assessing, teaching, and motivating ALL of the students in today's inclusive classrooms.

Lessons for Teachers: Strategies to Encourage Motivation

Until four basic conditions are met for every student and in every classroom, no motivational strategies will succeed. First, the classroom must be relatively organized and free from constant interruptions and disruptions. (Chapter 13 will give you the information you need to make sure this requirement is met.) Second, the teacher must be a patient, supportive person who never embarrasses the students because they made mistakes. Everyone in the class should view mistakes as opportunities for learning (Clifford, 1990, 1991). Third, the work must be challenging, but reasonable. If work is too easy or too difficult, students will have little motivation to learn. They will focus on finishing, not on learning. Finally, the learning tasks must be authentic. And as we have seen, what makes a task authentic is influenced by the students' culture (Bergin, 1999; Brophy & Kher, 1986; Stipek, 1993).

Once these four basic conditions are met, the influences on students' motivation to learn in a particular situation can be summarized in four questions: Can I succeed at this task? Do I want to succeed? What do I need to do to succeed? Do I belong? (Committee on Increasing High School Students' Engagement and Motivation to Learn, 2004; Eccles & Wigfield, 1985). We want students to have confidence in their ability so they will approach learning with energy and enthusiasm. We want them to see the value of the tasks involved and work to learn, not just try to get the grade or get finished. We want students to believe that success will come when they apply good learning strategies instead of believing that their only option is to use self-defeating, failure-avoiding, face-saving strategies. When things get difficult, we want students to stay focused on the task, and not get so worried about failure that they "freeze." And we want students to feel as though they belong in school—that their teachers and classmates care about them and can be trusted.

"Lessons for Teachers" are succinct and usable principles for teaching based on the research.

▼ CONNECT AND EXTEND TO LICENSURE

MULTIPLE-CHOICE QUESTIONS

1. Miss Johnson would like for her students to be motivated to do their work without bribing them with treats or promises of extra recess time. Which one of the following is the type of motivation should she encourage in her students?
   A. Extrinsic
   B. Intrinsic
   C. Locus of control
   D. Relatedness
   Hint: Intrinsic and Extrinsic Motivation
   Feedback: Intrinsic motivation is the natural human tendency to seek out and conquer challenges as we pursue personal interests and exercise our capabilities. When we are intrinsically motivated, we do not need incentives or punishments, because the activity itself is satisfying and rewarding (Anderman & Anderman, 2010; Deci & Ryan, 2002; Reiss, 2004).

4. Which of the following is true regarding extrinsic motivation?
   A. Extrinsic motivation should be avoided at all costs because it undermines a student's intrinsic desire.
   B. Extrinsic motivation is not associated with grades and incentives.
   C. Extrinsic motivation may be necessary to initially encourage students to engage in certain activities.
   D. Extrinsic motivation is more desirable than intrinsic motivation in the classroom as educators have increased control.
   Hint: Intrinsic and Extrinsic Motivation
   Feedback: To initially interest students in a topic, educators may use extrinsic measures such as quizzes. The ultimate goal, however, is for students to eventually realize the intrinsic satisfaction they acquire from engaging in certain activities or studying particular topics.

"Connect and Extend to Licensure" exercises appear at the end of every chapter, consisting of case studies with constructed-response questions, and multiple-choice questions, all mimicking the types of questions found on licensure exams such as the Praxis tests published by the Educational Testing Service (ETS).

SUPPLEMENTS

This Twelfth Edition of *Educational Psychology* provides a comprehensive and integrated collection of supplements to assist students and professors alike in maximizing learning and instruction. Together, these materials immerse students in the content of the text, allowing them and their instructors to benefit from a deeper and more meaningful learning experience. All of the instructor supplements are available at the Instructor Resource Center. To access the Instructor's Resource Manual, the PowerPoint lecture presentation, and the Assessment Package, go to the Instructor Resource Center at www.pearsonhighered.com and click on the "Educators" link. Here you will be able to login or complete a one-time registration for a user name and password.

Innovative Online Course—MyEducationLab

MyEducationLab™ THE POWER OF CLASSROOM PRACTICE In *Preparing Teachers for a Changing World,* Linda Darling-Hammond and her colleagues point out that grounding teacher education in real classrooms—among real teachers and students and among actual examples of students' and teachers' work—is an important, and perhaps even an essential, part of training teachers for the complexities of teaching in today's classrooms. MyEducationLab is an online learning solution that provides contextualized interactive exercises, simulations, and other resources designed to help you develop the knowledge and skills that teachers need. All of the activities and exercises in MyEducationLab are built around essential learning outcomes for teachers and are mapped to professional teaching standards. Utilizing classroom video, authentic student and teacher artifacts, case studies, and other resources and assessments, the scaffolded learning experiences in MyEducationLab offer you a unique and valuable education tool.

On the MyEducationLab for this course you will find the following features and resources.

STUDY PLAN AND BOOK RESOURCES SPECIFIC TO YOUR TEXT A MyEducationLab Study Plan provides students with the opportunity to take a self-assessment after reading each chapter of the text. Self-assessment questions are tied to learning outcomes, so the students are assessed on their knowledge and comprehension of all the concepts presented in each chapter. The quiz results automatically identify areas of the chapter that still need some additional study time. Students are then presented with Review, Practice, and Enrichment exercises to help ensure learning and to deepen understanding of chapter concepts—when just re-reading and studying chapter content is not enough. Flashcards for each chapter help students master definitions of key terms within each chapter. The study plan is designed to help each student perform well on exams and to promote deep understanding of chapter content.

In addition to the study plan, MyEducationLab resources specific to this book include:

- *AnitaTalks Podcasts:* Direct links to relevant selections from *Anita Talks about Teaching,* a selection of podcasts in which Dr. Woolfolk discusses how chapters of this text relate to the profession of teaching.
- *Connect and Extend to Licensure* exercises allow students to complete the licensure-style questions and activities shown at the end of each chapter of this text while receiving hints that help scaffold their correct responses, as well as feedback with which they can compare their responses.

CONNECTION TO NATIONAL STANDARDS Now it is easier than ever to see how coursework is connected to national standards. Each topic, activity and exercise on MyEducationLab lists intended learning outcomes connected to the appropriate national standards.

ASSIGNMENTS AND ACTIVITIES   Designed to enhance your understanding of concepts covered in class, these assignable exercises show concepts in action (through videos, cases, and/or student and teacher artifacts). They help you deepen content knowledge and synthesize and apply concepts and strategies you read about in the book. (Correct answers for these assignments are available to the instructor only.)

BUILDING TEACHING SKILLS AND DISPOSITIONS   These unique learning units help users practice and strengthen skills that are essential to effective teaching. After presenting the steps involved in a core teaching process, you are given an opportunity to practice applying this skill via videos, student and teacher artifacts, and/or case studies of authentic classrooms. Providing multiple opportunities to practice a single teaching concept, each activity encourages a deeper understanding and application of concepts, as well as the use of critical thinking skills. Feedback for the final quizzes is available to the instructor only.

IRIS CENTER RESOURCES   The IRIS Center at Vanderbilt University (http://iris. peabody.vanderbilt.edu), funded by the U.S. Department of Education's Office of Special Education Programs (OSEP), develops training enhancement materials for preservice and practicing teachers. The Center works with experts from across the country to create challenge-based interactive modules, case study units, and podcasts that provide research-validated information about working with students in inclusive settings. In your MyEducationLab course we have integrated this content where appropriate.

SIMULATIONS IN CLASSROOM MANAGEMENT   One of the most difficult challenges facing teachers today is how to balance classroom instruction with classroom management. These interactive cases focus on the classroom management issues teachers most frequently encounter on a daily basis. Each simulation presents a challenge scenario at the beginning and then offers a series of choices to solve each challenge. Along the way students receive mentor feedback on their choices and have the opportunity to make better choices if necessary. Upon exiting each simulation, you will have a clear understanding of how to address these common classroom management issues and will be better equipped to handle them in the classroom.

TEACHER TALK   This feature emphasizes the power of teaching through videos of master teachers, who each tell their own compelling stories of why they teach. These videos help you see the bigger picture and consider why the concepts and principles you are learning are important to your career as a teacher. Each of these featured teachers has been awarded the Council of Chief State School Officers Teachers of the Year award, the oldest and most prestigious award for teachers.

LESSON PLAN BUILDER   The **Lesson Plan Builder** is an effective and easy-to-use tool that you can use to create, update, and share quality lesson plans. The software also makes it easy to integrate state content standards into any lesson plan.

CERTIFICATION AND LICENSURE   The Certification and Licensure section is designed to help you pass your licensure exam by giving you access to state test requirements, overviews of what tests cover, and sample test items.
    The Certification and Licensure section includes the following:

- **State Certification Test Requirements:** Here, you can click on a state and will then be taken to a list of state certification tests.
- You can click on the **Licensure Exams** you need to take to find:
  - Basic information about each test
  - Descriptions of what is covered on each test
  - Sample test questions with explanations of correct answers

- **National Evaluation Series**™ by Pearson: Here, students can see the tests in the NES, learn what is covered on each exam, and access sample test items with descriptions and rationales of correct answers. You can also purchase interactive online tutorials developed by Pearson Evaluation Systems and the Pearson Teacher Education and Development group.
- **ETS Online Praxis Tutorials:** Here you can purchase interactive online tutorials developed by ETS and by the Pearson Teacher Education and Development group. Tutorials are available for the Praxis I exams and for select Praxis II exams.

Visit www.myeducationlab.com for a demonstration of this exciting new online teaching resource.

ONLINE INSTRUCTOR'S RESOURCE MANUAL The Online Instructor's Resource Manual synthesizes all of the resources available for each chapter and sifts through the materials to match the delivery method (e.g., semester, quarter) and areas of emphasis for the course. These materials can be used for traditional courses as well as online or online-supported courses. The Instructor's Resource Manual is available for download at www.pearsonhighered.com.

ONLINE TEST BANK Students learn better when they are held accountable for what they have learned. That is why we have developed a bank of hundreds of challenging questions in multiple-choice, fill-in-the-blanks, true/false, short-answer, and case study formats, along with detailed answer keys. The Test Bank is available online at www.pearsonhighered.com.

PEARSON MYTEST This is a powerful assessment generation program that helps instructors easily create and print quizzes and exams. Questions and tests are authored online, allowing ultimate flexibility and the ability to efficiently create and print assessments any time, anywhere! Instructors can access Pearson MyTest and their test bank files by going to www.pearsonmytest.com to log in, register, or request access. Features of Pearson MyTest include:

Premium assessment content

- Draw from a rich library of assessments that complement your Pearson textbook and your course's learning objectives.
- Edit questions or tests to fit your specific teaching needs.

Instructor-friendly resources

- Easily create and store your own questions, including images, diagrams, and charts using simple drag-and-drop and Word-like controls.
- Use additional information provided by Pearson, such as the question's difficulty level or learning objective, to help you quickly build your test.

Time-saving enhancements

- Add headers or footers and easily scramble questions and answer choices—all from one simple toolbar.
- Quickly create multiple versions of your test or answer key, and when ready, simply save to MS-Word or PDF format and print!
- Export your exams for import to Blackboard 6.0, CE (WebCT), or Vista (WebCT)!

ONLINE POWERPOINT SLIDES These visual aids display, summarize, and help explain core information presented in each chapter. They are available for download at www.pearsonhighered.com. All PowerPoint slides have been updated for consistency and to reflect current content in this new edition.

ACKNOWLEDGMENTS

During the years I have worked on this book, from initial draft to this most recent revision, many people have supported the project. Without their help, this text simply could not have been written.

Many educators contributed to this and previous editions. Carol Weinstein wrote the section in Chapter 13 on spaces for learning. Nancy Perry (University of British Columbia) and Philip Winne (Simon Frasier University) wrote sections of Chapter 11 on self-regulation. Brad Henry (The Ohio State University) crafted sections on technology in two chapters and also read every chapter with the digital world in mind to suggest updates. Michael Yough (Purdue University) looked over several chapters including the new one on Language Development, Language Learning, and Immigrant Education. That chapter was also improved by suggestions from Alan Hirvela, the Ohio State University. Gregg Schraw, the University of Nevada, Las Vegas, provided invaluable guidance for the chapters on cognitive learning. Gypsy M. Denzine (Northern Arizona University) is responsible for the *Test Bank*. The portraits of students in Chapters 1 and 6 were provided by Nancy Knapp (University of Georgia). The *Instructor's Resource Manual* and *PowerPoint™ Presentations* were created by Michael Yough (Purdue University) and Kate Kovach (The Ohio State University), future stars in our field.

As I made decisions about how to revise this edition, I benefited from the ideas of colleagues around the country who took the time to complete surveys, answer my questions, and review chapters.

For their revision reviews, thanks to: Frank D. Adams, Wayne State College; Karen J. Dreyer, University of Pittsburgh; Aleza Greene, University of Arkansas; Martin H. Jones, University of Memphis; Penny McGlawn, Harding University; Deborah Norland, Luther College; Susan Parault, St. Cloud State University; Joseph Polvere, Montclair State University; Anuradhaa Shastri, SUNY College of Oneonta; A. Sean Taylor, Des Moines Area Community College; Fredrick B. Van Sant, Ferris State University; Diane Ward, Roane State Community College.

Many classroom teachers across the country and around the world contributed their experience, creativity, and expertise to the *Teachers' Casebook*. I have thoroughly enjoyed my association with these master teachers, and I am grateful for the perspective they brought to the book: Madya Ayala, Campus Garza Sada, Monterrey, N. L. Mexico; Kelly McElroy Bonin, Klein Oaks High School, Spring, TX; Karen A. Boyarsky, Walter C. Black Elementary, Hightstown, NJ; Keith J. Boyle, Dunellen, NJ; Jane Campbell, Dunellen School District, Dunellen, NJ; Valerie Chilcoat, Glenmount School, Baltimore, MD; Katie Churchill, Oriole Parke Elementary School, Chicago, IL; Paula Colemere, McClintock High School, Tempe, AZ; Kelley Crockett, Meadowbrook Elementary School, Fort Worth, TX; Lou DeLauro, Dunellen School District, Dunellen, NJ; Paul Dragin, Columbus East High School, Columbus, OH; Aimee Fredette, Fisher Elementary School, Walpole, MA; Pam Gaskill, Riverside Elementary School, Dublin OH; Linda Glisson, St. James Episcopal Day School, Baton Rouge, LA; Jolita Harper, Weinland Park Elementary, Columbus, OH; Danielle Hartman, Claymont Elementary, Parkway School District, Ballwin, MO; Carla S. Higgins, Legend Elementary School, Newark, OH; Kelly L. Hoy, The Phillips Brooks School, Menlo Park, CA; Marie Hoffman Hurt, Pickerington Local Schools, Pickerington, OH; M. Denise Lutz, Grandview Heights High School, Columbus, OH; Jessica N. Mahtaban, Woodrow Wilson Middle School, Clifton, NJ; Jennifer Matz, Williams Valley Elementary School, Tower City, PA; Thomas Naismith, Slocum Independent School District, Slocum, TX; Allan Osborne, Snug Harbor Community School, Quincy, MA; Katie Piel, West Park School, Moscow, ID; Jennifer Pincoski, Lee County School District, Fort Myers, FL; Barbara Presley, C.W. Baker High School, Baldwinsville, NY; Lauren Rollins, Boulevard Elementary School, Shaker Heights, OH; Dr. Nancy Sheehan-Melzack, Snug Harbor Community School, Quincy, MA; Patricia Smith, Northside Independent School District, San Antonio, TX; Linda Sparks, John F. Kennedy Elementary School, Billerica, MA; Sara Vincent, Langley High School, McLean, VA; Jacalyn Walker, Treasure Mountain Middle School, Park City, UT; Michael Yasis, L.H. Tanglen Elementary School, Minnetonka, MN.

In a project of this size so many people make essential contributions. Becky Savage, Permissions Coordinator, worked diligently, often through weekends, to obtain permissions for the material reproduced in this text and the supplements. The text designer, Diane Lorenzo, and photo editor, Carol Sykes, made the look of this book the best yet—hard to do after 11 editions. Again, Kathy Smith, Project Manager, held all aspects of the project in her wonderfully ordered and intelligent mind. I will never forget that she found power for her computer using a neighbor's generator in the aftermaths of both the Katrina and Gustav hurricanes so that we could keep the chapters flowing. All the regular shipping services had stopped delivering but Kathy always delivers! She performed the impossible again this edition—wouldn't want to write without her! Mary Irvin, Production Editor, coordinated all aspects of the project, with amazing skill and grace. Somehow they brought sanity to what could have been chaos and fun to what might have been drudgery. Now the book is in the able hands of marketing manager Joanna Sabella and her staff. I can't wait to see what they are planning for me now! What a talented and creative group—I am honored to work with them all.

On this edition, I was again privileged to work with an outstanding editorial group. Their intelligence, creativity, sound judgment, style, and enduring commitment to quality can be seen on every page of this text. Kevin Davis, Publisher, guided the project from reviews to completion with the eye of an artist, the mind of a scholar, and the logistical capacity of high-powered computer. He proved to be an excellent collaborator with a wise grasp of the field and a sense of the future. Lauren Carlson, Editorial Assistant, kept everything running smoothly and kept my email humming. On this edition I was fortunate again to have the help of Alicia Reilly, an outstanding developmental editor with the perfect combination of vast knowledge, organizational ability, good humor, and creative thinking. Once again, she coordinated every aspect of the revision, always staying just ahead of whatever had to happen next, communicating with people around the world—remarkable! The text features, Teachers' Casebook, and excellent pedagogical supports would not exist without her tireless efforts.

Finally, I want to thank my family and friends for their kindness and support during the long days and nights that I worked on this book. To my family, Marion, Bob, Eric, Suzie, Lizzie, Wayne K., Marie, Kelly, Tom, Lisa, Lauren, Mike, and the newest member, Amaya—you are amazing.

And finally, to Wayne Hoy, my friend, colleague, inspiration, passion, husband—you are simply the best.

—*ANITA WOOLFOLK HOY*

BRIEF CONTENTS

CONTENTS

CHAPTER 3

THE SELF, SOCIAL, AND MORAL DEVELOPMENT 68

PART II LEARNING AND MOTIVATION

CHAPTER 7

BEHAVIORAL VIEWS OF LEARNING   244

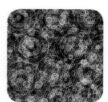

CHAPTER 10

THE LEARNING SCIENCES AND CONSTRUCTIVISM   354

CHAPTER 11

SOCIAL COGNITIVE VIEWS OF LEARNING AND MOTIVATION 396

CHAPTER 12

MOTIVATION IN LEARNING AND TEACHING 428

PART III TEACHING AND ASSESSING

CHAPTER 13

CREATING LEARNING ENVIRONMENTS 470

CHAPTER 14

TEACHING EVERY STUDENT 506

CHAPTER 15

CLASSROOM ASSESSMENT, GRADING, AND STANDARDIZED TESTING 546

SPECIAL FEATURES

POINT/COUNTERPOINT

chapter one

LEARNING, TEACHING, AND EDUCATIONAL PSYCHOLOGY

▶ **TEACHERS' CASEBOOK:** Leaving No Student Behind

It is your second year as a teacher in the Davis East school district. Over the last four years, the number of students from immigrant families has increased dramatically in your school. In your class, you have two students who speak Somali, one Hmong, one Farsi, and three Spanish sp0eakers. Some of them know a little English, but many have very few words other than "OK." If there had been more students from each of the language groups, the district would have given your school additional resources and special programs in each language, providing you extra help, but there are not quite enough students speaking most of the languages to meet the requirements. In addition, you have several students with special needs; learning disabilities, particularly problems in reading, seem to be the most common. Your state and district require you to prepare *all* your students for the achievement tests in the spring, and the national emphasis is on readiness for college and career by the end of high school—*for everyone*. Your only possible extra resource is a student intern from the local college.

CRITICAL THINKING

- What would you do to help all your students to progress and prepare for the achievement tests?
- How would you make use of the intern so that both she and your students learn?
- How could you involve the families of your non-English speaking students and students with learning disabilities to support their children's learning?

OVERVIEW AND OBJECTIVES

Like many students, you may begin this course with a mixture of anticipation and wariness. Perhaps you are required to take educational psychology as part of a program in teacher education, speech therapy, nursing, or counseling. You may have chosen this class as an elective. Whatever your reason for enrolling, you probably have questions about teaching, schools, students—or even about yourself—that you hope this course may answer. I have written the 12th edition of *Educational Psychology* with questions such as these in mind.

In this first chapter, we begin with education—more specifically, with student diversity in classrooms and federal legislation that impacts every teacher. Teachers have been both criticized as ineffective and lauded as the best hope for young people. Do teachers make a difference in students' learning? What characterizes good teaching, and what role does differentiated instruction play? Only when you are aware of the challenges and possibilities of teaching and learning today can you appreciate the contributions of educational psychology.

After a brief introduction to the world of the teacher, we turn to a discussion of educational psychology itself. How can principles identified by educational psychologists benefit teachers, therapists, parents, and others who are interested in teaching and learning? What exactly is the content of educational psychology, and where does this information come from? Finally, we consider an overview of a model that organizes research in educational psychology to identify the key student and school factors related to student learning (Lee & Shute, 2010). My goal is that you will become a confident and competent beginning teacher, so by the time you have completed this chapter, you should be able to:

Objective 1.1: Describe the key elements of and changes to the No Child Left Behind Act.

Objective 1.2: Discuss the essential features of effective teaching.

Objective 1.3: Describe the methods used to conduct research in the field of educational psychology.

Objective 1.4: Recognize key theories of development and learning that influence educational practice.

LEARNING AND TEACHING TODAY

Welcome to my favorite topic—educational psychology—the study of development, learning, motivation, teaching, and assessment in and out of schools. I believe this is the most important course you will take to prepare for your future as an educator in the classroom or the consulting office, whether your "students" are children or adults learning how to read or individuals discovering how to improve their diets. In fact, there is evidence that new teachers who have coursework in development and learning are twice as likely to stay in teaching (National Commission on Teaching and America's Future, 2003). This may be a required course for you, so let me make the case for educational psychology, first by introducing you to classrooms today.

Students Today: Dramatic Diversity and Remarkable Technology

Who are the students in American classrooms today? Here are a few statistics about the United States and Canada (taken from Children's' Defense Fund, 2008; Dewan, 2010; Freisen, 2010; Meece & Kurtz-Costes, 2001; U.S. Census Bureau, 2010a).

- In 2003, 12% of the people living in the United States were born in another country, and 18% spoke a language other than English at home—half of these families spoke Spanish.
- Today, 22% of children under the age of 18 are Latino. By 2050, Latinos will comprise about one quarter of the U.S. population (U.S. Census Bureau, 2010b).
- In Canada, projections are that by 2031, one in three Canadians will belong to a visible minority, with South Asians being the largest group represented. About 17% of the population report that their first language is not French or English, but instead one of over 100 other languages.
- One in five American children lives in poverty and one in twelve lives in extreme poverty, defined in 2011 by the United States Department of Health and Human Services as an income of $22,350 for a family of four ($27,940 in Alaska and $25,710 in Hawaii). The numbers are very similar for Canada.
- More than half of all children in poverty live in 8 states: California, Texas, New York, Florida, Illinois, Ohio, Georgia, and Michigan. A child is born into poverty in the United States every 33 seconds.

In contrast, because of the effects of mass media, these diverse students share many similarities today, particularly the fact that most are far more technologically literate than their teachers. For example:

- According to a recent survey, 29% of students in grades 3–5 and 56% of students in grades 9–12 had access to cell phones, 42% and 67% respectively had access to laptop computers, and the numbers were 55% and 85% for MP3 music players (Project Tomorrow, 2010).
- The students reported that the two greatest obstacles in using their technology in school were filters that stopped them from accessing the Web sites they needed for homework and bans on using their own mobile devices (namely cell phones) at school.

These statistics are dramatic, but a bit impersonal. As a teacher, counselor, recreational worker, speech therapist, or family member, you will encounter real children. In this book, you will meet many individuals such as Felipe, a 5th grade boy from a Spanish-speaking family who is working to learn school subjects and make friends in a language that is new to him; Ternice, an outspoken African American girl in an urban middle school who is hiding her giftedness; Benjamin, a good high school athlete diagnosed with ADHD whose wealthy parents have very high expectations for him and his teachers; Trevor, a 2nd-grade student who has trouble with the meaning of *symbol*; Allison, head of a popular clique and tormentor of the outcast Stephanie; Davy, a shy, struggling reader who is already falling behind in all his 2nd grade work; Eliot, a bright 6th grade student with severe learning disabilities; and Jessie, a student in a rural high school who just doesn't seem to care about her sinking GPA or school in general.

TEACHER EFFICACY Teachers' personal sense of efficacy is related to a school atmosphere of high expectations for teachers and students, administrative support, and real success with students.

Even though students in classrooms are increasingly diverse in race, ethnicity, language, and economic level, teachers are much less diverse—the percentage of White teachers is increasing (now about 91%), while the percentage of Black teachers is falling, down to about 7%. Clearly, it is important for all teachers to know and be able to work effectively with all their students. Several chapters in this book are devoted to understanding these diverse students. In addition, many times within each chapter, we will explore student diversity and inclusion through research, cases, and practical applications.

Confidence in Every Context

Schools are about teaching and learning; all other activities are secondary to these basic goals. But teaching and learning in the contexts described above can be challenging for both teachers and students. This book is about understanding the complex processes of development, learning, motivation, teaching, and assessment so that you can become a capable and confident teacher.

Much of my own research has focused on **teachers' sense of efficacy**, defined as a teacher's belief that he or she can reach even difficult students to help them learn. This confident belief appears to be one of the few personal characteristics of teachers that predict student achievement (Tschannen-Moran & Woolfolk Hoy, 2001; Tschannen-Moran, Woolfolk Hoy, & Hoy, 1998; Woolfolk & Hoy, 1990; Woolfolk Hoy, Hoy, & Davis, 2009). Teachers with a high sense of efficacy work harder and persist longer even when students are difficult to teach, in part because these teachers believe in themselves and in their students. Also, they are less likely to experience burnout and more likely to be satisfied with their jobs (Fives, Hamman, & Olivarez, 2005; Klassen & Chiu, 2010).

I have found that prospective teachers tend to increase in their personal sense of efficacy as a consequence of completing student teaching. But sense of efficacy may decline after the first year as a teacher, perhaps because the support that was there for you in student teaching is gone (Woolfolk Hoy & Burke-Spero, 2005). Teachers' sense of efficacy is higher in schools when the other teachers and administrators have high expectations for students and the teachers receive help from their principals in solving instructional and management problems (Capa, 2005; Hoy & Woolfolk, 1993). Another important conclusion from our research is that efficacy grows from real success with students, not just from the moral support or cheerleading of professors and colleagues. Any experience or training that helps you succeed in the day-to-day tasks of teaching will give you a foundation for developing a sense of efficacy in your career. This book was written to provide the knowledge and skills that form a solid foundation for an authentic sense of efficacy in teaching.

Teachers' sense of efficacy
A teacher's belief that he or she can reach even difficult students to help them learn.

High Expectations for Teachers and Students

On January 8, 2002, President George W. Bush signed into law the No Child Left Behind (NCLB) Act. Actually, NCLB was the most recent authorization of the Elementary and Secondary Education Act (ESEA), first passed in 1965. In a nutshell, NCLB requires that all students in grades 3 through 8 and once more in high school must take annual standardized achievement tests in reading and mathematics. In addition, they must be tested in science—one test a year in each of three grade spans (3–5, 6–9, 10–12). Based on these test scores, schools are judged to determine if their students are making adequate yearly progress (AYP) toward becoming proficient in the subjects tested. States have some say in defining proficiency and in setting AYP standards. But no matter how states define these standards, NCLB requires that all students must reach proficiency by the end of the 2013–2014 school year. Schools also must develop AYP goals and report scores separately for several groups, including racial and ethnic minority students, students with disabilities, students whose first language is not English, and students from low-income homes. As James Popham (2005a), an assessment expert, put it: "Today's public school teachers are now obligated to take part in an educational game whose rules have been dramatically altered because of a significant federal law. The NCLB Act, almost literally, seems likely to trump almost everything it touches" (p. 4).

NCLB was supposed to be reauthorized in 2007 or 2008. On March 13, 2010, the Obama Administration released *A Blueprint for Reform: The Reauthorization of the Elementary and Secondary Education Act* to describe a vision for the reauthorization of NCLB (see http://www2.ed.gov/policy/elsec/leg/blueprint/publicationtoc.html for a copy). One of the major changes suggested was to move from a punishment-based system to one that rewards excellent teaching and student growth. The Blueprint described five priorities (USDE, 2010):

1. **College- and Career-Ready Students:** Regardless of their income, race, ethnic or language background, or disability status, every student should graduate from high school ready for college or a career. To accomplish this goal, the Blueprint recommends *improved assessments* and *turnaround grants* to transform schools. In addition, Arne Duncan, the Secretary of Education, has waived the requirement to reach 100% proficiency for states that can demonstrate they have adopted their own testing and accountability programs and are making progress toward the goal of college or career readiness for all their high school graduates (Dillon, 2011).
2. **Great Teachers and Leaders in Every School:** "Research shows that top-performing teachers can make a dramatic difference in the achievement of their students, and suggests that the impact of being assigned to top-performing teachers year after year is enough to significantly narrow achievement gaps." (USDE, 2010, p. 13). To support this goal, the Blueprint proposes a Teacher and Leader Improvement Fund of competitive grants and new pathways for preparing educators. The focus of this book is to create great leaders in every school.
3. **Equity and Opportunity for All Students:** All students will be included in an accountability system that builds on college- and career-ready standards, rewards progress and success, and requires rigorous interventions in the lowest performing schools.
4. **Raise the Bar and Reward Excellence:** *Race to the Top*, a series of competitive grants for schools, has provided incentives for excellence by encouraging state and local leaders to work together on ambitious reforms, make tough choices, and develop comprehensive plans that change policies and practices to improve outcomes for students.
5. **Promote Innovation and Continuous Improvement:** In addition to the Race to the Top grants, an Investing in Innovation Fund will support local and nonprofit leaders as they develop and scale up programs that have demonstrated success, and discover the next generation of innovative solutions.

Time will tell how these proposals unfold, especially in the challenging economic environment we have experienced lately. It seems likely that capable and confident teachers will be required to reach these goals. Is that true? Do teachers make a difference? Good question.

Do Teachers Make a Difference?

You saw in the statistics presented earlier that in America there are many children growing up in poverty. For a while, some researchers concluded that wealth and social status, not teaching, were the major factors determining who learned in schools (e.g., Coleman, 1966). In fact, much of the early research on teaching was conducted by educational psychologists who refused to accept these claims that teachers were powerless in the face of poverty and societal problems (Wittrock, 1986).

How can you decide whether teaching makes a difference? Perhaps one of your teachers influenced your decision to become an educator. Even if you had such a teacher, and I hope you did, one of the purposes of educational psychology in general and this text in particular is to go beyond individual experiences and testimonies, powerful as they are, to examine larger groups. Three studies speak to the power of teachers in the lives of students. The first two focus on teacher–student relationships and the third examines the cost of poor teaching.

TEACHER–STUDENT RELATIONSHIPS.   Bridgett Hamre and Robert Pianta (2001) followed all the children who entered kindergarten one year in a small school district and continued in that district through the 8th grade. The researchers concluded that the quality of the teacher–student relationship in kindergarten (defined in terms of level of conflict with the child, the child's dependency on the teacher, and the teacher's affection for the child) predicted a number of academic and behavioral outcomes through the 8th grade, particularly for students with high levels of behavior problems. Even when the gender, ethnicity, cognitive ability, and behavior ratings of the student were accounted for, the relationship with the teacher still predicted aspects of school success. In a recent study that followed children from 3rd through 5th grade, Pianta and his colleagues found that two factors helped children with lower skills in mathematics begin to close the achievement gap. The factors were higher-level (not just basic skills) instruction and positive relationships with teachers (Crosnoe, Morrison, Burchinal, Pianta, Keating, Friedman, & Clarke-Stewart, 2010). Evidence is mounting for a strong association between the quality of teacher–child relationships and school performance. Also, students with significant behavior problems in the early years, are less likely to have problems later in school if their first teachers are sensitive to their needs and provide frequent, consistent feedback.

THE COST OF POOR TEACHING.   In a widely publicized study, researchers examined how students are affected by having several effective or ineffective teachers in a row (Sanders & Rivers, 1996). They looked at 5th graders in two large metropolitan school systems in Tennessee. Students who had highly effective teachers for 3rd, 4th, and 5th grades scored an average of 83rd percentile on a standardized mathematics achievement test in one district and 96th percentile in the other (99th percentile is the highest possible score). In contrast, students who had the least effective teachers three years in a row averaged 29th percentile in math achievement in one district and 44th percentile in the other—a difference of over 50 percentile points in both cases! Students who had average teachers or a mixture of teachers with low, average, and high effectiveness for the three years had math scores between these extremes. Sanders and Rivers concluded that the best teachers encouraged good-to-excellent gains in achievement for all students, but lower-achieving students were the first to benefit from good teaching. The effects of teaching were cumulative and residual—that is, better teaching in a later grade could partially make up for less effective teaching in earlier grades, but could not erase all the deficits. In fact, one study found that at least 7% of the differences in test score gains for students could be traced to their teachers (Hanushek, Rivkin, & Kain, 2005; Rivkin, Hanushek, & Kain, 2001).

RELATIONSHIPS MATTER Research has shown that the quality of the teacher–student relationship in kindergarten predicts a number of academic and behavioral outcomes, particularly for students with behavior problems, who are less likely to have problems later in school if their teachers are sensitive to their needs and provide frequent, consistent feedback.

Effective teachers who establish positive relationships with their students appear to be a powerful force in those students' lives. Students who have problems seem to benefit the most from good teaching. What makes a teacher effective? What is good teaching?

WHAT IS GOOD TEACHING?

Connect and Extend to PRAXIS II

Teacher Professionalism (IV, A2)
Begin your own development by reading educational publications. One widely read periodical is *Education Week*. You can access it online at www.edweek.com.

Educators, psychologists, philosophers, novelists, journalists, filmmakers, mathematicians, scientists, historians, policymakers, and parents, to name only a few groups, have examined this question; there are hundreds of answers. And good teaching is not confined to classrooms—it occurs in homes and hospitals, museums and sales meetings, therapists' offices, and summer camps. In this book, we are primarily concerned with teaching in classrooms, but much of what you will learn applies to other settings as well.

Inside Four Classrooms

To begin our examination of good teaching, let's step inside the classrooms of four outstanding teachers. The four situations are real. The first two teachers worked with my student teachers in local elementary schools and were studied by one of my colleagues, Carol Weinstein (Weinstein, Romano, & Mignano, 2011). The third teacher became an expert at helping students with severe learning difficulties, with the guidance of a consultant. The last example is a secondary school teacher who was the focus of a case study.

A BILINGUAL 1ST GRADE. Most of the 25 students in Viviana's class have recently emigrated from the Dominican Republic; the rest come from Nicaragua, Mexico, Puerto Rico, and Honduras. Even though the children speak little or no English when they begin school, by the time they leave in June, Viviana has helped them master the normal 1st grade curriculum for their district. She accomplishes this by teaching in Spanish early in the year to aid understanding, and then gradually introducing English as the students are ready. Viviana does not want her students segregated or labeled as disadvantaged. She encourages them to take pride in their Spanish-speaking heritage and uses every available opportunity to support their developing English proficiency.

Both Viviana's expectations for her students and her commitment to them are high. "With an energy level that is rare, she motivates, prods, instructs, models, praises, and captivates her students. The pace is brisk and Viviana clearly has a flair for the dramatic; she uses music, props, gestures, facial expressions, and shifts in voice tone to communicate the material" (Weinstein, Romano, & Mignano, 2011, p. 12). For Viviana, teaching is not just a job; it is a way of life.

A SUBURBAN 5TH GRADE. Ken teaches 5th grade in a suburban elementary school in central New Jersey. Students in the class represent a range of racial, ethnic, family income, and language backgrounds. Ken emphasizes "process writing." His students complete first drafts, discuss them with others in the class, revise, edit, and "publish" their work. The students also keep daily journals and often use them to share personal concerns with Ken. They tell him of problems at home, fights, and fears; he always takes the time to respond in writing. Ken also uses technology to connect lessons to real life. Students learn about ocean ecosystems by using a special interactive software program. For social studies, the class plays two simulation games that focus on history. One is about coming of age in Native American cultures and the other focuses on the colonization of America.

Throughout the year, Ken is very interested in the social and emotional development of his students; he wants them to learn about responsibility and fairness as well as science and social studies. This concern is evident in the way he develops his class rules at the beginning of the year. Rather than specifying dos and don'ts, Ken and his students devise a "Bill of Rights" for the class, describing the rights of the students. These rights cover most of the situations that might need a "rule."

AN INCLUSIVE CLASS. Eliot was bright and articulate. He easily memorized stories as a child, but he could not read by himself. His problems stemmed from severe learning difficulties with auditory and visual integration and long-term visual memory. When he tried to write, everything got jumbled. Dr. Nancy White worked with Eliot's teacher, Mia Russell, to tailor intensive tutoring that specifically focused on Eliot's individual learning patterns and his errors. With his teachers' help, over the next years, Eliot became an expert on his own learning and was transformed into an independent learner; he knew which strategies he had to use and when to use them. According to Eliot, "Learning that stuff is not fun, but it works!" (Hallahan & Kauffman, 2006, pp. 184–185).

AN ADVANCED MATH CLASS. Hilda Borko and Carol Livingston (1989) describe how Randy, an expert secondary school mathematics teacher, worked with his students' confusion to construct a review lesson about strategies for doing inte-

MENTORS MATTER Teaching is one of the few professions in which a new teacher must assume all of the responsibilities of an experienced "pro" during the first week on the job. Veteran teachers can be an excellent source of information and support during these early weeks.

grals. When one student said that a particular section in the book seemed "haphazard," Randy led the class through a process of organizing the material. He asked the class for general statements about useful strategies for doing integrals. He clarified their suggestions, elaborated on some, and helped students improve others. He asked the students to relate their ideas to passages in the text. Even though he accepted all reasonable suggestions, he listed only the key strategies on the board. By the end of the period, the students had transformed the disorganized material from the book into an ordered and useful outline to guide their learning. They also had a better idea about how to read and understand difficult material.

What do you see in these four classrooms? The teachers are confident and committed to their students. They must deal with a wide range of students: different languages, different home situations, and different abilities and learning challenges. They must adapt instruction and assessment to students' needs. They must make the most abstract concepts, such as integrals, real and understandable for their particular students. The whole time that these experts are navigating through the academic material, they also are taking care of the emotional needs of their students, propping up sagging self-esteem and encouraging responsibility. If we followed these teachers from the first day of class, we would see that they carefully plan and teach the basic procedures for living and learning in their classes. They can efficiently collect and correct homework, regroup students, give directions, distribute materials, collect lunch money, and deal with disruptions—and do all of this while also making a mental note to find out why one of their students is so tired. Finally, they are **reflective**—they constantly think back over situations to analyze what they did and why, and to consider how they might improve learning for their students.

SO WHAT IS GOOD TEACHING?   Is good teaching science or art, the application of research-based theories or the creative invention of specific practices? Is a good teacher an expert explainer—"a sage on the stage" or a great coach—"a guide by the side"? These debates have raged for years. In your other education classes, you probably will encounter criticisms of the scientific, teacher-centered sages. You will be encouraged to be inventive, student-centered guides. *But beware of either/or choices.* Teachers must be both knowledgeable and inventive. They must be able to use a range of strategies, and they must also be capable of inventing new strategies. They must have some basic research-based routines for managing classes, but they must also be willing and able to break from the routine when the situation calls for change. They must know the research on student

Reflective Thoughtful and inventive. Reflective teachers think back over situations to analyze what they did and why, and to consider how they might improve learning for their students.

development, "patterns common to particular ages, culture, social class, geography, and gender" (Ball, 1997, p. 773), and they also need to know their own particular students who are unique combinations of culture, gender, and geography. Personally, I hope you all become teachers who are both "sages" and "guides," wherever you stand.

Another answer to "What is good teaching?" involves a concept called *differentiated instruction*—fitting the teaching to the students. We look at this next.

Differentiated Instruction

STOP & THINK You are preparing a unit on habitats for your students. You decide to do as your educational psychology professor recommended and give an alternate form of the final unit test as a pretest to find out what the students already know about the subject. After you reassure them that the test won't be graded—you just want an idea about where to go in developing the lesson—the students settle in and seem to take the task seriously. Looking over the papers that night, you are dismayed. A quarter of the students make over 90% on the "final." Quite a few get around half of the questions right, but the rest of the class is clueless. The next day, when you ask Shanequa why she did so well on the test, she explains that in science class last year her group (and several others) chose habitats as the focus of their special project work. You stare at your lesson plans and realize that they fit practically no one in this class. What will you do? What would expert teachers such as Viviana, Ken, Mia, or Randy do? •

WHY DO WE NEED DIFFERENTIATED INSTRUCTION?   As you will see throughout this book, today's classrooms are diverse. Students differ in knowledge of the subjects being taught, language, socioeconomic status (SES), culture, race, and ethnicity. They bring different strengths, abilities, and challenges to the task of learning. Many educators believe that "classes should include students of diverse needs, achievement levels, interests, and learning styles, and instruction should be differentiated to take advantage of the diversity, not ignore it" (Jackson & Davis, 2000, p. 23). **Differentiated instruction** (Tomlinson, 2005b) is one way of going beyond accommodating these learner differences to seeing diversity as an array of strengths on which to build. The basic idea of differentiated instruction is that teachers must take into account not only the subjects they are teaching but also the students. In differentiated classrooms, students work at different paces, sometimes exercising varied learning options, and they are assessed using indicators that fit their interests and needs (George, 2005).

ELEMENTS OF DIFFERENTIATION.   Differentiated instruction conceives of all students as seeking purpose, challenge, affirmation, power, and the chance to contribute. The confident teacher views these different student needs as opportunities, not problems, and responds with invitation, investment, persistence, opportunity, and reflection. The teacher works to create curriculum and instruction for each student that is focused, engaging, demanding, important, and scaffolded. Carol Ann Tomlinson (2003) describes these characteristics as the *Cogs of Differentiation*. They are called *cogs* because they are interdependent and interlocking, like the inner workings of a clock. Each student's needs interact and connect with the differentiated curriculum and instruction created by the teacher for that student.

What are some examples of differentiation in curriculum and instruction (Tomlinson, 2003)? Let's assume students in a pre-algebra class have varied interests and often have difficulty understanding the value of what they are learning in math. The teacher can modify the content and product based on student interests by using examples from sports, business, medicine, technology, and other fields to illustrate how formulas are used. She also might guide students in interviewing people engaged in a range of jobs and hobbies to find out how they use formulas in their work and in sharing those examples with others in the class. In a second example—some students in Advanced Placement U.S. History are taking their first high-level course and occasionally they feel lost and discouraged by the course's demands. In response, the teacher might modify the learning environment and

Differentiated instruction Teaching that takes into account students' abilities, prior knowledge, and challenges so that instruction matches not only the subject being taught but also students' needs.

process based on student readiness and emotions by establishing study groups to help students prepare for both oral and written tests. Although much of the study group work takes place outside of class, the teacher conducts whole-class and small-group discussions about how the various groups approach studying, how the different approaches seem to work, and how students feel about their progress. The teacher also provides study guides to ensure the groups focus on critical facets of the content.

Is all this talk about expert teachers, science, art, and differentiated instruction making you a little nervous? Viviana, Ken, Mia, and Randy are experts at the science, art, and differentiating of teaching, but they have years of experience. What about you?

Beginning Teachers

STOP & THINK Imagine walking into your first day of teaching. List the concerns, fears, and worries you have. What assets do you bring to the job? What would build your confidence to teach? •

Beginning teachers everywhere share many concerns, including maintaining classroom discipline, motivating students, accommodating differences among students, evaluating students' work, dealing with parents, and getting along with other teachers (Conway & Clark, 2003; Melnick & Meister, 2008; Veenman, 1984). Many teachers also experience what has been called "reality shock" when they take their first job because they really cannot ease into their responsibilities. On the first day of their first job, beginning teachers face the same tasks as teachers with years of experience. Student teaching, while a critical element, does not really prepare prospective teachers for starting off a school year with a new class. If you listed any of these concerns in your response to the *Stop & Think* question above, you shouldn't be troubled. They come with the job of being a beginning teacher (Borko & Putnam, 1996; Cooke & Pang, 1991).

With experience, hard work, and good support, seasoned teachers can focus on the students' needs and judge their success by the accomplishments of their students (Fuller, 1969; Pigge & Marso, 1997). One experienced teacher described the shift from concerns about yourself to concerns about your students: "The difference between a beginning teacher and an experienced one is that the beginning teacher asks, 'How am I doing?' and the experienced teacher asks, 'How are the children doing?'" (Codell, 2001, p. 191).

My goal in writing this book is to give you the foundation for becoming an expert as you gain experience. One thing experts do is listen to their students. Table 1.1 shows some advice a 1st grade class gave to their student teacher: It looks like the students know about good teaching, too.

Connect and Extend to PRAXIS II

Teacher Professionalism (IV, A1)
Your professional growth relies on your becoming a member of a community of practice. The national organizations listed here have hundreds of affiliations and chapters across the country with regular conferences, conventions, and meetings to advance instruction in their areas. Take a look at their websites to get a feel for their approaches to issues related to professionalism.

- National Council of Teachers of English (www.ncte.org)
- International Reading Association (www.reading.org)
- National Science Teachers Association (www.nsta.org)
- National Council for the Social Studies (www.ncss.org)
- National Council of Teachers of Mathematics (www.nctm.org)

TABLE 1.1 • **Advice for Student Teachers from Their Students**

The students in Ms. Amato's elementary school class gave this advice as a gift to their student teacher on her last day.

1. Teach us as much as you can.
2. Give us homework.
3. Help us when we have problems with our work.
4. Help us to do the right thing.
5. Help us make a family in school.
6. Read books to us.
7. Teach us to read.
8. Help us write about faraway places.
9. Give us lots of compliments, like "Oh, that's so beautiful."
10. Smile at us.
11. Take us for walks and on trips.
12. Respect us.
13. Help us get our education.

Source: Nieto, Sonia, Affirming Diversity: The Sociopolitical Context of Multicultural Education, MyLabSchool Edition, 4th edition, © 2004. Reprinted by permission of Pearson Education, Inc. Upper Saddle River, NJ.

I began this chapter claiming that educational psychology is the most important course you will take. OK, maybe I am a bit biased—I have been teaching the subject for over four decades! So let me tell you more about my favorite topic.

THE ROLE OF EDUCATIONAL PSYCHOLOGY

For as long as the formal study of educational psychology has existed—over 100 years—there have been debates about what it really is. Some people believe educational psychology is simply knowledge gained from psychology and applied to the activities of the classroom. Others believe it involves applying the methods of psychology to study classroom and school life (Brophy, 2003; Wittrock, 1992). A quick look at history shows that educational psychology and teaching have been closely linked since the beginning.

In the Beginning: Linking Educational Psychology and Teaching

In one sense, educational psychology is very old. Issues Plato and Aristotle discussed—the role of the teacher, the relationship between teacher and student, methods of teaching, the nature and order of learning, the role of emotion in learning—are still topics in educational psychology today. But let's fast forward to recent history. From the beginning, psychology in the United States was linked to teaching. At Harvard in 1890, William James founded the field of psychology and developed a lecture series for teachers entitled *Talks to Teachers about Psychology*. These lectures were given in summer schools for teachers around the country and then published in 1899. James's student, G. Stanley Hall, founded the American Psychological Association. His dissertation was about children's understandings of the world; teachers helped him collect data. Hall encouraged teachers to make detailed observations to study their students' development—as his mother had done when she was a teacher. Hall's student, John Dewey, founded the Laboratory School at the University of Chicago and is considered the father of the progressive education movement (Berliner, 2006; Hilgard, 1996; Pajares, 2003). Another of William James's students, E. L. Thorndike, wrote the first educational psychology text in 1903 and founded the *Journal of Educational Psychology* in 1910.

In the 1940s and 1950s, the study of educational psychology concentrated on individual differences, assessment, and learning behaviors. In the 1960s and 1970s, the focus of research shifted to the study of cognitive development and learning, with attention to how students learn concepts and remember. More recently, educational psychologists have investigated how culture and social factors affect learning and development (Pressley & Roehrig, 2003).

Educational Psychology Today

What is educational psychology today? The view generally accepted is that **educational psychology** is a distinct discipline with its own theories, research methods, problems, and techniques. Educational psychologists do research on learning and teaching and, at the same time, work to improve educational practice (Pintrich, 2000). In order to understand as much as possible about learning and teaching, educational psychologists examine what happens when someone (a teacher or parent or software designer) teaches something (math or weaving or dancing) to someone else (student or co-worker or team) in some setting (classroom or theater or gym) (Berliner, 2006; Schwab, 1973). So educational psychologists study child and adolescent development; learning and motivation—including how people learn different academic subjects such as reading or mathematics; social and cultural influences on learning; teaching and teachers; and assessment, including testing (Alexander & Winne, 2006).

But even with all this research on so many topics, are the findings of educational psychologists really that helpful for teachers? After all, most teaching is just common sense, isn't it? Let's take a few minutes to examine these questions.

Educational psychology The discipline concerned with teaching and learning processes; applies the methods and theories of psychology and has its own as well.

Is It Just Common Sense?

In many cases, the principles set forth by educational psychologists—after spending much thought, time, and money—sound pathetically obvious. People are tempted to say, and usually do say, "Everyone knows that!" Consider these examples.

TAKING TURNS.   What method should a teacher use in selecting students to participate in a primary grade reading class?

Commonsense Answer.   Teachers should call on students randomly so that everyone will have to follow the lesson carefully. If a teacher were to use the same order every time, the students would know when their turn was coming up, and practice only that part.

ANSWER BASED ON RESEARCH.   Years ago, research by Ogden, Brophy, and Evertson (1977) found that the answer to this question is not so simple. In 1st grade reading classes, for example, going around the circle in order and giving each child a chance to read led to better overall achievement than calling on students randomly. The critical factor in going around the circle may be that each child gets a chance to participate. Without some system for calling on everyone, students can be overlooked or skipped. Research suggests there are better alternatives for teaching reading than going around the circle, but teachers should make sure that everyone has the chance for practice and feedback regardless of the approach used (Tierney, Readence, & Dishner, 1990).

HELPING STUDENTS.   When should teachers provide help for lower-achieving students as they do class work?

Commonsense Answer.   Teachers should offer help often. After all, these lower-achieving students may not know when they need help or they may be too embarrassed to ask for help.

ANSWER BASED ON RESEARCH.   Sandra Graham (1996) found that when teachers provide help before students ask, the students and others watching are more likely to conclude that the helped student does not have the ability to succeed. The student is more likely to attribute failures to lack of ability instead of lack of effort, so motivation suffers.

SKIPPING GRADES.   Should a school encourage exceptionally bright students to skip grades or to enter college early?

Commonsense Answer.   No! Very intelligent students who are several years younger than their classmates are likely to be social misfits. They are neither physically nor emotionally ready for dealing with older students and would be miserable in the social situations that are so important in school, especially in the later grades.

ANSWER BASED ON RESEARCH.   Maybe. In *A Nation Deceived: How Schools Hold Back America's Brightest Children* (2004), Nicholas Colangelo, Susan Assouline, and Miraca Gross list the 20 most important points from their report. The first two are: (1) Acceleration is the most effective curriculum intervention for gifted children, and (2) for bright students, acceleration has long-term beneficial effects, both academically and socially. Whether acceleration is the best solution for a student depends on many specific individual characteristics, including the intelligence and maturity of the student as well as the other available options. For some students, moving quickly through the material and working in advanced courses with older students is a very good idea. See Chapter 4 for more on adapting teaching to students' abilities.

OBVIOUS ANSWERS?   Lily Wong (1987) demonstrated that just seeing research results in writing can make them seem obvious. She selected 12 findings from research on teaching; one of them was the "taking turns" result noted above. She presented 6 of the findings in their correct form and 6 in exactly the opposite form to both college students and

RESEARCH MATTERS These students are participating in true "hands-on" cooperative learning. Will their knowledge of science improve using this approach? Are there better ways to learn this subject? Educational research should shed light on questions like these.

experienced teachers. Both the college students and the teachers rated about half of the wrong findings as "obviously" correct. In a follow-up study, another group of subjects was shown the 12 findings and their opposites and was asked to pick which ones were correct. For 8 of the 12 findings, the subjects chose the wrong result more often than the right one.

You may have thought that educational psychologists spend their time discovering the obvious. The preceding examples point out the danger of this kind of thinking. When a principle is stated in simple terms, it can sound simplistic. A similar phenomenon takes place when we see a gifted dancer or athlete perform; the well-trained performer makes it look easy. But we see only the results of the training, not all the work that went into mastering the individual movements. And bear in mind that any research finding—or its opposite—may sound like common sense. The issue is not what *sounds* sensible, but what is *demonstrated* when the principle is put to the test in research—our next topic (Gage, 1991).

Using Research to Understand and Improve Learning

STOP & THINK Quickly, list all the different research methods you can think of. •

Educational psychologists design and conduct many different kinds of research studies. Some of these are "descriptive," that is, their purpose is simply to describe events in a particular class or several classes.

DESCRIPTIVE STUDIES. Reports of **descriptive studies** often include survey results, interview responses, samples of actual classroom dialogue, or audio and video records of class activities. One descriptive approach, classroom **ethnography**, is borrowed from anthropology. Ethnographic methods involve studying the naturally occurring events in the life of a group and trying to understand the meaning of these events to the people involved. For example, the descriptions of Randy, the expert high school mathematics teacher earlier in this chapter, were taken from an ethnographic study by Borko and Livingston (1989). In some descriptive studies, the researcher uses **participant observation** and works within the class or school to understand the actions from the perspectives of the teacher and the students. Researchers also employ **case studies**. A case study investigates in depth how a teacher plans courses, for example, or how a student tries to learn specific material.

CORRELATION STUDIES. Often, the results of descriptive studies include reports of correlations. We will take a minute to examine this concept, because you will encounter many correlations in the coming chapters. A **correlation** is a number that indicates both the strength and the direction of a relationship between two events or measurements. Correlations range from 1.00 to –1.00. The closer the correlation is to either 1.00 or –1.00, the stronger the relationship. For example, the correlation between weight and height is about .70 (a strong relationship); the correlation between weight and number of languages spoken is about .00 (no relationship at all).

The sign of the correlation tells the direction of the relationship. A **positive correlation** indicates that the two factors increase or decrease together. As one gets larger, so does the other. Weight and height are positively correlated because greater weight tends to be

Descriptive studies Studies that collect detailed information about specific situations, often using observation, surveys, interviews, recordings, or a combination of these methods.

Ethnography A descriptive approach to research that focuses on life within a group and tries to understand the meaning of events to the people involved.

Participant observation A method for conducting descriptive research in which the researcher becomes a participant in the situation in order to better understand life in that group.

Case study Intensive study of one person or one situation.

Correlations Statistical descriptions of how closely two variables are related.

Positive correlation A relationship between two variables in which the two increase or decrease together. Example: calorie intake and weight gain.

associated with greater height. A **negative correlation** means that increases in one factor are related to decreases in the other, for example, the less you pay for a theater or concert ticket, the greater your distance from the stage. It is important to note that correlations do not prove cause and effect (see Figure 1.1). Weight and height are correlated—heavier people tend to be taller than lighter people. But gaining weight obviously does not cause you to grow taller. Knowing a person's weight simply allows you to make a general prediction about that person's height. Educational psychologists identify correlations so they can make predictions about important events in the classroom.

EXPERIMENTAL STUDIES. A second type of research—**experimentation**—allows educational psychologists to go beyond predictions and actually study cause and effect. Instead of just observing and describing an existing situation, the investigators introduce changes and note the results. First, a number of comparable groups of participants are created. In psychological research, the term **participants** (also called **subjects**) generally refers to the people being studied—such as teachers or 8th graders. One common way to make sure that groups of participants are essentially the same is to assign each person to a group using a random procedure. **Random** means each participant has an equal chance of being in any group. **Quasi-experimental studies** meet most of the criteria for true experiments, with the important exception that the participants are not assigned to groups at random. Instead, existing groups such as classes or schools participate in the experiments.

In experiments or quasi-experiments, for one or more of the groups studied, the experimenters change some aspect of the situation to see if this change or "treatment" has an expected effect. The results in each group are then compared. Usually, statistical tests are conducted. When differences are described as **statistically significant**, it means that they probably did not happen simply by chance. For example, if you see $p < .05$ in a study, this indicates that the result reported could happen by chance less than 5 times out of 100, and $p < .01$ means less than 1 time in 100.

A number of the studies we will examine attempt to identify cause-and-effect relationships by asking questions such as this: If some teachers receive training in how to teach spelling using morphology, the study of the smallest parts of words that contain meaning such as "s" or "ies" for making words plural (*cause*), will the trained teachers' students become better spellers than students whose teachers did not receive training in morphology (*effect*)? This actually was a *field experiment* because it took place in real

Negative correlation A relationship between two variables in which a high value on one is associated with a low value on the other. Example: height and distance from top of head to the ceiling.

Experimentation Research method in which variables are manipulated and the effects recorded.

Participants/Subjects People or animals studied.

Random Without any definite pattern; following no rule.

Quasi-experimental studies Studies that fit most of the criteria for true experiments, with the important exception that the participants are not assigned to groups at random. Instead, existing groups such as classes or schools participate in the experiments.

Statistically significant Not likely to be a chance occurrence.

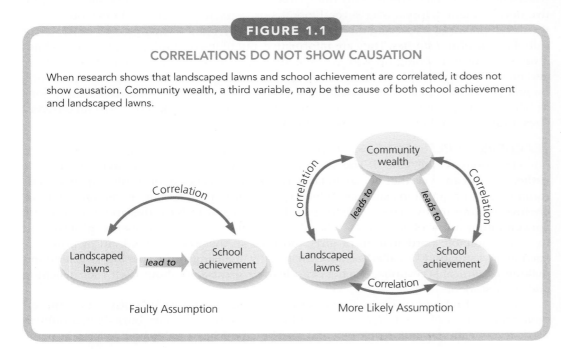

FIGURE 1.1

CORRELATIONS DO NOT SHOW CAUSATION

When research shows that landscaped lawns and school achievement are correlated, it does not show causation. Community wealth, a third variable, may be the cause of both school achievement and landscaped lawns.

Faulty Assumption

More Likely Assumption

classrooms and not a simulated laboratory situation. In addition, it was a *quasi-experiment* because the students were in existing classes and had not been randomly assigned to teachers, so we cannot be certain the experimental and control groups were the same before the teachers received their training. The researchers handled this by looking at improvement in spelling, not just final achievement level (Hurry et al., 2005).

SINGLE-SUBJECT EXPERIMENTAL DESIGNS.   The goal of **single-subject experimental studies** is to determine the effects of a therapy, teaching method, or other intervention. One common approach is to observe the individual for a baseline period (A) and assess the behavior of interest; try an intervention (B) and note the results; then remove the intervention and go back to baseline conditions (A); and finally reinstate the intervention (B). This form of single-subject design is called an ABAB experiment. For example, a teacher might record how much time students are out of their seats without permission during a week-long baseline period (A), and then try ignoring those who are out of their seats, but praising those who are seated and record how many are wandering out of their seats for the week (B). Next, the teacher returns to baseline conditions (A) and records results, and then reinstates the praise-and-ignore strategy (B) (Landrum & Kauffman, 2006). When this intervention was first tested, the praise-and-ignore strategy proved effective in increasing the time students spent in their seats (Madsen, Becker, Thomas, Koser, & Plager, 1968).

MICROGENETIC STUDIES.   The goal of **microgenetic studies** is to intensively study cognitive processes in the midst of change—while the change is actually occurring. For example, researchers might analyze how children learn a particular strategy for adding two-digit numbers over the course of several weeks. The microgenetic approach has three basic characteristics: the researchers (a) observe the entire period of the change—from when it starts to the time it is relatively stable; (b) make many observations, often using videotape recordings, interviews, and transcriptions of the exact words of the individuals being studied; (c) put the observed behavior "under a microscope," that is, they examine it moment by moment or trial by trial. The goal is to explain the underlying mechanisms of change—for example, what new knowledge or skills are developing to allow change to take place (Siegler & Crowley, 1991). This kind of research is expensive and time-consuming, so often only one or two children are studied.

THE ROLE OF TIME IN RESEARCH.   Another distinction is useful in understanding research—one based on time. Many things that psychologists want to study, such as cognitive development, happen over several months or years. Ideally, researchers would study the development by observing their subjects over many years as changes occur. These are called *longitudinal studies*. They are informative, but time-consuming, expensive, and not always practical: Keeping up with participants over a number of years as they grow up and move can be impossible. As a consequence, much research is *cross-sectional*, focusing on groups of children at different ages. For example, to study how children's conceptions of "alive" change from ages 3 to 16, researchers can interview children of several different ages, rather than following the same children for 14 years.

TEACHERS AS RESEARCHERS.   Research also can be a way to improve teaching in one classroom or one school. The same kind of careful observation, intervention, data gathering, and analysis that occurs in large research projects can be applied in any classroom to answer questions such as "Which writing prompts seem to encourage the most creative writing in my class?" "When does Kenyon seem to have the greatest difficulty concentrating on academic tasks?" "Would assigning task roles in science groups lead to more equitable participation of girls and boys in the work?" This kind of problem-solving investigation is called **action research**. By focusing on a specific problem and making careful observations, teachers can learn a great deal about both their teaching and their students.

You can find reports of the findings from all types of studies in journals that are referenced in this book. Table 1.2 provides a list of some of the major journals that publish work in educational and developmental psychology. I have published articles in many

Single-subject experimental studies Systematic interventions to study effects with one person, often by applying and then withdrawing a treatment.

Microgenetic studies Detailed observation and analysis of changes in a cognitive process as the process unfolds over a several-day or several-week period of time.

Action research Systematic observations or tests of methods conducted by teachers or schools to improve teaching and learning for their students.

TABLE 1.2 • **Examples of Journals in Educational Psychology and Child Development**

JOURNAL	ORGANIZATION/PUBLISHER	WEB SITE
Educational Psychologist	The Division of Educational Psychology (15) of the American Psychological Association	http://www.tandf.co.uk/journals/
Journal of Educational Psychology	American Psychological Association	http://www.apa.org/journals/edu/
Contemporary Educational Psychology	Elsevier	http://www.elsevier.com/
Educational Psychology Review	Springer	http://www.springer.com/
Theory Into Practice	Taylor Francis and The Ohio State University	http://ehe.osu.edu/tip/
The British Journal of Educational Psychology	British Psychological Society	http://www.bpsjournals.co.uk/
Learning and Instruction	European Association for Research on Learning and Instruction (EARLI)	http://www.elsevier.com/
Teaching and Teacher Education	Elsevier	http://www.elsevier.com/
The Elementary School Journal	University of Chicago Press	http://www.journals.uchicago.edu/
Psychology in the Schools	Wiley	http://www.wiley.com/WileyCDA/
School Psychology Quarterly	American Psychological Association	http://www.apa.org/journals/spq/
Child Development	Society for Research in Child Development	http://www.srcd.org/
Developmental Psychology	American Psychological Association	http://www.apa.org/journals/dev/
Journal of Applied Developmental Psychology	Elsevier	http://www.elsevier.com/
Developmental Review	Thompson Scientific	
Merrill Palmer Quarterly	Wayne State University	http://www.asu.edu/clas/ssfd/mpq/
Cognitive Development	Jean Piaget Society	http://www.piaget.org/
Early Childhood Research Quarterly	National Association for the Education of Young Children (NAEYC).	http://www.naeyc.org/

of these journals and also have reviewed manuscripts to decide what will be published. As I write this paragraph, I am editor of the *Theory Into Practice* journal. Our goal in that journal is just what the title says—to bring the most useful theories into educational practice and also to bring the wisdom of practice back to researchers who study education. I think *Theory Into Practice* is a great journal to inspire and guide action research in classrooms.

What Is Scientifically Based Research?

One of the requirements of the landmark No Child Left Behind Act was that educational programs and practices receiving federal money had to be consistent with "scientifically based research." The lawmakers believed that scientifically based research produces reliable and valid knowledge because the research is rigorous, systematic, and objective. In fact, the term *scientifically based research* appeared 110 times in the bill. Specifically, the NCLB Act stated that scientifically based research:

- Uses observations or experiments to systematically gather valid and reliable data.
- Involves rigorous and appropriate procedures for analyzing the data.
- Is clearly described so it can be repeated by others.
- Has been rigorously reviewed by appropriate, independent experts.

This description of scientifically based research fits the experimental approach described above better than other methods such as ethnographic research or case studies. Because schools are required to base their programs on scientifically based research as defined in the NCLB Act, there is continuing debate about what this means, as you will see in the *Point/Counterpoint*.

Theories for Teaching

As we saw earlier, the major goal of educational psychology is to understand what happens when someone teaches something to someone else in some setting (Berliner, 2006; Schwab, 1973). Reaching this goal is a slow process. There are very few landmark studies that answer a question once and for all. There are so many different kinds of students, teachers, tasks, and settings; and besides, human beings are pretty complicated. To deal with this complexity, research in educational psychology examines limited aspects of a situation—perhaps a few variables at a time or life in one or two classrooms. If enough studies are completed in a certain area and findings repeatedly point to the same conclusions, we eventually arrive at a **principle**. This is the term for an established relationship between two or more factors—between a certain teaching strategy, for example, and student achievement.

Another tool for building a better understanding of the teaching and learning processes is *theory*. The commonsense notion of theory (as in "Oh well, it was only a theory") is "a guess or hunch." But the scientific meaning of *theory* is quite different. "A **theory** in science is an interrelated set of concepts that is used to explain a body of data and to make predictions about the results of future experiments" (Stanovich, 1992, p. 21). Given a number of established principles, educational psychologists have developed explanations for the relationships among many variables and even whole systems of relationships. There are theories to explain how language develops, how differences in intelligence occur, and, as noted earlier, how people learn.

You will encounter many theories of development, learning, and motivation in this book. Theories are based on systematic research and they are the beginning and ending points of the research cycle. In the beginning, theories provide the research *hypotheses* to be tested or the questions examined. A **hypothesis** is a prediction of what will happen in a research study based on theory and previous research. For example, two different theories might suggest two competing predictions that could be tested. Piaget's theory might suggest that instruction cannot teach young children to think more abstractly, whereas Vygotsky's theory might suggest that this is possible. Of course, at times, psychologists don't know enough to make predictions, so they just ask *research questions*. An example question might be: "Is there a difference in Internet usage by male and female adolescents from different ethnic groups?"

Research is a continuing cycle that involves:

- Clear specification of hypotheses or questions based on current understandings or theories,
- Systematic gathering and analyzing of all kinds of information (data) about the questions from well-chosen research participants,

Evidenced-based practice in psychology (EBPP) Practices that integrate the best available research with the insights of expert practitioners and knowledge of the characteristics, culture, and preferences of the client.

Principle Established relationship between factors.

Theory Integrated statement of principles that attempts to explain a phenomenon and make predictions.

Hypothesis/Hypotheses A prediction of what will happen in a research study based on theory and previous research.

POINT/COUNTERPOINT: What Kind of Research Should Guide Education?

In the past decade, policies in both health care and in the treatment of psychological problems have emphasized evidenced-based practices (McHugh & Barlow, 2010). The American Psychological Association defines **evidenced-based practice in psychology (EBPP)** as "the integration of the best available research with clinical expertise in the context of patient characteristics, culture, and preferences" (American Psychological Association Task Force on Evidence-Based Practice for Children and Adolescents, 2008, p. 5). What does this mean in education?

POINT

▶ **Research should be scientific; educational reforms should be based on solid evidence.** According to Robert Slavin, "Education is on the brink of a scientific revolution that has the potential to profoundly transform policy, practice, and research" (Slavin, 2002, p. 15). Slavin paints a bright future for educational reform guided by scientifically based research:

It is possible that these policy reforms could set in motion a process of research and development on programs and practices affecting children everywhere. This process could create the kind of progressive, systematic improvement over time that has characterized successful parts of our economy and society throughout the 20th century, in fields such as medicine, agriculture, transportation, and technology. In each of these fields, processes of development, rigorous evaluation, and dissemination have produced a pace of innovation and improvement that is unprecedented in history. . . . These innovations have transformed the world. Yet education has failed to embrace this dynamic, and as a result, education moves from fad to fad. Educational practice does change over time, but the change process more resembles the pendulum swings of taste characteristic of art or fashion (think hemlines) rather than the progressive improvements characteristic of science and technology. (p. 16)

The major reason for extraordinary advances in medicine and agriculture, according to Slavin, is that these fields base their practices on scientific evidence. Randomized clinical trials and replicated experiments are the sources of the evidence.

In his Presidential Address to the First Conference of the International Mind, Brain, and Education Society, Kurt Fischer (2009, pp. 3–4) said:

What happened to education? If research produces useful knowledge for most of the industries and businesses of the world, then shouldn't it be serving the same function for education? Somehow education has been mostly exempt from this grounding in research. Dewey (1896) proposed the establishment of laboratory schools to ground education in research through combining research with practice in schools, ensuring both formative evaluation and democratic feedback. Unfortunately, his vision has never been realized. There is no infrastructure in education that routinely studies learning and teaching to assess effectiveness. If Revlon and Toyota can spend millions on research to create better products, how can schools continue to use alleged "best practices" without collecting evidence about what really works?

COUNTERPOINT

▶ **Experiments are not the only or even the best source of evidence.** David Olson (2004) disagrees strongly with Slavin's position. He claims that we cannot use medicine as an analogy to education. "Treatments" in education are much more complex and unpredictable than administering one drug or another in medicine. And every educational program is changed by classroom conditions and the way it is implemented. Patti Lather, a colleague of mine at Ohio State, says, "In improving the quality of practice, complexity and the messiness of practice-in-context cannot be fantasized away. To try to do so yields impoverishment rather than improvement. That loss is being borne by the children, teachers, and administrators in our schools" (2004, p. 30). David Berliner (2002) makes a similar point:

Doing science and implementing scientific findings are so difficult in education because humans in schools are embedded in complex and changing networks of social interaction. The participants in those networks have variable power to affect each other from day to day, and the ordinary events of life (a sick child, a messy divorce, a passionate love affair, migraine headaches, hot flashes, a birthday party, alcohol abuse, a new principal, a new child in the classroom, rain that keeps the children from a recess outside the school building) all affect doing science in school settings by limiting the generalizability of educational research findings. Compared to designing bridges and circuits or splitting either atoms or genes, the science to help change schools and classrooms is harder to do because context cannot be controlled.

Beyond Either/Or. Berliner concludes that a complex problem like education needs a whole range of methods for study— "ethnographic research is crucial, as are case studies, survey research, time series, design experiments, action research, and other means to collect reliable evidence for engaging in unfettered argument about education issues. A single method is not what the government should be promoting for educational researchers" (Berliner, 2002, p. 20).

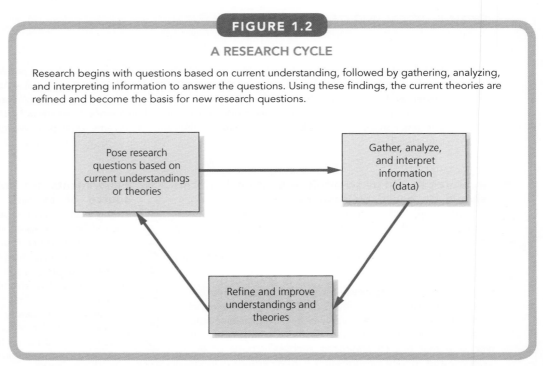

FIGURE 1.2

A RESEARCH CYCLE

Research begins with questions based on current understanding, followed by gathering, analyzing, and interpreting information to answer the questions. Using these findings, the current theories are refined and become the basis for new research questions.

Pose research questions based on current understandings or theories

Gather, analyze, and interpret information (data)

Refine and improve understandings and theories

Source: Woolfolk, Anita; Perry, Nancy E., Child and Adolescent Development, 1st Edition, © 2012. Reprinted by permission of Pearson Education, Inc., Upper Saddle River, NJ.

- Modification and improvement of explanatory theories based on the results of those analyses, and
- Formulation of new and better questions based on the improved theories … and on and on.

This empirical process of collecting data to test and improve theories is repeated over and over, as you can see in Figure 1.2. **Empirical** means "based on data." When researchers say that identifying an effective antibiotic or choosing a successful way to teach reading is an "empirical question," they mean that you need data and evidence to make the call. Constructing decisions from empirical analyses protects psychologists from developing theories based on personal biases, rumors, fears, faulty information, or preferences (Mertler & Charles, 2005). Answering questions with carefully gathered data means that science is self-correcting. If predictions do not play out or if answers to carefully formulated questions do not support current best understandings (theories), then the theories have to be changed. You can use the same kind of systematic and self-correcting thinking in your work with students.

Few theories explain and predict perfectly. In this book, you will see many examples of educational psychologists taking different theoretical positions and disagreeing on the overall explanations of such broad topics as learning and motivation. Because no one theory offers all the answers, it makes sense to consider what each has to offer.

So why, you may ask, is it necessary to deal with theories? Why not just stick to principles? The answer is that both are useful. Principles of classroom management, for example, will give you help with specific problems. A good theory of classroom management, on the other hand, will give you a new way of thinking about discipline problems; it will give you cognitive tools for creating solutions to many different problems and for predicting what might work in new situations. A major goal of this book is to provide you with the best and the most useful theories of development, learning, motivation, and teaching—those that have solid evidence behind them. Although you may prefer some theories to others, consider them all as ways of understanding the challenges teachers face.

Empirical Based on systematically collected data.

The theories you encounter in this text should be used as cognitive tools to help you examine, inspect, and interpret the claims you will hear and read about throughout your career (Leinhardt, 2001). No matter which theories or research methods we explore, education and psychology have had a long relationship. Educational psychology stands with a foot in two worlds: scholarship and practice. Merle Wittrock (1992, p. 138) sums it up well, saying that educational psychology focuses on "the psychological study of the everyday problems of education, from which one derives principles, models, theories, teaching procedures, and practical methods of instruction and evaluation, as well as research methods, statistical analyses, and measurement and assessment procedures appropriate for studying the thinking and affective processes of learners and the socially and culturally complex processes of schools." That about covers it.

I began this chapter by asserting that Educational Psychology is my favorite topic, as well as a key source of knowledge and skills for teaching. I end this chapter with one more bit of evidence for my enthusiasm. Educational Psychology will help you support student learning—the goal of all teaching.

Supporting Student Learning

In a recent article in the *Educational Psychologist*, a major journal in our field, Jihyun Lee and Valerie Shute (2010) sifted through thousands of studies of student learning conducted over the course of 60 years, seeking to identify those that had direct measures of student achievement in reading and mathematics. Then they narrowed their focus to studies with strong effects. About 150 studies met all their rigorous criteria. Using the results from these studies, Lee and Shute identified about a dozen variables that were directly linked to K–12 student achievement. The researchers grouped these factors into two categories: *student personal factors* and *school and social-contextual factors*, as you can see in Table 1.3. When I read this article, I was pleased to see that my favorite subject, educational psychology, provides a base for developing knowledge and skills in virtually every area except principal leadership (for that subject you have to consult a book I wrote with my husband on principals as instructional leaders).

As you can see in Table 1.3, this text should help you become a capable and confident teacher who can get students engaged in the classroom learning community—a community that respects its members. This book will guide you toward becoming a teacher who helps students develop into interested, motivated, self-regulated, and confident learners. As a consequence, you will be able to set high expectations for your students, rally the support of parents, and build your own sense of efficacy as a teacher.

TABLE 1.3 • **Research-Based Personal and Social-Contextual Factors That Support Student Achievement in K–12 Classrooms**

STUDENT PERSONAL FACTORS	EXAMPLES	WHERE IN THIS TEXT
Student Engagement		
Engaging Students' Behavior	Make sure students attend classes, follow rules, participate in school activities.	Chapters 5, 6, 7, 13
Engaging Students' Minds and Motivations	Design challenging tasks, tap intrinsic motivation, support student investment in learning, nurture student self-efficacy and other positive academic beliefs.	Chapters 2, 3, 10, 12
Engaging Students' Emotions	Connect to student interest, pique curiosity, foster a sense of belonging and class connections, diminish anxiety, and increase enjoyment in learning.	Chapters 3, 5, 6, 10, 12

continued

TABLE 1.3 • **Research-Based Personal and Social-Contextual Factors That Support Student Achievement in K–12 Classrooms (Continued)**

STUDENT PERSONAL FACTORS	EXAMPLES	WHERE IN THIS TEXT
Learning Strategies		
Cognitive Strategies	Directly teach knowledge and skills that support student learning and deep processing of valuable information (e.g., summarizing, inferring, applying, and reasoning).	Chapters 7, 8, 9, 14
Metacognitive Strategies	Directly teach students to monitor, regulate, and evaluate their own cognitive processes, strengths, and weaknessesas learners; teach them about when, where, why, and how to use specific strategies.	Chapters 7, 8, 9, 11
Behavioral Strategies	Directly teach students strategies and tactics for managing, monitoring, and evaluating their action, motivation, affect, and environment, such as skills in: • time management • test taking • help-seeking • note-taking • homework management	Chapters 7, 8, 9, 10, 11, 12, 13, 14
SOCIAL-CONTEXTUAL FACTORS	EXAMPLES	WHERE IN THIS TEXT
School Climate		
Academic Emphasis	Set high expectations for your students and encourage the whole school to do the same; emphasize positive relations with the school community.	Chapters 11, 12, 13
Teacher Variables	If possible, teach in a school with the positive qualities of collective efficacy, teacher empowerment, sense of affiliation.	Chapters 1, 11, 13
Principal Leadership	If possible, teach in a school with the positive qualities of collegiality, high morale, and clearly conveyed goals.	See Woolfolk Hoy & Hoy (2009)
Social-Familial Influences		
Parental Involvement	Support parents in supporting their children's learning.	Chapters 3, 4, 6, 12
Peer Influences	Create class and school norms that honor achievement, encourage peer support, and discourage peer conflict.	Chapters 10, 13, 15

Source: Based on Lee, J., & Shute, V. J. (2010). Personal and social-contextual factors in K–12 academic performance: An integrative perspective on student learning. Educational Psychologist, 45, 185–202.

▼ SUMMARY

Learning and Teaching Today (pp. 4–8)

What are classrooms like today? In 2003, 12% of the people living in the United States were born in another country, and 18% spoke a language other than English at home—half of these families speak Spanish. By 2050, there will be no majority race or ethnic group in the United States; every American will be a member of a minority group. Almost 20% of American children live in poverty. In 2008–2009, over half of school-age students with disabilities received most of their education in general education classrooms. Even though students in classrooms are increasingly diverse in race, ethnicity, language, and economic level, teachers are less diverse—the percentage of White teachers is increasing, while the percentage of Black teachers is falling. This book is about understanding the complex processes of development, learning, motivation, teaching, and assessment so that you can become a capable and confident teacher.

What is NCLB? The No Child Left Behind Act of 2002 requires standardized achievement testing in reading and mathematics every year for all students in grades 3 through 8, and once more in high school. Science is tested once in each grade span: elementary, middle, and high school. Based on these test scores, schools are judged to determine if their students are making Adequate Yearly Progress (AYP) toward becoming proficient in the subjects tested. The NCLB Act requires that all students in the schools must reach proficiency by the end of the 2013–2014 school year. NCLB was supposed to be reauthorized in 2007 or 2008. On March 13, 2010, The Obama Administration released *A Blueprint for Reform: The Reauthorization of the Elementary and Secondary Education Act* to describe a vision for the reauthorization of NCLB.

What evidence is there that teachers make a difference? Several studies speak to the power of teachers in the lives of students. The first found that the quality of the teacher–student relationship in kindergarten predicted several aspects of school success through the 8th grade. The second study found similar results for students from preschool through 5th grade. The third study examined math achievement for students in two large school districts as they moved through 3rd, 4th, and 5th grades. Again, the quality of the teacher made a difference: Students who had three high-quality teachers in a row were way ahead of peers who spent one or more years with less competent teachers. In a study that followed children from 3rd through 5th grade, two factors helped children with lower skills in mathematics begin to close the achievement gap: higher-level (not just basic skills) instruction and positive relationships with teachers.

What Is Good Teaching? (pp. 8–12)

What is good teaching? Good teachers are committed to their students. They must deal with a wide range of student abilities and challenges: different languages, different home situations, and different abilities and disabilities. They must adapt instruction and assessment to students' needs. The whole time that these experts are navigating through the academic material, they also are taking care of the emotional needs of their students, propping up sagging self-esteem and encouraging responsibility. From the first day of class, they carefully plan and teach the basic procedures for living and learning in their classes.

How does differentiated instruction help? Differentiated instruction is one way of going beyond accommodating learner differences to viewing diversity as an array of strengths on which to build. The basic idea of differentiated instruction is that teachers must take into account not only the subjects they are teaching but also the students. In differentiated classrooms, students work at different paces, sometimes exercising varied learning options, and they are assessed using indicators that fit their interests and needs. Differentiated instruction conceives of all students as seeking purpose, challenge, affirmation, power, and the chance to contribute. The confident teacher sees these different student needs as opportunities, not problems, and responds with invitation, investment, persistence, challenge, and reflection.

What are the concerns of beginning teachers? Learning to teach is a gradual process. The concerns and problems of teachers change as they grow in their ability. During the beginning years, attention tends to be focused on maintaining discipline, motivating students, accommodating differences among students, evaluating students' work, dealing with parents, and getting along with other teachers. Even with these concerns, many beginning teachers bring creativity and energy to their teaching and improve every year. The more experienced teacher can move on to concerns about professional growth and effectiveness in teaching a wide range of students.

The Role of Educational Psychology (pp. 12–22)

What is educational psychology? Educational psychology has been linked to teaching since it began in the United States over a century ago. The goals of educational psychology are to understand and to improve the teaching and learning processes. Educational psychologists develop knowledge and methods; they also use the knowledge and methods of psychology and other related disciplines to study learning and teaching in everyday situations. Educational psychologists examine what happens when someone/something (a teacher or parent or computer) teaches something (math or weaving or dancing) to someone else (student or co-worker or team) in some setting (classroom or theater or gym).

What are descriptive studies? Reports of descriptive studies often include survey results, interview responses, samples of actual classroom dialogue, or records of the class activities. Ethnographic methods involve studying the naturally occurring events in the life of a group and trying to understand the meaning of these events to the people involved. A case study investigates in depth how a teacher plans courses, for example, or how a student tries to learn specific material.

What are correlational, experimental, and quasi-experimental studies? A correlation is a number that indicates both the strength and the direction of a relationship between two events or measurements. The closer the correlation is to either 1.00 or −1.00, the stronger the relationship. Experimental studies can indicate cause-and-effect relationships and should help teachers implement useful changes. Instead of just observing and describing an existing situation, the investigators introduce changes and note the results. Quasi-experimental studies meet most of the criteria for true experiments, with the important exception being that the participants are not assigned to groups at random. Instead, existing groups such as classes or schools participate in the experiments.

What are single-subject and microgenetic studies? In single-subject experimental designs, researchers examine the effects of treatments on one person, often by using a baseline/intervention/baseline/intervention or ABAB approach. Microgenetic studies take many detailed observations of subjects to track the progression of change from the very beginning until a process becomes stable.

What is action research? When teachers or schools make systematic observations or test out methods to improve teaching and learning for their students, they are conducting action research.

What is scientifically based research? Scientifically based research systematically uses observations or experiments to gather valid and reliable data; involves rigorous and appropriate procedures for gathering and analyzing the data; is clearly described so it can be repeated by others; and has been rigorously reviewed by appropriate, independent experts.

Distinguish between principles and theories. A principle is an established relationship between two or more factors—between a certain teaching strategy, for example, and student achievement. A theory is an interrelated set of concepts that is used to explain a body of data and to make predictions. The principles from research offer a number of possible answers to specific problems, and the theories offer perspectives for analyzing almost any situation that may arise. Research is a continuing cycle that involves clear specification of hypotheses or questions based on good theory, systematic gathering and analyzing of data, modification and improvement of explanatory theories based on the results, and the formulation of new, better questions based on the improved theories.

What key factors support student learning? A synthesis of about 150 studies of student learning found two broad categories of influence: *student personal factors* and *school and social-contextual factors*. When I read this article, I was pleased to see that my favorite subject, educational psychology, provides a base for developing knowledge and skills in virtually every area except principal leadership.

▼ KEY TERMS

Action research (16)
Case study (14)
Correlations (14)
Descriptive studies (14)
Differentiated instruction (10)
Educational psychology (12)
Empirical (20)
Ethnography (14)

Evidence-based practice in psychology (EBPP) (18)
Experimentation (15)
Hypothesis/Hypotheses (18)
Microgenetic studies (16)
Negative correlation (15)
Participant observation (14)
Participants/Subjects (15)
Positive correlation (14)

Principle (18)
Quasi-experimental Studies (15)
Random (15)
Reflective (9)
Single-subject experimental studies (16)
Statistically significant (15)
Teachers' sense of efficacy (5)
Theory (18)

▼ CONNECT AND EXTEND TO LICENSURE

MULTIPLE-CHOICE QUESTIONS

1. Novice teachers face numerous tasks and scenarios with which they have little prior experience. For teachers currently entering the field, which of the following is not a challenge they are apt to encounter?
   A. Students who may exhibit superior technology skills as compared to their teachers
   B. An increasingly diverse population of students and families
   C. Inadequate resources to ensure the safety of their students while using technology in the classroom
   D. Students who face the challenges associated with living in poverty

2. Differentiated instruction makes accommodations for the unique qualities of each learner. For students embarking on a unit that explores animal species, which of the following would be the best example of differentiated instruction?
   A. Provide all students with the various vocabulary terms they are likely to encounter during the unit to best prepare them for future activities.

   B. Allow students to select their own species to research and require a standardized test upon completion of the unit to ensure learning has occurred.
   C. Have the students determine the manner in which they prefer to explore and be assessed upon the topic.
   D. Supply students with a variety of media options at different difficulty levels to explore the various animal species.

3. Both students and teachers work harder and persist longer when they have a high sense of efficacy. Which of the following does not enhance self-efficacy in both students and teachers?
   A. Formal school relationships that focus solely on skills
   B. Day-to-day success in achieving tasks
   C. High expectations from those in the environment
   D. Assistance from more knowledgeable partners

4. All the students in Ms. Clare's third grade class engage in weekly test reviews. Ms. Clare believes that these reviews will enhance student retention when standardized testing occurs in the

spring. Which of Ms. Clare's students under the No Child Left Behind Act will have his or her scores reported separately?

A. Susan Frasier who was recently identified with a learning disability
B. Brendan Kincaid who must wear corrected lenses in order to read
C. Miranda Ruiz whose English is excellent even though his parents moved to the United States from Mexico ten years ago
D. Lauren Stone who is a member of the third grade's gifted and talented cohort

CONSTRUCTED-RESPONSE QUESTIONS

Case

Sandra Chapman was determined to add to her repertoire of teaching skills as she entered her second year of teaching. Her first year as a high school teacher proved to be more of a challenge than she expected. Her school, located in the heart of the city, drew students from all walks of life and economic circumstances. Last year, she initially hoped that all of her students would master the history curriculum which she had inherited, but by midyear several of her students were not attending class on a regular basis. In an effort to increase attendance she took points off students' grades when they missed class and intentionally ignored them when they returned. She believed that by not taking an interest in where they were, she would not reinforce their "skipping" behavior. Miss Chapman also thought that by continually reminding students of how much they did not know, she would encourage them to study. Sadly, these methods did not work well and attendance only further declined. Sandra is now in the process of designing some new strategies.

5. Identify the methods Sandra Chapman uses to encourage attendance and explain why these methods might have been unsuccessful.
6. What advice would you offer Sandra Chapman as she prepares to develop new methods?

--- MyEducationLab™ ---

Go to Chapter 1 of the Book Specific Resources in MyEducationLab and click on "Connect and Extend to Licensure" to answer these questions. Compare your responses with the feedback provided.

▼ WHAT WOULD THEY DO?

TEACHERS' CASEBOOK: Leaving No Child Behind

Here is how several expert teachers said they would prepare a highly diverse group of students for spring achievement tests and readiness for college and career.

BARBARA PRESLEY • Transition/Work Study Coordinator—High School Level
B.E.S.T.T. Program (Baldwinsville Exceptional Student Training and Transition Program), C.W. Baker High School, Baldwinsville, NY

As the Transition/Work Study Coordinator and the originator of the BESTT Program, my responsibility was to prepare severely disabled students for life post high school. The philosophy of the Baldwinsville School District supported an employment model for training. Employment sites at local businesses were developed and Job Coaches were hired to work 1:1 with students in a "real-life" work environment with real work assignments and expectations.

While some, but not all of our students had to sit for exams, we found that the confidence they developed while at "work" and the work ethic they learned in that environment gave them the skills they needed to do their best in the testing situation. Job Coaches (interns) were invaluable in the "community classroom" not only because they taught our students the skills they needed to succeed, but also taught the community to recognize and appreciate our students for their capabilities rather than their disabilities. It is education that works two ways.

JENNIFER PINCOSKI • Learning Resource Teacher: K–12
Lee County School District, Fort Myers, FL

One of the advantages for teachers in this situation is that many of the strategies that are effective for students with learning disabilities are also effective for second-language learners. Even students who are meeting benchmarks will benefit from these supports. Some of these strategies include labeling items throughout the classroom for language/vocabulary acquisition, providing visual supports whenever possible, and using a variety of graphic organizers. Cooperative learning groups and the Total Physical Response (TPR) method can also help in the development of both language skills and content knowledge. Activities can be tiered to match students' levels of understanding, and to demonstrate their learning, students can be offered multiple assignment options from which to choose.

Exposing students to new vocabulary and content through auditory, visual, AND hands-on instruction will yield the best results. Broken down to its most basic level, this philosophy can be summarized by the proverb, "Tell me and I'll forget; show me and I'll remember; involve me and I'll understand." Students should be active participants in the learning process, not spectators.

JESSICA N. MAHTABAN • 8th Grade Math
Woodrow Wilson Middle School, Clifton, NJ

The first thing to address is survival. Each student must learn his/her name, address, and phone number. It is crucial for all students to know this information in case of any type of emergency. Afterward, the students will become familiar with the classroom routines and expectations. Once the students are comfortable with the routines and expectations, they will be able to focus on language. The intern, administration, parents, and I must meet frequently to work cooperatively on making projects and goals for each student.

During any lesson I would provide visual cues (gestures, pictures, objects) with verbal instruction. I would speak to the students in short sentences and give clear examples of what is expected from them. The intern and I will interact with students as they work independently or cooperatively during an activity. We will also check comprehension frequently, so that we can help any student that does not understand.

LAUREN ROLLINS • 1st Grade Teacher
Boulevard Elementary School, Shaker Heights, OH

As a teacher, my job is to do my best to meet the needs of every student in my classroom, regardless of what resources are available to me. This situation, while challenging, is no exception. If resources will not be provided to me by the school, it is my job to find them on my own or make them myself. Outside of the classroom, the first thing I would do is to contact any local agencies, community centers, or religious institutions that may be able to help me put together learning materials for the students from immigrant families. In the meantime, I would create labels for the classroom and for the homes of my students to expose them to as much English print as possible. I would use translation Web sites so that I could include the words in both English and their native languages. I would organize after school/evening meetings for these students and their families to provide as much additional exposure to the English language as possible. The role of the college intern would be to assist me in the differentiation of instruction so that the individual/small group needs of my students would be met. Together, she and I can create and implement skill-based lessons to help all of the students make meaningful progress with the curriculum and with test preparation.

PAUL DRAGIN • ESL Grades 9–12
Columbus East High School, Columbus OH

Multiple obstacles are posed in this situation. The scenario presents two pieces of information that I would key in on. One is that problems in reading seem to be the most common. This is the challenge I would place as the number one priority due to its preeminence in terms of predicting future academic success. Scoring well on the achievement tests and doing well in college are not realistic expectations without reading success. The other piece of information that is advantageous is the student intern from the local college. With reading as the focus, I would instruct the intern on some basic reading diagnostics to get a clearer picture of each student's reading level. From there, we could choose texts that would be appropriate to increase comprehension and fluency. With two instructors in the room, we would be better equipped for small-group instruction to target the various reading levels. This targeted reading instruction would be a benefit to the intern as well as the students since his or her services would be vital to instruction and together we would be assisting the students in their reading comprehension and subsequent language acquisition.

PAULA COLEMERE • Special Education Teacher–English, History
McClintock High School, Tempe, AZ

Before I even begin teaching this group of students, I would set my room up for success. Students can be distracted by too many things on the walls; therefore, everything I choose to display will be very deliberate. To do this, I would start with a blank slate and take everything off of the walls. I would label objects, such as the door, pencil sharpener, desks, etc., with signs to help the English Language Learners to build vocabulary. I would save an area to create a "word wall" for content area vocabulary; this will aid both the ELL students

and the students with special needs. It would be important to me to educate myself on the background of my students and where they come from. This would help me to make a personal connection with each student and it would help me to understand cultural differences when making contact with the family. It is also important to have an understanding as to what is happening in their home countries to try to make connections to learning based on their experiences. Finally, graphic organizers would be a key part of my lesson planning as it helps students to organize information.

SARA VINCENT • Special Education
Langley High School, McLean, VA

The classroom situation described requires the teacher to be creative. She must differentiate her lesson plans in order to accommodate the language barriers and the different learning styles. Since many of the students know a little English and others have reading troubles, a teacher can provide pictures with each lesson. For example, an assistive technology consultant can provide a teacher with computer programs, such as BoardMaker and PixWrite, which allow the teacher to compose lesson plans and accompanying assessments using words and pictures to convey ideas needed to help the students pass the end of the year achievement tests. As students become more proficient in English, some of the supports may be faded. The teacher should utilize the intern for students who are struggling and for those students who are achieving to move to a faster paced curriculum. The most important factors for this teacher are vigilance, flexibility, and creativity. A teacher with these characteristics will ensure that the needs of the students are met.

LINDA SPARKS • Grade 1
John F. Kennedy School, Billerica MA

I have found through the years that all students can learn, no matter what their backgrounds are, as long as they are given the right tools. I always start the new school year with all concrete, visual and "hands on" lessons. This way everyone is being introduced to the same skills in the same manner. During this time, I am trying to pick out each student's learning style and/or assessment needs. I have had many student teachers through the years and in the beginning I use them as my extra pair of eyes and hands and for assistance. Once trust has developed among the students, my student teachers, and me, I find I can begin to separate the students into smaller groups where I can better meet their needs. I also open the doors to families, offering them times to come in, whether it is before school, after school, or lunch times (adapting to their schedules) to help them better understand what is going on in the classroom and help their children at home. I have found this to be very helpful to the student and it provides me with a better understanding of the family. I show them materials I am using (unifix cubes for place value, pictures, models, symbols, etc …). Once the students are placed in groups, we can continue to teach according to their specific needs. I like to keep heterogeneous groups. That way, the students are more confident, and they don't have time to think about why they are in a specific group. My student teacher and I work together as a team to meet the needs of all of the students. I find that as long as the doors of communication are kept open, learning is possible for all students.

MyEducationLab™

Go to Topic #1, Research Methods and Teacher Reflection, in the MyEducationLab (www.myeducationlab. com) for *Educational Psychology*, where you can:

- Find learning outcomes for Research Methods and Teacher Reflection along with the national standards that connect to these outcomes.
- Complete Assignments and Activities that can help you more deeply understand the chapter content.
- Apply and practice your understanding of the core teaching skills identified in the chapter with the Building Teaching Skills and Dispositions learning units.
- Examine challenging situations and cases presented in the IRIS Center Resources.
- Access video clips of CCSSO National Teachers of the Year award winners responding to the question, "Why Do I Teach?" in the Teacher Talk section.
- Check your comprehension on the content covered in the chapter with the Study Plan. Here you will be able to take a chapter quiz, receive feedback on your answers, and then access Review, Practice, and Enrichment activities to enhance your understanding of chapter content.
- Find additional Teachers' Casebook scenarios and responses to them from practicing teachers.
- Use the Online Lesson Plan Builder to practice lesson planning and integrating national and state standards into your planning.

chapter two
COGNITIVE DEVELOPMENT

▶ **TEACHERS' CASEBOOK:** Symbols and Cymbals

The district curriculum guide calls for a unit on poetry, including lessons on *symbolism* in poems. You are concerned that many of your 4th grade students may not be ready to understand this abstract concept. To test the waters, you ask a few students what a *symbol* is.

"It's sorta like a big metal thing that you bang together." Tracy waves her hands like a drum major.

"Yeah," Sean adds, "My sister plays one in the high school band."

You realize they are on the wrong track here, so you try again. "I was thinking of a different kind of symbol, like a ring as a symbol of marriage or a heart as a symbol of love, or …"

You are met with blank stares.

Trevor ventures, "You mean like the Olympic torch?"

"And what does that symbolize, Trevor?" you ask.

"Like I said, a torch." Trevor wonders how you could be so dense.

CRITICAL THINKING

- What do these students' reactions tell you about children's thinking?
- How would you approach this unit?
- What more would you do to "listen" to your students' thinking so you could match your teaching to their level of thinking?
- How would you give your students concrete experiences with symbolism?
- How will you decide if the students are not developmentally ready for this material?

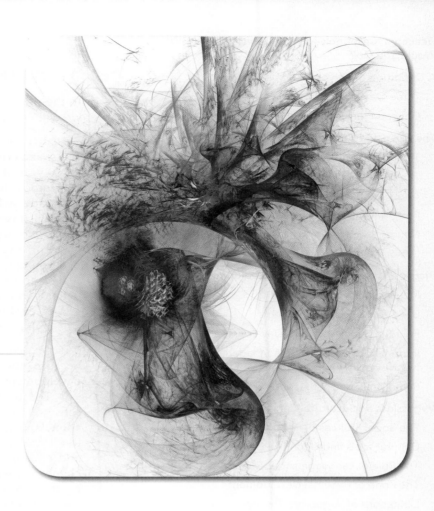

OVERVIEW AND OBJECTIVES

What is going on with Trevor? In this chapter, you will find out. We begin with a definition of development and examine three questions about development that psychologists have debated for many years: nature versus nurture, continuity versus discontinuity, and critical versus sensitive periods for development. Next we look at general principles of human development that most psychologists affirm. To understand cognitive development, we begin by studying how the brain works and then explore the ideas of two of the most influential cognitive developmental theorists, Jean Piaget and Lev Vygotsky. Piaget's ideas have implications for teachers about how their students think and what they can learn. We will consider criticisms of his ideas as well. The work of Lev Vygotsky, a Russian psychologist, highlights the important role teachers and parents play in the cognitive development of the child. Vygotsky's theory is becoming more and more influential in the field of child development. By the time you have completed this chapter, you should be able to:

Objective 2.1: Provide a definition of development that takes into account three agreed-upon principles.

Objective 2.2: Discuss three continuing debates about development, along with current consensus on these questions.

Objective 2.3: Summarize some current research on the physical development of the brain and possible implications for teaching.

Objective 2.4: Explain how the principles and stages presented in Piaget's theory of cognitive development influence current educational research and practice.

Objective 2.5: Explain how the principles presented in Vygotsky's theory of development influence current educational research and practice.

A DEFINITION OF DEVELOPMENT

In the next few chapters, as we explore how children develop, we will encounter some surprising situations.

- Leah, a 5-year-old, is certain that rolling out a ball of clay into a snake creates more clay.
- A 9-year-old child in Geneva, Switzerland, firmly insists that it is impossible to be Swiss and Genevan at the same time: "I'm already Swiss. I can't also be Genevan."
- Jamal, a very bright elementary school student, cannot answer the question "How would life be different if people did not sleep?" because he insists, "People HAVE TO SLEEP!"
- A young girl who once said her *feet* hurt, suddenly begins to refer to her *foots,* and then describes her *footses,* before she finally returns to talking about her *feet.*
- A 2-year-old brings his own mother to comfort a friend who is crying, even though the friend's mother is available, too.

What explains these interesting events? You will soon find out, because you are entering the world of child and adolescent development.

The term **development** in its most general psychological sense refers to certain changes that occur in human beings (or animals) between conception and death. The term is not applied to all changes, but rather to those that appear in orderly ways and remain for a reasonably long period of time. A temporary change caused by a brief illness, for example, is not considered a part of development. Human development can be divided into a number of different aspects. **Physical development**, as you might guess, deals with changes in the body. **Personal development** is the term generally used for changes in an individual's personality. **Social development** refers to changes in the way an individual relates to others. And **cognitive development** refers to changes in thinking, reasoning, and decision making.

Many changes during development are simply matters of growth and **maturation**. Maturation refers to changes that occur naturally and spontaneously and that are, to a large extent, genetically programmed. Such changes emerge over time and are relatively unaffected by environment, except in cases of malnutrition or severe illness. Much of a person's physical development falls into this category. Other changes are brought about through learning, as individuals interact with their environment. Such changes make up a large part of a person's social development. But what about the development of thinking and personality? Most psychologists agree that in these areas, both maturation and interaction with the environment (or *nature* and *nurture,* as they are sometimes called) are important, but they disagree about the amount of emphasis to place on each one. Nature versus nurture is one of three continuing discussions in theories of development.

Three Questions Across the Theories

Because there are many different approaches to research and theory, there are some continuing debates about key questions surrounding development.

WHAT IS THE SOURCE OF DEVELOPMENT? NATURE VERSUS NURTURE. Which is more important in development, the "nature" of an individual (heredity, genes, biological processes, maturation, etc.) or the "nurture" of environmental contexts (education, parenting, culture, social policies, etc.)? This debate has raged for at least 2,000 years and has accumulated many labels along the way, including "heredity versus environment," "biology versus culture," "maturation versus learning," and "innate versus acquired abilities." In earlier centuries, philosophers, poets, religious leaders, and politicians argued the question. Today scientists bring new tools to the discussion as they can map genes or trace the effects of drugs on brain activity, for example (Gottlieb, Wahlsten, & Lickliter, 2006). Even in scientific explanations, the pendulum has swung back and forth between nature and nurture (Cairns & Cairns, 2006; Overton, 2006).

Today the environment is seen as critical to development, but so are biological factors and individual differences. In fact, some psychologists assert that behaviors are determined 100% by biology and 100% by environment—they can't be separated (Miller, 2011). Current views emphasize complex **coactions** (joint actions) of nature and nurture. For example, a child born with a very easy-going, calm disposition will likely elicit different reactions from parents, playmates, and teachers than a child who is often upset and difficult to soothe; this shows that individuals are active in constructing their own environments. But environments shape individuals as well—if not, what good would education be? So today, the either/or debates about nature and nurture are of less interest to educational and developmental psychologists. As a pioneering developmental psychologist said over 100 years ago, the more exciting questions involve understanding how "both causes work together" (Baldwin, 1895, p. 77).

WHAT IS THE SHAPE OF DEVELOPMENT? CONTINUITY VERSUS DISCONTINUITY. Is human development a continuous process of increasing abilities, or are there leaps to new stages when abilities actually change? A continuous process would be like gradual improvement in your running endurance through systematic exercise. A discontinuous change (also called *qualitative*) would be like many of the changes in humans during puberty, such as the ability to reproduce—an entirely different ability. Qualitative changes are contrasted with purely quantitative change, such as the adolescent growing taller.

You can think of continuous or quantitative change like walking up a ramp to go higher and higher: Progress is steady. A discontinuous or qualitative change is more like walking up stairs: There are level periods, and then you ascend the next step all at once. Piaget's theory of cognitive development, described in the next section, is an example of *qualitative*, discontinuous change in children's thinking abilities. But other explanations of cognitive development based on learning theories emphasize gradual, continuous, *quantitative* change.

TIMING: IS IT TOO LATE? CRITICAL VERSUS SENSITIVE PERIODS. Are there critical periods during which certain abilities, such as language, need to develop? If those opportunities are missed, can the child still "catch up"? These are questions about timing and development. Many earlier psychologists, particularly those influenced by Freud, believed that early childhood experiences were critical, especially for emotional/social and cognitive development. But does early toilet training really set all of us on a particular life path? Probably not. More recent research shows that later experiences are powerful, too, and can change the direction of development (Kagan & Herschkowitz, 2005). Most psychologists today talk about **sensitive periods**—not critical periods. There are times when a person is especially ready for or responsive to certain experiences.

BEWARE OF EITHER/OR. As you might imagine, these debates about development proved too complicated to be settled by splitting alternatives into either/or possibilities (Griffins & Gray, 2005). Today, most psychologists view human development, learning, and motivation as a set of interacting and coacting contexts, from the inner biological structures and processes that influence development such as genes, cells, nutrition, and disease, to the external factors of families, neighborhoods, social relationships, educational and health institutions, public policies, time periods, historical events, and so on. So the effects of a childhood disease on the cognitive development of a child born in the 16th century to a poor family and treated by bloodletting or leeches will be quite different than the effect of the same disease on a child born in 2012 to a wealthy family and given

---

Development Orderly, adaptive changes we go through between conception and death and remain for a reasonably long period of time.

Physical development Changes in body structure and function over time.

Personal development Changes in personality that take place as one grows.

Social development Changes over time in the ways we relate to others.

Cognitive development Gradual orderly changes by which mental processes become more complex and sophisticated.

Maturation Genetically programmed, naturally occurring changes over time.

Coactions Joint actions of individual biology and the environment—each shapes and influences the other.

Sensitive periods Times when a person is especially ready for or responsive to certain experiences.

the best treatment available for that time period. Throughout the rest of this book, we will try to make sense of development, learning, motivation, and teaching without falling into the *either/or trap*.

General Principles of Development

Although there is disagreement about exactly how development takes place, there are a few general principles almost all theorists would support.

1. **People develop at different rates.** In your own classroom, you will have a whole range of examples of different developmental rates. Some students will be larger, better coordinated, or more mature in their thinking and social relationships. Others will be much slower to mature in these areas. Except in rare cases of very rapid or very slow development, such differences are normal and should be expected in any large group of students.
2. **Development is relatively orderly.** People develop abilities in a logical order. In infancy, they sit before they walk, babble before they talk, and see the world through their own eyes before they can begin to imagine how others see it. In school, they will master addition before algebra, Harry Potter before Shakespeare, and so on. But "orderly" does not necessarily mean linear or predictable—people might advance, stay the same for a period of time, or even go backwards.
3. **Development takes place gradually.** Very rarely do changes appear overnight. A student who cannot manipulate a pencil or answer a hypothetical question may well develop this ability, but the change is likely to take time.

THE BRAIN AND COGNITIVE DEVELOPMENT

If you have taken an introductory psychology class, you have read about the brain and nervous system. You probably remember that there are several different areas of the brain and that certain areas are involved in particular functions. For example, the feathery looking *cerebellum* coordinates and orchestrates balance and smooth, skilled movements—from the graceful gestures of the dancer to the everyday action of eating without stabbing yourself in the nose with a fork. The cerebellum may also play a role in higher cognitive functions such as learning. The *hippocampus* is critical in recalling new information and recent experiences, while the *amygdala* directs emotions. The *thalamus* is involved in our ability to learn new information, *particularly* if it is verbal. Figure 2.1 shows the various regions of the brain.

Advances in brain imaging techniques have allowed scientists remarkable access to the functioning brain. For example, **functional magnetic resonance imaging (fMRI)** shows how

Functional magnetic resonance imaging (fMRI) An MRI is an imaging technique that uses a magnetic field along with radio waves and a computer to create detailed pictures of the inside of the body. A functional MRI uses the MRI to measure the tiny changes that take place in the brain during brain activity.

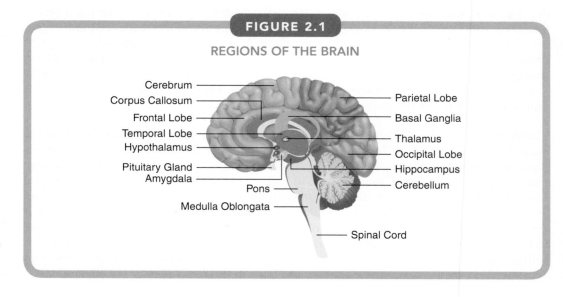

FIGURE 2.1

REGIONS OF THE BRAIN

Cerebrum
Corpus Callosum
Frontal Lobe
Temporal Lobe
Hypothalamus
Pituitary Gland
Amygdala
Pons
Medulla Oblongata

Parietal Lobe
Basal Ganglia
Thalamus
Occipital Lobe
Hippocampus
Cerebellum
Spinal Cord

blood flows within the brain when children or adults do different cognitive tasks. **Event-related potential (ERP)** measurements assess electrical activity of the brain through the skull or scalp as people perform activities such as reading or learning vocabulary words. **Positron emission tomography (PET)** scans can track brain activity under different conditions.

Let's begin our look at the brain by examining its tiny components—neurons, synapses, and glial cells.

The Developing Brain: Neurons

A newborn baby's brain weighs about one pound, barely one third of the weight of an adult brain. But this infant brain has billions of **neurons**, the specialized nerve cells that accumulate and transmit information (in the form of electrical activity) in the brain and other parts of the nervous system. Neurons are a grayish color, so they sometimes are called the *gray matter* of the brain. One neuron has the information processing capacity of a small computer. That means the processing power of one 3-pound human brain is likely greater than all the computers in the world. Of course, computers do many things, like calculate square roots of large numbers, much faster than humans can (Anderson, 2010). These incredibly important neuron cells are tiny—about 30,000 could fit on the head of a pin (Sprenger, 2010). Scientists once believed that all the neurons a person would ever have were present at birth, but now we know that the production of new neurons, **neurogenesis**, continues into adulthood (Johnson, 2003).

Neuron cells send out long arm- and branch-like fibers called *axons* and *dendrites* to connect with other neuron cells. The fiber ends from different neurons don't actually touch—there are tiny spaces between them, about one billionth of a meter in length, called **synapses**. Neurons share information by releasing chemicals that jump across the synapses. Axons transmit information out to muscles, glands, or other neurons; dendrites receive information and transmit it to the neuron cells themselves. Figure 2.2 shows these components of the neuron system (Anderson, 2010).

FIGURE 2.2

A SINGLE NEURON

Each neuron (nerve cell) includes dendrites that bring in messages and an axon that sends out messages. This is a single neuron, but each neuron is in a network with many others.

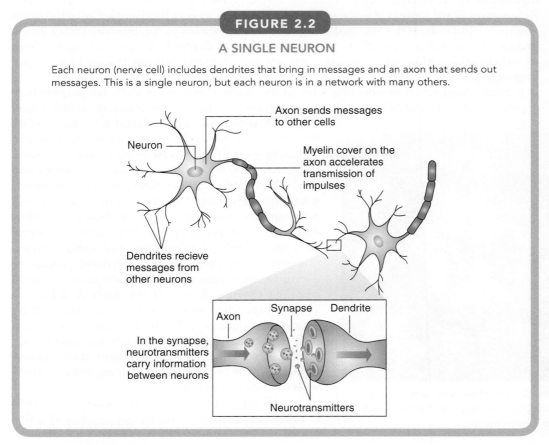

Axon sends messages to other cells

Neuron

Myelin cover on the axon accelerates transmission of impulses

Dendrites recieve messages from other neurons

In the synapse, neurotransmitters carry information between neurons

Axon   Synapse   Dendrite

Neurotransmitters

Event-related potential (ERP) Measurements that assess electrical activity of the brain through the skull or scalp.

Positron emission tomography (PET) A method of localizing and measuring brain activity using computer-assisted motion pictures of the brain.

Neurons Nerve cells that store and transfer information.

Neurogenesis The production of new neurons.

Synapses The tiny space between neurons—chemical messages are sent across these gaps.

At birth, each of the child's 100 to 200 billion neurons has about 2,500 synapses. However, the fibers that reach out from the neurons and the synapses between the fiber ends increase during the first years of life, perhaps into adolescence or longer. By ages 2 to 3, each neuron has around 15,000 synapses; children this age have many more synapses than they will have as adults. In fact, they are *oversupplied* with the neurons and synapses that they will need to adapt to their environments. However, only those neurons that are used will survive, and unused neurons will be "pruned." This pruning is necessary and supports cognitive development. Researchers have found that some developmental disabilities are associated with a gene defect that interferes with pruning (Bransford, Brown, & Cocking, 2000; Cook & Cook, 2009).

Two kinds of overproduction and pruning processes take place. One is called *experience-expectant* because synapses are overproduced in certain parts of the brain during specific developmental periods, awaiting (expecting) stimulation. For example, during the first months of life, the brain expects visual and auditory stimulation. If a normal range of sights and sounds occurs, then the visual and auditory areas of the brain develop. But children who are born completely deaf receive no auditory stimulation and, as a result, the auditory processing area of their brains becomes devoted to processing visual information. Similarly, the visual processing area of the brain for children blind from birth becomes devoted to auditory processing (Nelson, 2001; Neville, 2007).

Experience-expectant overproduction and pruning processes are responsible for general development in large areas of the brain and may explain why adults have difficulty with pronunciations that are not part of their native language. For example, the distinction between the sounds of *r* and *l* is important in English but not in Japanese, so by about 10 months, Japanese infants lose the ability to discriminate between *r* and *l*— *those neurons are pruned away.* As a result, Japanese adults learning these sounds require intense instruction and practice (Bransford et al., 2000; Hinton, Miyamoto, & Della-Chiesa, 2008).

The second kind of synaptic overproduction and pruning is called *experience-dependent*. Here, synaptic connections are formed based on the individual's experiences. New synapses are formed in response to neural activity in very localized areas of the brain when the individual is not successful in processing information. Again, more synapses are produced than will be kept after "pruning." Experience-dependent processes are involved in individual learning, such as mastering unfamiliar sound pronunciations in a second language you are studying.

Stimulating environments may help in the pruning process in early life (experience-expectant period) and also may support increased synapse development in adulthood (experience-dependent period) (Cook & Cook, 2009). In fact, animal studies have shown that rats raised in stimulating environments (with toys, tasks for learning, other rats, and human handling) develop and retain 25% more synapses than rats who are raised with little stimulation. Even though the research with rats may not apply directly to humans, it is clear that extreme deprivation can have negative effects on human brain development. But extra stimulation will not necessarily improve development for young children who are getting adequate or typical amounts (Byrnes & Fox, 1998; Kolb & Whishaw, 1998). So spending money on expensive toys or baby education programs probably offers more stimulation than is necessary. Pots and pans, blocks and books, sand and water all provide excellent stimulation— especially if accompanied by caring conversations with parents or teachers.

Look back at Figure 2.2. It appears that there is nothing between the neurons but air. Actually, this

SUPPORTING BRAIN DEVELOPMENT Studies of the brain indicate that stimulating environments and meaningful interactions with parents and teachers likely support better brain development.

is wrong. The spaces are filled with **glial cells**, the *white matter* of the brain. There are trillions of these cells—they greatly outnumber neurons. Glial cells appear to have many functions such as fighting infections, controlling blood flow and communication among neurons, and providing the *myelin* coating (see Figure 2.2) around axon fibers (Ormrod, 2011). **Myelination**, the coating of axon neuron fibers with an insulating fatty glial covering, influences thinking and learning. This process is something like coating bare electrical wires with rubber or plastic. This myelin coating makes message transmission faster and more efficient. Myelination happens quickly in the early years, but continues gradually into adolescence, with the child's brain doubling in volume in the first year of life and doubling again around puberty (Anderson, 2010).

The Developing Brain: Cerebral Cortex

Let's move from the neuron level to the brain itself. The outer 1/8-inch-thick covering is the cerebral cortex—the largest area of the brain. It is a thin sheet of neurons, but it is almost 3 square feet in area for adults. To get all that area in your head, the sheet is crumpled together with many folds and wrinkles (Anderson, 2010). In humans, this area of the brain is much larger than it is in lower animals. The cerebral cortex accounts for about 85% of the brain's weight in adulthood and contains the greatest number of neurons. The cerebral cortex allows the greatest human accomplishments, such as complex problem solving and language.

The cortex is the last part of the brain to develop, so it is believed to be more susceptible to environmental influences than other areas of the brain (Gluck, Mercado, & Myers, 2008; Schacter, Gilbert, & Wenger, 2009). Parts of the cortex mature at different rates. The region of the cortex that controls physical motor movement matures first, then the areas that control complex senses such as vision and hearing, and last, the frontal lobe that controls higher-order thinking processes. The temporal lobes of the cortex that play major roles in emotions, judgment, and language do not develop fully until the high school years and maybe later.

Different areas of the cortex seem to have distinct functions, as shown in Figure 2.3. Even though different functions are found in particular areas of the brain, these specialized functions are quite specific and elementary. To accomplish more complex functions

---

FIGURE 2.3

A VIEW OF THE CEREBRAL CORTEX

This is a simple representation of the left side of the human brain, showing the cerebral cortex. The cortex is divided into different areas, or lobes, each having a variety of regions with different functions. A few of the major functions are indicated here.

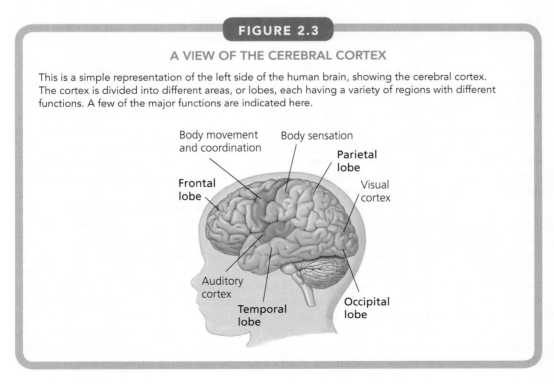

Glial cells The *white matter* of the brain. These cells greatly outnumber neurons and appear to have many functions such as fighting infections, controlling blood flow and communication among neurons, and providing the *myelin* coating around axon fibers.

Myelination The process by which neural fibers are coated with a fatty sheath called *myelin* that makes message transfer more efficient.

such as speaking or reading, the various areas of the cortex must communicate and work together (Anderson, 2010; Byrnes & Fox, 1998).

Another aspect of brain functioning that has implications for cognitive development is **lateralization**, or the specialization of the two hemispheres of the brain. We know that each half of the brain controls the opposite side of the body. Damage to the right side of the brain will affect movement of the left side of the body and vice versa. In addition, certain areas of the brain affect particular behaviors. For most of us, the left hemisphere of the brain is a major factor in language processing, and the right hemisphere handles much of our spatial-visual information and emotions (nonverbal information). For some left-handed people, the relationship may be reversed, but for most left-handers, and for females on average, there is less hemispheric specialization altogether (Anderson, 2010; O'Boyle & Gill, 1998). The brains of young children show more **plasticity** (adaptability) because they are not as specialized or lateralized as the brains of older children and adults. Young children with damage to the left side of the brain are somewhat able to overcome the damage, which allows language development to proceed. Different areas of the brain take over the functions of the damaged area. But in older children and adults, this compensation is less likely to occur after damage to the left brain hemisphere.

These differences in performance by the brain's hemispheres, however, are more relative than absolute; one hemisphere is just more efficient than the other in performing certain functions. Language is processed "differently, but simultaneously" by the left and right hemispheres (Alferink & Farmer-Dougan, 2010, p. 44). Nearly any task, particularly the complex skills and abilities that concern teachers, requires simultaneous participation of many different areas of the brain in constant communication with each other. For example, the right side of the brain is better at figuring out the meaning of a story, but the left side is where grammar and syntax are understood, so both sides of the brain have to work together in reading. Remember, no mental activity is exclusively the work of a single part of the brain—so there is no such thing as a "right-brained student" unless that individual has had the left hemisphere removed—a rare and radical treatment for some forms of epilepsy.

Adolescent Development and the Brain

The brain continues to develop throughout childhood and adolescence. During adolescence, changes in the brain increase individuals' abilities to control their behavior in both low-stress and high-stress situations, to be more purposeful and organized, and to inhibit impulsive behavior (Wigfield et al., 2006). But these abilities are not fully developed until the early 20s, so adolescents may "seem" like adults, at least in low-stress situations, but their brains are not fully developed. They often have trouble avoiding risks and controlling impulses. This is why adolescents' brains have been described as "high horse power, poor steering" (Organization for Economic Cooperation and Development [OECD], 2007, p. 6). One explanation looks to differences in the pace of development for two key systems involved in making sound decisions about risky behaviors and controlling impulsive behavior—the limbic system and the prefrontal cortex of the brain (Casey, Getz, & Galvan, 2008). The limbic system develops earlier; it is involved with emotions and reward-seeking/novelty/risk-taking/sensation-seeking behaviors. The prefrontal lobe takes more time to develop; it is involved with judgment and decision making.

As the limbic system matures, adolescents become more responsive to pleasure seeking and emotional stimulation. In fact, adolescents appear to need more intense emotional stimulation than either children or adults, so these young people are set up for taking risks and seeking thrills. Risk taking and novelty seeking can be positive factors for adolescent development as young people courageously try new ideas and behaviors—and learning is stimulated (McAnarney, 2008). But their less mature prefrontal lobe is not yet good at saying, "Whoa—that thrill is too risky!" So in emotional situations, thrill seeking wins out over caution, at least until the prefrontal lobe catches up and becomes more integrated with the limbic system toward the end of adolescence. Then risks can be evaluated in terms of long-term consequences, not immediate thrills (Casey et al., 2008; Steinberg, 2008). In addition, there are individual differences: Some adolescents are more prone than others to engage in risky behaviors.

Lateralization The specialization of the two hemispheres (sides) of the brain cortex.

Plasticity The brain's tendency to remain somewhat adaptable or flexible.

Teachers can take advantage of their adolescent students' intensity by helping them devote their energy and passion to areas such as politics, the environment, or social causes (Price, 2005) or by guiding them to explore emotional connections with characters in history or literature. Connections to family, school, community, and positive belief systems help adolescents "put the brakes" on reckless and dangerous behaviors (McAnarney, 2008).

Other changes in the neurological system during adolescence affect sleep; teenagers need about 9 hours of sleep per night, but many students' biological clocks are reset so it is difficult for them to fall asleep before midnight. Yet in many school districts, high school begins by 7:30, so 9 hours of sleep are impossible to get and students are continually sleep deprived. Classes that keep students in their seats, taking notes for the full period may literally "put the students to sleep." With no time for breakfast and little for lunch, these students' nutritional needs are often deprived as well (Sprenger, 2005).

Putting It All Altogether: How the Brain Works

What is your conception of the brain? Is the brain a culture-free container that holds knowledge the same way for everyone? Is the brain like a library of facts or a computer filled with information? Do you wake up in the morning, download what you need for the day, and then go merrily on your way? Is the brain like a pipe that transfers information from one person to another—a teacher to a student, for example? Kurt Fischer (2009) offers a different view, based on neuroscience research. Knowing is actively constructing understandings and actions. Knowledge is based in our activities:

> When animals and people do things in their worlds, they shape their behavior. Based on brain research, we know that likewise they literally shape the anatomy and physiology of their brains (and bodies). When we actively control our experience, that experience sculpts the way that our brains work, changing neurons, synapses, and brain activity. (p. 5)

Cultural differences in brain activity provide examples of how interactions in the world shape the brain. For example, in one study, when Chinese speakers added and compared Arabic numbers, they showed brain activity in the motor (movement) areas of their brains, whereas English speakers performing the same tasks had activity in the language areas of their brains (Tang et al., 2006). One explanation is that Chinese children are taught arithmetic using an abacus—a calculation tool that involves movement and spatial positions. As adults, these children retain a kind of visual-motor sense of numbers (Varma, McCandliss, & Schwartz, 2008). There also are cultural differences in how languages affect reading. For example, when they read, native Chinese speakers activate additional parts of their brain associated with spatial information processing, probably because the language characters used in written Chinese are pictures. But Chinese speakers also activate these spatial areas of the brain when they read English, demonstrating that reading proficiency can be reached through different neural pathways (Hinton, Miyamoto, & Della-Chiesa, 2008).

So the brain is ever changing, shaped by activity, culture, and context. We build knowledge as we do things, as we manipulate objects and ideas mentally and physically. What are the implications of this for teaching? Many publications for parents and teachers have useful ideas about the brain and education, but beware of suggestions that oversimplify. As you will see next, the jury still is out on many of these "brain-based" programs.

Neuroscience, Learning, and Teaching

There are many popular neuromyths about the brain, as you can see in Table 2.1 on the next page. We have to be careful about what we encounter in the media.

We know teaching can change the organization and structure of the brain. For example, individuals who are deaf and use sign language have different patterns of electrical activity in their brains than people who are deaf and do not use sign language (Varma, McCandliss, & Schwartz, 2008).

INSTRUCTION AND BRAIN DEVELOPMENT. Several studies have shown differences in brain activity associated with instruction. For example, the intensive instruction and practice provided to rehabilitate stroke victims can help them regain functioning by forming new connections and using new areas of the brain (Bransford, Brown, & Cocking, 2000;

TABLE 2.1 • **Myths About the Brain**

COMMON MYTHS	TRUTH
1. You use only 10 percent of your brain.	1. Use all your brain. That is why strokes are so devastating.
2. Listening to Mozart will make children smarter.	2. Listening won't, but learning to play a musical instrument is associated with increased cognitive achievement.
3. Some people are more "right brained," and others are more "left brained."	3. It takes both sides of your brain to do most things.
4. A young child's brain can only manage to learn one language at a time.	4. Children all over the world can and do learn two languages at once.
5. You can't change your brain.	5. Our brains are changing all the time.
6. Damage to the brain is permanent.	6. Most people recover well from minor brain injuries.
7. Playing games like Sudoku keeps your brain from aging.	7. Playing Sudoku makes you better at playing Sudoku and similar games. Physical exercise is a better bet to prevent decline.
8. The human brain is the biggest brain.	8. Sperm whales have brains 5 times heavier than those of humans.
9. Alcoholic beverages kill brain cells.	9. Heavy drinking does not kill brain cells but it can damage the nerve ends called dentrites and this causes problems with communicating messages in the brain. This damage is mostly reversible.
10. The adolescent's brain is the same as that of an adult.	10. There are critical differences between adolescents' and adults' brains: Adolescents' brains have "high horsepower, but poor steering" (Fischer, 2009).

Source: Adapted from Aamodt, S., & Wang, S. (2008); Fischer, K. W. (2009); Freeman, S. (2011); OECD (2007).

McKinley, 2011). In another example, Margarete Delazer and her colleagues (2005) compared students' brain activity as they learned new arithmetic operations, either by just memorizing the answers or by learning an algorithm strategy. Using functional magnetic resonance imaging (fMRI), the researchers found that students who simply memorized answers showed greater activity in the area of the brain that specializes in retrieving verbal information, whereas the students who used a strategy showed greater activity in the visual-spatial processing portion of the brain.

Bennett Shaywitz and his colleagues (2004) reported a dramatic demonstration of brain changes in children following instruction. The researchers studied 28 children ages 6 to 9 who were good readers and 49 children who were poor readers. Again, fMRIs showed differences in the brain activity of the two groups. The poor readers underused parts of their brains' left hemisphere and sometimes overused their right hemispheres. After over 100 hours of intensive instruction in letter–sound combinations, reading ability improved; the brains of the poor readers started to function more like those of the good readers and continued this functioning a year later. Poor readers who received the standard school remediation did not show the brain function changes.

In another dramatic example of how teaching can affect brain development, Fischer (2009) describes two children who each had one brain hemisphere removed as a treatment for severe epilepsy. Nico's right hemisphere was removed when he was 3, and his parents were told he would never have good visual-spatial skills. With strong and constant support and teaching, Nico grew up to be a skilled artist! Brooke's left hemisphere was removed when he was 11. His parents were told he would lose his ability to talk. Again, with strong support, he regained enough speaking and reading ability to finish high school and attend community college.

THE BRAIN AND LEARNING TO READ. Brain imaging research is revealing interesting differences among skilled and less skilled readers as they learn new vocabulary. For example, one imaging study showed that less skilled readers had trouble establishing high-quality representations of new vo-cabulary words in their brains, as indicated by *event-related potential (ERP)* measurements of electrical activity of the brain. When they encountered the new word later, less skilled readers' brains often didn't recognize that they had seen the word before, even though they had learned the words in an earlier lesson. If words you have learned seem unfamiliar later, you can see how it would be hard to understand what you read (Balass, Nelson, & Perfetti, 2010).

Reading is not innate or automatic—every brain has to be taught to read (Frey & Fisher, 2010). Reading is a complex integration of the systems in the brain that recognize sounds, written symbols, meanings, and sequences, and then connect with what the reader already knows. This has to happen quickly and automatically (Wolf et al., 2009). Will brain research help us teach reading more effectively? Judith Willis (2009), a neurobiologist who became a science teacher, cautions that

BRAIN RESEARCH AND READING Brain research may help us understand why strategies for teaching reading are or are not effective.

"Neuroimaging and the other brain monitoring systems used for reading research offer *suggestive* rather than completely empirical links between how the brain learns and metabolizes oxygen or glucose, conducts electricity, or changes its cellular density" (p. 333).

Although the strategies for teaching reading that are consistent with brain research are not completely new, the research may help us understand *why* these strategies work. What are some strategies suggested? Use multiple approaches that teach sounds, spelling, meanings, sequencing, and vocabulary through reading, writing, discussing, explaining, drawing, and modeling. Different students may learn in different ways, but all need practice in literacy.

EMOTIONS, LEARNING, AND THE BRAIN. Finally, another clear connection between the brain and classroom learning is in the area of emotions and stress. Let's step inside a high school math classroom described by Hinton, Miyamoto, and Della-Chiesa (2008, p. 91) for an example:

> Patricia, a high school student, struggles with mathematics. The last few times she answered a mathematics question she got it wrong and felt terribly embarrassed, which formed an association between mathematics . . . and negative emotions. . . . Her teacher had just asked her to come to the blackboard to solve a problem. This caused an immediate transfer of this emotionally-charged association to the amygdala, which elicits fear. Meanwhile, a slower, cortically-driven cognitive appraisal of the situation is occurring: she remembers her difficulty completing her mathematics homework last night, notices the problem on the board contains complicated graphs, and realizes that the boy she has a crush on is watching her from a front-row seat. These various thoughts converge to a cognitive confirmation that this is a threatening situation, which reinforces her progressing fear response and disrupts her ability to concentrate on solving the mathematics problem.

In Chapter 7 you will learn about how emotions can become paired with particular situations; and in Chapter 11, you will see that anxiety interferes with learning, whereas challenge, interest, and curiosity can support learning. If students feel unsafe and anxious, they are not likely to be able to focus attention on academics (Sylvester, 2003). But if students are not challenged or interested, learning suffers too. Keeping the level of challenge and support "just right" is a challenge for teachers. And helping students learn to regulate their own emotions and motivation is an important goal for education (see Chapter 10).

POINT/COUNTERPOINT: Brain-Based Education

Educators are hearing more and more about brain-based education, the importance of early stimulation for brain development, the "Mozart effect," and right- and left-brain activities. In fact, based on some research findings that listening to 10 minutes of Mozart can briefly improve spatial reasoning (Rauscher & Shaw, 1998; Steele, Bass, & Crook, 1999), a former governor of Georgia established a program to give a Mozart CD to every newborn. The scientists who had done the work couldn't believe how their research had been "applied" (Katzir & Pare-Blagoev, 2006). In fact, the governor apparently had confused experiments on infant brain development with studies of adults (Pinker, 2002). Are there clear educational implications from the neuroscience research on the brain?

POINT

▶ **No, the implications are not clear.** John Bruer, president of the James S. McDonnell Foundation, has written articles that are critical of the brain-based education craze (Bruer, 1999, 2002). He notes that many so-called applications of brain research begin with solid science, but then move to unwarranted speculation, and end in a sort of appealing folk tale about the brain and learning. He suggests that for each claim, the educator should ask, "Where does the science end and the speculation begin?" For example, one claim that Bruer questions is the notion of right-brain, left-brain learning.

"Right brain versus left brain" is one of those popular ideas that will not die. Speculations about the educational significance of brain laterality have been circulating in the education literature for 30 years. Although repeatedly criticized and dismissed by psychologists and brain scientists, the speculation continues. David Sousa devotes a chapter of How the Brain Learns to explaining brain laterality and presents classroom strategies that teachers might use to ensure that both hemispheres are involved in learning. . . . Now let's consider the brain sciences and how or whether they offer support for some of the particular teaching strategies Sousa recommends. To involve the right hemisphere in learning, Sousa writes, teachers should encourage students to generate and use mental imagery. . . . What brain scientists currently know about spatial reasoning and mental imagery provides counter examples to such simplistic claims as these. Such claims
arise out of a folk theory about brain laterality, not a neuroscientific one. . . . Different brain areas are specialized for different tasks, but that specialization occurs at a finer level of analysis than "using visual imagery." Using visual imagery may be a useful learning strategy, but if it is useful it is not because it involves an otherwise underutilized right hemisphere in learning. (Bruer, 1999, 653–654)

Ten years later, Kurt Fischer (2009), President of the International Mind, Brain, and Education Society, lamented:

Expectations for neuroscience and genetics to shape educational practice and policy have exploded far beyond what is merited by the state of the emerging field of MBE [mind body education] and the level of knowledge about how brains and genetics function . . . Many neuromyths " have entered popular discourse — beliefs about how the brain and body work that are widely accepted but blatantly wrong" (OECD, 2007b). Most of what is put forward as "brain based education" builds on these scientifically inaccurate myths: The one small way that neuroscience relates to most brain-based education is that the students have brains. There is no grounding for these claims in the young field of neuroscience.

No teacher doubts that the brain is important in learning. As Steven Pinker (2002), professor of psychology at Harvard University, observed, does anyone really think learning takes place somewhere else like the pancreas? But knowing that learning affects the brain does not tell us how to teach. All learning affects

---

Simply put, learning will be more effective "if educators help to minimize stress and fear at school, teach students emotional regulation strategies, and provide a positive learning environment that is motivating to students" (Hinton, Miyamoto, & Della-Chiesa, 2008).

As you can imagine, based on these and other amazing research results, educators have looked for applications of neuroscience research for their instruction. This has led to vigorous debate between the enthusiastic educational advocates of brain-based education and the skeptical neuroscience researchers who caution that studies of the brain do not really address major educational questions. See the *Point/Counterpoint* for a slice of this debate.

STOP & THINK As a teacher, you don't want to fall for overly simplistic "brain-based" teaching slogans. But obviously the brain and learning are intimately related—this is not a surprise. So how can you be a savvy, "neuroscientific" teacher (Murphy & Benton, 2010)?

Lessons for Teachers: General Principles

What can we learn from neuroscience? Here are some general teaching implications drawn from Driscoll (2005), Murphy and Benton (2010), Sprenger (2010), and Wolfe (2010):

the brain. ". . . this should be obvious, but nowadays any banality about learning can be dressed up in neurospeak and treated like a great revelation of science" (2002, p. 86). Virtually all of the so-called best practices for brain-based education are simple restatements of good teaching based on understandings of how people learn, not how their brain works. For example, we have known for over 100 years that it is more effective to learn in many shorter practice sessions as opposed to one long cramming session. To tie that fact to building more dendrites does not give teachers new strategies (Alferink & Farmer-Dougan, 2010). Finally, Richard Haier and Rex Jung (2008) look to the future: "Someday, we believe that our educational system will be informed by neuroscience knowledge, especially concerning intelligence, but how we get from here to there remains unclear" (p. 177).

may have trouble with sounds and sound patterns or with retrieving the names of very familiar letters, so there may be different bases for the reading disabilities (Katzir & Paré-Blagoev, 2006).

There are examples of applying knowledge of brain research to education. A reading improvement product called *FastForword* was developed by two neuroscientists, Dr. Michael Merzenich and Dr. Paula Tallal and is already in use today in classrooms around the country (see http://www.scilearn.com/results/success-stories/index.php). It specifically uses discoveries in neural plasticity to change the brain's ability to read the printed word (Tallal & Miller, 2003).

In his Presidential address for the First Conference of the International Mind, Brain, and Education Society, Kurt Fischer, a developmental psychologist and Harvard professor, noted:

COUNTERPOINT

▶ **Yes, teaching should be brain-based.** Articles in popular magazines such as *Newsweek* assert, " . . . it's naive to say that brain discoveries have no consequences for understanding how humans learn" (Begley, 2007). Do scientists agree? In their article on "Applying Cognitive Neuroscience Research to Education" in the *Educational Psychologist*, Tami Katzir and Juliana Paré-Blagoev (2006) concluded, "When applied correctly, brain science may serve as a vehicle for advancing the application of our understanding of learning and development. . . . Brain research can challenge common-sense views about teaching and learning by suggesting additional systems that are involved in particular tasks and activities" (p. 70). A number of universities, including Harvard, Cambridge, Dartmouth, the University of Texas at Arlington, University of Southern California, Beijing Normal University, Southeast University in Nanjing, and Johns Hopkins, have established training programs for educators in brain-education studies (Fischer, 2009; Wolfe, 2010).

Brain research is leading to much better understandings about learning disabilities. For example, neuroscience studies of people with reading disabilities have found that these individuals

The primary goal of the emerging field of Mind, Brain, and Education is to join biology, cognitive science, development, and education in order to create a sound grounding of education in research. The growing, worldwide movement needs to avoid the myths and distortions of popular conceptions of brain and genetics and build on the best integration of research with practice, creating a strong infrastructure that joins scientists with educators to study effective learning and teaching in educational settings. (2009, p. 3–16)

Fischer makes the point that we can go from understanding how the brain works to understanding cognitive processes, and then to developing educational practices. But jumping directly from knowledge about the brain to educational practices probably involves too much speculation.

Beware of Either/Or. Schools should not be run on curriculums based solely on the biology of the brain. However, to ignore what we do know about the brain would be equally irresponsible. Brain-based learning offers some direction for educators who want more purposeful, informed teaching. At the very least, the neuroscience research is helping us to understand why effective teaching strategies, such as distributed practice, work.

Resources: Podcast on understanding the brain: http://www.oecd.org/document/60/0,3343,en_2649_35845581_38811388_1_1_1_1,00.html

1. The brain can place some limits on learning in the form of brain anomalies in neural wiring or structure, but learning can occur through alternate pathways in the brain (as Nico and Brooke demonstrate). Thus, there are multiple ways both to teach and to learn a skill, depending on the student.
2. Many cognitive functions are differentiated—they are associated with different parts of the brain. Thus, learners are likely to have preferred modes of processing (visual or verbal, for example) as well as varying capabilities in these modes. Using a range of modalities for instruction and activities that draw on different senses may support learning—for example, using maps and songs to teach geography. Assessment should be differentiated, too.
3. The brain is relatively plastic, so enriched, active environments and flexible instructional strategies are likely to support cognitive development in young children and learning in adults.
4. Some learning disorders may have a neurological basis; neurological testing may assist in diagnosing and treating these disorders, as well as in evaluating the effects of various treatments.

5. The brain can change, but it takes time, so teachers must be consistent, patient, and compassionate in teaching and reteaching in different ways, as Nico's and Brooke's parents and teachers could tell you.

6. Learning from real life problems and concrete experiences helps students construct knowledge and also gives them multiple pathways for learning and retrieving information.

7. The brain seeks meaningful patterns and connections with existing networks, so teachers should tie new information to what students already understand and help them form new connections. Information that is not linked to existing knowledge will be easily forgotten.

8. It takes a long time to build and consolidate knowledge. Numerous visits in different contexts over time (not all at once) help to form strong, multiple connections.

9. Large, general concepts should be emphasized over small specific facts so students can build enduring, useful knowledge categories and associations that are not constantly changing.

10. Stories should be used in teaching. Stories engage many areas of the brain—memories, experiences, feelings, and beliefs. Stories also are organized and have a sequence—beginning, middle, end—so they are easier to remember than unrelated or unorganized information.

For the rest of the chapter, we turn from the brain and cognitive development to examine several major theories of cognitive development, the first offered by a biologist turned psychologist, Jean Piaget.

PIAGET'S THEORY OF COGNITIVE DEVELOPMENT

Swiss psychologist Jean Piaget was a real prodigy. In fact, in his teens, he published so many scientific papers on mollusks (marine animals such as oysters, clams, octopuses, snails, and squid) that he was offered a job as the curator of the mollusk collection at the Museum of Natural History in Geneva. He told the museum officials that he wanted to finish high school first. For a while, Piaget worked in Alfred Binet's laboratory in Paris developing intelligence tests for children. The reasons children gave for their wrong answers fascinated him, and this prompted him to study the thinking behind their answers—this question intrigued him for the rest of his life (Green & Piel, 2010). He continued to write until his death at the age of 84 (Miller, 2011).

During his long career, Piaget devised a model describing how humans go about making sense of their world by gathering and organizing information (Piaget, 1954, 1963, 1970a, 1970b). We will examine Piaget's ideas closely, because they provide an explanation of the development of thinking from infancy to adulthood.

STUDYING CHILDREN'S THINKING Jean Piaget was a Swiss psychologist whose insightful descriptions of children's thinking changed the way we understand cognitive development.

STOP & THINK Can you be in Pittsburgh, Pennsylvania, and the United States all at the same time? Is this a difficult question for you? How long did it take you to answer? •

According to Piaget (1954), certain ways of thinking that are quite simple for an adult, such as the Pittsburgh question above, are not so simple for a child. For example, do you remember the 9-year-old child at the beginning of the chapter who was asked if he could be a Genevan? He answered, *"No, that's not possible. I'm already Swiss, I can't also be Genevan"* (Piaget, 1965/1995, p. 252). Imagine teaching this student geography. The student has trouble with classifying one concept (Geneva) as a subset of another (Switzerland). There are other differences between adult and child thinking. Children's concepts of time may be different from your own. They may think, for example, that they will some day catch up to a sibling in age, or they may confuse the past and the future. Let's examine why.

Influences on Development

Cognitive development is much more than the addition of new facts and ideas to an existing store of information. According to Piaget, our thinking processes change radically, though slowly, from birth to maturity because we constantly strive to make sense of the world. Piaget identified four factors—biological maturation, activity, social experiences, and equilibration—that interact to influence changes in thinking (Piaget, 1970a). Let's briefly examine the first three factors. We'll return to a discussion of equilibration in the next section.

One of the most important influences on the way we make sense of the world is *maturation*, the unfolding of the biological changes that are genetically programmed. Parents and teachers have little impact on this aspect of cognitive development, except to be sure that children get the nourishment and care they need to be healthy.

Activity is another influence. With physical maturation comes the increasing ability to act on the environment and learn from it. When a young child's coordination is reasonably developed, for example, the child can discover principles about balance by experimenting with a seesaw. Thus, as we act on the environment—as we explore, test, observe, and eventually organize information—we are likely to alter our thinking processes at the same time.

As we develop, we are also interacting with the people around us. According to Piaget, our cognitive development is influenced by *social transmission*, or learning from others. Without social transmission, we would need to reinvent all the knowledge already offered by our culture. The amount people can learn from social transmission varies according to their stage of cognitive development.

Maturation, activity, and social transmission all work together to influence cognitive development. How do we respond to these influences?

Basic Tendencies in Thinking

As a result of his early research in biology, Piaget concluded that all species inherit two basic tendencies, or "invariant functions." The first of these tendencies is toward **organization**—the combining, arranging, recombining, and rearranging of behaviors and thoughts into coherent systems. The second tendency is toward **adaptation**, or adjusting to the environment.

ORGANIZATION. People are born with a tendency to organize their thinking processes into psychological structures. These psychological structures are our systems for understanding and interacting with the world. Simple structures are continually combined and coordinated to become more sophisticated and thus more effective. Very young infants, for example, can either look at an object or grasp it when it comes in contact with their hands. They cannot coordinate looking and grasping at the same time. As they develop, however, infants organize these two separate behavioral structures into a coordinated higher-level structure of looking at, reaching for, and grasping the object. They can, of course, still use each structure separately (Flavell, Miller, & Miller, 2002; Miller, 2011).

Piaget gave a special name to these structures: **schemes**. In his theory, schemes are the basic building blocks of thinking. They are organized systems of actions or thought that allow us to mentally represent or "think about" the objects and events in our world. Schemes can be very small and specific, for example, the sucking-through-a-straw scheme or the recognizing-a-rose scheme. Or they can be larger and more general, for example, the drinking scheme or the gardening scheme. As a person's thinking processes become more organized and new schemes develop, behavior also becomes more sophisticated and better suited to the environment.

ADAPTATION. In addition to the tendency to organize psychological structures, people also inherit the tendency to adapt to their environment. Two basic processes are involved in adaptation: assimilation and accommodation.

Organization Ongoing process of arranging information and experiences into mental systems or categories.

Adaptation Adjustment to the environment.

Schemes Mental systems or categories of perception and experience.

Assimilation takes place when we use our existing schemes to make sense of events in our world. Assimilation involves trying to understand something new by fitting it into what we already know. At times, we may have to distort the new information to make it fit. For example, the first time many children see a raccoon, they call it a "kitty." They try to match the new experience with an existing scheme for identifying animals.

Accommodation occurs when we must change existing schemes to respond to a new situation. If data cannot be made to fit any existing schemes, then more appropriate structures must be developed. We adjust our thinking to fit the new information, instead of adjusting the information to fit our thinking. Children demonstrate accommodation when they add the scheme for recognizing raccoons to their other systems for identifying animals.

People adapt to their increasingly complex environments by using existing schemes whenever these schemes work (assimilation) and by modifying and adding to their schemes when something new is needed (accommodation). In fact, both processes are required most of the time. Even using an established pattern such as sucking through a straw requires some accommodation if the straw is of a different size or length than the type you are used to. If you have tried drinking juice from box packages, you know that you have to add a new skill to your sucking-through-a-straw scheme—don't squeeze the box or you will shoot juice through the straw, straight up into the air and into your lap. Whenever new experiences are assimilated into an existing scheme, the scheme is enlarged and changed somewhat, so assimilation involves some accommodation (Mascolo & Fischer, 2005).

There are also times when neither assimilation nor accommodation is used. If people encounter something that is too unfamiliar, they may ignore it. Experience is filtered to fit the kind of thinking a person is doing at a given time. For example, if you overhear a conversation in a foreign language, you probably will not try to make sense of the exchange unless you have some knowledge of the language.

EQUILIBRATION. According to Piaget, organizing, assimilating, and accommodating can be viewed as a kind of complex balancing act. In his theory, the actual changes in thinking take place through the process of **equilibration**—the act of searching for a balance. Piaget assumed that people continually test the adequacy of their thinking processes in order to achieve that balance. Briefly, the process of equilibration works like this: If we apply a particular scheme to an event or situation and the scheme works, then equilibrium exists. If the scheme does not produce a satisfying result, then **disequilibrium** exists, and we become uncomfortable. This motivates us to keep searching for a solution through assimilation and accommodation, and thus our thinking changes and moves ahead. Of course, the level of disequilibrium must be just right or optimal—too little and we aren't interested in changing, too much and we may be discouraged or anxious and not change.

Four Stages of Cognitive Development

Now we turn to the actual differences that Piaget hypothesized for children as they grow. Piaget believed that all people pass through the same four stages in exactly the same order. The stages are generally associated with specific ages, as shown in Table 2.2, but these are only general guidelines, not labels for all children of a certain age. Piaget noted that individuals may go through long periods of transition between stages and that a person may show characteristics of one stage in one situation, but traits of a higher or lower stage in other situations. Therefore, remember that knowing a student's age is never a guarantee you will know how the child thinks (Orlando & Machado, 1996).

INFANCY: THE SENSORIMOTOR STAGE. The earliest period is called the **sensorimotor** stage, because the child's thinking involves seeing, hearing, moving, touching, tasting, and so on. During this period, infants develop **object permanence**, the understanding that objects exist in the environment whether they perceive them or not. This is the beginning of the important ability to construct a mental representation. As most parents discover, before infants develop object permanence, it is relatively easy to take something away from them. The trick is to distract them and remove the object while they are not looking—"out of sight, out of mind." The older infant who searches for the ball that has

---

Assimilation Fitting new information into existing schemes.

Accommodation Altering existing schemes or creating new ones in response to new information.

Equilibration Search for mental balance between cognitive schemes and information from the environment.

Disequilibrium In Piaget's theory, the "out-of-balance" state that occurs when a person realizes that his or her current ways of thinking are not working to solve a problem or understand a situation.

Sensorimotor Involving the senses and motor activity.

Object permanence The understanding that objects have a separate, permanent existence.

TABLE 2.2 • Piaget's Stages of Cognitive Development

STAGE	APPROXIMATE AGE	CHARACTERISTICS
Sensorimotor	0–2 years	Learns through reflexes, senses, and movement—actions on the environment. Begins to imitate others and remember events; shifts to symbolic thinking. Comes to understand that objects do not cease to exist when they are out of sight—object permanence. Moves from reflexive actions to intentional activity.
Preoperational	Begins about the time the child starts talking, to about 7 years old	Develops language and begins to use symbols to represent objects. Has difficulty with past and future—thinks in the present. Can think through operations logically in one direction. Has difficulties understanding the point of view of another person.
Concrete operational	Begins about first grade, to early adolescence, around 11 years old	Can think logically about concrete (hands-on) problems. Understands conservation and organizes things into categories and in series. Can reverse thinking to mentally "undo" actions. Understands past, present, and future.
Formal operational	Adolescence to adulthood	Can think hypothetically and deductively. Thinking becomes more scientific. Solves abstract problems in logical fashion. Can consider multiple perspectives and develops concerns about social issues, personal identity, and justice.

rolled out of sight is indicating an understanding that objects still exist even when they are not in view (Moore & Meltzoff, 2004). Some researchers suggest that infants as young as 3 to 4 months may know that an object still exists, but they do not have either the memory skills to "hold on" to the location of the object or the motor skills to coordinate a search (Baillargeon, 1999; Flavell et al., 2002).

A second major accomplishment in the sensorimotor period is the beginning of logical, **goal-directed actions**. Think of the familiar clear plastic container baby toy with a lid and several colorful items inside that can be dumped out and replaced. A 6-month-old baby is likely to become frustrated trying to get to the toys inside. An older child who has mastered the basics of the sensorimotor stage will probably be able to deal with the toy in an orderly fashion by building a "container toy" scheme: (1) get the lid off, (2) turn the container upside down, (3) shake if the items jam, and (4) watch the items fall. Separate lower-level schemes have been organized into a higher-level scheme to achieve a goal.

The child is soon able to reverse this action by refilling the container. Learning to reverse actions is a basic accomplishment of the sensorimotor stage. As we will soon see, however, learning to reverse thinking—that is, learning to imagine the reverse of a sequence of actions—takes much longer.

EARLY CHILDHOOD TO THE EARLY ELEMENTARY YEARS: THE PREOPERATIONAL STAGE. By the end of the sensorimotor stage, the child can use many action schemes. However, as long as these schemes remain tied to physical actions, they are of no use in recalling the past, keeping track of information, or planning. For this, children need what Piaget called **operations**, or actions that are carried out and reversed mentally rather than physically. At the **preoperational** stage the child is moving toward mastery, but has not yet mastered these mental operations (so thinking is preoperational).

Goal-directed actions Deliberate actions toward a goal.

Operations Actions a person carries out by thinking them through instead of literally performing the actions.

Preoperational The stage before a child masters logical mental operations.

"I can't tell you 'cause I'm wearin' my mittens."

Family Circus © 2002 Bil Keane, Inc.
King Features Syndicate

According to Piaget, the first type of thinking that is separate from action involves making action schemes symbolic. The ability to form and use symbols—words, gestures, signs, images, and so on—is thus a major accomplishment of the preoperational period and moves children closer to mastering the mental operations of the next stage. This ability to work with symbols to represent an object that is not present, such as using the word *horse* or a picture of a horse or even pretending to ride a broomstick horse, is called the **semiotic function**. In fact, the child's earliest use of symbols is in pretending. Children who are not yet able to talk will often use action symbols—pretending to drink from an empty cup or touching a comb to their hair, showing that they know what each object is for. This behavior also shows that their schemes are becoming more general and less tied to specific actions. The eating scheme, for example, can be used in playing house. During the preoperational stage, there is also rapid development of that very important symbol system, language. Between the ages of 2 and 4, most children enlarge their vocabulary from about 200 to 2,000 words.

As the child moves through the preoperational stage, the developing ability to think about objects in symbolic form remains somewhat limited to thinking in one direction only, or using one-way logic. It is very difficult for the child to "think backwards," or imagine how to reverse the steps in a task. **Reversible thinking** is involved in many tasks that are difficult for the preoperational child, such as the conservation of matter.

Conservation is the principle that the amount or number of something remains the same even if the arrangement or appearance is changed, as long as nothing is added and nothing is taken away. You know that if you tear a piece of paper into several pieces, you will still have the same amount of paper. To prove this, you know that you can reverse the process by taping the pieces back together. Here is a classic example of difficulty with conservation. Leah, a 5-year-old, is shown two identical glasses, both short and wide in shape. Both have exactly the same amount of colored water in them. She agrees that the amounts are "the same." The experimenter then pours the water from one of the glasses into a taller, narrower glass and asks, "Now, does one glass have more water, or are they the same?" Leah responds that the tall glass has more because "It goes up more here" (she points to higher level on taller glass).

Piaget's explanation for Leah's answer is that she is focusing, or *centering*, attention on the dimension of height. She has difficulty considering more than one aspect of the situation at a time, or **decentering**. The preoperational child cannot understand that decreased diameter compensates for increased height, because this would require taking into account two dimensions at once. Thus, children at the preoperational stage have trouble freeing themselves from their own immediate perceptions of how the world appears.

This brings us to another important characteristic of the preoperational stage. Preoperational children, according to Piaget, have a tendency to be **egocentric**, to see the world and the experiences of others from their own viewpoint. The concept of egocentrism, as Piaget intended it, does not mean selfish; it simply means children often assume that everyone else shares their feelings, reactions, and perspectives. For example, if a little girl at this stage is afraid of dogs, she may assume that all children share this fear. The 2-year-old at the beginning of this chapter who brought his own mother to comfort a distressed friend—even though the friend's mother was available—was simply seeing the situation through his own eyes. Very young children center on their own perceptions and on the way the situation appears to them. This is one reason it is difficult for preoperational children to understand that *your* right hand is not on the same side as theirs when you are facing them.

Research has shown that young children are not totally egocentric in every situation, however. Children as young as 2 describe more details about a situation to a parent who was not present than they provide to a parent who experienced the situation with them. So young children do seem quite able to take the needs and different perspectives of

Semiotic function The ability to use symbols—language, pictures, signs, or gestures—to represent actions or objects mentally.

Reversible thinking Thinking backward, from the end to the beginning.

Conservation Principle that some characteristics of an object remain the same despite changes in appearance.

Decentering Focusing on more than one aspect at a time.

Egocentric Assuming that others experience the world the way you do.

Helping Families Care for Preoperational Children

Encourage families to use concrete props and visual aids whenever possible.
Examples
1. When they use words such as *part*, *whole*, or *one half*, encourage families to demonstrate using objects in the house such as cutting an apple or pizza into parts.
2. Let children add and subtract with sticks, rocks, or colored chips. This technique also is helpful for early concrete-operational students.

Make instructions relatively short—not too many steps at once. Use actions as well as words.
Examples
1. When giving instructions such as how to feed a pet, first model the process, then ask the child to try it.
2. Explain a game by acting out one of the parts.

Help children develop their ability to see the world from someone else's point of view.
Examples
1. Ask children to imagine "how your sister felt when you broke her toy."

2. Be clear about rules for sharing or use of material. Help children understand the value of the rules and develop empathy by asking them to think about how they would like to be treated. Avoid long lectures on "sharing" or being "nice."

Give children a great deal of hands-on practice with the skills that serve as building blocks for more complex skills such as reading comprehension or collaboration.
Examples
1. Provide cut-out letters or letter magnets for the refrigerator to build words.
2. Do activities that require measuring and simple calculations—cooking, dividing a batch of popcorn equally.

Provide a wide range of experiences in order to build a foundation for concept learning and language.
Examples
1. Take trips to zoos, gardens, theaters, and concerts; encourage storytelling.
2. Give children words to describe what they are doing, hearing, seeing, touching, tasting, and smelling.

others into account, at least in certain situations (Flavell et al., 2002). And in fairness to young children, even adults can make assumptions that others feel or think like they do. For example, have you ever gotten a gift that the giver loved but was clearly inappropriate for you? The *Family and Community Partnerships Guidelines* give ideas for working with preoperational thinkers and for guiding families in supporting the cognitive development of their children.

LATER ELEMENTARY TO THE MIDDLE SCHOOL YEARS: THE CONCRETE-OPERATIONAL STAGE. Piaget coined the term **concrete operations** to describe this stage of "hands-on" thinking. The basic characteristics of the stage are the recognition of the logical stability of the physical world; the realization that elements can be changed or transformed and still conserve many of their original characteristics; and the understanding that these changes can be reversed.

Look at Figure 2.4, on the next page to see examples of the different tasks given to children to assess conservation and the approximate age ranges when most children can solve these problems. According to Piaget, the ability to solve conservation problems depends on having an understanding of three basic aspects of reasoning: identity, compensation, and reversibility. With a complete mastery of **identity**, the student knows that if nothing is added or taken away, the material remains the same. With an understanding of **compensation**, the student knows that an apparent change in one direction can be compensated for by a change in another direction. That is, if the glass is narrower, the liquid will rise higher in the glass. And with an understanding of reversibility, the student can mentally cancel out the change that has been made. Leah apparently knew it was the same water (identity), but lacked compensation and reversibility, so she was still moving toward conservation.

Concrete operations Mental tasks tied to concrete objects and situations.

Identity Principle that a person or object remains the same over time.

Compensation The principle that changes in one dimension can be offset by changes in another.

FIGURE 2.4

SOME PIAGETIAN CONSERVATION TASKS

In addition to the tasks shown here, other tasks involve the conservation of number, length, weight, and volume. These tasks are all achieved over the concrete-operational period.

	Suppose you start with this	→	Then you change the situation to this	→	The question you would ask a child is
(a) conservation of mass	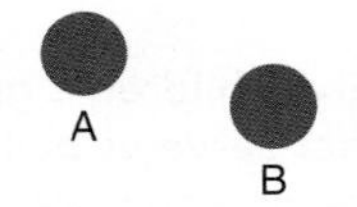 A B	Roll out clay ball B	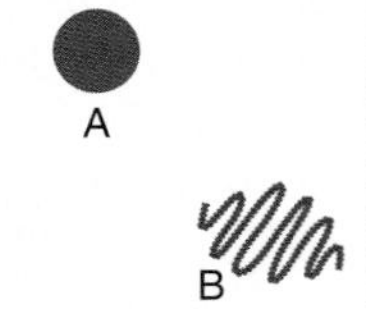 A B		Which is bigger, A or B?
(b) conservation of weight	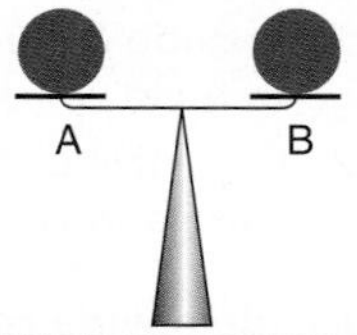 A B	Roll out clay ball B	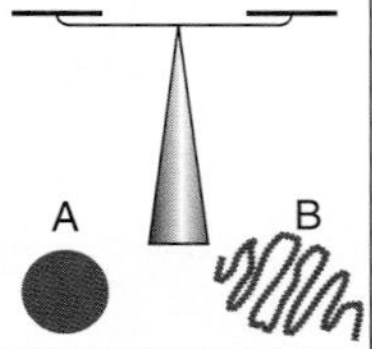 A B		Which will weigh more, A or B?
(c) conservation of volume	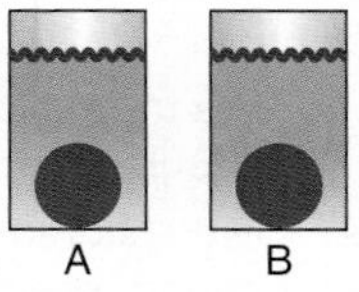 A B	Take clay ball out of water and roll out clay ball B	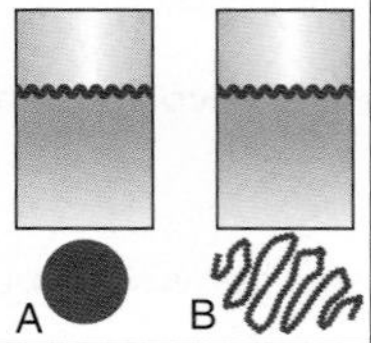 A B		When I put the clay back into the water beakers, in which beaker will the water be higher?
(d) conservation of continuous quantity	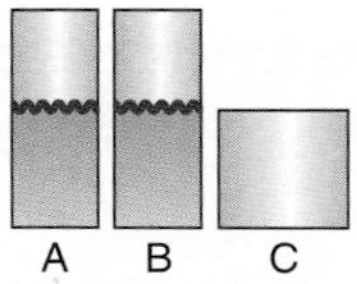 A B C	Pour water in beaker A into beaker C	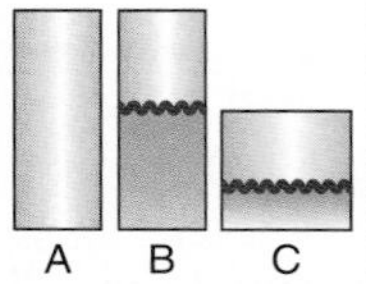 A B C		Which beaker has more liquid, B or C?
(e) conservation of number	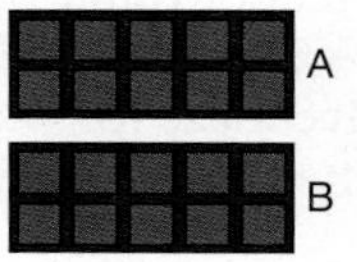 A B	Break candy bar B into pieces	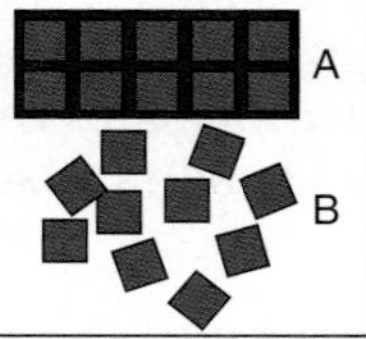 A B		Which is more candy? A or B

Another important operation mastered at this stage is **classification**. Classification depends on a student's abilities to focus on a single characteristic of objects in a set (for example, color) and group the objects according to that characteristic. More advanced classification at this stage involves recognizing that one class fits into another. A city can be in a particular state or province and also in a particular country, as you probably knew when I asked you earlier about Pittsburgh, Pennsylvania, USA. As children apply this advanced classification to locations, they often become fascinated with "complete" addresses such as Lee Jary, 5116 Forest Hill Drive, Richmond Hill, Ontario, Canada, North America, Northern Hemisphere, Earth, Solar System, Milky Way, Universe.

Classification is also related to **reversibility**. The ability to reverse a process mentally allows the concrete-operational student to see that there is more than one way to classify a group of objects. The student understands, for example, that buttons can be classified by color, and then reclassified by size or by the number of holes.

Classification Grouping objects into categories.

Reversibility A characteristic of Piagetian logical operations—the ability to think through a series of steps, then mentally reverse the steps and return to the starting point; also called *reversible thinking*.

Seriation is the process of making an orderly arrangement from large to small or vice versa. This understanding of sequential relationships permits a student to construct a logical series in which A < B < C (A is less than B is less than C) and so on. Unlike the preoperational child, the concrete-operational child can grasp the notion that B can be larger than A but still smaller than C.

With the abilities to handle operations such as conservation, classification, and seriation, the student at the concrete-operational stage has finally developed a complete and very logical system of thinking. However, this system of thinking is still tied to physical reality. The logic is based on concrete situations that can be organized, classified, or manipulated. Thus, children at this stage can imagine several different arrangements for the furniture in their rooms. They do not have to solve the problem strictly through trial and error by actually moving the furniture. However, the concrete-operational child is not yet able to reason about hypothetical, abstract problems that involve the coordination of many factors at once. This kind of coordination is part of Piaget's next and final stage of cognitive development.

In any grade you teach, knowledge of concrete-operational thinking will be helpful (see the *Guidelines*). In the early grades, the students are moving toward this logical system of thought. In the middle grades, it is in full flower, ready to be applied and extended

Seriation Arranging objects in sequential order according to one aspect, such as size, weight, or volume.

GUIDELINES

Teaching the Concrete-Operational Child

Continue to use concrete props and visual aids, especially when dealing with sophisticated material.
Examples
1. Use time lines in history and three-dimensional models in science.
2. Use diagrams to illustrate hierarchical relationships such as branches of government and the agencies under each branch.

Continue to give students a chance to manipulate and test objects.
Examples
1. Set up simple scientific experiments such as the following involving the relationship between fire and oxygen. What happens to a flame when you blow on it from a distance? (If you don't blow it out, the flame gets larger briefly, because it has more oxygen to burn.) What happens when you cover the flame with a jar?
2. Have students make candles by dipping wicks in wax, weave cloth on a simple loom, bake bread, set type by hand, or do other craft work that illustrates the daily occupations of people in the colonial period.

Make sure presentations and readings are brief and well organized.
Examples
1. Assign stories or books with short, logical chapters, moving to longer reading assignments only when students are ready.
2. Break up a presentation, giving students an opportunity to practice the first steps before introducing the next steps.

Use familiar examples to explain more complex ideas.
Examples
1. Compare students' lives with those of characters in a story. After reading *Island of the Blue Dolphins* (the true story of a girl who grew up alone on a deserted island), ask, "Have you ever had to stay alone for a long time? How did you feel?"
2. Teach the concept of area by having students measure two school rooms that are different sizes.

Give opportunities to classify and group objects and ideas on increasingly complex levels.
Examples
1. Give students slips of paper with individual sentences written on each paper and ask the students to group the sentences into paragraphs.
2. Compare the systems of the human body to other kinds of systems: the brain to a computer, the heart to a pump. Break down stories into components, from the broad to the specific: author, story, characters, plot, theme, place, time.

Present problems that require logical, analytical thinking.
Examples
1. Discuss open-ended questions that stimulate thinking: "Are the brain and the mind the same thing?" "How should the city deal with stray animals?" "What is the largest number?"
2. Use sports photos or pictures of crisis situations (Red Cross helping in disasters, victims of poverty or war, senior citizens who need assistance) to stimulate problem-solving discussions.

by your teaching. Students in high school and even adults still commonly use concrete-operational thinking, especially in areas that are new or unfamiliar.

HIGH SCHOOL AND COLLEGE: FORMAL OPERATIONS. Some students remain at the concrete-operational stage throughout their school years, even throughout life. However, new experiences, usually those that take place in school, eventually present most students with problems that they cannot solve using concrete operations.

- -

STOP & THINK You are packing for a long trip, but want to pack light. How many different three-piece outfits (slacks, shirt, jacket) will you have if you include three shirts, three slacks, and three jackets (assuming of course that they all go together in fashion perfection)? Time yourself to see how long it takes to arrive at the answer. •

- -

What happens when a number of variables interact, as in a laboratory experiment or the question above? Then a mental system for controlling sets of variables and working through a set of possibilities is needed. These are the abilities Piaget called **formal operations**.

At the level of formal operations, the focus of thinking can shift from what is to what might be. Situations do not have to be experienced to be imagined. You met Jamal at the beginning of this chapter. Even though he is a bright elementary school student, he could not answer the question, "How would life be different if people did not have to sleep?" because he insisted, "People HAVE TO SLEEP!" In contrast, the adolescent who has mastered formal operations can consider contrary-to-fact questions. In answering, the adolescent demonstrates the hallmark of formal operations—**hypothetico-deductive reasoning**. The formal-operational thinker can consider a hypothetical situation (people do not sleep) and reason *deductively* (from the general assumption to specific implications, such as longer workdays, more money spent on energy and lighting, smaller houses without bedrooms, or new entertainment industries). Formal operations also include *inductive* reasoning, or using specific observations to identify general principles. For example, the economist observes many specific changes in the stock market and attempts to identify general principles about economic cycles from this information.

Abstract formal-operational thinking is necessary for success in many advanced high school and college courses. For example, most math is concerned with hypothetical situations, assumptions, and givens: "Let $x = 10$," or "Assume $x2 + y2 = z2$," or "Given two sides and an adjacent angle … " Work in social studies and literature requires abstract thinking, too: "What did Wilson mean when he called World War I the 'war to end all wars'?" "What are some metaphors for hope and despair in Shakespeare's sonnets?" "What symbols of old age does T. S. Eliot use in *The Waste Land*?" "How do animals symbolize human character traits in Aesop's fables?"

The organized, scientific thinking of formal operations requires that students systematically generate different possibilities for a given situation. For example, if asked, "How many different shirt/slacks/jacket outfits can you make using three of each kind of clothing?" the child using formal operations can systematically identify the 27 possible combinations. (Did you get it right?) A concrete-operational thinker might name just a few combinations, using each piece of clothing only once. The underlying system of combinations is not yet available.

Another characteristic of this stage is **adolescent egocentrism**. Unlike egocentric young children, adolescents do not deny that other people may have different perceptions and beliefs; the adolescents just become very focused on their own ideas. They spend much time examining their own beliefs and attitudes. This leads to what Elkind (1981) calls the sense of an *imaginary audience*—the feeling that everyone is watching. Thus, adolescents believe that others are analyzing them: "Everyone noticed that I wore this shirt twice this week." "The whole class thought my answer was dumb!" You can see that social blunders or imperfections in appearance can be devastating if "everybody is watching." Luckily, this feeling of being "on stage" seems to peak in early adolescence by age 14 or 15, although in unfamiliar situations we all may feel our mistakes are being noticed.

Connect and Extend to PRAXIS II™

Reasoning (II, A1)
Be able to distinguish between inductive and deductive reasoning. Explain the role that each plays in the learning of concepts.

Formal operations Mental tasks involving abstract thinking and coordination of a number of variables.

Hypothetico-deductive reasoning A formal-operations problem-solving strategy in which an individual begins by identifying all the factors that might affect a problem and then deduces and systematically evaluates specific solutions.

Adolescent egocentrism Assumption that everyone else shares one's thoughts, feelings, and concerns.

The ability to think hypothetically, consider alternatives, identify all possible combinations, and analyze their own thinking has some interesting consequences for adolescents. Because they can think about worlds that do not exist, they often become interested in science fiction. Because they can reason from general principles to specific actions, they often are critical of people whose actions seem to contradict their principles. Adolescents can deduce the set of "best" possibilities and imagine ideal worlds (or ideal parents and teachers, for that matter). This explains why many students at this age develop interests in utopias, political causes, and social issues. They want to design better worlds, and their thinking allows them to do so. Adolescents also can imagine many possible futures for themselves and may try to decide which is best. Feelings about any of these ideals may be strong.

PLAYING FOR AN IMAGINARY AUDIENCE Adolescents may seem "alone in a crowd." They can become very focused on their own ideas and feel everyone is noticing their every mistake.

DO WE ALL REACH THE FOURTH STAGE? Most psychologists agree that there is a level of thinking more sophisticated than concrete operations. But there is a debate about how universal formal-operational thinking actually is, even among adults. The first three stages of Piaget's theory are forced on most people by physical realities. Objects really are permanent. The amount of water doesn't change when it is poured into another glass. Formal operations, however, are not so closely tied to the physical environment. Being able to use formal operations may be the result of practice in solving hypothetical problems and using formal scientific reasoning—abilities that are valued and taught in literate cultures, particularly in college. Even so, only about 30% to 40% of high school students can perform Piaget's formal-operational tasks (Meece & Daniels, 2008). The *Guidelines* will help you support the development of formal operations in your students.

GUIDELINES

Helping Students to Use Formal Operations

Continue to use concrete-operational teaching strategies and materials.
Examples
1. Use visual aids such as charts and illustrations as well as somewhat more sophisticated graphs and diagrams, especially when the material is new.
2. Compare the experiences of characters in stories to students' experiences.

Give students the opportunity to explore many hypothetical questions.
Examples
1. Have students write position papers, then exchange these papers with the opposing side and debate topical social issues such as the environment, the economy, and national health insurance.
2. Ask students to write about their personal vision of a utopia; write a description of a universe that has no sex differences; write a description of Earth after humans are extinct.

Give students opportunities to solve problems and reason scientifically.
Examples
1. Set up group discussions in which students design experiments to answer questions.
2. Ask students to justify two different positions on animal rights, with logical arguments for each position.

Whenever possible, teach broad concepts, not just facts, using materials and ideas relevant to the students' lives (Delpit, 1995).
Examples
1. When discussing the Civil War, consider racism or other issues that have divided the United States since then.
2. When teaching about poetry, let students find lyrics from popular songs that illustrate poetic devices, and talk about how these devices do or don't work well to communicate the meanings and feelings the songwriters intended.

Piaget himself (1974) suggested that most adults might only be able to use formal-operational thought in a few areas where they have the greatest experience or interest. Taking a college class fosters formal-operational abilities in that subject, but not necessarily in others (Lehman & Nisbett, 1990). So expect many students in your middle-school or high-school classes to have trouble thinking hypothetically, especially when they are learning something new. Sometimes, students find shortcuts for dealing with problems that are beyond their grasp; they may memorize formulas or lists of steps. These systems may be helpful for passing tests, but real understanding will take place only if students are able to go beyond this superficial use of memorization.

Information Processing, Neo-Piagetian, and Neuroscience Views of Cognitive Development

As you will see in Chapter 8, there are explanations for why children have trouble with conservation and other Piagetian tasks. These explanations focus on the development of information processing skills, such as attention, memory capacity, and learning strategies. As children mature and their brains develop, they are better able to focus their attention, process information more quickly, hold more information in memory, and use thinking strategies more easily and flexibly. Siegler (2000) proposes that as children grow older, they develop progressively better rules and strategies for solving problems and thinking logically. Teachers can help students develop their capacities for formal thinking by putting them in situations that challenge their thinking and reveal the shortcomings of their logic. Siegler's approach is called *rule assessment* because it focuses on understanding, challenging, and changing the rules that students use for thinking.

Some developmental psychologists have formulated **neo-Piagetian theories** that retain Piaget's insights about children's construction of knowledge and the general trends in children's thinking, but add findings from information processing theories about the role of attention, memory, and strategies. For example, Robbie Case (1992, 1998) devised an explanation of cognitive development suggesting that children develop in stages within specific domains such as numerical concepts, spatial concepts, social tasks, storytelling, reasoning about physical objects, and motor development. As children practice using the schemes in a particular domain (for example, using counting schemes in the number concept area), accomplishing the schemes requires less attention. The schemes become more automatic because the child does not have to "think so hard." This frees up mental resources and memory to do more, so the child is able to combine simple schemes into more complex ones and invent new schemes when needed (assimilation and accommodation in action).

Kurt Fischer (2009) connected cognitive development in different domains to research on the brain. He also examined development in different domains such as reading or math. You may remember Nico and Brooke, the remarkable children we met earlier in the chapter who each had one side of their brain removed to treat severe epilepsy, yet both still developed other pathways in their brains to recover lost spatial and verbal abilities. We have seen that one of the implications of research on the brain is that there are multiple pathways for learning.

Fischer has found, however, that even though their brains follow different pathways as they master skills in speaking, reading, and mathematics, children's growth patterns show a similar series of spurts and they go through predictable levels of development. When learning a new skill, children move through three tiers—from *actions* to *representations* to *abstractions*. Within each tier, the pattern is moving from accomplishing a single action to mapping or coordinating two actions together such as coordinating addition and multiplication in math, to creating whole systems of understanding. At the level of abstractions, they finally move to constructing explanatory principles. This may remind you of sensorimotor, concrete operations, and formal operations in Piaget's theory. Look at Table 2.3, which shows the movement through the tiers of *actions* to *representations* to *abstractions*.

For each skill level, the brain reorganizes itself, too. Table 2.3 shows this progression between birth and 30 years old for the skill of arithmetic operations: addition, subtraction, multiplication, and division. Notice the column that says "emergence of optimal level."

Neo-Piagetian theories More recent theories that integrate findings about attention, memory, and strategy use with Piaget's insights about children's thinking and the construction of knowledge.

TABLE 2.3 • **A Pattern of Cognitive Development over 30 Years**

As children develop skills in speaking, reading, and mathematics, their growth patterns show a similar series of spurts. In learning a new skill, children move from *actions* to *representations* to *abstractions*.

TIERS	LEVELS		AGE OF EMERGENCE OF OPTIMAL LEVEL	AGE OF FUNCTIONAL LEVEL
			23–25 yrs	30–45 yrs
Abstraction	Ab4. Principles		18–20	23–40
	Ab3. Systems		14–16	17–30
	Ab2. Mappings			
	Rp4./Ab1. Single Abstraction		10–12	13–20
Representations	Rp3 Systems		6–7	7–12
	Rp2 Mappings		3½–4½	4–8
	Sm4./Rp1. Single Representations		2	2–5
Actions	Sm3. Systems		11–13 mos	11–24 mos
	Sm2. Mappings		7–8	7–13
	Sm1. Single Actions		3–4	3–9

Source: Fischer, K. W. (2009). Mind, brain, and education: Building a scientific groundwork for learning and teaching. Mind, Brain, and Education, 3, 2–16.

This column shows the ages at which the skills will develop if the individuals have *quality support and the chance to practice*. The age the skill emerges without support and practice is shown in the last column. Support and practice are keys in another explanation of cognitive development we will discuss soon—Vygotsky's theory.

Some Limitations of Piaget's Theory

Although most psychologists agree with Piaget's insightful descriptions of *how* children think, many disagree with his explanations of *why* thinking develops as it does.

THE TROUBLE WITH STAGES. Some psychologists have questioned the existence of four separate stages of thinking, even though they agree that children do go through the changes that Piaget described (Mascolo & Fischer, 2005; Miller, 2011). One problem with the stage model is the lack of consistency in children's thinking. For example, children can conserve number (the number of blocks does not change when they are rearranged) a year or two before they can conserve weight (a ball of clay does not change when you flatten it). Why can't they use conservation consistently in every situation? In fairness, we should note that in his later work, even Piaget put less emphasis on stages of cognitive development and gave more attention to how thinking *changes* through equilibration (Miller, 2011).

Another problem with the idea of separate stages is that the processes may be more continuous than they seem. Changes may seem like discontinuous, qualitative leaps when we look across longer time periods. The 3-year-old persistently searching for a lost toy seems qualitatively different from the infant who doesn't seem to miss a toy or search when the toy rolls under a sofa. But if we watched a developing child very closely and observed moment-to-moment or hour-to-hour changes, we might see that indeed there are gradual, continuous changes. Rather than appearing all at once, the knowledge that a hidden toy still exists may be a product of the older child's more fully developed memory: He knows that the toy is under the sofa because he remembers seeing it roll there, whereas the infant can't hold on to that memory. The longer you require children to wait before searching—the longer you make them remember the object—the older they have to be to succeed (Siegler & Alibali, 2005).

CHILD EXPERTS One limitation of Piaget's theory appears to be the underestimation of young children's cognitive abilities. For instance, his theory does not explain how these young girls can play chess at the same level as many adults could.

Change can be both continuous and discontinuous, as described by a branch of mathematics called *catastrophe theory*. Changes that appear suddenly, like the collapse of a bridge, are preceded by many slowly developing changes such as gradual, continuous corrosion of the metal structures. Similarly, gradually developing changes in children can lead to large changes in abilities that seem abrupt (Dawson-Tunik, Fischer, & Stein, 2004; Siegler & Alibali, 2005).

UNDERESTIMATING CHILDREN'S ABILITIES. It now appears that Piaget underestimated the cognitive abilities of children, particularly younger ones. The problems he gave young children may have been too difficult and the directions too confusing. His subjects may have understood more than they could demonstrate when solving these problems. For example, work by Gelman and her colleagues (Gelman, 2000; Gelman & Cordes, 2001) shows that preschool children know much more about the concept of number than Piaget thought, even if they sometimes make mistakes or get confused. As long as preschoolers work with only 3 or 4 objects at a time, they can tell that the number remains the same, even if the objects are spread far apart or clumped close together. Mirjam Ebersbach (2009) demonstrated that most of the German kindergartners in her study considered all three dimensions—width, height, and length—when they estimated the volume of a wooden block (actually, how many small cubes it would take to make bigger blocks of different sizes). In other words, we may be born with a greater store of cognitive tools than Piaget suggested. Some basic understandings or core knowledge, such as the permanence of objects or the sense of number, may be part of our evolutionary equipment, ready for use in our cognitive development (Geary & Bjorklund, 2000; Woodward & Needham, 2009).

Piaget's theory does not explain how even young children can perform at an advanced level in certain areas where they have highly developed knowledge and expertise. An expert 9-year-old chess player may think abstractly about chess moves, whereas a novice 20-year-old player may have to resort to more concrete strategies to plan and remember moves (Siegler, 1998).

Finally, Piaget argued that the development of cognitive operations such as conservation or abstract thinking cannot be accelerated. He believed that children had to be developmentally ready to learn. Quite a bit of research, however, has shown that with effective instruction, children can learn to perform cognitive operations such as conservation. They do not have to naturally discover these ways of thinking on their own. Knowledge and experience in a situation affect the kind of thinking that students can do (Brainerd, 2003).

COGNITIVE DEVELOPMENT AND CULTURE. One final criticism of Piaget's theory is that it overlooks the important effects of the child's cultural and social group. Research across different cultures has generally confirmed that although Piaget was accurate about the sequence of the stages in children's thinking, the age ranges for the stages vary. Western children typically move to the next stage about 2 to 3 years earlier than children in non-Western societies. But careful research has shown that these differences across cultures depend on the subject or domain tested and whether the culture values and teaches knowledge in that domain. For example, children in Brazil who sell candy in the streets instead of attending school appear to fail a certain kind of Piagetian task—class inclusion (Are there more daisies, more tulips, or more flowers in the picture?). But when the tasks are phrased within concepts they understand—selling candy—then these children perform better than Brazilian children the same age who attend school (Saxe, 1999). When a culture or context emphasizes a cognitive ability, children growing up in that culture tend to acquire that ability sooner. In a study that compared Chinese 1st-, 3rd-, and 5th-grade students to American students in the same grades, the Chinese students mastered a Piagetian task that involved distance, time, and speed relationships about 2 years ahead of American students, most likely because the Chinese education system puts more emphasis on math and science in the early grades (Zhou, Peverly, Beohm, & Chongde, 2001).

Even concrete operations such as classification may develop differently in different cultures. For example, when individuals from the Kpelle people of Africa were asked to sort 20 objects, they created groups that made sense to them—a hoe with a potato, a knife with an orange. The experimenter could not get the Kpelle to change their categories; they said this way of sorting is how a wise man would do it. Finally, the experimenter asked in desperation, "Well, how would a fool do it?" Then the subjects promptly created the four neat classification piles the experimenter had expected—food, tools, and so on (Rogoff & Morelli, 1989).

There is another increasingly influential view of cognitive development. Proposed years ago by Lev Vygotsky and recently rediscovered, this theory ties cognitive development to culture.

VYGOTSKY'S SOCIOCULTURAL PERSPECTIVE

Psychologists today recognize that culture shapes cognitive development by determining what and how the child will learn about the world—the content and processes of thinking. For example, young Zinacanteco Indian girls of southern Mexico learn complicated ways of weaving cloth through informal instruction by adults in their communities. Cultures that prize cooperation and sharing teach these abilities early, whereas cultures that encourage competition nurture competitive skills in their children (Bakerman et al., 1990; Ceci & Roazzi, 1994). The stages observed by Piaget are not necessarily "natural" for all children because to some extent they reflect the expectations and activities of Western cultures, as the Kpelle people described above have taught us (Kozulin, 2003; Rogoff, 2003).

A major spokesperson for this **sociocultural theory** (also called *sociohistoric*) was a Russian psychologist who died almost 80 years ago. Lev Semenovich Vygotsky was only 38 when he died of tuberculosis, but during his brief life he produced over 100 books and articles. Some of the translations now available are Vygotsky (e.g., 1978, 1986, 1987a, 1987b, 1987c, 1993, 1997). Vygotsky began studying learning and development to improve his own teaching. He went on to write about language and thought, the psychology of art, learning and development, and educating students with special needs. His work was banned in Russia for many years because he referenced Western psychologists. But in the past 40 years, with the rediscovery of his writings, Vygotsky's ideas have become major influences in psychology and education and have provided alternatives to many of Piaget's theories (Gredler, 2009; Kozulin, 2003; Van Der Veer, 2007; Wink & Putney, 2002).

Vygotsky believed that human activities take place in cultural settings and that they cannot be understood apart from these settings. One of his key ideas was that our specific mental structures and processes can be traced to our interactions with others. These social interactions are more than simple influences on cognitive development—they actually create our cognitive structures and thinking processes (Palincsar, 1998). In fact, "Vygotsky conceptualized development as the transformation of socially shared activities into internalized processes" (John-Steiner & Mahn, 1996, p. 192). We will examine three themes in Vygotsky's writings that explain how social processes form learning and thinking: the social sources of individual thinking; the role of cultural tools in learning and development, especially the tool of language; and the zone of proximal development (Driscoll, 2005; Wertsch & Tulviste, 1992).

SOCIOCULTURAL THEORY Lev Vygotsky elaborated the sociocultural theory of development. His ideas about language, culture, and cognitive development have become major influences in the fields of psychology and education.

Sociocultural theory Emphasizes role in development of cooperative dialogues between children and more knowledgeable members of society. Children learn the culture of their community (ways of thinking and behaving) through these interactions.

The Social Sources of Individual Thinking

Vygotsky assumed that

> Every function in a child's cultural development appears twice: first, on the social level and later on the individual level; first between people (interpsychological) and then

inside the child (intrapsychological). This applies equally to voluntary attention, to logical memory, and to the formation of concepts. All the higher functions originate as actual relations between human individuals. (1978, p. 57)

In other words, higher mental processes, such as directing your own attention and thinking through problems, first are *co-constructed* during shared activities between the child and another person. Then these **co-constructed processes** are internalized by the child and become part of that child's cognitive development (Gredler, 2009). For example, children first use language in activities with others, to regulate the behavior of the others ("No nap!" or "I wanna cookie."). Later, however, the child can regulate her own behavior using private speech ("careful—don't spill"), as you will see in a later section. So, for Vygotsky, social interaction was more than influence; it was the origin of higher mental processes such as problem solving. Consider this example:

> A six-year-old has lost a toy and asks her father for help. The father asks her where she last saw the toy; the child says "I can't remember." He asks a series of questions—did you have it in your room? Outside? Next door? To each question, the child answers, "no." When he says "in the car?" she says "I think so" and goes to retrieve the toy. (Tharp & Gallimore, 1988, p. 14)

Who remembered? The answer is really neither the father nor the daughter, but the two together. The remembering and problem solving were co-constructed—between people—in the interaction. But the child (and the father) may have internalized strategies to use next time something is lost. At some point, the child will be able to function independently to solve this kind of problem. So, like the strategy for finding the toy, higher functions appear first between a child and a "teacher" before they exist within the individual child (Kozulin, 1990; 2003).

Here is another example of the social sources of individual thinking. Richard Anderson and his colleagues (2001) studied how 4th graders in small-group classroom discussions *appropriate* (take for themselves and use) argument stratagems that occur in the discussions. An *argument stratagem* is a particular form such as "I think [POSITION] because [REASON]," where the student fills in the position and the reason. For example, a student might say, "I think that the wolves should be left alone because they are not hurting anyone." Another strategy form is "If [ACTION], then [BAD CONSEQUENCE]," as in "If they don't trap the wolves, then the wolves will eat the cows." Other forms manage participation, for example, "What do you think [NAME]?" or "Let [NAME] talk."

Anderson's research identified 13 forms of talk and argument that helped to manage the discussion, get everyone to participate, present and defend positions, and handle confusion. The researchers found that the use of these different forms of talking and thinking *snowballed*: Once a useful argument was employed by one student, it spread to other students and the argument stratagem form appeared more and more in the discussions. Open discussions—students asking and answering each other's questions—were better than teacher-dominated discussion for the development of these argument forms. Over time, these ways of presenting, attacking, and defending positions could be internalized as mental reasoning and decision making for the individual students.

Both Piaget and Vygotsky emphasized the importance of social interactions in cognitive development, but Piaget saw a different role for interaction. He believed that interaction encouraged development by creating disequilibrium—that is, cognitive conflict motivated change. Thus, Piaget believed that the most helpful interactions were those between peers, because peers are on an equal basis and can challenge each other's thinking. Vygotsky, on the other hand, suggested that children's cognitive development is fostered by interactions with people who are more capable or advanced in their thinking—people such as parents and teachers (Moshman, 1997; Palinscar, 1998). Of course, students can learn from both adults and peers, and today, computers can play a role in supporting communication across distances or in different languages.

Cultural Tools and Cognitive Development

Vygotsky believed that **cultural tools**, including technical tools (such as printing presses, plows, rulers, abacuses, graph paper—today, we would add mobile devices, computers,

Co-constructed process A social process in which people interact and negotiate (usually verbally) to create an understanding or to solve a problem. The final product is shaped by all participants.

Cultural tools The real tools (computers, scales, etc.) and symbol systems (numbers, language, graphs) that allow people in a society to communicate, think, solve problems, and create knowledge.

the Internet, real-time translators for mobile devices and chats, search engines, digital organizers and calendars, assistive technologies for students with learning challenges…) and psychological tools (signs and symbol systems such as numbers and mathematical systems, Braille and sign language, maps, works of art, codes, and language) play very important roles in cognitive development. For example, as long as the culture provides only Roman numerals for representing quantity, certain ways of thinking mathematically—from long division to calculus—are difficult or impossible. But if a number system has a zero, fractions, positive and negative values, and an infinite quantity of numbers, then much more is possible. The number system is a psychological tool that supports learning and cognitive development—it changes the thinking process. This symbol system is passed from adult to child and from child to child through formal and informal interactions and teachings.

TECHNICAL TOOLS IN A DIGITAL AGE. The use of technical tools such as calculators and spell checkers has been somewhat controversial in education. Technology is increasingly "checking up" on us. I rely on the spell checker in my word processing program to protect me from embarrassment. But I also read student papers with spelling replacements that must have come from decisions made by the word processing program—without a "sense check" by the writer. Is student learning harmed or helped by these technology supports? Just because students learned mathematics in the past with paper-and-pencil procedures and practice does not mean that this is the best way to learn. For example, in the Third International Mathematics and Science Study (TIMSS, 1998), on every test at the advanced level, students who said that they used calculators in their daily math coursework performed much better than students who rarely or never used calculators. In fact, the research on calculators over the past decade has found that rather than eroding basic skills, calculator use has positive effects on students' problem-solving skills and attitudes toward math (Waits & Demana, 2000).

PSYCHOLOGICAL TOOLS. Vygotsky believed that all higher-order mental processes such as reasoning and problem solving are *mediated* by (accomplished through and with the help of) psychological tools. These tools allow children to transform their thinking by enabling them to gain greater and greater mastery of their own cognitive processes; thus they advance their own development as they use the tools. In fact, Vygotsky believed the essence of cognitive development is mastering the use of psychological tools such as language to accomplish the kind of advanced thinking and problem solving that could not be accomplished without those tools (Gredler, 2009; Karpov & Haywood, 1998). The process is something like this: As children engage in activities with adults or more capable peers, they exchange ideas and ways of thinking about or representing concepts—drawing maps, for example, as a way to represent spaces and places. Children internalize these co-created ideas. Thus, children's knowledge, ideas, attitudes, and values develop through appropriating or "taking for themselves" the ways of acting and thinking provided by both their culture and other members of their group (Wertsch, 2007).

In this exchange of signs and symbols and explanations, children begin to develop a "cultural tool kit" to make sense of and learn about their world (Wertsch, 1991). The kit is filled with technical tools such as graphing calculators or rulers directed toward the external world and psychological tools for acting mentally such as concepts, problem-solving strategies, and (as we saw earlier) argument strategems. Children do not just receive the tools, however. They transform the tools as they construct their own representations, symbols, patterns, and understandings. As we learned from Piaget, children's constructions of meaning are not the same as those of adults. In the exchange of signs and symbols such as language, children create their own understandings (a raccoon is a "kitty"). These understandings are gradually changed (a raccoon is a raccoon) as the children continue to engage in social activities and try to make sense of their world (John-Steiner & Mahn, 1996; Wertsch, 1991). In Vygotsky's theory, language is the most important symbol system in the tool kit, and it is the one that helps to fill the kit with other tools.

The Role of Language and Private Speech

Language is critical for cognitive development because it provides a way to express ideas and ask questions, the categories and concepts for thinking, and the links between the past and the future. Language frees us from the immediate situation to think about what was and what might be (Das, 1995; Driscoll, 2005). Vygotsky thought that:

> the specifically human capacity for language enables children to provide for auxiliary tools in the solution of difficult tasks, to overcome impulsive action, to plan a solution to a problem prior to its execution, and to master their own behavior. (1978, p. 28)

Vygotsky placed more emphasis than Piaget on the role of learning and language in cognitive development. He believed that "thinking depends on speech, on the means of thinking, and on the child's socio-cultural experience" (Vygotsky, 1987a, p. 120). In fact, Vygotsky believed that language in the form of private speech (talking to yourself) guides cognitive development.

PRIVATE SPEECH: VYGOTSKY'S AND PIAGET'S VIEWS COMPARED. If you have spent much time around young children, you know that they often talk to themselves as they play. This can happen when the child is alone or, even more often, in a group of children—each child talks enthusiastically, without any real interaction or conversation. Piaget called this the **collective monologue** and he labeled all of the children's self-directed talk "egocentric speech." He assumed that this egocentric speech is another indication that young children can't see the world through the eyes of others, so they chat away without taking into account the needs or interests of their listeners. As they mature, and especially as they have disagreements with peers, Piaget believed, children develop *socialized speech*. They learn to listen and exchange (or argue) ideas.

Vygotsky had very different ideas about young children's **private speech**. Rather than being a sign of cognitive immaturity, Vygotsky suggested that these mutterings play an important role in cognitive development because they move children in stages toward self-regulation: the ability to plan, monitor, and guide your own thinking and problem solving. First the child's behavior is regulated by others using language and other signs such as gestures. For example, the parent says, "No!" when the child reaches toward a candle flame. Next, the child learns to regulate the behavior of others using the same language tools. The child says "No!" to another child who is trying to take away a toy, often even imitating the parent's voice tone. The child also begins to use private speech to regulate her own behavior, saying "no" quietly to herself as she is tempted to touch the flame. Finally, the child learns to regulate her own behavior by using silent inner speech (Karpov & Haywood, 1998).

For example, in any preschool room you might hear 4- or 5-year-olds saying, "No, it won't fit. Try it here. Turn. Turn. Maybe this one!" while they do puzzles. Around the age of 7, children's self-directed speech goes underground, changing from spoken to whispered speech and then to silent lip movements. Finally, the children just "think" the guiding words. The use of private speech peaks at around age 9 and then decreases, although one study found that some students from ages 11 to 17 still spontaneously muttered to themselves during problem solving (McCafferty, 2004; Winsler, Carlton, & Barry, 2000; Winsler & Naglieri, 2003). Vygotsky called this inner speech "an internal plane of verbal thinking" (Vygotsky, 1934/1987c, p. 279)—a critical accomplishment on the road to higher-order thinking.

This series of steps from spoken words to silent inner speech is another example of how higher mental functions first appear between people as they communicate and regulate each other's behavior, and then emerge again within the individual as cognitive processes. Through this fundamental process, the child is using language to accomplish important cognitive activities such as directing attention, solving problems, planning, forming concepts, and gaining self-control. Research supports Vygotsky's ideas (Berk & Spuhl, 1995; Emerson & Miyake, 2003). Children and adults tend to use more private speech when they are confused, having difficulties, or making mistakes (Duncan & Cheyne, 1999). Have you ever thought to yourself something like, "Let's see, the first step is" or "Where did I use my glasses last?" or "If I read to the end of this page, then I can . . . "? You were using inner speech to remind, cue, encourage, or guide yourself.

Collective monologue Form of speech in which children in a group talk but do not really interact or communicate.

Private speech Children's self-talk, which guides their thinking and action. Eventually, these verbalizations are internalized as silent inner speech.

TABLE 2.4 • **Differences between Piaget's and Vygotsky's Theories of Egocentric or Private Speech**

	PIAGET	VYGOTSKY
	Represents an inability to take the perspective of another and engage in reciprocal communication.	Represents externalized thought; its function is to communicate with the self for the purpose of self-guidance and self-direction.
Course of Development	Declines with age.	Increases at younger ages and then gradually loses its audible quality to become internal verbal thought.
Relationship to Social Speech	Negative; least socially and cognitively mature children use more egocentric speech.	Positive; private speech develops out of social interaction with others.
Relationship to Environmental Contexts		Increases with task difficulty. Private speech serves a helpful self-guiding function in situations where more cognitive effort is needed to reach a solution.

Source: From "Development of Private Speech among Low-Income Appalachian Children," by L. E. Berk and R. A. Garvin, 1984, Developmental Psychology, 20, *p. 272. Copyright © 1984 by the American Psychological Association. Adapted with permission.*

This internal verbal thinking is not stable until about age 12, so children in elementary school may need to continue talking through problems and explaining their reasoning in order to develop their abilities to control their thinking (Gredler, 2009). Because private speech helps students regulate their thinking, it makes sense to allow, and even encourage, students to use private speech in school. Teachers' insisting on total silence when young students are working on difficult problems may make the work even harder for them. Take note when muttering increases in your class—this could be a sign that students need help.

Table 2.4 contrasts Piaget's and Vygotsky's theories of private speech. We should note that Piaget accepted many of Vygotsky's arguments and came to agree that language could be used in both egocentric and problem-solving ways (Piaget, 1962).

The Zone of Proximal Development

According to Vygotsky, at any given point in development, there are certain problems that a child is on the verge of being able to solve. The child just needs some structure, clues, reminders, help with remembering details or steps, encouragement to keep trying, and so on. Some problems, of course, are beyond the child's capabilities, even if every step is explained clearly. The **zone of proximal development (ZPD)** is the area between the child's current development level "as determined by independent problem solving" and the level of development that the child could achieve "through adult guidance or in collaboration with more capable peers" (Vygotsky, 1978, p. 86). It is a dynamic and changing space as student and teacher interact and understandings are exchanged. This is the area where instruction can succeed. Kathleen Berger (2012) called this area the "magic middle"—somewhere between what the student already knows and what the student isn't ready to learn.

PRIVATE SPEECH AND THE ZONE. We can see how Vygotsky's beliefs about the role of private speech in cognitive development fit with the notion of the zone of proximal development. Often, an adult uses verbal prompts and structuring to help a child solve a problem or accomplish a task. We will see later that this type of support has been called *scaffolding*. This support can be gradually reduced as the child takes over the guidance, perhaps first by giving the prompts as private speech and finally as inner speech. Let's move forward to a future day in the life of the girl in the example on page 56 who had lost her toy and listen to her *thoughts* when she realizes that a schoolbook is missing. They might sound something like this:

> "Where's my math book? Used it in class. Thought I put it in my book bag after class. Dropped my bag on the bus. That dope Larry kicked my stuff, so maybe..."

Zone of proximal development Phase at which a child can master a task if given appropriate help and support.

The girl can now systematically search for ideas about the lost book without help from anyone else.

THE ROLE OF LEARNING AND DEVELOPMENT. Piaget defined *development* as the active construction of knowledge and *learning* as the passive formation of associations (Siegler, 2000). He was interested in knowledge construction and believed that cognitive development has to come before learning—the child had to be cognitively "ready" to learn. He said that "learning is subordinated to development and not vice-versa" (Piaget, 1964, p. 17). Students can memorize, for example, that Geneva is in Switzerland, but still insist that they cannot be Genevan and Swiss at the same time. True understanding will take place only when the child has developed the operation of *class inclusion*—that one category can be included within another. But as we saw earlier, research has not supported Piaget's position on the need for cognitive development to precede learning (Brainerd, 2003).

In contrast, Vygotsky believed that learning is an active process that does not have to wait for readiness. In fact, "properly organized learning results in mental development and sets in motion a variety of developmental processes that would be impossible apart from learning" (Vygotsky, 1978, p. 90). He saw learning as a tool in development—learning pulls development up to higher levels and social interaction is a key in learning (Glassman, 2001; Wink & Putney, 2002). Vygotsky's belief that learning pulls development to higher levels means that other people, including teachers, play a significant role in cognitive development.

Limitations of Vygotsky's Theory

Vygotsky's theory added important considerations by highlighting the role of culture and social processes in cognitive development, but he may have gone too far. As we have seen in this chapter, we may be born with a greater store of cognitive tools than either Piaget or Vygotsky suggested. Some basic understandings, such as the idea that adding increases quantity, may be part of our biological predispositions, ready for use to guide our cognitive development. Young children appear to figure out much about the world before they have the chance to learn from either their culture or teachers (Schunk, 2008; Woodward & Needham, 2009). Also, Vygotsky did not detail the cognitive processes underlying developmental changes—for example, *which* cognitive processes allow students to engage in more advanced and independent participation in social activities? The major limitation of Vygotsky's theory, however, is that it consists mostly of general ideas; Vygotsky died before he could expand and elaborate on his ideas and pursue his research. His students continued to investigate his ideas, but much of that work was suppressed by Stalin's regime until the 1950s and 1960s (Gredler, 2005, 2009; Kozulin, 1990, 2003). A final limitation might be that Vygotsky did not have time to detail the applications of his theories for teaching, even though he was very interested in instruction. So, most of the applications described today have been created by others—and we don't even know if Vygotsky would agree with them.

IMPLICATIONS OF PIAGET'S AND VYGOTSKY'S THEORIES FOR TEACHERS

Piaget did not make specific educational recommendations and Vygotsky did not have enough time to develop a complete set of applications. But we can glean some guidance from both men.

Piaget: What Can We Learn?

Piaget was more interested in understanding children's thinking than in guiding teachers. He did express some general ideas about educational philosophy, however. He believed that the main goal of education should be to help children learn how to learn, and that education should "form not furnish" the minds of students (Piaget, 1969, p. 70). Piaget has taught us that we can learn a great deal about how children think by listening carefully and by paying close attention to their ways of solving problems. If we understand children's thinking, we will be better able to match teaching methods to children's current knowledge and abilities; in other words, we will be better able to differentiate instruction.

Even though Piaget did not design programs of education based on his ideas, his influence on current educational practice is huge (Hindi & Perry, 2007). For example, the National Association for the Education of Young Children has guidelines for developmentally appropriate practice (DAP) that incorporate Piaget's findings (Bredekamp, 2011; Bredekamp & Copple, 1997).

ACTIVE LEARNING The ability to manipulate concrete objects helps children understand abstract relationships such as the connection between symbols and quantity.

UNDERSTANDING AND BUILDING ON STUDENTS' THINKING. The students in any class will vary greatly in both their level of cognitive development and their academic knowledge. As a teacher, how can you determine whether students are having trouble because they lack the necessary thinking abilities or because they simply have not learned the basic facts? To do this, Case (1985b) suggests you observe your students carefully as they try to solve the problems you have presented. What kind of logic do they use? Do they focus on only one aspect of the situation? Are they fooled by appearances? Do they suggest solutions systematically or by guessing and forgetting what they have already tried? Ask your students how they tried to solve the problem. Listen to their strategies. What kind of thinking is behind repeated mistakes or problems? Students are the best sources of information about their own thinking (Confrey, 1990a).

Connect and Extend to PRAXIS II™

Implications of Piaget's Theory (I, A2)
The music, physical education, and art teachers in a rural, pre-K-to-8 school district work with students who characterize several of Piaget's stages. How should these three teachers adjust their teaching from level to level over the course of a week?

An important implication of Piaget's theory for teaching is what Hunt years ago (1961) called "the problem of the match." Students must be neither bored by work that is too simple nor left behind by teaching they cannot understand. According to Hunt, disequilibrium must be kept "just right" to encourage growth. Setting up situations that lead to unexpected results can help create an appropriate level of disequilibrium. When students experience some conflict between what they think should happen (a piece of wood should sink because it is big) and what actually happens (it floats!), they may rethink the situation, and new knowledge may develop.

Many materials and lessons can be understood at several levels and can be "just right" for a range of cognitive abilities. Classics such as *Alice in Wonderland*, myths, and fairy tales can be enjoyed at both concrete and symbolic levels. It is also possible for a group of students to be introduced to a topic together, and then work individually on follow-up activities matched to their learning needs. Using multi-level lessons is called *differentiated instruction* (Hipsky, 2011; Tomlinson, 2005b). We encountered this idea in Chapter 1 and will look at this approach more closely in Chapter 14.

ACTIVITY AND CONSTRUCTING KNOWLEDGE. Piaget's fundamental insight was that individuals construct their own understanding; learning is a constructive process. At every level of cognitive development, you will also want to see that students are actively engaged in the learning process. In Piaget's words:

> Knowledge is not a copy of reality. To know an object, to know an event, is not simply to look at it and make a mental copy or image of it. To know an object is to act on it. To know is to modify, to transform the object, and to understand the process of this transformation, and as a consequence to understand the way the object is constructed. (Piaget, 1964, p. 8)

This active experience, even at the earliest school levels, should not be limited to the physical manipulation of objects. It should also include mental manipulation of ideas that arise out of class projects or experiments (Gredler, 2005, 2009). For example, after a social studies lesson on different jobs, a primary-grade teacher might show students a picture of a woman and ask, "What could this person be?" After answers such as "teacher," "doctor," "secretary," "lawyer," "saleswoman," and so on, the teacher could suggest, "How about a daughter?" Answers such as "sister," "mother," "aunt," and "granddaughter" may follow. This should help the children switch dimensions in their classification and center on another aspect of the situation. Next, the teacher might suggest "American," "jogger," or "blonde." With older children, hierarchical classification might be involved: It is a picture of a woman, who is a human being; a human being is a primate, which is a mammal, which is an animal, which is a life form.

SCAFFOLDING LEARNING According to Vygotsky, much of children's learning is assisted or mediated by teachers or parents and tools in their environment, and most of this guidance is communicated through language.

Connect and Extend to PRAXIS II™

Implications of Vygotsky's Theory (I, A2)
Make a list of scaffolding techniques that would be appropriate with different instructional levels and content areas. Think of scaffolding techniques that others have used when you learned things outside of school (e.g., sports, hobbies).

Scaffolding Support for learning and problem solving. The support would be clues, reminders, encouragement, breaking the problem down into steps, providing an example or anything else that allows the student to grow in independence as a learner.

All students need to interact with teachers and peers in order to test their thinking, to be challenged, to receive feedback, and to watch how others work out problems. Disequilibrium is often set in motion quite naturally when the teacher or another student suggests a new way of thinking about something. As a general rule, students should act on, manipulate, observe, and then talk and/or write about (to the teacher and each other) what they have experienced. Concrete experiences provide the raw materials for thinking. Communicating with others makes students use, test, and sometimes change their thinking strategies.

Vygotsky: What Can We Learn?

Like Piaget, Vygotsky believed that the main goal of education was the development of higher mental functions, not simply filling students' memories with facts. So Vygotsky probably would oppose educational curricula that are an inch deep and a mile wide or seem like "trivial pursuit." As an example of this trivial pursuit curriculum, Margaret Gredler (2009) described a set of materials for a 9-week science unit that had 61 glossary terms such as *aqueous solution, hydrogen bonding,* and *fractional crystallization*—many terms described with only one or two sentences.

There are at least three ways that higher mental functions can be developed through cultural tools and passed from one individual to another: *imitative* learning (where one person tries to imitate the other), *instructed* learning (where learners internalize the instructions of the teacher and use these instructions to self-regulate), and *collaborative* learning (where a group of peers strives to understand each other and learning occurs in the process) (Tomasello, Kruger, & Ratner, 1993). Vygotsky was most concerned with the second type, *instructed* learning through direct teaching or by structuring experiences that encourage another's learning, but his theory supports learning through *imitation* or *collaboration* as well. Thus, Vygotsky's ideas are relevant for educators who teach directly, intentionally use modeling to teach, or create collaborative learning environments (Das, 1995; Wink & Putney, 2002). That pretty much includes all of us.

THE ROLE OF ADULTS AND PEERS. Vygotsky believed the child is not alone in the world "discovering" the cognitive operations of conservation or classification. This discovery is assisted or mediated by family members, teachers, peers, and even software tools (Puntambekar & Hubscher, 2005). Most of this guidance is communicated through language, at least in Western cultures. In some cultures, observing a skilled performance, not talking about it, guides the child's learning (Rogoff, 1990). Some people have called this adult assistance **scaffolding**, taken from Wood, Bruner, and Ross (1976). The idea is that children use the help for support while they build a firm understanding that will eventually allow them to solve the problems on their own. Actually, when Wood and his colleagues introduced the term *scaffolding*, they were talking about how teachers set up or structure learning environments, but Vygotsky's theory implies more dynamic exchanges between student and teacher that allow the teacher to support students in the parts of the task they cannot do alone—the interactions of assisted learning, as you will see next (Schunk, 2008).

ASSISTED LEARNING. Vygotsky's theory suggests that teachers need to do more than just arrange the environment so that students can discover on their own. Children cannot and should not be expected to reinvent or rediscover knowledge already available in their cultures. Rather, they should be guided and assisted in their learning (Karpov & Haywood, 1998).

Assisted learning, or guided participation, requires first learning from the student what is needed; then giving information, prompts, reminders, and encouragement at the right time and in the right amounts; and gradually allowing the students to do more and more on their own. Teachers can assist learning by adapting materials or problems to students' current levels; demonstrating skills or thought processes; walking students

TABLE 2.5 • **Strategies to Provide Scaffolding**

- Model the thought process for the students: Think out loud as you solve the problem or outline an essay, for example.
- Provide organizers or starters such as *who, what, why, how, what next?*
- Do part of the problem.
- Give hints and cues.
- Encourage students to set short-term goals and take small steps.
- Connect new learning to students' interests or prior learning.
- Use graphic organizers: timelines, charts, tables, categories, checklists, and graphs.
- Simplify the task, clarify the purpose, and give clear directions
- Teach key vocabulary and provide examples.

Sources: Adapted from http://projects.coe.uga.edu/epltt/index.php?title=Scaffolding#Sharing_a_Specific_Goal
http://condor.admin.ccny.cuny.edu/~group4/
http://k6educators.about.com/od/helpfornewteachers/a/scaffoldingtech.htm

through the steps of a complicated problem; doing part of the problem (for example, in algebra, the students set up the equation and the teacher does the calculations or vice versa); giving detailed feedback and allowing revisions; or asking questions that refocus students' attention (Rosenshine & Meister, 1992). Cognitive apprenticeships (Chapter 10) are examples. Look at Table 2.5 for examples of strategies that can be used in any lesson.

Reaching Every Student: Teaching in the "Magic Middle"

Both Piaget and Vygotsky probably would agree that students need to be taught in the magic middle (Berger, 2012) or the place of the "match" (Hunt, 1961)—where they are neither bored nor frustrated. Students should be put in situations where they have to reach to understand, but where support from other students or the teacher is also available. Sometimes the best teacher is another student who has just figured out how to solve the problem, because this student is probably operating in the learner's *zone of proximal development.*

Assisted learning Providing strategic help in the initial stages of learning, gradually diminishing as students gain independence.

GUIDELINES

Applying Vygotsky's Ideas in Teaching

Tailor scaffolding to the needs of students.
Examples
1. When students are beginning new tasks or topics, provide models, prompts, sentence starters, coaching, and feedback. As the students grow in competence, give less support and more opportunities for independent work.
2. Give students choices about the level of difficulty or degree of independence in projects; encourage them to challenge themselves, but to seek help when they are really stuck.

Make sure students have access to powerful tools that support thinking.
Examples
1. Teach students to use learning and organizational strategies, research tools, language tools (wikis, dictionaries, or computer searches), spreadsheets, and word-processing programs.
2. Model the use of tools; show students how you use an appointment book or electronic notebook to make plans and manage time, for example.

Build on the students' cultural funds of knowledge (Gonzales, Moll, & Amanti, 2005; Moll et al., 1992).
Examples
1. Identify family knowledge by having students interview each other's families about their work and home knowledge (agriculture, economics, manufacturing, household management, medicine and illness, religion, child care, cooking, etc.).
2. Tie assignments to these funds of knowledge and use community experts to evaluate assignments.

Capitalize on dialogue and group learning.
Examples
1. Experiment with peer tutoring; teach students how to ask good questions and give helpful explanations.
2. Experiment with cooperative learning strategies described in Chapter 10.

For more information about Vygotsky and his theories, see http://tip.psychology.org/vygotsky.html

Connect and Extend to PRAXIS II™

Distinctions Between Piaget's and Vygotsky's Theories (I, A2)
Consider how two teachers—one based in Vygotskian theory and one based in Piagetian theory—might differ in their concepts of learning and teaching and the instructional techniques that they might prefer.

Having a student work with someone who is just a bit better at the activity would be a good idea because both students benefit in the exchange of explanations, elaborations, and questions. In addition, students should be encouraged to use language to organize their thinking and to talk about what they are trying to accomplish. Dialogue and discussion are important avenues to learning (Karpov & Bransford, 1995; Kozulin & Presseisen, 1995; Wink & Putney, 2002). The *Guidelines* on the previous page gave more ideas for applying Vygotsky's insights.

Cognitive Development: Lessons for Teachers

In spite of cross-cultural differences in cognitive development and the different theories of development, there are some convergences. Piaget, Vygotsky, and more recent researchers studying cognitive development and the brain probably would agree with the following big ideas:

1. Cognitive development requires both physical and social stimulation.
2. To develop thinking, children have to be mentally, physically, and linguistically active. They need to experiment, talk, describe, reflect, write, and solve problems. But they also benefit from teaching, guidance, questions, explanations, demonstrations, and challenges to their thinking.
3. Teaching students what they already know is boring. Trying to teach what the student isn't ready to learn is frustrating and ineffective.
4. Challenge with support will keep students engaged but not fearful.

▼ SUMMARY

A Definition of Development (pp. 30–32)

What are the different kinds of development? Human development can be divided into physical development (changes in the body), personal development (changes in an individual's personality), social development (changes in the way an individual relates to others), and cognitive development (changes in thinking).

What are three questions about development and three general principles? For decades, psychologists and the public have debated whether development is shaped more by nature or nurture, whether change is a continuous process or involves qualitative differences or stages, and whether there are critical times for the development of certain abilities. We know today that these simple either/or distinctions cannot capture the complexities of human development where coactions and interactions are the rule. Theorists generally agree that people develop at different rates, that development is an orderly process, and that development takes place gradually.

The Brain and Cognitive Development (pp. 32–42)

What part of the brain is associated with higher mental functions? The cortex is a crumpled sheet of neurons that serves three major functions: receiving signals from sense organs (such as visual or auditory signals), controlling voluntary movement, and forming connections. The part of the cortex that controls physical motor movement develops or matures first, then the areas that control complex senses such as vision and hearing, and last, the frontal lobe, which controls higher-order thinking processes.

What is lateralization and why is it important? Lateralization is the specialization of the two sides, or hemispheres, of the brain. For most people, the left hemisphere is the major factor in language, and the right hemisphere is prominent in spatial and visual processing. Even though certain functions are associated with particular parts of the brain, the various parts and systems of the brain work together to learn and perform complex activities such as reading and constructing understanding.

What are some implications for teachers? Recent advances in both methods and findings in the neurosciences provide exciting information about brain activity during learning and brain activity differences among people with varying abilities and challenges and from different cultures. There are some basic implications for teaching based on these findings, but many of the strategies offered by "brain-based" advocates are simply good teaching. Perhaps we now know more about why these strategies work.

Piaget's Theory of Cognitive Development (pp. 42–55)

What are the main influences on cognitive development? Piaget's theory of cognitive development is based on the assumption that people try to make sense of the world and actively create knowledge through direct experiences with objects, people, and ideas. Maturation, activity, social transmission, and the need for equilibrium all influence the way thinking processes and knowledge develop. In response to these influences, thinking processes and knowledge develop through changes in the organization of thought (the development of schemes) and through adaptation—including the complementary processes of assimilation (incorporating into existing schemes) and accommodation (changing existing schemes).

What is a scheme? Schemes are the basic building blocks of thinking. They are organized systems of actions or thought that allow us to mentally represent or "think about" the objects and events in our world. Schemes may be very small and specific (grasping, recognizing a square), or they may be larger and more general (using a map in a new city). People adapt to their environment as they increase and organize their schemes.

As children move from sensorimotor to formal-operational thinking, what are the major changes? Piaget believed that young people pass through four stages as they develop: sensorimotor, preoperational, concrete-operational, and formal-operational. In the sensorimotor stage, infants explore the world through their senses and motor activity, and work toward mastering object permanence and performing goal-directed activities. In the preoperational stage, symbolic thinking and logical operations begin. Children in the stage of concrete operations can think logically about tangible situations and can demonstrate conservation, reversibility, classification, and seriation. The ability to perform hypothetico-deductive reasoning, coordinate a set of variables, and imagine other worlds marks the stage of formal operations.

How do neo-Piagetian and information processing views explain changes in children's thinking over time? Information processing theories focus on attention, memory capacity, learning strategies, and other processing skills to explain how children develop rules and strategies for making sense of the world and solving problems. Neo-Piagetian approaches also look at attention, memory, and strategies and at how thinking develops in different domains such as numbers or spatial relations. Research in neuroscience suggests that when learning a new skill, children move through three tiers—from *actions* to *representations* to *abstractions*. Within each tier, the pattern is moving from accomplishing a single action to mapping or coordinating two actions together such as coordinating addition and multiplication in math, to creating whole systems of understanding.

What are some limitations of Piaget's theory? Piaget's theory has been criticized because children and adults often think in ways that are inconsistent with the notion of invariant stages. It also appears that Piaget underestimated children's cognitive abilities; he insisted that children could not be taught the operations of the next stage, but had to develop them on their own. Alternative explanations place greater emphasis on students' developing information processing skills and ways teachers can enhance their development. Piaget's work is also criticized for overlooking cultural factors in child development.

Vygotsky's Sociocultural Perspective (pp. 55–60)

According to Vygotsky, what are three main influences on cognitive development? Vygotsky believed that human activities must be understood in their cultural settings. He believed that our specific mental structures and processes can be traced to our interactions with others; that the tools of the culture, especially the tool of language, are key factors in development; and that the zone of proximal development is the area where learning and development are possible.

What are psychological tools and why are they important? Psychological tools are signs and symbol systems such as numbers and mathematical systems, codes, and language that support learning and cognitive development—they change the thinking process by enabling and shaping thinking. Many of these tools are passed from adult to child through formal and informal interactions and teachings.

Explain how interpsychological development becomes intrapsychological development. Higher mental processes appear first between people as they are co-constructed during shared activities. As children engage in activities with adults or more capable peers, they exchange ideas and ways of thinking about or representing concepts. Children internalize these co-created ideas. Thus children's knowledge, ideas, attitudes, and values develop through appropriating, or "taking for themselves," the ways of acting and thinking provided by their culture and by the more capable members of their group.

What are the differences between Piaget's and Vygotsky's perspectives on private speech and its role in development? Vygotsky's sociocultural view asserts that cognitive development hinges on social interaction and the development of language. As an example, Vygotsky describes the role of children's self-directed talk in guiding and monitoring thinking and problem solving, whereas Piaget suggests that private speech is an indication of the child's egocentrism. Vygotsky, more than Piaget, emphasized the significant role played by adults and more able peers in children's learning. This adult assistance provides early support while students build the understanding necessary to solve problems on their own later.

What is a student's zone of proximal development? At any given point in development, there are certain problems that a child is on the verge of being able to solve and others that are beyond the child's capabilities. The zone of proximal development is the area where the child cannot solve a problem alone, but can be successful under adult guidance or in collaboration with a more advanced peer.

What are two criticisms or limitations of Vygotsky's theory? Vygotsky may have overemphasized the role of social interaction in cognitive development—children figure out quite a bit on their own. Also, because he died so young, Vygotsky was not able to develop and elaborate on his theories. His students and others since have taken up that work.

Implications of Piaget's and Vygotsky's Theories for Teachers (pp. 60–64)

What is the "problem of the match" described by Hunt? The "problem of the match" is that students must be neither bored by work that is too simple nor left behind by teaching they cannot understand. According to Hunt, disequilibrium must be carefully balanced to encourage growth. Situations that lead to errors can help create an appropriate level of disequilibrium.

What is active learning? Why is Piaget's theory of cognitive development consistent with active learning? Piaget's fundamental insight was that individuals construct their own understanding; learning is a constructive process. At every level of cognitive development, students must be able to incorporate information into their own schemes. To do this, they must act on the information in some way. This active experience, even at the earliest school levels, should include both physical manipulation of objects and mental manipulation of ideas. As a general rule, students should act, manipulate, observe, and then talk and/or write about what they have experienced. Concrete experiences provide the raw materials for thinking. Communicating with others makes students use, test, and sometimes change their thinking abilities.

What is assisted learning, and what role does scaffolding play? Assisted learning, or guided participation in the classroom, requires scaffolding—understanding the students' needs, giving information, prompts, reminders, and encouragement at the right time and in the right amounts, and then gradually allowing the students to do more and more on their own. Teachers can assist learning by adapting materials or problems to students' current levels, demonstrating skills or thought processes, walking students through the steps of a complicated problem, doing part of the problem, giving detailed feedback and allowing revisions, or asking questions that refocus students' attention.

▼ KEY TERMS

Accommodation (44)
Adaptation (43)
Adolescent egocentrism (50)
Assimilation (44)
Assisted learning (62)
Classification (48)
Co-constructed process (56)
Coactions (31)
Cognitive development (30)
Collective monologue (58)
Compensation (47)
Concrete operations (47)
Conservation (46)
Cultural tools (56)
Decentering (46)
Development (30)
Disequilibrium (44)
Egocentric (46)

Equilibration (44)
Event-related potential (ERP) (33)
Formal operations (50)
Functional magnetic resonance imaging (fMRI) (32)
Glial cells (35)
Goal-directed actions (45)
Hypothetico-deductive reasoning (50)
Identity (47)
Lateralization (36)
Maturation (30)
Myelination (35)
Neo-Piagetian theories (52)
Neurogenesis (33)
Neurons (33)
Object permanence (44)
Operations (45)
Organization (43)

Personal development (30)
Physical development (30)
Plasticity (36)
Positron emission tomography (PET) (33)
Preoperational (45)
Private speech (58)
Reversibility (48)
Reversible thinking (46)
Scaffolding (62)
Schemes (43)
Semiotic function (46)
Sensitive periods (31)
Sensorimotor (44)
Seriation (49)
Social development (30)
Sociocultural theory (55)
Synapses (33)
Zone of proximal development (59)

▼ CONNECT AND EXTEND TO LICENSURE

MULTIPLE-CHOICE QUESTIONS

1. Mr. Winstel was worried about his former star student, Ramon. As the seventh grade year progressed, Ramon was frequently being called into the principal's office for skateboard stunts that broke school rules and bordered on dangerous. Recently, Ramon's parents contacted Mr. Winstel to alert him to the fact Ramon had been skipping school to hang out with some older boys in the neighborhood. Which of the following answers would typically best describe what is happening with Ramon?

   A. Ramon's culture demands that boys of his age begin to engage in behaviors which reflect fearlessness.

   B. Ramon's limbic system is maturing but his prefrontal lobe has not yet caught up.

   C. Ramon is engaging in deviant behaviors as a cry for attention from his parents.

   D. Ramon is undergoing a period of synaptic pruning which causes adolescents to engage in risk taking behavior.

2. Miss McClintock discovered that five of the children in her class were developmentally advanced. All of the students' language skills were exploding! While many of the students still had trouble sharing, a few appeared to understand that by sharing everyone could be happy. Finally, there was even one child who could solve conservation problems. According to Piagetian theory, in what stage are the students in Miss McClintock' class?

   A. Formal Operations

   B. Concrete Operations

   C. Preoperational

   D. Sensorimotor

3. In introducing students to persuasive advertising methods, which of the following approaches would be most apt to lead to student retention?

   A. Determine what students already know about the topic and connect new information to their prior knowledge.

   B. Have students initially watch several commercials and take notes.

   C. Lecture students on the major persuasive techniques and have a quiz to assess learning.

   D. Have students form groups to research persuasive techniques.

4. Research studies involving the brain and learning indicate all but which one of the following statements is true?

   A. There is no such thing as "left brain" and "right brain" thinking.

   B. The production of new neurons continues into adulthood.

   C. Using different modalities for instruction and activities that draw on different senses may support learning.

   D. Pruning can damage heavily used cognitive pathways.

CONSTRUCTED-RESPONSE QUESTIONS

Case

Mr. Gething remembered that when planning for instruction students should be neither bored nor frustrated. Although this made sense to him, he was unsure how he would compensate for the diverse group of students he had in his second period language arts class. There were students who had difficulty with the English language and other students who planned to participate in the school's annual Shakespearean play. He knew that by grouping students of mixed ability, he could occasionally draw upon the talents of his knowledgeable students to assist the less advanced students. He also understood that without guidelines, students may not accomplish anything.

5. Explain the theory of learning Mr. Gething is initially drawing upon and the individual credited with it.

6. What is term for the assistance the more knowledgeable class members may provide to the less advanced students in order for them to succeed? List some strategies these students might use to assist their peers.

─── MyEducationLab™ ───

Go to Chapter 2 of the Book Specific Resources in MyEducationLab and click on "Connect and Extend to Licensure" to answer these questions. Compare your responses with the feedback provided.

▼ WHAT WOULD THEY DO?

TEACHERS' CASEBOOK: Symbols and Cymbals

Here is how several expert teachers said they would help their students understand abstract concepts.

LINDA GLISSON AND SUE MIDDLETON • 5th Grade Team Teachers
St. James Episcopal Day School, Baton Rouge, LA

To begin the lesson, I would have the students use a dictionary to define the word *symbolism* (root word—*symbol*) to discover that it means "something that stands for or represents something else." I would then give them a brief "across the curriculum" exercise in ways they incorporate symbols and symbolism into their thinking every day. For example (social studies, American history): The American flag is just a piece of cloth. Why then do we recite a pledge to it? Stand at attention when it passes in a parade? What does it stand for? (English, literature—fables and fairy tales): What does the wolf usually represent (stand for)? The lion? The lamb? (Art): What color stands for a glorious summer day? Evil? Goodness and purity? I would continue with math symbols, scientific symbols, and music symbols and lead the students toward contributing other examples such as symbols representing holidays. I would then tell them about their own examples of symbolism that I had recorded. The students' participation in and enthusiasm for the exercises would serve to determine whether they were ready for the material.

DR. NANCY SHEEHAN-MELZACK • Art and Music Teacher
Snug Harbor Community School, Quincy, MA

Even very young children can recognize symbols if the symbol is presented first and the explanation required second. A drawing of an octagon on a pole has always elicited the answer, "A stop sign," whenever I have shown it. Children recognize symbols, but the teacher needs to work from their concrete knowledge to the more abstract concept, and there are a great many symbols in their daily life on which one can draw. Children as young as 1st graders can recognize traffic sign shapes, letters of the alphabet, and numbers, and further recognize that they stand for directions, sounds, and how many. When they talk about these very common symbols, they can also realize they all use them for the same meaning.

VALERIE A. CHILCOAT • 5th/6th Grade Advanced Academics
Glenmount School, Baltimore, MD

Concrete examples of symbolism must come from the students' own world. Street signs, especially those with pictures and not words, are a great example. These concrete symbols, however, are not exactly the same as symbolism used in poetry. The link has to be made from the concrete to the abstract. Silly poetry is one way to do this. It is motivating to the students to read or listen to, and it can provide many examples of one thing acting as another. This strategy can also be used in lower grades to simply expose children to poetry containing symbolism.

KAREN BOYARSKY • 5th Grade Teacher
Walter C. Black Elementary School, Hightstown, NJ

You can tell a lot about students' thinking simply by interpreting their reactions. Knowing how to interpret students' reactions is just as important as any other assessment tool you might use. In this case, it is clear that the students are confused about the concept of symbolism. This is a difficult concept even for many 5th graders to understand and should be approached slowly. One approach to this topic would be to present students with pictures of familiar symbols, such as McDonald's Golden Arches, the Nike Swoosh, or the Target logo. Students could attempt to explain what each of these symbols mean. A discussion about why manufacturers choose to use symbols instead of words would follow. Another approach would be to have the students interpret comparisons that use *like* or *as*. For example, "Sue is as pretty as a flower." The teacher would guide the student to see that the author is using a flower to symbolize Sue's looks.

MyEducationLab™

Go to Topic 2, Cognitive and Linguistic Development, in the MyEducationLab (www.myeducationlab.com) for *Educational Psychology*, where you can:

- Find learning outcomes for Cognitive and Linguistic Development along with the national standards that connect to these outcomes.
- Complete Assignments and Activities that can help you more deeply understand the chapter content.
- Apply and practice your understanding of the core teaching skills identified in the chapter with the Building Teaching Skills and Dispositions learning units.
- Examine challenging situations and cases presented in the IRIS Center Resources.
- Access video clips of CCSSO National Teachers of the Year award winners responding to the question, "Why Do I Teach?" in the Teacher Talk section.
- Check your comprehension on the content covered in the chapter with the Study Plan. Here you will be able to take a chapter quiz, receive feedback on your answers, and then access Review, Practice, and Enrichment activities to enhance your understanding of chapter content.
- Find additional Teachers' Casebook scenarios and responses to them from practicing teachers.
- Use the Online Lesson Plan Builder to practice lesson planning and integrating national and state standards into your planning.

chapter three

THE SELF, SOCIAL, AND MORAL DEVELOPMENT

WHAT WOULD YOU DO?

▶ **TEACHERS' CASEBOOK:** Mean Girls

You have seen it before, but this year the situation in your middle-school classroom seems especially vicious. A clique of popular girls has made life miserable for several of their former friends—who are now "rejects." The discarded friends have committed the social sins of not fitting in—they wear the wrong clothes or aren't pretty enough or aren't interested in boys yet. To keep the status distinctions clear between themselves and "the others," the popular girls spread gossip about their former friends, often disclosing the intimate secrets revealed when the "out" girls and the "in" girls were *best* friends—only a few months ago. Today, you discover that Stephanie, one of the rejected girls, has written a long, heart-baring e-mail to her former best friend Alison, asking why Alison is "acting so mean." The now-popular Alison forwarded the e-mail to the entire school and Stephanie is humiliated. She has been absent for three days since the incident.

CRITICAL THINKING

- How would you respond to each of the girls?
- What—if anything—would you say to your other students?
- Are there ways you can address the issues raised by this situation in your classes?
- Reflecting on your years in school, were your experiences more like those of Alison or Stephanie?

OVERVIEW AND OBJECTIVES

Schooling involves more than cognitive development. As you think back on your years in school, what stands out—highlights of academic knowledge or memories of feelings, friendships, and fears? In this chapter, we examine the latter, which comprise personal, social, and moral development.

We begin by looking at a basic aspect of development that affects all the others—physical changes as students mature. Then we explore Urie Bronfenbrenner's bioecological theory and use it as a framework for examining the three major influences on children's personal and social development: families, peers, and teachers. Families today have gone through many transitions, and these changes affect the roles of teachers. Next, we explore ideas about how we come to understand ourselves by looking at self-concept and identity, including racial-ethnic identity. Erikson's theory of psychosocial development provides a lens for viewing these developments. Finally, we consider moral development. What factors determine our views about morality? What can teachers do to foster such personal qualities as honesty and cooperation? Why do students cheat in their academic work, and what can be done?

By the time you have completed this chapter, you should be able to:

Objective 3.1: Describe general trends and group differences in physical development through childhood and adolescence.

Objective 3.2: Discuss how the components of Bronfenbrenner's bioecological model influence development.

Objective 3.3: Discuss the relationship between parenting styles and children's development.

Objective 3.4: Describe general trends and group differences in the development of self-concept and identity.

Objective 3.5: Explain how positive peer relations (friendships) and negative peer relations (aggression) affect children's social development.

Objective 3.6: Explain current theories of moral development.

PHYSICAL DEVELOPMENT

This chapter is about personal and social development, but we begin with a kind of development that is a basic concern of all individuals and families—physical development.

STOP & THINK How tall are you? What grade were you in when you reached that height? Were you one of the tallest or shortest students in your middle or high school, or were you about average? Did you know students who were teased because of something about their physical appearance? How important was your physical development to your feelings about yourself? •

Physical and Motor Development

For most children, at least in the early years, growing up means getting bigger and stronger, and becoming more coordinated. It also can be a frightening, disappointing, exciting, and puzzling time.

YOUNG CHILDREN. Preschool children are very active. Their *gross-motor* (large muscle) skills improve greatly during these early years. Between ages 2 and about 4 or 5, preschoolers' muscles grow stronger, their brains develop to better integrate information about movements, their balance improves, and their center of gravity moves lower, so they are able to run, jump, climb, and hop. By age 2, most children stop "toddling." Their awkward, wide-legged gait becomes smooth and rhythmic—they have perfected walking. During their third year, most children learn to run, throw, and jump, but these activities are not well controlled until age 4 or 5. Most of these movements develop naturally if the child has normal physical abilities and the opportunity to play. Children with physical problems, however, may need special training to develop these skills. And because they can't always judge when to stop, many preschoolers need interludes of rest scheduled after periods of physical exertion (Darcey & Travers, 2006; Thomas & Thomas, 2008).

Fine-motor skills such as tying shoes or fastening buttons, which require the coordination of small movements, also improve greatly during the preschool years. Children should be given the chance to work with large paintbrushes, fat pencils and crayons, large pieces of drawing paper, large Legos, and soft clay or play-dough to accommodate their current skills. During this time, children will begin to develop a lifelong preference for their right or left hand. By age 5, about 90% of students prefer their right hand for most skilled work, and 10% or so prefer their left hand, with more boys than girls being left-handed (Feldman, 2004; Hill & Khanem, 2009). This is a genetically based preference, so don't try to make children switch.

ELEMENTARY SCHOOL YEARS. During the elementary-school years, physical development is fairly steady for most children. They become taller, leaner, and stronger, so they are better able to master sports and games. There is tremendous variation among children, however. A particular child can be much larger or smaller than average and still be perfectly healthy. Because children at this age are very aware of physical differences but are not the most tactful people, you may overhear comments such as "You're too little to be in fifth grade. What's wrong with you?" or "How come you're so fat?"

Throughout elementary school, many of the girls are likely to be as large as or larger than the boys in their classes. Between the ages of 11 and 14, girls are, on average, taller and heavier than boys of the same age. This size discrepancy can give girls an advantage in physical activities, but some girls may feel conflict over this and, as a result, downplay their physical abilities (Woolfolk & Perry, 2012).

THE ADOLESCENT YEARS. **Puberty** marks the beginning of sexual maturity. It is not a single event, but a series of changes involving almost every part of the body. The sex differences in physical development observed during the later elementary years become even more pronounced at the beginning of puberty. But these changes take time. The earliest visible signs of puberty in girls are the growth of nipples and budding of their breasts at around age 10 for European American and Canadian adolescents. At about the same time, boys' testes and scrotum begin to grow larger. On average, between ages 12 and 13, girls have their first menstrual period (called **menarche**) and boys have their first sperm ejaculation (called **spermarche**). Boys develop facial hair over the next several years, reaching their final beard potential by about age 18 or 19—with some exceptions who take longer to develop their final facial hair. Less welcome changes in puberty are increases in skin oiliness, skin acne, and body odor.

STUDENTS COME IN ALL SIZES The physical changes of adolescence have significant effects on the individual's identity. Psychologists have been particularly interested in the academic, social, and emotional differences they have found between adolescents who mature early and those who mature later.

Girls reach their final height by age 15 or 16, several years ahead of boys, so there is a time in middle school, as in late elementary school, when many girls are taller than their male classmates. Most boys continue growing until about age 19, but both boys and girls can continue to grow slightly until about age 25 (Thomas & Thomas, 2008; Wigfield, Byrnes, & Eccles, 2006). The ages for reaching maximum height are a bit younger for African American and Latino/a adolescents and a bit older for Asian Americans.

EARLY AND LATER MATURING. Psychologists have been particularly interested in the academic, social, and emotional differences they have found between adolescents who mature early and those who mature later. For girls, maturing way ahead of classmates can be a definite disadvantage. Being larger and more "developed" than everyone else your age is not a valued characteristic for girls in many cultures (Jones, 2004). Early maturation is associated with emotional difficulties such as depression, anxiety, and eating disorders, especially in societies that define thinness as attractive (Steinberg, 2005). Other problems for early maturing girls are lower achievement in school, drug and alcohol abuse, unplanned pregnancy, suicide, and greater risk of breast cancer in later life. Around the world, early menarche has been related to bulimia and alcohol use in Finland, suicide and alcohol use in Norway, and depression and anxiety in Australia (Mendle et al., 2007). In addition, researchers have found a correlation between age at menarche and adult **body mass index (BMI,** a measure of body fat); the younger the girl was when she had her first period, the greater her adult BMI, on average (Harris et al., 2008). Later-maturing girls seem to have fewer problems, but they may worry that something is wrong with them, so adult reassurance and support is important.

Early maturity in males is associated with popularity. The early maturer's taller, broad-shouldered body type fits the cultural stereotype for the male ideal; late-maturing boys may experience lower self-esteem because they are smaller and less muscular than the "ideal" for men. In fact, there is some evidence that the standards regarding physical appearance have increased (Harter, 2006). Even so, recent research points to more disadvantages than advantages for early maturation in boys (Westling, Andrews, Hampson, & Peterson, 2008). Early maturing boys tend to engage in more delinquent behavior—and this is true for White, African American, and Mexican American boys (Cota-Robles, Neiss, & Rowe, 2002). They also appear to be at greater risk for depression and for abusing alcohol and cigarettes (Westling et al., 2008).

Connect and Extend to PRAXIS II™

Human Development (I, A2)
Explain how development in one domain (e.g., physical, emotional) can affect development in other domains.

Puberty The physiological changes during adolescence that lead to the ability to reproduce.

Menarche The first menstrual period in girls.

Spermarche The first sperm ejaculation for boys.

Body mass index (BMI) A measure of body fat that evaluates weight in relation to height.

Dealing with Physical Differences in the Classroom

Address students' physical differences in ways that do not call unnecessary attention to the variations.
Examples

1. Try to seat smaller students so they can see and participate in class activities, but avoid seating arrangements that are obviously based on height.
2. Balance sports and games that rely on size and strength with games that reflect cognitive, artistic, social, or musical abilities, such as charades or drawing games.
3. Don't use, and don't allow students to use nicknames based on physical traits.
4. Make sure there is a good supply of left-handed scissors for preschool classes.

Help students obtain factual information on differences in physical development.
Examples

1. Set up science projects on sex differences in growth rates.
2. Have readings available that focus on differences between early and late maturers. Make sure that you present the positives and the negatives of each.

3. Find out the school policy on sex education and on informal guidance for students. Some schools, for example, encourage teachers to talk to girls who are upset about their first menstrual period, while other schools expect teachers to send the girls to talk to the school nurse (if your school still has one—budget cuts have eliminated many).
4. Give the students models in literature or in their community of accomplished and caring individuals who do not fit the culture's ideal physical stereotypes.

Accept that concerns about appearance and the opposite sex will occupy much time and energy for adolescents.
Examples

1. Allow some time at the end of class for socializing.
2. Deal with some of these issues in curriculum-related materials.

For more information about accommodations for physical differences in your classroom, see http://dos.claremontmckenna.edu/PhysicalLearningDiff.asp

Boys who mature late may have a more difficult time initially. However, some studies show that in adulthood, males who matured later tend to be more creative, tolerant, and perceptive. Perhaps the trials and anxieties of maturing late teach some boys to be better problem solvers (Brooks-Gunn, 1988; Steinberg, 2005). All adolescents can benefit from knowing that there is a very wide range for timing and rates in "normal" maturation and that there are advantages for both early and late maturers. The *Guidelines* give ideas for dealing with physical differences in the classroom.

Play, Recess, and Physical Activity

Maria Montessori once noted, "Play is children's work," and Piaget and Vygotsky would agree. More recently, the American Academy of Pediatrics stated, "Play is essential to development because it contributes to the cognitive, physical, social, and emotional well-being of children and youth" (Ginsburg, 2007, p. 182). The brain develops with stimulation, and play provides some of that stimulation at every age. In fact, some neuroscientists suggest that play might help in the important process of pruning brain synapses during childhood (Pellis, 2006). Other psychologists believe play allows children to experiment safely as they learn about their environment, try out new behaviors, solve problems, and adapt to new situations (Pellegrini, Dupuis, & Smith, 2007). Babies in the sensorimotor stage learn by exploring, sucking, pounding, shaking, throwing—acting on their environments. Preoperational preschoolers love make-believe play and use pretending to form symbols, explore language, and interact with others. They are beginning to play simple games with predictable rules. Elementary-school-age children also like fantasy, but are beginning to play more complex games and sports, and thus learn cooperation, fairness, negotiation, and winning and losing as well as developing more sophisticated language. As children grow into adolescents, play continues to be part of their physical and social development (Woolfolk & Perry, 2012).

PHYSICAL EXERCISE AND RECESS. There are good, academic reasons for encouraging children to exercise. Phillip Tomporowski and his colleagues (2008) reviewed the research on physical activity and cognitive development and concluded that "systematic exercise programs may actually enhance the development of specific types of mental processing known to be important for meeting challenges encountered both in academics and throughout the lifespan" (p. 127). Other researchers note that students in Asian countries, who consistently outperform U.S. students on international reading, science, and mathematics tests, have more frequent recess breaks throughout the school day. One study of 11,000 students who were 8 and 9 years old found that students who had daily recess of 15 minutes or longer every day were better behaved in class than students who had little or no recess. This was true even after controlling for student gender and ethnicity, public or private school setting, and class size (Barros, Silver, & Stein, 2009). These recess breaks may be especially important for students with attention-deficit hyperactive disorders (ADHD). In fact, if more breaks were provided, there might be fewer students, especially boys, diagnosed with ADHD (Pellegrini & Bohn, 2005).

Schools have a role in promoting physical activity. This can be especially important for students living in poverty and children with disabilities. Unfortunately, recess time is being cut to allow for more academic time focused on test preparation (Ginsburg, 2007; Pellegrini & Bohn, 2005). But the federal government has recognized the value of physical activity. In 2004, the United States Congress passed a law that requires educational agencies that receive federal aid, which covers most schools, to have a wellness policy. Different agencies, including the American Heart Association, recommend that as part of a wellness program, all children and youth should have a minimum of 30 minutes per day of moderate to vigorous physical activity (McKenzie & Kahan, 2008). One reason for concern about physical activity for children is the increase in childhood obesity, as you will see next.

Challenges in Physical Development

Physical development is public—everyone sees how tall, short, heavy, thin, muscular, or coordinated you are. As students move into adolescence, they feel "on stage," as if everyone is evaluating them; and physical development is part of what is being evaluated. So there are psychological consequences to physical development too (Thomas & Thomas, 2008).

OBESITY. If you have seen the news lately, you know that obesity is a growing problem in America, especially for children. In fact, since 1971, the incidence of childhood obesity has doubled in every age group from ages 2 to 19 (Centers for Disease Control, 2009). Obesity usually is defined as being more than 20% heavier than average compared to others of the same age, sex, and body build. Table 3.1 shows how the trend is increasing.

TABLE 3.1 • **The Increase in Childhood Obesity**

The data below are from the National Health and Nutrition Examination Survey (NHANES) completed by the National Center for Health Statistics.

PREVALENCE OF OVERWEIGHT AMONG U.S. CHILDREN AND ADOLESCENTS (AGED 2–19 YEARS)

	SURVEY PERIODS			
	1971–1974	1976–1980	1988–1994	2007–2008
Ages 2 through 5	5%	5%	7.2%	10.4%
Ages 6 through 11	4%	6.5%	11.3%	19.6%
Ages 12 through 19	6.1%	5%	10.5%	18.1%

Source: Centers for Disease Control and Prevention. http://www.cdc.gov/obesity/childhood/data.html

The consequences of obesity are serious for children and adolescents: diabetes, strain on bones and joints, respiratory problems, and a greater chance of heart problems as adults. Playing with friends or participating in sports can be affected negatively. In addition, children with obesity often are the targets of cruel teasing. Like everything else involving children's development, there probably are many interacting causes for this increase in obesity rates including poor diet, genetic factors, increased hours sitting in front of televisions and playing video games, and lack of exercise (Woolfolk & Perry, 2012). There is another challenge in physical development for many children that involves not too much weight, but too little.

EATING DISORDERS. Adolescents going through the changes of puberty are very concerned about their bodies. This has always been true, but today, the emphasis on fitness and appearance makes adolescents even more likely to worry about how their bodies "measure up." Both boys and girls can become dissatisfied with their bodies during adolescence because they don't match the cultural ideals in magazines and films. For girls, it also appears that conversations with friends about appearance can make dissatisfactions worse (Jones, 2004). For some, the concern becomes excessive. One consequence is eating disorders such as **bulimia** (binge eating) and **anorexia nervosa** (self-starvation), both of which are more common in females than in males. Bulimics often binge, eating an entire gallon of ice cream or a whole cake. Then, to avoid gaining weight, they force themselves to vomit or they use strong laxatives to purge themselves of the extra calories. Bulimics tend to maintain a normal weight, but the purging can permanently damage their digestive systems.

DON'T TURN AWAY FROM ME Students with anorexia usually require professional help—don't ignore the warning signs. A teacher may be the person who begins the chain of help for students with these tragic problems.

Anorexia is an even more dangerous disorder, for anorexics either refuse to eat or eat practically nothing while often exercising obsessively. In the process, they may lose 20% to 25% of their body weight, and some (about 20%) literally starve themselves to death. Anorexic students become very thin, and may appear pale, have brittle fingernails, and develop fine dark hairs all over their bodies. They are easily chilled because they have so little fat to insulate their bodies. They often are depressed, insecure, moody, and lonely. Girls may stop having their menstrual period. These eating disorders often begin in adolescence and are becoming more common— about 1% of adolescents (mostly, but not all girls) become anorexic (Rice & Dolgin, 2002). These students usually require professional help. Don't ignore the warning signs—less than one-third of people with eating disorders actually receive treatment (Stice & Shaw, 2004). A teacher may be the person who begins the chain of help for students with these tragic problems. The *Guidelines* give a few ideas for supporting positive body images in adolescents.

People certainly are more than physical bodies. The rest of this chapter is about personal and moral development, beginning with a theoretical frame to put that development in context.

Bulimia Eating disorder characterized by overeating, then getting rid of the food by self-induced vomiting or laxatives.

Anorexia nervosa Eating disorder characterized by very limited food intake.

GUIDELINES

Supporting Positive Body Images

Listen to adolescents talk about their health.
Examples

1. If they mention wanting to lose weight, seize the opportunity to talk about healthy weight, body image, and cultural influences on youth.
2. It they mention diets they or their friends are trying, provide them with nutritionally sound information about myths, misinformation, and dangers related to fad diets.
3. In general, be attentive. An adolescent may make a brief comment that could serve as a terrific entrance into a valuable conversation about body image.

Ask questions.
Examples

1. Are you concerned about your weight (or shape or size) at all? Do you think your friends are concerned about their weight? Do you or your friends talk a lot about your weight?
2. Do you know that diets are the worst way to lose or maintain weight? Have you ever dieted? Why?

3. Do you know that eating only low-fat or fat-free foods is NOT healthy eating? Do you know that you need fat in your diet, and that without it you can have all kinds of health problems?

Make available resources for adolescents who have body image issues.
Examples

1. Have accurate, youth-oriented resources available to read, look up on the Internet, or find in a library.
2. Encourage youth to continue conversations about these issues with you, their parents, a health professional, a trusted teacher, or a caring, knowledgeable adult.
3. Deal with some of these issues in curriculum-related materials.

For more information about adolescents and body image, see http://www.epi.umn.edu/let/pubs/img/adol_ch13.pdf

Source: Adapted from Story, M., & Stang, J. (2005). Nutrition needs of adolescents. In J. S. M. Story (Ed.), Guidelines for adolescent nutritional services. Minneapolis, MN: University of Minnesota, pp. 158–159.

BRONFENBRENNER: THE SOCIAL CONTEXT FOR DEVELOPMENT

We put the developing person in context by exploring the work of Urie Bronfenbrenner (1917–2005), who was born in Moscow, Russia, but moved with his family to the United States when he was 6. Bronfenbrenner completed a double major in psychology and music at Cornell in 1938 and a Ph.D. in psychology from the University of Michigan, in 1942. Over his long career in psychology he worked as a clinical psychologist in the U.S. Army and as a professor at the University of Michigan and at Cornell. He also helped to found the Head Start early childhood program.

The Importance of Context and the Bioecological Model

Educational and developmental psychologists are increasingly interested in the role of context. **Context** is the total situation that surrounds and interacts with an individual's thoughts, feelings, and actions to shape development and learning. There are contextual effects both internal and external to the developing individual. For example, hormone levels within the body are contexts for developing organs, including the brain, as well as for adolescents' self-concepts during puberty. In this book, however, we focus on the contexts outside the person. Children grow up in families and are members of particular ethnic, language, religious, and economic communities. They live in neighborhoods, attend schools, and are members of classes, teams, or glee clubs. The social and educational programs, along with the policies of governments affect their lives. These contexts influence the development of behaviors, beliefs, and knowledge by providing resources, supports, incentives and punishments, expectations, teachers, models, tools— all the building blocks of learning and development (Dodge, 2011; Lerner, Theokas, & Bobek, 2005).

Context Internal and external circumstances and situations that interact with the individual's thoughts, feelings, and actions to shape development and learning.

Contexts also affect how actions are interpreted. For example, if a stranger approaches a 7-month-old infant, the baby is likely to cry if the setting is unfamiliar, but she may not cry if the stranger is in her home. Adults are more likely to help a stranger in need in small towns as opposed to larger cities (Kagan & Herschkowitz, 2005). Think about a hearing a telephone ring. Is it 3:00 in the afternoon or 3:00 in the morning? Did you just call someone and leave a message asking for a return call? Has the phone been ringing off the hook, or is this the first call in days? Did you just sit down to dinner? The meaning of the ring and the feelings you have will vary, depending on the context.

Urie Bronfenbrenner's **bioecological model** of development (Bronfenbrenner, 1989; Bronfenbrenner & Morris, 2006) recognizes that the physical and social contexts in which we develop are ecosystems because they are constantly interacting with and influencing each other. Look at Figure 3.1. Every person lives within a microsystem, inside a mesosystem, embedded in an exosystem, all of which are a part of the macrosystem—like a set of Russian painted dolls, nested one inside the other. In addition, all development occurs in and is influenced by the time period—the chronosystem.

In the microsystem are the person's immediate relationships and activities. For a child, the microsystem might be the immediate family, friends, or teachers and the activities of play and school. Relationships in the microsystem are reciprocal—they flow in both directions. The child affects the parent and the parent influences the child, for example. The mesosystem is the set of interactions and relationships among all the elements of the microsystem—the family members interacting with each other or with the teacher. Again, all relationships are reciprocal—the teacher influences the parents and the parents affect the teacher, and

Bioecological model Bronfenbrenner's theory describing the nested social and cultural contexts that shape development. Every person develops within a *microsystem*, inside a *mesosystem*, embedded in an *exosystem*, all of which are a part of the *macrosystem* of the culture. All development occurs in and is influenced by the time period—the *chronosystem*.

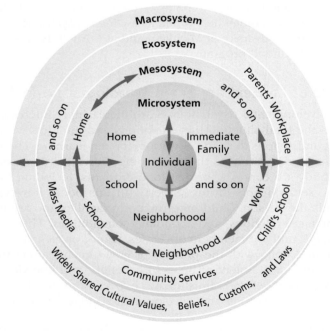

FIGURE 3.1

URIE BRONFENBRENNER'S BIOECOLOGICAL MODEL OF HUMAN DEVELOPMENT

Every person develops within a *microsystem* (family, friends, school activities, teacher, etc.) inside a *mesosystem* (the interactions among all the microsystem elements), embedded in an *exosystem* (social settings that affect the child, even though the child is not a direct member—community resources, parents' work place, etc.); all are part of the *macrosystem* (the larger society with its laws, customs, values, etc.). All development occurs in and is influenced by the time period—the *chronosystem*.

these interactions affect the child. The exosystem includes all the social settings that affect the child, even though the child is not a direct member of these systems. Examples are the teachers' relations with administrators and the school board; the parents' jobs; the community resources for health, employment, or recreation; or the family's religious affiliation. The macrosystem is the larger society—its values, laws, conventions, and traditions.

Families

The first context for child development is the mother's womb. Scientists are learning more about the effects of this first environment—the role of the expectant mother's level of stress, nutrition, smoking, alcohol and drug intake, exercise, and general health in her infant's development. Clearly, the influence of the family begins before birth, but many new influences follow (Woolfolk & Perry, 2012).

FAMILY STRUCTURE.   In the United States, the proportion of children growing up in a home with just one parent has doubled since the 1970s. About 10% of children have parents who never married, and most of these children (89%) live with their mothers. In fact, projections are that only about half of all children will grow up with two parents who

FAMILIES CAN BE MANY TYPES Only about 25% of all U.S. households are made up of a married husband and wife living with their biological children. Families also can include grandparents, adopted children, foster children, stepchildren, two moms or two dads, blended families, single parents, and many other possibilities.

stay married (Amato, 2006; Schoen & Canulas-Romo, 2006). Increasingly, children today may be part of **blended families**, with stepbrothers or stepsisters who move in and out of their lives. Some children live with an aunt, with grandparents, with one parent, in foster or adoptive homes, or with an older brother or sister. In some cultures such as Asian, Latin American, or African, children are more likely to grow up in **extended families**, with grandparents, aunts, uncles, and cousins living in the same household or at least in daily contact with each other. In addition, there are several million gay and lesbian parents in the United States (estimates are hard to determine because some parents conceal details about their sexual orientation to protect their children from bias and prejudice). Thus the best advice is to avoid the phrases "your parents" and "your mother and father" and instead to speak of "your family" when talking to students.

No matter who is doing the parenting, research has identified characteristic differences in parents' styles.

PARENTING STYLES. One well-known description of **parenting styles** is based on the research of Diane Baumrind (1991, 1996). Her early work focused on a careful longitudinal study of 100 (mostly European American, middle-class) preschool children. Through observation of children and parents and interviews with parents, Baumrind and the other researchers who built on her findings identified four parenting styles based on the parents' high or low levels of warmth and control:

- *Authoritative parents* (high warmth, high control) set clear limits, enforce rules, and expect mature behavior. But they are warm with their children. They listen to concerns, give reasons for rules, and allow more democratic decision making. There is less strict punishment and more guidance. Parents help children think through the consequences of their actions (Hoffman, 2001).
- *Authoritarian parents* (low warmth, high control) seem cold and controlling in their interactions with their children. The children are expected to be mature and to do what the parent says, "Because I said so!" There is not much talk about emotions. Punishments are strict, but not abusive. The parents love their children, but they are not openly affectionate.
- *Permissive parents* (high warmth, low control) are warm and nurturing, but they have few rules or consequences for their children and expect little in the way of mature behavior because "They're just kids."
- *Rejecting/Neglecting/Uninvolved parents* (low warmth, low control) don't seem to care at all and can't be bothered with controlling, communicating, or teaching their children.

Authoritarian, authoritative, and permissive parents love their children and are trying to do their best—they simply have different ideas about the best ways to parent. In broad strokes, there are differences in children's feelings and behavior associated with these three parenting styles. At least in European American, middle-class families, children of *authoritative* parents are more likely to do well in school, be happy with themselves, and relate well to others. Children of *authoritarian* parents are more likely to feel guilty or depressed, and children of *permissive* parents may have trouble interacting with peers—they are used to having their way (Berger, 2006; Spera, 2005).

Of course, the extreme of permissiveness becomes indulgence. Indulgent parents cater to their children's every whim—perhaps it is easier than being the adult who must make unpopular decisions. Both indulgent and rejecting/neglecting/uninvolved parenting styles can be harmful. For example, when 3,407 9th- through 12th-grade European American students described their parents' styles and their peer-group orientation, students, especially girls, who characterized their parents as uninvolved were more likely to be oriented toward "partyers" and "druggies" who did not endorse adult values (Durbin, Darling, Steinberg, & Brown, 1993).

CULTURE AND PARENTING. Much of the work on parenting styles has focused on European American middle-class families. But cultures differ in parenting styles. Research indicates that higher control, more authoritarian parenting is linked to better grades

Blended families Parents, children, and stepchildren merged into families through remarriages.

Extended families Different family members—grandparents, aunts, uncles, cousins, etc.—living in the same household or at least in daily contact with the children in the family.

Parenting styles The ways of interacting with and disciplining children.

Connect and Extend to PRAXIS II™

Families (I, B6)
Understand the influence of families, their culture, and values on student learning.

for Asian and African American students (Glasgow, Dornbusch, Troyer, Steinberg, & Ritter, 1997). Parenting that is strict and directive, with clear rules and consequences, combined with high levels of warmth and emotional support, is associated with higher academic achievement and greater emotional maturity for inner-city children (Garner & Spears, 2000; Jarrett, 1995). Differences in cultural values and in the danger level of some urban neighborhoods may make tighter parental control appropriate, and even necessary (Smetana, 2000). In addition, in cultures that have a greater respect for elders and a more group-centered rather than individualist philosophy, it may be a misreading of the parents' actions to perceive their demand for obedience as "authoritarian" (Lamb & Lewis, 2005; Nucci, 2001). In fact, research by Ruth Chao (2001; Chao & Tseng, 2002) has challenged Baumrind's conclusions for Asian families. Chao finds that an alternative parenting style of *chiao shun* (a Chinese term that Chao translates as "training") better characterizes parenting in Asian and Asian American families.

Research with Latino parents also questions whether studies of parenting styles based on European American families are helpful in understanding Latino families. Using a carefully designed observation system, Melanie Domenech Rodríguez and her colleagues included a third dimension of parenting—giving children more or less autonomy (freedom to make decisions). They found that almost all of the Latino parents they studied could be characterized as *protective* (high on warmth, high on control/demand, and low on granting autonomy) or *authoritative* (high on all three—warmth, control/demand, and granting autonomy). Also, these Latino parents tended to be more demanding and less likely to grant autonomy to their female children (Domenech Rodríguez, Donovick, & Crowley, 2009).

Whatever the structure of the families you work with, here are some *Family and Community Partnership Guidelines* for making connections.

STUDYING CULTURAL DIFFERENCES IN PARENTING The results of Ruth Chao's studies of Asian American parenting styles have challenged models of parenting based on European American parents and children. She is also studying whether serving as a translator or "language broker" for parents who do not speak English has an impact on the child's psychological well-being and relationship with the parents.

GUIDELINES — FAMILY AND COMMUNITY PARTNERSHIPS

Connecting with Families

1. Work with families to co-create methods for family involvement. Offer a range of possible participation methods. Make sure the plans are realistic and fit the lives of the families you are dealing with.

2. Remember that some students' families have had negative experiences with schools or may fear or mistrust schools and teachers. Find other places to collaborate: before or after ball games, or at a local church or recreation center. Go where families go; don't always expect them to come to school.

3. Maintain regular home–school contact through telephone calls or notes. If a family has no telephone, identify a contact person (relative or friend) who can take messages. If literacy is a problem, use pictures, symbols, and codes for written communication.

4. Make all communications positive, emphasizing growth, progress, and accomplishments.

5. With the families, design family–student celebrations of the student's efforts and successes (a movie, special meal, trip to the park or library, going out for ice cream or pizza).

6. On a regular basis, send home a note in word or picture form that describes the student's progress. Ask families to indicate how they celebrated the success and to return the note.

7. Follow up with a telephone call to discuss progress, answer questions, solicit family suggestions, and express appreciation for the families' contributions.

8. Make sure families feel welcome if they visit the classroom.

For more information on family school partnerships, see http://www.gse.harvard.edu/hfrp/projects/family.html

Source: From "Effects of Parent Involvement in Isolation or in Combination with Peer Tutoring on Student Self-Concept and Mathematics Achievement," by J. Fantuzzo, G. Davis, and M. Ginsburg, Journal of Educational Psychology, 87, pp. 272–281. Copyright © 1995 by the American Psychological Association. Adapted with permission of the APA.

ATTACHMENT. The emotional bond that forms between people is called **attachment**. The first attachment is between the child and parents or other caregivers. The quality of this bond appears to have implications for forming relationships throughout life (Thompson & Raikes, 2003). Children who form what are called secure attachments with caregivers receive comfort when needed and are more confident to explore their world, perhaps because they know they can count on the caregiver. Children who form insecure or disorganized attachments can be fearful, sad, anxious, clinging, rejecting, or angry in interactions with the caregivers. Some research indicates that authoritarian parenting styles are related to forming insecure attachments, but as we saw above, many factors influence the effects of parenting styles (Roeser, Peck, & Nasir, 2006).

The quality of attachment has implications for teachers. For example, in preschools, children who have formed secure attachments with parents/caregivers are less dependent on teachers and interact with other children appropriately. Secure attachment is positively related to achievement test scores, teacher assessments of social competence throughout the school years, and even to lower dropout rates (Roeser, Peck, & Nasir, 2006). As we will see later, researchers are currently examining students' attachment to teachers and schools as a positive force in their lives.

DIVORCE. The divorce rate in the United States is one of the highest in the world. Some analysts estimate that between 40% and 50% of first-time marriages that took place in the 1990s will end in divorce—and the divorce rate is even higher for second and third marriages (Amato, 2001; Schoen & Canulas-Romo, 2006). And as too many of us know from experiences in our own families, separation and divorce are stressful events for all participants, even under the best circumstances. The actual separation of the parents may have been preceded by years of conflict in the home or may come as a shock to all, including friends and children. During the divorce itself, conflict may increase as property and custody rights are being negotiated. After the divorce, more changes may disrupt the child's life as the custodial parent moves to a new neighborhood or works longer hours. For the child, this can mean leaving behind important friendships in the old neighborhood or school, just when support is needed the most. Even in those rare cases where there are few conflicts, ample resources, and the continuing support of friends and extended family, divorce is never easy for anyone. However it can be a better alternative for children than growing up in a home filled with conflict and discord. "Destructive conflict in any type of family undermines the well-being of parents and children" (Hetherington, 2006, p. 232).

The first two years after the divorce seem to be the most difficult period for both boys and girls and especially hard for young adolescents (ages 10–14). Recent research also indicates that divorce is harder on boys than girls, maybe because mothers still tend to get custody of children, which leaves boys without a male role model in the house (Fuller-Thomson & Dalton, 2011). Children may have problems in school or just skip school, lose or gain an unusual amount of weight, have trouble sleeping, or experience other difficulties. However, adjustment to divorce is an individual matter; some children respond with increased responsibility, maturity, and coping skills (Amato, 2006; Amato, Loomis, & Booth, 1995; APA, 2004). Over time, about 75% to 80% of children in divorced families adapt and become reasonably well adjusted (Hetherington & Kelly, 2003). See the *Guidelines* for ideas about how to help students dealing with divorce.

Peers

Children also develop within peer groups. Rubin and his colleagues (2005) distinguish between two kinds of peer groups: cliques and crowds. *Cliques* are relatively small, friendship-based groups (typically between 3 and a dozen members). Cliques are more evident in middle childhood. *Crowds* are less intimate, more loosely organized groups in which members may or may not interact with one another.

Attachment Forming an emotional bond with another person, initially a parent or family member.

- -

STOP & THINK Think back to high school—did you have friends in any of these groups: normals, populars, brains, jocks, partyers, druggies, others? What were the main "crowds" at your school? How did your friends influence you? •

- -

GUIDELINES

Helping Children of Divorce

Take note of any sudden changes in behavior that might indicate problems at home.
Examples

1. Be alert to physical symptoms such as repeated headaches or stomach pains, rapid weight gain or loss, fatigue or excess energy.
2. Be aware of signs of emotional distress such as moodiness, temper tantrums, difficulty in paying attention or concentrating.
3. Let parents know about the students' signs of stress.

Talk individually to students about their attitude or behavior changes. This gives you a chance to find out about unusual stress such as divorce.
Examples

1. Be a good listener. Students may have no other adult willing to hear their concerns.
2. Let students know you are available to talk, and let the student set the agenda.

Watch your language to make sure you avoid stereotypes about "happy" (two-parent) homes.
Examples

1. Simply say "your families" instead of "your mothers and fathers" when addressing the class.
2. Avoid statements such as "We need volunteers for room mother" or "Your father can help you."

Help students maintain self-esteem.
Examples

1. Recognize a job well done.
2. Make sure the student understands the assignment and can handle the workload. This is not the time to pile on new and very difficult work.

3. The student may be angry with his or her parents, but may direct the anger at teachers. Don't take the student's anger personally.

Find out what resources are available at your school.
Examples

1. Talk to the school psychologist, guidance counselor, social worker, or principal about students who seem to need outside help.
2. Consider establishing a discussion group, led by a trained adult, for students whose parents are going through a divorce.

Be sensitive to both parents' rights to information.
Examples

1. When parents have joint custody, both are entitled to receive information and attend parent–teacher conferences.
2. The noncustodial parent may still be concerned about the child's school progress. Check with your principal about state laws regarding the noncustodial parent's rights.

Be aware of long-term problems for students moving between two households.
Examples

1. Books, assignments, and gym clothes may be left at one parent's house when the student is currently on visitation with the other parent.
2. Parents may not show up for their turn to pick up their child at school or may miss a parent–teacher conference because the note never got home.

For ideas about helping children understand divorce, see
http://muextension.missouri.edu/xplor/hesguide/humanrel/gh6600.htm

---

CROWDS.   Adolescents are more likely to affiliate with larger crowds that provide them with an identity (e.g., Terrice is a jock, Lou's a brain, Olivia is a druggie). Laurence Steinberg and his colleagues have identified peer groups or crowds such as "jocks," "brains," "populars," and "druggies" that share common behaviors and attitudes (Durbin, Darling, Steinberg, & Brown, 1993; Steinberg, 1996, 1998). Based on a three-year study that surveyed 20,000 students in nine high schools in Wisconsin and California, Steinberg found that peers provide incentives for certain activities and ridicule others, which creates a school culture that affects the way the teachers behave. One in every five students Steinberg studied said that their friends made fun of people who tried to do well in school. Steinberg concluded that about 40% of the students were just going through the motions of learning. About 90% had copied someone else's homework and 66% had cheated on a test within the last year. Steinberg claims that this lack of investment is due in part to peer pressure because for many adolescents, "peers—not parents—are the chief determinants of how intensely they are invested in school and how much effort they devote to their education" (1998, p. 331). Let's look more closely at these powerful peer influences.

DRESS CODES AND MORE Peer cultures may set "rules" for how to dress and behave and in so doing determine which activities, music, or other students are in or out of favor.

PEER CULTURES. Different crowds or groups of students who have a set of "rules"—how to dress, talk, style their hair, and interact with others—are called **peer cultures**. The group determines which activities, music, or other students are in or out of favor. For example, when Jessica, a popular high school student, was asked to explain the rules that her group lives by, she had no trouble:

OK. No. 1: clothes. You cannot wear jeans any day but Friday, and you cannot wear a ponytail or sneakers more than once a week. Monday is fancy day—like black pants or maybe you bust out with a skirt. You have to remind people how cute you are in case they forgot over the weekend. No. 2: parties. Of course we sit down and discuss which ones we're going to because there is no point in getting all dressed up for a party that's going to be lame. (Talbot, 2002, p. 28)

These peer cultures encourage conformity to the group rules. When another girl in Jessica's group wore jeans on Monday, Jessica confronted her: "Why are you wearing jeans today? Did you forget it was Monday?" (Talbot, 2002, p. 28). Jessica explained that the group had to suspend this "rebel" several times, not allowing her to sit with them at lunch.

To understand the power of peers, we have to look at situations where the values and interests of parents clash with those of peers, and then see whose influence dominates. In these comparisons, peers usually win in matters of style and socializing. Parents and teachers still are influential in matters of morality, career choice, and religion (Harris, 1998). Also, not all aspects of peer cultures are bad or cruel. The norms in some groups are positive and support achievement in school.

CLIQUES AND FRIENDSHIPS. Friendships are central to students' lives. When there has been a falling-out or an argument, when rumors are started and pacts are made to ostracize someone (as with Alison and Stephanie at the beginning of the chapter), the results can be devastating. Beyond the immediate trauma of being "in" or "out" of the clique, peer relationships influence students' motivation and achievement in school (A. Ryan, 2001). In one study, 6th grade students without friends showed lower levels of academic achievement and fewer positive social behaviors and were more emotionally distressed, even two years later, than students with at least one friend (Wentzel, Barry, & Caldwell, 2004). The characteristics of friends and the quality of the friendships matter, too. Having stable, supportive relationships with friends who are socially competent and mature enhances social development, especially during difficult times such as parents' divorce or transition to new schools (Hartup & Stevens, 1999). Children who are rejected by their peers are less likely to participate in classroom learning activities, so their achievement suffers; they are more likely to drop out of school as adolescents and may even evidence more problems as adults. For example, rejected aggressive students are more likely to commit crimes as they grow older (Buhs, Ladd, & Herald, 2006; Coie & Dodge, 1998; Fredricks, Blumenthal, & Paris, 2004).

POPULARITY. What does it mean to be popular? We could answer this question by observing students or by using ratings from parents or teachers. But the most common way to assess popularity is to ask the students themselves two questions: Is this child liked? and What is this child like? Based on answers to these questions, we can identify four categories of children (see Table 3.2).

As you can see in Table 3.2, *popular* (highly rated) children may behave in positive or negative ways. *Rejected* children probably merit their low ratings because they are aggressive, immature, socially unskilled, or withdrawn. *Controversial* children get mixed reviews; they display both positive and negative social behaviors. Finally, *neglected* children are almost invisible—their peers simply do not mention them—but there is no consistent evidence that neglected children are anxious or withdrawn (Rubin et al., 2005).

Peer cultures Groups of children or adolescents with their own rules and norms, particularly about such things as dress, appearance, music, language, social values, and behavior.

TABLE 3.2 • **What Does It Take to Be Popular?**

POPULAR CHILDREN
Popular prosocial children: These children are both academically and socially competent. They do well in school and communicate well with peers. When they disagree with other children, they respond appropriately and have effective strategies for working things out. *Popular antisocial children:* This subgroup of children often includes boys who are aggressive. They may be athletic, and other children tend to think they are "cool" in the ways they bully other children and defy adult authority.
REJECTED CHILDREN
Rejected aggressive children: High rates of conflict and hyperactivity/impulsivity characterize the behaviors of this subgroup. These children have poor perspective-taking skills and self-control. They often misunderstand the intentions of others, assign blame, and act aggressively on their angry or hurt feelings. *Rejected withdrawn children:* These children are timid and withdrawn, often the targets of bullies. They are often socially awkward and withdraw from social interactions to avoid being scorned or attacked.
CONTROVERSIAL CHILDREN
As the descriptor implies, these children have both positive and negative social qualities and, as a result, their social status can change over time. They can be hostile and disruptive in some situations and then engage in positive prosocial behaviors in others. These children have friends and are generally happy with their peer relationships.
NEGLECTED CHILDREN
Perhaps surprisingly, most of these children are well adjusted and they are not less socially competent than other children. Peers tend to view them as shy, but they don't report being lonely or unhappy about their social lives. Apparently they don't experience the extreme social anxiety and wariness that withdrawn children do.

Source: Woolfolk, A., & Perry, N. E. (2012). Child and adolescent development. Columbus, OH: Pearson, P. 416.

WHO IS LIKELY TO HAVE PROBLEMS WITH PEERS? Children and adolescents are not always tolerant of differences. New students who are physically, intellectually, ethnically, racially, economically, or linguistically different may be rejected in classes with established cliques or crowds. Students who are aggressive, withdrawn, and inattentive-hyperactive are more likely to be rejected. But classroom context matters too, especially for aggressive or withdrawn students. In classrooms where the general level of aggression is high, being aggressive is less likely to lead to peer rejection. And in classrooms where solitary play and work are more common, being withdrawn is not as likely to lead to rejection. Thus, part of being rejected is just being too different from the norm. Also, being more attractive or engaging in prosocial behaviors such as sharing, cooperating, and friendly interactions are associated with peer acceptance, no matter what the classroom context. Many aggressive and withdrawn students lack these social skills; inattentive-hyperactive students often misread social cues or have trouble controlling impulses, so their social skills suffer, too (Coplan, Prakash, O'Neil, & Armer, 2004; Stormshak, Bierman, Bruschi, Dodge, & Coie, 1999). A teacher should be aware of how each student gets along with the group. Are there outcasts? Careful adult intervention can often correct such problems, especially at the late elementary and middle-school levels, as we will see next (Pearl, Leung, Acker, Farmer, & Rodkin, 2007).

Reaching Every Student: Teacher Support

Because they are the main adults in students' lives for many hours each week, teachers have opportunities to play a significant role in students' personal and social development. For students facing emotional or interpersonal problems, teachers are sometimes the best source of help. When students have chaotic and unpredictable home lives, they need a caring, predictable structure in school. They need teachers who set clear limits, are consistent, enforce rules firmly but not punitively, respect students, and show genuine concern. Being liked by teachers can offset the negative effects of peer rejection in middle school. And students who have few friends, but are not rejected—simply ignored by other students—can remain well adjusted academically and socially when they are liked and supported by teachers.

As a teacher, you can be available to your students if they want to talk about their personal problems without requiring them to do so. One of my student teachers gave a boy in her class a journal entitled "Very Hard Thoughts" so that he could write about his parents' divorce. Sometimes he talked to her about the journal entries, but at other times, he just recorded his feelings. The student teacher was very careful to respect the boy's privacy about his writings.

ACADEMIC AND PERSONAL CARING.   When researchers ask students to describe a "good teacher," three qualities are consistently at the center of their descriptions. Good teachers have positive interpersonal relationships—they care about their students. Second, good teachers keep the classroom organized and maintain authority without being rigid or "mean." Finally, good teachers are good motivators—they can make learning fun by being creative and innovative so students learn something. It appears that authoritative teaching strategies, like authoritative approaches to parenting, lead to positive relationships with students and enhance motivation for learning (Noguera, 2005; Woolfolk Hoy & Weinstein, 2006). We will look at motivation in Chapter 12 and at management in Chapter 13, so for now let's focus on caring and teaching.

For nearly two decades, research has documented the value and importance of positive relationships with teachers for students at every grade level (Davis, 2003). Teachers' behaviors that communicate liking and respect, such as eye contact, relaxed body posture, and smiling, are associated with students' liking of teachers, interest in courses, and motivation to achieve (Woolfolk & Perry, 2012). For example, one of my doctoral graduates studied middle-school mathematics classes and found that students' perceptions of their teachers' affective support and caring were related to the effort they invested in learning math (Sakiz, Pape, & Woolfolk Hoy, 2008). Tamera Murdock and Angela Miller (2003) found that 8th grade students' perceptions that their teachers cared about them were significantly related to the students' academic motivation, even after taking into account the motivational influences of parents and peers.

Students define caring in two ways. One is *academic caring*—setting high, but reasonable expectations and helping students reach those goals. The second is *personal caring*—being patient, respectful, humorous, willing to listen, interested in students' issues and personal problems. For higher-achieving students, academic caring is especially important, but for students who are placed at risk and often alienated from school, personal caring is critical (Cothran & Ennis, 2000; Woolfolk Hoy & Weinstein, 2006). In fact, in one study in a Texas high school, the Mexican and Mexican American students saw teacher caring as a prerequisite for their own caring about school; in other words, they needed to be *cared for* before they could *care about* school (Valenzuela, 1999). Unfortunately, in the same school, the mostly non-Latino teachers expected the students to care about school before they would invest their caring in the students. And for many teachers, caring about school meant behaving in more "middle-class" ways.

These contrasting student and teacher views can lead to a downward spiral of mistrust. Students withhold their cooperation until teachers "earn it" with their authentic caring. Teachers withhold caring until students "earn it" with respect for authority and cooperation. Marginalized students expect unfair treatment and behave defensively when they sense any unfairness. Teachers get tough and punish. Students feel correct about their mistrusting and become more guarded and defiant. Teachers feel correct in mistrusting and become more controlling and punitive, and on it goes (Woolfolk Hoy & Weinstein, 2006).

Of course, students need both academic and personal caring. Katz (1999) interviewed eight Latino immigrant students in a middle school and concluded:

> High expectations without caring can result in setting goals that are impossible for the student to reach without adult support and assistance. On the other hand, caring without high expectations can turn dangerously into paternalism in which teachers feel sorry for "underprivileged" youth but never challenge them academically. High expectations and caring in tandem, however, can make a powerful difference in students' lives. (p. 814)

In short, caring means not giving up on students in addition to demonstrating and teaching kindness in the classroom (Davis, 2003).

Teachers and Child Abuse

Certainly, one critical way to care about students is to protect their welfare and intervene in cases of abuse. Although accurate information about the number of abused children in the United States is difficult to find because many cases go unreported, every year about 3,000,000 cases of abuse and neglect are reported and 900,000 are confirmed. That means a child is abused or neglected every 35 seconds (Children's Defense Fund, 2010; U.S. Department of Health and Human Services, 2007). Of course, parents are not the only people who abuse children. Siblings, other relatives, and even teachers have been responsible for the physical and sexual abuse of children.

As part of your responsibilities as a teacher, you must alert your principal, school psychologist, or school social worker if you suspect abuse. In all 50 states, the District of Columbia, and the U.S. territories, the law requires certain professionals, often including teachers, to report suspected cases of child abuse. The legal definition of *abuse* has been broadened in many states to include neglect and failure to provide proper care and supervision. Be sure that you understand the laws in your state or province on this important issue, as well as your own moral responsibility. At least four children die of abuse or neglect each day in the United States, in many cases because no one would "get involved" (Children's Defense Fund, 2011). Even children who survive abuse pay a great price. In school alone, physically abused children are more likely to be aggressive in the classroom and are retained in grades and referred for special education services more often than children who were not abused (Roeser, Peck, & Nasir, 2006). What should you look for as indicators of abuse? Table 3.3 on the next page lists possible indicators.

Society and Media

All of the students you will teach grew up in a world of media, mobility, and machines. An astounding percentage, over 70% in 2010, had a television in their own bedroom. Many had computers and cell phones, even from early ages (Rideout, Foehr, & Roberts, 2010; Turkle, 2011). Each year their use of technology increases (Nielsen, 2010). In 2010, 75% of children ages 12 to 17 had cell phones. Figure 3.2 shows the different technologies that 12- and 17-year-olds use daily to keep in touch with friends.

A recent Nielsen Report documented that teens are sending or receiving an average of 3,339 text messages per month—over 100 per day (Nielsen, 2010). When do they have time

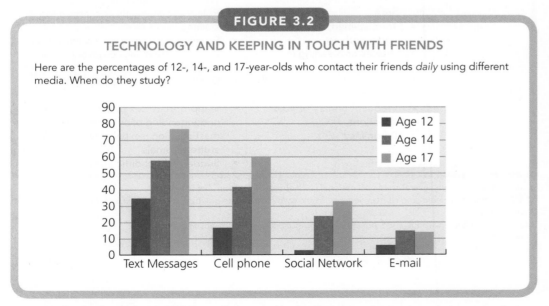

FIGURE 3.2

TECHNOLOGY AND KEEPING IN TOUCH WITH FRIENDS

Here are the percentages of 12-, 14-, and 17-year-olds who contact their friends *daily* using different media. When do they study?

Source: Based on data from Lenhart, A. (2010). Teens, cell phones and /texting: Text messages become the centerpiece communication. Washington, D.C.: Pew Research Center.

TABLE 3.3 • **Indicators of Child Abuse**

The following are some of the signs of abuse. Not every child with these signs is abused, but these indicators should be investigated. To learn about who must report child abuse, see http://www.childwelfare.gov/systemwide/laws_policies/statutes/manda.cfm

	PHYSICAL INDICATORS	BEHAVIORAL INDICATORS
Physical Abuse	• Unexplained bruises and welts (in various stages of healing), marks in the shape of belt buckles or electrical cords, human bite marks, puncture marks, bald spots, regularly appearing after absences or weekends • Unexplained burns, especially cigarette burns, burns in the shape of irons, rope burns, or immersion-burns (sock-like or glove-like) • Unexplained fractures, lacerations, or abrasions in various stages of healing • Injuries attributed to the child being "clumsy" or "accident-prone"	• Awkward movements, complains of soreness • Self-destructive • Withdrawn and aggressive—behavioral extremes • Uncomfortable with physical contact • Arrives at school early or stays late, as if afraid • Chronic runaway (adolescents) • Wears high neck, long sleeved clothing, not matching weather, to cover body • Frequent absences
Physical Neglect	• Abandonment • Unattended physical problems or medical needs • Constnt fatigue, lack of energy • Little or no supervision • Often hungry, dressed inappropriately for weather, poor hygiene • Lice, distended stomach, emaciation	• Falls asleep in class • Steals food, begs from classmates • Reports that no caretaker is at home • Frequently absent or tardy, or stays as long as possible at school • Self-destructive • Trouble with the law
Sexual Abuse	• Difficulty walking or sitting • Pain or itching in genital area • Torn, stained, or bloodied underclothing • Bruises or bleeding in external genitalia • Venereal disease, especially in pre-teens • Frequent urinary or yeast infections • Pregnancy	• Doesn't want to change for gym, PE • Withdrawn, chronic depression • Role reversal, overly concerned for siblings • Promiscuity, excessive seductiveness • Peer problems, lack of involvement • Massive weight change • Suicide attempts (especially adolescents) • Inappropriate sex play or premature understanding of sex, frequent masturbation, sexual play with dolls or stuffed animals • Sudden school difficulties

Source: Adapted from several state and national child abuse prevention Web sites:
U.S. Department of Health and Human Services: http://www.childwelfare.gov/pubs/usermanuals/sexabuse/sexabusec.cfm;
Pennsylvania:
http://www.pa-fsa.org/about_child_abuse__neglect/indicators_of_child_abuse.aspx;
New Jersey:
http://www.state.nj.us/dcf/abuse/indicators/.

for anything else? And these texts demand immediate attention. One high school sopho-more told Sherry Turkle (2011) that within his circle of friends, texts had to be answered as soon as possible, within 10 minutes, maximum. As he noted, "Texting is pressure" (p. 266). This pressure means that peers and even parents are always present—their messages demanding a response, even if the student is in class and must text in secret under the desk or with hands inside a backpack. Students and adults are spending more time with technology and less with each other. But these instant, superficial communications via cell phones, computers, iPads, and other electronic communication devices are not necessarily ties that bind students in deep relationships; instead, they are ties that preoccupy and dis-tract (Turkle, 2011). What will it be like to teach students who send and receive over 100 text messages a day, and who can't focus on your class when a Facebook posting appears? These are questions you will have to answer when you step into a classroom.

IDENTITY AND SELF-CONCEPT

What is identity? Is identity different from self-concept or self-esteem? How do we come to understand other people and ourselves? In this section we look at the development of identity and sense of self. You will see patterns similar to those noted in Chapter 2 for cog-nitive development. Children's understandings of themselves are concrete at first. Early views of self and friends are based on immediate behaviors and appearances. Children assume that others share their feelings and perceptions. Their thinking about themselves and others is simple, segmented, and rule-bound, not flexible or integrated into organized systems. In time, children are able to think abstractly about internal processes—beliefs, intentions, values, and motivations. With these developments in thinking, then, children can incorporate more abstract qualities into their knowledge of self, others, and situations (Harter, 2003; Woolfolk & Perry, 2012).

In this section you will encounter the term *identity* along with several *self-* terms: *self-concept, self-esteem,* and *self-worth.* The distinctions among these terms are not always sharp, and there is disagreement even among psycholo-gists about what each term means (Roeser, Peck, & Nasir, 2006). In general, *identity* is a broader concept than the *self-* terms. Identity includes people's general sense of themselves along with all their beliefs and attitudes. Identity integrates all the different aspects and roles of the self (Wigfield et al., 2006). But it is common for researchers to use *self-concept* and *identity* interchange-ably. To make matters easier, I will, too. We begin our consideration of identity/self-concept with the framework of Erik Erikson.

Erikson: Stages of Psychosocial Development

Like Piaget, Erik Erikson did not start his career as a psychologist. He skipped college, travelled around Europe, and ended up teaching in Vienna, where he studied psychoanalysis with Anna Freud, the daughter of Sigmund Freud. Soon after completing his training, he had to flee from the Nazis. He was denied citizenship in Denmark, so he moved to his second choice—New York City. Even though he had never attended college, on the basis of his groundbreak-ing work, he became a distinguished University Professor at Harvard. Later in his career he worked with the original Dr. Spock—Benjamin Spock, the widely read pediatrician whose books guided many baby boomers' parents, mine included (Green & Piel, 2010; Miller, 2011).

Erikson offered a basic framework for understanding the needs of young people in relation to the society in which they grow, learn, and later make their contribu-tions. Erikson's **psychosocial** theory emphasizes the emergence of the self, the search for identity, the individual's relationships with others, and the role of culture throughout life.

Like Piaget, Erikson regarded development as a passage through an interdependent series of stages, each with its particular goals, concerns, accomplishments, and dangers,

Erik Erikson proposed a theory of psychoso-cial development that describes tasks to be accomplished at different stages of life.

Psychosocial Describing the relation of the individual's emotional needs to the social environment.

TABLE 3.4 • **Erikson's Eight Stages of Psychosocial Development**

STAGES	APPROXIMATE AGE	IMPORTANT EVENT	DESCRIPTION
1. Basic trust versus basic mistrust	Birth to 12–18 months	Feeding	The infant must form a first loving, trusting relationship with the caregiver or develop a sense of mistrust.
2. Autonomy versus shame/ doubt	18 months to 3 years	Toilet training	The child's energies are directed toward the development of physical skills, including walking, grasping, controlling the sphincter. The child learns control but may develop shame and doubt if not handled well.
3. Initiative versus guilt	3 to 6 years	Independence	The child continues to become more assertive and to take more initiative but may be too forceful, which can lead to guilt feelings.
4. Industry versus inferiority	6 to 12 years	School	The child must deal with demands to learn new skills or risk a sense of inferiority, failure, and incompetence.
5. Identity versus role confusion	Adolescence	Peer relationships	The teenager must achieve identity in occupation, gender roles, politics, and religion.
6. Intimacy versus isolation	Young adulthood	Love relationships	The young adult must develop intimate relationships or suffer feelings of isolation.
7. Generativity versus stagnation	Middle adulthood	Parenting/ Mentoring	Each adult must find some way to satisfy and support the next generation.
8. Ego integrity versus despair	Late adulthood	Reflection on and acceptance of one's life	The culmination is a sense of acceptance of oneself and a sense of fulfillment.

Source: Lefton, Lester A., Psychology, 5th Edition, © 1994. Reprinted by permission of Pearson Education, Inc. Upper Saddle River, NJ.

as shown in Table 3.4 above. At each stage, Erikson suggests that the individual faces a **developmental crisis**. Each crisis can be resolved by embracing an extreme position or by the healthier and more productive stance of finding a balance between the extreme responses. The way in which the individual resolves each crisis influences resolution of future crises and has a lasting effect on that person's self-image and view of society. We will look briefly at all eight stages in Erikson's theory—or, as he called them, the "eight ages of man."

THE PRESCHOOL YEARS: TRUST, AUTONOMY, AND INITIATIVE. Erikson identifies trust versus mistrust as the basic conflict of infancy. According to Erikson, the infant will develop a sense of trust if its needs for food and care are met with comforting regularity and responsiveness from caregivers. In this first year, infants are in Piaget's sensorimotor stage and are just beginning to learn that they are separate from the world around them. This realization is part of what makes trust so important: Infants must trust the aspects of their world that are beyond their control (Miller, 2011; Posada et al., 2002). Having a secure

Developmental crisis A specific conflict whose resolution prepares the way for the next stage.

attachment (described earlier in this chapter) helps young children develop trust and also learn when mistrust is appropriate—either extreme of complete trust or mistrust is dysfunctional.

Erikson's second stage, **autonomy** *versus shame and doubt,* marks the beginning of self-control and self-confidence as young children begin to assume responsibilities for self-care such as feeding, toileting, and dressing. During this period, parents must tread a fine line in being protective—but not overprotective. If parents do not reinforce their children's efforts to master basic motor and cognitive skills, children may begin to feel shame; they may learn to doubt their abilities to manage the world. Erikson believes that children who experience too much doubt at this stage will lack confidence in their own abilities throughout life. Of course, some doubt is appropriate if the task is too difficult or dangerous—again the need for balance.

For Erikson, the next stage of **initiative** *versus guilt* "adds to autonomy the quality of undertaking, planning, and attacking a task for the sake of being active and on the move" (Erikson, 1963, p. 255). The challenge of this period is to maintain a balance between zest for activity and an understanding that not every impulse can be acted on. Again, adults must tread a fine line, this time in providing supervision without interference. If children are not allowed to do things on their own, a sense of guilt may develop; they may come to believe that what they want to do is always "wrong." The *Guidelines* on the next page suggest ways of encouraging initiative.

THE ELEMENTARY AND MIDDLE SCHOOL YEARS: INDUSTRY VERSUS INFERIORITY. Let's set the stage for the next phase. Between the ages of 5 and 7, when most children start school, cognitive development is proceeding rapidly. Children can process more information faster and their memory spans are increasing. They are moving from preoperational to concrete-operational thinking. As these internal changes progress, the children are spending hours every weekday in the new physical and social world of school. They must now reestablish Erikson's stages of psychosocial development in the unfamiliar school setting. They must learn to trust new adults, act autonomously in this more complex situation, and initiate actions in ways that fit the new rules of school.

The next psychosocial challenge for the school years is what Erikson calls **industry** *versus inferiority.* Students are beginning to see the relationship between perseverance and the pleasure of a job completed. In modern societies, children's ability to move between the worlds of home, neighborhood, and school, and to cope with academics, group activities, and friends will lead to a growing sense of competence. Difficulty with these challenges can result in feelings of inferiority. Children must master new skills and work toward new goals, at the same time they are being compared to others and risking failure.

The skills and concepts children learn in preschool and the early grades are critical. They set students on pathways toward achievement or failure for the rest of their school years (Paris, Morrison, & Miller, 2006). In fact, Entwisle and Alexander (1998) claim, "How well students do in the primary grades matters more for their future success than does their school performance at any other time" (p. 354). Because schools tend to reflect middle-class values and norms, making the transition to school and meeting the challenge of *industry versus inferiority* may be especially difficult for children who differ economically or culturally. The *Guidelines* on the next page give ideas for encouraging industry.

After elementary school, in the transition to middle school, students confront an increased focus on grades and performance as well as more competition on all fronts— academic, social, and athletic. Just when they are eager to make decisions and assume more independence, students encounter more rules, required courses, and assignments. They

DEVELOPING INITIATIVE Children need opportunities to learn things for themselves in order to develop a sense of initiative.

Connect and Extend to PRAXIS II™

Erikson's Psychosocial Theory of Development (I, A1, 2)
The school population spans four stages of Erikson's theory. Identify the major crisis of each of these stages. How can teachers support positive resolution of each of these stages? What are implications for negative resolution of these crises?

Autonomy Independence.

Initiative Willingness to begin new activities and explore new directions.

Industry Eagerness to engage in productive work.

GUIDELINES

Encouraging Initiative and Industry

Encourage children to make and to act on choices.
Examples

1. Have a free-choice time when children can select an activity or game.
2. As much as possible, avoid interrupting children who are very involved in what they are doing.
3. When children suggest an activity, try to follow their suggestions or incorporate their ideas into ongoing activities.
4. Offer positive choices: Instead of saying, "You can't have the cookies now," ask, "Would you like the cookies after lunch or after naptime?"

Make sure that each child has a chance to experience success.
Examples

1. When introducing a new game or skill, teach it in small steps.
2. Avoid competitive games when the range of abilities in the class is great.

Encourage make-believe with a wide variety of roles.
Examples

1. Have costumes and props that go along with stories the children enjoy. Encourage the children to act out the stories or make up new adventures for favorite characters.
2. Monitor the children's play to be sure no one monopolizes playing "teacher," "Mommy," "Daddy," or other heroes.

Be tolerant of accidents and mistakes, especially when children are attempting to do something on their own.
Examples

1. Use cups and pitchers that make it easy to pour and hard to spill.
2. Recognize the attempt, even if the product is unsatisfactory.
3. If mistakes are made, show students how to clean up, repair, or redo.

4. If a student consistently behaves in ways that are highly unusual or unacceptable, seek guidance from the school counselor or psychologist. The best time to help children deal with psychosocial problems is at an early age.

Make sure that students have opportunities to set and work toward realistic goals.
Examples

1. Begin with short assignments, then move on to longer ones. Monitor student progress by setting up progress checkpoints.
2. Teach students to set reasonable goals. Write down goals and have students keep a journal of progress toward these goals.

Give students a chance to show their independence and responsibility.
Examples

1. Tolerate honest mistakes.
2. Delegate to students tasks such as watering class plants, collecting and distributing materials, monitoring the computer lab, grading homework, keeping records of forms returned, and so on.

Provide support to students who seem discouraged.
Examples

1. Use individual charts and contracts that show student progress.
2. Keep samples of earlier work so students can see their improvements.
3. Have awards for most improved, most helpful, most hardworking.

---

change from a close connection with one teacher all year to more impersonal relations with numerous teachers in many different subjects across the year. They also go from being the most mature and highest status students in a small, familiar elementary school to being the "babies" in a large, impersonal middle school (Murdock, Hale, & Weber, 2001; Rudolph, Lambert, Clark, & Kurlakowsky, 2001; Wigfield, Eccles, MacIver, Rueman, & Midgley, 1991). In this demanding context, they face the next challenge—identity.

ADOLESCENCE: THE SEARCH FOR IDENTITY. As students move into adolescence, they are developing capabilities for abstract thinking and understanding the perspectives of others. Even greater physical changes are taking place as the students approach puberty. So, with developing minds and bodies, young adolescents must confront the central issue of constructing an **identity** that will provide a firm basis for adulthood. The individual has been developing a sense of self since infancy. But adolescence marks the first time that a conscious effort is made to answer the now-pressing question: "Who am I?" The conflict

Identity The complex answer to the question: "Who am I?"

defining this stage is *identity* versus *role confusion.* Identity refers to the organization of the individual's drives, abilities, beliefs, and history into a consistent image of self. It involves deliberate choices and decisions, particularly about work, values, ideology, and commitments to people and ideas (Miller, 2011; Penuel & Wertsch, 1995). If adolescents fail to integrate all these aspects and choices, or if they feel unable to choose at all, role confusion threatens.

STOP & THINK Have you decided on your career? What alternatives did you consider? Who or what was influential in shaping your decision? •

James Marcia (1991, 1994, 1999) expanded on Erikson's theory of identity formation. Specifically, he focused on two essential processes in achieving a mature identity: exploration and commitment. **Exploration** refers to the process by which adolescents consider and try out alternative beliefs, values, and behaviors in an effort to determine which will give them the most satisfaction. **Commitment** refers to individuals' choices concerning political and religious beliefs, for example, usually as a consequence of exploring the options. Then, Marcia identified four categories of identity status that arise from four patterns of exploration and commitment.

CONSTRUCTING AN IDENTITY With developing minds and bodies, young adolescents must confront the central issue of developing an identity that will provide a firm basis for adulthood. With adolescence comes a pressing question: "Who am I?"

The first, **identity achievement**, means that after *exploring* the realistic options, the individual has made choices and is *committed* to pursuing them. It appears that few students achieve this status by the end of high school; students who attend college may take even longer to decide. It is not uncommon for the explorations to continue into the early 20s. About 80% of students change their majors at least once (just ask my mom). And some adults may achieve a firm identity at one period in their lives, only to reject that identity and achieve a new one later. So identity, once achieved, may not be unchanging for everyone (Adams, Berzonsky, & Keating, 2006; Kroger, 2000; Nurmi, 2004).

Adolescents in the midst of struggling with choices are experiencing what Erikson called a **moratorium**. Erikson used the term *moratorium* to describe exploration with a delay in commitment to personal and occupational choices. This delay is very common, and probably healthy, for modern adolescents. Erikson believed that adolescents in complex societies have an identity crisis during moratorium. Today, the period is no longer referred to as a *crisis* because, for most people, the experience is a gradual exploration rather than a traumatic upheaval (Grotevant, 1998; Wigfield, Byrnes, & Eccles, 2006). Both identity-achieved and moratorium statuses are considered healthy.

Identity foreclosure is commitment without exploration. Foreclosed adolescents have not experimented with different identities or explored a range of options, but simply have committed themselves to the goals, values, and lifestyles of others—usually their parents, but sometimes cults or extremist groups. Foreclosed adolescents tend to be rigid, intolerant, dogmatic, and defensive (Frank, Pirsch, & Wright, 1990).

Identity diffusion occurs when individuals do not explore any options or commit to any actions. They reach no conclusions about who they are or what they want to do with their lives. Adolescents experiencing identity diffusion may be apathetic and withdrawn, with little hope for the future, or they may be openly rebellious. These adolescents often go along with the crowd, so they are more likely to abuse drugs (Archer & Waterman, 1990; Kroger, 2000).

Schools that give adolescents experiences with community service, real-world work, internships, and mentoring help to foster identity formation (Cooper, 1998). See the *Guidelines* on the next page for other ideas about supporting identity formation.

Exploration In Marcia's theory of identity statuses, the process by which adolescents consider and try out alternative beliefs, values, and behaviors in an effort to determine which will give them the most satisfaction.

Commitment In Marcia's theory of identity statuses, individuals' choices concerning political and religious beliefs, for example, usually as a consequence of exploring the options.

Identity achievement Strong sense of commitment to life choices after free consideration of alternatives.

Moratorium Identity crisis; suspension of choices because of struggle.

Identity foreclosure Acceptance of parental life choices without consideration of options.

Identity diffusion Uncenteredness; confusion about who one is and what one wants.

GUIDELINES

Supporting Identity Formation

Give students many models for career choices and other adult roles.
Examples

1. Point out models from literature and history. Have a calendar with the birthdays of eminent women, minority leaders, or people who made a little-known contribution to the subject you are teaching. Briefly discuss the person's accomplishments on his or her birthday.

2. Invite guest speakers to describe how and why they chose their professions. Make sure all kinds of work and workers are represented.

Help students find resources for working out personal problems.
Examples

1. Encourage them to talk to school counselors.

2. Discuss potential outside services.

Be tolerant of teenage fads as long as they don't offend others or interfere with learning.
Examples

1. Discuss the fads of earlier eras (neon hair, powdered wigs, love beads).

2. Don't impose strict dress or hair codes.

Give students realistic feedback about their work and support for improving. Adolescents may need many "second chances."
Examples

1. When students misbehave or perform poorly, make sure they understand the consequences of their behavior—the effects on themselves and others.

2. Give students model answers or show them other students' completed projects from previous years so they can compare their work to good examples.

3. Never use a student's work as a "bad" example. Create negative examples from multiple sources including mistakes you have made.

4. Because students are "trying on" roles, keep the roles separate from the person. Criticize the behavior without criticizing the student.

For more ideas about working with adolescents using Erikson's theory, see http://www.cde.ca.gov/ls/cg/pp/documents/erikson.pdf

IDENTITY AND TECHNOLOGY. Some scholars of technology have speculated that establishing a separate identity is complicated for adolescents today because they are constantly connected to others. Parents often give a cell phone to their children somewhere between the ages of 9 and 13, or even earlier, with the specific requirement that the children always answer a call from the parent. Sherry Turkle (2011) calls this happy recipient of a new cell phone a "tethered child," now able to participate in activities such as spending time at a mall or on the beach that would not have been allowed without the safety tether of the phone. But the price paid is that these children never navigate social and physical landscapes completely alone—parents and friends always are a speed dial away. The chance to solve problems, experience autonomy, and handle situations on your own is the basis for achieving identity and mature judgment. The tethered child is never alone. Texting means the tether is even shorter. The high school students Turkle interviewed talked about the "big mistake" of teaching their parents to text or IM. A friend of mine is a physician at a university heath center. She describes undergraduate patients who respond to her question, "What are your health concerns today?" with the answer, "My mom is on the phone—she'll tell you" and then the college student hands a cell phone to the doctor. Constant connectivity complicates achieving a separate identity and autonomy.

Connectivity also "offers new possibilities for experimenting with identity, particularly in adolescence, the sense of a free space, what Eric Erikson called the *moratorium*" (Turkle, 2011, p. 152). On Second Life or The Sims Online or other life simulations sites, adolescents can create whole new identities and keep multiple personalities "alive." Some people even talk about their "life mix," a mash up of what they live online and what they live in real life. For some adolescents, the boundaries may be unclear and easily crossed. Is the profile adolescents create on Facebook the "real" person, or as one high school senior described, the identity that you "mold" to present to the world? But with world-wide access to the self-presentation, a critical question arises, "How will the self I present be judged by others?" For connected and tethered adolescents today, Elkind's imaginary audience (discussed in Chapter 2) is now a real online audience. The consequences are not all positive, as another senior agonized:

> You have to know that everything you put up will be perused very carefully. And that makes it necessary for you to obsess over what you do put up and how you portray yourself. . . And when you have to think about what you come across as, that's just another way that. . . . you are thinking of yourself in a bad way. (Turkle, 2011, p. 184)

BEYOND THE SCHOOL YEARS. The crises of Erikson's stages of adulthood all involve the quality of human relations. **Intimacy** *versus isolation* refers to a willingness to relate to another person on a deep level, to have a relationship based on more than mutual need. Someone who has not achieved a sufficiently strong sense of identity tends to fear being overwhelmed or swallowed up by another person and may retreat into isolation. **Generativity** *versus stagnation* extends the ability to care for another person and involves concern and guidance for both the next generation and future generations. Productivity and creativity are essential features. Achieving **integrity** *versus despair* means consolidating your sense of self and fully accepting its unique and now unalterable history.

Erikson's work helped start the life-span development approach, and his theories have been especially useful in understanding adolescence and developing concepts of self. But feminists have criticized his notion that identity precedes intimacy, because their research indicates that for women, identity achievement is fused with achieving intimacy (Miller, 2011). And, as you will see next, recent research has focused on identity issues not fully explored by Erikson—racial and ethnic identity.

Racial-Ethnic Identity

As early as 1903, W.E.B. DuBois wrote about the "double consciousness" of African Americans. In essence, African Americans, like other ethnic or racial groups, are conscious of their ethnic identity as they negotiate being members of the larger culture as well. Ethnic minority students have to "sift through two sets of cultural values and identity options" to achieve a firm identity, so they may need more time to explore possibilities—a longer moratorium in Erikson's terms (Markstrom-Adams, 1992, p. 177). But the exploration is important; some psychologists consider ethnic identity a "master status," one that dominates all other identity concerns when judging the self (Charmaraman & Grossman, 2010; Herman, 2004).

ETHNIC IDENTITIES: OUTCOME AND PROCESS. Jean Phinney (1990, 2003) describes four outcomes for ethnic minority youth in their search for identity. They can try *assimilation*, fully adopting the values and behaviors of the majority culture and rejecting their ethnic culture. At the opposite end, they can be *separated*, associating only with members of their ethnic culture. A third possibility is *marginality*, living in the majority culture, but feeling alienated and uncomfortable in it and disconnected from the minority culture as well. The final alternative is *biculturalism* (sometimes called *integration*), maintaining ties to both cultures. And there are at least three ways to be bicultural. You could alternate between the two cultures, being fully "majority" in your behavior in one situation and fully "minority" in other situations. Or you could blend the two cultures by finding values and behaviors that are common to both and acting on them. Finally, you could fuse the two cultures by truly merging them into a new and complete whole (Phinney & Devich-Nevarro, 1997).

No matter what your identity outcome is, having strong positive feelings about your own ethnic group seems to be important for good mental health (Steinberg, 2005). In fact, Amy Marks and her colleagues (2011) determined that bicultural adolescents who form strong, positive multiethnic identities have higher self-esteem, fewer mental health problems, and higher academic achievement than peers with a single ethnic identity or an undeveloped multiethnic identity.

Intimacy Forming close, enduring relationships with others.

Generativity Sense of concern for future generations.

Integrity Sense of self-acceptance and fulfillment.

Some psychologists have used Marcia's identity statuses to understand the process of forming an ethnic identity. Children may begin with an unexamined ethnic identity, either because they have not explored at all (diffusion) or because they have accepted the identity encouraged by others (foreclosure). Many European American adolescents could fit the unexamined category. A period of ethnic identity exploration (moratorium) might be followed by a resolution of the conflict (identity achieved).

RACIAL IDENTITY: OUTCOME AND PROCESS.
William Cross (1991; Cross & Cross, 2007; DeCuir-Gunby, 2009) devised a framework that specifically addresses African American racial identity. The process he calls **nigrescence** has five stages:

KNOWING YOURSELF When majority adolescents are knowledgeable and secure about their own heritage, they are also more respectful of the heritage of others.

- *Pre-encounter:* At this stage, Cross says that an African American's attitude may range from ignoring race to feeling neutral about race, to actually being anti-Black. African Americans at this stage may adopt certain beliefs of White Americans, including the tendency to see "Whiteness" as superior. Some level of self-hate is a possible consequence. At the pre-encounter stage, people value other aspects of their identity, such as religion, profession, or social status.
- *Encounter:* This stage is often triggered by encounters with overt, covert, or institutional racism. For instance, when an African American is followed around in an upscale store, is assaulted by police, or sees news reports about such assaults, then his or her eyes are opened to the reality that race matters in society. The African American becomes attuned to his or her Blackness.
- *Immersion/Emersion:* Cross sees this as a transition—an in-between state that may cause people to be anxious about "becoming the 'right kind' of Black person" (Cross, 1991, p. 202). In response to encounters with discrimination, the individuals fill their lives with symbols of Blackness; they buy books about Black experiences and socialize mainly with other African Americans, for example. They are eager to understand their racial heritage more deeply.
- *Internalization:* Individuals are firmly connected to and secure in their sense of racial identity. They don't worry about what friends or outsiders think—they are confident in their own standards of Blackness.
- *Internalization-Commitment:* This stage is very closely connected with internalization. The main difference is a person's continued interest in and commitment to Black affairs. Such individuals chart their lives to connect to their Black racial identity; for example, a painter dedicates his life to painting Black images or a researcher dedicates her life to studying African American educational experiences.

Determining a racial identity may be even more complicated for biracial or multiracial adolescents. The parent they live with, the make-up of their neighborhood, their appearance, and experiences of discrimination or support can influence these adolescents' decisions about racial identity. Some psychologists think that these challenges help multiracial youth develop stronger and more complex identities, but other researchers argue that the challenges present an extra burden in an already tough process (Herman, 2004). Perhaps the outcome depends in part on the support adolescents receive in facing the challenges.

Nigrescence The process of developing a Black identity.

Racial and ethnic pride A positive self-concept about one's racial or ethnic heritage.

RACIAL AND ETHNIC PRIDE. For all students, pride in family and community is part of the foundation of a stable identity. Special efforts to encourage **racial and ethnic pride** are particularly important, so that students examining their identities do not get the message that differences are deficits (Spencer & Markstrom-Adams, 1990). In one study, researchers found that African American preschool students whose homes were rich with African American culture had more factual knowledge and better problem-solving skills. Parents who encouraged their children to be proud of their heritage reported fewer behavior problems with their children (Caughy, O'Campo, Randolph, & Nickerson, 2002). In other research, positive racial identity was found to be related to higher self-esteem and fewer emotional problems for both African American and White adolescents (DuBois, Burk-Braxton, Swenson, Tevendale, & Hardesty, 2002).

Each of us has an ethnic heritage. Janet Helms (1995) has written about stages in White identity development. Richard Milner (2003) has pointed to the importance of racial identity development and awareness, especially in teaching. When majority adolescents are knowledgeable and secure about their own heritage, they are also more respectful of the heritage of others. Thus, exploring the racial and ethnic roots of all students should foster both pride in self and acceptance of others (Rotherham-Borus, 1994).

In the next sections we move from overarching considerations of identity to more specific conceptions of self. In educational psychology, much research is focused on self-concept and self-esteem.

Self-Concept

The term *self-concept* is part of our everyday conversations. We talk about people who have a "low" self-concept or individuals whose self-concept is not "strong," as if self-concept were the oil level in a car or your abdominal muscles. These actually are misuses of the term. In psychology, **self-concept** generally refers to individuals' knowledge and beliefs about themselves—their ideas, feelings, attitudes, and expectations (Harter, 2006; Pajares & Schunk, 2001). We could consider self-concept to be our attempt to explain ourselves to ourselves, to build a scheme (in Piaget's terms) that organizes our impressions, feelings, and beliefs about ourselves. But this model or scheme is not permanent, unified, or unchanging. Our self-perceptions vary from situation to situation and from one phase of our lives to another.

THE STRUCTURE OF SELF-CONCEPT.   A student's overall self-concept is based on other, more specific concepts, including academic and nonacademic self-concepts. Herbert Marsh (2006) and his colleagues have identified up to 17 different self-concepts in nonacademic areas (e.g., physical appearance, popularity, trustworthiness, relations with parents, emotional stability) and academic areas (verbal, mathematics, problem solving, art, computers). For adolescents, both their overall academic self-concept (how quickly they learn or how well they do in school in general) and their subject-specific self-concept (how good they are in math) may influence their actions and motivation. For example, Martin Brunner and his colleagues (2010) suggest "students' educational aspirations (e.g., whether to go on to higher education) are driven by general academic self-concept, whereas the training program or college major chosen is influenced by the profile of subject-specific academic self-concepts" (p. 977). For adults, however, the separate, specific self-concepts are not necessarily integrated into an overall self-concept, so self-concept probably is more situation-specific in adults (Marsh & Ayotte, 2003; Marsh, Craven, & Martin, 2006; Schunk, Pintrich, & Meece, 2008).

HOW SELF-CONCEPT DEVELOPS.   The self-concept evolves through constant self-evaluation in different situations. Children and adolescents are continually asking themselves, in effect, "How am I doing?" They gauge the verbal and nonverbal reactions of significant people—parents and other family members in the early years, and friends, schoolmates, and teachers later—to make judgments (Harter, 1998, 2006).

Younger children tend to have positive and optimistic views of themselves. In one study, over 80% of the 1st graders surveyed thought they were the best students in their class (Stipek, 1981). With more experience in school, children make self-concept appraisals based on their own improvement. Researchers followed 60 students in New Zealand from the time they started school until the middle of their third year (Chapman, Tunmer, & Prochnow, 2000). In the first 2 months of school, differences in reading self-concept

Self-concept Individuals' knowledge and beliefs about themselves—their ideas, feelings, attitudes, and expectations.

began to develop, based on the ease or difficulty students had learning to read. Students who entered school with good knowledge about sounds and letters learned to read more easily and developed more positive reading self-concepts. Over time, differences in the reading performance of students with high and low reading self-concepts grew even greater. Thus, the children's early experiences with the important school task of reading had a strong impact on their self-concept.

As they mature, students become more realistic, but many are not accurate judges of their own abilities (Paris & Cunningham, 1996). In fact, some students suffer from "illusions of incompetence"—they seriously underestimate their own competence (Phillips & Zimmerman, 1990). As we have seen, during the middle-school years, students grow more self-conscious. At this age, self-concepts are tied to physical appearance and social acceptance as well as school achievement, so these years can be exceedingly difficult for students such as Stephanie, described at the opening of this chapter (Wigfield, Eccles, & Pintrich, 1996).

Both self and other comparisons shape self-concepts, at least in Western cultures. Students' self-concepts in math are shaped by how their math performance compares to their performance history. They also compare themselves to other math students (Altermatt, Pomerantz, Ruble, Frey, & Greulich, 2002; Schunk et al., 2008). Students who are strong in math in an average school feel better about their math skills than do students of equal ability in high-achieving schools. Marsh (1990; Marsh et al., 2008) calls this the "Big-Fish-Little-Pond Effect (BFLP)." Research that surveyed 265,180 15-year-old students in 10,221 schools across 41 countries around the world found the BFLP effect in every one of these countries (Seaton, Marsh, & Craven, 2009). Participation in a gifted and talented program seems to have a "Little-Fish-in-a-Big-Pond" effect: Students who participate in gifted programs, compared to similar students who remain in regular classes, tend to show declines in academic self-concepts over time, but no changes in nonacademic self-concepts (Marsh & Craven, 2002; Preckel, Goetz, & Frenzel, 2010).

CHOICES SHAPE FUTURES The courses selected in high school put students on a path toward the future, so self-concepts about particular academic subjects can be life-changing influences.

SELF-CONCEPT AND ACHIEVEMENT. Many psychologists consider self-concept to be the foundation of both social and emotional development. Research has linked self-concept to a wide range of accomplishments—from performance in competitive sports to job satisfaction to pride, enjoyment, and achievement in school (Byrne, 2002; Marsh & Hau, 2003; Goetz, Cronjaeger, Frenzel, Ludtke, & Hall, 2010; Möller & Pohlmann, 2010). Some evidence for the link between self-concept and school achievement is that performance in academic subjects is correlated with specific self-concepts in those areas, but not with social or physical self-concepts. For example, in one study, math self-concept correlated .77 with math test scores, .59 with grades, and .51 with coursework selection (Marsh et al., 2006; O'Mara, Marsh, Craven, & Debus, 2006).

That last correlation of math self-concept with course selection points to an important way self-concept affects learning in school. Think back to high school. When you had a chance to choose courses, did you pick your worst subjects—those where you felt least capable? Probably not. Herbert Marsh and Alexander Yeung (1997) examined how 246 boys in early high school in Sydney, Australia, chose their courses. Academic self-concept for a particular subject (mathematics, science, etc.) was the most important predictor of course selection—more important than previous grades in the subject or overall self-concept. The courses selected in high school put students on a path toward the future, so self-concepts about particular academic subjects can be life-changing influences.

Unfortunately, heavy emphasis on grade point averages (GPAs) for admission to some colleges can affect course choice as well, especially if students avoid classes to protect their GPAs because they see themselves as "no good" in math, science, world languages, or other challenging classes. Of course, we know from Chapter 1 that correlation is not cause—higher self-concept probably can encourage higher achievement but high achievement likely also leads to higher self-concept, so the causes work in both directions (Pinxten, De Fraine, Van Damme & D'Haenens, 2010).

Self-Esteem

STOP & THINK How strongly do you agree or disagree with the following statements?
   On the whole, I am satisfied with myself.
   I feel that I have a number of good qualities.
   I wish I could have more respect for myself.
   At times, I think that I am no good at all.
   I certainly feel useless at times.
   I take a positive attitude toward myself. •

These *Stop & Think* questions are taken from a widely used measure of self-esteem (Hagborg, 1993; Rosenberg, 1979). **Self-esteem** is an affective reaction—an overall judgment of self-worth that includes feeling confident and proud of yourself as a person. If people judge themselves positively—if they "like what they see"—we say that they have high self-esteem (Schunk, Pintrich, & Meece, 2008). Can you see the judgments of self-worth in the *Stop & Think* questions?

The terms *self-concept* and *self-esteem* are often used interchangeably, even though they have distinct meanings. Self-concept is a cognitive structure, a belief about who you are—for example, the belief that you are a good athlete. Self-esteem is an overall, general feeling of self-worth that incorporates your self-concepts in all areas of your life, so it is the "summary judgment" about your worth as a person (O'Mara, Marsh, Craven, & Debus, 2006). As you can see in the *Stop & Think* items above, the questions are pretty general; no specific areas such as academics or appearance are targeted. Self-esteem is influenced by whether the culture around you values your particular characteristics and capabilities (Bandura, 1997; Schunk et al., 2008). Some writers use *self-concept* and *self-esteem* interchangeably. But there is a conceptual difference—thinking versus valuing.

Do schools affect self-esteem: Is school important? As you can see from the *Point/Counterpoint* on the next page the school's role in student self-esteem has been hotly debated.

Over 100 years ago, William James (1890) suggested that self-esteem is determined by how successful we are in accomplishing tasks or reaching goals we value. If a skill or accomplishment is not important, incompetence in that area doesn't threaten self-esteem. Students must have legitimate success with tasks that matter to them. The reasons individuals give for their successes or failures also are important. In order to build self-esteem, students must attribute their successes to their own actions, not to luck or to special assistance.

Sex Differences in Self-Concept and Self-Esteem

Do girls and boys differ in their self-concepts? A study followed 761 middle-class, primarily European American students from 1st grade through high school (Jacobs, Lanza, Osgood, Eccles, & Wigfield, 2002). It is difficult to get longitudinal data, so this is a valuable study. In 1st grade, girls and boys had comparable perceptions of their own abilities in language arts, but boys felt significantly more competent in math and sports. Competence beliefs declined for both boys and girls across the grades, but boys fell faster in math, so that by high school, math competence beliefs were about the same for boys and girls. In language arts, boys' competence ratings fell more sharply than those of girls after 1st grade, but both leveled off during high school. In sports, competence ratings for both boys and girls dropped, but boys remained significantly more confident in their competence in sports throughout the entire 12 years.

Other studies have also found that girls tend to see themselves as more able than boys in reading and close friendships; boys are more confident about their abilities in math and athletics. Of course, some of these differences in self-confidence may reflect actual differences in achievement—girls tend to be better readers than boys, for example. As we have seen, many self-beliefs are reciprocally related to achievement—each affects the other (Eccles, Wigfield, & Schiefele, 1998; Pinxten, De Fraine, Van Damme & D'Haenens, 2010). When these results are examined together with Marsh and Yeung's (1997) findings

Connect and Extend to PRAXIS II™

Self-Esteem (I, A2)
Understand the bidirectional effects of school life and self-esteem on each other. What can teachers do to enhance students' self-esteem?

Self-esteem The value each of us places on our own characteristics, abilities, and behaviors.

POINT/COUNTERPOINT: What Should Schools Do to Encourage Students' Self-Esteem?

More than 2,000 books about how to increase self-esteem have been published. Schools and mental health facilities continue to develop self-esteem programs (Slater, 2002). The attempts to improve students' self-esteem have taken three main forms: personal development activities such as sensitivity training; self-esteem programs where the curriculum focuses directly on improving self-esteem; and structural changes in schools that place greater emphasis on cooperation, student participation, community involvement, and ethnic pride. Are these efforts valuable?

POINT

▶ **The self-esteem movement has problems.** Some people have accused schools of developing programs where the main objective is "to dole out a huge heaping of praise, regardless of actual accomplishments" (Slater, 2002, p. 45). But Erik Erikson (1980) warned years ago: "Children cannot be fooled by empty praise and condescending encouragement. They may have to accept artificial bolstering of their self-esteem in lieu of something better...." Erikson went on to explain that a strong and positive identity comes only from "wholehearted and consistent recognition of real accomplishment, that is, achievement that has meaning in their culture" (p. 95).

Frank Pajares and Dale Schunk (2002) point to another problem. "[W]hen what is communicated to children from an early age is that nothing matters quite as much as how they feel or how confident they should be, one can rest assured that the world will sooner or later teach a lesson in humility that may not easily be learned. An obsession with one's sense of self is responsible for an alarming increase in depression and other mental difficulties" (p. 16). Sensitivity training and self-esteem courses assume that we encourage self-esteem by changing the individual's beliefs, making the young person work harder against the odds. But what if the student's environment is truly unsafe, debilitating, and unsupportive? Some people have overcome tremendous problems, but to expect everyone to do so "ignores the fact that having positive self-esteem is almost impossible for many young people, given the deplorable conditions under which they are forced to live by the inequities in our society" (Beane, 1991, p. 27).

Worse yet, some psychologists are now contending that low self-esteem is not a problem, whereas high self-esteem may be. For example, they contend, people with high self-esteem are more willing to inflict pain and punishment on others (Baumeister, Campbell, Krueger, & Vohs, 2003; Slater, 2002). In addition, high self-esteem does not seem to predict academic learning. In a large study of adolescents, global self-esteem did not correlate with any of the nine academic outcomes measured (Marsh et al., 2006). And when people set self-esteem as a main goal, they may pursue that goal in ways that are harmful over the long run. They may, for example, avoid constructive criticisms or challenging tasks (Crocker & Park, 2004). Psychologist Lauren Slater (2002) in her article, "The Trouble with Self-Esteem" suggests that we rethink self-esteem and move toward honest self-appraisal

that will lead to self-control. She suggests, "Maybe self-control should replace self-esteem as a primary peg to reach for" (p. 47).

COUNTERPOINT

▶ **The self-esteem movement has promise.** A study that followed 322 6th grade students for two years found that students' satisfaction with school, their sense that classes were interesting and teachers cared, and teacher feedback and evaluations influenced students' self-esteem. In physical education, teachers' opinions were especially powerful in shaping students' conceptions of their athletic abilities (Hoge, Smit, & Hanson, 1990). Being placed in a low-ability group or being held back in school seems to have a negative impact on students' self-esteem, but learning in collaborative and cooperative settings seems to have a positive effect (Covington, 1992; Deci & Ryan, 1985). Interestingly, special programs such as "Student of the Month" or admission to advanced math classes had little effect on self-esteem. (Relate the latter to the "Big-Fish-Little-Pond Effect.")

Beyond the "feel-good psychology" of some aspects of the self-esteem movement is a basic truth: Self-esteem is a basic right of all humans. We deserve to respect ourselves, and schools should not undermine this right (Beane, 1991). If we view self-esteem accurately as a product of our thinking and our actions—our values, ideas, and beliefs as well as our interactions with others—then we see a significant role for the school. Practices that allow authentic participation, cooperation, problem solving, and accomplishment should replace policies that damage self-esteem, such as tracking and competitive grading.

Beyond Either/Or. Another possibility is to refocus on more specific self-concepts, because self-concepts in specific areas such as math are related to learning in math (O'Mara et al., 2006). Because self-concept and achievement probably affect each other, the researcher concluded:

In summary, whereas the optimal way to improve self-concept over the short-term is to focus interventions directly on self-concept enhancement, interventions that combine direct self-concept enhancement in concert with performance enhancement, coupled with appropriate feedback and praise, are likely to be advantageous when the goals of the intervention are to improve both self-concept and performance. (Marsh et al., 2006, p. 198)

that academic self-concept influences course selection, it seems that many students make decisions about courses that forever limit their future options.

For most ethnic groups (except African Americans), males are more confident about their abilities in math and science. Unfortunately, there are no long-term studies of other ethnic groups, so these patterns may be limited to European Americans.

Teachers' feedback, grading practices, evaluations, and communication of caring for students can make a difference in how students feel about their abilities in particular subjects. But the greatest increases in self-esteem come when students grow more competent in areas they value—including the social areas that become so important in adolescence. Thus, a teacher's greatest challenge is to help students achieve important understandings and skills.

UNDERSTANDING OTHERS AND MORAL DEVELOPMENT

As we seek our own identity and form images of ourselves, we are also learning about right and wrong. One aspect of moral development is understanding the "significant others" around us. How do we learn to interpret what others are thinking and feeling?

Theory of Mind and Intention

By the time they are 2 or 3 years old, children are beginning to develop a **theory of mind**, an understanding that other people are people too, with their own minds, thoughts, feelings, beliefs, desires, and perceptions (Astington & Dack, 2008; Flavell, Miller, & Miller, 2002; Miller, 2009). Children need a theory of mind to make sense of other people's behavior. Why is Sarah crying? Does she feel sad because no one will play with her? Children also need a theory of mind to understand that beliefs can differ from reality and that people can have different views. As you will see in Chapter 4, one explanation for autism is that children with this condition lack a theory of mind to help them understand their own or other people's emotions and behaviors.

Around the age of 2, children have a sense of intention, at least of their own intentions. They will announce, "I wanna peanut butter sandwich." As children develop a theory of mind, they also are able to understand that other people have intentions of their own. Older preschoolers who get along well with their peers are able to separate intentional from unintentional actions and to react accordingly. For example, they will not get angry when another child accidentally knocks over their block tower. But aggressive children have more trouble assessing intention. They are likely to attack anyone who topples their tower, even accidentally (Dodge & Pettit, 2003). As children mature, they are more able to assess and consider the intentions of others.

With a developing theory of mind, children are increasingly able to understand that other people have different feelings and experiences, and therefore may have a different viewpoint or perspective. This **perspective-taking ability** develops over time until it is quite sophisticated in adults. Being able to understand how others might think and feel is important in fostering cooperation and moral development, reducing prejudice, resolving conflicts, and encouraging positive social behaviors in general (Gehlbach, 2004). Some coaching in perspective-taking from the teacher might help if children mistreat peers and the mistreatment is not part of a deeper emotional or behavioral disorder (Woolfolk & Perry, 2012).

Moral Development

Along with a more advanced theory of mind and an understanding of intention, children also are developing a sense of right and wrong. In this section we focus on children's **moral reasoning**, their thinking about right and wrong and their active construction of moral judgments. Some of the earliest moral issues in classrooms involve dividing and sharing materials, or **distributive justice** (Damon, 1994). For young children (ages 5 to 6), fair distribution is based on equality; thus, teachers often hear, "Keshawn got more than I did—that's not fair!" In the next few years, children come to recognize that some people

Theory of mind An understanding that other people are people too, with their own minds, thoughts, feelings, beliefs, desires, and perceptions.

Perspective-taking ability Understanding that others have different feelings and experiences.

Moral reasoning The thinking process involved in judgments about questions of right and wrong.

Distributive justice Beliefs about how to divide materials or privileges fairly among members of a group; follows a sequence of development from equality to merit to benevolence.

should get more based on merit—they worked harder or performed better. Finally, around age 8, children are able to take need into account and to reason based on benevolence; they can understand that some students may get more time or resources from the teacher because those students have special needs.

Another area that involves moral development is an understanding of rules. If you have spent time with young children, you know that there is a period when you can say, "Eating in front of the TV is not allowed!" and get away with it. For young children, rules simply exist. Piaget (1965) called this the state of **moral realism**. At this stage, the child of 5 or 6 believes that rules about conduct or rules about how to play a game are absolute and can't be changed. If a rule is broken, the child believes that the punishment should be determined by how much damage is done, not by the intention of the child or by other circumstances. So, accidentally breaking three cups is worse than intentionally breaking one, and in the child's eyes, the punishment for the three-cup offense should be greater.

As children interact with others and see that different people have different rules, there is a gradual shift to a **morality of cooperation**. Children come to understand that people make rules and people can change them. When rules are broken, both the damage done and the intention of the offender are taken into account.

KOHLBERG'S THEORIES OF MORAL DEVELOPMENT.   Lawrence Kohlberg's (1963, 1975, 1981) theory of moral development is based in part on Piaget's ideas, described earlier.

- -

STOP & THINK A man's wife is dying. There is one drug that could save her, but it is very expensive, and the druggist who invented it will not sell it at a price low enough for the man to buy it. Finally, the man becomes desperate and considers stealing the drug for his wife. What should he do, and why? •

- -

Kohlberg evaluated the moral reasoning of both children and adults by presenting them with **moral dilemmas**, or hypothetical situations like the one above in which people must make difficult decisions and give their reasons. Based on their reasoning, Kohlberg proposed a detailed sequence of stages of moral reasoning, or judgments about right and wrong. He divided moral development into three levels: (1) *preconventional*, where judgment is based solely on a person's own needs and perceptions; (2) *conventional*, where the expectations of society and laws are taken into account; and (3) *postconventional*, where judgments are based on abstract, more personal principles of justice that are not necessarily defined by society's laws. Each of these three levels is further divided into two stages:

Preconventional Level

- Stage 1: *Obedience Orientation*—Obey rules to avoid punishments and bad consequences.
- Stage 2: *Rewards/Exchange Orientation*—Right and wrong is determined by personal needs and wants—"If I want it, it is right."

Conventional Level

- Stage 3: *Being Nice/Relationships Orientation*—Being good means being nice and pleasing others.
- Stage 4: *Law and Order Orientation*—Laws and authorities must be obeyed; the social system must be maintained.

Postconventional (Principled) Level

- Stage 5: *Social Contract Orientation*—The moral choice is determined by socially agreed upon standards—"the greatest good for the greatest number."

Moral realism Stage of development wherein children see rules as absolute.

Morality of cooperation Stage of development wherein children realize that people make rules and people can change them.

Moral dilemma Situations in which no choice is clearly and indisputably right.

- Stage 6: *Universal Ethical Principles Orientation*—There are universal principles of human dignity and social justice that individuals should uphold, no matter what the law or other people say.

Moral reasoning is related to both cognitive and emotional development. As we have seen, abstract thinking becomes increasingly important in the higher stages of moral development, as children move from decisions based on absolute rules to those based on abstract principles such as justice and mercy. The ability to see another's perspective, to judge intentions, and use formal-operational thinking to imagine alternative bases for laws and rules also enters into judgments at the higher stages.

CRITICISMS OF KOHLBERG'S THEORY. Even though there is evidence that the different levels of reasoning identified by Kohlberg do form a hierarchy, with each stage being an advancement in reasoning over the previous one (Boom, Brugman, & van der Heijden, 2001), his stage theory has been criticized. First, in reality, the stages do not seem to be separate, sequenced, and consistent. People often give reasons for moral choices that reflect several different stages simultaneously. Or a person's choices in one instance may fit one stage and his or her decisions in a different situation may reflect another stage. When asked to reason about helping someone else versus meeting their own needs, both children and adolescents reason at higher levels than when they are asked to reason about breaking the law or risking punishment (Arnold, 2000; Eisenberg et al., 1987; Sobesky, 1983).

Second, in everyday life, making moral choices involves more than reasoning. Emotions, competing goals, relationships, and practical considerations all affect choices. People may be able to reason at higher levels, but they may make choices at lower levels based on these other factors (Carpendale, 2000). Kohlberg emphasized cognitive reasoning about morality, but overlooked other aspects of moral maturity, such as character and virtue, that operate to solve moral problems in everyday life (Walker & Pitts, 1998).

GENDER DIFFERENCES: THE MORALITY OF CARING. One of the most hotly debated criticisms of Kohlberg's theory is that the stages are biased in favor of Western male values that emphasize individualism. His stages do not represent the way moral reasoning develops either in women or in other cultures, because the stage theory was based on a longitudinal study of American men only (Gilligan, 1982; Gilligan & Attanucci, 1988).

Carol Gilligan (1982) has proposed a different sequence of moral development, an "ethic of care." Gilligan suggests that individuals move from a focus on self-interest to moral reasoning based on commitment to specific individuals and relationships, and then to the highest level of morality based on the principles of responsibility and care for all people (which is a bit like Kohlberg's stage 3). If women never reach what Kohlberg considers the higher stages of justice, are they morally immature?

Some research supports this ethic of care and indicates that it is more typical of women's orientation to moral problem solving, especially when they reason about personal and real-life issues (Garmon, Basinger, Gregg, & Gibbs, 1996). However, a meta-analysis that combined the results of 113 studies found only small differences in moral orientation in line with Gilligan's theory (Jaffee & Hyde, 2000). The meta-analysis suggests both men and women use care to reason about interpersonal dilemmas and justice to reason about societal dilemmas. Moral reasoning was more strongly influenced by the context and content of the dilemma than by the gender of the reasoner. Even though men and women both seem to value caring and justice, there is some evidence that in everyday life, women feel more guilty about violating caring norms (being inconsiderate or untrustworthy) and men feel more guilty when they show violent behaviors (fighting or damaging property) (Williams & Bybee, 1994).

Caring for students and helping students learn to care has become a theme for many educators. For example, Nel Noddings (1995) urged that "themes of care" be used to organize the curriculum. Possible themes include "Caring for Self," "Caring for Family and Friends," and "Caring for Strangers and the World." Using the theme of "Caring for Strangers and the World," there could be units on crime, war, poverty, tolerance, ecology, or technology. The events after the massive tornado destruction in the Midwestern United States or

TABLE 3.5 **Using "Caring for Strangers and the World" as a Teaching Theme**

As part of a unit on "Caring for Strangers and the World," high-school students examine the issue of crime in several classes. In every class, the study of aspects of crime would be continually tied to the theme of caring and to discussions of safety, responsibility, trust in each other and in the community, and commitment to a safer future.

SUBJECT	ELEMENTS
Mathematics	Statistics: Gather data on the location and rates of crimes, ages of offenders, and costs of crime to society. Is there a correlation between severity of punishment and incidence of crime? What is the actual cost of a criminal trial?
English and Social Studies	Read *Oliver Twist*. Relate the characters to their social and historical context. What factors contributed to crime in 19th century England? Read popular mysteries. Are they literature? Are they accurate depictions of the criminal justice system?
Science	Genetics: Are criminal tendencies heritable? Are there sex differences in aggressive behavior? Are women less competent than men in moral reasoning (and why did some social scientists think so)? How would you test this hypothesis?
Arts	Is graffiti art really art?

Source: Based on "Teaching Themes of Care," by Nel Noddings, Phi Delta Kappan, 76, pp. 675–679.

earthquakes in Haiti and Japan that left thousands homeless might be a starting point for these units. Table 3.5 shows how a focus on crime and caring for strangers could be integrated into several high school classes.

Moral Judgments, Social Conventions, and Personal Choices

STOP & THINK
1. If there were no law against it, would it be OK to blind someone?
2. If there were no rule against it, would it be OK to chew gum in class?
3. Who should decide your favorite vegetable or how to style your hair? •

We probably could agree that it is wrong to blind someone, wrong to break class rules, and wrong to dictate food preferences or hairstyles for other people—but it is a different kind of "wrong" in each case. The first question is about actions that are inherently immoral. The answer to the question is concerned with conceptions of justice, fairness, human rights, and human welfare. Even young children know that it is not OK to hurt other people or steal from them—law or no law. But some rules, like no gum chewing in question 2, are **social conventions**—agreed-upon rules and ways of doing things in a particular situation. Students (mostly) avoid chewing gum when the class rules (conventions) say so. It is not inherently immoral to chew gum—it is just against the rules. Some classes—in college, for example—work well using different rules. And it is not immoral to dislike lima beans (at least I hope not) or to wear your hair long if you are a male; these are *personal choices*—individual preferences and private issues.

Other criticisms of Kohlberg's stages are that they mix up moral judgments with decisions about social conventions and also overlook personal choice. Larry Nucci (2001) offers an explanation of moral development that covers all three domains or areas: *moral judgments, social conventions*, and *personal choice*. Children's thinking and reasoning develops across all domains, but the pace of development may not be the same in every area.

Social conventions Agreed-upon rules and ways of doing things in a particular situation.

MORAL VERSUS CONVENTIONAL DOMAINS. For teachers, the most common "right and wrong" situations involve the moral and conventional domains. In the moral domain, beginning with a few basic ideas about right and wrong ("It is wrong to hurt others"), children move through the following stages: a sense that justice means equal treatment for all; an appreciation of equity and special needs; a more abstract integration of equity and equality along with a sense of caring in social relations; and finally, a sense as adults that morality involves beneficence and fairness and that moral principles are independent of the norms of any particular group.

In the *conventional domain*, children begin by believing that the regularities they see are real and right—for example, men have short hair and women have longer hair, so that is the way it should be. As they mature, children see the exceptions (men with pony tails, women with very short cuts) and realize that conventions are arbitrary. Next, children understand that rules, even though they are arbitrary, are made to maintain order and that people in charge make the rules. As students move through adolescence, they swing from understanding conventions as the appropriate ways to operate in a social system to viewing them as nothing but society's standards that have become set because they are widely applied and seldom challenged. Finally, adults realize that conventions are useful in coordinating social life, but changeable, too. So, compared to young children, older adolescents and adults generally are more accepting of others who think differently about conventions and customs.

IMPLICATIONS FOR TEACHERS. Nucci (2001) offers several suggestions for creating a moral atmosphere in your classroom. First, it is important to establish a community of mutual respect and warmth with a fair and consistent application of the rules. Without that kind of community, all your attempts to create a moral climate will be undermined. Second, teachers' responses to students should be appropriate to the domain of the behavior—moral or conventional. For example, here are some responses to moral issues (Nucci, 2001, p. 146):

1. When an act is inherently hurtful or unjust, emphasize the harm done to others: "John, that really hurt Jamal."
2. Encourage perspective-taking: "Chris, how would you feel if someone stole from you?"

   In contrast, here are two responses to rules or conventional issues:

3. Restate the rule: "Lisa, you are not allowed to be out of your seat during announcements."
4. Command: "Howie, stop swearing!"

In all four cases, the teacher's response fits the domain. To create an inappropriate response, just switch responses 1 or 2 with 3 or 4. For example, "Lisa, how would you feel if other people got out of their seat during announcements?" Lisa might feel just fine. And it is a weak response to a moral transgression to say, "John, it is against the rules to hit." It is more than against the rules—it hurts and it is wrong.

In the third domain—personal—children must sort out what decisions and actions are their personal choices and what decisions are outside personal choice. This process is the foundation for developing moral concepts related to individual rights, fairness, and democracy. Here, diverse cultures may have very different understandings about individual choice, privacy, and the role of individuality in the larger society.

Diversity in Moral Reasoning

There are a number of broad cultural distinctions that might influence moral reasoning. Some cultures can be considered more traditional, with greater emphasis on customs and rituals that change slowly over time. In contrast, traditions and customs tend to change more rapidly in modern cultures. Nucci (2001) suggests that in more traditional cultures, customs may become "moralized." For example, not wearing head coverings in some cultures may seem to be in the conventional domain to outsiders, but is closer to the moral domain for members of the culture, especially when religious beliefs are involved.

CREATING MORAL CLIMATES Educators can create a moral climate in their schools and classrooms by promoting and reinforcing a community of mutual respect.

Consider the findings of one study described by Nucci that asked devout Hindus to rate 35 behaviors that violated community norms. An eldest son eating chicken a day after his father's death was considered the worst violation and beating a disobedient wife was the least offensive. What seems like a convention (eating chicken) is a moral issue because the Hindus believed that the son's behavior would prevent his father from receiving salvation—a terrible and eternal fate. So, to understand what is convention and what is moral, we need to know about the beliefs of the culture.

In cultures that are more family-centered or group-oriented (often called *collectivist cultures*), the highest moral value might involve putting the opinions of the group before decisions based on individual conscience. Research has found that children's reasoning about moral, conventional, and personal domains is similar across cultures. Even in societies such as China that encourage deference to authority, Chinese children agree with Western children that adults have no right to dictate how children spend their free time. And people without authority, including children, should be obeyed when what they want you to do is fair and just, but disobeyed when what they dictate is immoral or unjust (Helwig, Arnold, Tan, & Boyd, 2003; Kim, 1998).

In the last years of his life, Kohlberg was studying moral behavior in schools. We turn to that topic now.

Connect and Extend to PRAXIS II™

Moral Development (I, A2)
Moral issues can have an important impact on the classroom. Identify major issues related to moral development and explain what a teacher can do to appropriately address these issues.

Moral Behavior: Aggression, and Cheating

Three important influences on moral behavior are modeling, internalization, and self-concept. First, children who have been consistently exposed to caring, generous adult models will tend to be more concerned for the rights and feelings of others (Eisenberg & Fabes, 1998; Woolfolk & Perry, 2012). Second, most theories of moral behavior assume that young children's moral behavior is first controlled by others through direct instruction, supervision, rewards and punishments, and correction. But in time, children **internalize** the moral rules and principles of the authority figures who have guided them; that is, children adopt the external standards as their own. If children are given reasons they can understand when they are corrected—particularly reasons that highlight the effects of actions on others—then they are more likely to internalize moral principles. They learn to behave morally even when "no one is watching" (Hoffman, 2000).

Finally, we must integrate moral beliefs and values into our total sense of who we are, our self-concept.

> The tendency for a person to behave morally is largely dependent on the extent to which moral beliefs and values are integrated in the personality, and in one's sense of self. The influence our moral beliefs have on our lives, therefore, is contingent on the personal importance that we as individuals attach to them—we must identify and respect them as our own. (Arnold, 2000, p. 372)

Internalize Process whereby children adopt external standards as their own.

Instrumental aggression Strong actions aimed at claiming an object, place, or privilege—not intended to harm, but may lead to harm.

AGGRESSION. Aggression should not be confused with assertiveness, which means affirming or maintaining a legitimate right. Saying, "You are sitting in my chair!" is assertive. Pushing the invader out of the chair is aggressive. There are several forms of aggression. The most common form is **instrumental aggression**, which is intended to gain an object or privilege, such as shoving to get a chair or snatching a book from another student. The intent is to get what you want, not to hurt the other child, but the hurt may happen anyway. A second kind is **hostile aggression**—inflicting intentional harm. Hostile aggression can take the form of either **overt aggression**, such as threats or physical attacks (as in, "I'm gonna beat you up!"), or **relational aggression**, which involves threatening or damaging social relationships (as in, "I'm never going to speak to you again!"). Boys are more likely to use overt aggression and girls, like Alison in the opening case, are more likely to use relational aggression, especially in middle school and beyond (Ostrov & Godleski, 2010). A final kind of hostile aggression is a growing concern today, **cyber aggression**—using e-mail, Twitter, Facebook, or other social media to spread rumors, make threats, or otherwise terrorize peers, as Stephanie's "friends" did in the case at the beginning of this chapter.

Aggressive students tend to believe that violence will be rewarded, and they use aggression to get what they want. They are more likely to believe that violent retaliation is acceptable: "It's OK to shove people when you're mad" (Egan, Monson, & Perry, 1998). Seeing violent acts go unpunished probably affirms and encourages these beliefs. In addition, some children, particularly boys, have difficulty reading the intentions of others (Dodge & Pettit, 2003; Zelli, Dodge, Lochman, & Laird, 1999). They assume another child "did it on purpose" when their block tower is toppled, they are pushed on the bus, or some other mistake is made. Retaliation follows and the cycle of aggression continues.

Children with more serious conduct problems often are identified during elementary school. But the problems are not new behaviors—usually they are behaviors the students have not outgrown from their early years (Petitclerc, Boivin, Dionne, Zoccolillo & Tremblay, 2009). So waiting for children to "outgrow" aggressive behaviors does not work. For example, one study in Finland asked teachers to rate students' aggression by answering "never," "sometimes," or "often" to statements such as "hurts another child when angry." Teacher-rated aggression when students were age 8 predicted school adjustment problems in early adolescence and long-term unemployment in adulthood (Kokko & Pulkkinen, 2000). Similar results were found in a study conducted in Canada, New Zealand, and the United States. Boys (but not girls) who were often physically aggressive in elementary school were at risk for continuing violent and nonviolent forms of delinquency through adolescence (Broidy et al., 2003).

It is clear that helping children handle aggression can make a lasting difference in their lives. One of the best approaches for preventing problems with aggression later in life is to intervene early. For example, one study found that aggressive children whose teachers taught them conflict management strategies were diverted from a life path of aggression and violence (Aber, Brown, & Jones, 2003). Sandra Graham (1996) has successfully experimented with approaches that help aggressive 5th and 6th grade boys become better judges of others' intentions. Strategies include engaging in role-play, participating in group discussions of personal experiences, interpreting social cues from photographs, playing pantomime games, making videos, and writing endings to unfinished stories. The boys in the 12-session training group showed clear improvement in reading the intentions of others and responding with less aggression.

RELATIONAL AGGRESSION. Insults, gossip, exclusion, taunts—all are forms of relational aggression, sometimes called *social aggression* because the intent is to harm social connections. After 2nd or 3rd grade, girls tend to engage in relational aggression more than boys, possibly because as girls become aware of gender stereotypes, they push their overt aggression underground into verbal, not physical, attacks. Relational aggression can be even more damaging than overt physical aggression—both to the victim and the aggressor. Victims, like Stephanie in the chapter opening, often are devastated. Teachers and other students may view relational aggressors as even more problematic than physical aggressors (Crick, Casas, & Mosher, 1997; Ostrov & Godleski, 2010). As early as preschool, children need to learn how to negotiate social relations without resorting to any kind of aggression. Interviews with adolescents reveal how much they count on their teachers and other adults in the school to protect them (Garbarino & deLara, 2002). We will examine more specific classroom strategies, especially strategies for handling bullying, in Chapter 13, *Creating Learning Environments*.

Hostile aggression Bold, direct action that is intended to hurt someone else; unprovoked attack.

Overt aggression A form of hostile aggression that involves physical attack.

Relational aggression A form of hostile aggression that involves verbal attacks and other actions meant to harm social relationships.

Cyber aggression Using e-mail, Twitter, Facebook, or other social media to spread rumors, make threats, or otherwise terrorize peers.

MEDIA, MODELING, AND AGGRESSION. Modeling plays an important role in the expression of aggression (Bandura, Ross, & Ross, 1963). Children who grow up in homes filled with harsh punishment and family violence are more likely to use aggression to solve their own problems (Patterson, 1997).

One very real source of aggressive models is found in almost every home in America—television. From ages 6 to 11, children spend an average of 28 hours a week watching television—more time than any other activity except sleep (Rideout, Foehr, & Roberts, 2010). With all this viewing, the possible influence of television violence is a real concern because in the United States, 82% of TV programs have at least some violence. The rate for children's programs is especially high—an average of 32 violent acts per hour, with cartoons being the worst. And in over 70% of the violent scenes, the violence goes unpunished (Kirsh, 2005; Mediascope, 1996). Does watching violent TV increase aggression? A panel of experts assembled by the U.S. Surgeon General to study media and violence reached a strong and clear conclusion: "Research on violent television and films, video games, and music reveals unequivocal evidence that media violence increases the likelihood of aggressive and violent behavior in both immediate and long-term contexts" (Anderson et al., 2003, p. 81).

You can reduce the negative effects of TV violence by stressing three points with your students: (1) most people do not behave in the aggressive ways shown on television; (2) the violent acts on TV are not real, but are created by special effects and stunts; and (3) there are better ways to resolve conflicts, and these are the ways most real people use to solve their problems (Huesmann et al., 2003). Also, avoid using TV viewing as a reward or punishment because that makes television even more attractive to children (Slaby et al., 1995). But television is not the only source of violent models. Students growing up in the inner cities see gang violence. Newspapers, magazines, and the radio are filled with stories of murders, rapes, and robberies. Many popular films are also filled with graphic depictions of violence, often performed by the "hero" who saves the day. And what about those video games?

VIDEO GAMES AND AGGRESSIVE BEHAVIOR. Recently researchers reviewed 130 reports based on over 130,000 participants from Western countries such as the United States, Australia, Germany, Italy, the Netherlands, Portugal, and the United Kingdom, as well as from Japan (Anderson et al., 2010). They found that playing violent video games is a causal factor for increased aggressive thoughts, feelings, and actions, along with decreased feelings of empathy. Culture and gender had very little impact on how susceptible players were to the effects of these games. But playing positive video games can increase prosocial behaviors, so it is not that games themselves are bad. It appears that we learn what we play, but there are few prosocial games and many violent ones. So an important issue facing teachers, parents, and our whole society is determining what we should do to limit the risks to children. The *Guidelines* give some ideas for dealing with aggression and encouraging cooperation.

MODELS OF AGGRESSION One very real source of aggressive models is television programming with a high degree of violent content.

CHEATING. About 80% to 90% of high school and college students cheat at some point in school. In fact, the rates of academic cheating have been rising for the past 30 years, perhaps in response to increased pressures and high-stakes testing (Murdock & Anderman, 2006).

There are some individual differences in cheating. Most studies of adolescent and college-age students find that males are more likely to cheat than females and lower-achieving students are more likely to cheat than higher achievers. Students focusing on performance goals (making good grades, looking smart) as opposed to learning goals, and

GUIDELINES

Dealing with Aggression and Encouraging Cooperation

Present yourself as a nonaggressive model.
Examples

1. Do not use threats of aggression to win obedience.
2. When problems arise, model nonviolent conflict-resolution strategies (see Chapter 13).

Ensure that your classroom has enough space and appropriate materials for every student.
Examples

1. Prevent overcrowding.
2. Make sure prized toys or resources are plentiful.
3. Remove or confiscate materials that encourage personal aggression, such as toy guns.
4. Avoid highly competitive activities and evaluations.

Make sure students do not profit from aggressive behaviors.
Examples

1. Comfort the victim of aggression and ignore the aggressor.
2. Use reasonable punishment, especially with older students.

Teach directly about positive social behaviors.
Examples

1. Incorporate lessons on social ethics/morality through reading selections and discussions.

2. Discuss the effects of antisocial actions such as stealing, bullying, and spreading rumors.
3. Provide models and encouragement—role-play appropriate conflict resolution.
4. Build self-esteem by building skills and knowledge.
5. Seek help for students who seem especially isolated and victimized.

Provide opportunities for learning tolerance and cooperation.
Examples

1. Emphasize the similarities among people rather than the differences.
2. Set up group projects that encourage cooperation.

For more ideas, see the National Youth Violence Prevention Resource Center: http://www.safeyouth.gov/Resources/Prevention/Pages/PreventionHome.aspx

---

students with a low sense of academic self-efficacy (a belief that they probably can't do well in school) are more likely to cheat. Finally, students who are impulsive may be more likely to cheat. (Anderman, Cupp, & Lane, 2009; Murdock & Anderman, 2006).

But cheating is not all about individual differences—the situation plays a role as well. In one study, the level of cheating decreased when students moved from math classes that emphasized competition and grades to classes that emphasized understanding and mastery (Anderman & Midgley, 2004). Students are less likely to cheat when they view their teacher as credible. If students trust the teacher as a credible source, they may be more likely to value the content being taught and therefore want to actually learn it (Anderman, Cupp, & Lane, 2009). In addition, students also are particularly likely to cheat when they are behind or "cramming for tests" or when they believe that their teachers do not care about them. For example, Erica had this perspective:

> I am a high school honors student, and I think there are different degrees of cheating. I'm a dedicated student, but when my history teacher bombards me with 50 questions due tomorrow or when a teacher gives me a fill-in-the-blanks worksheet on a night when I have swim practice, church, aerobics—and other homework—I'm going to copy from a friend! . . . Since I only do this when I need to, it isn't a habit. Every kid does this when they're in a pinch. (Jensen et al., 2002, p. 210)

Tamera Murdock and Eric Anderman (2006) have proposed a model for integrating what we know about cheating and doing research to learn more. They suggest that in deciding to cheat, students ask three questions: What is my goal? Can I do this? What are the costs? See Table 3.6 on the next page for some example answers to these questions that might be associated with decisions about whether to cheat, and some example strategies to support *not* cheating.

TABLE 3.6 • **When Do Students Cheat?**

Tamera Murdock and Eric Anderman have developed a model of academic cheating based on the answers to three questions.

QUESTIONS	LESS LIKELY TO CHEAT: EXAMPLE ANSWERS	MORE LIKELY TO CHEAT: EXAMPLE ANSWERS	WHAT CAN THE TEACHER DO? EXAMPLE STRATEGIES
What is my goal?	The goal is to learn, get smarter, and be the best I can be. It is my goal.	The goal is to look good, outperform others. The goal is imposed on me.	Communicate that the point of the class is to learn—everyone can get better.
Can I do it?	I can do it with reasonable effort.	I doubt my ability to do it.	Build students' confidence by helping them take small but successful steps. Point out students' past accomplishments.
What are the costs?	I will get caught and punished if I cheat. I will feel morally wrong or dishonored if I cheat.	I probably won't get caught and punished if I cheat. Everyone does it, so it can't be wrong. The pressure is too great—I can't fail. I have to cheat.	Make mistakes an opportunity to learn. Take the pressure out of assignments with the chance to revise. Monitor to prevent cheating and follow through with reasonable penalties.

Source: Adapted from Murdock and Anderman (2006).

The implications for teachers are straightforward. To prevent cheating, try to avoid putting students in high-pressure situations. Make sure they are well prepared for tests, projects, and assignments so they can do reasonably well without cheating. Be a trustworthy and credible source of information. Focus on learning and not on grades. Encourage collaboration on assignments and experiment with open-book, collaborative, or take-home tests. I often tell my students what concepts will be on the test and encourage them to discuss the concepts and their applications before the test. You might also make extra help available for those who need it. Be clear about your policies in regard to cheating, and enforce them consistently. Help students to resist temptation by monitoring them carefully during testing.

PERSONAL/SOCIAL DEVELOPMENT: LESSONS FOR TEACHERS

Certainly both Erikson and Bronfenbrenner stress that individuals are influenced by their social and cultural contexts. For example, here are a few big ideas:

1. Students whose parents are divorcing can benefit from authoritative teachers who are both warm and clear about requirements.
2. For all students, self-concepts are increasingly differentiated over time—they may feel competent in one subject, but not in others, or very capable as friends or family members, but not good about work in school.
3. For all students, it is a challenge to forge a meaningful identity that integrates their decisions about career, religion, ethnicity, gender roles, and connection to society. Teachers are in a position to support this quest.

4. Being rejected by peers is harmful for all students. Many students need guidance in developing social skills, in more accurately reading the intentions of others, in resolving conflicts, and in coping with aggression. Again, teachers can provide guidance.

5. When working under high pressure, with unreasonable workloads, and with little chance of being caught, many students will cheat. It is up to teachers and schools to avoid these conditions.

▼ SUMMARY

Physical Development (pp. 70–75)

Describe the changes in physical development of children in the preschool, elementary, and secondary grades. During the preschool years, there is rapid development of children's gross- and fine-motor skills. Physical development continues throughout the elementary-school years, with girls often ahead of boys in size. With adolescence comes puberty and emotional struggles to cope with all the related changes.

What are some of the consequences of early and late maturation for boys and girls? Females mature about two years ahead of males. Early-maturing boys are more likely to enjoy high social status; they tend to be popular and to be leaders. But they also tend to engage in more delinquent behavior—this is true for White, African American, and Mexican American boys. Early maturation is not generally beneficial for girls.

What is the role of recess and physical activity in development? Play supports brain development, language, and social development. Children release tensions, learn to solve problems, adapt to new situations, cooperate, and negotiate. The increase in childhood obesity is linked to inactivity and increased time spent watching TV and playing passive games such as video and Internet games.

What are some of the signs of eating disorders? Anorexic students may appear pale, have brittle fingernails, and have fine dark hairs developing all over their bodies. They are easily chilled because they have so little fat to insulate their bodies. They often are depressed, insecure, moody, and lonely. Girls may stop having their menstrual period.

Bronfenbrenner: The Social Context for Development (pp. 75–87)

Describe Bronfenbrenner's bioecological model of development. This model takes into account both the biological aspects internal to the individual and the nested social and cultural contexts that shape development. Every person develops within a microsystem (immediate relationships and activities) inside a mesosystem (relationships among microsystems), embedded in an exosystem (larger social settings such as communities); all of these are part of the macrosystem (culture). In addition, all development occurs in and is influenced by the time period—the chronosystem.

What are some aspects of the family that affect students in school? Students probably have experienced different parenting styles, and these styles can influence their social adjustment. At least in European American, middle-class families, children of authoritative parents are more likely to be happy with themselves and relate well to others, whereas children of authoritarian parents are more likely to feel guilty or depressed, and children of permissive parents may have trouble interacting with peers. But cultures also differ in parenting styles. Research indicates that higher-control parenting is linked to better grades for Asian and African American students.

How does divorce affect students? During the divorce itself, conflict may increase as property and custody rights are being decided. After the divorce, the custodial parent may have to move to a less expensive home, go to work for the first time, or work longer hours. For the child, this can mean leaving behind important friendships just when support is needed the most, having only one parent who has less time than ever to be with them, or adjusting to new family structures when parents remarry.

Why are peer relationships important? Peer relationships play a significant role in healthy personal and social development. There is strong evidence that adults who had close friends as children have higher self-esteem and are more capable of maintaining intimate relationships than adults who had lonely childhoods. Adults who were rejected as children tend to have more problems, such as dropping out of school or committing crimes.

What are peer cultures? Groups of students develop their own norms for appearance and social behavior. Group loyalties can lead to rejection for some students, leaving them upset and unhappy.

How can teachers' academic and personal caring affect students? Students value caring in teachers. Caring can be expressed as support for academic learning and as concern for personal problems. For higher-achieving and higher socioeconomic status students, academic caring may be more important, but for students who are alienated from school, personal caring may be more important.

What are some signs of child abuse? Signs of abuse or neglect include unexplained bruises, burns, bites, or other injuries and fatigue, depression, frequent absences, poor hygiene, inappropriate clothing, problems with peers, and many others. Teachers must report suspected cases of child abuse, and can be instrumental in helping students cope with other risks as well.

Self-Concept and Identity (pp. 87–99)

What are Erikson's stages of psychosocial development? Erikson's emphasis on the relationship between society and the individual is a psychosocial theory of development—a theory that connects personal development (psycho) to the social environment (social). Erikson believed that people go through eight life stages, each of which involves a central crisis. Adequate resolution of each crisis leads to greater personal and social competence and a stronger foundation for solving future crises. In the first two stages, an infant must develop a sense of trust over mistrust and a sense of autonomy over shame and doubt. In early childhood, the focus of the third stage is on developing initiative and avoiding feelings of guilt. In the child's elementary school years, the fourth stage involves achieving a sense of industry and avoiding feelings of inferiority. In the fifth stage, identity versus role confusion, adolescents consciously attempt to solidify their identity. According to Marcia, these efforts may lead to identity diffusion, foreclosure, moratorium, or achievement. Erikson's three stages of adulthood involve struggles to achieve intimacy, generativity, and integrity.

Describe the formation of ethnic and racial identities. Ethnic and racial minority students are confronted with the challenge of forming an identity while living in two worlds—the values, beliefs, and behaviors of their group and those of the larger culture. Most explanations for identity development describe stages moving from being unaware of differences between minority group and majority cultures, to different ways of negotiating the differences, and finally to an integration of cultures.

How does self-concept change as children develop? Self-concept (definition of self) becomes increasingly complex, differentiated, and abstract as we mature. Self-concept evolves through constant self-reflection, social interaction, and experiences in and out of school. Students develop a self-concept by comparing themselves to personal (internal) standards and social (external) standards. High self-esteem is related to better overall school experience, both academically and socially. Gender and ethnic stereotypes are significant factors as well.

Distinguish between self-concept and self-esteem. Both self-concept and self-esteem are beliefs about the self. Self-concept is our attempt to build a scheme that organizes our impressions, feelings, and attitudes about ourselves. But this model is not permanent. Self-perceptions vary from situation to situation and from one phase of our lives to another. Self-esteem is an evaluation of your self-worth. If people evaluate their worth positively, we say that they have high self-esteem. Self-concept and self-esteem are often used interchangeably, even though they have distinct meanings. Self-concept is a cognitive structure and self-esteem is an affective evaluation.

Are there differences in self-concepts for girls and boys? From 1st to 12th grade, competence beliefs decline for both boys and girls in math, language arts, and sports. By high school, boys and girls express about the same competence in math, girls are higher in language arts, and boys are higher in sports. In terms of general self-esteem, both boys and girls report declines in the transition to middle school, but boys' self-esteem goes up in high school while girls' self-esteem stays down.

Understanding Others and Moral Development (pp. 99–108)

What is a theory of mind and why is it important? A theory of mind is an understanding that other people are people too, with their own minds, thoughts, feelings, beliefs, desires, and perceptions. Children need a theory of mind to make sense of other people's behavior. As children develop a theory of mind, they also are able to understand that other people have intentions of their own.

How do perspective-taking skills change as students mature? An understanding of intentions develops as children mature, but aggressive students often have trouble understanding the intentions of others. Social perspective-taking also changes as we mature. Young children believe that everyone has the same thoughts and feelings they do. Later, they learn that others have separate identities and therefore separate feelings and perspectives on events.

What are the key differences among the preconventional, conventional, and postconventional levels of moral reasoning? Kohlberg's theory of moral development includes three levels: (1) a preconventional level, where judgments are based on self-interest; (2) a conventional level, where judgments are based on traditional family values and social expectations; and (3) a postconventional level, where judgments are based on more abstract and personal ethical principles. Critics suggest that Kohlberg's view does not account for possible cultural differences in moral reasoning or differences between moral reasoning and moral behavior.

Describe Gilligan's levels of moral reasoning. Carol Gilligan has suggested that because Kohlberg's stage theory was based on a longitudinal study of men only, it is very possible that the moral reasoning of women and the stages of women's development were not adequately represented. She has proposed an "ethic of care." Gilligan believes that individuals move from a focus on self-interest to moral reasoning based on commitment to specific individuals and relationships, and then to the highest level of morality based on the principles of responsibility and care for all people. Women are somewhat more likely to use a care orientation, but studies also show that both men and women can use both orientations.

How does thinking in the moral and conventional domains change over time? Beliefs about morality move from the young child's sense that justice means equal treatment for all to the adult's understanding that morality involves beneficence and fairness and that moral principles are independent of the norms of any particular group. In thinking about social conventions, children begin by believing that the regularities they see are real and right. After going through several stages, adults realize that conventions are useful in coordinating social life, but changeable too.

What influences moral behavior? Adults first control young children's moral behavior through direct instruction, supervision, rewards and punishments, and correction. A second important influence on the development of moral behavior is modeling. Children who have been consistently exposed to caring, generous adult models will tend to be more concerned for the rights and feelings of others.

What are the different types of aggression? Peer aggression can be instrumental (intended to gain an object or privilege), or hostile (intended to inflict harm). Hostile aggression can be either overt threats or physical attacks, or relational aggression, which involves threatening or damaging social relationships. Boys are more likely to use overt aggression and girls are more likely to use relational aggression. Today the many social media applications and sites provide other avenues for relational aggression.

How does ever-present media affect aggression and empathy? The world and the media provide many negative models of behavior. In time, children internalize the moral rules and principles of the authority figures who have guided them. If children are given reasons—particularly reasons that highlight the effects of actions on others—they can understand when they are corrected and then they are more likely to internalize moral principles. Some schools have adopted programs to increase students' capacity to care for others.

Why do students cheat? In schools, cheating is a common behavior problem that involves moral issues. The decision to cheat is based on three questions: What is my goal? Can I do this? What are the costs? Cheating is caused by both individual and situational factors, but if the pressure is great enough and the chance of getting caught is slim, many students will cheat.

▼ KEY TERMS

Anorexia nervosa (74)
Attachment (80)
Autonomy (89)
Bioecological model (76)
Blended families (78)
Body mass index (BMI) (71)
Bulimia (74)
Commitment (91)
Context (75)
Cyber aggression (105)
Developmental crisis (88)
Distributive justice (99)
Exploration (91)
Extended families (78)
Generativity (93)
Hostile aggression (105)

Identity (90)
Identity achievement (91)
Identity diffusion (91)
Identity foreclosure (91)
Industry (89)
Initiative (89)
Instrumental aggression (104)
Integrity (93)
Internalize (104)
Intimacy (93)
Menarche (71)
Moral dilemmas (100)
Moral realism (100)
Moral reasoning (99)
Morality of cooperation (100)
Moratorium (99)

Nigrescence (94)
Overt aggression (105)
Parenting styles (78)
Peer cultures (82)
Perspective-taking ability (99)
Psychosocial (87)
Puberty (71)
Racial and ethnic pride (94)
Relational aggression (105)
Self-concept (95)
Self-esteem (97)
Social conventions (102)
Spermarche (71)
Theory of mind (99)

▼ CONNECT AND EXTEND TO LICENSURE

MULTIPLE-CHOICE QUESTIONS

1. While several school districts limit the amount of time devoted to recess and play, the National Association for the Education of Young Children has recommended that children engage in play activities for all but which one of the following reasons?
   A. Play increases competence which children need to successfully navigate their world.
   B. Play engages many senses and children learn best when the whole self is involved.
   C. Children learn to appreciate that others have their own point of view through play.
   D. Play increases children's anxiety which prepares them for later challenges they may face.

2. Authoritative teaching strategies are associated with what students identify as "good teachers." Identify which one of the following educators is demonstrating authoritative techniques in the classroom.
   A. When Marcus failed to take his seat upon entering the room, Miss Thomas reminded him of the class rules and consequences.
   B. Paulo, a shy new student to the class, was forced by Mr. Hall on his first day in his new school to give a speech about his past experiences in Guatemala.
   C. Dina was allowed by her teacher to skip recess and play inside by herself because she did not have any friends.
   D. Mr. Krall allowed the students to have two free days at the beginning of the year in which to become acquainted with their peers in the classroom.

3. When a new student arrives in Ms. Taylor's class, she understands that they may initially have adjustment issues. In addition to pairing new students up with a partner to assist them in navigating Central Middle School, she also makes sure she addresses their psychosocial needs. Which one of the following strategies would be appropriate for a new student in Ms. Taylor's middle-school class?
   A. Allow the student to plan what they would like to do during their day at school.
   B. Encourage the student to take responsibility for their own personal needs.
   C. Provide support so that new students can feel a sense of competence and success.
   D. Let students know that the relationships they make in middle school are important to their emotional well-being and happiness later in life.

4. Research suggests that a majority of students cheat at one point in their academic career. Which one of the following is not a recommendation to reduce cheating in the classroom?
   A. Clear guidelines on what constitutes cheating accompanied by consequences which when imposed will deter other students due to their severity.
   B. Reduce the focus on grades and provide the material for students with which they must be familiar.
   C. Encourage collaboration with peers on assignments in order to provide support necessary and decrease anxiety.
   D. Ensure students are well prepared for assignments and tests.

CONSTRUCTED-RESPONSE QUESTIONS

Case

Suzanne Wilson entered Ms. Sullivan's class in the fall without any friends. While many of the third graders engaged in collaborative games on the playground, Suzanne would stand on the periphery and the other students did not include her. In class she appeared to be more typical of a younger child, sucking her thumb when she became upset and refusing to share during group activities. By December, Ms. Sullivan decided that steps should be taken to intervene. Mr. and Mrs. Wilson were called in for a parent meeting. When the Wilsons arrived, Suzanne was with them. What then transpired was shocking to Ms. Sullivan. Suzanne refused to allow her parents to talk with her teacher in private. Yelling above the crying and screaming, the Wilsons apologized and suggested they return on another day when Suzanne was feeling more agreeable.

1. Identify and explain the parenting style the Wilsons practice.

2. What strategies should Ms. Sullivan employ to assist Suzanne in her emotional development?

MyEducationLab™

Go to Chapter 3 of the Book Specific Resources in MyEducationLab and click on "Connect and Extend to Licensure" to answer these questions. Compare your responses with the feedback provided.

▼ WHAT WOULD THEY DO?

TEACHERS' CASEBOOK: Mean Girls

Here is how several expert teachers said they would address the situation with Alison and the clique of "mean girls."

THOMAS NAISMITH • Science Teacher Grades 7–12
Slocum Independent School District, Elkhart, TX

To bring civility to this classroom, I would address the situation in two stages. First, I would meet individually with the two girls involved in the most recent incident. I would make it very clear to Alison that her behavior was totally inappropriate and that such behavior was far beneath her. I would suggest to her that I was sure that it was just a temporary lapse of good judgment on her part and that I was sure that such an incident would not occur again. I would also ask her to play a role in helping to stop some of the other inappropriate behavior that was occurring in my classroom.

I would explain to Stephanie that she did not need to be embarrassed, because her classmates would appreciate the fact that she had made an effort to restore an old "friendship." I would comment on her positive qualities, explain that she should feel good about herself, and suggest that she seek the companionship of students who are open to her friendship.

The second step would be to address the class as a whole. I would be nonspecific in my comments, but I would make it very clear that the gossip and other "ugly" behavior would need to stop. I would explain that our classroom is a mini-society and that every member has the responsibility of treating others appropriately. I would further explain that they did not have to be "friends" with everyone, but should treat everyone with respect and dignity.

JACALYN D. WALKER • 8th Grade Science Teacher
Treasure Mountain Middle School, Park City, UT

Never work in a vacuum. This is especially important in a middle school or junior high school. Work with your school counselor, other grade level teachers, and parents. If you are doing this, you will have several options for dealing with this problem. You cannot fake caring about 12-, 13-, and 14-year-olds. They can spot a fake. You must be working with this age group because you truly like them as people. You appreciate their humor and their abilities. With a caring, trusting, and respectful relationship, students will be open to your help and guidance. Parents are often not involved in the classroom at these grade levels, but there are great programs available to get parents involved.

NANCY SCHAEFER • Grades 9–12
Cincinnati Hills Christian Academy High School, Cincinnati, OH

I would first make a phone call to Stephanie's home. Under the guise of calling about assignments because of the days she has missed, I would talk to one of her parents or guardians. My first goal would be to find out if the parents are aware of the situation. Sometimes girls like Stephanie are too embarrassed to tell their parents the whole story or even any of the real story. If the parents did not know the entire story, I might try to get Stephanie on the phone and help her tell her parents. Letting the adults around her know what has happened can relieve some of the shame she might be feeling.

I would then work with Stephanie and one or more of her parents to plan Stephanie's transition back to school. A school counselor might also be involved in this conversation. The adults would help Stephanie come up with a plan for how to handle possible difficult situations: face-to-face encounters with Alison, encounters with other old "friends," mean messages she might receive during the school day, or comments made to her by other students. We would help her think through these situations and practice how she could respond. I could talk to Stephanie's teachers to work on rearranging groups or seating to move the girls away from each other or to foster other friendships for Stephanie. Since almost everyone has stories about unfaithful friends, Stephanie might benefit from talking with a freshman or sophomore about that person's experiences and how they made new friends. Finally, I would try to arrange a brief and supervised meeting between Stephanie and Alison. Allowing an encounter to happen in a controlled environment would provide Stephanie an outlet to voice her hurt, without her having to resort to inappropriate actions.

During all of this, I would want to make sure that someone was also working with Alison, to prevent the escalation of events. This may be an administrator responsible for discipline, if school rules were violated, the school counselor, or another teacher with a good relationship with Alison. I would encourage the involvement of Alison's parents, especially if this were not the first vicious episode.

MyEducationLab™

Go to Topic #3, Personal, Social, and Moral Development, in the MyEducationLab (www.myeducationlab.com) for *Educational Psychology*, where you can:

- Find learning outcomes for Personal, Social, and Moral Development along with the national standards that connect to these outcomes.
- Complete Assignments and Activities that can help you more deeply understand the chapter content.
- Apply and practice your understanding of the core teaching skills identified in the chapter with the Building Teaching Skills and Dispositions learning units.
- Examine challenging situations and cases presented in the IRIS Center Resources.
- Access video clips of CCSSO National Teachers of the Year award winners responding to the question, "Why Do I Teach?" in the Teacher Talk section.
- Check your comprehension on the content covered in the chapter with the Study Plan. Here you will be able to take a chapter quiz, receive feedback on your answers, and then access Review, Practice, and Enrichment activities to enhance your understanding of chapter content.
- Find additional Teachers' Casebook scenarios and responses to them from practicing teachers.
- Use the Online Lesson Plan Builder to practice lesson planning and integrating national and state standards into your planning.

chapter four

LEARNER DIFFERENCES AND LEARNING NEEDS

▶ **TEACHERS' CASEBOOK:** Including Every Student

It is a new school year and your district has had a change in policy. "Special Education" programs have been discontinued and ALL students will now be included in general education classrooms full time. You knew that you were going to have students with a wide range of abilities, social skills, and motivation for learning in your classroom, but now you also have a student with severe asthma, a fairly high functioning student with Asperser's syndrome, a student with severe learning disabilities, and two students who are on medication for ADHD. It is not clear what resources will be available to you, but even so, you want to face this challenge with confidence and a sense of efficacy for teaching all students.

CRITICAL THINKING

- How will you design a standards-based curriculum that will allow all of the students to learn to their fullest potential and demonstrate proficiency toward the standards?

- What can you do to address the specific problems of your students who have been identified with special needs?

- How will you remain confident in you new situation?

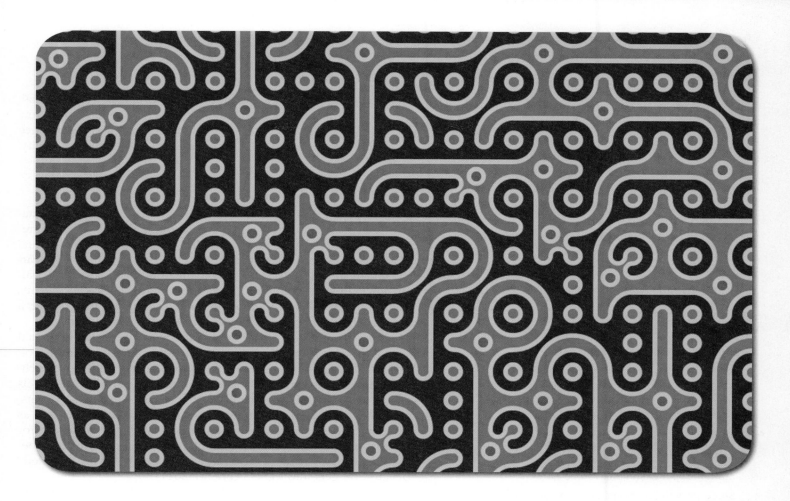

OVERVIEW AND OBJECTIVES

To answer the critical thinking questions, you need an understanding of individual differences. So far, we have talked little about individuals. We have discussed principles of development that apply to everyone—stages, processes, conflicts, and tasks. Our development as human beings is similar in many ways, but not in every way. Even among members of the same family, there are marked contrasts in appearance, interests, abilities, and temperament, and these differences have important implications for teaching. We will spend some time analyzing the concepts of intelligence and learning styles because these terms are so often misunderstood. You probably will have at least one student with special needs in your class, whatever grade you teach, so in this chapter we also explore both common and less frequently occurring learning problems that students may have. As we discuss each problem area, we will consider how a teacher might recognize problems, seek help, and plan instruction, including using the approach of response to intervention. By the time you have completed this chapter, you should be able to:

Objective 4.1:   Describe current hierarchical theories and multiple theories of intelligence.

Objective 4.2:   Explain how intelligence is measured, and discuss what these measurements tell teachers.

Objective 4.3:   Discuss the values and limitations of considering students' learning styles.

Objective 4.4:   Discuss the implications of the IDEA and Section 504 protections for contemporary education.

Objective 4.5:   Understand the special educational needs of students with learning challenges.

Objective 4.6:   Recognize the special educational needs of students who are gifted and talented.

INTELLIGENCE

Because the concept of intelligence is so important, so controversial, and so often misunderstood in education, we will spend quite a few pages discussing it. But before we begin, let's examine the practice of labeling people based on differences such as intelligence, ability, or disability.

Language and Labels

Every child is a distinctive collection of talents, abilities, and limitations. But some students also have learning disabilities, communication disorders, emotional or behavioral disorders, intellectual disabilities, physical disabilities, impaired vision or difficulties hearing, autism spectrum disorders, traumatic brain injury, or some combination of these challenges. Others have remarkable gifts and talents. Even though we will use terms like these throughout the chapter, a caution is in order: *Labeling students is a controversial issue.*

A label does not tell which methods to use with individual students. For example, few specific "treatments" automatically follow from a "diagnosis" of behavioral disorder; many different teaching strategies and materials are appropriate. Further, the labels can become self-fulfilling prophecies. Everyone—teachers, parents, classmates, and even the students themselves—may see a label as a stigma that cannot be changed. Finally, labels are mistaken for explanations, as in, "Santiago gets into fights because he has a behavior disorder." "How do you know he has a behavior disorder?" "Because he gets into fights." (Friend, 2011).

On the other hand, some educators argue that for younger students, at least, being labeled as "special needs" protects the child. For example, if classmates know a student has intellectual disabilities (once called *mental retardation*), they will be more willing to accept his or her behaviors. Of course, diagnostic labels still open doors to some programs, useful information, adaptive technology and equipment, or financial assistance. Labels probably both stigmatize and help students.

DISABILITIES AND HANDICAPS. A **disability** is just what the word implies—an inability to do something specific such as pronounce words or see or walk. A **handicap** is a disadvantage in certain situations. Some disabilities lead to handicaps, but not in all contexts. For example, being blind (a visual disability) is a handicap if you want to drive a car, but not when you are composing music or talking on the telephone. Stephen Hawking, the greatest living physicist, has Lou Gehrig's disease and no longer can walk or talk. He once said that he is lucky that he became a theoretical physicist "because it is all in the mind. So my disability has not been a serious handicap." It is important that we do not create *handicaps* for people by the way we react to their *disabilities*. Some educators have suggested that we drop the word *handicap* altogether because the source of the word is demeaning. *Handicap* came from the phrase "cap-in-hand," used to describe people with disabilities who once were forced to beg just to survive (Hardman, Drew, & Egan, 2005).

We can think of all human characteristics as being on a continuum, for instance, from very acute hearing to complete deafness. We all fall somewhere on that continuum, and our position on the continuum changes over our lifetimes. As we age, for example, there are likely to be changes in hearing, vision, and even some aspects of intellectual ability, as you will see later in this chapter.

Disability The inability to do something specific such as walk or hear.

Handicap A disadvantage in a particular situation, sometimes caused by a disability.

When speaking about a person with a disability, it is important that we avoid the language of pity, as in "confined to a wheelchair" or "victim of AIDS." Wheelchairs are not confining. They allow people to get around. Using "victim of" or "suffering with" makes the person seem powerless. On their resources Web site, the United Spinal Association offers a free pdf booklet with many ideas about disability. Every teacher should read it. See Figure 4.1 for an example.

Another way of showing respect to individuals with disabilities is to use "person-first" language, discussed next.

PERSON-FIRST LANGUAGE. Because everyone has a range of abilities, it makes sense to avoid labels such as "emotionally disturbed student" or "at-risk student." Describing a complex person with one or two words implies that the condition labeled is the most important aspect of the person. Actually, the individual has many characteristics and abilities, and to focus on the disability is to misrepresent the individual. An alternative is "person-first" language or speaking of "students with a behavior disorder" or "students placed at risk." Here, the emphasis is on the students first.

Students with learning disabilities	NOT	Learning disabled students
Students receiving special education	NOT	Special education students
A person with epilepsy	NOT	An epileptic
A child with a physical disability	NOT	A crippled child
Children diagnosed with autism	NOT	Autistic children or autistics

POSSIBLE BIASES IN THE APPLICATION OF LABELS. Even though there are many good tests and careful procedures for identifying students with disabilities and using labels properly, racial and ethnic minority students are overrepresented in the disability categories and underrepresented in gifted programs. For example, based on their actual

FIGURE 4.1

DISABILITY ETIQUETTE

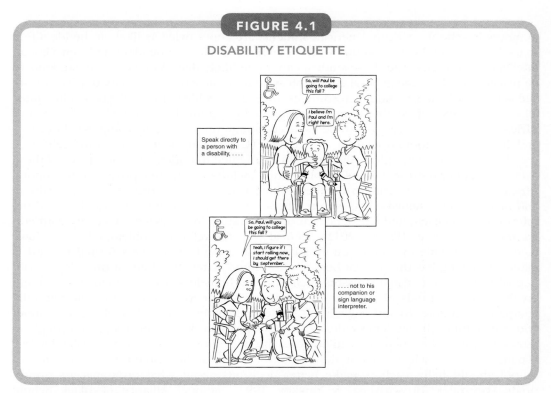

Source: Reprinted from "Disability Etiquette" © Permission granted by United Spinal Association. Go to www.unitedspinal.org for a free download of the full publication. Illustrations by Yvette Silver.

LABELS MAY PROMOTE FALSE STEREOTYPES When labels take precedence over individual characteristics, the labels themselves constitute a handicap. Stereotypes about people who use wheelchairs might interfere with recognition of this young girl's other characteristics and her individuality.

numbers in schools, African American students are about twice as likely to be identified as having a mental health condition and three times as likely to be identified as having an intellectual disability. And these students are more likely than White or Asian students to be placed outside of the general education system for most of their school day. The opposite is true for Latina/o and Asian students; they are less likely to be diagnosed in almost all categories except hearing impairments. Gifted programs have only about 8% each of African American and Latina/o students, even though these students comprise about 13% and 20% of the school population, respectively (U.S. Department of Education, 2007).

For almost four decades, educators have struggled to understand the causes of these over- and under-representations. Explanations include the higher poverty rates among African American and Latina/o families, which lead to poorer prenatal care, nutrition, and health care; systematic biases in teachers' attitudes, curriculum, instruction, and the referral process itself; and teachers' lack of preparation for working effectively with ethnic minority students (Friend, 2011). To deal with the referral problem, educators have recommended gathering more information about a student before a formal referral is made. How long has the student been in the United States? What about proficiency with English? Are there unusual stressors such as being homeless? Does the curriculum build on the student's funds of cultural knowledge (Chapter 5)? Is the classroom culturally compatible (Chapter 6) and engaging (Chapter 12)? Is the teacher knowledgeable about and respectful of the student's culture? Can the student's abilities be assessed through alternative approaches such as creativity tests and portfolios or performances (Chapter 15)? Having more knowledge about the student and his or her circumstances outside of school should help teachers make better decisions about what programs are appropriate (Gonzales, Brusca-Vega, & Yawkey, 1997; National Alliance of Black School Educators, 2002).

Intelligence is widely used in placement decisions and as a label in life in general. Let us begin with a basic question...

What Does Intelligence Mean?

STOP & THINK Who was the most intelligent person in your high school? Write down a name and the first 4 or 5 words that come to mind when you see that person in your mind's eye. What made you pick this individual? •

The idea that people vary in what we call **intelligence** has been with us for a long time. Plato discussed similar variations over 2,000 years ago. Most early theories about the nature of intelligence involved one or more of the following three themes: (1) the capacity to learn; (2) the total knowledge a person has acquired; and (3) the ability to adapt successfully to new situations and to the environment in general. A recent definition captures these elements and stresses higher-order thinking: "the ability to reason deductively or inductively, think abstractly, use analogies, synthesize information, and apply it to new domains" (Kanazawa, 2010, p. 281).

INTELLIGENCE: ONE ABILITY OR MANY? There are moderate to high correlations among scores on *all* mental tests. In fact, this consistent finding "is arguably both the best established and the most striking phenomenon in the psychological study of intelligence" (van der Mass et al., 2006, p. 855). Because of these persistent intercorrelations, some psychologists believe intelligence is a basic ability that affects performance on all cognitively oriented tasks, from solving mathematical problems to analyzing poetry to taking history essay examinations. What could explain these results? Charles Spearman (1927) suggested mental energy, which he called *g,* was used to perform any mental test. Spearman added that each test also requires some specific abilities as well—so ability to do any mental task is based on *g* + task-specific abilities. Today, psychologists generally agree that we can mathematically compute a common factor (*g*) across cognitive tests, but this computed factor is simply an indication or measure of **general intelligence**—it is not general intelligence itself (Kanazawa, 2010). Just having an overall mathematical indicator of intelligence isn't much help in understanding specific human abilities, so the notion of *g* does not have much explanatory power (Blair, 2006).

Raymond Cattell and John Horn's theory of fluid and crystallized intelligence is more helpful in providing explanations (Cattell, 1963; Horn, 1998; Kanazawa, 2010). **Fluid intelligence** is the mental efficiency and reasoning ability included in Kanazawa's definition of intelligence, quoted above. The neurophysiological underpinnings of fluid intelligence may be related to changes in brain volume, myelinization (coating of neural fibers that makes processing faster), the density of dopamine receptors, or processing abilities in the prefrontal lobe of the brain such as selective attention and especially *working memory* (Waterhouse, 2006), an aspect of brain functioning we will explore in Chapter 8. This aspect of intelligence increases until late adolescence (about age 22) because it is grounded in brain development, and then declines gradually with age. Fluid intelligence is sensitive to injuries and diseases.

In contrast, **crystallized intelligence** is the ability to apply the problem-solving methods appropriate in your cultural context—the "application to new domains" part of Kanazawa's definition of intelligence. Crystallized intelligence can increase throughout the life span because it includes learned skills and knowledge such as reading, facts, and how to hail a cab, make a quilt, or design a unit on symbolism in poetry. By investing fluid intelligence in solving problems, we develop our crystallized intelligence, but many tasks in life such as mathematical reasoning draw on both fluid and crystallized intelligence (Ferrer & McArdle, 2004; Finkel, Reynolds, McArdle, Gatz, & Pederson, 2003; Hunt, 2000).

The most widely accepted psychometric view today is that intelligence, like self-concept, has many facets and is a hierarchy of abilities, with general ability at the top and

Intelligence Ability or abilities to acquire and use knowledge for solving problems and adapting to the world.

General intelligence (*g*) A general factor in cognitive ability that is related in varying degrees to performance on all mental tests.

Fluid intelligence Mental efficiency, nonverbal abilities grounded in brain development.

Crystallized intelligence Ability to apply culturally approved problem-solving methods.

more specific abilities at lower levels of the hierarchy (Carroll, 1997; Sternberg, 2000). John Carroll (1997) identifies one general ability, a few broad abilities (such as fluid and crystallized abilities, learning and memory, visual and auditory perception, and processing speed), and at least 70 specific abilities such as language development, memory span, and simple reaction time. General ability may be related to the maturation and functioning of the frontal lobe of the brain, while specific abilities may be connected to other parts of the brain (Byrnes & Fox, 1998).

Multiple Intelligences

Connect and Extend to PRAXIS II™

Multiple Intelligences (I, B1)
Many teachers erroneously assume that they must address each of the 8 intelligences in each lesson they design. What are some of the realistic implications of the theory for classroom instruction?

While Howard Gardner was a developmental psychologist doing research with two very different groups—artistically gifted students at Harvard's Project Zero and patients with brain injuries at Boston's Veterans Administration Medical Center—he started thinking about a new theory of intelligence. Time and time again at the VA Medical Center, Gardner observed brain-injured patients who were lost spatially, but could do all kinds of verbal tasks, and other patients who had the opposite set of abilities and problems. He also worked with young children at Project Zero who could draw expertly but not craft a good sentence, and vice versa. Gardner concluded that there are several separate mental abilities, and developed his now-famous **theory of multiple intelligences** that describes at least eight separate intelligences (1983, 2003, 2009).

WHAT ARE THESE INTELLIGENCES? The eight intelligences in multiple intelligence (MI) theory are linguistic (verbal), musical, spatial, logical-mathematical, bodily-kinesthetic (movement), interpersonal (understanding others), intrapersonal (understanding self), and naturalist (observing and understanding natural and human-made patterns and systems). Gardner stresses that there may be more kinds of intelligence—eight is not a magic number. Recently, he has speculated that there may be a spiritual intelligence and an existential intelligence—the abilities to contemplate big questions about the meaning of life (Gardner, 2009). As Gardner witnessed firsthand in his early research with veterans and students, individuals may excel in one of these eight areas, but have no remarkable abilities, or may even have problems, in the other seven. Table 4.1 summarizes these eight intelligences.

Gardner believes that intelligence has a biological base. An intelligence is a "biopsychological potential to process information in certain ways in order to solve problems or create products that are valued in at least one culture or community" (Gardner, 2009, p. 5). Varying cultures and eras of history place different values on the eight intelligences. A naturalist intelligence is critical in farming cultures, whereas verbal and mathematical intelligences are important in technological cultures. In fact, Gardner suggests what industrialized cultures usually label as "intelligence" is just a combination of linguistic and logical mathematical skills, especially those taught in modern, secular schools (2009).

CRITICS OF MI THEORY. Gardner's MI theory has not received wide acceptance in the scientific community, even though many educators have embraced it. Lynn Waterhouse (2006) concluded that there have been no published studies that validate multiple intelligences theory. The eight intelligences are not independent; there are correlations among the abilities. In fact, logical-mathematical and spatial intelligences are highly correlated (Sattler, 2001). So, these "separate abilities" may not be so separate after all. Evidence linking musical and spatial abilities has prompted Gardner to consider that there may be connections among the intelligences (Gardner, 1998). In addition, some critics suggest that several intelligences are really talents (bodily-kinesthetic skill, musical ability) or personality traits (interpersonal ability). Other "intelligences" are not new at all. Many researchers have identified verbal and spatial abilities as elements of intelligence. Daniel Willingham (2004) has been even more blunt. "In the end, Gardner's theory is not that helpful. For scientists the theory is almost certainly incorrect. For educators, the daring applications forwarded by others in Gardner's name (and of which he disapproves) are unlikely to help students" (p. 24).

Theory of multiple intelligences In Gardner's theory of intelligence, a person's eight separate abilities: logical-mathematical, linguistic, musical, spatial, bodily-kinesthetic, interpersonal, intrapersonal, and naturalist.

TABLE 4.1 • **Eight Intelligences**

Howard Gardner's theory of multiple intelligences suggests that there are eight kinds of human abilities. An individual might have strengths or weaknesses in one or several areas.

INTELLIGENCE	END STATES	CORE COMPONENTS
Logical-mathematical	Scientist, Mathematician	Sensitivity to, and capacity to discern, logical or numerical patterns; ability to handle long chains of reasoning.
Linguistic	Poet, Journalist	Sensitivity to the sounds, rhythms, and meanings of words; sensitivity to the different functions of language.
Musical	Composer, Violinist	Abilities to produce and appreciate rhythm, pitch, and timbre; appreciation of the forms of musical expressiveness.
Spatial	Navigator, Sculptor	Capacities to perceive the visual-spatial world accurately and to perform transformations on one's initial perceptions.
Bodily-kinesthetic	Dancer, Athlete	Abilities to control one's body movements and to handle objects skillfully.
Interpersonal	Therapist, Salesman	Capacities to discern and respond appropriately to the moods, temperaments, motivations, and desires of other people.
Intrapersonal	Person with detailed, accurate self-knowledge	Access to one's own feelings and the ability to discriminate among them and draw on them to guide behavior; knowledge of one's own strengths, weaknesses, desires, and intelligence.
Naturalist	Botanist, Farmer, Hunter	Abilities to recognize plants and animals, to make distinctions in the natural world, to understand systems and define categories (perhaps even categories of intelligence).

Source: From "Multiple Intelligences Go to School," by H. Gardner and T. Hatch, Educational Researcher, 18(8), p. 6. Copyright © 1989 by the American Educational Research Association. Reproduced by permission of the publisher. Also Educational Information and Transformation, edited by J. Kane. Published by Prentice Hall. Copyright © 2002 by Prentice Hall. Reprinted by permission of Pearson Education, Inc., Upper Saddle River, NJ.

So there is not yet strong research evidence that adopting a multiple intelligences approach will enhance learning. In one of the few carefully designed evaluations, Callahan, Tomlinson, and Plucker (1997) found no significant gains in either achievement or self-concept for students who participated in START, a multiple intelligences approach to identifying and promoting talent in students who were at risk of failing.

GARDNER RESPONDS. In response to these criticisms, defenders of MI theory say that the critics have a very narrow view of intelligence and research about intelligence. Gardner based his theory on a set of criteria that integrated a wide range of research in psychology:

• Potential isolation by brain damage
• The existence of prodigies and other exceptional individuals who are experts in some areas and average or below in others
• An identifiable core operation or set of operations
• A distinctive developmental trajectory, culminating in expert performances

- An evolutionary history and evolutionary plausibility
- Support from experimental psychological tasks
- Evidence from psychometric findings
- Susceptibility to encoding in a symbol system (Gardner, 2009, p. 5)

Gardner's supporters believe newer research methods that look at dynamic models and study intelligence in cultural contexts will support MI theory (Chen, 2004; Gardner & Moran, 2006). In addition, Gardner (2003, 2009) also has responded to critics by identifying a number of myths, misconceptions, and misuses related to multiple intelligences theory and schooling. For example, he stresses that an intelligence is not the same as a sensory system—there is no "auditory intelligence" or "visual intelligence." Intelligences are not the same as learning styles. (Gardner doesn't believe that people actually have consistent learning styles.) Another misconception is that multiple intelligences theory disproves the idea of general intelligence. Gardner does not deny the existence of a general ability, but he does question how useful general intelligence is as an explanation for human achievements. Stay tuned for more developments.

MULTIPLE INTELLIGENCES GO TO SCHOOL. First let's consider a few misuses of MI theory in schools. Gardner particularly deplored an educational project in Australia that proclaimed different ethnic groups had certain specific intelligences but lacked others. Gardner went on television in Australia to call this program what it really was— "pseudoscience" and "veiled racism" (2009, p. 7). The project was cancelled. Another misuse is that some teachers embrace a simplistic version of Gardner's theory. They include every "intelligence" in every lesson, no matter how inappropriate.

A better way to use the theory is to focus on six Entry Points—narrative, logical-quantitative, aesthetic, experiential, interpersonal, and existential/foundational—in designing a curriculum (Gardner, 1991). For example, to teach about evolution, teachers might use the Entry Points as follows (Kornhaber, Fierros, & Veenema, 2004):

Narrative: Provide rich stories about Darwin's voyage to the Galapagos Islands or traditional folktales about the different plants and animals.

Logical-quantitative: Examine Darwin's attempts to map the distributions of the species or pose logical problems about what would happen to the ecosystem if one species disappeared.

Aesthetic: Examine Darwin's drawings of the species he studied on the Galapagos Islands.

Experiential: Do laboratory activities such as breeding fruit flies or completing virtual simulations of evolutionary processes.

Interpersonal: Form research teams or hold debates.

Existential/foundational: Consider questions about why species die out or what the purpose is for variation in species.

Multiple Intelligences: Lessons for Teachers

After 20 years of work on his multiple intelligences theory, Gardner believes two lessons are most important for teachers (2009). First, teachers should take the individual differences among students seriously and differentiate their instruction to connect with each student. Much of this book will help you do just that. Second, any discipline, skill, or concept should be taught in several appropriate ways (but not eight ways every time). Anything worth knowing has different representations and multiple connections to various ways of thinking. And understandings can be expressed in words, images, movements, tables, charts, numbers, equations, poetry, and on and on. These two big ideas should *guide* educational interventions, but Gardner stresses that his theory is not itself an educational intervention. The MI theory expands our thinking about abilities and avenues for teaching, but learning is still hard work, even if there are multiple paths to knowledge.

Intelligence as a Process

As you can see, the theories of Spearman, Cattell and Horn, Carroll, and Gardner tend to describe how individuals differ in the *content* of intelligence—different abilities. Work in cognitive psychology has emphasized instead the *information processing* that is common to all people. How do humans gather and use information to solve problems and behave intelligently? New views of intelligence are emerging from this work. The debates in the 2006 issue of *Behavioral and Brain Sciences* emphasized working memory capacity, the abilities to focus attention and inhibit impulses, and emotional self-regulation as aspects of fluid cognitive abilities.

Robert Sternberg's (1985, 2004; Stemler, Sternberg, Grigorenko, Jarvin, & Sharpes, 2009) **triarchic theory of successful intelligence** is a cognitive process approach to understanding intelligence. Sternberg uses the term *successful intelligence* to stress that intelligence is more than what is tested by mental abilities measures: Intelligence is about life success based on your own definition of success in your cultural context.

WHAT'S SMART? There has been considerable controversy over the meaning of intelligence, whether there is more than one way to be "smart," and how we should measure intelligence.

Sternberg believes the processes involved in intelligence are universal for humans. These processes are defined in terms of components—elementary information processes that are classified by the functions they serve and by how general they are. There are at least three different functions served. The first function—higher-order planning, strategy selection, and monitoring—is performed by *metacomponents* (sometimes called *executive processes*—see Chapter 8). A second function—implementing the strategies selected—is handled by *performance components*, such as taking notes to focus attention in class. The third function—gaining new knowledge—is performed by *knowledge-acquisition components*, such as separating relevant from irrelevant information as you try to understand a new concept. Some processes are specific; that is, they are necessary for only one kind of task, such as solving analogies. Other processes, such as monitoring progress and switching strategies, are very general and may be necessary in almost every cognitive task. This may help to explain the persistent correlations among all types of mental tests. People who are effective in selecting good problem-solving strategies, monitoring progress, and moving to a new approach when the first one fails are more likely to be successful on all types of tests.

Applying *metacomponents*, *performance components*, and *knowledge-acquisition components* allows individuals to solve problems in different situations and to develop three kinds of successful intelligence: analytic, creative, and practical. *Analytic intelligence* involves applying these components to situations with relatively familiar problems. *Creative intelligence* is necessary to cope successfully with new experiences in two ways: (1) using **insight**, or the ability to deal effectively with novel situations and find new solutions, and (2) using **automaticity**, the ability to become efficient and automatic in thinking and problem solving—the ability to quickly make the new solutions part of your cognitive tool kit, so to speak.

The third part of the triarchic theory, *practical intelligence*, highlights the importance of choosing an environment in which you can succeed, adapting to that environment, and reshaping it if necessary. People who are successful often seek situations in which their abilities will be valued, then work hard to capitalize on those abilities and compensate for any weaknesses. Thus, intelligence in this third sense involves practical matters

Triarchic theory of successful intelligence A three-part description of the mental abilities (thinking processes, coping with new experiences, and adapting to context) that lead to more or less intelligent behavior.

Insight The ability to deal effectively with novel situations.

Automaticity The result of learning to perform a behavior or thinking process so thoroughly that the performance is automatic and does not require effort.

TAKING AN INDIVIDUAL IQ TEST. This girl is completing a task like one she would encounter on the WISC-IV intelligence test. This assessment is conducted by a highly trained adult and takes an hour or two to complete, depending on how many subtests are given. Individual intelligence tests are more accurate and reliable than group tests.

such as career choice or social skills. In a field study in Voronezh, Russia, Elena Grigorenko and Robert Sternberg (2001) found that adults with higher practical and analytical intelligence coped better both mentally and physically with the stresses caused by rapid changes in that part of the world.

In recent years, Sternberg has added the concept of "wisdom" to his explanation of successful intelligence to create the *WICS theory* (Wisdom, Intelligence, Creativity Synthesized). According to WICS theory, the goal of education is to help citizens use: "(a) creativity to generate new ideas and problems as well as possible solutions to the problems, (b) analytical intelligence to evaluate the quality of these solutions, (c) practical intelligence to implement decisions and persuade others of their value, and (d) wisdom to ensure that these decisions help achieve a common good over the long and short terms" (Grigorenko et al., 2009, p. 965).

Even though there are many theories of intelligence, teachers, students, and parents are most familiar with intelligence as a number or score on an IQ test.

Measuring Intelligence

STOP & THINK How are an inch and a mile alike? What does *obstreperous* mean? Repeat these numbers backwards: 8 5 7 3 0 2 1 9 7. In what two ways is a lamp better than a candle? ●

These items, taken from Sattler (2001, p. 222), are similar to the verbal questions from a common individual intelligence test for children. Another part of the test asks the child to copy a design using blocks, find the missing part of a picture, or select from several pictures the two that go together. Even though psychologists do not agree about what intelligence is, they do agree that intelligence, as measured by standardized tests, is related to learning in school. Why is this so? It has to do in part with the way intelligence tests were first developed.

BINET'S DILEMMA. In 1904, Alfred Binet was confronted with the following problem by the minister of public instruction in Paris: How can students who will need special instruction and extra help be identified early in their school careers, before they fail in regular classes? Binet was also a political activist and very concerned about the rights of children. He believed that having an objective measure of learning ability could protect students living in poverty who might be forced to leave school because they were the victims of discrimination and assumed to be slow learners.

Binet and his collaborator Theodore Simon wanted to measure not merely school achievement, but also the intellectual skills students needed to do well in school. After trying many different tests and eliminating items that did not discriminate between successful and unsuccessful students, Binet and Simon finally identified 58 tests, several for each age group from 3 to 13. Binet's tests allowed the examiner to determine a **mental age** for a child. A child who succeeded on the items passed by most 6-year-olds, for example, was considered to have a mental age of 6, whether the child was actually 4, 5, 6, 7, or 8 years old.

Mental age In intelligence testing, a performance that represents average abilities for that age group.

GUIDELINES

Interpreting IQ Scores

Check to see if the score is based on an individual or a group test. Be wary of group test scores.
Examples
1. Individual tests include the Wechsler Scales (WPPSI–III, WISC-IV, WAIS-IV), the Stanford-Binet, the McCarthy Scales of Children's Abilities, the Woodcock-Johnson Psycho-Educational Battery, the Naglieri Nonverbal Ability Test—Individual, and the Kaufman Assessment Battery for Children.
2. Group tests include the Otis-Lennon School Abilities Tests, Slosson Intelligence Test, Raven Progressive Matrices, Naglieri Nonverbal Ability Test—Multiform, Differential Abilities Scales, and Wide Range Intelligence Test.

Remember that IQ tests are only estimates of general aptitude for learning.
Examples
1. Ignore small differences in scores among students.
2. Bear in mind that even an individual student's scores may change over time for many reasons, including measurement error.
3. Be aware that a total score is usually an average of scores on several kinds of questions. A score in the middle or average range may mean that the student performed at the average on every kind of question or that the student did quite well in some areas (for example, on verbal tasks) and rather poorly in other areas (for example, on quantitative tasks).

Remember that IQ scores reflect a student's past experiences and learning.
Examples
1. Consider these scores to be predictors of school abilities, not measures of innate intellectual abilities.
2. If a student is doing well in your class, do not change your opinion or lower your expectations just because one score seems low.
3. Be wary of IQ scores for minority students and for students whose first language was not English. Even scores on "culture-free" tests are lower for students placed at risk.
4. Remember that both adaptive skills and scores on IQ tests are used to determine intellectual abilities and disabilities.

For more about interpreting IQ scores, see
http://www.wilderdom.com/personality/L2-1UnderstandingIQ.html

---

The concept of **intelligence quotient**, or **IQ**, was added after Binet's test was brought to the United States and revised at Stanford University to give us the Stanford-Binet test. An IQ score was computed by comparing the mental-age score to the person's actual chronological age. The formula was

$$\text{Intelligence Quotient} = \text{Mental Age/Chronological Age} \times 100$$

The early Stanford-Binet test has been revised five times, most recently in 2003 (Roid, 2003). The practice of computing a mental age has proved to be problematic because IQ scores calculated on the basis of mental age do not have the same meaning as children get older. To cope with this problem, the concept of deviation IQ was introduced. The **deviation IQ** score is a number that tells exactly how much above or below the average a person scored on the test, compared to others in the same age group, as you will see in the next section.

WHAT DOES AN IQ SCORE MEAN? Most intelligence tests are designed so that they have certain statistical characteristics. For example, the average score is 100; 50% of the people from the general population who take the tests will score 100 or below, and 50% will score above 100. About 68% of the general population will earn IQ scores between 85 and 115. Only about 16% will receive scores below 85, and only 16% will score above 115. Note, however, that these figures hold true for White, native-born Americans whose first language is Standard English. Whether IQ tests should even be used with ethnic minority-group students is hotly debated.

GROUP VERSUS INDIVIDUAL IQ TESTS. The Stanford-Binet is an individual intelligence test. It has to be administered to one student at a time by a trained psychologist and it takes about two hours. Most of the questions are asked orally and do not require reading or writing. A student usually pays closer attention and is more motivated to do well when working directly with an adult. The *Guidelines* will help you interpret IQ scores realistically.

Connect and Extend to PRAXIS II™

Intelligence Testing (II, C1,4)
The public often misunderstands intelligence testing. Be prepared to respond to questions about the appropriate uses of intelligence tests. What are some inappropriate uses of these tests?

Intelligence quotient (IQ) Score comparing mental and chronological ages.

Deviation IQ Score based on a statistical comparison of an individual's performance with the average performance of others in that age group.

Psychologists also have developed group tests that can be given to whole classes or schools. Compared to an individual test, a group test is much less likely to yield an accurate picture of any one person's abilities. When students take tests in a group, they may do poorly because they do not understand the instructions, because they have trouble reading, because their pencils break or they lose their place on the answer sheet, because other students distract them, or because the answer format confuses them (Sattler, 2001). As a teacher, you should be very wary of IQ scores based on group tests.

THE FLYNN EFFECT: ARE WE GETTING SMARTER? Ever since IQ tests were introduced in the early 1900s, scores in 20 different industrialized countries and in some more traditional cultures have been rising (Daley, Whaley, Sigman, Espinosa, & Neumann, 2003). In fact, in a generation, the average score goes up about 18 points on standardized IQ tests—maybe you really are smarter than your parents! This is called the **Flynn effect** after James Flynn, a political scientist who documented the phenomenon. Some explanations include better nutrition and medical care for children and parents, increasing complexity in the environment that stimulates thinking, smaller families who give more attention to their children, increased literacy of parents, more and better schooling, and better preparation for taking tests. One result of the Flynn effect is that the norms used to determine scores (you will read more about norms in Chapter 15) have to be continually revised. In other words, to keep a score of 100 as the average, the test questions have to be made more difficult. This increasing difficulty has implications for any program that uses IQ scores as part of its entrance requirements. For example, some "average" students of the previous generation might be identified today as having intellectual disabilities because the test questions are harder (Kanaya, Scullin, & Ceci, 2003).

INTELLIGENCE AND ACHIEVEMENT. Scoring higher on IQ tests is related to school achievement for children in all ethnic groups. But standard IQ tests measure only analytic IQ, not practical or creative IQs. Elena Grigorenko and her colleagues (2009) used the usual standardized test scores and GPA to predict middle-school students' achievement in high school, but also included tests of students' abilities to manage their own learning and motivation, along with measures of practical and creative intelligence. Using this broader picture of students' abilities, the researchers were able to make better predictions, not only of achievement in high school but also of the rate of growth. So IQ test scores can provide some prediction of achievement, but if measures of self-regulated learning skills, practical intelligence, and creativity are included, more accurate predictions are likely.

But what about life after school? Do people who score high on IQ tests achieve more in life? Here the answer is less clear because life success and education are intertwined. High school graduates earn over $200,000 more than non-graduates in their lifetime; college graduates earn over $1,100,000 more; grads with doctoral degrees earn $2,400,000 more; and graduates with professional degrees (physicians, lawyers, etc.), over $3,400,000 more in their lifetime (Cheeseman Day & Burger, 2002). People with higher intelligence test scores tend to complete more years of school and to have higher-status jobs. However, when the number of years of education is held constant, the correlation decreases between IQ scores, income, and success in later life. Just as Grigorenko et al. (2009) found, other factors such as self-regulation, motivation, social skills, and luck may make the difference in life achievement (Goleman, 1995; Neisser et al., 1996.

Gender Differences in Intelligence

From infancy through the preschool years, most studies find few differences between boys and girls in overall mental and motor development or in specific abilities. During the school years and beyond, psychologists find no differences in general intelligence on the standard measures—these tests have been designed and standardized to minimize sex differences. However, scores on some tests of specific abilities show sex differences. Also, the scores of males tend to be slightly more variable in general, so there are more males than

Flynn effect Because of better health, smaller families, increased complexity in the environment, and more and better schooling, IQ test scores are steadily rising.

females with very high and very low scores on tests (Halpern et al., 2007; Lindberg, Hyde, Peterson, & Linn, 2010). In addition, there are more boys diagnosed with learning disabilities, ADHD, and autism. Diane Halpern and her colleagues (2007) summarize the research:

> By the end of grade school and beyond, females perform better on assessments of verbal abilities when assessments are heavily weighted with writing and the language-usage items cover topics with which females are familiar; sex differences favoring females are much larger in these conditions than when assessments of verbal abilities do not include writing. In contrast, males excel on certain visuospatial-ability measures. (p. 40)

There is a caution, however. In most studies of sex differences, race and ethnicity are not taken into account. For example, when ethnic groups are studied separately, there may be very small differences in mathematics performance favoring White males in high school and college, but slight differences favoring females among ethnic minority students. Also, there seem to be small differences in complex problem-solving skills favoring boys in high school, perhaps because problem solving is taught more in physics classes than in math, and boys are more likely than girls to take physics—another reason to encourage all students to get a good background in science (Lindberg et al., 2010).

Several recent international *meta-analyses* (analyses that combine data from many different studies on the same topic) have found few differences in mathematics achievement for boys and girls. For example, Sara Lindberg and her colleagues analyzed data from 242 studies that included 1.3 million elementary through high school students. Overall, they found that in the United States and some other nations, girls' and boys' performance in mathematics is comparable, but there are some differences by nations—girls scored higher than boys in several countries such as Russia, Bahrain, and Mexico, and boys' scores were higher in other countries such as Switzerland, the Netherlands, and African nations (Else-Quest, Hyde, & Linn, 2010; Lindberg et al., 2010). Also, the International Comparisons in Fourth-Grade Reading Literacy (Mullis, Martin, Gonzalez, & Kennedy, 2003) revealed that in 34 countries, 4th grade boys scored below girls in reading literacy. Finally, girls in general tend to get higher grades than boys in mathematics classes.

Males on average are better on tests that require mental rotation of a figure in space, prediction of the trajectories of moving objects, and navigating. Some researchers argue that evolution has favored these skills in males (Buss, 1995; Geary, 1995, 1999), but others relate these skills to males' more active play styles, their greater experience with video games, and their participation in athletics (Else-Quest et al., 2010; Stumpf, 1995). Some educational psychologists believe that spatial skills are neglected in school curriculums and that even a small amount of instruction can make a big difference for students (Uttal, Hand, & Newcombe, 2009). The cross-cultural comparisons suggest that much of the difference in mathematics scores comes from learning, not biology. And studies showing that adults rated a math paper attributed to "John T. McKay" a full point higher on a 5-point scale than the same paper attributed to "Joan T. McKay" suggests that discrimination and stereotyped expectations play a role as well (Angier & Chang, 2005).

Lindberg and her colleagues sum it up well: "Overall, it is clear that in the United States and some other nations, girls have reached parity with boys in mathematics performance. It is crucial that this information be made widely known to counteract stereotypes about female math inferiority held by gatekeepers such as parents and teachers and by students themselves" (2010, p. 1134). I agree that combating these stereotypes is critical. Melanie Steffens and her colleagues (2010) in Germany found that by age 9, girls already had developed implicit (out of awareness) math-gender stereotypes; the girls associated men with mathematics. These implicit beliefs grew stronger into adolescence, predicted girls' achievement in math, and affected their decisions to take elective math courses.

HEREDITY OR ENVIRONMENT?   Nowhere has the nature-versus-nurture debate raged so hard as in the area of intelligence. Should intelligence be seen as a potential, limited by our genetic makeup? Or does intelligence simply refer to an individual's current level of intellectual functioning, as influenced by experience and education?

Beware of either/or comparisons: It is impossible to separate intelligence "in the genes" from intelligence "due to experience." Today, most psychologists believe that differences in intelligence are the result of both heredity and environment, probably in about equal proportions for children (Petrill & Wilkerson, 2000). And environmental influences include everything from the health of a child's mother during pregnancy to the amount of lead in the child's home to the quality of teaching a child receives. For example, Japanese and Chinese students know much more mathematics than American students, but their intelligence test scores are quite similar. This superiority in math probably is related to differences in the way mathematics is taught and studied in the three countries and to the self-motivation skills of many Asian students (Baron, 1998; Stevenson & Stigler, 1992).

BEING SMART ABOUT IQ TESTS. We saw that intelligence tests originally were developed, in part, to protect the rights of children from poorer families who might be denied an education on the false grounds that they weren't able to learn. We also saw that intelligence tests predict school success equally accurately for students of different races and income levels. Even so, these tests can never be free of cultural content, so they always will have some biases built in. Keep this in mind when you see your students' scores on any test. Finally, remember that the results of every assessment for every student should be used to support that student's learning and development and to identify effective practices, not to deny the student access to resources or appropriate teaching. For all adults caring for children—parents, teachers, administrators, counselors, medical workers—it is especially important to realize that cognitive skills, like any other skills, are always improvable. *Intelligence is a current state of affairs, affected by past experiences and open to future changes.*

Now that you have a sense of what intelligence means, let's consider another kind of individual difference that often is misunderstood and misused in education—learning styles.

LEARNING AND THINKING STYLES

For many years, researchers have examined individual differences in "styles"—cognitive styles, learning styles, problem-solving styles, thinking styles, decision-making styles . . . the list goes on. Li-fang Zhang and Robert Sternberg (2005) organize the work on individual styles into three traditions. *Cognitive-centered* styles assess the ways people process information, for example, by being reflective or impulsive in responding (Kagan, 1976). *Personality-centered* styles assess more stable personality traits such as being extroverted versus being introverted or relying on thinking versus feeling (Myers & McCaulley, 1988). *Activity-centered* styles assess a combination of cognition and personality traits that affect how people approach activities, so these styles may be of special interest to teachers.

One theme in activity-centered approaches is the differences between surface and deep approaches to processing information in learning situations (Snow, Corno, & Jackson, 1996). Students who take a surface-processing approach focus on memorizing the learning materials, not understanding them. These students tend to be motivated by rewards, grades, external standards, and the desire to be evaluated positively by others. Individuals who have a deep-processing approach see the learning activities as a means for understanding some underlying concepts or meanings. They tend to learn for the sake of learning and are less concerned about how their performance is evaluated. Of course, the situation can encourage deep or surface processing, but there is evidence that individuals have tendencies to approach learning situations in characteristic ways (Biggs, 2001; Coffield, Moseley, Hall, & Ecclestone, 2004; Tait & Entwistle, 1998).

Learning Styles/Preferences

Here is another "style" term. You may have heard about **learning styles** or used the phrase yourself. Learning style usually is defined as the way a person approaches learning and studying. But beware—some conceptions of learning styles have little research support; others are based on solid studies. First—the cautions.

Connect and Extend to PRAXIS II™

Learning/Cognitive Styles (I, B1)
Familiarize yourself with the major issues involved with learning and cognitive styles, and understand their implications for classroom practice.

Learning styles Characteristic approaches to learning and studying.

CAUTIONS ABOUT LEARNING STYLES. Since the late 1970s, a great deal has been written about differences in students' "learning styles" (Dunn & Dunn, 1978, 1987; Dunn & Griggs, 2003; Gregorc, 1982; Keefe, 1982). But I believe **learning preferences** is a more accurate label because most of the research describes preferences for particular learning environments—for example, where, when, with whom, or with what lighting, food, or music you like to study. There are a number of instruments for assessing students' learning preferences—The Learning Style Inventory (Dunn, Dunn, & Price, 1989), Learning Styles Inventory (Revised) (Kolb, 1985), and the Learning Style Profile (Keefe & Monk, 1986).

Are these useful tools? Tests of learning style have been strongly criticized (Pashler, McDaniel, Rohrer, & Bjork, 2009). In fact, in an extensive examination of learning styles instruments, researchers at the Learning Skills Research Centre in England concluded, "with regard to work by Dunn and Dunn, Gregorc, and Riding, our examination of the reliability and validity of their learning style instruments strongly suggests that they should not be used in education or business" (Coffield, et al., 2004, p. 127). Most researchers are skeptical about the value of learning preferences. "The reason researchers roll their eyes at learning styles research is the utter failure to find that assessing children's learning styles and matching to instructional methods has any effect on their learning (Stahl, 2002, p. 99). In fact, an experimental study had college students self-assess their learning style as auditory, visual, or kinesthetic and then taught the students in keeping with their professed style (Kratzig & Arbuthnott, 2006). Matching learning with teaching styles did not improve learning. When the researchers examined how people identified their own learning styles, they concluded that people's judgments represented preferences rather than superior skills in using auditory, visual, or kinesthetic modalities. If college students have trouble identifying their own learning style, think about 4th or 9th graders!

In summary, the most recent review of learning styles research ends with these words: "The contrast between the enormous popularity of the learning-styles approach within education and the lack of credible evidence for its utility is, in our opinion, striking and disturbing. If classification of students' learning styles has practical utility, it remains to be demonstrated" (Pashler et al., 2009, p. 117).

So why are these ideas so popular? Part of the answer is that many thriving commercial companies are making large profits by providing advice to teachers, tutors, and managers about learning styles based on "inflated claims and sweeping conclusions which go beyond the current knowledge base" (Coffield et al., 2004, p. 127). Money talks.

THE VALUE OF CONSIDERING LEARNING STYLES. There is one learning styles distinction that has research support. Richard Mayer (e.g., Mayer & Massa, 2003) has been studying the distinction between visual and verbal learners, with a focus on learning from computer-based multimedia. Here, the assessment of learning styles is carefully done and more valid than assessments based on many of the commercial inventories. Mayer is finding that there is a visualizer–verbalizer dimension and that it has three facets: *cognitive spatial ability* (low or high), *cognitive style* (visualizer versus verbalizer), and *learning preference* (visual learner versus verbal learner), as shown in Table 4.2. So the picture is more complex than simply being a visual or a verbal learner. A student might have a preference for learning with pictures, but low spatial ability could make using pictures for learning less effective. To complicate matters even more, spatial abilities may be important for learning from static pictures, but less important for learning from animation—so the type of learning materials matters too (Hoeffler & Leutner, 2011). These differences can be reliably measured, but research has not identified the effects of teaching to these styles; certainly, presenting information in multiple modalities might be useful.

So before you try to accommodate all your students' learning styles, remember that students, especially younger ones, may not be the best judges of how they should learn. Preference for a particular style does not guarantee that using the style will be effective. Sometimes students, particularly poorer students, prefer what is easy and comfortable; real learning can be hard and uncomfortable. In some cases, students prefer to learn in a certain way because they have no alternatives; it is the only way they know how to approach the task. These students may benefit from developing new—and perhaps more

Learning preferences Preferred ways of studying and learning, such as using pictures instead of text, working with other people versus alone, learning in structured or in unstructured situations, and so on.

TABLE 4.2 • **Three Facets of the Visualizer-Verbalizer Dimension**

There are three dimensions to visual versus verbal learning: ability, style, and preference. Individuals can be high or low on any or all of these dimensions.

FACET	TYPES OF LEARNERS	DEFINITION
Cognitive Ability	High spatial ability	Good abilities to create, remember, and manipulate images and spatial information
	Low spatial ability	Poor abilities to create, remember, and manipulate images and spatial information
Cognitive Style	Visualizer	Thinks using images and visual information
	Verbalizer	Thinks using words and verbal information
Learning Preference	Visual learner	Prefers instruction using pictures
	Verbal learner	Prefers instruction using words

Source: From R. E. Mayer & L. J. Massa (2003). "Three Facets of Visual and Verbal Learners: Cognitive Ability, Cognitive Style and Learning Preference." Journal of Educational Psychology, 95(4), p. 838.

effective—ways to learn. Learning styles probably are a minor factor in learning; factors such as teaching strategies and social connections in classrooms likely play much larger roles (Kratzig & Arbuthnott, 2006).

Beyond Either/Or

Even though much of the work on matching learning styles and preferences to teaching is suspect, with unreliable measures and inflated claims, there is some value in thinking about learning styles. First, by helping students think about how they learn, you can develop thoughtful self-monitoring and self-awareness. In upcoming chapters, we will look at the value of such self-knowledge for learning and motivation. Second, looking at individual students' approaches to learning might help teachers appreciate, accept, and accommodate student differences and differentiate instruction (Coffield et al., 2004; Rosenfeld & Rosenfeld, 2004).

Schools can make available learning options, such as having quiet, private corners as well as large tables for working; comfortable cushions as well as straight chairs; brightly lighted desks along with darker areas; headphones for listening to music as well as earplugs; structured as well as open-ended assignments; and information available from visuals, podcasts, and DVDs as well as books. Will making these alterations lead to greater learning? Here the answer is not clear. Very bright students appear to need less structure and to prefer quiet, solitary learning (Torrance, 1986) and the visual–verbal distinction seems to be valid. If nothing else, some accommodation of student preferences may make your classroom more inviting and student-friendly and communicate to your students that you care about them as individuals.

Thus far, we have focused mostly on the varying abilities and styles of students. For the rest of the chapter, we will consider factors that can interfere with learning. It is important for all teachers to be aware of these issues because laws and policy changes over the past 40 years have expanded teachers' responsibilities in working with all students.

INDIVIDUAL DIFFERENCES AND THE LAW

STOP & THINK Have you ever had the experience of being the only one in a group who had trouble doing something? How would you feel if every day in school you faced the same kind of difficulty, while everyone else seemed to find the work easier than you? What kind of support and teaching would you need to keep trying? •

IDEA

Since 1975, in the United States, a series of laws, beginning with PL 94-142 (the Education of the Handicapped Act), has led to revolutionary changes in the education of children with disabilities. The legislation, now called the **Individuals with Disabilities Education Improvement Act (IDEA)** or sometimes **IDEIA**, was revised in 1990, 1997, and 2004. At the most general level, the law now requires states to provide a **free, appropriate public education (FAPE)** for all students with disabilities who participate in special education. There are no exceptions—the law requires **zero reject**. This policy also applies to students with communicable diseases such as AIDS. The expenses of meeting the special needs of these students are considered a public responsibility. Every state in the United States has a *child find* system to alert and educate the public about services for children with disabilities and to distribute useful information.

The definition of *disability* is specific in IDEA. The 13 categories of disabilities covered are listed in Table 4.3, along with the numbers of students in each category. About 13% of all students, ages 6 through 21, receive special education services under IDEA (National Center for Education Statistics, 2009). Most of these students spend some of their school day in general education classes. Table 4.3 also indicates the percentage of

TABLE 4.3 • **Students Ages 6–21 Served Under IDEA**

There are 13 categories of students served under IDEA. Below are the number of students in each category in 2008–2009 and the percentage of students in each category who are taught in general education classrooms at least 40% of their school day.

DISABILITY	NUMBER OF STUDENTS IN 2008–2009	PERCENTAGE OF THESE STUDENTS WHO SPEND AT LEAST 40% OF THE DAY IN GENERAL EDUCATION CLASSES
Specific learning disabilities	2,522,735	90
Speech/language impairments	1,121,496	92
Other health impairments (not orthopedic)	648,112	84
Intellectual disability (mental retardation)	475,713	44
Emotional disturbances	417,872	58
Autism spectrum disorders	292,638	54
Multiple disabilities	123,924	30
Developmental delay	96,853	83
Hearing impairments	70,682	71
Orthopedic impairments	62,332	68
Visual impairments	25,975	76
Traumatic brain injury	24,857	68
Deaf-blind	1,735	47
Total	5,884,924	

Source: Individual with Disabilities Education (IDEA) Act Data, Data Accountability Center, 2008. Available online https://www.ideadata.org/arc_toc10.asp#partbCC

Individuals with Disabilities Education Improvement Act (IDEA) Latest amendment of PL 94-142; guarantees a free public education to all children regardless of disability.

Free, appropriate public education (FAPE) Public funding to support appropriate educational programs for all students, no matter what their needs.

Zero reject A basic principle of IDEA specifying that no student with a disability, no matter what kind or how severe, can be denied a free public education.

ACCESS TO PUBLIC EDUCATION The Individuals with Disabilities Education Act (IDEA) guarantees a free and appropriate public education to all students regardless of disability.

these students who are taught in general education classes for at least 40% of their school day. You can see that no matter what grade or subject you teach, you will work with students with special needs.

Before we look at the different categories, let's examine the requirements in IDEA. There are three major points of interest to parents and teachers: the concept of "least restrictive placement"; the individualized education program (IEP); and the protection of the rights of both students with disabilities and their parents.

LEAST RESTRICTIVE ENVIRONMENT. IDEA requires states to develop procedures for educating each child in the **least restrictive environment**, a setting that is as close to the general education class setting as possible. Over the years, recommended approaches to achieve this have moved from **mainstreaming** (including children with special needs in a few regular education classes as convenient), to **integration** (fitting the child into existing class structures), to **inclusion** (restructuring educational settings to promote belonging for all students) (Avramidis, Bayliss, & Burden, 2000). Even though the IDEA legislation does not use the word *inclusion*, today the least restrictive environment is assumed to be inclusion as much as possible. In the end, successful inclusion probably depends on teachers being knowledgeable and well prepared, getting the support they need to teach, and being committed to inclusion. However, an emphasis on standardized testing may interfere with good teaching for included students (Friend, 2011; Idol, 2006; Kemp & Carter, 2006).

INDIVIDUALIZED EDUCATION PROGRAM. The drafters of the laws recognized that each student is unique and may need a specially tailored program to make progress. The **Individualized Education Program**, or **IEP**, is an agreement between parents and the school about the services that will be provided to the student. The IEP is written by a team that includes the student's parents or guardians, a general education teacher who works with the student, a special education teacher, a representative of the school district (often the principal), a qualified person who can interpret the student's evaluation results (often a school psychologist), and (if appropriate) the student. For students 16 and older, the team may include representatives from outside agencies who are providing services to help the student make transitions to life and support services after school. If the school and parents agree, the team could add other people who have special knowledge of the child (for example, a therapist). The program usually is updated each year. The IEP must state in writing:

Least restrictive environment (LRE) Educating each child with peers in the regular classroom to the greatest extent possible.

Mainstreaming Teaching children with disabilities in regular classes for part or all of their school day.

Integration Fitting the child with special needs into existing class structures.

Inclusion The integration of all students, including those with severe disabilities, into regular classes.

Individualized Education Program (IEP) Annually revised program for an exceptional student, detailing present achievement level, goals, and strategies, drawn up by teachers, parents, specialists, and (if possible) the student.

1. The student's present level of academic achievement and functional performance (sometimes referred to as *PLAAFP*).
2. Annual goals—measurable performance goals for the year. Students with significant needs or multiple disabilities may also have *short-term objectives* or *benchmarks* to make sure progress is continuous. The plan must tell how progress toward these goals and objectives will be measured. Parents must get progress reports at least as often as report cards are sent home for all students.
3. A statement of specific special education and related services to be provided to the student and details of when and where those services will be initiated. This statement can include descriptions of supplementary aids and assistive technologies (for example, using speech recognition software such as *Dragon*® to dictate answers or compose essays, or writing using a computer).
4. An explanation of how much of the student's program WILL NOT be in regular classroom and school settings.

GUIDELINES — FAMILY AND COMMUNITY PARTNERSHIPS

Productive Conferences

Plan and prepare for a productive conference.
Examples

1. Have a clear purpose and gather the needed information. If you want to discuss student progress, have work samples available.

2. Send home a list of questions, and ask families to bring the information to the conference. Sample questions from Friend and Bursuck (2002) are:
   - What is your child's favorite class activity?
   - Does your child have worries about any class activities? If so, what are they?
   - What are your priorities for your child's education this year?
   - What questions do you have about your child's education in my class this year?
   - How could we at school help make this the most successful year ever for your child?
   - Are there any topics you want to discuss at the conference that I might need to prepare for? If so, please let me know.
   - Would you like other individuals to participate in the conference? If so, please give me a list of their names.
   - Is there particular school information you would like me to have available? If so, please let me know.

During the conference, create and maintain an atmosphere of collaboration and respect.
Examples

1. Arrange the room for private conversation. Put a sign on your door to avoid interruptions. Meet around a conference table for better collaboration. Have tissues available.

2. Address families as "Mr." and "Ms.," not "Mom" and "Dad" or "Grandma." Use students' names.

3. Listen to families' concerns and build on their suggestions for their children.

After the conference, keep good records and follow up on decisions.
Examples

1. Make notes to yourself and keep them organized.

2. Summarize any actions or decisions in writing and send a copy to the family and any other teachers or professionals involved.

3. Communicate with families on other occasions, especially when there is good news to share.

For more information about parent conferences, see:
http://content.scholastic.com/browse/home.jsp *and search using "parent teacher conference."*

---

5. A statement about how the student will participate in state and district-wide assessments, particularly those required by the No Child Left Behind accountability procedures.

6. Beginning at age 14 and by age 16, a statement of needed transitional services to move the student toward further education or work in adult life. (Friend, 2011; Rosenberg, Westling, & McLeskey, 2011)

Figure 4.2 on the next page is an example of an individual transition planning (ITP) form for employment.

THE RIGHTS OF STUDENTS AND FAMILIES. Several stipulations in IDEA protect the rights of parents and students. Schools must have procedures for maintaining the confidentiality of student records. Testing practices must not discriminate against students from different cultural backgrounds. Parents have the right to see all records relating to the testing, placement, and teaching of their child. If they wish, parents may obtain an independent evaluation of their child. Parents may bring an advocate or representative to the meeting at which the IEP is developed. Students whose parents are unavailable must be assigned a surrogate parent to participate in the planning. Parents must receive written notice (in their native language) before any evaluation or change in placement is made. Finally, parents have the right to challenge the program developed for their child, and are protected by due process of law. Because teachers often have conferences with these families, I have provided some *Guidelines* to make the meetings more effective, but be aware that guidelines apply to meetings with all your students and their parents.

Connect and Extend to PRAXIS II™

Individual Education Programs (IEP) (I, B3)
When you sign an IEP, you are signing an important educational and legal document. Be sure that you can explain the purpose of an IEP, identify its components, and describe the kind of information that can be contained in one.

FIGURE 4.2

EXAMPLE OF A TRANSITION PLANNING FORM

This ITP was developed for a student who is moving toward work in a grocery store. The plan describes the needed services so the student can transition into supported employment.

ILLUSTRATIVE TRANSITION PLANNING FORM IN THE AREA OF EMPLOYMENT

Student: *Robert Brown*

Meeting Date: *January 20, 2003*

Graduation Date: *June, 2004*

IEP/Transition Planning Team Members: *Robert Brown (student), Mrs. Brown (parent), Jill Green (teacher), Mike Weatherby (Vocational Education), Dick Rose (Rehabilitation), Susan Marr (Developmental Disabilities Agency)*

TRANSITION PLANNING AREA: *Employment*

Student Preferences and Desired Postschool Goals:
: *Robert would like to work in a grocery store as a produce stocker.*

Present Levels of Performance:
: *Robert has held several work experience placements in local grocery stores (see attached placement summaries). He requires a self-management checklist using symbols to complete assigned work tasks. His rate of task completion is below the expected employer levels.*

Need Transition Services:
: *Robert will require job placement, training, and follow-along services from an employment specialist. In addition, he needs bus training to get to his job.*

ANNUAL GOAL: *Robert will work Monday through Friday from 1:00 to 4:00 p.m. at Smith's Food Center as a produce stocker, completing all assigned tasks without assistance from the employment specialist on ten consecutive weekly performance probes.*

Activities	Person	Completion Date
1. Place Robert on the state supported employment waiting list.	Susan Marr	May 1, 2003
2. Obtain a monthly bus pass.	Mrs. Brown	February 1, 2003
3. Schedule Robert for employee orientation training.		February 16, 2003

Source: McDonnell, John J.; Hardman, Michael L.; McDonnell Andrea P., Introduction to Persons With Moderate and Severe Disabilities: Educational and Social Issues, 2nd Edition, © 2003. Reprinted by permission of Pearson Education Inc., Upper Saddle River, NJ.

Section 504 Protections

Not all students who need special accommodations in school are covered by IDEA or are eligible for the services provided by the law. But these students' educational needs may be covered by other legislation. As a consequence of the civil rights movement in the 1960s and 1970s, the federal government passed the Vocational Rehabilitation Act of 1973. **Section 504** of that law prevents discrimination against people with disabilities in any program that receives federal money, such as public schools.

Through Section 504, all school-age children are ensured an equal opportunity to participate in school activities. The definition of *disability* is broad in Section 504. If a student has a condition that substantially limits participation in school, then the school still must develop a plan for giving that student access to education, even though the school gets no extra funds. To get assistance through Section 504, students must be assessed, often by a team, and a plan developed. Unlike IDEA, however, there are fewer rules about how this must happen, so individual schools design their own procedures (Friend, 2011). Look at Table 4.4 to see an example of the kinds of accommodations that might be made for a student. Many of these ideas seem to be "just good teaching." But I have been surprised to see how many teachers won't let students use calculators or audio recorders because "they should learn to do it like everyone else!" Two major groups are considered for Section 504 accommodations: students with medical or health needs (such as diabetes, drug addiction or alcoholism, severe allergies, communicable diseases, or temporary disabilities resulting from accidents) and students with attention-deficit hyperactivity disorder, if they are not already covered by IDEA.

The **Americans with Disabilities Act of 1990 (ADA)** prohibits discrimination against persons with disabilities in employment, transportation, public access, local government, and telecommunications. This comprehensive legislation extends the protections of Section 504 beyond the school and workplace to libraries, local and state government, restaurants, hotels, theaters, stores, public transportation, and many other settings.

TABLE 4.4 • **Examples of Accommodations Under Section 504**

The types of accommodations that can be written into a Section 504 plan are almost without limit. Some accommodations may relate to physical changes in the learning environment (for example, air filters are installed to remove allergens). However, many students who have Section 504 plans have functional impairments related to their learning or behavior, and their needs are somewhat similar to those of students with disabilities. The following is a sample of instructional accommodations that could be incorporated into a Section 504 plan:

- Seat the student nearest to where the teacher does most of his/her instruction.
- Have the student sit next to a peer who can help as needed.
- Seat the student away from the distractions of doorways or windows.
- Fold assignments in half so that the student is less overwhelmed by the quantity of work.
- Make directions telegraphic, that is, concise and clear.
- Allow use of a calculator or tape recorder.
- Use voice recognition software on the computer for written assignments.
- Mark right answers instead of wrong answers.
- Send a set of textbooks to be left at home so that the student does not have to remember to bring books from school.
- Provide books on tape so that the student can listen to assignments instead of reading them.

If you review these items, you can see that many of them just make good instructional sense. They are effective instructional practices that help learners with special needs succeed in your classroom.

Source: From Marilyn Friend & William D. Bursuck, Including Students with Special Needs: A Practical Guide for Classroom Teachers, 3e. Published by Allyn and Bacon, Boston, MA. Copyright © 2002 by Pearson Education. Adapted by permission of the publisher.

Section 504 A part of civil rights law that prevents discrimination against people with disabilities in programs that receive federal funds, such as public schools.

Americans with Disabilities Act of 1990 (ADA) Federal legislation prohibiting discrimination against persons with disabilities in employment, transportation, public access, local government, and telecommunications.

STUDENTS WITH LEARNING CHALLENGES

Before we look at some of the learning challenges children face, let's overview recent work on the neuroscience of learning difficulties. With all of the new technology, the amount of research on the brain and learning disabilities has grown exponentially.

Neuroscience and Learning Challenges

One of the early explanations for learning disabilities was minimal brain dysfunction. We now know that there are many other factors involved in the learning challenges children face, but certainly injuries or diseases of the brain can lead to disabilities in language, mathematics, attention, or behavior. In addition, there is some evidence that intensive teaching interventions can lead to changes in brain functioning (Simos et al., 2007). Studies of the brains of students with learning disabilities and with attention deficit disorders show some differences in structure and activity compared to those of students without problems. For example, people with attention disorders may have some areas of the brain that are smaller. The flow of blood appears to be lower than typical in the cerebellum and frontal lobes and the levels of electrical activity are different in certain brain areas, compared to people without attention deficits (Barkley, 2006). Elementary school students with specific language disabilities appear to have immature auditory systems—their brains process basic auditory information in a way similar to the brains of children 3 to 4 years younger (Goswami, 2004). The implications of these brain differences for instruction are still being worked out. It is difficult to determine exactly which came first, the learning problems or the brain differences (Friend, 2011).

Quite a bit of research on learning problems has focused on working memory (discussed in Chapter 8), partly because working memory capacity is a good predictor of a range of cognitive skills including language understanding, reading and mathematics abilities, and fluid intelligence (Bayliss, Jarrold, Baddeley, Gunn, & Leigh, 2005). In addition, some studies indicate that children who have learning disabilities in reading and mathematics problem solving have considerable difficulties with working memory (Siegel, 2003; Swanson & Saez, 2003). Specifically, some research shows that children with learning disabilities have problems using the system of working memory that holds verbal and auditory information while you work with it. Because children with learning disabilities have trouble holding on to words and sounds, it is difficult for them to put the words together to comprehend the meaning of a sentence or to figure out what a math story problem is really asking about.

An even more serious problem may be difficulties retrieving needed information from long-term memory, so it is hard for these children to simultaneously hold on to information (such as the result from the first two figures multiplied in an algebra problem) while they have to transform new incoming information, such as the next numbers to add. Important bits of information keep getting lost. Finally, children with learning disabilities in arithmetic and problem solving seem to have problems holding visual–spatial information such as number lines or quantity comparisons in working memory, so creating mental representations of "less than" and "greater than" problems is challenging (D'Amico & Guarnera, 2005).

As you saw in Table 4.3, almost one-half of all students receiving some kind of special education services in the public schools are diagnosed as having learning disabilities—by far the largest category of students with disabilities. We begin our exploration of learning challenges with these students.

Students with Learning Disabilities

Learning disability Problem with acquisition and use of language; may show up as difficulty with reading, writing, reasoning, or math.

How do you explain a student who struggles to read, write, spell, or learn math, even though he or she does not have intellectual disabilities, emotional problems, or educational disadvantages and has normal vision, hearing, and language capabilities? The student probably has a **learning disability**, but there is no fully agreed-upon definition of this term. One text on learning disabilities describes eight definitions (Hallahan et al., 2005), including the definition used in IDEA: "a disorder in one or more of the basic psychological processes involved in understanding or using language, spoken or written, that may manifest itself in imperfect ability to listen, think, speak, read, write, spell, or do mathematical calculation" (p. 15). Most definitions agree that students with learning disabilities perform significantly below what would be expected, given their other abilities.

Most educational psychologists believe there are both physiological and environmental bases for learning disabilities, such as brain injury, exposure to toxins before birth from mothers who smoked or drank while pregnant, poor nutrition, lead-based paint in the home, or even poor instruction (Smith, 2004). Genetics plays a role as well. If parents have a learning disability, their children have a 30% to 50% chance of having a learning disability too (Friend, 2011).

STUDENT CHARACTERISTICS. Students with learning disabilities are not all alike. The most common characteristics are specific difficulties in one or more academic areas; poor coordination; problems paying attention; hyperactivity and impulsivity; problems organizing and interpreting visual and auditory information; seeming lack of motivation; and difficulties making and keeping friends (Hallahan & Kauffman, 2006; Rosenberg et al., 2011). As you can see, many students with other disabilities (such as attention-deficit hyperactive disorder) and many normal students may have some of the same characteristics. To complicate the situation even more, not all students with learning disabilities will have these problems, and very few will have all of these characteristics. One student may be 3 years behind in reading but above grade level in math, while another student may have the opposite strengths and weaknesses and a third may have problems with organizing and studying that affect almost all subject areas.

Most students with learning disabilities have difficulties reading. Table 4.5 lists some of the most common problems, although these problems are not always signs of learning disabilities. For English-speaking students, these difficulties appear to be *phonemic awareness*—problems with relating sounds to letters that make up words, making spelling hard as well (Lyon, Shaywitz, & Shaywitz, 2003; Willcutt et al., 2001). For Chinese

TABLE 4.5 • **Reading Problems of Students with Learning Disabilities**

Do any of your students show these signs? They could be indications of learning disabilities.

ANXIETY AROUND READING
• Reluctant to read • Cries or acts out to avoid reading • Seems tense when reading
DIFFICULTY RECOGNIZING WORDS OR LETTERS
• Inserts an incorrect word, substitutes or skips words • Reverses letters or numbers—48 for 24, for example • Mispronounces words—"cape" for "cope" • Mixes up order of words in sentences: "I can bikes ride" for "I can ride bikes." • Reads very slowly and with little fluency—starts and stops often
POOR VOCABULARY SKILLS
• Can't read new vocabulary words • Has limited vocabulary
DIFFICULTY WITH UNDERSTANDING OR REMEMBERING WHAT WAS READ
• Can't recall basic facts from the reading • Can't make inferences or identify the main idea

Source: Based on information from Smith, D. D., & Tyler, N. C. (2010). Introduction to Special Education: Making a Difference (7th ed.). Columbus, OH: Merrill, and Helpguide.org. http://www.helpguide.org/mental/learning_disabilities.htm

speakers, reading disabilities seem to be related to *morphological awareness* or the ability to combine morphemes into words. Morphemes are the smallest units of meaning that make sense alone. For example, *books* has two morphemes: "book" and "s"—the "s" has meaning because it makes "book" plural. Recognizing units of meaning in Chinese characters is helpful in learning the language (Shu, McBride-Chang, Wu, & Liu, 2006).

Math, both computation and problem solving, is the second most common problem area for students with learning disabilities. Whereas English-speaking students with reading disabilities have trouble associating sounds with letters, students with some math disabilities have difficulty automatically associating numerals (1, 2, 3, etc.) with the correct magnitude—how many is 28, for example. So, before young students learn math computations, some may need extra practice to become automatic in associating numerals with the quantities they represent (Rubinsten & Henik, 2006).

The writing of some students with learning disabilities is virtually unreadable, and their spoken language can be halting and disorganized, as you can see in Figure 4.3. Students with learning disabilities often lack effective ways of approaching academic

FIGURE 4.3

WRITING SAMPLE FROM A STUDENT WITH LD

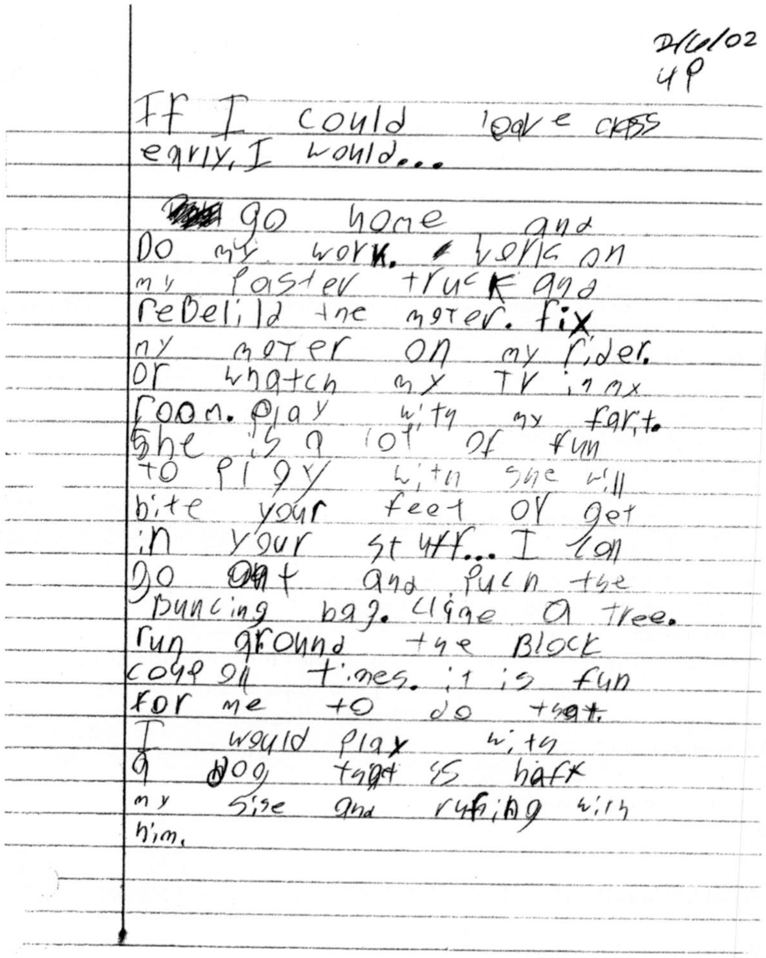

Source: From Friend, Marilyn, Special Education: Contemporary Perspectives for School Professionals, *2e. Published by Allyn and Bacon, Boston, MA. Copyright 2008 by Pearson Education. Adapted by permission of the publisher.*

tasks. They don't know how to focus on the relevant information, get organized, apply learning strategies and study skills, change strategies when the one being used isn't working, or evaluate their learning. They tend to be passive learners, in part because they don't know how to learn—they have failed so often. Working independently is especially trying, so homework and seatwork are often left incomplete (Hallahan et al., 2005).

TEACHING STUDENTS WITH LEARNING DISABILITIES. Early diagnosis is important so that students with learning disabilities do not become terribly frustrated and discouraged. The students themselves do not understand why they are having such trouble, and they may become victims of **learned helplessness**. This condition was first identified in learning experiments with animals. The animals were put in situations in which they received punishment (electric shocks) that they could not control. Later, when the situation was changed and they could have escaped the shocks or turned them off, the animals didn't even bother trying (Seligman, 1975). They had learned to be helpless victims. Students with learning disabilities may also come to believe that they cannot control or improve their own learning. This is a powerful belief. The students never exert the effort to discover that they can make a difference in their own learning, so they remain passive and helpless.

Students with learning disabilities may also try to compensate for their problems and develop bad learning habits in the process, or they may begin avoiding certain subjects out of fear of not being able to handle the work. To prevent these things from happening, teachers should refer the students to the appropriate professionals in the school as early as possible.

Two general approaches, preferably used together, are highly effective for students with learning disabilities (Friend, 2011). The first is *direct instruction*, described in Chapter 14. The basics of this approach are clear explanations and demonstrations of new material, teaching in small steps with practice after each step, immediate feedback, and teacher guidance and support. The second general approach is *strategy instruction*, described in Chapter 9. Strategies are specific rules for focusing attention and accomplishing tasks, such as **TREE** for supporting elementary students' persuasive writing.

> **T**opic sentence: Tell what you believe.
> **R**easons: Tell 3 or more reasons why you believe this. Will your readers believe this?
> **E**nding: Wrap it up!
> **E**xamine: Check for all 3 parts.

These strategies have to be taught using good direct instruction—explanation, examples, and practice with feedback. See Chapters 9 and 14 for more details about these two approaches.

Here are some other general strategies for working with students with learning disabilities. In the preschool and elementary years, keep verbal instructions short and simple; have students repeat directions back to you to be sure they understand; give multiple examples and repeat main points several times; allow more practice than usual, especially when the material is new. Many of these strategies are useful in secondary grades as well. In addition, directly teach older students self-monitoring strategies, such as cueing students to ask, "Was I paying attention?" Teach students to use external memory strategies such as note taking, and devices such as assignment books, to-do lists, or electronic calendars (Hardman, Drew, & Egan, 2005). In every grade, connect new material to knowledge students already have. You may be thinking that these are good ideas for many students who need more support and direct teaching of study skills. You are right.

Students with Hyperactivity and Attention Disorders

STOP & THINK If a student is struggling with time management and organization issues, what kind of accommodations would you provide? •

You probably have heard of and may even have used the term *hyperactivity*. The notion is a modern one; there were no "hyperactive children" 50 to 60 years ago.

Learned helplessness The expectation, based on previous experiences with a lack of control, that all of one's efforts will lead to failure.

Such children, like Mark Twain's Huckleberry Finn, were seen as rebellious, lazy, or "fidgety" (Nylund, 2000). Today, attention-deficit hyperactive disorder (ADHD) is common. Not too long ago, I opened the newspaper and saw the headline, "ADHD diagnoses soar in 4 years." The Centers for Disease Control now puts the number of children in the United States diagnosed with ADHD as 1 in 10 (Wechsler, 2010). But the United States is not alone. A report from the 2nd International Congress on ADHD (Thome & Reddy, 2009) noted evidence is increasing that ADHD is a worldwide problem and that people with ADHD have striking and consistent characteristics in every culture. The rates in different countries vary from 4% to 10% worldwide (Fabiano et al., 2009; Gerwe et al., 2009). Closer to home, many student teachers in my program have classes that include 5 or 6 students diagnosed as "hyperactive," and in one class, there are 10 students with that diagnosis. Even closer, several of my immediate family members have ADHD.

Connect and Extend to PRAXIS II™

ADHD (I, B2)
A new student's parent calls you to tell you that a neurologist has diagnosed her child with ADHD. What typical behaviors can you expect from the student? What can you do to support that student's development?

DEFINITIONS. Actually, hyperactivity is not one particular condition, but two kinds of problems that may or may not occur together—attention disorders and impulsive-hyperactivity problems. About half the children diagnosed in the United States have both conditions. Today, most psychologists agree that the main problem for children labeled hyperactive is directing and maintaining attention, not simply controlling their physical activity. The American Psychiatric Association (APA) has established a diagnostic category called **attention-deficit hyperactivity disorder (ADHD)** to identify children with this problem. APA defines ADHD as "a pervasive pattern of inattention, impulsivity and/or hyperactivity that is more frequent and severe than is typically observed in individuals at a comparable level of development" (American Psychiatric Association, DSM-IV-TR, 2000, p. 78). Some of the indicators listed in the DSM-IV-TR are:

- **Inattention:** Doesn't pay close attention to class activities, details of work, teacher directions, class discussions; can't organize work, notebooks, desk, assignments; easily distracted and forgetful.
- **Hyperactivity:** fidgets, and squirms; can't stay in assigned seat; can't move slowly, seems driven by a motor to go fast; talks excessively.
- **Impulsivity**: Blurts out answers; has trouble waiting for a turn; interrupts.

All children show some of these behaviors some of the time, but children with ADHD are likely to have some of these symptoms before age 7, the symptoms occur across many settings (not just school), and the symptoms lead to problems learning and getting along with others. ADHD usually is diagnosed in elementary school, but research suggests that problems with attention and hyperactivity may begin to show up as early as 3 years old (Friedman-Weieneth, Harvey, Youngswirth, & Goldstein, 2007). Even though about 2 to 3 times more boys than girls are identified as hyperactive, the gap appears to be narrowing. Girls have the same symptoms as boys, but tend to show the symptoms in less obvious ways, so they may not be identified as often and thus may miss getting appropriate support (Friend, 2011).

Just a few years ago, most psychologists thought that ADHD diminished as children entered adolescence, but now there is evidence that the problems can persist into adulthood for at least half of those with ADHD (Hirvikoski et al., 2011). Adolescence—with the increased stresses of puberty, transition to middle or high school, more demanding academic work, and more engrossing social relationships—can be an especially difficult time for students with ADHD (Taylor, 1998). When children diagnosed with ADHD become adults, about 30% have no more symptoms, 25% have persistent behavioral problems such as drug use or criminal behaviors, and around 25% develop major depression (Rosenberg et al., 2011).

TREATING ADHD WITH DRUGS. Today, there is an increasing reliance on drug therapy for ADHD, but there is controversy about this approach, as you can see in the *Point/Counterpoint*.

Attention-deficit hyperactivity disorder (ADHD) Current term for disruptive behavior disorders marked by overactivity, excessive difficulty sustaining attention, or impulsiveness.

POINT/COUNTERPOINT: Pills or Skills for Children With ADHD?

About 3% of school-age children in the United States (ages 6 to 18) take some kind of medication for ADHD. Should children with ADHD be given drugs?

POINT

▶ **Yes, drugs are helpful in ADHD.** Ritalin and other prescribed drugs such as Adderall, Focalin, Dexadrine, Vyvanse, and Cylert are stimulants, but in particular dosages, they tend to have paradoxical effects on many children with ADHD. Short-term effects include possible improvements in social behaviors such as cooperation, attention, and compliance. Research suggests that about 70% to 80% of children with ADHD are more manageable and better able to benefit from educational and social interventions when on medication (Hutchinson, 2009). In fact, both stimulants such as Adderall and Ritalin and nonstimulant treatments such as Strattera appear to have some helpful effects for many children and adolescents with ADHD (Kratchovil, 2009). Positive results also have been reported with Buspar, usually used to treat anxiety, and even some supplements such as pycnogenol (Trebaticka et al., 2009). There is also some evidence that Strattera might have positive effects on working memory, planning, and inhibition—at least for the Chinese children studied (Yang et al., 2009). German researchers studying the effects of longer-acting, once-a-day Concerta concluded that the transition from short-acting stimulants to Concerta was "associated with significant improvements in daily functioning in several areas of life, severity of disease, and in quality of life" (Gerwe et al., 2009, p. 185).

COUNTERPOINT

▶ **No, drugs should not be the first treatment tried with ADHD.** Many children experience negative side effects when taking these drugs, such as increased heart rate and higher blood pressure, interference with growth rate, insomnia, weight loss, and nausea (Smith & Tyler, 2010). For most children, these side effects are mild and can be controlled by adjusting the dosage. However, little is known about the long-term effects of drug therapy. A new drug called Strattera is not a stimulant, but may lead to increased thoughts of suicide. As a parent or teacher, you need to keep up with the research on treatments for ADHD.

Many studies have concluded that the improvements in behavior from the drugs *seldom* lead to improvements in academic learning or peer relationships, two areas where children with ADHD have great problems. Because children appear to improve dramatically in their behavior, parents and teachers, relieved to see change, may assume the problem has been cured. It hasn't. The children still need special help in learning, especially interventions focused on how to make *connections* among elements in readings or presentations in order to build coherent, accurate representations of the information (Bailey et al., 2009; Doggett, 2004; Purdie, Hattie, & Caroll, 2002).

Beware of Either/Or. The bottom line is that even if students in your class are on medication, it is critical that they also learn the academic and social skills they will need to succeed. They need to learn how and when to apply learning strategies and study skills. Also, they need to be encouraged to persist when challenged by difficult tasks and to see themselves as having control over their learning and behavior. Medication alone will not make this happen, but it may help. For learning to occur, medication needs to be paired with other effective interventions.

ALTERNATIVES/ADDITIONS TO DRUG TREATMENTS. Gregory A. Fabiano and his colleagues (2009) identified 174 studies conducted between 1967 and 2006 that included almost 3,000 participants in behavioral treatments for ADHD; all studies met rigorous standards of quality research. Behavioral treatments involve the application of methods derived from behavioral learning theories such as contingency management, time-out, shaping, self-regulation, and modeling (see Chapter 7). The researchers then compared treated with untreated groups or individuals before and after one or more different kinds of treatments. Their conclusion? Findings were clear and impressive. "Based on these results, there is strong and consistent evidence that behavioral treatments are effective for treating ADHD" (p. 129). In an interview, Gregory Fabiano said, "Our results suggest that efforts should be redirected from debating the effectiveness of behavioral interventions to dissemination, enhancing and improving the use of these programs in community, school and mental health settings." Researchers working with adults in Sweden also found that behavioral methods stressing a balance between accepting and changing ADHD symptoms and behaviors proved effective (Hirvikoski et al., 2011).

In sum, one large study in Australia concluded what you might guess—we should attack the problem on all fronts:

> Multimodal approaches to intervention have been found to be most effective in terms of lasting change. For most, but not all children and adolescents, treatment with psycho-stimulants has beneficial effects, provided that it is accompanied by remedial tuition, counseling, and behavior management by parents/teachers, as required. Thus, advice from several different professions may be necessary. (van Kraayenoord, Rice, Carroll, Fritz, Dillon, & Hill, 2001, p. 7)

Even if students in your class are on medication, it is critical that they also learn the academic and social skills they will need to survive. Again, this will not happen by itself, even if behavior improves with medication (Purdie et al., 2002).

Lessons for Teachers: Learning Disabilities and ADHD

Long assignments may overwhelm students with learning disabilities and attention deficits, so give them a few problems or paragraphs at a time with clear consequences for completion. Another promising approach combines instruction in learning and memory strategies with motivational training. The goal is to help students develop the "skill and will" to improve their achievement. They are also taught to monitor their own behavior and encouraged to be persistent and to see themselves as "in control" (Pfiffner, Barkley, & DuPaul, 2006).

The notion of being in control is part of a therapy strategy for dealing with ADHD, one that stresses personal agency. Rather than treating the problem child, David Nylund's (2000) SMART approach enlists the child's strengths to conquer his or her problems—to put the child in control. New metaphors for the situation are developed. Rather than seeing the problems as inside the child, Nylund helps everyone see ADHD, Trouble, Boredom, and other enemies of learning as outside the child—demons to be conquered or unruly spirits to be enlisted in the service of what the child wants to accomplish. The focus is on solutions. The steps of the **SMART** approach are:

Separating the problem of ADHD from the child
Mapping the influence of ADHD on the child and family
Attending to the exceptions to the ADHD story
Reclaiming special abilities of children diagnosed with ADHD
Telling and celebrating the new story. (Nylund, 2000, p. xix)

As a teacher, you can look for times when the student is engaged—even short times. What is different about these times? Discover the student's strengths and allow yourself to be amazed by them. Make changes in your teaching that support the changes the student is trying to make. Nylund gives the following example: Chris (age 9) and his teacher, Ms. Baker, became partners in putting Chris in control of his concentration in school. Ms. Baker moved Chris's seat to the front of the room. The two designed a subtle signal to get Chris back on track, and Chris organized his messy desk. These sound like some of the Section 504 accommodations in Table 4.4. When Chris's concentration improved, Chris received an award at a party given in his honor. Chris described how he was learning to listen in class: "You just have to have a strong mind and tell ADHD and Boredom not to bother you" (Nylund, 2000, p. 166). Students with ADHD have some suggestions, too, as you can see in Table 4.6 taken from Nylund (2000, pp. 202–203).

Students with Communication Disorders

Students with communication disorders who are between the ages of 6 and 21 are the second largest group served by special education. These students may have language disorders, speech disorders, or both. They make up about 19% of students receiving services. Communication disorders can arise from many sources, because so many different aspects of the individual are involved in learning language and using speech. A child with a hearing impairment will not learn to speak normally. Injuries can cause neurological problems that interfere with speech or language. Children who are not listened to, or whose perception of the world is distorted by emotional problems, will reflect these problems

TABLE 4.6 • **Students with ADHD Give Teachers Advice**

Students with ADHD make these recommendations for their teachers (Nylund, 2000):

- Use lots of pictures (visual clues) to help me learn.
- Recognize cultural and racial identity.
- Know when to bend the rules.
- Notice when I am doing well.
- Don't tell the other kids that I am taking Ritalin.
- Offer us choices.
- Don't just lecture—it's boring!
- Realize that I am intelligent.
- Let me walk around the classroom.
- Don't give tons of homework.
- More recess!
- Be patient.

in their language development. Because speaking involves movements, any impairment of the motor functions involved with speech can cause language disorders. And because language development and thinking are so interwoven, any problems in cognitive functioning can affect ability to use language.

SPEECH DISORDERS. Students who cannot produce sounds effectively for speaking are considered to have a **speech disorder**. About 5% of school age children have some form of speech impairment. Articulation problems and fluency disorders (stuttering) are the two most common problems.

Articulation disorders include distorting a sound like a lisp (*thumtimes* for *sometimes*), substituting one sound for another (*shairp* for *chair*), adding a sound (*chuch air* for *chair*), or omitting sounds (*chai* for *chair*) (Rosenberg et al., 2011). Keep in mind, however, that most children are 6 to 8 years old before they can successfully pronounce all English sounds in normal conversation. The sounds of the consonants *l, r, y, s, v,* and *z* and the consonant blends *sh, ch, ng, zh,* and *th* are the last to be mastered (Friend, 2011). Also, there are dialect differences based on geography that do not represent articulation problems. A child in your class who is from New England might say "ideer" for "idea," but have no speech impairment.

Stuttering generally appears between the ages of 3 and 4. Causes of stuttering are unknown, but might include emotional or neurological problems or learned behavior. If stuttering continues more than a year or so, the child should be referred to a speech therapist. Early intervention can make a big difference (Hardman et al., 2005). When you are working with a student who stutters, speak to the child often, privately, and without hurrying, interrupting, or finishing the child's words and sentences. Pause often, especially after the child finishes speaking—communicate that it is OK to take time to think before you speak. Notice when the stuttering is more and less frequent. Avoid pressuring the child to speak quickly. In class discussions, call on her or him early in the discussion so tension won't build up, and ask a question that can be answered with few words. Speak frankly about the stuttering, but assure the student it is nothing to be ashamed of—many successful people, including kings, have shared the challenge and learned to improve (Friend, 2011; Rosenberg et al. 2011).

Voicing problems, a third type of speech impairment, include speaking with an inappropriate pitch, quality, or loudness, or in a monotone. A student with any of these problems should be referred to a speech therapist. Recognizing the problem is the first step. Be alert for students whose pronunciation, loudness, voice quality, speech fluency, expressive range, or rate is very different from that of their peers. Pay attention also to students who seldom speak. Are they simply shy, or do they have difficulties with language?

LANGUAGE DISORDERS. Language differences are not necessarily language disorders. Students with language disorders are markedly deficient in their ability to understand or express language, compared with other students of their own age and cultural group

Speech disorder Inability to produce sounds effectively for speaking.

Articulation disorders Any of a variety of pronunciation difficulties, such as the substitution, distortion, or omission of sounds.

Voicing problems Inappropriate pitch, quality, loudness, or intonation.

TABLE 4.7 • **Encouraging Language Development**

- Talk about things that interest children.
- Follow the children's lead. Reply to their initiations and comments. Share their excitement.
- Don't ask too many questions. If you must, use questions such as *how did/do...*, *why did/do...*, and *what happened...* that result in longer explanatory answers.
- Encourage children to ask questions. Respond openly and honestly. If you don't want to answer a question, say so and explain why. (*I don't think I want to answer that question; it's very personal.*)
- Use a pleasant tone of voice. You need not be a comedian, but you can be light and humorous. Children love it when adults are a little silly.
- Don't be judgmental or make fun of children's language. If you are overly critical of children's language or try to catch and correct all errors, they will stop talking to you.
- Allow enough time for children to respond.
- Treat children with courtesy by not interrupting when they are talking.
- Include children in family and classroom discussions. Encourage participation and listen to their ideas.
- Be accepting of children and of their language. Hugs and acceptance can go a long way.
- Provide opportunities for children to use language and to have that language work for them to accomplish their goals.

Source: Adapted from information in Owens, Robert E. Jr. Language Disorders: A Functional Approach to Assessment and Intervention, 5e. Published by Allyn and Bacon, Boston, MA. Copyright © 2010 by Pearson Education. Adapted by permission of the publisher.

(Owens, 2012). Students who seldom speak, who use few words or very short sentences, or who rely only on gestures to communicate should be referred to a qualified school professional for observation or testing. Table 4.7 gives ideas for promoting language development for all students.

Students with Emotional or Behavioral Difficulties

Students with **emotional and behavioral disorders** can be among the most difficult to teach in a regular class, and they are a source of concern for many prospective teachers (Avramidis, Bayliss, & Burden, 2000). The future is not bright for students with emotional and behavioral disorders who do not get appropriate help. About one-third of these students are arrested during their school years and half are unemployed 3 to 5 years after leaving school (Rosenberg et al., 2011), so early intervention is really important.

Professionals in education define behavioral disorders as behaviors that deviate so much from the norm that they interfere with the child's own growth and development and/or the lives of others. The language in IDEA describes *emotional disturbances* (*ED*) that involve inappropriate behaviors, unhappiness or depression, fears and anxieties, and trouble with relationships. The American Psychological Association and the medical community refer to these behavioral difficulties as *mental disorders* (Friend, 2011). Table 4.8 describes a few of the specific disorders covered by the Diagnostic and Statistical Manual of Mental Disorders (4th edition, revised), also called the DSM-IV-TR.

However they are defined, what you will observe as a teacher are students who are aggressive, anxious, withdrawn, or depressed and who often have difficulty following rules, paying attention, or interacting with others. There are over 400,000 students with emotional disturbances in the United States, making this the 5th largest group receiving services. This number has increased about 20% since 1991–1992. As with learning disabilities and ADHD, there are more boys than girls diagnosed with these disorders—at least 3 times as many boys as girls identified. One troubling fact is that African American students are overrepresented in this category. They make up about 13% of the population, but about 26% of the students identified with emotional and behavioral disorders.

The range of possible emotional and behavioral disorders is wide. And students with other disabilities—learning disabilities, intellectual disabilities, or ADHD, for example—may also have emotional or behavioral problems as they struggle in school. Methods from applied behavioral analysis (Chapter 7) and direct teaching of self-regulation skills

Emotional and behavioral disorders Behaviors or emotions that deviate so much from the norm that they interfere with the child's own growth and development and/or the lives of others—inappropriate behaviors, unhappiness or depression, fears and anxieties, and trouble with relationships.

TABLE 4.8 • **Examples of Emotional and Behavioral Disorders from the *Diagnostic and Statistical Manual of Mental Disorders***

The definition of emotional and behavior disorders in IDEA is general: It does not list particular conditions. However, in the medical community many specific disorders have been identified, and these are included in the *Diagnostic and Statistical Manual of Mental Disorders* (fourth edition, text revision) (*DSM-IV-TR*). Instead of being called emotional and behavior disorders, they are referred to as mental disorders. The following list, although not complete, includes examples of mental disorders listed in that publication that educators would consider emotional and behavior disorders:

- **Anxiety disorders.** Anxiety disorders occur when students experience an overwhelming sense of fear or dread. One example is obsessive-compulsive disorder (OCD) in which students cannot stop themselves from worrying excessively about a specific concern, for example, germs. Other examples include phobias (fear of specific items, such as spiders, or fear of certain activities, such as going to school) and posttraumatic stress disorder (PTSD) in which students re-live in nightmares or flashbacks a traumatic event that they witnessed.
- **Disruptive behavior disorders.** This category includes three types of disorders:
  - *Attention deficit-hyperactivity disorder*. . . is characterized by inattention, a high level of activity and impulsivity, or a combination of these. Note, though, that it often is not considered a disability.
  - *Oppositional defiant disorder* (ODD) is diagnosed when students are defiant with adults and vindictive or blaming with peers to an excessive degree over a long period of time.
  - *Conduct disorders* are diagnosed when students fight, bully, display cruelty to animals or people, or otherwise repeatedly break serious rules.
- **Eating disorders.** The most common eating disorder is anorexia nervosa in which students believe they are overweight and refuse to eat, even when they are near starvation.
- **Mood disorders.** Also called affective disorders, this group includes depression . . . and bipolar disorder, also called manic depression, in which students' moods swing from extreme highs (manic) to extreme lows (depression).
- **Tic disorders.** Tics are involuntary, rapid, stereotyped movements of specific muscle groups. Students with tics may blink their eyes or repeatedly sniff. The most well known tic disorder is Tourette syndrome, a disorder that ranges from mild to severe and includes both facial or other physical tics as well as vocal tics, often "barking" or profanity.

Source: From Friend, Marilyn. Special Education: Contemporary Perspectives for School Professionals, 2e. *Published by Allyn and Bacon, Boston, MA. Copyright © 2008 by Pearson Education. Reprinted by permission of the publisher.*

(Chapter 11) are two useful approaches. Another possibility that has proved helpful for these students is to provide structure, organizational tools, and choices. Here are some ideas from Terri Swanson (2005):

- Structure the environment by minimizing visual and auditory stimulation, establishing clear visual boundaries between areas where different behaviors are expected, or organizing supplies in easy-to-use holders.
- Structure schedules by posting monthly and daily schedules, having clear starting and ending signals and clear procedures for turning in work.
- Structure activities by color-coding subject folders (blue for math, etc.), posting verbal instructions with visual prompts, or putting all materials needed for an activity in a "Science box."
- Structure rules and routines, for example, giving students a script to use in asking other students to play a game with them, writing rules out in a positive way, or preparing students for changes in routines such as spring break by reviewing pictures of what will be happening over the break.
- Offer choices by providing a short list of alternatives for completing assignments or projects.

Because students with emotional and behavioral disorders frequently break rules and push the limits, teachers often find themselves disciplining them. Be aware that there

GUIDELINES

Disciplining Students with Emotional Problems

Be careful not to violate due process rights of students—students and parents must know the behaviors expected and the consequences for misbehavior.

Examples

1. Communicate expectations clearly and in writing.
2. Ask parents and students to sign a copy of the classroom rules.
3. Post rules and consequences in class and on a class Web page.

Be very careful with severe punishments that remove students from class for a long time. These constitute a change in the child's educational program (IEP) and require due process.

Examples

1. Always follow due process for suspensions of more than 10 days.
2. Be aware of possible due process requirements for prolonged periods of time-out (in-school suspension).

Punishments for students with severe emotional problems must serve a clear educational purpose.

Examples

1. Give a rationale for punishment or correction that ties an action to a student's learning or the learning of others in the class.
2. Use written behavior contracts that include a rationale.

Make sure the rule and the punishment are reasonable.

Examples

1. Consider the student's age and physical condition.
2. Does the punishment match the offense and the way others in the class are treated?

3. Do other teachers handle similar situations in the same way?
4. Try less intrusive punishments first. Be patient. Move to more severe actions only when less severe procedures fail.

Keep good records and work collaboratively so all involved are informed.

Examples

1. Document the punishment of all students in a journal or log. List what precipitated the punishment, what procedures were used, how long the punishment lasted, the results, modifications to the punishment, and new results.
2. Note meetings with families, special education teachers, and the principal.
3. Make any changes involving management plans with families and other teachers.

Always use positive consequences in conjunction with negative ones.

Examples

1. If students lose points for breaking rules, give them ways to regain points through positive behavior.
2. Recognize genuine accomplishment and small steps—DON'T say, "Well, it's about time you . . ."

For more information on disciplining students with disabilities, see: http://www.nasponline.org/communications/spawareness/effdiscipfs.pdf

---

have been court rulings on disciplining students with serious emotional problems (Yell, 1990). The *Guidelines* may help when you are faced with these situations.

Let's consider an area where teachers may be able to detect problems and make a difference—suicide.

SUICIDE. Of course, not every student with emotional or behavioral problems will consider suicide, but depression often is associated with suicide. Up to 10% of adolescents have attempted suicide at some point, but even more have considered it. Native Americans and students living in rural communities are more likely to commit suicide. There are several general risk factors, and they seem to apply to both male and female African American, Latino, and White adolescents: depression and substance abuse, history of suicide in the family, being under stress, tendency to be impulsive or perfectionistic, belief that a person goes to a better place after dying, and family rejection or conflict. Having more than one of these risk factors is especially dangerous (Friend, 2011; Steinberg, 2005). In addition, there is concern today that some drugs prescribed for depression or ADHD may increase the risk of suicide in adolescents.

Suicide often comes as a response to life problems—problems that parents and teachers sometimes dismiss. There are many warning signs that trouble is brewing. Watch for changes in eating or sleeping habits, weight, grades, disposition, activity level, or interest in friends or activities that were once fun. Students at risk sometimes suddenly give away prized possessions such as iPads, books, clothing, or pets. They may seem depressed or hyperactive and may say things like "Nothing matters anymore," "I shouldn't be here," "If I died, people might love me more," "You won't have to worry about me anymore," or "I wonder what dying is like." They may start missing school or quit doing work. It is especially dangerous if the student not only talks about suicide but also has a plan for carrying it out.

If you suspect that there is a problem, talk to the student directly, ask about his or her concerns. One feeling shared by many people who attempt suicide is that no one cared enough to ask. Ask about specifics, and take the student seriously. You may need to become an advocate for the student with administrators, parents, or other adults who dismiss the warning signs. Also, be aware that teenage suicides often occur in clusters. After one student acts or when stories about a suicide are reported in the media, other teens are more likely to copy the suicide (Lewinsohn, Rohde, & Seeley, 1994; Rice & Dolgin, 2002). Table 4.9 lists common myths and facts about suicide.

DRUG ABUSE. Although drug abuse is not always associated with emotional or behavioral problems and people without these challenges may abuse drugs, many adolescents with emotional problems also abuse drugs. Abusing drugs is especially dangerous for African American males. In one study that followed a sample of adolescents from ages 19 to 27, about 33% of the African American young men who abused drugs died by age 27, compared to 3% for White males. The death rate for both African American and White females who abused drugs was 1% (Clark, Martin, & Cornelius, 2008).

TABLE 4.9 • **Myths and Facts about Suicide**

Myth:	People who talk about suicide don't kill themselves, they are just trying to get attention.
Fact:	People who die by suicide usually talk about it first. They are in pain and oftentimes reach out for help because they do not know what to do and have lost hope. Always take talk about suicide seriously. Always.
Myth:	Only certain types of people commit suicide.
Fact:	All types of people commit suicide—male and female, young and old, rich and poor, country people and city people. It happens in every racial, ethnic, and religious group.
Myth:	You should never ask people who are suicidal if they are thinking about suicide or if they have thought about a method, because just talking about it will give them the idea.
Fact:	Asking people if they are thinking about suicide does not give them the idea for suicide. And it is important to talk about suicide with people who are suicidal because you will learn more about their mindset and intentions, and allow them to diffuse some of the tension that is causing their suicidal feelings.
Myth:	Most people who kill themselves really want to die.
Fact:	The vast majority of people who are suicidal do not want to die. They are in pain, and they want to stop the pain. Suicide is often intended as a cry for help.
Myth:	Young people never think about suicide, they have their entire life ahead of them.
Fact:	Suicide is the third leading cause of death for young people ages 15–24. Sometimes children under 10 die by suicide.

Source: Adapted from information by Kevin Caruso, Suicide Myths, Suicide.org. Available online at http://www.suicide.org/suicide-myths.html

TABLE 4.10 • **Percentage of Students in the United States Grades 8 through 12 Who Reported Using These Drugs in the Past 30 Days**

DRUG	8TH GRADE	10TH GRADE	12TH GRADE	SIGNIFICANT INCREASE OVER ALL GRADES 2009–2010
Any illicit drug	9.5	18.5	23.8	
Marijuana	8.0	16.7	21.4	yes
Inhalants	3.6	2.0	1.4	
LSD	.6	.7	.8	
Ecstasy	1.1	1.9	1.4	yes
Cocaine	.6	.9	1.3	
Heroin	0.4	.4	.4	
Amphetamines	1.8	3.3	3.3	
Been drunk	5.0	14.7	26.8	
Cigarettes	7.1	13.6	19.2	
Smokeless tobacco	4.1	7.5	8.5	

Source: Drawn from data in Johnston, L. D., O'Malley, P. M., Bachman, J. G., & Schulenberg, J. E. (2011). Monitoring the Future National Results on Adolescent Drug Use: Overview of Key Findings, 2010. Ann Arbor: Institute for Social Research, The University of Michigan. Available online at http://www.monitoringthefuture.org/

Modern society makes growing up a very confusing process. Notice the messages from films and billboards. "Beautiful," popular, happy people drink alcohol and smoke cigarettes, with little concern for their health. Males are encouraged to "drink like a man!" We have over-the-counter drugs for almost every common ailment, and constant ads from drug companies broadcast the benefits of new prescription medications. Coffee or an "energy drink" wakes us up, and a pill helps us sleep. And then we tell students to "say no!" to drugs.

For many reasons, not just because of these contradictory messages, drug use has become a problem for students. Accurate statistics are hard to find, but estimates from the *Monitoring the Future* survey by researchers at the University of Michigan (Johnston, O'Malley, Bachman, & Schulenberg, 2011) indicate that 9.5% of 8th graders, 18.5% of 10th graders, and 23.8% of 12th graders reported using an illicit drug *in the past 30 days*, with marijuana being the most popular (see Table 4.10). In fact, marijuana use increased among teens from 2008 through 2010—the last data available when I wrote this chapter, with about 1% of 8th graders, 3% of 10th graders, and 6% of 12th graders reporting they use marijuana *daily*. Patterns of use for other drugs are inconsistent—use of ecstasy, cigarettes, and heroin is increasing for older students, but use of alcohol, cocaine, Vicodin, and sedatives is down. Use of many other drugs has leveled off—LSD, PCP, crack cocaine, OxyContin, methamphetamine, cough and cold medicines taken to get high, several so-called "club drugs" (Rohypnol, GHB, and ketamine), and anabolic steroids. Younger adolescents are more likely to use inhalants (glues, paint thinners, nail polish remover, aerosol sprays, etc.). They are inexpensive and available. And students don't realize that they are risking injury or death when they use inhalants.

Remarkably, about 15% of high school boys and 2% of girls have used some form of spit or other type of smokeless tobacco. The use of smokeless tobacco can cause cancers of the mouth, throat, larynx, esophagus, stomach, and pancreas; receding gums and gum disease (leading finally to tooth loss, pre-cancerous spots in the mouth), nicotine addiction, and possibly to heart disease and stroke (American Cancer Society, 2010).

PREVENTION. We should distinguish between experimentation and abuse. Many students try something at a party, but do not become regular users. Providing information or "scare" tactics such as the DARE drug prevention program seems to have little positive effect and may even encourage curiosity and experimentation (Dusenbury & Falco, 1995; Tobler & Stratton, 1997).

So what is more effective? Adam Fletcher and his colleagues analyzed research on school programs around the world. One overwhelmingly frequent finding was that after taking into account students' prior drug use and personal characteristics, "disengagement from school and poor teacher–student relations were associated with subsequent drug use and other risky health behaviors" (Fletcher, Bonell, & Hargreaves, 2008, p. 217). For example, the researchers describe one study that found, for young adolescents, being disconnected with school predicted their drug use 2 to 4 years later. One implication is that engaging adolescents in schools, forming positive relationships, and connecting the students to caring adults and peers is critical in creating a protective environment.

Students with Intellectual Disabilities

A word about terms. **Intellectual disability** is a more current name for *mental retardation*. You may also have heard the terms *cognitive impairment, general learning disability*, or *cognitive disability*. Intellectual disability is the preferred name, because the term *mental retardation* is considered offensive and stigmatizing; however, mental retardation still is used in the IDEA definitions and in many schools. In 2007, the American Association on Mental Retardation changed its name to the American Association on Intellectual and Developmental Disabilities (AAIDD) to reflect this rejection of the term *mental retardation*. The AAIDD definition of *intellectual disability* is "a disability characterized by significant limitations in both intellectual functioning and adaptive behavior as expressed in conceptual, social, and practical adaptive skills. This disability originates before age 18" (AAIDD.org).

Intellectual function is usually measured by IQ tests, with a score below 70 being one of the indicators. But an IQ score below the 70 range is not enough to diagnose a child as having intellectual disabilities. There must also be problems with adaptive behavior, day-to-day independent living, and social functioning. This caution is especially important when interpreting the scores of students from different cultures. Defining disability based on test scores alone can create what some critics call "the 6-hour retarded child"—students who are seen as disabled only for the part of the day they attend school.

Only about 1% of the population fit the AAIDD's definition of disability in both intellectual functioning and adaptive behavior. For years, this group was further divided into mild (IQ 50–69), moderate (IQ 35–49), severe (IQ 20–34), and profound levels (IQ below 20). Many school districts still use this system, and so does the World Health Organization. However, the IQ ranges are not perfect predictors of individuals' abilities to function, so the AAIDD now recommends a classification scheme based on the amount of support that a person requires to function at his or her highest level. Support varies from intermittent (e.g., as needed during stressful times), to limited (consistent support, but time-limited such as employment training), to extensive (daily care such as living in a group home), to pervasive (constant high-intensity care for all aspects of living) (Taylor, Richards, & Brady, 2005).

As a regular teacher, you may not have contact with children needing extensive or pervasive support unless your school is participating in a full inclusion program, but you probably will work with children needing intermittent or limited support. In the early grades, these students may simply learn more slowly than their peers. They need more time and more practice to learn, and they may have difficulty transferring learning from one setting to another or putting small skills together to accomplish a more complex task. They often have difficulties with metacognitive skills and executive functioning required to plan, monitor, and redirect attention and learning strategies (Simon, 2010), so very

Intellectual disabilities/Mental retardation Significantly below-average intellectual and adaptive social behavior, evident before age 18.

GUIDELINES

Teaching Students with Intellectual Disabilities

1. Develop specific learning objectives based on an analysis of each student's learning strengths and weaknesses. No matter what a student knows, he or she is ready to learn the next step.

2. Work on practical skills and concepts based on the demands of adult life.

3. Analyze the task the student will be learning—identify the specific steps involved in successful completion—don't overlook any steps in your planning.

4. State and present objectives simply.

5. Present material in small, logical steps. Practice extensively before going on to the next step. Use resources such as computer drill and practice exercises in class or have volunteers and family members continue guiding practice outside class.

6. Do not skip steps. Students with average intelligence can form conceptual bridges from one step to the next and make metacognitive judgments about how they are doing, but children with below-average intelligence need every step and bridge made explicit. Make connections for the student. Do not expect him or her to "see" the connections.

7. Be prepared to present the same idea in many different ways using different representations (verbal, visual, hands-on, etc.).

8. Go back to a simpler level if you see the student is not following.

9. Be especially careful to motivate the student and maintain attention. Allow and encourage different ways of expressing understanding—written, drawings, oral responses, gestures, etc.

10. Find materials that do not insult the student. A middle school boy may need the low vocabulary of "See Spot run," but will be insulted by the age of the characters and the content of the story.

11. Focus on a few target behaviors or skills so you and the student have a chance to experience success. Everyone needs positive reinforcement.

12. Be aware that students with below-average intelligence must overlearn, repeat, and practice more than children of average intelligence. They must be taught how to study, and they must frequently review and practice their newly acquired skills in different settings.

13. Pay close attention to social relations. Simply including students with below-average intelligence in a regular class will not guarantee that they will be accepted or that they will make and keep friends.

14. Establish peer tutoring programs and train all students in the class to serve as tutors and as tutees—see Chapter 10 for specifics.

For more information, see: http://www.aaidd.org/

structured and complete teaching and guidance makes sense. The *Guidelines* list more suggestions.

Learning goals for many students with intellectual disabilities who are between the ages of 9 and 13 include basic reading, writing, and arithmetic; learning about the local environment; social behavior; and personal interests. In middle and senior high school, the emphasis is on vocational and domestic skills, literacy for living (reading signs, labels, and newspaper ads; completing a job application), job-related behaviors such as courtesy and punctuality; health self-care; and citizenship skills. Today, there is a growing emphasis on **transition programming**—preparing the student to live and work in the community. As you saw earlier in the chapter, the law requires that schools design an IEP, or individualized educational program, for every child with disabilities. An ITP, or individualized transition plan, may be part of the IEP for students with intellectual disabilities (Friend, 2011).

Students with Health and Sensory Impairments

Some health impairments you may encounter are cerebral palsy, seizure disorders, asthma, HIV/AIDS, diabetes, visual impairments, and hearing impairments.

CEREBRAL PALSY AND MULTIPLE DISABILITIES. Damage to the brain before or during birth or during infancy can cause a child to have difficulty coordinating his or her body movements. The problem may be very mild, so the child simply appears a bit clumsy, or so severe that voluntary movement is practically impossible. The most common form of **cerebral palsy** is characterized by **spasticity** (overly tight or tense muscles). Many children

Transition programming Gradual preparation of students with special needs to move from high school into further education or training, employment, or community involvement.

Cerebral palsy Condition involving a range of motor or coordination difficulties due to brain damage.

Spasticity Overly tight or tense muscles, characteristic of some forms of cerebral palsy.

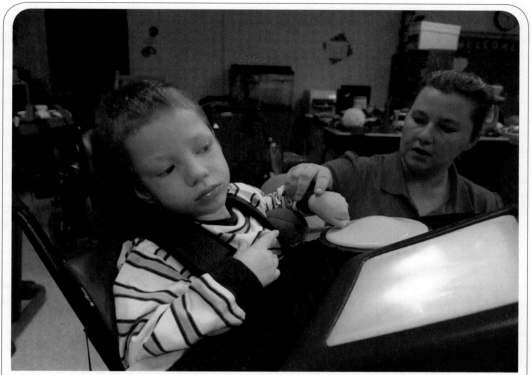

INSTRUCTIONAL ACCOMMODATIONS Physical and instructional accommodations can enable students with many kinds of disabilities to participate in general education classrooms. A specially designed desk enables this young child with cerebral palsy to work independently in class.

with cerebral palsy also have secondary handicaps. In the classroom, these secondary handicaps are the greatest concern—and these are generally what the regular teacher can help with most. For example, many children with cerebral palsy also have visual impairments or speech problems, and about 50% to 60% have mild to severe intellectual disabilities. But many students with cerebral palsy are average to well above average in measured intelligence (Pellegrino, 2002).

SEIZURE DISORDERS (EPILEPSY). A seizure is a cluster of behaviors that occurs in response to abnormal neurochemical activities in the brain (Hardman, Drew, & Egan, 2005). People with **epilepsy** have recurrent seizures, but not all seizures are the result of epilepsy; temporary conditions such as high fevers, infections, or withdrawal from drugs can also trigger seizures. Seizures take many forms and differ with regard to the length, frequency, and movements involved.

Most **generalized seizures** (once called *grand mal*) are accompanied by uncontrolled jerking movements that ordinarily last two to five minutes, possible loss of bowel or bladder control, and irregular breathing, followed by a deep sleep or coma. On regaining consciousness, the student may be very weary, confused, and in need of extra sleep. Most seizures can be controlled by medication. If a student has a seizure accompanied by convulsions in class, the teacher must take action so the student will not be injured. The major danger to a student having such a seizure is being injured from striking a hard surface during the violent jerking.

If a student has a seizure, stay calm and reassure the rest of the class. Do not try to restrain the child's movements; you can't stop the seizure once it starts. Lower the child gently to the floor, away from furniture or walls. Move hard objects away. Loosen scarves, ties, or anything that might make breathing difficult. Turn the child's head gently to the side, and put a soft coat or blanket under his or her head. Never put anything in the student's mouth—it is NOT true that people having seizures can swallow their tongues. Don't attempt artificial respiration unless the student does not start breathing again after

Epilepsy Disorder marked by seizures and caused by abnormal electrical discharges in the brain.

Generalized seizure A seizure involving a large portion of the brain.

the seizure stops. Find out from the student's parents how they deal with seizures. If one seizure follows another and the student does not regain consciousness in between, if the student is pregnant or has a medical ID that does not say "epilepsy, seizure disorder," if there are signs of injury, or if the seizure goes on for more than 5 minutes, get medical help right away (Friend, 2011).

Not all seizures are dramatic. Sometimes the student just loses contact briefly. The student may stare, fail to respond to questions, drop objects, and miss what has been happening for 1 to 30 seconds. These were once called *petit mal*, but they are now referred to as **absence seizures** and can easily go undetected. If a child in your class appears to daydream frequently, does not seem to know what is going on at times, or cannot remember what has just happened when you ask, you should consult the school psychologist or nurse. The major problem for students with absence seizures is that they miss the continuity of the class interaction—these seizures can occur as often as 100 times a day. If their seizures are frequent, students will find the lessons confusing. Question these students to be sure they are understanding and following the lesson. Be prepared to repeat yourself periodically.

OTHER SERIOUS HEALTH CONCERNS: ASTHMA, HIV/AIDS, AND DIABETES. There are many other health problems that affect students' learning, in great part because the students miss school, leading to lost instructional time and missed opportunities for friendships. Asthma is a chronic lung condition affecting 5 to 6 million children in America; it is more common for students in poverty. You probably have heard quite a bit about HIV/AIDS, a chronic illness in children that often can be controlled with medication. Luckily, we are making great progress in preventing HIV infection in children in the United States.

Type 2 diabetes is a chronic condition that affects the way the body metabolizes sugar (glucose). This condition needs to be taken seriously because it can affect almost every major organ in the body, including the heart, blood vessels, nerves, eyes, and kidneys (Mayo Clinic, 2009). For most children, this disease can be managed, or prevented altogether, by eating healthy foods, being physically active, and maintaining a healthy body weight. When diet and exercise modifications are not enough, children will need medications, such as insulin, to manage their blood sugar (Rosenberg et al., 2011; Werts, Culatta, & Tompkins, 2007).

With all health conditions, teachers need to talk to parents to find out how the problems are handled, what the signs are that a dangerous situation might be developing, and what resources are available for the student. Keep records of any incidents—they may be useful in the student's medical diagnosis and treatment.

STUDENTS WITH VISION IMPAIRMENTS. In the United States, only about 1 child in 1,000 has a visual impairment so serious that special educational services are needed. Most members of this group needing special services are classified as having **low vision**. This means they can read with the aid of a magnifying glass or large-print books. A small group of students, about 1 in every 2,500, is **educationally blind**. These students must use hearing and touch as their predominant learning channels (Kirk, Gallagher, & Anastasiow, 1993).

Students who have difficulty seeing often hold books either very close to or very far from their eyes. They may squint, rub their eyes frequently, or complain that their eyes burn or itch. The eyes may actually be swollen, red, or encrusted. Students with vision problems may misread material on the whiteboard or chalkboard, describe their vision as being blurred, be very sensitive to light, or hold their heads at an odd angle. They may become irritable when they have to do deskwork or lose interest if they have to follow an activity that is taking place across the room (Hunt & Marshall, 2002). Any of these signs should be reported to a qualified school professional.

Special materials and equipment that help these students to function in regular classrooms include large-print books; software that converts printed material to speech or to Braille; personal organizers that have talking appointment books or address books; special calculators; an abacus; three-dimensional maps, charts, and models; and special

Absence seizure A seizure involving only a small part of the brain that causes a child to lose contact briefly.

Low vision Vision limited to close objects.

Educationally blind Needing Braille materials in order to learn.

measuring devices. For students with visual problems, the quality of the print is often more important than the size, so watch out for hard-to-read handouts and blurry copies.

The arrangement of the room is also an issue. Students with visual problems need to know where things are, so consistency matters—a place for everything and everything in its place. Leave plenty of space for moving around the room, and make sure to monitor possible obstacles and safety hazards such as trash cans in aisles and open cabinet doors. If you rearrange the room, give students with visual problems a chance to learn the new layout. Also make sure these students have a buddy for fire drills or other emergencies (Friend & Bursuck, 2002).

STUDENTS WHO ARE DEAF. You will hear the term *hearing impaired* to describe these students, but the deaf community and researchers object to this label, so I will use their preferred terms, *deaf* and *hard of hearing*. The number of deaf students has been declining over the past three decades, but when the problem does occur, the consequences for learning are serious (Hunt & Marshall, 2002). Signs of hearing problems are turning one ear toward the speaker, favoring one ear in conversation, or misunderstanding conversation when the speaker's face cannot be seen. Other indications include not following directions, seeming distracted or confused at times, frequently asking people to repeat what they have said, mispronouncing new words or names, and being reluctant to participate in class discussions. Take note particularly of students who have frequent earaches, sinus infections, or allergies.

In the past, educators have debated whether oral or manual approaches are better for children who are deaf or hard of hearing. Oral approaches involve speech reading (also called *lip reading*) and training students to use whatever limited hearing they may have. Manual approaches include sign language and finger spelling. Research indicates that children who learn some manual method of communicating perform better in academic subjects and are more socially mature than students who are exposed only to oral methods. Today, the trend is to combine both approaches (Hallahan & Kauffman, 2006).

Another perspective suggests that people who are deaf are part of a different culture with a different language, values, social institutions, and literature. Hunt and Marshall (2002) quote one deaf professional: "How would women like to be referred to as male-impaired, or whites like to be called black-impaired? I'm not impaired; I'm deaf!" (p. 348). From this perspective, a goal is to help deaf children become bilingual and bicultural, to enable them to function effectively in both cultures. Technological innovations and the many avenues of communication through e-mail and the Internet have expanded communication possibilities for all people.

Autism Spectrum Disorders and Asperger Syndrome

You may be familiar with the term *autism*. In 1990 **autism** was added to the IDEA list of disabilities qualifying for special services. It is defined as "a developmental disability significantly affecting verbal and nonverbal communication and social interaction, generally evident before age three, that adversely affect the child's educational performance" (34 Federal Code of Regulations § 300.7). I will use the term preferred by professionals in the field, **autism spectrum disorders** to emphasize that autism includes a range of disorders from mild to major. You might also hear the term **pervasive developmental disorder (PDD)**, especially if you are talking with medical professionals. Estimates of the number of children with autism vary greatly, but are increasing dramatically. IDEA places the number on the autism spectrum at .25% of all children, ages 3 to 21. The most recent report from the Centers for Disease Control is 1 in every 310 girls and 1 in every 70 boys (CDC, 2010). Other estimates range as high a 1% of all children, ages 3 to 17 (Friend, 2011).

From early on, children with autism spectrum disorders may have difficulties in social relations. They do not form connections with others, avoid eye contact, or don't share feelings such as enjoyment or interest in others. Communication is impaired. About half of these students are nonverbal; they have no or very few language skills. Others make up their own language. They may obsessively insist on regularity and sameness in their environments—change is very disturbing. They may repeat behaviors or gestures and have restricted interests, watching the same DVD over and over, for example. They

Autism/Autism spectrum disorders Developmental disability significantly affecting verbal and nonverbal communication and social interaction, generally evident before age 3 and ranging from mild to major.

Pervasive developmental disorder (PDD) A term favored by the medical community to describe autism spectrum disorders.

SOME FACES OF ASPERGER SYNDROME In his book, *The Genesis of Artistic Creativity: Asperger Syndrome and the Arts*, Michael Fitzgerald (2005) speculates that the famous musicians Beethoven and Mozart, and the artists van Gogh and Warhol display behaviors associated with Asperger syndrome.

may be very sensitive to light, sound, touch, or other sensory information—sounds may be painful, for example, or the slight flickering of fluorescent lights may seem like constant bursts, causing severe headaches. They may be able to memorize words or steps in problem solving, but not use them appropriately or become very confused when the situation changes or questions are asked in a different way (Franklin, 2007; Friend, 2011; Matson, Matson, & Rivet, 2007).

Asperger syndrome is one of the disabilities included in the autism spectrum. Children with Asperger syndrome have many of the characteristics described above, but they have the greatest trouble with social relations. Language is less affected. Their speech may be fluent but unusual, mixing up pronouns of "I" and "you," for example. Many students with autism also have moderate to severe intellectual disabilities, but those with Asperger syndrome usually have average to above average intelligence (Friend, 2011).

THEORY OF MIND. One current explanation for autism and Asperger syndrome is that children with these disorders lack a theory of mind (Miller, 2009). We examined this concept briefly in Chapter 3—theory of mind is an understanding that you and other people have minds, thoughts, and emotions. Students with autism have difficulty explaining their own behaviors, appreciating that other people might have different feelings, and predicting how behaviors might affect emotions. So, for example, a student may not understand why classmates are bored by his constant repetition of stories or obscure facts about topics he finds fascinating. Or the student may stand too close or too far away when interacting, not realizing that she is making other people uncomfortable (Friend, 2011; Harris, 2006).

INTERVENTIONS. Early and intense interventions that focus on communications and social relations are particularly important for children with autism spectrum disorders. Without interventions, behaviors such as poor eye contact and odd-seeming mannerisms tend to increase over time (Matson et al., 2007). As they move into elementary school, some of these students will be in inclusive settings, others will be in specialized classes, and many will be in some combination of these two. Collaboration among teachers and the family is particularly important. Strategies such as providing smaller classes, offering structured environments, finding a class "buddy" to give support, maintaining a safe "home base" for times of stress, ensuring consistency in instruction and transition routines, implementing assistive technologies, and using visuals may be part of a collaborative plan (Friend, 2011; Harrower & Dunlap, 2001). Through adolescence and the transition to adulthood, instruction and guidance in life, work, and social skills are important educational goals.

Response to Intervention (RTI)

One of the problems for students with serious learning problems is that they have to struggle through the early grades, often falling farther and farther behind, until they are identified, assessed, qualified for an IDEA category, receive an individualized educational program (IEP), and finally get appropriate help. This has been called the "wait to fail" model. The reauthorization of IDEA in 2004 gave educators a new option for assessing and educating students who might have serious learning problems. The process is called **response to intervention** or **RTI**. The main goal of RTI is to make sure students get appropriate research-based instruction and support as soon as possible, in kindergarten if they need it, before they have fallen too far behind. A second goal is to make sure teachers are systematic in documenting the interventions they have tried with these students and describing how well each intervention worked. In addition, instead of using the discrepancy between IQ scores and student achievement to identify students with learning disabilities, educators can now use RTI criteria to determine who needs more intensive learning support (Klinger & Orosco, 2010). However, this last use of RTI has been criticized for not being a valid or reliable way of assessing students with learning disabilities because it does not provide a comprehensive and thorough picture of the student's strengths and weaknesses, including documenting other problems that might be present (Reynolds & Shaywitz, 2009).

RESPONSE TO INTERVENTION (RTI) One of the main goals of the response to intervention (RTI) process is to identify students who may have learning difficulties as early as possible so that they don't fall too far behind before problems are recognized. A second goal is to document what works and what doesn't with each student for planning.

One common way of reaching these RTI goals is to use a three-tiered system (sometimes a fourth tier is added). The first tier is to use a strong, well-researched way of teaching all students (we will look at these kinds of approaches in Chapter 14). Students who are struggling in the tier 1 curriculum, as identified by ongoing quality classroom assessments, are moved to the second tier and receive extra support and additional small-group instruction. If some students still make limited progress, they move to the third tier for additional one-to-one intensive help and perhaps a special needs assessment (Buffum, Mattos, & Weber, 2010). The approach has at least two advantages—students get extra help right away and the information gained based on their responses to the different interventions can be used for IEP planning, if the students reach the third stage of RTI. For more information on RTI, go to the Web site for the National Center on Response to Intervention (http://www.rti4success.org/).

We end the chapter with another group that has special needs, but is not covered by IDEA or Section 504—highly intelligent or talented students.

STUDENTS WHO ARE GIFTED AND TALENTED

Consider this situation, a true story.

> Latoya was already an advanced reader when she entered 1st grade in a large urban school district. Her teacher noticed the challenging chapter books Latoya brought to school and read with little effort. After administering a reading assessment, the school's reading consultant confirmed that Latoya was reading at the 5th grade level. Latoya's parents reported with pride that she had started to read independently when she was 3 years old and "had read every book she could get her hands on." (Reis et al., 2002)

In her struggling urban school, Latoya received no particular accommodations, and by 5th grade, she was still reading at just above the 5th grade level. Her 5th grade teacher had no idea that Latoya had ever been an advanced reader.

Response to intervention (RTI) A process to make sure students get appropriate research-based instruction and support as soon as possible and that teachers are systematic in documenting what interventions they have tried with these students so this information can be used in planning.

Here is another true story:

> Alex Wade's field is linguistics. In his search for the perfect language—and "annoyed," he says, with Esperanto—he has created 10 languages and 30 or 40 alphabets, including one language without verbs, just for the challenge. He's taking courses at the University of Nevada, Reno, in Basque, linguistics, and microbiology (because he also has a talent for science). . . . Alex is 13. (Kronholz, 2011)

Latoya and Alex are not alone. They are part of a group with special needs that is often overlooked by the schools: **gifted and talented students**. There is growing recognition that gifted students are being poorly served by most public schools. A national study found that more than one-half of all gifted students do not achieve in school at a level equal to their ability (Tomlinson-Keasey, 1990). Yet a survey of the states in 2008 by the National Association for Gifted Children (NAGC) found that at least a dozen states would not allow students to start kindergarten early, even if they were reading at a high level. At least 30 states allow only 11th and 12th graders to take college courses. What would that mean for students like Latoya and Alex (Kronholz, 2011)?

Who Are These Students?

There are many definitions of *gifted* because individuals can have many different gifts. Remember that Gardner (2003) identified eight separate "intelligences" and Sternberg (1997) suggests a triarchic model. Renzulli and Reis (2003) have a different three-part conception of giftedness: above-average general ability, a high level of creativity, and a high level of task commitment or motivation to achieve. The No Child Left Behind Act (2002) defines gifted students as those "who give evidence of high achievement capability in areas such as intellectual, creative, artistic, or leadership capacity, or in specific academic fields, and who need services or activities not ordinarily provided by the school in order to fully develop those capabilities" (p. 544). The College of William and Mary's Center for Gifted Education makes additional distinctions based on measured IQ: gifted learners score above 130 on IQ tests, the highly gifted score above 145, the exceptionally gifted above 160, and the profoundly gifted above 175 (Kronholz, 2011).

Truly gifted children are not the students who simply learn quickly with little effort. The work of gifted students is original, extremely advanced for their age, and potentially of lasting importance. These children may read fluently with little instruction by age 3 or 4. They may play a musical instrument like a skillful adult, turn a visit to the grocery store into a mathematical puzzle, and become fascinated with algebra when their friends are having trouble with simple addition (Winner, 2000). Recent conceptions widen the view of giftedness to include attention to the children's culture, language, and special needs (Association for the Gifted, 2001). These newer conceptions are more likely to identify children like Latoya.

What do we know about these remarkable individuals? A classic study of the characteristics of the academically and intellectually gifted was started decades ago by Lewis Terman and colleagues (1925, 1947, 1959; Holahan & Sears, 1995). This huge project followed the lives of 1,528 gifted males and females and continued until 2010. The subjects all had IQ scores in the top 1% of the population (140 or above on the Stanford-Binet individual test of intelligence). They were identified on the basis of these test scores and teacher recommendations.

Terman and colleagues found that these gifted children were larger, stronger, and healthier than the norm. They often walked sooner and were more athletic. They were more emotionally stable than their peers and became better-adjusted adults than the average individual. They had lower rates of delinquency, emotional difficulty, divorce, drug problems, and so on. Of course, the teachers in Terman's study who made the nominations may have selected students who were better adjusted initially. And remember, Terman's study just tells about academically gifted students. There are many other kinds of gifts.

WHAT IS THE ORIGIN OF THESE GIFTS? Studies of prodigies and geniuses in many fields document that deep and prolonged practice is necessary to achieve at the highest levels. For example, it took Newton 20 years to move from his first ideas to his ultimate

Gifted and talented students Very bright, creative, and talented students.

contribution (Howe, Davidson, & Sloboda, 1998; Winner, 2000). I remember listening to the early reports of Bloom's study of world-class concert pianists, sculptors, Olympic swimmers, research neurologists, mathematicians, and tennis champions, (1982). To study talent in tennis, Bloom's research team had interviewed the top tennis players in the world, their coaches, parents, siblings, and friends. One coach said that he would make a suggestion, and a few days later the young athlete would have mastered the move. Then the parents told how the child had practiced that move for hours on end after getting the coach's tip. So, focused, intense practice plays a role. Also, the families of prodigies tend to be child-centered and to devote hours to supporting the development of their child's gifts. Bloom's research team described tremendous sacrifices made by families: rising before dawn to drive their child to a swimming coach or piano teacher in another city, working two jobs, or even moving the whole family to another part of the country to find the best

ORIGINS OF GIFTEDNESS For years, researchers have debated the nature/nurture question about people with extraordinary abilities and talents. Studies of prodigies and geniuses in many fields document that deep and prolonged practice is necessary to achieve at the highest levels.

teachers or coaches. The children responded to the family's sacrifices by working harder and the families responded to the child's hard work by sacrificing more—an upward spiral of investment and achievement.

But hard work will never make me a world-class tennis player or a Newton. There is a role for nature as well. The children studied by Bloom showed early and clear talent in the areas they later developed. As children, great sculptors were constantly drawing and great mathematicians were fascinated with dials, gears, and gauges. Parents' investments in their children came after the children showed early high-level achievement (Winner, 2000, 2003). Recent research suggests that gifted children, at least those with extraordinary abilities in mathematics, music, and visual arts, may have unusual brain organization—which can have both advantages and disadvantages. Giftedness in mathematics, music, and visual arts appears to be associated with superior visual-spatial abilities and enhanced development of the right side of the brain. Children with these gifts are also more likely not to have right-hand dominance and to have language related-problems. These brain differences are evidence that "gifted children, child prodigies, and savants are not made from scratch but are born with unusual brains that enable rapid learning in a particular domain" (Winner, 2000, p. 160).

WHAT PROBLEMS DO THE GIFTED FACE? In spite of Bloom's and Terman's findings, it would be incorrect to say that every gifted student is superior in adjustment and emotional health. In fact, gifted adolescents, especially girls, are more likely to be depressed, and both girls and boys may be bored, frustrated, and isolated. Schoolmates may be consumed with baseball or worried about failing math, while the gifted child is fascinated with Mozart, focused on a social issue, or totally absorbed in computers, drama, or geology. Gifted children may be impatient with friends, parents, and even teachers who do not share their interests or abilities (Woolfolk & Perry, 2012). One researcher asked 13,000 gifted students in 7 states to name one word for their experiences. The most commonly used word was "waiting." "Waiting for teachers to move ahead, waiting for classmates to catch up, waiting to learn something new—always waiting" (Kronholz, 2011, p. 3).

Because their language is well developed, gifted students may be seen as show-offs when they are simply expressing themselves. They are sensitive to the expectations and feelings of others, so these students may be very vulnerable to criticisms and taunts. Because they are goal directed and focused, they may seem stubborn and uncooperative. Their keen sense of humor can be used as a weapon against teachers and other students

(Hardman, Drew, & Egan, 2005; Robinson & Clinkenbeard, 1998). Adjustment problems seem to be greatest for the most gifted, those in the highest range of academic ability (e.g., above 180 IQ). The chance of any teacher encountering a student in this highest IQ range is only about 1 in 80 over an entire 40-year career—but what if such a student walks into your class (Kronholz, 2011)?

Identifying Gifted Students

Identifying gifted children is not always easy, and teaching them well may be even more challenging. Many parents provide early educational experiences for their children. In middle and high school, some very able students deliberately earn lower grades, making their abilities even harder to recognize. Girls are especially likely to hide their abilities (Woolfolk & Perry, 2012).

RECOGNIZING GIFTS AND TALENTS. Here are a few questions to guide identification, suggested by Marilyn Friend (2011). Who can easily manipulate abstract symbol systems such as mathematics? Who can concentrate for long periods of time on personal interests? Who remembers easily? Who developed language and reading early, like Latoya described at the beginning of this section? Who is curious and has many interests? Whose work is original and creative? Certainly Alex's interests and creativity in inventing languages, described earlier, fit these last two critieria. These students may also prefer to work alone, have a keen sense of justice and fairness, be energetic and intense, form strong commitments to friends—often older students—and struggle with perfectionism.

Group achievement and intelligence tests tend to underestimate the IQs of very bright children. Group tests may be appropriate for screening, but they are not appropriate for making placement decisions. There is some evidence that using individual IQ tests such as the WISC-IV, which include evaluations of verbal comprehension and working memory, are the best predictors of achievement in reading and math for gifted students (Rowe, Kingsley, & Thompson, 2010). Many psychologists recommend a case study approach. This means gathering many kinds of information about the student in different contexts: test scores, grades, examples of work, projects and portfolios, letters or ratings from community or church members, self-ratings, nominations from teachers or peers, and so on (Renzulli & Reis, 2003). Especially for recognizing artistic talent, experts in the field can be called in to judge the merits of a child's creations. Science projects, exhibitions, performances, auditions, and interviews are all possibilities. Creativity tests and tests of self-regulation skills may identify some children not picked up by other measures, particularly minority students who may be at a disadvantage on the other types of tests (Grigorenko, et al., 2009). Remember, students with remarkable abilities in one area may have much less impressive abilities in others. In fact, there may be up to 180,000 students in American schools who are gifted *and* learning disabled. In addition, there are two other groups who are underrepresented in gifted education programs: girls and students living in poverty (Stormont, Stebbins, & Holliday, 2001). See Table 4.11 for ideas about identifying and supporting these students.

Teaching Gifted Students

Some educators believe that gifted students should be *accelerated*—moved quickly through the grades or through particular subjects. Other educators prefer *enrichment*—giving the students additional, more sophisticated, and more thought-provoking work, but keeping them with their age-mates in school. Actually, both may be appropriate (Torrance, 1986). One way of doing this is through *curriculum compacting*—assessing students' knowledge of the material in the instructional unit, then teaching only for those goals not yet reached (Reis & Renzulli, 2004). Using curriculum compacting, teachers may be able to eliminate about half of the usual curriculum content for some gifted students without any loss of learning. The time saved can be used for learning goals that include enrichment, sophistication, and novelty (Werts et al., 2007).

ACCELERATION. Many people object to acceleration, but most careful studies indicate that truly gifted students who begin primary, elementary, middle, or high school, college,

TABLE 4.11 • **Recognizing and Supporting All Students with Gifts and Talents**

Recognizing Gifted Students with Learning Disabilities. Here are some ideas for supporting gifted students with learning disabilities (McCoach, Kehle, Bray, & Siegle, 2001):
• Identify these students by looking longitudinally at achievement. • Remediate skill deficits, but also identify and develop talents and strengths. • Provide emotional support; it is important for all students, but especially for this group. • Help students learn to compensate directly for their learning problems, and assist them in "tuning in" to their own strengths and difficulties.
Recognizing Gifts in Girls. As young girls develop their identities in adolescence, they often reject being labeled as gifted—being accepted and popular and "fitting in" may become more important than achievement (Basow & Rubin, 1999; Stormont et al., 2001). How can teachers reach girls who are gifted?
• Notice when girls' test scores seem to decline in middle or high school. • Encourage assertiveness, achievement, high goals, and demanding work from all students. • Provide models of achievement through speakers, internships, or readings. • Look for and support gifts in arenas other than academic achievement.
Recognizing Gifted Students Who Live in Poverty. Health problems, lack of resources, homelessness, fears about safety and survival, frequent moves, and responsibilities for the care of other family members all make achievement in school more difficult. To identify students with gifts:
• Use alternative assessment, teacher nomination, and creativity tests. • Be sensitive to cultural differences in values about cooperative or solitary achievement (Ford, 2000). • Use multicultural strategies to encourage both achievement and the development of racial identities.

or even graduate school early do as well as, and usually better than, nongifted students who are progressing at the normal pace. Social and emotional adjustment does not appear to be impaired. Gifted students tend to prefer the company of older playmates (Davis, Rimm, & Siegle, 2011). In fact, Colangelo, Assouline, and Gross (2004) collected the research on the many benefits of acceleration and published two volumes called *A Nation Deceived: How Schools Hold Back America's Brightest Children*. These publications from the University of Iowa make a powerful case for acceleration.

An alternative to skipping grades is to accelerate students in one or two particular subjects or to allow concurrent enrollment in advanced placement or college courses, but keep them with peers for the rest of the time (Robinson & Clinkenbeard, 1998). For students who are extremely advanced intellectually (for example, those scoring 160 or higher on an individual intelligence test), the only practical solution likely is to accelerate their education (Davis, Rimm, & Siegle, 2011; Kronholz, 2011).

METHODS AND STRATEGIES. Teaching methods for gifted students should encourage abstract thinking (formal-operational thought), creativity, reading of high-level and original texts, and independence, not just the learning of greater quantities of facts. One approach that *does not* seem promising with gifted students is cooperative learning in mixed-ability groups. Gifted students tend to learn more when they work in groups with other high-ability peers (Fuchs, Fuchs, Hamlett, & Karns, 1998; Robinson & Clinkenbeard, 1998). In fact, students in gifted programs appear to be less bored when they are ability grouped with others like themselves. An interesting tradeoff for gifted students is that their academic self-concepts tend to decrease when they are grouped with other high-ability students—an example of the "Little-Fish-in-a-Big-Pond" effect described in Chapter 3 (Preckel, Goetz, & Frenzel, 2010).

In working with gifted and talented students, a teacher must be imaginative, flexible, tolerant, and unthreatened by the capabilities of these students. The teacher must ask: What do these children need most? What are they ready to learn? Who can help me to challenge them? Challenge and support are critical for all students. But challenging students who know more than anyone else in the school about history or music or science or math can be a challenge! Answers might come from faculty members at nearby colleges, retired professionals, books, museums, the Internet, or older students. Strategies might be as simple as letting the child do math with the next grade. Other options are summer institutes; courses at nearby colleges; classes with local artists, musicians, or dancers; independent research projects; selected classes in high school for younger students; honors classes; and special-interest clubs (Rosenberg, Westling, & McLeskey, 2011).

In the midst of providing challenge, don't forget the support. We all have seen the ugly sights of parents, coaches, or teachers forcing the joy out of their talented students by demanding practice and perfection beyond the child's interest. Just as we should not force children to stop investing in their talent ("Oh, Michelangelo, quit fooling with those sketches and go outside and play"), we also should avoid destroying intrinsic motivation with heavy doses of pressure and external rewards.

This has been a brief, selective look at the needs of children. If you decide that students in your class might benefit from special services of any kind, the first step is making a referral. How would you begin? Table 4.12 guides you through the referral process. In Chapter 14, when we discuss differentiated teaching, we will look at more ways to reach all your students.

TABLE 4.12 • **Making a Referral**

1. Contact the student's parents. It is very important that you discuss the student's problems with the parents *before* you refer.
2. Before making a referral, check *all* the student's school records. Has the student ever:

   - had a psychological evaluation?
   - qualified for special services?
   - been included in other special programs (e.g., for disadvantaged children; speech or language therapy)?
   - scored far below average on standardized tests?
   - been retained?

   Do the records indicate:

   - good progress in some areas, poor progress in others?
   - any physical or medical problem?
   - that the student is taking medication?

3. Talk to the student's other teachers and professional support personnel about your concern for the student. Have other teachers also had difficulty with the student? Have they found ways of dealing successfully with the student? Document the strategies that you have used in your class to meet the student's educational needs. Your documentation will be useful as evidence that will be helpful to or be required by the committee of professionals who will evaluate the student. Demonstrate your concern by keeping written records. Your notes should include items such as:

   - exactly what you are concerned about
   - why you are concerned about it
   - dates, places, and times you have observed the problem
   - precisely what you have done to try to resolve the problem
   - who, if anyone, helped you devise the plans or strategies you have used
   - evidence that the strategies have been successful or unsuccessful

   Remember that you should refer a student only if you can make a convincing case that the student may have a handicapping condition and probably cannot be served appropriately without special education. Referral for special education begins a time-consuming, costly, and stressful process that is potentially damaging to the student and has many legal ramifications.

▼ SUMMARY

Intelligence (pp. 116–128)

What are the advantages of and problems with labels? Labels and diagnostic classifications can easily become both stigmas and self-fulfilling prophecies, but they can also open doors to special programs and help teachers develop appropriate instructional strategies.

What is person-first language? "Person-first" language ("students with intellectual disabilities," "students placed at risk," etc.) is an alternative to labels that describe a complex person with one or two words, implying that the condition labeled is the most important aspect of the person. With person-first language, the emphasis is on the students first, not on the special challenges they face.

Distinguish between a disability and a handicap. A disability is an inability to do something specific such as see or walk. A handicap is a disadvantage in certain situations. Some disabilities lead to handicaps, but not in all contexts. Teachers must avoid imposing handicaps on disabled learners.

What is *g*? Spearman suggested there is one mental attribute, which he called *g* or general intelligence, that is used to perform any mental test, but that each test also requires some specific abilities in addition to *g*. A current version of the general plus specific abilities theory is Carroll's work identifying a few broad abilities (such as learning and memory, visual perception, verbal fluency) and at least 70 specific abilities. Fluid and crystallized intelligence are two of the broad abilities identified in most research.

What is Gardner's view of intelligence and his position on *g*? Gardner contends that an intelligence is a biological and psychological potential to solve problems and create outcomes that are valued by a culture. These intelligences are realized to a greater or lesser extent as a consequence of the experiential, cultural, and motivational factors in a person's environment. The intelligences are: linguistic, musical, spatial, logical-mathematical, bodily-kinesthetic, interpersonal, intrapersonal, naturalist, and perhaps existential. Gardner does not deny the existence of *g*, but questions how useful *g* is as an explanation for human achievements.

What are the elements in Sternberg's theory of intelligence? Sternberg's triarchic theory of intelligence is a cognitive process approach to understanding intelligence: Analytic/componential intelligence involves mental processes that are defined in terms of components: metacomponents, performance components, and knowledge-acquisition components. Creative/experiential intelligence involves coping with new experiences through insight and automaticity. Practical/contextual intelligence involves choosing to live and work in a context where success is likely, adapting to that context, and reshaping it if necessary. Practical intelligence is made up mostly of action-oriented tacit knowledge learned during everyday life.

How is intelligence measured, and what does an IQ score mean? Intelligence is measured through individual tests (Stanford-Binet, Wechsler, etc.) and group tests (Otis-Lennon School Abilities Tests, Slosson Intelligence Test, Raven Progressive Matrices, Naglieri Nonverbal Ability Test—Multiform, Differential Abilities Scales, Wide Range Intelligence Test, etc.). Compared to an individual test, a group test is much less likely to yield an accurate picture of any one person's abilities. The average score is 100. About 68% of

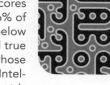

the general population will earn IQ scores between 85 and 115. Only about 16% of the population will receive scores below 85 or above 115. These figures hold true for White, native-born Americans whose first language is Standard English. Intelligence predicts success in school, but is less predictive of success in life when level of education is taken into account.

What is the Flynn effect and what are its implications? Since the early 1900s, IQ scores have been rising. To keep 100 as the average for IQ test scores, questions have to be made more difficult. This increasing difficulty has implications for any program that uses IQ scores as part of the entrance requirements. For example, students who were not identified as having learning problems a generation ago might be identified as having intellectual disabilities now because the test questions are harder.

Are there sex differences in cognitive abilities? Girls seem to be better on verbal tests, especially when writing is involved. Males seem to be superior on tasks that require mental rotation of objects. The scores of males tend to be more variable in general, so there are more males than females with very high and very low scores on tests. Research on the causes of these differences has been inconclusive, except to indicate that academic socialization and teachers' treatment of male and female students in mathematics classes may play a role.

Learning and Thinking Styles (pp. 128–130)

Distinguish between learning styles and learning preferences. Learning styles are the characteristic ways a person approaches learning and studying. Learning preferences are individual preferences for particular learning modes and environments. Even though learning styles and learning preferences are not related to intelligence or effort, they can affect school performance.

Should teachers match instruction to individual learning styles? Results of some research indicate that students learn more when they study in their preferred setting and manner, but most research does not show a benefit. Many students would do better to develop new—and perhaps more effective—ways to learn.

What learning style distinctions are the most well supported by research? One distinction that is repeatedly found in research is deep versus surface processing. Individuals who have a deep-processing approach see the learning activities as a means for understanding some underlying concepts or meanings. Students who take a surface-processing approach focus on memorizing the learning materials, not understanding them. A second is Mayer's visualizer–verbalizer dimension that has three facets: cognitive spatial ability (low or high), cognitive style (a visualizer versus a verbalizer), and learning preference (a verbal learner versus a visual learner).

Individual Differences and the Law (pp. 130–135)

Describe the main legal requirements that pertain to students with disabilities. Beginning with Public Law 94-142 (1975) and continuing with many reauthorizations including IDEA, the Individuals with Disabilities Education Act (2004), the requirements for teaching students with disabilities have been spelled out. Each learner or student with special needs (zero reject) should be educated in the least restrictive environment according to an individualized education program (IEP). The laws also protect the rights of students with special needs and their parents. In addition, Section 504 of the Vocational Rehabilitation Act of 1973 prevents discrimination against people with disabilities in any program that receives federal money, such as public schools. Through Section 504, all school-age children are ensured an equal opportunity to participate in school activities. The definition of disability is broad in Section 504 and in the Americans with Disabilities Act.

Students with Learning Challenges (pp. 136–155)

What does research in neuroscience tell us about learning problems? Studies of the brains of students with learning disabilities and with attention deficit disorders show some differences in structure and activity compared to those of students without problems. Students with learning disabilities have problems in using the system of working memory that holds verbal and auditory information while you work with it. Because children with learning disabilities have trouble holding on to words and sounds, it is difficult for them to put the words together to comprehend the meaning of a sentence or to figure out what a math story problem is really asking about. There also may be difficulties retrieving needed information from long-term memory while transforming new incoming information, such as the next numbers to add. Important bits of information keep getting lost.

What is a learning disability? Specific learning disabilities are disorders in one or more of the basic psychological processes involved in understanding or using spoken or written language. Listening, speaking, reading, writing, reasoning, or mathematical abilities might be affected. These disorders are intrinsic to the individual, presumed to be the result of central nervous system dysfunction, and may occur across the life span. Students with learning disabilities may become victims of learned helplessness when they come to believe that they cannot control or improve their own learning and therefore cannot succeed. A focus on learning strategies often helps students with learning disabilities.

What is ADHD and how is it handled in school? Attention-deficit hyperactivity disorder (ADHD) is the term used to describe individuals of any age with hyperactivity and attention difficulties. Use of medication to address ADHD is controversial, but currently on the rise. For many students there are negative side effects. In addition, little is known about the long-term effects of drug therapy. There also is no evidence that the drugs lead to improvement in academic learning or peer relationships. Approaches that combine motivational training with instruction in learning and memory strategies and behavior modification seem effective. The SMART approach that focuses on the abilities of children is another possibility.

What are the most common communication disorders? Common communication disorders include speech impairments (articulation disorders, stuttering, and voicing problems) and oral language disorders. If these problems are addressed early, great progress is possible.

What are the best approaches for students with emotional and behavioral disorders? Methods from applied behavioral analysis and direct teaching of social skills are two useful approaches. Students also may respond to structure and organization in the environment, schedules, activities, and rules.

What are some warning signs of potential suicide? Students at risk of suicide may show changes in eating or sleeping habits, weight, grades, disposition, activity level, or interest in friends. They sometimes suddenly give away prized possessions such as iPods, CDs, clothing, or pets. They may seem depressed or hyperactive and may start missing school or quit doing work. It is especially dangerous if the student not only talks about suicide, but also has a plan for carrying it out.

What defines intellectual disabilities? Before age 18, students must score below about 70 on a standard measure of intelligence and must have problems with adaptive behavior, day-to-day independent living, and social functioning. The AAIDD now recommends a classification scheme based on the amount of support that a person requires to function at his or her highest level. Support varies from intermittent (e.g., as needed during stressful times), to limited (consistent support, but time limited such as employment training), to extensive (daily care such as living in a group home), to pervasive (constant high-intensity care for all aspects of living).

How can schools accommodate the needs of students with physical disabilities? If the school has the necessary architectural features, such as ramps, elevators, and accessible rest rooms, and if teachers allow for the physical limitations of students, little needs to be done to alter the usual educational program. Identifying a peer to help with movements and transitions can be useful.

How would you handle a seizure in class? Do not restrain the child's movements. Lower the child gently to the floor, away from furniture or walls. Move hard objects away. Turn the child's head gently to the side, put a soft coat or blanket under the student's head, and loosen any tight clothing. Never put anything in the student's mouth. Find out from the student's parents how they deal with seizures. If one seizure follows another and the student does not regain consciousness in between, if the student is pregnant, or if the seizure goes on for more than 5 minutes, get medical help right away.

What are some signs of visual and hearing impairments? Holding books very close or far away, squinting, rubbing eyes, misreading the chalkboard, and holding the head at an odd angle are possible signs of visual problems. Signs of hearing problems are turning one ear toward the speaker, favoring one ear in conversation, or misunderstanding conversation when the speaker's face cannot be seen. Other indications include not following directions, seeming distracted or confused at times, frequently asking people to repeat what they have said, mispronouncing new words or names, and being reluctant to participate in class discussions.

How does autism differ from Asperger syndrome? Asperger syndrome is one of the autism spectrum disorders. Many students with autism also have moderate-to-severe intellectual disabilities, but those with Asperger syndrome usually have average-to-above-average intelligence and better language abilities than other children with autism.

What is Response to Intervention (RTI)? RTI is an approach to supporting students with learning problems as early as possible, not waiting for years to assess, identify, and plan a program. One RTI process is a three-tiered system. The first tier is to use a strong, well-researched way of teaching all students. Students who do not do well with these methods are moved to the second tier and receive extra support and additional small-group instruction. If some students still make limited progress, they move to the third tier for one-to-one intensive help and perhaps a special needs assessment.

Students Who Are Gifted and Talented (pp. 155–160)

What are the characteristics of gifted students? Gifted students learn easily and rapidly and retain what they have learned; use common sense and practical knowledge; know about many things that the other children don't; use a large number of words easily and accurately; recognize relations and comprehend meaning; are alert and keenly observant and respond quickly; are persistent and highly motivated on some tasks; and are creative or make interesting connections. Teachers should make special efforts to support underrepresented gifted students—girls, students who also have learning disabilities, and children living in poverty.

Is acceleration a useful approach with gifted students? Many people object to acceleration, but most careful studies indicate that truly gifted students who are accelerated do as well as and usually better than nongifted students who are progressing at the normal pace. Gifted students tend to prefer the company of older playmates and may be bored if kept with children their own age. Skipping grades may not be the best solution for a particular student, but for students who are extremely advanced intellectually (with a score of 160 or higher on an individual intelligence test), the only practical solution may be to accelerate their education.

▼ KEY TERMS

Absence seizure (152)
Americans with Disabilities Act of 1990 (ADA) (135)
Articulation disorders (143)
Attention-deficit hyperactivity disorder (ADHD) (140)
Autism/Autism spectrum disorders (153)
Automaticity (123)
Cerebral palsy (150)
Crystallized intelligence (119)
Deviation IQ (124)
Disability (116)
Educationally blind (152)
Emotional and behavioral disorders (144)
Epilepsy (151)
Fluid intelligence (119)
Flynn effect (126)

Free, appropriate public education (FAPE) (131)
General intelligence (*g*) (119)
Generalized seizure (151)
Gifted and talented students (156)
Handicap (116)
Inclusion (132)
Individualized Education Program (IEP) (132)
Individuals with Disabilities Education Improvement Act (IDEA) (131)
Insight (123)
Integration (132)
Intellectual disabilities/Mental retardation (149)
Intelligence (119)
Intelligence quotient (IQ) (124)
Learned helplessness (139)
Learning disability (136)

Learning preferences (129)
Learning styles (128)
Least restrictive environment (LRE) (132)
Low vision (152)
Mainstreaming (132)
Mental age (124)
Pervasive developmental disorder (PDD) (153)
Response to intervention (RTI) (155)
Section 504 (135)
Spasticity (150)
Speech disorder (143)
Theory of multiple intelligences (120)
Transition programming (150)
Triarchic theory of successful intelligence (123)
Voicing problems (143)
Zero reject (131)

▼ CONNECT AND EXTEND TO LICENSURE

MULTIPLE-CHOICE QUESTIONS

1. African American students are more likely to be identified for special education services and placed outside of the general education system than Caucasian students. All but which one of the following are attempts to explain this overrepresentation?
   A. High poverty rates which lead to poor prenatal care, nutrition, and health care.
   B. Teachers who are unprepared to work with ethnic minority students.
   C. Biases in teachers' attitudes and the curriculum.
   D. African American students comprise 80% of the gifted and talented population.

2. Developmental psychologist Howard Gardner's multiple intelligences theory continues to impact classrooms today in the United States based upon its reflection of which current classroom strategy?
   A. Differentiated instruction
   B. Sternberg's triarchic theory of successful intelligence
   C. Mainstreaming
   D. Response to Intervention (RTI)

3. When a student has been identified as needing special education services, the Individuals with Disabilities Education Act mandates all but which one of the following?

   A. Accommodations must be made during state standardized testing of all students receiving special education services.
   B. The law requires states to provide a free, appropriate public education (FAPE) for all students with disabilities who participate in special education.
   C. States are required to develop procedures for educating children in the least restrictive environment
   D. Students receiving special education services must have an Individualized Education Program.

4. Several students in Mr. Collins' kindergarten class appear to have deficits in their abilities. The school is unable to assess the children and begin providing special education services until next year. Which one of the following solutions would be the best?
   A. Mr. Collins should contact the parents of the students who need services and encourage them to work with their children at home.
   B. The school should wait until next year to begin services.
   C. Mr. Collins should begin Response to Intervention.
   D. The students in question should be sent to a school which specializes in special education services.

CONSTRUCTED-RESPONSE QUESTIONS

Case

Many beginning teachers become overwhelmed when they discover they have numerous students in their class with special needs. First year teacher Paige Morris was no exception. Of her twenty-five students, seven were identified as needing special education services. While Paige was certified in special education and elementary education, she felt ill-equipped to write and implement so many Individualized Education Plans. To make matters more concerning, three of her students were identified as ADHD. Miss Morris began to imagine herself trying to control a chaotic classroom without the tools she needed to succeed.

5. List the parts of an Individualized Education Program which must be in writing. Identify the aspect(s) of the IEP for which Paige is responsible.

6. Which parts of each child's program would assist Miss Morris in better understanding her students before they begin the school year?

— MyEducationLab™ ———

Go to Chapter 4 of the Book Specific Resources in MyEducationLab and click on "Connect and Extend to Licensure" to answer these questions. Compare your responses with the feedback provided.

▼ WHAT WOULD THEY DO?

TEACHERS' CASEBOOK: Including Every Student

Here is how several expert teachers said they would work with students with a wide range of abilities.

BARBARA PRESLEY • Transition/Work Study Coordinator—High School Level
B.E.S.T.T. Program (Baldwinsville Exceptional Student Training and Transition Program) C.W. Baker High School, Baldwinsville, NY

As a transition coordinator, it is my responsibility to link the special education standards to transition. Therefore, connecting work and tasks assigned at work sites to classroom standards was done in conjunction with classroom teachers. All requisite work skills and behaviors were reinforced in the classroom. Classroom instructional topics were integrated at each work site and reinforced by Job Coaches while students were at their work site. Job Coaches, teachers, and the transition coordinator communicate daily through goal books. Success breeds confidence for adults and students. For special needs students, the importance of linking and aligning classroom education with community education cannot be overstated.

JENNIFER PINCOSKI • Learning Resource Teacher: K–12
Lee County School District, Fort Myers, FL

One of the most important considerations when setting up the classroom is how to group students to maximize learning. Students should be assessed early on to provide the teacher with information on individual learning styles, interests, strengths, and needs; teachers who are prepared with this knowledge will be better able to group students appropriately.

Learning groups should be fluid, meaning that they will change often, depending on objectives and circumstances. Students may be grouped in a variety of ways, including: heterogeneously (a student with strengths in a skill area can assist a student who struggles), homogeneously by skill deficit (to provide interventions), by learning styles, and by areas of interest.

Part of the process of understanding students' needs also includes research. There are numerous resources available for teachers to educate themselves on support strategies for students with ADHD, Autism Spectrum Disorders, learning disabilities, and health impairments. These resources can include staff members on campus (counselor, nurse, special education teacher, etc.), as well as community advocacy groups, scholarly journals and literature (accessible at the local library), and, of course, the Internet.

Ultimately, the best way to support students is to learn about their strengths and challenges, and use this information to assist in the physical and educational organization of the classroom community.

JESSICA N. MAHTABAN • 8th Grade Math
Woodrow Wilson Middle School, Clifton, NJ

It is vital for me to become very familiar with all of the students' IEPs and to discuss the modifications that need to take place in the classroom with the special education teacher. Once everything has been reviewed, I can begin to construct the curriculum, which must accommodate all my students. Differentiated instruction will be integrated into the curriculum. Portfolios will be the major source of assessment for my students. Each student learns differently and at different a pace, which is why the portfolio would be the best assessment, since they show the individual growth of each student. Frequent contact with parents is the key component for helping each student succeed in the classroom and beyond.

AUREN ROLLINS • 1st Grade Teacher
Boulevard Elementary School, Shaker Heights, OH

Meeting the individual needs of all students is a challenging but essential part of teaching! In this situation, I would create differentiated learning centers, where students could work on curricular components in skill-based groups. The opportunity to work with smaller groups of students whose abilities are similar would allow me to differentiate the curriculum to best meet their academic needs. Groupings would need to be fluid and flexible to ensure that the students were continually being challenged by the curriculum. At each learning center, I would provide a variety of materials and literature related to the subject matter that are designed to meet the wide range of learning styles presented by the students. Additionally, I would allow the students working in the centers to choose which of the provided materials they would like to use to support their learning. Giving the students choices will help with student motivation. I would even consider enlisting their input as to which materials they would like in each center. Finally, I would enlist willing and able parent or community volunteers to assist me in managing the students at the learning centers. The combination of small, skill-based groups, engaging learning materials, and choice will allow students to tackle the curriculum to their fullest potential.

LINDA SPARKS • 1st Grade
John F. Kennedy School, Billerica MA

Most of our classes are inclusion classes, with limited resources for additional help. At the beginning of the year, I go through all of the records, IEPs, and 504 plans and write down my questions, concerns, and specific information that will help the student. Next, we all meet as a team with the teachers from the previous year and specialists who work with the students. I have found this very helpful in setting up a plan for the students in my class. Then, I don't spend time re-evaluating students in areas where team members already know how students can be most successful. I am given the resources needed to start the year, and we continue to meet throughout the year as additional resources are needed. We are also fortunate to have a volunteer program through the senior center, parent community, and local businesses. These adult volunteers commit to a specific number of hours a week, are trained by school staff for specific skills the students will need help with, and begin to implement these skills with the students.

PAUL DRAGIN • ESL Grades 9–12
Columbus East High School, Columbus OH

This situation has become the norm—at least in public schools in large urban areas. The special needs students who have been identified should have an IEP (Individualized Education Plan) that addresses specifics pertaining to the student's cognitive and/or behavioral issues. This would guide my instructional deviation to help ensure that I am providing the curriculum in a format that is more easily comprehended by those who may have challenges that are greater than mainstream students. The medical issue concerning the student with asthma is something that requires a greater sensitivity to ensure that I am alert to any possible medical emergency that may occur in the classroom. Confidence in this trying situation comes from attempting various strategies with the students and discovering, through trial and error, which are most effective at meeting their diverse educational needs.

PAULA COLEMERE • Special Education Teacher— English, History
McClintock High School, Tempe, AZ

It is every teacher's dream to have a room full of eager learners who are all on grade level. In my experience, this never happens! In any classroom, there are students who are below, at, or above grade level in their abilities. First, teachers need to know that fair doesn't mean equal. If I assign a five-paragraph essay to the class, but a student with a learning disability in writing struggles to write that much, I could either extend the due date or modify it to a three-paragraph essay. If the student is really low ability, I may only require a solid paragraph. Likewise, I would challenge the brightest students to go deeper. I would make sure my students knew I believed in them and would build their confidence in their abilities. Proximity is huge in classroom management; by constantly moving around the classroom, I can prompt my students to stay on task or to remind them of appropriate classroom behavior. This is done very quietly and privately. I also give a great deal of positive reinforcement as I walk around and point out all of the right things students are doing. The positive messages must outnumber negative messages.

MyEducationLab™

Go to Topic 4, Student Diversity, and Topic 5, Students with Special Needs, in the MyEducationLab (www.myeducationlab.com) for *Educational Psychology*, where you can:

- Find learning outcomes for student diversity and students with special needs along with the national standards that connect to these outcomes.
- Complete Assignments and Activities that can help you more deeply understand the chapter content.
- Apply and practice your understanding of the core teaching skills identified in the chapter with the Building Teaching Skills and Dispositions learning units.
- Examine challenging situations and cases presented in the IRIS Center Resources.
- Access video clips of CCSSO National Teachers of the Year award winners responding to the question, "Why Do I Teach?" in the Teacher Talk section.
- Check your comprehension on the content covered in the chapter with the Study Plan. Here you will be able to take a chapter quiz, receive feedback on your answers, and then access Review, Practice, and Enrichment activities to enhance your understanding of chapter content.
- Find additional Teachers' Casebook scenarios and responses to them from practicing teachers.
- Use the Online Lesson Plan Builder to practice lesson planning and integrating national and state standards into your planning.

chapter five

LANGUAGE DEVELOPMENT, LANGUAGE DIVERSITY, AND IMMIGRANT EDUCATION

▶ **TEACHERS' CASEBOOK:** Cultures Clash in the Classroom

Your high school classes this year are about equally divided among three groups—African Americans, Asians, and Latinos/as. Students from each of the three groups seem to stick together, rarely making friends with students from "outside." When you ask students to select partners for projects, the divisions are usually on ethnic lines. At times, there are insults exchanged between the groups, and the atmosphere of the class is becoming tense. Often the Asian or Latino students communicate in their native language—one you don't understand—and you assume that the joke is on you because of the looks and laughs directed your way. You realize that you are having trouble establishing positive relationships with many of the students whose language, culture, and background are very different from yours, and many other students, picking up on your discomfort, shy away from them too.

CRITICAL THINKING

- What is the real problem here?
- How would you help the students (and yourself) to feel more comfortable with each other?
- What are your first goals in working on this problem?
- How will these issues affect the grade levels you will teach?

OVERVIEW AND OBJECTIVES

Virtually all developed countries, and many developing ones, are becoming more diverse. Multiple languages fill many classrooms. For a range of reasons, including unrest across the globe, families are immigrating to find a better, safer life—and their children will likely be in your classrooms. In this new chapter of our book, we look at how the over 6,000 natural languages in the world developed, what role culture plays, the stages in language development, and the emergence of literacy. Next we consider diversity in language development and dual language development. But language diversity is more than bilingualism. Because all of us speak at least one dialect, we examine what teachers need to know about dialects and genderlects—a new term for me—along with the role of schools in second (or third) language learning. Finally we turn to the critical issue for you—how to become a capable and confident teacher of immigrant students and second language learners. What is the role of bilingual education and sheltered instruction? Do the emotions and concerns of these students affect their learning? How can you identify English language learners with special talents or special needs? By the time you have completed this chapter, you should be able to:

Objective 5.1: Understand how language develops and know how to support emergent literacy.

Objective 5.2: Discuss what happens when children develop two languages.

Objective 5.3: Address whether dialect differences affect learning and discuss what teachers can do.

Objective 5.4: Discuss whether English immersion or bilingual instruction is better for English language learners.

Objective 5.5: Explain who are the Generation 1.5 students and describe their learning characteristics.

Objective 5.6: Define sheltered instruction and explain how it works.

Objective 5.7: Discuss how teachers can recognize special learning needs and talents when they do not speak their students' first language.

THE DEVELOPMENT OF LANGUAGE

All children in every culture master the complicated system of their native language, unless severe deprivation or physical problems interfere. This knowledge is remarkable. To have a conversation, children must coordinate sounds, meanings, words and sequences of words, volume, voice tone, inflection, and turn-taking rules. Yet, by about age 4, most children have a vocabulary of thousands of words and knowledge of the grammar rules for basic conversations (Colledge et al., 2002).

What Develops? Language and Cultural Differences

There are over 6,000 natural languages in the world (Tomasello, 2006). In general, cultures develop words for the concepts that are important to them. For example, how many different shades of green can you name? Mint, olive, emerald, teal, sea foam, chrome, turquoise, chartreuse, lime, apple . . . An oil painting artist can add cobalt titanate green, cinnabar green, phthalo yellow green, viridian green, and many others. English-speaking countries have over 3,000 words for colors. In contrast, the Himba people of Namibia and a tribe of hunter-gatherer people in Papua New Guinea who speak Berinmo have five words for colors, even though they can recognize many color variations. But whether there are few or many color terms, children gradually acquire the color categories that are appropriate for their culture (Roberson, Davidoff, Davies, & Shapiro, 2004).

Languages change over time to reflect changing cultural needs and values. The Shoshoni Native Americans have one word that means, "to make a crunching sound walking on the sand." This word was valuable in the past to communicate about hunting, but today new words describing technical tools have been added to the Shoshoni language, as the group's life moves away from nomadic hunting. To hear hundreds of new 21st century tool words, listen to techies talk about computers (Price & Crapo, 2002).

THE PUZZLE OF LANGUAGE. It is likely that many factors—biological, cultural, and experiential—play a role in language development. To master a language, children must be able to (a) read the intentions of others so they can acquire the words, phrases, and concepts of their language and also (b) find patterns in the ways other people use these words and phrases to construct the grammar of their language (Tomasello, 2006). The important point is that children learn language as they develop other cognitive abilities by actively trying to make sense of what they hear and by looking for patterns and making up rules to put together the jigsaw puzzle of language.

In this process, humans may have built-in biases, rules, and constraints about language that restrict the number of possibilities considered. For example, young children seem to have a constraint specifying that a new label refers to a whole object, not just a part. Another built-in bias leads children to assume that the label refers to a class of similar objects. So the child learning about the rabbit is equipped naturally to assume that "rabbit" refers to the whole animal (not just its ears) and that other similar-looking animals are also rabbits (Jaswal & Markman, 2001; Markman, 1992). Reward and correction play a role in helping children learn correct language use, but the child's thinking in putting together the parts of this complicated system is very important (Waxman & Lidz, 2006).

Expressive vocabulary The words a person can speak.

Receptive vocabulary The words a person can understand in spoken or written words.

When and How Does Language Develop?

Table 5.1 shows the milestones of language development, ages 2 to 6, in Western cultures, along with ideas for encouraging development.

SOUNDS AND PRONUNCIATION. By about age 5, most children have mastered the sounds of their native language, but a few sounds may remain unconquered. You saw in the previous chapter that the sounds of the consonants *l, r, y, s, v,* and *z* and the consonant blends *sh, ch, ng, zh,* and *th* are the last to be mastered (Friend, 2011). Young children may understand and be able to use many words, but prefer to use the words they can pronounce easily. As children learn to hear differences in the sounds of language, they enjoy rhymes, songs, and general sound silliness. They like stories by Dr. Seuss partly because of the sounds, as is evidenced by the book titles—*All Aboard the Circus McGurkus* or *Wet Pet, Dry Pet, Your Pet, My Pet*. The young son of a friend of mine wanted to name his new baby sister Brontosaurus "just because it's fun to say."

THE DEVELOPMENT OF LANGUAGE The important point is that children learn language as they develop other cognitive abilities by actively trying to make sense of what they hear and by looking for patterns and making up rules to put together the jigsaw puzzle of language.

VOCABULARY AND MEANING. As you can see in Table 5.1, children between ages 2 and 3 can use about 450 words (**expressive vocabulary**) even though they can understand many more (**receptive vocabulary**). By age 6, children's expressive vocabularies will grow to about 2,600 words and their receptive vocabularies will be an impressive 20,000 plus words

TABLE 5.1 • Milestones in Early Childhood Language and Ways to Encourage Development

AGE RANGE	MILESTONE	STRATEGIES TO ENCOURAGE DEVELOPMENT
Between 2 and 3	Identifies body parts; calls self "me" instead of name; combines nouns and verbs; has a 450-word vocabulary; uses short sentences; matches 3–4 colors; knows *big* and *little*; likes to hear same story repeated; forms some plurals; answers "where" questions	• Help the child listen and follow instructions by playing simple games • Repeat new words over and over • Describe what you are doing, planning, thinking • Have the child deliver simple messages for you • Show the child you understand what he or she says by answering, smiling, and nodding your head • Expand what the child says. Child: "more juice." You say, "Chris wants more juice."
Between 3 and 4	Can tell a story; sentence length of 4–5 words; vocabulary about 1,000 words; knows last name, name of street, several nursery rhymes	• Talk about how objects are the same or different • Help the child to tell stories using books and pictures • Encourage play with other children Talk about places you've been or will be going
Between 4 and 5	Sentence length of 4–5 words; uses past tense; vocabulary of about 1,500 words; identifies colors, shapes; asks many questions like "why?" and "who?"	• Help the child sort objects and things (e.g., things to eat, animals) • Teach the child how to use the telephone • Let the child help you plan activities • Continue talking about the child's interests • Let the child tell and make up stories for you
Between 5 and 6 At every age	Sentence length of 5–6 words; average 6-year-old has vocabulary of about 10,000 words; defines objects by their use; knows spatial relations (like "on top" and "far") and opposites; knows address; understands *same* and *different*; uses all types of sentences	• Praise children when they talk about feelings, thoughts, hopes, fears • Sing songs, rhymes • Talk with them as you would an adult • Listen and show your pleasure when the child talks to you • Carry on conversations with the child • Ask questions to get the child to think and talk • Read books to the child every day, increasing in length as the child develops

Source: Reprinted from LDOnLine.org with thanks to the Learning Disabilities Association of America.

"WHEN I SAY 'RUNNED', YOU KNOW I MEAN 'RAN'. LET'S NOT QUIBBLE."

(Otto, 2010). Some researchers estimate that students in the early grades learn up to 20 words a day (Bloom, 2002). In the early elementary years, some children may have trouble with abstract words such as *justice* or *economy*. They also may not understand the subjunctive case ("If I were a butterfly") because they lack the cognitive ability to reason about things that are not true ("But you aren't a butterfly"). They may interpret all statements literally and thus misunderstand sarcasm or metaphor. For example, fables are understood concretely simply as stories instead of as moral lessons. Many children are in their preadolescent years before they are able to distinguish being kidded from being taunted, or before they know that a sarcastic remark is not meant to be taken literally. But by adolescence, students are able to use their developing cognitive abilities to learn abstract word meanings and to use poetic, figurative language (Owens, 2012).

Young children begin to elaborate their simple language by adding plurals; endings for verbs such as *-ed* and *-ing*; small words like *and, but*, and *in*; articles (*a, the*); and possessives (*the girl's hair*). A classic study by Jean Berko (1958) demonstrated that children could even apply these rules to make words that they had never encountered plural, possessive, or past tense. For example, when shown a picture of a single "wug," the preschool children in the study could answer correctly "wugs" when the researcher said, "Now there is another one. There are two of them. There are two _____." In the process of figuring out the rules governing these aspects of language, children make some very interesting mistakes.

GRAMMAR AND SYNTAX. For a brief time, children may use irregular forms of particular words properly, as if they are saying what they have heard. Then, as they begin to learn rules, they **overregularize** words by applying the rules to everything. Children who once said, "Our car is broken" begin to insist, "Our car is broked." A child who once talked about her *feet* may discover the *-s* for plurals and refer to her *foots* or *feets*, then learn about *-es* for plurals (*horses, kisses*) and describe her *footses*, before she finally returns to talking about her *feet* (Flavell et al., 2002). Parents often wonder why their child seems to be "regressing." Actually, these "mistakes" show how logical and rational children can be as they try to assimilate new words into existing schemes. Apparently these overregularizations happen in all languages, including American Sign Language. Because most languages have many irregular words, accommodation is necessary in mastering language. According to Joshua Hartshore and Michael Ullman (2006), girls tend to overregularize verb tenses more than boys, so they are more likely to say *holded* instead of *held*. The researchers speculate that because girls may have better memory for words, they have better access to similar words (*folded, molded, scolded*) and generalize to *holded*.

Early on, children master the basics of **syntax** (word order) in their native language, but overregularizing plays a role in mastering syntax too. For example, because the usual order in English is subject–verb–object, preschoolers just mastering the rules of language have trouble with sentences in any other order. If 4-year-old Justin hears a statement in the passive voice, like "The truck was bumped by the car," he probably thinks the truck did the bumping to the car because "truck" came first in the sentence. Interestingly, however, in languages where the passive voice is more important, such as the South African language Sesotho, children use this construction much earlier, as young as 3 or 4 (Demuth, 1990). So in talking with young children, in English at least, it is generally better to use direct language. By early elementary school, many children can understand the meaning of passive sentences, but they do not use such constructions in their normal conversations, unless the passive construction is common in their culture.

PRAGMATICS: USING LANGUAGE IN SOCIAL SITUATIONS. **Pragmatics** involves the appropriate use of language to communicate in social situations—how to enter a conversation, tell a joke, interrupt, keep a conversation going, or adjust your language for the listener. Children show an understanding of pragmatics when they talk in simpler sentences to younger children or command their pets to "Come here!" in louder, deeper voices, or provide more detail when describing an event to a parent who was absent from the event (Flavell et al., 2002; Rice, 1989). So even young children seem quite able to fit their language to the situation, at least with familiar people.

Overregularize To apply a rule of syntax or grammar in situations where the rule does not apply, e.g., "the bike was broked."

Syntax The order of words in phrases or sentences.

Pragmatics The rules for when and how to use language to be an effective communicator in a particular culture.

Rules for the appropriate use of language vary across cultures. For example, Shirley Brice Heath (1989) spent many hours observing White middle-class families and African American families who were poor. She found that the adults asked different kinds of questions and encouraged different kinds of "talk." White adults asked test-like questions with right answers, such as "How many cars are there?" or "Which car is bigger?" These questions seemed odd to African American children whose families don't ask about what they already know. The African American child might wonder, "Why would my aunt ask me how many cars? She can see there are 3." Instead, African American families encouraged rich storytelling and also teasing that hones their children's quick wit and assertive responses.

METALINGUISTIC AWARENESS.   Around the age of 5, students begin to develop **metalinguistic awareness**. This means their understanding about language and how it works becomes explicit. They have knowledge about language itself. They are ready to study and extend the rules that have been implicit—understood but not consciously expressed. This process continues throughout life, as we all become better able to use language. Learning to read and write, which begins with *emergent literacy*, encourages metalinguistic awareness.

Emergent Literacy

Today, in most languages, reading is a cornerstone of learning, and the foundation for reading is built in early childhood. Because young children vary greatly in their knowledge and skills related to reading, research has expanded to study what supports these emerging literacy skills (often called **emergent literacy**). Look at Figure 5.1, which shows a 6-year-old's story and grocery list, to see some emerging literacy skills.

FIGURE 5.1

A STORY AND A GROCERY LIST

This child knows quite a bit about reading and writing—letters make words that communicate meaning, writing goes from left to right and lists go down the page, and stories look different than shopping lists.

Emergent writing samples provided by Kalla Terpenning, who just turned 6.

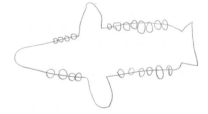

Me and Mommy went on the airplane. I saw the Librty BeL.

KALLA'S LiST UVe FRooTe
TOMMardoO Se.
AVooWCAdooeS.
OriNis.
APPLS.
PANYS.

Metalinguistic awareness Understanding about one's own use of language.

Emergent literacy The skills and knowledge, usually developed in the preschool years, that are the foundation for the development of reading and writing.

What are the most important skills that help literacy emerge? Here, the answers are not certain, but research has identified two broad categories of skills that are important for later reading: (1) skills related to understanding sounds and codes such as knowing that letters have names, that sounds are associated with letters, and that words are made up of sounds; and (2) oral language skills such as expressive and receptive vocabulary, knowledge of syntax, and the ability to understand and tell stories, for example (Dickinson et al., 2003; Storch & Whitehurst, 2002).

Some educators have emphasized decoding skills, others oral language, but a study by the National Institute of Child Health and Human Development (NICHD) Early Childhood Research Network (2005b) that followed over 1,000 children from age 3 through 3rd grade found that oral language skills at age 4½ predicted word decoding in 1st grade and reading comprehension in 3rd grade. The NICHD researchers concluded, "most recent investigations find that preschool oral language skills [for example, size of vocabulary, ability to use syntax, ability to understand and tell stories] play an important role along side code skills in predicting reading in the transition to school" (p. 439). Because this was not an experimental design (see Chapter 1), we cannot be sure that early decoding and oral language skills cause later reading achievement. But the results of this study suggest that decoding and oral language skills are likely an important part of the puzzle; these skills often support each other. *Beware of either/or choices* between emphasizing decoding versus oral language—both are important.

INSIDE-OUT AND OUTSIDE-IN SKILLS. One way to think about emergent literacy that captures both code and oral language skills for emergent literacy is the notion of **inside-out skills** and **outside-in skills** and processes, described in Table 5.2. This model, developed by Grover Whitehurst and Christopher Lonigan (1998) includes two interdependent sets of skills and processes.

> A reader must decode units of print into units of sound and units of sound into units of language. This is an inside-out process. However, being able to say a written word or series of written words is only a part of reading. The fluent reader must understand those auditory derivations, which involves placing them in the correct conceptual and contextual framework. This is an outside-in process. (p. 855)

For example, to understand even a simple sentence in print, such as "She ordered a camera from Amazon?" the reader must know about letters, sounds, grammar, and punctuation. The reader also has to remember the first words as he is reading the last ones. But these inside-out skills are not enough. To understand, the reader needs to have conceptual knowledge—what is a camera? What does it mean to order? Is this the Amazon River or Amazon online? Why the question mark? Who is asking? How does this sentence fit in the context of the story? Answering these questions takes outside-in skills and knowledge.

BUILDING A FOUNDATION. What builds this foundation of emergent literacy skills? Two related activities are critical: (1) conversations with adults that develop knowledge about language and (2) joint reading, using books as supports for talk about sounds, words, pictures, and concepts (NICHD Early Childhood Research Network, 2005a). Especially in the early years, the children's home experiences are central in the development of language and literacy (Burgess, Hecht & Lonigan, 2002; Sénéchal & LeFevre, 2002). In homes that promote literacy, parents and other adults value reading as a source of pleasure, and there are books and other printed materials everywhere. Parents read to their children, take them to bookstores and libraries, limit the amount of television everyone watches, and encourage literacy-related play such as setting up a pretend school or writing "letters" (Pressley, 1996; Snow, 1993; Whitehurst et al., 1994). Childcare workers and teachers can help. In a study that followed almost 300 low-income children from kindergarten to 5th grade, researchers found that the more families were involved with the school, the better their children's literacy development. School involvement was especially valuable when mothers had less education themselves (Dearing, Kreider, Simpkins, & Weiss, 2006).

Inside-out skills The emergent literacy skills of knowledge of graphemes, phonological awareness, syntactic awareness, phoneme-grapheme correspondence, and emergent writing.

Outside-in skills The emergent literacy skills of language, narrative, conventions of print, and emergent reading.

TABLE 5.2 • **Components of Emergent Literacy**

COMPONENT	BRIEF DEFINITION	EXAMPLE
Outside-in Processes		
Language	Semantic, syntactic, and conceptual knowledge	A child reads the word "bat" and connects the meaning to knowledge of baseball or flying mammals.
Narrative	Understanding and producing narrative	A child can tell a story, understands that books have stories.
Conventions of print	Knowledge of standard print formats	The child understands that print is read from left-to-right and front-to-back in English; understands the difference between pictures and print or the cover and the inside of the book.
Emergent reading	Pretending to read	Child takes a favorite book and retells the "story," often by using pictures as cues.
Inside-out Processes		
Knowledge of graphemes	Letter-name knowledge	A child can recognize letters and name letters.
Phonological awareness	Detection of rhyme; manipulation of syllables; manipulation of individual phonemes	A child can tell you words that rhyme with "hat." A child can clap as she says sounds in a word *cat*: /k/ /ă/ /t/
Syntactic awareness	Repair grammatical errors	A child says, "No! you say I *went* to the zoo, not I *goed* to the zoo."
Phoneme-grapheme correspondence	Letter-sound knowledge	The child can answer the question, "What sounds do these letters make?"
Emergent writing	Phonetic spelling	The child writes "eenuf," or "hambrgr."
Other Factors	Emergent literacy also depends on other factors such as short-term memory for sounds and sequences, the ability to recognize and name lists of letters, motivation, and interest.	

Source: Woolfolk, Anita; Perry, Nancy E., Child and Adolescent Development, 1st Edition, © 2012. Reprinted by permission of Pearson Education, Inc., Upper Saddle River, NJ.

Emergent Literacy and Bilingual Children

Emergent literacy skills are critical for school readiness, regardless of the child's language or languages (Hammer, Farkas, & Maczuga, 2010). Most school programs expect all children to learn to read in English. According to new research by Carol Hammer and her colleagues, this emphasis on reading only in English may not be necessary. In fact, one key factor may facilitate literacy development—growth in receptive language. You probably remember that *receptive* language is made up of the words and language structures you understand, even if you do not use them in your *expressive* language, the words and structures you actually use when you talk.

In one study, Hammer followed 88 children for two years in a Head Start program (Hammer, Lawrence, & Miccio, 2007). The mothers of all the children spoke the Puerto Rican dialect of Spanish. There actually were two groups of students—those who had been expected to speak both English and Spanish from birth and those who were not expected to learn English until they started Head Start at age 3. The researchers found that it was not a particular score on any test, but *growth in receptive language* in general during the program that predicted early reading outcomes—and it did not matter if the students spoke English and Spanish from birth or if they just started speaking English in school. They concluded "that growth in children's English receptive language abilities during Head Start, as opposed to the level of English they had achieved by the end of Head Start, positively predicted the children's emergent reading abilities in English and

GUIDELINES

Supporting Language and Promoting Literacy

FOR FAMILIES

Read with your children.
Examples

1. Help children understand that books contain stories, that they can visit the stories as often as they like, that the pictures in the books go along with the story meaning, and that the words are always the same when they visit the story—that's reading! (Hulit & Howard, 2006)
2. Have a night-time reading ritual.

Choose appropriate books and stories.
Examples

1. Choose books with simple plots and clear illustrations.
2. Make sure illustrations precede the text related to the illustration. This helps children learn to predict what is coming next.
3. Ensure that language is repetitive, rhythmic, and natural.

FOR TEACHERS

Use stories as a springboard for conversations.
Examples

1. Retell stories you have read with your students.
2. Talk about the words, activities, and objects in the books. Do the students have anything like these in their home or classroom?

Identify and build on strengths the families already have (Delpit, 2003).
Examples

1. What are the histories, stories, and skills of family members? Students can draw or write about these.
2. Show respect for the student's language by celebrating poems or songs from the language.

Provide home activities to be shared with family members.
Examples

1. Encourage family members to work with children to read and follow simple recipes, play language games, keep diaries or journals for the family, and visit the library. Get feedback from families or students about the activities.
2. Give families feedback sheets and ask them to help evaluate the child's schoolwork.

3. Provide lists of good children's literature available locally—work with libraries, clubs, and churches to identify sources.

FOR SCHOOL COUNSELORS AND ADMINISTRATORS

Communicate with families about the goals and activities of your program.
Examples

1. Have someone from the school district, the community, or even an older student translate into the language of the child's family any material you plan to send home.
2. At the beginning of school, send home a description of the goals to be achieved in your class—make sure it is in a clear and readable format.
3. As you start each unit, send home a newsletter describing what students will be studying—give suggestions for home activities that support the learning.

Involve families in decisions about curriculum.
Examples

1. Have planning workshops at times family members can attend—provide child care for younger siblings, but let children and families work together on projects.
2. Invite parents to come to class to read to students, take dictation of stories, tell stories, record or bind books, and demonstrate skills.

Make it easier for families to come to school.
Examples

1. Provide babysitting for younger children while families meet with teachers.
2. Consider transportation needs of families—can they get to school?

For more information on Family Literacy Partnerships, see http://www.famlit.org/

Source: Hulit, Lloyd M.; Howard, Merle R., Born to Talk: An Introduction to Speech and Language Development, 4th edition, © 2006. Reprinted by permission of Pearson Education, Inc., Upper Saddle River, NJ.

the children's ability to identify letters and words in English. This was the case regardless of the level of the children's prior exposure to English" (p. 243). In addition, growth in Spanish language abilities predicted reading performance in Spanish.

One implication is that teachers and parents should focus on continuing language development and not worry about rushing children into speaking English exclusively. As Hammer and her colleagues note, "If bilingual children's language growth is progressing well in either Spanish or English during the preschool years, positive early English and Spanish reading outcomes result in kindergarten" (p. 244). These findings are consistent with the recommendations of the Society for Research in Child Development: "Investing in dual-language instead of English-only programs and encouraging pre-kindergarten attendance can improve learning opportunities for Hispanic children and increase their chances of success" (SRCD, 2009, p. 1). The *Guidelines* give some ideas.

This brings us to a very important topic for teachers today—diversity in language development.

DIVERSITY IN LANGUAGE DEVELOPMENT

Many children learn two languages simultaneously while they are growing up. In fact, the United States is "one of the few countries in the world that takes pride in the fact that we speak only one language" (Noguera, 2005, p. 13).

Dual Language Development

If you mastered your own first language, then added a second or third language, you are an example of *additive bilingualism*—you kept your first language and added another. But if you lost your first language when you added a second one, you experienced *subtractive bilingualism* (Norbert, 2005). If family members and the community value a child's first language, he or she is more likely to keep that language when a second one is learned. But if a child experiences discrimination against the first language, he or she may leave the first language behind as proficiency is gained in a new language (Hamers & Blanc, 2000; Montrul, 2010). Immigrants are more likely to experience discrimination and therefore "subtract" their first language.

If they are exposed to two languages from birth, **bilingual** children (children who speak two languages) reach the language milestones in both languages on the same schedule as **monolingual** children (children learning only one language). Initially, bilingual children may have a larger vocabulary in the language that they are learning from the person with whom they spend the most time or have the closest bond, so a child who stays home all day with a Chinese-speaking parent will likely use more Chinese words. But over time, these children can become fully and equally bilingual if the dual language exposure (a) begins early in life (before age 5), (b) occurs across a wide and rich range of contexts, and (c) is systematic, consistent, and sustained in the home and community (Petitto, 2009; Petitto & Kovelman, 2002). Another requirement is that the second language must provide more than 25% of the child's language input; with less exposure, the child is unlikely to learn the second language (Pearson et al., 1997). Bilingual children may mix vocabularies of the two languages when they speak, but this is not necessarily a sign that they are confused because their bilingual parents often intentionally mix vocabularies as well, selecting the word that best expresses their intent (Creese, 2009). So, with consistent and sustained engagement in two languages, children can be fully bilingual.

Recent research on the brain and bilingualism shows that people who learn two languages before about age 5 process both languages in the same way as those who learn only one language and use the same parts of their brains (mostly in the left hemisphere). In contrast, people who learn a second language later have to use both hemispheres of their brain as well as the frontal lobe and working memory. They have to apply more cognitive effort. As Laura-Ann Petitto (2009) notes, "*Later* bilingual exposure does *change* the typical pattern of the brain's neural organization for language processing, but early bilingual exposure does not" (p. 191).

SECOND LANGUAGE LEARNING.
What if you didn't learn two languages as you were growing up? When and how should you learn a second language? To answer that question, you have to remember the distinction between **critical periods** for learning (if learning doesn't happen then, it never will) and **sensitive periods**, times when we are especially responsive to learning. There is no critical period that limits the possibility of language learning by adults (Marinova-Todd, Marshall, & Snow, 2000). In fact, older children go through the stages of language learning faster than young children. Adults have more learning strategies and greater knowledge of language in general to bring to bear in mastering a

Connect and Extend to PRAXIS II™

Bilingual Issues (IV, B4)
Identify the major issues related to the debate over bilingual education. Explain the major approaches to bilingual education, and describe steps that a teacher can take to promote the learning and language acquisition of non–English-speaking students.

Bilingual Speaking two languages and dealing appropriately with the two different cultures.

Monolingual Speaking only one language.

Critical periods If learning doesn't happen during these periods, it never will.

Sensitive periods Times when we are especially responsive to learning certain things.

second language (Diaz-Rico & Weed, 2002). But recent research on the brain and bilingualism suggests "*there is most definitely a 'sensitive period' for optimal bilingual language and reading exposure and mastery*. Age of first bilingual exposure predicts how strong a reader a bilingual child can and will become in each of their two languages" (Petitto, 2009, p. 192).

Even though there is no *critical* period for learning a language, there appears to be a critical period for learning accurate language pronunciation. The earlier people learn a second language, the more their pronunciation is near native. This is because from birth to about 4 months, infants can discriminate all the basic sound building blocks from any of the world's 6,000 or so languages. But after about 14 months they lose this capability and hone in on the sounds of the language they are learning. For children learning two languages at once, however, this developmental window seems to stay open longer, so these children can continue to differentiate sounds past 14 months (Petitto, 2009).

After adolescence it is almost impossible to learn a new language without speaking with an accent (Anderson & Graham, 1994). Even if a child overhears a language, without actually learning it formally, this can improve later learning. After studying college students learning Spanish, Terry Au and colleagues concluded that "Although waiting until adulthood to learn a language almost guarantees a bad accent, having overheard the target language during childhood seems to lessen this predicament substantially" (Au, Knightly, Jun, & Oh, 2002, p. 242). So the best time to acquire two languages on your own through exposure (and to learn native pronunciation for both languages) is early childhood (Au, Oh, Knightly, Jun, & Romo, 2008).

BENEFITS OF BILINGUALISM. There is no cognitive penalty for children who learn and speak two languages. In fact, there are benefits. Higher degrees of bilingualism are correlated with increased cognitive abilities in such areas as concept formation, creativity, theory of mind, cognitive flexibility, and understanding that printed words are symbols for language. In addition, these children have more advanced *metalinguistic* understanding of how language works; for example, they are more likely to notice grammar errors. Even more impressive, children from monolingual English-speaking families who attended bilingual schools and learned Spanish had better phoneme awareness and reading comprehension than their peers who were educated in an English-only program. Looking at all this research, Petitto (2009) concluded that "early bilingualism offers no disadvantages; on the contrary, young bilinguals may be afforded a linguistic and a reading advantage.... Moreover, learning to read in two languages may afford an advantage to children from monolingual homes in key phoneme awareness skills vital to reading success" (p. 193).

Heritage language The language spoken in the student's home or by members of the family.

DIVERSITY IN LANGUAGE DEVELOPMENT Higher degrees of bilingualism are correlated with increased cognitive abilities in such areas as concept formation, creativity, theory of mind, cognitive flexibility, and understanding that printed words are symbols for language.

These conclusions hold as long as there is no stigma attached to being bilingual and as long as children are not expected to abandon their first language in order to learn the second (Bialystok, 2001; Bialystok, Majumder, & Martin, 2003; Galambos & Goldin-Meadow, 1990; Hamers & Blanc, 2000). Laura Petitto and Ioulia Kovelman (2003) suggest that perhaps humans evolved to speak multiple languages because this would have survival value, so maybe the "contemporary pockets of civilization where one language is spoken are the aberrant deviation; in other words, perhaps our brains were neurologically set to be multilingual" (p. 14). In addition, speaking two languages is an asset when graduates enter the business world (Mears, 1998).

LANGUAGE LOSS. Even though the advantages of bilingualism seem clear, many children and adults are losing their heritage language (Montrul, 2010). **Heritage language** is the language spoken in a student's home or by older relatives when the larger society outside the home speaks a different language

(English in the United States). Often students who lose their heritage language were born in a new country after their parents or grandparents immigrated, so the students never lived in the country where everyone spoke their heritage language. In a large survey of 8th and 9th grade first- and second-generation children of immigrants in Miami and San Diego, Portes and Hao (1998) found that only 16% had retained the ability to speak their heritage language well. And 72% said they preferred to speak English. The languages of Native Americans are disappearing as well. Only about one-third still exist and 9 out of 10 of those are no longer spoken by the children (Krauss, 1992). Two Chinese American college students interviewed by Wong and Xiao (2010) expressed concerns this way:

> One of my biggest fears is that later on having kids and them not being able to speak Chinese, because my level of Chinese is not at the same level of my parents, and so I'm scared that it will get lost. (p. 161)
>
> My heritage language is definitely Toishan (Taishan), but even so, my parents don't always speak it fluently, so . . . I know somewhere down the line, I'm probably the last one to even speak it . . . and I feel like it is not my heritage anymore. (p. 165)

Rather than losing one language to gain another, the goal should be **balanced bilingualism**— being equally fluent in both languages (Gonzalez, 1999). Students' home language connects them to extended family and important cultural traditions, but outside their homes, English connects them to academic, social, and economic opportunities (Borrero & Yeh, 2010).

In many countries there are schools that focus on retaining heritage languages and cultures. Students attend these schools afternoons, weekends, or summers in addition to their regular public school. In Great Britain, these institutions are called *supplementary* or *complementary* schools. In Australia they are called *community language* or *ethnic schools*. In the United States and Canada, the name often is *heritage language schools* (Creese, 2009). Look at Table 5.3 for a sampling of these schools and their missions.

Balanced bilingualism Adding a second language capability without losing your heritage language.

TABLE 5.3 • **Schools That Support Heritage Languages in the United States and Canada**

LANGUAGE	SCHOOL	DESCRIPTION
German	German Heritage Language School, Halifax Nova Scotia http://www.german-language-school.ca/	Offers classes for adults and children. Lessons once a week for two hours on Thursday afternoons. German language skills (reading, writing, speaking, listening).
Chinese	Reidmount Saturday School, Markam, Ontario http://www.rhls.ca/	A co-educational Saturday school that offers Chinese (Mandarin and Cantonese), Chinese History, English (grammar and writing), Mathematics, Science, Communications, and Drawing for students from junior kindergarten to Grade 11.
Chinese	Chinese Heritage School, Monmouth Junction, NJ http://www.chsnj2000.org/	In addition to the regular language class, they also emphasize verbal conversation, Chinese Culture and family values. Their intention is to create a fun environment where children are motivated to study Chinese language, and feel proud to be Chinese.
Many languages	The Alliance for the Advancement of Heritage Languages in America http://www.cal.org/heritage/index.html	The mission of the Alliance is to promote the maintenance and development of heritage languages for the benefit of individuals, communities, and society.
Spanish	Grupo Educa http://www.elgrupoeduca.org/	Grupo Educa's mission is to enhance the Spanish language opportunities for children with a pre-existing knowledge of Spanish. Founded in June 2003 by a group of Southern California parents looking to expose their preschool-aged children to a dual-English/Spanish education.
Arabic and Hindi	Arabic and Hindi Heritage Language Classes, UCLA, Los Angeles http://www.international.ucla.edu/languages/programs/article.asp?parentid=105146	Intensive 5-week courses are for high school students who speak Hindi or Arabic at home and want to develop literacy and a deeper understanding of historical and contemporary South Asian culture. The project-based curriculum uses culturally relevant themes as a vehicle for listening, writing, speaking, and reading tasks.

Here are some ideas for learning about heritage schools in your area, suggested by Angela Creese (2009), a professor of educational linguistics at the University of Birmingham, United Kingdom:

- Find out which complementary/heritage schools are located in your area and make contact with them.
- When your students attend complementary/heritage schools, attend their awards ceremonies and presentations. Show your commitment to their bilingual and multicultural projects.
- Find out if teachers work in both the complementary/heritage and mainstream school sectors—ask them to undertake professional development workshops for other teachers in school.
- Ask a lead teacher of a complementary/heritage school to give an assembly.
- Encourage small-scale research and/or practical projects that would harness the potential links between complementary and mainstream schooling. (p. 272)

Signed Languages

People who can communicate in both a spoken and a signed language or in two different signed languages are considered bilingual (Petitto, 2009). There are a number of other parallels between spoken languages and the many signed languages used around the world, such as American Sign Language (ASL), Signed English (USA, Ireland, New Zealand, Australia, Great Britain), Lingua de Signos Nicaraguense (Nicaraguan Sign Language), Warlpiri Sign Language (Australia Aboriginal), and Langue des Signes Quebecoise (LSQ) or Quebec Sign Language. Each of these languages is distinct and not simply a derived version of a spoken language. For example, people using Quebec Sign Language and French Sign Language cannot understand each other, even though the French spoken language is common to both countries.

Both spoken and signed languages have large vocabularies and complex grammars. Laura Ann Petitto and Iugio Kovelman (2003) suggest that the same mechanisms for language acquisition are used for both spoken and signed languages. In addition, the milestones for signed language are the same as for spoken language. For example, children "say" their first words at about the same time, around 12 months, with both spoken and signed languages (Bloom, 2002). In fact, research with children learning a signed and a spoken language from infancy demonstrates that "being exposed to two languages from birth—and, in particular, being exposed to a signed and a spoken language from birth—does not cause a child to be language delayed or confused" (Petittto & Kovelman, 2003, p. 16). As with two spoken languages, children can become balanced bilinguals in a spoken and a signed language.

In the 1970s, language researchers were able to study the birth of a new socially shared signed language when Nicaragua established its first school for the deaf. The students came using their own unique invented sign languages. Over the years, a new language emerged that was based on the students' own sign languages. As the children developed the new Lingua de Signos Nicaraguense (Nicaraguan Sign Language), it became more systematic. The vocabulary expanded and the grammar grew more complex. New students learned the developing Nicaraguan Sign Language as their native language (Hoff, 2006; Senghaus & Coppola, 2001).

What Is Involved in Being Bilingual?

In the United States from 1995 to 2005 there was almost a 100% increase in the number of students who speak Asian languages and a 65% increase in the number of Spanish-speaking students. In fact, the United States has the 5th largest Spanish-speaking population in the world (Lessow-Hurley, 2005). The states with the largest number of English learners are Texas, California, Florida, New York, and Illinois, but numbers are surging in the Midwest, South, Nevada, and Oregon (Peregoy & Boyle, 2009). With these increased numbers come many misconceptions about bilingualism, as you can see in Table 5.4.

TABLE 5.4 • **Myths and Misconceptions about Being Bilingual**

In the table below, L1 means the original language and L2 means the second language.

MYTH	TRUTH
Learning a second language (L2) takes little time and effort.	Learning English as a second language takes 2–3 years for oral and 5–7 years for academic language use.
All language skills (listening, speaking, reading, writing) transfer from L1 to L2.	Reading is the skill that transfers most readily.
Code-switching is an indication of a language disorder.	Code-switching indicates high-level language skills in both L1 and L2.
All bilinguals easily maintain both languages.	It takes great effort and attention to maintain high-level skills in both languages.
Children do not lose their first language.	Loss of L1 and underdevelopment of L2 are problems for second language learners (semilingual in L1 and L2).
Exposure to English is sufficient for L2 learning.	To learn L2, students need to have a reason to communicate, access to English speakers, interaction, support, feedback, and time.
To learn English, students' parents need to speak only English at home.	Children need to use both languages in many contexts.
Reading in L1 is detrimental to learning English.	Literacy-rich environments in either L1 or L2 support development of necessary prereading skills.
Language disorders must be identified by tests in English.	Children must be tested in both L1 and L2 to determine language disorders.

Source: Brice, Alejandro E., The Hispanic Child: Speech, Language, Culture and Education, 1st Edition, © 2002. Reprinted by permission of Pearson Education, Inc., Upper Saddle River, NJ.

What does it really mean to be bilingual? Some definitions of *bilingualism* focus exclusively on a language-based meaning: Bilingual people, or bilinguals, speak two languages. Other definitions are more rigorous and define bilinguals as "adults who had early, intensive, and maintained dual language exposure and who use their two languages in their adult daily life" (Petitto, 2009, p. 186). But being bilingual and bicultural also means mastering the knowledge necessary to communicate in two cultures as well as dealing with potential discrimination (Borrero & Yeh, 2010). Consider these two students:

> A 9th-grade boy, who recently arrived in California from Mexico: "There is so much discrimination and hate. Even from other kids from Mexico who have been here longer. They don't treat us like brothers. They hate even more. It makes them feel more like natives. They want to be American. They don't want to speak Spanish to us; they already know English and how to act. If they are with us, other people will treat them more like wetbacks, so they try to avoid us." (Olsen, 1988, p. 36)
>
> Over 20 years later, a Chinese American college student is conflicted: 'Because I was born here, my parents . . . think that English is the language of the world, (but) I tell my mom that Mandarin is important, and she doesn't think so. She's kind of stuck in the old ways . . . like America is the only way to make money . . . I feel that as a Chinese American . . . second generation, I'm the first one to actually not follow what was followed before." (Wong & Xiao, 2010, p. 168)

The experiences of these two students show that you must also be able to move back and forth between two cultures and two languages while still maintaining a sense of your own identity, so bilingualism requires biculturalism as well (Lee, Wong, & Alvarez, 2008). Being a successful bilingual student has one more requirement—learning *academic language*.

TABLE 5.5 • **Common Errors and Accomplishments as Students Learn a Second Language**

LANGUAGE STAGE	COMMON ERRORS AND LIMITATIONS	ACCOMPLISHMENTS
During the first year of learning the language	• No speech at all • Only understands one word at a time • Mispronounces words • Leaves out words • One or two word responses • Relies heavily on context	• Uses pantomiming, gestures, pointing to communicate • Can use "yes," "no," or single words
During the second year of learning the language	• Basic pronunciation and grammar mistakes • Limited vocabulary	• Uses whole sentences • Good comprehension (in context) • Uses language to function well socially
During the third year and beyond of learning the language	• Some errors with complex grammar	• Can tell whole stories • Good comprehension • Beginning to understand and use academic language • Larger vocabulary

Source: Based on information from Miranda, T. Z. (2008). Bilingual Education for All Students: Still Standing after All These Years. In L. S. Verplaetse & N. Migliacci (Eds.), *Inclusive Pedagogy for English Language Learners: A Handbook of Research-Informed Practices* (pp. 257–275). New York: Erlbaum.

Contextualized and Academic Language

Proficiency in a second language has two separate aspects: face-to-face communication (known as *basic* or *contextualized language skills*) and academic uses of language such as reading and doing grammar exercises (known as *academic English*) (Fillmore & Snow, 2000; Garcia, 2002). **Academic language** is the entire range of language used in elementary, secondary, and university level schools. Academic language includes the general words and concepts used in many subjects such as *analyze, evaluate*, or *summarize*, as well as words and strategies specific to disciplines such as *angle, factor the equation*, or *derivative* in math, a *factor* in statistics, or a *derivative* in finance (you see how complicated this gets when the same word has two very different meanings in different fields). Academic language is associated with abstract, higher-order, complex concepts (Vogt, Echevarria, & Short, 2010).

It takes about 2 to 3 years in a good-quality program for children who are learning a new language to be able to use basic or contextualized language face to face in conversations. The stages for basic second language learning are shown in Table 5.5.

Mastering academic language skills such as reading texts in the new language takes much longer than three years—more like 5 to 10 years, depending on how much academic knowledge the student already had in his or her native language. So children who seem to "know" a second language in conversation may still have great difficulty with complex schoolwork in that language (Bialystok, 2001; Verplaetse & Migliacci, 2008). Here is how one Spanish-speaking international student, who went on to earn a doctoral degree and teach at a university, described her struggles with texts in college:

> I could not understand why I was doing so poorly. After all, my grammar and spelling were excellent. It took me a long time to realize that the way text is organized in English is considerably different from the way text is organized in a romance language, Spanish. The process involved a different set of rhetorical rules which were grounded in cultural

Academic language The entire range of language used in elementary, secondary, and university-level schools including words, concepts, strategies, and processes from academic subjects.

GUIDELINES

Promoting Language Learning

Provide structures, frameworks, scaffolds, and strategies.
Examples

1. "Think aloud" as you solve a problem by building on and clarifying the input of students.
2. Use visual organizers, story maps, or other aids to help students organize and relate information.

Teach relevant background knowledge and key vocabulary concepts.
Examples

1. Informally assess students' current background knowledge. Directly teach needed information, if missing.
2. Focus on key vocabulary words and use those words consistently.

Give focused and useful feedback.
Examples

1. Focus feedback on meaning, not grammar, syntax, or pronunciation.
2. Give frequent, brief, clear feedback—use words from the student's first language when you can.
3. Make sure to let students know when they are successful.
4. Break assignments and activities into smaller, "bite-sized pieces" with feedback after each "bite."

Keeps students involved and engaged.
Examples

1. Use small-group and pairs work.
2. Create situations where students talk at length.
3. Challenge students with clear higher-order questions—allow time to think and write out answers, maybe in pairs.

Show authentic respect for students' culture and language.
Examples

1. Learn about your students' personal and language background: What languages are spoken at home? When did the family arrive? How long have they lived in the United States? What schooling did they receive in other countries?
2. Learn about the students' religious background, food preferences and restrictions, and family customs; then incorporate students' experiences into writing and language arts activities.
3. Learn some key words in the students' languages.
4. View diversity as an asset; reject cultural deficit notions.

Sources: Adapted from Peregoy, S. F., &. Boyle, O. F. (2009). Reading, Writing, and Learning in ESL: A Resource Book for Teaching K–12 English Learners (5th ed.). Boston: Allyn & Bacon/Pearson; Echevarria, J., & Graves, A. (2011). Content Instruction: Teaching English Learners with Diverse Abilities (4th ed.). Columbus, OH: Pearson; and Gersten, R. (1996b). Literacy Instruction for Language-Minority Students: The Transition Years. The Elementary School Journal, 96, 217–220.

ways of being. I had never heard of the thesis statement, organizational rules, cohesion, coherence, or other features of discourse. (Sotillo, 2002, p. 280)

One 10th grader from Mexico described how her teacher helped her master academic language:

What I really love about my ESL teacher is that she explains how to organize our thoughts and how to write in school ways. She also teaches us what to do to be good, critical readers. That is so helpful in my other classes and I know it will be good for life. (Walqui, 2008, p. 111).

The *Guidelines* above give ideas for promoting language learning, but also keep cultural differences in mind as you teach. There are many ways that cultural differences might interfere with developing academic English and content understanding. For example, many Asian students come from a culture that believes asking the teacher questions is rude and inappropriate because questioning implies that the teacher has done a poor job of instruction. In Asian classrooms this might cause the teacher to lose face in front of the students—an entirely unacceptable situation. Thus teachers need to ask themselves why their English learners are not asking questions. For another example, class discussion may be considered a waste of time in cultures in which the teacher is viewed as the source of authoritative knowledge. How would students learn from other students who are not authorities? So beliefs about learning shaped by culture and previous experiences in different kinds of classrooms may explain why English learners seem quiet and reluctant to speak in class. English language learners also may think that their teachers are not very good because they do not explain everything. They also may strongly prefer memorization as a learning strategy if memorization was emphasized in their previous schools (thanks to Dr. Alan Hirvela at Ohio State University for pointing out these possible cultural differences in beliefs about schools and teachers).

We turn to other language teaching issues next, as we consider dialects.

DIALECT DIFFERENCES IN THE CLASSROOM

Communication is at the heart of teaching, but as we have seen in this chapter, culture affects communication. In this section, we will examine two kinds of language differences—dialect differences and genderlects.

Dialects

- -

STOP & THINK When you want a soft drink, what do you call it? Do you think people in other parts of the United States use the same term? •

- -

Growing up in Texas, we always asked, "Do you want a *coke*?" If the answer was yes, the next question was, "What kind—Coca-Cola, root beer, 7-Up, orange?" When I moved to New Jersey, I had to ask for a *soda*—if I asked for a coke, then that is just what I got. Twenty years later, at our moving-to-Ohio party, my colleague who had grown up in Columbus, Ohio, said, "You are going to have to learn to speak Midwestern and ask for a '*bottlapop*.'" Different regions have different ways of speaking—both in their accents and in their word usage.

A **dialect** is any variety of a language spoken by a particular group. Eugene Garcia (2002) defines a dialect as "a regional variation of language characterized by distinct grammar, vocabulary, and pronunciation" (p. 218). The dialect is part of the group's collective identity. Actually, every person reading this book speaks at least one dialect, maybe more, because there is no one absolute standard English. The English language has several dialects, for example, Australian, Canadian, British, and American. Within each of these dialects are variations. A few examples of dialects of American English are Southern, Bostonian, Cajun, and African American Vernacular (Garcia, 2002).

Dialects differ in their rules about pronunciation, grammar, and vocabulary, but it is important to remember that these differences are not errors. Each dialect is logical, complex, and rule-governed. An example of this is the use of the double negative. In many versions of American English, the double negative construction, such as "I don't have no more," is incorrect. But in many dialects, such as some varieties of African American Vernacular English, and in other languages (for instance, Russian, French, Spanish, and Hungarian), the double negative is part of the grammatical rules. To say "I don't want anything" in Spanish, you must literally say, "I don't want nothing," or "No quiero nada."

DIALECTS AND PRONUNCIATION.   Dialects also differ is pronunciation, which can lead to spelling problems. In some varieties of African American Vernacular English and in Southern dialects, for instance, there is less attention paid to pronouncing the ends of words. A lack of attention to final consonants, such as *s*, can lead to failure to indicate possession, third-person singular verbs, and plurals in the standard way. So *John's book* might be *John book*, and the singular and plural will sound the same for words such as *thinks*, *wasps*, and *lists*. When endings are not pronounced, there are more *homonyms* (words that sound alike but have different meanings) in the student's speech than the unknowing teacher may expect; *spent* and *spend* might sound alike, for example. Even without the confusions caused by dialect differences, there are many homonyms in English. Usually, special attention is given to words such as these when they come up in spelling lessons. If teachers are aware of the special homonyms in student dialects, they can teach these differences directly. Table 5.6 gives some other examples of dialect differences.

Dialect Any variety of a language spoken by a particular group.

TABLE 5.6 • **A Few Examples of Dialect Differences in African American English and Spanish Influenced English**

AREA OF LANGUAGE	STANDARD ENGLISH	AFRICAN AMERICAN ENGLISH
Sounds: Final consonants dropped	Hand, picked	Han, pick
Noun plurals	Two puppies	Two puppy
Noun possessives	Mama's house	Mama house
Past tense	John came.	John come.
Use of *being* verb	John is sick.	John sick.
Use of *bin* for remote past	She has been running for a long time.	She bin running.
Multiple negation	I don't ever have any problems.	I don't never have no problems.
AREA OF LANGUAGE	STANDARD ENGLISH	SPANISH INFLUENCED ENGLISH
Sounds: Alternate *ch* and *sh* sounds	Chair, snow	Share, chow
Sounds: Final consonants dropped	Start, least	Star, leas
Reflexive pronouns	Himself, themselves	Hisself, theirselves
Borrow for *lend*	Lend me a pencil.	Borrow me a pencil.
Barely for *recently*	They recently graduated from high school.	They barely graduated from high school.
Multiple negation	I don't have any pain.	I don't have no pain.
Using words from Spanish	15-year-old girl's coming out party	quinceñera

Source: Brice, Alejandro E.; Brice, Roanne, Language Development: Monolingual and Bilingual Acquisition, 1st Edition, © 2009. Reprinted by permission of Pearson Education, Inc., Upper Saddle River, NJ.

DIALECTS AND TEACHING. How can teachers cope with linguistic diversity in the classroom? First, they can be sensitive to their own possible negative stereotypes about children who speak a different dialect. Second, teachers can ensure comprehension by repeating instructions using different words and by asking students to paraphrase instructions or give examples. The best teaching approach seems to be to focus on understanding the students and accepting their language as a valid and correct system, but to teach the alternative forms of English (or whatever the dominant language is in your country) that are used in more formal work settings and writing so that the students will have access to a range of opportunities. For example, Lisa Delpit (1995) describes Martha Demientieff, a Native Alaskan teacher of Athabaskan children in a small village. The teacher's goal is for her students to become fluent in both their dialect, which she calls "Heritage English," and the "Formal English" of employers and others outside the village. She explains to her students that people outside the village will judge them by the way they talk and write. She goes on to explain:

> We have to feel sorry for them because they have only one way to talk. We're going to learn two ways to say things. One will be our Heritage way. The other will be Formal English. Then when we go to get jobs, we'll be able to talk like those people who only

DIALECT DIFFERENCES IN THE CLASSROOM Teachers should accept their linguistically diverse students' languages as valid and correct systems, but also teach the dominant language used in more formal work settings and writing so that the students will have access to a range of opportunities.

know and can only listen to one way. Maybe after we get the jobs we can help them to learn how it feels to have another language, like ours, that feels so good. We'll talk like them when we have to, but we'll always know our way is best. (p. 41)

Moving between two speech forms is called **code-switching**—something we all have learned to do. Sometimes, the code is formal speech for educational or professional communication. At other times, the code is informal for talk among friends and family. And occasionally, the codes are different dialects. Even young children recognize variations in codes. Delpit (1995) describes the reaction of one of her 1st grade students to her very first reading lesson. After she carefully recited the memorized introduction from the teacher's manual, a student raised his hand and asked, "Teacher, how come you talkin' like a white person? You talkin' just like my momma talk when she get on the phone."

Learning the alternative versions of a language is easy for most children, as long as they have good models, clear instruction, and opportunities for authentic practice.

Genderlects

If you had to guess what **genderlects** are, based on what you know about dialects, you probably would figure out that genderlects are different ways of talking for males and females. There are some small differences between boys and girls—girls tend to be slightly more talkative and affiliative in their speech (affiliative speech is talk intended to establish and maintain relationships). But much of the research has been conducted with White, middle-class children and the results do not necessarily hold for other groups and cultures. For example, some research reports that girls are more likely to cooperate and to talk about caring, whereas boys are more competitive and talk about rights and justice. But other studies have found that African American girls in one study were just as likely as boys to compete and talk about their rights in conversations (Leaper & Smith, 2004).

As with most aspects of language, there are cultural differences in genderlects. Interrupting is a good example. In America, boys interrupt more often than girls, but in Africa, the Caribbean, South America, and Eastern Europe, females interrupt males much more often than they do in America. And in Thailand, Hawaii, Japan, and Antigua, the style of speaking for boys and girls is overlapping—this overlapping talk is not interruption but cooperative turn taking (Owens, 2005).

TEACHING IMMIGRANT STUDENTS AND ENGLISH LANGUAGE LEARNERS

Code-switching Moving between two speech forms.

Genderlects Different ways of talking for males and females.

Felipe Vargas is a 5th grader who came with his family from Mexico to the United States more than three years ago so his father could take a job in a chicken-processing plant. Many Mexicans have come to work at the plant, and now there is a Spanish-speaking church, a Mexican grocery, and a Mexican bar and restaurant in the little northern Georgia town where they live. Felipe's mother, who takes care of the home and children, speaks no English, but his father and his older brother, Enrique, both speak a little. Enrique was 15 when the family came to this country. He left school after one year in an ESOL program, and went to work in the chicken plant. He is proud to be contributing to the family, but dreams of being a car mechanic; he spends all his free time fixing cars for neighbors and earns a little extra money that way. Felipe's oldest sister is 15 now, and, like him, spent two years in an ESOL program before transitioning to regular English-speaking classes. Her parents have chosen a husband for her from "back home," and she plans to leave school as soon as she turns 16, although she would rather not marry the man her parents have chosen. His two younger sisters are 8 and 4; the youngest is in a special Head Start class to learn English, and the other is repeating 2nd grade because she is having a hard time learning to read.

Felipe gets mostly Cs in school. He still struggles a bit with reading his textbooks, but he has many Anglo friends in his class and has no trouble talking English with them; in fact, he translates for his parents when they come to school for parent conferences, which they do whenever his father can get off

TEACHING IMMIGRANT STUDENTS AND ENGLISH LANGUAGE LEARNERS Most educational psychologists believe that no culture is deficient, but rather that there may be incompatibilities between the student's home culture and the expectations of the school.

work. Math is his real talent; he consistently gets As on his tests, and he is in the highest "math group," so he goes to another teacher for math. That teacher calls him "Phillip" and tells him he could be an accountant or maybe an engineer when he grows up. Felipe likes this idea, but his father says that college would cost too much money and reminds him that the family plans to go back to Mexico someday, when they have saved enough to buy a small farm, which is his father's dream.

There are so many students like Felipe and his siblings in America schools today. For the remainder of this chapter we explore ways of teaching these students so that their dreams of college and careers can come true wherever they finally live.

Immigrants and Refugees

In 2003, 12% of the people living in the United States were born in another country. Many of these children, like Felipe Vargas and his siblings, will be immigrants. **Immigrants** are people who voluntarily leave their country to become permanent residents in a new place. People from Mexico, like Felipe's family, are the largest U.S. immigrant group (Okagaki, 2006). **Refugees** are a special group of immigrants who also relocate voluntarily, but they are fleeing their home country because it is not safe. The United States requires that individuals seeking refugee status have "a well-founded fear of persecution on account of race, religion, nationality, membership in a particular social group, or political opinion" (U.S. Citizenship and Immigration Services, 2011). Since 1975, more than 3,000,000 refugees have permanently resettled in the United States, half of them children (Refugee Council USA, 2011).

In earlier decades, these new immigrants were expected to assimilate—that is, to enter the cultural **melting pot** and become like those who had arrived earlier. For years, the goal of American schools was to be the fire under the melting pot. Immigrant children who spoke different languages and had diverse religious and cultural heritages were expected to come to the schools, master English, and learn to become mainstream Americans. Of course, most schools were designed to serve European American middle-class children, so it was the immigrant children who were expected to do the adapting and changing—rather than the schools. *Involuntary immigrants*, descendants of the slaves forced to migrate to the United States, often were not welcome at all in the cultural melting pot.

Immigrants People who voluntarily leave their country to become permanent residents in a new place.

Refugees A special group of immigrants who also relocate voluntarily, but who are fleeing their home country because it is not safe.

Melting pot A metaphor for the absorption and assimilation of immigrants into the mainstream of society so that ethnic differences vanish.

In the 1960s and 1970s, some educators suggested that immigrants, students of color, and poor students had problems in school because they were "culturally disadvantaged" or "culturally handicapped." The assumption of this **cultural deficit model** was that the students' home culture was inferior because it had not prepared them to fit into the schools. Today, educational psychologists reject the idea of cultural deficits. They believe that no culture is deficient, but rather that there may be incompatibilities between the student's home culture and the expectations of the school (Gallimore & Goldenberg, 2001). Also, there is an increasing sense among many ethnic groups that they do not want to assimilate completely into mainstream American society. Rather, they want to maintain their culture and identity while still being a respected part of the larger society. Multiculturalism is the goal—more like a salad bowl filled with many ingredients instead of the prior melting pot idea (Banks, 1997, 2006; Stinson, 2006).

In past decades, most U.S. immigrants were concentrated in large urban areas and in California, Texas, Arizona, and New York. But today there are "New Ellis Islands" in many other cities and towns, particularly in the Midwestern states. Given the challenges of teaching students who have a range English speaking abilities coupled with the demands of accountability testing, it is clear that teachers everywhere are under pressure (Garcia & Tyler, 2010). And there is not much help--less than 1% of elementary and secondary school teachers are prepared to teach English as a Second Language (Aud et al., 2010).

Classrooms Today

English language learners are the fastest growing segment of the United States population. From 1994 to 2004, there was a 125% increase in students with limited English proficiency in Ohio where I teach (Newman, Samimy, & Romstedt, 2010). In 2008, nearly 21% of school-age children in the United States spoke a language other than English at home—almost three times as many as in 1979 (Aud et al., 2010). There are projections that by 2030, about 40% of the students in pre-kindergarten through high school will speak limited English (Guglielmi, 2008). By some estimates, Latinos alone will comprise about one quarter of the U.S. population by 2050 (U.S. Census Bureau, 2011). These changes are not limited to the United States. By 2031, it is projected that one in three Canadians will belong to a visible minority and one in four will be foreign born, so it is likely that the number of people who speak languages other than the official English and French will increase in Canada as well (Freisen, 2010). In fact, all the developed countries have many immigrant students. For example, more than half of the students under age 12 in the Amsterdam schools are from immigrant families (Crul & Holdaway, 2009).

Because immigrant families tend to live in particular neighborhoods, the schools in these communities generally have the largest number of immigrants and **English language learner (ELL)** students. Some of these students may not even be able to read and write in their native language. Clearly, schools serving these students need extra resources to hire and train native-language speaking teachers and aides, provide smaller classes, and purchase well-designed materials to teach complex academic subjects to students with limited English language skills (Crul & Holdaway, 2009). As you can guess, these extra resources are not always available.

FOUR STUDENT PROFILES.   Following are four general profiles of English learners in today's classrooms (Echevarria & Graves, 2011).

- *Balanced bilinguals.* These students speak, read, and write well both in their first language and in English. They have the academic knowledge needed to continue learning in both languages and the skills and attitudes to do so. These students may not present difficult teaching challenges, but they do need to maintain their skills in both languages and cultures.
- *Monolingual/literate students.* These students are literate in their native language (at or above grade level when working in their native language), but speak limited English.

Cultural deficit model A model that explains the school achievement problems of ethnic minority students by assuming that their culture is inadequate and does not prepare them to succeed in school.

English language learners (ELLs) Students who are learning English when their primary or heritage language is not English.

The teaching challenge here is to help the students develop English and continue to learn academic subjects.

- *Monolingual/preliterate students*. These students are not literate. They may not read or write in their native language or they may have very limited literacy skills. Some have never have attended school. In addition, they speak limited English. These students require the greatest support in learning both academic subjects and language.
- *Limited bilingual*. These students can converse well in both languages, but for some reason they have trouble learning academically. There may be underlying challenges such as learning disabilities or emotional problems. Further testing often is helpful to diagnose problems.

These student profiles are related to the distinction we encountered earlier in the chapter between contextualized conversational language and academic language. You may remember that it takes from 2 to 3 years to develop good conversational language, but 5 to 10 years to master academic language. *Conversational* skills include, for example, using appropriate vocabulary and sentences, asking and answering questions, starting and stopping conversations, listening, and understanding and using idioms.

Academic language includes reading and writing fluency; grammar and syntax; knowledge of specialized vocabulary; following written and oral directions; collaborating with other students on assignments; understanding different types of texts and forms of writing such as fiction, poetry, math problems, science charts and graphs, and timelines in history; and study skills such as outlining, summarizing, and reading comprehension (Echevarria & Graves, 2011). So to be successful in learning content, English language learners must put together an understanding of language with knowledge of terms, concepts, and conventions specific to a particular subject such as mathematics or biology. Figure 5.2 shows all the different domains of language that must come together for learning.

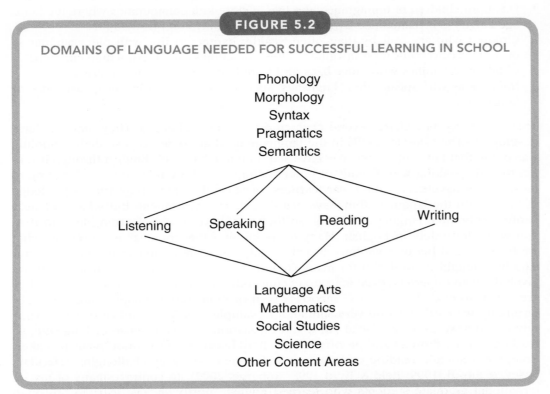

FIGURE 5.2

DOMAINS OF LANGUAGE NEEDED FOR SUCCESSFUL LEARNING IN SCHOOL

Phonology
Morphology
Syntax
Pragmatics
Semantics

Listening   Speaking   Reading   Writing

Language Arts
Mathematics
Social Studies
Science
Other Content Areas

Source: Echevarria, Jana J.; Graves, Anne, Sheltered Content Instruction: Teaching English Language Learners with Diverse Abilities, Coursesmart ETextbook, 4th Edition, © 2011. Reprinted by permission of Pearson Education, Inc., Upper Saddle River, NJ.

If you teach at a school with many English language learners, there probably will be school personnel who do formal assessments to provide appropriate placements for these students.

Generation 1.5: Students in Two Worlds

- -

STOP & THINK Imagine you are this person:

> You came to the United States at about the age of one. Your family was undocumented. You have a younger brother and sister who were born in the United States and are legal citizens, but you are not. Your parents and older siblings worked hard, often two jobs, so that the younger children could get a good education. You attended kindergarten, elementary, and high school in your family's new community in the United States. You graduated from high school with good grades and hoped to attend college, but soon discovered you did not qualify for scholarship support and would have to pay international student tuition, which you cannot afford. Even as a hardworking and promising student, you cannot legally work, vote, or drive in many states, in spite of the fact that you have lived virtually all your life in the United States and speak fluent English. •

- -

If you were this student, you would be a member of a large group, often called **Generation 1.5** because their characteristics, educational experiences, and language fluencies are somewhere in between those of students born in the United States and students who are recent immigrants (Gonzalez, 2010). They were not born in the United States, but have lived here most of their lives because they came with their families when they were young. The language spoken in their homes may not be English, but they often speak fluent conversational English, even if their academic English is not as well developed. Actually, there are several kinds of Generation 1.5 students, described by Dubarry and Lima (2003).

- Students from United States territories such as Puerto Rico, sometimes called "in-migrants."
- U.S.-born children of immigrants who live in close-knit communities where the heritage language is maintained by the residents for family and business life.
- Children who are sent by their often-wealthy parents to live with older siblings in order to receive education in United States, sometimes called "parachute children."
- Children of families who move back and forth between different countries.
- Immigrants who speak other "Englishes" such as English from Jamaica, East India, or Singapore.

These students may share several characteristics and challenges. They may not have developed strong literacy skills in the language used at home because their schooling was not in that language. They may have acquired much of their English through listening to and speaking with friends or older siblings, watching television, or listening to music. They have been called "ear learners" because they have built their knowledge of English on the language they have heard in their environment. But what they hear is often colloquial language or slang, so they may have trouble learning how to read and write accurately in English. Many of us know if the grammar is correct in what we hear or read because we have heard (mostly) accurate grammar all our lives—our ears have taught us well. But for many Generation 1.5 students, their ear learning has given them an imperfect, even inaccurate conception of English grammar. Because they are "ear learners," they may use incorrect verb or noun forms, mispronounce plurals, or mix up words that sound very similar, for example, *confident* and *confidence*. They rely on context, gestures, facial cues, and intonations to make sense of language, so reading is more difficult and proofreading is hard because they cannot "hear" mistakes. Complex academic reading and writing assignments are very challenging (Harklau, Losey, & Siegal, 1999; Reid & Byrd 1998; Roberge, 2002). In contrast, many of my international graduate students who learned English mostly as "eye learners" through reading, writing, and vocabulary and grammar exercises can write well, but they have

Generation 1.5 Students whose characteristics, educational experiences, and language fluencies are somewhere in between those of students born in the United States and students who are recent immigrants.

more difficulty with oral interactions. Knowing what kind of students you have and how they first learned English should help you understand the mistakes they make and the challenges they face.

Bilingual Education and English Learners

There are several terms associated with bilingual education. In the United States, students who are just learning English sometimes are called **limited-English-proficient** or **LEP**. More often, as we have seen, these students are called English language learners (ELLs), because their primary or heritage language is not English. **English as a Second Language (ESL)** is the name given to the *classes* devoted to teaching these students English. Limited proficiency in English often means lower academic achievement and poorer job prospects. So one issue around diversity in language development is how we should teach these students.

TWO APPROACHES TO ENGLISH LANGUAGE LEARNING. Virtually everyone agrees that all citizens should learn the official language of their country. But when and how should instruction in that language begin? Is it better to teach English language learners to read first in their native language or should they begin reading instruction in English? Do these children need some oral lessons in English before reading instruction can be effective? Should other subjects, such as mathematics and social studies, be taught in the primary (home) language until the children are fluent in English? As you can see in the *Point/Counterpoint* on the next page, debates about this question have raged for quite a while.

RESEARCH ON BILINGUAL EDUCATION. There are strong advantages for simultaneous bilingual learning. Remember Petitto's (2009) finding that monolingual English speakers who participated in a bilingual program excelled in the skills needed for reading in both languages. When the National Literacy Panel on Language—Minority Children and Youth reviewed studies of English-only *immersion* versus native language *maintenance* programs, they found that the students in the native language maintenance programs performed better on many different measured outcomes (Francis, Lesaux, & August, 2006). In a study that directly compared immersion and maintenance programs in 128 classrooms in Texas and California, Lee Branum-Martin and his colleagues (2010) found that the amount of teaching conducted in English and Spanish could not be predicted by type of program—there were many local variations. Some English immersion teachers used quite a bit of Spanish and some Spanish language maintenance programs taught quite a bit in English. Another finding was that Spanish language maintenance programs had a positive impact on English performance.

A study funded by the U.S. Department of Education (Gersten et al., 2007) identified five major recommendations for English learners, summarized here (Peregoy & Boyle, 2009).

1. Begin instruction with a formative assessment (see Chapter 15) of reading to determine exactly what the English learners know and what they are ready to learn, and to identify students who will need more help in reading.
2. Use small-group interventions to focus instruction on the areas of need identified in the assessments.
3. Target teaching essential vocabulary for the content in your curriculum as well as common words, phrases, and expressions used class.
4. Directly teach academic English—develop the students' abilities to read texts, write academic assignments, and use formal language and argument.
5. Make wide use of peer-assisted learning, particularly work in pairs, to complete academic tasks.

BILINGUALISM FOR ALL: TWO-WAY IMMERSION. Students in the United States need to master both conversational and academic English to achieve at high levels, but they

Limited-English-proficient (LEP) A term also used for students who are learning English when their primary or heritage language is not English—not the preferred term because of the negative connotations.

English as a Second Language (ESL) The classes devoted to teaching ELL students English.

POINT/COUNTERPOINT: What Is the Best Way to Teach English Language Learners?

There are two basic positions on this question, which have given rise to two contrasting teaching approaches: one that focuses on *immersion* in English-only teaching to make the transition to English as quickly as possible. The other approach attempts to *maintain or improve* the native language and use that language as the primary teaching language until English skills are more fully developed.

POINT

▶ **Structured English Immersion is the best approach for ELL students.** Proponents of the *immersion/fast transition* approach believe that English ought to be introduced as early and as intensively as possible; they argue that valuable learning time is lost if students are taught in their native language. Advocates cite the successes of the Canadian Immersion program as evidence that language immersion works (Baker, 1998). In an article for educational administrators, Kevin Clark claims: "These programs have the potential to accelerate ELLs' English language development and linguistic preparation for grade-level academic content" (2009, p. 42). Many schools today follow this line of thinking and offer **Structured English Immersion** or SEI. There are different perspectives on SEI, but usually it is defined as having two basic features: (1) teachers use English as much as possible in instruction, and (2) the level of the students' abilities in the class determines how teachers use and teach English: English use and teaching must be appropriate for student abilities (Ramirez, Yuen, & Ramey, 1991). There are at least three reasons why schools adopt this approach (Clark, 2009):

1. Some states have mandated this immersion by law and have limited the amount of teaching that can be done in the child's native language.

2. The accountability tests that all school districts in the United States must administer are in English. Schools where students don't score well on these tests face penalties, so getting the test takers to achieve English proficiency as fast as possible benefits the schools.

3. Schools are concerned that ELL students who do not get intensive and continuing English instruction may learn adequate conversational English but never develop the academic English needed for achievement in secondary schools and beyond.

Immersion in a language is the best way to learn a new language and is the basis for many language-learning programs around the world (Clark, 2009).

COUNTERPOINT

▶ **Students' native language should be maintained.** Teaching *in* English and hoping students will figure it out is not the same as *teaching* English. Proponents of *native-language maintenance instruction* raise four important issues (Gersten, 1996b; Goldenberg, 1996; Hakuta & Garcia, 1989).

1. Deep learning in the first language supports second language learning. For example, research on a large national sample that followed 8th graders for 12 years found that for Latino students, proficiency in the first language of Spanish predicted reading ability in English and English reading ability predicted achievement in school and in careers (Guglielmi, 2008). The metacognitive strategies and knowledge developed when students learn to read in their first language are transferred to reading in a second language as well (van Gelderen, Schoonen, Stoel, de Glopper, & Hulstijn, 2007). So maintaining and increasing proficiency in the first language is important. The learning strategies and academic content (math, science, history, etc.) that students learn in their native language are not forgotten when they learn English.

2. Children who are forced to try to learn math or science in an unfamiliar language are bound to have trouble. What if you had been forced to learn fractions or biology in a second language that you had studied for only a semester? Some psychologists believe students taught by this approach may become **semilingual**; that is, they are not proficient in either language. Being semilingual may be one reason the dropout rate is so high for low-SES Latino students (Ovando & Collier, 1998).

3. If the first language is neglected and the entire emphasis is on English, students may get the message that their home languages (and therefore, their families and cultures) are second class.

4. Years ago, Kenji Hakuta cited a "paradoxical attitude of admiration and pride for school-attained bilingualism on the one hand and scorn and shame for home-brewed immigrant bilingualism on the other" (1986, p. 229). Ironically, by the time students have mastered academic English and let their home language deteriorate, they reach secondary school and are encouraged to learn a "second" language. Sometimes native speakers of Spanish are encouraged to learn French or German, so they risk becoming semilingual in three languages (Miranda, 2008).

Beyond Either/Or. It is difficult to separate politics from practice in the debate about bilingual education. It is clear that high-quality bilingual education programs can have positive results. Students improve in the subjects that were taught in their native language, in their mastery of English, and in self-esteem as well (Crawford, 1997; Francis, Lesaux, & August, 2006). English as a second language (ESL) programs seem to have positive effects on reading comprehension (Proctor, August, Carlo, & Snow, 2006). But attention today is shifting from debate about general approaches to a focus on effective teaching strategies. As you will see many times in this book, a combination of clarity of learning goals and direct instruction in needed skills—including learning strategies and tactics, teacher- or peer-guided practice leading to independent practice, authentic and engaging tasks, opportunities for interaction and conversation that are academically focused, and warm encouragement from the teacher—seems to be effective (Chamot & O'Malley, 1996; Gersten, 1996b; Goldenberg, 1996).

should not sacrifice their native language in the process. The goal of schools should be balanced bilingualism. One approach to reaching this goal is to create two-way immersion classes that mix students who are learning a second language with students who are native speakers. The objective is for both groups to become fluent in both languages (Peregoy & Boyle, 2009; Sheets, 2005). My daughter spent a summer in such a program in Quebec and was ahead in every French class after that.

For truly effective education for ELLs, we will need many bilingual teachers. If you have a competence in another language, you might want to develop it fully for your teaching. Because there is only one qualified teacher for every 100 English language learners (Hawkins, 2004), promoting language learning is a responsibility for most teachers. Figure 5.3 shows teaching strategies that will support language and literacy development across the grade levels.

When students exit an immersion or a bilingual program with some English skills, they are not finished learning. The next phase for many students is sheltered instruction.

Sheltered Instruction

The challenge for most teachers working with immigrant and ELL students is to teach the subject matter and develop students' English language skills at the same time.

FIGURE 5.3

TEACHING STRATEGIES FOR PROMOTING LEARNING AND LANGUAGE ACQUISITION

Effective teaching for students in bilingual and ESL classrooms combines many strategies—direct instruction, mediation, coaching, feedback, modeling, encouragement, challenge, and authentic activities—many opportunities to read, write, and talk.

Strategies / Grade Level	K	1	2	3	4	5	6	7	8	9	10	11	12
Alphabet books	●—————————————→ (K–9)												
Assessment													
Formal				●—————→ (4–12)									
Informal	●—————————————→ (K–12)												
Dialogue journals	●—————————————→ (K–12)												
Drawing	●—————————————→ (K–12)												
Experiments	●—————————————→ (K–12)												
Invented spelling	●—————→ (K–6)												
Labeling	●—————————————→ (K–12)												
Language experience	●—————————————→ (K–12)												
Name charts	●—→ (K–2)												
Play centers	●—→ (K–2)												
Reading aloud	●—————————————→ (K–12)												
Shared reading	●———→ (K–4)												
Wall charts	●→ (K–1)												
Word recognition													
Sight words	●—→ (K–2)												
Phonics	●———→ (K–4)												
Context	●—————————————→ (K–12)												
Dictionary	●—————————————→ (K–12)												

Structured English immersion (SEI) An environment that teaches English rapidly by maximizing instruction in English and using English at a level appropriate to the abilities of the ELLs in the class.

Semilingual A lack of proficiency in any language; speaking one or more languages inadequately.

Source: Peregoy, Suzanne F.; Boyle, Owen F., Reading, Writing and Learning in ESL: A Resource Book for Teaching K-12 English Learners, 5th edition, © 2009. Reprinted by permission of Pearson Education, Inc., Upper Saddle River, NJ.

Sheltered instruction Approach to teaching that improves English language skills while teaching content to ELL students by putting the words and concepts of the content into context to make the content more understandable.

Sheltered Instruction Observation Protocol or SIOP® An observational system to check that each element of sheltered instruction is present for a teacher.

Sheltered instruction is one approach that has proved successful in reaching both goals. Sheltered instruction teaches content to ELL students by putting the words and concepts of the content into context to make the content more understandable. Strategies include simplifying and controlling language, giving attention to the relevant grammar and forms of English—helping students "crack the code," using visuals and gestures, and including real-life supports and examples. In addition, there is an emphasis on student talk and discussion instead of the teacher doing all the talking. In order to be clearer about what good sheltered instruction looks like, Jana Echevarría and her colleagues (2008) identified eight key elements: preparation, building background, comprehensibility, strategies, interaction, practice and application, lesson delivery, and review and assessment. Then the researchers developed an observational system to check that each element was included in teaching. The system is called the **Sheltered Instruction Observation Protocol or SIOP®**. Figure 5.4 gives some examples of what each element of SIOP® might include.

FIGURE 5.4

SOME EXAMPLES OF THE SHELTERED INSTRUCTION OBSERVATION PROTOCOL OR SIOP®

The SIOP® has 30 characteristics or areas to assess during observation. Each characteristic is rated from 4 (Highly Evident) to 0 (Not Evident) or NA (Not Applicable). These ratings are converted into a score.

Observer: _____   Teacher: _____
Date: _____   School: _____
Grade: _____   ESL level: _____
Class: _____   Lesson: Multi-day Single-day (circle one)

Directions: Circle the number that best reflects what you observe in a sheltered lesson. You may give a score from 0–4. Cite under "Comments" specific examples of the behaviors observed. Total Score: ☐ % Score ☐ Tape #:_____

	Highly Evident		Somewhat Evident		Not Evident	NA
Preparation	4	3	2	1	0	
1. **Content objectives** clearly defined, displayed, and reviewed with students	☐	☐	☐	☐	☐	☐
2. **Language objectives** clearly defined, displayed, and reviewed with students	☐	☐	☐	☐	☐	☐
3. **Content concepts** appropriate for age and educational background level of students	☐	☐	☐	☐	☐	☐
4. **Supplementary materials** used to a high degree, making the lesson clear and meaningful (e.g., computer programs, graphs, models, visuals)	☐	☐	☐	☐	☐	☐
5. **Adaptation of content** (e.g., text, assignment) to all levels of student proficiency	☐	☐	☐	☐	☐	☐
6. **Meaningful activities** that integrate lesson concepts (e.g., interviews, letter writing, simulations, models) with language practice opportunities for reading. writing, listening, and/or speaking *Comments:*	☐	☐	☐	☐	☐	☐
Building Background						
7. **Concepts explicitly linked** to students' background experiences	☐ ☐	☐ ☐	☐ ☐	☐ ☐	☐ ☐	☐ ☐
8. **Links explicitly made** between past learning and new concepts	☐	☐	☐	☐	☐	☐
9. **Key vocabulary emphasized** (e.g., introduced, written, repeated, and highlighted for students to see) *Comments:*						

	Highly Evident		Somewhat Evident		Not Evident	NA

Comprehensible

10. **Speech** appropriate for students' proficiency level (e.g., slower rate, enunciation and simple sentence structure for beginners) ☐ ☐ ☐ ☐ ☐ ☐

11. **Clear explanation** of academic tasks ☐ ☐ ☐ ☐ ☐ ☐

12. A variety of techniques used to make **content concepts** clear (e.g., modeling, visuals, hands-on activities, demonstration, gestures, body language)
Comments:

Strategies

13. Ample opportunities for students to use **learning strategies** ☐ ☐ ☐ ☐ ☐ ☐

14. **Scaffolding techniques** consistently used assisting and supporting student understanding (e.g., think-alouds) ☐ ☐ ☐ ☐ ☐ ☐

15. A variety of questions or tasks that promote **higher-order thinking skills** (e.g., literal, analytical, and interpretive questions) ☐ ☐ ☐ ☐ ☐ ☐
Comments:

Interaction

16. Frequent opportunities for **interaction** and discussion between teacher/student and among students, which encourage elaborated responses about lesson concepts ☐ ☐ ☐ ☐ ☐ ☐

17. **Grouping configurations** support language and content objectives of the lesson ☐ ☐ ☐ ☐ ☐ ☐

18. Sufficient **wait time for student response** consistently provided ☐ ☐ ☐ ☐ ☐ ☐

19. Ample opportunities for students to **clarify key concepts in L1** as needed with aide, peer, or L1 text
Comments:

Practice/Application

20. **Hands-on materials and/or manipulatives** provided for students to practice using new content knowledge ☐ ☐ ☐ ☐ ☐ ☐

21. Activities provided for students to **apply content and language knowledge** in the classroom ☐ ☐ ☐ ☐ ☐ ☐

22. Activities integrate all **language skills** (i.e., reading, listening, and speaking) ☐ ☐ ☐ ☐ ☐ ☐
Comments:

Lesson Delivery

23. **Content objectives** clearly supported by lesson delivery ☐ ☐ ☐ ☐ ☐ ☐

24. **Language objectives** clearly supported by lesson delivery ☐ ☐ ☐ ☐ ☐ ☐

25. **Students engaged** approximately 90–100% of the period ☐ ☐ ☐ ☐ ☐ ☐

26. **Pacing** of the lesson appropriate to the students' ability level ☐ ☐ ☐ ☐ ☐ ☐
Comments:

Review/Assessment

27. Comprehensive **review of key vocabulary** ☐ ☐ ☐ ☐ ☐ ☐

28. Comprehensive **review of key content concepts** ☐ ☐ ☐ ☐ ☐ ☐

29. Regular **feedback provided** to students on their output (e.g., language, content, work) ☐ ☐ ☐ ☐ ☐ ☐

30. **Assessment of student comprehension** and learning of all lesson objectives (e.g., spot checking, group response) throughout the lesson ☐ ☐ ☐ ☐ ☐ ☐
Comments:

Source: Echevarria, Jana J.; Graves, Anne, Sheltered Content Instruction: Teaching English Language Learners with Diverse Abilities, Coursesmart ETextbook, 4th Edition, © 2011. Reprinted by permission of Pearson Education, Inc., Upper Saddle River, NJ.

What might this look like? Here is an activity for a 7th grade language arts class in which students are learning the literary process of comparing and contrasting characters in stories (Vogt, Echevarria, & Short, 2010). In the same lesson, students also are learning some vocabulary specific to language arts content (*character traits*) as well as academic vocabulary used in many subjects (*compare, contrast*). Finally, the students are practicing higher order thinking skills by considering questions about situational behaviors and characters' traits such as, "Do people always act the same? Are shy people shy in every situation? Do motives affect behavior? Do traits affect behavior—always the same way?" The students have already read two stories, "Seventh Grade" by Gary Soto and "The Special Powers of Blossom Culp" by Richard Peck. To learn vocabulary about traits, the students explore a long list of traits, from "able" and "active" to "worried" and "young." They also complete a semantic feature analysis (SFA) of the main characters in the two stories—an example is shown in Figure 5.5.

Using the SFA, students can compare their analyses, look for patterns, and discuss their conclusions. They can work in pairs to write comparison-and-contrast essays so they have more opportunities to communicate. All of these activities involve English language learners in thinking, reading, speaking, and writing as they learn new content concepts, academic vocabulary, and comprehension strategies.

Affective and Emotional/Social Considerations

STOP & THINK You walk into one of your education classes. The instructor moves to the lectern and says:

> Mina-san, ohayō gozaimasu. Kyō wa, kyō iku shinrigaku no jū gyō ja arimasen. Kyō wa, nihon no bangō , ichi kara jū made benkyō -oshimasu. Soshite, kono kyōshitsu wa Amerika no kyōshitsu ja arimasen. Ima wa Nihon no kyōshitsu desu. Nihon no kyōshitsu dewa, shinakerebanaranai koto wa mittsu mo arimasu. Tatsu, rei, suwaru. Mina-san, tatte kudasai. Doshite tatteimasen ka? Wakarimasen ka?

The class continues in the same way until you are handed the "test" and told to "Do your best—this is 20% of your grade." You can't believe it! What would you do?

FIGURE 5.5

SEMANTIC FEATURE ANALYSIS OF CHARACTERS IN TWO SHORT STORIES

	confident	shy	eccentric	compassionate	easily embarrassed	cruel
Seventh Grade						
Victor	–	+	–	+	+	–
Teresa	+	–	–	+	NE	–
Michael	+	–	+	+	–	–
Mr. Bueller	+	–	–	+	–	–
The Special Powers of Blossom Culp						
Blossom	+	–	+	–	–	–
Blossom's Mama	+	–	+	–	–	–
Letty	+	–	–	–	NE	+
Miss Cartwright	+	NE	–	+	–	–

Source: Echevarria, Jana J.; Vogt, Maryellen J.; Short, Deborah J., The SIOP® Model for Teaching Mathematics to English Learners, 1st edition, © 2010. Reprinted by permission of Pearson Education, Inc., Upper Saddle River, NJ.

GUIDELINES

Providing Emotional Support and Increasing Self-Esteem for English Language Learners

Create learning activities that promote success in reading and writing.
Examples
1. Have weekly individual conferences with younger students and record their retelling of a story. Let students edit and revise the dictation and read it to a partner.
2. Do interactive journals with older students—collect each week and write back.

Make sure students have plenty of time to practice and get careful, targeted corrections.
Examples
1. Point out privately what is correct, almost correct, and wrong in written work.
2. Be sensitive about public oral corrections and build on what is correct, but do not accept clearly incorrect answers.

Connect teaching to relevant knowledge from students' lives.
Examples
1. Ask students to survey family members about favorite films— use film characters to discuss elements of literature—plot, point of view, etc.
2. Have students create construction firms and plan projects to learn math concepts.

Actively involve learners.
Examples
1. Use timelines in history compared to personal timelines based on family history.
2. Do projects in science based on animals or farming for rural students.

Use different grouping strategies.
Examples
1. Try pairs for writing stories and practicing oral presentations.
2. Create small teams to research recent immigrant groups' culture and language.

Provide native language support.
Examples
1. Learn and use as much of the students' language as possible—if they can learn, so can you.
2. Find Internet translation sources and local native speaking volunteers.
3. Bring native language magazines and books into the classroom.

Involve family and community members.
Examples
1. Bring in storytellers, local business owners, artists, craftspeople.
2. Create a Welcome Center for your class.

Hold high expectations for all students, and communicate these expectations clearly.
Examples
1. Keep scrapbooks of previous students who have gone on to careers or college.
2. Don't accept mediocre work.
3. Be a model of respect for diversity and an enemy of bigotry.

Source: Echevarria, Jana J.; Graves, Anne, Sheltered Content Instruction: Teaching English Language Learners with Diverse Abilities, Coursesmart ETextbook, 4th Edition, © 2011. Reprinted by permission of Pearson Education, Inc., Upper Saddle River, NJ.

Does this seem impossible? Actually, one of my doctoral students (Yough, 2010) designed this lesson (without the test) so his educational psychology class would experience how it feels to have important content taught in a language you don't speak (assuming your Japanese is a bit rusty!). Research on ELL students shows that they may experience severe challenges and stress in school. They may feel that they don't belong, and that others are making fun of them, or just ignoring them. Everyone else seems to know the rules and the right words. It takes courage and persistence to keep trying to communicate; it is easier to say as little as possible. So the practice in communicating that these students desperately need just doesn't happen.

What can teachers do to support students' courage and persistence in communicating? The first step is to create a classroom community that is caring and respectful. We explore strategies for creating classroom community in Chapter 13. Echevarria and Graves (2011) suggest additional steps to provide emotional support and increase self-esteem for ELL students, as you can see in the *Guidelines*.

Another problem is related to cultural differences. As we saw earlier, students who immigrate to the United States in their middle or high school years may have experienced very different educational systems and educational values "back home." They may have been very successful in those systems, perhaps by excelling in the memorizing required by the curriculum. When they encounter a different approach to education, suddenly they may struggle and feel as if they know little or nothing. As a teacher, you need to learn the strengths of these students and acknowledge their abilities—and build on their knowledge. We turn to that topic next.

Working with Families: Using the Tools of the Culture

Luis Moll and his colleagues wanted a better way to teach the children of working-class Mexican American families in the barrio schools of Tucson, Arizona (Moll et al., 1992). Rather than adopt a model of remediating the students' deficits, Moll decided to identify and build on the tools and cultural **funds of knowledge** of their families. By interviewing the families, the researchers identified their extensive knowledge about agriculture, economics, medicine, household management, mechanics, science, and religion. When teachers based their assignments on these funds of knowledge, students were more engaged and teachers were educated about their students' lives. For example, by participating in a Funds of Knowledge project, one teacher realized that she always had thought about her students in terms of deficits and problems—poor achievement, alienation, family troubles, and poverty. But then she got to know the families by focusing on their resources, not their limitations. She also learned that her students' actions often were misinterpreted:

> Strong family values and responsibility are characteristics of the families I visited. . . . My students were expected to participate in household chores such as cleaning house, car maintenance, food preparation, washing dishes, and caring for younger siblings. I learned what this insight meant when one of my students was unable to attend school drama and chorus rehearsals one day. In my journal entry detailing this project, I noted the following incident:
>
> -Wednesday (11/25/92) The music teacher commented (to me), "You know, Leticia has missed two chorus rehearsals." Before I could answer, the school drama teacher stepped in to add, "Oh, she's very irresponsible." She had signed up to be in the Drama Club and had only been to two meetings. I said "Wait a minute. . . ." I then told her how Leticia's younger brother was being hospitalized for a series of operations, and when the mother had to leave, she left Leticia in charge of caring for her two younger siblings. In fact, her missing after-school rehearsals was an act of responsibility, obedience and loyalty to her family. (Gonzales et al., 1993)

By engaging with students' families, this teacher learned about the valuable cognitive resources in the community, and her respect for her students and their families increased. Moll's work also was the basis for the Welcome Center project in a prekindergarten through 5th grade elementary school in the Southwest. Within four years the school had gone from 12% to 43% Latino/a, with most of these students recently arrived immigrants. The Welcome Center was a "social and instructional space where recent immigrant families in the school would come to trade a variety of expertise, meet each other, gather information about their children's education, and share general information on practical matters" (DaSilva Iddings, 2009, p. 207). The Center was a bright, comfortable, informal space with a small kitchen, picnic tables, computer and printer, books and magazines in Spanish and English, math manipulatives, showcases for children's work, and other welcoming features. Fifth graders offered homework assistance after school at the center. Spanish-speaking families taught classes in Spanish, cooking, and dancing for community members. English literacy activities were provided for adults and children learning together. The center produced many success stories—teachers who connected with students' families and came to appreciate the value of their students' language and culture, immigrant families who moved toward citizenship, and others who opened businesses and restaurants. Connections with families may be especially important for the success of immigrant students. The *Family and Community Partnerships Guidelines* have more ideas.

Funds of knowledge Knowledge that families and community members have acquired in many areas of work, home, and religious life that can become the basis for teaching.

GUIDELINES — FAMILY AND COMMUNITY PARTNERSHIPS

Welcoming All Families

Make sure communication with families is understandable.
Examples

1. Use the families' home languages wherever possible.
2. Use oral forms of communication—phone calls or home visits—whenever possible.

Balance positive and negative messages.
Examples

1. Send home notes or descriptions about their child's accomplishments or acts of kindness.
2. Explain disciplinary actions as ways of helping children succeed.

Establish systems for welcoming new families.
Examples

1. Assign more experienced "buddy" parents to communicate with new families.
2. Connect with multilingual media in your community to make announcements about school.

Make sure messages get through.
Examples

1. Establish telephone trees or texting networks.
2. Set the expectation that there will be a weekly note sent home so parents can ask their children about it.
3. Establish a class newsletter or Web site and incorporate multiple languages.

SPECIAL CHALLENGES: ENGLISH LANGUAGE LEARNERS WITH DISABILITIES AND SPECIAL GIFTS

If you remember the four profiles of ELLs described earlier, you know that one type of student may have learning disabilities, but it is very difficult to tell because the student's language is limited. English language learners with disabilities are difficult to diagnose—expert assessment is necessary (Garcia & Tyler, 2010). Sometimes students are inappropriately placed in special education just because they have problems with English, but other times, students who would benefit from special services are denied placement because their problems are assumed to be simply language learning issues (USDE, 2004). In addition, students with special talents and gifts may be difficult to recognize.

English Language Learners with Disabilities

As a teacher, one of your decisions will be whether to refer a struggling ELL student for testing. Of course, the first step is to use the best teaching approaches, incorporating sheltered instruction to develop both subject matter learning and English language development. But if progress seems much slower than usual, you might ask the following questions, suggested by George De George (2008): What is the student's educational background, and what is the background of his or her family? When did the student come to the United States? Being born in the United States but speaking another language at home or immigrating when very young actually can make learning in the early grades more difficult. Students who immigrate after successfully learning in their home country schools have literacy skills to build on. They know some academic content and they know they can learn in school. In contrast, the children who speak another language at home and have never been to school have no oral English to use as they learn the letters and sounds of written English. Bilingual instruction is the best strategy here.

Other questions to ask when considering a referral are: Were there any problems or complications during the mother's pregnancy? Has the child experienced any serious injuries or illnesses? Has the child moved around a great deal? Has the child had adequate opportunities to learn in a good bilingual or ESL program? Have the teachers who worked with the child been trained in teaching English as a second language? Is the student making progress, even if he or she is behind others the same age? Does the student have any talents or special skills to build on? These questions will help you determine if the student's difficulties are due to lack of learning opportunities, inadequate teaching, or a disability. No matter what the diagnosis—attention and appropriate teaching are needed. Students who have difficulties with English are much more likely to drop out of school (USDE, 2004).

Reaching Every Student: Recognizing Giftedness in Bilingual Students

Because they may be struggling with academic English, even though they are very knowledgeable, bilingual students may be overlooked for gifted and talented programs.

TABLE 5.7 • **Identifying Bilingual Students with Gifts and Talents**

Here are some ideas for identifying bilingual students with gifts and talents. Watch for students who:

_____ Learn English quickly
_____ Take risks in trying to communicate in English
_____ Practice English skills by themselves
_____ Initiate conversations with native English speakers
_____ Do not frustrate easily
_____ Are curious about new words or phrases and practice them
_____ Question word meanings; for example, "How can a bat be an animal and also something you use to hit a ball?"
_____ Look for similarities between words in their native language and English
_____ Are able to modify their language for less capable English speakers
_____ Use English to demonstrate leadership skills; for example, use English to resolve disagreements and to facilitate cooperative learning groups
_____ Prefer to work independently or with students whose level of English proficiency is higher than theirs
_____ Are able to express abstract verbal concepts with a limited English vocabulary
_____ Are able to use English in a creative way; for example, can make puns, poems, jokes, or original stories in English
_____ Become easily bored with routine tasks or drill work
_____ Have a great deal of curiosity
_____ Are persistent; stick to a task
_____ Are independent and self-sufficient
_____ Have a long attention span
_____ Become absorbed with self-selected problems, topics, and issues
_____ Retain, easily recall, and use new information
_____ Demonstrate social maturity, especially in the home or community

Source: Castellano, Jaime A.; Diaz, Eva, Reaching New Horizons: Gifted and Talented Education for Culturally and Linguistically Diverse Students, 1st Edition, © 2002. Reprinted by permission of Pearson Education, Inc., Upper Saddle River, NJ.

A 10th grade boy from Mexico, in the United States for two years, told an interviewer in Spanish:

> High school is hard for me because my English is so limited. …There are times when I feel a lot of pressure because I want to say something, but I don't know how to say it. There are many times when the teacher is asking questions, I know the answer, but I am afraid that people might laugh at me. (Walqui, 2008, p. 104)

This student might well be gifted. To identify gifted bilingual students, you can use a case study or portfolio approach in order to collect a variety of evidence, including interviews with parents and peers, formal and informal assessments, samples of student work and performances, and student self-assessments. The checklist in Table 5.7, from Castellano and Diaz (2002), is a useful guide.

▼ SUMMARY

The Development of Language (pp. 168–175)

How are humans predisposed to develop language? What roles do culture and learning play? Cultures create words for the concepts that are important to them. Children develop language as they build on other cognitive abilities by actively trying to make sense of what they hear, looking for patterns, and making up rules. In this process, built-in biases and rules may limit the search and guide the pattern recognition. Reward and correction play a role in helping children learn correct language use, but the child's thought processes are very important.

What are the elements of language? By age 5, most children have mastered almost all the sounds of their native language. In terms of vocabulary, we understand more words than we use. By age 6, children understand up to 20,000 words and use about 2,600 words. Understanding of words that express abstract ideas and hypothetical situations comes later as cognitive abilities develop. As children develop an understanding of grammar, they may apply new rules too widely, saying "broked" for "broken," for example. Understanding the passive voice in syntax develops after understanding active voice.

What are pragmatics and metalinguistic awareness? Pragmatics is knowledge about how to use language—when, where, how, and to whom to speak. Metalinguistic awareness, knowledge about your own use of language and how language works, begins around age 5 or 6 and grows throughout life.

What are the most important skills that help literacy emerge? Research has identified two broad categories of skills that are important for later reading: (1) understanding sounds and codes such as knowing that letters have names, that sounds are associated with letters, and that words are made up of sounds; and (2) oral language skills such as expressive and receptive vocabulary, knowledge of syntax, and the ability to understand and tell stories. One way to think about emergent literacy that captures both code and oral language skills for emergent literacy is the notion of inside-out skills (the ability to decode units of print into units of sound and units of sound into units of language) and outside-in skills and processes (the ability to understand those auditory derivations, which involves placing them in the correct conceptual and contextual framework). For bilingual Spanish-speaking students, growth in receptive language in Spanish or English predicts early reading outcomes. Parents and teachers can support emerging literacy by reading with children, retelling stories and talking about them, and limiting time spent watching television.

Diversity in Language Development (pp. 175–182)

What is involved in learning two languages? Children can learn two languages at once if they have adequate opportunities in both languages. There are cognitive advantages to learning more than one language, so it is valuable to retain your heritage language even as you learn another. The best time to learn accurate pronunciation is early childhood, but people of any age can learn a new language. Having overheard a language as a child can improve one's ability to learn that language as an adult. Even though the advantages of bilingualism seem clear, many children and adults are losing their heritage language. Rather than losing one language to gain another, the goal should be balanced bilingualism—being equally fluent in both languages. People who can communicate in both a spoken and a signed language or in two different signed languages are considered bilingual.

What does it mean to be truly bilingual? Some definitions of bilingualism focus exclusively on a language-based meaning: Bilingual people, or bilinguals, speak two languages. Other definitions are more rigorous and define bilinguals as adults who use their two languages effectively in their adult daily life, which includes being bicultural as well—moving back and forth between two cultures and two languages while still maintaining a sense of identity. Proficiency in a second language has two separate aspects: face-to-face communication (*contextualized language skills*) that take about two to three years in a good program to develop, and academic uses of language such as reading and doing grammar exercises (known as *academic English*) that take about 5 to 10 years to develop. Bilingual students also often struggle with social adjustment problems relating to biculturalism.

How do cultural differences affect bilingual students? Cultural differences might interfere with developing academic English and content understanding. For example, many Asian students come from a culture that believes asking the teacher questions is rude and inappropriate because questioning implies that the teacher has done a poor job of instruction. Thus teachers need to ask themselves why their English language learners are not asking questions. So beliefs about learning shaped by culture and previous experiences in different kinds of classrooms may explain why ELLs seem quiet and reluctant to speak in class. These students may also think that their teachers are not very good because the teachers do not explain everything. They also may strongly prefer memorization as a learning strategy if memorization was emphasized in their previous schools.

Dialect Differences in the Classroom (pp. 182–194)

What is a dialect? A dialect is any variety of a language spoken by a particular group. The dialect is part of the group's collective identity. Every person reading this book speaks at least one dialect, maybe more, because there is no one absolute standard English. Dialects differ in their rules about pronunciation, grammar, and vocabulary, but it is important to remember that these differences are not errors. Each dialect is logical, complex, and rule-governed. There are even some differences in how men and women talk, called genderlects.

How should teachers take dialects into account? Teachers can be sensitive to their own possible negative stereotypes about children who speak a different dialect. Teachers also can ensure comprehension by repeating instructions using different words and by asking students to paraphrase instructions or give examples. The best teaching approach seems to be to focus on understanding the students and to accept their language as a valid and correct system, but to teach the alternative forms of English (or whatever the dominant language is in your country) that are used in more formal work settings and writing so that the students will have access to a range of opportunities.

Teaching Immigrant Students and English language Learners (pp. 194–197)

Distinguish between the terms *immigrant* **and** *refugee.* Immigrants are people who voluntarily leave their country to become permanent residents in a new place. Refugees are a special group of immigrants who also relocate voluntarily, but they are fleeing their home country because it is not safe.

Distinguish between the "melting pot" and multiculturalism. Statistics point to increasing cultural diversity in American society. Old views—that minority group members and immigrants should lose their cultural distinctiveness and assimilate completely in the American "melting pot" or be regarded as culturally deficient—are being replaced by new emphases on multiculturalism, equal educational opportunity, and the celebration of cultural diversity.

What are four general profiles of English Language Learners? *Balanced bilinguals* speak, read, and write well both in their first language and in English. *Monolingual/literate students* are literate in their native language (at or above grade level when working in their native language), but speak limited English. *Monolingual/ preliterate students* are not literate. They may not read or write in their native language or they may have very limited literacy skills. *Limited bilingual* students can converse well in both languages, but for some reason they have trouble learning academically. There may be underlying challenges such as learning disabilities or emotional problems.

What is Gen 1.5? Generation 1.5 are students whose characteristics, educational experiences, and language fluencies are somewhere in between those of students born in the United States and students who are recent immigrants. They were not born in the United States, but have lived here most of their lives because they came with their families when they were young. The language spoken in their homes may not be English, but they often speak fluent conversational English, even if their academic English is not as well developed. They may tend to be "ear learners" who have mastered language by listening to and interacting with the language models around them.

What are the names related to English learners? English learners sometimes are called *limited-English-proficient* or *LEP*. More often, these students are called *English language learners (ELLs)*, because their primary or heritage language is not English. *English as a Second Language (ESL)* is the name given to the classes devoted to teaching these students English. Limited proficiency in English often means lower academic achievement and poorer job prospects. So one issue around diversity in language development is how we should teach these students.

What is bilingual education? Although there is much debate about the best way to help bilingual students master English, studies show it is best if they are not forced to abandon their first language. The more proficient students are in their first language, the faster they will master the second.

What is sheltered instruction? Sheltered instruction is one approach that has proved successful in teaching English and academic content. Sheltered instruction teaches content to ELLs by putting the words and concepts of the content into context to make the content more understandable. Strategies include simplifying and controlling language, giving attention to the relevant grammar and forms of English—helping students "crack the code," using visuals and gestures, and including real life supports and examples. In addition, there is an emphasis on student talk and discussion instead of the teacher doing all the talking. There are affective and emotional considerations for English language learners. They may experience severe challenges and stress in school. They may feel that they don't belong, that others are making fun of them, or just ignoring them. Building on students' funds of cultural knowledge is one way to make classrooms more supportive and teaching more effective.

Special Challenges: English Language Learners with Disabilities and Special Gifts (pp. 197–199)

How do teachers deal with the special needs of English language learners? As a teacher, one of your decisions will be whether to refer a struggling ELL student for testing. Of course, the first step is to use the best teaching approaches, incorporating sheltered instruction to develop both subject matter learning and English language development. But if progress seems much slower than usual, you might refer the student for observation or testing. No matter what the diagnosis—attention and appropriate teaching are needed. Students who have difficulties with English are much more likely to drop out of school. And because language differences can mask giftedness, teachers should make special efforts to identify bilingual students and English language learners who have gifts and talents.

▼ KEY TERMS

Academic language (180)
Balanced bilingualism (177)
Bilingual (175)
Code-switching (184)
Critical periods (175)
Cultural deficit model (186)
Dialect (182)
Emergent literacy (171)
English as a Second Language (ESL) (189)
English language learners (ELLs) (186)
Expressive vocabulary (169)

Funds of knowledge (196)
Genderlects (184)
Generation 1.5 (188)
Heritage language (176)
Immigrants (185)
Inside-out skills (172)
Limited-English-proficient (LEP) (189)
Melting pot (185)
Metalinguistic awareness (171)
Monolingual (175)
Outside-in skills (172)

Overregularize (170)
Pragmatics (170)
Receptive vocabulary (169)
Refugees (185)
Semilingual (190)
Sensitive periods (175)
Sheltered instruction (192)
Sheltered Instruction Observation Protocol
  or SIOP (192)
Structured English Immersion (SEI) (190)
Syntax (170)

▼ CONNECT AND EXTEND TO LICENSURE

MULTIPLE-CHOICE QUESTIONS

1. During the 1960s and 1970s, it was suggested by some educators that students of color and students living in poverty were culturally disadvantaged. The cultural deficit model implied students' home cultures were inferior because they failed to prepare them to fit into school. What is the current idea held by educational psychologists with respect to mismatches between students' home environments and school?

   A. There may be incompatibilities between the student's home culture and the expectations of the school.

   B. Deficits between the home culture and school can be compensated through special education services.

   C. Historically the gap between the home environment and the school environment is inconsequential.

   D. There is an increasing sense that ethnic groups should want to assimilate completely into mainstream American society.

2. Ms. Carney decided to visit the Mexican families of her ELL students to gain a better understanding of their backgrounds and culture. Drawing upon the research of Luis Moll and current best practice, what do you think Ms. Carney decided to do with the new information she gained from her family visits?

   A. She shared it with her supervisors and continued to remediate the students' deficits.

   B. She made notations about the information she gathered in her students' cumulative files.

   C. She decided to identify and build on the tools and cultural funds of knowledge of her students' families.

   D. She decided to not share the information as her supervisors may not have approved of her family visits.

3. Once Mr. Heney learned that his Asian ELL students consider it rude to ask the teacher questions because questioning implies that the teacher has done a poor job of teaching, he could generalize to which one of the following assumptions?

   A. If his English Language Learners are not asking questions he needs to ask them why.

   B. He should always quiz his Asian students as they may not be able to understand.

   C. Asian students are always very polite but their silence can mean they do not respect him as a teacher.

   D. Mr. Heney cannot make any generalizations about culture and learning.

4. One important way in which a teacher can motivate students is to show an interest in their lives. All but which one of the following are appropriate motivational strategies that demonstrate an interest in the lives of students from diverse backgrounds?

   A. Incorporate students' traditions into writing and language arts activities.

   B. Show respect for students' diversity by learning some key words in their language.

   C. Ask students to write a three-page essay in English about their family.

   D. Inquire about students' past experiences in their native country.

CONSTRUCTED-RESPONSE QUESTIONS
Case

Nick Takis was delighted that his portfolio had helped him land his first teaching job in Texas. Although he had never been to that state, he was excited about the prospect of his own classroom. When he arrived for his two week induction period in August his sunny mood began to wane. He learned that several of the students in his class were not fluent in English. To prepare for the challenge ahead, he drew upon what one of his favorite professors always suggested, "Break big projects down to bite size, and make sure you have all the information you need to make decisions."

5. What are the four general profiles of English learners in today's classroom with which Nick should familiarize himself?

6. What tips could you offer Nick Takis that would help him to promote language learning in his class?

─ **MyEducationLab™** ─

Go to Chapter 5 of the Book Specific Resources in MyEducationLab and click on "Connect and Extend to Licensure" to answer these questions. Compare your responses with the feedback provided.

▼ WHAT WOULD THEY DO?

TEACHERS' CASEBOOK: Cultures Clash in the Classroom

Here is how several expert teachers said they would establish positive relationships with the class described at the beginning of the chapter that included African American, Asian, and Latino/a students who did not get along.

JENNIFER PINCOSKI • Learning Resource Teacher: K–12
Lee County School District, Fort Myers, FL

The teacher has difficulty connecting with his/her students because the cultures are so different and the groups don't understand each other. The teacher's discomfort is evident, which is problematic because as the classroom leader, a teacher's attitude and behavior set the tone for everyone. Establishment of an inclusive and accepting learning environment starts at the top. It is important to model understanding and acceptance by respecting students as individuals, celebrating their differ ences, and showing a genuine interest in their lives.

    This is a good opportunity to get to know students on a more personal level. After assigning a quiet, independent task, the teacher can use this time to have brief conferences with each student one on one. Conferences should focus on becoming acquainted with the students, learning about their interests, and discussing goals. Not only does this help develop positive relationships, it also provides important information that can be used to plan future lessons and activities.

    Furthermore, in an effort to get students from different cultures to interact, the teacher may need to change the physical arrangement of the room and/or reassign seats. Rather than allowing students to choose their own groups, the teacher could either assign groups randomly or purposefully group students according to strengths, interests, learning styles, etc. Groups should change frequently, and assignments should be thoughtfully designed to complement students' individual characteristics.

LAUREN ROLLINS • 1st Grade Teacher
Boulevard Elementary School, Shaker Heights, OH

At the beginning of each school year, I set aside a significant amount of time to get to know my students, for them to get to know each other, and for them to get to know me. This is an integral part of building a classroom community. Familiarization with each group's culture is mandatory to achieve a successful outcome. It is also important that the groups of students learn to have mutual respect for each other. This is so important that it is worth suspending the curriculum until these goals are met. One activity would be to invite the students to share their backgrounds and cultures in a "show and tell" situation. Another activity would be to create "compliment charts" for each other. The students would write compliments, positive statements, and qualities that they like about each other on the charts. At the end of the activity, each student will walk away feeling respected and appreciated. It is a "feel good" activity and a big step toward respecting and appreciating the members of the classroom.

LINDA SPARKS • 1st Grade
John F. Kennedy School, Billerica, MA

Students are very quick to pick up on what a person thinks about them or how someone feels about them. I have not had this specific incident happen in my class as I am in an elementary school. But, I believe this can happen at any level, especially when the teacher feels uncomfortable in the setting. Students pick right up on how a teacher feels about them. They need to be respected in order to learn to be respectful, while building their trust and confidence. Once that trust is earned, the students are more willing to participate in activities in the classroom. I would have to do some flexible grouping as simple as "If you have green sneakers on, move to the left corner." They are not moving because they are of a specific ethnic group. I always have a jar with these quirky questions to move kids around, especially when I am changing desks. This also will maximize instruction because now they want their group to beat out their friends' group. When this happens, students will begin to get along socially while academic needs are being met.

PAULA COLEMERE • Special Education Teacher—English, History
McClintock High School, Tempe, AZ

My first goal is always to create a safe learning environment for my students. With underlying issues based on racial divisions in a class, it would be difficult for students to come to class prepared to learn. The hostility needs to be erased in this class. To work toward this goal, I would have the class do a team building activity. This activity would be built to show students that no matter how they look, they are much more alike than different. There is an activity I have done where students walk to the center line if they have ever experienced something. It starts simple, but gets deeper. For example, the facilitator might say, "Go to the center line if you know someone who has been murdered." Sadly, many students have experienced this and they will see they are not alone. Following this activity, I would have a discussion with the students about leaving our differences at the door. This is a teachable moment, as we will come across people throughout our lives that we don't like or who are different from us, but we have to find a way to make the relationship work to hold a job.

MyEducationLab™

Go to Topic 2, Cognitive and Linguistic Development and Topic 4, Student Diversity in the MyEducationLab (www.myeducationlab.com) for *Educational Psychology*, where you can:

- Find learning outcomes for Linguistic Development and Diversity along with the national standards that connect to these outcomes.
- Complete Assignments and Activities that can help you more deeply understand the chapter content.
- Apply and practice your understanding of the core teaching skills identified in the chapter with the Building Teaching Skills and Dispositions learning units.
- Examine challenging situations and cases presented in the IRIS Center Resources.
- Access video clips of CCSSO National Teachers of the Year award winners responding to the question, "Why Do I Teach?" in the Teacher Talk section.
- Check your comprehension on the content covered in the chapter with the Study Plan. Here you will be able to take a chapter quiz, receive feedback on your answers, and then access Review, Practice, and Enrichment activities to enhance your understanding of chapter content.
- Find additional Teachers' Casebook scenarios and responses to them from practicing teachers.
- Use the Online Lesson Plan Builder to practice lesson planning and integrating national and state standards into your planning.

chapter six
CULTURE AND DIVERSITY

► **TEACHERS' CASEBOOK:** White Girls Club

You teach in a fairly homogeneous primary school. In fact, most of your kindergarten–first grade students are middle- or upper middle-class and white. In January, a new student came to your school—the daughter of an African American professor who recently arrived to teach at the nearby college. After a few weeks, you notice that the new student is not being included in many activities. She sits alone in the library and plays alone at recess. No one sits with her at lunch, and at recess she is the last to be chosen for any team. This is troubling enough, but then one day you overhear two of your higher achieving girls talking about their "White Girls Club."

CRITICAL THINKING

- Would you investigate to learn more about this "Club"? How?
- If you found that your students had created a club that excluded nonwhite students, what would you do?
- If you teach older students, what can you do about student groups that define themselves by who *cannot* be members? ·

OVERVIEW AND OBJECTIVES

The cultural composition of American classrooms is changing. The same can be said for classrooms in many countries today. In a talk to the American Educational Research Association, Frank Pajares, one of the wisest educational psychologists I know, said, "The critical questions in education involve matters that cannot be settled by universal prescription. They demand attention to the cultural forces that shape our lives" (Pajares, 2000, p. 5). I believe he is right. In this chapter, we examine the many cultures that form the fabric of our society. We begin by considering some statistics about diversity in schools, and then meet four individuals whose stories bring the statistics to life—you met another one, Felipe, in Chapter 5. Next, we trace the schools' responses to different ethnic and cultural groups. With a broad conception of culture as a basis, we then examine three important dimensions of every student's identity: social class, race/ethnicity, and gender. Then, we turn to a consideration of multicultural education, a general process of school reform that incorporates and embraces diversity, and we look at approaches to creating culturally compatible and resilient classrooms. The last section presents three general principles for teaching every student. By the time you have completed this chapter, you should be able to:

Objective 6.1: Describe how social class, ethnicity, and race influence teaching and learning in a diverse society.

Objective 6.2: Explain the meaning of *stereotype threat*, and examine its possible effects on student achievement.

Objective 6.3: Describe the development of gender identity and the role of gender in teaching.

Objective 6.4: Define multicultural education.

Objective 6.5: Apply research on diversity to the creation of culturally compatible classrooms.

Connect and Extend to PRAXIS II™

The Larger Community (IV, B1,3)
Familiarize yourself with the predicted changes in the U.S. population over the next several decades. How are those changes likely to affect education? What can schools and teachers do to adjust positively to those changes?

Culture The knowledge, values, attitudes, and traditions that guide the behavior of a group of people and allow them to solve the problems of living in their environment.

TODAY'S DIVERSE CLASSROOMS

In this text we take a broad interpretation of cultural diversity, so we will examine social class, race, ethnicity, and gender as aspects of diversity. We begin with a look at the meaning of culture. Many people associate this concept with the "cultural events" section of the newspaper—art galleries, museums, Shakespeare festivals, classical music concerts, and so on. Culture has a much broader meaning; it embraces the whole way of life of a group of people.

American Cultural Diversity

There are many definitions of **culture**. Most include some or all of the following: the knowledge, skills, rules, norms, practices, traditions, self-definitions, institutions (educational, legal, communal, religious, political, etc.), language, and values that shape and guide beliefs and behavior in a particular group of people as well as the art, literature, folklore, and artifacts produced and passed down to the next generation (Cohen, 2009, 2010; Pai & Alder, 2001). The group constructs a culture—a program for living—and communicates the program to members. Groups can be defined along regional, ethnic, religious, racial, gender, social class, or other lines. Each of us is a member of many groups, so we all are influenced by many different cultures. Sometimes, the influences are incompatible or even contradictory. For example, if you are a feminist but also a Roman Catholic, you may have trouble reconciling the two different cultures' beliefs about the ordination of women as priests. Your personal belief will be based, in part, on how strongly you identify with each group.

There are many different cultures within every modern country. In the United States, students growing up in a small rural town in the Great Plains are part of a cultural group that is very different from that of students in a large Northeastern urban center or students in a Texas suburb. Within those small towns in the Great Plains, the son or daughter of a convenience store clerk grows up in a different culture from the child of the town doctor or dentist. Individuals of African, Asian, Hispanic, Native American, or European descent have distinctive histories and traditions. Everyone living within a particular country shares many common experiences and values, especially because of the influence of the mass media. But other aspects of their lives are shaped by differing cultural backgrounds.

Culture has been compared to an iceberg. One-third of the iceberg is visible; the rest is hidden and unknown. The visible signs of culture, such as costumes and marriage traditions, reflect only a small portion of the differences among cultures, as you can see in Figure 6.1.

Many of the differences are "below the surface." They are implicit, unstated, even unconscious biases and beliefs (Sheets, 2005). Cultures differ in rules for conducting interpersonal relationships, for example. In some groups, listeners give a slight affirmative nod of the head and perhaps an occasional "uh huh" to indicate they are listening carefully. But members of other cultures listen without giving acknowledgment, or with eyes downcast, as a sign of respect. In some cultures, high-status individuals initiate conversations and ask the questions, and low-status individuals only respond. In other cultures, the pattern is reversed.

Cultural influences are widespread and pervasive. Some psychologists even suggest that culture defines intelligence. For example, physical grace is essential in Balinese social life, so the ability to master physical movements is a mark of intelligence in that culture. Manipulating words and numbers is important in Western societies, so in these cultures such skills are indicators of intelligence (Gardner, 1983). Even symptoms of psychological disorders are affected by culture. In industrialized cultures where cleanliness

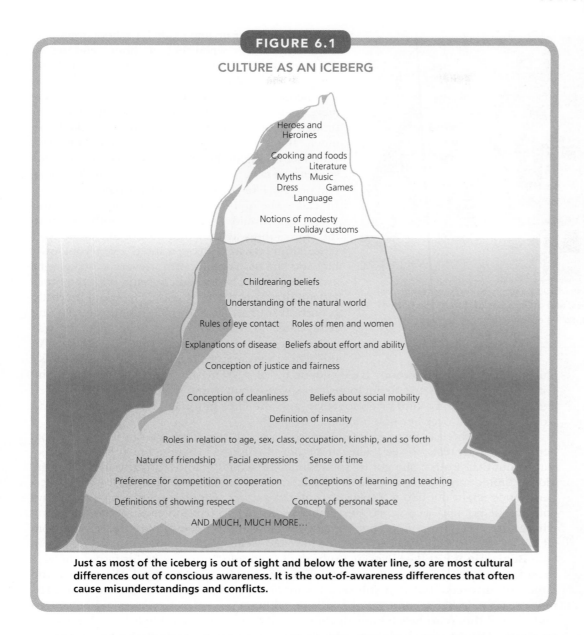

FIGURE 6.1

CULTURE AS AN ICEBERG

Heroes and
Heroines

Cooking and foods
Literature
Myths   Music
Dress   Games
Language

Notions of modesty
Holiday customs

Childrearing beliefs

Understanding of the natural world

Rules of eye contact   Roles of men and women

Explanations of disease   Beliefs about effort and ability

Conception of justice and fairness

Conception of cleanliness   Beliefs about social mobility

Definition of insanity

Roles in relation to age, sex, class, occupation, kinship, and so forth

Nature of friendship   Facial expressions   Sense of time

Preference for competition or cooperation   Conceptions of learning and teaching

Definitions of showing respect   Concept of personal space

AND MUCH, MUCH MORE...

Just as most of the iceberg is out of sight and below the water line, so are most cultural differences out of conscious awareness. It is the out-of-awareness differences that often cause misunderstandings and conflicts.

is emphasized, people with obsessive-compulsive disorders often become obsessed with cleaning their hands, whereas in Bali, where social networks are emphasized, people with obsessive-compulsive disorders often become obsessed with knowing all the details about the lives of their friends and family—their social network (Lemelson, 2003).

Let's get more specific about cultural diversity by meeting some students.

Meet Four More Students

In Chapter 1 you read some statistics about students in America. Look back at those statistics now to get a broad picture of American students today and tomorrow. As you can see, classrooms are becoming more diverse. But teachers do not work with statistics; they work with students—unique individuals, such as Felipe Vargas, the 5th grader you met in Chapter 5. Nancy Knapp from the University of Georgia invites us to meet four more individuals. These students are not specific people; they are composites of the characteristics of real people Nancy has known and taught. The names and schools are fictional, but the lives are very real.

Ternice Mattox is a 7th grader who lives with her mother and three younger siblings in a large city in the Northeast. Her mother works the 7:00–3:00 shift at a dry-cleaning plant and then cleans offices some nights and weekends to make ends meet, so Ternice gets her

JUST ONE CULTURE? Definitions of *culture* apply to regional, ethnic, religious, racial, gender, social class, and other areas of difference. Each of us is a member of many groups, so we all are influenced by many different cultures.

brothers and sister up and ready for school every day, feeds them dinner when they get home, and makes sure they do their homework at night; she has been doing this since she was 10.

School hasn't ever been very hard for Ternice; in elementary school she usually got Bs, even though a lot of the teachers said she talked too much. But she never really liked school until last year. Her 6th grade English teacher seemed to want students to talk. She had them reading stories about real people, like you could meet any day downtown. In class, she got people talking about what the characters should do and why the authors wrote the stories the way they did. Best of all, she let you write about whatever you wanted, even your own life; and she didn't count off for every mistake right away, but let you work with her and with the other kids until you had a final copy you could be really proud of. In that class, Ternice found out that she really liked to write, and her teacher said she was good at it; one of her stories even got published in the school newspaper. Ternice talked and wrote so much in that class that Anthony Bailey got on her about why she was "actin' so white." She got mad and told him that acting foolish was worse than acting white, but it still bothered her. She and Anthony kind of go together, and she likes him a lot; she has "Ternice and 'Tone" written all over her notebooks.

Her English class this year is not nearly as good. Her teacher from last year wants her to take some tests, to see if she can get into the gifted program, but Ternice is not so sure about that. Even if she got in, she's afraid she wouldn't know anyone; almost all the kids in "gifted" are white, and the few black kids are from another part of town. Besides, her friends might not like it, especially Anthony; at her school, "brains" don't go around with "regulars," and vice versa. Her mama wants her to try, and says there's no telling where she can go from there, but Ternice doesn't want to go anywhere that's away from all her friends. Still, she wishes she could have more classes like her English class last year.

Benjamin Whittaker lives in a suburb of Colorado Springs with his father, the vice president at a local bank and member of the board of a local hospital. His mother and father are divorced, but Ben still sees his mom every two weeks for the weekend. His older sister is in her second year of college, taking a pre-veterinary course. Ben started high school this year; he's taking algebra, world history, French, English, and freshman chemistry. His course schedule was his father's idea, especially the freshman chemistry. Ben feels completely out of his league in that class, but his father insisted that if he was going to get into pre-med in college, he had to get a jump-start on science. Ben's mother says medicine is where the money is, and she knows Ben can do it, if he just gets focused.

Ben's not so sure. He has never been a star student like his sister, and he really struggled at the beginning of middle school. He just couldn't get the hang of taking notes; either he couldn't figure out what was most important, so he'd try to write down everything the teachers said, or he'd get distracted by something, and miss whole sections of the lecture. He also had a hard time keeping track of his assignments, and when he did remember to do them, his notebooks and backpack were such a mess that sometimes he'd lose them before he got them turned in. At the end of the first semester, his homeroom teacher suggested he be evaluated for ADHD, and his family doctor put him on a trial dose of Ritalin, which seemed to help. With some additional coaching on organizational skills, Ben gradually improved and finished 8th grade with a solid B average. He still takes Ritalin on school days, but not on the weekends, which is when he does most of his artwork.

Art is what Ben really loves; since he was a little boy he has been drawing people and animals and whole scenes out of his imagination. Sometimes when he's working on a drawing, he loses all track of time; his mom calls it being "zoned in," and teases him that he'd forget to eat if she didn't come up and get him. Lately, he's been experimenting with the graphics program on his computer, and he's even drawn a few panels of his own Web comic. He's only shown it to some friends, but they thought it was pretty funny. It's weird, he never has trouble focusing on his art, but even with the Ritalin, he's having more and more trouble focusing on his schoolwork this year. He's worried his grades won't be very good; he may even flunk chemistry. Ben knows he could do better if he took a lighter load, especially if he could move out of the advanced track and take some art courses; but his parents say art is nice for a hobby, but it's no way to make a living.

Davy Walker is a 2nd grader who is worried he will be held back this year, but he's afraid to ask his teacher about it. He doesn't really like asking questions, anyway, because everyone looks at you, and sometimes they laugh if you ask a dumb one. The problem is, he just can't seem to catch on to reading the way most of the other kids do. He can read some of the words if he has enough time, especially if no one is listening to him, but he hates it when the teacher has them take turns reading aloud. Everyone else seems to read so much better and faster that he just freezes up and makes stupid mistakes.

His teacher had a conference with his mom and dad last fall, and told them he needed to read more at home. His parents own a family restaurant in the small town in Oregon where they live, and his mom and dad both work pretty long hours there; even his older sister helps out some on weekends. His mom tried for a while to get him to read to her when she put him to bed at night, but it didn't work out very well. He got sick of the baby books that were all he could read, and when she got him to try something harder, it went so slowly that she got impatient and quit. Davy was just as glad. When he grows up, he's going to run the restaurant for his dad. He can already clear tables and stack the dishes in the big dishwasher, and sometimes his dad lets him help run the cash register and make change. When he's older, he'll learn to take orders and work the grill. Davy doesn't see what reading has to do with running a good restaurant.

Jessie Kinkaid is a junior at Red Falls High School in Wisconsin. She lives with her mother, who works as a doctor's receptionist, in a small house in town. Her father owns the Ford car dealership, and lives just outside of town with his second wife and Jessie's 3-year-old half-brother, so she sees him pretty often.

Jessie is in the vocational track at school and mostly makes Cs, with a few Ds. Once in a while, she fails a course, but she'll have enough credits to graduate by the end of next year, which is all she really cares about. Her home economics teacher says she has a real flair for cooking, and wants Jessie to bring up her grades so she can apply to chef's school. Jessie likes to cook and knows she's good at it, but doesn't see any point in going to more school. She's only graduating to please her parents; she knows what she's going to do with her life. After graduation she's going to get a job in town some-where for a couple years to save up some money, and then she'll marry Walter Aiken. She and Walt have been going together since she was a freshman and he was a junior. Walt started this year at UW-Platteville to get a degree in animal science, and they plan to wait until he is finished before they get married. Then they'll move into the small house on the Aiken's farm until Walt's dad is ready to retire, probably in another three or four years. Then Walt will take over the farm, and they'll move into the big house; Jessie hopes they'll have at least one child by then.

So Jessie doesn't see any point in worrying about her grades, as long as she graduates. Her father agrees it would be foolish to waste time and money on extra schooling she'll never use. Jessie's mother, who left school at 17 to marry, is the one urging Jessie to think about going on. She says she just wants Jessie to "keep all her options open."

Felipe, Ternice, Ben, Davy, and Jessie are just five students, and there are millions more—unique collections of abilities and experiences. They speak different languages, have different ethnic and racial backgrounds, and live in different kinds of communities. Some come from families in poverty, others from families with power and privilege—but all face challenges in their education. For the remainder of the chapter we will look at the dimensions of cultural differences in schools today.

STOP & THINK Take a quick break from reading and turn on the television. (Don't do this if you won't come back to reading until next Tuesday!) Find a channel with commercials. (I know, it is harder to find one without.) Listen to about 15 commercials. For each one, is the voice or the character in the ad old or young? Economically privileged or poor? Male or a female? What is the character's ethnicity or race? Do a quick tally of how many instances you observe in each category. •

Connect and Extend to PRAXIS II™

Cultural and Gender Differences in the Classroom (III, B)
What are the sources of possible miscommunication between students and teachers in the classroom because of cultural or gender differences? Identify steps a teacher can take to minimize such problems.

Cautions: Interpreting Cultural Differences

Before we discuss cultural differences, two cautions are necessary. First, we will consider social class, ethnicity, race, and gender separately, because much of the available research focuses on only one of these variables. Of course, real children are not just African American, or middle class, or male; they are complex beings and members of many groups, just like the five students you met earlier.

The second caution is that group membership is not destiny. Just knowing a student is a member of a particular cultural group does not define what that student is like. People are individuals. For example, if a student in your class consistently arrives late, it may be that the student has a job before school, must walk a long distance, is responsible for getting younger siblings to school like Ternice, or even that he or she dreads school, much like Jessie.

CULTURAL CONFLICTS AND COMPATIBILITIES. The differences between cultures may be very obvious, tip-of-the iceberg characteristics such as holiday customs and dress, or they may be very subtle, below-the-surface differences such as how to get your turn in conversations. When subtle cultural differences meet, misunderstandings and conflicts are common. These conflicts can happen when the values and competencies of the dominant, mainstream culture are used to determine what is considered "normal" or appropriate behavior in schools. In these cases, children who have been socialized in a different culture may be perceived as acting inappropriately, not following the rules, or being rude and disrespectful.

Rosa Hernandez Sheets (2005) describes a 5-year-old Mexican American girl who tried to bring a bread roll, part of her school cafeteria lunch, home to give to her little brother every day. Her parents were proud of her for sharing, but the school officials made her throw the roll away, because it was against school rules to take food from the cafeteria. The girl was conflicted about following school rules versus honoring her family's cultural values. The teacher in this case solved the problem by talking to the cafeteria cook, putting the roll in a plastic bag, and placing the bag in the girl's backpack to be taken home after school.

Not all cultural differences lead to clashes in school, however. For example, compared to other ethnic groups, Asian Americans have the highest graduation rates from high school, college, and graduate school—so sometimes they are labeled as "model minorities" (Lee, 2006). Is this fair?

DANGERS IN STEREOTYPING. There are dangers in stereotyping both Asians and Asian Americans as model students—quiet, hardworking, and passive. Acting on these stereotypes can reinforce conformity and stifle assertiveness. Stacey Lee (2006) describes another stereotype confronting Asian Americans. They are seen as perpetual foreigners. No matter how many decades their families have lived in America, even 4th- or 5th-generation Asian American students are not seen as "real" Americans. In fact, Lee's research shows that teachers tend to refer to these students as "Asian," not "Asian American" or "American." That would be like calling me a German student because my great-grandfather came to Wisconsin from Germany. I was born in Texas and my knowledge of German culture is limited to my grandmother's recipe for pfefferneuse—excellent, by the way. Too often, students take these stereotypes to heart and feel "foreign" even in the country of their birth—America. One high school student told Lee (2004), "Watching MTV affected the way I acted very much. I wanted to be more Americanized. I changed my hair color. I got colored contact lenses" (p. 44). Later in this chapter, we will explore ways to make classrooms compatible with the home cultures of students. First, however, we need to examine some of the effects of cultural conflicts and discrimination on student achievement.

ECONOMIC AND SOCIAL CLASS DIFFERENCES

Even though most researchers would agree that social class is one of the most meaningful cultural dimensions in people's lives, those same researchers have great difficulty defining *social class* (Liu et al., 2004). Different terms are used—social class, socioeconomic status (SES), economic background, wealth, poverty, or privilege. Some people consider only economic differences; others add considerations of power, influence, mobility, control over resources, and prestige.

Social Class and SES

In modern societies, levels of wealth, power, and prestige are not always consistent. Some people—for instance, university professors—are members of professions that are reasonably high in terms of social status, but provide little wealth or power (believe me). Other people have political power even though they are not wealthy, or they may be members of the social register in a town, even though their family money is long gone. Most people are generally aware of their social class—that is, they perceive that some groups are above them in social class and some are below. They may even show a kind of *"classism"* (like racism or sexism), believing that they are "better" than members of lower social classes and avoiding association with them. For example, in an ethnographic study (see Chapter 1 if you don't remember what *ethnographic* means), Marissa, a member of the most popular and privileged clique in her high school, described the "grits"—the least popular group:

> Grits are poor. I think they mostly live in the country. We—[quickly correcting herself] some of my friends call them hicks or rednecks. I guess most live on the Hill—that's over on the west side of town. It's the slums. Grits smoke, do drugs, dress grungy. They have those hick accents. They usually get bad grades. They don't like school so I think they drop out a lot. They don't really fit in. They are troublemakers. I don't see them much; they aren't in any of my classes. (Brantlinger, 2004, pp. 109–110)

In addition to social class, there is another way of thinking about differences that is commonly used in research. Sociologists and psychologists combine variations in wealth, power, control over resources, and prestige into an index called **socioeconomic status**, or **SES**. In contrast to social class, most people are not conscious of their SES designation. SES is usually ascribed to people by researchers; different formulas for determining SES might lead to different assignments (Liu et al., 2004; Sirin, 2005). No single variable, not even income, is an effective measure of SES. Most researchers identify four general levels of SES: upper, middle, working, and lower. The main characteristics of these four levels are summarized in Table 6.1 on the next page. As you watched the commercials in the *Stop & Think* activity, how many people did you see who appeared to be in the lower-class SES?

Poverty and School Achievement

You saw in Chapter 1 that about 1 in 5 Americans under the age of 18 lives below the poverty level—$22,050 annual income for a family of four. That is 21% of all children in the United States. In fact, 9% of all children live in extreme poverty ($11,025 annual income). More than half of all poor children live in eight states (California, Texas, New York, Florida, Illinois, Georgia, Ohio, and Michigan). For a while, there were improvements. In 2000, the number of families in poverty was the lowest in 21 years—about 6.2 million (U.S. Census Bureau, September 25, 2001), but rates have been rising again since then to over 15 million. It is likely that 40% of all American children will live in poverty at some time in their lives (Koppelman, 2011).

In 2008, the absolute number of children living in poverty was similar for non-Hispanic White children (4.9 million), Latina/o children (5.6 million), and African American children (4.5 million). But the rate of poverty is higher for African American, Latino, and Native American children—35% of African American, 34% of Native American, and 31% of Latino children lived in poverty in 2008, whereas 13% of Asian and 11% of non-Hispanic White children were poor (National Poverty Center, 2011). African American and Latino families headed by single women have the highest poverty rate—about 50% (Moore, Redd, Burkhauser, Mbwana, & Collins, 2009). Contrary to many stereotypes, more poor

Connect and Extend to PRAXIS II™

Economic Conditions/ Socioeconomic Status (SES) (IV, B2) Be aware of the possible effects of socioeconomic status on student achievement. Consider what steps teachers can take to minimize those effects.

Socioeconomic status (SES) Relative standing in the society based on income, power, background, and prestige.

TABLE 6.1 • **Selected Characteristics of Different Social Classes**

	UPPER CLASS	MIDDLE CLASS	WORKING CLASS	LOWER CLASS
Income	$200,000+	$110,000–$200,000 (1/2) $50,000–$110,000 (1/2)	$25,000–$50,000	Below $25,000
Occupation	Corporate, professional, family money	White-collar, skilled blue-collar	Blue-collar	Minimum wage, unskilled labor
Education	Prestigious colleges and graduate schools	High school, college, or professional school	High school	High school or less
Home ownership	At least one home	Usually own home	About half own a home	Uncommon
Health coverage	Full	Usually	Limited	Uncommon
Neighborhoods	Exclusive or comfortable	Comfortable	Modest	Deteriorating
Afford children's college	Easily	Usually	Seldom	Uncommon
Political power	National, state, local	State or local	Limited	No

Source: Information from Macionis, J. J. (2010). Sociology (13th ed). Upper Saddle River, NJ: Pearson and Macionis, personal communication, 4/2/2010.

children live in suburban and rural areas than in central cities. But poverty rates are high in urban schools. In the 100 largest public school districts across the country, 56% of the students qualified for free and reduced-price lunches in 2008–2009, based on their low family income (NCES, 2011).

The average correlation between SES and achievement tests is moderate, about .30 to .40 (Sackett, Kuncel, Arneson, Cooper, & Waters, 2009; Sirin, 2005). In general, high-SES students of all ethnic groups show higher average levels of achievement on test scores and stay in school longer than low-SES students (Berliner, 2005; Gutman, Sameroff, & Cole, 2003). Poor children are at least twice as likely as non-poor children to be kept back in school. And the longer the child is in poverty, the stronger the impact is on achievement. For example, even when we take into account parents' education, the chance that children will be retained in grades or placed in special education classes increases by 2% to 3% for every year the children live in poverty (Ackerman, Brown, & Izard, 2004; Bronfenbrenner, McClelland, Wethington, Moen, & Ceci, 1996).

What are the effects of low socioeconomic status that might explain the lower school achievement of these students? No single cause is to blame (Evans, 2004). Poor health care for mother and child, dangerous or unhealthy home environments, limited resources, family stress, interruptions in schooling, exposure to violence, overcrowding, homelessness, discrimination, and other factors lead to school failures, low-paying jobs—and another generation born into poverty. Evans (2004), Jensen (2009), and McLoyd (1998) describe other possible explanations. Let's take a closer look at each of them.

HEALTH, ENVIRONMENT, AND STRESS. The negative effects of poverty begin even before a child is born. Families in poverty have less access to good prenatal and infant health care and nutrition. Over half of all adolescent mothers receive no prenatal care at all. Poor mothers and adolescent mothers are more likely to have premature babies, and prematurity is associated with many cognitive and learning problems. Children in poverty are more likely to be exposed to both legal drugs (nicotine, alcohol) and illegal drugs (cocaine, heroin) before birth. Children whose mothers take drugs during pregnancy can have problems with organization, attention, and language skills.

In the early years, children in poverty experience higher levels of stress hormones than children in middle-class and wealthy families. High levels of these hormones can interfere with the flow of blood in the brain as well as the development of synaptic connections (Shonkoff, 2006). In addition, stress hormones can deplete the body's supply of tryptophan (Richell, Deakin, & Anderson, 2005), an amino acid that calms impulsive and violent behaviors (Hudley & Novak, 2007). Poor children are four times as likely to experience stress due to evictions, lack of food, overcrowding, or utility disconnections. Increased stress is related to increased school absences, decreased attention and concentration, problems with memory and thinking, reduced motivation and effort, increased depression, and reduced neurogenesis (growth of new brain cells) (Jensen, 2009). As they grow, poor children breathe more polluted air and drink more contaminated water (Evans, 2004). They are at least twice as likely as non-poor children to suffer lead poisoning, which is associated with lower school achievement and long-term neurological impairment (McLoyd, 1998).

LOW EXPECTATIONS—LOW ACADEMIC SELF-CONCEPT. Because poor students may wear older clothes, speak in a dialect, or be less familiar with books and school activities, teachers and other students may assume that these students are not bright. The teacher may avoid calling on them, assuming they don't know the answer, set lower standards, and accept poor work. Thus, low expectations become institutionalized and the educational resources provided to these children are inadequate (Borman & Overman, 2004). Low expectations, along with a lower-quality educational experience, can lead to a sense of learned helplessness, described in Chapter 4. Low-SES children, particularly those who also encounter racial discrimination, may decide that school is a dead end. Without a high school diploma, these students find few rewards awaiting them in the work world. Many available jobs barely pay a living wage.

PEER INFLUENCES AND RESISTANCE CULTURES. Some researchers have suggested that low-SES students may become part of a **resistance culture**. To members of this culture, making it in school means selling out and trying to act "middle class." In order to maintain

Resistance culture Group values and beliefs about refusing to adopt the behaviors and attitudes of the majority culture.

WEALTH AND SCHOOL SUCCESS Wealthy students of all ethnic groups seem to show higher average levels of school success than poor students, who are also at least twice as likely to be kept back in school. The resources available to these groups of students are starkly different.

SUMMER SETBACKS. Children in poverty lose ground academically during the summers while middle- and upper-class families provide many educational experiences over the summer for their children. One study suggests that the four summer vacations between 2nd and 6th grade account for 80% of the achievement differences between poor and advantaged students.

their identity and their status within the group, low-SES students must reject the behaviors that would make them successful in school—studying, cooperating with teachers, even coming to class (Bennett, 2011; Ogbu, 1987, 1997). John Ogbu linked identification with a resistance culture to poor Latino American, Native American, and African American groups, but similar reactions have been noted for poor White students both in the United States and in England and high school students in Papua New Guinea (Woolfolk Hoy, Demerath, & Pape, 2002). This is not to say that all low-SES students resist achievement. Adolescents whose parents value academic achievement tend to select friends who also share those values (Berndt & Keefe, 1995). Many young people are high achievers in spite of either their economic situation or negative peer influences (O'Connor, 1997). And we should not forget that some aspects of schooling—competitive grading, public reprimands, stressful testing and assignments, and repetitive work that is too hard or too easy—can encourage resistance in all students (Okagaki, 2001). To focus solely on students' resistance is a way of blaming students for their lower achievement; instead, educators should focus on making school an inclusive place that does not invite resistance (Stinson, 2006).

HOME ENVIRONMENT AND RESOURCES. Families in poverty seldom have access to high-quality preschool care for their young children, the kind of care that enhances cognitive and social development (Duncan & Brooks-Gunn, 2000; Vandell, 2004). Poor children read less and spend more time watching television; they have less access to books, computers, libraries, trips, and museums (Evans, 2004; Kim & Guryan, 2010). Again, not all low-income families lack resources. Many families provide rich learning environments for their children. When parents of any SES level support and encourage their children—by reading to them, providing books and educational toys, taking the children to the library, making time and space for learning—the children tend to become better, more enthusiastic readers (Peng & Lee, 1992).

Home and neighborhood resources seem to have the greatest impact on children's achievement when school is not in session—during the summer or before students enter school.

SUMMER SETBACKS. Over the past decade, evidence has been mounting that students in poverty begin school about 6 months behind in reading skills compared to students from wealthier homes, but the difference between the groups grows to almost 3 years by 6th grade. One explanation for this growing gap is that the children from poorer homes, and especially those whose first language in not English, lose ground over the summer. Even though both groups make comparable achievement gains during the school year, every summer vacation creates about a 3-month reading achievement gap between poor and advantaged children (Kim & Guryan, 2010). One study suggested that the 4 summer vacations between 2nd and 6th grade accounted for 80% of the achievement differences between poor and advantaged students (Allington & McGill-Frazen, 2003, 2008). This truly is a case of the rich getting richer. Wealthier children have greater access to books all the time, but especially over the summer. They read more, and the more children read, the better readers they become—volume of reading matters.

POINT/COUNTERPOINT: Is Tracking an Effective Strategy?

Tracking students into different classes or strands (college prep, vocational, remedial, gifted, etc.) has been standard procedure in many schools for a long time, but does it work? Critics say tracking is harmful, whereas supporters claim it is useful, even though it presents challenges.

POINT ▶ Tracking is harmful and should be eliminated.

According to Tom Loveless, writing in the April 1999 issue of *Educational Leadership*, "Prominent researchers and prestigious national reports have argued that tracking stands in the way of equal educational opportunity" (p. 28).

Loveless goes on to cite the work of Braddock and Slavin (1993); Carnegie Council on Adolescent Development (1995); Oakes (1985); and Wheelock (1992)—all of whom make the argument against tracking. What is the basis for these claims? Surprisingly, the evidence is not clear or direct. For example, a few well-done and carefully designed studies found that tracking increases the gap between high and low achievers by depressing the achievement of low-track students and boosting the achievement of high-track students (Gamoran, 1987; Kerckhoff, 1986). And Gamoran also found that the achievement gap between low- and high-track students is greater than the gap between students who drop out of school and students who graduate. Because low-income students and students of color are overrepresented in the lower tracks, they suffer the greatest harm from tracking and should benefit the most from the elimination of tracking (Oakes, 1990b; Oakes & Wells, 2002). Is this likely? In an interview with Marge Scherer (1993), Jonathan Kozol described the cruel predictive side of tracking:

> [T]racking is so utterly predictive. The little girl who gets shoved into the low reading group in 2nd grade is very likely to be the child who is urged to take cosmetology instead of algebra in the 8th grade, and most likely to be in vocational courses, not college courses, in the 10th grade, if she hasn't dropped out by then. (p. 8)

COUNTERPOINT ▶ Eliminating tracking will hurt many students.

Researchers who have looked closely at tracking believe that tracking may be harmful for some students some of the time, but not for all students and not all of the time. First, as most people agree, tracking seems to have positive effects for the high-track students. Gifted programs, honors classes, and advanced placement classes seem to work (Fuchs, Fuchs, Hamlett, & Karns, 1998; Robinson & Clinkenbeard, 1998). No one, especially parents, wants to eliminate the positive effects of these programs. And the chance of being assigned to a high track is 10% greater for African American students (Gamoran & Mare, 1989), so detracking could be a special disservice to these students.

What would happen if schools were detracked? Loveless (1999) identifies some possible hidden costs. First, results of a large national study suggest that when low-track 10th graders are assigned to heterogeneous classes rather than low tracks, they gain about 5 percentage points in achievement. So far, so good. But average students lose 2 percentage points when put into heterogeneous classes and high-ability students lose about 5 points.

> The achievement gap is indeed narrowed, but apparently at the expense of students in regular and high tracks, representing about 70% of 10th graders in the United States. (Loveless, 1999, p. 29)

Another consequence of detracking is bright flight—the withdrawal of the brightest students from the schools. Both African American and White parents distrust mixed-ability classes to meet the needs of their children (Public Agenda Foundation, 1994).

Beware of Either/Or. In some classes, using a mixed-ability structure seems to hinder the achievement of all students. For example, students in heterogeneous algebra classes don't learn as much as students in tracked classes—whatever the ability level of the students (Epstein & MacIver, 1992). And a meta-analysis of student self-esteem found that students in low-track classes did *not* have lower self-esteem than students in heterogeneous classes (Kulik & Kulik, 1997).

So what is the answer? As usual, it is more complicated than simply detracking versus tracking. Careful attention to every student's achievement may mean different answers at different times.

TRACKING: POOR TEACHING. A final explanation for the lower achievement of many low-SES students is that these students experience **tracking** and therefore have a different academic socialization; that is, they are actually taught differently (Oakes, 1990b). If they are tracked into "low-ability," "general," "practical," or "vocational" classes, they may be taught to memorize and be passive. Middle-class students are more likely to be encouraged to think and be creative in their classes. Is tracking a problem? Read the *Point/Counterpoint* for the arguments.

Even if they are not tracked, low-income students are more likely to attend schools with inadequate resources and less-effective teachers (Evans, 2004). For example, in

Tracking Assignment to different classes and academic experiences based on achievement.

GUIDELINES

Teaching Students Who Live in Poverty

Educate yourself about the effects of poverty on student learning.
Examples
1. Read articles from good journals.
2. Seek reliable sources such as Eric Jensen's (2009), *Teaching with Poverty in Mind: What Being Poor Does to Kids' Brains and What Schools Can Do about It.*

Set and maintain high expectations.
Examples
1. Guard against feeling sorry for students, excusing poor work, and expecting less. Replace pity with empathy based on solid knowledge of your students.
2. Communicate to students that they can succeed with good effort.
3. Provide constructive criticism because you believe your students can do quality work.
4. Add challenging subjects and AP classes.

Develop caring relationships with your students.
Examples
1. Use inclusive language—"our class," "our projects," "our school," "our efforts."
2. Talk to students outside class. Make a point to identify their interests and abilities.
3. Attend sports or other events where your students participate.
4. Create a class welcome center for families (see Chapter 5).

Build learning and self-regulation skills as part of the curriculum.
Examples
1. Teach students how to organize work, focus attention, or seek appropriate help.
2. Include conflict management and social problem-solving skills in lessons.

Notice health problems.
Examples
1. Notice who seems to be absent or tardy often.
2. Check to see whether some students struggle to hear the class discussions. Can they see from the back of the room?
3. Model healthy eating and physical activity.

Assess student knowledge, start where they are, but don't stay there (Milner, 2010).
Examples
1. Use short ungraded assessments that target the learning objectives for each unit.
2. Differentiate instruction (Chapter 14) based on results.

Many examples adapted from Jensen, E. (2009). Teaching with Poverty in Mind: What Being Poor Does to Kids' Brains and What Schools Can do About It. Alexandria, VA: Association for Supervision and Curriculum Development.

---

high-poverty schools, over 50% of math teachers and over 60% of science teachers are inexperienced or teaching outside their subject expertise—they were not trained for the subjects they are teaching (Jensen, 2009). When low-SES students receive a substandard education, this gives them inferior academic skills and limits their life chances, beginning with not preparing them for higher education (Anyon, 1980; Knapp & Woolverton, 2003). See the *Guidelines* for a few ideas about quality teaching for students who live in poverty.

ETHNICITY AND RACE IN TEACHING AND LEARNING

The United States truly is a diverse society. By the year 2023, almost two-thirds of the school-age population will be African American, Asian, Latina/Latino, or from other ethnic groups (Children's Defense Fund, 2010). Before we look at the research on ethnicity and race, let's clarify some terms.

Terms: Ethnicity and Race

Ethnicity usually refers to a group's shared common cultural characteristics such as history, homeland, language, traditions, or religion. We all have some ethnic heritage, whether our background is Italian, Ukrainian, Hmong, Chinese, Japanese, Navajo, Hawaiian, Puerto Rican, Cuban, Hungarian, German, African, or Irish—to name only a few.

Ethnicity A cultural heritage shared by a group of people.

Race, on the other hand, is defined as "a category composed of men and women who share biologically transmitted traits that are defined as socially significant," such as skin color or hair texture (Macionis, 2003, p. 354). In effect, race is a label people apply to themselves and to others based on appearances. There are no biologically pure races. For any two humans chosen at random, an average of only .012% (about one-hundredth of one percent) of the alphabetic sequence of their genetic codes is different due to race (Myers, 2005). Today many psychologists emphasize that ethnicity and race are socially constructed ideas. Still, race is a powerful construct. At the individual level, race is part of our identity—how we understand ourselves and interact with others. At the group level, race is involved with economic and political structures (Omi & Winant, 1994).

Sociologists sometimes use the term **minority group** to label a group of people that receives unequal or discriminatory treatment. Strictly speaking, however, the term refers to a numerical minority compared to the total population. Referring to particular racial or ethnic groups as minorities is technically incorrect in some situations, because in certain places, such as Chicago or Mississippi, the "minority" group—African Americans—is actually the majority. This practice of referring to people as minorities because of their racial or ethnic heritage has been criticized because it is misleading and has negative historical connotations (Milner, 2010).

Ethnic and Racial Differences in School Achievement

A major concern in schools is that some ethnic groups consistently achieve below the average for all students (Matthews, Kizzie, Rowley, & Cortina, 2010; Uline & Johnson, 2005). This pattern of results tends to hold for all standardized achievement tests, but the gaps have been narrowing over the past four to five decades (Raudenbush, 2009). For example, as you can see in Figure 6.2 on the next page, on the National Assessment of Educational Progress in mathematics, the gap between scores of White and African American 4th graders has narrowed from 34 points in 1996 to 26 points in 2009. The gap between White and Hispanic 4th graders has narrowed from 25 in 1996 to 21 in 2009 (NCES, 2009).

Proponents of this notion of an "achievement gap" have been criticized for taking a narrow view, assuming that the scores of White, middle-class students are the norm that all other students must be compared to and measured by. Multicultural scholar H. Richard Milner (2010) reminds teachers that "people of color may experience a different type of 'normal' life and that excellence can and does emerge in multiple and varied forms: people of color from all walks of life are successful" (p. 9). He suggests that we think about other kinds of "gaps," such as teacher education and quality gaps, affordable housing gaps, challenging curriculum gaps, health care and nutrition gaps, school funding gaps, and quality childcare gaps—all culminating in *opportunity gaps* for many students of color.

Opportunity gaps lead to education completion gaps. Across all the United States in 2007, about 80% of White students graduated from high school, compared to 60% of African American students, 62% of Latino/a students, 91% of Asian/Pacific Islanders, and 61% of Native Americans. But again, these are averages across all the states. If we look state by state, we see some interesting differences. For example, Nevada had the lowest overall completion rate (52%), whereas Iowa, Nebraska, Vermont, and Wisconsin all had rates above 86%. In the other states, completion rates for White students ranged from 66% in South Carolina to 94% in Wisconsin; for African Americans from 51% in Florida and South Carolina to 100% in New Hampshire; Latino/a students from 44% in South Carolina to over 90% in West Virginia and Vermont; and Asian American students from 77% in Hawaii to 100% in Arkansas, Delaware, Idaho, Illinois, Maine, Missouri, Montana, New Hampshire, New Jersey, North Dakota, Oklahoma, South Dakota, and West Virginia (NCES, 2009).

Although there still are consistent differences among ethnic groups on tests of cognitive abilities, most researchers agree that the reasons for these differences are mainly the legacy of discrimination, the product of cultural mismatches and language differences, or a result of growing up in poverty. Because many students from ethnic groups are also

Race A socially constructed category based on appearances and ancestry.

Minority group A group of people who have been socially disadvantaged—not always a minority in actual numbers.

FIGURE 6.2

SCORES ON THE NATIONAL ASSESSMENT OF EDUCATIONAL PROGRESS IN 4TH GRADE MATHEMATICS

This figure compares the changes in the scores of White, African American, and Hispanic American 4th graders between 1990 and 2009.

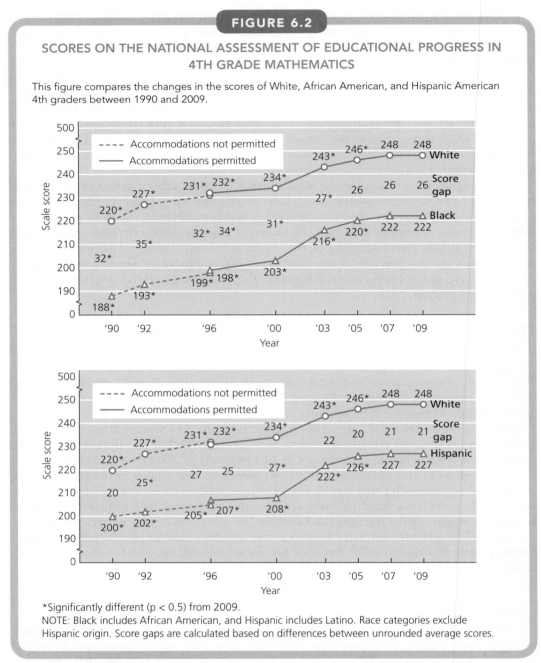

*Significantly different (p < 0.5) from 2009.
NOTE: Black includes African American, and Hispanic includes Latino. Race categories exclude Hispanic origin. Score gaps are calculated based on differences between unrounded average scores.

Source: National Assessment of Educational Progress (2011). National Report Card. Available online at http://nces.ed.gov/ nationsreportcard/pubs/main2009/2010451.asp Downloaded May 4, 2011.

economically disadvantaged, it is important to separate the effects of these two sets of influences on school achievement (Roberts, Mohammed, & Vaughn, 2010). For example, a recent study found that learning and self-regulation skills (such as attentiveness, persistence, organization, learning independence) explained the literacy development of African American boys from kindergarten to 5th grade, even after taking into account the effects of the boys' SES, home environment, and problem behaviors (Matthews, Kizzie, Rowley, & Cortina, 2010). So early development of these learning skills can help to close the opportunity gap, at least for African American boys, and probably for others.

Rather than focusing on achievement gaps, many educators have called for more research on the successes of African American and Latino/a students. Berry (2005) studied two middle-school-aged African American boys who were successful in mathematics. In the lives of those students, Berry found support and high expectations from family and teachers; positive math experiences in preschool and elementary school; connections to church and athletic extracurricular activities; and positive identities as math students. Berry encouraged educators and researchers "to focus on the success stories of those African American men and boys who are successful to identify the strengths, skills, and other significant factors it takes to foster success" (p. 61).

One final theme characterized the successful African American boys—their families had prepared them to understand and deal with discrimination, our next topic.

The Legacy of Discrimination

When we considered explanations for why low-SES students have trouble in school, we listed the limited educational opportunities and low expectations/biases of teachers and fellow students. This has been the experience of many ethnic minority students as well. For example, in some areas of the South in 1924, Black students attended their own separate schools for only 6 months out of the year because they were expected to work in the fields the other 6 months. White students continued in their separate schools a full 9 months. The highest grade available for the Black students was 8th (Raudenbush, 2009).

LINDA BROWN Nine-year-old Linda Brown, the plaintiff in *Brown v. Board of Education of Topeka*.

STOP & THINK Legal segregation came to an end in 1954. Take a moment to imagine you were living back then and the child described below was your own. What would you do?

[In] the city of Topeka, Kansas, a minister walked hand in hand with his seven-year-old daughter to an elementary school four blocks from their home. Linda Brown wanted to enroll in the 2nd grade, but the school refused to admit her. Instead, public school officials required her to attend another school two miles away. This meant that she had to walk six blocks to a bus stop, where she sometimes waited half an hour for the bus. In bad weather, Linda Brown would be soaking wet by the time the bus came; one day she became so cold at the bus stop that she walked back home. Why, she asked her parents, could she not attend the school only four blocks away? (Macionis, 2003, p. 353) •

Her parents' answer to this question, with the help of other concerned families, was to file a suit challenging the school policy. You know the outcome of the 1954 *Brown* v. *the Board of Education of Topeka* ruling. "Separate but equal" schools for Black children were declared inherently unequal. Even though segregation in schools became illegal nearly 60 years ago, about two-thirds of all African American students still attend schools where students of color make up at least 50% of the student body. Segregation in housing and neighborhoods persists, and some areas have drawn school boundary lines deliberately to separate school enrollments along racial lines (Kantor & Lowe, 1995; Ladson-Billings, 2004).

Years of research on the effects of desegregation have mostly shown that legally mandated integration is not a quick solution to the detrimental effects of centuries of racial inequality. In part because White students left integrated schools as the number of students of color increased, many urban schools today are more segregated than they were before the Supreme Court ordered busing and other desegregation measures. The schools in Los Angeles, Miami, Baltimore, Chicago, Dallas, Memphis, Houston, and Detroit have fewer than 11% non-Hispanic White students. And in almost 90% of the schools that have mostly African American and Latina/o students, at least half of the students live in poverty, so racial segregation becomes economic segregation as well (Ladson-Billings, 2004; Orfield & Frankenberg, 2005; Raudenbush, 2009).

Too often, even in integrated schools, minority-group students are resegregated in low-ability tracks. Simply putting people in the same building does not mean that they will come to respect each other or even that they will experience the same quality of education (Ladson-Billings, 2004; Pettigrew, 1998).

Doonesbury

BY GARRY TRUDEAU

WHAT IS PREJUDICE? The word *prejudice* is closely related to the word *prejudge*. **Prejudice** is a rigid and irrational generalization—a prejudgment—about an entire category of people. Prejudice is made up of beliefs, emotions, and tendencies toward particular actions. For example, you are prejudiced against people who are overweight if you think they are lazy (belief), feel disgusted (emotion), and refuse to date them (action) (Myers, 2010). Prejudice can be positive or negative; that is, you can have positive as well as negative irrational beliefs about a group, but the term usually refers to negative attitudes. Targets of prejudice can be based on race, ethnicity, religion, politics, geographic location, language, sexual orientation, gender, or appearance.

Racial prejudice is pervasive, and racism is not confined to one group (Clark, Anderson, Clark, & Williams, 1999). Blatant prejudice has decreased in the past four decades. For example, in 1970, over 50% of Americans agreed that it was all right to keep minorities out of their neighborhoods. By 1995, the number had dropped to about 10% (Myers, 2005). But subtle, below-the-surface racism continues. In response to several police shootings of unarmed Black men, researchers created a videogame that showed a series of White or Black men holding either a gun or a non-weapon such as a flashlight or wallet. Participants in the research were told to "shoot" whenever the person in the videogame held a weapon. Race was not mentioned. Nevertheless, participants shot armed targets more quickly and more frequently when those targets were Black, rather than White, but decided not to shoot unarmed targets more quickly and more frequently when they were White (Greenwald, Oakes, & Hoffman, 2003). When the participants in another study were actual police officers, they were more likely to mistakenly shoot unarmed Black suspects compared with unarmed White suspects (Plant & Peruche, 2005). Besides this obvious threat to well-being for those who are targets of prejudice, research in psychology shows that prejudice against individuals can undermine their mental and physical health, educational achievement, and success on the job (McKown, 2005).

THE DEVELOPMENT OF PREJUDICE. Prejudice starts early. By about age 6, over half the White children in a United States sample and 85% of students in a Canadian sample had significant pro-White, anti-Black biases. Two popular beliefs are that young children are innocently colorblind and that they will not develop biases unless their parents teach them to be prejudiced. Although these beliefs are appealing, they are not supported by research. Even without direct coaching from their parents, many young children develop racial prejudice. Current explanations of the development of prejudice combine personal, social, and societal factors (Katz, 2003; McKown, 2005).

One source of prejudice is the human tendency to divide the social world into two categories—us and them, or the in-group and the out-group. These divisions may be made on the basis of race, religion, sex, age, ethnicity, or even athletic team membership. We tend to see members of the out-group as inferior to and different from us, but similar to each other—"they all look alike" (Aboud, 2003; Lambert, 1995). Also, those who have more (more money, more social status, more prestige) may justify their privilege by assuming that they deserve to "have" because they are superior to the "have-nots." This can lead to blaming the victims: People who live in poverty or women who are raped are seen as causing their problems by their behavior—"they got what they deserved." Emotions play a part as well. When things go wrong, we look for someone or some whole group

Connect and Extend to PRAXIS II™

Racial Bias (IV, B4)
Describe the possible effects of racial discrimination and bias on minority students. What can teachers and schools do to address the lingering effects of this discrimination?

Prejudice Prejudgment or irrational generalization about an entire category of people.

to blame. For example, after the tragic events of 9/11, some people vented their anger by attacking innocent Arab Americans (Myers, 2010).

But prejudice is more than a tendency to form in-groups, a self-justification, or an emotional reaction—it is also a set of cultural values. Children learn about valued traits and characteristics from their families, friends, teachers, and the world around them. Think back to your analysis of commercials—did you observe many women or people of color? For years, most of the models presented in books, films, television, and advertising were European Americans. People of different ethnic and racial backgrounds were seldom the "heroes" (Ward, 2004). This is changing. In 2002, the Oscar awards for best actress and best actor went to African Americans, but Denzel Washington won for his portrayal of a villain. In 2005, Jamie Fox won an Oscar for his remarkable portrayal of Ray Charles—a hero. And of course, at the time I am writing, Barack Obama is President of the United States.

STOP & THINK List 3 traits most characteristic of:
College freshmen
Politicians
Athletes
Buddhists
Members of the National Rifle Association •

Prejudice is difficult to combat because it can be part of our thinking processes. You saw in Chapter 2 that children develop schemas—organized bodies of knowledge—about objects, events, and actions. We have schemas that organize our knowledge about people we know, and all our daily activities. We can also form schemas about groups of people. When I asked you to list the traits most characteristic of college freshmen, politicians, athletes, Buddhists, and members of the National Rifle Association, you probably could generate a list. That list would show that you have a **stereotype**—a schema—that organizes what you know (and believe) about the group.

As with any schema, we use our stereotypes to make sense of the world. You will see in Chapter 8 that having a schema allows you to process information more quickly and efficiently, but it also allows you to distort information to make it fit your schema better (Macrae, Milne, & Bodenhausen, 1994). This is the danger in racial, ethnic, and gender stereotypes. We notice information that confirms or agrees with our stereotype—our schema—and miss or dismiss information that does not fit. For example, if a juror has a negative stereotype of Asian Americans and is listening to evidence in the trial of an Asian American, the juror may interpret the evidence more negatively. The juror may actually forget testimony in favor of the defendant, and remember more damaging testimony instead. Information that fits the stereotype is even processed more quickly (Anderson, Klatzky, & Murray, 1990; Baron, 1998).

CONTINUING DISCRIMINATION. Prejudice consists of beliefs and feelings (usually negative) about an entire category of people. The third element of prejudice is a tendency to act, called *discrimination*. **Discrimination** is unequal treatment of particular categories of people. Clearly, many Americans face prejudice and discrimination in subtle or blatant ways every day. For example, Latinos, African Americans, and Native Americans make up about 35% of the U.S. population, but only 17% of the House of Representatives and 5% of the Senate (Koppelman, 2011). In the 2007–2008 school year, less than 4% of the doctorates awarded went to Latino students, 6% to African Americans, and .4% to Native Americans. In contrast, 27% of the doctorates were awarded to non-residents of the United States (NCES, 2010). Less than 9% of the scientists, engineers, and mathematicians in the United States are either African American or Hispanic American. Even though their attitudes toward science and math are more favorable than those of White students, Black and Hispanic students begin to lose out in science and math as early as elementary school. They are chosen less often for gifted classes and acceleration or enrichment programs. They are more likely to be tracked into "basic skills" classes. As they progress through middle school, high school, and college, their paths take them farther and farther out of

Stereotype Schema that organizes knowledge or perceptions about a category.

Discrimination Treating or acting unfairly toward particular categories of people.

the pipeline that produces our scientists. If they do persist and become scientists or engineers, they, along with women, will still be paid less than White employees for the same work (Mendoza & Johnson, 2000; National Science Foundation, 2011).

The families of racial and ethnic minority students often have to be vigilant about discrimination to protect their children. They may teach their children to notice and resist possible discrimination. Teachers may unintentionally offend these families if they are not sensitive to possible messages of discrimination. Carol Orange (2005) described a teacher who sent home a holiday worksheet that featured an alphabetical list of all the students in the class. Three students' names were not in the typed list, but were handwritten, out of order, and on the side of the sheet. Two of these students were Latino and one was African American. The mother of the African American student was very upset that her son was truly "marginalized" (written in the margins) on the list. These three students were added to the class (and hence, the list) later in the year, after the list was set up, but the teacher could have avoided this insult (unintended on her part) by redoing the list to give every student a place—a small but important symbol that she valued each one of them.

There is another problem caused by stereotypes and prejudice that can undermine academic achievement—stereotype threat.

Stereotype Threat

Stereotype threat is an "apprehensiveness about confirming a stereotype" (Aronson, 2002, p. 282). The basic idea is that when individuals are in situations in which a stereotype applies, they bear an extra emotional and cognitive burden—the possibility of confirming the stereotype, either in the eyes of others or in their own eyes. Thus, when girls are asked to solve complicated mathematics problems, for example, they are at risk of confirming widely held stereotypes that girls are inferior to boys in mathematics. It is not necessary that the individual believe the stereotype. All that matters is that the person is aware of the stereotype and cares about performing well enough to disprove its unflattering implications (Aronson, Lustina, Good, Keough, Steele, & Brown, 1999; Huguet & Régner, 2007). What are the results of stereotype threat? Recent research provides answers that should interest all teachers.

SHORT-TERM EFFECTS: TEST PERFORMANCE.   One review of the research on women, math, and stereotype threat concluded that very subtle clues that might activate anxiety, such as asking test takers to indicate their gender on an answer sheet before taking a math test, tend to lower math scores for women, especially when tests are difficult, the women are moderately identified with the math field, and being female is an important part of their identity. The differences are small on average—something like a female with average math ability scoring 450 instead of the expected average of 500 on an SAT- or GRE-type test. One study estimated that removing stereotype threat might mean an additional 6% of women getting a passing score on a high-stakes calculus test (Nguyen & Ryan, 2008; Wout, Dasco, Jackson, & Spencer, 2008). In other studies, girls in high school and college have scored below boys on a math test when stereotype threats are present, but the same as boys when these threats are not present (Smith & Hung, 2008). Just telling the girls that the math test they are about to take does not reveal gender differences is enough to eliminate any differences in scores.

In a series of experiments, Joshua Aronson, Claude Steele, and their colleagues demonstrated that when African American or Latino college students are put in situations that induce stereotype threat, their performance suffers (Aronson, 2002; Aronson & Steele, 2005; Okagaki, 2006). For example, African American and White undergraduate subjects in an experiment at Stanford University were told that the test they were about to take would precisely measure their verbal ability. A similar group of subjects was told that the purpose of the test was to understand the psychology of verbal problem solving and not to assess individual ability. As shown in Figure 6.3, when the test was presented as diagnostic of verbal ability, the African American students solved about half as many problems as the White students. In the non-threat situation, the two groups solved about the same number of problems.

All groups, not just minority-group students, can be susceptible to stereotype threat. In another study, the subjects were White male college students who were very strong in mathematics. One group was told that the test they were taking would help experimenters

Stereotype threat The extra emotional and cognitive burden that your performance in an academic situation might confirm a stereotype that others hold about you.

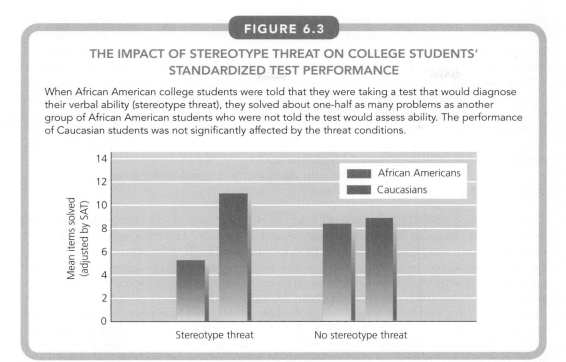

FIGURE 6.3

THE IMPACT OF STEREOTYPE THREAT ON COLLEGE STUDENTS' STANDARDIZED TEST PERFORMANCE

When African American college students were told that they were taking a test that would diagnose their verbal ability (stereotype threat), they solved about one-half as many problems as another group of African American students who were not told the test would assess ability. The performance of Caucasian students was not significantly affected by the threat conditions.

Source: Adapted from "The Effect of Stereotype Threat on the Standardized Test Performance of College Students," by J. Aronson, C. M. Steele, M. F. Salinas, & M. J. Lustina in Readings About the Social Animal, *10th ed. Worth Publishers. Reprinted by permission of Joshua Aronson, Ph.D.*

determine why Asian students performed so much better than Whites on that particular test. Another group just took the test. The group that faced the stereotype threat of confirming that "Asians are better in math" scored significantly lower on the test (Aronson et al., 1999). The individuals most vulnerable to stereotype threat are those who care the most and who are most deeply invested in high performance (Ryan & Ryan, 2005). The pressures of No Child Left Behind testing are likely to increase vulnerability.

Why does stereotype threat affect test performance? Anxiety is part of a model developed by Katherine Ryan and Allison Ryan (2005) to explain the links between stereotype threat and lower math performance for women and African Americans. When these students are in situations that evoke stereotype threats, such as high-pressure tests, they tend to adopt performance-avoidance goals. We will examine this kind of goal more deeply in Chapter 12, but the short version is that setting performance-avoidance goals means the students want to avoid looking dumb. Students who set these kinds of self-protective goals don't persist or use effective strategies. They tend to adopt self-handicapping strategies such as not trying or procrastinating—they just want to survive without looking stupid. But because they put off studying or didn't try, they are anxious and unprepared during the test. Ryan and Ryan sum up their model:

> Concerns about fulfilling a negative stereotype (females and Blacks do not do well in math) bring about a performance-avoid goal orientation towards the test-taking situation for students who are invested in doing well on the test. A performance-avoid goal will lead to an increase in the worry component of test anxiety, make self-efficacy vulnerable, and [lead] to cognitive disorganization or diminishment. (2005, p. 60)

Two other related explanations are that stereotype threat reduces working memory capacity—so students can't hold as much in their minds (Okagaki, 2006), and that it also decreases interest and engagement in the task—why get absorbed in something that will make you look incompetent? (Smith, Sansone, & White, 2007).

LONG-TERM EFFECTS: DISIDENTIFICATION. If students continue to adopt performance-avoidance goals and develop self-defeating strategies to avoid looking stupid, they may withdraw, claim to not care, exert little effort, or even drop out of school—they psychologically disengage from success and claim "math is for nerds" or "school is for losers." Once students define academics as "uncool," it is unlikely they will exert the effort needed for real learning. There is some evidence that Black male students are more likely than Black female students and White students to disidentify with academics—that is, to separate their sense of self-esteem from their academic achievement (Cokley, 2002; Major & Schmader, 1998; Steele, 1992). Other studies have questioned this disidentification connection, however. Historically, education has been valued among African American communities (Walker, 1996). One study found that African American adolescents who had strong Afrocentric beliefs also had higher achievement goals and self-esteem than adolescents who identified with the larger White culture (Spencer, Noll, Stoltzfus, & Harpalani, 2001).

The message for teachers is to help all students see academic achievement as part of their ethnic, racial, and gender identity.

COMBATING STEREOTYPE THREAT.   Aronson, Fried, and Good (2002) demonstrated the powerful effects of changing beliefs about intelligence. African American and White undergraduates were asked to write letters to "at-risk" middle-school students to encourage them to persist in school. Some of the undergraduates were given evidence that intelligence is improvable and encouraged to communicate this information to their pen pals. Others were given information about multiple intelligences, but not told that these multiple abilities can be improved. The middle-school students were not real, but the process of writing persuasive letters about improving intelligence proved powerful. The African American college students—and the White students to a lesser extent—who were encouraged to believe that intelligence can be improved had higher grade-point averages and reported greater enjoyment of and engagement in school when contacted at the end of the next school quarter. Changing their beliefs about the improvability of intelligence also led to higher year-end math achievement scores for middle-school girls (Good, Aronson, & Inzlicht, 2003). So, believing that intelligence can be improved might inoculate students against stereotype threat. In another study, reframing a threatening test as a "challenge" that "sharpens the mind" decreased the impact of stereotype threat for 4th to 6th grade African American students and for Princeton University students from high schools that rarely send students to Ivy League schools (Alter, Aaronson, Darley, Rodriguez, & Ruble, 2009).

In Chapter 12, we will discuss test anxiety and how to overcome the negative effects of anxiety. Many of these strategies are also appropriate for helping students resist stereotype threat.

Gender in Teaching and Learning

In this section, we examine the development of two related identities—sexual identity and gender-role identity. We particularly focus on how men and women are socialized and the role of teachers in providing an equitable education for both sexes.

Sex and Gender

The word *gender* usually refers to traits and behaviors that a particular culture judges to be appropriate for men and for women. In contrast, *sex* refers to biological differences (Brannon, 2002; Deaux, 1993). An individual's identity in terms of gender and sex has three components: gender identity, sexual orientation, and gender-role behaviors (Patterson, 1995; Ruble, Martin, & Berenbaum, 2006). **Gender identity** is a person's self-identification as male or female. *Gender-role behaviors* are those behaviors and characteristics that the culture associates with each gender, and *sexual orientation* involves the person's choice of a sexual partner.

Relations among these three elements are complex. For example, a woman may identify herself as a female (gender identity), but behave in ways that are not consistent with the gender role (play football or wrestle), and may be heterosexual, bisexual, or homosexual in her sexual orientation. So **sexual identity** is a complicated construction of beliefs, attitudes, and behaviors. Erikson and many other earlier psychologists thought

Gender identity The sense of self as male or female as well as the beliefs one has about gender roles and attributes.

Sexual identity A complex combination of beliefs about gender roles and sexual orientation.

that identifying your gender identity was straightforward; you simply realized that you were male or female and acted accordingly. But today, we know that some people experience conflicts about their gender. For example, transsexuals often report feeling trapped in the wrong body; they experience themselves as female, but their biological sex is male, or vice versa (Ruble et al., 2006; Yarhouse, 2001).

SEXUAL ORIENTATION. During adolescence, about 8% of boys and 6% of girls report engaging in some same-sex activity or feeling strong attractions to individuals of their own sex. Males are more likely than females to experiment with same-sex partners as adolescents, but females are more likely to experiment later, often in college. Fewer adolescents actually have a homosexual or bisexual orientation—about 4% of adolescents identify themselves as gay (males who choose male partners), lesbian (females who choose female partners), or bisexual (people who have partners of both sexes). This number increases to between 5% to 13% for adults (Savin-Williams, 2006).

Scientists debate the origins of homosexuality. Most of the research has been with men, so less is known about women. Evidence so far suggests that both biological and social factors are involved. For example, sexual orientation is more similar for identical twins than for fraternal twins, but not all identical twins have the same sexual orientation (Ruble et al., 2006).

There are quite a few models describing the development of sexual orientation as part of identity. Generally, the models include the following or similar stages (Yarhouse, 2001):

* *Feeling different*—Beginning around age 6, the child may be less interested in the activities of other children who are the same sex. Some children may find this difference troubling and fear being "found out." Others do not experience these anxieties.
* *Feeling confused*—In adolescence, as they feel attractions for peers of the same sex, students may be confused, upset, lonely, and unsure of what to do. They may lack role models and may try to change themselves by becoming involved in activities and dating patterns that fit heterosexual stereotypes.
* *Acceptance*—As young adults, many individuals sort through sexual orientation issues and identify themselves as gay, lesbian, or bisexual. They may or may not make their sexual orientation public, but might share the information with a few friends.

The problem with phase models of identity development is that the identity achieved is assumed to be final. Actually, newer models emphasize that sexual orientation can be flexible, complex, and multifaceted; it can change over the lifetime. For example, people may have dated or married opposite-sex partners at one point in their lives, but have same-sex attractions or partners later in their lives, or vice versa (Garnets, 2002).

Parents and teachers are seldom the first people to hear about the adolescent's sexual identity concerns. But if a student does seek your counsel, Table 6.2 on the next page provides some ideas for reaching out.

Gender Roles

Gender roles are expectations about how males and females should behave—about what is masculine and what is feminine. Gender roles vary by culture, time, and place. What was expected of women in the United States in the 1700s definitely has changed, even though women generally still are the primary caregivers and in charge of the home.

When and how do children develop gender roles? As early as age 2, children are aware of gender differences—they know whether they are girls or boys and that mommies are girls and daddies are boys. By age 3 or so, they realize that their sex cannot be changed; they will always be male or female. Biology plays a part in gender role development. Very early, hormones affect activity level and aggression, with boys tending to prefer active, rough, noisy play. Play styles lead young children to prefer same-sex play partners with similar styles, so by age 4, children spend three times as much play time with same-sex playmates as with opposite-sex playmates; by age 6, the ratio is 11 to 1 (Benenson, 1993; Hines, 2004; Maccoby, 1998).

TABLE 6.2 • **Reaching Out to Help Students Struggling with Sexual Identity**

These ideas come from the *Attic Speakers Bureau,* a program of The Attic Youth Center, where trained peer educators reach out to youth and youth-service providers in schools, organizations, and health-care facilities.

REACHING OUT
If a lesbian, gay, bisexual, or transgender youth or a youth questioning his or her own sexual orientation should come to you directly for assistance, remember the following simple, 5-point plan:
LISTEN It seems obvious, but the best thing that you can do in the beginning is allow that individual to vent and express what is going on in his or her life.
AFFIRM Tell them, "You are not alone." This is crucial. A lot of l/g/b/t/q youth feel isolated and lack peers with whom they can discuss issues around sexual orientation. Letting them know that there are others dealing with the same issues is invaluable. This statement is also important because it does not involve a judgment call on your part.
REFER You do not have to be the expert. A referral to someone who is trained to deal with these issues is a gift you are giving to that student, not a dismissal of responsibility.
ADDRESS Deal with harassers—do not overlook issues of verbal or physical harassment around sexual orientation. It is important to create and maintain an environment where all youth feel comfortable and welcome.
FOLLOW-UP Be sure to check in with the individual to see if the situation has improved and if there is anything further you may be able to do.
There are also some things that you as an individual can do to better serve l/g/b/t/q youth and youth dealing with issues around sexual orientation:
• Work on your own sense of comfort around issues of sexual orientation and sexuality.
• Get training on how to present information on sexual orientation effectively.
• Dispel myths around sexual orientation by knowing facts and sharing that information.
• Work on setting aside your own personal biases to better serve students dealing with issues around sexual orientation and sexuality.

Source: From Figure 3. Copyright © The Attic Speakers Bureau and Carrie E. Jacobs, Ph.D. Reprinted with permission.

But biology is not the whole story; boys and girls may be treated differently, too. Researchers have found that boys are given more freedom to roam the neighborhood and are allowed to tackle potentially dangerous activities earlier, such as crossing the street alone. Thus, independence and initiative seem to be encouraged more in boys than in girls. In fact, parents, peers, and teachers may reward behaviors that seem gender appropriate—gentle kindness in girls and strong assertiveness in boys (Brannon, 2002).

And then there are the toys! Walk through any store's toy section and see what is offered to girls and boys. Dolls and kitchen sets for girls and toy weapons for boys have been with us for decades. But we cannot blame the toy makers alone. Adults buying for children favor gender-typed toys; fathers also tend to discourage young sons from playing with "girl's" toys (Brannon, 2002).

Through their interactions with family, peers, teachers, toys, and the environment in general, children begin to form **gender schemas**, or organized networks of knowledge about what it means to be male or female. Gender schemas help children make sense of the world and guide their behavior (see Figure 6.4). So a young girl whose schema for "girls" includes "girls play with dolls and not with trucks" or "girls can't be scientists" will pay attention to, remember, and interact more with dolls than trucks, and she may avoid science activities (Golombok et al., 2006; Leaper, 2002; Liben & Signorella, 1993). Of course, these are averages, and individuals do not always fit the average. An individual girl might decide, for example, that the gender schema "trucks are for boys" doesn't matter to her. She plays with the truck if it interests her (Liben & Bigler, 2002).

By age 4, children have an initial sense of gender roles, and by 5 or so, they have developed a gender schema that describes what clothes, games, toys, behaviors, and careers are "right" for boys and girls—and these ideas can be quite rigid (Brannon, 2002). Even in this era of great progress toward equal opportunity, a preschool girl is more likely to

Gender schemas Organized cognitive structures that include gender-related information that influences how children think and behave.

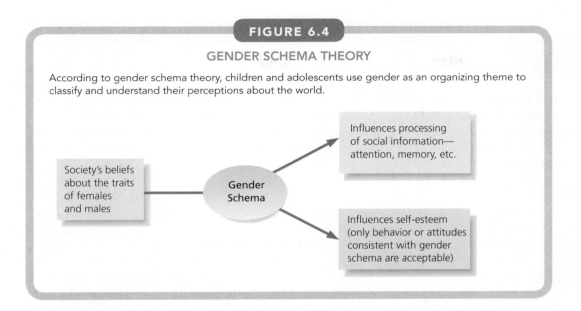

FIGURE 6.4

GENERAL SCHEMA THEORY

According to gender schema theory, children and adolescents use gender as an organizing theme to classify and understand their perceptions about the world.

tell you she wants to become a nurse than to say she wants to be an engineer. After she had given a lecture on the dangers of sex stereotyping in schools, a colleague of mine brought her young daughter to her college class. The students asked the little girl, "What do you want to be when you grow up?" The child immediately replied, "A doctor," and her professor/mother beamed with pride. Then the girl whispered to the students in the front row, "I really want to be a nurse, but my Mommy won't let me." Actually, this is a common reaction for young children. Preschoolers tend to have more stereotyped notions of sex roles than older children, and all ages seem to have more rigid and traditional ideas about male occupations than about what occupations females should pursue (Woolfolk & Perry, 2012). Later, as adolescents go through puberty, they may become even more focused on behaving in "masculine" or "feminine" ways, as defined by their peer culture. So many factors, from biology to cultural norms, play a role in gender role development. Beware of either/or explanations.

While I was proofreading this very page for a previous edition, riding cross-country on a train, the conductor stopped beside my seat. He said, "I'm sorry, dear, for interrupting your homework, but do you have a ticket?" I had to smile at his (I'm sure unintended) sexism. I doubt that he made the same comment to the man across the aisle who was writing on his legal pad. Like racial discrimination, messages of sexism can be subtle, and they can appear in classrooms.

Gender Bias in Curriculum Materials

Unfortunately, schools often foster **gender biases** in a number of ways. Publishers have established guidelines to prevent gender bias in teaching materials, but it still makes sense to check them for stereotypes. For example, even though children's books now have an equal number of males and females as central characters, there still are more males in the titles and the illustrations, and the characters (especially the boys) continue to behave in stereotypic ways. Boys are more aggressive and argumentative, and girls are more expressive and affectionate. Girl characters sometimes cross gender roles to be more active, but boy characters seldom show "feminine" expressive traits (Brannon, 2002; Evans & Davies, 2000). Also, video learning packages, virtual worlds, social media sites, and sources such as YouTube have not been carefully screened like most texts for gender, racial, ethnic, economic, religious, or age stereotypes and biases, and they can be sources of stereotyped messages (Henry, 2011). DVDs, computer programs, and testing materials often feature boys more than girls and include other biases. One look at the body builds of males and females in video combat games shows what unreal and unhealthy body images they promote.

Gender biases Different views of males and females, often favoring one gender over the other.

Another "text" that students read long before they arrive in your classroom is television. A content analysis of television commercials found that White male characters were more prominent than any other group (did you find that when you took the "commercial break" in the *Stop & Think* activity earlier?). Even when only the actor's voice could be heard, men were 10 times more likely to narrate commercials. And the same pattern of men as the "voice of authority" on television occurred in the United Kingdom, Europe, Australia, and Asia. Women were more likely than men to be shown as dependent on men and often were depicted at home (Brannon, 2002). So, both before and after going to school, students are likely to encounter texts that overrepresent males.

Connect and Extend to PRAXIS II™

Gender Bias (IV, B4)
There has been much debate in the news media over possible gender bias in schools. What can you as a teacher do to reduce or eliminate gender bias and its effects?

Gender Bias in Teaching

There has been quite a bit of research on teachers' treatment of male and female students. You should know, however, that most of these studies have focused on White students, so the results reported in this section hold mostly for White male and female students.

Many studies describe what seem like biases favoring boys. One of the best-documented findings of the past 30 years is that teachers have more overall interactions with boys than with girls; however, this includes more negative interactions with boys, but not more positive interactions (Jones & Dindia, 2004). This is true from preschool to college. Teachers ask more questions of males, give males more feedback (praise, criticism, and correction), and offer more specific and valuable comments to boys. The effect of these differences is that from preschool through college, girls, on the average, receive 1,800 fewer hours of attention and instruction than boys (Sadker, Sadker, & Klein, 1991). Of course, these differences are not evenly distributed. Some boys, generally high-achieving White students, receive more than their share, whereas high-achieving girls receive the least teacher attention.

Not all biases in school favor boys. In the past 10 years in North America, Western Europe, Australia, and some Asian countries, there have been questions about whether schools are serving boys well. This concern is fueled by data from many countries that seem to show underachievement in boys. For example, data from a U.S. government survey shows the average 11th grade boy writes at the level of an average 8th grade girl (Younger & Warrington, 2006). More dramatic accusations include that schools are trying to destroy "boys' culture" and force "feminine, frilly content" on boys.

Discrimination against girls has ended, the argument runs. Indeed, thanks to feminism, girls have special treatment and special programs. Now, what about the boys? It is boys who are slower to learn to read, more likely to drop out of school, more likely to be disciplined, more likely to be in programs for children with special needs. In school it is girls who are doing better, boys who are in trouble—and special programs for boys that are needed. (Connell, 1996, p. 207)

One explanation for why boys struggle in school is that the expectations of schooling do not fit the way boys learn (Gurian & Henley, 2001), particularly African American boys (Stinson, 2006). Another suggestion is that boys sabotage their own learning by resisting school expectations and rules to "display their masculinity and get respect" (Kleinfield, 2005, p. B6). Critics of the schools suggest that boys need smaller classes, more discussions, better discipline, mentoring programs, and more men in their schools—90% of elementary teachers are female (Svoboda, 2001).

GENDER-SPECIFIC TEACHING? Good teaching is good teaching; regardless of the gender of the students, the goal should be successful learning for everyone.

GUIDELINES

Avoiding Gender Bias in Teaching

Check to see if textbooks and other materials you are using present an honest view of the options open to both males and females.
Examples

1. Identify whether both males and females are portrayed in traditional and nontraditional roles at work, at leisure, and at home.
2. Discuss your analyses with students, and ask them to help you find sex-role biases in other materials—magazine advertising, TV programs, news reporting, for example.

Watch for any unintended biases in your own classroom practices.
Examples

1. Monitor whether you group students by sex for certain activities. Is the grouping appropriate?
2. Monitor whether you call on one sex or the other for certain answers—boys for math and girls for poetry, for example.
3. Monitor your metaphors. Don't ask students to "tackle the problem."

Look for ways in which your school may be limiting the options open to male or female students.
Examples

1. Find out what advice guidance counselors give to students in course and career decisions.
2. Look into whether there is a good sports program for both girls and boys.
3. See if girls are encouraged to take advanced placement courses in science and mathematics and if boys are encouraged in English and foreign language classes.

Use gender-free language as much as possible.
Examples

1. Make sure you speak of "law-enforcement officer" and "mail carrier" instead of "policeman" and "mailman."
2. Be sure you name a committee "head" instead of a "chairman."

Provide role models.
Examples

1. Assign articles in professional journals written by female research scientists or mathematicians.
2. Have recent female graduates who are majoring in science, math, engineering, or other technical fields come to class to talk about college.
3. Create electronic mentoring programs for both male and female students to connect them with adults working in areas of interest to the students.

Make sure all students have a chance to do complex, technical work.
Examples

1. Experiment with same-sex lab groups so girls do not always end up as the secretaries, boys as the technicians.
2. Rotate jobs in groups or randomly assign responsibilities.

What if you witness gender bias as a student teacher? See this site for ideas: http://www.tolerance.org/teach/magazine/features.jsp?p=0&is=36&ar=563#

A current suggestion for making schools more effective for both boys and girls is single-sex classrooms. A few years ago, the *New York Times Magazine* had a cover story about that topic (Weil, 2008). The research on this approach from around the world suggests that teaching boys and girls in separate classes can have positive effects on student learning, motivation, and engagement, but only if certain demanding conditions are met. Teachers must realize that there are no boy- or girl-specific teaching strategies—good teaching is good teaching. Regrouping students by sex does not make teaching easier; in fact, it can make class management more difficult. To succeed, both teachers and students must understand that the goal of their single-sex classrooms is better learning for everyone in an atmosphere that supports more open discussions with less concern about making impressions on peers (Younger & Warrington, 2006). The *Guidelines* provide additional ideas about avoiding gender bias for all students in your classes.

We have dealt with a wide range of differences in this chapter. How can teachers provide an appropriate education for all of their students? One answer is multicultural education with culturally compatible classrooms.

Connect and Extend to PRAXIS II™

Multicultural Education (III, B)
Know the major dimensions of
multicultural education. Describe
how these dimensions influence
each other.

MULTICULTURAL EDUCATION: CREATING CULTURALLY COMPATIBLE CLASSROOMS

Multicultural education is

> [a] process of comprehensive school reform and basic education for all students. It challenges and rejects racism and other forms of discrimination in schools and society and accepts and affirms the pluralism (ethnic, racial, linguistic, religious, economic, and gender, among others) that students, their communities, and their teachers reflect. (Nieto & Bode, 2008, p. 44)

James Banks (2006) suggests that multicultural education has five dimensions: *content integration, the knowledge construction process, prejudice reduction, an empowering school culture and social structure,* and an *equity pedagogy,* as shown in Figure 6.5. Many people are familiar only with the dimension of *content integration,* or using examples and content from a variety of cultures when teaching a subject. And because they believe that multicultural education is simply a change in content, some teachers assume that it is irrelevant for subjects such as science and mathematics. But if you consider the other four dimensions—helping students understand how knowledge is constructed, reducing prejudice, creating social structures in schools that support learning and development for all students, and using equity pedagogy or teaching methods that reach all students—then you will see that this view of multicultural education is relevant to all subjects and all students.

An examination of the alternative approaches to multicultural education is beyond the scope of an educational psychology text, but be aware that there is no general agreement about the "best" approach. Many educators have suggested that culturally relevant pedagogy should be an element in multicultural education reform.

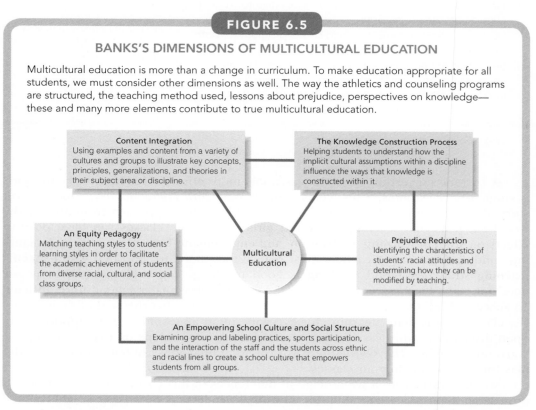

FIGURE 6.5

BANKS'S DIMENSIONS OF MULTICULTURAL EDUCATION

Multicultural education is more than a change in curriculum. To make education appropriate for all students, we must consider other dimensions as well. The way the athletics and counseling programs are structured, the teaching method used, lessons about prejudice, perspectives on knowledge—these and many more elements contribute to true multicultural education.

Source: Reprinted with the permission of James A. Banks from James A. Banks, An Introduction to Multicultural Education (4th edition). Boston: Allyn and Bacon, page 32.

Multicultural education Education that promotes equity in the schooling of all students.

Culturally Relevant Pedagogy

Several researchers have focused on teachers who are especially successful with students of color and students in poverty (Delpit, 1995; Ladson-Billings, 1994, 1995; Moll, Amanti, Neff, & Gonzalez, 1992; Siddle Walker, 2001). The work of Gloria Ladson-Billings (1990, 1992, 1995) is a good example. For three years, she studied excellent teachers in a California school district that served an African American community. In order to select the teachers, she asked parents and principals for nominations. Parents nominated teachers who respected them, created enthusiasm for learning in their children, and understood their children's need to operate successfully in two different worlds—the home community and the White world beyond. Principals nominated teachers who had few discipline referrals, high attendance rates, and high standardized test scores. Ladson-Billings was able to examine in depth 8 of the 9 teachers who were nominated by *both* parents and principals.

Based on her research, Ladson-Billings developed a conception of teaching excellence. She uses the term **culturally relevant pedagogy** to describe teaching that rests on three propositions.

1. *Students must experience academic success.* "Despite the current social inequities and hostile classroom environments, students must develop their academic skills. The ways those skills are developed may vary, but all students need literacy, numeracy, technological, social, and political skills in order to be active participants in a democracy" (Ladson-Billings, 1995, p. 160).
2. *Students must develop/maintain their cultural competence.* As they become more academically skilled, students still retain their cultural competence. "Culturally relevant teachers utilize students' culture as a vehicle for learning" (Ladson-Billings, 1995, p. 161). For example, one teacher used rap music to teach about literal and figurative meaning, rhyme, alliteration, and onomatopoeia in poetry. Another brought in a community expert known for her sweet potato pies to work with students. Follow-up lessons included investigations of George Washington Carver's sweet potato research, numerical analyses of taste tests, marketing plans for selling pies, and research on the educational preparation needed to become a chef.
3. *Students must develop a critical consciousness to challenge the status quo.* In addition to developing academic skills while retaining cultural competence, excellent teachers help students "develop a broader sociopolitical consciousness that allows them to critique the social norms, values, mores, and institutions that produce and maintain social inequities" (Ladson-Billings, 1995, p. 162). For example, in one school, students were upset that their textbooks were out of date. They mobilized to investigate the funding formulas that allowed middle-class students to have newer books, wrote letters to the newspaper editor to challenge these inequities, and updated their texts with current information from other sources.

Ladson-Billings (1995) noted that many people have said her three principles "are just good teaching." She agrees that she is describing good teaching, but questions "why so little of it seems to be occurring in classrooms populated by African American students" (p. 159). Geneva Gay (2000) uses the term *culturally responsive teaching* to describe a similar approach that uses the "cultural knowledge, prior experiences, frames of reference, and performance styles of ethnically diverse students to make learning encounters more relevant to and effective for them. It teaches to and through the strengths of these students. It is culturally validating and affirming" (p. 29).

Lisa Delpit (2003) describes three steps for teaching students of color that are consistent with culturally relevant pedagogy: (1) Teachers must be convinced of the inherent intellectual capability, humanity, and spiritual character of their students—they must believe in the children. There are many examples around the country of schools where low-income African American students are reading well above grade level and doing advanced math. When scores are low, the fault is not in the students, but in their education. (2) Teachers must fight the foolishness that high test scores or scripted lessons are evidence of good learning and good teaching. Successful instruction is "constant, rigorous, integrated across disciplines, connected to students' lived cultures, connected to their intellectual

Culturally relevant pedagogy Excellent teaching for students of color that includes academic success, developing/maintaining cultural competence, and developing a critical consciousness to challenge the status quo.

legacies, engaging, and designed for critical thinking and problem solving that is useful beyond the classroom" (p. 18). (3) Teachers must learn who their students are and the legacies they bring. Then, students can explore their own intellectual legacies and understand the important reasons for academic, social, physical, and moral excellence—not just to "get a job" but also "for our community, for your ancestors, for your descendents" (p. 19).

Michael Pressley and his colleagues (2004) did a case study of a very successful K–12 school for African American students. The characteristics of effective teaching at the school are shown in Table 6.3.

In the past, discussions of teaching low-income students from racial, ethnic, or language minority groups have focused on remediating problems or overcoming perceived deficits. But thinking today emphasizes teaching to the strengths and the resilience of these students.

TABLE 6.3 • **Research-Based Characteristics of Schools and Teachers Associated with Academic Achievement for African American Students**

CHARACTERISTICS OF SCHOOLS	CHARACTERISTICS OF EFFECTIVE TEACHING	OTHER CHARACTERISTICS
Strong administrative leadership	Dedicated teachers who are accountable to produce results	Much total academic time: A very long functional school day/week, including before-school-hours to after-school-hours interactions and tutoring, good use of almost every minute of every class hour, and summer school for students who need it
Frequent evaluation of student progress	Much teacher scaffolding, encouraging student self-regulation	Students who help one another with academics
Emphasis on academics	Curriculum and instruction emphasizing understanding	Strong family–school connections
Safe and orderly environment	Mentoring, especially with regard to college admissions	Donors and visibly supportive, successful alumni
High expectations for student achievement including selective recruitment/retention of students, with the school weeding out students who are not using the opportunity well in favor of students who will (i.e., weeding out misbehaving students, students not meeting academic standards)	Intentional, massive, and frequent attempts to motivate students, including use of the following mechanisms: Positive expectations Visible care by teachers and administrators Praise of specific accomplishments Generally positive atmosphere, encouragement of effort attributions Cooperative learning experiences Tangible rewards for achievements	Motivational mechanisms not often encountered in schools: Extreme community celebrations of academic achievements Encouragement of a possible self as college graduate and successful professional Discouragement of negative possible selves Development of informed pride in African American heritage and life

(Continued)

CHARACTERISTICS OF SCHOOLS	CHARACTERISTICS OF EFFECTIVE TEACHING	OTHER CHARACTERISTICS
Excellent classroom management in most classrooms, resulting in/including a high proportion of academic time on task.	Teachers who provide strong instructional supports for academic achievement (e.g., study guides, test expectations made apparent, informative, feedback on homework and before exams).	Many extracurricular and curricular-enrichment activities—almost all academically oriented or intended to increase commitment to academic pursuits.
		An attractive school building loaded with resources to support academic pursuits

Source: Adapted from Pressley, Raphael, DiBella, & Gallagher, 2004, pp. 234–235.

Fostering Resilience

In any given week, 12% to 15% of school-age children who have urgent needs for social and emotional support do not receive the help they need. Community and mental health services often don't reach the students who are at the highest risk. But many children at risk for academic failure not only survive—they thrive. They are resilient students. What can we learn from these students? What can teachers and schools do to encourage **resilience**?

RESILIENT STUDENTS. Students who seem able to thrive in spite of serious challenges are actively engaged in school. They have good interpersonal skills, confidence in their own ability to learn, positive attitudes toward school, pride in their ethnicity, and high expectations (Borman & Overman, 2004; Lee, 2005). Also, students who have high intelligence or valued talents are more protected from risks. Being easy-going and optimistic is associated with resilience as well. Factors outside the student—interpersonal relationships and social support—matter, too. It helps to have a warm relationship with a parent who has high expectations and supports learning by organizing space and time at home for study. But even without such a parent, a strong bond with someone competent—a grandparent, aunt, uncle, teacher, mentor, or other caring adult—can serve the same supportive function. Involvement in school, community, or religious activities can provide more connections to concerned adults and also teach lessons in social skills and leadership (Berk, 2005).

RESILIENT CLASSROOMS. You can't choose personalities or parents for your students. And if you could, stresses can build up for even the most resilient students. Beth Doll and her colleagues (2005) suggest that we have to change classrooms instead of kids because "alternative strategies will be more enduring and most successful when they are integrated into naturally occurring systems of support [like schools] that surround children" (p. 3). In addition, there is some evidence that changes in classrooms—such as reducing class size, creating an orderly and safe environment, and forming supportive relationships with teachers—have a greater impact on the academic achievement of African American students compared to Latino and White students (Borman & Overman, 2004). So how can you create a classroom that supports resilience?

In formulating their suggestions for characteristics of resilient classrooms, Doll and her colleagues (2005) drew on research in education and psychology on best practices for children in poverty and children with disabilities. There are two strands of elements that bind students to their classroom community: self-agency and connected relationships.

Resilience The ability to adapt successfully in spite of difficult circumstances and threats to development.

PROMOTING RESILIENCE Stresses can build up for even the most resilient students. How can you create a classroom community that supports resilience? One important factor is having connected relationships.

SELF-AGENCY STRAND

- **Academic self-efficacy,** a belief in your own ability to learn, is one of the most consistent predictors of academic achievement. As you will see in Chapter 11, self-efficacy emerges when students tackle challenging, meaningful tasks with the support needed to be successful and observe other students doing the same thing. Accurate and encouraging feedback from teachers also helps.
- **Behavioral self-control,** or student self-regulation, is essential for a safe and orderly learning environment. Chapters 7, 11, and 13 will give you ideas for helping students develop self-control.
- **Academic self-determination,** which includes making choices, setting goals, and following through, is the third element in the self-agency strand. As you will see in Chapter 12, students who are self-determined are more motivated and committed to learning.

RELATIONSHIP STRAND

- **Caring teacher–student relationships** are consistently associated with better school performance, especially for students who face serious challenges. We saw the power of caring teachers in Chapters 1 and 3, and we will continue to see the value of these relationships throughout this text.
- **Effective peer relations,** as we saw in Chapter 3, also are critical in connecting students to school.
- **Effective home–school relationships** are the final element in building a caring, connected network for students. In the School Development program, James Comer has found that when parents stay involved, their children's grades and test scores improve (Comer, Haynes, & Joyner, 1996). The *Family and Community Partnerships Guidelines* give some ideas for connecting with families.

Diversity in Learning

Over two decades ago Roland Tharp (1989) outlined several dimensions of classrooms that reflect the diversity of the students and can be tailored to better fit their backgrounds: social organization, cultural values, learning preferences, and sociolinguistics. His advice is still relevant today.

GUIDELINES — FAMILY AND COMMUNITY PARTNERSHIPS

Building Learning Communities

Joyce Epstein (1995) describes six types of family/school/community partnerships. The following guidelines are based on her six categories.

Parenting partnerships: Help all families establish home environments to support children as students.
Examples

1. Offer workshops, videos, courses, family literacy fairs, and other informational programs to help parents cope with parenting situations that they identify as important.
2. Establish family support programs to assist with nutrition, health, and social services.
3. Find ways to help families share information with the school about the child's cultural background, talents, and needs—learn from the families.

Communication: Design effective forms for school-to-home and home-to-school communication.
Examples

1. Make sure communications fit the needs of families. Provide translations, visual support, large print—whatever is needed to make communication effective.
2. Visit families in their neighborhoods after gaining their permission. Don't expect family members to come to school until a trusting relationship is established.
3. Balance messages about problems with communications of accomplishments and positive information.

Volunteering: Recruit and organize parent help and support.
Examples

1. Do an annual postcard survey to identify family talents, interests, times available, and suggestions for improvements.
2. Establish a structure (telephone tree, etc.) to keep all families informed. Make sure families without telephones are included.
3. If possible, set aside a room for volunteer meetings and projects.

Learning at home: Provide information and ideas for families about how to help children with schoolwork and learning activities.
Examples

1. Provide assignment schedules, homework policies, and tips on how to help with schoolwork without doing the work.
2. Get family input into curriculum planning—have idea and activity exchanges.
3. Send home learning packets and enjoyable learning activities, especially over holidays and summers.

Decision-making partnerships: Include families in school decisions, developing family and community leaders and representatives.
Examples

1. Create family advisory committees for the school with parent representatives.
2. Make sure all families are in a network with their representative.

Community partnerships: Identify and integrate resources and services from the community to strengthen school programs, family practices, and student learning and development.
Examples

1. Have students and parents research existing resources—build a database.
2. Identify service projects for students—explore service learning.
3. Identify community members who are school alumni and get them involved in school programs.

For more ideas on partnerships with parents, see http://www.projectappleseed.org/chklst.html

SOCIAL ORGANIZATION. "A central task of educational design is to make the organization of teaching, learning, and performance compatible with the social structures in which students are most productive, engaged, and likely to learn" (Tharp, 1989, p. 350). Social structure or social organization in this context means the ways people interact to accomplish a particular goal. For example, the social organization of Hawaiian society depends heavily on collaboration and cooperation. Children play together in groups of friends and siblings, with older children often caring for the younger ones. When cooperative work groups of four or five boys and girls were established in Hawaiian classrooms, student learning and participation improved (Okagaki, 2001, 2006). The teacher worked intensively with one group while the children in the remaining groups helped each other. But when the same structure was tried in a Navajo classroom, students would not work together. These children are socialized to be more solitary and not to play with children of the opposite sex. By setting up same-sex working groups of only two or three Navajo students, teachers encouraged them to help each other. If you have students from several cultures, you may need to provide choices and variety in grouping structures.

CULTURAL VALUES AND LEARNING PREFERENCES. Results of some research suggest that Hispanic American students are more oriented toward family and group loyalty. This may mean that these students prefer cooperative activities and dislike being made to compete with fellow students (Garcia, 1992; Vasquez, 1990). Four values shared by many Latina/o students are:

Familismo—tightly knit families. Discussing family problems or business may be seen as disloyal.
Simpatia—value of interpersonal harmony. Assertively voicing personal opinions or arguing may be seen as inappropriate.
Respecto—respect for people in authority, for example, teachers and government officials.
Personalismo—valuing of close interpersonal relationships; discomfort with distant, cold, professional relationships. (Dingfelder, 2005)

The learning styles of African Americans may be inconsistent with teaching approaches in most schools. Some of the characteristics of this learning style are a visual/ global approach rather than a verbal/analytic approach; a preference for reasoning by inference rather than by formal logic; a focus on people and relationships; a preference for energetic involvement in several activities simultaneously rather than routine, step-by-step learning; a tendency to approximate numbers, space and time; and a greater dependence on nonverbal communication. Students of color who identify with their traditional cultures tend to respond better to open-ended questions with more than one answer, as opposed to single, right-answer questions. Questions that focus on meaning or the "big picture" may be more productive than questions that focus on details (Bennett, 2011; Gay, 2000; Sheets, 2005).

Native Americans also appear to have a more global, visual style of learning. For example, Navajo students prefer hearing a story all the way through to the end before discussing parts of the story. Teachers who stop reading to ask comprehension questions seem odd to these students and interrupt their learning process (Tharp, 1989). Also, these students sometimes show strong preferences for learning privately, through trial and error, rather than having their mistakes made public (Vasquez, 1990).

There has been little research on the learning styles of Asian Americans, perhaps because they are viewed as a "model minority," as you saw earlier. Some educators suggest that Asian children tend to value teacher approval and to work well in structured, quiet learning environments where there are clear goals and social support (Manning & Baruth, 1996). Other research suggests that there are clear and deep differences in Asian and Western styles of learning. Students from Asian cultures tend be more interdependent and to value learning with others, which might explain some of their success in school. Western values emphasize independence and individual learning, which might explain some of the United States' successes in science, technology, and innovation (Chang et al., 2011). But, as you saw earlier, there are dangers in stereotyping any group, especially in terms of cultural learning styles.

CAUTIONS (AGAIN) ABOUT LEARNING STYLES RESEARCH. In considering this research on learning styles, you should keep two points in mind. First, the validity of some of the learning styles research has been strongly questioned, as we saw in the previous chapter. Second, there is a heated debate today about whether identifying ethnic group differences in learning styles and preferences is a dangerous, racist, sexist exercise. In our society, we are quick to move from the notion of "difference" to the idea of "deficits" and stereotypes (Gordon, 1991; O'Neil, 1990). I have included the information about learning style differences because I believe that, used sensibly, this information can help you better understand your students. But, it is dangerous and incorrect to assume that every individual in a group shares the same learning style (Sheets, 2005). The best advice for teachers is to be sensitive to individual differences in all your students and to make available alternative paths to learning. Never prejudge how a student will learn best based on assumptions about the student's ethnicity or race. Get to know the individual.

SOCIOLINGUISTICS.   **Sociolinguistics** is the study of "the courtesies and conventions of conversation across cultures" (Tharp, 1989, p. 351). Knowledge of sociolinguistics will help you understand why communication sometimes breaks down in classrooms. The classroom is a special setting for communicating; it has its own set of rules for when, how, to whom, about what subject, and in what manner to use language. Sometimes, the sociolinguistic skills of students do not fit the expectations of teachers or counselors, as we saw earlier.

In order to be successful, students must know the communication rules; that is, they must understand the **pragmatics** of the classroom—when, where, and how to communicate. This is not such an easy task. As class activities change, rules change. Sometimes you have to raise your hand (during the teacher's presentation), but sometimes you don't (during story time on the rug). Sometimes it is good to ask a question (during discussion), but other times it isn't so good (when the teacher is reprimanding you). These differing activity rules are called **participation structures,** and they define appropriate participation for each class activity. Most classrooms have many different participation structures. To be competent communicators in the classroom, students sometimes have to read very subtle, nonverbal cues telling them which participation structures are currently in effect. For example, when the teacher moves to the white board, students should look up and be ready for instructions.

SOURCES OF MISUNDERSTANDINGS.   Some children are simply better than others at reading the classroom situation because the participation structures of the school match the structures they have learned at home. The communication rules for most school situations are similar to those in middle-class homes, so children from these homes often appear to be more competent communicators. They know the unwritten rules. Students who are not White and middle class may not know the rules. For example, researchers found that Pueblo Indian students participated twice as much in classes where teachers waited longer to react. Waiting longer also helps girls to participate more freely in math and science classes (Grossman & Grossman, 1994). Students from different cultural backgrounds may have learned participation structures that conflict with the behaviors expected in school. For example, one study found that the home conversation style of Hawaiian children is to chime in with contributions to a story. In school, however, this overlapping style is viewed as "interrupting." When the teachers learned about these differences and made their reading groups more like their students' home conversation groups, the young Hawaiian children in their classes improved in reading (Au, 1980; Tharp, 1989).

It seems that even students who speak the same language as their teachers may still have trouble communicating, and thus learning school subjects. What can teachers do? Especially in the early grades, you should make communication rules for activities clear and explicit. Do not assume students know what to do. Use cues to signal students when changes occur. Explain and demonstrate appropriate behavior. I have seen teachers show young children how to use their "inside voice," "six-inch voice," or "whisper voice." One teacher said and then demonstrated, "If you have to interrupt me while I'm working with other children, stand quietly beside me until I can help you." Be consistent in responding to students. If students are supposed to raise their hands, don't call on those who break the rules. In these ways you will teach students how to learn in school.

Lessons for Teachers: Teaching Every Student

The goal of this chapter is to give you a sense of the diversity in today's and tomorrow's schools and to help you meet the challenges of teaching in a multicultural classroom. How will you understand and build on all the cultures of your students? How will you deal with many different languages? Here are three general teaching principles to guide you in finding answers to these questions.

Sociolinguistics The study of the formal and informal rules for how, when, about what, to whom, and how long to speak in conversations within cultural groups.

Pragmatics The rules for when and how to use language to be an effective communicator in a particular culture.

Participation structures The formal and informal rules for how to take part in a given activity.

REACHING EVERY STUDENT Know your students, respect your students, teach your students.

KNOW YOUR STUDENTS. We must learn who our students are and understand the legacies they bring (Delpit, 2003). Nothing you read in a chapter on cultural differences will teach you enough to understand the lives of all your students. If you can take other courses in college or read about other cultures, I encourage you to do it. But reading and studying are not enough. You should get to know your students' families and communities. Elba Reyes, a successful bilingual teacher for children with special needs, describes her approach:

Usually I find that if you really want to know a parent, you get to know them on their own turf. This is key to developing trust and understanding the parents' perspective. First, get to know the community. Learn where the local grocery store is and what the children do after school. Then schedule a home visit at a time that is convenient for the parents. The home environment is not usually as ladened with failure. I sometimes observed the child being successful in the home, for example, riding a bicycle or helping with dinner. (Bos & Reyes, 1996, p. 349)

Try to spend time with students and parents on projects outside school. Ask parents to help in class or to speak to your students about their jobs, their hobbies, or the history and heritage of their ethnic group. In the elementary grades, don't wait until a student is in trouble to have the first meeting with a family member. Watch for and listen to the ways that your students interact in large and small groups. Have students write to you, and write back to them. Eat lunch with one or two students. Spend some nonteaching time with them.

RESPECT YOUR STUDENTS. From knowledge ought to come respect for your students' learning strengths—for the struggles they face and the obstacles they have overcome. We must believe in our students (Delpit, 2003). For a child, genuine acceptance is a necessary condition for developing self-esteem. Sometimes the self-image and occupational aspirations of minority children actually decline in their early years in public school, probably because of the emphasis on majority culture values, accomplishments, and history. By presenting the accomplishments of particular members of an ethnic group or by bringing that group's culture into the classroom (in the form of literature, art, music, or any cultural knowledge), teachers can help students maintain a sense of pride in their cultural group. This integration of culture must be more than the "tokenism" of sampling ethnic foods or wearing costumes. Students should learn about the socially and intellectually important contributions of the various groups. There are many excellent references that provide background information, history, and teaching strategies for different groups of students (e.g., Banks, 2002; Gay, 2000; Irvine & Armento, 2001; Ladson-Billings, 1995).

TEACH YOUR STUDENTS. The most important thing you can do for your students is teach them to read, write, speak, compute, think, and create—through constant, rigorous, culturally connected instruction (Delpit, 2003). Too often, goals for low-SES or minority-group students have focused exclusively on basic skills. Students are taught words and sounds, but the meaning of the story is supposed to come later. Knapp, Turnbull, and Shields (1990, p. 5) make these suggestions:

- Focus on meaning and understanding from beginning to end—for example, by orienting instruction toward comprehending reading passages, communicating important ideas in written text, or understanding the concepts underlying number facts.
- Balance routine skill learning with novel and complex tasks from the earliest stages of learning.

GUIDELINES

Culturally Relevant Teaching

Experiment with different grouping arrangements to encourage social harmony and cooperation.
Examples

1. Try "study buddies" and pairs.
2. Organize heterogeneous groups of four or five.
3. Establish larger teams for older students.

Provide a range of ways to learn material to accommodate a range of learning styles.
Examples

1. Give students verbal materials at different reading levels.
2. Offer visual materials—charts, diagrams, and models.
3. Provide tapes for listening and viewing.
4. Set up activities and projects.

Teach classroom procedures directly, even ways of doing things that you thought everyone would know.
Examples

1. Tell students how to get the teacher's attention.
2. Explain when and how to interrupt the teacher if students need help.
3. Show which materials students can take and which require permission.
4. Demonstrate acceptable ways to disagree with or challenge another student.

Learn the meaning of different behaviors for your students.
Examples

1. Ask students how they feel when you correct or praise them. What gives them this message?

2. Talk to family and community members and other teachers to discover the meaning of expressions, gestures, or other responses that are unfamiliar to you.

Emphasize meaning in teaching.
Examples

1. Make sure students understand what they read.
2. Try storytelling and other modes that don't require written materials.
3. Use examples that relate abstract concepts to everyday experiences; for instance, relate negative numbers to being overdrawn in your checkbook.

Get to know the customs, traditions, and values of your students.
Examples

1. Use holidays as a chance to discuss the origins and meaning of traditions.
2. Analyze different traditions for common themes.
3. Attend community fairs and festivals.

Help students detect racist and sexist messages.
Examples

1. Analyze curriculum materials for biases.
2. Make students "bias detectives," reporting comments from the media.
3. Discuss the ways that students communicate biased messages about each other and decide what should be done when this happens.
4. Discuss expressions of prejudice such as anti-Semitism.

- Provide context for skill learning that establishes clear reasons for needing to learn the skills.
- Influence attitudes and beliefs about the academic content areas as well as skills and knowledge.
- Eliminate unnecessary redundancy in the curriculum (e.g., repeating instruction in the same mathematics skills year after year).

And finally, teach students directly about how to be students. In the early grades, this could mean directly teaching the courtesies and conventions of the classroom: how to get a turn to speak, how and when to interrupt the teacher, how to whisper, how to get help in a small group, how to give an explanation that is helpful. In the later grades, it may mean teaching the study skills that fit your subject. You can ask students to learn "how we do it in school" without violating principle number two above—respect your students. Ways of asking questions around the kitchen table at home may be different from ways of asking questions in school, but students can learn both ways, without deciding that either way is superior. And you can expand ways of doing it in school to include more possibilities. The *Guidelines* give more ideas.

▼ SUMMARY

Today's Diverse Classrooms (pp. 206–210)

What is culture? There are many conceptions of culture, but most include the knowledge, skills, rules, traditions, beliefs, and values that guide behavior in a particular group of people: Culture is a program for living. Everyone is a member of many cultural groups, defined in terms of geographic region, nationality, ethnicity, race, gender, social class, and religion. Membership in a particular group does not determine behavior or values, but makes certain values and kinds of behavior more likely. Wide variations exist within each group. You met four individuals, Ternice, Benjamin, Davy, and Jessie, who embody that diversity.

Economic and Social Class Differences (pp. 211–216)

What is SES, and how does it differ from social class? Social class reflects a group's prestige and power in a society. Most people are aware of the social class that they share with similar peers. Socioeconomic status (SES) is a term used by sociologists for variations in wealth, power, control over resources, and prestige. Socioeconomic status is determined by several factors—not just income—and often overpowers other cultural differences. No single variable is an effective measure of SES, but most researchers identify four general levels of SES: upper, middle, working, and lower classes. The main characteristics of these four levels are summarized in Table 6.1.

What is the relationship between SES and school achievement? Socioeconomic status and academic achievement are moderately correlated. High-SES students of all ethnic groups show higher average levels of achievement on test scores and stay in school longer than low-SES students. The longer the child is in poverty, the stronger the impact is on achievement. Why is there a correlation between SES and school achievement? Low-SES students may suffer from inadequate health care, teachers' lowered expectations of them, low self-esteem, learned helplessness, participation in resistance cultures, school tracking, understimulating home environments, and summer setbacks. This last striking finding is that low-SES children lose academic ground outside school over the summer, whereas higher-SES children continue to advance.

Ethnicity and Race in Teaching and Learning (pp. 216–224)

Distinguish between ethnicity and race. Ethnicity (culturally transmitted behavior) and race (biologically transmitted physical traits) are socially significant categories people use to describe themselves and others. Minority groups (either numerically or historically unempowered) are rapidly increasing in population.

How can differences in ethnicity of teachers and students affect school performance? Conflicts can arise from differences between teachers and students in culture-based beliefs, values, and expectations. Cultural conflicts are usually about below-the-surface differences, because when subtle cultural differences meet, misunderstandings are common. Students in some cultures learn attitudes and behaviors that are more consistent with school expectations. Differences among ethnic groups in cognitive and academic abilities are largely the legacy of racial segregation and continuing prejudice and discrimination.

Distinguish among *prejudice*, *discrimination*, and *stereotype threat*. Prejudice is a rigid and irrational generalization—a

prejudgment or attitude—about an entire category of people. Prejudice may target people in particular racial, ethnic, religious, political, geographic, or language groups, or it may be directed toward the gender or sexual orientation of the individual. Discrimination is unequal treatment of or actions toward particular categories of people. Stereotype threat is the extra emotional and cognitive burden that your performance in an academic situation might confirm a stereotype that others hold about you. It is not necessary that the individual even believe the stereotype. All that matters is that the person is aware of the stereotype and cares about performing well enough to disprove its unflattering implications. In the short run, the fear that you might confirm a negative stereotype can induce test anxiety and undermine performance. Over time, experiencing stereotype threat may lead to disidentification with schooling and academic achievement.

Gender in Teaching and Learning (pp. 224–229)

What are the stages of achieving a sexual orientation for gay and lesbian youth? Stages of achieving a sexual orientation for gay and lesbian students can also follow a pattern from discomfort to confusion to acceptance. Some researchers contend that sexual identity is not always permanent and can change over the years.

What are gender roles and how do they develop? Gender role is the image each individual has of himself or herself as masculine or feminine in characteristics—a part of self-concept. Biology (hormones) plays a role, as does the differential behavior of parents and teachers toward male and female children. Through their interactions with family, peers, teachers, and the environment in general, children begin to form gender schemas, or organized networks of knowledge about what it means to be male or female.

How are gender biases communicated? In children's books, there are more males in the titles and the illustrations, and the characters (especially the boys) continue to behave in stereotypic ways. Girl characters sometimes cross gender roles to be more active, but boy characters seldom show "feminine" expressive traits. Some overrepresentation of gender exists in television commercials too. Teachers interact more with boys in both positive and negative ways. Lately some educators have claimed that schools are not supportive of boys, and same-sex classrooms have been suggested as an answer. The research on the value of these classrooms is mixed.

Multicultural Education: Creating Culturally Compatible Classrooms (pp. 230–239)

What is multicultural education? Multicultural education is a field of study designed to increase educational equity for all students. According to the multicultural ideal, America should be transformed into a society that values diversity. James Banks suggests that multicultural education has five dimensions: integrating content, helping students understand how knowledge is influenced by beliefs, reducing prejudice, creating social structures in schools that support learning and development for all students, and using teaching methods that reach all students.

What is culturally relevant pedagogy? "Culturally relevant pedagogy is an approach to teaching that uses the cultural knowledge, prior experiences, frames of reference, and learning styles of ethnically diverse students to make learning encounters more relevant and effective for them. It teaches to and through the strengths of these students" (Gay, 2000). Gloria Ladson-Billings (1995, 2004) describes culturally relevant teaching that rests on three propositions: Students must experience academic success, develop/maintain their cultural competence, and develop a critical consciousness to challenge the status quo.

What are the elements of a resilient classroom? There are two strands of elements that bind students to their classroom community. One strand emphasizes the self-agency of students—their capacity to set and pursue goals. This includes academic self-efficacy, self-control, and self-determination. The second strand emphasizes caring and connected relationships with the teacher, peers, and the home.

▼ KEY TERMS

Culturally relevant pedagogy (231)
Culture (206)
Discrimination (221)
Ethnicity (216)
Gender biases (227)
Gender identity (224)
Gender schemas (226)

Minority group (217)
Multicultural education (230)
Participation structures (237)
Pragmatics (237)
Prejudice (220)
Race (217)
Resilience (233)

Resistance culture (213)
Sexual identity (224)
Socioeconomic status (SES) (211)
Sociolinguistics (237)
Stereotype (221)
Stereotype threat (222)
Tracking (215)

▼ CONNECT AND EXTEND TO LICENSURE

MULTIPLE-CHOICE QUESTIONS

1. Socioeconomic status and school achievement are often correlated. Which one of the following statements is not true regarding the relationship between SES and levels of achievement?
   A. The longer a child lives in poverty, the greater the impact is on achievement.
   B. Poor children are no more likely to be kept back in school than non-poor children.
   C. High-SES students of all ethnic groups generally show higher levels of achievement on test scores and stay in school longer than low-SES students.
   D. More poor children live in suburban and rural areas than in central cities.

2. Educators often believe students are not bright based upon inadequate resources at home. This inadequacy manifests itself as a lack of familiarity with school related activities. When this occurs, what is the likely outcome?
   A. These students work harder to prove themselves to their teachers.
   B. Teachers may have low expectations which negatively impact future academic success.
   C. The students will perform poorly because they will never catch up with their peers.
   D. Teachers understand that not all students will be able to academically achieve.

3. Damon, an African American student in Diane Collins' math class, pushed his math test away from him after a few minutes and proclaimed, "This is stupid. I don't know why we even have to do this." What should Ms. Collins consider?
   A. She should consider sending Damon to the Principal's office for insubordination.
   B. She might have made the test too difficult for her African American students so she should make an easier test next time.
   C. Damon may be exhibiting performance-avoidance goals because he doesn't want to look dumb.
   D. Damon's high self-efficacy has caused him to determine that testing is a waste of his time.

4. In an effort to avoid gender bias in his fourth grade classroom, Mr. Bonner used gender-free language, provided positive role models, and ensured all students had opportunities to engage in various activities by rotating classroom jobs and activities. His school was also experimenting with single-sex classrooms. Next year, Mr. Bonner thought he might opt to teach in one of those classrooms. All but which of the following are true concerning single-sex classrooms?
   A. There are positive effects on learning, motivation, and engagement if certain conditions are met.
   B. Teaching is not easier when regrouping students by sex.
   C. Teachers must realize there are specific boy and girl teaching strategies.
   D. There is often less concern about making impressions on peers.

CONSTRUCTED-RESPONSE QUESTIONS

Case

Paulo Nzambi moved from his home in Angola to the United States in the fifth grade. While his English and schooling were adequate, his teacher Katie Wyant worried about his social adjustment. His quiet demeanor and soft voice were, in many ways, the opposite of his male peers. Paulo appeared hesitant when interacting with her as if he was unsure about how to behave. As the year progressed, Katie noticed he had not made any progress in adjusting to the classroom. She decided she needed to be proactive in finding a solution.

5. In order to acquire a better understanding of Paulo and make school a more positive experience, what three types of relationships would assist Paulo as well as Miss Wyant?
6. What aspects of culturally relevant teaching might Katie Wyant employ to assist Paulo Nzambi in his transition to an American classroom?

MyEducationLab™

Go to Chapter 6 of the Book Specific Resources in MyEducationLab and click on "Connect and Extend to Licensure" to answer these questions. Compare your responses with the feedback provided.

▼ WHAT WOULD THEY DO?
TEACHERS' CASEBOOK: White Girls Club

Here is how some expert teachers responded to the situation described at the beginning of the chapter about the "White Girls Club."

JENNIFER PINCOSKI • Learning Resource Teacher: K–12
Lee County School District, Fort Myers, FL

All teachers feel the pressure of high-stakes testing and meeting academic standards, and unfortunately, this leaves little time to provide character education and team-building activities. Even kindergarten classrooms have sacrificed social skills/ friendship lessons for additional academic instruction, even though many students come to school not knowing how to appropriately interact with peers.

In the face of No Child Left Behind and Race to the Top mandates, briefly suspending content instruction to teach kindness and build a respectful classroom community may sound like a waste of valuable academic time. However, teachers who establish a positive learning environment where students feel safe and valued ultimately spend less time redirecting and correcting misbehaviors. Students who feel accepted and appreciated will demonstrate longer time on task and greater interest in learning than those who don't.

In this case, the entire class could benefit from lessons on diversity, respect, and tolerance. School counselors are a great resource for these types of activities, and are often available to teach or co-teach the lessons.

In the long run, a proactive approach is far more efficient than a reactive one. Taking the time to build rapport and establish a sense of community will preserve hours of instruction that would have been lost to peer conflict, off-task behaviors, and non-compliance.

LAUREN ROLLINS • 1st Grade Teacher
Boulevard Elementary School, Shaker Heights, OH

Discrimination of any kind will not be tolerated in my classroom! I would attack this unfortunate situation through a variety of different approaches—whole-class instruction, private small-group discussions, and one-on-one meetings with my new student and her parents. I would start my whole-class lesson by passing out candy (or some other desired object—stickers, pencils, etc.) to one chosen group of people—only boys, students with brown eyes, etc. I would purposely choose a group that excluded the girls who have formed the "White Girls Club." This activity would spark a conversation with the class about how unfair it is that one group of students got to do something that another group did not. We would talk about how the excluded group felt by this slight and why it is important not to discriminate against people for any reason. I would also include a read-aloud of a children's book that supported this topic. I would stop throughout my reading to discuss the feelings of the different characters in the book. Next, I would meet privately with the girls who have formed the club. I would remind them that excluding people from a group is unacceptable and will not be tolerated by me. Either everyone gets to play, or no one does. Lastly, I would meet with my new student and her parents. I would ask her to give me the names of a few students in my class with whom she would be interested in building a relationship. I would encourage her parents to set up one-on-one play dates for their daughter outside of school with the hope of them building relationships.

LINDA SPARKS • Grade 1
John F. Kennedy School, Billerica MA

We begin each year setting up classroom rules and expectations. We write them down and all students sign the "contract." It is then posted in a visible place in the classroom. Throughout the year we will go over the rules. The first one always states that we treat others the way we want to be treated. We have had these "clubs" pop up, from "only boys can play a sport at recess" to "the way a child looks." When I notice a change in classroom climate, I always begin with a generalized scenario (e.g., out at recess, the principal noticed that only the boys were playing basketball but some of the girls were watching and wanting to play). We would then brainstorm a list of what the principal could do to help let the girls play. It is amazing the wonderful ideas that come up when the student is not being put on the spot, but rather the whole class is getting the chance to share their thoughts. I find that starting this way, students will start to think of specific times when this has happened to them and how it was resolved. It is amazing how quickly these "clubs" or "groups" disappear once the lesson has been presented. We have a few programs we use in our school for teaching tolerance. We have Second Step in which scenarios are presented and students role play the scene. This is one of their favorites. Another is a bucket filler, where students can be caught doing something good either by another student or by a staff member. The person who catches them fills out a bucket-filling slip and it gets put into a big silver bucket. No one wants to be a bucket dipper by making people feel sad or left out. No matter what the age, clubs can quickly dissipate when the students are the ones who are given the chance to resolve the problem.

PAULA COLEMERE • Special Education Teacher—English, History
McClintock High School, Tempe, AZ

In one of my favorite lessons for the beginning of the year I give each student five mixed beans and have students choose which is the "best" one. We then discuss why they chose the bean as the best and discuss the differences in beans before connecting to people. After the discussion, we role play different scenarios that deal with diversity; this is a good lesson because it addresses self-esteem in addition to diversity. While all students can use a boost to self-esteem, it would hopefully help the new girl to feel better about the situation. This lesson can be tailored to younger or older students. Since these students are young, I would hope this would be a gentle way for the girls in the "club" to see that what they have been doing is wrong. My next step would be to conference with the girls and mediate if necessary.

PAUL DRAGIN • ESL Grades 9–12
Columbus East High School, Columbus OH

Based on the observations, I would not hesitate to act quickly in this situation of exclusion. Based on the age group of the students, I would attack this problem two ways initially. I would spend classroom time talking about building community and present some scenarios and videos about how it feels to be excluded or left out. With children at this impressionable age, this troubling dilemma may leave an indelible mark on some if handled in such a way that they internalize the feelings that the excluded student is inevitably confronted with being the "other." I would contact the parents of the girls who made the "White girls club" comment and let them know what I overheard and witnessed regarding the new student. Hopefully, this could turn an unfortunate situation into a great learning opportunity that would stick with the students whenever they are confronted with someone racially, ethnically, or culturally different from them.

JESSICA N. MAHTABAN • 8th Grade Math
Woodrow Wilson Middle School, Clifton, NJ

My immediate response would be to investigate the "club." I could talk to each girl individually and ask why she started the club as well as why they felt it was important to exclude people from their club. Also, I must make sure the parents, administration, and counselors are aware of the situation as well.

It is my job to explain to my students as best I can that it's not polite to exclude anyone. I would give them different scenarios about exclusion and ask for them to reflect on their personal feelings for each scenario. We would discuss in groups as well as the whole class about the scenarios and their feelings. Problem solving together would be the best approach to finding various solutions to problems as well as figuring out who can help them in different situations. Hopefully, by the end of these lessons each student will understand that our classroom is a family, and that, as a family, we celebrate differences—not segregate.

BARBARA PRESLEY • Transition/Work Study Coordinator—High School Level, B.E.S.T.T. Program (Baldwinsville Exceptional Student Training and Transition Program)
C.W. Baker High School, Baldwinsville, NY

Eliminating bias can only be achieved through exposure, knowledge, and experience. In my work with severely disabled students, I found that special needs students' peers were less judgmental and exclusionary when they were given the opportunity to interact with our students. I would definitely find out about any "club" that has the potential to be destructive. We created situations where the skills and aptitudes of our special needs students were spotlighted; they then invited typical peers to join them. Almost everyone wants to share in a success, so our students' peers joined in and the prejudice and malice diminished.

SARA VINCENT • Special Education
Langley High School, McLean, VA

Discrimination and racism often occur because of ignorance. The best solution to minimize discrimination is educating individuals about diverse cultures. The teacher can invite the new student's family into the classroom to talk about their backgrounds and experiences, or she can have the entire class complete a project on family history. Once the other students in the classroom learn more about the new student's culture, they will be more likely to accept her differences and understand that she is not much different from them. In addition, the teacher can have the new student be team leader at recess or in the classroom so that she will not be picked last. This will help her gain confidence in befriending her peers. While the teacher attempts to focus on positive aspects of educating her students, she should make the administration aware of the "White Girls Club" situation. Administrators should intervene and bring attention to the situation if the troubling behaviors of the other girls continue.

MyEducationLab™

Go to Topic 4, Student Diversity, in the MyEducationLab (www.myeducationlab.com) for *Educational Psychology*, where you can:

- Find learning outcomes for Student Diversity along with the national standards that connect to these outcomes.
- Complete Assignments and Activities that can help you more deeply understand the chapter content.
- Apply and practice your understanding of the core teaching skills identified in the chapter with the Building Teaching Skills and Dispositions learning units.
- Examine challenging situations and cases presented in the IRIS Center Resources.
- Access video clips of CCSSO National Teachers of the Year award winners responding to the question, "Why Do I Teach?" in the Teacher Talk section.
- Check your comprehension on the content covered in the chapter with the Study Plan. Here you will be able to take a chapter quiz, receive feedback on your answers, and then access Review, Practice, and Enrichment activities to enhance your understanding of chapter content.
- Find additional Teachers' Casebook scenarios and responses to them from practicing teachers.
- Use the Online Lesson Plan Builder to practice lesson planning and integrating national and state standards into your planning.

chapter seven

BEHAVIORAL VIEWS OF LEARNING

▶ **TEACHERS' CASEBOOK:** Sick of Class

One of your students asks for permission to see the school nurse at least twice a week. According to the nurse, most of his complaints have been groundless. True, once he was coming down with the flu, but 9 out of 10 times, there has been nothing wrong at all. Recently you have noticed that he tends to "get sick" during oral assignments or when he has to speak before the class. What steps would you take to deal with this situation?

CRITICAL THINKING

- Could this be a case of a classically conditioned phobia? If so, what would you do?
- What functions might be this behavior be serving?
- How would you support more positive behaviors and help the student find other ways to meet his needs?
- Would giving rewards or administering punishments be useful in this situation? Why or why not?

OVERVIEW AND OBJECTIVES

We begin this chapter with a general definition of learning that takes into account the opposing views of different theoretical groups. We will highlight one group, the behavioral theorists, in this chapter and another major group, the cognitive theorists, in Chapters 8 and 9; then, we will look at constructivism in Chapter 10 and social cognitive views in Chapter 11. As you can see, there are many ways to look at learning, and each has something to offer educators.

Our discussion in this chapter will focus on four behavioral learning processes: contiguity, classical conditioning, operant conditioning, and observational learning, with the greatest emphasis placed on the last two processes. After examining the implications of applied behavior analysis for teaching, we look at a recent direction in behavioral approaches to learning—self-management. Finally, we investigate Bandura's challenge to behavioral views of learning as well as other criticisms, cautions, and ethical considerations for educators.

By the time you have completed this chapter, you should be able to:

Objective 7.1: Define learning, and distinguish among the processes involved in learning through contiguity, classical conditioning, and operant conditioning.

Objective 7.2: Distinguish between positive and negative reinforcement and presentation and removal punishment.

Objective 7.3: Apply behavioral approaches to modifying behavior in and out of the classroom.

Objective 7.4: Describe newer approaches to applied behavioral analysis, including functional behavioral assessment and self-management.

Objective 7.5: Discuss contemporary challenges to behavioral theories of learning and address concerns about their application.

UNDERSTANDING LEARNING

When we hear the word *learning,* most of us think of studying and school. We think about subjects or skills we intend to master, such as algebra, Spanish, chemistry, or karate. But learning is not limited to school. We learn every day of our lives. Babies learn to kick their legs to make the mobile above their cribs move, young girls learn the lyrics to all their favorite Taylor Swift songs, middle-aged people like me learn to change their diet and exercise patterns, and every few years we all learn to find a new style of dress attractive when the old styles (the ones we once loved) go out of fashion. This last example shows that learning is not always intentional. We don't try to like new styles and dislike old ones; it just seems to happen that way. We don't intend to become nervous when we hear a teacher call our name or when we step onto a stage, yet many of us do. So what is this powerful phenomenon called *learning*?

In the broadest sense, **learning** occurs when experience (including practice) causes a relatively permanent change in an individual's knowledge or behavior. The change may be deliberate or unintentional, for better or for worse, correct or incorrect, and conscious or unconscious (Mayer, 2011; Schunk, 2012). To qualify as learning, this change must be brought about by experience—by the interaction of a person with his or her environment. Changes simply caused by maturation, such as growing taller or turning gray, do not qualify as learning. Temporary changes resulting from illness, fatigue, drugs, or hunger are also excluded from a general definition of learning. A person who has gone without food for two days does not learn to be hungry, and a person who is ill does not learn to move more slowly. Of course, learning plays a part in how we respond to hunger or illness.

Our definition specifies that the changes resulting from learning take place in the individual's knowledge or behavior. Most psychologists would agree with this statement, but some tend to emphasize the change in knowledge, whereas others focus on the change in behavior. Cognitive psychologists, who focus on changes in knowledge, believe learning is an internal mental activity that cannot be observed directly. As you will see in the next chapter, cognitive psychologists studying learning are interested in unobservable mental activities such as thinking, remembering, and solving problems (Schwartz, Wasserman, & Robbins, 2002).

The psychologists discussed in this chapter, on the other hand, favor **behavioral learning theories**. The behavioral view generally assumes that the outcome of learning is a change in behavior, and it emphasizes the effects of external events on the individual. Some early behaviorists such as J. B. Watson took the radical position that because thinking, intentions, and other internal mental events could not be seen or studied rigorously and scientifically, these "mentalisms," as he called them, should not even be included in an explanation of learning.

Neuroscience of Behavioral Learning

You saw in Chapter 2 that we are learning more and more about the brain. Researchers conducting animal and human studies have discovered quite a bit about the areas of the brain that are involved with learning new behaviors. For example, parts of the cerebellum are involved in simple reflex learning, like learning to blink following a particular tone, and that other parts of the brain are involved in learning how to avoid painful stimulation such as shock (Schwartz, Wasserman, & Robbins, 2002). Other lines of research ask why animals and people will behave in certain ways to gain stimulation or reinforcers. Stimulation to

Learning Process through which experience causes permanent change in knowledge or behavior.

Behavioral learning theories Explanations of learning that focus on external events as the cause of changes in observable behaviors.

certain parts of the brain will cause hungry rats to ignore food and keep doing whatever it takes to keep the stimulation coming. These same brain systems are associated with the pleasures people experience from many things, including food and music. It is likely that many parts of the brain and complex patterns of activity allow us to enjoy some experiences, "learn to want them, and learn how to get them" (Bernstein & Nash, 2008, p. 187).

Before we look in depth at behavioral explanations of learning, let's step into an actual classroom and note the possible results of learning.

Learning Is Not Always What It Seems

After weeks of working with her cooperating teacher in an 8th grade social studies class, Elizabeth was ready to take over on her own. As she moved to the front of the room, she saw another adult approach the classroom door. It was Mr. Ross, her supervisor from college. Elizabeth's neck and facial muscles suddenly became very tense.

WHAT IS LEARNING? Behavioral views of learning generally assume that the outcome of learning is a change in behavior. The focus is on what can be observed.

"I've stopped by for my first observation," Mr. Ross said. "I couldn't reach you last night to tell you."

Elizabeth tried to hide her reaction, but her hands trembled as she gathered the notes for the lesson.

"Let's start today with a kind of game. I will say some words, then I want you to tell me the first words you can think of and I will write them on the board. Don't all speak at once, though. Wait until someone else has finished to say your word. Okay, here is the first word: Slavery."

"Civil War." "Lincoln." "Freedom." "Emancipation Proclamation." The answers came quickly, and Elizabeth was relieved to see that the students understood the game.

"All right, very good," she said. "Now try another one: South."

"South Carolina." "South Dakota." "South Park," "No, the Confederacy, you dummy." "*Cold Mountain*." "Jude Law." With this last answer, a ripple of laughter moved across the room.

"Jude Law!" Elizabeth sighed dreamily. "*Cold Mountain* was on television last week." Then she laughed too. Soon all the students were laughing. "Okay, settle down," Elizabeth said. "Here is another word: North."

"Bluebellies." The students continued to laugh. "Jelly Bellies." "Belly-dancers." More laughter and a few inappropriate gestures.

"Just a minute," Elizabeth pleaded. "These ideas are getting a little off base!"

"Off base? Baseball," shouted the boy who had first mentioned Jude Law. He stood up and started throwing balls of paper to a friend in the back of the room, simulating the style of Tim Lincecum.

"The San Francisco Giants." "No, the Red Sox." "Ball games." "Hot dogs." "Popcorn." "Movies." "Netflix." "*Cold Mountain*." "Jude Law." The responses now came too fast for Elizabeth to stop them. For some reason, the Jude Law line got an even bigger laugh the second time around, and Elizabeth suddenly realized she had lost the class.

"Okay, because you know so much about the Civil War, close your books and take out a pen," Elizabeth said, obviously angry. She passed out the worksheet that she had planned as a cooperative, open-book project. "You have 20 minutes to finish this test!"

"You didn't tell us we were having a test!" "This isn't fair!" "We haven't even covered this stuff yet!" "I didn't do anything wrong!" There were moans and disgusted looks, even from the most mellow students. "I'm reporting you to the principal; it's a violation of students' rights!"

This last comment hit hard. The class had just finished discussing human rights as preparation for this unit on the Civil War. As she listened to the protests, Elizabeth felt terrible. How was she going to grade these "tests"? The first section of the worksheet involved facts about events during the Civil War, and the second section asked students to create a news-style program interviewing ordinary people touched by the war.

"All right, all right, it won't be a test. But you do have to complete this worksheet for a grade. I was going to let you work together, but your behavior this morning tells me that you are not ready for group work. If you can complete the first section of the sheet working quietly and seriously, you may work together on the second section." Elizabeth knew that her students would like to work together on writing the script for the news interview program.

Elizabeth was afraid to look back at her supervisor. What was he writing on his observation form?

It appears, on the surface at least, that very little learning of any sort was taking place in Elizabeth's classroom. In fact, Elizabeth had some good ideas, but she also made some mistakes in her application of learning principles. We will return to this episode several times in the chapter to analyze various aspects of what took place. To get us started, four events can be singled out, each possibly related to a different learning process.

First, the students were able to associate the words *Carolina, Dakota,* and *Park* with the word *South.* Second, Elizabeth's hands trembled when her college supervisor entered the room. Third, one student continued to disrupt the class with inappropriate responses. And fourth, after Elizabeth laughed at a student's comment, the class joined in her laughter. The four learning processes represented are contiguity, classical conditioning, operant conditioning, and observational learning. In the following pages we will examine these four kinds of learning, starting with contiguity.

EARLY EXPLANATIONS OF LEARNING: CONTIGUITY AND CLASSICAL CONDITIONING

One of the earliest explanations of learning came from Aristotle (384–322 B.C.). He said that we remember things together (1) when they are similar, (2) when they contrast, and (3) when they are contiguous. This last principle is the most important, because it is included in all explanations of learning by association. The principle of **contiguity** states that whenever two or more sensations occur together often enough, they will become associated. Later, when only one of these sensations (a **stimulus**) occurs, the other will be remembered too (a **response**) (Rachlin, 1991; Schwartz et al., 2002). For example, when Elizabeth said "South," students associated the words "Carolina" and "Dakota." They had heard these words together many times. Other processes may also be involved when students learn these phrases, but contiguity is a factor. Contiguity also plays a major role in another learning process best known as *classical conditioning.*

STOP & THINK Close your eyes and focus on a vivid image of the following: The smell of French fries cooking. A time you were really embarrassed in school. The taste of chocolate fudge. The sound of a dentist's drill. What did you notice as you formed these images? •

If you are like me, imagining the sound of the dentist's drill tightens your neck muscles. I can actually salivate when I imagine salty fries or smooth rich chocolate (especially because it is 7:00 PM and I haven't had dinner yet). The first embarrassing school incident I remembered was falling flat as I did a cartwheel in front of the whole high school. A small cringe still accompanies the memory. **Classical conditioning** focuses on the learning of involuntary emotional or physiological responses such as fear, increased muscle tension, salivation, or sweating. These sometimes are called **respondents** because they are automatic responses to stimuli. Through the process of classical conditioning, humans and animals can be trained to react involuntarily to a stimulus that previously had no effect—or a very different effect—on them. The stimulus comes to elicit, or bring forth, the response automatically.

Classical conditioning was discovered in the 1920s by Ivan Pavlov, a Russian physiologist who was trying to determine how long it took a dog to secrete digestive juices after it had been fed. But the intervals of time kept changing. At first, the dogs salivated as expected while they were being fed. Then the dogs began to salivate as soon as they saw the food and finally they salivated as soon as they heard the scientists walking toward the lab. Pavlov decided to make a detour from his original experiments and examine these unexpected interferences or "psychic reflexes" as he called them at first.

Connect and Extend to PRAXIS II™

Learning by Association (I, A1) Quite a bit of classroom learning can be attributed to contiguity (i.e., learning by association). What are some things that you might have learned because your teacher paired certain stimuli (e.g., names of the letters of the alphabet)?

Contiguity Association of two events because of repeated pairing.

Stimulus Event that activates behavior.

Response Observable reaction to a stimulus.

Classical conditioning Association of automatic responses with new stimuli.

Respondents Responses (generally automatic or involuntary) elicited by specific stimuli.

GUIDELINES

Applying Classical Conditioning

Associate positive, pleasant events with learning tasks.
Examples

1. Emphasize group competition and cooperation over individual competition. Many students have negative emotional responses to individual competition that may generalize to other learning.

2. Make division drills fun by having students decide how to divide refreshments equally, then letting them eat the results.

3. Make voluntary reading appealing by creating a comfortable reading corner with pillows, colorful displays of books, and reading props such as puppets (see Morrow & Weinstein, 1986, for more ideas).

Help students to risk anxiety-producing situations voluntarily and successfully.
Examples

1. Assign a shy student the responsibility of teaching two other students how to distribute materials for map study.

2. Devise small steps toward a larger goal. For example, give ungraded practice tests daily, and then weekly, to students who tend to "freeze" in test situations.

3. If a student is afraid of speaking in front of the class, let the student read a report to a small group while seated, then read it while standing, then give the report from notes instead of reading it verbatim. Next, move in stages toward having the student give a report to the whole class.

Help students recognize differences and similarities among situations so they can discriminate and generalize appropriately.
Examples

1. Explain that it is appropriate to avoid strangers who offer gifts or rides, but safe to accept favors from adults when parents are present.

2. Assure students who are anxious about taking college entrance exams that this test is like all the other achievement tests they have taken.

If you would like to learn more about classical conditioning, see
http://www.class.uidaho.edu/psyc390/lessons/lesson02/lesson2.htm

---

In one of his first experiments, Pavlov began by sounding a tuning fork and recording a dog's response. As expected, there was no salivation. At this point, the sound of the tuning fork was a **neutral stimulus** because it brought forth no salivation. Then Pavlov fed the dog. The response was salivation. The food was an **unconditioned stimulus (US)** because no prior training or "conditioning" was needed to establish the natural connection between food and salivation. The salivation was an **unconditioned response (UR)**, again because it was elicited automatically—no conditioning required.

Using these three elements—the food, the salivation, and the tuning fork—Pavlov demonstrated that a dog could be *conditioned* to salivate after hearing the tuning fork. He did this by contiguous pairing of the sound with food. He sounded the fork and then quickly fed the dog. After Pavlov repeated this several times, the dog began to salivate after hearing the sound, but before receiving the food. Now the sound had become a **conditioned stimulus (CS)** that could bring forth salivation by itself. The response of salivating after the tone was now a **conditioned response (CR)**.

If you think that Pavlovian conditioning is of historical interest only, consider this excerpt from *USA Today* describing an advertising campaign for products aimed at "Gen Y," those people born between 1977 and 1994:

> Mountain Dew executives have their own term for this [advertising strategy]: the Pavlovian connection. By handing out samples of the brand at surfing, skateboard and snowboard tournaments, "There's a Pavlovian connection between the brand and the exhilarating experience," says Dave Burwich, a top marketing executive at Pepsi, which makes Mountain Dew. (Horovitz, April 22, 2002, p. B2)

Maybe they could hand out math homework too! The *Guidelines* above give some other ideas.

It is possible that many of our emotional reactions to various situations are learned in part through classical conditioning. Physicians have a term, "white coat syndrome," that describes people whose blood pressure (an involuntary response) goes up when it is tested in the doctor's office, usually by someone in a white coat. Another example,

Neutral stimulus Stimulus not connected to a response.

Unconditioned stimulus (US) Stimulus that automatically produces an emotional or physiological response.

Unconditioned response (UR) Naturally occurring emotional or physiological response.

Conditioned stimulus (CS) Stimulus that evokes an emotional or physiological response after conditioning.

Conditioned response (CR) Learned response to a previously neutral stimulus.

Elizabeth's trembling hands when she saw her college supervisor, might be traced to previous unpleasant experiences during past evaluations of her performance. Now just the thought of being observed elicits a pounding heart and sweaty palms. Classical conditioning has implications for teachers as well as marketing managers. Remember that emotions and attitudes as well as facts and ideas are learned in classrooms. This emotional learning can sometimes interfere with academic learning. Procedures based on classical conditioning also can be used to help people learn more adaptive emotional responses, as the *Guidelines* on the previous page suggest.

OPERANT CONDITIONING: TRYING NEW RESPONSES

Connect and Extend to PRAXIS II™

Basics of Operant Conditioning (I, A1)
Be able to explain learning from the behavioral perspective. Incorporate concepts of *reward* and *punishment* into your explanation. Have a firm grasp of the effects of reinforcement schedules on learning.

So far, we have concentrated on the automatic conditioning of reflex-like responses such as salivation and fear. Clearly, not all human learning is so unintentional and not all behaviors are so automatic. People actively "operate" on their environment. These deliberate actions are called **operants**. The learning process involved in operant behavior is called **operant conditioning** because we learn to behave in certain ways as we operate on the environment.

The person generally thought to be responsible for developing the concept of operant conditioning is B. F. Skinner (1953). Skinner began with the belief that the principles of classical conditioning account for only a small portion of learned behaviors. Many human behaviors are operants, not respondents. Classical conditioning describes only how existing responses might be paired with new stimuli; it does not explain how new operant behaviors are acquired.

Behavior, like response or action, is simply a word for what a person does in a particular situation. Conceptually, we may think of a behavior as sandwiched between two sets of environmental influences: those that precede it (its **antecedents**) and those that follow it (its **consequences**) (Skinner, 1950). This relationship can be shown very simply as antecedent–behavior–consequence, or A–B–C (Kazdin, 2008). As behavior is ongoing, a given consequence becomes an antecedent for the next ABC sequence. Research in operant conditioning shows that operant behavior can be altered by changes in the antecedents, the consequences, or both. Early work focused on consequences, often using rats or pigeons as subjects.

Types of Consequences

Operants Voluntary (and generally goal-directed) behaviors emitted by a person or an animal.

Operant conditioning Learning in which voluntary behavior is strengthened or weakened by consequences or antecedents.

Antecedents Events that precede an action.

Consequences Events that follow an action.

Reinforcement Use of consequences to strengthen behavior.

Reinforcer Any event that follows a behavior and increases the chances that the behavior will occur again.

STOP & THINK Think back over teachers you have had who used rewards or punishments. *Try to remember different types of rewards:*
  Concrete rewards (stickers, food, prizes, certificates)
  Activity rewards (free time, puzzles, free reading)
  "Exemption" rewards (no homework, no weekly test)
  Social rewards (praise, recognition)
  What about punishments?
  Loss of privileges (cannot sit where you want, cannot work with friends)
  Fines (lost points, grades, money)
  Extra work (homework, laps, push-ups) •

According to the behavioral view, consequences determine to a great extent whether a person will repeat the behavior that led to the consequences. The type and timing of consequences can strengthen or weaken behaviors. We will look first at consequences that strengthen behavior.

REINFORCEMENT. Although **reinforcement** is commonly understood to mean "reward," this term has a particular meaning in psychology. A **reinforcer** is any consequence that strengthens the behavior it follows. So, by definition, reinforced behaviors increase in frequency or duration. Whenever you see a behavior persisting or increasing over time, you can assume the consequences of that behavior are reinforcers for the individual involved (Alberto & Troutman, 2009; Landrum & Kauffman, 2006). The reinforcement process can be diagrammed as follows:

$$\text{Behavior} \xrightarrow{\text{CONSEQUENCE}} \text{Reinforcer} \xrightarrow{\text{EFFECT}} \text{Strengthened or repeated behavior}$$

We can be fairly certain that food will be a reinforcer for a hungry animal, but what about people? It is not clear why an event acts as a reinforcer for an individual, but there are many theories about why reinforcement works. For example, some psychologists suggest that reinforcers are preferred activities or that they satisfy needs, whereas other psychologists believe that reinforcers reduce tension or stimulate a part of the brain (Rachlin, 1991; Schwartz et al., 2002). Whether the consequences of any action are reinforcing probably depends on the individual's perception of the event and the meaning it holds for her or him. For example, students who repeatedly get sent to the principal's office for misbehaving may be indicating that something about this consequence is reinforcing for them, even if it doesn't seem desirable to you. By the way, Skinner did not speculate about why reinforcers increase behavior. He believed that it was useless to talk about "imaginary constructs" such as meaning, expectations, needs, or tensions. Skinner simply described the tendency for a given operant behavior to increase after certain consequences (Skinner, 1953, 1989).

There are two types of reinforcement. The first, called **positive reinforcement**, occurs when the behavior produces a new stimulus. Examples include a pigeon's pecking on the red key, producing food; your wearing a new outfit, producing many compliments; or a student falling out of his chair, producing cheers and laughter from classmates.

Notice that positive reinforcement can occur even when the behavior being reinforced (falling out of a chair) is not "positive" from the teacher's point of view. In fact, positive reinforcement of inappropriate behaviors occurs unintentionally in many classrooms. Teachers help maintain problem behaviors by inadvertently reinforcing them. For example, Elizabeth may have unintentionally reinforced problem behavior in her class by laughing the first time the boy answered, "Jude Law." The problem behavior may have persisted for other reasons, but the consequence of Elizabeth's laughter could have played a role.

When the consequence that strengthens a behavior is the *appearance* (addition) of a new stimulus, the situation is defined as *positive reinforcement*. In contrast, when the consequence that strengthens a behavior is the *disappearance* (subtraction) of a stimulus, the process is called **negative reinforcement**. If a particular action leads to avoiding or escaping an **aversive** situation, the action is likely to be repeated in a similar situation. A common example is the car seatbelt buzzer. As soon as you put on your seatbelt, the irritating buzzer stops. You are likely to *repeat* this "buckling up" action in the future (so the process is *reinforcement*) because the behavior made an aversive buzzing stimulus *disappear* (so the kind of reinforcement is *negative*).

Consider our opening case student who continually "gets sick" right before a test or oral presentation and then is sent to the nurse's office. This behavior allows him to escape aversive situations—tests—so getting "sick" is being maintained, in part, through negative reinforcement. It is negative because the stimulus (the test or report) disappears; it is reinforcement because the behavior that caused the stimulus to disappear (getting "sick") increases or repeats. It is also possible that classical conditioning plays a role. The student may have been conditioned to experience unpleasant physiological reactions to tests.

It is important to remember that the "negative" in negative reinforcement does not imply that the behavior being reinforced is necessarily negative or bad. The meaning is closer to that of "negative" numbers—*something is subtracted*. Try to associate positive and negative reinforcement with the *consequence* of adding or subtracting something following a behavior that has the *effect* of strengthening (reinforcing) the behavior.

Positive reinforcement Strengthening behavior by presenting a desired stimulus after the behavior.

Negative reinforcement Strengthening behavior by removing an aversive stimulus when the behavior occurs.

Aversive Irritating or unpleasant.

PUNISHMENT.   Negative reinforcement is often confused with punishment. To avoid this mistake, remember that the process of reinforcement (positive or negative) always involves strengthening behavior. **Punishment,** on the other hand, involves *decreasing* or *suppressing* behavior. A behavior followed by a punisher is less likely to be repeated in similar situations in the future. Again, it is the effect that defines a consequence as punishment, and different people have different perceptions of what is punishing. One student may find suspension from school punishing, whereas another student wouldn't mind the break at all. The process of punishment is diagrammed as follows:

CONSEQUENCE   EFFECT
Behavior ———→ Punisher ———→ Weakened or decreased behavior

Like reinforcement, punishment may take one of two forms. The first type has been called Type I punishment, but this name isn't very informative, so I use the term **presentation punishment**. It occurs when presenting or adding a stimulus following the behavior suppresses or decreases the behavior. When teachers reprimand students, assign extra work, or make students run extra laps, and so on, they are using presentation punishment. I call the other type of punishment (Type II punishment) **removal punishment** because it involves removing a stimulus. When teachers or parents take away privileges after a young person has behaved inappropriately, they are applying removal punishment. With both types, the effect is to decrease the behavior that led to the punishment. Figure 7.1 summarizes the processes of reinforcement and punishment.

Reinforcement Schedules

When individuals are learning a new behavior, they will learn it faster if they are reinforced for every correct response. This is a **continuous reinforcement schedule**. Then, when

Punishment Process that weakens or suppresses behavior.

Presentation punishment Decreasing the chances that a behavior will occur again by presenting an aversive stimulus following the behavior; also called *Type I punishment.*

Removal punishment Decreasing the chances that a behavior will occur again by removing a pleasant stimulus following the behavior; also called *Type II punishment.*

Continuous reinforcement schedule Presenting a reinforcer after every appropriate response.

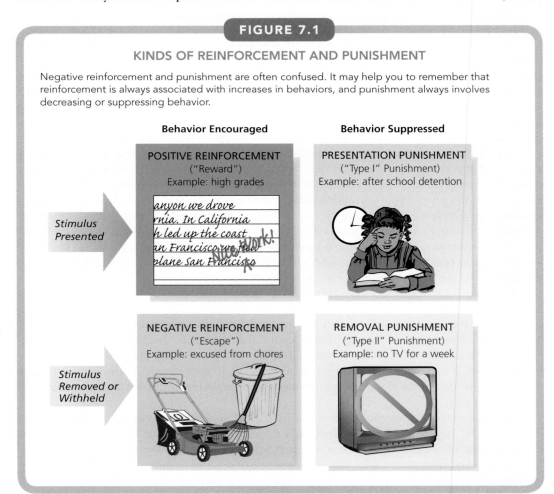

FIGURE 7.1

KINDS OF REINFORCEMENT AND PUNISHMENT

Negative reinforcement and punishment are often confused. It may help you to remember that reinforcement is always associated with increases in behaviors, and punishment always involves decreasing or suppressing behavior.

Behavior Encouraged	Behavior Suppressed
POSITIVE REINFORCEMENT ("Reward") Example: high grades	**PRESENTATION PUNISHMENT** ("Type I" Punishment) Example: after school detention
NEGATIVE REINFORCEMENT ("Escape") Example: excused from chores	**REMOVAL PUNISHMENT** ("Type II" Punishment) Example: no TV for a week

Stimulus Presented

Stimulus Removed or Withheld

the new behavior has been mastered, they will maintain it best if they are reinforced intermittently rather than every time. An **intermittent reinforcement schedule** helps students to maintain skills without expecting constant reinforcement.

There are two basic types of intermittent reinforcement schedules. One—called an **interval schedule**—is based on the amount of time that passes between reinforcers. The other—a **ratio schedule**—is based on the number of responses learners give between reinforcers. Interval and ratio schedules may be either fixed (predictable) or variable (unpredictable). Table 7.1 summarizes the five possible reinforcement schedules (the continuous schedule and the four kinds of intermittent schedules).

What are the effects of different schedules? Speed of performance depends on control. If reinforcement is based on the number of responses you give, then you have more control over the reinforcement: The faster you accumulate the correct number of responses, the faster the reinforcement will come. A teacher who says, "As soon as you complete these 10 problems correctly, you may listen to your music," can expect higher rates of performance than a teacher who says, "Work on these ten problems for the next 20 minutes. Then I will check your papers and those with 10 correct may listen to their music."

Persistence in performance depends on unpredictability. Continuous reinforcement and both kinds of fixed reinforcement (ratio and interval) are quite predictable. We come

TABLE 7.1 • **Five Reinforcement Schedules**

SCHEDULE	DEFINITION	EXAMPLE	RESPONSE PATTERN	REACTION WHEN REINFORCEMENT STOPS
Continuous	Reinforcement after every response	Turning on the television	Rapid learning of response	Very little persistence; rapid disappearance of response
Fixed-interval	Reinforcement after a set period of time	Weekly quiz	Response rate increases as time for reinforcement approaches, then drops after reinforcement	Little persistence; rapid drop in response rate when time for reinforcement passes and no reinforcer appears
Variable-interval	Reinforcement after varying lengths of time	Pop quizzes	Slow, steady rate of responding; very little pause after reinforcement	Greater persistence; slow decline in response rate
Fixed-ratio	Reinforcement after a set number of responses	Piece work Bake sale	Rapid response rate; pause after reinforcement	Little persistence; rapid drop in response rate when expected number of responses are given and no reinforcer appears
Variable-ratio	Reinforcement after a varying number of responses	Slot machines	Vary high response rate; little pause after reinforcement	Greatest persistence; response rate stays high and gradually drops off

Intermittent reinforcement schedule Presenting a reinforcer after some but not all responses.

Interval schedule Length of time between reinforcers.

Ratio schedule Reinforcement based on the number of responses between reinforcers.

Source: From Achieving Educational Excellence: Behavior Analysis for School Personnel *(Figure, p. 89), by B. Sulzer-Azaroff and G. R. Mayer, 1994, San Marcos, CA: Western Image, P.O. Box 427. Copyright © 1994 by Beth Sulzer-Azaroff and G. Roy Mayer. Reprinted by permission of the authors.*

INTERMITTENT REINFORCEMENT Casino slot machines are a good example of the effectiveness of intermittent reinforcement: People "learn" to persist in losing their money, because they might be rewarded with a jackpot, albeit infrequently and unpredictably.

to expect reinforcement at certain points and are generally quick to give up when the reinforcement does not meet our expectations. To encourage persistence of response, variable schedules are most appropriate. A great example of student persistence on a variable schedule was presented in an article about Valorie Lewis, a member of the *USA Today* All-USA teacher team. Describing Lewis's 3rd grade class, one of her colleagues said that the students are "afraid to be absent because they don't want to take the chance they will miss anything. Mrs. Lewis doesn't tell them when she is planning something special, so they have to be there every day just in case" (Johnson, 2008, p. 7D). In fact, if the reinforcement schedule is gradually changed until it becomes very "lean"—meaning that reinforcement occurs only after many responses or a after a long time interval—then people can learn to work for extended periods without any reinforcement at all. Just watch gamblers playing slot machines to see how powerful a lean reinforcement schedule can be.

Reinforcement schedules influence how persistently we will respond when reinforcement is withheld. What happens when reinforcement is completely withdrawn?

EXTINCTION.   In classical conditioning, the conditioned response is extinguished (disappears) when the conditioned stimulus appears, but the unconditioned stimulus does not follow (tone, but no food). In operant conditioning, a person or an animal will not persist in a certain behavior if the usual reinforcer is withheld long enough. The behavior will eventually be extinguished (stop). For example, if you repeatedly e-mail a professor but never get a reply, you may give up. Removal of reinforcement altogether leads to **extinction**. The process may take a while, however, as you know if you have tried to extinguish a child's tantrums by withholding your attention. Often the child wins—because you give up ignoring her—and instead of extinction, intermittent reinforcement occurs. This, of course, may encourage even more persistent tantrums in the future.

Antecedents and Behavior Change

In operant conditioning, antecedents—the events preceding behaviors—provide information about which behaviors will lead to positive consequences and which will lead to unpleasant ones. Skinner's pigeons learned to peck for food when a light was on, but not to bother when the light was off, because no food followed pecking when the light was off. In other words, they learned to use the antecedent light as a cue to discriminate the likely consequence of pecking. The pigeons' pecking was under **stimulus control**, that is, controlled by the discriminative stimulus of the light. This happens in humans too. For example, I found myself (more than once) about to turn into my old office parking lot, even after my department had been relocated to a new building across town. As I drove, the old landmark cues kept me heading automatically to the old office. Another example is the supposedly true story of a getaway car driver in a bank robbery who sped through town, only to be caught by the police when she dutifully stopped at a red light. The stimulus of the red light had come to have automatic control.

We all learn to discriminate—to read situations. When should you ask to borrow your roommate's car—after a major disagreement or after you both have had a great time at a party? The antecedent cue of a school principal standing in the hall helps students discriminate the probable consequences of running or attempting to break into a locker. We often respond to such antecedent cues without fully realizing that they are influencing our behavior. But teachers can use cues deliberately in the classroom.

Extinction The disappearance of a learned response.

Stimulus control Capacity for the presence or absence of antecedents to cause behaviors.

EFFECTIVE INSTRUCTION DELIVERY (EID). One important antecedent to increase positive student responses is the type of instructions you give. Research on **effective instruction delivery** has found instructions that are concise, clear, and specific, and that communicate an expected result are more effective than vague directions. Statements work better than questions. You should be within a few feet of the students; directions shouted from across the room are less likely to work. Ideally, you should make eye contact with the students first, and then give the directions (Roberts, Tingstrom, Olmi, & Bellipanni, 2008).

CUEING. By definition, **cueing** is the act of providing an antecedent stimulus just before a specific behavior is supposed to take place. Cueing is particularly useful in setting the stage for behaviors that must occur at a given time, but are easily forgotten. In working with young people, teachers often find themselves correcting behaviors after the fact, asking students, "When are you going to start remembering to . . . ?" These reminders often lead to irritation. The mistake is already made, and the young person is left with only two choices: to promise to try harder or to think, "Why don't you leave me alone?" Neither response is very satisfying. Presenting a nonjudgmental cue can help prevent such negative confrontations. When a student performs the appropriate behavior after a cue, the teacher can reinforce the student's accomplishment instead of punishing failure.

PROMPTING. Sometimes students need help learning to respond to a cue in an appropriate way so the cue becomes a discriminative stimulus. One approach is to provide an additional cue, called a **prompt**, following the first cue. There are two principles for using a cue and a prompt to teach a new behavior. First, make sure the environmental stimulus that you want to become a cue occurs immediately before the prompt you are using, so students will learn to respond to the cue and not rely only on the prompt. Second, fade (gradually reduce or delay) the prompt as soon as possible so students do not become dependent on it (Alberto & Troutman, 2009).

One way to incorporate cueing and prompting is by providing students with a checklist or reminder sheet. Figure 7.2 is a checklist for the steps in peer tutoring. Working in pairs

> **Effective instruction delivery** Instructions that are concise, clear, and specific, and that communicate an expected result. Statements work better than questions.
>
> **Cueing** Providing a stimulus that "sets up" a desired behavior.
>
> **Prompt** A reminder that follows a cue to make sure the person reacts to the cue.

FIGURE 7.2

WRITTEN PROMPTS: A PEER-TUTORING CHECKLIST

By using this checklist, students are reminded how to be effective tutors. As they become more proficient, the checklist may be less necessary.

 Remember to...

 _____ 1. Have the lesson ready.

 _____ 2. Talk clearly.

 _____ 3. Be friendly.

 _____ 4. Tell the student when the answer is right.

 _____ 5. STOP! Correct mistakes.

 _____ 6. Praise good work!

 _____ 7. Make the lesson fun.

 _____ 8. Do not give TOO MUCH help.

 _____ 9. Fill out the daily sheet.

_____ 10. Can you add a suggestion?

Source: From Achieving Educational Excellence: Behavior Analysis for School Personnel (Figure, p. 89), by B. Sulzer-Azaroff and G. R. Mayer, 1994, San Marcos, CA: Western Image, P.O. Box 427. Copyright © 1994 by Beth Sulzer-Azaroff and G. Roy Mayer. Reprinted by permission of the authors.

is the cue; the checklist is the prompt. As students learn the procedures, the teacher may stop using the checklist, but may remind the students of the steps. When no written or oral prompts are necessary, the students have learned to respond appropriately to the environmental cue of working in pairs—they have learned how to behave in peer tutoring situations. However, the teacher should continue to monitor the process, recognize good work, and correct mistakes. Before a peer tutoring session, the teacher might ask students to close their eyes and "see" the checklist, focusing on each step. As students work, the teacher could listen to their interactions and continue to provide coaching as they improve their peer tutoring skills.

What would these principles look like in action? We turn to that next.

APPLIED BEHAVIOR ANALYSIS

Connect and Extend to PRAXIS II™

Applied Behavior Analysis (I, C4) When teachers need to change inappropriate or ineffective classroom behaviors that have not changed in response to standard behavioral techniques (e.g., response cost), they often employ applied behavior analysis. Familiarize yourself with the steps in developing and implementing an intervention based on that technique.

Applied behavior analysis is the application of behavioral learning principles to change behavior. The method is sometimes called **behavior modification**, but this term has negative connotations for many people and is often misunderstood (Alberto & Troutman, 2009; Kazdin, 2001, 2008).

Ideally, applied behavior analysis requires clear specification of the behavior to be changed; careful measurement of the behavior; analysis of the antecedents and reinforcers that might be maintaining inappropriate or undesirable behavior; interventions based on behavioral principles to change the behavior; and careful measurement of changes. In research on applied behavior analysis, an ABAB design (described in Chapter 1) is common. That is, researchers take a baseline measurement of the behavior (A), then apply the intervention (B), then stop the intervention to see if the behavior goes back to the baseline level (A), and then reintroduce the intervention (B).

In classrooms, teachers usually cannot follow all the ABAB steps, but they can do the following:

1. Clearly specify the behavior to be changed and note the current level. For example, if a student is "careless," does this mean 2, 3, 4, or more computation errors for every 10 problems?
2. Plan a specific intervention using antecedents, consequences, or both. For example, offer the student one extra minute of computer time for every problem completed with no errors.
3. Keep track of the results, and modify the plan if necessary.

Let's consider some specific methods for accomplishing step 2—the intervention.

Methods for Encouraging Behaviors

As we discussed earlier, to encourage behavior is to reinforce it. There are several specific ways to encourage existing behaviors or teach new ones. These include teacher attention and praise, the Premack principle, shaping, and positive practice.

REINFORCING WITH TEACHER ATTENTION. Many psychologists advise teachers to "accentuate the positive"—praise students for good behavior, while ignoring misbehavior. In fact, some researchers believe that "the systematic application of praise and attention may be the most powerful motivational and classroom management tool available to teachers" (Alber & Heward, 1997, p. 277; Alber & Heward, 2000). A related strategy is *differential reinforcement*, or ignoring inappropriate behaviors, while being sure to reinforce appropriate behaviors as soon as they occur. For example, if a student is prone to making irrelevant comments ("When is the game this Friday?"), you should ignore the off-task comment, but recognize a task-related contribution as soon as it occurs (Landrum & Kauffman, 2006).

This praise-and-ignore approach can be helpful, but don't expect it to solve all classroom management problems. Several studies have shown that disruptive behaviors persist when teachers use positive consequences (mostly praise) as their only classroom

Applied behavior analysis The application of behavioral learning principles to understand and change behavior.

Behavior modification Systematic application of antecedents and consequences to change behavior.

GUIDELINES

Using Praise Appropriately

Be clear and systematic in giving praise.
Examples

1. Make sure praise is tied directly to appropriate behavior.
2. Make sure the student understands the specific action or accomplishment that is being praised. Say, "I am impressed that you made sure everyone in your group got a chance to speak," not, "Good job leading the group."

Make praise "appreciative" not "evaluative" (Ginott, 1972).
Examples

1. Praise and appreciate the student's efforts, accomplishments, and actions—especially when the actions help others.
2. Don't evaluate the student's character or personality—praise the action, not the person.

Set standards for praise based on individual abilities and limitations.
Examples

1. Praise progress or accomplishment in relation to the individual student's past efforts.
2. Focus the student's attention on his or her own progress, not on comparisons with others.

Attribute the student's success to effort and ability so the student will gain confidence that success is possible again.
Examples

1. Don't imply that the success may be based on luck, extra help, or easy material.

2. Ask students to describe the problems they encountered and how they solved them.

Make praise really reinforcing.
Examples

1. Don't attempt to influence the rest of the class by singling out some students for praise. This tactic frequently backfires, because students know what's really going on. In addition, you risk embarrassing the student you have chosen to praise.
2. Don't give undeserved praise to students simply to balance failures. It is seldom consoling and calls attention to the student's inability to earn genuine recognition.
3. Don't use "caboosing"—tacking a criticism on at the end, as in "Good job on completing your homework this week. Why can't you do that every week?" (Kazdin, 2008).

Recognize genuine accomplishments.
Examples

1. Reward the attainment of specified goals, not just participation.
2. Do not reward uninvolved students just for being quiet and not disrupting the class.
3. Tie praise to students' improving competence or to the value of their accomplishment. Say, "I noticed that you double-checked all your problems. Your score reflects your careful work."

For more information on teacher praise, see:
http://moodle.ed.uiuc.edu/wiked/index.php/Praise

management strategy (McGoey & DuPaul, 2000; Pfiffner & O'Leary, 1987; Sullivan & O'Leary, 1990). Also, if attention from other students is reinforcing the problem behaviors, the teacher's ignoring them won't help much.

There is a second consideration in using praise. The positive results found in research occur when teachers carefully and systematically praise their students (Landrum & Kauffman, 2006). Merely "handing out compliments" will not improve behavior. To be effective, praise must (1) be contingent on the behavior to be reinforced, (2) specify clearly the behavior being reinforced, and (3) be believable (O'Leary & O'Leary, 1977). In other words, the praise should be sincere recognition of a well-defined behavior so students understand what they did to warrant the recognition. Teachers who have not received special training often violate these conditions (Brophy, 1981). Ideas for using praise effectively, based on Brophy's extensive review of the subject and Alan Kazdin's (2008) work with parents and teachers, are presented in the *Guidelines*.

Some psychologists have suggested that teachers' use of praise tends to focus students on learning to win approval rather than on learning for its own sake. Perhaps the best advice is to be aware of the potential dangers of the overuse or misuse of praise and to navigate accordingly.

SELECTING REINFORCERS: THE PREMACK PRINCIPLE. In most classrooms, there are many readily available reinforcers other than teacher attention, such as the chance

GRANDMA'S RULE "First, do what I want you to do, and then you may do what you want to do." According to the Premack principle, by making preferred activities contingent on learning and positive behavior, teachers can greatly increase both.

Connect and Extend to PRAXIS II™

Encouraging/Discouraging Behaviors (I, B2)
Understand the appropriate uses of techniques to encourage or discourage various classroom behaviors. Know the limitations and problems associated with these types of interventions.

to talk to other students, work at computers, or feed the class animals. However, teachers tend to offer these opportunities in a rather haphazard way. Just as with praise, by making privileges and rewards directly contingent on learning and positive behavior, the teacher can greatly increase both learning and desired behavior.

A helpful guide for choosing the most effective reinforcers is the **Premack principle**, named for David Premack (1965). According to the Premack principle, a high-frequency behavior (a preferred activity) can be an effective reinforcer for a low-frequency behavior (a less-preferred activity). This is sometimes referred to as "Grandma's rule": First, do what I want you to do, and then you may do what you want to do. Elizabeth used this principle in her class when she told them they could work together on their Civil War news program after they quietly completed the first section of the worksheet on their own.

If students didn't have to study, what would they do? The answers to this question may suggest many possible reinforcers. For most students, talking, moving around the room, sitting near a friend, being exempt from assignments or tests, reading magazines, using the computer, or playing games are preferred activities. The best way to determine appropriate reinforcers for your students may be to watch what they do in their free time. (See http://www.interventioncentral.org/tools/jackpot_reinforcer_survey_generator for more ideas.)

For the Premack principle to be effective, the low-frequency (less preferred) behavior must happen first. In the following dialogue, observe how the teacher loses a perfect opportunity to use the Premack principle:

Students: Oh, no! Do we have to work on grammar again today? The other classes got to discuss the play we saw in the auditorium this morning.

Teacher: But the other classes finished the lesson on sentences yesterday. We're almost finished too. If we don't finish the lesson, I'm afraid you'll forget the rules we reviewed yesterday.

Students: Why don't we finish the sentences at the end of the period and talk about the play now?

Teacher: Okay, if you promise to complete the sentences later.

Discussing the play could have served as a reinforcer for completing the lesson. As it is, the class may well spend the entire period discussing the play. Just as the discussion becomes fascinating, the teacher will have to end it and insist that the class return to the grammar lesson.

SHAPING. What happens when students continually fail to gain reinforcement because they simply cannot perform a skill in the first place? Consider these examples:

- A 4th grade student looks at the results of the latest mathematics test. "No credit on almost half of the problems again because I made one dumb mistake in each problem. I hate math!"
- A 10th grade student finds some excuse each day for avoiding the softball game in gym class. The student cannot catch a ball and now refuses to try.

In both situations, the students are receiving no reinforcement for their work because the end product of their efforts is not good enough. A safe prediction is that the

Premack principle Principle stating that a more-preferred activity can serve as a reinforcer for a less-preferred activity.

students will soon learn to dislike the class, the subject, and perhaps the teacher and school in general. One way to prevent this problem is the strategy of **shaping**, also called **successive approximations**. Shaping involves reinforcing progress instead of waiting for perfection.

In order to use shaping, the teacher must take the final complex behavior the student is expected to master and break it down into a number of small, manageable steps. One approach that identifies the small steps is **task analysis**, originally developed by R. B. Miller (1962) to help the armed services train personnel. Miller's system begins with a definition of the final performance requirement—what the trainee (or student) must be able to do at the end of the program or unit. Then, the steps that will lead to the final goal are specified. The procedure simply breaks skills and processes down into subskills and subprocesses—small steps to success.

Consider an example of task analysis in which students must write a position paper based on research. If the teacher assigned the position paper without analyzing the task, what could happen? Some of the students might not know how to do systematic computer research. They might read one or two entries in Wikipedia, and then write about their position based only on this brief reading. Another group of students might know how to use computers and search engines to do research online and how to find information from indexes in books, but have difficulty integrating information to reach conclusions. They might hand in lengthy papers listing summaries of different ideas without any synthesis or conclusions. Another group of students might be able to draw conclusions, but their written presentations might be so confusing and grammatically incorrect that the teacher could not understand what they were trying to say. Each of the groups would have failed to fulfill the assignment, but for different reasons.

A task analysis gives a picture of the logical sequence of steps leading toward the final goal. An awareness of this sequence can help teachers make sure that students have the necessary skills before they move to the next step. In addition, when students have difficulty, the teacher can pinpoint problem areas. Many behaviors can be improved through shaping, especially the acquisition of skills that involve persistence, endurance, increased accuracy, greater speed, or extensive practice to master. Because shaping is a time-consuming process, however, it should not be used if success can be attained through simpler methods such as cueing.

POSITIVE PRACTICE. In **positive practice**, students replace one behavior with another. This approach is especially appropriate for dealing with academic errors. When students make a mistake, they must correct it as soon as possible and practice the correct response. The same principle can be applied when students break classroom rules. Instead of being punished, the student might be required to practice the correct alternative action, for example, entering the room and immediately putting backpacks in assigned places. This process sometimes is called *positive practice overcorrection* because the correct behavior is practiced until it becomes almost automatic (Cole, Montgomery, Wilson, & Milan, 2000; Marvin, Rapp, Stenske, Rojas, Swanson, & Bartlett, 2010).

The *Guidelines* on the next page summarize approaches encouraging positive behavior.

Handling Undesirable Behavior

No matter how successful you are at accentuating the positive, there are times when you must cope with undesirable behavior, either because other methods fail or because the behavior itself is dangerous and calls for direct action. For this purpose, negative reinforcement, reprimands, response cost, and social isolation all offer possible solutions.

NEGATIVE REINFORCEMENT. Recall the basic principle of negative reinforcement: If an action stops or avoids something unpleasant, then that action is likely to occur again in similar situations. Negative reinforcement was operating in Elizabeth's classroom. When they moaned and complained, her students escaped the test, so negative reinforcement probably increased the frequency of complaining in the future.

Shaping Reinforcing each small step of progress toward a desired goal or behavior.

Successive approximations Small components that make up a complex behavior.

Task analysis System for breaking down a task hierarchically into basic skills and subskills.

Positive practice Practicing correct responses immediately after errors.

GUIDELINES

Encouraging Positive Behaviors

Make sure you recognize positive behavior in ways that students value.
Examples

1. When presenting class rules, set up positive consequences for following rules as well as negative consequences for breaking rules.
2. Recognize honest admissions of mistakes by giving a second chance: "Because you admitted that you copied your paper from a book, I'm giving you a chance to rewrite it."
3. Offer desired rewards for academic efforts, such as extra recess time, exemptions from homework or tests, or extra credit on major projects.

When students are tackling new material or trying new skills, give plenty of reinforcement.
Examples

1. Find and comment on something right in every student's first life drawing.
2. Reinforce students for encouraging each other. "French pronunciation is difficult and awkward at first. Let's help each other by eliminating all giggles when someone is brave enough to attempt a new word."

After new behaviors are established, give reinforcement on an unpredictable schedule to encourage persistence.
Examples

1. Offer surprise rewards for good participation in class.
2. Start classes with a short, written extra-credit question. Students don't have to answer, but a good answer will add points to their total for the semester.
3. Make sure the good students get compliments for their work from time to time. Don't take them for granted.

Use the Premack principle to identify effective reinforcers.
Examples

1. Watch what students do with their free time.

2. Notice which students like to work together. The chance to work with friends is often a good reinforcer.

Use cueing to help establish new behaviors.
Examples

1. Put up humorous signs in the classroom to remind students of rules.
2. At the beginning of the year, as students enter class, call their attention to a chart posted on the board listing all of the materials they should have with them when they come to class.

Make sure all students, even those who often cause problems, receive some praise, privileges, or other rewards when they do something well.
Examples

1. Review your class list occasionally to make sure all students are receiving some reinforcement.
2. Set standards for reinforcement so that all students will have a chance to be rewarded.
3. Check your biases. Are boys getting more opportunities for reinforcement than girls, or vice versa? How about students of different races?

Establish a variety of reinforcers.
Examples

1. Let students suggest their own reinforcers or choose from a "menu" of reinforcers with "weekly specials."
2. Talk to other teachers or parents about ideas for reinforcers.

For more ideas about building positive behaviors, see this site:
http://www.afcec.org/tipsforteachers/tips_c4.html

Negative reinforcement can also be used to enhance learning. To do this, you place students in mildly unpleasant situations so they can "escape" when their behavior improves. Consider these examples:

Teacher to a 3rd-grade class: "When the supplies are put back in the cabinet and each of you is sitting quietly, we will go outside. Until then, we will miss our recess."

High-school teacher to a student who seldom finishes in-class assignments: "As soon as you complete the assignment, you may join the class in the auditorium. But until you finish, you must work in the study hall."

Antonio Banderas in the film, *Take the Lead:* Working with a group of totally uncooperative students, Banderas blasts the students with music they hate, only turning it off when the entire class is lined up and ready to practice their ballroom dance moves.

Actually, a true behaviorist might object to identifying these situations as examples of negative reinforcement because too much student thinking and understanding is required to make the negative reinforcers work. Teachers cannot treat students like lab animals, subjecting them to loud noises or cold environments until they give a right answer. But teachers can make sure that unpleasant situations improve when student behavior improves.

You may wonder why the negative reinforcement examples above are not considered punishment. Surely staying in during recess, not accompanying the class to a special program, or being subjected to music you hate is punishing. But the focus in each case is on strengthening specific behaviors (putting away supplies, finishing in-class assignments, lining up and cooperating with the teacher). The teacher strengthens (reinforces) the behaviors by removing something aversive as soon as the desired behaviors occur. Because the consequence involves removing or "subtracting" a stimulus, the reinforcement is negative.

Negative reinforcement also gives students a chance to exercise control. Missing recess or hearing music you hate are unpleasant situations, but in each case, the students retain control. As soon as they perform the appropriate behavior, the unpleasant situation ends. In contrast, punishment occurs after the fact, and a student cannot so easily control or terminate it.

DELIVERING REPRIMANDS Research has shown that scolding a student in front of the entire class may actually reinforce his or her disruptive behavior by drawing more attention to it; thus, calm, private reprimands may be more effective.

There are several rules for negative reinforcement: Describe the desired change in a positive way. Don't bluff. Make sure you can enforce your unpleasant situation. Follow through despite complaints. Insist on action, not promises. If the unpleasant situation terminates when students promise to be better next time, you have reinforced making promises, not making changes (Alberto & Troutman, 2009; O'Leary, 1995).

REPRIMANDS. In the *Junction Journal,* my daughter's elementary school newspaper, I read the following lines in a story called "Why I Like School," written by a 4th grader: "I also like my teacher. She helps me understand and learn. She is nice to everyone. I like it when she gets mad at somebody, but she doesn't yell at them in front of the class, but speaks to them privately."

Soft, calm, private **reprimands** are more effective than loud, public reprimands in decreasing disruptive behavior (Landrum & Kauffman, 2006). Research has shown that when reprimands are loud enough for the entire class to hear, disruptions increase or continue at a constant level. Some students enjoy public recognition for misbehavior, or they don't want classmates to see them "lose" to the teacher. If they are not used too often, and if the classroom is generally a positive, warm environment, then students usually respond quickly to private reprimands (Kaplan, 1991).

RESPONSE COST. The concept of **response cost** is familiar to anyone who has ever paid a fine. For certain infractions of the rules, people must lose some reinforcer—money, time, privileges (Walker, Shea, & Bauer, 2004). In a class, the concept of response cost can be applied in a number of ways. The first time a student breaks a class rule, the teacher gives a warning. The second time, the teacher makes a mark beside the student's name in the grade book. The student loses 2 minutes of recess for each mark accumulated. For older students, a certain number of marks might mean losing the privilege of working in a group or using the computers.

SOCIAL ISOLATION. One of the most controversial behavioral methods for decreasing undesirable behavior is the strategy of **social isolation**, often called **time out** from reinforcement. The process involves removing a highly disruptive student from the

Reprimands Criticisms for misbehavior; rebukes.

Response cost Punishment by loss of reinforcers.

Social isolation Removal of a disruptive student for 5 to 10 minutes.

Time out Technically, the removal of all reinforcement. In practice, isolation of a student from the rest of the class for a brief time.

classroom for 5 to 10 minutes. The student is placed in an empty, uninteresting room alone—the punishment is brief isolation from other people. A trip to the principal's office or confinement to a chair in the corner of the regular classroom does not have the same effect as sitting alone in an empty room. But beware. If a brief time out does not help improve the situation, don't try a longer time out. Alan Kazdin (2008), who has been helping teachers and parents work positively with children for decades, says, "If you are giving longer and longer time-outs, it means your strategy is failing. The answer is not to escalate—just the opposite in fact. If you are giving more and longer time-outs, this should tell you that you need to do more to positively reinforce good behaviors to replace the unwanted behaviors" (p. 10)—good advice for any form of punishment.

SOME CAUTIONS ABOUT PUNISHMENT. Unfortunately, punishment seems to be a very common part of parenting and schooling. I say *unfortunately* because study after study shows that punishment by itself, as usually practiced in homes and schools, just doesn't work. It tells children what to stop doing (often, they knew that already), but it does not teach them what to do instead (Kazdin, 2008). Whenever you consider the use of punishment, you should make it part of a two-pronged attack. The first goal is to carry out the punishment and suppress the undesirable behavior. The second goal is to make clear what the student should be doing instead and to provide reinforcement for those desirable actions. Thus, while the problem behaviors are being suppressed, positive alternative responses are being strengthened. As you will see in the next section, recent approaches really emphasize supporting positive behaviors. The *Guidelines* give ideas for using punishment for positive purposes.

Let me repeat. Punishment in and of itself does not lead to any positive behavior. Harsh punishment communicates to students that "might makes right" and may encourage retaliation. In addition, punishment works best when the potential punisher—the teacher—is around. Students learn to "be good" when the teacher is in the room, but when the teacher leaves or there is a substitute teacher, the system might fall apart. Punishment tends to focus students on the consequences of their actions for themselves instead of challenging them to think about the impact of their behavior on others; as a result punishment does not instill compassion or empathy for others. Finally, punishment can interfere with developing a caring relationship with your students (Alberto & Troutman, 2009; Hardin, 2008; Kohn, 1996a, 1996b, 2005; Walker et al., 2004).

PUTTING IT ALL TOGETHER: BEHAVIORAL APPROACHES TO TEACHING AND MANAGEMENT

Connect and Extend to PRAXIS II™

Teaching and Management (I, A1; II, A3; I, C4)
Identify major approaches to teaching and classroom management that are based on behavioral principles. Understand the advantages and disadvantages of each.

The behavioral approach to learning has inspired several important contributions to instruction, including systems for specifying learning objectives and direct instruction (we will look at these topics in Chapter 14 when we discuss teaching) and class management systems such as group consequences, contingency contracts, and token economies (Landrum & Kauffman, 2006). These approaches are useful when the goal is to learn explicit information or change behaviors and when the material is sequential and factual.

Remember, there is one element that is part of every behavioral learning program—specific practice of correct behaviors. Contrary to popular wisdom, practice does not make perfect. Instead, practice makes permanent the behaviors practiced, so practicing accurate behaviors is important. As other examples of a behavioral approach, consider group consequences, contingency contracts, and token reinforcement.

Group Consequences

A teacher can base reinforcement for the class on the behavior of selected target students (for example, "If Jamarcus, Evan, and Mei stay on their mats until the end of nap time, then we will have a special snack"). Also, the class can earn rewards based on the collective behavior of everyone in the class, usually by adding each student's points to a class or a team total. The **good behavior game** is an example of this approach. Teachers and students discuss what would make the classroom a better place. Then, they identify

Good behavior game Arrangement where a class is divided into teams and each team receives demerit points for breaking agreed-upon rules of good behavior.

GUIDELINES

Using Punishment

Try to structure the situation so you can use negative reinforcement rather than punishment.
Examples

1. Allow students to escape unpleasant situations (completing additional workbook assignments, weekly tests of math facts) when they reach a level of competence.
2. Insist on actions, not promises. Don't let students convince you to change the terms of the agreement.

If you do use punishment, keep it mild and brief—then pair it with doing the right thing.
Examples

1. Time out for young children—no more than 2 to 5 minutes; loss of points—no more than 1 sticker if the student can earn 5 in a day (Kazdin, 2008).
2. Pair the brief, mild punishment with reinforcement for doing the right thing or restitution. If a student writes graffiti in the restroom, use brief punishment plus cleaning off the graffiti.

Be consistent in your application of punishment.
Examples

1. Avoid inadvertently reinforcing the behavior you are trying to punish. Keep confrontations private, so that students don't become heroes for standing up to the teacher in a public showdown.
2. Let students know in advance the consequences of breaking the rules by posting major class rules for younger students or outlining rules and consequences in a course syllabus for older students.
3. Tell students they will receive only one warning before punishment is given. Give the warning in a calm way, and then follow through.
4. Make punishment as unavoidable and immediate as is reasonably possible.
5. Don't punish when you are angry—you may be too harsh, then need to take it back later—which shows a lack of consistency.

Focus on the students' actions, not on the students' personal qualities.
Examples

1. Reprimand in a calm but firm voice.
2. Avoid vindictive or sarcastic words or tones of voice. You might hear your own angry words later when students imitate your sarcasm.
3. Stress the need to end the problem behavior instead of expressing any dislike you might feel for the student.
4. Be aware that students of color are disproportionately punished, sent to detention, and expelled from school. Are your policies fair?

Adapt the punishment to the infraction.
Examples

1. Ignore minor misbehaviors that do not disrupt the class, or stop these misbehaviors with a disapproving glance or a move toward the student.
2. Make sure the punishment isn't worse than the crime—don't take away all the free time a student has earned for one infraction of the rules, for example (Landrum & Kauffman, 2006). Less punishment is more effective, as long as it is paired with reinforcement for doing the right thing.
3. Don't use homework as a punishment for misbehaviors such as talking in class.
4. When a student misbehaves to gain peer acceptance, removal from the group of friends can be effective, because this is really time out from a reinforcing situation.
5. If the problem behaviors continue, analyze the situation and try a new approach. Your punishment may not be very punishing, or you may be inadvertently reinforcing the misbehavior.

For more information on punishment, see
http://www.ext.vt.edu/pubs/family/350-111/350-111.html

---

behaviors that get in the way of learning. Based on this discussion, class rules are developed and the class is divided into two or three teams. Each time a student breaks one of the rules, that student's team is given a mark. The team with the fewest marks at the end of the period receives a special reward or privilege (longer recess, first to lunch, the team "spaceship" is moved closer to the "moon," and so on). If all teams earn fewer than a preestablished number of marks, all receive the reward. Sometimes a class needs a "no tattling" rule so the teams don't spend all their time pointing out each other's mistakes. Most studies indicate that even though the game generates only small improvements in academic achievement, it can produce definite improvements in the behaviors listed in the good behavior rules and it can prevent many behavior problems (Embry, 2002; Tingstrom, Sterling-Turner, & Wilczynski, 2006).

What happens if we add interventions that target academic achievement to the proven power of the Good Behavior Game? Catherine Bradshaw and her colleagues did just that (Bradshaw, Zmuda, Kellam, & Ialongo, 2009). They followed 678 mostly African American students from urban 1st grade classes through their high school years. In 1st grade these students participated in either a control group or one of two specific programs: (a) a classroom-centered intervention that combined the Good Behavior Game with an enhanced academic curriculum (read-alouds, journal writing, Reader's Theater, critical thinking skills, Mimosa math, small group activities, etc.) or (b) a family-centered intervention that promoted parent involvement in home reading and math activities and helped parents develop better child management strategies. Students who participated in the classroom intervention that combined the Good Behavior Game with an enhanced academic curriculum in 1st grade had higher scores on standardized achievement tests in grade 12, reduced referrals for special education services, higher rates of high school graduation, and higher rates of college attendance 12 years later! The parent involvement program had positive but not significant effects on all these measures and a small significant effect on reading test scores. So early investment in helping students learn positive behaviors and academic skills can make a difference for years to come.

You can also use **group consequences** without dividing the class into teams; that is, you can base reinforcement on the behavior of the whole class. However, caution is needed using group approaches—the whole group should not suffer for the misbehavior or mistakes of one individual if the group has no real influence over that person. I once saw an entire class break into cheers when the teacher announced that one boy was transferring to another school. The chant "No more points! No more points!" filled the room. The "points" referred to the teacher's system of giving one point to the whole class each time anyone broke a rule. Every point meant 5 minutes of recess lost. The boy who was transferring had been responsible for the loss of many recess periods. He was not very popular to begin with, and the point system, though quite effective in maintaining order, had made the boy an outcast in his own class.

Peer pressure in the form of support and encouragement, however, can be a positive influence. Group consequences are recommended when students care about the approval of their peers (Theodore, Bray, Kehle, & Jenson, 2001). If the misbehavior of several students seems to be encouraged by the attention and laughter of other students, then group consequences could be helpful. Teachers might show students how to give support and constructive feedback to classmates. If a few students seem to enjoy sabotaging the system, those students may need separate arrangements such as putting all the saboteurs together in their own group.

Contingency Contracts and Token Reinforcement

In a **contingency contract** program, the teacher draws up an individual contract with each student, describing exactly what the student must do to earn a particular privilege or reward. In some programs, students suggest behaviors to be reinforced and the rewards that can be gained. The negotiating process itself can be an educational experience, as students learn to set reasonable goals and abide by the terms of a contract. And, if students participate in setting the goals, they often are more committed to reaching them (Locke & Latham, 2002; Schunk, 2011; Schunk, Pintrich, & Meece, 2008).

An example of a contract for completing assignments that is appropriate for intermediate and upper-grade students is presented in Figure 7.3. This chart serves as a contract, assignment sheet, and progress record. Information about progress can support student motivation. Something like this might even help you keep track of assignments and due dates in your college classes.

- -

STOP & THINK Have you ever participated in a program where you earned points or credits that you could exchange for a reward? Are you a member of a frequent flyer club, or do you get points on your credit card? Do you get one free coffee for every 10 coffee purchases or a free smoothie when you fill a punch card? Does being a part of such a program affect your buying habits? How? I know I pay for everything I can with my credit card to get the points and always try fly on one airline for the same reason. •

- -

Group consequences Rewards or punishments given to a class as a whole for adhering to or violating rules of conduct.

Contingency contract A contract between the teacher and a student specifying what the student must do to earn a particular reward or privilege.

FIGURE 7.3

A CONTINGENCY CONTRACT FOR COMPLETING ASSIGNMENTS

The teacher and student agree on the due dates for each assignment, marking them in blue on the chart. Each time an assignment is turned in, the date of completion is marked in black on the chart. As long as the actual completion line is above the planned completion line, the student earns free time or other contracted rewards.

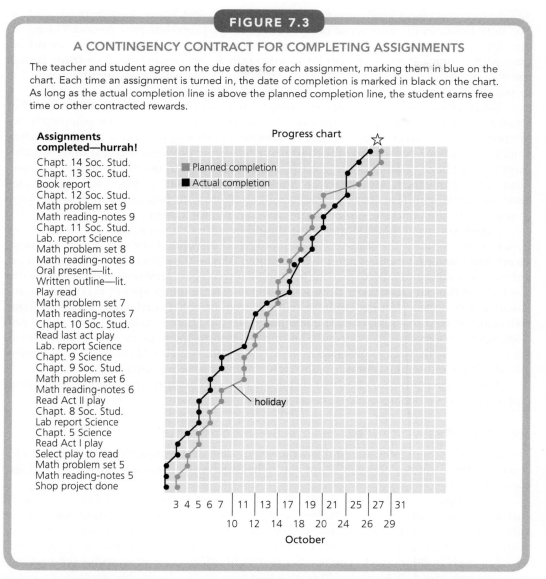

Assignments completed—hurrah!

Chapt. 14 Soc. Stud.
Chapt. 13 Soc. Stud.
Book report
Chapt. 12 Soc. Stud.
Math problem set 9
Math reading-notes 9
Chapt. 11 Soc. Stud.
Lab. report Science
Math problem set 8
Math reading-notes 8
Oral present—lit.
Written outline—lit.
Play read
Math problem set 7
Math reading-notes 7
Chapt. 10 Soc. Stud.
Read last act play
Lab. report Science
Chapt. 9 Science
Chapt. 9 Soc. Stud.
Math problem set 6
Math reading-notes 6
Read Act II play
Chapt. 8 Soc. Stud.
Lab report Science
Chapt. 5 Science
Read Act I play
Select play to read
Math problem set 5
Math reading-notes 5
Shop project done

Progress chart

Planned completion
Actual completion

holiday

3 4 5 6 7 | 11 | 13 | 17 | 19 | 21 | 25 | 27 | 31
10 12 14 18 20 24 26 29
October

Source: From Achieving Educational Excellence: Behavior Analysis for School Personnel *(Figure, p. 89), by B. Sulzer-Azaroff and G. R. Mayer, 1994, San Marcos, CA: Western Image, P.O. Box 427. Copyright © 1994 by Beth Sulzer-Azaroff and G. Roy Mayer. Reprinted by permission of the authors.*

Often, it is difficult to provide positive consequences for all the students who deserve them. A **token reinforcement system** can help solve this problem by allowing all students to earn tokens for both academic work and positive classroom behavior. The tokens may be points, checks, holes punched in a card, chips, play money, or anything else that is easily identified as the student's property. Periodically, the students exchange the tokens they have earned for some desired reward (Alberto & Troutman, 2009; Kazdin, 2001).

Depending on the age of the student, the rewards could be small toys, school supplies, free time, special class jobs, positive notes sent home, time to listen to music, or other privileges. When a "token economy," as this kind of system is called, is first established, the tokens should be given out on a fairly continuous schedule, with chances to exchange the tokens for rewards available early and often. Once the system is working well, however, tokens should be distributed on an intermittent schedule and saved for longer periods of time before they are exchanged for rewards.

Another variation is to allow students to earn tokens in the classroom and then exchange them for rewards at home. These plans are very successful when parents are

Token reinforcement system
System in which tokens earned for academic work and positive classroom behavior can be exchanged for some desired reward.

willing to cooperate. Usually a note or report form is sent home daily or twice a week. The note indicates the number of points earned in the preceding time period. The points may be exchanged for minutes of television viewing, access to special toys, or private time with parents. Points can also be saved up for larger rewards such as trips. Do not use this procedure, however, if you suspect the child might be pressured for perfection or punished for poor reports (Jurbergs, Palcic, & Kelly, 2007).

Token reinforcement systems are complicated and time-consuming. Generally, they should be used in only three situations: (1) to motivate students who are completely uninterested in their work and have not responded to other approaches; (2) to encourage students who have consistently failed to make academic progress; and (3) to deal with a class that is out of control. Some groups of students seem to benefit from token economies more than others. Students with intellectual disabilities, children who have failed often, students with few academic skills, and students with behavior problems all seem to respond to the concrete, direct nature of token reinforcement.

Before you try a token system, you should be sure that your teaching methods and materials are right for the students. Sometimes, class disruptions or lack of motivation indicate that teaching practices need to be changed. Maybe the class rules are unclear or are enforced inconsistently. Perhaps your instructions are vague. Maybe the text is too easy or too hard or the pace is wrong. If these problems exist, a token system may improve the situation temporarily, but the students will still have trouble learning the academic material. Improve your teaching first. The few pages devoted here to token reinforcement and contingency contracts can offer only an introduction to these programs. If you want to set up a large-scale reward program in your classroom, you should probably seek professional advice. Often, the school psychologist, counselor, or principal can help.

The next section describes two examples that successfully applied behavioral principles to improve behaviors of students with special needs.

Reaching Every Student: Severe Behavior Problems

Students with severe behavior problems provide some of the most difficult challenges for teachers. Three studies show how applied behavioral principles can be useful in helping these students.

Lea Theodore and her colleagues (2001) worked with the teacher of five adolescent males who were diagnosed as having severe emotional disorders. A short list of clear rules was established (e.g., use no obscene words, comply with the teacher's requests within five seconds, make no verbal putdowns). The rules were written on index cards taped to each student's desk. The teacher had a checklist on his desk with each student's name to note any rule breaking. This checklist was easily observable, so students could monitor their own and each other's performance. At the end of the 45-minute period, a student chose a "criterion" from a jar. The possible criteria were: performance of the whole group, student with the highest score, student with the lowest score, the average of all students, or a random single student. If the student or students selected to be the criterion had five checks or fewer for rule-breaking, then the whole class got a reward, also chosen randomly from a jar. The possible rewards were things like a power drink, a bag of chips, a candy bar, or a late-to-class pass. An ABAB design was used—baseline, two-week intervention, two-week withdrawal of intervention, and two-week return to group consequences. All students showed clear improvement in following the rules when the reward system was in place. Students liked the approach and the teacher found it easy to implement.

In the second study, Kara McGoey and George DuPaul (2000) worked with teachers in three preschool classrooms to address problem behaviors of four students diagnosed as having Attention-Deficit Hyperactive Disorder. The teachers tried both a token reinforcement program (students earned small and large buttons on a chart for following class rules), and a response cost system (students began with five small buttons and one large button per activity each day and lost buttons for not following rules). Both procedures were effective in lowering rule breaking, but the teachers found the response cost system easier to implement.

Behavioral interventions are often used with children with autism (see Bartlett, Rapp, Krueger, & Henrickson, 2011; Hall, Grundon, Pope, & Romero, 2010; Soares, Vannest, & Harrison, 2009). For example, Sara Bartlett and her colleagues tested a *response cost* strategy to treat the problem of spitting by Evan, an 8-year-old boy with autism who had very limited verbal abilities. The researchers let the boy listen to a radio, identified as a favorite toy by his teachers, as he worked at a table in a therapy room in his school. When the boy spit, the radio was removed for 10 seconds, and then replaced. Evan's spitting went to near zero rates during these training sessions. Then the researchers stopped the response cost strategy and the radio was not removed when Evan spit. The rates of spitting went back up. Next the researchers reinstituted the response cost, removing the radio for 10 seconds, and Evan's spitting went back down again to near zero. (Notice this also is an example of an ABAB research design—baseline, treatment, return to baseline, reinstate treatment.) The researchers moved Evan back into the classroom and conducted his training sessions there. Finally they taught Evan's teachers to use the strategy and Evan's spitting stayed at near zero in his regular classroom through the entire 4-month follow-up period.

FUNCTIONAL BEHAVIORAL ASSESSMENT These approaches focus on the "why" of student behavior ... or misbehavior. Teachers observe student behaviors in context and may interview the student, peers, and parents.

Functional Behavioral Assessment and Positive Behavior Supports

Teachers in both regular and special education classes have had success with a new approach that begins by asking, "What are students getting out of their problem behaviors—what functions do these behaviors serve?" The focus is on the *why* of the behavior, not on the *what* (Lane, Falk, & Wehby, 2006; Stage et al., 2008; Warren et al., 2006). The reasons for problem behaviors generally fall into four categories (Barnhill, 2005; Maag & Kemp, 2003). Students act out to:

1. Receive attention from others—teachers, parents, or peers.
2. Escape from some unpleasant situation—an academic or social demand.
3. Get a desired item or activity.
4. Meet sensory needs, such as stimulation from rocking or flapping arms for some children with autism.

If the reason for the behavior is known, then the teacher can devise ways of supporting positive behaviors that will serve the same "why" function. For example, I once worked with a middle-school principal who was concerned about a boy who had lost his father a few years earlier and was having trouble in a number of subjects, especially math. The student disrupted math class at least twice a week and ended up in the principal's office. There, the boy enjoyed the principal's undivided attention. After a scolding, they talked about sports because the principal liked the student and was concerned that he had no male role models. It is easy to spot the function of the classroom disruptions—they always led to (1) escape from math class (negative reinforcement) and (2) one-on-one time with the principal (positive reinforcement after a little bit of reprimanding). The principal, teacher, and I developed a way to support the student's positive behaviors in math by getting him some extra tutoring and by giving him time with the principal when he completed math problems instead of when he acted up in class. The new positive behaviors served many of the same functions as the old problem behaviors.

DISCOVERING THE "WHY": FUNCTIONAL BEHAVIORAL ASSESSMENTS. The process of understanding the "why" of a problem behavior is known as **functional behavioral assessment (FBA)**. Using a wide range of procedures to map the A-B-Cs of the situation—the antecedents, behaviors, and consequences—teachers try to identify the reason for

Functional behavioral assessment (FBA) Procedures used to obtain information about antecedents, behaviors, and consequences to determine the reason or function of the behavior.

the behavior (Barnhill, 2005). Many different procedures might help you determine the functions of a behavior. You can begin by interviewing students about their behaviors. In one study, students were asked to describe what they did that got them in trouble in school, what happened just before they acted out, and what happened right after. Even though the students were not always sure why they acted out, they seemed to benefit from talking to a concerned adult who was trying to understand their situation, not just reprimand them (Murdock, O'Neill, & Cunningham, 2005). But you will need to do more than just talk to students. You might also talk to parents or other teachers. You could conduct an A-B-C observation with these questions in mind: When and where does the problem behavior occur? What people or activities are involved? What happens right before—what do others do or say and what did the target student do or say? What happens right after the behavior—what did you, other students, or the target student do or say? What does the target student gain or escape from by engaging in the behavior—what changes after the student acts out? A more structured approach is shown in Figure 7.4—an observation guide for functional behavioral assessment based on a simple ABC analysis. Using this information, the teacher found out that the student acted out whenever the class was transitioning to another activity. The sources of reinforcement for the student are clear too.

The same behaviors may serve different functions for different students. For example, a functional behavioral assessment of three preschool students found that two of the students were aggressive and uncooperative in order to gain the teacher's attention, but the third child actually was trying to escape or avoid teacher attention (Dufrene, Doggett, Henington, & Watson, 2007). With information from a functional behavioral assessment, teachers developed an intervention package, including **positive behavior supports** for each child. Two students met specific standards to get the teacher attention they wanted, but the third child got to be "left alone" as long as he met certain standards.

POSITIVE BEHAVIOR SUPPORTS. The Individuals with Disabilities Education Act (IDEA, 2004) discussed in Chapter 4 requires positive behavior supports (PBS) for students with disabilities and those at risk for special education placement. Positive behavior supports are the actual interventions designed to replace problem behaviors with new actions that serve the same purpose for the student.

Positive behavior supports can help students with disabilities succeed in inclusion classrooms. For example, the disruptive behavior of a 5-year-old boy with an intellectual disability was nearly eliminated in a relatively short time through a PBS intervention that was based on a functional assessment conducted by the regular teaching staff and the special education teacher. The intervention included making sure the tasks assigned were at the right difficulty level, providing assistance with these tasks, teaching the student

Positive behavior supports (PBS) Interventions designed to replace problem behaviors with new actions that serve the same purpose for the student.

FIGURE 7.4

A SIMPLE STRUCTURED OBSERVATION GUIDE FOR FUNCTIONAL BEHAVIORAL ANALYSIS USING THE ABC FRAME

Student Name: Denton R.
Location: Math—Mrs. B
Start time: 1:02

Date: 2/25/2012
Observer: Mr. B.
Stop time: 1:15

A: Antecedents	B: Behaviors	C: Consequences
1:03 Students get out books and open to begin class.	D. pulls out his cap and puts it on.	Students around D. start laughing and saying "Hey."
1:05 Teacher notices D. and tells him to remeove his cap.	D. stands, slowly removes his cap, and bows.	Students applaud.
1:14 Teacher asks D. a question.	D. says, "man, I don't know."	Another student says, "Yeah, you're stupid." Others laugh.

Source: Friend, Marilyn; Bursuck, William D., Including Students with Special Needs: A Practical Guide for Classroom Teachers, 6th Edition, © 2012. Reprinted by permission of Pearson Education, Inc., Upper Saddle River, NJ.

how to request assistance, and teaching the student how to request a break from assigned work (Soodak & McCarthy, 2006; Umbreit, 1995).

But these approaches are not only for students with special needs. Research shows that disciplinary referrals decrease when the whole school uses these approaches for all students (Lewis, Sugai, & Colvin, 1998). Because about 5% of students account for about 50% of the discipline referrals, it makes sense to develop interventions for those students. Positive behavior interventions based on functional assessments can reduce these behavior problems by 80% (Crone & Horner, 2003). At the classroom level, teachers are encouraged to use such preventive strategies as **precorrection**, which involves identifying the context for a student's misbehavior, clearly specifying the alternative expected behavior, modifying the situation to make the problem behavior less likely—for example, providing a cue or moving the student away from tempting distractions—then rehearsing the expected positive behaviors in the new context and providing powerful reinforcers when the positive behaviors occur. There is an emphasis on keeping students engaged, providing a positive focus, consistently enforcing school/class rules, correcting disruptive behavior proactively, and planning for smooth transitions (Freiberg, 2006).

Positive behavior supports also can be part of a school-wide program. At the school level, the teachers and administrators can:

- Agree on a common approach for supporting positive behaviors and correcting problems.
- Develop a few positively stated, specific behavioral expectations and procedures for teaching these expectations to all students.
- Identify a continuum of ways (from small and simple, to more complex and stronger) to acknowledge appropriate behaviors and correct behavioral errors.
- Integrate the positive behavior support procedures with the school's discipline policy.

Research on school-wide positive behavior supports is limited, but results so far have been good. A study comparing middle-school students in a behavior support program with students outside the program showed that program students reported more positive reinforcement for appropriate behavior. Disciplinary referrals as well as verbal and physical aggression significantly decreased. In addition, students' perceptions of school safety improved (Metzler, Biglan, Rusby & Sprague, 2001). Studies of school-wide PBS efforts also indicate decreases in disciplinary referrals (Lewis, Sugai, & Colvin, 1998, 1997; Soodak & McCarthy, 2006).

Even with new approaches such as PBS, in recent years, most behavioral psychologists have found that operant conditioning offers too limited an explanation of learning. As behavioral approaches to learning developed, some researchers added a new element—thinking about behavior.

Self-Management

- -

STOP & THINK What area of your life needs some self-management? Write down one behavior you would like to increase and one behavior you would like to eliminate. •

- -

As you will see throughout this book, the role of students in managing their own learning is a major concern of psychologists and educators today. This concern is not restricted to any one group or theory. Different areas of research and theory all converge on one important idea: that the responsibility and the ability to learn rest within the student. Students must be active—no one can learn for someone else (Mace, Belfiore, & Hutchinson, 2001; Manning & Payne, 1996; Winne, 1995; Zimmerman & Schunk, 2004). From a behavioral perspective, students may be involved in any or all of the steps in a basic behavior change program. They may help set goals, observe their own work, keep records of it, and evaluate their own performance. Finally, they can select and deliver reinforcement.

GOAL SETTING. It appears that the goal-setting phase is very important in **self-management** (Reeve, 1996; Schunk, Pintrich, & Meece, 2008). In fact, some research suggests that setting

Precorrection A tool for positive behavior support that involves identifying the context for a student's misbehavior, clearly specifying the alternative expected behavior, modifying the situation to make the problem behavior less likely, then rehearsing the expected positive behaviors in the new context and providing powerful reinforcers.

Self-management Use of behavioral learning principles to change your own behavior.

specific goals and making them public may be the critical elements of self-management programs. For example, S. C. Hayes and his colleagues identified college students who had serious problems with studying and taught them how to set specific study goals. Students who set goals and announced them to the experimenters performed significantly better on tests covering the material they were studying than students who set goals privately and never revealed them to anyone (Hayes, Rosenfarb, Wulfert, Munt, Korn, & Zettle, 1985). A review of 20 years of research on self-management found that adults most often set the goals for students (Briesch & Chafouleas, 2009).

Higher standards tend to lead to higher performance (Locke & Latham, 2002). Unfortunately, student-set goals have a tendency to reflect increasingly lower expectations. Teachers can help students maintain high standards by monitoring the goals set and reinforcing high standards.

MONITORING AND EVALUATING PROGRESS.   Students may also participate in the monitoring and evaluation phases of a behavior change program. In fact, these are the elements of self-management that most often are handled by the students themselves (Briesch & Chafouleas, 2009; Mace, Belfiore, & Hutchinson, 2001). Some examples of behaviors that are appropriate for self-monitoring are the number of assignments completed, time spent practicing a skill, number of books read, number of problems correct, and time taken to run a mile. Tasks that must be accomplished without teacher supervision, such as homework or private study, are also good candidates for self-monitoring. Students keep a chart, diary, or checklist that records the frequency or duration of the behaviors in question. A progress record card can help older students break down assignments into small steps, determine the best sequence for completing the steps, and keep track of daily progress by setting goals for each day. The record card itself serves as a prompt that can be faded out.

Self-evaluation is somewhat more difficult than simple self-recording because it involves making a judgment about quality. Students can evaluate their behavior with reasonable accuracy, especially if they learn standards for judging a good performance or product. One key to accurate self-evaluation seems to be for the teacher to periodically check students' assessments and give reinforcement for accurate judgments. Older students may learn accurate self-evaluation more readily than younger students. Again, bonus points can be awarded when the teachers' and students' evaluations match (Kaplan, 1991). Self-correction can accompany self-evaluation. Students first evaluate, then alter and improve their work, and finally, compare the improvements to the standards again (Mace, Belfiore, & Hutchinson, 2001).

SELF-REINFORCEMENT.   The last step in self-management is **self-reinforcement**. There is some disagreement, however, as to whether this step is actually necessary. Some psychologists believe that setting goals and monitoring progress alone are sufficient and that self-reinforcement adds nothing to the effects (Hayes et al., 1985). Others believe that rewarding yourself for a job well done can lead to higher levels of performance than simply setting goals and keeping track of progress (Bandura, 1986). If you are willing to be tough and really deny yourself something you want until your goals are reached, then perhaps the promise of the reward can provide extra incentive for work. With that in mind, you may want to think of some way to reinforce yourself when you finish reading this chapter. A similar approach helped me write the chapter in the first place.

Sometimes, teaching students self-management can solve a problem for teachers and provide fringe benefits as well. For example, the coaches of a competitive swim team with members ages 9 to 16 were having difficulty persuading swimmers to maintain high work rates. Then the coaches drew up four charts indicating the training program to be followed by each member and posted the charts near the pool. The swimmers were given the responsibility of recording both their numbers of laps and their completion of each training unit. Because the recording was public, swimmers could see their own and their teammates' progress and keep accurate track of the work units completed. Work output increased by 27%. The coaches also liked the system because swimmers could begin to work immediately without waiting for instructions (McKenzie & Rushall, 1974).

Self-reinforcement Controlling your own reinforcers.

GUIDELINES — FAMILY AND COMMUNITY PARTNERSHIPS

Student Self-Management

Introduce the system to parents and students in a positive way.
Examples

1. Invite family participation and stress possible benefits to all family members.
2. Consider starting the program just with volunteers.
3. Describe how you use self-management programs yourself.

Help families and students establish reachable goals.
Examples

1. Have examples of possible self-management goals for students such as starting homework early in the evening, or keeping track of books read.
2. Show families how to post goals and keep track of progress. Encourage everyone in the family to work on a goal.

Give families ways to record and evaluate their child's progress (or their own).
Examples

1. Divide the work into easily measured steps.
2. Provide models of good work where judgments are more difficult, such as in creative writing.

3. Give families a record form or checklist to keep track of progress.

Encourage families to check the accuracy of student records from time to time, and help their children to develop forms of self-reinforcement.
Examples

1. Have many checkups when students are first learning, and fewer later.
2. Have siblings check one another's records.
3. Where appropriate, test the skills that students are supposed to be developing at home and reward students whose self-evaluations match their test performances.
4. Have students brainstorm ideas with their families for rewarding themselves for jobs well done.

For more about self-management, see:
http://www.selfmanagementforkids.org/

At times, families can be enlisted to help their children develop self-management abilities. Working together, teachers and parents can focus on a few goals and, at the same time, support the growing independence of the students. The *Family and Community Partnerships Guidelines* give some ideas.

CHALLENGES, CAUTIONS, AND CRITICISMS

In this section we look at some of the challenges to earlier behavioral approaches to learning as well as some important criticisms and cautions.

Beyond Behaviorism: Bandura's Challenge

Over 35 years ago, Albert Bandura (1977) noted that the traditional behavioral view of learning had many limitations. Sometimes Bandura has been characterized as a neo-behaviorist, but he has corrected that label:

> At the time of my graduate training, the entire field of psychology was behaviorally oriented with an almost exclusive focus on the phenomenon of learning. But I never really fit the behavioral orthodoxy. At the time virtually all of the theorizing and research centered on learning through the effects of reinforcing outcomes. In my first major program of research, I argued against the primacy of conditioning in favor of observational learning, in which people neither emit responses nor receive reinforcements during the process of learning. (quoted in Pajares, 2008, p. 1)

In his early work, called **social learning theory**, Bandura pointed out two key distinctions between enactive and observational learning and between learning and performance.

Social learning theory Theory that emphasizes learning through observation of others.

OBSERVATIONAL LEARNING Observational theories of learning consider the importance of learning by doing and learning by observing others.

ENACTIVE AND OBSERVATIONAL LEARNING. Bandura distinguished between enactive and vicarious or observational learning. **Enactive learning** is learning by doing and experiencing the consequences of your actions. This may sound like operant conditioning all over again, but it is not, and the difference has to do with the role of consequences. Proponents of operant conditioning believe that consequences strengthen or weaken behavior. In enactive learning, however, consequences are seen as providing information. Bandura emphasized reinforcement does not "stamp in" responses, but instead instills expectations about outcomes—what will happen if I do that behavior? He explained this position in his early book, *Social Learning Theory* (1977). In other words, our interpretations of the consequences create expectations, influence motivation, and shape beliefs (Schunk, 2012).

Vicarious learning is learning by observing others, so it often is called **observational learning**. People and animals can learn merely by observing another person or animal learn, and this fact challenges the behaviorist idea that cognitive factors are unnecessary in an explanation of learning. If people can learn by watching, they must be focusing their attention, constructing images, remembering, analyzing, and making decisions that affect learning. Thus, much is going on mentally before performance and reinforcement can even take place. Cognitive apprenticeships, discussed in Chapter 10, are examples of vicarious learning—learning by observing others.

LEARNING AND PERFORMANCE. To explain some limitations of the behavioral model, Bandura also distinguished between the acquisition of knowledge (learning) and the observable performance based on that knowledge (behavior). In other words, Bandura suggested that we all may know more than we show. An example is found in one of Bandura's early studies (1965). Preschool children saw a film of a model kicking and punching an inflatable "Bobo" doll. One group saw the model rewarded for the aggression, another group saw the model punished, and a third group observed no consequences. When they were moved to a room with the Bobo doll, the children who had seen the punching and kicking reinforced on the film were the most aggressive toward the doll. Those who had seen the attacks punished were the least aggressive. But when the children were promised rewards for imitating the model's aggression, all of them demonstrated that they had learned the behavior.

Thus, incentives can affect performance. Even though learning may have occurred, it may not be demonstrated until the situation is appropriate or there are incentives to perform. This might explain why some students don't perform "bad behaviors" such as swearing or smoking that they all see modeled by adults, peers, and the media. Personal consequences may discourage them from performing the behaviors. In other examples, children may have learned how to write the alphabet, but perform badly because their fine motor coordination is limited, or they may have learned how to simplify fractions, but perform badly on a test because they are anxious. In these cases, their performance is not an indication of their learning.

Bandura provided an alternative to the behavioral theories of the time. His work continued as he developed *social cognitive theory*—one of the most influential theories of learning and motivation in educational psychology today. We will devote Chapter 11 to a closer look at social cognitive theory.

Enactive learning Learning by doing and experiencing the consequences of your actions.

Observational learning Learning by observation and imitation of others—vicarious learning.

Criticisms of Behavioral Methods

This chapter gave you an overview of several strategies for changing classroom behavior. However, you should be aware that these strategies are tools that can be used either responsibly or irresponsibly. What, then, are some issues you should keep in mind?

POINT/COUNTERPOINT: Should Students Be Rewarded for Learning?

For years, educators and psychologists have debated whether students should be rewarded for schoolwork and academic accomplishments. In the early 1990s, Paul Chance and Alfie Kohn exchanged opinions in several issues of *Phi Delta Kappan* (March 1991; November 1992; June 1993). Then, Judy Cameron and W. David Pierce (1996) published an article on reinforcement in the *Review of Educational Research* that precipitated extensive criticisms and rebuttals in the same journal from Mark Lepper, Mark Keavney, Michael Drake, Alfie Kohn, Richard Ryan, and Edward Deci (Kohn, 1996; Lepper, Keavney, & Drake, 1996; Ryan & Deci, 1996). Many of the same people exchanged opinions in the November 1999 issue of *Psychological Bulletin* (Deci, Koestner, & Ryan, 1999; Eisenberg, Pierce, & Cameron, J., 1999). What are the arguments?

POINT

▶ **Students are punished by rewards.** Alfie Kohn (1993) argues, "Applied behaviorism, which amounts to saying, 'do this and you'll get that,' is essentially a technique for controlling people. In the classroom it is a way of doing things to children rather than working *with* them" (p. 784). He contends that rewards are ineffective because when the praise and prizes stop, the behaviors stop too. After analyzing 128 studies of extrinsic rewards, Edward Deci, Richard Koestner, and Richard Ryan (1999) concluded that "tangible rewards tend to have a substantial effect on intrinsic motivation, with the limiting conditions we have specified. Even when tangible rewards are offered as indicators of good performance, they typically decrease intrinsic motivation for interesting activities" (pp. 658–659).

The problem with rewards does not stop here. According to Kohn, rewarding students for learning actually makes them less interested in the material:

All of this means that getting children to think about learning as a way to receive a sticker, a gold star, or a grade—or even worse, to get money or a toy for a grade, which amounts to an extrinsic motivator for an extrinsic motivator—is likely to turn learning from an end into a means. Learning becomes something that must be gotten through in order to receive the reward. Take the depressingly pervasive program by which children receive certificates for pizzas when they have read a certain number of books. John Nicholls of the University of Illinois comments, only half in jest, that the likely consequence of this program is "a lot of fat kids who don't like to read." (p. 785)

Source: From "Sticking Up for Rewards," by P. Chance, June 1993, Phi Delta Kappan, pp. 787–790. Copyright © 1993 by Phi Delta Kappan. Reprinted with permission of Phi Delta Kappan and the author. From "Rewards versus Learning: A Response to Paul Chance," by A. Kohn, June 1993, Phi Delta Kappan, pp. 783 and 785. Copyright © 1993 by Alfie Kohn. Reprinted from Phi Delta Kappan with the author's permission.

COUNTERPOINT

▶ **Learning should be rewarding.** According to Paul Chance (1993):

Behavioral psychologists in particular emphasize that we learn by acting on our environment. As B. F. Skinner put it: "[People] act on the world, and change it, and are changed in turn by the consequences of their actions." Skinner, unlike Kohn, understood that people learn best in a responsive environment. Teachers who praise or otherwise reward student performance provide such an environment. . . . If it is immoral to let students know they have answered questions correctly, to pat students on the back for a good effort, to show joy at a student's understanding of a concept, or to recognize the achievement of a goal by providing a gold star or a certificate— if this is immoral, then count me a sinner. (p. 788)

Do rewards undermine interest? In their review of research, Cameron and Pierce (1994) concluded, "When tangible rewards (e.g., gold star, money) are offered contingent on performance on a task [not just on participation] or are delivered unexpectedly, intrinsic motivation is maintained" (p. 49). In a later review of research, Eisenberg, Pierce, and Cameron (1999) added "Reward procedures requiring specific high task performance convey a task's personal or social significance, increasing intrinsic motivation" (p. 677). Even psychologists such as Edward Deci and Mark Lepper who suggest that rewards might undermine intrinsic motivation agree that rewards can also be used positively. When rewards provide students with information about their growing mastery of a subject or when the rewards show appreciation for a job well done, then the rewards bolster confidence and make the task more interesting to the students, especially students who lacked ability or interest in the task initially. Nothing succeeds like success. As Chance points out, if students master reading or mathematics with the support of rewards, they will not forget what they have learned when the praise stops. Would they have learned without the rewards? Some would, but some might not. Would you continue working for a company that didn't pay you, even though you liked the work? Will freelance writer Alfie Kohn, for that matter, lose interest in writing because he gets paid fees and royalties?

STOP & THINK During your job interview, the principal asks, "A teacher last year got in trouble for bribing his students with homework exemptions to get them to behave in class. What do you think about using rewards and punishments in teaching?" What will you say? •

While you think about your answer to this question, look at the *Point/Counterpoint* on "Should Students Be Rewarded for Learning?" to see two different perspectives. Properly used, the strategies in this chapter can be effective tools to help students learn academically and grow in self-sufficiency. Effective tools, however, do not automatically produce excellent work, and behavioral strategies are often implemented haphazardly, inconsistently, incorrectly, or superficially (Landrum & Kauffman, 2006). The indiscriminate use of even the best tools can lead to difficulties.

Some psychologists fear that rewarding students for all learning will cause them to lose interest in learning for its own sake (Deci, 1975; Deci & Ryan, 1985; Kohn, 1993, 1996b; Lepper & Greene, 1978; Lepper, Keavney, & Drake, 1996; Ryan & Deci, 1996). Studies have suggested that using reward programs with students who are already interested in the subject matter may, in fact, cause students to be less interested in the subject when the reward program ends, as you saw in the *Point/Counterpoint*. In addition, there is some evidence that praising students for being intelligent when they succeed can undermine their motivation if they do not perform as well the next time. After they fail, students who had been praised for being smart may be less persistent and enjoy the task less compared to students who had been praised earlier for working hard (Mueller & Dweck, 1998).

Just as you must take into account the effects of a reward system on the individual, you must also consider its impact on other students. Using a reward program or giving one student increased attention may have a detrimental effect on the other students in the classroom. Is it possible that other students will learn to be "bad" in order to be included in the reward program? Most of the evidence on this question suggests that using individual adaptations such as reward programs does not have any adverse effects on students who are not participating if the teacher believes in the program and explains the reasons for using it to the nonparticipating students. After interviewing 98 students in grades 1 through 6, Cindy Fulk and Paula Smith (1995) concluded, "Teachers may be more concerned about equal treatment of students than students are" (p. 416). If the conduct of some students does seem to deteriorate when their peers are involved in special programs, many of the same procedures discussed in this chapter should help them return to previous levels of appropriate behavior (Chance, 1992, 1993).

"Hey wait a minute! You're cleaning erasers as a punishment? I'm cleaning them as a reward!"

© 1991 Tony Saltzmann. Reprinted by permission.

Ethical Issues

The ethical questions related to the use of the strategies described in this chapter are similar to those raised by any process that seeks to influence people. What are the goals? How do these goals fit with those of the school as a whole? What effect will a strategy have on the individuals involved? Is too much control being given to the teacher, or to a majority?

GOALS.   The strategies described in this chapter could be applied exclusively to teaching students to sit still, raise their hands before speaking, and remain silent at all other times (Winett & Winkler, 1972). This certainly would be an unethical use of the techniques. It is true that a teacher may need to establish some organization and order, but stopping with improvements in conduct will not ensure academic learning. On the other hand, in some situations, reinforcing academic skills may lead to improvements in conduct. Whenever possible, emphasis should be placed on academic learning. Academic improvements generalize to other situations more successfully than do changes in classroom conduct.

STRATEGIES.   Punishment can have negative side effects: It can serve as a model for aggressive responses, and it can encourage negative emotional reactions. Punishment is unnecessary and even unethical when positive approaches, which have fewer potential dangers, might work as well. When simpler, less-restrictive procedures fail, then more complicated procedures should be tried.

A second consideration in the selection of a strategy is the impact of the strategy on the individual student. For example, some teachers arrange for students to be rewarded at home with a gift or special activities based on good work in school. But if a student has a history of being severely punished at home for bad reports from school, a home-based reinforcement program might be very harmful to that student. Reports of unsatisfactory progress at school could lead to increased abuse at home.

Behavioral Approaches: Lessons for Teachers

There is great diversity in the learning histories of students. Every person in your class will come to you with different fears and anxieties. Some students may be terrified of speaking in public or of failing at competitive sports. Others will be anxious around various animals. Different activities or objects will serve as reinforcers for some students, but not others. Some students will work for the promise of good grades—others could care less. All of your students will have learned different behaviors in their homes, neighborhoods, churches, or communities.

The research and theories presented in this chapter should help you understand how the learning histories of your students might have taught them to respond automatically to tests with sweaty palms and racing hearts—possible classical conditioning at work. Their learning histories might have included being reinforced for persistence, or for whining—operant conditioning at work. The chance to work in a group may be a reinforcer for some students and a punisher for others. Remember, what works for one student may not be right for another. And students can get "too much of a good thing"; reinforcers can lose their potency if they are overused.

Even though your students will have many different learning histories, there are some convergences—principles that apply to all people:

1. No one eagerly repeats behaviors that have been punished or ignored. Without some sense of progress, it is difficult to persist.
2. When actions lead to consequences that are positive for the person involved, those actions are likely to be repeated.
3. Teachers often fail to use reinforcement to recognize appropriate behavior; they respond instead to inappropriate behaviors, sometimes providing reinforcing attention in the process.
4. To be effective, praise must be a sincere recognition of a real accomplishment.
5. Whatever their current level of functioning, students can learn to be more self-managing.

▼ SUMMARY

Understanding Learning (pp. 246–248)

What is learning? Although theorists disagree about the definition of learning, most would agree that learning occurs when experience causes a change in a person's knowledge or behavior. Changes simply caused by maturation, illness, fatigue, or hunger are excluded from a general definition of learning. Behavioral theorists emphasize the role of environmental stimuli in learning and focus on behavior—observable responses. Behavioral learning processes include contiguity learning, classical conditioning, operant conditioning, and observational learning.

Early Explanations of Learning: Contiguity and Classical Conditioning (pp. 248–250)

How does a neutral stimulus become a conditioned stimulus? In classical conditioning, which was discovered by Pavlov, a previously neutral stimulus is repeatedly paired with a stimulus that evokes an emotional or physiological response. Later, the previously neutral stimulus alone evokes the response—that is, the neutral stimulus is conditioned to bring forth a conditioned response. The neutral stimulus has become a conditioned stimulus.

What are some everyday examples of classical conditioning? Here are a few; add your own: Salivating when you smell your favorite foods, tension when you hear a dentist's drill, nervousness when you step on stage.

Operant Conditioning: Trying New Responses (pp. 250–256)

What defines a consequence as a reinforcer? As a punisher? According to Skinner's concept of operant conditioning, people learn through the effects of their deliberate responses. For an individual, the effects of consequences following an action may serve as either reinforcers or punishers. A consequence is defined as a reinforcer if it strengthens or maintains the response that brought it about, but as a punishment if it decreases or suppresses the response that brought it about.

Negative reinforcement is often confused with punishment. How are they different? The process of reinforcement (positive or negative) always involves strengthening behavior. The teacher strengthens (reinforces) desired behaviors by removing something aversive as soon as the desired behaviors occur. Because the consequence involves removing or "subtracting" a stimulus, the reinforcement is negative. Punishment, on the other hand, involves decreasing or suppressing behavior. A behavior followed by a "punisher" is less likely to be repeated in similar situations in the future.

How can you encourage persistence in a behavior? Ratio schedules (based on the number of responses) encourage higher rates of response, and variable schedules (based on varying numbers of responses or varying time intervals) encourage persistence of responses.

What is the difference between a cue and a prompt? A cue is an antecedent stimulus just before a particular behavior is to take place. A prompt is an additional cue following the first cue. Make sure the environmental stimulus that you want to become a cue occurs immediately before the prompt you are using, so students will learn to respond to the cue and not rely only on the prompt. Then, fade the prompt as soon as possible so students do not become dependent on it.

Applied Behavior Analysis (pp. 256–262)

What are the steps in applied behavior analysis? The steps are: (1) Clearly specify the behavior to be changed and note the current level. (2) Plan a specific intervention using antecedents, consequences, or both. (3) Keep track of the results, and modify the plan if necessary.

How can the Premack principle help you identify reinforcers? The Premack principle states that a high-frequency behavior (a preferred activity) can be an effective reinforcer for a low-frequency behavior (a less-preferred activity). The best way to determine appropriate reinforcers for your students may be to watch what they do in their free time. For most students, talking, moving around the room, sitting near a friend, being exempt from assignments or tests, computer time, or playing games are preferred activities.

When is shaping an appropriate approach? Shaping helps students develop new responses a little at a time, so it is useful for building complex skills, working toward difficult goals, and increasing persistence, endurance, accuracy, or speed. Because shaping is a time-consuming process, however, it should not be used if success can be attained through simpler methods such as cueing.

What are some cautions in using punishment? Punishment in and of itself does not lead to any positive behavior or compassion for others and it may interfere with developing caring relationships with students. Thus, whenever you consider the use of punishment, you should make it part of a two-pronged attack. First, carry out the punishment and suppress the undesirable behavior. Second, make clear what the student should be doing instead and provide reinforcement for those desirable actions. Thus, while the problem behaviors are being suppressed, positive alternative responses are being strengthened.

Putting it All Together: Behavioral Approaches to Teaching and Management (pp. 262–271)

Describe the managerial strategies of group consequences, contingency contracts, and token programs. Using group consequences involves basing reinforcement for the whole class on the behavior of the whole class. In a contingency contract program, the teacher draws up an individual contract with each student, describing exactly what the student must do to earn a particular privilege or reward. In token programs, students earn tokens (points, checks, holes punched in a card, chips, etc.) for both academic work and positive classroom behavior. Periodically, the students exchange the tokens they have earned for some desired reward. A teacher must use these programs with caution, emphasizing learning and not just "good" behavior.

How can functional behavioral assessment and positive behavior supports be used to improve student behaviors? In doing a functional behavioral assessment, a teacher studies the antecedents and consequences of problem behaviors to determine the reason or function of the behavior. Then, positive behavior supports are designed to replace problem behaviors with new actions that serve the same purpose for the student, but do not have the same problems.

What are the steps in self-management? Students can apply behavior analysis on their own to manage their own behavior. Teachers can encourage the development of self-management skills by allowing students to participate in setting goals, keeping track of progress, evaluating accomplishments, and selecting and giving their own reinforcers.

Challenges, Cautions, and Criticisms (pp. 271–275)

What was Bandura's challenge to behavioral learning? Bandura believed that the traditional behavioral view of learning had many limitations. Even though he was educated during a time when behavioral learning was dominant, he never really fit the behavioral orthodoxy. He argued in favor of observational learning, in which people neither emit responses nor receive reinforcements during the process of learning.

Distinguish between enactive and vicarious (observational) learning. Enactive learning is learning by doing and experiencing the consequences of your actions. Vicarious (observational) learning is learning by observing, which challenges the behaviorist idea that cognitive factors are unnecessary in an explanation of learning. Much is going on mentally before performance and reinforcement can even take place. In behavioral views, reinforcement and punishment directly affect behavior. In social learning theory, seeing another person, a model, reinforced or punished can have similar effects on the observer's behavior. Social cognitive theory expanded social learning theory to include cognitive factors such as beliefs, expectations, and perceptions of self.

Distinguish between learning and performance. Social learning theory recognized the differences between learning and performance—in other words, we all may know more than we show. You can learn something, but not perform it until the situation and incentives are right. Even though learning may have occurred, it may not be demonstrated until the situation is appropriate or there are incentives to perform.

What are the main criticisms of behavioral approaches? The misuse or abuse of behavioral learning methods is unethical. Critics of behavioral methods also point out the danger that reinforcement could decrease interest in learning by overemphasizing rewards and could have a negative impact on other students. Teachers can use behavioral learning principles appropriately and ethically.

▼ KEY TERMS

Antecedents (250)
Applied behavior analysis (256)
Aversive (251)
Behavior modification (256)

Behavioral learning theories (246)
Classical conditioning (248)
Conditioned response (CR) (249)
Conditioned stimulus (CS) (249)

Consequences (250)
Contiguity (248)
Contingency contract (264)
Continuous reinforcement schedule (252)

▼ CONNECT AND EXTEND TO LICENSURE

MULTIPLE-CHOICE QUESTIONS

1. After a long spring time with many bee stings, several of the kindergartners at Teddy Bear Cave Kindergarten refused to go outside for activities on the playground. Once an exterminator found and removed the nest, Miss Cochran announced the bees were gone. Later that day when Miss Cochran lined up the children to go to the playground, several of the students burst into tears and begged to not go. Which of the following would be an explanation for this event?

    A. Operant conditioning
    B. Successive approximations
    C. Classical conditioning
    D. Response cost

2. Which one of the following behavioral principles does NOT apply to all people?

    A. No one eagerly repeats behaviors that have been punished or ignored. Without some sense of progress, it is difficult to persist.
    B. When actions lead to consequences that are positive for the person involved, those actions are likely to be repeated.
    C. To be effective, praise must be general in nature.
    D. Teachers often fail to use reinforcement to recognize appropriate behavior; they respond instead to inappropriate behaviors, sometimes providing reinforcing attention in the process.

3. Several of the students in Mr. Camp's class had difficulty behaving in line. He thought he had managed to get them under control with reinforcement. He had been giving them a token every time they lined up in an orderly fashion. While it initially worked like magic, now the students were falling back into their old patterns. What type of reinforcement schedule should Mr. Camp have used after his students had mastered lining up in an orderly fashion?

    A. Shaping
    B. Intermittent
    C. Continuous
    D. Applied behavior analysis

4. Applied behavior analysis requires several steps for a behavior to be changed. Which of the following steps is not one of the required?

    A. Clear specification of the behavior to be changed and careful measurement of the behavior
    B. Analysis of the antecedents and reinforcers that might be maintaining inappropriate or undesirable behavior
    C. Interventions based on behavioral principles to change the behavior
    D. Concrete reinforcement for good behavior

CONSTRUCTED-RESPONSE QUESTIONS

Case

Haley Williams sat in Dr. Karr's office, once again, having to explain why she could not get along with her teacher. "I don't know why she picks on me in front of the class. All I know is that when she starts to yell at me, I lose my temper. I'm not even sure what I am supposed to do! It seems like *everything* I do is wrong according to Miss Kemp. I know we have talked about getting along and how that would be better for everyone, but Dr. Karr, I just don't like her and she does not like me. Can't I be switched to another class?

1. Is Miss Kemp doing anything that actually contributes to Haley's poor behavior? Explain your answer.

2. What could one assume about Miss Kemp's reprimands if Haley's behavior has not decreased?

─── MyEducationLab™ ───

Go to Chapter 7 of the Book Specific Resources in MyEducationLab and click on "Connect and Extend to Licensure" to answer these questions. Compare your responses with the feedback provided.

▼ WHAT WOULD THEY DO?

TEACHERS' CASEBOOK: Sick of Class

Here is how some expert teachers responded to the situation described at the beginning of the chapter about the disruptive student.

PAULA COLEMERE • Special Education Teacher—English, History
McClintock High School, Tempe, AZ

If this is a chronic issue, I would conduct a Functional Behavioral Analysis (FBA) and develop a Behavior Intervention Plan (BIP) to address the student's needs. The real problem here is the student avoiding a task that he does not want to participate in. I would work with this student to find a way to make the task less daunting and try to ease his fears. If the student is just nervous about speaking in front of class, as many students are, maybe he can present in front of a smaller group. This way, the student is still working on the skill. I have had students who are terrified to read in class practice a small part of a passage with me to build confidence, and then I call on them in class to read in front of peers. If just escaping class is the function of the behavior, I would look to find a replacement for seeing the nurse. This would be tied to completing the task first. For example, "After you answer your question, you can deliver this to the office." This offers the student the movement as a reward for completing the task.

LINDA SPARKS • 1st Grade
John F. Kennedy School, Billerica MA

Every year, we always have a few "frequent flyers" to the nurse. Some just need to take a walk, while others try to remove themselves from an uncomfortable situation in the class where they think they may be made fun of, talked about, or put down. I always let them go in the beginning until the nurse or I have time to just observe and ask different questions. I find that when a child is away from the situation, he is more comfortable sharing what is going on. Sometimes it is as simple as he didn't complete an assignment, he is afraid he will make a mistake, or maybe something is happening at home. I had one student who tried to make himself sick daily. It was a new behavior and we were trying to figure out what was going on. We called home and the parents assured us nothing had changed. We eventually found out that the parents were selling their home and the student overheard them talking on the phone about moving and looking at houses. After days of trying to put this together, he finally shared with me that he was afraid to be at school because he thought his mommy and daddy were going to move while he was at school and no one would be home when he got there. This is another instance where time is needed, trust needs to be earned, and compassion needs to be present.

JENNIFER L. MATZ • 6th Grade
Williams Valley Elementary, Tower City, PA

This type of behavior in students is usually attention seeking or avoidance of a situation. First, speak to the student privately. Tell him he seems to ask to see the nurse frequently. This causes him to miss valuable instruction time. Is there something about class that he doesn't like? When he opens up, explain that many adults say their biggest fear in life is public speaking. This shows him he is not alone. Explain to him that unfortunately in life, there will be times you will have to do it. Share with him from your experience. Explain that some students have worked out a "signal" that he can use when he knows the answer and is ready to speak. Work this out between the two of you so no one else would know. It could be something as simple as tugging on your earlobe, touching the tip of your nose, etc. The signal should be something that is not obvious to anyone but you and the student. Make a deal with him that at first he must volunteer once a day. As he progresses, gradually increase how many times a day he should be volunteering.

JENNIFER PINCOSKI • Learning Resource Teacher: K–12
Lee County School District, Fort Myers, FL

The student's apparent anxiety over public speaking needs to be acknowledged. Punishing him or forcing him to participate will only worsen the situation. Steps can be taken to help the student become more comfortable with oral presentations, but in the meantime, alternate activities should be provided for him to demonstrate his knowledge.

Several things can be done to ease the student's anxiety. The teacher can meet with him beforehand to go over the assignment and let him practice without an audience. Students can then be divided into pairs so they only have to present to one other person; the first time, he can even be permitted to select his own partner (discussed privately, so he does not feel embarrassed). The pairs can gradually be increased to groups of 3, 4, etc. Pairs and groups can be rotated so the student presents to all of his classmates, a few at a time. Students can also be paired up to work on the assignment and present it together.

The process of increasing this student's confidence with oral presentations will take time; patience and positive reinforcement are critical. Ultimately, it is most important to make sure he has adequate means of demonstrating his learning and being assessed on content objectives.

JESSICA N. MAHTABAN • 8th Grade Math
Woodrow Wilson Middle School, Clifton, NJ

I would first to speak to the student alone and discuss my concerns. Together we would try to find a way for him to come up with various solutions to facing his fear. Maybe the student could start by just presenting to me and gradually we could add more people to the group until he is comfortable with the whole class. Or the student could tape record his presentation and play it to the class as part of the group presentation. If it were a severe case of a phobia, I would involve the school counselor, administration, school psychiatrist, the student, and, of course, his parents. Together we could address the child's needs. I don't feel rewards or punishment would help this situation. Students need to learn how to handle their problems on their own without always having a reward once the task is accomplished. Nor is it fair to feel the pressure of being punished if the task is not completed. The goal is to have all students be intrinsically motivated; in turn, this will help them to be prepared for the real world.

LAUREN ROLLINS • 1st Grade Teacher
Boulevard Elementary School, Shaker Heights, OH

This student is clearly uncomfortable speaking in class. Punishing him for this would be a huge mistake! Instead, I would have an individual conference with him. During our meeting, I would tell him that I have noticed his frequent trips to the nurse when public speaking situations occur, and I would like to help him to overcome his fear. I would start by assuring him that his thoughts are important to me and offering him the opportunity to respond by writing his answers down, rather than sharing them aloud. I would also offer him the opportunity to give his oral presentations to me privately. Then, I would slowly raise my expectations for his class participation—asking him to contribute one response aloud each week, then twice, etc. I would praise him and reward him for this in a way that would be motivating and meaningful to him. I would continue to add to my expectations until he felt comfortable being a participant in class discussions. As for oral presentations, as he became comfortable presenting to me one on one, I would ask him to invite one or two friends to his presentations and then a small group. My goal would be for him to slowly feel more and more comfortable presenting to a group of his choice. Eventually, my expectations for him would be the same as my expectations for the rest of his peers.

SARA VINCENT • Special Education
Langley High School, McLean, VA

The student is exhibiting task avoidance behavior. In order to extinguish the behavior of the student, modifications should first be made to the assignment. The student should have the choice to either perform the oral assignments in front of the teacher only or record his work in a location that is comfortable to him. Over time, the student can be introduced to a slightly larger group and given rewards when he completes the work. The rewards can slowly be faded until the student is comfortable with speaking in front of the class.

PAUL DRAGIN • ESL grades 9–12
Columbus East High School, Columbus OH

After speaking with the nurse and determining that there is no merit to the repeated trips, I would speak with the student and try to get him to open up about the possible fear that the classroom activity is provoking. Assuming that it is the fear of public speaking, I would propose some strategies to slowly integrate him into the oral activities by modifying the requirements and affirming his attempts. Fear of public speaking is common, and I would acknowledge this fact with all of the students and communicate why it is so important to practice this skill in the classroom setting.

MyEducationLab™

Go to Topic 8, Behaviorist Perspectives, in the MyEducationLab (www.myeducationlab.com) for *Educational Psychology*, where you can:

- Find learning outcomes for Behaviorist Perspectives along with the national standards that connect to these outcomes.
- Complete Assignments and Activities that can help you more deeply understand the chapter content.
- Apply and practice your understanding of the core teaching skills identified in the chapter with the Building Teaching Skills and Dispositions learning units.
- Examine challenging situations and cases presented in the IRIS Center Resources.
- Access video clips of CCSSO National Teachers of the Year award winners responding to the question, "Why Do I Teach?" in the Teacher Talk section.
- Check your comprehension on the content covered in the chapter with the Study Plan. Here you will be able to take a chapter quiz, receive feedback on your answers, and then access Review, Practice, and Enrichment activities to enhance your understanding of chapter content.
- Find additional Teachers' Casebook scenarios and responses to them from practicing teachers.
- Use the Online Lesson Plan Builder to practice lesson planning and integrating national and state standards into your planning. Go to Chapter 6 of the Book Specific Resources in MyEducationLab and click on "Connect and Extend to Licensure" to answer these questions. Compare your responses with the feedback provided.

chapter eight
COGNITIVE VIEWS OF LEARNING

▶ **TEACHERS' CASEBOOK:** Remembering the Basics

You have just graded the first large unit test of the year. About two-thirds of the students seem to have mastered the material and understood the key ideas. The other third, however, seems to be totally lost. Somehow they failed to remember the basic vocabulary and facts—the foundation they must know before they can move on to the more complicated work in the next unit. These students often have trouble remembering key information from one day or week to the next.

CRITICAL THINKING

- How could you help these students retain and retrieve the necessary information?
- What are your options besides a rote memory approach?
- How would you use what the students already know to help them learn in better, more meaningful ways?
- How will these issues affect the grade levels you will teach?

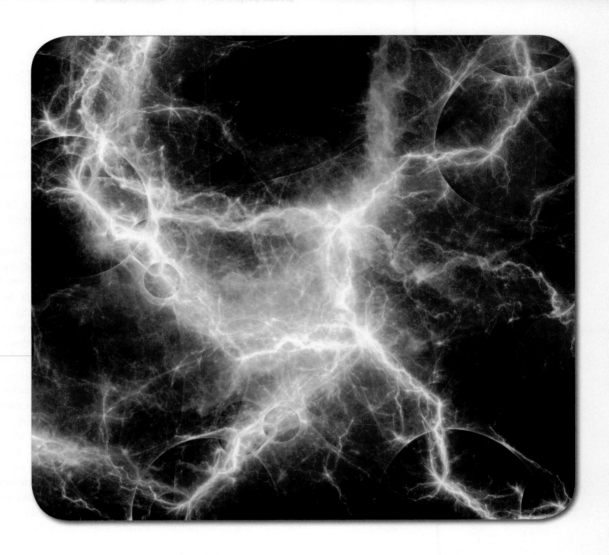

OVERVIEW AND OBJECTIVES

We turn from behavioral theories of learning to the cognitive perspective in this chapter. This means a shift from "viewing the learners and their behaviors as products of incoming environmental stimuli" to seeing the learners as "sources of plans, intentions, goals, ideas, memories, and emotions actively used to attend to, select, and construct meaning from stimuli and knowledge from experience" (Wittrock, 1982, pp. 1–2). We will begin with a discussion of the general cognitive approach to learning and memory and the importance of knowledge in learning. To understand memory, we will consider early information processing models of memory, along with the recent improvements on those models suggested by findings in the interdisciplinary fields of cognitive science. These new models point to key processes of working memory, cognitive load, and knowledge. Then, we turn to ideas about how teachers can help their students become more knowledgeable. By the time you have completed this chapter, you should be able to:

Objective 8.1: Differentiate between behavioral and cognitive views of learning.

Objective 8.2: Explain early information processing models of memory and recent cognitive science models, including working memory and cognitive load theory.

Objective 8.3: Discuss the role of different kinds of knowledge in learning and remembering.

Objective 8.4: Describe the processes involved in storing and retrieving different types of information from long-term memory.

Objective 8.5: Identify some developmental and individual differences in memory.

Objective 8.6: Describe processes and strategies involved in becoming knowledgeable.

ELEMENTS OF THE COGNITIVE PERSPECTIVE

The cognitive perspective is both the oldest and one of the youngest members of the psychological community. It is old because discussions of the nature of knowledge, the value of reason, and the contents of the mind date back at least to the ancient Greek philosophers (Gluck, Mercado, & Myers, 2008). From the late 1800s until several decades ago, however, cognitive studies fell from favor and behaviorism thrived. Today, there is renewed interest in learning, thinking, and problem solving. The focus is the scientific study of memory and cognition—broadly defined as "the mental events and knowledge we use when we recognize an object, remember a name, have an idea, understand a sentence, or solve a problem" (Ashcraft & Radvansky, 2010, p. 2). The emphasis is on everyday thinking, even though the study of abnormal thinking (as in schizophrenia) can help us understand cognition better at times. The **cognitive view of learning** can be described as a generally agreed-upon philosophical orientation. Most importantly, cognitive psychologists assume that mental processes exist, that they can be studied scientifically, and that humans are active information processors.

In the past few years, the study of memory and cognition has become interdisciplinary and often is called **cognitive science**—the study of thinking, language, and, increasingly, the brain. Cognitive science views cognition as the operation of a very complex but coordinated system of multiple memory components interacting rapidly and simultaneously (Ashcraft & Radvansky, 2010). In Chapter 10 we will look more closely at cognitive science, or as it is sometimes called even more broadly, *the learning sciences*.

Comparing Cognitive and Behavioral Views

The cognitive and behavioral views differ in their assumptions about what is learned. According to the cognitive view, knowledge and strategies are learned, then changes in knowledge and strategies make changes in behavior possible. According to the behavioral view, the new behaviors themselves are learned. Both behavioral and cognitive theorists believe reinforcement is important in learning, but for different reasons. The strict behaviorist maintains that reinforcement strengthens responses; cognitive theorists perceive reinforcement as a source of information about what is likely to happen if behaviors are repeated or changed.

VIEWS OF LEARNING. In the cognitive view, learning is extending and transforming the understanding we already have, not simply writing associations on the blank slates of our brains (Greeno, Collins, & Resnick, 1996). Instead of being passively influenced by environmental events, people actively choose, practice, pay attention, ignore, reflect, and make many other decisions as they pursue goals. Older cognitive views emphasized the acquisition of knowledge, but newer approaches stress its construction (Anderson, Reder, & Simon, 1996; Mayer, 2011).

GOALS. The goal of behavioral researchers is to identify a few general laws of learning that apply to all higher organisms—including humans, regardless of age, intelligence, or other individual differences. Cognitive psychologists, on the other hand, study a wide range of learning situations. Because of their focus on individual and developmental differences in cognition, they have not been as concerned with general laws of learning. This is one of the reasons that there is no single cognitive model or theory of learning that represents the entire field.

Cognitive view of learning A general approach that views learning as an active mental process of acquiring, remembering, and using knowledge.

Cognitive science The interdisciplinary study of thinking, language, intelligence, knowledge creation, and the brain.

282

The Brain and Cognitive Learning

The brain continues to change throughout life, and learning affects those changes. One study found that part of the brain hippocampus is larger in taxi drivers than in other car drivers, and this increased size is related to the length of time the person has been driving a taxi. The explanation is that part of the brain grew larger because it was used more in navigating around the city (Maguire et al., 2000). In another study, when people learned to read musical notations, they developed an automatic response to just looking at a sheet of music—they read it without being told to and their motor cortex prepared to play the notes (Stewart, Henson, Kampe, Walsh, Turner, & Firth, 2003). Observing and visualizing also support learning because the brain automatically responds. For example, when observing someone perform an action, the area of the observer's brain that would be involved in the action is activated just by watching—the brain rehearses the action it sees another person perform. These areas of the brain that fire both during perception of an action and when performing the action have been called *mirror neurons* in monkeys (where they were first discovered) and **mirror systems** in humans because the activated areas in humans contain millions of neurons (Ehnrenfeld, 2011; Rizzolatti, Fadiga, Gallese, & Fogassi, 1996). When you actually look at an object, a certain area of the brain is activated. Just mentally visualizing the object activates at least two-thirds of the same area of the brain (Ganis, Thompson, & Kosslyn, 2004).

COGNITIVE VIEWS These students are literally building their understanding as they try to construct models and solve problems.

Clearly the brain is involved whenever learning takes place. As Blakemore and Frith (2005) note in their book on lessons for education from research in neuroscience: "We start with the idea that the brain has evolved to educate and be educated, often instinctively and effortlessly" (p. 459). The brain shapes and is shaped by cognitive processing activities. Even at the neural level, new synapses are formed a few minutes after a child is unsuccessful at processing information. So unsuccessful processing triggers development, too (Siegler, 2004).

Because of the continuing development of the brain, particularly as the prefrontal cortex matures, children become more able to integrate past and present experiences. An infant or a toddler reacts impulsively, but the 8-year-old can remember and reflect. Analysis, control, abstraction, memory space, speed of processing, and interconnection of information make self-regulation and continuing cognitive development possible. Many of these developmental and brain changes involve knowledge—a key element in the cognitive perspective.

The Importance of Knowledge in Cognition

STOP & THINK Quickly, list 10 terms that pertain to educational psychology. Now list 10 terms that relate to ceramic engineering. •

Unless you are studying ceramic engineering, it probably took you longer to list 10 terms from that field than from educational psychology. Some of you may still be asking, "What is ceramic engineering anyway?" Your answers depend on your knowledge. (Hint: Think fiber optics, ceramic teeth and bones, ceramic semi-conductors for computers, heat-shielding tiles for space shuttles.)

Knowledge and knowing are the outcomes of learning. When we learn the history of cognitive psychology, the products of ceramic engineering, or the rules of tennis, we know something new. However, knowing is more than the end product of previous learning; it also guides new learning. The cognitive approach suggests that one of the most important elements in the learning process is what the individual brings to new learning situations. What we already know is the foundation and frame for constructing all future learning. Knowledge determines to a great extent what we will pay attention to,

Mirror systems Areas of the brain that fire both during perception of an action by someone else and when performing the action.

perceive, learn, remember, and forget (Bransford, Brown, & Cocking, 2000; Sawyer, 2006). For example, compared to 4th graders with little knowledge of soccer, 4th graders who were soccer experts learned and remembered far more new soccer terms, even though the abilities of the two groups to learn and remember nonsoccer terms were the same. The difference was the soccer experts used their soccer knowledge to organize and cluster the soccer terms, which helped them remember (Schneider & Bjorklund, 1992).

GENERAL AND SPECIFIC KNOWLEDGE. Knowledge in the cognitive perspective includes both subject-specific understandings (math, history, soccer, etc.) and general cognitive abilities, such as planning, solving problems, and comprehending language (Greeno, Collins, & Resnick, 1996). So, there are different kinds of knowledge. Some is **domain-specific knowledge** that pertains to a particular task or subject. For example, knowing that the shortstop plays between second and third base is specific to the domain of baseball. Some knowledge, on the other hand, is general—it applies to many different situations. For example, **general knowledge** about how to read or use a computer or focus attention is useful both in and out of school.

Of course, there is no absolute line between general and domain-specific knowledge. When you were first learning to read, you may have studied specific facts about the sounds of letters. At that time, knowledge about letter sounds was specific to the domain of reading. But now you can use both knowledge about letter sounds and the ability to read in more general ways (Bruning, Schraw, & Norby, 2011; Schunk, 2008). And learning in school generally requires both domain-specific and domain-general knowledge and skills. For example, Steven Hecht and Kevin Vagi (2010) followed students from 4th through 5th grade as the students were learning about fractions. Difficulty mastering fractions was associated both with lack of specific knowledge about fractions and lack of general knowledge about how to behave and pay attention in class.

To have knowledge of something is to remember it over time and to be able to find it when you need it. Cognitive psychologists have studied memory extensively and have learned more about knowledge in the process. Let's see what they have learned.

COGNITIVE VIEWS OF MEMORY

There are a number of theories of memory, but the most common are the information processing explanations (Ashcraft & Radvansky, 2010; Bruning et al., 2011; Sternberg & Sternberg, 2012). We will use this well-researched framework for examining learning and memory.

Early **information processing** views of memory used the computer as a model. Like the computer, the human mind takes in information, performs operations on it to change its form and content, stores the information, retrieves it when needed, and generates responses to it. But for most cognitive psychologists, the computer model is only a metaphor for human mental activity. Figure 8.1 is a schematic representation of an early information processing model of memory (Atkinson & Shiffrin, 1968).

According to this model, stimuli from the environment (input) flow into the sensory registers, one for each sensing modality (seeing, hearing, tasting, etc.). From there, some information is encoded and moves to short-term memory. Short-term memory holds information very briefly, combines it with information from long-term memory, and with enough effort, moves some information into long-term memory storage. Short-term memory is also responsible for generating responses or output.

This model proved helpful, but also incomplete. For example, in the model, information moved through the system mostly in one way, from sensory registers to long-term memory, but research indicated many more interactions and connections among the processes. The model could not explain how out-of-awareness memories or knowledge could influence learning or how several cognitive processes could happen simultaneously—like many small computers operating in parallel. A more recent cognitive science information processing model retains some of the features of the old approach, but emphasizes the role of working memory, attention, and the interactions among the elements of the system, as shown in Figure 8.2, which is based on several sources (Ashcraft & Radvansky, 2010; Bruning et al., 2011; Sternberg & Sternberg, 2012).

In order to understand this model, let's examine each element more carefully.

Domain-specific knowledge Information that is useful in a particular situation or that applies mainly to one specific topic.

General knowledge Information that is useful in many different kinds of tasks; information that applies to many situations.

Information processing The human mind's activity of taking in, storing, and using information.

FIGURE 8.1

THE EARLY INFORMATION PROCESSING SYSTEM

Information is encoded in sensory memory, where attention determines what will be held in short-term memory for further use. In short-term memory, new information connects with knowledge from long-term memory. Thoroughly processed and connected information becomes part of long-term memory, and can be activated to return to short-term memory.

Maintenance Rehearsal

Input → Sensory Register Sounds, images, etc. → Attention → Short-Term Memory → Encoding → Long-Term Memory
Long-Term Memory → Retrieval → Short-Term Memory
Short-Term Memory ↓ Responses

FIGURE 8.2

A RECENT VERSION OF THE INFORMATION PROCESSING SYSTEM

Information is encoded in sensory memory, where perception and attention determine what will be held in working memory for further use. In working memory, executive processes manage the flow of information and integrate new information with knowledge from long-term memory. Thoroughly processed and connected information becomes part of long-term memory, and when activated again, becomes part of working memory. Implicit memories are formed without conscious effort. All three elements of the system interact with each other to guide perception; represent, organize, and interpret information; apply and modify propositions, concepts, images, schemas, and strategies; construct knowledge; and solve problems. Attention has a role in all three memory processes and in the interactions among them.

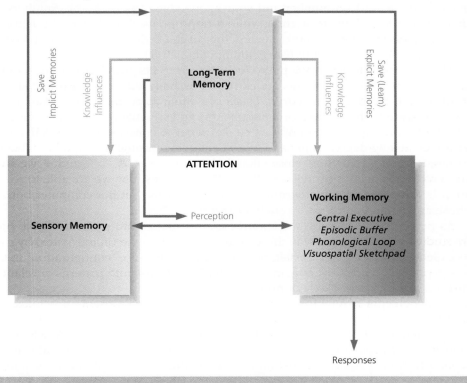

Save Implicit Memories
Knowledge Influences
Long-Term Memory
Knowledge Influences
Save (Learn) Explicit Memories

ATTENTION

Sensory Memory ← Perception → Working Memory

Working Memory
*Central Executive
Episodic Buffer
Phonological Loop
Visuospatial Sketchpad*

Responses

Sensory Memory

Stimuli from the environment (sights, sounds, smells, etc.) constantly bombard our body's mechanisms for seeing, hearing, tasting, smelling, and feeling. **Sensory memory** is the initial processing that transforms these incoming stimuli into information so we can make sense of them. Other names for the sensory memory are *sensory buffer, iconic memory* (for images), and *echoic memory* (for sounds).

CAPACITY, DURATION, AND CONTENTS OF SENSORY MEMORY. The capacity of sensory memory is very large, and it can take in more information than we can possibly handle at once. But this vast amount of sensory information is fragile in duration. It lasts less than three seconds.

- -

STOP & THINK Wave a pencil (or your finger) back and forth before your eyes while you stare straight ahead. What exactly do you see? Pinch your arm and let go. What do you feel just after you let go? •

- -

You just experienced this brief holding of sensory information in your own sensory memory. You could see a trace of the pencil after the actual stimulus had been removed and feel the pinch after you let go. The sensory memory held information about the stimuli very briefly after the actual stimulus had left (Lindsay & Norman, 1977).

The information content of sensory memory resembles the sensations from the original stimulus. Visual sensations are coded briefly as images, almost like photographs. Auditory sensations are coded as sound patterns, similar to echoes. It may be that the other senses also have their own codes. Thus, for a second or so, a wealth of data from sensory experience remains intact. In these moments, we have a chance to select and organize information for further processing. Perception and attention are critical at this stage.

PERCEPTION. The process of detecting a stimulus and assigning meaning to it is called **perception**. This meaning is constructed based on both physical representations from the world and our existing knowledge. For example, consider these marks: I3. If asked what the letter is, you would say "B." If asked what the number is, you would say "13." The actual marks remain the same; their meaning changes in keeping with your expectation to recognize a letter or a number and your knowledge of what Arabic numbers and the Latin alphabet look like. To a child without appropriate knowledge, the marks would probably be meaningless. Context matters too. In the series **A 13 C**, 13 is a *letter,* but in the series **12 13 14**, it is a *number* (Bruning et al., 2011).

The process from sensory input to recognized objects probably goes through several stages. In the first phase, features are extracted or analyzed to give a rough sketch. This feature analysis has been called *data-driven* or **bottom-up processing** because the stimulus must be analyzed into features or components and assembled into a meaningful pattern "from the bottom up." For example, a capital letter A consists of two relatively straight lines joined at a 45-degree angle and a horizontal line through the middle. Whenever we see these features, or anything close enough, including A, A, **A**, A, Ⴈ, and *A*, we are on the road to recognizing an A (Anderson, 2010). This explains how we are able to read words written in other people's handwriting, and why humans, but not computer bots, can fill in those annoying security codes such as axqᏫℛ. .

As perception continues, the features are organized into patterns. These processes were studied in Germany early in this century (and later in the United States) by psychologists called *Gestalt theorists*. **Gestalt,** which means "pattern" or "configuration" in German, refers to people's tendency to organize sensory information into patterns or relationships. Figure 8.3 presents a few Gestalt principles.

If all perception relied only on feature analysis and Gestalt principles, learning would be very slow. At the last stage of perception, the features and patterns detected are combined in light of the context of the situation and our existing knowledge—called **top-down** or conceptually driven processing. So to recognize patterns rapidly, in addition to noting features, we use context and what we already know about the situation—our

Connect and Extend to PRAXIS II™

Attention (I, A1)
Attention has an important place in instructional activities. What steps can a teacher take to gain and maintain student attention during instruction?

Sensory memory System that holds sensory information very briefly.

Perception Interpretation of sensory information.

Bottom-up processing Perceiving based on noticing separate defining features and assembling them into a recognizable pattern.

Gestalt German for *pattern* or *whole*. Gestalt theorists hold that people organize their perceptions into coherent wholes.

Top-down Making sense of information by using context and what we already know about the situation; sometimes called *conceptually drivien perception*.

FIGURE 8.3

EXAMPLES OF GESTALT PRINCIPLES

Gestalt principles of perception explain how we "see" patterns in the world around us.

a. Figure-ground
What do you see? Faces or a vase? Make one figure—the other ground.

b. Proximity
You see these lines as 3 groups because of the proximity of the lines.

c. Similarity
You see these lines as an alternating pattern because of the similarity in height of lines.

d. Closure
You perceive a circle instead of a series of curved lines.

Source: Schunk, Dale H., Learning Theories: An Educational Perspective , 2nd Edition, © 1996. Reprinted by permission of Pearson Education, Inc., Upper Saddle River, NJ.

knowledge about words or pictures or the way the world generally operates. For example, you would not have seen the earlier marks as the letter A if you had no knowledge of the Latin alphabet. So, what you know also affects what you are able to perceive. In Figure 8.2, the role of knowledge in perception is represented by the double arrow between long-term memory (stored knowledge), working memory, and sensory memory.

THE ROLE OF ATTENTION.   If every variation in color, movement, sound, smell, temperature, and other features ended up in working memory, life would be impossible. But **attention** is selective. By paying attention to selected stimuli and ignoring others, we limit the possibilities of what we will perceive and process. What we pay attention to is guided to a certain extent by what we already know and what we need to know, so attention is involved in and influenced by all three memory processes shown in Figure 8.2. Attention is also affected by what else is happening at the time, by the type and complexity of the task, by the resources you bring to the situation, and by your ability to control or focus your attention. Some students with attention-deficit disorder have great difficulty focusing attention or ignoring competing stimuli.

But attention takes effort and is a limited resource. I imagine you have to work a bit to pay attention to these words about attention! We can pay attention to only one cognitively demanding task at a time (Sternberg & Sternberg, 2012). For example, when I was learning to drive, I couldn't listen to the radio and drive at the same time. After some practice, I could listen, but I had to turn the radio off when traffic was heavy. After years of practice, I can plan a class, listen to the radio, and carry on a conversation as I drive. This is possible because many processes that initially require attention and concentration become automatic with practice. Actually, **automaticity** probably is a matter of degree; we are not completely automatic, but rather more or less automatic in our performances depending on how much practice we have had, the situation, and whether we are intentionally focusing our attention and directing our own cognitive processing. For example, even experienced drivers might become very attentive and focused during a blinding blizzard—and no one should text or talk on a cell phone while driving. But the AAA Foundation for Traffic Safety found that over half of the adult drivers in the United States admit to using a phone while driving, even though research has shown that driving while chatting is equivalent to driving while drinking. Estimates are that about 2,600 deaths, 330,000 injuries, and 1.5 million instances of property damage in the United States result each year from driver cell phone use (Cohen & Graham, 2003). Other studies show that using a cell phone while driving increases your risk of having an accident by 400% and hands free sets do not make any improvement in safety (Novotney, 2009).

Attention Focus on a stimulus.

Automaticity The ability to perform thoroughly learned tasks without much mental effort.

EYES (AND ATTENTION) ON THE ROAD The girl in the picture has it right. You can talk to passengers, but a text or phone conversation while driving is dangerous for everyone because the demands on attention are too great.

ATTENTION AND MULTITASKING. Drivers who text or chat say they are multitasking, and often they think all is fine. You may be multitasking right now. Adolescents are multitasking more than ever, perhaps because they have access to so much technology. In one survey of 8- to 18-year-olds, about one-third of them reported multitasking with multimedia while they do their homework (Azzam, 2006). These students reported using media about 6 to 7 hours each day on average, but with the multitasking, they actually were exposed to more than 8 to 9 hours of media.

Is multitasking a good idea? Research by David Meyer and his colleagues at the Brain, Cognition, and Actions Laboratory of Michigan University says it depends (Hamilton, 2009). Actually, there are two types of multitasking—*sequential multitasking*, in which you switch back and forth from one task to another, but focus on only one at a time, and *simultaneous multitasking*, in which there is overlapping focus on several tasks at time. Also, the content of the tasks makes a difference. Some tasks, such as walking and chewing gum, call on different cognitive and physical resources—and both walking and chewing are pretty automatic. But other complex tasks, such as driving and talking on the phone, require some of the same cognitive resources—paying attention to traffic and paying attention to what the caller is saying. The problem with multitasking comes with *simultaneous, complex* tasks.

For tasks that are at all complicated, no matter how good you have become at multitasking, your performance of the task will suffer (David Meyer interviewed by Hamilton, 2009, p. 1). In fact, it can take up to 400% longer to do a homework assignment if you are multitasking (Paulos, 2007). In complicated situations, the brain prioritizes and focuses on one thing. You may be able to listen to quiet instrumental music in the background while you study, but favorite songs with words will steal your attention away and it will take time to get back to what you were doing.

ATTENTION AND TEACHING. The first step in learning is paying attention. Students cannot process information that they do not recognize or perceive (Lachter, Forster, & Ruthruff, 2004). But how successfully information is processed depends on several things, not just attention. Some tasks are *resource-limited*. Performance on those tasks will improve if we allocate more resources, for example, turn off the iPod and give the complicated lecture your full attention. Other tasks are *data-limited*, which means that successful processing depends on the amount and quality of the data available. If the quality of the information available is inadequate, then no matter how hard we focus attention, we will not be successful. For example, if you just can't hear the lecture or you know very few of the terms being used, more focused attention will not help you understand. We have already discussed a third kind of task—*automated*—that happens without much attention because we have practiced it so thoroughly, for example, the way an expert musician moves her fingers on the strings of a guitar (Bruning et al., 2011).

Many factors in the classroom influence student attention. Bright colors, underlining, highlighting of written or spoken words, calling students by name, surprise events, intriguing questions, variety in tasks and teaching methods, and changes in voice level, lighting, or pacing can all be used to *gain* attention. But then students have to *maintain* attention—they have to stay focused on the important features of the learning situation. The *Guidelines* offer ideas for capturing and maintaining students' attention.

Working Memory

Working memory The information that you are focusing on at a given moment.

Working memory is the "workbench" of the memory system, the interface where new information is held temporarily and combined with knowledge from long-term memory to solve problems or comprehend a lecture, for example. Working memory "contains"

GUIDELINES

Gaining and Maintaining Attention

Use signals.
Examples

1. Develop a signal that tells students to stop what they are doing and focus on you. Some teachers move to a particular spot in the room, flick the lights, tap the table, or play a chord on the class piano. Mix visual and auditory signals.
2. Avoid distracting behaviors, such as tapping a pencil while talking, that interfere with both signals and attention to learning.
3. Give short, clear directions before, not during, transitions.
4. Be playful with younger children: Use a dramatic voice, sensational hat, or clapping game (Miller, 2005).

Reach out rather than call out (Miller, 2005).
Examples

1. Walk to the child, look into his or her eyes.
2. Speak in a firm but nonthreatening voice.
3. Use the child's name.

Make sure the purpose of the lesson or assignment is clear to students.
Examples

1. Write the goals or objectives on the board and discuss them with students before starting. Ask students to summarize or restate the goals.
2. Explain the reasons for learning, and ask students for examples of how they will apply their understanding of the material.
3. Tie the new material to previous lessons—show an outline or map of how the new topic fits with previous and upcoming material.

Incorporate variety, curiosity, and surprise.
Examples

1. Arouse curiosity with questions such as "What would happen if?"
2. Create shock by staging an unexpected event such as a loud argument just before a lesson on communication.
3. Alter the physical environment by changing the arrangement of the room or moving to a different setting.
4. Shift sensory channels by giving a lesson that requires students to touch, smell, or taste.
5. Use movements, gestures, and voice inflection—walk around the room, point, and speak softly and then more emphatically. (My husband has been known to jump up on his desk to make an important point in his college classes!)

Ask questions and provide frames for answering.
Examples

1. Ask students why the material is important, how they intend to study, and what strategies they will use.
2. Give students self-checking or self-editing guides that focus on common mistakes or have them work in pairs to improve each other's work—sometimes it is difficult to pay attention to your own errors.

For more ideas about gaining student attention, see http://www.atozteacherstuff.com/Tips/Attention_Getters/

---

what you are thinking about at the moment. For this reason, some psychologists consider the working memory to be synonymous with "consciousness" (Sweller, van Merrienboer, & Paas, 1998). Unlike sensory memory or long-term memory, working memory capacity is very limited—something many of your professors seem to forget as they race through a lecture while you work to hold on to and make sense of their words and PowerPoints.

In Figure 8.1 you saw **short-term memory**. Short-term memory is not exactly the same as working memory. Working memory includes both temporary storage and active processing—the workbench of memory—where active mental effort is applied to both new and old information. But short-term memory usually means just storage, the immediate memory for new information that can be held about 15 to 20 seconds (Baddeley, 2001). Early experiments suggested that the capacity of short-term memory was only about 5 to 9 (the "magic 7," + or −2) separate new bits of information at once (Miller, 1956). Later, we will see that this limitation can be overcome using strategies such as chunking or grouping, but the 5 to 9 limit generally holds true in everyday life. It is quite common to remember a new phone number after finding it on the Internet, as you make the call. But what if you have two phone calls to make in succession? Two new phone numbers (14 digits) probably cannot be stored simultaneously.

Short-term memory Component of memory system that holds information for about 20 seconds.

Connect and Extend to PRAXIS II™

Memory and Instruction (II, A1)
To maximize the learning derived from instructional activities, a teacher should be aware of the characteristics of working memory. Consider the techniques or tactics a teacher can employ that complement those characteristics.

Alan Baddeley and his colleagues are responsible for the model of working memory that is central to our current understanding of human cognition. In this model, working memory is composed of at least four elements: *the central executive* that controls attention and other mental resources (the "worker" of working memory), the *phonological loop* that holds verbal and acoustical (sound) information, the *visuospatial sketchpad* for visual and spatial information, and the *episodic buffer* where information from the phonological loop, visuospatial sketchpad, and long-term memory is integrated together to create representations based on verbal, spatial, and visual information. The phonological loop and visuospatial sketchpad are short-term memory storage for sounds and images, so they are like what was considered short-term memory in earlier information processing models. The phonological loop, visuospatial sketchpad, and episodic buffer do some lower-level work for the central executive—holding on to and combining information. Baddeley also said there may be other lower-level worker/storage systems for different information, but phonological loop, visuospatial sketchpad, and episodic buffer are the ones we know about (Baddeley, 2007; Baddeley, Hitch, & Allen, 2009; Jarrold, Tam, Baddeley, & Harvey, 2011). Figure 8.4 shows the working memory system—let's experience that system in action.

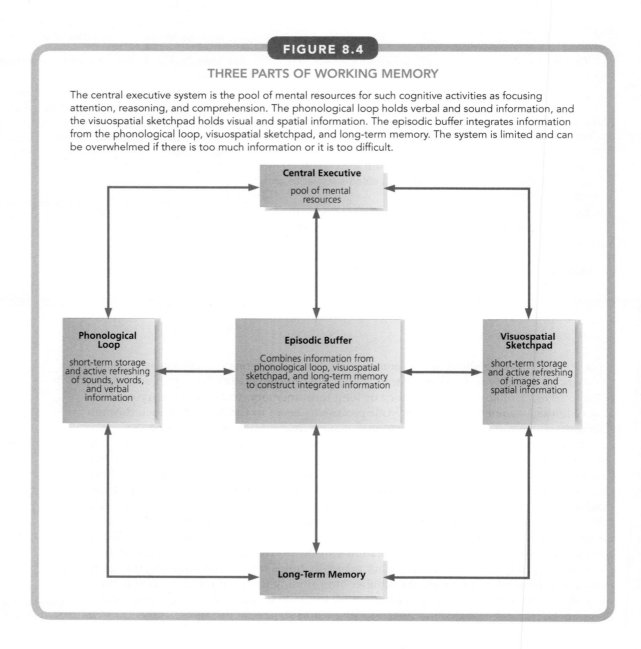

FIGURE 8.4

THREE PARTS OF WORKING MEMORY

The central executive system is the pool of mental resources for such cognitive activities as focusing attention, reasoning, and comprehension. The phonological loop holds verbal and sound information, and the visuospatial sketchpad holds visual and spatial information. The episodic buffer integrates information from the phonological loop, visuospatial sketchpad, and long-term memory. The system is limited and can be overwhelmed if there is too much information or it is too difficult.

Central Executive
pool of mental resources

Phonological Loop
short-term storage and active refreshing of sounds, words, and verbal information

Episodic Buffer
Combines information from phonological loop, visuospatial sketchpad, and long-term memory to construct integrated information

Visuospatial Sketchpad
short-term storage and active refreshing of images and spatial information

Long-Term Memory

STOP & THINK Solve this problem from Ashcraft and Radvansky (2010, p. 161) and pay attention to how you go about the process:

$$\frac{(4 + 5) \times 2}{3 + (12/4)} \bullet$$

THE CENTRAL EXECUTIVE. As you solved the problem above, the central executive of your working memory focused your attention on the facts that you needed (what is 4 + 5? what is 12/4?), retrieved rules for which operations to do first, and recalled how to divide. The **central executive** supervises attention, makes plans, and decides what information to retrieve and how to allocate resources, as you can see in Figure 8.4.

THE PHONOLOGICAL LOOP. The **phonological loop** is a speech- and sound-related system for holding and rehearsing (refreshing) words and sounds in short-term memory. It briefly holds verbal information and keeps it active by keeping it "in the loop"—rehearsing and paying attention to the information. The short-term storage of the phonological loop is where you put the "18" (4 + 5 = 9; 9 × 2 = 18) from the top line of the problem while you calculated the 3 + (12/4) on the bottom of the problem. Baddeley (2001, 2007) suggests that we can hold as much in the phonological loop as we can rehearse (say to ourselves) in 1.5 to 2 seconds. The 7-digit telephone number fits this limitation. But what if you tried to hold these 7 words in mind: *disentangle appropriation gossamer anti-intellectual preventative foreclosure documentation* (Gray, 2011)? Besides being a mouthful, these words take longer than 2 seconds to rehearse and are more difficult to hold in working memory than 7 single digits or 7 short words. In addition, some of the words may be unfamiliar to you, so they are harder to rehearse.

Remember—put in your working memory—that we are discussing temporarily holding new information. In daily life we certainly can hold more than 5 to 9 bits or 1.5 seconds of information at once. While you are keying in that 7-digit phone number you just looked up, you are bound to have other things "on your mind"—in your memory—such as how to use a telephone, whom you are calling, and why. You don't have to pay attention to these things; they are not new knowledge. Some of the processes, such as using the keypad on the phone, are *automated* tasks. However, because of the working memory's limitations, if you were in a foreign country and were attempting to use an unfamiliar telephone system, you might very well have trouble remembering the phone number because your central executive was searching for strategies to use the phone system at the same time. Even a few bits of new information can be too much to remember if the new information is very complex or unfamiliar or if you have to integrate several elements to make sense of a situation (Sweller, van Merrienboer, & Paas, 1998).

THE VISUOSPATIAL SKETCHPAD. Now try this problem.

STOP & THINK If you rotate a *d* 180 degrees clockwise, do you get a *b* or a *p*? •

Most people answer this question by creating a visual image of a "d" and rotating it. The **visuospatial sketchpad** is the place in your mind where you manipulated the image (after your central executive retrieved the meaning of "180 degrees," and "clockwise" of course). Working in the visuospatial sketchpad has some of the same aspects as actually looking at a picture or object. If you have to solve the "d" problem and also pay attention to an image on a screen, you will be slowed down just like you would be if you had to look back and forth between two different objects. But if you had to solve the "d" problem while repeating digits, there is little slow down. You can use your phonological loop and your visuospatial sketchpad at the same time, but each is quickly filled and easily overburdened. In fact, each kind of task—verbal and visual—appears to happen in different areas of the brain and there are some individual differences in the capacities of these systems, too (Ashcraft & Radvansky, 2010; Gray, 2011).

Central executive The part of working memory that is responsible for monitoring and directing attention and other mental resources.

Phonological loop Part of working memory. A speech- and sound-related system for holding and rehearsing (refreshing) words and sounds in short-term memory for about 1.5 to 2 seconds.

Visuospatial sketchpad Part of working memory. A holding system for visual and spatial information.

THE EPISODIC BUFFER. If working memory is the workbench of memory, the episodic buffer is the workbench of working memory. The **episodic buffer** is the process that brings together and integrates information from the phonological loop, visuospatial sketchpad, and long-term memory under the supervision of the central executive, to create complex memories, such as storing the appearance, voice, words, and actions of an actor in a film to create a complete character.

THE DURATION AND CONTENTS OF WORKING MEMORY. It is clear that the duration of information in the working memory system is short, about 5 to 20 seconds, unless you keep rehearsing the information or process it in some other way. It may seem to you that a memory system with a 20-second time limit is not very useful, but, without this system, you would have already forgotten what you read in the first part of this sentence before you came to these last few words. This would clearly make understanding sentences difficult.

The contents of information in working memory may be in the form of sounds and images that resemble the representations in sensory memory, or the information may be structured more abstractly, based on meaning.

Cognitive Load and Retaining Information

Let's get back to that professor who raced through a lecture, taxing your working memory. Some tasks make more demands than others on working memory. **Cognitive load** is a term that refers to the amount of mental resources, mostly working memory, required to perform a particular task. The concept is only about 25 years old, but in 2010 there was an entire special issue of *Educational Psychology Review* dedicated to Cognitive Load Theory (van Gog, Paas, & Sweller, 2010).

THREE KINDS OF COGNITIVE LOAD. The cognitive load of a task is not an absolute "weight." The extent of cognitive load in a given situation depends on many things, including what the person already knows about the task and what supports are available. There are three kinds of cognitive load. One is unavoidable, one gets in the way, and one is valuable.

Intrinsic cognitive load is unavoidable—it is the amount of cognitive processing required to figure out the material. That amount depends on how many elements you have to take into account, how complicated the interactions among the elements are, and your level of expertise in problem area (Antonenko, Paas, Grabner, & van Gog, 2010). Even though working memory can hold 5 to 9 new bits of information, it can process only about 2 to 4 at a time, so if you have to understand how many separate elements interact in a complex system, such as grasping the structure and function of DNA, you will be in trouble unless you already understand some of the parts—vocabulary, concepts, procedures, and so on (van Merriënboer & Sweller, 2005). Intrinsic cognitive load is essential to the task—it cannot be eliminated. But good instruction can help manage intrinsic load.

Extraneous cognitive load is the cognitive capacity you use to deal with problems not related to the learning task, like trying to get your roommate (spouse, children, partner) to quit interrupting you or struggling with a disorganized lecture or a poorly written textbook (not this one of course!). Instruction can help manage extraneous load by providing supports, focusing attention on the main ideas, and generally supplying scaffolding (see Chapter 2).

The good cognitive load is called *germane* because it is directly related to (germane to) high quality learning. **Germane cognitive load** comes from deep processing of relevant information—organizing and integrating the material with what you already know and forming new understandings. Instruction can support this process by asking students to explain the material to each other or to themselves, draw or chart their understandings, take useful notes, and use other strategies we will discuss in upcoming chapters (Berthold & Renkl, 2009; Mayer, 2011, van Gog et al., 2010). The three kinds of cognitive load are summarized in Table 8.1. Just a note: Some psychologists suggest that there is no practical distinction between intrinsic and germane load—a student must deal with both to learn (Kalyuga, 2011).

Episodic buffer The process that brings together and integrates information from the phonological loop, visuospatial sketchpad, and long-term memory under the supervision of the central executive.

Cognitive load The volume of resources necessary to complete a task.

Intrinsic cognitive load The resources required by the task itself, regardless of other stimuli.

Extraneous cognitive load The resources required to process stimuli irrelevant to the task.

Germane cognitive load Deep processing of information related to the task, including the application of prior knowledge to a new task or problem.

TABLE 8.1 • **Three Kinds of Cognitive Load**

There are three types of cognitive load that make demands during learning, with different causes and effects.

TYPE OF COGNITIVE LOAD	WHAT IS IT?	WHAT CAUSES IT?	WHAT'S AN EXAMPLE?	WHAT HAPPENS?
Intrinsic	*Unavoidable*: the essential processing needed to attend to and represent the material	Caused by the inherent complexity of the task: the more complex, the more basic processing needed	More intrinsic processing needed to recognize and organize a complicated task such as quadratic equations	Processing focuses attention and begins to organize learning, rote learning possible
Extraneous	*Avoidable or manageable*: unhelpful processing needed to deal with problems that are not related to the learning task itself	Caused by poor learning strategies, divided attention and distractibility, poor instruction, inadequate background knowledge	Students scan back and forth between the text and a graph, but don't know how to read the graph or integrate the visual and verbal information	Inappropriate processing, no learning, possible discouragement
Germane	*Desirable*: the deep processing (organizing, integrating, connecting to prior knowledge) required to generate understandings	Learner motivation to understand, make strong effort, try new strategies when first attempts fall short	Learner diagrams relationships in a problem, connects to key ideas in the text	Appropriate organizing, elaborating, and visualizing lead to deep learning

Source: Adapted from Bruning, R. H., Schraw, G. J., & Norby, M. M. (2011). Cognitive Psychology and Instruction (5th ed.). Boston: Pearson, pp. 220–224; Mayer, R. E. (2011). Applying the Science of Learning. Boston: Pearson, pp. 62–71.

RETAINING INFORMATION IN WORKING MEMORY. Information in working memory must be kept activated in order for it to be retained. Activation is high as long as you are focusing on information, but activation decays or fades quickly when attention shifts away. Holding information in working memory is like a circus performer keeping a series of plates spinning on top of several poles. The performer gets one plate spinning, moves to the next plate, and the next, but has to return to the first plate before it slows down too much and falls off its pole. If we don't keep the information "spinning" in working memory—keep it activated—it will "fall off" (Anderson, 1995, 2010). When activation fades, forgetting follows.

To keep information activated, most people continue rehearsing the information mentally. There are two types of rehearsal. **Maintenance rehearsal** involves repeating the information in your phonological loop or refreshing information in your visuospatial sketchpad. As long as you revisit the information, it can be maintained in working memory indefinitely. Maintenance rehearsal is useful for retaining something you plan to use and then forget, such as a phone number or a location on a map.

Maintenance rehearsal Keeping information in working memory by repeating it to yourself.

Elaborative rehearsal involves connecting the information you are trying to remember with something you already know—with knowledge from long-term memory. For example, if you meet someone at a party whose name is the same as your brother's, you don't have to repeat the name to keep it in memory; you just have to make the connection. This kind of rehearsal not only retains information in working memory but also helps create long-term memories. Rehearsal is a process the central executive controls to manage the flow of information through the information processing system (Ashcraft & Radvansky, 2010).

The limited capacity of working memory can also be somewhat circumvented by the process of **chunking**. Because the number of bits of information, not the size of each bit, is a limitation for working memory, you can retain more information if you can group individual bits of information. You can experience this effect of chunking by trying to hold these letters in memory:

HBOUSACIALOLATM

Now try these:

HBO USA CIA LOL ATM

You just used chunking to group the string of letters into memorable (and meaningful) chunks, so you could hold more in memory. Also, you brought your knowledge of the world to bear on the memory task. Chunking helps you remember a password or social security number.

FORGETTING.   Information may be lost from working memory through *interference* or *decay*. **Interference** is fairly straightforward: Processing new information interferes or gets confused with old information. As new thoughts accumulate, old information is lost from working memory. Information is also lost by time **decay**. If you don't continue to pay attention to information, the activation level decays (weakens) and finally drops so low that the information cannot be reactivated—it disappears altogether. Some cognitive psychologists argue that interference is the main factor in forgetting in working memory—your mind starts processing other information and the previous information is "written over" (Sternberg & Sternberg, 2012).

Actually, forgetting is very useful. Without forgetting, people would quickly overload their working memories and learning would cease. Also, it would be a problem if you remembered permanently every sentence you ever read, every sound you ever heard, every picture you ever saw . . . you get the idea. Finding a particular bit of information in all that sea of knowledge would be impossible. It is helpful to have a system that provides temporary storage and that "weeds out" some information from everything you experience.

Individual Differences and Working Memory

As you might expect, there are both developmental and individual differences in working memory. Let's examine a few.

DEVELOPMENTAL DIFFERENCES.   There are three basic aspects of memory: memory span or the amount of information that can be held in short-term/working memory, memory processing efficiency, and speed of processing. As they get older, children can process many different kinds of information—verbal, visual, mathematical, etc.—faster, so increased speed of processing seems to be a general factor. In addition, the increase in speed with age is the same for American and Korean children, so increasing processing speed with age may be universal (Kail, 2000; Kail & Park, 1994).

These three basic capacities act together and influence each other; more efficient processing allows greater amounts to be held in memory, for example (Demetriou, Christou, Spanoudis, & Platsidou, 2002). You experienced this effect of efficient processing when you remembered HBOUSACIALOLATM by chunking the letters into HBO USA CIA LOL ATM. Your more efficient and faster processing expanded your memory span. Young children have fewer strategies and less knowledge, so they have more trouble with memorizing a longer series. But as they grow older, children develop more effective strategies for remembering information. Most children spontaneously discover rehearsal around age 5 or 6 and continue to use it. Also around age 6, most children discover the value of using

Elaborative rehearsal Keeping information in working memory by associating it with something else you already know.

Chunking Grouping individual bits of data into meaningful larger units.

Interference Processing new information interferes or gets confused with old information.

Decay The weakening and fading of memories with the passage of time.

organizational strategies, and by 9 or 10, they use these strategies spontaneously. So, given the following words to learn:

couch, orange, rat, lamp, pear, sheep, banana, rug, pineapple, horse, table, dog

an older child or an adult might organize the words into three short lists of furniture, fruit, and animals. Also remember that expertise in an area helps you use categories to organize and remember, as we saw with the expert soccer players earlier. Younger children can be taught to use rehearsal or organization to improve memory, but they probably won't apply the strategies unless they are reminded. Children also become more able to use elaboration as they mature, but this strategy develops late in childhood. Creating images or stories to assist in remembering ideas is more likely for older elementary school students and adolescents (Siegler, 1998).

In terms of strategies, for young children, using a new strategy or operation—such as reaching for a toy, counting, or finding a word—takes up a large portion of their working memory. But once an operation is mastered and becomes more automatic, there is more working memory available for short-term storage of new information (Johnson, 2003). So, through changes in the brain, faster processing of information, the development and automating of strategies, and added knowledge, working memory increases in capacity from ages 4 through adolescence (Alloway, Gathercole, & Pickering, 2006; Gathercole, Pickering, Ambridge, & Wearing, 2004). Children are 10 to 11 years old before they have adult-like memories (Bauer, 2006).

DEVELOPMENTAL DIFFERENCES There are several developmental differences in how students process information in working and long-term memory.

INDIVIDUAL DIFFERENCES. Besides developmental differences, there are other individual variations in working memory, and these differences have implications for learning. Try this:

STOP & THINK Read the following sentences and words in caps out loud once:
For many years my family and friends have been working on the farm. SPOT
Because the room was stuffy, Bob went outside for some fresh air. TRAIL
We were fifty miles out to sea before we lost sight of the land. BAND
Now cover the sentences and answer these questions (be honest):
Name the words that were in all caps. Who was in the stuffy room? Who worked on the farm? •

You have just taken a few items from a test of working memory span (Engle, 2001). The test required you to both process and store—process the meaning of the sentences and store the words. How did you do?

The more educational psychologists study working memory, the more we realize how important it is in learning and development at every age (Alloway, Banner, & Smith, 2010; Welsh, Nix, Blair, Bierman, & Nelson, 2010). For adolescents and adults, the correlation between scores on a test of working memory span (like the one you just took in the *Stop & Think* exercise above) and the verbal portion of the Scholastic Assessment Test (SAT) is about .59. But there is no correlation between the SAT and simple short-term memory span (repeating digits). For elementary school students, growth in working memory (but not simple short-term memory) is related to reading abilities and reading comprehension; problems with working memory are associated with reading disabilities. Working memory is related to academic achievement, math computation, and solving complex word problems in math in elementary school. For young children, growth in working memory and attention control during the preschool years predicts emergent literacy and number skills.

Working-memory span is also related to scores on intelligence tests. If a task requires controlled attention or higher-level thinking, then working memory probably is a factor in performing that task (Ackerman, Beier, & Boyle, 2005; Hambrick, Kane, & Engle, 2005; Unsworth & Engle, 2005). Some people seem to have more efficient working memories than others (Cariglia-Bull & Pressley, 1990; DiVesta & Di Cintio, 1997; Jurden, 1995), and differences in working memory may be associated with giftedness in math and verbal areas.

We turn next to long-term memory. Because this is such an important topic for teachers, we will spend quite a bit of time on it.

LONG-TERM MEMORY

Working memory holds the information that is currently activated, such as the name of the person you just met. **Long-term memory** holds the information that is well learned, such as the names of all the people you know.

Capacity, Duration, and Contents of Long-Term Memory

There are a number of differences between working and long-term memory. Information enters working memory very quickly, but it takes time and effort to store memories for the long term. Whereas the capacity of working memory is limited, the capacity of long-term memory appears to be, for all practical purposes, unlimited. In addition, once information is securely stored in long-term memory, it can remain there permanently. Our access to information in working memory is immediate because we are thinking about the information at that very moment. But gaining access to information in long-term memory requires time and effort.

Recently, some psychologists have suggested that there are not two separate memory stores (working and long term). Rather, working memory is the part of long-term memory that works on (processes) currently activated information. The difference between working memory and long-term memory just may be in how activated or inactive a particular memory is (Anderson, 2010; Wilson, 2001). This model sees memory as a set of nested systems with very short-term storage (phonological loop, visuospatial sketchpad, other brief holding areas) nested in working memory, which is just the active part of long-term memory that does the integrating of old and new information (Sternberg & Sternberg, 2012).

CONTENTS OF LONG-TERM-MEMORY: DECLARATIVE, PROCEDURAL, AND SELF-REGULATORY KNOWLEDGE. Earlier, we talked about general and specific knowledge. Another way to categorize knowledge is as *declarative*, *procedural*, or *self-regulatory* (Schraw, 2006).

Declarative knowledge is knowledge that can be declared, through words and symbol systems of all kinds—Braille, sign language, dance or musical notation, mathematical symbols, and so on. Declarative knowledge is "knowing that" something is the case. The range of declarative knowledge is tremendous. You can know very specific facts (the atomic weight of gold is 196.967), or generalities (leaves of some trees change color in autumn), or personal preferences (I don't like lima beans), or rules (to divide fractions, invert the divisor and multiply). Small units of declarative knowledge can be organized into larger units; for example, principles of reinforcement and punishment can be organized in your thinking into a theory of behavioral learning.

Procedural knowledge is "knowing how" to do something such as divide fractions or design a website—it is knowledge in action. Procedural knowledge must be demonstrated. Notice that repeating the rule "to divide fractions, invert the divisor and multiply" shows declarative knowledge—the student can state the rule. But to show procedural knowledge, the student must act. When faced with a fraction to divide, the student must divide correctly. Students demonstrate procedural knowledge when they translate a passage into Spanish, correctly categorize a geometric shape, or craft a coherent paragraph.

Self-regulatory knowledge is knowing how to manage your learning—knowing how and when to use your declarative and procedural knowledge (Schraw, 2006). It takes self-regulatory knowledge to know when to read every word in a text and when to skim or when to apply a strategy for overcoming procrastination. Self-regulatory knowledge

Long-term memory Permanent store of knowledge.

Declarative knowledge Verbal information; facts; "knowing that" something is the case.

Procedural knowledge Knowledge that is demonstrated when we perform a task; "knowing how."

Self-regulatory knowledge Knowing how to manage your learning, or knowing how and when to use your declarative and procedural knowledge.

TABLE 8.2 • **Kinds of Knowledge**

	GENERAL KNOWLEDGE	**DOMAIN-SPECIFIC KNOWLEDGE**
Declarative	Hours the library is open Rules of grammar	The definition of "hypotenuse" The lines of the poem "The Raven"
Procedural	How to use your cell phone How to drive	How to solve an oxidation-reduction equation How to throw a pot on a potter's wheel

Conditional	When to give up and try
	  another approach
	When to skim and when to read
	  carefully
		When to use the formula for calculating volume
		When to rush the net in tennis

has also been called *conditional knowledge* (Paris & Cunningham, 1996). For many students, this kind of knowledge is a stumbling block. They have the facts and can do the procedures, but they don't seem to understand how to apply what they know at the appropriate time. Self-regulatory knowledge can be specific to a subject area (when to use the formula for calculating area, not perimeter, in geometry) or more general (how to summarize key points or use diagrams to organize information). In fact, all three kinds of knowledge—declarative, procedural, and self-regulatory—can be either general or domain-specific, as you can see in Table 8.2 (Schraw, 2006).

Most cognitive psychologists distinguish between two categories of long-term memory, explicit and implicit, with subdivisions under each category, as shown in Figure 8.5. **Explicit memory** is knowledge from long-term memory that can be recalled and consciously considered. We are aware of these memories—we know we have remembered them. **Implicit memory**, on the other hand, is knowledge that we are not conscious of recalling, but that influences behavior or thought without our awareness. These different kinds of memory are associated with different parts of the brain (Ashcraft & Radvansky, 2010; Gray, 2011).

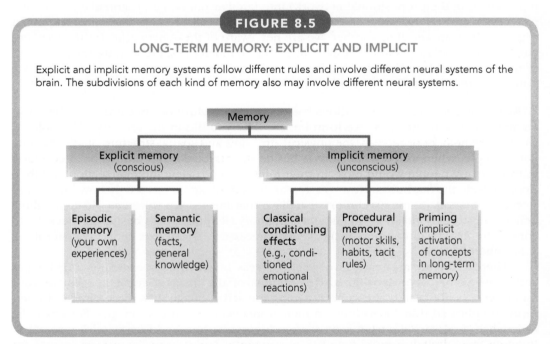

FIGURE 8.5

LONG-TERM MEMORY: EXPLICIT AND IMPLICIT

Explicit and implicit memory systems follow different rules and involve different neural systems of the brain. The subdivisions of each kind of memory also may involve different neural systems.

Memory
- Explicit memory (conscious)
  - Episodic memory (your own experiences)
  - Semantic memory (facts, general knowledge)
- Implicit memory (unconscious)
  - Classical conditioning effects (e.g., conditioned emotional reactions)
  - Procedural memory (motor skills, habits, tacit rules)
  - Priming (implicit activation of concepts in long-term memory)

Explicit memory Long-term memories that involve deliberate or conscious recall.

Implicit memory Knowledge that we are not conscious of recalling, but that influences our behavior or thought without our awareness.

This view has been challenged recently. Lynne Reder and her colleagues claim that implicit and explicit are not different memory systems, but just different kinds of tasks that are accomplished with one memory system (Reder, Park, & Kieffaber, 2009). Stay tuned as new theories develop. For now, we will stick with the idea of explicit and implicit systems, and look at explicit memories first.

Explicit Memories: Semantic and Episodic

In Figure 8.5, you will see that explicit memories can be either semantic (based on meaning) or episodic (based the sequence of events).

Semantic memory, very important in schools, is memory for meaning, including words, facts, theories, and concepts—*declarative* knowledge, so sometimes the name *declarative memory* is used. These memories are not tied to particular experiences and are represented and stored as propositions, images, concepts, and schemas (Anderson, 2010; Schraw, 2006).

PROPOSITIONS AND PROPOSITIONAL NETWORKS. How do we represent the meaning of sentences and pictures in our memories? One answer is with propositions connected in networks. A proposition is the smallest unit of knowledge that can be judged true or false. Anderson (2010, p. 123) gives this example of a statement with three propositions: "Lincoln, who was president of the United States during a bitter war, freed the slaves." The three basic propositions are:

1. Lincoln was president of the United States during a war.
2. The war was bitter.
3. Lincoln freed the slaves.

Propositions that share information are linked in what cognitive psychologists call **propositional networks**. It is the meaning, not the exact words or word order, that is stored in the network. The same propositional network would apply to the sentence: "The slaves were freed by Lincoln, who, during a bitter war, was president of the United States." The meaning is the same, and it is this meaning that is stored in memory as a set of relationships among propositions.

It is possible that most information is stored and represented in propositional networks. When we want to recall a bit of information, we can translate its meaning (as represented in the propositional network) into familiar phrases and sentences, or mental pictures. Also, because propositions are networked, recall of one bit of information can trigger or activate recall of another. We are not aware of these networks, for they are not part of our conscious memory (Anderson, 2010). In much the same way, we are not aware of underlying grammatical structure when we form a sentence in our own language; we don't have to diagram a sentence in order to say it.

IMAGES. **Images** are representations based on the structure or appearance of the information (Anderson, 2010). As we form images (like you did in the rotating "d" problem), we try to remember or recreate the physical attributes and spatial structure of information. For example, when asked what store is beside the Starbucks at a particular intersection in town, many people would look "in their mind's eye" to view the intersection and then "look" beside the Starbucks. However, researchers don't agree on exactly how images are stored in memory. Some psychologists believe that images are stored as pictures; others believe we store propositions in long-term memory (Radio Shack is beside Starbucks) and convert to pictures in working memory when necessary. The debate continues (Sternberg & Sternberg, 2012).

There probably are features of each process involved—some memory for images and some verbal or propositional descriptions of the image. Seeing images "in your mind's eye" is not exactly the same as seeing the actual image. It is more difficult to perform complicated transformations on mental images than on real images. For example, if you had a plastic "d" magnet on your refrigerator, you could very quickly rotate it. Rotating mentally takes more time for most people. And it is easier to form images for some words or concepts than others—it is probably easier for you to form an image of

Semantic memory Memory for meaning.

Propositional network Set of interconnected concepts and relationships in which long-term knowledge is held.

Images Representations based on the physical attributes—the appearance—of information.

Starbucks than one of *justice*, for example. Nevertheless, images are useful in making many practical decisions such as how a sofa might look in your living room or how to line up a golf shot. Images may also be helpful in abstract reasoning. Physicists, such as Faraday and Einstein, report creating images to reason about complex new problems. Einstein claimed that he was visualizing chasing a beam of light and catching up to it when the concept of relativity came to him (Kosslyn & Koenig, 1992).

TWO ARE BETTER THAN ONE: WORDS AND IMAGES. Allan Paivio's (1986, 2006; Clark & Paivio, 1991) **dual coding theory** suggests that information is stored in long-term memory as either visual images or verbal units, or both. Psychologists who agree with this point of view believe that information coded both visually and verbally is easiest to learn (Butcher, 2006). This may be one reason why explaining an idea with words and then representing it visually in a figure, as we do in textbooks, has proved helpful to students.

STOP & THINK What makes a cup a cup? List the characteristics of *cupness*. What is a fruit? Is a banana a fruit? Is a tomato a fruit? How about a squash? A watermelon? A sweet potato? An olive? A coconut? How did you learn what makes a fruit a fruit? •

CONCEPTS. Most of what we know about cups and fruits and the world involves concepts and relations among concepts (Ashcraft & Radvansky, 2010). But what exactly is a concept? A **concept** is a category used to group similar events, ideas, objects, or people. When we talk about a particular concept such as *student*, we refer to a category of people who are similar to one another—they all study a subject. The people may be old or young, in school or not; they may be studying basketball or Bach, but they all can be categorized as students. Concepts are abstractions. They do not exist in the real world. Only individual examples of concepts exist. Concepts help us organize vast amounts of information into manageable units. For instance, there are about 7.5 million distinguishable differences in colors. By categorizing these colors into some dozen or so groups, we manage to deal with this diversity quite well (Bruner, 1973).

In early research, psychologists assumed that people create concepts based on rules about **defining attributes**, or distinctive features. For example, books all contain pages that are bound together in some way (but what about "eBooks"?). Your concept of a cat might include defining attributes such as a round head on a small body, triangle-shaped ears, whiskers, four legs, and fur. This concept enables you to identify cats whether they are calico or Siamese without relearning "cat" each time you encounter a new cat. The defining attributes theory of concepts suggests that we recognize specific examples by noting key required features.

Since about 1970, however, these views about the nature of concepts have been challenged (Ashcraft & Radvansky, 2010). Although some concepts, such as equilateral triangle, have clear-cut defining attributes, most concepts do not. Take the concept of *party*. What are the defining attributes? You might have difficulty listing these attributes, but you probably recognize a party when you see or hear one (unless, of course we are talking about political parties, or the other party in a lawsuit, where the sound might not help you recognize the "party"). What about the concept of *bird*? Your first thought might be that birds are animals that fly. But is an ostrich a bird? What about a penguin? A bat?

PROTOTYPES, EXEMPLARS, AND THEORY-BASED CATEGORIES. One current view of concept learning suggests that we have in our minds a prototype of a party or a bird or the letter A—an image that captures the essence of each concept. A **prototype** is the best representative of its category. For instance, the best representative of the "birds" category

CHANGING CONCEPTS Concepts have many attributes and may not remain constant. Recent technological applications such as text messaging have changed the concept of "conversation."

Connect and Extend to PRAXIS II

Teaching Concepts (II, A2)
Teachers devote much effort to the development of concepts that are vital in learning subject matter and skills. Understand the major approaches to teaching concepts and be able to describe their strengths and limitations.

Dual coding theory Suggests that information is stored in long-term memory as either visual images or verbal units, or both.

Concept A category used to group similar events, ideas, objects, or people.

Defining attribute Qualities that connect members of a group to a specific concept.

Prototype A best example or best representative of a category.

for many North Americans might be a robin (Rosch, 1973). Other members of the category may be very similar to the prototype (sparrow) or similar in some ways but different in others (chicken, ostrich). At the boundaries of a category, it may be difficult to determine if a particular instance really belongs. For example, is a television "furniture"? Is an elevator a "vehicle"? Is an olive a "fruit"? Whether something fits into a category is a matter of degree or graded membership. Thus, categories have fuzzy boundaries. Some events, objects, or ideas are simply better examples of a concept than others (Ashcraft & Radvansky, 2010).

Another explanation of concept learning suggests that we identify members of a category by referring to exemplars. **Exemplars** are our actual memories of specific birds, parties, furniture, and so on that we use to compare with an item in question to see if that item belongs in the same category as our exemplar. Prototypes probably are built from experiences with many exemplars. This happens naturally because memories of particular events (episodic memories) tend to blur together over time, creating an average or typical sofa prototype from all the sofa exemplars you have experienced (Smith & Kosslyn, 2007).

There are some drawbacks to prototype and exemplar theories. For example, how do you know what "bird experiences " to blur or average together to create a bird concept if you don't already have a bird concept? One answer is that our classifications are essentially **theory-based** ideas about the world that we create to make sense of things. So a *brick,* a *rock,* and a *shoe* are in the same category if the category is "things to pound a nail with if I don't have a hammer." Our theory of what might work creates the "things to pound with" category. Some of the knowledge used to create concepts based on theories may be implicit and out of awareness, for example, what makes for "good music"—I just know it when I hear it (Ashcraft & Radvansky, 2010; Sternberg & Sternberg, 2012).

Jacob Feldman (2003) suggests a final aspect of concept formation—the simplicity principle. Feldman says that when humans are confronted with examples, they induce the simplest category or rule that would cover all the examples. Sometimes it is easy to come up with a simple rule (triangles) and sometimes it is more difficult (fruit), but humans seek a simple hypothesis for collecting all the examples under one concept. Feldman suggests that this simplicity principle is one of the oldest ideas in cognitive psychology: "organisms seek to understand their environment by reducing incoming information to a simpler, more coherent, and more useful form" (p. 231). Does this remind you of the Gestalt principles of perception?

SCHEMAS. Propositions, concepts, and single images are fine for representing single ideas and simple relationships, but often our knowledge about a topic combines many concepts, images, and propositions. To explain this kind of complex knowledge, psychologists developed the idea of a schema. **Schemas** (sometimes called **schemata**) are abstract knowledge structures that organize vast amounts of information. A schema (the singular form) is a mental framework that guides our perception and helps us make sense of our experience based on what we already know and what we expect to happen (Sternberg & Sternberg, 2012). Figure 8.6 is a partial representation of a schema for knowledge about reinforcement.

The schema tells you what features are typical of a category, what to expect about an object or situation. The pattern has "slots" that are filled with specific information as we apply the schema in a particular situation. And schemas are personal. For example, my schema of reinforcement is less richly developed than Skinner's schema must have been. You encountered a very similar concept of *scheme* in the discussion of Piaget's theory of cognitive development in Chapter 2.

When you hear the sentence, "Lincoln, who was president of the United States during a bitter war, freed the slaves," you know even more about it than the three propositions. You probably can infer that reuniting the country after the war was difficult based on your schema for a "bitter" conflict. Your schema for "slaves" gives you some sense of the kind of life they were freed from. None of this information was explicitly stated in the sentence.

Schematic knowledge helps us to form and understand concepts. How do we know that counterfeit money is not "real" money, even though it perfectly fits our "money" prototype and exemplars and looks like real money? We know because of its history.

Exemplar An actual memory of a specific object.

Theory-based An explanation for concept formation that suggests our classifications are based on ideas about the world that we create to make sense of things.

Schemas (singular, *schema*) Basic structures for organizing information; concepts.

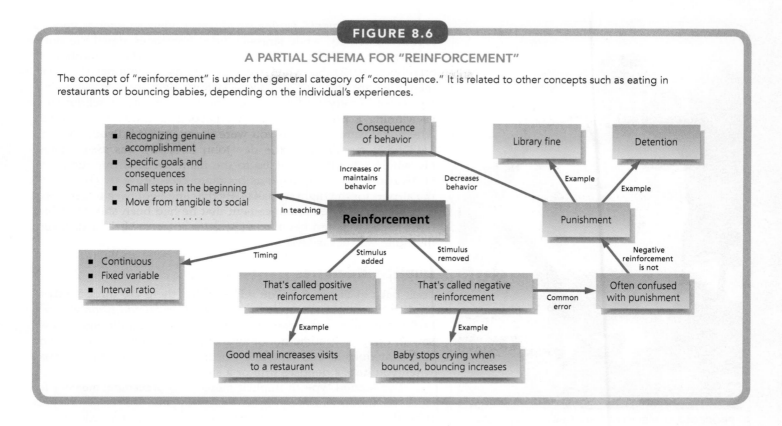

FIGURE 8.6

A PARTIAL SCHEMA FOR "REINFORCEMENT"

The concept of "reinforcement" is under the general category of "consequence." It is related to other concepts such as eating in restaurants or bouncing babies, depending on the individual's experiences.

The "wrong" people printed the money. So our understanding of the concept of money is connected with concepts of crime, forgery, the federal treasury, and many others in a larger schema for "money."

Another type of schema, a **story grammar** (sometimes called a *schema for text* or *story structure*) helps students to understand and remember stories. A general story grammar is: setting, initiating events, reactions, goals, actions, outcomes, and endings (van den Broek, Lorch, & Thurlow, 1996). A more specific story grammar could be something like this: murder discovered, search for clues, murderer's fatal mistake identified, trap set to trick suspect into confessing, murderer takes bait . . . mystery solved! To comprehend a story, we select a schema that seems appropriate. Then, we use this framework to decide which details are important, what information to seek, and what to remember. It is as though the schema is a theory about what should occur in the story. The schema guides us in "interrogating" the text, pointing to the specific information we expect to find so that the story makes sense. If we activate our "murder mystery schema," we may be alert for either clues or a murderer's fatal mistake. Without an appropriate schema, trying to understand a story, textbook, or classroom lesson is a very slow, difficult process, something like finding your way through a new town without a map or GPS.

To review, propositions, images, concepts, and schemas are all explicit *semantic* memories. The second kind of explicit memory is *episodic*.

EPISODIC MEMORY. Memory for information tied to a particular place and time, especially information about the events or episodes of your own life, is called **episodic memory**. Episodic memory is about events we have experienced, so we often can explain when the event happened. In contrast, we usually can't describe when we acquired a semantic memory. For example, you may have a difficult time remembering when you developed semantic memories for the meaning of the word *injustice*, but you can easily remember a time that you felt unjustly treated. Episodic memory also keeps track of the order of things, so it is a good place to store jokes, gossip, or plots from films.

Memories for dramatic or emotional moments in your life are called **flashbulb memories**. These memories are vivid and complete, as if your brain demanded that you

Story grammar Typical structure or organization for a category of stories.

Episodic memory Long-term memory for information tied to a particular time and place, especially memory of the events in a person's life.

Flashbulb memories Clear, vivid memories of emotionally important events in your life.

"record this moment." Under stress, more glucose energy goes to fuel brain activity, while stress-induced hormones signal the brain that something important is happening (Myers, 2005; Sternberg & Sternberg, 2012). So when we have intense emotional reactions, memories are stronger and more lasting. Many people have vivid memories of very positive or very negative events in school such as winning a prize or being humiliated. You probably know just where you were and what you were doing on 9/11. People over 50 have vivid memories of the day John Kennedy was assassinated. My whole school had walked to the main street of our suburb of Ft. Worth, Texas, to applaud as his motorcade drove by en route to the airport for the flight to Dallas. By the time I got back to geometry class, we heard the announcement that he had been shot in Dallas. My friend, who had been at a press breakfast with him that very morning, was devastated.

Implicit Memories

Look back at Figure 8.5. You will see that there are three kinds of implicit or out-of-awareness memories: *classical conditioning, procedural memory,* and *priming effects.* In classical conditioning, as we saw in Chapter 7, some out-of-awareness memories may cause you to feel anxious as you take a test or make your heart rate increase when you hear a dentist's drill or a siren.

The second type of implicit memory is **procedural memory** for skills, habits, and how to perform tasks—in other words, memory for procedural knowledge. It may take a while to learn a procedure—such as how to ski, factor an equation, or design a teaching portfolio, but once learned, this knowledge tends to be remembered for a long time. Procedural knowledge is represented as scripts and condition-action rules, sometimes called *productions.*

Scripts are action sequences or plans for actions stored in memory (Schraw, 2006). We all have scripts for events like ordering food in restaurants and these scripts differ depending on whether the restaurant is a four-star bistro or a fast-food drive-through. Even young children have scripts for how to behave during snack time at preschool or at a friend's birthday party, as you can see in Figure 8.7. In fact, for very young children, scripts seem to help them organize and remember the predictable aspects of their world. This frees up some working memory to learn new things and recognize when something is out of place in the situation. In terms of human survival, it probably is useful to remember what is likely to keep happening and to notice when something is out of place (Nelson & Fivush, 2004).

Productions specify what to do under certain conditions: If A occurs, then do B. A production might be something like, "If you want to snow ski faster, lean back slightly," or "If your goal is to increase student attention and a student has been paying attention a bit longer than usual, then praise the student." People can't necessarily state all their scripts and condition-action rules, and they don't even realize that

PROCEDURAL MEMORY Procedural memory applies to skills, habits, and "how to do things." It may take a while to learn a procedure, such as serving a tennis ball, but once learned, the procedure tends to be remembered for a long time.

Procedural memory Long-term memory for how to do things.

Script Schema or expected plan for the sequence of steps in a common event such as buying groceries or ordering pizza.

Productions The contents of procedural memory; rules about what actions to take, given certain conditions.

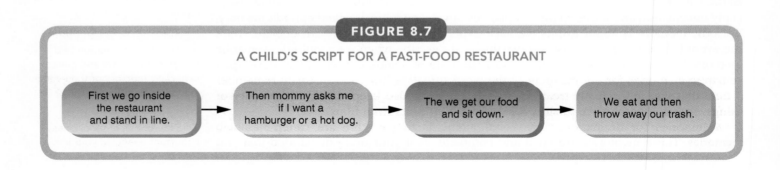

FIGURE 8.7

A CHILD'S SCRIPT FOR A FAST-FOOD RESTAURANT

| First we go inside the restaurant and stand in line. | → | Then mommy asks me if I want a hamburger or a hot dog. | → | The we get our food and sit down. | → | We eat and then throw away our trash. |

they are following these rules, but they act on them nevertheless. The more practiced the procedure, the more automatic the action and the more implicit the memory (Anderson, 2010; Schraw, 2006).

STOP & THINK Fill in these blanks: MEM _ _ _ •

The final type of implicit memory involves **priming**, or activating information that already is in long-term memory through some out-of-awareness process. You might have seen an example of priming in the fill-in-the-blank question above. If you wrote MEMORY instead of MEMOIR or MEMBER, or other MEM words, then priming may have played a role because the word *memory* has occurred many times in this chapter. Priming may be the fundamental process for retrieval as associations are activated and spread through the memory system (Ashcraft & Radvansky, 2010).

Storing and Retrieving Information in Long-Term Memory

Just what is done to "save" information permanently—to create explicit and implicit memories? How can we make the most effective use of our practically unlimited capacity to learn and remember? The way you learn information in the first place—the way you process it in working memory at the outset—strongly affects its recall later. One important requirement is that you integrate new information with existing knowledge as you construct an understanding. Here, *elaboration, organization, imagery,* and *context* play a role.

Elaboration is adding meaning to new information by connecting with already existing knowledge. In other words, we apply our schemas and draw on already existing knowledge to construct an understanding. Frequently, we change our existing knowledge in the process. We often elaborate automatically. For example, a paragraph about an historic figure in ancient Rome tends to activate our existing knowledge about that period; we use the old knowledge to understand the new.

Material that is elaborated when first learned will be easier to recall later. First, as we saw earlier, elaboration is a form of rehearsal. It keeps the information activated in working memory long enough to have a chance for the new information to be integrated with knowledge in long-term memory. Second, elaboration builds extra links to existing knowledge. The more one bit of information or knowledge is associated with other bits, the more routes there are to follow to get to the original bit. To put it another way, you have several "handles" or priming/retrieval cues to "pick up" or recognize the information you might be seeking (Bruning et al., 2011).

The more students elaborate new ideas, the more they "make them their own," the deeper their understanding and the better their memory for the knowledge will be. We help students to elaborate when we ask them to:

- translate information into their own words
- create examples
- explain to a peer

- create a metaphor
- draw a diagram of the situation
- act out the relations
- apply the information to new problems

Of course, if students elaborate new information by developing misguided explanations, these misconceptions will be remembered, too.

Organization is a second element of processing that improves learning. Material that is well organized is easier to learn and to remember than bits and pieces of information, especially if the material is complex or extensive. Chunking is one kind of organization—putting small bits of information into larger, more meaningful chunks. Placing a concept in a structure also will help you learn and remember both general definitions and specific examples. The structure serves as a guide back to the information when you need it. For example, Table 8.2 organizes information about types of knowledge and Figure 8.6 organizes my knowledge about reinforcement. The *Family and Community Partnerships Guidelines* give ideas for working with families to give all your students more support and practice in organizing learning.

Connect and Extend to PRAXIS II™

Memory and Recall (I, A1)
Cognitivists emphasize the role that elaboration, organization, and context have in effective encoding of information into long-term memory. Be aware of techniques that make use of those processes.

Priming Activating a concept in memory or the spread of activation from one concept to another.

Elaboration Adding and extending meaning by connecting new information to existing knowledge.

Organization Ordered and logical network of relations.

Organizing Learning

Give families specific strategies to help their children practice and remember.
Examples

1. Develop "super learner" homework assignments that include material to be learned and a "parent coaching card" with a description of a simple memory strategy—appropriate for the material—that parents can teach their child.
2. Provide a few comprehension check questions so a family member can review reading assignments and check the child's understanding.
3. Describe the value of distributed practice and give family members ideas for how and when to work skills practice into home conversations and projects.

Ask family members to share their strategies for organizing and remembering.
Examples

1. Create a family calendar.

2. Encourage planning discussions in which family members help students break large tasks into smaller jobs, identify goals, and find resources.

Discuss the importance of attention in learning.
Examples

1. Encourage families to create study spaces that are away from distractions.
2. Make sure parents know the purpose of homework assignments.

For a Web site dedicated to high-school study skills that might help parents, see http://www.mtsu.edu/~studskl/hsindex.html

---

IMAGERY. You may remember that the dual coding theory of memory suggests that information coded both visually and verbally is easiest to learn (Butcher, 2006; Paivio, 2006). Imagery can support memory if the information to be learned lends itself to images—it is easier to form an image for *car* than for *internal combustion*, for example, at least for me. Also the ability to form and use mental images appears to vary among individuals—some people are simply better at this task than others (Bruning et al., 2011). That said, is a picture worth 1,000 words in teaching? Richard Mayer (2001, 2005) has studied this question for several years and has found that the right combination of pictures and words can make a significant difference in students' learning, at least for older students. Mayer's cognitive theory of multimedia learning includes three ideas that should be familiar to you now:

Dual Coding: Visual and verbal materials are processed in different systems (Clark & Paivio, 1991).
Limited Capacity: Working memory for verbal and visual material is severely limited. Cognitive load has to be managed (Baddeley, 2001; van Merriënboer & Sweller, 2005).
Generative Learning: Meaningful learning happens when students focus on relevant information and generate or build connections (Mayer, 2008, 2011).

The problem: How to build complex understandings that integrate information from visual (pictures, diagrams, graphs, animations, films) and verbal (text, lecture) sources, given the limitations of working memory. *The solution:* Make sure the information is available at the same time or in focused small bites. Mayer and Gallini (1990) provide an example. They used three kinds of texts to explain how a bicycle pump works. One text used only words, the second had pictures that just showed the parts of the pump system and the steps, and the third (this one improved student learning and recall) showed both the "on" and the "off" states of the pumps with labels right on the illustration for each step in the pumping process, as you can see in Figure 8.8.

There are several cautions about using multiple representations to teach, however. First, Vernon Hall and his colleagues (1997) found that students who drew their own illustrations of how a pump works did as well as students who were provided Mayer's illustrations. Second, the students in both Mayer's and Hall's studies were in college. When

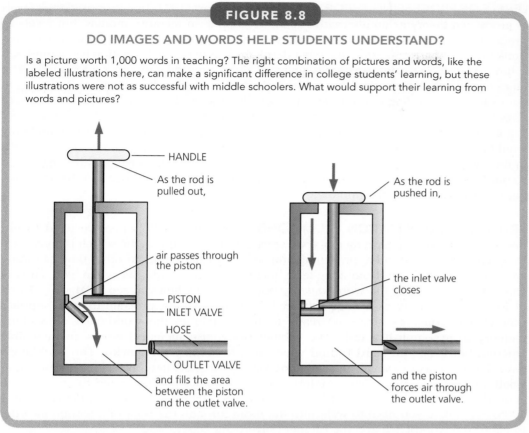

FIGURE 8.8

DO IMAGES AND WORDS HELP STUDENTS UNDERSTAND?

Is a picture worth 1,000 words in teaching? The right combination of pictures and words, like the labeled illustrations here, can make a significant difference in college students' learning, but these illustrations were not as successful with middle schoolers. What would support their learning from words and pictures?

HANDLE

As the rod is pulled out,

As the rod is pushed in,

air passes through the piston

the inlet valve closes

PISTON
INLET VALVE

HOSE

OUTLET VALVE

and fills the area between the piston and the outlet valve.

and the piston forces air through the outlet valve.

Source: Based on Mayer and Gallini (1990).

Erin McTigue (2009) tried to replicate these kinds of results with middle school students in life and physical sciences, the labeled pictures led to small improvements in students' understanding for life science texts, but not for physical science texts.

So research has shown that just using multiple representations (words, pictures, diagrams, charts, animations, etc.) does not necessarily lead to better learning. Students, especially younger ones, need supports such as color coding to draw attention to relevant relations in pictures and diagrams, or frequent checks for understanding with corrections if they are forming misconceptions (Bertgild & Renkl, 2009). The moral of the story? Give students multiple ways to understand—pictures and explanations. But don't overload working memory—"package" the visual and verbal information together in bite-size (or memory-size) pieces and teach students directly how to learn from illustrations or how to draw their own.

Context is a fourth element of processing that influences learning. Aspects of physical and emotional context—places, rooms, moods, who is with us—are learned along with other information. Later, if you try to remember the information, it will be easier if the current context is similar to the original one (Ashcraft & Radvansky, 2010). Context is a kind of priming that activates the information. For example, in a classic study, scuba divers who learned a list of words underwater and then were tested underwater remembered more than scuba divers who learned underwater but were tested on dry land (Godden & Baddeley, 1975). In another study, students who learned material in one type of room performed better on tests taken in a similar room than they did on comparable tests taken in a very different-looking room (Smith, Glenberg, & Bjork, 1978). So, studying for a test under "test-like" conditions (not at McDonald's, for example) may result in improved performance. Of course, you can't always go back to the same place or a similar one in order to recall something. But if you can picture the setting, the time of day, and your companions, you may eventually reach the information you seek.

Context The physical or emotional backdrop associated with an event.

LEVELS OF PROCESSING THEORY. Craik and Lockhart (1972) first proposed their **levels of processing theory** as an alternative to short-/long-term memory models, but levels of processing theory is particularly related to the notion of elaboration described earlier. Craik and Lockhart suggested that what determines how long information is remembered is how extensively the information is analyzed and connected with other information. The more completely information is processed, the better are our chances of remembering it. For example, according to the levels of processing theory, if I ask you to sort pictures of dogs based on the color of their coats, you might not remember many of the pictures later. But if I ask you to rate each dog on how likely it is to chase you as you jog, you probably would remember more of the pictures. To rate the dogs, you must pay attention to details in the pictures, relate features of the dogs to characteristics associated with danger, and so on. This rating procedure requires deeper processing and more focus on the *meaning*, not surface features, of the photos.

RETRIEVING INFORMATION FROM LONG-TERM MEMORY. When we need to use information from long-term memory, we search for it. Sometimes, the search is conscious, as when you see a friend approaching and search for her name. At other times, locating and using information from long-term memory is automatic, as when you enter a computer password or the word *memory* pops to mind when you see MEM _ _ _. Think of long-term memory as a huge cabinet full of tools (skills, procedures) and supplies (knowledge, concepts, schemas) ready to be brought to the workbench of working memory to accomplish a task. The cabinet (long-term memory) stores an incredible amount, but it may be hard to find what you are looking for quickly. The workbench (working memory) is small, but anything on it is immediately available. Because it is small, however, supplies (bits of information) sometimes are lost when the workbench is overloaded or when one bit of information covers (interferes with) another (E. Gagné, 1985). Of course you have to walk into the room through the door of attention in order to get to the workbench and the cabinet (Silverman, 2008).

SPREADING ACTIVATION. The size of the network in long-term memory is huge, but only small parts from it are activated at any one time—in fact, as you saw earlier, some psychologists say the smaller activated part of long-term memory *is* working memory. Information is retrieved in this network through **spreading activation**. When a particular proposition or image is active—when we are thinking about it—other closely associated knowledge can be primed or triggered as well, and activation can spread through the network (Anderson, 2010). Thus, as I focus on the propositions, "I'd like to go for a drive to see the fall leaves," related ideas such as, "I should rake leaves," and "The car needs an oil change," come to mind. As activation spreads from the "car trip" to the "oil change," the original thought, or active memory, disappears from working memory because of the limited space. Thus, **retrieval** from long-term memory occurs partly through the spreading of activation from one bit of knowledge to related ideas in the network.

RECONSTRUCTION. In long-term memory, the information is still available, even when it is not activated, even when you are not thinking about it at the moment. If spreading activation does not "find" the information we seek, then we might still come up with an answer through **reconstruction**, a cognitive tool or problem-solving process that makes use of logic, cues, and other knowledge to construct a reasonable answer by filling in any missing parts (Koriat, Goldsmith, & Pansky, 2000). Sometimes reconstructed recollections are incorrect. For example, in 1932, F. C. Bartlett conducted a series of famous studies on remembering stories. He read a complex, unfamiliar Native American tale to students at England's Cambridge University and, after various lengths of time, asked the students to recall the story. Stories the students recalled were generally shorter than the original and were translated into the concepts and language of the Cambridge student culture. The story told of a seal hunt, for instance, but many students remembered (reconstructed)

Levels of processing theory Theory that recall of information is based on how deeply it is processed.

Spreading activation Retrieval of pieces of information based on their relatedness to one another. Remembering one bit of information activates (stimulates) recall of associated information.

Retrieval Process of searching for and finding information in long-term memory.

Reconstruction Recreating information by using memories, expectations, logic, and existing knowledge.

a "fishing trip," an activity closer to their experiences and more consistent with their schemas.

FORGETTING AND LONG-TERM MEMORY. Over 100 years ago, Hermann Ebbinghaus (1885/1964), a pioneer in studying memory for verbal information, said simply, "All sorts of ideas, if left to themselves, are gradually forgotten. This fact is generally known" (p. 62). Information appears to be lost from long-term memory through time decay and interference. For example, memory for Spanish–English vocabulary decreases for about 3 years after a person's last course in Spanish, then stays level for about 25 years, then drops again for the next 25 years. One explanation for this decline is that neural connections, like muscles, grow weak without use. After 25 years, it may be that the memories are still somewhere in the brain, but they are too weak to be reactivated. Also, the physiological deterioration that comes with age could account for the later declines because some neurons simply die (Anderson, 2010). Finally, newer memories may interfere with or obscure older memories, and older memories may interfere with memory for new material.

Even with decay and interference, long-term memory is remarkable. Information in working memory can be lost and forgotten, but information stored in long-term memory may be available for a long time, given the right cues (Erdelyi, 2010). Teaching strategies that encourage student engagement, deeper processing of information, and higher levels of initial learning are associated with longer retention. Examples of such strategies are frequent reviews and tests, elaborated feedback, high standards, mastery learning, and active involvement in learning projects.

Individual Differences and Long-Term Memory

The major individual difference that affects long-term memory is knowledge. As we saw with the young soccer experts, when people have more domain-specific declarative and procedural knowledge, they are better at learning and remembering material in that domain (Alexander, 1997). Think about what it is like to read a very technical textbook in an area you know little about. Every line is difficult. You have to stop and look up words or turn back to earlier sections to read about concepts you don't understand. It is hard to remember what you are reading because you are trying to understand and remember at the same time. But with a good basis of knowledge, learning and remembering become easier; the more you know, the easier it is to know more. This may be why classes in your major seem easier than the required classes outside your major. Another factor could be interest. To develop expert understanding and recall in a domain requires the "continuous interplay of skill (i.e., knowledge) and thrill (i.e., interest)" (Alexander, Kulikowich, & Schulze, 1994, p. 334).

Now let's turn to the really important question: How can teachers support the development of long-lasting knowledge?

BECOMING KNOWLEDGEABLE: SOME BASIC PRINCIPLES

We will discuss the development of *declarative* and *procedural* knowledge separately, but keep in mind that real learning is a combination and integration of these elements. We look at developing the third type, *self-regulatory* knowledge, in the next chapter when we discuss metacognition.

Reaching Every Student: Development of Declarative Knowledge

As you have seen, people learn best when they have a good base of knowledge in the area they are studying. With many well-elaborated schemas and scripts to guide them, new material makes more sense, and there are many possible spots in the long-term memory network for connecting new information with old. What are some possible strategies? Perhaps the best single method for helping students learn is to make each lesson as meaningful as possible.

MAKING IT MEANINGFUL. Meaningful lessons are presented in vocabulary that makes sense to the students. New terms are clarified through ties with more familiar words and ideas. Meaningful lessons are well organized, with clear connections between the different elements of the lesson. Finally, meaningful lessons make natural use of old information to help students understand new information through examples or analogies.

The importance of meaningful lessons is emphasized below in an example presented years ago by Smith (1975).

STOP & THINK Look at the three lines below. Begin by covering all but the first line. Look at it for a second, close the book, and write down all the letters you remember. Then repeat this procedure with the second and third lines.
   1.   KBVODUWGPJMSQTXNOGMCTRSO
   2.   READ JUMP WHEAT POOR BUT SEEK
   3.   KNIGHTS RODE HORSES INTO WAR •

Each line has the same number of letters, but the chances are great that you remembered all the letters in the third line, a good number of letters in the second line, and very few in the first line. The first line makes no sense. There is no way to organize it in a brief glance. Working memory is simply not able to hold and process all those bits of information quickly. The second line is more meaningful. You do not have to see each letter because your long-term memory brings prior knowledge of spelling rules and vocabulary to the task. The third line is the most meaningful. Just a glance and you can probably remember all of it because you bring to this task prior knowledge not only of spelling and vocabulary but also of rules about syntax and probably some historical information about knights (they didn't ride in tanks). This sentence is meaningful because you have existing schemas for assimilating it (Sweller, van Merriënboer, & Paas, 1998).

The challenge for teachers is to make lessons less like learning the first line and more like learning the third line. Although this may seem obvious, think about the times when you have read a sentence in a text or heard an explanation from a professor that might just as well have been KBVODUWGPJMSQTXNOGMCTRSO. But beware, attempts to change the ways that students are used to learning—moving from memorizing to meaningful—are not always greeted with student enthusiasm. Students may be concerned about their grades; at least when memorization gains an A, they know what is expected. Meaningful learning can be riskier and more challenging. In Chapters 9, 10, and 11 we will examine a variety of ways in which teachers can support meaningful learning and understanding.

What can you do when students don't have a good base of knowledge? Mnemonics is a memory strategy for getting started.

MNEMONICS. **Mnemonics** are systematic procedures for improving memory (Atkinson et al., 1999; Levin, 1994; Rummel, Levin, & Woodward, 2003). When information has little inherent meaning, mnemonic strategies build in meaning by connecting what is to be learned with established words or images.

The **loci method** derives its name from the plural of the Latin word *locus,* meaning "place." To use loci, you must first imagine a very familiar place, such as your own house or apartment, and pick out particular locations to serve as "pegs" to "hang" memories. For instance, let's say you want to remember to buy milk, bread, butter, and cereal at the store. Imagine a giant jug of milk blocking the entry hall, a lazy loaf of bread sleeping on the living room couch, a stick of butter melting all over the dining room table, and cereal covering the kitchen floor. When you want to remember the items, all you have to do is take an imaginary walk through your house.

If you need to remember information for long periods of time, an acronym may be the answer. An **acronym** is a form of abbreviation—a word formed from the first letter of each word in a phrase, for example, HOMES to remember the Great Lakes (Huron, Ontario, Michigan, Erie, Superior). Another method forms phrases or

Connect and Extend to PRAXIS II™

Prior Knowledge (I, A1)
Prior knowledge strongly influences how we build and reorganize new knowledge. Be familiar with the role of schemas and propositional networks in the construction of knowledge and how they affect learning.

Mnemonics Techniques for remembering; the art of memory.

Loci method Technique of associating items with specific places.

Acronym Technique for remembering by using the first letter of each word in a phrase to form a new, memorable word.

sentences out of the first letter of each word or item in a list, for example, Every Good Boy Does Fine to remember the lines on the G clef—E, G, B, D, F. Because the words must make sense as a sentence, this approach also has some characteristics of **chain mnemonics**, methods that connect the first item to be memorized with the second, the second item with the third, and so on. In one type of chain method, each item on a list is linked to the next through some visual association or story. Another chain-method approach is to incorporate all the items to be memorized into a jingle such as "i before e except after c."

The mnemonic system that has been most extensively researched in teaching is the **keyword method**. Joel Levin and his colleagues use a mnemonic (the 3 Rs) to teach the keyword mnemonic method:

- ***R****ecode* the to-be-learned vocabulary item as a more familiar, concrete keyword—this is the keyword.
- ***R****elate* the keyword clue to the vocabulary item's definition through a sentence.
- ***R****etrieve* the desired definition.

The keyword method has been used extensively in foreign language learning. For example, the Spanish word *carta* (meaning "letter") sounds like the English word *cart. Cart* becomes the keyword: You imagine a shopping cart filled with letters on its way to the post office, or you make up a sentence such as "The cart full of letters tipped over" (Pressley, Levin, & Delaney, 1982). A similar approach has been used to help students connect artists with particular aspects of their paintings. For example, students are told to imagine that the heavy dark lines of paintings by Rouault are made with a *ruler* (Rouault) dipped in black paint (Carney & Levin, 2000, 2002).

Vocabulary learned with keywords can be easily forgotten if students are given keywords and images instead of being asked to supply words and images that are relevant to them. When the teacher provides the memory links, these associations may not fit the students' existing knowledge and may be forgotten or confused later; as a result, remembering suffers (Wang & Thomas, 1995; Wang, Thomas, & Ouellette, 1992). Younger students have some difficulty forming their own images. For them, memory aids that rely on auditory cues—rhymes such as "Thirty days hath September" seem to work better (Willoughby, Porter, Belsito, & Yearsley, 1999). Not all educators agree, however, as you will see in the *Point/Counterpoint*.

Until we have some knowledge to guide learning, it may help to use some mnemonic approaches to build vocabulary and facts.

ROTE MEMORIZATION. Very few things need to be learned by rote. The greatest challenge teachers face is to help students think and understand, not just memorize. Unfortunately, many students view **rote memorizing** and learning as the same thing (Iran-Nejad, 1990).

On rare occasions we do have to memorize something word for word, such as lines in a song, poem, or play. How would you do it? If you have tried to memorize a list of items that are all similar to one another, you may have found that you tended to remember items at the beginning and at the end of the list, but forgot those in the middle. This is called the **serial-position effect**. **Part learning**, breaking the list into smaller segments, can help prevent this effect, because breaking a list into several shorter lists means there will be fewer middle items to forget.

Another strategy for memorizing a long selection or list is the use of **distributed practice**. A student who studies Hamlet's soliloquy intermittently throughout the weekend will probably do much better than a student who tries to memorize the entire speech on Sunday night. Studying for an extended period is called *massed practice*. **Massed practice** leads to cognitive overload, fatigue, and lagging motivation. Distributed practice gives time for deeper processing and strengthens the connections in the neural network of the brain (Mumford, Costanza, Baughman, Threlfall, & Fleishman, 1994; Paul, 2011). What is

Connect and Extend to PRAXIS II™

Memory Strategies (II, A1)
Medical students often use mnemonics to remember the vast amounts of information they encounter in their studies. Be familiar with the major mnemonic methods and the kinds of information that they are most suitable for.

Chain mnemonics Memory strategies that associate one element in a series with the next element.

Keyword method System of associating new words or concepts with similar-sounding cue words and images.

Rote memorization Remembering information by repetition without necessarily understanding the meaning of the information.

Serial-position effect The tendency to remember the beginning and the end, but not the middle of a list.

Part learning Breaking a list of items into shorter lists.

Distributed practice Practice in brief periods with rest intervals.

Massed practice Practice for a single extended period.

POINT/COUNTERPOINT: What's Wrong with Memorizing?

For years, students have relied on memorization to learn vocabulary, procedures, steps, names, and facts. Is this a bad idea?

POINT

▶ **Rote memorization creates inert knowledge.** Years ago William James (1912) described the limitations of rote learning by telling a story about what can happen when students memorize but do not understand:

A friend of mine, visiting a school, was asked to examine a young class in geography. Glancing at the book, she said: "Suppose you should dig a hole in the ground, hundreds of feet deep, how should you find it at the bottom—warmer or colder than on top?" None of the class replying, the teacher said: "I'm sure they know, but I think you don't ask the question quite rightly. Let me try." So, taking the book, she asked: "In what condition is the interior of the globe?" And received the immediate answer from half the class at once. "The interior of the globe is in a condition of igneous fusion." (p. 150)

The students had memorized the answer, but they had no idea what it meant. Perhaps they didn't understand the meaning of "interior," "globe," or "igneous fusion." At any rate, the knowledge was useful to them only when they were answering test questions, and only then when the questions were phrased exactly as they had been memorized. Students often resort to memorizing the exact words of definitions when they have no hope for actually understanding the terms or when teachers count off for definitions that are not exact.

Howard Gardner has been a vocal critic of rote memorization and a champion of "teaching for understanding." In an interview in *Phi Delta Kappan* (Siegel & Shaughnessy, 1994), Gardner says:

My biggest concern about American education is that even our better students in our better schools are just going through the motions of education. In The Unschooled Mind, I review ample evidence that suggests an absence of understanding—the inability of students to take knowledge, skills, and other apparent attainments and apply them successfully in new situations. In the absence of such flexibility and adaptability, the education that the students receive is worth little. (pp. 563–564)

COUNTERPOINT

▶ **Rote memorization can be effective.** Memorization may not be such a bad way to learn new information that has little inherent meaning, such as foreign language vocabulary. Alvin Wang, Margaret Thomas, and Judith Ouellette (1992) compared learning Tagalog (the national language of the Philippines) using either rote memorization or the keyword approach for associating new words with existing words and images. In their study, even though the keyword method led to faster and better learning initially, long-term forgetting was *greater* for students who had used the keyword method than for students who had learned by rote memorization.

A study of preservice teachers found that they believed memorization is valuable for young children to build basic skills (Beghetto, 2008). There are times when students must memorize and we do them a disservice if we don't teach them how. For example, "memorization in simple mathematics or word reading activities in the early grades may be desirable and promote future academic success; constructivist, problem-based learning by itself may not be as successful as a combination of both constructivist problem solving and memorization together" (Chang et al, 2011, p. 25).

Beware of Either/Or. Every discipline has its own terms, names, facts, and rules. As adults, we want to work with physicians who have memorized the correct names for the bones and organs of the body or the drugs needed to combat particular infections. Of course, they can look up some information or research certain conditions, but they have to know where to start. We want to work with accountants who give us accurate information about the new tax codes, information they probably had to memorize because it changes from year to year in ways that are not necessarily rational or meaningful. We want to deal with computer salespeople who have memorized their stock and know exactly which printers will work with our computer. Just because something was learned through memorization does not mean it is inert knowledge. The real question, as Gardner points out, is whether you can *use* the information flexibly and effectively to solve new problems.

forgotten after one session can be relearned in the next with distributed practice. Still, there is debate in education about how much memorization should be encouraged, as you can see in the *Point/Counterpoint.*

Development of Procedural Knowledge

One characteristic that distinguishes experts from novices in every arena, from reading to medical diagnosis, is that the experts' declarative knowledge has become "proceduralized," that is, incorporated into routines they can apply automatically without making many demands on working memory. Explicit memories have become implicit and the expert is no longer aware of them. Skills that are applied without conscious thought are called **automated basic skills**. An example is shifting gears in a standard transmission car. At first, you have to think about every step, but as you become more expert (if you do), the procedure becomes automatic. But not all procedures can be automatic, even for experts in a particular domain. For example, no matter how expert you are in driving, you still have to consciously watch the traffic around you. This kind of conscious procedure is called a *domain-specific strategy*. Automated basic skills and domain-specific strategies are learned in different ways (Gagné, Yekovich, & Yekovich, 1993).

AUTOMATED BASIC SKILLS. Most psychologists identify three stages in the development of an automated skill: *cognitive, associative,* and *autonomous* (Anderson, 2010; Fitts & Posner, 1967). At the cognitive stage, when we are first learning, we rely on declarative knowledge and general problem-solving strategies to accomplish our goal. For example, to learn how to assemble a bookshelf, we might try to follow steps in the instruction manual, putting a check beside each step as we complete it to keep track of progress. At this stage, we have to "think about" every step and perhaps refer back to the pictures of parts to see what a "4-inch metal bolt with lock nut" looks like. The cognitive load on working memory is heavy. There can be quite a bit of trial-and-error learning at this stage when, for example, the bolt we chose doesn't fit.

At the *associative stage*, individual steps of a procedure are combined or "chunked" into larger units. We reach for the right bolt and put it into the right hole. One step smoothly cues the next. With practice, the associative stage moves to the *autonomous stage*, where the whole procedure can be accomplished without much attention. So if you assemble enough bookshelves, you can have a lively conversation as you do, paying little attention to the assembly task. This movement from the cognitive to the associative to the autonomous stage holds for the development of basic cognitive skills in any area, but science, medicine, chess, and mathematics have been most heavily researched. One thing is clear—it takes many hours of successful practice to make skills automatic.

What can teachers do to help their students pass through these three stages and become more expert learners? In general, it appears that two factors are critical: *prerequisite knowledge* and *practice with feedback*. First, if students don't have the essential prior knowledge (concepts, schemas, skills, etc.), the cognitive load on working memory will be too great. Second, practice with feedback allows you to form associations, recognize cues automatically, and combine small steps into larger condition-action rules or **productions**. Even from the earliest stage, some of this practice should include a simplified version of the whole process in a real context. Practice in real contexts helps students learn not only *how* to do a skill but also *why and when* (Collins, Brown, & Newman, 1989; Gagné, Yekovich, & Yekovich, 1993). Of course, as every athletic coach knows, if a particular step, component, or process is causing trouble, that element might be practiced alone until it is more automatic, and then put back into the whole sequence, to lower the cognitive load on working memory (Anderson, Reder, & Simon, 1996; Ericsson, 2011).

DOMAIN-SPECIFIC STRATEGIES.   As we saw earlier, some procedural knowledge, such as monitoring the traffic while you drive, is not automatic because conditions are constantly changing. Once you decide to change lanes, the maneuver may be fairly automatic, but the decision to change lanes was conscious, based on the traffic conditions around you. **Domain-specific strategies** are consciously applied skills that organize thoughts and actions to reach a goal. To support this kind of learning, teachers need to provide opportunities for practice in many different situations—for example, practice reading with package labels, magazines, books, letters, operating manuals, web pages and so on. In the next chapter's discussion of problem-solving and study strategies, we will examine other ways to help students develop domain-specific strategies. For now, let's summarize these ideas for developing declarative and procedural knowledge in a set of *Guidelines*. We will spend quite a bit of time in the next chapter on developing self-regulatory knowledge.

Connect and Extend to PRAXIS II™

Developing Basic Skills (II, A3) Efficient and effective performance as a learner requires the automatic use of basic skills. Describe what teachers can do to help students develop automatic basic skills.

Automated basic skills Skills that are applied without conscious thought.

Productions Units of knowledge that combine conditions with actions in "if this happens, do that" relationships that often are automatic.

Domain-specific strategies Consciously applied skills to reach goals in a particular subject or problem.

GUIDELINES

Helping Students Understand and Remember

Make sure you have the students' attention.
Examples

1. Develop a signal that tells students to stop what they are doing and focus on you. Make sure students respond to the signal—don't let them ignore it. Practice using the signal.
2. Move around the room, use gestures, and avoid speaking in a monotone.
3. Begin a lesson by asking a question that stimulates interest in the topic.
4. Regain the attention of individual students by walking closer to them, using their names, or asking them a question.

Help students separate essential from nonessential details and focus on the most important information.
Examples

1. Summarize instructional objectives to indicate what students should be learning. Relate the material you are presenting to the objectives as you teach: "Now I'm going to explain exactly how you can find the information you need to meet Objective One on the board—determining the tone of the story."
2. When you make an important point, pause, repeat, ask a student to paraphrase, note the information on the board in colored chalk, or tell students to highlight the point in their notes or readings.

Help students make connections between new information and what they already know.
Examples

1. Review prerequisites to help students bring to mind the information they will need to understand new material: "Who can tell us the definition of a quadrilateral? Now, what is a rhombus? Is a square a quadrilateral? Is a square a rhombus? What did we say yesterday about how you can tell? Today we are going to look at some other quadrilaterals."
2. Use an outline or diagram to show how new information fits with the framework you have been developing. For example,

"Now that you know the duties of the FBI, where would you expect to find it in this diagram of the branches of the U.S. government?"

3. Give an assignment that specifically calls for the use of new information along with information already learned.

Provide for repetition and review of information.
Examples

1. Begin the class with a quick review of the homework assignment.
2. Give frequent, short tests.
3. Build practice and repetition into games, or have students work with partners to quiz each other.

Present material in a clear, organized way.
Examples

1. Make the purpose of the lesson very clear.
2. Give students a brief outline to follow. Put the same outline on an overhead transparency so you can keep yourself on track. When students ask questions or make comments, relate these to the appropriate section of the outline.
3. Use summaries in the middle and at the end of the lesson.

Focus on meaning, not memorization.
Examples

1. In teaching new words, help students associate the new word to a related word they already understand: "*Enmity* is from the same base as *enemy.*"
2. In teaching about remainders, have students group 12 objects into sets of 2, 3, 4, 5, 6, and ask them to count the "leftovers" in each case.

For more information on information processing, see:
http://www.edpsyinteractive.org/topics/cognition/infoproc.html

▼ SUMMARY

Elements of the Cognitive Perspective (pp. 282–284)

Contrast cognitive and behavioral views of learning in terms of what is learned and the role of reinforcement. According to the cognitive view, knowledge is learned, and changes in knowledge make changes in behavior possible. According to the behavioral view, the new behaviors themselves are learned. Both behavioral and cognitive theorists believe reinforcement is important in learning, but for different reasons. The strict behaviorist maintains that reinforcement strengthens responses; cognitive theorists see reinforcement as a source of feedback about what is likely to happen if behaviors are repeated or changed—as a source of information.

How does knowledge affect learning? The cognitive approach suggests that one of the most important elements in the learning process is knowledge the individual brings to the learning situation. What we already know determines to a great extent what we will pay attention to, perceive, learn, remember, and forget.

What is the brain's role in cognition? The human brain seems to both impact and be impacted by learning. For example, individuals who regularly complete tasks such as taxi driving develop certain regions of the brain more than others who do not engage in such activities. Research also suggests that learning changes communication among neurons. These changes enable children to engage in complex tasks such as integrating past and present experiences by approximately age 7.

Cognitive Views of Memory (pp. 284–296)

Describe the path from sensory input to recognizing objects. The first phase in the process is feature analysis, or bottom-up processing, because the stimulus must be analyzed into features or components and assembled into a meaningful pattern. The

Gestalt principles are one explanation for how features are organized into patterns. In addition to noting features and using these Gestalt principles, to recognize patterns rapidly, we use what we already know about the situation, information from the context, and our knowledge of prototypes or best examples.

What is working memory? Working memory is both short-term storage in the phonological loop and visuospatial sketchpad and processing in the episodic buffer, guided by the central executive—it is the workbench of conscious thought. To keep information activated in working memory for longer than 20 seconds, people use maintenance rehearsal (mentally repeating) and elaborative rehearsal (making connections with knowledge from long-term memory). Elaborative rehearsal also helps move new information to long-term memory. The limited capacity of working memory can also be somewhat circumvented by the control process of chunking. There are individual differences in working memory, and working memory span is related to performance on tasks that require higher-level thinking and controlled attention such as IQ tests and the SAT.

What is cognitive load and how does it impact information processing? Cognitive load refers to the volume of cognitive resources, including perception, attention and memory, necessary to perform a task. These resources must be devoted not only to organizing and understanding the task, but also to analyzing the solution and ignoring irrelevant stimuli. If cognitive load is high, it can decrease or even inhibit one's ability to perform a task.

Long-Term Memory (pp. 296–307)

Compare declarative, procedural, and self-regulatory knowledge. Declarative knowledge is knowledge that can be declared, usually in words or other symbols. Declarative knowledge is "knowing that" something is the case. Procedural knowledge is "knowing how" to do something; it must be demonstrated. Self-regulatory knowledge is "knowing when and why" to apply your declarative and procedural knowledge.

How is information represented in long-term memory, and what role do schemas play? Memories may be explicit (semantic or episodic) or implicit (procedural, classical conditioning, or priming). In long-term memory, bits of information may be stored and interrelated in terms of propositional networks, images, concepts, and schemas. A concept is a category used to group similar events, ideas, objects, or people such as books, students, or cats. Concepts provide a manner of organizing diversity among members of a group. Concepts are often represented by prototypes (an ideal example) and exemplars (a representative memory). Long-term memories include concepts that enable people to identify and recognize members of a group. To organize propositions, images, and concepts, we have schemas, which are data structures that allow us to represent large amounts of complex information, make inferences, and understand new information. Today some psychologists suggest that working memory is just the part of long-term memory that is currently activated—that you are thinking about at any given time.

What learning processes improve long-term memory? The way you learn information in the first place affects its recall later. One important requirement is to integrate new material with knowledge already stored in long-term memory using elaboration, organization, imagery, and context. The dual coding theory suggests that information coded both verbally and visually is easier to remember. Pictures and words help students learn as long as they are well organized and do not overload working memory. Another view of memory is the levels of processing theory, in which recall of information is determined by how completely it is processed.

Why do we forget? Information lost from working memory truly disappears, but information in long-term memory may be available, given the right cues. Information appears to be lost from long-term memory through time decay (neural connections, like muscles, grow weak without use) and interference (newer memories may obscure older memories, and older memories may interfere with memory for new material).

Becoming Knowledgeable: Some Basic Principles (pp. 307–312)

Describe three ways to develop declarative knowledge. Declarative knowledge develops as we integrate new information with our existing understanding. The most useful and effective way to learn and remember is to understand and use new information. Making the information to be remembered meaningful is important and often is the greatest challenge for teachers. Mnemonics are memorization aids: They include approaches such as the loci method, acronyms, chain mnemonics, and the keyword method. A powerful but limiting way to accomplish this is rote memorization, which can best be supported by part learning and distributed practice.

Describe some methods for developing procedural knowledge. Automated basic skills and domain-specific strategies—two types of procedural knowledge—are learned in different ways. There are three stages in the development of an automated skill: cognitive (following steps or directions guided by declarative knowledge), associative (combining individual steps into larger units), and autonomous (where the whole procedure can be accomplished without much attention). Prerequisite knowledge and practice with feedback help students move through these stages. Domain-specific strategies are consciously applied skills of organizing thoughts and actions to reach a goal. To support this kind of learning, teachers need to provide opportunities for practice and application in many different situations.

▼ KEY TERMS

Acronym (308)
Attention (287)
Automated basic skills (310)
Automaticity (287)
Bottom-up processing (286)
Central executive (291)
Chain mnemonics (308)
Chunking (294)
Cognitive load (292)
Cognitive science (282)
Cognitive view of learning (282)
Concept (299)
Context (305)
Decay (294)
Declarative knowledge (296)

Defining attribute (299)
Distributed practice (309)
Domain-specific knowledge (284)
Domain-specific strategies (312)
Dual coding theory (299)
Elaboration (303)
Elaborative rehearsal (296)
Episodic buffer (292)
Episodic memory (301)
Exemplar (300)
Explicit memory (297)
Extraneous cognitive load (292)
Flashbulb memories (301)
General knowledge (284)
Germane cognitive load (292)

Gestalt (286)
Images (298)
Implicit memory (297)
Information processing (284)
Interference (294)
Intrinsic cognitive load (292)
Keyword method (309)
Levels of processing theory (306)
Loci method (308)
Long-term memory (296)
Maintenance rehearsal (293)
Massed practice (309)
Mirror systems (283)
Mnemonics (308)
Organization (303)

▼ CONNECT AND EXTEND TO LICENSURE

MULTIPLE-CHOICE QUESTIONS

1. Rachel had been practicing her multiplication tables for weeks before her yearly standardized test. She knew all of her facts completely. This type of knowledge that Rachel now has attained does not require attention and concentration. This process is known as which one of the following?
   A. Declarative memory
   B. Flashbulb memory
   C. Automaticity
   D. Schema

2. Elaboration occurs when one adds meaning to new information by connecting with already existing knowledge. In other words, we apply our schemas and draw on already existing knowledge to construct an understanding. Which of the following is NOT true of elaboration?
   A. Elaboration can occur automatically.
   B. Material that is elaborated when first learned will be easier to recall later.
   C. Elaboration can limit the number of links to stored knowledge.
   D. The more students elaborate new ideas, the deeper their understanding and the better their memory for the knowledge will be.

3. Miss Campbell wanted to ensure that her driver's education students were safe under all circumstances. To ensure this, she had her students drive in the rain and snow. She also made sure they had adequate practice for driving in traffic and on the highway. Miss Campbell was encouraging the development of which of the following strategies?
   A. Domain-specific
   B. Mnemonic
   C. Declarative
   D. Elaborative

4. Cognitive load is a term that refers to the amount of mental resources, mostly working memory, required to perform a particular task. Of the three types of cognitive load, which can instruction support by asking students to explain the material to each other or to themselves, drawing or charting their understandings, or taking useful notes?
   A. Intrinsic cognitive load
   B. Extraneous cognitive load
   C. Germane cognitive load
   D. Working cognitive load

CONSTRUCTED-RESPONSE QUESTIONS

Case

Reflecting on his first year as a teacher, Mr. Beech was a little embarrassed at how little he understood the teaching and learning process when he began teaching. He remembered handing back a math test and admonishing his students with the following words. "Everybody in this room knew the test was today. I can't believe not one of you passed it. All I can say is, you had better master these concepts before we get into the testing season. Thirty percent of the standardized test is on algebra. I know we did several chapters quickly this time, more than you were used to, but we have to finish this book. And, no, I will not let you retake this test."

5. Explain the three types of knowledge Mr. Beech's students probably had to use while taking the algebra test.

6. In addition to not overloading his students with new information, how else can Mr. Beech assist his students in understanding and remembering in the future?

MyEducationLab™

Go to Chapter 8 of the Book Specific Resources in MyEducationLab and click on "Connect and Extend to Licensure" to answer these questions. Compare your responses with the feedback provided.

▼ WHAT WOULD THEY DO?

TEACHERS' CASEBOOK: Remembering the Basics

Here is how a number of expert teachers responded to the situation at the beginning of the chapter about students who often have trouble remembering key information from one day or week to the next.

PAULA COLEMERE • Special Education Teacher—English, History
McClintock High School, Tempe, AZ

I always evaluate my test results to see if student mistakes came from a poorly written question. If a number of students are missing the same test question, I review the answers to see what went wrong. This helps me to see if I need to alter my test or alter my instruction. As a teacher, I am constantly reflecting on my successes and defeats. Did I set a purpose for learning at the beginning of the unit? Did I make connections to prior knowledge? Before giving this unit test, was there sufficient formative assessment along the way? It makes more sense to pay attention during lessons to see what students understand and where they need more instruction. For students who are struggling along the way, I would spend a little more time on a concept and offer extra help during lunch or after school to help them gain a better understanding. I would teach them how to organize information and how to study. Chunking information is another good strategy to help students who struggle. I also teach test-taking skills to help students build confidence in their test-taking abilities.

LAUREN ROLLINS • 1st Grade
Boulevard Elementary School, Shaker Heights, OH

I promote different styles of teaching and learning in my classroom. However, I usually present some material, such as vocabulary words, math facts, and sight words, using a rote memory approach. In this situation, that method seemed to work well for the majority of the students, but not all of them. Therefore, it is my job as the teacher to create opportunities for those students to work with the material in a different way. In the example of the vocabulary, I would help the students create their own dictionaries where they would define each vocabulary word in a way that makes sense to them and provide examples that they would remember. Once the vocabulary becomes more meaningful to them, it will be easier for them to remember. In my classroom, I try to provide the students with a variety of methods to practice these types of concepts. Coloring pages, matching activities, word/number searches, secret codes, games, books, etc. are available to my students to help them practice sight words and math facts every day. I encourage my students to serve as peer tutors and enlist parents to work one on one with students as well. Every little bit helps!

SARA VINCENT • Special Education
Langley High School, McLean, VA

Every individual learns differently. The teacher in this scenario should first take time to identify how the students learn material effectively. Their inability to master the material may stem from a note-taking problem; students may benefit more from a cloze note-taking format rather than attempting to decipher what information is important. In addition, the teacher should administer smaller assessments more frequently prior to the final test in order to determine if all students are grasping the information. The teacher could then provide remediation to those students who are still struggling with the material. Every day, a teacher should evaluate her delivery of the information. She should also assess if the students are learning the material. In other words, no one can be a perfect teacher; effective teaching is always a work in progress.

JESSICA N. MAHTABAN • 8th Grade Math
Woodrow Wilson Middle School, Clifton, NJ

Mind mapping would be a great tool to help students retain and retrieve information. It is a fast and fun way to take visual notes, expand students' visual thinking skills, and make learning meaningful. Graphic organizers are another phenomenal instrument to use that steers the students away from just memorizing facts. A graphic organizer expands students' higher level thinking skills and helps them make connections. A student's prior knowledge helps him or her build upon lessons and make connections with new information. When a student can relate to the content and have meaningful connections, a whole new classroom emerges!

The next step would be to teach students how to comprehend the material rather than just retain the material. Teachers need to provide students with strategies they can use in order to comprehend all the subjects. Also, teachers need to provide students with plenty of modeling! Modeling all the strategies students can use in order to comprehend material will benefit the students the most!

JENNIFER L. MATZ • Grade 6
Williams Valley Elementary, Tower City, PA

I review vocabulary every day at the start of the lesson. This only takes a few minutes. My students make "flip books." Flip books are better than flash cards because students can test themselves and flash cards can be lost. We write the definition, but then we write it in "kid" words too. I ask them to explain words or events in their own words.

Some review ideas are: Make up two sets of cards: one set with the words, the other set with the definition. Pass out both sets to the class and ask "word people" to find their "matching definition." Another is to have a student come to the front and cover his eyes. Write the word on the board and have the class give him clues. They may not say the word—he must guess it.

Make up songs to help students remember information. When I taught second grade, we had an array of grammar songs and rhymes to remember nouns, pronouns, etc. My students made up movements. You can pair students who have mastered material with those who have not. Students often have better ways of remembering things than we can teach them.

— **MyEducationLab** —

Go to Topic 6, Memory and Cognitive Processes, in the MyEducationLab (www.myeducationlab.com) for *Educational Psychology*, where you can:

- Find learning outcomes for Memory and Cognitive Processes along with the national standards that connect to these outcomes.
- Complete Assignments and Activities that can help you more deeply understand the chapter content.
- Apply and practice your understanding of the core teaching skills identified in the chapter with the Building Teaching Skills and Dispositions learning units.
- Examine challenging situations and cases presented in the IRIS Center Resources.
- Access video clips of CCSSO National Teachers of the Year award winners responding to the question, "Why Do I Teach?" in the Teacher Talk section.
- Check your comprehension on the content covered in the chapter with the Study Plan. Here you will be able to take a chapter quiz, receive feedback on your answers, and then access Review, Practice, and Enrichment activities to enhance your understanding of chapter content.
- Find additional Teachers' Casebook scenarios and responses to them from practicing teachers.
- Use the Online Lesson Plan Builder to practice lesson planning and integrating national and state standards into your planning.

chapter nine
COMPLEX COGNITIVE PROCESSES

▶ **TEACHERS' CASEBOOK:** Uncritical Thinking

This year's class is worse than any you've ever had. You assigned a research paper and you find more and more students are using the Web for their information. In itself, using the Web is not bad, but the students appear to be completely uncritical about what they find on the Internet. "If it is on the Web, it must be right" is the attitude of most students. Their first drafts are filled with quotes that seem very biased to you, but there are no sources cited or listed. It is not just that students don't know how to reference their work. You are more concerned that they cannot critically evaluate what they are reading. And all they are reading is the Net!

CRITICAL THINKING

- How would you help your students evaluate the information they are finding on the Web?

- Beyond this immediate issue, how will you help students think more critically about the subjects you are teaching?

- How will you take into account the cultural beliefs and values of your students as you support their critical thinking?

OVERVIEW AND OBJECTIVES

In the previous chapter we focused on the development of knowledge—how people make sense of and remember information and ideas. In this chapter, we consider complex cognitive processes that lead to understanding. Understanding is more than memorizing. It is more than retelling in your own words. Understanding involves appropriately transforming and using knowledge, skills, and ideas. These understandings are considered "higher-level cognitive objectives" in a commonly used system of educational objectives (Anderson & Krathwohl, 2001; Bloom, Engelhart, Frost, Hill, & Krathwohl, 1956). We will focus on the implications of cognitive theories for the day-to-day practice of teaching.

Because the cognitive perspective is a philosophical orientation and not a unified theoretical model, teaching methods derived from it are varied. In this chapter, we will first examine the complex cognitive process of metacognition—using knowledge and skills about learning, motivation, and yourself to plan and regulate your own learning. Next we explore four important areas in which cognitive theorists have made suggestions for learning and teaching: learning strategies, problem solving, creativity, and critical thinking, including argumentation. Finally, we will consider the question of how to encourage the transfer of learning from one situation to another to make learning more useful.

By the time you have completed this chapter, you should be able to:

Objective 9.1: Discuss the roles of metacognition in learning and remembering.

Objective 9.2: Describe several learning and study strategies that help students develop their metacognitive abilities.

Objective 9.3: Explain the processes involved in problem solving and the factors that can interfere with successful problem solving.

Objective 9.4: Explain how creativity is defined, assessed, and encouraged in the classroom.

Objective 9.5: Identify factors that influence students' abilities to think critically and to form and support arguments.

Objective 9.6: Discuss how, why, and when knowledge learned in one situation might be applied to new situations and problems.

METACOGNITION

In Chapter 8 we discussed a number of **executive control processes**, including attention, rehearsal, organization, imagery, and elaboration. These executive control processes are sometimes called *metacognitive* skills, because they can be intentionally used to regulate cognition.

Metacognitive Knowledge and Regulation

Emily Fox and Michelle Riconscente define **metacognition** simply as "knowledge or awareness of self as knower" (2008, p. 373). Metacognition literally means cognition about cognition—or thinking about thinking—something William James wrote about over 100 years ago (although he did not give it that name). The term was introduced into discussions of child development by John Flavell and his colleagues in the early 1970s. Metacognition is higher-order knowledge about your own thinking as well as your ability to use this knowledge to manage your own cognitive processes such as comprehension and problem solving (Bruning et al., 2011). People differ in how well and how quickly they learn because they differ in their metacognitive knowledge and skills.

Metacognition involves all three kinds of knowledge we discussed earlier: (1) *declarative knowledge* about yourself as a learner, the factors that influence your learning and memory, and the skills, strategies, and resources needed to perform a task—*knowing what* to do; (2) *procedural knowledge* or *knowing how* to use the strategies; and (3) *self-regulatory knowledge* to ensure the completion of the task—*knowing the conditions*, when and why, to apply the procedures and strategies (Bruning et al., 2011). Metacognition is the strategic application of this declarative, procedural, and self-regulatory knowledge to accomplish goals and solve problems (Schunk, 2012). Metacognition also includes knowledge about the value of applying cognitive strategies in learning (Pressley & Harris, 2006).

Metacognition regulates thinking and learning (Brown, 1987; Nelson, 1996). There are three essential skills: *planning*, *monitoring*, and *evaluating*. *Planning* involves deciding how much time to give to a task, which strategies to use, how to start, which resources to gather, what order to follow, what to skim and what to give intense attention to, and so on. *Monitoring* is the real-time awareness of "how I'm doing." Monitoring is asking, "Is this making sense? Am I trying to go too fast? Have I studied enough?" *Evaluating* involves making judgments about the processes and outcomes of thinking and learning. "Should I change strategies? Get help? Give up for now? Is this paper (painting, model, poem, plan, etc.) finished?" The notion of *reflection* in teaching—thinking back on what happened in class and why, and thinking forward to what you might do next time—is really about metacognition in teaching (Sawyer, 2006).

Of course, we don't have to be metacognitive all the time. Some actions become routine or habits. Metacognition is most useful when tasks are challenging, but not too difficult. And even when we are planning, monitoring, and evaluating, these processes are not necessarily conscious, especially in adults. We may use them automatically without being aware of our efforts (Perner, 2000). Experts in a particular field plan, monitor, and evaluate as second nature; they have difficulty describing their metacognitive knowledge and skills (Pressley & Harris, 2006; Reder, 1996).

Executive control processes Processes such as selective attention, rehearsal, elaboration, and organization that influence encoding, storage, and retrieval of information in memory.

Metacognition Knowledge about our own thinking processes.

Individual Differences in Metacognition

Some differences in metacognitive abilities are the result of development. Younger children, for example, may not be aware of the purpose of a lesson—they may think the point is simply to finish. They also may not be good at gauging the difficulty of a task—they may think that reading for fun and reading a science book are the same (Gredler, 2009). As children grow older, they are more able to exercise executive control over strategies. For example, they are more able to determine if they have understood instructions or if they have studied enough to remember a set of items. Metacognitive abilities begin to develop around ages 5 to 7 and improve throughout school (Flavell, Green, & Flavell, 1995; Woolfolk & Perry, 2012).

Not all differences in metacognitive abilities have to do with age or maturation. Some individual differences in metacognitive abilities are probably caused by differences in biology or learning experiences. In fact, many students diagnosed as having learning disabilities have problems monitoring their attention (Hallahan & Kauffman, 2006), particularly with long tasks. Working to improve metacognitive skills can be especially important for students who often have trouble in school (Schunk, 2012; Swanson, 1990).

Lessons for Teachers: Developing Metacognition

Like any knowledge or skill, metacognitive knowledge and skills can be learned and improved.

METACOGNITION Metacognition involves choosing the best way to approach a learning task. Students with good metacognitive skills set goals, organize their activities, select among various approaches to learning, and change strategies if needed.

METACOGNITIVE DEVELOPMENT FOR YOUNGER STUDENTS.

In his 2nd grade classroom in Queens, New York, Daric Desautel (2009) worked with mostly Latino/a and Asian students. As part of teaching literacy, Desautel decided to focus on student metacognitive knowledge and skills such as setting goals, planning, evaluating achievements, and self-reflection to help students develop the habit of "looking in" at their own thinking. He also included self-reflections to help students evaluate their writing and gain insight into themselves as readers and writers. For example, one self-reflection included a checklist asking:

- Did you pick a topic that you know all about?
- Did you write a special beginning that makes the reader want more?
- Did you organize your thoughts and make a Table of Contents?
- Did you pick the right kind of paper and illustrate your book clearly?
- Did you re-read your work to check for SOUND, SENSE, ORDER, and GOOFS?

Desautel was successful in helping all his students, not just the most verbal and advanced, develop metacognitive knowledge. One student noted in his reflection, "I worked hard and did my best to make this book. I like nonfiction books better than stories. Next time, I would write about a different sport."

In her work with 1st and 2nd graders, Nancy Perry found that asking students two questions helped them become more metacognitive. The questions were "What did you learn about yourself as a reader/writer today?" and "What did you learn that you can do again and again and again?" When teachers asked these questions regularly during class, even young students demonstrated fairly sophisticated levels of metacognitive understanding and action (Perry et al., 2000).

Many of the cooperating teachers I work with use a strategy called **KWL** to guide reading and inquiry in general. This general frame can be used with most grade levels. The steps are:

K What do I already know about this subject?
W What do I want to know?
L At the end of the reading or inquiry, what have I learned?

KWL A strategy to guide reading and inquiry: Before—What do I already *know*? What do I *want* to know? After—What have I *learned*?

The KWL frame encourages students to "look within" and identify what they bring to each learning situation, where they want to go, and what they actually achieved—a very metacognitive approach to learning. Marilyn Friend and William Bursuck (2002, pp. 362–363) describe how one teacher used modeling and discussion to teach the KWL strategy. After reviewing the steps, the teacher models an example and a nonexample of using KWL to learn about "crayons."

> **Teacher:** What do we do now that we have a passage assigned to read? First, I brainstorm, which means I try to think of anything I already know about the topic and write it down.

The teacher writes on the board or overhead known qualities of crayons, such as "made of wax," "come in many colors," "can be sharpened," "several different brands."

> **Teacher:** I then take this information I already know and put it into categories, like "what crayons are made of" and "crayon colors." Next, I write down any questions I would like to have answered during my reading, such as "Who invented crayons? When were they invented? How are crayons made? Where are they made?" At this point, I'm ready to read, so I read the passage on crayons. Now I must write down what I learned from this passage. I must include any information that answers the questions I wrote down before I read and any additional information. For example, I learned that colored crayons were first made in the United States in 1903 by Edwin Binney and E. Harold Smith. I also learned that the Crayola Company owns the company that made the original magic markers. Last, I must organize this information into a map so I can see the different main points and any supporting points.

At this point, the teacher draws a map on the chalkboard or overhead.

> **Teacher:** Let's talk about the steps I used and what I did before and after I read the passage.

A class discussion follows.

> **Teacher:** Now I'm going to read the passage again, and I want you to evaluate my textbook reading skills based on the KWL Plus strategy we've learned.

The teacher then proceeds to demonstrate the strategy *incorrectly*.

> **Teacher:** The passage is about crayons. Well, how much can there really be to know about crayons besides there are hundreds of colors and they always seem to break in the middle? Crayons are for little kids, and I'm in junior high so I don't need to know that much about them. I'll just skim the passage and go ahead and answer the question. Okay, how well did I use the strategy steps?

The class discusses the teacher's inappropriate use of the strategy. Notice how the teacher provides both an *example* and a *nonexample*—good teaching.

METACOGNITIVE DEVELOPMENT FOR SECONDARY AND COLLEGE STUDENTS (LIKE YOU). For older students, teachers can incorporate metacognitive questions into their lessons, lectures, and assignments. For example, David Jonassen (2011) suggests that instructional designers incorporate these questions into hypermedia learning environments to help students be more self-reflective:

KWL One cooperative learning strategy used by many teachers to guide reading and inquiry is called KWL: What do I know? What do I want to know? What have I learned?

What are my intellectual strengths and weaknesses?

How can I motivate myself to learn when I need to?

How good am I at judging how well I understand something?

How can I focus on the meaning and significance of new information?

How can I set specific goals before I begin a task?

What questions should I ask about the material before I begin?

How well have I accomplished my goals once I'm finished?

Have I learned as much as I could have once I finish a task?

Have I considered all options after I solve a problem?

Metacognition includes knowledge about using many strategies in learning—our next topic.

LEARNING STRATEGIES

Most teachers will tell you that they want their students to "learn how to learn." Years of research indicate that using good learning strategies helps students learn and that these strategies can be taught (Hamman, Berthelot, Saia, & Crowley, 2000; Pressley & Harris, 2006). But were you taught "how to learn"? Powerful and sophisticated learning strategies and study skills are seldom taught directly until high school or even college, so most students have little practice with them. In contrast, early on, students usually discover repetition and rote learning on their own, so they have extensive practice with these strategies. And, unfortunately, some teachers think that memorizing is learning (Beghetto, 2008; Woolfolk Hoy & Murphy, 2001). This may explain why many students cling to flash cards and memorizing—they don't know what else to do (Willoughby, Porter, Belsito, & Yearsley, 1999).

As we saw in Chapter 8, the way something is learned in the first place greatly influences how readily we remember the information and how appropriately we can apply the knowledge later. First, students must be *cognitively engaged* in order to learn—they have to *focus attention* on the relevant or important aspects of the material. Second, they have to *invest effort*, make connections, elaborate, translate, invent, organize, and reorganize in order to think and *process deeply*—the greater the practice and processing, the stronger the learning. Finally, students must *regulate and monitor* their own learning—keep track of what is making sense and notice when a new approach is needed, that is, they must be *metacognitive*. The emphasis today is on helping students develop effective learning strategies that focus attention and effort, process information deeply, and monitor understanding.

Being Strategic About Learning

Learning strategies are a special kind of procedural knowledge—*knowing how* to do something. There are thousands of strategies. Some are general and taught in school, such as summarizing or outlining. Others are specific to a subject, such as using a mnemonic to remember the order of the planets: "My Very Educated Mother Just Served Us Nachos" for Mercury, Venus, Earth, Mars, Jupiter, Saturn, Uranus, and Neptune. Other strategies may be unique, invented by an individual to learn Chinese characters, for example. Learning strategies can be cognitive (summarizing, identifying the main idea), metacognitive (monitoring comprehension—do I understand?), or behavioral (using an Internet dictionary, setting a timer to work till time's up) (Cantrell, Almasi, Carter, Rintamaa, & Madden, 2010). All are ways of accomplishing a learning task that are intentionally applied when usual methods have not worked and strategic effort is needed (Harris, Alexander, & Graham, 2008). Over time, as you become more expert at using the strategies, less intentional effort is needed. Ultimately you may become more automatic in applying the strategies; in other words, the strategies will become your usual way of accomplishing that kind of task, until they don't work and new strategies are needed.

Skilled learners have a wide range of learning strategies that they can apply fairly automatically. Using learning strategies and study skills is related to higher GPAs in high

Connect and Extend to PRAXIS II™

Learning Strategies (I, A1)
For suggestions about their effective use, take a look at the study skills site developed by the Virginia Polytechnic Institute (http://www.ucc.vt.edu/stdysk/stdyhlp.html), and also see http://www.studygs.net/ for more ideas.

Learning strategies A special kind of procedural knowledge—*knowing how* to approach learning tasks.

school and persistence in college (Robbins et al., 2004). Researchers have identified several important principles:

1. Students must be exposed to a number of different strategies, not only general learning strategies but also very specific strategies for particular subjects, such as the graphic strategies described later in this section.
2. Students should be taught self-regulatory (conditional) knowledge about when, where, and why to use various strategies. Although this may seem obvious, teachers often neglect this step. A strategy is more likely to be maintained and employed if students know when, where, and why to use it.
3. Students may know when and how to use a strategy, but unless they also develop the desire to employ these skills, general learning ability will not improve. Several learning strategy programs include a motivational training component.
4. Students need to believe that they can learn new strategies, that the effort will pay off, and that they can "get smarter" by applying these strategies.
5. Students need some background knowledge and useful schemas in the area being studied to make sense of learning materials. It will be difficult to find the main idea in a paragraph about *ichthyology*, for example, if you don't know much about fish. So students may need direct instruction in schematic (content) knowledge along with strategy training. Table 9.1 summarizes several learning strategies.

DECIDING WHAT IS IMPORTANT. You can see from the first entry in Table 9.1 that learning begins with focusing attention—deciding what is important. But distinguishing the main idea from less important information is not always easy. Often students focus on the "seductive details" or the concrete examples, perhaps because these are more interesting (Gardner, Brown, Sanders, & Menke, 1992). You may have had the experience of remembering a joke or an intriguing example from a lecture, but not being clear about the larger point the professor was trying to make. Finding the central idea is especially difficult if you lack prior knowledge in an area and the amount of new information provided

TABLE 9.1 • **Examples of Learning Strategies**

	EXAMPLES
Planning and Focusing Attention	Setting goals and timetables
	Underlining and highlighting
	Skimming, looking for headings and topic sentences
Organizing and Remembering	Making organizational charts
	Creating flowcharts, Venn diagrams
	Using mnemonics, imagery
Comprehension	Concept mapping, webs
	Summarizing, outlining and note-taking
	Creating examples
	Explaining to a peer
Cognitive Monitoring	Making predictions
	Self-questioning and self-testing
	Identifying what doesn't make sense
Practice	Using part practice
	Using whole practice

is extensive. Teachers can give students practice using signals in texts such as headings, bold words, outlines, or other indicators to identify key concepts and main ideas (Lorch, Lorch, Ritchey, McGovern, & Coleman, 2001).

SUMMARIES. Creating summaries can help students learn, but students have to be taught how to summarize (Byrnes, 1996; Palincsar & Brown, 1984). Jeanne Ormrod (2004) summarizes these suggestions for helping students create summaries. Ask students to:

- Find or write a topic sentence for each paragraph or section.
- Identify big ideas that cover several specific points.
- Find some supporting information for each big idea.
- Delete any redundant information or unnecessary details.

Begin by doing summaries of short, easy, well-organized readings. Introduce longer, less organized, and more difficult passages gradually. Ask students to compare their summaries and discuss what ideas they thought were important and why—what's their evidence?

Two other study strategies that are based on identifying key ideas are underlining texts and taking notes.

- -

STOP & THINK How do you make notes as you read? Look back over the past several pages of this chapter. Are my words highlighted yellow or pink? Are there marks or drawings in the margins and if so, do the notes pertain to the chapter or are they grocery lists and doodles?

- -

UNDERLINING AND HIGHLIGHTING. Do you underline or highlight key phrases in textbooks? Underlining and note-taking are probably two of the most frequent but ineffectively used strategies among college students. One common problem is that students underline or highlight too much. It is far better to be selective. In studies that limit how much students can underline—for example, only one sentence per paragraph—learning has improved (Snowman, 1984). In addition to being selective, you also should actively transform the information into your own words as you underline or take notes. Don't rely on the words of the book. Note connections between what you are reading and other things you already know. Draw diagrams to illustrate relationships. Finally, look for organizational patterns in the material and use them to guide your underlining or note-taking.

TAKING NOTES. Taking good lecture notes is not an easy task. You have to hold the lecture information in working memory; select, organize, and transform the important ideas and themes before the information "falls off" your working memory workbench; and write down the ideas and themes—all while you are still following the lecture (Peverly et al., 2007). As you fill your notebook with words and try to keep up with a lecturer, you may wonder if taking notes makes a difference. It does, if the strategy is used well.

- Taking notes focuses attention during class. Of course, if taking notes distracts you from actually listening to and making sense of the lecture, then note-taking may not be effective (Kiewra, 1989, 2002; Van Meter, Yokoi, & Pressley, 1994).
- Taking notes makes you construct meaning from what you are hearing, seeing, or reading, so you elaborate, translate into your own words, and remember (Armbruster, 2000). Even if students don't review notes before a test, taking them in the first place appears to aid learning, especially for those who lack prior knowledge in an area.
- Notes provide extended external storage that allows you to return and review. Students who use their notes to study tend to perform better on tests, especially if they take many high-quality notes—more is better as long as you are capturing key ideas, concepts, and relationships, not just intriguing details (Kiewra, 1985, 1989; Peverly, Brobst, Graham, & Shaw, 2003).
- Expert students match notes to their anticipated use and modify strategies after tests or assignments; use personal codes to flag material that is unfamiliar or difficult; fill in holes by consulting relevant sources (including other students in the class); and record information verbatim only when a verbatim response will be required. In other words, they are *strategic* about taking and using notes (Van Meter, Yokoi, & Pressley, 1994).

Even though taking notes is valuable from middle school through graduate school, students with learning disabilities often have trouble (Boyle, 2010a, 2010b). Middle school and high school students with learning disabilities who used a strategic note-taking form recalled and understood significantly more key ideas from science lectures than students in control groups who used conventional note-taking methods (Boyle, 2010b; Boyle & Weishaar, 2001). For an example of this kind of form see http://www.ldonline.org/article/6210/. Figure 9.1 is a general form that can be used in many note-taking situations. Dividing up the page is an idea from Cornell notes, an idea devised by Walter Pauk of Cornell University, who wrote the classic guide, *How to Study in College* in the 1950s. It

---

FIGURE 9.1

A FORM FOR TAKING NOTES MORE STRATEGICALLY

Topic:	What do I already know about this topic?
Key Points/ Key Terms	Notes

Summaries: Write 3 to 5 sentences that capture the main ideas.

1.

2.

3.

4.

5.

Questions: What is still confusing or unclear?

Source: Based on ideas from Pauk, Walter; Owens, Ross J. Q. (2010) [1962], *How to Study in College* (10th ed.). Florence, KY: Cengage Learning; http://academic.cuesta.edu/acasupp/as/618.htm; and http://www.ldonline.org/article/6210/

is still available (Pauk & Owens, 2010). This form could be useful for any student who needs extra guidance in note-taking,

Visual Tools for Organizing

To use underlining and note-taking effectively, you must identify main ideas. In addition, you must understand the organization of the text or lecture—the connections and relationships among ideas. Some visual strategies have been developed to help students with this key organizational element (Van Meter, 2001). A **concept map** is a drawing that charts the relations among ideas, as shown in Figure 9.2, which is a concept map describing a Web site for creating concept maps! You may have referred to these interconnected ideas as *webs*.

In a review of 55 studies with students from 4th grade to graduate school and subjects ranging from science to statistics to nursing, John Nesbit and Olusola Adesope (2006) concluded that, "in comparison with activities such as reading text passages, attending lectures, and participating in class discussions, concept mapping activities are more effective for attaining knowledge retention and transfer" (p. 434). "Mapping" relationships by noting causal connections, comparison/contrast connections, and examples improves recall. My students at Ohio State use **Cmaps,** the free downloadable tools from the Web site shown in Figure 9.2, for creating concept maps—one even planned his dissertation and organized all the reading for his doctoral examinations with tools from the Web site. Computer Cmaps can be linked to the Internet, and students in different classrooms and schools all over the world can collaborate on them. Students should compare their filled-in "maps" and discuss the differences in their thinking with each other.

Connect and Extend to PRAXIS II™

Concept Mapping (II, A2)
For advice and additional information about the creation and use of concept maps, go to the Web site *Graphic Organizers* (http://www.graphic.org/concept.html).

Concept map A drawing that charts the relationships among ideas.

Cmaps Tools for concept mapping developed by the Institute for Human and Machine Cognition that are connected to many knowledge maps and other resources on the Internet.

FIGURE 9.2

THE WEB SITE FOR THE INSTITUTE FOR HUMAN AND MACHINE COGNITION CMAP TOOLS AT HTTP://CMAP.IHMC.US/

At this site, you can download concept mapping tools to construct, share, and criticize knowledge on any subject.

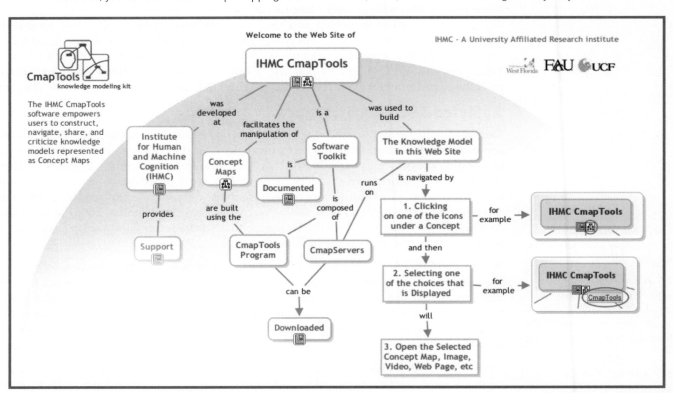

Source: Institute for Human and Machine Cognition Cmap Tools home page. http://cmap.ihmc.us. Reprinted with permission from the IHMC.

There are other ways to visualize organization, such as Venn diagrams, which show how ideas or concepts overlap, and tree diagrams, which show how ideas branch off each other. Time lines organize information in sequence and are useful in classes such as history or geology.

Reading Strategies

As we saw above, effective learning strategies should help students *focus attention*, invest effort (connect, elaborate, translate, organize, summarize) so they *process information deeply*, and *monitor* their understanding. There are a number of strategies that support these processes in reading. Many use mnemonics to help students remember the steps involved. For example, one strategy that can be used for any grade above later elementary is **READS:**

R Review headings and subheadings.
E Examine boldface words.
A Ask, "What do I expect to learn?"
D Do it—Read!
S Summarize in your own words. (Friend & Bursuck, 2012)

A strategy that can be used in reading literature is **CAPS:**
C Who are the characters?
A What is the aim of the story?
P What problem happens?
S How is the problem solved?

There are several reasons why these strategies are effective. First, following the steps makes students more aware of the organization of a given chapter. How often have you skipped reading headings entirely and thus missed major clues about the way the information was organized? Next, these steps require students to study the chapter in sections instead of trying to learn all the information at once. This makes use of *distributed practice*. Answering questions about the material forces students to process the information more deeply and with greater elaboration.

No matter what strategies you use, students have to be taught how to use them. *Direct teaching, explanation, modeling*, and *practice with feedback* are necessary and are especially important for students with learning challenges and students whose first language is not English. For an example of direct teaching of strategies with explanations, modeling, and practice with feedback, see the KWL discussion earlier in this chapter.

Applying Learning Strategies

One of the most common findings in research on learning strategies is what are known as **production deficiencies**. Students learn strategies, but do not apply them when they could or should (Pressley & Harris, 2006). This is especially a problem for students with learning disabilities. For these students, executive control processes (that is, metacognitive strategies) such as planning, organizing, monitoring progress, and making adaptations often are underdeveloped (Kirk, Gallagher, Anastasiow, & Colemen, 2006). It makes sense to teach these strategies directly. To insure that students actually use the strategies they learn, several conditions must be met.

APPROPRIATE TASKS. First, of course, the learning task must be *appropriate*. Why would students use more complex learning strategies when the task set by the teacher is to "learn and return" the exact words of the text or lecture? With these tasks, memorizing will be rewarded and the best strategies involve distributed practice and perhaps mnemonics (described in Chapter 8). But we hope that there are few of these kinds of tasks in contemporary teaching, so if the task is *understanding*, not memorizing, what else is necessary?

VALUING LEARNING. The second condition for using sophisticated strategies is that students must *care* about learning and understanding. They must have goals that can be reached using effective strategies (Zimmerman & Schunk, 2001). I was reminded of this in my educational psychology class one semester when I enthusiastically shared an article

Production deficiency Students learn problem-solving strategies, but do not apply them when they could or should.

READS A five-step reading strategy: *Review* headings; *Examine* boldface words; *Ask*, "What do I expect to learn?"; *Do* it—Read; *Summarize* in your own words.

CAPS A strategy that can be used in reading literature: *Characters*, *Aim* of story, *Problem*, *Solution*.

GUIDELINES

Becoming an Expert Student

Make sure you have the necessary declarative knowledge (facts, concepts, ideas) to understand new information.
Examples
1. Keep definitions of key vocabulary available as you study.
2. Review required facts and concepts before attempting new material.

Find out what type of test the teacher will give (essay, short answer), and study the material with that in mind.
Examples
1. For a test with detailed questions, practice writing answers to possible questions.
2. For a multiple-choice test, use mnemonics to remember definitions of key terms.

Make sure you are familiar with the organization of the materials to be learned.
Examples
1. Preview the headings, introductions, topic sentences, and summaries of the text.
2. Be alert for words and phrases that signal relationships, such as *on the other hand, because, first, second, however, since.*

Know your own cognitive skills and use them deliberately.
Examples
1. Use examples and analogies to relate new material to something you care about and understand well, such as sports, hobbies, or films.
2. If one study technique is not working, try another—the goal is to stay involved, not to use any particular strategy.

Study the right information in the right way.
Examples
1. Be sure you know exactly what topics and readings the test will cover.
2. Spend your time on the important, difficult, and unfamiliar material that will be required for the test or assignment.
3. Keep a list of the parts of the text that give you trouble, and spend more time on those pages.
4. Process the important information thoroughly by using mnemonics, forming images, creating examples, answering questions, making notes in your own words, and elaborating on the text. Do not try to memorize the author's words—use your own.

Monitor your own comprehension.
Examples
1. Use questioning to check your understanding.
2. When reading speed slows down, decide if the information in the passage is important. If it is, note the problem so you can reread or get help to understand. If it is not important, ignore it.
3. Check your understanding by working with a friend and quizzing one another.

For more resources on studying,
see: http://www.ucc.vt.edu/stdysk/stdyhlp.html or
http://www.d.umn.edu/student/loon/acad/strat/
Source: From "Research Synthesis on Study Skills" by B. B. Armbruster and T. H. Anderson. Educational Leadership, 39. Copyright © 1993 by the American Association for Supervision and Curriculum Development. Reprinted with permission from ASCD. All rights reserved. The Association for Supervision and Curriculum Development is a worldwide community of educators advocating sound policies and sharing best practices to achieve the success of each learner. To learn more, visit ASCD at www.ascd.org.

about study skills from the newspaper, *USA Today*. The gist of the article was that students should continually revise and rewrite their notes from a course, so that by the end, all their understanding could be captured in one or two pages. Of course, the majority of the knowledge at that point would be reorganized and connected well with other knowledge. "See," I told the class, "these ideas are real—not just trapped in texts. They can help you study smarter in college." After a heated discussion, one of the best students said in exasperation, "I'm carrying 18 hours—I don't have time to *learn* this stuff!" She did not believe that her goal—to survive the 18 hours—could be reached by using time-consuming study strategies.

EFFORT AND EFFICACY.   My student also was concerned about effort. The third condition for applying learning strategies is that students must believe the effort and investment required to apply the strategies are reasonable, given the likely return (Winne, 2001). And of course, students must believe they are capable of using the strategies; that is, they must have self-efficacy for using the strategies to learn the material in question (Schunk, 2012). This is related to another condition: Students must have a base of knowledge and/or experience in the area. No learning strategies will help students accomplish tasks that are completely beyond their current understandings.

The *Guidelines* provide a summary of ideas for you and your students.

Reaching Every Student: Learning Strategies for Struggling Students

Reading is key in all learning. Strategy instruction can help many struggling readers. As you have seen, some approaches make use of mnemonics to help students remember the steps. For example, Susan Cantrell (2010) and her colleagues identified 862 students in 6th and 9th grade who were at least two years behind in reading. The students were from 23 different schools. Students were randomly assigned to either a Learning Strategies Curriculum (Deshler & Schumaker, 2005) or the traditional curriculum. The Learning Strategies Curriculum focused on six strategies: word identification, visual imagery, self-questioning, LINCS vocabulary strategy, sentence writing, and paraphrasing. The **LINCS Vocabulary Strategy** uses stories and imagery to help students learn how to identify, organize, define, and remember words, which increases their ownership of their learning. The LINCS steps are:

L: "List the parts." Identify the vocabulary word and key information.
I: "Identify a reminding word." Pick a known word that reminds them of the vocabulary word.
N: "Note a LINCing story." Create a story that bridges the vocabulary word with the known word.
C: "Create a LINCing picture." Draw a picture that represents the story.
S: "Self-test." Check their learning of the vocabulary word by reciting all the parts of their LINCS.

After a year, the 6th graders who had participated in the Learning Strategies Curriculum performed significantly better on reading comprehension and strategy use, but there were no differences for 9th graders. It is possible that reading strategy instruction is most effective in elementary and early middle school when students are learning how to learn through reading (Cantrell, Almasi, Carter, Rintamaa, & Madden, 2010).

Of course, you have to do more than just tell students about the strategy—you have to teach it. Michael Pressley and Vera Woloshyn (1995) developed the Cognitive Strategies Model as a guide for teaching students to improve their metacognitive strategies. Table 9.2 describes the steps in teaching these strategies.

PROBLEM SOLVING

STOP & THINK You're interviewing with the district superintendent for a position as a school psychologist. The superintendent is known for his unorthodox interview questions. He hands you a pad of paper and a ruler and says, "Tell me, what is the exact thickness of a single sheet of paper?" •

TABLE 9.2 • **Teaching Strategies for Improving Students' Metacognitive Knowledge and Skills**

These eight guidelines taken from Pressley and Woloshyn (1995) should help you in teaching any metacognitive strategy.

- Teach a few strategies at a time, intensively and extensively as part of the ongoing curriculum.
- Model and explain new strategies.
- If parts of the strategy were not understood, model again and re-explain strategies in ways that are sensitive to those confusing or misunderstood aspects of strategy use.
- Explain to students where and when to use the strategy.
- Provide plenty of practice, using strategies for as many appropriate tasks as possible.
- Encourage students to monitor how they are doing when they are using strategies.
- Increase students' motivation to use strategies by heightening their awareness that they are acquiring valuable skills—skills that are at the heart of competent functioning.
- Emphasize reflective processing rather than speedy processing; do everything possible to eliminate high anxiety in students; encourage students to shield themselves from distractions so they can attend to academic tasks.

For a list of strategies and how to teach them see: http://www.unl.edu/csi/bank.html

Source: Adapted from Pressley, M., & Woloshyn, V. (1995). Cognitive Strategy Instruction That Really Improves Children's Academic Performance. Cambridge, MA: Brookline Books, p. 18.

LINCS Vocabulary Strategy A strategy that uses stories and imagery to help students learn how to identify, organize, define, and remember words and their meanings.

This is a true story—I was asked the paper thickness question in an interview years ago. The answer was to measure the thickness of the entire pad and divide by the number of pages in the pad. I got the answer and the job, but what a tense moment that was. I suppose the superintendent was interested in my ability to solve problems—under pressure!

A **problem** has an initial state (the current situation), a goal (the desired outcome), and a path for reaching the goal (including operations or activities that move you toward the goal). Problem solvers often have to set and reach subgoals as they move toward the final solution. For example, if your goal is to drive to the beach, but at the first stop sign you skid through the intersection, you may have to reach a subgoal of fixing your brakes before you can continue toward the original goal (Schunk, 2012). Also, problems can range from *well structured* to *ill structured*, depending on how clear-cut the goals are and how much structure is provided for solving them. Most arithmetic problems are well structured, but finding the right college major is ill structured—many different solutions and paths to solutions are possible. Life presents many ill-structured problems.

Connect and Extend to PRAXIS II™

Problem Solving (II, A1)
Be prepared to identify the steps in the general problem-solving process. Describe the techniques that students can employ to build useful representations of problems.

Problem solving is usually defined as formulating new answers, going beyond the simple application of previously learned rules to achieve a goal. Problem solving is what happens when no solution is obvious—when, for example, you can't afford new brakes for the car that skidded on the way to the beach (Mayer & Wittrock, 2006). Some psychologists suggest that most human learning involves problem solving (Anderson, 1993).

There is a debate about problem solving. Some psychologists believe that effective problem-solving strategies are specific to the problem area. That is, the problem-solving strategies in mathematics are unique to math; the strategies in art are unique to art, and so on. The other side of the debate claims that there are some general problem-solving strategies that can be useful in many areas. General problem-solving strategies usually include the steps of *identifying* the problem, *setting goals*, *exploring* possible solutions and consequences, *acting,* and finally *evaluating* the outcome.

Actually, there is evidence for the value of both general and specific strategies. In their research with 4th and 5th graders, Steven Hecht and Kevin Vargi (2010) found that both domain-specific and general factors affected performance on problems involving fractions. The influences were specific conceptual knowledge about fractions and the general information processing skill of attentive classroom behavior. Another study with children in 3rd grade found that both specific arithmetic knowledge and general attention-focusing skills were related to arithmetic problem solving (Fuchs et al., 2006). Finally, Robert Kail and Lynda Hall (1999) found that both domain-specific arithmetic knowledge and general information processing skills, including reading and information processing time, were related to success in solving word problems.

It appears that people move between general and specific approaches, depending on the situation and their level of expertise. Early on, when we know little about a problem area or domain, we can rely on general learning and problem-solving strategies to make sense of the situation. As we gain more domain-specific knowledge (particularly procedural knowledge about how to do things in the domain), we consciously apply the general strategies less and less; our problem solving becomes more automatic. But if we encounter a problem outside our current knowledge, we may return to relying on general strategies to attack the problem (Alexander, 1992, 1996).

A key first step in any problem solving—general or specific—is identifying that a problem exists (and perhaps treating the problem as an opportunity).

Identifying: Problem Finding

Problem identification is not always straightforward. I am reminded of a story about tenants who were angry because the elevators in their building were slow. Consultants hired to "fix the problem" reported that the elevators were no worse than average and improvements would be very expensive. One day, as the building supervisor watched people waiting impatiently for an elevator, he realized that the problem was not slow elevators, but the fact that people were bored; they had nothing to do while they waited.

Problem Any situation in which you are trying to reach some goal and must find a means to do so.

Problem solving Creating new solutions for problems.

When the boredom problem was identified and seen as an opportunity to improve the "waiting experience," the simple solution of installing a mirror by the elevator on each floor eliminated complaints.

Even though problem identification is a critical first step, research indicates that people often "leap" to naming the first problem that comes to mind ("the elevators are too slow!"). Experts in a field are more likely to spend time carefully considering the nature of the problem (Bruning, Schraw, & Norby, 2011). Finding a solvable problem and turning it into an opportunity is the process behind many successful inventions, such as the ballpoint pen, garbage disposal, appliance timer, alarm clock, self-cleaning oven, and thousands of others.

Once a solvable problem is identified, what next?

Defining Goals and Representing the Problem

Let's take a real problem: The machines designed to pick tomatoes are damaging the tomatoes. What should we do? If we represent the problem as a faulty machine design, then the goal is to improve the machine. But if we represent the problem as a faulty design of the tomatoes, then the goal is to develop a tougher tomato. The problem-solving process follows two entirely different paths, depending on which representation and goal are chosen (Bransford & Stein, 1993). To represent the problem and set a goal, you have to *focus attention* on relevant information, *understand the words* of the problem, and *activate the right schema* to understand the whole problem.

STOP & THINK If you have black socks and white socks in your drawer, mixed in the ratio of four to five, how many socks will you have to take out to make sure you have a pair the same color (adapted from Sternberg & Davidson, 1982)? •

FOCUSING ATTENTION ON WHAT IS RELEVANT. Representing the problem often requires finding the relevant information and ignoring the irrelevant details. For example, what information was relevant in solving the above sock problem? Did you realize that the information about the four-to-five ratio of black socks to white socks is irrelevant? As long as you have only two different colors of socks in the drawer, you will have to remove only three socks before two of them match.

UNDERSTANDING THE WORDS. The second task in representing a problem is understanding the meaning of the words, sentences, and factual information in the problem. So problem solving requires comprehension of the language and relations in the problem. In math word problems, it also involves assigning mathematical operators (addition, division, etc.) to relations among numbers (Jitendra et al., 2010; Lee, Ng, & Ng, 2009). All this makes a demand on working memory. For example, the main stumbling block in representing many word problems is the students' understanding of part-whole relations (Cummins, 1991). Students have trouble figuring out what is part of what, as is evident in this dialogue between a teacher and a 1st grader:

> **Teacher:** Pete has three apples. Ann also has some apples. Pete and Ann have nine apples altogether. How many apples does Ann have?
>
> **Student:** Nine.
>
> **Teacher:** Why?
>
> **Student:** Because you just said so.
>
> **Teacher:** Can you retell the story?
>
> **Student:** Pete had three apples. Ann also had some apples. Ann had nine apples. Pete also has nine apples. (Adapted from De Corte & Verschaffel, 1985, p. 19)

The student interprets "altogether" (the whole) as "each" (the parts).

A common difficulty for older students is understanding that ratio and proportion problems are based on multiplicative relations, not additive relations (Jitendra et al., 2010). So to solve

$$2: 14 = ? : 35$$

many students subtract to find the difference between 2 and 14 ($14 - 2 = 12$) and then subtract 12 from 35 to get 23, giving them the (wrong) answer

$$2 : 14 = 23 : 35$$

The real question is about the *proportional* relationship between 2 and 14. How many times larger than 2 is 14? The answer: 7 times larger. Then the real question is "35 is 7 times larger than what number?" The answer is 5 ($7 \times 5 = 35$). So

$$2 : 14 + 5 : 35$$

Sometimes, students are taught to search for key words (*more, less, greater*, etc.), pick a strategy or formula based on the key words (*more* means "add"), and apply the formula. Actually, this gets in the way of forming a conceptual understanding of the whole problem—the next challenge (Van de Walle, Kary, & Bay-Williams, 2010).

UNDERSTANDING THE WHOLE PROBLEM. The third task in representing a problem is to assemble all the relevant information and sentences into an accurate understanding or translation of the total problem. This means that students need to form a conceptual model of the problem—they have to understand what the problem is *really asking* (Jonassen, 2003). Consider this example.

STOP & THINK Two train stations are 50 miles apart. At 2 P.M. one Saturday afternoon, two trains start toward each other, one from each station. Just as the trains pull out of the stations, a bird springs into the air in front of the first train and flies ahead to the front of the second train. When the bird reaches the second train, it turns back and flies toward the first train. The bird continues to do this until the trains meet. If both trains travel at the rate of 25 miles per hour and the bird flies at 100 miles per hour, how many miles will the bird have flown before the trains meet? (Posner, 1973) •

Your interpretation of the problem is called a *translation* because you translate the problem into a schema that you understand. If you translate this as a *distance* problem (activate a distance schema) and set a goal ("I have to figure out how far the bird travels before it meets the oncoming train and turns around, then how far it travels before it has to turn again, and finally add up all the trips back and forth"), then you have a very difficult task on your hands. But there is a better way to structure the problem. You can represent it as a question of *time* and focus on the time the bird is in the air. The solution could be stated like this:

> The trains are going the same speed so they will meet in the middle, 25 miles from each station. This will take one hour because they are traveling 25 mph. In an hour, the bird will cover 100 miles because it is flying at 100 miles per hour. Easy!

Research shows that students can be too quick to decide what a problem is asking. Once a problem is categorized—"Aha, it's a distance problem!"—a particular schema is activated. The schema directs attention to relevant information and sets up expectations for what the right answer should look like. For example, if you use a distance schema in the above problem, the right answer looks like adding up many small distance calculations (Kalyuga, Chandler, Tuovinen, & Sweller, 2001; Reimann & Chi, 1989).

When students lack the necessary schemas to represent problems, they often rely on surface features of the situation and represent the problem incorrectly, like the student who wrote "15 + 24 = 39" as the answer to, "Joan has 15 bonus points and Louise has 24. How many more does Louise have?" This student saw two numbers and the word *more*, so he applied the *add to get more* procedure. When students use the wrong schema, they

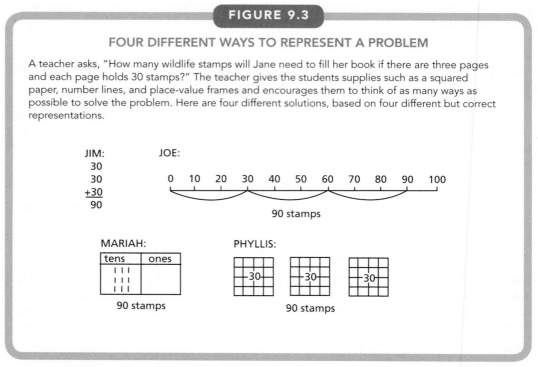

FIGURE 9.3

FOUR DIFFERENT WAYS TO REPRESENT A PROBLEM

A teacher asks, "How many wildlife stamps will Jane need to fill her book if there are three pages and each page holds 30 stamps?" The teacher gives the students supplies such as a squared paper, number lines, and place-value frames and encourages them to think of as many ways as possible to solve the problem. Here are four different solutions, based on four different but correct representations.

Source: Riedesel, C. Alan, Schwartz, James E., Essentials of Elementary Mathematics, 2nd Edition, © 1999. Reprinted by permission of Pearson Education, Inc., Upper Saddle River, NJ.

overlook critical information, use irrelevant information, and may even misread or misremember critical information so that it fits the schema. But when students use the proper schema to represent a problem, they are less likely to be confused by irrelevant information or tricky wording, such as the presence of the word *more* in a problem that really requires *subtraction* (Fenton, 2007; Resnick, 1981). Figure 9.3 gives examples of different ways students might represent a simple mathematics problem. Exposure to different ways of representing and solving problems helps develop mathematical understanding (Star & Rittle-Johnson, 2009).

How can students who lack a good base of knowledge improve their translation and schema selection? To answer this question, we usually have to move to area-specific problem-solving strategies because schemas are specific to content areas.

TRANSLATION AND SCHEMA TRAINING: DIRECT INSTRUCTION IN SCHEMAS. For students with little knowledge in an area, teachers can begin by directly teaching the necessary schema using demonstration, modeling, and "think-alouds." As we just saw, ratio/proportion problems like the following are a big challenge for many students.

> Ernesto and Dawn worked separately on their social studies projects this weekend. The ratio of the number of hours Ernesto spent on the project to the number of hours Dawn spent on the project was 2:3. If Ernesto spent 16 hours on the project, how many hours did Dawn spend on the project? (Jitendra et al., 2010, p. 257)

The teacher used a "think-aloud" to focus students on the key schema for solving this problem, so she said, "**First,** I figure this is a ratio problem, because it compared the number of hours that Ernesto worked **to** the number of hours Dawn worked. This is a **part-part ratio** that tells about a **multiplicative relationship** (2 : 3) between the hours Ernesto and Dawn worked." The teacher went on to think aloud, "**Next,** I represented the information. . . ." **Finally**, I used the equivalent fractions strategy and . . . ." The think-aloud demonstration can be followed by providing students with many *worked examples*. In mathematics and physics it appears that in the *early stages* of learning, students benefit from seeing many different kinds of example problems worked out correctly for them (Moreno, Ozogul, & Reisslein, 2011). But before we explore worked examples in the next section, a caution is in order. Students with advanced knowledge improve when they solve new problems, not when they focus on already worked out examples. Worked examples can actually interfere with the learning of more expert students. This has been called the *expert reversal effect* because what works for experts is the *reverse* of what works for beginners (Kalyuga, & Renkl, 2010).

TRANSLATION AND SCHEMA TRAINING: WORKED EXAMPLES. Worked examples reflect all the stages of problem solving—identifying the problem, setting goals, exploring solutions, solving the problem, and finally evaluating the outcome (Schworm & Renkl, 2007; van Gog, Paas, & Sweller, 2010). Worked examples are useful in many subject areas. Adrienne Lee and Laura Hutchinson (1998) found that undergraduate students learned more when they were provided with examples of chemistry problem solutions that were annotated to show an expert problem solver's thinking at critical

WORKED OUT EXAMPLES Students benefit from seeing many different kinds of example problems worked out correctly for them, especially when they show an expert problem solver's thinking at critical steps.

steps. In Australia, Slava Kalyuga and colleagues (2001) found that worked-out examples helped apprentices to learn about electrical circuits when the apprentices had less experience in the area. Silke Schworm and Alexander Renkl (2007) used video examples to help student teachers learn how to make convincing arguments for or against a position.

Why are examples effective? Part of the answer is in *cognitive load theory*, discussed in the previous chapter. When students lack specific knowledge in domains—for example, fractions or proportions—they try to solve the problems using general strategies such as looking for key words or applying rote procedures. But these approaches put great strain on working memory—too much to "keep in mind" at once. In contrast, worked examples chunk some of the steps, provide cues and feedback, focus attention on relevant information, and make fewer demands on memory, so the students can use cognitive resources to understand instead of searching randomly for solutions (Wittwer & Renkl, 2010).

To get the most benefit from worked examples, however, students have to actively engage—just "looking over" the examples is not enough. This is not too surprising when you think about what supports learning and memory. You need to pay attention, process deeply, and connect with what you already know. Students should explain the examples to themselves. This *self-explanation* component is a critical part of making learning from worked examples active, not passive. Examples of self-explanation strategies include trying to predict the next step in a solution, then checking to see if you are right or trying to identify an underlying principle that explains how to solve the problem. In their study with student teachers, Schworm and Renkl (2007) embedded prompts that required the student teachers to think about and explain elements of the arguments they saw on the tape, such as, "Which argumentative elements does this sequence contain? How is it related to Kirsten's statement?" (p. 289). Students have to be mentally engaged in making sense of the examples—and self-explanation is one key to engagement (Atkinson & Renkl, 2007; Wittwer & Renkl, 2010).

Another way to use worked examples is to have students compare examples that reach a right answer, but are worked out in different ways. What is the same about each solution? What is different? Why? (Rittle-Johnson & Star, 2007). Also, worked-out examples should deal with one source of information at a time rather than having students move between text passages, graphs, tables, and so on. The cognitive load will be too heavy for beginners if they have to integrate many sources of information to make sense of the worked examples (Marcus, Cooper, & Sweller, 1996).

Worked examples can serve as analogies or models for solving new problems. But beware. Without explanations and coaching, novices may remember the surface features of a worked example or case instead of the deeper meaning or the structure. It is the meaning or structure, not the surface similarities, that helps in solving new, analogous problems (Gentner, Lowenstein, & Thompson, 2003). I have heard students complain that the test preparation problems in their math classes were about boats and river currents, but the test asked about airplanes and wind speed. They protested, "There were no problems about boats on the test!" In fact, the problems on the test about wind were solved in exactly the same way as the "boat" problems, but the students were focusing only on the surface features. One way to overcome this tendency is to have students compare examples or cases so they can develop a problem-solving schema that captures the common structure, not the surface features, of the cases (Gentner et al., 2003).

How else might students develop the schemas they will need to represent problems in a particular subject area? Mayer (1983) has recommended giving students practice in the following: (1) recognizing and categorizing a variety of problem types; (2) representing problems—either concretely in pictures, symbols, or graphs, or in words; and (3) selecting relevant and irrelevant information in problems.

THE RESULTS OF PROBLEM REPRESENTATION.   There are two main outcomes of the problem representation stage of problem solving, as shown in Figure 9.4. If your representation of the problem suggests an immediate solution, your task is done. In one sense, you haven't really solved a new problem; you have simply recognized the new problem as a "disguised" version of an old problem that you already knew how to solve. This has been called **schema-driven problem solving**. In terms of Figure 9.4, you can use the schema-activated route and proceed directly to a solution.

But what if you have no existing way of solving the problem or your activated schema fails? Time to search for a solution!

Exploring Possible Solution Strategies

In conducting your search for a solution, you have available two general kinds of procedures: algorithmic and heuristic. Both of these are forms of procedural knowledge (Schraw, 2006).

Schema-driven problem solving
Recognizing a problem as a "disguised" version of an old problem for which one already has a solution.

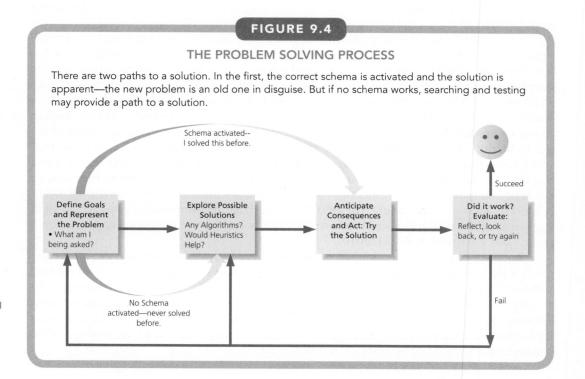

FIGURE 9.4

THE PROBLEM SOLVING PROCESS

There are two paths to a solution. In the first, the correct schema is activated and the solution is apparent—the new problem is an old one in disguise. But if no schema works, searching and testing may provide a path to a solution.

ALGORITHMS. An **algorithm** is a step-by-step prescription for achieving a goal. It usually is domain specific; that is, it is tied to a particular subject area. In solving a problem, if you choose an appropriate algorithm (e.g., to find the mean, you add all the scores, then divide by the number of scores) and implement it properly, a right answer is guaranteed. Unfortunately, students often apply algorithms unsystematically, trying out one first, and then another. They may even happen on the right answer, but not understand how they got there, or they may forget the steps they used to find the answer. For some students, applying algorithms haphazardly could be an indication that formal operational thinking and the ability to work through a set of possibilities systematically (as described by Piaget) is not yet developed. But many problems cannot be solved by algorithms. What then?

HEURISTICS. A **heuristic** is a general strategy that might lead to the right answer (Schoenfeld, 2011). Because many of life's problems (careers, relationships, etc.) are not straightforward and have ill-defined problem statements and no apparent algorithms, the discovery or development of effective heuristics is important (Korf, 1999). Let's examine a few.

In **means-ends analysis,** the problem is divided into a number of intermediate goals or subgoals, and then a means of solving each intermediate subgoal is figured out. For example, writing a 20-page term paper can loom as an insurmountable problem for some students. They would be better off breaking this task into several intermediate goals, such as selecting a topic, locating sources of information, reading and organizing the information, making an outline, and so on. As they attack a particular intermediate goal, they may find that other goals arise. For example, locating information may require that they find someone to refresh their memory about using the library computer search system. Keep in mind that psychologists have yet to discover an effective heuristic for students who are just starting their term paper the night before it is due.

Some problems lend themselves to a **working-backward strategy,** in which you begin at the goal and move back to the unsolved initial problem. Working backward is sometimes an effective heuristic for solving geometry proofs. It can also be a good way to set intermediate deadlines ("Let's see, if I have to submit this chapter in four weeks, I should have a first draft finished by the 11th, and that means I better stop searching for new references and start writing by....").

Another useful heuristic is **analogical thinking** (Copi, 1961; Gentner et al., 2003), which limits your search for solutions to situations that have something in common with the one you currently face. When submarines were first designed, for example, engineers had to figure out how battleships could determine the presence and location of vessels hidden in the depths of the sea. Studying how bats solve an analogous problem of navigating in the dark led to the invention of sonar. Take note, however, that to use analogies effectively, you must focus on meaning and not surface similarities, so focusing on bats' appearance would not have helped to solve the communication problem.

The possible analogies students bring to the classroom are bound to vary, based on their experience and culture. For example, Zhe Chen and his colleagues (2004) wondered if college students might use familiar folk tales—one kind of cultural knowledge—as analogies to solve problems. That is just what happened. Chinese students were better at solving a problem of weighing a statue because the problem was similar to their folk tale about how to weigh an elephant (by water displacement). American students were better at solving a problem of finding the way out of a cave (leaving a trail), by using an analogy to Hansel and Gretel, a common American folk tale.

Putting your problem-solving plan into words and giving reasons for selecting it can lead to successful problem solving (Lee & Hutchinson, 1998). You may have discovered the effectiveness of this **verbalization** process accidentally, when a solution popped into your head as you were explaining a problem to someone else.

Anticipating, Acting, and Looking Back

After representing the problem and exploring possible solutions, the next step is to select a solution and anticipate the consequences. For example, if you decide to solve the damaged tomato problem by developing a tougher tomato, how will consumers react? If you take

Algorithm Step-by-step procedure for solving a problem; prescription for solutions.

Heuristic General strategy used in attempting to solve problems.

Means-ends analysis Heuristic in which a goal is divided into subgoals.

Working-backward strategy Heuristic in which one starts with the goal and moves backward to solve the problem.

Analogical thinking Heuristic in which one limits the search for solutions to situations that are similar to the one at hand.

Verbalization Putting your problem-solving plan and its logic into words.

time to learn a new graphics program to enhance your term paper (and your grade), will you still have enough time to finish the paper?

After you choose a solution strategy and implement it, evaluate the results by checking for evidence that confirms or contradicts your solution. Many people tend to stop working before they reach the best solution and simply accept an answer that works in some cases. In mathematical problems, evaluating the answer might mean applying a checking routine, such as adding to check the result of a subtraction problem or, in a long addition problem, adding the column from bottom to top instead of top to bottom. Another possibility is estimating the answer. For example, if the computation was 11×21, the answer should be around 200, because 10×20 is 200. A student who reaches an answer of 2,311 or 32 or 562 should quickly realize these answers cannot be correct. Estimating an answer is particularly important when students rely on calculators or computers, because they cannot go back and spot an error in the figures.

Factors That Hinder Problem Solving

Sometimes problem solving requires looking at things in new ways. People may miss out on a good solution because they fixate on conventional uses for materials. This difficulty is called **functional fixedness** (Duncker, 1945). In your everyday life, you may often exhibit functional fixedness. Suppose a screw on a dresser-drawer handle is loose. Will you spend 10 minutes searching for a screwdriver or will you fix it with a ruler edge or a dime?

Another kind of fixation that blocks effective problem solving is **response set,** getting stuck on one way of representing a problem. Try this:

In each of the four matchstick arrangements below, move only one stick to change the equation so that it represents a true equality such as V = V.

V = VII   VI = XI   XII = VII   VI = II

You probably figured out how to solve the first example quite quickly. You simply move one matchstick from the right side over to the left to make VI = VI. Examples two and three can also be solved without too much difficulty by moving one stick to change the V to an X or vice versa. But the fourth example (taken from Raudsepp & Haugh, 1977) probably has you stumped. To solve this problem, you must change your response set or switch schemas, because what has worked for the first three problems will not work this time. The answer here lies in changing from Roman numerals to Arabic numbers and using the concept of square root. By overcoming response set, you can move one matchstick from the right to the left to form the symbol for square root; the solution reads $\sqrt{1} = 1$, which is simply the symbolic way of saying that the square root of 1 equals 1. Recently, a creative reader of this text e-mailed some other solutions. Jamaal Allan, then a masters' student at Pacific University, pointed out that you could use any of the matchsticks to change the = sign to ≠. Then, the last example would be V ≠ II or 5 does not equal 2, an accurate statement. He suggested that you also might move one matchstick to change = to < or > and the statements would still be true (but not equalities as specified in the problem above). Bill Wetta, a student at Ashland University, offered another solution that used both Arabic and Roman numerals. You can move one matchstick to make the first V an X. Then VI = II becomes XI = II, or eleven (in Roman numerals) equals 11 (in Arabic numerals). Just this morning I received another creative approach from Ray Partlow, an educational psychology student in Newark, Ohio. He noted, "Simply remove a matchstick from the V from the left-hand side, and place it directly on top of the I, getting II = II." Covering one matchstick with another opens up a whole new set of possibilities! Can you come up with any other solutions? Be creative!

SOME PROBLEMS WITH HEURISTICS. We often apply heuristics automatically to make quick judgments; that saves us time in everyday problem solving. The mind can react automatically and instantaneously, but the price we often pay for this efficiency may be bad problem solving, which can be costly. Making judgments by invoking stereotypes leads even smart people to make dumb decisions. For example, we might use **representativeness heuristics** to make judgments about possibilities based on our prototypes—what we think is representative of a category. Consider this:

Response set Rigidity; the tendency to respond in the most familiar way.

Functional fixedness Inability to use objects or tools in a new way.

Representativeness heuristic Judging the likelihood of an event based on how well the events match your prototypes—what you think is representative of the category.

If I ask you whether a slim, short stranger who enjoys poetry is more likely to be a truck driver or an Ivy League classics professor, what would you say?

You might be tempted to answer based on your prototypes of truck drivers or professors. But consider the odds. With about 10 Ivy League schools and 4 or so classics professors per school, we have 40 professors. Say 10 are both short and slim, and half of those like poetry—we are left with 5. But there are at least 400,000 truck drivers in the United States. If only 1 in every 800 of those truck drivers were short, slim poetry lovers, we have 500 truck drivers who fit the description. With 500 truck drivers versus 5 professors, it is 100 times more likely that our stranger is a truck driver (Myers, 2005).

Teachers and students are busy people, and they often base their decisions on what they have in their minds at the time. When judgments are based on the availability of information in our memories, we are using the **availability heuristic.** If instances of events come to mind easily, we think they are common occurrences, but that is not necessarily the case; in fact, it is often wrong. People remember vivid stories and quickly come to believe that such events are the norm, but again, they often are wrong. For example, you may be surprised to learn the average family in poverty has only 2.2 children (Children's Defense Fund, 2005a, 2005b) if you have vivid memories from viewing a powerful film about a large, poor family. Data may not support a judgment, but **belief perseverance,** or the tendency to hold on to our beliefs, even in the face of contradictory evidence, may make us resist change.

The **confirmation bias** is the tendency to search for information that confirms our ideas and beliefs: This arises from our eagerness to get a good solution. You have often heard the saying "Don't confuse me with the facts." This aphorism captures the essence of the confirmation bias. Most people seek evidence that supports their ideas more readily than they search for facts that might refute them. For example, once you decide to buy a certain car, you are likely to notice reports about the good features of the car you chose, not the good news about the cars you rejected. Our automatic use of heuristics to make judgments, our eagerness to confirm what we like to believe, and our tendency to explain away failure combine to generate *overconfidence*. Students usually are overconfident about how fast they can get their papers written; it typically takes twice as long as they estimate (Buehler, Griffin, & Ross, 1994). In spite of their underestimation of their completion time, they remain overly confident of their next prediction.

The *Guidelines* on the next page give some ideas for helping students become good problem solvers.

Expert Knowledge and Problem Solving

Most psychologists agree that effective problem solving is based on having an ample store of knowledge about the problem area (Schoenfeld, 2011). In order to solve the matchstick problem, for example, you had to understand Roman and Arabic numbers as well as the concept of square root. You also had to know that the square root of 1 is 1. Let's take a moment to examine this expert knowledge.

KNOWING WHAT IS IMPORTANT. Experts know where to focus their attention. For example, knowledgeable baseball fans (I am told) pay attention to the moves of the shortstop to learn if the pitcher will throw a fastball, curveball, or slider. But those with little knowledge about baseball may never see the movements of the shortstop, unless a hit is headed toward that part of the field (Bruning, Schraw, & Norby, 2011). In general, experts know what to pay attention to when judging a performance or product such as an Olympic high dive or a prize-winning chocolate cake. To nonexperts, most good dives or cakes look about the same, unless of course they "flop"!

MEMORY FOR PATTERNS AND ORGANIZATION. The modern study of expertise began with investigations of chess masters (Simon & Chase, 1973). Results indicated that masters can quickly recognize about 50,000 different arrangements of chess pieces. They can look at one of these patterns for a few seconds and remember where every piece on the board was placed. It is as though they have a "vocabulary" of 50,000 patterns. Michelene Chi (1978) demonstrated that 3rd through 8th grade chess experts had

Availability heuristic Judging the likelihood of an event based on what is available in your memory, assuming those easily remembered events are common.

Belief perseverance The tendency to hold on to beliefs, even in the face of contradictory evidence.

Confirmation bias Seeking information that confirms our choices and beliefs, while disconfirming evidence.

GUIDELINES

Problem Solving

Ask students if they are sure they understand the problem.
Examples
1. Can they separate relevant from irrelevant information?
2. Are they aware of the assumptions they are making?
3. Encourage them to visualize the problem by diagramming or drawing it.
4. Ask them to explain the problem to someone else. What would a good solution look like?

Encourage attempts to see the problem from different angles.
Examples
1. Suggest several different possibilities yourself, and then ask students to offer some.
2. Give students practice in taking and defending different points of view on an issue.

Let students do the thinking; don't just hand them solutions.
Examples
1. Offer individual problems as well as group problems, so that each student has the chance to practice.

2. Give partial credit if students have good reasons for "wrong" solutions to problems.
3. If students are stuck, resist the temptation to give too many clues. Let them think about the problem overnight.

Help students develop systematic ways of considering alternatives.
Examples
1. Think out loud as you solve problems.
2. Ask, "What would happen if?"
3. Keep a list of suggestions.

Teach heuristics.
Examples
1. Use analogies to solve the problem of limited parking in the downtown area. How are other "storage" problems solved?
2. Use the working backward strategy to plan a party.

For more resources on problem solving, see
http://www.hawaii.edu/suremath/home.html

---

a similar ability to remember chess piece arrangements. For all the masters, patterns of pieces are like words. If you were shown any word from your vocabulary store for just a few seconds, you would be able to remember every letter in the word in the right order (assuming you could spell the word). But a series of letters arranged randomly is hard to remember, as you saw in Chapter 8. An analogous situation holds for chess masters. When chess pieces are placed on a board randomly, masters are no better than average players at remembering the positions of the pieces. The master's memory is for patterns that make sense or could occur in a game.

A similar phenomenon occurs in other fields. There may be an intuition about how to solve a problem based on recognizing patterns and knowing the "right moves" for those patterns. Experts in physics, for example, organize their knowledge around central principles (e.g., Boyle's or Newton's laws), whereas beginners organize their smaller amounts of physics knowledge around the specific details stated in the problems (e.g., levers or pulleys) (Ericsson, 1999; Fenton, 2007).

PROCEDURAL KNOWLEDGE. In addition to representing a problem very quickly, experts know what to do next and are able do it. They have a large store of *productions* or if-then schemas about what action to take in various situations. Thus, the steps of understanding the problem and choosing a solution happen simultaneously and fairly automatically (Ericsson & Charness, 1999). Of course, this means

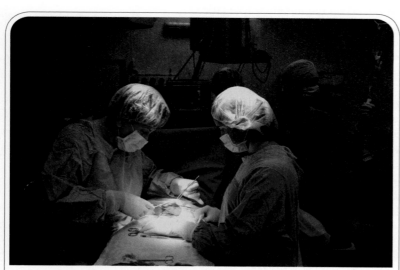

EXPERT KNOWLEDGE large part of becoming an expert is simply acquiring a great store of *domain knowledge* or knowledge that is particular to a field. This surgeon has likely invested years of deliberate, focused, sustained practice to become an expert.

that they must have many, many schemas available. A large part of becoming an expert is simply acquiring a great store of *domain knowledge* or knowledge that is particular to a field (Alexander, 1992). To do this, you must encounter many different kinds of problems in that field, observe others solving problems, and practice solving many yourself. Some estimates are that it takes 10 years or 10,000 hours of deliberate, focused, sustained practice to become an expert in most fields (Ericsson, 2011; Ericsson & Charness, 1994; Simon, 1995). Experts' rich store of knowledge is elaborated and well practiced, so that it is easy to retrieve from long-term memory when needed (Anderson, 1993).

PLANNING AND MONITORING. Experts spend more time analyzing problems, drawing diagrams, breaking large problems down into subproblems, and making plans. Whereas a novice might begin immediately—writing equations for a physics problem or drafting the first paragraph of a paper, experts plan out the whole solution and often make the task simpler in the process. As they work, experts monitor progress, so time is not lost pursuing dead ends or weak ideas (Schunk, 2012).

So what can we conclude? Experts (1) know where to focus their attention, (2) perceive large, meaningful patterns in given information and are not confused by surface features and details, (3) hold more information in working and long-term memories, in part because they have organized the information into meaningful chunks and procedures, (4) take a great deal of time to analyze a given problem, (5) have automatic procedures for accomplishing pieces of the problem, and (6) are better at monitoring their performance. When the area of problem solving is fairly well defined, such as chess or physics or computer programming, then these skills of expert problem solvers hold fairly consistently. But when the problem-solving area is less well defined and has fewer clear underlying principles, such as problem solving in economics or psychology, then the differences between experts and novices are not as clear-cut (Alexander, 1992).

CREATIVITY AND CREATIVE PROBLEM SOLVING

STOP & THINK Consider this student. He had severe dyslexia—a learning disability that made reading and writing exceedingly difficult. He described himself as an "underdog." In school, he knew that if the reading assignment would take others an hour, he had to allow two or three hours. He knew that he had to keep a list of all of his most frequently misspelled words in order to be able to write at all. He spent hours alone in his room. Would you expect his writing to be creative? Why or why not? •

The person described in the box above is John Irving, celebrated author of what one critic called "wildly inventive" novels such as *The World According to Garp*, *The Cider House Rules*, and *A Prayer for Owen Meany* (Amabile, 2001). How do we explain his amazing creativity? What is creativity?

Defining Creativity

Creativity is the ability to produce work that is original, but still appropriate and useful (Plucker, Beghetto, & Dow, 2004). Most psychologists agree that there is no such thing as "all-purpose creativity"; people are creative in a particular area, as John Irving was in writing fiction. But to be creative, the "invention" must be intended. An accidental spilling of paint that produces a novel design is not creative unless the artist recognizes the potential of the "accident," or she uses the spilling technique intentionally to create new works (Weisberg, 1993). Although we frequently associate the arts with creativity, any subject can be approached in a creative manner.

Assessing Creativity

STOP & THINK How many uses can you list for a brick? Take a moment and brainstorm—write down as many as you can. •

Creativity Imaginative, original thinking or problem solving.

SOCIAL ACCEPTANCE OF CREATIVITY History is filled with examples of creative breakthroughs rejected in their time (for example, Galileo's theory of the sun as the center of the solar system). Is today's society ready to welcome creative contributions in the field of alternative energies?

Like the author John Irving, Paul Torrance had a learning disability. He became interested in educational psychology when he was a high school English teacher (Neumeister & Cramond, 2004). Torrance was known as the "Father of Creativity." He developed two types of creativity tests: verbal and graphic (Torrance, 1972; Torrance & Hall, 1980). In the verbal test, you might be instructed to think up as many uses as possible for a brick (as you did above) or asked how a particular toy might be changed to make it more fun. On the graphic test, you might be given 30 circles and asked to create 30 different drawings, with each drawing including at least one circle. Figure 9.5 shows the creativity of an 8-year-old girl in completing this task.

These tests require **divergent thinking,** an important component of many conceptions of creativity. Divergent thinking is the ability to propose many different ideas or answers. **Convergent thinking** is the more common ability to identify only one answer. Responses to all these creativity tasks are scored for originality, fluency, and flexibility—three aspects of divergent thinking. *Originality* is usually determined statistically. To be original, a response must be given by fewer than 5 or 10 people out of every 100 who take the test. *Fluency* is the number of different responses. *Flexibility* is generally measured by the number of different categories of responses. For instance, if you listed 20 uses of a brick, but each was to build something, your fluency score might be high, but your flexibility score would be low. Of the three measures, fluency—the number of responses—is the best predictor of divergent thinking, but there is more to real-life creativity than divergent thinking (Plucker et al., 2004).

A few possible indicators of creativity in your students are curiosity, concentration, adaptability, high energy, humor (sometimes bizarre), independence, playfulness, nonconformity, risk taking, attraction to the complex and mysterious, willingness to fantasize and daydream, intolerance for boredom, and inventiveness (Sattler & Hoge, 2006).

What Are the Sources of Creativity?

Researchers have studied cognitive processes, personality factors, motivational patterns, and background experiences to explain creativity (Simonton, 2000). Teresa Amabile (1996) proposes a three-component model of creativity. Individuals or groups must have:

1. *Domain-relevant skills* including talents and competencies that are valuable for working in the domain, such as Michelangelo's skills in shaping stone, developed when he lived with a stonecutter's family as a child.
2. *Creativity-relevant processes* including work habits and personality traits such as John Irving's habit of working 10-hour days to write and rewrite and rewrite until he perfected his stories.
3. *Intrinsic task motivation* or a deep curiosity and fascination with the task. This aspect of creativity can be greatly influenced by teachers and parents who support autonomy, stimulate curiosity, encourage fantasy, and provide challenge.

CREATIVITY AND COGNITION.   Having a rich store of knowledge in an area is the basis for creativity, but something more is needed. For many problems, that "something more" is the ability to see things in a new way—**restructuring** the problem, which leads to a sudden **insight.** Often this happens when a person has struggled with a problem or project, and then sets it aside for a while. Some psychologists believe that time away allows for *incubation*, a kind of unconscious working through the problem. Actually, it is more complex than that. Incubation seems to help more on divergent thinking tasks than on verbal or visual tasks. Also incubation is more helpful when a longer preparation period precedes the individual's setting the problem aside (Sio & Ormerod, 2009). Leaving the problem for a time probably interrupts rigid ways of thinking so you can restructure your view of the situation and think more divergently (Gleitman, Fridlund,

Divergent thinking Coming up with many possible solutions.

Convergent thinking Narrowing possibilities to a single answer.

Restructuring Conceiving of a problem in a new or different way.

Insight Sudden realization of a solution.

FIGURE 9.5

A GRAPHIC ASSESSMENT OF THE CREATIVITY OF AN EIGHT-YEAR-OLD

The titles she gave her drawings, from left to right, are as follows: "Dracula," "one-eyed monster," "pumpkin," "Hula-Hoop," "poster," "wheelchair," "earth," "moon," "planet," "movie camera," "sad face," "picture," "stoplight," "beach ball," "the letter O," "car," "glasses."

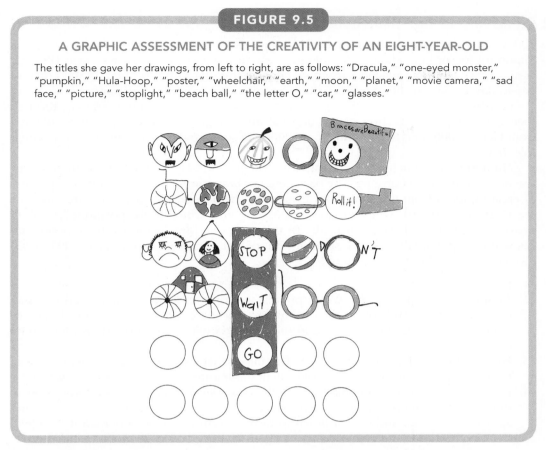

Source: "A Graphic Assessment of the Creativity of an Eight-Year-Old," from The Torrance Test of Creative Thinking by E.P. Torrance, 1986, 2000. Reprinted with permission of Scholastic Testing Service, Inc., Bensonville, IL 60106 USA.

& Reisberg, 1999). Creativity requires extensive knowledge, flexibility, and the continual reorganizing of ideas. And we saw that motivation, persistence, and social support play important roles as well.

CREATIVITY AND DIVERSITY. As Dean Simonton said, even with years of research on creativity, "Psychologists still have a long way to go before they come anywhere close to understanding creativity in women and minorities" (2000, p. 156). Thus far, white males have been the focus of creativity research and writing over the years. However, patterns of creativity in other groups are complex—sometimes matching and sometimes diverging from patterns found in traditional research.

In another connection between creativity and culture, research suggests that being on the outside of mainstream society, being bilingual, or being exposed to other cultures might encourage creativity (Simonton, 2000). In fact, true innovators often break rules. "Creators have a desire to shake things up" (Winner, 2000, p. 167). In addition, even for those who are not outside the mainstream, it appears that participation in multicultural experiences fosters creativity. Angela Ka-Yee Leung and her colleagues (2008; Maddux, Leung, Chui, & Galinsky, 2009) reviewed theory and research, including experimental studies that exposed participants to information and images about other cultures. The researchers concluded that multicultural experiences support both creative processes, such as retrieving novel or unconventional ideas from memory, and creative performance, such as generating insightful solutions to problems. These effects are especially strong when people open themselves up to divergent ideas, and when the situation does not emphasize finding quick, firm answers. Multicultural individuals are particularly willing to consider and build on unfamiliar ideas, entertain conflicting alternatives, and make unlikely connections between ideas (Leung & Chiu, 2010; Maddux & Galinsky, 2009). So even though your students may not be able to travel to Tibet or Turkey, they still could become more creative problem solvers if they learned about different cultures.

Creativity in the Classroom

Today's and tomorrow's complex problems require creative solutions. And creativity is important for an individual's psychological, physical, social, and career success (Plucker et al., 2004). How can teachers promote creative thinking? All too often, in the crush of day-to-day classroom life, teachers stifle creative ideas without realizing what they are doing. Teachers are in an excellent position to encourage or discourage creativity through their acceptance or rejection of the unusual and imaginative. The *Guidelines*, adapted from Fleith (2000) and Sattler and Hoge (2006), describe other possibilities for encouraging creativity.

In addition to encouraging creativity through everyday interactions with students, teachers can try brainstorming. The basic tenet of **brainstorming** is to separate the process of creating ideas from the process of evaluating them because evaluation often inhibits creativity (Osborn, 1963). Evaluation, discussion, and criticism are postponed until all possible suggestions have been made. In this way, one idea inspires others; people do not withhold potentially creative solutions out of fear of criticism. John Baer (1997, p. 43) gives these rules for brainstorming:

1. Defer judgment.
2. Avoid ownership of ideas. When people feel that an idea is "theirs," egos sometimes get in the way of creative thinking. They are likely to be more defensive later when ideas are critiqued, and they are less willing to allow their ideas to be modified.
3. Feel free to "hitchhike" on other ideas. This means that it's okay to borrow elements from ideas already on the table, or to make slight modifications of ideas already suggested.
4. Encourage wild ideas. Impossible, totally unworkable ideas may lead someone to think of other, more possible, more workable ideas. It's easier to take a wildly imaginative bad idea and tone it down to fit the constraints of reality than it is to take a boring bad idea and make it interesting enough to be worth thinking about.

Individuals as well as groups may benefit from brainstorming. In writing this book, for example, I have sometimes found it helpful to list all the different topics that could be covered in a chapter, then leave the list and return to it later to evaluate the ideas.

The Big C: Revolutionary Innovation

Ellen Winner (2000) describes the "big-C creativity" or innovation that establishes a new field or revolutionizes an old one. Even child prodigies do not necessarily become adult innovators. Prodigies have mastered well-established domains very early, but innovators change the entire domain. "Individuals who ultimately make creative breakthroughs tend from their earliest days to be explorers, innovators, and tinkerers. Often this adventurousness is interpreted as insubordination, though more fortunate tinkerers receive from teachers or peers some form of encouragement for their experimentation" (Gardner, 1993, pp. 32–33). What can parents and teachers do to encourage these potential creators? Winner (2000) lists four dangers to avoid:

1. Avoid pushing so hard that the child's intrinsic passion to master a field becomes a craving for extrinsic rewards.
2. Avoid pushing so hard that the child later looks back on a missed childhood.
3. Avoid freezing the child into a safe, technically perfect way of performing that has led to lavish rewards.
4. Be aware of the psychological wounds that can follow when the child who can perform perfectly becomes the forgotten adult who can do nothing more than continue to perform perfectly—without ever creating something new.

Finally, teachers and parents can encourage students with outstanding abilities and creative talents to give back to the society—service learning, discussed in Chapter 10, is one opportunity.

We may not all be revolutionary in our creativity, but we all can be experts in one area—critical thinking.

Brainstorming Generating ideas without stopping to evaluate them.

GUIDELINES

Encouraging Creativity

Accept and encourage divergent thinking.
Examples

1. During class discussion, ask: "Can anyone suggest a different way of looking at this question?"
2. Reinforce attempts at unusual solutions to problems, even if the final product is not perfect.
3. Offer choices in topics for projects or modes of presentation (written, oral, visual or graphic, using technology).

Tolerate dissent.
Examples

1. Ask students to support dissenting opinions.
2. Make sure nonconforming students receive an equal share of classroom privileges and rewards.

Encourage students to trust their own judgment.
Examples

1. When students ask questions you think they can answer, rephrase or clarify the questions and direct them back to the students.
2. Give ungraded assignments from time to time.

Emphasize that everyone is capable of creativity in some form.
Examples

1. Avoid describing the feats of great artists or inventors as if they were superhuman accomplishments.

2. Recognize creative efforts in each student's work. Have a separate grade for originality on some assignments.

Provide time, space, and materials to support creative projects.
Examples

1. Collect "found" materials for collages and creations—buttons, stones, shells, paper, fabric, beads, seeds, drawing tools, clay—try flea markets and friends for donations. Have mirrors and pictures for drawing faces.
2. Make a well-lighted space available where children can work on projects, leave them, and come back to finish them.
3. Follow up on memorable occasions (field trips, news events, holidays) with opportunities to draw, write, or make music.

Be a stimulus for creative thinking.
Examples

1. Use class brainstorming sessions whenever possible.
2. Model creative problem solving by suggesting unusual solutions for class problems.
3. Encourage students to delay judging a particular suggestion for solving a problem until all the possibilities have been considered.

For more ideas, see
http://ceep.crc.uiuc.edu/eecearchive/digests/1995/edward95.html

CRITICAL THINKING AND ARGUMENTATION

Many educational psychologists believe that good thinking can and should be developed in school. One way to develop students' thinking is to create a *culture of thinking* in your classrooms (Perkins, Jay, & Tishman, 1993). This means that there is a spirit of inquisitiveness and critical thinking, a respect for reasoning and creativity, and an expectation that students will learn to make and counter arguments based on evidence.

Developing Critical Thinking

Critical thinking skills are useful in almost every life situation—even in evaluating the media ads that constantly bombard us. When you see a group of gorgeous people extolling the virtues of a particular brand of orange juice as they frolic in skimpy bathing suits, you must decide if sex appeal is a relevant factor in choosing a fruit drink (remember Pavlovian advertising from Chapter 7).

No matter what approach you use to develop critical thinking, it is important to follow up with additional practice. One lesson is not enough. For example, if your class examined a particular historical document to determine if it reflected bias or propaganda, you should follow up by analyzing other written historical documents, contemporary advertisements, or news stories. Unless thinking skills become overlearned and relatively

Connect and Extend to PRAXIS II™

Thinking Skills (II, A1)
A nearly universal goal of educational programs across the country is the development of thinking skills. Describe what a teacher can do to cultivate these skills in the classroom. Read *Teaching Thinking Skills* (http://www.nwrel.org/scpd/sirs/6/cu11.html) for a concise overview of research, issues, and key factors related to this topic.

Critical thinking Evaluating conclusions by logically and systematically examining the problem, the evidence, and the solution.

automatic, they are not likely to be transferred to new situations (Mayer & Wittrock, 2006). Instead, students will use these skills only to complete the lesson in social studies, not to evaluate the claims made by friends, politicians, car manufacturers, or diet plans. Table 9.3 describes the characteristics of a critical thinker.

Critical Thinking in Specific Subjects

The characteristics of critical thinkers in Table 9.3 would be useful in any subject. But some critical thinking skills are specific to a particular subject. For example, to teach history, Jeffrey Nokes and his colleagues investigated (1) using traditional texts versus multiple readings, and (2) direct teaching of critical thinking skills versus no direct teaching of critical thinking skills (Nokes, Dole, & Hacker, 2007). The multiple texts included historical fiction, excerpts from speeches, government documents, photographs, charts and historical data, and short sections from texts. The history critical thinking skills taught were:

- **Sourcing:** Looking at the source of the document before reading and using that information to help interpret and make inferences about the reading. Is the source biased? Can I trust it?
- **Corroboration:** Making connections between the information in different texts and noting similarities and contradictions.
- **Contextualization:** Imaging the time, place, people, and culture that is the context for the event, with all the political and social forces that might be operating.

Students who learned with multiple texts instead of traditional textbooks actually learned more history content. Also, students were able to learn and apply two of the three critical thinking skills, *sourcing* and *corroboration*, when they were *directly taught* how to use the skills. Contextualization proved more difficult, perhaps because the students lacked the background knowledge to fill in contextual information. So critical thinking for specific subjects can be taught along with the subject. But as you can see in the *Point/Counterpoint*, educators don't agree about the best way to foster critical thinking in schools.

Argumentation

The ability to construct and support a position is essential in science, politics, persuasive writing, and critical thinking, to name just a few areas. The heart of **argumentation** (the process of debating a claim with someone else) is supporting your position with evidence and understanding, and then refuting your opponent's claims and evidence. Children are not good at argumentation, adolescents are a bit better, and adults are better still, but not perfect. Children don't pay very much attention to the claims and evidence of the other person in the debate. Adolescents understand that their opponent in a debate has a different position, but they tend to spend much more time presenting their own position than they do trying to understand and critique their opponent's claims. It is as if the adolescents believe "winning an argument" means making a better presentation, but

TABLE 9.3 • **What Is a Critical Thinker?**

Assuming that critical thinking is reasonable reflective thinking focused on deciding what to believe or do, a critical thinker:

1. Is open minded and mindful of alternatives.
2. Tries to be well informed.
3. Judges well the credibility of sources.
4. Identifies conclusions, reasons, and assumptions.
5. Judges well the quality of an argument, including the acceptability of its reasons, assumptions, and evidence.
6. Can well develop and defend a reasonable position.
7. Asks appropriate clarifying questions.
8. Formulates plausible hypotheses; plans experiments well.
9. Defines terms in a way appropriate for the context.
10. Draws conclusions when warranted, but with caution.
11. Integrates all items in this list when deciding what to believe or do.

Source: Adapted from Robert H. Ennis: http://faculty.ed.uiuc.edu/rhennis/index.html, Downloaded 5.26/2011.

POINT/COUNTERPOINT: Should Schools Teach Critical Thinking and Problem Solving?

The question of whether schools should focus on process or content, problem-solving skills or core knowledge, higher-order thinking skills or academic information has been debated for years. Some educators suggest that students must be taught how to think and solve problems, while other educators assert that students cannot learn to "think" in the abstract. They must be thinking about something—some content. Should teachers focus on knowledge or thinking?

POINT ▶ Problem solving and higher-order thinking can and should be taught.

An article in the April, 28, 1995, issue of the *Chronicle of Higher Education* makes this claim:

Critical thinking is at the heart of effective reading, writing, speaking, and listening. It enables us to link together mastery of content with such diverse goals as self-esteem, self-discipline, multicultural education, effective cooperative learning, and problem solving. It enables all instructors and administrators to raise the level of their own teaching and thinking. (p. A-71)

Closer to home for you, Peter Facione (2011) claims that critical thinking is related to GPA in college and to reading comprehension. How can students learn to think critically? Some educators recommend teaching thinking skills directly with widely used techniques such as the Productive Thinking Program or CoRT (Cognitive Research Trust). Other researchers argue that learning computer programing languages will improve students' minds and teach them how to think logically. Finally, because expert readers automatically apply certain metacognitive strategies, many educators and psychologists recommend directly teaching novice or poor readers how to apply these strategies. Michael Pressley's Good Strategy User model (Pressley & Harris, 2006) and Palincsar and Brown's (1984) reciprocal teaching approach are successful examples of direct teaching of metacognitive skills. Research on these approaches generally shows improvements in achievement and comprehension for students of all ages who participate (Pressley & Harris, 2006; Rosenshine & Meister, 1994).

COUNTERPOINT ▶ Thinking and problem-solving skills do not transfer.

According to E. D. Hirsch, a vocal critic of critical thinking programs:

But whether such direct instruction of critical thinking or self-monitoring does in fact improve performance is a subject of debate in the research community. For instance, the research regarding critical thinking is not reassuring. Instruction in critical thinking has been going on in several countries for over a hundred years. Yet researchers found that students from nations as varied as Israel, Germany, Australia, the Philippines, and the United States, including those who have been taught critical thinking continue to fall into logical fallacies. (1996, p. 136)

The CoRT program has been used in over 5,000 classrooms in 10 nations. But Polson and Jeffries (1985) report that "after 10 years of widespread use we have no adequate evidence concerning the effectiveness of the program" (p. 445). In addition, Mayer and Wittrock (1996) note that field studies of problem solving in real situations show that people often fail to apply the mathematical problem-solving approaches they learn in school to actual problems encountered in the grocery store or home.

Even though educators have been more successful in teaching metacognitive skills, critics still caution that there are times when such teaching hinders rather than helps learning. Robert Siegler (1993) suggests that teaching self-monitoring strategies to low-achieving students can interfere with the students' development of adaptive strategies. Forcing students to use the strategies of experts may put too much burden on working memory as the students struggle to use an unfamiliar strategy and miss the meaning or content of the lesson. For example, rather than teach students strategies for figuring out words from context, it may be helpful for students to focus on learning more vocabulary words.

Beware of Either/Or. One clear message from current research on learning is that both subject specific knowledge and learing strategies are important. Students today need to be critical consumers of all kinds of knowledge, but critical thinking alone is not enough. Students need the knowledge, vocabulary, and concepts to understand what they are reading, seeing and hearing. The best teachers can teach math content and how to learn math at the same time, or history and how to critically assess history sources.

they don't appreciate the need to understand and weaken the opponent's claims (Kuhn & Dean, 2004).

Children and adolescents focus more on their own positions because it is too demanding to remember and process both their own and their opponent's claims and evidence at the same time—the *cognitive load* is just too much. In addition, argumentation skills are not natural. They take both time and instruction to learn (Kuhn, Goh, Iordanou, & Shaenfield, 2008; Udell, 2007).

But what has to be learned? In order to make a case while understanding and refuting the opponent's case, you must be aware of what you are saying, what your opponent is saying, and how to refute your opponent's claims. This takes planning, evaluating how the plan is going, reflecting on what the opponent has said, and changing strategies as needed—in other words, *metacognitive knowledge and skills for argumentation*. Deanna Kuhn and her colleagues (2008) designed a process for developing metacognitive argumentation skills. They presented a 6th grade class with the following dilemma.

> The Costa family has moved to the edge of town from far away Greece with their 11-year-old son Nick. Nick was a good student and soccer player back home in Greece. Nick's parents have decided that in this new place, they want to keep Nick at home with them, and not have him be at the school with the other children. The family speaks only Greek, and they think Nick will do better if he sticks to his family's language and doesn't try to learn English. They say they can teach him everything he needs at home. What should happen? Is it okay for the Costa family to live in the town but keep Nick at home, or should they be required to send their son to the town school like all the other families do? (p. 1313)

Based on their initial position on the dilemma, the 28 students in the class were divided into two groups—"Nick should go to school" or "Nick should be taught at home." These two groups were divided again into same-gender pairs and all the "Nick should go to school" pairs moved to a room next door to their class. For about 25 minutes, each pair from one side "debated" a pair in the other room using instant messaging (IM). Later in the week the process was repeated, but with different pairs debating. In all, there were seven IM debates, so every "go to school" pair debated every "stay home" pair over several weeks. After four of the seven sessions, the pairs were given a transcript of the dialogue from their last debate, along with worksheets that scaffolded their *reflection* on their own arguments or the arguments of their opponents. The students evaluated their arguments and tried to improve them, with some adults coaching. These reflective sessions were repeated three times.

Next, there was a "showdown" debate—the entire "go to school" team debated the entire "stay home" team via one computer per team and a smart board. For this debate, half of each team prepared as experts on their position and half as experts *on the opponent's arguments*. After winter break and again after spring break, the whole process was repeated with new dilemmas.

You can see that there were three techniques employed in the study, supported by technology, to help students become more metacognitive about argumentation. First, they had to work in pairs to collaborate and agree on each communication with the opposing pair. Second, the researchers provided the pairs with transcripts of parts of their dialogue with the opponents so the partners could reflect on the discussions. Third, the dialogues were conducted via instant messaging, so the pairs had a permanent record of the discussion.

So what happened? The pairs, IM, and reflection strategies were successful for most students in helping them take into account the opponent's position and create strategies for rebutting the opponent's arguments. Working in pairs seemed to be especially helpful. When adolescents and even adults work alone, they often are not successful at creating effective counterarguments and rebuttals (Kuhn & Franklin, 2006).

TEACHING FOR TRANSFER

STOP & THINK Think back for a moment to a class in one of your high school subjects that you have not studied in college. Imagine the teacher, the room, the textbook. Now remember what you actually learned in class. If it was a science class, what were some of the formulas you learned? Oxidation reduction? Boyle's law? •

If you are like most of us, you may remember *that* you learned these things, but you will not be quite sure exactly *what* you learned. Were those hours wasted? This question relates to the important topic of learning transfer. Let's begin with a definition of *transfer*.

Whenever something previously learned influences current learning or when solving an earlier problem affects how you solve a new problem, **transfer** has occurred. Erik De Corte (2003) calls transfer "the productive use of cognitive tools and motivations" (p. 142). This meaning of *transfer* emphasizes doing something new (productive), not just

Argumentation The process of debating a claim with someone else.

reproducing a previous application of the tools. If students learn a mathematical principle in one class and use it to solve a physics problem days or weeks later in another class, then transfer has taken place. However, the effect of past learning on present learning is not always positive. Functional fixedness and response set (described earlier in this chapter) are examples of negative transfer because they are attempts to apply familiar but *inappropriate* strategies to a new situation.

Actually, there are several dimensions of transfer (Barnett & Ceci, 2002). You can transfer learning across subjects (math skills used in science problems), across physical contexts (learned in school, used on the job), across social contexts (learned alone, used with your family or team), across time periods (learned in college, used months or years later), across functions (learned for academics, used for hobbies and recreation), and across modalities (learned from watching the Home and Garden cable channel, used to discuss ideas for a patio with a landscape architect). So transfer can refer to many different examples of applying knowledge and skills beyond where, when, and how you learned them.

The Many Views of Transfer

Transfer has been a focus of research in educational psychology for over 100 years. After all, the productive use of knowledge, skills, and motivations across a lifetime is a fundamental goal of education (Pugh & Bergin, 2006; Shaffer, 2010). Early work focused on specific transfer of skills and the general transfer of *mental discipline* gained from studying rigorous subjects such as Greek or mathematics. But in 1924, E. L. Thorndike demonstrated that there was no mental discipline benefit from learning Greek. Learning Greek just helped you learn more Greek. So, thanks to Thorndike, you were not required to take Greek in high school.

More recently, researchers have distinguished between the automatic, direct use of skills such as reading or writing in everyday applications and the thoughtful transfer of knowledge and strategies to arrive at creative solutions to problems (Bereiter, 1995; Bransford & Schwartz, 1999; Salomon & Perkins, 1989). The key to thoughtful transfer is *mindful abstraction*, or the deliberate identification of a principle, main idea, strategy, or procedure that is not tied to one specific problem or situation, but could apply to many. Such an abstraction becomes part of your metacognitive knowledge, available to guide future learning and problem solving. Bransford and Schwartz (1999) added another key—a resource-rich environment that supports productive, appropriate transfer. Table 9.4 summarizes the types of transfer.

Connect and Extend to PRAXIS II™

Transfer of Learning
Successful transfer of learning from the school to other contexts is evidence of superior instruction. What can teachers do to optimize transfer of knowledge and skills to the broader world?

TABLE 9.4 • **Kinds of Transfer**

	DIRECT-APPLICATION	**PREPARATION FOR FUTURE LEARNING**
Definition	Automatic transfer of highly practiced skill	Conscious application of abstract knowledge to a new situation Productive use of cognitive tools and motivations
Key Conditions	Extensive practice Variety of settings and conditions Overlearning to automaticity	Mindful focus on abstracting a principle, main idea, or procedure that can be used in many situations Learning in powerful teaching-learning environments
Examples	Driving many different cars Finding your gate in an airport	Applying KWL or READS strategies Applying procedures from math in designing a page layout for the school newspaper

Transfer Influence of previously learned material on new material; the productive (not reproductive) uses of cognitive tools and motivations.

HIGHER LEVEL TRANSFER Students will be more likely to transfer knowledge to new situations if they have been actively involved in the learning process. They should be encouraged to form abstractions that they will apply later, so the students know transfer is an important goal.

Teaching for Positive Transfer

Years of research and experience show that students will master new knowledge, problem-solving procedures, and learning strategies, but usually they will not use them unless prompted or guided. For example, studies of real-world mathematics show that people do not always apply math procedures learned in school to solve practical problems in their homes or at grocery stores (Lave, 1988; Lave & Wenger, 1991). This happens because learning is *situated*—tied to specific situations. Because knowledge is learned as a tool to solve particular problems, we may not realize that the knowledge is relevant when we encounter a problem that seems different, at least on the surface (Driscoll, 2005; Singley & Anderson, 1989). How can you make sure your students will use what they learn, even when situations change?

WHAT IS WORTH LEARNING? First, you must answer the question "What is worth learning?" The learning of basic skills such as reading, writing, computing, cooperating, and speaking will definitely transfer to other situations, because these skills are necessary for later work both in and out of school—writing job applications, reading novels, paying bills, working on a team, locating and evaluating health care services, among others. All later learning depends on positive transfer of these basic skills to new situations.

Teachers must also be aware of what the future is likely to hold for their students, both as a group and as individuals. What will society require of them as adults? As a child growing up in Texas in the 1950s and 1960s, I studied nothing about computers, even though my father was a computer systems analyst; yet now I spend hours at my Mac each day. Back then I learned to use a slide rule. Now, calculators and computers have made this skill obsolete. My mom encouraged me to take advanced math and physics instead of typing in high school. Those were great classes, but I struggle with typing every day at my computer—who knew? Undoubtedly, changes as extreme and unpredictable as these await the students you will teach. For this reason, the general transfer of principles, attitudes, learning strategies, self-motivation, time management skills, and problem solving will be just as important for your students as the specific transfer of basic skills.

HOW CAN TEACHERS HELP? For basic skills, greater transfer can also be ensured by **overlearning,** practicing a skill past the point of mastery. Many of the basic facts students learn in elementary school, such as the multiplication tables, are traditionally overlearned. Overlearning helps students develop automated basic skills as we saw in Chapter 8.

For higher-level transfer, students must first learn and understand. Students will be more likely to transfer knowledge to new situations if they have been actively involved in the learning process. Students should be encouraged to form abstractions that they will apply later, so they know transfer is an important goal. It also helps if students form deep connections between the new knowledge and their existing structures of knowledge as well as connections to their everyday experiences (Pugh & Bergin, 2007). Erik De Corte (2003) believes that teachers support transfer, the productive use of cognitive tools and motivations, when they create powerful teaching-learning environments using these design principles:

- The environments should support constructive learning processes in all students.
- The environments should encourage the development of student self-regulation, so that teachers gradually give over more and more responsibilities to the students.
- Learning should involve interaction and collaboration.
- Learners should deal with problems that have personal meaning for them, that are similar to those they will face in the future.

Overlearning Practicing a skill past the point of mastery.

GUIDELINES — FAMILY AND COMMUNITY PARTNERSHIPS

Promoting Transfer

Keep families informed about their child's curriculum so they can support learning.
Examples
1. At the beginning of units or major projects, send a letter summarizing the key goals, a few of the major assignments, and some common problems students have in learning the material for that unit.
2. Ask parents for suggestions about how their child's interests could be connected to the curriculum topics.
3. Invite parents to school for an evening of "strategy learning." Have the students teach their family members one of the strategies they have learned in school.

Give families ideas for how they might encourage their children to practice, extend, or apply learning from school.
Examples
1. To extend writing, ask parents to encourage their children to write letters or e-mails to companies or civic organizations asking for information or free products. Provide a shell letter form for structure and ideas and include addresses of companies that provide free samples or information.
2. Ask family members to include their children in some projects that require measurement, halving or doubling recipes, or estimating costs.

3. Suggest that students work with grandparents to do a family memory book. Combine historical research and writing.

Show connections between learning in school and life outside school.
Examples
1. Ask families to talk about and show how they use the skills their children are learning in their jobs, hobbies, or community involvement projects.
2. Ask family members to come to class to demonstrate how they use reading, writing, science, math, or other knowledge in their work.

Make families partners in practicing learning strategies.
Examples
1. Focus on one learning strategy at a time—ask families to simply remind their children to use a particular strategy with homework that week.
2. Develop a lending library of books and videotapes to teach families about learning strategies.
3. Give parents a copy of the Becoming an Expert Student Guidelines on page 327, rewritten for your grade level.

For more information on promoting transfer, see: http://education.calumet.purdue.edu/vockell/edPsybook/Edpsy6/edpsy6_transfer.htm

---

- The classroom culture should encourage students to become aware of and develop their cognitive and motivational processes. In order to be productive users of these tools, students must know about and value them.

The next three chapters delve in depth about how to support constructive learning, motivation, self-regulation, collaboration, and self-awareness in all students. For now, the *Family and Community Partnerships Guidelines* give ideas for enlisting the support of families in encouraging transfer.

There is one last kind of transfer that is especially important for students—the transfer of the *learning strategies* we encountered earlier. Learning strategies are meant to be applied across a wide range of situations.

STAGES OF TRANSFER FOR STRATEGIES. Gary Phye (1992, 2001; Phye & Sanders, 1994) describes three stages in developing strategic transfer. In the *acquisition phase*, students should not only receive instruction about a strategy and how to use it, but also rehearse the strategy and practice being aware of when and how they are using it. In the *retention phase*, more practice with feedback helps students hone their strategy use. In the *transfer phase*, students should be given new problems that can be solved with the same strategy, even though the problems appear different on the surface. To enhance motivation, teachers should point out to students how using the strategy will help them solve many problems and accomplish different tasks. These steps help build both procedural and self-regulatory knowledge—*how* to use the strategy as well as *when and why*.

For all students, there is a positive relationship between using learning strategies and academic gains such as high school GPA and retention in college (Robbins, Le, & Lauver,

2005). Some students will learn productive strategies on their own, but all students can benefit from direct teaching, modeling, and practice of learning strategies and study skills. This is one important way to prepare all of your students for the future. Newly mastered concepts, principles, and strategies must be applied in a wide variety of situations and with many types of problems (Chen & Mo, 2004). Positive transfer is encouraged when skills are practiced under authentic conditions, similar to those that will exist when the skills are needed later. Students can learn to write by corresponding with e-mail pen pals in other countries. They can learn historical research methods by studying their own family history. Some of these applications should involve complex, ill-defined, unstructured problems, because many of the problems to be faced in later life, both in school and out, will not come to students complete with instructions.

▼ SUMMARY

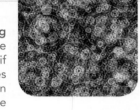

Metacognition (pp. 318–321)

What are the three metacognitive skills? The three metacognitive skills used to regulate thinking and learning are planning, monitoring, and evaluating. Planning involves deciding how much time to give to a task, which strategies to use, how to start, and so on. Monitoring is the real-time awareness of "how I'm doing." Evaluating involves making judgments about the processes and outcomes of thinking and learning and acting on those judgments.

What are some sources of individual differences in metacognition? Individual differences in metacognition may result from different paces of development (maturation) or biological differences among learners. For example, young students may not be able to understand a lesson's purpose as well as older students.

How can teachers help students develop metacognitive knowledge and skills? With younger students, teachers can help students "look inside" to identify what they do to read, write, or learn better. Systems such as KWL can help, if teachers demonstrate, explain, and model the strategy. For older students, teachers can build self-reflective questions into assignments and learning materials.

Learning Strategies (pp. 321–328)

What are learning strategies? Learning strategies are a special kind of procedural knowledge—*knowing how* to do something. A strategy for learning might include mnemonics to remember key terms, skimming to identify the organization, and then writing answers to possible essay questions. Use of strategies and tactics reflects metacognitive knowledge.

What key functions do learning strategies play? Learning strategies help students become cognitively engaged—focus attention on the relevant or important aspects of the material. Second, they encourage students to invest effort, make connections, elaborate, translate, organize, and reorganize in order to think and process deeply—the greater the practice and processing, the stronger the learning. Finally, strategies help students regulate and monitor their own learning—keep track of what is making sense and notice when a new approach is needed.

Describe some procedures for developing learning strategies. Expose students to a number of different strategies, not only general learning strategies but also very specific tactics, such as the graphic strategies. Teach conditional knowledge about when, where, and why to use various strategies. Develop motivation to use the strategies and tactics by showing students how their learning and performance can be improved. Provide direct instruction in content knowledge needed to use the strategies.

When will students apply learning strategies? If they have appropriate strategies, students will apply them if they are faced with a task that requires good strategies, value doing well on that task, think the effort to apply the strategies will be worthwhile, and believe that they can succeed using the strategies. Also, to apply deep processing strategies, students must assume that knowledge is complex and takes time to learn and that learning requires their own active efforts.

Problem Solving (pp. 328–339)

What is problem solving? Problem solving is both general and domain specific. Also, problems can range from *well structured* to *ill structured*, depending on how clear cut the goal is and how much structure is provided for solving the problem. General problem-solving strategies usually include the steps of *identifying* the problem, *setting goals*, *exploring* possible solutions and consequences, *acting*, and finally *evaluating* the outcome. Both general and specific problem solving are valuable and necessary.

Why is the representation stage of problem solving so important? To represent the problem accurately, you must understand both the whole problem and its discrete elements. Schema training may improve this ability. The problem-solving process follows entirely different paths, depending on what representation and goal are chosen. If your representation of the problem suggests an immediate solution, the task is done; the new problem is recognized as a "disguised" version of an old problem with a clear solution. But if there is no existing way of solving the problem or if the activated schema fails, then students must search for a solution. The application of algorithms and heuristics—such as means-ends analysis, working backward, analogical thinking, and verbalization—may help students solve problems.

Describe factors that can interfere with problem solving. Factors that hinder problem solving include functional fixedness or rigidity (response set). These disallow the flexibility needed to represent problems accurately and to have insight into solutions. Also, as we make decisions and judgments, we may overlook important information because we base judgments on what seems representative of a category (representativeness heuristic) or what is available in memory (availability heuristic), then pay attention only to information that confirms our choices (confirmation bias) so that we hold on to beliefs, even in the face of contradictory evidence (belief perseverance).

What are the differences between expert and novice knowledge in a given area? Expert problem solvers have a rich store of declarative, procedural, and conditional knowledge. They organize this knowledge around general principles or patterns that apply to large classes of problems. They work faster, remember relevant information, and monitor their progress better than novices.

Creativity and Creative Problem Solving (pp. 339–343)

What is creativity and how is it assessed? Creativity is a process that involves independently restructuring problems to see things in new, imaginative ways. Creativity is difficult to measure, but tests of divergent thinking can assess originality, fluency, and flexibility. Originality is usually determined statistically. To be original, a response must be given by fewer than 5 or 10 people out of every 100 who take the test. Fluency is the number of different responses. The number of different categories of responses measures flexibility.

What can teachers do to support creativity in the classroom? Multicultural experiences appear to help students think flexibly and creatively. Teachers can encourage creativity in their interactions with students by accepting unusual, imaginative answers, modeling divergent thinking, using brainstorming, and tolerating dissent.

Critical Thinking and Argumentation (pp. 343–346)

What is critical thinking? Critical thinking skills include defining and clarifying the problem, making judgments about the consistency and adequacy of the information related to a problem, and drawing conclusions. No matter what approach you use to develop critical thinking, it is important to follow up activities with additional practice. One lesson is not enough—overlearning will help students use critical thinking in their own lives.

What is argumentation? The heart of argumentation (the process of debating a claim with someone else) is supporting your position with evidence and understanding, and then refuting your opponent's claims and evidence. Argumentation skills are not natural. They take both time and instruction to learn. It is especially difficult for children and adolescents to pay attention to, understand, and refute the opponent's position with evidence.

Teaching for Transfer (pp. 346–350)

What is transfer? Transfer occurs when a rule, fact, or skill learned in one situation is applied in another situation; for example, applying rules of punctuation to write a job application letter. Transfer also involves applying to new problems the principles learned in other, often dissimilar situations.

What are some dimensions of transfer? Information can be transferred across a variety of contexts. Some examples include transfer from one subject to another, one physical location to another or one function to another. These types of transfer make it possible to use skills developed in one area for many other tasks.

Distinguish between automatic and mindful, intentional transfer. Spontaneous application of well-learned knowledge and skills is automatic transfer. Mindful, intentional transfer involves reflection and conscious application of abstract knowledge to new situations. Learning environments should support active constructive learning, self-regulation, collaboration, and awareness of cognitive tools and motivational processes. In addition, students should deal with problems that have meaning in their lives. In addition, teachers can help students transfer learning strategies by teaching strategies directly, providing practice with feedback, and then expanding the application of the strategies to new and unfamiliar situations.

▼ KEY TERMS

Algorithm (335)
Analogical thinking (335)
Argumentation (344)
Availability heuristic (337)
Belief perseverance (337)
Brainstorming (342)
CAPS (326)
Cmaps (325)
Concept map (325)
Confirmation bias (337)
Convergent thinking (340)
Creativity (339)

Critical thinking (343)
Divergent thinking (340)
Executive control processes (318)
Functional fixedness (336)
Heuristic (335)
Insight (340)
KWL (319)
Learning strategies (321)
LINCS vocabulary strategy (328)
Means-ends analysis (335)
Metacognition (318)
Overlearning (348)

Problem (329)
Problem solving (329)
Production deficiency (326)
READS (326)
Representativeness heuristic (336)
Response set (336)
Restructuring (340)
Schema-driven problem solving (334)
Transfer (346)
Verbalization (335)
Working-backward strategy (335)

▼ CONNECT AND EXTEND TO LICENSURE

MULTIPLE-CHOICE QUESTIONS

1. What higher-order knowledge can make the difference between how well and quickly one's students learn material?
   A. Declarative
   B. Rote
   C. Metacognition
   D. Procedural

2. Knowing the importance of metacognition, Joanna Pappas decided she would try to focus her young students' attention on their own thinking skills. Joanna knew by having her students "think" about their thinking they would eventually increase their metacognitive skills. Which one of the following strategies should Joanna employ?
   A. Insight
   B. A KWL chart
   C. An algorithm
   D. Overlearning

3. Teachers often neglect to teach their students about when, where, and why they should use various strategies. A strategy is more apt to be retained and appropriately used when educators directly teach which type of knowledge?

   A. Declarative
   B. Procedural
   C. Self-regulatory
   D. Rote

4. Fourth graders, Richard and Bruce, sat on the stoop outside of the school. They had missed their bus and now had to make the decision whether to walk taking a short-cut or just wait until their mothers notice they had not arrived home. "I think we should start walking on the path and maybe we will get there before they notice we missed the bus."

   "I think we should wait. If we walk on the path and our mothers come to get us, they won't see us and they'll worry. Missing the bus is bad enough. If my mom can't find me, she'll be really mad!" In what type of problem solving are the two boys engaged?

   A. Heuristic
   B. Schema-driven
   C. Algorithm
   D. CAPS

CONSTRUCTED-RESPONSE QUESTIONS

Case

Karen Slagle walked away from her friends on the playground. She had just had an argument over who would win the spot as class president. "I know my brother will win. He has more friends and that equals more votes."

"Karen, you can't be serious. What about the issues such as school policies and procedures?"

"Those issues don't matter. Regina Hoyt won because she was popular last year. The only real issue is popularity."

"What about the year before last when the captain of the football team lost because his campaign didn't deal with anything but sports issues?"

"That was a fluke. Look at our freshman year. That popular basketball player won."

5. How is Karen Slagle's argument an example of confirmation bias?

6. In the current argument Karen Slagle is not practicing critical thinking. What types of strategies do critical thinkers employ?

MyEducationLab™

Go to Chapter 9 of the Book Specific Resources in MyEducationLab and click on "Connect and Extend to Licensure" to answer these questions. Compare your responses with the feedback provided.

▼ WHAT WOULD THEY DO?

TEACHERS' CASEBOOK: Uncritical Thinking

Here is how some practicing teachers would help students learn to critically evaluate the information they find on the Internet.

PAUL DRAGIN • ESL grades 9–12
Columbus East High School, Columbus OH

This common problem does not have an easy fix. A few years ago, a student completed a research paper about 9/11, and the paper was filled with conspiracy theories that the student reported as fact. This dramatic example of undocumented, unsubstantiated research opened my eyes to the need to teach research methods far more explicitly to my students. A general strategy to help ensure more quality research is as follows. After allowing the students to explore using Google and other common search engines to get some familiarity with their topic, I direct them to a reference database such as EBSCOhost or ProQuest, which, in our city, can be accessed with a library card via the public library Web site. By limiting the databases they can use, it reduces the likelihood that inaccurate and highly biased information makes its way into their reports. Demonstrating to them the difference between research-based, scholarly information and general information can go a long way in producing a product that demonstrates actual research.

SARA VINCENT • Special Education
Langley High School, McLean, VA

The Internet is a useful tool for students, but it is filled with a plethora of bad information. Luckily, the teacher in the described scenario can fix the problem prior to the students' submission of their final drafts. As an English teacher, I often encounter this problem, but find that the majority of the students will comply if I set strict citation guidelines. Upon returning the first drafts to the students, I would devote the next lesson to using credible sources rather than using less reliable sources. I would show examples of absurd claims from Internet Web sites. I would also show the students how to find appropriate information. The students would then exchange papers and complete a peer editing lesson. In this lesson, students would critique areas of their peers' drafts in which the sources were weak or nonexistent. In order to create strict citation guidelines, I tell my students that they were not allowed to use any Web site that ends in ".com." Instead, they only are allowed to use Web sites that end in ".edu" or ".gov," or they could use online databases such as JSTOR. If a student chose to use an inappropriate site, then he would automatically fail the assignment. If other teachers use these strict guidelines, the students in the class are highly likely to choose credible Web sites.

PAULA COLEMERE • Special Education Teacher—English, History
McClintock High School, Tempe, AZ

I usually teach my research unit after we have done persuasive reading and writing. Since I teach students how to evaluate information for bias during the persuasive unit, I know they have some prior knowledge before we tackle research. I show examples from scholarly journals, books, and general Web sites like Wikipedia. Then, as we discuss, I think aloud to model for students why I would or would not use a source. I typically do not allow my students to use any Web sources and keep them to the sites that are pre-approved in our library's database. If I were to allow a Web-based source, it would be limited to one. It is extremely helpful to students if you can show them sample research papers that are excellent, satisfactory, and poor. This way, they have an idea of what the finished product should look like. Another strategy would be to read a passage as a class and critically evaluate it together. Thinking critically is a skill that needs to be modeled and taught to kids. It is a mistake to assume they know how to do this on their own.

JESSICA N. MAHTABAN • 8th Grade Math
Woodrow Wilson Middle School, Clifton, NJ

The best way to show students how to evaluate information from Web sites is by modeling. I have a PowerPoint presentation that explains to students how to evaluate authenticity of what they are reading on the Internet. Once the students become familiar with all the key points of how to evaluate Web sites, then I can show various Web sites on the Smart board, and as a class we can discuss and review the validity of the site.

We need to teach students how to articulate their thoughts by expanding on their ideas. Teachers can add "Why or why not?" or "explain" to the end of questions. If students are exposed to higher-level thinking questions and learn how to ask and answer these questions, then they can think more critically about school subjects.

JENNIFER PINCOSKI • Learning Resource Teacher: K–12
Lee County School District, Fort Myers, FL

Understanding that the Internet plays such a significant role in students' lives and that it does provide reliable information, the class needs to be taught how to appropriately use the Web for research. This involves teaching strategies on how to identify credible information, and providing ample opportunities for practice.

In order to understand that not all information on the Internet is accurate, students need to see real examples—examples that are relevant to them. This could be as simple as exposing them to several different sites that post conflicting information about the same topic, and then asking them to define how they would decide which information to believe.

Once students recognize that they need to exercise discretion when retrieving information from the Internet, they can be taught HOW to do so. The teacher can provide a list of guiding questions that will help students critically evaluate their sources. The ultimate goal is for students to use the guiding questions independently and apply them across settings; however, in the beginning, students will require a much higher level of support. An "I do, we do, you do" approach is probably the best way to assist students in the development and practice of these skills.

LAUREN ROLLINS • 1st Grade Teacher
Boulevard Elementary School, Shaker Heights, OH

The Internet is a fantastic resource when it is used properly. Unfortunately, because anyone can post information on the Internet, it is not always reliable or factual. With respect to evaluating information found on the Internet, I would encourage my students to visit multiple sites with multiple viewpoints so they could weigh the relative merits of each. In this way, they practice their critical thinking skills.

Using examples of "factual" information found on Web sites that contradict clearly accepted facts will teach the students that they must evaluate information in the context of what they know to be true. This will help them to understand that multiple sources, not just the Internet, should be used. In addition, I would also devote some time to teaching my students how to properly cite sources from the Internet and other sources. This is an important skill and also a necessary one so that they will not be suspected of plagiarism.

LINDA SPARKS • 1st Grade
John F. Kennedy School, Billerica MA

Whenever I assign a new research project, I begin with a specific list of resource instructions. For example, I might state that I want 2 books, 2 magazine articles and 3 Web sites. After the topic is picked, I have the students pull together their resources and come to me so that I can check them to make sure each student is headed in the right direction. It also gives me a better understanding of what they are researching and I can find out if there are any misconceptions about the project. I find I get better results this way, as the students know I am aware of what they are researching and that I have their lists of resources. (Even if they are not going to use them all, I want them to see what is available for them.) I also am more prepared to teach specific writing skills. The first skill I teach before I assign a project as they practice reading articles is how to take that information and transfer it into their own words. Limiting the number of quotes is a way to have a higher thinking process taking place. Many times, when given the chance, students are more creative than the writers of the articles they read.

BARBARA PRESLEY • Transition/Work Study Coordinator—High School Level
C.W. Baker High School, Baldwinsville, NY

To me, discussion is key: whole-group discussion, small-group discussion, and 1:1 discussion, all the time being prepared to defend or criticize (with legitimate corroboration) topics raised. Students learn well from their mistakes as long as the correction is respectful and meaningful to them personally. They can't learn to think critically until someone questions their premises and they have to defend their position—as long as the discussions are conducted without malice. They are gaining experience in critical thinking through the process of criticism, both given and received.

MyEducationLab™

Go to Topic 7, Knowledge Construction, in the MyEducationLab (www.myeducationlab.com) for *Educational Psychology*, where you can:

- Find learning outcomes for Knowledge Construction along with the national standards that connect to these outcomes.
- Complete Assignments and Activities that can help you more deeply understand the chapter content.
- Apply and practice your understanding of the core teaching skills identified in the chapter with the Building Teaching Skills and Dispositions learning units.
- Examine challenging situations and cases presented in the IRIS Center Resources.
- Access video clips of CCSSO National Teachers of the Year award winners responding to the question, "Why Do I Teach?" in the Teacher Talk section.
- Check your comprehension on the content covered in the chapter with the Study Plan. Here you will be able to take a chapter quiz, receive feedback on your answers, and then access Review, Practice, and Enrichment activities to enhance your understanding of chapter content.
- Find additional Teachers' Casebook scenarios and responses to them from practicing teachers.
- Use the Online Lesson Plan Builder to practice lesson planning and integrating national and state standards into your planning.

chapter ten

THE LEARNING SCIENCES
AND CONSTRUCTIVISM

▶ **TEACHERS' CASEBOOK:** Learning to Cooperate

You want to use cooperative learning with your middle-school students. Many students have worked in groups, but few seem to have participated in true cooperative learning. When you surveyed the class members about their experiences, most rolled their eyes and groaned. You take it that their experiences have not been very positive. These students have a wide range of abilities, including some who are truly gifted and talented, several who are just learning English, and a few who are very shy; and then there are others who would take over and dominate every discussion if you let them. You believe that collaboration is a crucial 21st century skill for all students and that learning together can deepen understanding as students question, explain, and build on each other's thinking. No matter what, you want the experience of learning together to build your students' confidence and your sense of efficacy as a teacher, so you want authentic successes.

CRITICAL THINKING

- How would you begin to introduce cooperative learning to your students?
- What tasks will you choose to start?
- How will you establish groups?
- What will you watch and listen for to be sure the students are making the most of the experience?

OVERVIEW AND OBJECTIVES

For the past three chapters, we have analyzed different aspects of learning. We considered behavioral, information processing, and cognitive science explanations of what and how people learn. We have examined complex cognitive processes such as metacognitive skills and problem solving. These explanations of learning focus on the individual and what is happening in his or her "head." In this chapter, we expand our investigation of learning to include insights from a relatively recent interdisciplinary approach called the *learning sciences*. This approach brings together work in many fields that study learning, including educational psychology, computer science, neuroscience, and anthropology. One of the foundations of the learning sciences is constructivism, a broad perspective that calls attention to two critical aspects of learning: social and cultural factors. In this chapter, we examine the role of other people and the cultural context in learning. Sociocultural constructivist theories have roots in cognitive perspectives, but have moved well beyond these early explanations. We will explore a number of teaching strategies and approaches that are consistent with cognitive perspectives—inquiry, problem-based learning, cooperative learning, cognitive apprenticeships, and service learning. Finally, we will examine learning in this digital age, including the considerations about learning in technology-rich environments.

By the time you have completed this chapter, you should be able to:

Objective 10.1: Describe the collaborative approach that led to the interdisciplinary field of learning sciences.

Objective 10.2: Explain different perspectives on constructivism as a theory of learning and teaching.

Objective 10.3: Identify the common elements in most contemporary constructivist theories.

Objective 10.4: Apply constructivist principles to classroom practice.

Objective 10.5: Evaluate the use of community-based activities/service learning.

Objective 10.6: Describe positive and negative influences of technology on the learning and development of children and adolescents.

Learning sciences An interdisciplinary science of learning, based on research in psychology, education, computer science, philosophy, sociology, anthropology, neuroscience, and other fields that study learning.

THE LEARNING SCIENCES

In the previous three chapters, psychologists were responsible for most of the theory and research we discussed. But many other people have also studied learning: Today, there are multiple perspectives included in the learning sciences.

What Are the Learning Sciences?

The interdisciplinary field of the **learning sciences** encompasses research in psychology, education, computer science, philosophy, sociology, anthropology, neuroscience, and other fields that study learning. You already have explored some of the foundations of the learning sciences in Chapters 8 and 9, including the make-up of working memory and the role of cognitive load in learning; how information is represented in complex structures such as schemas; what experts know and how their knowledge is different from that of novices; metacognition; problem solving; thinking and reasoning; and how knowledge transfers (or doesn't transfer) from the classroom to the world beyond.

No matter what their focus, all knowledge workers in the learning sciences are interested in how deep knowledge in subjects like science, mathematics, and literacy is actually acquired and applied in the real world of scientists and mathematicians and writers. In the *Cambridge Handbook of Learning Sciences*, R. Keith Sawyer (2006) contrasts what it takes for deep learning to occur with traditional classroom practices that have dominated schooling in many countries for decades. Look at Table 10.1 to see the differences.

Basic Assumptions of the Learning Sciences

Even though the different fields in the learning sciences approach their study from varying perspectives, there is growing agreement about some basic assumptions (Sawyer, 2006):

- **Experts have deep conceptual knowledge.** Experts know many facts and procedures, but just learning facts and procedures will not make you an expert. Experts have deep conceptual understanding that allows them to put their knowledge into action; they are able to apply and modify their knowledge to fit each situation. Experts' deep conceptual knowledge generates problem finding and problem solving.
- **Learning comes from the learner.** Better instruction alone will not transfer deep understandings from teachers to students. Learning is more than receiving and processing information transmitted by teachers or texts. Rather, students must actively participate in their own personal construction of knowledge. We are knowledge inventors, not copy machines (de Koek, Sleegers, & Voeten, 2004).
- **Schools must create effective learning environments.** It is the job of the school to create environments where students are active in constructing their own deep understandings so they can reason about real-world problems and transfer their learning from school to their lives beyond the school walls.
- **Prior knowledge is key.** Students come into our classrooms filled with knowledge and beliefs about how the world works. Some of these preconceptions are right, some are part right, and some are wrong. If teaching does not begin with what the students "know," then the students will learn what it takes to pass the test, but their knowledge and beliefs about the world will not change.

TABLE 10.1 • **How Deep Learning Contrasts with Learning in Traditional Classrooms**

LEARNING IN TRADITIONAL CLASSROOMS	BUT FINDINGS FROM COGNITIVE SCIENCE SHOW THAT DEEP LEARNING REQUIRES THAT:
Class material is not related to what students already know. Example: Teacher says, *"Igneous rocks are . . .*	Learners relate new understandings to what they already know and believe. Example: Teacher says, *"Have any of you seen granite counter tops on TV home shows or maybe you have one in your house? What do they look like . . .?"*
Class material presented and learned as disconnected bits of knowledge. *"The definition of metamorphic rocks is. . . ."*	Learners integrate and interconnect their knowledge in expanding conceptual systems. *"We already have learned about two kinds of rocks. We also learned last week about how the earth has changed over the centuries, with some ocean floors becoming land areas. Today we will learn about how marble and diamonds. . . . "*
Lessons involve memorizing facts and doing procedures without understanding how or why. *"To divide fractions, invert and multiply . . ."*	Learners search for patterns and recognize or invent underlying principles. *"Remind me what it means to divide. . . . Ok, so ¾ divided by ½ means how many sets of what are in. . . .?"*
Learners have trouble understanding ideas that are not straight from the textbook or explained in the same way. *"What does your textbook say about . . ."*	Learners evaluate new ideas, even if not in the text, and integrate them into their thinking. *"On TV yesterday there was a story about a new drug that is effective in curing one out of 8 cases of. . . . What is the probability of a cure?"*
Authorities and experts are the source of unchanging and accurate facts and procedures. *"Scientists agree. . . ."*	Learners understand that knowledge is socially constructed by people, so ideas require critical examination. *"Here is an excerpt from the Presidential debates last week. Let's think about how you would determine what statements are more supported by evidence . . .?"*
Learners simply memorize everything instead of thinking about the purpose of learning and the best strategies for that purpose. *"This will be on the test."*	Learners think about why they are learning, monitor their understanding, and reflect on their own learning processes. *"How could you use this concept in your own life? How can you tell if you are understanding it?"*

Source: Based on Sawyer, K. (2006). The new science of learning. In R. K. Sawyer (Ed.). The Cambridge handbook of the learning sciences (p. 4). New York: The Cambridge University Press. New York: Oxford University Press.

• **Reflection is necessary to develop deep conceptual knowledge.** Students need to express and perform the knowledge they are developing through writing, conversations, drawings, projects, skits, portfolios, reports, and so on. But the performance is not enough. To develop deep conceptual knowledge, students need to reflect—thoughtfully analyze their own work and progress.

Embodied Cognition

Recently a new theme has emerged in the cognitive and learning sciences—**embodied cognition.** This is awareness that "the way we think about and represent information reflects the fact that we need to interact with the world" (Ashcraft & Radvansky, 2010, p. 32).

Embodied cognition Theory stating that cognitive processes develop from real-time, goal-directed interactions between humans and their environment.

These interactions occur through our senses and bodies, and the way our bodies interact with the world to achieve our goals affects our thinking. In other words, our cognitive processes have deep roots in the interactions of our bodies with the real world—what develops cognitively depends on our sensorimotor engagement with the world. In this view of cognition, the body, not the mind, is primary, but the body needs the mind to successfully interact in the world. In some ways, this perspective is similar to Piaget's idea that thinking emerges early on from the infant's sensorimotor interaction in the world. Instead of being just simple conduits for outside world sounds and images, our senses and motor responses are central to how we think. So we have to understand how our physical body interacts with the world in order to understand our mind (Wilson, 2002).

Actually, it appears that humans are capable of both real-time, situation-by-situation, adaptive, ever-changing interactions (where the *mind is serving the body* to succeed, for example, driving in traffic or doing a jigsaw puzzle) and abstract thinking using symbols and representations developed in earlier times to solve current problems (where *the body—brain control system—is serving the mind*, for example, *in using images or analogies to learn a new language*). Humans' ability to mentally represent and manipulate symbols that are not present in real time is critical. In fact, Margret Wilson (2002) suggests:

> This takeover by the mind, and the concomitant ability to mentally represent what is distant in time or space, may have been one of the driving forces behind the runaway train of human intelligence that separated us from other hominids. (p. 635)

In educational psychology, these fundamental assumptions of the learning sciences and embodied cognition all lead to the conclusion that thinking is constructive. In the next section we look at both cognitive and social constructivism—topics you will hear about repeatedly in your preparation for teaching.

COGNITIVE AND SOCIAL CONSTRUCTIVISM

Consider this situation:

> A young child who has never been to the hospital is in her bed in the pediatric wing. The nurse at the station down the hall calls over the intercom above the bed, "Hi Chelsea, how are you doing? Do you need anything?" The girl looks puzzled and does not answer. The nurse repeats the question with the same result. Finally, the nurse says emphatically, "Chelsea, are you there? Say something!" The little girl responds tentatively, "Hello wall—I'm here."

Chelsea encountered a new situation—a talking wall. The wall is persistent. It sounds like a grown-up wall. She shouldn't talk to strangers, but she is not sure about walls. She uses what she knows and what the situation provides to construct meaning and to act.

Here is another example of constructing meaning. This time, Kate and her 9-year-old son Ethan co-construct understandings as they buy groceries:

Ethan: (running to get a shopping cart) Do we need the big one?

Kate: We might—better too big than not big enough. Here is our list—where do we go first?

Ethan: We need ice cream for the party! (Ethan heads toward frozen foods)

Kate: Whoa! What happened to the ice cream carton you left out on the kitchen counter?

Ethan: It melted and it wasn't out that long. I promise!

Kate: Right and we may be in this store a while, so let's start with things that won't melt while we are shopping—I usually buy produce first.

Ethan: What's "produce"?

Kate: Things that grow—fruits and vegetables "produced" by farmers.

Ethan: OK, the list says cucumbers. Here they are. Wait there are two kinds. Which do you want? The little ones say "local." What's local?

Kate: Local means from around here—close to us, close to our "location." Hmmm.—the big ones are 75 cents *each* and these smaller ones are $1.15 *a pound*. How would you decide which is a better deal?.

Ethan: I guess bigger is better, right? Or is local better?

Kate: Well, I wonder if they cost the same for the amount you get—per pound. How could you figure that out?

Ethan: I don't know—the price for a pound isn't on the big ones, just the price each.

Kate: When the doctor wants to know how many pounds you weigh, she puts you on a scale. What if you weighed a big cucumber over there on that food scale?

Ethan: OK—it weighs ½ a pound.

Kate: So half a pound costs 75 cents—what would a whole pound cost—that's 2 halves make a whole?

Ethan: 75 cents plus 75 cents—$1.50—Gee the bigger ones are more expensive. So the smaller ones are better and they are "local"—that's good too, right?

Kate: Maybe. I like to support our local farmers. Where are the small cucumbers from—look at the tiny print on the label.

Ethan: Virginia—is that close to us?

Kate: Not really—it is about a 6-hour drive from here…

Look at the knowledge being co-constructed about planning ahead, vocabulary, math, problem solving, and even geography. Constructivist theories of learning focus on how people make meaning, both on their own like Chelsea and in interaction with others like Ethan.

Constructivist Views of Learning

Constructivism is a broad term used by philosophers, curriculum designers, psychologists, educators, and others. Ernst von Glasersfeld calls it "a vast and woolly area in contemporary psychology, epistemology, and education" (1997, p. 204). Constructivist perspectives are grounded in the research of Piaget; Vygotsky; the Gestalt psychologists; Bartlett, Bruner, and Rogoff; as well as the philosophy of John Dewey and the work in anthropology of Jean Lave, to mention just a few intellectual roots.

There is no one constructivist theory of learning, but most constructivist theories agree on two central ideas:

Central Idea 1: Learners are active in constructing their own knowledge.
Central Idea 2: Social interactions are important in this knowledge construction process (Bruning, Schraw, & Norby, 2011).

Constructivist approaches in science and mathematics education, in educational psychology and anthropology, and in computer-based education all embrace these two ideas. But even though many psychologists and educators use the term *constructivism,* they often mean very different things (Martin, 2006; McCaslin & Hickey, 2001; Phillips, 1997).

One way to organize constructivist views is to talk about two forms of constructivism: psychological and social construction (Palincsar, 1998; Phillips, 1997). We could oversimplify a bit and say that psychological constructivists focus on how individuals use information, resources, and even help from others to build and improve their mental models and problem-solving strategies—see Central Idea #1. In contrast, social constructivists view learning as increasing our abilities to participate with others in activities that are meaningful in the culture—see Central Idea #2 (Windschitl, 2002). Let's look a bit closer at each type of constructivism.

PSYCHOLOGICAL/INDIVIDUAL/COGNITIVE CONSTRUCTIVISM.
Many psychological theories include some kind of constructivism because these theories embrace the idea that individuals construct their own cognitive structures as they interpret their experiences in particular situations (Palincsar, 1998). These psychological constructivists "are concerned

Constructivism View that emphasizes the active role of the learner in building understanding and making sense of information.

CONSTRUCTIVIST VIEWS Constructivist theories are based on the ideas that learners actively develop their knowledge, rather than passively receive it, in package form, from teachers or outside sources.

with how individuals build up certain elements of their cognitive or emotional apparatus" (Phillips, 1997, p. 153). Because they study individual knowledge, beliefs, self-concept, or identity, they are sometimes called *individual constructivists* or *cognitive constructivists;* they all focus on the inner psychological life of people. When Chelsea talked to the wall in the previous section, she was making meaning using her own individual knowledge and beliefs about how to respond when someone (or something) talks to you. She was using what she knew to impose intellectual structure on her world (Piaget, 1971; Windschitl, 2002). When children observe that most plants need soil to grow and then conclude that plants "eat dirt," they are using what they know about how eating supports life to make sense of plant growth (Linn & Eylon, 2006).

Using these standards, the most recent information processing theories are constructivist because they are concerned with how individuals construct internal representations (propositions, images, concepts, schemas) that can be remembered and retrieved (Mayer, 1996). The outside world is viewed as a source of input, but once the sensations are perceived and enter working memory, the important work is assumed to be happening "inside the head" of the individual (Schunk, 2012; Vera & Simon, 1993). Some psychologists, however, believe that information processing is "trivial" or "weak" constructivism because the individual's only constructive contribution is to build accurate internal representations of the outside world (Derry, 1992; Garrison, 1995; Marshall, 1996; Windschitl, 2002).

In contrast, Piaget's psychological (cognitive) constructivist perspective is less concerned with "correct" representations and more interested in meaning as it is constructed by the individual. As we saw in Chapter 2, Piaget proposed that as children develop, their thinking becomes more organized and adaptive and less tied to concrete events. Piaget's special concern was with logic and the construction of universal knowledge that cannot be learned directly from the environment—knowledge such as conservation or reversibility (Miller, 2011). Such knowledge comes from reflecting on and coordinating our own cognitions or thoughts, not from mapping external reality. Piaget saw the social environment as an important factor in development, but did not believe that social interaction was the main mechanism for changing thinking (Moshman, 1997). Some educational and developmental psychologists have referred to Piaget's kind of constructivism as **first wave constructivism** or "solo" constructivism, with its emphasis on Central Idea 1, individual meaning making (DeCorte, Greer, and Verschaffel, 1996; Paris, Byrnes, & Paris, 2001).

At the extreme end of individual constructivism is the notion of **radical constructivism.** This perspective holds that there is no reality or truth in the world, only the individual's perceptions and beliefs. Each of us constructs meaning from our own experiences, but we have no way of understanding or "knowing" the reality of others (Woods & Murphy, 2002). A difficulty with this position is that, when pushed to the extreme of relativism, all knowledge and all beliefs are equal because they are all valid individual perceptions. There are problems with this thinking for educators. First, teachers have a professional responsibility to emphasize some values, such as honesty or justice, over others, such as bigotry and deception. All perceptions and beliefs are not equal. As teachers, we ask students to work hard to learn. If learning cannot advance understanding because all understandings are equally good, then, as David Moshman (1997) notes, "we might just as well let students continue to believe whatever they believe" (p. 230). Also, it appears that some knowledge, such as

First wave constructivism A focus on the individual and psychological sources of knowing, as in Piaget's theory.

Radical constructivism Knowledge is assumed to be the individual's construction; it cannot be judged right or wrong.

counting and one-to-one correspondence, is not constructed, but universal. Knowing one-to-one correspondence is part of being human (Geary, 1995; Schunk, 2012).

VYGOTSKY'S SOCIAL CONSTRUCTIVISM. As you also saw in Chapter 2, Vygotsky emphasized Central Idea 2 above, that social interaction, cultural tools, and activity shape individual development and learning, just as Ethan's interactions and activities in the grocery store with his mother shaped his learning about anticipating possible consequences (running out of space in the shopping cart and melted ice cream), the meaning of "produce" and "local," how to calculate price per pound, and geography (Martin, 2006). By participating in a broad range of activities with others, learners *appropriate* the outcomes produced by working together; these outcomes could include both new strategies and knowledge. **Appropriating** means being able to reason, act, and participate using cultural tools—for example, using conceptual tools such as "force" and "acceleration" to reason in physics (Mason, 2007). In psychological (cognitive) constructivism, learning means individually possessing knowledge, but in social constructivism, learning means belonging to a group and participating in the social construction of knowledge (Mason, 2007). Putting learning in social and cultural contexts is known as **second wave constructivism** (Paris, Byrnes, & Paris, 2001).

Because his theory relies heavily on social interactions and the cultural context to explain learning, most psychologists classify Vygotsky as a social constructivist (Palincsar, 1998; Prawat, 1996). However, some theorists categorize him as a psychological constructivist because he was primarily interested in development within the individual (Moshman, 1997; Phillips, 1997). In a sense, Vygotsky was both. One advantage of Vygotsky's theory of learning is that it gives us a way to consider both the psychological and the social: He bridges both camps. For example, Vygotsky's concept of the *zone of proximal development*—the area in which a child can solve a problem with the help (scaffolding) of an adult or more able peer—has been called a place where culture and cognition create each other (Cole, 1985). Culture creates cognition when the adult uses tools and practices from the culture (language, maps, computers, looms, or music) to steer the child toward goals the culture values (reading, writing, weaving, dance). Cognition creates culture as the adult and child together generate new practices and problem solutions to add to the cultural group's repertoire (Serpell, 1993). So people are both products and producers of their societies and cultures (Bandura, 2001). One way of integrating individual and social constructivism is to think of knowledge as both *individually constructed* and *socially mediated* (Windschitl, 2002).

The term **constructionism** is sometimes used to describe how public knowledge is created. Although this is not our main concern in educational psychology, it is worth a quick look.

CONSTRUCTIONISM. Social constructionists do not focus on individual learning. Their concern is how public knowledge in disciplines such as science, math, economics, or history is constructed. Beyond this kind of academic knowledge, constructionists also are interested in how common-sense ideas, everyday beliefs, and commonly held understandings about people and the world are communicated to new members of a sociocultural group (Gergen, 1997; Phillips, 1997). Questions raised might include who determines what constitutes history, what is the proper way to behave in public, or how to get elected class president. Social constructionists believe all knowledge is socially constructed, and, more important, some people have more power than others to define what constitutes such knowledge. Relationships between and among teachers, students, families, and the community are the central issues. Collaboration to understand diverse viewpoints is encouraged, and traditional bodies of knowledge often are challenged (Gergen, 1997). The philosophies of Jacques Dierrida and Michel Foucault are important sources for constructionists. Vygotsky's theory, with its attention to the way cognition creates culture, has some elements in common with constructionism.

These different perspectives on constructivism raise some general questions, and they disagree on the answers. These questions can never be fully resolved, but different theories tend to favor different positions. Let's consider the questions.

Appropriating Being able to internalize or take for yourself knowledge and skills developed in interaction with others or with cultural tools.

Second wave constructivism A focus on the social and cultural sources of knowing, as in Vygotsky's theory.

Constructionism How public knowledge in disciplines such as science, math, economics, or history is constructed.

How Is Knowledge Constructed?

One tension among different approaches to constructivism is based on how knowledge is constructed. Moshman (1982) describes three explanations.

1. *The realities and truths of the external world direct knowledge construction.* Individuals reconstruct outside reality by building accurate mental representations such as propositional networks, concepts, cause-and-effect patterns, and condition-action production rules that reflect "the way things really are." The more the person learns, the deeper and broader his or her experience is, the closer that person's knowledge is to objective reality. Information processing holds this view of knowledge (Cobb & Bowers, 1999).

2. *Internal processes such as Piaget's organization, assimilation, and accommodation direct knowledge construction.* New knowledge is abstracted from old knowledge. Knowledge is not a mirror of reality, but rather an abstraction that grows and develops with cognitive activity. Knowledge is not true or false; it just grows more internally consistent and organized with development.

3. *Both external and internal factors direct knowledge construction.* Knowledge grows through the interactions of internal (cognitive) and external (environmental and social) factors. Vygotsky's description of cognitive development through the appropriation and use of cultural tools such as language is consistent with this view (Bruning, Schraw, & Norby, 2011). Another example is Bandura's theory of reciprocal interactions among people, behaviors, and environments described in Chapter 11 (Schunk, 2012). Table 10.2 summarizes the three general explanations about how knowledge is constructed.

TABLE 10.2 • **How Knowledge Is Constructed**

TYPE	ASSUMPTIONS ABOUT LEARNING AND KNOWLEDGE	EXAMPLE THEORIES
External Direction	Knowledge is acquired by constructing a representation of the outside world. Direct teaching, feedback, and explanation affect learning. Knowledge is accurate to the extent that it reflects the "way things really are" in the outside world.	Information processing
Internal Direction	Knowledge is constructed by transforming, organizing, and reorganizing previous knowledge. Knowledge is not a mirror of the external world, even though experience influences thinking and thinking influences knowledge. Exploration and discovery are more important than teaching.	Piaget
Both External and Internal Direction	Knowledge is constructed based on social interactions and experience. Knowledge reflects the outside world as filtered through and influenced by culture, language, beliefs, interactions with others, direct teaching, and modeling. Guided discovery, teaching, models, and coaching as well as the individual's prior knowledge, beliefs, and thinking affect learning.	Vygotsky

Knowledge: Situated or General?

A second question that cuts across many constructivist perspectives is whether knowledge is internal, general, and transferable, or bound to the time and place in which it is constructed. Psychologists who emphasize the social construction of knowledge and situated learning affirm Vygotsky's notion that learning is inherently social and embedded in a particular cultural setting (Cobb & Bowers, 1999). What is true in one time and place—such as the "fact" before Columbus's time that the earth was flat—becomes false in another time and place. Particular ideas may be useful within a specific **community of practice**, such as 15th-century navigation, but useless outside that community. What counts as new knowledge is determined in part by how well the new idea fits with current accepted practice. Over time, the current practice may be questioned and even overthrown, but until such major shifts occur, current practice will shape what is considered valuable.

Situated learning emphasizes that learning in the real world is not like studying in school. It is more like an apprenticeship where novices, with the support of an expert guide and model, take on more and more responsibility until they are able to function independently. Proponents of this view believe situated learning explains learning in factories, around the dinner table, in high school halls, in street gangs, in the business office, and on the playground.

Situated learning is often described as "enculturation," or adopting the norms, behaviors, skills, beliefs, language, and attitudes of a particular community. The community might be mathematicians or gang members or writers or students in your 8th grade class or soccer players—any group that has particular ways of thinking and doing. Knowledge is viewed not as individual cognitive structures, but rather as a creation of the community over time. The practices of the community—the ways of interacting and getting things done, as well as the tools the community has created—constitute the knowledge of that community. Learning means becoming more able to participate in those practices and use the tools (Greeno, Collins, & Resnick, 1996; Mason, 2007; Rogoff, 1998).

At the most basic level, "situated learning emphasizes the idea that much of what is learned is specific to the situation in which it is learned" (Anderson, Reder, & Simon, 1996, p. 5). Thus, some would argue, learning to do calculations in school may help students do more school calculations, but it may not help them balance a checkbook, because the skills can be applied only in the context in which they were learned—namely school (Lave, 1997; Lave & Wenger, 1991). But it also appears that knowledge and skills can be applied across contexts that were not part of the initial learning situation, as when you use your ability to read and calculate to do your income taxes, even though income tax forms were not part of your high school curriculum (Anderson, Reder, & Simon, 1996).

Learning that is situated in school does not have to be doomed or irrelevant (Bereiter, 1997). As you saw in Chapter 9, a major question in educational psychology—and education in general—concerns the transfer of knowledge from one situation to another. How can you encourage this transfer from one situation to another? Help is on the way in the next section.

Common Elements of Constructivist Student-Centered Teaching

STOP & THINK What makes a lesson student centered? List the characteristics and features that put the student in the center of learning. •

We have looked at some areas of disagreement among the constructivist perspectives, but what about areas of agreement? All constructivist theories assume that knowing develops as learners, like Chelsea and Ethan, try to make sense of their experiences. "Learners, therefore, are not empty vessels waiting to be filled, but rather active organisms seeking meaning" (Driscoll, 2005, p. 487). Humans construct mental models or schemas and continue to revise them to make better sense of their experiences. Again, we are knowledge inventors, not filing cabinets. Our constructions do not necessarily resemble external

Community of practice Social situation or context in which ideas are judged useful or true.

Situated learning The idea that skills and knowledge are tied to the situation in which they were learned and that they are difficult to apply in new settings.

Connect and Extend to PRAXIS II™

Student-Centered Learning (II, A3)
Many of the major initiatives to reform content-area curricula (e.g., science, mathematics) emphasize student-centered/constructivist approaches to learning. Describe the major principles of these approaches and explain how they differ from teacher-centered approaches.

reality; rather, they are our unique interpretations, like Chelsea's friendly, persistent wall. This doesn't mean that all constructions are equally useful or viable. Learners test their understandings against experience and the understandings of other people—they negotiate and co-construct meanings like Ethan did with his mother.

Constructivists share similar goals for learning. They emphasize knowledge *in use* rather than the *storing* of inert facts, concepts, and skills. Learning goals include developing abilities to find and solve ill-structured problems, critical thinking, inquiry, self-determination, and openness to multiple perspectives (Driscoll, 2005). Even though there is no single constructivist theory, many constructivist approaches recommend five conditions for learning:

1. Embed learning in complex, realistic, and relevant learning environments.
2. Provide for social negotiation and shared responsibility as a part of learning.
3. Support multiple perspectives and use multiple representations of content.
4. Nurture self-awareness and an understanding that knowledge is constructed.
5. Encourage ownership in learning. (Driscoll, 2005; Marshall, 1992)

Before we discuss particular teaching approaches, let's look more closely at these dimensions of constructivist teaching.

Complex learning environments Problems and learning situations that mimic the ill-structured nature of real life.

Social negotiation Aspect of learning process that relies on collaboration with others and respect for different perspectives.

Intersubjective attitude A commitment to build shared meaning with others by finding common ground and exchanging interpretations.

COMPLEX LEARNING ENVIRONMENTS AND AUTHENTIC TASKS. Constructivists believe that students should not be given stripped-down, simplified problems and basic skills drills, but instead should encounter **complex learning environments** that deal with "fuzzy," ill-structured problems. The world beyond school presents few simple problems or step-by-step directions, so schools should be sure that every student has experience solving complex problems. Complex problems are not just difficult ones; rather, they have many parts. There are multiple, interacting elements in complex problems and multiple possible solutions. There is no one right way to reach a conclusion, and each solution may bring a new set of problems.

These complex problems should be embedded in authentic tasks and activities, the kinds of situations that students would face as they apply what they are learning to the real world (Needles & Knapp, 1994). Students may need support (*scaffolding*) as they work on these complex problems, with teachers helping them find resources, keeping track of their progress, breaking larger problems down into smaller ones, and so on. This aspect of constructivist approaches is consistent with situated learning in emphasizing learning in situations where the knowledge will be applied.

SOCIAL NEGOTIATION. Many constructivists share Vygotsky's belief that higher mental processes develop through **social negotiation** and interaction, so collaboration in learning is valued. A major goal of teaching is to develop students' abilities to establish and defend their own positions while respecting the positions of others and working together to negotiate or co-construct meaning. To accomplish this exchange, students must talk and listen to each other. It is a challenge for children in cultures that are individualistic and competitive, such as the United States, to adopt what has been called an **intersubjective attitude**—a commitment to build shared meaning by finding common ground and exchanging interpretations.

AUTHENTIC TASKS AND SOCIAL INTERACTIONS Constructivist approaches recommend that educators emphasize complex, realistic, and relevant learning environments, as well as the importance of social interactions in the learning process. For example, the students here are collaborating to create a household budget.

MULTIPLE PERSPECTIVES AND REPRESENTATIONS OF CONTENT. When students encounter only one model, one analogy, one way of understanding complex content, they often oversimplify as they try to apply that one approach to every situation. I saw this happen in my educational psychology class when six students were presenting an example of guided discovery learning. The students' presentation was a near copy of a guided discovery demonstration I had given earlier in the semester, but with some major misconceptions. My students knew only one way to represent discovery learning. Resources for the class should have provided **multiple representations of content** using different analogies, examples, and metaphors. This idea is consistent with Jerome Bruner's (1966) **spiral curriculum,** a structure for teaching that introduces the fundamental structure of all subjects—the "big ideas"—early in the school years, then revisits the subjects in more and more complex forms over time.

UNDERSTANDING THE KNOWLEDGE CONSTRUCTION PROCESS.   Constructivist approaches emphasize making students aware of their own role in constructing knowledge. The assumptions we make, our beliefs, and our experiences shape what each of us comes to "know" about the world. Different assumptions and different experiences lead to different knowledge, as we saw in Chapter 6 when we explored the role of cultural differences in shaping knowledge. If students are aware of the influences that shape their thinking, they will be more able to choose, develop, and defend positions in a self-critical way while respecting the positions of others.

STUDENT OWNERSHIP OF LEARNING.   "While there are several interpretations of what [constructivist] theory means, most agree that it involves a dramatic change in the focus of teaching, putting the students' own efforts to understand at the center of the educational enterprise" (Prawat, 1992, p. 357). Student ownership does not mean that the teacher abandons responsibility for instruction. Because the design of teaching is a central issue in this book, we will spend the rest of this chapter discussing examples of *ownership of learning* and *student-centered instruction*.

APPLYING CONSTRUCTIVIST PERSPECTIVES

Even though there are many applications of constructivist views of learning, we can recognize constructivist approaches by the activities of the teacher and the students. Mark Windschitl (2002) suggests that the following activities encourage meaningful learning:

- Teachers elicit students' ideas and experiences in relation to key topics, then fashion learning situations that help students elaborate on or restructure their current knowledge.
- Students are given frequent opportunities to engage in complex, meaningful, problem-based activities.
- Teachers provide students with a variety of information resources as well as the tools (technological and conceptual) necessary to mediate learning.
- Students work collaboratively and are given support to engage in task-oriented dialogue with one another.
- Teachers make their own thinking processes explicit to learners and encourage students to do the same through dialogue, writing, drawings, or other representations.
- Students are routinely asked to apply knowledge in diverse and authentic contexts, explain ideas, interpret texts, predict phenomena, and construct arguments based on evidence, rather than focus exclusively on the acquisition of predetermined "right answers."
- Teachers encourage students' reflective and autonomous thinking in conjunction with the conditions listed above.
- Teachers employ a variety of assessment strategies to understand how students' ideas are evolving and to give feedback on the processes as well as the products of their thinking. (p. 137)

In addition, constructivist approaches include **scaffolding** to support students' developing expertise. One implication of Vygotsky's theory of cognitive development is that deep understanding requires that students grapple with problems in their zone of

Multiple representations of content Considering problems using various analogies, examples, and metaphors.

Spiral curriculum Bruner's design for teaching that introduces the fundamental structure of all subjects early in the school years, then revisits the subjects in more and more complex forms over time.

Scaffolding Teachers and students make meaningful connections between what the teacher knows and what the students know and need in order to help the students learn more.

proximal development; they need scaffolding in order to work in that zone. Here is a good definition of scaffolding that emphasizes the dynamic interactive nature of scaffolding as well as the knowledge that both teacher and student bring—both are experts on something: "Scaffolding is a powerful conception of teaching and learning in which teachers and students create meaningful connections between teachers' cultural knowledge and the everyday experience and knowledge of the student" (McCaslin & Hickey, 2001, p. 137). Look back at the grocery store conversation between Ethan and his mother at the beginning of the previous section. Notice how the mother used the melted ice cream on the kitchen counter and the scale in the doctor's office—connections to Ethan's experience and knowledge—to scaffold Ethan's understanding.

Even though there are different views of scaffolding, most educational psychologists agree on three characteristics (van de Pol, Volman, & Beishuizen, 2010):

1. **Contingency Support**: The teacher is constantly adjusting, differentiating, and tailoring responses to the student.
2. **Fading**: The teacher gradually withdraws support as the student's understanding and skills deepen.
3. **Transferring Responsibility**: Students assume more and more responsibility for their own learning.

In the next sections, we will examine three specific teaching approaches that put the student at the center and provide scaffolding: inquiry and problem-based learning, cognitive apprenticeships, and cooperative learning.

Inquiry and Problem-Based Learning

John Dewey described the basic **inquiry learning** format in 1910. There have been many adaptations of this strategy, but the form usually includes the following elements (Echevarria, 2003; Lashley, Matczynski, & Rowley, 2002). The teacher presents a puzzling event, question, or problem. The students:

- formulate hypotheses to explain the event or solve the problem,
- collect data to test the hypotheses,
- draw conclusions, and
- reflect on the original problem and the thinking processes needed to solve it.

EXAMPLES OF INQUIRY.   Shirley Magnusson and Annemarie Palincsar have developed a teachers' guide for planning, implementing, and assessing different phases of inquiry science units, called *Guided Inquiry Supporting Multiple Literacies or GisML* (Hapgood, Magnusson, & Palincsar, 2004; Palincsar, Magnusson, Collins, & Cutter, 2001; Palincsar, Magnusson, Marano, Ford, & Brown, 1998). The teacher first identifies a curriculum area and some general guiding questions, puzzles, or problems. For example, the teacher chooses *communication* as the area and asks this general question: "How and why do humans and animals communicate?" Next, several specific focus questions are posed. "How do whales communicate?" "How do gorillas communicate?" The focus questions have to be carefully chosen to guide students toward important understandings. One key idea in understanding animal communication is the relationship among the animal's structures, survival functions, and habitat. Animals have specific *structures* such as large ears or echo-locators, which function to find food, attract mates, or identify predators, and these structures and functions are related to the animals' *habitats—large ears for navigating in the dark for example*. Thus, focus questions must ask about animals with different structures for communication, different functional needs for survival, and different habitats. Questions about animals with the same kinds of structures or the same habitats would not be good focus points for inquiry (Magnusson & Palincsar, 1995).

The next phase is to engage students in the inquiry, perhaps by playing different animal sounds, having students make guesses and claims about communication, and asking the students questions about their guesses and claims. Then, the students conduct both first-hand and second-hand investigations. First-hand investigations are direct experiences and experiments, for example, measuring the size of bats' eyes and ears

Connect and Extend to PRAXIS II™

Inquiry Learning (II, A2, 3)
Inquiry learning is a student-centered approach to learning that predates many "traditional" forms of instruction. Describe the basic structure of this approach to learning. What are its strengths and limitations? What roles does the teacher have?

Inquiry learning Approach in which the teacher presents a puzzling situation and students solve the problem by gathering data and testing their conclusions.

in relation to their bodies (using pictures or videos—not real bats!). In second-hand investigations, students consult books, the Internet, interviews with experts, and other resources to find specific information or get new ideas. As part of their investigating, the students begin to identify patterns. The curved line in Figure 10.1 shows that cycles can be repeated. In fact, students might go through several cycles of investigating, identifying patterns, and reporting results before moving on to constructing explanations and making final reports. Another possible cycle is to evaluate explanations before reporting by making and then checking predictions, applying the explanation to new situations.

Inquiry teaching allows students to learn content and process at the same time. In the examples given above, students learned about how animals communicate and how structures are related to habitats. In addition, they learned the inquiry process itself—how to solve problems, evaluate solutions, and think critically.

PROBLEM-BASED LEARNING. Whereas inquiry learning grew out of practices in science, problem-based learning grew out of research on expert knowledge in medicine (Schmidt, van der Molen, te Winkel, &. Wijnen, 2009). The goals of **problem-based learning** are to help students develop knowledge that is useful and flexible, not inert. Inert knowledge is information that is memorized but seldom applied (Cognition and Technology Group at Vanderbilt [CTGV], 1996; Whitehead, 1929). Other goals of problem-based learning are to enhance intrinsic motivation and skills in problem solving, collaboration, evidence-based decision making, and self-directed lifelong learning.

In problem-based learning, students are confronted with a problem that launches their inquiry as they collaborate to find solutions. The students identify and analyze the problem based on the facts from the scenario; and then they begin to generate hypotheses about solutions. As they suggest hypotheses, they identify missing information—what do they need to know to test their solutions? This launches a phase of research. Then,

Connect and Extend to PRAXIS II™

Discovery Learning (I, A1)
Many teachers, especially in mathematics and science, believe that meaningful learning in their areas is best supported by discovery learning. Be prepared to answer questions about the assumptions, techniques, strengths, and limitations of this instructional strategy.

FIGURE 10.1

A MODEL TO GUIDE TEACHER THINKING ABOUT INQUIRY-BASED SCIENCE INSTRUCTION

The straight lines show the sequence of phases in instruction and the curved lines show cycles that might be repeated during instruction.

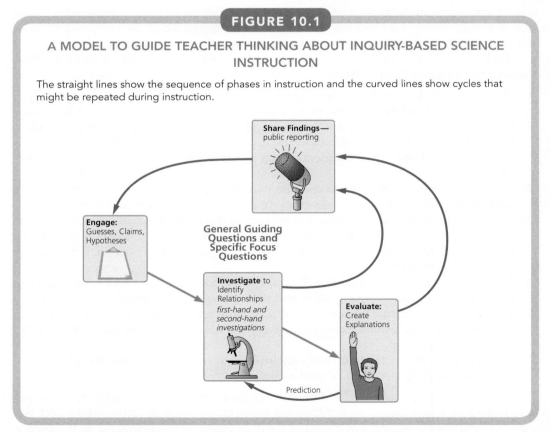

Source: Based on "Designing a Community of Practice: Principles and Practices of the GisML Community," by A. S. Palincsar, S. J. Magnusson, N. Marano, D. Ford, and N. Brown, 1998, Teaching and Teacher Education, 14, p. 12. Adapted with permission from Elsevier.

Problem-based learning Methods that provide students with realistic problems that don't necessarily have "right" answers.

students apply their new knowledge, evaluate their problem solutions, recycle to research again if necessary, and finally reflect on the knowledge and skills they have gained. Throughout the entire process, students are not alone or unguided. Their thinking and problem solving is scaffolded by the teacher, computer software supports, models, coaching, expert hints, guides and organizational aids, or other students in the collaborative groups—so working memory is not overloaded. For example, as students work, they may have to fill in a diagram that helps them distinguish between "claims" and "reasons" in a scientific argument (Derry, Hmelo-Silver, Nagarajan, Chernobilsky, & Beitzel, 2006; Hmelo-Silver, Ravit, & Chinn, 2007).

In true problem-based learning, the problem is real and the students' actions matter. For example, during the 2010 Deepwater oil spill, many teachers used the problem as a springboard for learning. Their students researched how this spill compared to others in size, location, costliness, causes, and attempted solutions. What could be done? How do currents and tides play a role? What locations, businesses, and wildlife are in the greatest danger? What will the short-term and long-term financial and environmental impacts be? What actions can students take to play a positive role? A number of teachers blogged about using the oil spill in problem-based learning and collected resources for other teachers (see http://www.edutopia.org/blog/oil-spill-project-based-learning-resources).

Some problems are not authentic because they do not directly affect the students' lives, but they are engaging. For example, in a computer simulation called the *River of Life Challenge* (Sherwood, 2002), students meet Billy and his lab partner Suzie, who are analyzing the quality of water from a local river. Suzie is concerned that Billy's conclusions are careless and incomplete. Billy is challenged to research the issue in more depth by the *Legacy League*, a multi-ethnic group of characters who raise questions and direct Billy and Suzie to helpful resources so they can research the answers. The format for the challenge in the STAR Legacy Cycle includes six phases: encounter the challenge, generate ideas, consider multiple perspectives, research and revise your ideas, test your mettle (check your understanding), and go public about your conclusions. Undergraduate science education students who used this simulation improved their graph-reading skills as well as their conceptual understanding of several topics such as the composition of air and classes of organisms in a river ecosystem (Kumar & Sherwood, 2007).

Let's look at these phases more closely as they might take place in an upper-level science class (Klein & Harris, 2007).

1. The cycle begins with an *intriguing challenge* to the whole class. For example, in biomechanics it might be "Assume you are a living cell in a bioreactor. What things will influence how long you live?" or "Your grandmother is recovering from a broken hip. In which hand should she hold the cane to help her balance?" The question is framed in a way that makes students bring to bear their current knowledge and preconceptions.
2. Next, students *generate ideas* to compile what they currently know and believe using individual, small-group, or whole-group brainstorming or other activities.
3. *Multiple perspectives* are added to the process in the form of outside experts (live, on video, or from texts), Web sites, magazine or journal articles, or a CD on the subject. In the river challenge above, the Legacy League guided Billy and Suzie to explore multiple perspectives.
4. Students go deeper to *research and revise*. They consult more sources or hear class lectures, all the while revising ideas and perhaps journaling about their thinking.
5. Students *test their mettle* by getting feedback from other students or the teacher about their tentative conclusions. Some formative (ungraded) tests might check their understanding at this point.
6. Students *go public* with their final conclusions and solutions in the form of an oral presentation, poster/project, or final exam.

Project-based science is a multimedia learning environment similar to problem-based learning that focuses on K-12 grades (Krajcik & Czerniak, 2007). MyProject is a web-based science learning environment used in college (Papanikolaou & Boubouka, 2011). The teacher's role in problem-based learning is to identify engaging problems and appropriate resources, orient students to the problem by describing objectives and rationales; organize the students by helping them set goals and define tasks; support, coach, and mentor students as they gather information, craft solutions, and prepare artifacts (models, reports, videos, PowerPoints, portfolios, etc.); and support student reflection on their own learning outcomes and processes (Arends & Kilcher, 2010).

RESEARCH ON INQUIRY AND PROBLEM-BASED LEARNING. Does using inquiry or problem-based learning activities lead to greater achievement? The debate has waged for years. Some research results say "yes." For example, using an open-ended and software-supported inquiry science approach called GenScope™ that explores genetics, students in high school science classrooms learned significantly more compared to students in traditional classrooms (Hickey et al., 1999, 2000). In a study of almost 20,000 middle-school students in a large urban district who used inquiry-based materials, those who participated in inquiry learning had significantly higher passing rates on standardized tests. African American boys especially benefited from these methods (Geier et al., 2008). Several other studies point to increases in student engagement and motivation with inquiry learning (Hmelo-Silver et al., 2007), as long as the learning is supported and students have adequate background knowledge. But not every educational psychologist agrees that problem-based learning is valuable, at least for all students, as you can see in the *Point/Counterpoint* on the next page.

Another constructivist approach that relies heavily on scaffolding is cognitive apprenticeships.

Cognitive Apprenticeships and Reciprocal Teaching

Over the centuries, apprenticeships have proved to be an effective form of education. By working alongside a master and perhaps other apprentices, young people have learned many skills, trades, and crafts. Knowledgeable guides provide models, demonstrations, and corrections, as well as a personal bond that is motivating. The performances required of the learner are real and important and grow more complex as the learner becomes more competent (Collins, 2006; Linn & Eylon, 2006; Hung, 1999). With *guided participation* in real tasks comes *participatory appropriation*—students appropriate the knowledge, skills, and values involved in doing the tasks (Rogoff, 1995, 1998). In addition, both the newcomers to learning and the old-timers contribute to the community of practice by mastering and remastering skills—and sometimes improving these skills in the process (Lave & Wenger, 1991).

Allan Collins (2006) suggests that knowledge and skills learned in school have become too separated from their use in the world beyond school. To correct this imbalance, some educators recommend that schools adopt many of the features of apprenticeships. But rather than learning to sculpt or dance or build a cabinet, apprenticeships in school would focus on cognitive objectives such as reading comprehension, writing, or mathematical problem solving. There are many **cognitive apprenticeship** models, but most share six features:

- Students observe an expert (usually the teacher) *model* the performance.
- Students get external support through *coaching* or tutoring (including hints, tailored feedback, models, and reminders).
- Students receive conceptual *scaffolding*, which is then gradually faded as the student becomes more competent and proficient.
- Students continually *articulate* their knowledge—putting into words their understanding of the processes and content being learned.
- Students *reflect* on their progress, comparing their problem solving to an expert's performance and to their own earlier performances.
- Students are required to *explore* new ways to apply what they are learning—ways that they have not practiced at the master's side.

As students learn, they are challenged to master more complex concepts and skills and to perform them in many different settings.

Cognitive apprenticeship A relationship in which a less experienced learner acquires knowledge and skills under the guidance of an expert.

POINT/COUNTERPOINT: Are Inquiry and Problem-Based Learning Effective Teaching Approaches?

Inquiry, discovery learning, and problem-based learning are very appealing, but are they effective? Specifically, does problem-based learning lead to deep understanding for most students?

POINT

▶ **Problem-Based Learning is overrated.** Paul Kirschner and his colleagues were clear and critical in their article in the *Educational Psychologist*. Even the title of the article was blunt: "Why minimal guidance during instruction does not work: An analysis of the failure of constructivist, discovery, problem-based, experiential, and inquiry-based teaching." They argued:

Although unguided or minimally guided instructional approaches are very popular and intuitively appealing, the point is made that these approaches ignore both the structures that constitute human cognitive architecture and evidence from empirical studies over the past half-century that consistently indicate that minimally guided instruction is less effective and less efficient than instructional approaches that place a strong emphasis on guidance of the student learning process. (Kirschner, Sweller, & Clark, 2006, p. 75)

These respected researchers (and others more recently) cited decades of research demonstrating that unguided discovery/inquiry and problem-based learning are ineffective, especially for students with limited prior knowledge (Kalyuga, 2011; Klahr & Nigam, 2004; Tobias, 2010). Louis Alfieri and his colleagues (2011) examined the results from 108 studies going back over 50 years and found that explicit teaching was more beneficial than unassisted discovery, especially for studies published in the most well-rated journals. Their conclusion: "unassisted discovery generally does not benefit learning" (p. 12).

But what about problem-based learning in particular? Much of the research on problem-based learning has taken place in medical schools, and results have been mixed. In one study, students learning through problem-based instruction were better at clinical skills such as problem formation and reasoning, but they were worse in their basic knowledge of science and felt less prepared in science (Albanese & Mitchell, 1993). A review of problem-based learning curricula in medical schools concluded that this approach was not effective in promoting higher levels of student knowledge (Colliver, 2000).

COUNTERPOINT

▶ **Problem-Based Learning is a powerful teaching approach.** Problem-based learning has some advantages. In another study, medical students who learned with problem-based approaches created more accurate and coherent solutions to medical problems (Hmelo, 1998). In an extensive study of a problem-based medical program in the Netherlands, Schmidt and his colleagues (2009) concluded that, compared to graduates of conventional programs, graduates of the problem-based learning program performed better in practical medical and interpersonal skills, took less time to graduate, and had small positive differences in their medical knowledge and diagnostic reasoning. MBA students who learned a concept using problem-based methods were better at explaining the concept than students who had learned the concept from lecture and discussion (Capon & Kuhn, 2004). Students who are better at self-regulation may

---

How can teaching provide cognitive apprenticeships? Mentoring in teaching is one example. Another is cross-age grouping. In the Key School, an inner-city public elementary school in Indianapolis, Indiana, students of different ages work side by side for part of every day on a "pod" designed to have many of the qualities of an apprenticeship. The pods might focus on a craft or a discipline. Examples include gardening, architecture, and "making money." Many levels of expertise are evident in the students of different ages, so students can move at a comfortable pace, but still have the model of a master available. Community volunteers, including many parents, visit to demonstrate a skill that is related to the pod topic.

Alan Schoenfeld's (1989, 1994) teaching of mathematical problem solving is another example of the cognitive apprenticeship instructional model.

COGNITIVE APPRENTICESHIPS IN READING: RECIPROCAL TEACHING. The goal of **reciprocal teaching** is to help students understand and think deeply about what they read (Palincsar, 1986; Palincsar & Brown, 1984, 1989). To accomplish this goal, students in small reading groups learn four strategies: *summarizing* the content of a passage, *asking a question* about the central point, *clarifying* the difficult parts of the material, and *predicting* what will come next. These are strategies skilled readers apply almost automatically, but poor readers seldom do—or they don't know how. To use the strategies effectively, poorer readers need direct instruction, modeling, and practice in actual reading situations.

First, the teacher introduces these strategies, perhaps focusing on one strategy each day. As the expert, the teacher explains and models each strategy and encourages

Reciprocal teaching Designed to help students understand and think deeply about what they read.

benefit more from problem-based methods (Evensen, Salisbury-Glennon, & Glenn, 2001), but using problem-based methods over time can help all students to develop self-directed learning skills.

Cindy Hmelo-Silver (2004; Hmelo-Sliver et al., 2007) reviewed the research and found good evidence that problem-based learning supports the construction of flexible knowledge and the development of problem-solving and self-directed learning skills, but there is less evidence that participating in problem-based learning is intrinsically motivating or that it teaches students to collaborate. In studies of high school economics and mathematics, recent research favors problem-based approaches for learning more complex concepts and solving multistep word problems.

Beware of Either/Or. You don't have to choose between inquiry and content-focused methods. The best approach in elementary and secondary schools may be a balance of content-focused and inquiry or problem-based methods. For example, Eva Toth, David Klahr, and Zhe Chen (2000) tested a balanced approach for teaching 4th graders how to use the controlled variable strategy in science to design good experiments. The method had three phases: (1) in small groups, students conducted exploratory experiments to identify variables that made a ball roll farther down a ramp; (2) the teacher led a discussion, explained the controlled variable strategy, and modeled good thinking about experiment design; and (3) the students designed and conducted application experiments to isolate which variables caused the ball to roll farther. The combination of inquiry, discussion, explanation, and modeling was successful in helping the students understand the concepts. Clearly scaffolding supports are key factors in successful inquiry and problem-based learning.

The difference seems to come down to completely unguided discovery versus guided, supported, and well-scaffolded inquiry. Alfieri and his colleagues (2011) concluded:

> Overall, the effects of unassisted-discovery tasks seem limited, whereas enhanced-discovery tasks requiring learners to be actively engaged and constructive seem optimal. On the basis of the current analyses, optimal approaches should include at least one of the following: (a) guided tasks that have scaffolding in place to assist learners, (b) tasks requiring learners to explain their own ideas and ensuring that these ideas are accurate by providing timely feedback, or (c) tasks that provide worked examples of how to succeed in the task. (p. 13)

student apprentices to practice. Next, the teacher and the students read a short passage silently. Then, the teacher again provides a model by summarizing, questioning, clarifying, or predicting based on the reading. Everyone reads another passage, and the students gradually begin to assume the teacher's role. The teacher becomes a member of the group, and may finally leave, as the students take over the teaching. Often, the students' first attempts are halting and incorrect. But the teacher gives clues, guidance, encouragement, support doing parts of the task (such as providing question stems), modeling, and other forms of scaffolding to help the students master these strategies. The goal is for students to learn to apply these strategies independently as they read so they can make sense of text.

APPLYING RECIPROCAL TEACHING. Although reciprocal teaching seems to work with almost any age student, most of the research has been done with younger adolescents who can read aloud fairly accurately, but who are far below average in reading comprehension. After 20 hours of practice with this approach, many students who were in the bottom quarter of their class moved up to the average level or above on tests of reading comprehension. Palincsar has identified three guidelines for effective reciprocal teaching ("When Student Becomes Teacher," 1986):

1. *Shift gradually*. The shift from teacher to student responsibility must be gradual.
2. *Match demands to abilities*. The difficulty of the task and the responsibility must match the abilities of each student and grow as these abilities develop.

NURTURING INDEPENDENT READERS The concept of scaffolding and gradually moving the student toward independent and fluid reading comprehension is a critical component in reciprocal teaching and cognitive apprenticeships.

3. *Diagnose thinking.* Teachers should carefully observe the "teaching" of each student for clues about how the student is thinking and what kind of instruction he or she needs.

In contrast to some approaches that try to teach 40 or more strategies, an advantage of reciprocal teaching is that it focuses attention on four powerful strategies. But these strategies must be taught—not all students develop them on their own. One study of reciprocal teaching spanning over three years found that questioning was the strategy used most often, but that students had to be taught how to ask higher-level questions because most student questions were literal or superficial (Hacker & Tenent, 2002). Another advantage of reciprocal teaching is that it emphasizes practicing these four strategies in the context of actual reading—reading literature and reading texts. Finally, the idea of scaffolding and gradually moving the student toward independent and fluid reading comprehension is a critical component in reciprocal teaching and cognitive apprenticeships in general (Rosenshine & Meister, 1994).

Collaboration and Cooperation

Even with all the concern today about academic standards, performance on proficiency tests, and international comparisons of student achievement, schooling has always been about more than academic learning. Of course, academics are the prime directive, but an education also prepares students to live and work cooperatively with all kinds of people:

> Most corporations are looking for employees who are not only good at the mastery of a particular set of academic skills but who also have the ability to work harmoniously with a wide variety of coworkers as a cooperative team, to demonstrate initiative and responsibility, and to communicate effectively. (Aronson, 2000, p. 91)

For the past four decades, researchers have examined collaboration and cooperation in schools. Although there are some inconsistencies, the majority of the studies indicate that truly cooperative groups have positive effects—from preschool to college—on students' empathy, tolerance for differences, feelings of acceptance, friendships, self-confidence, awareness of the perspectives of others, higher-level reasoning, problem solving, and even school attendance (Galton, Hargreaves, & Pell, 2009; Gillies & Boyle, 2011; Solomon, Watson, & Battistich, 2001). It is even argued that cooperative learning experiences are crucial in preventing many of the social problems that plague children and adolescents (Gillies, 2003, 2004).

COLLABORATION, GROUP WORK, AND COOPERATIVE LEARNING.

The terms *collaboration, group work,* and *cooperative learning* often are used as if they mean the same thing. Certainly there is some overlap, but there are differences as well. The distinctions between collaboration and cooperation are not always clear. Ted Panitz (1996) suggests **collaboration** is a philosophy about how to relate to others—how to learn and work. Collaboration is a way of dealing with people that respects differences, shares authority, and builds on the knowledge that is distributed among other people. **Cooperation,** on the other hand, is a way of working with others to attain a shared goal (Gillies, 2003). Collaborative learning has roots in the work of British teachers who wanted their students to respond to literature in more active ways as they learned. Cooperative learning has American roots in the work of psychologists John Dewey and Kurt Lewin. You could say that *cooperative* learning is one way to *collaborate* in schools.

Group work, on the other hand, is simply several students working together—they may or may not be cooperating. Many activities can be completed in groups. For example,

Connect and Extend to PRAXIS II™

Characteristics of Cooperative Learning (II, A2)
Many instructional strategies labeled as *cooperative learning* lack one or more qualities that are essential components of such techniques. List those essential qualities and explain the role of each.

Collaboration A philosophy about how to relate to others—how to learn and work.

Cooperation Way of working with others to attain a shared goal.

students can work together to conduct a local survey. How do people feel about the plan to build a new mall that will bring more shopping and more traffic? Would the community support or oppose the building of a nuclear power plant? If students must learn 10 new definitions in a biology class, why not let them divide up the terms and definitions and teach one another? Be sure, however, that everyone in the group can handle the task. Sometimes, one or two students end up doing the work of the entire group.

Group work can be useful, but true cooperative learning requires much more than simply putting students in groups and dividing up the work. Angela O'Donnell and Jim O'Kelly, colleagues of mine from Rutgers University, describe a teacher who claimed to be using "cooperative learning" by asking students to work in pairs on a paper, each writing one part. Unfortunately, the teacher allowed no time to work together and provided no guidance or preparation in cooperative social skills. Students got a grade for their individual part and a group grade for the whole project. One student received an A for his part, but a C for the group project because his partner earned an F—he never turned in any work. So one student was punished with a C for a situation he could not control while the other was rewarded with a C for doing no work at all. This was not cooperative learning—it wasn't even group work (O'Donnell & O'Kelly, 1994).

COOPERATION: A WORTHY GOAL While academics are the key goal, education also prepares students to live and work cooperatively with all kinds of people. Studies of cooperative learning indicate its positive influence on students' empathy, tolerance, friendships, self-confidence, and even school attendance.

BEYOND GROUPS TO COOPERATION. David and Roger Johnson (2009a), two of the founders of cooperative learning in the United States, define formal **cooperative learning** as "students working together, for one class period to several weeks, to achieve shared learning goals and complete jointly specific tasks and assignments" (p. 373). Cooperative learning has a long history in American education, moving in and out of favor over the years. Today, evolving constructivist perspectives have fueled a growing commitment to learning situations that rely on elaboration, interpretation, explanation, and argumentation— that is, cooperative learning (Webb & Palincsar, 1996, p. 844). David and Roger Johnson (2009a) note:

> From being discounted and ignored, cooperative learning has steadily progressed to being one of the dominant instructional practices throughout the world. Cooperative learning is now utilized in schools and universities throughout most of the world in every subject area and from preschool through graduate school and adult training programs. (p. 365)

Different learning theory approaches favor cooperative learning for different reasons (O'Donnell, 2002, 2006). Information processing theorists point to the value of group discussion in helping participants rehearse, elaborate, and expand their knowledge. As group members question and explain, they have to organize their knowledge, make connections, and review—all processes that support information processing and memory. Advocates of a Piagetian perspective suggest the interactions in groups can create the cognitive conflict and disequilibrium that lead an individual to question his or her understanding and try out new ideas—or, as Piaget (1985) said, "to go beyond his current state and strike out in new directions" (p. 10). Those who favor Vygotsky's theory suggest that social interaction is important for learning because higher mental functions such as reasoning, comprehension, and critical thinking originate in social interactions and are then appropriated and internalized by individuals. Students can accomplish mental tasks with social support before they can do them alone. Thus, cooperative learning provides the social support and scaffolding students need to move learning forward. To benefit from these dimensions of cooperative learning, groups must be cooperative—all members must participate. But, as any teacher or parent knows, cooperation is not automatic when students are put into groups.

Cooperative learning Situations in which elaboration, interpretation, explanation, and argumentation are integral to the activity of the group and where learning is supported by other individuals.

WHAT CAN GO WRONG: MISUSES OF GROUP LEARNING. Without careful planning and monitoring by the teacher, group interactions can hinder learning and reduce rather than improve social relations in classes (Gillies & Boyle, 2011). For example, if there is pressure in a group for conformity—perhaps because rewards are being misused or one student dominates the others—interactions can be unproductive and unreflective. Misconceptions might be reinforced, or the worst, not the best, ideas may be combined to construct a superficial or even incorrect understanding (Battistich, Solomon, & Delucci, 1993). Students who work in groups but arrive at wrong answers may be more confident that they are right—a case of "two heads are worse than one" (Puncochar & Fox, 2004). Also, the ideas of low-status students may be ignored or even ridiculed while the contributions of high-status students are accepted and reinforced, regardless of the merit of either set of ideas (Anderson, Holland, & Palincsar, 1997; Cohen, 1986). Mary McCaslin and Tom Good (1996) list several other disadvantages of group learning:

- Students often value the process or procedures over the learning. Speed and finishing early take precedence over thoughtfulness and learning.
- Rather than challenging and correcting misconceptions, students support and reinforce misunderstandings.
- Socializing and interpersonal relationships may take precedence over learning.
- Students may simply shift dependency from the teacher to the "expert" in the group—learning is still passive and what is learned can be wrong.
- Status differences may be increased rather than decreased. Some students learn to "loaf" because the group progresses with or without their contributions. Others become even more convinced that they are unable to understand without the support of the group.

The next sections examine how teachers can avoid these problems and encourage true cooperation.

Tasks for Cooperative Learning

Like so many other decisions in teaching, plans for using cooperative groups begin with a goal. What are students supposed to accomplish? Successful teachers interviewed in one study emphasized that group activities must be well planned, students need to be prepared to work in groups, and teachers' expectations for the task have to be explicitly stated (Gillies & Boyle, 2011). What is the task? Is it a true group task—one that builds on the knowledge and skills of several students—or is the task more appropriate for individuals (Cohen, 1994; O'Donnell, 2006)?

Tasks for cooperative groups may be more or less structured. Highly structured tasks include work that has specific answers—drill and practice, applying routines or procedures, answering questions from readings, computations in mathematics, and so on. Ill-structured complex tasks have multiple answers and unclear procedures, requiring problem finding and higher-order thinking. These ill-structured problems are true group tasks; that is, they are likely to require the resources (knowledge, skills, problem-solving strategies, creativity) of all the group members to accomplish, whereas individuals often can accomplish highly structured tasks just as effectively as groups. These distinctions are important because ill-structured, complex, true group tasks appear to require more and higher-quality interactions than routine tasks if learning and problem solving are to occur (Cohen, 1994; Gillies, 2004; Gillies & Boyle, 2011).

HIGHLY STRUCTURED, REVIEW, AND SKILL-BUILDING TASKS. A relatively structured task such as reviewing previously learned material for an exam might be well served by a structured technique such as STAD (Student Teams Achievement Divisions), in which teams of four students compete to determine which team's members can amass the greatest improvement over previous achievement levels (Slavin, 1995). Praise, recognition, or extrinsic rewards can enhance motivation, effort, and persistence under these conditions, and thus increase learning. Focusing the dialogue by assigning narrow roles also may help students stay engaged when the tasks involve practice or review.

ILL-STRUCTURED, CONCEPTUAL, AND PROBLEM-SOLVING TASKS. If the task is ill structured and more cognitive in nature, then an open exchange and elaborated discussion will be more helpful (Cohen, 1994; Ross & Raphael, 1990). Thus, strategies that encourage extended and productive interactions are appropriate when the goal is to develop higher-order thinking and problem solving. In these situations, a tightly structured process, competition among groups for rewards, and rigid assignment of roles are likely to inhibit the richness of the students' interactions and to interfere with progress toward the goal. Open-ended techniques such as reciprocal questioning (King, 1994), reciprocal teaching (Palincsar & Brown, 1984; Rosenshine & Meister, 1994), pair-share (Kagan, 1994), or Jigsaw (Aronson, 2000) should be more productive because, when used appropriately, they encourage more extensive interaction and elaborative thought in situations where students are being exposed to complex materials. In these instances, the use of rewards may well divert the group away from the goal of in-depth cognitive processing. When rewards are offered, the goal often becomes achieving the reward as efficiently as possible, which could mean having the highest achieving students do all the work (Webb & Palincsar, 1996).

SOCIAL SKILLS AND COMMUNICATION TASKS. When the goal of peer learning is enhanced social skills or increased intergroup understanding and appreciation of diversity, the assignment of specific roles and functions within the group might support communication (Cohen, 1994; Kagan, 1994). In these situations, it can be helpful to rotate leadership roles so that minority group students and females have the opportunity to demonstrate and develop leadership skills; in addition, all group members can experience the leadership capabilities of each individual (Miller & Harrington, 1993). Rewards probably are not necessary, and they may actually get in the way because the goal is to build community, a sense of respect, and responsibility for all team members.

Preparing Students for Cooperative Learning

David and Roger Johnson (2009a) explain five elements that define true cooperative learning groups:

- Positive interdependence
- Promotive interaction
- Individual accountability
- Collaborative and social skills
- Group processing

Group members experience *positive interdependence*. The members believe they can attain their goals only if the others in the group attain their goals as well, so they need each other for support, explanations, and guidance. *Promotive interaction* means that group members encourage and facilitate each other's efforts. They usually interact face to face and close together, not across the room, but they also could interact via digital media around the world. Even though they feel a responsibility to the group to work together and help each other, students must ultimately demonstrate learning on their own; they are held *individually accountable* for learning, often through individual tests or other assessments. *Collaborative and social skills* are necessary for effective group functioning. Often, these skills, such as giving constructive feedback, reaching consensus, and involving every member, must be taught and practiced before the groups tackle a learning task. Finally, members monitor *group processes* and relationships to make sure the group is working effectively and to learn about the dynamics of groups. They take time to ask, "How are we doing as a group? Is everyone working together? What should we do more or less of next time?"

Research in grades 8 through 12 in Australia found that students in cooperative groups that were structured to require positive interdependence and mutual helping learned more in math, science, and English than students in unstructured learning groups (Gillies, 2003). In addition, compared to students in the unstructured groups, students in the structured groups also said learning was more fun.

SETTING UP COOPERATIVE GROUPS.   How large should a cooperative group be? Again, the answer depends on your learning goals. If the purpose is for the group members to review, rehearse information, or practice, 4 to 5 or 6 students is about the right size. But if the goal is to encourage each student to participate in discussions, problem solving, or computer learning, then groups of 2 to 4 members work best. Also, when setting up cooperative groups, it often makes sense to balance the number of boys and girls. Some research indicates that when there are just a few girls in a group, they tend to be left out of the discussions unless they are the most able or assertive members. By contrast, when there are only one or two boys in the group, they tend to dominate and be "interviewed" by the girls unless these boys are less able than the girls or are very shy. In some studies, but not all, of mixed-gender groups, girls avoided conflict and boys dominated discussion (O'Donnell & O'Kelly, 1994; Webb & Palincsar, 1996). Whatever the case, teachers must monitor groups to make sure everyone is contributing and learning.

If a group includes some students who are perceived as different or who are often rejected, then it makes sense to be sure that there are group members who are tolerant and kind. One successful teacher interviewed by Gillies and Boyle (2011) put it this way:

> I also try to make sure that there are one or two people in the group who have the ability to be tolerant. At least the kid in question will know that, while the other group members may not be his best friends, they won't give him a hard time. I try to put the least reactive kids in the group with the child in question. This year I've had a couple of girls who have been very good with difficult kids. They don't put up with nonsense but they don't over-react and are prepared to demonstrate some good social skills. (p. 72)

GIVING AND RECEIVING EXPLANATIONS.   In practice, the effects of learning in a group vary, depending on what actually happens in the group and who is in it. If only a few people take responsibility for the work, these people will learn, but the nonparticipating members probably will not. Students who ask questions, get answers, and attempt explanations are more likely to learn than students whose questions go unasked or unanswered. In fact, there is evidence that the more a student provides elaborated, thoughtful explanations to other students in a group, the more the *explainer* learns. Giving good explanations appears to be even more important for learning than receiving explanations (O'Donnell, 2006; Webb, Farivar, & Mastergeorge, 2002). In order to explain, you have to organize the information, put it into your own words, think of examples and analogies (which connect the information to things you already know), and test your understanding by answering questions. These are excellent learning strategies (King, 1990, 2002; O'Donnell & O'Kelly, 1994).

Good explanations are relevant, timely, correct, and elaborated enough to help the listener correct misunderstandings; the best explanations tell why (Webb et al., 2002; Webb & Mastergeorge, 2003). For example, in a middle-school mathematics class, students worked in groups on the following problem:

> Find the cost of a 30-minute telephone call to the prefix 717 where the first minute costs $0.22 and each additional minute costs $0.13.

The level of explanation and help students received was significantly related to learning; the higher the level of explanation, the more learning took place. Table 10.3 shows the different levels of help. Of course, the students must pay attention to and use the help in order to learn. And the help-receiver also has responsibilities if learning is to go well. For example, if a helper says, "13 times 29," then the receiver should say, "Why is it 29?" Asking good questions and giving clear explanations are critical, and usually these skills must be taught.

ASSIGNING ROLES.   Some teachers assign roles to students to encourage cooperation and full participation. Several roles are described in Table 10.4. If you use roles, be sure that they support learning. In groups that focus on social skills, roles should support listening, encouragement, and respect for differences. In groups that focus on practice, review, or mastery of basic skills, roles should support persistence, encouragement, and

TABLE 10.3 • **Levels of Help in Cooperative Groups**

Students are more likely to learn if they give and get higher-level help.

LEVEL	DESCRIPTION AND EXAMPLE
Highest	
6	Verbally labeled explanation of how to solve part or all of the problem ("Multiply 13 cents by 29, because 29 minutes are left after the first minute.")
5	Numerical rule with no verbal labels for the numbers ("This is 30, so you minus 1.")
4	Numerical expression or equation ("13 times 29.")
3	Numbers to write or copy ("Put 13 on top, 29 on the bottom. Then you times it.")
2	Answer to part or all of the problem ("I got $3.77.")
1	Non-content or non-informational response ("Just do it the way she said.")
0	No response
Lowest	

Source: Adapted from Webb, N M., Troper, J. D., & Fall, R. (1995). Constructive activity and learning in collaborative small groups. Journal of Educational Psychology, 87, p. 411.

participation. In groups that focus on higher-order problem solving or complex learning, roles should encourage thoughtful discussion, sharing of explanations and insights, probing, brainstorming, and creativity. Make sure that you don't communicate to students that the major purpose of the groups is simply to do the procedures—the roles. Roles are supports for learning, not ends in themselves (Woolfolk Hoy & Tschannen-Moran, 1999).

Often, cooperative learning strategies include group reports to the entire class. If you have been on the receiving end of these class reports, you know that they can be

TABLE 10.4 • **Possible Student Roles in Cooperative Learning Groups**

Depending on the purpose of the group and the age of the participants, having these assigned roles might help students cooperate and learn. Of course, students may have to be taught how to enact each role effectively, and roles should be rotated so students can participate in different aspects of group learning.

ROLE	DESCRIPTION
Encourager	Encourages reluctant or shy students to participate
Praiser/Cheerleader	Shows appreciation of others' contributions and recognizes accomplishments
Gate Keeper	Equalizes participation and makes sure no one dominates
Coach	Helps with the academic content, explains concepts
Question Commander	Makes sure all students' questions are asked and answered
Checker	Checks the group's understanding
Taskmaster	Keeps the group on task
Recorder	Writes down ideas, decisions, and plans
Reflector	Keeps group aware of progress (or lack of progress)
Quiet Captain	Monitors noise level
Materials Monitor	Picks up and returns materials

Source: Based on Cooperative Learning by S. Kagan. Published by Kagan Publishing, San Clemente, CA. Copyright © 1994 by Kagan Publishing.

deadly dull. To make the process more useful for the audience as well as the reporters, Annemarie Palincsar and Leslie Herrenkohl (2002) taught the class members to use *intellectual roles* as they listened to reports. These roles were based on the scientific strategies of predicting and theorizing, summarizing results, and relating predictions and theories to results. Some audience members were assigned the role of checking the reports for clear relationships between predictions and theories. Other students in the audience listened for clarity in the findings. And the rest of the students were responsible for evaluating how well the group reports linked prediction, theories, and findings. Research shows that using these roles promotes class dialogue, thinking and problem solving, and conceptual understanding (Palincsar & Herrenkohl, 2002). Table 10.5 summarizes the considerations in designing cooperative learning, based on the goals of the group.

TABLE 10.5 • **What Should You Consider in Planning and Doing Cooperative Learning?**

CONSIDERATIONS	SOCIAL SKILLS TASKS: TEAM BUILDING, COOPERATION SKILLS	STRUCTURED TASKS: REVIEW, PRACTICE FACTS, AND SKILLS	UNSTRUCTURED TASKS: CONCEPTUAL, PROBLEM SOLVING, THINKING AND REASONING
Group Size and Composition	2–5 students, common interest groups, mixed groups, random groups	2–4 students, mixed ability, high with medium and medium with low	2–4 students, select members to encourage interaction
Why Assign Roles?	to monitor participation and conflict, rotate leadership	to monitor engagement and ensure low-status students have resources to offer, i.e., Jigsaw	roles may interfere—use only to encourage interaction, divergent thinking, and extended, connected discourse, i.e., debate sides, group facilitator
Extrinsic Rewards/ Incentives	not necessary, may be helpful	to support motivation, effort, persistence	not necessary
Teacher's Role	model, encourager	model, director, coach	model facilitator
Student Skills Needed	listening, turn-taking, encouraging, managing conflict	questioning, explaining, encouraging, content knowledge, learning strategies	questioning, explaining, elaborating, probing, divergent thinking, providing rationales, synthesizing
What Supports Learning? Watch and Listen for...	modeling and practice	giving multiple, elaborated explanations, attention and practice	quantity and quality of interactions, using and connecting knowledge resources, probing, and elaboration
Potential Problems	unproductive conflict, nonparticipation	poor help-giving skills, disengaged or excluded students	disengaged or excluded students, cognitive loafing, superficial thinking, avoiding controversy
Averting Problems	simpler task, direct teaching of social skills, team building, conflict resolution skills, discuss group process	structure interdependence and individual accountability, teach helping and explaining	structure controversy, assign "thinking roles," allow adequate time
Small Start	one or two skills, i.e., listening and paraphrasing	pairs of students quizzing each other	numbered heads together

Source: From "Implications of cognitive approaches to peer learning for teacher education," by A. Woolfolk Hoy & M. Tschannen-Moran in *Cognitive perspectives on peer learning*, A. O'Donnell and A. King (Eds.), 1999, p. 278. Adapted with permission of Taylor and Francis Group, LLC, a division of Imforma plc.

TABLE 10.6 • **Question Stems to Encourage Dialogue in Reciprocal Questioning**

After participating in a lesson or studying an assignment on their own, students use these stems to develop questions, create and compare answers, and collaborate to create the best response.

> What is an everyday application of ...?
> How would you define .... in your own words.?
> What are the advantages and disadvantages of ...?
> What do you already know about ...?
> Explain why .... applies to ....?
> How does ..... influence ......?
> What is the value of ...?
> What are the reasons for ....?
> What are some arguments for and against .....?
> What is the your first choice about ...? Your second choice? ....? Why?
> What is the best ... and why?
> Compare ... and ... based only on ....
> How would .... be different if ....?
> Do you agree or disagree with this claim ...? What is your evidence?

Designs for Cooperation

Developing deep understandings in cooperative groups requires that all the group members *participate* in *high-quality discussions*. Discussions that support learning include talk that interprets, connects, explains, and uses evidence to support arguments. We now turn to different strategies that build in structures to support both participation and high-quality discussions.

RECIPROCAL QUESTIONING.   **Reciprocal questioning** requires no special materials or testing procedures and can be used with a wide range of ages. After a lesson or presentation by the teacher, students work in pairs or triads to ask and answer questions about the material (King, 1990, 1994, 2002). The teacher provides question stems (see Table 10.6), and then students are taught how to develop specific questions on the lesson material using the generic question stems. The students create questions, and then take turns asking and answering. This process has proved more effective than traditional discussion groups because it seems to encourage deeper thinking about the material. Questions such as those in Table 10.6, which encourage students to make connections between the lesson and previous knowledge or experience, seem to be the most helpful.

For example, using question stems like those in Table 10.6, a small group in Mr. Garcia's 9th grade world cultures class had the following discussion about the concept of culture:

Sally: In your own words, what does culture mean?

Jim: Well, Mr. Garcia said in the lesson that a culture is the knowledge and understandings shared by the members of a society. I guess it's all the things and beliefs and activities that people in a society have in common. It includes things like religion, laws, music, medical practices, stuff like that.

Sally: And dance, art, family roles.

Barry: Knowledge includes language. So, I guess cultures include language, too.

Jim: I guess so. Actually, I have a question about that: How does a culture influence the language of a society?

Barry: Well, for one thing, the language is made up of words that are important to the people of that culture. Like, the words name things that the people care about, or need, or use. And so, different cultures would have different vocabularies. Some cultures may not even have a word for *telephone,* because they don't have any. But, phones are important in our culture, so we have lots of different words for phones, like *cell phone, digital phone, desk phone, cordless phone, phone machine,* and . . .

Reciprocal questioning Students work in pairs or triads to ask and answer questions about lesson material.

Jim (laughing): I'll bet desert cultures don't have any words for *snow* or *skiing*.

Sally (turning to Barry): What's your question?

Barry: I've got a great question! You'll never be able to answer it. What would happen if there were a group somewhere without any spoken language? Maybe they were all born not being able to speak, or something like that. How would that affect their culture, or could there even be a culture?

Sally: Well, it would mean they couldn't communicate with each other.

Jim: And they wouldn't have any music! Because they wouldn't be able to sing.

Barry: But wait! Why couldn't they communicate? Maybe they would develop a nonverbal language system, you know, the way people use hand signals, or the way deaf people use sign language. (King, 2002, pp. 34–35)

JIGSAW. Elliot Aronson and his graduate students invented the **Jigsaw Classroom** when Aronson was a professor of social psychology (and I was a student) at the University of Texas at Austin. Some of my friends worked on his research team. Aronson developed the approach "as a matter of absolute necessity to help defuse a highly explosive situation" (Aronson, 2000, p. 137). The Austin schools had just been desegregated by court order. White, African American, and Hispanic students were together in classrooms for the first time. Hostility and turmoil ensued, with fistfights in corridors and classrooms. Aronson's answer was the Jigsaw Classroom.

In Jigsaw, each group member is given part of the material to be learned by the whole group. Students become "expert" on their piece. Because students have to learn and be tested on every piece of the larger "puzzle," everyone's contribution is important—the students truly are interdependent. A more recent version, Jigsaw II, adds expert groups in which the students who are responsible for the same material from each learning group confer to make sure they understand their assigned part and then plan ways to teach the information to their learning group members. Next, students return to their learning groups, bringing their expertise to the sessions. In the end, students take an individual test covering all the material and earn points for their learning team score. Teams can work for rewards or simply for recognition (Aronson, 2000; Slavin, 1995).

STRUCTURED CONTROVERSIES. Constructive conflict resolution is essential in classrooms because conflicts are inevitable and even necessary for learning. Piaget's theory tells us that developing knowledge requires cognitive conflict. David and Roger Johnson (2009b) make a powerful case for constructive intellectual conflict:

> Conflict is to student learning what the internal combustion engine is to the automobile. The internal combustion engine ignites the fuel and the air with a spark to create the energy for movement and acceleration. Just as the fuel and the air are inert without the spark, so, ideas in the classroom are inert without the spark of intellectual conflict. (p. 37)

One study of 10th graders found that students who were wrong, but for different reasons, were sometimes able to correct their misunderstandings if they argued together about their conflicting wrong answers (Schwarz, Neuman, & Biezuner, 2000). Individuals trying to exist in groups will have interpersonal conflicts, too, which also can lead to learning. In fact, research over the last 40 years demonstrates that constructive controversy in classrooms can lead to greater learning, open-mindedness, seeing the perspectives of others, creativity, motivation, engagement, and self-esteem (Johnson & Johnson, 2009b). Table 10.7 shows how academic and interpersonal conflicts can be positive forces in a learning community.

As you can see in Table 10.7, the structured part of **structured controversies** is that students work in pairs within their four-person cooperative groups to research a particular controversy, such as whether lumber companies should be allowed to cut down trees in national forests. Each pair of students researches the issue, develops a pro or con position, presents their position and evidence to the other pair, discusses the issue, and then reverses positions and argues for the other perspective. Then, the group develops a final report that summarizes the best arguments for each position and reaches a consensus (Johnson & Johnson, 2009b; O'Donnell, 2006).

Connect and Extend to PRAXIS II™

Forms of Cooperative Learning (II, A2)
STAD and Jigsaw are just two of many cooperative learning techniques, each designed for certain instructional purposes. Go to *Cooperative Learning* (http://www.utc.edu/Teaching-Resource-Center/CoopLear.html), sponsored by the University of Tennessee at Chattanooga, to learn about techniques and uses for cooperative learning.

Jigsaw Classroom A learning process in which each student is part of a group and each group member is given part of the material to be learned by the whole group. Students become "expert" on their piece and then teach it to the others in their group.

Structured controversy Students work in pairs within their four-person cooperative groups to research a particular controversy.

TABLE 10.7 • **Structured Controversies: Learning from Academic and Interpersonal Conflicts**

Conflict, if handled well, can support learning. Academic conflicts can lead to critical thinking and conceptual change. Conflicts of interest are unavoidable, but can be handled so no one is the loser.

ACADEMIC CONTROVERSY	CONFLICTS OF INTEREST
One person's ideas, information, theories, conclusions, and opinions are incompatible with those of another, and the two seek to reach an agreement.	The actions of one person attempting to maximize benefits prevents, blocks or interferes with another person maximizing her or his benefits.
Controversy Procedure	*Integrative (Problem-Solving) Negotiations*
Research and prepare positions	Describe wants
Present and advocate positions	Describe feelings
Refute opposing position and refute attacks on own position	Describe reasons for wants and feelings
Reverse perspectives	Take other's perspective
Synthesize and integrate best evidence and reasoning from all sides	Invent three optional agreements that maximize joint outcomes Choose one and formalize agreement

Source: From "The Three Cs of School and Classroom Management," by D. Johnson and R. Johnson. In H. J. Freiberg (Ed.), Beyond Behaviorism: Changing the Classroom Management Paradigm. *Boston: Allyn and Bacon. Copyright © 1999 by Allyn & Bacon. Adapted with permission.*

In addition to these approaches, Spencer Kagan (1994) has developed many cooperative learning structures designed to accomplish different kinds of academic and social tasks. The *Guidelines* on the next page give you ideas for incorporating cooperative learning in to your classes.

Reaching Every Student: Using Cooperative Learning Wisely

Cooperative learning always benefits from careful planning, but sometimes including students with special needs requires extra attention to planning and preparation. For example, cooperative structures such as scripted questioning and peer tutoring depend on a balanced interaction between the person taking the role of questioner or explainer and the student who is answering or being taught. In these interactions, you want to see and hear explaining and teaching, not just telling or giving right answers. But many students with learning disabilities have difficulties understanding new concepts, so both the explainer and the student can get frustrated, and social rejection for the student with learning disabilities might follow. Because students with learning disabilities often have problems with social relations, it is not a good idea to put them in situations where more rejection is likely. So, when you are teaching new or difficult-to-grasp concepts, cooperative learning might not be the best choice for students with learning disabilities (Kirk et al., 2006). In fact, research has found that cooperative learning in general is not always effective for students with learning disabilities (Smith, 2006).

Gifted students also may not benefit from cooperative learning when groups are mixed in ability. The pace often is too slow, the tasks too simple, and there is just too much repetition. In addition, gifted students often fall into the role of teacher or end up just doing the work quickly for the whole group. If you use mixed-ability groups and include gifted students, the challenges are to use complex tasks that allow work at different levels and keep gifted students engaged without losing the rest of the class (Smith, 2006).

Cooperative learning may be an excellent choice for English language learners (ELLs), however. The Jigsaw cooperative structure is especially helpful because all students in the group, including the ELL students, have information that the group needs, so they also must talk, explain, and interact. In fact, the Jigsaw approach was developed in response to the need to create high interdependence in diverse groups. In many classrooms today, there are 4, 5, 6, or more languages represented. Teachers can't be expected to master every heritage language spoken by all of their students every year. In these classrooms, cooperative groups can help as students work together on academic tasks. Students who speak two languages can help translate and explain lessons to others in

GUIDELINES

Using Cooperative Learning

Fit group size and composition to your learning goals.
Examples

1. For social skills and team-building goals, use groups of 2–5, common interest groups, mixed groups, or random groups.
2. For structured fact and skill-based practice and review tasks, use groups of 2–4, mixed ability such as high-middle and middle-low or high-low and middle-middle group compositions.
3. For higher-level conceptual and thinking tasks, use groups of 2–4; select members to encourage interaction.

Assign appropriate roles.
Examples

1. For social skills and team-building goals, assign roles to monitor participation and conflict; rotate leadership of the group.
2. For structured fact and skill-based practice and review tasks, assign roles to monitor engagement and insure low-status students have resources to offer, as in Jigsaw.
3. For higher-level conceptual and thinking tasks, assign roles only to encourage interaction, divergent thinking, and extended, connected discourse, as in debate teams, or group facilitator. Don't let roles get in the way of learning.

Make sure you assume a supporting role as the teacher.
Examples

1. For social skills and team-building goals, be a model and encourager.
2. For structured fact and skill-based practice and review tasks, be a model, director, or coach.
3. For higher-level conceptual and thinking tasks, be a model and facilitator.

Move around the room and monitor the groups.
Examples

1. For social skills and team-building goals, watch for listening, turn-taking, encouraging, and managing conflict.
2. For structured fact and skill-based practice and review tasks, watch for questioning, giving multiple elaborated explanations, attention, and practice.
3. For higher-level conceptual and thinking tasks, watch for questioning, explaining, elaborating, probing, divergent thinking, providing rationales, synthesizing, using and connecting knowledge sources.

Start small and simple until you and the students know how to use cooperative methods.
Examples

1. For social skills and team-building goals, try one or two skills, such as listening and paraphrasing.
2. For structured fact and skill-based practice and review tasks, try pairs of students quizzing each other.
3. For higher-level conceptual and thinking tasks, try reciprocal questioning using pairs and just a few question stems.

For more information on cooperative learning, see: http://www.co-operation.org/ http://edtech.kennesaw.edu/intech/cooperativelearning.htm

Source: Adapted from "Implications of Cognitive Approaches to Peer Learning for Teacher Education," by A. Woolfolk Hoy and M. Tschannen-Moran, 1999. In A. O'Donnell and A. King (Eds.), Cognitive Perspectives on Peer Learning *(pp. 257–284). Mahwah, NJ: Lawrence Erlbaum.*

the group. Speaking in a smaller group may be less anxiety provoking for students who are learning another language; thus, ELL students may get more language practice with feedback in these groups (Smith, 2006).

Cooperative learning is only as good as its design and implementation. Cooperative methods probably are both misused and underused in schools, in part because using cooperative learning well requires time and investment in teaching students how to learn in groups (Blatchford, Baines, Rubie-Davis, Bassett, & Chowne, 2006).

Dilemmas of Constructivist Practice

Years ago, Larry Cremin (1961) observed that progressive, innovative pedagogies require infinitely skilled teachers. Today, the same could be said about constructivist teaching. We have already seen that there are many varieties of constructivism and many practices that flow from these different conceptions. We also know that all teaching today happens in a context of high-stakes testing and accountability. In these situations, constructivist teachers face many challenges. Mark Windschitl (2002) identified four teacher dilemmas of constructivism in practice, summarized in Table 10.8. The first is conceptual: How do I make sense of cognitive versus social conceptions of constructivism and reconcile

TABLE 10.8 • **Teachers' Dilemmas of Constructivism in Practice**
Teachers face conceptual, pedagogical, cultural, and political dilemmas as they implement constructivist practices. Here are explanations of these dilemmas and some representative questions that teachers face as they confront them.

TEACHERS' DILEMMA CATEGORY	REPRESENTATIVE QUESTIONS OF CONCERN
I. *Conceptual dilemmas:* Grasping the underpinnings of cognitive and social constructivism; reconciling current beliefs about pedagogy with the beliefs necessary to support a constructivist learning environment.	Which version of constructivism is suitable as a basis for my teaching? Is my classroom supposed to be a collection of individuals working toward conceptual change or a community of learners whose development is measured by participation in authentic disciplinary practices? If certain ideas are considered correct by experts, should students internalize those ideas instead of constructing their own?
II. *Pedagogical dilemmas:* Honoring students' attempts to think for themselves while remaining faithful to accepted disciplinary ideas; developing deeper knowledge of subject matter; mastering the art of facilitation; managing new kinds of discourse and collaborative work in the classroom.	Do I base my teaching on students' existing ideas rather than on learning objectives? What skills and strategies are necessary for me to become a facilitator? How do I manage a classroom where students are talking to one another rather than to me? Should I place limits on students' construction of their own ideas? What types of assessments will capture the learning I want to foster?
III. *Cultural dilemmas:* Becoming conscious of the culture of your classroom; questioning assumptions about what kinds of activities should be valued; taking advantage of experiences, discourse patterns, and local knowledge of students with varied cultural backgrounds.	How can we contradict traditional, efficient classroom routines and generate new agreements with students about what is valued and rewarded? How do my own past images of what is proper and possible in a classroom prevent me from seeing the potential for a different kind of learning environment? How can I accommodate the worldviews of students from diverse backgrounds while at the same time transforming my own classroom culture? Can I trust students to accept responsibility for their own learning?
IV. *Political dilemmas:* Confronting issues of accountability with various stakeholders in the school community; negotiating with key others the authority and support to teach for understanding.	How can I gain the support of administrators and parents for teaching in such a radically different and unfamiliar way? Should I make use of approved curriculums that are not sensitive enough to my students' needs, or should I create my own? How can diverse problem-based experiences help students meet specific state and local standards? Will constructivist approaches adequately prepare my students for high-stakes testing for college admissions?

Source: M. Windschitl (2002). Framing constructivism in practice as the negotiation of dilemmas: An analysis of the conceptual, pedagogical, cultural, and political challenges facing teachers. Review of Educational Research, 72, p. 133. Copyright © 2002 by the American Educational Research Association. Reproduced with permission of the publisher.

these different perspectives with my practice? The second dilemma is pedagogical: How do I teach in truly constructivist ways that both honor my students' attempts to think for themselves, but still insure that they learn the academic material? Third are cultural dilemmas: What activities, cultural knowledge, and ways of talking will build a community in a diverse classroom? Finally, there are political dilemmas: How can I teach for deep understanding and critical thinking, but still satisfy the accountability demands of parents and the requirements of No Child Left Behind?

SERVICE LEARNING

Service learning combines academic learning with personal and social development for secondary and college students (Woolfolk Hoy, Demerath, & Pape, 2002). A more formal definition of **service learning** is "a teaching and learning strategy that integrates meaningful

Service learning Combines academic learning with personal and social development for secondary and college students.

GUIDELINES — FAMILY AND COMMUNITY PARTNERSHIPS

Service Learning

The service should be ongoing, not just a brief project.
Examples

1. Instead of having a two-week food drive with a party for the class that collected the most, encourage a longer commitment to cook or serve food at shelters for homeless families.
2. Contact local agencies to identify real needs that your students could address or search online by zip code: http://www.volunteermatch.org/

Consider virtual volunteering. See http://www.serviceleader .org/virtual
Examples

1. Translate a document into another language.
2. Provide multimedia expertise, such as preparing a PowerPoint™, QuickTime™ or other computer-based presentation.
3. Design an agency's newsletter or brochure, or copyedit an agency's publication or proposal.
4. Proofread drafts of papers and online publications.
5. Research and write articles for brochures, newsletters, Web sites.
6. Design a logo for an agency or program, or fill other illustration needs.

Be aware of service learning projects in school. Make sure learning is at the center.
Examples

1. Have clear learning objectives for the projects.
2. Examine grade-level standards in science, history, health, literature, and other areas to see how some might be

met through service projects—for example, how might concepts in biology be learned through designing a nutrition education project for senior citizens or preschool students?

3. Do students reflect over time about their experiences, keep journals, write or draw what they have learned, and include these reflections in class discussions?

Make sure the service draws on your child's talents and skills so that it is actually valuable to the recipients and he or she gains a sense of accomplishment and usefulness from applying skills to help others.
Examples

1. Youth who have artistic talents might help redecorate a game room at a senior citizens' center.
2. Individuals who are good storytellers could work with children at a day care center or in a children's clinic.
3. Students who are bilingual might help teachers translate school newsletters into the languages of fellow students' families or serve as translators at local clinics.

Design service learning opportunities so they are inclusive (Dymond, Renzaglia, & Chun, 2007).
Examples

1. Consider transportation needs for children with disabilities.
2. Link service learning projects to life skills such as social skills on the job, safety, and punctuality.
3. Encourage teachers to monitor interactions in groups for all students; be aware of how students with special needs are included.

For more ideas, see:
http://www.service-learningpartnership.org/site/PageServer

---

community service with instruction and reflection to enrich the learning experience, teach civic responsibility, and strengthen communities" (National Service Learning Clearing House, n.d.). About half of American high schools have some form of service learning (Dymond, Renzaglia, & Chun, 2007). The Alliance for Service Learning in Education Reform (1993) lists several characteristics of service learning. The activities:

- Are organized and meet actual community needs.
- Are integrated into the student's curriculum.
- Provide time to reflect and write about the service experience.
- Provide opportunities to apply newly learned academic skills and knowledge.
- Enhance both academic learning and a sense of caring for others.

Service learning activities may involve direct service (tutoring, serving meals at homeless shelters), indirect service (collecting food for shelters, raising money), or advocacy (designing and distributing posters about a food drive, writing newspaper articles) (Johnson & Notah, 1999). Service learning also could be a form of problem-based learning.

Participation in service learning can promote political and moral development for adolescents. Through service learning projects, adolescents experience their own competence and agency by working with others in need. Students see themselves as political and moral agents, rather than as merely good citizens (Youniss & Yates, 1997). In addition, service learning can help adolescents think in new ways about their relationships with people who are unlike them, and thus can lead them to become more tolerant of differences (Tierney, 1993). Finally, service learning experiences foster an "ethic of care" that can result in a growing commitment to confront difficult social problems (Rhodes, 1997). In this sense, student involvement in service learning can motivate and empower adolescents to critically reflect on their role in society (Woolfolk Hoy, Demerath, & Pape, 2002). A number of schools now have participation in service learning as a graduation requirement, but some educators question if "required" service is fair or appropriate. At least three of the school requirements have been challenged in court. but, so far, the requirements have been upheld (Johnson & Notah, 1999).

SERVICE LEARNING Community service projects can promote adolescents' moral development, feelings of competence and agency, and tolerance of differences, and encourage them to reflect critically on their roles in society.

Studies of service learning have produced mixed results. Some studies have found modest gains on measures of social responsibility, tolerance for others, empathy, attitude toward adults, and self-esteem (Solomon et al., 2001). A case study at an urban parochial high school describes a successful service learning experience program that was required for juniors and was part of a yearlong course on social justice (Youniss & Yates, 1999). In the class, students examined the moral implications of current social issues such as homelessness, poverty, exploitation of immigrant laborers, and urban violence. Students also were required to serve four times (approximately 20 hours) at an inner-city soup kitchen. The researchers concluded that students emerged from the course with "a deeper awareness of social injustice, a greater sense of commitment to confront these injustices, and heightened confidence in their abilities overall" (Yates & Youniss, 1999, p. 64).

Your students may be involved in service learning both inside and outside the school. You might share the *Family and Community Partnership Guidelines* with families and use them yourself. Many are taken from Richard Sagor (2003) and Elias and Schwab (2006).

LEARNING IN A DIGITAL WORLD

It seems that computers, smart phones, iPods, iPads, iTouches, tablets, digital readers, and interactive video games, along with iCloud, Facebook, Twitter, Google, Yahoo, … , and other digital tools and media have changed life for everyone. Homes and schools are filled with media. For students, doing homework often involves exchanging messages with friends via e-mail, texting, or cell phones, searching the Web, and downloading resources—all the time listening to music via an iPod or watching television (Roberts, Foehr, & Rideout, 2005). Over 35% of children *ages 6 months to 3 years* have a TV in their own bedroom. There are DVD players in 95% of homes, and 27% of the children have a DVD player in their bedrooms. The television is on an average of 6 hours a day (Rideout et al. 2003; Rosen, 2010). Vandewater et al. (2005) found that the TV was on all day or most of the day in 35% of the homes they studied. In fact, children spend more time watching television than they do in any other activity except sleep.

Learning Environments and Technology

With all the technology available today, there is growing interest in *technology-rich learning environments* or TREs. These environments include virtual worlds, computer simulations that support problem-based learning such as the *River of Life Challenge* described earlier, intelligent tutoring systems, educational games, audio recordings, hand-held wireless devices, and multimedia environments—to name just a few.

There are three kinds of uses for technology in schools. First, teachers can design technology-based activities for their classrooms, for virtual learning environments, or for blended models using both in-class and virtual environments. Second, students can interact with technologies in a variety of ways, such as by using a computer or tablet to complete assignments, or by collaborating in a virtual environment with other students or teachers using interactive **cloud computing** applications. Cloud computing allows computer users online access to applications such as a Google documents or Microsoft Web Mail along with computing assets such as network-accessible data storage and processing. Finally, administrators use technology to track teacher, class, and student information in school, district, or statewide systems. You could be involved with any or all three uses of technology in your teaching.

The primary goal for integrating technology into a classroom is to support student learning. The process may seem difficult and troublesome at first, especially for teachers with few technological skills. Starting points include researching your school or district technology policies and procedures, identifying internal resources such as technology integration teams, seeking out training resources, and working with teachers who already use technology in their classes. Becoming familiar with available technological resources will help you to identify and include new technologies that will enhance your teaching. A golden rule for technology integration in any classroom is that you do not need to re-invent the wheel. Focus on identifying centers of expertise where existing resources are available to adapt and build on.

Virtual Learning Environments

Virtual Learning Environments (VLEs) is a broad term that describes many ways of learning in virtual systems. The most traditional VLE is referred to as a **Learning Management System (LMSs)**. LMSs deliver e-learning using applications such as Moodle, BlackBoard, RCampus, and Desire2Learn. Learning management systems are large, complex, and costly—my university uses a system we call "Carmen" to support every course on campus. My Carmen sites have readings, discussion groups, class-built Wikis, PowerPoints, weblinks, a calendar, and many other resources. We taught classes without these assets for decades, but the learning management system has expanded our teaching and learning options. To deal with costs, some institutions use free *open-source software* to construct virtual learning environments. Tools that support open-source software include Moodle, Google Apps, Microsoft SharePoint, and PBWorks.

There are different kinds of virtual learning environments. A **Personal Learning Environment (PLE)** framework provides tools that support individualized learning in a variety of contexts and situations; the learners assume control of how and when their learning occurs. Students working in personal learning environments can download an assignment at Panera, read the material on the bus, and then post an analysis on the discussion board at 4:00 A.M. from their room—learning is asynchronous, it takes place any time and anywhere. Complex personal learning environments include tools that assess learners' knowledge and then adapt the next content to fit their needs. Tools that support PLEs include computer-based training modules, e-books, cognitive tutors, quizzes, and self-assessment tools.

A **Personal Learning Network (PLN)** is a framework in which knowledge is constructed through online peer interactions. PLNs consist of both synchronous (real time) and asynchronous technologies using interactive Web conferencing, hybrid classes, or online discussions. A PLN can be used for K–12 instructional purposes and also as a resource for professional development. Social networking tools such as Facebook, Twitter, Edutopia, and EdWeb allow the instruction to move outside the school, city, and even country to include learners with similar interests around the globe. Tools that support personal learning networks include: Web conferencing tools, such as Adobe Connect and Elluminate, instant messaging, interactive video and audio messaging, social networking, discussion boards, and blogs.

Cloud computing Allows computer users to access applications, such as a Google document or Microsoft Web Mail, as well as computing assets such as network-accessible data storage and processing to use online applications.

Virtual Learning Environments (VLE) A broad term that describes many ways of learning in virtual or online systems.

Learning Management System (LMS) Systems that deliver e-learning, provide tools and learning materials, keep records, administer assessments, and manage learning.

Personal Learning Environment (PLE) Provides tools that support individualized learning in a variety of contexts and situations.

Personal Learning Network (PLN) Framework in which knowledge is constructed through online peer interactions.

The most complex VLE is an **Immersive Virtual Learning Environment (IVLE).** The IVLE is a simulation of a real-world environment. The purpose is to learn through enculturation, for example by being eco explorers in the rainforest or reporters covering a story about an outbreak of food poisoning in a local school (Gee, 2003; Gibson, Aldrich, & Prensky, 2006; Hamilton, 2011; Shaffer et al., 2009). Immersive Virtual Learning Environments are designed to be domain specific using realistic scenarios (Bagley & Shaffer, 2009; Shaffer et al., 2009). IVLE experiences mimic tasks required in a professional practicum, such as interviewing sources for a news story about food poisoning, following leads to identify the source of a problem, and crafting an accurate engaging article, thus blending real-world engagement in a virtual scenario. These immersive environments often include *cognitive tutors*—the technology is programmed to interact as a tutor by providing prompts after analyzing the student's response.

Massive Multi-player Online Games (MMOGs) are interactive gaming environments constructed in virtual worlds in which the learner assumes a character role of avatar. Virtual world simulations incorporating MMOGs have been used for experiential and didactic learning in the medical field for several years and quickly are gaining attention in PK–12 classrooms. The pedagogic value in good gaming design is the ability to create complex scenarios by developing lessons using modeling and problem-based learning scenarios as alternative methods of instruction (Gee, 2008). For example, Project Evoke is a game developed by the World Bank (http://www.urgentevoke.com/). As they play the game, adolescents from around the world work collectively to solve major world problems such as hunger. Stay tuned for more exciting learning worlds.

Developmentally Appropriate Computer Activities for Young Children

Digital media are appealing, but are they appropriate for preschool children? This is a hotly debated issue. Computers should not be used to do solitary drill-and-practice activities. Developmentally appropriate ways to use computers with 3- and 4-year-olds are different from the ways we use computers in kindergarten and the primary grades (http://www.kidsource.com/education/computers.children.html). With developmentally appropriate computer activities, young children can benefit cognitively without sustaining losses in creativity (Haugland & Wright, 1997). Software for children should include simple spoken directions; the activities should be open-ended and encourage discovery, exploration, problem solving, and understanding of cause and effect. Children should be able to remain in control of the activities through a variety of responses. Finally, the content should be appropriate for and respectful of diverse cultures, ages, and abilities (Fischer & Gillespie, 2003; Frost, Wortham, & Reifel, 2005). Linda Tsantis and her colleagues suggest that you ask this question about any program you are considering: "Does this software program help create learning opportunities that did not exist without it?" (Tsantis, Berwick, & Thouvebelle, 2003).

There is another important consideration—does the program's multimedia features (e.g., embedded videos, zoom-ins, music, added sounds, images) add to learning or take away from it? One danger is that programs will include attractive visuals or sound effects that actually interrupt and interfere with the development of important concepts. For example, do the sounds of a buzz saw and the thud of a falling tree in a Peter Rabbit storytelling program foster distractibility and interfere with understanding the story, plot, and characters? Maybe (Tsantis et al., 2003).

Immersive Virtual Learning Environment (IVLE) A simulation of a real-world environment that immerses students in tasks like those required in a professional practicum.

Massive Multi-player Online Games (MMOG) Interactive gaming environments constructed in virtual worlds where the learner assumes a character role of avatar.

MEDIA MULTITASKERS For older students, doing homework often involves exchanging messages with friends via e-mail or cell phones, searching the Web, and downloading resources—all the time listening to music via an iPod or watching television.

Dealing with all of this stimulation might make children better at multitasking, but also worse at deeper thought processes such as developing perspective-taking skills and understanding the plot, theme, and sequence of the story. So children learn to do several things at once, but have a superficial understanding of what they are doing (Carpenter, 2000).

Research in the Netherlands, however, demonstrated that multimedia storybooks can provide support for understanding stories and remembering linguistic information for kindergarten students from families with low educational levels who are behind in language and literacy skills (Verhallen, Bus, & de Jong, 2006). The difference in this study seemed to be that the multimedia features of the story supported understanding and memory by providing multiple pathways to meaning, giving visual and verbal representations of key story elements, focusing attention on important information, and reinforcing key ideas. This extra scaffolding may be especially important for students with limited language and literacy skills. So the bottom line is that multimedia elements should focus on meaning and not just provide attractive "bells and whistles."

Computers and Older Students

There is evidence that using computers—especially games that require multiple activities, visual attention, imagery, and fast action—supports the development of visual skills, as long as the tasks fit the student's level of ability (Subrahmanyam, Greenfield, Kraut, & Gross, 2001). But does computer use support academic learning? The answer is complex and even surprising. After reviewing hundreds of studies, including five other research reviews, Roschelle, Pea, Hoadley, Gordon, and Means (2000) concluded that there were no strong conclusions. Using computer tutorial programs appeared to improve achievement test scores for K–12 students, but simulations and enrichment programs had few effects—perhaps another example that when you teach and test specific skills, children learn the skills. More recent research reports similar results. Computers may be more useful in improving mathematics and science skills than other subjects and not very successful in improving reading (Slavin, Lake, Chambers Cheung, & Davis, 2009). Like any teaching tool, computers can be effective if used well, but just being on a computer will not automatically increase academic achievement, especially achievement as measured by standardized tests (Richtell, 2011). Roschelle and colleagues concluded that computers are more likely to increase achievement if they support the basic processes that lead to learning: active engagement, frequent interaction with feedback, authenticity and real-world connection, and productive group work (Jackson et al., 2006). See the *Guidelines* for more ideas.

DIGITALLY DISADVANTAGED? Many students have limited access to technology at home or in their communities. This split in access to technology has been called the *digital divide*.

Media/Digital Literacy

With the advent of digital media comes a new concern with literacy—media or digital literacy. Today, to be literate—that is to be able to read, write, and communicate—children have to read and write in many media, not just printed words. Films, videos, DVDs, computers, photographs, artwork, magazines, music, television, billboards, and more communicate through images and sounds. How do children read these messages? This is a new area of research and application in educational and developmental psychology (Hobbs, 2004).

As an example of practice, consider Project Look Sharp at Ithaca College, directed by Cynthia Scheibe, a developmental psychologist (http://www.ithaca.edu/looksharp/). The goal of the project is to provide materials, training, and support as teachers

GUIDELINES

Using Computers

IF YOU HAVE ONLY ONE COMPUTER IN YOUR CLASSROOM

Provide convenient access.
Examples

1. Find a central location if the computer is used to display material for the class.
2. Find a spot on the side of the room that allows seating and view of the screen, but does not crowd or disturb other students if the computer is used as a workstation for individuals or small groups.

Be prepared.
Examples

1. Check to be sure software needed for a lesson or assignment is installed and working.
2. Make sure instructions for using the software or doing the assignment are in an obvious place and clear.
3. Provide a checklist for completing assignments.

Create "trained experts" to help with computers.
Examples

1. Train student experts, and rotate experts.
2. Use adult volunteers—parents, grandparents, aunts and uncles, older siblings—anyone who cares about the students.

Develop systems for using the computer.
Examples

1. Make up a schedule to insure that all students have access to the computer and no students monopolize the time.
2. Create standard ways of saving student work.

IF YOU HAVE MORE THAN ONE COMPUTER IN YOUR CLASSROOM

Plan the arrangement of the computers to fit your instructional goals.
Examples

1. For cooperative groups, arrange so students can cluster around their group's computer.
2. For different projects at different computer stations, allow for easy rotation from station to station.

Experiment with other models for using computers.
Examples

1. Navigator Model—4 students per computer: One student is the (mouse and keyboard) driver, another is the "navigator." "Back-seat driver 1" manages the group's progress and "back-seat driver 2" serves as the timekeeper. The navigator attends a 10-minute to 20-minute training session in which the facilitator provides an overview of the basics of particular software. Navigators cannot touch the mouse. Driver roles are rotated.
2. Facilitator Model—6 students per computer: the facilitator has more experience, expertise, or training—serves as the guide or teacher.
3. Collaborative Group Model—7 students per computer: Each small group is responsible for creating some component of the whole group's final product. For example, one part of the group writes a report, another creates a map, and a third uses the computer to gather and graph census data.

NO MATTER HOW MANY COMPUTERS YOU HAVE IN YOUR CLASSROOM

Select developmentally appropriate programs that encourage learning, creativity, and social interaction.
Examples

1. Encourage two children to work together rather than having children work alone.
2. Check the implicit messages in programs. For example, some drawing programs allow children to "blow up" their projects if they don't like them, so instead of solving a problem they just destroy it. Tsantis et al. (2003) recommend a recycle metaphor instead of a "blow it up" option.
3. Look for programs that encourage discovery, exploration, problem solving, and multiple responses.

Monitor children as they work at computers.
Examples

1. Make sure computers are in areas where adults can observe them.
2. Discuss with children why some programs or Web sites are off limits.
3. Balance computer time with active play such as hands-on projects, blocks, sand, water, and art.

Keep children safe as they work at computers.
Examples

1. Teach children to shield their identity on the Internet and monitor any "friends" they may be communicating with.
2. Install filtering software to protect children from inappropriate content.

Sources: Suggestions are taken from Frost, J. L., Wortham, S. C., & Reifel, S. (2005). Play and child development (2nd ed.). Upper Saddle River, NJ: Prentice-Hall, pp. 76–80 and Tsantis, L. A., Bewick, C. J., & Thouvenelle, S. (2003, November). Examining some common myths about computer use in the early years. Beyond the Journal: Young Children on the Web (pp. 1–9).

GUIDELINES

Supporting the Development of Media Literacy

Use media to practice general observation, critical thinking, analysis, perspective-taking, and production skills.
Examples

1. Ask students to think critically about the information presented in advertising, "news" programs, and textbooks—would different people interpret the messages in differing ways?
2. Foster creativity by having students produce their own media on a topic you are studying.
3. Ask students to compare ways information might be presented in a documentary, TV news report, advertisement, public service announcement, etc.
4. Give examples of how word selection, background music, camera angles, color, etc. can be used to set a mood or bias a message.

Use media to stimulate interest in a new topic.
Examples

1. Analyze a magazine article about the topic.
2. Read sections from a novel or view film clips on the topic.

Help students identify what they already know or believe about a topic based on popular media content. Help them identify erroneous beliefs.
Examples

1. What do students "know" about space travel?
2. What have they learned about biology from advertisements?

Use media as a standard pedagogical tool.
Examples

1. Provide information about a topic through many different media sources—Internet, books, DVDs, audio recordings, online newspapers, etc.
2. Assign homework that makes use of different media.
3. Have students express opinions or attempt to persuade using different media—photographs, collages, videos, poems, songs, animated films, etc.

Analyze the effects that media had on historical events.
Examples

1. How were Native Americans portrayed in art and in films?
2. What sources of information were available 50 years ago? 100 years ago?

For more ideas, see:
http://www.ithaca.edu/looksharp/

integrate media literacy and critical thinking about media into their class lessons. Teachers participating in the project help their students become critical readers of media. One group of elementary school students studied ants in science, and then viewed the animated film, *Antz*. In the discussion after the movie, students were challenged to describe what was accurate and inaccurate in the film's portrayal of ants. What were the messages of the film? How was product placement (e.g., an ant drinking a bottle of Pepsi) used? Tests immediately and 6 months later indicated that the children performed best on the questions related to the discussion about the accuracy of the film (Scheibe, 2005). Project Look Sharp suggests these questions to guide discussion of media:

1. Who made—and who sponsored—this message, and what is their purpose?
2. Who is the target audience and how is the message specifically tailored to that audience?
3. What are the different techniques used to inform, persuade, entertain, and attract attention?
4. What messages are communicated (and/or implied) about certain people, places, events, behaviors, lifestyles, and so forth?
5. How current, accurate, and credible is the information in this message?
6. What is left out of the message that might be good to know? (p. 63)

The *Guidelines* give more ideas from Scheibe and Rogow (2004) for supporting the development of media literacy in your students.

▼ SUMMARY

The Learning Sciences (pp. 356–358)

What are some basic assumptions of the learning sciences? Key assumptions in the learning sciences are that experts develop deep conceptual knowledge, learning comes from the learner, creating learning environments is the responsibility of the school, students' prior knowledge is key, and reflection is a critical component of learning. These common assumptions enable researchers from a variety of disciplines to address the same issues of learning from a variety of perspectives.

Cognitive and Social Constructivism (pp. 358–365)

Describe two kinds of constructivism and distinguish these from constructionism. *Psychological* constructivists such as Piaget are concerned with how individuals make sense of their world, based on individual knowledge, beliefs, self-concept, or identity—also called *first wave constructivism*. *Social* constructivists such as Vygotsky believe that social interaction, cultural tools, and activity shape individual development and learning—also called *second wave constructivism*. By participating in a broad range of activities with others, learners appropriate the outcomes produced by working together; they acquire new strategies and knowledge of their world. Finally, constructionists are interested in how public knowledge in academic disciplines is constructed as well as how everyday beliefs about the world are communicated to new members of a sociocultural group.

In what ways do constructivist views differ about knowledge sources, accuracy, and generality? Constructivists debate whether knowledge is constructed by mapping external reality, by adapting and changing internal understandings, or by an interaction of external forces and internal understandings. Most psychologists believe there is a role for both internal and external factors, but differ in how much they emphasize one or the other. Also, there is discussion about whether knowledge can be constructed in one situation and applied to another or whether knowledge is situated, that is, specific and tied to the context in which it was learned. What is meant by thinking as enculturation? Enculturation is a broad and complex process of acquiring knowledge and understanding consistent with Vygotsky's theory of mediated learning. Just as our home culture taught us lessons about the use of language, the culture of a classroom can teach lessons about thinking by giving us models of good thinking; providing direct instruction in thinking processes; and encouraging practice of those thinking processes through interactions with others.

What are some common elements in most constructivist views of learning? Even though there is no single constructivist theory, many constructivist approaches recommend complex, challenging learning environments and authentic tasks; social negotiation and co-construction; multiple representations of content; understanding that knowledge is constructed; and student ownership of learning.

Applying Constructivist Perspectives (pp. 365–383)

Distinguish between inquiry methods and problem-based learning. The inquiry strategy begins when the teacher presents a puzzling event, question, or problem. The students ask questions (only yes-no questions in some kinds of inquiry) and then formulate hypotheses to explain the event or solve the problem; collect data to test the hypotheses about casual relationships; form conclusions and generalizations; and reflect on the original problem and the thinking processes needed to solve it. Problem-based learning may follow a similar path, but the learning begins with an authentic problem—one that matters to the students. The goal is to learn math or science or history or some other important subject while seeking a real solution to a real problem.

Describe six features that most cognitive apprenticeship approaches share. Students observe an expert (usually the teacher) model the performance; get external support through coaching or tutoring; and receive conceptual scaffolding, which is then gradually faded as the student becomes more competent and proficient. Students continually articulate their knowledge—putting into words their understanding of the processes and content being learned. They reflect on their progress, comparing their problem solving to an expert's performance and to their own earlier performances. Finally, students explore new ways to apply what they are learning—ways that they have not practiced at the master's side.

Describe the use of dialogue in reciprocal teaching. The goal of reciprocal teaching is to help students understand and think deeply about what they read. To accomplish this goal, students in small reading groups learn four strategies: summarizing the content of a passage, asking a question about the central point, clarifying the difficult parts of the material, and predicting what will come next. These strategies are practiced in a classroom dialogue about the readings. Teachers first take a central role, but as the discussion progresses, the students take more and more control.

What are the differences between collaboration and cooperation? One view is that collaboration is a philosophy about how to relate to others—how to learn and work. Collaboration is a way of dealing with people that respects differences, shares authority, and builds on the knowledge that is distributed among other people. Cooperation, on the other hand, is a way of working together with others to attain a shared goal.

What are the learning theory underpinnings of cooperative learning? Learning can be enhanced in cooperative groups through rehearsal and elaboration (information processing theories), creation and resolution of disequilibrium (Piaget's theory), or scaffolding of higher mental processes (Vygotsky's theory).

Describe five elements that define true cooperative learning. Students interact face-to-face and close together, not across the room. Group members experience positive interdependence—they need each other for support, explanations, and guidance. Even though they work together and help each other, members of the group must ultimately demonstrate learning on their own—they are held individually accountable for learning, often through individual tests or other assessments. If necessary, the collaborative skills important for effective group functioning, such as giving constructive feedback, reaching consensus, and involving every member, are taught and practiced before the groups tackle a learning task. Finally, members monitor group processes and relationships to make sure the group is working effectively and to learn about the dynamics of groups.

How should tasks match design in cooperative learning? A relatively structured task works well with a structured technique; extrinsic rewards can enhance motivation, effort, and persistence under these conditions; roles, especially those that focus attention on the work to be accomplished, also may be productive. On the other hand, strategies that encourage extended and productive interactions are appropriate when the goal is to develop higher-order thinking and problem solving. The use of rewards may well divert the group away from the goal of in-depth cognitive processing. When the goal of peer learning is enhanced social skills or increased intergroup understanding and appreciation of diversity, the assignment of specific roles and functions within the group might support communication. Rewards probably are not necessary and may actually get in the way because the goal is to build community, a sense of respect, and responsibility for team members.

What are some possible strategies for cooperative learning? Strategies include reciprocal questioning, Jigsaw, structured controversy, and many cooperative structures described by Spencer Kagan.

Service Learning (pp. 383–385)

What are some key characteristics of service learning? Service learning activities should be organized around and designed to meet actual community needs, and integrated into the student's curriculum. Teachers should provide time for students to reflect on and write about their service experience, offer opportunities to apply newly learned academic skills and knowledge, and strive to enhance both academic learning and a sense of caring for others. Service learning activities ought not be supplementary to students' regular activities, but instead should be an integral part of their learning.

Learning in a Digital World (pp. 385–390)

What are some possible uses of technology in education? Technology such as computers, iPods, smart phones, digital readers, and interactive gaming systems are extremely popular among young people. In fact, the many ways of communicating and interacting with others through technology may even shape the way students think about what it means to socialize. These technologies can be useful teaching tools, but they do have limitations. First, technology cannot necessarily replace the teacher when it comes to direct instruction (and not all programs are able to bring about learning). Classrooms of the future may take greater advantage of learning environments that immerse students in virtual worlds where they work alone or with others to solve problems, create projects, simulate the skills of experts, visit historical sites, tour world class museums, or play games that teach and apply academic skills. The results of research on technology-enhanced learning emphasize that technology by itself will not guarantee improvement in academic achievement—like any tool, technology must be used well by confident, competent teachers.

▼ KEY TERMS

Appropriating (361)
Cloud computing (386)
Cognitive apprenticeship (369)
Collaboration (372)
Community of practice (363)
Complex learning environments (364)
Constructionism (361)
Constructivism (359)
Cooperation (372)
Cooperative learning (373)
Embodied cognition (357)
First wave constructivism (360)

Immersive Virtual Learning Environment (IVLE) (387)
Inquiry learning (366)
Intersubjective attitude (364)
Jigsaw Classroom (380)
Learning Management System (LMS) (386)
Learning sciences (356)
Massive Multi-player Online Games (MMOG) (387)
Multiple representations of content (365)
Personal Learning Environment (PLE) (386)
Personal Learning Network (PLN) (386)

Problem-based learning (367)
Radical constructivism (360)
Reciprocal questioning (379)
Reciprocal teaching (370)
Scaffolding (365)
Second wave constructivism (361)
Service learning (383)
Situated learning (363)
Social negotiation (364)
Spiral curriculum (365)
Structured controversy (380)
Virtual Learning Environments (VLE) (386)

▼ CONNECT AND EXTEND TO LICENSURE

MULTIPLE-CHOICE QUESTIONS

1. All but which one of the following activities would be consistent with a constructivist environment?
   A. Students are given frequent opportunities to engage in complex, meaningful, problem-based activities
   B. Students work collaboratively and are given support to engage in task-oriented dialogue with one another
   C. Teachers elicit students' ideas and experiences in relationship to key topics, then fashion learning situations that assist students in elaborating on or restructuring their current knowledge
   D. Teachers employ limited assessment strategies and give feedback on products rather than processes

2. In Mr. Lawrence's classroom students are engaged in learning the art of driving. They watch Mr. Lawrence model techniques,

receive hints and feedback from him on their performance, and are encouraged to put into words the new skills they are practicing. This type of learning is best referred to as which one of the following?

    A. Reciprocal teaching

    B. Cognitive apprenticeship

    C. Cooperative learning

    D. Schema building

3. Group activities must be well planned. Students need to be prepared to work in groups, and teachers have to be explicit in stating their expectations. Which one of the following strategies is NOT an element which defines true cooperative learning?

    A. Positive interdependence and individual accountability

    B. Group processing

    C. Competition

    D. Collaborative and social skills

4. Research demonstrates that constructive controversy can lead to greater learning, open-mindedness, seeing the perspectives of others, creativity, motivation, and engagement. Which one of the following is the set up for activities that engage students in structured controversies?

    A. Students work in pairs within their four-person cooperative groups to research a particular argument.

    B. Each student is part of a group and each group member is given part of the material to be learned by the whole group. Students become experts on their piece and then teach it to the others in their group.

    C. Students intuitively understand the design that helps them think deeply about what they read.

    D. A combination of academic learning with personal and social development for secondary and college students is created.

CONSTRUCTED-RESPONSE QUESTIONS

Case

In order to infuse her class with constructivist strategies, Brenda Rhodes planned several problem-based learning scenarios. One of the scenarios required students to find a solution for their city's homeless population. Over the past few years the number of homeless individuals and families had grown alarmingly quickly. Social service agencies, shelters and businesses in the central city were struggling to deal with the challenge. Brenda believed her students would find the topic interesting and that it met the criteria for problem-based learning.

5. Does Brenda Rhodes' activity of finding a solution for the city's homeless population as a topic meet the requirements for problem-based learning? Explain your answer.

6. Identify several types of scaffolding the students might use to help them solve their problem.

MyEducationLab™

Go to Chapter 10 of the Book Specific Resources in MyEducationLab and click on "Connect and Extend to Licensure" to answer these questions. Compare your responses with the feedback provided.

▼ WHAT WOULD THEY DO?

TEACHERS' CASEBOOK: Learning to Cooperate

Here is how some practicing teachers responded to the situation described at the beginning of the chapter about the class that hated cooperative learning.

PAULA COLEMERE • Special Education Teacher—English, History
McClintock High School, Tempe, AZ

First, cooperative learning should be introduced early in the year and used in a variety of ways. Simple activities such as "think-pair-share" or "tell partner two things you learned" are basic ways of having students learn cooperatively. In addition, Socratic seminars are a great way to get students to dialogue together and gain deeper understanding of a concept. A Socratic seminar begins with the facilitator posing an open-ended question to the group. Participants are encouraged to learn through a meaningful discussion rather than memorizing bits of information. This takes practice, but if introduced early and practiced throughout the year, students will gain higher-level thinking skills. Finally, when having students do a team activity in class, groups need to be placed together thoughtfully and deliberately by the teacher. Team members need to be taught skills necessary for successful group work

such as active listening and how to give and receive constructive criticism. Groups should have a variety of abilities and students should be assigned specific tasks within the group so everyone has a role and purpose.

PAUL DRAGIN • ESL Grades 9–12
Columbus East High School, Columbus OH

To introduce cooperative learning, I will begin with some exercises that require no talking, such as puzzles that can only be completed by group cooperation and sharing without any verbal communication. Each group member receives pieces that make up a puzzle; the catch is that some of the pieces belong to another group member's puzzle. By trading pieces strategically and rapidly, the goal is to be the first group to complete all puzzles. This sets the stage for a discussion about the need to work together, since each person in the group needs something that another team member has in order to complete his or her puzzle. All effective cooperative learning requires the input of each member, and without that input, the activity has no chance of reaching its full potential. The establishment of groups is open to myriad options and this is a good thing. Randomly assigning students as well as strategically assigning students to work together is an important learning opportunity for each student and better mimics real-world situations where we don't get to choose our co-workers.

JENNIFER PINCOSKI • Learning Resource Teacher, K–12
Lee County School District, Fort Myers, FL

In order to have effective groups, students need to respect each other and feel accepted by their peers. Therefore, it is important to incorporate some class-building and team-building exercises before the groups jump into academic content. The purpose of these activities is to acquaint students with one another and create a sense of community.

It will be easier to establish groups if the teacher collects information about the students first. This information can include anything from preferred learning style to favorite subject to career aspirations. It is also important to understand the students' levels of academic proficiency. Groups should be fluid, because different types of groups will accomplish different outcomes.

Teachers need to identify the objectives of an activity before creating the groups for that activity. In some situations, it might be appropriate to group students who are strong in a skill with students who have deficits in that skill. In other cases, it might be more effective to group together students with similar interests or career goals. It is up to the teacher to determine which type of group will result in the most worthwhile outcome for students.

LAUREN ROLLINS • 1st Grade
Boulevard Elementary School, Shaker Heights, OH

Group work is an important part of the curriculum and a teaching/learning method that I use with my students on a daily basis starting from the beginning of the school year. As I am getting to know my students and they are getting to know each other, cooperative learning activities are very simple and structured. These experiences allow them to build cooperative skills. Groups and the tasks for which each member is responsible are both assigned by me. As the school year progresses, I use cooperative learning to focus on specific skills, to facilitate peer tutoring, to accomplish a task, to play a game, etc. Depending on what I want the students to gain from the learning activity, groups are chosen at random, picked by the students, or selected by me. My students enjoy the opportunity to learn in these different types of groupings. As groups are working, I rotate through the classroom, making sure that the groups are on task and that each member is contributing to the learning activity. I spend a few minutes with each group to get a sense of how successfully the students are working together to accomplish the given task. I help facilitate when needed.

BARBARA PRESLEY • Transition/Work Study Coordinator—High School Level
B.E.S.T.T. Program (Baldwinsville Exceptional Student Training and Transition Program), C.W. Baker High School, Baldwinsville, NY

Throughout their high school experience, as students prepare for their life post high school, I send the youngest and newest students to "intern" with an older student who is secure and successful at their job site. The younger student is more comfortable going into a new situation with the company and support of one of their older peers. The older student gains confidence and takes pride in and ownership of the task of sharing knowledge and skills with his/her trainee. Entry-level job skills are practically universal, so each student gains from the experience.

LINDA SPARKS • 1st Grade
John F. Kennedy School, Billerica MA

I have used cooperative learning groups a lot through the years. There are so many things that can be learned and shared from working together. There is always frustration with some students, but overall it seems to work. I also try to set it up in a variety of ways, from letting them select their own groups, picking names out of a hat, passing out different topics and forming groups based on the topics. I will use assessments to organize a group as well as make sure that each student has a specific task. (Project editor, information manager, organizer, reporter, researcher, etc.) There always seems to be one student ready to take a back seat and let the others in the group do all of the work. We go over the social skills needed to work in a group. We often will post a list in the classroom of simple rules: using appropriate language, speaking quietly and respectfully while working, listening and encouraging team members, and asking for help when needed. While they work in their groups, I will walk around the class and take notes on what is being worked on. I want to make sure there are no misconceptions about the project. After the project is completed, I grade them in a variety of ways. I give a grade to each participant for his/her contribution to the project, a group grade for the project and or presentation, and a grade for group participation for the project. Students learn more when they are directly involved in what is being taught. This is yet another style of learning.

JESSICA N. MAHTABAN • 8th Grade Math
Woodrow Wilson Middle School, Clifton, NJ

The lesson would begin with a definition of cooperative learning as well as a real-world example. The first activity would be simple; it is called Numbered Heads Together (taken from Kagan in a cooperative learning class). Students number off in their teams so each teammate has a different number; then the teacher asks a question and provides think time. Students put their "heads together" to discuss the question. The teacher calls a number and the student with that number from each group shares with the class the group's answer. The activities would get more difficult as students get comfortable with cooperative learning.

In order to group students in the classroom, ideally there would be four students per group facing each other. On one side would be a high student (based on grades); next to them would be medium high student; across from this student would be a low student; and next to the low student would a medium low student. The high student would rarely interact with the low student because when paired off for activities they would only work with medium high and medium low students. Based on my 10 years of teaching experience the high student rarely has the patience to work with a low student, but the medium high and medium low students will work very well with the low student. Another method of grouping students is according to personality as well as heterogeneously.

─── MyEducationLab™ ───

Go to Topic Topic 7, Knowledge Constructiion, in the MyEducationLab (www.myeducationlab.com) for Educational Psychology, where you can:

- Find learning outcomes for Knowledge Construction along with the national standards that connect to these outcomes.
- Complete Assignments and Activities that can help you more deeply understand the chapter content.
- Apply and practice your understanding of the core teaching skills identified in the chapter with the Building Teaching Skills and Dispositions learning units.
- Examine challenging situations and cases presented in the IRIS Center Resources.
- Access video clips of CCSSO National Teachers of the Year award winners responding to the question, "Why Do I Teach?" in the Teacher Talk section.
- Check your comprehension on the content covered in the chapter with the Study Plan. Here you will be able to take a chapter quiz, receive feedback on your answers, and then access Review, Practice, and Enrichment activities to enhance your understanding of chapter content.
- Find additional Teachers' Casebook scenarios and responses to them from practicing teachers.
- Use the Online Lesson Plan Builder to practice lesson planning and integrating national and state standards into your planning.

chapter eleven

SOCIAL COGNITIVE VIEWS OF LEARNING AND MOTIVATION

► **TEACHERS' CASEBOOK:** Failure To Self-Regulate

You know that your students need to be organized and self-regulating to do well in both their current and their future classes. But many of the students just don't seem to know how take charge of their own learning. They have trouble completing larger projects—many wait until the last minute. They can't organize their work or decide what is most important. Some can't even keep up with assignments. Their book bags are disaster areas—filled with long overdue assignment sheets and class handouts from last semester crumbled in with school newsletters and permission slips for field trips. You are concerned because they will need to be much more organized and on top of their work as they progress through their education. You have so much material to cover to meet district guidelines, but many of your students are drowning in the amount of work they already have.

CRITICAL THINKING

- What organizational skills do students need to be successful in your subject or class?

- What could you do to teach these skills, while still covering the material that will be on the proficiency or achievement tests the students will have to take in the spring?

- How would you help students develop an authentic sense of efficacy for guiding their own learning?

OVERVIEW AND OBJECTIVES

For the past four chapters, we have analyzed different aspects of learning. We considered behavioral and information processing explanations of what and how people learn. We have examined cognitive science and complex cognitive processes such as concept learning and problem solving. These explanations of learning focus on the individual and what is happening in his or her "head." Recent perspectives have called attention to two other aspects of learning that are critical: social and cultural factors. In the previous chapter, we examined social constructivism and the interdisciplinary learning sciences. In this chapter, we look at social cognitive theory—a current view of learning and motivation that discusses dynamic interactions among many of the behavioral, personal, and cultural factors involved in learning and motivation.

Social cognitive theory has its roots in Bandura's early criticisms of behavioral views of learning, as you read in Chapter 7. Social cognitive theory moved beyond behaviorism to focus on humans as self-directed agents who make choices and marshal resources to reach goals. Concepts such as self-efficacy and self-regulated learning are key in social cognitive theories. These concepts are important in understanding motivation as well, so this chapter provides a good path from learning to the discussion of motivation in the next chapter. We end the chapter with a look back at our tour through different models of instruction. Rather than debating the merits of each approach, we will consider the contributions of these different models of instruction, grounded in different theories of learning. Don't feel that you must choose the "best" approach—there is no such thing. Even though theorists argue about which model is best, excellent teachers don't debate. They apply all the approaches, using each one when appropriate.

By the time you have completed this chapter, you should be able to:

Objective 11.1: Define the basic principles of social cognitive theories of learning and motivation including triarchic reciprocal causality, modeling/observational learning, self-efficacy, and agency.

Objective 11.2: Discuss the roles of observation and self-efficacy in learning.

Objective 11.3: Describe important components of self-regulated learning.

Objective 11.4: Apply self-regulated learning principles to teaching.

SOCIAL COGNITIVE THEORY

As we saw in Chapter 7, in the early 1960s, Albert Bandura demonstrated that people can learn by observing both the actions of others and the consequences of those actions. Most of what is known today as *social cognitive theory* is based on the work begun by Albert Bandura in the 1950s at Stanford University. Before we talk about the theory, let's meet the man.

A Self-Directed Life: Albert Bandura

Albert Bandura's life story should be a movie. You could say he lived the American dream, except that he is from Canada. His parents were immigrants from Eastern Europe; they chose the rugged land of northern Alberta for their family farm. Bandura's parents never went to school, but they valued education. His father taught himself to read in three languages, giving young Albert a great model of self-regulated learning—a concept that figures prominently in social cognitive theory today. On the way to finishing high school, Bandura worked many jobs, including a stint as a carpenter at a furniture factory and one as a road worker on the Alaska Highway in the Yukon. He finished his undergraduate degree at the University of British Columbia in three years, even though he had to cram all his classes into the morning to have time for his afternoon jobs. Because he needed a morning class to fill one time slot, he enrolled in introductory psychology and found his future profession (Bandura, 2007, p. 46). His next stop was graduate school at the epicenter of psychological research in 1950—the University of Iowa. After earning his Ph.D. (in three years again), Bandura joined the faculty at Stanford in 1953—he was 28 years old. He is still at Stanford nearly 60 years later, and now teaches some of the children of his former students.

When I read Bandura's autobiography (see http://www.des.emory.edu/mfp/bandurabio.html for a summary with pictures), I was struck by how much his theories reflected his life as a self-directed, self-regulating learner growing up in a challenging environment. Describing his experiences in his two-teacher high school, Bandura said:

> We had to take charge of our own learning. Self-directed learning was an essential means of academic self-development, not a theoretical abstraction. The paucity of educational resources turned out to be an enabling factor that has served me well rather than an insurmountable handicapping one. The content of courses is perishable, but self-regulatory skills have lasting functional value whatever the pursuit might be. (p. 45)

In the next section we will look at the key features of Albert Bandura's work and social cognitive theory by considering four topics: moving beyond behaviorism, the concept of triarchic reciprocal causality, the power of observational learning, and the key beliefs of agency and self-efficacy.

Beyond Behaviorism

Bandura's early **social learning theory** emphasized modeling and observing others being reinforced or punished for particular behaviors. But as you know from Chapter 7, he found basic behaviorism to be too limited. In his autobiography, Bandura (2007) describes the shortcomings of behaviorism and the need to put people in social context:

Social learning theory Theory that emphasizes learning through observation of others.

I found this behavioristic theorizing discordant with the obvious social reality that much of what we learn is through the power of social modeling. I could not imagine a culture in which its language; mores; familial customs and practices; occupational competencies; and educational, religious, and political practices were gradually shaped in each new member by rewarding and punishing consequences of their trial-and-error performances. (p. 55)

Over time, Bandura's explanations of learning included more attention to cognitive factors such as *expectations* and *beliefs* in addition to the social influences of models (Bandura, 1986, 1997, 2001). His current perspective, **social cognitive theory**, retains an emphasis on the role of other people serving as models and teachers (the *social* part of social cognitive theory), but includes thinking, believing, expecting, anticipating, self-regulating, and making comparisons and judgments (the *cognitive* part). Social cognitive theory is a *dynamic system* that explains human adaptation, learning, and motivation. The theory addresses how people develop social, emotional, cognitive, and behavioral capabilities; how people regulate their own lives; and what motivates them (Bandura, 2007; Bandura & Locke, 2003). In fact, many of the concepts from this chapter will help you understand motivation in the upcoming chapter.

ALBERT BANDURA You may remember Albert Bandura from Chapter 7. Pictures from his famous Bobo doll experiment on observational learning are in the background. Most of what we know today as social cognitive theory is based on the work he began in the 1950s at Stanford University.

Triarchic Reciprocal Causality

I claimed that social cognitive theory describes a system. This system, called **triarchic reciprocal causality**, is the dynamic interplay among three kinds of influences: personal, environmental, and behavioral, as shown in Figure 11.1. Personal factors (beliefs, expectations, attitudes, and knowledge), the physical and social environment (resources, consequences of actions, other people, models and teachers, and physical settings), and behavior (individual actions, choices, and verbal statements) all influence and are influenced by each other.

Figure 11.1 shows the interaction of person, environment, and behavior in learning settings (Schunk, Pintrich, & Meece, 2008). External factors such as models,

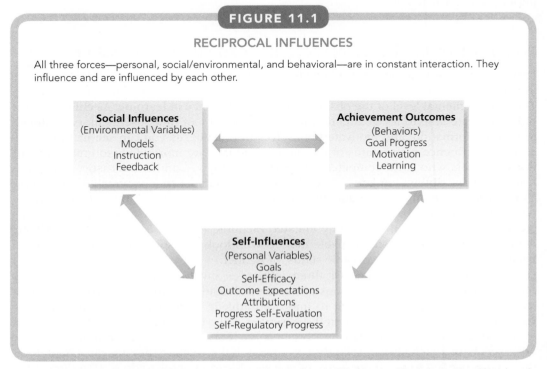

FIGURE 11.1

RECIPROCAL INFLUENCES

All three forces—personal, social/environmental, and behavioral—are in constant interaction. They influence and are influenced by each other.

Social Influences
(Environmental Variables)
Models
Instruction
Feedback

Achievement Outcomes
(Behaviors)
Goal Progress
Motivation
Learning

Self-Influences
(Personal Variables)
Goals
Self-Efficacy
Outcome Expectations
Attributions
Progress Self-Evaluation
Self-Regulatory Progress

Sources: From "Social-Self Interaction and Achievement Behavior" by D. H. Schunk, 1999, Educational Psychologist, 34, p. 221. Adapted with permission of Lawrence Erlbaum Associates, Inc. and the author.

Social cognitive theory Theory that adds concern with cognitive factors such as beliefs, self-perceptions, and expectations to social learning theory.

Triarchic reciprocal causality An explanation of behavior that emphasizes the mutual effects of the individual and the environment on each other.

instructional strategies, or teacher feedback (elements of the environment for students) can affect student personal factors such as goals, sense of efficacy for the task (described in the next section), attributions (beliefs about causes for success and failure), and processes of self-regulation such as planning, monitoring, and controlling distractions. For example, teacher feedback can lead students to feel either more confident or more discouraged, and then the students adjust their goals accordingly. Environmental and personal factors encourage behaviors such as effort and persistence that lead to learning. But these behaviors also reciprocally impact personal factors. For example, as students achieve through increased effort (behavior), their confidence and interest increase (personal). And behaviors also affect the social environment. For example, if students do not persist or if they seem to misunderstand, teachers may change instructional strategies or learning group assignments, thus changing the learning environment for the students.

Think for a minute about the power of reciprocal causality in classrooms. If personal factors, behaviors, and the environment are in constant interaction, then cycles of events are progressive and self-perpetuating. Suppose a student who is new to the school walks into class late because he got lost in the unfamiliar building. The student has a tattoo and several visible pierced body parts. He is anxious about his first day and hopes to do better at this new school, but the teacher's initial reaction to his late entry and dramatic appearance is a bit hostile. The student feels insulted and responds in kind, so the teacher begins to form expectations about him and acts more vigilant, less trusting. The student senses the distrust. He decides that this school will be just as worthless as his previous one—and wonders why he should bother to try. The teacher sees the student's disengagement, invests less effort in teaching him, and the cycle continues. These reciprocal effects are more than hypothetical. When Trevor and Kitty Williams (2010) examined data on high school students' confidence in mathematics and achievement in mathematics in 30 different countries, they found evidence that math confidence and math achievement reciprocally influenced each other in 26 of the countries, just as Bandura would predict.

Two key elements of social cognitive theory are observational learning and self-efficacy. We will examine each of these more closely, with special emphasis on their implications for teaching.

MODELING: LEARNING BY OBSERVING OTHERS

Learning by observing others is a key element of social cognitive theory. What causes an individual to learn and perform modeled behaviors and skills? Several factors play a role. The developmental level of the observer makes a difference in learning. As children grow older, they are able to focus attention for longer periods of time, use memory strategies to retain information, and motivate themselves to practice, as you can see in Table 11.1. A second influence is the status of the model. Children are more likely to imitate the actions of others who seem competent, powerful, prestigious, and enthusiastic, so parents, teachers, older siblings, athletes, action heroes, rock stars, or film personalities may serve as models, depending on the age and interests of the child. Third, by watching others, we learn about what behaviors are appropriate for people like ourselves, so models who are seen as similar are more readily imitated (Schunk, Pintrich, & Meece, 2008). All students need to see successful, capable models who look and sound like them, no matter what their ethnicity, socioeconomic status, or gender.

Look at Table 11.1. The last three influences involve goals and expectations. If observers expect that certain actions of models will lead to particular outcomes (such as specific practice regimens leading to improved athletic performance) and the observers value those outcomes or goals, then the observers will pay attention to the models and try to reproduce their behaviors. Finally, observers are more likely to learn from models if the observers have a high level of self-efficacy—that is, if they believe they are capable of doing the actions needed to reach the goals, or at least of learning how to do so (Bandura, 1997; Schunk, Pintrich, & Meece, 2008).

TABLE 11.1 • **Factors That Affect Observational Learning**

CHARACTERISTIC	EFFECTS ON MODELING PROCESS
Developmental Status	Improvements with development include longer attention and increased capacity to process information, use strategies, compare performances with memorial representations, and adopt intrinsic motivators.
Model Prestige and Competence	Observers pay greater attention to competent, high-status models. Consequences of modeled behaviors convey information about functional value. Observers attempt to learn actions they believe they will need to perform.
Vicarious Consequences	Consequences to models convey information about behavioral appropriateness and likely outcomes of actions. Valued consequences motivate observers. Similarity in attributes or competence signals appropriateness and heightens motivation.
Outcome Expectations	Observers are more likely to perform modeled actions they believe are appropriate and will result in rewarding outcomes.
Goal Setting	Observers are likely to attend to models who demonstrate behaviors that help observers attain goals.
Self-efficacy	Observers attend to models when they believe they are capable of learning or performing the modeled behavior. Observation of similar models affects self-efficacy ("If they can do it, I can too").

Source: From Learning Theories: An Education Perspective *(4th ed.), by D. H. Schunk. Published by Prentice Hall. Copyright © 2004 by Prentice Hall. Reprinted by permission of Pearson Education, Inc., Upper Saddle River, NJ.*

Elements of Observational Learning

STOP & THINK Your interview for a position in the middle school is going well. The next question is: "Who are your models as teachers? Do you hear yourself saying or see yourself doing things that other teachers have done? Are there teachers from films or books that you would like to emulate?" •

Through observational learning, we learn not only *how* to perform a behavior but also what will happen to us in specific situations if we perform it. Observation can be a very efficient learning process. The first time children hold hairbrushes, cups, or tennis rackets, they usually brush, drink, or swing as well as they can, given their current muscle development and coordination. Let's take a closer look at how observational learning occurs. Bandura (1986) notes that observational learning includes four elements: paying attention, retaining information or impressions, producing behaviors, and being motivated to repeat the behaviors.

ATTENTION. In order to learn through observation, we have to pay attention. In teaching, you will have to ensure students' attention to the critical features of the lesson by making clear presentations and highlighting important points. In demonstrating a skill (for example, threading a sewing machine or operating a lathe), you may need to have students look over your shoulder as you work. Seeing your hands from the same perspective as they see their own directs their attention to the right features of the situation and makes observational learning easier.

RETENTION. In order to imitate the behavior of a model, you have to remember it. This involves mentally representing the model's actions in some way, probably as verbal steps ("Hwa-Rang, the eighth form in Tae Kwan Do karate, is a palm-heel block, then a middle riding stance punch, then . . ."), or as visual images, or both. Retention can be improved by mental rehearsal (imagining imitating the behavior) or by actual practice. In the retention phase of observational learning, practice helps us remember the elements of the desired behavior, such as the sequence of steps.

PRODUCTION. Once we "know" how a behavior should look and remember the elements or steps, we still may not perform it smoothly. Sometimes, we need a great deal of practice, feedback, and coaching about subtle points before we can reproduce the behavior of the model. In the production phase, practice makes the behavior smoother and more expert.

MOTIVATION AND REINFORCEMENT. As you saw in Chapter 7, social learning theory distinguishes between acquisition and performance. We may acquire a new skill or behavior through observation, but we may not perform that behavior until there is some motivation or incentive to do so. Reinforcement can play several roles in observational learning. If we anticipate being reinforced for imitating the actions of a model, we may be more motivated to pay attention, remember, and reproduce the behaviors. In addition, reinforcement is important in maintaining learning. A person who tries a new behavior is unlikely to persist without reinforcement (Schunk, 2008). For example, if an unpopular student adopted the dress of the "in" group, but was ignored or ridiculed, it is unlikely that the imitation would continue.

Bandura identifies three forms of reinforcement that can encourage observational learning. First, of course, the observer may reproduce the behaviors of the model and receive direct reinforcement, as when a gymnast successfully executes a front flip/round-off combination and the coach/model says, "Excellent!"

But the reinforcement need not be direct—it may be **vicarious reinforcement**. The observer may simply see others reinforced for a particular behavior and then increase his or her production of that behavior. For example, if you compliment two students on the attractive illustrations in their lab reports, several other students who observe your compliments may turn in illustrated lab reports next time. Most TV ads hope for this kind of effect. People in commercials become deliriously happy when they drive a particular car or drink a specific energy drink, and the viewer is supposed to do the same; the viewer's behavior is reinforced vicariously by the actors' obvious pleasure. Punishment can also be vicarious: You may slow down on a stretch of highway after seeing several people get speeding tickets there.

The final form of reinforcement is **self-reinforcement**, or controlling your own reinforcers. This sort of reinforcement is important for both students and teachers. In fact, if one goal of education is to produce people who are capable of educating themselves, then students must learn to manage their own lives, set their own goals, and provide their own reinforcement. In adult life, rewards are sometimes vague and goals often take a long time to reach. Think about how many small steps are required to complete an education and find your first job. As a teacher, sometimes self-reinforcement is all that keeps you going. Life is filled with tasks that call for this sort of self-regulation—a topic we will address later in this chapter (Rachlin, 2004).

Social cognitive theory has some powerful implications for teaching. In this section, we will look more closely at using observational learning in teaching.

Observational Learning in Teaching

Vicarious reinforcement Increasing the chances that we will repeat a behavior by observing another person being reinforced for that behavior.

Self-reinforcement Controlling (selecting and administering) your own reinforcers.

STOP & THINK How would you incorporate observational learning into your teaching? What are the skills, attitudes, and strategies that can be modeled in teaching your subject? •

There are five possible outcomes of observational learning: directing attention, encouraging existing behaviors, changing inhibitions, teaching new behaviors and attitudes, and arousing emotions. Let's look at each of these as they occur in classrooms.

DIRECTING ATTENTION. By observing others, we not only learn about actions but also notice the objects involved in the actions. For example, in a preschool class, when one child plays enthusiastically with a toy that has been ignored for days, many other children may want to have the toy, even if they play with it in different ways or simply carry it around. This happens, in part, because the children's attention has been drawn to that particular toy.

FINE-TUNING ALREADY-LEARNED BEHAVIORS. All of us have had the experience of looking for cues from other people when we find ourselves in unfamiliar situations. Observing the behavior of others tells us which of our already-learned behaviors to use: the proper fork for eating the salad, when to leave a gathering, what kind of language is appropriate, and so on. Adopting the dress and grooming styles of TV or music idols is another example of this kind of effect.

STRENGTHENING OR WEAKENING INHIBITIONS. If class members witness one student breaking a class rule and getting away with it, they may learn that undesirable consequences do not always follow rule breaking. If the rule breaker is a well-liked, high-status class leader, the effect of the modeling may be even more pronounced. This **ripple effect** (Kounin, 1970) can work for the teacher's benefit. When the teacher deals effectively with a rule breaker, especially a class leader, the idea of breaking this rule may be inhibited for the other students viewing the interaction. This does not mean that teachers must reprimand each student who breaks a rule, but once a teacher has called for a particular action, following through is an important part of capitalizing on the ripple effect.

TEACHING NEW BEHAVIORS. Modeling has long been used, of course, to teach dance, sports, and crafts, as well as skills in subjects such as food science, chemistry, and welding. Modeling can also be applied deliberately in the classroom to teach mental skills and to broaden horizons—to teach new ways of thinking. Teachers serve as models for a vast range of behaviors, from pronouncing vocabulary words, to reacting to the seizure of a student with epilepsy, to being enthusiastic about learning. For example, a teacher might model critical thinking skills by thinking "out loud" about a student's question. Or a high school teacher concerned about girls who seem to have stereotyped ideas about careers might invite women with nontraditional jobs to speak to the class. Studies indicate that modeling can be most effective when the teacher makes use of all the elements of observational learning—attention, retention, production, and especially reinforcement and practice.

Models who are the same age as the students may be particularly effective. For example, Schunk and Hanson (1985) compared two methods for teaching subtraction to 2nd graders who had difficulties learning this skill. One group of students observed other 2nd graders learning the procedures, while another group watched a teacher's demonstration. Then, both groups participated in the same instructional program. The students who observed peer models learning not only scored higher on tests of subtraction after instruction but also gained more confidence in their own ability to learn. For students who doubt their own abilities, a good model is a low-achieving peer who keeps trying and finally masters the material (Schunk, 2004).

Connect and Extend to PRAXIS II™

Observational Learning (II, B2)
Identify situations in which observational learning may be a wise approach, and describe the essential elements of effective observational learning.

Ripple effect "Contagious" spreading of behaviors through imitation.

DO AS I DO . . . Modeling has long been used to teach dance, sports, and crafts, and skills such cooking, chemistry, and welding. Modeling can also be applied deliberately in the classroom to teach mental skills and to broaden horizons—to teach new ways of thinking.

GUIDELINES

Using Observational Learning

Model behaviors and attitudes you want your students to learn.
Examples

1. Show enthusiasm for the subject you teach.
2. Be willing to demonstrate both the mental and the physical tasks you expect the students to perform. I once saw a teacher sit down in the sandbox while her 4-year-old students watched her demonstrate the difference between "playing with sand" and "throwing sand."
3. When reading to students, model good problem solving. Stop and say, "Now let me see if I remember what happened so far," or "That was a hard sentence. I'm going to read it again."
4. Model good problem solving—think out loud as you work through a difficult problem.

Use peers, especially class leaders, as models.
Examples

1. In group work, pair students who do well with those who are having difficulties.
2. Ask students to demonstrate the difference between "whispering" and "silence—no talking."

Make sure students see that positive behaviors lead to reinforcement for others.
Examples

1. Point out the connections between positive behavior and positive consequences in stories.
2. Be fair in giving reinforcement. The same rules for rewards should apply to both the students with problems and the students who do not cause trouble.

Enlist the help of class leaders in modeling behaviors for the entire class.
Examples

1. Ask a well-liked student to be friendly to an isolated, fearful student.
2. Let high-status students lead an activity when you need class cooperation or when students are likely to be reluctant at first. Popular students can model dialogues in foreign-language classes or be the first to tackle dissection procedures in biology.

For more information on observational learning, see: http://www.readwritethink.org/lessons/lesson_view.asp?id=275

AROUSING EMOTION. Finally, through observational learning, people may develop emotional reactions to situations they have never experienced personally, such as flying or driving. A child who watches a friend fall from a swing and break an arm may become fearful of swings. After the terrible events of September 11, 2001, children may be anxious when they see airplanes flying close to the ground. News reports of shark attacks have many of us anxious about swimming in the ocean. Note that hearing and reading about a situation are also forms of observation. Some terrible examples of modeling occur with "copy-cat killings" or suicide clusters in schools. When frightening things happen to people who are similar in age or circumstances to your students, they may need to be given an opportunity to talk about their emotions.

The *Guidelines* will give you some ideas about using observational learning in the classroom.

Self-efficacy is a key element of social cognitive theory that is especially important in learning and teaching.

SELF-EFFICACY AND AGENCY

Self-efficacy A person's sense of being able to deal effectively with a particular task.

Human agency The capacity to coordinate learning skills, motivation, and emotions to reach your goals.

Bandura (1986, 1994, 1997) suggests that predictions about possible outcomes of behavior are critical for learning because they affect goals, effort, persistence, strategies, and resilience. "Will I succeed or fail? Will I be liked or laughed at?" "Will I be more accepted by teachers in this new school?" These predictions are affected by **self-efficacy**—our beliefs about our personal competence or effectiveness in a given area. Bandura (1994) defines self-efficacy as "people's beliefs about their capabilities to produce designated levels of performance that exercise influence over events that affect their lives" (p. 71).

Bandura's more recent efforts (2006) and the work of many other researchers have focused on the role of self-efficacy in **human agency**—the *exercising influence over life events* part of the definition above. Agency involves the ability to make intentional choices and action plans, design appropriate courses of action, and then motivate and regulate the execution of these plans and actions. When we discuss self-regulation later in the chapter, you will see how students and teachers can become more *agentic*—more self-directing and in charge of their own learning and motivation.

Self-Efficacy, Self-Concept, and Self-Esteem

Most people assume self-efficacy is the same as self-concept or self-esteem, but it isn't. *Self-efficacy* is future-oriented, "a context-specific assessment of competence to perform a specific task" (Pajares, 1997, p. 15). *Self-concept* is a more global construct that contains many perceptions about the self, including self-efficacy. Self-concept is developed as a result of external and internal comparisons, using other people or other aspects of the self as frames of reference. But self-efficacy focuses on your ability to successfully accomplish a particular task with no need for comparisons—the question is whether *you* can do it, not whether others would be successful. Also, self-efficacy beliefs are strong predictors of behavior, but self-concept has weaker predictive power (Anderman & Anderman, 2009; Bandura, 1997).

Self-efficacy is "context specific," which means it varies, depending on the subject or task. For example, my sense of efficacy for singing is really low, but I feel confident in my ability to read a map and navigate (except in certain cities that are hopeless). Even young students have different efficacy beliefs for different tasks. One study found that by the 1st grade, students already differentiated among their sense of efficacy for reading, for writing, and for spelling (Wilson & Trainin, 2007).

Self-efficacy is concerned with judgments of personal competence; self-esteem is concerned with judgments of self-worth. There is no direct relationship between self-esteem and self-efficacy. It is possible to feel highly efficacious in one area and still not have a high level of self-esteem, or vice versa (Valentine, DuBois, & Cooper, 2004). For example, as I confessed earlier, I have very low self-efficacy for singing, but my self-esteem is not affected, probably because my life does not require singing. But if my self-efficacy for teaching a particular class started dropping after several bad experiences, I know my self-esteem would suffer because I value teaching.

CAN I DO IT? Self-efficacy refers to the knowledge of one's own ability to successfully accomplish a particular task with no need for comparisons with others' ability—the question is "Can I do it?" not "Are others better than I am?"

Connect and Extend to PRAXIS II™

Modeling (II, B2)
Teachers often utilize modeling to teach students new behaviors. Identify the characteristics that tend to make models effective in instructional context.

Sources of Self-Efficacy

Bandura identified four sources of self-efficacy expectations: mastery experiences, physiological and emotional arousal, vicarious experiences, and social persuasion. **Mastery experiences** are our own direct experiences—usually the most powerful source of efficacy information. Successes raise efficacy beliefs, while failures lower efficacy. Level of **arousal** affects self-efficacy, depending on how the arousal is interpreted. As you face the task, are you anxious and worried (lowers efficacy) or excited and "psyched" (raises efficacy) (Bandura, 1997; Schunk, Pintrich, & Meece, 2008; Usher & Pajares, 2009)?

In **vicarious experiences**, someone else models accomplishments. The more closely the student identifies with the model, the greater the impact on self-efficacy will be. When the model performs well, the student's efficacy is enhanced, but when the model performs poorly, efficacy expectations decrease. Although mastery experiences generally are acknowledged as the most influential source of efficacy beliefs in adults, Keyser and Barling (1981) found that children (6th graders in their study) rely more on **modeling** as a source of self-efficacy information.

Social persuasion can be a "pep talk" or specific performance feedback. Social persuasion alone can't create enduring increases in self-efficacy, but a persuasive boost in self-efficacy can lead a student to make an effort, attempt new strategies, or try hard enough to succeed (Bandura, 1982). Social persuasion can counter occasional setbacks that might have instilled self-doubt and interrupted persistence. The potency of persuasion depends on the credibility, trustworthiness, and expertise of the persuader (Bandura, 1997). Table 11.2 summarizes the sources of self-efficacy.

Self-Efficacy in Learning and Teaching

STOP & THINK On a scale from 1 to 100, how confident are you that you will finish reading this chapter today? •

Let's assume your sense of efficacy is around 90 for completing this chapter. Greater efficacy leads to greater effort and persistence in the face of setbacks, so even if you are interrupted in your reading, you are likely to return to the task. I believe I can finish writing this section today, so I have resumed work on it after my computer crashed and I had to start over on several pages. Of course, that could make for a late night, because I am going to a San Francisco Giants baseball game at 7:00 tonight and may have to finish the section after the game.

Self-efficacy also influences motivation through goal setting. If we have a high sense of efficacy in a given area, we will set higher goals, be less afraid of failure, and find new strategies when old ones fail. If your sense of efficacy for reading this chapter is high, you are likely to set high goals for completing the chapter—maybe you will take some notes,

Mastery experiences Our own direct experiences—the most powerful source of efficacy information.

Arousal Physical and psychological reactions causing a person to feel alert, excited, or tense.

Vicarious experiences Accomplishments that are modeled by someone else.

Modeling Changes in behavior, thinking, or emotions that happen through observing another person—a model.

Social persuasion A "pep talk" or specific performance feedback—one source of self-efficacy.

TABLE 11.2 • **Sources of Self-Efficacy**

SOURCE	EXAMPLE
Mastery Experiences	Past successes and failures in similar situations, as perceived by the individual. To increase efficacy, the success must be attributed to the ability, effort, choices, and strategies of the individual—not to luck or extensive help from others.
Vicarious Experiences	Seeing other people like you succeed on a task or reach a goal that is similar to the one you face.
Social Persuasion	Encouragement, informational feedback, useful guidance from a trusted source.
Physiological Arousal	Positive or negative arousal—excitement and a feeling of being "psyched" and ready (increases efficacy) or a sense of anxiety and foreboding (decreases efficacy).

GUIDELINES

Encouraging Self-Efficacy

Emphasize students' progress in a particular area.
Examples
1. Return to earlier material in reviews and show how "easy" it is now.
2. Encourage students to improve projects when they have learned more.
3. Keep examples of particularly good work in portfolios.

Set learning goals for your students, and model a mastery orientation for them.
Examples
1. Recognize progress and improvement.
2. Share examples of how you have developed your abilities in a given area and provide other models of achievement who are similar to your students—no supermen or superwomen whose accomplishments seem unattainable.
3. Read stories about students who overcame physical, mental, or economic challenges.
4. Don't excuse failure because a student has problems outside school. Help the student succeed inside school.

Make specific suggestions for improvement, and revise grades when improvements are made.
Examples
1. Return work with comments noting what the students did right, what they did wrong, and why they might have made the mistakes.
2. Experiment with peer editing.
3. Show students how their revised, higher grade reflects greater competence and raises their class average.

Stress connections between past efforts and past accomplishments.
Examples
1. Have individual goal-setting and goal-review conferences with students, in which you ask students to reflect on how they solved difficult problems.
2. Confront self-defeating, failure-avoiding strategies directly.

For more information on self-efficacy, see:
http://www.emory.edu/EDUCATION/mfp/self-efficacy.html

too. If your sense of efficacy is low, however, you may avoid the reading altogether or give up easily when problems arise or you are interrupted with a better offer (Bandura, 1993, 1997; Pajares & Schunk, 2001). See the *Guidelines* for ideas about encouraging self-efficacy.

What is the most motivating level of efficacy? Should students be accurate, optimistic, or pessimistic in their predictions? There is evidence that a higher sense of self-efficacy supports motivation, even when the efficacy is an overestimation. Children and adults who are optimistic about the future are more mentally and physically healthy, less depressed, and more motivated to achieve (Flammer, 1995; Seligman, 2006). After examining almost 140 studies of motivation, Sandra Graham concluded that these qualities characterize many African Americans. She found that the African Americans studied had strong self-concepts and high expectations, even in the face of difficulties (Graham, 1994, 1995).

As you might expect, there are dangers in underestimating abilities because then students are more likely to put out a weak effort and give up easily. But there are dangers in continually overestimating performance as well. Students who think that they are better readers than they actually are may not be motivated to go back and repair misunderstandings as they read. They don't discover that they did not really understand the material until it is too late (Pintrich & Zusho, 2002).

In schools, we are particularly interested in self-efficacy for learning mathematics, writing, history, science, sports, and other subjects, as well as self-efficacy for using learning strategies and for the many other challenges that classrooms present. For example, in research with students, self-efficacy is related to writing and math performance for students from 3rd grade through high school (Fast et al., 2010; Kenney-Benson, Pomerantz, Ryan, & Patrick, 2006; Pajares, 2002), life satisfaction for adolescents (Vecchio, Gerbino, Pastorelli, Del Bove, & Caprara, 2007), use of deep processing learning strategies for college students (Prat-Sala & Redford, 2010), choice of college major (Pajares, 2002), and performance in college for older students (Elias & MacDonald, 2007). The value of self-efficacy seems to be cross-cultural. For example, self-efficacy is related to math/science goals and interests for Mexican American youth (Navarro, Flores, & Worthington, 2007), academic achievement in math for both male and female middle-school students (Kenney-Benson, Pomerantz, Ryan, & Patrick, 2006), and mathematics achievement for both Anglo and South Asian Canadian middle-school students (Klassen, 2004).

So, maybe you are thinking, sure higher self-efficacy is related to higher achievement because students who have more ability have higher self-efficacy. But these relationships between self-efficacy and achievement hold even when we take ability into account. For example, when students with the same ability in math are compared, the ones with higher self-efficacy for math perform better in math (Wigfield & Wentzel, 2007).

Research indicates that performance in school is improved and self-efficacy is increased when students (a) adopt short-term goals so it is easier to judge progress; (b) are taught to use specific learning strategies such as outlining or summarizing that help them focus attention; and (c) receive rewards based on achievement, not just engagement, because achievement rewards signal increasing competence (Graham & Weiner, 1996).

Teachers' Sense of Efficacy

You saw in Chapter 1 that much of my own research has focused on **teachers' sense of efficacy**, defined as a teacher's belief that he or she can reach even difficult students to help them learn. This confident belief appears to be one of the few personal characteristics of teachers that predict student achievement (Tschannen-Moran & Woolfolk Hoy, 2001; Tschannen-Moran, Woolfolk Hoy, & Hoy, 1998; Woolfolk Hoy & Burke-Spero, 2005; Woolfolk Hoy, Hoy, & Davis, 2009). As with any kind of efficacy, there may be both benefits and dangers in overestimating abilities. Optimistic teachers probably set higher goals, work harder, reteach when necessary, and persist in the face of problems. But some benefits might follow from having doubts about your efficacy. The *Point/Counterpoint* looks at both sides of teachers' efficacy judgments.

It takes self-efficacy to be self-regulated. We turn to this issue next to explore how you can help your students lead a self-directed life.

Teachers' sense of efficacy A teacher's belief that he or she can reach even the most difficult students and help them learn.

TEACHER SELF-EFFICACY Research shows that teachers' sense of efficacy grows from real success with students. Experience or training that helps teachers succeed in the day-to-day tasks of teaching will contribute to their sense of efficacy.

POINT/COUNTERPOINT: Are High Levels of Teacher Efficacy Beneficial?

Based on Bandura's research on self-efficacy, we probably would assume that high sense of efficacy for teachers is a good thing. But not everyone agrees. Here is the debate.

▶ **Higher efficacy is better than lower.** The research on teachers' sense of efficacy points to many positive outcomes related to higher efficacy. With my husband and a colleague, I summarized this research (Woolfolk Hoy, Hoy, & Davis, 2009). Here are a few of the findings we identified. Teachers with a strong sense of efficacy tend be more enthusiastic and spend more time teaching in subject areas where their sense of efficacy is higher, and they tend to avoid subjects when efficacy is lower. Teachers with higher efficacy judgments tend to be more open to new ideas; more willing to experiment with new methods to better meet the needs of their students; more likely to use powerful but potentially difficult-to-manage methods such as inquiry and small-group work; and less likely to use easy-to-adopt but weaker methods such as lectures. Higher efficacy teachers are less likely to criticize students and more persistent in following up on incorrect student answers. Teachers with a higher sense of efficacy tend to select strategies that support student learning rather than those that simply cover the curriculum. Compared to low efficacy teachers, those who report a higher sense of efficacy tend to be more active in monitoring seatwork and maintaining academic focus, and they respond quickly to student misbehavior by redirecting attention without showing anger or becoming threatened. What about the students? In addition to being related to student achievement, teachers' sense of efficacy has been associated with other student outcomes such as motivation and students' own sense of efficacy.

▶ **There are problems with high efficacy.** In spite of the large body of literature describing positive outcomes associated with higher self-efficacy, several researchers have questioned whether higher is always better. For example, Karl Wheatley (2002, 2005) suggested that several forms of teacher self-efficacy might be problematic. One is the excessive optimism of beginning teachers that interferes with their ability to accurately judge their own effectiveness. In an analysis of students who were about to begin their student teaching, Carol Weinstein (1988) found a strong sense of "unrealistic optimism"—the tendency to believe that problems experienced by others would not happen to them. Interestingly, the unrealistic optimism was greatest for activities having to do with controlling students (e.g., maintaining discipline, and establishing and enforcing class rules). These findings are consistent with Emmer and Hickman's (1991) observations that student teachers who had trouble managing their classes still reported high levels of classroom management efficacy. Another problematic consequence of higher efficacy is resistance to acquiring new knowledge and skills and a tendency to "stick with what works"—with the ways of teaching that have provided the sense of mastery in the past. Overconfident efficacy may quickly be followed by giving up if the task proves more difficult than first thought. Wheatley (2002) believes "lower efficacy beliefs are essential for teacher learning; doubt motivates change" (p. 18).

Beyond Either/Or. It is true that persistent high efficacy perceptions in the face of poor performance (unrealistic optimism) can produce avoidance rather than action and interfere with teacher learning, but I believe that a sense of *efficacy for learning to teach* would be necessary to respond in these positive ways to the doubts described above. The challenge is to develop an authentic sense of self-efficacy—one that is accurate or just a bit optimistic.

SELF-REGULATED LEARNING

As you may remember from the beginning of this chapter, Albert Bandura said his early education in a tiny school in Canada had given him self-regulation skills that lasted a lifetime. He also noted:

> A major goal of formal education is to equip students with the intellectual tools, self-beliefs, and self-regulatory capabilities to educate themselves throughout their lifetime. The rapid pace of technological change and accelerated growth of knowledge are placing a premium on capability for self-directed learning. (Bandura, 2007, p. 10)

Today, people change jobs an average of seven times before they retire. Many of these career changes require new learning that must be self-initiated and self-directed (Martinez-Pons, 2002). Thus, one goal of teaching, as Bandura noted, should be to free students from the need for teachers, so the students can continue to learn independently throughout their lives. To continue learning independently throughout life, you must be self-regulated—what we refer to in conversations as a *self-starter*.

STOP & THINK Think about the class you are taking where you are using this textbook. On a 7-point scale—from 1 = *not at all true of me*, to 7 = *very true of me*—answer the following questions:

1. When I study for a test, I try to put together the information from class and from the book.
2. When I do homework, I try to remember what the teacher said in class so I can answer the questions correctly.
3. I know I will be able to learn the material for this class.
4. I expect to do well in this class.
5. I ask myself questions to make sure I know the material I have been studying.
6. Even when study materials are dull and uninteresting, I keep working until I finish. •

You have just answered six items from the Motivated Strategies for Learning Questionnaire (MSLQ) (Midgley, et al., 1998; Pintrich & De Groot, 1990). This questionnaire has been used in hundreds of studies to assess students' self-regulated learning and motivation. How did you do? The first two questions assess your use of *cognitive strategies*, like those we discussed in Chapter 9. The second two questions assess your *sense of efficacy* for this class. But the last two questions (5 and 6) specifically assess **self-regulation**, defined by Barry Zimmerman and Dale Schunk (2011) as the process we use to activate and sustain our thoughts, behaviors, and emotions in order to reach our goals. Bandura (2007) summarizes self-regulation as setting goals and mobilizing the efforts and resources needed to reach those goals. When the goals involve learning, we talk about *self-regulated learning* (Dinsmore, Alexander, & Loughlin, 2008). Self-regulated learners are "metacognitive, motived to learn, and strategic" (Perry & Rahim, 2011, p. 122).

Self-regulated learners have a combination of academic learning skills and self-control that makes learning easier, so they are more motivated; in other words, they have the skill and the will to learn (Murphy & Alexander, 2000; Schunk, 2005). Self-regulated learners transform their mental abilities, whatever they are, into academic skills and strategies (Zimmerman & Schunk, 2011). Many studies link strategy use to different measures of academic achievement, especially for middle-school and high school students (Fredricks et al., 2004). For younger students, self-regulation of attention and emotion are critical for learning and achieving in school (Valiente, Lemery-Chalfant, & Swanson, 2010).

What Influences Self-Regulation?

The concept of self-regulated learning integrates much of what is known about effective learning and motivation. As you can see from the processes described above, three factors influence skill and will: knowledge, motivation, and self-discipline or volition. In addition, there are developmental differences among students.

KNOWLEDGE. To be self-regulated learners, students need knowledge about themselves, the subject, the task, strategies for learning, and the contexts in which they will apply their learning. "Expert" students know about themselves and how they learn best. For example, they know their preferred learning approaches; what is easy and what is hard for them; how to cope with the difficult parts; what their interests and talents are; and how to use their strengths. These experts also know quite a bit about the subject being studied—and the more they know, the easier it is to learn more (Alexander, Schallert, & Reynolds, 2009). They probably understand that different learning tasks require different approaches on their part. A simple memory task, for example, might require a mnemonic strategy (see Chapter 8), whereas a complex comprehension task might be approached by means of concept maps of the key ideas (see Chapter 9). Also, these self-regulated learners know that learning is often difficult and knowledge is seldom absolute; there usually are different ways of looking at problems as well as different solutions (Greene, Muis, & Pieschl, 2010; Winne, 1995).

These expert students not only know what each task requires but also can apply the strategy needed. They can skim or read carefully. They can use memory strategies

Self-regulation Process of activating and sustaining thoughts, behaviors, and emotions in order to reach goals.

or reorganize the material. As they become more knowledgeable in a field, they apply many of these strategies automatically. In short, they have mastered a large, flexible repertoire of learning strategies (see Chapter 9). Finally, self-regulated learners think about the contexts in which they will apply their knowledge—when and where they will use their learning—so they can set motivating goals and connect present work to future accomplishments (Weinstein, 1994; Winne, 1995).

MOTIVATION. Self-regulated learners are motivated to learn (see Chapter 12). They find many tasks in school interesting because they value learning, not just performing well in the eyes of others. They believe their own intelligence and abilities are improvable. Even if they are not intrinsically motivated by a particular task, they are serious about getting the intended benefit from it. They focus their attention and other cognitive and emotional resources on the task at hand. They know why they are studying, so their actions and choices are self-determined and not controlled by others (Zimmerman, 2011). However, knowledge and motivation are not always enough. Self-regulated learners need volition or self-discipline. "Where motivation denotes commitment, volition denotes follow-through" (Corno, 1992, p. 72).

VOLITION. I am two months behind in this project. I have been writing almost all day, 6 days a week since last January. I am barely awake, but I want to keep writing because the deadline for this chapter is very near. I have knowledge and motivation, but to keep going I need a good dose of volition. **Volition** is an old-fashioned word for will-power. The more technical definition for volition is *protecting opportunities to reach goals*. Self-regulated learners know how to protect themselves from distractions—where to study, for example, so they are not interrupted. They know how to cope when they feel anxious, drowsy, or lazy (Corno, 2011; Snow, Corno, & Jackson, 1996). And they know what to do when they are tempted to stop working and have (another) cup of coffee—the temptation I'm facing now—that, and a beautiful San Francisco day that beckons me to pull weeds in the backyard (pulling weeds always looks appealing when I face a tough writing job— cleaning closets is a close second).

Volition is deliberate and effortful, but with practice it can become more automatic— a habit or a "work ethic" (Corno, 2011). William James knew this over 100 years ago. One of my favorite James quotes is about making volition a habit. He said: "do every day or two something for no other reason than that you would rather not do it, so that when the hour of dire need draws nigh, it may find you not unnerved and untrained to stand the test" (James, 1890, IV, p. 126).

Volition Will power; self-discipline; work styles that protect opportunities to reach goals by applying self-regulated learning.

Co-regulation A transitional phase during which students gradually appropriate self-regulated learning and skills through modeling, direct teaching, feedback, and coaching from teachers, parents, or peers.

Shared regulation Students working together to regulate each other through reminders, prompts, and other guidance.

DEVELOPMENT OF SELF-REGULATION. There are developmental differences in self-regulation. Self-regulation generally improves over time. In the early grades, girls may be better than boys in self-regulation (Greene, Muis, & Pieschl, 2010; Matthews, Ponitz, & Morrison, 2009).

How do students develop knowledge, motivation, and volition? Two social processes support the development of self-regulation: co-regulation and shared regulation. **Co-regulation** is a transitional phase during which students gradually appropriate self-regulated learning and skills through modeling, direct teaching, feedback, and coaching from teachers, parents, or peers. **Shared regulation** happens when students work together to regulate each other through reminders, prompts, and other guidance.

What does self-regulation look like when it has developed? Let's examine some models.

THE SKILL AND THE WILL Self-regulated learners have a combination of academic learning skills and self-control that makes learning easier; they have the *skill* and the *will* to learn.

Models of Self-Regulated Learning and Agency

Albert Bandura may have gone from high-school graduate to professor at Stanford in 6 years using his self-regulated learning knowledge and skills, but not all of your students will be Banduras with established *habits of volition*. In fact, some psychologists suggest that you think of this capacity as one of many characteristics that distinguish individuals (Snow, Corno, & Jackson, 1996). Some students are much better at it than others. How can you help more students become self-regulated learners in school? What is involved in being self-regulated?

Theoretical models of **self-regulated learning** describe how learners—like you!—set goals and mobilize the efforts and resources needed to reach those goals. There are several models of self-regulated learning, but all agree that the cognitive processes needed for self-regulated learning require effort (Greene, Muis, & Pieschl, 2010; Puustinen & Pulkkinen, 2001; Winne, 2011). Let's look at one developed by Phil Winne and Allyson Hadwin (1998), shown in Figure 11.2. This depiction of self-regulated learning has many facets, as it should when the topic at hand is how you manage your academic life.

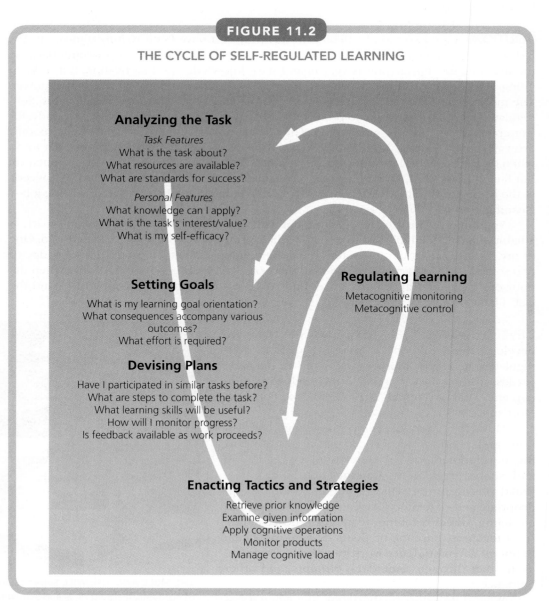

FIGURE 11.2

THE CYCLE OF SELF-REGULATED LEARNING

Analyzing the Task

Task Features
What is the task about?
What resources are available?
What are standards for success?

Personal Features
What knowledge can I apply?
What is the task's interest/value?
What is my self-efficacy?

Setting Goals

What is my learning goal orientation?
What consequences accompany various outcomes?
What effort is required?

Devising Plans

Have I participated in similar tasks before?
What are steps to complete the task?
What learning skills will be useful?
How will I monitor progress?
Is feedback available as work proceeds?

Regulating Learning

Metacognitive monitoring
Metacognitive control

Enacting Tactics and Strategies

Retrieve prior knowledge
Examine given information
Apply cognitive operations
Monitor products
Manage cognitive load

Source: "The Cycle of Self-Regulated Learning" from Educational Psychology (3rd Canadian ed.) by A. E. Woolfolk, P. H. Winne, and N. E. Perry. Toronto: Pearson, 2006, p. 307, Fig 8.9. Adapted with permission of Pearson Education Canada and Philip Winne.

Self-regulated learning A view of learning as skills and will applied to analyzing learning tasks, setting goals and planning how to do the task, applying skills, and especially making adjustments about how learning is carried out.

The model of self-regulated learning in Figure 11.2 is based on the belief that learners are *agents*. As we saw earlier, agency is the capacity to coordinate learning skills, motivation, and emotions to reach your goals. Agents are not puppets on strings held by teachers, textbook authors, or Web page designers. Instead, agents control many factors that influence how they learn. Self-regulating learners exercise agency as they engage in a cycle with four main stages: analyzing the task, setting goals and devising plans, enacting strategies and regulating learning by making needed adjustments.

1. *Analyzing the learning task.* You are familiar with this stage of self-regulated learning. What do you do when a professor announces there will be a test? You ask about conditions you believe will influence how you'll study. Is it essay or multiple-choice? Is your best friend up to date on the material to be tested and available to study with you? In general, learners examine whatever information they think is relevant in order to construct a sense of what the task is about, what resources to bring to bear, and how they feel about the work to be done—are they interested? confident? anxious? knowledgeable? clueless?

2. *Setting goals and devising plans.* Knowing conditions that influence work on tasks provides information that learners use to create goals for learning. Then, plans can be developed about how to reach those goals. What goals for studying might you set for a quiz covering only one chapter that counts just 3% toward your course grade? Would your goals change if the test covered the last six chapters and counted 30% toward your course grade? What targets are identified in these goals—repeating definitions, being able to discuss how a teacher could apply findings from key research studies described in the textbook, or critiquing theoretical positions? Choosing goals affects the shape of a learner's plans for how to study. Is practicing definitions the best approach? Is a better plan to create examples and applications of key concepts?

3. *Enacting strategies to accomplish the task.* In this phase, self-regulated learners consider what they know or need to know that will help them be successful with these strategies. They are especially alert as they enact their plan to monitor how well the plan is working. They ask themselves these questions: Is the cognitive load too great? Am I getting overwhelmed? What can I do to manage all this complex information? Is the approach I'm taking too effortful for the results I'm are achieving? Am I reaching my goals? Is my progress rate fast enough to be prepared for the test?

4. *Regulating learning.* This is metacognitive monitoring and control (see Chapter 9). In this phase, learners come to decisions about whether changes are needed in any of the three preceding phases. For example, if learning is slow, they ask these questions: Should I study with my best friend? Do I need to review some prior material that provides the foundation for the content I am now studying? Do I need to start over—identifying what the task really is and then setting new (higher, lower, different) goals?

An Individual Example of Self-Regulated Learning

Students today are faced with constant distractions. Barry Zimmerman (2002, p. 64) describes Tracy, a high-school student who is devoted to Facebook and Twitter:

> An important mid-term math exam is two weeks away, and she had begun to study while listening to popular music "to relax her." Tracy has not set any study goals for herself—instead she simply tells herself to do as well as she can on the test. She uses no specific learning strategies for condensing and memorizing important material and does not plan out her study time, so she ends up cramming for a few hours before the test. She has only vague self-evaluative standards and cannot gauge her academic preparation accurately. Tracy attributes her learning difficulties to an inherent lack of mathematical ability and is very defensive about her poor study methods. However, she does not ask for help from others because she is afraid of "looking stupid," or seek out supplementary materials from the library because she "already has too much to learn." She finds studying to be anxiety-provoking, has little self-confidence in achieving success, and sees little intrinsic value in acquiring mathematical skill.

Clearly, Tracy is unlikely to do well on the test. What would help? For an answer, let's consider Zimmerman's cycle of self-regulated learning. His cycle has three phases—*forethought, performance, reflection*—and is consistent with the Winne and Hadwin model described above. In Zimmerman's phase 1, the *forethought phase* (like Winne and Hadwin's steps 1 and 2 of analyzing the task and setting goals), Tracy needs to set clear, reasonable goals and plan a few strategies for accomplishing those goals. And Tracy's beliefs about motivation make a difference at this point, too. If Tracy had a sense of self-efficacy for applying the strategies that she planned, if she believed that using those strategies would lead to math learning and success on the test, if she saw some connections between her own interests and the math learning, and if she were trying to master the material—not just look good or avoid looking bad—then she would be on the road to self-regulated learning.

Moving from forethought to Zimmerman's *performance phase* (similar to Winne and Hadwin's step 3 of enacting the strategies) brings new challenges. Now Tracy must have a repertoire of self-control (volitional) and learning strategies, including using imagery, mnemonics, attention focusing, and other techniques such as those described in Chapters 8 and 9 (Kiewra, 2002). She also will need to self-observe, that is, monitor how things are going so she can change strategies if needed. Actual recording of time spent, problems solved, or pages written may provide clues about when or how to make the best use of study time. Turning off the music would help, too.

Finally, Tracy needs to move to Zimmerman's phase 3 of *reflection* (similar to Winne and Hadwin's step 4 of regulating learning) by looking back on her performance and reflecting on what happened. It will help her develop a sense of efficacy if she attributes successes to effort and good strategy use and avoids self-defeating actions and beliefs such as making weak efforts, pretending not to care, or assuming she is "no good at math."

Both Zimmerman's and Winne and Hadwin's models emphasize the cyclical nature of self-regulated learning: Each phase flows into the next, and the cycle continues as students encounter new learning challenges. Both models begin with being informed about the task so you can set good goals. Having a repertoire of learning strategies and tactics also is necessary in both models. And self-monitoring of progress followed by modifying plans if needed are critical to both. Notice also that the way students think about the task and their ability to do it—their *sense of efficacy for self-regulation*—is key as well (Zimmerman, 2011).

Two Classrooms

Students differ in their self-regulation knowledge and skills. But teachers must work with an entire classroom, and still "reach every student." Here are two examples of real situations where teachers did just that. The first involves writing, the second math problem solving—both complex tasks.

WRITING.   Carol is a 2nd grade student described by Nancy Perry and Lynn Drummond (2002). Ms. Lynn was Carol's teacher; she characterizes Carol as "a very weak writer." Carol has difficulty finding facts and then transforming those facts into meaningful prose for a research report. Also, she has difficulty with the mechanics of writing, which, according to Ms. Lynn, "holds her back."

Over the course of the year, Ms. Lynn involved her grade 2 and 3 students in three projects about animals. Through this writing, she wanted students to learn how to: (a) do research, (b) write expository text, (c) edit and revise their writing, and (d) use the computer as a tool for researching and writing. For the first report, the class worked on one topic together (Chipmunks). They did the fact-finding and writing together, because Ms. Lynn needed to show them how to do research and write a report. Also, the class developed frameworks for working collaboratively as a community of learners. When they wrote the second report (on Penguins), Ms. Lynn offered students many more choices and encouraged them to depend more on themselves and one another. Finally, for the third report, students chose an animal, conducted a self-regulated research project, and wrote a report. Now that they knew how to do research and write a report, they could work alone or together and be successful at this complex task.

Carol worked with a student in grade 3 who was doing research on a related topic. He showed Carol how to use a table of contents, and offered advice about how to phrase ideas in her report. Also, Carol underlined words she thought were misspelled so she could check them later when she met with Ms. Lynn to edit her report. Unlike many low-achieving students who have not learned strategies for self-regulating learning, Carol was not afraid to attempt challenging tasks, and she was confident about her ability to develop as a writer. Reflecting on her progress across the school year, Carol said, "I learned a lot from when I was in grade 1 because I had a lot of trouble then."

MATH PROBLEM SOLVING. Lynn Fuchs and her colleagues (2003) assessed the value of incorporating self-regulated learning strategies into math problem-solving lessons in real classrooms. The researchers worked with 24 teachers. All of the teachers taught the same content in their 3rd grade classes. Some of these teachers (randomly chosen) taught in their usual way. Another randomly chosen group incorporated strategies to encourage problem-solving transfer—using skills and knowledge learned in the lessons to solve problems in other situations and classes. The third group of teachers added transfer and self-regulated learning strategies to their units on math problem solving. Here are a few of the transfer and self-regulated learning strategies that were taught:

- Using a key, students scored their homework and gave it to a homework collector (a peer).
- Students graphed their completion of homework on a class report.
- Students used individual thermometer graphs that were kept in folders to chart their daily scores on individual problems.
- At the beginning of each session, students inspected their previous charts and set goals to beat their previous scores.
- Students discussed with partners how they might apply problem-solving strategies outside class.
- Before some lessons, students reported to the group about how they had applied problem-solving skills outside class.

Both transfer and self-regulated learning strategies helped students learn mathematical problem solving and apply this knowledge to new problems. The addition of self-regulated learning strategies was especially effective when students were asked to solve problems that were very different from those they encountered in the lessons. Students at every achievement level as well as students with learning disabilities benefited from learning the strategies.

Technology and Self-Regulation

In the previous chapter, we saw some examples of using technology-rich environments to explore complex concepts. But to learn in these rich environments, students need metacognitive and self-regulatory skills so they won't get lost in a sea of information. If the concepts they are learning are challenging and complicated, then some scaffolding is needed to support the students' developing understandings (Azevedo, 2005; Azevedo, Johnson, Chauncey, & Graesser, 2011). For example, Roger Azevedo and his colleagues (2004) studied undergraduate students who were learning about the circulatory system using a hypermedia encyclopedia. The materials available to them included texts, diagrams, photographs, video clips, and animated examples of how the circulatory system works. There were three different learning conditions. One group of students was told just to learn all they could about the circulatory system. A second group got the same instructions, but, in addition, they had a list of 10 subgoals to guide their learning. The third group had the list of subgoals plus a self-regulation "coach," who helped them plan their learning, monitor their developing understanding, try different strategies, and handle problems when they arose. Students in all three conditions were asked to "think out loud" as they used the hypermedia materials—describing what they were thinking as they went through the materials. Students who had the support of a self-regulation coach who focused on task analysis, goal setting, using strategies, and monitoring progress developed more complete and complex mental models of the circulatory system.

Supporting Self-Regulation at Home and in School

Emphasize the value of encouragement.
Examples

1. Teach students to encourage each other.
2. Tell families about the areas that are most challenging for their child—those that will be the most in need of encouragement.

Model self-regulation.
Examples

1. Target small steps for improving an academic skill. Tailor goals to the student's current achievement level.
2. Discuss with your students how you set goals and monitor progress.
3. Ask parents and caregivers to show their children how they set goals for the day or week, write to-do lists, or keep appointment books.

Make families a source of good strategy ideas.
Examples

1. Have short, simple materials describing a "strategy of the month" that students can practice at home.

2. Create a lending library of books about goal setting, motivation, learning, and time-management strategies for students.
3. Encourage families to help their children focus on problem-solving processes and not turn immediately to the answers at the back of the book when doing homework.

Provide self-evaluation guidelines.
Examples

1. Develop rubrics for self-evaluation with students (see Chapter 15). Model how to use them.
2. Provide record-keeping sheets for assignments early in the year; then gradually have students develop their own.
3. Encourage parents and caregivers to model self-evaluation as they focus on areas they want to improve.
4. For family conferences, have examples of materials other families have successfully used to keep track of progress.

For more ideas to share with parents and caregivers, see: http://www.pbs.org/wholechild/parents/building.html

---

How could you provide this kind of self-regulation teaching and coaching for your students? Maybe peer coaches would be one way, or enlisting the help of families.

Reaching Every Student: Families and Self-Regulation

Children begin to learn self-regulation in their homes. Families can teach and support self-regulated learning through modeling, encouragement, facilitation, rewarding of goal setting, good strategy use, and other processes described in the next section (Martinez-Pons, 2002). The *Family and Community Partnerships Guidelines* give some ideas for helping students become more self-regulating.

Another Approach to Self-Regulation: Cognitive Behavior Modification

When some psychologists were studying a behavior modification approach called *self-management*—using reinforcement and punishment to manage your own behavior—Donald Meichenbaum (1977) was having success teaching impulsive students to "talk themselves through" tasks. Meichenbaum called his method *cognitive behavior modification* (Manning & Payne, 1996). **Cognitive behavior modification** focuses on self-talk to regulate behavior.

You may remember from Chapter 2 that there is a stage in cognitive development when young children seem to guide themselves through a task using private speech. They talk to themselves, often repeating the words of a parent or teacher. In cognitive behavior modification, students are taught directly how to use this **self-instruction**. Meichenbaum (1977) outlined the steps:

1. An adult model performs a task while talking to him- or herself out loud (cognitive modeling).
2. The child performs the same task under the direction of the model's instructions (overt, external guidance).

Cognitive behavior modification Procedures based on both behavioral and cognitive learning principles for changing your own behavior by using self-talk and self-instruction.

Self-instruction Talking oneself through the steps of a task.

SELF-REGULATION BEGINS AT HOME Parents can teach and support self-regulated learning through modeling, encouragement, facilitation, and rewarding of goal setting, in order to help children become more self-regulating.

3. The child performs the task while instructing him- or herself aloud (overt, self-guidance).
4. The child whispers the instructions to him- or herself as he/she goes through the task (faded, overt self-guidance).
5. The child performs the task while guiding his/her performance via private speech (covert self-instruction). (p. 32)

Brenda Manning and Beverly Payne (1996) list four skills that can increase student learning: listening, planning, working, and checking. How might cognitive self-instruction help students develop these skills? One possibility is to use personal booklets or class posters that prompt students to "talk to themselves" about these skills. For example, one 5th grade class designed a set of prompts for each of the four skills and posted the prompts around the classroom. The prompts for listening included "Does this make sense?" "Am I getting this?" "I need to ask a question now before I forget." "Pay attention!" "Can I do what he's saying to do?" Planning prompts were "Do I have everything together?" "Do I have my friends tuned out for right now?" "Let me get organized first." "What order will I do this in?" "I know this stuff!" Posters for these and the other two skills, working and checking, are shown in Figure 11.3 on the next page. Part of the power of this process is in getting students involved in thinking about and creating their own guides and prompts. Having the discussion and posting the ideas makes students more self-aware and in control of their own learning.

Actually, cognitive behavior modification as it is practiced by Meichenbaum and others has many more components than just teaching students to use self-instruction. Meichenbaum's methods also include dialogue and interaction between teacher and student, modeling, guided discovery, motivational strategies, feedback, careful matching of the task with the student's developmental level, and other principles of good teaching. The student is even involved in designing the program (Harris, 1990; Harris & Pressley, 1991). Given all this, it is no surprise that students seem to be able to generalize the skills developed with cognitive behavior modification to new learning situations (Harris, Graham, & Pressley, 1992).

Today, there are entire school intervention programs based on cognitive behavior modification. For example, the *Coping Power Program* includes training for both parents and their children, beginning in the last half of one academic year and continuing through the entire next school year. The training for students often focuses on anger and aggression. Different training sessions emphasize personal goal-setting, awareness of feelings

Connect and Extend to PRAXIS II™

Self-Regulation (II, A1)
Take a look at *The Learning Base* (http://www.allkindsofminds .org/library/challenges/ GTPSelfregulatingLearning.htm) for tips to help students develop the goals, metacognitive skills, and self-regulatory practices that can support a lifelong devotion to learning.

FIGURE 11.3

POSTERS TO REMIND STUDENTS TO "TALK THEMSELVES THROUGH"
LISTENING, PLANNING, WORKING, AND CHECKING IN SCHOOL

These four posters were designed by a 5th-grade class to help them remember to use self-instruction. Some of the reminders reflect the special world of these preadolescents.

Poster 1

While Listening:
1. Does this make sense?
2. Am I getting this?
3. I need to ask a question now before I forget.
4. Pay attention.
5. Can I do what he's saying to do?

Poster 3

While Working:
1. Am I working fast enough?
2. Stop staring at my girlfriend and get back to work.
3. How much time is left?
4. Do I need to stop and start over?
5. This is hard for me, but I can manage.

Poster 2

While Planning:
1. Do I have everything together?
2. Do I have my friends tuned out for right now?
3. Let me get organized first.
4. What order will I do this in?
5. I know this stuff!

Poster 4

While Checking:
1. Did I finish everything?
2. What do I need to recheck?
3. Am I proud of this work?
4. Did I write all the words? Count them.
5. I think I finished. I organized myself. Did I daydream too much?

Source: Manning M. Lee, Payne, Beverly D., *Self-Talk for Teachers and Students: Metacognitive Strategies for Personal and Classroom Use,* 1st edition, © 1994. Reprinted by permission of Pearson Education, Inc., Upper Saddle River, NJ.

(especially anger), learning to relax and change the focus away from the angry feelings, making coping self-statements, developing organizational and study skills, seeing the perspectives of others, developing social problem-solving skills, and dealing with peer pressure by practicing how to say no (Lochman & Wells, 2003). Another similar approach is *Tools for Getting Along* (Daunic, Smith, Brank, & Penfield, 2006). Both programs have been effective in helping aggressive middle-school students to "get along" with their classmates and teachers. In addition, in psychotherapy, tools based on cognitive behavior modification have proved to be some of the most effective ways of dealing with psychological problems such as depression.

Both the *Coping Power Program* and *Tools for Getting Along* include emotional self-regulation skills. We turn to this area of self-regulation next.

Emotional Self-Regulation

Social and emotional competences and self-regulation are critical for both academic and personal development. The Collaborative for Academic, Social, and Emotional Learning (CASEL) lists five core social and emotional skills and competencies:

- **Self-awareness**—accurately assessing your feelings, interests, values, and strengths; maintaining a well-grounded sense of self-confidence
- **Self-management**—regulating your emotions to handle stress, control impulses, and persevere in overcoming obstacles; setting and monitoring progress toward personal and academic goals; expressing emotions appropriately

- **Social awareness**—taking the perspective of and empathizing with others; recognizing and appreciating individual and group similarities and differences; recognizing and using family, school, and community resources
- **Relationship skills**—establishing and maintaining healthy and rewarding relationships based on cooperation; resisting inappropriate social pressure; preventing, managing, and resolving interpersonal conflict; seeking help when needed
- **Responsible decision-making**—making decisions based on consideration of ethical standards, safety concerns, appropriate social norms, respect for others, and likely consequences of various actions; applying decision-making skills to academic and social situations; contributing to the well-being of one's school and community (http://casel.org/why-it-matters/what-is-sel/skills-competencies/)

A number of studies that followed students over several years in the United States and in Italy have found that prosocial behaviors and social competence in the early grades are related to academic achievement and popularity with peers as many as five years later (Elias & Schwab, 2006). Developing emotional self-regulation is especially important in the early years when students are learning how to learn in schools. For example, Carlos Valiente and his colleagues (2010) followed almost 300 students through kindergarten to assess the relations between effortful self-control, emotionality, and academic achievement. They found that students' anger, sadness, and shyness were negatively related to achievement and that self-control was positively related to achievement, particularly for students who showed lower levels of negative emotions. So helping students develop emotional self-regulation can set them on a good path for learning in school, and probably can help them in social relations with their peers as well. How can teachers help students develop these skills? The *Guidelines* give some ideas.

GUIDELINES

Encouraging Emotional Self-Regulation

Create a climate of trust in your classroom.
Examples

1. Avoid listening to "tattle tale" stories about students.
2. Follow through with fair consequences.
3. Avoid unnecessary comparisons and give students opportunities to improve their work.

Help students recognize and express their feelings.
Examples

1. Provide a vocabulary of emotions and note descriptions of emotions in characters or stories.
2. Be clear and descriptive about your own emotions.
3. Encourage students to write in journals about their own feelings. Protect the privacy of these writings (see trust above).

Help students recognize emotions in others.
Examples

1. For young children, "Look at Chandra's face. How do you think she feels when you say those things?"
2. For older students, use readings, analysis of characters in literature, films, or role reversals to help them identify the emotions of others.

Provide strategies for coping with emotions.
Examples

1. Discuss or practice alternatives such as stopping to think how the other person feels, seeking help, and using anger management strategies such as self-talk or leaving the scene.
2. Model strategies for students. Talk about how you handle anger, disappointment, or anxiety.

Help students recognize cultural differences in emotional expression.
Examples

1. Have students write about or discuss how they show emotions in their family.
2. Teach students to "check it out"—ask the other people how they are feeling.

For ideas about promoting emotional competence, see http://casel.org/

TEACHING TOWARD SELF-EFFICACY AND SELF-REGULATED LEARNING

STOP & THINK How are you studying right now? What goals have you set for your reading today? What is your plan for learning, and what strategies are you using right now to learn? How did you learn those strategies? •

Most teachers agree that students need to develop skills and attitudes for independent, lifelong learning (*self-regulated learning* and a *sense of efficacy for learning*). Fortunately, there is a growing body of research that offers guidance about how to design tasks and structure classroom interactions to support students' development of and engagement in self-regulated learning (Neuman & Roskos, 1997; Perry, 1998; Sinatra & Taasoobshirazi, 2011; Stoeger & Ziegler, 2011; Wharton-McDonald et al., 1997; Zimmerman & Schunk, 2011). This research indicates that students develop academically effective forms of self-regulated learning (SRL) and a sense of efficacy for learning when teachers involve them in *complex meaningful tasks* that extend over *long periods of time*, much like the constructivist activities described in Chapter 10. Also, to develop self-regulated learning and self-efficacy for learning, students need to have some *control over their learning processes and products*—they need to make choices about what to work on, where, and with whom. They also need to have *control over the difficulty* of the task—how much to read or write, at what pace, and with what level of support. And because self-monitoring and self-evaluation are key to effective SRL and a sense of efficacy, teachers can help students develop SRL by involving them in *setting criteria* for evaluating their learning processes and products, and then giving them opportunities to *reflect* on and make judgments about their progress using those standards. It helps to work in *collaboration* with peers and seek feedback from them. As you saw earlier, this has been called *shared regulation*. Throughout the entire process, teachers must *co-regulate* the task by "providing just enough and just in time information and support to facilitate students' acquisition and application of SRL" (Perry & Rahim, 2011, p. 130). Let's examine each of these more closely.

Complex Tasks

Teachers don't want to assign students tasks that are too difficult and that lead to frustration. This is especially true when students have learning difficulties or disabilities. In fact, research indicates that the most motivating and academically beneficial tasks for students are those that challenge, but don't overwhelm them (Rohrkemper & Corno, 1988; Turner, 1997); complex tasks need not be overly difficult for students.

The term *complex* refers to the design of tasks, not their level of difficulty. From a design point of view, tasks are complex when they address multiple goals and involve large chunks of meaning—for example, projects and thematic units. Furthermore, complex tasks extend over long periods of time, engage students in a variety of cognitive and metacognitive processes, and allow for the production of a wide range of products (Perry, VandeKamp, Mercer, & Nordby, 2002; Wharton-McDonald et al., 1997). For example, a study of Egyptian pyramids might result in the production of written reports, maps, diagrams, skits, and models.

Even more important, complex tasks provide students with information about their learning progress. These tasks require them to engage in deep, elaborative thinking and problem solving. In the process, students develop and refine their cognitive and metacognitive strategies. Furthermore, succeeding at such tasks increases students' self-efficacy and intrinsic motivation (McCaslin & Good, 1996; Turner, 1997). Rohrkemper and Corno (1988) advised teachers to design complex tasks that provide opportunities for students to modify the learning conditions in order to cope with challenging problems. Learning to cope with stressful situations and make adaptations is an important educational goal. Remember from Chapter 4, that according to Sternberg, one aspect of intelligence is choosing or adapting environments so that you can succeed.

Control

Teachers can share control with students by giving them choices. When students have choices (e.g., about what to produce, how to produce it, where to work, whom to work with), they are more likely to anticipate a successful outcome (increased self-efficacy) and consequently increase effort and persist when difficulty arises (Turner & Paris, 1995). Also, by involving students in making decisions, teachers invite them to take responsibility for learning by planning, setting goals, monitoring progress, and evaluating outcomes (Turner, 1997). These are qualities of highly effective, self-regulating learners.

Giving students choices creates opportunities for them to adjust the level of challenge that particular tasks present (e.g., they can choose easy or more challenging reading materials, determine the nature and amount of writing in a report, supplement writing with other expressions of learning). But what if students make poor academic choices? Highly effective, high-SRL teachers carefully consider the choices they give to students. They make sure students have the knowledge and skills they need to operate independently and make good decisions (Perry & Rahim, 2011). For example, when students are learning new skills or routines, teachers can offer choices with constraints (e.g., students must write a minimum of four sentences/paragraphs/pages, but they can choose to write more; they must demonstrate their understanding of an animal's habitat, food, and babies, but they can write, draw, or speak their knowledge).

Highly effective teachers also teach and model good decision making. For example, when students are choosing partners, teachers can ask them to consider what they need from their partner (e.g., shared interest and commitment, perhaps knowledge or skills that they need to develop). When students are making choices about how best to use their time, these teachers ask, "What can you do when you're finished? What can you do if you are waiting for my help?" Often, lists are generated and posted, so students can refer to them while they work. Finally, highly effective teachers give students feedback about the choices they make and tailor the choices they give to suit the unique characteristics of particular learners. For example, they might encourage some students to select research topics for which resources are readily available and written at a level that is accessible to the learner. Alternatively, they might encourage some students to work collaboratively versus independently to ensure they have the support and shared regulation they need to be successful.

DEVELOPING STUDENT CONTROL In order to develop self-regulated learning and self-efficacy for learning, students need to have some control over their learning processes and products; teachers can help by involving students in evaluating their learning processes, products, and progress.

Self-Evaluation

Evaluation practices that support SRL are nonthreatening. They are embedded in ongoing activities, emphasize process as well as products, focus on personal progress, and help students to interpret errors as opportunities for learning to occur. In these contexts, students enjoy and actually seek challenging tasks because the cost of participation is low (Paris & Ayres, 1994). Involving students in generating evaluation criteria and evaluating their own work also reduces the anxiety that often accompanies assessment by giving students a sense of control over the outcome. Students can judge their work in relation to a set of qualities both they and their teachers identify as "good" work. They can consider the effectiveness of their approaches to learning and alter their behaviors in ways that enhance it (Winne, 2011; Winne & Perry, 2000).

In high-SRL classrooms, there are both formal and informal opportunities for students to evaluate their learning. For example, one student teacher asked 4th- and 5th-grade students to submit reflections journals describing the games they designed with a partner or small group of collaborators for a probability and statistics unit (Perry, Phillips, & Dowler, 2004). Their journals explained their contribution to the group's process and product, and described what they learned from participating. The student teacher took these reflections into account when she evaluated the games. More informally, teachers ask students "What have you learned about yourself as a writer today?" "What do good researchers and writers do?" "What can we do that we couldn't do before?" Questions like these, posed to individuals or embedded in class discussions, prompt students' metacognition, motivation, and strategic action—the components of SRL.

Collaboration

The Committee on Increasing High School Students' Motivation to Learn (2004) concluded that when students can put their heads together, they are more receptive to challenging assignments—the very kind of complex task that develops self-regulation. The Committee added:

> Collaborative work also can help students develop skills in cooperation. Furthermore, it helps create a community of learners who have responsibility for each other's learning, rather than a competitive environment, which is alienating to many students, particularly those who do not perform as well as their classmates. (p. 51)

The most effective uses of cooperative/collaborative relationships to support SRL are those that reflect a climate of community and shared problem solving (Perry & Drummond, 2002; Perry, VandeKamp, Mercer, & Nordby, 2002). In these contexts, teachers and students actually co-regulate one another's learning (McCaslin & Good, 1996), offering support, whether working alone, in pairs, or small groups. This support is instrumental to individuals' development and use of metacognition, intrinsic motivation, and strategic action (e.g., sharing ideas, comparing strategies for solving problems, identifying everyone's area of expertise). High-SRL teachers spend time at the start of each school year teaching routines and establishing norms of participation (e.g., how to give constructive feedback and how to interpret and respond to peers' suggestions). As you will see in Chapter 13, developing useful management and learning procedures and routines takes time at the beginning of the year, but it is time well spent. Once routines and patterns of interaction are established, students can focus on learning and teachers can attend to teaching academic skills and the curriculum.

BRINGING IT ALL TOGETHER: THEORIES OF LEARNING

How can we make sense of the diversity in perspectives on learning we have explored for the last four chapters? We have considered behavioral, cognitive, constructivist (individual and social), and social cognitive explanations of what people learn and how they learn it. Table 11.3 presents a summary of several of these perspectives on learning.

TABLE 11.3 • **Four Views of Learning**

There are variations within each of these views of learning and overlaps as well, especially in constructivist views.

	BEHAVIORAL	COGNITIVE	CONSTRUCTIVIST		SOCIAL COGNITIVE
	Applied Behavioral Analysis *B. F. Skinner*	Information Processing *J. Anderson*	Individual *Jean Piaget*	Social/Situated *Lev Vygotsky*	Social Cognitive Theory *Albert Bandura*
Knowledge	Fixed body of knowledge to acquire Stimulated from outside	Fixed body of knowledge to acquire Stimulated from outside Prior knowledge influences how information is processed	Changing body of knowledge, individually constructed in social world Built on what learner brings	Socially constructed knowledge Built on what participants contribute, construct together	Changing body of knowledge, constructed in interaction with others and the environment
Learning	Acquisition of facts, skills, concepts Occurs through drill, guided practice	Acquisition of facts, skills, concepts, and strategies Occurs through the effective application of strategies	Active construction, restructuring prior knowledge Occurs through multiple opportunities and diverse processes to connect to what is already known	Collaborative construction of socially defined knowledge and values Occurs through socially constructed opportunities	Active construction of knowledge based on observation, interacting in the physical and social world, and developing agency— becoming more self-regulating
Teaching	Transmission presentation (Telling)	Transmission Guide students toward more "accurate" and complete knowledge	Challenge, guide thinking toward more complete understanding	Co-construct knowledge with students	Presenting models, demonstrating, supporting self-efficacy and self-regulation
Role of Teacher	Manager, supervisor Correct wrong answers	Teach and model effective strategies Correct misconceptions	Facilitator, guide Listen for student's current conceptions, ideas, thinking	Facilitator, guide Co-participant Co-construct different interpretation of knowledge; listen to socially constructed conceptions	Model, facilitator, motivator Model of self-regulated learning
Role of Peers	Not usually considered	Not necessary but can influence information processing	Not necessary but can stimulate thinking, raise questions	Ordinary and necessary part of process of knowledge construction	Serve as models Ordinary and necessary part of process of knowledge construction
Role of Student	Passive recipient of information Active listener, direction-follower	Active processor of information, strategy user Organizer and reorganizer of information Rememberer	Active construction (within mind) Active thinker, explainer, interpreter, questioner	Active co-construction with others and self Active thinker, explainer, interpreter, questioner Active social participator	Active co-construction with others and self Active thinker, explainer, interpreter, questioner Active social participator

Rather than debating the merits of each approach, consider their contributions to understanding learning and improving teaching. Don't feel that you must choose the "best" approach—there is no such thing. Chemists, biologists, and nutritionists rely on different theories to explain and improve health. Different views of learning can be used together to create productive learning environments for the diverse students you will teach. Behavioral theory helps us understand the role of cues in setting the stage for behaviors and the role of consequences and practice in encouraging or discouraging particular behaviors. But much of humans' lives and learning is more than behaviors. Language and higher-order thinking require complex information processing and memory—something the cognitive models help us understand. And what about the person as a creator and constructor of knowledge, not just a processor of information? Here, constructivist perspectives have much to offer. Finally, social cognitive theory highlights the important role of agency and self-direction. Life requires self-regulated learning.

I like to think of the four main learning theories in Table 11.3 as four pillars for teaching. Students must first understand and make sense of the material (constructivist); then, they must remember what they have understood (cognitive—information processing); then, they must practice and apply (behavioral) their new skills and understanding to make them more fluid and automatic—a permanent part of their repertoire. Finally, they must take charge of their own learning (social cognitive). Failure to attend to any part of the process results in lower-quality learning.

▼ SUMMARY

Social Cognitive Theory (pp. 398–400)

Distinguish between social learning and social cognitive theories. Social learning theory expanded behavioral views of reinforcement and punishment. In behavioral views, reinforcement and punishment directly affect behavior. In social learning theory, observing another person, a model, being reinforced or punished can have similar effects on the observer's behavior. Social cognitive theory expands social learning theory to include cognitive factors such as beliefs, expectations, and perceptions of self. Current social cognitive theory is a dynamic system that explains human adaptation, learning, and motivation. The theory addresses how people develop social, emotional, cognitive, and behavioral capabilities; how people regulate their own lives; and what motivates them.

What is triarchic reciprocal causality? Triarchic reciprocal causality is the dynamic interplay between three kinds of influences: personal, environmental, and behavioral. Personal factors (beliefs, expectations, attitudes, and knowledge), the physical and social environment (resources, consequences of actions, other people, models and teachers, and physical settings), and behavior (individual actions, choices, and verbal statements) all influence and are influenced by each other.

Modeling: Learning from Others (pp. 400–404)

What is modeling? Learning by observing others is a key element of social cognitive theory. Modeling is influenced by the developmental characteristics of the observer, the status and prestige of the model, the consequences of the model's actions as seen by the observer, the observer's expectations about performing the observed behaviors (will I be rewarded?), the links that the observers perceive between their goals and the models' behaviors (will doing what the model does get me what I want?), and the observer's self-efficacy (can I do it?).

What kinds of outcomes can observational learning encourage? Observational learning can lead to five possible outcomes, including

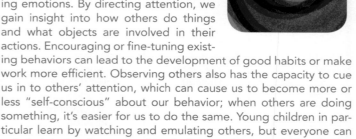

directing attention, encouraging existing behaviors, changing inhibitions, teaching new behaviors and attitudes, and arousing emotions. By directing attention, we gain insight into how others do things and what objects are involved in their actions. Encouraging or fine-tuning existing behaviors can lead to the development of good habits or make work more efficient. Observing others also has the capacity to cue us in to others' attention, which can cause us to become more or less "self-conscious" about our behavior; when others are doing something, it's easier for us to do the same. Young children in particular learn by watching and emulating others, but everyone can gain insight into how something is done well (or poorly) by observing someone else do it. Finally, observing can lead to the association of emotions with certain activities. If others are observed enjoying an activity, the observer may learn to enjoy the activity as well.

Self-Efficacy and Agency (pp. 404–409)

What is self-efficacy, and how is it different from other self-schemas? Self-efficacy is distinct from other self-schemas in that it involves judgments of capabilities specific to a particular task. Self-concept is a more global construct that contains many perceptions about the self, including self-efficacy. Compared to self-esteem, self-efficacy is concerned with judgments of personal capabilities; self-esteem is concerned with judgments of self-worth.

What are the sources of self-efficacy? Four sources are mastery experiences (direct experiences), level of arousal as you face the task, vicarious experiences (accomplishments are modeled by someone else), and social persuasion (a "pep talk" or specific performance feedback).

How does self-efficacy affect motivation? Greater efficacy leads to greater effort, persistence in the face of setbacks, higher goals, and finding new strategies when old ones fail. If sense of efficacy is low, however, people may avoid a task altogether or give up easily when problems arise.

What is teachers' sense of efficacy? One of the few personal characteristics of teachers related to student achievement is a teacher's efficacy belief that he or she can reach even difficult students to help them learn. Teachers with a high sense of efficacy work harder, persist longer, and are less likely to experience burnout. Teachers' sense of efficacy is higher in schools where the other teachers and administrators have high expectations for students and where teachers receive help from their principals in solving instructional and management problems. Efficacy grows from real success with students, so any experience or training that helps you succeed in the day-to-day tasks of teaching will give you a foundation for developing a sense of efficacy in your career. There may be some benefits to lower efficacy, if this encourages teachers to pursue professional development and improvement.

Self-Regulated Learning (pp. 409–419)

What factors are involved in self-regulated learning? One important goal of teaching is to prepare students for lifelong learning. To reach this goal, students must be self-regulated learners; that is, they must have a combination of the knowledge, motivation to learn, and volition that provides the skill and will to learn independently and effectively. Knowledge includes an understanding of self, subject, task, learning strategy, and contexts for application. Motivation to learn provides the commitment, and volition is the follow-through that combats distraction and protects persistence.

What is the self-regulated learning cycle? There are several models of self-regulated learning. Winne and Hadwin describe a four-phase model: analyzing the task, setting goals and designing plans, enacting strategies to accomplish the task, and regulating learning. Zimmerman notes three similar phases: forethought (which includes setting goals, making plans, self-efficacy, and motivation); performance (which involves self-control and self-monitoring); and reflection (which includes self-evaluation and adaptations, leading to the forethought/planning phase again).

What are some examples of teaching students to be more self-regulating? Self-regulating learners engage in four types of activities: analyzing the task, setting goals and designing plans, engaging in learning, and adjusting their approach to learning. Teaching students to be more self-regulating might take the form of providing opportunities to identify and analyze the task at hand. Students should ask themselves: What is the task? What is an ideal outcome of the task? Students may also benefit from goal-setting practice; they may ask: What are my short-term goals? What are my long-term goals? Learning strategies such as identifying important details and developing a big picture of material is the next step in the process. Finally, students need to reflect on whether they were successful and devise strategies for overcoming shortcomings in their self-regulation process. They may ask themselves:

Where was I successful? Where do I need to improve in order to meet my goals in the future?

What is cognitive behavior modification? Cognitive behavior modification is a process in which self-talk is used to regulate behavior. Cognitive behavior modification may take many forms, including helping to keep students engaged in their learning or helping them deal effectively with anger and aggression. Some research has identified four skills that are particularly helpful self-talk strategies: listening, planning, working, and checking. Cognitive behavior modification can be used with students of all ages, but helping students engage in self-talk may require more adult assistance and guidance for younger children, or those who have not had opportunities to practice good self-regulation strategies.

What are the skills involved in emotional self-regulation? Emotionally self-regulating individuals are aware of their own emotions and the feelings of others—realizing that inner emotions can differ from outward expressions. They can talk about and express emotions in ways that are appropriate for their cultural group. They can feel empathy for others in distress and also cope with their own distressing emotions—they can handle stress. These individuals know that relationships are defined in part by how emotions are communicated within the relationship. All these skills come together to produce a capacity for emotional self-regulation.

Teaching Toward Self-Efficacy and Self-Regulated Learning (pp. 419–422)

How can teachers support the development of self-efficacy and self-regulated learning? Teachers should involve students in complex meaningful tasks that extend over long periods of time; provide them control over their learning processes and products—they need to make choices. They should involve students in setting criteria for evaluating their learning processes and products, and then give them opportunities to make judgments about their progress using those standards. Finally, teachers should encourage students to work collaboratively with and seek feedback from peers.

Bringing It All Together: Theories of Learning (pp. 422–424)

What is the value of the four different perspectives on learning? The behavioral, cognitive, constructivist, and social cognitive learning theories are four pillars for teaching. Students must first understand and make sense of the material (constructivist); then, they must remember what they have understood (cognitive—information processing); then, they must practice and apply (behavioral) their new skills and understanding to make them more fluid and automatic—a permanent part of their repertoire. Finally, they must take charge of their own learning (social cognitive). Failure to attend to any part of the process results in lower-quality learning.

▼ KEY TERMS

Arousal (406)
Co-regulation (411)
Cognitive behavior modification (416)
Human agency (404)
Mastery experiences (406)
Modeling (406)
Ripple effect (403)
Self-efficacy (404)

Self-instruction (416)
Self-regulated learning (412)
Self-regulation (410)
Self-reinforcement (402)
Shared regulation (411)
Social cognitive theory (399)
Social learning theory (398)
Social persuasion (406)

Teachers' sense of efficacy (408)
Triarchic reciprocal causality (399)
Vicarious experiences (406)
Vicarious reinforcement (402)
Volition (411)

▼ CONNECT AND EXTEND TO LICENSURE

MULTIPLE-CHOICE QUESTIONS

1. "I believe I will do well in this class." Chris declared to her brother. "I received a perfect score on the verbal part of the SAT, and I have always excelled in my literature classes." Chris is demonstrating which of the following?
   A. High self-esteem
   B. High levels of empathy
   C. High self-efficacy in English
   D. Low self-efficacy in English

2. Modeling is defined as changes in behavior, thinking, or emotions that happen through observing another person. Which theory and theorist is associated with learning through observation?
   A. Behaviorist Theory, Skinner
   B. Constructivist Theory, Piaget
   C. Social Cognitive Theory, Bandura
   D. Sociocultural Theory, Vygotsky

3. Miss Hutton turned around with a scowl on her face and addressed her second graders. "What do you think you're doing Johnny? Did I tell you to get out of your seat? Don't you ever let me catch you up without permission." The class sat silently with their eyes wide. When the lunch bell rang an hour later not one of the children dared to move from their seats. This is an example of which one of the following?
   A. Self-regulation
   B. Self-efficacy
   C. Reciprocal causality
   D. Vicarious learning

4. Through observational learning, one learns how to perform a behavior and also what will happen in specific situations if one performs it. Observation can be a very efficient learning process. What four elements must be met in order to learn from observation?
   A. Attention, retention, production, and motivation/reinforcement
   B. Attention, cognition, belief, and value
   C. Observation, desire, developmental capability, and suitability
   D. Observation, motivation, abstraction, and reinforcement

CONSTRUCTED-RESPONSE QUESTIONS

Case

"Marcus! Look how well you did on your spelling test!" Mr. Bonner smiled at Marcus, who beamed in response. "I knew when we started to chart your progress you would really do well. You have had three perfect scores on the last three tests. It just goes to show, you studied every night for a few minutes and your grade has gone up, up, up! I'm looking at the chart we made at the beginning of the year and I think it really helped."

"Mr. Bonner, I would like to do the same thing in math. I think if I practice every night and chart my progress, I'll get perfect grades in math too! I'll make a chart and pick out some math games I can play at home to improve."

5. How is Mr. Bonner encouraging Marcus' self-efficacy?

6. How is Marcus' response to Mr. Bonner an example of self-regulated learning?

— MyEducationLab™ —

Go to Chapter 11 of the Book Specific Resources in MyEducationLab and click on "Connect and Extend to Licensure" to answer these questions. Compare your responses with the feedback provided.

▼ WHAT WOULD THEY DO?

TEACHERS' CASEBOOK: Failure to Self-Regulate

Here is how several expert teachers responded to the situation at the beginning of the chapter of the teacher with a class of disorganized students.

JANE W. CAMPBELL • 2nd Grade Teacher
John P. Faber Elementary School, Dunellen, NJ

To begin the year, I teach several routines that help students to become more independent and successful. First they are introduced to a homework folder labeled with the classroom number and school name. Ownership is important, so they write their own names on the label too. There are also designated sections for parent signatures, homework to be returned to school, and homework to be kept at home. Each day students put their things into the proper section. I check the students' success by walking through the room and looking at their folders. As different students become proficient, they become student helpers to help spot check other students as well. Organizing the students takes time, but once the routine is established, most students can successfully complete the task. As the routine is practiced and established, the students become successful and more self-reliant. Everyone is happy: the students, the parents, and the teacher.

CARLA S. HIGGINS • K–5 Literacy Coordinator
Legend Elementary School, Newark, OH

I don't make assumptions about my students' organizational skills. Instead, I explicitly teach them skills that work for our class and support future organization such as using a structured folder for class paperwork, frequent checkpoints, and an assignment calendar or agenda. I would include students in planning due dates by considering what it would take to complete each assignment. For longer assignments, I ask students to help create a reasonable time-line for completing steps of the project and offer frequent checks for completion of the steps. Finally, since we live in a culture where technology drives much of our communication, I would set up a Web site or e-mail reminder system to provide additional support for students and to communicate with parents to keep them involved.

MARIE HOFFMAN HURT • 8th Grade Foreign Language
Teacher (German & French)
Pickerington Local Schools, Pickerington, OH

Part of being a good teacher is learning how to teach the "process" of learning alongside the required content material. In the grand scheme of teaching, content-specific learning is only a small percentage of what I teach—something I didn't expect when I started my career in education. A large part of succeeding in life (and on achievement tests!), rather than just knowing how to conjugate a French verb, is knowing the habits, routines, and learning skills that students master WHILE learning those French verbs. With this in mind, it is much easier to keep the task at hand in perspective. If a teacher focuses on fundamental strategies such as organization and planning, and inextricably links these strategies to the operation of the classroom, these concepts become second nature to the students. Students are better able to absorb and learn the content-specific material because they have the tools necessary to do so.

KELLY L. HOY • 5th Grade
The Phillips Brooks School, Menlo Park, CA

In an elementary school classroom, organizational skills are central to alleviating stress for students, teachers, and even parents. From the desk to the binder to the backpack, somehow students' paperwork mysteriously disappears. There are ways to battle the infamous "black hole" book bag or desk. Teachers should take time at the end of each period to clearly state where the assignment should be placed and each child can give a signal that his/her paper is in the correct place. For time-sensitive projects, having different dates in which notes, drafts, and final projects are due will help students learn time management. Students can check off that they have the correct materials in assignment logs and get a teacher's initials. Periodic "book bag checks" can help students organize their book bags for homework.

PATRICIA A. SMITH • High School Math
Earl Warren High School, San Antonio, TX

In my high school mathematics classes, I spend the first two months of the school year training my students in organizational skills. All of my students are given a schedule that outlines topics of discussion, assignment due dates, and quiz and test dates. I also give each of them a "scorecard" where they keep track of their own grades. This serves as a double check for me as the teacher as well as providing a sense of ownership of earned grades to the students.

All my students have a three-ring binder with a plastic cover—their schedule fits inside the plastic cover. Early in the year, I start every class with a look at the schedule and question students on assignment due dates. In addition, I collect all assignments and tests in colored folders unique to each class section. When the students walk into my classroom and see their designated color of folder on my desk, they know that something is due. Most of my quizzes are the take-home variety. I place them on a table in the back of the room and students are responsible for locating, completing, and returning them. In fact, I put them out several days in advance and do not accept late quizzes, thereby increasing student responsibility and organization. Graded papers are also processed in the same manner, thereby perpetuating the new and orderly system and disabling the old unorganized ways.

MyEducationLab™

Go to Topic 9, Social Cognitive Perspectives, in the MyEducationLab (www.myeducationlab.com) for *Educational Psychology*, where you can:

- Find learning outcomes for Social Cognitive Perspectives along with the national standards that connect to these outcomes.
- Complete Assignments and Activities that can help you more deeply understand the chapter content.
- Apply and practice your understanding of the core teaching skills identified in the chapter with the Building Teaching Skills and Dispositions learning units.
- Examine challenging situations and cases presented in the IRIS Center Resources.
- Access video clips of CCSSO National Teachers of the Year award winners responding to the question, "Why Do I Teach?" in the Teacher Talk section.
- Check your comprehension on the content covered in the chapter with the Study Plan. Here you will be able to take a chapter quiz, receive feedback on your answers, and then access Review, Practice, and Enrichment activities to enhance your understanding of chapter content.
- Find additional Teachers' Casebook scenarios and responses to them from practicing teachers.
- Use the Online Lesson Plan Builder to practice lesson planning and integrating national and state standards into your planning.

chapter twelve

MOTIVATION in LEARNING and TEACHING

▶ **TEACHERS' CASEBOOK:** Motivating Students When Resources Are Thin

It is July and you have finally gotten a teaching position. The district wasn't your first choice, but job openings were really tight, so you're pleased to have a job in your field. You are discovering that the teaching resources in your school are slim to none; the only materials available are some aging texts and the workbooks that go with them. Every idea you have suggested for software, simulation games, DVDs, field trips, or other more active teaching materials has been met with the same response, "There's no money in the budget for that." As you look over the texts and workbooks, you wonder how the students could be anything but bored by them. To make matters worse, the texts look pretty high level for your students. But the objectives in the workbooks are important. Besides, the district curriculum requires these units. Students will be tested on them in district-wide assessments next spring.

CRITICAL THINKING

- How would you arouse student curiosity and interest about the topics and tasks in the workbooks?
- How would you establish the value of learning this material?
- How would you handle the difficulty level of the texts?
- What do you need to know about motivation to solve these problems?
- What do you need to know about your students in order to motivate them?

OVERVIEW AND OBJECTIVES

Most educators agree that motivating students is one of the critical tasks of teaching. In order to learn, students must be cognitively, emotionally, and behaviorally engaged in productive class activities. We begin with the question "What is motivation?" and examine many of the answers that have been proposed, including a discussion of intrinsic and extrinsic motivation and five general theories of motivation: behavioral, humanistic, cognitive, social cognitive, and sociocultural. Next, we consider more closely several personal factors that frequently appear in discussions of motivation: needs, goal orientations, beliefs and self-perceptions, interests and curiosity, emotions, and anxiety.

How do we put all this information together in teaching? How do we create environments, situations, and relationships that encourage motivation and engagement in learning? First, we consider how the personal influences on motivation come together to support motivation to learn. Then, we examine how motivation is influenced by the academic work of the class, the value of the work, and the setting in which the work must be done. Finally, we discuss a number of strategies for developing motivation as a constant state in your classroom and as a permanent trait in your students.

By the time you have completed this chapter, you should be able to:

Objective 12.1: Define motivation and differentiate among five theoretical explanations for learner motivation.

Objective 12.2: Explain how learners' needs influence their motivation to learn.

Objective 12.3: Describe the different kinds of goal orientations and their influences on motivation.

Objective 12.4: Discuss how students' beliefs and attributions can influence motivation.

Objective 12.5: Describe the roles of interests, curiosity, emotions, and anxiety in motivation.

Objective 12.6: Explain how teachers can influence and encourage students' motivation to learn.

Motivation An internal state that arouses, directs, and maintains behavior.

We began examining motivation in the previous chapter when we explored students' beliefs about their capabilities—their self-efficacy. We will spend another chapter on motivation because students' motivation has a direct and powerful impact on their social interactions and academic achievement in your classroom. Students with the same abilities and prior knowledge may perform quite differently, based on their motivation (Wigfield & Wentzel, 2007). So how does that work? Let's start with a basic question.

WHAT IS MOTIVATION?

Motivation is usually defined as an internal state that arouses, directs, and maintains behavior. Psychologists studying motivation have focused on five basic questions:

1. What choices do people make about their behavior? Why do some students, for example, focus on their homework and others watch television?
2. How long does it take to get started? Why do some students start their homework right away, while others procrastinate?
3. What is the intensity or level of involvement in the chosen activity? Once the backpack is opened, is the student engrossed and focused or is he just going through the motions?
4. What causes someone to persist or to give up? Will a student read the entire Shakespeare assignment or just a few pages?
5. What is the person thinking and feeling while engaged in the activity? Is the student enjoying Shakespeare, feeling competent, or worrying about an upcoming test (Graham & Weiner, 1996; Pintrich, Marx, & Boyle, 1993)?

Meeting Some Students

Many factors influence motivation and engaged learning. To get a sense of the complexity of motivation, let's step into a high-school science classroom just after the teacher has given directions for a lab activity. The student profiles are adapted from Stipek (2002).

Hopeless Geraldo won't even start the assignment—as usual. He just keeps saying, "I don't understand," or "This is too hard." When he answers your questions correctly, he "guessed" and he "doesn't really know." Geraldo spends most of his time staring into space; he is falling farther and farther behind.

Safe Sumey checks with you about every step—she wants to be perfect. You once gave her bonus points for doing an excellent color drawing of the apparatus, and now she produces a work of art for lab every time. But Sumey won't risk getting a B. If it isn't required or on the test, Sumey isn't interested in doing the work.

Satisfied Spenser, on the other hand, is interested in this project. In fact, he knows more than you do about it. Evidently he spends hours reading about chemistry and performing experiments. But his overall grade in your class is between B⁻ and C because he never turns in homework. Spenser is satisfied with the C he can get on tests without even trying.

Defensive Daleesha doesn't have her lab manual—again, so she has to share with another student. Then she pretends to be working, but spends most of her time making fun of the assignment or trying to get answers from other students when your back is turned. She is afraid to try because if she makes an effort and fails, she fears that everyone will know she is "dumb."

Anxious Amee is a good student in most subjects, but she freezes on science tests and "forgets" everything she knows when she has to answer questions in class. Her parents are scientists and expect her to become one too, but her prospects for this future look dim.

- -

STOP & THINK Each of these students has problems with at least one of the five areas of motivation: (1) choices, (2) getting started, (3) intensity, (4) persistence, or (5) thoughts and feelings. Can you diagnose the problems? The answers are on page 432 •

- -

Each student presents a different motivational challenge, yet you have to figure out how to motivate and teach the entire class. In the next few pages, we will look more closely at the meaning of motivation so we can better understand these students.

Intrinsic and Extrinsic Motivation

We all know how it feels to be motivated, to move energetically toward a goal or to work hard, even if we are bored by the task. What energizes and directs our behavior? The explanation could be drives, basic desires, needs, incentives, fears, goals, social pressure, self-confidence, interests, curiosity, beliefs, values, expectations, and more. Some psychologists have explained motivation in terms of personal *traits* or individual characteristics. Certain people, so the theory goes, have a strong need to achieve, a fear of tests, a curiosity about mechanical objects, or an enduring interest in art, so they work hard to achieve, avoid tests, tinker endlessly in their garages, or spend hours in art galleries. Other psychologists see motivation more as a *state*, a temporary situation. If, for example, you are reading this paragraph because you have a test tomorrow, you are motivated (at least for now) by the situation. Of course, the motivation we experience at any given time usually is a combination of trait and state. You may be studying because you value learning *and* because you are preparing for a test.

A classic distinction is made between intrinsic and extrinsic motivation. **Intrinsic motivation** is the natural human tendency to seek out and conquer challenges as we pursue personal interests and exercise our capabilities. When we are intrinsically motivated, we do not need incentives or punishments, because the activity itself is satisfying and rewarding (Anderman & Anderman, 2010; Deci & Ryan, 2002; Reiss, 2004). Satisfied Spenser studies chemistry outside school simply because he loves learning about chemistry; no one makes him do it. Intrinsic motivation is associated with many positive outcomes in school such as academic achievement, creativity, reading comprehension and enjoyment, and using deep learning strategies (Corpus, McClintic-Gilbert, & Hayenga, 2009).

In contrast, when we do something in order to earn a grade, avoid punishment, please the teacher, or for some other reason that has very little to do with the task itself, we experience **extrinsic motivation**. We are not really interested in the activity for its own sake; we care only about what it will gain us. Safe Sumey works for the grade; she has little interest in the subject itself. Extrinsic motivation has been associated with negative emotions, poor academic achievement, and maladaptive learning strategies (Corpus et al., 2009).

According to psychologists who adopt the intrinsic/extrinsic concept of motivation, it is impossible to tell just by looking if a behavior is intrinsically or extrinsically motivated. The essential difference between the two types of motivation is the student's *reason* for acting, that is, whether the **locus of causality** for the action (the location of the cause) is internal or external—inside or outside the person. Students who read or practice their backstroke or paint may be reading, swimming, or painting because they freely chose the activity based on personal interests (*internal locus of causality/intrinsic motivation*), or because someone or something else outside is influencing them (*external locus of causality/extrinsic motivation*) (Reeve, 2002; Reeve & Jang, 2006a, 2006b).

As you think about your own motivation, you probably realize that the dichotomy between intrinsic and extrinsic motivation is too either/or—too all-or-nothing. There are two explanations that avoid either/or thinking. One is that our activities fall along a continuum from fully self-determined (intrinsic motivation) to fully determined by others

Intrinsic motivation Motivation associated with activities that are their own reward.

Extrinsic motivation Motivation created by external factors such as rewards and punishments.

Locus of causality The location—internal or external—of the cause of behavior.

FOR THE MEDAL ONLY? Is this athlete motivated just by a piece of metal hanging from a ribbon, or is he also likely intrinsically motivated to achieve what he has in his sport?

Connect and Extend to PRAXIS II™

Promoting Intrinsic Motivation to Learn (I, C2, 3)
For a set of practical tips, guidelines, and suggestions for boosting and maintaining motivation to learn, go to *Increasing Student Engagement and Motivation: From Time-on-Task to Homework* (http://www.nwrel.org/request/oct00/textonly.html).

(extrinsic motivation). For example, students may freely choose to work hard on activities that they don't find particularly enjoyable because they know the activities are important in reaching a valued goal—such as spending hours studying educational psychology in order to become a good teacher. Is this intrinsic or extrinsic motivation? Actually, it is in between—the person is freely choosing to accept outside causes such as licensure requirements and then is trying to get the most benefit from the requirements. The person has *internalized an external cause* (Vansteenkiste, Lens, & Deci, 2006).

A second explanation is that intrinsic and extrinsic motivations are not two ends of a continuum. Instead, intrinsic and extrinsic tendencies are two independent possibilities, and, at any given time, we can be motivated by some aspects of each (Covington & Mueller, 2001). Teaching can create intrinsic motivation by connecting to students' interests and supporting growing competence. But you know this won't work all the time. Did you find fractions inherently interesting? Was your curiosity piqued by irregular verbs? If teachers count on intrinsic motivation to energize all their students all of the time, they will be disappointed. There are situations where incentives and external supports are necessary. Teachers must encourage and nurture intrinsic motivation, while making sure that extrinsic motivation supports learning (Anderman & Anderman, 2010; Brophy, 2003). To do this, they need to know about the factors that influence motivation.

Five General Approaches to Motivation

STOP & THINK Why are you reading this chapter? Are you curious about motivation and interested in the topic? Or is there a test in your near future? Do you need this course to earn a teaching license or to graduate? Maybe you believe that you will do well in this class, and that belief keeps you working. Perhaps it is some combination of these reasons. What motivates you to study motivation? •

Motivation is a vast and complicated subject encompassing many theories. Some theories were developed through work with animals in laboratories. Others are based on research with humans in situations that used games or puzzles. The work done in clinical or industrial psychology inspired additional theories as well. Our examination of the field will be selective; otherwise we would never finish.

STOP & THINK ANSWERS Hopeless Geraldo has trouble with getting started (2) and with a sense of despair (5); during the activity he feels defeated and helpless. Safe Sumey makes good choices (1), gets started right away (2), and persists (4). But she is not really engaged and takes little pleasure in the work (4 and 5). As long as he is following his own choices (1), Satisfied Spenser is prompt in getting started (2), engaged (3), persistent (4), and enjoys the task (5). Defensive Daleesha makes poor choices (1), procrastinates (2), avoids engagement (3), and gives up easily (4) because she is so concerned about how others will judge her (5). Anxious Amee's problems have to do with what she thinks and how she feels as she works (5). Her worry and anxiety may lead her to make poor choices (1) and procrastinate (2), which only makes her more anxious at test time. •

Reward An attractive object or event supplied as a consequence of a behavior.

Incentive An object or event that encourages or discourages behavior.

BEHAVIORAL APPROACHES TO MOTIVATION. According to the behavioral view, an understanding of student motivation begins with a careful analysis of the incentives and rewards present in the classroom. A **reward** is an attractive object or event supplied as a consequence of a particular behavior. For example, Safe Sumey was *rewarded* with bonus points when she drew an excellent diagram. An **incentive** is an object or event that encourages or discourages behavior. The promise of an A+ was an *incentive* to Sumey. Actually receiving the grade was a *reward*. Providing grades, stars, stickers, and other reinforcers for learning—or demerits for misbehavior—is an attempt to motivate students by extrinsic means of incentives, rewards, and punishments.

HUMANISTIC APPROACHES TO MOTIVATION. In the 1940s, proponents of humanistic psychology such as Carl Rogers argued that neither of the dominant schools of psychology, behavioral or Freudian, adequately explained why people act as they do. **Humanistic interpretations** of motivation emphasize such intrinsic sources of motivation as a person's needs for "self-actualization" (Maslow, 1968, 1970), the inborn "actualizing tendency" (Rogers & Freiberg, 1994), or the need for "self-determination" (Deci, Vallerand, Pelletier, & Ryan, 1991). So, from the humanistic perspective, to motivate means to encourage people's inner resources—their sense of competence, self-esteem, autonomy, and self-actualization. Maslow's theory and Deci and Ryan's self-determination theory, discussed later, are influential humanistic explanations of motivation.

COGNITIVE APPROACHES TO MOTIVATION. In cognitive theories, people are viewed as active and curious, searching for information to solve personally relevant problems. Thus, cognitive theorists emphasize intrinsic motivation. In many ways, cognitive theories of motivation also developed as a reaction to the behavioral views. Cognitive theorists believe that behavior is determined by our thinking, not simply by whether we have been rewarded or punished for the behavior in the past (Stipek, 2002). Behavior is initiated and regulated by plans (Miller, Galanter, & Pribram, 1960), goals (Locke & Latham, 2002), schemas (Ortony, Clore, & Collins, 1988), expectations (Vroom, 1964), and attributions (Weiner, 2010). We will look at goals, expectations, and attributions later in this chapter.

SOCIAL COGNITIVE THEORIES. Many influential social cognitive explanations of motivation can be characterized as **expectancy × value theories**. This means that motivation is seen as the product of two main forces: the individual's *expectation* of reaching a goal and the *value* of that goal to him or her. In other words, the important questions are, "If I try hard, can I succeed?" and "If I succeed, will the outcome be valuable or rewarding to me?" Motivation is a product of these two forces, because if either factor is zero, then there is no motivation to work toward the goal. For example, if I believe I have a good chance of making the basketball team (high expectation), and if making the team is very important to me (high value), then my motivation should be strong. But if either factor is zero (I believe I haven't a prayer of making the team, or I couldn't care less about playing basketball), then my motivation will be zero, too (Tollefson, 2000).

Jacqueline Eccles and Allan Wigfield add the element of *cost* to the expectancy × value equation. Values have to be considered in relation to the cost of pursuing them. How much energy will be required? What could I be doing instead? What are the risks if I fail? Will I look stupid (Eccles, 2009; Eccles & Wigfield, 2002)?

SOCIOCULTURAL CONCEPTIONS OF MOTIVATION. Finish this sentence: I am a/an _____. What is your identity? With what groups do you identify most strongly? **Sociocultural views of motivation** emphasize participation in communities of practice. People engage in activities to maintain their identities and their interpersonal relations within the community. Thus, students are motivated to learn if they are members of a classroom or school community that values learning. Just as we learn through socialization to speak or dress or order food in restaurants—by watching and learning from more capable members of the culture—we also learn to be students by watching and learning from members of our school community. In other words, we learn by the company we keep (Eccles, 2009; Hickey, 2003; Rogoff, Turkanis, & Bartlett, 2001). When we see ourselves as soccer players, or sculptors, or engineers, or teachers, or psychologists, we are claiming an identity within

Humanistic interpretation
Approach to motivation that emphasizes personal freedom, choice, self-determination, and striving for personal growth.

Expectancy × value theories
Explanations of motivation that emphasize individuals' expectations for success combined with their valuing of the goal.

Sociocultural views of motivation
Perspectives that emphasize participation, identities, and interpersonal relations within communities of practice.

TABLE 12.1 • **Five Views of Motivation**

	BEHAVIORAL	HUMANISTIC	COGNITIVE	SOCIAL COGNITIVE	SOCIOCULTURAL
Source of Motivation	Extrinsic	Intrinsic	Intrinsic	Intrinsic and Extrinsic	Intrinsic
Important Influences	Reinforcers, rewards, incentives, and punishers	Need for self-esteem, self-fulfillment, and self-determination	Beliefs, attributions for success and failure, expectations	Goals, expectations, intentions, self-efficacy	Engaged participation in learning communities; maintaining identity through participation in activities of group
Key Theorists	Skinner	Maslow Deci	Weiner Graham	Locke & Latham Bandura	Lave Wenger

a group. In building an identity in the group, we move from legitimate peripheral participation to central participation. **Legitimate peripheral participation** means that beginners are genuinely involved in the work of the group, even if their abilities are undeveloped and their contributions are small. The novice weaver learns to dye wool before spinning and weaving, and the novice teacher learns to tutor one child before working with the whole group. Each task is a piece of the real work of the expert. The identities of both the novice and the expert are bound up in their participation in the community. They are motivated to learn the values and practices of the community to keep their identity as community members (Lave & Wenger, 1991; Wenger, 1998).

The behavioral, humanistic, cognitive, social cognitive, and sociocultural approaches to motivation are summarized in Table 12.1. These theories differ in their answers to the question, "What is motivation?" but each contributes in its own way toward a comprehensive understanding.

To organize the many ideas about motivation in a way that is useful for teaching, let's examine four broad areas. Most contemporary explanations of motivation include a discussion of needs, goals, beliefs, and finally, the emotional "hot" side of motivation–interests, curiosity, emotions, and anxiety (Murphy & Alexander, 2000).

NEEDS

Early research in psychology conceived of motivation in terms of trait-like needs or consistent personal characteristics. Three of the main needs studied extensively in this earlier work were the needs for *achievement, power,* and *affiliation* (Pintrich, 2003). Abraham Maslow's influential theory emphasized a hierarchy that included all these needs and more.

Maslow's Hierarchy of Needs

Maslow (1970) suggested that humans have a **hierarchy of needs** ranging from lower-level needs for survival and safety to higher-level needs for intellectual achievement and finally self-actualization. **Self-actualization** is Maslow's term for self-fulfillment, the realization of personal potential. Each of the lower needs must be met before the next higher need can be addressed.

Maslow (1968) called the four lower-level needs—for survival, then safety, followed by belonging, and then self-esteem—**deficiency needs**. When these needs are satisfied, the motivation for fulfilling them decreases. He labeled the three higher-level needs—intellectual achievement, then aesthetic appreciation, and finally self-actualization—**being needs**. When

Legitimate peripheral participation Genuine involvement in the work of the group, even if your abilities are undeveloped and contributions are small.

Hierarchy of needs Maslow's model of seven levels of human needs, from basic physiological requirements to the need for self-actualization.

Self-actualization Fulfilling one's potential.

Deficiency needs Maslow's four lower-level needs, which must be satisfied first.

Being needs Maslow's three higher-level needs, sometimes called *growth needs*.

they are met, a person's motivation does not cease; instead, it increases to seek further fulfillment. Unlike the deficiency needs, these being needs can never be completely filled. For example, the more successful you are in your efforts to develop as a teacher, the harder you are likely to strive for even greater improvement.

Maslow's theory has been criticized for the very obvious reason that people do not always appear to behave as the theory would predict. Most of us move back and forth among different types of needs and may even be motivated by many needs at the same time. Some people deny themselves safety or friendship in order to achieve knowledge, understanding, or greater self-esteem.

Criticisms aside, Maslow's theory does give us a way of looking at the whole student, whose physical, emotional, and intellectual needs are all interrelated. A child whose feelings of safety and sense of belonging are threatened by divorce may have little interest in learning how to divide fractions. If school is a fearful, unpredictable place where neither teachers nor students know where they stand, they are likely to be more concerned with security and less with learning or teaching. Belonging to a social group and maintaining self-esteem within that group, for example, are important to students. If doing what the teacher says conflicts with group rules, students may choose to ignore the teacher's wishes or even defy the teacher.

Self-determination theory is a more recent approach to motivation that focuses on human needs (Deci & Ryan, 2002; Reeve, 2009).

Self-Determination: Need for Competence, Autonomy, and Relatedness

Self-determination theory suggests that we all need to feel competent and capable in our interactions in the world, to have some choices and a sense of control over our lives, and to be connected to others—to belong to a social group. Notice that these are similar to earlier conceptions of basic needs: *competence* (achievement), *autonomy and control* (power), and *relatedness* (affiliation). Because different cultures have divergent conceptions of self, some psychologists have asked whether the needs for competence, autonomy, and relatedness are universal. In a series of studies, Hyungshim Jang and her colleagues (2009) found that experiences of competence, autonomy, and relatedness were associated with satisfying learning experiences for Korean high school students, so even in a collectivistic culture, these needs may be important.

Need for autonomy is central to self-determination because it is the desire to have our own wishes, rather than external rewards or pressures, determine our actions (Deci & Ryan, 2002; Reeve, 2009; Reeve, Deci, & Ryan, 2004). People strive to have authority in their lives, to be in charge of their own behavior. They constantly struggle against pressure from external controls such as the rules, schedules, deadlines, orders, and limits imposed by others. Sometimes, even help is rejected so that the individual can remain in command (deCharms, 1983).

SELF-DETERMINATION IN THE CLASSROOM. Classroom environments that support student self-determination and autonomy are associated with greater student interest and curiosity (even interest in homework assignments), sense of competence, creativity, conceptual learning, grades, school attendance and satisfaction, engagement, use of self-regulated learning strategies, psychological well-being, and preference for challenge. These relationships appear to hold from 1st grade through graduate school (Jang, Reeve, & Deci, 2010; Moller, Deci, & Ryan, 2006; Reeve, 2009; Shih, 2008). When students have the authority to make choices, they are more likely to believe that the work is important, even if it is not "fun." Thus, they tend to internalize educational goals and take them as their own.

In contrast to autonomy-supporting classrooms, controlling environments tend to improve performance only on rote recall tasks. When students are pressured to perform, they often seek the quickest, easiest solution. But even though controlling styles of teaching are less effective, teachers are under pressure from administrators, accountability requirements, and cultural expectations to be "in charge," along with parents' expectations

Connect and Extend to PRAXIS II™

Maslow (I, C1)
Consider how problems with satisfying Maslow's hierarchy of needs can affect student learning. Link these ideas to direct or vicarious experiences you might have had in school.

Connect and Extend to PRAXIS II™

Self-Determination (I, C3)
Understand how self-determination can boost or diminish motivation and describe practical steps that teachers can take to establish a sense of self-determination in students.

Need for autonomy The desire to have our own wishes, rather than external rewards or pressures, determine our actions.

SELF-DETERMINED STUDENTS Classroom environments that support student self-determination and autonomy are associated with greater student interest and curiosity, sense of competence, creativity, conceptual learning, and preference for challenge.

for class "discipline." In addition, students often are passive and un-engaged or even defiant. Finally, some teachers equate control with useful structure or feel more comfortable with a controlling style (Reeve, 2009). Assuming you are willing to resist those pressures, how can you support student autonomy? One answer is to focus on information, not control, in your interactions with students.

INFORMATION AND CONTROL. **Cognitive evaluation theory** (Deci & Ryan, 2002) explains how students' experiences such as being praised or criticized, reminded of deadlines, assigned grades, given choices, or lectured about rules can influence their intrinsic motivation by affecting their sense of self-determination and competence. According to this theory, all events have two aspects: *controlling* and *informational*. If an event is highly controlling, that is, if it pressures students to act or feel a certain way, then students will experience less control and their intrinsic motivation will be diminished. If, on the other hand, the event provides information that increases the students' sense of competence, then intrinsic motivation will increase. Of course, if the information provided makes students feel less competent, it is likely that motivation will decrease (Pintrich, 2003). Here is an example of a more *controlling* communication:

> Your paper is due on Monday. Today, we are going to the school library. In the library, you will find information from books and Internet sites to use for your paper. Don't waste your time; don't goof off; make sure to get your work done. In the library, you may work by yourself or with a partner. (Reeve, 2009, p. 169)

This teacher may believe that he is supporting autonomy because he offered a *choice*. Contrast his message with the following statement that gives *information* about why the library visit is valuable:

> Your paper is due on Monday. As a way of helping you write a well-researched paper, we are going to where the information is—the school library. The reason we are going to the library is to find the information you need from books and Internet sites. While there, you may be tempted to goof off, but students in the past have found that a trip to the library was a crucial part of writing an excellent paper. To help you write your best possible paper, you may work in the way you wish—by yourself or with a partner. (Reeve, 2009, p. 169)

As a teacher, what can you do to support student needs for autonomy and competence? An obvious first step is to limit your controlling messages to students because controlling language (*must, ought, have* to, *should...*) can undermine student motivation (Vansteenkiste, Simons, Lens, Sheldon, & Deci, 2004). Make sure the information you provide highlights students' growing competence. The *Guidelines* give some ideas.

THE NEED FOR RELATEDNESS. The need for relatedness is the desire to establish close emotional bonds and attachments with others. When teachers and parents are responsive and demonstrate that they care about the children's interests and well-being, the children show high intrinsic motivation. Students who feel a sense of relatedness to teachers, parents, and peers are more emotionally engaged in school (Furrer & Skinner, 2003).

Cognitive evaluation theory Suggests that events affect motivation through the individual's perception of the events as controlling behavior or providing information.

GUIDELINES

Supporting Self-Determination and Autonomy

Allow and encourage students to make choices.
Examples

1. Design several different ways to meet a learning objective (e.g., a paper, a compilation of interviews, a test, a news broadcast) and let students choose one. Encourage them to explain the reasons for their choice.
2. Appoint student committees to make suggestions about streamlining procedures such as caring for class pets or distributing equipment.
3. Provide time for independent and extended projects.
4. Allow students to choose work partners as long as they focus on the task.

Help students plan actions to accomplish self-selected goals.
Examples

1. Experiment with goal cards. Students list their short- and long-term goals and then record 3 or 4 specific actions that will move them toward the goals. Goal cards are personal—like credit cards.
2. Encourage middle and high school students to set goals in each subject area, record them in a goal book or on a thumb drive, and check progress toward the goals on a regular basis.

Hold students accountable for the consequences of their choices.
Examples

1. If students choose to work with friends and do not finish a project because too much time was spent socializing, grade the project as it deserves and help the students see the connection between lost time and poor performance.
2. When students choose a topic that captures their imagination, discuss the connections between their

investment in the work and the quality of the products that follow.

Provide rationales for limits, rules, and constraints.
Examples

1. Explain reasons for rules.
2. Respect rules and constraints in your own behavior.

Acknowledge that negative emotions are valid reactions to teacher control.
Examples

1. Communicate that it is okay (and normal) to feel bored waiting for a turn, for example.
2. Communicate that sometimes important learning involves frustration, confusion, weariness.
3. Acknowledge students' perspective: "Yes, this problem is difficult." Or "I can understand why you might feel that way."

Use noncontrolling, positive feedback.
Examples

1. See poor performance or behavior as a problem to be solved, not a target of criticism.
2. Avoid controlling language, "should," "must," "have to."

For more information on self-determination theory see: http://www.psych.rochester.edu/SDT/

Source: From 150 Ways to Increase Intrinsic Motivation in the Classroom, *by James P. Raffini. Published by Allyn and Bacon, Boston, MA. Copyright © 1996 by Pearson Education and from* Motivating Others: Nurturing Inner Motivational Resources *by Johnmarshall Reeve. Published by Allyn and Bacon, Boston, MA. Copyright © 1996 by Pearson Education. Adapted by permission of the publisher.*

All students need caring teachers, but students placed at risk have an even greater need for this kind of teacher. Positive relationships with teachers increase the likelihood that students will succeed in high school and go onto college (Stipek, 2006; Thompson, 2008; Woolfolk Hoy & Weinstein, 2006). In addition, emotional and physical problems—ranging from eating disorders to suicide—are more common among individuals who lack social relationships (Baumeister & Leary, 1995). Relatedness is similar to a sense of belonging, discussed in Chapter 3 (Osterman, 2000).

Needs: Lessons for Teachers

From infancy to old age, people want to be competent, connected, and in control. Students are more likely to participate in activities that help them grow more competent and less likely to engage in activities that hold the possibility of failure. This means that your students need appropriately challenging tasks—not too easy, but not impossible either. They also benefit from watching their competence grow, perhaps through self-monitoring systems or portfolios. To be connected, students need to feel that people in school care about them and can be trusted to help them learn.

What else matters in motivation? Many theories include goals as key elements.

GOAL ORIENTATIONS

A **goal** is an outcome or attainment an individual is striving to accomplish (Locke & Latham, 2002). When students strive to read a chapter or make a 4.0 GPA, they are involved in goal-directed behavior. In pursuing goals, students are generally aware of some current condition (I haven't even opened my book), some ideal condition (I have understood every page), and the discrepancy between the two. Goals motivate people to act in order to reduce the discrepancy between "where they are" and "where they want to be." Goal setting is usually effective for me. In addition to the routine tasks, such as eating lunch, which will happen without much attention, I often set goals for each day. For example, today I intend to finish this section, walk on the treadmill, schedule a dentist appointment, and wash another load of clothes (I know—not too exciting). Having decided to do these things, I will feel uncomfortable if I don't complete the list.

According to Locke and Latham (2002), there are four main reasons why goal setting improves performance. Goals:

1. Direct attention to the task at hand and away from distractions. Every time my mind wanders from this chapter, my goal of finishing the section helps direct my attention back to the writing.
2. Energize effort. The more challenging the goal, to a point, the greater the effort.
3. Increase persistence. When we have a clear goal, we are less likely to give up until we reach the goal: Hard goals demand effort and tight deadlines lead to faster work.
4. Promote the development of new knowledge and strategies when old strategies fall short. For example, if your goal is making an A and you don't reach that goal on your first quiz, you might try a new study approach for the next quiz, such as explaining the key points to a friend.

Types of Goals and Goal Orientations

The types of goals we set influence the amount of motivation we have to reach them. Goals that are *specific, elaborated, moderately difficult,* and *likely to be reached* in the near future tend to enhance motivation and persistence (Schunk, Pintrich, & Meece, 2008; Stipek, 2002).

Specific, elaborated goals provide clear standards for judging performance. If performance falls short, we keep going. For example, Ralph Ferretti and his colleagues (2009) gave 4th and 6th grade students either a general goal for writing a persuasive essay ("write a letter to a teacher about whether or not students should be given more out-of-class assignments...") or the general goal elaborated with specific subgoals such as:

* You need to say very clearly what your opinion or viewpoint is;
* You need to think of two or more reasons to back up your opinion;
* You need to explain why those reasons are good reasons for your opinion (p. 580)

Both students with and without learning disabilities wrote more persuasive essays when they were given specific subgoals.

Moderate difficulty provides a challenge, but not an unreasonable one. Finally, goals that can be reached *fairly soon* are not likely to be pushed aside by more immediate concerns. Groups such as Alcoholics Anonymous show they are aware of the motivating value of short-term goals when they encourage their members to stop drinking "one day at a time."

STOP & THINK On a scale from 1 (Strongly Agree) to 5 (Strongly Disagree), how would you answer these questions:

I feel really pleased in school when

___ I solve problems by working hard   ___ All the work is easy

___ I know more than the others   ___ I learn something new

___ I don't have to work hard   ___ I am the only one who gets an A

___ I keep busy   ___ I am with my friends •

___ I finish first

Goal What an individual strives to accomplish.

FOUR ACHIEVEMENT GOAL ORIENTATIONS IN SCHOOL. Goals are specific targets. **Goal orientations** are patterns of beliefs about goals related to achievement in school. Goal orientations include the reasons we pursue goals and the standards we use to evaluate progress toward those goals. For example, your target might be to make an A in this course. Are you doing so in order to *master* educational psychology—to learn all about it, or to *perform*—to look good in the eyes of your friends and family? There are four main goal orientations—mastery (learning), performance (looking good), work-avoidance, and social (Schunk, Pintrich, & Meece, 2008). In the *Stop & Think* exercise you just completed, can you tell which goal orientations are reflected in the different answers? Most of the questions were adapted from a study on students' theories about learning mathematics (Nicholls, Cobb, Wood, Yackel, & Patashnick, 1990).

The most common distinction in research on students' goals is between mastery goals (also called *task goals* or *learning goals*) and performance goals (also called *ability goals* or *ego goals*). The point of a **mastery goal** is to improve, to learn, no matter how awkward you appear. When students set mastery goals, the quality of their engagement in the task is higher—they are more invested. Students with mastery goals tend to seek challenges, persist when they encounter difficulties, and feel better about their work (Midgley, 2001). They focus on the task at hand and are not worried about how their performance "measures up" in comparison to others in the class. We often say that these people "get lost in their work." In addition, they are more likely to seek appropriate help, use deeper cognitive processing strategies, apply better study strategies, and generally approach academic tasks with confidence (Anderman & Patrick, 2012; Kaplan & Maehr, 2007).

The second kind of goal is a performance goal. Students with **performance goals** care about demonstrating their ability to others. They may be focused on getting good test scores and grades, or they may be more concerned with winning and beating other students. Students whose goal is outperforming others may do things

"MEASURING UP" ISN'T THE POINT When students set mastery goals, the quality of their engagement in the task is higher—they are more invested. They are less worried about how their performance compares to that of others in the class.

to look smart, such as reading easy books in order to "read the most books." The evaluation of their performance by others, not what they learn, is what matters. Students with performance goals may act in ways that actually interfere with learning. For example, they may cheat or use short-cuts to get finished, work hard only on graded assignments, be upset and hide papers with low grades, choose tasks that are easy, and be very uncomfortable with assignments that have unclear evaluation criteria (Anderman & Anderman, 2010; Stipek, 2002).

WAIT—ARE PERFORMANCE GOALS ALWAYS BAD? Performance goals sound pretty dysfunctional, don't they? Earlier research indicated that performance goals generally were detrimental to learning, but like extrinsic motivation, a performance goal orientation may not be all bad, all of the time. In fact, some research indicates that both mastery and performance goals are associated with using active learning strategies and high self-efficacy (Midgley, Kaplan, & Middleton, 2001; Stipek, 2002). For college students, pursuing performance goals has been related to higher achievement. And, as is the case with intrinsic and extrinsic motivation, students can, and often do pursue mastery and performance goals at the same time (Anderman & Patrick, 2012).

To account for these recent findings, educational psychologists have added the distinction of approach/avoidance to the mastery/performance distinction. In other words, students may be motivated to either approach mastery or avoid misunderstanding. They may approach performance or avoid looking dumb. Table 12.2 on the next page shows examples and the effects of each kind of goal orientation. Where do you see the most problems? Do you agree that the real problems are with avoidance? Students who fear misunderstanding (mastery avoid) may be perfectionist—focused on getting it exactly

Goal orientations Patterns of beliefs about goals related to achievement in school.

Mastery goal A personal intention to improve abilities and learn, no matter how performance suffers.

Performance goal A personal intention to seem competent or perform well in the eyes of others.

TABLE 12.2 • **Goal Orientations**
Students may have either an approach or an avoidance focus for mastery and performance goal orientations.

GOAL ORIENTATION	APPROACH FOCUS	AVOIDANCE FOCUS
Mastery	*Focus:* Mastering the task, learning, understanding *Standards Used:* Self-improvement, progress, deep understanding (task-involved)	*Focus:* Avoiding misunderstanding or not mastering the task *Standards Used:* Just don't be wrong; perfectionists don't make mistakes
Performance	*Focus:* Being superior, winning, being the best *Standards Used:* Normative—getting the highest grade, winning the competition (ego-involved goal)	*Focus:* Avoiding looking stupid, avoiding losing *Standards Used:* Normative—don't be the worst, get the lowest grade, or be the slowest (ego-involved goal)

Source: From Pintrich, Paul R. and Dale H. Schunk. Motivation in Education: Theory, Research and Applications, 2e. Published by Allyn and Bacon, Boston, MA. Copyright © 2002 by Pearson Education. Adapted by permission of the publisher.

right. Students who avoid looking dumb (performance avoid) may adopt defensive, failure-avoiding strategies like Defensive Daleesha described earlier—they pretend not to care, make a show of "not really trying," or cheat (Harackiewiz, Barron, Pintrich, Elliot, & Thrash, 2002; Harackiewiz & Linnenbrink, 2005).

One final caution—performance approach goals can turn into performance avoidance goals if students are not successful in looking smart or winning. The path might lead from performance approach (trying to win), to performance avoidance (saving face and trying not to look dumb), to learned helplessness (I give up!). So teachers are wise to avoid trying to motivate using competition and social comparisons (Brophy, 2005).

BEYOND MASTERY AND PERFORMANCE. Some students don't want to learn, look smart, or avoid looking dumb; they just want to finish fast or avoid work altogether. These students try to complete assignments and activities as quickly as possible without exerting much effort (Schunk, Pintrich, & Meece, 2008). John Nicholls called these students **work-avoidant learners**—they feel successful when they don't have to try hard, when the work is easy, or when they can "goof off" (Nicholls & Miller, 1984).

A final category of goals becomes more important as students get older—**social goals**. As students move into adolescence, their social networks change to include more peers. Nonacademic activities such as athletics, dating, and "hanging out" compete with schoolwork. Social goals include a wide variety of needs and motives that have different relationships to learning—some help, but others hinder learning. For example, adolescents' goal of maintaining friendly relations can get in the way of learning when cooperative learning group members don't challenge wrong answers or misconceptions because they are afraid to hurt each other's feelings (Anderson, Holland, & Palincsar, 1997). Certainly, pursuing social goals such as having fun with friends or avoiding being labeled a "nerd" can get in the way of learning. But the goal of bringing honor to your family or team by working hard or being part of a peer group that values academics certainly can support learning (Pintrich, 2003; A. Ryan, 2001; Urdan & Maehr, 1995).

We talk about goals in separate categories, but students can and do pursue several goals at once (Bong, 2009; Darnon, Dompnier, Gillieron, & Butera, 2010). They have to coordinate their goals so they can make decisions about what to do and how to act. What if social and academic goals are incompatible? For example, if students do not see a connection between achievement in school and success in life, particularly because

Work-avoidant learners Students who don't want to learn or to look smart, but just want to avoid work.

Social goals A wide variety of needs and motives to be connected to others or part of a group.

discrimination prevents them from succeeding, then they are not likely to set academic achievement as a goal. Such anti-academic peer groups probably exist in every high school (Committee on Increasing High School Students' Engagement and Motivation to Learn, 2004; Wentzel, 1999). Sometimes, succeeding in the peer group means not achieving in school—and succeeding in the peer group is important. The need for social relationships is basic and strong for most people.

GOALS IN SOCIAL CONTEXT. You have seen in other chapters that current thinking in educational psychology puts people in context. Goal orientation theory is no exception. The people in the situation socially construct the meaning of an activity, such as an assignment in a biology class; goals set for the activity will reflect the participants' understanding of "what they are doing." So, in a highly competitive classroom climate, students might be more likely to adopt performance goals. In contrast, in a supportive, learner-centered classroom, even a student with a lower sense of self-efficacy might be encouraged to aim for higher mastery goals. Goals are constructed as part of the triadic reciprocal interaction of person, environment, and behavior described by social cognitive theory—"interlocking perceptions of 'meaning,' 'purpose,' and 'self' in guiding and framing action, thought and emotion" (Kaplan & Maehr, 2007).

The way students perceive their class defines the *classroom goal structure*—the goals that students think are emphasized in the class (Murayama & Elliot, 2009). Lisa Fast and her colleagues (2010) found that 4th through 6th grade students had significantly higher levels of self-efficacy and mathematics achievement when they perceived their math classes as caring, challenging, and mastery oriented. So challenge, support, and a focus on learning, not looking good, seem to create a positive classroom environment.

Feedback, Goal Framing, and Goal Acceptance

Besides having specific goals and creating supportive social relationships, there are three additional factors that make goal setting in the classroom effective. The first is *feedback*. In order to be motivated by a discrepancy between "where you are" and "where you want to be," you must have an accurate sense of both your current status and how far you have to go. There is evidence that feedback emphasizing progress is the most effective. In one study, feedback to adults emphasized either that they had accomplished 75% of the standards set or that they had fallen short of the standards by 25%. When the feedback highlighted accomplishment, the subjects' self-confidence, analytic thinking, and performance were all enhanced (Bandura, 1997).

The second factor affecting motivation to pursue a goal is *goal framing*. Activities or assignments can be explained or framed as helping students' intrinsic goals, such as growing competence, self-determination, positive relationships with friends or teachers, or well-being. The alternative is portraying activities as helping students reach extrinsic goals such as working for a grade, meeting requirements, getting ready for classes next year, and so on. When activities are linked to students' intrinsic goals of becoming more competent, self-directed, and connected with others, then the students process information more deeply and persist longer to gain a conceptual (not superficial) understanding. Linking activities to the extrinsic goals of meeting someone else's standards promotes rote learning, but not deep understanding or persistence (Vansteenkiste, Lens, & Deci, 2006).

The third factor is *goal acceptance*. Commitment matters: The relationship between higher goals and better performance is strongest when people are committed to the goals (Locke & Latham, 2002). If students reject goals set by others or refuse to set their own goals, then their motivation will suffer. Generally, students are more willing to commit to the goals of others if the goals seem realistic, reasonably difficult, and meaningful—and if the goals are validated by connecting activities to students' intrinsic interests (Grolnick, Gurland, Jacob, & Decourcey, 2002).

Goals: Lessons for Teachers

Students are more likely to work toward goals that are clear, specific, reasonable, moderately challenging, and attainable within a relatively short period of time. If teachers focus on student performance, high grades, and competition, they may encourage students to set performance goals. This could undermine the students' ability to learn and become task-involved and set them on a path toward alienation from learning in school and learned helplessness (Anderman & Maehr, 1994; Brophy, 2005). Students may not yet be expert at setting their own goals or keeping these goals in mind, so encouragement and accurate feedback are necessary. If you use any reward or incentive systems, be sure the goal you set is to learn and improve in some area, not just to perform well or look smart. And be sure the goal is not too difficult. Students, like adults, are unlikely to stick with tasks or respond well to teachers who make them feel insecure or incompetent, which leads us to our next topic—the power of beliefs in motivation.

BELIEFS AND SELF-PERCEPTIONS

Thus far, we have talked about needs and goals, but there is another factor that must be considered in explaining motivation. What do students believe about learning and about themselves—their competence and the causes for success or failure? Let's start with a basic question—What do they believe about knowing?

Beliefs About Knowing: Epistemological Beliefs

What students believe about knowledge and learning (their **epistemological beliefs**) will influence their motivation and the kinds of strategies that they use.

- -

STOP & THINK How would you answer these questions taken from Chan & Sachs (2001)?

1. Which of the following is the most important thing in learning math? (a) remember what the teacher has taught you, (b) practice lots of problems, (c) understand the problems you work on.

2. Which of the following is the important thing to do in learning science? (a) faithfully do the work the teacher tells you, (b) try to see how the explanation makes sense, (c) try to remember everything you are supposed to know.

3. If you wanted to know everything there is about something, say animals, how long would you have to study it? (a) less than a year if you study hard, (b) about one or two years, (c) forever.

4. What happens when you learn more and more about something? (a) the questions get more and more complex, (b) the questions get easier and easier, (c) the questions all get answered. •

- -

Using questions like those above, researchers have identified several dimensions of epistemological beliefs (Chan & Sachs, 2001; Schommer, 1997; Schommer-Aikins, 2002; Schraw & Olafson, 2002). For example:

- **Structure of Knowledge:** Is knowledge in a field a simple set of facts or a complex structure of concepts and relationships?
- **Stability/Certainty of Knowledge:** Is knowledge fixed or does it evolve over time?
- **Ability to Learn:** Is the ability to learn fixed (based on innate ability) or changeable?
- **Speed of Learning:** Can we gain knowledge quickly or does it take time to develop knowledge?
- **Nature of Learning:** Does learning mean memorizing facts passed down from authorities and keeping the facts isolated, or does it mean developing your own integrated understandings?

Students' beliefs about knowing and learning affect the goals they set and the learning strategies they apply. For example, if you believe that knowledge should be gained quickly, you are likely to try one or two quick strategies (read the text once, spend two minutes trying to solve the word problem) and then stop. If you believe that learning means developing integrated understandings, you will process the material more deeply, connect to existing knowledge, create your own examples, or draw diagrams, and generally elaborate on the information to make it your own (Kardash & Howell, 2000; Muis &

Epistemological beliefs Beliefs about the structure, stability, and certainty of knowledge, and how knowledge is best learned.

Franco, 2009). In one study, elementary school students (grades 4 and 6) who believed that learning is understanding processed science texts more deeply than others who believed that learning is reproducing facts (Chan & Sachs, 2001). The *Stop & Think* questions you just answered were used in that study to assess the students' beliefs. The answers associated with a belief in complex, evolving knowledge that takes time to understand and grows from active learning are 1c, 2b, 3c, and 4a.

Beliefs about one dimension discussed above—ability to learn—are particularly powerful. Read on.

Beliefs About Ability

STOP & THINK Rate these statements taken from Dweck (2000) on a scale from 1 (Strongly Agree) to 6 (Strongly Disagree).

____ You have a certain amount of intelligence and you really can't do much to change it.

____ You can learn new things, but you can't really change your basic intelligence.

____ No matter who you are, you can change your intelligence a lot.

____ No matter how much intelligence you have, you can always change it quite a bit. •

Some of the most powerful beliefs affecting motivation in school are about ability. Adults use two basic concepts of ability (Dweck, 2002, 2006). An **entity view of ability** assumes that ability is a stable, uncontrollable trait—a characteristic of the individual that cannot be changed. According to this view, some people have more ability than others, but the amount each person has is set. An **incremental view of ability**, on the other hand, suggests that ability is unstable and controllable—"an ever-expanding repertoire of skills and knowledge" (Dweck & Bempechat, 1983, p. 144). By hard work, study, or practice, knowledge can be increased and thus ability can be improved. What is your view of ability? Look back at your answers to the *Stop & Think* questions.

Young children tend to hold an exclusively incremental view of ability. Through the early elementary grades, most students believe that effort is the same as intelligence. Smart people try hard, and trying hard makes you smart. If you fail, you aren't smart and you didn't try hard (Dweck, 2000; Stipek, 2002). At around age 11 or 12, children can differentiate among effort, ability, and performance. At about this time, they come to believe that someone who succeeds without working at all must be really smart. This is when beliefs about ability begin to influence motivation (Anderman & Anderman, 2010).

Students who hold an *entity* (unchangeable) view of intelligence tend to set performance avoid goals to avoid looking bad in the eyes of others. They seek situations where they can look smart and protect their self-esteem. Like Safe Sumey, they keep doing those things they can do well without expending too much effort or risking failure, because either one—working hard or failing—indicates (to them) low ability. To work hard but still fail would be devastating. Students with learning disabilities are more likely to hold an entity view.

In contrast, holding an *incremental* view of ability is associated with greater motivation and learning. Believing that you can improve your ability helps you focus on the *processes* of problem solving and applying good strategies, instead of on the *products* of test scores and grades (Chen & Pajares, 2010).

Teachers who hold *entity* views are quicker to form judgments about students and slower to modify their opinions when confronted with contradictory evidence (Stipek, 2002). Teachers who hold *incremental* views, in contrast, tend to set mastery goals and seek situations in which students can improve their skills, because improvement means getting smarter. Failure is not devastating; it simply indicates more work is needed. Ability is not threatened. Incremental theorists tend to set moderately difficult goals, the kind we have seen are the most motivating.

Beliefs about ability are related to other beliefs about what you can and cannot control in learning.

Entity view of ability Belief that ability is a fixed characteristic that cannot be changed.

Incremental view of ability Belief that ability is a set of skills that can be changed.

Beliefs About Causes and Control: Attribution Theory

One well-known explanation of motivation begins with the assumption that we try to make sense of our own behavior and the behavior of others by searching for explanations and causes. To understand our own successes and failures, particularly unexpected ones, we all ask, "Why?" Students ask themselves, "Why did I flunk my midterm?" or "Why did I do so well this grading period?" They may attribute their successes and failures to ability, effort, mood, knowledge, luck, help, interest, clarity of instructions, the interference of others, unfair policies, and so on. To understand the successes and failures of others, we also make attributions—that the others are smart or lucky or work hard, for example. **Attribution theories** of motivation describe how the individual's explanations, justifications, and excuses influence motivation (Anderman & Anderman, 2010).

Bernard Weiner is one of the main educational psychologists responsible for relating attribution theory to school learning (Weiner, 2000, 2010). According to Weiner, most of the attributed causes for successes or failures can be characterized in terms of three dimensions:

1. **Locus** (location of the cause—internal or external to the person). For example, attributing a great piano performance to your musical talent or hard work are internal attributions. Explaining that the performance is based on coaching from a great teacher is an external attribution.
2. **Stability** (whether the cause of the event is the same across time and in different situations). For example, talent is stable, but effort can change.
3. **Controllability** (whether the person can control the cause). For example, effort and finding a great teacher are controllable, but innate musical talent is not.

Every cause for success or failure can be categorized on these three dimensions. For instance, luck is external (locus), unstable (stability), and uncontrollable (controllability). In attribution theory, ability is usually considered stable and uncontrollable, but incremental theorists (described earlier) would argue that ability is unstable and controllable. Weiner's locus and controllability dimensions are closely related to Deci's concept of locus of causality.

Weiner believes that these three dimensions have important implications for motivation because they affect expectancy and value. The *stability* dimension, for example, seems to be closely related to expectations about the future. If students attribute their failure to stable factors such as the difficulty of the subject or an unfair teacher, they will expect to keep failing in that subject or with that teacher. But if they attribute the outcome to unstable factors such as mood or luck, they can hope for better outcomes next time. The *internal/external locus* seems to be closely related to feelings of self-esteem. If success or failure is attributed to internal factors, success will lead to pride and increased motivation, whereas failure will diminish self-esteem. The *controllability* dimension is related to emotions such as anger, pity, gratitude, or shame. If we feel responsible for our failures, we may feel guilt; if we feel responsible for successes, we may feel proud. Failing at a task we cannot control can lead to shame or anger (Weiner, 2010).

Feeling in control of your own learning seems to be related to choosing more difficult academic tasks, putting out more effort, using better strategies, and persisting longer in school work (Schunk, 2000; Weiner, 1994a, 1994b). Factors such as continuing discrimination against women, people of color, and individuals with special needs can affect these individuals' perceptions of their ability to control their lives (van Laar, 2000).

ATTRIBUTIONS IN THE CLASSROOM.   People with a strong sense of **self-efficacy** (see Chapter 11) for a given task ("I'm good at math") tend to attribute their failures to lack of effort ("I should have double-checked my work"), misunderstanding directions, or just not studying enough. These are internal, controllable attributions. As a consequence, they usually focus on strategies for succeeding next time. This response often leads to achievement, pride, and a greater feeling of control. But people with a low sense of self-efficacy ("I'm terrible at math") tend to attribute their failures to lack of ability ("I'm just dumb").

The greatest motivational problems arise when students attribute failures to stable, uncontrollable causes. Such students may seem resigned to failure, depressed, helpless—what we

Connect and Extend to PRAXIS II™

Attribution Theory (I, C1)
Go to the *Encyclopedia of Psychology* (http://www.psychology.org/links/Environment_Behavior_Relationships/Motivation/) and follow its link for Attribution Theory to learn more about using principles derived from this theory to boost intrinsic motivation to learn.

Attribution theories Descriptions of how individuals' explanations, justifications, and excuses influence their motivation and behavior.

Self-efficacy Beliefs about personal competence in a particular situation.

generally call "unmotivated" (Weiner, 2000, 2010). These students respond to failure by focusing even more on their own inadequacy; their attitudes toward schoolwork may deteriorate even further. Apathy is a logical reaction to failure if students believe the causes are stable, unlikely to change, and beyond their control anyway. In addition, students who view their failures in this light are less likely to seek help; they believe nothing and no one can help, so they conceal their needs for help. This creates a downward spiral of failure and concealment—"the motivationally 'poor' children, by concealing their difficulties, become 'poorer'" (Marchland & Skinner, 2007). You can see that if a student held an en-tity view (ability cannot be changed) and a low sense of self-efficacy, motivation would be destroyed when failures were attributed to lack of ability ("I just can't do this and I'll never be able to learn") (Bandura, 1997; Schunk, Pintrich, & Meece, 2008; Stipek, 2002).

UNMOTIVATED? The greatest motivational problems arise when students attribute failures to uncontrollable causes and focus on their own inad-equacy. Apathy is a logical reaction if students believe the causes of failure are beyond their control.

TEACHER ACTIONS AND STUDENT ATTRIBUTIONS. We also make attributions about the causes of other people's successes and failures. When a teacher assumes that student failure is attributable to forces beyond the student's control, the teacher tends to respond with sympathy and avoid giving punishments. If, however, the failures are attributed to a controllable factor such as lack of effort, the teacher's response is more likely to be irrita-tion or anger, and reprimands may follow. These tendencies seem to be consistent across time and cultures (Weiner, 1986, 2000).

What do students make of these reactions from their teachers? Sandra Graham (1991, 1996) gives some surprising answers. There is evidence that when teachers respond to students' mistakes with pity, praise for a "good try," or unsolicited help, the students are more likely to attribute their failure to an uncontrollable cause—usually lack of ability. Does this mean that teachers should be critical and withhold help? Of course not! But it is a reminder that over-solicitous help can give unintended messages. Graham (1991) sug-gests that many minority group students could be the victims of well-meaning pity from teachers. Seeing the very real problems that the students face, teachers may "ease up" on requirements so the students will "experience success." But a subtle communication may accompany the pity, praise, and extra help: "You don't have the ability to do this, so I will overlook your failure." Graham says, "The pertinent question for blacks is whether their own history of academic failure makes them more likely to be the targets of sympathetic feedback from teachers and thus the recipients of low-ability cues" (1991, p. 28). This kind of benevolent feedback, even if well intended, can be a subtle form of racism.

Beliefs About Self-Worth

Whatever the label, most theorists agree that a sense of efficacy, control, or self-determination is critical if people are to feel intrinsically motivated.

LEARNED HELPLESSNESS. When people come to believe that the events and out-comes in their lives are mostly uncontrollable, they have developed **learned helplessness** (Seligman, 1975). To understand the power of learned helplessness, consider this classic experiment (Hiroto & Seligman, 1975): Subjects received either solvable or unsolvable puzzles. In the next phase of the experiment, all subjects were given a series of solvable puzzles. The subjects who struggled with unsolvable puzzles in the first phase of the ex-periment usually solved significantly fewer puzzles in the second phase. They had learned that they could not control the outcome, so why even try?

Learned helplessness appears to cause three types of deficits: *motivational, cogni-tive*, and *affective*. Students who feel hopeless, like Hopeless Geraldo described earlier,

Learned helplessness The expectation, based on previous experiences with a lack of control, that all one's efforts will lead to failure.

TABLE 12.3 • **Mastery-Oriented, Failure-Avoiding, and Failure-Accepting Students**

	ATTITUDE TOWARD FAILURE	GOALS SET	ATTRIBUTIONS	VIEW OF ABILITY	STRATEGIES
Mastery-Oriented	Low fear of failure	Learning goals: moderately difficult and challenging	Effort, use of right strategy, sufficient knowledge is cause of success	Incremental; improvable	Adaptive strategies; e.g., try another way, seek help, practice/study more
Failure-Avoiding	High fear of failure	Performance goals; very hard or very easy	Lack of ability is cause of failure	Entity; set	Self-defeating strategies; e.g., make a feeble effort, pretend not to care
Failure-Accepting	Expectation of failure; depression	Performance goals or no goals	Lack of ability is cause of failure	Entity; set	Learned helplessness; likely to give up

expect to fail, so why should they even try—thus *motivation* suffers. Because they are pessimistic about learning, these students miss opportunities to practice and improve skills and abilities, so they develop *cognitive* deficits. Finally, they often suffer from *affective* problems such as depression, anxiety, and listlessness (Alloy & Seligman, 1979). Once established, it is very difficult to reverse the effects of learned helplessness.

SELF-WORTH. What are the connections between attributions and beliefs about ability, self-efficacy, and self-worth? Covington and his colleagues suggest that these factors come together in three kinds of motivational sets: *mastery oriented, failure avoiding*, and *failure accepting*, as shown in Table 12.3 (Covington, 1992; Covington & Mueller, 2001).

Mastery-oriented students tend to value achievement and see ability as improvable (an incremental view), so they focus on mastery goals in order to increase their skills and abilities. They are not fearful of failure, because failing does not threaten their sense of competence and self-worth. This allows them to set moderately difficult goals, take risks, and cope with failure constructively. They generally attribute success to their own effort, and thus they assume responsibility for learning and have a strong sense of self-efficacy. They learn fast, have more self-confidence and energy, are more aroused, welcome concrete feedback (it does not threaten them), and are eager to learn "the rules of the game" so that they can succeed. All of these factors make for persistent, successful learning (Covington & Mueller, 2001; McClelland, 1985).

Failure-avoiding students tend to hold an entity (fixed) view of ability, so they set performance goals. They lack a strong sense of their own competence and self-worth separate from their performance. In other words, they feel only as smart as their last test grade, so they never develop a solid sense of self-efficacy. In order to feel competent, they must protect themselves (and their self-worth) from failure. If they have been generally successful, they may seek to avoid failure like Safe Sumey, simply by taking few risks and "sticking with what they know." If, on the other hand, they have experienced a good bit of failure, then they, like Defensive Daleesha, may adopt self-defeating strategies such as feeble efforts, setting very low or ridiculously high goals, or claiming not to care. Just before a test, a student might say, "I didn't study at all!" or "All I want to do is pass." Then, any grade above passing is a success. Procrastination is another example. Low grades do not imply low ability if the student can claim, "I did okay considering I didn't start the term paper until last night." All these are **self-handicapping** strategies because the students are imposing handicaps on their own achievement. Very little learning is going on.

Mastery-oriented students Students who focus on learning goals because they value achievement and see ability as improvable.

Failure-avoiding students Students who avoid failure by sticking to what they know, by not taking risks, or by claiming not to care about their performance.

Self-handicapping Students may engage in behavior that blocks their own success in order to avoid testing their true ability.

GUIDELINES

Encouraging Self-Worth

Emphasize that abilities are not set, but are always improvable.
Examples
1. Share examples of how you have improved your knowledge and skills, for example in writing, at a sport, or doing a craft.
2. Tell about your own failures that became successes when you tried new strategies or got the right help.
3. Save first drafts and finished products from students in previous classes to show how much the students improved with effort and support.

Teach directly about the difference between learning goals and performance goals.
Examples
1. Encourage students to set a small-step goal for one subject.
2. Recognize improvements often with private authentic praise.
3. Use personal best goals, not between-student competition.

Make the classroom a place where failure is just diagnostic—failure tells what needs to be improved.
Examples
1. If a student gives a wrong answer in class, say "I bet others would give that answer too. Let's examine why that is not

the best answer. This gives us a chance to dig deeper—excellent!"
2. Encourage revising, improving, polishing, and redoing with an emphasis on improvement.
3. Show students connections between their revised work and a higher grade, but emphasize their growing competence.

Encourage help seeking and help giving.
Examples
1. Teach students how to ask explicit questions about what they do not understand.
2. Recognize students who are helpful.
3. Train class experts for some ongoing needs such as technology guides or progress checkers.

For more information on self-worth, see:
http://honolulu.hawaii.edu/intranet/committees/FacDevCom/guidebk/teachtip/motiv.htm

---

Unfortunately, failure-avoiding strategies generally lead to the very failure the students were trying to avoid. If failures continue and excuses wear thin, the students may finally decide that they are incompetent. Their sense of self-worth and self-efficacy deteriorates. They give up and thus become **failure-accepting students**. They are convinced that their problems are due to low ability. As we saw earlier, those students who attribute failure to low ability and believe ability is fixed are likely to become depressed, apathetic, and helpless. Like Hopeless Geraldo, they have little hope for change.

Teachers may be able to prevent some failure-avoiding students from becoming failure accepting by using multiple outcome measures and setting a number of goals. In this way all students have a realistic chance of succeeding on some outcome measures and reaching at least a few goals (Chen, Wu, Kee, Lin, & Shui, 2009). Also, many students may need support in aspiring to higher levels in the face of sexual or ethnic stereotypes about what they "should" want or what they "should not" be able to do well. This kind of support could make all the difference. Instead of pitying or excusing these students, teachers can teach them how to learn and then hold them accountable for their learning. This will help the students develop a sense of self-efficacy for learning and avoid learned helplessness. The *Guidelines* discuss how to encourage self-worth.

Beliefs and Attributions: Lessons for Teachers

If students believe they lack the ability to understand higher mathematics, they will probably act on this belief even if their actual abilities are well above average. These students are likely to have little motivation to tackle trigonometry or calculus, because they expect to do poorly in these areas. If students believe that failing means they are stupid, they are likely to adopt many self-handicapping, self-defeating strategies. And teachers who stress performance, grades, and competition can encourage self-handicapping without realizing they are doing so (Anderman & Anderman, 2010). Just telling students to "try harder" is not particularly effective. Students need real evidence that effort will pay off,

Failure-accepting students Students who believe their failures are due to low ability and there is little they can do about it.

that setting a higher goal will not lead to failure, that they can improve, and that abilities can be changed. They need authentic mastery experiences.

What else do we know about motivation? Feelings matter.

INTERESTS, CURIOSITY, EMOTIONS, AND ANXIETY

Do you remember starting school? Were you curious about what might be in store, excited about your new world, interested and challenged? Many children are. But a common concern of parents and teachers is that this curiosity and excitement about learning is replaced by a sense of drudgery and disinterest. School becomes a job you have to do—a workplace where the work is not that interesting (Wigfield & Wentzel, 2007). In fact, interest in school decreases over time from elementary to high school, with boys showing greater declines than girls. The transition to middle school is particularly linked to a decline in interest. These declines are troubling because results of research on learning in school show that interest is related to students' attention, goals, grades, and depth of learning (Dotterer, McHale, & Vrouter, 2009; Hidi & Renninger, 2006).

Tapping Interests

STOP & THINK As part of your interview for a job in a large high school, the principal asks, "How would you get students interested in learning? Could you tap their interests in your teaching?" •

There are two kinds of interests—*personal* (individual) and *situational*—the trait and state distinction again. Personal or individual interests are more long-lasting aspects of the person, such as an enduring tendency to be attracted to or to enjoy subjects such as languages, history, or mathematics, or activities such as sports, music, or films. Students with individual interests in learning in general seek new information and have more positive attitudes toward schooling. Situational interests are more short-lived aspects of the activity, text, or materials that catch and keep the student's attention. Both personal and situational interests are related to learning from texts—greater interest leads to more positive emotional responses to the material, then to greater persistence in learning, deeper processing, better remembering of the material, and higher achievement (Ainley, Hidi, & Berndorf, 2002; Hofer, 2010; Pintrich, 2003). And interests increase when students feel competent, so even if students are not initially attracted to a subject or activity, they may develop interests as they experience success (Stipek, 2002).

Ann Renninger (2009) describes a four-phase model of interest development:

situational interest triggered → situational interest maintained →
emerging individual interest → well-developed individual interest

For example, consider Julia, a graduating senior in college described by Hidi and Renninger (2006). As she waits nervously in the dentist's office, flipping through a magazine, her attention is drawn (*situational interest trigger*) to an article about a man who left his engineering job to become a facilitator in legal conflict resolution. When she is called to the dentist's chair, she is still reading the article, so she marks her place and returns to finish reading after her appointment (*situational interest maintained*). She takes notes, and, over the next weeks, searches the Internet, visits the library, and meets with her advisor to get more information about this career option (*emerging individual interest*). Four years later, Julia is enjoying her job as a facilitator as she handles more and more arbitration cases for a law firm (*well-developed, enduring individual interest*).

In the early stages of this four-phase model, emotions play a big role—feelings of excitement, pleasure, fun, and curiosity. Situational interest may be triggered by positive feelings, as when Julia started reading. Curiosity followed and helped Julia stay engaged

INTEREST AND EXCITEMENT Students' interest in and excitement about what they're learning are two of the most important factors in education.

as she learned more about becoming a facilitator. As Julia added knowledge to her curiosity and positive feelings, her personal interest emerged, and the *cycle of positive feelings, curiosity, and knowledge* continued to build enduring interest.

CATCHING AND HOLDING INTERESTS. Whenever possible, it helps to connect academic content to students' enduring individual interests. But given that the content you will teach is determined by standards in most classrooms today, it will be difficult to tailor lessons to each student's interests. You will have to rely more on triggering and maintaining situational interest. Here, the challenge is to not only *catch* but also *hold* students' interest (Pintrich, 2003). For example, Mathew Mitchell (1993) found that using computers, groups, and puzzles caught students' interest in secondary mathematics classes, but the interests did not hold. Lessons that held the students' interest over time included math activities that were related to real-life problems and active participation in laboratory activities and projects. Another source of interest is fantasy. Cordova and Lepper (1996) found that students learned more math facts during a computer exercise in which they were challenged, as captains of star ships, to navigate through space by solving math problems. The students got to name their ships, stock the (imaginary) galley with their favorite snacks, and name all the crew members after their friends. In a study of math learning with older adolescents, Durik and Harachkiewicz (2007) concluded that catching interest by using colorful learning materials with pictures was helpful for students with low initial interest in mathematics, but not for students who were already interested. For the interested students, holding interest by showing how math could be personally useful was more effective.

There are other cautions in responding to students' interests, as you can see in the *Point/Counterpoint*.

Curiosity: Novelty and Complexity

Nearly 50 years ago, psychologists suggested that individuals are naturally motivated to seek novelty, surprise, and complexity (Berlyne, 1966). Exploration probably is innate; infants must explore the world to learn about it (Bowlby, 1969). More recently, Reiss

POINT/COUNTERPOINT: Does Making Learning Fun Make for Good Learning?

When many beginning teachers are asked about how to motivate students, they often mention making learning fun. But is it necessary for learning to be fun?

POINT

▶ **Teachers should make learning fun.** When I searched "making learning fun" on Google.com, I found 10 pages of resources and references. Clearly, there is interest in making learning fun. Research shows that passages in texts that are more interesting are remembered better (Schunk, Pintrich, & Meece, 2008). For example, students who read books that interested them spent more time reading, read more words in the books, and felt more positively about reading (Guthrie & Alao, 1997).

Games and simulations can make learning more fun, too. For example, when my daughter was in the 8th grade, all the students in her grade spent three days playing a game her teachers had designed called ULTRA. Students were divided into groups and formed their own "countries." Each country had to choose a name, symbol, national flower, and bird. They wrote and sang a national anthem and elected government officials. The teachers allocated different resources to the countries. To get all the materials needed for the completion of assigned projects, the countries had to establish trade with one another. There was a monetary system and a stock market. Students had to work with their fellow citizens to complete cooperative learning assignments. Some countries "cheated" in their trades with other nations, and this allowed debate about international relations, trust, and war. Liz says she had fun—but she also learned how to work in a group without the teacher's supervision and gained a deeper understanding of world economics and international conflicts.

A highly motivating 3rd grade teacher in another study had her class set up a post office for the whole school. Each classroom in the school had an address and zip code. Students had jobs in the post office, and everyone in the school used the post office to deliver letters to students and teachers. Students designed their own stamps and set postal rates. The teacher said that the system "improves their creative writing without them knowing it" (Dolezal, Welsh, Pressley, & Vincent, 2003, p. 254).

COUNTERPOINT

▶ **Fun can get in the way of learning.** As far back as the early 1900s, educators warned about the dangers of focusing on fun in learning. None other than John Dewey, who wrote extensively about the role of interest in learning, cautioned that you can't make boring lessons interesting by mixing in fun like you can make bad chili good by adding some spicy hot sauce. Dewey wrote, "When things have to be made interesting, it is because interest itself is wanting. Moreover, the phrase itself is a misnomer. The thing, the object, is no more interesting than it was before" (Dewey, 1913, pp. 11–12).

There is a good deal of research now indicating that adding interest by incorporating fascinating but irrelevant details actually gets in the way of learning the important information. These "seductive details," as they have been called, divert the readers' attention from the less interesting main ideas (Harp & Mayer, 1998). For example, students who read biographies of historical figures remembered more very interesting—but unimportant—information compared to interesting main ideas (Wade, Schraw, Buxton, & Hayes, 1993).

Shannon Harp and Richard Mayer (1998) found similar results with high school science texts. These texts added emotional interest and seductive details about swimmers and golfers who are injured by lightning to a lesson on the process of lightning. They concluded that, "in the case of emotional interest versus cognitive interest, the verdict is clear. Adjuncts aimed at increasing emotional interest failed to improve understanding of scientific explanations" (p. 100). The seductive details may have disrupted students' attempts to follow the logic of the explanations and thus interfered with their comprehending the text. Harp and Mayer conclude that "the best way to help students enjoy a passage is to help them understand it" (p. 100).

(2004) listed curiosity as one of the 16 basic human motivations, and Flum and Kaplan (2006) made the case that schools should target developing an exploratory orientation in students as a major goal.

Interest and curiosity are related. Curiosity can be defined as a tendency to be interested in a wide range of areas (Pintrich, 2003). According to Renninger's (2009) four-phase model of interest described in the previous section, our individual interests begin to emerge as we raise and answer "curiosity questions" that help us organize our knowledge about a topic. In order for situational interests to develop into long-term individual interests, curiosity and the desire for exploration are necessary.

George Lowenstein (1994) suggests that curiosity arises when attention is focused on a gap in knowledge. These information gaps cause a sense of deprivation—a need to know that we call "curiosity." This idea is similar to Piaget's concept of disequilibrium, discussed in Chapter 2, and has a number of implications for teaching. First, students need some base of knowledge before they can experience gaps in that knowledge leading to curiosity. Second, students must be aware of the gaps in order for curiosity to result. In other words, they need a metacognitive awareness of what they know and don't know (Hidi, Renninger, & Krapp, 2004). Asking students to make guesses and then providing

GUIDELINES

Building on Students' Interests and Curiosity

Relate content objectives to student experiences.
Examples

1. With a teacher in another school, establish pen pals across the classes. Through writing letters, students exchange personal experiences, photos, drawings, written work, and ask and answer questions ("Have you learned cursive writing yet?" "What are you doing in math now?" "What are you reading?"). Letters can be mailed in one large mailer to save stamps or sent via email.

2. Identify classroom experts for different assignments or tasks. Who knows how to use the computer for graphics? How to search the Net? How to cook? How to use an index?

3. Have a "Switch Day" when students exchange roles with a school staff or support person. Students must research the role by interviewing their staff member, prepare for the job, dress the part for the day they take over, and then evaluate their success after the switch.

Identify student interests, hobbies, and extracurricular activities that can be incorporated into class lessons and discussions.
Examples

1. Have students design and conduct interviews and surveys to learn about each other's interests.

2. Keep the class library stocked with books that connect to students' interests and hobbies.

3. Allow choices (stories in language arts or projects in science) based on students' interests.

Support instruction with humor, personal experiences, and anecdotes that show the human side of the content.
Examples

1. Share your own hobbies, interests, and favorites.

2. Tell students there will be a surprise visitor; then dress up as the author of a story and tell about "yourself" and your writing.

Use original source material with interesting content or details.
Examples

1. Letters and diaries in history.

2. Darwin's notes in biology.

Create surprise and curiosity.
Examples

1. Have students predict what will happen in an experiment, then show them whether they were right or wrong.

2. Provide quotes from history and ask students to guess who said it.

For more information on students' interests and motivation, see: http://mathforum.org/~sarah/Discussion.Sessions/biblio.motivation.html

Source: From 150 Ways to Increase Intrinsic Motivation in the Classroom, *by James P. Raffini. Published by Allyn and Bacon, Boston, MA. Copyright © 1996 by Pearson Education. Adapted by permission of the publisher. Also Motivation in Education (2nd ed.) by P. Pintrich and D. Schunk, 2002, Merrill/Prentice-Hall, pp. 298–299.*

feedback can be helpful. Also, proper handling of mistakes can stimulate curiosity by pointing to missing knowledge. Finally, the more we learn about a topic, the more curious we may become about that subject. As Maslow (1970) predicted, fulfilling the need to know increases, not decreases, the need to know more. See the *Guidelines* for more about building interest and curiosity in the classroom.

Emotions and Anxiety

How do you feel about learning? Excited, bored, curious, fearful? Today, researchers emphasize that learning is not just about the *cold cognition* of reasoning and problem solving. Learning and information processing also are influenced by emotion, so *hot cognition* plays a role in learning as well (Pintrich, 2003). Research on emotions, learning, and motivation is expanding, in part because we know more about the brain and emotion.

NEUROSCIENCE AND EMOTION. In mammals, including humans, stimulation to a small area of the brain called the *amygdala* seems to trigger emotional reactions such as the "fight or flight" response. The responses in nonhuman animals can be strong. But human emotions are the outcome of physiological responses triggered by the brain, combined with interpretations of the situation and other information. So, hearing startling sounds during an action movie might cause a brief emotional reaction, but hearing the same sounds in the middle of the night as you are walking through a dark alley could lead to stronger and more lasting emotional reactions. Even though the amygdala plays a key role in emotions, many other brain regions are also involved. Emotions are a "constant interplay between cognitive assessments, conscious feelings, and bodily responses, with each able to influence the other" (Gluck, Mercado, & Myers, 2007, p. 418). Humans are more likely to pay attention to, learn about, and remember events, images, and readings that provoke emotional responses (Murphy & Alexander, 2000; Cowley & Underwood, 1998; Reisberg & Heuer, 1992). Emotions can affect learning by changing brain dopamine levels that influence long-term memory and by directing attention toward one aspect of the situation (Pekrun, Elliott, & Maier, 2006). Sometimes, emotions interfere with learning by taking up attention or working memory space that could be used for learning (Pekrun, Goetz, Titz, & Perry, 2002).

In teaching, we are concerned about a particular kind of emotions—those related to achievement in school. Experiences of success or failure can provoke achievement emotions such as pride, hope, boredom, anger, or shame (Pekrun, Elliot, & Maier, 2006). How can we use these findings to support learning in school?

ACHIEVEMENT EMOTIONS. In the past, with the exception of anxiety, emotions generally were overlooked in research on learning and motivation (Linnenbrink-Garcia & Pekrun, 2011). But as you saw above, research in the neurosciences has shown that emotions are both causes and consequences of learning processes. Reinhard Pekrun and his colleagues (2006, 2010) have tested a model that relates different goal orientations to boredom and other emotions in older adolescents from the United States and Germany. The goal orientations are those we discussed earlier: mastery, performance approach, and performance avoidance.

With a *mastery goal*, students focused on an activity. They valued the activity as a way to get smarter, and they felt in control. They were not afraid of failing, so they could focus on the task at hand. The researchers found that having mastery goals predicted enjoyment in learning, hope, and pride. Students with mastery goals were less likely to feel angry or bored about learning. Boredom is a big problem in classrooms because it is associated with difficulties in paying attention, lack of intrinsic motivation, weak effort, shallow processing of information, and poor self-regulated learning (Pekrun et al., 2010)

With a *performance-approach goal*, students wanted to look good or be the best, and they focused their attention on positive outcomes. Performance-approach goals were related mostly to pride. Students with *performance-avoidance goals* focused on the fear of failing and the possibility of looking stupid. Performance-avoidance goals predicted feelings of anxiety, hopelessness, and shame. These findings are summarized in Table 12.4.

TABLE 12.4 • **How Different Achievement Goals Influence Achievement Emotions**

Different goals are associated with different emotions that can impact motivation.

GOAL ORIENTATION	STUDENT EMOTIONS
Mastery Focus on activity, controllability, positive value of activity	Increases: enjoyment of activity, pride, hope Decreases: boredom, anger
Performance-approach Focus on outcome, controllability, positive outcome value	Increases: pride
Performance-avoidance Focus on outcome, lack of controllability, negative outcome value	Increases: anxiety, hopelessness, shame

Source: Adapted from Pekrun, R., Elliot, A. J., & Maier, M. A. (2006). Achievement goals and discrete achievement emotions: A theoretical model and prospective test. Journal of Educational Psychology, 98, 583–597.

How can you increase positive achievement emotions and decrease boredom in the subject you teach? Students are more likely to feel bored if they believe they have little control over the learning activities and they don't value the activities. Matching challenge to the students' skill levels and giving choices can increase the students' sense of control. In addition, efforts to build student interest and show the value of the activities also help to fight boredom. And remember, achievement emotions are domain specific. The fact that students enjoy and feel proud of their work in math does not mean they will enjoy English or history (Goetz, Frenzel, Hall, & Pekrun, 2008; Pekrun et al., 2010). In addition, teachers who enjoy their subjects tend to be more enthusiastic and encourage student enjoyment, so make sure, as much as possible, that you are teaching from your own interests and passions (Brophy, 2008; Frenzel, Goetz, Lüdtke, Pekrun, & Sutton, 2009).

AROUSAL AND ANXIETY. Just as we all know how it feels to be motivated, we all know what it is like to be aroused. **Arousal** involves both psychological and physical reactions—changes in brain wave patterns, blood pressure, heart rate, and breathing rate. We feel alert, wide awake, even excited.

To understand the effects of arousal on motivation, think of two extremes. The first is late at night. You are trying for the third time to understand a required reading, but you are so sleepy. Your attention drifts as your eyelids droop. You decide to go to bed and get up early to study (a plan that you know seldom works). At the other extreme, imagine that you have a critical test tomorrow—one that determines whether you will get into the school you want. You feel tremendous pressure from everyone to do well. You know that you need a good night's sleep, but you are wide awake. In the first case, arousal is too low and in the second, too high. Psychologists have known for years that there is an optimum level of arousal for most activities (Yerkes & Dodson, 1908). Generally speaking, higher levels of arousal are helpful on simple tasks such as sorting laundry, but lower levels of arousal are better for complex tasks such as taking the SAT or GRE.

ANXIETY IN THE CLASSROOM. At one time or another, everyone has experienced **anxiety**, or a general uneasiness, a feeling of self-doubt, and sense of tension. The effects of anxiety on school achievement are clear. Anxiety can be both a cause and an effect of school failure—students do poorly because they are anxious, and their poor performance increases their anxiety. Anxiety probably is both a *trait* and a *state*. Some students tend to be anxious in many situations (trait anxiety), but some situations are especially anxiety provoking (state anxiety) (Covington, 1992; Zeidner, 1998).

Anxiety seems to have both cognitive and affective components. The cognitive side includes worry and negative thoughts—thinking about how bad it would be to fail and worrying that you will, for example. The affective side involves physiological and emotional reactions such as sweaty palms, upset stomach, racing heartbeat, or fear (Jain & Dowson, 2009; Schunk, Pintrich, & Meece, 2008). Whenever there are pressures to perform, severe consequences for failure, and competitive comparisons among students, anxiety may be encouraged (Wigfield & Eccles, 1989). Research with school-age children shows a relationship between the quality of sleep (how quickly and how well you sleep) and anxiety. Better-quality sleep is associated with positive arousal or an "eagerness" to learn. Poor-quality sleep, on the other hand, is related to debilitating anxiety and decreased school performance. You may have discovered these relationships for yourself in your own school career (Meijer & van den Wittenboer, 2004).

HOW DOES ANXIETY INTERFERE WITH ACHIEVEMENT? Anxiety interferes with learning and test performance at three points: focusing attention, learning, and testing. When students are learning new material, they must pay attention to it. Highly anxious students evidently divide their attention between the new material and their preoccupation with how worried and nervous they are feeling. Instead of concentrating, they keep noticing the tight feelings in their chest, thinking, "I'm so tense, I'll never understand this stuff!" From the beginning, anxious students may miss much of the information they are supposed to learn because their thoughts are focused on their own worries (Cassady & Johnson, 2002).

Connect and Extend to PRAXIS II™

Test Anxiety (I, C3)
Test Taking and Anxiety (http://www.ulrc.psu.edu/studyskills/test_taking.html) provides tips and insights into addressing the problems associated with test anxiety. (And the tips might be useful for doing well on the PRAXIS II™ exam!)

Arousal Physical and psychological reactions causing a person to be alert, attentive, wide awake.

Anxiety General uneasiness, a feeling of tension.

But the problems do not end here. Even if they are paying attention, many anxious students have trouble learning material that is somewhat disorganized and difficult—material that requires them to rely on their memory. Unfortunately, much material in school could be described this way. In addition, many highly anxious students have poor study habits. Simply learning to be more relaxed will not automatically improve these students' performance; their learning strategies and study skills must be improved as well (Jain & Dowson, 2009; Naveh-Benjamin, 1991).

Finally, anxious students often know more than they can demonstrate on a test. They may lack critical test-taking skills, or they may have learned the material, but "freeze and forget" on tests (Naveh-Benjamin, McKeachie, & Lin, 1987).

Reaching Every Student: Coping with Anxiety

Some students, particularly those with learning disabilities or emotional disorders, may be especially anxious in school. When students face stressful situations such as tests, they can use three kinds of coping strategies: problem-focused self-regulating learning strategies, emotional management, and avoidance. *Problem-focused self-regulating strategies* might include planning a study schedule, borrowing good notes, or finding a protected place to study. *Emotion-focused strategies* are attempts to reduce the anxious feelings, for example, by using relaxation exercises or describing the feelings to a friend. Of course, the latter might become an *avoidance strategy*, along with going out for pizza or suddenly launching an all-out desk-cleaning attack (can't study until you get organized!). Different strategies are helpful at different points—for example, self-regulated learning before and emotion management during an exam. Different strategies fit different people and situations (Zeidner, 1995, 1998).

Teachers should help highly anxious students to set realistic goals, because these individuals often have difficulty making wise choices. They tend to select either extremely difficult or extremely easy tasks. In the first case, they are likely to fail, which will increase their sense of hopelessness and anxiety about school. In the second case, they will probably succeed on the easy tasks, but they will miss the sense of satisfaction that could encourage greater effort and ease their fears about schoolwork. Goal cards, progress charts, or goal-planning journals may help here. In addition, directly teaching students self-regulated learning strategies and supporting their self-efficacy can help them be more in control of their learning and their anxiety (Jain & Dowson, 2009).

Curiosity, Interests, and Emotions: Lessons for Teachers

Make efforts to keep the level of arousal right for the task at hand. If students are going to sleep, energize them by introducing variety, piquing their curiosity, surprising them, or giving them a brief chance to be physically active. Learn about their interests and incorporate these interests into lessons and assignments. If arousal is too great, follow the *Guidelines* for dealing with anxiety.

How can we put together all this information about motivation? How can teachers create environments, situations, and relationships that encourage motivation? We address these questions next.

MOTIVATION TO LEARN IN SCHOOL: ON TARGET

Teachers are concerned about developing a particular kind of motivation in their students—the **motivation to learn**, defined as "a student tendency to find academic activities meaningful and worthwhile and to try to derive the intended academic benefits from them" (Brophy, 1988, pp. 205–206). Motivation to learn involves more than wanting or intending to learn. It includes the quality of the student's mental efforts. For example, reading the text 11 times may indicate persistence, but motivation to learn implies more thoughtful, active study strategies, such as summarizing, elaborating the basic ideas, outlining in your own words, drawing graphs of the key relationships, and so on (Brophy, 1988).

Motivation to learn The tendency to find academic activities meaningful and worthwhile and to try to benefit from them.

GUIDELINES

Coping with Anxiety

Use competition carefully.
Examples
1. Monitor activities to make sure no students are being put under undue pressure.
2. During competitive games, make sure all students involved have a reasonable chance of succeeding.
3. Experiment with cooperative learning activities.

Avoid situations in which highly anxious students will have to perform in front of large groups.
Examples
1. Ask anxious students questions that can be answered with a simple yes or no, or some other brief reply.
2. Give anxious students practice in speaking before smaller groups.

Make sure all instructions are clear. Uncertainty can lead to anxiety.
Examples
1. Write test instructions on the board or on the test itself instead of giving them orally.
2. Check with students to make sure they understand. Ask several students how they would do the first question, exercise, or sample question on a test. Correct any misconceptions.
3. If you are using a new format or starting a new type of task, give students examples or models to show how it is done.

Avoid unnecessary time pressures.
Examples
1. Give occasional take-home tests.
2. Make sure all students can complete classroom tests within the period given.

Remove some of the pressures from major tests and exams.
Examples
1. Teach test-taking skills; give practice tests; provide study guides.
2. Avoid basing most of a report-card grade on one test.
3. Make extra-credit work available to add points to course grades.
4. Use different types of items in testing because some students have difficulty with particular formats.

Develop alternatives to written tests.
Examples
1. Try oral, open-book, or group tests.
2. Have students do projects, organize portfolios of their work, make oral presentations, or create a finished product.

Teach students self-regulation strategies (Schutz & Davis, 2000).
Examples
1. Before the test: Encourage students to see the test as an important and challenging task that they have the capabilities to prepare for. Help students stay focused on the task of getting as much information as possible about the test.
2. During the test: Remind students that the test is important (but not overly important). Encourage task focus—pick out the main idea in the question, slow down, stay relaxed.
3. After the test: Think back on what went well and what could be improved. Focus on controllable attributions—study strategies, effort, careful reading of questions, relaxation strategies.

For more information about test anxiety, see:
http://www.counselingcenter.uiuc.edu/?page_id=193

It would be wonderful if all our students came to us filled with the motivation to learn, but they don't. As teachers, we have three major goals. The first is to get students productively involved with the work of the class; in other words, to *catch* their interest and create a *state* of motivation to learn. The second and longer-term goal is to develop in our students enduring individual interests and the *trait* of being motivated to learn so they will be able to educate themselves for the rest of their lives. And finally, we want our students to be *cognitively engaged*—to think deeply about what they study. In other words, we want them to be thoughtful (Blumenfeld, Puro, & Mergendoller, 1992).

Earlier in this chapter we examined the roles of intrinsic and extrinsic motivation, attributions, goals, beliefs, self-perceptions, interests, curiosity, and emotions in motivation. Table 12.5 on the next page shows how each of these factors contributes to motivation to learn.

The central question for the remainder of the chapter is: How can teachers use their knowledge about attributions, goals, beliefs, self-perceptions, interests, and emotions to

TABLE 12.5 • **Building a Concept of Motivation to Learn**
Motivation to learn is encouraged when the following five elements come together.

SOURCE OF MOTIVATION	OPTIMUM CHARACTERISTICS OF MOTIVATION TO LEARN	CHARACTERISTICS THAT DIMINISH MOTIVATION TO LEARN
Type of Goal Set	INTRINSIC: Personal factors such as needs, interests, curiosity, enjoyment	EXTRINSIC: Environmental factors such as rewards, social pressure, punishment
Type of Involvement	LEARNING GOAL: Personal satisfaction in meeting challenges and improving; tendency to choose moderately difficult and challenging goals TASK-INVOLVED: Concerned with mastering the task	PERFORMANCE GOAL: Desire for approval for performance in others' eyes; tendency to choose very easy or very difficult goals EGO-INVOLVED: Concerned with self in others' eyes
Achievement Motivation	Motivation to ACHIEVE: Mastery orientation	Motivation to AVOID FAILURE: Prone to anxiety
Likely Attributions	Successes and failures attributed to CONTROLLABLE effort and ability	Successes and failures attributed to UNCONTROLLABLE causes
Beliefs about Ability	INCREMENTAL VIEW: Belief that ability can be improved through hard work and added knowledge and skills	ENTITY VIEW: Belief that ability is a stable, uncontrollable trait

Connect and Extend to PRAXIS II™

Target (I, C1,2,3)
Describe the major features of the TARGET model and identify related strategies that are likely to boost motivation.

increase motivation to learn? To organize our discussion, we will use the TARGET model (Ames, 1992; Epstein, 1989), identifying six areas where teachers make decisions that can influence student motivation to learn.

T: task that students are asked to do
A: autonomy or authority students are allowed in working
R: recognition for accomplishments
G: grouping practices
E: evaluation procedures
T: time in the classroom

Tasks for Learning

To understand how an **academic task** can affect students' motivation, we need to analyze the task. Tasks have different values for students.

Academic tasks The work the student must accomplish, including the content covered and the mental operations required.

Importance/Attainment value The importance of doing well on a task; how success on the task meets personal needs.

TASK VALUE. As you probably recall, many theories suggest that the strength of our motivation in a particular situation is determined by both our *expectation* that we can succeed and the *value* of that success to us. Perceptions of task value predict the choices students make, such as whether to enroll in advanced science classes or join the track team. Efficacy expectations predict achievement in actually doing the task—how well the students will perform in the science class or on the track team (Wigfield & Eccles, 2002b).

We can think of task value as having four components: importance, interest, utility, and cost (Eccles & Wigfield, 2002; Hulleman, Godes, Hendricks, & Harackiewicz, 2010). **Importance or attainment value** is the significance of doing well on the task; this is closely tied to the needs of the individual (the need to be well liked, athletic, etc.).

For instance, if someone has a strong need to appear smart and believes that a high grade on a test proves you are smart, then the test has high attainment value for that person. A second component is **interest or intrinsic value**. This is simply the enjoyment one gets from the activity itself. Some people like the experience of learning. Others enjoy the feeling of hard physical effort or the challenge of solving puzzles. Tasks also can have **utility value**; that is, they help us achieve a short-term or long-term goal such as earning a degree. Finally, tasks have costs—negative consequences that might follow from doing the task such as not having time to do other things or looking awkward as you perform the task.

You can see from our discussion of task value that personal and environmental influences on motivation interact constantly. The task we ask students to accomplish is an aspect of the environment; it is external to the student. But the value of accomplishing the task is bound up with the internal needs, beliefs, and goals of the individual. Because task value has to do with choices, positive values toward academic tasks can be life-changing because choices about courses in high school and education after high school affect career and life opportunities (Durik, Vida, & Eccles, 2006).

BEYOND TASK VALUE TO GENUINE APPRECIATION. Jere Brophy (2008, p. 140) reminds teachers that there is more to value than interest or utility—there is the power of knowing: "Powerful ideas expand and enrich the quality of students' subjective lives." These ideas give us lenses for viewing the world, tools for making decisions, and frames for appreciating the beauty in words and images. An entire issue of *Theory Into Practice*, the journal I edit, is devoted to Jere's ideas about engaging students in the value and appreciation of learning (Turner, Patrick, & Meyer, 2011). One way to build appreciation is with authentic tasks.

AUTHENTIC TASKS. Recently, there has been a great deal written about the use of authentic tasks in teaching. An **authentic task** has some connection to the real-life problems and situations that students will face outside the classroom, both now and in the future. If you ask students to memorize definitions they will never use, to learn the material only because it is on the test, or to repeat work they already understand, then there can be little motivation to learn. But if the tasks are authentic, students are more likely to see the genuine utility value of the work and are also more likely to find the tasks meaningful and interesting (Pugh & Phillips, 2011). **Problem-based learning** and service learning (Chapter 10) are two examples of the use of authentic tasks in teaching. For example, a physics teacher might use skateboarding as a basis for problems and examples, knowing that skateboarding is an authentic task for many of her students (Anderman & Anderman, 2010). For younger students, compare these two teachers described by Anderman and Anderman (2010):

> Mrs. Byrnes gives her class an initial lesson on halves and quarters, divides students into groups of three, and gives each group two Twinkies and a plastic knife. She asks the students to cut one Twinkie into two equally-sized pieces, and the other Twinkie into four equally-sized pieces. Next comes the challenge–use the Twinkie pieces to determine which fraction is bigger, one-half (1/2) or three-fourths (3/4). Mrs. Byrnes then visits each group; the members must explain their work to her. When they are correct, they get to eat the Twinkies.
>
> Mr. Fletcher gives the same initial lesson on halves and quarters. He then provides each student with a worksheet with a few simple questions that are designed to help the students to learn about fractions. For these questions, the students are supposed to imagine that they have several pieces of paper, and that they cut the paper with scissors into various quantities (e.g., they cut one paper into four equal-size pieces, they cut another paper into two equal-size pieces). The students are then asked to demonstrate whether one-half (1/2) or three-fourths (3/4) is the bigger fraction. They then have to write down their answer, along with a brief explanation.

The students in Mrs. Byrnes's class were involved in a more authentic (and tasty) task involving cutting and dividing food, cooperating with others, and enjoying the fruits (or Twinkies) of their labor. They also had to figure out how to share two halves and four quarters equally among three people—advanced cooperation.

Interest or intrinsic value The enjoyment a person gets from a task.

Utility value The contribution of a task to meeting one's goals.

Authentic task Tasks that have some connection to real-life problems the students will face outside the classroom.

Problem-based learning Methods that provide students with realistic problems that don't necessarily have right answers.

Supporting Autonomy and Recognizing Accomplishment

The second area in the TARGET model involves how much choice and autonomy students are allowed. Choice and control in schools are not the norm. Children and adolescents spend literally thousands of hours in schools where other people decide what will happen. Yet we know that self-determination and a sense of internal locus of causality are critical to maintaining intrinsic motivation and student engagement (Jang, Reeve, & Deci, 2010; Reeve, Nix, & Hamm, 2003). What can teachers do to support choice without creating chaos?

SUPPORTING CHOICES.   Choices should provide a range of selections that allow students to follow their interests and pick an option that is important and relevant to them (Katz & Assor, 2007). But beware of giving too many choices. Like totally unguided discovery or aimless discussions, unstructured or unguided choices can be counterproductive for learning (Garner, 1998). I know that graduate students in my classes find it disconcerting if I ask them to design a final project that will determine their grade, just as I panic when I am asked to give a talk on "whatever you want."

The alternative is *bounded choice*—giving students a range of options that set valuable tasks for them, but also allow them to follow personal interests. The balance must be just right: "too much autonomy is bewildering and too little is boring" (Guthrie et al., 1998, p. 185). Students can have input about work partners, seating arrangements, how to display work, or suggestions for class rules. But the most important kind of autonomy support teachers can provide probably is cognitive autonomy support—giving students opportunities to discuss different cognitive strategies for learning, approaches to solving problems, or positions on an issue (Stefanou, Perencevich, DiCinto, & Turner, 2004). Students also can exercise autonomy about how they receive feedback from the teacher or from classmates. Figure 12.1 describes a strategy called "Check It Out," in which students specify the skills that they want to have evaluated in a particular assignment. Over the

---

FIGURE 12.1

STUDENT AUTONOMY: CHECK IT OUT

Using this technique to support student autonomy, the teacher decides on a set of skills that will be developed over a unit, but the student decides which skill(s) will be evaluated on any given assignment. Over the course of the unit, all the skills have to be "checked out." This student has indicated that she wants the teacher to "check out" her creativity and verb tense.

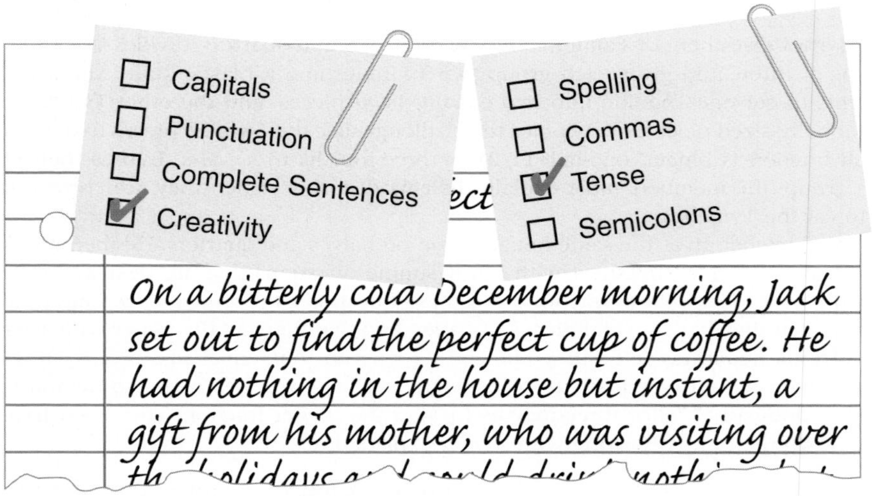

☐ Capitals
☐ Punctuation
☐ Complete Sentences
☑ Creativity

☐ Spelling
☐ Commas
☑ Tense
☐ Semicolons

On a bitterly cold December morning, Jack set out to find the perfect cup of coffee. He had nothing in the house but instant, a gift from his mother, who was visiting over

course of a unit, all the skills have to be "checked out," but students choose when each one is evaluated.

RECOGNIZING ACCOMPLISHMENT. The third TARGET area is recognition for accomplishments. Students should be recognized for improving on their own personal best, for tackling difficult tasks, for persistence, and for creativity—not just for performing better than others. In Chapter 7 we noted that giving students rewards for activities that they already enjoy can undermine intrinsic motivation. What sort of recognition leads to engagement? One answer comes from a study by Ruth Butler (1987). Students in the 5th and 6th grades were given interesting divergent thinking tasks that were followed up by one of the following teacher responses: individual personalized comments, standardized praise ("very good"), grades, or no feedback. Interest, performance, attributions to effort, and task involvement were higher after personalized comments. Ego-involved motivation (the desire to look good or do better than others) was greater after grades and standard praise.

Grouping, Evaluation, and Time

You may remember a teacher who made you want to work hard—someone who made a subject come alive. Or you may remember how many hours you spent practicing as a member of a team, orchestra, choir, or theater troupe. If you do, then you know the motivational power of relationships with other people.

GROUPING AND GOAL STRUCTURES. Motivation can be greatly influenced by the ways we relate to the other people who are also involved in accomplishing a particular goal. Johnson and Johnson (2009a) have labeled this interpersonal factor the **goal structure** of the task. There are three goal structures: cooperative, competitive, and individualistic, as shown in Table 12.6.

When the task involves complex learning and problem-solving skills, cooperation leads to higher achievement than competition, especially for students with lower abilities. Students learn to set attainable goals and negotiate. They become more altruistic. The interaction with peers that students enjoy so much becomes a part of the learning process. The result? The need for belonging described by Maslow is more likely to be met and motivation is increased (Stipek, 2002; Webb & Palincsar, 1996). There are many

TABLE 12.6 • **Different Goal Structures**
Each goal structure is associated with a different relationship between the individual and the group. This relationship influences motivation to reach the goal.

	COOPERATIVE	COMPETITIVE	INDIVIDUALISTIC
Definition	Students believe their goal is attainable only if other students will also reach the goal.	Students believe they will reach their goal if and only if other students do not reach the goal.	Students believe that their own attempt to reach a goal is not related to other students' attempts to reach the goal.
Examples	Team victories—each player wins only if all the team members win: a relay race, a quilting bee, a barn raising, a symphony, a play.	Golf tournament, singles tennis match, a 100-yard dash, valedictorian, Miss America pageant.	Lowering your handicap in golf, jogging, learning a new language, enjoying a museum, losing or gaining weight, stopping smoking.

Source: Based on Learning Together and Alone: Cooperation, Competition, and Individualization (5th ed.), by D. Johnson & R. Johnson. Published by Allyn and Bacon, Boston, MA. Copyright © 1999 by Pearson Education.

Goal structure The way students relate to others who are also working toward a particular goal.

approaches to peer learning or group learning, as you saw in Chapter 11. For example, to encourage motivation with a cooperative goal structure, form reading groups based on student interests instead of abilities and change the groups every month (Anderman & Anderman, 2010).

EVALUATION.   The greater the emphasis on competitive evaluation and grading, the more students will focus on performance goals rather than mastery. And low-achieving students who have little hope of either performing well or mastering the task may simply want to get it over with (Brophy, 2005). How can teachers prevent students from simply focusing on the grade or doing the work "just to get finished"? The most obvious answer is to de-emphasize grades and to emphasize learning in the class. Students need to understand the value of the work. Instead of saying, "You will need to know this for the test," tell students how the information will be useful in solving problems they want to solve. Suggest that the lesson will answer some interesting questions. Communicate that understanding is more important than finishing. Unfortunately, many teachers do not follow this advice.

TIME.   Most experienced teachers know that there is too much work and not enough time in the school day. Even if they become engrossed in a project, students must stop and turn their attention to another class when the bell rings or when the teacher's schedule indicates it's time to move on to a new subject. Furthermore, students must progress as a group. If particular individuals can move faster or if they need more time, they may still have to follow the pace of the whole group. So scheduling often interferes with motivation by making students move faster or slower than would be appropriate or by interrupting their involvement. It is difficult to develop persistence and a sense of self-efficacy when students are not allowed to stick with a challenging activity. As a teacher, will you be able to make time for engaged and persistent learning? Some elementary classrooms have *DEAR* time—Drop Everything And Read—to give extended periods when everyone, even the teacher, reads. Some middle and high schools have *block scheduling* in which teachers work in teams to plan larger blocks of class time.

PUTTING IT ALL TOGETHER.   We can see how these motivational elements come together in real classrooms. Sara Dolezal and her colleagues observed and interviewed 3rd grade teachers in eight Catholic schools and determined if their students were low, moderate, or high in their level of motivation (Dolezal, Welsh, Pressley, & Vincent, 2003). Table 12.7 summarizes the dramatic differences in these classrooms between the use of strategies that support motivation and those that undermine it. Students in the *low-engagement* classes were restless and chatty as they faced their easy, undemanding seatwork. The classrooms were bare, unattractive, and filled with management problems. Instruction was disorganized. The class atmosphere was generally negative. The *moderately engaged* classrooms were organized to be "student friendly," with reading areas, group work areas, posters, and student artwork. The teachers were warm and caring, and they connected lessons to students' background knowledge. Management routines were smooth and organized, and the class atmosphere was positive. The teachers were good at catching student attention, but they had trouble *holding* attention, probably because the tasks were too easy. *Highly engaging* teachers had all the positive qualities of student-friendly classrooms—but they added more challenging tasks along with the support the students needed to succeed. These excellent motivators did not rely on one or two approaches to motivate their students; they applied a large repertoire of strategies from Table 12.7.

Diversity in Motivation

Because students differ in terms of language, culture, economic privilege, personality, knowledge, and experience, they will also differ in their needs, goals, interests, emotions, and beliefs. Teachers encourage motivation to learn by taking this diversity into account using TARGET—designing tasks, supporting autonomy, recognizing accomplishments, grouping, making evaluations, and managing time. Take interest, for example. Embedding

TABLE 12.7 • **Strategies That Support and Undermine Motivation in the Classroom**

A FEW STRATEGIES THAT SUPPORT MOTIVATION	
STRATEGY	**EXAMPLE**
Messages of accountability and high expectations	The teacher asks students to have parents review and sign some assignments.
Teacher communicates importance of work	"We need to check it for at least 1 minute, which means looking over it carefully."
Clear goals/directions	The teacher explains exactly how the students are to separate into groups and complete their nominations for their favorite book.
Connections across the curriculum	The teacher relates the concept of ratios in math to compare/contrast skills in reading.
Opportunities to learn about and practice dramatic arts	After studying about historical figures, students write and produce their own plays.
Attributions to effort	During a word game, the teacher says to a student, "Did you study last night?" The student nods. "See how it helps?"
Encouraging risk-taking	"I need a new shining face. Someone I haven't called on yet. I need a risk-taker."
Uses games and play to reinforce concept or review material	During a math lesson using balance, students spend 5 minutes weighing the favorite toy they were asked to bring in that day.
Home–school connections	As part of math science unit, a recycling activity asks families to keep a chart of everything they recycle in a week.
Multiple representations of a task	The teacher uses 4 ways to teach multiplication: "magic multipliers," sing-along multiplication facts, whole-class flash card review, "Around-the-World" game.
Positive classroom management, praise, private reprimands	"Thumbs up when you are ready to work. Table 7 has thumbs up. I like the way table 7 is waiting patiently."
Stimulating creative thought	"We are going to use our imaginations today. We are going to take a trip to an imaginary theater in our heads."
Opportunities for choice	Students can choose to use prompts for their journal writing or pick their own topic.
Teacher communicates to students that they can handle challenging tasks	"This is hard stuff and you are doing great. I know adults who have trouble with this."
Value students—communicate caring	The teacher allows a new student to sit with a buddy for the day.
A FEW STRATEGIES THAT DO NOT SUPPORT MOTIVATION TO LEARN	
Attributions to intellect rather than effort	When students remark during a lesson, "I'm stupid" or "I'm a dork," the teacher says nothing, then replies, "Let's have someone who is smart."
Teacher emphasizes competition rather than working together	The teacher conducts a poetry contest where students read poems to the class and the class members hold up cards with scores rating how well each student performed.
No scaffolding for learning a new skill	The teacher is loud and critical when students have trouble: "Just look back in the glossary and don't miss it because you are too lazy to look it up."
Ineffective/negative feedback	"Does everyone understand?" A few students say yes and the teacher moves on.
Lack of connections	On Martin Luther King Day, the teacher leads a brief discussion of King, then the remainder of the activities are about Columbus.
Easy tasks	The teacher provides easy work and "fun" activities that teach little.

A FEW STRATEGIES THAT DO NOT SUPPORT MOTIVATION TO LEARN *(continued)*	
Negative class atmosphere	"Excuse me, I said page number. If you follow and listen, you would know."
Punitive classroom management	The teacher threatens bad grades if students do not look up words in the glossary.
Work that is much too difficult	The teacher assigns independent math work that only one or two students can do.
Slow pacing	The pace is set for the slowest students—others finish and have nothing to do.
Emphasis on finishing, not learning	The teacher communicates the purpose is to finish, not learn or use the vocabulary.
Sparse, unattractive classroom	There are no decorated bulletin boards, maps, charts, or displays of student work.
Poor planning	Missing handouts force the teacher to have large instead of smaller work groups.
Public punishment	All students stand, and the teacher reads a list of those who finished the assignment and they sit down. The teacher gives public lecture on responsibility to those left standing.

Source: Adapted from "How do nine third-grade teachers motivate their students?" by S. E. Dolezal, L. M. Welsh, M. Pressley, & M. Vincent. Elementary School Journal, *2003, 103, pp. 247–248.*

student writing tasks in cultural contexts is one way to catch and hold situational interest (Alderman, 2004; Bergin, 1999). When Latina/o immigrant students in middle-school classes moved from writing using worksheets and standard assignments to writing about such topics as immigration, bilingualism, and gang life—issues that were important to them and to their families—their papers got longer and the writing quality was better (Rueda & Moll, 1994).

Language is a central factor in students' connections with the school. When bilingual students are encouraged to draw on both English and their heritage language, motivation and participation can increase. Robert Jimenez (2000) found in his study of bilingual Latino/a students that successful readers viewed reading as a process of making sense; they used both of their languages to understand the material. For instance, they might look for Spanish word parts in English words to help them translate. Less-successful students had a different goal. They believed that reading just meant saying the words correctly in English. It is likely their interest and sense of efficacy for reading in English would be less, too.

Lessons for Teachers: Strategies to Encourage Motivation

Until four basic conditions are met for every student and in every classroom, no motivational strategies will succeed. First, the classroom must be relatively organized and free from constant interruptions and disruptions. (Chapter 13 will give you the information you need to make sure this requirement is met.) Second, the teacher must be a patient, supportive person who never embarrasses the students because they made mistakes. Everyone in the class should view mistakes as opportunities for learning (Clifford, 1990, 1991). Third, the work must be challenging, but reasonable. If work is too easy or too difficult, students will have little motivation to learn. They will focus on finishing, not on learning. Finally, the learning tasks must be authentic. And as we have seen, what makes a task authentic is influenced by the students' culture (Bergin, 1999; Brophy & Kher, 1986; Stipek, 1993).

Once these four basic conditions are met, the influences on students' motivation to learn in a particular situation can be summarized in four questions: Can I succeed at this task? Do I want to succeed? What do I need to do to succeed? Do I belong? (Committee on Increasing High School Students' Engagement and Motivation to Learn, 2004; Eccles & Wigfield, 1985). We want students to have confidence in their ability so they will approach learning with energy and enthusiasm. We want them to see the value of the tasks involved and work to learn, not just try to get the grade or get finished. We want students to believe that success will come when they apply good learning strategies instead of believing that their only option is to use self-defeating, failure-avoiding, face-saving strategies. When things get difficult, we want students to stay focused on the task, and not get so worried about failure that they "freeze." And we want students to feel as though they belong in school—that their teachers and classmates care about them and can be trusted.

CAN I DO IT? BUILDING CONFIDENCE AND POSITIVE EXPECTATIONS.   No amount of encouragement or "cheerleading" will substitute for real accomplishment. To ensure genuine progress:

1. *Begin work at the students' level and move in small steps.* One possibility is to have very easy and very difficult questions on every test and assignment, so all students are both successful and challenged. When grades are required, make sure all the students in class have a chance to make at least a C if they work hard.
2. *Make sure learning goals are clear, specific, and possible to reach in the near future.* Break long-term projects into subgoals. If possible, give students a range of goals at different levels of difficulty and let them choose.
3. *Stress self-comparison, not comparison with others.* Give specific feedback and corrections. Tell students what they are doing right as well as what is wrong and why it is wrong. Periodically, give students a question or problem that was once hard for them but now seems easy. Point out how much they have improved.
4. *Communicate to students that academic ability is improvable* and specific to the task at hand. In other words, the fact that a student has trouble in algebra doesn't necessarily mean that geometry will be difficult. Don't undermine your efforts to stress improvement by displaying only the 100% papers on the bulletin board.
5. *Model good problem solving,* especially when you have to try several approaches. Students need to see that learning is not smooth and error-free, even for the teacher.

DO I WANT TO DO IT? SEEING THE VALUE OF LEARNING.   Teachers can use intrinsic and extrinsic motivation strategies to help students see the value of the learning task.

Attainment and Intrinsic Value.   To establish attainment value, we must connect the learning task with the needs of the students. It must be possible for students to meet their needs for safety, belonging, and achievement in our classes. Many students are quietly wounded by their teachers' words or school practices that embarrass, label, or demean (Olson, 2008). We must make it clear that both women and men can be high achievers in all subjects: no subjects are the territory of only one sex. It is not "unfeminine" to be strong in mathematics, car mechanics, or sports. It is not "unmasculine" to be good in literature, art, or French.

There are many strategies for encouraging intrinsic (interest) motivation. Several of the following are taken from Brophy (1988).

1. *Tie class activities to student interests* in sports, music, current events, pets, common problems or conflicts with family and friends, fads, television, and movie personalities, or other significant features of their lives (Schiefele, 1991).
2. *Arouse curiosity.* Point out puzzling discrepancies between students' beliefs and the facts. For example, Stipek (1993) describes a teacher who asked her 5th grade class if there were "people" on some of the other planets. When the students said yes, the teacher asked if people needed oxygen to breathe. Because the students had just learned this fact, they responded yes. Then the teacher told them that there is no oxygen in the atmosphere of the other planets. This surprising discrepancy between what the children knew about oxygen and what they believed about life on other planets led to a rousing discussion of the atmospheres of other planets.

3. *Make the learning task fun.* Many lessons can be taught through simulations or games (see the *Point/Counterpoint*). Used appropriately so that the activity connects with learning, these experiences can be very worthwhile and fun, too.

4. *Make use of novelty and familiarity.* Don't overuse a few teaching approaches or motivational strategies. We all need some variety. Varying the goal structures of tasks (cooperative, competitive, individualistic) can help. When the material being covered in class is abstract or unfamiliar to students, try to connect it to something they know and understand. For example, talk about the size of a large area, such as the Acropolis in Athens, in terms of football fields.

Instrumental Value. Sometimes it is difficult to encourage intrinsic motivation, and so teachers must rely on the utility or "instrumental" value of tasks. It is important to learn many skills because they will be needed in more advanced classes or for life outside school.

1. When these connections are not obvious, you should *explain the connections* to your students or ask them to explain how the material will be important in their lives (Hulleman, Godes, Hendricks, & Harackiewicz, 2010).

2. In some situations, teachers can *provide incentives and rewards* for learning (see Chapter 7). Remember, though, that giving rewards when students are already interested in the activity may undermine intrinsic motivation.

3. *Use ill-structured problems and authentic tasks* in teaching. Connect problems in school to real problems outside, such as buying your first car, making decisions about mobile phone plans, or writing a persuasive letter to a potential employer.

WHAT DO I NEED TO DO TO SUCCEED? STAYING FOCUSED ON THE TASK. When students encounter difficulties, as they must if they are working at a challenging level, they need to keep their attention on the task. If the focus shifts to worries about performance, fear of failure, or concern with looking smart, then motivation to learn is lost.

1. *Give students frequent opportunities to respond* through questions and answers, short assignments, or demonstrations of skills and correct problems quickly. You don't want students to practice errors too long.

2. When possible, *have students create a finished product.* They will be more persistent and focused on the task when the end is in sight. For example, I often begin a house-painting project thinking I will work for just an hour and then find myself still painting hours later because I want to see the finished product.

3. *Avoid heavy emphasis on grades and competition.* An emphasis on grades forces students to focus on performance, not learning. Anxious students are especially hard hit by highly competitive evaluation.

4. *Reduce the task risk without oversimplifying it.* When tasks are risky (failure is likely and the consequences of failing are grave), student motivation suffers. For difficult, complex, or ambiguous tasks, provide students with plenty of time, support, resources, help, and the chance to revise or improve work.

5. *Model motivation to learn* for your students. Talk about your interest in the subject and how you deal with difficult learning tasks.

6. *Teach the particular learning strategies* that students will need to master the material being studied. Show students how to learn and remember so they won't be forced to fall back on self-defeating strategies or rote memory.

DO I BELONG IN THIS CLASSROOM? This last question will take more than a page or two to address, so I have devoted a large part of Chapter 13 to the notion of creating learning communities. The support of families can be helpful as you design strategies for your students. The *Family and Community Partnerships Guidelines* give ideas for working with families.

Motivation to Learn

Understand family goals for children.
Examples

1. In an informal setting, around coffee or snacks, meet with families individually or in small groups to listen to what their goals are for their children.
2. Mail out questionnaires or send response cards home with students, asking what skills the families believe their children most need to work on. Pick one goal for each child and develop a plan for working toward the goal both inside and outside school. Share the plan with the families and ask for feedback.

Identify student and family interests that can be related to goals.
Examples

1. Ask a member of the family to share a skill or hobby.
2. Identify "family favorites"—favorite foods, music, vacations, sports, activities, hymns, movies, games, snacks, recipes, memories. Tie class lessons to interests.

Give families a way to track progress toward goals.
Examples

1. Provide simple "progress charts" or goal cards that can be posted on the refrigerator.
2. Ask for parents' or caregivers' feedback (and mean it) about your effectiveness in helping their children.

Work with families to build confidence and positive expectations.
Examples

1. Avoid comparing one child in a family to another during conferences and discussions with family members.

2. Ask family members to highlight strong points of homework assignments. They might attach a note to assignments describing the three best aspects of the work and one element that could be improved.

Make families partners in showing the value of learning.
Examples

1. Invite family members to the class to demonstrate how they use mathematics or writing in their work.
2. Involve parents or caregivers in identifying skills and knowledge that could be applied at home and prove helpful to the family right now, for example, keeping records on service agencies, writing letters of complaint to department stores or landlords, or researching vacation destinations.

Provide resources that build skill and will for families.
Examples

1. Give family members simple strategies for helping their children improve study skills.
2. Involve older students in a "homework hotline" telephone network for helping younger students.

Have frequent celebrations of learning.
Examples

1. Invite families to a "museum" at the end of a unit on dinosaurs. Students create the museum in the auditorium, library, or cafeteria. After visiting the museum, families go to the classroom to examine their child's portfolio for the unit.
2. Place mini-exhibits of student work at local grocery stores, libraries, or community centers.

▼ SUMMARY

What Is Motivation? (pp. 430–434)

Define motivation. Motivation is an internal state that arouses, directs, and maintains behavior. The study of motivation focuses on how and why people initiate actions directed toward specific goals, how long it takes them to get started in the activity, how intensively they are involved in the activity, how persistent they are in their attempts to reach these goals, and what they are thinking and feeling along the way.

What is the difference between intrinsic and extrinsic motivation? Intrinsic motivation is the natural tendency to seek out and conquer challenges as we pursue personal interests and exercise capabilities—it is motivation to do something when we don't have

to. Extrinsic motivation is based on factors not related to the activity itself. We are not really interested in the activity for its own sake; we care only about what it will gain us.

How does locus of causality apply to motivation? The essential difference between intrinsic and extrinsic motivation is the person's reason for acting, that is, whether the locus of causality for the action is inside or outside the person. If the locus is internal, the motivation is intrinsic; if the locus is external, the motivation is extrinsic. Most motivation has elements of both. In fact, intrinsic and extrinsic motivation may be two separate tendencies—both can operate at the same time in a given situation.

What are the key factors in motivation according to a behavioral viewpoint? A humanistic viewpoint? A cognitive viewpoint? A social cognitive viewpoint? A sociocultural viewpoint? Behaviorists tend to emphasize extrinsic motivation caused by incentives, rewards, and punishment. Humanistic views stress the intrinsic motivation created by the need for personal growth, fulfillment, and self-determination. Cognitive views stress a person's active search for meaning, understanding, and competence, and the power of the individual's attributions and interpretations. Social cognitive theories take into account both the behaviorists' concern with the consequences of behavior and the cognitivists' interest in the impact of individual beliefs and expectations. Many influential social cognitive explanations of motivation can be characterized as expectancy × value theories. Sociocultural views emphasize legitimate engaged participation and identity within a community.

What are expectancy × value theories? Expectancy × value theories suggest that motivation to reach a goal is the product of our expectations for success and the value of the goal to us. If either is zero, our motivation is zero also.

What is legitimate peripheral participation? Legitimate peripheral participation means that beginners are genuinely involved in the work of the group, even if their abilities are undeveloped and their contributions are small. The identities of the novice and the expert are bound up in their participation in the community. They are motivated to learn the values and practices of the community to keep their identity as community members.

Needs (pp. 434–437)

Distinguish between deficiency needs and being needs in Maslow's theory. Maslow called four lower-level needs—survival, safety, belonging, and self-esteem—deficiency needs. When these needs are satisfied, the motivation for fulfilling them decreases. He labeled the three higher-level needs—intellectual achievement, aesthetic appreciation, and self-actualization—being needs. When they are met, a person's motivation increases to seek further fulfillment.

What are the basic needs that affect motivation, and how does self-determination affect motivation? Self-determination theory suggests that motivation is affected by the need for competence, autonomy and control, and relatedness. When students experience self-determination, they are intrinsically motivated—they are more interested in their work, have a greater sense of self-esteem, and learn more. Whether students experience self-determination depends in part on if the teacher's communications with students provide information or seek to control them. In addition, teachers must acknowledge the students' perspective, offer choices, provide rationales for limits, and treat poor performance as a problem to be solved rather than a target for criticism.

Goal Orientations (pp. 438–442)

What kinds of goals are the most motivating? Goals increase motivation if they are specific, moderately difficult, and able to be reached in the near future.

Describe mastery, performance, work-avoidant, and social goals. A mastery goal is the intention to gain knowledge and master skills, leading students to seek challenges and persist when they encounter difficulties. A performance goal is the intention to get good grades or to appear smarter or more capable than others, leading students to be preoccupied with themselves and how they appear (ego-involved learners). Students can approach or avoid these two kinds of goals—the problems are greatest with avoidance. Another kind of avoidance is evident with work-avoidant learners, who simply want to find the easiest way to handle the situation. Students with social goals can be supported or hindered in their learning, depending on the specific goal (i.e., have fun with friends or bring honor to the family).

What makes goal setting effective in the classroom? In order for goal setting to be effective in the classroom, students need accurate feedback about their progress toward goals and they must accept the goals set. Generally, students are more willing to adopt goals that seem realistic, reasonably difficult, meaningful, and validated by activities connecting them to their intrinsic interests.

Beliefs and Self-Perceptions (pp. 442–448)

What are epistemological beliefs and how do they affect motivation? Epistemological beliefs are ways of understanding how you think and learn. Individuals' epistemological beliefs can impact their approach to learning, their expectations of themselves and the work they do, and the extent to which they engage in academic tasks. Specifically, epistemological beliefs include your understanding of the structure, stability, and certainty of knowledge. A belief that knowledge can be organized into a grand scheme in which all things are related, for example, may lead students to try to connect all new knowledge with previous knowledge in a meaningful way. If the task proves excessively challenging, these students may believe the new information is not relevant to them or worth understanding.

How do beliefs about ability affect motivation? When people hold an entity theory of ability—that is, they believe that ability is fixed—they tend to set performance goals and strive to protect themselves from failure. When they believe ability is improvable (an incremental theory), however, they tend to set mastery goals and handle failure constructively.

What are the three dimensions of attributions in Weiner's theory? According to Weiner, most of the attributed causes for successes or failures can be characterized in terms of three dimensions: locus (location of the cause internal or external to the person), stability (whether the cause stays the same or can change), and responsibility (whether the person can control the cause). The greatest motivational problems arise when students attribute failures to stable, uncontrollable causes. These students may seem resigned to failure, depressed, helpless—what we generally call "unmotivated."

What is learned helplessness and what deficits does it cause? When people come to believe that the events and outcomes in their lives are mostly uncontrollable, they have developed learned helplessness, which is associated with three types of deficits: motivational, cognitive, and affective. Students who feel hopeless will be unmotivated and reluctant to attempt work. They miss opportunities to practice and improve skills and abilities, so they develop cognitive deficits and they often suffer from affective problems such as depression, anxiety, and listlessness.

How does self-worth influence motivation? Mastery-oriented students tend to value achievement and see ability as improvable, so they focus on mastery goals, take risks, and cope with failure constructively. A low sense of self-worth seems to be linked with the failure-avoiding and failure-accepting strategies intended to protect the individual from the consequences of failure. These strategies may seem to help in the short term, but are damaging to motivation and self-esteem in the long run.

Interests, Curiosity, Emotions, and Anxiety (pp. 448–454)

How do interests and emotions affect learning? Learning and information processing are influenced by emotion. Students are more likely to pay attention to, learn, and remember events, images, and readings that provoke emotional responses or that are related to their personal interests. However, there are cautions in responding to students' interests. "Seductive details," interesting bits of information that are not central to the learning, can hinder learning.

How does curiosity affect learning, and what can teachers do to stimulate curiosity in their subject area? Curiosity is the tendency toward interest in a variety of things. Students' curiosity is guided by their interests, and thus provides them with a self-driven motivation to explore new ideas and concepts. As a result, curiosity can be a powerful motivational tool that captures and maintains students' attention in school. Teachers can foster curiosity by tapping into students' interests, illustrating connections between course material and applications that may be interesting to students, and allowing students to find these connections for themselves. An example might include asking students to identify which simple machines are at work in a skateboard or rollercoaster.

What is the role of arousal in learning? There appears to be an optimum level of arousal for most activities. Generally speaking, a higher level of arousal is helpful on simple tasks, but lower levels of arousal are better for complex tasks. When arousal is too low, teachers can stimulate curiosity by pointing out gaps in knowledge or using variety in activities. Severe anxiety is an example of arousal that is too high for optimal learning.

How does anxiety interfere with learning? Anxiety can be the cause or the result of poor performance; it can interfere with attention to, learning of, and retrieval of information. Many anxious students need help in developing effective test-taking and study skills.

Motivation to Learn in School: On TARGET (pp. 454–465)

Define motivation to learn. Teachers are interested in a particular kind of motivation—student motivation to learn. Student motivation to learn is both a trait and a state. It involves taking academic work seriously, trying to get the most from it, and applying appropriate learning strategies in the process.

What does TARGET stand for? TARGET is an acronym for the six areas in which teachers make decisions that can influence student motivation to learn: the nature of the *task* that students are asked to do, the *autonomy* students are allowed in working, how students are *recognized* for their accomplishments, *grouping* practices, *evaluation* procedures, and the scheduling of *time* in the classroom.

How do tasks affect motivation? The tasks that teachers set affect motivation. When students encounter tasks that are related to their interests, stimulate their curiosity, or are connected to real-life situations, they are more likely to be motivated to learn. Tasks can have attainment, intrinsic, or utility value for students. Attainment value is the importance to the student of succeeding. Intrinsic value is the enjoyment the student gets from the task. Utility value is determined by how much the task contributes to reaching short-term or long-term goals.

Distinguish between bounded and unbounded choices. Like totally unguided discovery or aimless discussions, unstructured or unbounded choices can be counterproductive for learning. The alternative is bounded choice—giving students a range of options that set out valuable tasks for them, but also allow them to follow personal interests. The balance must be just right so that students are not bewildered by too much choice or bored by too little room to explore.

How can recognition undermine motivation and a sense of self-efficacy? Recognition and reward in the classroom will support motivation to learn if the recognition is for personal progress rather than competitive victories. Praise and rewards should focus on students' growing competence. At times, praise can have paradoxical effects when students use the teacher's praise or criticism as cues about capabilities.

List three goal structures and distinguish among them. How students relate to their peers in the classroom is influenced by the goal structure of the activities. Goal structures can be competitive, individualistic, or cooperative. Cooperative goal structures can encourage motivation and increase learning, especially for low-achieving students.

How does the evaluative climate affect goal setting? The more competitive the grading, the more students set performance goals and focus on "looking competent," that is, they are more ego-involved. When the focus is on performing rather than learning, students often see the goal of classroom tasks as simply finishing, especially if the work is difficult.

What are some effects of time on motivation? In order to foster motivation to learn, teachers should be flexible in their use of time in the classroom. Students who are forced to move faster or slower than they should or who are interrupted as they become involved in a project are not likely to develop persistence for learning.

▼ KEY TERMS

Academic tasks (456)
Anxiety (453)
Arousal (453)
Attribution theories (444)
Authentic task (457)
Being needs (434)
Cognitive evaluation theory (436)
Deficiency needs (434)
Entity view of ability (443)
Epistemological beliefs (442)

Expectancy × value theories (433)
Extrinsic motivation (431)
Failure-accepting students (447)
Failure-avoiding students (446)
Goal (438)
Goal orientations (439)
Goal structure (459)
Hierarchy of needs (434)
Humanistic interpretation (433)
Importance/Attainment value (456)

Incentive (432)
Incremental view of ability (443)
Interest or intrinsic value (457)
Intrinsic motivation (431)
Learned helplessness (445)
Legitimate peripheral participation (434)
Locus of causality (431)
Mastery goal (439)
Mastery-oriented students (446)
Motivation (430)

▼ CONNECT AND EXTEND TO LICENSURE

MULTIPLE-CHOICE QUESTIONS

1. Miss Johnson would like for her students to be motivated to do their work without bribing them with treats or promises of extra recess time. Which one of the following is the type of motivation she should encourage in her students?
   A. Extrinsic
   B. Intrinsic
   C. Locus of control
   D. Relatedness

2. Why should educators concern themselves with Abraham Maslow's Hierarchy of Needs?
   A. The stages in students' development might determine their ability to be successful in certain subjects.
   B. Social and emotional growth can impact students in their ability to cooperate with their peers.
   C. Deficiencies in students' lives can impact their ability to succeed academically.
   D. Parenting styles determine whether students succeed academically or not.

3. Teachers who select all content for their students and insist upon students accomplishing their assignments on their own neglect which of the following aspects of self-determination?
   A. Autonomy and competence
   B. Autonomy and relatedness
   C. Relatedness and competence
   D. Autonomy, relatedness and competence

4. Which of the following is true regarding extrinsic motivation?
   A. Extrinsic motivation should be avoided at all costs because it undermines a student's intrinsic desire.
   B. Extrinsic motivation is not associated with grades and incentives.
   C. Extrinsic motivation may be necessary to initially encourage students to engage in certain activities.
   D. Extrinsic motivation is more desirable than intrinsic motivation in the classroom as educators have increased control.

CONSTRUCTED-RESPONSE QUESTIONS

Case

Stephanie Wilson had been educated in "old school methods." Her teachers insisted on straight rows of seated students who did not talk during lectures or complain about assignments. While Stephanie had been successful in this model, not all of her past classmates flourished in such a rigid environment. As a new teacher she wanted a more student friendly environment. She envisioned a classroom where students were stimulated by the activities and worked collaboratively. "I want my students to look forward to coming to school. I want them to be agents in the learning process, not just passive recipients of my curriculum." She imagined designing learning situations in which her students could all achieve. Step by step they could all learn! As her students progress, she would see when they got off the track and manage to remediate before they started to do poorly. In this way, Stephanie thought, none of her students would be failures.

5. Explain why Stephanie's plan to provide early remediation when students are struggling is a good idea.

6. How can Stephanie Wilson support self-determination and autonomy in her classroom?

--- MyEducationLab™ ---

Go to Chapter 12 of the Book Specific Resources in MyEducationLab and click on "Connect and Extend to Licensure" to answer these questions. Compare your responses with the feedback provided.

▼ WHAT WOULD THEY DO?

TEACHERS' CASEBOOK: Motivating Students When Resources Are Thin

Here is how some practicing teachers responded to motivate students when resources are slim.

AIMEE FREDETTE • 2nd Grade
Fisher Elementary School, Walpole, MA

A very effective way that I use to get the children curious and interested is to pose a question to the class before the start of a lesson. This gives the children a focus for the lesson. As the year progresses, the children begin coming up with questions of their own. Another very successful way to spark interest and curiosity is the use of three-column activators, a brainstorming activity that the teacher and students do together. The students brainstorm WHAT WE THINK WE KNOW about the topic. The teacher records all responses, writing them on chart paper. Then the children brainstorm WHAT WE WANT TO KNOW about the topic. Again the teacher would record their responses. The third column, titled WHAT WE HAVE LEARNED, is added to as the theme progresses. The first two columns are referred to as the children learn about the theme.

DANIELLE HARTMAN • 2nd Grade

Claymont Elementary School, Ballwin, MO

First of all, don't get discouraged. You don't need a textbook in order to be a successful teacher. Look over the district's curriculum guides and see what the objectives are for each unit you will be teaching. Once you know the objectives, get creative. Keeping the students motivated and interested in learning is essential. By giving them choice and using a variety of teaching methods you will allow them to stay actively engaged in their learning. You will be amazed at what the students will come up with when they are given choices.

MICHAEL YASIS

L.H. Tanglen Elementary School, Minnetonka, MN

Most learning is acquired through active learning and participation. Therefore, the workbooks that focus on drill and practice, if given as the primary source of learning, most likely would bore the students. I would approach this situation by first engaging the students in a discussion to assess their prior knowledge. I would then challenge and extend their understanding of the concepts through guided discovery, building on similar examples from the "boring" workbooks. While they work on the concepts independently in their workbooks, their confidence and self-esteem will increase.

KELLY MCELROY BONIN • High School Counselor

Klein Oak High School, Spring, TX

Simply being excited to be working with the 3rd graders and showing interest and enthusiasm for the subject matter should arouse the students' interest and encourage them to learn. How many times have you heard it said, "Mrs. Energy was the best teacher I ever had. She took the most boring, difficult subject and made it fun and interesting." I have heard this so many times both as a student and as a teacher, and it proves my point. Just the fact that

the teacher is excited about the material shows the students that this is important information that they need, plus they are curious about the material when they respect and like their teacher. If I felt like the difficulty level of the textbooks was too great, I would have to break the lessons down into smaller increments and use different techniques—discussion, re-teaching, group projects, etc.—to enrich the students and adapt to their level of learning. When your students are motivated, they can accomplish anything—it doesn't matter what materials are available to them, what the difficulty level of the textbook is, and so on. Kids will be motivated when their teacher truly cares about them, is passionate about the material, and makes school interesting.

PAM GASKILL • 2nd Grade

Riverside Elementary School, Dublin, OH

Teaching is inherently creative. Use your time and creativity this summer to acquaint yourself with the required objectives and think about ways in which you can make them meaningful and relevant to your students. Explore other available resources in the community, such as libraries, speakers' bureaus, and resource centers. Plan to incorporate a variety of activities such as videos, group work, field trips, projects, and speakers so that your students will remain interested and involved. Utilize materials that your students have access to from home—books, videos, artifacts, Internet printouts. It is amazing how cooperative parents can be when asked to help in specified ways. You might even make use of the old workbook pages, not in the traditional way, but for cooperative work. You can facilitate student success by pairing weaker readers with more competent readers to discuss and complete the worksheets. Stress that everyone needs to work together to learn the material. Active participation and engagement with the materials will help your students to construct their own meanings more effectively.

MyEducationLab™

Go to Topic 10, Motivation and Affect, in the MyEducationLab (www.myeducationlab.com) for *Educational Psychology*, where you can:

- Find learning outcomes for motivation and affect along with the national standards that connect to these outcomes.
- Complete Assignments and Activities that can help you more deeply understand the chapter content.
- Apply and practice your understanding of the core teaching skills identified in the chapter with the Building Teaching Skills and Dispositions learning units.
- Examine challenging situations and cases presented in the IRIS Center Resources.
- Access video clips of CCSSO National Teachers of the Year award winners responding to the question, "Why Do I Teach?" in the Teacher Talk section.
- Check your comprehension on the content covered in the chapter with the Study Plan. Here you will be able to take a chapter quiz, receive feedback on your answers, and then access Review, Practice, and Enrichment activities to enhance your understanding of chapter content.
- Find additional Teachers' Casebook scenarios and responses to them from practicing teachers.
- Use the Online Lesson Plan Builder to practice lesson planning and integrating national and state standards into your planning.

chapter thirteen

CREATING LEARNING ENVIRONMENTS

▶ **TEACHERS' CASEBOOK:** Bullies and Victims

Two boys are terrorizing one of your students. These boys are larger, stronger, and older than the boy in your class, who is small for his age and shy. Unfortunately, the bullies are fairly popular, in part because they are successful athletes. There are incidents on the bus before and after school, in the gym, in the hallways, and at lunch—including intimidation, extortion of lunch money, tripping, shoving, and verbal taunts—"fag" is a favorite chant. You do not have the two bullies in any of your classes. Your student has started to miss school routinely, and when he is in class, the quality of his work is declining.

CRITICAL THINKING

- How would you handle this situation?
- Who should be involved?
- What would you do about the verbal homophobic insults?
- What would you do if the bullies were in your classes?
- What would you do if the bullies and victim were girls?

OVERVIEW AND OBJECTIVES

This chapter looks at the ways that teachers create social and physical environments for learning by examining classroom management—one of the main concerns of teachers, particularly beginning teachers. The very nature of classes, teaching, and students makes good management a critical ingredient of success, and we will investigate why this is true. Successful managers create more time for learning, involve more students, and help students to become self-managing.

A positive learning environment must be established and maintained throughout the year. One of the best ways to accomplish this is by working to prevent problems from occurring at all. But when problems arise—as they always do—an appropriate response is important. What will you do when students challenge you openly in class, when one student asks your advice on a difficult personal problem, or when another withdraws from all participation? We will examine the ways that teachers can communicate effectively with their students in these and many other situations.

By the time you have completed this chapter, you should be able to:

Objective 13.1: Relate academic learning time and student cooperation to creating and maintaining a classroom climate conducive to academic achievement and socio-emotional well-being.

Objective 13.2: Summarize the research on the roles of rules, procedures, and consequences in classroom management.

Objective 13.3: Explain how the physical environment can support or interfere with learning, and plan an appropriate arrangement for your classroom.

Objective 13.4: Identify strategies for preventing and addressing student misbehaviors, including bullying.

Objective 13.5: Characterize successful teacher–student communication.

THE NEED FOR ORGANIZATION

In study after study of the factors related to student achievement, classroom management stands out as the variable with the largest impact (Marzano & Marzano, 2003). Knowledge of and skill in classroom management are marks of expertise in teaching; and stress and exhaustion from managerial difficulties are precursors of burnout in teaching (Emmer & Stough, 2001). What is it about classrooms that makes management so critical?

Classes are particular kinds of environments. They have distinctive features that influence their inhabitants no matter how the students or the desks are organized or what the teacher believes about education (Doyle, 2006). Classrooms are *multidimensional*. They are crowded with people, tasks, and time pressures. Many individuals—all with differing goals, preferences, and abilities—must share resources, use and reuse materials without losing them, move in and out of the room, and so on. In addition, actions can have multiple effects. Calling on low-ability students may encourage their participation and thinking, but may also lead to management problems if the students are unable to answer your questions. And events occur *simultaneously*—everything happens at once and the pace is fast. Teachers have literally hundreds of exchanges with students during a single day.

In this rapid-fire existence, events are *unpredictable*. Even when plans are carefully made, a lesson can still be interrupted by a technology glitch or a loud, angry discussion right outside the classroom. Because classrooms are *public*, the way the teacher handles these unexpected intrusions is seen and judged by all. Students are always noticing if the teacher is being "fair." Is there favoritism? What happens when a rule is broken? Finally, classrooms have *histories*. The meaning of a particular teacher's or student's actions depends in part on what has happened before. The fifteenth time a student arrives late requires a different teacher response compared to the first late arrival. In addition, the history of the first few weeks of school affects life in the class for the rest of the year.

The Basic Task: Gain Their Cooperation

The basic management task for teachers is to achieve order and harmony by gaining and maintaining student cooperation in class activities (Doyle, 2006). Given the multidimensional, simultaneous, fast-paced, unpredictable, public, and historical nature of classrooms, this is quite a challenge. Gaining student cooperation means planning activities, having materials ready, making appropriate behavioral and academic demands on students, giving clear signals, accomplishing transitions smoothly, foreseeing problems and stopping them before they start, selecting and sequencing activities so that flow and interest are maintained—and much more. Also, different activities require different managerial skills. For example, a new or complicated activity may be a greater threat to classroom management than a familiar or simple activity.

Obviously, gaining the cooperation of kindergartners is not the same task as gaining the cooperation of high school seniors. During kindergarten and the first few years of elementary school, direct teaching of classroom rules and procedures is important. For children in the middle elementary years, many classroom routines have become relatively automatic, but new procedures for a particular activity may have to be taught directly, and the entire system still needs monitoring and maintenance. Toward the end of elementary school, some students begin to test and defy authority. The management challenges at

COOPERATION IS KEY Gaining student cooperation is the first task of classroom management. There are lessons, materials, time, space, and people to coordinate to keep learning on track.

this stage are to deal productively with these disruptions and to motivate students who are becoming less concerned about teachers' opinions and more interested in their social lives. By the end of high school, the challenges are to manage the curriculum, fit academic material to students' interests and abilities, and help students become more self-managing (Emmer & Evertson, 2013; Evertson & Emmer, 2013).

The Goals of Classroom Management

STOP & THINK You are interviewing for a job in a great district—it is known for innovation. The assistant principal looks at you for a moment and then asks, "What is classroom management?" How would you answer? •

The aim of **classroom management** is to maintain a positive, productive learning environment. But order for its own sake is an empty goal. As we discussed in Chapter 7, it is unethical to use classroom management techniques just to keep students docile and quiet. What, then, is the point of working so hard to manage classrooms? There are at least three reasons.

ACCESS TO LEARNING. Each classroom activity has its own rules for participation. Sometimes these rules are clearly stated by the teacher, but often they are implicit and

Classroom management Techniques used to maintain a healthy learning environment, relatively free of behavior problems.

unstated. Teacher and students may not even be aware that they are following different rules for different activities (Berliner, 1983). For example, in a reading group, students may have to raise their hands to make a comment, but in a show-and-tell circle in the same class, they may simply have to catch the teacher's eye.

As we saw in Chapter 6, the rules defining who can talk, what they can talk about, when and to whom they can talk, and how long they can talk are often called **participation structures**. In order to participate successfully in a given activity, students must understand the participation structure. Some students, however, seem to come to school less able to participate than others. The participation structures they learn at home in interactions with siblings, parents, and other adults do not match the participation structures of school activities (Cazden, 2001). What can we conclude? To reach the first goal of good classroom management—giving all students access to learning—you must make sure everyone knows how to participate in class activities. The key is awareness. What are your rules and expectations? Are they understandable, given your students' cultural backgrounds and home experiences? What unspoken rules or values may be operating? Are you clearly signaling appropriate ways to participate? For some students, particularly those with behavioral and emotional challenges, direct teaching and practicing of important behaviors may be required (Emmer & Stough, 2001).

MORE TIME FOR LEARNING. I once used a stopwatch to time the commercials during a TV quiz show. I was amazed to find that half of the program was devoted to commercials. Actually, very little quizzing took place. If you used a similar approach in classrooms, timing all the different activities throughout the day, you might be surprised by how little actual teaching takes place. Many minutes each day are lost through interruptions, disruptions, late starts, and rough transitions. Obviously, students can only learn what they encounter. Almost every study examining time and learning has found a significant relationship between time spent on content and student learning (Weinstein, Romano, & Mignano, 2011). Thus, one important goal of classroom management is to expand the sheer number of minutes available for learning. This is sometimes called **allocated time**.

Simply making more time for learning will not automatically lead to achievement. To be valuable, time must be used effectively. As you saw in the chapters on cognitive learning, the way students process information is a central factor in what they learn and remember. Basically, students will learn what they practice and think about. Time spent actively involved in specific learning tasks often is called **engaged time**, or sometimes **time on task**.

Again, however, engaged time doesn't guarantee learning. Students may be struggling with material that is too difficult or they may be using the wrong learning strategies. When students are working with a high rate of success—really learning and understanding—we call the time spent **academic learning time**. So the second goal of class management is to increase academic learning time by keeping students actively engaged in worthwhile, appropriate learning activities. Figure 13.1 shows how the 1,000+ hours of time mandated for school in most states can become only about 333 hours of quality academic learning time for a typical student.

Getting students engaged in learning early in their school careers can make a big difference. Several studies have shown that teachers' rating of students' on-task, persistent engagement in 1st grade predicts achievement test score gains and grades through 4th grade, as well as the decision to drop out of high school (Fredricks, Blumenfeld, & Paris, 2004).

MANAGEMENT FOR SELF-MANAGEMENT. The third goal of any management system is to help students become better able to manage themselves. If teachers focus on student compliance, they will spend much of the teaching/learning time monitoring and correcting. Students come to perceive the purpose of school as just following rules, not constructing deep understanding of academic knowledge. And complex learning structures such as cooperative or problem-based learning require student *self-management*. Compliance with rules is not enough to make these learning structures work (McCaslin & Good, 1998).

Participation structures Rules defining how to participate in different activities.

Allocated time Time set aside for learning.

Engaged time/Time on task Time spent actively engaged in the learning task at hand.

Academic learning time Time when students are actually succeeding at the learning task.

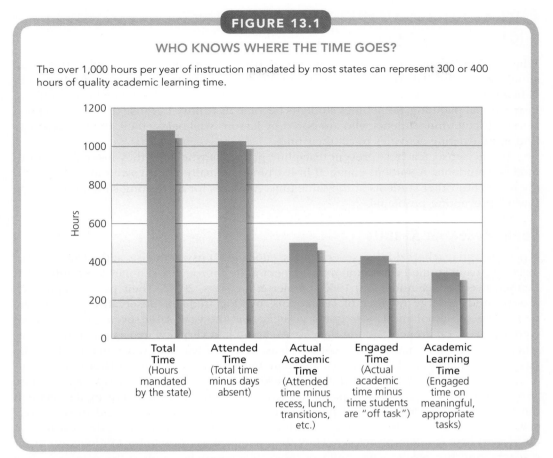

FIGURE 13.1

WHO KNOWS WHERE THE TIME GOES?

The over 1,000 hours per year of instruction mandated by most states can represent 300 or 400 hours of quality academic learning time.

Source: From Elementary Classroom Management *(4th ed.), by C.S. Weinstein and A.J. Mignano, Jr., New York: McGraw-Hill. Copyright © 2007 by The McGraw-Hill Companies. Adapted with permission of the McGraw-Hill Companies, Inc.*

The movement from demanding obedience to teaching self-regulation and self-control is a fundamental shift in discussions of classroom management today (Evertson & Weinstein, 2006). Tom Savage (1999) says simply, "the most fundamental purpose of discipline is the development of self-control. Academic knowledge and technological skill will be of little consequence if those who possess them lack self-control" (p. 11). Through self-control, students demonstrate responsibility—the ability to fulfil their own needs without interfering with the rights and needs of others (Glasser, 1990). Students learn self-control by making choices and dealing with the consequences, setting goals and priorities, managing time, collaborating to learn, mediating disputes and making peace, and developing trusting relations with trustworthy teachers and classmates (Bear, 2005; Rogers & Frieberg, 1994).

Encouraging **self-management** requires extra time, but teaching students how to take responsibility is an investment well worth the effort. There is good evidence for this claim. Nancy Perry and Rebecca Collie (2011) compared a preservice preparation program that instructed student teachers about how to coach their students to be self-regulated learners with other programs that did not emphasize self-regulation. The student teachers who developed self-regulation knowledge and skills were more confident, less stressed, and more engaged during their student teaching compared to other prospective teachers who did not learn how to help their students to become self-regulated. This makes sense—if you teach your students to manage their own behavior and learning, you should have fewer management problems, less stress, and more time to teach, which would support your growing sense of teacher efficacy. When elementary and secondary teachers have very effective class management systems but neglect to set student self-management as a goal, their students often find that they have trouble working independently after they graduate from these "well-managed" classes.

Self-management Management of your own behavior and acceptance of responsibility for your own actions.

CREATING A POSITIVE LEARNING ENVIRONMENT

When making plans for your class, much of what you have already learned in this book should prove helpful. You know, for example, that problems are prevented when individual variations such as those discussed in Chapters 2 through 6 are taken into account in instructional planning. Sometimes students become disruptive because the work assigned is too difficult. And students who are bored by lessons well below their ability levels may find more exciting activities to fill their time.

In one sense, teachers prevent discipline problems whenever they make an effort to motivate students. A student engaged in learning is usually not involved in a clash with the teacher or other students at the same time. All plans for motivating students are steps toward preventing problems.

Some Research Results

What else can teachers do? For several years, educational psychologists at the University of Texas at Austin studied classroom management quite thoroughly (Emmer & Stough, 2001; Emmer, Evertson, & Anderson, 1980; Emmer & Gerwels, 2006). Their general approach was to study a large number of classrooms, making frequent observations during the first weeks of school and less frequent visits later in the year. After several months, there were dramatic differences among the classes. Some had very few management problems, whereas others had many. The most and least effective teachers were identified on the basis of the quality of classroom management and student achievement later in the year.

Next, the researchers looked at their observation records of the first weeks of class to see how the effective teachers *got started*. Other comparisons were made between the teachers who ultimately had harmonious, high-achieving classes and those whose classes were fraught with problems. On the basis of these comparisons, the researchers developed management principles. They then taught these principles to a new group of teachers, and the results were quite positive. Teachers who applied the principles had fewer problems; their students spent more time learning and less time disrupting; and achievement was higher. The findings of these studies formed the basis for two books on classroom management (Emmer & Evertson, 2009, 2013; Evertson & Emmer, 2009, 2013). Many of the ideas in the following pages are from these books.

Routines and Rules Required

Connect and Extend to PRAXIS II™

Procedures and Routines (I, C4)
Efficient procedures and routines reduce confusion and opportunities for misbehavior and they save time that can be devoted to learning tasks. Identify frequent activities or classroom events that would benefit from well-structured procedures or routines. Explain principles for establishing procedures and routines so that students are likely to observe them.

- -

STOP & THINK What are the three or four most important rules you will have for your classroom? •

- -

At the elementary school level, teachers must lead 20 to 30 students of varying abilities through many different activities each day. Without efficient rules and procedures, a great deal of time is wasted dealing with the same questions and issues over and over. "My pencil broke. How can I do my math?" "I'm finished with my experiment. What should I do now?" "Carlos tripped me!" "I left my homework in my locker."

At the secondary school level, teachers must meet daily with over 100 students who use dozens of materials and often change rooms. Secondary school students are also more likely to challenge teachers' authority. The effective managers studied by Emmer, Evertson, and their colleagues had planned *procedures* and *rules* for coping with these situations.

ROUTINES AND PROCEDURES. How will materials and assignments be distributed and collected? Under what conditions can students leave the room? How will grades be determined? What are the special routines for handling equipment and supplies in science, art, or vocational classes? **Procedures** and **routines** describe how activities are accomplished in classrooms, but they are seldom written down; they are simply the ways of getting

Procedures/routines Prescribed steps for an activity.

GUIDELINES

Establishing Class Routines

Determine procedures for student upkeep of desks, classroom equipment, and other facilities.
Examples

1. Set aside a cleanup time each day or once a week in self-contained classes.
2. Demonstrate and have students practice how to push chairs under the desk, take and return materials stored on shelves, sharpen pencils, use the sink or water fountain, assemble lab equipment, and so on.
3. Put a rotating monitor in charge of equipment or materials.

Decide how students will be expected to enter and leave the room.
Examples

1. Have a procedure for students to follow as soon as they enter the room. Some teachers have a standard assignment ("Have your homework out and be checking it over").
2. Inform students under what conditions they can leave the room, and make sure they understand when they need to ask for permission to do so.
3. Tell students how they should gain admission to the room if they are late.
4. Set up a policy about class dismissal. Many teachers require students to be in their seats and quiet before they can leave at the end of class. The teacher, not the bell, dismisses class.

Establish signals for getting students' attention and teach them to your students.
Examples

1. In the classroom, flick the lights on and off, sound a chord on a piano or recorder, sound a bell like the "ring bell for service" at a sales counter, move to the podium and stare silently at the class, use a phrase like "Eyes, please," take out your grade book, or move to the front of the class.
2. In the halls, raise a hand, clap once, or use some other signal to indicate "Stop."

3. On the playground, raise a hand or whistle to indicate "Line up."

Set routines for student participation in class.
Examples

1. Decide whether you will have students raise their hands for permission to speak or simply require that they wait until the speaker has finished.
2. Determine a signal to indicate that you want everyone to respond at once. Some teachers raise a cupped hand to their ear. Others preface the question with "Everyone."
3. Make sure you are clear about differences in procedures for different activities: reading group, learning center, discussion, teacher presentation, seatwork, video watching, peer learning group, library, and so forth.
4. Establish how many students at a time can be at the pencil sharpener, teacher's desk, learning center, sink, bookshelves, reading corner, or bathroom.

Determine how you will communicate, collect, and return assignments.
Examples

1. Establish a place for listing assignments. Some teachers reserve a particular corner of the board for listing assignments. Others write assignments in colored chalk. For younger students, it may be better to prepare assignment sheets or folders, color-coding them for math workbook, reading packet, and science kit.
2. Be clear about how and where assignments should be collected. Some teachers collect assignments in a box or bin; others have a student collect work while they introduce the next activity.

For ideas about involving students in developing rules and procedures, see http://www.educationworld.com/a_lesson/lesson/lesson274.shtml

---

things done in class. Carol Weinstein and Andy Mignano (Weinstein & Novodvorsky, 2011; Weinstein, Romano, & Mignano, 2011) suggest that teachers establish routines to cover the following areas:

1. *Administrative routines,* such as taking attendance
2. *Student movement,* such as entering and leaving or going to the bathroom
3. *Housekeeping,* such as watering plants or storing personal items
4. *Lesson-running routines,* such as how to collect assignments or return homework
5. *Interactions between teacher and student,* such as how to get the teacher's attention when help is needed
6. *Talk among students,* such as giving help or socializing

You might use these six areas as a framework for planning your class routines. The *Guidelines* should help you as you plan.

Connect and Extend to PRAXIS II™

Rules (I, C4)
Fair, consistently enforced rules can have a positive effect on motivation to learn by promoting a safe and warm classroom environment. Describe how to establish and maintain effective rules. Keep in mind age-related concerns.

RULES. Unlike routines, rules are often written down and posted, because **rules** specify expected and forbidden actions in the class. They are the dos and don'ts of classroom life. In establishing rules, you should consider what kind of atmosphere you want to create. What student behaviors will help you teach effectively? What limits do the students need to guide their behavior? The rules you set should be consistent with school rules, and also in keeping with principles of learning. For example, we know from the research on small-group learning that students benefit when they explain work to peers. They learn as they teach. A rule that forbids students to help each other may be inconsistent with good learning principles. Or a rule that says, "No erasures when writing" may make students focus more on preventing mistakes than on communicating clearly in their writing (Burden, 1995; Emmer & Stough, 2001; Weinstein, Romano, & Mignano, 2011).

Rules should be positive and observable (raise your hand to be recognized). Having a few general rules that cover many specifics is better than listing all the dos and don'ts. But, if specific actions are forbidden, such as leaving the campus or smoking in the bathrooms, then a rule should make this clear (Emmer & Gerwels, 2006).

RULES FOR ELEMENTARY SCHOOL. Evertson and Emmer (2009) give four examples of general rules for elementary school classes:

1. *Respect and be polite to all people.* Give clear explanations of what you mean by "polite," including not hitting, fighting, or teasing. Examples of polite behavior include waiting your turn, saying "please" and "thank you," and not calling names. This applies to behavior toward adults (including substitute teachers) and peers.
2. *Be prompt and prepared.* This rule highlights the importance of the academic work in the class. Being prompt includes the beginning of the day as well as transitions between activities.
3. *Listen quietly while others are speaking.* This applies to the teacher and other students, in both large-class lessons and small-group discussions.
4. *Obey all school rules.* This reminds students that all school rules apply in your classroom. Then students cannot claim, for example, that they thought it was okay to chew gum or listen to an iPod in your class, even though these are against school rules, "because you never made a rule against it for us."

Whatever the rule, students need to be taught the behaviors that the rule includes and excludes. Examples, practice, and discussion will be needed before learning is complete.

As you've seen, different activities often require different rules. This can be confusing for elementary students until they have thoroughly learned all the rules. To prevent confusion, you might consider making signs that list the rules for each activity. Then, before the activity, you can post the appropriate sign as a reminder. This provides clear and consistent cues about participation structures so all students, not just the "well behaved," know what is expected. Of course, these rules must be explained and discussed before the signs can have their full effect.

RULES FOR SECONDARY SCHOOL. Emmer and Evertson (2009) suggest six examples of rules for secondary students:

1. *Bring all needed materials to class.* The teacher must specify the type of pen, pencil, paper, notebook, texts, and so on.
2. *Be in your seat and ready to work when the bell rings.* Many teachers combine this rule with a standard beginning procedure for the class, such as a warm-up exercise on the board or a requirement that students have paper with a proper heading ready when the bell rings.
3. *Respect and be polite to all people.* This covers fighting, verbal abuse, and general troublemaking. All people includes the teacher.
4. *Listen and stay seated while someone else is speaking.* This applies when the teacher or other students are talking.

Rules Statements specifying expected and forbidden behaviors; dos and don'ts.

5. *Respect other people's property*. This means property belonging to the school, the teacher, or other students.
6. *Obey all school rules*. As with the elementary class rules, this covers many behaviors and situations, so you do not have to repeat every school rule for your class. It also reminds the students that you will be monitoring them inside and outside your class. Make sure you know all the school rules. Some secondary students are very adept at convincing teachers that their misbehavior "really isn't against the rules."

These rules are more than ways to maintain order. In their study of 34 middle-school classrooms, Lindsay Matsumura and her colleagues (2008) found that having explicit rules about respecting others in the classroom predicted the number of students who participated in class discussion, so it seems clear that respect is a gateway to student engagement with the academic material and class dialogue that supports learning.

CONSEQUENCES. As soon as you decide on your rules and procedures, you must consider what you will do when a student breaks a rule or does not follow a procedure. It is too late to make this decision after the rule has been broken. For many infractions, the logical consequence is going back to "do it right." Students who run in the hall may have to return to where they started and walk properly. Incomplete papers can be redone. Materials left out should be put back. You can use **natural or logical consequences** to support social/emotional development by doing the following (Elias & Schwab, 2006):

RULES PROMOTE RESPECT Classroom rules that are understood clearly by all students can help maintain a classroom environment that is respectful and more conducive to effective learning.

- Separate the deed from the doer in your response—the problem is the behavior, not the student.
- Emphasize to students that they have the power to choose their actions and thus avoid losing control.
- Encourage student reflection, self-evaluation, and problem solving—avoid teacher lecturing.
- Help students identify and give a rationale for what they could do differently next time in a similar situation.

The main point here is that decisions about penalties (and rewards) must be made early on, so students know before they break a rule or use the wrong procedure what this will mean for them. I encourage my student teachers to get a copy of the school rules and their cooperating teacher's rules, and then plan their own. Sometimes, consequences are more complicated. In their case studies of four expert elementary school teachers, Weinstein, Romano, and Mignano (2011) found that the teachers' negative consequences fell into seven categories, as shown in Table 13.1 on the next page.

WHO SETS THE RULES AND CONSEQUENCES? If you are going to involve students in setting rules or creating a constitution, you may need to wait until you have established a sense of community in your classroom. Before students can contribute meaningfully to the class rules, they need to trust the teacher and the situation (Elias & Schwab, 2006). In the first chapter, I described Ken, an expert teacher who worked with his students to establish a students' "Bill of Rights" instead of defining rules. These

Natural/logical consequences Instead of punishing, have students redo, repair, or in some way face the consequences that naturally flow from their actions.

TABLE 13.1 • **Seven Categories of Penalties for Students**

1. **Expressions of disappointment.** If students like and respect their teacher, then a serious, sorrowful expression of disappointment may cause students to stop and think about their behavior.
2. **Loss of privileges.** Students can lose free time. If they have not completed homework, for example, they can be required to do it during a free period or recess.
3. **Time-Out: Exclusion from the group.** Students who distract their peers or fail to cooperate can be separated from the group until they are ready to cooperate. Some teachers give a student a pass for 10 to 15 minutes. The student must go to another class or study hall, where the other students and teachers ignore the offending student for that time.
4. **Written reflections on the problem.** Students can write in journals, write essays about what they did and how it affected others, or write letters of apology—if this is appropriate. Another possibility is to ask students to describe objectively what they did; then the teacher and the student can sign and date this statement. These records are available if parents or administrators need evidence of the students' behavior.
5. **Visits to the principal's office.** Expert teachers tend to use this penalty rarely, but they do use it when the situation warrants. Some schools require students to be sent to the office for certain offenses, such as fighting. If you tell a student to go to the office and the student refuses, you might call the office saying the student has been sent. Then the student has the choice of either going to the office or facing the principal's penalty for "disappearing" on the way.
6. **Detentions.** Detentions can be very brief meetings after school, during a free period, or at lunch. The main purpose is to talk about what has happened. (In high school, detentions are often used as punishments; suspensions and expulsions are available as more extreme measures.)
7. **Contacting parents.** If problems become a repeated pattern, most teachers contact the student's family. This is done to seek support for helping the student, not to blame the parents or punish the student.

Source: From Elementary Classroom Management (4th ed.), by C.S. Weinstein and A.J. Mignano, Jr., New York: McGraw-Hill. Copyright © 2007 by The McGraw-Hill Companies. Adapted with permission of the McGraw-Hill Companies, Inc.

"rights" cover most situations that might require a "rule" and help the students move toward the goal of becoming self-managing. In a recent class, the Bill of Rights included the rights to whisper when the teacher is not talking, be treated politely, have a two-minute break between working periods, make choices about the day's schedule, have privacy and not have people take your things, and chew gum without blowing bubbles, among several others.

Developing rights and responsibilities rather than rules makes an important point to students. "Teaching children that something is wrong because there is a rule against it is not the same as teaching them that there is a rule against it because it is wrong, and helping them to understand why this is so" (Weinstein, 1999, p. 154). Students should understand that the rules are developed so that everyone can work and learn together. I might add that when Ken has had some very difficult classes, he and his students have had to establish some "laws" that protect students' rights, as you can see in Table 13.2.

Another kind of planning that affects the learning environment is designing the physical arrangement of the class furniture, materials, and learning tools.

TABLE 13.2 • **Laws to Protect Our Rights**

1. Follow directions the first time.
2. Speak nicely, be courteous, and respect other people, their feelings and their things. Follow the Bill of Rights.
3. Laugh at the right time for the right time.
4. Respect others' right to learn. Do not distract others. Don't be nosy. Don't yell. Remember to get quiet at countdown.
5. Talk at the right times with the right tone of voice and volume.
6. Transitions and movements are calm, quiet, careful and elegant.
7. Follow all classroom and school procedures, like: bathroom; pencil; lunch and recess; morning; dismissal; and . . .

Source: From Elementary Classroom Management (4th ed., p. 108), by C.S. Weinstein and A.J. Mignano, Jr., New York: McGraw-Hill. Copyright © 2007 by The McGraw-Hill Companies. Adapted with permission of the McGraw-Hill Companies, Inc.

Planning Spaces for Learning

STOP & THINK Think back over all the rooms in all the schools you have attended. Which ones stand out as inviting or exciting? Which ones were cold and empty? Did one teacher have a design that let students do different things in various parts of the room? •

Spaces for learning should invite and support the activities you plan for your classes, and they should respect the inhabitants of the space. This respect begins at the door for young children by helping them identify their classroom. One school that has won awards for its architecture paints each classroom door a different bright color, so young children can find their "home" (Herbert, 1998). Once inside, spaces can be created that invite quiet reading, group collaboration, or independent research. If students are to use materials, they should be able to reach them. In an interview with Marge Scherer (1999), Herb Kohl describes how he creates a positive environment in his classes.

> What I do is put up the most beautiful things I know—posters, games, puzzles, challenges—and let the children know these are provocations. These are ways of provoking them into using their minds. You have to create an environment that makes kids walk in and say, "I really want to see what's here. I would really like to look at this." (p. 9)

In terms of classroom arrangement, there are two basic ways of organizing space: personal territories and interest areas.

PERSONAL TERRITORIES. Can the physical setting influence teaching and learning in classrooms organized by territories? A front seat location does seem to increase participation for students who are predisposed to speak in class, whereas a seat in the back will make it more difficult to participate and easier to sit back and daydream (Woolfolk & Brooks, 1983). But the **action zone** where participation is greatest may be in other areas such as on one side, or near a particular learning center (Good, 1983a; Lambert, 1994). To "spread the action around," Weinstein, Romano, and Mignano (2011) suggest that teachers move around the room when possible, establish eye contact with and direct questions to students seated far away, and vary the seating so the same students are not always consigned to the back.

Horizontal rows share many of the advantages of the traditional row and column arrangements. Both are useful for independent seatwork and teacher, student, or media presentations; they encourage students to focus on the presenter and simplify housekeeping. Horizontal rows also permit students to work more easily in pairs. However, this is a poor arrangement for large-group discussion.

Clusters of four or circle arrangements are best for student interaction. Circles are especially useful for discussions but still allow for independent seatwork. Clusters permit students to talk, help one another, share materials, and work on group tasks. Both arrangements, however, are poor for whole-group presentations and may make class management more difficult.

The *fishbowl or stack* special formation, where students sit close together near the focus of attention (the back row may even be standing), should be used only for short periods of time, because it is not comfortable and can lead to discipline problems. On the other hand, the fishbowl can create a feeling of group cohesion and is helpful when the teacher wants students to watch a demonstration, brainstorm on a class problem, or see a small visual aid.

INTEREST AREAS. The design of interest areas can influence the way the areas are used by students. For example, working with a classroom teacher, Carol Weinstein (1977) was able to make changes in interest areas that helped the teacher meet her objectives of having more girls involved in the science center and having all students experiment more with a variety of manipulative materials. In a second study, changes in a library corner led to

Connect and Extend to PRAXIS II™

Classroom Space (I, C4)
The physical organization of a class has an effect on student behavior and learning. Describe how the physical layout of classrooms can affect the learning environment. Apply principles of classroom organization to enhance learning and minimize disruption.

Action zone Area of a classroom where the greatest amount of interaction takes place.

GUIDELINES

Designing Learning Spaces

Note the fixed features and plan accordingly.
Examples

1. Remember that the audiovisual center and computers need electrical outlets.
2. Keep art supplies near the sink, small-group work by a blackboard.

Create easy access to materials and a well-organized place to store them.
Examples

1. Make sure materials are easy to reach and visible to students.
2. Have enough shelves so that materials need not be stacked.

Provide students with clean, convenient surfaces for studying.
Examples

1. Put bookshelves next to the reading area, games by the game table.
2. Prevent fights by avoiding crowded work spaces.

Avoid dead spaces and "racetracks."
Examples

1. Don't have all the interest areas around the outside of the room, leaving a large dead space in the middle.
2. Avoid placing a few items of furniture right in the middle of this large space, creating a "racetrack" around the furniture.

Arrange things so you can see your students and they can see all instructional presentations.
Examples

1. Make sure you can see over partitions.
2. Design seating so that students can see instruction without moving their chairs or desks.

Make sure work areas are private and quiet.
Examples

1. Make sure there are no tables or work areas in the middle of traffic lanes; a person should not have to pass through one area to get to another.
2. Keep noisy activities as far as possible from quiet ones. Increase the feeling of privacy by placing partitions, such as bookcases or pegboards, between areas or within large areas.

Provide choices and flexibility.
Examples

1. Establish private cubicles for individual work, open tables for group work, and cushions on the floor for whole-class meetings.
2. Give students a place to keep their personal belongings. This is especially important if students don't have personal desks.

Try new arrangements; then evaluate and improve.
Examples

1. Have a "two-week arrangement"; then evaluate.
2. Enlist the aid of your students. They have to live in the room, too, and designing a classroom can be a very challenging educational experience.

For more ideas on classroom design, see http://www.edfacilities.org/rl/classroom_design.cfm

---

more involvement in literature activities throughout the class (Morrow & Weinstein, 1986). If you design interest areas for your class, keep the *Guidelines* in mind.

Personal territories and interest areas are not mutually exclusive; many teachers use a design that combines these types of organization. Individual students' desks—their territories—are placed in the center, with interest areas in the back or around the periphery of the room. This allows the flexibility needed for both large- and small-group activities. Figure 13.2 shows an elementary classroom that combines interest area and personal territory arrangements.

Getting Started: The First Weeks of Class

Determining a room design, rules, and procedures are the first steps toward having a well-managed class, but how do effective teachers gain students' cooperation in those early critical days and weeks? One study carefully analyzed the first weeks' activities of effective and ineffective elementary teachers, and found striking differences (Emmer, Evertson, & Anderson, 1980). By the second or third week of school, students in the ineffective teachers' classrooms were more and more disruptive, and less and less on task.

FIGURE 13.2

AN ELEMENTARY CLASSROOM ARRANGEMENT

This 4th grade teacher has designed a space that allows teacher presentations and demonstrations, small group work, computer interactions, math manipulatives activities, informal reading, art, and other projects without requiring constant rearrangements.

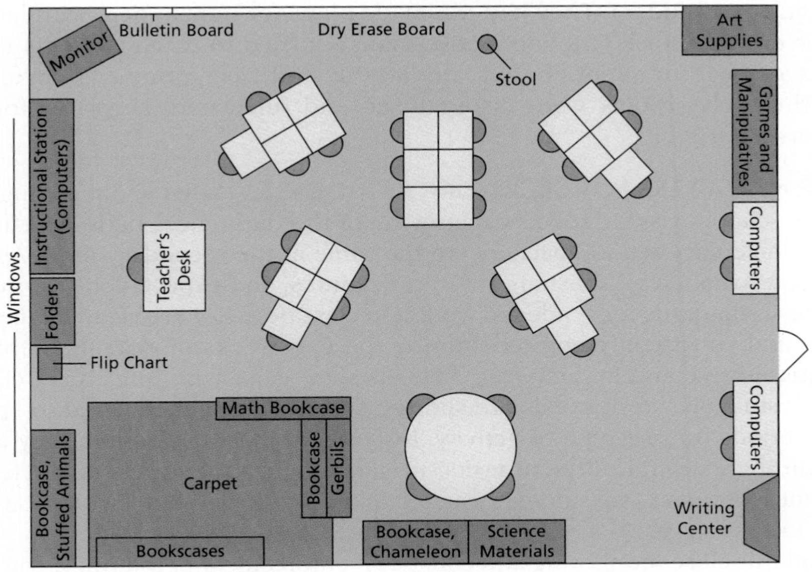

Source: From Elementary Classroom Management (4th ed.), by C.S. Weinstein and A.J. Mignano, Jr., New York: McGraw-Hill. Copyright © 2007 by The McGraw-Hill Companies. Adapted with permission of the McGraw-Hill Companies, Inc.

EFFECTIVE MANAGERS FOR ELEMENTARY STUDENTS. In the *effective teachers' classrooms*, the very first day was well organized. Nametags were ready. There was something interesting for each child to do right away. Materials were set up. The teachers had planned carefully to avoid any last-minute tasks that might take them away from their students. These teachers dealt with the children's pressing concerns first. "Where do I put my things?" "How do I pronounce my teacher's name?" "Can I whisper to my neighbor?" "Where is the bathroom?" The effective teachers were explicit about their expectations. They had a workable, easily understood set of rules and taught the students the most important rules right away. They taught the rules like any other subject—with lots of explanation, examples, and practice.

Throughout the first weeks, the effective managers continued to spend quite a bit of time teaching rules and procedures. Some used guided practice to teach procedures; others used rewards to shape behavior. Most taught students to respond to a bell or some other signal to gain their attention. These teachers worked with the class as a whole on enjoyable academic activities. They did not rush to get students into small groups or to start them in readers. This whole-class work gave the teachers a better opportunity to continue monitoring all students' learning of the rules and procedures. Misbehavior was stopped quickly and firmly, but not harshly.

In the *poorly managed classrooms*, the first weeks were quite different. Rules were not workable; they were either too vague or very complicated. For example, one teacher made a rule that students should "be in the right place at the right time." Students were not told what this meant, so their behavior could not be guided by the rule. Neither positive nor negative behaviors had clear, consistent consequences. After students broke a rule, ineffective managers might give a vague criticism, such as "Some of my children are too noisy," or issue a warning, but not follow through with the threatened consequence.

In the poorly managed classes, procedures for accomplishing routine tasks varied from day to day and were never taught or practiced. Instead of dealing with these obvious needs, ineffective managers spent time on procedures that could have waited. For example, one teacher had the class practice for a fire drill the first day, but left unexplained other procedures that would be needed every day. Students wandered around the classroom aimlessly and had to ask each other what they should be doing. Often the students talked to one another because they had nothing productive to do. Ineffective teachers frequently left the room. Many became absorbed in paperwork or in helping just one student. They had not made plans for how to deal with late-arriving students or interruptions. One ineffective manager tried to teach students to respond to a bell as a signal for attention, but later let the students ignore it. All in all, the first weeks in these classrooms were disorganized and filled with surprises for teachers and students alike.

EFFECTIVE MANAGERS FOR SECONDARY STUDENTS.   What about getting started in a secondary school class? It appears that many of the differences between effective and ineffective elementary school teachers are the same at the secondary level. Again, *effective managers* focus on establishing rules, procedures, and expectations on the first day of class. These standards for academic work and class behavior are clearly communicated to students and consistently enforced during the first weeks of class. Student behavior is closely monitored, and infractions of the rules are dealt with quickly. In classes with lower-ability students, work cycles are shorter; students are not required to spend long, unbroken periods on one type of activity. Instead, during each period, they are moved smoothly through several different tasks. In general, effective teachers carefully follow each student's progress, so students cannot avoid work without facing consequences (Emmer & Evertson, 1982).

With all this close monitoring and consistent enforcement of the rules, you may wonder if effective secondary teachers have to be grim and humorless. Not necessarily. The effective managers in one classic study also smiled and joked more with their students (Moskowitz & Hayman, 1976). As any experienced teacher can tell you, there is much more to smile about when the class is cooperative.

Maintaining a Good Environment for Learning

A good start is just that—a beginning. Effective teachers build on this beginning. They maintain their management system by preventing problems and keeping students engaged in productive learning activities. We have discussed several ways to keep students engaged. In the previous chapter on motivation, for example, we considered stimulating curiosity, relating lessons to student interests, establishing learning goals instead of performance goals, and having positive expectations. What else can teachers do?

Encouraging Engagement

STOP & THINK What activities keep you completely engaged—the time just seems to disappear? What is it about those activities that keeps you focused? •

Connect and Extend to PRAXIS II™

Promoting Student Engagement (I, C4)
A principle of educational psychology is that the more students are cognitively engaged in an activity, the more they are likely to learn. What tactics can teachers employ to maximize their students' cognitive engagement during learning tasks?

In general, as teacher supervision increases, students' engaged time also increases. One study found that elementary students working directly with a teacher were on task 97% of the time, whereas students working on their own were on task only 57% of the time (Frick, 1990). This does not mean that teachers should eliminate independent work for students. It simply means that this type of activity usually requires careful planning and monitoring.

When the task provides continuous cues for the student about what to do next, involvement will be greater. Activities with clear steps are likely to be more absorbing, because one step leads naturally to the next. When students have all the materials they need to complete a task, they tend to stay involved. If their curiosity is piqued, students will be motivated to continue seeking an answer. And, as you now know, students will be

GUIDELINES

Keeping Students Engaged

Make basic work requirements clear.

Examples

1. Specify and post the routine work requirements for headings, paper size, pen or pencil use, and neatness.
2. Establish and explain rules about late or incomplete work and absences. If a pattern of incomplete work begins to develop, deal with it early; speak with parents if necessary.
3. Make due dates reasonable, and stick to them unless the student has a very good excuse for lateness.

Communicate the specifics of assignments.

Examples

1. With younger students, have a routine procedure for giving assignments, such as writing them on the board in the same place each day. With older students, assignments may be dictated, posted, or given in a syllabus.
2. Remind students of upcoming assignments.
3. With complicated assignments, give students a sheet describing what to do, what resources are available, due dates, and so on. Older students should also be told your grading criteria.
4. Demonstrate how to do the assignment, do the first few questions together, or provide a sample worksheet.

Monitor work in progress.

Examples

1. When you give an assignment in class, make sure each student gets started correctly. If you check only students who raise their hands for help, you will miss those who think they know what to do but don't really understand, those who are too shy to ask for help, and those who don't plan to do the work at all.
2. Check progress periodically. In discussions, make sure everyone has a chance to respond.

Give frequent academic feedback.

Examples

1. Elementary students should get papers back the day after they are handed in.
2. Good work can be displayed in the classroom and graded papers sent home to parents each week.
3. Students of all ages can keep records of grades, projects completed, and extra credits earned.
4. For older students, break up long-term assignments into several phases, giving feedback at each point.

For more ideas, see http://trc.virginia.edu/Publications/Teaching_Concerns/TC_Topic/Engaging_Students.htm

---

more engaged if they are involved in authentic tasks—activities that have connections to real life. Also, activities are more engaging when the level of challenge is higher and when students' interests are incorporated into the tasks (Emmer & Gerwels, 2006).

Of course, teachers can't supervise every student all the time, or rely on curiosity to keep students motivated. Something else must keep students working on their own. In their study of elementary and secondary teachers, Evertson, Emmer, and their colleagues found that effective class managers at both levels had well-planned systems for encouraging students to manage their own work (Emmer & Evertson, 2009, 2013; Evertson & Emmer, 2009, 2013). The *Guidelines* are based on their findings.

Prevention Is the Best Medicine

The ideal way to manage problems, of course, is to prevent them in the first place. In a classic study, Jacob Kounin (1970) examined classroom management by comparing effective teachers, whose classes were relatively free of problems, with ineffective teachers, whose classes were continually plagued by chaos and disruption. Observing both groups in action, Kounin found that the teachers were not very different in the way they handled discipline *once problems arose*. The difference was that the successful managers were much better at preventing problems. Kounin concluded that effective classroom managers were especially skilled in four areas: "withitness," overlapping activities, group focusing, and movement management. More recent research confirms the importance of these factors (Emmer & Stough, 2001).

WITHITNESS. **Withitness** means communicating to students that you are aware of everything that is happening in the classroom—that you aren't missing anything. "With-it"

Withitness According to Kounin, awareness of everything happening in a classroom.

teachers seem to have eyes in the back of their heads. They avoid becoming absorbed by distractions or interacting with only a few students, because this encourages the rest of the class to wander. These teachers are always scanning the room, making eye contact with individual students, so the students know they are being monitored (Charles, 2011; Weinstein, Romano, & Mignano, 2011).

These teachers prevent minor disruptions from becoming major. They also know who instigated the problem, and they make sure they deal with the right people. In other words, they do not make what Kounin called *timing errors* (waiting too long before intervening) or *target errors* (blaming the wrong student and letting the real perpetrators escape responsibility for their behavior).

If two problems occur at the same time, effective managers deal with the more serious one first. For example, a teacher who tells two students to stop whispering, but ignores even a brief shoving match at the pencil sharpener communicates a lack of awareness. Students begin to believe they can get away with almost anything if they are clever.

OVERLAPPING AND GROUP FOCUS.
Overlapping means keeping track of and supervising several activities at the same time. For example, a teacher may have to check the work of an individual and at the same time keep a small group working by saying, "Right, go on," and stop an incident in another group with a quick "look" or reminder (Burden, 1995; Charles, 2011).

Maintaining a **group focus** means keeping as many students as possible involved in appropriate class activities and avoiding narrowing in on just one or two students. All students should have something to do during a lesson. For example, the teacher might ask everyone to write the answer to a question, and then call on individuals to respond while the other students compare their answers. Choral responses might be required while the teacher moves around the room to make sure everyone is participating. During a grammar lesson the teacher might say, "Everyone who thinks the answer is *have run,* hold up the red side of your card. If you think the answer is *has run,* hold up the green side" (Hunter, 1982). This is one way teachers can ensure that all students are involved and that everyone understands the material.

MOVEMENT MANAGEMENT.
Movement management means keeping lessons and the group moving at an appropriate (and flexible) pace, with smooth transitions and variety. The effective teacher avoids abrupt transitions, such as announcing a new activity before gaining the students' attention or starting a new activity in the middle of something else. In these situations, one-third of the class will be doing the new activity, many will be working on the old lesson, several will be asking other students what to do, some will be taking the opportunity to have a little fun, and most will be confused. Another transition problem Kounin noted is the slowdown, or taking too much time to start a new activity. Sometimes teachers give too many directions. Problems also arise when teachers have students work one at a time while the rest of the class waits and watches.

STUDENT SOCIAL SKILLS AS PREVENTION.
But what about the students? What can they do? When students lack social and emotional skills such as being able to share materials, read the intentions of others, or handle frustration, classroom management problems often follow. So all efforts to teach social and emotional self-regulation are steps toward preventing management problems. Over the short term, educators can teach and model these skills, and then give students feedback and practice using them in a variety of settings. Over the long term, teachers can help to change attitudes that value aggression over cooperation and compromise (Elias & Schwab, 2006).

Debra Stipek and her colleagues (1999) describe many ways teachers embed social skills lessons into school subjects and informal discussions. For example, class rules emphasize respect ("there are no stupid questions"); students learn to give "put ups" not "put downs"; the lives of historical figures provide opportunities to discuss choices and how to deal with stresses; and student conflicts become life lessons in relationships. In addition,

Overlapping Supervising several activities at once.

Group focus The ability to keep as many students as possible involved in activities.

Movement management Keeping lessons and the group moving at an appropriate (and flexible) pace, with smooth transitions and variety.

students are given a "Toolbox of Coping Skills" that contains concrete objects to be used to address problems. The Toolbox includes Post-it® notes to record student concerns and troubling situations so the incidents can be dealt with at an appropriate time. Exit and U-turn signs remind students that the best strategy may be to "exit" the situation. "Exiting to a safe place, without explanation, is taught as one appropriate face-saving, and possibly life-saving, response" (Stipek et al., 1999, p. 443). Indicators are that students do learn to use these skills.

Caring Relationships: Connections with School

All efforts directed toward building positive relationships with students and creating a classroom community are steps toward preventing management problems. Students respect teachers who maintain their authority without being rigid or harsh, who are fair and honest with them, who make sure they understand the material, who ask if something is wrong when they seem upset, and who use creative instructional practices to "make learning fun." Students also value teachers who show academic and personal caring by acting like real people (not just as teachers), sharing responsibility, minimizing the use of external controls, including everyone, searching for students' strengths, communicating effectively, and showing an interest in their students' lives and pursuits (Elias & Schwab, 2006; Wentzel, 2002; Woolfolk Hoy & Weinstein, 2006).

SCHOOL CONNECTIONS. Students who feel connected with school are happier, more engaged in school work, more self-disciplined, and less likely to be involved in dangerous behaviors such as substance abuse, violence, and early sexual activity (Freiberg, 2006; McNeely, Nonnemaker, & Blum, 2002; Pointz, Rimm-Kaufman, Grimm, & Curby, 2009). In fact, in a synthesis of 119 studies published in either English or German conducted from 1948 to 2004, Jeffrey Cornelius-White (2007) concluded that positive, warm, encouraging relationships with teachers are related to many valuable student outcomes, including higher participation in class, greater critical thinking skills, lower drop-out rates, higher self-esteem, increased motivation, less disruptive behavior, and better attendance. When Barbara Bartholomew (2008) asked a veteran special education teacher what keeps students engaged and motivated, the teacher replied without hesitation, "Students need to know that no matter what, you will never give up on them" (p. 58).

An example of respect for students and their lives comes from first-year teacher Esme Codell. "Madame Esme" (the name she preferred) had a morning ritual:

> In the morning, three things happen religiously. I say good morning, real chipper, to every single child and make sure they say good morning back. Then I collect "troubles" in a "Trouble Basket," a big green basket into which the children pantomime unburdening their home worries so they can concentrate on school. Sometimes a kid has no troubles. Sometimes a kid piles it in, and I in turn pantomime bearing the burden. This way, too, I can see what disposition the child is in when he or she enters. Finally, before they can come in, they must give me a word, which I print on a piece of tag board and keep in an envelope. It can be any word, but preferably one that they heard and don't really know or one that is personally meaningful. We go over the words when we do our private reading conferences. (Codell, 2001, p. 30)

If students perceive their schools are competitive places where they are treated differently based on race, gender, or ethnicity, then they are more likely to act out or withdraw altogether. But when

"DON'T GIVE UP ON ME" Students who feel connected with school are happier, more self-disciplined, and less likely to engage in negative behaviors. Believing that they matter and that their teachers are "on their side" helps keep students engaged and motivated.

they feel that they have choices, that the emphasis is on personal improvement and not comparisons, and that they are respected and supported by teachers, students are more likely to bond with schools (Osterman, 2000). One way of expressing respect and caring is by connecting with students' families and home lives. For example, students in China describe their teachers as high on caring. This may be because Chinese teachers spend quite a bit of time in students' homes, learning about their home life, and offering help outside school. These teachers show respect for the families and cultures of their students by their willingness to visit and to help (Jia et al., 2009; Suldo et al., 2009).

CREATING COMMUNITIES OF CARE FOR ADOLESCENTS.   The transition to high school is a particularly important time to maintain caring teacher–student relationships. Students have more teachers and fewer close relationships, just at a time when emotional, social, and academic stresses are increasing. One diverse urban school with over 2,000 students confronted this problem by creating small communities of care. These were interdisciplinary teams of students and teachers who shared common interests and participated in a Freshman Focus class during the first 9 weeks of school. The class helped students adjust to high school, get oriented to the building, and develop school skills like taking notes, social skills, and even skills for getting along with parents. The programs led to the development of positive teacher beliefs about students, supportive teacher–student relationships, and the promotion of academic and life skills (Ellerbrock & Kiefer, 2010).

DEALING WITH DISCIPLINE PROBLEMS

Being an effective manager does not mean publicly correcting every minor infraction of the rules. This kind of public attention may actually reinforce the misbehavior, as we saw in Chapter 7. The key is being aware of what is happening and knowing what is important so you can prevent problems.

Stopping Problems Quickly

Most students comply quickly when the teacher gives a *desist* (a "stop doing that") or redirects behavior. But some students are the targets of more than their share of desists. One study found that these disruptive students seldom complied with the first teacher request to stop. Often, the disruptive students responded negatively, leading to an average of 4 to 5 cycles of teacher desists and student responses before the student complied (Nelson & Roberts, 2000). Emmer and Evertson (2009) and Levin and Nolan (2000) suggest seven simple ways to stop misbehavior quickly, moving from least to most intrusive:

- *Make eye contact* with, or move closer to, the offender. Other nonverbal signals, such as pointing to the work students are supposed to be doing, might be helpful. Make sure the student actually stops the inappropriate behavior and gets back to work. If you do not, students will learn to ignore your signals.
- *Try verbal hints* such as "name-dropping" (simply insert the student's name into the lecture), asking the student a question, or making a humorous (not sarcastic) comment such as, "I must be hallucinating. I swear I heard someone shout out an answer, but that can't be because I haven't called on anyone yet!"
- *Ask students* if they are aware of the negative effects of their actions or send an "I" message, described later in the chapter.
- If they are not performing a class procedure correctly, *remind the students* of the procedure and have them follow it correctly. You may need to quietly collect a toy, comb, magazine, or note that is competing with the learning activities, while privately informing the students that their possessions will be returned after class.
- In a calm, unhostile way, ask the student to *state the correct rule or procedure* and then to follow it. Glasser (1969) proposes three questions: "What are you doing? Is it against the rules? What should you be doing?"
- *Tell the student* in a clear, assertive, and unhostile way to stop the misbehavior. (Later in the chapter, we will discuss assertive messages to students in more detail.) If students "talk back," simply repeat your statement.

GUIDELINES

Imposing Penalties

Delay the discussion of the situation until you and the students involved are calmer and more objective.
Examples

1. Say calmly to a student, "Sit there and think about what happened. I'll talk to you in a few minutes," or, "I don't like what I just saw. Talk to me during your free period today."

2. Say, "I'm really angry about what just happened. Everybody take out journals; we are going to write about this." After a few minutes of writing, the class can discuss the incident.

Impose penalties privately.
Examples

1. Make arrangements with students privately. Stand firm in enforcing arrangements.

2. Resist the temptation to "remind" students in public that they are not keeping their side of the bargain.

3. Move close to a student who must be disciplined and speak so that only the student can hear.

After imposing a penalty, reestablish a positive relationship with the student immediately.
Examples

1. Send the student on an errand or ask him or her for help.

2. Compliment the student's work or give symbolic "pat on the back" when the student's behavior warrants. Look hard for such an opportunity.

Set up a graded list of penalties that will fit many occasions.
Example

1. For not turning in homework: (1) receive reminder; (2) receive warning; (3) hand homework in before close of school day; (4) stay after school to finish work; (5) participate in a teacher–student-parent conference to develop an action plan.

Always teach problem-solving strategies along with penalties to help students learn what to do next time (Elias & Schwab, 2006).
Examples

1. Use Problem Diaries, where students record what they were feeling, identify the problem and their goal, then think of other possible ways to solve the problem and achieve the goal.

2. Try Keep Calm 5-2-5: At the first physical signs of anger, students say to themselves: "Stop. Keep Calm," then take several slow breaths, counting to 5 breathing in, 2 holding breath, and 5 breathing out.

For more ideas, see http://www.stopbullyingnow.com *or* http://www.cfchildren.org

---

- *Offer a choice.* For example, when a student continued to call out answers no matter what the teacher tried, the teacher said, "John, you have a choice. Stop calling out answers immediately and begin raising your hand to answer or move your seat to the back of the room and you and I will have a private discussion later. You decide" (Levin & Nolan, 2000, p. 177).

Many teachers prefer the use of *logical consequences*, described earlier, as opposed to penalties. For example, if one student has harmed another, you can require the offending student to make an "Apology of Action," which includes a verbal apology plus somehow repairing the damage done. This helps offenders develop empathy and social perspective taking as they think about what would be an appropriate "repair" (Elias & Schwab, 2006).

There is a caution about penalties. Never use lower achievement status (moving to a lower reading group, giving a lower grade, giving excess homework) as a punishment for breaking class rules. These actions should be done only if the benefit of the action outweighs the possible risk of harm. As Carolyn Orange (2000) notes, "Effective, caring teachers would not use low achievement status, grades, or the like as a means of discipline. This strategy is unfair and ineffective. It only serves to alienate the student" (p. 76).

If you must impose penalties, the *Guidelines*, taken from Weinstein and Novodvorsky (2011) and Weinstein, Romano, and Mignano (2011), give ideas about how to do it. The examples are taken from the actual words of the expert teachers described in their book.

Bullying and Cyber-Bullying

Bullying is a type of aggression characterized by systematic and repeated abuse of power intended to harm the victim (Merrell, Isava, Gueldner, & Ross, 2008). The line between good-natured exchanges and hostile teasing may seem thin, but a rule of thumb is that teasing someone who is less powerful or less popular or using any racial, ethnic, or religious slur should *not* be tolerated. Between 10% and 30% of children and youth are involved in bullying, and this seems to be the case around the world (Cook, Williams, Guerra, Kim, & Sadek, 2010; Guerra, Williams, & Sadek, 2011). Both bullies and victims are at risk for long-term academic, psychological, and behavioral problems (Swearer, Espelage, Vaillancourt, & Hymel, 2010).

VICTIMS.   Studies from both Europe and the United States indicate that about 10% of children are chronic victims—the constant targets of physical or verbal attacks. One kind of victim tends to have low self-esteem and to feel anxious, lonely, insecure, and unhappy. These students often are prone to crying and withdrawal; in general, when attacked, they won't defend themselves. These victims may believe that they are rejected because they have flaws that they cannot change or control—no wonder they are depressed and helpless! There is a second kind of victim—highly emotional and hot-tempered students who seem to provoke aggressive reactions from their peers. Members of this group have few friends (Pellegrini, Bartini, & Brooks, 1999).

Garbarino and deLara (2002) estimate that 160,000 children avoid school every day and thousands more drop out of school altogether because they are always afraid. Children who have been chronic victims through elementary and middle school are more depressed and more likely to attempt suicide as young adults (Graham, 1998; Hodges & Perry, 1999). And students who kill or injure others in schools are more often victims than bullies (Reinke & Herman, 2002a, 2002b). In the past years, we have seen tragic consequences when bullied students turned guns on their tormentors in schools in the United States and in Europe.

BULLYING AND TEASING.   A longitudinal study that followed a representative sample of 1st through 6th grade students for two years found that aggressive children whose teachers taught them conflict management strategies were moved away from a life path of aggression and violence (Aber, Brown, & Jones, 2003). But when teachers are silent about aggression and teasing, students may "hear" the teacher's agreement with the insult (Weinstein & Novodvorsky, 2011). Table 13.3 presents a list of dos and don'ts about teasing in schools.

Besides following these guidelines, research has shown that having a strong sense of community in your classroom is associated with more student empathy for the victims of bullying and less "blaming the victim" for being attacked (Gini, 2008). So anything you do to develop class community based on fairness and trust will be a step toward dealing with bullying. In a study of over 2,500 students in 59 schools, Nancy Guerra and her colleagues (2011) found that providing opportunities for success, promoting achievement and self-esteem, and improving teacher–student relationships also help to prevent bullying.

Unfortunately, the results are mixed on the effectiveness of many school-wide bullying prevention programs. And another discouraging finding is that administrators prefer to adopt anti-bullying programs that they heard about from colleagues rather than determine if there was any scientific evidence that the programs worked—and many don't (Swearer et al., 2010).

CHANGING ATTRIBUTIONS.   Cynthia Hudley and her colleagues (2007) at UCLA have developed a program to reduce physical aggression in elementary schools. The program,

TABLE 13.3 • **Dos and Don'ts about Teasing**

Teasing has led to some tragic situations. Talk about what to do in your class.

DO	DON'T
1. Be careful of others' feelings. 2. Use humor gently and carefully. 3. Ask whether teasing about a certain topic hurts someone's feelings. 4. Accept teasing from others if you tease. 5. Tell others if teasing about a certain topic hurts your feelings. 6. Know the difference between friendly gentle teasing and hurtful ridicule or harassment. 7. Try to read others' "body language" to see if their feelings are hurt—even when they don't tell you. 8. Help a weaker student when he or she is being ridiculed.	1. Tease someone you don't know well. 2. [If you are a boy] tease girls about sex. 3. Tease about a person's body. 4. Tease about a person's family members. 5. Tease about a topic when a student has asked you not to. 6. Tease someone who seems agitated or whom you know is having a bad day. 7. Be thin-skinned about teasing that is meant in a friendly way. 8. Swallow your feelings about teasing—tell someone in a direct and clear way what is bothering you.

Source: From Middle and Secondary Classroom Management: Lessons from Research and Practice *(4th ed.), by C.S. Weinstein. Published by McGraw-Hill. Copyright © 2007 by McGraw-Hill. Adapted with permission from the McGraw-Hill Companies, Inc.*

which is called BrainPower, is grounded in attribution theory, discussed in Chapter 12. The central goal of BrainPower is to teach aggressive students "to start from a presumption of accidental causes. When a social encounter with a peer results in a negative outcome (a spilled lunch tray, a bump in the lunch line, missing homework, etc.) the child will begin with the assumption that the outcome was due to accidental causes rather than intentional hostility from peers" (www.brainpowerprogram.com/index-1.html). The program also teaches accurate reading of social cues, so that students recognize when aggression against them is intentional. After students become more skillful at judging social cues, they learn and practice appropriate responses such as asking questions, being assertive—not aggressive, or seeking adult help. Two decades of research on this program shows it has been successful in changing many students' attributions and behaviors (Hudley, Graham, & Taylor, 2007).

CYBER-BULLYING.   With all the possibilities of technology come problems, too. Now bullies have new ways to torment victims using email, text messaging, Twitter, Facebook, cell phones, YouTube, Web blogs, online voting booths, and more (Weinstein & Novodvorsky, 2011). For example, when 16-year-old Denise broke up with her boyfriend, he sought revenge by posting her email address and cell phone number on Web sites and blogs devoted to sex. For months, she got embarrassing and frightening phone calls and messages (Strom & Strom, 2005). This kind of bullying is difficult to combat because the perpetrators can hide, but the damage can be long term. Table 13.4 on the next page has some ideas for dealing with cyber-bullying.

Special Problems with High School Students

Many secondary students never complete their schoolwork. Because students at this age have many assignments and teachers have many students, both teachers and students may lose track of what has and has not been turned in. It often helps to teach students how to use a daily planner—paper or electronic. In addition, teachers must keep accurate records. The most important thing is to enforce the established consequences for incomplete work. Do not pass a student because you know he or she is "bright enough" to pass. Make it clear to these students that the choice is theirs: They can do the work and pass, or they can refuse to do the work and face the consequences. You might also

Connect and Extend to PRAXIS II™

Student Misbehavior (I, C4)
Even the most well-managed classroom will have instances of student misbehavior. Explain the principles for dealing with common student misbehaviors. What strategies can teachers employ to deal fairly and effectively with those problems?

TABLE 13.4 • **Ideas for Dealing with Cyber-Bullying**

- Develop an explicit policy for acceptable in-school use of the Internet and include it in the school handbook (or your class rules). The policy should spell out what constitutes cyber-bullying and list consequences.
- Make sure that children and young people are aware that bullying will be dealt with seriously.
- Ensure that parents/guardians who express cyber-bullying concerns are taken seriously.
- Explain to students that they
  - Should never share or give out personal information, PIN numbers, phone numbers, etc.
  - Should not delete messages; they do not have to read them, but they should show them to an adult they trust. Messages can be used to take action against cyber-bullies.
  - Should not open a message from someone they don't know.
  - Should *never* reply to the message.
  - Can block the sender's message if they are being bullied through e-mail or instant messaging.
  - Can forward the messages to their Internet Service Provider.
  - Should tell an adult.
  - Should show the message to the police if it contains physical threats.
  - Should speak out against cyber-bullying.
  - Should never send messages when they are angry.
  - Should never send messages they wouldn't want others to see.
- Make parents aware of the fact that all of the major Internet Service Providers offer some form of parental controls. For example, AOL has developed "AOL Guardian," which reports with whom youngsters exchange messages and what Web sites they visit and monitors chat rooms for children 13 and under.
- Encourage parents to keep computers in a public room in the house.
- Invite members of the local police department to come to school to speak with parents and students about proper Internet use.
- Make sure ethics is included in any computer instruction given at your school.

Source: From Middle and Secondary Classroom Management: Lessons from Research and Practice *(4th ed.), by C.S. Weinstein. Published by McGraw-Hill. Copyright © 2007 by McGraw-Hill. Adapted with permission from the McGraw-Hill Companies, Inc.*

ask, in a private moment, if there is anything interfering with the student's ability to get the work done.

There is also the problem of students who continually break the same rules, always forgetting materials, for example, or getting into fights. What should you do? Seat these students away from others who might be influenced by them. Try to catch them before they break the rules, but if rules are broken, be consistent in applying established consequences. Do not accept promises to do better next time (Levin & Nolan, 2000). Teach the students how to monitor their own behavior; some of the self-regulation techniques described in Chapter 11 should be helpful. Finally, remain friendly with the students. Try to catch them in a good moment so you can talk to them about something other than their rule breaking.

A defiant, hostile student can pose serious problems. If there is an outburst, try to get out of the situation as soon as possible; everyone loses in a public power struggle. One possibility is to give the student a chance to save face and cool down by saying, "It's your choice to cooperate or not. You can take a minute to think about it." If the student complies, the two of you can talk later about controlling the outbursts. If the student refuses to cooperate, you can tell him or her to wait in the hall until you get the class started on work, then step outside for a private talk. If the student refuses to leave, send another class member for the assistant principal. Again, follow through. If the student complies before help arrives, do not let him or her off the hook. If outbursts occur frequently, you might have a conference with the counselor, family members, or other teachers. If the problem is an irreconcilable clash of personalities, the student should be transferred to another teacher. There is quite a bit of discussion today about zero tolerance for rule breaking in the schools. Is this a good idea? The *Point/Counterpoint* looks at both sides.

POINT/COUNTERPOINT: Is Zero Tolerance a Good Idea?

With the very visible violence in schools today, some districts have instituted "zero-tolerance" policies for rule breaking. One result? Two 8-year-old boys in New Jersey were suspended for making "terrorist threats." They had pointed paper guns at their classmates while playing. Do zero-tolerance policies make sense?

POINT

▶ **Zero tolerance means zero common sense.** An Internet search using keywords ["zero-tolerance" and schools] will locate a wealth of information about the policy—much of it against. For example, Oren Dorrell reported this incident in the November 2, 2009 edition of *USA Today*:

The most recent high-profile case [of zero tolerance] involved Zachary Christie, a 6-year-old who was suspended for five days on Sept. 29 after he brought a camping utensil that was part knife, fork and spoon to Downes Elementary in Newark, Del. School officials considered it a dangerous instrument and suspended the boy, adding that he couldn't return to Downes until he completed at least 45 days at an alternative school.

What does the research say? In 2006, the American Psychological Association set up a Zero Tolerance Task force to answer that question (Reynolds et al., 2008). Analyzing a decade of research, they reached the following conclusions:

- Schools are not any safer or more effective in disciplining students now than before they instituted zero tolerance.
- The higher rates of suspension caused by zero tolerance have not led to less racial bias in disciplining students.
- Zero tolerance policies can actually lead to increases in bad behavior that then lead to higher dropout rates.

In addition, zero tolerance policies can discourage students from informing teachers when the students learn that a classmate is "planning to do something dangerous." The zero tolerance rules get in the way of trusting relationships between teachers and students (Syvertsen, Flanagan, & Stout, 2009). Adolescents need both structure and support, but zero tolerance policies can create a highly structured, rigid environment that ignores the need for support. Finally, many of the popular zero-tolerance interventions such as increased security guards, hallway monitors, and the introduction of metal detectors have no apparent effect on the incidence of school bullying (Hyman et al., 2006; NCES, 2003).

COUNTERPOINT

▶ **Zero tolerance is necessary for now.** The arguments for zero tolerance focus on school safety and the responsibilities of schools and teachers to protect the students and themselves. Of course, many of the incidents reported in the news seem like overreactions to childhood pranks or worse, overzealous application of zero tolerance to innocent mistakes or lapses of memory. But how do school officials separate the innocent from the dangerous? For example, it has been widely reported that Andy Williams (the boy who killed two classmates in Santee, California) assured his friends before the shootings that he was only joking about "pulling a Columbine."

On January 13, 2003, I read a story in *USA Today* by Gregg Toppo entitled "School Violence Hits Lower Grades: Experts Who See Violent Behavior in Younger Kids Blame Parents, Prenatal Medical Problems and an Angry Society; Educators Search for Ways to Cope." The story opened with these examples: a 2nd-grader in Indiana takes off his shoe and attacks his teacher with it, a Philadelphia kindergartner hits a pregnant teacher in the stomach, and an 8-year-old in Maryland threatens to use gasoline (he knew exactly where he would pour it) to burn down his suburban elementary school. Toppo noted, "Elementary school principals and safety experts say they're seeing more violence and aggression than ever among their youngest students, pointing to what they see as an alarming rise in assaults and threats to classmates and teachers" (p. A2). Toppo cited statistics indicating that, although the incidence of school violence has decreased overall, attacks on elementary school teachers have actually increased.

Beyond Either/Or. Surely we can ask adults to use good judgment in applying rules in dangerous situations, but not feeling trapped by the rules when student actions are not intended to harm and are not dangerous.

It sometimes is useful to keep records of these incidents by logging the student's name, words and actions, date, time, place, and teacher's response. These records may help identify patterns and can prove useful in meetings with administrators, families, or special services personnel (Burden, 1995). Some teachers have students sign each entry to verify the incidents.

Fighting or destruction of property is a difficult and potentially dangerous problem. The first step is to send for help and get the names of participants and witnesses. Then, remove any students who may have gathered to watch; an audience will only make things worse. Do not try to break up a fight without help. Make sure the school office is aware of the incident; usually the school has a policy for dealing with these situations. What else can you do? The *Guidelines* on the next page for handling potentially explosive situations are taken from Weinstein and Novodvorsky (2011).

GUIDELINES

Handling Potentially Explosive Situations

Move slowly and deliberately toward the problem situation.
Examples
1. Walk slowly; then be as still as possible.
2. Establish eye-level position.

Be respectful.
Examples
1. Keep a reasonable distance.
2. Do not crowd the student. Do not get "in the student's face."
3. Speak respectfully. Use the student's name.
4. Avoid pointing or gesturing.

Be brief.
Examples
1. Avoid long-winded statements or nagging.
2. Stay with the agenda. Stay focused on the problem at hand. Do not get sidetracked.
3. Deal with less severe problems later.

Avoid power struggles.
Examples
1. Speak privately if possible.
2. Do not get drawn into "I won't, you will" arguments.
3. Don't make threats or raise your voice.

Inform the student of the expected behavior and the negative consequence as a choice or decision for the student to make. Then withdraw from the student and allow some time for the student to decide.
Examples
1. "Michael, you need to return to your desk, or I will have to send for the principal. You have a few seconds to decide." The teacher then moves away, perhaps attending to other students.
2. If Michael does not choose the appropriate behavior, deliver the negative consequences. ("You are choosing to have me call the principal.") Follow through with the consequence.

For more ideas, see: http://www.njcap.org/templated/Programs.html

Source: From Middle and Secondary Classroom Management: Lessons from Research and Practice *(4th ed.), by C.S. Weinstein. Published by McGraw-Hill. Copyright © 2007 by McGraw-Hill. Adapted with permission from the McGraw-Hill Companies, Inc.*

THE NEED FOR COMMUNICATION

STOP & THINK A student says to you, "That book you assigned is really stupid—I'm not reading it!" What do you say? •

Communication between teacher and students is essential when problems arise. Communication is more than "teacher talks—student listens." It is more than the words exchanged between individuals. We communicate in many ways. Our actions, movements, voice tone, facial expressions, and many other nonverbal behaviors send messages to our students. Many times, the messages we intend to send are not the messages our students receive.

Message Sent—Message Received

Teacher: Carl, where is your homework?

Carl: I left it in my Dad's car this morning.

Teacher: Again? You will have to bring me a note tomorrow from your father saying that you actually did the homework. No grade without the note.

Message Carl receives: I can't trust you. I need proof you did the work.

***

Teacher: Sit at every other desk. Put all your things under your desk. Jane and Laurel, you are sitting too close together. One of you move!

Message Jane and Laurel receive: I expect you two to cheat on this test.

***

A new student comes to Ms. Lincoln's kindergarten. The child is messy and un-washed. Ms. Lincoln puts her hand lightly on the girl's shoulder and says, "I'm glad you are here." Her muscles tense, and she leans away from the child.

Message student receives: I don't like you. I think you are bad.

In all interactions, a message is sent and a message is received. Sometimes teachers believe they are sending one message, but their voices, body positions, choices of words, and gestures may communicate a different message.

Students may hear the hidden message and respond to it. For example, a student may respond with hostility if she or he feels insulted by the teacher (or by another student), but may not be able to say exactly where the feeling of being insulted came from. Perhaps it was in the teacher's tone of voice, not the words actually spoken. But the teacher feels attacked for no reason. The first principle of communication is that people respond to what they think was said or meant, not necessarily to the speaker's intended message or actual words.

Students in my classes have told me about one instructor who encourages accurate communication by using the **paraphrase rule**. Before any participant, including the teacher, is allowed to respond to any other participant in a class discussion, he or she must summarize what the previous speaker said. If the summary is wrong, indicating the speaker was misunderstood, the speaker must explain again. The respondent then tries again to paraphrase. The process continues until the speaker agrees that the listener has heard the intended message.

Paraphrasing is more than a classroom exercise. It can be the first step in communicating with students. Before teachers can deal appropriately with any student problem, they must know what the real problem is. A student who says, "This book is really dumb! Why did we have to read it?" may really be saying, "The book was too difficult for me. I couldn't read it, and I feel dumb."

Diagnosis: Whose Problem Is It?

As a teacher, you may find many student behaviors unacceptable, unpleasant, or troubling. It is often difficult to stand back from these problems, take an objective look, and decide on an appropriate response. According to Thomas Gordon (1981), the key to good teacher–student relationships is determining why you are troubled by a particular behavior and who "owns" the problem. The answer to these questions is critical. If it is really the student's problem, the teacher must become a counselor and supporter, helping the student find his or her own solution. But if the teacher "owns" the problem, it is the teacher's responsibility to find a solution through problem solving with the student.

Diagnosing who owns the problem is not always straightforward. Let's look at three troubling situations to get some practice in this skill:

1. A student writes obscene words and draws sexually explicit illustrations in a school encyclopedia.
2. A student tells you that his parents had a bad fight and he hates his father.
3. A student quietly reads a newspaper in the back of the room.

Why are these behaviors troubling? If you cannot accept the student's behavior because it has a serious effect on you as a teacher—if you are blocked from reaching your goals by the student's action—then you own the problem. It is your responsibility to confront the student and seek a solution. A teacher-owned problem appears to be present in the first situation described above—the young pornographer—because teaching materials are damaged.

If you feel annoyed by the behavior because it is getting in the student's own way or because you are embarrassed for the child, but the behavior does not directly interfere with your teaching, then it is probably the student's problem. The student who hates his father would not prevent you from teaching, even though you might wish the student felt differently. The problem is really the student's, and he must find his own solution.

Connect and Extend to PRAXIS II™

Teacher–Student Communication (III, A)
A well-managed classroom requires a bidirectional line of communication between the teacher and students. Describe the various communication styles that teachers employ when interacting with students, and explain how those styles affect student behavior.

Paraphrase rule Policy whereby listeners must accurately summarize what a speaker has said before being allowed to respond.

The third situation is more difficult to diagnose. One argument is that the teacher is not interfered with in any way, so it is the student's problem. But teachers might find the student reading the paper distracting during a lecture, so it is their problem, and they must find a solution. In a gray area such as this, the answer probably depends on how the teacher actually experiences the student's behavior.

Having decided who owns the problem, it is time to act.

Counseling: The Student's Problem

Let's pick up the situation in which the student found the reading assignment "dumb." How might a teacher handle this positively?

Student: This book is really dumb! Why did we have to read it?

Teacher: You're pretty upset. This seemed like a worthless assignment to you. [Teacher paraphrases the student's statement, trying to hear the emotions as well as the words.]

Student: Yeah! Well, I guess it was worthless. I mean, I don't know if it was. I couldn't exactly read it.

Teacher: It was just too hard to read, and that bothers you.

Student: Sure, I felt really dumb. I know I can write a good report, but not with a book this tough.

Teacher: I think I can give you some hints that will make the book easier to understand. Can you see me after school today?

Student: Okay.

Here the teacher used **empathetic listening** to allow the student to find a solution. (As you can see, this approach relies heavily on paraphrasing.) By trying to hear the student and by avoiding the tendency to jump in too quickly with advice, solutions, criticisms, reprimands, or interrogations, the teacher keeps the communication lines open. Here are a few *unhelpful* responses the teacher might have made:

- I chose the book because it is the best example of the author's style in our library. You will need to have read it before your English II class next year. (The teacher justifies the choice; this prevents the student from admitting that this "important" assignment is too difficult.)
- Did you really read it? I bet you didn't do the work, and now you want out of the assignment. (The teacher accuses; the student hears, "The teacher doesn't trust me!" and must either defend herself or himself or accept the teacher's view.)
- Your job is to read the book, not ask me why. I know what's best. (The teacher pulls rank, and the student hears, "You can't possibly decide what is good for you!" The student can rebel or passively accept the teacher's judgment.)

Empathetic, active listening is more than a parroting of the student's words; it should capture the emotions, intent, and meaning behind them. Sokolove, Garrett, Sadker, and Sadker (1986, p. 241) have summarized the components of active listening: (1) blocking out external stimuli; (2) attending carefully to both the verbal and nonverbal messages; (3) differentiating between the intellectual and the emotional content of the message; and (4) making inferences regarding the speaker's feelings.

When students realize they really have been heard and not evaluated negatively for what they have said or felt, they begin to trust the teacher and to talk more openly. Sometimes the true problem surfaces later in the conversation.

Confrontation and Assertive Discipline

Now let's assume a student is doing something that actively interferes with teaching. The teacher decides the student must stop. The problem is the teacher's. Confrontation, not counseling, is required.

Empathetic listening Hearing the intent and emotions behind what another says and reflecting them back by paraphrasing.

"I" MESSAGES. Gordon (1981) recommends sending an **"I" message** in order to intervene and change a student's behavior. Basically, this means telling a student in a straightforward, assertive, and nonjudgmental way what she or he is doing, how it affects you as a teacher, and how you feel about it. The student is then free to change voluntarily, and often does so. Here are two "I" messages:

If you leave your book bags in the aisles, I might trip and hurt myself.
When you all call out, I can't concentrate on each answer, and I'm frustrated.

ASSERTIVE DISCIPLINE. Lee and Marlene Canter (1992; Canter, 1996) suggest other approaches for dealing with a teacher-owned problem. They call their method **assertive discipline.** Many teachers are ineffective with students because they are either wishy-washy and passive or hostile and aggressive (Charles, 2011).

EMPATHETIC LISTENING When students realize they really have been heard and not evaluated negatively for what they have said or felt, they begin to trust the teacher and to talk more openly. Sometimes the true problem surfaces later in the conversation.

Instead of telling the student directly what to do, *passive* teachers tell, or often ask, the student to *try* or to *think about* the appropriate action. The passive teacher might comment on the problem behavior without actually telling the child what to do differently: "Why are you doing that? Don't you know the rules?" or "Sam, are you disturbing the class?" Or teachers may clearly state what should happen, but never follow through with the established consequences, giving the students "one more chance" every time. Finally, teachers may ignore behavior that should receive a response or they may wait too long before responding.

A *hostile response style* involves different mistakes. Teachers may make "you" statements that condemn the student without stating clearly what the student should be doing: "You should be ashamed of the way you're behaving!" or "You never listen!" or "You are acting like a baby!" Teachers may also threaten students angrily, but follow through too seldom, perhaps because the threats are too vague—"You'll be very sorry you did that when I get through with you!"—or too severe. For example, a teacher tells a student in a physical education class that he will have to "sit on the bench for three weeks." A few days later, the team is short one member and the teacher lets the student play, never returning him to the bench to complete the three-week sentence. Often a teacher who has been passive becomes hostile and explodes when students persist in misbehaving.

In contrast with both the passive and hostile styles, an *assertive response* communicates to the students that you care too much about them and the process of learning to allow inappropriate behavior to persist. Assertive teachers clearly state what they expect. To be most effective, the teachers often look into a student's eyes when speaking and address the student by name. Assertive teachers' voices are calm, firm, and confident. They are not sidetracked by accusations such as "You just don't understand!" or "You don't like me!" Assertive teachers do not get into a debate about the fairness of the rules. They expect changes, not promises or apologies.

Not all educators believe that assertive discipline is useful. Earlier critics questioned the penalty-focused approach and emphasized that assertive discipline undermined student self-management (Render, Padilla, & Krank, 1989). John Covaleskie (1992) observed, "What helps children become moral is not knowledge of the rules, or even obedience to the rules, but discussions about the reasons for acting in certain ways" (p. 56). These critics have had an impact. More recent versions of assertive discipline focus on teaching

"I" message Clear, nonaccusatory statement of how something is affecting you.

Assertive discipline Clear, firm, unhostile response style.

students how to behave responsibly and working to establish mutual respect and trust (Charles, 2011).

CONFRONTATIONS AND NEGOTIATIONS. If "I" messages or assertive responses fail and a student persists in misbehaving, teacher and student are in a conflict. Several pitfalls now loom. The two individuals become less able to perceive each other's behavior accurately. Research has shown that the more angry you get with another person, the more you see the other as the villain and yourself as an innocent victim. Because you feel the other person is in the wrong, and he or she feels just as strongly that the conflict is all your fault, very little mutual trust is possible. A cooperative solution to the problem is almost impossible. In fact, by the time the discussion has gone on a few minutes, the original problem is lost in a sea of charges, countercharges, and self-defense (Baron & Byrne, 2003).

There are three methods of resolving a conflict between a teacher and a student. One is for the teacher to impose a solution. This may be necessary during an emergency, as when a defiant student refuses to go to the hall to discuss a public outburst, but it is not a good solution for most conflicts. The second method is for the teacher to give in to the student's demands. You might be convinced by a particularly compelling student argument, but again, this should be used sparingly. It is generally a bad idea to be talked out of a position, unless the position was wrong in the first place. Problems arise when either the teacher or the student gives in completely.

Gordon recommends a third approach, which he calls the "no-lose method." Here, the needs of both the teacher and the student are taken into account in the solution. No one person is expected to give in completely; all participants retain respect for themselves and each other. The no-lose method is a six-step, problem-solving strategy:

1. *Define the problem.* What exactly are the behaviors involved? What does each person want? (Use active listening to help students pinpoint the real problem.)
2. *Generate many possible solutions.* Brainstorm, but remember, don't allow any evaluations of ideas yet.
3. *Evaluate each solution.* Any participant may veto any idea. If no solutions are found to be acceptable, brainstorm again.
4. *Make a decision.* Choose one solution through consensus—no voting. In the end, everyone must be satisfied with the solution.
5. *Determine how to implement the solution.* What will be needed? Who will be responsible for each task? What is the timetable?
6. *Evaluate the success of the solution.* After trying the solution for a while, ask, "Are we satisfied with our decision? How well is it working? Should we make some changes?"

Many of the conflicts in classrooms can be important learning experiences for all concerned.

Reaching Every Student: Peer Mediation and Negotiation

Handling conflict is difficult for most of us—and for young people it can be even harder. Nearly 40 years ago, a large study of more than 8,000 junior and senior high students and 500 faculty from three major cities concluded that 90% of the conflicts among students are resolved in destructive ways or are never resolved at all (DeCecco & Richards, 1974). The few studies conducted since that time have reached similar conclusions. Avoidance, force, and threats seem to be the major strategies for dealing with conflict (Johnson et al., 1995). But there are better ways—like peer mediation and negotiation strategies that teach lifelong lessons.

David Johnson and his colleagues (1995) provided conflict resolution training to 227 students in 2nd through 5th grade. Students learned a five-step negotiating strategy:

1. *Jointly define the conflict.* Separate the person from the problem and the actions involved, avoid win–lose thinking, and get both parties' goals clear.
2. *Exchange positions and interests.* Present a tentative proposal and make a case for it; listen to the other person's proposal and feelings; and stay flexible and cooperative.

3. *Reverse perspectives.* See the situation from the other person's point of view and reverse roles and argue for that perspective.
4. *Invent at least three agreements that allow mutual gain.* Brainstorm, focus on goals, think creatively, and make sure everyone has power to invent solutions.
5. *Reach an integrative agreement.* Make sure both sets of goals are met. If all else fails, flip a coin, take turns, or call in a third party—a mediator.

In addition to learning conflict resolution, all students in Johnson and Johnson's study were trained in mediation strategies. The role of the mediator was rotated—every day the teacher chose two students to be the class mediators and to wear the mediators' T-shirts. Johnson and his colleagues found that students learned the conflict resolution and mediation strategies and used them successfully to handle conflicts in a more productive way, both in school and at home.

Peer mediation has also been successful with older students and those with serious problems (Sanchez & Anderson, 1990). In one program, selected gang members were given mediation training, and then all members were invited to participate voluntarily in the mediation process, supervised by school counselors. Strict rules governed the process leading to written agreements signed by gang representatives. Sanchez and Anderson (1990) found that gang violence in the school was reduced to a bare minimum—"The magic of the mediation process was communication" (p. 56).

Even if you do not have formal peer mediation training in your school, you can help your students handle conflict more productively. For example, Esme Codell, the excellent first-year teacher you met earlier in this chapter, taught her 5th graders a simple four-step process and posted the steps on a bulletin board: "1. Tell person what you didn't like. 2. Tell person how it made you feel. 3. Tell person what you want in the future. 4. Person responds with what they can do. Congratulations! You are a Confident Conflict Conqueror!" (Codell, 2001, p. 23).

We have looked at quite a few perspectives on classroom management. Clearly, there is not a one-size-fits-all strategy for creating social and physical spaces for learning. What does the research tell us? Are some better than others?

Research on Management Approaches

Research provides some guidance. Emmer and Aussiker (1990) conducted a meta-analysis of three general perspectives on management: *influencing* students through listening and problem solving, as described by Gordon (1981); *group management* through class meetings and student discussion, as advocated by Glasser (1969, 1990); and *control* through rewards and punishments, as exemplified by Canter and Canter (1992). No clear conclusions could be drawn about the impact of these approaches on student behaviors. However, some evaluations have found positive effects for Freiberg's (2012; Freiberg & Lamb, 2009) Consistency Management program and for programs that use rewards and punishments (Lewis, 2001).

INTEGRATING IDEAS.   In a study conducted in Australia, Ramon Lewis (2001) found that recognizing and rewarding appropriate student behaviors, talking with students about how their behavior affects others, involving students in class discipline decisions, and providing nondirective hints and descriptions about unacceptable behaviors were associated with students taking greater responsibility for their own learning. It is interesting that these interventions represent all three of the general approaches reviewed by Emmer and Aussiker: *influence, group management,* and *control.* In a study of over 3,000 9th grade students in Singapore, Youyan Nie and Shun Lau (2009) found that both caring and control were positively related to student engagement, so blending control, influence, caring, and group management strategies may be necessary in order to create positive learning environments. This is not always easy. Lewis also concluded that teachers sometimes find using caring, influence, and group management difficult when students are aggressive—and most in need of these positive approaches. When teachers feel threatened, it can be difficult for them to do what students need, but that may be the most important time to act positively and combine caring with control.

GUIDELINES — FAMILY AND COMMUNITY PARTNERSHIPS

Classroom Management

Make sure families know the expectations and rules of your class and school.
Examples

1. At a Family Fun Night, have your students do skits showing the rules—how to follow them and what breaking them "looks like" and "sounds like."
2. Make a poster for the refrigerator at home that describes, in a light way, the most important rules and expectations.
3. For older students, give families a list of due dates for the major assignments, along with tips about how to encourage quality work by pacing the effort—avoiding last minute panic. Some schools require family members to sign a paper indicating they are aware of the due dates.
4. Communicate in appropriate ways—use the family's first language when possible. Tailor messages to the reading level of the home.

Make families partners in recognizing good citizenship.
Examples

1. Send positive notes home when students, especially students who have had trouble with classroom management, work well in the classroom.

2. Give ideas for ways any family, even those with few economic resources, can celebrate accomplishment—a favorite food; the chance to choose a game to play; a comment to a special person such as an aunt, grandparent, or minister; the chance to read to a younger sibling.

Identify talents in the community to help build a learning environment in your class.
Examples

1. Have students write letters to carpet and furniture stores asking for donations of remnants to carpet a reading corner.
2. Find family members who can build shelves or room dividers, paint, sew, laminate manipulatives, write stories, repot plants, or network computers.
3. Contact businesses for donations of computers, printers, or other equipment.

Seek cooperation from families when behavior problems arise.
Examples

1. Talk to families over the phone or in their home. Keep good records about the problem behavior.
2. Listen to family members and solve problems with them.

COMMUNICATING WITH FAMILIES ABOUT CLASSROOM MANAGEMENT. As we have seen throughout this book, families are important partners in education. This statement applies to classroom management as well. When parents and teachers share the same expectations and support each other, they can create a more positive classroom environment and more time for learning. The *Family and Community Partnerships Guidelines* provide ideas for working with families and the community.

DIVERSITY: CULTURALLY RESPONSIVE MANAGEMENT

Research on discipline shows that African Americans and Latino/a Americans, especially males, are punished more often and more harshly than other students. These students lose time from learning as they spend more hours in detention or suspension (Gay, 2006; Monroe & Obidah, 2002; Skiba, Michael, Nardo, & Peterson, 2000). Why?

The notion that African Americans and Latino/a students are punished more because they commit more serious offenses is NOT supported by the data. Instead, these students are punished more severely for minor offenses such as rudeness or defiance—words and actions that are interpreted by teachers as meriting severe punishment. One explanation is a lack of cultural synchronization between teachers and students. "The language, style of walking, glances, and dress of black children, particularly males, have engendered fear, apprehension, and overreaction among many teachers and school administrators" (Irvine, 1990, p. 27). African American students may be disciplined for behaviors that were never intended to be disruptive or disrespectful. Teachers do their students and themselves a service if they work at becoming bicultural—helping their students to learn how to function in both mainstream and home cultures, but also learning the meaning of their students' words and actions—so they do not misinterpret and then punish their students' unintended insults (Gay, 2006).

Culturally responsive management is simply a part of the larger concept of culturally relevant teaching. Geneva Gay (2006) sums it up:

> If the classroom is a comfortable, caring, embracing, affirming, engaging, and facilitative place for students then discipline is not likely to be much of an issue. It follows then that both classroom management and school achievement can be improved for students from different ethnic, racial, social, and linguistic backgrounds by ensuring that curriculum and instruction are culturally relevant and personally meaningful for them.

I once asked a gifted educator in an urban New Jersey high school which teachers were most effective with the really tough students. He said there are two kinds: teachers who can't be intimidated or fooled and expect their students to learn, and teachers who really care about the students. When I asked, "Which kind are you?" he answered "Both!" He is an example of a "warm demander," a teacher who seems to be most effective with students placed at risk (Irvine & Armento, 2001; Irvine and Fraser, 1998). Sometimes these **warm demanders** appear harsh to outside observers (Burke-Spero, 1999; Burke-Spero & Woolfolk Hoy, 2002). Carla Monroe and Jennifer Obidah (2002) studied Ms. Simpson, an African American teacher working with her 8th grade science class. She describes herself as having high expectations for academics and behavior in her classes—so much so that she believed her students perceived her as "mean." Yet she often used humor and dialect to communicate her expectations, as in the following exchange:

Ms. Simpson [addressing the class]: If you know you're going to act the fool just come to me and say, "I'm going to act the fool at the pep rally," so I can go ahead and send you to wherever you need to go. [Class laughs.]

Ms. Simpson: I'm real serious. If you know you're having a bad day, you don't want anybody touching you, you don't want nobody saying nothing to you, somebody bump into you you're going to snap—you need to come up to me and say, "I'm going to snap and I can't go to the pep rally." [The students start to call out various comments.]

Ms. Simpson: Now, I just want to say I expect you to have the best behavior because you're the most mature students in the building . . . don't make me stop the pep rally and ask the 8th graders to leave.

Edward: We'll have silent lunch won't we? [Class laughs.]

Ms. Simpson: You don't want to dream about what you're going to have. [Class laughs.] Ok, 15 minutes for warm ups. [The students begin their warm-up assignment.]

Many African American students may be more accustomed to a directive kind of management and discipline outside of school. Their families might say, "Put down that candy" or "Go to bed," whereas White parents might ask, "Can we eat candy before dinner?" or "Isn't it time for bed?" As H. Richard Milner (2006, p. 498) says, "The question should not be which approach is right or wrong but which approach works with and connects with the students' prior knowledge and ways of knowing."

Culturally responsive management Taking cultural meanings and styles into account when developing management plans and responding to students.

Warm demanders Effective teachers with African American students who show both high expectations and great caring for their students.

▼ SUMMARY

The Need for Organization (pp. 472–475)

What are the challenges of classroom management? Classrooms are by nature multidimensional, full of simultaneous activities, fast-paced and immediate, unpredictable, public, and affected by the history of students' and teachers' actions. A teacher must juggle all these elements every day. Productive classroom activity requires students' cooperation. Maintaining cooperation is different for each age group. Young students are learning how to "go to school" and need to learn the general procedures of school. Older students need to learn the specifics required for working in different subjects. Working with adolescents requires teachers to understand the power of the adolescent peer group.

What are the goals of effective classroom management? The goals of effective classroom management are to make ample time for learning; improve the quality of time use by keeping students actively engaged; make sure participation structures are clear, straightforward, and consistently signaled; and encourage student self-management, self-control, and responsibility.

Creating a Positive Learning Environment (pp. 476–484)

Distinguish between rules and procedures. Rules are the specific dos and don'ts of classroom life. They usually are written down or posted. Procedures cover administrative tasks, student movement, housekeeping, and routines for accomplishing lessons, interactions between students and teachers, and interactions among students. Rules can be written in terms of rights and students may benefit from participating in establishing these rules. Consequences should be established for following and breaking the rules and procedures so that the teacher and the students know what will happen.

Distinguish between personal territories and interest-areas spatial arrangements. There are two basic kinds of spatial organization, territorial (the traditional classroom arrangement) and functional (dividing space into interest or work areas). Flexibility is often the key. Access to materials, convenience, privacy when needed, ease of supervision, and a willingness to reevaluate plans are important considerations in the teacher's choice of physical arrangements.

Contrast the first school week of effective and ineffective classroom managers. Effective classroom managers spent the first days of class teaching a workable, easily understood set of rules and procedures by using lots of explanation, examples, and practice. Students were occupied with organized, enjoyable activities, and they learned to function cooperatively in the group. Quick, firm, clear, and consistent responses to infractions of the rules characterized effective teachers. The teachers had planned carefully to avoid any last-minute tasks that might have taken them away from their students. These teachers dealt with the children's pressing concerns first. In contrast, for ineffective managers, procedures for accomplishing routine tasks varied from day to day and were never taught or practiced. Students talked to one another because they had nothing productive to do. Ineffective teachers frequently left the room. Many became absorbed in paperwork or in helping just one student. They had not made plans for how to deal with typical problems such as late-arriving students or interruptions.

Maintaining a Good Environment for Learning (pp. 484–488)

How can teachers encourage engagement? In general, as teacher supervision increases, students' engaged time also increases. When the task provides continuous cues for the student about what to do next, involvement will be greater. Activities with clear steps are likely to be more absorbing, because one step leads naturally to the next. Making work requirements clear and specific, providing needed materials, and monitoring activities all add to engagement.

Explain the factors identified by Kounin that prevent management problems in the classroom. To create a positive environment and prevent problems, teachers must take individual differences into account, maintain student motivation, and reinforce positive behavior. Successful problem preventers are skilled in four areas described by Kounin: "withitness," overlapping, group focusing, and movement management. When penalties have to be imposed, teachers should impose them calmly and privately. In addition to applying Kounin's ideas, teachers can prevent problems by establishing a caring classroom community and teaching students to use social skills and emotional self-regulation skills.

How do teachers help students form connections with schools? To get started on building connections, teachers should make expectations for both academic work and student behaviors clear. Respect for students' needs and rights should be at the center of class procedures. Students know that their teachers care about them when teachers try to make classes interesting, are fair and honest with them, make sure they understand the materials, and have ways to cope with students' concerns and troubles.

Dealing with Discipline Problems (pp. 488–494)

Describe seven levels of intervention in misbehavior. Teachers can first make eye contact with the student or use other nonverbal signals, then try verbal hints such as simply inserting the student's name into the lecture. Next the teacher asks if the offender is aware of the negative effects of the actions, then reminds the student of the procedure and has her or him follow it correctly. If this does not work, the teacher can ask the student to state the correct rule or procedure and then to follow it, and then move to telling the student in a clear, assertive, and unhostile way to stop the misbehavior. If this fails too, the teacher can offer a choice—stop the behavior or meet privately to work out the consequences.

What can teachers do about bullying, teasing, and cyberbullying? Teachers often underestimate the amount of peer conflict and bullying that happens in schools. Bullying involves both an imbalance of power between students and repeated attempts at harm and may take place in a variety of settings—including those in which students are not face-to-face with one another at school. Teachers can think of bullying as a form of violence and approach strategies for overcoming bullying as they would strategies to overcoming other violent acts. For example, prevention of bullying can take the form of developing a respectful classroom community and discussing conflict.

What are some challenges in secondary classrooms? Teachers working in secondary schools should be prepared to handle students who don't complete schoolwork, repeatedly break the same rule, or openly defy teachers. These students may also be experiencing new and powerful stressors. As a result, secondary students may benefit if teachers provide opportunities or point out resources for these students to seek out help and support. Teachers might also find consultation with guidance counselors and parents or caregivers helpful.

The Need for Communication (pp. 494–500)

What is meant by "empathetic listening"? Communication between teacher and student is essential when problems arise. All interactions between people, even silence or neglect, communicate some meaning. Empathetic, active listening can be a helpful response when students bring problems to teachers. Teachers must reflect back to the students what they hear them saying. This reflection is more than a parroting of words; it should capture the emotions, intent, and meaning behind them.

Distinguish among passive, hostile, and assertive response styles. The passive style can take several forms. Instead of telling the student directly what to do, the teacher simply comments on the behavior, asks the student to think about the appropriate action, or threatens but never follows through. In a hostile response style, teachers may make "you" statements that condemn the student without stating clearly what the student should be doing. An assertive response communicates to the students that the teacher cares too much about them and the process of learning to allow inappropriate behavior to persist. Assertive teachers clearly state what they expect.

What is peer mediation? Peer mediation is one good possibility for preventing violence in schools. The steps for peer mediation are: (1) Jointly define the conflict. (2) Exchange positions and interests. (3) Reverse perspectives. (4) Invent at least three agreements that allow mutual gain. (5) Reach an integrative agreement.

Diversity: Culturally Responsive Management (pp. 500–501)

What is culturally responsive management and why is it needed? African Americans and Latino/a Americans, especially males, are punished more often and more harshly than other students, but they do not commit more serious offenses. Instead, these students are punished more severely for minor offenses such as rudeness or defiance—words and actions that are interpreted by teachers as meriting severe punishment. One explanation is a lack of cultural synchronization between teachers and students. Culturally responsive management combines high expectaions for students' appropriate behavior with warmth and caring for the students as individuals.

▼ KEY TERMS

Academic learning time (474)
Action zone (481)
Allocated time (474)
Assertive discipline (497)
Classroom management (473)
Culturally responsive
   management (501)

Empathetic listening (496)
Engaged time/Time on task (474)
Group focus (486)
"I" message (497)
Movement management (486)
Natural/logical consequences (479)
Overlapping (486)

Paraphrase rule (495)
Participation structures (474)
Procedures/routines (476)
Rules (478)
Self-management (475)
Warm demanders (501)
Withitness (485)

▼ CONNECT AND EXTEND TO LICENSURE

MULTIPLE-CHOICE QUESTIONS

1. What is the aim of classroom management?
    A. To keep an orderly classroom
    B. To establish the primacy of the teacher
    C. To sustain a quiet and disciplined environment
    D. To maintain a positive productive learning environment

2. Which of the following is NOT a benefit of teaching students to be self-regulated?
    A. Students demonstrate the ability to fulfill their own needs without interfering with the rights and needs of others
    B. Teachers have fewer management problems, less stress, and more time to teach
    C. Students require increased teacher attention; therefore they learn more
    D. It requires extra time initially but leads to greater teacher self-efficacy

3. Mr. Ruiz was constantly plagued by students disrupting his English class. Determined to finally gain control, he resorted to afterschool detention, dropping letter grades, and belittling his students. When his evaluation by the principal occurred at the end of the term, he received low scores on his classroom management skills. His principal, Dr. Simon, provided feedback based upon research. Which one of the following would not be consistent with ideal ways to deal with Mr. Ruiz's problems?
    A. Teachers should begin the school year with severe consequences so students understand the teacher controls the classroom
    B. Teachers should aim to prevent classroom problems before they occur
    C. Teachers should exhibit withitness and overlapping in their activities
    D. Teachers must understand and practice movement management

4. Which of the following techniques is recommended for approaching and disciplining a student who may be prone to explosive behavior?
    A. Move swiftly and get as close to the misbehaving student as possible
    B. Ensure that there are several witnesses to the confrontation
    C. Be respectful and brief
    D. Use a loud voice to establish power

CONSTRUCTED-RESPONSE QUESTIONS
Case

It happened every day. Ginny Harding had to reprimand two boys in her class continually. Instead of feeling like a coach and mentor, Ginny started to feel like a nag. It wore on both boys and also on her. The boys were not malicious, they were just third graders being third graders. She remembered hearing an adage, one should not continue to do the same thing and expect different results. Over the next weekend Ginny decided to develop a more effective manner of handling this latest challenge.

5. List several simple ways in which Ginny Harding can quickly stop the boys from misbehaving.

6. Routines and procedures can also reduce the incidents of misbehavior by assisting students in smooth transitions from one activity to another. List several classroom operations and activities which should have an established routine or procedure.

MyEducationLab™

Go to Chapter 13 of the Book Specific Resources in MyEducationLab and click on "Connect and Extend to Licensure" to answer these questions. Compare your responses with the feedback provided.

▼ WHAT WOULD THEY DO?
TEACHERS' CASEBOOK: Bullies and Victims

Here is how some practicing teachers responded to the problems with bullies at school.

JOLITA HARPER • 3rd Grade
Preparing Academic Leaders Academy, Maple Heights, OH

I believe that the entire learning community has a clear role in preventing acts of intimidation between students, and that this is best accomplished with clear communication between all parties. Care should be taken to spread awareness between colleagues as to the nature of the situation. Classroom teachers who are alert to these instances of bullying are then able to provide an additional presence in situations, such as in hallways and the lunchroom, where this is likely to take place. Further, communication between individual classroom teachers and the victim of this bullying is essential. I would make certain to provide a sensitive ear to this student's plight as we work together to formulate alternatives toward improving the situation. Finally, in the event that the two bullying students were in my classes, I would communicate with them in such a way as to make clear the effect of their actions on others in an effort to promote empathy for their victim and, hopefully, initiate a change in their behaviors.

KEITH J. BOYLE • English Teacher, Grades 9–12
Dunellen High School, Dunellen, NJ

Errant behavior throughout the middle school may be indicative of future behavioral problems and, as many things in life, the more this misbehavior is allowed to exist, the longer it will have a chance to thrive. In this case of a child being continually bullied by two other children (gender having no bearing in this situation), the knowledge of this wrongdoing must not be ignored or isolated. I would interview both the victim and the bullies, separately, to glean as much information as possible. If this were a singular incident, I would attempt to handle it myself via contact with the pertinent parents. However, if this were a recurring problem, the administration must be made aware. Any administrator will acknowledge that to be left in the dark about a serious situation within the environs of his/her responsibility is precarious. The appropriate guidance counselor should also be involved. The gravity of abusive behavior toward fellow students must be emphasized to the offenders. Significant punitive action is integral in order to send a message to the entire community that their school is indeed a haven in which one can feel the uninhibited freedom to learn.

DAN DOYLE • History Teacher, Grade 11
St. Joseph's Academy, Hoffman, IL

As a high school teacher I'd be especially concerned about the existence of bullying among older students. While such behavior in elementary school is hurtful and damaging, it can become downright dangerous as students get older (and bigger!). I'd also be frustrated to think that, perhaps, early warning signs among these children may have been ignored or under-addressed at the elementary level, when teachers and/or parents are better positioned to get a grip on them. My first step would be to alert school personnel, particularly those who monitor hallways, the cafeteria, and other common areas, to be on the lookout for any type of bullying behavior. I'd put those responsible in communication with the guidance counselor's office; the counselor would determine whether the parents needed to be involved from there. Events in our society in recent years preclude the option of taking this sort of behavior lightly, or assuming it will take care of itself.

KELLEY CROCKETT
Meadowbrook Elementary School, Fort Worth, TX

Bullying cannot be tolerated. No school, no teacher, no administrator can afford a climate in which abusive behavior is allowed to germinate. Any incident of victimization must be immediately documented and submitted to the Principal. As well, I would schedule a conference that same day with the school counselor for my student in order to both allow another avenue of documentation and reinforce support that the problem is being aggressively addressed.

How I handle the next step depends on the administration in place but the important issue to remember is that there is a next step. The teacher must follow up with the student. Within 48 hours I would privately ask my student if there have been any further incidents. If he hesitates or acknowledges continued harassment I would direct him to write it down and I would document any questions I had asked him and his responses. I would then include his statement and my own in another report for both the Principal and the counselor.

As teachers, we hold the front line. To the children in our care we represent one of the first relationships with authority and civilize society. We can do no less than lend our voice and action to the betterment of our world.

MyEducationLab™

Go to Topic 12, Classroom Management, in the MyEducationLab (www.myeducationlab.com)
for *Educational Psychology*, where you can:

- Find learning outcomes for classroom management along with the national standards that connect to these outcomes.
- Complete Assignments and Activities that can help you more deeply understand the chapter content.
- Apply and practice your understanding of the core teaching skills identified in the chapter with the Building Teaching Skills and Dispositions learning units.
- Examine challenging situations and cases presented in the IRIS Center Resources.
- Access video clips of CCSSO National Teachers of the Year award winners responding to the question, "Why Do I Teach?" in the Teacher Talk section.
- Check your comprehension on the content covered in the chapter with the Study Plan. Here you will be able to take a chapter quiz, receive feedback on your answers, and then access Review, Practice, and Enrichment activities to enhance your understanding of chapter content.
- Find additional Teachers' Casebook scenarios and responses to them from practicing teachers.
- Use the Online Lesson Plan Builder to practice lesson planning and integrating national and state standards into your planning.

chapter fourteen

TEACHING EVERY STUDENT

▶ **TEACHERS' CASEBOOK:** Reaching and Teaching Every Student

You have started a new job in a high school in your hometown. When you were in school, the students were fairly homogeneous—White, working to middle class, and English speaking. There was a "special education" class for students who had serious learning or developmental problems. But in the classes you are teaching, you find a wide range of reading levels, family incomes, and learning problems. Two of your students are virtually ready for college, whereas several others can barely read the texts—and their writing is impossible to decipher. Reading English texts is a challenge for some of your ELL students, although they seem to speak English with little trouble.

CRITICAL THINKING

- How would you differentiate instruction for these very dissimilar students?
- Do different philosophies of teaching provide different answers to this question?
- How will you grade work if you have successfully differentiated instruction?

OVERVIEW AND OBJECTIVES

Much of this text has been about learning and learners. In this chapter, we focus on teaching and teachers. Are there particular characteristics that distinguish effective from ineffective teachers? Research on whole-class teaching points to the importance of several factors that we will explore.

What else do we know about teaching? We look at how teachers plan, including how to use taxonomies of learning objectives or themes as a basis for planning.

With this foundation of knowing how to set goals and make plans, as well as an understanding of the characteristics of effective teachers, we move to a consideration of some general teacher-centered strategies: lecturing, seatwork, homework, questioning, recitation, and group discussion.

In the final section of this chapter, we will focus on how to match teaching to the needs and abilities of students through differentiated instruction, flexible grouping, and adaptive teaching. Finally we explore how teachers' beliefs about their students' abilities—teacher expectations—might influence student learning and teacher–student relationships.

By the time you have completed this chapter, you should be able to:

Objective 14.1: Identify the characteristics of effective teachers and effective classroom climates.

Objective 14.2: Develop learning objectives using Bloom's taxonomy.

Objective 14.3: Describe the processes involved in planning a lesson and differentiate among basic formats for putting plans into action.

Objective 14.4: Discuss the appropriate uses of direct instruction, homework, questioning, and group discussion.

Objective 14.5: Define differentiated instruction and adaptive teaching, and apply the approach to teaching a diverse group of students.

Objective 14.6: Explain the possible effects of teacher expectations and know how to avoid the negative implications.

RESEARCH ON TEACHING

This chapter is about teaching, so we will start with findings from several decades of research.

How would you go about identifying the keys to successful teaching? You might ask students, principals, college professors of education, or experienced teachers to list the characteristics of good teachers. Or you could do intensive case studies of a few classrooms over a long period. You might observe classes, rate different teachers on certain characteristics, and then see which characteristics were associated with teachers whose students either achieved the most or were the most motivated to learn. (To do this, of course, you would have to decide how to assess achievement and motivation.) You could identify teachers whose students, year after year, learned more than students working with other teachers; then you could observe the more successful teachers and note what they do. You might also train teachers to apply several different strategies to teach the same lesson and then determine which strategy led to the greatest student learning. You could videotape teachers, and then ask them to view the tapes and report what they were thinking about as they taught and what influenced their decisions while teaching, called *stimulated recall*. You might study transcripts of classroom dialogue to learn what helped students understand the material. You might use the relationships identified between teaching and learning as the basis for developing teaching approaches and testing these approaches in *design experiments*.

All of these approaches and more have been used to investigate teaching (Floden, 2001; Greeno, Collins, and Resnick, 1996; Gröschner, Seidel, & Shavelson, 2012). Let's examine some of the specific knowledge about teaching gained from these projects.

Characteristics of Effective Teachers

STOP & THINK Think about the most effective teacher you ever had—the one that you learned the most from. What were the characteristics of that person? What made that teacher so effective? •

Some of the earliest research on effective teaching focused on the personal qualities of the teachers themselves. Results revealed some lessons about three teacher characteristics: clarity, warmth, and knowledge. Recent research has focused on knowledge, so we will spend some extra time on that characteristic.

CLARITY AND ORGANIZATION. When Barak Rosenshine and Norma Furst (1973) reviewed about 50 studies of teaching, they concluded that *clarity* was the most promising teacher behavior for future research on effective teaching. Teachers who provide clear presentations and explanations tend to have students who learn more and who rate their teachers more positively (Comadena, Hunt, & Simonds, 2007; Hines, Cruickshank, & Kennedy, 1985). The clearer and less vague the teacher's explanations and instructions are, the more the students learn (Evertson & Emmer, 2009; 2012).

WARMTH AND ENTHUSIASM. As you are well aware, some teachers are much more enthusiastic than others. Some studies have found that ratings of teachers' enthusiasm for their subject are correlated with student achievement gains (Keller, Neumann, &

EFFECTIVE TEACHERS Effective teachers know how to transform their knowledge into examples, explanations, illustrations, and activities.

Fischer, 2012), whereas warmth, friendliness, and understanding seem to be the teacher traits most strongly associated with students' liking the teacher and the class in general (Hamann, Baker, McAllister, & Bauer, 2000; Madsen, 2003; Soar & Soar, 1979). But notice: These are correlational studies. The results do not tell us that teacher enthusiasm causes student learning or that warmth causes positive attitudes, only that the two variables tend to occur together. Two possible connections are that when teachers are enthusiastic, they capture and hold student attention, and that enthusiastic teachers model engagement and interest in learning. Student attention, interest, and engagement lead to learning. Of course, it is easier to be an enthusiastic teacher when your students are learning (Keller et al., 2012).

What about another important teacher characteristic—knowledge?

Knowledge for Teaching

As you saw in Chapters 8 and 9, knowledge is the defining characteristic of expertise. **Expert teachers** have elaborate systems of knowledge for understanding problems in teaching. For example, when a beginning teacher is faced with students' wrong answers on math or history tests, all of these answers may seem about the same—wrong. But for an expert teacher, wrong answers are part of a rich system of knowledge that could include how to recognize several types of wrong answers, the misunderstanding or lack of information behind each kind of mistake, the best way to reteach and correct the misunderstanding, materials and activities that have worked in the past, and several ways to test whether the reteaching was successful. This unique kind of teacher knowledge that combines mastery of *academic content* with knowing *how to teach* the content and how to match instruction to *student differences* is called **pedagogical content knowledge** (Gess-Newsome, 2012). In addition, expert teachers have clear goals and take individual differences into account when planning for their students. These teachers are **reflective** practitioners, constantly trying to understand and improve their work with students (Hogan, Rabinowitz, & Craven, 2003).

Expert teachers Experienced, effective teachers who have developed solutions for classroom problems. Their knowledge of teaching process and content is extensive and well organized.

Pedagogical content knowledge Teacher knowledge that combines mastery of *academic content* with knowing *how to teach* the content and how to match instruction to *student differences*.

Reflective Thoughtful and inventive. Reflective teachers think back over situations to analyze what they did and why and to consider how they might improve learning for their students.

What do expert teachers know that allows them to be so successful? Lee Shulman (1987) has studied this question, and he has identified seven areas of professional knowledge. Expert teachers know:

1. The academic subjects they teach—their content knowledge is deep and interconnected.
2. General teaching strategies that apply in all subjects (such as the principles of classroom management, effective teaching, and evaluation that you will discover in this book).
3. The curriculum materials and programs appropriate for their subject and grade level.
4. Subject-specific knowledge for teaching: special ways of teaching certain students and particular concepts, such as the best ways to explain negative numbers to lower-ability students.
5. The characteristics and cultural backgrounds of learners.
6. The settings in which students learn—pairs, small groups, teams, classes, schools, and the community.
7. The goals and purposes of teaching.

This is quite a list. Obviously, one course cannot give you all the information you need to teach. In fact, a whole program of courses won't make you an expert. That takes time and experience. But studying educational psychology has added to your professional knowledge because at the heart of educational psychology is a concern with learning wherever it occurs.

Do teachers who know more about their subject have a more positive impact on their students? It depends on the subject. When Hill, Rowan, and Ball (2005) tested U.S. 1st and 3rd grade teachers' specific knowledge of the math concepts that they actually teach and their understanding of how to teach those concepts, they found that teachers with greater *content* and *pedagogical content knowledge* had students who learned more mathematics. High school students appear to learn more mathematics from teachers with degrees or significant coursework in mathematics (Wayne & Youngs, 2003). Studies in German high schools have found that math teachers with more pedagogical content knowledge have students who are more cognitively engaged and more supported in learning, and this higher quality instruction predicts higher student math achievement (Baumert et al., 2010).

When we look at teachers' knowledge of facts and concepts in other subjects, as measured by test scores and college grades, the relationship to student learning is unclear and may be indirect (Aloe & Becker, 2009). We know from Darling-Hammond and Youngs' (2002) work that the quality of teachers—as measured by whether the teachers were fully certified and have a major in their teaching field—is related to student performance. When we look at scores on teacher certification tests, there is a modest positive relationship between teachers' scores and students' achievement—the strongest evidence for this relationship is again in mathematics (Boyd, Goldhaber, Lankford, & Wyckoff, 2008).

The indirect effects are that teachers who know more may make clearer presentations and recognize student difficulties more easily. They are ready for any student questions and do not have to be evasive or vague in their answers. Thus, knowledge is necessary for effective teaching because being more knowledgeable helps teachers be *clearer*, more *organized*, and more *responsive* to student questions.

Recent Research on Teaching

A program of large-scale, longitudinal research by Robert Pianta and his colleagues (2005, 2008; Crosnoe et al., 2010; Jerome, Harme, & Pianta, 2009; Luckner & Pianta, 2011) has identified three aspects of classroom climate that are related to the development and learning of preschool and elementary school students. These three dimensions are consistent with the characteristics of teachers identified in earlier research on teaching, and they cover affective, behavioral, and cognitive dimensions, as you can see in Table 14.1. The *affective* dimension in Pianta's model is teacher *emotional support*, similar to teacher warmth and enthusiasm identified in early research. The *cognitive* dimension is instructional support, which includes concept development (activities and discussions that promote student higher-order thinking) and quality feedback that is specific and focused on the learning process. Concept development and quality feedback may be easier for teachers with greater knowledge for teaching. Pianta's third dimension is classroom organization, which includes *behavioral* concerns such as classroom and lesson management, with clear activities and routines that make more time for student learning and are really engaging—similar to the teacher characteristics of clarity and organization.

Now let's get to the specifics of teaching—the first step is planning.

TABLE 14.1 • **Dimensions of Classroom Climate**

AREA OF TEACHING	CLASSROOM CLIMATE DIMENSION	COMPONENTS	DEFINITIONS AND EXAMPLES
Affective	**Emotional Support**	*Positive Climate*	Warmth, mutual respect, positive emotional connections between teacher and students
		Negative Climate (negative predictor of learning)	Disrespect, anger, hostility
		Teacher Sensitivity	Consistency and effectiveness in responding to students' academic and emotional needs
		Regard for Students' Perspectives	Activities encourage student autonomy and emphasize students' interests, motivations, and points of view
Cognitive	**Instructional Support**	*Concept Development*	Activities and discussion promote higher-order thinking skills and cognition
		Quality of Feedback	Consistency in providing specific, process-oriented feedback and back-and-forth exchanges to extend students' learning
Behavioral	Classroom Organization	*Behavior Management*	Teachers' effectiveness in monitoring, preventing, and redirecting misbehavior
		Productivity	How consistently learning is maximized with clear activities and routines, teacher preparation, efficient transitions, and minimal disruptions
		Instructional Learning Formats	How well materials, modalities, and activities are used to engage students in learning

Source: Based on Brown, J. L., Jones, S. M., LaRusso, M. D., & Aber, J. L. (2010). Improving classroom quality: Teacher influences and experimental impacts of the 4Rs Program. Journal of Educational Psychology, 102, 153–167.

THE FIRST STEP: PLANNING

STOP & THINK Greta Morine-Dershimer (2006) asks which of the following are true about teacher planning:

Time is of the essence.   A little planning goes a long way.

Plans are made to be broken.   You can do it yourself.

Don't look back.   One size fits all. •

Research on Planning

When you thought about the "What Would You Do?" challenge at the beginning of this chapter, you were planning. In the past few years, educational researchers have become very interested in teachers' planning. They have interviewed teachers about how they plan, asked teachers to "think out loud" while planning or to keep journals describing their plans, and even studied teachers intensively for months at a time. What do you think they have found?

First, planning influences what students will learn, because planning transforms the available time and curriculum materials into activities, assignments, and tasks for students—*time is of the essence planning*. When a teacher decides to devote 7 hours to language arts and 15 minutes to science in a given week, the students in that class will learn more language than science. Planning done at the beginning of the year is particularly important, because many routines and patterns, such as time allocations, are established early. So, *a little planning does go a long way* in terms of what will be taught and what will be learned.

Second, teachers engage in several levels of planning—by the year, term, unit, week, and day. All the levels must be coordinated. Accomplishing the year's plan requires breaking the work into terms, the terms into units, and the units into weeks and days. For experienced teachers, unit planning seems to be the most important level, followed by weekly and then daily planning. As you gain experience in teaching, it will be easier to coordinate these levels of planning and incorporate the state and district curriculum standards as well (Morine-Dershimer, 2006).

Third, plans reduce—but do not eliminate—uncertainty in teaching. Planning must allow flexibility. There is some evidence that when teachers "overplan"—fill every minute and stick to the plan no matter what—their students do not learn as much as students whose teachers are flexible (Shavelson, 1987). So *plans are not made to be broken—but sometimes they need to be bent a bit.*

In order to plan creatively and flexibly, teachers need to have wide-ranging knowledge about students, their interests, and their abilities; the subjects being taught; alternative ways to teach and assess understanding; how to apply and adapt materials and texts; and how to pull all this knowledge together into meaningful activities. The plans of beginning teachers sometimes don't work because they lack knowledge about the students or the subject—they can't estimate how long it will take students to complete an activity, for example, or they stumble when asked for an explanation or a different example (Calderhead, 1996).

EXPERT PLANNING In planning, you can go it alone, but collaboration is better. Sharing ideas with colleagues can be one of the best experiences in teaching.

In planning, *you can do it yourself—but collaboration is better.* Working with other teachers and sharing ideas is one of the best experiences in teaching. Some educators think that a collaborative approach to planning used in Japan called *kenshu* or "mastery through study" is one reason why Japanese students do so well on international tests. A basic part of the kenshu process involves a small group of teachers developing a lesson and then videotaping one of the group members teaching the lesson. Next, all members review the tape, analyze student responses, and improve the lesson further. Other teachers try the revised lesson and more improvements follow. At the end of the school year, all the study groups may publish the results of their work. In the United States, this process is called **lesson study** (Morine-Dershimer, 2006). To learn about this approach, search the Internet using the keywords "lesson study." Then, explore some of the lesson plans available using the keywords "lesson plans," or search by subject or grade—for example, "math lesson plans" or "4th grade lesson plans."

"And then, of course, there's the possibility of being just the slightest bit too organized."

By permission of Glen Dines. From *Phi Delta Kappan.*

But even great lesson plans taken from a terrific Web site on science have to be adapted to your situation. Some of the adaptation comes before you teach and some comes after. In fact, much of what experienced teachers know about planning comes from looking back—reflecting—on what worked and what didn't, so *DO look back* on your plans and grow professionally in the process. Collaborative reflection and revising lessons are major components of the lesson study approach to planning.

Finally, there is no one model for effective planning. *One size does NOT fit all* in planning. Planning is a creative problem-solving process for experienced teachers; they know how to complete many lessons and are able to teach segments of lessons effectively. They know what to expect and how to proceed, so they don't necessarily continue to follow the detailed lesson-planning models they learned during their teacher preparation programs. Planning is more informal—"in their heads." However, many experienced teachers think it was helpful to learn this detailed system as a foundation (Clark & Peterson, 1986).

No matter how you plan, you must have a learning goal in mind. In the next section, we consider the range of goals that you might have for your students.

Objectives for Learning

We hear quite a bit today about visions, goals, outcomes, and standards. At a very general, abstract level are the grand goals society may have for graduates of public schools such as preparing them "to succeed in college and the workplace and to compete in the global economy" (USDE, Race to The Top, 2009, p. 2). But very general goals are meaningless as potential guidelines for instruction. States may turn these grand goals into *standards* and *indicators*, such as the Colorado standard that students will "Use comprehension skills such as previewing, predicting, inferring, comparing and contrasting, rereading and self-monitoring, summarizing, etc." At this level, the indicators are close to being instructional objectives (Airasian, 2005). You can find your state's standards at http://www.educationworld.com/standards/state/index.shtml.

AN EXAMPLE OF STANDARDS: TECHNOLOGY. Here is an example of standards that relate to you—the teacher—and what you should know about technology. Two widely adopted technology standards are from the International Society for Technology in Education (ISTE) and the Partnership for 21st Century Skills. The ISTE produced the National Education Technology Standards for teachers shown below (NETS-T; http://www.iste.org/standards/nets-for-teachers/nets-for-teachers-2008.aspx):

1. **Facilitate and Inspire Student Learning and Creativity***
   Teachers use their knowledge of subject matter, teaching and learning, and technology to facilitate experiences that advance student learning, creativity, and innovation in both face-to-face and virtual environments.

National Educational Technology Standards for Teachers. Second edtion © 2008 ISTE ® (International Society of Technology in Education), www.iste.org. All rights reserved.

Lesson study As a group, teachers develop, test, improve, and retest lessons until they are satisfied with the final version.

2. **Design and Develop Digital-Age Learning Experiences and Assessments**
   Teachers design, develop, and evaluate authentic learning experiences and assessment incorporating contemporary tools and resources to maximize content learning in context and to develop the knowledge, skills, and attitudes identified in the NETS•S.

3. **Model Digital-Age Work and Learning**
   Teachers exhibit knowledge, skills, and work processes representative of an innovative professional in a global and digital society.

4. **Promote and Model Digital Citizenship and Responsibility**
   Teachers understand local and global societal issues and responsibilities in an evolving digital culture and exhibit legal and ethical behavior in their professional practices.

5. **Engage in Professional Growth and Leadership**
   Teachers continuously improve their professional practice, model lifelong learning, and exhibit leadership in their school and professional community by promoting and demonstrating the effective use of digital tools and resources.

But what about your teaching? Let's move into the classroom.

CLASSROOMS: INSTRUCTIONAL OBJECTIVES.   Norman Gronlund and Susan Brookhart (2009) define **instructional objectives** as intended learning outcomes. Objectives are the performances expected of students after instruction in order to demonstrate their learning. Objectives written by people with behavioral views focus on observable and measurable changes in the learner. Behavioral objectives use terms such as *list, define, add,* or *calculate*. Cognitive objectives, on the other hand, emphasize thinking and comprehension, so they are more likely to include words such as *understand, recognize, create,* or *apply*. Let's look at one well-developed method of writing specific behavioral objectives.

MAGER: START WITH THE SPECIFIC.   Robert Mager (1975, 1997) developed a very influential system for writing instructional objectives. His idea is that objectives ought to describe what students will be doing when demonstrating their achievement and show how teachers will know they are doing it, so these are generally regarded as **behavioral objectives**. According to Mager, a good objective has three parts. First, it describes the intended *student behavior*. What must the student do? Second, it lists the *conditions* under which the behavior will occur: How will this behavior be recognized or tested? Third, it gives the *criteria* for acceptable performance on the test. For example, an objective in social studies might be: "Given a recent article from an online political blog [*conditions*], the student will mark each statement with an F for fact or an O for opinion [*observable student behavior*], with 75% of the statements correctly marked [*criteria*]." With this emphasis on final behavior, Mager's system requires a very explicit statement. Mager contends that often students can teach themselves if they are given well-stated objectives.

GRONLUND: START WITH THE GENERAL.   Gronlund and Brookhart (2009) offer a different approach, which is often used for writing **cognitive objectives**. They believe an objective should be stated first in general terms (*understand, solve, appreciate,* etc.). Then, the teacher should clarify by listing a few sample behaviors that would provide evidence that the student has attained the objective. Look at the example in Table 14.2. The goal here is comprehension of a scientific concept. A teacher could never list all the behaviors that might be involved in "comprehension," but stating an initial, general objective along with specific examples makes the purpose clear.

The most recent research on instructional objectives tends to favor approaches similar to Gronlund's. James Popham (2005a), a former proponent of very specific objectives, makes this recommendation:

> Strive to come up with a half dozen or so truly salient, broad, yet measurable instructional objectives for your own classroom. Too many small-scope, hyperspecific objectives will be of scant value to you because, if you're at all normal, you'll soon disregard [them]. On the other hand, a small number of intellectually manageable, broad, yet measurable objectives will not only prove helpful to you instructionally but will also help you answer the what-to-assess question. (pp. 104–105)

Connect and Extend to PRAXIS II™

Instructional Objectives (II, B1)
Describe the key elements of behavioral and instructional objectives. Be able to write each type of objective for a content area that you expect to teach.

Instructional objectives Clear statement of what students are intended to learn through instruction.

Behavioral objectives Instructional objectives stated in terms of observable behaviors.

Cognitive objectives Instructional objectives stated in terms of higher-level thinking operations.

TABLE 14.2 • **A Combined Method for Creating Objectives**

GENERAL OBJECTIVE
Comprehends scientific concepts.
SPECIFIC EXAMPLES
1. Describes the concept in his or her own words. 2. Gives an example of the concept [that is new]. 3. States hypotheses based on the concept. 4. Describes how the process functions in a given situation. 5. Describes an experiment that illustrates the process.

Source: Norman E. Gronlund & Susan M. Brookhart, Gronlund's writing instructional objectives (8th ed.), Upper Saddle River, NJ: Pearson © 2009. Adapted by permission of Pearson Education, Inc.

Flexible and Creative Plans—Using Taxonomies

Connect and Extend to PRAXIS II™

STOP & THINK Think about your assignments for one of your classes. What kind of thinking is involved in doing the assignments?

Remembering facts and terms?

Understanding key ideas?

Applying information to solve problems?

Analyzing a situation, task, or problem?

Making evaluations or giving opinions?

Creating or designing something new? •

Taxonomies of Educational Objectives (II, B1) Taxonomies influence every aspect of instruction from textbook design to lesson planning. List the major objectives of each of the taxonomies, and describe the focus of each objective. Be able to incorporate these objectives into instructional objectives that you design.

Almost 60 years ago, a group of experts in educational evaluation led by Benjamin Bloom set out to improve college and university examinations. The impact of their work has touched education at all levels around the world (Anderson & Sosniak, 1994). Bloom and his colleagues developed a **taxonomy**, or classification system, of educational objectives. Objectives were divided into three domains: *cognitive, affective*, and *psychomotor*. A handbook describing the objectives in each area was eventually published. In real life, of course, behaviors from these three domains occur simultaneously. While students are writing (psychomotor), they are also remembering or reasoning (cognitive), and they are likely to have some emotional response to the task as well (affective).

THE COGNITIVE DOMAIN. Bloom's taxonomy of the thinking or **cognitive domain** is considered one of the most significant educational writings of the 20th century (Anderson & Sosniak, 1994). The six basic objectives in Bloom's taxonomy are *knowledge, comprehension, application, analysis, synthesis,* and *evaluation* (Bloom, Engelhart, Frost, Hill, & Krathwohl, 1956).

It is common in education to consider these objectives as a hierarchy, each skill building on those below, but this is not entirely accurate. Some subjects, such as mathematics, do not fit this structure very well (Kreitzer & Madaus, 1994). Still, you will hear many references to *lower-level* and *higher-level* objectives, with knowledge, comprehension, and application considered lower level and the other categories considered higher level. As a rough way of thinking about objectives, this can be helpful (Gronlund & Brookhart, 2009). The taxonomy of objectives can also be helpful in planning assessments because different procedures are appropriate for objectives at the various levels, as you will see in Chapter 15.

Taxonomy Classification system.

Cognitive domain In Bloom's taxonomy, memory and reasoning objectives.

In 2001, a group of educational researchers published the first major revision of the cognitive taxonomy and this is the one we use today (Anderson & Krathwohl, 2001).

1. *Remembering*: Remembering or recognizing something without necessarily understanding, using, or changing it.
2. *Understanding*: Understanding the material being communicated without necessarily relating it to anything else.
3. *Applying*: Using a general concept to solve a particular problem.
4. *Analyzing*: Breaking something down into its parts.
5. *Evaluating*: Judging the value of materials or methods as they might be applied in a particular situation.
6. *Creating*: Creating something new by combining different ideas.

The 2001 revision of Bloom's taxonomy added a new dimension—to recognize that cognitive processes must process *something*—you have to remember or understand or apply some form of knowledge. If you look at Table 14.3, you will see the result. We now have the six processes of *remembering, understanding, applying, analyzing, evaluating,* and *creating* acting on four kinds of knowledge—*factual, conceptual, procedural,* and *metacognitive.*

Consider how this revised taxonomy might suggest objectives for a social studies/language arts class. An objective that targets analyzing conceptual knowledge is:

> After reading an historical account of the battle of the Alamo, students will be able to explain the author's point of view or bias.

An objective for evaluating metacognitive knowledge might be:

> Students will reflect on and describe their strategies for identifying the biases of the author.

See http://projects.coe.uga.edu/epltt/index.php?title=Bloom%27s_Taxonomy for more explanations and examples.

Affective domain Objectives focusing on attitudes and feelings.

THE AFFECTIVE DOMAIN. The objectives in the taxonomy of the **affective domain**, or domain of emotional response, have not yet been revised from the original version. These

---

TABLE 14.3 • **A Revised Taxonomy in the Cognitive Domain**

The revised taxonomy includes cognitive processes operating on different kinds of knowledge. The verbs in the chart are examples of what might be used to create objectives.

THE KNOWLEDGE DIMENSION	THE COGNITIVE PROCESS DIMENSION					
	1. REMEMBER	2. UNDERSTAND	3. APPLY	4. ANALYZE	5. EVALUATE	6. CREATE
A. Factual Knowledge	list	summarize	classify	order	rank	combine
B. Conceptual Knowledge	describe	interpret	experiment	explain	assess	plan
C. Procedural Knowledge	tabulate	predict	calculate	differentiate	conclude	compose
D. Metacognitive Knowledge	appropriate use	execute	select strategy	change strategy	reflect	invent

Source: From Anderson, Lorin W., David R. Krathwohl, et al., A Taxonomy for Learning, Teaching, and Assessing. Published by Allyn and Bacon, Boston, MA. Copyright © 2001 by Pearson Education. Reprinted by permission of the publisher.

objectives run from least to most committed (Krathwohl, Bloom, & Masia, 1964). At the lowest level, a student would simply pay attention to a certain idea. At the highest level, the student would adopt an idea or a value and act consistently with that idea. There are five basic objectives in the affective domain:

1. *Receiving*: Being aware of or attending to something in the environment. This is the I'll-listen-to-the-concert-but-I-won't-promise-to-like-it level.
2. *Responding*: Showing some new behavior as a result of experience. At this level, a person might applaud after the concert or hum some of the music the next day.
3. *Valuing*: Showing some definite involvement or commitment. At this point, a person might choose to go to a concert instead of a film.
4. *Organization*: Integrating a new value into one's general set of values, giving it some ranking among one's general priorities. This is the level at which a person would begin to make long-range commitments to concert attendance.
5. *Characterization by value*: Acting consistently with the new value. At this highest level, a person would be firmly committed to a love of music and demonstrate it openly and consistently.

Like the basic objectives in the cognitive domain, these five objectives are very general. To write specific learning objectives, you must state what students will actually be doing when they are receiving, responding, valuing, and so on. For example, an objective for a nutrition class at the valuing level (showing involvement or commitment) might be stated: After completing the unit on food contents and labeling, at least 50% of the class will commit to the junk-food boycott project by giving up fast food for a month.

THE PSYCHOMOTOR DOMAIN.   Until recently, the **psychomotor domain**, or realm of physical ability objectives, has been mostly overlooked by teachers who were not directly involved with physical education. There are several taxonomies in this domain (e.g., Harrow, 1972; Simpson, 1972) that generally move from basic perceptions and reflex actions to skilled, creative movements. James Cangelosi (1990) provides a useful way to think about objectives in the psychomotor domain as either (1) voluntary muscle capabilities that require endurance, strength, flexibility, agility, or speed, or (2) the ability to perform a specific skill.

Objectives in the psychomotor domain should be of interest to a wide range of educators, including those in fine arts, vocational-technical education, and special education. Many other subjects, such as chemistry, physics, and biology, also require specialized movements and well-developed hand–eye coordination. Using lab equipment, the mouse on a computer, or art materials means learning new physical skills. Here are two psychomotor objectives:

Four minutes after completing a one-mile run in eight minutes or under, your heart rate will be below 120.

Use a computer mouse effectively to "drag and drop" files.

Whatever your instructional objectives are for your students, Terry TenBrink (2006, p. 57) suggests these criteria. Objectives should be:

1. Student-oriented (emphasis on what the student is expected to do).
2. Descriptive of an appropriate learning outcome (both developmentally appropriate and appropriately sequenced, with more complex objectives following prerequisite objectives).
3. Clear and understandable (not too general or too specific).
4. Observable (avoid outcomes you can't see such as "appreciating" or "realizing").

The *Guidelines* on the next page should help you if you use objectives for every lesson or even for just a few assignments.

Psychomotor domain Physical ability and coordination objectives.

GUIDELINES

Using Instructional Objectives

Avoid "word magic"—phrases that sound noble and important, but say very little, such as "Students will become deep thinkers."
Examples

1. Keep the focus on specific changes that will take place in the students' knowledge and skills.
2. Ask students to explain the meaning of the objectives. If they can't give specific examples of what you mean, the objectives are not communicating your intentions to your students.

Suit the activities to the objectives.
Examples

1. If the goal is the memorization of vocabulary, give the students memory aids and practice exercises.
2. If the goal is the ability to develop well-thought-out positions, consider position papers, debates, projects, or mock trials.

3. If you want students to become better writers, give many opportunities for writing and rewriting.

Make sure your tests are related to your objectives.
Examples

1. Write objectives and rough drafts for tests at the same time—revise these drafts of tests as the units unfold and objectives change.
2. Weight the tests according to the importance of the various objectives and the time spent on each.

For additional ideas, see
http://www.personal.psu.edu/staff/b/x/bxb11/Objectives/ or
http://edtech.tennessee.edu/~bobannon/objectives.html

Connect and Extend to PRAXIS II™

Planning Thematic Units (II, A2)
Thematic learning units that integrate two or more content areas have become common in modern classrooms. Describe the principles involved in designing these activities, and explain how student learning can be assessed.

Planning from a Constructivist Perspective

STOP & THINK Think about the same course assignments you analyzed in the previous *Stop & Think*. What are the big ideas that run through all those assignments? What other ways could you learn about those ideas besides the assignments? •

Traditionally, it has been the teacher's responsibility to do most of the planning for instruction, but new ways of planning are emerging. In **constructivist approaches**, planning is shared and negotiated. The teacher and students together make decisions about content, activities, and approaches. Rather than having specific student behaviors and skills as objectives, the teacher has overarching goals—"big ideas" or themes—that guide planning (Borich, 2011). These goals are understandings or abilities that the teacher returns to again and again. For the last decade, teaching with themes and integrated content have been major elements in planning and designing lessons and units, from kindergarten (Roskos & Neuman, 1998) through high school (Clarke & Agne, 1997). For example, Elaine Homestead and Karen McGinnis (middle-school teachers) and Elizabeth Pate (a college professor) designed a unit on "Human Interactions" that included studying racism, world hunger, pollution, and air and water quality. Students researched issues by reading textbooks and outside sources, learning to use databases, interviewing local officials, and inviting guest speakers into class. Students had to develop knowledge in science, mathematics, and social studies. They learned to write and speak persuasively, and, in the process, raised money for hunger relief in Africa (Pate, McGinnis, & Homestead, 1995).

Elementary-age students can benefit from integrated planning, too. There is no reason to work on spelling skills, then listening skills, then writing skills, and then social studies or science. All these abilities can be developed together if students work to solve authentic problems. Some topics for integrating themes with younger children are people, friendship, communications, habitats, communities, and patterns. Possibilities for older students are given in Table 14.4.

Constructivist approach View that emphasizes the active role of the learner in building understanding and making sense of information.

TABLE 14.4 • **Some Themes for Integrated Planning for Middle and High School Students**

Courage	Time and Space
Mystery	Groups and Institutions
Survival	Work
Human Interaction	Motion
Communities of the Future	Cause and Effect
Communication/Language	Probability and Prediction
Human Rights and Responsibilities	Change and Conservation
Identity/Coming of Age	Diversity and Variation
Interdependence	Autobiography

Sources: Based on Curriculum Development; Interdisciplinary High School Teaching by J. H. Clarke and R. M. Agne, 1997, Boston: Allyn & Bacon; and Teaching through Themes by G. Thompson, 1991, New York: Scholastic. See Thompson for resources and strategies to develop some of these themes in elementary school and Clarke and Agne for ideas at the high school level.

Let's assume you have an idea of what you want students to understand, but how do you teach to encourage understanding? You still need to decide what's happening on Monday. You need to design teaching that is appropriate for the objectives.

TEACHING APPROACHES

In this section we will provide some basic formats for putting plans into action. The first challenge is to match your teaching methods to your objectives. We begin with strategies for teaching explicit facts and concepts.

Direct Instruction

For many people, "teaching" means an instructor explaining material to students—lecture is a classic form. There was an explosion of research in the 1970s and 1980s that focused on these more traditional forms of teaching. The results of all this work identified a model of teaching that was related to improved student learning. Barak Rosenshine and Robert Stevens (1986) call this approach **direct instruction** or **explicit teaching**. Tom Good (1983a) uses the term **active teaching** to describe a similar approach.

The direct instruction model fits a specific set of circumstances because it was derived from a particular approach to research. Researchers identified the elements of direct instruction by comparing teachers whose students learned more than expected (based on entering knowledge) with teachers whose students performed at an expected or average level. The researchers focused on existing practices in American classrooms. Because the focus was on traditional forms of teaching, the research could not identify successful innovations. Effectiveness was usually defined as average improvement in standardized test scores for a whole class or school. So the results hold for large groups, but not necessarily for every student in the group. Even when the average achievement of a group improves, the achievement of some individuals may decline (Good, 1996; Shuell, 1996).

Given these conditions, you can see that direct instruction applies best to the teaching of **basic skills**—clearly structured knowledge and essential skills, such as science facts, mathematics computations, reading vocabulary, and grammar rules (Rosenshine & Stevens, 1986). These skills involve tasks that are relatively unambiguous; they can be taught step by step and evaluated by standardized tests. Franz Weinert and Andreas Helmke (1995) describe direct instruction as having the following features:

(a) the teacher's classroom management is especially effective and the rate of student interruptive behaviors is very low; (b) the teacher maintains a strong academic focus and

Connect and Extend to PRAXIS II™

Teacher-Centered Instruction (II, A3) Teacher-centered instruction is often thought of as the "traditional" approach to instruction. In what situations is this instructional format most effective? What are the basic steps involved in carrying out this form of instruction?

Direct instruction/Explicit teaching Systematic instruction for mastery of basic skills, facts, and information.

Active teaching Teaching characterized by high levels of teacher explanation, demonstration, and interaction with students.

Basic skills Clearly structured knowledge that is needed for later learning and that can be taught step by step.

uses available instructional time intensively to initiate and facilitate students' learning activities; (c) the teacher insures that as many students as possible achieve good learning progress by carefully choosing appropriate tasks, clearly presenting subject-matter information and solution strategies, continuously diagnosing each student's learning progress and learning difficulties, and providing effective help through remedial instruction. (p. 138)

To this list, Xin Ma (2012) adds moving at a brisk pace and having a warm and accepting classroom climate.

How would a teacher turn these themes into actions?

ROSENSHINE'S SIX TEACHING FUNCTIONS. Rosenshine and his colleagues (Rosenshine, 1988; Rosenshine & Stevens, 1986) have identified six teaching functions based on the research on effective instruction. These could serve as a checklist or framework for teaching basic skills.

1. *Review and check the previous day's work.* Reteach if students misunderstood or made errors.
2. *Present new material.* Make the purpose clear, teach in small steps, and provide many examples and nonexamples of the ideas and concepts you are teaching.
3. *Provide guided practice.* Question students, give practice problems, and listen for misconceptions and misunderstandings. Reteach if necessary. Continue guided practice until students answer about 80% of the questions correctly.
4. *Give feedback and correctives based on student answers.* Reteach if necessary. (Remember, Pianta and colleagues' [2005, 2008] class climate component of instructional support included quality feedback.)
5. *Provide independent practice.* Let students apply the new learning on their own, in seatwork, cooperative groups, or homework. The success rate during independent practice should be about 95%. This means that students must be well prepared for the work by the presentation and guided practice and that assignments must not be too difficult. The point is for the students to practice until the skills become overlearned and automatic—until the students are confident. Hold students accountable for the work they do—check it.
6. *Review weekly and monthly to consolidate learning.* Include some review items as homework. Test often, and reteach material missed on the tests.

These six functions are not steps to be followed in a particular order, but all of them are elements of effective instruction. For example, feedback, review, or reteaching should occur whenever necessary and should match the abilities of the students. Also, keep in mind the age and prior knowledge of your students. The younger or the less prepared your students are, the briefer your explanations should be. Use more and shorter cycles of presentation, guided practice, feedback, and correctives.

Connect and Extend to PRAXIS II™

Advance Organizers (II, A3)
The advance organizer is an important element in many teacher-centered/expository approaches to instruction. Be able to explain the role of the advance organizer in these approaches, and identify the basic types of organizers.

ADVANCE ORGANIZERS. Teachers using direct instruction often begin with an **advance organizer**. This is an introductory statement broad enough to encompass all the information that will follow. The organizers can serve three purposes: They direct your attention to what is important in the coming material, they highlight relationships among ideas that will be presented, and they remind you of relevant information you already have.

Advance organizers fall into one of two categories, comparative and expository (Mayer, 1984). *Comparative organizers* activate (bring into working memory) already existing schemas. They remind you of what you already know, but may not realize is relevant. A comparative advance organizer for a history lesson on revolutions might be a statement that contrasts military uprisings with the physical and social changes involved in the Industrial Revolution; you could also compare the common aspects of the French, English, Mexican, Russian, Iranian, Egyptian, and American revolutions (Salomon & Perkins, 1989).

In contrast, *expository organizers* provide new knowledge that students will need in order to understand the upcoming information. In an English class, you might begin a large thematic unit on rites of passage in literature with a very broad statement of the theme and why it has been so central in literature—something like, "A central character coming of age

Advance organizer Statement of inclusive concepts to introduce and sum up material that follows.

must learn to know himself or herself, often makes some kind of journey of self-discovery, and must decide what in the society is to be accepted and what should be rejected." Such an organizer might precede reading novels such as *The Adventures of Huckleberry Finn*.

The general conclusion of research on advance organizers is that they do help students learn, especially when the material to be learned is quite unfamiliar, complex, or difficult—as long as two conditions are met (Langan-Fox, Waycott, & Albert, 2000; Morin & Miller, 1998). First, to be effective, the organizer must be understood by the students. This was demonstrated dramatically in a classic study by Dinnel and Glover (1985). They found that instructing students to paraphrase an advance organizer—which, of course, requires them to understand its meaning—increased the effectiveness of the organizer. Second, the organizer must really be an organizer: It must indicate relations among the basic concepts and terms that will be used. Concrete models, diagrams, or analogies seem to be especially good organizers (Robinson, 1998; Robinson & Kiewra, 1995).

ADVANCE ORGANZERS Advance organizers remind students of information they already know that will help them understand the new material or present key concepts they will need. This teacher is helping students bring to mind what they already know about bones in the human body before launching into the lesson.

WHY DOES DIRECT INSTRUCTION WORK?   Well-organized presentations with clear explanations, the use of advance organizers, explanatory links, and reviews can all help students perceive connections among ideas. If done well, therefore, a direct instruction lesson could be a resource that students use to construct understanding. For example, reviews and advance organizers activate prior knowledge, so the student is ready to understand. Brief, clear presentations and guided practice avoid overloading the students' information processing systems and taxing their working memories. Numerous examples and nonexamples that highlight similarities and differences give many pathways and associations for building networks of concepts. Guided practice can also give the teacher a snapshot of the students' thinking as well as their misconceptions, so these can be addressed directly as misconceptions rather than simply as "wrong answers."

Every subject, even college English or chemistry, requires some direct instruction. Noddings (1990) reminds teachers that students may need some direct instruction in how to use various manipulative materials so they can actually learn from (not just play with) the materials. Students working in cooperative groups may need guidance, modeling, and practice in how to ask questions and give explanations. And to solve difficult problems, students may need some direct instruction in possible problem-solving strategies.

Some studies have found that teachers' presentations take up one-sixth to one-fourth of all classroom time. Teacher explanation is appropriate for communicating a large amount of material to many students in a short period of time, introducing a new topic, giving background information, or motivating students to learn more on their own. Teacher presentations are therefore most appropriate for cognitive and affective objectives at the lower levels of the taxonomies described earlier: for remembering, understanding, applying, receiving, responding, and valuing (Arends, 2001; Kindsvatter, Wilen, & Ishler, 1992).

EVALUATING DIRECT INSTRUCTION.   Direct instruction, particularly when it involves extended teacher presentations or lectures, has some disadvantages. You may find that some students have trouble listening for more than a few minutes at a time and that they simply tune you out. Teacher presentations can put the students in a passive position by doing much of the cognitive work for them; this may prevent students from asking

GUIDELINES

Teaching Effectively

Use advance organizers.
Examples

1. English: Shakespeare used the social ideas of his time as a framework for his plays—Julius Caesar, Hamlet, and Macbeth deal with concepts of natural order, a nation as the human body, etc.
2. Social studies: Geography dictates economy in preindustrialized regions or nations.
3. History: Important concepts during the Renaissance were symmetry, admiration of the classical world, the centrality of the human mind.

Use a number of examples.
Examples

1. In mathematics class, ask students to point out all the examples of right angles that they can find in the room.
2. In teaching about islands and peninsulas, use maps, slides, models, postcards.

Organize your lessons carefully.
Examples

1. Provide objectives that help students focus on the purpose of the lesson.
2. Begin lessons by writing a brief outline on the board, or work on an outline with the class as part of the lesson.
3. If possible, break the presentation into clear steps or stages.
4. Review periodically.

Anticipate and plan for difficult parts in the lesson.
Examples

1. Plan a clear introduction to the lesson that tells students what they are going to learn and how they will learn it.
2. Do the exercises and anticipate student problems—consult the teachers' manual for ideas.
3. Have definitions ready for new terms, and prepare several relevant examples for concepts.
4. Think of analogies that will make ideas easier to understand.
5. Organize the lesson in a logical sequence; include checkpoints that incorporate oral or written questions or problems to make sure the students are following the explanations.

Strive for clear explanations.
Examples

1. Avoid vague words and ambiguous phrases: Steer clear of "the *somes*"—*something, someone, sometime, somehow;*

"the *not verys*"—*not very much, not very well, not very hard, not very often;* and other unspecific fillers, such as *most, not all, sort of,* and so on, *of course, as you know, I guess, in fact, or whatever,* and *more or less.*

2. Use specific (and, if possible, colorful) names instead of *it, them,* and *thing.*
3. Refrain from using pet phrases such as *you know, like,* and *Okay?*
4. Record one of your lessons to check yourself for clarity.
5. Give explanations at several levels so all students, not just the brightest, will understand.
6. Focus on one idea at a time and avoid digressions.

Make clear connections by using explanatory links such as *because, if–then,* or *therefore*.
Examples

1. "The North had an advantage in the Civil War because its economy was based on manufacturing."
2. Explanatory links are also helpful in labeling visual material such as graphs, concept maps, or illustrations.

Signal transitions from one major topic to another with phrases.
Examples

1. "The next area," "Now we will turn to," or "The second step is."
2. Outline topics, listing key points, drawing concept maps on the board, or using an overhead projector.

Communicate an enthusiasm for your subject and the day's lesson.
Examples

1. Tell students why the lesson is important. Have a better reason than "This will be on the test" or "You will need to know it next year." Emphasize the value of the learning itself.
2. Be sure to make eye contact with the students.
3. Vary your pace and volume in speaking. Use silence for emphasis.

For more ideas about effective teaching, see
http://www.education.ky.gov/KDE/Instructional+Resources/Highly+Effective+Teaching+and+Learning

---

Scripted cooperation Learning strategy in which two students take turns summarizing material and criticizing the summaries.

or even thinking of questions (Freiberg & Driscoll, 2005). **Scripted cooperation** is one way of incorporating active learning into lectures. Several times during the presentation, the teacher asks students to work in pairs. One person is the summarizer and the other critiques the summary, then they switch roles for the next summary/critique. This gives

TABLE 14.5 ● **Active Learning and Teacher Presentations**

Here are some ideas I use for keeping students cognitively engaged in lessons. They can be adapted for many ages.

Write an Answer: Pose a question, ask everyone to write a brief answer, then call on students to share what they wrote.	**Voting:** Pose two alternative explanations; ask how many agree with each (may be a good idea to ask the student to close their eyes and vote so they won't be swayed by the votes of others).
I used to think_____, but now I know_____: After a lesson, ask students to fill in the blanks, then share their results with the person beside them	**Choral Response:** Have the whole class restate in unison important facts and ideas, such as "In a right triangle, $a^2 + b^2 = c^2$"
Think-Pair-Share: Pose a question, students think of an answer on their own, then consult with a neighbor to improve the answer, then volunteers share their ideas.	**One-Minute-Write:** After a section of the lesson, students write for one minute to summarize the key points or raise a question about what is not clear to them.

students a chance to check their understanding, organize their thinking, and translate ideas into their own words. Other possibilities are described in Table 14.5.

Critics also claim that direct instruction is based on the wrong theory of learning. Teachers break material into small segments, present each segment clearly, and reinforce or correct, thus transmitting accurate understandings from teacher to student. The student is viewed as an "empty vessel" waiting to be filled with knowledge, rather than an active constructor of knowledge (Berg & Clough, 1991; Driscoll, 2005). These criticisms of direct instruction echo the criticisms of behavioral learning theories.

There is ample evidence, however, that direct instruction and explanation can help students learn actively, not passively (Leinhardt, 2001). For younger and less prepared learners, student-controlled learning without teacher direction and instruction can lead to systematic deficits in the students' knowledge. Without guidance, the understandings that students construct can be incomplete and misleading (Sweller, Kirschner, & Clark, 2007). For example, Harris and Graham (1996) describe the experiences of their daughter Leah in a whole-language/progressive education school, where the teachers successfully developed their daughter's creativity, thinking, and understanding.

> Skills, on the other hand, have been a problem for our daughter and for other children. At the end of kindergarten, when she had not made much progress in reading, her teacher said she believed Leah had a perceptual problem or a learning disability. Leah began asking what was wrong with her, because other kids were reading and she wasn't. Finally, an assessment was done. (p. 26)

The testing indicated no learning disability, strong comprehension abilities, and poor word attack skills. Luckily, Leah's parents knew how to teach word attack skills. Direct teaching of these skills helped Leah become an avid and able reader in about six weeks. Deep understanding and fluid performance—whether in reading or dance or mathematical problem solving or reading—require models of expert performance and extensive practice with feedback (Anderson, Reder, & Simon, 1995). Guided and independent practice with feedback are at the heart of the direct instruction model. See the *Guidelines* for more ideas about teaching effectively.

Seatwork and Homework

SEATWORK.   The conclusions of the limited research on **seatwork** (independent classroom-desk work) are clear; this technique is often overused. For example, a summary of research from 1975 to 2000 found that students with learning disabilities, who often have trouble improving without teacher guidance, were spending about 40% of their time on individual seatwork (Vaughn, Levy, Coleman, & Bos, 2002).

Seatwork Independent classroom work.

Seatwork should follow up a lesson and give students supervised practice. It should not be the main mode of instruction. Unfortunately, many workbook pages and worksheets do little to support the learning of important objectives. Before you assign work, ask yourself, "Does doing this work help students learn anything that matters?" Students should see the connection between the seatwork and the lesson. Tell them why they are doing the work. The objectives should be clear, all the materials that might be needed should be provided, and the work should be easy enough that students can succeed on their own. Success rates should be high—near 100%. When seatwork is too difficult, students often resort to guessing or copying just to finish.

There are several alternatives to workbooks and worksheets, such as reading silently and reading aloud to a partner; writing for a "real" audience; writing letters or journals; transcribing conversations and punctuating them properly; making up problems; working on long-term projects and reports; solving brainteasers and puzzles; and computer activities (Weinstein, Romano, & Mignano, 2011). One of my favorites is creating a group story. Two students begin a story on the computer. Then two more add a paragraph. The story grows with each new pair's addition. The students are reading and writing, editing and improving. With so many different authors, each writer may spark the creative thinking of other contributors.

Any independent work requires careful monitoring. Being available to students doing seatwork is more effective than offering students help before they ask for it. Short, frequent contacts are best (Brophy & Good, 1986). Sometimes you may be working with a small group while other students do seatwork. In these situations, it is especially important for students to know what to do if they need help. One expert teacher described by Weinstein, Romano, and Mignano (2011) taught students a rule, "Ask three, then me." Students have to consult three classmates before seeking help from the teacher. This teacher also spends time early in the year showing students how to help each other—how to ask questions and how to explain.

STOP & THINK Think back to your elementary and high school days. Do you remember any homework assignments? What sticks in your mind about those assignments? •

HOMEWORK. In contrast to the limited research on seatwork, educators have been studying the effects of homework for over 75 years (Cooper, 2004; Cooper, Robinson, & Patall, 2006; Corno, 2000; Trautwein, 2007).

To benefit from homework, students must understand the assignment. It may help to do the first few questions as a class, to clear up any misconceptions. This is especially important for students who may have no one at home to consult if they have problems with the assignment. A second way to keep students involved is to hold them accountable for completing the work correctly, not just for filling in the page. This means the work should be checked, the students given a chance to correct the errors or revise work, and the results counted toward the class grade. Expert teachers often have ways of correcting homework quickly during the first minutes of class by having students check each other's or their own work. There are other concerns about making homework effective, as you can see in the *Point/Counterpoint*.

If students get stuck on homework, they need help at home, someone who can scaffold their work without just "giving the answer" (Pressley, 1995). But many families don't know how to help (Hoover-Dempsey et al., 2001). The *Family and Community Partnerships Guidelines* on page 526 provide ideas for helping families deal with homework.

Questioning and Discussion

Teachers pose questions, students answer. This form of teaching, sometimes called *recitation,* has been with us for many years (Weinstein et al., 2011). The teacher's questions develop a framework for the subject matter involved. The pattern from the teacher's point of view consists of *initiation* (teacher asks questions), *response* (student answers), and *evaluation/reaction* (praising, correcting, probing, or expanding) or IRE (Burbules & Bruce, 2001). These steps are repeated over and over.

Connect and Extend to PRAXIS II™

Questioning (III, C)
Effective questioning skills are among the most valuable skills that a teacher can possess—and among the more difficult to develop. For guidance on asking effective questions in the classroom, read *Question Types* (http://www.unl.edu/teaching/teachquestions.html).

POINT/COUNTERPOINT: Is Homework a Valuable Use of Time?

Like so many methods in education, homework has moved in and out of favor. In the early 1900s, homework was seen as an important path to mental discipline, but by the 1940s, homework was criticized as too much drill and low-level learning. Then, in the 1950s, homework was rediscovered as a way to catch up with the Soviet Union in science and mathematics, only to be seen as putting too much pressure on students during the more laid-back 1960s. By the 1980s, homework was in again as a way to improve the standing of American children compared to students around the world (Cooper & Valentine, 2001). Today, homework is increasing in early elementary schools (Hofferth & Sandberg, 2000). Everyone has done homework—were those hours well spent?

POINT

▶ **Homework does not help students learn.** No matter how interesting an activity is, students will eventually get bored with it—so why give them work both in and out of school? They will simply grow weary of learning. And important opportunities are lost for community involvement or leisure activities that would create well-rounded citizens. When parents help with homework, they can do more harm than good—sometimes confusing their children or teaching them incorrectly. And students from poorer families often must work, so they miss doing the homework; then the learning discrepancy between the rich and poor grows even greater. Besides, the research is inconsistent about the effects of homework. For example, one study found that in-class work was better than homework in helping elementary students learn (Cooper & Valentine, 2001). In his book, *The Homework Myth: Why Our Kids Get Too Much of a Bad Thing*, Alfie Kohn (2006) suggests the schools adopt no homework as the default policy. "Changing the default to no homework would likely have two practical consequences: The number of assignments would decline and the quality of those assignments would rise. Both of these, I believe, represent significant improvements in our children's education" (p. 168).

Harris Cooper and his colleagues reviewed many studies of homework and concluded that there is little relationship between homework and learning for young students, but the relationship between homework and achievement grows progressively stronger for older students. Most of the studies involved math and reading or English homework, however, not social studies, science, or other subjects.

COUNTERPOINT

▶ **Well-planned homework can work for many students.** There is recent evidence that students in high school who do more homework (and watch less television after school) have higher grades, even when other factors such as gender, grade level, ethnicity, SES, and amount of adult supervision are taken into consideration (Cooper, Robinson, & Patall, 2006; Cooper & Valentine, 2001; Cooper, Valentine, Nye, & Kindsay, 1999). Consistent with all these findings, the National PTA makes these recommendations:

> [F]or children in grades K–2, homework is most effective when it does not exceed 10–20 minutes each day; older students, in grades 3–6, can handle 30–60 minutes a day; in junior and senior high school, the amount of homework will vary by subject. (Henderson, 1996, p. 1)

Most research examines the relationship between amount of time spent on homework (as reported by students or parents) and achievement in terms of grades or achievement tests. Another approach is to focus on effort instead of time. Students' self-reported effort on homework is consistently and positively related to student achievement (Trautwein, Schnyder, Niggli, Neuman, & Lüdtke, 2009). "High homework effort means that a student does his or her best to solve the tasks assigned. There need not be a close relationship between effort and time on homework: A student putting as much effort as possible into a homework assignment might finish in 5 min or still be working after an hour" (Trautwein & Lüdtke, 2007, p. 432). Students are more likely to put in effort if they see the homework as interesting, valuable, reasonably challenging, and not anxiety provoking—this could require some differentiated homework assignments (Dettmers, Trautwein, Ludtke, Kunter, & Baumert, 2010). So the challenge is to get students to put their best efforts into appropriate homework and not assign homework that is low quality.

Let us consider the heart of recitation, the soliciting or questioning phase. Effective questioning techniques may be among the most powerful tools that teachers employ during lessons. An essential element of contemporary learning techniques is keeping students cognitively engaged—and that is where skillful questioning strategies are especially effective. Questions play several roles in cognition. They can help students rehearse information for effective recall. They can work to identify gaps in students' knowledge base, and provoke curiosity and long-term interest. They can initiate cognitive conflict and promote the disequilibrium that results in a changed knowledge structure. They can serve as cues, tips, or reminders as an expert guides a novice in a learning experience. And students as well as teachers should learn to question effectively. I tell my students that the first step in doing a good research project is asking a good question.

GUIDELINES FAMILY AND COMMUNITY PARTNERSHIPS

Homework

Make sure families know what students are expected to learn.
Examples

1. At the beginning of a unit, send home a list of the main objectives, examples of major assignments, key due dates, a homework "calendar," and a list of free resources available at libraries or on the Internet.
2. Provide a clear, concise description of your homework policy—how homework is counted toward class grades; consequences for late, forgotten, or missing homework, etc.

Help families find a comfortable and helpful role in their child's homework.
Examples

1. Remind families that "helping with homework" means encouraging, listening, monitoring, praising, discussing, brainstorming—not necessarily teaching and never doing the work for their child.
2. Encourage families to set aside a quiet time and place for everyone in the family to study. Make this time a regular part of the daily routine.
3. Have some homework assignments that are fun and involve the whole family—puzzles, family albums, watching a television program together and doing a "review."
4. In conferences, ask families how you could help them to support their child in completing and learning from homework. Check lists? Background reading? Web sites? Explanations of study skills?

Solicit and use suggestions from families about homework.
Examples

1. Find out what responsibilities the child has at home—how much time is available for homework.

2. Periodically, have a "homework hotline" for call-in questions and suggestions.

If no one is at home to help with homework, set up other support systems.
Examples

1. Assign study buddies who can be available over the phone.
2. If students have computers, provide lists of Internet help lines.
3. Locate free help in public libraries and make these resources known.

Take advantage of family and community "funds of knowledge" to connect homework with life in the community and life in the community with lessons in school (Moll et al., 1992).
Examples

1. Create a class lesson about how family members use math and reading in sewing and in housing construction (Epstein & Van Voorhis, 2001).
2. Design interactive homework projects that families do together to evaluate needed products for their home, for example, deciding on the best buy on shampoo or paper towels.

For more ideas, see
http://www.slideshare.net/stanfreeda/unit-7-homework-strategies-parental-involvement-notes

---

For now, we will focus on teachers' questions. Many of the beginning teachers I work with are surprised to discover how valuable good questions can be and how difficult they are to create.

STOP & THINK Think back to your most recent class. What kinds of questions does your professor ask? What sort of thinking is required to answer the questions? Remembering, understanding, applying, analyzing, evaluating, or creating? How long does the professor wait for an answer? •

KINDS OF QUESTIONS.   Some educators have estimated the typical teacher asks between 30 and 120 questions an hour, or about 1,500,000 questions over a teaching career (Sadker & Sadker, 2006). What are these questions like? Many can be categorized in terms of Bloom's taxonomy of objectives in the cognitive domain. Table 14.6 offers examples of questions at the different taxonomic levels.

TABLE 14.6 • **Classroom Questions for Objectives in the Cognitive Domain**

Questions can be posed that encourage thinking at every level of Bloom's taxonomy in the cognitive domain. Of course, the thinking required depends on what has gone before in the discussion.

CATEGORY	TYPE OF THINKING EXPECTED	EXAMPLES
Knowledge (Remembering)	Recalling or recognizing information as learned	Define. . . . What is the capital of . . . ? What did the text say about . . . ?
Comprehension (Understanding)	Demonstrating understanding of the materials; transforming, reorganizing, or interpreting	Explain in your own words. . . . Compare. . . What is the main idea of . . . ? Describe what you saw. . . .
Application (Applying)	Using information to solve a problem with a single correct answer	Which principle is demonstrated in . . . ? Calculate the area of. . . . Apply the rule of . . . to solve. . . .
Analysis (Analyzing)	Critical thinking; identifying reasons and motives; making inferences based on specific data; analyzing conclusions to see if supported by evidence	What influenced the writings of . . . ? Why was Washington, D.C. chosen . . . ? Which of the following are facts and which are opinions . . . ? Based on your experiment, what is the chemical . . . ?
Synthesis (Creating)	Divergent, original thinking; original plan, proposal, design, or story	What's a good name for . . . ? How could we raise money for . . . ? What would the United States be like if the South had won . . . ?
Evaluation (Evaluating)	Judging the merits of ideas, offering opinions, applying standards	Which U.S. senator is the most effective? Which painting do you believe to be better? Why? Why would you favor . . . ?

Source: Based on "Questioning Skills" by M. Sadker and D. Sadker, in J. Cooper (Ed.), CLASSROOM TEACHING SKILLS: A HANDBOOK (3rd ed.) (pp. 143–160), 1986, Boston, D. C. Heath.

Another way to categorize questioning is in terms of **convergent questions** (only one right answer) or **divergent questions** (many possible answers). Questions about concrete facts are convergent: "Who ruled England in 1540?" "Who wrote the original Peter Pan?" Questions dealing with opinions or hypotheses are divergent: "In this story, which character is most like you and why?" "In 100 years, which of the past five presidents will be most admired?"

FITTING THE QUESTIONS TO THE STUDENTS. All kinds of questions can be effective (Barden, 1995). Different patterns seem to be better for certain types of students, however. The best pattern for younger students and for lower-ability students of all ages is simple questions that allow a high percentage of correct answers, ample encouragement, help when the student does not have the correct answer, and praise. For high-ability students, the successful pattern includes harder questions at both higher and lower levels and more critical feedback (Berliner, 1987; Good, 1988).

Convergent questions Questions that have a single correct answer.

Divergent questions Questions that have no single correct answer.

Whatever their age or ability, all students should have some experience with thought-provoking questions and, if necessary, help in learning how to answer them. As we saw in Chapter 9, to master critical thinking and problem-solving skills, students must have a chance to practice those skills. They also need time to think about their answers. But classic research shows that teachers wait an average of only one second for students to answer (Rowe, 1974). When teachers learn to pose a question, then wait at least 3 to 5 seconds before calling on a student to answer, students tend to give longer answers; more students are likely to participate, ask questions, and volunteer appropriate answers; student comments involving analysis, synthesis, inference, and speculation tend to increase; and the students generally appear more confident in their answers (Berliner, 1987; Sadker & Sadker, 2006).

This seems like a simple improvement in teaching, but 5 seconds of silence is not that easy to handle. It takes practice. You might try asking students to jot down ideas or even discuss the question with another student and formulate an answer together. This makes the wait more comfortable and gives students a chance to think. Of course, if it is clear that students are lost or don't understand the question, waiting longer will not help. When your question is met with blank stares, rephrase the question or ask if anyone can clarify it. However, there is some evidence that extending wait times does not affect learning in university classes (Duell, 1994), so with advanced high-school students, you might conduct your own evaluation of wait time.

A word about selecting students to answer questions. If you call only on volunteers, then you may get the wrong idea about how well students understand the material. Also, the same people volunteer over and over again. Many expert teachers have some systematic way of making sure that they call on everyone: They pull names from a jar or check names off a list as each student speaks (Weinstein & Novodvorsky, 2011; Weinstein, Romano, & Mignano, 2011). Another possibility is to put each student's name on an index card, then shuffle the cards and go through the deck as you call on people. You can use the card to make notes about the quality of students' answers or any extra help they seem to need.

RESPONDING TO STUDENT ANSWERS. What do you do after the student answers? The most common response, occurring about 50% of the time in most classrooms, is simple acceptance—"OK" or "Uh-huh" (Sadker & Sadker, 2006). But there are better reactions, depending on whether the student's answer is correct, partially correct, or wrong. If the answer is quick, firm, and correct, simply accept the answer or ask another question. If the answer is correct but hesitant, give the student feedback about why the answer is correct: "That's right, Chris, the Senate is part of the legislative branch of government because the Senate. . . ." This allows you to explain the material again. If this student is unsure, others may be confused as well. If the answer is partially or completely wrong but the student has made an honest attempt, you should probe for more information, give clues, simplify the question, review the previous steps, or reteach the material. If the student's wrong answer is silly or careless, however, it is better simply to correct the answer and go on (Good, 1988; Rosenshine & Stevens, 1986).

John Hattie and Helen Timperley (2007) reviewed several decades of research on feedback and constructed a model to guide teachers. The model proposes three feedback questions: "Where am I going?" "How am I going?" and "Where to next?" The first question is about goals and goal clarity. The second is about progress—movement toward goals. The third question is about moving forward to improve understandings when goals are not met yet or to build on attained goals. The Hattie and Timperley model also considers the focus of the feedback on four levels: task, process, self-regulation, and self-feedback. Here are some examples (p. 90):

Task Feedback: "You need to include more about the Treaty of Versailles."
Process Feedback: "This page may make more sense if you use the strategies we talked about earlier."
Self-Regulation Feedback: "You already know the key features of the opening of an argument. Check to see whether you have incorporated them in your first paragraph."
Self-Feedback: "You are a great student." "That's an intelligent response, well done."

Hattie and Timperley argue that feedback about *process* and *self-regulation* is the most powerful because it helps students move toward deep understanding, mastery, and self-direction in learning. Feedback about self (usually praise) is common in classes, but is not effective unless the praise provides information about how effort, persistence, or self-regulation moved the student forward, as in "You are terrific—you stuck with this, revised again, and now this essay makes a powerful argument."

GROUP DISCUSSION. **Group discussion** is in some ways similar to the recitation strategy. A teacher may pose questions, listen to student answers, react, and probe for more information, but in a true group dialogue, the teacher does not have a

GROUP DISCUSSIONS Small group discussions allow greater student participation and exchange of ideas, but students may need help in staying focused.

dominant role. Students ask questions, answer each other's questions, and respond to each other's answers (Beck, McKeown, Worthy, Sandora, & Kucan, 1996; Burbules & Bruce, 2001; Parker & Hess, 2001).

There are many advantages to group discussions. The students are directly involved and have the chance to participate. They learn to express themselves clearly, to justify opinions, and to tolerate different views. Group discussion also gives students a chance to ask for clarification, examine their own thinking, follow personal interests, and assume responsibility by taking leadership roles in the group. Thus, group discussions help students evaluate ideas and synthesize personal viewpoints. Discussions are also useful when students are trying to understand difficult concepts that go against common sense. By thinking together, challenging each other, and suggesting and evaluating possible explanations, students are more likely to reach a genuine understanding.

Of course, there are disadvantages. Class discussions are quite unpredictable and may easily digress into exchanges of ignorance. You may have to do a good deal of preparation to ensure that participants have enough background knowledge for the discussion. Some members of the group may have great difficulty participating and may become anxious if forced to speak. And large groups are often unwieldy. In many cases, a few students will dominate the discussion while the others daydream (Arends, 2004; Freiberg & Driscoll, 2005).

Are discussions effective learning tools? In a major review of research conducted from 1964 to 2003 on the value of discussing texts for improving student comprehension, Karen Murphy and her colleagues (2009) reached some surprising conclusions. They examined a wide range of discussion formats including Instructional Conversations, Junior Great Books Shared Inquiry, Questioning the Author, Literature Circles, Book Club, and Grand Conversation—to name just a few. They found many of these approaches were very successful in increasing student talk, limiting teacher talk, and promoting students' literal interpretations of the texts they discussed. But getting students to talk more did not necessarily promote their critical thinking, reasoning, or argumentation skills. Also, discussion was more effective for students whose comprehension abilities are below average, perhaps because average and higher-ability students already have the skills to comprehend texts. A few discussion structures, such as Junior Great Books Shared Inquiry, used over a longer period of time seemed to support both comprehension of text and critical thinking. The researchers concluded, "Simply putting students into groups and encouraging them to talk is not enough to enhance comprehension and learning; it is but a step in the process" (p. 760). The *Guidelines* give some ideas for facilitating a productive group discussion.

Group discussion Conversation in which the teacher does not have the dominant role; students pose and answer their own questions.

GUIDELINES

Productive Group Discussions

Invite shy children to participate.
Examples
1. "What's your opinion, Joel?" or "Does anyone have another opinion?"
2. Don't wait until there is a deadly silence to ask shy students to reply. Most people, even those who are confident, hate to break a silence.

Direct student comments and questions back to another student.
Examples
1. "That's an unusual idea, Steve. Kim, what do you think of Steve's idea?"
2. "That's an important question, John. Maura, do you have any thoughts about how you'd answer that?"
3. Encourage students to look at and talk to one another rather than wait for your opinion.

Make sure that you understand what a student has said. If you are unsure, other students may be unsure as well.
Examples
1. Ask a second student to summarize what the first student said; then, the first student can try again to explain if the summary is incorrect.
2. "Karen, I think you're saying . . . Is that right, or have I misunderstood?"

Probe for more information.
Examples
1. "That's a strong statement. Do you have any evidence to back it up?"

2. "Did you consider any other alternatives?"
3. "Tell us how you reached that conclusion. What steps did you go through?"

Bring the discussion back to the subject.
Examples
1. "Let's see, we were discussing . . . and Sarah made one suggestion. Does anyone have a different idea?"
2. "Before we continue, let me try to summarize what has happened thus far."

Give time for thought before asking for responses.
Example
1. "How would your life be different if television had never been invented? Jot down your ideas on paper, and we will share reactions in a minute." After a minute: "Hiromi, will you tell us what you wrote?"

When a student finishes speaking, look around the room to judge reactions.
Examples
1. If other students look puzzled, ask them to describe why they are confused.
2. If students are nodding assent, ask them to give an example of what was just said.

For more ideas, see
http://www.podnetwork.org/publications/teachingexcellence/09-10/V21_N1_Takayama.pdf or http://www.extension.umn.edu/distribution/citizenship/components/00018e.html

Fitting Teaching to Your Goals

In the midst of all our discussions about methods, we have to keep in mind that the first questions should be: What should students learn? and What is worth knowing today? Then, we can match methods to goals. Deanna Kuhn (2007) said it well:

> As for direct instruction, of course it has a place. Each young student does not need to reinvent knowledge from the ground up. The challenge is to formulate what we want direct instruction to be. In doing so, it is well to keep in mind that it is students who construct meaning from such instruction and decide what it is that they will learn. (p. 112)

There is no one best way to teach. Different goals and student needs require different teaching methods. Direct instruction often leads to better performance on achievement tests, whereas the open, informal methods such as discovery learning or inquiry approaches are associated with better performance on tests of creativity, abstract thinking, and problem solving. In addition, the open methods are better for improving attitudes toward school and for stimulating curiosity, cooperation among students, and lower absence rates (Borich, 2011; Walberg, 1990). According to these conclusions, when the goals of teaching involve problem solving, creativity, understanding, and mastering processes, many approaches besides direct instruction should be effective. These guidelines are in keeping with Tom Good's conclusion that teaching should become less direct as students mature and when the goals involve affective development and problem solving or critical thinking (Good, 1983a). Every student may require direct, explicit teaching for some learning goals some of the time, but all students also need to experience more open, constructivist, student-centered teaching as well. So far, we have talked about approaches to teaching—general strategies. But in today's diverse classrooms, one size does not fit all. Within the general approach, teachers have to fit their instruction to the needs and abilities of their students—they have to differentiate instruction.

DIFFERENTIATED INSTRUCTION

We introduced **differentiated instruction** in Chapter 1. Actually, the idea of adapting teaching to the abilities and needs of the learner is an ancient one. To prove it, Lyn Corno (2008, p. 161) quotes these words of Quintilian from the 5th century BC:

> Some students are slack and need to be encouraged; others work better when given a freer rein. Some respond best when there is some threat or fear; others are paralyzed by it. Some apply themselves to the task over time, and learn best; others learn best by concentration and focus in a single burst of energy. (Quintilian, trans. 1921)

Obviously Quintilian appreciated the need for fitting instruction to the student. One way to do this when teachers have many students is to use appropriate groupings.

Within-Class and Flexible Grouping

It is not unusual to have 3- to 5-year ability differences in any given classroom (Castle, Deniz, & Tortora, 2005). But even if you decided to simply forge ahead (against Quintilian's advice) and teach the same material in the same way to your entire class, you would not be alone. Differences in students' prior knowledge are a major challenge for teachers, especially in subjects that build on previous knowledge and skills such as math and science (Loveless, 1998). One answer has been ability grouping, but that also poses a number of problems.

THE PROBLEMS WITH ABILITY GROUPING. Students in many classes and schools are grouped by ability, even though there is no clear evidence that this **within-class ability grouping** is superior to other approaches. In a random sample of primary grade teachers in the United States, 63% reported using within-class ability groups for reading. Students in lower-ability groups were less likely to be asked critical comprehension questions and were given fewer opportunities to make choices about what to read (Chorzempa & Graham, 2006). For schools with lower-SES students, grouping often means that these students are segregated into lower-ability tracks. According to Paul George (2005):

> In my 3 decades of experience with this issue, when homogenous grouping is the primary strategy for organizing students in schools with significant racial and ethnic diversity in the population, the result is almost always deep, and often starkly obvious, division of students on the basis of race, ethnicity, and social class. (p. 187)

Thoughtfully constructed and well-taught ability groups in math and reading can be effective, but the point of any grouping strategy should be to provide appropriate challenge and support—that is, to reach children within their "zone of proximal development" (Vygotsky, 1997). Flexible grouping is one possible answer.

FLEXIBLE GROUPING. In **flexible grouping**, students are grouped and regrouped based on their learning needs. Assessment is continuous so that students are always working within their zone of proximal development. Arrangements might include small groups, partners, individuals, and even the whole class—depending on which grouping best supports each student's learning of the particular academic content. Flexible grouping approaches include high-level instruction and high expectations for all students, regardless of their group placement (Corno, 2008). One 5-year longitudinal study of flexible grouping in a high-needs urban elementary school found 10% to 57% increases in students who reached mastery level, depending on the subject area and grade level. Teachers received training and support in the assessment, grouping, and teaching strategies needed, and by

Connect and Extend to PRAXIS II™

The Teacher's Role in Student-Centered Instruction (II, A3)
The teacher's role in student-centered instruction is significantly different from that in teacher-centered instruction.

Differentiated instruction A flexible approach to teaching that matches content, process, and product based on student differences in readiness, interests, and learning needs.

Within-class ability grouping System of grouping in which students in a class are divided into two or three groups based on ability in an attempt to accommodate student differences.

Flexible grouping Grouping and regrouping students based on learning needs.

GUIDELINES

Using Flexible Grouping

Form and re-form groups based on accurate diagnosis of students' current performance in the subject being taught.
Examples

1. Use scores on the most recent reading assessments to establish reading groups, and rely on current math performance to form math groups.
2. Assess continuously. Change group placement frequently when students' achievement changes.

Make sure different groups get appropriately different instruction, not just the same material. Make sure teachers, methods, and pace are adjusted to fit the needs of the group.
Examples

1. Vary more than pace; fit teaching to students' interests and knowledge.
2. Assign all groups research reports, but have some be written, and others oral or PowerPoint presentations.
3. Organize and teach groups so that low-achieving students get appropriate extra instruction—not just the same material again. Make lower achieving groups smaller so students get extra attention.
4. Make sure all work is meaningful and respectful—no worksheets for lower ability groups while the higher ability groups do experiments and projects.
5. Try alternatives. For example, DeWayne Mason and Tom Good (1993) found that supplementing whole-class

instruction in math with remediation and enrichment for students when they needed it worked better than dividing the class into two ability groups and teaching these groups separately.

Discourage comparisons between groups and encourage students to develop a whole-class spirit.
Examples

1. Don't seat groups together outside the context of their reading or math group.
2. Avoid naming ability groups—save the names for mixed-ability or whole-class teams.

Group by ability for one, or, at the most, two subjects.
Examples

1. Make sure there are many lessons and projects that mix members from the groups.
2. Experiment with learning strategies in which cooperation is stressed (described in Chapter 10).
3. Keep the number of groups small (two or three at most) so that you can provide as much direct teaching as possible—leaving students alone for too long leads to less learning.

For more information about classroom grouping, see these two sites:
http://www.eduplace.com/science/profdev/articles/valentino.html

---

the end of the study, 95% of the teachers were using flexible grouping. The teachers in the study believed that some of the gains came because students were more focused on learning and more confident (Castle et al., 2005).

Another way to use flexible grouping is in a nongraded elementary school. Students of several ages (for example, 6, 7, and 8) are together in one class, but they are flexibly grouped within the class for instruction based on achievement, motivation, or interest in different subjects. This cross-grade grouping seems to be effective for students of all abilities as long as the grouping allows teachers to give more direct instruction to the groups. But be sensible about cross-age grouping. Mixing 3rd, 4th, and 5th graders for math or reading class based on what they are ready to learn makes sense. However, sending a large 4th grader to the 2nd grade, where he is the only older student and stands out like a sore thumb, isn't likely to work well. Also, when cross-age classes are created just because there are too few students for one grade—and not in order to better meet the students' learning needs—the results are not positive (Veenman, 1997). As we have seen repeatedly throughout this text, working at a challenging level, but one you can master with effort and support, is more likely to encourage learning and motivation.

If you ever decide to use flexible grouping in your class, the *Guidelines* should make the approach more effective (Arends, 2007; Good & Brophy, 2008).

Adaptive Teaching

Adaptive teaching Provides all students with challenging instruction and uses supports when needed, but removes these supports as students become able to handle more on their own.

Lyn Corno (2008) has developed a model of **adaptive teaching** that also addresses learner differences. In this approach, teachers see "learner variation as an opportunity for learning from teaching rather than as obstacles to be overcome" (p. 171). Adaptive teaching provides all students with challenging instruction and uses supports when needed, but removes those supports as students become able to handle more on their own. Figure 14.1 shows the continuum of support and type of instruction that matches students' needs. As shown on the far left of the figure, when students are novices in an area or have little prior knowledge and skills, the teaching is more direct and includes well-designed motivational strategies to keep them engaged. At the same time, students are taught how to apply appropriate cognitive strategies, to give them the "skills" to learn. There are short cycles of teaching, checking for understanding, and reteaching. As students develop aptitudes in the subject, teaching moves to modeling, guided practice, and coaching. By this time, students should have improved their cognitive "skills" strategies, so teaching can also focus on motivational and volitional strategies—the "will" to learn. Finally as students gain more knowledge and skills, teaching can move to guided discovery, independent study, and peer tutoring, with an emphasis on self-regulated learning—the kind of learning the students will need for the rest of their lives.

Adaptive teaching makes sure that everyone is challenged. For example, one teacher at a magnet school described how he "iced" his curriculum with some content "just beyond the reach" of even his most advanced students. He wanted to be sure all his students found some assignments difficult. He believed "everyone needs to stretch in my class" (Corno, 2008, p. 165).

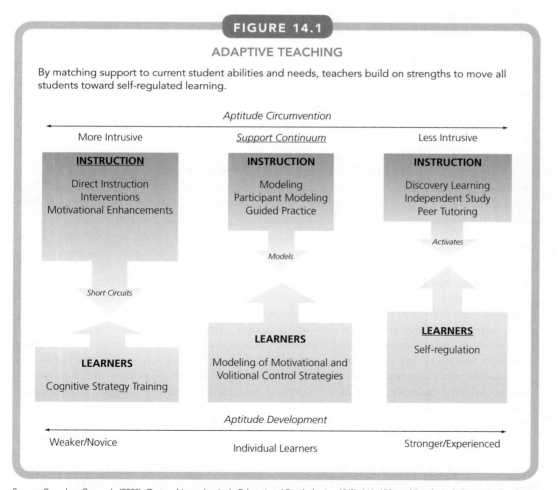

FIGURE 14.1

ADAPTIVE TEACHING

By matching support to current student abilities and needs, teachers build on strengths to move all students toward self-regulated learning.

Aptitude Circumvention

More Intrusive	*Support Continuum*	Less Intrusive
INSTRUCTION	**INSTRUCTION**	**INSTRUCTION**
Direct Instruction Interventions Motivational Enhancements	Modeling Participant Modeling Guided Practice	Discovery Learning Independent Study Peer Tutoring

Short Circuits *Models* *Activates*

| **LEARNERS** Cognitive Strategy Training | **LEARNERS** Modeling of Motivational and Volitional Control Strategies | **LEARNERS** Self-regulation |

Aptitude Development

| Weaker/Novice | Individual Learners | Stronger/Experienced |

Source: Based on Corno, L. (2008). On teaching adaptively. Educational Psychologist, 43(3), 161–173; and Randi, J., & Corno, L., Teaching and learner variation, in Pedagogy—Learning from Teaching, British Journal of Educational Psychology, Monograph Series II(3), pp. 47–69.

Reaching Every Student: Differentiated Instruction in Inclusive Classrooms

STOP & THINK When you think about teaching in an inclusive classroom, what are your concerns? Do you have enough training? Will you get the support you need from school administrators or specialists? Will working with the students with disabilities take time away from your other responsibilities? •

These questions are common ones, and sometimes such concerns are justified. But effective teaching for students with disabilities does not require a unique set of skills. It is a combination of good teaching practices and sensitivity to all your students. Students with disabilities need to learn the academic material, and they need to be full participants in the day-to-day life of the classroom.

To accomplish the first goal of academic learning, students with learning disabilities appear to benefit from using extended practice distributed over days and weeks and from advanced organizers such as focusing students on what they already know or stating clear objectives (Swanson, 2001).

To accomplish the second goal of integrating students with disabilities into the day-to-day life of the classroom, Marilyn Friend and William Bursuck (2002) recommend the INCLUDE strategy:

Identify the environmental, curricular, and instructional demands of your classroom.
Note students' learning strengths and needs.
Check for potential areas of student success.
Look for potential problem areas.
Use information gathered to brainstorm instructional adaptations.
Decide which adaptations to try.
Evaluate student progress.

Table 14.7 shows how the INCLUDE strategy might be applied to students with learning and behavioral disabilities.

When students have special needs, they may be referred for evaluation to child study teams, school psychologists, or teachers of students with special needs. (See Table 4.12 on page 160 for guidelines about referring students for evaluation.) The outcome of this process sometimes includes the preparation of an individualized education program or IEP, as described in Chapter 4. Figure 14.2 on page 536 is an excerpt from the IEP of a boy who had difficulty managing anger and complying with teacher requests. You may help to develop these programs for students in your classes. Well-designed programs should provide guidance for you in your planning and teaching.

Technology and Differentiation

IDEA requires that all students eligible for special education services must be considered for assistive technology. **Assistive technology** is any product, piece of equipment, or system that is used to increase, maintain, or improve the functional capabilities of individuals with disabilities (Goldman, Lawless, Pellegrino, & Plants, 2006). For students who require small steps and many repetitions to learn a new concept, computers are the perfect patient tutors, repeating steps and lessons as many times as necessary. A well-designed computer instructional program is engaging and interactive—two important qualities for students who have problems paying attention or a history of failure that has eroded motivation. For example, a math or spelling program might use images, sounds, and gamelike features to maintain the attention of a student with an attention-deficit disorder. Interactive digital media programs teach hearing people how to use sign language. Many programs do not involve sound, so students with hearing impairments can get the full benefit from the lessons. Students who have trouble reading can use programs that will "speak" a word for them if they touch the unknown word. With this immediate access to help, the students are much more likely to get the reading practice they need to prevent falling farther and farther behind. Other devices actually convert printed pages and typed texts to spoken words for students who are blind or others who benefit from hearing

Assistive technology Devices, systems, and services that support and improve the capabilities of individuals with disabilities.

TABLE 14.7 • **Making Adaptations for Students with Learning and Behavior Disabilities Using Steps in the INCLUDE Strategy**

IDENTIFY CLASSROOM DEMANDS	NOTE STUDENT STRENGTHS AND NEEDS	CHECK FOR POTENTIAL SUCCESSES/LOOK FOR POTENTIAL PROBLEMS	DECIDE ON ADAPTATIONS
Student desks in clusters of four	*Strengths* Good vocabulary skills *Needs* Difficulty attending to task	*Success* Student understands instruction if on task *Problem* Student off task—does not face instructor as she teaches	Change seating so student faces instructor
Small-group work with peers	*Strengths* Good handwriting *Needs* Oral expressive language—problem with word finding	*Success* Student acts as secretary for cooperative group *Problem* Student has difficulty expressing self in peer learning groups	Assign as secretary of group Place into compatible small group Develop social skills instruction for all students
Expect students to attend class and be on time	*Strengths* Good drawing skills *Needs* Poor time management	*Success* Student uses artistic talent in class *Problem* Student is late for class and frequently does not attend at all	Use individualized student contract for attendance and punctuality—if goals met, give student artistic responsibility in class
Textbook difficult to read	*Strengths* Good oral communication skills *Needs* Poor reading accuracy Lacks systematic strategy for reading text	*Success* Student participates well in class Good candidate for class dramatizations *Problem* Student is unable to read text for information	Provide taped textbooks Highlight student text
Lecture on women's suffrage movement to whole class	*Strengths* Very motivated and interested in class *Needs* Lack of background knowledge	*Success* Student earns points for class attendance and effort *Problem* Student lacks background knowledge to understand important information in lecture	Give student video to view before lecture Build points for attendance and working hard into grading system
Whole-class instruction on telling time to the quarter hour	*Strengths* Good coloring skills *Needs* Cannot identify numbers 7–12 Cannot count by fives	*Success* Student is able to color clock faces used in instruction *Problem* Student is unable to acquire telling time skills	Provide extra instruction on number identification and counting by fives

Source: From Including Students with Special Needs: A Practical Guide for Classroom Teachers, *3/e by Marilyn Friend & William D. Bursuck. Published by Allyn and Bacon, Boston, MA. Copyright © 2002 by Pearson Education. Adapted by permission of the publisher.*

information. For the student with a learning disability whose writing can't be read, word processors produce perfect penmanship so the ideas can finally get on paper. Once the ideas are recorded, the student can reorganize and improve his or her writing without the agony of rewriting by hand (Hallahan, Kauffman, & Pullen, 2009).

With these tremendous advances in technology have come new barriers, however. Many computers have graphic interfaces. Manipulating the programs requires precise "mouse movements," as you may remember when you first learned to point and click. These maneuvers are often difficult for students with motor problems or visual impairments. And

FIGURE 14.2

AN EXCERPT FROM AN IEP—INDIVIDUALIZED EDUCATION PROGRAM

This IEP was developed for a 15-year-old boy to help him manage anger and comply with teacher requests.

Student: __Curt__   Age: __15__   Grade: __9__   Date: __10/12/94__

Unique Characteristics/ Needs	Special Education, Related Services, Modifications	(begin duration)	Present Levels, Objectives, Annual Goals (Objectives to include procedure, criteria, schedule)
Social Needs: ■ To learn anger management skills, especially regarding swearing ■ To learn to comply with requests Present Level: Lashes out violently when not able to complete work, uses profane language, and refuses to follow further directions from adults	1. Teacher and/or counselor consult with behavior specialists regarding techniques and programs for teaching social skills, especially anger management.	30 min., 3 x week	Goal: During the last quarter of the academic year, Curt will have 2 or fewer detentions for any reason. Objective 1: At the end of the 1st quarter, Curt will have had 10 or fewer detentions.
	2. Provide anger management training for Curt.	30 min., 2 x week	Objective 2: At the end of 2nd quarter, Curt will have had 7 or fewer detentions.
	3. Establish a peer group which involves role playing, etc. so Curt can see positive role models and practice newly learned anger management skills.		Objective 3: At the end of 3rd quarter, Curt will have had 4 or fewer detentions. Goal: Curt will manage his behavior and language in a reasonably acceptable manner as reported by faculty/peers.
	4. Develop a behavior plan for Curt which gives him responsibility for charting his own behavior.		Objective 1: At 2 weeks, asked at end of class if Curt's behavior language was acceptable or not, 3 out of 5 teachers will say "acceptable."
	5. Provide a teacher or some other adult mentor to spend time with Curt (could be talking; game play, physical activity).	30 min., 2 x week	Objective 2: At 6 weeks, asked same question, 4 out of 6 teachers will say "acceptable."
	6. Provide training for the mentor regarding Curt's needs/goals.		Objective 3: At 12 weeks. 6 out of 6 will say "acceptable."

Adaptations to regular program:

■ In all classes, Curt should be near front of class
■ Curt should be called on often to keep him involved and on task
■ All teachers should help Curt with study skills as trained by spelling/language specialist and resource room teacher
■ Teachers should monitor Curt's work closely in the beginning weeks/months of his program

Source: From Better IEPs, 4th ed. (p. 127) by Barbara D. Bateman. Copyright 1996, 2006 by Barbara D. Bateman. Reprinted by permission of the author and Attainment Company, Inc.

the information available on the Internet often is unusable for students with visual problems. Researchers are working on the problem—trying to devise ways for people to access the information nonvisually (Hallahan, Kauffman, & Pullen, 2009). For example, in 2010 the learning management system called *Canvas* was awarded the national Federation of the Blind—Nonvisual Accessibility Gold Level Certification because the system is equally accessible to blind and sighted users (NFB, 2010). One current trend is **universal design**—considering the needs of all users in the design of new tools, learning programs, or Web sites (Pisha & Coyne, 2001).

For gifted students, computers can be a connection with databases and computers in universities, museums, and research labs. Computer networks allow students to work on projects and share information with others across the country. It is also possible to have

Universal design Considering the needs of all users in the design of new tools, learning programs, or Web sites.

GUIDELINES

Teachers as Mentors

Beware of stereotypes in your thinking and teaching.
Examples

1. See every student as an individual and communicate that clearly to the student.
2. Analyze curriculum materials for biases and teach students to become bias detectors.

Take advantage of technology.
Examples

1. Use a Web program like *Eyes to the Future,* which link middle school girls with high school girls in their districts who have stayed interested in math and science as well as women who use science, math, and technology in their careers. The purpose is to help middle school girls see how their work at school relates to "real life." (http://etf.terc.edu/)
2. Establish "email pals" for students, with retired adults or successful former students as their mentors.
3. Download resources from NWREL's National Mentoring Center, especially their school-based mentoring and tutoring materials (http://www.nwrel.org/mentoring/topic_pubs.php#5).

Let students know you believe in them.
Examples

1. Set standards high and give critical feedback, but also provide support and encouragement.
2. Showcase accomplishments of former students.

Take the time to establish and maintain relationships.
Examples

1. Don't expect trust right away; you may have to earn it.
2. Stay in touch with students and keep the door open to provide guidance in the future.
3. Spend some time with students outside academics—before or after school, as part of clubs or extracurricular activities. Have some fun together. Find common interests.

If you set up a more formal mentoring system, be sure participants are trained and monitored.
Examples

1. Use materials from national mentor groups for training, for example, Elements of Effective Practice from MENTOR/ National Mentoring Partnership (http://www.mentoring.org/ start_a_program/planning_and_design/).
2. Have regular times to provide ongoing training and to deal with problems that may arise.

gifted students write programs for students and teachers. Quite a few principals around the country rely on their students to keep the technology networks in their schools working smoothly. These are just a few examples of what technology can do. Check with the resource teachers in your district to find out what is available in your school.

Mentoring Students as a Way of Differentiating Teaching

One way to make all instruction more appropriate and effective is to know your students and develop trusting relationships with them. The knowledge you gain about the students should help in adapting your teaching, and the positive relationship you establish will help students stay engaged in learning. See the *Guidelines* for ideas.

No matter how you differentiate instruction, there is one part of your teaching that should be the same for all your students—*appropriate high expectations*.

TEACHER EXPECTATIONS

Over 40 years ago, a study by Robert Rosenthal and Lenore Jacobson (1968) captured the attention of the national media in a way that few studies by psychologists have since then. The study also caused great controversy within the professional community. Debate about the meaning of the results continues (De Boer, Bosker, & van der Werf, 2010; Jussim, 2012; Jussim, Robustelli, & Cain , 2009; Rosenthal, 1995; Snow, 1995).

What did Rosenthal and Jacobson say that caused such a stir? They randomly chose several students in a number of elementary school classrooms, and then told the teachers that these students probably would make significant intellectual gains during the year. The students did indeed make larger gains than normal that year. The researchers presented data suggesting the existence of a "**Pygmalion effect**" or self-fulfilling prophecy in the classroom. A **self-fulfilling prophecy** is a groundless expectation that leads to behaviors that then make the original expectation come true (Merton, 1948). An example is a false belief that a bank is failing; this leads to a rush of patrons withdrawing money, which then causes the bank to fail as expected.

STOP & THINK When you thought about the most effective teacher you ever had, was one of the characteristics that the teacher believed in you or demanded the best from you? How did the teacher communicate that belief? •

Two Kinds of Expectation Effects

Actually, two kinds of expectation effects can occur in classrooms. In the self-fulfilling prophecy described above, the teacher's beliefs about the students' abilities have no basis in fact, but student behavior comes to match the initially inaccurate expectation. The second kind of expectation effect occurs when teachers are fairly accurate in their initial reading of students' abilities and respond to students appropriately. The problems arise when students show some improvement, but teachers do not alter their expectations to take account of the improvement. This is called a **sustaining expectation effect**, because the teacher's unchanging expectation sustains the student's achievement at the expected level. The chance to raise expectations, provide more appropriate teaching, and thus encourage greater student achievement is lost. In practice, self-fulfilling prophecy effects seem to be stronger in the early grades, and sustaining effects are more likely in the later grades (Kuklinski & Weinstein, 2001).

Sources of Expectations

There are many possible sources of teachers' expectations, including intelligence test scores (especially if they are not interpreted appropriately); gender (more behavior problems for boys and higher academic achievement for girls); notes from previous teachers; the medical or psychological reports in students' permanent files; prior knowledge about older brothers and sisters; appearance (higher expectations for attractive students); previous achievement; socioeconomic status; race and ethnicity; and the actual behaviors of the student (Van Matre, Valentine, & Cooper, 2000). Even the student's after-school activities can be a source of expectations. Teachers tend to hold higher expectations for students who participate in extracurricular activities than for students who do nothing after school. And recent research shows that some teachers may even hold expectations at the class level, that is, they have higher or lower expectations for all the students in a particular class (Rubie-Davies, 2010).

Some students are more likely than others to be the recipients of sustaining expectations. For example, withdrawn children provide little information about themselves, so teachers may sustain their expectations about these children for lack of new input (Jones & Gerig, 1994). Also, self-fulfilling prophecy effects tend to be stronger for students from lower-SES families and for African American students (De Boer, Bosker, & van der Werf, 2010). In a synthesis of over 50 studies, Harriet Tenenbaum and Martin Ruck (2007) found that teachers held higher expectation for and directed more positive questions and encouragement toward European American compared to African American and Latino/a students. The highest expectations were reserved for Asian American students. It appears that early childhood teachers may hold higher expectations for students who are more socially competent (Hinnant, O'Brien, & Ghazarian, 2009). For example, in another study of 110 students whose development was followed from age 4 to age 18, Jennifer Alvidrez and Rhona Weinstein (1999) found that teachers tended to overestimate the abilities of preschool children they rated as independent and interesting and to underestimate the abilities of children perceived as immature and anxious.

Expectations and beliefs focus attention and organize memory, so teachers may pay attention to and remember the information that fits their initial expectations (Fiske,

Pygmalion effect Exceptional progress by a student as a result of high teacher expectations for that student; named for mythological king, Pygmalion, who made a statue, then caused it to be brought to life.

Self-fulfilling prophecy A groundless expectation that is confirmed because it has been expected.

Sustaining expectation effect Student performance is maintained at a certain level because teachers don't recognize improvements.

1993; Hewstone, 1989). Even when student performance does not fit expectations, the teacher may rationalize and attribute the performance to external causes beyond the student's control. For example, a teacher may assume that the low-ability student who did well on a test must have cheated and that the high-ability student who failed must have been upset that day. In both cases, behavior that seems out of character is dismissed. It may take many instances of supposedly uncharacteristic behavior to change the teacher's beliefs about a particular student's abilities. Thus, expectations often remain in the face of contradictory evidence (Brophy, 1998).

Do Teachers' Expectations Really Affect Students' Achievement?

The answer to this question is more complicated than it might seem. There are two ways to investigate the issue. One is to give teachers unfounded expectations about their students and note if these baseless expectations have any effects. The other approach is to identify the naturally occurring expectations of teachers and study the effects of these expectations. The answer to the question of whether teacher expectations affect student learning depends in part on which approach is taken to study the question.

The original Rosenthal and Jacobson experiment used the first approach—giving teachers groundless expectations and noting the effects. A careful analysis of the results revealed that even though 1st through 6th grade students participated in the study, the self-fulfilling prophecy effects could be traced to dramatic changes in just five students in grades one and two. After reviewing the research on teacher expectations, Raudenbush (1984) concluded that these expectations have only a small effect on student IQ scores (the outcome measure used by Rosenthal and Jacobson) and only in the early years of a new school setting—in the first years of elementary school and then again in the first years of middle school.

SOURCES OF TEACHER EXPECTATIONS Students' extracurricular activities can be sources of expectations. Teachers tend to hold higher expectations for students who participate in extracurricular activities than for students who "just hang out" after school.

But what about the second approach—naturally occurring expectations? Research shows that teachers do indeed form beliefs about students' capabilities. Many of these beliefs are accurate assessments based on the best available data and are corrected as new information is collected (Jussim & Haber, 2005). But inaccuracies can make a difference. In the longitudinal study by Alvidrez and Weinstein (1999), teachers' judgments of student ability at age 4 predicted student grade-point average at age 18. The strongest predictions were for students whose abilities were *underestimated*. If teachers decide that some students are less able, and if the teachers lack effective strategies for working with lower-achieving students, then students may experience a double threat—low expectations and inadequate teaching (Good & Brophy, 2008).

Even though it is clear that teacher expectations can affect student achievement, the effects are modest on average and tend to dissipate somewhat over the years (Jussim, 2012). The power of the expectation effect depends on the age of the students (generally speaking, younger students are more susceptible) and on how differently a teacher treats high- versus low-expectation students, an issue we turn to next (Kuklinski & Weinstein, 2001). Teachers may use different instructional strategies and also have different relationships with students based on expectations.

INSTRUCTIONAL STRATEGIES. Different grouping processes may well have a marked effect on students because different groups get different instruction (De Boer, Bosker, & van der Werf, 2010). And some teachers leave little to the imagination; they make their expectations all too clear. For example, Alloway (1984) recorded comments such as these directed to low-achieving groups:

"I'll be over to help you slow ones in a minute." "The blue group will find this hard."

Avoiding the Negative Effects of Teacher Expectations

Use information about students from tests, cumulative folders, and other teachers very carefully.
Examples
1. Avoid reading cumulative folders early in the year.
2. Be critical and objective about the reports you hear from other teachers.
3. Be flexible in your expectations—a student's label or your judgment might be wrong.

Be flexible in your use of grouping strategies.
Examples
1. Review work of students often and experiment with new groupings.
2. Use different groups for different subjects.
3. Use mixed-ability groups in cooperative exercises.

Provide both challenge and support.
Examples
1. Don't say, "This is easy, I know you can do it."
2. Offer a wide range of problems, and encourage all students to try a few of the harder ones for extra credit. Find something positive about these attempts.
3. Make sure your high expectations come with academic and emotional support for students' struggles. "Holding high standards without providing a warm environment is merely harsh. A warm environment without high standards lacks backbone" (Jussim, 2012).

Be especially careful about how you respond to low-achieving students during class discussions.
Examples
1. Give them prompts, cues, and time to answer.
2. Give ample praise for good answers.
3. Call on low achievers as often as high achievers.

Use materials that show a wide range of ethnic groups.
Examples
1. Check readers and library books. Is there ethnic diversity?
2. Ask students to research and create their own materials, based on community or family sources.

Make sure that your teaching does not reflect racial, ethnic, or sexual stereotypes or prejudice.
Examples
1. Use a checking system to be sure you call on and include all students.
2. Monitor the content of the tasks you assign. Do boys get the "hard" math problems to work at the board? Do you avoid having students with limited English give oral presentations?

Be fair in evaluation and disciplinary procedures.
Examples
1. Make sure equal offenses receive equal punishment. Find out from students in an anonymous questionnaire whether you seem to be favoring certain individuals.
2. Try to grade student work without knowing the identity of the student. Ask another teacher to give you a "second opinion" from time to time.

Communicate to all students that you believe they can learn—and mean it.
Examples
1. Return papers that do not meet standards with specific suggestions for improvements.
2. If students do not have the answers immediately, wait, probe, and then help them think through an answer.

Involve all students in learning tasks and in privileges.
Examples
1. Use some system to make sure you give each student practice in reading, speaking, and answering questions.
2. Keep track of who gets to do what job. Are some students always on the list, whereas others seldom make it?

Monitor your nonverbal behavior.
Examples
1. Do you lean away or stand farther away from some students? Do some students get smiles when they approach your desk, whereas others get only frowns?
2. Does your tone of voice vary with different students?

For more information see
http://chiron.valdosta.edu/whuitt/files/teacherexpect.html

In these remarks, the teacher not only tells the students that they lack ability, but also communicates that finishing the work, not understanding, is the goal.

Once teachers divide students into ability groups, they usually differentiate by assigning different learning activities. To the extent that teachers choose activities that challenge students and increase achievement, these differences are probably necessary. Activities become inappropriate, however, when students who are ready for more challenging work are not given the opportunity to try it because teachers believe they cannot handle it. This is an example of a *sustaining expectation effect*.

TEACHER–STUDENT INTERACTIONS.   However the class is grouped and whatever the assignments are, the quantity and the quality of teacher–student interactions are likely to affect the students. Students who are expected to achieve tend to be asked more and harder questions, to be given more chances and a longer time to respond, and to be interrupted less often than students who are expected to do poorly. Teachers also give these high-expectation students cues and prompts, communicating their belief that the students can answer the question (Good & Brophy, 2008; Rosenthal, 1995). They tend to smile at these students more often and to show greater warmth through such nonverbal responses as leaning toward the students and nodding their heads as the students speak (Woolfolk & Brooks, 1983, 1985).

In contrast, with low-expectation students, teachers ask easier questions, allow less time for answering, and are less likely to give prompts. They are more likely to respond with sympathetic acceptance or even praise for inadequate answers from low-achieving students, but to criticize these same students for wrong answers. Even more disturbing, low-achieving students receive less praise than high-achieving students for similar correct answers. This inconsistent feedback can be very confusing for low-ability students. Imagine how hard it would be to learn if your wrong answers were sometimes praised, sometimes ignored, and sometimes criticized, and your right answers received little recognition (Good 1983a, 1983b; Hattie & Timperley, 2007). Even though the effects of these communications may be small each day, there can be huge effects as the expectation differences build year after year with many teachers (Trouilloud, Sarrazin, Bressoux, & Bois, 2006).

Lessons for Teachers: Communicating Appropriate Expectations

Of course, not all teachers form inappropriate expectations or act on their expectations in unconstructive ways (Babad, Inbar, & Rosenthal, 1982). The *Guidelines* may help you avoid some of these problems. But avoiding the problem may be more difficult than it seems. In general, low-expectation students also tend to be the most disruptive students. (Of course, low expectations can reinforce their desire to disrupt or misbehave.) Teachers may call on these students less, wait a shorter time for their answers, and give them less praise for right answers, partly to avoid the wrong, careless, or silly answers that can cause disruptions, delays, and digressions. The challenge is to deal with these very real threats to classroom management without communicating low expectations to some students or fostering their own low expectations of themselves. And sometimes, low expectations become part of the culture of the school—beliefs shared by teachers and administrators alike (Weinstein, Madison, & Kuklinski, 1995).

▼ SUMMARY

Research on Teaching (pp. 508–511)

What methods have been used to study teaching? For years, researchers have tried to unravel the mystery of effective teaching using classroom observation, case studies, interviews, experimentation with different methods, stimulated recall (teachers view videotapes and explain their teaching), analysis of lesson transcripts, and other approaches to study teaching in real classrooms.

What are the general characteristics of good teaching? A variety of teacher qualities are related to good teaching. Research suggests teachers who receive proper training and certification have more successful students. Although it is important, teacher knowledge of a subject is not sufficient for effective teaching. Thorough knowledge does lead to greater clarity and better organization, which are both tied to good teaching. Teachers who provide clear presentations and explanations tend to have students who learn more and who rate their teachers more positively. Teacher warmth,

friendliness, and understanding seem to be the traits most strongly related to positive student attitudes about the teacher and the course in general.

What do expert teachers know? It takes time and experience to become an expert teacher. These teachers have a rich store of well-organized knowledge about the many specific situations of teaching. This includes knowledge about the subjects they teach, their students, general teaching strategies, subject-specific ways of teaching, settings for learning, curriculum materials, and the goals of education. Expert teachers also know how to be reflective practitioners—how to use their experience as a way to grow and improve in their teaching.

What does the new latest research on teaching show? A program of large-scale, longitudinal research has identified three aspects of classroom climate that are related to the development and learning of preschool and elementary school students. These three dimensions are consistent with the characteristics of teachers identified in earlier research on teaching and cover affective, behavioral, and cognitive dimensions. The *affective* dimension is teacher *emotional support*, similar to teacher warmth and enthusiasm identified in early research. The *cognitive* dimension is instructional support, which includes concept development (activities and discussions that promote student higher-order thinking) and quality feedback that is specific and focused on the learning process. The third dimension is classroom organization, which includes *behavioral* concerns such as classroom and lesson management with clear activities and routines that make more time for learning and really engage students—similar to the teacher characteristics of clarity and organization.

The First Step: Planning (pp. 512–519)

What are the levels of planning, and how do they affect teaching? Teachers engage in several levels of planning—by the year, term, unit, week, and day. All the levels must be coordinated. The plan determines how time and materials will be turned into activities for students. There is no single model of planning, but all plans should allow for flexibility. Planning is a creative problem-solving process for experienced teachers. It is more informal—"in their heads."

What is an instructional objective? An instructional objective is a clear and unambiguous description of your educational intentions for your students. Mager's influential system for writing behavioral objectives states that a good objective has three parts—the intended student behavior, the conditions under which the behavior will occur, and the criteria for acceptable performance. Gronlund's alternative approach suggests that an objective should be stated first in general terms, and then the teacher should clarify by listing sample behaviors that would provide evidence that the student has attained the objective. The most recent research on instructional objectives tends to favor approaches similar to Gronlund's.

Describe the three taxonomies of educational objectives. Bloom and others have developed taxonomies categorizing basic objectives in the cognitive, affective, and psychomotor domains. In real life, of course, behaviors from these three domains occur simultaneously. A taxonomy encourages systematic thinking about relevant objectives and ways to evaluate them. Six basic objectives are listed in the cognitive domain: remembering, understanding, applying, analyzing, evaluating, and creating, acting on four kinds of knowledge: factual, conceptual, procedural, and metacognitive. Objectives in the affective domain run from least committed to most committed. Objectives in the psychomotor domain generally move from basic perceptions and reflex actions to skilled, creative movements.

Describe constructivist planning. Planning is shared and negotiated in student-centered, or constructivist, approaches. Rather than having specific student behaviors as objectives, the teacher has overarching goals or "big ideas" that guide planning. Integrated content and teaching with themes are often part of the planning. Assessment of learning is ongoing and mutually shared by teacher and students.

Teaching Approaches (pp. 519–531)

What is direct instruction? Direct instruction is appropriate for teaching basic skills and explicit knowledge. It includes the teaching functions of review/overview, presentation, guided practice, feedback and correctives (with reteaching if necessary), independent practice, and periodic reviews. The younger or less able the students, the shorter the presentation should be, with more cycles of practice and feedback.

Distinguish between convergent and divergent and high-level versus low-level questions. Convergent questions have only one right answer. Divergent questions have many possible answers. Higher-level questions require analyzing, evaluating, and creating—students have to think for themselves. The best pattern for younger students and for lower-ability students of all ages is simple questions that allow a high percentage of correct answers, ample encouragement, help when the student does not have the correct answer, and praise. For high-ability students, the successful pattern includes harder questions at both higher and lower levels and more critical feedback. Whatever their age or ability, all students should have some experience with thought-provoking questions and, if necessary, help in learning how to answer them.

How can wait time affect student learning? When teachers pose a question and then learn to wait at least 3 to 5 seconds before calling on a student to answer, students tend to give longer answers; more students are likely to participate, ask questions, and volunteer appropriate answers; student comments involving analysis, synthesis, inference, and speculation tend to increase; and the students generally appear more confident in their answers.

What are the uses and disadvantages of group discussion? Group discussion helps students participate directly, express themselves clearly, justify opinions, and tolerate different views. Group discussion also gives students a chance to ask for clarification, examine their own thinking, follow personal interests, and assume responsibility by taking leadership roles in the group. Thus, group discussions help students evaluate ideas and synthesize personal viewpoints. However, discussions are quite unpredictable and may easily digress into exchanges of ignorance.

How can you match teaching to your goals? Different goals and student needs require different teaching methods. Direct instruction often leads to better performance on achievement tests, whereas the open, informal methods such as discovery learning or inquiry approaches are associated with better performance on tests of creativity, abstract thinking, and problem solving. In addition, the open methods are better for improving attitudes toward school and for stimulating curiosity, cooperation among students, and lower absence rates.

Differentiated Instruction (pp. 531–537)

What are the problems with ability grouping? Academic ability groupings can have disadvantages and advantages for students and teachers. Student in higher ability groups may benefit, but students in lower ability groups are less likely to be asked critical comprehension questions and are given fewer opportunities to make choices about readings and assignments. For schools with lower-SES students, grouping often means that these students are segregated even in their own classes, so ability grouping can create segregation within diverse schools.

What are the alternatives available for grouping in classes, including flexible grouping? Cross-age grouping by subject can be an effective way to deal with ability differences in a school. Within-class ability grouping, if handled sensitively and flexibly, can have positive effects, but alternatives such as cooperative learning may be better.

What is adaptive teaching? Adaptive teaching provides all students with challenging instruction and uses supports when needed, but removes those supports as students are able to handle more on their own.

What characterizes effective teaching for students with disabilities? Effective teaching for students with disabilities does not require a unique set of skills. It is a combination of good teaching practices and sensitivity to all students. Students with disabilities need to learn the academic material, and they need to be full participants in the day-to-day life of the classroom.

What resources do teachers have to work effectively with students with disabilities? When students have special needs, they may be referred for evaluation to specialists such as child study teams, school psychologists, or teachers of students with special needs. The outcome of this process sometimes includes the preparation of an individualized educational program or IEP, as described in Chapter 4, which will have teaching ideas and guidelines. In addition, differentiated instruction can improve learning for all students and developing mentoring relationships with students can help teachers connect with student abilities and needs.

Teacher Expectations (pp. 537–541)

What are some sources of teacher expectations? Sources include intelligence test scores, gender, notes from previous teachers, medical or psychological reports found in cumulative folders, ethnic background, prior knowledge about older brothers and sisters, physical characteristics, previous achievement, socioeconomic status, and the actual behaviors of the student.

What are the two kinds of expectation effects and how do they happen? The first is the self-fulfilling prophecy, in which the teacher's beliefs about the students' abilities have no basis in fact, but student behavior comes to match the initially inaccurate expectation. The second is a sustaining expectation effect, in which teachers are fairly accurate in their initial reading of students' abilities and respond to students appropriately, but they do not alter their expectations to take account of any improvement. When this happens, the teacher's unchanging expectation can sustain the student's achievement at the expected level. In practice, sustaining effects are more common than self-fulfilling prophecy effects.

What are the different avenues for communicating teacher expectations? Some teachers tend to treat students differently, depending on their own views of how well the students are likely to do. Differences in treatment toward low-expectation students may include setting less challenging tasks, focusing on lower-level learning, giving fewer choices, providing inconsistent feedback, and communicating less respect and trust. Students may behave accordingly, fulfilling teachers' predictions or staying at an expected level of achievement.

▼ KEY TERMS

Active teaching (519)
Adaptive teaching (532)
Advance organizer (520)
Affective domain (516)
Assistive technology (534)
Basic skills (519)
Behavioral objectives (514)
Cognitive domain (515)
Cognitive objectives (514)
Constructivist approach (518)

Convergent questions (527)
Differentiated instruction (531)
Direct instruction/Explicit teaching (519)
Divergent questions (527)
Expert teachers (509)
Flexible grouping (531)
Group discussion (529)
Instructional objectives (514)
Lesson study (513)
Pedagogical content knowledge (509)

Psychomotor domain (517)
Pygmalion effect (538)
Reflective (509)
Scripted cooperation (522)
Seatwork (523)
Self-fulfilling prophecy (538)
Sustaining expectation effect (538)
Taxonomy (515)
Universal design (536)
Within-class ability grouping (531)

▼ CONNECT AND EXTEND TO LICENSURE

MULTIPLE-CHOICE QUESTIONS

1. Direct instruction is best used when teachers do which one of the following.
   A. Teach basic skills
   B. Have their students explore numerous pathways to solve a mathematics problem
   C. Encourage their students to refine their creativity in art
   D. Assign critical thinking exercises

2. Homework has long been a staple of education. In order for students to gain the most from their homework experience, all but which one of the following suggestions should be followed?
   A. Establish that students understand the assignment
   B. Hold students accountable for completing the work correctly
   C. Check students' work and allow for corrections and revisions
   D. Require a parent signature to ensure collaboration with home

3. Ellen Baker knew that her new job in a middle school would require that she understand differentiated instruction. By utilizing this strategy, her students would be more apt to progress and master the concepts they needed to be successful throughout their school years. One of the techniques she decided to use involved grouping students on their learning needs. In this manner, students who had scored poorly on their fractions tests would be grouped with similar students to remediate and develop that skill. She likened this type of differentiated instruction to having students continually work in their zone of proximal development. The type of strategy Ellen Baker wants to use is referred to as which one of the following.
   A. Flexible Grouping
   B. Jigsaw
   C. Collaborative group work
   D. Peer tutoring

4. Teachers sometimes make determinations about their students' abilities based upon little evidence. When teachers expect their students will not do well, their words and actions can actually

make that expectation come true regardless of the validity. This effect is referred to as which one of the following.

A. Self-fulfilling prophecy
B. The zone of proximal development
C. Professional license
D. Supportive withdraw

CONSTRUCTED-RESPONSE QUESTIONS

Case

Although Casey Yost had done well in her college classes, she was having a difficult time with her student teaching. Her mentor teacher continually scolded her for not correctly writing her objectives and rushing through lessons. Casey didn't understand how she could both make her lessons clear and manage to cover the material necessary for the students' upcoming standardized tests. "Casey, if your students don't understand the material, it won't make a difference if you cover the material or not. Let's

review one of your objectives for the upcoming lesson. 'Students will understand fractions'. This objective is too general. How can you measure if your students 'understand'? You need to select words that correspond to specific actions that you can observe or measure. Let's try to develop a few objectives that are more specific in nature."

5. In what ways can Casey Yost avoid writing objectives that are too general?

6. In order to teach her students more effectively, list several strategies Casey can employ during instruction.

MyEducationLab™

Go to Chapter 14 of the Book Specific Resources in MyEducationLab and click on "Connect and Extend to Licensure" to answer these questions. Compare your responses with the feedback provided.

▼ WHAT WOULD THEY DO?

TEACHERS' CASEBOOK: Reaching and Teaching Every Student

Here is how some practicing teachers would differentiate instruction for the class described at the beginning of the chapter.

LOU DE LAURO • 5th Grade Language Arts
John P. Faber School, Dunellen, NJ

In your hometown you probably know a lot of people. To be successful you are going to have to use the town to help you. If you plan properly, you should be able to secure one guest a week for the entire school year. The kids will love meeting new people each week and reading with them. But you need more than a guest a week to visit your classroom. So ask the businesses in town. Maybe a business can run a fundraiser so you can purchase alternative texts for your students. Maybe the local library can introduce you to their biggest donor who might donate texts to you. Maybe you can apply for a grant with the local educational foundation to get new materials.

But you need more help. You are a teacher; you were probably a strong student who connected with your former teachers. Visit any teachers that are still teaching and get their advice on what to do. What has worked in the past may work well now, too.

Devote many hours after school to your students. Small-group instruction will help these kids. Get the two students who are practically ready for college small stipends donated by a local business so they stay after school and help you with your challenging students. I think that if you fully take advantage of your home court, this is one situation in which you can easily prevail.

MARIE HOFFMAN HURT • 8th Grade Foreign Language
Teacher (German & French)
Pickerington Local Schools, Pickerington, OH

To start, I would encourage a teacher to look beyond the general classifications of "white, working, middle class, and English speaking." Even in a class full of students who fit this demographic, there is an array of individuals. Each student learns differently and has different interests. A good teacher will recognize this and challenge students as people, not as groups. Do your best to layer as much as

you can throughout your lessons. Give students choices. Use what resources you have—in this case particularly ESL resources. Even praising students' individual characteristics and accomplishments outside the classroom sets the tone. Finally, keep in mind that you are only one person and can only give your best. Don't overwork yourself and burn out—you are no good to your students or your family if you are wiped out.

M. DENISE LUTZ • Technology Coordinator
Grandview Heights High School, Columbus, OH

Studies have shown that student success is directly related to teacher effectiveness. In today's diverse classrooms a teacher must develop effective classroom pedagogy that incorporates effective instructional strategies, uses effective classroom management strategies, and designs effective classroom curriculum to meet the needs of all learners. It is necessary to communicate learning goals for all students, track individual progress, and celebrate successes. Under the guidance of the teacher, students should learn to work collaboratively in small groups and as a cohesive class encouraging and helping one another to be successful. A teacher who establishes and maintains classroom rules and procedures while acknowledging students who do and do not follow these rules and procedures fosters this kind of environment. Consistency, trust, and authenticity will help to advance the development of effective relationships between the teacher, the home, and among class members. Effective classroom curriculum always begins with the end in mind. The teacher should have a clear picture of what mastery of content would look like for each of his or her students. Understanding the big idea and defining essential questions will guide the collection of activities and lessons that will move each student in the direction of success. The direction of success will remain the same for all students, but lessons and activities may present different paths for individuals to traverse. Today's teacher must work from day one to get to know each individual and to establish a culture of collaboration among the group.

PATRICIA A. SMITH • *High School Math*
Earl Warren High School, San Antonio, TX

Because this new teacher is a product of the same school system, it will be imperative to begin classroom instruction with absolutely no preconceived opinions toward any particular student. Likewise, a diverse population requires the teacher to resolve student situations discreetly and judiciously, and not publicly. The initial goals of the teacher would be to facilitate student work in a cooperative manner and engender teacher trust. Planning and organizing icebreaker exercises the first few days of the school year could prove extremely profitable.

With a wide range of reading levels, small groups would work to the teacher's advantage. I would not suggest grouping students according to reading level at all times, but would opt to appoint a recognized student leader to orchestrate daily oral recitations. Moreover, I would select reading materials suited to all students and keep the assignments brief to avoid overwhelming struggling readers. The student leader could also design questions to gauge comprehension and give the group a follow-up spelling test. Initially, the spelling test would be composed of five to ten simple words that students could either print or write. Subsequently, as the students gain confidence and experience success, the readings could be assigned as homework and the students would be required to write a short paragraph answering a reading comprehension question.

If the teacher remains well organized, the instructional time allotted for small group interaction should not extend over 15 minutes in a single class period. Thus, the teacher would not forfeit traditional grammar lessons for the entire class but would still provide limited individualized instruction. I would also supplement SAT reading and English practice for all college bound students.

MyEducationLab™

Go to Topic 11, Planning and Instruction, in the MyEducationLab (www.myeducationlab.com) for *Educational Psychology*, where you can:

- Find learning outcomes for planning and instruction along with the national standards that connect to these outcomes.
- Complete Assignments and Activities that can help you more deeply understand the chapter content.
- Apply and practice your understanding of the core teaching skills identified in the chapter with the Building Teaching Skills and Dispositions learning units.
- Examine challenging situations and cases presented in the IRIS Center Resources.
- Access video clips of CCSSO National Teachers of the Year award winners responding to the question, "Why Do I Teach?" in the Teacher Talk section.
- Check your comprehension on the content covered in the chapter with the Study Plan. Here you will be able to take a chapter quiz, receive feedback on your answers, and then access Review, Practice, and Enrichment activities to enhance your understanding of chapter content.
- Find additional Teachers' Casebook scenarios and responses to them from practicing teachers.
- Use the Online Lesson Plan Builder to practice lesson planning and integrating national and state standards into your planning.

chapter fifteen

CLASSROOM ASSESSMENT, GRADING, AND STANDARDIZED TESTING

TEACHERS' CASEBOOK: Giving Meaningful Grades

Your school requires that you give letter grades to your class. You can use any method you want, as long as an A, B, C, D, or F appears for each of the subject areas on every student's report card, every grading period. Some teachers are using worksheets, quizzes, homework, and tests. Others are assigning group work and portfolios. A few teachers are individualizing standards by grading on progress and effort more than final achievement. Some are trying contract approaches and experimenting with longer-term projects, while others are relying almost completely on daily class work. Two teachers who use group work are considering giving credit toward grades for being a "good group member" or competitive bonus points for the top-scoring group. Others are planning to use improvement points for class rewards, but not for grades. Your only experience with grading was using written comments and a mastery approach that rated the students as making satisfactory or unsatisfactory progress toward particular objectives. You want a system that is reliable, fair and manageable, but also encourages learning, not just performance. And you want a system that gives the students feedback they can use to prepare for the proficiency tests required by NCLB.

CRITICAL THINKING

- What would you choose as your major graded assignments and projects?
- Would you include credit for behaviors such as group participation or effort?
- How would you put all the elements together to determine a grade for every student for every marking period?
- How would you justify your system to the principal and to the students' families, especially when the teachers in your school are using so many different criteria?
- What do you think of the wide range of criteria being used by different teachers—is this fair to students?
- How will these issues affect the grade levels you will teach?

WHAT WOULD YOU DO?

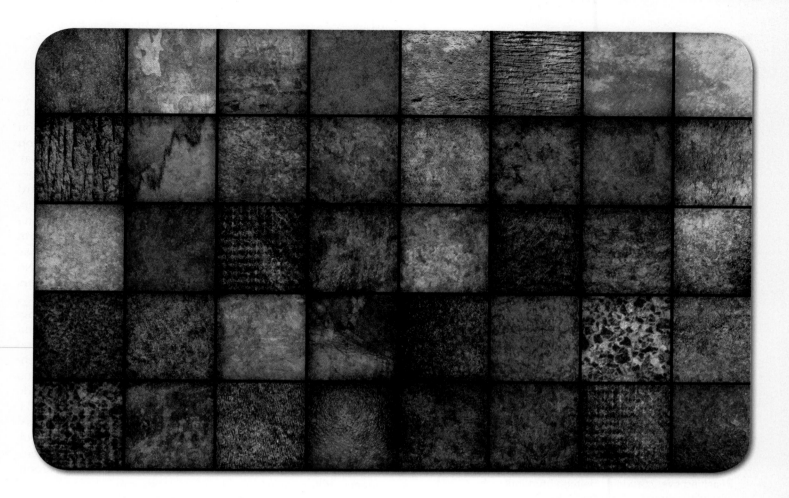

OVERVIEW AND OBJECTIVES

As you read this chapter, you will examine assessment, testing, and grading, focusing not only on the effects they are likely to have on students, but also on practical ways to develop better methods for testing and grading.

We begin with a consideration of the basic concepts in assessment including validity and reliability. Next we examine the many types of tests teachers prepare each year and approaches to assessment that don't rely on traditional testing. Then, we explore the effects grades are likely to have on students and the very important topic of communication with students and families. How will you justify the grades you give? Finally, because standardized tests are so important today, we spend some time looking at testing, the meaning of test scores, and alternatives to traditional testing.

By the time you have completed this chapter, you should be able to:

Objective 15.1: Distinguish among evaluation, measurement, and assessment, including the functions of each.

Objective 15.2: Distinguish between norm-referenced and criterion-referenced assessments.

Objective 15.3: Describe how reliability, validity, and absence of bias are used to understand and judge assessments.

Objective 15.4: Describe two kinds of traditional classroom testing, and how authentic assessment can be used as an alternative to traditional assessments.

Objective 15.5: Describe the effects of grading on students and the types of strategies teachers can use to communicate to parents about grades.

Objective 15.6: Explain how to interpret common standardized test scores (percentile rank, stanine, grade-equivalent, scale score).

Objective 15.7: Identify some of the current issues in standardized testing.

BASICS OF ASSESSMENT

Would it surprise you to learn that published tests, such as college entrance exams and IQ tests, are creations of the 20th century? In the early to mid-1900s, college entrance was generally based on grades, essays, and interviews. From your own experience, you know that testing has come a long way since then—too far, say some critics. Published tests today are called **standardized tests** because they are administered, scored, and interpreted in a standard manner—same directions, time limits, and scoring for all (Popham, 2011). Standard methods of developing items, administering the test, scoring it, and reporting the scores are all implied by the term *standardized test*. The schools where you teach probably will use standardized tests, especially to meet the requirements of the No Child Left Behind (NCLB) Act. In most schools, however, teachers do not have much say in selecting these tests.

Classroom assessments, on the other hand, are created and selected by teachers. Classroom assessments can take many different forms—unit tests, essays, portfolios, projects, performances, oral presentations—the list is long. Assessments are critical because teaching involves making many kinds of judgments—decisions based on values: "Is this software appropriate for my students?" "Will Jacob do better if he repeats the 1st grade?" "Should Emily get a B– or a C+ on the project?" This chapter is about judgments that involve measurement, testing, and grading, and all forms of assessment. We look at both classroom assessment and standardized testing, with an emphasis on the former, because teachers are responsible for classroom assessments. Before we look at either classroom or standardized assessments, let's examine some key distinctions that apply to both, beginning with the difference between measurement and assessment.

Measurement and Assessment

Measurement is quantitative—the description of an event or characteristic using numbers. Measurement tells how much, how often, or how well by providing scores, ranks, or ratings. Instead of saying, "Sarah doesn't seem to understand addition," a teacher might say, "Sarah answered only 2 of the 15 problems correctly in her addition homework." Measurement also allows a teacher to compare one student's performance on a particular task with either a specific standard or the performances of other students on the same task.

Not all the decisions made by teachers involve measurement. Some decisions are based on information that is difficult to express numerically: student preferences, discussions with families, previous experiences, even intuition. But measurement does play a large role in many classroom decisions, and, when properly done, it can provide unbiased data for decision making.

Increasingly, measurement specialists are using the term *assessment* to describe the process of gathering information about students' learning. **Assessment** is broader than testing and measurement because it includes all kinds of ways to sample and observe students' skills, knowledge, and abilities (Linn & Miller, 2005). Assessments can be formal, such as unit tests, or informal, such as observing who emerges as a leader in group work. Assessments can be designed by classroom teachers or by local, state, or national agencies such as school districts or the Educational Testing Service. And today, assessments can go well beyond paper-and-pencil exercises to judgments based on students' performances, portfolios, projects, or products (Popham, 2011).

FORMATIVE AND SUMMATIVE ASSESSMENT.   There are two general uses or functions for assessment: formative and summative. **Formative assessment** occurs before or during instruction. The purposes of formative assessment are to guide the teacher in planning and improving instruction and to help students improve learning. In other words, formative assessment helps *form* instruction and provides feedback that is "nonevaluative, supportive, timely, and specific" (Shute, 2008, p. 153). Often students are given a formative test prior to instruction, a **pretest** that helps the teacher determine what students already know. Sometimes a test is given during instruction to see what areas of weakness remain so teaching can be directed toward the problem areas. These formative tests are not graded, so students who tend to be very anxious about "real" tests may find this low-pressure practice in test taking especially helpful.

Summative assessment occurs at the end of instruction. Its purpose is to let the teacher and the students know the level of accomplishment attained. Summative assessment, therefore, provides a summary of accomplishment. The final exam is a classic example.

SUMMATIVE ASSESSMENT The final exam is a classic example of a summative assessment. This type of assessment occurs at the end of instruction and provides a summary of accomplishment.

The distinction between formative and summative assessment is based on how the results are used. And any kind of assessment—traditional, performance, project, oral, portfolio, and so on—can be used for either formative or summative purposes. If the purpose of the assessment is to improve your teaching and help students guide their own learning, then the evaluation is *formative*. But if the purpose is to evaluate final achievement (and help determine a course grade), the assessment is *summative* (Nitko & Brookhart, 2011). In fact, the same assessment could be used as a formative evaluation at the beginning of the unit and as a summative evaluation at the end. Table 15.1 gives some examples of different uses of assessment.

The formative uses of assessment are really the most important in teaching. In fact, Popham believes "any teacher who uses tests dominantly to determine whether students get high or low grades should receive a solid F in classroom assessment" (2008, p. 256). Tests and all assessments should be used to help teachers make better instructional decisions.

TABLE 15.1 • Using Tests to Make Instructional Decisions

The best use of assessment is to plan, guide, and target instruction. Here are some decisions that can benefit from assessment results.

DECISION CATEGORY	TYPICAL ASSESSMENT STRATEGY	DECISION OPTIONS
What to teach in the first place?	Preassessment before instruction	Whether to provide instruction for specific objectives?
How long to keep teaching toward a particular instructional objective?	En route assessments of students' progress	Whether to continue or cease instruction for an objective either for an individual or for the whole class?
How effective was an instructional sequence?	Comparing students' posttest to pretest performances	Whether to retain, discard, or modify a given instructional sequence the next time it's used?

Source: From Popham, W. James, Classroom Assessment: What Teachers Need to Know, 4/e. Published by Allyn and Bacon, Boston, MA. Copyright © 2005 by Pearson Education. Adapted by permission of the publisher.

Measurement An evaluation expressed in quantitative (number) terms.

Assessment Procedures used to obtain information about student performance.

Formative assessment Ungraded testing used before or during instruction to aid in planning and diagnosis.

Pretest Formative test for assessing students' knowledge, readiness, and abilities.

Summative assessment Testing that follows instruction and assesses achievement.

Connect and Extend to PRAXIS II™

Criterion-/Norm-Referenced Tests (II, C5)
The ERIC Digest *Norm- and Criterion-Referenced Testing* (http://www.ericdigests.org/1998–1/norm.htm) describes the purposes, content, and issues related to criterion- and norm-referenced tests. Giving accurate feedback to parents is part of a teacher's job. When talking with a parent about a child's abilities, do you think the use of norm-referenced or criterion-referenced test results is more desirable?

The answers given on any type of test have no meaning by themselves; we must make some kind of comparison in order to interpret test results. There are two basic types of comparisons: In the first, a test score is compared to the scores obtained by other people who have taken the same test. (This is called a *norm-referenced comparison*.) The second type is *criterion-referenced*. Here, the score is compared to a fixed standard or minimum passing score. Actually, the same test can be interpreted either in a norm-referenced or criterion-referenced way.

NORM-REFERENCED TEST INTERPRETATIONS. In **norm-referenced testing** and grading, the people who have taken the test provide the norms for determining the meaning of a given individual's score. You can think of a *norm* as being the typical level of performance for a particular group. By comparing the individual's raw score (the actual number correct) to the norm, we can determine if the score is above, below, or around the average for that group. There are at least three types of **norm groups** (comparison groups) in education—the class or school itself, the school district, and national samples. Students in national norm groups used for large-scale assessment programs are tested one year and then the scores for that group serve as comparisons or norms every year for several years until the test is revised or renormed. The norm groups are selected so that all socioeconomic status (SES) groups are included in the sample. Because high-SES students tend to do better on many standardized tests, a high-SES school district will almost always have higher scores compared to the norm group.

Norm-referenced tests cover a wide range of general objectives. They are especially appropriate when only the top few candidates can be admitted to a program. However, norm-referenced measurement has its limitations. The results of a norm-referenced test do not tell you whether students are ready to move on to more advanced material. For instance, knowing that a student is in the top 3% of the class on a test of algebraic concepts will not tell you if he or she is ready to move on to advanced math; everyone else in the class may have a limited understanding of the algebraic concepts.

Nor are norm-referenced tests particularly appropriate for measuring affective and psychomotor objectives. To measure individuals' psychomotor learning, you need a clear description of standards. (Even the best gymnast in school performs certain exercises better than others and needs specific guidance about how to improve.) In the affective area, attitudes and values are personal; comparisons among individuals are not really appropriate. For example, how could we measure an "average" level of political values or opinions? Finally, norm-referenced tests tend to encourage competition and comparison of scores. Some students compete to be the best. Others, realizing that being the best is impossible, may compete to be the worst. Both goals have their casualties.

CRITERION-REFERENCED TEST INTERPRETATIONS. When test scores are compared, not to the scores of others, but to a given criterion or standard of performance, this is **criterion-referenced testing** or grading. To decide who should be allowed to drive a car, it is important to determine just what standard of performance works for selecting safe drivers. It does not matter how your test results compare to the results of others. If your performance on the test was in the top 10%, but you consistently ran through red lights, you would not be a good candidate for receiving a license, even though your score was high.

Criterion-referenced tests measure the mastery of very specific objectives. The results of a criterion-referenced test should tell the teacher exactly what the students can and cannot do, at least under certain conditions. For example, a criterion-referenced test would be useful in measuring the students' ability to add three-digit numbers. A test could be designed with 20 different problems, and the standard for mastery could be set at 17 correct out of 20. (The standard is often somewhat arbitrary and may be based on such things as the teacher's experience.) If two students receive scores of 7 and 11, it does not matter that one student did better than the other because neither met the standard of 17. Both need more help with addition.

In teaching basic skills, there are many instances where comparison to a preset standard is more important than comparison to the performance of others. It is not very comforting to know, as a parent, that your child is better in reading than most of

Norm-referenced testing Testing in which scores are compared with the average performance of others.

Norm group Large sample of students serving as a comparison group for scoring tests.

Criterion-referenced testing Testing in which scores are compared to a set performance standard.

the students in her class if none of the students is reading at grade level. Sometimes standards for meeting the criterion must be set at 100% correct. You would not like to have your appendix removed by a surgeon who left surgical instruments inside the body *only* 10% of the time.

Criterion-referenced tests are not appropriate for every situation, however. Many subjects cannot be broken down into a set of specific objectives. Moreover, although standards are important in criterion-referenced testing, they can often be arbitrary, as you have already seen. When deciding whether a student has mastered the addition of three-digit numbers comes down to the difference between 16 or 17 correct answers, it seems difficult to justify one particular standard over another. Finally, at times, it is valuable to know how the students in your class compare to other students at their grade level both locally and nationally. You can see that each type of test is well suited for certain situations, but each also has its limitations.

VALIDITY AND RELIABILITY The validity and reliability decisions based on tests may be affected by the extent to which the tests measure intelligence, knowledge, motivation, or differences in life experiences.

Assessing the Assessments: Reliability and Validity

One of the most common problems with the use of assessments, especially tests, is mis-interpretation of results. This often happens when people believe tests are precise measurements of a student's ability. No test provides a perfect picture of a person's abilities; a test is only one small sample of behavior. Three factors are important in developing good tests and interpreting results: *reliability, validity,* and *absence of bias.*

RELIABILITY OF TEST SCORES.   Scores are reliable if a test gives a consistent and stable "reading" of a person's ability from one occasion to the next, assuming the person's ability remains the same. A reliable thermometer works in a similar manner, giving you a reading of 100°C each time you measure the temperature of boiling water. Measuring **reliability** this way, by giving the test on two different occasions, indicates *stability* or *test-retest reliability.* If a group of people take two equivalent versions of a test and the scores on both tests are comparable, this indicates *alternate-form reliability.* Reliability can also refer to the *internal consistency* or the precision of a test. This type of reliability, known as *split-half reliability,* is calculated by comparing performance on half of the test questions with performance on the other half. If, for example, someone did quite well on all the odd-numbered items and not at all well on the even-numbered items, we could assume that the items were not very consistent or precise in measuring what they were intended to measure.

There are several ways to compute reliability, but all the possibilities give numbers between 0.0 and 1.0, like a correlation coefficient. Above .90 is considered very reliable; .80 to .90 is good, and below .80 is not very good reliability for commercially produced standardized tests such as the SAT or ACT (Haladyna, 2002). Generally speaking, longer tests are more reliable than shorter ones.

ERROR IN SCORES.   All tests are imperfect estimators of the qualities or skills they are trying to measure. There are errors in every testing situation. There are sources of error related to the student such as mood, motivation, test-taking skills, or even cheating. Sometimes the errors are in your favor and you score higher than your ability might warrant; sometimes the errors go against you. There are also sources of error related to the test itself—the directions are unclear, the reading level is too high, the items are ambiguous, or the time limits are wrong.

The score each student receives always includes some amount of error. How can error be reduced? As you might guess, this returns us to the question of reliability. The

Reliability Consistency of test results.

more reliable the test scores are, the less error there will be in the score actually obtained. On standardized tests, test developers take this into consideration and make estimations of how much the students' scores would probably vary if they were tested repeatedly. This estimation is called the **standard error of measurement**. Thus, a reliable test can also be defined as one with a small standard error of measurement.

CONFIDENCE INTERVAL.   Never base an opinion of a student's ability or achievement on the exact score the student obtains. For standardized tests, many test companies now report scores using a **confidence interval**, or "standard error band," that encloses the student's actual score. This makes use of the standard error of measurement and allows a teacher to consider the range of scores that might include a student's **true score**—the score the student would get if the measurement were completely accurate and error-free.

Let us assume, for example, that two students in your class take a standardized achievement test in Spanish. The standard error of measurement for this test is 5. One student receives a score of 79 and the other, a score of 85. At first glance, these scores seem quite different. But when you consider the standard error bands around the scores, not just the scores alone, you see that the bands overlap. The first student's true score might be anywhere between 74 and 84 (that is, the actual score of 79 plus and minus the standard error of 5). The second student's true score might be anywhere between 80 and 90. Both students could have the same true score of 80, 81, 82, 83, or 84 because the score bands overlap at those numbers. It is crucial to keep in mind the idea of standard error bands when selecting students for special programs. No child should be rejected simply because the score obtained missed the cutoff by one or two points. The student's true score might well be above the cutoff point. See Figure 15.5 for a report with these score bands.

VALIDITY.   If test scores are sufficiently reliable, the next question is whether the scores are valid, or more accurately, whether the judgments and decisions based on the test scores are valid. To have **validity**, the decisions and inferences based on the test must be supported by evidence. This means that validity is judged in relation to a particular use or purpose, that is, in relation to the actual decision being made and the evidence for that decision. A particular test might be valid for one purpose, but not for another (Frisbie, 2005; Oosterhof, 2009; Popham, 2011).

There are different kinds of evidence to support a particular judgment. If the purpose of a test is to measure the skills covered in a course or unit, then we would hope to see test questions on all the important topics and not on extraneous information. If this condition is met, we would have *content-related evidence of validity*. Have you ever taken a test that dealt only with a few ideas from one lecture or just a few pages of the textbook? Then decisions based on that test (like your grade) certainly lacked content-related evidence of validity.

Some tests are designed to predict outcomes. The SATs, for example, are intended to predict performance in college. If SAT scores correlate with academic performance in college as measured by, say, grade-point average in the first year, then we have *criterion-related evidence of validity* for the use of the SAT in admissions decisions.

Most standardized tests are designed to measure some psychological characteristic or "construct" such as reasoning ability, reading comprehension, achievement motivation, intelligence, creativity, and so on. It is a bit more difficult to gather *construct-related evidence of validity*, yet this is a very important requirement—probably the most important. Construct-related evidence of validity is gathered over many years. It is indicated by a pattern of scores. For example, older children can answer more questions on intelligence tests than younger children can. This fits with our *construct* of intelligence. If the average 5-year-old answered as many questions correctly on a test as the average 13-year-old, we would doubt that the test really measured intelligence. Construct-related evidence for validity can also be demonstrated when the results of a test correlate with the results of other well-established, valid measures of the same construct.

Today, many psychologists suggest that construct validity is the broadest category and that gathering content- and criterion-related evidence is another way of determining if the test actually measures the construct it was designed to measure. Nearly 40 years ago,

Standard error of measurement Hypothetical estimate of variation in scores if testing were repeated.

Confidence interval Range of scores within which an individual's particular score is likely to fall.

True score The score the student would get if the measurement were completely accurate and error-free.

Validity Degree to which a test measures what it is intended to measure.

Sam Messick (1975) raised two important questions to consider in making any decisions about using a test: *Is the test a good measure of the characteristic it is assumed to assess? Should the test be used for the proposed purpose?* The first question is about construct validity; the second is about ethics and values.

A test must be reliable in order to be valid. For example, if an intelligence test yields different results each time it is given to the same child over the course of a few months, then, by definition, it is not reliable. Certainly, it couldn't be a valid measure of intelligence because intelligence is assumed to be fairly stable, at least over a short period of time. However, reliability will not guarantee validity. If that intelligence test gave the same score every time for a particular child, but didn't predict school achievement, speed of learning, or other characteristics associated with intelligence, then performance on the test would not be a true indicator of intelligence. The test would be reliable—but invalid. Reliability and validity are issues with all assessments, not just standardized tests. Classroom tests should yield scores that are *reliable*, that are as free from error as possible, and *valid*—accurately measure what they are supposed to.

ABSENCE OF BIAS. The third important criterion for judging assessments is absence of bias. **Assessment bias** "refers to qualities of an assessment instrument that offend or unfairly penalize a group of students because of the students' gender, ethnicity, socio-economic status, religion, or other such group-defining characteristic" (Popham, 2011, p. 111). Biases are aspects of the test such as content, language, or examples that might distort the performance of a group—either for better or for worse. For example, if a reading test used passages that described boxing or football scenarios, we might expect males on average to do better than females.

Two forms of assessment bias are *unfair penalization* and *offensiveness*. The reading assessment with heavy sports content is an example of unfair penalization—girls may be penalized for their lack of boxing or football knowledge. Offensiveness occurs when a particular group might be insulted by the content of the assessment. Offended, angry students may not perform at their best.

What about biases based on ethnicity or social class? Research on test bias shows that most standardized tests predict school achievement equally well across all groups of students (Sattler, 2001). But even so, many people believe that the tests still can be unfair to some groups. Tests may not have *procedural fairness*; that is, some groups may not have an equal opportunity to show what they know on the test. Here are a few examples:

1. The language of the test and the tester is often different from the languages of the students.
2. Answers that support middle-class values are often rewarded with more points.
3. On individually administered intelligence tests, being very verbal and talking a lot is rewarded. This favors students who feel comfortable in that particular situation.

Also, tests may not be fair because different groups have had different opportunities to learn the material tested. The questions asked tend to center on experiences and facts more familiar to the dominant culture than to minority-group students. Consider this test item for 4th graders described by Popham (2011, p. 371):

> My uncle's field is computer programming.

Look at the sentences below. In which sentence does the word *field* mean the same as it does in the boxed sentence above?

> A. The softball pitcher knew how to field her position.
> B. They prepared the field by spraying and plowing it.
> C. I know the field I plan to enter when I finish college.
> D. The doctor used a wall chart to examine my field of vision.

Items like this are included on most standardized and textbook tests. But not all families describe their work as a field of employment. If your parents work in professional fields such as computers, medicine, law, or education, the item would make sense, but what if

Assessment bias Qualities of an assessment instrument that offend or unfairly penalize a group of students because of the students' gender, SES, race, ethnicity, etc.

your parents worked at a grocery store or a car repair shop? Are these fields? Life outside class has prepared some students, but not others, for this item.

Concern about cultural bias in testing has led some psychologists to try to develop **culture-fair** or **culture-free tests**. These efforts have not been very successful. On many of the so-called culture-fair tests, the performance of students from lower-SES backgrounds and ethnic groups has been the same as or worse than their performance on the standard Wechsler and Binet Intelligence scales (Sattler, 2001). And when you think about it, how can you separate culture from cognition? Every student's learning is embedded in his or her culture and every test question emerges from some kind of cultural knowledge.

Today, most standardized tests are checked carefully for assessment bias, but teacher-made tests may have biased content as well. It makes sense to have colleagues check your tests for bias, especially when you are getting started in teaching (Popham, 2011).

With this background in the basic concepts of formative and summative assessments; norm-referenced and criterion-referenced interpretations; and attention to reliability, validity, and absence of bias, we are ready to enter the classroom, where *learning is supported by frequent assessments using cumulative questions that ask students to apply and integrate knowledge.*

CLASSROOM ASSESSMENT: TESTING

STOP & THINK Think back to your most recent test. What was the format? Did you feel that the test results were an accurate reflection of your knowledge or skills? Have you ever had to design a test? What makes a good, fair test? •

Connect and Extend to PRAXIS II™

Traditional Assessment (II C1, 2, 4) Objective and essay tests continue to have important roles in effective assessment and evaluation programs. Describe the appropriate uses of these types of tests. Identify the advantages and limitations of each.

When most people think of assessments in a classroom, they usually think of testing. As you will see shortly, teachers today have many other options, but testing is still a significant activity in most classrooms. In this section, we will examine how to evaluate the tests that accompany standard curriculum materials and show you how to write your own test questions.

Using the Tests from Textbooks

Most elementary and secondary school texts today come complete with supplemental materials such as teaching manuals and ready-made tests. Using these tests can save time, but is this good teaching practice? The answer depends on your objectives for your students, the way you teach the material, and the quality of the tests provided. If the textbook test is of high quality, matches your testing plan, and fits the instruction you actually provided for your students, then it may be the right test to use. Check the reading level of the items provided and be prepared to revise/improve them (Airasian, 2005; McMillan, 2004). Table 15.2 gives key points to consider in evaluating textbook tests.

What if there are no tests available for the material you want to cover, or the tests provided in your teachers' manuals are not appropriate for your students? Then it's time for you to create your own tests. We will consider the two major kinds of traditional tests—objective and essay.

Objective Testing

Culture-fair/culture-free test A test without cultural bias.

Objective testing Multiple-choice, matching, true/false, short-answer, and fill-in tests; scoring answers does not require interpretation.

Multiple-choice questions, matching exercises, true/false statements, and short-answer or fill-in items are all types of **objective testing**. The word *objective* in relation to testing means "not open to many interpretations," or "not subjective." The scoring of these types of items is relatively straightforward compared to the scoring of essay questions because the answers are more clear-cut than essay answers.

How should you decide which item format is best for a particular test? Use the one that provides the most direct measure of the learning outcome you intended for your students (Gronlund & Waugh, 2009). In other words, if you want to see how well students can write a letter, have them write a letter, don't ask multiple-choice questions about letters. But if many different item formats will work equally well, then use multiple-choice

TABLE 15.2 • **Key Points to Consider in Judging Textbook Tests**

1. The decision to use a textbook test or pre-made standard achievement test must come *after* a teacher identifies the objective that he or she has taught and now wants to assess.
2. Textbook and standard tests are designed for the typical classroom, but since few classrooms are typical, most teachers deviate somewhat from the text in order to accommodate their pupils' needs.
3. The more classroom instruction deviates from the textbook, the less valid the textbook tests are likely to be.
4. The main consideration in judging the adequacy of a textbook or standard achievement test is the match between its test questions and what pupils were taught in their classes:
   a. Are questions similar to the teacher's objectives and instructional emphases?
   b. Do questions require pupils to perform the behaviors they were taught?
   c. Do questions cover all or most of the important objectives taught?
   d. Is the language level and terminology appropriate for pupils?
   e. Does the number of items for each objective provide a sufficient sample of pupil performance?

Source: From Classroom Assessment: Concepts and Applications *(5th ed.) by P. W. Airasian (2005). New York: McGraw-Hill, p. 161. With permission from The McGraw-Hill Companies.*

questions because they are easier to score fairly and can cover many topics. Switch to other formats if writing good multiple-choice items for the material is not possible or appropriate. For example, if related concepts such as terms and definitions need to be linked, then a matching item is a better format than multiple-choice. If it is difficult to come up with several wrong answers for a multiple-choice item, try a true/false question instead. Alternatively, ask the student to supply a short answer that completes a statement (fill in the blank). Variety in objective testing can lower students' anxiety because the entire grade does not depend on one type of question that a particular student may find difficult. We will look closely at the multiple-choice format because it is the most versatile—and the most difficult to use well.

USING MULTIPLE-CHOICE TESTS.   Even though about three-fourths of education professors reject the use of multiple-choice tests in determining students' grades, about half of public school teachers endorse these tests (Banks, 2005), so you should know how to use these tests well. In fact, many schools require teachers to give students experience answering multiple-choice tests in order to prepare them for NCLB testing (McMillan, 2004). Of course, multiple-choice items can test facts, but these items can assess more than recall and recognition if they require the student to deal with new material by applying or analyzing the concept or principle being tested (Gronlund & Waugh, 2009; McMillan, 2004). For example, the following multiple-choice item is designed to assess students' ability to recognize unstated assumptions, one of the skills involved in analyzing an idea:

An educational psychology professor states, "A z score of $+1$ on a test is equivalent to a percentile rank of approximately 84." Which of the following assumptions is the professor making?

1. The scores on the test range from 0 to 100.
2. The standard deviation of the test scores is equal to 3.4.
3. The distribution of scores on the test is normal. (Correct answer)
4. The test is valid and reliable.

If you did not know the correct answer above, don't worry. We will get to z scores later in this chapter and it will all make sense.

WRITING MULTIPLE-CHOICE QUESTIONS.   All test items require skillful construction, but good multiple-choice items are a real challenge. Some students jokingly refer to multiple-choice tests as "multiple-guess" tests—a sign that these tests are often poorly designed. Your goal in writing test items is to design them so that they measure student achievement, not test-taking and guessing skills.

GUIDELINES

Writing Objective Test Items

Make the stem clear and simple, and present only a single problem. Unessential details should be left out.
Example

Poor	*Better*
There are several different kinds of standard or derived scores. An IQ score is especially useful because	An advantage of an IQ score is

State the problem in the stem in positive terms. Negative language is confusing. If you must use words such as *not*, *no*, or *except*, underline them or type them in all capitals.
Example

Poor	*Better*
Which of the following is not a standard score?	Which of the following is NOT a standard score?

Do not expect students to make extremely fine discriminations among answer choices.
Example
The percentage of area in a normal curve falling between +1 and −1 standard deviations is about:

Poor
a. 66%   b. 67%
c. 68%   d. 69%.

Better
a. 14%   b. 34%
c. 68%   d. 95%.

Make sure each alternative answer fits the grammatical form of the stem, so that no answers are obviously wrong.
Example

Poor
The Stanford-Binet test yields an
a. IQ score.
b. reading level.
c. vocational preference.
d. mechanical aptitude.

Better
The Stanford-Binet is a test of
a. intelligence.
b. reading level.
c. vocational preference.
d. mechanical aptitude.

Avoid including two distractors that have the same meaning.
If only one answer can be right and if two answers are the same, then these two must both be wrong. This narrows down the choices considerably.

Avoid using categorical words such as *always, all, only,* or *never* unless they can appear consistently in all the alternatives.
Most smart test takers know that categorical answers are usually wrong.

Avoid using the exact wording found in the textbook.
Poor students may recognize the answers without knowing what they mean.

Avoid overuse of *all of the above* and *none of the above*.
Such choices may be helpful to students who are simply guessing. In addition, using *all of the above* may trick a quick student who sees that the first alternative is correct and does not read on to discover that the others are correct, too.

Avoid obvious patterns on a test—they aid students who are guessing.
The position of the correct answer should be varied, as should its length.

The **stem** of a multiple-choice item is the part that asks the question or poses the problem. The choices that follow are called *alternatives*. The wrong answers are called **distractors** because their purpose is to distract students who have only a partial understanding of the material. If there were no good distractors, students with only a vague understanding would have no difficulty in finding the right answer. The *Guidelines* should help you write good stems and alternatives.

Stem The question part of a multiple-choice item.

Distractors Wrong answers offered as choices in a multiple-choice item.

Essay Testing

The best way to measure some learning objectives is to ask students to create answers on their own; essay questions are one way to accomplish this. The most difficult part of essay testing is judging the quality of the answers, but writing good, clear questions is not particularly easy, either. We will look at writing, administering, and grading essay tests.

We will also consider factors that can bias the scoring of essay questions and ways you can overcome these problems.

CONSTRUCTING ESSAY TESTS.   Because answering takes time, true essay tests cover less material than objective tests. Thus, for efficiency, essay tests should be limited to the assessment of important, complex learning outcomes. A good essay question gives students a clear and precise task and indicates the elements to be covered in the answer. The students should know how extensive their answer needs to be and about how much time they should spend on each question. Evaluate these two essay questions from Popham (2011, pp. 183–184):

1. (High school level) You have just viewed a videotape containing three widely seen television commercials. What is the one classic propaganda technique present in all three commercials?
2. (Middle school level) Thinking back over the mathematics lesson and homework assignments you had during the past 12 weeks, what conclusions can you draw? Take no more than one page for your response.

Question 1 is pretty clear (do you agree?), but some indication of desired length would be helpful. Question 2 gives a page limit, but would you know what is being asked? What is the specific question here?

Students need ample time for answering. If more than one essay is assigned in the same class period, you may want to suggest time limits for each question. Remember, however, that time pressure increases anxiety and may prevent accurate assessment of some students. Whatever your approach, do not try to make up for the limited amount of material an essay test can cover by including a large number of questions. It would be better to plan on more frequent testing than to include more than two or three essay questions in a single class period. Combining an essay question with a number of objective items is one way to avoid the problem of limited sampling of course material (Gronlund & Waugh, 2009).

EVALUATING ESSAYS.   Gronlund and Waugh (2009) offer several strategies for grading essays. When possible, a good first step is to construct a set of scoring criteria or a rubric (more on this later) and share it with students. Then, decide what type of information should be in every answer. Here is an example from TenBrink (2003, p. 326).

Question: Defend or refute the following statement: Civil wars are necessary to the growth of a developing country. Cite reasons for your argument, and use examples from history to help substantiate your claim.
Scoring Rubric: All answers, regardless of the position taken, should include (1) a clear statement of the position, (2) at least five logical reasons, (3) at least four examples from history that clearly substantiate the reasons given.

Once you have set your expectations for answers, you can assign points to the various parts of the essay. You might also give points for the organization of the answer and the internal consistency of the essay. You can then assign grades such as 1 to 5 or A, B, C, D, and F, and sort the papers into piles by grade. As a final step, skim the papers in each pile to see if they are comparable in quality. These techniques will help ensure fairness and accuracy in grading.

When grading essay tests that contain several questions, it makes sense to grade all responses to one question before moving on to the next. This helps prevent the quality of a student's answer to one question from influencing your reaction to the student's other answers. After you finish reading and scoring the first question, shuffle the papers so that no students end up having all their questions graded first (when you may be taking more time to give feedback or are applying stricter standards, for example) or last (when you may be tired of writing feedback or more lax in your standards). You may achieve greater objectivity if you ask students to put their names on the back of the paper, so that grading is anonymous. A final check on your fairness as a grader is to have another teacher who is equally familiar with your goals and subject matter look over a few of your tests without

NONTRADITIONAL ASSESSMENTS Alternatives to traditional testing have emerged that address what are seen as its limits, including that it emphasizes recall of facts instead of thinking and problem solving. Alternative approaches include authentic assessment, student exhibitions, and student portfolios.

knowing what grades you have assigned. This can give you valuable insights into areas of bias in your grading practices.

THE VALUE OF TRADITIONAL TESTING. Right answers are important. Even though schooling is about learning to think and solve problems, it is also about knowledge. Students must have something to think about—facts, ideas, concepts, principles, theories, explanations, arguments, images, opinions. Well-designed traditional tests can evaluate students' knowledge effectively and efficiently (Airasian, 2005). Some educators believe that traditional testing should play an even greater role than it currently does. Educational policy analysts suggest that American students, compared to students in many other developed countries, lack essential knowledge because American schools emphasize process—critical thinking, self-esteem, problem solving—more than content. In order to teach more about content, teachers will need to determine how well their students are learning the content, and traditional testing provides useful information about content learning. Tests are also valuable in motivating and guiding students' learning. There is research evidence that frequent testing encourages learning and retention. In fact, taking more frequent tests improves learning, even if there is no feedback from the test—bad teaching, but a powerful result (Roediger & Karpicke, 2006)

CRITICISMS OF TRADITIONAL TESTS.   Traditional testing has been under fire since at least the 1990s. As Grant Wiggins (1991) noted then:

> We do not judge Xerox, the Boston Symphony, the Cincinnati Reds, or Dom Perignon vineyards on the basis of indirect, easy to test, and common indicators. Nor would the workers in those places likely produce quality if some generic, secure test served as the only measure of their success in meeting a standard. Demanding and getting quality, whether from students or adult workers, means framing standards in terms of the work that we undertake and value. (p. 22)

Wiggins continues to argue for assessment that makes sense, that tests knowledge as it is applied in real-world situations. Understanding cannot be measured by tests that ask students to use skills and knowledge out of context.

Your stand on traditional testing is part of your philosophy of teaching. Let's look at a few alternative approaches to classroom assessment.

AUTHENTIC CLASSROOM ASSESSMENTS

Authentic assessments ask students to apply skills and abilities as they would in real life. For example, they might use fractions to enlarge or reduce recipes. Grant Wiggins (1989) made this argument over 20 years ago:

> If tests determine what teachers actually teach and what students will study for—and they do—then the road to reform is a straight but steep one: test those capabilities and habits we think are essential, and test them in context. Make [tests] replicate, within reason, the challenges at the heart of each academic discipline. Let them be—authentic. (p. 41)

Wiggins goes on to say that if our instructional goals for students include the abilities to write, speak, listen, create, think critically, do research, solve problems, or apply knowledge,

Authentic assessments
Assessment procedures that test skills and abilities as they would be applied in real-life situations.

then our tests should ask students to write, speak, listen, create, think, research, solve, and apply. How can this happen?

Many educators suggest we look to the arts and sports for analogies to solve this problem. If we think of the "test" as being the recital, exhibition, game, mock court trial, or other performance, then teaching to the test is just fine. All coaches, artists, and musicians gladly "teach" to these "tests" because performing well on these tests is the whole point of instruction. Authentic assessment asks students to perform. The performances may be thinking performances, physical performances, creative performances, or other forms. So **performance assessment** is any form of assessment that requires students to carry out an activity or produce a product in order to demonstrate learning (Airasian, 2005).

It may seem odd to talk about thinking as a performance, but there are many parallels. Serious thinking is risky, because real-life problems are not well defined. Often, the outcomes of our thinking are public—others evaluate our ideas. Like a dancer auditioning for a Broadway show, we must cope with the consequences of being evaluated. Like a potter looking at a lump of clay, a student facing a difficult problem must experiment, observe, redo, imagine, and test solutions, apply both basic skills and inventive techniques, make interpretations, decide how to communicate results to the intended audience, and often accept criticism and improve the initial solution (Eisner, 1999; Herman, 1997).

Portfolios and Exhibitions

The concern with authentic assessment has led to the development of several approaches based on the goal of performance in context. Instead of circling answers to "factual" questions about nonexistent situations, students are required to solve real problems. Facts are used in a context where they apply—for example, instead of asking students, "If you bought a toy for 69 cents and gave the clerk a dollar, how much change would you get back?" have students work in pairs with real money to role play making different purchases or set up a mock class store and have students make purchases and give change (Gronlund & Waugh, 2009, p. 151). The following is taken from the New York State Alternative Assessment in Science Project, 9–12th Grade Performance assessment (http://butterfly.ctl.sri.com/pals/tasks/9-12/Perspiration/admin.html).

Description:
Students collect data on the cooling of water in two different test tubes—one wrapped in wet newspaper and one in dry newspaper. They then identify trends in their data, make predictions, and describe how their experiment is similar to the body's perspiration. The task assesses students' abilities to make simple observations, gather and collect data, identify trends and make predictions, and demonstrate their understanding by relating the experiment to real life.

Overall Task Content Area:
Life Science

Specific Knowledge Areas:
Regulation and behavior

Performance Expectations:
- conducting investigations
- using equipment
- gathering, organizing, and representing data
- formulating conclusions from investigational data
- applying scientific principles to develop explanations and solve new problems

Students completing this "test" will use scientific knowledge to understand a real-life phenomenon—perspiration. In the process, they will have to think critically and write persuasively. Every year, most states release some of the items from past tests to the public. The Center for Technology in Learning of SRI International, a nonprofit science research

Connect and Extend to PRAXIS II™

Authentic Tests (II, C1, 2, 4)
The emphasis on student-centered learning has been accompanied by an emphasis on authentic tests. Understand the purpose, value, and advantages of these forms of assessment. Describe their characteristics and the potential problems with their use.

Performance assessments Any form of assessment that requires students to carry out an activity or produce a product in order to demonstrate learning.

institute, also provides an online resource bank of performance-based assessments linked to the National Science Education Standards. The resource is called PALS (Performance Assessment Links in Science). Go to http://butterfly.ctl.sri.com/pals/index.html; see the performance tasks for kindergarten through 12th grade. You can select tasks by standard and grade level. Each task comes with directions for students, a guide for administrators, and a scoring guide or rubric. Many also have examples of student work. The Life Science task on the previous page came from that site.

Portfolios and exhibitions are two approaches to assessment that require performance in context. With these approaches, it is difficult to tell where instruction stops and assessment starts because the two processes are interwoven (Oosterhof, 2009; Popham, 2011).

Connect and Extend to PRAXIS II™

Portfolio Assessment (II, C1, 2)
For a discussion of the advantages, limitations, design, and implementation of portfolio programs, and to examine samples of portfolio checklists, go to Teachervision.com (http://www.teachervision.com/lesson-plans/lesson-4536.html).

PORTFOLIOS. For years, photographers, artists, models, and architects have had portfolios to display their skills and show to prospective employers. A **portfolio** is a systematic collection of work, often including work in progress, revisions, student self-analyses, and reflections on what the student has learned. Written work or artistic pieces are common contents of portfolios, but student portfolios might also include letters to the portfolio readers describing each entry and its importance, graphs, diagrams, pictures or digital slideshows, PowerPoint presentations, recordings of the students reading their work, unedited and final drafts of persuasive essays or poems, lists of books read, annotated Web site addresses, peer comments, videotapes, laboratory reports, and computer programs—anything that demonstrates learning in the area being taught and assessed (Popham, 2011). There is a distinction between process portfolios and final or "best work" portfolios. The distinction is similar to the difference between formative and summative evaluation. Process portfolios document learning and show progress. Best work portfolios showcase final accomplishments (Johnson & Johnson, 2002). Table 15.3 shows some examples for both individuals and groups.

EXHIBITIONS. An **exhibition** is a performance test that has two additional features. First, it is public, so students preparing exhibitions must take the audience into account; communication and understanding are essential. Second, an exhibition often requires many hours of preparation, because it is the culminating experience of a whole program of study. Thomas Guskey and Jane Bailey (2001) suggest that exhibits help students understand the qualities of good work and recognize those qualities in their own productions and performances. Students also benefit when they select examples of their work to exhibit and articulate their reasons for making the selections. Being able to judge quality can encourage student motivation by setting clear goals. The *Guidelines* on page 562 give some ideas for using portfolios in your teaching.

Evaluating Portfolios and Performances

Checklists, rating scales, and scoring rubrics are helpful when you assess performances, because assessments of performances, portfolios, and exhibitions are criterion-referenced, not norm-referenced. In other words, the students' products and performances are compared to established public standards, not ranked in relation to other students' work (Wiggins, 1991).

Portfolio A collection of the student's work in an area, showing growth, self-reflection, and achievement.

Exhibition A performance test or demonstration of learning that is public and usually takes an extended time to prepare.

Scoring rubrics Rules that are used to determine the quality of a student's performance.

SCORING RUBRICS. A checklist or rating scale gives specific feedback about elements of a performance. **Scoring rubrics** are rules that are used to determine the quality of a student performance, often on a 4-point scale from "excellent" (4) to "inadequate" (1) or on a scale that assigns points to each category—10 points for excellent, 6 for good, and so on (Mabry, 1999). For example, a rubric describing excellent *delegation of responsibility* in a group research project might be:

> Each student in the group can clearly explain what information is needed by the group, what information s/he is responsible for locating, and when the information is needed.

This rubric was generated using Rubistar (http://rubistar.4teachers.org/index.php), an online service for educators that allows you to select a subject area and category, then create a rubric. To get the above rubric, I chose the subject of writing—"group planning

TABLE 15.3 • **Process and Best Works Portfolios for Individuals and Groups**

Here are a few examples of how to use portfolios in different subjects.

THE PROCESS PORTFOLIO		
Subject Area	**Individual Student**	**Cooperative Group**
Science	Documentation (running records or logs) of using the scientific method to solve a series of laboratory problems	Documentation (observation checklists) of using the scientific method to solve a series of laboratory problems
Mathematics	Documentation of mathematical reasoning through double-column mathematical problem solving (computations on the left side and running commentary explaining thought processes on the right side)	Documentation of complex problem solving and use of higher-level strategies
Language Arts	Evolution of compositions from early notes through outlines, research notes, response to others' editing, and final draft	Rubrics and procedures developed to ensure high-quality peer editing
THE BEST WORKS PORTFOLIO		
Subject Area	**Individual Student**	**Cooperative Group**
Language Arts	The best compositions in a variety of styles—expository, humor/satire, creative (poetry, drama, short story), journalistic (reporting, editorial columnist, reviewer), and advertising copy	The best dramatic production, video project, TV broadcast, newspaper, advertising display
Social Studies	The best historical research paper, opinion essay on historical issue, commentary on current event, original historical theory, review of a historical biography, account of academic controversy participated in	The best community survey, paper resulting from academic controversy, oral history compilation, multidimensional analysis of historical event, press corps interview with historical figure
Fine Arts	The best creative products such as drawings, paintings, sculptures, pottery, poems, thespian performance	The best creative products such as murals, plays written and performed, inventions thought of and built

Source: From D.W. Johnson and R.T. Johnson, Meaningful Assessment: A Meaningful and Cooperative Process. *Published by Allyn and Bacon, Boston, MA.*

and research project"—and the category of "delegation of responsibility." The *Guidelines* on the next page give more ideas; some are taken from Goodrich (1997), Johnson and Johnson (2002), and Popham (2011).

Performance assessment requires careful judgment on the part of teachers and clear communication to students about what is good and what needs improving. In some ways, the approach is similar to the clinical method first introduced by Binet to assess intelligence: It is based on observing the student perform a variety of tasks and comparing his or her performance to a standard. Just as Binet never wanted to assign a single number to represent the child's intelligence, teachers who use authentic assessments do not try to assign one score to the student's performance. Even if rankings, ratings, and grades have to be given, these judgments are not the ultimate goals—improvement of learning is.

Connect and Extend to PRAXIS II™

Scoring Rubrics (II, C3)
Kathy Schrock's Guide for Educators (http://school.discovery.com/schrockguide/assess.html) provides information about every aspect of the use of scoring rubrics in the classroom as well as an extensive collection of rubrics that can be used or adapted by teachers.

GUIDELINES

Creating Portfolios

Involve students in selecting the pieces that will make up their portfolios.
Examples

1. During the unit or semester, ask each student to select work that fits certain criteria, such as "my most difficult problem," "my best work," "my most improved work," or "three approaches to."
2. For their final submissions, ask students to select pieces that best show how much they have learned.

Make sure the portfolios include information that shows student self-reflection and self-criticism.
Examples

1. Ask students to include a rationale for their selections.
2. Have each student write a "guide" to his or her portfolio, explaining how strengths and weaknesses are reflected in the work included.
3. Include self- and peer critiques, indicating specifically what is good and what might be improved.
4. Model self-criticism of your own productions.

Make sure the portfolios reflect the students' activities in learning.
Examples

1. Include a representative selection of projects, writings, drawings, and so forth.
2. Ask students to relate the goals of learning to the contents of their portfolios.

Be aware that portfolios can serve different functions at different times of the year.
Examples

1. Early in the year, it might hold unfinished work or "problem pieces."
2. At the end of the year, it should contain only what the student is willing to make public.

Be certain portfolios demonstrate students' growth.
Examples

1. Ask students to make a "history" of their progress along certain dimensions and to illustrate points in their growth with specific works.
2. Ask students to include descriptions of activities outside class that reflect the growth illustrated in the portfolio.

Teach students how to create and use portfolios.
Examples

1. Keep models of very well done portfolios as examples, but stress that each portfolio is an individual statement.
2. Examine your students' portfolios frequently, especially early in the year when they are just getting used to the idea. Give constructive feedback.

For more ideas about using portfolios, see http://www.teachervision.fen.com/assessment/teaching-methods/20153.html

---

GUIDELINES

Developing a Rubric

1. **Look at models:** Show students examples of good and not-so-good work based on composites of work not linked to individual students. Identify the characteristics that make the good ones good and the bad ones bad.
2. **List criteria:** Use the discussion of models to begin a list of what counts in quality work.
3. **Articulate gradations of quality:** Describe the best and worst levels of quality; then fill in the middle levels based on your knowledge of common problems and the discussion of not-so-good work.
4. **Practice on models:** Have students use the rubrics to evaluate the models you gave them in Step 1.
5. **Use self- and peer-assessment:** Give students their task. As they work, stop them occasionally for self- and peer-assessment.
6. **Revise:** Always give students time to revise their work based on the feedback they get in Step 5.

7. **Use teacher assessment:** In your grading, be sure to use the same rubric students used to assess their work.

Note: Step 1 may be necessary only when you are asking students to engage in a task with which they are unfamiliar. Steps 3 and 4 are useful but time consuming; you can do these on your own, especially when you've been using rubrics for a while. A class experienced in rubric-based assessment can streamline the process so that it begins with listing criteria, after which the teacher writes out the gradations of quality, checks them with the students, makes revisions, then uses the rubric for self-, peer, and teacher assessment.

For a great explanation of using rubrics, see http://pareonline.net/getvn.asp?v=7&n=25

The article includes several links such as http://www.teach-nology.com/web_tools/rubrics/ *and* http://rubistar.4teachers.org/ *that allow you to create and customize rubrics for your class.*

It is often helpful to have students join in the development of rating scales and scoring rubrics. When students participate, they are challenged to decide what quality work looks or sounds like in a particular area. They know in advance what is expected. As students gain practice in designing and applying scoring rubrics, their work and their learning often improve. Figure 15.1 gives three alternatives—numerical, graphic, and descriptive—for rating an oral presentation.

RELIABILITY, VALIDITY, GENERALIZABILITY.   Because the teacher's personal judgment plays such a central role in evaluating performances, issues of reliability, validity, and generalizability are critical considerations. One teacher's "excellent" could be another teacher's "adequate." Research shows that when raters are experienced and scoring rubrics are well developed and refined, reliability may improve (Herman & Winters, 1994; LeMahieu, Gitomer, & Eresh, 1993). Some of this improvement in reliability occurs because a rubric focuses the raters' attention on a few dimensions of the work and gives limited scoring levels to choose from. If scorers can give only a rating of 1, 2, 3, or 4, they are more likely to agree than if they could score based on a 100-point scale. So the rubrics may achieve

---

FIGURE 15.1

THREE WAYS OF RATING AN ORAL PRESENTATION

Numerical Rating Scale

Directions:
Indicate how often the pupil performs each of these behaviors while giving an oral presentation. For each behavior circle **1** if the pupil **always** performs the behavior, **2** if the pupil **usually** performs the behavior, **3** if the pupil **seldom** performs the behavior, and **4** if the pupil **never** performs the behavior.

Physical Expression

A. Stands straight and faces audience.
    1 2 3 4
B. Changes facial expression with change in the tone of the presentation.
    1 2 3 4

Graphic Rating Scale

Directions:
Place an **X** on the line that shows how often the pupil did each of the behaviors listed while giving an oral presentation.

Physical Expression

A. Stands straight and faces audience.

| always | usually | seldom | never |

B. Changes facial expression with change in the tone of the presentation.

| always | usually | seldom | never |

Descriptive Rating Scale

Directions:
Place an **X** on the line at the place that best describes the pupil's performance of each behavior.

Physical Expression

A. Stands straight and faces audience.

| stands straight, always looks at audience | weaves, fidgets, eyes roam from audience to ceiling | constant, distracting movements, no eye contact with audience |

B. Changes facial expression with change in the tone of the presentation.

| matches facial expressions to content and emphasis | facial expressions usually appropriate, occasional lack of expression | no match between tone and facial expression; expression distracts |

Source: From Classroom Assessment: Concepts and applications (5th ed.) by P. W. Airasian (2005). New York: McGraw-Hill, p. 251. With permission of The McGraw-Hill Companies.

reliability not because they capture underlying agreement among raters, but because the rubrics limit options and thus limit variability in scoring (Mabry, 1999).

In terms of validity, there is some evidence that students who are classified as "master" writers on the basis of portfolio assessment are judged less capable using standard writing assessments. Which form of assessment is the best reflection of enduring qualities? It is hard to say. In addition, when rubrics are developed to assess specific tasks, the results of applying them may not predict performance on anything except very similar tasks, so we do not know whether a student's performance on a specific task will generalize to the larger area of study (Haertel, 1999; Herman & Winters, 1994; McMillan, 2004).

DIVERSITY AND BIAS IN PERFORMANCE ASSESSMENT.   Equity is an issue in all assessment and no less so with performances and portfolios. With a public performance, there could be bias effects based on a student's appearance and speech or the student's access to expensive audio, video, or graphic tools. Performance assessments have the same potential as other tests to discriminate unfairly against students who are not wealthy or who are culturally different (McDonald, 1993). And the extensive group work, peer editing, and out-of-class time devoted to portfolios means that some students may have access to greater networks of support and outright help. Many students in your classes will come from families that have sophisticated computer graphics and desktop publishing capabilities. Others may have little support from home. These differences can be sources of bias and inequity, especially in portfolios and exhibitions.

Informal Assessments

Informal assessments are ungraded (formative) assessments that gather information from multiple sources to help teachers make decisions (Banks, 2005). Early on in the unit, assessments should be formative (provide feedback, but not count toward a grade), saving the actual graded assessments for later in the unit when all students have had the chance to learn the material (Tomlinson, 2005a). Some examples of informal assessment are journals, student observations and checklists, questioning, and student self-assessment.

JOURNALS.   Journals are very flexible and widely used informal assessments. Students usually have personal or group journals and write in them on a regular basis. In their study, Michael Pressley and his colleagues (2007) found that excellent 1st grade literacy teachers used journaling for three purposes:

- As communication tools that allowed students to express their own thoughts and ideas.
- As an opportunity to apply what they have learned.
- As an outlet to encourage fluency and creative expression in language usage.

Teachers may use journals to learn about their students in order to better connect their teaching to the students' concerns and interests. But often journals focus on academic learning, usually through responses to prompts. Banks (2005) describes one high school physics teacher who asked his students to respond to these three questions in their journals:

1. How can you determine the coefficient of friction if you know only the angle of the inclined plane?
2. Compare and contrast magnetic, electronic, and gravitational fields.
3. If you were to describe the physical concept of sound to your best friend, what music would you use to demonstrate this concept?

When he read the students' journals, the teacher realized that many of the students' basic assumptions about friction, acceleration, and velocity came from personal experiences and not from scientific reasoning. His approach to teaching had to change to reach the students. The teacher never would have known to make the changes in his instruction without reading the journals (Banks, 2005).

There are many other kinds of informal assessments—keeping notes and observations about student performance, rating scales, and checklists. Every time teachers ask questions or watch students perform skills, the teachers are conducting informal assessments. Look at Table 15.4, which summarizes the possibilities and limitations of aligning different assess-

Informal assessments Ungraded (formative) assessments that gather information from multiple sources to help teachers make decisions.

ment tools with their targets. One major message in this chapter is the importance of correctly matching the type of assessment tools used to the target—to what is being assessed.

INVOLVING STUDENTS IN ASSESSMENTS.   One way to connect teaching and assessment while developing students' sense of efficacy for learning is to involve the students in the assessment process. Students can keep track of their own progress and assess their improvement. Here are other ideas, some taken from Stiggins and Chappuis (2005). Students might:

- Learn about the criteria for judging work by examining and discussing with a peer examples of good, average, and poor products or performances. Then pick a poor example and revise to improve it.
- Describe to the teacher or a peer (orally or in writing) the way they approached an assignment, the problems they encountered, the options they considered, and the final result.
- Analyze their strengths and weaknesses before starting a project, then discuss with the teacher or peers how they will use their strengths and overcome their weaknesses as they work on the project.
- In pairs, make up questions that might be on the test, explain why those are good questions, and then answer them together.

TABLE 15.4 • Aligning Different Assessment Tools with Their Targets

Different learning outcomes require different assessment methods.

ASSESSMENT METHOD				
Target to Be Assessed	**Selected Response**	**Essay**	**Performance Assessment**	**Personal Communication**
Knowledge Mastery	Multiple-choice, true/false, matching, and fill-in can sample mastery of elements of knowledge	Essay exercises can tap understanding of relationships among elements of knowledge	Not a good choice for this target—three other options preferred	Can ask questions, evaluate answers, and infer mastery—but a time-consuming option
Reasoning Proficiency	Can assess understanding of basic patterns of reasoning	Written descriptions of complex problem solutions can provide a window into reasoning proficiency	Can watch students solve some problems and infer about reasoning proficiency	Can ask student to "think aloud" or can ask follow-up questions to probe reasoning
Skills	Can assess mastery of the prerequisites of skillful performance—but cannot tap the skill itself	Can assess mastery of the prerequisites of skillful performance—but cannot tap the skill itself	Can observe and evaluate skills as they are being performed	Strong match when skill is oral communication proficiency; also can assess mastery of knowledge prerequisite to skillful performance
Ability to Create Products	Can assess mastery of knowledge prerequisite to the ability to create quality products—but cannot assess the quality of products themselves	Can assess mastery of knowledge prerequisite to the ability to create quality products—but cannot assess the quality of products themselves	A strong match can assess: (a) proficiency in carrying out steps in product development and (b) attributes of the product itself	Can probe procedural knowledge and knowledge of attributes of quality products—but not product quality

- Look back at earlier work and analyze how they have grown by describing "I used to think . . . but now I know. . . ." After doing a few of these analyses, summarize using a frame such as: What did I know before I started? What did I learn? What do I want to learn next
- Before a major test, do a free write on these prompts "What exactly will be on the test?" "What kinds of questions will be asked (multiple-choice, essay, etc.)?" "How well will I do?" "What do I need to study to make sure I am ready?"

One last idea—the teacher arranges items on a test according to specific learning targets, and prepares a "test analysis" chart for students, with three boxes: "My strengths," "Quick review," and "Further study." After handing back the corrected test, students identify learning targets they have mastered and write them in the "My strengths" box. Next, students categorize their wrong answers as either "simple mistake" or "further study." Then, students list the simple mistakes in the "Quick review" box. Last, students write the rest of the learning targets represented by wrong answers in the "Further study" box.

No matter how you assess students, ultimately you will assign grades. We turn to that job next.

GRADING

- -

STOP & THINK Think back on your report cards and grades over the years. Did you ever receive a grade that was lower than you expected? How did you feel about yourself, the teacher, the subject, and school in general as a result of the lower grade? What could the teacher have done to help you understand and profit from the experience? •

- -

In determining a final grade, the teacher must make a major decision. Should a student's grade reflect the student's status in comparison with the rest of the class, or should the grade reflect the amount of material learned and how well it has been learned? In other words, should grading be *norm-referenced* or *criterion-referenced?*

Norm-Referenced versus Criterion-Referenced Grading

In **norm-referenced grading**, the major influence on a grade is the student's standing in comparison with others who also took the course. If a student studies very hard and almost everyone else does too, the student may receive a disappointing grade, perhaps a C or D. One common type of norm-referenced grading is called **grading on the curve.** How you feel about this approach probably depends on where your grades generally fall along that "curve." There is good evidence that this type of grading damages the relationships among students and between teachers and students and also diminishes motivation for most students (Krumboltz & Yeh, 1996). When you think about it, if the curve arbitrarily limits the number of good grades that can be given, then, in the game of grading, most students will be losers (Guskey & Bailey, 2001; Haladyna, 2002; Kohn, 1996b). Over 30 years ago, Benjamin Bloom (of Bloom's taxonomy) and his colleagues (1981) pointed out the fallacy of grading on the curve:

> There is nothing sacred about the normal curve. It is the distribution most appropriate to chance and random activity. Education is a purposeful activity, and we seek to have students learn what we have to teach. If we are effective in our instruction, the distribution of achievement should be very different from the normal curve. In fact, we may even insist that our educational efforts have been unsuccessful to the extent that the distribution of achievement approximates the normal distribution. (pp. 52–53)

In **criterion-referenced grading**, the grade represents a list of accomplishments. If clear objectives have been set for the course, the grade may represent a certain number of objectives met satisfactorily. When a criterion-referenced system is used, criteria for each grade generally are spelled out in advance. It is then up to the student to earn the grade she or he wants to receive. Theoretically, in this system, all students can achieve an A if

Norm-referenced grading Assessment of students' achievement in relation to one another.

Grading on the curve Norm-referenced grading that compares students' performance to an average level.

Criterion-referenced grading Assessment of each student's mastery of course objectives.

they reach the criteria. Criterion-referenced grading has the advantage of relating judgments about a student to the achievement of clearly defined instructional goals. Some school districts have developed reporting systems where report cards list objectives along with judgments about the student's attainment of each. Reporting is done at the end of each unit of instruction. The elementary school report card shown in Figure 15.2 demonstrates the relationship between assessment and the goals of the unit.

Most schools have a specified grading system, so we won't spend time here on the many possible systems. Let's consider a different question—one with research behind it. What is the effect of grades on students?

FIGURE 15.2

A CRITERION-REFERENCED REPORT CARD

This is one example of a criterion-referenced report card. Other forms are possible, but all criterion-referenced reports indicate student progress toward specific goals.

LINCOLN ELEMENTARY SCHOOL
GRADE 5

Student ________________ Teacher ________________ Principal Muriel Simms Quarter 2 3 4

E = Excellent S = Satisfactory P = Making Progress N = Needs improvement

READING PROGRAM

Materials Used: ________

___ Reads with understanding
___ Is able to write about what is read
___ Completes reading group work accurately and on time
___ Shows interest in reading

Reading Skills

___ Decodes new words
___ Understands new words

Independent Reading Level
Below/At Grade Level/Above

LANGUAGE ARTS

___ Uses oral language effectively
___ Listens carefully
___ Masters weekly spelling

Writing skills

___ Understands writing as process
___ Creates a rough draft
___ Makes meaningful revisions
___ Creates edited, legible final draft

Editing skills

___ Capitalizes
___ Punctuates
___ Uses complete sentences
___ Uses paragraphs
___ Demonstrates dictionary skills

Writing skill level:
Below/At Grade Level/Above

MATHEMATICS

Problem Solving

___ Solves teacher-generated problems
___ Solves self-/student-generated problems
___ Can create story problems

Interpreting Problems

___ Uses appropriate strategies
___ Can use more than one strategy
___ Can explain strategies in written form
___ Can explain strategies orally

Math Concepts

Understands Base Ten
Beginning/Developing/Sophisticated

Multiplication, Basic facts
Beginning/Developing/Sophisticated

2-Digit Multiplications
Beginning/Developing/Sophisticated

Division
Beginning/Developing/Sophisticated

Geometry
Beginning/Developing/Sophisticated

Overall Math Skill Level:
Beginning/Developing/Sophisticated

Attitude/Work Skills

___ Welcomes a challenge
___ Persistent
___ Takes advantage of learning from others
___ Listens to others
___ Participates in discussion

It Figures
Is working on: ________

Goals: ________
Is working on achieving goal: ________

SOCIAL STUDIES

___ Understands subject matter
___ Shows curiosity and enthusiasm
___ Contributes to class discussions
___ Uses map skills
___ Demonstrates control of reading skills by interpreting text

Topics covered: individual cultures, Columbus–first English colonies

SCIENCE

___ Shows curiosity about scientific subject matter
___ Asks good scientific questions
___ Shows knowledge of scientific method
___ Uses knowledge of scientific method to help set up and run experiment(s)
___ Makes good scientific observations
___ Has researched scientific topic(s)
Topic(s) ________

I Wonder
Is currently working on ________

WORKING SKILLS

___ Listens carefully
___ Follows directions
___ Works neatly and carefully
___ Checks work
___ Completes work on time
___ Uses time wisely
___ Works well independently
___ Works well in a group
___ Takes risks in learning
___ Welcomes a challenge

HOMEWORK

___ Self-selects homework
___ Completes work accurately
___ Completes work on time

PRESENTATIONS/PROJECTS

____
____

HUMAN RELATIONS

___ Shows courtesy
___ Respects rights of others
___ Shows self-control
___ Interacts well with peers
___ Shows a cooperative and positive attitude in class
___ Shows a cooperative attitude when asked to work with other students
___ Is willing to help other students
___ Works well with other adults (subs, student teacher, parents, etc.)

Attendance

	1st	2nd	3rd	4th
Present				
Absent				
Tardy				

Placement for next year: ________

Source: From Lincoln Elementary School, Grade 5, Madison, WI. Used with permission.

EFFECTS OF FEEDBACK Students often need help figuring out why their answers are incorrect; without such feedback they are likely to make the same mistakes again.

Effects of Grading on Students

When we think of grades, we often think of competition. Highly competitive classes may be particularly hard on anxious students, students who lack self-confidence, and students who are less prepared. So, although high standards and competition do tend to be generally related to increased academic learning, it is clear that a balance must be struck between high standards and a reasonable chance to succeed. Rick Stiggins and Jan Chappuis (2005) observe:

> From their very earliest school experiences, our students draw life-shaping conclusions about themselves as learners on the basis of the information we provide to them as a result of their teachers' classroom assessments. As the evidence accumulates over time, they decide if they are capable of succeeding or not. They decide whether the learning is worth the commitment it will take to attain it. They decide . . . whether to risk investing in the schooling experience. These decisions are crucial to their academic well-being. (p. 11)

It may sound as though low grades and failure should be avoided in school. But the situation is not that simple.

THE VALUE OF FAILING? After reviewing many years of research on the effects of failure from several perspectives, Margaret Clifford (1990, 1991) concluded:

> It is time for educators to replace easy success with challenge. We must encourage students to reach beyond their intellectual grasp and allow them the privilege of learning from mistakes. There must be a tolerance for error-making in every classroom, and gradual success rather than continual success must become the yardstick by which learning is judged. (1990, p. 23)

Some level of failure may be helpful for most students, especially if teachers help the students see connections between hard work and improvement. Efforts to protect students from failure and to guarantee success may be counterproductive. Carol Tomlinson, an expert on differentiated instruction, puts it this way: "Students whose learning histories have caused them to believe that excellence can be achieved with minimal effort do not learn to expend effort, and yet perceive that high grades are an entitlement for them" (2005b, p. 266). So maybe not failure, but accurate and critical feedback can be especially important for students who are used to easy As (Shute, 2008).

RETENTION IN GRADE. So far, we have been talking about the effects of failing a test or perhaps a course. But what about the effect of failing an entire grade—that is, of being "held back"? One study in North Carolina found that kindergarten retention had more than doubled from 1992 to 2002, with over 6% of students retained in 2002. About 10% of U.S. students ages 16–19 have been retained at least once (Wu, West, & Hughes, 2010). Retained children are more likely to be male, members of minority groups, living in poverty, and younger, and less likely to have participated in early childhood programs (Beebe-Frankenberger, Bovina, Macmillan, & Gresham, 2004; Hong & Raudenbush, 2005). Is retention a good policy? See the *Point/Counterpoint* to examine the issue.

Grades and Motivation

If you are relying on grades to motivate students, you had better think again (Smith, Smith, & De Lisi, 2001). The assessments you give should support students' motivation to learn—not their motivation to work for a good grade. But is there really a difference between working for a grade and working to learn? The answer depends in part on how a grade is determined. If you test only at a simple but detailed level of knowledge, you

POINT/COUNTERPOINT: Should Children Be Held Back?

For the last 100 years, parents and educators have debated about the value of retention versus *social promotion* (passing students on to the next grade with their peers). What does the evidence say? What are the arguments?

POINT

▶ **Yes, it just makes sense.** Retention in kindergarten for children considered "not ready" for 1st grade is a common practice. Compared to students who are relatively younger (January to August birthdays), students who are relatively older (born September to November) have higher achievement in school on average (Cobley, McKenna, Baker, & Wattie, 2009). In fact, some parents hold their son or daughter back to give the child an edge over peers in each grade thereafter or because the child was born late in the year—a practice sometimes called "academic red-shirting." In the mid-1960s, 96% of 6-year-olds were enrolled in 1st grade in the United States. By 2008, the number was 84% (Barnard-Brak, 2008). The results on academic red-shirting are mixed. Some studies have found benefits for students who have been held back by their parents, but other studies have found no benefits.

With the increased emphasis on high standards and accountability, the idea of social promotion has come under fire and retention is seen as the better way. Guanglei Hong and Stephen Raudenbush (2005) summarize this and other arguments that have been made in favor of retention:

> A widely endorsed argument is that, when low-achieving students are retained in a grade, the academic status of children in a classroom will become more homogeneous, easing the teacher's task of managing instructional activities (Byrnes, 1989; also see Shepard & Smith, 1988, for a review). In particular, retaining some children in kindergarten may allow the first-grade teacher to teach at a higher level, benefiting those who would be promoted under the policy. Meanwhile, children who view grade retention as a punishment may study harder to avoid being retained in the future. Some have argued that, in comparison with the social promotion policy, repeating a grade is perhaps developmentally more appropriate and may make learning more meaningful for children who are struggling (Plummer & Graziano, 1987; Smith & Shepard, 1988). If these arguments are correct, adopting a policy of grade retention will benefit those promoted and those retained, thus boosting achievement overall. (p. 206)

COUNTERPOINT

▶ **No, retention is not effective.** After summarizing the arguments in favor of kindergarten retention, Hong and Raudenbush (2005) review the findings of almost a century of research. They note that even though there are a small number of studies that support the value of retention, the weight of the evidence indicates that it is not helpful and may even be harmful. Most research finds that grade retention is associated with poor long-term outcomes such as dropping out of school, higher arrest rates, fewer job opportunities, lower self-esteem (Jimerson, 1999; Jimerson, Anderson, & Whipple, 2002; Jimerson & Ferguson, 2007; Shepard & Smith, 1989). Lucy Barnard-Brak (2008) studied a national sample of 986 children who had been identified as having learning disabilities and concluded, "delayed kindergarten entrance was not associated with better academic achievement for children with learning disabilities across time" (p. 50).

The study by Hong and Raudenbush (2005) examined data on 11,843 kindergarten students who participated in a longitudinal study that followed them to the end of 1st grade. The researchers were able to compare retained and promoted students from schools that practice retention as well as promoted students from schools that practice social promotion. They found no evidence that retention improved either reading or mathematics achievement. In addition, retention did not seem to improve instruction in the 1st grade by making the class more similar in academic ability. After one year, the retained students were an average of one year behind, and evidence indicated that these children would have done better if promoted. The researchers concluded that retention "seemed to have constrained the learning potential for all but the highest-risk children" (p. 220). Another study that followed retained and promoted students for 4 years found some short-term advantages for retained students in social and behavioral skills, followed by long-term problems and vulnerabilities. The authors suggest that the "struggle-succeed-struggle" pattern may undermine academic motivation for retained students and interfere with peer relations (Wu, West, & Hughes, 2010).

Beware of Either/Or: Using Research for Children. No matter what, children who are having trouble should get help, whether they are promoted or retained. However, just covering the same material again in the same way won't solve the children's academic or social problems. As Jeannie Oakes (1999) has said, "No sensible person advocates social promotion as it is currently framed—simply passing incompetent children on to the next grade" (p. 8). The best approach may be to promote the children along with their peers, but to give them special remediation during the summer or over the next year (Mantzicopoulos & Morrison, 1992). In addition, because the inability to focus attention and self-regulate is an important aspect of readiness to learn (Blair, 2002), help should also focus on improving these skills as well. An even better approach would be to prevent the problems before they occur by providing extra resources in the early years (McCoy & Reynolds, 1999).

GUIDELINES

Using Any Grading System

Explain your grading policies to students early in the course and remind them of the policies regularly.
Examples

1. Give older students a handout describing the assignments, tests, grading criteria, and schedule.
2. Explain to younger students in a low-pressure manner how their work will be evaluated.

Base grades on clearly specified, reasonable standards.
Examples

1. Specify standards by developing a rubric with students—have anonymous examples of poor, good, and excellent work from previous classes.
2. Discuss workload and grading standards with more experienced teachers.
3. Give a few formative tests to get a sense of your students' abilities before you give a graded test.
4. Take tests yourself first to gauge the difficulty of the test and to estimate the time your students will need.

Base your grades on as much objective evidence as possible.
Examples

1. Plan in advance how and when you will test.
2. Keep a portfolio of student work. This may be useful in student or parent conferences.

Be sure students understand test directions.
Examples

1. Outline the directions on the board.
2. Ask several students to explain the directions.
3. Go over a sample question first.

Correct, return, and discuss test questions as soon as possible.
Examples

1. Have students who wrote good answers read their responses for the class; make sure they are not the same students each time.
2. Discuss why wrong answers, especially popular wrong choices, are incorrect.
3. As soon as students finish a test, give them the answers to questions and the page numbers where answers are discussed in the text.

As a rule, do not change a grade.
Examples

1. Make sure you can defend the grade in the first place.
2. DO change any clerical or calculation errors.

Guard against bias in grading.
Examples

1. Ask students to put their names on the backs of their papers.
2. Use an objective point system or model papers when grading essays.

Keep pupils informed of their standing in the class.
Examples

1. Write the distribution of scores on the board after tests.
2. Schedule periodic conferences to go over work from previous weeks.

may force students to choose between complex learning and a good grade. But when a grade reflects meaningful learning, working for a grade and working to learn become the same thing. As a teacher, you can use grades to motivate the kind of learning you intend students to achieve in your course. Finally, low grades generally do not encourage greater efforts. Students receiving low grades are more likely to withdraw, blame others, decide that the work is "dumb," or feel responsible for the low grade but helpless to make improvements. They give up on themselves or on school (Tomlinson, 2005b). Rather than assigning a failing grade, you might consider the work incomplete and give students support in revising or improving. Maintain high standards and give students a chance to reach them (Guskey, 2011; Guskey & Bailey, 2001).

Another effect on motivation that occurs in high schools is the race for valedictorian. Sometimes, students and families find clever ways to move ahead of the competition—but the strategies have little to do with learning. As Tom Guskey and Jane Bailey (2001) note, when a valedictorian wins by a 1/1,000 of decimal point, how meaningful is the learning behind the difference? Some high schools now name multiple valedictorians—as many as meet the highest standards of the school—because they believe that the educators' job is "not to select talent, but, rather, to develop talent" (Guskey & Bailey, 2001, p. 39).

The *Guidelines* give ideas for using any grading system in a fair and reasonable way.

Give students the benefit of the doubt. All measurement techniques involve error.
Examples

1. Unless there is a very good reason not to, give the higher grade in borderline cases.
2. If a large number of students miss the same question in the same way, revise the question for the future and consider throwing it out for that test.

Avoid reserving high grades and high praise for answers that conform to your ideas or to those in the textbook.
Examples

1. Give extra points for correct and creative answers.
2. Withhold your opinions until all sides of an issue have been explored.
3. Reinforce students for disagreeing in a rational, productive manner.
4. Give partial credit for partially correct answers.

Make sure each student has a reasonable chance to be successful, especially at the beginning of a new task.
Examples

1. Pretest students to make sure they have prerequisite abilities.
2. When appropriate, provide opportunities for students to retest to raise their grades, but make sure the retest is as difficult as the original.
3. Consider failing efforts as "incomplete" and encourage students to revise and improve.
4. Base grades more on work at the end of the unit; give ungraded work in the beginning of the unit.

Balance written and oral feedback.
Examples

1. Consider giving short, lively written comments with younger students and more extensive written comments with older students.
2. When the grade on a paper is lower than the student might have expected, be sure the reason for the lower grade is clear.
3. Tailor comments to the individual student's performance; avoid writing the same phrases over and over.
4. Note specific errors, possible reasons for errors, ideas for improvement, and work done well.

Make grades as meaningful as possible.
Examples

1. Tie grades to the mastery of important objectives.
2. Give ungraded assignments to encourage exploration.
3. Experiment with performances and portfolios.

Base grades on more than just one criterion.
Examples

1. Use essay questions as well as multiple-choice items on a test.
2. Grade oral reports and class participation.

For more thoughts about grading, see
http://teaching.berkeley.edu/bgd/grading.html

Source: General conferencing guidelines adapted from Problems in Middle and High School Teaching: A Handbook for Student Teachers and Beginning Teachers *(pp. 182–187), by A. M. Drayer, 1979, Boston: Allyn and Bacon. Copyright © 1979 by Allyn and Bacon. Adapted by permission of the author and publisher.*

Beyond Grading: Communicating with Families

No number or letter grade conveys the totality of a student's experience in a class or course. Students, families, and teachers sometimes become too focused on the end point—the grade. But communicating with families should involve more than just sending home grades. There are a number of ways to communicate with and report to families. Many teachers I know have a beginning-of-the-year newsletter or student handbook that communicates homework, behavior, and grading policies to families. Other options described by Guskey & Bailey (2001) are:

- Notes attached to report cards
- Phone calls, especially "Good News" calls
- School open houses
- Student-led conferences
- Portfolios or exhibits of student work
- Homework hotlines
- School or class Web pages
- Home visits

Conferences with parents or caregivers are often expected of teachers in elementary school and can be equally important in middle and high school. Clearly, the more skilled teachers are at communicating, the more effective they will be at conducting these conferences. Listening and problem-solving skills such as those discussed in Chapter 13 can be particularly important. When you are dealing with families or students who are angry or upset, make sure you really hear their concerns, not just their words. The atmosphere should be friendly and unrushed. Any observations about the student should be as factual as possible, based on observation or information from assignments. Information gained from a student or a parent/caregiver should be kept confidential.

One kind of information that will interest parents is their child's standardized test scores. In the next section we look at these tests.

STANDARDIZED TESTING

For as long as I can remember, educators and policy makers have been concerned about the test performance of American students. In 1983, the National Commission on Excellence in Education published *A Nation at Risk: The Imperative for Educational Reform*. According to this report, standardized test scores were at a 25-year low. More recently, politicians point to the Trends in International Mathematics and Science Study (TIMSS) data collected in 1995, 1999, 2003, and 2007 showing that the United States is behind many other developed countries in math and science test scores. These tests were repeated in Spring 2011—stay tuned for the results beginning in December of 2012 (http://timss.bc.edu/timss2011/index.html).

Part of the response to these test results has been more testing. In 2002, President Bush signed the No Child Left Behind Act that requires each state to create content standards in reading, mathematics, and science and assessments to measure student achievement linked to those standards (Linn, Baker, & Betebenner, 2002). Even though the Obama administration allowed exemptions and extensions to the strict requirements, the increase in testing and assessments will affect you, no matter what grade you teach. So teachers must be knowledgeable about testing. Understanding what standardized test scores really mean and how they can be used (or misused) is a good start. Let's look first at the results you will see from testing—the scores.

Types of Scores

STOP & THINK At your first parent conference, a mother and father are concerned about their child's percentile rank of 86. They say that they expect their child to "get close to 100 percent. We know she should be able to do that because her grade-equivalent score is half a year above her grade!" What would you say? Do they understand the meaning of these scores? •

To understand the scores from tests, you need to know some basics about different types of scores and what they tell you, but first you need to know some (easy) statistics.

MEASUREMENTS OF CENTRAL TENDENCY AND STANDARD DEVIATION. You have probably had a great deal of experience with means. A **mean** is simply the arithmetical average of a group of scores. To calculate the mean, you add the scores and divide the total by the number of scores in the distribution. The mean offers one way of measuring **central tendency**, the score that is typical or representative of the whole distribution of scores. Very high or very low scores affect the mean. Two other measures of central tendency are the median and the mode. The **median** is the middle score in a ranked list of scores, the point at which half the scores are larger and half are smaller. When there are a few very high or low scores, the median may be a better representative of the central tendency of a group than the mean. The **mode** is the score that occurs most often.

The measure of central tendency gives a score that is representative of the group of scores, but it does not tell you anything about how the scores are distributed. Two groups of scores may both have a mean of 50, but be alike in no other way. One group might contain the scores 50, 45, 55, 55, 45, 50, 50; the other group might contain the scores 100, 0, 50, 90, 10, 50, 50. In both cases, the mean, median, and mode are all 50, but the distributions are quite different.

The **standard deviation** is a measure of how widely the scores vary from the mean. The larger the standard deviation, the more spread out the scores are in the distribution. The smaller the standard deviation, the more the scores are clustered around the mean.

Connect and Extend to PRAXIS II™

Concepts of Standardized Testing (II, C5)
Be able to define norm groups, measures of central tendency, standard deviation, normal distribution, reliability, and validity, and explain their roles in standardized tests.

Mean Arithmetical average.

Central tendency Typical score for a group of scores.

Median Middle score in a group of scores.

Mode Most frequently occurring score.

Standard deviation Measure of how widely scores vary from the mean.

For example, in the distribution 50, 45, 55, 55, 45, 50, 50, the standard deviation is much smaller than in the distribution 100, 0, 50, 90, 10, 50, 50. Another way of saying this is that distributions with very small standard deviations have less **variability** in the scores.

Knowing the mean and the standard deviation of a group of scores gives you a better picture of the meaning of an individual score. For example, suppose you received a score of 78 on a test. You would be very pleased with the score if the mean of the test were 70 and the standard deviation were 4. In this case, your score would be 2 standard deviations above the mean, a score well above average.

Consider the difference if the mean of the test had remained at 70, but the standard deviation had been 20. In the second case, your score of 78 would be less than 1 standard deviation from the mean. You would be much closer to the middle of the group, with a score above average, but not high. Knowing the standard deviation tells you much more than simply knowing the **range** of scores. No matter how the majority scored on the tests, one or two students may do very well or very poorly and thus make the range very large.

THE NORMAL DISTRIBUTION.   Standard deviations are very useful in understanding test results. They are especially helpful if the results of the tests form a **normal distribution**. You may have encountered the normal distribution before. It is the bell-shaped curve, the most famous frequency distribution because it describes many naturally occurring physical and social phenomena. Many scores fall in the middle, giving the curve its bell appearance. You find fewer and fewer scores as you look out toward the end points, or *tails*, of the distribution. The normal distribution has been thoroughly analyzed by statisticians. The mean of a normal distribution is also its midpoint. Half the scores are above the mean, and half are below it. In a normal distribution, the mean, median, and mode are all the same point.

Another convenient property of the normal distribution is that the percentage of scores falling within each area of the curve is known, as you can see in Figure 15.3. A person scoring within 1 standard deviation of the mean obviously has company. Many scores pile up here. In fact, 68% of all scores are located in the area from 1 standard deviation below to 1 standard deviation above the mean. About 16% of the scores are higher than 1 standard deviation above the mean. Of this higher group, only 2% are higher than 2 standard deviations above the mean. Similarly, only about 16% of the scores are less than 1 standard deviation below the mean, and of that group only about 2% are lower than 2 standard deviations below the mean. At 2 standard deviations from the mean in either direction, the scorer has left the pack.

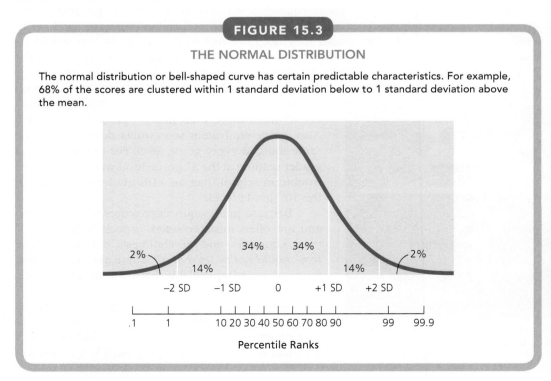

FIGURE 15.3

THE NORMAL DISTRIBUTION

The normal distribution or bell-shaped curve has certain predictable characteristics. For example, 68% of the scores are clustered within 1 standard deviation below to 1 standard deviation above the mean.

Percentile Ranks

Variability Degree of difference or deviation from mean.

Range Distance between the highest and the lowest scores in a group.

Normal distribution The most commonly occurring distribution, in which scores are distributed evenly around the mean.

The SAT college entrance exam is one example of a normal distribution. The mean of the SAT is 500 and the standard deviation is 100. If you know people who made scores of 700, you know they did very well. Only about 2% of the people who take the test do that well, because only 2% of the scores are better than 2 standard deviations above the mean in a normal distribution. Your score of 78 would be in the top 2% on a test with a mean of 70 and a standard deviation of 4.

Now we are ready to look at different kinds of test scores.

PERCENTILE RANK SCORES.

Ranking is the basis for one very useful kind of score reported on standardized tests, a **percentile rank** score. In percentile ranking, each student's *raw score* (actual number correct) is compared with the raw scores of the students in the *norm group* (comparison group). The percentile rank shows the percentage of students in the norm group that scored at or below a particular raw score. If a student's score were the same as or better than three-quarters of the students in the norm group, the student would score in the *75th percentile* or have a percentile rank of 75. You can see that this does not mean that the student had a raw score of 75 correct answers or even that the student answered 75% of the questions correctly. Rather, the 75 refers to the percentage of people in the norm group whose scores on the test were equal to or below this student's score. A percentile rank of 50 means that a student has scored as well as or better than 50% of the norm group and has achieved an average score.

There is one caution in interpreting percentile scores. Differences in percentile ranks do not mean the same thing in terms of raw score points in the middle of the scale as they do at the fringes. For example, the difference between the 50th and 60th percentile might be just 2 raw points, whereas the difference on the same test between the 90th and 99th percentile could be about 10 points. So a few answers right or wrong can make a bigger difference in percentile scores if you are near the middle.

GRADE-EQUIVALENT SCORES.

Grade-equivalent scores are generally obtained from separate norm groups for each grade level. The average of the scores of all the 10th graders in the norm group defines the 10th grade equivalent score. Suppose the raw-score average of the 10th grade norm group is 38. Any student who attains a raw score of 38 on that test will be assigned a grade-equivalent score of 10th grade. Grade-equivalent scores are generally listed in numbers such as 8.3, 4.5, 7.6, 11.5, and so on. The whole number gives the grade. The decimals stand for tenths of a year, but they are usually interpreted as months.

Suppose a student with the grade-equivalent score of 10 is a 7th grader. Should this student be promoted immediately? Probably not. Different forms of tests are used at different grade levels, so the 7th grader may not have had to answer items that would be given to 10th graders. The high score may represent superior mastery of material at the 7th grade level rather than a capacity for doing advanced work. Even though an average 10th grader could do as well as our 7th grader on this particular test, the 10th grader would certainly know much more than this 7th grade test covered. Also, grade-equivalent score units do not mean the same thing at every grade level. For example, a 2nd grader reading at the 1st grade level would have more trouble in school than an 11th grader who reads at the 10th grade level.

Because grade-equivalent scores are misleading and are often misinterpreted, especially by parents, most educators and psychologists strongly believe *they should not be used at all*. There are several other forms of reporting available that are more appropriate.

STANDARD SCORES.

As you may remember, one problem with percentile ranks is the difficulty in making comparisons among ranks. A discrepancy of a certain number of raw-score points has a different

Percentile rank Percentage of those in the norming sample who scored at or below an individual's score.

Grade-equivalent score Measure of grade level based on comparison with norming samples from each grade.

STANDARDIZED TESTS You can tell these students are concentrating. What will their scores tell us? What do they mean?

meaning at different places on the scale. With standard scores, on the other hand, a difference of 10 points is the same everywhere on the scale.

Standard scores are based on the standard deviation. A very common standard score is called the **z score**. A *z* score tells how many standard deviations above or below the average a raw score is. In the example described earlier, in which you were fortunate enough to get a 78 on a test where the mean was 70 and the standard deviation was 4, your *z* score would be +2, or 2 standard deviations above the mean. If a person were to score 64 on this test, the score would be 1.5 standard deviation units below the mean, and the *z* score would be −1.5. A *z* score of 0 would be no standard deviations above the mean—in other words, right on the mean. Measurements similar to *z* scores are used when you take a bone density test. Your score will compare your bone density to that of a healthy 30-year-old. If your score is below −1, you are moving toward osteoporosis. Below −2, you are there.

To calculate the *z* score for a given raw score, subtract the mean from the raw score and divide the difference by the standard deviation. The formula is:

$$z = \frac{\text{Raw Score} - \text{Mean}}{\text{Standard Deviation}}$$

Because it is often inconvenient to use negative numbers, other standard scores have been devised to eliminate this difficulty. The **T score** has a mean of 50 and uses a standard deviation of 10. Thus, a *T* score of 50 indicates average performance. If you multiply the *z* score by 10 (which eliminates the decimal) and add 50 (which gets rid of the negative number), you get the equivalent *T* score as the answer. The person whose *z* score was −1.5 would have a *T* score of 35.

First multiply the z score by 10:   −1.5 × 10 = −15
Then add 50:   −15 + 50 = 35

As you saw, the scoring of the SAT test is based on a similar procedure, with a mean score set at 500, and a standard deviation of 100. Most IQ tests have a mean score of 100 and a standard deviation of 15. Different states have different ways of determining standards-based scores. For example, scale scores for each grade and subject on the California Standards Tests (CSTs) range from 150 to 600 (http://star.cde.ca.gov/star2009/help_scoreexplanations.asp).

Before we leave this section on types of scores, we should mention one other widely used method. **Stanine scores** (the name comes from "standard nine") are standard scores. There are only nine possible scores on the stanine scale, the whole numbers 1 through 9. The mean is 5, and the standard deviation is 2. Each unit from 2 to 8 is equal to half a standard deviation.

Stanine scores provide a method of considering a student's rank, because each of the nine scores includes a specific range of percentile scores in the normal distribution. For example, a stanine score of 1 is assigned to the bottom 4% of scores in a distribution. A stanine of 2 is assigned to the next 7%. Of course, some raw scores in this 7% range are better than others, but they all get a stanine score of 2.

Each stanine score represents a wide range of raw scores. This has the advantage of encouraging teachers and parents to view a student's score in more general terms instead of making fine distinctions based on a few points. Figure 15.4 on the next page compares the four types of standard scores we have considered, showing how each would fall on a normal distribution curve.

Interpreting Standardized Test Reports

STOP & THINK Look at the test printout in Figure 15.5. on page 577. What are this student's strengths and weaknesses? How do you know? •

What specific information can teachers expect from achievement test results? Test publishers usually provide individual profiles for each student, showing scores on each subtest. Figure 15.5 is an example of a Student Report for a 4th grader, Sally Valenzuela, on the *Stanford Achievement Test, 10th Edition*. Note that the Student Report has three sections.

Standard scores Scores based on the standard deviation.

z score Standard score indicating the number of standard deviations above or below the mean.

T score Standard score with a mean of 50 and a standard deviation of 10.

Stanine scores Whole number scores from 1 to 9, each representing a wide range of raw scores.

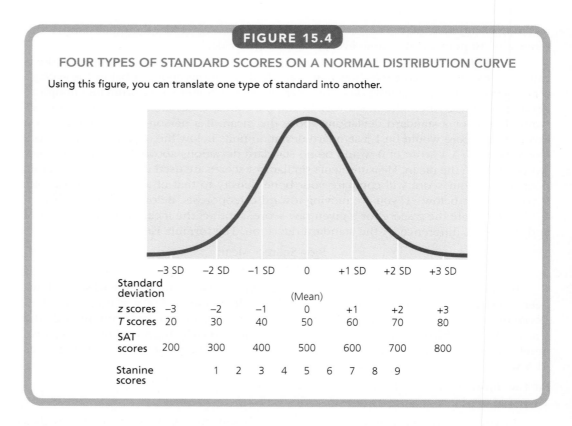

FIGURE 15.4

FOUR TYPES OF STANDARD SCORES ON A NORMAL DISTRIBUTION CURVE

Using this figure, you can translate one type of standard into another.

	−3 SD	−2 SD	−1 SD	0	+1 SD	+2 SD	+3 SD
Standard deviation				(Mean)			
z scores	−3	−2	−1	0	+1	+2	+3
T scores	20	30	40	50	60	70	80
SAT scores	200	300	400	500	600	700	800
Stanine scores	1	2 3	4	5	6	7 8	9

Connect and Extend to PRAXIS II™

Interpreting Achievement Tests (II, C4)
Accurate information from the teacher is essential for students' academic progress. The ERIC Digest *Explaining Test Results to Parents* (http://www.ericdigests.org/pre-9210/parents.htm) will help with this task. See Chapter 6 for a discussion of how to use praise effectively. These guidelines apply to written feedback as well.

The first, (About This Student's Performance), is a brief narrative explanation that may include a Lexile Measure™, which is computed from the Reading Comprehension score and helps teachers identify Sally's reading level in order to select appropriate texts.

The second section (Subtests and Totals) attempts to paint a picture of the student's achievement in *Reading, Mathematics, Language, Spelling, Science, Social Science, Listening,* and *Thinking Skills.* That section also includes total scores on the battery of tests and scores on the Otis-Lennon School Ability test—a kind of group IQ or scholastic aptitude test. Some of the subtests are further divided into more specific assessments. For example, *Reading* is broken down into "word study skills," "reading vocabulary," and "reading comprehension." Next to each subtest are several different ways of reporting Sally's score. The school decides which scores are reported, based on a list of possible reporting formats. This school chose the following types of scores:

Number Correct: Under the second column is the number of items that Sally answered correctly for that subtest (the total number of items on the subtest is in the first column).

Scale Score: This is basic score used to derive all the other scores, sometimes called a *growth score* because it describes growth in achievement that typically occurs as students move through the grades. For example, the average score for 3rd graders might be 585, whereas the average score for 10th graders might be 714 on tests with possible scores that range from 0 to 1000 across the entire K–12 grades. Often, the difficulty of items is included in calculating scale scores. Schools are increasingly using this score because they can compare across years, classes, or schools in the district (Popham, 2005a).

National PR-S (National Percentile Rank and Stanine): This score tells us where Sally stands in relation to students at her grade level across the country in terms of percentile rank (percent with the same score or lower) and stanine.

National NCE (Normal Curve Equivalent): This is a standard score derived from the percentile rank, with a range of 1 to 99, a mean of 50, and a standard deviation of 21.

Grade Equivalent Score: This indicates that Sally's scaled score is the same as an average student in the indicated grade and month of school. Beware of the problems with grade-equivalent scores described earlier.

AAC (Achievement/Ability Comparison) Range: The ACC score compares Sally's achievement on each subtest to a norm group of other students who have her same ability as measured by the Otis-Lennon School Ability test. The ACC range categorizes Sally's ACC score as HIGH, MIDDLE, or LOW. You can see that Sally is in the middle on most of the subtests, so her achievement is in the middle compared to students with abilities similar to hers.

National Grade Percentile Bands: The range of national percentile scores in which Sally's true score is likely to fall. You may remember from our discussion of true scores that this range, or confidence interval, is determined by adding and subtracting the standard error of the test from Sally's actual score. Chances are high that Sally's true score is within this range. Bands that do not overlap indicate likely differences in achievement.

The bottom of Figure 15.5 (Clusters) breaks Sally's subtests down into even more specific skills. For each skill we see the number of questions possible to answer (NP), the number Sally attempted (NA), and the number she got correct (NC). The check marks beside the skills indicate if she is average, above average, or below average in each. Notice that some skills are assessed with only a few (3 to 8) questions. Remember that fewer items means less reliability.

FIGURE 15.5

A TYPICAL SCORE REPORT

A sample test score report, with no actual test data used.

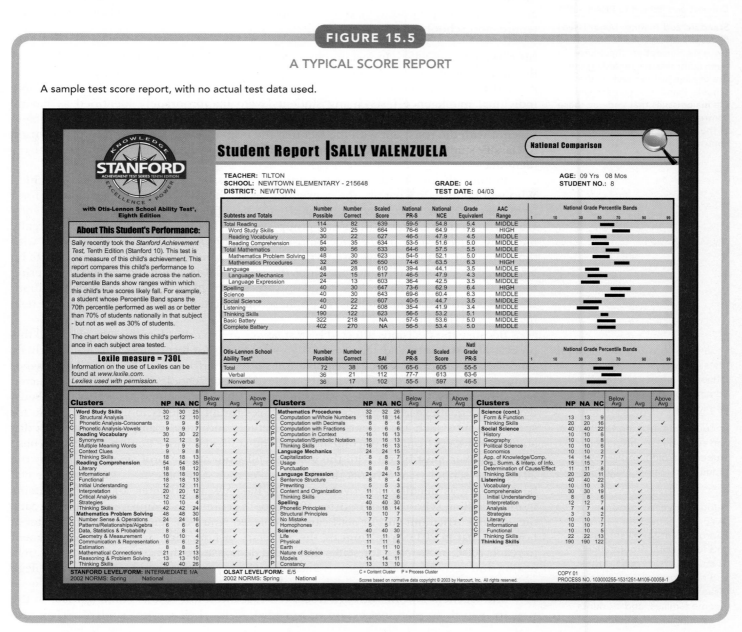

DISCUSSING TEST RESULTS WITH FAMILIES. Teachers often have formal conferences and informal talks with parents or caregivers. Often the topic is testing results. At times, you will be expected to explain or describe test results to your students' families. The *Family and Community Partnerships Guidelines* give some ideas.

Accountability and High-Stakes Testing

STOP & THINK How has standardized testing affected your life so far? What opportunities have been opened or closed to you based on test scores? Was the process fair? •

Every day, there are many decisions made about individuals that are based on the results of tests. Should Russell be issued a driver's license? How many and which students from the 8th grade would benefit from an accelerated program in science? Who needs extra tutoring? Who will be admitted to college or professional school? Test scores may affect "admission" to 1st grade, promotion from one grade to the next, high school graduation, access to special programs, placement in special education classes, teacher licensure and tenure, and school funding.

MAKING DECISIONS. In making these decisions, it is important to distinguish between the *quality* of the test itself and the way the test is *used*. Even the best assessments can be, and have been, misused. Years ago, for example, using otherwise valid and reliable individual intelligence tests, many students were inappropriately identified as having mental retardation, the term used at that time (Snapp & Woolfolk, 1973). The problem was not with the tests, but with the fact that the test score was the only information used to classify students. Much more information is always needed to make this type of placement decision.

Behind all the statistics and terminology are issues related to values and ethics. Who will be tested? What are the consequences of choosing one test over another for a particular purpose with a given group? What is the effect of the testing on the students? How will the test scores of minority-group students be interpreted? What do we really mean by *intelligence, competence,* and *scholastic aptitude*? Do our views agree with those implied by the tests we use to measure these constructs? How will test results be integrated with other information about the individual to make judgments? Answering these questions requires choices based on values, as well as accurate information about what tests can and cannot tell us. Keep these values issues in mind as we examine testing uses and decisions.

Because the decisions affected by test scores are so critical, many educators call this process **high-stakes testing**. One of the high-stakes uses for test results is to hold teachers, schools, and administrators **accountable** for student performance. For example, teacher bonuses might be tied to their students' achievement or schools' funding may be affected by testing results. One of the provisions in the No Child Left Behind Act is that states must develop **adequate yearly progress (AYP)** objectives for all students in general and also for specific groups such as students from major ethnic and racial groups, students with disabilities, students from low-income families, and students whose English is limited. These AYP objectives must be set with the goal that all students are proficient or better by the 2013–2014 school year. Schools that fail to meet their AYP objectives for two years will be identified as needing improvement (Linn, Baker, & Betebenner, 2002). The students in these "failing schools" can transfer. If a school's scores don't improve after three years, the school curriculum and/or staff can be replaced. You may remember from Chapter 1, however, that in 2011 Arne Duncan, the Secretary of Education, waived the requirement to reach 100% proficiency for states that could demonstrate they have adopted their own testing and accountability programs and are making progress toward the goal of college or career readiness for all their high school graduates (Dillion, 2011).

The teachers I work with are frustrated that often test results come too late in the year to help them plan instruction or remediation for their current students. They also

Connect and Extend to PRAXIS II™

Standardized Testing: Major Issues (II, C5)
Since their inception, there have been controversies regarding the use of standardized tests in the schools. Familiarize yourself with the major issues that underlie these controversies. Explain the positions of the different camps in these controversies.

High-stakes testing Standardized tests whose results have powerful influences when used by school administrators, other officials, or employers to make decisions.

Accountable Making teachers and schools responsible for student learning, usually by monitoring learning with high-stakes tests.

Adequate yearly progress (AYP) Objectives for yearly improvement for all students and for specific groups such as students from major ethnic and racial groups, students with disabilities, students from low-income families, and students whose English is limited.

GUIDELINES — FAMILY AND COMMUNITY PARTNERSHIPS

Conferences and Explaining Test Results

GENERAL CONFERENCING GUIDELINES

Decide on a few clear goals for the conference.
Examples
Gathering information about the student to help in your instruction
Explaining grades or test results
Letting parents know what is coming during the next unit or marking period
Soliciting help from parents
Making suggestions for use at home

Begin and end with a positive statement.
Examples
"Jacob is a natural leader."
"Eve really enjoys the science center."
"Yesim is really supportive when other students are upset."
"Ashanti's sense of humor keeps the class positive."

Listen actively.
Examples
Accept the emotions of parents or caregivers. Don't try to talk them out of what they feel.
"You seem to feel frustrated when Lee doesn't do his homework."

Respect family members' time and their concern about their child—Establish a partnership.
Examples
Speak plainly, briefly, and avoid jargon.
Be tactful, but don't avoid talking about tough issues.
Ask families to follow through on class goals at home: "Ask Leona for her homework checklist and help her keep it up to date. I will do the same at school."

Learn from the family members.
Examples
What are the students' strengths as revealed in hobbies or extracurricular activities?
What are the students' interests?

Follow-up and follow through.
Examples
Send a brief note thanking the family members for attending.
Share student successes through notes or e-mail messages.
Keep families informed before problems develop.

EXPLAINING AND USING TEST RESULTS

Explain in nontechnical terms, what each type of score on the test report means and why tests are not "perfect."
Examples
1. If the test is norm-referenced, know what the comparison group was (National? State? Local district?). Explain that the child's score shows how he or she performed in relation to the other students in the comparison group.
2. If the test is criterion-referenced, explain that the scores show how well their child performs specific tasks such as word problems or reading comprehension.
3. Encourage parents to think of the score not as a single point, but as a range or band that includes the score.
4. Ignore small differences between scores.

For norm-referenced tests, use percentile scores. They are the easiest to understand.
Examples
1. Percentile scores tell what percent of students in the comparison group made the same score or lower—higher percentiles are better and 99 is as high as you can get: 50 is average.
2. Percentile scores do not tell the "percent correct," so scores that would be bad on a classroom test (say 65% to 75% or so) often are above average—even good—as percentile scores.

Avoid using grade-equivalent scores.
Examples
1. If parents want to focus on the "grade level" of their child, tell them that high grade-equivalent scores reflect a thorough understanding of the current grade level and NOT the capacity to do higher grade-level work.
2. Tell parents that the same grade-equivalent score has different meanings in different subjects—reading versus mathematics, for example.

Source: Based on ideas from The Successful Classroom: Management Strategies for Regular and Special Education Teachers by D. P. Fromberg & M. Driscoll. Published by Teachers College, Columbia University; Scholastic. (2011). Planning for parent conferences, http://www2.scholastic.com/browse/article.jsp?id=4194; and Kennedy, K. (2009). Teacher tips: Explaining achievement test results to parents,http://www.helium.com/items/1636565-parents-and-achievement-tests

For more help explaining tests to parents, see
http://pareonline.net/getvn.asp?v=1&n=1

are troubled by the amount of time that testing takes—to prepare for the tests and to give them. They complain that the tests cover material that their curriculum does not include. Are they right?

DOCUMENTED PROBLEMS WITH HIGH-STAKES TESTING. When so much rides on the results of a test, you would assume that the test actually measured what had been taught. In the past, this match has been a problem. Recently, the overlap between what is taught and what is tested has been improving, but it still makes sense to be aware of possible mismatches.

What about time? Studies have found that in some states, 80% of the elementary schools spend about 20% of their instructional time preparing for the end-of-grade tests (Abrams & Madaus, 2003). Studies of the actual high-stakes tests in action show other troubling consequences. Testing narrows the curriculum. In fact, after examining the results of years of testing, Lisa Abrams and George Madaus (2003) concluded "In every setting where a high-stakes test operates, the exam content eventually defines the curriculum" (p. 32). For example, using the Texas Assessment of Academic Skills has led to curriculum changes that overemphasize what is tested and neglect other areas. In addition, it seems that the test of mathematics is also a test of reading. Students with poor reading ability have trouble with the math test, especially if their first language is not English.

Another unintended consequence of the early-warning testing in elementary school is to "push out" students who believe they are going to fail the high school graduation test. If they won't graduate anyway, they see no point in continuing to attend school (McNeil & Valenzuela, 2000). For example, in the 2000–2001 school year, about one-third of the English Language Learners dropped out of high school in New York. The main reason given was their inability to pass the required Regents Exam (Medina, 2002). No matter how good the test, some uses of high-stakes tests are not appropriate. Table 15.5 describes some of them.

USING HIGH-STAKES TESTING WELL. To be valuable, testing programs must have a number of characteristics. Of course, the tests used must be reliable, valid for the purposes used, and free of bias. In addition, the testing program must:

1. Match the content standards of the district—this is a vital part of validity.
2. Be part of the larger assessment plan. No individual test provides all the necessary information about student achievement. It is critical that schools avoid making pass/fail decisions based on a single test.
3. Test complex thinking, not just skills and factual knowledge.
4. Provide alternate assessment strategies for students with identifiable disabilities.
5. Provide opportunities for retesting when the stakes are high.
6. Include all students in the testing, but also provide informative reports of the results that make the students' situations clear if they have special challenges or circumstances such as disabilities.
7. Provide appropriate remediation when students fail.
8. Make sure all students taking the test have adequate opportunities to learn the material being tested.
9. Take into account the student's language. Students who have difficulty reading or writing in English will not perform well on tests that require English proficiency.
10. Use test results for children, not against them (Haladyna, 2002).

This is important, so I will repeat it: High-stakes standardized **achievement tests** must be chosen so that the items on the test actually measure knowledge gained in the classes. Also, students must have the necessary skills to take the test. If students score low on a science test not because they lack knowledge about science, but because they have difficulty reading the questions, don't speak English fluently, or have too little time to finish, then the test is not a valid measure of science achievement for those students.

Connect and Extend to PRAXIS II™

Alternatives to Standardized Testing (II, C1)
For an overview of the major forms of authentic testing, go to Teachervision.com (http://www.teachervision.com/lesson-plans/lesson-6385.html).

Achievement tests Standardized tests measuring how much students have learned in a given content area.

TABLE 15.5 • **Inappropriate Uses for High-Stakes Test Results**

Beware of some uses for standardized test results. Tests were not designed for these purposes.

Pass/Fail Decisions	In order to deny students graduation from any grade, there must be strong evidence that the test used is valid, reliable, and free of bias. Some tests, for example, the *Texas Assessment of Academic Skills* (TAAS), have been challenged in the courts and found to meet these standards, but not all tests are good enough to make pass/fail decisions.
State-to-State Comparisons	You cannot really compare states using standardized test scores. States do not have the same curriculum, tests, resources, or challenges. If comparisons are made, they usually tell us what we already know—some states have more funding for schools and families with higher incomes or education levels.
Evaluation of Teachers or Schools	Many influences on test scores—family and community resources—are outside the control of teachers and schools. Often students move from school to school, so many students taking a test in spring may have been in the school only for a few weeks.
Identifying Where to Buy a House	Generally speaking, the schools with the highest test scores are in the neighborhoods where families have the highest levels of education and income. They may not be the "best schools" in terms of teaching, programs, or leadership, but they are the schools lucky enough to have the "right" students.

Source: From Essentials of Standardized Achievement Testing: Validity and Accountability. *T. H. Haladyna, Published by Allyn and Bacon, Boston, MA. Copyright © 2002 by Pearson Education. Adapted by permission of the publisher.*

Reaching Every Student: Helping Students with Disabilities Prepare for High-Stakes Tests

Erik Carter and his colleagues (2005) tested a procedure for preparing students with learning disabilities, mild intellectual disabilities, and language impairments for a high-stakes state test The students were ages 15 to 19; over half were African American males and all had IEPs (Individual Educational Programs—see Chapter 4) to guide their education. None had passed the state-required achievement tests. Over six class periods, an instructor taught the students strategies such as filling in bubbles on answer sheets completely, sorting problems by difficulty and doing the easy ones first, using rounding to estimate answers in math, identifying exactly what the question is asking by underlining key words and phrases, and strategies for eliminating alternatives that have redundant information or extreme qualifiers.

The good news is that after completing the preparation program, students improved their scores significantly on the tests. But the bad news is that the increases were not large enough to bring most of the students to the passing level. The authors recommend that preparation for testing should occur much earlier for students with disabilities. At an average age of 16, the students in this study already were discouraged. The strategies taught should be closely aligned with the specific types of problems that the students will encounter on the test and should be embedded in good content instruction. Finally, these

GUIDELINES

Preparing Yourself and Your Students for Testing

ADVICE FOR TEACHERS

Make sure the test actually covers the content of the unit of study.
Examples

1. Compare test questions to course objectives. Make sure that there is good overlap.
2. Check to see if the test is long enough to cover all important topics.
3. Find out if there are any difficulties your students experience with the test, such as not enough time, too difficult a level of reading, and so on. If there are, discuss these problems with appropriate school personnel.

Make sure students know how to use all the test materials.
Examples

1. Several days before the testing, do a few practice questions with a similar format.
2. Demonstrate the use of the answer sheets, especially computer-scored answer sheets.
3. Check with new students, shy students, slower students, and students who have difficulty reading to make sure they understand the questions.
4. Make sure students know if and when guessing is appropriate.

Follow instructions for administering the test exactly.
Examples

1. Practice giving the test before you actually use it.
2. Follow the time limits exactly.

Make students as comfortable as possible during testing.
Examples

1. Do not create anxiety by making the test seem like the most important event of the year.
2. Help the class relax before beginning the test, perhaps by telling a joke or having everyone take a few deep breaths. Don't be tense yourself!
3. Make sure the room is quiet.
4. Discourage cheating by monitoring the room. Don't become absorbed in your own paperwork.

ADVICE FOR STUDENTS

Use the night before the test effectively.
Examples

1. Study the night before the exam, ending with a final look at a summary of the key points, concepts, and relationships.
2. Get a good night's sleep. If you know you generally have trouble sleeping the night before an exam, try getting extra sleep on several previous nights.

Set the situation so you can concentrate on the test.
Examples

1. Give yourself plenty of time to eat and get to the exam room.
2. Don't sit near a friend. It may make concentration difficult. If your friend leaves early, you may be tempted to do so, too.

Make sure you know what the test is asking.
Examples

1. Read the directions carefully. If you are unsure, ask the instructor or proctor for clarification.
2. Read each question carefully to spot tricky words, such as *not, except, all of the following but one.*
3. On an essay test, read every question first, so you know the size of the job ahead of you and can make informed decisions about how much time to spend on each question.
4. On a multiple-choice test, read every alternative, even if an early one seems right.

Use time effectively.
Examples

1. Begin working right away and move as rapidly as possible while your energy is high.
2. Do the easy questions first.
3. Don't get stuck on one question. If you are stumped, mark the question so you can return to it easily later, and go on to questions you can answer more quickly.
4. On a multiple-choice test, if you know you will not have time to finish, fill in all the remaining questions with the same letter if there is no penalty for guessing.
5. If you are running out of time on an essay test, do not leave any questions blank. Briefly outline a few key points to show the instructor you knew the answer but needed more time.

Know when to guess on multiple-choice or true-false tests.
Examples

1. Always guess when only right answers are scored.
2. Always guess when you can eliminate some of the alternatives.
3. Don't guess if there is a penalty for guessing, unless you can confidently eliminate at least one alternative.
4. Are correct answers always longer? shorter? in the middle? more likely to be one letter? more often true than false?
5. Does the grammar give the right answer away or eliminate any alternatives?

Check your work.
Examples

1. Even if you can't stand to look at the test another minute, reread each question to make sure you answered the way you intended.

2. If you are using a machine-scored answer sheet, check occasionally to be sure the number of the question you are answering corresponds to the number of the answer on the sheet.

On essay tests, answer as directly as possible.
Examples

1. Avoid flowery introductions. Answer the question in the first sentence and then elaborate.
2. Don't save your best ideas till last. Give them early in the answer.
3. Unless the instructor requires complete sentences, consider listing points, arguments, and so on by number in your answer. It will help you organize your thoughts and concentrate on the important aspects of the answer.

Learn from the testing experience.
Examples

1. Pay attention when the teacher reviews the answers. You can learn from your mistakes, and the same question may reappear in a later test.
2. Notice if you are having trouble with a particular kind of item; adjust your study approach next time to handle this type of item better.

For more test-taking strategies see http://www.eop.mu.edu/study/ or http://www.testtakingtips.com/

---

students often are anxious about the negative consequences of failing—not receiving a regular diploma, or no access to college or trade school. The best way to deal with this anxiety is to better equip the students with the academic skills they will need to succeed (Carter et al., 2005). The *Guidelines* should help you and all your students prepare for high-stakes testing.

Lessons for Teachers: Quality Assessment

Quality teaching and quality assessment share the same basic principles, and these principles hold for all students. Carol Tomlinson (2005b, pp. 265–266) suggests that good instruction and good grading both depend on a teacher who:

• Is aware of and responds to student differences.
• Specifies clear learning outcomes.
• Uses pretests and formative assessments to monitor student progress toward learning goals.
• Adapts instruction in a variety of ways to ensure, as much as possible, that each student continues to progress.
• Makes sure students know the criteria for success on summative assessments that are tightly aligned to the stated learning goals.
• Provides varied forms of assessment to ensure that students have an unobstructed opportunity to express what they have learned.

▼ SUMMARY

Basics of Assessment (pp. 548–554)

Distinguish between measurement and assessment. Measurement is the description of an event or characteristic using numbers. Assessment includes measurement, but is broader because it includes all kinds of ways to sample and observe students' skills, knowledge, and abilities.

Distinguish between formative and summative assessment. In the classroom, assessment may be formative (ungraded, diagnostic) or summative (graded). Formative assessment helps form instruction, and summative assessment summarizes students' accomplishments.

Distinguish between norm-referenced and criterion-referenced tests. In norm-referenced tests, a student's performance is compared to the average performance of others. In criterion-referenced tests, scores are compared to a pre-established standard. Norm-referenced tests cover a wide range of general objectives. However, results of norm-referenced tests do not tell whether students are ready for advanced material, and they are not appropriate for affective and psychomotor objectives. Criterion-referenced tests measure the mastery of very specific objectives.

What is test reliability? Some tests are more reliable than others; that is, they yield more stable and consistent estimates. Care must be taken in the interpretation of test results. Each test is only a sample of a student's performance on a given day. The score is only an estimate of a student's hypothetical true score. The standard error of measurement takes into account the possibility for error and is one index of test reliability.

What is test validity? The most important consideration about a test is the validity of the decisions and judgments that are based on the test results. Evidence of validity can be related to content, criterion, or construct. Construct-related evidence for validity is the broadest category and encompasses the other two categories of content and criterion. Tests must be reliable to be valid, but reliability does not guarantee validity.

What is absence of bias? Tests must be free of assessment bias. Bias occurs when tests include material that offends or unfairly penalizes a group of students because of the students' gender, SES, race, or ethnicity. Culture-fair tests have not proved to solve the problem of assessment bias.

Classroom Assessment: Testing (pp. 554–558)

How can testing support learning? Learning is supported by frequent testing using cumulative questions that ask students to apply and integrate knowledge. With the goals of assessment in mind, teachers are in a better position to design their own tests or evaluate the tests provided by textbook publishers.

Describe two kinds of traditional testing. Two traditional formats for testing are the objective test and the essay test. Objective tests, which can include multiple-choice, true/false, fill-in, and matching items, should be written with specific guidelines in mind. Writing and scoring essay questions requires careful planning, in addition to criteria to discourage bias in scoring.

Authentic Classroom Assessments (pp. 558–566)

What is authentic assessment? Critics of traditional testing believe that teachers should use authentic tests and other authentic assessment procedures. Authentic assessment requires students to perform tasks and solve problems that are similar to the real-life performances that will be expected of them outside of school.

Describe portfolios and exhibitions. Portfolios and exhibitions are two examples of authentic assessment. A portfolio is a collection of the student's work, sometimes chosen to represent growth or improvement or sometimes featuring "best work." Exhibitions are public performances of the student's understandings. With portfolios and exhibitions, there is an emphasis on performing real-life tasks in meaningful contexts.

What are the issues of reliability, validity, and equity with portfolios and performance assessment? Using authentic assessments does not guarantee reliability, validity, and equity (absence of bias). Using rubrics is one way to make assessment more reliable and valid. But the results from assessment based on rubrics may not predict performance on related tasks. Also, rater bias based on the appearance, speech, or behavior of minority-group students or a lack of resources may place minority-group students at a disadvantage in performance assessments or projects.

How can teachers use informal assessments? Informal assessments are ungraded (formative) assessments that gather information from multiple sources to help teachers make decisions. Some examples of informal assessment are student observations and checklists, questioning, and student self-assessment. Journals are very flexible and widely used informal assessments. Students usually have personal or group journals and write in them on a regular basis.

Grading (pp. 566–572)

Describe two kinds of grading. Grading can be either norm-referenced or criterion-referenced. One popular norm-referenced system is grading on the curve, based on a ranking of students in relation to the average performance level. This is not recommended. Criterion-referenced report cards usually indicate how well the individual student has met each of several objectives.

How can failure support learning? Students need experience in coping with failure, so standards must be high enough to encourage effort. Occasional failure can be positive if appropriate feedback is provided. Students who never learn how to cope with failure and still persist in learning may give up quickly when their first efforts are unsuccessful.

Which is better, "social promotion" or being "held back"? Simply retaining or promoting a student who is having difficulty will not guarantee that the student will learn. Unless the student is very young or emotionally immature compared to others in the class, the best approach may be to promote, but provide extra support such as tutoring or summer school sessions. Differentiated instruction could prevent problems.

Can grades promote learning and motivation? Written or oral feedback that includes specific comments on errors or faulty strategies, but that balances this criticism with suggestions about how to improve along with comments on the positive aspects of the work, increases learning. Grades can encourage students' motivation to learn if they are tied to meaningful learning.

How can communications with families support learning? Not every communication from the teacher needs to be tied to a grade. Communication with students and families can be important in helping a teacher understand students and present effective instruction by creating a consistent learning environment. Students and families have a legal right to see all the information in the students' records, so the contents of files must be appropriate, accurate, and supported by evidence.

Standardized Testing (pp. 572–583)

What are mean, median, mode, and standard deviation? The mean (arithmetical average), median (middle score), and mode (most common score) are all measures of central tendency. The standard deviation reveals how scores spread out around the mean. A normal distribution is a frequency distribution represented as a bell-shaped curve. Many scores cluster in the middle; the farther from the midpoint, the fewer the scores.

Describe different kinds of scores. There are several basic types of standardized test scores: percentile rankings, which indicate the percentage of others who scored at or below an individual's score; grade-equivalent scores, which indicate how closely a student's performance matches average scores for a given grade; and standard scores, which are based on the standard deviation. T and z scores are both common standard scores. A stanine score is a standard score that incorporates elements of percentile rankings.

What are some current issues in testing? Controversy over standardized testing has focused on the role and interpretation of tests, the widespread use of tests to evaluate schools, the problems with accountability based on test scores, and the testing of teachers. If the test matches important objectives of the curriculum, is given to students who actually studied the curriculum for a reasonable period of time, is free of bias, fits the students' language capabilities, and was administered properly, then test results provide some information about the effectiveness of the school. But studies of the actual tests in action show troubling consequences such as narrowing the curriculum and pushing some students out of school early. Teachers should use results to improve instruction, not to stereotype students or justify lowered expectations.

Can students become better test takers? How? Performance on standardized tests can be improved if students gain experience with this type of testing and are given training in study skills and problem solving. Many students can profit from direct instruction about how to prepare for and take tests. Involving students in designing these test preparation programs can be helpful. Students with learning challenges may benefit from intensive and ongoing preparation for taking tests, particularly if the test-taking strategies are tied to specific problems and content learned and tested.

▼ KEY TERMS

Accountable (578)
Achievement tests (580)
Adequate yearly progress (AYP) (578)
Assessment (549)
Assessment bias (553)
Authentic assessments (558)
Central tendency (572)
Classroom assessments (548)
Confidence interval (552)
Criterion-referenced grading (566)
Criterion-referenced testing (550)
Culture-fair/culture-free test (554)
Distractors (556)
Exhibition (560)
Formative assessment (549)
Grade-equivalent score (574)

Grading on the curve (566)
High-stakes testing (578)
Informal assessments (564)
Mean (572)
Measurement (549)
Median (572)
Mode (572)
Norm group (550)
Norm-referenced grading (566)
Norm-referenced testing (550)
Normal distribution (573)
Objective testing (554)
Percentile rank (574)
Performance assessments (559)
Portfolio (560)
Pretest (549)

Range (573)
Reliability (551)
Scoring rubrics (560)
Standard deviation (572)
Standard error of measurement (552)
Standard scores (575)
Standardized tests (548)
Stanine scores (575)
Stem (556)
Summative assessment (549)
T score (575)
True score (552)
Validity (552)
Variability (573)
z score (575)

▼ CONNECT AND EXTEND TO LICENSURE

MULTIPLE-CHOICE QUESTIONS

1. Which of the following assessment methods provides feedback that is nonevaluative, occurs before or during instruction, and guides teachers in planning and improving instruction?
   A. Summative
   B. Criterion referenced
   C. Formative
   D. Norm referenced

2. The yearly standardized test in Mr. Taylor's class is given in the spring. By the summer, Mr. Taylor's students received their scores in the mail. Many of the parents were upset and contacted Mr. Taylor regarding their children's 'low scores'. "Mr. Taylor, I don't understand how my daughter could be in Honors classes and have scores on her standardized test in the 70s?"
   "Your daughter's scores are above the average nationally. The average score would be a 50." What type of scoring is being utilized in the yearly tests Mr. Taylor's class must take?
   A. Criterion referenced
   B. Norm referenced
   C. Raw scores
   D. Authentic scoring

3. Maria had proven to be a very good student in Mr. Rhodes' class despite having just moved to the United States from another country. So, it came as a surprise when Maria performed poorly on her tests. When Mr. Rhodes consulted another teacher who also had Maria as a student, he learned that maybe his test questions had something to do with it. His colleague explained that Maria comes from a relatively primitive area which does not have television. Her exposure to concepts which draw upon a wide variety of cultural experiences was limited. This indicated to Mr. Rhodes that his tests unfairly penalized Maria. This type of assessment which unfairly penalizes a student for his or her lack of resources or culture is known as which one of the following?
   A. Attribution bias
   B. Assessment bias
   C. Reliability bias
   D. Validity bias

4. Which one of the follow types of assessments would be most beneficial for assessing a student's ability to debate?
   A. Formative assessment
   B. Portfolio assessment
   C. Summative assessment
   D. Performance assessment

CONSTRUCTED-RESPONSE QUESTIONS

Case

"How will you grade our oral book reports Miss Wren?"

"We are going to both grade them! We will develop what is called a rubric. It is a list of items on which you should focus while preparing and presenting your book report."

"How will we be involved?"

"You will help me make the rubric. What are some of the things you think should be included in your oral report?"

"I think we should have to have audience participation or else it gets too boring!"

"Good idea, Terry. What else?" The class continued to add to the rubric until there were six aspects on which to focus. "Class, you will also assist me in grading your performance by using the rubric. By making the rubric and using it to grade yourself, you should do very well."

"There are no surprises that way!" Lisa shouted.

5. In addition to listing the criteria for what constitutes quality work and having students self-assess, list some additional guidelines for Miss Wren to remember when developing a rubric.

6. Grades, a form of extrinsic reinforcement, can be a source of celebration for Miss Wren's students or a punishment. In order to make the most of grades and increase her students' chances for success, what should Miss Wren keep in mind when grading her students?

MyEducationLab™

Go to Chapter 15 of the Book Specific Resources in MyEducationLab and click on "Connect and Extend to Licensure" to answer these questions. Compare your responses with the feedback provided.

▼ WHAT WOULD THEY DO?

TEACHERS' CASEBOOK: Giving Meaningful Grades

Here is how some practicing teachers responded to the grading challenge at the beginning of the chapter.

KATIE CHURCHILL • 3rd Grade Teacher
Oriole Parke Elementary School, Chicago, IL

I would use a combination of assessment tools to evaluate my students. Using a rubric that students and parents alike are familiar with provides an easy-to-follow-and-understand grading system. The rubric needs to remain in a focal area in the classroom as a constant reminder to the students of what their expectations are.

By differentiating instruction consistently to cover all learning styles and modalities, the students would hopefully become more involved and invested in their own learning and, as a result, produce better quality work and exceed expectations.

Several factors would play a part in obtaining a particular letter grade. The letter grade would be earned through a combination of group work, completing objectives, and following the rubric guidelines for quality work.

MADYA AYALA • High School Teacher of Preperatoria
Eugenio Garza Lagüera, Campus Garza Sada, Monterrey, N. L. Mexico

I think it is important to assess a cross-section of student work. First, portfolios can be a useful way to gather various types of work throughout the year. Using a portfolio, a teacher can then attach a letter grade to student progress and achievement. It is important to grade children not only on progress, but also on their understanding of material. I would use meaningful, written assessments to test for retention and understanding of my students' knowledge. Finally, I would grade various projects and experiments so that the students who are better project-based learners will be graded fairly. I also like the idea of using a rubric system to grade students on writing or projects. Under a rubric system, a teacher allocates a certain number of points to each content area. It is then easy to attach a letter grade based on the number of points received.

KATIE PIEL • Kindergarten–6th Grade Teacher
West Park School, Moscow, ID

Students should be given the latitude to express achievement in different ways like group projects, daily class work, tests, and individual projects. All students would be held accountable for demonstrating their own learning. With each teacher grading on a different standard, the teachers must also take on the responsibility of collaborating with their peers. Communicating to other teachers the skills a student can be expected to bring with him or her to the next level is crucial.

AIMEE FREDETTE • 2nd Grade Teacher
Fisher Elementary School, Walpole, MA

I believe that students are not all smart in the same ways. I give the students a variety of ways to demonstrate their knowledge. I also focus on the students' ability to take their knowledge and integrate it into other subject areas across the curriculum.

I use a student portfolio for each child, compiled throughout the year and used to show growth and development. Each time I correct papers I choose a couple of pieces of work that each child has done. I put these papers in the portfolio folder. I try to choose a variety of work, not necessarily their "prize work." At the end of the year the children receive the entire folder to keep.

ALLAN OSBORNE • Assistant Principal
Snug Harbor Community School, Quincy, MA

Any grading system should consider a student's progress and effort. Grading systems also should be individualized to account for a student's unique strengths and weaknesses. Thus, a mainstreamed special education student should not be held to the same expectations as a gifted student.

The most critical aspect of any successful grading system is that it is fair. Fairness dictates that students and their parents be given information in advance about class requirements and expectations, along with a description of grading criteria. A system that is fair can be easily justified. It is also important to keep accurate and detailed records of student progress. In addition to recording grades on tests, quizzes, and projects, anecdotal records describing a student's typical performance should be kept. These records can be valuable if a report card grade is questioned.

Although group assignments can be an important learning experience, I would be reluctant to place too much emphasis on a group project grade. As we all know, each member of the group does not participate equally, and thus, a group grade does not reflect the contribution of each individual member.

MyEducationLab™

Go to Topic 13, Assessment, in the MyEducationLab (www.myeducationlab.com) for *Educational Psychology*, where you can:

- Find learning outcomes for assessment along with the national standards that connect to these outcomes.
- Complete Assignments and Activities that can help you more deeply understand the chapter content.
- Apply and practice your understanding of the core teaching skills identified in the chapter with the Building Teaching Skills and Dispositions learning units.
- Examine challenging situations and cases presented in the IRIS Center Resources.
- Access video clips of CCSSO National Teachers of the Year award winners responding to the question, "Why Do I Teach?" in the Teacher Talk section.
- Check your comprehension on the content covered in the chapter with the Study Plan. Here you will be able to take a chapter quiz, receive feedback on your answers, and then access Review, Practice, and Enrichment activities to enhance your understanding of chapter content.
- Find additional Teachers' Casebook scenarios and responses to them from practicing teachers.
- Use the Online Lesson Plan Builder to practice lesson planning and integrating national and state standards into your planning.

LICENSURE APPENDIX

Part 1
Licensure Examination Study Guide

You probably will have to take a licensure examination in order to become a teacher in your state. In almost 40 states the Praxis II™ test is the required licensure examination. This section highlights the concepts from each chapter that may be on your licensure test.

Chapter 1

Developing relationships with professionals: Until you become a teacher, it will be difficult to establish a working relationship with other practitioners. However, you might find this site beneficial: K–12 Professional Circle (http://nces.ed.gov/practitioners/teachers.asp).

Keeping current with educational issues: Education Week (http://www.edweek.org/) will keep you up to date about innovations in teaching, policy initiatives, and changes in public laws related to education. These issues are often highly complex. The use of critical thinking skills is essential when making judgments about the information you will encounter in this type of publication.

Chapter 2

For Piagetian and Vygotskian theories of development, you should understand:

- Basic assumptions of each
- How students build their unique knowledge bases
- How students acquire skills
- Important terms and concepts related to each
- The key steps, mechanisms, or milestones related to each theory
- The limitations of each theory

Chapter 3

Understand the major concepts and progressions related to:

- Bronfenbrenner and the Social Context for Development
- Erikson's theory of psychosocial development
- Piaget's and Kohlberg's perspectives on moral development
- Gilligan's theory of caring

Design or choose strategies that:

- support optimal social and emotional development of students
- help students cope with major life transitions and challenges to safety, physical, and mental health
- help students build a sense of self-concept, self-esteem, and self-identity (including racial identity)

Recognize signs or behaviors that indicate sexual abuse or child abuse

Chapter 4

Explain the effects of legislation on public education:

- Americans with Disabilities Act
- Individuals with Disabilities Education Improvement Act
- Section 504
- Individualized Education Plans
- Inclusion, Mainstreaming and Least Restrictive Environment
- Inclusion, Mainstreaming and Least Restrictive Environment

Understand views of intelligence and describe its measurement:

- Types of intelligence tests and their uses
- Multiple intelligences

- Interpreting intelligence scores
- Modifications to testing

Accommodate the needs of students with exceptionalities:

- Attention-Deficit Hyperactivity Disorder
- Visual, speech, and physical difficulties
- Learning disabilities
- Intellectual disabilities/mental retardation

Chapter 5

For the development of language, you should understand:

- Basic assumptions of major theories
- The major accomplishments of language development of school-age children
- The relationship between language and literacy
- Basic steps that teachers can take to enhance literacy among their students
- Strategies that support English acquisition in non-English speaking students

Chapter 6

Recognize the influences that ethnicity, socioeconomic status, and community values may have on:

- Student–teacher relationships/parent–teacher relationships
- Student learning styles
- Academic achievement
- Attitudes, self-esteem, and expectations for success
- Opportunities for quality educational experiences

Understand the influences that gender may have on:

- Teachers' attention to students
- Differences in mental abilities

Devise strategies that:

- Eliminate sexist teaching practices
- Promote positive school–home relationships
- Reduce or eliminate racial and ethnic stereotypes and biases

Chapter 7

Understand the basic assumptions and contributions of these behaviorists:

- Pavlov
- Skinner

Determine appropriate behavioral techniques to:

- Establish efficient classroom routines and procedures
- Foster appropriate classroom conduct
- Help students monitor and regulate learning

Understand basic processes of operant conditioning and their roles in learning, including:

- Antecedents and consequences
- Types of reinforcement and reinforcement schedules
- Punishment
- Shaping

Chapter 8

Understand how memory and recall are affected by:

- The limitations, capacities, and capabilities of the various structures of human memory (e.g., memory stores)
- The manner in which humans process information
- Prior knowledge of a topic
- Executive control processes

Explain how students and teachers can enhance learning through the use of:

- Elaboration and mnemonic devices
- Organized presentations
- Meaningful learning and instructional activities

Chapter 9

Focus on each of these major topics:

- Metacognitive knowledge and learning
- Learning strategies
  - Basic principles of teaching these strategies
  - Cognitive processes involved in various strategies
  - Appropriate uses of different strategies
- Problem solving
  - General problem-solving strategies/heuristics and algorithms
  - The value of problem representation
  - Factors that impede problem solving
- Creativity
  - Meaning of creativity
  - Encouraging student creativity
- Critical Thinking
- Transfer of learning
  - Types of transfer/promoting transfer

Chapter 10

Explain the advantages and appropriate uses of major student-centered approaches to learning and instruction:

- Inquiry method
- Problem-based learning
- Cognitive apprenticeships
- Cooperative learning
- Service learning

Understand important concepts related to student-centered models of instruction:

- Situated learning
- Complex learning environments
- Authentic tasks
- Multiple representations of content
- Piaget and Vygotsky: Theories of constructivism

Chapter 11

Focus on these major topics:

- Bandura
- Modeling and Observational Learning
- Social Cognitive Theory
- Self Regulated Learning
- Self-Efficacy
- Teachers' Sense of Efficacy

Chapter 12

Describe the theoretical foundations of the major approaches to motivation.

- Identify and define important terms related to motivation including goals, attributions, intrinsic and extrinsic motivation, self-determination.
- Use your knowledge of motivation to:
  — identify situations and conditions that can enhance or diminish student motivation to learn.
  — design strategies to support individual and group work in the classroom.
  — implement practices that help students become self-motivated.

Chapter 13

Understand principles of classroom management that promote positive relationships by:

- Establishing daily procedures and routines
- Responding effectively to minor student misbehavior
- Implementing reasonable rules, penalties, and rewards
- Keeping students actively engaged in purposeful learning

Diagnose problems and prevent or reduce inappropriate behaviors by:

- Communicating with students and parents
- Addressing misbehaviors in the least intrusive way possible
- Confronting disruptive behaviors in an effective, efficient manner

Chapter 14

Develop plans for instruction and consider:

- The role of objectives in instruction
- Writing behavioral and cognitive objectives
- The use of educational taxonomies to design effective objectives
- The role of independent practice (i.e., seatwork and homework)
- Direct instruction and expository teaching
  — Basic assumptions
  — Inductive reasoning/deductive reasoning
  — Appropriate uses/principles of implementation

Understand the basic principles of teacher-centered and student-centered forms of instruction, including:

- Appropriate uses and limitations
- The role of the teacher
- Effective questioning techniques
- Whole group discussions
- Recitation
- Thematic/interdisciplinary instruction
- Differentiated instruction

Chapter 15

Describe the characteristics and purposes of major types of tests:

- Criterion-referenced and norm-referenced tests
- Achievement, aptitude, and diagnostic tests

Explain the major issues related to concerns about standardized testing, including:

- High-stakes testing
- Bias in testing
- Test-taking programs

Understand major concepts related to classroom assessment and grading:

- Formative and summative assessment
- Reliability and validity
- Criterion-referenced and norm-referenced grading

Describe the characteristics, uses, and limitations of major assessment techniques, including:

- Multiple-choice items
- Essays
- Portfolios
- Exhibitions

Design a scoring rubric for an authentic learning task that possesses:

- Validity
- Reliability
- Generalizability
- Equity

Part 2
Correlating Text Content to the PRAXIS II™ Principles of Learning and Teaching Tests and Intasc Standards

Each state in the country has its own set of licensure requirements that new teachers must meet in order to work in the classroom. An increasing number of states are basing their requirements on standards developed by INTASC (Interstate New Teacher Assessment and Support Consortium). These standards are based on ten principles of effective teaching that INTASC has identified as essential for optimal student learning. Many states assess new teachers' knowledge of those principles through the use of tests from the PRAXIS II™ series published by the Educational Testing Service. Within the PRAXIS II™ series are three *Principles of Learning and*

Teaching (PLT) tests, one each for grades K–6, 5–9, and 7–12. Each PLT test assesses students' knowledge of educational psychology and its application in the classroom.

The following table is designed to help you study for your PLT test and meet the Knowledge standards for each of INTASC's ten principles of effective teaching. The left-hand column of the table lists the topics assessed in a PLT test. The right-hand column contains INTASC's Knowledge standards. In the center column, you will find the chapters, sections, and page numbers in this textbook that correspond to the PLT tests and INTASC standards.

PRAXIS II™ Topics	Woolfolk Text Connections	INTASC Principles
I. Students as Learners **A. Student Development and the Learning Process**		
1. Theoretical foundations about how learning occurs: how students construct knowledge, acquire skills, and develop habits of mind	*Chapters 2, 7–12* (entire chapters)	1(d) The teacher understands how learning occurs—how students construct knowledge, acquire skills, and develop habits of mind—and knows how to use instructional strategies that promote student learning.
■ Examples of important theorists:		
• Jean Piaget	*Chapter 2*/Piaget's Theory of Cognitive Development (pp. 42–55)	
• Lev Vygotsky	*Chapter 2*/Vygotsky's Sociocultural Perspective (pp. 55–60)	
• Howard Gardner	*Chapter 4*/Multiple Intelligences (pp. 120–122)	
• Robert Sternberg	*Chapter 4*/Intelligence as a Process (pp. 123–124)	
• Albert Bandura	*Chapter 7*/Behavioral Views of Learning (pp. 244–276)	
• Urie Bronfenbrenner	*Chapter 3*/Bronfenbrenner: The Social Context for Development (pp. 75–87)	
■ Important terms that relate to learning theory:		
• Adaptation	*Chapter 2*/Basic Tendencies in Thinking (pp. 43–44)	
• Conservation	*Chapter 2*/Basic Tendencies in Thinking (pp. 43–44)	
• Constructivism	*Chapter 2*/Implications of Piaget's and Vygotsky's Theories for Teachers (pp. 60–64); *Chapter 10*/Constructivist Views of Learning (pp. 363–365)	
• Equilibration	*Chapter 2*/Basic Tendencies in Thinking (pp. 43–44)	
• Co-constructed process	*Chapter 2*/The Social Sources of Individual Thinking (pp. 55–56)	
• Private speech	*Chapter 2*/The Role of Language and Private Speech (pp. 58–59)	
• Scaffolding	*Chapter 2*/Assisted Learning (pp. 62–65); *Guidelines:* Applying Vygotsky's Ideas in Teaching (pp. 63); *Chapter 10*/Cognitive Apprenticeships and Reciprocal Teaching (pp. 369–372)	

PRAXIS II™ Topics	Woolfolk Text Connections	INTASC Principles
• Zone of proximal development	*Chapter 2*/The Zone of Proximal Development (pp. 59–60)	
• Learning	*Chapter 7*: Understanding Learning (pp. 246–248) *Chapter 8*/Comparing Cognitive and Behavioral Views (p. 282) *Chapter 10*/Cognitive and Reciprocal Teaching (pp. 369–372) *Chapter 12*/Motivation in Teaching and Learning (pp. 430–466)	
• Knowledge	*Chapter 2*/The Social Sources of Individual Thinking (pp. 55–56); Activity and Constructing Knowledge (pp. 61–62) *Chapter 8*/The Importance of Knowledge in Cognition (pp. 283–283); Becoming Knowledgeable: Some Basic Principles (pp. 307–313) *Chapter 10*/How Is Knowledge Constructed? (p. 362); Knowledge: Situated or General? (p. 363)	
• Memory	*Chapter 8*/Sensory Memory (pp. 286–288); Working Memory (pp. 288–292); Long-Term Memory (pp. 296–307)	
• Schemas	*Chapter 8*/Schemas (pp. 300–301)	
• Transfer	*Chapter 8*/Teaching for Transfer (pp. 346–350); The Many Views of Transfer (p. 347)	
2. Human development in the physical, social, emotional, moral, and cognitive domains		1(f) The teacher is aware of expected developmental progressions and ranges of individual variation within each domain (physical, social, emotional, moral, and cognitive), can identify levels of readiness in learning, and understands how development in any one domain may affect performance in others.
■ Contributions of important theorists:		
• Jean Piaget	*Chapter 2*/Piaget's Theory of Cognitive Development (pp. 42–55)	
• Lev Vygotsky	*Chapter 2*/Vygotsky's Sociocultural Perspective (pp. 55–60)	
• Erik Erikson	*Chapter 3*/Erikson: Stages of Psychosocial Development (pp. 87–93)	
• Lawrence Kohlberg	*Chapter 3*/Kohlberg's Theories of Moral Development (pp. 100–101)	
• Carol Gilligan	*Chapter 3*/Gender Differences: The Morality of Caring (pp. 101–102)	

PRAXIS II™ Topics	Woolfolk Text Connections	INTASC Principles
■ Major progressions in each developmental domain and the ranges of individual variation within each domain	*Chapter 2*/Four Stages of Cognitive Development (pp. 44–51); Some Limitations of Piaget's Theory (pp. 53–55); Information Processing, Neo-Piagetian, and Neuroscience Views of Cognitive Development (pp. 52–53); The Social Sources of Individual Thinking (pp. 55–56) *Chapter 3*/Physical Development (pp. 70–74); Young Children (p. 70); Elementary School (p. 70); Adolescence (p. 71); Moral Development (pp. 99–102) *Chapter 5*/The Development of Language (pp.168–175)	1(e) The teacher understands that students' physical, social, emotional, moral and cognitive development influence learning and knows how to address these factors when making instructional decisions.
■ Impact of students' physical, social, emotional, moral, and cognitive development on their learning and ways to address these factors when making decisions	*Chapter 2*/Four Stages of Cognitive Development (pp. 44–51); Some Limitations of Piaget's Theory (pp. 53–55); *Guidelines*: Helping Families Care for Preoperational Children (p. 47); *Guidelines*: Teaching the Concrete-Operational Child (p. 49); *Guidelines*: Helping Students to Use Formal Operations (p. 51); The Social Sources of Individual Thinking (pp. 55–56); Assisted Learning (pp. 62–63); The Zone of Proximal Development (pp. 59–60); *Chapter 3*/Physical Development (pp. 70–74); The Preschool Years: Trust, Autonomy, and Initiative (pp. 88–89); Elementary and Middle School Years: Industry versus Inferiority (pp. 89–90); Adolescence: The Search for Identity (pp. 90–91); Kohlberg's Stages of Moral Development (pp. 100–101); Self-Concept and Self-Esteem (pp. 95–97); School Life and Self-Esteem (p. 97); Diversity and Perception of Self (pp. 93–95); Theory of Mind and Intention (p. 99); Moral Judgment, Social Conventions, and Personal Choices (pp. 102–103) *Chapter 5*/The Development of Language (pp. 168–175) *Chapter 13*/Maintaining a Good Environment for Learning (pp. 484–488)	
■ How development in one domain, such as physical, may affect performance in another domain, such as social	*Chapter 2*/General Principles of Development (p. 32); The Brain and Cognitive Development (pp. 32–42); Influences on Development (p. 43) *Chapter 3*/Physical Development (pp. 70–74)	

B. Students as Diverse Learners

1. Differences in the ways students learn and perform	*Chapter 4*/Learner Differences and Learning Needs (entire chapter) *Chapter 6*/Culture and Diversity (entire chapter)	2(g) The teacher understands and can identify differences in approaches to learning and performance, including different learning styles, multiple intelligences, and performance modes, and can design instruction that helps use students' strengths as the basis for growth.
• Learning styles	*Chapter 4*/Learning Styles/Preferences (pp. 128–130) *Chapter 6*/Diversity in Learning (pp. 234–237)	
• Multiple intelligences	*Chapter 4*/Multiple Intelligences (pp. 120–122)	

PRAXIS II™ Topics	Woolfolk Text Connections	INTASC Principles
• Performance modes	*Chapter 2*/Later Elementary to the Middle-School Years: The Concrete-Operational Stage (pp. 47–50); *Guidelines*: Teaching the Concrete-Operational Child (p. 49)	
— Concrete operational thinking	*Chapter 4*/Learning and Thinking Styles (pp. 128–130)	
— Visual and aural learners	*Chapter 4*/Students with Learning Challenges (pp. 136–155)	
• Gender differences	*Chapter 3*/Gender Differences: The Morality of Caring (pp. 101–102) *Chapter 6*/Gender in Teaching and Learning (pp. 224–229); *Guidelines*: Avoiding Gender Bias in Teaching (p. 229)	
• Cultural expectations and styles	*Chapter 6*/Today's Diverse Classrooms (pp. 206–210); Ethnicity and Race in Teaching and Learning (pp. 216–224); *Guidelines*: Culturally Relevant Teaching (p. 239) *Chapter 14*/Teacher Expectations (pp. 537–441)	
2. Areas of exceptionality in students' learning	*Chapter 4*/Learner Differences (Full chapter)	2(h) The teacher knows about areas of exceptionality in learning—including learning disabilities, visual and perceptual difficulties, and special physical or mental challenges.
• Special physical or sensory challenges	*Chapter 4*/Students with Communication Disorders (pp. 142–144); Students with Health and Sensory Impairments (pp. 150–153); Students Who Are Deaf (p. 153)	
• Learning disabilities	*Chapter 4*/Students with Learning Disabilities (pp. 136–139); Individual Education Programs (pp. 132–133); Section 504 (p. 135)	
• ADHD	*Chapter 4*/Students with Hyperactivity and Attention Disorders (pp. 139–141)	
• Functional and mental retardation	*Chapter 4*/Students with Intellectual Disabilities (pp. 149–150); *Guidelines*: Teaching Students with Intellectual Disabilities (p. 150)	
3. Legislation and institutional responsibilities relating to exceptional students	*Chapter 4*/Individual Differences and the Law (pp. 130–135); Section 504 (p. 135)	9(g) The teacher understands and implements laws related to students' rights and teacher responsibilities (e.g., for equal education, appropriate education for handicapped students, confidentiality, privacy, appropriate treatment of students, reporting in situations related to possible child abuse).
• Americans with Disabilities Act (ADA), Individuals with Disabilities Education Act (IDEA); Section 504 Protections for Students		
• Inclusion, mainstreaming, and "least restrictive environment"	*Chapter 4*/Individual Differences and the Law (pp. 130–135); Least Restrictive Environment (p. 132) *Chapter 14*/Reaching Every Student: Differentiated Instruction in Inclusive Classrooms (p. 584)	
4. Approaches for accommodating various learning styles and intelligences	*Chapter 4*/Learner Differences; focus on: Multiple Intelligences Go to School (p. 122); Teaching Gifted Students (pp. 158–160); Individual Differences and the Law (pp. 130–135)	2(g) The teacher understands and can identify differences in approaches to learning and performance, including different learning styles, multiple intelligences, and performance modes, and can design instruction that uses students' strengths as the basis for growth.

PRAXIS II™ Topics	Woolfolk Text Connections	INTASC Principles
• Differentiated instruction	*Chapter 14*/Differentiated Instruction (pp. 531–537); Technology and Differentiation (pp. 534–537); Reaching Every Student: Effective Teaching in Inclusive Classrooms (pp. 584)	
• Alternative assessment	*Chapter 15*/Informal Assessment (pp. 564–566); Authentic Classroom Assessment (pp. 558–566); Portfolios and Exhibitions (pp. 559–560); *Guidelines*: Creating Portfolios (p. 562); *Guidelines*: Developing a Rubric (p. 562)	
• Testing modifications	*Chapter 15*/Reaching Every Student: Helping Students with Disabilities Prepare for High-Stakes Testing (pp. 581–583)	
5. Process of second language acquisition and strategies to support the learning of students	*Chapter 5*/Dialects (pp. 182–184); Bilingualism (pp. 175–178)	2(i) The teacher knows about the process of second language acquisition and about strategies to support the learning of students whose first language is not English.
6. Understanding of influences of individual experiences, talents, and prior learning, as well as language, culture, family, and community values on students' learning		
• Multicultural backgrounds	*Chapter 6*/American Cultural Diversity (pp. 206–207); Ethnic and Racial Differences in School Achievement (pp. 217–219)	2(j) The teacher understands how students' learning is influenced by individual experiences, talents, and prior learning, as well as language, culture, family and community values. 2(k) The teacher has a well-grounded framework for understanding cultural and community diversity and knows how to learn about and incorporate students' experiences, cultures, and community resources into instruction.
• Age-appropriate knowledge and behaviors	*Chapter 2*/Four Stages of Cognitive Development (pp. 44–51); Vygotsky's Sociocultural Perspective (pp. 55–60); Implications of Piaget's and Vygotsky's Theories for Teachers (pp. 61–64) *Chapter 3*/entire Chapter—focus on: The Preschool Years: Trust, Autonomy, and Initiative (pp. 88–89); Elementary and Middle School Years: Industry versus Inferiority (pp. 89–90); Adolescence: The Search for Identity (pp. 90–91); Emotional and Moral Development (pp. 99–104)	
• The student culture at the school	*Chapter 3*/Bronfenbrenner: The Social Context for Development (pp. 75–87); Peers (pp. 80–83) *Chapter 12*/Learned Helplessness (p. 445–446)	
• Family backgrounds	*Chapter 3*/Families (pp. 77–80) *Family and Community Partnership Guidelines* (all chapters)	
• Linguistic patterns and differences	*Chapter 4*/Students with Language and Communication Disorders (pp. 142–144) *Chapter 5*/The Development of Language (pp. 168–175); Dialects (pp. 182–184); Bilingualism (pp. 175–178)	1(g). The teacher understands communication theory, language development, and the role of language in learning.
• Cognitive patterns and differences	*Chapter 4*/Learning and Thinking Styles (pp. 128–130) *Chapter 8*/Long-Term Memory (pp. 296–307)	
• Social and emotional issues	*Chapter 3*/Moral Behavior (pp. 104–108) *Chapter 4*/Students with Emotional or Behavioral Difficulties (pp. 144–149)	

PRAXIS II™ Topics	Woolfolk Text Connections	INTASC Principles
C. Student Motivation and the Learning Environment		
1. Theoretical foundations about human motivation and behavior	*Chapter 12*/What Is Motivation? (pp. 430–434); Five General Approaches to Motivation (pp. 432–434)	3(i). The teacher can use knowledge about human motivation and behavior drawn from the foundational sciences of psychology, anthropology, and sociology to develop strategies for organizing and supporting individual and group work.
• Important terms that relate to motivation and behavior	*Chapter 7*/Operant Conditioning: Trying New Responses (pp. 250–256); Reinforcement Schedules (pp. 252–254); *Chapter 11*/Motivation in Learning and Teaching (entire chapter); *Chapter 12*/(entire chapter) *Chapter 14*/Teacher Expectations (pp. 537–541)	
2. How knowledge of human emotion and behavior should influence strategies for organizing and supporting individual and group work in the classroom	*Chapter 12*/Emotions and Anxiety (pp. 451–454); *Guidelines*: Coping with Anxiety (p. 455); *Guidelines*: Supporting Self-Determination and Autonomy (p. 437) *Chapter 14*/Teacher Expectations (pp. 537–541)	3(i) The teacher can use knowledge about human motivation and behavior drawn from the foundational sciences of psychology, anthropology, and sociology to develop strategies for organizing and supporting individual and group work.
3. Factors and situations that are likely to promote or diminish students' motivation to learning, and how to help students to become self-motivated	*Chapter 12*/Needs: Lessons for Teachers (p. 437); Goals: Lessons for Teachers (pp. 441–442); Curiosity, Interests and Emotions: Lessons for Teachers (p. 454); Supporting Autonomy and Recognizing Accomplishment (pp. 458–459)	3(j). The teacher recognizes factors and situations that are likely to promote or diminish intrinsic motivation and knows how to help students become self-motivated.
4. Principles of effective management and strategies to promote positive relationships, cooperation, and purposeful learning	*Chapter 7*/Methods for Encouraging Behavior (pp. 256–259); *Guidelines*: Encouraging Positive Behaviors (p. 260); Handling Undesirable Behavior (pp. 259–262); Functional Behavioral Assessment and Positive Behavior Supports (p. 267–269); Reaching Every Student: Severe Behavior Problems (pp. 266–267)	3(k) The teacher understands the principles of effective classroom management and can use a range of strategies to promote positive relationships, cooperation, and purposeful learning in the classroom.
• Establishing daily procedures and routines		
• Establishing classroom rules, punishments, and rewards	*Chapter 13*/Routines and Rules Required (pp. 476–480); *Guidelines*: Establishing Class Routines (p. 477); Prevention Is the Best Medicine (pp. 485–487); *Reaching Every Student*: Peer Mediation and Negotiation (pp. 498–499) *Chapter 14*/Teacher Expectations (pp. 537–541)	
• Giving timely feedback	*Chapter 7*/Guidelines: Using Praise Appropriately (p. 257) *Chapter 13*/The Need for Communication (pp. 494–500) *Chapter 14*/Responding to Student Answers (pp. 526–527) *Chapter 15*/Effects of Grading on Students (p. 568)	
• Maintaining accurate records	*Chapter 15*/Portfolios and Exhibitions (pp. 559–560); *Guidelines*: Creating Portfolios (p. 562); Evaluating Portfolios and Performances (pp. 560–561)	
• Communicating with parents and caregivers	*Chapters 2–15*/Family and Community Partnerships	
• Using objective behavior descriptions	*Chapter 7*/Applied Behavior Analysis (pp. 256–262);	

PRAXIS II™ Topics	Woolfolk Text Connections	INTASC Principles
• Responding to student misbehavior	*Chapters 7*/Handling Undesirable Behavior (pp. 259–262); *Guidelines*: Using Punishment (p. 263); Group Consequences (pp. 262–264) *Chapter 13*/Dealing with Discipline Problems (pp. 488–493); Special Problems with High School Students (pp. 491–493); *Guidelines:* Imposing Penalties (p. 489); Counseling: The Students' Problem (p. 496); Confrontation and Assertive Discipline (pp. 496–498); Handling Potentially Explosive Situations (p. 494)	
• Arranging classroom space	*Chapter 13*/Planning Spaces for Learning (pp. 481–482); *Guidelines*: Designing Learning Spaces (p. 482)	
• Pacing and the structure of the lesson	*Chapter 13*/Encouraging Engagement (pp. 484–485); *Guidelines:* Keeping Students Engaged (p. 485); Withitness (pp. 485–486); Overlapping and Group Focus (p. 486); Movement Management (p. 486) *Chapter 14*/Clarity and Organization (p. 508); *Guidelines*: Teaching Effectively (p. 522)	

II. Instruction and Assessment

A. Instructional Strategies

1. Major cognitive processes associated with student learning

• Critical thinking	*Chapter 9*/Creativity and Creative Problem Solving (pp. 339–342); *Guidelines*: Encouraging Creativity (p. 343)	8(j) The teacher understands the cognitive processes associated with various kinds of learning (e.g., critical and creative thinking, problem structuring and problem solving, invention, memorization and recall) and how these processes can be stimulated.
• Creative thinking		
• Inductive and deductive thinking		
• Problem structuring and problem solving	*Chapter 9*/Problem Solving (pp. 328–339)	
• Invention	*Chapter 9*/Creativity and Creative Problem Solving (pp. 339–342)	
• Memorization and recall	*Chapter 8*/Cognitive Views of Learning (focus on sections related to memory)	

2. Major categories, advantages, and appropriate uses of instructional strategies

• Cooperative learning	*Chapter 10*/Collaboration and Cooperation (pp. 372–374); *Guidelines*: Using Cooperative Learning (p. 382)	8(k) The teacher understands principles and techniques, along with advantages and limitations, associated with various instructional strategies (e.g., cooperative learning, direct instruction, discovery learning, whole-group discussion, independent study, interdisciplinary instruction).
• Direct instruction (often referred to as *teacher-centered instruction*)	*Chapter 14*/Direct Instruction (pp. 519–523)	
• Discovery learning	*Chapter 10*/Inquiry and Problem-Based Learning (pp. 366–369)	4(k). The teacher understands how students' conceptual frameworks and their misconceptions for an area of knowledge can influence their learning.
• Whole-group discussion	*Chapter 14*/Group Discussion (p. 529); *Guidelines*: Productive Group Discussions (p. 530)	
• Independent study	*Chapter 9*/Learning Strategies (pp. 321–328); *Guidelines*: Becoming an Expert Student (p. 327) *Chapter 11*/Models of Self-Regulated Learning and Agency (pp. 412–413);	

PRAXIS II™ Topics	Woolfolk Text Connections	INTASC Principles
• Interdisciplinary instruction (sometimes referred to as *thematic instruction*)	*Chapter 10*/Inquiry and Problem-Based Learning (pp. 366–369); *Chapter 14*/Planning from a Constructionist Perspective (p. 518)	
• Questioning	*Chapter 14* and Discussion (pp. 524–529)	
3. Principles, techniques, and methods associated with major instructional strategies		
• Direct instruction (*often referred to as teacher-centered instruction*)	*Chapter 14*/Direct Instruction (pp. 519–523); Questioning and Discussion (pp. 524–529); Rosenshine's Six Teaching Functions (p. 520)	8(k) The teacher understands principles and techniques, along with advantages and limitations, associated with various instructional strategies (e.g., cooperative learning, direct instruction, discovery learning, whole-group discussion, independent study, interdisciplinary instruction).
• Student-centered models	*Chapter 10*/Cognitive and Social Constructivism (pp. 358–365); Applying Constructivist Perspectives (pp. 365–383)	
4. Methods for enhancing student learning through the use of a variety of resources and materials	*Chapter 10*/Service Learning (pp. 383–385) *Chapter 14*/Technology and Differentiation (pp. 524–526)	8(n). The teacher knows how to enhance learning through the use of a wide variety of materials as well as human and technological resources (e.g., computers, audio-visual technologies, videotapes and discs, local experts, primary documents and artifacts, texts, reference books, literature, and other print resources).

B. Planning Instruction

PRAXIS II™ Topics	Woolfolk Text Connections	INTASC Principles
1. Techniques for planning instruction to meet curriculum goals, including the incorporation of learning theory, subject matter, curriculum development, and student development		
• National and state learning standards • State and local curriculum frameworks • State and local curriculum guides	*Chapter 15*/Issues in Standardized Testing (pp. 551–552)	7(g). The teacher understands learning theory, subject matter, curriculum development, and student development and knows how to use this knowledge in planning instruction to meet curriculum goals.
• Scope and sequence in specific disciplines • Units and lessons	*Chapter 14*/The First Step: Planning (pp. 512–519); Planning from a Constructivist Perspective (pp. 518–519)	
• Behavioral objectives: affective, cognitive, and psychomotor • Learner objectives and outcomes	*Chapter 14*/Objectives for Learning (pp. 513–514); The Cognitive Domain (pp. 515–516); The Affective Domain (pp. 516–517); The Psychomotor Domain (p. 517); *Guidelines*: Using Instructional Objectives (p. 518)	
2. Techniques for creating effective bridges between curriculum goals and students' experiences		7(j). The teacher knows how to take contextual considerations (instructional materials, individual student interests, needs, and aptitudes, and community resources) into account in planning instruction that creates an effective bridge between curriculum goals and students' experiences.
• Modeling	*Chapter 7*/Social Learning Theory (pp. 271–272)	
• Guided practice	*Chapter 2*/Assisted Learning (pp. 62–63) *Chapter 10*/Cognitive Apprenticeships and Reciprocal Teaching (pp. 369–372) *Chapter 14*/Rosenshine's Six Teaching Functions (p. 520)	
• Independent practice, including homework	*Chapter 11*/Models of Self-Regulated Learning and Agency (pp. 412–413); *Family and Community Partnerships*: Supporting Self-Regulation at Home and at School (p. 417) *Chapter 14*/Seatwork and Homework (pp. 523–524)	

PRAXIS II™ Topics	Woolfolk Text Connections	INTASC Principles
• Transitions	*Chapter 13*/Overlapping and Group Focus (p. 486); Movement Management (p. 486); *Guidelines*: Keeping Students Engaged (p. 485)	
• Activating students' prior knowledge	*Chapter 8*/The Importance of Knowledge in Cognition (pp. 283–284); Capacity, Duration, and Contents of Long-Term Memory (pp. 296–298) *Chapter 9*/Defining Goals and Representing the Problem (pp. 330–334)	
• Anticipating preconceptions	*Chapter 9*/Factors That Hinder Problem Solving (pp. 336–337)	
• Encouraging exploration and problem solving	*Chapter 2*/Implications of Piaget's Theory for Teachers (pp. 61–64) *Chapter 9*/Problem Solving (pp. 328–339); Creativity and Creative Problem Solving (pp. 339–342) *Chapter 11*/Models of Self-Regulated Learning and Agency (pp. 412–413)	
• Building new skills on those previously acquired	*Chapter 2*/Basic Tendencies in Thinking (pp. 43–44); *Chapter 4*/Students with Intellectual Disabilities (pp. 149–150); *Guidelines*: Teaching Students with Intellectual Disabilities (p. 150) *Chapter 8*/Capacity and Duration and Contents of Long-Term Memory (pp. 296–298); Development of Declarative Knowledge (pp. 307–309); Procedural and Conditional Knowledge (pp. 310–313) *Chapter 11*/Observational Learning in Teaching (pp. 402–404);	

C. Assessment Strategies

PRAXIS II™ Topics	Woolfolk Text Connections	INTASC Principles
1. Types of assessments	*Chapter 15*/Norm-Referenced versus Criterion-Referenced Grading (pp. 566–567); Authentic Classroom Assessments (pp. 558–566); Formative and Summative Assessment (pp. 548–550); Objective Testing (pp. 554–556); Essay Tests (pp. 556–558); Portfolios and Exhibitions (pp. 559–560); Informal Assessments (pp. 564–566)	6(j). The teacher understands the characteristics, uses, advantages, and limitations of different types of assessments (e.g., criterion-referenced and norm-referenced instruments, traditional standardized and performance-based tests, observation systems, and assessments of student work) for evaluating how students learn, what they know and are able to do, and what kinds of experiences will support their further growth and development.
2. Characteristics of assessments	*Chapter 15*/Reliability (p. 551); Validity (pp. 552–553); Writing Multiple-Choice Questions (pp. 555–556); Constructing Essays (p. 557); Reliability, Variability, Generalizability, (pp. 563–564); *Guidelines*: Developing a Rubric (p. 562)	6(k) The teacher knows how to select, construct, and use assessment strategies and instruments appropriate to the learning outcomes being evaluated and to other diagnostic purposes.
3. Scoring assessments	*Chapter 15*/Using Multiple-Choice Tests (p. 555); Evaluating Essays: (p. 557); Evaluating Essays: Methods (pp. 557–558); Evaluating Portfolios and Performances (pp. 560–564); Guidelines: Developing a Rubric (p. 562)	
4. Uses of assessments	*Chapter 15*/Norm-Referenced versus Criterion-Referenced Grading (pp. 566–567) Accountability and High Stakes (pp. 578–580); Formative and Summative Assessment (pp. 548–551); Alternatives to Traditional Assessment (pp. 558–566)	
5. Understanding of measurement theory and assessment-related issues	*Chapter 15*/Norm-Referenced versus Criterion-Referenced Grading (pp. 566–567)	6(k) The teacher understands measurement theory and assessment-related issues, such as validity, reliability, bias, and scoring concerns.

PRAXIS II™ Topics	Woolfolk Text Connections	INTASC Principles
III. Communication Techniques		
A. Basic, effective verbal and nonverbal communication techniques	*Chapter 13*/The Need for Communication (pp. 494–500) *Chapter 13*/Teacher Expectations (pp. 485–488)	8(m). The teacher recognizes the importance of nonverbal as well as verbal communication. 6D. The teacher knows about and can use effective verbal, nonverbal, and media communication techniques.
B. Effect of cultural and gender differences on communications in the classroom	*Chapter 5*/Language Differences in the Classroom (pp. 182–184); Sociolinguistics (p. 237)	3(e). The teacher understands how cultural and gender differences can affect communication in the classroom.
C. Types of questions that can stimulate discussion in different ways for different purposes	*Chapter 14*/Questioning and Discussion (pp. 524–526)	5(n). The teacher knows about and can use effective verbal, nonverbal, and media communication techniques.
• Probing for learner understanding	*Chapter 14*/Questioning and Discussion (pp. 524–526)	
• Helping students articulate their ideas and thinking processes	*Chapter 9*/Guidelines: Problem Solving (p. 338); *Chapter 14*/Group Discussion (pp. 529–530); Guidelines: Positive Group Discussions (p.530);	
• Promoting risk-taking and problem solving		
• Facilitating factual recall	*Chapter 14*/Questioning and Discussion (pp. 524–526)	
• Encouraging convergent and divergent thinking	*Chapter 9*/Assessing Creativity (pp. 339–340) *Chapter 14*/Kinds of Questions (pp. 526–527)	
• Stimulating curiosity	*Chapter 12*/Tapping Interests (pp. 448–449); *Guidelines*: Building on Students' Interests (p. 398); Curiosity, Novelty and Complexity (pp. 449–451)	
• Helping students to question	*Chapter 14*/Fitting the Questions to the Students (pp. 527–528)	
IV. Profession and Community		
A. The Reflective Practitioner		
1. Types of resources available for professional development and learning	MyEducationLab	10(h). The teacher is aware of major areas of research on teaching and of resources available for professional learning (e.g., professional literature, colleagues, professional associations, professional development activities).
• Professional literature		
• Colleagues	*Chapters 2–15*/Teachers' Casebook (opening and closing sections of each chapter)	
2. Ability to read and understand articles about current views, ideas, and debates regarding best teaching practices	*Chapter 1*/Using Research to Understand and Improve Teaching (pp. 14–17) *Chapters 2–15*/Point/Counterpoint (one per chapter)	10(h). The teacher is aware of major areas of research on teaching and of resources available for professional learning (e.g., professional literature, colleagues, professional associations, professional development activities).
3. Why personal reflection on teaching practices is critical, and approaches that can be used to achieve this	*Chapters 2–15*/Point/Counterpoint (one per chapter)	4(j). The teacher understands major concepts, assumptions, debates, processes of inquiry, and ways of knowing that are central to the discipline(s) s/he teaches.
B. The Larger Community		
1. Role of the school as a resource to the larger community	*Chapter 6*/Culture and Diversity (entire chapter) *Chapter 13*/The Classroom Community (pp. 487–488)	10(i). The teacher understands schools as organizations within the larger community context and understands the operations of the relevant aspects of the system(s) within which s/he works.

PRAXIS II™ Topics	Woolfolk Text Connections	INTASC Principles
2. Factors in the students' environment outside of school (family circumstances, community environments, health, and economic conditions) that may influence students' life and learning	*Chapter 3*/Families (pp. 77–80); Peers (pp. 80–83); *Chapter 4*/Children with Learning Challenges (pp. 150–152)	10(m). The teacher understands how factors in the students' environment outside of school (e.g., family circumstances, community environments, health and economic conditions) may influence students' life and learning.
3. Basic strategies for involving parents/guardians and leaders in the community in the educational process	*Chapter 6*/Culture and Diversity (entire chapter) *Chapter 10*/ Service Learning *Chapters 2–14/Family and Community Partnerships*: (one in each chapter)	
4. Major laws related to students' rights and teacher responsibilities • Equal education • Appropriate education for handicapped children • Confidentiality and privacy • Appropriate treatment of students Reporting situations related to possible child abuse	*Chapter 4*/ Individual Differences and the Law (pp. 130–135) *Chapter 4*/The Rights of Students and Families (p. 133) *Chapter 13*/The Need for Communication (pp. 494–499) *Chapter 3*/Child Abuse (p. 85)	9(j). The teacher understands and implements laws related to students' rights and teacher responsibilities (e.g., for equal education, appropriate education for handicapped students, confidentiality, privacy, appropriate treatment of students, reporting in situations related to possible child abuse).

The Interstate New Teacher Assessment and Support Consortium (INTASC) standards were developed by the Council of Chief State School Officers and member states. Copies may be downloaded from the Council's website at http://www.ccsso.org.

Council of Chief State School Officers. (1992). Model standards for beginning teacher licensing, assessment, and development: A resource for state dialogue. Washington, DC: Author. http://www.ccsso.org/content/pdfs/corestrd.pdf.

Glossary

Absence seizure A seizure involving only a small part of the brain that causes a child to lose contact briefly.

Academic language The entire range of language used in elementary, secondary, and university-level schools including words, concepts, strategies, and processes from academic subjects.

Academic learning time Time when students are actually succeeding at the learning task.

Academic tasks The work the student must accomplish, including the product expected, resources available, and the mental operations required.

Accommodation Altering existing schemes or creating new ones in response to new information.

Accountable Making teachers and schools responsible for student learning, usually by monitoring learning with high-stakes tests.

Achievement tests Standardized tests measuring how much students have learned in a given content area.

Acronym Technique for remembering by using the first letter of each word in a phrase to form a new, memorable word.

Action research Systematic observations or tests of methods conducted by teachers or schools to improve teaching and learning for their students.

Action zone Area of a classroom where the greatest amount of interaction takes place.

Active teaching Teaching characterized by high levels of teacher explanation, demonstration, and interaction with students.

Adaptation Adjustment to the environment.

Adaptive teaching Provides all students with challenging instruction and uses supports when needed, but removes these supports as students become able to handle more on their own.

Adequate yearly progress (AYP) Objectives for yearly improvement for all students and for specific groups such as students from major ethnic and racial groups, students with disabilities, students from low-income families, and students whose English is limited.

Adolescent egocentrism Assumption that everyone else shares one's thoughts, feelings, and concerns.

Advance organizer Statement of inclusive concepts to introduce and sum up material that follows.

Affective domain Objectives focusing on attitudes and feelings.

Algorithm Step-by-step procedure for solving a problem; prescription for solutions.

Allocated time Time set aside for learning.

Americans with Disabilities Act of 1990 (ADA) Federal legislation prohibiting discrimination against persons with disabilities in employment, transportation, public access, local government, and telecommunications.

Analogical thinking Heuristic in which one limits the search for solutions to situations that are similar to the one at hand.

Anorexia nervosa Eating disorder characterized by very limited food intake.

Antecedents Events that precede an action.

Anxiety General uneasiness, a feeling of tension.

Applied behavior analysis The application of behavioral learning principles to understand and change behavior.

Appropriating Being able to internalize or take for yourself knowledge and skills developed in interaction with others or with cultural tools.

Argumentation The process of debating a claim with someone else.

Arousal Physical and psychological reactions causing a person to feel alert, attentive, wide awake, excited, or tense.

Articulation disorders Any of a variety of pronunciation difficulties, such as the substitution, distortion, or omission of sounds.

Assertive discipline Clear, firm, unhostile response style.

Assessment Procedures used to obtain information about student performance.

Assessment bias Qualities of an assessment instrument that offend or unfairly penalize a group of students because of the students' gender, SES, race, ethnicity, etc.

Assimilation Fitting new information into existing schemes.

Assisted learning Providing strategic help in the initial stages of learning, gradually diminishing as students gain independence.

Assistive technology Devices, systems, and services that support and improve the capabilities of individuals with disabilities.

Attachment Forming an emotional bond with another person, initially a parent or family member.

Attention Focus on a stimulus.

Attention-deficit hyperactivity disorder (ADHD) Current term for disruptive behavior disorders marked by overactivity, excessive difficulty sustaining attention, or impulsiveness.

Attribution theories Descriptions of how individuals' explanations, justifications, and excuses influence their motivation and behavior.

Authentic assessments Assessment procedures that test skills and abilities as they would be applied in real-life situations.

Authentic task Tasks that have some connection to real-life problems the students will face outside the classroom.

Autism/Autism spectrum disorders Developmental disability significantly affecting verbal and nonverbal communication and social interaction, generally evident before age 3 and ranging from mild to major.

Automated basic skills Skills that are applied without conscious thought.

Automaticity The ability to perform thoroughly learned tasks without much mental effort. The result of learning to perform a behavior or thinking process so thoroughly that the performance is automatic and does not require effort.

Autonomy   Independence.

Availability heuristic   Judging the likelihood of an event based on what is available in your memory, assuming those easily remembered events are common.

Aversive   Irritating or unpleasant.

Balanced bilingualism   Adding a second language capability without losing your heritage language.

Basic skills   Clearly structured knowledge that is needed for later learning and that can be taught step by step.

Behavior modification   Systematic application of antecedents and consequences to change behavior.

Behavioral learning theories   Explanations of learning that focus on external events as the cause of changes in observable behaviors.

Behavioral objectives   Instructional objectives stated in terms of observable behaviors.

Being needs   Maslow's three higher-level needs, sometimes called *growth needs*.

Belief perseverance   The tendency to hold on to beliefs, even in the face of contradictory evidence.

Bilingual   Speaking two languages and dealing appropriately with the two different cultures.

Bioecological model   Bronfenbrenner's theory describing the nested social and cultural contexts that shape development. Every person develops within a *microsystem*, inside a *mesosystem*, embedded in an *exosystem*, all of which are a part of the *macrosystem* of the culture. All development occurs in and is influenced by the time period—the *chronosystem*.

Blended families   Parents, children, and stepchildren merged into families through remarriages.

Body mass index (BMI)   A measure of body fat that evaluates weight in relation to height.

Bottom-up processing   Perceiving based on noticing separate defining features and assembling them into a recognizable pattern.

Brainstorming   Generating ideas without stopping to evaluate them.

Bulimia   Eating disorder characterized by overeating, then getting rid of the food by self-induced vomiting or laxatives.

CAPS   A strategy that can be used in reading literature: *Characters, Aim* of story, *Problem, Solution*.

Case study   Intensive study of one person or one situation.

Central executive   The part of working memory that is responsible for monitoring and directing attention and other mental resources.

Central tendency   Typical score for a group of scores.

Cerebral palsy   Condition involving a range of motor or coordination difficulties due to brain damage.

Chain mnemonics   Memory strategies that associate one element in a series with the next element.

Chunking   Grouping individual bits of data into meaningful larger units.

Classical conditioning   Association of automatic responses with new stimuli.

Classification   Grouping objects into categories.

Classroom assessments   Classroom assessments are selected and created by teachers and can take many different forms—unit tests, essays, portfolios, projects, performances, oral presentations, etc.

Classroom management   Techniques used to maintain a healthy learning environment, relatively free of behavior problems.

Cloud computing   Allows computer users to access applications, such as Google documents or Microsoft Web Mail, as well as computing assets such as network-accessible data storage and processing to use online applications.

Cmaps   Tools for concept mapping developed by the Institute for Human and Machine Cognition that are connected to many knowledge maps and other resources on the Internet.

Coactions   Joint actions of individual biology and the environment—each shapes and influences the other.

Co-constructed process   A social process in which people interact and negotiate (usually verbally) to create an understanding or to solve a problem. The final product is shaped by all participants.

Code-switching   Moving between two speech forms.

Cognitive apprenticeship   A relationship in which a less experienced learner acquires knowledge and skills under the guidance of an expert.

Cognitive behavior modification   Procedures based on both behavioral and cognitive learning principles for changing your own behavior by using self-talk and self-instruction.

Cognitive development   Gradual orderly changes by which mental processes become more complex and sophisticated.

Cognitive domain   In Bloom's taxonomy, memory and reasoning objectives.

Cognitive evaluation theory   Suggests that events affect motivation through the individual's perception of the events as controlling behavior or providing information.

Cognitive load   The volume of resources necessary to complete a task.

Cognitive objectives   Instructional objectives stated in terms of higher-level thinking operations.

Cognitive science   The interdisciplinary study of thinking, language, intelligence, knowledge creation, and the brain.

Cognitive view of learning   A general approach that views learning as an active mental process of acquiring, remembering, and using knowledge.

Collaboration   A philosophy about how to relate to others—how to learn and work.

Collective monologue   Form of speech in which children in a group talk but do not really interact or communicate.

Commitment   In Marcia's theory of identity statuses, individuals' choices concerning political and religious beliefs, for example, usually as a consequence of exploring the options.

Community of practice   Social situation or context in which ideas are judged useful or true.

Compensation   The principle that changes in one dimension can be offset by changes in another.

Complex learning environments   Problems and learning situations that mimic the ill-structured nature of real life.

Concept   A category used to group similar events, ideas, objects, or people.

Concept map   A drawing that charts the relationships among ideas.

Concrete operations Mental tasks tied to concrete objects and situations.

Conditioned response (CR) Learned response to a previously neutral stimulus.

Conditioned stimulus (CS) Stimulus that evokes an emotional or physiological response after conditioning.

Confidence interval Range of scores within which an individual's true score is likely to fall.

Confirmation bias Seeking information that confirms our choices and beliefs, while disconfirming evidence.

Consequences Events that follow an action.

Conservation Principle that some characteristics of an object remain the same despite changes in appearance.

Constructionism How public knowledge in disciplines such as science, math, economics, or history is constructed.

Constructivism/Constructivist approach View that emphasizes the active role of the learner in building understanding and making sense of information.

Context Internal and external circumstances and situations that interact with the individual's thoughts, feelings, and actions to shape development and learning. The physical or emotional backdrop associated with an event.

Contiguity Association of two events because of repeated pairing.

Contingency contract A contract between the teacher and a student specifying what the student must do to earn a particular reward or privilege.

Continuous reinforcement schedule Presenting a reinforcer after every appropriate response.

Convergent questions Questions that have a single correct answer.

Convergent thinking Narrowing possibilities to a single answer.

Cooperation Way of working with others to attain a shared goal.

Cooperative learning Situations in which elaboration, interpretation, explanation, and argumentation are integral to the activity of the group and where learning is supported by other individuals.

Co-regulation A transitional phase during which students gradually appropriate self-regulated learning and skills through modeling, direct teaching, feedback, and coaching from teachers, parents, or peers.

Correlations Statistical descriptions of how closely two variables are related.

Creativity Imaginative, original thinking or problem solving.

Criterion-referenced grading Assessment of each student's mastery of course objectives.

Criterion-referenced testing Testing in which scores are compared to a set performance standard.

Critical periods If learning doesn't happen during these periods, it never will.

Critical thinking Evaluating conclusions by logically and systematically examining the problem, the evidence, and the solution.

Crystallized intelligence Ability to apply culturally approved problem-solving methods.

Cueing Providing a stimulus that "sets up" a desired behavior.

Cultural deficit model A model that explains the school achievement problems of ethnic minority students by assuming that their culture is inadequate and does not prepare them to succeed in school.

Cultural tools The real tools (computers, scales, etc.) and symbol systems (numbers, language, graphs) that allow people in a society to communicate, think, solve problems, and create knowledge.

Culturally relevant pedagogy Excellent teaching for students of color that includes academic success, developing/maintaining cultural competence, and developing a critical consciousness to challenge the status quo.

Culturally responsive management Taking cultural meanings and styles into account when developing management plans and responding to students.

Culture The knowledge, values, attitudes, and traditions that guide the behavior of a group of people and allow them to solve the problems of living in their environment.

Culture-fair/culture-free test A test without cultural bias.

Cyber aggression Using e-mail, Twitter, Facebook, or other social media to spread rumors, make threats, or otherwise terrorize peers.

Decay The weakening and fading of memories with the passage of time.

Decentering Focusing on more than one aspect at a time.

Declarative knowledge Verbal information; facts; "knowing that" something is the case.

Deficiency needs Maslow's four lower-level needs, which must be satisfied first.

Defining attribute Qualities that connect members of a group to a specific concept.

Descriptive studies Studies that collect detailed information about specific situations, often using observation, surveys, interviews, recordings, or a combination of these methods.

Development Orderly, adaptive changes we go through between conception and death and remain for a reasonably long period of time.

Developmental crisis A specific conflict whose resolution prepares the way for the next stage.

Deviation IQ Score based on a statistical comparison of an individual's performance with the average performance of others in that age group.

Dialect Any variety of a language spoken by a particular group.

Differentiated instruction A flexible approach to teaching that matches content, process, and product based on student differences in readiness, interests, and learning needs. Teaching that takes into account students' abilities, prior knowledge, and challenges so that instruction matches not only the subject being taught but also students' needs.

Direct instruction/Explicit teaching Systematic instruction for mastery of basic skills, facts, and information.

Disability The inability to do something specific such as walk or hear.

Discrimination Treating or acting unfairly toward particular categories of people.

Disequilibrium In Piaget's theory, the "out-of-balance" state that occurs when a person realizes that his or her current ways of thinking are not working to solve a problem or understand a situation.

Distractors Wrong answers offered as choices in a multiple-choice item.

Distributed practice Practice in brief periods with rest intervals.

Distributive justice Beliefs about how to divide materials or privileges fairly among members of a group; follows a sequence of development from equality to merit to benevolence.

Divergent questions Questions that have no single correct answer.

Divergent thinking Coming up with many possible solutions.

Domain-specific knowledge Information that is useful in a particular situation or that applies mainly to one specific topic.

Domain-specific strategies Consciously applied skills to reach goals in a particular subject or problem.

Dual coding theory Suggests that information is stored in long-term memory as either visual images or verbal units, or both.

Educational psychology The discipline concerned with teaching and learning processes; applies the methods and theories of psychology and has its own as well.

Educationally blind Individuals who have very little or no functionalal vision for learning and primarily use Braille, audio, and tactile aids, and other assistive technologies in their learning.

Effective instruction delivery Instructions that are concise, clear, and specific, and that communicate an expected result. Statements work better than questions.

Egocentric Assuming that others experience the world the way you do.

Elaboration Adding and extending meaning by connecting new information to existing knowledge.

Elaborative rehearsal Keeping information in working memory by associating it with something else you already know.

Embodied cognition Theory stating that cognitive processes develop from real-time, goal-directed interactions between humans and their environment.

Emergent literacy The skills and knowledge, usually developed in the preschool years, that are the foundation for the development of reading and writing.

Emotional and behavioral disorders Behaviors or emotions that deviate so much from the norm that they interfere with the child's own growth and development and/or the lives of others—inappropriate behaviors, unhappiness or depression, fears and anxieties, and trouble with relationships.

Empathetic listening Hearing the intent and emotions behind what another says and reflecting them back by paraphrasing.

Empirical Based on systematically collected data.

Enactive learning Learning by doing and experiencing the consequences of your actions.

Engaged time/Time on task Time spent actively engaged in the learning task at hand.

English as a Second Language (ESL) The classes devoted to teaching ELL students English.

English language learners (ELLs) Students who are learning English when their primary or heritage language is not English.

Entity view of ability Belief that ability is a fixed characteristic that cannot be changed.

Epilepsy Disorder marked by seizures and caused by abnormal electrical discharges in the brain.

Episodic buffer The process that brings together and integrates information from the phonological loop, visuospatial sketchpad, and long-term memory under the supervision of the central executive.

Episodic memory Long-term memory for information tied to a particular time and place, especially memory of the events in a person's life.

Epistemological beliefs Beliefs about the structure, stability, and certainty of knowledge, and how knowledge is best learned.

Equilibration Search for mental balance between cognitive schemes and information from the environment.

Ethnicity A cultural heritage shared by a group of people.

Ethnography A descriptive approach to research that focuses on life within a group and tries to understand the meaning of events to the people involved.

Event-related potential (ERP) Measurements that assess electrical activity of the brain through the skull or scalp.

Evidenced-based practice in psychology (EBPP) Practices that integrate the best available research with the insights of expert practitioners and knowledge of the characteristics, culture, and preferences of the client.

Executive control processes Processes such as selective attention, rehearsal, elaboration, and organization that influence encoding, storage, and retrieval of information in memory.

Exemplar An actual memory of a specific object.

Exhibition A performance test or demonstration of learning that is public and usually takes an extended time to prepare.

Expectancy X value theories Explanations of motivation that emphasize individuals' expectations for success combined with their valuing of the goal.

Experimentation Research method in which variables are manipulated and the effects recorded.

Expert teachers Experienced, effective teachers who have developed solutions for classroom problems. Their knowledge of teaching process and content is extensive and well organized.

Explicit memory Long-term memories that involve deliberate or conscious recall.

Exploration In Marcia's theory of identity statuses, the process by which adolescents consider and try out alternative beliefs, values, and behaviors in an effort to determine which will give them the most satisfaction.

Expressive vocabulary The words a person can use in speaking.

Extended families Different family members—grandparents, aunts, uncles, cousins, etc.—living in the same household or at least in daily contact with the children in the family.

Extinction The disappearance of a learned response.

Extraneous cognitive load The resources required to process stimuli irrelevant to the task.

Extrinsic motivation Motivation created by external factors such as rewards and punishments.

Failure-accepting students Students who believe their failures are due to low ability and there is little they can do about it.

Failure-avoiding students Students who avoid failure by sticking to what they know, by not taking risks, or by claiming not to care about their performance.

First wave constructivism A focus on the individual and psychological sources of knowing, as in Piaget's theory.

Flashbulb memories Clear, vivid memories of emotionally important events in your life.

Flexible grouping Grouping and regrouping students based on learning needs.

Fluid intelligence   Mental efficiency, nonverbal abilities grounded in brain development.

Flynn effect   Because of better health, smaller families, increased complexity in the environment, and more and better schooling, IQ test scores are steadily rising.

Formal operations   Mental tasks involving abstract thinking and coordination of a number of variables.

Formative assessment   Ungraded testing used before or during instruction to aid in planning and diagnosis.

Free, appropriate public education (FAPE)   Public funding to support appropriate educational programs for all students, no matter what their needs.

Functional behavioral assessment (FBA)   Procedures used to obtain information about antecedents, behaviors, and consequences to determine the reason or function of the behavior.

Functional fixedness   Inability to use objects or tools in a new way.

Functional magnetic resonance imaging (fMRI)   An MRI is an imaging technique that uses a magnetic field along with radio waves and a computer to create detailed pictures of the inside of the body. A functional MRI uses the MRI to measure the tiny changes that take place in the brain during brain activity.

Funds of knowledge   Knowledge that families and community members have acquired in many areas of work, home, and religious life that can become the basis for teaching.

Gender biases   Different views of males and females, often favoring one gender over the other.

Gender identity   The sense of self as male or female as well as the beliefs one has about gender roles and attributes.

Gender schemas   Organized cognitive structures that include gender-related information that influences how children think and behave.

Genderlects   Different ways of talking for males and females.

General intelligence (g)   A general factor in cognitive ability that is related in varying degrees to performance on all mental tests.

General knowledge   Information that is useful in many different kinds of tasks; information that applies to many situations.

Generalized seizure   A seizure involving a large portion of the brain.

Generation 1.5   Students whose characteristics, educational experiences, and language fluencies are somewhere in between those of students born in the United States and students who are recent immigrants.

Generativity   Sense of concern for future generations.

Germane cognitive load   Deep processing of information related to the task, including the application of prior knowledge to a new task or problem.

Gestalt   German for *pattern* or *whole*. Gestalt theorists hold that people organize their perceptions into coherent wholes.

Gifted and talented students   Very bright, creative, and talented students.

Glial cells   The *white matter* of the brain. These cells greatly outnumber neurons and appear to have many functions such as fighting infections, controlling blood flow and communication among neurons, and providing the *myelin* coating around axon fibers.

Goal   What an individual strives to accomplish.

Goal orientations   Patterns of beliefs about goals related to achievement in school.

Goal structure   The way students relate to others who are also working toward a particular goal.

Goal-directed actions   Deliberate actions toward a goal.

Good behavior game   Arrangement where a class is divided into teams and each team receives demerit points for breaking agreed-upon rules of good behavior.

Grade-equivalent score   Measure of grade level based on comparison with norming samples from each grade.

Grading on the curve   Norm-referenced grading that compares students' performance to an average level.

Group consequences   Rewards or punishments given to a class as a whole for adhering to or violating rules of conduct.

Group discussion   Conversation in which the teacher does not have the dominant role; students pose and answer their own questions.

Group focus   The ability to keep as many students as possible involved in activities.

Handicap   A disadvantage in a particular situation, sometimes caused by a disability.

Heritage language   The language spoken in the student's home or by members of the family.

Heuristic   General strategy used in attempting to solve problems.

Hierarchy of needs   Maslow's model of seven levels of human needs, from basic physiological requirements to the need for self-actualization.

High-stakes testing   Standardized tests whose results have powerful influences when used by school administrators, other officials, or employers to make decisions.

Hostile aggression   Bold, direct action that is intended to hurt someone else; unprovoked attack.

Human agency   The capacity to coordinate learning skills, motivation, and emotions to reach your goals.

Humanistic interpretation   Approach to motivation that emphasizes personal freedom, choice, self-determination, and striving for personal growth.

Hypothesis/Hypotheses   A prediction of what will happen in a research study based on theory and previous research.

Hypothetico-deductive reasoning   A formal-operations problem-solving strategy in which an individual begins by identifying all the factors that might affect a problem and then deduces and systematically evaluates specific solutions.

"I" message   Clear, nonaccusatory statement of how something is affecting you.

Identity   Principle that a person or object remains the same over time. (Piaget) The complex answer to the question: "Who am I?" (Erikson)

Identity achievement   Strong sense of commitment to life choices after free consideration of alternatives.

Identity diffusion   Uncenteredness; confusion about who one is and what one wants.

Identity foreclosure   Acceptance of parental life choices without consideration of options.

Images   Representations based on the physical attributes—the appearance—of information.

Immersive Virtual Learning Environment (IVLE)   A simulation of a real-world environment that immerses students in tasks like those required in a professional practicum.

Immigrants   People who voluntarily leave their country to become permanent residents in a new place.

Implicit memory   Knowledge that we are not conscious of recalling, but that influences our behavior or thought without our awareness.

Importance/Attainment value   The importance of doing well on a task; how success on the task meets personal needs.

Incentive   An object or event that encourages or discourages behavior.

Inclusion   The integration of all students, including those with severe disabilities, into regular classes.

Incremental view of ability   Belief that ability is a set of skills that can be changed.

Individualized Education Program (IEP)   Annually revised program for an exceptional student, detailing present achievement level, goals, and strategies, drawn up by teachers, parents, specialists, and (if possible) the student.

Individuals with Disabilities Education Improvement Act (IDEA)   Latest amendment of PL 94-142; guarantees a free public education to all children regardless of disability.

Industry   Eagerness to engage in productive work.

Informal assessments   Ungraded (formative) assessments that gather information from multiple sources to help teachers make decisions.

Information processing   The human mind's activity of taking in, storing, and using information.

Initiative   Willingness to begin new activities and explore new directions.

Inquiry learning   Approach in which the teacher presents a puzzling situation and students solve the problem by gathering data and testing their conclusions.

Inside-out skills   The emergent literacy skills of knowledge of graphemes, phonological awareness, syntactic awareness, phoneme-grapheme correspondence, and emergent writing.

Insight   In problem solving, the sudden realization of a solution. In the triarchic theory of intelligence, the ability to deal effectively with novel situations.

Instructional objectives   Clear statement of what students are intended to learn through instruction.

Instrumental aggression   Strong actions aimed at claiming an object, place, or privilege—not intended to harm, but may lead to harm.

Integration   Fitting the child with special needs into existing class structures.

Integrity   Sense of self-acceptance and fulfillment.

Intellectual disabilities/Mental retardation   Significantly below-average intellectual and adaptive social behavior, evident before age 18.

Intelligence quotient (IQ)   Score comparing mental and chronological ages.

Intelligence   Ability or abilities to acquire and use knowledge for solving problems and adapting to the world.

Interest or intrinsic value   The enjoyment a person gets from a task.

Interference   The process that occurs when remembering certain information is hampered by the presence of other information.

Intermittent reinforcement schedule   Presenting a reinforcer after some but not all responses.

Internalize   Process whereby children adopt external standards as their own.

Intersubjective attitude   A commitment to build shared meaning with others by finding common ground and exchanging interpretations.

Interval schedule   Length of time between reinforcers.

Intimacy   Forming close, enduring relationships with others.

Intrinsic cognitive load   The resources required by the task itself, regardless of other stimuli.

Intrinsic motivation   Motivation associated with activities that are their own reward.

Jigsaw Classroom   A learning process in which each student is part of a group and each group member is given part of the material to be learned by the whole group. Students become "expert" on their piece and then teach it to the others in their group.

Keyword method   System of associating new words or concepts with similar-sounding cue words and images.

KWL   A strategy to guide reading and inquiry: Before—What do I already *know*? What do I *want* to know? After—What have I *learned?*

Lateralization   The specialization of the two hemispheres (sides) of the brain cortex.

Learned helplessness   The expectation, based on previous experiences with a lack of control, that all of one's efforts will lead to failure.

Learning   Process through which experience causes permanent change in knowledge or behavior.

Learning disability   Problem with acquisition and use of language; may show up as difficulty with reading, writing, reasoning, or math.

Learning Management System (LMS)   Systems that deliver e-learning, provide tools and learning materials, keep records, administer assessments, and manage learning.

Learning preferences   Preferred ways of studying and learning, such as using pictures instead of text, working with other people versus alone, learning in structured or in unstructured situations, and so on.

Learning sciences   An interdisciplinary science of learning, based on research in psychology, education, computer science, philosophy, sociology, anthropology, neuroscience, and other fields that study learning.

Learning strategies   A special kind of procedural knowledge—*knowing how* to approach learning tasks.

Learning styles   Characteristic approaches to learning and studying.

Least restrictive environment (LRE)   Educating each child with peers in the regular classroom to the greatest extent possible.

Legitimate peripheral participation   Genuine involvement in the work of the group, even if your abilities are undeveloped and contributions are small.

Lesson study   As a group, teachers develop, test, improve, and retest lessons until they are satisfied with the final version.

Levels of processing theory   Theory that recall of information is based on how deeply it is processed.

Limited-English-proficient (LEP)   A term also used for students who are learning English when their primary or heritage language is not English—not the preferred term because of the negative connotations.

LINCS Vocabulary Strategy   A strategy that uses stories and imagery to help students learn how to identify, organize, define, and remember words and their meanings.

Loci method   Technique of associating items with specific places.

Locus of causality   The location—internal or external—of the cause of behavior.

Long-term memory   Permanent store of knowledge.

Low vision   Vision limited to close objects.

Mainstreaming   Teaching children with disabilities in regular classes for part or all of their school day.

Maintenance rehearsal   Keeping information in working memory by repeating it to yourself.

Massed practice   Practice for a single extended period.

Massive Multi-player Online Games (MMOG)   Interactive gaming environments constructed in virtual worlds where the learner assumes a character role or avatar.

Mastery experiences   Our own direct experiences—the most powerful source of efficacy information.

Mastery goal   A personal intention to improve abilities and learn, no matter how performance suffers.

Mastery-oriented students   Students who focus on learning goals because they value achievement and see ability as improvable.

Maturation   Genetically programmed, naturally occurring changes over time.

Mean   Arithmetical average.

Means-ends analysis   Heuristic in which a goal is divided into subgoals.

Measurement   An evaluation expressed in quantitative (number) terms.

Median   Middle score in a group of scores.

Melting pot   A metaphor for the absorption and assimilation of immigrants into the mainstream of society so that ethnic differences vanish.

Menarche   The first menstrual period in girls.

Mental age   In intelligence testing, a performance that represents average abilities for that age group.

Metacognition   Knowledge about our own thinking processes.

Metalinguistic awareness   Understanding about one's own use of language.

Microgenetic studies   Detailed observation and analysis of changes in a cognitive process as the process unfolds over a several-day or several-week period of time.

Minority group   A group of people who have been socially disadvantaged—not always a minority in actual numbers.

Mirror systems   Areas of the brain that fire both during perception of an action by someone else and when performing the action.

Mnemonics   Techniques for remembering; the art of memory.

Mode   Most frequently occurring score.

Modeling   Changes in behavior, thinking, or emotions that happen through observing another person—a model.

Monolingual   Speaking only one language.

Moral dilemma   Situations in which no choice is clearly and indisputably right.

Moral realism   Stage of development wherein children see rules as absolute.

Moral reasoning   The thinking process involved in judgments about questions of right and wrong.

Morality of cooperation   Stage of development wherein children realize that people make rules and people can change them.

Moratorium   Identity crisis; suspension of choices because of struggle.

Motivation   An internal state that arouses, directs, and maintains behavior.

Motivation to learn   The tendency to find academic activities meaningful and worthwhile and to try to benefit from them.

Movement management   Keeping lessons and the group moving at an appropriate (and flexible) pace, with smooth transitions and variety.

Multicultural education   Education that promotes equity in the schooling of all students.

Multiple representations of content   Considering problems using various analogies, examples, and metaphors.

Myelination   The process by which neural fibers are coated with a fatty sheath called *myelin* that makes message transfer more efficient.

Natural/logical consequences   Instead of punishing, have students redo, repair, or in some way face the consequences that naturally flow from their actions.

Need for autonomy   The desire to have our own wishes, rather than external rewards or pressures, determine our actions.

Negative correlation   A relationship between two variables in which a high value on one is associated with a low value on the other. Example: height and distance from top of head to the ceiling.

Negative reinforcement   Strengthening behavior by removing an aversive stimulus when the behavior occurs.

Neo-Piagetian theories   More recent theories that integrate findings about attention, memory, and strategy use with Piaget's insights about children's thinking and the construction of knowledge.

Neurogenesis   The production of new neurons.

Neurons   Nerve cells that store and transfer information.

Neutral stimulus   Stimulus not connected to a response.

Nigrescence   The process of developing a Black identity.

Norm group   Large sample of students serving as a comparison group for scoring tests.

Normal distribution   The most commonly occurring distribution, in which scores are distributed evenly around the mean.

Norm-referenced grading   Assessment of students' achievement in relation to one another.

Norm-referenced testing   Testing in which scores are compared with the average performance of others.

Object permanence   The understanding that objects have a separate, permanent existence.

Objective testing   Multiple-choice, matching, true/false, short-answer, and fill-in tests; scoring answers does not require interpretation.

Observational learning   Learning by observation and imitation of others—vicarious learning.

Operant conditioning   Learning in which voluntary behavior is strengthened or weakened by consequences or antecedents.

Operants   Voluntary (and generally goal-directed) behaviors emitted by a person or an animal.

Operations   Actions a person carries out by thinking them through instead of literally performing the actions.

Organization   Ongoing process of arranging information and experiences into mental systems or categories. Ordered and logical network of relations.

Outside-in skills   The emergent literacy skills of language, narrative, conventions of print, and emergent reading.

Overlapping   Supervising several activities at once.

Overlearning   Practicing a skill past the point of mastery.

Overregularize   To apply a rule of syntax or grammar in situations where the rule does not apply, e.g., "the bike was broked."

Overt aggression   A form of hostile aggression that involves physical attack.

Paraphrase rule   Policy whereby listeners must accurately summarize what a speaker has said before being allowed to respond.

Parenting styles   The ways of interacting with and disciplining children.

Part learning   Breaking a list of items into shorter lists.

Participant observation   A method for conducting descriptive research in which the researcher becomes a participant in the situation in order to better understand life in that group.

Participants/Subjects   People or animals studied.

Participation structures   The formal and informal rules for how to take part in a given activity.

Pedagogical content knowledge   Teacher knowledge that combines mastery of *academic content* with knowing *how to teach* the content and how to match instruction to *student differences*.

Peer cultures   Groups of children or adolescents with their own rules and norms, particularly about such things as dress, appearance, music, language, social values, and behavior.

Percentile rank   Percentage of those in the norming sample who scored at or below an individual's score.

Perception   Interpretation of sensory information.

Performance assessments   Any form of assessment that requires students to carry out an activity or produce a product in order to demonstrate learning.

Performance goal   A personal intention to seem competent or perform well in the eyes of others.

Personal development   Changes in personality that take place as one grows.

Personal Learning Environment (PLE)   Provides tools that support individualized learning in a variety of contexts and situations.

Personal Learning Network (PLN)   Framework in which knowledge is constructed through online peer interactions.

Perspective-taking ability   Understanding that others have different feelings and experiences.

Pervasive developmental disorder (PDD)   A term favored by the medical community to describe autism spectrum disorders.

Phonological loop   Part of working memory. A speech- and sound-related system for holding and rehearsing (refreshing) words and sounds in short-term memory for about 1.5 to 2 seconds.

Physical development   Changes in body structure and function over time.

Plasticity   The brain's tendency to remain somewhat adaptable or flexible.

Portfolio   A collection of the student's work in an area, showing growth, self-reflection, and achievement.

Positive behavior supports (PBS)   Interventions designed to replace problem behaviors with new actions that serve the same purpose for the student.

Positive correlation   A relationship between two variables in which the two increase or decrease together. Example: calorie intake and weight gain.

Positive practice   Practicing correct responses immediately after errors.

Positive reinforcement   Strengthening behavior by presenting a desired stimulus after the behavior.

Positron emission tomography (PET)   A method of localizing and measuring brain activity using computer-assisted motion pictures of the brain.

Pragmatics   The rules for when and how to use language to be an effective communicator in a particular culture.

Precorrection   A tool for positive behavior support that involves identifying the context for a student's misbehavior, clearly specifying the alternative expected behavior, modifying the situation to make the problem behavior less likely, then rehearsing the expected positive behaviors in the new context and providing powerful reinforcers.

Prejudice   Prejudgment or irrational generalization about an entire category of people.

Premack principle   Principle stating that a more-preferred activity can serve as a reinforcer for a less-preferred activity.

Preoperational   The stage before a child masters logical mental operations.

Presentation punishment   Decreasing the chances that a behavior will occur again by presenting an aversive stimulus following the behavior; also called *Type I punishment*.

Pretest   Formative test for assessing students' knowledge, readiness, and abilities.

Priming   Activating a concept in memory or the spread of activation from one concept to another.

Principle   Established relationship between factors.

Private speech   Children's self-talk, which guides their thinking and action. Eventually, these verbalizations are internalized as silent inner speech.

Problem   Any situation in which you are trying to reach some goal and must find a means to do so.

Problem solving   Creating new solutions for problems.

Problem-based learning   Students are confronted with a problem that launches their inquiry as they collaborate to find solutions and learn valuable information and skills in the process.

Procedural knowledge   Knowledge that is demonstrated when we perform a task; "knowing how."

Procedural memory   Long-term memory for how to do things.

Procedures/routines   Prescribed steps for an activity.

Production deficiency   Students learn problem-solving strategies, but do not apply them when they could or should.

Productions   The contents of procedural memory; rules about what actions to take, given certain conditions. Units of knowledge that combine conditions with actions in "if this happens, do that" relationships that often are automatic.

Prompt   A reminder that follows a cue to make sure the person reacts to the cue.

Propositional network   Set of interconnected concepts and relationships in which long-term knowledge is held.

Prototype   A best example or best representative of a category.

Psychomotor domain   Physical ability and coordination objectives.

Psychosocial   Describing the relation of the individual's emotional needs to the social environment.

Puberty   The physiological changes during adolescence that lead to the ability to reproduce.

Punishment   Process that weakens or suppresses behavior.

Pygmalion effect   Exceptional progress by a student as a result of high teacher expectations for that student; named for mythological king, Pygmalion, who made a statue, then caused it to be brought to life.

Quasi-experimental studies   Studies that fit most of the criteria for true experiments, with the important exception that the participants are not assigned to groups at random. Instead, existing groups such as classes or schools participate in the experiments.

Race   A socially constructed category based on appearances and ancestry.

Racial and ethnic pride   A positive self-concept about one's racial or ethnic heritage.

Radical constructivism   Knowledge is assumed to be the individual's construction; it cannot be judged right or wrong.

Random   Without any definite pattern; following no rule.

Range   Distance between the highest and the lowest scores in a group.

Ratio schedule   Reinforcement based on the number of responses between reinforcers.

READS   A five-step reading strategy: *Review* headings; *Examine* boldface words; *Ask,* "What do I expect to learn?"; *Do* it—Read; *Summarize* in your own words.

Receptive vocabulary   The words a person can understand in spoken or written words.

Reciprocal questioning   Students work in pairs or triads to ask and answer questions about lesson material.

Reciprocal teaching   Learning to apply the strategies of questioning, summarizing, predicting, and clarifying; designed to help students understand and think deeply about what they read.

Reconstruction   Recreating information by using memories, expectations, logic, and existing knowledge.

Reflective   Thoughtful and inventive. Reflective teachers think back over situations to analyze what they did and why, and to consider how they might improve learning for their students.

Refugees   A special group of immigrants who also relocate voluntarily, but who are fleeing their home country because it is not safe.

Reinforcement   Use of consequences to strengthen behavior.

Reinforcer   Any event that follows a behavior and increases the chances that the behavior will occur again.

Relational aggression   A form of hostile aggression that involves verbal attacks and other actions meant to harm social relationships.

Reliability   Consistency of test results.

Removal punishment   Decreasing the chances that a behavior will occur again by removing a pleasant stimulus following the behavior; also called *Type II punishment*.

Representativeness heuristic   Judging the likelihood of an event based on how well the events match your prototypes—what you think is representative of the category.

Reprimands   Criticisms for misbehavior; rebukes.

Resilience   The ability to adapt successfully in spite of difficult circumstances and threats to development.

Resistance culture   Group values and beliefs about refusing to adopt the behaviors and attitudes of the majority culture.

Respondents   Responses (generally automatic or involuntary) elicited by specific stimuli.

Response   Observable reaction to a stimulus.

Response cost   Punishment by loss of reinforcers.

Response set   Rigidity; the tendency to respond in the most familiar way.

Response to intervention (RTI)   A process to make sure students get appropriate research-based instruction and support as soon as possible and that teachers are systematic in documenting what interventions they have tried with these students so this information can be used in planning.

Restructuring   Conceiving of a problem in a new or different way.

Retrieval   Process of searching for and finding information in long-term memory.

Reversibility   A characteristic of Piagetian logical operations—the ability to think through a series of steps, then mentally reverse the steps and return to the starting point; also called reversible thinking.

Reversible thinking   Thinking backward, from the end to the beginning.

Reward   An attractive object or event supplied as a consequence of a behavior.

Ripple effect   "Contagious" spreading of behaviors through imitation.

Rote memorization   Remembering information by repetition without necessarily understanding the meaning of the information.

Rules   Statements specifying expected and forbidden behaviors; dos and don'ts.

Scaffolding   Support for learning and problem solving. The support could be clues, reminders, encouragement, breaking the problem down into steps, providing an example or anything else that allows the student to grow in independence as a learner. Teachers and students make meaningful connections between what the teacher knows and what the students know and need in order to help the students learn more.

Schema-driven problem solving   Recognizing a problem as a "disguised" version of an old problem for which one already has a solution.

Schemas (singular, *schema*)   Basic structures for organizing information; concepts.

Schemes   Mental systems or categories of perception and experience.

Scoring rubrics   Rules that are used to determine the quality of a student's performance.

Script   Schema or expected plan for the sequence of steps in a common event such as buying groceries or ordering pizza.

Scripted cooperation   Learning strategy in which two students take turns summarizing material and criticizing the summaries.

Seatwork   Independent classroom work.

Second wave constructivism   A focus on the social and cultural sources of knowing, as in Vygotsky's theory.

Section 504   A part of civil rights law that prevents discrimination against people with disabilities in programs that receive federal funds, such as public schools.

Self-actualization   Fulfilling one's potential.

Self-concept   Individuals' knowledge and beliefs about themselves—their ideas, feelings, attitudes, and expectations.

Self-efficacy   A person's sense of being able to deal effectively with a particular task. Beliefs about personal competence in a particular situation.

Self-esteem   The value each of us places on our own characteristics, abilities, and behaviors.

Self-fulfilling prophecy   A groundless expectation that is confirmed because it has been expected.

Self-handicapping   Students may engage in behavior that blocks their own success in order to avoid testing their true ability.

Self-instruction   Talking oneself through the steps of a task.

Self-management   Management of your own behavior and acceptance of responsibility for your own actions. Also the use of behavioral learning principles to change your own behavior.

Self-regulated learning   A view of learning as skills and will applied to analyzing learning tasks, setting goals and planning how to do the task, applying skills, and especially making adjustments about how learning is carried out.

Self-regulation   Process of activating and sustaining thoughts, behaviors, and emotions in order to reach goals.

Self-regulatory knowledge   Knowing how to manage your learning, or knowing how and when to use your declarative and procedural knowledge.

Self-reinforcement   Controlling (selecting and administering) your own reinforcers.

Semantic memory   Memory for meaning.

Semilingual   A lack of proficiency in any language; speaking one or more languages inadequately.

Semiotic function   The ability to use symbols—language, pictures, signs, or gestures—to represent actions or objects mentally.

Sensitive periods   Times when a person is especially ready to learn certain things or responsive to certain experiences.

Sensorimotor   Involving the senses and motor activity.

Sensory memory   System that holds sensory information very briefly.

Serial-position effect   The tendency to remember the beginning and the end, but not the middle of a list.

Seriation   Arranging objects in sequential order according to one aspect, such as size, weight, or volume.

Service learning   A teaching strategy that invites students to identify, research, and address real community challenges, using knowledge and skills learned in the classroom.

Sexual identity   A complex combination of beliefs about gender roles and sexual orientation.

Shaping   Reinforcing each small step of progress toward a desired goal or behavior.

Shared regulation   Students working together to regulate each other through reminders, prompts, and other guidance.

Sheltered instruction   Approach to teaching that improves English language skills while teaching content to ELL students by putting the words and concepts of the content into context to make the content more understandable.

Sheltered Instruction Observation Protocol or SIOP®   An observational system to check that each element of sheltered instruction is present for a teacher.

Short-term memory   Component of memory system that holds information for about 20 seconds.

Single-subject experimental studies   Systematic interventions to study effects with one person, often by applying and then withdrawing a treatment.

Situated learning   The idea that skills and knowledge are tied to the situation in which they were learned and that they are difficult to apply in new settings.

Social cognitive theory   Theory that adds concern with cognitive factors such as beliefs, self-perceptions, and expectations to social learning theory.

Social conventions   Agreed-upon rules and ways of doing things in a particular situation.

Social development   Changes over time in the ways we relate to others.

Social goals   A wide variety of needs and motives to be connected to others or part of a group.

Social isolation   Removal of a disruptive student for 5 to 10 minutes.

Social learning theory   Theory that emphasizes learning through observation of others.

Social negotiation   Aspect of learning process that relies on collaboration with others and respect for different perspectives.

Social persuasion   A "pep talk" or specific performance feedback—one source of self-efficacy.

Sociocultural theory   Emphasizes role in development of cooperative dialogues between children and more knowledgeable members of society. Children learn the culture of their community (ways of thinking and behaving) through these interactions.

Sociocultural views of motivation   Perspectives that emphasize participation, identities, and interpersonal relations within communities of practice.

Socioeconomic status (SES)   Relative standing in the society based on income, power, background, and prestige.

Sociolinguistics   The study of the formal and informal rules for how, when, about what, to whom, and how long to speak in conversations within cultural groups.

Spasticity   Overly tight or tense muscles, characteristic of some forms of cerebral palsy.

Speech disorder   Inability to produce sounds effectively for speaking.

Spermarche   The first sperm ejaculation for boys.

Spiral curriculum   Bruner's design for teaching that introduces the fundamental structure of all subjects early in the school years, then revisits the subjects in more and more complex forms over time.

Spreading activation Retrieval of pieces of information based on their relatedness to one another. Remembering one bit of information activates (stimulates) recall of associated information.

Standard deviation Measure of how widely scores vary from the mean.

Standard error of measurement Hypothetical estimate of variation in scores if testing were repeated.

Standard scores Scores based on the standard deviation.

Standardized tests Tests given, usually nationwide, under uniform conditions and scored according to uniform procedures.

Stanine scores Whole number scores from 1 to 9, each representing a wide range of raw scores.

Statistically significant Not likely to be a chance occurrence.

Stem The question part of a multiple-choice item.

Stereotype Schema that organizes knowledge or perceptions about a category.

Stereotype threat The extra emotional and cognitive burden that your performance in an academic situation might confirm a stereotype that others hold about you.

Stimulus Event that activates behavior.

Stimulus control Capacity for the presence or absence of antecedents to cause behaviors.

Story grammar Typical structure or organization for a category of stories.

Structured controversy Students work in pairs within their four-person cooperative groups to research a particular controversy.

Structured English immersion (SEI) An environment that teaches English rapidly by maximizing instruction in English and using English at a level appropriate to the abilities of the ELLs in the class.

Successive approximations Reinforcing small steps to reach a goal; the small component steps that make up a complex behavior.

Summative assessment Testing that follows instruction and assesses achievement.

Sustaining expectation effect Student performance is maintained at a certain level because teachers don't recognize improvements.

Synapses The tiny space between neurons—chemical messages are sent across these gaps.

Syntax The order of words in phrases or sentences.

_T_ score Standard score with a mean of 50 and a standard deviation of 10.

Task analysis System for breaking down a task hierarchically into basic skills and subskills.

Taxonomy Classification system.

Teachers' sense of efficacy A teacher's belief that he or she can reach even the most difficult students and help them learn.

Theory Integrated statement of principles that attempts to explain a phenomenon and make predictions.

Theory of mind An understanding that other people are people too, with their own minds, thoughts, feelings, beliefs, desires, and perceptions.

Theory of multiple intelligences In Gardner's theory of intelligence, a person's eight separate abilities: logical-mathematical, linguistic, musical, spatial, bodily-kinesthetic, interpersonal, intrapersonal, and naturalist.

Theory-based An explanation for concept formation that suggests our classifications are based on ideas about the world that we create to make sense of things.

Time out Technically, the removal of all reinforcement. In practice, isolation of a student from the rest of the class for a brief time.

Token reinforcement system System in which tokens earned for academic work and positive classroom behavior can be exchanged for some desired reward.

Top-down Making sense of information by using context and what we already know about the situation; sometimes called _conceptually driven perception_.

Tracking Assignment to different classes and academic experiences based on achievement.

Transfer Influence of previously learned material on new material; the productive (not reproductive) uses of cognitive tools and motivations.

Transition programming Gradual preparation of students with special needs to move from high school into further education or training, employment, or community involvement.

Triarchic reciprocal causality An explanation of behavior that emphasizes the mutual effects of the individual and the environment on each other.

Triarchic theory of successful intelligence A three-part description of the mental abilities (thinking processes, coping with new experiences, and adapting to context) that lead to more or less intelligent behavior.

True score The score the student would get if the measurement were completely accurate and error-free.

Unconditioned response (UR) Naturally occurring emotional or physiological response.

Unconditioned stimulus (US) Stimulus that automatically produces an emotional or physiological response.

Universal design Considering the needs of all users in the design of new tools, learning programs, or Web sites.

Utility value The contribution of a task to meeting one's goals.

Validity Degree to which a test measures what it is intended to measure.

Variability Degree of difference or deviation from mean.

Verbalization Putting your problem-solving plan and its logic into words.

Vicarious experiences Accomplishments that are modeled by someone else.

Vicarious reinforcement Increasing the chances that we will repeat a behavior by observing another person being reinforced for that behavior.

Virtual Learning Environments (VLE) A broad term that describes many ways of learning in virtual or online systems.

Visuospatial sketchpad Part of working memory. A holding system for visual and spatial information.

Voicing problems Inappropriate pitch, quality, loudness, or intonation.

Volition Will power; self-discipline; work styles that protect opportunities to reach goals by applying self-regulated learning.

Warm demanders Effective teachers with African American students who show both high expectations and great caring for their students.

Within-class ability grouping   System of grouping in which students in a class are divided into two or three groups based on ability in an attempt to accommodate student differences.

Withitness   According to Kounin, awareness of everything happening in a classroom.

Work-avoidant learners   Students who don't want to learn or to look smart, but just want to avoid work.

Working memory   The brain system that provides temporary holding and processing of information to accomplish complex cognitive tasks as language comprehension, learning, and reasoning; the information that you are focusing on at a given moment.

Working-backward strategy   Heuristic in which one starts with the goal and moves backward to solve the problem.

z score   Standard score indicating the number of standard deviations above or below the mean that a particular score falls.

Zero reject   A basic principle of IDEA specifying that no student with a disability, no matter what kind or how severe, can be denied a free public education.

Zone of proximal development   Phase at which a child can master a task if given appropriate help and support.

References

Aamodt, S., & Wang, S. (2008). *Welcome to your brain: Why you lose your car keys but never forget how to drive and other puzzles of everyday life*. New York, NY: Bloomsbury.

Aber, J. L., Brown, J. L., & Jones, S. M. (2003). Developmental trajectories toward violence in middle childhood: Course, demographic differences, and response to school-based intervention. *Developmental Psychology, 39*, 324–348.

Aboud, F. E. (2003). The formation of in-group favoritism and out-group prejudice in young children: Are they distinct attitudes? *Developmental Psychology, 39*, 48–60.

Abrams, I. M., & Madaus, G. F. (2003). The lessons of high stakes testing. *Educational Leadership, 61*(32), 31–35.

Ackerman, B. P., Brown, E. D., & Izard, C. E. (2004). The relations between contextual risk, earned income, and the school adjustment of children from economically disadvantaged families. *Developmental Psychology, 40*, 204–216.

Ackerman, P. L., Beier, M. E., & Boyle, M. O. (2005). Working memory and intelligence: The same or different constructs? *Psychological Bulletin, 131*, 30–60.

Adams, G. R., Berzonsky, M. D., & Keating, L. (2006). Psychosocial resources in first-year university students: The role of identity processes and social relationships. *Journal of Youth and Adolescence, 35*(1), 78–88.

Ainley, M., Hidi, S., & Berndorf, D. (2002). Interest, learning, and the psychological processes that mediate their relationship. *Journal of Educational Psychology, 94*, 545–561.

Airasian, P. W. (2005). *Classroom assessment: Concepts and applications* (5th ed.). New York, NY: McGraw-Hill.

Albanese, M. A., & Mitchell, S. A. (1993). Problem-based learning: A review of literature on its outcomes and implementation issues. *Academic Medicine, 68*, 52–81.

Alber, S. R., & Heward, W. L. (1997). Recruit it or lose it! Training students to recruit positive teacher attention. *Intervention in School and Clinic, 32*, 275–282.

Alber, S. R., & Heward, W. L. (2000). Teaching students to recruit positive attention: A review and recommendations. *Journal of Behavioral Education, 10*, 177–204.

Alberto, P. A., & Troutman, A. C. (2009). *Applied behavior analysis for teachers* (8th ed.). Boston, MA: Pearson.

Alderman, M. K. (2004). *Motivation for achievement: Possibilities for teaching and learning*. Mahwah, NJ: Erlbaum.

Alexander, P. A. (1992). Domain knowledge: Evolving themes and emerging concerns. *Educational Psychologist, 27*, 33–51.

Alexander, P. A. (1996). The past, present, and future of knowledge research: A reexamination of the role of knowledge in learning and instruction. *Educational Psychologist, 31*, 89–92.

Alexander, P. A. (1997). Mapping the multidimensional nature of domain learning: The interplay of cognitive, motivational, and strategic forces. *Advances in Motivation and Achievement, 10*, 213–250.

Alexander, P. A., Kulikowich, J. M., & Schulze, S. K. (1994). How subject-matter knowledge affects recall and interest. *American Educational Research Journal, 31*, 313–337.

Alexander, P. A., Schallert, D. L., & Reynolds, R. E. (2009). What is learning anyway? A topographical perspective considered. *Educational Psychologist, 44*, 176–192.

Alexander, P. A., & Winne, P. H. (2006). *Handbook of educational psychology* (2nd ed.). Mahwah, NJ: Erlbaum.

Alferink, L. A., & Farmer-Dougan, V. (2010). Brain-(not) based education: Dangers of misunderstanding and misapplication of neuroscience research. *Exceptionality, 18*, 42–52.

Alfieri, L., Brooks, P. J., Aldrich, N. J., & Tenenbaum, H. R. (2011). Does discovery-based instruction enhance learning? *Journal of Educational Psychology, 103*, 1–18.

Alliance for Service Learning in Education Reform. (1993). Standards of quality for school based service learning. *Equity and Excellence in Education, 26*(2), 71–77.

Allington, R. L., & McGill-Frazen, A. (2003). The impact of summer setback on the reading achievement gap. *Phi Delta Kappan, 85*(1), 68–75.

Allington, R. L., & McGill-Frazen, A. (2008). Got books? *Educational Leadership, 65*(7), 20–23.

Alloway, N. (1984). *Teacher expectations*. Paper presented at the meetings of the Australian Association for Research in Education, Perth, Australia.

Alloway, T. P, Banner, G. E., & Smith, P. (2010). Working memory and cognitive styles in adolescents' attainment. *British Journal of Educational Psychology, 80*, 567–581.

Alloway, T. P., Gathercole, S. E., & Pickering, S. J. (2006). Verbal and visuo-spatial short-term and working memory in children: Are they separable? *Child Development, 77*, 1698–1716.

Alloy, L. B., & Seligman, M. E. P. (1979). On the cognitive component of learned helplessness and depression. *The Journal of Learning and Motivation, 13*, 219–276.

Aloe, A. M., & Becker, B. J. (2009). Teacher verbal ability and school outcomes: Where is the evidence? *Educational Researcher, 38*, 612–624.

Alter, A. L., Aaronson, J., Darley, J. M., Rodriguez, C., & Ruble, D. N. (2009). Rising to the threat: Reducing stereotype threat by reframing the threat as a challenge. *Journal of Experimental Social Psychology, 46*, 166–171.

Altermatt, E. R., Pomerantz, E. M., Ruble, D. N., Frey, K. S., & Greulich, F. K. (2002). Predicting changes in children's self-perceptions of academic competence: A naturalistic examination of evaluative discourse among classmates. *Developmental Psychology, 38*, 903–917.

Alvidrez, J., & Weinstein, R. S. (1999). Early teacher perceptions and later student academic achievement. *Journal of Educational Psychology, 91*, 731–746.

Amabile, T. M. (1996). *Creativity in context*. Boulder, CO: Westview Press.

Amabile, T. M. (2001). Beyond talent: John Irving and the passionate craft of creativity. *American Psychologist, 56*, 333–336.

Amato, L. F., Loomis, L. S., & Booth, A. (1995). Parental divorce, marital conflict, and offspring well-being during early adulthood. *Social Forces, 73*, 895–915.

Amato, P. R. (2001). Children of divorce in the 1990s: An update of the Amato and Keith (1991) meta-analysis. *Journal of Family Psychology, 15*, 355–370.

Amato, P. R. (2006). Marital discord, divorce, and children's well-being. In A. Clarke-Stewart & J. Dunn (Eds.), *Families count: Effects on child and adolescent development* (pp. 179–202). New York, NY: Cambridge University Press.

American Association on Intellectual and Developmental Disabilities (AAIDD). (2010). Definition of intellectual disability. Available online at: http://www.aamr.org/content_100. cfm?navID_21

American Cancer Society. (2010). Child and teen tobacco use: Understanding the problem. Atlanta, GA: Author. Available online at: http://www.cancer.org/cancer/cancercauses/ tobaccocancer/childandteentobaccouse/ child-and-teen-tobacco-use

American Psychiatric Association. (2000). *Diagnostic and statistical manual of mental disorders* (4th ed., text revision) *DSM-IV-TR*. Washington, DC: Author.

American Psychological Association. (2001). Making stepfamilies work. Available online at: http://www.apa.org/helpcenter/stepfamily.aspx. APA Psychology Help Center.

American Psychological Association. (2004). An Overview of the psychological literature on the effects of divorce on children. Available online at: http://www.apa.org/about/gr/issues/cyf/ divorce.aspx

American Psychological Association Task Force on Evidence-Based Practice for Children and Adolescents. (2008). *Disseminating evidence-based practice for children and adolescents: A systems approach to enhancing care*. Washington, DC: Author. Available online at: www.apa. org/pi/cyf/evidence.html

Ames, C. (1992). Classrooms: Goals, structures, and student motivation. *Journal of Educational Psychology, 84*, 261–271.

Anderman, E. M., & Anderman, L. H. (2009). *Motivating children and adolescents in schools*. Columbus, OH: Merrill/Prentice Hall.

Anderman, E. M., & Anderman, L. H. (2010). *Motivating children and adolescents in schools*. Columbus, OH: Merrill/Prentice Hall.

Anderman, E. M., Cupp, P. K., & Lane, D. (2009). Impulsivity and academic cheating. *Journal of Experimental Education, 78*, 135–150.

Anderman, E. M., & Maehr, M. L. (1994). Motivation and schooling in the middle grades. *Review of Educational Research, 64*, 287–310.

Anderman, E. M., & Midgley, C. (2004). Changes in self-reported academic cheating across the transition from middle school to high school. *Contemporary Educational Psychology, 29,* 499–517.

Anderman, E. M., & Patrick, H. (2012). Achievement goal theory, conceptualization of ability/intelligence, and classroom climate. In S. L. Christenson, A. L. Reschly, & C. Wylie (Eds.), *The handbook of research on student engagement.* New York, NY: Springer Science.

Anderson, C. A., Berkowitz, L., Donnerstein, E., Huesmann, L. R., Johnson, J. D., Linz, D., & Wartella, E. (2003). The influence of media violence on youth. *Psychological Science in the Public Interest, 4,* 81–110.

Anderson, C. A., Shibuya, Al, Ihori, N., Swing, E. L., Bushman, B. J., Sakamoto, A., … Saleem, M. (2010). Violent video game effects on aggression, empathy, and prosocial behavior in eastern and western countries: A meta-analytic review. *Psychological Bulletin, 136,* 151–173.

Anderson, C. W., Holland, J. D., & Palincsar, A. S. (1997). Canonical and sociocultural approaches to research and reform in science education: The story of Juan and his group. *The Elementary School Journal, 97,* 359–384.

Anderson, J. R. (1993). Problem solving and learning. *American Psychologist, 48,* 35–44.

Anderson, J. R. (1995). Cognitive psychology and its implications (4th ed.). New York, NY: Freeman.

Anderson, J. R. (2010). *Cognitive psychology and its implications* (7th ed.). New York, NY: Worth.

Anderson, J. R., Reder, L. M., & Simon, H. A. (1995). *Applications and misapplication of cognitive psychology to mathematics education.* Unpublished manuscript. Available online at http://www.psy.cmu.edu/~mm4b/misapplied.html

Anderson, J. R., Reder, L. M., & Simon, H. A. (1996). Situated learning and education. *Educational Researcher, 25,* 5–11.

Anderson, L. W., & Krathwohl, D. R. (Eds.). (2001). *A taxonomy for learning, teaching, and assessing: A revision of Bloom's taxonomy of educational objectives.* New York, NY: Longman.

Anderson, L. W., & Sosniak, L. A. (Eds.). (1994). *Bloom's taxonomy: A forty-year retrospective.* Ninety-third yearbook for the National Society for the Study of Education: Part II. Chicago, IL: University of Chicago Press.

Anderson, P. J., & Graham, S. M. (1994). Issues in second-language phonological acquisition among children and adults. *Topics in Language Disorders, 14,* 84–100.

Anderson, R. C., Nguyen-Jahiel, K., McNurlen, B., Archodidou, A., Kim, S-Y., Reznitskaya, A., et al. (2001). The snowball phenomenon: Spread of ways of talking and ways of thinking across groups of children. *Cognition and Instruction, 19,* 1–46.

Anderson, S. M., Klatzky, R. L., & Murray, J. (1990). Traits and social stereotypes: Efficiency differences in social information processing. *Journal of Personality and Social Psychology, 59,* 192–201.

Angier, N., & Chang, K. (2005, January 24). Gray matter and the sexes: Still a scientific gray area. *The New York Times,* A1+.

Antonenko, P., Paas, F., Grabner, R., & van Gog, T. (2010). Using electroencephalography to measure cognitive load. *Educational Psychology Review, 22,* 425–438.

Anyon, J. (1980). Social class and the hidden curriculum of work. *Journal of Education, 162,* 67–92.

Archer, S. L., & Waterman, A. S. (1990). Varieties of identity diffusions and foreclosures: An exploration of the subcategories of the identity statuses. *Journal of Adolescent Research, 5,* 96–111.

Arends, R. I. (2001). *Learning to teach* (5th ed.). New York, NY: McGraw-Hill.

Arends, R. I. (2004). *Learning to teach* (6th ed.). New York, NY: McGraw-Hill.

Arends, R. I. (2007). *Learning to teach* (7th ed.). New York, NY: McGraw-Hill.

Arends, R. I., & Kilcher, A. (2010). *Teaching for student learning: Becoming an accomplished teacher.* New York, NY: Routeledge.

Armbruster, B. B. (2000). Taking notes from lectures. In R. F. Flippo & D. C. Caverly (Eds.), *Handbook of college reading and study strategy research* (pp. 175–200). Mahwah, NJ: Lawrence Erlbaum.

Arnold, M. L. (2000). Stage, sequence, and sequels: Changing conceptions of morality, post-Kohlberg. *Educational Psychology Review, 12,* 365–383.

Aronson, E. (2000). *Nobody left to hate: Teaching compassion after Columbine.* New York, NY: Worth.

Aronson, J. (2002). Stereotype threat: Contending and coping with unnerving expectations. In J. Aronson & D. Cordova (Eds.), *Improving education: Classic and contemporary lessons from psychology* (pp. 279–301). New York, NY: Academic Press.

Aronson, J., Fried, C. B., & Good, C. (2002). Reducing the effects of stereotype threat on African American college students: The role of theories of intelligence. *Journal of Experimental Social Psychology, 33,* 113–125.

Aronson, J., Lustina, M. J., Good, C., Keough, K., Steele, C. M., & Brown, J. (1999). When White men can't do math: Necessary and sufficient factors in stereotype threat. *Journal of Experimental Social Psychology, 35,* 29–46.

Aronson, J., & Steele, C. M. (2005). Stereotypes and the fragility of human competence, motivation, and self-concept. In C. Dweck & E. Elliot (Eds.), *Handbook of competence and motivation.* New York, NY: Guilford.

Aronson, J., Steele, C. M., Salinas, M. F., & Lustina, M. J. (1999). The effect of stereotype threat on the standardized test performance of college students. In E. Aronson (Ed.), *Readings about the social animal* (8th ed.). New York, NY: Freeman.

Ashcraft, M. H., & Radvansky, G. A. (2010). *Cognition* (5th ed.). Upper Saddle River, NJ: Prentice-Hall/Pearson.

Ashton, P. (2009). Learning in infant development: Promising paradigm shift or another swing of the pendulum? (2009). *PsycCRITIQUES, 54*(4): doi: 10.1037/a0014993

Associated Press. (2001, February 21). ABA recommends dropping zero-tolerance in schools. Available online at: http://www.cnn.com/2001/fyi/teachers.ednews/02/21/zero.tolerance.ap

Association for the Gifted. (2001). *Diversity and developing gifts and talents: A national action plan.* Arlington, VA: Author.

Astington, J. W., & Dack, L. A. (2008). Theory of mind. In M. M. Haith & J. B. Benson (Eds.), *Encyclopedia of infant and early childhood development* (Vol. 3, pp. 343–356). San Diego, CA: Academic Press.

Atkinson, R. C., & Shiffrin, R. M. (1968). Human memory: A proposed system and its control processes. In K. Spence & J. Spence (Eds.), *The psychology of learning and motivation* (Vol. 2, pp. 89–195). New York, NY: Academic Press.

Atkinson, R. K., Levin, J. R., Kiewra, K. A., Meyers, T., Atkinson, L. A., Renandya, W. A., & Hwang, Y. (1999). Matrix and mnemonic text-processing adjuncts: Comparing and combining their components. *Journal of Educational Psychology, 91,* 242–257.

Atkinson, R. K., & Renkl, A. (2007). Interactive example-based learning environments: Using interactive elements to encourage effective processing of worked examples. *Educational Psychology Review, 19,* 375–386.

Au, K. H. (1980). Participation structures in a reading lesson with Hawaiian children: Analysis of a culturally appropriate instructional event. *Anthropology and Education Quarterly, 11,* 91–115.

Au, T. K., Knightly, L. M., Jun, S., & Oh, J. S. (2002). Overhearing a language during childhood. *Psychological Science, 13,* 238–243.

Au, T. K., Oh, J. S., Knightly, L. M., Jun, S-A., & Romo, L. F. (2008). Salvaging a child language. *Journal of Memory and Language, 58,* 998–1011.

Aud, S., Hussar, W., Planty, M., Snyder, T., Bianco, K., Fox, M., Frohlich, L., Kemp, J., & Drake, L. (2010). *The condition of education 2010* (NCES 2010-028). National Center for Education Statistics, U.S. Department of Education. Washington, DC: U.S. Government Printing Office.

Aufderheide, P., & Firestone, C. (1993). *Media literacy: A report of the national leadership conference on media literacy.* Queenstown, MD: Aspen Institute.

Avramidis, E., Bayliss, P., & Burden, R. (2000). Student teachers' attitudes toward the inclusion of children with special education needs in the ordinary school. *Teaching and Teacher Education, 16,* 277–293.

Azevedo, R. (2005). Using hypermedia as a metacognitive tool for enhancing student learning? The role of self-regulated learning. *Educational Psychologist, 40,* 199–209.

Azevedo, R., Johnson, A., Chauncey, A. & Graesser, A. (2011). Use of hypermedia to assess and convey self-regulated learning. In B. Zimmerman & D. Schunk (Eds*.), Handbook of self-regulation of learning and performance* (pp. 102–121). New York, NY: Routledge.

Azzam, A. M. (2006, April). A generation immersed in media. *Educational Leadership,* 92–93.

Babad, E. Y., Inbar, J., & Rosenthal, R. (1982). Pygmalion, Galatea, and the Golem: Investigations of biased and unbiased teachers. *Journal of Educational Psychology, 74,* 459–474.

Baddeley, A. D. (1986). *Working memory.* Oxford, UK: Clarendon Books.

Baddeley, A. D. (2001). Is working memory still working? *American Psychologist, 56,* 851–864.

Baddeley, A. D.. (2007). *Working memory, thought, and action.* New York, NY: Oxford University Press.

Baddeley, A. D., Hitch, G. J., Allen, R. J. (2009). Working memory and binding in sentence recall. *Journal of Memory and Language, 61,* 438–456.

Baer, J. (1997). *Creative teachers, creative students.* Boston, MA: Allyn & Bacon.

Bagley, E., & Shaffer, D. W. (2009). When people get in the way: Promoting civic thinking through epistemic gameplay. *International Journal of Gaming and Computer-mediated Simulations, 1,* 36–52.

Bailey, U. L., Lorch, E. P., Milich, R., & Charnigo, R. (2009). Developmental changes in attention and comprehension among children with attention deficit hyperactivity disorder. *Child Development, 80*, 1842–1855.

Baillargeon, R. (1999). Young infants' expectations about hidden objects: A reply to three challenges. *Developmental Psychology, 2*, 115–132.

Baker, K. (1998). Structured English immersion breakthrough in teaching limited-English-proficient students. *Phi Delta Kappan, 80*(3), 199–204. Available online at: http://pdkintl.org/kappan/kbak9811.htm

Bakerman, R., Adamson, L. B., Koner, M., & Barr, R. G. (1990). !Kung infancy: The social context of object exploration. *Child Development, 61*, 794–809.

Balass, M., Nelson, J. R., & Perfetti, C. A. (2010). Word learning: An ERP investigation of word experience effects on recognition and word processing. *Contemporary Educational Psychology, 35*, 126–140.

Baldwin, J. M. (1895). *Mental development in the child and the race: Methods and processes.* New York, NY: Macmillan.

Ball, D. L. (1997). What do students know? Facing challenges of distance, context, and desire in trying to hear children. In B. J. Biddle, T. L. Good, & I. F. Goodson (Eds.), *The international handbook of teachers and teaching* (pp. 769–818). Dordrecht, the Netherlands: Kluwer.

Bandura, A. (1965). Influence of models' reinforcement contingencies on the acquisition of imitative responses. *Journal of Personality and Social Psychology, 1*, 589–595.

Bandura, A. (1977). *Social learning theory.* Englewood Cliffs, NJ: Prentice-Hall.

Bandura, A. (1982). Self-efficacy mechanisms in human agency. *American Psychologist, 37*, 122–147.

Bandura, A. (1986). *Social foundations of thought and action.* Englewood Cliffs, NJ: Prentice-Hall.

Bandura, A. (1993). Perceived self-efficacy in cognitive development and functioning. *Educational Psychologist, 28*, 117–148.

Bandura, A. (1994). Self-efficacy. In V. S. Ramachaudran (Ed.), *Encyclopedia of human behavior* (Vol. 4, pp. 71–81). New York, NY: Academic Press.

Bandura, A. (1997). *Self-efficacy: The exercise of control.* New York, NY: Freeman.

Bandura, A. (2001). Social cognitive theory: An agentic perspective. *Annual review of psychology* (Vol. 52, pp. 1–26). Palo Alto, CA: Annual Reviews, Inc.

Bandura, A. (2006). Adolescent development from an agentic perspective. In F. Pajares & T. Urdan (Eds.), *Self-efficacy beliefs of adolescents.* Greenwich, CT: Information Age.

Bandura, A. (2007). Albert Bandura. In L. Gardner & W. M. Runyan (Eds.). *A history of psychology in autobiography* (Vol. IX, pp. 43–75). Washington, DC: American Psychological Association.

Bandura, A., & Locke, E. (2003). Negative self-efficacy and goal effects revisited. *Journal of Applied Psychology, 88*, 87–99.

Bandura, A., Ross, D., & Ross, S. A. (1963). Vicarious reinforcement and imitative learning. *Journal of Abnormal and Social Psychology, 67*, 601–607.

Banks, J. A. (1997). *Teaching strategies for ethnic studies* (6th ed.). Boston, MA: Allyn & Bacon.

Banks, J. A. (2002). *An introduction to multicultural education* (3rd ed.). Boston, MA: Allyn & Bacon.

Banks, J. A. (2006). *Cultural diversity and education: Foundations, curriculum, and teaching* (5th ed.). Boston, MA: Allyn & Bacon.

Banks, S. R. (2005). *Classroom assessment: Issues and practice.* Boston, MA: Allyn & Bacon.

Barden, L. M. (1995). Effective questioning and the ever-elusive higher-order question. *American Biology Teacher, 57*, 423–426.

Barkley, R. A. (Ed.). (2006). *Attention-deficit hyperactivity disorder: A handbook for diagnosis and treatment* (3rd ed., pp. 547–588). New York, NY: Guilford.

Barnard-Brak, L. (2008). Academic red-shirting among children with learning disabilities. *Learning Disabilities: A Contemporary Journal, 6*, 43–54.

Barnett, M. S., & Ceci, S. J. (2002). When and where do we apply what we learn? A taxonomy for far transfer. *Psychological Bulletin, 128*, 612–637.

Barnhill, G. P. (2005). Functional behavioral assessment in schools. *Intervention in School and Clinic, 40*, 131–143.

Baron, R. A. (1998). *Psychology* (4th ed.). Boston, MA: Allyn & Bacon.

Baron, R. A., & Byrne, D. (2003). *Social psychology* (10th ed.). Boston, MA: Allyn & Bacon.

Barros, E., Silver, J., & Stein. R. E. K. (2009). School recess and group classroom behavior. *Pediatrics, 123*, 431–436.

Bartholomew, B. (2008). Sustaining the fire. *Educational Leadership, 65*(6), 55–60.

Bartlett, F. C. (1932). *Remembering: A study in experimental and social psychology.* New York, NY: Macmillan.

Bartlett, S. M., Rapp, J. T., Krueger, T. K., & Henrickson, M. L. (2011). The use of response cost to treat spitting by a child with autism. *Behavioral Interventions, 26*, 76–83.

Basow, S. A., & Rubin, L. R. (1999). Gender influences on adolescent development. In N. G. Johnson, M. C. Roberts, & J. Worell (Eds.), *Beyond appearance: A new look at adolescent girls* (pp. 25–52). Washington, DC: American Psychological Association.

Battistich, V., Solomon, D., & Delucci, K. (1993). Interaction processes and student outcomes in cooperative groups. *Elementary School Journal, 94*, 19–32.

Bauer, P. J. (2006). Event memory. In D. Kuhn & R. S. Siegler (Eds.), *Cognition, perception, and language* (6th ed., Vol. 2, pp. 373–425). New York, N Y: Wiley.

Baumeister, R. F., Campbell, J. D., Krueger, J. L., & Vohs, K. D. (2003). Does high self-esteem cause better performance, interpersonal success, happiness, or healthier lifestyles? *Psychological Science in the Public Interest, 4*, 1–44.

Baumeister, R. F., & Leary, M. R. (1995). The need to belong: Desire for interpersonal attachments as a fundamental human motivation. *Psychological Bulletin, 117*, 497–529.

Baumert, J., Kunter, M., Blum, W., Brunner, M., Voss, T., Jordan, A., Klusmann, U., Krauss, S., Neubrand, M., & Tsai, Y.-M. (2010). Teachers' mathematical knowledge, cognitive activation in the classroom, and student progress. *American Educational Research Journal, 47*(1), 133–180.

Baumrind, D. (1991). Effective parenting during early adolescent transitions. In P. A. Cowan & M. Hetherington (Eds.),. *Family transitions* (pp. 111–165). Hillsdale, NJ: Erlbaum.

Baumrind, D. (1996). The discipline controversy revisited. *Family Relations, 45*, 405–414.

Bayliss, D. M., Jarrold, C., Baddeley, A. D., Gunn, D., & Leigh, E. (2005). Mapping the developmental constraints on working memory span performance. *Developmental Psychology, 41*, 579–597.

Beane, J. A. (1991). Sorting out the self-esteem controversy. *Educational Leadership, 49*(1), 25–30.

Bear, G. G. (with Cavalier, A. R., & Manning, M. A.). (2005). *Developing self-discipline and preventing and correcting misbehavior.* Boston, MA: Allyn & Bacon.

Beck, I. L., McKeown, M. G., Worthy, J., Sandora, C. A., & Kucan, L. (1996). Questioning the author: A yearlong classroom implementation to engage students with text. *The Elementary School Journal, 96*, 385–414.

Beebe-Frankenberger, M., Bocian, K. L., MacMillan, D. L., & Gresham, F. M. (2004). Sorting second grade students with academic deficiencies: Characteristics differentiating those retained in grade from those promoted to third grade. *Journal of Educational Psychology, 96*, 204–215.

Beghetto, R. A. (2008). Prospective teachers' beliefs about imaginative thinking in K–12 schooling. *Thinking Skills and Creativity, 3*, 134–142.

Begley, S. (2007, October). The case for chutes and ladders. *Newsweek.* Available online at: http://www.newsweek.com/2007/10/13/the-case-for-chutes-and-ladders.html

Benenson, J. F. (1993). Greater preference among females than males for dyadic interaction in early childhood. *Child Development, 64*, 544–555.

Bennett, C. I. (2011). Comprehensive multicultural education: Theory and practice (7th ed.). Boston, MA: Allyn & Bacon.

Bereiter, C. (1995). A dispositional view of transfer. In A. McKeough, J. Lupart, & A. Marini (Eds.), *Teaching for mastery: Fostering generalization in learning* (pp. 21–34). Mahwah, NJ: Erlbaum.

Bereiter, C. (1997). Situated cognition and how I overcome it. In D. Kirshner & J. A. Whitson (Eds.), *Situated cognition: Social, semiotic, and psychological perspectives* (pp. 281–300). Mahwah, NJ: Erlbaum.

Berg, C. A., & Clough, M. (1991). Hunter lesson design: The wrong one for science teaching. *Educational Leadership, 48*(4), 73–78.

Berger, K. S. (2006). The developing person through childhood and adolescence (7th ed.). New York, NY: Worth.

Berger, K. S. (2012). The developing person through the life span (8th ed.). New York, NY: Worth.

Bergin, D. (1999). Influences on classroom interest. *Educational Psychologist, 34*, 87–98.

Berk, L. E. (2001). *Awakening children's minds: How parents and teachers can make a difference.* New York, NY: Oxford University Press.

Berk, L. E. (2005). *Infants, children, and adolescents* (5th ed.). Boston, MA: Allyn & Bacon.

Berk, L. E., & Spuhl, S. T. (1995). Maternal interaction, private speech, and task performance in preschool children. *Early Childhood Research Quarterly, 10*, 145–169.

Berko, J. (1958). The child's learning of English morphology. *Word, 14*, 150–177.

Berliner, D. C. (1983). Developing concepts of classroom environments: Some light on the T in studies of ATI. *Educational Psychologist, 18*, 1–13.

Berliner, D. C. (1987). But do they understand? In V. Richardson-Koehler (Ed.), *Educators' handbook: A research perspective* (pp. 259–293). New York, NY: Longman.

Berliner, D. C. (1988). Simple views of effective teaching and a simple theory of classroom instruction. In D. Berliner & B. Rosenshine (Eds.), *Talks to teachers* (pp. 93–110). New York, NY: Random House.

Berliner, D. C. (2002). Educational research: The hardest science of all. *Educational Researcher, 31*(8), 18–20.

Berliner, D. C. (2005). Our impoverished view of educational reform. *The Teachers College Record, 108*, 949–995.

Berliner, D. C. (2006). Educational psychology: Searching for essence throughout a century of influence. In P. A. Alexander & P. H. Winne (Eds.), *Handbook of educational psychology* (2nd ed., pp. 3–27). Mahwah, NJ: Erlbaum.

Berlyne, D. (1966). Curiosity and exploration. *Science, 153*, 25–33.

Berndt, T. J., & Keefe, K. (1995). Friends' influence on adolescents' adjustment to school. *Child Development, 66*, 1312–1329.

Bernstein, D. A., & Nash, P. W. (2008). *Essentials of psychology* (4th ed.). Boston, MA: Houghton-Mifflin.

Berry, R. Q., III. (2005). Voices of success: Descriptive portraits of two successful African American male middle school mathematics students. *Journal of African American Studies, 8*(4), 46–62.

Berthold, K., & Renkl, A. (2009). Instructional aids to support a conceptual understanding of multiple representations. *Journal of Educational Psychology, 101*, 70–87.

Bialystok, E. (2001). *Bilingualism in development: Language, literacy, and cognition.* New York, NY: Cambridge University Press.

Bialystok, E., Majumder, S., & Martin, M. M. (2003). Developing phonological awareness: Is there a bilingual advantage? *Applied Linguistics, 24*, 27–44.

Biggs, J. (2001). Enhancing learning: A matter of style of approach. In R. Sternberg & L. Zhang (Eds.), *Perspectives on cognitive, learning, and thinking styles* (pp. 73–102). Mahwah, NJ: Erlbaum.

Blair, C. (2002). School readiness: Integrating cognition and emotion in a neurobiological conceptualization of children's functioning at school entry. *American Psychologist, 57*, 111–127.

Blair, C. (2006). How similar are fluid cognition and general intelligence? A developmental neuroscience perspective on fluid cognition as an aspect of human cognition. Main article with commentaries. *Behavioral and Brain Sciences, 29*, 109–160.

Blakemore, S. K., & Frith, U. (2005). The learning brain: Lessons for education: a precis. *Developmental Science, 8*, 459–461.

Blatchford, P., Baines, E., Rubie-Davis, C., Bassett, P., & Chowne, A. (2006). The effect of a new approach to group work on pupil-pupil and teacher-interactions. *Journal of Educational Psychology, 98*, 750–765.

Bloom, B. S. (1981). *All our children learning: A primer for parents, teachers, and other educators.* New York, NY: McGraw-Hill.

Bloom, B. S. (1982). The role of gifts and markers in the development of talent. *Exceptional Children, 48*, 510–522.

Bloom, B. S., Engelhart, M. D., Frost, E. J., Hill, W. H., & Krathwohl, D. R. (1956). *Taxonomy of educational objectives. Handbook I: Cognitive domain.* New York, NY: David McKay.

Bloom, P. (2002). *How children learn the meanings of words.* Cambridge, MA: MIT Press.

Blumenfeld, P. C., Puro, P., & Mergendoller, J. R. (1992). Translating motivation into thoughtfulness. In H. Marshall (Ed.), *Redefining student learning: Roots of educational change* (pp. 207–240). Norwood, NJ: Ablex.

Bong, M. (2009). Age-related differences in achievement goal differentiation. *Journal of Educational Psychology, 101*, 879–896.

Boom, J., Brugman, D., & van der Heijden, P. G. (2001). Hierarchical structure of moral stages assessed by a sorting task. *Child Development, 72*, 535–548.

Borich, G. D. (2011). *Effective teaching methods: Research-based practice* (7th ed.). Columbus, OH: Pearson.

Borko, H., & Livingston, C. (1989). Cognition and improvisation: Differences in mathematics instruction by expert and novice teachers. *American Educational Research Journal, 26*, 473–498.

Borko, H., & Putnam, R. (1996). Learning to teach. In D. Berliner & R. Calfee (Eds.), *Handbook of educational psychology* (pp. 673–708). New York, NY: Macmillan.

Borman, G. D., & Overman, L. T. (2004). Academic resilience in mathematics among poor and minority students. *The Elementary School Journal, 104*, 177–195.

Borrero, N. E., & Yeh, C. J. (2010). Ecoogical English language learning among ethnic minority youth. *Educational Researcher, 39*, 571–581.

Bos, C. S., & Reyes, E. I. (1996). Conversations with a Latina teacher about education for language-minority students with special needs. *The Elementary School Journal, 96*, 344–351.

Bowlby, J. (1969). *Attachment and loss: Attachment.* New York, NY: Basic Books.

Boyd, D., Goldhaber, D., Lankford, H., & Wyckoff, J., (2008). The effect of certification and preparation on teacher quality. *The Future of Children, 17*(1), 45.

Boyle, J. R. (2010a). Note-taking skills of middle school students with and without learning disabilities. *Journal of Learning Disabilities, 43*, 530–540.

Boyle, J. R. (2010b). Strategic note-taking for middle school students with learning disabilities in science classes. *Learning Disabilities Quarterly, 33*, 93–109.

Boyle, J. R., & Weishaar, M. (2001). The effects of a strategic note-taking technique on the comprehension and long term recall of lecture information for high school students with LD. *Learning Disabilities Research and Practice, 16*, 125–133.

Braddock, J., II, & Slavin, R. E. (1993). Why ability grouping must end: Achieving excellence and equity in American education. *Journal of Intergroup Relations, 20*(2), 51–64.

Bradshaw, C. P., Zmuda, J. H., Kellam, S. G., & Ialongo, N. S. (2009). Longitudinal impact of two universal preventive interventions in first grade on educational outcomes in high school. *Journal of Educational Psychology, 101*, 926–937.

Brainerd, C. J. (2003). Jean Piaget, learning research, and American education. In B. J. Zimmerman & D. H. Schunk (Eds.), *Educational psychology: A century of contributions* (pp. 251–287). Mahwah, NJ: Erlbaum.

Brannon, L. (2002). *Gender: Psychological perspectives* (3rd ed.). Boston, MA: Allyn & Bacon.

Bransford, J. D., Brown, A. L., & Cocking, R. R. (2000). *How people learn: Brain, mind, experience, and school.* Washington, DC: National Academy Press.

Bransford, J. D., & Schwartz, D. (1999). Rethinking transfer: A simple proposal with multiple implications. In A. Iran-Nejad & P. D. Pearson (Eds.), *Review of research in education* (Vol. 24, pp. 61–100). Washington, DC: American Educational Research Association.

Bransford, J. D., & Stein, B. S. (1993). *The IDEAL problem solver: A guide for improving thinking, learning, and creativity* (2nd ed.). New York, NY: Freeman.

Brantlinger, E. (2004). Who wins and who loses? Social class and students' identities. In M. Sadowski (Ed.), *Adolescents at school: Perspectives on youth, identity, and education* (pp. 107–126). Cambridge, MA: Harvard University Press.

Branum-Martin, L., Foorman, B. R., Francis, D. J., & Mehta, P. D. (2010). Contextual effects of bilingual programs on beginning reading. *Journal of Educational Psychology, 102*, 341–355.

Bredekamp, S. (2011).*Effective practices in early childhood education: Building a foundation.* Columbus, OH: Merrill.

Bredekamp, S., & Copple, C. (1997). *Developmentally appropriate practice in early childhood programs.* Washington, DC: National Association for the Education of Young Children.

Briesch, A. M., & Chafouleas, S. M. (2009). Review and analysis of literature on self-management interventions to promote appropriate classroom behaviors (1988–2008). *School Psychology Quarterly, 24*, 106–118.

Broidy, L. M., Nagin, D. S., Tremblay, R. E., Bates, J. E., Brame, B., Dodge, K., . . . Vitaro, F. (2003). Developmental trajectories of childhood disruptive behaviors and adolescent delinquency: A six site, cross-national study. *Developmental Psychology, 39*, 222–245.

Bronfenbrenner, U. (1989). Ecological systems theory. In R. Vasta (Ed.), *Annals of child development* (Vol. 6, pp.187–249). Boston, MA: JAI Press, Inc.

Bronfenbrenner, U., McClelland, P., Wethington, E., Moen, P., & Ceci, S. (1996). *The state of Americans: This generation and the next.* New York, NY: Free Press.

Bronfenbrenner, U., & Morris, P. A. (2006). The bioecological model of human development. In W. Damon & R. M. Lerner (Eds.), *Handbook of child psychology: Theoretical models of human development* (6th ed., Vol. 1, pp. 793–827). Hoboken, NJ: Wiley.

Brooks-Gunn, J. (1988). Antecedents and consequences of variations in girls' maturational timing. In M. D. Levin & E. R. McAnarney (Eds.), *Early adolescent transitions* (pp. 101–121). Lexington, MA: Lexington Books.

Brophy, J. E. (1981). Teacher praise: A functional analysis. *Review of Educational Research, 51*, 5–21.

Brophy, J. E. (1988). On motivating students. In D. Berliner & B. Rosenshine (Eds.), *Talks to teachers* (pp. 201–245). New York, NY: Random House.

Brophy, J. E. (1998). *Motivating students to learn.* New York, NY: McGraw-Hill.

Brophy, J. E. (2003). An interview with Jere Brophy by B. Gaedke, & M. Shaughnessy. *Educational Psychology Review, 15*, 199–211.

Brophy, J. E. (2005). Goal theorists should move on from performance goals. *Educational Psychologist, 40*, 167–176.

Brophy, J. E. (2008). Developing students' appreciation for what is taught in school, *Educational Psychologist, 43*, 132–141.

Brophy, J. E., & Evertson, C. (1978). Context variables in teaching. *Educational Psychologist, 12*, 310–316.

Brophy, J. E., & Good, T. (1986). Teacher behavior and student achievement. In M. Wittrock (Ed.), *Handbook of research on teaching* (3rd ed.) (pp. 328–375). New York, NY: Macmillan.

Brophy, J. E., & Kher, N. (1986). Teacher socialization as a mechanism for developing student motivation to learn. In R. Feldman (Ed.), *Social psychology applied to education* (pp. 256–288). New York, NY: Cambridge University Press.

Brown, A. (1987). Metacognition, executive control, self-regulation, and other more mysterious mechanisms. In F. Weinert & R. Kluwe (Eds.), *Metacognition, motivation, and understanding* (pp. 65–116). Hillside, NJ: Erlbaum.

Brown, J. L., Jones, S. M., LaRusso, M. D., & Aber, J. L. (2010). Improving classroom quality: Teacher influences and experimental impacts of the 4Rs Program. *Journal of Educational Psychology, 102*, 153–167.

Bruer, J. T. (1999). In search of . . . brain-based education. *Phi Delta Kappan, 80*, 648–657.

Bruer, J. T. (2002). Avoiding the pediatrician's error: How neuroscientists can help educators (and themselves). *Nature Neuroscience, 5*, 1031–1033.

Bruner, J. S. (1966). *Toward a theory of instruction.* New York, NY: Norton.

Bruner, J. S. (1973). *Beyond the information given: Studies in the psychology of knowing.* New York, NY: Norton.

Brunner, M., Keller, U., Dierendinck, C., Reichert, M., Ugen, S., Fischbach, A., & Martin, R. (2010). The structure of academic self-concepts revisited: The nested Marsh/Shavelson model. *Journal of Educational Psychology, 102*, 964–981.

Bruning, R. H., Schraw, G. J., & Norby, M. M. (2011). *Cognitive psychology and instruction* (5th ed.). Boston, MA: Pearson.

Buffum, A., Mattos, M., & Weber, C. (2010). The why behind RTI. *Educational Leadership, 68*(2), 10–16.

Buhs, E. S., Ladd, G. W., & Herald, S. L. (2006). Peer exclusion and victimization: Processes that mediate the relation between peer group rejection and children's classroom engagement. *Journal of Educational Psychology, 98*, 1–13.

Burbules, N. C., & Bruce, B. C. (2001). Theory and research on teaching as dialogue. In V. Richardson (Ed.), *Handbook of research on teaching* (4th ed., pp. 1102–1121). Washington, DC: American Educational Research Association.

Burden, P. R. (1995). *Classroom management and discipline: Methods to facilitate cooperation and instruction.* White Plains, NY: Longman.

Burgess, S. R., Hecht, S. A., & Lonigan, C. J. (2002). Relations of the home literacy environment (HLE) to the development of reading-related abilities: A one-year longitudinal study. *Reading Research Quarterly, 37*, 408–426.

Burke-Spero, R. (1999). Toward a model of "civitas" through an ethic of care: A qualitative study of preservice teachers' perceptions about learning to teach diverse populations (Doctoral dissertation, The Ohio State University, 1999). *Dissertation Abstracts International, 60*, 11A, 3967.

Burke-Spero, R., & Woolfolk Hoy, A. (2002). *The need for thick description: A qualitative investigation of developing teacher efficacy.* Unpublished manuscript, University of Miami.

Burt, S. A. (2010). Are there shared environmental influences on attention-deficit/hyperactivity disorder? Reply to Wood, Buitelaar, Rijsdijk, Asherson, and Kuntsi (2010). *Psychological Bulletin, 136*, 341–343.

Buss, D. M. (1995). Psychological sex differences: Origin through sexual selection. *American Psychologist, 50*, 164–168.

Bussey, K. (2011). The influence of gender on students' self-regulated learning and performance. In B. Zimmerman & D. Schunk (Eds.*), Handbook of self-regulation of learning and performance* (pp. 426–441) New York, NY: Routledge.

Butcher, K. R. (2006). Learning from text with diagrams: Promoting mental model development and inference generation. *Journal of Educational Psychology, 98*, 182–197.

Butler, R. (1987). Task-involving and ego-involving properties of evaluation: Effects of different feedback conditions on motivational perceptions, interest, and performance. *Journal of Educational Psychology, 79*, 474–482.

Byrne, B. M. (2002). Validating the measurement and structure of self-concept: Snapshots of past, present, and future research. *American Psychologist, 57*, 897–909.

Byrnes, D. A. (1989). Attitudes of students, parents, and educators toward repeating a grade. In L. A. Shepard & M. L. Smith (Eds.), *Flunking grades: Research and policies on retention* (pp. 108–131). Philadelphia, PA: Falmer.

Byrnes, J. P. (1996). *Cognitive development and learning in instructional contexts.* Boston, MA: Allyn & Bacon.

Byrnes, J. P., & Fox, N. A. (1998). The educational relevance of research in cognitive neuroscience. *Educational Psychology Review, 10*, 297–342.

Cairns, R. B., & Cairns, B. D. (2006). The making of developmental psychology. In R. M. Lerner (Ed.), *Handbook of child psychology* (6th ed., Vol. 1: Theoretical models of human development, pp. 89–165). New York, NY: Wiley.

Calderhead, J. (1996). Teacher: Beliefs and knowledge. In D. Berliner & R. Calfee (Eds.), *Handbook of educational psychology* (pp. 709–725). New York, NY: Macmillan.

Callahan, C. M., Tomlinson, C. A., & Plucker, J. (1997). *Project STATR using a multiple intelligences model in identifying and promoting talent in high-risk students.* Storrs, CT: National Research Center for Gifted and Talented. University of Connecticut Technical Report.

Cameron, J., & Pierce, W. D. (1994). Reinforcement, reward, and intrinsic motivation: A meta-analysis. *Review of Educational Research, 64*, 363–423.

Cameron, J., & Pierce, W. D. (1996). The debate about rewards and intrinsic motivation: Protests and accusations do not alter the results. *Review of Educational Research, 66*, 39–52.

Cangelosi, J. S. (1990). *Designing tests for evaluating student achievement.* New York, NY: Longman.

Canter, L. (1996). First the rapport—then the rules. *Learning, 24*(5), 12+.

Canter, L., & Canter, M. (1992). *Lee Canter's Assertive Discipline: Positive behavior management for today's classroom.* Santa Monica, CA: Lee Canter and Associates.

Cantrell, S. C., Almasi, J. F., Carter, J. S., Rintamaa, M., & Madden, A. (2010). The impact of a strategy-based intervention on the comprehension and strategy use of struggling adolescent readers. *Journal of Educational Psychology, 102*, 257–280.

Capa, Y. (2005). *Novice teachers' sense of efficacy.* Doctoral dissertation, The Ohio State University, Columbus, OH.

Capon, N., & Kuhn, D. (2004). What's so good about problem-based learning? *Cognition and Instruction, 22*, 61–79.

Cariglia-Bull, T., & Pressley, M. (1990). Short-term memory differences between children predict imagery effects when sentences are read. *Journal of Experimental Child Psychology, 49*, 384–398.

Carnegie Council on Adolescent Development. (1995). *Great transitions: Preparing adolescents for a new century.* New York, NY: Carnegie Corporation of New York.

Carney, R. N., & Levin, J. R. (2000). Mnemonic instruction, with a focus on transfer. *Journal of Educational Psychology, 92*, 783–790.

Carney, R. N., & Levin, J. R. (2002). Pictorial illustrations *still* improve students' learning from text. *Educational Psychology Review, 14*, 5–26.

Carpendale, J. I. M. (2000). Kohlberg and Piaget on stages and moral reasoning. *Developmental Review, 20*, 181–205.

Carpenter, S. (2000). In the digital age experts pause to examine the effects on kids. *Monitor on Psychology, 31*(11), 48–49.

Carroll, J. B. (1997). The three-stratum theory of cognitive abilities. In D. P. Flanagan, J. L. Genshaft, & P. L. Harrison (Eds.), *Contemporary intellectual assessment: Theories, tests, and issues* (pp. 122–130). New York, NY: Guilford.

Carter, E. W., Wehby, J., Hughes, C., Johnson, S. M., Plank, D. R., Barton-Arwood, S. M., & Lunsford, L. B. (2005). Preparing adolescents with high-incidence disabilities for high-stakes testing with strategy instruction. *Preventing School Failure, 49*(2), 55–62.

Case, R. (1985). A developmentally-based approach to the problem of instructional design. In R. Glaser, S. Chipman, & J. Segal (Eds.), *Teaching thinking skills* (Vol. 2, pp. 545–562). Hillsdale, NJ: Erlbaum.

Case, R. (1992). *The mind's staircase: Exploring the conceptual underpinnings of children's thought and knowledge.* Mahwah, NJ: Erlbaum.

Case, R. (1998). The development of conceptual structures. In D. Kuhn & R. S. Siegler (Eds.), *Handbook of child psychology: Vol. 2: Cognition, perception, and language* (pp. 745–800). New York, NY: Wiley.

Casey, B. J., Getz, S., & Galvan, A. (2008). The adolescent brain. *Developmental Review, 28*, 62–77.

Cassady, J. C., & Johnson, R. E. (2002). Cognitive anxiety and academic performance. *Contemporary Educational Psychology 27*, 270–295.

Castellano, J. A., & Diaz, E. I. (Eds.). (2002). *Reaching new horizons. Gifted and talented education for culturally and linguistically diverse students.* Boston, MA: Allyn & Bacon.

Castle, S., Deniz, C. B., & Tortora, M. (2005). Flexible grouping and student learning in a high-needs school. *Education and Urban Society, 37,* 139–150.

Cattell, R. B. (1963). Theory of fluid and crystallized intelligence: A critical experiment. *Journal of Educational Psychology, 54,* 1–22.

Caughy, M. O., O'Campo, P. J., Randolph, S. M., & Nickerson, K. (2002). The influence of racial socialization practices on the cognitive and behavioral competence of African American preschoolers. *Child Development, 73,* 1611–1625.

Cazden, C. (2001). *Classroom discourse: The language of teaching and learning* (2nd ed.). Portsmouth, NH: Heinemann.

Ceci, S. J., & Roazzi, A. (1994). The effects of context on cognition: Postcards from Brazil. In R. J. Sternberg (Ed.), *Mind in context* (pp. 74–101). New York, NY: Cambridge University Press.

Center for American Progress. (2010, September 10). *Child poverty by the numbers: New data shows largest number of people in poverty on record.* Available online at: http://www.americanprogress.org/issues/2010/09/poverty_numbers.html

Centers for Disease Control. (2009). *Defining childhood overweight and obesity.* Retrieved from http://www.cdc.gov/obesity/childhood/defining.html

Centers for Disease Control. (2010). *Community report from the autism and developmental disabilities monitoring (ADDM) network.* Atlanta, GA: Author. Available online at: http://www.cdc.gov/ncbddd/autism/states/ADDMCommunityReport2009.pdf

Chamot, A. U., & O'Malley, J. M. (1996). The Cognitive Academic Language Learning Approach: A model for linguistically diverse classrooms. *The Elementary School Journal, 96,* 259–274.

Chan, C. K., & Sachs, J. (2001). Beliefs about learning in children's understanding of science texts. *Contemporary Educational Psychology, 26,* 192–210.

Chance, P. (1991). Backtalk: A gross injustice. *Phi Delta Kappan, 72,* 803.

Chance, P. (1992). The rewards of learning. *Phi Delta Kappan, 73,* 200–207.

Chance, P. (1993). Sticking up for rewards. *Phi Delta Kappan, 74,* 787–790.

Chang, L., Mak, M. C K., Li, T., Wu, B. P., Chen, B. B., & Lu, H. J. (2011). Cultural adaptations to environmental variability: An evolutionary account of East–West differences. *Educational Psychology Review, 23,* 99–129.

Chao, R. (2001). Extending research on the consequences of parenting style for Chinese Americans and European Americans. *Child Development, 72,* 1832–1843.

Chao, R., & Tseng, V. (2002). Parenting of Asians. In M. H. Bornstein (Ed.), *Handbook of parenting: Social conditions and applied parenting* (2nd ed., Vol. 4, pp. 59–93). Mahwah, NJ: Erlbaum.

Chapman, J. W., Tunmer, W. E., & Prochnow, J. E. (2000). Early reading-related skills and performance, reading self-concept, and the development of academic self-concept: A longitudinal study. *Journal of Educational Psychology, 92,* 703–708.

Charles, C. M. (2011). *Building classroom discipline* (10th ed.). Boston, MA: Allyn & Bacon.

Charmaraman, L., & Grossman, J. M. (2010). Importance of race and ethnicity: An exploration of Asian, Black, Latino, and multiracial adolescent identity. *Cultural Diversity and Ethnic Minority Psychology, 16,* 144–151.

Cheeseman Day, J., & Newburger, E. C. (2002). The big payoff: Educational attainment and synthetic estimates of work-life earnings. Washington DC: U.S. Bureau of the Census. Available online at: http://usgovinfo.about.com/od/moneymatters/a/edandearnings.htm

Chen, J. A., & Pajares, F. (2010). Implicit theories of ability of Grade 6 science students: Relation to epistemological beliefs and academic motivation and achievement in science. *Contemporary Educational Psychology, 35,* 75–87.

Chen, J.-Q. (2004) Theory of multiple intelligences: Is it a scientific theory? *Teachers College Record, 106,* 17–23.

Chen, L. H., Wu, C-H, Kee, Y. H., Lin, M-S., & Shui, S-H. (2009). Fear of failure, 2 × 2 achievement goal and self-handicapping: An examination of the hierarchical model of achievement motivation in physical education. *Contemporary Educational Psychology, 34,* 298–305.

Chen, Z., & Mo, L. (2004). Schema induction in problem solving: A multidimensional analysis. *Journal of Experimental Psychology: Learning, Memory, and Cognition, 30,* 583–600.

Chen, Z., Mo, L., & Honomichl, R. (2004). Having the memory of an elephant: Long-term retrieval and the use of analogues in problem solving. *Journal of Experimental Psychology: General, 133,* 415–433.

Chenoweth, K. (2010). Leaving nothing to chance. *Educational Leadership, 68*(3), 16–21.

Chi, M. T. H. (1978). Knowledge structures and memory development. In R. Siegler (Ed.), *Children's thinking: What develops?* (pp. 73–96). Hillsdale, NJ: Erlbaum.

Children's Defense Fund. (2005a). Child poverty. Washington, DC: Author.

Children's Defense Fund. (2005b, January). The minimum wage will not support a family of four. Washington, DC: Author.

Children's Defense Fund. (2008, June). Each day in America. Available online at: http://www.childrensdefense.org/site/PageServer?pagename=research_national_data_each_day.

Children's Defense Fund. (2010). *The state of America's children: 2010.* Washington DC: Author. Available online at: http://www.childrensdefense.org/child-research-data-publications/data/state-of-americas-children-2010-report.html

Chorzempa, B. F., & Graham, S. (2006). Primary-grade teachers' use of within-class ability grouping in reading. *Journal of Educational Psychology, 98,* 529–541.

Clark, C. M., & Peterson, P. L. (1986). Teachers' thought processes. In M. Wittrock (Ed.), *Handbook of research on teaching* (3rd ed.) (pp. 255–296). New York, NY: Macmillan.

Clark, D. B., Martin, C. S., & Cornelius, J. R. (2008). Adolescent-onset substance use disorders predict young adult mortality. *Journal of Adolescent Health, 42,* 637–639.

Clark, J. M., & Paivio, A. (1991). Dual coding theory and education. *Educational Psychology Review, 3,* 149–210.

Clark, K. (2009). The case for Structured English Immersion. *Educational Leadership, 66*(7), 42–46.

Clark, R., Anderson, N. B., Clark, V. R., & Williams, D. R. (1999). Racism as a stressor for African Americans. *American Psychologist, 54,* 805–816.

Clarke, J. H., & Agne, R. M. (1997). *Curriculum development; Interdisciplinary high school teaching.* Boston, MA: Allyn & Bacon.

Clifford, M. M. (1990). Students need challenge, not easy success. *Educational Leadership, 48*(1), 22–26.

Clifford, M. M. (1991). Risk taking: Empirical and educational considerations. *Educational Psychologist, 26,* 263–298.

Cobb, P., & Bowers, J. (1999). Cognitive and situated learning: Perspectives in theory and practice. *Educational Researcher, 28*(2), 4–15.

Cobley, S., McKenna, J., Baker, J., & Wattie, N. (2009). How pervasive are relative age effects in secondary school education? *Journal of Educational Psychology, 101,* 520–528.

Codell, E. R. (2001). *Educating Esme: Diary of a teacher's first year.* Chapel Hill, NC: Algonquin Books.

Coffield, F. J., Moseley, D. V., Hall, E., & Ecclestone, K. (2004). *Learning styles and pedagogy in post–16 learning: A systematic and critical review.* London, England: Learning and Skills Research Centre/University of Newcastle upon Tyne.

Cognition and Technology Group at Vanderbilt. (1996). Looking at technology in context: A framework for understanding technology and educational research. In D. Berliner & R. Calfee (Eds.), *Handbook of educational psychology* (pp. 807–840). New York, NY: Macmillan.

Cohen, A. B. (2009). Many forms of culture. *American Psychologist, 64,* 194–204.

Cohen, A. B. (2010). Just how many different forms of culture are there? *American Psychologist, 65,* 59–61.

Cohen, E. G. (1986). *Designing group work: Strategies for the heterogeneous classroom.* New York, NY: Teachers College Press.

Cohen, E. G. (1994). *Designing group work* (2nd ed.). New York, NY: Teachers College Press.

Cohen, M. R., & Graham, J. D. (2003). A revised economic analysis of restrictions on the use of cell phones while driving. *Risk Analysis, 23,* 5–17.

Coie, J. D., & Dodge, K. A. (1998). Aggression and antisocial behavior. In N. Eisenberg (Ed.), *Handbook of child psychology: Vol. 3. Social, emotional, and personality development* (5th ed., pp. 779–862). New York, NY: Wiley.

Cokley, K. O. (2002). Ethnicity, gender, and academic self-concept: A preliminary examination of academic disidentification and implications for psychologists. *Cultural Diversity and Ethnic Minority Psychology, 8,* 378–388.

Colangelo, N., Assouline, S. G. & Gross, M. U. M. (2004). *A nation deceived: How schools hold back America's brightest children (Vols. 1& 2).* The Connie Belin & Jacqueline N. Blank International Center for Gifted Education and Talent Development, College of Education, The University of Iowa, Ames, Iowa. Available online at: http://www.accelerationinstitute.org/Nation_Deceived/Get_Report.aspx

Cole, G. A., Montgomery, R. W., Wilson, K. M., & Milan, M. A. (2000). Parametric analysis of overcorrection duration effects: Is longer really better than shorter? *Behavior Modification, 24,* 359–378.

Cole, M. (1985). The zone of proximal development: Where culture and cognition create each other. In J. V. Wertsch (Ed.), *Culture, communication, and cognition: Vygotskian perspectives* (pp. 146–161). New York, NY: Cambridge University Press.

Coleman, J. S. (1966). *Equality of educational opportunity*. Washington, DC: U.S. Government Printing Office.

Colledge, E., Bishop, D. V. M., Koeppen-Schomerus, G., Price, T. S., Happe, F., Eley, T., … Plomin, R. (2002). The structure of language abilities at 4 Years: A twin study. *Developmental Psychology, 38*, 749–757.

Collins, A. (2006). Cognitive apprenticeship. In R. K. Sawyer (Ed.), *The Cambridge handbook of the learning sciences* (pp. 47–77). New York, NY: The Cambridge University Press.

Collins, A., Brown, J. S., & Newman, S. E. (1989). Cognitive apprenticeship: Teaching the crafts of reading, writing, and mathematics. In L. B. Resnick (Ed.), *Knowing, learning, and instruction: Essays in honor of Robert Galser* (pp. 453–494). Hillsdale, NJ: Erlbaum.

Collins, W. A., Maccoby, E. E., Steinberg, L., Hetherington, E. M., & Bornstein, M. H. (2000). Contemporary research on parenting: The case for nature and nurture. *American Psychologist, 55*, 218–232.

Colliver, J. A. (2000). Effectiveness of problem-based learning curricula: Research and theory. *Academic Medicine, 75*, 259–266.

Comadena, M. E., Hunt, S. K., & Simonds, C. J. (2007). The effects of teacher clarity, nonverbal immediacy, and caring on student motivation, affective and cognitive learning. *Communication Research Reports, 24*, 241–248.

Comer, J. P., Haynes, N. M., & Joyner, E. T. (1996). The School Development Program. In J. P. Comer, N. M. Haynes, E. T. Joyner, & M. Ben-Avie (Eds.), *Rallying the whole village: The Comer process for reforming education* (pp. 1–26). New York, NY: Teachers College Press.

Committee on Increasing High School Students' Engagement and Motivation to Learn. (2004). *Engaging schools: Fostering high school students' motivation to learn*. Washington, DC: The National Academies Press.

Confrey, J. (1990). A review of the research on students' conceptions in mathematics, science, and programming. *Review of Research in Education, 16*, 3–56.

Connell, R. W. (1996). Teaching the boys: New research on masculinity, and gender strategies for schools. *Teachers College Record, 98*, 206–235.

Conway, P. F., & Clark, C. M. (2003). The journey inward and outward: A re-examination of Fuller's concerns-based model of teacher development. *Teaching and Teacher Education 19*, 465–482.

Cook, C. R., Williams, K. R., Guerra, N. G., Kim, T. E., & Sadek, S. (2010). Predictors of bullying and victimization in childhood: A meta-analytic investigation. *School Psychology Quarterly, 25*, 65–83.

Cook, J. L., & Cook, G. (2009). *Child development: Principles and perspectives* (2nd ed.). Boston, MA: Allyn & Bacon.

Cooke, B. L., & Pang, K. C. (1991). Recent research on beginning teachers: Studies of trained and untrained novices. *Teaching and Teacher Education, 7*, 93–110.

Cooper, C. R. (1998). *The weaving of maturity: Cultural perspectives on adolescent development*. New York, NY: Oxford University Press.

Cooper, H. M. (2004). Special Issue: Homework. *Theory Into Practice, 43*(3).

Cooper, H. M., Robinson, J. C., Patall, E. A. (2006). Does homework improve academic achievement? A synthesis of research, 1987–2003. *Review of Educational Research, 76*, 1–62.

Cooper, H. M., & Valentine, J. C. (Eds.). (2001). Special Issue: Homework. *Educational Psychologist, 36*(3), Summer.

Cooper, H. M., Valentine, J. C., Nye, B., & Kindsay, J. J. (1999). Relationships between five after-school activities and academic achievement. *Journal of Educational Psychology, 91*, 369–378.

Copi, I. M. (1961). *Introduction to logic*. New York, NY: Macmillan.

Coplan, R. J., Prakash, K., O'Neil, K., & Armer, M. (2004). Do you "want" to play? Distinguishing between conflicted shyness and social disinterest in early childhood. *Developmental Psychology, 40*, 244–258.

Cordova, D. I., & Lepper, M. R. (1996). Intrinsic motivation and the process of learning: Beneficial effects of contextualization, personalization, and choice. *Journal of Educational Psychology, 88*, 715–730.

Cornelius-White, J. (2007). Learner-centered teacher–student relationships are effective: A meta-analysis. *Review of Educational Research, 77*, 113–143.

Corno, L. (2000). Looking at homework differently. *Elementary School Journal, 100*, 529–548.

Corno, L. (2008). On teaching adaptively. *Educational Psychologist, 43*, 161–173.

Corno, L. (2011). Studying self-regulation habits. In B. Zimmerman & D. Schunk (Eds.), *Handbook of self-regulation of learning and performance* (pp. 361–375) New York, NY: Routledge.

Corpus, J. H., McClintic-Gilbert, M. S., & Hayenga, A. O. (2009). Within-year changes in children's intrinsic and extrinsic motivational orientations: Contextual predictors and academic outcomes. *Contemporary Educational Psychology, 34*, 154–166.

Cota-Robles, S., Neiss, M., & Rowe, D. C. (2002). The role of puberty in violent and nonviolent delinquency among Anglo American, Mexican American and African American boys. *Journal of Adolescent Research*, 17, 364–376.

Cothran, D. J., & Ennis, C. D. (2000). Building bridges to student engagement: Communicating respect and care for students in urban high school. *Journal of Research and Development in Education, 33*(2), 106–117.

Covaleskie, J. F. (1992). Discipline and morality: Beyond rules and consequences. *The Educational Forum, 56*(2), 56–60.

Covington, M. V. (1992). Making the grade: A self-worth perspective on motivation and school reform. New York, NY: Holt, Rinehart, & Winston.

Covington, M. V., & Mueller, K. J. (2001). Intrinsic versus extrinsic motivation: An approach/avoidance reformulation. *Educational Psychology Review, 13*, 157–176.

Cowley, G., & Underwood, A. (1998, June 15). Memory. *Newsweek, 131*(24), 48–54.

Craik, F. I. M., & Lockhart, R. S. (1972). Levels of processing: A framework for memory research. *Journal of Verbal Learning and Verbal Behavior, 11*, 671–684.

Crawford, J. (1997). *Best evidence: Research foundations of the Bilingual Education Act*. Washington, DC: National Clearinghouse for Bilingual Education.

Creese, A. (2009). Building on young people's linguistic and cultural continuity: Complementary schools in the United Kingdom. *Theory Into Practice, 48*, 267–273.

Cremin, L. (1961). *The transformation of the school: Progressivism in American education, 1876–1957*. New York, NY: Vintage.

Crick, N. R., Casas, J. F., & Mosher M. (1997). Relational and overt aggression in preschool. *Developmental Psychology, 33*, 579–588.

Crisci, P. E. (1986). The Quest National Center: A focus on prevention of alienation. *Phi Delta Kappan, 67*, 440–442.

Crocker, J., & Park, L. E. (2004). Reaping the benefits of pursuing self-esteem without the costs. *Psychological Bulletin, 130*, 392–414.

Crone, D. A., & Horner, R. H. (2003). *Building positive behavior support systems in schools: Functional behavioral assessment*. New York, NY: The Guilford Press.

Crosnoe, R., Morrison, F., Burchinal, M., Pianta, R., Keating, D., Friedman, S. L., & Clarke-Stewart, K. A. (2010). Instruction, teacher–student relations, and math achievement trajectories in elementary school. *Journal of Educational Psychology, 102*, 407–417.

Cross, W. E. (1991). *Shades of black: Diversity in African-American identity*. Philadelphia, PA: Temple University Press.

Cross, W. E., Jr., & Cross, T. B. (2007). Theory, research, and models. In S. M. Quintana & C. McKown (Eds.), *Race, racism and developing child* (pp. 154–181). New York, NY: Wiley.

Crul, M., & Holdaway, J. (2009). Children of immigrants in schools in New York and Amsterdam: The factors shaping attainment. *Teachers College Record, 111*(6), 1476–1507.

Cummins, D. D. (1991). Children's interpretation of arithmetic word problems. *Cognition and Instruction, 8*, 261–289.

D'Agostino, J. V., & Powers, S. J. (2009). Predicting teacher performance with test scores and grade point average: A meta-analysis. *American Educational Research Journal, 46*(1), 146–182.

Daley, T. C., Whaley, S. E., Sigman, M. D., Espinosa, M. P., & Neumann, C. (2003). IQ on the rise: The Flynn Effect in rural Kenyan children. *Psychological Science, 14*(3), 215–219.

D'Amico, A., & Guarnera, M. (2005). Exploring working memory in children with low arithmetical achievement. *Learning and Individual Differences, 15*, 189–202.

Damon, W. (1994). Fair distribution and sharing: The development of positive justice. In B. Puka (Ed.), Fundamental research in moral development (pp. 189–254). *Moral development: A compendium, Vol. 2*. New York, NY: Garland Publishing.

Darcey, J. S., & Travers, J. F. (2006). *Human development across the lifespan* (6th ed.). New York, NY: McGraw-Hill.

Darling-Hammond, L., & Youngs, P. (2002). Defining "Highly Qualified Teachers": What does "Scientifically-Based Research" actually tell us? *Educational Researcher*, 13–25.

Darnon, C., Dompnier, B., Gillieron, O., & Butera, F. (2010). The interplay of mastery and performance goals in social comparison: A multiple-goal perspective. *Journal of Educational Psychology, 102*, 212–222.

Das, J. P. (1995). Some thoughts on two aspects of Vygotsky's work. *Educational Psychologist, 30*, 93–97.

DaSilva Idings, A. C. (2009). Bridging home and school literacy practices: Empowering families of recent immigrant children. *Theory Into Practice, 48*, 304–311.

Daunic, A. P., Smith. S. W., Brank, E. M., & Penfield, R. D. (2006). Classroom based cognitive-behavioral intervention to prevent aggression: Efficacy and social validity. *Journal of School Psychology, 44*, 123–139.

Davis, G. A., Rimm, S. B., & Siegle, D. (2011). *Education of the gifted and talented* (6th ed.). Boston, MA: Pearson.

Davis, H. A. (2003). Conceptualizing the role and influence of student–teacher relationships on children's social and cognitive development, *Educational Psychologist, 38*, 207–234.

Dawson-Tunik, T., Fischer, K. W., & Stein, Z. (2004). Do stages belong at the center of developmental theory? *New Ideas in Psychology, 22*, 255–263.

De Boer, H., Bosker, R. J., & van der Werf, M. P. C. (2010). Sustainability of teacher expectation bias effects on long-term student performance. *Journal of Educational Psychology, 102*, 168–179.

De Corte, E. (2003). Transfer as the productive use of acquired knowledge, skills, and motivations. *Current Directions in Psychological Research, 12*, 142–146.

De Corte, E., Greer, B., & Verschaffel, L. (1996). Mathematics learning and teaching. In D. Berliner & R. Calfee (Eds.), *Handbook of educational psychology* (pp. 491–549). New York, NY: Macmillan.

De Corte, E., & Verschaffel, L. (1985). Beginning first graders' initial representation of arithmetic word problems. *Journal of Mathematical Behavior, 4*, 3021.

De George, G. (2008). Is it language or is it special needs? Appropriately diagnosing English language learners having achievement difficulties. In L. S. Verplaetse & N. Migliacci (Eds.), *Inclusive pedagogy for English language learners: A handbook of research-informed practices* (pp. 277–303). New York, NY: Erlbaum.

de Kock, A., Sleegers, P., & Voeten, M. J. M. (2004). New learning and the classification of learning environments in secondary education. *Review of Educational Research, 74*(2), 141–170.

Dearing, E., Kreider, H., Simpkins, S., & Weiss, H. B. (2006). Family involvement in school and low-income children's literacy: Longitudinal associations between and within families. *Journal of Educational Psychology, 98*, 653–664.

Deaux, K. (1993). Commentary: Sorry, wrong number: A reply to Gentile's call. *Psychological Science, 4*, 125–126.

DeCecco, J., & Richards, A. (1974). *Growing pains: Uses of school conflicts*. New York, NY: Aberdeen.

deCharms, R. (1983). Intrinsic motivation, peer tutoring, and cooperative learning: Practical maxims. In J. Levine & M. Wang (Eds.), *Teacher and student perceptions: Implications for learning* (pp. 391–398). Hillsdale, NJ: Erlbaum.

Deci, E. L. (1975). *Intrinsic motivation*. New York, NY: Plenum.

Deci, E. L., Koestner, R., & Ryan, R. M. (1999). A meta-analytic review of experiments examining the effects of extrinsic rewards on intrinsic motivation. *Psychological Bulletin, 125*, 627–668.

Deci, E. L., & Ryan, R. M. (1985). *Intrinsic motivation and self-determination in human behavior*. New York, NY: Plenum.

Deci, E. L., & Ryan, R. M. (Eds.). (2002). *Handbook of self-determination research*. Rochester, NY: University of Rochester Press.

Deci, E. L., Vallerand, R. J., Pelletier, L. G., & Ryan, R. M. (1991). Motivation and education: The self-determination perspective. *Educational Psychologist, 26*, 325–346.

DeCuir-Gunby, J. T. (2009). A review of the racial identity development of African American adolescents: The role of education. *Review of Educational Research, 79*, 103–124.

Delazer, M., Ischebeck, A., Domahs, F., Zamarian, L., Koppelstaetter, F., Siednetoph, C. M., . . . Benke, T. (2005). Learning by strategies and learning by drill: Evidence from an fMRI study. *NeuroImage, 25*, 838–849.

Delpit, L. (1995). *Other people's children: Cultural conflict in the classroom*. New York, NY: The New York Press.

Delpit, L. (2003). Educators as "Seed People": Growing a new future. *Educational Researcher, 7*(32), 14–21.

Demetriou, A., Christou, C., Spanoudis, G., & Platsidou, M. (2002). The development of mental processing: Efficiency, working memory and thinking. *Monographs of the Society for Research in Child Development, 67*(1).

Demuth, K. (1990). Subject, topic, and Sesotho passive. *Journal of Child Language, 17*, 67–84.

Derry, S. J. (1992). Beyond symbolic processing: Expanding horizons for educational psychology. *Journal of Educational Psychology, 84*, 413–419.

Derry, S. J., Hmelo-Silver, C. E., Nagarajan, A., Chernobilsky, E., & Beitzel, B. (2006). Cognitive transfer revisited: Can we exploit new media to solve old problems on a large scale? *Journal of Educational Computing Research, 35*, 145–162.

Desautel, D, (2009). Becoming a thinking thinker: Metacognition, self-reflection, and classroom practice. *Teachers College Record, 111*, 1997–2020. http://www.tcrecord.org ID Number: 15504.

Deshler, D., & Schumaker, J. (2005). *Teaching adolescents to be strategic learners*. Thousand Oaks, CA: Corwin Press.

Dettmers, S., Trautwein, U, Lüdtke, O., Kunter, M., & Baumert, J. (2010). Homework works if homework quality is high: Using multilevel modeling to predict the development of achievement in mathematics. *Journal of Educational Psychology, 102*, 467–482.

Dewan, S. (2010, January 10). Southern schools mark two minorities. *New York Times*, p. A19+.

Dewey, J. (1896). The university school. *University Record (University of Chicago), 1* , 417–419.

Dewey, J. (1913). *Interest and effort in education*. Boston, MA: Houghton-Mifflin.

Diaz-Rico, L. T., & Weed, K. Z. (2002). *The cross-cultural, language, and academic development handbook* (2nd ed.). Boston, MA: Allyn & Bacon.

Dickinson, D., McCabe, A., Anastopoulos, L., Peisner-Feinberg, E., & Poe, M. (2003). The comprehensive language approach to early literacy: The interrelationships among vocabulary, phonological sensitivity, and print knowledge among preschool-aged children. *Journal of Educational Psychology, 95*, 465–481.

Dillon, S. (2011, August 8). Overriding a key education law: Waivers offered to sidestep a 100 percent proficiency rule. *New York Times*, A11.

Dingfelder, S. F. (2005). Closing the gap for Latino patients. *Monitor on Psychology, 36*(1), 58–61.

Dinnel, D., & Glover, J. A. (1985). Advance organizers: Encoding manipulations. *Journal of Educational Psychology, 77*, 514–522.

Dinsmore, D. L., Alexander, P. A., & Loughlin, S. M. (2008). Focusing the conceptual lens on meta-cognition, self-regulation, and self-regulated learning. *Educational Psychology Review, 20*, 391–409.

DiVesta, F. J., & Di Cintio, M. J. (1997). Interactive effects of working memory span and text comprehension on reading comprehension and retrieval. *Learning and Individual Differences, 9*, 215–231.

Dodge, K. A. (2011). Context matters in child and family policy. *Child Development, 82*, 433–442.

Dodge, K. A., & Pettit, G. S. (2003). A biopsychosocial model of the development of chronic conduct problems in adolescence. *Developmental Psychology, 39*, 349–371.

Doggett, A. M. (2004). ADHD and drug therapy: Is it still a valid treatment? *Child Health Care, 8*, 69–81.

Dolezal, S. E., Welsh, L. M., Pressley, M., & Vincent, M. (2003). How do nine third-grade teachers motivate their students? *Elementary School Journal, 103*, 239–267.

Doll, B., Zucker, S., & Brehm, K. (2005). *Resilient classrooms: Creating healthy environments for learning*. New York, NY: Guilford.

Domenech Rodriguez, M. M., Donovick, M. R., & Crowley, S. L. (2009). Parenting styles in a cultural context: Observations of protective parenting in first-generation Latinos. *Family Process, 48*(2), 195–210.

Dotterer, A. M., McHale, S. M., & Crouter, A. C. (2009). The development and correlates of academic interests from childhood through adolescence. *Journal of Educational Psychology, 101*, 509–519.

Doyle, W. (2006). Ecological approaches to classroom management. In C. Evertson & C. S. Weinstein (Eds.), *Handbook for classroom management: Research, practice, and contemporary issues*. Mahwah, NJ: Erlbaum.

Driscoll, MP. (2005). *Psychology of learning for instruction* (3rd ed.). Boston, MA: Allyn & Bacon.

Dubarry, M., & Alves de Lima, D. (2003). *Notes on Generation 1.5*. De Anza College, Cupertino, CA. Available online at: http://faculty.deanza.edu/alvesdelimadiana/stories/storyReader$438

DuBois, D. L., Burk-Braxton, C., Swenson, L. P., Tevendale, H. D., & Hardesty, J. L. (2002). Race and gender influences on adjustment in early adolescence: Investigation of an integrative model. *Child Development, 73*, 1573–1592.

Duell, O. K. (1994). Extended wait time and university student achievement. *American Educational Research Journal, 31*, 397–414.

Dufrene, B. A., Doggett, R. A., Henington, C., & Watson, T. S. (2007). Functional assessment and intervention for disruptive classroom behaviors in preschool and Head Start classrooms. *Journal of Behavioral Education, 16*, 368–388.

Duncan, G. J., & Brooks-Gunn, J. (2000). Family poverty, welfare reform, and child development. *Child Development, 71*, 188–196.

Duncan, R. M., & Cheyne, J. A. (1999). Incidence and functions of self-reported private speech in young adults: A self-verbalization questionnaire. *Canadian Journal of Behavioural Sciences, 31*, 133–136.

Duncker, K. (1945). On solving problems. *Psychological Monographs, 58*(5, Whole No. 270).

Dunn, K., & Dunn, R. (1978). *Teaching students through their individual learning styles*. Reston, VA: National Council of Principals.

Dunn, K., & Dunn, R. (1987). Dispelling outmoded beliefs about student learning. *Educational Leadership, 44*(6), 55–63.

Dunn, R., Dunn, K., & Price, G. E. (1989). *Learning Styles Inventory (LSI): An inventory for identification of how individuals in grades 3 through 12 prefer to learn.* Lawrence, KS: Price Systems.

Dunn, R., & Griggs, S. (2003). *Synthesis of the Dunn and Dunn Learning-Style Model Research: Who, what, when, where, and so what?* New York, NY: St. John's University.

Durbin, D. L., Darling, N., Steinberg, L., & Brown, B. B. (1993). Parenting style and peer group membership among European-American adolescents. *Journal of Research on Adolescence, 3,* 87–100.

Durik, A. M., & Harackiewicz, J. M. (2007). Different strokes for different folks: How individual interest moderates the effects of situational factors on task interest. *Journal of Educational Psychology, 99,* 597–610.

Durik, A. M., Vida, M., & Eccles, J. S. (2006). Task values and ability beliefs as predictors of high school literacy choices: A developmental analysis. *Journal of Educational Psychology, 98*(2), 382–393.

Dusenbury, L., & Falco, M. (1995). Eleven components of effective drug abuse prevention curricula. *Journal of School Health, 65,* 420–425.

Dweck, C. S. (2000). *Self-theories: Their role in motivation, personality, and development.* Philadelphia, PA: Routledge Press.

Dweck, C. S. (2002). The development of ability conceptions. In A. Wigfield & J. Eccles (Eds.), *The development of achievement motivation.* San Diego, CA: Academic Press.

Dweck, C. S. (2006). *Mindset: The new psychology of success.* New York, NY: Random House.

Dweck, C. S., & Bempechat, J. (1983). Children's theories on intelligence: Consequences for learning. In S. Paris, G. Olson, & W. Stevenson (Eds.), *Learning and motivation in the classroom* (pp. 239–256). Hillsdale, NJ: Erlbaum.

Dymond, S. K., Renzaglia, A., & Chun, E. (2007). Elements of effective high school service learning programs that include students with and without disabilities. *Remedial and Special Education, 28,* 227–243.

Ebbinghaus, H. (1964). *Memory* (H. A. Ruger & C. E. Bussenius, Trans.). New York, NY: Dover. (Original work published 1885)

Ebersbach, M. (2009). Achieving a new dimension: Children integrate three stimulus dimensions in volume estimations. *Developmental Psychology, 45,* 877–883.

Eccles, J. (2009) Who am I and what am I going to do with my life? Personal and collective identities as motivators of action. *Educational Psychologist, 44,* 78–89.

Eccles, J., & Wigfield, A. (1985). Teacher expectations and student motivation. In J. Dusek (Ed.), *Teacher expectancies* (pp. 185–226). Hillsdale, NJ: Erlbaum.

Eccles, J. & Wigfield, A. (2002). Motivational beliefs, values, goals. *Annual Review of Psychology, 53,* 109–132.

Eccles, J., Wigfield, A., & Schiefele, U. (1998). Motivation to succeed. In W. Damon (Series Ed.) & N. Eisenberg (Volume Ed.), *Handbook of child psychology: Vol. 3. Social, emotional, and personality development* (5th ed., pp. 1017–1095). New York, NY: Wiley.

Echevarria, J., & Graves, A. (2011). *Sheltered content instruction: Teaching English learners with diverse abilities* (4th ed.). Columbus, OH: Pearson.

Echevarria, M. (2003). Anomalies as a catalyst for middle school students' knowledge construction and scientific reasoning during science inquiry. *Journal of Educational Psychology, 95,* 357–374.

Egan, S. K., Monson, T. C., & Perry, D. G. (1998). Social-cognitive influences on change in aggression over time. *Developmental Psychology, 34,* 996–1006.

Ehrenfeld, T. (2001). Reflections on mirror neurons. *Observer: Association for Psychological Science, 24*(3), 11–13.

Eisenberg, N., & Fabes, R. A. (1998). Prosocial development. In W. Damon (Series Ed.) & N. Eisenberg (Vol. Ed.), *Handbook of child psychology: Vol. 3. Social, emotional, and personality development* (5th ed., pp. 701–778). New York, NY: Wiley.

Eisenberg, N., Shell, R., Pasernack, J., Lennon, R., Beller, R., & Mathy, R. M. (1987). Prosocial development in middle childhood: A longitudinal study. *Developmental Psychology, 23,* 712–718.

Eisenberg, R., Pierce, W. D., & Cameron, J. (1999). Effects of rewards on intrinsic motivation— Negative, neutral, and positive: Comment on Deci, Koestner, and Ryan (1999). *Psychological Bulletin, 125,* 677–691.

Eisner, E. W. (1999). The uses and limits of performance assessments. *Phi Delta Kappan, 80,* 658–660.

Elias, M. J., & Schwab, Y. (2006). From compliance to responsibility: Social and emotional learning and classroom management. In C. Evertson & C. S. Weinstein (Eds.), *Handbook for classroom management: Research, practice, and contemporary issues.* Mahwah, NJ: Erlbaum.

Elias, S. M., & MacDonald, S. (2007). Using past performance, proxy efficacy, and academic self-efficacy to predict college performance. *Journal of Applied Social Psychology, 37,* 2518–2531.

Elkind, D. (1981). Obituary—Jean Piaget (1896–1980). *American Psychologist, 36,* 911–913.

Ellerbrock, C. R., & Kiefer, S. M. (2010). Creating a ninth-grade community of care. *The Journal of Educational Research, 103,* 393–406.

Else-Quest, N. M., Hyde, J. S., & Linn, M. C. (2010). Cross-national patterns of gender differences in mathematics: A meta-analysis. *Psychological Bulletin, 136,* 103–127.

Embry, D. D. (2002). The Good Behavior Game: A best practice candidate as a universal behavior vaccine. *Clinical Child and Family Psychology Review, 5,* 273–297.

Emerson, M. J., & Miyake, A. (2003). The role of inner speech in task switching: A dual-task investigation. *Journal of Memory and Language, 48,* 148–168.

Emmer, E. T., & Aussiker, A. (1990). School and classroom discipline problems: How well do they work? In O. Moles (Ed.), *Student discipline strategies: Research and practice.* Albany, NY: SUNY Press.

Emmer, E. T., & Evertson, C. M. (1982). Effective classroom management at the beginning of the school year in junior high school classes. *Journal of Educational Psychology, 74,* 485–498.

Emmer, E. T., & Evertson, C. M., (2009). *Classroom management for middle and high school teachers* (8th ed.). Boston, MA: Allyn & Bacon.

Emmer, E. T., & Evertson, C. M., (2013). *Classroom management for middle and high school teachers* (9th ed.). Boston, MA: Allyn & Bacon.

Emmer, E. T., Evertson, C. M., & Anderson, L. M. (1980). Effective classroom management at the beginning of the school year. *Elementary School Journal, 80,* 219–231.

Emmer, E. T., & Gerwels, M. C. (2006). Classroom management in middle school and high school classrooms. In C. Evertson & C. S. Weinstein (Eds.), *Handbook for classroom management: Research, practice, and contemporary issues.* Mahwah, NJ: Erlbaum.

Emmer, E. T., & Stough, L. M. (2001). Classroom management: A critical part of educational psychology with implications for teacher education. *Educational Psychologist, 36,* 103–112.

Engle, R. W. (2001). What is working memory capacity? In H. Roediger, J. Nairne, I. Neath, & A. Suprenant (Eds.), *The nature of remembering: Essays in honor of Robert G. Crowder* (pp. 297–314). Washington, DC: American Psychological Association.

Entwistle, D. R., & Alexander, K. L. (1998). Facilitating the transition to first grade: The nature of transition and research on factors affecting it. *The Elementary School Journal, 98,* 351–364.

Epstein, J. L. (1989). Family structure and student motivation. In R. E. Ames & C. Ames (Eds.), *Research on motivation in education: Vol. 3. Goals and cognitions* (pp. 259–295). New York, NY: Academic Press.

Epstein, J. L. (1995). School/Family/Community partnerships: Caring for the children we share. *Phi Delta Kappan, 76,* 701–712.

Epstein, J. L., & MacIver, D. J. (1992). *Opportunities to learn: Effects on eighth graders of curriculum offerings and instructional approaches.* (Report No. 34). Baltimore, MD: Center for Research on Elementary and Middle Schools, Johns Hopkins University.

Epstein, J. L., & Van Voorhis, F. L. (2001). More than minutes: Teachers' roles in designing homework. *Educational Psychologist, 36,* 181–193.

Erdelyi, M. H. (2010). The ups and downs of memory. *American Psychologist, 65,* 623–633.

Ericsson, A. (2011, August). *Deliberate practice and the future of education and professional training.* Keynote address at the European Association for Research on Learning and Instruction, University of Exeter, UK.

Ericsson, K. A. (1999). Expertise. In R. Wilson & F. Keil (Eds.), *The MIT encyclopedia of the cognitive sciences* (pp. 298–300). Cambridge, MA: MIT Press.

Ericsson, K. A., & Charness, N. (1994). Expert performance: Its structure and acquisition. *American Psychologist, 49*(8), 725–747.

Ericsson, K. A., & Charness, N. (1999). Expert performance: Its structure and acquisition. In S. Ceci & W. Williams (Eds.), The nature-nurture debate: The essential readings. *Essential readings in developmental psychology.* Malden, MA: Blackwell.

Erikson, E. H. (1963). *Childhood and society* (2nd ed.). New York, NY: Norton.

Erikson, E. H. (1968). *Identity, youth, and crisis.* New York, NY: Norton.

Erikson, E. H. (1980). *Identity and the life cycle* (2nd ed.). New York, NY: Norton.

Evans, G. W. (2004). The environment of childhood poverty. *American Psychologist, 59,* 77–92.

Evans, L., & Davies, K. (2000). No sissy boys here: A content analysis of the representation of masculinity in elementary school reading texts. *Sex Roles, 42,* 255–270.

Evensen, D. H., Salisbury-Glennon, J. D., & Glenn, J. (2001). A qualitative study of six medical students in a problem-based curriculum: Toward a situated model of self-regulation. *Journal of Educational Psychology, 93*, 659–676.

Evertson, C. M., & Emmer, E. T. (2009). *Classroom management for elementary school teachers* (8th ed.). Boston, MA: Allyn & Bacon.

Evertson, C. M., & Emmer, E. T. (2013). *Classroom management for elementary school teachers* (9th ed.). Boston, MA: Allyn & Bacon.

Evertson, C. M., & Weinstein, C. S. (Eds.). (2006). *Handbook of classroom management: Research, practice, and contemporary issues.* Mahwah, NJ: Erlbaum.

Fabiano, G. A., Pelham, W. E., Coles, E. K., Gnagy, E. M., Chronis-Tuscano, A., & O'Connor, B. C. (2009). A meta-analysis of behavioral treatments for attention-deficit/hyperactivity disorder. *Clinical Psychology Review, 29*, 129–140.

Facione, P. A. (2011). *Think critically.* Boston, MA: Pearson.

Fantuzzo, J., Davis, G., & Ginsburg, M. (1995). Effects of parent involvement in isolation or in combination with peer tutoring on student self-concept and mathematics achievement. *Journal of Educational Psychology, 87*, 272–281.

Fast, L. A., Lewis, J. L., Bryant, M. J., Bocian, K. A., Cardullo, R. A., Rettig, M., & Hammond, K. A. (2010). Does math self-efficacy mediate the effect of the perceived classroom environment on standardized math test performance? *Journal of Educational Psychology, 102*, 729–740.

Feldman, J. (2003). The simplicity principle in human concept learning. *Current Directions in Psychological Science, 12*, 227–232.

Feldman, R. S. (2004). *Child development* (3rd ed.). Upper Saddle River, NJ: Prentice-Hall.

Fenton, D. F. (2007). The implications of research on expertise for curriculum and pedagogy. *Educational Psychology Review, 19*, 91–110.

Ferrer, E., & McArdle, J. J. (2004). An experimental analysis of dynamic hypotheses about cognitive abilities and achievement from childhood to early adulthood. *Developmental Psychology, 40*, 935–952.

Ferretti, R. P., Lewis, W. E., & Andrews-Weckerly, S. (2009). Do goals affect the structure of students' argumentative writing strategies? *Journal of Educational Psychology, 101*, 577–589.

Fillmore, L.W., & Snow, C. (2000). What teachers need to know about language. Available online at: http://citeseerx.ist.psu.edu/viewdoc/download?doi=10.1.1.92.9117&rep=rep1&type=pdf

Finkel, D., Reynolds, C. A., McArdle, J. J., Gatz, M., & Pedersen, N. L. (2003). Latent growth curve analyses of accelerating decline in cognitive abilities in adulthood. *Developmental Psychology, 39*, 535–550.

Fischer, K. W. (2009). Mind, brain, and education: Building a scientific groundwork for learning and teaching. *Mind, Brain, and Education, 3*, 2–16.

Fischer, M. A., & Gillespie, C. S. (2003). Computers and young children's development. *Young Children, 58*(4), 85–91.

Fiske, S. T. (1993). Social cognition and social perception. *Annual Review of Psychology, 44*, 155–194.

Fitts, P. M., & Posner, M. I. (1967). *Human performance.* Belmont, CA: Brooks Cole.

Fives, H. R., Hamman, D., & Olivarez, A. (2005, April). *Does burnout begin with student teaching? Analyzing efficacy, burnout, and support during the student-teaching semester.* Paper presented at the Annual Meeting of the American Educational Research Association, Montreal, CA.

Flavell, J. H., Green, F. L., & Flavell, E. R. (1995). Young children's knowledge about thinking. *Monographs of the Society for Research in Child Development, 60*(1) (Serial No. 243).

Flavell, J. H., Miller, P. H., & Miller, S. A. (2002). *Cognitive development* (4th ed.). Upper Saddle River, NJ: Prentice-Hall.

Fleith, D. (2000). Teacher and student perceptions of creativity in the classroom environment. *Roeper Review, 22*, 148–153.

Fletcher, A., Bonell, C., & Hargreaves, J. (2008). School effects on young people's drug use: A systematic review of intervention and observational studies. *Journal of Adolescent Health, 42*, 209–220.

Floden, R. E. (2001). Research on effects of teaching: A continuing model for research on teaching. In V. Richardson (Ed.), *Handbook of research on teaching* (4th ed., pp. 3–16). Washington, DC: American Educational Research Association.

Flum, H., & Kaplan, A. (2006). Exploratory orientation as an educational goal. *Educational Psychologist, 41*, 99–110.

Ford, D. Y. (2000). *Infusing multicultural content into the curriculum for gifted students.* (ERIC EC Digest #E601). Arlington, VA: The ERIC Clearinghouse on Disabilities and Gifted Education.

Fox, E., & Riconscente, M. (2008). Metacognition and Self-Regulation in James, Piaget, and Vygotsky. *Educational Psychology Review, 20*, 373–389.

Francis, D. J., Lesaux, N., & August, D. (2006). Language of instruction. In D. August & T. Shanahan (Eds.), *Developing literacy in second language learners: Report of the national literacy panel on language-minority children and youth* (pp. 365–413). Mahwah, NJ: Erlbaum.

Frank, S. J., Pirsch, L. A., & Wright, V. C. (1990). Late adolescents' perceptions of their parents: Relationships among deidealization, autonomy, relatedness, and insecurity and implications for adolescent adjustment and ego identity status. *Journal of Youth and Adolescence, 19*, 571–588.

Franklin, J. (2007). Achieving with autism: Dispelling common misconceptions is essential for success. *Education Update, 49*(7), 1–9.

Fredricks, J. A., Blumenfeld, P. C., & Paris, A. H. (2004). School engagement: Potential of the concept, state of the evidence. *Review of Educational Research, 74*, 59–109.

Freeman, S. (2011). *Top 10 Myths About the Brain, How Stuff Works.* Available online at: http://health.howstuffworks.com/human-body/systems/nervous-system/10-brain-myths.htm

Freiberg, H. J., (in press). Classroom management and student achievement. In J. Hattie and E. Anderman (Eds.). *International Handbook of Student Achievement.* New York, NY: Routledge.

Freiberg, H. J., & Driscoll, A. (2005). *Universal teaching strategies* (4th ed.). Boston, MA: Allyn & Bacon.

Freiberg, H. J., & Lamb, S. M. (2009). Dimensions of person-centered classroom management. *Theory Into Practice, 48*, 99–105.

Freiberg, J. (2006). Research-based programs for preventing and solving discipline problems. In C. Evertson & C. S. Weinstein (Eds.), *Handbook for classroom management: Research, practice, and contemporary issues.* Mahwah, NJ: Erlbaum.

Freisen, J. (2010, March 10). The hanging face of Canada: Booming minority populations by 2031. *The Globe and Mail: National.*

Frenzel, A. C., Goetz, T., Lüdtke, O., Pekrun, R., & Sutton, R. E. (2009). Emotional transmission in the classroom: Exploring the relationship between teacher and student enjoyment. *Journal of Educational Psychology, 101*, 705–716.

Frey, N., & Fisher, D. (2010). Reading and the brain: What early childhood educators need to know. *Early Childhood Education Journal, 38*, 103–110.

Frick, T. W. (1990). Analysis of patterns in time: A method of recording and quantifying temporal relations in education. *American Educational Research Journal, 27*, 180–204.

Friedman-Weieneth, J. L., Harvey, E. A., Youngswirth, S. D., & Goldstein, L. H. (2007). The relation between 3-year-old-children's skills and their hyperactivity, inattention, and aggression. *Journal of Educational Psychology, 99*, 671–681.

Friend, M. (2006). *Special education: Contemporary perspectives for school professionals.* Boston, MA: Allyn & Bacon.

Friend, M. (2011). *Special education: Contemporary perspectives for school professionals* (3rd ed.). Boston, MA: Allyn & Bacon/Pearson.

Friend, M., & Bursuck, W. D. (2002). *Including students with special needs* (3rd ed.). Boston, MA: Allyn & Bacon.

Friend, M., & Bursuck, W. D. (2009). *Including students with special needs: A practical guide for classroom teachers* (5th ed.). Boston, MA: Allyn & Bacon/Pearson.

Friend, M., & Bursuck, W. D. (2012). *Including students with special needs: A practical guide for classroom teachers* (6th ed.). Boston, MA: Allyn & Bacon/Pearson.

Frisbie, D. A. (2005). Measurement 101: Some fundamentals revisited. *Educational Measurement: Issues and Practices, 24*(2), 21–28.

Frost, J. L., Wortham, S. C., & Reifel, S. (2005). *Play and child development* (2nd ed.). Upper Saddle River, NJ: Prentice-Hall.

Fuchs, L. S., Fuchs, D., Compton, D. L., Rowell, S. R., Seethaler, P. M., Capizzi, A. M, ... Fletcher, J. M. (2006). The cognitive correlates of third-grade skill in arithmetic, algorithmic, computation, and arithmetic work problems. *Journal of Educational Psychology, 98*, 29–43.

Fuchs, L. S., Fuchs, D., Hamlett, C. L., & Karns, K. (1998). High-achieving students' interactions and performance on complex mathematical tasks as a function of homogeneous and heterogeneous pairings. *American Educational Research Journal, 35*, 227–268.

Fulk, C. L., & Smith, P. J. (1995). Students' perceptions of teachers' instructional and management adaptations for students with learning or behavior problems. *The Elementary School Journal, 95*(5), 409–419.

Fuller, F. G. (1969). Concerns of teachers: A developmental conceptualization. *American Educational Research Journal, 6*, 207–226.

Fuller-Thomson, E., & Dalton, A. (2011, January 5) Suicidal ideation among individuals whose parents have divorced: Findings from a representative Canadian community survey. *Psychiatry Research.* Available online at: http://www.ncbi.nlm.nih.gov/pubmed/21251718

Furrer, C., & Skinner, E. (2003). Sense of relatedness as a factor in children's academic engagement and performance. *Journal of Educational Psychology, 95*(11), 148–161.

Gage, N. L. (1991). The obviousness of social and educational research results. *Educational Researcher, 20*(A), 10–16.

Gagné, E. D. (1985). *The cognitive psychology of school learning.* Boston, MA: Little, Brown.

Gagné, E. D., Yekovich, C. W., & Yekovich, F. R. (1993). *The cognitive psychology of school learning* (2nd ed.). New York, NY: Harper-Collins.

Galambos, S. J., & Goldin-Meadow, S. (1990). The effects of learning two languages on metalinguistic development. *Cognition, 34,* 1–56.

Gallagher, M. (2001, June 11). More on zero-tolerance in schools. *NewsMax.com.* Available online at: http://www.newsmax.com/archives/articles/2001/6/11/123253.shtml

Gallimore, R., & Goldenberg, C. (2001). Analyzing cultural models and settings to connect minority achievement and school improvement research. *Educational Psychologist, 36,* 45–56.

Galton, M., Hargreaves, L., & Pell, T. (2009). Group work and whole-class teaching with 11–14-year-olds compared. *Cambridge Journal of Education, 39,* 119–140.

Gamoran, A. (1987). The stratification of high school learning opportunities. *Sociology of Education, 60,* 135–155.

Gamoran, A., & Mare, R. D. (1989). Secondary school tracking and educational inequality: Compensation, reinforcement, or neutrality. *American Journal of Sociology, 94,* 146–183.

Ganis, G., Thompson, W. L., & Kosslyn, S. M. (2004). Brain areas underlying visual mental imagery and visual perception: An fMRI study. *Cognitive Brain Research, 20,* 226–241.

Garbarino, J., & deLara, E. (2002). *And words can hurt forever: How to protect adolescents from bullying, harassment, and emotional violence.* New York, NY: Free Press.

Garcia, E. E. (1992). "Hispanic" children: Theoretical, empirical, and related policy issues. *Educational Psychology Review, 4,* 69–94.

Garcia, E. E. (2002). *Student cultural diversity: Understanding the meaning and meeting the challenge.* Boston, MA: Houghton Mifflin.

Garcia, S. B., & Tyler, B-J. (2010). Meeting the needs of English language learners with learning disabilities in the general curriculum. *Theory Into Practice, 49,* 113–120.

Gardner, H. (1975). *The shattered mind: The person after brain damage.* New York, NY: Knopf.

Gardner, H. (1983). *Frames of mind: The theory of multiple intelligences.* New York, NY: Basic Books.

Gardner, H. (1991). *The unschooled mind: How children think and how schools should teach.* New York, NY: Basic Books.

Gardner, H. (1993). *Creating minds: An anatomy of creativity seen through the lives of Freud, Einstein, Picasso, Stravinsky, Elliot, Graham, and Gandhi.* New York, NY: Basic Books.

Gardner, H. (1998). Reflections on multiple intelligences: Myths and messages. In A. Woolfolk (Ed.), *Readings in educational psychology* (2nd ed.) (pp. 61–67). Boston, MA: Allyn & Bacon.

Gardner, H. (2003, April 21). *Multiple intelligence after twenty years.* Paper presented at the American Educational Research Association, Chicago, IL.

Gardner, H. (2009). Birth and the spreading of a meme. In J-Q Chen, S. Moran, & H. Gardner (Eds.), *Multiple intelligences around the world* (pp. 3–16). San Francisco, CA: Wiley.

Gardner, H., & Moran, S. (2006). The science of multiple intelligences theory: A response to Lynn Waterhouse. *Educational Psychologist, 41,* 227–232.

Gardner, R., Brown, R., Sanders, S., & Menke, D. J. (1992). "Seductive details" in learning from text. In K. A. Renninger, S. Hidi, & A. Krapp (Eds.), *The role of interest in learning and development* (pp. 239–254). Hillsdale, NJ: Erlbaum.

Garmon, L. C., Basinger, K. S., Gregg, V. R., & Gibbs, J. C. (1996). Gender differences in stage and expression of moral judgment. *Merrill-Palmer Quarterly, 42,* 418–437.

Garner, P. W., & Spears, F. M. (2000). Emotion regulation in low-income preschool children. *Social Development, 9,* 246–264.

Garner, R. (1998). Choosing to learn and not-learn in school. *Educational Psychology Review, 10,* 227–238.

Garnets, L. (2002). Sexual orientations in perspective. *Cultural Diversity and Ethnic Minority Psychology, 8,* 115–129.

Garrison, J. (1995). Deweyan pragmatism and the epistemology of contemporary social constructivism. *American Educational Research Journal, 32,* 716–741.

Gathercole, S. E., Pickering, S. J., Ambridge, B., & Wearing, H. (2004). The structure of working memory from 4 to 15 years of age. *Developmental Psychology, 40,* 177–190.

Gay, G. (2000). *Culturally responsive teaching: Theory, research, and practice.* New York, NY: Teachers College Press.

Gay, G. (2006). Connections between classroom management and culturally responsive teaching. In C. Evertson & C. S. Weinstein (Eds.), *Handbook for classroom management: Research, practice, and contemporary issues.* Mahwah, NJ: Erlbaum.

Geary, D. C. (1995). Sexual selection and sex differences in spatial cognition. *Learning and Individual Differences, 7,* 289–303.

Geary, D. C. (1999). Evolution and developmental sex differences. *Current Directions in Psychological Science, 8,* 115–120.

Geary, D. C., & Bjorklund, D. F. (2000). Evolutionary developmental psychology. *Child Development, 7,* 57–65.

Gee, J. P., (2008). Learning and games. In K. Salen (Ed.), *The ecology of games: Connecting youth, games, and learning* (pp. 21–40). Cambridge, MA: The MIT Press, The John D. and Catherine T. MacArthur Foundation Series on Digital Media and Learning. doi:10.1162/dmal.9780262693646.021

Gehlbach, H. (2004). A new perspective on perspective taking: A multidimensional approach to conceptualizing an aptitude. *Educational Psychology Review, 16,* 207–234.

Geier, R., Blumenfeld, P., Marx, R., Krajcik, J., Fishman, B., & Soloway, E., & Clay-Chambers, J. (2008). Standardized test outcomes for students engaged in inquiry based science curriculum in the context of urban reform. *Journal of Research in Science Teaching, 45,* 922–939.

Gelman, R. (2000). The epigenesis of mathematical thinking. *Journal of Applied Developmental Psychology, 21,* 27–37.

Gelman, R., & Cordes, S. A. (2001). Counting in animals and humans. In E. Dupoux (Ed.), *Essay in honor of Jacques Mehler.* Cambridge, MA: MIT Press.

Gentner, D., Loewenstein, J., & Thompson, L. (2003). Learning and transfer: A general role for analogical encoding. *Journal of Educational Psychology, 95,* 393–408.

George, P. S. (2005). A rationale for differentiated instruction in the regular classroom. *Theory Into Practice, 44,* 185–193.

Gergen, K. J. (1997). Constructing constructivism: Pedagogical potentials. *Issues in Education: Contributions from Educational Psychology, 3,* 195–202.

Gersten, R. (1996a). The language-minority students in transition: Contemporary instructional research. *The Elementary School Journal, 96,* 217–220.

Gersten, R. (1996b). Literacy instruction for language-minority students: The transition years. *The Elementary School Journal, 96,* 217–220.

Gersten, R., Baker, S. K., Shanahan, T., Linan-Thompson, S., Collins, P., & Scarcella, R.. (2007). *Effective literacy and English language instruction for English learners in the elementary grades.* IES Practice Guide. Princeton, NJ: What Works Clearinghouse.

Gerwe, M., Stollhoff, K., Mossakowski, J., Kuehle, H-J., Goertz, U., Schaefer, C., . . . Heger, S. (2009). Tolerability and effects of OROS® MPH (Concerta ®) on functioning, severity of disease and quality of life in children and adolescents with ADHD: Results from a prospective, non-interventional trial. *Attention Deficit Hyperactive Disorder, 1,* 175–186.

Gess-Newsome, J. (2012). Pedagogical content knowledge. In J. Hattie & E. Anderman (Eds.), *International handbook of student achievement.* New York, NY: Routledge.

Gibson, D., Aldrich, C., & Prensky, M. (Eds.). (2006). *Games and simulations in online learning: Research and development frameworks.* Hershey, PA: Information Science Publishing.

Gillies, R. (2003). The behaviors, interactions, and perceptions of junior high school students during small-group learning. *Journal of Educational Psychology, 96,* 15–22.

Gillies, R. (2004). The effects of cooperative learning on junior high school students during small group learning. *Learning and Instruction, 14,* 197–213.

Gillies, R., & Boyle, M. (2011). Teachers' reflections of cooperative learning (CL): A two-year follow-up. *Teaching Education, 22,* 63–78.

Gilligan, C. (1982). *In a different voice: Psychological theory and women's development.* Cambridge, MA: Harvard University Press.

Gilligan, C., & Attanucci, J. (1988). Two moral orientations: Gender differences and similarities. *Merrill-Palmer Quarterly, 34,* 223–237.

Gini, G. (2008). Italian elementary and middle school students' blaming the victim of bullying and perception of school moral atmosphere. *The Elementary School Journal, 108,* 335–354.

Ginott, H. G. (1972). *Teacher and child: A book for parents and teachers.* New York, NY: Collier Books.

Ginsburg, K. R. (2007). The importance of play in promoting healthy child development and maintaining strong parent-child bonds. *Pediatrics, 119,* 182–191.

Glasgow, K. L., Dornbusch, S. M., Troyer, L., Steinberg, L., & Ritter, P. L. (1997). Parenting styles, adolescents' attributions, and educational outcomes in nine heterogeneous high schools. *Child Development, 68,* 507–523.

Glasser, W. (1969). *Schools without failure.* New York, NY: Harper & Row.

Glasser, W. (1990). *The quality school: Managing students without coercion.* New York, NY: Harper & Row.

Glassman, M. (2001). Dewey and Vygotsky: Society, experience, and inquiry in educational practice. *Educational Researcher, 30*(4), 3–14.

Gleitman, H., Fridlund, A. J., & Reisberg, D. (1999). *Psychology* (5th ed.). New York, NY: Norton.

Gluck, M. A., Mercado, E., & Myers, C. E. (2008). *Learning and memory: From brain to behavior.* New York, NY: Worth.

Godden, D. R., & Baddeley, A. D. (1975). Context-dependent memory in two natural environments: On land and underwater. *British Journal of Psychology, 66,* 325–331.

Goetz, T., Cronjaeger, H., Frenzel, A. C., Ludtke, O., & Hall, N. (2010). Academic self-concept and emotion relations: Domain specificity and age effects. *Contemporary Educational Psychology, 35,* 44–58.

Goetz, T., Frenzel, A. C., Hall, N. C., & Pekrun, R. (2008). Antecedents of academic emotions: Testing the internal/external frame of reference model for academic enjoyment. *Contemporary Educational Psychology, 33,* 9–33.

Goldenberg, C. (1996). The education of language-minority students: Where are we, and where do we need to go? *The Elementary School Journal, 96,* 353–361.

Goldman, S. R., Lawless, K., Pellegrino, J. W., & Plants, R. (2006). Technology for teaching and learning with understanding. In J. Cooper (Ed.), *Classroom teaching skills* (8th ed., pp. 104–150). Boston, MA: Houghton-Mifflin.

Goleman, D. (1995). *Emotional intelligence.* New York, NY: Bantam.

Golombok, S., Rust, J., Zervoulis, K., Croudace, T., Golding, J., & Hines, M. (2008). Developmental trajectories of sex-typed behavior in boys and girls: A longitudinal general population study of children aged 2.5–8 years. *Child Development, 79,* 1583–1593.

Gonzales, N., Moll, L. C., Floyd-Tenery, M., Rivera, A., Rendon, P., Gonzales, R., & Amanti, C. (1993). *Teacher research on funds of knowledge: Learning from households.* Washington, DC: The Georgetown University National Center for Research on Cultural Diversity and Second Language Learning. Available online at: http://www.ncela.gwu.edu/pubs/ncrcdsll/epr6.htm

Gonzalez, A. L. (2010, June). *Hispanics in the US: A new generation.* BBC News: US and Canada. Available online at: http://www.bbc.co.uk/news/10209099

Gonzalez, N., Moll, L. C., & Amanti, C. (2005). *Funds of knowledge: Theorizing practices in households and classrooms.* Mahwah, NJ: Erlbaum.

Gonzalez, V. (1999). *Language and cognitive development in second language learning: Educational implications for children and adults.* Boston, MA: Allyn & Bacon.

Gonzalez, V., Brusca-Vega, R., & Yawkey, T. (1997). *Assessment and instruction of culturally diverse students with or at-risk of learning problems: From research to practice.* Boston, MA: Allyn & Bacon.

Good, C., Aronson, J., & Inzlicht, M. (2003). Improving adolescents' standardized test performance: An intervention to reduce the effects of stereotype threat. *Journal of Applied Developmental Psychology, 24,* 645–662.

Good, T. L. (1983a). Classroom research: A decade of progress. *Educational Psychologist, 18,* 127–144.

Good, T. L. (1983b). Research on classroom teaching. In L. Shulman & G. Sykes (Eds.), *Handbook of teaching and policy* (pp. 42–80). New York, NY: Longman.

Good, T. L. (1988). Teacher expectations. In D. Berliner & B. Rosenshine (Eds.), *Talks to teachers* (pp. 159–200). New York, NY: Random House.

Good, T. L. (1996). Teaching effects and teacher evaluation. In J. Sikula (Ed.), *Handbook of research on teacher education* (pp. 617–665). New York, NY: Macmillan.

Good, T. L., & Brophy, J. E. (2008). *Looking in classrooms* (10th ed.). New York, NY: Longman.

Goodrich, H. (1997). Understanding rubrics. *Educational Leadership, 54*(4), 14–17.

Gordon, E. W. (1991). Human diversity and pluralism. *Educational Psychologist, 26,* 99–108.

Gordon, T. (1981). Crippling our children with discipline. *Journal of Education, 163,* 228–243.

Goswami, U. (2004). Neuroscience, education, and special education. *British Journal of Special Education, 31,* 175–183.

Gottlieb, G., Wahlsten, D., & Lickliter, R. (2006). The significance of biology for human development: A developmental psychobiological systems view. In R. M. Lerner (Ed.), *Handbook of child psychology* (6th ed., Vol. 1: Theoretical models of human development, pp. 210–257). New York, NY: Wiley.

Graham, S. (1991). A review of attribution theory in achievement contexts. *Educational Psychology Review, 3,* 5–39.

Graham, S. (1996). How causal beliefs influence the academic and social motivation of African-American children. In G. G. Brannigan (Ed.), *The enlightened educator: Research adventures in the schools* (pp. 111–126). New York, NY: McGraw-Hill.

Graham, S. (1998). Self-blame and peer victimization in middle school: An attributional analysis. *Developmental Psychology, 34,* 587–599.

Graham, S., & Weiner, B. (1996). Theories and principles of motivation. In D. Berliner & R. C. Calfee (Eds.), *Handbook of educational psychology* (pp. 63–84). New York, NY: Macmillan.

Gray, P. (2002). *Psychology* (4th ed.). New York, NY: Worth.

Gray, P. (2011). *Psychology* (6th ed.). New York, NY: Worth.

Gredler, M. E. (2005). *Learning and instruction: Theory into practice* (5th ed.). Boston, MA: Allyn & Bacon.

Gredler, M. E. (2009). Hiding in plain sight: The stages of mastery/self-regulation in Vygotsky's cultural-historical theory. *Educational Psychologist, 44,* 1–19.

Gredler, M. E. (2009). *Learning and instruction: Theory into practice* (6th ed.). Columbus, OH: Merrill.

Green, M., & Piel, J. A. (2010). *Theories of human development: A comparative approach* (2nd ed.). Boston, MA: Allyn & Bacon.

Greene, J. A., Muis, K. R., & Pieschl, S. (2010) The role of epistemic beliefs in students' self-regulated learning with computer-based learning environments: Conceptual and methodological issues. *Educational Psychologist, 45,* 245–257.

Greeno, J. G., Collins, A. M., & Resnick, L. B. (1996). Cognition and learning. In D. Berliner & R. Calfee (Eds.), *Handbook of educational psychology* (pp.15–46). New York, NY: Macmillan.

Greenwald, A. G., Oakes, M. A., & Hoffman, H. G. (2003). Targets of discrimination: Effects of race on responses to weapons holders. *Journal of Experimental Social Psychology, 39,* 399–405.

Gregorc, A. F. (1982). *Gregorc Style Delineator: Development, technical, and administrative manual.* Maynard, MA: Gabriel Systems.

Griffins, P. E., & Gray, R. D. (2005). Discussion: Three ways to misunderstand developmental systems theory. *Biology and Philosophy, 20,* 417–425.

Grigorenko, E. L., Jarvin, L., Diffley III, R., Goodyear, J., Shanahan, E. J., & Sternberg, R. J. (2009). Are SSATs and GPA enough? A theory-based approach to predicting academic success in secondary school. *Journal of Educational Psychology, 101,* 964–981.

Grigorenko, E. L., & Sternberg, R. J. (2001). Analytical, creative, and practical intelligence as predictors of self-reported adaptive functioning: A case study in Russia. *Intelligence, 29,* 57–73.

Grolnick, W. S., Gurland, S. T., Jacob, K. F., & DeCourcey, W. (2002). The development of self-determination in middle childhood and adolescence. In A. Wigfield & J. Eccles (Eds.), *Development of achievement motivation* (pp. 147–171). New York, NY: Academic Press.

Gronlund, N. E., & Brookhart, S. M. (2009). *Gronlund's writing instructional objectives* (8th ed.). Columbus, OH: Pearson.

Gronlund, N. E., & Waugh, C. K. (2009). *Assessment of student achievement* (9th ed.). Columbus, OH: Pearson.

Gröschner, A., Seidel, T., & Shavelson, R. S. (2012). Methods for studying teacher and teaching effectiveness. In J. Hattie & E. Anderman (Eds.), *International handbook of student achievement.* New York, NY: Routledge.

Grossman, H., & Grossman, S. H. (1994). *Gender issues in education.* Boston, MA: Allyn & Bacon.

Grotevant, H. D. (1998). Adolescent development in family contexts. In N. Eisenberg (Ed.), *Handbook of child psychology: Vol 3. Social, emotional, and personality development* (5th ed.) (pp. 1097–1149). New York, NY: Wiley.

Guerra, N. G., Williams, K. R., & Sadek, S. (2011). Understanding bullying and victimization during childhood and adolescence: A mixed methods study. *Child Development, 82,* 295–310.

Guglielmi, R. S. (2008). Native language proficiency, English literacy, academic achievement, and occupational attainment in limited-English-proficient students: A latent growth modeling perspective. *Journal of Educational Psychology, 100,* 322–342.

Guilford, J. P. (1988). Some changes in the Structure-of-Intellect model. *Educational and Psychological Measurement, 48,* 1–4.

Gurian, M., & Henley, P. (2001). *Boys and girls learn differently: A guide for teachers and parents.* San Francisco, CA: Jossey-Bass.

Guskey, T. R. (1994). Making the grade: What benefits students? *Educational Leadership, 52*(2), 14–21.

Guskey, T. R. (2011). Five obstacles to grading reform. Educational Leadership, 69(3), 17-21.

Guskey, T. R., & Bailey, J. M. (2001). *Developing grading and reporting systems for student learning.* Thousand Oaks, CA: Corwin Press.

Guthrie, J. T., & Alao, S. (1997). Designing contexts to increase motivations of reading. *Educational Psychologist, 32,* 95–105.

Guthrie, J. T., Cox, K. E., Anderson, E., Harris, K., Mazzoni, S., & Rach, L. (1998). Principles of integrated instruction for engagement in reading. *Educational Psychology Review, 10,* 227–238.

Gutman, L. M., Sameroff, A., & Cole, R. (2003). Academic growth curve trajectories from 1st grade to 12th grade: Effects of multiple social risk factors and preschool child factors. *Developmental Psychology, 39,* 777–790.

Hacker, D. J., & Tenent, A. (2002). Implementing reciprocal teaching in the classroom: Overcoming obstacles and making modifications. *Journal of Educational Psychology, 94,* 699–718.

Haertel, E. H. (1999). Performance assessment and educational reform. *Phi Delta Kappan, 80,* 662–666.

Hagborg, W. J. (1993). Rosenberg Self-Esteem Scale and Harter's Self-Perception Profile for Adolescents: A concurrent validity study. *Psychology in Schools, 30,* 132–136.

Haier, R. J., & Jung, R. E. (2008). Brain imaging studies of intelligence and creativity: What is the picture for education? *Roeper Review, 30,* 171–180.

Hakuta, K. (1986). *Mirror of language: The debate on bilingualism.* New York, NY: Basic Books.

Hakuta, K., & Garcia, E. E. (1989). Bilingualism and education. *American Psychologist, 44,* 374–379.

Haladyna, T. H. (2002). *Essentials of standardized achievement testing: Validity and accountability.* Boston, MA: Allyn & Bacon.

Hall, L. J., Grundon, G. S., Pope, C., & Romero, A. B. (2010). Training paraprofessionals to use behavioral strategies when educating learners with autism spectrum disorders across environments. *Behavioral Interventions, 25,* 37–51.

Hall, V. C., Bailey, J., & Tillman, D. (1997). Can student-generated illustrations be worth ten thousand words? *Journal of Educational Psychology, 89,* 677–681.

Hallahan, D. P., & Kauffman, J. M. (2006). *Exceptional learners: Introduction to special education* (10th ed.). Boston, MA: Allyn & Bacon.

Hallahan, D. P., Kauffman, J. M., & Pullen, P. C. (2009). *Exceptional learners: Introduction to special education* (11th ed.). Boston, MA: Allyn & Bacon.

Hallahan, D. P., Lloyd, J. W., Kauffman, J. M., Weiss, M. P., & Martinez, E. A. (2005). *Introduction to learning disabilities* (5th ed.). Boston, MA: Allyn & Bacon.

Halpern, D. F., Benbow, C. P., Geary. D. C., Gur, R. C., Hyde, J. S., & Gernsbacher, M. A. (2007). The science of sex differences in science and mathematics. *Psychological Science in the Public Interest, 8,* 1–51.

Hamann, D. L., Baker, D. S., McAllister, P. A., & Bauer, W. I. (2000). Factors affecting university music students' perceptions of lesson quality and teaching effectiveness. *Journal of Research in Music Education, 48,* 102–113.

Hambrick, D. Z., Kane, M. J., & Engle, R. W. (2005). The role of working memory in higher-level cognition. In R. Sternberg & J. E. Pretz (Eds.), *Cognition and intelligence: Identifying the mechanisms of the mind* (pp. 104–121). New York, NY: Cambridge University Press.

Hamers, J. F., & Blanc, M. H. A. (2000). *Bilinguality and bilingualism* (2nd ed.). Cambridge, England: Cambridge University Press.

Hamilton, J. (2009). Multitasking teens may be muddling their brains. Available online at: http://www.npr.org/templates/story/story.php?storyId_95524385

Hamman, D., Berthelot, J., Saia, J., & Crowley, E. (2000). Teachers' coaching of learning and its relation to students' strategic learning. *Journal of Educational Psychology, 92,* 342–348.

Hammer, C. S., Lawrence, F. R., & Miccio, A. W. (2007). Bilingual children's language abilities and reading outcomes in Head Start and kindergarten. *Language, Speech and Hearing Services in Schools, 38,* 237–248.

Hamre, B. K., & Pianta, R. C. (2001). Early teacher–child relationships and the trajectory of children's school outcomes through eighth grade. *Child Development, 72,* 625–638.

Hanushek, E. A., Rivkin, S. G., & Kain, J. J. (2005). Teachers, schools and academic achievement, *Econometrica 73,* 417–458.

Hapgood, S., Magnusson, S. J., & Palincsar, A. S. (2004). Teacher, text, and experience: A case of young children's scientific inquiry. *The Journal of the Learning Sciences, 13,* 455–505.

Harackiewicz, J. M., Barron, K. E., Pintrich, P. R., Elliot, A. J., & Thrash, T. M. (2002). Revision of achievement goal theory: Necessary and illuminating. *Journal of Educational Psychology, 94,* 562–575.

Harackiewicz, J. M., & Linnenbrink, E. A. (2005). Multiple achievement goals and multiple pathways for learning: The agenda and impact of Paul R. Pintrich. *Educational Psychologist, 40,* 75–84.

Hardin, C. J. (2008). *Effective classroom management: Models and strategies for today's classrooms* (2nd ed.). Columbus, OH: Merrill/Prentice-Hall.

Hardman, M. L., Drew, C. J., & Egan, M. W. (2005). *Human exceptionality: Society, school, and family* (8th ed.). Boston, MA: Allyn & Bacon.

Harklau, L., Losey, K. M., & Siegal, M. (Eds.) (1999). *Generation 1.5 Meet college composition: Issues in the teaching of writing to U.S.-educated learners of ESL.* Mahwah, NJ: Lawrence Erlbaum Associates.

Harmer, C. S., Farkas, G., & Maczuga, S. (2010). The language and literacy development of Head Start children: A study using the family and child experiences survey database. *Language, Speech, and Hearing Services in Schools, 41,* 70–83.

Harp, S. F., & Mayer, R. E. (1998). How seductive details do their damage: A theory of cognitive interest in science learning. *Journal of Educational Psychology, 90,* 414–434.

Harris, J. R. (1998). *The nurture assumption: Why children turn out the way they do: Parents matter less than you think and peers matter more.* New York, NY: Free Press.

Harris, K. R., Alexander, P., & Graham, S. (2008). Michael Pressley's contributions to the history and future of strategies research. *Educational Psychologist, 43,* 86–96.

Harris, K. R., & Graham, S. (1996). Memo to constructivist: Skills count too. *Educational Leadership, 53*(5), 26–29.

Harris, M. A., Prior, J. C., & Koehoom, M. (2008). Age at menarche in the Canadian population: Secular trends and relationship to adulthood BMI. *Journal of Adolescent Health, 43,* 548–554.

Harris, P. L. (2006). Social cognition. In D. Kuhn & R. Siegler (Eds.), *Handbook of child psychology* (6th ed., Vol. 2). New York, NY: Wiley.

Harrow, A. J. (1972). *A taxonomy of the psychomotor domain: A guide for developing behavior objectives.* New York, NY: David McKay.

Harrower, J. K., & Dunlap, G. (2001). Including children with autism in general classrooms. *Behavior Modification, 25,* 762–784.

Harter, S. (1998). The development of self-representations. In N. Eisenberg (Ed.), *Handbook of child psychology: Vol. 3. Social, emotional, and personality development* (5th ed., pp. 553–618). New York, NY: Wiley.

Harter, S. (2003). The development of self-representation during childhood and adolescence. In M. R. Leary & J. P. Tangney (Eds.), *Handbook of self and identity* (pp. 610–642). New York, NY: Guilford.

Harter, S. (2006). The self. In W. Damon & R. M. Lerner (Series Eds.) *Social, emotional and personality development* (6th ed., pp. 646–718). New York, NY: Wiley.

Hartshore, J. K., & Ullman, M. T. (2006). Why girls say "holded" more than boys. *Developmental Science, 9,* 21–32.

Hartup, W. W., & Stevens, N. (1999). Friendships and adaptation across the lifespan. *Current Directions in Psychological Science, 8,* 76–79.

Hatfield, D. (2011). *The right kind of telling: An Analysis of feedback and learning in a journalism epistemic game.* Dissertation, University of Wisconsin-Madison.

Hattie, J., & Timperley, H. (2007). The power of feedback. *Review of Educational Research, 77,* 81–112.

Haugland, S. W., & Wright, J. L. (1997). *Young children and technology: A world of discovery.* Boston, MA: Allyn & Bacon.

Hawkins, M. R. (2004). Researching English language and literacy development in schools. *Educational Researcher, 33*(3), 14–25.

Hawley, W. D., & Nieto, S. (2010). Another inconvenient truth: Race and ethnicity matter. *Educational Leadership, 68*(3), 66–71.

Hayes, S. C., Rosenfarb, I., Wulfert, E., Munt, E. D., Korn, Z., & Zettle, R. D. (1985). Self-reinforcement effects: An artifact of social standard setting? *Journal of Applied Behavior Analysis, 18,* 201–214.

Heath, S. B. (1989). Oral and literate traditions among black Americans living in poverty. *American Psychologist, 44,* 367–373.

Hecht, S. A., & Vagi, K. J. (2010). Sources of group and individual differences in emerging fraction skills. *Journal of Educational Psychology, 102,* 843–859.

Helms, J. E. (1995). An update of Helms's White and People of Color racial identity models. In J. G. Ponterotto, J. M. Casas, L. A. Suzuki, & C. M. Alexander (Eds.), *Handbook of multicultural counseling* (pp. 181–198). Thousand Oaks, CA: Sage.

Helwig, C. C., Arnold, M. L., Tan, D., & Boyd, D. (2003). Chinese adolescents' reasoning about democratic and authority-based decision making in peer, family, and school contexts. *Child Development, 74,* 783–800.

Henderson, M. (1996). *Helping your students get the most out of homework* [Brochure]. Chicago, IL: National Parent–Teacher Association.

Henry, B. (2011, May 2). Personal communication.

Herbert, E. A. (1998). Design matters: How school environment affects children. *Educational Leadership, 56*(1), 69–71.

Herman, J. (1997). Assessing new assessments: How do they measure up? *Theory Into Practice, 36,* 197–204.

Herman, J., & Winters. L. (1994). Portfolio research: A slim collection. *Educational Leadership, 52*(2), 48–55.

Herman, M. (2004). Forced to choose: Some determinants of racial identification in multiracial adolescents, *Child Development, 75,* 730–748.

Hetherington, E. M. (2006). The influence of conflict, marital problem solving and parenting on children's adjustment in nondivorced, divorced and remarried families. In A. Clarke-Stewart &

J. Dunn (Eds.), *Families count: Effects on child and adolescent development* (pp. 203–237). New York, NY: Cambridge University Press.

Hetherington, E. M., & Kelly, J. (2003). *For better or for worse: Divorce reconsidered*. New York, NY: W. W. Norton.

Hewstone, M. (1989). Changing stereotypes with disconfirming information. In D. Bar-Tal, C. Graumann, A. Kruglanski, & W. Stroebe (Eds.), *Stereotyping and prejudice: Changing conceptions* (pp. 207–223). New York, NY: Springer-Verlag.

Hickey, D. T. (2003). Engaged participation vs. marginal non-participation: A stridently sociocultural model of achievement motivation. *Elementary School Journal, 103*(4), 401–429.

Hickey, D. T., Kindfield, A. C. H., Horwitz, P., & Christie, M. A. (1999). Advancing educational theory by enhancing practice in a technology supported genetics learning environment. *Journal of Education, 181*, 25–55.

Hickey, D. T., Wolfe, E. W., & Kindfield, A. C. H. (2000). Assessing learning in a technology-supported genetics environment: Evidential and consequential validity issues. *Educational Assessment, 6*, 155–196.

Hidi, S., & Renninger, K. A. (2006). The four-phase model of interest development. *Educational Psychologist, 41*, 111–127.

Hidi, S., Renninger, K. A., & Krapp, A. (2004). Interest, a motivational variable that combines affective and cognitive functioning. In D. Y. Dai & R. J. Sternberg (Eds.), *Motivation, emotion, and cognition: Integrative perspectives on intellectual functioning and development* (pp. 89–115). Mahwah, NJ: Erlbaum.

Hilgard, E. R. (1996). History of educational psychology. In R. Calfee & D. Berliner (Eds.), *Handbook of educational psychology* (pp. 990–1004). New York, NY: Macmillan.

Hill, E. L., & Khanem, F. (2009). The development of hand preference in children: The effect of task demands and links with manual dexterity. *Brain and Cognition, 71*, 99–107. doi:10.1016/j.bandc.2009.04.006

Hill, H. C., Rowan, B., & Ball, D. L. (2005). Effects of teachers' mathematics knowledge for teaching on student achievement. *American Educational Research Journal, 42*, 371–406.

Hill, W. F. (2002). *Learning: A survey of psychological interpretations* (7th ed.). Boston, MA: Allyn & Bacon.

Hindi, E. R., & Perry, N. (2007). Elementary teachers' application of Jean Piaget's theories of cognitive development during social studies curriculum debates in Arizona. *The Elementary School Journal, 108*, 64–79.

Hines, C. V., Cruickshank, D. R., & Kennedy, J. J. (1985). Teacher clarity and its relation to student achievement and satisfaction. *American Educational Research Journal, 22*, 87–99.

Hines, M. (2004) *Brain gender*. New York, NY: Oxford University Press.

Hinnant, J. B., O'Brien, M, & Ghazarian, S. R. (2009). The longitudinal relations of teacher expectations to achievement in the early school years. *Journal of Educational Psychology, 101*, 662–670.

Hinton, C., Miyamoto, K., & Della-Chiesa, B. (2008). Brain research, learning and emotions: Implications for education research, policy and practice. *European Journal of Education, 43*, 87–103.

Hipsky, S. (2011). *Differentiated literacy and language arts strategies for the elementary classroom*. Columbus, OH: Merrill.

Hiroto, D. S., & Seligman, M. E. P. (1975). Generality of learned helplessness in man. *Journal of Personality and Social Psychology, 31*, 311–327.

Hirsch, E. D., Jr. (1996). *The schools we need: Why we don't have them*. New York, NY: Doubleday.

Hirvikoski, T., Waaler, E., Alfredsson, J., Pihlgren, C. Holmström, A., Johnson, A., . . . Nordström, A. L. (2011). Reduced ADHD symptoms in adults with ADHD after structured skills training group: Results from a randomized controlled trial. *Behavioural Research and Therapy, 49*, 175–185.

Hmelo, C. E. (1998). Problem-based learning: Effects on the early acquisition of cognitive skill in medicine. *Journal of the Learning Sciences, 7*, 173–208.

Hmelo-Silver, C. E. (2004). Problem-based learning: What and how do students learn? *Educational Psychology Review, 16*, 235–266.

Hmelo-Silver, C. E., Ravit, G. D., & Chinn, C. A. (2007). Scaffolding and achievement in problem-based and inquiry learning: A response to Kirschner, Sweller, and Clark (2006). *Educational Psychologist, 42*, 99–107.

Hobbs, R. (2004). A review of school-based initiatives in media literacy education. *American Behavioral Scientist, 48*, 42–59.

Hodges, E. V. E., & Perry, D. G. (1999). Personal and interpersonal antecedents and consequences of victimization by peers. *Journal of Personality and Social Psychology, 76*, 677–685.

Hoeffler, T. N., & Leutner, D. (2011). The role of spatial ability in learning from instructional animations – Evidence for an ability-as-compensator hypothesis. *Computers in Human Behavior, 27*, 209–216.

Hofer, M. (2010). Adolescents' development of individual interests: A product of multiple goal regulation? *Educational Psychologist, 45*(3), 149–166.

Hoff, E. (2006). How social contexts support and shape language development. *Developmental Review, 26*, 55–88.

Hofferth, S. L., & Sandberg, J. F. (2000). *Changes in American children's time, 1981–1997*. Ann Arbor, MI: University of Michigan Population Studies Center.

Hoffman, M. L. (2000). *Empathy and moral development*. New York, NY: Cambridge University Press.

Hoffman, M. L. (2001). A comprehensive theory of prosocial moral development. In A. Bohart & D. Stipek & (Eds.), *Constructive and destructive behavior* (pp. 61–86). Washington, DC: American Psychological Association.

Hogan, T., Rabinowitz, M., & Craven, J. A. III. (2003). Representation in teaching: Inferences from research of expert and novice teachers. *Educational Psychologist, 38*, 235–247.

Hoge, D. R., Smit, E. K., & Hanson, S. L. (1990). School experiences predicting changes in self-esteem of sixth- and seventh-grade students. *Journal of Educational Psychology, 82*, 117–126.

Holahan, C., & Sears, R. (1995). *The gifted group in later maturity*. Stanford, CA: Stanford University Press.

Hong, G., & Raudenbush, S. W. (2005). Effects of kindergarten retention policy on children's cognitive growth in reading and mathematics. *Educational Evaluation and Policy Analysis, 27*, 205–224.

Hoover-Dempsey, K. V., Battiato, A. C., Walker, J. M. T., Reed, R. P., DeJong, J. M., & Jones, K. P. (2001). Parental involvement in homework. *Educational Psychologist, 36*, 195–209.

Horn, J. L. (1998). A basis for research on age differences in cognitive capabilities. In J. J. McArdle & R. W. Woodcock (Eds.), *Human cognitive theories in theory and practice* (pp. 57–87). Mahwah, NJ: Erlbaum.

Horovitz, B. (2002, April 22). Gen Y: A tough crowd to sell. *USA Today*, pp. B1–2.

Howe, M. J. A., Davidson, J. W., & Sloboda, J. A. (1998). Innate talents: Reality or myth? *Behavioral and Brain Sciences, 21*, 399–406.

Hoy, W. K., & Woolfolk, A. E. (1993). Teachers' sense of efficacy and the organizational health of schools. *Elementary School Journal, 93*, 355–372.

Hudley, C., & Novak, A. (2007). Environmental influences, the developing brain, and aggressive behavior. *Theory Into Practice, 46*, 121–129.

Hudley, C., Graham, S., & Taylor, A. (2007). Reducing aggressive behavior and increasing motivation in school: The evolution of an intervention to strengthen school adjustment. *Educational Psychologist, 42*, 251–260.

Huesmann, L. R., Moise-Titus, J., Podolski, C. P., & Eron, L. D. (2003). Longitudinal relations between children's exposure to TV violence and their aggressive and violent behavior in young adulthood: 1977–1992. *Developmental Psychology, 39*, 201–221.

Huguet, P., & Régner, I. (2007). Stereotype threat among schoolgirls in quasi-ordinary classroom circumstances. *Journal of Educational Psychology, 99*, 345–360.

Hulit, L., & Howard, M. (2006). *Born to talk: An introduction to speech and language development* (4th ed.). Boston, MA: Allyn & Bacon.

Hulleman, C. S., Godes, O., Hendricks, B. L., & Harackiewicz, J. M. (2010). Enhancing interest and performance with a utility value intervention. *Journal of Educational Psychology, 102*, 880–895.

Hung, D. W. L. (1999). Activity, apprenticeship, and epistemological appropriation: Implications from the writings of Michael Polanyi. *Educational Psychologist, 34*, 193–205.

Hunt, E. (2000). Let's hear it for crystallized intelligence. *Learning and Individual Differences, 12*, 123–129.

Hunt, J. McV. (1961). *Intelligence and experience*. New York, NY: Ronald.

Hunt, N., & Marshall, K. (2002). *Exceptional children and youth: An introduction to special education* (3rd ed.). Boston, MA: Houghton Mifflin.

Hunter, M. (1982). *Mastery teaching*. El Segundo, CA: TIP Publications.

Hurry, J., Nunes, T., Bryant, P., Pretzlik, U., Parker, M., Curno, C., & Midgley, L. (2005) Transforming research on morphology into teacher practice *Research Papers In Education, 20*(2), 187–206.

Hutchinson, N. L. (2009). *Inclusion of exceptional learners in Canadian classrooms: A practical handbook for teachers* (3rd ed.). Toronto, Canada: Prentice Hall.

Hyman, I., Kay, B., Tabori, A, Weber, M., Mahon, M., & Cohen, I. (2006). Bullying: Theory, research and interventions about student victimization. In C. Evertson & C. S. Weinstein (Eds.), *Handbook for classroom management: Research, practice, and contemporary issues*. Mahwah, NJ: Erlbaum.

IDEA. (1997). Available online at: http://www.ed.gov/policy/speced/guid/idea/idea2004.html

Idol, L. (2006). Toward inclusion of special education students in general education: A program evaluation of eight schools. *Remedial and Special Education, 27*, 77–94.

Iran-Nejad, A. (1990). Active and dynamic self-regulation of learning processes. *Review of Educational Research, 60*, 573–602.

Irvine, J. J. (1990). *Black students and school failure: Policies, practices, and prescriptions.* New York, NY: Praeger.

Irvine, J. J., & Armento, B. J. (2001). *Culturally responsive teaching: Lesson planning for elementary and middle grades.* New York, NY: McGraw-Hill.

Irvine, J. J., & Fraser, J. W. (1998, May). Warm demanders. *Education Week.* Available online at: http://www.edweek.org/ew/ewstory.cfm?slug=35irvine.h17&keywords=Irvine

Irving, O., & Martin, J. (1982). Withitness: The confusing variable. *American Educational Research Journal, 19*, 313–319.

Jackson, A., & Davis, G. (2000). *Turning points 2000: Educating adolescents in the 21st century.* New York, NY: Teachers College Press.

Jackson, L. A., von Eye, A., Biocca, F. A., Barbatsis, G., Zhao, Y., & Fitzgerald, H. E. (2006). Does home Internet use influence the academic performance of low-income children? *Developmental Psychology, 42*, 429–435.

Jacobs, J. E., Lanza, S., Osgood, D. W., Eccles, J. S., & Wigfield, A. (2002). Changes in children's self-competence and values: Gender and domain differences across grades one through twelve. *Child Development, 73*, 509–527.

Jaffee, S., & Hyde, J. S. (2000). Gender differences in moral orientation. *Psychological Bulletin, 126*, 703–726.

Jain, S., & Dowson, M. (2009), Mathematics anxiety as a function of multidimensional self-regulation and self-efficacy. *Contemporary Educational Psychology, 34*, 240–249.

James, W. (1890). *The principles of psychology* (Vol. 2). New York, NY: Holt.

James, W. (1912). *Talks to teachers on psychology: And to students on some of life's ideals.* New York, NY: Holt.

Jang, H., Reeve, J., & Deci, E. L. (2010). Engaging students in learning activities: It is not autonomy support or structure but autonomy support and structure. *Journal of Educational Psychology, 102*, 588–600.

Jang, H., Reeve, J., Ryan, R. M., & Kim. A. (2009). Can self-determination theory explain what underlies the productive, satisfying learning experiences of collectivistically oriented Korean students? *Journal of Educational Psychology, 101*, 644–661.

Jarrett, R. (1995). Growing up poor: The family experiences of socially mobile youth in low-income African American neighborhoods. *Journal of Adolescent Research, 10*, 111–135.

Jarrold, C., Tam, H., Baddeley, A. D., & Harvey, C. E. (2011). How does processing affect storage in working memory tasks? Evidence for both domain-general and domain-specific effects. *Journal of Experimental Psychology: Learning, Memory, and Cognition, 37*, 688–705.

Jaswal, V. K., & Markman, E. M. (2001). Learning proper and common names in inferential versus ostensive contexts. *Child Development, 72*, 787–802.

Jensen, E. (2009). *Teaching with poverty in mind: What being poor does to kids' brains and what schools can do about it.* Alexandria, VA:

Association for Supervision and Curriculum Development.

Jensen, L. A., Arnett, J. J., Feldman, S. S., & Cauffman, E. (2002). It's wrong but everybody does it: Academic dishonesty among high school and college students. *Contemporary Educational Psychology, 27*, 209–228.

Jerome, E. M., Hamre, B. K., & Pianta, R. C. (2009). Teacher—child relationships from kindergarten to sixth grade: Early childhood predictors of teacher-perceived conflict and closeness. *Social Development, 18*(4), 915–945.

Jia, Y., Way, N., Ling, G., Yoshikawa, H., Chen, X., & Hughes, D. (2009). The influence of student perceptions of school climate on socioemotional and academic adjustment: A comparison of Chinese and American adolescents. *Child Development, 80*, 1514–1530.

Jimenez, R. (2000). Literacy and identity development of Latina/o students who are successful English readers: Opportunities and obstacles. *American Educational Research Journal, 37*, 971–1000.

Jimerson, S. R. (1999). On the failure of failure: Examining the association between early grade retention and education and employment outcomes during late adolescence. *Journal of School Psychology, 37*, 243–272.

Jimerson, S. R., Anderson, G. E., & Whipple, A. D. (2002). Winning the battle and losing the war: Examining the relation between grade retention and dropping out of high school. *Psychology in the Schools, 39*, 441–457.

Jimerson, S. R., & Ferguson, P. (2007). A longitudinal study of grade retention: Academic and behavioral outcomes of retained students through adolescence. *School Psychology Quarterly, 22*, 314–339.

Jitendra, A. K., Star, J. R., Starosta, K., Leh J. M., Sood, S., Caskie, G., ... Mack, T. R. (2009). Improving seventh grade students' learning of ratio and proportion: The role of schema-based instruction. *Contemporary Educational Psychology, 34*, 250–264.

Johnson, A. (2003). Procedural memory and skill acquisition. In A. F. Healy & R. W. Proctor (Eds.), *Experimental psychology* (Vol. 4, pp. 499–523). New York, NY: Wiley.

Johnson, A. M., & Notah, D. J. (1999). Service learning: History, literature, review, and a pilot study of eighth graders. *The Elementary School Journal, 99*, 453–467.

Johnson, D. W., & Johnson, R. T. (1999). *Learning together and alone: Cooperation, competition, and individualization* (5th ed.). Boston, MA: Allyn & Bacon.

Johnson, D. W., & Johnson, R. T. (1999). The three Cs of school and classroom management. In H. J. Freiberg (Ed.), *Beyond behaviorism: Changing the classroom management paradigm* (pp. 119–144). Boston, MA: Allyn & Bacon.

Johnson, D. W., & Johnson, R. T. (2002). *Meaningful assessment: A meaningful and cooperative process.* Boston, MA: Allyn & Bacon.

Johnson, D. W., & Johnson, R. T. (2009a). An educational psychology success story: Social interdependence theory and cooperative learning. *Educational Researcher, 38*, 365–379.

Johnson, D. W., & Johnson, R. T. (2009b). Energizing learning: The instructional power of conflict. *Educational Researcher, 38*, 37–51.

Johnson, D. W., Johnson, R. T., Dudley, B., Ward, M., & Magnuson, D. (1995). The impact of peer mediation training on the management of

school and home conflicts. *American Educational Research Journal, 32*, 829–844.

Johnson, M. H. (2003). Development of human brain functions. *Biological Psychiatry, 54*, 1312–1316.

Johnson, S. (2008, January 14). A childhood in poverty informs her teaching. *USA Today*, p. 7D.

John-Steiner, V., & Mahn, H. (1996). Sociocultural approaches to learning and development: A Vygotskian framework. *Educational Psychologist, 31*, 191–206.

Johnston, L. D., O'Malley, P. M., Bachman, J. G., & Schulenberg, J. E. (2011). *Monitoring the Future national results on adolescent drug use: Overview of key findings, 2010.* Ann Arbor, MI: Institute for Social Research, The University of Michigan.

Jonassen, D. H. (2003). Designing research-based instruction for story problems. *Educational Psychology Review, 15*, 267–296.

Jonassen, D. H. (2011). Ask systems: Interrrogative access to multiple ways of thinking. *Education Technology Research and Development, 59*, 159–175.

Jones, D. C. (2004). Body image among adolescent girls and boys: A longitudinal study. *Developmental Psychology, 40*, 823–835.

Jones, M. C. (1965). Psychological correlates of somatic development. *Child Development, 36*, 899–911.

Jones, M. G., & Gerig, T. M. (1994). Silent sixth-grade students: Characteristics, achievement, and teacher expectations. *Elementary School Journal, 95*, 169–182.

Jones, M. S., Levin, M. E., Levin, J. R., & Beitzel, B. D. (2000). Can vocabulary-learning strategies and pair-learning formats be profitably combined? *Journal of Educational Psychology, 92*, 256–262.

Jones, S. M., & Dindia, K. (2004). A meta-analytic perspective on sex equity in the classroom. *Review of Educational Research, 74*, 443–471.

Jurbergs, N., Palcic, J., & Kelly, M. L. (2007). School-home notes with and without response cost: Increasing attention and academic performance in low-income children with attention deficit/hyperactivity disorder. *School Psychology Quarterly, 22*, 358–379.

Jurden, F. H. (1995). Individual differences in working memory and complex cognition. *Journal of Educational Psychology, 87*, 93–102.

Jussim, L. (2012). Teachers' expectations. In J. Hattie & E. Anderman (Eds.), *International handbook of student achievement.* New York, NY: Routledge.

Jussim, L., & Harber, K. (2005). Teacher expectations and self-fulfilling prophecies: Knowns and unknowns; resolved and unresolved controversies. *Personality and Social Psychology Review, 9*, 131–135.

Jussim, L., Robustelli, S., & Cain, T. (2009). Teacher expectations and self-fulfilling prophecies. In A. Wigfield and K. Wentzel (Eds), *Handbook of motivation at school* (pp. 349–380). Mahwah, NJ: Erlbaum.

Kagan, J. (1976). Commentary on reflective and impulsive children: Strategies of information processing underlying differences in problem solving. *Monograph of the Society for Research in Child Development, 41*(5) (Ser. No. 168).

Kagan, J., & Herschkowitz, N. (2005). *A young mind in a growing brain.* Mahwah, NJ: Erlbaum.

Kagan, S. (1994). *Cooperative learning.* San Juan Capistrano, CA: Kagan Cooperative Learning.

Kail, R. (2000). Speed of processing: Developmental change and links to intelligence. *Journal of School Psychology, 38,* 51–61.

Kail, R., & Hall, L. K. (1999). Sources of developmental change in children's word-problem performance. *Journal of Educational Psychology, 91,* 600–668.

Kail, R., & Park, Y. (1994). Processing time, articulation time, and memory span. *Journal of Experimental Child Psychology, 57,* 281–291.

Kalyuga, S. (2011). Cognitive load theory: How many types of load does it really need? *Educational Psychology Review, 23,* 1–19.

Kalyuga, S., Chandler, P., Tuovinen, J., & Sweller, J. (2001). When problem solving is superior to studying worked examples. *Journal of Educational Psychology, 93,* 579–588.

Kalyuga, S., & Renkl, A. (2010). Expertise reversal effect and its instructional implications: Introduction to the special issue. *Instructional Science, 38,* 209–215.

Kanaya, T., Scullin, M. H., & Ceci, S. J. (2003). The Flynn effect and U.S. policies: The impact of rising IQ scores on American society via mental retardation diagnoses. *American Psychologist, 58,* 1–13.

Kanazawa, S. (2010). Evolutionary psychology and intelligence research. *American Psychologist, 65*(4), 279–289.

Kantor, H., & Lowe, R. (1995). Class, race, and the emergence of federal education policy: From the New Deal to the Great Society. *Educational Researcher, 24*(3), 4–11.

Kaplan, A., & Maehr, M. L. (2007). The contributions and prospects of goal orientation theory. *Educational Psychology Review, 19,* 141–184.

Kaplan, J. S. (1991). *Beyond behavior modification* (2nd ed.). Austin, TX: Pro-Ed.

Kardash, C. M., & Howell, K. L. (2000). Effects of epistemological beliefs and topic-specific beliefs on undergraduates' cognitive and strategic processing of dual-positional text. *Journal of Educational Psychology, 92,* 524–535.

Karpov, Y. V., & Bransford, J. D. (1995). L. S. Vygotsky and the doctrine of empirical and theoretical learning. *Educational Psychologist, 30,* 61–66.

Karpov, Y. V., & Haywood, H. C. (1998). Two ways to elaborate Vygotsky's concept of mediation implications for instruction. *American Psychologist, 53,* 27–36.

Katz, I., & Assor, A. (2007). When choice motivates and when it does not. *Educational Psychology Review, 19,* 429–442.

Katz, P. A. (2003). Racists or tolerant multiculturalists? How do they begin? *American Psychologist, 58,* 897–909.

Katz, S. R. (1999). Teaching in tensions: Latino immigrant youth, their teachers, and the structures of schooling. *Teachers College Record, 100*(4), 809–840.

Katzir, T., & Paré-Blagoev, J. (2006). Applying cognitive neuroscience research to education: The case of literacy. *Educational Psychologist, 4,* 53–74.

Kazdin, A. E. (2001). *Behavior modification in applied settings* (6th ed.). Belmont, CA: Wadsworth.

Kazdin, A. E. (2008). *The Kazdin method for parenting the defiant child.* Boston, MA: Houghton-Mifflin.

Keefe, J. W. (1982). Assessing student learning styles: An overview. In *Student learning styles and brain behavior.* Reston, VA: National Association of Secondary School Principals.

Keefe, J. W., & Monk, J. S. (1986). *Learning style profile examiner's manual.* Reston, VA: National Association of Secondary School Principals.

Keller, M., Neumann, K., & Fischer, H. E. (2012). Teacher enthusiasm and student learning. In J. Hattie & E. Anderman (Eds.), *International handbook of student achievement.* New York, NY: Routledge.

Keller, P., & El-Sheikh, M. (2011). Children's emotional security and sleep: Longitudinal relations and directions of effects. *Journal of Child Psychology and Psychiatry, 52*(1), 64–71. doi: 10.1111/j.1469-7610.2010.02263.x

Kemp, C., & Carter, M. (2006). The contribution of academic skills to the successful inclusion of children with disabilities. *Journal of Developmental and Physical Disabilities, 18,* 123–146.

Kerckhoff, A. C. (1986). Effects of ability grouping in British secondary schools. *American Sociological Review, 51,* 842–858.

Kiewra, K. A. (1985). Investigating notetaking and review: A depth of processing alternative. *Educational Psychologist, 20,* 23–32.

Kiewra, K. A. (1989). A review of note-taking: The encoding storage paradigm and beyond. *Educational Psychology Review, 1,* 147–172.

Kiewra, K. A. (2002). How classroom teachers can help students learn and teach them how to learn. *Theory Into Practice, 41,* 71–80.

Kim, J. S., & Guryan, J. (2010). The efficacy of a voluntary summer book reading intervention for low-income Latino children from language minority families. *Journal of Educational Psychology, 102,* 20–31.

Kim, K. M. (1998). Korean children's perceptions of adult and peer authority and moral reasoning. *Developmental Psychology, 5,* 310–329.

Kindsvatter, R., Wilen, W., & Ishler, M. (1992). *Dynamics of effective teaching* (2nd ed.). New York, NY: Longman.

King, A. (1990). Enhancing peer interaction and learning in the classroom through reciprocal questioning. *American Educational Research Journal, 27,* 664–687.

King, A. (1994). Guiding knowledge construction in the classroom: Effects of teaching children how to question and how to explain. *American Educational Research Journal, 31,* 338–368.

King, A. (2002). Structuring peer interactions to promote high-level cognitive processing. *Theory Into Practice, 41,* 31–39.

Kirk, S., Gallagher, J. J., & Anastasiow, N. J. (1993). *Educating exceptional children* (7th ed.). Boston, MA: Houghton Mifflin.

Kirk, S. A., Gallagher, J. J., Anastasiow, N. J., & Coleman, M. R. (2006). *Educating exceptional children* (11th ed.). Boston, MA: Houghton Mifflin.

Kirschner, P. A., Sweller, J., & Clark, R. E. (2006). Why minimal guidance during instruction does not work: An analysis of the failure of constructivist, discovery, problem-based, experiential, and inquiry-based teaching. *Educational Psychologist, 41,* 75–86.

Kirsh, S. J. (2005). Cartoon violence and aggression in youth. *Aggression and Violent Behavior, 11,* 547–557.

Kirst, M. (1991). Interview on assessment issues with James Popham. *Educational Researcher, 20*(2), 24–27.

Klahr, D., & Nigram, M. (2004). Equivalence of learning paths in early science instruction: Effects of direct instruction and discovery learning. *Psychological Science, 15,* 661–667.

Klassen, R. M. (2004). A cross-cultural investigation of the efficacy beliefs of South Asian immigrant and Anglo Canadian nonimmigrant early adolescents. *Journal of Educational Psychology, 96,* 731–742.

Klassen, R. M., & Chiu, M. M. (2010). Effects on teachers' self-efficacy and job satisfaction: Teacher gender, years of experience, and job stress. *Journal of Educational Psychology, 10,* 741–756. doi: 10.1037/a0019237

Klein, S. S., & Harris, A. H. (2007). A users guide to the Legacy Cycle. *Journal of Education and Human Development, 1.* Available online at: http://www.scientificjournals.org/journals2007/articles/1088.pdf

Kleinfeld, J. (2005). Culture fuels boys learning problems. *Alaska Daily News,* p. B6.

Kling, K. C., Hyde, J. S., Showers, C. J., & Buswell, B. N. (1999). Gender differences in self-esteem: A meta-analysis. *Psychological Bulletin, 125,* 470–500.

Klinger, J., & Orosco, M. J. (2010). This issue: Response to intervention. *Theory Into Practice, 49,* 247–249.

Knapp, M., Turnbull, B. J., & Shields, P. M. (1990). New directions for educating children of poverty. *Educational Leadership, 48*(1), 4–9.

Knapp, M. S., & Woolverton, S. (2003). Social class and schooling. In J. A. Banks & C. A. Banks (Eds.), *Handbook of research on multicultural education.* San Francisco, CA: Jossey-Bass.

Kohlberg, L. (1963). The development of children's orientations toward moral order: Sequence in the development of moral thought. *Vita Humana, 6,* 11–33.

Kohlberg, L. (1975). The cognitive-developmental approach to moral education. *Phi Delta Kappan, 56,* 670–677.

Kohlberg, L. (1981). *The philosophy of moral development.* New York, NY: Harper & Row.

Kohn, A. (1993). Rewards versus learning: A response to Paul Chance. *Phi Delta Kappan, 74,* 783–787.

Kohn, A. (1996a). *Beyond discipline: From compliance to community.* Alexandria, VA: Association for Supervision and Curriculum Development.

Kohn, A. (1996b). By all available means: Cameron and Pierce's defense of extrinsic motivators. *Review of Educational Research, 66,* 1–4.

Kohn, A. (2005). Unconditional teaching. *Educational Leadership, 62,* 12–17.

Kohn. A. (2006). *The homework myth: Why our kids get too much of a bad thing.* Cambridge, MA: Da Capo Press.

Kokko, K., & Pulkkinen, L. (2000). Aggression in childhood and long-term unemployment in adulthood: A cycle of maladaptation and some protective factors. *Developmental Psychology, 36,* 463–472.

Kolb, G., & Whishaw, I. Q. (1998). Brain plasticity and behavior. In J. T. Spence, J. M. Darley, & D. J. Foss (Eds.), *Annual review of psychology* (pp. 43–64). Palo Alto, CA: Annual Reviews.

Koppleman, K. L. (2011). *Understanding human differences: Multicultural education for a diverse America* (3rd ed.). Boston, MA: Pearson.

Korf, R. (1999). Heuristic search. In R. Wilson & F. Keil (Eds.), *The MIT encyclopedia of the cognitive sciences* (pp. 372–373). Cambridge, MA: MIT Press.

Koriat, A., Goldsmith, M., & Pansky, A. (2000). Toward a psychology of memory accuracy. In S. Fiske (Ed.), *Annual review of psychology* (pp. 481–537). Palo Alto, CA: Annual Reviews.

Kornhaber, M., Fierros, E., & Veenema, S. (2004). *Multiple intelligences: Best ideas for research and practice*. Boston, MA: Allyn & Bacon.

Kosslyn, S. M., & Koenig, O. (1992). *Wet mind: The new cognitive neuroscience*. New York, NY: Free Press.

Kounin, J. S. (1970). *Discipline and group management in classrooms*. New York, NY: Holt, Rinehart & Winston.

Kozulin, A. (1990). *Vygotsky's psychology: A biography of ideas*. Cambridge, MA: Harvard University Press.

Kozulin, A., (2003). Psychological tools and mediated learning. In A. Kouzlin, B. Gindis, V. Ageyev, & S. M. Miller (Eds.), *Vygotsky's educational theory in cultural context* (pp. 15–38). Cambridge, UK: Cambridge University Press.

Kozulin, A. (Ed.). (2003). *Vygotsky's educational theory in cultural context*. Cambridge, UK: Cambridge University Press.

Kozulin, A., & Presseisen, B. Z. (1995). Mediated learning experience and psychological tools: Vygotsky's and Feuerstein's perspectives in a study of student learning. *Educational Psychologist, 30*, 67–75.

Krajcik, J., & Czerniak, C. (2007). *Teaching science in elementary and middle school classrooms: A project-based approach* (3rd ed.). Mahwah, NJ: Erlbaum.

Kratchovil, C. J. (2009). Current pharmacotherapy for ADHD. 2nd International Congress on ADHD. From Childhood to Adult Disease. May 21-24, 2009, Vienna, Austria. *Attention Deficit and Hyperactivity Disorders, 1*: 61.

Krathwohl, D. R., Bloom, B. S., & Masia, B. B. (1964). *Taxonomy of educational objectives. Handbook II: Affective domain*. New York, NY: David McKay.

Kratzig, G. P., & Arbuthnott, K. D. (2006). Perceptual learning style and learning proficiency: A test of the hypothesis. *Journal of Educational Psychology, 98*, 238–246.

Krauss, M. (1992). Statement of Michael Krauss, representing the Linguistic Society of America. In U.S. Senate, *Native American Languages Act of 1991: Hearing before the Select Committee onIndian Affairs* (pp. 18–22). Washington, DC: U.S. Government Printing Office.

Kreitzer, A. E., & Madaus, G. F. (1994). Empirical investigations of the hierarchical structure of the taxonomy. In L. W. Anderson & L. A. Sosniak (Eds.), *Bloom's taxonomy: A forty-year retrospective*. Ninety-third yearbook for the National Society for the Study of Education: Part II (pp. 64–81). Chicago, IL: University of Chicago Press.

Kroger, J. (2000). *Identity development: Adolescence through adulthood*. Thousand Oaks, CA: Sage.

Kronholz, J. (2011), Challenging the gifted: Nuclear chemistry and Sartre draw the best and brightest to Reno. *Education Next, 11*(2), 1-8. Available online at: http://educationnext.org/challenging-the-gifted/

Krumboltz, J. D., & Yeh, C. J. (1996). Competitive grading sabotages good teaching. *Phi Delta Kappan, 78*, 324–326.

Kuhn, D. (2007). Is direct instruction an answer to the right question? *Educational Psychologist, 42*, 109–113.

Kuhn, D., & Dean, D. (2004). Connecting scientific reasoning with casual inference. *Journal of Cognition and Development, 5*, 261–288.

Kuhn, D., & Franklin, S. (2006). The second decade: What develops (and how). In D. Kuhn &

R. S. Siegler (Eds.), *Cognition, perception, and language* (6th ed., Vol. 2, pp. 953–993). New York, NY: Wiley.

Kuhn, D., Goh, W., Iordanou, K., & Shaenfield, D. (2008). Arguing on the computer: A microgenetic study of developing argument skills in a computer-supported environment. *Child Development, 79*, 1310–1328.

Kuklinski, M. R., & Weinstein, R. S. (2001). Classroom and developmental differences in a path model of teacher expectancy effects. *Child Development, 72*, 1554–1578.

Kulik, J. A., & Kulik, C. L. (1997). Ability grouping. In N. Colangelo & G. Davis (Eds.), *Handbook of gifted education* (2nd ed., pp. 230–242). Boston, MA: Allyn & Bacon.

Kumar, D. D., & Sherwood, R. D. (2007). Effect of problem-based simulation on the conceptual understanding of undergraduate science educational majors. *Journal of Science Education and Technology, 16*, 239–246.

Kuo, L., & Anderson, R. C. (2006). Morphological awareness and learning to read: A cross-language perspective. *Educational Psychologist, 41*, 161–180.

Lachter, J., Forster, K. I., & Ruthruff, K. I. (2004). Forty-five years after Broadbent (1958): Still no identification without attention. *Psychological Review, 111*, 880–913.

Ladson-Billings, G. (1990). Like lightning in a bottle: Attempting to capture the pedagogical excellence of successful teachers of Black students. *Qualitative Studies in Education, 3*, 335–344.

Ladson-Billings, G. (1992). Culturally relevant teaching: The key to making multicultural education work. In C. A. Grant (Ed.), *Research and multicultural education* (pp. 106–121). London: Falmer Press.

Ladson-Billings, G. (1994). *The dream keepers*. San Francisco, CA: Jossey-Bass.

Ladson-Billings, G. (1995). But that is just good teaching! The case for culturally relevant pedagogy. *Theory Into Practice, 34*, 161–165.

Ladson-Billings, G. (2004). Landing on the wrong note: The price we paid for Brown. *Educational Researcher, 33*(7), 3–13.

Lamb, M. E., & Lewis, C. (2005). The role of parent-child relationships in child development. In M. H. Bornstein & M. E. Lamb (Eds.), *Developmental science: An advanced textbook* (5th ed., pp. 429–468). Mahwah, NJ: Erlbaum.

Lambert, N. M. (1994). Seating arrangement in classrooms. *The International Encyclopedia of Education* (2nd ed.) *9*, 5355–5359.

Landrum, T. J., & Kauffman, J. M. (2006). Behavioral approaches to classroom management. In C. M. Evertson & C. S. Weinstein (Eds.), *Handbook of classroom management: Research, practice, and contemporary issues*. Mahwah, NJ: Erlbaum.

Lane, K., Falk, K., & Wehby, J. (2006). Classroom management in special education classrooms and resource rooms. In C. M. Evertson & C. S. Weinstein (Eds.), *Handbook of classroom management: Research, practice, and contemporary issues*. Mahwah, NJ: Erlbaum.

Langan-Fox, J., Waycott, J. L., & Albert, K. (2000). Linear and graphic organizers: Properties and processing. *International Journal of Cognitive Ergonomics, 4*(1), 19–34.

Lashley, T. J., II, Matczynski, T. J., & Rowley, J. B. (2002). *Instructional models: Strategies for teaching in a diverse society* (2nd ed.). Belmont, CA: Wadsworth/ Thomson Learning.

Lather, P. (2004). Scientific research in education: A critical perspective. *Journal of Curriculum and Supervision, 20*, 14–30.

Lave, J. (1988). *Cognition in practice: Mind, mathematics, and culture in everyday life*. New York, NY: Cambridge University Press.

Lave, J. (1997). The culture of acquisition and the practice of understanding. In D. Kirshner & J. A. Whitson (Eds.), *Situated cognition: Social, semiotic, and psychological perspectives* (pp. 17–35). Mahwah, NJ: Erlbaum.

Lave, J., & Wenger, E. (1991). *Situated learning: Legitimate peripheral participation*. Cambridge, MA: Cambridge University Press.

Leaper, C. (2002). Parenting girls and boys. In M. H. Bornstein (Ed.), *Handbook of parenting, Vol. 1: Children and parenting* (2nd ed., pp. 127–152). Mahwah, NJ: Erlbaum.

Leaper, C., & Smith, T. S. (2004). A meta-analytic review of gender variations in children's language use: Talkativeness, affiliative speech, and assertive speech. *Developmental Psychology, 40*, 993–1027.

Lee, A. Y., & Hutchinson, L. (1998). Improving learning from examples through reflection. *Journal of Experimental Psychology: Applied, 4*, 187–210.

Lee, C. (2008). Synthesis of research on the role of culture in learning among African American youth: The contributions of Asa G. Hilliard, III. *Review of Educational Research, 78*, 797–827.

Lee, J., & Shute, V. J. (2010). Personal and social-contextual factors in K–12 academic performance: An integrative perspective on student learning, *Educational Psychologist, 45*, 185–202.

Lee, K., Ng, E. L., & Ng, S. F. (2009). The contributions of working memory and executive functioning to problem representation and solution generation in algebraic word problems. *Journal of Educational Psychology, 101*, 373–387.

Lee, R. M. (2005). Resilience against discrimination: Ethnic identity and other-group orientation as protective factors for Korean Americans. *Journal of Counseling Psychology, 52*, 36–44.

Lee, S. J. (2004). Model minorities and perpetual foreigners: The impact of stereotyping on Asian American students. In M. Sadowski (Ed.), *Adolescents at school: Perspectives on youth, identity, and education* (pp. 41–49). Cambridge, MA: Harvard University Press.

Lee, S. J., Wong, N-W. A., & Alvarez, A. N. (2008). The model minority and the perpetual foreigner: Stereotypes of Asian Americans. In N. Tewari & A. Alvarez (Eds.), *Asian American psychology: Current perspectives* (pp. 69–84). Boca Raton, FL: CRC Press.

Lefton, L. (1994). *Psychology* (5th ed.). Boston, MA: Allyn & Bacon.

Lehman, D. R., & Nisbett, R. E. (1990). A longitudinal study of the effects of undergraduate training on reasoning. *Developmental Psychology, 26*, 952–960.

Leinhardt, G. (2001). Instructional explanations: A commonplace for teaching and location for contrasts. In V. Richardson (Ed.), *Handbook of research on teaching* (4th ed., pp. 333–357). Washington, DC: American Educational Research Association.

LeMahieu, P., Gitomer, D. H., & Eresh, J. T. (1993). *Portfolios in large-scale assessment: Difficult but not impossible*. Unpublished manuscript, University of Delaware.

Lemelson, R. (2003). Obsessive-compulsive disorder in Bali. *Transcultural Psychiatry, 40*, 377–408.

Leming, J. S. (1981). Curriculum effectiveness in value/moral education. *Journal of Moral Education, 10*, 147–164.

Lenhart, A. (2010). *Teens, cell phones and /texting: Text messages become the centerpiece communication*. Washington, DC: Pew Research Center. Available online at: http://pewresearch.org/pubs/1572/teens-cell-phones-text-messages

Lepper, M. R., & Greene, D. (1978). *The hidden costs of rewards: New perspectives on the psychology of human motivation*. Hillsdale, NJ: Erlbaum.

Lepper, M. R., Keavney, M., & Drake, M. (1996). Intrinsic motivation and extrinsic reward: A commentary on Cameron and Pierce's meta-analysis. *Review of Educational Research, 66*, 5–32.

Lerner, R. M., Theokas, C., & Bobek, D. L. (2005). Concepts and theories of human development: Historical and contemporary dimensions. In M. H. Bornstein & M. E. Lamb (Eds.), *Developmental science: An advanced textbook* (5th ed., pp. 3–43). Mahwah, NJ: Erlbaum.

Lessow-Hurley, J. (2005). *The foundations of dual language development*. Boston, MA: Allyn & Bacon.

Leung, A. K-y., & Chiu, C-y. (2010). Multicultural experience, idea receptiveness, and creativity. *Journal of Cross-Cultural Psychology, 41*, 723–741.

Leung, A. K., Maddux, W. W., Galinsky, A. D., & Chiu, C. (2008). Multicultural experience enhances creativity: The when and how. *American Psychologist, 63*, 169–181.

Levin, J. R. (1994). Mnemonic strategies and classroom learning: A twenty-year report card. *Elementary School Journal, 94*, 235–254.

Levin, J. R., & Nolan, J. F. (2000). *Principles of classroom management: A professional decision-making model*. Boston, MA: Allyn & Bacon.

Lewinsohn, P. M., Rohde, P., & Seeley, J. R. (1994). Psychological risk factors for future attempts. *Journal of Consulting and Clinical Psychology, 62*, 297–305.

Lewis, R. (2001). Classroom discipline and student responsibility: The students' view. *Teaching and Teacher Education, 17*, 307–319.

Lewis, T. J., Sugai, G., & Colvin, G. (1998). Reducing problem behavior through a school-wide system of effective behavioral support: Investigation of a school-wide social skills training program and contextual interventions. *School Psychology Review, 27*, 446–459.

Liben, L. S., & Bigler, R. S. (2002). The developmental course of gender differentiation: Conceptualizing, measuring, and evaluating constructs and pathways. *Monographs of the Society for Research in Child Development, 67*(2), 1–187.

Liben, L. S., & Signorella, M. L. (1993). Gender-schematic processing in children: The role of initial interpretations of stimuli. *Developmental Psychology, 29*, 141–149.

Lindberg, S. M., Hyde, J. S., Peterson, J. L., & Linn, M. C. (2010). New trends in gender and mathematics performance: A meta-analysis. *Psychological Bulletin, 136*, 1123–1135.

Lindsay, P. H., & Norman, D. A. (1977). *Human information processing: An introduction to psychology* (2nd ed.). New York, NY: Academic Press.

Linn, M. C., & Eylon, B. S. (2006). Science education: Integrating views of learning and instruction. In P. A. Alexander & P. H. Winne (Eds.), *Handbook of educational psychology* (2nd ed., pp. 511–544). Mahwah, NJ: Erlbaum.

Linn, R. L., Baker, E. L., & Betebenner, D. W. (2002). Accountability systems: Implications of requirements of the No Child Left Behind Act of 2001. *Educational Researcher, 31*(6), 3–16.

Linn, R. L., & Miller , M. D. (2005). *Measurement and assessment in teaching* (9th ed.). Upper Saddle River, NJ: Prentice-Hall/Merrill.

Linnenbrink-Garcia, L., & Pekrun, R. (2011). Students' emotions and academic engagement: Introduction to the special issue. *Contemporary Educational Psychology, 36*, 1–3.

Liu, W. M., Ali, S. R., Soleck, G., Hopps, J., Dunston, K., & Pickett, T., Jr. (2004). Using social class in counseling psychology research. *Journal of Counseling Psychology, 51*, 3–18.

Lochman, J. E., & Wells, K. C. (2003). The Coping Power program for preadolescent aggressive boys and their parents: Effects at the one-year follow-up. *Journal of Consulting and Clinical Psychology, 72*, 571–578.

Locke, E. A., & Latham, G. P. (2002). Building a practically useful theory of goal setting and task motivation: A 35-year odyssey. *American Psychologist, 57*, 705–717.

Lorch, R. F., Lorch, E. P., Ritchey, K., McGovern, L., & Coleman, D. (2001). Effects of headings on text summarization. *Contemporary Educational Psychology, 26*, 171–191.

Loveless, T. (1998). The tracking and ability grouping debate. *Fordham Report, 2*(88), 1–27.

Loveless, T. (1999). Will tracking reform promote social equity? *Educational Leadership, 56*(7), 28–32.

Lowenstein, G. (1994). The psychology of curiosity: A review and reinterpretation. *Psychological Bulletin, 117*, 75–98.

Luckner, A. E., & Pianta, R. C. (2011). Teacher student interactions in fifth grade classrooms: Relations with children's peer behavior. *Journal of Applied Developmental Psychology, 32*, 257–266. doi:10.1016/j.appdev.2011.02.010.

Lyon, G. R., Shaywitz, S. E., & Shaywitz, B. A. (2003). A definition of dyslexia. *Annals of Dyslexia, 53*, 1–14.

Ma, X. (2012). The relation of teacher characteristics to student achievement. In J. Hattie & E. Anderman (Eds.), *International handbook of student achievement*. New York, NY: Routledge.

Maag, J. W., & Kemp, S. E. (2003). Behavioral intent of power and affiliation: Implications for functional analysis. *Remedial and Special Education, 24*, 57–64.

Mabry, L. (1999). Writing to the rubrics: Lingering effects of traditional standardized testing on direct writing assessment. *Phi Delta Kappan, 80*, 673–679.

Maccoby, E. E. (1998). *The two sexes: Growing up apart, coming together*. Cambridge, MA: Harvard University Press.

Mace, F. C., Belfiore, P. J., & Hutchinson, J. M. (2001). Operant theory and research on self-regulation. In B. Zimmerman & D. Schunk (Eds.), *Self-regulated learning and academic achievement: Theoretical perspectives* (2nd ed.). Mahwah, NJ: Erlbaum.

Macionis, J. J. (2003). *Sociology* (9th ed.). Upper Saddle River, NJ: Prentice-Hall.

Macionis, J. J. (2010). *Sociology* (13th ed.). Upper Saddle River, NJ: Prentice-Hall.

Macrae, C. N., Milne, A. B., & Bodenhausen, C. V. (1994). Stereotypes as energy-saving devices: A peek inside the cognitive toolbox. *Journal of Personality and Social Psychology, 66*, 37–47.

Maddux, W. W., & Galinsky, A. D. (2009). Cultural borders and mental barriers: Living in and adapting to foreign cultures facilitates creativity. *Journal of Personality and Social Psychology, 96*, 1047–1061.

Madsen, C. H., Becker, W. C., Thomas, D. R., Koser, L., & Plager, E. (1968). An analysis of the reinforcing function of "sit down" commands. In R. K. Parker (Ed.), *Readings in educational psychology*. Boston, MA: Allyn & Bacon.

Madsen, K. (2003). The effect of accuracy of instruction, teacher delivery, and student attentiveness on musicians' evaluation of teacher effectiveness. *Journal of Research in Music Education, 51*, 38–51.

Mager, R. (1975). *Preparing instructional objectives* (2nd ed.). Palo Alto, CA: Fearon.

Mager, R. F. (1997). Preparing instructional objectives: A critical tool in the development of effective instruction (3rd Ed.). Atlanta, GA: Center for Effective Performance.

Magnusson, S. J., & Palincsar, A. S. (1995). The learning environment as a site of science reform. *Theory Into Practice, 34*, 43–50.

Maguire, E. A., Gadian, D. G., Johnsrude, I. S., Good, C. D., Ashburner, J., Frackowiak, R. S., & Frith, C. D. (2000). Navigation-related structural change in the hippocampi of taxi drivers. *Proceedings of the National Academy of Science, USA, 97*(8), 4398–4403.

Major, B., & Schmader, T. (1998). Coping with stigma through psychological disengagement. In J. Swim & C. Stangor (Eds.), *Stigma: The target's perspective* (pp. 219–241). New York, NY: Academic Press.

Manning, B. H., & Payne, B. D. (1996). *Self-talk for teachers and students: Metacognitive strategies for personal and classroom use*. Boston, MA: Allyn & Bacon.

Manning, M. L., & Baruth, L. G. (1996). *Multicultural education of children and adolescents* (2nd ed.). Boston, MA: Allyn & Bacon.

Mantzicopolos, P., & Morrison, D. (1992). Kindergarten retention: Academic and behavioral outcomes through the end of second grade. *American Educational Research Journal, 29*, 182–198.

Marchland, G., & Skinner, E. A. (2007). Motivational dynamics of children's academic help-seeking and concealment. *Journal of Educational Psychology, 99*, 65–82.

Marcia, J. E. (1991). Identity and self development. In R. Lerner, A. Peterson, & J. Brooks-Gunn (Eds.), *Encyclopedia of adolescence* (Vol. 1). New York, NY: Garland.

Marcia, J. E. (1994). The empirical study of ego identity. In H. Bosma, T. Graafsma, H. Grotebanc, & D. DeLivita (Eds.), *The identity and development*. Newbury Park, CA: Sage.

Marcia, J. E. (1999). Representational thought in ego identity, psychotherapy, and psychosocial development. In I. E. Sigel (Ed.), *Development of mental representation: Theories and applications*. Mahwah, NJ: Erlbaum.

Marcus, N., Cooper, M., & Sweller, J. (1996). Understanding instructions. *Journal of Educational Psychology, 88*, 49–63.

Marinova-Todd, S., Marshall, D., & Snow, C. (2000). Three misconceptions about age and L2 learning. *TESOL Quarterly, 34*(1), 9–34.

Markman, E. M. (1992). Constraints on word learning: Speculations about their nature, origins, and domain specificity. In M. Gunnar & M. Maratsos (Eds.), *Minnesota symposium on child psychology* (Vol. 25, pp. 59–101). Hillsdale, NJ: Erlbaum.

Marks, A. K, Patton, F., & Coll, C. G. (2011). Being bicultural: A mixed - methods study of adolescents' implicitly and explicitly measured multiethnic identities. *Developmental Psychology, 47*, 270–288.

Markstrom-Adams, C. (1992). A consideration of intervening factors in adolescent identity formation. In G. R. Adams, R. Montemayor, & T. Gullotta (Eds.), *Advances in adolescent development: Vol. 4. Adolescent identity formation* (pp. 173–192). Newbury Park, CA: Sage.

Marsh, H. W. (1990). Influences of internal and external frames of reference on the formation of math and English self-concepts. *Journal of Educational Psychology, 82*, 107–116.

Marsh, H. W., & Ayotte, V. (2003). Do multiple dimensions of self-concept become more differentiated with age? The differential distinctiveness hypothesis. *Journal of Educational Psychology, 95*, 687–706.

Marsh, H. W., & Craven, R. (2002). The pivotal role of frames of reference in academic self-concept formation: The Big Fish Little Pond Effect. In F. Pajares & T. Urdan (Eds.), *Adolescence and Education* (Volume II, pp. 83–123). Greenwich, CT: Information Age.

Marsh, H. W., Craven, R. G., & Martin, A. (2006). What is the nature of self-esteem: Unidimensional and multidimensional perspectives. In M. Kernis (Ed.), *Self-esteem: Issues and answers* (pp. 16–25). New York, NY: Psychology Press.

Marsh, H. W., & Hau, K-T. (2003). Big-Fish-Little-Pond effect on academic self-concept. *American Psychologist, 58*, 364–376.

Marsh, H. W., Seaton M., Trautwein, U., Lüdtke, O., Hau, K. T., O'Mara, A. J., & Craven, R. G. (2008). The Big-fish–little-pond-effect stands up to critical scrutiny: Implications for theory, methodology, and future research. *Educational Psychology Review, 20*, 319–350.

Marsh, H. W., Trautwein, U., Lüdtke, O., Köller, O., & Baumert, J. (2006). Integration of multidimensional self-concept and core personality constructs: Construct validation and relations to well-being and achievement. *Journal of Personality, 74*, 403–456.

Marsh, H. W., & Yeung, A. S. (1997). Coursework selection: Relation to academic self-concept and achievement. *American Educational Research Journal, 34*, 691–720.

Marshall, H. H. (Ed.). (1992). *Redefining student learning: Roots of educational change*. Norwood, NJ: Ablex.

Marshall, H. H. (1996). Implications of differentiating and understanding constructivist approaches. *Journal of Educational Psychology, 31*, 235–240.

Martin, J. (2006). Social cultural perspectives in educational psychology. In P. A. Alexander & P. H. Winne (Eds.), *Handbook of educational psychology* (2nd ed., pp. 595–614). Mahwah, NJ: Erlbaum.

Martinez-Pons, M. (2002). A social cognitive view of parental influence on student academic self-regulation. *Theory Into Practice, 61*, 126–131.

Marvin, K. L., Rapp, J. T., Stenske, M. T., Rojas, N. R., Swanson, G. J., & Bartlett, S. M. (2010). Response repetition as an error-correction procedure for sight-word reading: A replication and extension. *Behavioral Interventions, 25*, 109–127.

Marzano, R. J., & Marzano, J. S. (2003, September). The key to classroom management. *Educational Leadership, 61*(1), 6–13.

Mascolo, M. F., & Fischer, K. W. (2005). Constructivist theories. In B. Hopkins (Ed.), *The Cambridge encyclopedia of child development*. New York, NY: Cambridge University Press.

Maslow, A. H. (1968). *Toward a psychology of being* (2nd ed.). New York, NY: Van Nostrand.

Maslow, A. H. (1970). *Motivation and personality* (2nd ed.). New York, NY: Harper and Row.

Mason, D. A., & Good, T. L. (1993). Effects of two-group and whole-class teaching on regrouped elementary students' mathematics achievement. *American Educational Research Journal, 30*, 328–360.

Mason, L. (2007). Introduction: Bridging the cognitive and sociocultural approaches in research on conceptual change: Is it possible? *Educational Psychologist, 42*, 1–7.

Matson, J. L., Matson, M. L., & Rivet, T. T. (2007). Social-skills treatments for children with autism spectrum disorders. *Behavior Modification, 31*, 682–707.

Matsumara, L. C., & Crosson, A. (2008). Classroom climate, rigorous instruction and curriculum, and students' interactions in urban middle schools. *The Elementary School Journal, 108*, 293–312.

Matsumara, L. C., Slater, S. C., & Crosson, A. (2008). Classroom climate, rigorous instruction and curriculum, and students' interactions in urban middle schools. *The Elementary School Journal, 108*, 293–312.

Matthews, J. S., Kizzie, K. T., Rowley, S. J., & Cortina, K. (2010). African Americans and boys: Understanding the literacy gap, tracing academic trajectories, and evaluating the role of learning-related skills. *Journal of Educational Psychology, 102*, 757–771.

Matthews, J. S., Ponitz, C. C., & Morrison, F. J. (2009). Early gender differences in self-regulation and academic achievement. *Journal of Educational Psychology, 101*, 689–704.

Mayer, R. E. (1983). *Thinking, problem solving, cognition*. San Francisco, CA: Freeman.

Mayer, R. E. (1984). Twenty-five years of research on advance organizers. *Instructional Science, 8*, 133–169.

Mayer, R. E. (1996). Learners as information processors: Legacies and limitations of educational psychology's second metaphor. *Journal of Educational Psychology, 31*, 151–161.

Mayer, R. E. (2001). *Multimedia learning*. New York, NY: Cambridge University Press.

Mayer, R. E. (2005). Cognitive theory of multimedia learning. In R. E. Mayer (Ed.), *The Cambridge handbook of multimedia learning* (pp. 31–48). New York, NY: Cambridge University Press.

Mayer, R. E. (2008). *Learning and instruction* (2nd ed.). Columbus, OH: Merrill/Prentice-Hall.

Mayer, R. E. (2011). *Applying the science of learning*. Boston, MA: Pearson.

Mayer, R. E., & Gallini, J. K. (1990). When is an illustration worth ten thousand words? *Journal of Educational Psychology, 82*, 715–726.

Mayer, R. E., & Massa, L. J. (2003). Three facets of visual and verbal learners: Cognitive ability, cognitive style and learning preference. *Journal of Educational Psychology, 95*(4), 833–846.

Mayer, R. E., & Wittrock, M. C. (1996). Problem-solving transfer. In D. Berliner & R. Calfee (Eds.), *Handbook of educational psychology* (pp. 47–62). New York, NY: Macmillan.

Mayer, R. E., & Wittrock, M. C. (2006). Problem solving. In P. A. Alexander & P. H. Winne (Eds.), *Handbook of educational psychology* (2nd ed., pp. 287–303). Mahwah, NJ: Erlbaum.

Mayo Clinic. (2009). *Type 2 diabetes: Complications*. Available online at: http://www.mayoclinic.com/health/type-2-diabetes/DS00585/DSECTION_complications

McAnarney, E. R. (2008). Adolescent brain development: Forging new links. *Journal of Adolescent Health, 42*, 321–323.

McCafferty, S. G. (2004). Introduction. *International Journal of Applied Linguistics, 14*(1), 1–6.

McCaslin, M., & Good, T. (1996). The informal curriculum. In D. Berliner & R. Calfee (Eds.), *Handbook of educational psychology* (pp. 622–670). New York, NY: Macmillan.

McCaslin, M., & Good, T. L. (1998). Moving beyond management as sheer compliance: Helping students to develop goal coordination strategies. *Educational Horizons, 76*, 169–176.

McCaslin, M., & Hickey, D. T. (2001). Self-regulated learning and academic achievement: A Vygotskian view. In B. Zimmerman & D. Schunk (Eds.), *Self-regulated learning and academic achievement: Theoretical perspectives* (2nd ed., pp. 227–252). Mahwah, NJ: Erlbaum.

McClelland, D. (1985). *Human motivation*. Glenview, IL: Scott, Foresman.

McCoach, D. B., Kehle, T. J., Bray, M. L., & Siegle, D. (2001). Best practices in the identification of gifted students with learning disabilities. *Psychology in the Schools, 38*, 403–411.

McCoy, A. R., & Reynolds, A. J. (1999). Grade retention and school performance: An extended investigation. *Journal of School Psychology, 37*, 273–298.

McDonald, J. P. (1993). Three pictures of an exhibition: Warm, cool, and hard. *Phi Delta Kappan, 6*, 480–485.

McGoey, K. E., & DuPaul, G. J. (2000). Token reinforcement and response cost procedures: Reducing disruptive behavior of children with attention-deficit/hyperactivity disorder. *School Psychology Quarterly, 15*, 330–343.

McHugh, J. R., & Barlow, D. H. (2010). The Dissemination and implementation of evidence-based psychological treatments: A review of current efforts. *American Psychologist, 65*(2), 73–84. DOI: 10.1037/a0018121.

McKenzie, T. L., & Kahan, D. (2008). Physical activity, public health, and elementary schools. *The Elementary School Journal, 108*, 171–180.

McKenzie, T. L., & Rushall, B. S. (1974). Effects of self-recording on attendance and performance in a competitive swimming training environment. *Journal of Applied Behavior Analysis, 7*, 199–206.

McKinley, J. C. (2011, January 24). Shot in the head, but getting back on his feet and on with his life. *New York Times*, A-16. Available online at: http://www.nytimes.com/2011/01/24/us/24rehab.html?scp=7&sq=Houston%20rehabilitation&st=cse.

McKown, C. (2005). Applying ecological theory to advance the science and practice of school-based prejudice reduction interventions. *Educational Psychologist, 40*, 177–189.

McLoyd, V. C. (1998). Economic disadvantage and child development. *American Psychologist, 53*, 185–204.

McMillan, J. H. (2004). *Classroom assessment: Principles and practice for effective instruction* (3rd ed.). Boston, MA: Allyn & Bacon.

McNeely, C. A., Nonnemaker, J. M., & Blum, R. W. (2002). Promoting school connectedness:

Evidence from the National Longitudinal Study of Adolescent Health. *Journal of School Health, 72*(4), 138–146.

McNeil, L. M., & Valenzuela, A. (2000). *The harmful impact of the TAAS system of testing in Texas: Beneath the accountability rhetoric.* Cambridge, MA: Harvard University Civil Rights Project. Available online at: www.law.harvard.edu/groups/civil-rights/testing.html

McTigue, E. M. (2009). Does multimedia learning theory extend to middle-school students? *Contemporary Educational Psychology, 34,* 143–153.

Mears, T. (1998). Saying 'Si' to Spanish. *Boston Globe,* April 12.

Mediascope. (1996). *National television violence study: Executive summary 1994–1995.* Studio City, CA: Author.

Medina, J. (2002, June 23). Groups say Regents Exam push immigrants to drop out. *The New York Times,* p. A28.

Meece, J. L., & Daniels, D. H. (2008). *Child and adolescent development for educators* (3rd ed.). New York, NY: McGraw-Hill.

Meece, J. L., & Kurtz-Costes, B. (2001). Introduction: The schooling of ethnic minority children and youth. *Educational Psychologist, 36,* 1–7.

Meijer, A. M., & Wittenboer, G. L. H. van den. (2004). The joint contribution of sleep, intelligence and motivation to school performance, *Personality and Individual Differences,37,* 95–106.

Melnick, S. A., & Meister, D. G. (2008). A comparison of beginning and experienced teacher concerns. *Education Research Quarterly, 31*(3), 39–56.

Mendle, J., Turkheimer, E., & Emery, R. E. (2007). Detrimental psychological outcomes associated with early pubertal timing in adolescent girls. *Developmental Review, 27,* 151–171.

Mendoza, E. M., & Johnson, K. O. (2000). Land of Plenty: Diversity as America's competitive edge in science, engineering, and technology. Washington DC: Congressional Commission on the Advancement of Women and Minorities in Science, Engineering and Technology Development.

Merrell, K. W., Isava, D. M., Gueldner, B. A., & Ross, S. W. (2008). How effective are school bullying intervention programs? A meta-analysis of intervention research. *School Psychology Quarterly, 23,* 26–42.

Mertler, C. A., & Charles, C. M. (2005). *Introduction to educational research* (5th ed.). Boston, MA: Allyn & Bacon.

Merton, R. K. (1948). The self-fulfilling prophecy. *Antioch Review, 8,* 193–210.

Messick, S. (1975). The standard problem: Meaning and values in measurement and evaluation. *American Psychologist, 35,* 1012–1027.

Metzler, C. W., Biglan, A., Rusby, J. C., & Sprague, J. R. (2001). Evaluation of a comprehensive behavior management program to improve school-wide positive behavior support. *Education and Treatment of Children, 24*(4), 448–470.

Midgley, C. (2001). A goal theory perspective on the current status of middle level schools. In T. Urdan & F. Pajares (Eds.), *Adolescence and education* (pp. 33–59). Volume I. Greenwich, CT: Information Age Publishing.

Midgley, C., Kaplan, A., & Middleton, M. (2001). Performance-approach goals: Good for what, for whom, under what circumstances, and at what cost? *Journal of Educational Psychology, 93,* 77–86.

Midgley, C., Kaplan, A., Middleton, M., Maehr, M. L., Urdan, T., Anderman, L. H., … Roser, R. (1998). The development and validation of scales assessing students' achievement goal orientations. *Contemporary Educational Psychology, 23,* 113–131.

Miller, G. A. (1956). The magical number seven, plus or minus two: Some limits on our capacity for processing information. *Psychological Review, 63,* 81–97.

Miller, G. A., Galanter, E., & Pribram, K. H. (1960). *Plans and the structure of behavior.* New York, NY: Holt, Rinehart & Winston.

Miller, M. D., Linn, R. L., & Gronlund, N. E. (2009). *Measurement and assessment in education* (10th ed.) Boston, MA: Pearson.

Miller, N., & Harrington, H. J. (1993). Social categorization and intergroup acceptance: Principles for the development an design of cooperative learning teams. In R. Hertz-Lasarowitz & N. Miller (Eds.), *Interaction in cooperative groups: The theoretical anatomy of group learning* (pp. 203–227). New York, NY: Cambridge University Press.

Miller, P. H. (2011). *Theories of developmental psychology* (5th ed.). New York, NY: Worth.

Miller, R. B. (1962). Analysis and specification of behavior for training. In R. Glaser (Ed.), *Training research and education: Science edition.* New York, NY: Wiley.

Miller, S. A. (2005). Tips for getting children's attention. *Early Childhood Today,* 19.

Miller, S. A. (2009). Children's understanding of second-order mental statuses. *Psychological Bulletin, 135,* 749–773.

Milner, H.R. (2003). Teacher reflection and race in cultural contexts: History, meaning, and methods in teaching. *Theory into Practice 42*(3), 173–180.

Milner, H. R. (2006). Classroom management in urban classrooms. In C. M. Evertson & C. S. Weinstein, (Eds.), *Handbook of classroom management: Research, practice, and contemporary issues* (pp. 491–522). Mahwah, NJ: Erlbaum.

Milner, H. R IV. (2010). *Start where you are but don't stay there: Understanding diversity, opportunity gaps, and teaching in today's schools.* Cambridge, MA: Harvard Education Press.

Miranda, T. Z. (2008). Bilingual education for all students: Still standing after all these years. In L. S. Verplaetse & N. Migliacci (Eds.), *Inclusive pedagogy for English language learners: A handbook of research-informed practices* (pp. 257–275). New York, NY: Erlbaum.

Mitchell, M. (1993). Situational interest: Its multifaceted structure in the secondary school mathematics classroom. *Journal of Educational Psychology. 85,* 424–436.

Moll, L. C., Amanti, C., Neff, D., & Gonzalez, N. (1992). Funds of knowledge for teaching: Using a qualitative approach to connect homes and classrooms. *Theory into Practice, 31,* 132–141.

Moller, A. C., Deci, E. L., & Ryan, R. M. (2006). Choice and ego-depletion: The moderating role of autonomy. *Personality and Social Psychology Bulletin, 32*(8), 1024–1036.

Möller, J., & Pohlmann, B. (2010). Achievement differences and self-concept differences: Stronger associations for above or below average students? *British Journal of Educational Psychology, 80,* 435–450.

Monroe, C. R., & Obidah, J. E. (2002, April). *The impact of cultural synchronization on a teacher's perceptions of disruption: A case study of an African American middle school classroom.* Paper presented at the American Educational Research Association, New Orleans, LA.

Montrul, S. (2010). Dominant language transfer in adult second language learners and heritage speakers. *Second Language Research, 26,* 293–327.

Moore, K. A., Redd, Z. Burkhauser, M., Mbwana, K., & Collins, A. (2009). *Children in poverty: Trends, consequences, and policy options.* Washington DC: Child Trends, #2009–11.

Moore, M. K., & Meltzoff, A. N. (2004). Object permanence after a 24-hr delay and leaving the locale of disappearance: the role of memory, space, and identity. *Developmental Psychology, 40,* 606–620.

Moreno, R., Ozogul, G., & Reisslein, M. (2011). Teaching with concrete and abstract visual representations: Effects on students' problem solving, problem representations, and learning perceptions. *Journal of Educational Psychology, 103,* 32–47.

Morin, V. A., & Miller, S. P. (1998). Teaching multiplication to middle school students with mental retardation. *Education & Treatment of Children, 21,* 22–36.

Morine-Dershimer, G. (2006). Instructional planning. In J. Cooper (Ed.), *Classroom teaching skills* (7th ed., pp. 20–54). Boston, MA: Houghton-Mifflin.

Morrow, L. M., & Weinstein, C. (1986). Encouraging voluntary reading: The impact of a literature program on children's use of library centers. *Reading Research Quarterly, 21,* 330–346.

Moshman, D. (1982). Exogenous, endogenous, and dialectical constructivism. *Developmental Review, 2,* 371–384.

Moshman, D. (1997). Pluralist rational constructivism. *Issues in Education: Contributions from Educational Psychology, 3,* 229–234.

Moskowitz, G., & Hayman, M. L. (1976). Successful strategies of inner-city teachers: A year-long study. *Journal of Educational Research, 69,* 283–289.

Mueller, C. M., & Dweck, C. S. (1998). Praise for intelligence can undermine children's motivation and performance. *Journal of Personality and Social Psychology, 75,* 33–52.

Muis, K. R., & Franco, G. M. (2009). Epistemic beliefs: Setting the standards for self-regulated learning. *Contemporary Educational Psychology, 34,* 306–318.

Mullis, I. V. S., Martin, M. O., Gonzalez, E., & Kennedy, A. M. (2003). *PIRLS 2001 International report: IEA's study of reading literacy achievement in primary schools.* Chestnut Hill, MA: Boston College. Available online at:. http://timss.bc.edu/pirls2001i/PIRLS2001_Pubs_IR.html

Mumford, M. D., Costanza, D. P., Baughman, W. A., Threlfall, V., & Fleishman, E. A. (1994). Influence of abilities on performance during practice: Effects of massed and distributed practice. *Journal of Educational Psychology, 86,* 134–144.

Murayama, K., & Elliot, A. J. (2009). The joint influence of personal achievement goals and classroom goal structures on achievement-relevant outcomes. *Journal of Educational Psychology, 101,* 432–447.

Murdock, S. G., O'Neill, R. E., & Cunningham, E. (2005). A comparison of results and acceptability of functional behavioral assessment procedures with a group of middle school students with emotional/behavioral disorders (E/BD). *Journal of Behavioral Education, 14*, 5–18.

Murdock, T. A., & Anderman, E. M. (2006). Motivational perspectives on student cheating: Toward an integrated model of academic dishonesty. *Educational Psychologist, 42*, 129–145.

Murdock, T. B., Hale, N. M., & Weber, M. J. (2001). Predictors of cheating among early adolescents: Academic and social motivations. *Contemporary Educational Psychology, 26*, 96–115.

Murdock, T. B., & Miller, A. (2003). Teachers as sources of middle school students' motivational identity: Variable-centered and person-centered analytic approaches. *Elementary School Journal, 103*, 383–399.

Murphy, P. K., & Alexander, P. A. (2000). A motivated exploration of motivation terminology. *Contemporary Educational Psychology, 25*, 3–53.

Murphy, P. K., & Benton, S. L. (2010).The new frontier of educational neuropsychology: Unknown opportunities and unfulfilled hopes. *Contemporary Educational Psychology, 35*, 153–155.

Murphy, P. K., Wilkinson, I. A. G., Soter, A. O., Hennessey, M. N., & Alexander, J. F. (2009). Examining the effects of classroom discussion on students' comprehension of text: A meta-analysis. *Journal of Educational Psychology, 101*, 740–764.

Myers, D. G. (2005). *Exploring psychology* (6th ed. in modules). New York, NY: Worth.

Myers, D. G. (2010). *Psychology* (9th ed.). New York, NY: Worth.

Myers, I. B., & McCaulley, M. H. (1988). *Manual: A guide to the development and use of the Myers-Briggs Type Indicator*. Palo Alto, CA: Consulting Psychologists.

National Alliance of Black School Educators. (2002). *Addressing over-representations of African American students in special education: The prereferral intervention process*. Arlington, VA: Council for Exceptional Education.

National Association for the Education of Young Children. (2006). *The value of recess and outdoor play*. Available online at: http://www.naeyc.org/ece/1998/08.asp.

National Center for Educational Statistics. (2003). *Indicators of school crime and safety 2002*. Available online at: http://nces.ed.gov/pubs2003/schoolcrime/6.asp?nav=1

National Center for Education Statistics. (2009). *Number and percentage distribution of 3- to 21-year-olds served under the Individuals with Disabilities Education Act (IDEA), Part B, and number served as a percentage of total public school enrollment, by type of disability: Selected school years, 1980–81 through 2008–09*. Washington, DC: U.S. Department of education. Available online at: http://nces.ed.gov/programs/coe/tables/table-cwd-1.asp

National Center for Education Statistics. (2009). *The nation's report card: Mathematics 2009 (NCES 2010–451)*. Institute of Education Sciences, U.S. Department of Education, Washington, DC.

National Center for Education Statistics. (2010). *Condition of education 2010, indicator 23 (NCES 2010–028)*. Institute of Education Sciences, U.S. Department of Education, Washington, DC.

National Center for Educational Statistics.(2011). *Characteristics of the 100 largest public elementary and secondary school districts in the United States: 2008–09*. Washington, DC: Author. Available online at: http://nces.ed.gov/pubs2010/100largest0809/how.asp

National Commission on Excellence in Education. (1983). *A nation at risk: The imperative for educational reform*. Washington, DC: Author. Available online at: http://www.ed.gov/pubs/NatAtRisk/index.html

National Commission on Teaching and America's Future. (2003). *No dream denied: A pledge to America's children*. Washington, DC: Author.

National Federation of the Blind (NFB). (2010). *NFB nonvisual accessibility web certification granted to Instructure Learning Management System*. Available online at: http://www.disabled-world.com/disability/accessibility/websitedesign/learning-management-system.php#ixzz1ZYiOqF56.

National Poverty Center. (2011). *Poverty in the United States: Frequently asked questions*. The University of Michigan, Gerald R. Ford School of Public Policy, Ann Arbor, MI. Available online at: http://npc.umich.edu/poverty/

National Science Foundation, Division of Science Resources Statistics. (2011). *Women, minorities, and persons with disabilities in science and engineering: 2011*. Special Report NSF 11-309. Arlington, VA. Available online at: http://www.nsf.gov/statistics/wmpd/

National Service Learning Clearinghouse. (n.d.). *Service learning is . . . .* Available online at: http://www.servicelearning.org/welcome_to_service-learning/service-learning_is/index.php

Navarro, R. L., Flores, L. Y., & Worthington, R. L. (2007). Mexican American middle school students' goal intentions in mathematics and science: A test of social cognitive career theory. *Journal of Counseling Psychology, 54*, 320–335.

Naveh-Benjamin, M. (1991). A comparison of training programs intended for different types of test-anxious students: Further support for an information-processing model. *Journal of Educational Psychology, 83*, 134–139.

Naveh-Benjamin, M., McKeachie, W. J., & Lin, Y. (1987). Two types of test-anxious students: Support for an information processing model. *Journal of Educational Psychology, 79*, 131–136.

Needles, M., & Knapp, M. (1994). Teaching writing to children who are underserved. *Journal of Educational Psychology, 86*, 339–349.

Neisser, U., Boodoo, G., Bouchard, A., Boykin, W., Brody, N., Ceci, . . . Urbina, S. (1996). Intelligence: Knowns and unknowns. *American Psychologist, 51*, 77–101.

Nelson, C.A. (2001). The development and neural bases of face recognition. *Infant and Child Development, 10*, 3–18.

Nelson, J. R., & Roberts, M. L. (2000). Ongoing reciprocal teacher-student interactions involving disruptive behaviors in general education classrooms. *Journal of Emotional and Behavioral Disorders, 4*, 147–161.

Nelson, K., & Fivush, R. (2004). The emergence of autobiographical memory: A social cultural developmental theory. *Psychological Review, 111*, 486–511.

Nelson, T. O. (1996). Consciousness and metacognition. *American Psychologist, 51*, 102–116.

Nesbit, J. C., & Adesope, O. O. (2006). Learning with concept and knowledge maps: A meta-analysis. *Review of Educational Research, 76*, 413–448.

Neumeister, K. L. S., & Cramond, B. (2004). E. Paul Torrance (1915–2003). *American Psychologist, 59*, 179.

Neville, H. (2007, March). *Experience shapes human brain development and function*. Paper presented at the biennial meeting of the Society for Research in Child Development, Boston.

Newcombe, N., & Baenninger, M. (1990). The role of expectations in spatial test performance: A meta-analysis. *Sex Roles, 16*, 25–37.

Newman, K. L., Samimy, K., & Romstedt, K. (2010). Developing a training program for secondary teachers of English language learners in Ohio. *Theory Into Practice, 49*, 152–161.

Nguyen, H.-H. D., & Ryan, A. M. (2008). Does stereotype threat affect test performance of minorities and women? A meta-analysis of experimental evidence. *Journal of Applied Psychology, 93*, 1314–1334.

NICHD Early Child Care Research Network. (2005a). *Child care and child development*. New York, NY: Guilford Press.

NICHD Early Child Care Research Network. (2005b). Pathways to reading: The role of oral language in the transition to reading. *Developmental Psychology, 41*(2), 428–442.

Nicholls, J., Cobb, P., Wood, T., Yackel, E., & Patashnick, M. (1990). Assessing student's theories of success in mathematics: Individual and classroom differences. *Journal for Research in Mathematics Education, 21*, 109–122.

Nicholls, J. G., & Miller, A. (1984). Conceptions of ability and achievement motivation. In R. Ames & C. Ames (Eds.), *Research on motivation in education. Vol. 1: Student Motivation* (pp. 39–73). New York, NY: Academic Press.

Nie, Y., & Lau, S. (2009). Complementary roles of care and behavioral control in classroom management: The self-determination theory perspective. *Contemporary Educational Psychology, 34*, 185–194.

Nielsen. (2010). *U.S. teen mobile report: Calling yesterday, texting today, using apps tomorrow*. New York, NY: The Nielsen Company. Available online at: http://blog.nielsen.com/nielsenwire/online_mobile/u-s-teen-mobile-report-calling-yesterday-texting-today-using-apps-tomorrow/

Nieto, S. (2004). *Affirming diversity: The sociopolitical context of multicultural education* (4th ed.). Boston, MA: Allyn & Bacon.

Nieto, S., & Bode, P. (2008). *Affirming diversity: The sociopolitical context of multicultural education* (5th ed.). Boston, MA: Allyn & Bacon.

Nitko, A. J., & Brookhart, S. M. (2011). *Educational assessment of students* (6th ed.). Boston, MA: Pearson.

No Child Left Behind Act. (2002). P. L. 107–110, Title IX, Part A, Section 9101 (22), pp. 544, 20 U.S. C. 7802.

Noddings, N. (1990). Constructivism in mathematics education. In R. Davis, C. Maher, & N. Noddings (Eds.), *Constructivist views on the teaching and learning of mathematics* (pp. 7–18). Monograph 4 of the National Council of Teachers of Mathematics, Reston, VA.

Noddings, N. (1995). Teaching themes of care. *Phi Delta Kappan, 76*, 675–679.

Noguera, P. (2005). The racial achievement gap: How can we assume an equity of outcomes. In L. Johnson, M. E. Finn, & R. Lewis (Eds.), *Urban education with an attitude*. Albany, NY: SUNY Press.

Nokes, J. D., Dole, J. A., & Hacker, D. J. (2007). Teaching high school students to use heuristics while reading historical texts. *Journal of Educational Psychology, 99*, 492–504.

Norbert, F. (2005). Research findings on early first language attrition: Implications for the discussion of critical periods in language acquisition. *Language Learning, 55*(3), 491–531.

Novotney, A. (2009). Dangerous distraction. *Monitor on Psychology, 40*, 32. Available online at: http://www.apa.org/monitor/2009/02/dangerous.aspx

Novotney, A. (2011). Coed versus single-sex schools. *Monitor on Psychology, 42*(2), 58–62.

Nucci, L. P. (2001). *Education in the moral domain*. New York, NY: Cambridge Press.

Nurmi, J. (2004). Socialization and self-development: Channeling, selection, adjustment, and reflection. In R. Lerner & L. Steinberg (Eds.), *Handbook of adolescent psychology*. New York, NY: Wiley.

Nylund, D. (2000). *Treating Huckleberry Finn: A new narrative approach to working with kids diagnosed ADD/ADHD*. San Francisco: Jossey-Bass.

O'Boyle, M. W., & Gill, H. S. (1998). On the relevance of research findings in cognitive neuroscience to educational practice. *Educational Psychology Review, 10*, 397–410.

O'Connor, C. (1997). Dispositions toward (collective) struggle and educational resilience in the inner city: A case analysis of six African American high school students. *American Educational Research Journal, 34*, 593–629.

O'Donnell, A. M. (Ed.). (2002, Winter). Promoting thinking through peer learning. Special issue of *Theory Into Practice, 61*(1).

O'Donnell, A. M. (2006). The role of peers and group learning. In P. A. Alexander & P. H. Winne (Eds.), *Handbook of educational psychology* (2nd ed., pp. 781–802). Mahwah, NJ: Erlbaum.

O'Donnell, A. M., & O'Kelly, J. (1994). Learning from peers: Beyond the rhetoric of positive results. *Educational Psychology Review, 6*, 321–350.

O'Leary, K. D., & O'Leary, S. (Eds.). (1977). *Classroom management: The successful use of behavior modification* (2nd ed.). Elmsford, NY: Pergamon.

O'Leary, S. (1995). Parental discipline mistakes. *Current Directions in Psychological Science, 4*, 11–13.

O'Mara, A. J., Marsh, H. W., Craven, R. G., & Debus, R. L. (2006). Do self-concept interventions make a difference? A synergistic blend of construct validation and meta-analysis. *Educational Psychologist, 41*, 181–206.

O'Neil, J. (1990). Link between style, culture proves divisive. *Educational Leadership, 48*(2), 8.

Oakes, J. (1985). *Keeping track*. New Haven, CT: Yale University Press.

Oakes, J. (1990a). Opportunities, achievement, and choice: Women and minority students in science and math. *Review of Research in Education, 16*, 153–222.

Oakes, J. (1990b). *Multiplying inequities: The effects of race, social class, and tracking on opportunities to learn mathematics and science*. Santa Monica, CA: Rand.

Oakes, J. (1999). Promotion or retention: Which one is social? *Harvard Education Letter, 15*(1), 8.

Oakes, J., & Wells, A. S. (2002). Detracking for high student achievement. In L. Abbeduto (Ed.), *Taking sides: Clashing views and controversial issues in educational psychology* (2nd ed., pp. 26–30). Guilford, CT: McGraw-Hill Duskin.

Ogbu, J. U. (1987). Variability in minority school performance: A problem in search of an explanation. *Anthropology and Education Quarterly, 18*, 312–334.

Ogbu, J. U. (1997). Understanding the school performance of urban blacks: Some essential background knowledge. In H. Walberg, O. Reyes, & R. P. Weissberg (Eds.), *Children and youth: Interdisciplinary perspectives* (pp. 190–240). Norwood, NJ: Ablex.

Ogden, C., & Carroll, M. (2010). Prevalence of obesity among children and adolescents: United States, trends 1963–1965 through 2007–2008. Washington, DC: Center for Disease Statistics. Available online at: http://www.cdc.gov/nchs/data/hestat/obesity_child_07_08/obesity_child_07_08.htm

Ogden, J. E., Brophy, J. E., & Evertson, C. M. (1977, April). *An experimental investigation of organization and management techniques in first-grade reading groups*. Paper presented at the annual meeting of the American Educational Research Association, New York.

Okagaki, L. (2001). Triarchic model of minority children's school achievement. *Educational Psychologist, 36*, 9–20.

Okagaki, L. (2006). Ethnicity, learning. In P. Alexander & P. Winne (Eds.), *Handbook of educational psychology* (2nd ed., pp. 615–634). Mahwah, NJ: Erlbaum.

Olsen, L. (1988). *Crossing the schoolhouse border: Immigrant students and the California public schools*. San Francisco, CA: California Tomorrow.

Olson, D. R. (2004). The triumph of hope over experience in the search for "what works": A response to Slavin. *Educational Researcher, 33*(1), 24–26.

Olson, K. (2008). The wounded student. *Educational Leadership, 65*(6), 46–48.

Omi, M., & Winant, H. (1994). *Racial formation in the United States: From the 1960s to the 1990s* (2nd ed.). New York, NY: Routledge.

Oosterhof, A. (2009). *Developing and using classroom assessments* (4th ed.). Columbus, OH: Pearson/Merrill.

Orange, C. (2000). *25 biggest mistakes teachers make and how to avoid them*. Thousand Oaks, CA: Corwin.

Orange, C. (2005). *44 smart strategies for avoiding classroom mistakes*. Thousand Oaks, CA: Corwin Press.

Orfield, G., & Frankenberg, E. (2005). Where are we now? In F. Shultz (Ed.), *Annual editions: Multicultural education* (pp. 10–12). Dubuque, IA: McGraw-Hill/Dushkin.

Orfield, G., Frankenberg, E., & Siegel-Hawley, G. (2010). Integrated schools: Finding a new path. *Educational Leadership, 68*(3), 22–27.

Organization for Economic Cooperation and Development. (2007). *Understanding the brain: The birth of a learning science*. Paris: Author OECD.

Orlando L., & Machado, A. (1996). In defense of Piaget's theory: A reply to 10 common criticisms. *Psychological Review, 103*, 143–164.

Ormrod, J. E. (2004). *Human learning* (4th ed.). Columbus, OH: Merrill/Prentice-Hall.

Ormrod, J. E. (2012). *Human learning* (6th ed.). Boston, MA: Pearson.

Ortony, A., Clore, G. L., & Collins, A. (1988). *The cognitive structure of emotions*. Cambridge, UK: Cambridge University Press.

Osborn, A. F. (1963). *Applied imagination* (3rd ed.). New York, NY: Scribner's.

Osterman, K. F. (2000). Students' need for belonging in the school community. *Review of Educational Research, 70*, 323–367.

Ostrov, J. M., & Godleski, S. A. (2010). Toward an integrated gender-linked model of aggression subtypes in early and middle childhood. *Psychological Bulletin, 117*, 233–242.

Otto, B. (2010). *Language development in early childhood* (5th ed.). Columbus, OH: Merrill.

Ovando, C. J., & Collier, V. P. (1998). *Bilingual and ESL classrooms: Teaching in multicultural contexts* (2nd ed.). Boston, MA: McGraw-Hill.

Overton, W. F. (2006). Developmental psychology: Philosophy, concepts, and methodology. In R. M. Lerner (Ed.), *Handbook of child psychology* (6th ed., Vol. 1: Theoretical models of human development, pp. 18–88). New York, NY: Wiley.

Owens, R. E. (2005). *Language development: An introduction* (6th ed.). Boston, MA: Allyn & Bacon.

Owens, R. E. (2010). *Language disorders: A functional approach to assessment and intervention* (5th ed.). Boston, MA: Allyn & Bacon.

Owens, R. E. (2012). *Language development: An introduction* (8th ed.). Boston, MA: Allyn & Bacon.

Pai, Y., & Adler, S. A. (2001). *Cultural foundations of education* (3rd ed.). Upper Saddle River, NJ: Merrill.

Paivio, A. (2006). *Mind and its evolution; A dual coding theoretical interpretation*. Mahwah, NJ: Lawrence Erlbaum Associates, Inc.

Pajares, F. (1997). Current directions in self-efficacy research. In M. L. Maehr & P. R. Pintrich (Eds.), *Advances in motivation and achievement* (Vol. 10, pp. 1–49). Greenwich, CT: JAI Press.

Pajares, F. (2000, April). *Seeking a culturally attentive educational psychology*. Paper presented at the annual meeting of the American Educational Research Association, New Orleans, LA. Available online at: http://www.emory.edu/EDUCATION/mfp/AERA2000Discussant.html

Pajares, F. (2003). William James: Our father who begot us. In B. J. Zimmerman & D. H. Schunk (Eds.), *Educational psychology: A century of contributions* (pp. 41–64). Mahwah, NJ: Erlbaum.

Pajares, F. (2008). Self-efficacy information. Retrieved from: http://www.des.emory.edu/mfp/banconversion.html

Pajares, F., & Schunk, D. H. (2001). Self-beliefs and school success: Self-efficacy, self-concept, and school achievement. In R. Riding & S. Rayner (Eds.), *Perception* (pp. 239–266). Westport, CT: Ablex Publishing.

Pajares, F., & Schunk, D. H. (2002). Self and self-belief in psychology and education: An historical perspective. In J. Aronson & D. Cordova (Eds.), *Psychology of education: Personal and interpersonal forces* (pp. 1–19). New York, NY: Academic Press.

Palincsar, A. S. (1986). The role of dialogue in providing scaffolded instruction. *Educational Psychologist, 26*, 73–98.

Palincsar, A. S. (1998). Social constructivist perspectives on teaching and learning. In J. T. Spence, J. M. Darley, & D. J. Foss (Eds.), *Annual Review of Psychology* (pp. 345–375). Palo Alto, CA: Annual Reviews.

Palincsar, A. S., & Brown, A. L. (1984). Reciprocal teaching of comprehension-fostering and monitoring activities. *Cognition and Instruction, 1*, 117–175.

Palincsar, A. S., & Brown, A. L. (1989). Classroom dialogues to promote self-regulated comprehension. In J. Brophy (Ed.), *Advances in research on teaching* (Vol. 1, pp. 35–67). Greenwich, CT: JAI Press.

Palincsar, A. S., & Herrenkohl, L. R. (2002). Designing collaborative learning contexts. *Theory Into Practice, 61,* 26–32.

Palincsar, A. S., Magnusson, S. J., Collins, K. M., & Cutter, J. (2001). Promoting deep understanding of science in students with disabilities in inclusion classrooms. *Learning Disabilities Quarterly, 24*(1), 15–32.

Palincsar, A. S., Magnuson, S. J., Marano, N., Ford, D., & Brown, N. (1998). Designing a community of practice: Principles and practices of the GIsML community. *Teaching and Teacher Education, 14,* 5–19.

Panitz, T. (1996). *A definition of collaborative vs cooperative learning.* Available online at: http://www.londonmet.ac.uk/deliberations/collaborative-learning/panitz-paper.cfm

Papanikolaou, K., & Boubouka, M. (2010-2011). Promoting collaboration in a project-based e-learning context. *Journal of Research on Technology in Education, 43,* 135–155.

Paris, S. G., Byrnes, J. P., & Paris, A. H. (2001). Constructing theories, identities, and actions of self-regulated learners. In B. J. Zimmerman & D. H. Schunk (Eds.), *Self-regulated learning and academic achievement: Theoretical perspectives* (2nd ed., pp. 253–287). Mahwah, NJ: Erlbaum.

Paris, S. G., & Cunningham, A. E. (1996). Children becoming students. In D. Berliner & R. Calfee (Eds.), *Handbook of educational psychology* (pp. 117–146). New York, NY: Macmillan.

Paris, S. G., Morrison, F. J., & Miller, K. F. (2006). Academic pathways from preschool through elementary school. In P. A. Alexander & P. H. Winne (Eds.), *Handbook of educational psychology* (2nd ed., pp. 61–85). Mahwah, NJ: Erlbaum.

Parker, W. C., & Hess, D. (2001). Teaching with and for discussion. *Teaching and Teacher Education, 17,* 273–289.

Pashler, H., McDaniel, M., Rohrer, D., & Bjork, R. (2009). Learning styles: Concepts and evidence. *Psychological Science in the Public Interest, 9,* 105–119.

Patall, E. A., Cooper, H., & Wynn, S. R. (2010). The effectiveness and relative importance of choice in the classroom. *Journal of Educational Psychology, 102,* 896–915.

Pate, P. E., McGinnis, K., & Homestead, E. (1995). Creating coherence through curriculum integration. In M. Harmin (1994), *Inspiring active learning: A handbook for teachers* (pp. 62–70). Alexandria, VA: Association for Supervision and Curriculum Development.

Patterson, C. (1995). Lesbian & gay parenting. Available online at: http://www.apa.org/pi/lgbt/resources/parenting.aspx

Patterson, G. R. (1997). Performance models for parenting: A social interactional perspective. In J. Grusec & L. Kuczynski (Eds.), *Parenting and the socialization of values: A handbook of contemporary theory* (pp. 193–235). New York, NY: Wiley.

Paul, A. M. (2011, September 10). The trouble with homework. *New York Times,* Sunday Review Section, p. 6.

Paulos, L. (2007). Multitasking madness. *Scholastic Choices, 23*(1), 10–13.

Pearl, R., Leung, M. C., Acker, R. V., Farmer, T. W., & Rodkin, P. C. (2007). Fourth- and fifth-grade teachers' awareness of their classrooms' social networks. *The Elementary School Journal, 108,* 25–39.

Pearson, B. Z., Fernandez, S. C., Lewedeg, V., & Oller, D. K. (1997). The relation of input factors to lexical learning by bilingual infants. *Applied Linguistics, 18,* 41–58.

Pekrun, R., Elliot, A. J., & Maier, M. A. (2006). Achievement goals and discrete achievement emotions: A theoretical model and prospective test. *Journal of Educational Psychology, 98,* 583–597.

Pekrun, R., Goetz, T., Daniels, L. M., Stupinsky, R. H., & Perry, R. P. (2010). Boredom in achievement settings: Exploring control–value antecedents and performance outcomes of a neglected emotion. *Journal of Educational Psychology, 102,* 531–549.

Pekrun, R., Goetz, T., Titz, W., & Perry, R. P. (2002). Academic emotions in students' self-regulated learning and achievement. A program of qualitative and quantitative research. *Educational Psychologist, 37,* 91–105.

Pellegrini, A. D., Bartini, M., & Brooks, F. (1999). School bullies, victims, and aggressive victims: Factors relating to group affiliation and victimization in early adolescence. *Journal of Educational Psychology, 91,* 216–224.

Pellegrini, A. D., & Bohn, C. M. (2005). The role of recess in children's cognitive performance and school adjustment. *Educational Researcher, 34,* 13–19.

Pellegrini, A. D., Dupuis, D., & Smith, P. K. (2007). Play in evolution and development. *Developmental Review, 27,* 261–276.

Pellegrino, L. (2002). Cerebral palsy. In M. L. Batshaw (Ed.), *Children with disabilities.* Baltimore, MD: Brookes.

Pellis, S. (2006). The effects of orbital frontal cortex damage on the modulation of defensive responses by rats in playful and nonplayful social contexts. *Behavioral Neuroscience, 120,* 72–84.

Peng, S., & Lee, R. (1992, April). *Home variables, parent–child activities, and academic achievement: A study of 1988 eighth graders.* Paper presented at the annual meeting of the American Educational Research Association, San Francisco, CA.

Penuel, W. R., & Wertsch, J. V. (1995). Vygotsky and identity formation: A sociocultural approach. *Educational Psychologist, 30,* 83–92.

Peregoy, S. F., &. Boyle, O. F. (2009. *Reading, writing, and learning in ESL: A resource book for teaching K–12 English learners* (5th ed.). Boston, MA: Allyn & Bacon/Pearson.

Perkins, D. N., Jay, E., & Tishman, S. (1993). New conceptions of thinking: From ontology to education. *Educational Psychologist, 28,* 67–85.

Perner, J. (2000). Memory and theory of mind. In E. Tulving & F. I. M. Craik (Eds.), *The Oxford handbook of memory* (pp. 297–312). New York, NY: Oxford.

Perry, N. E., & Collie, R. J. (2011, April). School climate and social and emotional learning: Predictors of early career teacher well-being and efficacy. Paper presented at the annual meeting of the American Educational Research Association, New Orleans, LA.

Perry, N. E., & Drummond, L. (2002). Helping young students become self-regulated researchers and writers. *The Reading Teacher, 56,* 298–310.

Perry, N. E., Phillips, L., & Dowler, J. (2004). Examining features of tasks and their potential to promote self-regulated learning. *Teachers College Record, 106,* 1854–1878.

Perry, N. E., & Rahim, A. (2011) Studying self-regulated learning in classrooms. In B. Zimmerman & D. Schunk (Eds.), *Handbook of self-regulation of learning and performance* (pp. 122–136) New York, NY: Routledge.

Perry, N. E., VandeKamp, K. O., & Mercer, L. K. (2000, April). *Investigating teacher-student interactions that foster self-regulated learning.* In N. E. Perry (Chair), Symposium conducted at the meeting of the American Educational Research Association, New Orleans, LA.

Perry, N. E., VandeKamp, K. O., Mercer, L. K., & Nordby, C. J. (2002). Investigating teacher-student interactions that foster self-regulated learning. *Educational Psychologist, 37,* 5–15.

Peter, M., Glück, J., & Beiglböck, W. (2010). Map understanding as a developmental marker in childhood. *Journal of Individual Differences, 31,* 64–67.

Petitclerc, A., Boivin, M., Dionne, G., Zoccolillo, M., & Tremblay, R. E. (2009). Disregard for rules: The early development and predictors of a specific dimension of disruptive behavior disorders. *Journal of Child Psychology and Psychiatry, 50,* 1477–1484.

Petitto, L. A. (2009). New discoveries from the bilingual brain and mind across the life span: Implications for education. *Brain, Mind, and Education, 3,* 185–197.

Petitto, L. A., & Kovelman, I. (2003). The bilingual paradox: How signing-speaking bilingual children help us resolve bilingual issues and teach us about the brain's mechanisms underlying all language acquisition. *Language Learning, 8*(3), 5–18.

Petrill, S. A., & Wilkerson, B. (2000). Intelligence and achievement: A behavioral genetic perspective. *Educational Psychology Review, 12,* 185–199.

Pettigrew, T. (1998). Intergroup contact theory. In J. T. Spence, J. M. Darley, & D. J. Foss (Eds.), *Annual review of psychology* (pp. 65–85). Palo Alto, CA: Annual Reviews.

Peverly, S. T., Brobst, K., Graham, M., & Shaw, R. (2003). College adults are not good at self-regulation: A study on the relationship of self-regulation, note-taking, and test-taking. *Journal of Educational Psychology, 95,* 335–346.

Peverly, S. T., Ramaswamy, V., Brown, C., Sumowski, J., & Alidoost, M., & Garner, J. (2007). What predicts skill in lecture note taking? *Journal of Educational Psychology, 99,* 167–180.

Pfiffner, L., Barkley, R. A., & DuPaul, G. J. (2006). Treatment of ADHD in school settings. In R. A. Barkley (Ed.), *Attention-deficit hyperactivity disorder: A handbook for diagnosis and treatment* (3rd ed., pp. 547–588). New York, NY: Guilford.

Pfiffner, L. J., & O'Leary, S. G. (1987). The efficacy of all positive management as a function of the prior use of negative consequences. *Journal of Applied Behavior Analysis, 20,* 265–271.

Phillips, D. (1997). How, why, what, when, and where: Perspectives on constructivism and education. *Issues in Education: Contributions from Educational Psychology, 3,* 151–194.

Phillips, D., & Zimmerman, M. (1990). The developmental course of perceived competence and incompetence among competent children. In R. Sternberg & J. Kolligian (Eds.), *Competence considered* (pp. 41–66). New Haven, CT: Yale University Press.

Phinney, J. S. (1990). Ethnic identity in adolescents and adults: Review of research. *Psychological Bulletin, 108*(3), 499–514.

Phinney, J. S. (2003). Ethnic identity and acculturation. In K. Chun, P. Ball, & Marin, G. (Eds.),

Acculturation: Advances in theory, measurement, and applied research (pp. 63–81). Washington, DC: American Psychological Association.

Phinney, J. S., & Devich-Navarro, M. (1997). Variations in bicultural identification among African American and Mexican American adolescents. *Journal of Research on Adolescence, 7,* 3–32.

Phye, G. D. (1992). Strategic transfer: A tool for academic problem solving. *Educational Psychology Review, 4,* 393–421.

Phye, G. D. (2001). Problem-solving instruction and problem-solving transfer: The correspondence issue. *Journal of Educational Psychology, 93,* 571–578.

Phye, G. D., & Sanders, C. E. (1994). Advice and feedback: Elements of practice for problem solving. *Contemporary Educational Psychology, 17,* 211–223.

Piaget, J. (1954). *The construction of reality in the child* (M. Cook, Trans.). New York, NY: Basic Books.

Piaget, J. (1962). *Comments on Vygotsky's critical remarks concerning "The language and thought of the child" and "Judgment and reasoning in the child."* Cambridge, MA: MIT Press.

Piaget, J. (1963). *Origins of intelligence in children.* New York, NY: Norton.

Piaget, J. (1964). Development and learning. In R. Ripple & V. Rockcastle (Eds.), *Piaget rediscovered* (pp. 7–20). Ithaca, NY: Cornell University Press.

Piaget, J. (1965). *The moral judgment of the child.* New York, NY: Free Press.

Piaget, J. (1965/1995). *Sociological studies.* New York, NY: Routledge. (Original work published in 1965.)

Piaget, J. (1969). *Science of education and the psychology of the child.* New York, NY: Viking.

Piaget, J. (1970a). Piaget's theory. In P. Mussen (Ed.), *Handbook of child psychology* (3rd ed.) (Vol. 1, pp. 703–732). New York, NY: Wiley.

Piaget, J. (1970b). *The science of education and the psychology of the child.* New York, NY: Orion Press.

Piaget, J. (1971). *Biology and knowledge.* Edinburgh, UK: Edinburgh Press.

Piaget, J. (1974). *Understanding causality* (D. Miles and M. Miles, Trans.). New York, NY: Norton.

Piaget, J. (1985). *The equilibrium of cognitive structures: The central problem of intellectual development* (T. Brown & K. L. Thampy, Trans.). Chicago, IL: University of Chicago Press.

Pianta, R. C., Belsky, J., Vandergrift, N., Houts, R., & Morrison, F. J. (2008). Classroom effects on children's achievement trajectories in elementary school. *American Educational Research Journal, 45,* 365–397.

Pianta, R. C., Howes, C., Burchinal, M., Bryant, D. M., Clifford, R. M., Early, D. M., & Barbarin, O. (2005). Features of pre-kindergarten programs, classrooms, and teachers: Do they predict observed classroom quality and child–teacher interactions? *Applied Developmental Science, 9*(3), 144–159.

Pigge, F. L., & Marso, R. N. (1997). A seven-year longitudinal multi-factor assessment of teaching concerns development through preparation and early teaching. *Teaching and Teacher Education, 13,* 225–235.

Pinker, S. (2002). *The blank slate: The modern denial of human nature.* New York, NY: Penguin.

Pintrich, P. R. (2000). Educational psychology at the millennium: A look back and a look forward. *Educational Psychologist, 35,* 221–226.

Pintrich, P. R. (2003). A motivational science perspective on the role of student motivation in learning and teaching. *Journal of Educational Psychology, 95,* 667–686.

Pintrich, P. R., Marx, R. W., & Boyle, R. A. (1993). Beyond cold conceptual change: The role of motivational beliefs and classroom contextual factors in the process of conceptual change. *Review of Educational Research, 63,* 167–199.

Pintrich, P. R., & Schunk, D. H. (2002). *Motivation in education: Research and applications* (2nd ed.). Boston, MA: Allyn and Bacon.

Pintrich, P. R., & Zusho, A. (2002). The development of academic self-regulation: The role of cognitive and motivational factors. In A. Wigfield & J. Eccles (Eds.), *Development of achievement motivation* (pp. 249–284). San Diego, CA: Academic Press.

Pinxten, M., De Fraine, B., Van Damme, J., & D'Haenens, E. (2010). Causal ordering of academic self-concept and achievement: Effects of type of achievement measure. *British Journal of Educational Psychology, 80,* 689–709.

Pisha, B., & Coyne, P. (2001). Smart for the start: The promise of universal design for learning. *Remedial and Special Education, 22,* 197–203.

Plant, E. A., & Peruche, B. M. (2005). The consequences of race for police officers' responses to criminal suspects. *Psychological Science, 16,* 180–183.

Plucker, J. A., Beghetto, R. A., & Dow, G. T. (2004). Why isn't creativity more important to educational psychologists? Potential pitfalls and future directions in creativity research. *Educational Psychology, 39*(2), 83–96.

Plummer, D. L, & Graziano, W. G. (1987). Impact of grade retention on the social development of elementary school children." *Developmental Psychology, 23,* 267–275.

Polson, P. G., & Jeffries, R. (1985). Instruction in general problem-solving skills: An analysis of four approaches. In J. Segal, S. Chipman, & R. Glaser (Eds.), *Thinking and learning skills* (Vol. 1, pp. 417–455). Mahwah, NJ: Erlbaum.

Ponitz, C. C., Rimm-Kaufman, S. E., Grimm, K. J., & Curby, T. W. (2009). Kindergarten classroom quality, behavioral engagement, and reading achievement. *School Psychology Review, 38,* 102–120.

Popham, W. J. (2005a). *Classroom assessment: What teachers need to know* (4th ed.). Boston, MA: Allyn & Bacon.

Popham, W. J. (2008). *Classroom assessment: What teachers need to know* (5th ed.). Boston, MA: Allyn & Bacon.

Popham, W. J. (2011). *Classroom assessment: What teachers need to know* (6th ed.). Boston, MA: Allyn & Bacon.

Portes, A., & Hao, L. (1998). E pluribus unum: Bilingualism and loss of language in the second generation. *Sociology of Education*, 71: 269–294.

Posada, G., Jacobs, A., Richmond, M., Carbonell, O. A., Alzate, G., Bustamante, M. R., & Quiceno, J. (2002). Maternal care giving and infant security in two cultures. *Developmental Psychology, 38,* 67–78.

Posner, M. I. (1973). *Cognition: An introduction.* Glenview, IL: Scott, Foresman.

Prat-Sala, M., & Redford, P. (2010). The interplay between motivation, self-efficacy, and

approaches to studying. *British Journal of Educational Psychology, 80,* 283–305.

Prawat, R. S. (1992). Teachers beliefs about teaching and learning: A constructivist perspective. *American Journal of Education, 100,* 354–395.

Prawat, R. S. (1996). Constructivism, modern and postmodern. *Issues in Education: Contributions from Educational Psychology, 3,* 215–226.

Preckel, T., Goetz, T., & Frenzel, A. (2010). Ability grouping of gifted students: Effects on academic self-concept and boredom. *British Journal of Educational Psychology, 80,* 451–472.

Premack, D. (1965). Reinforcement theory. In D. Levine (Ed.), *Nebraska symposium on motivation* (Vol. 13, pp. 123–180). Lincoln, NE: University of Nebraska Press.

Pressley, M. (1995). More about the development of self-regulation: complex, long-term, and thoroughly social. *Educational Psychologist, 30,* 207–212.

Pressley, M. (1996, August). *Getting beyond whole language: Elementary reading instruction that makes sense in light of recent psychological research.* Paper presented at the annual meeting of the American Psychological Association, Toronto.

Pressley, M., & Harris, K. A. (2006). Cognitive strategies instruction: From basic research to classroom instruction. In P. A. Alexander & P. H. Winne (Eds.), *Handbook of educational psychology* (2nd ed., pp. 265–286). Mahwah, NJ: Erlbaum.

Pressley, M., Levin, J., & Delaney, H. D. (1982). The mnemonic keyword method. *Review of Research in Education, 52,* 61–91.

Pressley, M., Mohan, L., Raphael, L. M., & Fingeret, L. (2007). How does Bennett Woods Elementary School produce such high reading and writing achievement? *Journal of Educational Psychology, 99,* 221–240.

Pressley, M., Raphael, L., Gallagher, J. D., & DiBella, J. (2004). Providence St. Mel School: How a school that works for African American students works. *Journal of Educational Psychology, 96*(2), 216–235.

Pressley, M., & Roehrig, A. (2003). Educational psychology in the modern era: 1960 to the present. In B. J. Zimmerman & D. H. Schunk (Eds.), *Educational psychology: A century of contributions* (pp. 333–366). [A Project of Division 15 (Educational Psychology) of the American Psychological Association]. Mahwah, NJ: Erlbaum.

Pressley, M., & Woloshyn, V. (1995). *Cognitive strategy instruction that really improves children's academic performance.* Cambridge, MA: Brookline Books.

Price, L. F. (2005). The biology of risk taking. *Educational Leadership, 62*(7), 22–27.

Price, W. F., & Crapo, R. H. (2002). *Cross-cultural perspectives in introductory psychology* (4th ed.). Pacific Grove, CA: Wadsworth.

Proctor, C. P., August, D., Carlo, M. S., & Snow, C. (2006). The intriguing role of Spanish language vocabulary knowledge in predicting English reading comprehension. *Journal of Educational Psychology, 98,* 159–169.

Project Tomorrow. (2010). *The new 3 E's of education: Enabled, engaged, empowered. How today's students are leveraging emerging technologies for learning.* Irvine, CA: Project Tomorrow. Available online at: http://www.tomorrow.org/about/team.html

Public Agenda Foundation. (1994). *First things first: What Americans expect from public schools.* New York, NY: Author.

Pugh, K. J., & Bergin, D. A. (2006). Motivational influences on transfer. *Educational Psychologist, 41,* 147–160.

Pugh, K. J., & Phillips, M. M. (2011). Content appreciation: Why it matters and how you can foster it. *Theory Into Practice, 50.*

Puncochar, J., & Fox, P. W. (2004). Confidence in individual and group decision-making: When "Two Heads" are worse than one. *Journal of Educational Psychology, 96,* 582–591.

Puntambekar, S., & Hubscher, R. (2005). Tools for scaffolding students in a complex learning environment: What have we gained and what have we missed? *Educational Psychologist, 40,* 1–12.

Purdie, N., Hattie, J., & Carroll, A. (2002). A review of the research on interventions for Attention Deficit Hyperactivity Disorder: What works best? *Review of Educational Research, 72,* 61–99.

Puustinen, M., & Pulkkinen, L. (2001). Models of self-regulated learning: A review. *Scandinavian Journal of Educational Research, 45,* 269–286.

Rachlin, H. (1991). Introduction to modern behaviorism (3rd ed.). New York, NY: W. H. Freeman.

Rachlin, H. (2004). *The science of self-control.* Cambridge, MA: Harvard University Press.

Ramirez, J. D., Yuen, S. D., & Ramey, D. R. (1991). *Final report: Longitudinal study of structured immersion strategy, early-exit, and late-exit transitional bilingual education programs for language-minority children.* San Mateo, CA: Aguirre International.

Raudenbush, S. (1984). Magnitude of teacher expectancy effects on pupil IQ as a function of the credibility of expectancy induction: A synthesis of findings from 18 experiments. *Journal of Educational Psychology, 76,* 85–97.

Raudenbush, S.W. (2009). The *Brown* Legacy and the O'Connor Challenge: Transforming schools in the images of children's potential. *Educational Researcher, 38,* 169–180.

Raudsepp, E., & Haugh, G. P. (1977). *Creative growth games.* New York, NY: Harcourt Brace Jovanovich.

Rauscher, F. H., & Shaw, G. L. (1998). Key components of the Mozart effect. *Perceptual and Motor Skills, 86,* 835–841.

Reder, L. M. (1996). Different research programs on metacognition: Are the boundaries imaginary? *Learning and Individual Differences, 8,* 383–390.

Reder, L. M., Park, H., & Kieffaber, P. D. (2009). Memory systems do not divide on consciousness: reinterpreting memory in terms of activation and binding. *Psychological Bulletin, 135,* 23–49.

Reed, S. K. (2006). Cognitive architecture for multimedia learning. *Educational Psychologist, 41,* 87–98.

Reeve, J. (1996). *Motivating others: Nurturing inner motivational resources.* Boston, MA: Allyn & Bacon.

Reeve, J. (2002). Self-determination theory applied to educational settings. In E. L. Deci & R. M. Ryan (Eds.), *Handbook of self-determination research* (pp. 183–203). Rochester, NY: University of Rochester Press.

Reeve, J. (2009). Why teachers adopt a controlling motivating style toward students and how they can become more autonomy supportive. *Educational Psychologist, 44,* 159–175.

Reeve, J., Deci, E. L., & Ryan, R. M. (2004). *Self-determination theory: A dialectical framework for understanding the sociocultural influences on motivation and learning: Big theories revisited* (Vol. 4, pp. 31–59). Greenwich, CT: Information Age Press.

Reeve, J., & Jang, H. (2006a). Teachers as facilitators: What autonomy-supportive teachers do and why their students benefit. *Elementary School Journal, 106,* 225–236.

Reeve, J., & Jang, H. (2006b). What teachers say and do to support students' autonomy during a learning activity. *Journal of Educational Psychology, 98,* 209–218.

Reeve, J., Nix, G., & Hamm, D. (2003). The experience of self-determination in intrinsic motivation and the conundrum of choice. *Journal of Educational Psychology, 95,* 347–392.

Refugee Council USA. (2011). History of the U.S. refugee resettlement program. Washington DC: Refugee Council USA. Available online at: http://www.rcusa.org/index.php?page=history

Reid, J. M., & Byrd, P. (1998). *Grammar in the composition classroom.* New York, NY: Heinle & Heinle Publisher.

Reimann, P., & Chi, M. T. H. (1989). Human expertise. In K. J. Gilhooly (Ed.), *Human and machine problem solving* (pp. 161–191). New York, NY: Plenum Press.

Reinke, W. M., & Herman, K. C. (2002a). A research agenda for school violence prevention. *American Psychologist, 57,* 796–797.

Reinke, W. M., & Herman, K. C. (2002b). Creating school environments that deter antisocial behaviors in youth. *Psychology in the Schools, 39,* 549–560.

Reis, S. M., Kaplan, S. N., Tomlinson, C. A., Westberg, K. L., Callahan, C. M., & Cooper, C. R. (2002). Equal does not mean identical. In L. Abbeduto (Ed.), *Taking sides: Clashing on controversial issues in educational psychology* (pp. 31–35). Guilford, CT: McGraw-Hill/Duskin.

Reis, S. M., & Renzulli, J. S. (2004). Current research on the social and emotional development of gifted and talented students: Good news and future possibilities. *Psychology in the Schools, 41,* published online in Wiley InterScience (www.interscience.wiley.com).

Reisberg, D., & Heuer, F. (1992). Remembering the details of emotional events. In E. Winograd & U. Neisser (Eds.), *Affect and accuracy in recall: Studies of "flashbulb" memories.* Cambridge, UK: Cambridge University Press.

Reiss, S. (2004). Multifaceted nature of intrinsic motivation: The theory of 16 basic desires. *Review of General Psychology, 8,* 179–193.

Render, G. F., Padilla, J. N. M., & Krank, H. M. (1989). What research really shows about assertive discipline. *Educational Leadership, 46*(6), 72–75.

Renninger, K. A. (2009). Interest and identity development in instruction: An inductive model. *Educational Psychologist, 44,* 105–118.

Renzulli, J. S., & Reis, S. M. (2003). The schoolwide enrichment model: Developing creative and productive giftedness. In N. Colangelo & G. A. Davis (Eds.), *Handbook of gifted education* (pp. 184–203). Boston, MA: Allyn & Bacon.

Resnick, L. B. (1981). Instructional psychology. *Annual Review of Psychology, 32,* 659–704.

Reynolds, C. R., & Shaywitz, S. E. (2009). Response to Intervention: Ready or not? Or, from wait-to-fail to watch-them-fail. *School Psychology Quarterly, 24,* 130–145.

Rhodes, R. A. (1997). *Community service and higher learning: Explorations of the caring self.* Albany, NY: State University of New York Press.

Rice, F. P., & Dolgin, K. G. (2002). *The adolescent: Development, relationships, and culture* (10th ed.). Boston, MA: Allyn & Bacon.

Rice, M. L. (1989). Children's language acquisition. *American Psychologist, 44,* 149–156.

Richell, R., Deakin, J., & Anderson, I. (2005). Effect of acute tryptophan depletion on the response to controllable and uncontrollable noise stress. *Biological Psychiatry, 57,* 295–300.

Richtell, M. (2011, September 3). In classroom of the future, stagnant score. *New York Times,* A1.

Rideout, V. J., Foehr, U. G., & Roberts, D. F. (2010, January). Generation M: Media in the lives of 8–18 year-olds. Kaiser Family Foundation. Available online at: http://www.kff.org/entmedia/upload/8010.pdf

Rideout, V. J., Vandewater, E. A., & Wartella, E. A. (2003). *Zero to six: Electronic media in the lives of infants, toddlers, and preschoolers* (No. 3378). Menlo Park, CA: Henry J. Kaiser Family Foundation and the Children's Digital Media Centers (CDMC).

Riggs, N. R., Sakuma, K. K., & Pentz, M. A. (2007). Preventing risk for obesity by promoting self-regulation and decision-making skills: Pilot results from the PATHWAYS to health program (PATHWAYS). *Education Review, 31,* 287–310.

Rittle-Johnson, B., & Star, J. R. (2007). Does comparing solution methods facilitate conceptual and procedural knowledge? An experimental study on learning to solve equations. *Journal of Educational Psychology, 99,* 561–574.

Rivkin, S. G., Hanushek, E. A., & Kain, J. F. (2001). *Teachers, schools, and academic achievement.* Amherst, MA: Amherst College.

Rizzolatti, G., Fadiga, L., Gallese, V., & Fogassi, L. (1996). Premotor cortex and the recognition of motor actions. *Brain Research: Cognitive Brain Research, 3*(2), 131–141.

Robbins, S. B., Lauver, K., Davis, H. L., Davis, D., Langley, R., & Carlstrom, A. (2004). Psychosocial and study skill factors predict college outcomes? A meta-analysis. *Psychological Bulletin, 130,* 261–288.

Robbins, S. B., Le, L., & Lauver, K. (2005). Promoting successful college outcomes for all students: Reply to Weissberg and Owen (2005). *Psychological Bulletin, 131,* 410–411.

Roberge, M. M. (2002). California's Generation 1.5 immigrants: What experiences, characterisitcs, and needs do they bring to our English classes? *The CATESOL Journal, 14*(1), 107–129.

Roberson, D., Davidoff, J., Davies, I. R. L., & Shapiro, L. R. (2004). The development of color categories in two languages: A longitudinal study. *Journal of Experimental Psychology: General, 133,* 554–571.

Roberts, D. F., Foehr, U. G., & Rideout, V. (2005). *Generation M: Media in the lives of 8–18 year-olds.* Technical Reports 7250/7251. Menlo Park, CA: Kaiser Family foundation. Available online at: http://www.kff.org/entmedia/7251.cfm

Roberts, D. S., Tingstrom, D. H., Olmi, D. J., & Bellipanni, K. D. (2008). Positive antecedent and consequent components in child compliance training. *Behavior Modification, 32,* 21–38.

Roberts, G., Mohammed, S. S., & Vaughn, S. (2010). Reading achievement across three language groups: Growth estimates for overall reading and reading subskills obtained with the early childhood longitudinal survey. *Journal of Educational Psychology, 102*, 668–686.

Robinson, A., & Clinkenbeard, P. R. (1998). Giftedness: An exceptionality examined. In J. T. Spence, J. M. Darley, & D. J. Foss (Eds.), *Annual review of psychology* (pp. 117–139). Palo Alto, CA: Annual Reviews.

Robinson, D. H. (1998). Graphic organizers as aids to test learning. *Reading Research and Instruction, 37*, 85–105.

Robinson, D. H., & Kiewra, K. A. (1995). Visual argument: Graphic outlines are superior to outlines in improving learning from text. *Journal of Educational Psychology, 87*, 455–467.

Roediger, H. L., & Karpicke, J. D. (2006). The power of testing memory, *Perspectives on Psychological Science, 1*, 181–210.

Roeser, R. W., Peck, S. C., & Nasir, N. S. (2006). Self and identity processes in school motivation, learning, and achievement. In P. A. Alexander & P. H. Winne (Eds.), *Handbook of educational psychology* (2nd ed., pp. 391–424). Mahwah, NJ: Erlbaum.

Rogers, C. R., & Freiberg, H. J. (1994). *Freedom to learn* (3rd ed.). Columbus, OH: Merrill.

Rogoff, B. (1990). *Apprenticeship in thinking: Cognitive development in social context.* New York, NY: Oxford University Press.

Rogoff, B. (1995). Observing sociocultural activity on three planes: Participatory appropriation, guided participation, and apprenticeship. In J. Wertsch, P. del Rio, & A. Alverez (Eds.), *Sociocultural studies of mind* (pp. 139–164). Cambridge, UK: Cambridge University Press.

Rogoff, B. (1998). Cognition as a collaborative process. In W. Damon (Series Ed.) and D. Kuhn & R. S. Siegler (Vol. Eds.), *Handbook of child psychology: Vol. 2* (5th ed., pp. 679–744). New York, NY: Wiley.

Rogoff, B. (2003). *The cultural nature of human development.* New York, NY: Oxford University Press.

Rogoff, B., & Morelii, G. (1989). Perspectives on children's development from cultural psychology. *American Psychologist, 44*, 343–348.

Rogoff, B., Turkanis, C. G., & Bartlett, L. (2001). *Learning together: Children and adults in a school community.* New York, NY: Oxford.

Roid, G. H. (2003). *Stanford-Binet Intelligence Scales, Fifth Edition.* Itasca, IL: Riverside Publishing.

Rop, C. (1997/1998). Breaking the gender barrier in the physical sciences. *Educational Leadership, 55*(4), 58–60.

Rosch, E. H. (1973). On the internal structure of perceptual and semantic categories. In T. Moore (Ed.), *Cognitive development and the acquisition of language* (pp. 111–144). New York, NY: Academic Press.

Roschelle, J. M., Pea, R. D., Hoadley, C. M., Gordon, D. N., & Means, B. M. (2000, Fall/Winter). Changing how and what children learn in school with computer-based technologies. *Children and Computer Technology, 10*(2), 76–101.

Rosen, L. (2010). *Rewired: Understanding the iGeneration and the way they learn.* New York, NY: Palgrave Macmillan.

Rosenberg, M. (1979). *Conceiving the self.* New York, NY: Basic Books.

Rosenberg, M. S., Westling, D. L., & McLeskey, J. (2011). *Special education for today's teachers: An introduction.* Boston, MA: Allyn & Bacon/Pearson.

Rosenfeld, M., & Rosenfeld, S. (2004). Developing teacher sensitivities to individual learning differences. *Educational Psychology, 24*, 465–486.

Rosenshine, B. (1988). Explicit teaching. In D. Berliner & B. Rosenshine (Eds.), *Talks to teachers* (pp. 75–92). New York, NY: Random House.

Rosenshine, B., & Furst, N. (1973). The use of direct observation to study teaching. In R. Travers (Ed.), *Second handbook of research on teaching.* Chicago, IL: Rand McNally.

Rosenshine, B., & Meister, C. (1992, April). *The uses of scaffolds for teaching less structured academic tasks.* Paper presented at the annual meeting of the American Educational Research Association, San Francisco, CA.

Rosenshine, B., & Meister, C. (1994). Reciprocal teaching: A review of the research. *Review of Educational Research, 64*, 479–530.

Rosenshine, B., & Stevens, R. (1986). Teaching functions. In M. Wittrock (Ed.), *Handbook of research on teaching* (3rd ed., pp. 376–391). New York, NY: Macmillan.

Rosenthal, R. (1995). Critiquing Pygmalion: A 25-year perspective. *Current Directions in Psychological Science, 4*, 171–172.

Rosenthal, R., & Jacobson, L. (1968). *Pygmalion in the classroom.* New York, NY: Holt, Rinehart, Winston.

Roskos, K., & Neuman, S. B. (1998). Play as an opportunity for literacy. In O. N. Saracho & B. Spodek (Eds.), *Multiple perspectives on play in early childhood education* (pp. 100–115). Albany, NY: State University of New York Press.

Ross, J. A., & Raphael, D. (1990). Communication and problem solving achievement in cooperative learning groups. *Journal of Curriculum Studies, 22*, 149–164.

Rotherham-Borus, M. J. (1994). Bicultural reference group orientations and adjustment. In M. Bernal & G. Knight (Eds.), *Ethnic identity.* Albany, NY: State University of New York Press.

Rowe, E. W., Kingsley, J. M., & Thompson, D. F. (2010). Predictive ability of the general ability index (GAI) versus the full scale IQ among gifted referrals. *School Psychology Quarterly, 25*, 119–128.

Rowe, M. B. (1974). Wait-time and rewards as instructional variables: Their influence on language, logic, and fate control. Part 1: Wait-time. *Journal of Research in Science Teaching, 11*, 81–94.

Rubie-Davies, C. M. (2010). Teacher expectations and perceptions of student attributes: Is there a relationship? *British Journal of Educational Psychology, 80*, 121–135.

Rubin, K. H., Coplan, R., Chen, X., Buskirk, A. A., & Wojslawowicz, J. C. (2005). Peer relationships in childhood. In M. H. Bornstein & M. E. Lamb (Eds.), *Developmental science: An advanced textbook* (pp. 469–512). Mahwah, NJ: Erlbaum.

Rubinsten, O., & Henik, A. (2006). Double dissociations of functions in developmental dyslexia and dyscalculia. *Journal of Educational Psychology, 98*, 854–867.

Ruble, D. N., Martin, C. L., & Berenbaum, S. A. (2006). Gender development. In *Handbook of child psychology* (Vol. 3, pp. 858–932). Hoboken, NJ: John Wiley & Sons.

Rudolph, K. D., Lambert, S. F., Clark, A. G., & Kurlakowsky, K. D. (2001). Negotiating the transition to middle school: The role of self-regulatory processes. *Child Development, 72*, 926–946.

Rueda, R., & Moll, L. C. (1994) A sociocultural perspective on motivation. In F. O'Neil Jr. & M. Drillings (Eds.), *Motivation: Theory and research* (pp. 117–137). Hillsdale, NJ: Erlbaum.

Rummel, N., Levin, J. R., & Woodward, M. M. (2003). Do pictorial mnemonic text-learning aids give students something worth writing about? *Journal of Educational Psychology, 95*, 327–334.

Ryan, A. (2001). The peer group as a context for development of young adolescents' motivation and achievement. *Child Development, 72*, 1135–1150.

Ryan, K. E., & Ryan, A. M. (2005). Psychological processes underlying stereotype threat and standardized math test performance. *Educational Psychologist, 40*, 53–63.

Ryan, R. M., & Deci, E. L. (1996). When paradigms clash: Comments on Cameron and Pierce's claim that rewards do not undermine intrinsic motivation. *Review of Educational Research, 66*, 33–38.

Ryan, R. M., & Deci, E. L. (2000). Intrinsic and extrinsic motivation: Classic definitions and new directions. *Contemporary Educational Psychology, 25*, 54–67.

Sackett, P. R., Hardison, C. M., & Cullen, M. J. (2004). On the value of correcting mischaracterizations of stereotype threat. *American Psychologist, 59*, 48–49.

Sackett, P. R., Kuncel, N. R., Arneson, J. J., Cooper, S. R., & Waters, S. D. (2009). Does socioeconomic status explain the relationship between admissions tests and post-secondary academic performance? *Psychological Bulletin, 135*, 1–22.

Sadker, M., & Sadker, D. (1986). Questioning skills. In J. Cooper (Ed.), *Classroom Teaching Skills: A Handbook* (3rd ed., pp.143–160). Boston, MA: D. C. Heath.

Sadker, M., & Sadker, D. (2006). Questioning skills. In J. Cooper (Ed.), *Classroom teaching skills* (8th ed., pp. 104–150). Boston, MA: Houghton-Mifflin.

Sadker, M., Sadker, D., & Klein, S. (1991). The issue of gender in elementary and secondary education. *Review of Research in Education, 17*, 269–334.

Sagor, R. (2003). *Motivating students and teachers in an era of standards.* Alexandria, VA: Association for Supervision and Curriculum Development.

Sakiz, G., Pape, S., & Woolfolk Hoy, A. (2008, March). Does teacher affective support matter? The role of affective support in middle school mathematics classrooms. Paper presented at the annual meeting of the American Educational Research Association, New York, NY.

Salomon, G., & Perkins, D. N. (1989). Rocky roads to transfer: Re-thinking mechanisms of a neglected phenomenon. *Educational Psychologist, 24*, 113–142.

Sanchez, F., & Anderson, M. L. (1990, May). Gang mediation: A process that works. *Principal*, 54–56.

Sanders, W. L., & Rivers, J. C. (1996). *Cumulative and residual effects of teachers on student academic achievement.* Knoxville, TN: University of Tennessee Value-Added Research and Assessment Center.

Sattler, J. M. (2001). *Assessment of children: Cognitive applications* (4th ed.). San Diego, CA: Jerome M. Sattler, Inc.

Sattler, J. M., & Hoge, R. D. (2006). *Assessment of children: Behavioral, social, and clinical foundations.* La Mesa, CA: Jerome M. Sattler Publisher.

Savage, T. V. (1999). *Teaching self-control through management and discipline*. Boston, MA: Allyn & Bacon.

Savin-Williams, R. C. (2006). Who's gay? Does it matter? *Current Directions in Psychological Science, 15*(1), 40–44.

Sawyer, R. K. (2006). *Explaining creativity: The science of human motivation*. New York, NY: Oxford University Press.

Sawyer, R. K. (2006). Introduction: The new science of learning. In R. K. Sawyer (Ed.), *The Cambridge handbook of the learning sciences* (pp. 1–16). New York, NY: Cambridge.

Saxe, G. B. (1999). Source of concepts: A cross cultural-developmental perspective. In E. K. Scholnick, K. Nelson, S. A. Gelman, & P. H. Miller (Eds.), *Conceptual development: Piaget's legacy* (pp. 253–267). Mahwah, NJ: Erlbaum.

Schacter, D. L., Gilbert, D. T., & Wenger, D. M. (2009). *Psychology*. New York, NY: Worth.

Scheibe, C., & Rogow, F. (2004). *12 basic principles for incorporating media literacy and critical thinking into any curriculum* (2nd ed.). Ithaca, NY: Project Look Sharp—Ithaca College.

Scherer, M. (1993). On savage inequalities: A conversation with Jonathan Kozol. *Educational Leadership, 50*(4), 4–9.

Scherer, M. (1999). The discipline of hope: A conversation with Herb Kohl. *Educational Leadership, 56*(1), 8–13.

Schiefele, U. (1991). Interest, learning, and motivation. *Educational Psychologist, 26*, 299–324.

Schmidt, H. G., van der Molen, H. T., te Winkel, W. W. R., & Wijnen, W. H. F. W. (2009). Constructivist, problem-based learning does work: A meta-analysis of curricular comparisons involving a single medical school. *Educational Psychologist, 44*, 227–249.

Schneider, W., & Bjorklund, D. F. (1992). Expertise, aptitude, and strategic remembering. *Child Development, 63*, 416–473.

Schoen, R., & Canudas-Romo, V. (2006). Timing effects on divorce: 20th century experience in the United States. *Journal of Marriage and the Family, 68*, 749–758.

Schoenfeld, A. H. (1989). Teaching mathematical thinking and problem solving. In L. B. Resnick & L. E. Klopfer (Eds.), *Toward the thinking curriculum: Current cognitive research* (pp. 83–103). Alexandria, VA: ASCD.

Schoenfeld, A. H. (1994). *Mathematics thinking and problem solving*. Hillsdale, NJ: Erlbaum.

Schoenfeld, A. H. (2011). *How we think: The theory of goal-oriented decision making and its educational applications*. New York, NY: Routledge.

Scholastic. (2011). Planning for parent conferences. Available online at: http://www2.scholastic.com/browse/article.jsp?id=4194

Schommer, M. (1997). The development of epistemological beliefs among secondary students: A longitudinal study. *Journal of Educational Psychology, 89*, 37–40.

Schommer-Aikins, M. (2002). An evolving theoretical framework for an epistemological belief system. In B. K. Hofer & P. R. Pintrich (Eds.), *Personal epistemology: The psychology of beliefs about knowledge and knowing* (pp. 103–118). Mahwah, NJ: Erlbaum.

Schraw, G. (2006). Knowledge: Structures and processes. In P. A. Alexander & P. H. Winne (Eds.), *Handbook of educational psychology* (2nd ed., pp. 825–847). Mahwah, NJ: Erlbaum.

Schraw, G., & Olafson, L. (2002). Teachers' epistemological world views and educational practices. *Issues in Education, 8*, 99–148.

Schunk, D. H. (2000). *Learning theories: An educational perspective* (3rd ed.). Columbus, OH: Merrill.

Schunk, D. H. (2004). *Learning theories: An educational perspective* (4th ed.). Columbus, OH: Merrill.

Schunk, D. H. (2008). *Learning theories: An educational perspective* (5th ed.). Columbus, OH: Merrill.

Schunk, D. H. (2012). *Learning theories: An educational perspective* (6th ed.). Boston, MA: Allyn & Bacon/Pearson.

Schunk, D. H., & Hanson, A. R. (1985). Peer models: Influence on children's self-efficacy and achievement. *Journal of Educational Psychology, 77*, 313–322.

Schunk, D. H., Pintrich, P. R., & Meece, J. L. (2008). *Motivation in education: Theory, research, and applications* (3rd ed.). Columbus, OH: Merrill.

Schutz, P. A., & Davis, H. A. (2000). Emotions and self-regulations during test-taking. *Educational Psychologist, 35*, 243–256.

Schwab, J. J. (1973). The Practical 3: Translation into curriculum. *School Review, 81*, 501–522.

Schwartz, B., Wasserman, E. A., & Robbins, S. J. (2002). *Psychology of learning and behavior* (5th ed.). New York, NY: W. W. Norton.

Schwarz, B. B., Neuman, Y., & Biezuner, S. (2000). Two wrongs may make a right . . . if they argue together! *Cognition and Instruction, 18*, 461–494.

Schworm, S., & Renkl, A. (2007). Learning argumentation skills through the use of prompts for self-explaining examples. *Journal of Educational Psychology, 99*, 285–295.

Seaton, M., Marsh, H. W., & Craven, R. G. (2009). Earning its place as a pan-human theory: Universality of the Big-Fish-Little-Pond effect across 41 culturally and economically diverse countries. *Journal of Educational Psychology, 101*, 403–419.

Seligman, M. E. P. (1975). *Helplessness: On depression, development, and death*. San Francisco, CA: Freeman.

Seligman, M. E. P. (2006). *Learned optimism: How to change your mind and your life* (2nd ed.). New York, NY: Pocket Books.

Selman, R. L. (1980). *The growth of interpersonal understanding*. New York, NY: Academic Press.

Sénéchal, M., & LeFevre, J. A. (2002). Parental involvement in the development of children's reading skills: A five-year longitudinal study. *Child Development, 73*, 445–460.

Senghas, A., & Coppola, M. (2001). Children creating language: How Nicaraguan Sign Language acquired a spatial grammar. *Psychological Review, 96*, 323–328.

Serpell, R. (1993). Interface between sociocultural and psychological aspects of cognition. In E. Forman, N. Minick, & C. A. Stone (Eds.), *Contexts for learning: Sociocultural dynamics in children's development* (pp. 357–368). New York, NY: Oxford University Press.

Shaffer, D. W. (2010). *The Bicycle Helmets of "Amsterdam": Computer games and the problem of transfer* (Epistemic Games Group Working Paper No. 2010-01). Madison, WI: University of Wisconsin-Madison.

Shaffer, D. W., Hatfield, D., Svarovsky, G. N., Nash, P., Nulty, A., Bagley, E., . . . Mislevy, R. J. (2009). Epistemic network analysis: A prototype for 21st century assessment of learning. *International Journal of Learning Media, 1*(2), 33–53.

Shavelson, R. J. (1987). Planning. In M. Dunkin (Ed.), *The international encyclopedia of teaching and teacher education* (pp. 483–486). New York, NY: Pergamon Press.

Shaywitz, B. A., Shaywitz, S. E., Blachman, B. A., Pugh, K. R., Fulbright, R. K., Skudlarski, P., . . . Gore, J. C. (2004). Development of left occipitotemporal systems for skilled reading in children after a phonologically-based intervention. *Biological Psychiatry, 55*, 926–933.

Sheets, R. H. (2005). *Diversity pedagogy: Examining the role of culture in the teaching-learning process*. Boston, MA: Allyn & Bacon.

Shepard, L. A., & Smith, M. L. (1988). Escalating academic demand in kindergarten: Counterproductive policies. *Elementary School Journal, 89*(2), 135–145.

Shepard, L. A., & Smith, M. L. (1989). Academic and emotional effects of kindergarten retention. In L. Shepard & M. Smith (Eds.), *Flunking grades: Research and policies on retention* (pp. 79–107). Philadelphia, PA: Falmer Press.

Sherwood, R. D. (2002). Problem-based multimedia software for middle grade science: Development issues and an initial field study. *Journal of Computers in Mathematics and Science Teaching, 21*, 147–165.

Shih, S. S. (2008). The relation of self-determination and achievement goals to Taiwanese eighth graders' behavioral and emotional engagement in schoolwork. *The Elementary School Journal, 108*, 313–334.

Shonkoff, J. P. (2006). A promising opportunity for developmental and behavioral pediatrics at the interface of neuroscience, psychology, and social policy: Remarks on receiving the 2005 C. Anderson Aldrich Award. *Pediatrics, 118*, 2187–2191.

Shu, H., McBride-Chang, C., Wu, S., & Liu, H. (2006). Understanding Chinese developmental dyslexia: Morphological awareness as a core cognitive construct. *Journal of Educational Psychology, 98*, 122–133.

Shuell, T. J. (1996). Teaching and learning in a classroom context. In D. Berliner & R. Calfee (Eds.), *Handbook of educational psychology* (pp. 726–764). New York, NY: Macmillan.

Shulman, L. S. (1987). Knowledge and teaching: Foundations of the new reform. *Harvard Educational Review, 19*(2), 4–14.

Shute, V. J. (2008). Focus on formative feedback. *Review of Educational Research, 78*, 153–189.

Siddle Walker, V. (2001). African American teaching in the South: 1940–1960. *Review of Educational Research, 38*, 751–779.

Siegel, J., & Shaughnessy, M. F. (1994). Educating for understanding: An interview with Howard Gardner. *Phi Delta Kappan, 75*, 536–566.

Siegel, L. S. (2003). Basic cognitive processes and reading disabilities. In H. L. Swanson, K. R. Harris, & S. Graham (Eds.), *Handbook of learning disabilities* (pp. 158–181). New York, NY: Guilford Press.

Siegler, R. S. (1993). Adaptive and non-adaptive characteristics of low-income children's mathematical strategy use. In B. Penner (Ed.), *The challenge in mathematics and science education: Psychology's response* (pp. 341–366). Washington, DC: American Psychological Association.

Siegler, R. S. (1998). *Children's thinking* (3rd ed.). Upper Saddle River, NJ: Prentice-Hall.

Siegler, R. S. (2000). The rebirth of children's learning. *Child Development, 71*, 26–35.

Siegler, R. S. (2004). Turning memory development inside out. *Developmental Review, 24*, 469–475.

Siegler, R. S., & Alibali, M. W. (2005). *Children's thinking* (4th ed.). Upper Saddle River, NJ: Prentice-Hall.

Siegler, R. S., & Crowley, K. (1991). The microgenetic method: A direct means for studying cognitive development. *American Psychologist, 56*, 606–620.

Silverman, S. K. (2008, April, 11). Personal communication, Columbus, Ohio.

Simon, D. P., & Chase, W. G. (1973). Skill in chess. *American Scientist, 61*, 394–403.

Simon, H. A. (1995). The information-processing view of mind. *American Psychologist, 50*, 507–508.

Simon, T. (2010). Rewards and challenges of cognitive neuroscience studies of persons with intellectual and developmental disabilities. Special Issue for the *American Journal on Intellectual and Developmental Disabilities, 115*, 79-82. doi: 10.1352/1944-7558-115.2.79

Simonton, D. K. (1999). Creativity from a historiometric perspective. In R. J. Sternberg (Ed.), *Handbook of creativity* (pp. 116–133). New York, NY: Cambridge University Press.

Simonton, D. K. (2000). Creativity: Cognitive, personal, developmental, and social aspects. *American Psychologist, 55*, 151–158.

Simos, P. G., Fletcher, J. M., Sarkari, S., Billingsley-Marshall, R., Denton, C. A., & Papanicolaou, A. C. (2007). Intensive instruction affects brain magnetic activity associated with oral word reading in children with persistent reading disabilities. *Journal of Learning Disabilities, 40* (1), 37–48.

Simpson, E. J. (1972). The classification of educational objectives in the psychomotor domain. *The Psychomotor Domain. Vol. 3*. Washington, DC: Gryphon House.

Sinatra, G. M., & Mason, L. (2008). Beyond knowledge: Learner characteristics influencing conceptual change. In S. Vosniadou (Ed.), *International handbook of research on conceptual change*. Mahwah, NJ: Erlbaum.

Sinatra, G. M., & Taasoobshirazi, G. (2011). Intentional conceptual change: The self-regulation of sciene learning. In B. Zimmerman & D. Schunk (Eds.), *Handbook of self-regulation of learning and performance* (pp. 203–216). New York, NY: Routledge.

Singley, K., & Anderson, J. R. (1989). *The transfer of cognitive skill*. Cambridge, MA: Harvard University Press.

Sio, U. N., & Ormerod, T. C. (2009). Does incubation enhance problem solving? A meta-analytic review. *Psychological Bulletin, 135*, 94–120.

Sirin, S. R. (2005). Socioeconomic status and academic achievement: A meta-analytic review of research. *Review of Educational Research, 75*, 417–453.

Skiba, R. J., Michael, R. S., Nardo, A. C., & Peterson, R. (2000). *The color of discipline: Sources of racial and gender disproportionality in school punishment* (Report #SRS1). Bloomington, IN: Indiana Education Policy Center.

Skinner, B. F. (1950). Are theories of learning necessary? *Psychological Review, 57*, 193–216.

Skinner, B. F. (1953). *Science and human behavior*. New York, NY: Macmillan.

Skinner, B. F. (1989). The origins of cognitive thought. *American Psychologist, 44*, 13–18.

Slaby, R. G., Roedell, W. C., Arezzo, D., & Hendrix, K. (1995). *Early violence prevention*. Washington, DC: National Association for the Education of Young Children.

Slater, L. (2002, February 3). The trouble with self-esteem. *The New York Times Magazine*, pp. 44–47.

Slavin, R. E. (1995). *Cooperative learning* (2nd ed.). Boston, MA: Allyn & Bacon.

Slavin, R. E. (2002). Evidence-based education policies: Transforming education practice and research. *Educational Researcher, 31*(7), 15–21.

Slavin, R. E., Lake, C., Chambers, B., Cheung, A., & Davis, S. (2009). Effective reading programs for elementary grades: A best–evidence synthesis. *Review of Educational Resaerch, 79*, 1391–1465.

Smetana, J. G. (2000). Middle-class African American adolescents' and parents' conceptions of parental authority and parenting practices: A longitudinal investigation. *Child Development, 71*, 1672–1686.

Smith, C. R. (2004). *Learning disabilities: The interaction of learner, task, and setting* (5th ed.). Boston, MA: Allyn & Bacon.

Smith, C. S., & Hung, L-C. (2008). Stereotype threat: Effects on education. *Social Psychology of Education, 11*, 243–257.

Smith, D. D. (2006). *Introduction to special education: Teaching in an age of opportunity* (5th ed.). Boston, MA: Allyn & Bacon.

Smith, D. D., & Tyler, N. C. (2010). *Introduction to special education: Making a difference* (7th ed.). Columbus, OH: Merrill.

Smith, E. E., & Kosslyn, S. M. (2007). *Cognitive psychology: Mind and brain*. Upper Saddle River, NJ: Pearson/Prentice-Hall.

Smith, F. (1975). *Comprehension and learning: A conceptual framework for teachers*. New York, NY: Holt, Rinehart & Winston.

Smith, J. K., Smith, L. F., & De Lisi, R. (2001). *Natural classroom assessment: Designing seamless instruction and assessment*. Thousand Oaks, CA: Corwin Press.

Smith, J. L., Sansone, C., & White, P. H. (2007). The stereotyped task process: The role of interest and achievement motivation. *Journal of Educational Psychology, 88*, 99–114.

Smith, S. M., Glenberg, A., & Bjork, R. A. (1978). Environmental context and human memory. *Memory and Cognition, 6*, 342–353.

Snapp, M., & Woolfolk, A. E. (1973, March). *An examination of children in special education over a thirteen-year period*. Paper presented at the National Association of School Psychologists, 5th Annual Meeting, New York, NY.

Snow, C. E. (1993). Families as social contexts for literacy development. In C. Daiute (Ed.), *New directions for child development* (No. 61, pp. 11–24). San Francisco, CA: Jossey-Bass.

Snow, R. E. (1995). Pygmalion and intelligence. *Current Directions in Psychological Science, 4*, 169–171.

Snow, R. E., Corno, L., & Jackson, D. (1996). Individual differences in affective and cognitive functions. In D. Berliner & R. Calfee (Eds.), *Handbook of educational psychology* (pp. 243–310). New York, NY: Macmillan.

Snowman, J. (1984). Learning tactics and strategies. In G. Phye & T. Andre (Eds.), *Cognitive instructional psychology* (pp. 243–275). Orlando, FL: Academic Press.

Soar, R. S., & Soar, R. M. (1979). Emotional climate and management. In P. Peterson & H. Walberg (Eds.), *Research on teaching: Concepts, findings,*

and implications (pp. 97–119). Berkeley, CA: McCutchan.

Soares, D. A., Vannest, K. J., & Harrison, J. (2009). Computer aided self-monitoring to increase academic production and reduce self-injurious behavior in a child with autism. *Behavioral Interventions, 24*, 171–183.

Sobesky, W. E. (1983). The effects of situational factors on moral judgment. *Child Development, 54*, 575–584.

Society for Research in Child Development (SRCD). (2009). Young Hispanic children: Boosting opportunities for learning. *Society for Research in Child Development: Social Policy Report Briefs, 23*(2), 1–2.

Sokolove, S., Garrett, J., Sadker, D., & Sadker, M. (1986). Interpersonal communications skills. In J. Cooper (Ed.), *Classroom teaching skills: A handbook* (pp. 233–278). Lexington, MA: D. C. Heath.

Solomon, D., Watson, M. S., & Battistich, V. A. (2001). Teaching and schooling effects on moral/prosocial development. In V. Richardson (Ed.), *Handbook of research on teaching* (4th ed., pp. 566–603). Washington, DC: American Educational Research Association.

Soodak, L. C., & McCarthy, M. R. (2006). Classroom management in inclusive settings. In C. M. Evertson & C. S. Weinstein (Eds.), *Handbook of classroom management: Research, practice, and contemporary issues*. Mahwah, NJ: Erlbaum.

Sotillo, S. M. (2002). Finding our voices, finding ourselves: Becoming bilingual and bicultural. In G. S. Boutte (Ed.), *Resounding voices: School experiences of people from diverse ethnic backgrounds* (pp. 275–307). Boston, MA: Allyn & Bacon.

Spearman, C. (1927). *The abilities of man: Their nature and measurement*. New York, NY: Macmillan.

Spencer, M. B., & Markstrom-Adams, C. (1990). Identity processes among racial and ethnic-minority children in America. *Child Development, 61*, 290–310.

Spencer, M. B., Noll, E., Stoltzfus, J., & Harpalani, V. (2001). Identity and school adjustment: Questioning the "Acting White" assumption. *Educational Psychologist, 36*(1), 21–30.

Spera, C. (2005). A review of the relationship among parenting practices, parenting styles, and adolescent school achievement. *Educational Psychology Review, 17*, 125–146.

Spörer, N., & Brunstein, J. C. (2009). Fostering the reading comprehension of secondary school students through peer-assisted learning: Effects on strategy knowledge, strategy use, and task performance. *Contemporary Educational Psychology, 34*, 289–297.

Sprenger, M. (2005). Inside Amy's brain. *Educational Leadership, 62*(7), 28–32.

Sprenger, M. (2010). *Brain-based teaching in the digital age*. Alexandria, VA: Association for Supervision and Curriculum Development.

Stage, S. A., Jackson, H. G., Erickson M. J., Moscovitz, K. K., Bush, J. W., Violette, H. D., . . . Pious, C. (2008). A validity study of functionally-based behavioral consultation with students with emotional/behavioral disabilities. *School Psychology Quarterly, 23*, 327–353.

Stahl, S. A. (2002). Different strokes for different folks? In L. Abbeduto (Ed.), *Taking sides: Clashing on controversial issues in educational psychology* (pp. 98–107). Guilford, CT: McGraw-Hill/Duskin.

Stanovich, K. E. (1992). *How to think straight about psychology* (3rd ed.). Glenview, IL: Scott, Foresman.

Star, J. R., & Rittle-Johnson, B. (2009). It pays to compare: An experimental study on computational estimation. *Journal of Experimental Child Psychology, 102,* 408–426.

Steele, C. (1992). Race and the schooling of African-Americans. *Atlantic Monthly, 269*(4), 68–78.

Steele, K. M., Bass, K. E., & Crook, M. D. (1999). The mystery of the Mozart effect: Failure to replicate. *Psychological Science, 10,* 366–368.

Stefanou, C. R., Perencevich, K. C., DiCintio, M., & Turner, J. C. (2004). Supporting autonomy in the classroom: Ways teachers encourage student decision making and ownership. *Educational Psychologist, 39,* 97–110.

Steffens, M. C., Jelenec, P., & Noack, P. (2010). On the leaky math pipeline: Comparing implicit math-gender stereotypes and math withdrawal in female and male children and adolescents. *Journal of Educational Psychology, 102,* 947–963.

Steinberg, L. (1996). *Beyond the classroom: Why schools are failing and what parents need to do.* New York, NY: Simon & Schuster.

Steinberg, L. (1998). Standards outside the classroom. In D. Ravitch (Ed.), *Brookings papers on educational policy* (pp. 319–358). Washington, DC: Brookings Institute.

Steinberg, L. (2005). *Adolescence* (7th ed.). New York, NY: McGraw-Hill.

Steinberg, L. (2008). A social neuroscience perspective on adolescent risk-taking. *Developmental Review, 28,* 78–106.

Stemler, S. E., Sternberg, R. J., Grigorenko, E. L., Jarvin, L., & Sharpes, K. (2009). Using the theory of successful intelligence as a framework for developing assessments in AP physics. *Contemporary Educational Psychology, 34,* 195–209.

Sternberg, R. J. (1985). *Beyond IQ: A triarchic theory of human intelligence.* New York, NY: Cambridge University Press.

Sternberg, R. J. (1997). *Successful intelligence.* New York, NY: Plume.

Sternberg, R. J. (1999). A propulsion model of types of creative contribution. *Review of General Psychology, 3,* 83–100.

Sternberg, R. J. (2000). *Handbook of human intelligence.* New York, NY: Cambridge University Press.

Sternberg, R. J. (2004). Culture and intelligence. *American Psychologist, 59,* 325–338.

Sternberg, R. J., & Davidson, J. (1982, June). The mind of the puzzler. *Psychology Today,* 37–44.

Sternberg, R. J., & Sternberg, K. (2012). *Cognitive psychology* (6th ed.). Belmont, CA: Wadsworth.

Stevenson, H. W., & Stigler, J. W. (1992). *The learning gap.* New York, NY: Summit Books.

Stewart, L., Henson, R., Kampe, K., Walsh, V., Turner, R., & Frith, U. (2003). Brain changes after learning to read and play music. *NeuroImage, 20*(1), 71–83.

Stice, E., & Shaw, H. (2004). Eating disorder prevention programs: A meta-analytic review. *Psychological Bulletin, 130,* 206–227.

Stiggins, R. J., & Chappuis, J. (2005). Using student-involved classroom assessment to close achievement gaps. *Theory Into Practice, 44,* 11–18.

Stigler, J. W., Lee, S., & Stevenson, H. W. (1987). Mathematics classrooms in Japan, Taiwan, and the United States. *Child Development, 58,* 1272–1285.

Stinson, D. W. (2006). African American male adolescents, schooling, (an mathematics): Deficiency, rejection, and achievement. *Review of Educational Research, 76,* 477–506.

Stipek, D. J. (1981). Children's perceptions of their own and their peers' academic competence. *Journal of Educational Psychology, 73,* 404–410.

Stipek, D. J. (1993). *Motivation to learn* (2nd ed.). Boston, MA: Allyn & Bacon.

Stipek, D. J. (2002). *Motivation to learn: Integrating theory and practice* (4th ed.). Boston, MA: Allyn & Bacon.

Stipek, D. (2006). Relationships matter. *Educational Leadership, 64*(1), 46–49.

Stipek, D., de la Sota, A., & Weishaupt, L. (1999). Life lessons: An embedded classroom approach to preventing high-risk behaviors among preadolescents. *The Elementary School Journal, 99,* 433–451.

Stodolsky, S. S. (1988). *The subject matters: Classroom activity in math and social studies.* Chicago, IL: University of Chicago Press.

Stoeger, H., & Ziegler, A. (2011). Self-regulatory training through elementary-school students' homework completion. In B. Zimmerman & D. Schunk (Eds.), *Handbook of self-regulation of learning and performance* (pp. 87–101) New York, NY: Routledge.

Storch, S., & Whitehurst, G. (2002). Oral language and code-related precursors to reading: Evidence from a longitudinal structural model. *Developmental Psychology, 38,* 934–947.

Stormont, M., Stebbins, M. S., & Holliday, G. (2001). Characteristics and educational support needs of underrepresented gifted adolescents. *Psychology in the Schools, 38,* 413–423.

Stormshak, E. A., Bierman, K. L., Bruschi, C., Dodge, K. A., Coie, J. D., et al. (1999). The relation between behavior problems and peer preference in different classrooms. *Child Development, 70,* 169–182.

Story, M., & Stang, J. (2005). Nutrition needs of adolescents. In J. S. M. Story (Ed.), *Guidelines for adolescent nutritional services* (pp. 158–159). Minneapolis, MN: University of Minnesota Press.

Strayer, D. L., & Drews, F. A. (2007). Cell-phone induced driver distraction. *Current Directions in Psychological Science, 16,* 128–131.

Strom, P. S., & Strom, R. D. (2005). Cyberbullying by adolescents: A preliminary assessment. *The Educational Forum, 70*(1), 21–36.

Stumpf, H. (1995). Gender differences on test of cognitive abilities: Experimental design issues and empirical results. *Learning and Individual Differences, 7,* 275–288.

Subrahmanyam, K., Greenfield, P., Kraut, R., & Gross, E. (2001). The impact of computer use on children's and adolescents' development. *Applied Developmental Psychology, 22,* 7–30.

Suldo, S. M., Friedrich, A. A., White, T., Farmer, J., Minch, D., & Michalowski, J. (2009). Teacher support and adolescents' subjective well-being: A mixed-methods investigation. *School Psychology Review, 38,* 67–85.

Sullivan, M. A., & O'Leary, S. G. (1990). Maintenance following reward and cost token programs. *Behavior Therapy, 21,* 139–149.

Sulzer-Azaroff, B., & Mayer, G. R. (1986). *Achieving educational excellence using behavioral strategies.* New York, NY: Holt, Rinehart & Winston.

Sunburst Software. (1999). *A Field Trip to the Sea.*

Svoboda, J. S. (2001). Review of *Boys and girls learn differently.*The Men's Resource Network.

Available online at: http://mensightmagazine.com/reviews/Svoboda/boysandgirls.htm

Swanson, H. L. (1990). The influence of meta-cognitive knowledge and aptitude on problem solving. *Journal of Educational Psychology, 82,* 306–314.

Swanson, H. L. (2001). Research on interventions for adolescents with learning disabilities: A meta-analysis of outcomes related to higher-order processing. *The Elementary School Journal, 101,* 332–348.

Swanson H. L., & Saez, L. (2003). Memory difficulties in children and adults with learning disabilities. In H. L. Swanson, S. Graham, & K. R. Harris (Eds.), *Handbook of learning disabilities* (pp. 182–198). New York, NY: Guilford Press.

Swanson, T. C. (2005). Providing structure for children with learning and behavior problems. *Intervention in School and Clinic, 40,* 182–187.

Swearer, S. M., Espelage, D. L., Vaillancourt, T., & Hymel, S. (2010). What can be done about school bullying? Linking research to educational practice. *Educational Researcher, 39,* 38–47.

Sweeney, W. J., Salva, E., Cooper, J. O., & Talbert-Johnson, C. (1993). Using self-evaluation to improve difficult to read handwriting for secondary students. *Journal of Behavioral Education, 3,* 427–443.

Sweller, J., Kirschner, P. A., & Clark, R. E. (2007). Why minimally guided teaching techniques do not work: A reply to commentaries. *Educational Psychologist, 42,* 115–121.

Sweller, J., van Merrienboer, J. J. G., & Paas, F. G. W. C. (1998). Cognitive architecture and instructional design. *Educational Psychology Review, 10,* 251–296.

Sylvester, R. (2003). *A biological brain in a cultural classroom* (2nd ed.). Thousand Oaks, CA: Sage.

Tait, H., & Entwistle, N. J. (1998). Identifying students at risk through ineffective study strategies. *Higher Education, 31,* 97–116.

Talbot, M. (2002, February 24). Girls just want to be mean. *The New York Times Magazine,* pp. 24–29+.

Tallal, P., & Miller, S. L. (2003). How the brain learns to read. *Middle Matters, 12*(1), 7.

Tang, Y., Zhang, W., Chen, K., Feng, S., Ji, Y. Shen, J,. et al. (2006). Arithmetic processing in the brain shaped by culture. *Proceedings of the National Academy of Sciences USA, 103,* 10775–10780.

Taylor, E. (1998). Clinical foundation of hyperactivity research. *Behavioural Brain Research, 94,* 11–24.

Taylor, R. L., Richards, S. B., & Brady, M. P. (2005). *Mental retardation: Historical perspectives, current practices, and future directions.* Boston, MA: Allyn & Bacon.

TenBrink, T. D. (2003). Assessment. In J. Cooper (Ed.), *Classroom teaching skills* (7th ed., pp. 311–353). Boston, MA: Houghton-Mifflin.

TenBrink, T. D. (2006). Assessment. In J. Cooper (Ed.), *Classroom teaching skills* (8th ed., pp. 55–78). Boston, MA: Houghton-Mifflin.

Tenenbaum, H. R., & Ruck, M. D. (2007). Are teachers' expectations different for racial minority than for European American students? A meta-analysis. *Journal of Educational Psychology, 99,* 253–273.

Terman, L. M., Baldwin, B. T., & Bronson, E. (1925). Mental and physical traits of a thousand gifted children. In L. M. Terman (Ed.), *Genetic studies of genius* (Vol. 1). Stanford, CA: Stanford University Press.

Terman, L. M., & Oden, M. H. (1947). The gifted child grows up. In L. M. Terman (Ed.), *Genetic studies of genius* (Vol. 4). Stanford, CA: Stanford University Press.

Terman, L. M., & Oden, M. H. (1959). The gifted group in mid-life. In L. M. Terman (Ed.), *Genetic studies of genius* (Vol. 5). Stanford, CA: Stanford University Press.

Tesser, A., Stapel, D. A., & Wood, J. V. (2002). *Self and motivation:Emerging psychological perspectives*. Washington, DC: American Psychological Association.

Tharp, R. G. (1989). Psychocultural variables and constants: Effects on teaching and learning in schools. *American Psychologist, 44*, 349–359.

Tharp, R. G., & Gallimore, R. (1988). *Rousing minds to life: Teaching, learning, and schooling in social context*. New York, NY: Cambridge University Press.

Theodore, L. A., Bray, M. A., Kehle, T. J., & Jenson, W. R. (2001). Randomization of group contingencies and reinforcers to reduce classroom disruptive behavior. *Journal of School Psychology, 39*, 267–277.

Thomas, K. T., & Thomas, J. R. (2008). Principles of motor development for elementary school physical education. *The Elementary School Journal, 108*, 181–195.

Thome, J., & Reddy, D. P. (2009). The current status of research into attention deficit hyperactivity disorder: Proceedings of the 2nd International Congress on ADHD: From childhood to adult disease. *Attention Deficit Hyperactive Disorder, 1*, 165–174.

Thompson, G. (1991). *Teaching through themes*. New York, NY: Scholastic.

Thompson, G. (2008). Beneath the apathy. *Educational Leadership, 65*(6), 50–54.

Thompson, R. A., & Raikes, H. A. (2003). Toward the next quarter-century: Conceptual and methodological challenges for attachment theory. *Development and Psychopathology, 15*, 691–718.

Tierney, R. J., Readence, J. E., & Dishner, E. K. (1990). *Reading strategies and practices: A compendium* (3rd ed.). Boston, MA: Allyn & Bacon.

Tierney, W. G. (1993). *Building communities of difference: Higher education in the twenty-first century*. Westport, CT: Bergin and Garvey.

TIMSS. (1998). *Third International Mathematics and Science Study*. Washington, DC: National Center for Educational Statistics. Available online at: http://nces.ed.gov/timss/

TIMSS. (2008). Fourth International Mathematics and Science Study. Available online at: http://ncesed.gov/timss/

Tingstrom, D. H., Sterling-Turner, H. E., & Wilczynski, S. M. (2006). The Good Behavior Game: 1962–2002. *Behavior Modification, 30*, 225–253.

Tobias, S. (2010). Generative learning theory, paradigm shifts, and constructivism in educational psychology: A tribute to Merl Wittrock. *Educational Psychologist, 45*, 51–54.

Tobler, N., & Stratton, H. (1997). Effectiveness of school-based drug prevention programs: A metaanalysis of the research. *Journal of Primary Prevention, 18*, 71–128.

Tollefson, N. (2000). Classroom applications of cognitive theories of motivation. *Education Psychology Review, 12*, 63–83.

Tomasello, M. (2006). Acquiring linguistic constructions. In D. Kuhn & R. S. Siegler (Eds.), *Handbook of child psychology* (6th ed., Vol. 2: Cognition, language, and perception, pp. 255–298). New York, NY: Wiley.

Tomasello, M., Kruger, A. C., & Ratner, H. H. (1993). Cultural learning. *Behavioral and Brain Sciences, 16*, 495–552.

Tomlinson, C. A. (2003). *Fulfilling the promise of the differentiated classroom*. Alexandria, VA: Association for Supervision and Curriculum Development.

Tomlinson, C. A. (2005a). Grading and differentiation: Paradox or good practice? *Theory Into Practice, 44*, 262–269.

Tomlinson, C. A. (2005b, Summer). Differentiating instruction. *Theory Into Practice, 44*(3).

Tomlinson-Keasey, C. (1990). Developing our intellectual resources for the 21st century: Educating the gifted. *Journal of Educational Psychology, 82*, 399–403.

Tomporowski, P., Davis, C. L., Miller, P. H., & Naglieri, J. A. (2008). Exercise and children's intelligence, cognitive and academic achievement. *Educational Psychology Review, 20*, 111–131.

Toppo, G. (2003, January 13). School violence hits lower grades: Experts who see violent behavior in younger kids blame parents, prenatal medical problems and an angry society; educators search for ways to cope. *USA Today*. Available online at: http://www.usatoday.com/educate/college/education/articles/20030119.htm

Torrance, E. P. (1972). Predictive validity of the Torrance tests of creative thinking. *Journal of Creative Behavior, 6*, 236–262.

Torrance, E. P. (1986). Teaching creative and gifted learners. In M. Wittrock (Ed.), *Handbook of research on teaching* (3rd ed., pp. 630–647). New York, NY: Macmillan.

Torrance, E. P., & Hall, L. K. (1980). Assessing the future reaches of creative potential. *Journal of Creative Behavior, 14*, 1–19.

Toth, E., Klahr, D., & Chen, Z. (2000). Bridging research and practice: A cognitively based classroom intervention for teaching experimentation to elementary school children. *Cognition and Instruction, 18*, 423–459.

Trautwein, U. (2007). The homework–achievement relation reconsidered: Differentiating homework time, homework frequency, and homework effort. *Learning and Instruction, 17*, 372–388.

Trautwein, U., & Koller, O. (2003). The relationship between homework and achievement—Still a mystery. *Educatonal Psychology Review, 15*, 115–145.

Trautwein, U., & Lüdtke, O. (2007). Students' self-reported effort and time on homework in six school subjects: Between-students differences and within-student variation. *Journal of Educational Psychology, 99*, 232–234.

Trautwein, U., Schnyder, I., Niggli, A, Neuman, M., & Lüdtke, O. (2009). Chameleon effects in homework research: The homework–achievement association depends on the measures used and the level of analysis chosen. *Contemporaty Educational Psychology, 34*, 77–88.

Trebaticka, J., Paduchova, Z., Suba, J. et al. (2009). Markers of oxidative stress in ADHD and their modulation by Polyhenolic extract, Pycnogenal. From Childhood to Adult Disease. May 21–24, 2009, Vienna, Austria. *Attention Deficit and Hyperactivity Disorders, 1*: 33.

Trouilloud, D., Sarrazin, P., Bressoux, P., & Bois, J. (2006). Relation between teachers' early expectations and students' later perceived competence in physical education classes: autonomy-supportive climate as a moderator. *Journal of Educational Psychology, 98*, 75–86.

Tsantis, L. A., Bewick, C. J., & Thouvenelle, S. (2003). Examining some common myths about computer use in the early years [Electronic Version]. *Beyond the Journal: Young Children on the Web*, 1-9. Available online at: http://journal.naeyc.org/btj/200311/CommonTechnoMyths.pdf

Tschannen-Moran, M., & Woolfolk Hoy, A. (2001). Teacher efficacy: Capturing an elusive construct. *Teaching and Teacher Education, 17*, 783–805.

Tschannen-Moran, M., Woolfolk Hoy, A., & Hoy, W. K. (1998). Teacher efficacy: Its meaning and measure. *Review of Educational Research, 68*, 202–248.

Turkle, S. (2011). *Alone together: Why we expect more from technology and less from ourselves*. New York, NY: Basic Books.

Turner, J., Patrick, H., & Meyer, D. (2011). Engaging students in learning: A Special Issue dedicated to Jere Brophy. *Theory Into Practice, 50*.

Twenge, J. M., & Campbell, W. K. (2001). Age and birth cohort differences in self-esteem: A cross temporal meta-analysis. *Journal of Personality and Social Psychology Review, 5*, 321–344.

Uline, C. L., & Johnson, J. F. (2005). Closing the achievement gap: What will it take? Special Issue of *Theory Into Practice, 44*(1), Winter.

Umbreit, J. (1995). Functional analysis of disruptive behavior in an inclusive classroom. *Journal of Early Intervention, 20*(1), 18–29.

Unsworth, N., & Engle, R. W. (2005). Working memory capacity and fluid abilities: Examining the correlation between Operation Span and Raven. *Intelligence, 33*, 67–81.

Urdan, T. C., & Maehr, M. L. (1995). Beyond a two-goal theory of motivation and achievement: A case for social goals. *Review of Educational Research, 65*, 213–243.

U.S. Bureau of the Census. (2010a). *State and country quick facts*. Available online at: http://quickfacts.census.gov/qfd/states/00000.html

U.S. Bureau of the Census. (2010b). *Hispanic population of the United States: Projections*. Available online at: http://www.census.gov/population/www/socdemo/hispanic/hispanic_pop_presetation.html

U.S Bureau of the Census. (2011). *Children below poverty level by race and Hispanic origin*. Available online at: http://www.census.gov/compendia/statab/2011/tables/11s0711.pdf

U.S. Bureau of the Census. (2011). U.S. population projections 2010–2050. Available online at: http://www.census.gov/population/www/projections/summarytables.html.

U.S. Citizenship and Immigration Services. (2011). Home page. Available online at: http://www.uscis.gov/portal/site/uscis.

U.S. Department of Education. (2004). *26th Annual report to Congress on the implementation of the Individuals with Disabilities Act, 2005*. Washington DC: Office of Special Education and Rehabilitative Services.

U.S. Department of Education. (2007). *27th Annual report to Congress on the implementation of the Individuals with Disabilities Act, 2005*. Washington DC: Office of Special Education and Rehabilitative Services.

U.S.Department of Education. (2009, November). *Race to the Top Program: Executive summary*. U. S. Department of Education, Washington, D. C. Available online at http://www2.ed.gov/programs/racetothetop/executive-summary.pdf

U.S. Department of Education. (2010, March). *ESEA Blueprint for Reform*. Washington, DC: USDE, Office of Planning, Evaluation and Policy

Development. http://www2.ed.gov/programs/racetothetop/index.html

U.S. Department of Health and Human Services. (2007). *Frequently asked questions: Administration for Children and Families.* Available online at: http://www.acf.hhs.gov/acf_services.html#caan

Usher, E. L., & Pajares, F. (2009). Sources of self-efficacy in mathematics: A validation study. *Contemporary Educational Psychology, 34,* 89–101.

Uttal, D. H., Hand, L. L., & Newcombe, N. S. (2009, April). *Malleability of spatial cognition: Results of a meta-analysis.* Paper presented at the biennial meeting of the Society for Research in Child Development, Denver, CO.

Valentine, J. C., DuBois, D. L., & Cooper, H. (2004). The relations between self-beliefs and academic achievement: A systematic review. *Educational Psychologist, 39,* 111–133.

Valenzuela, A. (1999). *Subtractive schooling: U.S.–Mexican youth and the politics of caring.* Albany, NY: SUNY Press.

Valiente, C., Lemery-Chalfant, K., & Swansos, J. (2010). Prediction of kindergartners' academic achievement from their effortful control and emotionality: Evidence for direct and moderated relations. *Journal of Educational Psychology, 102,* 550–560.

van den Broek, P., Lorch, E. P., & Thurlow, R. (1996). Children's and adults' memory for television stories: The role of causal factors, story-grammar categories, and hierarchical level. *Child Development, 67,* 3010–3028.

van de Pol, J., Volman, M., & Beishuizen, J. (2010). Scaffolding in teacher–student interaction: A decade of research. *Educational Psychology Review, 22,* 271–296.

van der Mass, H. L. J., Dolan, C. V., Grasman, R. P. P. P., Wicherts, J. M., Huizenga, H. M., & Raijmakers, M. E. J. (2006). A dynamic model of general intelligence: The positive manifold of intelligence by mutualism. *Psychological Review, 113,* 842–861.

Van Der Veer, R. (2007). Vygotsky in context: 1900–1935. In H. Daniels, M. Cole, & J. V. Wertsch (Eds.), *The Cambridge companion to Vygotsky* (pp. 21–49). New York, NY: Cambridge University Press.

Van de Walle, J. A., Karp, K. S., & Bay-Williams, J. M. (2010). *Elementary and middle school mathematics: Teaching developmentally* (7th ed.). Boston, MA: Pearson Education, Inc.

van Gelderen, A., Schoonen, R., Stoel, R. D., de Glopper, K., & Hulstijn, J. (2007). Development of adolescent reading comprehension in language 1 and language 2: A longitudinal analysis of constituent components. *Journal of Educational Psychology, 99,* 477–491.

van Gog, T., Pass, F., & Sweller, J. (2010). Cognitive load theory: Advances in research on worked examples, animations, and cognitive load measurement. *Educational Psychology Review, 22,* 375–378.

van Kraayenoord, C. E., Rice, D., Carroll, A., Fritz, E., Dillon, L., & Hill, A. (2001). *Attention deficit hyperactivity disorder: Impact and implications for Queensland.* Queensland, Australia: Queensland Disability Services. Available online at: www.families.qld.gov.au

van Laar, C. (2000). The paradox of low academic achievement but high self-esteem in African American students: An attributional account. *Educational Psychology Review, 12,* 33–61.

Van Matre, J. C., Valentine, J. C., & Cooper, H. (2000). Effect of students' after-school activities on teachers' academic expectations. *Contemporary Educational Psychology, 25,* 167–183.

Van Merriënboer, J. J. G., & Sweller, J. (2005). Cognitive load and complex learning: Recent developments and future directions. *Educational Psychology Review, 17,* 147–177.

Van Meter, P. (2001). Drawing construction as a strategy for learning from text. *Journal of Educational Psychology, 93,* 129–140.

Van Meter, P., Yokoi, L., & Pressley, M. (1994). College students' theory of note-taking derived from their perceptions of note-taking. *Journal of Educational Psychology, 86,* 323–338.

Vandell, D. L. (2004). Early child care: The known and the unknown. *Merrill-Palmer Quarterly, 50,* 387–414.

Vandewater, E. A., Bickham, D. S., Lee, J. H., Cummings, H. M., Wartella, E. A., & Rideout, V. J. (2005). When the television is always on: Heavy television exposure and young children's development. *American Behavioral Scientist, 48,* 562–567.

Vansteenkiste, M., Lens, W., & Deci, E. L. (2006). Intrinsic versus extrinsic goal contents in self-determination theory: Another look at the quality of academic motivation. *Educational Psychologist, 41,* 19-31.

Vansteenkiste, M., Simons, J., Lens, W., Sheldon, K. M., & Deci, E. L. (2004). Motivating learning, performance, and persistence: The synergistic role of intrinsic goals and autonomy-support. *Journal of Personality and Social Psychology, 87,* 246–260.

Varma, S., McCandliss, B. D., & Schwartz, D. L. (2008). Scientific and pragmatic challenges for bridging education and neuroscience. *Educational Researcher, 37,* 140–152.

Vasquez, J. A. (1990). Teaching to the distinctive traits of minority students. *The Clearing House, 63,* 299–304.

Vaughn, S., Levy, S., Coleman, M., & Bos, C. S. (2002). Reading instruction for students with LD and EBD: A synthesis of observation studies. *Journal of Special Education, 36*(1), 2–13.

Vecchio, G. M., Gerbino, M., Pastorelli, C., Del Bove, G., & Caprara, G. V. (2007). Multi-faceted self-efficacy beliefs as predictors of life satisfaction in late adolescence. *Personality and Individual Differences, 43,* 1807–1818.

Veenman, S. (1984). Perceived problems of beginning teachers. *Review of Educational Research, 54,* 143–178.

Veenman, S. (1997). Combination classes revisited. *Educational Research and Evaluation, 65*(4), 319–381.

Vélez, C. E., Wolchik, S. A., Tein, J Y., & Sandler, I. (2011). Protecting children from the consequences of divorce: A longitudinal study of the effects of parenting on children's coping processes. *Child Development, 82,* 244–257. doi: 10.1111/j.1467-8624.2010.01553.x

Vera, A. H., & Simon, H. A. (1993). Situated action: A symbolic interpretation. *Cognitive Science, 17,* 7–48.

Verhallen, M. J. A. J., Bus, A. G., & de Jong, M. T. (2006). The promise of multimedia stories for kindergarten children at risk. *Journal of Educational Psychology, 98,* 410–419.

Verplaetse, L. S., & Migliacci, N. (2008). Inclusive pedagogy: An introduction. In L. S. Verplaetse & N. Migliacci (Eds.), *Inclusive pedagogy for English language learners: A handbook of research-informed practices* (pp. 3–13). New York, NY: Erlbaum.

Vispoel, W. P., & Austin, J. R. (1995). Success and failure in junior high school: A critical incident approach to understanding students' attributional beliefs. *American Educational Research Journal, 32,* 377–412.

Vogt, M. E., Echevarria, J, & Short, D. J. (2010). *The SIOP® Model for teaching English-language arts to English learners.* Boston, MA: Pearson.

Volkow, N. D., Wang, G. J., Newcorn, J., Fowler, J. S., Telang, F., Solanto, M. V., . . . Pradhan, K. (2007). Brain dopamine transporter levels in treatment and drug naïve adults with ADHD. *NeuroImage, 34,* 1182–1190.

von Glaserfeld, E. (1997). Amplification of a constructivist perspective. *Issues in Education: Contributions from Educational Psychology, 3,* 203–210.

Vroom, V. (1964). *Work and motivation.* New York, NY: Wiley.

Vygotsky, L. S. (1978). *Mind in society: The development of higher mental process.* Cambridge, MA: Harvard University Press.

Vygotsky, L. S. (1986). *Thought and language.* Cambridge, MA: MIT Press.

Vygotsky, L. S. (1987a). The genetic roots of thinking and speech. In R. W. Rieber & A. S. Carton (Eds.), *Problems of general psychology, Vol. 1. Collected works* (pp. 101–120). New York, NY: Plenum. (Work originally published in 1934.)

Vygotsky, L. S. (1987b). *Problems of general psychology.* New York, NY: Plenum.

Vygotsky, L. S. (1987c). Thought and word. In R.W. Rieber & A. S. Carton (Eds.), *Collected works of L. S. Vygotsky: Vol. 1. Problems of general psychology* (pp. 243–285). New York, NY: Plenum. (Work originally published in 1934.)

Vygotsky, L. S. (1993). *The collected works of L. S. Vygotsky: Vol. 2* (J. Knox & C. Stevens, Trans.). New York, NY: Plenum.

Vygotsky, L. S. (1997). *Educational psychology* (R. Silverman, Trans.). Boca Raton, FL: St. Lucie.

Wade, S. E., Schraw, G., Buxton, W. M., & Hayes, M. T. (1993). Seduction of the strategic reader: Effects of interest on strategies and recall. *Reading Research Quarterly, 28,* 3–24.

Waits, B. K., & Demana, F. (2000). Calculators in mathematics teaching and learning: Past, present, future. In M. J. Burke & F. R. Curcio (Eds.), *Learning mathematics for a new century: NCTM 2000 Yearbook* (pp. 51–66). Reston, VA: National Council of Teachers of Mathematics.

Walberg, H. J. (1990). Productive teaching and instruction: Assessing the knowledge base. *Phi Delta Kappan, 72,* 470–478.

Wald, J. (2001, August 29). The failure of zero tolerance. *Salon Magazine.* Available online at: http://www.salon.com/mwt/feature/2001/08/29/zero_tolerance/index.html?sid=1046257

Walker, J. E., Shea, T. M., & Bauer, A. M. (2004). *Behavior management: A practical approach for educators.* Upper Saddle River, NJ: Merrill/Prentice Hall.

Walker, L. J., & Pitts, R. C. (1998). Naturalistic conceptions of moral maturity. *Developmental Psychology, 34,* 403–419.

Walker, V. S. (1996). *Their highest potential.* Chapel Hill: University of North Carolina Press.

Walqui, A. (2008). The development of teacher expertise to work with adolescent English learners: A model and a few priorities. In L. S. Verplaetse & N. Migliacci (Eds.), *Inclusive pedagogy for English language learners: A handbook of research-informed practices* (pp. 103–125). New York, NY: Lawrence Erlbaum.

Wang, A. Y., & Thomas, M. H. (1995). Effects of keywords on long-term retention: Help or hindrance? *Journal of Educational Psychology, 87*, 468–475.

Wang, A. Y., Thomas, M. H., & Ouellette, J. A. (1992). Keyword mnemonic and retention of second-language vocabulary words. *Journal of Educational Psychology, 84*, 520–528.

Ward, L. M. (2004). Wading through the stereotypes: Positive and negative associations between media use and Black adolescents' conception of self. *Developmental Psychology, 40*, 284–294.

Warren, J. S., Bohanon-Edmonson, H. M., Turnbull, A. P., Sailor, W., Wickham, D., Griggs, P., & Beech, S. E. (2006). School-wide positive behavior support: Addressing behavior problems that impede student learning. *Educational Psychology Review, 18*, 187–198.

Waterhouse, L. (2006). Multiple intelligences, the Mozart effect, and emotional intelligence: A critical review. *Educational Psychologist, 41*, 207–225.

Watt, H. M. G., & Richardson, P. W. (2012). Teacher motivation and student achievement outcomes. In J. A. C. Hattie & E. M. Anderman (Eds.), *The international handbook of student achievement.* New York, NY: Routledge.

Waxman, S. R., & Lidz, J. L. (2006). Early word learning. In D. Kuhn & R. S. Siegler (Eds.), *Handbook of child psychology* (6th ed., Vol. 2: Cognition, perception, and language, pp. 299–335). New York, NY: Wiley.

Wayne, A. J., & Youngs, P. (2003). Teacher characteristics and student achievement gains: A review. *Review of Educational Research, 73*, 89–122.

Webb, N. M., Farivar, S. H., & Mastergeorge, A. M. (2002). Productive helping in cooperative groups. *Theory Into Practice, 41*, 13–20.

Webb, N. M., & Mastergeorge, A. M. (2003). The development of students' helping behavior and learning in peer-directed small groups. *Cognition and Instruction, 21*, 361–428.

Webb, N. M., & Palincsar, A. (1996). Group processes in the classroom. In D. C. Berliner & R. C. Calfee (Eds.), *Handbook of educational psychology* (pp. 841–876). New York, NY: Macmillan.

Wechsler, P. (2010, November 12). ADHD diagnoses soar in 4 years. *Columbus Dispatch*, Columbus, OH. Available online at: http://www.dispatch.com/content/stories/national_world/2010/11/12/adhd-diagnoses-soar-in-4-years.html.

Weil, E. (2008, March 2). Should boys and girls be taught separately? *The New York Times Magazine*, pp. 33–45+.

Weiner, B. (1986). *An attributional theory of motivation and emotion.* New York, NY: Springer.

Weiner, B. (1994a). Ability versus effort revisited: The moral determinants of achievement evaluation an achievement as a moral system. *Educational Psychologist, 29*, 163–172.

Weiner, B. (1994b). Integrating social and persons theories of achievement striving. *Review of Educational Research, 64*, 557–575.

Weiner, B. (2000). Interpersonal and intrapersonal theories of motivation from an attributional perspective. *Educational Psychology Review, 12*, 1–14.

Weiner, B. (2010). The development of an attribution-based theory of motivation: A history of ideas. *Educational Psychologist, 45*, 28–36.

Weinert, F. E., & Helmke, A. (1995). Learning from wise mother nature or big brother instructor: The wrong choice as seen from an educational perspective. *Educational Psychologist, 30*, 135–143.

Weinstein, C. S. (1977). Modifying student behavior in an open classroom through changes in the physical design. *American Educational Research Journal, 14*, 249–262.

Weinstein, C. S. (1999). Reflections on best practices and promising programs: Beyond assertive classroom discipline. In H. J. Freiberg (Ed.), *Beyond behaviorism: Changing the classroom management paradigm* (pp. 147–163). Boston, MA: Allyn & Bacon.

Weinstein, C. S., & Mignano, A. (2007). *Elementary classroom management: Lessons from research and practice* (4th ed.). New York, NY: McGraw-Hill.

Weinstein, C. S., & Novodvorsky, I. (2011). *Middle and secondary classroom management: Lessons from research and practice* (5th ed.). New York, NY: McGraw-Hill.

Weinstein, C. S., Romano, M. E., & Mignano, A. J. (2011). *Elementary classroom management: Lessons from research and practice* (5th ed.). New York, NY: McGraw-Hill.

Weinstein, R. S., Madison, S. M., & Kuklinski, M. R. (1995). Raising expectations in schools: Obstacles and opportunities for change. *American Educational Research Journal, 32*, 121–159.

Weisberg, R. W. (1993). *Creativity: Beyond the myth of genius.* New York, NY: W. H. Freeman.

Welsh, J. A., Nix, R. L., Blair, C., Bierman, K. L., & Nelson, K. E. (2010). The development of cognitive skills and gains in academic school readiness for children from low-income families. *Journal of Educational Psychology, 102*, 43–53.

Wenger, E. (1998). *Communities of practice: learning, meaning, and identity.* New York, NY: Cambridge University Press.

Wentzel, K. R. (1999). Social-motivational processes and interpersonal relations: Implications for understanding motivation in school. *Journal of Educational Psychology, 91*, 76–97.

Wentzel, K. R. (2002). Are effective teachers like good parents? Teaching styles and student adjustment in early adolescence. *Child Development, 73*, 287–301.

Wentzel, K. R., Barry, C. M., & Caldwell, K. A. (2004). Friendships in middle school: Influences on motivation and school adjustment. *Journal of Educational Psychology, 96*, 195–203.

Werts, M. G., Culatta, A., & Tompkins, J. R. (2007). *Fundamentals of special education: What every teacher should know* (3rd ed.). Columbus, OH: Pearson/Allyn & Bacon-Merrill.

Wertsch, J. V. (1991). *Voices of the mind: A sociocultural approach to mediated action.* Cambridge, MA: Harvard University Press.

Wertsch, J. V. (2007). Mediation. In H. Daniels, M. Cole, & J. V. Wertsch (Eds.), *The Cambridge companion to Vygotsky* (pp. 178–192). New York, NY: Cambridge University Press.

Wertsch, J. V., & Tulviste, P. (1992). L. S. Vygotsky and contemporary developmental psychology. *Developmental Psychology, 28*, 548–557.

Westberg, K. L., Archambault, F. X., Dodyns, S. M., & Slavin, T. J. (1993). The classroom practices observation study. *Journal of the Education of the Gifted, 16*(2), 120–146.

Westling, E., Andrews, J. A., Hampson, S. E., & Peterson, M. (2008). Pubertal timing and substance use: The effects of gender, parental monitoring and deviant peers. *Journal of Adolescent Health, 42*, 555–563.

Wheatley, K. F. (2002). The potential benefits of teacher efficacy doubts for educational reform. *Teaching and Teacher Education, 18*, 5–22.

Wheatley, K. F. (2005). The case for reconceptualizing teacher efficacy research. *Teaching and Teacher Education, 21*, 747–766.

Wheelock, A. (1992). *Crossing the tracks: How untracking can save America's schools.* New York, NY: The New Press.

Whitehead, A. N. (1929). *The aims of education.* New York, NY: Macmillan.

Whitehurst, G. J., Epstein, J. N., Angell, A. L., Payne, A. C., Crone, D. A., & Fischel, J. E. (1994). Outcomes of an emergent literacy program in headstart. *Journal of Educational Psychology, 86*, 542–555.

Whitehurst, G. J., & Lonigan, C. J. (1998). Child development and emergent literacy. *Child Development, 69*, 845–872.

Wigfield, A., Byrnes, J. P., & Eccles, J. S. (2006). Development during early and middle adolescence. In P. A. Alexander & P. H. Winne (Eds.), *Handbook of educational psychology* (2nd ed., pp. 87–113). Mahwah, NJ: Erlbaum.

Wigfield, A., & Eccles, J. (1989). Test anxiety in elementary and secondary school students. *Educational Psychologist, 24*, 159–183.

Wigfield, A., & Eccles, J. (2002). The development of competence beliefs, expectancies of success, and achievement values from childhood through adolescence. In A. Wigfield & J. Eccles (Eds.), *Development of achievement motivation* (pp. 91–120). San Diego, CA: Academic Press.

Wigfield, A., Eccles, J., MacIver, D., Rueman, D., & Midgley, C. (1991). Transitions at early adolescence: Changes in children's domain-specific self-perceptions and general self-esteem across the transition to junior high school. *Developmental Psychology, 27*, 552–565.

Wigfield, A., Eccles, J. S., & Pintrich, P. R. (1996). Development between the ages of 11 and 25. In D. Berliner & R. Calfee (Eds.), *Handbook of educational psychology* (pp. 148–185). New York, NY: Macmillan.

Wigfield, A., & Wentzel, K. R. (2007). Introduction to motivation at school: Interventions that work. *Educational Psychologist, 42*, 191–196.

Wiggins, G. (1989). Teaching to the authentic test. *Educational Leadership, 46*(7), 41–47.

Wiggins, G. (1991). Standards, not standardization: Evoking quality student work. *Educational Leadership, 48*(5), 18–25.

Willcutt, E. G., Pennington, B. F., Boada, R., Ogline, J. S., Tunick, R. A., Chhabildas, N. A., & Olson, R. K. (2001). A comparison of the cognitive deficits in reading disability and attention-deficit/hyperactivity disorder. *Journal of Abnormal Psychology, 110*, 157–172.

William, D. (2010) Standardized testing and school accountability. *Educational Psychologist, 45*, 107–122.

Williams, C., & Bybee J. (1994). What do children feel guilty about? Developmental and gender differences. *Developmental Psychology, 30*, 617–623.

Williams, T., & Williams, K. (2010). Self-efficacy and performance in mathematics: Reciprocal feterminism in 33 nations. *Journal of Educational Psychology, 102*, 453–466.

Willingham, D. T. (2004). Reframing the mind. *Education Next, 4*(3), 19–24.

Willis, J. (2007). Which brain research can educators trust? *Phi Delta Kappan, 88*, 697–699.

Willis, J. (2009). What brain research suggests for teaching reading strategies. *Educational Forum, 73,* 333–346.

Willoughby, T., Porter, L., Belsito, L., & Yearsley, T. (1999). Use of elaboration strategies by grades two, four, and six. *Elementary School Journal, 99,* 221–231.

Wilson, M. (2001). The case for sensorimotor coding in working memory. *Psychonomic Bulletin and Review, 8,* 44–57.

Wilson, M. (2002). Six views of embodied cognition. *Psychonomic Bulletin and Review, 9,* 625–636.

Wilson M., & Trainin, G. (2007). First-grade students' motivation and achievement for reading, writing, and spelling. *Reading Psychology, 28,* 257–282.

Windschitl, M. (2002). Framing constructivism in practice as the negotiation of dilemmas: An analysis of the conceptual, pedagogical, cultural, and political challenges facing teachers. *Review of Educational Research, 72,* 131–175.

Winett, R. A., & Winkler, R. C. (1972). Current behavior modification in the classroom: Be still, be quiet, be docile. *Journal of Applied Behavior Analysis, 15,* 499–504.

Wink, J., & Putney, L. (2002). *A vision of Vygotsky.* Boston, MA: Allyn & Bacon.

Winne, P. H. (1995). Inherent details in self-regulated learning. *Educational Psychologist, 30,* 173–188.

Winne, P. H. (2001). Self-regulated learning viewed from models of information processing. In B. J. Zimmerman & D. H. Schunk (Eds.), *Self-regulated learning and academic achievement: Theoretical perspectives* (2nd ed., pp. 153–189). Mahwah, NJ: Erlbaum.

Winne. P. H. (2011). A cognitive and metacognitive analysis of self-regulated learning. In B. Zimmerman & D. Schunk, (Eds.) *Handbook of self-regulation of learning and performance* (pp. 15–32). New York, NY: Routledge.

Winne, P. H., & Hadwin, A. F. (1998). Studying as self-regulated learning. In D. J. Hacker, J. Dunlosky, & A. C. Graesser (Eds.), *Metacognition in educational theory and practice* (pp. 277–304). Mahwah, NJ: Erlbaum.

Winne, P. H., & Perry, N. E. (2000). Measuring self-regulated learning. In P. Pintrich, M. Boekaerts, & M. Zeidner (Eds.), *Handbook of self-regulation* (pp. 531–566). Orlando, FL: Academic Press.

Winner, E. (2000). The origins and ends of giftedness. *American Psychologist, 55,* 159–169.

Winner, E. (2003). Musical giftedness. *Bulletin of Psychology and the Arts, 4,* 1, 2–5.

Winsler, A., Carlton, M. P., & Barry, M. J. (2000). Age-related changes in preschool children's systematic use of private speech in a natural setting. *Journal of Child Language, 27,* 665–687.

Winsler, A., & Naglieri, J. A. (2003). Overt and covert verbal problem-solving strategies: Developmental trends in use, awareness, and relations with task performance in children age 5 to 17. *Child Development, 74,* 659–678.

Winters, F. I., Greene, J. A., & Costich, C. M. (2008). Self-regulation of learning within computer-based learning environments: A critical analysis. *Educational Psychology Review* doi:10.1007/s10648-008-9080-9.

Wittrock, M. C. (1982, March). *Educational implications of recent research on learning and memory.* Paper presented at the annual meeting of the American Educational Research Association, New York.

Wittrock, M. C. (Ed.). (1986). *Handbook of research on teaching* (3rd ed.). New York, NY: Macmillan.

Wittrock, M. C. (1992). An empowering conception of educational psychology. *Educational Psychologist, 27,* 129–142.

Wittwer, J., & Renkl, A. (2010). How effective are instructional explanations in example-based learning? A meta-analytic review. *Educational Psychology Review, 22,* 393–409.

Wolf, M., Barzillai, M., Gottwald, S., Miller, L., Spencer, K., Norton, E. , . . . Morris, R. (2009). The RAVE-O intervention: Connecting neuroscience to the classroom. *Mind, Brain, and Education, 3,* 84–93.

Wolfe, P. (2010). *Brain matters: Translating research into classroom practice* (2nd ed.). Alexandria, VA: Association for Supervision and Curriculum Development.

Wong, K. F., & Xiao, Y. (2010). Diversity and difference: Identity Issues of Chinese heritage language learners from dialect backgrounds. *Heritage Language Journal, 7,* 153–187.

Wong, L. (1987). Reaction to research findings: Is the feeling of obviousness warranted? *Dissertation Abstracts International, 48/12,* 3709B (University Microfilms #DA 8801059).

Wood, D., Bruner, J., & Ross, S. (1976). The role of tutoring in problem solving. *British Journal of Psychology, 66,* 181–191.

Woods, B. S., & Murphy, P. K. (2002). Thickening the discussion: What can William James tell us about constructivism? *Educational Theory, 52,* 443–449.

Woodward, A., & Needham, A. (Eds.) (2009). *Learning and the infant mind.* New York, NY: Oxford University Press.

Woolfolk, A. E., & Brooks, D. (1983). Nonverbal communication in teaching. In E. Gordon (Ed.), *Review of research in education* (Vol. 10, pp. 103–150). Washington, DC: American Educational Research Association.

Woolfolk, A. E., & Brooks, D. (1985). The influence of teachers' nonverbal behaviors on students' perceptions and performance. *Elementary School Journal, 85,* 514–528.

Woolfolk, A. E., & Hoy, W. K. (1990). Prospective teachers' sense of efficacy and beliefs about control. *Journal of Educational Psychology, 82,* 81–91.

Woolfolk, A., E. & Perry, N. E. (2012). *Child development.* Boston Allyn & Bacon/Pearson.

Woolfolk, A. E., Perry, N., & Winne, P. (2006). *Educational psychology: Third Canadian edition* (3rd ed.). Toronto, CA: Pearson.

Woolfolk, A. E., Rosoff, B., & Hoy, W. K. (1990). Teachers' sense of efficacy and their beliefs about managing students. *Teaching and Teacher Education, 6,* 137–148.

Woolfolk Hoy, A., & Burke-Spero, R. (2005). Changes in teacher efficacy during the early years of teaching: A comparison of four measures. *Teaching and Teacher Education, 21,* 343–356.

Woolfolk Hoy, A., Davis, H., & Pape, S. (2006). Teachers' knowledge, beliefs, and thinking. In P. A. Alexander & P. H, Winne (Eds.), *Handbook of educational psychology* (2nd ed., pp. 715–737). Mahwah, NJ: Erlbaum.

Woolfolk Hoy, A., Demerath, P., & Pape, S. (2002). Teaching adolescents: Engaging developing selves. In T. Urdan & F. Pajares (Eds.), *Adolescence and education* (pp. 119–169, Volume I). Greenwich, CT: Information Age Publishing.

Woolfolk Hoy, A., Hoy, W. K., & Davis, H. (2009). Teachers' self-efficacy beliefs. In K. Wentzel & A. Wigfield (Eds.), *Handbook of motivation in school.* Mahwah, NJ: Erlbaum.

Woolfolk Hoy, A., & Murphy, P. K. (2001). Teaching educational psychology to the implicit mind. In R. Sternberg & B. Torff (Eds.), *Understanding and teaching the implicit mind* (pp. 145–185). Mahwah, NJ: Erlbaum.

Woolfolk Hoy, A., Pape, S., & Davis, H. (2006). Teachers' knowledge, beliefs, and thinking. In P. A. Alexander & P. H, Winne (Eds.), *Handbook of educational psychology* (2nd ed.). Mahwah, NJ: Erlbaum.

Woolfolk Hoy, A., & Tschannen-Moran. M. (1999). Implications of cognitive approaches to peer learning for teacher education. In A. O'Donnell & A. King (Eds.), *Cognitive perspectives on peer learning* (pp. 257–284). Mahwah, NJ: Erlbaum.

Woolfolk Hoy, A., & Weinstein, C. S. (2006). Students' and teachers' perspectives about classroom management. In C. Evertson & C. S. Weinstein (Eds.), *Handbook for classroom management: Research, practice, and contemporary issues.* Mahwah, NJ: Erlbaum.

Wout, D., Dasco, H., Jackson, J., & Spencer, S. (2008). The many faces of stereotype threat: Group- and self-threat. *Journal of Experimental Social Psychology, 44,* 792–799.

Wu, W., West, S. G., & Hughes, J. N. (2010). Effect of grade retention in first grade on psychosocial outcomes. *Journal of Educational Psychology, 102,* 135–152.

Yang, L., Shuai, L., Du, Q., et al. (2009). Atomoxetine and executive functioning in Chinese ADHD children. From Childhood to Adult Disease. May 21–24, 2009, Vienna, Austria. *Attention Deficit and Hyperactivity Disorders, 1,* 135.

Yarhouse, M. A. (2001). Sexual identity development: The influence of valuative frameworks on identity synthesis. *Psychotherapy, 38*(3), 331–341.

Yell, M. L. (1990). The use of corporal punishment, suspension, expulsion, and timeout with behaviorally disordered students in public schools: Legal considerations. *Behavioral Disorders, 15,* 100–109.

Yerkes, R. M., & Dodson, J. D. (1908). The relation of strength of stimulus to rapidity of habit formation. *Journal of Comparative Neurology, 18,* 459–482.

Yough, M. (2010, August). *An intervention: Teaching candidates' beliefs and linguistic minority students.* Paper presented at the American Psychological Association Annual Convention, San Diego, CA.

Younger, M. R., & Warrington, M. (2006). Would Harry and Hermione have done better in single-sex teaching in coeducational secondary schools in the United Kingdom? *American Educational Research Journal, 43,* 579–620.

Youniss, J., & Yates, M. (1997). *Community service and social responsibility in youth.* Chicago, IL: University of Chicago Press.

Zeidner, M. (1995). Adaptive coping with test situations. *Educational Psychologist, 30,* 123–134.

Zeidner, M. (1998). *Test anxiety: The state of the art.* New York, NY: Plenum.

Zelli, A., Dodge, K. A., Lochman, J. E., & Laird, R. D. (1999). The distinction between beliefs legitimizing aggression and deviant processing of social cues: Testing measurement validity and the hypothesis that biased processing mediates the effects of beliefs on aggression. *Journal of Personality and Social Psychology, 77,* 150–166.

Zhang, L., & Sternberg, R. J. (2005). The threefold model of intellectual styles. *Educational Psychology Review, 17,* 1–53.

Zhou, Z., Peverly, S. T., Beohm, A. E., & Chongde, L. (2001). American and Chinese children's understanding of distance, time, and speed interrelations. *Cognitive Development, 15,* 215–240.

Zimmerman, B. (2011). Motivational sources and outcomes of self-regulated learning and performance. In B. Zimmerman & D. Schunk, (Eds.), *Handbook of self-regulation of learning and performance* (pp. 49–64). New York, NY: Routledge.

Zimmerman, B. J., & Schunk, D. H. (Eds.). (2001). *Self-regulated learning and academic achievement: Theoretical perspectives* (2nd ed.). Mahwah, NJ: Erlbaum.

Zimmerman, B. J., & Schunk, D. H. (2004). Self-regulating intellectual processes and outcomes: A social cognitive perspective. In D. Y. Dao & R. J. Sternberg (Eds.), *Motivation, emotion, and cognition: Integrative perspectives on intellectual functioning and development* (pp. 323–350). Mahwah, NJ: Erlbaum.

Zimmerman, B., & Schunk, D. (Eds.). (2011). *Handbook of self-regulation of learning and performance.* New York, NY: Routledge.

NAME INDEX

SUBJECT INDEX

Photo Credits

FUNDAMENTALS
OF MANAGEMENT

ESSENTIAL CONCEPTS AND APPLICATIONS

FUNDAMENTALS OF MANAGEMENT 8e

ESSENTIAL CONCEPTS AND APPLICATIONS

STEPHEN P. ROBBINS

San Diego State University

DAVID A. DECENZO

Coastal Carolina University

MARY COULTER

Missouri State University

PEARSON

Boston   Columbus   Indianapolis   New York   San Francisco   Upper Saddle River
Amsterdam   Cape Town   Dubai   London   Madrid   Milan   Munich   Paris   Montréal   Toronto
Delhi   Mexico City   Sao Paulo   Sydney   Hong Kong   Seoul   Singapore   Taipei   Tokyo

Editorial Director: Sally Yagan
Senior Acquisitions Editor: Kim Norbuta
Editorial Project Manager: Claudia Fernandes
Director of Marketing: Maggie Moylan
Senior Marketing Manager: Nikki Ayana Jones
Marketing Assistant: Ian Gold
Senior Managing Editor: Judy Leale
Production Project Manager: Kelly Warsak
Senior Operations Supervisor: Arnold Vila
Operations Specialist: Cathleen Petersen
Creative Director: Blair Brown
Senior Art Director: Kenny Beck
Text Designer: Michael Fruhbeis
Cover Designer: Michael Fruhbeis
Cover Art: LCI Design
Manager, Rights and Permissions: Hessa Albader
Medial Project Manager, Production: Lisa Rinaldi
Senior Media Project Manager: Denise Vaughn
Full-Service Project Management: Sharon Anderson/BookMasters, Inc.
Composition: Integra Software Services
Printer/Binder: Courier/Kendallville
Cover Printer: Lehigh-Phoenix Color
Text Font: 10/12 Times

Credits and acknowledgments borrowed from other sources and reproduced, with permission, in this textbook appear on appropriate page within text.

Microsoft® and Windows® are registered trademarks of the Microsoft Corporation in the U.S.A. and other countries. Screen shots and icons reprinted with permission from the Microsoft Corporation. This book is not sponsored or endorsed by or affiliated with the Microsoft Corporation.

Many of the designations by manufacturers and seller to distinguish their products are claimed as trademarks. Where those designations appear in this book, and the publisher was aware of a trademark claim, the designations have been printed in initial caps or all caps.

Library of Congress Cataloging-in-Publication Data

Robbins, Stephen P.,
  Fundamentals of management: essential concepts and applications / Stephen P. Robbins,
David A. DeCenzo, Mary Coulter. — 8th ed.
    p. cm.
  Includes bibliographical references and index.
  ISBN 978-0-13-262053-6
  1. Management.   I. DeCenzo, David A.   II. Coulter, Mary K.   III. Title.
HD31.R5643 2013
658—dc23

2011043635

10 9 8 7 6 5 4 3 2 1

ISBN 10:   0-13-262053-7
ISBN 13: 978-0-13-262053-6

To my wife, Laura

Steve

....

To my family who continue to help me understand what life is about, who are there through thick and thin, and who demonstrate what is good about people today. To Terri, Mark, Meredith, Gabriella, and Natalie, thank you for making me the person I am today.

Dave

....

To Brooklynn...my sweet baby girl!

Mary

Brief Contents

Contents

A Short Note to Students

Get Experienced!

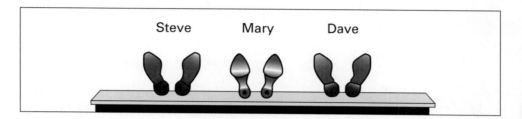

Steve   Mary   Dave

While we have your "first-page" attention, we want to ask you a few important questions.

1. Did you ever wish you could experience a course in a way that best suits your learning style and your schedule?
2. Wouldn't it be nice to find out exactly what you know or don't know?
3. How would you like to create your own study plan, one that lets you monitor your own learning progress, where—at a glance—you could see exactly which topics you need to review?
4. Did you ever wish that you could have this study plan linked to a variety of interactive content to help you learn the material?
5. What about having it all online 24/7?

If you answered *Yes* to any of the above, then **MyManagementLab**, the online homework tool that is available for this book, is for you. It was built with your course and your unique learning style in mind. No complicated registration, no complicated interface, just a straightforward, read it, learn it, and experience it.

Go ahead. Get experienced.

Good luck this semester and we hope you enjoy reading this book as much as we did writing it for you.

Steve Robbins   Mary Coulter   Dave De Cenzo

Preface

Welcome to the eighth edition of *Fundamentals of Management!* A lot has changed in the world since *FOM* was first published in 1994. However, we haven't changed our commitment to providing you with the most engaging and up-to-date introduction to management paperback on the market. And how do we do this? By covering the essential concepts of management; providing a sound foundation for understanding the key issues; offering a strong, practical focus, including the latest research; and doing these with a writing style that you and your students will find interesting and straightforward.

This book continues the exciting design introduced in the last edition. We love the way it looks and the way management concepts are presented! And we hope you do, too! It's a self-contained learning package. In addition to the end-of-chapter summaries and review questions, we've organized all the chapter self-assessments, skills modules, hands-on manager's inbox exercises, and case applications into an easy-to-find and easy-to-use section at the back of the book. In addition, the text is supported by the most comprehensive Web site and supplement package, although your students will find the essential elements they need to understand and apply management concepts within the text itself. You have the choice about how best to use the materials: text only, online only, or text and online. It's your decision!

What Key Changes Have We Made in the Eighth Edition?

You might not think that there could be too much new to put in a book . . . especially an eighth edition one! But that's the great thing about a book that discusses managers and management! It's always easy to find new material just by paying attention to what's happening in the news! New issues and ideas are always confronting managers.

We also took a major step forward by adding a complete, self-contained section on developing management skills. It's one thing to *know* something. It's another to be able to *use* that knowledge. The skill-building exercises included in the *Your Turn to Be the Manager* section at the end of this book have been added to help you apply and use management concepts. The 18 skills selected were chosen because of their relevance to developing management competence and their linkage to one or more of the topic areas in this book.

For each of these 18 skills, we provide the following: (1) a self-assessment test, (2) a brief interpretation of what the self-assessment results mean, (3) a review of basic skill concepts and specific behaviors associated with developing competence in the skill, (4) a short, in-class application designed to provide you with an opportunity to practice the behaviors associated with the skill, and (5) several reinforcement activities to give you additional opportunities to practice and learn the behaviors associated with the skill.

In addition to this comprehensive skills material, take a look at some of the other new "things" we've included in this book:

- A new chapter on integrative managerial issues
- *Your Turn to Be a Manager* section at the end of the book, which includes by chapter a self-contained self-assessment/skills/skills practice module, a manager's in-box exercise, and a case application
- Quantitative Decision-Making Aids module

In addition, here is a chapter-by-chapter list of the topic additions and changes in the eighth edition:

Chapter 1—Managers and Management

- New chapter opener (Symantec)
- New material on managerial roles
- New material on managerial competencies
- New examples
- New Right or Wrong ethics box (Derek Jeter)
- New Technology and the Manager's Job box (managing robots)
- New statistics in And the Survey Says box
- Added "Think About" questions to boxes
- New "Your Turn to Be the Manager" section with skills assessment and practice, experiential exercise, and case application
- 37 percent of chapter endnotes include 2009–2011 references

Chapter 2—The Management Environment

- New chapter opener (Zappos)
- New material on external environment
- Updated information on economic component of external environment
- Added material on omnipotent and symbolic views of management
- Added material on demographics component of external environment
- Added material on how external environment affects managers (jobs and unemployment, environmental uncertainty, and stakeholder relationships)
- Moved organizational culture material to this chapter
- Added material on how culture affects managers
- New examples
- Updated Right or Wrong ethics box (Steve Jobs, Apple, and medical leave)
- New From the Past to the Present box
- New statistics in the And the Survey Says box
- Added "Think About" questions to boxes
- New "Your Turn to Be the Manager" section with skills assessment and practice, experiential exercise, and case application
- 50 percent of chapter endnotes include 2010–2011 references

Chapter 3—Integrative Managerial Issues

- New chapter opener (Deutsche Telecom)
- Rearranged material in social responsibility section
- New material on how SR affects a company's financial performance
- New material on sustainability
- Included ethics material and discussion of three views of ethics in a separate section
- Added discussions of ethical leadership and ethics training
- Included diversity material in separate section
- Added material on different types of workforce diversity
- New examples

- New Right or Wrong box (McDonald's and its targeted Web sites)
- New statistics in the And the Survey Says box
- Added "Think About" questions to boxes
- New "Your Turn to Be the Manager" section with skills assessment and practice, experiential exercise, and case application
- 29 percent of chapter endnotes include 2010–2011 references

Chapter 4—Foundations of Decision Making

- New chapter opener (NASA)
- New examples
- New Right or Wrong box (MTV and its new show *Skins*)
- Added "Think About" questions to boxes
- New "Your Turn to Be the Manager" section with skills assessment and practice, experiential exercise, and case application
- 21 percent of chapter endnotes include 2010–2011 references

Chapter 5—Foundations of Planning

- New chapter opener (Flip video camera and Cisco Systems)
- New examples
- New Right or Wrong box (sobriety checkpoint smartphone app)
- Added "Think About" questions to boxes
- New "Your Turn to Be the Manager" section with skills assessment and practice, experiential exercise, and case application
- 25 percent of chapter endnotes include 2010–2011 references

Chapter 6—Organizational Structure and Design

- New chapter opener ("volunteer" workers and Verizon)
- New examples
- New section on flexible work arrangements
- New Right or Wrong box (ethical hacking of Apple iPad)
- Added "Think About" questions to boxes
- New "Your Turn to Be the Manager" section with skills assessment and practice, experiential exercise, and case application
- 16 percent of chapter endnotes include 2010–2011 references

Chapter 7—Managing Human Resources

- New chapter opener (UPS and driver training)
- New examples and updated statistics
- New Right or Wrong box (medical marijuana use in workplaces)
- Added "Think About" questions to boxes
- New "Your Turn to Be the Manager" section with skills assessment and practice, experiential exercise, and case application
- 28 percent of chapter endnotes include 2010–2011 references

Chapter 8—Managing Change and Innovation

- New chapter opener (France Telecom and employee suicides)
- New examples and updated statistics
- Updated Right or Wrong box (organizational stress programs)
- Added "Think About" questions to boxes
- New "Your Turn to Be the Manager" section with skills assessment and practice, experiential exercise, and case application
- 26 percent of chapter endnotes include 2010–2011 references

Chapter 9—Foundations of Individual Behavior

- New chapter opener (HCL Technologies)
- New examples and updated statistics
- Updated Right or Wrong box (employees trying to look good)
- Added "Think About" questions to boxes
- New "Your Turn to Be the Manager" section with skills assessment and practice, experiential exercise, and case application
- 38 percent of chapter endnotes include 2010–2011 references

Chapter 10—Understanding Groups and Managing Work Teams

- New chapter opener (Intel's Israel Development Center)
- New examples and updated statistics
- New Right or Wrong box (team coworkers sharing too much personal information)
- Added "Think About" questions to boxes
- New "Your Turn to Be the Manager" section with skills assessment and practice, experiential exercise, and case application
- 29 percent of chapter endnotes include 2010–2011 references

Chapter 11—Motivating and Rewarding Employees

- New chapter opener (Google)
- New examples and updated statistics
- Added new material on motivating employees during rough economic conditions
- New Right or Wrong box (Borders paying bonuses to managers)
- Added "Think About" questions to boxes

- New "Your Turn to Be the Manager" section with skills assessment and practice, experiential exercise, and case application
- 25 percent of chapter endnotes include 2010–2011 references

Chapter 12—Leadership and Trust

- New chapter opener (Navy commander)
- New examples and updated statistics
- Added new material on leader-member exchange (LMX) theory
- Added "Think About" questions to boxes
- New "Your Turn to Be the Manager" section with skills assessment and practice, experiential exercise, and case application
- 25 percent of chapter endnotes include 2010–2011 references

Chapter 13—Managing Communication and Information

- New chapter opener (Best Buy)
- New examples and updated statistics
- Added new material on contemporary issues in communication
- New Right or Wrong box (office/workplace gossip)
- Added "Think About" questions to boxes
- New "Your Turn to Be the Manager" section with skills assessment and practice, experiential exercise, and case application
- 19 percent of chapter endnotes include 2010–2011 references

Chapter 14—Foundations of Control

- New chapter opener (BP's Deepwater Horizon)
- New examples and updated statistics
- Added "Think About" questions to boxes
- New "Your Turn to Be the Manager" section with skills assessment and practice, experiential exercise, and case application
- 38 percent of chapter endnotes include 2010–2011 references

Chapter 15—Operations Management

- New chapter opener (Starbucks)
- New examples and updated statistics
- New Right or Wrong box (reserved parking spaces)
- Added "Think About" questions to boxes
- New "Your Turn to Be the Manager" section with skills assessment and practice, experiential exercise, and case application
- 19 percent of chapter endnotes include 2010–2011 references

Instructor Supplements

At the Instructor Resource Center, www.pearsonhighered.com/irc, instructors can access a variety of print, digital, and presentation resources available with this text in downloadable format. Registration is simple and gives you immediate access to new titles and new editions. As a registered faculty member, you can download resource files and receive immediate access to and instructions for installing course management content on your campus server.

In case you ever need assistance, our dedicated technical support team is ready to help with the media supplements that accompany this text. Visit http://247.pearsoned.com for answers to frequently asked questions and toll-free user support phone numbers.

The following supplements are available for download to adopting instructors:

- Instructor's Resource Manual
- Test Bank
- TestGen® Computerized Test Bank (test-generating program)
- PowerPoint Presentations

VIDEOS ON DVD. Video segments that illustrate the most pertinent topics in management today and highlight relevant issues that demonstrate how people lead, manage, and work effectively. Contact your Pearson representative for the DVD.

AACSB Learning Standards Tags in the Test Item File

WHAT IS THE AACSB? AACSB is a not-for-profit corporation of educational institutions, corporations, and other organizations devoted to the promotion and improvement of higher education in business administration and accounting. A collegiate institution offering degrees in business administration or accounting can volunteer for AACSB accreditation review. The AACSB makes initial accreditation decisions and conducts periodic reviews to promote continuous quality improvement in management education. Pearson Education is a proud member of the AACSB and is pleased to help you apply AACSB Learning Standards.

WHAT ARE AACSB LEARNING STANDARDS? One of the criteria for AACSB accreditation is the quality of the curricula. Although no specific courses are required, the AACSB expects a curriculum to include learning experiences in the following categories:

- Communication abilities
- Ethical understanding and reasoning abilities
- Analytic skills
- Use of information technology
- Dynamics of the global economy
- Multicultural and diversity understanding
- Reflective thinking skills

These seven categories are AACSB Learning Standards. Questions that test skills relevant to those standards are tagged with the appropriate standard. For example, a question testing the moral questions associated with externalities would receive the ethical understanding and reasoning abilities tag.

HOW CAN I USE THESE TAGS? Tagged questions help you measure whether students are grasping the course content that aligns with the AACSB categories. In addition, the tagged questions may help to identify potential applications of these skills. This, in turn, may suggest enrichment activities or other educational experiences to help students achieve these goals.

Student Supplements

CourseSmart eTextbook

CourseSmart eTextbooks were developed for students looking to save on required or recommended textbooks. Students simply select their eText by title or author and purchase immediate access to the content for the duration of the course using any major credit card. With a CourseSmart eText, students can search for specific keywords or page numbers, take notes online, print out reading assignments that incorporate lecture notes, and bookmark important passages for later review. For more information or to purchase a CourseSmart eTextbook, visit www.coursesmart.com.

MyManagementLab

MyManagementLab (www.mymanagementlab.com) is an easy-to-use online tool that personalizes course content and provides robust assessment and reporting to measure individual and class performance. All of the resources that students need for course success are in one place—flexible and easily adapted for your students' course experience.

Self-Assessment Library (S.A.L.)

If you are interested in additional self-assessments for your students, this valuable tool includes 67 individual self-assessment exercises that allow students to assess their know-ledge, beliefs, feelings, and actions in regard to a wide range of personal skills, abilities, and interests. Provided scoring keys allow for immediate, individual analysis. S.A.L. is available as a printed workbook, a CD-ROM, and by an access code, so students have a choice of how they want to complete the assessments. Contact your Pearson representative to have S.A.L. packaged with this textbook—S.A.L. ISBN 0-13-608376-5.

Acknowledgments

Writing and publishing a textbook requires the talents of a number of people whose names never appear on the cover. We'd like to recognize and thank a phenomenal team of talented people who provided their skills and abilities in making this book a reality.

This team includes: Kim Norbuta, our senior acquisitions editor; Kelly Warsak, our senior production project manager; Nikki Jones, our senior marketing manager; Claudia Fernandes, our senior editorial project manager; Sally Yagan, our editorial director; and Nancy Moudry, our highly talented and gifted photo researcher.

We also want to thank our reviewers—past and present—for the insights they have provided us:

David Adams, *Manhattanville College*
Lorraine P. Anderson, *Marshall University*
Maria Aria, *Camden Community College*
Marcia Marie Bear, *University of Tampa*
Barbara Ann Boyington, *Brookdale Community College*
Reginald Bruce, *University of Louisville*
Elena Capella, *University of San Francisco*
James Carlson, *Manatee Community College*
Pam Carstens, *Coe College*
Casey Cegielski, *Auburn University*
Michael Cicero, *Highline Community College*
Evelyn Delanee, *Daytona Beach Community College*
Kathleen DeNisco, *Erie Community College, South Campus*
Jack Dilbeck, *Ivy Tech State College*
Fred J. Dorn, *University of Mississippi*
Myra Ellen Edelstein, *Salve Regina University*
Deborah Gilliard, *Metropolitan State College, Denver*
Robert Girling, *Sonoma State University*
Patricia Green, *Nassau Community College*
Gary Greene, *Manatee Community College, Venice Campus*
Kenneth Gross, *The University of Oklahoma*
Aaron Hines, *SUNY New Paltz*

Edward A. Johnson, *University of North Florida*
Kim Lukaszewski, *SUNY New Paltz*
Brian Maruffi, *Fordham University*
Mantha Vlahos Mehallis, *Florida Atlantic University*
Christine Miller, *Tennessee Technological University*
Diane Minger, *Cedar Valley College*
James H. Moore, *Arizona State University*
Francine Newth, *Providence College*
Leroy Plumlee, *Western Washington University*
Pollis Robertson, *Kellogg Community College*
Cynthia Ruszkowski, *Illinois State University*
Thomas J. Shaughnessy, *Illinois Central College*
Andrea Smith-Hunter, *Siena College*
Martha Spears, *Winthrop University*
Jeff Stauffer, *Ventura College*
Kenneth R. Tillery, *Middle Tennessee State University*
Robert Trumble, *Virginia Commonwealth University*
Philip Varca, *University of Wyoming*
Margaret Viets, *University of Vermont*
Lucia Worthington, *University of Maryland University College*
Seokhwa Yun, *Montclair State University*

Thank You!

Steve, Dave, and I would like to thank you for considering and choosing our book for your management course. All of us have several years of teaching under our belt, and we know how challenging yet rewarding it can be. Our goal is to provide you with the best resources available to help you excel in the classroom!

About the Authors

STEPHEN P. ROBBINS received his Ph.D. from the University of Arizona. He previously worked for the Shell Oil Company and Reynolds Metals Company and has taught at the University of Nebraska at Omaha, Concordia University in Montreal, the University of Baltimore, Southern Illinois University at Edwardsville, and San Diego State University. He is currently professor emeritus in management at San Diego State.

Dr. Robbins's research interests have focused on conflict, power, and politics in organizations, behavioral decision making, and the development of effective interpersonal skills. His articles on these and other topics have appeared in such journals as *Business Horizons*, the *California Management Review, Business and Economic Perspectives, International Management, Management Review, Canadian Personnel and Industrial Relations*, and *The Journal of Management Education*.

Dr. Robbins is the world's best-selling textbook author in the areas of management and organizational behavior. His books have sold more than 5 million copies and have been translated into 20 languages. His books are currently used at more than 1,500 U.S. colleges and universities, as well as hundreds of schools throughout Canada, Latin America, Australia, New Zealand, Asia, and Europe.

Dr. Robbins also participates in masters track competition. Since turning 50 in 1993, he's won 23 national championships and 14 world titles. He was inducted into the U.S. Masters Track & Field Hall of Fame in 2005 and is currently the world record holder at 100m and 200m for men 65 and over.

DAVID A. DECENZO (Ph.D., West Virginia University) is president of Coastal Carolina University in Conway, South Carolina. In his capacity as president, Dr. DeCenzo is responsible for the overall vision and leadership of the university. He has been at Coastal since 2002 when he took over leadership of the E. Craig Wall Sr. College of Business. Since then, the college established an economics major and developed an MBA program. During that period, student enrollment and faculty positions nearly doubled. The college also established significant internship opportunities locally, nationally, and internationally in major *Fortune* 100 companies. As provost, Dr. DeCenzo worked with faculty leadership to pass a revised general education core curriculum as well as institute a minimum salary level for the university's faculty members. Before joining the Coastal faculty in 2002, he served as director of partnership development in the College of Business and Economics at Towson University in Maryland. He is an experienced industry consultant, corporate trainer, and public speaker. Dr. DeCenzo is the author of numerous textbooks that are used widely at colleges and universities throughout the United States and the world.

Dr. DeCenzo and his wife, Terri, have four children and reside in Pawleys Island, South Carolina.

MARY COULTER (Ph.D., University of Arkansas) held different jobs including high school teacher, legal assistant, and city government program planner before completing her graduate work. She has taught at Drury University, the University of Arkansas, Trinity University, and Missouri State University. She is currently professor emeritus of management at Missouri State University. Dr. Coulter's research interests were focused on competitive strategies for not-for-profit arts organizations and the use of new media in the educational process. Her research on these and other topics has appeared in such journals as *International Journal of Business Disciplines, Journal of Business Strategies, Journal of Business Research, Journal of Nonprofit and Public Sector Marketing,* and *Case Research Journal*. In additional to *Fundamentals of Management*, Dr. Coulter has published other books with Prentice Hall including *Management* (with Stephen P. Robbins), *Strategic Management in Action,* and *Entrepreneurship in Action*.

When she's not busy writing, Dr. Coulter enjoys puttering around in her flower gardens, trying new recipes, reading all different types of books, and enjoying many different activities with Ron, Sarah and James, Katie and Matt, and especially with her new granddaughter, Brooklynn. Love ya' my sweet baby girl!

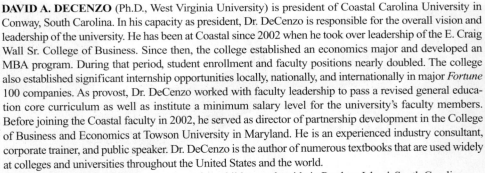

CHAPTER
1

Managers
and
Management

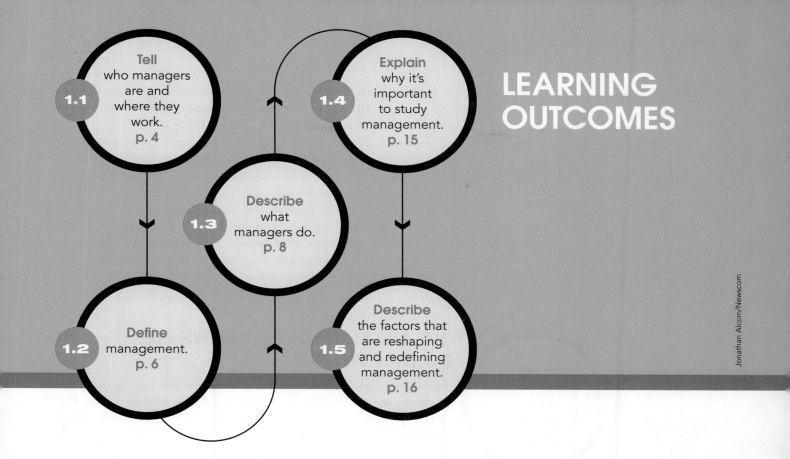

1.1 Tell who managers are and where they work. p. 4

1.3 Describe what managers do. p. 8

1.4 Explain why it's important to study management. p. 15

1.2 Define management. p. 6

1.5 Describe the factors that are reshaping and redefining management. p. 16

Jonathan Alcorn/Newscom

Saving the World

"Imagine what life would be like if your product were never finished, if your work were never done, if your market shifted 30 times a day."[1] Sounds pretty crazy, doesn't it? However, the computer-virus hunters at Symantec Corporation don't have to imagine . . . that's the reality of their daily work. At the company's well-obscured Dublin facility (one of three around the globe), operations manager Patrick Fitzgerald must keep his engineers and researchers focused 24/7 on identifying and combating what the bad guys are throwing out there. Right now, they're trying to stay ahead of the biggest virus threat, Stuxnet, which targets computer systems running the environmental controls in industrial facilities, such as temperature in power plants, pressure in pipelines, automated timing, and so forth. The consequences of someone intent on doing evil getting control over such critical functions could be disastrous. That's why the virus hunters' work is never done. And it's why those who manage the virus hunters have such a challenging job.

Symantec's Patrick Fitzgerald seems to be a good example of a successful manager—that is, a manager successfully guiding employees as they do their work—in today's world. The key word here is example. There's no one universal model of what a successful manager is. Managers today can be under age 18 or over age 80. They may be women as well as men, and they can be found in all industries and in all countries. They manage small businesses, large corporations, government agencies, hospitals, museums, schools, and not-for-profit enterprises. Some hold top-level management jobs while others are middle managers or first-line supervisors.

Although most managers don't deal with employees who could, indeed, be saving the world, all managers have important jobs to do. This book is about the work they do. In this chapter, we introduce you to managers and management: who they are, where they work, what management is, what they do, and why you should spend your time studying management. Finally, we'll wrap up the chapter by looking at some factors that are reshaping and redefining management.

1.1 Tell who managers are and where they work.

WHO ARE MANAGERS AND WHERE DO THEY WORK?

Managers work in organizations. So before we can identify who managers are and what they do, we need to define what an **organization** is: a deliberate arrangement of people brought together to accomplish some specific purpose. Your college or university is an organization. So are the United Way, your neighborhood convenience store, the Dallas Cowboys football team, fraternities and sororities, the Cleveland Clinic, and global companies such as Nestlé, Nokia, and Nissan. These organizations share three common characteristics. (See Exhibit 1–1.)

What Three Characteristics Do All Organizations Share?

The first characteristic of an organization is that it has a distinct purpose, which is typically expressed in terms of a goal or set of goals. For example, Bob Iger, Disney's president and CEO, has said his company's goal is to "focus on what creates the most value for our shareholders by delivering high-quality creative content and experiences, balancing respect for our legacy with the demand to be innovative, and maintaining the integrity of our people and products."[2] That purpose or goal can only be achieved with people, which is the second common characteristic of organizations. An organization's people make decisions and engage in work activities to make the goal(s) a reality. Finally, the third characteristic is that all organizations develop a deliberate and systematic structure that defines and limits the behavior of its members. Within that structure, rules and regulations might guide what people can or cannot do, some members will

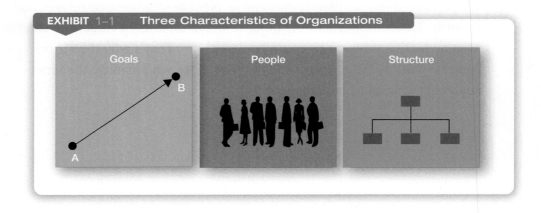

EXHIBIT 1–1 **Three Characteristics of Organizations**

Goals | People | Structure

supervise other members, work teams might be formed, or job descriptions might be created so organizational members know what they're supposed to do.

How Are Managers Different from Nonmanagerial Employees?

Although managers work in organizations, not everyone who works in an organization is a manager. For simplicity's sake, we'll divide organizational members into two categories: nonmanagerial employees and managers. **Nonmanagerial employees** are people who work directly on a job or task and have no responsibility for overseeing the work of others. The employees who ring up your sale at Home Depot, make your burrito at Chipotle, or process your course registration in your college's registrar's office are all nonmanagerial employees. These nonmanagerial employees may be referred to by names such as associates, team members, contributors, or even employee partners. **Managers**, on the other hand, are individuals in an organization who direct and oversee the activities of other people in the organization. This distinction doesn't mean, however, that managers don't ever work directly on tasks. Some managers do have work duties not directly related to overseeing the activities of others. For example, regional sales managers for Motorola also have responsibilities in servicing some customer accounts in addition to overseeing the activities of the other sales associates in their territories.

What Titles Do Managers Have?

Identifying exactly who the managers are in an organization isn't difficult, but be aware that they can have a variety of titles. Managers are usually classified as top, middle, or first-line. (See Exhibit 1–2.) **Top managers** are those at or near the top of an organization. For instance, as the CEO of Kraft Foods Inc., Irene Rosenfeld is responsible for making decisions about the direction of the organization and establishing policies and philosophies that affect all organizational members. Top managers typically have titles such as vice president, president, chancellor, managing director, chief operating officer, chief executive officer, or chairperson of the board. **Middle managers** are those managers found between the lowest and top levels of the organization. For example, the plant manager at the Kraft manufacturing facility in Springfield, Missouri, is a middle manager. These individuals often manage other managers and maybe some nonmanagerial employees and are typically responsible for translating the goals set by top managers into specific details that lower-level managers will

RIGHT ? WRONG

Managers at all levels have to deal with ethical dilemmas and those ethical dilemmas are found in all kinds of circumstances. For instance, New York Yankees shortstop Derek Jeter, who is regarded as an upstanding and outstanding player in Major League Baseball, admitted that in a September 2010 game against the Tampa Bay Devil Rays he faked being hit by a pitch in order to get on base.[3] According to game rules, a hit batter automatically moves to first base. In this case, the ball actually hit the knob of Jeter's bat, but he acted as if the pitch had actually struck him. Jeter later scored a run, although the Yankees ultimately lost the game. Such ethical dilemmas are part and parcel of being a manager and although they're not easy, you'll learn how to recognize such dilemmas and appropriate ways of responding.

Think About:

- What do you think? Were Jeter's actions acceptable (i.e., ethical)?

- Does the fact that theatrics are part of all sports competitions make it acceptable?

- Was it the umpire's "fault" for missing the call?

- Did the team manager have any responsibility to respond to Jeter's action?

- What if the Yankees had actually won the game by one run? Would that make a difference in how you feel about this?

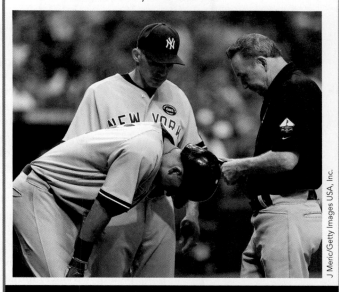

J Meric/Getty Images USA, Inc.

---

organization
A systematic arrangement of people brought together to accomplish some specific purpose

nonmanagerial employees
People who work directly on a job or task and have no responsibility for overseeing the work of others

managers
Individuals in an organization who direct the activities of others

top managers
Individuals who are responsible for making decisions about the direction of the organization and establishing policies that affect all organizational members

middle managers
Individuals who are typically responsible for translating goals set by top managers into specific details that lower-level managers will see get done

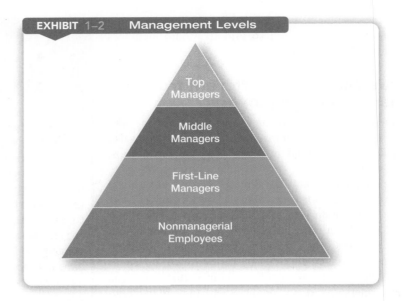

EXHIBIT 1–2   Management Levels

see get done. Middle managers may have such titles as department or agency head, project leader, unit chief, district manager, division manager, or store manager. **First-line managers** are those individuals responsible for directing the day-to-day activities of nonmanagerial employees. For example, the third-shift manager at the Kraft manufacturing facility in Springfield is a first-line manager. First-line managers are often called supervisors, team leaders, coaches, shift managers, or unit coordinators.

WHAT IS MANAGEMENT?

1.2 Define management.

Simply speaking, management is what managers do. But that simple statement doesn't tell us much. A better explanation is that **management** is the process of getting things done, effectively and efficiently, with and through other people. We need to look closer at some key words in this definition.

A *process* refers to a set of ongoing and interrelated activities. In our definition of management, it refers to the primary activities or functions that managers perform. We'll explore these functions more in the next section.

Efficiency and effectiveness have to do with the work being done and how it's being done. **Efficiency** means doing a task correctly ("doing things right") and getting the most output from the least amount of inputs. Because managers deal with scarce inputs—including resources such as people, money, and equipment—they're concerned with the efficient use of those resources. Managers want to minimize resource usage and thus resource costs.

It's not enough, however, just to be efficient. Managers are also concerned with completing activities. In management terms, we call this **effectiveness**. Effectiveness means "doing the right things" by doing those work tasks that help the organization reach its goals. Whereas efficiency is concerned with the *means* of getting things done, effectiveness is concerned with the *ends*, or attainment of organizational goals. (See Exhibit 1–3.)

Although *efficiency* and *effectiveness* are different, they are interrelated. For instance, it's easier to be effective if you ignore efficiency. If Hewlett-Packard disregarded labor and material input costs, it could produce more sophisticated and longer-lasting toner cartridges for its laser printers. Similarly, some government agencies have been regularly criticized for being reasonably effective but extremely inefficient. Our conclusion: Poor management is most often due to both inefficiency and ineffectiveness or to effectiveness achieved without regard for efficiency. Good management is concerned with both attaining goals (effectiveness) and doing so as efficiently as possible.

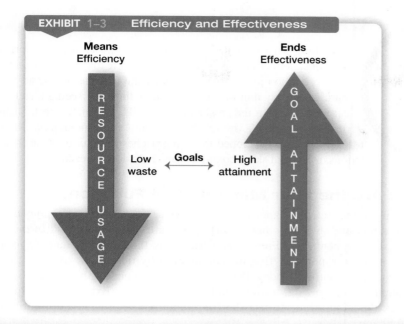

EXHIBIT 1-3   Efficiency and Effectiveness

From the Past to the Present

Where did the terms *management* or *manager* originate?[4] The terms are actually centuries old. One source says that the word *manager* originated in 1588 to describe one who manages. The specific use of the word as "one who conducts a house of business or public institution" is said to have originated in 1705. Another source says that the origin (1555–1565) is from the word *maneggiare*, which meant to handle or train horses, and was a derivative of the word *mano*, which is from the Latin word for hand, *manus*. That origin arose from the way that horses were guided, controlled, or directed where to go—that is, through using one's hand. As used in the way we've defined it in terms of overseeing and directing organizational members, however, the words *management* and *manager* are more appropriate to the early-twentieth-century time period. Peter Drucker, the late management writer, studied and wrote about management for more than 50 years. He said, "When the first business schools in the United States opened around the turn of the twentieth century, they did not offer a single course in management. At about that same time, the word 'management' was first popularized by Frederick Winslow Taylor." Let's look at what Taylor contributed to what we know about management today.

In 1911, Taylor's book *Principles of Scientific Management* was published. Its contents were widely embraced by managers around the world. The book described the theory of **scientific management**: the use of scientific methods to define the "one best way" for a job to be done. Taylor worked at the Midvale and Bethlehem Steel Companies in Pennsylvania. As a mechanical engineer with a Quaker and Puritan background, he was continually appalled by workers' inefficiencies. Employees used vastly different techniques to do the same job. They often "took it easy" on the job,

and Taylor believed that worker output was only about one-third of what was possible. Virtually no work standards existed. Workers were placed in jobs with little or no concern for matching their abilities and aptitudes with the tasks they were required to do. Taylor set out to remedy that by applying the scientific method to shop-floor jobs. He spent more than two decades passionately pursuing the "one best way" for such jobs to be done. Based on his groundbreaking studies of manual workers using scientific principles, Taylor became known as the "father" of scientific management. His ideas spread in the United States and to other countries and inspired others to study and develop methods of scientific management. These early management writers paved the way for our study of management, an endeavor that continues today as you'll discover as you read and study the materials in this textbook.

Think About:

- How do the origins of the words *manager* and *management* relate to what we know about managers and management today?

- What kind of workplace do you think Taylor would create?

- How have Taylor's views contributed to how management is practiced today?

- Could scientific management principles help you be more efficient? Choose a task you do regularly (such as laundry, grocery shopping, studying for exams, etc.). Analyze it by writing down the steps involved in completing that task. See if there are activities that could be combined or eliminated. Find the "one best way" to do this task. And the next time you have to do this task, try the scientifically managed way! See if you become more efficient—keeping in mind that changing habits isn't easy to do.

---

first-line managers
Supervisors responsible for directing the day-to-day activities of nonmanagerial employees

management
The process of getting things done, effectively and efficiently, through and with other people

efficiency
Doing things right, or getting the most output from the least amount of inputs

effectiveness
Doing the right things, or completing activities so that organizational goals are attained

scientific management
The use of scientific methods to define the "one best way" for a job to be done

WHAT DO MANAGERS DO?

1.3 **Describe** what managers do.

Describing what managers do isn't easy because, just as no organizations are alike, neither are managers' jobs. Despite that fact, managers do share some common job elements, whether the manager is a head nurse in the cardiac surgery unit of the Cleveland Clinic overseeing a staff of critical care specialists or the president of O'Reilly Automotive establishing goals for the company's more than 44,000 team members. Management researchers have developed three approaches to describe what managers do: functions, roles, and skills/competencies. Let's look at each.

What Are the Four Management Functions?

According to the functions approach, managers perform certain activities or functions as they direct and oversee others' work. What are these functions? In the early part of the twentieth century, a French industrialist by the name of Henri Fayol proposed that all managers perform five management activities: plan, organize, command, coordinate, and control.[5] Today, these management functions have been condensed to four: planning, organizing, leading, and controlling. (See Exhibit 1–4.) Most management textbooks continue to use the four functions approach. Let's look briefly at each function.

Because organizations exist to achieve some purpose, someone has to define that purpose and find ways to achieve it. A manager is that someone and does this by planning. **Planning** includes defining goals, establishing strategy, and developing plans to

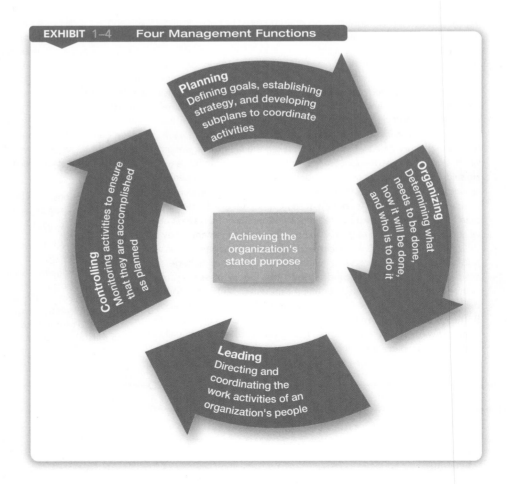

EXHIBIT 1–4   Four Management Functions

Planning
Defining goals, establishing strategy, and developing subplans to coordinate activities

Organizing
Determining what needs to be done, how it will be done, and who is to do it

Controlling
Monitoring activities to ensure that they are accomplished as planned

Leading
Directing and coordinating the work activities of an organization's people

Achieving the organization's stated purpose

coordinate activities. Setting goals, establishing strategy, and developing plans ensures that the work to be done is kept in proper focus and helps organizational members keep their attention on what is most important.

Managers are also responsible for arranging and structuring work to accomplish the organization's goals. This function is called **organizing**. Organizing includes determining what tasks are to be done and by whom, how tasks are to be grouped, who reports to whom, and who will make decisions.

We know that every organization has people. And it's part of a manager's job to direct and coordinate the work activities of those people. This is the **leading** function. When managers motivate employees, direct the activities of others, select the most effective communication channel, or resolve conflicts among members, they're leading.

The fourth and final management function is **controlling**, which involves monitoring, comparing, and correcting work performance. After the goals are set, the plans formulated, the structural arrangements determined, and the people hired, trained, and motivated, there has to be some evaluation to see if things are going as planned. Any significant deviations will require that the manager get work back on track.

Just how well does the functions approach describe what managers do? Is it an accurate description of what managers actually do? Some have argued that it isn't.[6] So, let's look at another perspective on describing what managers do.

As president and CEO of the Johnny Rockets restaurant chain, John Fuller develops plans to achieve the company's widespread expansion strategy. Fuller's vision is to extend the chain's focus of providing customers with an entertaining dining experience and classic American food such as burgers, fries, and shakes. Fuller plans to increase the chain's market penetration by launching new store concepts and by entering new domestic and international markets such as India and South Korea. Concepts for new restaurants include sports lounges, mobile kitchens, and a model that offers a streamlined menu and a create-your-own-burger option. Fuller is shown here with Johnny Rockets restaurant servers who are known for dancing on the job.

What Are Management Roles?

Fayol's original description of management functions wasn't derived from careful surveys of managers in organizations. Rather, it simply represented his observations and experiences in the French mining industry. In the late 1960s, Henry Mintzberg did an empirical study of five chief executives at work.[7] What he discovered challenged long-held notions about the manager's job. For instance, in contrast to the predominant view that managers were reflective thinkers who carefully and systematically processed information before making decisions, Mintzberg found that the managers he studied engaged in a number of varied, unpatterned, and short-duration activities. These managers had little time for reflective thinking because they encountered constant interruptions and their activities often lasted less than nine minutes. In addition to these insights, Mintzberg provided a categorization scheme for defining what managers do based on the managerial roles they use at work. These **managerial roles** referred to specific categories of managerial actions or behaviors expected of a manager. (To help you better understand this concept, think of the different roles you play—such as student, employee, volunteer, bowling team member, sibling, and so forth—and the different things you're expected to do in those roles.)

planning
Includes defining goals, establishing strategy, and developing plans to coordinate activities

organizing
Includes determining what tasks are to be done, who is to do them, how the tasks are to be grouped, who reports to whom, and who will make decisions

leading
Includes motivating employees, directing the activities of others, selecting the most effective communication channel, and resolving conflicts

controlling
Includes monitoring performance, comparing it with goals, and correcting any significant deviations

managerial roles
Specific categories of managerial behavior; often grouped around interpersonal relationships, information transfer, and decision making

Mintzberg concluded that managers perform 10 different but interrelated roles. These 10 roles, as shown in Exhibit 1–5, are grouped around interpersonal relationships, the transfer of information, and decision making. The **interpersonal roles** are ones that involve people (subordinates and persons outside the organization) and other duties that are ceremonial and symbolic in nature. The three interpersonal roles are figurehead, leader, and liaison. The **informational roles** involve collecting, receiving, and disseminating information. The three information roles include monitor, disseminator, and spokesperson. Finally, the **decisional roles** entail making decisions or choices. The four decisional roles are entrepreneur, disturbance handler, resource allocator, and negotiator.

Recently, Mintzberg completed another intensive study of managers at work and concluded that, "Basically, managing is about influencing action. It's about helping organizations and units to get things done, which means action."[8] Based on his observations, Mintzberg said managers do this in three ways: (1) by managing actions directly (for instance, negotiating contracts, managing projects, etc.), (2) by managing people who take action (for example, motivating them, building teams, enhancing the organization's culture, etc.), or (3) by managing information that propels people to take action (using budgets, goals, task delegation, etc.). According to Mintzberg, a manager has two roles—framing, which defines how a manager approaches his or her job; and scheduling, which "brings the frame to life" through the distinct tasks the manager does. A manager "performs" these roles while managing actions directly, managing people who take action, or managing information. Mintzberg's newest study gives us additional insights on the manager's job, adding to our understanding of what it is that managers do.

So which approach is better—functions or roles? Although each does a good job of describing what managers do, the functions approach still seems to be the generally accepted way of describing the manager's job. Its continued popularity is a tribute to its clarity and simplicity. "The classical functions provide clear and discrete methods of classifying the thousands of activities that managers carry out and the techniques they use in terms of the functions they perform for the achievement of goals."[9] However, Mintzberg's initial roles approach and newly developed model of managing do offer us other insights into what managers do.

EXHIBIT 1–5   **Mintzberg's Managerial Roles**

INTERPERSONAL ROLES

- Figurehead
- Leader
- Liaison

INFORMATIONAL ROLES

- Monitor
- Disseminator
- Spokesperson

DECISIONAL ROLES

- Entrepreneur
- Disturbance handler
- Resource allocator
- Negotiator

Source: Based on Mintzberg, Henry, *The Nature of Managerial Work,* 1st edition, © 1973.

What Skills and Competencies Do Managers Need?

The final approach we're going to look at for describing what managers do is by looking at the skills and competencies they need in managing. Dell Inc. is a company that understands the importance of management skills.[10] Its first-line managers go through an intensive five-day offsite skills training program. One of the company's directors of learning and development thought this was the best way to develop "leaders who can build that strong relationship with their front-line employees." What have the supervisors learned from the skills training? Some things mentioned included how to communicate more effectively and how to refrain from jumping to conclusions when discussing a problem with a worker. Management researcher Robert L. Katz and others have proposed that managers must possess and use four critical management skills in managing.[11]

Conceptual skills are the skills managers use to analyze and diagnose complex situations. They help managers see how things fit together and facilitate making good decisions. Interpersonal skills are those skills involved with working well with other people both individually and in groups. Because managers get things done with and through other people, they must have good interpersonal skills to communicate, motivate, mentor, and delegate. Additionally, all managers need technical skills, which are the job-specific knowledge and techniques needed to perform work tasks. These abilities are based on specialized knowledge or expertise. For top-level managers, these abilities tend to be related to knowledge of the industry and a general understanding of the organization's processes and products. For middle- and lower-level managers, these abilities are related to the specialized knowledge required in the areas where they work—finance, human resources, marketing, computer systems, manufacturing, information technology, and so forth. Finally, managers need and use political skills to build a power base and establish the right connections. Organizations are political arenas in which people compete for resources. Managers who have and know how to use political skills tend to be better at getting resources for their groups.

More recent studies have focused on the competencies managers need in their positions as important contributors to organizational success. One such study identified nine managerial competencies including: *traditional functions* (encompassing tasks such as decision making, short-term planning, goal setting, monitoring, team building, etc.); *task orientation* (including elements such as urgency, decisiveness, initiative, etc.); *personal orientation* (including things such as compassion, assertiveness, politeness, customer focus, etc.); *dependability* (involving aspects such as personal responsibility, trustworthiness, loyalty, professionalism, etc.); *open-mindedness* (encompassing elements such as tolerance, adaptability, creative thinking, etc.); *emotional control*, which included both resilience and stress management; *communication* (including aspects such as listening, oral communication, public presentation, etc.); *developing self and others* (including tasks such as performance assessment, self-development, providing developmental feedback, etc.); and *occupational acumen and concerns* (involving aspects such as technical proficiency, being concerned with quality and quantity, financial concern, etc.).[12] As you can see from this list of competencies, "what" a manager does is quite broad and varied.

---

interpersonal roles
Involving people (subordinates and persons outside the organization) and other duties that are ceremonial and symbolic in nature

informational roles
Involving collecting, receiving, and disseminating information

decisional roles
Entailing making decisions or choices

conceptual skills
A manager's ability to analyze and diagnose complex situations

interpersonal skills
A manager's ability to work with, understand, mentor, and motivate others, both individually and in groups

technical skills
Job-specific knowledge and techniques needed to perform work tasks

political skills
A manager's ability to build a power base and establish the right connections

Finally, a recent study that examined the work of some 8,600 managers found that what these managers did could be put into three categories of competencies: conceptual, interpersonal, and technical/administrative.[13] As you can see, these research findings agree with the list of management skills identified by Katz and others.

Is the Manager's Job Universal?

So far, we've discussed the manager's job as if it were a generic activity. That is, a manager is a manager regardless of where he or she manages. If management is truly a generic discipline, then what a manager does should be essentially the same whether he or she is a top-level executive or a first-line supervisor, in a business firm or a government agency; in a large corporation or a small business; or located in Paris, Texas, or Paris, France. Is that the case? Let's take a closer look at the generic issue.

LEVEL IN THE ORGANIZATION.   Although a supervisor in a claims department at Aetna may not do exactly the same things that the president of Aetna does, it doesn't mean that their jobs are inherently different. The differences are of degree and emphasis but not of activity.

As managers move up in the organization, they do more planning and less direct overseeing of others. (See Exhibit 1–6.) All managers, regardless of level, make decisions. They do planning, organizing, leading, and controlling activities, but the amount of time they give to each activity is not necessarily constant. In addition, the content of the managerial activities changes with the manager's level. For example, as we'll demonstrate in Chapter 6, top managers are concerned with designing the overall organization's structure, whereas lower-level managers focus on designing the jobs of individuals and work groups.

PROFIT VERSUS NOT-FOR-PROFIT.   Does a manager who works for the U.S. Postal Service, the Memorial Sloan-Kettering Cancer Center, or the Red Cross do the same things that a manager at Amazon or Symantec does? That is, is the manager's job the same in both profit and not-for-profit organizations? The answer, for the most part, is yes. All managers make decisions, set goals, create workable organization structures, hire and motivate employees, secure legitimacy for their organization's existence, and

---

TECHNOLOGY
AND THE MANAGER'S JOB

IS IT STILL MANAGING WHEN WHAT YOU'RE MANAGING ARE ROBOTS?

"The office of tomorrow is likely to include workers that are faster, smarter, more responsible—and happen to be robots."[14] Are you at all surprised by this statement? Although robots have been used in factory and industrial settings for a long time, it's becoming more common to find robots in the office and it's bringing about new ways of looking at how work is done and at what and how managers manage. So what *would* the manager's job be like managing robots? And even more intriguing is how these "workers" might affect how human coworkers interact with them.

As machines have become smarter and smarter—did any of you watch Watson take on the human *Jeopardy* challengers—researchers have been looking at human-machine interaction and "how people relate to the increasingly smart devices that surround them." One conclusion is that people find it easy to bond with a robot,

even one that doesn't look or sound anything like a real person. "All a robot had to do was move around in a purposeful way, and people thought of it, in some ways, as a coworker." People will give their robots names and even can describe the robot's moods and tendencies. As telepresence robots become more common, the humanness becomes even more evident. For example, when Erwin Deininger, the electrical engineer at Reimers Electra Steam, a small company in Clear Brook, Virginia, moved to the Dominican Republic when his wife's job transferred her there, he was able to still be "present" at the company via his VGo robot. Now Deininger "wheels easily from desk to desk and around the shop floor, answering questions and inspecting designs." The company's president was "pleasantly surprised at how useful the robot has proven" and even more surprised at how he acts around it. "He finds it hard to not think of the robot as, in a very

real sense, Deininger himself. After a while, he says, it's not a robot anymore."

There's no doubt that robot technology will continue to be incorporated into organizational settings. The manager's job will become even more exciting and challenging as humans and machines work together to accomplish the organization's goals.

Think About:

· Look back at our definitions of manager and management. Do they fit the organizational office setting described here? Explain.

· Do some research on telepresence and telepresence robots. How might this technology change how workers and managers work together?

· What's your response to the title of this box: *Is* it still managing when what you're managing are robots? Discuss.

· If you had to "manage" people and robots, how do you think your job as manager might be different than what the chapter describes? (Think in terms of functions, roles, and skills/competencies.)

EXHIBIT 1–6 Management Activities by Organizational Level

First-Level Managers
Organizing 24%
Planning 15%
Controlling 10%
Leading 51%

Middle Managers
Organizing 33%
Planning 18%
Controlling 13%
Leading 36%

Top Managers
Planning 28%
Organizing 36%
Controlling 14%
Leading 22%

Source: Based on T. A. Mahoney, T. H. Jerdee, and S. J. Carroll, "The Job(s) of Management," *Industrial Relations*, 4, no. 2 (1965), p. 103.

develop internal political support in order to implement programs. Of course, the most important difference between the two is how performance is measured. Profit, or the "bottom line," is an unambiguous measure of a business organization's effectiveness. Not-for-profit organizations don't have such a universal measure, making performance measurement more difficult. But don't interpret this difference to mean that managers in those organizations can ignore the financial side of their operations. Even not-for-profit organizations need to make money to continue operating. It's just that in not-for-profit organizations, "making a profit" for the "owners" is not the primary focus.

SIZE OF ORGANIZATION.   Would you expect the job of a manager in a local print shop that employs 12 people to be different from that of a manager who runs a 1,200-person printing facility for the *Washington Times*? This question is best answered by looking at the jobs of managers in small businesses and comparing them with our previous discussion of managerial roles. First, however, let's define a small business.

No commonly agreed-upon definition of a small business is available because different criteria are used to define *small*. For example, an organization can be classified as a small business using such criteria as number of employees, annual sales, or total assets. For our purposes, we'll describe a **small business** as an independent business having fewer than 500 employees that doesn't necessarily engage in any new or innovative practices and has relatively little impact on its industry.[15] So, is the job of managing a small business different from that of managing a large one? Some differences appear to exist. As Exhibit 1–7 shows, the small business manager's

Like many small business managers, Jessica and Emily Leung spend much of their time in the entrepreneurial activities of searching for new opportunities and stimulating change. The twin sisters launched their e-commerce business Hey Lady Shoes, a designer shoe company to market footwear that is stylish yet comfortable, or, as they put it, "to have a killer shoe that isn't a killer shoe." In looking for new business opportunities, the Hey Lady founders are shown here at a two-day technical business conference where they joined hundreds of other small business owners to learn how to apply new technology such as social media and other online tools to grow their business.

w49/Newscom

small business
An independent business having fewer than 500 employees that doesn't necessarily engage in any new or innovative practices and has relatively little impact on its industry

EXHIBIT 1-7   Managerial Roles in Small and Large Businesses

IMPORTANCE OF ROLES

Roles Played by Managers in Small Firms		Roles Played by Managers in Large Firms
	High ↑	
Spokesperson		Resource allocator
Entrepreneur Figurehead Leader	Moderate	Liaison Monitor Disturbance handler Negotiator
Disseminator	Low ↓	Entrepreneur

Source: Based on J. G. P. Paolillo, "The Manager's Self-Assessments of Managerial Roles: Small vs. Large Firms," *American Journal of Small Business* (January–March 1984), pp. 61–62.

most important role is that of spokesperson. He or she spends a great deal of time performing outwardly directed actions such as meeting with customers, arranging financing with bankers, searching for new opportunities, and stimulating change. In contrast, the most important concerns of a manager in a large organization are directed internally—deciding which organizational units get what available resources and how much of them. Accordingly, the entrepreneurial role—looking for business opportunities and planning activities for performance improvement—appears to be least important to managers in large firms, especially among first-level and middle managers.

Compared with a manager in a large organization, a small business manager is more likely to be a generalist. His or her job will combine the activities of a large corporation's chief executive with many of the day-to-day activities undertaken by a first-line supervisor. Moreover, the structure and formality that characterize a manager's job in a large organization tend to give way to informality in small firms. Planning is less likely to be a carefully orchestrated ritual. The organization's design will be less complex and structured, and control in the small business will rely more on direct observation than on sophisticated, computerized monitoring systems. Again, as with organizational level, we see differences in degree and emphasis but not in the activities that managers do. Managers in both small and large organizations perform essentially the same activities, but how they go about those activities and the proportion of time they spend on each are different.

MANAGEMENT CONCEPTS AND NATIONAL BORDERS. The last generic issue concerns whether management concepts are transferable across national borders. If managerial concepts were completely generic, they would also apply universally in any country in the world, regardless of economic, social, political, or cultural differences. Studies that have compared managerial practices between countries have not generally supported the universality of management concepts. In Chapter 3, we'll examine some specific differences between countries and describe their effect on managing. At this point, it's important for you to understand that most of the concepts discussed in the following chapters primarily apply to the United States, Canada, Great Britain, Australia, and other English-speaking countries. Managers likely will have to modify these concepts if they want to apply them in India, China, Chile, or other countries whose economic, political, social, or cultural environments differ from that of the so-called free-market democracies.

WHY STUDY MANAGEMENT?

At this point in the chapter, you may be wondering why you need to take a management class. Maybe you're majoring in accounting or marketing or information technology and may not understand how studying management is going to help you in your career. Let's look at some reasons why you may want to understand more about management.

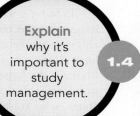

Explain why it's important to study management.

1.4

First, all of us have a vested interest in improving the way organizations are managed. Why? Because we interact with them every day of our lives and an understanding of management offers insights into many organizational aspects. When you renew your driver's license, are you frustrated that a seemingly simple task takes so long? Were you surprised when well-known businesses you thought would never fail went bankrupt or were you angry when entire industries had to rely on government bailout money to survive changing economic conditions? Are you annoyed when you call an airline three times and its representatives quote three different prices for the same trip? Such problems are mostly the result of managers doing a poor job of managing.

Organizations that are well managed—such as Walmart, Apple, Tata, Starbucks, McDonald's, Singapore Airlines, and Google—develop a loyal following and find ways to prosper even in economically challenging times. Poorly managed organizations may find themselves with a declining customer base and reduced revenues and may even have to file for bankruptcy protection. For instance, Gimbel's, W. T. Grant, Hollywood Video, Dave & Barry's, Circuit City, Eastern Airlines, and Enron were once thriving corporations. They employed tens of thousands of people and provided goods and services on a daily basis to hundreds of thousands of customers. Today those companies no longer exist. Poor management did them in. You can begin to recognize poor management and know what good managers should be doing by studying management.

The second reason for studying management is the reality that for most of you, once you graduate from college and begin your career, you will either manage or be managed. For those who plan to be managers, an understanding of management forms the foundation on which to build your management skills and abilities. For those of you who don't see yourself managing, you're still likely to have to work with managers. Also, assuming that you'll have to work for a living and recognizing that you're likely to work in an organization, you'll probably have some managerial responsibilities even if you're not a manager. Our experience tells us that you can gain a great deal of insight into the way your boss (and fellow employees) behave and how organizations function by studying management. Our point is that you don't have to aspire to be a manager to gain valuable information from a course in management.

In this photo, Starbucks managers and employees cheer their fellow workers as they compete in the Ambassador's Cup contest at company headquarters in Seattle to determine which employees are the best coffee experts. The study of management is important because it provides insights into successful organizations like Starbucks that are well-managed and have developed a loyal customer base as well as unsuccessful organizations that are poorly managed and lose customers. For students pursuing a career in management and for those who will be managed, the study of management provides knowledge about manager skills and responsibilities, how organizations function, and how people behave in the workplace.

Erika Schultz/Newscom

WHAT FACTORS ARE RESHAPING AND REDEFINING MANAGEMENT?

"At Best Buy's headquarters, more than 60 percent of employees are now judged only on tasks or results. Salaried people put in as much time as it takes to do their work. Those employees report better relationships with family and friends, more company loyalty, and more focus and energy. Productivity has increased by 35 percent. Employees say they don't know whether they work fewer hours—they've stopped counting. Perhaps more important, they're finding new ways to become efficient."[17] Welcome to the new world of management!

In today's world, managers are dealing with changing workplaces, ethical and trust issues, global economic and political uncertainties, and changing technology. For example, although people still need to purchase food during tough economic times, grocery stores have struggled to retain their customer base and to keep costs down. At Publix Super Markets, the large grocery chain in the southeastern United States, everyone, including managers, is looking for ways to better serve customers. The company's president, Todd Jones, who started his career bagging groceries at a Publix in New Smyrna Beach, Florida, is guiding the company through these challenges by keeping everyone's focus—from baggers to checkers to stockers—on exceptional customer service.[18] Or consider the management challenges faced by Roger Oglesby, the then-publisher and editor of the *Seattle Post-Intelligencer* (P-I). The P-I, like many other newspapers, had struggled to find a way to be successful in an industry that was losing readers and revenues at an alarming rate. The decision was made to go all-digital and in early 2009, the P-I became an Internet-only news source. Difficult actions followed as the news staff was reduced from 165 to about 20 people. In its new "life" as a digital news source, the organization faces other challenges—challenges for Michelle Nicolosi, now the manager who needs to plan, organize, lead, and control in this changed environment.[19]

Managers everywhere are likely to have to manage in changing circumstances, and the fact is that *how* managers manage is changing. Throughout the rest of this book, we'll be discussing these changes and how they're affecting the way managers plan, organize, lead, and control. We want to highlight two of these changes: the increasing importance of customers and innovation.

The success of Trader Joe's specialty retail chain is built on outstanding customer service. Understanding that employee attitudes and behaviors play a big role in customer satisfaction, the company hires people who are warm, friendly, energetic, enthusiastic, and fun-loving. New hires receive customer service training in product knowledge, communication skills, teamwork, and leadership. The employees shown here beginning their day with stretching exercises in preparation of a new store opening embody the attitudes and behaviors focused on listening to customers and responding to their requests. As frontline employees, they are the driving force behind Trader Joe's high customer satisfaction ratings.

Why Are Customers Important to the Manager's Job?

John Chambers, CEO of Cisco Systems, likes to listen to voice mails forwarded to him from dissatisfied customers. He said, "E-mail would be more efficient, but I want to hear the emotion, I want to hear the frustration, I want to hear the caller's level of comfort with the strategy we're employing. I can't get that through e-mail."[20] This is a manager who understands the importance of customers. Organizations need customers. Without them, most organizations would cease to exist. Yet, focusing on the customer has long been thought to be the responsibility of marketing people. "Let the marketers worry about the customers" is how many managers felt. We're discovering, however, that employee attitudes and behaviors play a big role in customer satisfaction. Think of the times you've been treated poorly (or superbly) by an employee during a service encounter and how that affected the way you felt about the situation.

Managers are recognizing that delivering consistent high-quality customer service is essential for survival and success in today's competitive environment and that employees are an important part of that equation.[21] The implication is clear—they must create a customer-responsive organization where employees are friendly and courteous, accessible, knowledgeable, prompt in responding to customer needs, and willing to do what's necessary to please the customer.[22]

Why Is Innovation Important to the Manager's Job?

"Nothing is more risky than not innovating."[23] Innovation means doing things differently, exploring new territory, and taking risks. And innovation isn't just for high-tech or other technologically sophisticated organizations; innovative efforts are needed in all types of organizations. You'd expect companies like Apple, Facebook, Google, and Nike to be on a list of the world's 50 most innovative companies.[24] But what about the likes of ESPN, the sports programming channel? It has been a leader in integrating new technology with products like ESPN 3D, the first 3-D channel on cable; live streaming on-demand video on Microsoft's Xbox Live; and use of virtual technology to highlight various sports events, people, and feats. Or what about donorschoose.org, an online way to connect kids who need school supplies with donors who want to help. In 2010, the number of donors on the Web site grew to 250,000, who gave away some $30 million to support 60,000 classroom projects. In today's challenging environment, innovation *is* critical and managers need to understand what, when, where, how, and why innovation can be fostered and encouraged throughout an organization. For example, during a presentation by the manager in charge of Walmart's global business, he explained his recipe for success (personal and organizational) as continually looking for new ways to do his job better; that is, to be innovative. Managers not only need to be innovative personally, but encourage their employees to be innovative.

As you can see, being a manager is both challenging and exciting. One thing we feel strongly about is that managers do matter to organizations. The Gallup Organization, which has polled millions of employees and tens of thousands of managers, has found that the single most important variable in employee productivity and loyalty isn't pay or benefits or workplace environment; it's the quality of the relationship between employees and their direct supervisors. Gallup also found that relationship with their manager is the largest factor in *employee engagement*—which is when employees are connected to, satisfied with, and enthusiastic about their jobs—accounting for at least 70 percent of an employee's level of engagement.[25] Recently, however, one factor that has affected how employees view their manager is the lingering global recession. For instance, a report from Towers Watson, a global consulting firm, found that "relationship with supervisor/manager" was the top-ranked reason *employers* gave for why employees leave an organization. However, the manager relationship wasn't even in the top five reasons given by *employees,* who cited factors such as stress levels and base pay.[26] Since the economic downturn has threatened the very survival of organizations, employees may be more concerned with that and less concerned with their managers. However, Towers Watson also found that the way a company manages its people can significantly affect its financial performance.[27] What can we conclude from such reports? That managers *do* matter and will continue to matter to organizations!

employee engagement
When employees are connected to, satisfied with, and enthusiastic about their jobs

1 Review

CHAPTER SUMMARY

1.1 Tell who managers are and where they work. Managers are individuals who work in an organization directing and overseeing the activities of other people. Managers are usually classified as top, middle, or first-line. Organizations, which are where managers work, have three characteristics: goals, people, and a deliberate structure.

1.2 Define management. Management is the process of getting things done, effectively and efficiently, with and through other people. Efficiency means doing a task correctly ("doing things right") and getting the most output from the least amount of inputs. Effectiveness means "doing the right things" by doing those work tasks that help the organization reach its goals.

1.3 Describe what managers do. What managers do can be described using three approaches: functions, roles, and skills/competencies. The functions approach says that managers perform four functions: planning, organizing, leading, and controlling. Mintzberg's roles approach says that what managers do is based on the 10 roles they use at work, which are grouped around interpersonal relationships, the transfer of information, and decision making. The skills/competencies approach looks at what managers do in terms of the skills and competencies they need and use. Four

critical management skills are conceptual, interpersonal, technical, and political. Additional managerial competencies include aspects such as dependability, personal orientation, emotional control, communication, and so forth. All managers plan, organize, lead, and control although how they do these activities and how often they do them may vary according to level in the organization, whether the organization is profit or not-for-profit, the size of the organization, and the geographic location of the organization.

1.4 Explain why it's important to study management. One reason it's important to study management is that all of us interact with organizations daily so we have a vested interest in seeing that organizations are well managed. Another reason is the reality that in your career you will either manage or be managed. By studying management you can gain insights into the way your boss and fellow employees behave and how organizations function.

1.5 Describe the factors that are reshaping and redefining management. In today's world, managers are dealing with changing workplaces, ethical and trust issues, global economic and political uncertainties, and changing technology. Two areas of critical importance to managers are delivering high-quality customer service and encouraging innovative efforts.

MyManagementLab   For more resources, please visit **www.mymanagementlab.com**

UNDERSTANDING THE CHAPTER

1. What is an organization and why are managers important to an organization's success?
2. How do managers differ from nonmanagerial employees?
3. In today's environment, which is more important to organizations—efficiency or effectiveness? Explain your choice.
4. Using any of the popular business periodicals (such as *BusinessWeek, Fortune, Wall Street Journal, Fast Company*), find examples of managers doing each of the four management functions. Write up a description and explain how these are examples of that function.
5. Is your course instructor a manager? Discuss in terms of planning, organizing, leading, and controlling. Also discuss using Mintzberg's managerial roles approach.
6. Is there one best "style" of management? Why or why not?
7. Is business management a profession? Why or why not? Do some external research in answering this question.

8. Are managers important to organizations? Does what they do "matter?" Discuss and be specific in explaining your answer.
9. Using current business periodicals, find five examples of managers you would describe as *master managers.* Write a paper describing these individuals as managers and why you think they deserve this title.
10. An article by Gary Hamel in the February 2009 issue of *Harvard Business Review* addresses how management must be reinvented to be more relevant to today's world. Get a copy of that article. Choose one of the 25 grand challenges identified. Discuss what it is and what it means for the way that organizations are managed.

Go to p. 402

YOUR TURN ᵀᴼ A MANAGER for Chapter 1.

Endnotes

1. Based on D. Waller, "The Virus Hunters," *Management Today,* December 2010, p. 98; A. Ricadela, "Symantec Forecast Tops Estimates on Business Spending," *Businessweek.com,* October 28, 2010; J. Brandon, "Doing Battle with Online Threats," *Inc.,* October 2010, p. 46; "Hackers Seeking Trade Secrets," *Information Management,* May–June 2010, p. 9; and S. Kirsner, "Sweating in the Hot Zone," *Fast Company,* October 2005, pp. 60–65.
2. The Walt Disney Company, Letter to Shareholders, *2010 Annual Report,* pp. 1–3; and *2008 Annual Report,* pp. 2–3.
3. Right or Wrong box based on C. Hausman, "Top Sports News of Week Revolves Around Ethics," *Ethics Newsline,* www.globalethics.org/newsline (September 20, 2010); P. Rogers, "Was It OK for Jeter to Fake Getting Hit by Pitch?" *Chicago Tribune Online,* September 16, 2010; and G. Shelton, "Derek Jeter's Dramatics in Faking Being Hit by Pitch Were Over the Line," *St. Petersburg Times Online,* September 16, 2010.
4. From the Past to the Present box based on Dictionary.com Unabridged, based on the Random House Dictionary, © Random House, Inc. 2009, http://dictionary.reference.com/browse/manage; Online Etymology Dictionary, www.etymonline.com (June 5, 2009); P. F. Drucker, *Management: Revised Edition* (New York: HarperCollins Publishers, 2008); and F. W. Taylor, *Principles of Scientific Management* (New York: Harper, 1911), p. 44. For other information on Taylor, see S. Wagner-Tsukamoto, "An Institutional Economic Reconstruction of Scientific Management: On the Lost Theoretical Logic of Taylorism," *Academy of Management Review,* January 2007, pp. 105–117; R. Kanigel, *The One Best Way: Frederick Winslow Taylor and the Enigma of Efficiency* (New York: Viking, 1997); and M. Banta, *Taylored Lives: Narrative Productions in the Age of Taylor, Veblen, and Ford* (Chicago: University of Chicago Press, 1993).
5. H. Fayol, *Industrial and General Administration* (Paris: Dunod, 1916).
6. For a comprehensive review of this question, see C. P. Hales, "What Do Managers Do? A Critical Review of the Evidence," *Journal of Management* (January 1986), pp. 88–115.
7. H. Mintzberg, *The Nature of Managerial Work* (New York: Harper & Row, 1973).
8. "What Managers Really Do," *Wall Street Journal,* August 17, 2009, p. R2; and H. Mintzberg, *Managing* (San Francisco: Berrett Koehler), 2009.
9. S. J. Carroll and D. A. Gillen, "Are the Classical Management Functions Useful in Describing Managerial Work?" *Academy of Management Review*, January 1987, p. 48.
10. E. White, "Firms Step Up Training for Front-Line Managers," *Wall Street Journal,* August 27, 2007, p. B3.
11. See, for example, J. G. Harris, D. W. DeLong, and A. Donnellon, "Do You Have What It Takes to Be an E-Manager?" *Strategy and Leadership* (August 2001), pp. 10–14; C. Fletcher and C. Baldry, "A Study of Individual Differences and Self-Awareness in the Context of Multi-Source Feedback," *Journal of Occupational and Organizational Psychology* (September 2000), pp. 303–319; and R. L. Katz, "Skills of an Effective Administrator," *Harvard Business Review,* September–October 1974, pp. 90–102.
12. R. P. Tett, H. A. Guterman, A. Bleier, and P. J. Murphy, "Development and Content Validation of a 'Hyperdimensional' Taxonomy of Managerial Competence," *Human Performance,* vol. 13, no. 3 (2000), pp. 205–251.
13. E. C. Dierdorff, R. S. Rubin, and F. P. Morgeson, "The Milieu of Managerial Work: An Integrative Framework Linking Work Context to Role Requirements," *Journal of Applied Psychology* (July 2009), pp. 972–988.
14. Technology and the Manager's Job box based on D. Bennett, "I'll Have My Robots Talk to Your Robots," *Bloomberg BusinessWeek* (February 21–27, 2011), pp. 52–62; E. Spitznagel, "The Robot Revolution Is Coming," *Bloomberg BusinessWeek,* January 17–23, 2011, pp. 69–71; G. A. Fowler, "Holiday Hiring Call: People vs. Robots," *Wall Street Journal,* December 20, 2010, pp. B1+; A. Schwartz, "Bring Your Robot to Work Day," *Fast Company.com* (November 2010), pp. 72–74; and P. J. Hinds, T. L. Roberts, and H. Jones, "Whose Job Is It Anyway? A Study of Human- Robot Interaction in a Collaborative Task," *Human-Computer Interaction* (March 2004), pp. 151–181.

15. "Frequently Asked Questions," *U.S. Small Business Administration,* www.sba.gov/advo (September 2008); T. L. Hatten, *Small Business: Entrepreneurship and Beyond* (Upper Saddle River, NJ: Prentice Hall, 1997), p. 5; L. W. Busenitz, "Research on Entrepreneurial Alertness," *Journal of Small Business Management* (October 1996), pp. 35–44; and J. W. Carland, F. Hoy, W. R. Boulton, and J. C. Carland, "Differentiating Entrepreneurs from Small Business Owners: A Conceptualization," *Academy of Management Review,* vol. 9, no. 2 (1984), pp. 354–359.

16. And the Survey Says box based on C. Kincaid, "On the Front Lines," *Training* (June 2009), pp. 48–49; "Dear Workforce," *Workforce Management Online* (July 1, 2010); J. Yang and A. Gonzalez, "Boss as a Friend?" *USA Today,* November 2, 2010, p. 1B; "Who's Your TV Boss?" *Training* (November–December 2010), p. 8; "Generation Gap: On Their Bosses, Millennials Happier Than Boomers," *Wall Street Journal,* November 15, 2010, p. B6; J. Light, "Bosses Overestimate Their Managing Skills," *Wall Street Journal,* November 1, 2010, p. B10; and J. MacIntyre, "Leadership Perspectives," *Springfield Business Journal,* February 14–20, 2011, p. 11.

17. T. Shelton, "Best Buy's New ROLE," *Training* (June 2009), pp. 24–28; and T. J. Erickson, "Task, Not Time: Profile of a Gen Y Job," *Harvard Business Review,* February 2008, p. 19.

18. T. W. Martin, "May I Help You?" *Wall Street Journal,* April 23, 2009, p. R4.

19. Hearst Seattle Media Staff Directory, www.seattlepi.com/facts/pistaff.shtml (February 23, 2011); and W. Yardley and R. Perez-Peña, "Seattle Paper Shifts Entirely to the Web," *New York Times Online* (March 17, 2009).

20. F. F. Reichheld, "Lead for Loyalty," *Harvard Business Review,* July–August 2001, p. 76.

21. See, for instance, H. Ernst, W. D. Hoyer, M. Krafft, and K. Krieger, "Customer Relationship Management and Company Performance—The Mediating Role of New Product Performance," *Journal of the Academy of Marketing Science* (April 2011), pp. 290–306; J. P. Dotson and G. M. Allenby, "Investigating the Strategic Influence of Customer and Employee Satisfaction on Firm Financial Performance," *Marketing Science* (September–October 2010), pp. 895–908; R. Grewal, M. Chandrashekaran, and A. V. Citrin, "Customer Satisfaction Heterogeneity and Shareholder Value," *Journal of Marketing Research* (August 2010), pp. 612–626; M. Riemann, O. Schilke, and J. S. Thomas, "Customer Relationship Management and Firm Performance: The Mediating Role of Business Strategy," *Journal of the Academy of Marketing Science* (Summer 2010), pp. 326–346; and K. A. Eddleston, D. L. Kidder, and B. E. Litzky, "Who's the Boss? Contending with Competing Expectations from Customers and Management," *Academy of Management Executive* (November 2002), pp. 85–95.

22. See, for instance, C. B. Blocker, D. J. Flint, M. B. Myers, and S. F. Slater, "Proactive Customer Orientation and Its Role for Creating Customer Value in Global Markets," *Journal of the Academy of Marketing Science* (April 2011), pp. 216–233; G. A. Gorry and R. A. Westbrook, "Once More, With Feeling: Empathy and Technology in Customer Care," *Business Horizons* (March–April 2011), pp. 125–134; M. Dixon, K. Freeman, and N. Toman, "Stop Trying to Delight Your Customers," *Harvard Business Review,* July–August 2010, pp. 116–122; D. M. Mayer, M. G. Ehrhart, and B. Schneider, "Service Attribute Boundary Conditions of the Service Climate-Customer Satisfaction Link," *Academy of Management Journal* (October 2009), pp. 1034–1050; B. A. Gutek, M. Groth, and B. Cherry, "Achieving Service Success Through Relationships and Enhanced Encounters," *Academy of Management Executive* (November 2002), pp. 132–144; Eddleston, Kidder, and Litzky, "Who's the Boss? Contending With Competing Expectations From Customers and Management"; S. D. Pugh, J. Dietz, J. W. Wiley, and S. M. Brooks, "Driving Service Effectiveness Through Employee-Customer Linkages," *Academy of Management Executive* (November 2002), pp. 73–84; S. D. Pugh, "Service with a Smile: Emotional Contagion in the Service Encounter," *Academy of Management Journal* (October 2001), pp. 1018–1027; W. C. Tsai, "Determinants and Consequences of Employee Displayed Positive Emotions," *Journal of Management,* vol. 27, no. 4 (2001), pp. 497–512; Naumann and Jackson, Jr., "One More Time: How Do You Satisfy Customers?"; and M. D. Hartline and O. C. Ferrell, "The Management of Customer-Contact Service Employees: An Empirical Investigation," *Journal of Marketing* (October 1996), pp. 52–70.

23. R. A. Hattori and J. Wycoff, "Innovation DNA," *Training and Development* (January 2002), p. 24.

24. *Fast Company* Staff, "World's 50 Most Innovative Companies," *Fast Company,* March 2011, pp. 66+.

25. E. Frauenheim, "Managers Don't Matter," *Workforce Management Online* (April 6, 2010); and K. A. Tucker and V. Allman, "Don't Be a Cat-and-Mouse Manager," The Gallup Organization, www.brain.gallup.com (September 9, 2004).

26. Frauenheim, 2010.

27. "WorkUSA® 2004/2005: Effective Employees Drive Financial Results," Watson Wyatt Worldwide, Washington, DC.

History Module

A BRIEF HISTORY OF MANAGEMENT'S ROOTS

Henry Ford once said, "History is more or less bunk." Well . . . he was wrong! History is important because it can put current activities in perspective. We propose that you need to know management history because it can help you understand what today's managers do. In this module, you'll find an annotated timeline that discusses key milestones in management theory. Then, in each chapter's "From the Past to the Present" box feature, we highlight a key person and his or her contributions or a key historical factor and its effect on contemporary management concepts. We believe this approach will help you better understand the origins of many contemporary management concepts.

○ Early Management

Management has been practiced a long time. Organized endeavors directed by people responsible for planning, organizing, leading, and controlling activities have existed for thousands of years. Regardless of what these individuals were called, someone had to perform those functions.

3000 – 2500 B.C.E.

The Egyptian pyramids are proof that projects of tremendous scope, employing tens of thousands of people were completed in ancient times.[1] It took more than 100,000 workers some 20 years to construct a single pyramid. Someone had to plan what was to be done, organize people and materials to do it, make sure those workers got the work done, and impose some controls to ensure that everything was done as planned. That someone was managers.

Stephen Sudd/Getty Images USA, Inc.

1400s

At the arsenal of Venice, warships were floated along the canals, and at each stop, materials and riggings were added to the ship.[2] Sounds a lot like a car "floating" along an assembly line, doesn't it? In addition, the Venetians used warehouse and inventory systems to keep track of materials, human resource management functions to manage the labor force (including wine breaks), and an accounting system to keep track of revenues and costs.

1780s – Mid 1800s

The **Industrial Revolution** may be the most important pre-twentieth-century influence on management. Why? Because with the industrial age came the birth of the corporation. With large, efficient factories pumping out products, someone needed to forecast demand, make sure adequate supplies of materials were available, assign tasks to workers, and so forth. Again, that someone was managers! It was indeed a historical event for two reasons: (1) because of all the organizational aspects (hierarchy, control, job specialization, and so forth) that became a part of the way work was done, and (2) because management had become a necessary component to ensure the success of the enterprise.

Getty Images USA, Inc.

1776

Although this is an important date in U.S. history, it's also important because it's the year Adam Smith's *Wealth of Nations* was published. In it, he argued the economic advantages of the **division of labor** (or **job specialization**)—that is, breaking down jobs into narrow, repetitive tasks. Using division of labor, individual productivity could be increased dramatically. Job specialization continues to be a popular way to determine how work gets done in organizations. But as you'll see in Chapter 6, it does have its drawbacks.

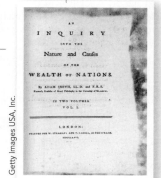
Getty Images USA, Inc.

3000 BC – 1776	1911 – 1947	Late 1700s – 1950s	1940s – 1950s	1960s – present
Early Management	Classical Approaches	Behavioral Approach	Quantitative Approach	Contemporary Approaches

Classical Approaches

Beginning around the turn of the twentieth century, the discipline of management began to evolve as a unified body of knowledge. Rules and principles were developed that could be taught and used in a variety of settings. These early management proponents were called classical theorists.

Corbis Images

1911

That's the year Frederick W. Taylor's *Principles of Scientific Management* was published. His groundbreaking book described a theory of **scientific management**—the use of scientific methods to determine the "one best way" for a job to be done. His theories were widely accepted and used by managers around the world and Taylor became known as the "father" of scientific management.[3] Other major contributors to scientific management were Frank and Lillian Gilbreth (early proponents of time-and-motion studies and parents of the large family described in the original book *Cheaper by the Dozen*) and Henry Gantt (whose work on scheduling charts was the foundation for today's project management). Taylor's work is profiled in Chapter 1's "From the Past to the Present" box.

Getty Images USA, Inc.

1916 – 1947

Unlike Taylor who focused on an individual production worker's job, Henri Fayol and Max Weber looked at organizational practices by focusing on what managers do and what constituted good management. This approach is known as **general administrative theory.** Fayol was introduced in Chapter 1 as the person who first identified five management functions. He also identified 14 **principles of management**—fundamental rules of management that could be applied to all organizations.[4] (See Exhibit HM–1 for a list of these 14 principles.) Weber is known for his description and analysis of bureaucracy, which he believed was an ideal, rational form of organization structure, especially for large organizations. In Chapter 6, we elaborate on these two important management pioneers.

EXHIBIT HM–1   Fayol's Fourteen Principles of Management

1 **Division of Work.** This principle is the same as Adam Smith's "division of labor." Specialization increases output by making employees more efficient.

2 **Authority.** Managers must be able to give orders. Authority gives them this right. Along with authority, however, goes responsibility. Whenever authority is exercised, responsibility arises.

3 **Discipline.** Employees must obey and respect the rules that govern the organization. Good discipline is the result of effective leadership, a clear understanding between management and workers regarding the organization's rules, and the judicious use of penalties for infractions of the rules.

4 **Unity of Command.** Every employee should receive orders from only one superior.

5 **Unity of Direction.** Each group of organizational activities that have the same objective should be directed by one manager using one plan.

6 **Subordination of Individual Interests to the General Interest.** The interests of any one employee or group of employees should not take precedence over the interests of the organization as a whole.

7 **Remuneration.** Workers must be paid a fair wage for their services.

8 **Centralization.** Centralization refers to the degree to which subordinates are involved in decision making. Whether decision making is centralized (to management) or decentralized (to subordinates) is a question of proper proportion. The task is to find the optimum degree of centralization for each situation.

9 **Scalar Chain.** The line of authority from top management to the lowest ranks represents the scalar chain. Communications should follow this chain. However, if following the chain creates delays, cross-communications can be allowed if agreed to by all parties and if superiors are kept informed. Also called chain of command.

10 **Order.** People and materials should be in the right place at the right time.

11 **Equity.** Managers should be kind and fair to their subordinates.

12 **Stability of Tenure of Personnel.** High employee turnover is inefficient. Management should provide orderly personnel planning and ensure that replacements are available to fill vacancies.

13 **Initiative.** Employees who are allowed to originate and carry out plans will exert high levels of effort.

14 **Esprit de Corps.** Promoting team spirit will build harmony and unity within the organization.

Behavioral Approach o

The behavioral approach to management focused on the actions of workers. How do you motivate and lead employees in order to get high levels of performance?

Late 1700s – Early 1900s

Managers get things done by working with people. Several early management writers recognized how important people are to an organization's success.[5] For instance, Robert Owen, who was concerned about deplorable working conditions, proposed an idealistic workplace. Hugo Munsterberg, a pioneer in the field of industrial psychology, suggested using psychological tests for employee selection, learning theory concepts for employee training, and studies of human behavior for employee motivation. Mary Parker Follett was one of the first to recognize that organizations could be viewed from both individual *and* group behavior. She thought that organizations should be based on a group ethic rather than on individualism.

1960s – Today

An organization's people continue to be an important focus of management research. The field of study that researches the actions (behaviors) of people at work is called **organizational behavior (OB)**. OB researchers do empirical research on human behavior in organizations. Much of what managers do today when managing people—motivating, leading, building trust, working with a team, managing conflict, and so forth—has come out of OB research. These topics are explored in depth in Chapters 9–13.

Relay Assembly Operation

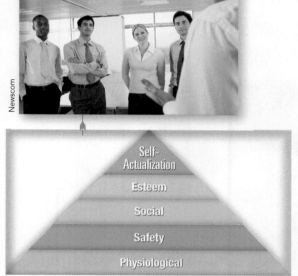

Self-Actualization
Esteem
Social
Safety
Physiological

1924 – Mid-1930s

The **Hawthorne studies**, a series of studies that provided new insights into individual and group behavior, were without question the most important contribution to the behavioral approach to management.[6] Conducted at the Hawthorne (Cicero, Illinois) Works of the Western Electric Company, the studies were initially designed as a scientific management experiment. Company engineers wanted to see the effect of various lighting levels on worker productivity. Using control and experimental groups of workers, they expected to find that individual output in the experimental group would be directly related to the intensity of the light. However, much to their surprise, they found that productivity in both groups varied with the level of lighting. Not able to explain it, the engineers called in Harvard professor Elton Mayo. Thus began a relationship that lasted until 1932 and encompassed numerous experiments in the behavior of people at work. What were some of their conclusions? Group pressures can significantly affect individual productivity, and people behave differently when they're being observed. Scholars generally agree that the Hawthorne studies had a dramatic impact on management beliefs about the role of people in organizations and led to a new emphasis on the human behavior factor in managing organizations.

1930s – 1950s

The human relations movement is important to management history because its supporters never wavered from their commitment to making management practices more humane. Proponents of this movement uniformly believed in the importance of employee satisfaction—a satisfied worker was believed to be a productive worker.[7] So they offered suggestions like employee participation, praise, and being nice to people to increase employee satisfaction. For instance, Abraham Maslow, a humanistic psychologist, who's best known for his description of a hierarchy of five needs (a well-known theory of employee motivation), said that once a need was substantially satisfied, it no longer served to motivate behavior. Douglas McGregor developed Theory X and Theory Y assumptions, which related to a manager's beliefs about an employee's motivation to work. Even though both Maslow's and McGregor's theories were never fully supported by research, they're important because they represent the foundation from which contemporary motivation theories were developed. Both are described more fully in Chapter 11.

○ Quantitative Approach

The quantitative approach, which focuses on the application of statistics, optimization models, information models, computer simulations, and other quantitative techniques to management activities, provided tools for managers to make their jobs easier.

1940s

The **quantitative approach** to management—which is the use of quantitative techniques to improve decision making—evolved from mathematical and statistical solutions developed for military problems during World War II. After the war was over, many of these techniques used for military problems were applied to busi-nesses.[8] For instance, one group of military officers, dubbed the "Whiz Kids," joined Ford Motor Company in the mid-1940s and immediately began using statistical methods to improve decision making at Ford. You'll find more information on these quantitative applications in Chapter 15.

1950s

After World War II, Japanese organi-zations enthusiastically embraced the concepts espoused by a small group of quality experts, the most famous being W. Edwards Deming (photo below) and Joseph M. Duran. As these Japanese manu-facturers began beating U.S. com-petitors in quality comparisons, Western managers soon took a more serious look at Deming's and Juran's ideas.[9] Their ideas became the basis for **total quality management (TQM),** which is a management philosophy devoted to continual improvement and responding to customer needs and expectations. We'll look closer at Deming and his beliefs about TQM in Chapter 15.

Bert Hardy/Getty Images USA, Inc.

AP Images

Contemporary Approaches ⭘

Most of the early approaches to management focused on managers' concerns inside the organization. Starting in the 1960s, management researchers began to look at what was happening in the external environment outside the organization.

1960s

Although Chester Barnard, a telephone company executive, wrote in his 1938 book *The Functions of the Executive* that an organization functioned as a cooperative system, it wasn't until the 1960s that management researchers began to look more carefully at systems theory and how it related to organizations.[10] The idea of a system is a basic concept in the physical sciences. As related to organizations, the **systems approach** views systems as a set of interrelated and interdependent parts arranged in a manner that produces a unified whole. Organizations function as **open systems**, which means they are influenced by and interact with their environment. Exhibit HM–2 illustrates an organization as an open system. A manager has to efficiently and effectively manage all parts of the system in order to achieve established goals. See Chapter 2 for additional information on the external and internal factors that affect how organizations are managed.

Frederick Brown/Newscom

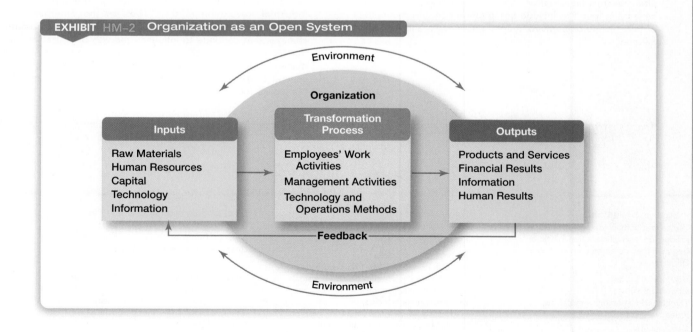

EXHIBIT HM–2   **Organization as an Open System**

Environment — Organization

Inputs	Transformation Process	Outputs
Raw Materials Human Resources Capital Technology Information	Employees' Work Activities Management Activities Technology and Operations Methods	Products and Services Financial Results Information Human Results

Feedback

Environment

O Contemporary Approaches

Newscom

1960s

Early management theorists proposed manage-ment principles that they generally assumed to be universally applicable. Later research found exceptions to many of these principles. The **contingency approach** (or situational approach) says that organizations, employees, and situations are different and require different ways of managing. A good way to describe contingency is "if . . . then." *If* this is the way my situation is, *then* this is the best way for me to manage in this situation. One of the earliest contingency studies was done by Fred Fiedler and looked at what style of leadership was most effective in what situation.[11] Popular contingency variables have been found to include organization size, the routineness of task technology, environmental uncertainty, and individual differences.

1980s – Present

Although the dawn of the information age is said to have begun with Samuel Morse's telegraph in 1837, the most dramatic changes in information technology have occurred in the latter part of the twentieth century and have directly affected the manager's job.[12] Managers now may manage employees who are working from home or working halfway around the world. An organization's computing resources used to be mainframe computers locked away in temperature-controlled rooms and only accessed by the experts. Now, practically everyone in an organization is connected—wired or wireless—with devices no larger than the palm of the hand. Just like the impact of the Industrial Revolution in the 1700s on the emergence of management, the information age has brought dramatic changes that continue to influence the way organizations are managed. The impact of information technology on how managers do their work is so profound that we've included in several chapters a boxed feature on "Technology and the Manager's Job."

Industrial Revolution
The advent of machine power, mass production, and efficient transportation begun in the late eighteenth century in Great Britain

division of labor (or job specialization)
The breakdown of jobs into narrow repetitive tasks

scientific management
The use of the scientific method to define the one best way for a job to be done

general administrative theory
Descriptions of what managers do and what constitutes good management practice

principles of management
Fayol's fundamental or universal principles of management practice

Hawthorne studies
Research done in the late 1920s and early 1930s devised by Western Electric industrial engineers to examine the effect of different work environment changes on worker productivity, which led to a new emphasis on the human factor in the functioning of organizations and the attainment of their goals

organizational behavior (OB)
The field of study that researches the actions (behaviors) of people at work

quantitative approach
The use of quantitative techniques to improve decision making

total quality management (TQM)
A managerial philosophy devoted to continual improvement and responding to customer needs and expectations

systems approach
An approach to management that views an organization as a system, which is a set of interrelated and interdependent parts arranged in a manner that produces a unified whole

open systems
Systems that dynamically interact with their environment

contingency approach (or situational approach)
An approach to management that says that individual organizations, employees, and situations are different and require different ways of managing

Endnotes

1. C. S. George, Jr., *The History of Management Thought,* 2d ed. (Upper Saddle River, NJ: Prentice Hall, 1972), p. 4.
2. Ibid., pp. 35–41.
3. F. W. Taylor, *Principles of Scientific Management* (New York: Harper, 1911), p. 44. For other information on Taylor, see S. Wagner-Tsukamoto, "An Institutional Economic Reconstruction of Scientific Management: On the Lost Theoretical Logic of Taylorism," *Academy of Management Review,* January 2007, pp. 105–117; R. Kanigel, *The One Best Way: Frederick Winslow Taylor and the Enigma of Efficiency* (New York: Viking, 1997); and M. Banta, *Taylored Lives: Narrative Productions in the Age of Taylor, Veblen, and Ford* (Chicago: University of Chicago Press, 1993).
4. H. Fayol, *Industrial and General Administration* (Paris: Dunod, 1916); M. Weber, *The Theory of Social and Economic Organizations*, ed. T. Parsons, trans. A. M. Henderson and T. Parsons (New York: Free Press, 1947); and M. Lounsbury and E. J. Carberry, "From King to Court Jester? Weber's Fall from Grace in Organizational Theory," *Organization Studies,* vol. 26, no. 4 (2005), pp. 501–525.
5. R. A. Owen, *A New View of Society* (New York: E. Bliss and White, 1825); H. Munsterberg, *Psychology and Industrial Efficiency* (Boston: Houghton Mifflin, 1913); and M. P. Follett, *The New State: Group Organization the Solution of Popular Government* (London: Longmans, Green, 1918).
6. E. Mayo, *The Human Problems of an Industrial Civilization* (New York: Macmillan, 1933); and F. J. Roethlisberger and W. J. Dickson, *Management and the Worker* (Cambridge, MA: Harvard University Press, 1939). Also see G. W. Yunker, "An Explanation of Positive and Negative Hawthorne Effects: Evidence from the Relay Assembly Test Room and Bank Wiring Observation Room Studies," paper presented, Academy of Management Annual Meeting, August 1993, Atlanta, Georgia; S. R. Jones, "Was There a Hawthorne Effect?" *American Sociological Review*, November 1992, pp. 451–468; and S. R. G. Jones, "Worker Interdependence and Output: The Hawthorne Studies Reevaluated," *American Sociological Review*, April 1990, pp. 176–190; J. A. Sonnenfeld, "Shedding Light on the Hawthorne Studies,"

Journal of Occupational Behavior (April 1985), pp. 111–130; B. Rice, "The Hawthorne Defect: Persistence of a Flawed Theory," *Psychology Today*, February 1982, pp. 70–74; R. H. Franke and J. Kaul, "The Hawthorne Experiments: First Statistical Interpretations," *American Sociological Review*, October 1978, pp. 623–643; and A. Carey, "The Hawthorne Studies: A Radical Criticism," *American Sociological Review*, June 1967, pp. 403–416.
7. A. Maslow, "A Theory of Human Motivation," *Psychological Review,* July 1943, pp. 370–396; see also A. Maslow, *Motivation and Personality* (New York: Harper & Row, 1954); and D. McGregor, *The Human Side of Enterprise* (New York: McGraw-Hill, 1960).
8. P. Rosenzweig, "Robert S. McNamara and the Evolution of Management," *Harvard Business Review,* December 2010, pp. 86–93; and C. C. Holt, "Learning How to Plan Production, Inventories, and Work Force," *Operations Research,* January–February 2002, pp. 96–99.
9. T. A. Stewart, "A Conversation with Joseph Juran," *Fortune,* January 11, 1999, pp. 168–170; J. R. Hackman and R. Wageman, "Total Quality Management: Empirical, Conceptual, and Practical Issues," *Administrative Science Quarterly,* June 1995, pp. 309–342; B. Krone, "Total Quality Management: An American Odyssey," *The Bureaucrat,* Fall 1990, pp. 35–38; and A. Gabor, *The Man Who Discovered Quality* (New York: Random House, 1990).
10. C. I. Barnard, *The Functions of the Executive* (Cambridge: Harvard University Press, 1938); and K. B. DeGreene, *Sociotechnical Systems: Factors in Analysis, Design, and Management* (Upper Saddle River, NJ: Prentice Hall, 1973), p. 13.
11. F. E. Fiedler, *A Theory of Leadership Effectiveness* (New York: McGraw-Hill, 1967).
12. "Information Age: People, Information & Technology—An Exhibition at the National Museum of American History," *Smithsonian Institution,* http://photo2.si.edu/infoage/infoage.html (June 11, 2009); and P. F. Drucker, *Management, Revised Edition* (New York: HarperCollins Publishers, 2008).

CHAPTER 2

The
Management
Environment

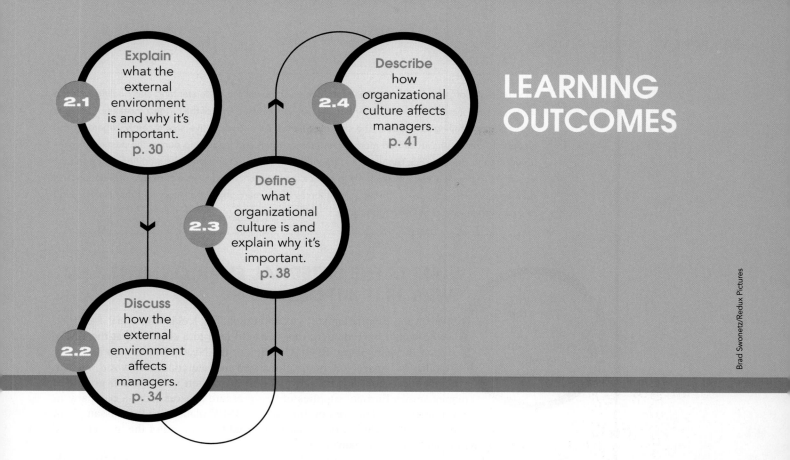

LEARNING OUTCOMES

2.1 Explain what the external environment is and why it's important. p. 30

2.4 Describe how organizational culture affects managers. p. 41

2.3 Define what organizational culture is and explain why it's important. p. 38

2.2 Discuss how the external environment affects managers. p. 34

Brad Swonetz/Redux Pictures

Going to Extremes

No. 1 best e-retailer. For those of you who have shopped on Zappos.com, that number one ranking probably isn't a surprise.[1] For those of you who haven't shopped on Zappos.com, it wouldn't take long for you to see why Zappos deserves that accolade. And it's more than the fact that Zappos has a great selection of products, super-fast shipping, and free returns. The real secret to its success is its people who make the Zappos shopping experience truly unique and outstanding. The company, which began selling shoes and other products online in 1999, has put "extraordinary effort into building a desirable organizational culture, which has provided a sure path to business success." As part of its culture, Zappos espouses 10 corporate values. At the top of that list is "Deliver WOW through service." And do they ever deliver the WOW! Even through the recent economic challenges, Zappos has continued to thrive—a sure sign its emphasis on organizational culture is paying off.

No successful organization, or its managers, can operate without understanding and dealing with the dynamic environment—external and internal—that surrounds it. One of the biggest mistakes managers make today is failing to adapt to the changing world. As one executive said recently, regarding the economic crisis, "I have learned more about management and leadership during the past six months than I had in the previous ten years."[2] Organizations that are too bound by tradition and don't (or refuse to) change are less and less likely to survive the turbulence in today's world. To better understand this issue, we need to look at the important forces in the management environment that are affecting the way organizations are managed today.

WHAT IS THE EXTERNAL ENVIRONMENT AND WHY IS IT IMPORTANT?

2.1 Explain what the external environment is and why it's important.

When the Eyjafjallajökull volcano erupted in Iceland on April 14, 2010, who would have thought that it would lead to a shutdown at the BMW plant in Spartanburg, South Carolina or the Nissan Motor auto assembly facility in Japan?[3] Yet, in our globalized and interconnected world, such an occurrence shouldn't be surprising at all. When volcanic ash grounded planes across Europe, supplies of tire-pressure sensors from a company in Ireland couldn't be delivered on time to the BMW plant or to the Nissan plant. Because we live in a "connected" world, managers need to be aware of the impact of the external environment on their organization.

The term external environment refers to factors, forces, situations, and events outside the organization that affect its performance. As shown in Exhibit 2–1, it includes several different components. The economic component encompasses factors such as interest rates, inflation, changes in disposable income, stock market fluctuations, and business cycle stages. The demographic component is concerned with trends in population characteristics such as age, race, gender, education level, geographic location, income, and family composition. The technological component is concerned with scientific or industrial innovations. The sociocultural component is concerned with societal and cultural factors such as values, attitudes, trends, traditions, lifestyles, beliefs, tastes, and patterns of behavior. The

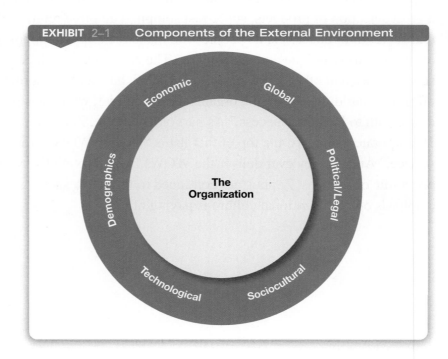

EXHIBIT 2–1   **Components of the External Environment**

Economic · Global · Political/Legal · Sociocultural · Technological · Demographics

The Organization

political/legal component looks at federal, state, and local laws, as well as laws of other countries and global laws. It also includes a country's political conditions and stability. And the global component encompasses those issues (like a volcano eruption) associated with globalization and a world economy. Although all these components potentially constrain managers' decisions and actions, we're going to look closely at only two of the components—economic and demographic.

How Has the Economy Changed?

You knew the economic context had changed when a blue-ribbon company like General Motors went bankrupt, the Organization for Economic Cooperation and Development predicted some 25 million unemployed individuals globally, the U.S. unemployment rate hovered around 9 percent, and an economic vocabulary included terminology like *toxic assets, collateralized debt obligations, TARP, bailouts, underwater homeowners, economic stabilization, wraparound mortgages,* and *stress tests.*[4] The recent economic crisis—called the "Great Recession" by some analysts—began with turmoil in home mortgage markets in the United States as many homeowners found themselves unable to make their payments. The problems also soon affected businesses as credit markets collapsed. All of a sudden, credit was no longer readily available to fund business activities. Due to our globally connected world, it didn't take long for economic troubles in the United States to spread to other countries.

What led to the massive problems? Experts cited a long list of factors including excessively low interest rates for a long period of time, fundamental flaws in the U.S. housing market, and massive global liquidity. All these factors led businesses and consumers to become highly leveraged, which wasn't an issue when credit was easily available.[5] However, as liquidity dried up, the worldwide economic system sputtered and nearly collapsed. With trillions lost in home value, millions of home foreclosures, a huge public debt burden in many countries, and widespread social problems due to job losses, it's clear that the U.S. and global economic environments have changed.

In the U.S. economic system, which is based mostly on capitalistic principles, trade and industry are controlled privately rather than by the government. But as we've seen time and time again in such a system, people sometimes make bad, even disastrous, decisions. The esteemed economist John Maynard Keynes once said, "Capitalism is the astounding belief that the most wickedest of men will do the most wickedest of things for the greatest good of everyone."[6] Despite this cynical view, modern capitalism has created "unprecedented wealth in our lifetime, shown its power to lift people out of poverty, and spread a culture of competitive genius."[7] It's also been called the "most productive economic engine invented."[8] Since the early 1900s, the U.S. approach has been the most important model for organizing business activities. It brought the world the corporate model of ownership and organization, large-scale operations based on mass production techniques, open markets, formal organization structures with hierarchies and multiple business divisions, and labor-management collective bargaining. Business organizations in many countries have patterned themselves after this model. However, as the economic problems of the past few years have shown, it's by no means perfect.

Experts believe that as the U.S. economy emerges from recession, the way businesses operate will not be the way it's always been. As the U.S. Secretary of the Treasury said, "Capitalism will be different."[9] The biggest change is likely to be in the role of government, especially in financial markets and in consumer protection. Also, government spending as a share of the U.S. economy is likely to remain at levels not seen since World War II. Beyond that, more government intervention is likely to mean more regulations or at the least, increased enforcement and oversight of regulations already in place. However, some believe

external environment
Factors, forces, situations, and events outside the
organization that affect its performance

From the Past to the Present

In February 2010, when Ford Motor Company surpassed General Motors in sales for the first time in at least 50 years, GM announced an overhaul in its top management ranks. GM's North American president said that "he could see clear as day that the mix and the structure of people weren't right and that these changes were necessary for GM to move faster and win."[10] Just how much difference *does* a manager make in how an organization performs? Management theory proposes two perspectives in answering this question: the omnipotent view and the symbolic view.

In Chapter 1, we stressed how important managers were to organizations. The dominant view in management theory is that managers are directly responsible for an organization's success or failure. This perspective is called the **omnipotent view of management**. Differences in an organization's performance are assumed to be due to decisions and actions of its managers. Good managers anticipate change, exploit opportunities, correct poor performance, and lead their organizations. When profits are up, managers take the credit and are rewarded with bonuses, stock options, and the like. When profits are down, top managers are often fired in the belief that "new blood" will bring improved results. In this view, someone has to be held accountable when organizations perform poorly regardless of the reasons, and that "someone" is the manager. Of course, when things go well, managers also get the credit—even if they had little to do with achieving the positive outcomes. And this view isn't limited to business organizations. It also explains turnover among college and professional sports coaches, who are considered the "managers" of their teams. Coaches who lose more games than they win are usually fired and replaced by new coaches who are expected to correct the poor performance.

In contrast, others have argued that much of an organization's success or failure is due to external forces outside managers' control. This perspective is called the **symbolic view of management**. The symbolic view says that a manager's ability to affect performance outcomes is influenced and constrained by external factors. According to this view, it's unreasonable to expect managers to significantly affect an organization's performance. Instead, performance is influenced by factors over which managers have little control such as the economy, customers, governmental policies, competitors' actions, industry conditions, and decisions made by previous managers. This view is labeled "symbolic" because it's based on the belief that managers symbolize control and influence. How? By developing plans, making decisions, and engaging in other managerial activities to make sense out of random, confusing, and ambiguous situations. However, the actual part that managers play in organizational success or failure is limited.

In reality, managers are neither all-powerful nor helpless. But their decisions and actions are constrained. External constraints come from the organization's external environment and internal constraints come from the organization's culture.

Think About:

- Why do you think these two perspectives on management are important?

- How are the omnipotent and the symbolic views of management similar? Different?

The home mortgage problems that began in the United States and affected businesses as credit markets collapsed had an enormous economic impact that nearly collapsed the global economic system. During the recent global recession, millions of jobs were eliminated, unemployment rates rose to levels not seen in many years, and unemployed individuals reached 25 million worldwide. This photo shows unemployed Japanese people searching through job vacancies at an employment bureau in Tokyo, where the unemployment rate soared. In our globalized and interconnected world, managers need to stay informed about the economy because it poses constraints and challenges for them in the areas of jobs and employment.

Kazuhiro Nogi/Newscom

that more governmental oversight isn't the answer. For example, social scientist Amitai Etzioni said, "The world economy consists of billions of transactions every day. There can never be enough inspectors, accountants, customs officers, and police to ensure that all or even most of these transactions are properly carried out. Moreover, those charged with enforcing regulations are themselves not immune to corruption, and hence, they too must be supervised and held accountable to others—who also have to be somehow regulated. The upshot is that regulation cannot be the linchpin of attempts to reform our economy. What is needed is something far more sweeping: for people to internalize a different sense of how one ought to behave, and act on it because they believe it is right."[11] We've also seen a shift in public opinion as more people have expressed concerns about the growing budget deficit and increased government intervention in the economy. In a poll by the *Wall Street Journal,* some 49 percent of the respondents said they had a great deal of concern about a greater government role in the economy and business.[12] Keep in mind that over time, this "new" normal will no longer be new—it will have become "the norm."[13] What's important for managers is to stay informed about what's happening not only in the economic component but in the other external environmental components as well. In fact, there is one other important external component we need to look at: demographics.

What Role Do Demographics Play?

Have you ever heard the phrase "demography is destiny"? What this phrase means is that the size and characteristics of a country's population can have a significant effect on what it's able to achieve. For instance, experts say that by 2050, "emerging economies led by India and China will collectively be larger than the developed economies."[14] Small European nations with low birth rates, such as Austria, Belgium, Denmark, Norway, and Sweden, will drop off the list of the 30 biggest economies. **Demographics**, the characteristics of a population used for purposes of social studies, can and do have a significant impact on how managers manage. Those population characteristics include things such as

TECHNOLOGY AND THE MANAGER'S JOB | CHANGING AND IMPROVING THE WAY MANAGERS MANAGE

One positive aspect of this changed economy comes from the vast possibilities associated with continuing advancements in technology.[15] **Technology** includes any equipment, tools, or operating methods that are designed to make work more efficient. One area where technology has had an impact is in the process where inputs (labor, raw materials, and the like) are transformed into outputs (goods and services to be sold). In years past, this transformation was usually performed by human labor. With technology, however, human labor has been replaced with electronic and computer equipment. From robots in offices to online banking systems to social networks where employees interact with customers, technology has made the work of creating and delivering goods and services more efficient and effective.

Another area where technology has had a major impact is in information. Information technology (IT) has created the ability to circumvent the physical confines of working only in a specified organizational location. With notebook and desktop computers, fax machines, smartphones, organizational intranets, and other IT tools, organizational members who work mainly with information can do that work from any place at any time.

Finally, technology is also changing the way managers manage, especially in terms of how they interact with employees who may be working anywhere and anytime. Effectively communicating with individuals in remote locations and ensuring that work goals are being met are challenges that managers must address. Throughout the rest of the book, we'll look at how managers are meeting those challenges in the ways they plan, organize, lead, and control.

Think About:

· Is management easier or harder with all the available technology? What do you think?

· What benefits does technology provide and what problems does technology pose for (a) employees and (b) managers?

· Which technologies have been most useful to you personally thus far? Why? Do you think they will remain useful to you as you begin your career? Why or why not?

omnipotent view of management
The view that managers are directly responsible for an organization's success or failure

symbolic view of management
The view that much of an organization's success or failure is due to external forces outside managers' control

demographics
The characteristics of a population used for purposes of social studies

technology
Any equipment, tools, or operating methods that are designed to make work more efficient

Age is an important demographic for Michelle Zubizarreta (center), chief administrative officer of Zubi Advertising, a Hispanic agency in Coral Gables, Florida. Surrounded by some of the Gen Y employees whom she manages, Zubizarreta values the enthusiasm and the contributions of her young workers. With the economic recession creating the need for new ways to generate revenue, Zubizarreta asked her tech-savvy, multitasking young staffers for their creative input. She allowed them to use Facebook to conduct consumer surveys, and she formed innovation groups by setting up teams to develop advertising-related iPhone apps and to generate other money-making ideas.

age, income, sex, race, education level, ethnic makeup, employment status, geographic location, and so forth—pretty much the types of information collected on governmental census surveys.

Age is a particularly important demographic for managers since the workplace often has different age groups all working together. *Baby Boomers. Gen X. Gen Y. Post-Millennials.* Maybe you've heard or seen these terms before. They're names given by population researchers to four well-known age groups found in the U.S. population. Baby Boomers are those individuals born between 1946 and 1964. You've heard so much about "boomers" because there are so many of them. The sheer numbers of people in that cohort means they've had a significant impact on every aspect of the external environment (from the educational system to entertainment/lifestyle choices to the Social Security system and so forth) as they've gone through various life cycle stages. Gen X is used to describe those individuals born between 1965 and 1977. This age group has been called the baby bust generation since it followed the baby boom and is one of the smaller age cohorts. Gen Y (or the "Millennials") is an age group typically considered to encompass those individuals born between 1978 and 1994. As the children of the Baby Boomers, this age group is also large in number and making its imprint on external environmental conditions as well. From technology to clothing styles to work attitudes, Gen Y is impacting organizational workplaces. Then, there are the Post-Millennials—the youngest identified age group, basically teens and middle-schoolers.[16] This group also has been called the iGeneration, primarily because they've grown up with technology that customizes everything to the individual. Another name given to this age group is Generation C, since it's a group that's always been digitally connected. One thing that characterizes this group is that "many of their social interactions take place on the Internet, where they feel free to express their opinions and attitudes." It's the first group to have "never known any reality other than that defined and enabled by the Internet, mobile devices, and social networking."[17] Population experts say it's too early to tell whether elementary school-aged children and younger are part of this demographic group or whether the world they live in will be so different that they'll comprise a different demographic cohort.

Demographic age cohorts are important to our study of management because large numbers of people at certain stages in the life cycle can constrain decisions and actions taken by businesses, governments, educational institutions, and other organizations. Studying demographics doesn't only involve current statistics, but also looks to the future. For instance, recent analysis of birth rates shows that more than 80 percent of babies being born worldwide are from Africa and Asia.[18] And here's an interesting fact: India has one of the world's youngest populations with more males under the age of 5 than the entire population of France. And by 2050, it's predicted that China will have more people age 65 and older than the rest of the world combined.[19] Just imagine the impact of these population trends on global organizations.

HOW DOES THE EXTERNAL ENVIRONMENT AFFECT MANAGERS?

2.2 Discuss how the external environment affects managers.

Knowing *what* the various components of the external environment are and examining certain aspects of that environment are important for managers. However, understanding *how* the environment affects managers is equally as important. We're going to look at three ways the external environment constrains and challenges managers—first, through its impact on jobs and employment; next, through the environmental uncertainty that is present; and finally, through the various stakeholder relationships that exist between an organization and its external constituencies.

JOBS AND EMPLOYMENT.   As any or all of the external environmental conditions change, one of the most powerful constraints managers face is the impact of such changes on jobs and employment—both in poor conditions and in good conditions. The power of this constraint became painfully obvious during the recent global recession as millions of jobs were eliminated and unemployment rates rose to levels not seen in many years. Economists now predict that about a quarter of the 8.4 million jobs eliminated in the United States during this most recent economic downturn won't come back and will instead be replaced by other types of work in growing industries.[20] Other countries face the same issues. Although such readjustments aren't bad in and of themselves, they do create challenges for managers who must balance work demands and having enough people with the right skills to do the organization's work.

Not only do changes in external conditions affect the types of jobs that are available, they affect how those jobs are created and managed. For instance, many employers are using flexible work arrangements with work tasks done by freelancers hired to work on an as-needed basis or by temporary workers who work full-time but are not permanent employees or by individuals who share jobs.[21] Keep in mind that these approaches are being used because of the constraints from the external environment. As a manager, you'll need to recognize how such work arrangements affect the way you plan, organize, lead, and control. Flexible work arrangements have become so prevalent that we'll discuss them in other chapters as well.

ASSESSING ENVIRONMENTAL UNCERTAINTY.   Another constraint posed by external environments is the amount of uncertainty found in that environment, which can affect organizational outcomes. **Environmental uncertainty** refers to the degree of change and complexity in an organization's environment. The matrix in Exhibit 2–2 shows these two aspects.

EXHIBIT 2–2   **Environmental Uncertainty Matrix**

		Degree of Change	
		Stable	**Dynamic**
Degree of Complexity	**Simple**	**Cell 1** Stable and predictable environment Few components in environment Components are somewhat similar and remain basically the same Minimal need for sophisticated knowledge of components	**Cell 2** Dynamic and unpredictable environment Few components in environment Components are somewhat similar but are continually changing Minimal need for sophisticated knowledge of components
	Complex	**Cell 3** Stable and predictable environment Many components in environment Components are not similar to one another and remain basically the same High need for sophisticated knowledge of components	**Cell 4** Dynamic and unpredictable environment Many components in environment Components are not similar to one another and are continually changing High need for sophisticated knowledge of components

environmental uncertainty
The degree of change and complexity in an organization's environment

RIGHT ? OR WRONG

For the second time in two years, Apple's CEO Steve Jobs has taken a medical leave a year and a half after his return following a liver transplant. "The leave raises questions about both his long-term prognosis and the leadership of the world's most valuable technology company." Jobs has said he would remain chief executive and that he hoped to return to Apple as soon as he could. During his first absence, Jobs remained in almost daily telephone contact with other top executives as he monitored the progress of both the iPhone 4 and the iPad. An analyst with a financial firm has said that "regardless of whether Mr. Jobs returned to Apple, the company would probably continue doing well for the foreseeable future, although its long-term prospects were more uncertain." Jobs did return briefly to introduce the iPad2. However, many feel that because Jobs is so closely linked with the firm's creative vision, the company (and Steve Jobs) should be required to release more medical information.[27]

Note: Steve Jobs, who resigned his CEO position in August 2011, passed away on October 5, 2011.

Think About:

- What do you think about this?
- Do the heads of publicly traded firms have a right to medical privacy? Why or why not?
- What stakeholders do you think are most important in this situation?
- What responsibilities do organizations have to stakeholders in situations like this?
- What ethical implications might arise in such a situation?

Jim Wilson/Redux Pictures

The first dimension of uncertainty is the degree of unpredictable change. If the components in an organization's environment change frequently, it's a *dynamic* environment. If change is minimal, it's a *stable* one. A stable environment might be one in which there are no new competitors, few technological breakthroughs by current competitors, little activity by pressure groups to influence the organization, and so forth. For instance, Zippo Manufacturing, best known for its Zippo lighters, faces a relatively stable environment.[22] There are few competitors and little technological change. The main external concern for the company is probably the declining trend in tobacco usage. In contrast, the recorded music industry faces a dynamic (highly uncertain and unpredictable) environment. Digital formats, apps, and music-downloading sites have turned the industry upside down and brought high levels of uncertainty.

The other dimension of uncertainty describes the degree of **environmental complexity**, which looks at the number of components in an organization's environment and the extent of the knowledge that the organization has about those components. An organization that has few competitors, customers, suppliers, or government agencies to deal with, or that needs little information about its environment, has a less complex and thus less uncertain environment.

How does the concept of environmental uncertainty influence managers? Looking again at Exhibit 2–2, each of the four cells represents different combinations of degree of complexity and degree of change. Cell 1 (stable-simple environment) represents the lowest level of environmental uncertainty and cell 4 (dynamic and complex environment) the highest. Not surprisingly, managers have the greatest influence on organizational outcomes in cell 1 and the least in cell 4. Because uncertainty is a threat to an organization's effectiveness, managers try to minimize it. Given a choice, managers would prefer to operate in the least uncertain environments, but they rarely control that choice. In addition, the nature of the external environment today is that most industries are facing more dynamic change, making their environments more uncertain.

MANAGING STAKEHOLDER RELATIONSHIPS. What has made MTV a popular cable channel for young adults year after year? One reason is that it understands the importance of building relationships with its various stakeholders: viewers, reality show participants, music celebrities, advertisers, affiliate TV stations, public service groups, and others. The nature of stakeholder relationships is another way in which the environment influences managers. The more obvious and secure these relationships, the more influence managers will have over organizational outcomes.

Stakeholders are any constituencies in an organization's environment that are affected by that organization's decisions and actions. These groups have a stake in or are significantly influenced by what the organization does. In turn, these groups can influence the organization. For example, think of the groups that might be affected by the decisions and actions of Starbucks—coffee bean farmers, employees, specialty coffee competitors, local communities, and so forth. Some of these stakeholders also, in turn, may impact decisions and actions of Starbucks' managers. The idea that organizations have stakeholders is now widely accepted by both management academics and practicing managers.[23]

Exhibit 2–3 identifies the most common stakeholders that an organization might have to deal with. Note that these stakeholders do include internal and external groups. Why? Because both can affect what an organization does and how it operates.

Why should managers even care about managing stakeholder relationships?[24] For one thing, it can lead to desirable organizational outcomes such as improved predictability of environmental changes, more successful innovations, greater degree of trust among stakeholders, and greater organizational flexibility to reduce the impact of change. For instance, social media company Facebook is spending more on lobbying and meeting with governmental officials as lawmakers and regulators look at sweeping changes to online privacy law. The company is "working to shape its image on Capitol Hill and avert measures potentially damaging to its information-sharing business."[25]

Can stakeholder management affect organizational performance? The answer is yes! Management researchers who have looked at this issue are finding that managers of high-performing companies tend to consider the interests of all major stakeholder groups as they make decisions.[26]

Another reason for managing external stakeholder relationships is that it's the "right" thing to do. Because an organization depends on these external groups as sources of inputs (resources) and as outlets for outputs (goods and services), managers should consider the interests of stakeholders as they make decisions. We'll address this issue in more detail in the next chapter when we look at corporate social responsibility.

m42/Newscom

Some 5,000 employees congregating at a Boston Scientific Corporation meeting were thanked by patients treated with the firm's medical devices they helped produce. Speaking in person and projected on two huge video screens, the patients and their family members expressed gratitude to the employees for products and procedures that either saved their lives or improved the quality of their lives. Along with hospitals and physicians, these patients are stakeholders who are influenced by what the medical technology company does. Hearing the stories of patients also benefits Boston Scientific. Knowing that their work helps other people and saves lives is a key motivating factor for employees.

EXHIBIT 2–3   **Organizational Stakeholders**

- Employees
- Customers
- Unions
- Social and Political Action Groups
- Shareholders
- Organization
- Competitors
- Communities
- Trade and Industry Associations
- Suppliers
- Governments
- Media

environmental complexity
The number of components in an organization's environment and the extent of knowledge that the organization has about those components

stakeholders
Any constituencies in an organization's environment that are affected by that organization's decisions and actions

As we've tried to make clear throughout this section, it's not going to be "business as usual" for organizations or for managers. Managers will have hard decisions to make about how they do business and about their people. It's important that you understand how changes in the external environment will affect your organizational and management experiences. Now, we need to switch gears and look at the internal aspects of the organization, specifically, its culture.

2.3 Define what organizational culture is and explain why it's important.

WHAT IS ORGANIZATIONAL CULTURE AND WHY IS IT IMPORTANT?

Each of us has a unique personality—traits and characteristics that influence the way we act and interact with others. When we describe someone as warm, open, relaxed, shy, or aggressive, we're describing personality traits. An organization, too, has a personality, which we call its *culture.*

At Vanguard Group Inc., CEO William McNabb recently received an e-mail from one of his sales reps that a longtime client wanted to have lunch with him.[28] "At the end of the e-mail was a simple request: Please do not suit up." The client specifically asked that the CEO not wear a suit because it made the client feel uncomfortable. Despite being more than 100 miles from the formalities of Wall Street, Vanguard had always required its employees worldwide to dress in business attire—jacket and tie for men and professional dress for women. Not anymore. McNabb announced on his blog that Vanguard was going "business appropriate," meaning that employees would no longer need to suit up unless they were meeting with clients. And employees have embraced the new dress code. Expectations of appropriate work dress are one of the more visible elements of an organization's culture.

What Is Organizational Culture?

Organizational culture has been described as the shared values, principles, traditions, and ways of doing things that influence the way organizational members act. In most organizations, these shared values and practices have evolved over time and determine, to a large extent, how "things are done around here."[29]

Our definition of culture implies three things. First, culture is a *perception*. It's not something that can be physically touched or seen, but employees perceive it on the basis of what they experience within the organization. Second, organizational culture is *descriptive*. It's concerned with how members perceive or describe the culture, not with whether they like it. Finally, even though individuals may have different backgrounds or work at different organizational levels, they tend to describe the organization's culture in similar terms. That's the *shared* aspect of culture.

A culture of youthfulness describes the personality of the YOHO brand of e-commerce, online interactive community, and fashion magazine ventures founded by Liang Chao, CEO of New Power Corporation. Chao created a casual, fun-loving, and fast-paced environment for his young college graduate staffers who share similar lifestyles and the belief that "being young is an attitude." Focusing on the fashions of youth, highly energetic and imaginative employees are committed to YOHO's goal of becoming the biggest portal for Chinese young people and are the key factors in attracting young readers and customers. Shown here are staffers holding an online ordering meeting for YOHO's e-commerce Web site at company offices in Nanjing, China.

Chen Qi/Newscom

How Can Culture Be Assessed?

Research suggests that seven dimensions describe an organization's culture.[30] These dimensions (shown in Exhibit 2–4) range from low to high, meaning it's not typical of the culture (low) or is especially typical of the culture (high). Describing an organization using these seven dimensions gives a composite picture of the organization's culture. In many organizations, one cultural dimension often is emphasized more than the others and essentially shapes the organization's personality and the way organizational members work. For instance, at Sony Corporation the focus is product innovation (innovation

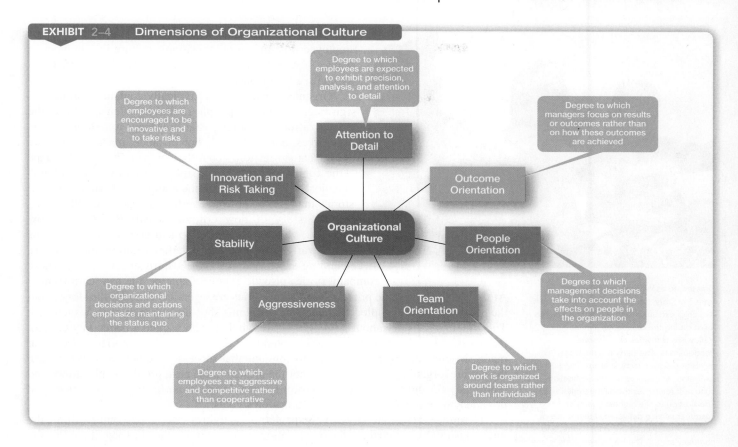

EXHIBIT 2–4 Dimensions of Organizational Culture

and risk taking). The company "lives and breathes" new product development and employees' work behaviors support that goal. In contrast, Southwest Airlines has made its employees a central part of its culture (people orientation) and shows this through the way it treats them.

Where Does an Organization's Culture Come From?

An organization's culture usually reflects the vision or mission of the organization's founders. Because the founders had the original idea, they also had biases on how to carry out the idea. They were not constrained by previous customs or ideologies. The founders established the early culture by projecting an image of what the organization should be and what its values were. The small size of most new organizations also helped the founders impose their vision on all organization members. An organization's culture, then, results from the interaction between (1) the founders' biases and assumptions, and (2) what the first employees learn subsequently from their own experiences. For example, the founder of IBM, Thomas Watson, established a culture based on "pursuing excellence, providing the best customer service, and respect for employees." Ironically, some 85 years later, in an effort to revitalize the ailing IBM, CEO Louis Gerstner enhanced that culture with his strong, "customer-oriented sensibility," recognizing the urgency the marketplace imposes on having customers' expectations met. And at Southwest Airlines, former CEO Herb Kelleher reinforced the company's "people culture" by implementing certain practices— such as compensation and benefits above industry averages—to make employees happy.

organizational culture
The shared values, principles, traditions, and ways of doing things that influence the way organizational members act

Matt Nager/Redux Pictures

Dressed up as Woody, the pull-string doll from *Toy Story*, Southwest Airlines chairman and chief executive Gary Kelly (right) enjoys a skit during the company's annual Halloween festivities at corporate headquarters. The party is a ritual that celebrates Southwest's energized and exuberant employees and free-wheeling culture. It reinforces the airline's mission of "dedication to the highest quality of customer service delivered with a sense of warmth, friendliness, individual pride, and company spirit." The Halloween party is one of eight annual corporate events that bring employees together and help keep the company's fun-loving culture alive.

AND THE SURVEY SAYS... [40]

67 percent of corporate leaders surveyed say that resilience is important in keeping your job during uncertain times.

57 percent of workers surveyed said that the additional job responsibilities they've assumed in the current economy are a burden.

63 percent of Americans polled said that what they were most angry about was the economy.

32 percent of workers surveyed said that acclimating to a different corporate culture could pose the greatest challenge when reentering the workforce.

67 percent of men never wear a tie to work.

61 percent of senior managers surveyed said their organization was somewhat prepared to deal with a sudden loss of a key senior manager.

35 percent of CEOs said their biggest challenge during a recession is retaining employee talent.

How Do Employees Learn the Culture?

Employees "learn" an organization's culture in a number of ways. The most common are stories, rituals, material symbols, and language.

Organizational *"stories"* typically contain a narrative of significant events or people including such things as the organization's founders, rule breaking, reactions to past mistakes, and so forth.[31] For instance, managers at Nike feel that stories told about the company's past help shape the future. Whenever possible, corporate "storytellers" (senior executives) explain the company's heritage and tell stories that celebrate people getting things done. When they tell the story of how cofounder Bill Bowerman (now deceased) went to his workshop and poured rubber into his wife's waffle iron to create a better running shoe, they're celebrating and promoting Nike's spirit of innovation. These company stories provide examples that people can learn from.[32] At the 3M Company, the product innovation stories are legendary. There's the story about the 3M scientist who spilled chemicals on her tennis shoe and came up with Scotchgard. Then, there's the story about Art Fry, a 3M researcher, who wanted a better way to mark the pages of his church hymnal and invented the Post-it Note. These stories reflect what made 3M great and what it will take to continue that success.[33] To help employees learn the culture, organizational stories anchor the present in the past, provide explanations and legitimacy for current practices, exemplify what is important to the organization, and provide compelling pictures of an organization's goals.[34]

Corporate *rituals* are repetitive sequences of activities that express and reinforce the important values and goals of the organization.[35] For example, the "Passing of the Pillars" is an important ritual at Boston Scientific's facility near Minneapolis. When someone has a challenging assignment, they're "awarded" a small two-foot high plaster-of-Paris pillar to show that they've got support from all their colleagues.[36]

When you walk into different businesses, do you get a "feel" for what type of work environment it is—formal, casual, fun, serious, and so forth? These reactions demonstrate the power of *material symbols* or *artifacts* in creating an organization's personality.[37] The layout of an organization's facilities, how employees dress, the types of automobiles provided to top executives, and the availability of corporate aircraft are examples of material symbols. Others include the size of offices, the elegance of furnishings, executive "perks" (extra benefits provided to managers, such as health club memberships, use of company-owned facilities, and so forth), employee fitness centers or on-site dining facilities, and reserved parking spaces for certain employees. At WorldNow, an important material symbol is an old dented drill that the founders purchased for $2 at a thrift store. The drill symbolizes the company's culture of "drilling down to solve problems." When an employee is presented with the drill in recognition of outstanding work, he or she is expected to personalize the drill in some way and devise a new rule for caring for it. One employee installed a Bart Simpson trigger; another made the drill wireless by adding an antenna. The company's "icon" carries on the culture even as the organization evolves and changes.[38] Material symbols convey to employees who is important and the kinds of behavior (for example, risk taking, conservative, authoritarian, participative, individualistic, and so forth) that are expected, appropriate, and rewarded.

Many organizations and units within organizations use *language* as a way to identify and unite members of a culture. By learning this language, members attest to their acceptance of the culture and their willingness to help preserve it. At Cranium, a Seattle board game company, "chiff" is used to remind employees of the need to be incessantly innovative in everything they do. "Chiff" stands for "clever, high-quality, innovative, friendly, fun."[39] Over time, organizations often develop unique terms to describe equipment, key personnel, suppliers, customers, processes, or products related to its business. New employees are frequently overwhelmed with acronyms and jargon that, after a short period of time, become a natural part of their language. Once learned, this language acts as a common denominator that bonds members.

HOW DOES ORGANIZATIONAL CULTURE AFFECT MANAGERS?

Marjorie Kaplan, president of the Animal Planet and Science networks, understands the power of organizational culture and how it affects her as a manager. She says that one of her company's stated goals is "to make it the place where, when you come to work you feel like you have the opportunity to bring your best self and you're also challenged to bring your best self."[41] And she's trying to create and maintain a culture that does just that for her employees and for herself.

> Describe how organizational culture affects managers.
>
> **2.4**

The two main ways that an organization's culture affects managers are (1) its effect on what employees do and how they behave, and (2) its effect on what managers do.

How Does Culture Affect What Employees Do?

An organization's culture has an effect on what employees do, depending on how strong, or weak, the culture is. Strong cultures—those in which the key values are deeply held and widely shared—have a greater influence on employees than do weaker cultures. The more employees accept the organization's key values and the greater their commitment to those values, the stronger the culture is. Most organizations have moderate to strong cultures; that is, there is relatively high agreement on what's important, what defines "good" employee behavior, what it takes to get ahead, and so forth. The stronger a culture becomes, the more it affects what employees do and the way managers plan, organize, lead, and control.[42]

Also, in organizations with a strong culture, that culture can substitute for the rules and regulations that formally guide employees. In essence, strong cultures can create predictability, orderliness, and consistency without the need for written documentation. Therefore, the stronger an organization's culture, the less managers need to be concerned with developing formal rules and regulations. Instead, those guides will be internalized in employees when they accept the organization's culture. If, on the other hand, an organization's culture is weak—if no dominant shared values are present—its effect on employee behavior is less clear.

How Does Culture Affect What Managers Do?

Houston-based Apache Corp. has become one of the best performers in the independent oil drilling business because it has fashioned a culture that values risk taking and quick decision making. Potential hires are judged on how much initiative they've shown in getting projects done at other companies. And company employees are handsomely rewarded if they meet profit and production goals.[43] Because an organization's culture constrains what they can and cannot do and how they manage, it's particularly relevant to managers. Such constraints are rarely explicit. They're not written down. It's unlikely they'll even be spoken. But they're there, and all managers quickly learn what to do and not do in their organization. For instance, you won't find the following values written down, but each comes from a real organization.

strong cultures
Cultures in which the key values are deeply held and widely shared

The strong culture of Honest Tea Company is all about honesty. Seth Goldman, cofounder and "TeaEO" of Honest Tea, started the company with a mission to create truly healthy, organic beverages. In growing his company, Goldman used the same authenticity, integrity, and purity in crafting his products as he did in conducting his business and creating relationships with employees, suppliers, and customers. Key values of Honest Tea include communicating with openness and trust, engaging employees in all aspects of the business, focusing on corporate social responsibility, and committing to high environmental standards. Goldman is shown here holding a tea tasting of new products with employees and a supplier at company headquarters.

- Look busy even if you're not.
- If you take risks and fail around here, you'll pay dearly for it.
- Before you make a decision, run it by your boss so that he or she is never surprised.
- We make our product only as good as the competition forces us to.
- What made us successful in the past will make us successful in the future.
- If you want to get to the top here, you have to be a team player.

The link between values such as these and managerial behavior is fairly straightforward. Take, for example, a so-called "ready-aim-fire" culture. In such an organization, managers will study and analyze proposed projects endlessly before committing to them. However, in a "ready-fire-aim" culture, managers take action and then analyze what has been done. Or, say an organization's culture supports the belief that profits can be increased by cost cutting and that the company's best interests are served by achieving slow but steady increases in quarterly earnings. Managers are unlikely to pursue programs that are innovative, risky, long term, or expansionary. In an organization whose culture conveys a basic distrust of employees, managers are more likely to use an authoritarian leadership style than a democratic one. Why? The culture establishes for managers appropriate and expected behavior. For example, Banco Santander, whose headquarters are located 20 kilometers from downtown Madrid, has been described as a "risk-control freak." The company's managers adhered to "banking's stodgiest virtues—conservatism and patience." However, it's those values that triggered the company's growth from the sixth largest bank in Spain to the largest bank in the euro zone.[44]

As shown in Exhibit 2–5, a manager's decisions are influenced by the culture in which he or she operates. An organization's culture, especially a strong one, influences and constrains the way managers plan, organize, lead, and control.

EXHIBIT 2–5   Managerial Decisions Affected by Culture

PLANNING

- The degree of risk that plans should contain
- Whether plans should be developed by individuals or teams
- The degree of environmental scanning in which management will engage

ORGANIZING

- How much autonomy should be designed into employees' jobs
- Whether tasks should be done by individuals or in teams
- The degree to which department managers interact with each other

LEADING

- The degree to which managers are concerned with increasing employee job satisfaction
- What leadership styles are appropriate
- Whether all disagreements—even constructive ones—should be eliminated

CONTROLLING

- Whether to impose external controls or to allow employees to control their own actions
- What criteria should be emphasized in employee performance evaluations
- What repercussions will occur from exceeding one's budget

Mary Calvert/The New York Times/Redux Pictures

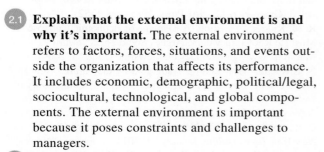

Review

CHAPTER SUMMARY

2.1 **Explain what the external environment is and why it's important.** The external environment refers to factors, forces, situations, and events outside the organization that affects its performance. It includes economic, demographic, political/legal, sociocultural, technological, and global components. The external environment is important because it poses constraints and challenges to managers.

2.2 **Discuss how the external environment affects managers.** There are three ways that the external environment affects managers: its impact on jobs and employment, the amount of environmental

uncertainty, and the nature of stakeholder relationships.

2.3 **Define what organizational culture is and explain why it's important.** Organizational culture is the shared values, principles, traditions, and ways of doing things that influence the way organizational members act. It's important because of the impact it has on decisions, behaviors, and actions of organizational employees.

2.4 **Describe how organizational culture affects managers.** Organizational culture affects managers in two ways: through its effect on what employees do and how they behave, and through its effect on what managers do as they plan, organize, lead, and control.

MyManagementLab   For more resources, please visit **www.mymanagementlab.com**

UNDERSTANDING THE CHAPTER

1. How much impact do managers actually have on an organization's success or failure?

2. Describe the six external environment components. Why is it important for managers to understand these components?

3. How has the changed economy affected what managers do? Find two or three examples in current business periodicals of activities and practices that organizations are using. Discuss them in light of the changed environment.

4. Why is it important for managers to pay attention to demographic trends and shifts?

5. What is environmental uncertainty? What impact does it have on managers and organizations? Find two examples in current business periodicals that

illustrate how environmental uncertainty affects organizations.

6. "Businesses are built on relationships." What do you think this statement means? What are the implications for managing the external environment?

7. Is organizational culture an asset to an organization? Explain. Can it ever be a liability? Explain.

8. How is an organization's culture formed and maintained?

9. Discuss the impact of a strong culture on organizations and managers.

10. Pick two organizations that you interact with frequently (as an employee or as a customer) and assess their culture according to the dimensions shown in Exhibit 2–4.

Go to p. 406
YOUR TURN ᵀᴼ BE A MANAGER for Chapter 2.

Endnotes

1. "100 Best Companies to Work For," *Fortune,* February 7, 2011, pp. 91+; V. Nayar, "Employee Happiness: Zappos vs. HCL," *Businessweek.com,* January 5, 2011; D. Richards, "At Zappos, Culture Pays," *Strategy+Business Online,* Autumn 2010; T. Hseih, "Zappos's CEO on Going to Extremes for Customers," *Harvard Business Review,* July–August 2010, pp. 41–45; A. Perschel, "Work-Life Flow: How Individuals, Zappos, and Other Innovative Companies Achieve High Engagement," *Global Business & Organizational Excellence,* July 2010, pp. 17–30; T. Hseih, "Why I Sold Zappos," *Inc.,* June 2010, pp. 100–104; T. Hseih, "Happy Feet," *Newsweek,* June 21, 2010, p. 10; M. Betts, "Zappos Earns No. 1 Ranking for E-retailing," *Computerworld,* June 7, 2010, p. 4; S. Elliott, "Tireless Employees Get Their Tribute, Even If It's in Felt and Polyester," *New York Times Online,* March 4, 2010; C. Palmeri, "Now for Sale, Zappos Culture," *Bloomberg BusinessWeek,* January 11, 2010, p. 57; and E. Frauenheim, "Can Zappos Culture Survive the Amazon Jungle?" *Workforce Management Online,* September 14, 2009.
2. J. Robison, "What Leaders Must Do Next," *The Gallup Management Journal Online,* http://gmj.com/ (June 11, 2009).
3. C. Matlack, "The Growing Peril of a Connected World," *Bloomberg BusinessWeek,* December 6–12, 2010, pp. 63–64.
4. C. Rampell, "Big Jump in Private Jobs Bolsters Recovery Hopes," *New York Times Online,* March 4, 2011; D. Das, Gaea News Network, "Men Lost More Jobs Than Women Worldwide: Accenture," *Reuters,* March 9, 2010; P. Izzo, "Economists Expect Shifting Work Force," *Wall Street Journal Online,* February 11, 2010; and BBC News, "Recession May See 25m Jobs Lost," *BBC News Online,* September 16, 2009.
5. S. Reddy, M. Walker, and A. Batson, "Factories Revive Economy," *Wall Street Journal,* April 2, 2010, pp. A1+; and S. Shinn, "Banking on Customers," *BizEd,* March–April 2010, pp. 16–21.
6. N. Gibbs, "25 People to Blame," *BusinessWeek,* February 23, 2009, p. 20.
7. Ibid.
8. F. Zakaria, "Greed Is Good (To a Point)," *Newsweek,* June 22, 2009, pp. 41–47.
9. M. E. Porter and M. R. Kramer, "Shared Value," *Harvard Business Review,* January–February 2011, pp. 63–77; and Zakaria, 2009.
10. From the Past to the Present box based on S. Terlep and N. E. Boudette, "Feeling Heat from Ford, GM Reshuffles Managers," *Wall Street Journal Online,* March 3, 2010; "Why CEO Churn Is Healthy," *BusinessWeek*, November 13, 2000, p. 230; T. M. Hout, "Are Managers Obsolete?" *Harvard Business Review*, March–April 1999, pp. 161–168; S. M. Puffer and J. B. Weintrop, "Corporate Performance and CEO Turnover: The Role of Performance Expectations," *Administrative Science Quarterly*, March 1991, pp. 1–19; C. R. Schwenk, "Illusions of Management Control? Effects of Self-Serving Attributions on Resource Commitments and Confidence in Management," *Human Relations*, April 1990, pp. 333–347; J. R. Meindl and S. B. Ehrlich, "The Romance of Leadership and the Evaluation of Organizational Performance," *Academy of Management Journal* (March 1987), pp. 91–109; J. A. Byrne, "The Limits of Power," *BusinessWeek*, October 23, 1987, pp. 33–35; D. C. Hambrick and S. Finkelstein, "Managerial Discretion: A Bridge between Polar Views of Organizational Outcomes," in L. L. Cummings and

B. M. Staw (eds.), *Research in Organizational Behavior*, vol. 9 (Greenwich, CT: JAI Press, 1987), pp. 369–406; and J. Pfeffer, "Management as Symbolic Action: The Creation and Maintenance of Organizational Paradigms," in L. L. Cummings and B. M. Staw (eds.), *Research in Organizational Behavior*, vol. 3 (Greenwich, CT: JAI Press, 1981), pp. 1–52.
11. R. M. Kidder, "Cleaning Up Damage of Economic Collapse Must Be Rooted in Values, Argues Sociologist," *Ethics Newsline,* www.globalethics.org/newsline (June 15, 2009).
12. N. F. Koehn, "How to Stop Trading Away the Future," *New York Times Online,* March 5, 2011; and L. Meckler, "Public Wary of Deficit, Economic Intervention," *Wall Street Journal,* June 18, 2009, pp. A1+.
13. C. Rampell, "The 'New Normal' Is Actually Pretty Old," *New York Times Online,* January 11, 2011; R. Farzad, "Normal," *Bloomberg BusinessWeek,* December 20, 2010–January 2, 2011, pp. 15–18; and N. H. Tseng, "Five 'New Normals' That Really Will Stick," *CNNMoney.com,* August 20, 2010.
14. P. Coy, "If Demography Is Destiny, Then India Has the Edge," *Bloomberg BusinessWeek,* January 17–23, 2011, pp. 9–10.
15. Managing Technology box based on R. M. Kesner, "Running Information Services as a Business: Managing IS Commitments within the Enterprise," *Information Strategy,* Summer 2002, pp. 15–35.
16. M. Richtel, "Growing Up Digital, Wired for Distraction," *New York Times Online,* November 21, 2010; S. Jayson, "iGeneration Has No Off Switch," *USA Today,* February 10, 2010, pp. 1D+; and L. Rosen, *Rewired: Understanding the iGeneration and the Way They Learn* (Palgrave-McMillan), 2010.
17. R. Friedrich, M. Peterson, and A. Koster, "The Rise of Generation C," *Strategy+Business,* Spring 2011, pp. 1–8.
18. S. Cardwell, "Where Do Babies Come From?" *Newsweek,* October 19, 2009, p. 56.
19. Y. Hori, J-P. Lehmann, T. Ma Kam Wah, and V. Wang, "Facing Up to the Demographic Dilemma," *Strategy+Business Online,* Spring 2010; and E. E. Gordon, "Job Meltdown or Talent Crunch?" *Training* (January 2010), p. 10.
20. R. Hampson, "The Changing Face of American Jobs," *USA Today,* January 13, 2011, pp. 1A+; P. Izzo, "Economists Expect Shifting Work Force," *Wall Street Journal Online,* February 11, 2010; and J. Lanhart, "Even In a Recovery, Some Jobs Won't Return," *Wall Street Journal,* January 12, 2010, p. A15.
21. E. Frauenheim, "Companies Focus Their Attention on Flexibility," *Workforce Management Online,* February 2011; P. Davidson, "Companies Do More with Fewer Workers," *USA Today,* February 23, 2011, pp. 1B+; K. Bennhold, "Working Part-Time in the 21st Century," *New York Times Online,* December 29, 2010; M. Rich, "Weighing Costs, Companies Favor Temporary Help," *New York Times Online,* December 19, 2010; P. Davidson, "Temporary Workers Reshape Companies, Jobs," *USA Today,* October 13, 2010, pp. 1A+; P. Davidson, "More Temp Workers Are Getting Hired," *USA Today,* March 8, 2010, p. 1B; S. Reddy, "Wary Companies Rely on Temporary Workers," *Wall Street Journal,* March 6–7, 2010, p. A4; P. Davidson, "Cuts in Hours Versus Cuts in Jobs," *USA Today,* February 25, 2010, p. 1B; and S. A. Hewlett, L. Sherbin, and K. Sumberg, "How Gen Y and Boomers Will Reshape Your Agenda," *Harvard Business Review,* July–August, 2009, pp. 71–76.

22. J. R. Hagerty, "Zippos Preps for a Post-Smoker World," *Wall Street Journal,* March 8, 2011, pp. B1+.

23. J. P. Walsh, "Book Review Essay: Taking Stock of Stakeholder Management," *Academy of Management Review*, April 2005, pp. 426–438; R. E. Freeman, A. C. Wicks, and B. Parmar, "Stakeholder Theory and The Corporate Objective Revisited," *Organization Science*, 15 (2004), pp. 364–369; T. Donaldson and L. E. Preston, "The Stakeholder Theory of the Corporation: Concepts, Evidence, and Implications," *Academy of Management Review*, January 1995, pp. 65–91; and R. E. Freeman, *Strategic Management: A Stakeholder Approach* (Boston: Pitman/Ballinger), 1984.

24. J. S. Harrison and C. H. St. John, "Managing and Partnering with External Stakeholders," *Academy of Management Executive*, May 1996, pp. 46–60.

25. J. Swartz, "Facebook Changes Its Status in Washington," *USA Today,* January 13, 2011, p. 1B+.

26. S. L. Berman, R. A. Phillips, and A. C. Wicks, "Resource Dependence, Managerial Discretion, and Stakeholder Performance," *Academy of Management Proceedings* Best Conference Paper, August 2005; A. J. Hillman and G. D. Keim, "Shareholder Value, Stakeholder Management, and Social Issues: What's the Bottom Line?" *Strategic Management Journal* (March 2001), pp. 125–139; J. S. Harrison and R. E. Freeman, "Stakeholders, Social Responsibility, and Performance: Empirical Evidence and Theoretical Perspectives," *Academy of Management Journal* (July 1999), pp. 479–487; and J. Kotter and J. Heskett, *Corporate Culture and Performance* (New York: The Free Press, 1992).

27. Right or Wrong box based on M. Helft, "Jobs Returns to Introduce a New iPad," *New York Times Online,* March 2, 2011; R. Pyrillis, "Apple Won't Say Who Will Eventually Take Jobs' Job," *Workforce Management Online,* February 25, 2011; A. Satariano, "Apple Challenged by Investors on Jobs Succession Planning," *Bloomberg BusinessWeek Online,* February 23, 2011; J. Sonnenfeld, "The Genius Dilemma," *Newsweek,* January 31, 2011, pp. 12–17; C. Hausman, "Ethics Questions After Steve Jobs Takes Medical Leave from Apple," *Ethics Newsline Online,* January 31, 2011; A. Satariano, "The Essence of Apple," *Bloomberg BusinessWeek,* January 24–30, 2011, pp. 6–8; J. S. Lublin, "Investors Want Right to Know," *Wall Street Journal,* January 24, 2011, p. B7; G. Strauss, J. Swartz, and J. Graham, "As Jobs Steps Away, It's a Test for Apple," *USA Today,* January 18, 2011, pp. 1A+; Y. I. Kane and J. S. Lublin, "Apple Chief to Take Leave," *Wall Street Journal,* January 18, 2011, pp. A1+; B. Weinstein, "How Truthful Must CEO Steve Jobs Be?" *Bloomberg BusinessWeek Online,* January 18, 2011; S. Lohr, "Can Apple Find More Hits Without Its Tastemaker?" *New York Times Online,* January 18, 2011; and M. Helft, "Jobs Takes Sick Leave at Apple Again, Stirring Questions," *New York Times Online,* January 17, 2011.

28. J. Toonkel, "Vanguard CEO to Employees: Let's Lose the Suits," *Workforce Management Online,* December 3, 2010.

29. K. Shadur and M. A. Kienzle, "The Relationship Between Organizational Climate and Employee Perceptions of Involvement," *Group & Organization Management*, December 1999, pp. 479–503; M. J. Hatch, "The Dynamics of Organizational Culture," *Academy of Management Review*, October 1993, pp. 657–693; D. R. Denison, "What Is the Difference between Organizational Culture and Organizational Climate? A Native's Point of View on a Decade of Paradigm Wars," paper presented at Academy of Management Annual Meeting, 1993, Atlanta, GA; and L. Smircich, "Concepts of Culture and Organizational Analysis," *Administrative Science Quarterly*, September 1983, p. 339.

30. J. A. Chatman and K. A. Jehn, "Assessing the Relationship between Industry Characteristics and Organizational Culture: How Different Can You Be?" *Academy of Management Journal* (June 1994), pp. 522–553; and C. A. O'Reilly III, J. Chatman, and D. F. Caldwell, "People and Organizational Culture: A Profile Comparison Approach to Assessing Person-Organization Fit," *Academy of Management Journal* (September 1991), pp. 487–516.

31. P. Guber, "The Four Truths of the Storyteller," *Harvard Business Review,* December 2007, pp. 53–59; S. Denning, "Telling Tales," *Harvard Business Review*, May 2004, pp. 122–129; T. Terez, "The Business of Storytelling," *Workforce*, May 2002, pp. 22–24; J. Forman, "When Stories Create an Organization's Future," *Strategy & Business*, Second Quarter 1999, pp. 6–9; C. H. Deutsch, "The Parables of Corporate Culture," *New York Times*, October 13, 1991, p. F25; and D. M. Boje, "The Storytelling Organization: A Study of Story Performance in an Office-Supply Firm," *Administrative Science Quarterly*, March 1991, pp. 106–126.

32. E. Ransdell, "The Nike Story? Just Tell It!" *Fast Company*, January–February 2000, pp. 44–46.

33. J. Useem, "Jim McNerney Thinks He Can Turn 3M from a Good Company into a Great One—With a Little Help from His Former Employer, General Electric," *Fortune*, August 12, 2002, pp. 127–132.

34. Denning, 2004; and A. M. Pettigrew, "On Studying Organizational Cultures," *Administrative Science Quarterly*, December 1979, p. 576.

35. M. T. Dacin, K. Munir, and P. Tracey, "Formal Dining at Cambridge Colleges: Linking Ritual Performance and Institutional Maintenance," *Academy of Management Journal* (December 2010), pp. 1393–1418.

36. D. Drickhamer, "Straight to the Heart," *Industry Week*, October 2003, pp. 36–38.

37. E. H. Schein, "Organizational Culture," *American Psychologist,* February 1990, pp. 109–119.

38. M. Zagoski, "Here's the Drill," *Fast Company*, February 2001, p. 58.

39. "Slogans That Work," *Forbes.com Special*, January 7, 2008, p. 99.

40. And the Survey Says box based on "Best Leaders Bounce Back," *Training,* July–August 2010, p. 7; J. Yang and P. Trap, "Burden vs. Opportunity," *USA Today,* October 13, 2010, p. 1B; C. Hausman, "Harris Asks the U.S. Public What It's Angry About," *Ethics Newsline Online,* November 15, 2010; J. MacIntyre, "Hurdles to Re-Entry," *Springfield, Missouri Business Journal*, August 16–22, 2010, p. 16; G. Kranz, "Fit to Be Tied? Recession May Inspire More Formal Work Attire," *Workforce Management Online,* October 18, 2008; J. Light, "Sudden Leader Loss Leaves Firms in Limbo," *Wall Street Journal,* January 24, 2011, p. B7; and J. Yang and A. Gonzalez, "CEO Challenges," *USA Today,* December 23, 2008, p. 1B.

41. A. Bryant, "Chaos and Order: How to Strike the Best Balance," *New York Times Online,* March 5, 2011.

42. E. H. Schein, *Organizational Culture and Leadership* (San Francisco: Jossey-Bass, 1985), pp. 314–315.

43. C. Palmeri, "The Fastest Drill in the West," *BusinessWeek*, October 24, 2005, pp. 86–88.

44. J. Levine, "Dare to Be Boring," *Time,* February 1, 2010, pp. Global Business 1–2.

CHAPTER
3
Integrative
Managerial
Issues

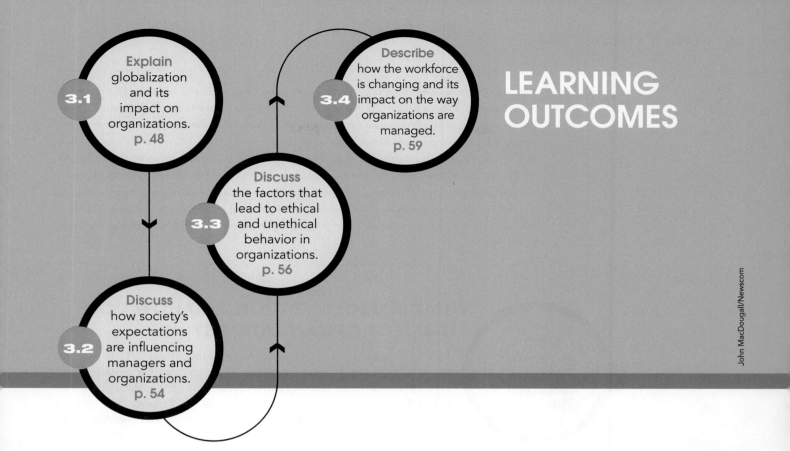

LEARNING OUTCOMES

3.1 **Explain** globalization and its impact on organizations. p. 48

3.4 **Describe** how the workforce is changing and its impact on the way organizations are managed. p. 59

3.3 **Discuss** the factors that lead to ethical and unethical behavior in organizations. p. 56

3.2 **Discuss** how society's expectations are influencing managers and organizations. p. 54

A Level Playing Field?

Companies across the globe have a problem—a large gender gap in leadership.[1] Men far outnumber women in senior business leadership positions. This sexism exists despite efforts and campaigns to improve equality in the workplace. However, one European company—Deutsche Telekom—is tackling the problem head-on. It says that it intends to "more than double the number of women who are managers within five years." In addition, it plans to increase the number of women in senior and middle management to 30 percent by the end of 2015, up from 12 percent today. With this announcement, the company becomes the first member of the DAX 30 index of blue-chip German companies to introduce a gender quota. Deutsche's chief executive René Obermann said, "Taking on more women in management positions is not about the enforcement of misconstrued egalitarianism. Having a greater number of women at the top will quite simply enable us to operate better."

Although Deutsche Telekom's goal of bringing more women into leadership positions is admirable, it's not alone in its inability to diversify its management ranks. Even in the United States, where women have been graduating with advanced professional degrees in record numbers, the number of women in senior leadership positions remains low—only 3 percent of Fortune 500 companies have female CEOs.[2] The issue of employing and engaging a diverse global workforce is an important one for today's managers. However, managers also face other important issues associated with globalization and with doing business in an ethical and responsible way. Because each of these topics—diversity, globalization, and ethics/social responsibility—are integrated throughout many aspects of what managers do and how they manage, we're going to look closer at these integrative managerial issues in this chapter.

WHAT IS GLOBALIZATION AND HOW DOES IT AFFECT ORGANIZATIONS?

3.1 Explain globalization and its impact on organizations.

"It's like being in an emergency room, doing triage." That was the response of Tony Prophet, a senior vice president for operations at Hewlett-Packard after learning that a catastrophic earthquake and tsunami had hit Japan. Not long after getting the news, Mr. Prophet "had set up a virtual 'situation room' so managers in Japan, Taiwan, and America could instantly share information." The analogy of an emergency room was very apt, according to experts, because "modern global supply chains mirror complex biological systems. . . . They can be remarkably resilient and self-healing, yet at times quite vulnerable to some specific seemingly small weakness." Normally, the global flow of goods routinely adapts, day in and day out, to all kinds of glitches and setbacks. However, when a major disaster strikes (for instance, an earthquake in Japan or New Zealand, a volcano in Iceland, labor unrest in China, political upheavals in the Middle East, floods in India, or a hurricane in the United States), the fragility of the global supply chain becomes more apparent.[3]

An important issue that managers must deal with is globalization. Recall from our discussion in Chapter 2 that one important component of the external environment was the global arena. Major events such as catastrophic natural disasters and the global economic meltdown of the past few years have created challenges for managers doing business globally. Despite such challenges, globalization isn't about to disappear. Nations and businesses have been trading with each other for centuries through all kinds of disasters and economic ups and downs. Over the last couple of decades, we've seen an explosion of companies operating almost anywhere in the world. National borders mean little when it comes to doing business. Avon, a so-called American company, gets 79 percent of its annual revenues from sales outside North America. BMW, a German-owned firm, builds cars in South Carolina. McDonald's sells hamburgers in China. Tata, an Indian company, purchased the Jaguar brand—which started as a British company—from Ford Motor Company. Although the world is still a **global village**—that is, a boundaryless world where goods and services are produced and marketed worldwide—how managers do business in that global village is changing. To be effective in this boundaryless world, managers need to adapt to this changed environment, as well as continue to foster an understanding of cultures, systems, and techniques that are different from their own.

What Does It Mean to Be "Global"?

Organizations are considered global if they exchange goods and services with consumers in other countries. Such marketplace globalization is the most common approach to being global. However, many organizations, especially high-tech organizations, are considered global because they use managerial and technical employee talent from other countries. One factor that affects talent globalization is immigration laws and regulations. Managers must be alert to changes in those laws. Finally, an organization can be considered global if it uses financial sources and resources outside its home country, which is known as financial globalization.[4] As might be expected, the global economic slowdown severely affected the availability of financial resources globally. And even as countries' economies began the slow process of recovery, the impact continued to be felt globally.

What Are the Different Types of Global Organizations?

In the mid-1960s, **multinational corporations (MNCs)** became commonplace and initiated rapid growth in international trade. MNCs are any type of international company that maintains operations in multiple countries. Today, companies such as Procter & Gamble, Walmart, Exxon, Coca-Cola, and Aflac are among a growing number of U.S.-based firms that earn significant portions of their annual revenues from foreign operations.

One type of MNC is a **multidomestic corporation**, which decentralizes management and other decisions to the local country in which it is operating. A multidomestic corporation doesn't attempt to replicate its domestic successes by managing foreign operations from its home country. Instead, local employees typically are hired to manage the business and marketing strategies are tailored to that country's unique characteristics. Many consumer product companies organize their global businesses using this approach because they must adapt their products to meet the needs of local markets. For example, Switzerland-based Nestlé operates as a multidomestic corporation. With operations in almost every country on the globe, its managers are responsible for making sure the company's products fit its consumers wherever they are. In parts of Europe, Nestlé sells products that are not available in the United States or Latin America.

Another type of MNC is a **global corporation**, which centralizes its management and other decisions in the home country. These companies treat the world market as an integrated whole and focus on the need for global efficiency. Although these companies may have considerable global holdings, management decisions with company-wide implications are made from headquarters in the home country. Some examples of global companies include Sony, Deutsche Bank AG, and Merrill Lynch (now a subsidiary of Bank of America).

Other companies use an arrangement that eliminates artificial geographical barriers. This type of MNC is often called a **transnational** or **borderless organization**.[5] For example, IBM dropped its organizational structure based on country and reorganized into industry groups. Ford Motor Company is pursuing the One Ford concept as it integrates its global operations. Another company, Thomson SA, which is legally incorporated in France, has eight major locations around the globe. The CEO said, "We don't want people to think we're based anyplace."[6] Managers choose this approach to increase efficiency and effectiveness in a competitive global marketplace.[7]

This young man enjoying a Coke in Copenhagen, Denmark, is consuming one of 1.7 billion servings a day of a beverage brand owned by The Coca-Cola Company. A multinational manufacturer, distributor, and marketer, the company produces more than 400 brands and 3,500 different products, including soft drinks, water, juices and juice drinks, sports and energy drinks, sparkling beverages, and tea and coffee. Based in Atlanta, Georgia, it operates in more than 200 countries and generates almost 80 percent of its revenue from operations outside of the United States. The Coca-Cola Company is a global business that operates on a local scale with hundreds of bottling partners worldwide in achieving its mission "to refresh the world."

Francis Dean/Newscom

---

global village
A boundaryless world where goods and services are produced and marketed worldwide

multinational corporation (MNC)
Any type of international company that maintains operations in multiple countries

multidomestic corporation
An MNC that decentralizes management and other decisions to the local country where it's doing business

global corporation
An MNC that centralizes management and other decisions in the home country.

transnational (borderless) organization
A structural arrangement for global organizations that eliminates artificial geographical barriers

How Do Organizations Go Global?

When organizations do go global, they often use different approaches. (See Exhibit 3–1.) At first, managers may want to get into a global market with minimal investment. At this stage, they may start with **global sourcing** (also called global outsourcing), which is purchasing materials or labor from around the world wherever it is cheapest. The goal: take advantage of lower costs in order to be more competitive. For instance, Massachusetts General Hospital uses radiologists in India to interpret CT scans.[8] Although global sourcing may be the first step to going international for many companies, they often continue using this approach because of the competitive advantages it offers. However, as the current economic crisis accelerated, many organizations reconsidered their decisions to source globally. For instance, Dell, Apple, and American Express are just a few that have scaled back some of their offshore customer service operations. One analyst said that companies rethinking their global sourcing decisions are trying to make "choices about the best place to do a given piece of work—be it offshore, onshore, or nearshore. As this transformation occurs, work is being spread throughout the world and companies are globalizing to keep up."[9] When a company wants to take that next step in going global, each successive stage beyond global sourcing requires more investment and thus entails more risk for the organization.

The next step in going global may involve **exporting** the organization's products to other countries—that is, making products domestically and selling them abroad. In addition, an organization might do **importing**, which involves acquiring products made abroad and selling them domestically. Both usually entail minimal investment and risk, which is why many small businesses often use these approaches to doing business globally.

Finally, managers might use **licensing** or **franchising**, which are similar approaches involving one organization giving another organization the right to use its brand name, technology, or product specifications in return for a lump sum payment or a fee that is usually based on sales. The only difference is that licensing is primarily used by manufacturing organizations that make or sell another company's products, and franchising is primarily used by service organizations that want to use another company's name and operating methods. For example, New Delhi consumers can enjoy Subway sandwiches, Namibians can dine on KFC fried chicken, and Russians can consume Dunkin' Donuts— all because of *franchises* in these countries. On the other hand, Anheuser-Busch InBev *licensed* the right to brew and market its Budweiser beer to brewers such as Labatt in Canada, Modelo in Mexico, and Kirin in Japan.

Once an organization has been doing business internationally for a while and has gained experience in international markets, managers may decide to make more of a direct investment. One way to do this is through a **global strategic alliance**, which is a partnership between an organization and a foreign company partner or partners in which both

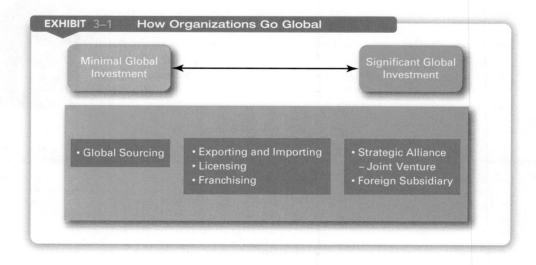

EXHIBIT 3–1   How Organizations Go Global

Minimal Global Investment ⟷ Significant Global Investment

- Global Sourcing
- Exporting and Importing
- Licensing
- Franchising
- Strategic Alliance
  – Joint Venture
- Foreign Subsidiary

share resources and knowledge in developing new products or building production facilities. For example, Honda Motor and General Electric teamed up to produce a new jet engine. A specific type of strategic alliance in which the partners form a separate, independent organization for some business purpose is called a **joint venture**. For example, Hewlett-Packard has had numerous joint ventures with various suppliers around the globe to develop different components for its computer equipment. These partnerships provide a relatively easy way for companies to compete globally.

Finally, managers may choose to directly invest in a foreign country by setting up a **foreign subsidiary** as a separate and independent facility or office. This subsidiary can be managed as a multidomestic organization (local control) or as a global organization (centralized control). As you can probably guess, this arrangement involves the greatest commitment of resources and poses the greatest amount of risk. For instance, United Plastics Group of Westmont, Illinois, built three injection-molding facilities in Suzhou, China. The company's executive vice president for business development says that level of investment was necessary because "it fulfilled our mission of being a global supplier to our global accounts."[10]

These young employees pose for a picture at the official opening of Intel's new assembly plant and test facilities in Ho Chi Minh City, Vietnam. While building the complex, Intel's managers faced many challenges in recruiting and training young workers for the new plant due to cultural differences between the United States and Vietnam. For example, the work culture in Vietnam is based on a hierarchical system of power, status, and authority, in contrast to Intel's culture of teamwork. By understanding these differences and knowing that Vietnamese youth love American pop culture, managers used team-building exercises such as Karaoke Fridays to teach the young trainees how to become team players.

What Do Managers Need to Know About Managing in a Global Organization?

A global world brings new challenges for managers, especially in managing in a country with a different national culture.[11] A specific challenge comes from the need to recognize the differences that might exist and then find ways to make interactions effective.

U.S. managers once held (and some still do hold) a rather parochial view of the world of business. **Parochialism** is a narrow focus in which managers see things only through their own eyes and from their own perspectives. They don't recognize that people from other countries have different ways of doing things or that they live differently from Americans. This view can't succeed in a global village—nor is it the dominant view held today. Changing such perceptions requires understanding that countries have different cultures and environments.

All countries have different values, morals, customs, political and economic systems, and laws, all of which can affect how a business is managed. For instance, in the United States, laws guard against employers taking action against employees solely on the basis of their age. Similar laws can't be found in all other countries. Thus, managers must be aware of a country's laws when doing business there.

The most important and challenging differences for managers to understand, however, are those related to a country's social context or culture. For example, status is perceived

---

global sourcing
Purchasing materials or labor from around the world, wherever it is cheapest

exporting
Making products domestically and selling them abroad

importing
Acquiring products made abroad and selling them domestically

licensing
An agreement in which an organization gives another the right, for a fee, to make or sell its products, using its technology or product specifications

franchising
An agreement in which an organization gives another organization the right, for a fee, to use its name and operating methods

global strategic alliance
A partnership between an organization and a foreign company partner(s) in which both share resources and knowledge in developing new products or building production facilities

joint venture
A specific type of strategic alliance in which the partners agree to form a separate, independent organization for some business purpose

foreign subsidiary
A direct investment in a foreign country that involves setting up a separate and independent facility or office

parochialism
A narrow focus in which managers see things only through their own eyes and from their own perspective

---

From the Past to the Present

An illuminating study of the differences in cultural environments was conducted by Geert Hofstede in the 1970s and 1980s.[12] He surveyed more than 116,000 IBM employees in 40 countries about their work-related values. He found that managers and employees vary on five value dimensions of national culture:

- *Power distance.* The degree to which people in a country accept that power in institutions and organizations is distributed unequally. Ranges from relatively low (low power distance) to extremely unequal (high power distance).

- *Individualism versus collectivism.* Individualism is the degree to which people in a country prefer to act as individuals rather than as members of groups. Collectivism is the equivalent of low individualism.

- *Quantity of life versus quality of life.* Quantity of life is the degree to which values such as assertiveness, the acquisition of money and material goods, and competition are important. Quality of life is the degree to which people value relationships and show sensitivity and concern for the welfare of others.

- *Uncertainty avoidance.* This dimension assesses the degree to which people in a country prefer structured over unstructured situations and whether people are willing to take risks.

- *Long-term versus short-term orientation.* People in cultures with long-term orientations look to the future and value thrift and persistence. A short-term orientation values the past and present and emphasizes respect for tradition and fulfilling social obligations.

Here are a few highlights of four of Hofstede's cultural dimensions and how different countries rank on those dimensions:

Think About:

- Look at the ratings for Mexico and the United States. How do you think a team-based rewards program might work in each country?

- Look at the ratings for Italy and the United States. How do you think encouraging employees to take risks and to think "outside the box" might work in each country?

- What does this information tell you about the importance of understanding cultural differences?

COUNTRY	INDIVIDUALISM/ COLLECTIVISM	POWER DISTANCE	UNCERTAINTY AVOIDANCE	ACHIEVEMENT/ NURTURING[a]
Australia	Individual	Small	Moderate	Strong
Canada	Individual	Moderate	Low	Moderate
England	Individual	Small	Moderate	Strong
France	Individual	Large	High	Weak
Greece	Collective	Large	High	Moderate
Italy	Individual	Moderate	High	Strong
Japan	Collective	Moderate	High	Strong
Mexico	Collective	Large	High	Strong
Singapore	Collective	Large	Low	Moderate
Sweden	Individual	Small	Low	Weak
United States	Individual	Small	Low	Strong
Venezuela	Collective	Large	High	Strong

[a]A weak achievement score is equivalent to high nurturing.
Source: Based on G. Hofstede, "Motivation, Leadership, and Organization: Do American Theories Apply Abroad?" *Organizational Dynamics*, Summer 1980, pp. 42–63.

---

differently in different countries. In France, status is often the result of factors important to the organization, such as seniority, education, and the like. In the United States, status is more a function of what individuals have accomplished personally. Managers need to understand societal issues (such as status) that might affect business operations in another country and recognize that organizational success can come from a variety of managerial practices. Fortunately, managers have help in this regard by turning to the research that has been done on the differences in cultural environments.

HOFSTEDE'S FRAMEWORK.   Geert Hofstede's framework is one of the most widely referenced approaches for analyzing cultural variations. His work has had a major impact on what we know about cultural differences among countries and is highlighted in our From the Past to the Present box.

GLOBE FINDINGS.   Although Hofstede's work has provided the basic framework for differentiating among national cultures, most of the data are over 30 years old. Another more recent research program, called Global Leadership and Organizational Behavior Effectiveness (GLOBE), is an ongoing cross-cultural investigation of leadership and national culture. Using data from more than 17,000 managers in 62 societies around the world, the GLOBE research team (led by Robert House) has identified nine dimensions on which national cultures differ.[13] For each of these dimensions, we have indicated which countries rated high, which rated moderate, and which rated low.

◆ *Assertiveness.* The extent to which a society encourages people to be tough, confrontational, assertive, and competitive versus modest and tender. (*High:* Spain, United States, and Greece. *Moderate:* Egypt, Ireland, and Philippines. *Low:* Sweden, New Zealand, and Switzerland.)

◆ *Future orientation.* The extent to which a society encourages and rewards future-oriented behavior such as planning, investing in the future, and delaying gratification. (*High:* Denmark, Canada, and Netherlands. *Moderate:* Slovenia, Egypt, and Ireland. *Low:* Russia, Argentina, and Poland.)

◆ *Gender differentiation.* The extent to which a society maximizes gender role differences. (*High:* South Korea, Egypt, and Morocco. *Moderate:* Italy, Brazil, and Argentina. *Low:* Sweden, Denmark, and Slovenia.)

◆ *Uncertainty avoidance.* As defined in Hofstede's landmark research, the GLOBE team defined this term as a society's reliance on social norms and procedures to alleviate the unpredictability of future events. (*High:* Austria, Denmark, and Germany. *Moderate:* Israel, United States, and Mexico. *Low:* Russia, Hungary, and Bolivia.)

◆ *Power distance.* As in the original research, the GLOBE team defined this as the degree to which members of a society expect power to be unequally shared. (*High:* Russia, Spain, and Thailand. *Moderate:* England, France, and Brazil. *Low:* Denmark, Netherlands, and South Africa.)

◆ *Individualism/collectivism.* Again, this term was defined similarly to the original research as the degree to which individuals are encouraged by societal institutions to be integrated into groups within organizations and society. A low score is synonymous with collectivism. (*High:* Greece, Hungary, and Germany. *Moderate:* Hong Kong, United States, and Egypt. *Low:* Denmark, Singapore, and Japan.)

◆ *In-group collectivism.* In contrast to focusing on societal institutions, this dimension encompasses the extent to which members of a society take pride in membership in small groups such as their family and circle of close friends and the organizations in which they are employed. (*High:* Egypt, China, and Morocco. *Moderate:* Japan, Israel, and Qatar. *Low:* Denmark, Sweden, and New Zealand.)

◆ *Performance orientation.* This dimension refers to the degree to which a society encourages and rewards group members for performance improvement and excellence. (*High:* United States, Taiwan, and New Zealand. *Moderate:* Sweden, Israel, and Spain. *Low:* Russia, Argentina, and Greece.)

◆ *Humane orientation.* This cultural aspect is the degree to which a society encourages and rewards individuals for being fair, altruistic, generous, caring, and kind to others. (*High:* Indonesia, Egypt, and Malaysia. *Moderate:* Hong Kong, Sweden, and Taiwan. *Low:* Germany, Spain, and France.)

The GLOBE studies confirm that Hofstede's dimensions are still valid, and extend his research rather than replace it. GLOBE's added dimensions provide an expanded and updated measure of countries' cultural differences. It's likely that cross-cultural studies of human behavior and organizational practices will increasingly use the GLOBE dimensions to assess differences between countries. For instance, GLOBE's research dimensions are being used in creating and assessing international advertising.[14]

GLOBE
The Global Leadership and Organizational Behavior Effectiveness research program, a program that studies cross-cultural leadership behaviors

3.2 Discuss how society's expectations are influencing managers and organizations.

WHAT DOES SOCIETY EXPECT FROM ORGANIZATIONS AND MANAGERS?

It's an incredibly simple but potentially world-changing idea.[15] For each pair of shoes sold, a pair is donated to a child in need. That's the business model followed by TOMS Shoes. During a visit to Argentina in 2006 as a contestant on the CBS reality show *The Amazing Race,* Blake Mycoskie, founder of TOMS, "saw lots of kids with no shoes who were suffering from injuries to their feet." He was so moved by the experience that he wanted to do something.

That something is what TOMS Shoes does now by blending charity with commerce. Those shoe donations—now over 1 million pairs—have been central to the success of the TOMS brand. And the brand's popularity is likely to increase as Mary-Kate and Ashley Olsen have partnered with TOMS Shoes in selling a special line of fashionable sandals.

What *does* society expect from organizations and managers? That may seem like a hard question to answer, but not for Blake Mycoskie. He believes that society expects organizations and managers to be respon-sible and ethical. However, as we saw in the publicized stories of notorious financial scandals at Enron, Bernard Madoff Investment Securities, HealthSouth, and others, managers don't always act responsibly or ethically.

How Can Organizations Demonstrate Socially Responsible Actions?

Few terms have been defined in as many different ways as *social responsibility.* Some of the more popular meanings include profit maximization, going beyond profit making, voluntary activities, and concern for the broader social system.[16] On one side is the classical—or purely economic—view that management's only social responsibility is to maximize profits.[17] On the other side is the socioeconomic position, which holds that management's responsibility goes beyond making profits to include protecting and improving society's welfare.[18]

When we talk about **social responsibility** (also known as **corporate social responsibility,** or **CSR**), we mean a business firm's intention, beyond its legal and economic obligations, to do the right things and act in ways that are good for society. Note that this definition assumes that a business obeys the law and pursues economic interests. But also note that this definition views a business as a moral agent. In its effort to do good for society, it must differentiate between right and wrong.

We can understand social responsibility better if we compare it to two similar concepts. **Social obligations** are those activities a business firm engages in to meet certain economic and legal responsibilities. It does the minimum that the law requires and only pursues social goals to the extent that they contribute to its economic goals. **Social responsiveness** is characteristic of the business firm that engages in social actions in response to some popular social need. Managers in these companies are guided by social norms and values and make practical, market-oriented decisions about their actions.[19] A U.S. business that meets federal pollution standards or safe packaging regulations is meeting its social obligation because laws mandate these actions. However, when it provides on-site child-care facilities for employees or packages products using recycled paper, it's being socially respon-sive to working parents and environmentalists who have voiced these social concerns and demanded such actions. For many businesses, their social actions are probably better viewed as being socially responsive rather than socially responsible, at least according to our defini-tions. However, such actions are still good for society. Social responsibility adds an ethical imperative to do those things that make society better and to not do those that could make it worse.

College students surround Blake Mycoskie, the TOMS Shoes founder who believes that management's responsibility goes beyond making profits to include improving society's welfare. TOMS gives shoes to children in need by working with charitable giving partners throughout the world that are already established in countries where TOMS shoes are given. These partners must also meet TOMS criteria for responsible giving. They include giving shoes to the same children on a regular basis as they grow, being considerate of the local economy so giving shoes does not have a negative socioeconomic impact on communities, and incorporating the giving of shoes into their existing health, education, hygiene, and community development programs.

a27/Newscom

EXHIBIT 3–2	Arguments For and Against Social Responsibility

FOR

Public expectations
Public opinion now supports businesses pursuing economic and social goals.

Long-run profits
Socially responsible companies tend to have more secure long-run profits.

Ethical obligation
Businesses should be socially responsible because responsible actions are the right thing to do.

Public image
Businesses can create a favorable public image by pursuing social goals.

Better environment
Business involvement can help solve difficult social problems.

Discouragement of further governmental regulation
By becoming socially responsible, businesses can expect less government regulation.

Balance of responsibility and power
Businesses have a lot of power, and an equally large amount of responsibility is needed to balance against that power.

Stockholder interests
Social responsibility will improve a business's stock price in the long run.

Possession of resources
Businesses have the resources to support public and charitable projects that need assistance.

Superiority of prevention over cures
Businesses should address social problems before they become serious and costly to correct.

AGAINST

Violation of profit maximization
Business is being socially responsible only when it pursues its economic interests.

Dilution of purpose
Pursuing social goals dilutes business's primary purpose—economic productivity.

Costs
Many socially responsible actions do not cover their costs and someone must pay those costs.

Too much power
Businesses have a lot of power already and if they pursue social goals they will have even more.

Lack of skills
Business leaders lack the necessary skills to address social issues.

Lack of accountability
There are no direct lines of accountability for social actions.

Should Organizations Be Socially Involved?

The importance of corporate social responsibility surfaced in the 1960s when social activists questioned the singular economic objective of business. Even today, good arguments can be made for and against businesses being socially responsible. (See Exhibit 3–2.) Yet, arguments aside, times have changed. Managers regularly confront decisions that have a dimension of social responsibility: philanthropy, pricing, employee relations, resource conservation, product quality, and doing business in countries with oppressive governments are just a few. To address these issues, managers may reassess packaging design, recyclability of products, environmental safety practices, outsourcing decisions, foreign supplier practices, employee policies, and the like.

Another way to look at this issue is whether social involvement affects a company's economic performance, which numerous studies have done.[20] Although most found a

social responsibility (corporate social responsibility, or CSR)
A business firm's intention, beyond its legal and economic obligations, to do the right things and act in ways that are good for society

social obligation
When a business firm engages in social actions because of its obligation to meet certain economic and legal responsibilities

social responsiveness
When a business firm engages in social actions in response to some popular social need

small positive relationship, no generalizable conclusions can be made because these studies have shown that relationship is affected by various contextual factors such as firm size, industry, economic conditions, and regulatory environment.[21] Other researchers have questioned causation. If a study showed that social involvement and economic performance were positively related, this didn't necessarily mean that social involvement *caused* higher economic performance. It could simply mean that high profits afforded companies the "luxury" of being socially involved.[22] Such concerns can't be taken lightly. In fact, one study found that if the flawed empirical analyses in these studies were "corrected," social responsibility had a neutral impact on a company's financial performance.[23] Another found that participating in social issues not related to the organization's primary stakeholders had a negative effect on shareholder value.[24] Despite all these concerns, after re-analyzing several studies, other researchers have concluded that managers can afford to be (and should be) socially responsible.[25]

What Is Sustainability and Why Is It Important?

It's the world's largest retailer with almost $422 billion in annual sales, 2.1 million employees, and 8,400 stores. Yes, we're talking about Walmart. And considering its size, Walmart is probably the last company that you'd think about in a section describing sustainability. However, Walmart announced in early 2010 that it would "cut some 20 million metric tons of greenhouse gas emissions from its supply chain by the end of 2015—the equivalent of removing more than 3.8 million cars from the road for a year."[27] This corporate action affirms that sustainability has become a mainstream issue for managers.

What's emerging in the twenty-first century is the concept of managing in a sustainable way, which has had the effect of widening corporate responsibility not only to managing in an efficient and effective way, but also to responding strategically to a wide range of environmental and societal challenges.[28] Although "sustainability" means different things to different people, in essence, according to the World Business Council for Sustainable Development (2005), it is concerned with "meeting the needs of people today without compromising the ability of future generations to meet their own needs." From a business perspective, **sustainability** has been defined as a company's ability to achieve its business goals and increase long-term shareholder value by integrating economic, environmental, and social opportunities into its business strategies.[29] Sustainability issues are now moving up the agenda of business leaders and the boards of thousands of companies. Like the managers at Walmart are discovering, running an organization in a more sustainable way will mean that managers have to make informed business decisions based on thorough communication with various stakeholders, understanding their requirements, and factoring economic, environmental, and social aspects into how they pursue their business goals.

The idea of practicing sustainability affects many aspects of business, from the creation of products and services to their use and subsequent disposal by consumers. Following sustainability practices is one way in which organizations can show their commitment to being responsible. In today's world where many individuals have diminishing respect for businesses, few organizations can afford the bad press or potential economic ramifications of being seen as socially irresponsible. Managers also want to be seen as ethical, which is the topic we're going to look at next.

WHAT FACTORS DETERMINE ETHICAL AND UNETHICAL BEHAVIOR?

3.3 Discuss the factors that lead to ethical and unethical behavior in organizations.

- Employees at a law firm in Florida that handled foreclosures for Freddie Mac and Fannie Mae changed thousands of documents and hid them in a room when company officials came to conduct audits.
- A Paris court found Jérôme Kerviel, a former financial trader at French bank Société Générale, guilty of triggering a massive trading scandal

that created severe financial problems for his employer. Mr. Kerviel claims that the company turned a blind eye to his questionable but hugely profitable methods.

◆ According to the NFL Players Association, "352 players were placed on the season-ending injured reserve list in the 2010–11 season. That's 21 percent."[30] Hundreds more players suffered lesser injuries, from concussions to dislocations, keeping them from playing for at least one game.

You might be wondering about the connection among these three unrelated stories. When you read about these decisions, behaviors, and actions, you might be tempted to conclude that businesses just aren't ethical. Although that isn't the case, managers do face ethical issues and dilemmas.

Ethics commonly refers to a set of rules or principles that defines right and wrong conduct.[31] Right or wrong behavior, though, may at times be difficult to determine. Most recognize that something illegal is also unethical. But what about questionable "legal" areas or strict organizational policies? For instance, what if you managed an employee who worked all weekend on a rush project and you told him to take off two days sometime later and mark it down as "sick days" because your company had a clear policy that overtime would not be compensated for any reason?[32] Would that be wrong? As a manager, how will you handle such situations?

In What Ways Can Ethics Be Viewed?

To better understand what's involved with managerial ethics, we need to first look at three different perspectives on how managers make ethical decisions.[33] The **utilitarian view of ethics** says that ethical decisions are made solely on the basis of their outcomes or consequences. The goal of utilitarianism is to provide the greatest good for the greatest number. In the **rights view of ethics**, individuals are concerned with respecting and protecting individual liberties and privileges such as the right of free consent, the right to privacy, the right of free speech, and so forth. Making ethical decisions under this view is fairly simple because the goal is to avoid interfering with the rights of others who might be affected by the decision. Finally, under the **theory of justice view of ethics**, an individual imposes and enforces rules fairly and impartially. For instance, a manager would be using the theory of justice perspective by deciding to pay individuals who are similar in their levels of skills, performance, or responsibility the same and not base that decision on arbitrary differences such as gender, personality, or personal favorites. The goal of this approach is to be equitable, fair, and impartial in making decisions.

Regardless of which view you think is most appropriate, whether a manager (or any employee, for that matter) acts ethically or unethically will depend on several factors. These factors include an individual's morality, values, personality, and experiences; the organization's culture; and the ethical issue being faced.[34] People who lack a strong moral sense are much less likely to do the wrong things if they are constrained by rules, policies, job descriptions, or strong cultural norms that discourage such behaviors. For example, suppose that someone in your class stole the final exam and is selling a copy for $50. You need to do well on the exam or risk failing the course. You suspect that some classmates have bought copies, which could affect any results because your professor grades on a curve. Do you buy a copy because you fear that without it you'll be disadvantaged, do you refuse to buy a copy and

In this photo, employees at a General Mills plant load boxes of cereal onto a community food bank truck as part of the company's commitment to Feeding America, a hunger relief organization. Doing things that make society better is an ethical imperative at General Mills, because it's the right thing to do. Each employee receives a Code of Conduct that outlines ethical expectations and gives examples for how to act with integrity in every decision and action. The company provides ethics training programs, an intranet site for compliance information, and an Ethics Line available 24/7 for help with ethical questions and for reporting violations. General Mills depends on its global workforce to act consistently with local laws and the company's values and ethical policies.

try your best, or do you report your knowledge to your instructor? This example of the final exam illustrates how ambiguity over what is ethical can be a problem for managers.

How Can Managers Encourage Ethical Behavior?

At a Senate hearing exploring the accusations that Wall Street firm Goldman Sachs deceived its clients during the housing-market meltdown, Arizona senator John McCain said, "I don't know if Goldman has done anything illegal, but there's no doubt their behavior was unethical."[35] You have to wonder what the firm's managers were thinking or doing while such ethically questionable decisions and actions were occurring. It's pretty obvious that they weren't encouraging ethical behaviors!

Managers can do a number of things if they're serious about encouraging ethical behaviors—hire employees with high ethical standards, establish codes of ethics, lead by example, link job goals and performance appraisal, provide ethics training, and implement protective mechanisms for employees who face ethical dilemmas. By themselves, such actions won't have much of an impact. But if an organization has a comprehensive ethics program in place, it can potentially improve an organization's ethical climate. The key variable, however, is *potentially*. A well-designed ethics program does not guarantee the desired outcome. Sometimes corporate ethics programs are mostly public relations gestures that do little to influence managers and employees. For instance, even Enron, often thought of as the "poster child" of corporate wrongdoing, outlined values in its final annual report that most would consider ethical—communication, respect, integrity, and excellence. Yet the way top managers behaved didn't reflect those values at all.[36] We want to look at three ways that managers can encourage ethical behavior and create a comprehensive ethics program.

CODES OF ETHICS. Codes of ethics are popular tools for attempting to reduce employee ambiguity about what's ethical and what's not.[37] A **code of ethics** is a formal document that states an organization's primary values and the ethical rules it expects managers and nonmanagerial employees to follow. Ideally, these codes should be specific enough to guide organizational members in what they're supposed to do yet loose enough to allow for freedom of judgment. Research shows that 97 percent of organizations with more than 10,000 employees have written codes of ethics. Even in smaller organizations, nearly 93 percent have them.[38] And codes of ethics are becoming more popular globally. Research by the Institute for Global Ethics says that shared values such as honesty, fairness, respect, responsibility, and caring are embraced worldwide.[39]

The effectiveness of such codes depends heavily on whether management supports them and ingrains them into the corporate culture, and how individuals who break the codes are treated.[40] If management considers them to be important, regularly reaffirms their content, follows the rules themselves, and publicly reprimands rule breakers, ethics codes can be a strong foundation for an effective corporate ethics program.[41]

ETHICAL LEADERSHIP. In 2007, Peter Löscher was hired as CEO of German company Siemens to clean up a global bribery scandal that cost the company a record-setting $1.34 billion in fines. His approach: "Stick to your principles. Have a clear ethical north. Be trusted and be the role model of your company . . . true leaders have a set of core values they publicly commit to and live by in good times and bad."[42] Doing business ethically requires a commitment from managers. Why? Because they're the ones who uphold the shared values and set the cultural tone. Managers must be good ethical role models both in words *and,* more importantly, in actions. What you *do* is far more important than what you *say* in getting employees to act ethically. For example, if managers take company

EXHIBIT 3–3   **Being an Ethical Leader**

- Be a good role model by being ethical and honest.
- Tell the truth always.
- Don't hide or manipulate information.
- Be willing to admit your failures.
- Share your personal values by regularly communicating them to employees.
- Stress the organization's or team's important shared values.
- Use the reward system to hold everyone accountable to the values.

resources for their personal use, inflate their expense accounts, or give favored treatment to friends, they imply that such behavior is acceptable for all employees.

Managers also set the tone by their reward and punishment practices. The choices of whom and what are rewarded with pay increases and promotions send a strong signal to employees. As we said earlier, when an employee is rewarded for achieving impressive results in an ethically questionable manner, it indicates to others that those ways are acceptable. When an employee does something unethical, managers must punish the offender and publicize the fact by making the outcome visible to everyone in the organization. This practice sends a message that doing wrong has a price and it's not in employees' best interests to act unethically! (See Exhibit 3–3 for suggestions on being an ethical leader.)

ETHICS TRAINING.   Yahoo! used an off-the-shelf online ethics training package, but employees said that the scenarios used to demonstrate different concepts didn't resemble those that might come up at Yahoo! and were too middle-American and middle-aged for the global company with a youthful workforce. So the company changed its ethics training! The new ethics training package is more animated and interactive and has more realistic storylines for the industry. The 45-minute training module covers the company's code of conduct and resources available to help employees understand it.[43]

Like Yahoo!, more and more organizations are setting up seminars, workshops, and similar ethics training programs to encourage ethical behavior. Such training programs aren't without controversy as the primary concern is whether ethics can be taught. Critics stress that the effort is pointless because people establish their individual value systems when they're young. Proponents note, however, several studies have shown that values can be learned after early childhood. In addition, they cite evidence that shows that teaching ethical problem solving can make an actual difference in ethical behaviors;[44] that training has increased individuals' level of moral development;[45] and that, if nothing else, ethics training increases awareness of ethical issues in business.[46]

WHAT IS TODAY'S WORKFORCE LIKE AND HOW DOES IT AFFECT THE WAY ORGANIZATIONS ARE MANAGED?

Describe how the workforce is changing and its impact on the way organizations are managed. **3.4**

Walking through the lobby of one of MGM Mirage's hotels, Brenda Thompson, the company's director of diversity and leadership education noted that, "It's amazing all the different languages I can hear. . . . Our guests come from all over the world, and it makes us realize the importance of reflecting that diversity in our workplace." And Thompson has been instrumental in developing a program at MGM that is all "about maximizing 100 percent inclusion of everyone in the organization."[47] Such diversity

code of ethics
A formal document that states an organization's primary values and the ethical rules it expects managers and nonmanagerial employees to follow

The Toronto Star/Newscom

Michael Bach (right) created an inclusive environment at accounting firm KPMG in Canada by launching a diversity initiative that he heads as the National Director of Diversity, Equity, and Inclusion. Bach introduced programs and formalized policies designed to find, attract, and develop diverse talents that benefit KPMG by engaging its entire workforce. He developed diversity training for employees and formed social clubs, including an international club where members meet regularly to support employees who are new to the country. Among the many employee networks he created are networks for women, for parents with special needs children, and for religious groups, Bach is shown here with members of the firm's Asian network.

can be found in many organizational workplaces domestically and globally, and managers in those workplaces are looking for ways to value and develop that diversity, just as Brenda Thompson is doing.

What Is Workplace Diversity?

Look around your classroom (or your workplace). You're likely to see young/old, male/female, tall/short, blonde/brunette, blue-eyed/brown-eyed any number of races, and any variety of dress styles. You'll see people who speak up in class and others who are content to keep their attention on taking notes or daydreaming. Have you ever noticed your own little world of diversity where you are right now? Many of you may have grown up in an environment that included diverse individuals, while others may have not had that experience. We want to focus on *workplace* diversity, so let's look at what it is.

Diversity has been "one of the most popular business topics over the last two decades. It ranks with modern business disciplines such as quality, leadership, and ethics. Despite this popularity, it's also one of the most controversial and least understood topics."[48] With its basis in civil rights legislation and social justice, the word "diversity" often invokes a variety of attitudes and emotional responses in people. Diversity has traditionally been considered a term used by human resources departments, associated with fair hiring practices, discrimination, and inequality. But diversity today is considered to be so much more.

We're defining **workforce diversity** as the ways in which people in an organization are different from and similar to one another. Notice that our definition not only focuses on the differences, but the similarities of employees, reinforcing our belief that managers and organizations should view employees as having qualities in common as well as differences that separate them. It doesn't mean that those differences are any less important, but that our focus as managers is in finding ways to develop strong relationships with and engage our entire workforce.

What Types of Diversity Are Found in Workplaces?

Diversity is a big issue, and an important issue, in today's workplaces. What types of diversity do we find in those workplaces? Exhibit 3–4 lists several types of workplace diversity.

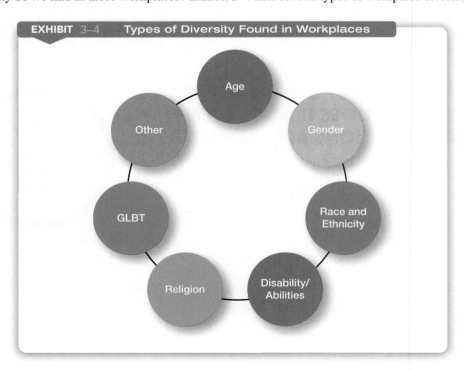

EXHIBIT 3–4 **Types of Diversity Found in Workplaces**

AGE.   The aging of the population is a major critical shift taking place in the workforce. With many of the nearly 85 million baby boomers still employed and active in the workforce, managers must ensure that those employees are not discriminated against because of age. Both Title VII of the Civil Rights Act of 1964 and the Age Discrimination in Employment Act of 1967 prohibit age discrimination. The Age Discrimination Act also restricts mandatory retirement at specific ages. In addition to complying with these laws, organizations need programs and policies in place that provide for fair and equal treatment of their older employees.

GENDER.   Women (49.8%) and men (50.2%) now each make up almost half of the workforce.[49] Yet, as our chapter opener showed, gender diversity issues are still quite prevalent in organizations. These issues include the gender pay gap, career start and progress, and misconceptions about whether women perform their jobs as well as men do. It's important for managers and organizations to explore the strengths that both women and men bring to an organization and the barriers they face in contributing fully to organizational efforts.

RACE AND ETHNICITY.   There's a long and controversial history in the United States and in other parts of the world over race and how people react to and treat others of a different race. Race and ethnicity are important types of diversity in organizations. We're going to define **race** as the biological heritage (including physical characteristics such as one's skin color and associated traits) that people use to identify themselves. Most people identify themselves as part of a racial group and such racial classifications are an integral part of a country's cultural, social, and legal environments. **Ethnicity** is related to race, but it refers to social traits—such as one's cultural background or allegiance—that are shared by a human population.

The racial and ethnic diversity of the U.S. population is increasing and at an exponential rate. We're also seeing this same effect in the composition of the workforce. Most of the research on race and ethnicity as they relate to the workplace has looked at hiring decisions, performance evaluations, pay, and workplace discrimination. Managers and organizations need to make race and ethnicity issues a key focus in effectively managing workforce diversity.

DISABILITY/ABILITIES.   For persons with disabilities, 1990 was a watershed year—the year the Americans with Disabilities Act (ADA) became law. ADA prohibits discrimination against persons with disabilities and also requires employers to make reasonable accommodations so their workplaces are accessible to people with physical or mental disabilities and enable them to effectively perform their jobs. With the law's enactment, individuals with disabilities became a more representative and integral part of the U.S. workforce.

RIGHT ? OR WRONG

In August 2009, a viral campaign against McDonald's Web site, 365black.com, began to spread.[50] Anger over the Web site grew as news commentators discovered an additional McDonald's Web site targeting the Asian community, called MyInspirAsian.com. One individual said, "Even if the idea was a good one and truly was promoting Black cultural heritage, it really does come off as manipulation and stereotyping." Check out both Web sites.

Think About:

- What do you think? Do you think these targeted sites are manipulative and stereotypical? Why or why not? Is there anything else the company could or should be doing?

- Go to McDonald's corporate Web site. Find the information on diversity. Make a short list of what McDonald's is doing with respect to diversity programs and actions.

© Directphoto.org/Alamy.

---

workforce diversity
Ways in which people in a workforce are similar and different from one another in terms of gender, age, race, sexual orientation, ethnicity, cultural background, and physical abilities and disabilities

race
The biological heritage (including physical characteristics, such as one's skin color and associated traits) that people use to identify themselves

ethnicity
Social traits, such as one's cultural background or allegiance, that are shared by a human population

In effectively managing a workforce with disabled employees, managers need to create and maintain an environment in which employees feel comfortable disclosing their need for accommodation. Those accommodations, by law, enable individuals with disabilities to perform their jobs but they also need to be perceived as equitable by those not disabled. It's the balancing act that managers face.

RELIGION. Hani Khan, a college sophomore, had worked for three months as a stock clerk at a Hollister clothing store in San Francisco.[51] One day, she was told by her supervisors to remove the head scarf that she wears in observance of Islam (known as a *hijab*) because it violated the company's "look policy" (which instructs employees on clothing, hair styles, makeup, and accessories they may wear to work). She refused on religious grounds and was fired one week later. Like a number of other Muslim women, she filed a federal job discrimination complaint. A spokesperson for Abercrombie & Fitch (Hollister's parent company) said that, "If any Abercrombie associate identifies a religious conflict with an Abercrombie policy . . . the company will work with the associate in an attempt to find an accommodation."

Title VII of the Civil Rights Act prohibits discrimination on the basis of religion (as well as race/ethnicity, country of origin, and sex). However, you'd probably not be surprised to find out that the number of religious discrimination claims has been growing in the United States.[52] In accommodating religious diversity, managers need to recognize and be aware of different religions and their beliefs, paying special attention to when certain religious holidays fall. Businesses benefit when they can accommodate, if possible, employees who have special needs or requests in a way that other employees don't view it as "special treatment."

GLBT—SEXUAL ORIENTATION AND GENDER IDENTITY. The acronym GLBT—which refers to gay, lesbian, bisexual, and transgender people—is being used more frequently and relates to the diversity of sexual orientation and gender identity.[53] Sexual orientation has been called the "last acceptable bias."[54] We want to emphasize that we're not condoning this perspective; what this comment refers to is that most people understand that racial and ethnic stereotypes are "off-limits." Unfortunately, it's not unusual to hear derogatory comments about gays or lesbians. U.S. federal law does not prohibit discrimination against employees on the basis of sexual orientation, although many states and municipalities do. However, in Europe, the Employment Equality Directive required all European Union member states to introduce legislation making it unlawful to discriminate on grounds of sexual orientation.[55] Despite the progress that's been made in making workplaces more accommodating of gays and lesbians, obviously much more needs to be done. One study found that more than 40 percent of gay and lesbian employees indicated they had been unfairly treated, denied a promotion, or pushed to quit their job because of their sexual orientation.[56]

As with most of the types of diversity we've discussed in this section, managers need to look at how best to meet the needs of their GLBT employees. They need to respond to employees' concerns while also creating a safe and productive work environment for all.

OTHER TYPES OF DIVERSITY. As we said earlier, diversity refers to *any* dissimilarities or differences that might be present in a workplace. Other types of workplace diversity that managers might confront and have to deal with include socioeconomic background (social class and income-related factors), team members from different functional areas or organizational units, physical attractiveness, obesity/thinness, job seniority, or intellectual abilities. Each of these types of diversity also can affect how employees are treated in the workplace. Again, managers need to ensure that all employees—no matter the similarities or dissimilarities—are treated fairly and given the opportunity and support to do their jobs to the best of their abilities.

How Are Organizations and Managers Adapting to a Changing Workforce?

Since organizations wouldn't be able to do what they're in business to do without employees, managers have to adapt to the changes taking place in the workforce. They're responding with diversity initiatives such as work-life balance programs, contingent jobs, and recognition of generational differences.

WORK-LIFE BALANCE PROGRAMS.   The typical employee in the 1960s or 1970s showed up at the workplace Monday through Friday and did his or her job in eight- or nine-hour chunks of time. The workplace and hours were clearly specified. That's not the case anymore for a large segment of the workforce. Employees are increasingly complaining that the line between work and nonwork time has blurred, creating personal conflicts and stress.[57] Several factors have contributed to this blurring between work and personal life. One is that in a world of global business, work never ends. At any time and on any day, for instance, thousands of Caterpillar employees are working somewhere in the company's facilities. The need to consult with colleagues or customers 8 or 10 time zones away means that many employees of global companies are "on call" 24 hours a day. Another factor is that communication technology allows employees to do their work at home, in their cars, or on the beach in Tahiti. Although this capability allows those in technical and professional jobs to do their work anywhere and at anytime, it also means there's no escaping from work. Another factor is that as organizations have had to lay off employees during the economic downturn, "surviving" employees find themselves working longer hours. It's not unusual for employees to work more than 45 hours a week, and some work more than 50. Finally, fewer families today have a single wage earner. Today's married employee is typically part of a dual-career couple, which makes it increasingly difficult for married employees to find time to fulfill commitments to home, spouse, children, parents, and friends.[58]

More and more, employees recognize that work is squeezing out their personal lives, and they're not happy about it. Today's progressive workplaces must accommodate the varied needs of a diverse workforce. In response, many organizations are offering **family-friendly benefits**, benefits that provide a wide range of scheduling options that allow employees more flexibility at work, accommodating their need for work-life balance. They've introduced programs such as on-site child care, summer day camps, flextime, job sharing, time off for school functions, telecommuting, and part-time employment. Younger people, particularly, put a higher priority on family and a lower priority on jobs and are looking for organizations that give them more work flexibility.[59]

CONTINGENT JOBS.   "Companies want a workforce they can switch on and off as needed."[60] Although this quote may shock you, the truth is that the labor force already has begun shifting away from traditional full-time jobs toward a **contingent workforce**—part-time, temporary, and contract workers who are available for

Ernst & Young is a progressive firm that accommodates the needs of its diverse employees by providing family-friendly benefits. Flexible work plans offered by this accounting and tax service firm include telecommuting, reduced work schedules, compressed workweeks, and day-to-day work-hour flexibility. Family-support programs include low-cost backup child and adult care, a college coach program that helps parents and high school students prepare for college, family medical leave, parental leave, and adoption assistance. Young employees, such as the workers at Ernst & Young's Boston office shown here, place a high priority on work-life balance and value organizations that give them flexible work options.

Mary K Merrill/Newscom

---

family-friendly benefits
Benefits that provide a wide range of scheduling options and allow employees more flexibility at work, accommodating their needs for work-life balance

contingent workforce
Part-time, temporary, and contract workers who are available for hire on an as-needed basis

hire on an as-needed basis. In today's economy, many organizations have responded by converting full-time permanent jobs into contingent jobs. It's predicted that by the end of the next decade the number of contingent employees will have grown to about 40 percent of the workforce. (It's at 30 percent today.)[61] In fact, one compensation and benefits expert says that "a growing a number of workers will need to structure their careers around this model," which could likely include you![62]

What are the implications for managers and organizations? Because contingent employees are not "employees" in the traditional sense of the word, managing them has its own set of challenges and expectations. Managers must recognize that because contingent workers lack the stability and security of permanent employees, they may not identify with the organization or be as committed or motivated. Managers may need to treat contingent workers differently in terms of practices and policies. However, with good communication and leadership, an organization's contingent employees can be just as valuable a resource to an organization as permanent employees are. Today's managers must recognize that it will be their responsibility to motivate their entire workforce, full-time and contingent, and to build their commitment to doing good work!

GENERATIONAL DIFFERENCES. Managing generational differences presents some unique challenges, especially for baby boomers and Gen Y. Conflicts and resentment can arise over issues ranging from appearance to technology and management style.

What *is* appropriate office attire? That answer may depend on who you ask, but more importantly, it depends on the type of work being done and the size of the organization. To accommodate generational differences in what is considered appropriate, the key is flexibility. For instance, a guideline might be that when an employee is not interacting with someone outside the organization, more casual wear (with some restrictions) is acceptable.

What about technology? Gen Y has grown up with ATMs, DVDs, cell phones, e-mail, texting, laptops, and the Internet. When they don't have information they need, they just enter a few keystrokes to get it. They're content to meet virtually to solve problems, while baby boomers expect important problems to be solved with in-person meetings. Baby boomers complain about Gen Y's inability to focus on one task, while Gen Y'ers see nothing wrong with multitasking. Again, flexibility and understanding from both is the key in working together effectively and efficiently.

Finally, what about management style? Gen Y employees want bosses who are open-minded; experts in their field, even if they aren't tech savvy; organized; teachers, trainers, and mentors; not authoritarian or paternalistic; respectful of their generation; understanding of their need for work-life balance; providing constant feedback; communicating in vivid and compelling ways; and providing stimulating and novel learning experiences.[63]

Because Gen Y employees have a lot to offer organizations in terms of their knowledge, passion, and abilities, managers have to recognize and understand the behaviors of this group in order to create an environment in which work can be done efficiently, effectively, and without disruptive conflict.

3 Review

CHAPTER SUMMARY

3.1 **Explain globalization and its impact on organizations.** Organizations are considered global if they exchange goods and services with consumers in other countries, if they use managerial and technical employee talent from other countries, or if they use financial sources and resources outside their home country. Businesses going global are usually referred to as multinational corporations (MNCs). As an MNC, they may operate as a multidomestic corporation, a global corporation, or a transnational or borderless organization. When a business goes global, it may start with global sourcing, move to exporting or importing, use licensing or franchising, pursue a global strategic alliance, or set up a foreign subsidiary. In doing business globally, managers need to be aware of different laws and political and economic systems. But the biggest challenge is in understanding the different country cultures. Two cross-cultural frameworks that managers can use are Hofstede's and GLOBE.

3.2 **Discuss how society's expectations are influencing managers and organizations.** Society expects organizations and managers to be responsible and ethical. An organization's social involvement can be from the perspective of social obligation, social responsiveness, or social responsibility. After much analysis, researchers have concluded that managers can afford

to be (and should be) socially responsible. Sustainability has become an important societal issue for managers and organizations.

3.3 **Discuss the factors that lead to ethical and unethical behavior in organizations.** Ethics can be viewed from the utilitarian view, the rights view, or the theory of justice view. Whether a manager acts ethically or unethically depends on his or her morality, values, personality, and experiences; the organization's culture; and the ethical issue being faced. Managers can encourage ethical behavior by hiring employees with high ethical standards, establishing a code of ethics, leading by example, linking job goals and performance appraisal, providing ethics training, and implementing protective mechanisms for employees who face ethical dilemmas.

3.4 **Describe how the workforce is changing and its impact on the way organizations are managed.** The workforce continues to reflect increasing diversity. Types of workforce diversity include age, gender, race and ethnicity, disability/abilities, religion, and sexual orientation and gender identity. Organizations and managers are responding to the changing workforce with work-life balance programs, contingent jobs, and recognition of generational differences.

MyManagementLab   For more resources, please visit **www.mymanagementlab.com**

UNDERSTANDING THE CHAPTER

1. How does the concept of a global village affect organizations and managers?

2. Describe the different types of global organizations and the ways that organizations can go global.

3. What are the managerial implications of Hofstede's research on cultural environments? The GLOBE study?

4. How are social responsibility, social obligation, and social responsiveness different? Similar?

5. What is sustainability, and how can organizations practice it?

6. Describe how a manager would approach ethical decisions according to each of the three views on ethics.

7. Discuss specific ways managers can encourage ethical behavior.

8. What is workforce diversity, and why is it an important issue for managers?

9. Describe the six types of diversity found in workplaces.

10. Describe and discuss the three ways that organizations and managers are adapting to a changing workforce.

Go to p. 409
YOUR TURN ᵀᴼ BE A MANAGER for Chapter 3.

Endnotes

1. C. Skrzypinski, "Study: Employers Fall Short Developing Female Business Leaders," *SHRM Online,* March 15, 2011; L. Stevens and J. Espinoza, "Deutsche Telekom Sets Women-Manager Quota," *Wall Street Journal Online,* March 22, 2010; J. Blaue, "Deutsche Telekom Launches Quota for Top Women Managers," www.german-info.com/business_shownews; N. Clark, "Goal at Deutsche Telekom: More Women as Managers," *New York Times Online,* March 15, 2010; R. Foroohar and S. H. Greenberg, "Working Women Are Poised to Become the Biggest Economic Engine the World Has Ever Known," *Newsweek,* November 2, 2009, pp. B2–B5; News Release, "Women Still Hold Less Than a Quarter of Senior Management Positions in Privately Held Businesses," *Grant Thornton International,* www.gti.org (March 5, 2009); and Catalyst Research Report, *Different Cultures, Similar Perceptions: Stereotyping of Western European Business Leaders,* www.catalyst.org (2006).

2. N. M. Carter and C. Silva, "Pipeline's Broken Promise," *Catalyst,* www.catalyst.org (2010), p. 1; and "Women in Management in the United States, 1950–Present," *Catalyst,* www.catalyst.org (April 2010).

3. S. Lohr, "Stress Test for the Global Supply Chain," *New York Times Online,* March 19, 2011; D. Jolly, "Long Pause for Japanese Industry Raises Concerns About Supply Chain," *New York Times Online,* March 16, 2011; and M. Helft and N. Bunkley, "Disaster in Japan Batters Suppliers," *New York Times Online,* March 14, 2011.

4. E. Beinhocker, I. Davis, and L. Mendonca, "The 10 Trends You Have to Watch," *Harvard Business Review,* July–August 2009, pp. 55–60.

5. P. F. Drucker, "The Global Economy and the Nation-State," *Foreign Affairs,* September–October, 1997, pp. 159–171.

6. P. Dvorak, "Why Multiple Headquarters Multiply," *Wall Street Journal,* November 19, 2007, pp. B1+.

7. D. A. Aaker, *Developing Business Strategies,* 5th ed. (New York: John Wiley & Sons, 1998); and J. A. Byrne et al., "Borderless Management," *BusinessWeek*, May 23, 1994, pp. 24–26.

8. B. Davis, "Migration of Skilled Jobs Abroad Unsettles Global-Economy Fans," *Wall Street Journal,* January 26, 2004, p. A1.

9. A. Pande, "How to Make Onshoring Work," *Harvard Business Review,* March 2011, p. 30; P. Davidson, "Some Manufacturing Heads Back to USA," *USA Today,* August 6, 2010, pp. 1B+; and V. Couto, A. Divakaran, and M. Mani, "Is Backshoring the New Offshoring?" *Strategy & Business,* October 21, 2008, pp. 1–3.

10. J. Teresko, "United Plastics Picks China's Silicon Valley," *Industry Week,* January 2003, p. 58.

11. "Global Business: Getting the Frameworks Right," *Organization for Economic Cooperation and Development*, April 2000, p. 20.

12. From the Past to the Present box based on D. Holtbrügge and A. T. Mohr, "Cultural Determinants of Learning Style Preferences," *Academy of Management Learning & Education,* December 2010, pp. 622–637; G. Hofstede, "The GLOBE Debate: Back to Relevance," *Journal of International Business Studies* (November 2010), pp. 1339–1346; G. A. Gelade, P. Dobson, and K. Auer, "Individualism, Masculinity, and the Sources of Organizational Commitment," *Journal of Cross-Cultural Psychology* (September 2008), pp. 599–617; G. Hofstede, "The Cultural Relativity of Organizational Practices and Theories," *Journal of International Business Studies* (Fall 1983), pp. 75–89; and G. Hofstede, *Culture Consequences: International Differences in Work-Related Values* (Beverly Hills, CA: Sage Publications, 1980), pp. 25–26. For an interesting discussion of collectivism and teams, see C. Gomez, B. L. Kirkman, and D. Shapiro, "The Impact of Collectivism and In-Group Membership on the Evaluation Generosity of Team Members," *Academy of Management Journal* (December 2000), pp. 1097–1106. Hofstede's term for what we've called quantity of life and quality of life was actually "masculinity versus femininity," but we've changed his terms because of their strong sexist connotation.

13. R. J. House, N. R. Quigley, and M. S. deLuque, "Insights from Project GLOBE: Extending Advertising Research Through a Contemporary Framework," *International Journal of Advertising,* 29, no. 1 (2010), pp. 111–139; R. R. McRae, A. Terracciano, A. Realo, and J.Allik, "Interpreting GLOBE Societal Practices Scale," *Journal of Cross-Cultural Psychology* (November 2008), pp. 805–810; J. S. Chhokar, F. C. Brodbeck, and R. J. House, *Culture and Leadership Across the World: The GLOBE Book of In-Depth Studies of 25 Societies* (Philadelphia: Lawrence Erlbaum Associates), 2007; and R. J. House, P. J. Hanges, M. Javidan, P. W. Dorfman, and V. Gupta, *Culture, Leadership, and Organizations: The GLOBE Study of 62 Societies* (Thousand Oaks, CA: Sage Publications), 2004.

14. R. J. House, N. R. Quigley, and M. S. deLuque, 2010.

15. M. Karimzadeh, "Olsens Collaborate with Toms Shoes," *Women's Wear Daily,* February 14, 2011, p. 11b; J. Schechtman, "Good Business," *Newsweek,* October 11, 2010, p. 50; "Toms Shoes to Donate One-Millionth Pair," *Women's Wear Daily,* August 9, 2010, p. 9–10; "Ten Companies With Social Responsibility at the Core," *Advertising Age,* April 19, 2010, p. 88; C. Binkley, "Charity Gives Shoe Brand Extra Shine," *Wall Street Journal,* April 1, 2010, p. D7; J. Shambora, "How I Got Started: Blake Mycoskie, Founder of TOMS Shoes," *Fortune,* March 22, 2010, p. 72; and "Making A Do-Gooder's Business Model Work," *BusinessWeek Online,* January 26, 2009.

16. D. Dearlove and S. Crainer, "Enterprise Goes Social," *Chief Executive*, March 2002, p. 18; and "Bronze Winner: Ben & Jerry's Citizen Cool," *Brandweek,* March 18, 2002, p. R-24.

17. M. Friedman, *Capitalism and Freedom* (Chicago: University of Chicago Press, 1962); and M. Friedman, "The Social Responsibility of Business Is to Increase Profits," *New York Times Magazine,* September 13, 1970, p. 33.

18. See, for instance, N. A. Ibrahim, J. P. Angelidis, and D. P. Howell, "The Corporate Social Responsiveness Orientation of Hospital Directors: Does Occupational Background Make a Difference?" *Health Care Management Review,* Spring 2000, pp. 85–92.

19. See, for example, D. J. Wood, "Corporate Social Performance Revisited," *Academy of Management Review,* October 1991, pp. 703–708; and S. L. Wartick and P. L. Cochran, "The Evolution of the Corporate Social Performance Model," *Academy of Management Review,* October 1985, p. 763.

20. See, for instance, R. Lacy and P. A. Kennett-Hensel, "Longitudinal Effects of Corporate Social Responsibility on Customer Relationships," *Journal of Business Ethics* (December 2010), pp. 581–597; S. Arendt and M. Brettel, "Understanding the Influence of Corporate Social Responsibility on Corporate Identity,

Image, and Firm Performance," *Management Decision,* 48, no. 10 (2010), pp. 1469–1492; J. Peloza, "The Challenge of Measuring Financial Impacts from Investments in Corporate Social Performance," *Journal of Management* (December 2009), pp. 1518–1541; J. D. Margolis and H. Anger Elfenbein, "Do Well by Doing Good? Don't Count on It," *Harvard Business Review,* January 2008, pp. 19–20; M. L. Barnett, "Stakeholder Influence Capacity and the Variability of Financial Returns to Corporate Social Responsibility," 2007; D. O. Neubaum and S. A. Zahra, "Institutional Ownership and Corporate Social Performance: The Moderating Effects of Investment Horizon, Activism, and Coordination," *Journal of Management* (February 2006), pp. 108–131; B. A. Waddock and S. B. Graves, "The Corporate Social Performance–Financial Performance Link," *Strategic Management Journal* (April 1997), pp. 303–319; J. B. McGuire, A. Sundgren, and T. Schneeweis, "Corporate Social Responsibility and Firm Financial Performance," *Academy of Management Journal* (December 1988), pp. 854–872; K. Aupperle, A. B. Carroll, and J. D. Hatfield, "An Empirical Examination of the Relationship Between Corporate Social Responsibility and Profitability," *Academy of Management Journal* (June 1985), pp. 446–463; and P. Cochran and R. A. Wood, "Corporate Social Responsibility and Financial Performance," *Academy of Management Journal* (March 1984), pp. 42–56.

21. Peloza, "The Challenge of Measuring Financial Impacts from Investments in Corporate Social Performance."

22. B. Seifert, S. A. Morris, and B. R. Bartkus, "Having, Giving, and Getting: Slack Resources, Corporate Philanthropy, and Firm Financial Performance," *Business & Society,* June 2004, pp. 135–161; and McGuire, Sundgren, and Schneeweis, "Corporate Social Responsibility and Firm Financial Performance."

23. A. McWilliams and D. Siegel, "Corporate Social Responsibility and Financial Performance: Correlation or Misspecification?" *Strategic Management Journal* (June 2000), pp. 603–609.

24. A. J. Hillman and G. D. Keim, "Shareholder Value, Stakeholder Management, and Social Issues: What's the Bottom Line?" *Strategic Management Journal,* 22 (2001), pp. 125–139.

25. M. Orlitzky, F. L. Schmidt, and S. L. Rynes, "Corporate Social and Financial Performance," *Organization Studies,* 24, no. 3 (2003), pp. 403–441.

26. And the Survey Says box based on *Blowing the Whistle on Workplace Conduct,* Ethics Resource Center, www.ethics.org (December 2010); G. M. Maddock and R. L. Viton, "Co-Creating Planet-Friendly Profits," *Bloomberg Businessweek Online,* December 21, 2010; B. Leonard, "When HR Goes Bad," *HR Magazine,* January 2011, pp. 28–32; C. Hausman, "Ethics Books More Likely Than Other Works To Be Stolen from Libraries," *Global Ethics Newsline Online,* December 20, 2010; "Strong Ethical Culture Helps Bottom Line," *HR Magazine,* December 2010, p. 21; J. Yang and P. Trap, "If Granted Access to a Confidential Document Accidently I'd . . . ," *USA Today,* September 13, 2010, p. 1B; and R. M. Kidder, "Ask Not for Whom the Students Cheat: They Cheat for Thee," *Global Ethics Newsline Online,* February 28, 2011.

27. S. Rosenbloom, "Wal-Mart Unveils Plan to Make Supply Chain Greener," *New York Times Online,* February 26, 2010.

28. G. Unruh and R. Ettenson, "Growing Green," *Harvard Business Review,* June 2010, pp. 94–100; G. Zoppo, "Corporate Sustainability," *DiversityInc,* May 2010, pp. 76–80; and KPMG Global Sustainability Services, *Sustainability Insights,* October 2007.

29. *Symposium on Sustainability: Profiles in Leadership,* New York, October 2001.

30. C. Hausman, "Ethics, Economics, and Injuries Dominate Sports News," *Ethics Newsline Online,* February 7, 2011; S. Armour and T. Frank, "Ex-Worker: Law Firm Ran 'Foreclosure Mill,'" *USA Today,* October 19, 2010, p. 3B; and N. Clark, "Rogue Trader at Société Générale Gets Jail Term," *New York Times Online,* October 5, 2010.

31. S. A. DiPiazza, "Ethics in Action," *Executive Excellence,* January 2002, pp. 15–16.

32. This example is based on J. F. Viega, T. D. Golden, and K. Dechant, "Why Managers Bend Company Rules," *Academy of Management Executive* (May 2004), pp. 84–90.

33. G. F. Cavanaugh, D. J. Moberg, and M. Valasquez, "The Ethics of Organizational Politics," *Academy of Management Journal* (June 1981), pp. 363–374.

34. J. Liedtka, "Ethics and the New Economy," *Business and Society Review,* Spring 2002, p. 1.

35. R. M. Kidder, "Can Disobedience Save Wall Street?" *Ethics Newsline,* www.globalethics.org (May 3, 2010).

36. P. M. Lencioni, "Make Your Values Mean Something," *Harvard Business Review,* July 2002, p. 113.

37. D. H. Schepers, "Setting Global Standards: Guidelines for Creating Codes of Conduct in Multinational Corporations," *Business and Society,* December 2003, p. 496; and B. R. Gaummitz and J. C. Lere, "Contents of Codes of Ethics of Professional Business Organizations in the United States," *Journal of Business Ethics* (January 2002), pp. 35–49.

38. M. Weinstein, "Survey Says: Ethics Training Works," *Training* (November 2005), p. 15.

39. J. E. Fleming, "Codes of Ethics for Global Corporations," *Academy of Management News,* June 2005, p. 4.

40. T. F. Shea, "Employees' Report Card on Supervisors' Ethics: No Improvement," *HR Magazine,* April 2002, p. 29.

41. See also A. G. Peace, J. Weber, K. S. Hartzel, and J. Nightingale, "Ethical Issues in eBusiness: A Proposal for Creating the eBusiness Principles," *Business and Society Review,* Spring 2002, pp. 41–60.

42. D. Jones, "CEO's Moral Compass Steers Siemens," *USA Today,* February 15, 2010, p. 3B.

43. E. Finkel, "Yahoo Takes New 'Road' on Ethics Training," *Workforce Management Online,* July 2010.

44. T. A. Gavin, "Ethics Education," *Internal Auditor,* April 1989, pp. 54–57.

45. L. Myyry and K. Helkama, "The Role of Value Priorities and Professional Ethics Training in Moral Sensitivity," *Journal of Moral Education,* 31, no. 1 (2002), pp. 35–50; W. Penn and B. D. Collier, "Current Research in Moral Development as a Decision Support System," *Journal of Business Ethics* (January 1985), pp. 131–136.

46. J. A. Byrne, "After Enron: The Ideal Corporation," *BusinessWeek,* August 19, 2002, pp. 68–71; D. Rice and C. Dreilinger, "Rights and Wrongs of Ethics Training," *Training & Development Journal* (May 1990), pp. 103–109; and J. Weber, "Measuring the Impact of Teaching Ethics to Future Managers: A Review, Assessment, and

Recommendations," *Journal of Business Ethics* (April 1990), pp. 182–190.

47. S. Caminiti, "The Diversity Factor," *Fortune,* October 19, 2007, pp. 95–105; and B. Velez, "People and Places," *DiversityInc Online,* www.diversityinc.com (October 2006).

48. R. Anand and M. Frances Winters, "A Retrospective View of Corporate Diversity Training from 1964 to the Present," *Academy of Management Learning & Education,* September 2008, pp. 356–372.

49. N. Gibbs, "What Women Want Now," *Time,* October 26, 2009, pp. 24–33.

50. Right or Wrong box based on DiversityInc Staff, "Does McDonald's Web Site Stereotype Blacks?" *DiversityInc.com Online,* www.diversityinc.com (August 25, 2009).

51. M. Bello, USA Today, "Controversy Shrouds Scarves," *Springfield, Missouri News-Leader,* April 17, 2010, p. 8A.

52. "Facts & Figures: Number of Religious Discrimination Complaints Received," *DiversityInc,* November–December 2009, p. 52.

53. P. Wang and J. L. Schwartz, "Stock Price Reactions to GLBT Nondiscrimination Policies," *Human Resource Management,* March–April 2010, pp. 195–216.

54. L. Sullivan, "Sexual Orientation—The Last 'Acceptable' Bias," *Canadian HR Reporter,* December 20, 2004, pp. 9–11.

55. F. Colgan, T. Wright, C. Creegan, and A. McKearney, "Equality and Diversity in the Public Services: Moving Forward on Lesbian, Gay and Bisexual Equality?" *Human Resource Management Journal,* 19, no. 3 (2009), pp. 280–301.

56. J. Hempel, "Coming Out in Corporate America," *BusinessWeek,* December 15, 2003, pp. 64–72.

57. See, for instance, P. Cappelli, J. Constantine, and C. Chadwick, "It Pays to Value Family: Work and Family Trade-Offs Reconsidered," *Industrial Relations,* April 2000, pp. 175–198; R. C. Barnett and D. T. Hall, "How to Use Reduced Hours to Win the War for Talent," *Organizational Dynamics,* March 2001, p. 42; and M. A. Verespej, "Balancing Act," *Industry Week,* May 15, 2000, pp. 81–85.

58. M. Conlin, "The New Debate over Working Moms," *BusinessWeek,* November 18, 2000, pp. 102–103.

59. M. Elias, "The Family-First Generation," *USA Today,* December 13, 2004, p. 5D.

60. J. Revell, C. Bigda, and D. Rosato, "The Rise of Freelance Nation," *CNNMoney,* cnnmoney.com (June 12, 2009).

61. Ibid.

62. Ibid.

63. S. Armour, "Generation Y: They've Arrived at Work with a New Attitude," *USA Today,* November 6, 2005, pp. 1B+; B. Moses, "The Challenges of Managing Gen Y," *Globe and Mail,* March 11 2005, p. C1; and C. A. Martin, *Managing Generation Y* (Amherst, MA: HRD Press, 2001).

CHAPTER 4

Foundations of Decision Making

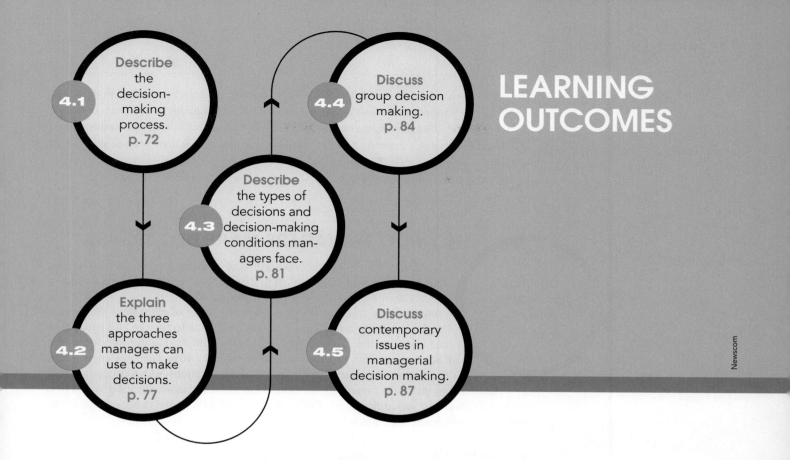

4.1 Describe the decision-making process. p. 72

4.4 Discuss group decision making. p. 84

4.3 Describe the types of decisions and decision-making conditions managers face. p. 81

4.2 Explain the three approaches managers can use to make decisions. p. 77

4.5 Discuss contemporary issues in managerial decision making. p. 87

Newscom

Lift Off

Over the years, NASA (National Aeronautics and Space Administration) has provided us with some spectacular moments—from Neil Armstrong's first steps on the moon to the Hubble Telescope's mesmerizing photos of distant stars and galaxies.[1] NASA's vision—to understand and protect our home planet, to explore the Universe and search for life, and to inspire the next generation of explorers—has guided its management team over the years as decisions were made about projects, missions, and programs. When the space shuttle program—NASA's main project mission—ended in 2011, the organization floundered. In fact, one agency program manager described NASA's future as "a period of sustained ambiguity." Possible new goals for NASA proposed by the president included getting to an asteroid by 2025 and putting astronauts on Mars by 2030. It's clear that NASA needs to chart a new course. As its managers contemplate that future, decision making will be crucial to plotting a course that takes the organization efficiently and effectively in a desirable direction.

Making decisions, especially during times of uncertainty when there are no precedents to guide you, can't be easy. However, that doesn't mean that managers can just forget about or ignore making decisions. Rather, as illustrated by the situation that decision makers at NASA face, even when decisions are difficult or complex, you gather the best information you can and just do it. Managers make a lot of decisions—minor and major. The overall quality of those decisions goes a long way in determining an organization's success or failure. In this chapter, we examine the basics of decision making.

HOW DO MANAGERS MAKE DECISIONS?

4.1 Describe the decision-making process.

Decision making is typically described as choosing among alternatives, but this view is overly simplistic. Why? Because decision making is a process rather than the simple act of choosing among alternatives. Exhibit 4–1 illustrates the **decision-making process** as a set of eight steps that begins with identifying a problem; it moves through selecting an alternative that can alleviate the problem and concludes with evaluating the decision's effectiveness. This process is as applicable to your decision about what you're going to do on spring break as it is to the decisions NASA executives will make as they shape the organization's future. The process can also be used to describe both individual and group decisions. Let's take a closer look at the process in order to understand what each step entails.

What Defines a Decision Problem?

The decision-making process begins with the identification of a **problem** (step 1) or, more specifically, a discrepancy between an existing and a desired state of affairs.[2] Let's develop an example illustrating this point to use throughout this section. For the sake of simplicity, we'll make it an example most of us can relate to: the decision to buy a car. Take the case of a new-product manager for the Netherlands-based food company Royal Ahold. The manager spent nearly $6,000 on auto repairs over the past few years, and now the car has a blown engine. Repair estimates indicate that it is not economical to repair the car. Furthermore, convenient public transportation is unavailable.

So now we have a problem that results from the disparity between the manager's need to have a car that works and the fact that her current one doesn't. Unfortunately, this example doesn't tell us much about how managers identify problems. In the real world, most problems don't come with neon signs identifying them as such. A blown engine is a clear signal to the manager that she needs a new car, but few problems are that obvious. Instead, problem identification is subjective. Furthermore, the manager who mistakenly solves the wrong problem perfectly is just as likely to perform poorly as the manager who fails to identify the right problem and does nothing. Problem identification is neither a simple nor

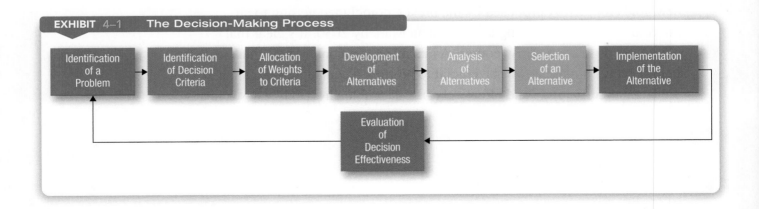

EXHIBIT 4–1   The Decision-Making Process

Identification of a Problem → Identification of Decision Criteria → Allocation of Weights to Criteria → Development of Alternatives → Analysis of Alternatives → Selection of an Alternative → Implementation of the Alternative → Evaluation of Decision Effectiveness

an unimportant part of the decision-making process.[3] How do managers become aware they have a discrepancy? They have to make a comparison between the current state of affairs and some standard, which can be past performance, previously set goals, or the performance of some other unit within the organization or in other organizations. In our car-buying example, the standard is previous performance—a car that runs.

What Is Relevant in the Decision-Making Process?

Once a manager has identified a problem that needs attention, the decision criteria that will be important in solving the problem must be identified (step 2).

In our vehicle-buying example, the product manager assesses the factors that are relevant in her decision, which might include criteria such as price, model (two-door or four-door), size (compact or intermediate), manufacturer (French, Japanese, South Korean, German, American), optional equipment (navigation system, side-impact protection, leather interior), and repair records. These criteria reflect what she thinks is relevant in her decision. Every decision maker has criteria—whether explicitly stated or not—that guide his or her decision making. Note that in this step in the decision-making process, what is not identified is as important as what is. If the product manager doesn't consider fuel economy to be a criterion, then it will not influence her choice of car. Thus, if a decision maker does not identify a particular factor in this second step, it's treated as irrelevant.

The steps involved in buying a vehicle provide a good example of the decision-making process, which applies to both individual and group decisions. For this young woman, the process starts with a problem: She needs a car to drive to a new job. Then she identifies decision criteria (price, color, size, and performance); assigns priorities to the criteria; develops, analyzes, and selects alternatives; and implements the alternative. In the last step of the decision-making process she evaluates the effectiveness of her decision.

How Does the Decision Maker Weight the Criteria and Analyze Alternatives?

In many decision-making situations, the criteria are not all equally important.[4] It's necessary, therefore, to allocate weights to the items listed in step 2 in order to give them their relative priority in the decision (step 3). A simple approach is to give the most important criterion a weight of 10 and then assign weights to the rest against that standard. Thus, in contrast to a criterion that you gave a 5, the highest-rated factor would be twice as important. The idea is to use your personal preferences to assign priorities to the relevant criteria in your decision as well as to indicate their degree of importance by assigning a weight to each. Exhibit 4–2 lists the criteria and weights that our manager developed for her vehicle

EXHIBIT 4–2	**Important Criteria and Weights in a Car-Buying Decision**

CRITERION	WEIGHT
Price	10
Interior comfort	8
Durability	5
Repair record	5
Performance	3
Handling	1

decision-making process
A set of eight steps that includes identifying a problem, selecting a solution, and evaluating the effectiveness of the solution

problem
A discrepancy between an existing and a desired state of affairs

decision criteria
Factors that are relevant in a decision

| | | | EXHIBIT 4-3 | Assessment of Possible Car Alternatives | | | |

ALTERNATIVES	INITIAL PRICE	INTERIOR COMFORT	DURABILITY	REPAIR RECORD	PERFORMANCE	HANDLING	TOTAL
Jeep Compass	2	10	8	7	5	5	37
Ford Focus	9	6	5	6	8	6	40
Hyundai Elantra	8	5	6	6	4	6	35
Ford Fiesta SES	9	5	6	7	6	5	38
Volkswagen Golf	5	6	9	10	7	7	44
Toyota Prius	10	5	6	4	3	3	31
Mazda 3 MT	4	8	7	6	8	9	42
Kia Soul	7	6	8	6	5	6	38
BMW 335	9	7	6	4	4	7	37
Nissan Cube	5	8	5	4	10	10	42
Toyota Camry	6	5	10	10	6	6	43
Honda Fit Sport MT	8	6	6	5	7	8	40

replacement decision. Price is the most important criterion in her decision, with performance and handling having low weights.

Then the decision maker lists the alternatives that could succeed in resolving the problem (step 4). No attempt is made in this step to appraise these alternatives, only to list them.[5] Let's assume that our manager has identified 12 cars as viable choices: Jeep Compass, Ford Focus, Hyundai Elantra, Ford Fiesta SES, Volkswagen Golf, Toyota Prius, Mazda 3 MT, Kia Soul, BMW 335, Nissan Cube, Toyota Camry, and Honda Fit Sport MT.

Once the alternatives have been identified, the decision maker must critically analyze each one (step 5). Each alternative is evaluated by appraising it against the criteria. The strengths and weaknesses of each alternative become evident as they're compared with the criteria and weights established in steps 2 and 3. Exhibit 4–3 shows the assessed values that the manager put on each of her 12 alternatives after she had test-driven each car. Keep in mind that the ratings shown in Exhibit 4–3 are based on the assessment made by the new-product manager. Again, we're using a scale of 1 to 10. Some assessments can be achieved in a relatively objective fashion. For instance, the purchase price represents the best price the manager can get from local dealers, and consumer magazines report data from owners on frequency of repairs. However, the assessment of handling is clearly a personal judgment. Our point: most decisions contain judgments. They're reflected in the criteria chosen in step 2, the weights given to the criteria, and the evaluation of alternatives. The influence of personal judgment explains why two car buyers with the same amount of money may look at two totally distinct sets of alternatives or even look at the same alternatives and rate them differently.

Exhibit 4–3 shows only an assessment of the 12 alternatives against the decision criteria; it does not reflect the weighting done in step 3. If one choice had scored 10 on every criterion, you wouldn't need to consider the weights. Similarly, if the weights were all equal, you could evaluate each alternative merely by summing up the appropriate lines in Exhibit 4–3. For instance, the Ford Fiesta SES would have a score of 38, and the Toyota Camry a score of 43. If you multiply each alternative assessment against its weight, you get the figures in Exhibit 4–4. For instance, the Kia Soul scored a 40 on durability, which was determined by multiplying the weight given to durability [5] by the manager's appraisal of Kia on this criterion [8]. The sum of these scores represents an evaluation of each alternative against the previously established criteria and weights. Notice that the weighting of the criteria has changed the ranking of alternatives in our example. The Volkswagen Golf, for example, has gone from first to third. From our analysis, both initial price and interior comfort worked against the Volkswagen.

What Determines the Best Choice?

Step 6 is the critical act of choosing the best alternative from among those assessed. Since we determined all the pertinent factors in the decision, weighted them appropriately, and identified the viable alternatives, we merely have to choose the alternative that generated

	INITIAL PRICE [10]		INTERIOR COMFORT [8]		DURABILITY [5]		REPAIR RECORD [5]		PERFORMANCE [3]		HANDLING [1]		TOTAL
ALTERNATIVES														
Jeep Compass	2	20	10	80	8	40	7	35	5	15	5	5	195
Ford Focus	9	90	6	48	5	25	6	30	8	24	6	6	223
Hyundai Elantra	8	80	5	40	6	30	6	30	4	12	6	6	198
Ford Fiesta SES	9	90	5	40	6	30	7	35	6	18	5	5	218
Volkswagen Golf	5	50	6	48	9	45	10	50	7	21	7	7	221
Toyota Prius	10	100	5	40	6	30	4	20	3	9	3	3	202
Mazda 3 MT	4	40	8	64	7	35	6	30	8	24	9	9	202
Kia Soul	7	70	6	48	8	40	6	30	5	15	6	6	209
BMW 335	9	90	7	56	6	30	4	20	4	12	7	7	215
Nissan Cube	5	50	8	64	5	25	4	20	10	30	10	10	199
Toyota Camry	6	60	5	40	10	50	10	50	6	18	6	6	224
Honda Fit Sport MT	8	80	6	48	6	30	5	25	7	21	8	8	212

EXHIBIT 4-4 Evaluation of Car Alternatives: Assessment Criteria × Criteria Weight

the highest score in step 5. In our vehicle example (Exhibit 4–4), the decision maker would choose the Toyota Camry. On the basis of the criteria identified, the weights given to the criteria, and the decision maker's assessment of each car on the criteria, the Toyota scored highest [224 points] and, thus, became the best alternative.

What Happens in Decision Implementation?

Although the choice process is completed in the previous step, the decision may still fail if it's not implemented properly (step 7). Therefore, this step is concerned with putting the decision into action. Decision implementation includes conveying the decision to those affected and getting their commitment to it.[6] The people who must carry out a decision are most likely to enthusiastically endorse the outcome if they participate in the decision-making process. Also, as we'll discuss later in this chapter, groups or committees can help a manager achieve commitment.

What Is the Last Step in the Decision Process?

In the last step in the decision-making process (step 8), managers appraise the result of the decision to see whether the problem was resolved. Did the alternative chosen in step 6 and implemented in step 7 accomplish the desired result? Evaluating the results of a decision is part of the managerial control process, which we'll discuss in Chapter 14.

What Common Errors Are Committed in the Decision-Making Process?

When managers make decisions, they not only use their own particular style, but may use "rules of thumb" or heuristics, to simplify their decision making.[7] Rules of thumb can be useful because they help make sense of complex, uncertain, and ambiguous information. Even though managers may use rules of thumb, that doesn't mean those rules are reliable. Why? Because they may lead to errors and biases in processing and evaluating information. Exhibit 4–5 identifies 12 common decision errors and biases that managers make. Let's look briefly at each.[8]

When decision makers tend to think they know more than they do or hold unrealistically positive views of themselves and their performance, they're exhibiting the *over-confidence bias*. The *immediate gratification bias* describes decision makers who tend to want immediate rewards and to avoid immediate costs. For these individuals, decision

decision implementation
Putting a decision into action

heuristics
Judgmental shortcuts or "rules of thumb" used to simplify decision making

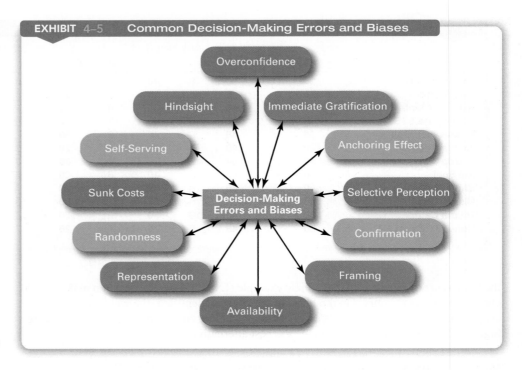

EXHIBIT 4-5   Common Decision-Making Errors and Biases

- Overconfidence
- Hindsight
- Immediate Gratification
- Self-Serving
- Anchoring Effect
- Sunk Costs
- Selective Perception
- Randomness
- Confirmation
- Representation
- Framing
- Availability

Decision-Making Errors and Biases

As sales manager of Prudential Realty in Brea, California, Tom Pelton makes decisions every day in performing the functions of planning, organizing, leading, and controlling. With home sales at his office dropping to an average of 54 sales per month, Pelton decided to develop a plan for attracting more first-time buyers and investors and then issued a challenge to his 75 agents to motivate them to sell 100 homes in a month. If they reached the goal, Pelton promised he would wear a dress to work. Pelton's decisions resulted in 102 home sales, setting a record for the office. The 6-foot-5, 260-pound Pelton made good on his promise by sashaying into the office with Aerosmith's "Dude Looks like a Lady" blaring over a loudspeaker, while his colleagues cheered, laughed, and took pictures to capture the fun-loving moment.

choices that provide quick payoffs are more appealing than those in the future. The *anchoring effect* describes when decision makers fixate on initial information as a starting point and then, once set, fail to adequately adjust for subsequent information. First impressions, ideas, prices, and estimates carry unwarranted weight relative to information received later. When decision makers selectively organize and interpret events based on their biased perceptions, they're using the *selective perception bias*. This influences the information they pay attention to, the problems they identify, and the alternatives they develop. Decision makers who seek out information that reaffirms their past choices and discount information that contradicts past judgments exhibit the *confirmation bias*. These people tend to accept at face value information that confirms their preconceived views and are critical and skeptical of information that challenges these views. The *framing bias* happens when decision makers select and highlight certain aspects of a situation while excluding others. By drawing attention to specific aspects of a situation and highlighting them, while at the same time downplaying or omitting other aspects, they distort what they see and create incorrect reference points. The *availability bias* occurs when decision makers tend to remember events that are the most recent and vivid in their memory. The result? It distorts their ability to recall events in an objective manner and results in distorted judgments and probability estimates. When decision makers assess the likelihood of an event based on how closely it resembles other events or sets of events, that's the *representation bias*. Managers exhibiting this bias draw analogies and see identical situations where they don't exist. The *randomness bias* describes when decision makers try to create meaning out of random events. They do this because most decision makers have difficulty dealing with chance even though random events happen to everyone and there's nothing that can be done to predict them. The *sunk costs error* takes place when decision makers forget that current choices can't correct the past. They incorrectly fixate on past expenditures of time, money, or effort in assessing choices rather than on future consequences. Instead of ignoring sunk costs, they can't forget them. Decision makers who are quick to take credit for their successes and to blame failure on outside factors are exhibiting the *self-serving bias*. Finally, the *hindsight bias* is the tendency for decision makers to falsely believe that they would have accurately predicted the outcome of an event once that outcome is actually known.

Managers can avoid the negative effects of these decision errors and biases by being aware of them and then not using them! Beyond that, managers also should pay attention to "how" they make decisions and try to identify the heuristics they typically use and critically evaluate how appropriate those are. Finally, managers could ask colleagues to help identify weaknesses in their decision-making style and then work on improving those weaknesses.

WHAT ARE THREE APPROACHES MANAGERS CAN USE TO MAKE DECISIONS?

Although everyone in an organization makes decisions, decision making is particularly important to managers. As Exhibit 4–6 shows, it's part of all four managerial functions. In fact, that's why we say that decision making is the essence of management.[9] And that's why managers—as they plan, organize, lead, and control—are called *decision makers*.

The fact that almost everything a manager does involves making decisions doesn't mean that decisions are always time-consuming, complex, or evident to an outside observer. Most decision making is routine. Every day of the year you make a decision about what to eat for dinner. It's no big deal. You've made the decision thousands of times before. It's a pretty simple decision and can usually be handled quickly. It's the type of

Explain the three approaches managers can use to make decisions. 4.2

EXHIBIT 4–6 Decisions Managers May Make

PLANNING
- What are the organization's long-term objectives?
- What strategies will best achieve those objectives?
- What should the organization's short-term objectives be?
- How difficult should individual goals be?

ORGANIZING
- How many employees should I have report directly to me?
- How much centralization should there be in the organization?
- How should jobs be designed?
- When should the organization implement a different structure?

LEADING
- How do I handle employees who appear to be low in motivation?
- What is the most effective leadership style in a given situation?
- How will a specific change affect worker productivity?
- When is the right time to stimulate conflict?

CONTROLLING
- What activities in the organization need to be controlled?
- How should those activities be controlled?
- When is a performance deviation significant?
- What type of management information system should the organization have?

decision you almost forget *is* a decision. And managers also make dozens of these routine decisions every day, such as, for example, which employee will work what shift next week, what information should be included in a report, or how to resolve a customer's complaint. Keep in mind that even though a decision seems easy or has been faced by a manager a number of times before, it still is a decision. Let's look at three perspectives on how managers make decisions.

What Is the Rational Model of Decision Making?

When Hewlett-Packard (HP) acquired Compaq, the company did no research on how customers viewed Compaq products until "months after then-CEO Carly Fiorina publicly announced the deal and privately warned her top management team that she didn't want to hear any dissent pertaining to the acquisition."[10] By the time they discovered that customers perceived Compaq products as inferior—just the opposite of what customers felt about HP products—it was too late. HP's performance suffered and Fiorina lost her job.

We assume that managers' decision making will be **rational decision making**; that is, they'll make logical and consistent choices to maximize value.[11] After all, managers have all sorts of tools and techniques to help them be rational decision makers. (See the Technology and the Manager's Job box for additional information.) But as the HP example illustrates, managers aren't always rational. What does it mean to be a "rational" decision maker?

A rational decision maker would be fully objective and logical. The problem faced would be clear and unambiguous, and the decision maker would have a clear and specific goal and know all possible alternatives and consequences. Finally, making decisions rationally would consistently lead to selecting the alternative that maximizes the likelihood of achieving that goal. These assumptions apply to any decision—personal or managerial. However, for managerial decision making, we need to add one additional assumption— decisions are made in the best interests of the organization. These assumptions of rationality aren't very realistic, but the next concept can help explain how most decisions get made in organizations.

TECHNOLOGY AND THE MANAGER'S JOB — MAKING BETTER DECISIONS WITH TECHNOLOGY

Information technology is providing managers with a wealth of decision-making support, including expert systems, neural networks, groupware, and specific problem-solving software.[12] *Expert systems* use software programs to encode the relevant experience of an expert and allow a system to act like that expert in analyzing and solving ill-structured problems. The essence of expert systems is that (1) they use specialized knowledge about a particular problem area rather than general knowledge that would apply to all problems; (2) they use qualitative reasoning rather than numerical calculations; and (3) they perform at a level of competence that is higher than that of nonexpert humans. They guide users through problems by asking them a set of sequential questions about the situation and drawing conclusions based on the answers given. The conclusions are based on programmed rules that have been modeled on the actual reasoning processes of experts who have confronted similar problems before. Once in place, these systems allow employees and lower-level managers to make high-quality decisions that previously could have been made only by senior managers.

Neural networks are the next step beyond expert systems. They use computer software to imitate the structure of brain cells and connections among them. Sophisticated robotics use neural networks for their intelligence. Neural networks are able to distinguish patterns and trends too subtle or complex for human beings. For instance, people can't easily assimilate more than two or three variables at once, but neural networks can perceive correlations among hundreds of variables. As a result, they can perform many operations simultaneously, recognizing patterns, making associations, generalizing about problems they haven't been exposed to before, and learning through experience. For instance, most banks today use neural networks to flag potential credit card fraud. In the past they relied on expert systems to track millions of credit card transactions, but these earlier systems could look at only a few factors, such as the size of a transaction. Consequently, thousands of potential defrauding incidents were "flagged," most of which were false positives. Now with neural networks, significantly fewer numbers of cases are being identified as problematic—and it's more likely now that the majority of those identified will be actual cases of fraud. Furthermore, with the neural network system, fraudulent activities on a credit card can be uncovered in a matter of hours, rather than the two to three days it took prior to the implementation of neural networks. This is just one example of the power of IT to enhance an organization's—and its managers'—decision-making capabilities.

Think About:

· Can a manager have too much data when making decisions? Explain.

· Does information technology, such as expert systems and neural networks, make decisions, or is it simply a tool for managers? Discuss.

· How can technology help managers make better decisions?

· "Decision making is both science and art." Do you agree? Why or why not?

From the Past to the Present

Herbert A. Simon, who won a Nobel Prize in economics for his work on decision making, was primarily concerned with how people use logic and psychology to make choices.[13] He proposed that individuals were limited in their ability to "grasp the present and anticipate the future," and this bounded rationality made it difficult for them to "achieve the best possible decisions." Thus, people made "good enough" or "satisficing" choices. He went on to describe all administrative activity as group activity in which an organization took some decision-making autonomy from the individual and substituted it for an organizational decision-making process. Simon believed that such a process was necessary since it was impossible for any single individual to achieve any "high degree of objective rationality."

Simon's important contributions to management thinking came through his belief that to study and understand organizations meant studying the complex network of decisional processes that were inherent. His work in bounded rationality helps us make sense of how managers can behave rationally and still make satisfactory decisions, even given the limits of their capacity to process information.

Think About:

• Do you think satisficing is settling for second best? Discuss.

• In what decisions have you made "satisficing" choices? Were you happy with those choices?

• How does knowing about bounded rationality help make you a better decision maker?

What Is Bounded Rationality?

Despite the unrealistic assumptions, managers are expected to act rationally when making decisions.[14] They understand that "good" decision makers are supposed to do certain things and exhibit good decision-making behaviors as they identify problems, consider alternatives, gather information, and act decisively but prudently. When they do so, they show others that they're competent and that their decisions are the result of intelligent deliberation. However, a more realistic approach to describing how managers make decisions is the concept of bounded rationality, which says that managers make decisions rationally, but are limited (bounded) by their ability to process information.[15] Because they can't possibly analyze all information on all alternatives, managers satisfice, rather than maximize. That is, they accept solutions that are "good enough." They're being rational within the limits (bounds) of their ability to process information. Let's look at an example.

Suppose that you're a finance major and upon graduation you want a job, preferably as a personal financial planner, with a minimum salary of $45,000 and within a hundred miles of your hometown. You accept a job offer as a business credit analyst— not exactly a personal financial planner but still in the finance field—at a bank 50 miles from home at a starting salary of $39,000. If you had done a more comprehensive job search, you would have discovered a job in personal financial planning at a trust company only 25 miles from your hometown and starting at a salary of $43,000. You weren't a perfectly rational decision maker because you didn't maximize your decision by searching all possible alternatives and then choosing the best. But because the first job offer was satisfactory (or "good enough"), you behaved in a bounded rationality manner by accepting it.

Most decisions that managers make don't fit the assumptions of perfect rationality, so managers satisfice. However, keep in mind that their decision making is also likely influenced by the organization's culture, internal politics, power considerations, and by a phenomenon called escalation of commitment, which is an increased commitment to a previous decision despite evidence that it may have been wrong.[16] You'll read about a

rational decision making
Describes choices that are consistent and value-maximizing within specified constraints

bounded rationality
Making decisions that are rational within the limits of a manager's ability to process information

satisfice
Accepting solutions that are "good enough"

escalation of commitment
An increased commitment to a previous decision despite evidence that it may have been a poor decision

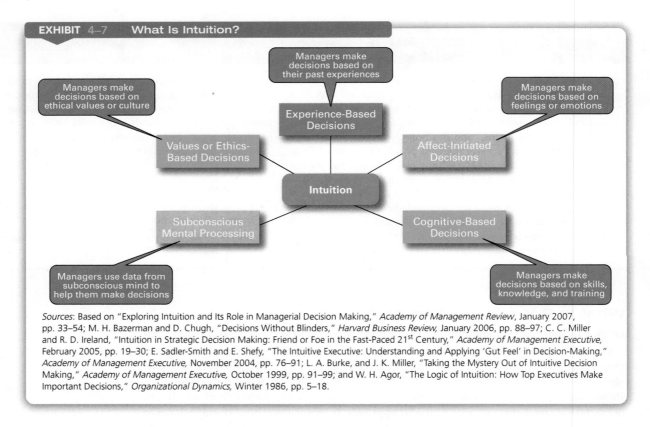

EXHIBIT 4–7   What Is Intuition?

Managers make decisions based on ethical values or culture

Managers make decisions based on their past experiences

Managers make decisions based on feelings or emotions

Experience-Based Decisions

Values or Ethics-Based Decisions

Affect-Initiated Decisions

Intuition

Subconscious Mental Processing

Cognitive-Based Decisions

Managers use data from subconscious mind to help them make decisions

Managers make decisions based on skills, knowledge, and training

Sources: Based on "Exploring Intuition and Its Role in Managerial Decision Making," *Academy of Management Review*, January 2007, pp. 33–54; M. H. Bazerman and D. Chugh, "Decisions Without Blinders," *Harvard Business Review*, January 2006, pp. 88–97; C. C. Miller and R. D. Ireland, "Intuition in Strategic Decision Making: Friend or Foe in the Fast-Paced 21st Century," *Academy of Management Executive*, February 2005, pp. 19–30; E. Sadler-Smith and E. Shefy, "The Intuitive Executive: Understanding and Applying 'Gut Feel' in Decision-Making," *Academy of Management Executive*, November 2004, pp. 76–91; L. A. Burke, and J. K. Miller, "Taking the Mystery Out of Intuitive Decision Making," *Academy of Management Executive*, October 1999, pp. 91–99; and W. H. Agor, "The Logic of Intuition: How Top Executives Make Important Decisions," *Organizational Dynamics*, Winter 1986, pp. 5–18.

real-life example of escalation of commitment in this chapter's Case Application on p. 415 as we take a closer look at NASA's decision making on occasions when decision makers escalated commitment to a bad decision, actions that led to disastrous outcomes. Why would decision makers escalate commitment to a bad decision? Because they don't want to admit that their initial decision may have been flawed. Rather than search for new alternatives, they simply increase their commitment to the original solution.

What Role Does Intuition Play in Managerial Decision Making?

When Diego Della Valle, chairman of Italy-based Tod's luxury shoe empire, wants to know if a new style of shoes will work in the marketplace, he doesn't use focus groups or poll testing. Nope . . . he wears them. After a few days, if they're not to his liking, he renders his verdict: "These won't go into production." His intuitive decision approach has helped him turn Tod's into a successful multinational, multibillion-dollar company.[17] Like Della Valle, managers often use their intuition to help their decision making. What is **intuitive decision making**? It's making decisions on the basis of experience, feelings, and accumulated judgment. It's been described as "unconscious reasoning."[18] Researchers studying managers' use of intuitive decision making have identified five different aspects of intuition, which we describe in Exhibit 4–7.[19] How common is intuitive decision making? One survey found that almost half of the executives surveyed "used intuition more often than formal analysis to run their companies."[20]

Intuitive decision making can complement both rational and boundedly rational decision making.[21] First of all, a manager who has had experience with a similar type of problem or situation often can act quickly with what appears to be limited information because of that past experience. In addition, a recent study found that individuals who experienced intense feelings and emotions when making decisions actually achieved higher decision-making performance, especially when they understood their feelings as they were making decisions. The old belief that managers should ignore emotions when making decisions may not be the best advice.[22]

WHAT TYPES OF DECISIONS AND DECISION-MAKING CONDITIONS DO MANAGERS FACE?

Laura Ipsen is a senior vice president and general manager at Smart Grid, a business unit of Cisco Systems, which is working on helping utility companies find ways to build open, interconnected systems. She describes her job as "like having to put together a 1,000-piece puzzle, but with no box top with the picture of what it looks like and with some pieces missing."[23] Decision making in that type of environment is quite different from decision making done by a manager of a local Gap outlet store.

Describe the types of decisions and decision-making conditions managers face.

4.3

The types of problems managers face in decision-making situations often determine how a problem is treated. In this section, we present a categorization scheme for problems and for types of decisions. Then we show how the type of decision making a manager uses should reflect the characteristics of the problem.

How Do Problems Differ?

Some problems are straightforward. The goal of the decision maker is clear, the problem familiar, and information about the problem easily defined and complete. Examples might include a supplier who is late with an important delivery, a customer who wants to return an Internet purchase, a TV news team that has to respond to an unexpected and fast-breaking event, or a university that must help a student who is applying for financial aid. Such situations are called structured problems. They align closely with the assumptions underlying perfect rationality.

Many situations faced by managers, however, are unstructured problems. They are new or unusual. Information about such problems is ambiguous or incomplete. Examples of unstructured problems include the decision to enter a new market segment, to hire an architect to design a new office park, or to merge two organizations. So, too, is the decision to invest in a new, unproven technology. For instance, when Andrew Mason founded his online coupon start-up Groupon, he faced a situation best described as an unstructured problem.[24]

How Does a Manager Make Programmed Decisions?

Just as problems can be divided into two categories, so, too, can decisions. Programmed, or routine, decision making is the most efficient way to handle structured problems. However, when problems are unstructured, managers must rely on nonprogrammed decision making in order to develop unique solutions.

An auto mechanic damages a customer's rim while changing a tire. What does the manager do? Because the company probably has a standardized method for handling this type of problem, it is considered a programmed decision. For example, the manager may replace the rim at the company's expense. Decisions are programmed to the extent that they are repetitive and routine and to the extent that a specific approach has been worked out for handling them. Because the problem is well structured, the manager does not have to go to the trouble and expense of an involved decision process. Programmed decision making is relatively simple and tends to rely heavily on previous solutions. The develop-the-alternatives stage in the decision-making process is either nonexistent or given little attention. Why? Because once the structured problem is defined, its solution is usually

intuitive decision making
Making decisions on the basis of experience, feelings, and accumulated judgment

structured problem
A straightforward, familiar, and easily defined problem

unstructured problem
A problem that is new or unusual for which information is ambiguous or incomplete

programmed decision
A repetitive decision that can be handled using a routine approach

Policies for programmed decisions provide guidelines to channel a manager's thinking in a specific direction. Nestlé has corporate policies that guide decision making in the areas of nutrition, health, and wellness; consumer communication; and quality assurance and product safety. The company's quality policy covers all Nestlé products, including these Swiss chocolate cows made at a Nestlé plant in Switzerland. The quality policy is "to build trust by offering products and services that match consumer expectation and preference, and to comply with all internal and external food safety, regulatory, and quality requirements."

self-evident or at least reduced to only a few alternatives that are familiar and that have proved successful in the past. In many cases, programmed decision making becomes decision making by precedent. Managers simply do what they and others have done previously in the same situation. The damaged rim does not require the manager to identify and weight decision criteria or develop a long list of possible solutions. Rather, the manager falls back on a systematic procedure, rule, or policy.

PROCEDURES. A procedure is a series of interrelated sequential steps that a manager can use when responding to a well-structured problem. The only real difficulty is identifying the problem. Once the problem is clear, so is the procedure. For instance, a purchasing manager receives a request from computing services for licensing arrangements to install 250 copies of Norton Antivirus Software. The purchasing manager knows that a definite procedure is in place for handling this decision. Has the requisition been properly filled out and approved? If not, he can send the requisition back with a note explaining what is deficient. If the request is complete, the approximate costs are estimated. If the total exceeds $8,500, three bids must be obtained. If the total is $8,500 or less, only one vendor need be identified and the order placed. The decision-making process is merely the execution of a simple series of sequential steps.

RULES. A rule is an explicit statement that tells a manager what he or she ought—or ought not—to do. Rules are frequently used by managers who confront a structured problem because they're simple to follow and ensure consistency. In the preceding example, the $8,500 cutoff rule simplifies the purchasing manager's decision about when to use multiple bids.

POLICIES. A third guide for making programmed decisions is a policy. It provides guidelines to channel a manager's thinking in a specific direction. The statement that "we promote from within, whenever possible" is an example of a policy. In contrast to a rule, a policy establishes parameters for the decision maker rather than specifically stating what should or should not be done. It's at this point that one's ethical standards will come into play. As an analogy, think of the Ten Commandments as rules and the U.S. Constitution as policy. The latter requires judgment and interpretation; the former do not.

How Do Nonprogrammed Decisions Differ from Programmed Decisions?

Examples of nonprogrammed decisions include deciding whether to acquire another organization, deciding which global markets offer the most potential, or deciding whether to sell off an unprofitable division. Such decisions are unique and nonrecurring. When a manager confronts an unstructured problem, no cut-and-dried solution is available. A custom-made, nonprogrammed response is required.

The creation of a new organizational strategy is a nonprogrammed decision. This decision is different from previous organizational decisions because the issue is new; a different set of environmental factors exists, and other conditions have changed. For example, Amazon.com's Jeff Bezos's strategy to "get big fast" helped the company grow tremendously. But this strategy came at a cost—perennial financial losses. To turn a profit, Bezos made decisions regarding "sorting orders, anticipating demand, more efficient shipping, foreign partnerships, and opening a marketplace allowing other sellers to sell their books at Amazon." As a result, for the first time in company history, Amazon is profitable.[25]

How Are Problems, Types of Decisions, and Organizational Level Integrated?

Exhibit 4–8 describes the relationship among types of problems, types of decisions, and level in the organization. Structured problems are responded to with programmed decision making. Unstructured problems require nonprogrammed decision making. Lower-level managers essentially confront familiar and repetitive problems; therefore, they most typically rely on programmed decisions such as standard operating procedures. However, the problems confronting managers are likely to become less structured as they move up the organizational hierarchy. Why? Because lower-level managers handle the routine decisions themselves and pass upward only decisions that they find unique or difficult. Similarly, managers pass down routine decisions to their employees in order to spend their time on more problematic issues.

Few managerial decisions in the real world are either fully programmed or fully nonprogrammed. Most decisions fall somewhere in between. Few programmed decisions eliminate individual judgment completely. At the other extreme, even the most unusual situation requiring a nonprogrammed decision often can be helped by programmed routines. A final point we want to make is that organizational efficiency is facilitated by programmed decision making—a fact that may explain its wide popularity. Whenever possible, management decisions are likely to be programmed. Obviously, this approach isn't too realistic at the top of the organization, because most of the problems that top-level managers confront are of a nonrecurring nature. However, the necessity to control costs and other variables motivate them to create policies, standard operating procedures, and rules to guide other lower-level managers.

Programmed decisions minimize the need for managers to exercise discretion. This factor is important because discretion costs money. The more nonprogrammed decision making a manager is required to do, the greater the judgment needed. Because sound judgment is an uncommon quality, it costs more to acquire the services of managers who possess it.

What Decision-Making Conditions Do Managers Face?

When making decisions, managers may face three different conditions: certainty, risk, and uncertainty. Let's look at the characteristics of each.

The ideal situation for making decisions is one of **certainty**, which is a situation where a manager can make accurate decisions because the outcome of every alternative is known. For example, when South Dakota's state treasurer decides where to deposit excess state

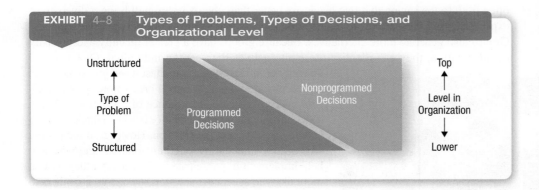

EXHIBIT 4–8   Types of Problems, Types of Decisions, and Organizational Level

---

procedure
A series of interrelated, sequential steps used to respond to a structured problem

rule
An explicit statement that tells employees what can or cannot be done

policy
A guideline for making decisions

nonprogrammed decision
A unique and nonrecurring decision that requires a custom-made solution

certainty
A situation in which a decision maker can make accurate decisions because all outcomes are known

funds, he knows exactly the interest rate being offered by each bank and the amount that will be earned on the funds. He is certain about the outcomes of each alternative. As you might expect, most managerial decisions aren't like this.

A far more common situation is one of **risk**, conditions in which the decision maker is able to estimate the likelihood of certain outcomes. Under risk, managers have historical data from past personal experiences or secondary information that lets them assign probabilities to different alternatives.

What happens if you face a decision where you're not certain about the outcomes and can't even make reasonable probability estimates? We call this condition **uncertainty**. Managers do face decision-making situations of uncertainty. Under these conditions, the choice of alternative is influenced by the limited amount of available information and by the psychological orientation of the decision maker.

4.4 Discuss group decision making.

HOW DO GROUPS MAKE DECISIONS?

Do managers make a lot of decisions in groups? You bet they do! Many decisions in organizations, especially important decisions that have far-reaching effects on organizational activities and personnel, are typically made in groups. It's a rare organization that doesn't at some time use committees, task forces, review panels, work teams, or similar groups as vehicles for making decisions. Why? In many cases, these groups represent the people who will be most affected by the decisions being made. Because of their expertise, these people are often best qualified to make decisions that affect them.

Studies tell us that managers spend a significant portion of their time in meetings. Undoubtedly, a large portion of that time is involved with defining problems, arriving at solutions to those problems, and determining the means for implementing the solutions. It's possible, in fact, for groups to be assigned any of the eight steps in the decision-making process.

What Are the Advantages of Group Decision Making?

Individual and group decisions have their own set of strengths. Neither is ideal for all situations. Let's begin by reviewing the advantages that group decisions have over individual decisions.

Group decisions provide more complete information than do individual ones.[27] There is often truth to the saying that two heads are better than one. A group will bring a diversity of experiences and perspectives to the decision process that an individual acting alone cannot.[28] Groups also generate more alternatives. Because groups have a greater quantity and diversity of information, they can identify more alternatives than can an individual. Quantity and diversity of information are greatest when group members represent different specialties. Furthermore, group decision making increases acceptance of a solution.[29] Many decisions fail after the final choice has been made because people do not accept the solution. However, if the people who will be affected by a certain solution, and who will help implement it, participate in the decision they will be more likely to accept the decision and encourage others to accept it. And, finally, this process increases legitimacy. The group decision-making process is consistent with democratic ideals; therefore, decisions made by groups may be perceived as more legitimate than decisions made by a single person. The fact that the individual decision maker has complete power and has not consulted others can create a perception that a decision was made autocratically and arbitrarily.

An advantage of group decision making is that it brings a diversity of experiences and perspectives to the decision process. Group decision making is more effective than individual decision making at WLC Architects, where multiethnic design teams of professionals from various disciplines work on complex design and construction projects ranging from schools to civic centers. The group members representing many different specialties of architects and engineers generate more decision alternatives because they have a greater quantity and diversity of information. The decisions resulting from WLC's integrated team approach determine the success of its projects in terms of affordability, functionality, and creativity.

PhotoEdit

What Are the Disadvantages of Group Decision Making?

If groups are so good, how did the phrase "a camel is a racehorse put together by a committee" become so popular? The answer, of course, is that group decisions are not without their drawbacks. First, they're *time-consuming*. It takes time to assemble a group. In addition, the interaction that takes place once the group is in place is frequently inefficient. Groups almost always take more time to reach a solution than an individual would take to make the decision alone. They may also be subject to *minority domination*, where members of a group are never perfectly equal.[30] They may differ in rank in the organization, experience, knowledge about the problem, influence on other members, verbal skills, assertiveness, and the like. This imbalance creates the opportunity for one or more members to dominate others in the group. A minority that dominates a group frequently has an undue influence on the final decision.

Another problem focuses on the *pressures to conform* in groups. For instance, have you ever been in a situation in which several people were sitting around discussing a particular item and you had something to say that ran contrary to the consensus views of the group, but you remained silent? Were you surprised to learn later that others shared your views and also had remained silent? What you experienced is what Irving Janis called **groupthink**.[31] In this form of conformity, group members withhold deviant, minority, or unpopular views in order to give the appearance of agreement. As a result, groupthink undermines critical thinking in the group and eventually harms the quality of the final decision. And, finally, *ambiguous responsibility* can become a problem. Group members share responsibility, but who is actually responsible for the final outcome?[32] In an individual decision, it's clear who is responsible. In a group decision, the responsibility of any single member is watered down.

Groupthink affects a group's ability to appraise alternatives objectively and may jeopardize the arrival at a quality decision. Because of pressures for conformity, groups often deter individuals from critically appraising unusual, minority, or unpopular views. Consequently, an individual's mental efficiency, reality testing, and moral judgment deteriorate. How does groupthink occur? The following are examples of situations in which groupthink is evident:

◆ Group members rationalize any resistance to the assumptions they have made.
◆ Members apply direct pressures on those who momentarily express doubts about any of the group's shared views or who question the validity of arguments favored by the majority.
◆ Those members who have doubts or hold differing points of view seek to avoid deviating from what appears to be group consensus.
◆ An illusion of unanimity is pervasive. If someone does not speak, it is assumed that he or she is in full accord.

Does groupthink really hinder decision making? Yes. Several research studies have found that groupthink symptoms were associated with poorer quality decision outcomes. But groupthink can be minimized if the group is cohesive, fosters open discussion, and has an impartial leader who seeks input from all members.[33]

When Are Groups Most Effective?

Whether groups are more effective than individuals depends on the criteria you use for defining effectiveness, such as accuracy, speed, creativity, and acceptance. Group decisions tend to be more accurate. On average, groups tend to make better decisions than individuals, although groupthink may occur.[34] However, if decision effectiveness is defined in terms of speed, individuals are superior. If creativity is important, groups tend to

risk
A situation in which a decision maker is able to estimate the likelihood of certain outcomes

uncertainty
A situation in which a decision maker has neither certainty nor reasonable probability estimates available

groupthink
When a group exerts extensive pressure on an individual to withhold his or her different views in order to appear to be in agreement

RIGHT ? WRONG

Newscom

be more effective than individuals. And if effectiveness means the degree of acceptance the final solution achieves, the nod again goes to the group.

The effectiveness of group decision making is also influenced by the size of the group. The larger the group, the greater the opportunity for heterogeneous representation. On the other hand, a larger group requires more coordination and more time to allow all members to contribute. This factor means that groups probably should not be too large: A minimum of five to a maximum of about fifteen members is best. Groups of five to seven individuals appear to be the most effective. Because five and seven are odd numbers, decision deadlocks are avoided. Effectiveness should not be considered without also assessing efficiency. Groups almost always stack up as a poor second in efficiency to the individual decision maker. With few exceptions, group decision making consumes more work hours than does individual decision making. In deciding whether to use groups, then, primary consideration must be given to assessing whether increases in effectiveness are more than enough to offset the losses in efficiency.

How Can You Improve Group Decision Making?

Three ways of making group decisions more creative are brainstorming, the nominal group technique, and electronic meetings.

WHAT IS BRAINSTORMING? Brainstorming is a relatively simple idea-generating process that specifically encourages any and all alternatives while withholding any criticism of those alternatives.[36] In a typical brainstorming session, a half-dozen to a dozen people sit around a table. Of course, technology is changing where that "table" is. The group leader states the problem in a clear manner that is understood by all participants. Members then "freewheel" as many alternatives as they can in a given time. No criticism is allowed, and all the alternatives are recorded for later discussion and analysis.[37] Brainstorming, however, is merely a process for generating ideas. The next method, the nominal group technique, helps groups arrive at a preferred solution.[38]

HOW DOES THE NOMINAL GROUP TECHNIQUE WORK? The nominal group technique restricts discussion during the decision-making process, hence the term. Group members must be present, as in a traditional committee meeting, but they are required to operate independently. They secretly write a list of general problem areas or potential solutions to a problem. The chief advantage of this technique is that it permits the group to meet formally but does not restrict independent thinking, as so often happens in the traditional interacting group.[39]

HOW CAN ELECTRONIC MEETINGS ENHANCE GROUP DECISION MAKING? The most recent approach to group decision making blends the nominal group technique with computer technology and is called the electronic meeting.

Once the technology for the meeting is in place, the concept is simple. Numerous people sit around a table that's empty except for a series of computer terminals. Issues are presented to the participants, who type their responses onto their computer screens. Individual comments, as well as aggregate votes, are displayed on a projection screen in the room.

The major advantages of electronic meetings are anonymity, honesty, and speed.[40] Participants can anonymously type any message they want, and it will flash on the screen for all to see with a keystroke. It allows people to be brutally honest with no penalty. And it is fast—chitchat is eliminated, discussions do not digress, and many participants can "talk" at once without interrupting the others.

Electronic meetings are significantly faster and much cheaper than traditional face-to-face meetings.[41] Nestlé, for instance, continues to use the approach for many of its meetings, especially globally focused meetings.[42] However, as with all other forms of group activities, electronic meetings do experience some drawbacks. Those who type quickly can outshine those who may be verbally eloquent but lousy typists; those with the best ideas don't get credit for them; and the process lacks the informational richness of face-to-face oral communication. However, group decision making is likely to include extensive usage of electronic meetings.[43]

A variation of the electronic meeting is the videoconference. By linking together media from different locations, people can have face-to-face meetings even when they are thousands of miles apart. This capability has enhanced feedback among the members, saved countless hours of business travel, and ultimately saved companies such as Nestlé and Logitech hundreds of thousands of dollars. As a result, they're more effective in their meetings and have increased the efficiency with which decisions are made.[44] Many companies utilized these approaches during the global recession.

WHAT CONTEMPORARY DECISION-MAKING ISSUES DO MANAGERS FACE?

Discuss contemporary issues in managerial decision making.

4.5

Today's business world revolves around making decisions, often risky ones, usually with incomplete or inadequate information, and under intense time pressure. Most managers make one decision after another; and as if that weren't challenging enough, more is at stake than ever before. Bad decisions can cost millions. We're going to look at two important issues—national culture and creativity—that managers face in today's fast-moving and global world.

How Does National Culture Affect Managers' Decision Making?

Research shows that, to some extent, decision-making practices differ from country to country.[45] The way decisions are made—whether by group, by team members, participatively, or autocratically by an individual manager—and the degree of risk a decision maker is willing to take are just two examples of decision variables that reflect a country's cultural environment. For example, in India, power distance and uncertainty avoidance (see Chapter 3) are high. There, only very senior-level managers make decisions, and they are likely to make safe decisions. In contrast, in Sweden, power distance and uncertainty avoidance are low. Swedish managers are not afraid to make risky decisions. Senior managers in Sweden also push decisions down in the ranks. They encourage lower-level

brainstorming
An idea-generating process that encourages alternatives while withholding criticism

nominal group technique
A decision-making technique in which group members are physically present but operate independently

electronic meeting
A type of nominal group technique in which participants are linked by computer

Aira Vehaskari/Newscom

Creativity based on expertise in developing video games made an important contribution to decision making at Rovio Mobile, the Finnish firm that created the Angry Birds game. One decision that led to Angry Birds' success was to invest time and money during the game's development to produce an innovative physics-based game that made it easy to learn, created depth for advanced players in later stages, and appealed to people of all ages. After studying the iPhone apps system, Rovio decided to launch the game on iPhone where it quickly became the most popular paid application in 61 countries. Rovio also decided to focus on player retention by issuing free regular game updates. Shown here is an Angry Bird on display at Rovio's offices.

managers and employees to take part in decisions that affect them. In countries such as Egypt, where time pressures are low, managers make decisions at a slower and more deliberate pace than managers do in the United States. And in Italy, where history and traditions are valued, managers tend to rely on tried and proven alternatives to resolve problems.

Decision making in Japan is much more group oriented than in the United States.[46] The Japanese value conformity and cooperation. Before making decisions, Japanese CEOs collect a large amount of information, which is then used in consensus-forming group decisions called **ringisei**. Because employees in Japanese organizations have high job security, managerial decisions take a long-term perspective rather than focusing on short-term profits, as is often the practice in the United States.

Senior managers in France and Germany also adapt their decision styles to their countries' cultures. In France, for instance, autocratic decision making is widely practiced, and managers avoid risks. Managerial styles in Germany reflect the German culture's concern for structure and order. Consequently, German organizations generally operate under extensive rules and regulations. Managers have well-defined responsibilities and accept that decisions must go through channels.

As managers deal with employees from diverse cultures, they need to recognize common and accepted behavior when asking them to make decisions. Some individuals may not be as comfortable as others with being closely involved in decision making, or they may not be willing to experiment with something radically different. Managers who accommodate the diversity in decision-making philosophies and practices can expect a high payoff if they capture the perspectives and strengths that a diverse workforce offers.

Why Is Creativity Important in Decision Making?

A decision maker needs creativity: the ability to produce novel and useful ideas. These ideas are different from what's been done before but are also appropriate to the problem or opportunity presented. Why is creativity important to decision making? It allows the decision maker to appraise and understand the problem more fully, including "seeing" problems others can't see. However, creativity's most obvious value is in helping the decision maker identify all viable alternatives.

Most people have creative potential that they can use when confronted with a decision-making problem. But to unleash that potential, they have to get out of the psychological ruts most of us get into and learn how to think about a problem in divergent ways.

We can start with the obvious. People differ in their inherent creativity. Einstein, Edison, Dali, and Mozart were individuals of exceptional creativity. Not surprisingly, exceptional creativity is scarce. A study of lifetime creativity of 461 men and women found that fewer than 1 percent were exceptionally creative. But 10 percent were highly creative, and about 60 percent were somewhat creative. These findings suggest that most of us have creative potential, if we can learn to unleash it.

Given that most people have the capacity to be at least moderately creative, what can individuals and organizations do to stimulate employee creativity? The best answer to this question lies in the three-component model of creativity based on an extensive body of research.[47] This model proposes that individual creativity essentially requires expertise, creative-thinking skills, and intrinsic task motivation. Studies confirm that the higher the level of each of these three components, the higher the creativity.

Expertise is the foundation of all creative work. Dali's understanding of art and Einstein's knowledge of physics were necessary conditions for them to be able to make creative contributions to their fields. And you wouldn't expect someone with a minimal knowledge of programming to be highly creative as a software engineer. The potential for creativity is enhanced when individuals have abilities, knowledge, proficiencies, and similar expertise in their fields of endeavor.

The second component is *creative-thinking skills*. It encompasses personality characteristics associated with creativity, the ability to use analogies, as well as the talent to see the familiar in a different light. For instance, the following individual traits have been found to be associated with the development of creative ideas: intelligence, independence, self-confidence, risk taking, internal locus of control, tolerance for ambiguity, and perseverance in the face of frustration. The effective use of analogies allows decision makers to apply an idea from one context to another. One of the most famous examples in which analogy resulted in a creative breakthrough was Alexander Graham Bell's observation that it might be possible to take concepts that operate in the ear and apply them to his "talking box." He noticed that the bones in the ear are operated by a delicate, thin membrane. He wondered why, then, a thicker and stronger piece of membrane shouldn't be able to move a piece of steel. Out of that analogy the telephone was conceived. Of course, some people have developed their skill at being able to see problems in a new way. They're able to make the strange familiar and the familiar strange. For instance, most of us think of hens laying eggs. But how many of us have considered that a hen is only an egg's way of making another egg?

The final component in our model is *intrinsic task motivation*—the desire to work on something because it's interesting, involving, exciting, satisfying, or personally challenging. This motivational component is what turns creative *potential* into *actual* creative ideas. It determines the extent to which individuals fully engage their expertise and creative skills. So creative people often love their work, to the point of seeming obsessed. Importantly, an individual's work environment and the organization's culture (we'll look at organization culture in the next chapter) can have a significant effect on intrinsic motivation. Specifically, five organizational factors have been found that can impede your creativity: (1) expected evaluation—focusing on how your work is going to be evaluated; (2) surveillance—being watched while you're working; (3) external motivators—emphasizing external, tangible rewards; (4) competition—facing win–lose situations with your peers; and (5) constrained choices—being given limits on how you can do your work.

ringisei
Japanese consensus-forming group decisions

creativity
The ability to produce novel and useful ideas

4 Review

CHAPTER SUMMARY

4.1 **Describe the decision-making process.** The decision-making process consists of eight steps: (1) identify a problem, (2) identify decision criteria, (3) weight the criteria, (4) develop alternatives, (5) analyze alternatives, (6) select alternative, (7) implement alternative, and (8) evaluate decision effectiveness. As managers make decisions, they may use heuristics to simplify the process, which can lead to errors and biases in their decision making. The 12 common decision-making errors and biases include overconfidence, immediate gratification, anchoring, selective perception, confirmation, framing, availability, representation, randomness, sunk costs, self-serving bias, and hindsight.

4.2 **Explain the three approaches managers can use to make decisions.** The first approach is the rational model. The assumptions of rationality are as follows: the problem is clear and unambiguous; a single, well-defined goal is to be achieved; all alternatives and consequences are known; and the final choice will maximize the payoff. The second approach, bounded rationality, says that managers make rational decisions but are bounded (limited) by their ability to process information. In this approach, managers satisfice, which is when decision makers accept solutions that are good enough. Finally, intuitive decision making is making decisions on the basis of experience, feelings, and accumulated judgment.

4.3 **Describe the types of decisions and decision-making conditions managers face.** Programmed decisions are repetitive decisions that can be handled by a routine approach and are used when the problem being resolved is straightforward, familiar, and easily defined (structured). Nonprogrammed decisions are unique decisions that require a custom-made solution and are used when the problems are new or unusual (unstructured) and for which information is ambiguous or incomplete. Certainty involves a situation in which a manager can make accurate decisions because all outcomes are known. With risk, a manager can estimate the likelihood of certain outcomes in a situation. Uncertainty is a situation in which a manager is not certain about the outcomes and can't even make reasonable probability estimates.

4.4 **Discuss group decision making.** Groups offer certain advantages when making decisions—more complete information, more alternatives, increased acceptance of a solution, and greater legitimacy. On the other hand, groups are time-consuming, can be dominated by a minority, create pressures to conform, and cloud responsibility. Three ways of improving group decision making are brainstorming (utilizing an idea-generating process that specifically encourages any and all alternatives while withholding any criticism of those alternatives), the nominal group technique (a technique that restricts discussion during the decision-making process), and electronic meetings (the most recent approach to group decision making, which blends the nominal group technique with sophisticated computer technology).

4.5 **Discuss contemporary issues in managerial decision making.** As managers deal with employees from diverse cultures, they need to recognize common and accepted behavior when asking them to make decisions. Some individuals may not be as comfortable as others with being closely involved in decision making, or they may not be willing to experiment with something radically different. Also, managers need to be creative in their decision making because creativity allows them to appraise and understand the problem more fully, including "seeing" problems that others can't see.

MyManagementLab   For more resources, please visit **www.mymanagementlab.com**

UNDERSTANDING THE CHAPTER

1. Why is decision making often described as the essence of a manager's job?

2. Describe the eight steps in the decision-making process.

3. All of us bring biases to the decisions we make. What would be the drawbacks of having biases? Could there be any advantages to having biases? Explain. What are the implications for managerial decision making?

4. "Because managers have software tools to use, they should be able to make more rational decisions." Do you agree or disagree with this statement? Why?

5. Is there a difference between wrong decisions and bad decisions? Why do good managers sometimes make wrong decisions? Bad decisions? How might managers improve their decision-making skills?

6. Describe a decision you've made that closely aligns with the assumptions of perfect rationality. Compare this decision with the process you used to select your college. Did you depart from the rational model in your college decisions? Explain.

7. Explain how a manager might deal with making decisions under conditions of uncertainty.

8. Why do you think organizations have increased the use of groups for making decisions? When would you recommend using groups to make decisions?

9. Find two examples each of procedures, rules, and policies. Bring your examples to class and be prepared to share them.

10. Do a Web search on the phrase "dumbest moments in business" and get the most current version of this list. Choose three of the examples and describe what happened. What's your reaction to each example? How could the managers in each have made better decisions?

Go to p. 412
YOUR TURN TO BE A MANAGER for Chapter 4.

Endnotes

1. J. Dean, "Boldness of '81 Test Flight Unlikely to Be Repeated," *USA Today*, April 11, 2011, p. 7A; G. Griffin, "As Shuttle Retires, A Vote for Commercial Space Flight," *USA Today*, April 6, 2011, p. 9A; A. K. Donahue, "More to Learn from NASA About Learning, Unlearning, and Forgetting," *Journal of Public Administration Research* (April 2011), pp. 391–395; C. Chaplain, "Additional Cost Transparency and Design Criteria Needed for National Aeronautics and Space Administration (NASA) Projects," *GAO Reports*, March 3, 2011, pp. 1–11; A. Pasztor, "U.S. News: NASA Budget Plan Restricts Spending on Private Rockets," *Wall Street Journal*, February 14, 2011, p. A2; "NASA's Space-Shuttle Program Ends," *Fast Company*, February 2011, p. 22; H. Hickam, "How About a Moon Base?" *Wall Street Journal*, December 14, 2010, p. A19; J. Penn, "NASA's Plan Is Not Sustainable," *Aviation Week & Space Technology*, December 6, 2010, p. 74; P. M. Barrett, "Lost in Space," *Bloomberg BusinessWeek*, November 1–7, 2010, pp. 66–73; A. Pasztor, "NASA Chief Bolden Seeks 'Plan B' for the Space Agency," *Wall Street Journal*, March 4, 2010, p. A6; A. Pasztor, "NASA Gets Flak on New Course," *Wall Street Journal*, March 1, 2010, p. A6; B. Mintz Testa, "New Workforce Orbit-Relaunch at NASA," *Workforce Management Online*, February 16, 2010; L. B. Jabs, "Communicative Rules and Organizational Decision Making," *Journal of Business Communication* (July 2005), pp. 265–288; T. M. Garrett, "Whither *Challenger*, Wither *Columbia*: Management Decision Making and the Knowledge Analytic," *American Review of*

   Public Administration, December 2004, pp. 389–402; M. Maier "Teaching from Tragedy: An Interdisciplinary Module on the Space Shuttle *Challenger*," *THE Journal* (September 1993), pp. 91–94; and G. Moorhead, R. Ference, and C. P. Neck, "Group Decision Fiascoes Continue: Space Shuttle *Challenger* and a Revised Groupthink Framework," *Human Relations*, June 1991, pp. 539–550.

2. See, for example, A. Nagurney, J. Dong, and P. L. Mokhtarian, "Multicriteria Network Equilibrium Modeling with Variable Weights for Decision-Making in the Information Age with Applications to the Telecommuting and Teleshopping," *Journal of Economic Dynamics and Control* (August 2002), pp. 1629–1650.

3. J. Flinchbaugh, "Surfacing Problems Daily: Advice for Building a Problem-Solving Culture," *Industry Week*, April 2011, p. 12; "Business Analysis Training Helps Leaders Achieve an Enterprise-Wide Perspective," *Leader to Leader*, Fall 2010, pp. 63–65; D. Okes, "Common Problems with Basic Problem Solving," *Quality*, September 2010, pp. 36–40; J. Sawyer, "Problem-Solving Success Tips," *Business and Economic Review*, April–June 2002, pp. 23–24.

4. See J. Figueira and B. Ray, "Determining the Weights of Criteria in the Electre Type of Methods with a Revised Simons' Procedure," *European Journal of Operational Research*, June 1, 2002, pp. 317–326.

5. For instance, see M. Elliott, "Breakthrough Thinking," *IIE Solution*, October 2001, pp. 22–25; and B. Fazlollahi and

R. Vahidov, "A Method for Generation of Alternatives by Decision Support Systems," *Journal of Management Information Systems* (Fall 2001), pp. 229–250.

6. D. Miller, Q. Hope, R. Eisenstat, N. Foote, and J. Galbraith, "The Problem of Solutions: Balancing Clients and Capabilities," *Business Horizons,* March–April 2002, pp. 3–12.

7. E. Teach, "Avoiding Decision Traps," *CFO,* June 2004, pp. 97–99; and D. Kahneman and A. Tversky, "Judgment Under Uncertainty: Heuristics and Biases," *Science* 185 (1974), pp. 1124–1131.

8. Information for this section taken from S. P. Robbins, *Decide & Conquer* (Upper Saddle River, NJ: Financial Times/Prentice Hall, 2004).

9. T. A. Stewart, "Did You Ever Have to Make Up Your Mind?" *Harvard Business Review,* January 2006, p. 12; and E. Pooley, "Editor's Desk," *Fortune,* June 27, 2005, p. 16.

10. J. Pfeffer and R. I. Sutton, "Why Managing by Facts Works," *Strategy & Business,* Spring 2006, pp. 9–12.

11. See T. Shavit and A. M. Adam, "A Preliminary Exploration of the Effects of Rational Factors and Behavioral Biases on the Managerial Choice to Invest in Corporate Responsibility," *Managerial and Decision Economics,* April 2011, pp. 205–213; A. Langley, "In Search of Rationality: The Purposes Behind the Use of Formal Analysis in Organizations," *Administrative Science Quarterly*, December 1989, pp. 598–631; and H. A. Simon, "Rationality in Psychology and Economics," *Journal of Business* (October 1986), pp. 209–224.

12. Technology and the Manager's Job box based on M. Xu, V. Ong, Y. Duan, and B. Mathews, "Intelligent Agent Systems for Executive Information Scanning, Filtering, and Interpretation: Perceptions and Challenges," *Information Processing & Management,* March 2011, pp. 186–201; J. P. Kallunki, E. K. Laitinen, and H. Silvola, "Impact of Enterprise Resource Planning Systems on Management Control Systems and Firm Performance," *International Journal of Accounting Information Systems* (March 2011), pp. 20–39; H. W. K. Chia, C. L. Tan, and S. Y. Sung, "Enhancing Knowledge Discovery via Association-Based Evolution of Neural Logic Networks," *IEEE Transactions on Knowledge and Data Engineering* (July 2006), pp. 889–901; F. Harvey, "A Key Role in Detecting Fraud Patterns: Neural Networks," *Financial Times,* January 23, 2002, p. 3; D. Mitchell and R. Pavur, "Using Modular Neural Networks for Business Decisions," *Management Decision,* January–February 2002, pp. 58–64; B. L. Killingsworth, M. B. Hayden, and R. Schellenberger, "A Network Expert System Management System of Multiple Domains," *Journal of Information Science* (March–April 2001), p. 81; and S. Balakrishnan, N. Popplewell, and M. Thomlinson, "Intelligent Robotic Assembly," *Computers & Industrial Engineering,* December 2000, p. 467.

13. From the Past to the Present box based on M. Ibrahim, "Theory of Bounded Rationality," *Public Management,* June 2009, pp. 3–5; D. A. Wren, *The Evolution of Management Thought* Fourth Edition (New York: John Wiley & Sons, Inc., 1994), p. 291; and H. A. Simon, *Administrative Behavior* (New York: Macmillan Company, 1945).

14. J. G. March, "Decision-Making Perspective: Decisions in Organizations and Theories of Choice," in A. H. Van de Ven and W. F. Joyce (eds.), *Perspectives on Organization Design and Behavior* (New York: Wiley-Interscience, 1981), pp. 232–233.

15. See D. R. A. Skidd, "Revisiting Bounded Rationality," *Journal of Management Inquiry* (December 1992), pp. 343–347; B. E.

Kaufman, "A New Theory of Satisficing," *Journal of Behavioral Economics* (Spring 1990), pp. 35–51; and N. McK. Agnew and J. L. Brown, "Bounded Rationality: Fallible Decisions in Unbounded Decision Space," *Behavioral Science,* July 1986, pp. 148–161.

16. See, for example, G. McNamara, H. Moon, and P. Bromiley, "Banking on Commitment: Intended and Unintended Consequences of an Organization's Attempt to Attenuate Escalation of Commitment," *Academy of Management Journal* (April 2002), pp. 443–452; V. S. Rao and A. Monk, "The Effects of Individual Differences and Anonymity on Commitment to Decisions," *Journal of Social Psychology* (August 1999), pp. 496–515; C. F. Camerer and R. A. Weber, "The Econometrics and Behavioral Economics of Escalation of Commitment: A Re-examination of Staw's Theory," *Journal of Economic Behavior and Organization* (May 1999), pp. 59–82; D. R. Bobocel and J. P. Meyer, "Escalating Commitment to a Failing Course of Action: Separating the Roles of Choice and Justification," *Journal of Applied Psychology* (June 1994), pp. 360–363; and B. M. Staw, "The Escalation of Commitment to a Course of Action," *Academy of Management Review,* October 1981, pp. 577–587.

17. L. Alderman, "A Shoemaker That Walks but Never Runs," *New York Times Online,* October 8, 2010.

18. C. Flora, "When to Go with Your Gut," *Women's Health,* June 2009, pp. 68–70.

19. See J. Evans, "Intuition and Reasoning: A Dual-Process Perspective," *Psychological Inquiry,* October–December 2010, pp. 313–326; T. Betsch and A. Blockner, "Intuition in Judgment and Decision Making: Extensive Thinking Without Effort," *Psychological Inquiry,* October–December 2010, pp. 279–294; R. Lange and J. Houran, "A Transliminal View of Intuitions in the Workplace," *North American Journal of Psychology,* 12, no. 3 (2010), pp. 501–516; E. Dane and M. G. Pratt, "Exploring Intuition and Its Role in Managerial Decision Making," *Academy of Management Review,* January 2007, pp. 33–54; M. H. Bazerman and D. Chugh, "Decisions Without Blinders," *Harvard Business Review,* January 2006, pp. 88–97; C. C. Miller and R. D. Ireland, "Intuition in Strategic Decision Making: Friend or Foe in the Fast-Paced 21st Century," *Academy of Management Executive,* February 2005, pp. 19–30; E. Sadler-Smith and E. Shefy, "The Intuitive Executive: Understanding and Applying 'Gut Feel' in Decision-Making," *Academy of Management Executive,* November 2004, pp. 76–91; and L. A. Burke and M. K. Miller, "Taking the Mystery Out of Intuitive Decision Making," *Academy of Management Executive,* October 1999, pp. 91–99.

20. C. C. Miller and R. D. Ireland, "Intuition in Strategic Decision Making: Friend or Foe," p. 20.

21. E. Sadler-Smith and E. Shefy, "Developing Intuitive Awareness in Management Education," *Academy of Management Learning & Education,* June 2007, pp. 186–205.

22. M. G. Seo and L. Feldman Barrett, "Being Emotional During Decision Making—Good or Bad? An Empirical Investigation," *Academy of Management Journal* (August 2007), pp. 923–940.

23. "Next: Big Idea," *Fast Company,* December 2010–January 2011, pp. 39–40.

24. B. Stone and D. Macmillan, "Groupon's $6 Billion Snub," *Bloomberg BusinessWeek,* December 13–19, 2010, pp. 6–7; E. M. Rusli and J. Wortham, "Google Gambit for Groupon Raises Concerns," *New York Times Online,* November 30, 2010;

D. Lyons, "Click and Save," *Newsweek,* November 29, 2010, p. 25; and J. Goltz, "Doing the Math on a Groupon Deal," *New York Times Online,* November 23, 2010.

25. R. D. Hof and H. Green, "How Amazon Cleared That Hurdle," *BusinessWeek*, February 4, 2002, p. 59.

26. And the Survey Says box based on P. Wang, "To Make Better Choices, Choose Less," *Money,* June 2010, pp. 111–114; B. Dumaine, "The Trouble with Teams," *Fortune,* September 5, 1994, pp. 86–92; A. S. Wellner, "A Perfect Brainstorm," *Inc.,* October 2003, pp. 31–35; "The Poll," *BusinessWeek,* August 21–28, 2006, p. 44; "Hurry Up and Decide," *BusinessWeek,* May 14, 2001, p. 16; J. MacIntyre, "Bosses and Bureaucracy," *Springfield, Missouri Business Journal,* August 1–7, 2005, p. 29; J. Crick, "Hand Jive," *Fortune,* June 13, 2005, pp. 40–41; and "On the Road to Invention," *Fast Company,* February 2005, p. 16.

27. See, for instance, S. Schulz-Hardt, A. Mojzisch, F. C. Brodbeck, R. Kerschreiter, and D. Frey, "Group Decision Making in Hidden Profile Situations: Dissent as a Facilitator for Decision Quality," *Journal of Personality and Social Psychology,* (December 2006), pp. 1080–1083; and C. K. W. DeDreu and M. A. West, "Minority Dissent and Team Innovation: The Importance of Participation in Decision Making." *Journal of Applied Psychology* (December 2001), pp. 1191–1201.

28. S. Mohammed, "Toward an Understanding of Cognitive Consensus in a Group Decision-Making Context," *Journal of Applied Behavioral Science* (December 2001), p. 408.

29. M. J. Fambrough and S. A. Comerford, "The Changing Epistemological Assumptions of Group Theory," *Journal of Applied Behavioral Science* (September 2006), pp. 330–349.

30. R. A. Meyers, D. E. Brashers, and J. Hanner, "Majority-Minority Influence: Identifying Argumentative Patterns and Predicting Argument-Outcome Links," *Journal of Communication* (Autumn 2000), pp. 3–30.

31. I. L. Janis, *Groupthink* (Boston: Houghton Mifflin, 1982). See also J. Chapman, "Anxiety and Defective Decision Making: An Elaboration of the Groupthink Mode," *Management Decision,* October 2006, pp. 1391–1404.

32. See, for instance, T. Horton, "Groupthink in the Boardroom," *Directors and Boards,* Winter 2002, p. 9.

33. See, for example, T. W. Costello and S. S. Zalkind, eds., *Psychology in Administration: A Research Orientation* (Upper Saddle River, NJ: Prentice Hall, 1963), pp. 429–430; R. A. Cooke and J. A. Kernaghan, "Estimating the Difference Between Group versus Individual Performance on Problem Solving Tasks," *Group and Organization Studies,* September 1987, pp. 319–342; and L. K. Michaelsen, W. E. Watson, and R. H. Black, "A Realistic Test of Individual Versus Group Consensus Decision Making," *Journal of Applied Psychology* (October 1989), pp. 834–839. See also J. Hollenbeck, D. R. Ilgen, J. A. Colquitt, and A. Ellis, "Gender Composition, Situational Strength, and Team Decision-Making Accuracy: A Criterion Decomposition Approach," *Organizational Behavior and Human Decision Processes,* May 2002, pp. 445–475.

34. See, for example, L. K. Michaelsen, W. E. Watson, and R. H. Black, "A Realistic Test of Individual versus Group Consensus Decision Making," *Journal of Applied Psychology* (October 1989), pp. 834–839; and P. W. Pease, M. Beiser, and M. E. Tubbs, "Framing Effects and Choice Shifts in Group Decision Making," *Organizational Behavior and Human Decision Processes,* October 1993, pp. 149–165.

35. Right or Wrong box based on C. A. MacKenzie, "MTV Cancels 'Skins'; Season 2 Not Happening," *From Inside the Box Blog* [http://blog.zap2it.com/frominsidethebox/2011/06/mtv-cancels-skins-season-2-not-happening.html (June 9, 2011); J. Hibbard, "MTV's *Skins* Rises for Finale, but Will TV's Most Controversial Drama Return?" www.insidetv.ew.com (March 22, 2011); J. Alston, "Why *The Real World* Still Matters," *The Daily Beast Blog,* March 9, 2011; D. Groner, "As MTV Premiers Its 25th Season, Critics Ask If *The Real World* Is Still Relevant?" www.mediaite.com/tv (March 9, 2011); D. Holloway, "Barely Legal," *Back Stage,* February 17, 2011, pp. 2–3; B. Grossman, "On Corporate Responsibility," *Broadcasting & Cable,* February 7, 2011, p. 26; A. Silver, "Brief History: Sex on TV," *Time,* February 7, 2011, p. 19; L. A. E. Schuker, "Skins Audience Flattens Out," *Wall Street Journal Online,* February 2, 2011; J. Lafayette, "MTV Upfront: More Than *Skins* Deep," *Broadcasting & Cable,* January 31, 2011, p. 16; L. A. E. Schuker, "Skins Audience Sinks 51%," *Wall Street Journal,* January 26, 2011, p. B8; S. Roberts, "Skins Is Not Being Canceled by MTV, Despite Ratings Drop from 3.3 to 1.6 Million: Network Rep," *New York Daily News Online,* January 26, 2011; C. Hausman, "Teen Drama Pushes Envelope on Depictions of Sex, Drug Use," *Ethics Newsline Online,* January 24, 2011; and D. Carr, "MTV's Naked Calculation Gone Bad," *New York Times Online,* January 23, 2011.

36. J. Wagstaff, "Brainstorming Requires Drinks," *Far Eastern Economic Review,* May 2, 2002, p. 34.

37. T. Kelley, "Six Ways to Kill a Brainstormer," *Across the Board,* March–April 2002, p. 12.

38. K. L. Dowling and R. D. St. Louis, "Asynchronous Implementation of the Nominal Group Technique: Is It Effective," *Decision Support Systems,* October 2000, pp. 229–248.

39. See also B. Andersen and T. Fagerhaug, "The Nominal Group Technique," *Quality Progress,* February 2000, p. 144.

40. J. Burdett, "Changing Channels: Using the Electronic Meeting System to Increase Equity in Decision Making," *Information Technology, Learning, and Performance Journal* (Fall 2000), pp. 3–12.

41. "Fear of Flying," *Business Europe,* October 3, 2001, p. 2.

42. "VC at Nestlé," *Business Europe,* October 3, 2001, p. 3.

43. M. Roberti, "Meet Me on the Web," *Fortune: Tech Supplement,* Winter 2002, p. 10.

44. See also, J. A. Hoxmeier and K. A. Kozar, "Electronic Meetings and Subsequent Meeting Behavior: Systems as Agents of Change," *Journal of Applied Management Studies* (December 2000), pp. 177–195.

45. See, for instance, P. Berthon, L. F. Pitt, and M. T. Ewing, "Corollaries of the Collective: The Influence of Organizational Culture and Memory Development on Perceived Decision-Making Context," *Academy of Marketing Science Journal* (Spring 2001), pp. 135–150.

46. J. de Haan, M. Yamamoto, and G. Lovink, "Production Planning in Japan: Rediscovering Lost Experiences or New Insights," *International Journal of Production Economics* (May 6, 2001), pp. 101–109.

47. T. M. Amabile, "Motivating Creativity in Organizations," *California Management Review* (Fall 1997), pp. 39–58.

Quantitative Module

QUANTITATIVE DECISION-MAKING AIDS

In this module we'll look at several decision-making aids and techniques, as well as some popular tools for managing projects.[1] Specifically, we'll introduce you to payoff matrices, decision trees, break-even analysis, ratio analysis, linear programming, queuing theory, and economic order quantity. The purpose of each method is to provide managers with a tool to assist in the decision-making process and to provide more complete information to make better-informed decisions.

Payoff Matrices

In Chapter 4 we introduced you to the topic of uncertainty and how it can affect decision making. Although uncertainty plays a critical role by limiting the amount of information available to managers, another factor is their psychological orientation. For instance, the optimistic manager will typically follow a *maximax* choice (maximizing the maximum possible payoff); the pessimist will often pursue a *maximin* choice (maximizing the minimum possible payoff); and the manager who desires to minimize his "regret" will opt for a *minimax* choice. Let's briefly look at these different approaches using an example.

Consider the case of a marketing manager at Visa International in New York. He has determined four possible strategies (we'll label these S1, S2, S3, and S4) for promoting the Visa card throughout the northeastern United States. However, he is also aware that one of his major competitors, American Express, has three competitive strategies (CA1, CA2, and CA3) for promoting its own card in the same region. In this case, we'll assume that the Visa executive has no previous knowledge that would allow him to place probabilities on the success of any of his four strategies. With these facts, the Visa card manager formulates the matrix in Exhibit QM–1 to show the various Visa strategies and the resulting profit to Visa, depending on the competitive action chosen by American Express.

In this example, if our Visa manager is an optimist, he'll choose S4 because that could produce the largest possible gain ($28 million). Note that this choice maximizes the maximum possible gain (maximax choice). If our manager is a pessimist, he'll assume only the worst can occur. The worst outcome for each strategy is as follows: S1 = $11 million; S2 = $9 million; S3 = $15 million; and S4 = $14 million. Following the maximin choice, the pessimistic manager would maximize the minimum payoff—in other words, he'd select S3.

In the third approach, managers recognize that once a decision is made it will not necessarily result in the most profitable payoff. What could occur is a "regret" of profits forgone (given up)—regret referring to the amount of money that could have been made had a different strategy been used. Managers calculate regret by subtracting all possible payoffs in each category from the maximum possible payoff for each given—in this case, for each

EXHIBIT QM–1 Payoff Matrix for Visa			
VISA MARKETING STRATEGY	AMERICAN EXPRESS'S RESPONSE (in $millions)		
	CA1	CA2	CA3
S1	13	14	11
S2	9	15	18
S3	24	21	15
S4	18	14	28

EXHIBIT QM–2 Regret Matrix for Visa

VISA MARKETING STRATEGY	AMERICAN EXPRESS'S RESPONSE (in $millions)		
	CA1	CA2	CA3
S1	11	7	17
S2	15	6	10
S3	0	0	13
S4	6	7	0

competitive action. For our Visa manager, the highest payoff, given that American Express engages in CA1, CA2, or CA3, is $24 million, $21 million, or $28 million, respectively (the highest number in each column). Subtracting the payoffs in Exhibit QM–1 from these figures produces the results in Exhibit QM–2.

The maximum regrets are S1 = $17 million; S2 = $15 million; S3 = $13 million; and S4 = $7 million. The minimax choice minimizes the maximum regret, so our Visa manager would choose S4. By making this choice, he'll never have a regret of profits forgone of more than $7 million. This result contrasts, for example, with a regret of $15 million had he chosen S2 and American Express had taken CA1.

Decision Trees

Decision trees are a useful way to analyze hiring, marketing, investment, equipment purchases, pricing, and similar decisions that involve a progression of decisions. They're called decision trees because, when diagrammed, they look a lot like a tree with branches. Typical decision trees encompass expected value analysis by assigning probabilities to each possible outcome and calculating payoffs for each decision path.

Exhibit QM–3 illustrates a decision facing Harrington, the midwestern region site selection supervisor for Walden bookstores. Becky supervises a small group of specialists

EXHIBIT QM–3

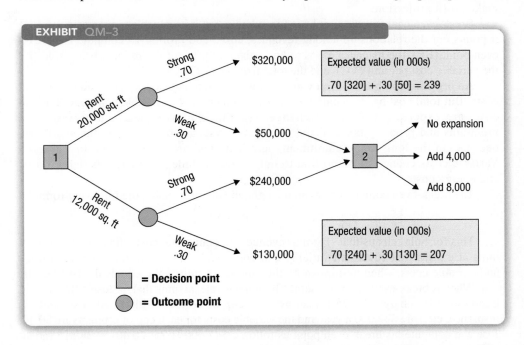

decision trees
A diagram used to analyze a progression of decisions. When diagrammed, a decision tree looks like a tree with branches.

who analyze potential locations and make store site recommendations to the midwestern region's director. The lease on the company's store in Winter Park, Florida, is expiring, and the property owner has decided not to renew it. Becky and her group have to make a relocation recommendation to the regional director. Becky's group has identified an excellent site in a nearby shopping mall in Orlando. The mall owner has offered her two comparable locations: one with 12,000 square feet (the same as she has now) and the other a larger, 20,000-square-foot space. Becky's initial decision concerns whether to recommend renting the larger or smaller location. If she chooses the larger space and the economy is strong, she estimates the store will make a $320,000 profit. However, if the economy is poor, the high operating costs of the larger store will mean that the profit will be only $50,000. With the smaller store, she estimates the profit at $240,000 with a good economy and $130,000 with a poor one.

As you can see from Exhibit QM–3, the expected value for the larger store is $239,000 [(.70 × 320) + (.30 × 50)]. The expected value for the smaller store is $207,000 [(.70 × 240) + (.30 × 130)]. Given these projections, Becky is planning to recommend the rental of the larger store space. What if Becky wants to consider the implications of initially renting the smaller space and then expanding if the economy picks up? She can extend the decision tree to include this second decision point. She has calculated three options: no expansion, adding 4,000 square feet, and adding 8,000 square feet. Following the approach used for Decision Point 1, she could calculate the profit potential by extending the branches on the tree and calculating expected values for the various options.

Break-Even Analysis

How many units of a product must an organization sell in order to break even—that is, to have neither profit nor loss? A manager might want to know the minimum number of units that must be sold to achieve his or her profit objective or whether a current product should continue to be sold or should be dropped from the organization's product line. **Break-even analysis** is a widely used technique for helping managers make profit projections.[2]

Break-even analysis is a simplistic formulation, yet it is valuable to managers because it points out the relationship among revenues, costs, and profits. To compute the break-even point (BE), the manager needs to know the unit price of the product being sold (P), the variable cost per unit (VC), and the total fixed costs (TFC).

An organization breaks even when its total revenue is just enough to equal its total costs. But total cost has two parts: a fixed component and a variable component. Fixed costs are expenses that do not change, regardless of volume, such as insurance premiums and property taxes. Fixed costs, of course, are fixed only in the short term because, in the long run, commitments terminate and are, thus, subject to variation. Variable costs change in proportion to output and include raw materials, labor costs, and energy costs.

The break-even point can be computed graphically or by using the following formula:

$$BE = [TFC/(P - VC)]$$

This formula tells us that (1) total revenue will equal total cost when we sell enough units at a price that covers all variable unit costs, and (2) the difference between price and variable costs, when multiplied by the number of units sold, equals the fixed costs.

When is break-even analysis useful? To demonstrate, assume that, at Jose's Bakersfield Espresso, Jose charges $1.75 for an average cup of coffee. If his fixed costs (salary, insurance, etc.) are $47,000 a year and the variable costs for each cup of espresso are $0.40, Jose can compute his break-even point as follows: $47,000/(1.75 – 0.40) = 34,815 (about 670 cups of espresso sold each week), or when annual revenues are approximately $60,926. This same relationship is shown graphically in Exhibit QM–4.

How can break-even analysis serve as a planning and decision-making tool? As a planning tool, break-even analysis could help Jose set his sales objective. For example, he could establish the profit he wants and then work backward to determine what sales level is needed

EXHIBIT QM-4

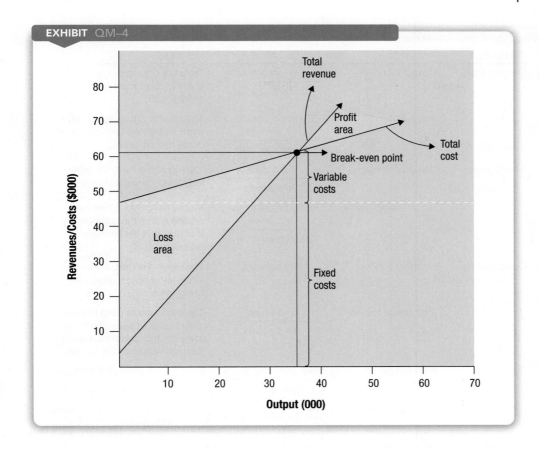

to reach that profit. As a decision-making tool, break-even analysis could also tell Jose how much volume has to increase in order to break even if he is currently operating at a loss, or how much volume he can afford to lose and still break even if he is currently operating profitably. In some cases, such as the management of professional sports franchises, break-even analysis has shown the projected volume of ticket sales required to cover all costs to be so unrealistically high that management's best choice is to sell or close the business.

Ratio Analysis

We know that investors and stock analysts make regular use of an organization's financial documents to assess its worth. These documents can be analyzed by managers as planning and decision-making aids.

Managers often want to examine their organization's balance sheet and income statements to analyze key ratios, that is, to compare two significant figures from the financial statements and express them as a percentage or ratio. This practice allows managers to compare current financial performance with that of previous periods and other organizations in the same industry. Some of the more useful ratios evaluate liquidity, leverage, operations, and profitability. These ratios are summarized in Exhibit QM–5.

What are liquidity ratios? *Liquidity* is a measure of the organization's ability to convert assets into cash in order to meet its debt obligations. The most popular liquidity ratios are the current ratio and the acid test ratio.

The *current ratio* is defined as the organization's current assets divided by its current liabilities. Although there is no magic number that is considered safe, the accountant's rule

break-even analysis
A technique foridentifying the point at which total revenue is just sufficient to cover total costs.

EXHIBIT QM–5 **Popular Financial Controls**

OBJECTIVE	RATIO	CALCULATION	MEANING
Liquidity test	Current ratio	$\dfrac{\text{Current assets}}{\text{Current liabilities}}$	Tests the organization's ability to meet short-term obligations
	Acid test	$\dfrac{\text{Current assets less inventories}}{\text{Current liabilities}}$	Tests liquidity more accurately when inventories turn over slowly or are difficult to sell
Leverage test	Debt to assets	$\dfrac{\text{Total debt}}{\text{Total assets}}$	The higher the ratio, the more leveraged the organization
	Times interest earned	$\dfrac{\text{Profits before interest and taxes}}{\text{Total interest charges}}$	Measures how far profits can decline before the organization is unable to meet its interest expenses
Operations test	Inventory turnover	$\dfrac{\text{Cost of sales}}{\text{Inventory}}$	The higher the ratio, the more efficiently inventory assets are being used
	Total assets turnover	$\dfrac{\text{Revenues}}{\text{Total assets}}$	The fewer assets used to achieve a given level of sales, the more efficiently management is using the organization's total assets
Profitability	Profit margin on revenues	$\dfrac{\text{Net profit after taxes}}{\text{Total revenues}}$	Identifies the profits that various products are generating
	Return on investment	$\dfrac{\text{Net profit after taxes}}{\text{Total assets}}$	Measures the efficiency of assets to generate profits

of thumb for the current ratio is 2:1. A significantly higher ratio usually suggests that management is not getting the best return on its assets. A ratio at or below 1:1 indicates potential difficulty in meeting short-term obligations (accounts payable, interest payments, salaries, taxes, etc.).

The *acid test ratio* is the same as the current ratio except that current assets are reduced by the dollar value of inventory held. When inventories turn slowly or are difficult to sell, the acid test ratio may more accurately represent the organization's true liquidity. That is, a high current ratio heavily based on an inventory that is difficult to sell overstates the organization's true liquidity. Accordingly, accountants typically consider an acid test ratio of 1:1 to be reasonable.

Leverage ratios refer to the use of borrowed funds to operate and expand an organization. The advantage of leverage occurs when funds can be used to earn a rate of return well above the cost of those funds. For instance, if management can borrow money at 8 percent and can earn 12 percent on it internally, it makes good sense to borrow, but there are risks to overleveraging. The interest on the debt can be a drain on the organization's cash resources and can, in extreme cases, drive an organization into bankruptcy. The objective, therefore, is to use debt wisely. Leverage ratios such as *debt to assets ratio* (computed by dividing total debt by total assets) or the *times interest earned ratio* (computed as profits before interest and taxes divided by total interest charges) can help managers control debt levels.

Operating ratios describe how efficiently management is using the organization's resources. The most popular operating ratios are inventory turnover and total assets turnover. The *inventory turnover ratio* is defined as revenue divided by inventory. The higher the ratio, the more efficiently inventory assets are being used. Revenue divided by total assets represents an organization's *total assets turnover ratio*. It measures the level of assets needed to generate the organization's revenue. The fewer the assets used to achieve a given level of revenue, the more efficiently management is using the organization's total assets.

Profit-making organizations want to measure their effectiveness and efficiency. Profitability ratios serve such a purpose. The better known of these ratios are profit margin on revenues and return on investment.

Managers of organizations that have a variety of products want to put their efforts into those products that are most profitable. The *profit margin on revenues ratio*, computed as net profit after taxes divided by total revenues, is a measure of profits per dollar revenues.

One of the most widely used measures of a business firm's profitability is the *return on investment ratio*. It's calculated by dividing net profits by total assets. This percentage recognizes that absolute profits must be placed in the context of assets required to generate those profits.

Linear Programming

Matt Free owns a software development company. One product line involves designing and producing software that detects and removes viruses. The software comes in two formats: Windows and Mac versions. He can sell all of these products that he can produce, which is his dilemma. The two formats go through the same production departments. How many of each type should he make to maximize his profits?

A close look at Free's operation tells us he can use a mathematical technique called **linear programming** to solve his resource allocation dilemma. As we will show, linear programming is applicable to his problem, but it cannot be applied to all resource allocation situations. Besides requiring limited resources and the objective of optimization, it requires that there be alternative ways of combining resources to produce a number of output mixes. A linear relationship between variables is also necessary, which means that a change in one variable will be accompanied by an exactly proportional change in the other. For Free's business, this condition would be met if it took exactly twice the time to produce two diskettes—irrespective of format—as it took to produce one.

Many different types of problems can be solved with linear programming. Selecting transportation routes that minimize shipping costs, allocating a limited advertising budget among various product brands, making the optimum assignment of personnel among projects, and determining how much of each product to make with a limited number of resources are just a few. To give you some idea of how linear programming is useful, let's return to Free's situation. Fortunately, his problem is relatively simple, so we can solve it rather quickly. For complex linear programming problems, computer software has been designed specifically to help develop solutions.

First, we need to establish some facts about the business. He has computed the profit margins to be $18 for the Windows format and $24 for the Mac. He can, therefore, express his objective function as maximum profit = $18R + $24S, where R is the number of Windows-based CDs produced and S is the number of Mac CDs. In addition, he knows how long it takes to produce each format and the monthly production capacity for virus software: 2,400 hours in design and 900 hours in production (see Exhibit QM–6). The

EXHIBIT QM–6 **Production Data for Virus Software**

	NUMBER OF HOURS REQUIRED PER UNIT		
DEPARTMENT	WINDOWS VERSION	MAC VERSION	MONTHLY PRODUCT CAPACITY (HOURS)
Design	4	6	2,400
Manufacture	2.0	2.0	900
Profit per unit	$18	$24	

linear programming
A mathematical technique that solves resource allocation problems.

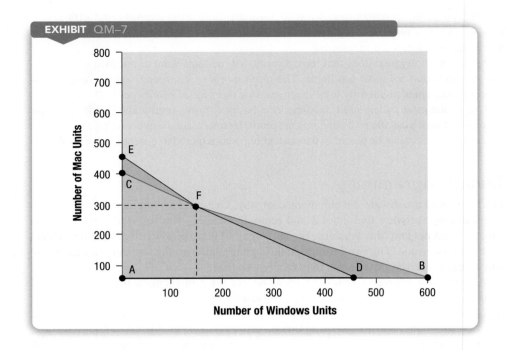

EXHIBIT QM–7

production capacity numbers act as constraints on his overall capacity. Now Free can establish his constraint equations:

$$4R + 6S < 2,400$$
$$2R + 2S < 900$$

Of course, because a software format cannot be produced in a volume less than zero, Matt can also state that $R > 0$ and $S > 0$. He has graphed his solution as shown in Exhibit QM–7. The beige shaded area represents the options that do not exceed the capacity of either department. What does the graph mean? We know that total design capacity is 2,400 hours. So if Matt decides to design only the Windows format, the maximum number he can produce is 600 (2,400 hours ÷ 4 hours of design for each Windows version). If he decides to produce all Mac versions, the maximum he can produce is 400 (2,400 hours ÷ 6 hours of design for Mac). This design constraint is shown in Exhibit QM–7 as line BC. The other constraint Matt faces is that of production. The maximum of either format he can produce is 450, because each takes two hours to copy, verify, and package. This production constraint is shown in the exhibit as line DE.

Free's optimal resource allocation will be defined at one of the corners of this feasibility region (area ACFD). Point F provides the maximum profits within the constraints stated. At point A, profits would be zero because neither virus software version is being produced. At points C and D, profits would be $9,600 (400 units @ $24) and $8,100 (450 units @ $18), respectively. At point F profits would be $9,900 (150 Windows units @ $18 + 300 Mac units @ $24).[3]

Queuing Theory

You are a supervisor for a branch of Bank of America outside of Cleveland, Ohio. One of the decisions you have to make is how many of the six teller stations to keep open at any given time. Queuing theory, or what is frequently referred to as waiting line theory, could help you decide.

A decision that involves balancing the cost of having a waiting line against the cost of service to maintain that line can be made more easily with queuing theory. These types of common situations include determining how many gas pumps are needed at gas stations, tellers at bank windows, toll takers at toll booths, or check-in lines at airline ticket counters. In each situation, management wants to minimize cost by having as few stations open as possible yet not so few as to test the patience of customers. In our teller example, on certain days (such as the first of every month and Fridays) you could open all six windows and keep waiting time to a minimum, or you could open only one, minimize staffing costs, and risk a riot.

The mathematics underlying queuing theory is beyond the scope of this book, but you can see how the theory works in our simple example. You have six tellers working for you, but you want to know whether you can get by with only one window open during an average morning. You consider 12 minutes to be the longest you would expect any customer to wait patiently in line. If it takes 4 minutes, on average, to serve each customer, the line should not be permitted to get longer than three deep (12 minutes ÷ 4 minutes per customer = 3 customers). If you know from past experience that, during the morning, people arrive at the average rate of two per minute, you can calculate the probability (P) of customers waiting in line as follows:

$$P_n = \left[1 - \left(\frac{\text{Arrival rate}}{\text{Service rate}} \right) \right] \times \left[\frac{\text{Arrival rate}}{\text{Service rate}} \right]^n$$

where n = 3 customers, arrival rate = 2 per minute, and service rate = 4 minutes per customer.

Putting these numbers into the foregoing formula generates the following:

$$P_n = [1 - 2/4] \times [2/4]^3 = (1/2) \times (8/64) = (8/128) = 0.0625$$

What does a P of 0.0625 mean? It tells you that the likelihood of having more than three customers in line during the average morning is 1 chance in 16. Are you willing to live with four or more customers in line 6 percent of the time? If so, keeping one teller window open will be enough. If not, you will have to assign more tellers to staff more windows.

Economic Order Quantity Model

When you order checks from a bank, have you noticed that the reorder form is placed about two-thirds of the way through your supply of checks? This practice is a simple example of a **fixed-point reordering system**. At some preestablished point in the process, the system is designed to "flag" the fact that the inventory needs to be replenished. The objective is to minimize inventory carrying costs while at the same time limiting the probability of *stocking out* of the inventory item. In recent years, retail stores have increasingly been using their computers to perform this reordering activity. Their cash registers are connected to their computers, and each sale automatically adjusts the store's inventory record. When the inventory of an item hits the critical point, the computer tells management to reorder.

One of the best-known techniques for mathematically deriving the optimum quantity for a purchase order is the **economic order quantity (EOQ)** model (see Exhibit QM–8). The EOQ model seeks to balance four costs involved in ordering and carrying inventory: the purchase costs (purchase price plus delivery charges less discounts); the ordering costs (paperwork, follow-up, inspection when the item arrives, and other processing costs); carrying costs (money tied up in inventory, storage, insurance, taxes, etc.); and stock-out costs (profits forgone from orders lost, the cost of reestablishing goodwill, and additional

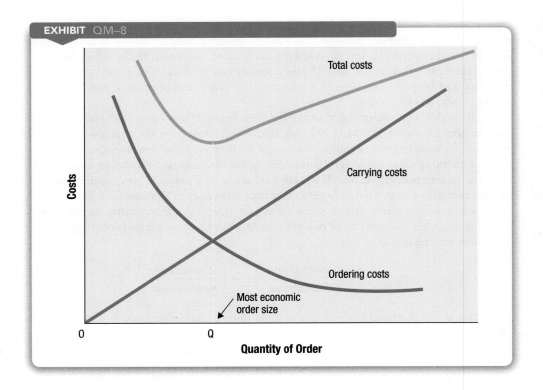

EXHIBIT QM–8

expenses incurred to expedite late shipments). When these four costs are known, the model identifies the optimal order size for each purchase.

The objective of the economic order quantity (EOQ) model is to minimize the total costs associated with the carrying and ordering costs. As the amount ordered gets larger, average inventory increases and so do carrying costs. For example, if annual demand for an inventory item is 26,000 units, and a firm orders 500 each time, the firm will place 52 [26,000/500] orders per year. This order frequency gives the organization an average inventory of 250 [500/2] units. If the order quantity is increased to 2,000 units, fewer orders (13) [26,000/2,000] will be placed. However, average inventory on hand will increase to 1,000 [2,000/2] units. Thus, as holding costs go up, ordering costs go down, and vice versa. The optimum economic order quantity is reached at the lowest point on the total cost curve. That's the point at which ordering costs equal carrying costs—or the economic order quantity (see point Q in Exhibit QM–8).

To compute this optimal order quantity, you need the following data: forecasted demand for the item during the period (D); the cost of placing each order (OC); the value or purchase price of the item (V); and the carrying cost (expressed as a percentage) of maintaining the total inventory (CC). Given these data, the formula for EOQ is as follows:

$$EOQ = \sqrt{\frac{2 \times D \times OC}{V \times CC}}$$

Let's work an example of determining the EOQ. Take, for example, Barnes Electronics, a retailer of high-quality sound and video equipment. The owner, Sam Barnes, wishes to determine the company's economic order quantities of high-quality sound and video equipment. The item in question is a Sony compact voice recorder. Barnes forecasts sales of 4,000 units a year. He believes that the cost for the sound system should be $50. Estimated costs of placing an order for these systems are $35 per order and annual insurance, taxes, and other carrying costs at 20 percent of the recorder's value. Using the EOQ formula, and the preceding information, he can calculate the EOQ as follows:

$$EOQ = \sqrt{\frac{2 \times 4{,}000 \times 35}{50 \times .20}}$$

$$EOQ = \sqrt{28{,}000}$$

$$EOQ = 167.33 \text{ or } 168 \text{ units}$$

The inventory model suggests that it's most economical to order in quantities or lots of approximately 168 recorders. Stated differently, Barnes should order about 24 [4,000/168] times a year. However, what would happen if the supplier offers Barnes a 5 percent discount on purchases if he buys in minimum quantities of 250 units? Should he now purchase in quantities of 168 or 250? Without the discount, and ordering 168 each time, the annual costs for these recorders would be as follows:

With the 5 percent discount for ordering 250 units, the item cost [$50 × ($50 × 0.05)]

Purchase cost:	$50 × $4,000	=	$200,000
Carrying cost (average number of inventory units times value of item times percentage):	168/2 × $50 × 0.2	=	840
Ordering costs (number of orders times cost to place order):	24 × $35	=	840
Total cost:		=	$201,680

would be $47.5. The annual inventory costs would be as follows:

Purchase cost:	$47.50 × $4,000	=	$190,000.00
Carrying cost:	250/2 × $47.50 × 0.2	=	1,187.50
Ordering cost:	16 × $35	=	560.00
Total cost:		=	$191,747.50

These calculations suggest to Barnes that he should take advantage of the 5 percent discount. Even though he now has to stock larger quantities, the annual savings amounts to nearly $10,000. A word of caution, however, needs to be added. The EOQ model assumes that demand and lead times are known and constant. If these conditions can't be met, the model shouldn't be used. For example, it generally shouldn't be used for manufactured component inventory because the components are taken out of stock all at once, in lumps, or odd lots, rather than at a constant rate. Does this caveat mean that the EOQ model is useless when demand is variable? No. The model can still be of some use in demonstrating trade-offs in costs and the need to control lot sizes. However, more sophisticated lot sizing models are available for handling demand and special situations. The mathematics for EOQ, like the mathematics for queuing theory, go far beyond the scope of this text.

Endnotes

1. Readers are encouraged to see B. Render, R. M. Stair, and M. E. Hanna, *Quantitative Analysis for Management*, 9th ed. (Upper Saddle River, NJ: Prentice Hall, 2005).
2. J. Schmid, "Getting to Breakeven," *Catalog Age*, November 2001, pp. 89–90.
3. We want to acknowledge and thank Professor Jeff Storm of Virginia Western Community College for his assistance in this example.

CHAPTER
5

Foundations
of **Planning**

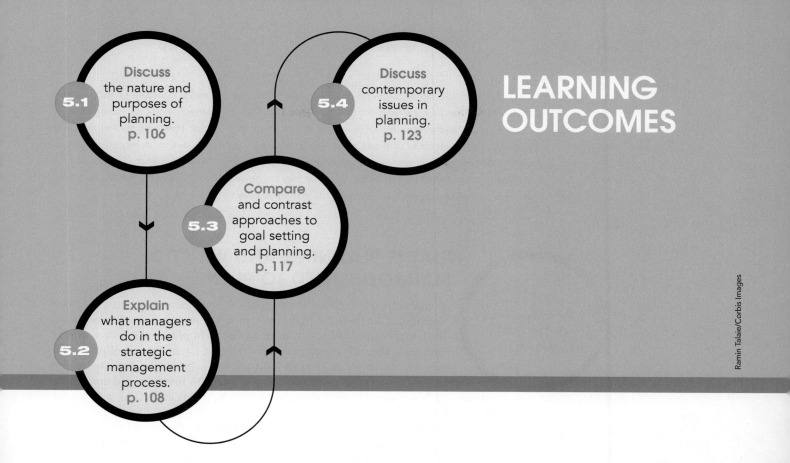

Ramin Talaie/Corbis Images

Flip Flop

You've probably seen them at weddings or graduations, and maybe even at parties. No, they're not "crashers," they're the handheld Flip video camcorder. Flip was the brainchild of some San Francisco entrepreneurs whose idea was to create a pocket-size, inexpensive, and easy-to-use video camera. Considering that most video cameras were big, bulky, complicated, and expensive, that idea seemed right on target. And it was! When Flip went on sale in 2007, it quickly dominated the camcorder market as some 2 million were sold in the first two years. "Then, in 2009, the founders cashed out and sold to Cisco Systems, the computer networking giant, for $590 million." Not a bad payday, huh! For Cisco, the acquisition was a key to its strategy of expanding in the consumer market, especially as homes became more media-enabled. However, two years later, in April 2011, Cisco announced it was "killing" Flip and laying off 550 employees. Even in the frenetic, chaotic tech world, that was a fast flip flop. As one analyst said, "It's a testament to the pace of innovation in consumer electronics and smartphone technology. More and more functionality is being integrated into smartphones."[1]

Cisco Systems, like other organizations, has a purpose, people, and a structure to support and enable those people in carrying out that purpose. Also, like other organizations, its managers must develop plans and strategies for how best to achieve that purpose. However, sometimes after evaluating the outcomes of those plans and strategies, managers have to change direction as conditions change. This chapter presents the basics of planning. You'll learn what planning is, how managers use strategic management, and how they set goals and establish plans. Finally, we'll look at some of the contemporary planning issues managers have to deal with.

WHAT IS PLANNING AND WHY DO MANAGERS NEED TO PLAN?

5.1 Discuss the nature and purposes of planning.

Planning is often called the primary management function because it establishes the basis for all the other things managers do as they organize, lead, and control. What is meant by the term *planning?* As we said in Chapter 1, planning encompasses defining the organization's objectives or goals, establishing an overall strategy for achieving those goals, and developing a comprehensive hierarchy of plans to integrate and coordinate activities. It's concerned with ends (*what* is to be done) as well as with means (*how* it's to be done).

Planning can be further defined in terms of whether it's *formal* or *informal*. All5managers plan, even if it's only informally. In informal planning, very little, if anything, is written down. What is to be accomplished is in the heads of one or a few people. Furthermore, the organization's goals are rarely verbalized. Informal planning generally describes the planning that takes place in many smaller businesses. The owner-manager has an idea of where he or she wants to go and how he or she expects to get there. The planning is general and lacks continuity. Of course, you'll see informal planning in some large organizations, while some small businesses will have sophisticated formal plans.

When we use the term *planning* in this book, we're referring to formal planning. In formal planning, specific goals covering a specific time period are defined. These goals are written down and made available to organization members. Using these goals, managers develop specific plans that clearly define the path the organization will take to get from where it is to where it wants to be.

Why Should Managers Formally Plan?

Managers should plan for at least four reasons. (See Exhibit 5–1.) First, planning establishes coordinated effort. It gives direction to managers and nonmanagerial employees. When all organizational members understand where the organization is going and what they must contribute to reach the goals, they can begin to coordinate their activities, thus fostering teamwork and cooperation. On the other hand, a lack of planning can cause organizational members or work units to work against one another and keep the organization from moving efficiently toward its goals.

Second, by forcing managers to look ahead, anticipate change, consider the impact of change, and develop appropriate responses, planning reduces uncertainty. It also clarifies the consequences of the actions managers might take in response to change. Planning, then, is precisely what managers need in a changing environment.

Third, planning reduces overlapping and wasteful activities. Coordination before the fact is likely to uncover waste and redundancy. Furthermore, when means and ends are clear, inefficiencies become obvious.

Finally, planning establishes the goals or standards that facilitate control. If organizational members are unsure of what they are attempting to achieve, how can they assess whether they've achieved it? When managers plan, they develop goals and plans. When they

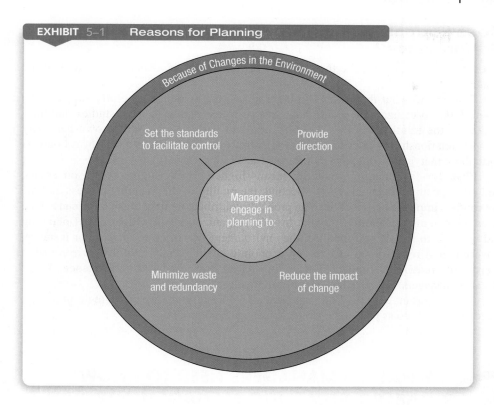

EXHIBIT 5-1   Reasons for Planning

Because of Changes in the Environment

Managers engage in planning to:

Set the standards to facilitate control

Provide direction

Minimize waste and redundancy

Reduce the impact of change

control, they see whether the plans have been carried out and the goals met. If significant deviations are identified, corrective action can be taken. Without planning, there would be no goals against which to measure or evaluate work efforts.

What Are Some Criticisms of Formal Planning?

Although it makes sense for an organization to establish goals and direction, critics have challenged some of the basic assumptions of planning.[2]

1. *Planning may create rigidity.* Formal planning efforts can lock an organization into specific goals to be achieved within specific timetables. Such goals may have been set under the assumption that the environment wouldn't change. Forcing a course of action when the environment is random and unpredictable can be a recipe for disaster. Instead, managers need to remain flexible and not be tied to a course of action simply because it's the plan.

2. *Formal plans can't replace intuition and creativity.* Successful organizations are typically the result of someone's vision, but these visions have a tendency to become formalized as they evolve. If formal planning efforts reduce the vision to a programmed routine, that too can lead to disaster. Planning should enhance and support intuition and creativity, not replace it.

3. *Planning focuses managers' attention on today's competition, not on tomorrow's survival.* Formal planning, especially strategic planning (which we'll discuss shortly), has a tendency to focus on how to best capitalize on existing business opportunities within the industry. Managers may not look at ways to re-create or reinvent the industry. Instead, when managers plan, they should be open to forging into uncharted waters if there are untapped opportunities.

4. *Formal planning reinforces success, which may lead to failure.* The American tradition has been that success breeds success. After all, if it's not broken, don't fix it. Right? Well maybe not! Success may, in fact, breed failure in an uncertain environment. It's hard to change or discard successful plans—to leave the comfort of what works for the uncertainty (and anxiety) of the unknown. Still, managers may need to face that unknown and be open to doing things in new ways to be even more successful.

Does Formal Planning Improve Organizational Performance?

Does it pay to plan? Or have the critics of planning won the debate? Let's look at the evidence.

Contrary to what the critics of planning say, the evidence generally supports the position that organizations should have formal plans. Although most studies that have looked at the relationship between planning and performance have shown generally positive relationships, we can't say that organizations that formally plan *always* outperform those that don't.[3] But what can we conclude?

First, formal planning generally means higher profits, higher return on assets, and other positive financial results. Second, the quality of the planning process and the appropriate implementation of the plan probably contribute more to high performance than does the extent of planning. Finally, in those organizations in which formal planning did not lead to higher performance, the environment was often to blame. For instance, governmental regulations, unforeseen economic challenges, and other environmental constraints reduce the impact of planning on an organization's performance. Why? Because managers will have fewer viable alternatives.

One important aspect of an organization's formal planning is strategic planning, which managers do as part of the strategic management process.

5.2 Explain what managers do in the strategic management process.

WHAT DO MANAGERS NEED TO KNOW ABOUT STRATEGIC MANAGEMENT?

German engineering giant Siemens AG is rethinking its strategic goal of becoming a major player in the nuclear power industry. U.K. drug maker GlaxoSmithKline PLC has decided to sell off Alli, its over-the-counter diet drug. Best Buy Co. is shrinking its "big-box store" strategy to better position itself to compete online against Amazon.com. Burberry Group PLC is outfitting its stores in China with the latest digital technology including touch screens for customers and iPads for staff in an attempt to win over younger customers.[4] These are just a few of the business news stories from a single week, and each one is about a company's strategies. Strategic management is very much a part of what managers do.

What Is Strategic Management?

Strategic management is what managers do to develop an organization's strategies. What are an organization's **strategies**? They're the plans for how the organization will do what it's in business to do, how it will compete successfully, and how it will attract and satisfy its customers in order to achieve its goals.

Why Is Strategic Management Important?

Unlike many other mall-based clothing chains experiencing disastrous sales declines, retailer Buckle Inc. suffered from weak sales only during the last stages of the recent economic downturn. And it didn't take long for Buckle to regain its footing. What's the company's strategy? One important part has been its location strategy. Only a few of its 400-plus stores were located in states that suffered the worst from the recession. Another part of its strategy was to offer customer perks such as custom pants fittings and free hemming on its jeans. Such "customer-service investments can go a long way in differentiating Buckle in the congested teen market."[5] This company's managers obviously understand why strategic management is important!

Why *is* strategic management so important? One reason is that it can make a difference in how well an organization performs. Why do some businesses succeed and others fail, even when faced with the same environmental conditions? Research has found a generally positive relationship between strategic planning and performance.[6] Those companies that plan strategically appear to have better financial results than those organizations that don't.

Another reason it's important has to do with the fact that managers in organizations of all types and sizes face continually changing situations (recall our discussion in Chapter 2). They cope with this uncertainty by using the strategic management process to examine relevant factors in planning future actions.

Finally, strategic management is important because organizations are complex and diverse. Each part needs to work together to achieve the organization's goals; strategic management helps do this. For example, with more than 2.1 million employees worldwide working in various departments, functional areas, and stores, Walmart uses strategic management to help coordinate and focus employees' efforts on what's important.

Strategic management isn't just for business organizations. Even organizations such as government agencies, hospitals, educational institutions, and social agencies need strategic management. For example, the skyrocketing costs of a college education, competition from for-profit companies offering alternative educational environments, state budgets being slashed because of declining revenues, and cutbacks in federal aid for students and research have led many university administrators to assess their colleges' aspirations and identify a market niche in which they can survive and prosper.

What Are the Steps in the Strategic Management Process?

The **strategic management process** (see Exhibit 5–2) is a six-step process that encompasses strategy planning, implementation, and evaluation. Although the first four steps describe the planning that must take place, implementation and evaluation are just as important! Even the best strategies can fail if management doesn't implement or evaluate them properly.

China is playing a significant role in the strategic plans of British fashion house Burberry Group PLC. Recognizing that young Chinese shoppers are driving the growth of the global luxury industry, Burberry's CEO Angela Ahrendts has selected China as the first market to launch the firm's digital retail model in a worldwide campaign that targets young consumers. Winning Chinese customers is critical to Burberry's growth strategy, with China expected to become the world's largest market for luxury goods by 2020. Shown here addressing the World Retail Congress, Ahrendts describes how Burberry is using in-store digital technology plus its own online shopping site, Chinese social networking sites, and Internet television to attract young buyers.

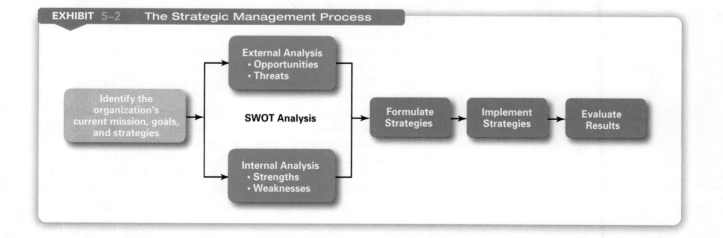

EXHIBIT 5–2   The Strategic Management Process

Identify the organization's current mission, goals, and strategies → External Analysis • Opportunities • Threats / Internal Analysis • Strengths • Weaknesses (SWOT Analysis) → Formulate Strategies → Implement Strategies → Evaluate Results

strategic management
What managers do to develop an organization's strategies

strategies
Plans for how the organization will do what it's in business to do, how it will compete successfully, and how it will attract its customers in order to achieve its goals

strategic management process
A six-step process that encompasses strategy planning, implementation, and evaluation

---

EXHIBIT 5-3	**What a Mission Statement Includes**

Customers: Who are the firm's customers?

Markets: Where does the firm compete geographically?

Concern for survival, growth, and profitability: Is the firm committed to growth and financial stability?

Philosophy: What are the firm's basic beliefs, values, and ethical priorities?

Concern for public image: How responsive is the firm to societal and environmental concerns?

Products or services: What are the firm's major products or services?

Technology: Is the firm technologically current?

Self-concept: What are the firm's major competitive advantage and core competencies?

Concern for employees: Are employees a valuable asset of the firm?

Source: Based on F. David, *Strategic Management,* 11th ed. (Upper Saddle River, NJ: Prentice Hall, 2007), p. 70.

STEP 1: **Identifying the organization's current mission, goals, and strategies.** Every organization needs a mission—a statement of its purpose. Defining the mission forces managers to identify what it's in business to do. For instance, the mission of Avon is "To be the company that best understands and satisfies the product, service, and self-fulfillment needs of women on a global level." The mission of Facebook is "a social utility that connects you with the people around you." The mission of the National Heart Foundation of Australia is to "reduce suffering and death from heart, stroke, and blood vessel disease in Australia." These statements provide clues to what these organizations see as their purpose. What should a mission statement include? Exhibit 5–3 describes some typical components.

It's also important for managers to identify the current goals and strategies. Why? So managers have a basis for assessing whether they need to be changed.

STEP 2: **Doing an external analysis.** We discussed the external environment in Chapter 2. Analyzing that environment is a critical step in the strategic management process. Managers do an external analysis so they know, for instance, what the competition is doing, what pending legislation might affect the organization, or what the labor supply is like in locations where it operates. In an external analysis, managers should examine all components of the environment (economic, demographic, political/legal, sociocultural, technological, and global) to see the trends and changes.

Once they've analyzed the environment, managers need to pinpoint opportunities that the organization can exploit and threats that it must counteract or buffer against. Opportunities are positive trends in the external environment; threats are negative trends.

STEP 3: **Doing an internal analysis.** Now we move to the internal analysis, which provides important information about an organization's specific resources and capabilities. An organization's resources are its assets—financial, physical, human, and intangible—that it uses to develop, manufacture, and deliver products to its customers. They're "what" the organization has. On the other hand, its capabilities are its skills and abilities in doing the work activities needed in its business—"how" it does its work. The major value-creating capabilities of the organization are known as its core competencies.[7] Both resources and core competencies determine the organization's competitive weapons.

After completing an internal analysis, managers should be able to identify organizational strengths and weaknesses. Any activities the organization does well or any unique resources that it has are called strengths. Weaknesses are activities the organization doesn't do well or resources it needs but doesn't possess.

The combined external and internal analyses are called the SWOT analysis because it's an analysis of the organization's *s*trengths, *w*eaknesses, *o*pportunities, and *t*hreats. After completing the SWOT analysis, managers are ready to formulate appropriate strategies—that is, strategies that (1) exploit an organization's strengths and external opportunities, (2) buffer or protect the organization from external threats, or (3) correct critical weaknesses.

STEP 4: Formulating strategies. As managers formulate strategies, they should consider the realities of the external environment and their available resources and capabilities and design strategies that will help an organization achieve its goals. Managers typically formulate three main types of strategies: corporate, business, and functional. We'll describe each shortly.

STEP 5: Implementing strategies. Once strategies are formulated, they must be implemented. No matter how effectively an organization has planned its strategies, performance will suffer if the strategies aren't implemented properly.

STEP 6: Evaluating results. The final step in the strategic management process is evaluating results. How effective have the strategies been at helping the organization reach its goals? What adjustments are necessary? For instance, when Anne Mulcahy, Xerox's former CEO, was first named to that post, she assessed the results of previous strategies and determined that changes were needed. She made strategic adjustments—cutting jobs, selling assets, and reorganizing management—to regain market share and improve her company's bottom line.

Baofan/Photoshot Holdings

In examining the external environment to assess trends and changes, Baidu's chief executive Robin Li sees opportunities for his company to grow. Baidu is the largest Chinese language search engine. With more than two-thirds of China's population not yet Internet users, Li believes search advertising will continue as the company's main growth driver for the next decade. Li also sees China's fast-growing mobile Internet market as a huge opportunity for Baidu due to the rapid growth in the number of mobile phone subscribers. According to Li, the decision of competitor Google to move its China search engine service to Hong Kong benefited Baidu because it drew attention to the search business and helped educate the advertisers that search is one of the best ways for them to reach their targeted consumers.

What Strategies Do Managers Use?

Strategies need to be formulated for all levels in the organization: corporate, business, and functional (see Exhibit 5–4). Let's look closer at each of these types of strategies.

CORPORATE STRATEGY. A *corporate strategy* is an organizational strategy that specifies what businesses a company is in or wants to be in and what it wants to do with those businesses. It's based on the mission and goals of the organization and the roles that each business unit of the organization will play. We can see both of these aspects with PepsiCo, for instance. Its mission is: To be the world's premier consumer products company focused on convenient foods and beverages. It pursues that mission with a corporate strategy that has put it in different businesses including PepsiCo Americas Beverage, PepsiCo International, Frito-Lay North America, Quaker Foods North America, and Latin America Foods. The other part of corporate strategy is when top managers decide what to do with those businesses. The three main types of corporate strategies are growth, stability, and renewal.

mission
A statement of an organization's purpose

opportunities
Positive trends in the external environment

threats
Negative trends in the external environment

resources
An organization's assets that it uses to develop, manufacture, and deliver products to its customers

capabilities
An organization's skills and abilities in doing the work activities needed in its business

core competencies
The major value-creating capabilities of an organization

strengths
Any activities the organization does well or any unique resources that it has

weaknesses
Activities the organization doesn't do well or resources it needs but doesn't possess

SWOT analysis
The combined external and internal analyses

corporate strategy
An organizational strategy that specifies what businesses a company is in or wants to be in and what it wants to do with those businesses

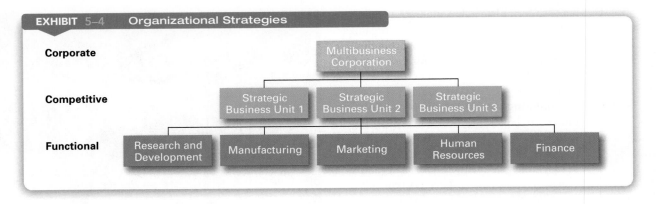

EXHIBIT 5-4   Organizational Strategies

Growth Strategy.   Even though Walmart is the world's largest retailer, it continues to grow internationally and in the United States. A **growth strategy** is when an organization expands the number of markets served or products offered, either through its current business(es) or through new business(es). Because of its growth strategy, an organization may increase revenues, number of employees, or market share. Organizations grow by using concentration, vertical integration, horizontal integration, or diversification.

An organization that grows using *concentration* focuses on its primary line of business and increases the number of products offered or markets served in this primary business. For instance, Beckman Coulter, Inc., a Fullerton, California-based organization with annual revenues of almost $3.7 billion has used concentration to become one of the world's largest medical diagnostics and research equipment companies. The company has been so successful at this strategy that its largest rival acquired it for nearly $7 billion.

A company also might choose to grow by *vertical integration*, either backward, forward, or both. In backward vertical integration, the organization becomes its own supplier so it can control its inputs. For instance, eBay owns an online payment business that helps it provide more secure transactions and control one of its most critical processes. In forward vertical integration, the organization becomes its own distributor and is able to control its outputs. For example, Apple has some 380 retail stores around the globe to distribute its product.

In *horizontal integration*, a company grows by combining with competitors. For instance, French cosmetics giant L'Oréal acquired The Body Shop. Horizontal integration has been used in a number of industries in the last few years—financial services, consumer products, airlines, department stores, and software, among others. The U.S. Federal Trade Commission usually scrutinizes these combinations closely to see if consumers might be harmed by decreased competition. Other countries may have similar restrictions. For instance, managers at Oracle Corporation had to get approval from the European Commission, the "watchdog" for the European Union, before it could acquire rival business-software maker PeopleSoft.

Finally, an organization can grow through *diversification*, either related or unrelated. Related diversification is when a company combines with other companies in different, but related, industries. For example, American Standard Companies is in a variety of businesses including bathroom fixtures, air conditioning and heating units, plumbing parts, and pneumatic brakes for trucks. Although this mix of businesses seems odd, the company's "strategic fit" is the efficiency-oriented manufacturing techniques developed in its primary business of bathroom fixtures, which it has transferred to all its other businesses. Unrelated diversification is when a company combines with firms in different and unrelated industries. For instance, the Tata Group of India has businesses in chemicals, communications and IT, consumer products, energy, engineering, materials, and services. Again, an odd mix. But in this case, no strategic fit exists among the businesses. Each business is expected to compete and thrive on its own.

Stability Strategy.   During periods of economic uncertainty, many companies choose to maintain things as they are. In this **stability strategy**, an organization continues to do what it is currently doing. Examples of this strategy include continuing to serve the same clients by offering the same product or service, maintaining market share, and sustaining the organization's current business operations. The organization doesn't grow, but doesn't fall behind, either.

Renewal Strategy. In 2010, Federal National Mortgage Association (Fannie Mae) lost $14 billion after losing almost $72 billion in 2009. Its "brother" Freddie Mac (Federal Home Loan Mortgage Corporation) lost $14 billion in 2010 and $21.5 billion in 2009. Hitachi had a loss of $1.1 billion in 2010 and over $8 billion in 2009. When an organization is in trouble, something needs to be done. Managers need strategies that address declining performance. These strategies are called renewal strategies, of which there are two main types. A *retrenchment strategy* is a short-run renewal strategy used for minor performance problems. This strategy helps it stabilize operations, revitalize organizational resources and capabilities, and prepare to compete once again. When an organization's problems are more serious, more drastic action—the *turnaround strategy*—is needed. Managers do two things for both renewal strategies: cut costs and restructure organizational operations. However, in a turnaround strategy, these measures are more extensive than in a retrenchment strategy.

COMPETITIVE STRATEGY. A competitive strategy is a strategy for how an organization will compete in its business(es). For a small organization in only one line of business or a large organization that has not diversified into different products or markets, its competitive strategy describes how it will compete in its primary or main market. For organizations in multiple businesses, however, each business will have its own competitive strategy that defines its competitive advantage, the products or services it will offer, the customers it wants to reach, and the like. For example, the French company LVMH-Moët Hennessy Louis Vuitton SA has different competitive strategies for its businesses, which include Bliss cosmetics, Donna Karan fashions, Louis Vuitton leather goods, Guerlain perfume, TAG Heuer watches, Dom Perignon champagne, and other luxury products. Its selective retail division includes Sephora cosmetics stores, Le Bon Marché Paris department stores, and a majority holding of DFS Group duty-free shops. When an organization is in several different businesses, those single businesses that are independent and formulate their own competitive strategies are often called strategic business units (SBUs).

RIGHT ? WRONG

Choose healthy groceries. Create fabulous Web sites. Destroy green pigs with angry birds. There are phone apps to do just about everything. Even knowing how to avoid sobriety checkpoints—locations where law enforcement officials stop some drivers and perform breath tests on those suspected of being drunk.[8] In March 2011, U.S. senators Harry Reid, Charles E. Schumer, Frank R. Lautenberg, and Tom Udall sent a letter to Apple, Google, and Research In Motion (BlackBerry's parent company) requesting that these companies remove those apps from their online stores. The senators believed that the apps were "harmful to public safety" because it made it too easy for intoxicated drivers to avoid the checkpoints. BlackBerry agreed to pull its apps not long after receiving the letter and thanked the group for bringing these apps to their attention. Apple and Google did not respond. One point to make is that these apps do nothing illegal in supplying the precise locations of sobriety checkpoints. However, the vice president for policy at Mothers Against Drunk Driving said, "There's a difference between a broad announcement that there will be sobriety checkpoints in a general location versus a specific location that can be downloaded to your smartphone with the intent of allowing a drunk driver to evade a checkpoint."

Think About:

- What do you think? Are these apps ethical? Why or why not?
- When crafting strategy, should managers ever consider whether the strategy being implemented is offensive, objectionable, questionable, or unacceptable? Is it more acceptable or less acceptable when your company is considered an industry icon to continue with such strategies? Or does it matter?
- What stakeholders are most important in this situation, and what concerns might those stakeholders have?

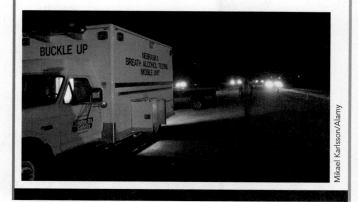
Mikael Karlsson/Alamy

The Role of Competitive Advantage. Michelin has mastered a complex technological process for making superior radial tires. Coca-Cola has created the world's best brand using specialized marketing and merchandising capabilities. The Ritz-Carlton hotels have a unique ability to deliver personalized customer service. Each of these companies has created a competitive advantage.

Developing an effective competitive strategy requires an understanding of **competitive advantage**, which is what sets an organization apart; that is, its distinctive edge. That distinctive edge comes from the organization's core competencies by doing something that others cannot do or doing it better than others can do it. For example, Southwest Airlines has a competitive advantage because of its skills at giving passengers what they want—convenient, reliable, and inexpensive service. Or competitive advantage can come from the company's resources—the organization has something that its competitors do not have. For instance, Walmart's state-of-the-art information system allows it to monitor and control inventories and supplier relations more efficiently than its competitors, which Walmart has turned into a cost advantage.

Choosing a Competitive Strategy. One of the leading researchers in strategy formulation is Michael Porter of Harvard's Graduate School of Business. His competitive strategies framework argues that managers can choose among three generic competitive strategies.[9] According to Porter, no firm can successfully achieve an above-average profitability by trying to be all things to all people. Rather, Porter proposed that managers must choose a competitive strategy that will give it a distinct advantage by capitalizing on the strengths of the organization and the industry it is in. His three competitive strategies are cost-leadership, differentiation, and focus.

When an organization competes on the basis of having the lowest costs in its industry, it's following a **cost leadership strategy**. A low-cost leader is highly efficient. Overhead is kept to a minimum, and the firm does everything it can to cut costs. You won't find expensive art or interior décor at offices of low-cost leaders. For example, at Walmart's headquarters in Bentonville, Arkansas, office furnishings are functional, not elaborate, maybe not what you'd expect for the world's largest retailer. Although a low-cost leader doesn't place a lot of emphasis on "frills," its product must be perceived as comparable in quality to that offered by rivals or at least be acceptable to buyers.

A company that competes by offering unique products that are widely valued by customers is following a **differentiation strategy**. Product differences might come from exceptionally high quality, extraordinary service, innovative design, technological capability, or an unusually positive brand image. Practically any successful consumer product or service can be identified as an example of the differentiation strategy; for instance, Nordstrom's (customer service); 3M Corporation (product quality and innovative design); Coach (design and brand image); and Apple (product design).

Although these two competitive strategies are aimed at the broad market, the final type of competitive strategy—the **focus strategy**—involves a cost advantage (cost focus) or a differentiation advantage (differentiation focus) in a narrow segment or niche. Segments can be based on product variety, customer type, distribution channel, or geographical location. For example, Denmark's Bang & Olufsen, whose revenues are more than $455 million, focuses on high-end audio equipment sales. Whether a focus strategy is feasible depends on the size of the segment and whether the organization can make money serving that segment.

By offering unique products that are widely valued by customers, Whole Foods Market uses a differentiation strategy for competing in the retail food industry. Since its inception, Whole Foods has focused on selling the highest-quality natural and organic products that benefit customers' health and following environment-friendly operating practices. This competitive strategy reflects the company's motto of "Whole Foods—Whole People—Whole Planet." The retailer is committed to buying fruits and vegetables from local farmers who are dedicated to sustainable agriculture. In this photo a mom and her kids shopping at a Whole Foods store pick up their fresh vegetables grown by a small local farmer.

What happens if an organization can't develop a cost or differentiation advantage? Porter called that being *stuck in the middle* and warned that it's not a good place to be.

Sustaining Competitive Advantage. Every organization has resources (assets) and capabilities (how work gets done). So what makes some organizations more successful than others? Why do some professional baseball teams consistently win championships or draw large crowds? Why do some organizations have consistent and continuous growth in revenues and profits? Why do some colleges, universities, or departments experience continually increasing enrollments? Why do some companies consistently appear at the top of lists ranking the "best," or the "most admired," or the "most profitable"? The answer is that not every organization is able to effectively exploit its resources and to develop the core competencies that can provide it with a competitive advantage. And it's not enough simply to create a competitive advantage. The organization must be able to sustain that advantage; that is, to keep its edge despite competitors' actions or evolutionary changes in the industry. But that's not easy to do! Market instabilities, new technology, and other changes can challenge managers' attempts at creating a long-term, sustainable competitive advantage. However, by using strategic management, managers can better position their organizations to get a sustainable competitive advantage.

FUNCTIONAL STRATEGY. The final type of strategy managers use is the **functional strategy**, which includes those strategies used by an organization's various functional departments to support the competitive strategy. For instance, when Starbucks found itself facing increased competition from the likes of McDonald's and Dunkin' Donuts, it put additional emphasis on its marketing, product research and development, and customer service strategies. We don't cover specific functional strategies here since you'll cover them in other business courses you take.

What Strategic Weapons Do Managers Have?

In today's intensely competitive and chaotic marketplace, organizations are looking for whatever "weapons" they can use to do what they're in business to do and to achieve their goals. Some of these weapons include customer service, employee skills and loyalty, innovation, and quality. We've covered customer service in previous chapters and will discuss employee-related matters in Chapters 7 and 9 through 13. Look for a discussion related to innovation and strategy in the Technology and the Manager's Job box. That leaves quality, which we need to look at.

QUALITY AS A STRATEGIC WEAPON. When W. K. Kellogg started manufacturing his cornflake cereal in 1906, his goal was to provide his customers with a high-quality, nutritious product that was enjoyable to eat. That emphasis on quality is still important today. Every Kellogg employee has a responsibility to maintain the high quality of its products.

Many organizations are employing quality practices to build competitive advantage and attract and hold a loyal customer base. If implemented properly, quality can be a way for an organization to create a sustainable competitive advantage.[11] And if a business is

---

competitive advantage
What sets an organization apart; its distinctive edge

cost leadership strategy
When an organization competes on the basis of having the lowest costs in its industry

differentiation strategy
When an organization competes on the basis of having unique products that are widely valued by customers

focus strategy
When an organization competes in a narrow segment or niche with either a cost focus or a differentiation focus

functional strategy
Strategy used in an organization's various functional departments to support the competitive strategy

TECHNOLOGY AND THE MANAGER'S JOB — IT AND STRATEGY

How important is IT to a company's strategy?[10] Very important . . . as two examples will illustrate! Harrah's Entertainment, the world's largest gaming company, is fanatical about customer service, and for good reason. Company research showed that customers who were satisfied with the service they received at a Harrah's casino increased their gaming expenditures by 10 percent, and those who were extremely satisfied increased their gaming expenditures by 24 percent. It discovered this important customer service–expenditures connection because of its incredibly sophisticated information system. But an organization's IT may not always have such a positive payoff as the

next example shows! At Prada's Manhattan flagship store, store designers were hoping for a "radically new shopping experience" that combined "cutting-edge architecture and twenty-first-century customer service." Or at least that was the strategy. Prada invested almost one-fourth of the new store's budget into IT, including wireless networks linked to an inventory database. As envisioned, sales staff would roam the store armed with PDAs so they could check whether items were in stock. Even the dressing rooms would have touch screens so customers could do the same. But the strategy didn't work as planned. The equipment malfunctioned and the staff was overwhelmed with trying to

cope with crowds and equipment that didn't work. It's no wonder the multimillion-dollar investment might not have been the best strategy. When an organization's IT "works," it can be a very powerful strategic tool!

Think About:

· How should managers ensure that their IT efforts contribute to their strategies?

· Could the problems at Prada have been prevented? How might goals and plans have prevented these problems?

· How do IT applications help you be a better planner in your personal life? (Think smartphone organizers and calendars, text and voice messaging, etc.)

---

able to continuously improve the quality and reliability of its products, it may have a competitive advantage that can't be taken away.[12] Incremental improvement is something that becomes an integrated part of an organization's operations and can develop into a considerable advantage.

BENCHMARKING TO PROMOTE QUALITY. Managers in such diverse industries as health care, education, and financial services are discovering what manufacturers have long recognized—the benefits of **benchmarking**, which is the search for the best practices among competitors or noncompetitors that lead to their superior performance. The basic idea of benchmarking is that managers can improve quality by analyzing and then copying the methods of the leaders in various fields.

In 1979, Xerox undertook what is widely regarded as the first benchmarking effort in the United States. Until then, the Japanese had been aggressively copying the successes of others by traveling around, watching what others were doing, and then using their new knowledge to improve their products and processes. Xerox's managers couldn't figure out how Japanese manufacturers could sell midsized copiers in the United States for considerably less than Xerox's production costs. So the company's head of manufacturing took a team to Japan to make a detailed study of its competition's costs and processes. The team got most of their information from Xerox's own joint venture partner, Fuji-Xerox, which knew its competition well. What the team found was shocking. Their Japanese rivals were light-years ahead of Xerox in efficiency. Benchmarking those efficiencies was the beginning of Xerox's recovery in the copier field. Today, many organizations use benchmarking practices. For instance, the American Medical Association developed more than 100 standard performance measures to improve medical care. Carlos Ghosn, CEO of Nissan, benchmarked Walmart's operations in purchasing, transportation, and logistics. And Southwest Airlines studied Indy 500 pit crews, who can change a race car's tire in under 15 seconds, to see how their gate crews could make their gate turnaround times even faster.[13]

Once managers have the organization's strategies in place, it's time to set goals and develop plans to pursue those strategies.

Teachers participating in the Weightless Flights of Discovery program are helping Northrop Grumman Foundation achieve its goal of inspiring more students to pursue careers in science, technology, engineering, and math. Concerned about our nation's shortage of future engineers and technologists, the aerospace and defense firm launched its program for middle school math and science teachers so they can bring unique learning opportunities to their classrooms. The program puts teachers in a zero-gravity aircraft flight where they learn about the physics of weightlessness, conduct experiments captured by a video camera, and then use their videotaped experience to show their students how math and science can be the basis for a fascinating career.

HOW DO MANAGERS SET GOALS AND DEVELOP PLANS?

Compare and contrast approaches to goal setting and planning.

5.3

Planning involves two important aspects: goals and plans. **Goals (objectives)** are desired outcomes or targets. They guide managers' decisions and form the criteria against which work results are measured. **Plans** are documents that outline how goals are going to be met. They usually include resource allocations, budgets, schedules, and other necessary actions to accomplish the goals. As managers plan, they develop both goals and plans.

What Types of Goals Do Organizations Have and How Do They Set Those Goals?

Although it might seem that organizations have a single goal—for businesses, to make a profit and for not-for-profit organizations, to meet the needs of some constituent group(s)—an organization's success can't be determined by a single goal. In reality, all organizations have multiple goals. For instance, businesses may want to increase market share, keep employees motivated, or work toward more environmentally sustainable practices. And a church provides a place for religious practices, but also assists economically disadvantaged individuals in its community and acts as a social gathering place for church members.

TYPES OF GOALS. Most company's goals can be classified as either strategic or financial. Financial goals are related to the financial performance of the organization while strategic goals are related to all other areas of an organization's performance. For instance, McDonald's financial targets include 3 to 5 percent average annual sales and revenue growth, 6 to 7 percent average annual operating income growth, and returns on invested capital in the high teens.[14] An example of a strategic goal would be the request by Nissan's CEO for the company's GT-R supercar: match or beat the performance of Porsche's 911 Turbo.[15] These goals are **stated goals**—official statements of what an organization says, and what it wants its stakeholders to believe, its goals are. However, stated goals—which can be found in an organization's charter, annual report, public relations announcements, or in public statements made by managers—are often conflicting and influenced by what various stakeholders think organizations should do. Such statements can be vague and probably better represent management's public relations skills instead of being meaningful guides to what the organization is actually trying to accomplish. It shouldn't be surprising then to find that an organization's stated goals are often irrelevant to what's actually done.[16]

If you want to know an organization's **real goals**—those goals an organization actually pursues—observe what organizational members are doing. Actions define priorities. Knowing that real and stated goals may differ is important for recognizing what you might otherwise think are inconsistencies.

SETTING GOALS. As we stated earlier, goals provide the direction for all management decisions and actions and form the criterion against which actual accomplishments are measured. Everything organizational members do should be oriented toward achieving goals. These goals can be set either through a process of traditional goal setting or by using management by objectives.

---

benchmarking
The search for the best practices among competitors or noncompetitors that lead to their superior performance

goals (objectives)
Desired outcomes or targets

plans
Documents that outline how goals are going to be met

stated goals
Official statements of what an organization says, and wants its stakeholders to believe, its goals are

real goals
Those goals an organization actually pursues as shown by what the organization's members are doing

EXHIBIT 5-5 Traditional Goal Setting

Traditional Goal Setting. In **traditional goal setting**, goals set by top managers flow down through the organization and become subgoals for each organizational area. (See Exhibit 5–5.) This traditional perspective assumes that top managers know what's best because they see the "big picture." And the goals passed down to each succeeding level guide individual employees as they work to achieve those assigned goals. Take a manufacturing business, for example. The president tells the vice president of production what he expects manufacturing costs to be for the coming year and tells the marketing vice president what level he expects sales to reach for the year. These goals are passed to the next organizational level and written to reflect the responsibilities of that level, passed to the next level, and so forth. Then, at some later time, performance is evaluated to determine whether the assigned goals have been achieved. Or that's the way it's supposed to happen. But in reality, it doesn't always do so. Turning broad strategic goals into departmental, team, and individual goals can be a difficult and frustrating process.

Another problem with traditional goal setting is that when top managers define the organization's goals in broad terms—such as achieving "sufficient" profits or increasing "market leadership"—these ambiguous goals have to be made more specific as they flow down through the organization. Managers at each level define the goals and apply their own interpretations and biases as they make them more specific. Clarity is often lost as the goals make their way down from the top of the organization to lower levels. But it doesn't have to be that way. For example, at Tijuana-based dj Orthopedics de Mexico, employee teams see the impact of their daily work output on company goals. The company's human resource manager says, "When people get a close connection with the result of their work, when they know every day what they are supposed to do and how they achieved the goals, that makes a strong connection with the company and their job."[17]

When the hierarchy of organizational goals *is* clearly defined, as it is at dj Orthopedics, it forms an integrated network of goals, or a **means-ends chain**. Higher-level goals (or ends) are linked to lower-level goals, which serve as the means for their accomplishment. In other words, the goals achieved at lower levels become the means to reach the goals (ends) at the next level. And the accomplishment of goals at that level becomes the means to achieve the goals (ends) at the next level and on up through the different organizational levels. That's how traditional goal setting is supposed to work.

Management by Objectives. Instead of using traditional goal setting, many organizations use **management by objectives (MBO)**, a process of setting mutually agreed-upon goals and using those goals to evaluate employee performance. If a manager were to use this approach, he would sit down with each member of his team and set goals and periodically review whether progress was being made toward achieving those goals. MBO programs have four elements: goal specificity, participative decision making, an

From the Past to the Present

Management by objectives (MBO) is not new. The concept can be traced back to Peter Drucker, who first popularized the term in his 1954 book *The Practice of Management*.[18] Its appeal lies in its emphasis on converting overall objectives into specific objectives for organizational units and individual members.

MBO makes goals operational by a process in which they cascade down through the organization. The organization's overall objectives are translated into specific objectives for each succeeding level—division, departmental, individual—in the organization. The result is a hierarchy that links objectives at one level to those at the next level. For the individual employee, MBO provides specific personal performance objectives. If all the individuals achieve their goals, then the unit's goals will be attained. Likewise, if all the units attain their goals, then the divisional goals will be met until ultimately the organization's overall goals will become a reality.

Does MBO work? Assessing the effectiveness of MBO is a complex task. But goal-setting research can give us some answers. For instance, research has shown that specific, difficult-to-achieve goals produce a higher level of output than do no goals or generalized goals such as "do your best." Also, feedback favorably affects performance because it lets a person know whether his or her level of effort is sufficient or needs to be increased. These findings are consistent with MBO's emphasis on specific goals and feedback. What about participation, though, since MBO strongly advocates that goals be set participatively? Research comparing participatively set goals with assigned goals has not shown any strong or consistent relationship to performance. One critical factor in the success of any MBO program, however, is top management commitment to the process. When top managers had a high commitment to MBO and were personally involved in its implementation, productivity gains were higher than if this commitment was lacking.

Think About:

- Why do you think management commitment is so important to the success of MBO programs?

- Do you set goals for yourself? Do you feel that setting goals helps you perform better? Discuss.

- Could MBO be useful in your personal life? How? What would you need to do to set up an MBO-like approach to your personal goals?

explicit time period, and performance feedback.[19] Instead of using goals to make sure employees are doing what they're supposed to be doing, MBO uses goals to motivate them as well. The appeal is that it focuses on employees working to accomplish goals they've had a hand in setting. (See the From the Past to the Present box for more information on MBO.)

Studies of actual MBO programs have shown that it can increase employee performance and organizational productivity. For example, one review of MBO programs found productivity gains in almost all of them.[20] But is MBO relevant for today's organizations? If it's viewed as a way of setting goals, then yes, research shows that goal setting can be an effective approach to motivating employees.[21]

Characteristics of Well-Written Goals. No matter which approach is used, goals have to be written, and some goals more clearly indicate what the desired outcomes are. Managers should develop well-written goals. Exhibit 5–6 lists the characteristics.[22] With these characteristics in mind, managers are now ready to actually set goals.

EXHIBIT 5–6   **Well-Written Goals**

- Written in terms of outcomes rather than actions
- Measurable and quantifiable
- Clear as to a time frame
- Challenging yet attainable
- Written down
- Communicated to all necessary organizational members

traditional goal setting
Goals set by top managers flow down through the organization and become subgoals for each organizational area

means-ends chain
An integrated network of goals in which higher-level goals are linked to lower-level goals, which serve as the means for their accomplishment

management by objectives (MBO)
A process of setting mutually agreed-upon goals and using those goals to evaluate employee performance

Steps in Goal Setting.   Managers should follow six steps when setting goals.

1. *Review the organization's mission and employees' key job tasks.* An organization's mission statement will provide an overall guide to what organizational members think is important. Managers should review the mission before writing goals because goals should reflect that mission. In addition, it's important to define what you want employees to accomplish as they do their tasks.

2. *Evaluate available resources.* You don't want to set goals that are impossible to achieve given your available resources. Even though goals should be challenging, they should be realistic. After all, if the resources you have to work with won't allow you to achieve a goal no matter how hard you try or how much effort is exerted, you shouldn't set that goal. That would be like the person with a $50,000 annual income and no other financial resources setting a goal of building an investment portfolio worth $1 million in three years. No matter how hard he or she works at it, it's not going to happen.

3. *Determine the goals individually or with input from others.* The goals reflect desired outcomes and should be congruent with the organizational mission and goals in other organizational areas. These goals should be measurable, specific, and include a time frame for accomplishment.

4. *Make sure goals are well-written and then communicate them to all who need to know.* Writing down and communicating goals forces people to think them through. The written goals also become visible evidence of the importance of working toward something.

5. *Build in feedback mechanisms to assess goal progress.* If goals aren't being met, change them as needed.

6. *Link rewards to goal attainment.* It's natural for employees to ask "What's in it for me?" Linking rewards to goal achievement will help answer that question.

Once the goals have been established, written down, and communicated, managers are ready to develop plans for pursuing the goals.

What Types of Plans Do Managers Use and How Do They Develop Those Plans?

Managers need plans to help them clarify and specify how goals will be met. Let's look first at the types of plans managers use.

TYPES OF PLANS.   The most popular ways to describe plans are in terms of their *breadth* (strategic versus tactical), *time frame* (long term versus short), *specificity* (directional versus specific), and *frequency of use* (single-use versus standing). As Exhibit 5–7 shows, these types of plans aren't independent. That is, strategic plans are usually long term, directional, and single-use. Let's look at each type of plan.

Breadth.   Strategic plans are those that apply to an entire organization and encompass the organization's overall goals. Tactical plans (sometimes referred to as operational plans) specify the details of how the overall goals are to be achieved. When McDonald's invested in its Redbox kiosk business, it was the result of strategic planning. Deciding when, where, and how to actually operate the business was the result of tactical plans in marketing, logistics, finance, and so forth.

Time Frame.   The number of years used to define short-term and long-term plans has declined considerably due to environmental uncertainty. *Long term* used to mean anything

EXHIBIT 5–7	Types of Plans		
BREADTH OF USE	**TIME FRAME**	**SPECIFICITY**	**FREQUENCY OF USE**
Strategic	Long term	Directional	Single-use
Tactical	Short term	Specific	Standing

over seven years. Try to imagine what you're likely to be doing in seven years. It seems pretty distant, doesn't it? Now, you can begin to understand how difficult it is for managers to plan that far in the future. Thus, long-term plans are now defined as plans with a time frame beyond three years. Short-term plans cover one year or less.

Specificity. Intuitively, it would seem that specific plans would be preferable to directional, or loosely guided, plans. Specific plans are plans that are clearly defined and leave no room for interpretation. For example, a manager who wants to increase his work unit's output by 8 percent over the next 12 months might establish specific procedures, budget allocations, and work schedules to reach that goal. However, when uncertainty is high and managers must be flexible in order to respond to unexpected changes, they'd likely use directional plans, flexible plans that set general guidelines. For example, Sylvia Rhone, president of Motown Records, had a simple goal—to "sign great artists."[23] She could create a specific plan to produce and market 10 albums from new artists this year. Or she might formulate a directional plan to use a network of people around the world to alert her to new and promising talent so she can increase the number of artists she has under contract. Sylvia, and any manager who engages in planning, must keep in mind that you have to weigh the flexibility of directional plans against the clarity you can get from specific plans.

Frequency of Use. Some plans that managers develop are ongoing, while others are used only once. A single-use plan is a one-time plan specifically designed to meet the needs of a unique situation. For instance, when Dell began developing a pocket-sized device for getting on the Internet, managers used a single-use plan to guide their decisions. In contrast, standing plans are ongoing plans that provide guidance for activities performed repeatedly. For example, when you register for classes for the upcoming semester, you're using a standardized registration plan at your college or university. The dates change, but the process works the same way semester after semester.

DEVELOPING PLANS. The process of developing plans is influenced by three contingency factors and by the planning approach followed.

Contingency Factors in Planning. Look back at our chapter-opening case. How will Cisco executives proceed now that the decision has been made to abandon its Flip business? Three contingency factors affect the choice of plans: organizational level, degree of environmental uncertainty, and length of future commitments.[24]

Exhibit 5–8 shows the relationship between a manager's level in the organization and the type of planning done. For the most part, lower-level managers do operational (or tactical) planning while upper-level managers do strategic planning.

The second contingency factor is environmental uncertainty. When uncertainty is high, plans should be specific, but flexible. Managers must be prepared to change or amend plans as they're implemented. For example, at Continental Airlines, the former CEO and his management team established a specific goal of focusing on what customers wanted most—on-time flights—to help the company become more competitive in the highly uncertain airline industry. Because of that uncertainty, the management team identified a "destination, but not a flight plan," and changed plans as necessary to achieve its goal of on-time service.

strategic plans
Plans that apply to the entire organization and encompass the organization's overall goals

tactical plans
Plans that specify the details of how the overall goals are to be achieved

long-term plans
Plans with a time frame beyond three years

short-term plans
Plans with a time frame of one year or less

specific plans
Plans that are clearly defined and leave no room for interpretation

directional plans
Plans that are flexible and set general guidelines

single-use plan
A one-time plan specifically designed to meet the needs of a unique situation

standing plans
Plans that are ongoing and provide guidance for activities performed repeatedly

EXHIBIT 5-8   Planning and Organizational Level

The last contingency factor also is related to the time frame of plans. The **commitment concept** says that plans should extend far enough to meet those commitments made when the plans were developed. Planning for too long or too short a time period is inefficient and ineffective. We can see the importance of the commitment concept, for example, with the plans that organizations make to increase their computing capabilities. At the data centers where companies' computers are housed, many have found their "power-hungry computers" generate so much heat that their electric bills have skyrocketed because of the increased need for air conditioning.[25] How does this illustrate the commitment concept? As organizations expand their computing technology, they're "committed" to whatever future expenses are generated by that plan. They have to live with the plan and its consequences.

Approaches to Planning.   Federal, state, and local government officials are working together on a plan to boost populations of wild salmon in the northwestern United States. Managers in the Global Fleet Graphics division of the 3M Company are developing detailed plans to satisfy increasingly demanding customers and to battle more aggressive competitors. Emilio Azcárraga Jean, chairman, president, and CEO of Grupo Televisa, gets input from many different people before setting company goals and then turns over the planning for achieving the goals to various executives. In each of these situations, planning is done a little differently. *How* an organization plans can best be understood by looking at *who* does the planning.

In the traditional approach, planning is done entirely by top level managers who often are assisted by a **formal planning department**, a group of planning specialists whose sole responsibility is to help write the various organizational plans. Under this approach, plans developed by top-level managers flow down through other organizational levels, much like the traditional approach to goal-setting. As they flow down through the organization, the plans are tailored to the particular needs of each level. Although this approach makes managerial planning thorough, systematic, and coordinated, all too often the focus is on developing "the plan," a thick binder (or binders) full of meaningless information, that's stuck away on a shelf and never used by anyone for guiding or coordinating work efforts. In fact, in a survey of managers about formal top-down organizational planning processes, over 75 percent said that their company's planning approach was unsatisfactory.[26] A common complaint was that "plans are documents that you prepare for the corporate planning staff and later forget." Although this traditional top-down approach to planning is used by many organizations, it can be effective only if managers understand the importance of creating documents that organizational members actually use, not documents that look impressive but are never used.

Another approach to planning is to involve more organizational members in the process. In this approach, plans aren't handed down from one level to the next, but instead are developed by organizational members at the various levels and in the various work units to meet their specific needs. For instance, at Dell, employees from production, supply management, and channel management meet weekly to make plans based on current product demand and supply. In addition, work teams set their own daily schedules and track their progress against those schedules. If a team falls behind, team members develop "recovery" plans to try to get back on schedule.[28] When organizational members are more actively involved in planning, they see that the plans are more than just something written down on paper. They can actually see that the plans are used in directing and coordinating work.

WHAT CONTEMPORARY PLANNING ISSUES DO MANAGERS FACE?

We conclude this chapter by addressing two contemporary issues in planning. Specifically, we're going to look at planning effectively in dynamic environments and then at how managers can use environmental scanning, especially competitive intelligence.

Discuss contemporary issues in planning.

5.4

How Can Managers Plan Effectively in Dynamic Environments?

As we saw in Chapter 2, the external environment is continually changing. For instance, Wi-Fi has revolutionized all kinds of industries from airlines to automobile manufacturing to supermarkets. Social networking sites are being used by companies for connecting with customers. Amounts spent on eating out instead of cooking at home are predicted to decline. And experts believe that China and India are transforming the twenty-first-century global economy.

How can managers effectively plan when the external environment is continually changing? We already discussed uncertain environments as one of the contingency factors that affect the types of plans managers develop. Because dynamic environments are more the norm than the exception, let's look at how they can effectively plan in such environments.

In an uncertain environment, managers should develop plans that are specific, but flexible. Although this may seem contradictory, it's not. To be useful, plans need some specificity, but the plans should not be set in stone. Managers need to recognize that planning is an ongoing process. The plans serve as a road map although the destination may change due to dynamic market conditions. They should be ready to change directions if environmental conditions warrant. This flexibility is particularly important as plans are implemented. Managers need to stay alert to environmental changes that may impact implementation and respond as needed. Keep in mind, also, that even when the environment is highly uncertain, it's important to continue formal planning in order to see any effect on organizational performance. It's the persistence in planning that contributes to significant performance improvement. Why? It seems that, as with most activities, managers "learn to plan" and the quality of their planning improves when they continue to do it.[29] Finally, make the organizational hierarchy flatter to effectively plan in dynamic environments. A flatter hierarchy means lower organizational levels can set goals and develop plans because organizations have little time for goals and plans to flow down from the top. Managers should teach their employees how to set goals and to plan and then trust them to do it. And you need look no further than Bangalore, India, to find a company that effectively understands this. Just a decade ago, Wipro Limited was "an anonymous conglomerate selling cooking oil and personal computers, mostly in India." Today, it's a $6 billion-a-year global company with most of its business (over 75 percent) coming from information-technology services.[30] Accenture, EDS, IBM, and the big U.S. accounting firms know all too well the competitive threat Wipro represents. Not only are Wipro's

---

commitment concept
The idea that plans should extend far enough to meet those commitments made when the plans were developed

formal planning department
A group of planning specialists whose sole responsibility is to help write the various organizational plans

Jagdeesh Nv/PhotoLibrary/Index Stock Imagery

Knowledgeable and skilled employees play an important role in planning at Wipro, a global information technology services company serving more than 800 clients including governments, educational institutions, and business enterprises. Operating in a dynamic environment, Wipro empowers its customer engagement managers to set goals and make plans in analyzing clients' ever-changing business needs and devising innovative solutions that help them function faster, simpler, and more efficiently. Giving these frontline employees responsibility for planning is part of Wipro's ownership-oriented approach of empowering them to function as mini-CEOS. Shown here are Wipro employees at company headquarters in Bangalore, India.

employees economical, they're knowledgeable and skilled. And they play an important role in the company's planning. Since the information services industry is continually changing, employees are taught to analyze situations and to define the scale and scope of a client's problems in order to offer the best solutions. These employees are the ones on the front line with the clients and it's their responsibility to establish what to do and how to do it. It's an approach that positions Wipro for success no matter how the industry changes.

How Can Managers Use Environmental Scanning?

A manager's analysis of the external environment may be improved by **environmental scanning**, which involves screening large amounts of information to detect emerging trends. One of the fastest-growing forms of environmental scanning is **competitive intelligence**, which is accurate information about competitors that allows managers to anticipate competitors' actions rather than merely react to them.[31] It seeks basic information about competitors: Who are they? What are they doing? How will what they're doing affect us?

Many who study competitive intelligence suggest that much of the competitor-related information managers need to make crucial strategic decisions is available and accessible to the public.[32] In other words, competitive intelligence isn't organizational espionage. Advertisements, promotional materials, press releases, reports filed with government agencies, annual reports, want ads, newspaper reports, information on the Internet, and industry studies are readily accessible sources of information. Specific information on an industry and associated organizations is increasingly available through electronic databases. Managers can literally tap into this wealth of competitive information by purchasing access to databases. Attending trade shows and debriefing your own sales staff also can be good sources of information on competitors. In addition, many organizations even regularly buy competitors' products and ask their own employees to evaluate them to learn about new technical innovations.[33]

In a changing global business environment, environmental scanning and obtaining competitive intelligence can be quite complex, especially when information must be gathered from around the world. However, managers could subscribe to news services that review newspapers and magazines from around the globe and provide summaries to client companies.

Managers do need to be careful about the way information, especially competitive intelligence, is gathered to prevent any concerns about whether it's legal or ethical. For instance, Starwood Hotels sued Hilton Hotels alleging that two former employees stole trade secrets and helped Hilton develop a new line of luxury, trendy hotels designed to appeal to a young demographic.[34] The court filing said, "This is the clearest imaginable case of corporate espionage, theft of trade secrets, unfair competition, and computer fraud." Competitive intelligence becomes illegal corporate spying when it involves the theft of proprietary materials or trade secrets by any means. The Economic Espionage Act makes it a crime in the United States to engage in economic espionage or to steal a trade secret.[35] Difficult decisions about competitive intelligence arise because often there's a fine line between what's considered *legal and ethical* and what's considered *legal but unethical*. Although the top manager at one competitive intelligence firm contends that 99.9 percent of intelligence gathering is legal, there's no question that some people or companies will go to any lengths—some unethical—to get information about competitors.[36]

environmental scanning
An analysis of the external environment, which involves screening large amounts of information to detect emerging trends

competitive intelligence
A type of environmental scanning that gives managers accurate information about competitors

5 Review

CHAPTER SUMMARY

5.1 Discuss the nature and purposes of planning.
As the primary management function, planning establishes the basis for all the other things that managers do. The planning we're concerned with is formal planning; that is, specific goals covering a specific time period are defined and written down and specific plans are developed to make sure those goals are met. There are four reasons why managers should plan: (1) it establishes coordinated efforts; (2) it reduces uncertainty; (3) it reduces overlapping and wasteful activities; and (4) it establishes the goals or standards that are used in controlling work. Although criticisms have been directed at planning, the evidence generally supports the position that organizations benefit from formal planning.

5.2 Explain what managers do in the strategic management process. Managers develop the organization's strategies in the strategic management process, which is a six-step process encompassing strategy planning, implementation, and evaluation. The six steps are as follows: (1) Identify the organization's current mission, goals, and strategies; (2) do an external analysis; (3) do an internal analysis; steps 2 and 3 together are called SWOT analysis; (4) formulate strategies; (5) implement strategies; and (6) evaluate results. The end result of this process is a set of corporate, competitive, and functional strategies that allow the organization to do what it's in business to do and to achieve its goals.

5.3 Compare and contrast approaches to goal setting and planning. Most company's goals are classified as either strategic or financial. We can also look at goals as either stated or real. In traditional goal setting, goals set by top managers flow down through the organization and become subgoals for each organizational area. Organizations could also use management by objectives, which is a process of setting mutually agreed-upon goals and using those goals to evaluate employee performance. Plans can be described in terms of their breadth, time frame, specificity, and frequency of use. Plans can be developed by a formal planning department or by involving more organizational members in the process.

5.4 Discuss contemporary issues in planning. One contemporary planning issue is planning in dynamic environments, which usually means developing plans that are specific but flexible. Also, it's important to continue planning even when the environment is highly uncertain. Finally, because there's little time in a dynamic environment for goals and plans to flow down from the top, lower organizational levels should be allowed to set goals and develop plans. Another contemporary planning issue is using environmental scanning to help do a better analysis of the external environment. One form of environmental scanning, competitive intelligence, can be especially helpful in finding out what competitors are doing.

MyManagementLab For more resources, please visit www.mymanagementlab.com

---

UNDERSTANDING THE CHAPTER

1. Contrast formal with informal planning. Discuss why planning is beneficial.

2. Describe in detail the six-step strategic management process.

3. What is a SWOT analysis, and why is it important to managers?

4. "Organizations that fail to plan are planning to fail." Do you agree or disagree with this statement? Explain your position.

5. Under what circumstances do you believe MBO would be most useful? Discuss.

6. Find examples in current business periodicals of each of Porter's generic strategies. Name the company, describe the strategy being used, and explain why it's an example of that strategy. Be sure to cite your sources.

7. "The primary means of sustaining a competitive advantage is to adjust faster to the environment than

your competitors do." Do you agree or disagree with this statement? Explain your position.

8. What types of planning do you do in your personal life? Describe these plans in terms of being (a) strategic or operational, (b) short term or long term, (c) specific or directional, and (d) single-use or standing.

9. Do a personal SWOT analysis. Assess your personal strengths and weaknesses (skills, talents, abilities). What are you good at? What are you not so good at? What do you enjoy doing? Not enjoy doing? Then, identify career opportunities and threats by

researching job prospects in the industry you're interested in. Look at trends and projections. You might want to check out the information the Bureau of Labor Statistics provides on job prospects. Once you have all this information, write a specific career action plan. Outline five-year career goals and what you need to do to achieve those goals.

10. "The concept of competitive advantage is as important for not-for-profit organizations as it is for for-profit organizations." Do you agree or disagree with this statement? Explain, using examples to make your case.

Go to p. 416

YOUR TURN TO BE A MANAGER for Chapter 5.

Endnotes

1. R. Cheng and D. Clark, "Cisco Flips Consumer Strategy," *Wall Street Journal,* April 13, 2011, p. B3; J. Swartz, "Cisco to Close Flip Video-Camera Business," *USA Today,* April 13, 2011, p. 2B; S. Grobart and E. M. Rusli, "For Flip Video Camera, Four Years from Hot Start-Up to Obsolete," *New York Times Online,* April 12, 2011; D. Goldman, "Cisco Kills Flip, Cuts 550 Workers," *CNNMoney.com,* April 12, 2011; C. Tuna, "Head of Cisco's Consumer Business to Depart," *Wall Street Journal Online,* February 11, 2011; "Recognizing Excellence," *New Zealand Management,* December 2010, pp. 97–101; T. Dreier, "Cheap Flicks," *Money,* July 2010, p. 18; R. Karlgaard, "Three Joy-Giving Products," *Forbes,* June 22, 2009, p. 21; "Cisco Buying Flip Video Camera Maker," *Networkworld.com,* March 23, 2009, p. 10; S. H. Wildstrom, "Cisco Pushes Further into Consumer Technology," *BusinessWeek Online,* March 20, 2009; and K. Boehret, "The Mossberg Solution: An Easier Way to Make and Share Videos," *Wall Street Journal,* September 12, 2007, p. D3.

2. M. C. Mankins and R. Steele, "Stop Making Plans—Start Making Decisions," *Harvard Business Review,* January 2006, pp. 76–84; L. Bossidy and R. Charan, *Execution: The Discipline of Getting Things Done* (New York: Crown/Random House), 2002; P. Roberts, "The Art of Getting Things Done," *Fast Company,* June 2000, p. 162; H. Mintzberg, *The Rise and Fall of Strategic Planning* (New York: Free Press, 1994); G. Hamel and C. K. Prahalad, *Competing for the Future* (Boston: Harvard Business School Press, 1994); and D. Miller, "The Architecture of Simplicity," *Academy of Management Review*, January 1993, pp. 116–138.

3. See, for example, F. Delmar and S. Shane, "Does Business Planning Facilitate the Development of New Ventures?" *Strategic Management Journal* (December 2003), pp. 1165–1185; R. M. Grant, "Strategic Planning in a Turbulent Environment: Evidence from the Oil Majors," *Strategic Management Journal*

(June 2003), pp. 491–517; P. J. Brews and M. R. Hunt, "Learning to Plan and Planning to Learn: Resolving the Planning School/Learning School Debate," *Strategic Management Journal* (December 1999), pp. 889–913; C. C. Miller and L. B. Cardinal, "Strategic Planning and Firm Performance: A Synthesis of More Than Two Decades of Research," *Academy of Management Journal* (March 1994), pp. 1649–1685; N. Capon, J. U. Farley, and J. M. Hulbert, "Strategic Planning and Financial Performance: More Evidence," *Journal of Management Studies* (January 1994), pp. 22–38; D.K. Sinha, "The Contribution of Formal Planning to Decisions," *Strategic Management Journal* (October 1990), pp. 479–492; J. A. Pearce II, E. B. Freeman, and R. B. Robinson Jr., "The Tenuous Link Between Formal Strategic Planning and Financial Performance," *Academy of Management Review*, October 1987, pp. 658–675; L. C. Rhyne, "Contrasting Planning Systems in High, Medium, and Low Performance Companies," *Journal of Management Studies* (July 1987), pp. 363–385; and J. A. Pearce II, K. K. Robbins, and R. B. Robinson, Jr., "The Impact of Grand Strategy and Planning Formality on Financial Performance," *Strategic Management Journal* (March–April 1987), pp. 125–134.

4. V. Fuhrmans, "Siemens Rethinks Nuclear Ambitions," *Wall Street Journal,* April 15, 2011, p. B1+; J. Whalen, "Glaxo to Shed Its OTC Diet Drug, Alli," *Wall Street Journal,* April 15, 2011, p. B1; M. Bustillo, "Best Buy to Shrink 'Big-Box' Store Strategy," *Wall Street Journal,* April 15, 2011, p. B7; and L. Burkitt, "Burberry Dresses Up China Stores with Digital Strategy," *Wall Street Journal,* April 14, 2011, p. B9.

5. A. J. Karr, "December Comp Crux," *Women's Wear Daily,* January 7, 2011, p. 4; A. Steigrad, "Specialty Retailers Show Weak Spots in Quarter," *Women's Wear Daily,* August 20, 2010, p. 14; K. Peterson, "Buckle Bends as Claiborne, Orbitz Climb, Ambow Sinks," *Wall Street Journal,* August 6, 2010, p. C6;

N. Casey, "Teen Idols: Aeropostale, Buckle Post Big Gains as Rivals Swoon," *Wall Street Journal,* May 22, 2009, p. B8; V. Dagher, "Hot Topic Goes Cold, Buckle Wears a Smile," *Wall Street Journal,* May 22, 2009, p. C6; and J. B. Stewart, "A Retailer Bucks a Trend with Sales Success in Its Jeans," *Wall Street Journal,* May 13, 2009, p. D1.

6. M. Gruber, F. Heinemann, M. Brettel, and S. Hungeling, "Configurations of Resources and Capabilities and Their Performance Implications: An Exploratory Study on Technology Ventures," *Strategic Management Journal* (December 2010), pp. 1337–1356; T. H. Poister, "The Future of Strategic Planning in the Public Sector: Linking Strategic Management and Performance," *Public Administration Review,* December 2010, pp. S246–S254; J. González-Benito and Isabel Suárez-González, "A Study of the Role Played by Manufacturing Strategic Objectives and Capabilities in Understanding the Relationship Between Porter's Generic Strategies and Business Performance," *British Journal of Management,* vol. 21, (2010), pp. 1027–1043; J. A. Parnell and E. B. Dent, "The Role of Luck in the Strategy-Performance Relationship," *Management Decision,* vol. 47, no. 6, (2009), pp. 1000–1021; H. J. Cho and V. Pucik, "Relationship Between Innovativeness, Quality, Growth, Profitability, and Market Value," *Strategic Management Journal* (June 2005), pp. 555–575; W. F. Joyce, "What Really Works," *Organizational Dynamics,* May 2005, pp. 118–129; M. A. Roberto, "Strategic Decision-Making Processes," *Group & Organization Management,* December 2004, pp. 625–658; A. Carmeli and A. Tischler, "The Relationships Between Intangible Organizational Elements and Organizational Performance," *Strategic Management Journal* (December 2004), pp. 1257–1278; D. J. Ketchen, C. C. Snow, and V. L. Street, "Improving Firm Performance by Matching Strategic Decision-Making Processes to Competitive Dynamics," *Academy of Management Executive,* November 2004, pp. 29–43; E. H. Bowman and C. E. Helfat, "Does Corporate Strategy Matter?" *Strategic Management Journal,* 22 (2001), pp. 1–23; P. J. Brews and M. R. Hunt, "Learning to Plan and Planning to Learn: Resolving the Planning School-Learning School Debate," *Strategic Management Journal,* 20 (1999), pp. 889–913; D. J. Ketchen Jr., J. B. Thomas, and R. R. McDaniel Jr., "Process, Content and Context; Synergistic Effects on Performance," *Journal of Management,* 22, no. 2 (1996), pp. 231–257; C. C. Miller and L. B. Cardinal, "Strategic Planning and Firm Performance: A Synthesis of More Than Two Decades of Research," *Academy of Management Journal* (December 1994), pp. 1649–1665; and N. Capon, J. U. Farley, and J. M. Hulbert, "Strategic Planning and Financial Performance: More Evidence," *Journal of Management Studies* (January 1994), pp. 105–110.

7. C. K. Prahalad and G. Hamel, "The Core Competence of the Corporation," *Harvard Business Review*, May–June 1990, pp. 79–91.

8. Right or Wrong box based on R. Stross, "Helping Drunken Drivers Avoid Tickets, But Not Wrecks," *New York Times Online,* April 16, 2011; "Senators Ask App Stores to End DUI Evasion Aids," *Telecommunications Reports,* April 1, 2011, p. 24; J. R. Quain, "DUI Checkpoint Apps Draw Ire and Fire," *Fox News.com,* March 29, 2011; M. Esteban and KOMO Staff, "App Designed to Sniff Out DUI Checkpoints Snuffed Out by Senators," *KOMO News.com,* March 25, 2011; and Associated Press, "Group Urges Sobriety Checkpoints," *Wall Street Journal,* January 13, 2005, p. A1.

9. C. H. Green, "Competitive Theory and Business Legitimacy," *BusinessWeek Online,* June 23, 2010; S. Parthasarathy, "Business Strategy" *Financial Management,* June 2010, pp. 32–33; M. E. Porter, *On Competition, Updated and Expanded Edition* (Boston: Harvard Business School), 2008; O. Ormanidhi and O. Stringa, "Porter's Model of Generic Competitive Strategies," *Business Economics,* July 2008, pp. 55–64; M. E. Porter, "The Five Competitive Forces That Shape Strategy," *Harvard Business Review,* January 2008, pp. 78–93; N. Argyres and A. M. McGahan, "Introduction: Michael Porter's Competitive Strategy," *Academy of Management Executive,* May 2002, pp. 41–42; and N. Argyres and A. M. McGahan, "An Interview with Michael Porter," *Academy of Management Executive,* May 2002, pp. 43–52.

10. Managers and Technology box based on D. McGinn, "From Harvard to Las Vegas," *Newsweek,* April 18, 2005, pp. E8–E14; G. Lindsay, "Prada's High-Tech Misstep," *Business 2.0,* March 2004, pp. 72–75; G. Loveman, "Diamonds in the Data Mine," *Harvard Business Review,* May 2003, pp. 109–113; and L. Gary, "Simplify and Execute: Words to Live By in Times of Turbulence," *Harvard Management Update,* January 2003, p. 12.

11. N. A. Shepherd, "Competitive Advantage: Mapping Change and the Role of the Quality Manager of the Future," *Annual Quality Congress,* May 1998, pp. 53–60; T. C. Powell, "Total Quality Management as Competitive Advantage: A Review and Empirical Study," *Strategic Management Journal* (January 1995), pp. 15–37; and R. D. Spitzer, "TQM: The Only Source of Sustainable Competitive Advantage," *Quality Progress,* June 1993, pp. 59–64.

12. See R. J. Schonenberger, "Is Strategy Strategic? Impact of Total Quality Management on Strategy," *Academy of Management Executive*, August 1992, pp. 80–87; C. A. Barclay, "Quality Strategy and TQM Policies: Empirical Evidence," *Management International Review*, Special Issue 1993, pp. 87–98; R. Jacob, "TQM: More Than a Dying Fad?" *Fortune*, October 18, 1993, pp. 66–72; R. Krishnan, A. B. Shani, R. M. Grant, and R. Baer, "In Search of Quality Improvement Problems of Design and Implementation," *Academy of Management Executive*, November 1993, pp. 7–20; B. Voss, "Quality's Second Coming," *Journal of Business Strategy*, March–April 1994, pp. 42–46; and special issue of *Academy of Management Review* devoted to TQM, July 1994, pp. 390–584.

13. R. Pear, "A.M.A. to Develop Measure of Quality of Medical Care," *New York Times Online,* February 21, 2006; and A. Taylor III, "Double Duty," *Fortune,* March 7, 2005, pp. 104–110.

14. McDonald's Annual Report 2007, www.mcdonalds.com (April 21, 2008).

15. S. Zesiger Callaway, "Mr. Ghosn Builds His Dream Car," *Fortune,* February 4, 2008, pp. 56–58.

16. See, for instance, J. Pfeffer, *Organizational Design* (Arlington Heights, IL: AHM Publishing, 1978), pp. 5–12; and C. K. Warriner, "The Problem of Organizational Purpose," *Sociological Quarterly* (Spring 1965), pp. 139–146.

17. D. Drickhamer, "Braced for the Future," *Industry Week,* October 2004, pp. 51–52.

18. From the Past to the Present box based on P. F. Drucker, *The Practice of Management* (New York: Harper & Row, 1954); J. F. Castellano and H. A. Roehm, "The Problem with

Managing by Objectives and Results," *Quality Progress,* March 2001, pp. 39–46; J. Loehr and T. Schwartz, "The Making of a Corporate Athlete," *Harvard Business Review,* January 2001, pp. 120–128; A. J. Vogl, "Drucker, of Course," *Across the Board,* November–December 2000, p. 1. For information on goals and goal setting, see, for example, E. A. Locke, "Toward a Theory of Task Motivation and Incentives," *Organizational Behavior and Human Performance*, May 1968, pp. 157–189; E. A. Locke, K. N. Shaw, L. M. Saari, and G. P. Latham, "Goal Setting and Task Performance: 1969–1980," *Psychological Bulletin,* July 1981, pp. 12–52; E. A. Locke and G. P. Latham, *A Theory of Goal Setting and Task Performance* (Upper Saddle River, NJ: Prentice Hall, 1990); P. Ward and M. Carnes, "Effects of Posting Self-Set Goals on Collegiate Football Players' Skill Execution During Practice and Games," *Journal of Applied Behavioral Analysis,* (Spring 2002), pp. 1–12; D. W. Ray, "Productivity and Profitability," *Executive Excellence,* October 2001, p. 14; D. Archer, "Evaluating Your Managed System," *CMA Management,* January 2000, pp. 12–14; and C. Antoni, "Management by Objectives: An Effective Tool for Teamwork," *International Journal of Human Resource Management* (February 2005), pp. 174–184. For information on participation in goal setting, see, for example, T. D. Ludwig and E. S. Geller, "Intervening to Improve the Safety of Delivery Drivers: A Systematic Behavioral Approach," *Journal of Organizational Behavior Management* (April 4, 2000), pp. 11–24; P. Latham and L. M. Saari, "The Effects of Holding Goal Difficulty Constant on Assigned and Participatively Set Goals," *Academy of Management Journal* (March 1979), pp. 163–168; M. Erez, P. C. Earley, and C. L. Hulin, "The Impact of Participation on Goal Acceptance and Performance: A Two Step Model," *Academy of Management Journal* (March 1985), pp. 50–66; and G. P. Latham, M. Erez, and E. A. Locke, "Resolving Scientific Disputes by the Joint Design of Crucial Experiments by the Antagonists: Application to the Erez Latham Dispute Regarding Participation in Goal Setting," *Journal of Applied Psychology* (November 1988), pp. 753–772. For information on effectiveness of MBO, see, for example, F. Dahlsten, A. Styhre, and M. Williander, "The Unintended Consequences of Management by Objectives: The Volume Growth Target at Volvo Cars," *Leadership & Organization Development Journal* (July 2005), pp. 529–541; J. R. Crow, "Crashing with the Nose Up: Building a Cooperative Work Environment," *Journal for Quality and Participation* (Spring 2002), pp. 45–50; and E. C. Hollensbe and J. P. Guthrie, "Group Pay-for-Performance Plans: The Role of Spontaneous Goal Setting," *Academy of Management Review,* October 2000, pp. 864–72.

19. P. N. Romani, "MBO by Any Other Name Is Still MBO," *Supervision,* December 1997, pp. 6–8; and A. W. Schrader and G. T. Seward, "MBO Makes Dollar Sense," *Personnel Journal* (July 1989), pp. 32–37.

20. R. Rodgers and J. E. Hunter, "Impact of Management by Objectives on Organizational Productivity," *Journal of Applied Psychology* (April 1991), pp. 322–336.

21. G. P. Latham, "The Motivational Benefits of Goal-Setting," *Academy of Management Executive,* November 2004, pp. 126–129.

22. For additional information on goals, see, for instance, P. Drucker, *The Executive in Action* (New York: HarperCollins Books, 1996), pp. 207–214; and E. A. Locke and G. P. Latham,

A Theory of Goal Setting and Task Performance (Upper Saddle River, NJ: Prentice Hall, 1990).

23. J. L. Roberts, "Signed, Sealed, Delivered?" *Newsweek,* June 20, 2005, pp. 44–46.

24. Several of these factors were suggested by R. K. Bresser and R. C. Bishop, "Dysfunctional Effects of Formal Planning: Two Theoretical Explanations," *Academy of Management Review*, October 1983, pp. 588–599; and J. S. Armstrong, "The Value of Formal Planning for Strategic Decisions: Review of Empirical Research," *Strategic Management Journal*, (July–September 1982), pp. 197–211.

25. K. Garber, "Powering the Information Age," *U.S. News & World Report,* April 2009, pp. 46–48; and S. Hamm, "It's Too Darn Hot," *BusinessWeek,* March 31, 2008, pp, 60–63.

26. A. Campbell, "Tailored, Not Benchmarked: A Fresh Look at Corporate Planning," *Harvard Business Review*, March–April 1999, pp. 41–50.

27. And the Survey Says box based on American Management Association, "Mercer Study Shows Workforce Priorities for 2010," www.amanet.org (October 21, 2009); M. Weinstein, "Coming Up Short? Join the Club," *Training* (April 2006), p. 14; J. Yang and M. E. Mullins, "Employee's Concerns in Mergers and Acquisitions," *USA Today,* June 6, 2007, p. 1B; J. Choi, D. Lovallo, and A. Tarasova, "Better Strategy for Business Units: A McKinsey Global Survey," *McKinsey Quarterly Online,* www.mckinseyquarterly.com (July 2007); G. Kranz, "Workers Unprepared," *Workforce Management Online,* March 13, 2008; and American Management Association, "2003 Survey on Leadership Challenges," www.amanet.org.

28. J. H. Sheridan, "Focused on Flow," *IW,* October 18, 1999, pp. 46–51.

29. Brews and Hunt, "Learning to Plan and Planning to Learn: Resolving the Planning School/Learning School Debate."

30. R. J. Newman, "Coming and Going," *U.S. News and World Report,* January 23, 2006, pp. 50–52; T. Atlas, "Bangalore's Big Dreams," *U.S. News and World Report,* May 2, 2005, pp. 50–52; and K. H. Hammonds, "Smart, Determined, Ambitious, Cheap: The New Face of Global Competition," *Fast Company,* February 2003, pp. 90–97.

31. See, for example, P. Tarraf and R. Molz, "Competitive Intelligence," *SAM Advanced Management Journal* (Autumn 2006), pp. 24–34; W. M. Fitzpatrick, "Uncovering Trade Secrets: The Legal and Ethical Conundrum of Creative Competitive Intelligence," *SAM Advanced Management Journal* (Summer 2003), pp. 4–12; L. Lavelle, "The Case of the Corporate Spy," *BusinessWeek,* November 26, 2001, pp. 56–58; C. Britton, "Deconstructing Advertising: What Your Competitor's Advertising Can Tell You About Their Strategy," *Competitive Intelligence,* January/February 2002, pp. 15–19; and L. Smith, "Business Intelligence Progress in Jeopardy," *InformationWeek,* March 4, 2002, p. 74.

32. S. Greenbard, "New Heights in Business Intelligence," *Business Finance,* March 2002, pp. 41–46; K. A. Zimmermann, "The Democratization of Business Intelligence," *KN World,* May 2002, pp. 20–21; and C. Britton, "Deconstructing Advertising: What Your Competitor's Advertising Can Tell You About Their Strategy," *Competitive Intelligence,* January–February 2002, pp. 15–19.

33. C. Hausman, "Business-Ethics News Featured in World-Press Reports," *Ethics Newsline,* March 14, 2011; and L. Weathersby, "Take This Job and ***** It," *Fortune,* January 7, 2002, p. 122.

34. P. Lattiman, "Hilton and Starwood Settle Dispute," *New York Times Online,* December 22, 2010; "Starwood vs. Hilton," *Hotels' Investment Outlook,* June 2009, p. 14; R. Kidder, "Hotel Industry Roiled by Corporate Espionage Claim," *Ethics Newsline,* www.globalethicslorg/newsline; Reuters, "Hilton Hotels Is Subpoenaed in Espionage Case," *New York Times Online,* April 22, 2009; T. Audi, "U.S. Probes Hilton Over Theft Claims," *Wall Street Journal,* April 22, 2009, p. B1; and T. Audi, "Hilton Is Sued Over Luxury Chain," *Wall Street Journal,* April 17, 2009, p. B1.

35. B. Rosner, "HR Should Get a Clue: Corporate Spying Is Real," *Workforce,* April 2001, pp. 72–75.

36. K. Western, "Ethical Spying," *Business Ethics,* September–October 1995, pp. 22–23.

CHAPTER 6

Organizational Structure and Design

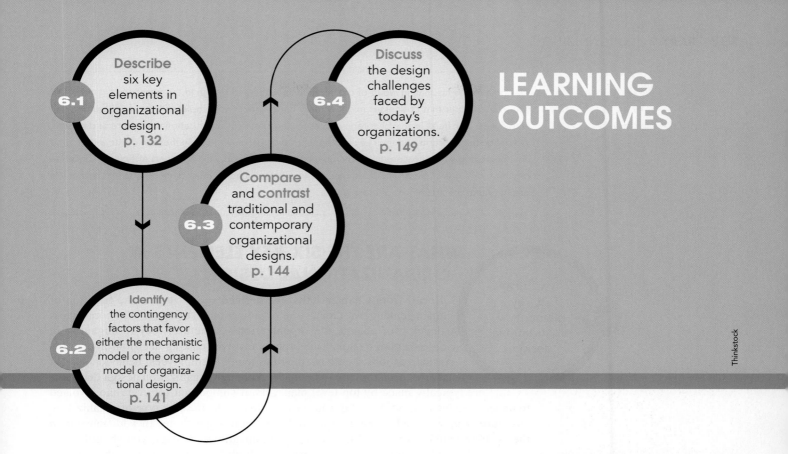

LEARNING
OUTCOMES

6.1 Describe six key elements in organizational design. p. 132

6.2 Identify the contingency factors that favor either the mechanistic model or the organic model of organizational design. p. 141

6.3 Compare and contrast traditional and contemporary organizational designs. p. 144

6.4 Discuss the design challenges faced by today's organizations. p. 149

Thinkstock

Volunteers Work

They're individuals you might never have thought of as being part of an organization's structure, but for many organizations, volunteers provide a much-needed source of labor.[1] Maybe you've volunteered at a Habitat for Humanity build, a homeless shelter, or some nonprofit organization. However, what if the volunteer assignment was at a for-profit business and the job description read like this: "Spend a few hours a day, at your computer, supplying answers online to customer questions about technical matters like how to set up an Internet home network or how to program a new high-definition television," all for no pay. Many large corporations, start-up companies, and venture capitalists are betting that this "emerging corps of Web-savvy helpers will transform the field of customer service."

Welcome to the fascinating world of organization structure and design in the twenty-first century! Did you ever consider that businesses might actually have work tasks completed by someone other than employees...for free? In this chapter, we present the basics of organizational structure and design. We define the concepts and their key components and how managers use these to create a structured environment in which organizational members can do their work efficiently and effectively. Once the organization's goals, plans, and strategies are in place, managers must develop a structure that will best facilitate the attainment of those goals.

WHAT ARE THE SIX KEY ELEMENTS IN ORGANIZATIONAL DESIGN?

6.1 Describe six key elements in organizational design.

Recall from Chapter 1 that we defined **organizing** as the function of management that creates the organization's structure. When managers develop or change the organization's structure, they're engaging in **organization design**. This process involves making decisions about how specialized jobs should be, the rules to guide employees' behaviors, and at what level decisions are to be made. Although organization design decisions are typically made by top-level managers, it's important for everyone involved to understand the process. Why? Because each of us works in some type of organization structure, and we need to know how and why things get done. In addition, given the changing environment and the need for organizations to adapt, you should begin understanding what tomorrow's structures may look like—they will be the settings you'll be working in.

Few topics in management have undergone as much change in the past few years as that of organizing and organizational structure. Managers are reevaluating traditional approaches and exploring new structural designs that best support and facilitate employees doing the organization's work—designs that can achieve efficiency but are also flexible.

The basic concepts of organization design formulated by management writers such as Henri Fayol and Max Weber offered structural principles for managers to follow. Almost 80 years have passed since many of those principles were originally proposed. Given that length of time and all the changes that have taken place, you'd think that those principles would be mostly worthless today. Surprisingly, they're not. They still provide valuable insights into designing effective and efficient organizations. Of course, we've also gained a great deal of knowledge over the years as to their limitations. In the following sections, we discuss the six basic elements of organizational structure: work specialization, departmentalization, authority and responsibility, span of control, centralization versus decentralization, and formalization.

What Is Work Specialization?

At the Wilson Sporting Goods factory in Ada, Ohio, workers make every football used in the National Football League and most of those used in college and high school football games. To meet daily output goals, the workers specialize in job tasks such as molding, stitching and sewing, lacing, and so forth.[2] This is an example of **work specialization**, which is dividing work activities into separate job tasks. Individual employees "specialize" in doing part of an activity rather than the entire activity in order to increase work output. It's also known as division of labor.

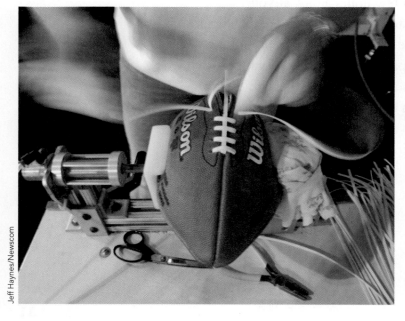

Wilson Sporting Goods Company uses work specialization in making some 700,000 footballs a year for the Pee Wee leagues to the National Football Association. The activities involved in handcrafting a Wilson football are divided into 13 separate job tasks, beginning with cutting panels from leather and ending with putting the balls into a form and filling them with high pressure. Shown here is an employee specializing in the task of lacing the ball. Also known as division of labor, work specialization is an organizing mechanism that helps employees boost their productivity and makes efficient use of workers' diverse skills.

Jeff Haynes/Newscom

Work specialization allows organizations to efficiently use the diversity of skills that workers have. In most organizations, some tasks require highly developed skills; others can be performed by employees with lower skill levels. If all workers were engaged in all the steps of, say, a manufacturing process, all would need the skills necessary to perform both the most demanding and the least demanding jobs. Thus, except when performing the most highly skilled or highly sophisticated tasks, employees would be working below their skill levels. In addition, skilled workers are paid more than unskilled workers, and, because wages tend to reflect the highest level of skill, all workers would be paid at highly skilled rates to do easy tasks—an inefficient use of resources. This concept explains why you rarely find a cardiac surgeon closing up a patient after surgery. Instead, doctors doing their residencies in open-heart surgery and learning the skill usually stitch and staple the patient after the surgeon has finished the surgery.

Early proponents of work specialization believed that it could lead to great increases in productivity. At the beginning of the twentieth century, that generalization was reasonable. Because specialization was not widely practiced, its introduction almost always generated higher productivity. But a good thing can be carried too far. At some point, the human diseconomies—boredom, fatigue, stress, low productivity, poor quality, increased absenteeism, and high turnover—exceed the economic advantages (see Exhibit 6–1).[3]

WHAT IS TODAY'S VIEW OF SPECIALIZATION? Most managers today see work specialization as an important organizing mechanism because it helps employees be more efficient. For example, McDonald's uses high specialization to get its products made and delivered to customers efficiently. However, managers also have to recognize its limitations. That's why companies such as Avery-Dennison, Ford Australia, Hallmark, and American Express use minimal work specialization and instead give employees a broad range of tasks to do.

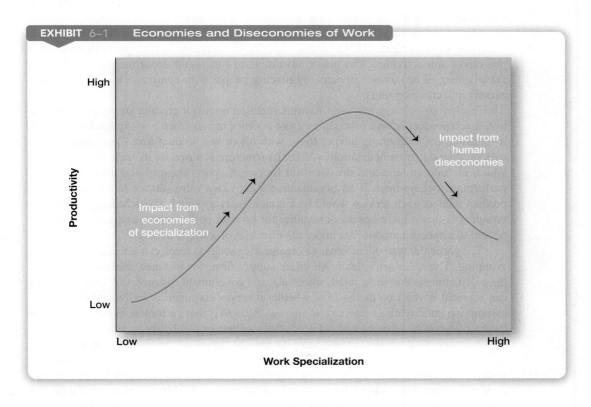

EXHIBIT 6–1   **Economies and Diseconomies of Work**

---

organizing
The function of management that creates the organization's structure

organization design
When managers develop or change the organization's structure

work specialization
Dividing work activities into separate job tasks; also called division of labor

EXHIBIT 6–2	Types of Departmentalization
• **Functional**	Groups employees based on work performed (e.g., engineering, accounting, information systems, human resources)
• **Product**	Groups employees based on major product areas in the corporation (e.g., women's footwear, men's footwear, and apparel and accessories)
• **Customer**	Groups employees based on customers' problems and needs (e.g., wholesale, retail, government)
• **Geographic**	Groups employees based on location served (e.g., North, South, Midwest, East)
• **Process**	Groups employees based on the basis of work or customer flow (e.g., testing, payment)

What Is Departmentalization?

Early management writers argued that after deciding what job tasks will be done by whom, common work activities needed to be grouped back together so work gets done in a coordinated and integrated way. How jobs are grouped together is called departmentalization. There are five common forms of departmentalization (see Exhibit 6–2) although an organization may use its own unique classification. No single method of departmentalization was advocated by the early writers. The method or methods used should reflect the grouping that would best contribute to the attainment of the goals of the organization and the individual units.

HOW ARE ACTIVITIES GROUPED?   One of the most popular ways to group activities is by functions performed, or functional departmentalization. A manager might organize the workplace by separating engineering, accounting, information systems, human resources, and purchasing specialists into departments. Functional departmentalization can be used in all types of organizations. Only the functions change to reflect the organization's objectives and activities. The major advantage to functional departmentalization is the achievement of economies of scale by placing people with common skills and specializations into common units.

Product departmentalization focuses attention on major product areas in the corporation. Each product is under the authority of a senior manager who is a specialist in, and is responsible for, everything having to do with his or her product line. One company that uses product departmentalization is Nike. Its structure is based on its varied product lines, which include athletic and dress/casual footwear, sports apparel and accessories, and performance equipment. If an organization's activities were service related rather than product related, each service would be autonomously grouped. The advantage of product grouping is that it increases accountability for product performance, because all activities related to a specific product are under the direction of a single manager.

The particular type of customer an organization seeks to reach can also dictate employee grouping. The sales activities in an office supply firm, for instance, can be divided into three departments that serve retail, wholesale, and government customers. A large law office can segment its staff on the basis of whether it serves corporate or individual clients. The assumption underlying customer departmentalization is that customers in each department have a common set of problems and needs that can best be met by specialists.

Another way to departmentalize is on the basis of geography or territory—geographic departmentalization. The sales function might have western, southern, midwestern, and eastern regions. If an organization's customers are scattered over a large geographic area, this form of departmentalization can be valuable. For instance, the organization structure of Coca-Cola reflects the company's operations in two broad geographic areas—the North American sector and the international sector (which includes the Pacific Rim, the European Community, Northeast Europe and Africa, and Latin America).

The final form of departmentalization is called process departmentalization, which groups activities on the basis of work or customer flow—like that found in many states' motor vehicle offices or in health care clinics. Units are organized around common skills needed to complete a certain process. If you've ever been to a state motor vehicle office to get a driver's license, you've probably experienced process departmentalization. With separate departments to handle applications, testing, information and photo processing, and payment collection, customers "flow" through the various departments in sequence to get their licenses.

WHAT IS TODAY'S VIEW OF DEPARTMENTALIZATION? Most large organizations continue to use most or all of the departmental groups suggested by the early management writers. Black & Decker, for instance, organizes its divisions along functional lines, its manufacturing units around processes, its sales around geographic regions, and its sales regions around customer groupings. However, many organizations use **cross-functional teams**, which are

teams made up of individuals from various departments and that cross traditional departmental lines. These teams have been useful especially as tasks have become more complex and diverse skills are needed to accomplish those tasks.[4]

Finally, today's competitive environment has refocused the attention of management on its customers. To better monitor the needs of customers and to be able to respond to changes in those needs, many organizations are giving greater emphasis to customer departmentalization.

What Are Authority and Responsibility?

To understand authority and responsibility, you also have to be familiar with the **chain of command**, the line of authority extending from upper organizational levels to lower levels, which clarifies who reports to whom. Managers need to consider it when organizing work because it helps employees with questions such as "Who do I report to?" or "Who do I go to if I have a problem?" So, what *are* authority and responsibility?

Authority refers to the rights inherent in a managerial position to give orders and expect the orders to be obeyed. Authority was a major concept discussed by the early management writers as they viewed it as the glue that held an organization together.[5] It was delegated downward to lower-level managers, giving them certain rights while prescribing certain limits within which to operate. Each management position had specific inherent rights that incumbents acquired from the position's rank or title. Authority, therefore, is related to one's position within an organization and has nothing to do with the personal characteristics of an individual manager. When a position of authority is vacated, the person who has left the position no longer has any authority. The authority remains with the position and its new incumbent.

When managers delegate authority, they must allocate commensurate **responsibility**. That is, when employees are given rights, they also assume a corresponding obligation to perform. And they should be held accountable for their performance! Allocating authority without responsibility and accountability creates opportunities for abuse. Likewise, no one should be held responsible or accountable for something over which he or she has no authority.

At Dell, customer departmentalization allows the computer firm to better understand its customers and respond to their needs. Dell organizes its customers into eight segments: home and home office, small and medium business, large business, state and local government, federal government, K through 12 institutions, higher education institutions, and health care. To reach more home and home-office users, Dell has adopted a retail strategy that enables consumers to buy its personal computers in retail outlets worldwide. Through a partnership with Gome Group, China's largest electronics retailer, Dell plans to expand its laptop and desktop sales. Shown here are Dell products on display at a Gome store in Beijing.

---

departmentalization
How jobs are grouped together

functional departmentalization
Grouping activities by functions performed

product departmentalization
Grouping activities by major product areas

customer departmentalization
Grouping activities by customer

geographic departmentalization
Grouping activities on the basis of geography or territory

process departmentalization
Grouping activities on the basis of work or customer flow

cross-functional teams
Teams made up of individuals from various departments and that cross traditional departmental lines

chain of command
The line of authority extending from upper organizational levels to lower levels, which clarifies who reports to whom

authority
The rights inherent in a managerial position to give orders and expect the orders to be obeyed

responsibility
An obligation to perform assigned duties

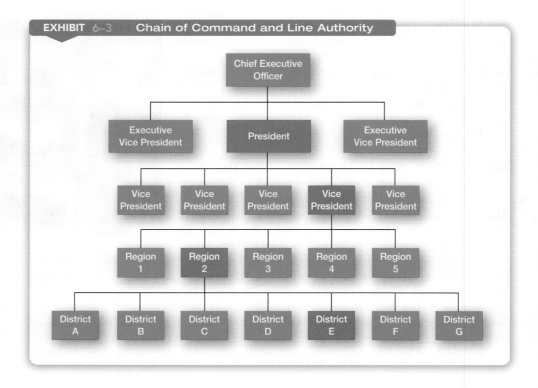

EXHIBIT 6–3   Chain of Command and Line Authority

WHAT ARE THE DIFFERENT TYPES OF AUTHORITY RELATIONSHIPS?   The early management writers distinguished between two forms of authority: line authority and staff authority. Line authority entitles a manager to direct the work of an employee. It is the employer–employee authority relationship that extends from the top of the organization to the lowest echelon, according to the chain of command, as shown in Exhibit 6–3. As a link in the chain of command, a manager with line authority has the right to direct the work of employees and to make certain decisions without consulting anyone. Of course, in the chain of command, every manager is also subject to the direction of his or her superior.

Keep in mind that sometimes the term *line* is used to differentiate line managers from staff managers. In this context, *line* refers to managers whose organizational function contributes directly to the achievement of organizational objectives. In a manufacturing firm, line managers are typically in the production and sales functions, whereas managers in human resources and payroll are considered staff managers with staff authority. Whether a manager's function is classified as line or staff depends on the organization's objectives. For example, at Staff Builders, a supplier of temporary employees, interviewers have a line function. Similarly, at the payroll firm of ADP, payroll is a line function.

As organizations get larger and more complex, line managers find that they do not have the time, expertise, or resources to get their jobs done effectively. In response, they create staff authority functions to support, assist, advise, and generally reduce some of their informational burdens. The hospital administrator cannot effectively handle the purchasing of all the supplies the hospital needs, so she creates a purchasing department, a staff department. Of course, the head of the purchasing department has line authority over the purchasing agents who work for him. The hospital administrator might also find that she is overburdened and needs an assistant. In creating the position of her assistant, she has created a staff position. Exhibit 6–4 illustrates line and staff authority.

WHAT IS UNITY OF COMMAND?   An employee who has to report to two or more bosses might have to cope with conflicting demands or priorities.[6] Accordingly, the early writers believed that each employee should report to only one manager, a term called unity of command. In those rare instances when the unity of command had to be violated, a clear separation of activities and a supervisor responsible for each was always explicitly designated.

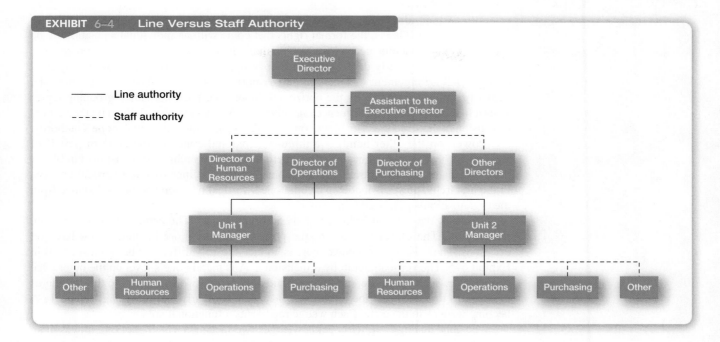

EXHIBIT 6-4   Line Versus Staff Authority

Unity of command was logical when organizations were relatively simple. Under some circumstances it is still sound advice and organizations continue to adhere to it. But advances in technology, for instance, allow access to organizational information that was once accessible only to top managers. Moreover, with computers, employees can communicate with anyone else in the organization without going through the formal communication channels of the chain of command. As such, in some instances, strict adherence to the unity of command creates a degree of inflexibility that hinders an organization's performance.

HOW DOES TODAY'S VIEW OF AUTHORITY AND RESPONSIBILITY DIFFER FROM THE HISTORICAL VIEW?   The early management writers were enamored of authority. They assumed that the rights inherent in one's formal position in an organization were the sole source of influence, and they believed that managers were all-powerful. This assumption might have been true 60 or even 30 years ago. Organizations were simpler. Staff was less important. Managers were only minimally dependent on technical specialists. Under such conditions, influence is the same as authority. And the higher a manager's position in the organization, the more influence he or she had. However, those conditions no longer exist. Researchers and practitioners of management now recognize that you don't have to be a manager to have power and that power is not perfectly correlated with one's level in the organization.

Authority is an important concept in organizations, but an exclusive focus on authority produces a narrow, unrealistic view of influence. Today, we recognize that authority is but one element in the larger concept of power.

HOW DO AUTHORITY AND POWER DIFFER?   Authority and power are often considered the same thing, but they're not. Authority is a right. Its legitimacy is based on an authority figure's position in the organization. Authority goes with the job. **Power**, on the other hand,

---

line authority
Authority that entitles a manager to direct the work of an employee

staff authority
Positions with some authority that have been created to support, assist, and advise those holding line authority

unity of command
Structure in which each employee reports to only one manager

power
An individual's capacity to influence decisions

refers to an individual's capacity to influence decisions. Authority is part of the larger concept of power. That is, the formal rights that come with an individual's position in the organization are just one means by which an individual can affect the decision process.

Exhibit 6–5 visually depicts the difference between authority and power. The two-dimensional arrangement of boxes in part A portrays authority. The area in which the authority applies is defined by the horizontal dimension. Each horizontal grouping represents a functional area. The influence one holds in the organization is defined by the vertical dimension in the structure. The higher one is in the organization, the greater one's authority.

Power, on the other hand, is a three-dimensional concept (the cone in part B of Exhibit 6–5). It includes not only the functional and hierarchical dimensions but also a third dimension called centrality. Although authority is defined by one's vertical position in the hierarchy, power is made up of both one's vertical position and one's distance from the organization's power core or center.

Think of the cone in Exhibit 6–5 as an organization. The center of the cone is the power core. The closer you are to the power core, the more influence you have on decisions. The existence of a power core is, in fact, the only difference between A and B in Exhibit 6–5. The vertical hierarchy dimension in A is merely one's level on the outer edge of the cone. The top of the cone corresponds to the top of the hierarchy, the middle of the cone to the middle of the hierarchy, and so on. Similarly, the functional groups in A become wedges in the cone. Each wedge represents a functional area.

The cone analogy explicitly acknowledges two facts: (1) The higher one moves in an organization (an increase in authority), the closer one moves to the power core; and (2) it is not necessary to have authority in order to wield power because one can move horizontally inward toward the power core without moving up. For instance, assistants often are

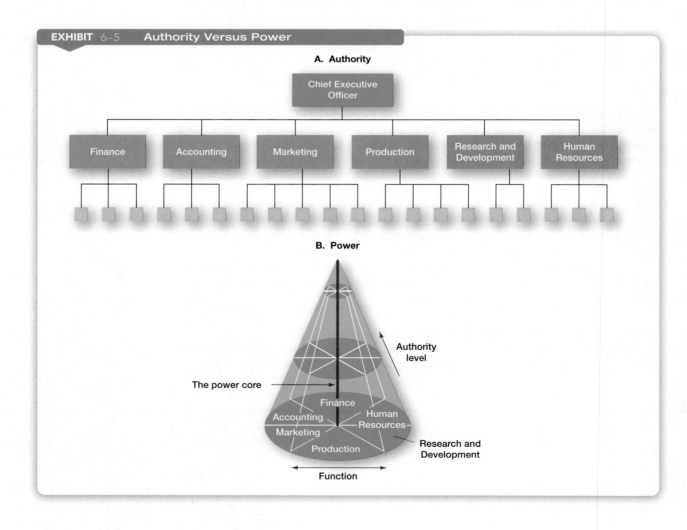

EXHIBIT 6–5   Authority Versus Power

A. Authority

Chief Executive Officer

Finance   Accounting   Marketing   Production   Research and Development   Human Resources

B. Power

Authority level

The power core

Finance
Accounting
Marketing
Human Resources
Production
Research and Development

Function

EXHIBIT 6–6	Types of Power
Coercive power	Power based on fear.
Reward power	Power based on the ability to distribute something that others value.
Legitimate power	Power based on one's position in the formal hierarchy.
Expert power	Power based on one's expertise, special skill, or knowledge.
Referent power	Power based on identification with a person who has desirable resources or personal traits.

powerful in a company even though they have little authority. As gatekeepers for their bosses, these assistants have considerable influence over whom their bosses see and when they see them. Furthermore, because they're regularly relied upon to pass information on to their bosses, they have some control over what their bosses hear. It's not unusual for a $105,000-a-year middle manager to tread carefully in order not to upset the boss's $45,000-a-year administrative assistant. Why? Because the assistant has power. This individual may be low in the authority hierarchy but close to the power core.

Likewise, low-ranking employees who have relatives, friends, or associates in high places might also be close to the power core. So, too, are employees with scarce and important skills. The lowly production engineer with 20 years of experience in a company might be the only one in the firm who knows the inner workings of all the old production machinery. When pieces of this old equipment break down, only this engineer understands how to fix them. Suddenly, the engineer's influence is much greater than it would appear from his or her level in the vertical hierarchy. What do these examples tell us about power? They indicate that power can come from different areas. French and Raven identified five sources, or bases, of power: coercive, reward, legitimate, expert, and referent.[7] We summarize them in Exhibit 6–6.

What Is Span of Control?

How many employees can a manager efficiently and effectively supervise? This question of **span of control** received a great deal of attention from early management writers. Although early writers came to no consensus on a specific number, most favored small spans—typically no more than six workers—in order to maintain close control.[8] However, several writers did acknowledge level in the organization as a contingency variable. They argued that as a manager rises in an organization, he or she has to deal with a greater number of unstructured problems, so top managers need a smaller span than do middle managers, and middle managers require a smaller span than do supervisors. Over the last decade, however, we've seen some change in theories about effective spans of control.[9]

Many organizations are increasing their spans of control. The span for managers at such companies as General Electric and Kaiser Aluminum has expanded significantly in the past decade. It has also expanded in the federal government, where efforts to increase the span of control are being implemented to save time in making decisions.[10] The span of control is increasingly being determined by looking at contingency variables. It's obvious that the more training and experience employees have, the less direct supervision they need. Managers who have well-trained and experienced employees can function with a wider span. Other contingency variables that determine the appropriate span include similarity of employee tasks, the complexity of those tasks, the physical

Decentralization is key to the success of the Nordstrom department store chain. Empowering employees, like the managers and salespeople at a new store opening shown here, is a primary reason why Nordstrom stands out as the model of customer service in the retail industry. Nordstrom has built a strong corporate culture that empowers buyers, store managers, department managers, and salespeople to make decisions in the best interest of their customers. Buyers are given the freedom to acquire merchandise that reflects local lifestyles and tastes, salespeople are empowered to accept returned merchandise, and department managers have the authority to make decisions about hiring, training, and evaluating their sales teams.

Jeff Gritchen/Newscom

span of control
The number of employees a manager can efficiently and effectively supervise

RIGHT ? WRONG

It's probably an understatement to say that people were excited about the introduction of Apple's iPad.[11] Then the news broke that a small group of computer experts calling themselves Goatse Security had hacked into AT&T's Web site and found numbers that identified iPads connected to AT&T's mobile network and those numbers allowed the group to uncover 114,000 e-mail addresses of thousands of first-adopter iPad customers including prominent officials in companies, politics, and the military. AT&T called it an act of malice, condemned the hackers, and apologized to its affected customers. The group that exposed the flaw said that it did a "public service." One analyst for CNET also said that the group did a good thing. "Ethical hacking" was a phrase used. "Security researchers often disclose holes to keep vendors honest. Many sources complain that they notify companies of security vulnerabilities and that the companies take months, or even years, to provide a fix to customers. In the meantime, malicious hackers could have discovered the same hole and used it to steal data, infect computers, or attack systems without the computer owner knowing there is even a risk."

Think About:

- What do you think? Is there such a thing as "ethical hacking"?
- What ethical issues do you see here?
- What are the implications for various stakeholders in this situation?

proximity of employees, the degree to which standardized procedures are in place, the sophistication of the organization's management information system, the strength of the organization's value system, and the preferred managing style of the manager.[12]

How Do Centralization and Decentralization Differ?

One of the questions that needs to be answered when organizing is "At what level are decisions made?" **Centralization** is the degree to which decision making takes place at upper levels of the organization. **Decentralization** is the degree to which lower-level managers provide input or actually make decisions. Centralization-decentralization is not an either-or concept. Rather, it's a matter of degree. What we mean is that no organization is completely centralized or completely decentralized. Few, if any, organizations could effectively function if all their decisions were made by a select few people (centralization) or if all decisions were pushed down to the level closest to the problems (decentralization). Let's look, then, at how the early management writers viewed centralization as well as at how it exists today.

Early management writers proposed that centralization in an organization depended on the situation.[13] Their goal was the optimum and efficient use of employees. Traditional organizations were structured in a pyramid, with power and authority concentrated near the top of the organization. Given this structure, historically centralized decisions were the most prominent, but organizations today have become more complex and responsive to dynamic changes in their environments. As such, many managers believe that decisions need to be made by those individuals closest to the problems, regardless of their organizational level. In fact, the trend over the past several decades—at least in U.S. and Canadian organizations—has been a movement toward more decentralization in organizations.[14]

WHAT IS TODAY'S VIEW OF CENTRALIZATION-DECENTRALIZATION? Today, managers often choose the amount of centralization or decentralization that will allow them to best implement their decisions and achieve organizational goals.[15] What works in one organization, however, won't necessarily work in another, so managers must determine the amount of decentralization for each organization and work units within it. When managers empower employees and delegate to them the authority to make decisions on those things that affect their work and to change the way that they think about work, that's decentralization. Notice, however, that it doesn't imply that top-level managers no longer make decisions.

What Is Formalization?

Formalization refers to how standardized an organization's jobs are and the extent to which employee behavior is guided by rules and procedures. In highly formalized organizations, there are explicit job descriptions, numerous organizational rules, and clearly defined procedures covering work processes. Employees have little discretion over what's done, when it's done, and how it's done. However, where formalization is low, employees have more discretion in how they do their work. Early management writers expected organizations to be fairly formalized, as formalization went hand-in-hand with bureaucratic-style organizations.

WHAT IS TODAY'S VIEW OF FORMALIZATION?   Although some formalization is necessary for consistency and control, many organizations today rely less on strict rules and standardization to guide and regulate employee behavior. For instance, consider the following situation:

> A customer comes into a branch of a large national drug store chain and drops off a roll of film for same-day developing 37 minutes after the store's cut-off time. Although the sales clerk knows he's supposed to follow the rules, he also knows he could get the film developed with no problem and wants to accommodate the customer. So he accepts the film and hopes that his manager won't find out.[16]

Did this employee do something wrong? He did "break" the rule. But by "breaking" the rule, he actually brought in revenue and provided good customer service.

Considering there are numerous situations where rules may be too restrictive, many organizations have allowed employees some latitude, giving them sufficient autonomy to make those decisions that they feel are best under the circumstances. It doesn't mean throwing out all organizational rules because there always *will* be rules that are important for employees to follow—and these rules should be explained so employees understand why it's important to adhere to them. But for other rules, employees may be given some leeway.[17]

WHAT CONTINGENCY VARIABLES AFFECT STRUCTURAL CHOICE?

The most appropriate structure to use will depend on contingency factors. In this section, we address two generic organization structure models and then look at the more popular contingency variables—strategy, size, technology, and environment.

Identify the contingency factors that favor either the mechanistic model or the organic model of organizational design.

6.2

How Is a Mechanistic Organization Different from an Organic Organization?

Exhibit 6–7 describes two organizational forms.[18] The mechanistic organization (or bureaucracy) was the natural result of combining the six elements of structure. Adhering to the chain-of-command principle ensured the existence of a formal hierarchy of authority, with each person controlled and supervised by one superior. Keeping the span of control small at increasingly higher levels in the organization created tall, impersonal structures. As the distance between the top and the bottom of the organization expanded, top management would increasingly impose rules and regulations. Because top managers couldn't control lower-level activities through direct observation and ensure the use of standard practices, they substituted rules and regulations. The early management writers' belief in a high degree of work specialization created jobs that were simple, routine, and standardized. Further specialization through the use of

centralization
The degree to which decision making takes place at upper levels of the organization

decentralization
The degree to which lower-level managers provide input or actually make decisions

formalization
How standardized an organization's jobs are and the extent to which employee behavior is guided by rules and procedures

mechanistic organization
A bureaucratic organization; a structure that's high in specialization, formalization, and centralization

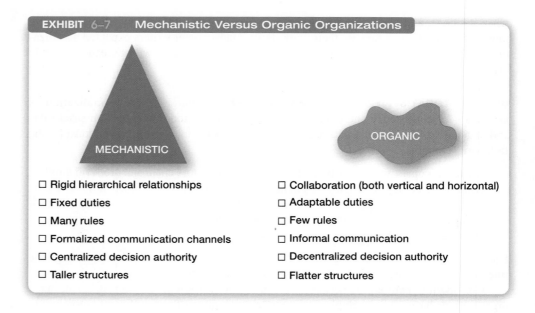

EXHIBIT 6–7   Mechanistic Versus Organic Organizations

MECHANISTIC

- ☐ Rigid hierarchical relationships
- ☐ Fixed duties
- ☐ Many rules
- ☐ Formalized communication channels
- ☐ Centralized decision authority
- ☐ Taller structures

ORGANIC

- ☐ Collaboration (both vertical and horizontal)
- ☐ Adaptable duties
- ☐ Few rules
- ☐ Informal communication
- ☐ Decentralized decision authority
- ☐ Flatter structures

departmentalization increased impersonality and the need for multiple layers of management to coordinate the specialized departments.

The **organic organization** is a highly adaptive form that is as loose and flexible as the mechanistic organization is rigid and stable. Rather than having standardized jobs and regulations, the organic organization's loose structure allows it to change rapidly as required.[19] It has division of labor, but the jobs people do are not standardized. Employees tend to be professionals who are technically proficient and trained to handle diverse problems. They need few formal rules and little direct supervision because their training has instilled in them standards of professional conduct. For instance, a petroleum engineer doesn't need to be given procedures on how to locate oil sources miles offshore. The engineer can solve most problems alone or after conferring with colleagues. Professional standards guide his or her behavior. The organic organization is low in centralization so that the professional can respond quickly to problems and because top-level managers cannot be expected to possess the expertise to make necessary decisions.

Top managers typically put a great deal of thought into designing an appropriate structure. What that appropriate structure is depends on four contingency variables: the organization's strategy, size, technology, and degree of environmental uncertainty. Let's look at these contingency variables.

How Does Strategy Affect Structure?

An organization's structure should facilitate goal achievement. Because goals are an important part of the organization's strategies, it's only logical that strategy and structure are closely linked. Alfred Chandler initially researched this relationship.[20] He studied several large U.S. companies and concluded that changes in corporate strategy led to changes in an organization's structure that supported the strategy. Specifically, he found that organizations usually begin with a single product or line. The simplicity of the strategy required only a simple or loose form of structure to execute it. As such, decisions could be centralized in the hands of a single senior manager, and complexity and formalization were low. However, as organizations grew, their strategies become more ambitious and elaborate.

Research has shown that certain structural designs work best with different organizational strategies.[21] For instance, the flexibility and free-flowing information of the organic structure works well when an organization is pursuing meaningful and unique innovations. The mechanistic organization with its efficiency, stability, and tight controls works best for companies wanting to tightly control costs.

How Does Size Affect Structure?

There's considerable evidence that an organization's size affects its structure.[22] Large organizations—typically considered to be those with more than 2,000 employees—tend to have more specialization, departmentalization, centralization, and rules and regulations than do small organizations. However, once an organization grows past a certain size, size has less influence on structure. Why? Essentially, once there are around 2,000 employees, it's already fairly mechanistic. Adding another 500 employees won't impact the structure much. On the other hand, adding 500 employees to an organization that has only 300 employees is likely to make it more mechanistic.

How Does Technology Affect Structure?

Every organization uses some form of technology to convert its inputs into outputs. For instance, workers at Whirlpool's Brazilian facility build microwave ovens and air conditioners on a standardized assembly line. Employees at FedEx Kinko's do custom design and print jobs for individual customers. And employees at Bayer's facility in Pakistan make pharmaceutical products using a continuous-flow production line. The initial research on technology's effect on structure can be traced to Joan Woodward.[23] For more information on her ground-breaking work, see the From the Past to the Present box.

From the Past to the Present

Joan Woodward, a British management scholar, studied small manufacturing firms in southern England to determine the extent to which structural design elements were related to organizational success.[24] She couldn't find any consistent pattern until she divided the firms into three distinct technologies that had increasing levels of complexity and sophistication. The first category, **unit production**, described the production of items in units or small batches. The second category, **mass production**, described large-batch manufacturing. Finally, the third and most technically complex group, **process production**, included continuous-process production. A summary of her findings regarding technology and appropriate organizational structure is shown in Exhibit 6–8.

Woodward's study of technology and organizational structure is one of the earliest studies of contingency theory. Her answer to the "it depends on" question would be that appropriate organizational design depends on what the organization's technology is. Other more recent studies also have shown that organizations adapt their structures to their technology depending on how routine their technology is for transforming inputs into outputs. In general, the more routine the technology, the more mechanistic the structure can be, and organizations with more nonroutine technology are more likely to have organic structures.

Think About:

- Give some examples of products produced by each of the three distinct technologies.
- Why would a mechanistic structure be more appropriate for an organization with a routine technology?
- Likewise, why would an organic structure be more appropriate for an organization with a nonroutine technology?
- Do you think Woodward's framework would still apply to today's organizations? Why or why not?

EXHIBIT 6–8   Woodward's Findings on Technology and Structure

	UNIT PRODUCTION	MASS PRODUCTION	PROCESS PRODUCTION
Structural characteristics:	Low vertical differentiation	Moderate vertical differentiation	High vertical differentiation
	Low horizontal differentiation	High horizontal differentiation	Low horizontal differentiation
	Low formalization	High formalization	Low formalization
Most effective structure:	Organic	Mechanistic	Organic

organic organization
A structure that's low in specialization, formalization, and centralization

unit production
The production of items in units or small batches

mass production
Large-batch manufacturing

process production
Continuous flow or process production

How Does the Environment Affect Structure?

In Chapter 2, we discussed the organization's environment as a constraint on managerial discretion. It also has a major effect on an organization's structure. Essentially, mechanistic organizations are most effective in stable environments. Organic organizations are best matched with dynamic and uncertain environments.

The evidence on the environment–structure relationship helps to explain why so many managers have restructured their organizations to be lean, fast, and flexible.[25] Global competition, accelerated product innovation by competitors, knowledge management, and increased demands from customers for higher quality and faster deliveries are examples of dynamic environmental forces.[26] Mechanistic organizations tend to be ill equipped to respond to rapid environmental change. As a result, managers, such as those at Samsung Electronics, are redesigning their organizations in order to make them more organic.[27]

6.3 Compare and **contrast** traditional and contemporary organizational designs.

WHAT ARE SOME COMMON ORGANIZATIONAL DESIGNS?

In making structural decisions, managers have some common designs from which to choose: traditional ones and more contemporary ones. Let's look at some of the various types of organization designs.

What Traditional Organizational Designs Can Managers Use?

When designing a structure, managers may choose one of the traditional organizational designs. These structures—simple, functional, and divisional—tend to be more mechanistic in nature. (See Exhibit 6–9 for a summary of the strengths and weaknesses of each.)

WHAT IS THE SIMPLE STRUCTURE?   Most companies start as entrepreneurial ventures using a simple structure, which is an organizational design with low departmentalization, wide spans of control, authority centralized in a single person, and little formalization.[28] The simple structure is most widely used in smaller businesses and its strengths should be obvious. It's fast, flexible, and inexpensive to maintain, and accountability is clear. However, it becomes increasingly inadequate as an organization grows, because its few policies or rules to guide operations and its high centralization result in information overload at the top. As size increases, decision making becomes slower and can eventually come to a standstill as the single executive tries to continue making all the decisions. If the

---

EXHIBIT 6–9   **Traditional Organization Designs**

Simple Structure
- **Strengths:** Fast; flexible; inexpensive to maintain; clear accountability.
- **Weaknesses:** Not appropriate as organization grows; reliance on one person is risky.

Functional Structure
- **Strengths:** Cost-saving advantages from specialization (economies of scale, minimal duplication of people and equipment); employees are grouped with others who have similar tasks.
- **Weaknesses:** Pursuit of functional goals can cause managers to lose sight of what's best for the overall organization; functional specialists become insulated and have little understanding of what other units are doing.

Divisional Structure
- **Strengths:** Focuses on results—division managers are responsible for what happens to their products and services.
- **Weaknesses:** Duplication of activities and resources increases costs and reduces efficiency.

structure is not changed and adapted to its size, the firm can lose momentum and is likely to eventually fail. The simple structure's other weakness is that it's risky: Everything depends on one person. If anything happens to the owner-manager, the organization's information and decision-making center is lost. As employees are added, however, most small businesses don't remain as simple structures. The structure tends to become more specialized and formalized. Rules and regulations are introduced, work becomes specialized, departments are created, levels of management are added, and the organization becomes increasingly bureaucratic. Two of the most popular bureaucratic design options grew out of functional and product departmentalizations and are called the functional and divisional structures.

WHAT IS THE FUNCTIONAL STRUCTURE?   A functional structure is an organizational design that groups similar or related occupational specialties together. You can think of this structure as functional departmentalization applied to the entire organization. For example, Revlon, Inc., is organized around the functions of operations, finance, human resources, and product research and development.

The strength of the functional structure lies in the advantages that accrue from work specialization. Putting like specialties together results in economies of scale, minimizes duplication of personnel and equipment, and makes employees comfortable and satisfied because it gives them the opportunity to talk the same language as their peers. The most obvious weakness of the functional structure, however, is that the organization frequently loses sight of its best interests in the pursuit of functional goals. No one function is totally responsible for results, so members within individual functions become insulated and have little understanding of what people in other functions are doing.

WHAT IS THE DIVISIONAL STRUCTURE?   The divisional structure is an organizational structure made up of separate business units or divisions.[29] In this structure, each division has limited autonomy, with a division manager who has authority over his or her unit and is responsible for performance. In divisional structures, however, the parent corporation typically acts as an external overseer to coordinate and control the various divisions, and often provides support services such as financial and legal. Health care giant Johnson & Johnson, for example, has three divisions: pharmaceuticals, medical devices and diagnostics, and consumer products. In addition, it has several subsidiaries that also manufacture and market diverse health care products.

The chief advantage of the divisional structure is that it focuses on results. Division managers have full responsibility for a product or service. The divisional structure also frees the headquarters staff from being concerned with day-to-day operating details so that they can pay attention to long-term and strategic planning. The major disadvantage of the divisional structure is duplication of activities and resources. Each division, for instance, may have a marketing research department. If there weren't any divisions, all of an organization's marketing research might be centralized and done for a fraction of the cost that divisionalization requires. Thus, the divisional form's duplication of functions increases the organization's costs and reduces efficiency.

What Contemporary Organizational Designs Can Managers Use?

Managers are finding that the traditional designs often aren't appropriate for today's increasingly dynamic and complex environment. Instead, organizations need to be lean, flexible, and innovative; that is, more organic. So managers are finding creative ways to

---

simple structure
An organizational design with low departmentalization, wide spans of control, authority centralized in a single person, and little formalization

functional structure
An organizational design that groups similar or related occupational specialties together

divisional structure
An organizational structure made up of separate business units or divisions

---

EXHIBIT 6–10   Contemporary Organization Designs

TEAM STRUCTURE

- **What it is:** A structure in which the entire organization is made up of work groups or teams.
- **Advantages:** Employees are more involved and empowered. Reduced barriers among functional areas.
- **Disadvantages:** No clear chain of command. Pressure on teams to perform.

MATRIX-PROJECT STRUCTURE

- **What it is:** Matrix is a structure that assigns specialists from different functional areas to work on projects but who return to their areas when the project is completed. Project is a structure in which employees continuously work on projects. As one project is completed, employees move on to the next project.
- **Advantages:** Fluid and flexible design that can respond to environmental changes. Faster decision making.
- **Disadvantages:** Complexity of assigning people to projects. Task and personality conflicts.

BOUNDARYLESS STRUCTURE

- **What it is:** A structure that is not defined by or limited to artificial horizontal, vertical, or external boundaries; includes *virtual* and *network* types of organizations.
- **Advantages:** Highly flexible and responsive. Utilizes talent wherever it is found.
- **Disadvantages:** Lack of control. Communication difficulties.

---

structure and organize work and are using designs such as team-based structures, matrix and project structures, and boundaryless structures.[30] (See Exhibit 6–10 for a summary of these designs.)

WHAT ARE TEAM STRUCTURES?   Larry Page and Sergey Brin, co-founders of Google, have created a corporate structure that "tackles most big projects in small, tightly focused teams."[31] A **team structure** is one in which the entire organization is made up of work teams that do the organization's work.[32] In this structure, employee empowerment is crucial because there is no line of managerial authority from top to bottom. Rather, employee teams design and do work in the way they think is best, but are also held responsible for all work performance results in their respective areas. In large organizations, the team structure complements what is typically a functional or divisional structure. This allows the organization to have the efficiency of a bureaucracy while providing the flexibility of teams. For instance, companies such as Amazon, Boeing, Hewlett-Packard, Louis Vuitton, Motorola, and Xerox extensively use employee teams to improve productivity.

Although team structures have been positive, simply arranging employees into teams is not enough. Employees must be trained to work on teams, receive cross-functional skills training, and be compensated accordingly. Without a properly implemented team-based pay plan, many of the benefits of a team structure may be lost.[33] We'll cover teams more thoroughly in Chapter 10.

WHAT ARE MATRIX AND PROJECT STRUCTURES?   In addition to team-based structures, other popular contemporary designs are the matrix and project structures. The **matrix structure** assigns specialists from different functional departments to work on projects led by a project manager. When employees finish work on an assigned project, they go back to their functional departments. One unique aspect of this design is that it creates a *dual chain of command* since employees in a matrix organization have two managers: their functional area manager and their product or project manager, who share authority.

These Google employees gather for a team meeting in the offices of the Internet search engine's European headquarters in Dublin, Ireland. At offices around the globe, Googlers work in small focused teams to perform organizational tasks, create new ideas, and resolve problems. Google's team structure is critical to the firm's focus on innovation. The company's commitment to innovation depends on team members sharing ideas and opinions, testing them, and putting them into practice. Google gives empowered team members the authority to make decisions that will get innovations to market as quickly as possible.

John Cogill/AP Images

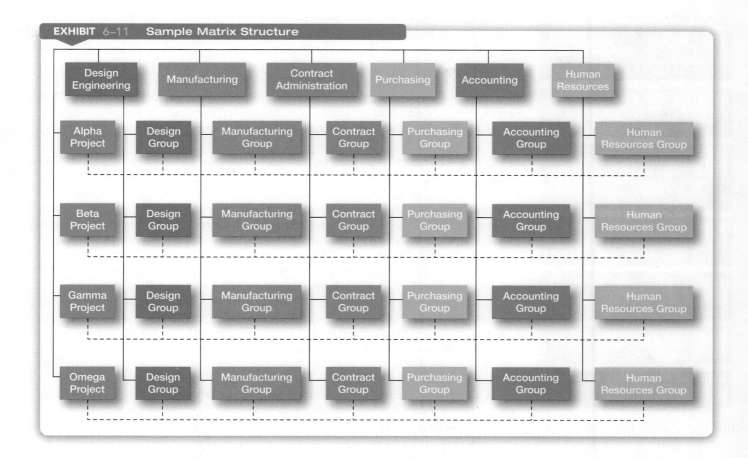

EXHIBIT 6–11   Sample Matrix Structure

(See Exhibit 6–11.) The project manager has authority over the functional members who are part of his or her project team in areas related to the project's goals. However, any decisions about promotions, salary recommendations, and annual reviews typically remain the functional manager's responsibility. To work effectively, both managers have to communicate regularly, coordinate work demands on employees, and resolve conflicts together.

The primary strength of the matrix is that it can facilitate coordination of a multiple set of complex and interdependent projects while still retaining the economies that result from keeping functional specialists grouped together. The major disadvantages of the matrix are the confusion it creates and its propensity to foster power struggles. When you dispense with the chain of command and unity of command principles, you significantly increase ambiguity. Confusion can arise over who reports to whom. The confusion and ambiguity, in turn, are what trigger the power struggles.

Instead of a matrix structure, many organizations are using a **project structure**, in which employees continuously work on projects. Unlike the matrix structure, a project structure has no formal departments where employees return at the completion of a project. Instead, employees take their specific skills, abilities, and experiences to other projects. Also, all work in project structures is performed by teams of employees. For instance, at design firm IDEO, project teams form, disband, and form again as the work requires. Employees "join" project teams because they bring needed skills and abilities to that project. Once a project is completed, however, they move on to the next one.[34]

team structure
A structure in which the entire organization is made up of work teams

matrix structure
A structure in which specialists from different functional departments are assigned to work on projects led by a project manager

project structure
A structure in which employee continuously work on projects

Project structures tend to be more flexible organizational designs. The major advantage of that is that employees can be deployed rapidly to respond to environmental changes. Also, there's no departmentalization or rigid organizational hierarchy to slow down making decisions or taking action. In this structure, managers serve as facilitators, mentors, and coaches. They eliminate or minimize organizational obstacles and ensure that teams have the resources they need to effectively and efficiently complete their work. The two major disadvantages of the project structure are the complexity of assigning people to projects and the inevitable task and personality conflicts that arise.

WHAT IS A BOUNDARYLESS ORGANIZATION? Another contemporary organizational design is the boundaryless organization, which is an organization whose design is not defined by, or limited to, the horizontal, vertical, or external boundaries imposed by a predefined structure.[36] Former GE chairman Jack Welch coined the term because he wanted to eliminate vertical and horizontal boundaries within GE and break down external barriers between the company and its customers and suppliers. Although the idea of eliminating boundaries may seem odd, many of today's most successful organizations are finding that they can operate most effectively by remaining flexible and *un*structured: that the ideal structure for them is *not* having a rigid, bounded, and predefined structure.[37]

What do we mean by "boundaries"? There are two types: (1) *internal*—the horizontal ones imposed by work specialization and departmentalization and the vertical ones that separate employees into organizational levels and hierarchies; and (2) *external*—the boundaries that separate the organization from its customers, suppliers, and other stakeholders. To minimize or eliminate these boundaries, managers might use virtual or network structural designs.

A virtual organization consists of a small core of full-time employees and outside specialists temporarily hired as needed to work on projects.[38] An example is StrawberryFrog, a global advertising agency with offices in New York, Amsterdam, Mumbai, and Saõ Paulo. Work gets done with a minimal administrative staff and a global network of freelancers who are assigned client work. By relying on these freelancers, the company enjoys a network of talent without all the unnecessary overhead and structural complexity.[39] The inspiration for this structural approach comes from the film industry. There, people are essentially "free agents" who move from project to project applying their skills—directing, talent casting, costuming, makeup, set design, and so forth—as needed.

Another structural option for managers wanting to minimize or eliminate organizational boundaries is a network organization, which is one that uses its own employees to do some work activities and networks of outside suppliers to provide other needed product components or work processes.[40] This organizational form is sometimes called a modular organization by manufacturing firms.[41] This structural approach allows organizations to concentrate on what they do best by contracting out other activities to companies that do those activities best. Many companies are using such an approach for certain organizational work activities. For instance, the head of development for Boeing's 787 airplane manages thousands of employees and some 100 suppliers at more than 100 sites in different countries.[42] Sweden's Ericsson contracts its manufacturing and even some of its research and development to more cost-effective contractors in New Delhi, Singapore, California, and other global locations.[43] And at Penske Truck Leasing, dozens of business processes such as securing permits and titles, entering data from drivers' logs, and processing data for tax filings and accounting have been outsourced to Mexico and India.[44]

STAR Collaborative is a virtual staffing network launched by cofounders Ed Lefkow (left in photo) and Dan Olson. STAR is a specialty consultant group comprised of 150-plus freelance project and change management professionals who help primarily *Fortune* 500 companies achieve business results by finding ways to increase communication, foster collaboration, and develop leadership. A virtual structure enables STAR to provide the high-quality resources of skilled and experienced consultants offered by large consulting firms without the unnecessary overhead and structural complexity. In this photo, Lefkow and Olson conduct business in a coffee shop, one of many virtual offices they work from so they can be close to their clients.

WHAT ARE TODAY'S ORGANIZATIONAL DESIGN CHALLENGES?

Discuss the design challenges faced by today's organizations.

6.4

As managers look for organizational designs that will best support and facilitate employees doing their work efficiently and effectively, there are certain challenges with which they must contend. These include keeping employees connected, managing global structural issues, building a learning organization, and designing flexible work arrangements.

How Do You Keep Employees Connected?

Many organizational design concepts were developed during the twentieth century when work tasks were fairly predictable and constant, most jobs were full-time and continued indefinitely, and work was done at an employer's place of business under a manager's supervision.[45] That's not what it's like in many organizations today, as you saw in our preceding discussion of virtual and network organizations. A major structural design challenge for managers is finding a way to keep widely dispersed and mobile employees connected to the organization. The Technology and the Manager's Job box describes ways that information technology can help.

How Do Global Differences Affect Organizational Structure?

Are there global differences in organizational structures? Are Australian organizations structured like those in the United States? Are German organizations structured like those in France or Mexico? Given the global nature of today's business environment, this is an issue

---

TECHNOLOGY AND THE MANAGER'S JOB   THE CHANGING WORLD OF WORK

It's fair to say that the world of work will never be like it was 10 years ago.[46] IT has opened up new possibilities for employees to do their work in locations as remote as Patagonia or in the middle of downtown Seattle. Although organizations have always had employees who traveled to distant corporate locations to take care of business, these employees no longer have to find the nearest pay phone or wait to get back to "the office" to see what problems have cropped up. Instead, mobile computing and communication have given organizations and employees ways to stay connected and to be more productive. Let's look at some of the technologies that are changing the way work is done.

· Handheld devices with e-mail, calendars, and contacts can be used anywhere there's a wireless network. And these devices can be used to log into corporate databases and company intranets.

· Employees can videoconference using broadband networks and Webcams.

· Many companies are giving employees key fobs with constantly changing encryption codes that allow them to log onto the corporate network to access e-mail and company data from any computer hooked up to the Internet.

· Cell phones switch seamlessly between cellular networks and corporate Wi-Fi connections.

The biggest issue in doing work anywhere, anytime is security. Companies must protect their important and sensitive information. However, software and other disabling devices have minimized security issues considerably. Even insurance providers are more comfortable giving their mobile employees access to information. For instance, Health Net Inc. gave BlackBerrys to many of its managers so they can tap into customer records from anywhere. As one tech company CEO said, "Companies now can start thinking about innovative apps [applications] they can create and deliver to their workers anywhere."

Think About:

· What benefits do you see with being able to do work anywhere, anytime? (Think in terms of benefits for an organization and for its human resources.)

· What other issues, besides security, do you see with being able to do work anywhere, anytime? (Again, think about this for an organization and for its employees.)

· How do you use IT to do your work as a student?

· What challenges do you find in doing so?

---

boundaryless organization
An organization whose design is not defined by, or limited to, boundaries imposed by a predefined structure

virtual organization
An organization that consists of a small core of full-time employees and outside specialists temporarily hired as needed to work on projects

network organization
An organization that uses its own employees to do some work activities and networks of outside suppliers to provide other needed product components or work processes

with which managers need to be familiar. Researchers have concluded that the structures and strategies of organizations worldwide are similar, "while the behavior within them is maintaining its cultural uniqueness."[47] What does this mean for designing effective and efficient structures? When designing or changing structure, managers may need to think about the cultural implications of certain design elements. For instance, one study showed that formalization—rules and bureaucratic mechanisms—may be more important in less economically developed countries and less important in more economically developed countries where employees may have higher levels of professional education and skills.[48] Other structural design elements may be affected by cultural differences as well.

How Do You Build a Learning Organization?

Doing business in an intensely competitive global environment, British retailer Tesco realized how important it was for its stores to run well behind the scenes. And it does so using a proven "tool" called Tesco in a Box, which promotes consistency in operations as well as being a way to share innovations. Tesco is an example of a **learning organization**, an organization that has developed the capacity to continuously learn, adapt, and change.[49] The concept of a learning organization doesn't involve a specific organizational design per se, but instead describes an organizational mind-set or philosophy that has significant design implications. In a learning organization, employees are practicing knowledge management by continually acquiring and sharing new knowledge and are willing to apply that knowledge in making decisions or performing their work. Some organizational design theorists even go so far as to say that an organization's ability to learn and to apply that learning as they perform the organization's work may be the only sustainable source of competitive advantage.

What would a learning organization look like? As you can see in Exhibit 6–12, the important characteristics of a learning organization revolve around organizational design, information sharing, leadership, and culture. Let's take a closer look at each.

What types of organizational design elements would be necessary for learning to take place? In a learning organization, it's critical for members to share information and collaborate on work activities throughout the entire organization—across different functional specialties and even at different organizational levels—through minimizing or eliminating the existing structural and physical boundaries. In this type of boundaryless environment, employees are free to work together and collaborate in doing the organization's work the

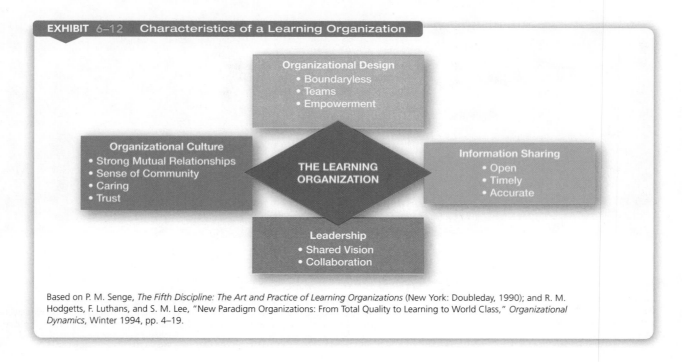

EXHIBIT 6–12 Characteristics of a Learning Organization

Organizational Design
- Boundaryless
- Teams
- Empowerment

Organizational Culture
- Strong Mutual Relationships
- Sense of Community
- Caring
- Trust

THE LEARNING ORGANIZATION

Information Sharing
- Open
- Timely
- Accurate

Leadership
- Shared Vision
- Collaboration

Based on P. M. Senge, *The Fifth Discipline: The Art and Practice of Learning Organizations* (New York: Doubleday, 1990); and R. M. Hodgetts, F. Luthans, and S. M. Lee, "New Paradigm Organizations: From Total Quality to Learning to World Class," *Organizational Dynamics*, Winter 1994, pp. 4–19.

best way they can, and to learn from each other. Because of this need to collaborate, teams also tend to be an important feature of a learning organization's structural design. Employees work in teams on whatever activities need to be done, and these employee teams are empowered to make decisions about doing their work or resolving issues. Empowered employees and teams have little need for "bosses" who direct and control. Instead, managers serve as facilitators, supporters, and advocates for employee teams.

Learning can't take place without information. For a learning organization to "learn," information must be shared among members; that is, organizational employees must engage in knowledge management by sharing information openly, in a timely manner, and as accurately as possible. Because few structural and physical barriers exist in a learning organization, the environment is conducive to open communication and extensive information sharing.

Leadership plays an important role as an organization moves toward becoming a learning organization. What should leaders do in a learning organization? One of their most important functions is facilitating the creation of a shared vision for the organization's future and then keeping organizational members working toward that vision. In addition, leaders should support and encourage the collaborative environment that's critical to learning. Without strong and committed leadership throughout the organization, it would be extremely difficult to be a learning organization.

Finally, the organizational culture is an important aspect of being a learning organization. In a learning organization's culture, everyone agrees on a shared vision and everyone recognizes the inherent interrelationships among the organization's processes, activities, functions, and external environment. It also fosters a strong sense of community, caring for each other, and trust. In a learning organization, employees feel free to communicate openly, share, experiment, and learn without fear of criticism or punishment.

How Can Managers Design Efficient and Effective Flexible Work Arrangements?

Accenture consultant Keyur Patel's job arrangement is becoming the norm, rather than the exception.[50] During a recent consulting assignment, he had three clocks on his desk: one set to Manila time (where his software programmers were), one to Bangalore (where another programming support team worked), and the third for San Francisco, where he was spending four days a week helping a major retailer implement IT systems to track and improve sales. And his cell phone kept track of the time in Atlanta, his home, where he headed on Thursday evenings.

For this new breed of professionals, life is a blend of home and office, work and leisure. Thanks to technology, work can now be done anywhere, anytime. As organizations adapt their structural designs to these new realities, we see more of them adopting flexible working arrangements. Such arrangements not only exploit the power of technology, but give organizations the flexibility to deploy employees when and where needed. In this section, we're going to take a look at some different types of flexible work arrangements including telecommuting; compressed workweeks, flextime, and job sharing; and contingent workforce. As with the other structural options we've looked at, managers must evaluate these in light of the implications for decision making, communication, authority relationships, work task accomplishment, and so forth.

WHAT'S INVOLVED IN TELECOMMUTING?   Information technology has made telecommuting possible and external environmental changes have made it necessary for many organizations. Telecommuting is a work arrangement in which employees work at home and are linked to the workplace by computer. Needless to say, not every job is a candidate for telecommuting. But many are.

---

learning organization
An organization that has developed the capacity to continuously learn, adapt, and change

telecommuting
A work arrangement in which employees work at home and are linked to the workplace by computer

Justin Lane/PhotoLibrary/Index Stock Imagery

When you call to book a flight with JetBlue Airlines, there's a good chance that you'll make a reservation with an agent working from home. That's because 80 percent of JetBlue's reservation agents are telecommuters. JetBlue reports that allowing its agents to work from home saves the company money and expensive office space and increases worker productivity. Telecommuting also gives JetBlue the flexibility to deploy more employees when call volume is high and fewer employees during slow call periods. The flexible work arrangement is a popular initiative with employees because it saves them traveling time and gas money and gives them more time to spend with their family.

Working from home used to be considered a "cushy perk" for a few lucky employees and such an arrangement wasn't allowed very often. Now, many businesses view telecommuting as a business necessity. For instance, at SCAN Health Plan, the company's chief financial officer said that getting more employees to telecommute provided the company a way to grow without having to incur any additional fixed costs such as office buildings, equipment, or parking lots.[51] In addition, some companies view the arrangement as a way to combat high gas prices and to attract talented employees who want more freedom and control over their work.

Despite its apparent appeal, many managers are reluctant to have their employees become "laptop hobos."[52] They argue that employees might waste time surfing the Internet or playing online games instead of working, ignore clients, and desperately miss the camaraderie and social exchanges of the workplace. In addition, managers worry about how they'll "manage" these employees? How do you interact with an employee and gain his or her trust when they're not physically present? And what if their work performance isn't up to par? How do you make suggestions for improvement? Another significant challenge is making sure that company information is kept safe and secure when employees are working from home.

Employees often express the same concerns about working remotely, especially when it comes to the isolation of not being "at work." At Accenture, where employees are scattered around the world, the chief human resources officer says that it isn't easy to maintain that esprit de corps.[53] However, the company put in place a number of programs and processes to create that sense of belonging for its workforce including webconferencing tools, assigning each employee to a career counselor, and holding quarterly community events at its offices. In addition, the telecommuter employee may find that the line between work and home becomes even more blurred, which can be stressful.[54] These are important organizing issues and ones that managers and organizations must address when moving toward having employees telecommute.

HOW CAN ORGANIZATIONS USE COMPRESSED WORKWEEKS, FLEXTIME, AND JOB SHARING?

During the most recent economic crisis in the United Kingdom, accounting firm KPMG needed to reduce costs and decided to use flexible work options as a way of doing so.[55] The company's program, called Flexible Futures, offered employees four options to choose from: a four-day workweek with a 20 percent salary reduction; a two-to-twelve-week sabbatical at 30 percent of pay; both options; or continue with their regular schedule. Some 85 percent of the U.K. employees agreed to the reduced-work-week plan. "Since so many people agreed to the flexible work plans, KPMG was able to cap the salary cut at about 10 percent for the year in most cases." The best thing, though, was that as a result of the plan, KPMG didn't have to do large-scale employee layoffs.

As this example shows, organizations sometimes find they need to restructure work using other forms of flexible work arrangements. One approach is a compressed workweek in which employees work longer hours per day but fewer days per week. The most common arrangement is four 10-hour days (a 4-40 program). Another alternative is flextime (also known as flexible work hours), which is a scheduling system in which employees are required to work a specific number of hours a week but are free to vary those hours within certain limits. In a flextime schedule, most companies designate certain common core hours when all employees are required to be on the job, but starting, ending, and lunch-hour times are flexible. Another type of job scheduling is called job sharing—the practice of having two or more people split a full-time job. Organizations might offer job sharing to professionals who want to work but don't want the demands and hassles of a full-time position. For instance, at Ernst & Young, employees in many of the company's locations can choose from a variety of flexible work arrangements including job sharing. Many companies use job sharing during economic downturns to avoid employee layoffs.[56]

WHAT IS A CONTINGENT WORKFORCE? "When Julia Lee first heard of Tongal, she thought it was a scam. Tongal pays people—anyone with a good idea, really—to create online videos for companies such as Mattel, Allstate, and Popchips."[57] Tongal divides projects into stages and pays cash for the top-five ideas. On Lee's first submission—which only took three hours of work—she got $1,000. On another, she earned $4,000. In a year's time, she's earned some $6,000 for about 100 hours of work. Tongal isn't the only business doing this. The idea of breaking up a job into small pieces and using the Internet to find workers to do those tasks was pioneered by LiveOps about a decade ago and followed by Amazon.com's Mechanical Turk in 2005.

"Companies want a workforce they can switch on and off as needed."[58] Although this quote may shock you, the truth is that the labor force already has begun shifting away from traditional full-time jobs toward contingent workers—temporary, freelance, or contract workers whose employment is *contingent* upon demand for their services. In today's economy, many organizations have responded by converting full-time permanent jobs into contingent jobs. It's predicted that by the end of the next decade the number of contingent employees will have grown to about 40 percent of the workforce. (It's at 30 percent today.)[59] In fact, one compensation and benefits expert says that "a growing a number of workers will need to structure their careers around this model."[60] That's likely to include you!

What are the implications for managers and organizations? Since contingent employees are not "employees" in the traditional sense of the word, managing them has its own set of challenges and expectations. Managers must recognize that because contingent workers lack the stability and security of permanent employees, they may not identify with the organization or be as committed or motivated. Managers may need to treat contingent workers differently in terms of practices and policies. However, with good communication and leadership, an organization's contingent employees can be just as valuable a resource to an organization as permanent employees are. Today's managers must recognize that it will be their responsibility to motivate their entire workforce, full-time and contingent, and to build their commitment to doing good work![61]

No matter what structural design managers choose for their organizations, the design should help employees do their work in the best, most efficient and effective way they can. The structure needs to help, not hinder, organizational members as they carry out the organization's work. After all, the structure is simply a means to an end.

---

compressed workweek
A workweek where employees work longer hours per day but fewer days per week

flextime (also known as flexible work hours)
A work scheduling system in which employees are required to work a specific number of hours per week but can vary when they work those hours within certain limits

job sharing
When two or more people split a full-time job

contingent workers
Temporary, freelance, or contract workers whose employment is *contingent* upon demand for their services

6 Review

CHAPTER SUMMARY

6.1 Describe six key elements in organizational design. The first element, *work specialization*, refers to dividing work activities into separate job tasks. The second, *departmentalization,* is how jobs are grouped together, which can be one of five types: functional, product, customer, geographic, or process. The third—*authority, responsibility, and power* all have to do with getting work done in an organization. Authority refers to the rights inherent in a managerial position to give orders and expect those orders to be obeyed. Responsibility refers to the obligation to perform when authority has been delegated. Power is the capacity of an individual to influence decisions and is not the same as authority. The fourth, *span of control*, refers to the number of employees a manager can efficiently and effectively manage. The fifth, *centralization and decentralization*, deals with where the majority of decisions are made—at upper organizational levels or pushed down to lower-level managers. The sixth, *formalization*, describes how standardized an organization's jobs are and the extent to which employees' behavior is guided by rules and procedures.

6.2 Identify the contingency factors that favor either the mechanistic model or the organic model of organizational design. A *mechanistic* organization design is quite bureaucratic whereas an *organic* organization design is more fluid and flexible. The *strategy*-determines-structure factor says that as organizational strategies move from single product to product diversification, the structure will move from organic to mechanistic. As an organization's *size* increases, so does the need for a more mechanistic structure. The more nonroutine the *technology*, the more organic a structure should be. Finally, stable *environments*

are better matched with mechanistic structures, but dynamic ones fit better with organic structures.

6.3 Compare and contrast traditional and contemporary organizational designs. Traditional structural designs include simple, functional, and divisional. A *simple structure* is one with low departmentalization, wide spans of control, authority centralized in a single person, and little formalization. A *functional structure* is one that groups similar or related occupational specialties together. A *divisional structure* is one made up of separate business units or divisions. Contemporary structural designs include *team-based structures* (the entire organization is made up of work teams); *matrix and project structures* (where employees work on projects for short periods of time or continuously); and *boundaryless organizations* (where the structural design is free of imposed boundaries). A boundaryless organization can either be a virtual or a network organization.

6.4 Discuss the design challenges faced by today's organizations. One design challenge lies in keeping employees connected, which can be accomplished through using information technology. Another challenge is understanding the global differences that affect organizational structure. Although structures and strategies of organizations worldwide are similar, the behavior within them differs, which can influence certain design elements. Another challenge is designing a structure around the mind-set of being a learning organization. Finally, managers are looking for organizational designs with efficient and effective flexible work arrangements. They're using options such as telecommuting, compressed workweeks, flextime, job sharing, and contingent workers.

MyManagementLab For more resources, please visit **www.mymanagementlab.com**

UNDERSTANDING THE CHAPTER

1. Describe what is meant by the term *organization design.*

2. Discuss the traditional and contemporary views of each of the six key elements of organizational design.

3. Can an organization's structure be changed quickly? Why or why not? Should it be changed quickly? Why or why not?

4. "An organization can have no structure." Do you agree or disagree with this statement? Explain.

5. Contrast mechanistic and organic organizations.

6. Explain the contingency factors that affect organizational design.

7. With the availability of information technology that allows employees to work anywhere, anytime, is organizing still an important managerial function? Why or why not?

8. Researchers are now saying that efforts to simplify work tasks actually have negative results for both companies and their employees. Do you agree? Why or why not?

9. "The boundaryless organization has the potential to create a major shift in the way we work." Do you agree or disagree with this statement? Explain.

10. Draw an organization chart of an organization with which you're familiar (where you work, a student organization to which you belong, your college or university, etc.). Be very careful in showing the departments (or groups) and especially be careful to get the chain of command correct. Be prepared to share your chart with the class.

Go to p. 420

YOUR TURN TO BE A MANAGER for Chapter 6.

Endnotes

1. A. Fox, "Pave the Way for Volunteers," *HR Magazine,* June 2010, pp. 70–74; G. Morse, "The Power of Unwitting Workers," *Harvard Business Review,* October 2009, pp. 27–27; S. Lohr, "Customer Service? Ask a Volunteer," *New York Times Online,* April 26, 2009; and B. Xu, D. R. Jones, and B. Shao, "Volunteers' Involvement in Online Community Based Software Development," *Information & Management,* April 2009, pp. 151–158.

2. M. Boyle, "Super Bucks," *Fortune,* February 4, 2008, pp. 8–9; and M. Hiestand, "Making a Stamp on Football," *USA Today,* January 25, 2005, pp. 1C+.

3. S. E. Humphrey, J. D. Nahrgang, and F. P. Morgeson, "Integrating Motivational, Social, and Contextual Work Design Features: A Meta-Analytic Summary and Theoretical Expansion of the Work Design Literature," *Journal of Applied Psychology* (September 2007), pp. 1332–1356.

4. E. Kelly, "Keys to Effective Virtual Global Teams," *Academy of Management Executive,* May 2001, pp. 132–133; and D. Ancona, H. Bresman, and K. Kaeufer, "The Comparative Advantage of X-Team," *MIT Sloan Management Review,* Spring 2002, pp. 33–39.

5. R. S. Benchley, "Following Orders," *Chief Executive,* March 2002, p. 6.

6. R. Preston, "Inside Out," *Management Today,* September 2001, p. 37; and R. D. Clarke, "Over Their Heads," *Black Enterprise,* December 2000, p. 79.

7. See J. R. P. French and B. Raven, "The Bases of Social Power," in D. Cartwright and A. F. Zander, eds., *Group Dynamics: Research and Theory* (New York: Harper & Row, 1960), pp. 607–623.

8. L. Urwick, *The Elements of Administration* (New York: Harper & Row, 1944), pp. 52–53. See also, J. H. Gittel, "Supervisory Span, Relational Coordination, and Flight Departure Performance: A Reassessment of Post-Bureaucracy Theory," *Organizational Science,* July–August 2001, pp. 468–483.

9. S. Harrison, "Is There a Right Span of Control? Simon Harrison Assesses the Relevance of the Concept of Span of Control to Modern Businesses," *Business Review,* February 2004, pp. 10–13.

10. P. C. Light, "From Pentagon to Pyramids: Whacking at Bloat," *Government Executive,* July 2001, p. 100.

11. Right or Wrong box based on C. Bray, "Hackers Are Arrested in iPad Breach," *Wall Street Journal,* January 19, 2011, p. B1; C. Hausman, "Was AT&T's iPad Security Breach 'Ethical' Hacking?" *Ethics Newsline,* www.globalethics.org (June 21, 2010); S. E. Ante and B. Worthen, "FBI to Probe iPad Breach— Group That Exposed AT&T Flaw to See Addresses Says It Did a Public Service," *Wall Street Journal,* June 11, 2010, p. B1; and S. E. Ante, "AT&T Discloses Breach of iPad Owner Data," *Wall Street Journal Online,* June 9, 2010.

12. See, for instance, D. Van Fleet, "Span of Management Research and Issues," *Academy of Management Journal* (September 1983), pp. 546–552; and S. H. Cady and P. M. Fandt, "Managing Impressions with Information: A Field Study of Organizational Realities," *Journal of Applied Behavioral Science* (June 2001), pp. 180–204.

13. Henri Fayol, *General and Industrial Management*, trans. C. Storrs (London: Pitman Publishing, 1949), pp. 19–42.

14. J. Zabojnik, "Centralized and Decentralized Decision Making in Organizations," *Journal of Labor Economics* (January 2002), pp. 1–22.

15. See P. Kenis and D. Knoke, "How Organizational Field Networks Shape InterOrganizational Tie-Formation Rates," *Academy of Management Review,* April 2002, pp. 275–293.

16. E. W. Morrison, "Doing the Job Well: An Investigation of Pro-Social Rule Breaking," *Journal of Management* (February 2006), pp. 5–28.

17. Ibid.

18. T. Burns and G. M. Stalker, *The Management of Innovation* (London: Tavistock, 1961).

19. D. Dougherty, "Re-imagining the Differentiation and Integration of Work for Sustained Product Innovation," *Organization Science,* September–October 2001, pp. 612–631.

20. A. D. Chandler, Jr., *Strategy and Structure: Chapters in the History of the Industrial Enterprise* (Cambridge, MA: MIT Press, 1962).

21. See, for instance, L. L. Bryan and C. I. Joyce, "Better Strategy Through Organizational Design," *McKinsey Quarterly,* no. 2 (2007), pp. 21–29; D. Jennings and S. Seaman, "High and Low Levels of Organizational Adaptation: An Empirical Analysis of Strategy, Structure, and Performance," *Strategic Management Journal* (July 1994), pp. 459–475; D. C. Galunic and K. M. Eisenhardt, "Renewing the Strategy-Structure-Performance Paradigm," in B. M. Staw and L. L. Cummings (eds.), *Research in Organizational Behavior*, vol. 16 (Greenwich, CT: JAI Press, 1994), pp. 215–255; R. Parthasarthy and S. P. Sethi, "Relating Strategy and Structure to Flexible Automation: A Test of Fit and Performance Implications," *Strategic Management Journal*, 14, no. 6 (1993), pp. 529–549; H. A. Simon, "Strategy and Organizational Evolution," *Strategic Management Journal* (January 1993), pp. 131–142; H. L. Boschken, "Strategy and Structure: Re-conceiving the Relationship," *Journal of Management* (March 1990), pp. 135–150; D. Miller, "The Structural and Environmental Correlates of Business Strategy," *Strategic Management Journal* (January–February 1987), pp. 55–76; and R. E. Miles and C. C. Snow, *Organizational Strategy, Structure, and Process* (New York: McGraw-Hill, 1978).

22. See, for instance, P. M. Blau and R. A. Schoenherr, *The Structure of Organizations* (New York: Basic Books, 1971); D. S. Pugh, "The Aston Program of Research: Retrospect and Prospect," in A. H. Van de Ven and W. F. Joyce (eds.), *Perspectives on Organization Design and Behavior* (New York: John Wiley, 1981), pp. 135–166; and R. Z. Gooding and J. A. Wagner III, "A Meta-Analytic Review of the Relationship Between Size and Performance: The Productivity and Efficiency of Organizations and Their Subunits," *Administrative Science Quarterly*, December 1985, pp. 462–481.

23. J. Woodward, *Industrial Organization: Theory and Practice* (London: Oxford University Press, 1965).

24. From the Past to the Present box based on J. Woodward, *Industrial Organization: Theory and Practice.* Also, see, for instance, C. Perrow, "A Framework for the Comparative Analysis of Organizations," *American Sociological Review,* April 1967, pp. 194–208; J. D. Thompson, *Organizations in Action* (New York: McGraw-Hill, 1967); J. Hage and M. Aiken, "Routine Technology, Social Structure, and Organizational Goals," *Administrative Science Quarterly,* September 1969, pp. 366–377; C. C. Miller, W. H. Glick, Y. D. Wang, and G. Huber, "Understanding Technology-Structure Relationships: Theory Development and Meta-Analytic Theory Testing," *Academy of Management Journal* (June 1991), pp. 370–399; D. M. Rousseau and R. A. Cooke, "Technology and Structure: The Concrete, Abstract, and Activity Systems of Organizations," *Journal of Management* (Fall–Winter 1984), pp. 345–361; and D. Gerwin, "Relationships between Structure and Technology," in P.C. Nystrom and W. H. Starbuck (eds.), *Handbook of Organizational Design,* vol. 2 (New York: Oxford University Press, 1981), pp. 3–38.

25. See, for example, H. M. O'Neill, "Restructuring, Reengineering and Rightsizing: Do the Metaphors Make Sense?" *Academy of Management Executive* 8, no. 4 (1994), pp. 9–30; R. K. Reger, J. V. Mullane, L. T. Gustafson, and S. M. Demarie, "Creating Earthquakes to Change Organizational Mindsets," *Academy of Management Executive* 8, no. 4 (1994), pp. 31–41; and J. Tan, "Impact of Ownership Type on Environment–Strategy Linkage and Performance: Evidence from a Transitional Company," *Journal of Management Studies* (May 2002), pp. 333–354.

26. J. C. Linder and S. Cantrell, "It's All in the Mind(set)," *Across the Board,* May–June 2002, pp. 38–42; and B. Holland, "Management's Sweet Spot," *New Zealand Management,* March 2002, pp. 60–61.

27. M. Song, "Samsung Electronics Net Rises 54%," *Wall Street Journal,* April 22, 2002, p. B4.

28. H. Mintzberg, *Structure in Fives: Designing Effective Organizations* (Upper Saddle River, NJ: Prentice Hall, 1983), p. 157.

29. D. A. Garvin and L. C. Levesque, "The Multiunit Enterprise," *Harvard Business Review,* June 2008, pp. 106–117; and R. J. Williams, J. J. Hoffman, and B. T. Lamont, "The Influence of Top Management Team Characteristics on M-Form Implementation Time," *Journal of Managerial Issues* (Winter 1995), pp. 466–480.

30. See, for example, R. Greenwood and D. Miller, "Tackling Design Anew: Getting Back to the Heart of Organization Theory," *Academy of Management Perspectives,* November 2010, pp. 78–88; G. J. Castrogiovanni, "Organization Task Environments: Have They Changed Fundamentally Over Time?" *Journal of Management,* vol. 28, no. 2 (2002), pp. 129–150; D. F. Twomey, "Leadership, Organizational Design, and Competitiveness for the 21st Century," *Global Competitiveness,* Annual 2002, pp. S31–S40; M. Hammer, "Processed Change: Michael Hammer Sees Process as 'the Clark Kent of Business Ideas'—A Concept That Has the Power to Change a Company's Organizational Design," *Journal of Business Strategy,*

(November–December 2001), pp. 11–15; T. Clancy, "Radical Surgery: A View from the Operating Theater," *Academy of Management Executive,* February 1994, pp. 73–78; I. I. Mitroff, R. O. Mason, and C. M. Pearson, "Radical Surgery: What Will Tomorrow's Organizations Look Like?" *Academy of Management Executive,* February 1994, pp. 11–21; and R. E. Hoskisson, C. W. L. Hill, and H. Kim, "The Multidivisional Structure: Organizational Fossil or Source of Value?" *Journal of Management* 19, no. 2 (1993), pp. 269–298.

31. Q. Hardy, "Google Thinks Small," *Forbes,* November 14, 2005, pp. 198–202.

32. See, for example, D. R. Denison, S. L. Hart, and J. A. Kahn, "From Chimneys to Cross-Functional Teams: Developing and Validating a Diagnostic Model," *Academy of Management Journal* (December 1996), pp. 1005–1023; D. Ray and H. Bronstein, *Teaming Up: Making the Transition to a Self-Directed Team-Based Organization* (New York: McGraw Hill, 1995); J. R. Katzenbach and D. K. Smith, *The Wisdom of Teams* (Boston: Harvard Business School Press, 1993); J. A. Byrne, "The Horizontal Corporation," *BusinessWeek,* December 20, 1993, pp. 76–81; B. Dumaine, "Payoff from the New Management," *Fortune,* December 13, 1993, pp. 103–110; and H. Rothman, "The Power of Empowerment," *Nation's Business,* June 1993, pp. 49–52.

33. C. Garvey, "Steer Teams with the Right Pay," *HR Magazine,* May 2002, pp. 70–78.

34. P. Kaihla, "Best-Kept Secrets of the World's Best Companies," *Business 2.0,* April 2006, p. 83; C. Taylor, "School of Bright Ideas," *Time Inside Business,* April 2005, pp. A8–A12; and B. Nussbaum, "The Power of Design," *Business Week,* May 17, 2004, pp. 86–94.

35. And the Survey Says box based on J. Schramm, "At Work in a Virtual World," *HR Magazine,* June 2010, p. 152; J. Yang and A. Gonzalez, "Top Peeves About Someone Working from Home," *USA Today,* May 27, 2010, p. 1B; J. Jusko, "A Team Effort," *Industry Week,* January 2007, pp. 42+; P. Coy, M. Conlin, and M. Herbst, "The Disposable Worker," *Bloomberg BusinessWeek,* January 18, 2010, p. 36; "Employee Loyalty Increases During Recession," *Workforce Management Online,* March 9, 2010; "Study: Flexibility Programs Gain Ground in Hard Times," *Workforce Management Online,* July 23, 2009; and J. Hyatt, "Taking It Personally," *CFO,* July–August 2009, p. 29.

36. See, for example, G. G. Dess, A. M. A. Rasheed, K. J. McLaughlin, and R. L. Priem, "The New Corporate Architecture," *Academy of Management Executive,* August 1995, pp. 7–20.

37. For additional readings on boundaryless organizations, see Rausch and Birkinshaw, June 2008; M. F. R. Kets de Vries, "Leadership Group Coaching in Action: The Zen of Creating High Performance Teams," *Academy of Management Executive,* February 2005, pp. 61–76; J. Child and R. G. McGrath, "Organizations Unfettered: Organizational Form in an Information-Intensive Economy," *Academy of Management Journal* (December 2001), pp. 1135–1148; M. Hammer and S. Stanton, "How Process Enterprises Really Work," *Harvard Business Review,* November–December 1999, pp. 108–118; T. Zenger and W. Hesterly, "The Disaggregation of Corporations: Selective Intervention, High-Powered Incentives,

and Modular Units," *Organization Science,* vol. 8 (1997), pp. 209–222; R. Ashkenas, D. Ulrich, T. Jick, and S. Kerr, *The Boundaryless Organization: Breaking the Chains of Organizational Structure* (San Francisco: Jossey-Bass, 1997); R. M. Hodgetts, "A Conversation with Steve Kerr," *Organizational Dynamics*, Spring 1996, pp. 68–79; and J. Gebhardt, "The Boundaryless Organization," *Sloan Management Review*, Winter 1996, pp. 117–119. For another view of boundaryless organizations, see B. Victor, "The Dark Side of the New Organizational Forms: An Editorial Essay," *Organization Science*, November 1994, pp. 479–482.

38. See, for instance, Y. Shin, "A Person-Environment Fit Model for Virtual Organizations," *Journal of Management* (December 2004), pp. 725–743; D. Lyons, "Smart and Smarter," *Forbes,* March 18, 2002, pp. 40–41; W. F. Cascio, "Managing a Virtual Workplace," *Academy of Management Executive,* August 2000, pp. 81–90; G. G. Dess, A. M. A. Rasheed, K. J. McLaughlin, and R. L. Priem, "The New Corporate Architecture"; H. Chesbrough and D. Teece, "When Is Virtual Virtuous: Organizing for Innovation," *Harvard Business Review,* January–February 1996, pp. 65–73; and W. H. Davidow and M. S. Malone, *The Virtual Corporation* (New York: Harper Collins, 1992).

39. "Could Your Brand Pass the Tee Shirt Test?" *Fortune,* May 28, 2007, p. 122; M. Maddever, "The New School: An Inconvenient Truth," www.strategymag.com (April 2007); K. Hugh, "Goodson Forecasts Future Shock," www.adweek.com (March 5, 2007); J. Ewing, "Amsterdam's Red-Hot Ad Shops," *BusinessWeek,* December 18, 2006, p. 52; and T. Howard, "Strawberry Frog Hops to a Different Drummer," *USA Today,* October 10, 2005 p. 4B.

40. R. E. Miles, C. C. Snow, J. A. Matthews, G. Miles, and H. J. Coleman, Jr., "Organizing in the Knowledge Age: Anticipating the Cellular Form," *Academy of Management Executive,* November 1997, pp. 7–24; C. Jones, W. Hesterly, and S. Borgatti, "A General Theory of Network Governance: Exchange Conditions and Social Mechanisms," *Academy of Management Review,* October 1997, pp. 911–945; R. E. Miles and C. C. Snow, "The New Network Firm: A Spherical Structure Built on Human Investment Philosophy," *Organizational Dynamics,* Spring 1995, pp. 5–18; and R. E. Miles and C. C. Snow, "Causes of Failures in Network Organizations," *California Management Review,* vol. 34, no. 4 (1992), pp. 53–72.

41. G. Hoetker, "Do Modular Products Lead to Modular Organizations?" *Strategic Management Journal* (June 2006), pp. 501–518; C. H. Fine, "Are You Modular or Integral?" *Strategy & Business,* Summer 2005, pp. 44–51; D. A. Ketchen, Jr. and G. T. M. Hult, "To Be Modular or Not to Be? Some Answers to the Question," *Academy of Management Executive,* May 2002, pp. 166–167; M. A. Schilling, "The Use of Modular Organizational Forms: An Industry-Level Analysis," *Academy of Management Journal* (December 2001), pp. 1149–1168; D. Lei, M. A. Hitt, and J. D. Goldhar, "Advanced Manufacturing Technology: Organizational Design and Strategic Flexibility," *Organization Studies,* vol. 17 (1996), pp. 501–523; R. Sanchez and J. Mahoney, "Modularity Flexibility and Knowledge Management in Product and Organization Design," *Strategic Management Journal,* vol. 17 (1996), pp. 63–76; and R. Sanchez, "Strategic Flexibility in Product Competition," *Strategic Management Journal,* vol. 16 (1995), pp. 135–159.

42. C. Hymowitz, "Have Advice, Will Travel," *Wall Street Journal,* June 5, 2006, pp B1+.

43. S. Reed, A. Reinhardt, and A. Sains, "Saving Ericsson," *BusinessWeek,* November 11, 2002, pp. 64–68.

44. P. Engardio, "The Future of Outsourcing," *BusinessWeek,* January 30, 2006, pp. 50–58.

45. C. E. Connelly and D. G. Gallagher, "Emerging Trends in Contingent Work Research," *Journal of Management* (November 2004), pp. 959–983.

46. Technology and the Manager's Job box based on R. Cheng, "So You Want to Use Your iPhone for Work? How the Smartest Companies Are Letting Employees Use Their Personal Gadgets to Do Their Jobs," *Wall Street Journal,* April 25, 2011, pp. R1+; B. Roberts, "Mobile Workforce Management," *HR Magazine,* March 2011, pp. 67–70; D. Darlin, "Software That Monitors Your Work, Wherever You Are," *New York Times Online* www.nytimesonline.com (April 12, 2009); D. Pauleen and B. Harmer, "Away from the Desk...Always," *Wall Street Journal,* December 15, 2008, p. R8; J. Marquez, "Connecting a Virtual Workforce," *Workforce Management Online* www.workforce.com (September 22, 2008); R. Yu, "Work Away from Work Gets Easier with Technology," *USA Today,* November 28, 2006, p. 8B; M. Weinstein, "GOing Mobile," *Training,* September 2006, pp. 24–29; C. Cobbs, "Technology Helps Boost Multitasking," *Springfield, Missouri News-Leader,* June 15, 2006, p. 5B; C. Edwards, "Wherever You Go, You're On the Job," *BusinessWeek,* June 20, 2005, pp. 87–90; and S. E. Ante, "The World Wide Work Space," *BusinessWeek,* June 6, 2005, pp. 106–108.

47. N. M. Adler, *International Dimensions of Organizational Behavior,* 5th ed. (Cincinnati, OH: South-Western), 2008, p. 62.

48. P. B. Smith and M. F. Peterson, "Demographic Effects on the Use of Vertical Sources of Guidance by Managers in Widely Differing Cultural Contexts," *International Journal of Cross Cultural Management* (April 2005), pp. 5–26.

49. P. Olson, "Tesco's Landing," *Forbes,* June 4, 2007, pp. 116–118; and P. M. Senge, *The Fifth Discipline: The Art and Practice of Learning Organizations* (New York: Doubleday, 1990).

50. J. Marquez, "Connecting a Virtual Workforce," *Workforce Management Online,* February 3, 2009.

51. M. Conlin, "Home Offices: The New Math," *BusinessWeek,* March 9, 2009, pp. 66–68.

52. Ibid.

53. J. Marquez, "Connecting a Virtual Workforce."

54. S. Jayson, "Working at Home: Family-Friendly," *USA Today,* April 15, 2010, pp. 1A+; T. D. Hecht and N. J. Allen, "A Longitudinal Examination of the Work-Nonwork Boundary Strength Construct," *Journal of Organizational Behavior* (October 2009), pp. 839–862; and G. E. Kreiner, E. C. Hollensbe, and M. L. Sheep, "Balancing Borders and Bridges: Negotiating the Work-Home Interface via Boundary Work Tactics," *Academy of Management Journal* (August 2009), pp. 704–730.

55. J. T. Marquez, "The Future of Flex," *Workforce Management Online,* January 2010.

56. S. Greenhouse, "Work-Sharing May Help Companies Avoid Layoffs," *New York Times Online,* June 16, 2009.

57. R. King, "Meet the Microworkers," *Bloomberg BusinessWeek Online,* February 1, 2011; and R. King, "Mechanical Serfdom Is Just That," *Bloomberg BusinessWeek Online,* February 1, 2011.

58. K. Bennhold, "Working (Part-Time) in the 21st Century," *New York Times Online,* December 29, 2010; and J. Revell, C. Bigda, and D. Rosato, "The Rise of Freelance Nation," *CNNMoney,* cnnmoney.com, June 12, 2009.

59. Revell, Bigda, and Rosato, "The Rise of Freelance Nation."

60. Ibid.

61. H. G. Jackson, "Flexible Workplaces: The Next Imperative," *HR Magazine,* March 2011, p. 8; E. Frauenheim, "Companies Focus Their Attention on Flexibility," *Workforce Management Online,* February 2011; P. Davidson, "Companies Do More with Fewer Workers," *USA Today,* February 23, 2011, pp. 1B+; M. Rich, "Weighing Costs, Companies Favor Temporary Help," *New York Times Online,* December 19, 2010; and P. Davidson, "Temporary Workers Reshape Companies, Jobs," *USA Today,* October 13, 2010, pp. 1B+.

CHAPTER 7 Managing Human Resources

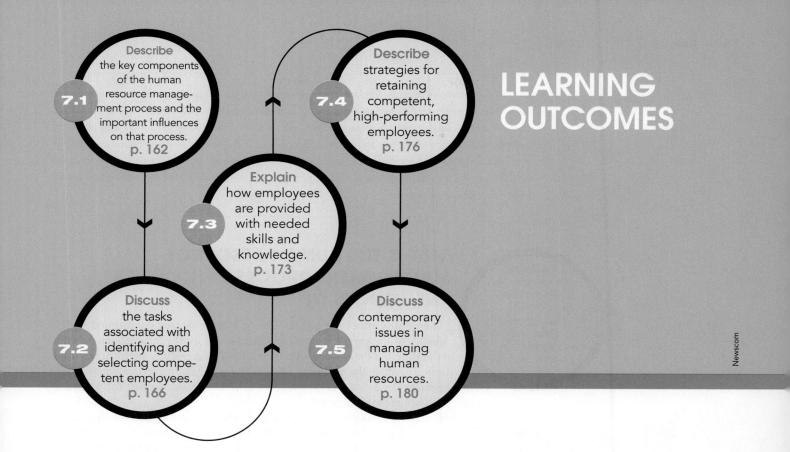

7.1 Describe the key components of the human resource management process and the important influences on that process. p. 162

7.4 Describe strategies for retaining competent, high-performing employees. p. 176

7.3 Explain how employees are provided with needed skills and knowledge. p. 173

7.2 Discuss the tasks associated with identifying and selecting competent employees. p. 166

7.5 Discuss contemporary issues in managing human resources. p. 180

Newscom

Thinking Outside the Box

It's the world's largest package delivery company with the instantly recognizable brown trucks.[1] Every day United Parcel Service (UPS) transports some 15 million packages and documents throughout the United States and to more than 215 countries and territories (and more than 430 million packages alone during the month before Christmas). And delivering those packages quickly and correctly is what it gets paid to do. In fact, UPS has been described as an "efficiency freak." That massive effort wouldn't be possible without its 99,000-plus drivers. However, UPS recognizes that it has an HR challenge: hiring and training some 25,000 drivers over the next five years to replace retiring Baby Boomers. But the company has a plan in place that combines its tested business model of uniformity and efficiency (for instance, drivers are trained to hold their keys on a pinky finger so they don't waste time fumbling in their pockets for the keys) with a new approach to driver training.

With an organization's structure in place, managers then have to find people to fill the jobs that have been created or to remove people from jobs if business circumstances require it. And like UPS is experiencing, those people have to be recruited, selected, and then trained to do their jobs efficiently and effectively. That's where human resource management (HRM) comes in. It's an important task that involves having the right number of the right people in the right place at the right time. In this chapter, we'll look at the process managers use to do just that. In addition, we'll look at some contemporary HRM issues facing managers.

7.1 Describe the key components of the human resource management process and the important influences on that process.

WHAT IS THE HUMAN RESOURCE MANAGEMENT PROCESS AND WHAT INFLUENCES IT?

The quality of an organization is to a large degree determined by the quality of the people it employs. Success for most organizations depends on finding the employees with the skills to successfully perform the tasks required to attain the company's strategic goals. Staffing and human resource management decisions and methods are critical to ensuring that the organization hires and keeps the right people.

Some of you may be thinking, "Sure, personnel decisions are important. But aren't most of them made by people who specifically handle human resource issues?" It's true that, in many organizations, a number of the activities grouped under the label **human resource management (HRM)** are done by specialists. In other cases, HRM activities may be outsourced to companies, domestic or global. Not all managers have HRM staff support, though. Many small business managers, for instance, frequently must do their own hiring without the assistance of HRM specialists. Even managers in larger organizations are often involved in recruiting candidates, reviewing application forms, interviewing applicants, orienting new employees, making decisions about employee training, providing career advice to employees, and evaluating employees' performance. So, even if an organization provides HRM support activities, every manager is involved with human resource decisions in his or her unit.[2]

Exhibit 7–1 introduces the key components of an organization's HRM process. It represents eight activities (the yellow boxes) that, if properly executed, will staff an organization with competent, high-performing employees who are capable of sustaining their performance level over the long term.

After an organization's strategy has been established and the organization structure designed, it's time to add the people. That's one of the most critical roles for HRM and one that has increased the importance of human resource managers to the organization. The first three activities in the HRM process represent employment planning: the addition of staff through recruitment, the reduction in staff through downsizing, and selection. When executed properly, these steps lead to the identification and selection of competent employees and assist organizations in achieving their strategic directions.

Once you select competent people, you need to help them adapt to the organization and ensure that their job skills and knowledge are kept current. These next two activities in the HRM process are accomplished through orientation and training. The last steps in the HRM process are designed to identify performance goals, correct performance problems if necessary, and help employees sustain a high level of performance over their entire work life. The activities involved include performance appraisal, and compensation and benefits. HRM also includes safety and health issues, but we're not covering those topics in this book.

Notice in Exhibit 7–1 that the entire process is influenced by the external environment. Many of the factors introduced in Chapter 2 directly affect all management practices, but their effect is felt most in managing the organization's human resources, because whatever happens to an organization ultimately influences what happens to its

EXHIBIT 7-1   The Human Resource Management Process

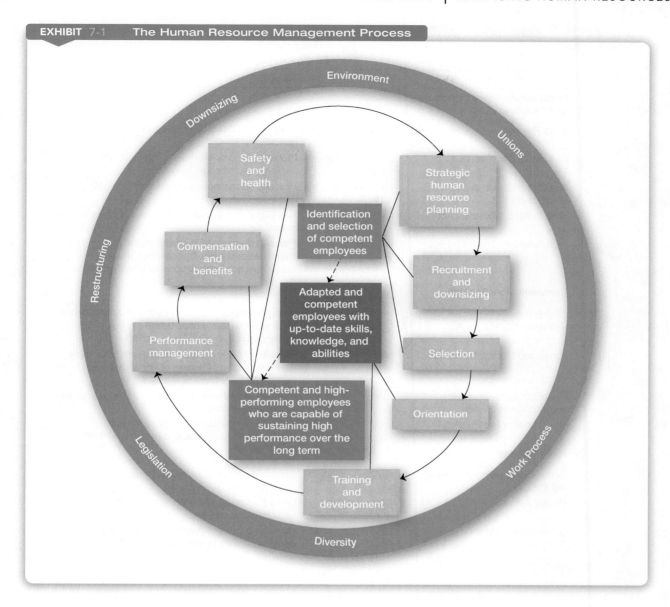

EXHIBIT 7-1   The Human Resource Management Process

employees. So, before we review the HRM process, let's examine one primary environmental force that affects it—the legal environment, and employment and discrimination laws in particular.

What Is the Legal Environment of HRM?

HRM practices are governed by laws, which vary from country to country. Within countries, state or provincial and local regulations further influence specific practices. Consequently, it's impossible to provide you with all the information you need about the relevant regulatory environment. As a manager, it will be important for you to know what you can and cannot do, legally.

EXHIBIT 7-2	Major HRM Laws	

LAWS

LAW OR RULING	YEAR	DESCRIPTION
Equal Employment Opportunity and Discrimination		
Equal Pay Act	1963	Prohibits pay differences for equal work based on gender
Civil Rights Act, Title VII	1964 (amended in 1972)	Prohibits discrimination based on race, color, religion, national origin, or gender
Age Discrimination in Employment Act	1967 (amended in 1978)	Prohibits discrimination against employees 40 years and older
Vocational Rehabilitation Act	1973	Prohibits discrimination on the basis of physical or mental disabilities
Americans with Disabilities Act	1990	Prohibits discrimination against individuals who have disabilities or chronic illnesses; also requires reasonable accommodations for these individuals
Compensation/Benefits		
Worker Adjustment and Retraining Notification Act	1990	Requires employers with more than 100 employees to provide 60 days' notice before a mass layoff or facility closing
Family and Medical Leave Act	1993	Gives employees in organizations with 50 or more employees up to 12 weeks of unpaid leave each year for family or medical reasons
Health Insurance Portability and Accountability Act	1996	Permits portability of employees' insurance from one employer to another
Lilly Ledbetter Fair Pay Act	2009	Changes the statute of limitations on pay discrimination to 180 days from each paycheck
Health/Safety		
Occupational Safety and Health Act (OSHA)	1970	Establishes mandatory and health standards in organizations
Privacy Act	1974	Gives employees the legal right to examine personnel files and letters of reference
Consolidated Omnibus Reconciliation Act (COBRA)	1985	Requires continued health coverage following termination (paid by employee)

WHAT ARE THE PRIMARY U.S. LAWS AFFECTING HRM? Since the mid-1960s, the federal government in the United States has greatly expanded its influence over HRM by enacting a number of laws and regulations (see Exhibit 7–2 for examples). Although we've not seen many laws enacted recently at the federal level, many state laws have been passed that add to the provisions of the federal laws. For instance, in many states today, it's illegal to discriminate against an individual based on sexual orientation. As a result, today's employers must ensure that equal employment opportunities exist for job applicants and current employees. Decisions regarding who will be hired, for example, or which employees will be chosen for a management training program must be made without regard to race, sex, religion, age, color, national origin, or disability. Exceptions can occur only when special circumstances exist. For instance, a community fire department can deny employment to a firefighter applicant who is confined to a wheelchair, but if that same individual is applying for a desk job, such as a fire department dispatcher, the disability cannot be used as a reason to deny employment. The issues involved, however, are rarely that clear-cut. For example, employment laws protect most employees whose religious beliefs require a specific style of dress—robes, long shirts, long hair, and the like. However, if the specific style of dress may be hazardous or unsafe in the work setting (e.g., when operating machinery), a company could refuse to hire a person who would not adopt a safer dress code.

From the Past to the Present

Hugo Munsterberg was a pioneer in the field of industrial psychology and is "generally credited with creating the field."[3] As an admirer of Frederick W. Taylor and the scientific management movement, Munsterberg stated that "Taylor had introduced most valuable suggestions which the industrial world cannot ignore." Drawing on Taylor's works, Munsterberg stressed "the importance of efficiently using workers to achieve economic production." His research and work in showing organizations ways to improve the performance and well-being of workers was fundamental to the emerging field of management in the early 1900s.

Today, industrial-organizational psychology is defined as the scientific study of the workplace. Industrial-organizational (I/O) psychologists use scientific principles and research-based designs to generate knowledge about workplace issues. (Check out the Society for Industrial and Organizational Psychology at www.siop.org.) They study organizational topics such as job performance, job analysis, performance appraisal, compensation, work/life balance, work sample tests, employee training, employment law, personnel recruitment and selection, and so forth. Their research has contributed much to the field that we call human resource management. And all of this is due to the early work done by Hugo Munsterberg.

Think About:

• Why is it important to scientifically study the workplace?

• Do you think it's easier today to scientifically study the workplace than it was back in Munsterberg's days? Why or why not?

• How has I/O psychology contributed to HRM?

• Go to the SIOP Web site. Find the student section and the discussion of what I/O psychologists really do. In a bulleted list, summarize one of the individual profiles.

Trying to balance the "shoulds and should-nots" of these laws often falls within the realm of **affirmative action programs.** Many organizations operating in the United States have affirmative action programs to ensure that decisions and practices enhance the employment, upgrading, and retention of members from protected groups such as minorities and females. These organizations refrain from discrimination and actively seek to enhance the status of members from protected groups.

U.S. managers are not completely free to choose whom they hire, promote, or fire. Although these regulations have significantly helped to reduce employment discrimination and unfair employment practices, they have, at the same time, reduced management's discretion over HR decisions.

ARE HRM LAWS THE SAME GLOBALLY?   HRM laws aren't the same globally. You need to know the laws and regulations that apply in your locale. Let's look at some of the federal legislation in countries such as Canada, Mexico, Australia, and Germany.

Canadian HRM laws closely parallel those in the United States. The Canadian Human Rights Act prohibits discrimination on the basis of race, religion, age, marital status, sex, physical or mental disability, or national origin. This law governs practices throughout the country. Canada's HRM environment, however, is somewhat different from that in the United States in that it involves more decentralization of lawmaking to the provincial level. For example, discrimination on the basis of language is not prohibited anywhere in Canada except in Quebec.

In Mexico, employees are more likely to be unionized than they are in the United States. Labor issues in Mexico are governed by the Mexican Federal Labor Law. One hiring law states that an employer has 28 days to evaluate a new employee's work performance. After that period, the employee is granted job security and termination is quite difficult and expensive. Those who violate the Mexican Federal Labor Law are subject to severe penalties, including criminal action that can result in steep fines and even jail sentences for employers who fail to pay, for example, the minimum wage.

Australia's discrimination laws were not enacted until the 1980s, and generally apply to discrimination and affirmative action for women. Yet, gender opportunities for women in Australia appear to lag behind those in the United States. In Australia,

affirmative action programs
Programs that ensure that decisions and practices
enhance the employment, upgrading, and retention
of members of protected groups

however, a significant proportion of the workforce is unionized. The higher percentage of unionized workers has placed increased importance on industrial relations specialists in Australia, and reduced the control of line managers over workplace labor issues. However, in 1997, Australia overhauled its labor and industrial relations laws with the objective of increasing productivity and reducing union power. The Workplace Relations Bill gives employers greater flexibility to negotiate directly with employees on pay, hours, and benefits. It also simplifies federal regulation of labor–management relations.

Our final example, Germany, is similar to most Western European countries when it comes to HRM practices. Legislation requires companies to practice representative participation, in which the goal is to redistribute power within the organization, putting labor on a more equal footing with the interests of management and stockholders. The two most common forms of representative participation are work councils and board representatives. **Work councils** link employees with management. They are groups of nominated or elected employees who must be consulted when management makes decisions involving personnel. **Board representatives** are employees who sit on a company's board of directors and represent the interest of the firm's employees.

7.2 Discuss the tasks associated with identifying and selecting competent employees.

HOW DO MANAGERS IDENTIFY AND SELECT COMPETENT EMPLOYEES?

Every organization needs people to do whatever work is necessary for doing what the organization is in business to do. How do organizations get those people? And more importantly what can they do to ensure they get competent, talented people? This first phase of the HRM process involves three tasks: employment planning, recruitment and downsizing, and selection.

What Is Employment Planning?

Internet start-ups across Silicon Valley are struggling to compete for talent as more-established companies such as Facebook, Twitter, and Zynga are looking to add employees as business continues to grow. During the last economic downturn, Boeing cut more than 3,000 jobs, mostly from its commercial airplanes unit. During the same time, it added 106 employees to its defense unit and was looking for several hundred more.[4] Like many companies, these start-ups and Boeing are juggling the supply of human resources to meet demand.

Employment planning is the process by which managers ensure that they have the right number and kinds of people in the right places at the right times, people who are capable of effectively and efficiently completing those tasks that will help the organization achieve its overall goals. Employment planning, then, translates the organization's mission and goals into an HR plan that will allow the organization to achieve those goals. The process can be condensed into two steps: (1) assessing current human resources and future human resource needs, and (2) developing a plan to meet those needs.

HOW DOES AN ORGANIZATION CONDUCT AN EMPLOYEE ASSESSMENT? Managers begin by reviewing the current human resource status. This review is typically done by generating a **human resource inventory**. It's not difficult to generate an inventory in most organizations since the information for it is derived from forms completed by employees. Such inventories might list the name, education, training, prior employment, languages spoken, capabilities, and specialized skills of each employee in the organization. This inventory allows managers to assess what talents and skills are currently available in the organization.

Another part of the current assessment is **job analysis**. Whereas the human resources inventory is concerned with telling management what individual employees can do, job analysis is more fundamental. It's typically a lengthy process, one in which workflows are analyzed and skills and behaviors that are necessary to perform jobs are identified. For instance, what does an international reporter who works for the *Wall Street Journal* do? What minimal knowledge, skills, and abilities are necessary for the adequate performance of this job? How do the job requirements for an international reporter compare with those for a domestic reporter or for a newspaper editor? Job analysis can answer these questions. Ultimately, the purpose of job analysis is to determine the kinds of skills, knowledge, and attitudes needed to successfully perform each job. This information is then used to develop or revise job descriptions and job specifications.

A **job description** is a written statement that describes the job—what a job holder does, how it's done, and why it's done. It typically portrays job content, environment, and conditions of employment. The **job specification** states the minimum qualifications that a person must possess to perform a given job successfully. It focuses on the person and identifies the knowledge, skills, and attitudes needed to do the job effectively. The job description and job specification are important documents when managers begin recruiting and selecting. For instance, the job description can be used to describe the job to potential candidates. The job specification keeps the manager's attention on the list of qualifications necessary for an incumbent to perform a job and assists in determining whether candidates are qualified. Furthermore, hiring individuals on the basis of the information contained in these two documents helps ensure that the hiring process does not discriminate.

3M Company needs a constant flow of creative scientists and engineers into its organization in order to achieve its goal of continually inventing new products through technological innovation. In a typical year, 3M hires several hundred scientists and technical experts. But faced with a future shortage of employees in these fields, 3M has developed a plan to replenish its supply of scientists. Part of the plan is an educational program that brings public high school students to 3M headquarters where they learn directly about science and technology from the company's researchers. In this photo, a 3M research specialist (left) works with a student in the company's adhesives laboratory.

HOW ARE FUTURE EMPLOYEE NEEDS DETERMINED? Future human resource needs are determined by the organization's strategic direction. Demand for human resources (employees) is a result of demand for the organization's products or services. On the basis of an estimate of total revenue, managers can attempt to establish the number and mix of people needed to reach that revenue. In some cases, however, the situation may be reversed. When particular skills are necessary and in scarce supply, the availability of needed human resources determines revenues. For example, managers of an upscale chain of assisted-living retirement facilities who find themselves with abundant business opportunities are limited in growing revenues by whether they can hire a qualified nursing staff to fully meet the needs of the residents. In most cases, however, the overall organizational goals and the resulting revenue forecast provide the major input in determining the organization's HR requirements.

After assessing both current capabilities and future needs, managers can estimate shortages—both in number and in kind—and highlight areas in which the organization is overstaffed. They can then develop a plan that matches these estimates with forecasts of future labor supply. Employment planning not only guides current staffing needs but also projects future employee needs and availability.

work councils
Groups of nominated or elected employees who must be consulted when management makes decisions involving personnel

board representatives
Employees who sit on a company's board of directors and represent the interest of employees

employment planning
The process by which managers ensure they have the right numbers and kinds of people in the right places at the right time

human resource inventory
A report listing important information about employees such as name, education, training, skills, languages spoken, and so forth

job analysis
An assessment that defines jobs and the behaviors necessary to perform them

job description
A written statement that describes a job

job specification
A written statement of the minimum qualifications that a person must possess to perform a given job successfully

How Do Organizations Recruit Employees?

Once managers know their current staffing levels—understaffed or overstaffed—they can begin to do something about it. If vacancies exist, they can use the information gathered through job analysis to guide them in **recruitment**—that is, the process of locating, identifying, and attracting capable applicants. On the other hand, if employment planning indicates a surplus, managers may want to reduce the labor supply within the organization and initiate downsizing or restructuring activities.

WHERE DOES A MANAGER RECRUIT APPLICANTS? Applicants can be found by using several sources, including the Internet. Exhibit 7–3 offers some guidance. The source that's used should reflect the local labor market, the type or level of position, and the size of the organization.

Which recruiting sources tend to produce superior applicants? Most studies have found that employee referrals generally produce the best applicants.[5] Why? First, applicants referred by current employees are prescreened by those employees. Because the recommenders know both the job and the person being recommended, they tend to refer well-qualified applicants.[6] Second, because current employees often feel that their reputation in the organization is at stake with a referral, they tend to make referrals only when they are reasonably confident that the referral won't make them look bad. However, managers shouldn't always opt for the employee-referred applicant; such referrals may not increase the diversity and mix of employees.

How Does a Manager Handle Layoffs?

Nokia reduces its global workforce by 7,000 (nearly 5% of its total workforce). Panasonic, the biggest Japanese maker of consumer electronic goods, cuts 17,000 jobs as it "adapts its business to a changing global environment." MySpace lays off 500 employees, cutting its staff count by 47 percent.[7]

In the past decade, and especially during the last couple of years, most global organizations, as well as many government agencies and small businesses, have been forced to shrink the size of their workforce or restructure their skill composition. Downsizing has become a relevant strategy for meeting the demands of a dynamic environment.

EXHIBIT 7-3   Recruiting Sources

SOURCE	ADVANTAGE	DISADVANTAGE
Internal searches	Low cost; build employee morale; candidates are familiar with organization	Limited supply; may not increase proportion of protected group employees
Advertisements	Wide distribution can be targeted to specific groups	Generate many unqualified candidates
Employee referrals	Knowledge about the organization provided by current employees; can generate strong candidates because a good referral reflects on the recommender	May not increase the diversity and mix of employees
Public employment agencies	Free or nominal cost	Candidates tend to be lower skilled, although some skilled employees available
Private employment agencies	Wide contacts; careful screening; short-term guarantees often given	High cost
School placement	Large, centralized body of candidates	Limited to entry-level positions
Temporary help services	Fill temporary needs	Expensive
Employee leasing and independent contractors	Fill temporary needs but usually for more specific, longer-term projects	Little commitment to an organization other than current project

EXHIBIT 7-4	Downsizing Options
OPTION	DESCRIPTION
Firing	Permanent involuntary termination
Layoffs	Temporary involuntary termination; may last only a few days or extend to years
Attrition	Not filling openings created by voluntary resignations or normal retirements
Transfers	Moving employees either laterally or downward; usually does not reduce costs but can reduce intraorganizational supply–demand imbalances
Reduced workweeks	Having employees work fewer hours per week, share jobs, or through furloughs perform their jobs on a part-time basis
Early retirements	Providing incentives to older and more-senior employees for retiring before their normal retirement date
Job sharing	Having employees, typically two part-timers, share one full-time position

WHAT ARE DOWNSIZING OPTIONS?   Obviously, people can be fired, but other restructuring choices may be more beneficial to the organization. Exhibit 7–4 summarizes a manager's major downsizing options. Keep in mind that, regardless of the method chosen, employees may suffer. We discuss downsizing more fully—for both victims and survivors—later in this chapter.

How Do Managers Select Job Applicants?

Once the recruiting effort has developed a pool of applicants, the next step in the HRM process is to determine who is best qualified for the job. In essence, then, the selection process is a prediction exercise: It seeks to predict which applicants will be "successful" if hired; that is, who will perform well on the criteria the organization uses to evaluate its employees. In filling a network administrator position, for example, the selection process should be able to predict which applicants will be capable of properly installing, debugging, and managing the organization's computer network. For a position as a sales representative, it should predict which applicants will be successful at generating high sales volumes. Consider, for a moment, that any selection decision can result in four possible outcomes. As shown in Exhibit 7–5, two outcomes would indicate correct decisions, and two would indicate errors.

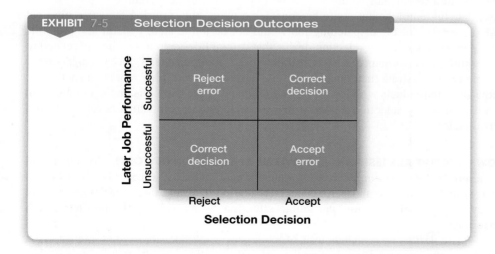

EXHIBIT 7-5   Selection Decision Outcomes

A decision is correct (1) when the applicant who was predicted to be successful (was accepted) and later proved to be successful on the job, or (2) when the applicant who was predicted to be unsuccessful (was rejected) and, if hired, would not have been able to do the job. In the former case, we have successfully accepted; in the latter case, we have successfully rejected. Problems occur, however, when we reject applicants who, if hired, would have performed successfully on the job (called *reject errors*) or accept those who subsequently perform poorly (*accept errors*). These problems are, unfortunately, far from insignificant. A generation ago, reject errors only meant increased selection costs because more applicants would have to be screened. Today, selection techniques that result in reject errors can open the organization to charges of employment discrimination, especially if applicants from protected groups are disproportionately rejected. Accept errors, on the other hand, have obvious costs to the organization, including the cost of training the employee, the costs generated or profits forgone because of the employee's incompetence, and the cost of severance and the subsequent costs of additional recruiting and selection screening. The major intent of any selection activity is, therefore, to reduce the probability of making reject errors or accept errors while increasing the probability of making correct decisions. We do this by using selection procedures that are both reliable and valid.

WHAT IS RELIABILITY?   Reliability addresses whether a selection device measures the same characteristic consistently. For example, if a test is reliable, any individual's score should remain fairly stable over time, assuming that the characteristics it is measuring are also stable. The importance of reliability should be self-evident. No selection device can be effective if it's low in reliability. Using such a device would be the equivalent of weighing yourself every day on an erratic scale. If the scale is unreliable—randomly fluctuating, say, 10 to 15 pounds every time you step on it—the results will not mean much. To be effective predictors, selection devices must possess an acceptable level of consistency.

WHAT IS VALIDITY?   Any selection device that a manager uses—such as application forms, tests, interviews, or physical examinations—must also demonstrate validity. Validity is based on a proven relationship between the selection device used and some relevant measure. For example, we mentioned earlier a firefighter applicant who was wheelchair bound. Because of the physical requirements of a firefighter's job, someone confined to a wheelchair would be unable to pass the physical endurance tests. In that case, denying employment could be considered valid, but requiring the same physical endurance tests for the dispatching job would not be job related. Federal law prohibits managers from using any selection device that cannot be shown to be directly related to successful job performance. That constraint goes for entrance tests, too; managers must be able to demonstrate that, once on the job, individuals with high scores on such a test outperform individuals with low scores. Consequently, the burden is on the organization to verify that any selection device it uses to differentiate applicants is related to job performance.

HOW EFFECTIVE ARE TESTS AND INTERVIEWS AS SELECTION DEVICES?   Managers can use a number of selection devices to reduce accept and reject errors. The best-known devices include written and performance-simulation tests and interviews. Let's briefly review each device, giving particular attention to its validity in predicting job performance.

Typical *written tests* include tests of intelligence, aptitude, ability, and interest. Such tests have long been used as selection devices, although their popularity has run in cycles. Written tests were widely used after World War II, but beginning in the late 1960s, they fell out of favor. They were frequently characterized as discriminatory, and many organizations could not validate that their written tests were job related. Today, written tests have made a comeback although most of them are now Internet based.[8] Managers are increasingly aware that poor hiring decisions are costly and that properly designed tests can reduce the likelihood of making such decisions. In addition, the cost of developing and validating a set of written tests for a specific job has declined significantly.

A review of the evidence finds that tests of intellectual ability, spatial and mechanical ability, perceptual accuracy, and motor ability are moderately valid predictors for many semiskilled and unskilled operative jobs in an industrial organization.[9] However, an enduring criticism of written tests is that intelligence and other tested characteristics can be somewhat removed from the actual performance of the job itself.[10] For example, a high score on an intelligence test is not necessarily a good indicator that the applicant will perform well as a computer programmer. This criticism has led to an increased use of *performance-simulation tests*.

What better way to find out whether an applicant for a technical writing position at Apple can write technical manuals than to ask him or her to do it? That's why there's an increasing interest in **performance-**

Chris Seward/Newscom

simulation tests. Undoubtedly, the enthusiasm for these tests lies in the fact that they're based on job analysis data and, therefore, should more easily meet the requirement of job relatedness than do written tests. Performance-simulation tests are made up of actual job behaviors rather than substitutes. The best-known performance-simulation tests are work sampling (a miniature replica of the job) and assessment centers (simulating real problems one may face on the job). The former is suited to persons applying for routine jobs, the latter to managerial personnel.

The advantage of performance simulation over traditional testing methods should be obvious. Because its content is essentially identical to job content, performance simulation should be a better predictor of short-term job performance and should minimize potential employment discrimination allegations. Additionally, because of the nature of their content and the methods used to determine content, well-constructed performance-simulation tests are valid predictors.

The *interview*, along with the application form, is an almost universal selection device. Few of us have ever gotten a job without undergoing one or more interviews. The irony of this is that the value of an interview as a selection device has been the subject of considerable debate.[11]

Interviews can be reliable and valid selection tools, but too often they're not. When interviews are structured and well organized, and when interviewers are held to relevant questioning, interviews are effective predictors.[12] But those conditions don't characterize many interviews. The typical interview in which applicants are asked a varying set of essentially random questions in an informal setting often provides little in the way of valuable information.

All kinds of potential biases can creep into interviews if they're not well structured and standardized. To illustrate, a review of the research leads us to the following conclusions:

- ◆ Prior knowledge about the applicant will bias the interviewer's evaluation.
- ◆ The interviewer tends to hold a stereotype of what represents a good applicant.
- ◆ The interviewer tends to favor applicants who share his or her own attitudes.
- ◆ The order in which applicants are interviewed will influence evaluations.
- ◆ The order in which information is elicited during the interview will influence evaluations.

The Container Store's business mission is to sell products that save customers space and time. The retailer hires salespeople who are energetic, display a positive and helpful attitude, love to sell, and can solve customers' one-of-a-kind storage and organization problems. To make interviews more valid and reliable, store managers use the behavioral or situational interview. In this photo, a Container Store recruiting manager leads a job candidate in a role-playing exercise as part of the interview. The recruiter presents the candidate with a realistic selling situation and then observes what she says and how she behaves. For The Container Store, the behavioral interview is an effective way to predict successful job performance.

---

reliability
The degree to which a selection device measures the same thing consistently

validity
The proven relationship between a selection device and some relevant criterion

performance-simulation tests
Selection devices based on actual job behaviors

◆ Negative information is given unduly high weight.

◆ The interviewer may make a decision concerning the applicant's suitability within the first four or five minutes of the interview.

◆ The interviewer may forget much of the interview's content within minutes after its conclusion.

◆ The interview is most valid in determining an applicant's intelligence, level of motivation, and interpersonal skills.

◆ Structured and well-organized interviews are more reliable than unstructured and unorganized ones.[13]

What can managers do to make interviews more valid and reliable? A number of suggestions that have been made over the years include reviewing the job description and job specification to help in assessing the applicant; preparing a structured set of questions to ask all applicants for the job; reviewing an applicant's résumé before meeting him or her; asking questions and listening carefully to the applicant's answer; and writing your evaluation of the applicant while the interview is still fresh in your mind.

One last popular modification to interviews has been the behavioral or situation interview.[14] In this type of interview, applicants are observed not only for what they say, but also how they behave. Applicants are presented with situations—often complex problems involving role playing—and are asked to "deal" with the situation. This type of interview provides an opportunity for interviewers to see how a potential employee will behave and how he or she will react under stress. Proponents of behavioral interviewing indicate such a process is much more indicative of an applicant's performance than simply having the individual tell the interviewer what he or she has done. In fact, research in this area indicates that behavioral interviews are nearly eight times more effective for predicting successful job performance.[15]

HOW CAN YOU "CLOSE THE DEAL"? Interviewers who treat the recruiting and hiring of employees as if the applicants must be sold on the job and exposed only to an organization's positive characteristics are likely to have a workforce that is dissatisfied and prone to high turnover.[16]

During the hiring process, every job applicant acquires a set of expectations about the company and about the job for which he or she is interviewing. When the information an applicant receives is excessively inflated, a number of things happen that have potentially negative effects on the company. First, mismatched applicants are less likely to withdraw from the search process. Second, because inflated information builds unrealistic expectations, new employees are likely to become quickly dissatisfied and to resign prematurely. Third, new hires are prone to become disillusioned and less committed to the organization when they face the unexpected harsh realities of the job. In many cases, these individuals feel that they were misled during the hiring process and may become problem employees.

To increase job satisfaction among employees and reduce turnover, managers should consider a **realistic job preview (RJP)**.[17] An RJP includes both positive and negative information about the job and the company. For example, in addition to the positive comments typically expressed in the interview, the applicant is told of the less attractive aspects of the job. For instance, he or she might be told that there are limited opportunities to talk to coworkers during work hours, that chances of being promoted are slim, or that work hours fluctuate so erratically that employees may be required to work during what are usually off hours (nights and weekends). Research indicates that applicants who have been given a realistic job preview hold lower and more realistic job expectations for the jobs they will be performing and are better able to cope with the frustrating elements of the job than are applicants who have been given only inflated information. The result is fewer unexpected resignations by new employees. For managers, realistic job previews offer a major insight into the HRM process. That is, it's just as important to *retain* good people as it is to *hire* them in the first place. Presenting only positive job aspects to an applicant may initially entice him or her to join the organization, but it may be a decision that both parties quickly regret.

HOW ARE EMPLOYEES PROVIDED WITH NEEDED SKILLS AND KNOWLEDGE?

If we've done our recruiting and selecting properly, we should have hired competent individuals who can perform successfully on the job. But successful performance requires more than possessing certain skills. New hires must be acclimated to the organization's culture and be trained and given the knowledge to do the job in a manner consistent with the organization's goals. To achieve this, HRM uses orientation and training.

Explain how employees are provided with needed skills and knowledge. 7.3

How Are New Hires Introduced to the Organization?

Once a job candidate has been selected, he or she needs to be introduced to the job and organization. This introduction is called **orientation**.[18] The major goals of orientation are to reduce the initial anxiety all new employees feel as they begin a new job; to familiarize new employees with the job, the work unit, and the organization as a whole; and to facilitate the outsider–insider transition. *Job orientation* expands on the information the employee obtained during the recruitment and selection stages. The new employee's specific duties and responsibilities are clarified as well as how his or her performance will be evaluated. Orientation is also the time to correct any unrealistic expectations new employees might hold about the job. *Work unit orientation* familiarizes an employee with the goals of the work unit, makes clear how his or her job contributes to the unit's goals, and provides an introduction to his or her coworkers. *Organization orientation* informs the new employee about the organization's goals, history, philosophy, procedures, and rules. This information includes relevant HR policies such as work hours, pay procedures, overtime requirements, and benefits. And a tour of the organization's physical facilities is often part of this orientation.

Managers have an obligation to make the integration of a new employee into the organization as smooth and anxiety-free as possible. Successful orientation, whether

TECHNOLOGY AND THE MANAGER'S JOB — DIGITAL HR

HR has gone digital.[19] Using software that automates many basic HR processes associated with recruiting, selecting, orienting, training, appraising performance, and storing and retrieving employee information, HR departments have cut costs and optimized service. One HR area where IT has contributed is in pre-employment assessments. For instance, at KeyBank, a Cleveland-based financial services organization, virtual "job tryout simulations" have been used in order to reduce 90-day turnover rates and create more consistency in staffing decisions. These simulations create an interactive multimedia experience and mimic key job tasks for competencies such as providing client service, adapting to change, supporting team members, following procedures, and working efficiently. Before using these virtual assessments, the bank was losing 13 percent of new tellers and call center associates in their first 90 days. After implementing the virtual assessments, that number dropped to 4 percent.

Another area where IT has had a significant impact is in training. In a survey by the American Society for Training and Development, 95 percent of the responding companies reported using some form of e-learning. Using technology to deliver needed knowledge, skills, and attitudes has had many benefits. As one researcher said, "The ultimate purpose of e-learning is not to reduce the cost of training, but to improve the way your organization does business." And in many instances, it seems to do that! For example, when Hewlett-Packard looked at how its customer service was affected by a blend of e-learning and other instructional methods, rather than just classroom training, it found that "sales representatives were able to answer questions more quickly and accurately, enhancing customer-service provider relations." And Unilever found that after e-learning training for sales employees, sales increased by several million dollars.

Think About:

· HR is supposed to be a "people-oriented" profession. Does the use of all this technology make it less so? Why or why not?

· Have you ever applied for a job on one of the many online job sites? What was your experience like? What benefits do these sites offer? What drawbacks do they have?

· You want a job after graduating from college. Knowing that you're likely to encounter online recruitment and selection procedures, how can you best prepare for making yourself stand out in the process?

realistic job preview (RJP)
A preview of a job that provides both positive and negative information about the job and the company

orientation
Introducing a new employee to the job and the organization

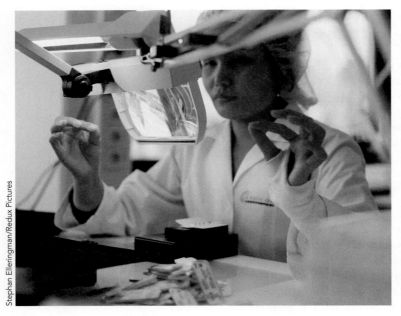

Stephan Elleringman/Redux Pictures

Ethicon, a subsidiary of Johnson & Johnson, is a global medical device firm that places a high priority on employee training. Working at an Ethicon plant in Germany, the employee shown here joins together under a microscope extremely fine threads and needles—finer than a human eyelash—that surgeons use during optical, neuron, and vascular surgery. Training for this type of work that requires great dexterity and accuracy takes about six months. Extensive and intensive employee training by Ethicon and other firms that make medical devices used by health care practitioners is important in promoting healing and speeding the recovery of millions of patients.

formal or informal, results in an outsider–insider transition that makes the new member feel comfortable and fairly well-adjusted, lowers the likelihood of poor work performance, and reduces the probability of a surprise resignation by the new employee only a week or two into the job.[20]

What Is Employee Training?

On the whole, planes don't cause airline accidents, people do. Most collisions, crashes, and other airline mishaps—nearly three-quarters of them—result from errors by the pilot or air traffic controller, or from inadequate maintenance. Weather and structural failures typically account for the remaining accidents.[21] We cite these statistics to illustrate the importance of training in the airline industry. Such maintenance and human errors could be prevented or significantly reduced by better employee training, as shown by the amazing "landing" of US Airways Flight 1549 in the Hudson River in January 2009 with no loss of life. Pilot Captain Chesley Sullenberger attributed the positive outcome to the extensive and intensive training that all pilots and flight crews undergo.[22]

Employee training is a learning experience that seeks a relatively permanent change in employees by improving their ability to perform on the job. Thus, training involves changing skills, knowledge, attitudes, or behavior.[23] This change may involve what employees know, how they work, or their attitudes toward their jobs, coworkers, managers, and the organization. It's been estimated, for instance, that U.S. business firms spend billions each a year on formal courses and training programs to develop workers' skills.[24] Managers, of course, are responsible for deciding when employees are in need of training and what form that training should take.

Determining training needs typically involves answering several questions. If some of these questions sound familiar, you've been paying close attention. It's precisely the type of analysis that takes place when managers develop an organizational structure to achieve their strategic goals—only now the focus is on the people.[25]

The questions in Exhibit 7–6 suggest the kinds of signals that can warn a manager when training may be necessary. The more obvious ones are related directly to productivity. Indications that job performance is declining include decreases in production numbers, lower quality, more accidents, and higher scrap or rejection rates. Any of these outcomes might suggest that worker skills need to be fine-tuned. Of course, we're assuming that an employee's performance decline is in no way related to lack of effort. Managers, too, must also recognize that training may be required because the workplace is constantly evolving. Changes imposed on employees as a result of job redesign or a technological breakthrough also require training.

HOW ARE EMPLOYEES TRAINED? Most training takes place on the job. Why? It's simple and it usually costs less. However, on-the-job training can disrupt the workplace and result in an increase in errors while learning takes place. Also, some skill training is too complex to learn on the job and must take place outside the work setting.

Many different types of training methods are available. For the most part, we can classify them as on-the-job or off-the-job training. The more popular training methods are summarized in Exhibit 7–7.

HOW CAN MANAGERS ENSURE THAT TRAINING IS WORKING? It's easy to generate a new training program, but if training efforts aren't evaluated, any can be rationalized. It would be nice if all companies could boast the returns on investments in training that Neil Huffman Auto Group executives do; they claim they receive $230 in increased

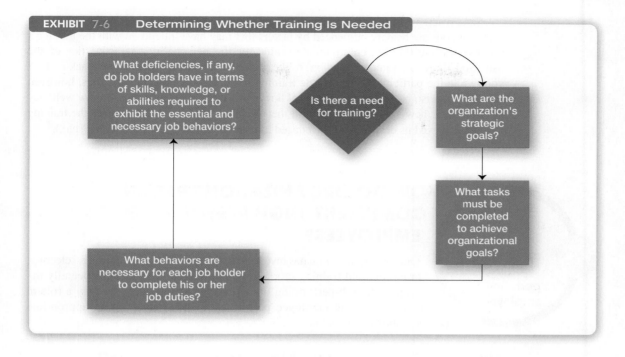

EXHIBIT 7-6   Determining Whether Training Is Needed

What deficiencies, if any, do job holders have in terms of skills, knowledge, or abilities required to exhibit the essential and necessary job behaviors?

Is there a need for training?

What are the organization's strategic goals?

What tasks must be completed to achieve organizational goals?

What behaviors are necessary for each job holder to complete his or her job duties?

productivity for every dollar spent on training.[26] But such a claim cannot be made unless training is properly evaluated.

How are training programs typically evaluated? The following approach is probably generalizable across organizations: Several managers, representatives from HRM, and a group of workers who have recently completed a training program are asked for their opinions. If the comments are generally positive, the program may get a favorable evaluation and it's continued until someone decides, for whatever reason, that it should be eliminated or replaced.

EXHIBIT 7-7   Typical Training Methods

SAMPLE ON-THE-JOB TRAINING METHODS

Job rotation	Lateral transfers allowing employees to work at different jobs. Provides good exposure to a variety of tasks.
Understudy assignments	Working with a seasoned veteran, coach, or mentor. Provides support and encouragement from an experienced worker. In the trades industry, this may also be an apprenticeship.

SAMPLE OFF-THE-JOB TRAINING METHODS

Classroom lectures	Lectures designed to convey specific technical, interpersonal, or problem-solving skills.
Films and videos	Using media to explicitly demonstrate technical skills that are not easily presented by other training methods.
Simulation exercises	Learning a job by actually performing the work (or its simulation). May include case analyses, experiential exercises, role-playing, and group interaction.
Vestibule training	Learning tasks on the same equipment that one actually will use on the job but in a simulated work environment.

employee training
A learning experience that seeks a relatively permanent change in employees by improving their ability to perform on the job

Such reactions from participants or managers, while easy to acquire, are the least valid. Their opinions are heavily influenced by factors that may have little to do with the training's effectiveness—difficulty, entertainment value, or the personality characteristics of the instructor. However, trainees' reactions to the training may, in fact, provide feedback on how worthwhile the participants viewed the training to be. Beyond general reactions, however, training must also be evaluated in terms of how much the participants learned; how well they are using their new skills on the job (did their behavior change?); and whether the training program achieved its desired results (reduced turnover, increased customer service, etc.).[27]

7.4 Describe strategies for retaining competent, high-performing employees.

HOW DO ORGANIZATIONS RETAIN COMPETENT, HIGH-PERFORMING EMPLOYEES?

Once an organization has invested significant dollars in recruiting, selecting, orienting, and training employees, it wants to keep them, especially the competent, high-performing ones! Two HRM activities that play a role in this are managing employee performance and developing an appropriate compensation and benefits program.

What Is a Performance Management System?

It's important for managers to get their employees to achieve performance levels that the organization considers desirable. How do managers ensure that employees are performing as well as they're supposed to? In organizations, the formal means of assessing the work of employees is through a systematic performance appraisal process.

A **performance management system** is a process of establishing performance standards and evaluating performance in order to arrive at objective human resource decisions—such as pay increases and training needs—as well as to provide documentation to support any personnel actions. But how do you evaluate an employee's performance? We list specific appraisal techniques in Exhibit 7–8.

The *written essay* requires no complex forms or extensive training to complete. However, a "good" or "bad" appraisal may be determined as much by the evaluator's writing skill as by the employee's actual level of performance. The use of *critical incidents* focuses the evaluator's attention on critical or key behaviors. The appraiser writes down anecdotes describing whatever the employee did that was especially effective or ineffective. The key here is that specific behaviors are cited, not vaguely defined personality traits. One of the oldest and most popular methods of appraisal is by *adjective rating scales*. This method lists a set of performance factors such as quantity and quality of work, job knowledge,

EXHIBIT 7-8	Performance Appraisal Methods	
METHOD	**ADVANTAGE**	**DISADVANTAGE**
Written essay	Simple to use	More a measure of evaluator's writing ability than of employee's actual performance
Critical incidents	Rich examples; behaviorally based	Time-consuming; lack quantification
Graphic rating scales	Provide quantitative data; less time-consuming than others	Do not provide depth of job behavior assessed
BARS	Focus on specific and measurable job behaviors	Time-consuming; difficult to develop measures
Multiperson	Compares employees with one another	Unwieldy with large number of employees
MBO	Focuses on end goals; results oriented	Time-consuming
360° appraisal	More thorough	Time-consuming

cooperation, loyalty, attendance, honesty, and initiative. The evaluator then goes down the list and rates each factor on an incremental scale. An approach that has received renewed attention involves *behaviorally anchored rating scales (BARS)*.[28] These scales combine major elements from the critical incident and adjective rating scale approaches. The appraiser rates an employee according to items along a numerical scale, but the items are examples of actual behavior on a given job rather than general descriptions or traits.[29]

Finally, an appraisal device that seeks performance feedback from such sources as the person being rated, bosses, peers, team members, customers, and suppliers has become popular in organizations. It's called the **360-degree appraisal**.[30] It's being used in approximately 90 percent of *Fortune* 1000 firms, including such companies as Otis Elevator, DuPont, Nabisco, Pfizer, ExxonMobil, Cook Children's Health Care System, General Electric, UPS, and Nokia.[31]

In today's dynamic organizations, traditional performance evaluation systems may be outdated.[32] Downsizing has given supervisors greater responsibility and more employees who report directly to them. Accordingly, it may be next to impossible for supervisors to have extensive job knowledge of each of their employees. Furthermore, the growth of project teams and employee involvement places the responsibility for evaluation where people are better able to make accurate assessments.[33]

The 360-degree feedback process also has some positive benefits for development concerns.[34] Many managers simply do not know how their employees view them and the work they have done. Research studies into the effectiveness of 360-degree performance appraisals report positive results including more accurate feedback, empowering employees, reducing the subjective factors in the evaluation process, and developing leadership in an organization.[35]

SHOULD PEOPLE BE COMPARED TO ONE ANOTHER OR AGAINST A SET OF STANDARDS?   The methods previously identified have one thing in common. They require us to evaluate employees on the basis of how well their performance matches established or absolute criteria. Multiperson comparisons, on the other hand, compare one person's performance with that of one or more individuals. These are relative, not absolute, measuring devices. The three most popular forms of this method are group-order ranking, individual ranking, and paired comparison.

The *group-order ranking* requires the evaluator to place employees into a particular classification such as "top fifth" or "second fifth." If a rater has 20 employees, only four can be in the top fifth, and, of course, four must be relegated to the bottom fifth. The *individual ranking* approach requires the evaluator to list the employees in order from highest to lowest. Only one can be "best." In an appraisal of 30 employees, the difference between the first and second employee is assumed to be the same as that between the twenty-first and twenty-second. Even though some employees may be closely grouped, no ties are allowed. In the *paired comparison*

Home Depot replaced a qualitative and subjective performance evaluation system that varied from region to region and store to store with a new companywide evaluation process based on mostly quantitative criteria. The new process includes the 360-degree appraisal for Home Depot's managers. Employees, customers, suppliers, and other sources now review managers by assigning points for specific behaviors such as "displays character" and "drives change." The new review has given Home Depot more accurate feedback and has reduced subjective factors in the process. Shown here talking with managers and employees who participate in the 360-degree appraisal is Ann-Marie Campbell, president of Home Depot's southern division.

performance management system
A system that establishes performance standards that are used to evaluate employee performance

360-degree appraisal
An appraisal device that seeks feedback from a variety of sources for the person being rated

approach, each employee is compared with every other employee in the comparison group and rated as either the superior or weaker member of the pair. After all paired comparisons are made, each employee is assigned a summary ranking based on the number of superior scores he or she achieved. Although this approach ensures that each employee is compared against every other employee, it can become unwieldy when large numbers of employees are being assessed.

WHAT ABOUT MBO AS AN APPRAISAL APPROACH? We introduced management by objectives during our discussion of planning in Chapter 5. However, MBO is also a mechanism for appraising performance.

Employees are evaluated by how well they accomplish a specific set of objectives that are critical to the successful completion of their jobs. As you'll recall from our discussion in Chapter 5, these objectives need to be tangible, verifiable, and measurable. MBO's popularity among managerial personnel is probably due to its focus on end goals. Managers tend to emphasize such results-oriented outcomes as profit, sales, and costs. This emphasis meshes with MBO's concern with quantitative measures of performance. Because MBO emphasizes ends rather than means, this appraisal method allows managers to choose the best path for achieving their goals.

What Happens If an Employee's Performance Is Not Up to Par?

So far this discussion has focused on the performance management system. But what if an employee is not performing in a satisfactory manner? What can you do?

If, for some reason, an employee is not meeting his or her performance goals, a manager needs to find out why. If it's because the employee is mismatched for the job (a hiring error) or because he or she does not have adequate training, the fix is relatively simple. The manager can either reassign the individual to a job that better matches his or her skills or train the employee to do the job more effectively. If the problem is associated with an employee's lack of desire to do the job, not with his or her abilities, it becomes a **discipline** problem. In that case, a manager can try counseling and, if necessary, take disciplinary action such as verbal and written warnings, suspensions, and even terminations.

Employee counseling is a process designed to help employees overcome performance-related problems. Rather than viewing the performance problem from a punitive standpoint (discipline), employee counseling attempts to uncover why employees have lost their desire or ability to work productively. More importantly, it's designed to find ways to fix the problem. In many cases, employees don't go from being productive one day to being unproductive the next. Rather, the change happens gradually and may be a function of what's occurring in their personal lives. Employee counseling attempts to assist employees in getting help to resolve whatever is bothering them. The premise behind employee counseling is fairly simple: It's beneficial to both the organization and the employee. Just as it's costly to have an employee quit shortly after being hired, it's costly to fire someone. The time spent recruiting and selecting, orienting, training, and developing employees translates into money. If, however, an organization can help employees overcome personal problems and get them back on the job quickly, it can avoid these costs. But make no mistake about it, employee counseling is not intended to lessen the effect of an employee's poor performance, nor is it intended to reduce his or her responsibility to change inappropriate work behavior. If the employee can't or won't accept help, then disciplinary actions must be taken.

How Are Employees Compensated?

Executives at Discovery Communications Inc. had an employee morale problem on their hands. Many of the company's top performers were making the same salaries as the poorer performers and the company's compensation program didn't allow for giving raises to people who stayed in the same position. The only way for managers to reward the top performers was to give them a bonus or promote them to another position. Executives were discovering that not only was that unfair, it was counterproductive. So they overhauled the program.[37]

Although there are exceptions, most of us work for money. What our jobs pay and what benefits we get fall under the heading of compensation and benefits. Determining levels of compensation isn't easy. However, most of us expect to receive appropriate compensation from our employer. Developing an effective and appropriate compensation system is an important part of the HRM process.[38] It can help attract and retain competent and talented individuals who help an organization accomplish its mission and goals. In addition, an organization's compensation system has been shown to have an impact on its strategic performance.[39] Managers must develop a compensation system that reflects the changing nature of work and the workplace in order to keep people motivated.

HOW ARE PAY LEVELS DETERMINED? How does management decide who gets paid $15.85 an hour and who receives $325,000 a year? The answer lies in **compensation administration**. The goals of compensation administration are to design a cost-effective pay structure that will attract and retain competent employees and to provide an incentive for these individuals to exert high energy levels at work. Compensation administration also attempts to ensure that pay levels, once determined, will be perceived as fair by all employees. Fairness means that the established pay levels are adequate and consistent for the demands and requirements of the job. Therefore, the primary determination of pay is the kind of job an employee performs. Different jobs require different kinds and levels of skills, knowledge, and abilities, and these factors vary in their value to the organization. So, too, do the responsibility and authority of various positions. In short, the higher the skills, knowledge, and abilities—and the greater the authority and responsibility—the higher the pay.

So, how do managers determine who gets paid what? Several factors influence the compensation and benefit packages that different employees receive. Exhibit 7–9 summarizes

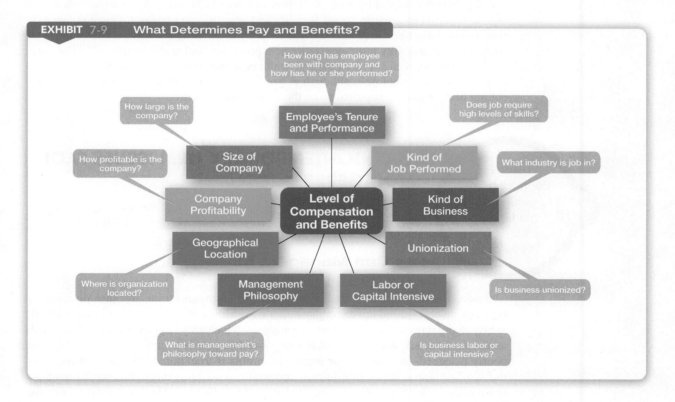

EXHIBIT 7-9 **What Determines Pay and Benefits?**

---

discipline
Actions taken by a manager to enforce an organization's standards and regulations

employee counseling
A process designed to help employees overcome performance-related problems

compensation administration
The process of determining a cost-effective pay structure that will attract and retain employees, provide an incentive for them to work hard, and ensure that pay levels will be perceived as fair

these factors, which are job-based and business or industry-based. One factor that's critical is the organization's philosophy toward compensation. Some organizations, for instance, don't pay employees any more than they have to. In the absence of a union contract that stipulates wage levels, those organizations only have to pay minimum wage for most of their jobs. On the other hand, some organizations are committed to a compensation philosophy of paying their employees at or above area wage levels in order to emphasize that they want to attract and keep the best pool of talent.

Many organizations are using alternative approaches to determining compensation including skill-based pay and variable pay. **Skill-based pay** systems reward employees for the job skills and competencies they can demonstrate. Under this type of pay system, an employee's job title doesn't define his or her pay category, skills do.[40] Research shows that these types of pay systems tend to be more successful in manufacturing organizations than in service organizations and in organizations pursuing technical innovations.[41] On the other hand, many organizations use **variable pay** systems, in which an individual's compensation is contingent on performance—90 percent of U.S. organizations use variable pay plans, and 81 percent of Canadian and Taiwanese organizations do.[42]

WHY DO ORGANIZATIONS OFFER EMPLOYEE BENEFITS?   When an organization designs its overall compensation package, it has to look further than just an hourly wage or annual salary. It has to take into account another element, **employee benefits**, which are nonfinancial rewards designed to enrich employees' lives. They have grown in importance and variety over the past several decades. Once viewed as "fringes," today's benefit packages reflect efforts to provide something that each employee values.

The benefits offered by an organization vary widely in scope. Most organizations are legally required to provide Social Security and workers' and unemployment compensation, but organizations may also provide an array of benefits such as paid time off from work, life and disability insurance, retirement programs, and health insurance.[43] The costs of some of these, such as retirement and health insurance benefits, may be paid by both the employer and the employee, although as you'll see in the next section, organizations are cutting back or putting stipulations on these two costly benefits.

Discuss contemporary issues in managing human resources.

7.5

WHAT CONTEMPORARY HRM ISSUES FACE MANAGERS?

HR issues that face today's managers include downsizing, workforce diversity, sexual harassment, workplace spirituality, and HR costs.

How Can Managers Manage Downsizing?

Downsizing is the planned elimination of jobs in an organization. Because downsizing typically involves shrinking the organization's workforce, it's an important issue in HRM. When an organization has too many employees—which may happen when it's faced with an economic crisis, declining market share, overly aggressive growth, or when it's been poorly managed—one option for improving profits is to eliminate excess workers. Over the last few years, many well-known companies have gone through several rounds of downsizing—Boeing, Volkswagen, Microsoft, Dell, General Motors, Unisys, Siemens, Merck, and Toyota, among others. How can managers best manage a downsized workforce?

After downsizing, disruptions in the workplace and in employees' personal lives are to be expected. Stress, frustration, anxiety, and anger are typical reactions of both individuals being laid off and the job survivors. And it may surprise you to learn that both victims and survivors experience those feelings.[44] Many organizations have

EXHIBIT 7-10   Tips for Managing Downsizing

- Communicate openly and honestly:
  - Inform those being let go as soon as possible
  - Tell surviving employees the new goals and expectations
  - Explain impact of layoffs
- Follow any laws regulating severance pay or benefits
- Provide support/counseling for surviving employees
- Reassign roles according to individuals' talents and backgrounds
- Focus on boosting morale:
  - Offer individualized reassurance
  - Continue to communicate, especially one-on-one
  - Remain involved and available

helped layoff victims by offering a variety of job-help services, psychological counseling, support groups, severance pay, extended health insurance benefits, and detailed communications. Although some individuals react negatively to being laid off (the worst cases involve individuals returning to their former organization and committing a violent act), offers of assistance reveal that an organization does care about its former employees. While those being laid off get to start over with a clean slate and a clear conscience, survivors don't. Unfortunately, the "survivors" who retain their jobs and have the task of keeping the organization going or even of revitalizing it seldom receive attention. One negative consequence appears to be what is being called **layoff-survivor sickness**, a set of attitudes, perceptions, and behaviors of employees who survive involuntary staff reductions.[45] Symptoms include job insecurity, perceptions of unfairness, guilt, depression, stress from increased workload, fear of change, loss of loyalty and commitment, reduced effort, and an unwillingness to do anything beyond the required minimum.

To show concern for job survivors, managers may want to provide opportunities for employees to talk to counselors about their guilt, anger, and anxiety.[46] Group discussions can be a way for the survivors to vent their feelings. Some organizations have used downsizing as the spark to implement increased employee participation programs such as empowerment and self-managed work teams. In short, to keep morale and productivity high, managers should make every attempt to ensure that those individuals still working in the organization know that they're valuable and much-needed resources. Exhibit 7–10 summarizes some ways that managers can reduce the trauma associated with downsizing.[47]

How Can Workforce Diversity Be Managed?

Although we discussed the changing makeup of the workforce in Chapter 3, workforce diversity also affects such basic HRM activities as recruitment, selection, and orientation.[48]

Improving workforce diversity requires managers to widen their recruiting net. For example, the popular practice of relying on current employee referrals as a source of new job applicants tends to produce candidates who have similar characteristics to those of present employees. So managers have to look for applicants in places where they haven't typically looked before. To increase diversity, managers are increasingly

skill-based pay
A pay system that rewards employees for the job skills they demonstrate

variable pay
A pay system in which an individual's compensation is contingent on performance

employee benefits
Membership-based rewards designed to enrich employees' lives

downsizing
The planned elimination of jobs in an organization

layoff-survivor sickness
A set of attitudes, perceptions, and behaviors of employees who survive layoffs

RIGHT ? WRONG

It's likely to be a challenging issue for HR managers.[49] "It" is the use of medical marijuana by employees. Fourteen states and the District of Columbia have laws or constitutional amendments that allow patients with certain medical conditions such as cancer, glaucoma, or chronic pain to use marijuana without fear of being prosecuted. Federal prosecutors have been directed by the current administration not to bring criminal charges against marijuana users who follow their states' laws. However, that puts employers in a difficult position as they try to accommodate state laws on medical marijuana use while having to enforce federal rules or company drug-use policies that are based on federal law. Although courts have generally ruled that companies do not have to accommodate medical marijuana users, legal guidance is still not all that clear. Legal experts have warned employers to "not run afoul of disability and privacy laws." In addition to the legal questions, employers are concerned about the challenge of maintaining a safe workplace.

Think About:

- What ethical issues do you see in this?

- How might this issue affect HR processes such as recruitment, selection, performance management, compensation and benefits, and safety and health?

- What other stakeholders might be impacted by this? In what ways might they be impacted?

ZUMA Press/Newscom

turning to nontraditional recruitment sources such as women's job networks, over-50 clubs, urban job banks, disabled people's training centers, ethnic newspapers, and gay rights organizations. This type of outreach should enable an organization to broaden its pool of applicants.

Once a diverse set of applicants exists, efforts must be made to ensure that the selection process does not discriminate. Moreover, applicants need to be made comfortable with the organization's culture and be made aware of management's desire to accommodate their needs. For instance, at TGI Friday's, company managers work diligently to accommodate differences and create workplace choices for a diverse workforce; so, too, do companies such as Sodexo, Johnson & Johnson, Ernst & Young, Marriott International, IBM, and Bank of America.[50]

Finally, orientation is often difficult for women and minorities. Many organizations, such as Lotus and Hewlett-Packard, provide special workshops to raise diversity consciousness among current employees as well as programs for new employees that focus on diversity issues. The thrust of these efforts is to increase individual understanding of the differences each of us brings to the workplace. A number of companies also have special mentoring programs to deal with the reality that lower-level female and minority managers have few role models with whom to identify.[51]

What Is Sexual Harassment?

Sexual harassment is a serious issue in both public and private sector organizations. Some 12,000 complaints are filed with the EEOC each year,[52] with more than 16 percent of the complaints filed by males.[53] Settlements in some of these cases incurred a substantial cost to the companies in terms of litigation. It's estimated that sexual harassment is the single largest financial risk facing companies today—and can result in decreases (sometimes greater than 30%) in a company's stock price.[54] At Mitsubishi, for example, the company paid out more than $34 million to 300 women for the rampant sexual harassment to which they were exposed.[55] But it's more than just jury awards. Sexual harassment results in millions lost in absenteeism, low productivity, and turnover.[56] Sexual harassment, furthermore, is not just a U.S. phenomenon. It's a global issue. For instance, nearly 10 percent of workers responding to a global survey reported that they had been harassed sexually or physically at work. The survey covered countries such as India, China, Saudi Arabia, Sweden, France, Belgium, Germany, Great Britain, and Poland, among others.[57] Even though discussions of sexual harassment cases often focus on the large awards granted by a court, employers face other concerns. Sexual harassment creates an unpleasant work environment for organization members and undermines their ability to perform their jobs. But just what is sexual harassment?

Any unwanted action or activity of a sexual nature that explicitly or implicitly affects an individual's employment, performance, or work environment can be regarded as **sexual harassment**. It can occur between members of the opposite or of the same sex—between employees of the organization or between employee and nonemployee.[58] Although such an activity has been generally prohibited under Title VII (sex discrimination) in the United States, in recent years this problem has gained more recognition. By most accounts, prior to the mid-1980s, occurrences were generally viewed as isolated incidents, with the individual committing the act being solely responsible (if at all) for his or her actions.[59] Today, charges of sexual harassment continue to appear in the headlines on an almost regular basis.

Much of the problem associated with sexual harassment is determining what constitutes this illegal behavior.[60] In 1993, the EEOC cited three situations in which sexual harassment can occur. In these instances, verbal or physical conduct toward an individual:

1. Creates an intimidating, offensive, or hostile environment.
2. Unreasonably interferes with an individual's work.
3. Adversely affects an employee's employment opportunities.

For many organizations, it's the offensive or hostile environment issue that's problematic.[61] What constitutes such an environment? Challenging hostile environment situations gained much support from the Supreme Court case of *Meritor Savings Bank v. Vinson*.[62] This case stemmed from a situation in which Ms. Vinson initially refused the sexual advances of her boss. However, out of fear of reprisal, she ultimately conceded. But according to court records, it didn't stop there. Vinson's boss continued to harass Vinson, subjecting her to severe hostility that affected her job.[63] In addition to supporting hostile environment claims, the *Meritor* case also identified employer liability; that is, in sexual harassment cases, an organization can be held liable for sexual harassment actions by its managers, employees, and even customers![64]

Although the *Meritor* case has implications for organizations, how do organizational members determine whether something is offensive? For instance, does sexually explicit language in the office create a hostile environment? How about off-color jokes? Pictures of women totally undressed? The answer is it could! It depends on the people in the organization and the environment in which they work. The point here is that we all must be attuned to what makes fellow employees uncomfortable—and if we don't know, then we should ask! Organizational success will, in part, reflect how sensitive each employee is toward another in the company. At DuPont, for example, the corporate culture and diversity programs are designed to eliminate sexual harassment through awareness and respect for all individuals.[65] It means understanding one another and, most importantly, respecting others' rights. Similar programs exist at FedEx, General Mills, and Levi-Strauss, among other companies.

If sexual harassment carries with it potential costs to the organization, what can a company do to protect itself?[66] The courts want to know two things—did the organization know about, or should it have known about, the alleged behavior? And what did managers do to stop it?[67] With the number and dollar amounts of the awards today, it's even more important for organizations and managers to educate all employees on sexual harassment matters and to have mechanisms available to monitor employees. Furthermore, "victims" no longer have to prove that their psychological well-being is seriously affected.

Kathleen Lange/AP Images

A peer-training program at the U.S. Naval Academy is designed to prevent sexual harassment, a high-profile problem not only at the military college but also in the U.S. Navy and U.S. Marine Corps. The Sexual Harassment and Assault Prevention Education (SHAPE) program is an open forum that gives midshipmen the opportunity to learn about and discuss many different aspects of sexual harassment, including gender discrimination and inappropriate language that can instigate harassment. Shown here are two student trainers guiding a class, one of 16 the midshipmen complete during their four years at the academy.

---

sexual harassment
Any unwanted action or activity of a sexual nature that explicitly or implicitly affects an individual's employment, performance, or work environment

The U.S. Supreme Court ruled in 1993, in the case of *Harris v. Forklift Systems, Inc.*, that victims do not have to suffer substantial mental distress to receive a jury award. Furthermore, in June 1998, the Supreme Court ruled that sexual harassment may have occurred even if the employee had not experienced any "negative" job repercussions. In this case, Kimberly Ellerth, a marketing assistant at Burlington Industries, filed harassment charges against her boss because he "touched her, suggested she wear shorter skirts, and told her during a business trip that he could make her job 'very hard or very easy.'" When Ellerth refused, the harasser never "punished" her; in fact, she even received a promotion during the time the harassment was ongoing. What the Supreme Court's decision in this case indicates is that "harassment is defined by the ugly behavior of the manager, not by what happened to the worker subsequently."[68]

Finally, in a sexual harassment matter, managers must remember that the harasser may have rights, too.[69] No action should be taken against someone until a thorough investigation has been conducted. Furthermore, the results of the investigation should be reviewed by an independent and objective individual before any action against the alleged harasser is taken. Even then, the harasser should be given an opportunity to respond to the allegation and have a disciplinary hearing if desired. Additionally, an avenue for appeal should also exist for the alleged harasser—an appeal heard by someone at a higher level of management who is not associated with the case.

What Is Workplace Spirituality?

What do organizations such as Southwest Airlines, Ford Motor Company, Tom's of Maine, Herman Miller, Tyson Foods, or Hewlett-Packard have in common? Among other characteristics, they're among a number of organizations that have embraced workplace spirituality.

Workplace spirituality is not about organized religious practices, theology, or one's spiritual leader.[70] Rather, **workplace spirituality** is about recognizing that employees have an inner life that nourishes and is nourished by meaningful work that takes place in the context of an organizational community. A recent study of the concept identified three factors: interconnection with a higher power, interconnection with human beings, and interconnection with nature and all living things.[71] Organizations that promote a spiritual culture recognize that employees have both a mind and a spirit, seek to find meaning and purpose in their work, and possess a desire to connect with other employees and be part of a community.

WHY THE EMPHASIS ON SPIRITUALITY IN TODAY'S ORGANIZATIONS? Historical management models had no room for spirituality.[72] These models typically focused on organizations that were efficiently run without feelings toward others. Similarly, concern about an employee's inner life had no role in managing organizations. But just as we've come to realize that the study of emotions improves our understanding of how and why people act the way they do in organizations, an awareness of spirituality can help one better understand employee work behavior in the twenty-first-century organization.

WHAT DOES A SPIRITUAL ORGANIZATION LOOK LIKE? The concept of spirituality draws on the ethics, values, motivation, work/life balance, and leadership elements of an organization. Spiritual organizations are concerned with helping employees develop and reach their full potential. They're also concerned with addressing problems created by work/life conflicts.

What differentiates spiritual organizations from their nonspiritual counterparts? Although research is fairly new in this arena, several characteristics tend to be associated with a spiritual organization.[73] We list them in Exhibit 7–11.

Although workplace spirituality has generated some interest in many organizations, it's not without its critics. Those who argue against spirituality in organizations

EXHIBIT 7-11   **Characteristics of a Spiritual Organization**

CHARACTERISTIC	DESCRIPTION
Strong sense of purpose	Organizational members know why the organization exists and what it values.
Focus on individual development	Employees are valuable and need to be nurtured to help them grow; this characteristic also includes a sense of job security.
Trust and openness	Organizational member relationships are characterized by mutual trust, honesty, and openness.
Employee empowerment	Employees are allowed to make work-related decisions that affect them, highlighting a strong sense of delegation of authority.
Tolerance of employee expression	The organizational culture encourages employees to be themselves and to express their moods and feelings without guilt or fear of reprimand.

typically focus on two issues. First is the question of legitimacy. Specifically, do organizations have the right to impose spiritual values on their employees? Second is the question of economics. Are spirituality and profits compatible? Let's briefly look at these issues.

The potential for an emphasis on spirituality to make some employees uneasy is clear. Critics argue that organizations have no business imposing spiritual values on employees. This criticism is undoubtedly valid when spirituality is defined as bringing religion and God into the workplace.[74] However, the criticism appears less stinging when the goal is limited to helping employees find meaning in their work lives.

The issue of whether spirituality and profits are compatible goals is certainly relevant for anyone in business. The evidence, although limited, indicates that the two may be compatible. Several studies show that organizations that have introduced spirituality into the workplace have witnessed improved productivity, reduced turnover, greater employee satisfaction, and increased organizational commitment.[75]

WHAT DOES HRM HAVE TO DO WITH SPIRITUALITY?   Ironically, introducing spirituality into the organization is nothing new for HR. In actuality, many of the areas that HRM addresses, and has done so for many years, are many of the same things that support spirituality.[76] For instance, matters such as work/life balances, proper selection of employees, setting performance goals and rewarding people for the work they do, are all components of making the organization more "spiritual." In fact, as you review the characteristics of a spiritual organization, in every case, HRM is either the leader in making such things happen, or is the vehicle by which the organization helps employees understand their responsibilities and offers the requisite training to make things happen. In the end, it's HRM that will make the workplace a supportive work environment, one where communication abounds and employees feel free to express themselves.

How and Why Are Organizations Controlling HR Costs?

HR costs are skyrocketing, especially those associated with employee health care and employee pensions. Organizations are looking for ways to control these costs.

workplace spirituality
A spiritual culture where organizational values promote a sense of purpose through meaningful work that takes place in the context of community

WHAT ABOUT EMPLOYEE HEALTH CARE COSTS?   Employees at Paychex who undergo a confidential health screening and risk assessment, and for those who smoke who agree to enroll in a smoking cessation program, can get free annual physicals, colonoscopies, and 100 percent coverage of preventive care as well as lower deductibles and costs. At Black and Decker Corporation, employees and dependents who certify in an honor system that they have been tobacco-free for at least six months pay $75 less per month for their medical and dental coverage. At Amerigas Propane, employees were given an ultimatum: get their medical checkups or lose their health insurance. Some 67 percent of employers are concerned about the effects of obesity on medical claims expenses.[77]

All these examples illustrate how companies are trying to control skyrocketing employee health care costs. Since 2002, health care costs have risen an average of 15 percent a year and are expected to double by the year 2016 from the $2.2 trillion spent in 2007. The new federal health care mandates are expected to also add to those costs.[78] And smokers cost companies even more—about 25 percent more for health care than nonsmokers do.[79] However, the biggest health care cost for companies is obesity—an estimated $73 billion a year in medical expenditures and absenteeism.[80] A study of manufacturing organizations found that presenteeism, which is defined as employees not performing at full capacity, was 1.8 percent higher for workers with moderate to severe obesity than for all other employees. The reason for the lost productivity is likely the result of reduced mobility because of body size or pain problems such as arthritis. Another study found that injuries sustained by obese workers often require substantially more medical care and are more likely to lead to permanent disabilities than similar injuries suffered by employees who were not obese.[81]

Is it any wonder that organizations are looking for ways to control their health care costs? How? First, many organizations are providing opportunities for employees to lead healthy lifestyles. From financial incentives to company-sponsored health and wellness programs, the goal is to limit rising health care costs. About 41 percent of companies use some type of positive incentives aimed at encouraging healthy behavior, up from 34 percent in 1996.[82] Another study indicated that nearly 90 percent of companies surveyed planned to aggressively promote healthy lifestyles to their employees during the next three to five years.[83] Many are starting sooner: Google, Yamaha Corporation of America, Caterpillar, and others are putting health food in company break rooms, cafeterias, and vending machines; providing deliveries of fresh organic fruit; and putting "calorie taxes" on fatty foods. At Wegmans Food Markets, employees are challenged to eat five cups of fruits and vegetables and walk 10,000 steps a day. And the "competition" between departments and stores has proved to be very popular and effective.[84] In the case of smokers, however, some companies have taken a more aggressive stance by increasing the amount smokers pay for health insurance or by firing them if they refuse to stop smoking.

WHAT ABOUT EMPLOYEE PENSION PLAN COSTS?   The other area where organizations are looking to control costs is employee pension plans. Corporate pensions have been around since the nineteenth century.[85] But the days when companies could afford to give employees a broad-based pension that provided them a guaranteed retirement income have changed. Pension commitments have become such an enormous burden that companies can no longer afford them. In fact, the corporate pension system has been described as "fundamentally broken."[86] It's not just struggling companies that have eliminated employee pension plans. Lots of reasonably sound companies—for instance, NCR, FedEx, Lockheed Martin, and Motorola—no longer provide pensions. Only 42 *Fortune* 100 companies now offer pension plans to their new hires. Even IBM, which closed its pension plan to new hires in December 2004, told employees that their pension benefits would be frozen.[87] Obviously, the pension issue is one that directly affects HR decisions. On the one hand, organizations want to attract talented, capable employees by offering them desirable benefits such as pensions. But on the other hand, organizations have to balance that with the costs of providing such benefits.

7 Review

7.1 Describe the key components of the human resource management process and the important influences on that process. The HRM process consists of eight activities that will staff an organization with competent, high-performing employees who are capable of sustaining their performance level over the long term. The first three HR activities involve employment planning and include recruitment, downsizing, and selection. The next two steps involve helping employees adapt to the organization and ensuring that their skills and knowledge are kept current, and include the HR activities of orienting and training. The last steps involve identifying performance goals, correcting performance problems, and helping employees sustain high levels of performance. These are done using the HR activities of performance appraisal, compensation and benefits, and safety and health. The main influences on the HRM process are legal although other environmental conditions such as restructuring, downsizing, diversity, and so forth can impact it as well.

7.2 Discuss the tasks associated with identifying and selecting competent employees. The first task is employment planning, which involves job analysis and the creation of job descriptions and job specifications. Then, if job needs are indicated, recruitment involves attempts to develop a pool of potential job candidates. Downsizing is used to reduce the labor supply. Selection involves determining who is best qualified for the job. Selection devices need to be both reliable and valid. Managers may want to give potential employees a realistic job preview.

7.3 Explain how employees are provided with needed skills and knowledge. New hires must be acclimated to the organization's culture and be trained and given the knowledge to do the job in a manner consistent with the organization's goals. Orientation—job, work unit, and organizational—provides new employees with information to introduce them to the job. Training is used to help employees improve their ability to perform on the job.

7.4 Describe strategies for retaining competent, high-performing employees. Two HRM activities that play a role in this are managing employee performance and developing an appropriate compensation and benefits program. Managing employee performance involves establishing performance standards and then appraising performance to see if those standards have been met. There are various performance appraisal techniques managers can use. If an employee's performance is not up to par, managers need to assess why and take action. Compensation and benefits programs can help attract and retain competent and talented individuals. Managers have to determine who gets paid what and what benefits will be offered.

7.5 Discuss contemporary issues in managing human resources. Downsizing is the planned elimination of jobs and must be managed from the perspective of layoff victims and job survivors. Workforce diversity must be managed through HRM activities including recruitment, selection, and orientation. Sexual harassment is a significant concern of organizations and managers, which mean programs and mechanisms must be in place to educate all employees about it. Workplace spirituality involves attempts by organizations to make work more meaningful to employees. Finally, organizations are looking for ways to control HR costs, especially health care costs and pension costs.

MyManagementLab   For more resources, go to www.mymanagementlab.com

UNDERSTANDING THE CHAPTER

1. How does HRM affect all managers?
2. Should an employer have the right to choose employees without governmental interference? Support your position.
3. Some critics claim that corporate HR departments have outlived their usefulness and are not there to help employees but to shield the organization from legal problems. What do you think? What benefits are there to having a formal HRM process? What are the drawbacks?
4. Do you think it's ethical for a prospective employer to delve into an applicant's life by means of interviews, tests, and background investigations? What if those

investigations involved looking at your Facebook page or personal blogs? Explain your position.

5. Discuss the advantages and drawbacks of the various recruiting sources.

6. Discuss the advantages and drawbacks of the various selection devices.

7. What are the benefits and drawbacks of realistic job previews? (Consider this question from both the perspective of the organization *and* the perspective of a potential employee.)

8. List the factors that influence employee compensation and benefits.

9. What, in your view, constitutes sexual harassment? Describe how companies can minimize sexual harassment in the workplace.

10. Research your chosen career by finding out what it's going to take to be successful in this career in terms of education, skills, experience, and so forth. Write a personal career guide that details this information.

Go to p. 423

YOUR TURN ᴛᴏ ʙᴇ A MANAGER for Chapter 7.

Endnotes

1. A. Schwartz, "Leadership Development in a Global Environment: Lessons Learned from One of the World's Largest Employers," *Industrial and Commercial Training,* vol. 43, no. 1 (2011), pp. 13–16; "HR Trendbook 2011: Games at Work," *HR Magazine,* 2011, p. 70; "UPS to Deliver 430m Parcels in Month Before Christmas," *Commercial Motor,* December 2, 2010, p. 14; M. J. Credeur, "Squeezing More Green Out of Brown," *Bloomberg BusinessWeek,* September 20, 2010, p. 43; J. Casale, "Thorough Training Delivers Safer Drivers," *Business Insurance,* July 12, 2010, p. 1; J. Levitz, "UPS Thinks Outside the Box on Driver Training," *Wall Street Journal,* April 6, 2010, pp. B1+; and K. Kingsbury, "Road to Recovery," *Time,* March 8, 2010, pp. Global 14–16.

2. Material for this chapter is drawn from D. A. DeCenzo and S. P. Robbins, *Fundamentals of Human Resources Management,* 10th ed. (Hoboken, NJ: John Wiley & Sons, 2010).

3. From the Past to the Present box based on D. A. Wren and A. G. Bedeian, *The Evolution of Management Thought,* 6th ed. (Hoboken, NJ: John Wiley & Sons, 2009), pp. 198–200; "Building Better Organizations: Industrial-Organizational Psychology in the Workplace," *Society for Industrial and Organizational Psychology,* www.siop.org (July 13, 2009); and M. Munsterberg, *Hugo Munsterberg: His Life and Work* (New York: Appleton-Century-Crofts, 1922).

4. P. W. Tam and S. Woo, "Talent War Crunches Start-Ups," *Wall Street Journal,* February 28, 2011, pp. B1+; and C. Tuna, "Many Companies Hire as They Fire," *Wall Street Journal,* May 11, 2009, p. B6.

5. J. J. Salopek, "Employee Referrals Remain a Recruiter's Best Friend," *Workforce Management Online,* December 2010; L. G. Klaff, "New Internal Hiring Systems Reduce Cost and Boost Morale," *Workforce Management,* March 2004, pp. 76–79; M. N. Martinez, "The Headhunter Within," *HR Magazine,* August 2001, pp. 48–55; "Even Non-Recruiting Companies Must Maintain Hiring Networks," *HR Focus,* November 2001, p. 8; and L. Greenhalgh, A. T. Lawrence, and

R. I. Sutton, "Determinants of Work Force Reduction Strategies in Declining Organizations," *Academy of Management Review,* April 1988, pp. 241–254.

6. J. J. Salopek, "Employee Referrals Remain a Recruiter's Best Friend"; "Employee Referral Programs: Highly Qualified New Hires Who Stick Around," *Canadian HR Reporter,* June 4, 2001, p. 21; and C. Lachnit, "Employee Referral Saves Time, Saves Money, Delivers Quality," *Workforce,* June 2001, pp. 66–72.

7. C. Lawton, "Nokia to Cut 7,000 Globally," *Wall Street Journal,* April 28, 2011, p. B3; D. Jolly, "Panasonic to Cut 17,000 Jobs," *New York Times Online,* April 28, 2011; and L. Segall, "MySpace Slashes Its Staff in Half," *CNNMoney.com,* January 11, 2011.

8. J. Mooney, "Pre-Employment Testing on the Internet: Put Candidates a Click Away and Hire at Modem Speed," *Public Personnel Management,* Spring 2002, pp. 41–52.

9. See, for instance, R. D. Arvey and J. E. Campion, "The Employment Interview: A Summary and Review of Recent Research," *Personnel Psychology,* Summer 1982, pp. 281–322; and M. M. Harris, "Reconsidering the Employment Interview: A Review of Recent Literature and Suggestions for Future Research," *Personnel Psychology,* Winter 1989, pp. 691–726; J. H. Prager, "Nasty or Nice: 56-Question Quiz," *Wall Street Journal,* February 22, 2000, p. A4; and M. K. Zachary, "Labor Law for Supervisors," *Supervision,* March 2001, pp. 23–26.

10. See, for instance, G. Nicholsen, "Screen and Glean: Good Screening and Background Checks Help Make the Right Match for Every Open Position," *Workforce,* October 2000, p. 70.

11. R. A. Posthuma, F. P. Morgeson, and M. A. Campion, "Beyond Employment Interview Validity: A Comprehensive Narrative Review of Recent Research and Trends Over Time," *Personnel Psychology,* Spring 2002, pp. 1–81.

12. A. I. Huffcutt, J. M. Conway, P. L. Roth, and N. J. Stone, "Identification and Meta-Analysis Assessment of Psychological Constructs Measured in Employment Interviews," *Journal of Applied Psychology* (October 2001), pp. 897–913; and

A. I. Huffcutt, J. A. Weekley, W. H. Wiesner, T. G. Degroot, and C. Jones, "Comparison of Situational and Behavioral Description Interview Questions for Higher-Level Positions," *Personnel Psychology,* Autumn 2001, pp. 619–644.

13. See C. H. Middendorf and T. H. Macan, "Note-Taking in the Employment Interview: Effects on Recall and Judgments," *Journal of Applied Psychology* (April 2002), pp. 293–303; D. Butcher, "The Interview Rights and Wrongs," *Management Today,* April 2002, p. 4; P. L. Roth, C. H. Can Iddekinge, A. I. Huffcutt, C. E. Eidson, and P. Bobko, "Corrections for Range Restriction in Structured Interview Ethnic Group Differences: The Value May Be Larger than Researchers Thought," *Journal of Applied Psychology* (April 2002), pp. 369–376; and E. Hermelin and I. T. Robertson, "A Critique and Standardization of Meta-Analytic Coefficients in Personnel Selection," *Journal of Occupational and Organizational Psychology* (September 2001), pp. 253–277.

14. See J. Merritt, "Improv at the Interview," *BusinessWeek,* February 3, 2003, p. 63; P. J. Taylor and B. Small, "Asking Applicants What They Would Do Versus What They Did Do: A Meta-Analysis Comparison of Situation and Past Behavior Employment Interview Questions," *Journal of Occupational and Organizational Psychology* (September 2002), pp. 277–295; S. D. Mauer, "A Practitioner-Based Analysis of Interviewer Job Expertise and Scale Format as Contextual Factors in Situational Interviews," *Personnel Psychology,* Summer 2002, pp. 307–328; and J. M. Barclay, "Improving Selection Interviews with Structure: Organizations' Use of Behavioral Interviews," *Personnel Review* 30, no. 1 (2001), pp. 81–95.

15. J. Merrit, "Improv at the Interview," p. 63.

16. S. H. Applebaum and M. Donia, "The Realistic Downsizing Preview: A Management Intervention in the Prevention of Survivor Syndrome (Part II)," *Career Development International,* January 2001, pp. 5–19.

17. D. Zielinski, "Effective Assessments," *HRMagazine,* January 2011, pp. 61–64; W. L. Gardner, B. J. Reithel, R. T. Foley, C. C. Cogliser, and F. O. Walumbwa, "Attraction to Organizational Culture Profiles: Effects of Realistic Recruitment and Vertical and Horizontal Individualism-Collectivism," *Management Communication Quarterly,* February 2009, pp. 437–472; and S. L. Premack and J. P. Wanous, "A Meta-Analysis of Realistic Job Preview Experiments," *Journal of Applied Psychology* (November 1985), pp. 706–720.

18. C. Garvey, "The Whirlwind of a New Job," *HR Magazine,* June 2001, pp. 110–118.

19. Technology and the Manager's Job box based on D. Zielinski, "Effective Assessments;" R. E. DeRouin, B. A. Fritzsche, and E. Salas, "E-Learning in Organizations," *Journal of Management* (December 2005), pp. 920–940; K. O'Leonard, *HP Case Study: Flexible Solutions for Multi-Cultural Learners,* (Oakland: CA: Bersin & Associates), 2004; S. Greengard, "The Dawn of Digital HR," *Business Finance,* October 2003, pp. 55–59; and J. Hoekstra, "Three in One," *Online Learning,* vol. 5 (2001), pp. 28–32.

20. B. P. Sunoo, "Results-Oriented Customer Service Training," *Workforce* (May 2001), pp. 84–90.

21. See, for instance, E. G. Tripp, "Aging Aircraft and Coming Regulations: Political and Media Pressures Have Encouraged the FAA to Expand Its Pursuit of Real and Perceived Problems of Older Aircraft and Their Systems. Operators Will Pay," *Business and Commercial Aviation,* March 2001, pp. 68–75.

22. "A&S Interview: Sully's Tale," *Air & Space Magazine,* www.airspacemag.com (February 18, 2009); A. Altman, "Chesley B. Sullenberger III," *Time,* www.time.com (January 16, 2009); and K. Burke, P. Donohue, and C. Siemaszko, "US Airways Airplane Crashes in Hudson River—Hero Pilot Chesley Sullenberger III Saves All Aboard," *New York Daily News,* www.nydailynews.com (January 16, 2009).

23. C. S. Duncan, J. D. Selby-Lucas, and W. Swart, "Linking Organizational Goals and Objectives to Employee Performance: A Quantitative Perspective," *Journal of American Academy of Business* (March 2002), pp. 314–318.

24. "Training Expenditures," *Training* (November–December 2010), p. 19.

25. R. Langlois, "Fairmont Hotels: Business Strategy Starts with People," *Canadian HR Reporter,* November 5, 2001, p. 19.

26. M. Dalahoussaye, "Show Me the Results," *Training* (March 2002), p. 28.

27. See, for example, R. E. Catalano and D. L. Kirkpatrick, "Evaluating Training Programs: The State of the Art," *Training and Development Journal* (May 1968), pp. 2–9.

28. A. Tziner, C. Joanis, and K. R. Murphy, "A Comparison of Three Methods of Performance Appraisal with Regard to Goal Properties, Goal Perception, and Rate Satisfaction," *Group and Organization Management,* June 2000, pp. 175–190; and T. W. Kent and T. J. Davis, "Using Retranslation to Develop Operational Anchored Scales to Assess the Motivational Context of Jobs," *International Journal of Management* (March 2002), pp. 10–16.

29. See, also, C. A. Ramus and U. Steger, "The Roles of Supervisory Support Behaviors and Environmental Policy in Employee 'Ecoinitiatives' at Leading-Edge European Companies," *Academy of Management Journal* (August 2000), pp. 605–626.

30. See R. de Andrés, J. L. Garcia-Lapresta, and J. González-Pachón, "Performance Appraisal Based on Distance Function Methods," *European Journal of Operational Research* (December 2010), pp. 1599–1607; and L. Atwater and J. Brett, "Feedback Format: Does It Influence Manager's Reaction to Feedback," *Journal of Occupational and Organizational Psychology* (December 2006), pp. 517–532.

31. See "Performance Appraisals," *Business Europe,* April 3, 2002, p. 3.

32. M. A. Peiperl, "Getting 360 Feedback Right," *Harvard Business Review,* January 2001, pp. 142–147.

33. T. J. Maurer, D. R. D. Mitchell, and F. G. Barbeite, "Predictors of Attitudes Toward a 360-Degree Feedback System and Involvement in Post-Feedback Management Development Activity," *Journal of Occupational and Organizational Psychology* (March 2002), pp. 87–107.

34. A. Evans, "From Every Angle," *Training* (September 2001), p. 22.

35. R. de Andrés, J. L. Garcia-Lapresta, and J. González-Pachón, "Performance Appraisal Based on Distance Function Methods," *European Journal of Operational Research* (December 2010), pp. 1599–1607; J. Nelson, "How to Ace Your Yearly Review," *Canadian Business,* December 7, 2010, p. 94; G. P. Sillup and R. Klimberg, "Assessing the Ethics of Implementing Performance Appraisal Systems," *Journal of Management Development,* vol. 29, no. 1 (2010), pp. 38–55; T. Maylett, "360-Degree Feedback Revisited: The Transition from Development to Appraisal," *Compensation & Benefits Review,*

September–October 2009, pp. 52–59; P. Kamen, "The Way That You Use It: Full Circle Can Build Better Organizations with the Right Approach," *CMA Management,* April 2003, pp. 10–13; M. Kennett, "First Class Coach," *Management Today* (December 2001), p. 84; and T. A. Beehr, L. Ivanitsjaya, C. P. Hansen, D. Erofeev, and D. M. Gudanowski, "Evaluation of 360-Degree Feedback Ratings: Relationships with Each Other and with Performance and Selection Predictors," *Journal of Organizational Behavior* (November 2001), pp. 775–788.

36. By the Numbers box based on "Survey: 21 Percent of Job Seekers Dropped After Reference Checks," *Workforce Management Online,* June 23, 2010; J. Yang and A. Lewis, "Doing Jobs Without Training," *USA Today,* October 20, 2008, p. 1B; F. Di Meglio, "Dream Jobs: College Students Get Real," *Bloomberg BusinessWeek Online,* April 30, 2010; E. A. Grant, "Cookie Monster," *Fast Company,* June 2010, pp. 58–60; "Hiring for Fit," *Workforce Management Online,* May 28, 2010; J. Yang and A. Gonzalez, "Most Appealing Career Model for Me Is To . . ." *USA Today,* May 5, 2010, p. 1B; J. Yang and V. Salazar, "Most Neglected Grooming for Interviews," *USA Today,* December 31, 2009, p. 1B; and J. Yang and K. Simmons, "Preferred Résumé Format," *USA Today,* November 16, 2009, p. 1B.

37. J. D. Glater, "Seasoning Compensation Stew," *New York Times,* March 7, 2001, pp. C1+.

38. This section based on R. I. Henderson, *Compensation Management in a Knowledge-Based World,* 9th ed. (Upper Saddle River, NJ: Prentice Hall, 2003).

39. M. P. Brown, M. C. Sturman, and M. J. Simmering, "Compensation Policy and Organizational Performance: The Efficiency, Operational and Financial Implications of Pay Levels and Pay Structure," *Academy of Management Journal* (December 2003), pp. 752–762; J. D. Shaw, N. P. Gupta, and J. E. Delery, "Pay Dispersion and Workforce Performance: Moderating Effects of Incentives and Interdependence," *Strategic Management Journal* (June 2002), pp. 491–512; E. Montemayor, "Congruence between Pay Policy and Competitive Strategy in High-Performing Firms," *Journal of Management,* vol. 22, no. 6 (1996), pp. 889–908; and L. R. Gomez-Mejia, "Structure and Process of Diversification, Compensation Strategy, and Firm Performance," *Strategic Management Journal,* 13 (1992), pp. 381–397.

40. J. D. Shaw, N. Gupta, A. Mitra, and G. E. Ledford, Jr., "Success and Survival of Skill-Based Pay Plans," *Journal of Management* (February 2005), pp. 28–49; C. Lee, K. S. Law, and P. Bobko, "The Importance of Justice Perceptions on Pay Effectiveness: A Two-Year Study of a Skill-Based Pay Plan," *Journal of Management,* vol. 26, no. 6 (1999), pp. 851–873; G. E. Ledford, "Paying for the Skills, Knowledge and Competencies of Knowledge Workers," *Compensation and Benefits Review*, July–August 1995, pp. 55–62; and E. E. Lawler III, G. E. Ledford Jr., and L. Chang, "Who Uses Skill-Based Pay and Why," *Compensation and Benefits Review*, March–April 1993, p. 22.

41. J. D. Shaw, N. Gupta, A. Mitra, and G. E. Ledford Jr., "Success and Survival of Skill-Based Pay Plans."

42. Information from Hewitt Associates Studies: "As Fixed Costs Increase, Employers Turn to Variable Pay Programs as Preferred Way to Reward Employees," August 21, 2007; "Hewitt Study Shows Pay-for-Performance Plans Replacing Holiday Bonuses," December 6, 2005; "Salaries Continue to Rise in Asia Pacific, Hewitt Annual Study Reports," November 23, 2005; and "Hewitt Study Shows Base Pay Increases Flat for 2006 with Variable Pay Plans Picking Up the Slack," Hewitt Associates, LLC, www.hewittassociates.com (August 31, 2005).

43. "Mandated Benefits: 2002 Compliance Guide," *Employee Benefits Journal* (June 2002), p. 64; and J. J. Kim, "Smaller Firms Augment Benefits, Survey Shows," *Wall Street Journal,* June 6, 2002, p. D2.

44. P. P. Shah, "Network Destruction: The Structural Implications of Downsizing," *Academy of Management Journal* (February 2000), pp. 101–112.

45. See, for example, K. A. Mollica and B. Gray, "When Layoff Survivors Become Layoff Victims: Propensity to Litigate," *Human Resource Planning,* January 2001, pp. 22–32.

46. S. Koudsi, "You're Stuck," *Fortune,* December 10, 2001, pp. 271–274.

47. S. Berfield, "After the Layoff, The Redesign," *Business Week,* April 14, 2008, pp. 54–56; L. Uchitelle, "Retraining Laid-Off Workers, But for What?" *New York Times Online,* March 26, 2006; D. Tourish, N. Paulsen, E. Hobman, and P. Bordia, "The Downsides of Downsizing: Communication Processes and Information Needs in the Aftermath of a Workforce Reduction Strategy," *Management Communication Quarterly,* May 2004, pp. 485–516; J. Brockner, G. Spreitzer, A. Mishra, W. Hochwarter, L. Pepper, and J. Weinberg, "Perceived Control As an Antidote to the Negative Effects of Layoffs on Survivors' Organizational Commitment and Job Performance," *Administrative Science Quarterly,* 49 (2004), pp. 76–100; and E. Krell, "Defusing Downsizing," *Business Finance,* December 2002, pp. 55–57.

48. A. Joshi, "Managing the Organizational Melting Pot: Dilemmas of Workplace Diversity," *Administrative Science Quarterly,* December 2001, pp. 783–784.

49. Right or Wrong box based on R. Pyrillis, "Workers Using Medical Marijuana Hold Their Breath, but Employers Worry They'll Take a Hit," *Workforce Management Online,* April 2011; "Puffing Up Over Pot in Workplace," *Workforce Management,* March 2011, p. 41; D. Cadrain, "The Marijuana Exception," *HR Magazine,* November 2010, pp. 40–42; D. Cadrain, "Do Medical Marijuana Laws Protect Usage by Employees?" *HR Magazine,* November 2010, p. 12; A. K. Wiwi and N. P. Crifo, "The Unintended Impact of New Jersey's New Medical Marijuana Law on the Workplace," *Employee Relations Law Journal,* Summer 2010, pp. 33–37; S. Simon, "At Work, a Drug Dilemma," *Wall Street Journal,* August 3, 2010l, p. D1; and J. Greenwald, "Medical Marijuana Laws Create Dilemma for Firms," *Business Insurance,* February 15, 2010, pp. 1–20.

50. Top 50 Companies for Diversity, *DiversityInc,* June 2010, pp. 18–19.

51. See, for instance, K. Iverson, "Managing for Effective Workforce Diversity," *Cornell Hotel and Restaurant Administration Quarterly,* April 2000, pp. 31–38.

52. U.S. Equal Employment Opportunity Commission, "Sexual Harassment Charges EEOC and FEPAs Combined: FY 1997–FY 2010," http://www.eeoc.gov/eeoc/statistics/enforcement/sexual_harassment.

53. Ibid.

54. N. F. Foy, "Sexual Harassment Can Threaten Your Bottom Line," *Strategic Finance* (August 2000), pp. 56–57.

55. "Federal Monitors Find Illinois Mitsubishi Unit Eradicating Harassment," *Wall Street Journal* (September 7, 2000), p. A8.

56. L. J. Munson, C. Hulin, and F. Drasgow, "Longitudinal Analysis of Dispositional Influences and Sexual Harassment: Effects on Job and Psychological Outcomes," *Personnel Psychology* (Spring 2000), p. 21.

57. B. Leonard, "Survey: 10% of Employees Report Harassment at Work," *HR Magazine,* October 2010, p. 18.

58. "*Nichols v. Azteca Restaurant Enterprises,*" *Harvard Law Review,* May 2002, p. 2074; A. J. Morrell, "Non-Employee Harassment," *Legal Report* (January–February 2000), p. 1. See also S. Lim and L. M. Cortina, "Interpersonal Mistreatment in the Workplace: The Interface and Impact of General Incivility and Sexual Harassment," *Journal of Applied Psychology* (May 2005), pp. 483–496.

59. Although the male gender is referred to here, it is important to note that sexual harassment may involve people of either sex or the same sex. (See, for instance, *Oncale v. Sundowner Offshore Service, Inc.*, 118 S. Ct. 998.)

60. See also A. M. O'Leary-Kelly, L. Bowes-Sperry, C. A. Bates, and E. R. Lean, "Sexual Harassment at Work: A Decade (Plus) of Progress," *Journal of Management* (June 2009), pp. 503–536; M. Rotundo, D. H. Nguyen, and P. R. Sackett, "A Meta-Analytic Review of Gender Differences in Perceptions of Sexual Harassment," *Journal of Applied Psychology* (October 2001), pp. 914–922.

61. R. L. Wiener and L. E. Hurt, "How Do People Evaluate Social Sexual Conduct at Work? A Psychological Model," *Journal of Applied Psychology* (February 2000), p. 75.

62. *Meritor Savings Bank v. Vinson*, 477 U.S. 57 (1986).

63. R. D. Lee and P. S. Greenlaw, "Employer Liability for Employee Sexual Harassment: A Judicial Policy-Making Study," *Public Administration Review* (March–April 2000), p. 127.

64. Ibid.

65. "You and DuPont: Diversity," DuPont Company Documents (1999–2000), http://www.dupont.com/careers/you/diverse.html; and "DuPont Announces 2000 Dr. Martin Luther King, Days of Celebration," DuPont Company Documents, http://www.dupont.com/corp/whats-news/releases/00/001111.html (January 11, 2000).

66. It should be noted here that under the Title VII and the Civil Rights Act of 1991, the maximum award that can be given, under the Federal Act, is $300,000. However, many cases are tried under state laws that permit unlimited punitive damages.

67. J. W. Janove, "Sexual Harassment and the Big Three Surprises," *HR Magazine,* November 2001, pp. 123–130; and L. A. Baar, and J. Baar, "Harassment Case Proceeds Despite Failure to Report," *HR Magazine,* June 2005, p. 159.

68. W. L. Kosanovich, J. L. Rosenberg, and L. Swanson, "Preventing and Correcting Sexual Harassment: A Guide to the Ellerth/Faragher Affirmative Defense," *Employee Relations Law Journal* (Summer 2002), pp. 79–99; M. Zall, "Workplace Harassment and Employer Liability," *Fleet Equipment,* January 2000, p. B1. See also, "Ruling Allows Defense in Harassment Cases," *HR Magazine,* August 2004, p. 30.

69. See, for instance, P. W. Dorfman, A. T. Cobb, and R. Cox, "Investigations of Sexual Harassment Allegations: Legal Means Fair—Or Does It?" *Human Resources Management,* Spring 2000, pp. 33–39.

70. C. H. Liu and P. J. Robertson, "Spirituality in the Workplace," *Journal of Management Inquiry* (March 2011), pp. 35–50; and C. Cash and G. R. Gray, "A Framework for Accommodating Religion and Spirituality in the Workplace," *The Academy of Management Executive,* 14, no. 3 (August 2000), p. 124.

71. Liu and Robertson, "Spirituality in the Workplace;" and D. P. Ashmos and D. Duchon, "Spirituality at Work: A Conceptualization and Measure," *Journal of Management Inquiry* (June 2000), p. 139.

72. A. A. Mohamed, J. Wisnieski, M. Askar, and I. Syed, "Toward a Theory of Spirituality in the Workplace," *Competitiveness Review* 14, no. 1 (Winter–Fall 2004), pp. 102–107.

73. See F. Warner, "Professionals Tap a Higher Power in the Workplace," *Workforce Management Online,* April 2011; Liu and Robertson, "Spirituality in the Workplace;" E. J. Kutcher, J. D. Bragger, O. Rodriguez-Srednicki, and J. L. Masco, "The Role of Religiosity in Stress, Job Attitudes, and Organizational Citizenship Behavior," *Journal of Business Ethics* (August 2010), pp. 319–337; I. A. Mitroff and E. A. Denton, *A Spiritual Audit of Corporate America: A Hard Look at Spirituality, Religion, and Values in the Workplace* (San Francisco, CA: Jossey-Bass, 1999); J. Milliman, J. Ferguson, D. Trickett, and B. Condemi, "Spirit and Community at Southwest Airlines: An Investigation of a Spiritual Values-Based Model," *Journal of Organizational Change Management* 12, no. 3 (1999), pp. 221–233; E. H. Burack, "Spirituality in the Workplace," *Journal of Organizational Change Management* 12, no. 3 (1999), pp. 280–291; and F. Wagner-Marsh and J. Conley, "The Fourth Wave: The Spirituality-Based Firm," *Journal of Organizational Change Management* 12, no. 3 (1999), pp. 292–302.

74. M. Conlin, "Religion in the Workplace: The Growing Presence of Spirituality in Corporate America," *BusinessWeek,* November 1, 1999, pp. 151–158; and P. Paul, "A Holier Holiday Season," *American Demographics,* December 2001, pp. 41–45.

75. For a thorough review of the benefits of workplace spirituality, see J. Marques, S. Dhiman, and R. King, "Spirituality in the Workplace: Developing an Integral Model and a Comprehensive Definition," *Journal of American Academy of Business* (September 2005), pp. 81–92. See, also, M. Conlin, "Religion in the Workplace," p. 153; C. P. Neck and J. F. Milliman, "Thought Leadership: Finding Spiritual Fulfillment in Organizational Life," *Journal of Managerial Psychology* 9, no. 8 (1984), p. 9; D. W. McCormick, "Spirituality and Management," *Journal of Managerial Psychology* 9, no. 6 (1994), p. 5; E. Brandt, "Corporate Pioneers Explore Spirituality Peace," *HR Magazine,* April 1996, p. 82; P. Leigh, "The New Spirit at Work," *Training and Development* (February 1997), p. 193; and J. Milliman, A Czaplewski, and J. Ferguson, "An Exploratory Empirical Assessment of the Relationship Between Spirituality and Employee Work Attitudes," paper presented at the national Academy of Management meeting, Washington, D.C. (August 2001).

76. See, for example, J. Marques, "HR's Crucial Role in the Establishment of Spirituality in the Workplace," *Journal of Academy of Business* (September 2005), pp. 27–31.

77. These examples taken from S. J. Wells, "Does Work Make You Fat?" *HR Magazine,* October 2010, pp. 26–32; R. King, "Slimming Down Employees to Cut Costs"; C. Tkaczyk, "Lowering Health-Care Costs," *Fortune,* November 23, 2009, p. 16; and A. W. Matthews, "When All Else Fails: Forcing Workers into Healthy Habits," *Wall Street Journal,* July 8, 2009, pp. D1+.

78. D. Mattioli, "Firms Feel Pain from Health Law," *Wall Street Journal,* December 13, 2010, pp. B1; L. Cornwell, "More Companies Penalize Workers with Health Risks," The Associated Press, *Springfield, Missouri News-Leader,* September 10, 2007, p. 10A; and A. Zimmerman, Matthews, and Hudson, "Can Employers Alter Hiring Policies to Cut Health Costs?"

79. B. Pyenson and K. Fitch, "Smoking May Be Hazardous to Your Bottom Line," *Workforce Online,* www.workforce.com (December 2007); and L. Cornwell, The Associated Press, "Companies Tack on Fees on Insurance for Smokers," *Springfield, Missouri News-Leader,* February 17, 2006, p. 5B.

80. J. Wojcik, "Research Shows Cost of Employee Obesity," *Business Insurance,* October 18, 2010, p. 24.

81. R. Ceniceros, "Obesity Can Exacerbate Workplace Injuries, Study Notes," *Workforce Management Online,* December 15, 2010; and "Obesity Weighs Down Production," *Industry Week,* March 2008, pp. 22–23.

82. J. Appleby, "Companies Step Up Wellness Efforts," *USA Today,* August 1, 2005, pp. 1A+.

83. G. Kranz, "Prognosis Positive: Companies Aim to Get Workers Healthy," *Workforce Management,* www.workforce.com (April 15, 2008).

84. S. J. Wells, "Does Work Make You Fat?"; and M. Conlin, "Hide the Doritos! Here Comes HR," *BusinessWeek,* April 28, 2008, pp. 94–96.

85. J. Fox, "Good Riddance to Pensions," *CNN Money,* January 12, 2006.

86. M. Adams, "Broken Pension System in Crying Need of a Fix," *USA Today,* November 15, 2005, p. 1B+.

87. "Prevalence of Retirement Plans by Type in the *Fortune* 100," *Pension Benefits,* September 2010, pp. 1–2; D. Kansas, "Has the 401(k) Failed?" *Fortune,* June 22, 2009, pp. 94–98; S. Block, "Company Pensions Are Out on a Limb," *USA Today,* May 22, 2009, pp. 1B+; A. Feldman, "Retiring the 401(k) Contribution," *BusinessWeek,* November 24, 2008, p. 32; J. Appleby, "Traditional Pensions Are Almost Gone. Is Employer-Provided Health Insurance Next?" *USA Today,* November 13, 2007, pp.1A+; S. Kelly, "FedEx, Goodyear Make Big Pension Plan Changes," *Workforce Management,* www.workforce.com, (March 1, 2007); G. Colvin, "The End of a Dream," *Fortune,* www.cnnmoney.com (June 22, 2006); E. Porter and M. Williams Nash, "Benefits Go the Way of Pensions," *NY Times Online,* February 9, 2006; and J. Fox, "Good Riddance to Pensions."

Career Module

BUILDING YOUR CAREER

The term *career* has several meanings. In popular usage, it can mean advancement ("she is on a management career track"), a profession ("he has chosen a career in accounting"), or a lifelong sequence of jobs ("his career has included 12 jobs in six organizations"). For our purposes, we define a **career** as the sequence of work positions held by a person during his or her lifetime. Using this definition, it's apparent that we all have, or will have, a career. Moreover, the concept is as relevant to unskilled laborers as it is to software designers or physicians. But career development isn't what it used to be!

What Was Career Development Like, Historically?

Although career development has been an important topic in management courses for years, some dramatic changes have occurred in the concept. Career development programs used to be designed to help employees advance their work lives within a specific organization. The focus of such programs was to provide employees the information, assessment, and training needed to help them realize their career goals. Career development was also a way for organizations to attract and retain highly talented people. This approach has all but disappeared in today's workplace. Now, organizations that have such traditional career programs are few and far between. Downsizing, restructuring, and other organizational adjustments have brought us to one significant conclusion about career development: You—not the organization—will be responsible for designing, guiding, and developing your own career.

What Is Career Development Like, Now?

This idea of increased personal responsibility for one's career has been described as a **boundaryless career**. The challenge is that few hard-and-fast rules are available to guide you.

One of the first decisions you have to make is career choice. The optimum choice is one that offers the best match between what you want out of life and your interests, your abilities and personality, and market opportunities. Good career choices should result in a series of jobs that give you an opportunity to be a good performer, make you want to maintain your commitment to your career, lead to highly satisfying work, and give you the proper balance between work and personal life. A good career match, then, is one in which you are able to develop a positive self-concept, to do work that you think is important, and to lead the kind of life you desire. In a recent survey by Capital One Financial Corporation, 66 percent of college graduates said that a comprehensive benefits package (including, for example, health care, 401(k) program, child care, and domestic partner benefits) was the

---

career
The sequence of work positions held by a person during his or her lifetime

boundaryless career
When an individual takes personal responsibility for his or her own career

most important factor in their job search. Starting salary ranked second at 64 percent, with job location ranked third at 60 percent. Today's college grads are also looking to be rewarded or compensated (with comp time or matching donations, for instance) for their volunteer and philanthropic activities.

Once you've identified a career choice, it's time to initiate the job search. However, we aren't going to get into the specifics of job hunting, writing a résumé, or interviewing successfully, although those things are important. Let's fast-forward through all that and assume that your job search was successful. It's time to go to work! How do you survive and excel in your career?

How Can I Have a Successful Career?

What can you do to improve your chances for career success? You're already doing the *most* important thing: You're getting a college education! It's the surest way to increase your lifetime earnings. Currently, the average high school graduate earns $27,915 a year. His or her counterpart with a college degree earns $51,206. College graduates earn, on average, $800,000 more than high school graduates over their working career. Investing in your education and training is one of the best investments you'll make in your lifetime. What *else* can you do? The following suggestions are based on extensive research into career management.

Assess Your Personal Strengths and Weaknesses

Where do your natural talents lie? What can you do, relative to others, that gives you a competitive advantage? Are you particularly good with numbers? Have strong people skills? Good with your hands? Write better than most people? Everyone has some things that they do better than others and some areas where they're weak. Play to your strengths.

Identify Market Opportunities

Where are tomorrow's job opportunities? Regardless of your strengths, certain job categories are likely to decline in the coming decades—for instance, bank tellers, small farmers, movie projectionists, travel agents, and secretaries. In contrast, abundant opportunities are more likely to be created by an increasingly aging society, continued emphasis on technology, increased spending on education and training, and concern with personal security. These factors are likely to create excellent opportunities for jobs in gerontological counseling, network administration, training consultants, and security-alarm installers.

Take Responsibility for Managing Your Own Career

Historically, companies tended to assume responsibility for their employees' careers. Today, this is the exception rather than the rule. Employees are increasingly expected to take responsibility for their own careers.

Think of your career as your business and you're its CEO. To survive, you have to monitor market forces, head off competitors, and be ready to quickly take advantage of opportunities when they surface. You have to protect your career from harm and position yourself to benefit from changes in the environment.

Develop Your Interpersonal Skills

Interpersonal skills, especially the ability to communicate, top the list of almost every employer's "must have" skills. Whether it's getting a new job or a promotion, strong interpersonal skills are likely to give you a competitive edge.

Practice Makes Perfect

There's an increasing amount of evidence indicating that super-high achievers aren't fundamentally different from the rest of us. They just work harder and smarter. It's been found, based on studies of world-class performers in music, sports, chess, science, and business, that people like Tiger Woods, Mozart, and Bill Gates put in about 10,000 hours (or 10 years at 1,000 hours a year) of persistent, focused training and experience before they hit their peak performance level. If you want to excel in any field, you should expect to have to put in a lot of deliberate practice—consistently engaging in repeated activity specifically designed to improve performance beyond your current comfort and ability level.

Stay Up-to-Date

In today's dynamic world, skills can become obsolete quickly. To keep your career on track, you need to make learning a lifetime commitment. You should be continually "going to school"—if not taking formal courses, then reading books and journals to ensure that you don't get caught with obsolete skills.

Network

Networking refers to creating and maintaining beneficial relationships with others in order to accomplish your goals. It helps to have friends in high places. It also helps to have contacts who can keep you informed of changes that are going on in your organization and in your industry. Go to conferences. Maintain contact with former college friends and alumni. Get involved in community activities. Cultivate a broad set of relationships. And in today's increasingly interconnected world, join online business networking groups such as LinkedIn, Spoke, and Talkbiznow.

Stay Visible

Networking can increase your visibility. So, too, can writing articles in your professional journals, teaching classes or giving talks in your area of expertise, attending conferences and professional meetings, and making sure your accomplishments are properly promoted. You increase your mobility and value in the marketplace by keeping visible.

Seek a Mentor

Employees with mentors are likely to have enhanced mobility, increased knowledge of the organization's inside workings, greater access to senior executives, increased satisfaction, and increased visibility. For women and minorities, having mentors has been shown to be particularly helpful in promoting career advancement and success.

Leverage Your Competitive Advantage

Develop skills that will give you a competitive advantage in the marketplace. Especially focus on skills that are important to employers, skills that are scarce, and areas where you have limited competition. Try to avoid a worst-case scenario: You have a job that anyone can learn in 30 minutes. Remember that the harder it is for you to learn and develop a highly prized skill, the harder it'll also be for others to acquire it. Generally speaking, the more training necessary to do a job and the fewer people who have that training, the greater your security and influence.

Here's an insight from many years as a student and a professor: To succeed in school, you have to be a generalist and excel at everything. For instance, to earn a 4.0 GPA, you need to be a star in English, math, science, geography, languages, and so on. The "real world," on the other hand, rewards specialization. You don't have to be good at everything. You just need to be good at something that others aren't and that society values. You can be lousy in math or science and still be a very successful opera singer, artist, salesperson, or writer. You don't have to excel in English to be a computer programmer or electrician. The secret to life success is identifying your comparative advantage and then developing it. And as we've noted previously, you need to invest approximately 10,000 hours in honing your skills to achieve optimum proficiency.

Don't Shun Risks

Don't be afraid to take risks, especially when you're young and you don't have much to lose. Going back to school, moving to a new state or country, or quitting a job to start your own business can be the decision that will set your life in a completely new direction. Great accomplishments almost always require taking the path less traveled; and the road to nowhere is paved with fears of the unknown.

It's OK to Change Jobs

Past generations often believed "you don't leave a good job." That advice no longer applies. In today's fast-changing job market, staying put often only means that you're staying behind. Employers no longer expect long-term loyalty. And to keep your skills fresh, your income increasing, and your job tasks interesting, it will be increasingly likely that you'll need to change employers.

Opportunities, Preparation, and Luck = Success

Successful people are typically ambitious, intelligent, and hardworking. But they are also lucky. It's not by chance that many of the biggest technology success stories—Bill Gates and Paul Allen at Microsoft, Steve Jobs at Apple, Scott McNealy at Sun Microsystems, Eric Schmidt at Novell and Google—were born in a narrow three-year period between June 1953 and March 1956. They were smart. They were interested in computers and technology. But they were also lucky. They reached their teens and early 20s in 1975—at the dawn of the personal computer age. Those people with similar interests and talents but born in the mid-1940s were likely to have joined a firm like IBM out of college and been enamored with mainframe computers. Had they been born in the early 1960s, they would have missed getting in on the ground floor of the revolution.

Success is a matter of matching up opportunities, preparation, and luck. It's been suggested that few of us get more than a couple of special opportunities in our lifetime. If you're lucky, you will recognize those opportunities, have made the proper preparations, and then act on them.

You can't control when you were born, where you were born, your parents' finances, or the like. Those are the luck factors. But what you can control is your preparation and willingness to act when opportunity knocks.

Sources: Managing Your Career Module based on J. H. Greenhaus, V. M. Godstalk, and G. A. Callahan, *Career Management*, 3rd ed. (Cincinnati, OH: South–Western, 2000); K. A. Ericsson, "Deliberate Practice and the Modifiability of Body and Mind," *International Journal of Sports Psychology* (January–March 2007), pp. 4–34; J. P. Newport, "Mastery, Just 10,000 Hours Away," *Wall Street Journal*, March 14–15, 2009, p. W6; "Capital One Survey Highlights What Today's College Graduates Want from Employers," www.businesswire.com (June 10, 2008); M. Gladwell, *Outliers: The Story of Success* (New York: Little, Brown, 2008); R. N. Boles, *What Color Is Your Parachute? 2009: A Practical Manual for Job-Hunters and Career-Changers* (Berkeley, CA: Ten Speed Press, 2009); D. E. Super and D. T. Hall, "Career Development: Exploration and Planning," in M. R. Rosenzweig and L.W. Porter (eds.), *Annual Review of Psychology*, vol. 29 (Palo Alto, CA: Annual Reviews, 1978), p. 334; and M. B. Arthur and D. M. Rousseau, *The Boundaryless Career: A New Employment Principle for a New Organizational Era* (New York: Oxford University Press, 1996).

Managing Change and Innovation

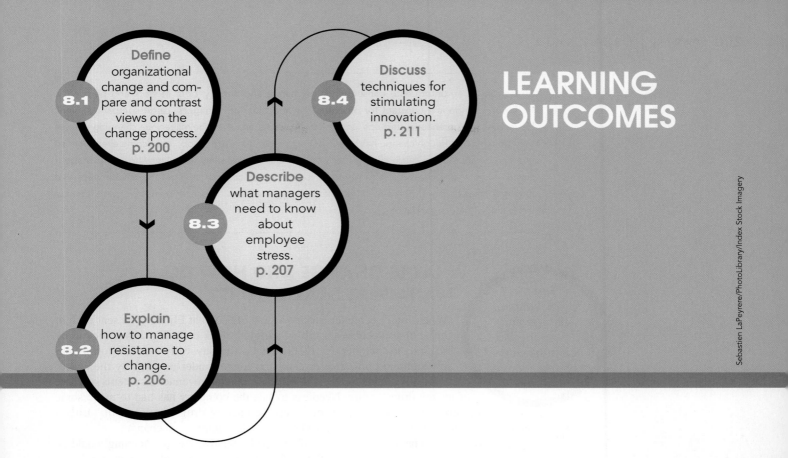

LEARNING OUTCOMES

8.1 Define organizational change and compare and contrast views on the change process. p. 200

8.4 Discuss techniques for stimulating innovation. p. 211

8.3 Describe what managers need to know about employee stress. p. 207

8.2 Explain how to manage resistance to change. p. 206

Stress Kills

We know that too much stress can be bad for our health and well-being. That connection proved itself painfully and tragically at France Télécom.[1] Since early 2008, there have been more than 50 suicides of people who worked for the company. The situation captured the attention of the worldwide media, the public, and the French government because many of the suicides and more than a dozen failed suicide attempts were attributed to work-related problems. The masks worn by these protesting Telecom employees say "Lombard has killed me." Didier Lombard was the chairman of the board and chief executive officer of France Telecom when the suicides took place. Although France has a higher suicide rate than any other large Western country, this scenario was particularly troublesome. The spate of suicides highlighted a quirk at the heart of French society: "Even with robust labor protection, workers see themselves as profoundly insecure in the face of globalization, with many complaining about being pushed beyond their limits." France isn't the only country dealing with worker suicides. Workplace conditions at China's Foxconn, the world's largest maker of electronic components (including the iPhone, iPod, and iPad), were strongly criticized after 11 Foxconn employees committed suicide.

Stress can be an unfortunate consequence of change and anxiety, both at work and personally. However, change is a constant for organizations and thus for managers. Large companies, small businesses, entrepreneurial start-ups, universities, hospitals, and even the military are changing the way they do things. Although change has always been a part of a manager's job, it's become even more so in recent years. And because change can't be eliminated, managers must learn how to manage it successfully. In this chapter, we're going to look at organizational change efforts, the ways that managers can deal with the stress that exists in organizations, and how managers can stimulate innovation in their organizations.

WHAT IS CHANGE AND HOW DO MANAGERS DEAL WITH IT?

8.1 Define organizational change and compare and contrast views on the change process.

When John Lechleiter assumed the CEO's job at Eli Lilly, he sent each of his senior executives a gift—"a digital clock counting down, second by second, to October 23, 2011. That's the day Lilly's $5 billion-a-year schizophrenia pill, Zyprexa, was no longer under patent." By the end of 2016, Lilly stands to lose $10 billion in annual revenues as patents on three of its key drugs expire. Needless to say, the company has had to make some organizational changes as it picks up the pace of drug development.[2] Lilly's managers are doing what managers everywhere must do—implement change!

If it weren't for change, a manager's job would be relatively easy. Planning would be easier because tomorrow would be no different from today. The issue of organization design would be solved because the environment would be free from uncertainty and there would be no need to adapt. Similarly, decision making would be dramatically simplified because the outcome of each alternative could be predicted with near pinpoint accuracy. It would also simplify the manager's job if competitors never introduced new products or services, if customers didn't make new demands, if government regulations were never modified, if technology never advanced, or if employees' needs always remained the same. But that's not the way it is.

Change is an organizational reality. Most managers, at one point or another, will have to change some things in their workplace. We classify these changes as **organizational change**, which is any alteration of an organization's people, structure, or technology. (See Exhibit 8–1.) Let's look more closely at each of these three areas.

Changing *structure* includes any alteration in authority relationships, coordination mechanisms, degree of centralization, job design, or similar organization structure variables. For instance, in previous chapters, we've mentioned that work process engineering, restructuring, and empowering result in decentralization, wider spans of control, reduced work specialization, and work teams. These structural components give employees the authority and means to implement process improvements. For instance, the creation of work teams that cut across departmental lines allows those people who understand a problem best to solve that problem. In addition, cross-functional work teams encourage cooperative problem solving rather than "us versus them" situations. All of these situations may involve some type of structural change.

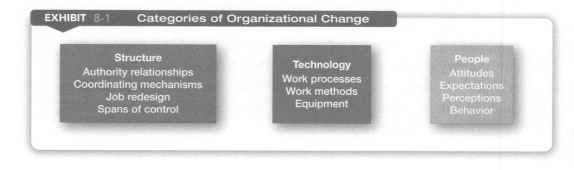

EXHIBIT 8-1   **Categories of Organizational Change**

Structure	Technology	People
Authority relationships	Work processes	Attitudes
Coordinating mechanisms	Work methods	Expectations
Job redesign	Equipment	Perceptions
Spans of control		Behavior

Changing *technology* encompasses modifications in the way work is done or the methods and equipment used. One organizational area, in particular, where managers deal with changing technology is continuous improvement initiatives, which are directed at developing flexible processes to support better-quality operations. Employees committed to continuous improvements are constantly looking for things to fix. Thus, work processes must be adaptable to continual change and fine-tuning. Such adaptability requires an extensive commitment to educating and training workers. Employees need skills training in problem solving, decision making, negotiation, statistical analysis, and team-building, and they must be able to analyze and act on data. For example, Campbell Soup Co. uses both technology and employee training to maintain its market-leading position in the soup industry.[3]

Changes in *people* refer to changes in employee attitudes, expectations, perceptions, or behaviors. The human dimension of change requires a workforce that's committed to quality and continuous improvement. Again, proper employee education and training are needed, as is a performance evaluation and reward system that supports and encourages those improvements. For example, successful programs put quality goals into bonus plans for executives and incentives for employees.

Why Do Organizations Need to Change?

In Chapter 2 we pointed out that both external and internal forces constrain managers. These same forces also bring about the need for change. Let's briefly review these factors.

WHAT EXTERNAL FORCES CREATE A NEED TO CHANGE? The external forces that create the need for organizational change come from various sources. In recent years, the *marketplace* has affected firms such as AT&T and Lowe's because of new competition. AT&T, for example, faces competition from local cable companies and from free Internet services such as Skype. Lowe's, too, must now contend with a host of aggressive competitors such as Home Depot and Menard's. *Government laws and regulations* are also an impetus for change. For example, when the Americans with Disabilities Act was signed into law, thousands of businesses were required to widen doorways, reconfigure restrooms, and add ramps. Even today, organizations continue to deal with the requirements of improving accessibility for the disabled.

Technology also creates the need for organizational change. The Internet has changed the way we get information, how products are sold, and how we get our work done. Technological advancements have created significant economies of scale for many organizations. For instance, technology allows Scottrade to offer its clients the opportunity to make online trades without a broker. The assembly line in many industries has also undergone dramatic change as employers replace human labor with technologically advanced mechanical robots. Also, the fluctuation in *labor markets* forces managers to initiate changes. For example, the shortage of registered nurses in the United States has led many hospital administrators to redesign nursing jobs and to alter their rewards and benefits packages for nurses, as well as join forces with local universities to address the nursing shortage.

As the news headlines remind us, *economic* changes affect almost all organizations. For instance, prior to the mortgage market meltdown, low interest rates led to significant growth in the housing market. This growth meant more jobs, more employees hired, and significant increases in sales in other businesses that supported the building industry. However, as the economy soured, it had the opposite effect on the housing industry and other industries as credit markets dried up and businesses found it difficult to get the capital they needed to operate. And although it's been over a decade since 9/11, the airline industry is still dealing with the organizational changes forced on it by increased security measures and other environmental factors such as high fuel costs.

organizational change
Any alteration of an organization's people, structure, or technology

Changes in the economic environment created a need for internal change at Intuit, Inc., a developer of tax-preparation and financial software. When the economic recession slowed the sales of Intuit's QuickBooks, Quicken, and TurboTax software, the firm's senior executives created an environment and established workplace practices that facilitated employee innovation. Developing an internal innovation program has transformed Intuit from a software maker to a provider of Web sites and new online and mobile software that are driving the company's long-term growth. Shown here at a business technology event is an Intuit vice president of innovation sharing how his firm boosted sales with new products and services.

WHAT INTERNAL FORCES CREATE A NEED TO CHANGE? Internal forces can also create the need for organizational change. These internal forces tend to originate primarily from the internal operations of the organization or from the impact of external changes. (It's also important to recognize that such changes are a normal part of the organizational life cycle.)[4]

When managers redefine or modify an organization's *strategy*, that action often introduces a host of changes. For example, Nokia bringing in new equipment is an internal force for change. Because of this action, employees may face job redesign, undergo training to operate the new equipment, or be required to establish new interaction patterns within their work groups. Another internal force for change is that the *composition of an organization's workforce* changes in terms of age, education, gender, nationality, and so forth. A stable organization in which managers have been in their positions for years might need to restructure jobs in order to retain more ambitious employees by affording them some upward mobility. The compensation and benefits systems might also need to be reworked to reflect the needs of a diverse workforce and market forces in which certain skills are in short supply. *Employee attitudes*, such as increased job dissatisfaction, may lead to increased absenteeism, resignations, and even strikes. Such events will, in turn, often lead to changes in organizational policies and practices.

Who Initiates Organizational Change?

Organizational changes need a catalyst. People who act as catalysts and assume the responsibility for managing the change process are called **change agents**.[5]

Any manager can be a change agent. When we talk about organizational change, we assume that it's initiated and carried out by a manager within the organization. However, the change agent could be a nonmanager—for example, an internal staff specialist or an outside consultant whose expertise is in change implementation. For major systemwide changes, an organization will often hire outside consultants for advice and assistance. Because these consultants come from the outside, they offer an objective perspective that insiders usually lack. However, the problem is that outside consultants may not understand the organization's history, culture, operating procedures, and personnel. They're also prone to initiating more drastic changes than insiders—which can be either a benefit or a disadvantage—because they don't have to live with the repercussions after the change is implemented. In contrast, internal managers who act as change agents may be more thoughtful (and possibly more cautious) because they must live with the consequences of their actions.

How Does Organizational Change Happen?

We often use two metaphors to clarify the change process.[6] The **"calm waters" metaphor** envisions the organization as a large ship crossing a calm sea. The ship's captain and crew know exactly where they're going because they've made the trip many times before. Change appears as the occasional storm, a brief distraction in an otherwise calm and predictable trip. In the **"white-water rapids" metaphor**, the organization is seen as a small raft navigating a raging river with uninterrupted white-water rapids. Aboard the raft are half a dozen people who have never worked together before, who are totally unfamiliar with the river, who are unsure of their eventual destination, and who, as if things weren't bad enough, are traveling at night. In the white-water rapids metaphor, change is the status quo and managing change is a continual process.

These two metaphors represent distinctly different approaches to understanding and responding to change. Let's look closer at each one.

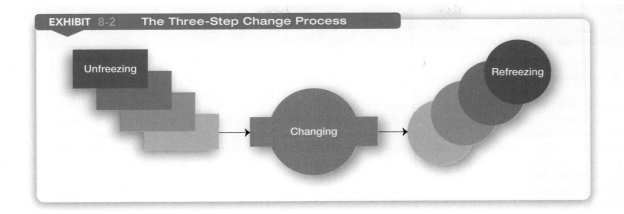

EXHIBIT 8-2   The Three-Step Change Process

WHAT IS THE "CALM WATERS" METAPHOR?   Until recently, the "calm waters" metaphor dominated the thinking of practicing managers and academics. The prevailing model for handling change in such circumstances is best illustrated in Kurt Lewin's three-step description of the change process.[7] (See Exhibit 8–2.)

According to Lewin, successful change requires unfreezing the status quo, changing to a new state, and freezing the new change to make it permanent. The status quo can be considered an equilibrium state. Unfreezing is necessary to move from this equilibrium. It can be achieved in one of three ways:

◆ The driving forces, which direct behavior away from the status quo, can be increased.
◆ The restraining forces, which hinder movement from the existing equilibrium, can be decreased.
◆ The two approaches can be combined.

Once the situation has been unfrozen, the change itself can be implemented. However, the mere introduction of change doesn't ensure that it will take hold. The new situation, therefore, needs to be frozen so that it can be sustained over time. Unless this last step is done, it's likely that the change will be short-lived and employees will revert to the previous equilibrium state. The objective of freezing the entire equilibrium state, then, is to stabilize the new situation by balancing the driving and restraining forces.

Note how Lewin's three-step process treats change as a break in the organization's equilibrium state.[8] The status quo has been disturbed, and change is necessary to establish a new equilibrium state. Although this view might have been appropriate to the relatively calm environment faced by most organizations during the twentieth century, it's increasingly obsolete as a description of the kinds of "seas" that current managers have to navigate. (See the From the Past to the Present box for more information on Lewin and his organizational research.)

WHAT IS THE "WHITE-WATER RAPIDS" METAPHOR?   Susan Whiting is the chair of Nielsen Media Research, the company best known for its television ratings, which are frequently used to determine how much advertisers pay for TV commercials. The media research business isn't what it used to be, however, as the Internet, video on demand, cell phones, iPods, digital video recorders, and other changing technologies have made data collection much more challenging. Whiting says, "If you look at a typical week I have, it's a combination of trying to lead a company in change in an industry in change."[9] That's a

---

change agents
People who act as change catalysts and assume the responsibility for managing the change process

"calm waters" metaphor
A description of organizational change that likens that change to a large ship making a predictable trip across a calm sea and experiencing an occasional storm

"white-water rapids" metaphor
A description of organizational change that likens that change to a small raft navigating a raging river

---

○ From the Past to the Present ○

"There is nothing so practical as a good theory."

"If you want truly to understand something, try to change it."

These two quotes by Kurt Lewin provide unique insights into who he was and how he approached studying management.[10] Lewin, who's often called the father of modern social psychology (a discipline that uses scientific methods to "understand and explain how the thought, feeling, and behavior of individuals are influenced by the actual, imagined, or implied presence of other human beings"), made his name in management circles through his studies of group dynamics. His approach was based on the belief that "group behavior is an intricate set of symbolic interactions and forces that not only affect group structure but also modify individual behavior."

One of his research studies that looked at modifying family food habits during World War II provided new and important insights into introducing change. He found that "changes were more easily induced through group decision making than through lectures and individual appeals." So what did this mean? His findings suggested that changes would be more readily accepted when people felt they had an opportunity to be involved in the change rather than when

they were simply asked or told to change. That's an important lesson for any manager, even today, to learn and apply.

Finally, another of Lewin's major contributions was the idea of force field analysis, a framework for looking at the factors (forces) that influenced a situation. Those forces could either be *driving* movement toward a goal or *blocking* movement toward a goal. When you view this idea in terms of managing change, you can see how this process also could contribute to understanding the dynamics of what makes change work and how managers can overcome resistance to change; that is, increase the driving forces, decrease the blocking forces, or both.

Think About:

- Using your own words, explain each of the two Lewin quotes above.

- Explain force field analysis and how it can be used in organizational change.

- What advice do you see in this information about Lewin's ideas that managers might use?

---

pretty accurate description of what change is like in our second change metaphor—white-water rapids. It's also consistent with a world that's increasingly dominated by information, ideas, and knowledge.[11]

To get a feeling of what managing change might be like in a white-water rapids environment, consider attending a college that had the following rules: Courses vary in length. When you sign up, you don't know how long a course will run. It might go for 2 weeks or 30 weeks. Furthermore, the instructor can end a course at any time with no prior warning. If that isn't challenging enough, the length of the class changes each time it meets: Sometimes the class lasts 20 minutes; other times it runs for 3 hours. And the time of the next class meeting is set by the instructor during this class. There's one more thing. All exams are unannounced, so you have to be ready for a test at any time. To succeed in this type of environment, you'd have to respond quickly to changing conditions. Students who were overly structured or uncomfortable with change wouldn't succeed.

DOES EVERY MANAGER FACE A WORLD OF CONSTANT AND CHAOTIC CHANGE?
No, not every manager faces such a world. However, the numbers who don't is dwindling. The stability and predictability of the calm waters metaphor don't exist. Disruptions in the status quo are not occasional and temporary, and they are not followed by a return to calm waters. Many managers never get out of the rapids. Like Susan Whiting, just described, they face constant forces in the environment (external *and* internal) that bring about the need for organizational change.

HOW DO ORGANIZATIONS IMPLEMENT PLANNED CHANGES? At the Wyndham Peachtree Conference Center in Georgia, businesses bring groups of employees to try their hand at the ancient Chinese water sport of dragon boat racing. Although the physical exercise is an added benefit, it's the team-building exercise in which participants learn about communication, collaboration, and commitment that's meant to be the longest-lasting benefit.[12]

We know that most changes employees experience in an organization don't happen by chance. Often managers make a concerted effort to alter some aspect of the organization. Whatever happens—in terms of structure or technology—ultimately affects organizational members. Efforts to assist organizational members with a planned change are referred to as **organization development (OD).**

In facilitating long-term, organization-wide changes, OD focuses on constructively changing the attitudes and values of organization members so that they can more readily adapt to and be more effective in achieving the new directions of the organization.[13] When OD efforts are planned, organization leaders are, in essence, attempting to change the organization's culture.[14] However, a fundamental issue of OD is its reliance on employee participation to foster an environment in which open communication and trust exist.[15] Persons involved in OD efforts acknowledge that change can create stress for employees. Therefore, OD attempts to involve organizational members in changes that will affect their jobs and seeks their input about how the change is affecting them (just as Lewin suggested).

Any organizational activity that assists with implementing planned change can be viewed as an OD technique. However, the more popular OD efforts in organizations rely heavily on group interactions and cooperation and include survey feedback, process consultation, team-building, and intergroup development.

Survey feedback efforts are designed to assess employee attitudes about and perceptions of the change they are encountering. Employees are generally asked to respond to a set of specific questions regarding how they view such organizational aspects as decision making, leadership, communication effectiveness, and satisfaction with their jobs, coworkers, and management.[16] The data that a change agent obtains are used to clarify problems that employees may be facing. As a result of this information, the change agent takes some action to remedy the problems.

In **process consultation**, outside consultants help managers to perceive, understand, and act on organizational processes with which they must deal.[17] These elements might include, for example, workflow, informal relationships among unit members, and formal communications channels. Consultants give managers insight into what is going on. It's important to recognize that consultants are not there to solve these problems. Rather, they act as coaches to help managers diagnose the interpersonal processes that need improvement. If managers, with the consultants' help, cannot solve the problem, the consultants will often help managers find experts who can.

Organizations are made up of individuals working together to achieve some goals. Because organizational members must frequently interact with peers, a primary function of OD is to help them become a team. **Team-building** is generally an activity that helps work groups set goals, develop positive interpersonal relationships, and clarify the roles and responsibilities of each team member. It's not always necessary to address each area because the group may be in agreement and understand what's expected of it. The primary focus of team-building is to increase members' trust and openness toward one another.[18]

Whereas team-building focuses on helping a work group become more cohesive, **intergroup development** attempts to achieve the same results among different work groups. That is, intergroup development attempts to change attitudes, stereotypes, and perceptions that one group may have toward another group. In doing so, better coordination among the various groups can be achieved.

Xyratex, a data storage firm based in the United Kingdom, brings its managers and employees from around the world together to participate in philanthropic team-building events. This photo shows coworkers who gathered in Sacramento, California, for a team-building exercise to assemble bicycles and then give them to kids from local Boys & Girls Clubs. Team-building helps Xyratex employees increase their trust and openness toward one another and deepen their commitment to the firm's mission of "advancing digital innovation." By combining team building with philanthropy, Xyratex gives employees the opportunity to achieve a corporate goal of helping children who live near the firm's operations in Europe, Asia, and North America.

Randall Benton/Newscom

organization development (OD)
Efforts that assist organizational members with a planned change by focusing on their attitudes and values

survey feedback
A method of assessing employees' attitudes toward and perceptions of a change

process consultation
Using outside consultants to assess organizational processes such as workflow, informal intra-unit relationships, and formal communication channels

team-building
Using activities to help work groups set goals, develop positive interpersonal relationships, and clarify the roles and responsibilities of each team member

intergroup development
Activities that attempt to make several work groups more cohesive

8.2 Explain how to manage resistance to change.

HOW DO MANAGERS MANAGE RESISTANCE TO CHANGE?

We know that it's better for us to eat healthy and to be active, yet few of us follow that advice. We resist making changes in our lifestyle. Volkswagen Sweden and ad agency DDB Stockholm did an experiment to see if they could get people to change their behavior and take the healthier option of using the stairs instead of riding an escalator.[19] How? They put a working piano keyboard on a stairway in a Stockholm subway station (you can see a video of it on YouTube) to see if commuters would use it. The experiment was a resounding success as stair traffic rose 66 percent. The lesson—people can change if you make the change appealing.

Managers should be motivated to initiate change because they're concerned with improving their organization's effectiveness. But change isn't easy in any organization. It can be disruptive and scary. Organizations, and people within them, can build up inertia that causes them to resist any change, even if the change might be beneficial. In this section, we review why people in organizations resist change and what can be done to lessen that resistance.

Why Do People Resist Organizational Change?

It's often said that most people hate any change that doesn't jingle in their pockets. This resistance to change is well documented.[20] Why *do* people resist organizational change? The main reasons include uncertainty, habit, concern over personal loss, and the belief that the change is not in the organization's best interest.[21]

Change replaces the known with uncertainty. No matter how much you may dislike attending college (or certain classes), at least you know what's expected of you. When you leave college for the world of full-time employment, you'll trade the known for the unknown. Employees in organizations are faced with similar uncertainty. For example, when quality control methods based on statistical models are introduced into manufacturing plants, many quality control inspectors have to learn the new methods. Some may fear that they'll be unable to do so and may develop a negative attitude toward the change or behave poorly if required to use them.

Another cause of resistance is that we do things out of habit. Every day when you go to school or work you probably get there the same way, if you're like most people. We're creatures of habit. Life is complex enough—we don't want to have to consider the full range of options for the hundreds of decisions we make every day. To cope with this complexity, we rely on habits or programmed responses. But when confronted with change, our tendency to respond in our accustomed ways becomes a source of resistance.

The third cause of resistance is the fear of losing something already possessed. Change threatens the investment you've already made in the status quo. The more that people have invested in the current system, the more they resist change. Why? They fear losing status, money, authority, friendships, personal convenience, or other economic benefits that they value. This helps explain why older workers tend to resist change more than younger workers since they generally have more invested in the current system and more to lose by changing.

A final cause of resistance is a person's belief that the change is incompatible with the goals and interests of the organization. For instance, an employee who believes that a proposed new job procedure will reduce product quality can be expected to resist the change. This type of resistance can actually be beneficial to the organization if expressed in a positive way.

What Are Some Techniques for Reducing Resistance to Organizational Change?

At an annual 401(k) enrollment meeting, the CEO of North American Tool, frustrated at his employees' disinterest in maxing out their investments, brought in a big bag, unzipped it, and upended it over a table.[23] Cash poured out—$9,832 to be exact—the amount employees had failed to claim the prior year. He gestured at the money and said, "This is your money. It should be in your pocket. Next year, do you want it on the table or in your

EXHIBIT 8-3	Techniques for Reducing Resistance to Change		
TECHNIQUE	**WHEN USED**	**ADVANTAGE**	**DISADVANTAGE**
Education and communication	When resistance is due to misinformation	Clear up misunderstandings	May not work when mutual trust and credibility are lacking
Participation	When resisters have the expertise to make a contribution	Increase involvement and acceptance	Time-consuming; has potential for a poor solution
Facilitation and support	When resisters are fearful and anxiety-ridden	Can facilitate needed adjustments	Expensive; no guarantee of success
Negotiation	When resistance comes from a powerful group	Can "buy" commitment	Potentially high cost; opens doors for others to apply pressure too
Manipulation and co-optation	When a powerful group's endorsement is needed	Inexpensive, easy way to gain support	Can backfire, causing change agent to lose credibility
Coercion	When a powerful group's endorsement is needed	Inexpensive, easy way to gain support	May be illegal; may undermine change agent's credibility

pocket?" When the 401(k) enrollment forms were distributed, several individuals signed up. Sometimes to get people to change, you first have to get their attention.

When managers see resistance to change as dysfunctional, what can they do? Several strategies have been suggested in dealing with resistance to change. These approaches include education and communication, participation, facilitation and support, negotiation, manipulation and co-optation, and coercion. These tactics are summarized here and described in Exhibit 8–3. Managers should view these techniques as tools and use the most appropriate one depending on the type and source of the resistance.

Education and communication can help reduce resistance to change by helping employees see the logic of the change effort. This technique, of course, assumes that much of the resistance lies in misinformation or poor communication.

Participation involves bringing those individuals directly affected by the proposed change into the decision-making process. Their participation allows these individuals to express their feelings, increase the quality of the process, and increase employee commitment to the final decision.

Facilitation and support involve helping employees deal with the fear and anxiety associated with the change effort. This help may include employee counseling, therapy, new skills training, or a short paid leave of absence.

Negotiation involves exchanging something of value for an agreement to lessen the resistance to the change effort. This resistance technique may be quite useful when the resistance comes from a powerful source.

Manipulation and co-optation refer to covert attempts to influence others about the change. They may involve twisting or distorting facts to make the change appear more attractive.

Finally, *coercion* can be used to deal with resistance to change. Coercion involves the use of direct threats or force against the resisters.

WHAT REACTION DO EMPLOYEES HAVE TO ORGANIZATIONAL CHANGE?

For many employees, change creates stress. A dynamic and uncertain environment characterized by restructurings, downsizings, empowerment, and personal-life matters has caused large numbers of employees to feel overworked and "stressed out." As our opening case described, sometimes the stress gets to be so intense that individuals respond in a drastic (and tragic) way. In this section, we'll review specifically what is meant by the term *stress*, what the symptoms of stress are, what causes stress, and what managers can do to reduce anxiety.

Describe what managers need to know about employee stress. **8.3**

What Is Stress?

Stress is the adverse reaction people have to excessive pressure placed on them from extraordinary demands, constraints, or opportunities.[24] Stress isn't always bad. Although it's often discussed in a negative context, stress can be positive, especially when it offers a potential gain. For instance, functional stress allows an athlete, stage performer, or employee to perform at his or her highest level at crucial times.

However, stress is more often associated with constraints and demands. A constraint prevents you from doing what you desire; demands refer to the loss of something desired. When you take a test at school or have your annual performance review at work, you feel stress because you confront opportunity, constraints, and demands. A good performance review may lead to a promotion, greater responsibilities, and a higher salary. But a poor review may keep you from getting a promotion. An extremely poor review might lead to your being fired.

One other thing to understand about stress is that just because the conditions are right for stress to surface doesn't always mean it will. Two conditions are necessary for *potential* stress to become *actual* stress.[25] First, there must be uncertainty over the outcome, and second, the outcome must be important.

What Are the Symptoms of Stress?

We see stress in a number of ways. For instance, an employee who is experiencing high stress may become depressed, accident prone, or argumentative; may have difficulty making routine decisions; may be easily distracted, and so on. As Exhibit 8–4 shows, stress symptoms can be grouped under three general categories: physical, psychological, and behavioral. All of these can significantly affect an employee's work.

Too much stress can also have tragic consequences. In Japan, there's a stress phenomenon called **karoshi** (pronounced kah-roe-she), which is translated literally as "death from overwork." During the late 1980s, "several high-ranking Japanese executives still in their prime years suddenly died without any previous sign of illness."[26] As public concern increased, even the Japanese Ministry of Labour got involved, and it now publishes statistics on the number of karoshi deaths. As Japanese multinational companies expand operations to China, Korea, and Taiwan, it's feared that the karoshi culture may follow.

What Causes Stress?

Stress can be caused by personal factors and by job-related factors called **stressors**. Clearly, change of any kind—personal or job-related—has the potential to cause stress because it involves demands, constraints, or opportunities. Organizations have no shortage of factors that can cause stress. Pressures to avoid errors or complete tasks in

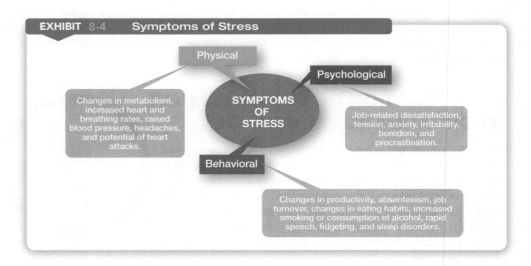

EXHIBIT 8-4   **Symptoms of Stress**

Physical — Changes in metabolism, increased heart and breathing rates, raised blood pressure, headaches, and potential of heart attacks.

Psychological — Job-related dissatisfaction, tension, anxiety, irritability, boredom, and procrastination.

SYMPTOMS OF STRESS

Behavioral — Changes in productivity, absenteeism, job turnover, changes in eating habits, increased smoking or consumption of alcohol, rapid speech, fidgeting, and sleep disorders.

a limited time period, changes in the way reports are filed, a demanding supervisor, and unpleasant coworkers are a few examples. Let's look at five categories of organizational stressors: task, role, and interpersonal demands; organization structure; and organizational leadership.

Task demands are factors related to an employee's job. They include the design of a person's job (autonomy, task variety, degree of automation), working conditions, and the physical work layout. Work quotas can put pressure on employees when their "outcomes" are perceived as excessive.[27] The more interdependence between an employee's tasks and the tasks of others, the more potential stress there is. *Autonomy*, on the other hand, tends to lessen stress. Jobs in which temperatures, noise, or other working conditions are dangerous or undesirable can increase anxiety. So, too, can working in an overcrowded room or in a visible location where interruptions are constant.

Role demands relate to pressures placed on an employee as a function of the particular role he or she plays in the organization. **Role conflicts** create expectations that may be hard to reconcile or satisfy. **Role overload** is experienced when the employee is expected to do more than time permits. **Role ambiguity** is created when role expectations are not clearly understood and the employee is not sure what he or she is to do.

Interpersonal demands are pressures created by other employees. Lack of social support from colleagues and poor interpersonal relationships can cause considerable stress, especially among employees with a high social need.

Organization structure can increase stress. Excessive rules and an employee's lack of opportunity to participate in decisions that affect him or her are examples of structural variables that might be potential sources of stress.

Organizational leadership represents the supervisory style of the organization's managers. Some managers create a culture characterized by tension, fear, and anxiety. They establish unrealistic pressures to perform in the short run, impose excessively tight controls, and routinely fire employees who don't measure up. This style of leadership filters down through the organization and affects all employees.

Personal factors that can create stress include family issues, personal economic problems, and inherent personality characteristics. Because employees bring their personal problems to work with them, a full understanding of employee stress requires a manager to be understanding of these personal factors.[28] Evidence also indicates that employees' personalities have an effect on how susceptible they are to stress. The most commonly used labels for these personality traits are Type A and Type B.

Chris Crisman/Redux Pictures

These top global executives of the JWT advertising agency have highly stressful jobs. As senior corporate executives leading an agency with more than 200 offices in 90 countries, they have a career that ranks high on the list of the most stressful jobs. Role and task demands make the jobs of senior executives stressful because as leaders they are expected to develop strategies and make decisions that keep their company profitable. This complex task requires an extensive knowledge of business and an understanding of industry trends, technological developments, and competitors' plans. On average, business leaders work 11 hours a day and face daily pressure to make decisions that affect employees, shareholders, and other stakeholders.

---

stress
The adverse reaction people have to excessive pressure placed on them from extraordinary demands, constraints, or opportunities

karoshi
A Japanese term that refers to a sudden death caused by overworking

stressors
Factors that cause stress

role conflicts
Work expectations that are hard to satisfy

role overload
Having more work to accomplish than time permits

role ambiguity
When role expectations are not clearly understood

RIGHT ? WRONG

One in five companies offers some form of stress management program.[29] Although such programs are available, many employees may choose not to participate. They may be reluctant to ask for help, especially if a major source of that stress is job insecurity. After all, there's still a stigma associated with stress. Employees don't want to be perceived as being unable to handle the demands of their job. Although they may need stress management now more than ever, few employees want to admit that they're stressed.

Think About:

- What can be done about this paradox?

- Do organizations even *have* an ethical responsibility to help employees deal with stress?

Madis Uudam/Shutterstock

The **Type A personality** is characterized by chronic feelings of a sense of time urgency, an excessive competitive drive, and difficulty accepting and enjoying leisure time. The opposite of Type A is the **Type B personality**. Type Bs never suffer from time urgency or impatience. Until quite recently, it was believed that Type As were more likely to experience stress on and off the job. A closer analysis of the evidence, however, has produced new conclusions. Studies show that only the hostility and anger associated with Type A behavior are actually associated with the negative effects of stress. And Type Bs are just as susceptible to the same anxiety-producing elements. For managers, what is important is to recognize that Type A employees are more likely to show symptoms of stress, even if organizational and personal stressors are low.

How Can Stress Be Reduced?

As mentioned earlier, not all stress is dysfunctional. Even though stress can never be totally eliminated from a person's life, managers want to reduce the stress that leads to dysfunctional work behavior. How? Through controlling certain organizational factors to reduce job-related stress, and to a more limited extent, offering help for personal stress.

Things that managers can do in terms of job-related factors begin with employee selection. Managers need to make sure that an employee's abilities match the job requirements. When employees are in over their heads, their stress levels typically will be high. A realistic job preview during the selection process can minimize stress by reducing ambiguity over job expectations. Improved organizational communications will keep ambiguity-induced stress to a minimum. Similarly, a performance planning program such as MBO will clarify job responsibilities, provide clear performance goals, and reduce ambiguity through feedback. Job redesign is also a way to reduce stress. If stress can be traced to boredom or to work overload, jobs should be redesigned to increase challenge or to reduce the workload. Redesigns that increase opportunities for employees to participate in decisions and to gain social support also have been found to lessen stress.[30] For instance, at U.K. pharmaceutical maker GlaxoSmithKline, a team-resilience program in which employees can shift assignments depending on people's workload and deadlines, has helped reduce work-related stress by 60 percent.[31]

No matter what you do to eliminate organizational stressors, some employees will still be "stressed out." And stress from an employee's personal life raises two problems. First, it's difficult for the manager to control directly. Second, there are ethical considerations. Specifically, does the manager have the right to intrude—even in the most subtle ways—in an employee's personal life? If a manager believes it's ethical and the employee is receptive, there are a few approaches the manager can consider.

To help deal with these issues, many companies offer employee assistance and wellness programs.[32] These employer-sponsored programs are designed to assist employees in areas where they might be having difficulties such as financial planning, legal matters, health, fitness, or stress.[33]

Contemporary **employee assistance programs (EAPs)** are extensions of programs that began in U.S. companies in the 1940s.[34] Companies such as DuPont, Standard Oil, and Kodak recognized that a number of their employees were experiencing problems with alcohol. Formal programs were implemented on the company's site to educate these workers about the dangers of alcohol and to help them overcome their addiction. The rationale for these programs, which still holds today, is getting a productive employee back on the job as quickly as possible. An organization also can benefit in terms of a return on investment. It's estimated that U.S. companies spend almost $1 billion each year on EAP programs. Studies suggest that most of these companies save up to $5 to $16 for every EAP dollar spent.[35] That's a significant return on investment!

In addition to EAP, many organizations are implementing wellness programs. A **wellness program** is designed to keep employees healthy.[36] These programs vary and may focus on such things as smoking cessation, weight control, stress management, physical fitness, nutrition education, high-blood-pressure control, violence protection, work team problem intervention, and so on.[37] Wellness programs are designed to help cut employer health costs and to lower absenteeism and turnover by preventing health-related problems.[38]

HOW CAN MANAGERS ENCOURAGE INNOVATION IN AN ORGANIZATION?

Discuss techniques for stimulating innovation.

8.4

"Innovation is the key to continued success." "We innovate today to secure the future."[39] These two quotes (the first by Ajay Banga, the CEO of MasterCard, and the second by Sophie Vandebroek, chief technology officer of Xerox Innovation Group) reflect how important innovation is to organizations. Success in business today demands innovation. In the dynamic, chaotic world of global competition, organizations must create new products and services and adopt state-of-the-art technology if they're going to compete successfully.[40]

What companies come to mind when you think of successful innovators? Maybe Apple with all its cool work and entertainment gadgets. Maybe Facebook for its 800 million-plus users. Maybe Nissan for creating the Leaf, the first mass-market all-electric car. Or even maybe Zynga (a company founded in 2007 and now worth over $500 million) for creating wildly popular games and dominating the social gaming market.[41] What's the secret to the success of these innovator champions? What can other managers do to make their organizations more innovative? In the following pages, we'll try to answer those questions as we discuss the factors behind innovation.

How Are Creativity and Innovation Related?

Creativity refers to the ability to combine ideas in a unique way or to make unusual associations between ideas.[42] A creative organization develops unique ways of working or novel solutions to problems. For instance, at Mattel, company officials introduced "Project Platypus," a special group that brings people from all disciplines—engineering, marketing, design, and sales—and tries to get them to "think outside the box" in order to "understand the sociology and psychology behind children's play patterns." To help make this kind of thinking happen, team members embarked on such activities as imagination exercises, group crying, and stuffed-bunny throwing. What does throwing stuffed bunnies have to do with creativity? It's part of a juggling lesson where team members tried to learn to juggle two balls and a stuffed bunny. Most people can easily learn to juggle two balls but can't let go of that third object. Creativity, like juggling, is learning to let go—that is, to "throw the bunny."[43] But creativity by itself isn't enough. The outcomes of the creative process need to be turned into useful products or work methods, which is defined as **innovation**. Thus,

---

Type A personality
People who have a chronic sense of urgency and an excessive competitive drive

Type B personality
People who are relaxed and easygoing and accept change easily

employee assistance programs (EAPs)
Programs offered by organizations to help employees overcome personal and health-related problems

wellness programs
Programs offered by organizations to help employees prevent health problems

creativity
The ability to produce novel and useful ideas

innovation
The process of taking a creative idea and turning it into a useful product, service, or method of operation

Michael Tercha/Newscom

Groupon is an innovative organization that channeled creativity into a useful outcome. Company founder and CEO Andrew Mason describes his Groupon.com innovation as a "hybrid of local advertising and local commerce." An online group discount service targeted to local communities, Groupon has been called "the most exciting thing to happen to retail since eBay." The service offers daily deals from local merchants through group coupons, giving businesses a new way to advertise their products and services and giving consumers the chance to try new things at a huge discount. Shown here are employees of Groupon in Chicago, where the company was started in 2008 and has since expanded to cities throughout the world.

the innovative organization is characterized by its ability to channel creativity into useful outcomes. When managers talk about changing an organization to make it more creative, they usually mean they want to stimulate and nurture innovation.

What's Involved in Innovation?

Some people believe that creativity is inborn; others believe that with training, anyone can be creative. The latter group views creativity as a fourfold process consisting of perception, incubation, inspiration, and innovation.[44]

Perception involves the way you see things. Being creative means seeing things from a unique perspective. One person may see solutions to a problem that others cannot or will not see at all. The movement from perception to reality, however, doesn't occur instantaneously. Instead, ideas go though a process of *incubation*. Sometimes employees need to sit on their ideas, which doesn't mean sitting and doing nothing. Rather, during this incubation period, employees should collect massive amounts of data that are stored, retrieved, studied, reshaped, and finally molded into something new. During this period, it's common for years to pass. Think for a moment about a time you struggled for an answer on a test. Although you tried hard to jog your memory, nothing worked. Then suddenly, like a flash of light, the answer popped into your head. You found it! *Inspiration* in the creative process is similar. Inspiration is the moment when all your efforts successfully come together.

Although inspiration leads to euphoria, the creative work isn't complete. It requires an innovative effort. *Innovation* involves taking that inspiration and turning it into a useful product, service, or way of doing things. Thomas Edison is often credited with saying that "Creativity is 1 percent inspiration and 99 percent perspiration." That 99 percent, or the innovation, involves testing, evaluating, and retesting what the inspiration found. It's usually at this stage that an individual involves others more in what he or she has been working on. Such involvement is critical because even the greatest invention may be delayed, or lost, if an individual cannot effectively deal with others in communicating and achieving what the creative idea is supposed to do.

How Can a Manager Foster Innovation?

The systems model (inputs → transformation process → outputs) can help us understand how organizations become more innovative.[45] If an organization wants innovative products and work methods (*outputs*), it has to take its *inputs* and *transform* them into those outputs. Those *inputs* include creative people and groups within the organization. But as we said earlier, having creative people isn't enough. The *transformation process* requires having the right environment to turn those inputs into innovative products or work methods. This "right" environment—that is, an environment that stimulates innovation—includes three variables: the organization's structure, culture, and human resource practices. (See Exhibit 8–5.)

HOW DO STRUCTURAL VARIABLES AFFECT INNOVATION? When Carol Bartz joined Yahoo! Inc. as CEO, one of the first things she noticed was how the organization's structure got in the way of innovation. Employees didn't know, when they wanted to try something different, whether they got to make the decision or somebody else did and what would happen if they went for it. Bartz's philosophy was that, "There's a freedom when you organize around the idea that you're clearly in charge and go for it." Today, Yahoo!'s structure has been changed so that there are clearer lines of responsibility and the freedom to make mistakes.[46]

Research into the effect of structural variables on innovation shows five things.[47] First, an organic-type structure positively influences innovation. Because this structure is

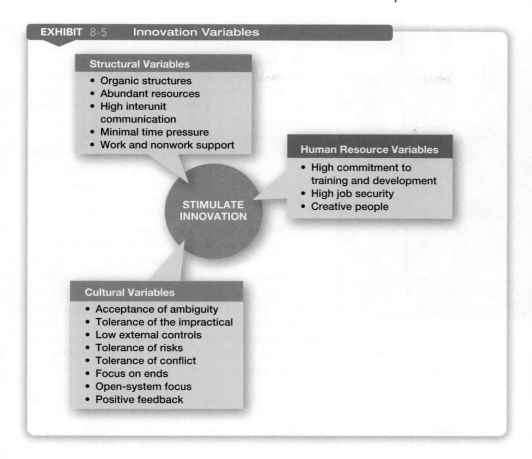

EXHIBIT 8-5   Innovation Variables

Structural Variables
- Organic structures
- Abundant resources
- High interunit communication
- Minimal time pressure
- Work and nonwork support

Human Resource Variables
- High commitment to training and development
- High job security
- Creative people

STIMULATE INNOVATION

Cultural Variables
- Acceptance of ambiguity
- Tolerance of the impractical
- Low external controls
- Tolerance of risks
- Tolerance of conflict
- Focus on ends
- Open-system focus
- Positive feedback

low in formalization, centralization, and work specialization, it facilitates the flexibility and sharing of ideas that are critical to innovation. Second, the availability of plentiful resources provides a key building block for innovation. With an abundance of resources, managers can afford to purchase innovations, can afford the cost of instituting innovations, and can absorb failures. Third, frequent communication between organizational units helps break down barriers to innovation.[48] Cross-functional teams, task forces, and other such organizational designs facilitate interaction across departmental lines and are widely used in innovative organizations. Fourth, innovative organizations try to minimize extreme time pressures on creative activities despite the demands of white-water-rapids-type environments. Although time pressures may spur people to work harder and may make them feel more creative, studies show that it actually causes them to be less creative.[49] Finally, studies have shown that when an organization's structure explicitly supports creativity, employees' creative performance can be enhanced. Beneficial kinds of support include encouragement, open communication, readiness to listen, and useful feedback.[50]

HOW DOES AN ORGANIZATION'S CULTURE AFFECT INNOVATION?   Innovative organizations tend to have similar cultures.[51] They encourage experimentation; reward both successes and failures; and celebrate mistakes. An innovative organization is likely to have the following characteristics.

◆ *Accepts ambiguity.* Too much emphasis on objectivity and specificity constrains creativity.
◆ *Tolerates the impractical.* Individuals who offer impractical, even foolish, answers to what-if questions are not stifled. What at first seems impractical might lead to innovative solutions.
◆ *Keeps external controls minimal.* Rules, regulations, policies, and similar organizational controls are kept to a minimum.

Jim Wilson/Redux Pictures

Giving employees a sense of creative ownership is key to the innovation process at Zynga, a social network game developer. Shown here at company headquarters in San Francisco, Zynga's co-founder and chief executive Mark Pincus established "Be CEO: Own outcomes" as a core value to guide employees in how they do their jobs. Another core value—"Build games you and your friends love to play"—is supported by Zynga's organizational culture that gives employees the freedom to experiment, tolerates risk and conflict, and holds rules and regulations at a minimum. By also providing positive feedback and encouragement, Zynga supports employees' creative ideas that result in the development of popular games such as *CityVille*.

◆ *Tolerates risk.* Employees are encouraged to experiment without fear of consequences should they fail. Mistakes are treated as learning opportunities.

◆ *Tolerates conflict.* Diversity of opinions is encouraged. Harmony and agreement between individuals or units are *not* assumed to be evidence of high performance.

◆ *Focuses on ends rather than means.* Goals are made clear, and individuals are encouraged to consider alternative routes toward meeting the goals. Focusing on ends suggests that there might be several right answers to any given problem.

◆ *Uses an open-system focus.* Managers closely monitor the environment and respond to changes as they occur. For example, at Starbucks, product development depends on "inspiration field trips to view customers and trends." When Michelle Gass (who's now the president of Starbucks' division, Seattle's Best Coffee) was in charge of Starbucks marketing, she "took her team to Paris, Düsseldorf, and London to visit local Starbucks and other restaurants to get a better sense of local cultures, behaviors, and fashions." She says, "You come back just full of different ideas and different ways to think about things than you would had you read about it in a magazine or e-mail."[52]

◆ *Provides positive feedback.* Managers provide positive feedback, encouragement, and support so employees feel that their creative ideas receive attention. For instance, at Research In Motion, Mike Lazaridis, president and co-CEO says, "I think we have a culture of innovation here, and [engineers] have absolute access to me. I live a life that tries to promote innovation."[53]

WHAT HUMAN RESOURCE VARIABLES AFFECT INNOVATION? In this category, we find that innovative organizations actively promote the training and development of their members so their knowledge remains current; offer their employees high job security to reduce the fear of getting fired for making mistakes; and encourage individuals to become **idea champions**, actively and enthusiastically supporting new ideas, building support, overcoming resistance, and ensuring that innovations are implemented. Research finds that idea champions have common personality characteristics: extremely high self-confidence, persistence, energy, and a tendency toward risk taking. They also display characteristics associated with dynamic leadership. They inspire and energize others with their vision of the potential of an innovation and through their strong personal conviction in their mission. They're also good at gaining the commitment of others to support their mission. In addition, idea champions have jobs that provide considerable decision-making discretion. This autonomy helps them introduce and implement innovations in organizations.[54]

idea champions
Individuals who actively and enthusiastically support new ideas, build support for, overcome resistance to, and ensure that innovations are implemented

8 Review

CHAPTER SUMMARY

8.1 Define organizational change and compare and contrast views on the change process. Organizational change is any alteration of an organization's people, structure, or technology. The "calm waters" metaphor of change suggests that change is an occasional disruption in the normal flow of events and can be planned and managed as it happens, using Lewin's three-step change process (unfreezing, changing, and freezing). The "white-water rapids" view of change suggests that change is ongoing, and managing it is a continual process.

8.2 Explain how to manage resistance to change. People resist change because of uncertainty, habit, concern about personal loss, and the belief that a change is not in the organization's best interests. Techniques for managing resistance to change include education and communication (educating employees about and communicating to them the need for the change), participation (allowing employees to participate in the change process), facilitation and support (giving employees the support they need to implement the change), negotiation (exchanging something of value to reduce resistance), manipulation and co-optation (using negative actions to influence), selecting people who are open to and accept change, and coercion (using direct threats or force).

8.3 Describe what managers need to know about employee stress. Stress is the adverse reaction people have to excessive pressure placed on them from extraordinary demands, constraints, or opportunities.

The symptoms of stress can be physical, psychological, or behavioral. Stress can be caused by personal factors and by job-related factors. To help employees deal with stress, managers can address job-related factors by making sure an employee's abilities match the job requirements, improving organizational communications, using a performance planning program, or redesigning jobs. Addressing personal stress factors is trickier, but managers could offer employee counseling, time management programs, and wellness programs.

8.4 Discuss techniques for stimulating innovation. Creativity is the ability to combine ideas in a unique way or to make unusual associations between ideas. Innovation is turning the outcomes of the creative process into useful products or work methods. An innovative environment encompasses structural, cultural, and human resource variables.

Important structural variables include an organic-type structure, abundant resources, frequent communication between organizational units, minimal time pressure, and support. Important cultural variables include accepting ambiguity, tolerating the impractical, keeping external controls minimal, tolerating risk, tolerating conflict, focusing on ends not means, using an open-system focus, and providing positive feedback. Important human resource variables include high commitment to training and development, high job security, and encouraging individuals to be idea champions.

MyManagementLab   For more resources, please visit **www.mymanagementlab.com**

UNDERSTANDING THE CHAPTER

1. Why is managing change an integral part of every manager's job?

2. Contrast the calm waters and white-water rapids metaphors of change. Which of these would you use to describe your current life? Why is that one your choice?

3. Describe Lewin's three-step change process. How is it different from the change process needed in the white-water rapids metaphor of change?

4. How are opportunities, constraints, and demands related to stress? Give an example of each.

5. Organizations typically have limits to how much change they can absorb. As a manager, what signs would you look for that might suggest your organization has exceeded its capacity to change?

6. Why is organization development planned change? Explain how planned change is important for organizations in today's dynamic environment.

7. How do creativity and innovation differ? Give an example of each.

8. Research information on how to be a more creative person. Write down suggestions in a bulleted list format and be prepared to present your information in class.

9. How does an innovative culture make an organization more effective? Do you think an innovative culture could ever make an organization less effective? Why or why not?

10. When you find yourself experiencing dysfunctional stress, write down what's causing the stress, what stress symptoms you're exhibiting, and how you're dealing with the stress. Keep this information in a journal and evaluate how well your stress reducers are working and how you could handle stress better. Your goal is to get to a point where you recognize that you're stressed and can take positive actions to deal with the stress.

Go to p. 426
YOUR TURN TO BE A MANAGER for Chapter 8.

Endnotes

1. K. Dunn, "Employee Turnover and Suicide: It Turns Out the Response to Either Is the Same," *HR Capitalist Online,* May 9, 2011; S. Mahoney, "Stress Less, Accomplish More," *Good Housekeeping,* May 2010, p. 57; A. Chrisafis, "France Telecom Worker Kills Himself in Office Car Park," www.guardian.co.uk (April 27, 2011); Reuters, "France Telecom to Probe Employee Suicide by Fire," www.trust.org (April 27, 2011); A. R. Carey and P. Trap, "Aspect of the Job That Workers Find the Most Stressful," *USA Today,* April 20, 2011, p. 1A; "Survey," *Shape,* April 2011, p. 48; M. V. Rafter, "The Yawning of New Era," *Workforce Management Online,* December 2010; C. Hausman, "Millions of U.K. Workers Lie to Bosses About Stress-Induced Days," *Global Ethics Online,* November 8, 2010; E. Holbrook, "Beneath the Bell Jar: Companies Confront a Rise in Workplace Suicides," *Risk Management,* November 2010, pp. 6–8; "Survey: 30 Percent of Managers Under More Stress," *Workforce Management Online,* September 22, 2010; M. Colchester, "France Télécom Faces Inquiry Over Suicides," *New York Times Online,* April 12, 2010; M. Saltmarsh, "France Télécom Suicides Prompt an Investigation," *New York Times Online,* April 9, 2010; E. Frauenheim, "Suicides Spur Management Shake-Up at France Télécom," *Workforce Management,* March 2010, pp. 6–8; C. Stievenard, "France's Approach to Workplace 'Bullying,'" *Workforce Management Online,* www.workforce.com (March 2010); R. Bender and M. Colchester, "Morale Is Priority for France Télécom," *Wall Street Journal,* February 4, 2010, p. B2; The Associated Press, "Executive Quits After Suicides at France Télécom," *New York Times Online,* October 6, 2009; and D. Jolly and M. Saltmarsh, "Suicides in France Put Focus on Workplace," *New York Times Online,* September 30, 2009.

2. A. Weintraub and M. Tirrell, "Eli Lilly's Drug Assembly Line," *Bloomberg BusinessWeek,* March 8, 2010, pp. 56–57.

3. J. Katz, "Campbell Soup Cooking Up a New Recipe?" *Industry Week,* January 2011, p. 51.

4. K. Grzbowska, "The Social Aspect of Introducing Changes into the Organization," *International Journals of Human Resources Development and Management,* February 2, 2007, p. 67; and I. M. Jawahar and G. L. McLaughlin, "Toward a Descriptive Stakeholder Theory: An Organizational Life Cycle Approach," *Academy of Management Review,* July 2001, pp. 397–415.

5. E. Shannon, "Agent of Change," *Time,* March 4, 2002, p. 17; B. Kenney, "SLA Head Shaffer Resigns Abruptly: Did 'Change Agent' Move Too Fast in Aggressive Restructuring?" *Library Journal,* March 15, 2002, pp. 17–19; and T. Mudd, "Rescue Mission," *Industry Week,* May 1, 2000, pp. 30–37.

6. The idea for these metaphors came from P. Vaill, *Managing as a Performing Art: New Ideas for a World of Chaotic Change* (San Francisco: Jossey Bass, 1989).

7. K. Lewin, *Field Theory in Social Science* (New York: Harper & Row, 1951).

8. R. E. Levasseur, "People Skills: Change Management Tools— Lewin's Change Model," *Interfaces,* August 2001, pp. 71–74.

9. D. Lieberman, "Nielsen Media Has Cool Head at the Top," *USA Today,* March 27, 2006, p. 3B.

10. From the Past to the Present box based on D. A. Wren and A. G. Bedeian, *The Evolution of Management Thought,* 6th ed. (Hoboken, NJ: John Wiley & Sons, Inc., 2009); "Biography and Quotes of Kurt Lewin," *About.com,* psychology.about.com (July 15, 2009); and K. T. Lewin, "The Dynamics of Group Action," *Educational Leadership,* January 1944, pp. 195–200.

11. L. S. Lüscher and M. W. Lewis, "Organizational Change and Managerial Sensemaking: Working Through Paradox," *Academy of Management Journal* (April 2008), pp. 221–240; F. Buckley and K. Monks, "Responding to Managers' Learning Needs in an Edge-of-Chaos Environment: Insights from Ireland," *Journal of Management* (April 2008), pp. 146–163; and G. Hamel, "Take It Higher," *Fortune,* February 5, 2001, pp. 169–170.

12. L. Freifeld, "Paddle to Collaborate," *Training* (November– December 2010), p. 6.

13. S. Hicks, "What Is Organization Development?" *Training and Development* (August 2000), p. 65; and H. Hornstein, "Organizational Development and Change Management: Don't Throw the Baby Out with the Bath Water," *Journal of Applied Behavioral Science* (June 2001), pp. 223–227.

14. J. Wolfram and S. Minahan, "A New Metaphor for Organization Development," *Journal of Applied Behavioral Science* (June 2006), pp. 227–243.

15. See, for instance, H. B. Jones, "Magic, Meaning, and Leadership: Weber's Model and the Empirical Literature." *Human Relations,* June 2001, p. 753.

16. G. Akin and I. Palmer, "Putting Metaphors to Work for a Change in Organizations," *Organizational Dynamics,* Winter 2000, pp. 67–79.

17. J. Grieves, "Skills, Values or Impression Management: Organizational Change and the Social Processes of Leadership, Change Agent Practice, and Process Consultation," *Journal of Management Development* (May 2000), p. 407.

18. M. McMaster, "Team Building Tips," *Sales & Marketing Management,* January 2002, p. 140; and "How To: Executive Team Building," *Training and Development* (January 2002), p. 16.

19. S. Shinn, "Stairway to Reinvention," *BizEd,* January–February 2010, p. 6; M. Scott, "A Stairway to Marketing Heaven," *BusinessWeek,* November 2, 2009, p. 17; and The Fun Theory, http://thefuntheory.com (November 10, 2009).

20. See, for example, J. Robison and D. Jones, "Overcoming the Fear of Change," *Gallup Management Journal Online,* January 7, 2011; J. D. Ford, L. W. Ford, and A. D'Amelio, "Resistance to Change: The Rest of the Story," *Academy of Management Review,* April 2008, pp. 362–377; A. Deutschman, "Making Change: Why Is It So Hard to Change Our Ways?" *Fast Company,* May 2005, pp. 52–62; S. B. Silverman, C. E. Pogson, and A. B. Cober, "When Employees at Work Don't Get It: A Model for Enhancing Individual Employee Change in Response to Performance Feedback," *Academy of Management Executive,* May 2005, pp. 135–147; C. E. Cunningham, C. A. Woodward, H. S. Shannon, J. MacIntosh, B. Lendrum, D. Rosenbloom, and J. Brown, "Readiness for Organizational Change: A Longitudinal Study of Workplace, Psychological and Behavioral Correlates," *Journal of Occupational and Organizational Psychology* (December 2002), pp. 377–392; M. A. Korsgaard, H. J. Sapienza, and D. M. Schweiger, "Beaten Before Begun: The Role of Procedural Justice in Planning Change," *Journal of Management* 28, no. 4 (2002), pp. 497–516; R. Kegan and L. L. Lahey, "The Real Reason People Won't Change," *Harvard Business Review,* November

2001, pp. 85–92; S. K. Piderit, "Rethinking Resistance and Recognizing Ambivalence: A Multidimensional View of Attitudes Toward an Organizational Change," *Academy of Management Review,* October 2000, pp. 783–794; C. R. Wanberg and J. T. Banas, "Predictors and Outcomes of Openness to Changes in a Reorganizing Workplace," *Journal of Applied Psychology* (February 2000), pp. 132–142; A. A. Armenakis and A. G. Bedeian, "Organizational Change: A Review of Theory and Research in the 1990s," *Journal of Management* 25, no. 3 (1999), pp. 293–315; and B. M. Staw, "Counterforces to Change," in P.S. Goodman and Associates (eds.), *Change in Organizations* (San Francisco: Jossey-Bass, 1982), pp. 87–121.

21. A. Reichers, J. P. Wanous, and J. T. Austin, "Understanding and Managing Cynicism about Organizational Change," *Academy of Management Executive*, February 1997, pp. 48–57; P. Strebel, "Why Do Employees Resist Change?" *Harvard Business Review,* May–June 1996, pp. 86–92; and J. P. Kotter and L.A. Schlesinger, "Choosing Strategies for Change," *Harvard Business Review*, March–April 1979, pp. 107–109.

22. And the Survey Says box based on based on S. Schomer, "Under Pressure," *Fast Company,* April 2010, p. 112; "Organizational Change: Facebook Poll," *Harvard Business Review,* March 2010, p. 16; J. Yang and S. Ward, "I'd Rather Give Up," *USA Today,* March 4, 2010, p. 1B; M. Weinstein, "Missing Something," *Training* (January 2010), p. 6; J. MacIntyre, "Hard At Work," *Springfield Business Journal,* November 30–December 6, 2009, p. 16; J. MacIntyre, "Accidental Innovation," *Springfield Business Journal,* September 28–October 4, 2009, p. 22; and M. Healy and S. Ward, "Workplace Worries," *USA Today,* August 28, 2008, p. 1D.

23. D. Heath and C. Heath, "Passion Provokes Action," *Fast Company,* February 2011, pp. 28–30.

24. Adapted from the UK National Work-Stress Network, www.workstress.net.

25. R. S. Schuler, "Definition and Conceptualization of Stress in Organizations," *Organizational Behavior and Human Performance,* April 1980, p. 191.

26. A. Kanai, "Karoshi (Work to Death) in Japan," *Journal of Business Ethics* (January 2009) Supplement 2, pp. 209–216; The Associated Press, "Overwork Cited in Death of Japanese Worker," *New York Times Online,* July 10, 2008; "Jobs for Life," *Economist,* www.economist.com (December 19, 2007); and B. L. de Mente, "Karoshi: Death from Overwork," Asia Pacific Management Forum, www.apmforum.com (May 2002).

27. See, for example, "Stressed Out: Extreme Job Stress: Survivors' Tales," *Wall Street Journal* January 17, 2001, p. B1.

28. See, for instance, S. Bates, "Expert: Don't Overlook Employee Burnout," *HR Magazine,* August 2003, p. 14.

29. Right or Wrong? box based on D. Cole, "The Big Chill," *US News & World Report,* December 6, 2004, pp. EE2–EE5.

30. H. Benson, "Are You Working Too Hard?" *Harvard Business Review,* November 2005, pp. 53–58; B. Cryer, R. McCraty, and D. Childre, "Pull the Plug on Stress," *Harvard Business Review,* July 2003, pp. 102–107; C. Daniels, "The Last Taboo"; C. L. Cooper and S. Cartwright, "Healthy Mind, Healthy Organization—A Proactive Approach to Occupational Stress," *Human Relations,* April 1994, pp. 455–471; C. A. Heaney et al., "Industrial Relations, Worksite Stress Reduction and Employee Well-Being: A Participatory Action Research Investigation," *Journal of Organizational Behavior* (September 1993),

pp. 495–510; C. D. Fisher, "Boredom at Work: A Neglected Concept," *Human Relations,* March 1993, pp. 395–417; and S. E. Jackson, "Participation in Decision Making as a Strategy for Reducing Job-Related Strain," *Journal of Applied Psychology* (February 1983), pp. 3–19.

31. C. Mamberto, "Companies Aim to Combat Job-Related Stress," *Wall Street Journal,* August 13, 2007, p. B6.

32. T. Barton, "Brave Face," *Employee Benefits,* January 2011, p. 41; and "Employee Assistance Programs," *HR Magazine,* May 2003, p. 143.

33. S. Barrett, "Employee Assistance Programs," *Employee Benefits,* January 2011, pp. 49–52; "EAPs with the Most," *Managing Benefits Plans,* March 2003, p. 8; and K. Tyler, "Helping Employees Cope with Grief," *HR Magazine,* September 2003, pp. 55–58.

34. N. Faba, "The EAP Problem," *Benefits Canada,* March 2011, p. 7; D. A. Masi, "Redefining the EAP Field," *Journal of Workplace Behavioral Health* (January–March 2011), pp. 1–9; R. M. Weiss, "Brinksmanship Redux: Employee Assistance Programs' Precursors and Prospects," *Employee Responsibilities & Rights Journal* (December 2010), pp. 325–343; and F. Hansen, "Employee Assistance Programs (EAPs) Grow and Expand Their Reach," *Compensation and Benefits Review,* March–April 2000, p. 13.

35. F. Phillips, "Employee Assistance Programs: A New Way to Control Health Care Costs," *Employee Benefit Plan Review,* August 2003, pp. 22–24.

36. K. Lee, "EAP Diversity Detracts from Original Focus, Some Say," *Employee Benefits News,* July 1, 2003, p. 1.

37. See, for instance, P. Petesch, "Workplace Fitness or Workplace Fits?" *HR Magazine,* July 2001, pp. 137–140.

38. C. Petersen, "Value of Complementary Care Rises, But Poses Challenges," *Managed HealthCare,* November 2000, pp. 47–48.

39. A. Saha-Bubna and M. Jarzemsky, "MasterCard President Is Named CEO," *Wall Street Journal* April 13, 2010, p. C3; and S. Vandebook, "Quotable," *IndustryWeek,* April 2010, p. 18.

40. R. M. Kanter, "Think Outside the Building," *Harvard Business Review,* March 2010, p. 34; T. Brown, "Change By Design," *BusinessWeek,* October 5, 2009, pp. 54–56; J. E. Perry-Smith and C. E. Shalley, "The Social Side of Creativity: A Static and Dynamic Social Network Perspective," *Academy of Management Review,* January 2003, pp. 89–106; and P. K. Jagersma, "Innovate or Die: It's Not Easy, But It Is Possible to Enhance Your Organization's Ability to Innovate," *Journal of Business Strategy* (January–February 2003), pp. 25–28.

41. *Fast Company* staff, "The World's 50 Most Innovative Companies," *Fast Company,* March 2011, pp. 66+; and G. Colvin, "The World's Most Admired Companies," *Fortune,* March 21, 2011, pp. 109+.

42. These definitions are based on T. M. Amabile, *Creativity in Context* (Boulder, CO: Westview Press, 1996).

43. C. Salter, "Mattel Learns to 'Throw the Bunny,'" *Fast Company,* November 2002, p. 22; and L. Bannon, "Think Tank in Toyland," *Wall Street Journal,* June 6, 2002, pp. B1, B3.

44. C. Vogel and J. Cagan, *Creating Breakthrough Products: Innovation from Product Planning to Program Approval* (Upper Saddle River, NJ: Prentice Hall, 2002).

45. R. W. Woodman, J. E. Sawyer, and R. W. Griffin, "Toward a Theory of Organizational Creativity," *Academy of Management Review,* April 1993, pp. 293–321.

46. K. Swisher, "A Question of Management," *Wall Street Journal* June 2, 2009, p. R4.

47. T. M. Egan, "Factors Influencing Individual Creativity in the Workplace: An Examination of Quantitative Empirical Research," *Advances in Developing Human Resources,* May 2005, pp. 160–181; N. Madjar, G. R. Oldham, and M. G. Pratt, "There's No Place Like Home? The Contributions of Work and Nonwork Creativity Support to Employees' Creative Performance," *Academy of Management Journal* (August 2002), pp. 757–767; T. M. Amabile, C. N. Hadley, and S. J. Kramer, "Creativity Under the Gun," *Harvard Business Review,* August 2002, pp. 52–61; J. B. Sorensen and T. E. Stuart, "Aging, Obsolescence, and Organizational Innovation," *Administrative Science Quarterly*, March 2000, pp. 81–112; G.R. Oldham and A. Cummings, "Employee Creativity: Personal and Contextual Factors at Work," *Academy of Management Journal* (June 1996), pp. 607–634; and F. Damanpour, "Organizational Innovation: A Meta-Analysis of Effects of Determinants and Moderators," *Academy of Management Journal* (September 1991), pp. 555–590.

48. P. R. Monge, M. D. Cozzens, and N. S. Contractor, "Communication and Motivational Predictors of the Dynamics of Organizational Innovations," *Organization Science*, May 1992, pp. 250–274.

49. T. M. Amabile, C. N. Hadley, and S. J. Kramer, "Creativity Under the Gun."

50. N. Madjar, G. R. Oldham, and M. G. Pratt, "There's No Place Like Home? The Contributions of Work and Nonwork Creativity Support to Employees' Creative Performance."

51. See, for instance, J. E. Perry-Smith, "Social Yet Creative: The Role of Social Relationships in Facilitating Individual Creativity," *Academy of Management Journal* (February 2006), pp. 85–101; C. E. Shalley, J. Zhou, and G. R. Oldham, "The Effects of Personal and Contextual Characteristics on Creativity: Where Should We Go from Here?" *Journal of Management,* 30, no. 6 (2004), pp. 933–958; J. E. Perry-Smith and C. E. Shalley, "The Social Side of Creativity: A Static and Dynamic Social Network Perspective"; J. M. George and J. Zhou, "When Openness to Experience and Conscientiousness Are Related to Creative Behavior: An Interactional Approach," *Journal of Applied Psychology* (June 2001), pp. 513–524; J. Zhou, "Feedback Valence, Feedback Style, Task Autonomy, and Achievement Orientation: Interactive Effects on Creative Behavior," *Journal of Applied Psychology,* 83 (1998), pp. 261–276; T. M. Amabile, R. Conti, H. Coon, J. Lazenby, and M. Herron, "Assessing the Work Environment for Creativity," *Academy of Management Journal* (October 1996), pp. 1154–1184; S. G. Scott and R. A. Bruce, "Determinants of Innovative People: A Path Model of Individual Innovation in the Workplace," *Academy of Management Journal* (June 1994), pp. 580–607; R. Moss Kanter, "When a Thousand Flowers Bloom: Structural, Collective, and Social Conditions for Innovation in Organization," in B. M. Staw and L. L. Cummings (eds.), *Research in Organizational Behavior*, vol. 10 (Greenwich, CT: JAI Press, 1988), pp. 169–211; and Amabile, *Creativity in Context.*

52. J. McGregor, "The World's Most Innovative Companies," *BusinessWeek,* April 24, 2006, p. 70.

53. Ibid.

54. J. Ramos, "Producing Change That Lasts," *Across the Board*, March 1994, pp. 29–33; T. Stjernberg and A. Philips, "Organizational Innovations in a Long-Term Perspective: Legitimacy and Souls-of-Fire as Critical Factors of Change and Viability," *Human Relations*, October 1993, pp. 1193–2023; and J. M. Howell and C. A. Higgins, "Champions of Change," *Business Quarterly*, Spring 1990, pp. 31–32.

CHAPTER 9

Foundations of Individual Behavior

LEARNING OUTCOMES

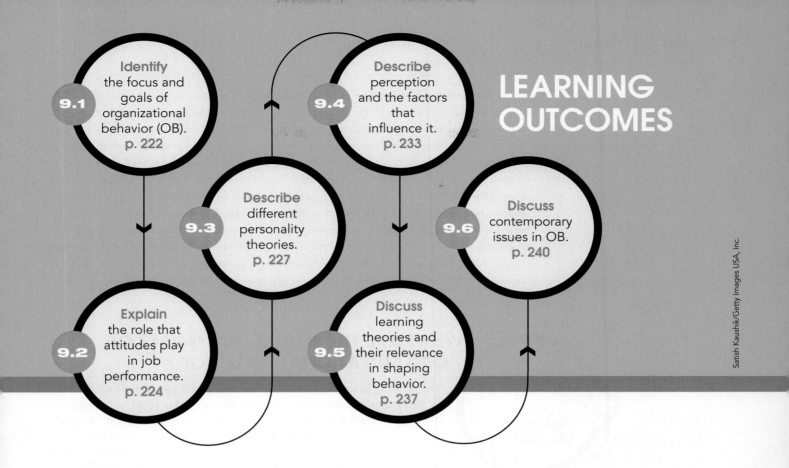

9.1 Identify the focus and goals of organizational behavior (OB). p. 222

9.4 Describe perception and the factors that influence it. p. 233

9.3 Describe different personality theories. p. 227

9.6 Discuss contemporary issues in OB. p. 240

9.2 Explain the role that attitudes play in job performance. p. 224

9.5 Discuss learning theories and their relevance in shaping behavior. p. 237

Satish Kaushik/Getty Images USA, Inc.

Employees First

"Employees first." That's the most important and crucial cultural value that HCL Technologies CEO Vineet Nayar believes will take his company into the future.[1] Although most managers think that customers should come first, Nayar's philosophy is that employee satisfaction needs to be the top priority.

As one of the largest companies in India, HCL sells various information technology product services, such as laptop, custom software development, and technology consulting. Luring and keeping top talent is one of the challenges HCL faces. And at its size, it doesn't have the atmosphere of a fun and quirky start-up.

Part of that "employee first" philosophy is a no-layoff policy, which was difficult to uphold during the pressures of the economic downturn. Like its competitors, HCL had excess employees and had suspended raises. But HCL kept its promise and didn't lay off any HCLite (Nayar's name for HCL employees). As business has picked up, however, employees begin looking at competitors' job offers. During the first quarter alone of 2010, HCL lost 22 percent of its workforce. Maybe it's time to monitor and track employee satisfaction.

Although most managers will not go as far as Vineet Nayar to promote employee satisfaction, many organizations are concerned with the attitudes of their employees. Like him, they want to attract and retain employees with the right attitudes and personality. They want people who show up and work hard, get along with coworkers and customers, have good attitudes, and exhibit good work behaviors in other ways. But as you're probably already aware, people don't always behave like that "ideal" employee. They job hop at the first opportunity or they may post critical comments in blogs. People differ in their behaviors and even the same person can behave one way one day and a completely different way another day. For instance, haven't you seen family members, friends, or coworkers behave in ways that prompted you to wonder: Why did they do that? In this chapter, we look at four psychological aspects—attitudes, personality, perception, and learning—and demonstrate how these things can help managers understand the behavior of those people with whom they have to work. We conclude the chapter by looking at contemporary behavioral issues facing managers.

WHAT ARE THE FOCUS AND GOALS OF ORGANIZATIONAL BEHAVIOR?

9.1 Identify the focus and goals of organizational behavior (OB).

The material in this and the next four chapters draws heavily on the field of study that's known as *organizational behavior (OB)*. Although it's concerned with the subject of behavior—that is, the actions of people— organizational behavior is the study of the actions of people at work.

One of the challenges in understanding organizational behavior is that it addresses issues that aren't obvious. Like an iceberg, OB has a small visible dimension and a much larger hidden portion. (See Exhibit 9–1.) What we see when we look at an organization is its visible aspects: strategies, objectives, policies and procedures, structure, technology, formal authority relationships, and chain of command. But under the surface are other elements that managers need to understand—elements that also influence how employees behave at work. As we'll show, OB provides managers with considerable insights into these important, but hidden, aspects of the organization.

What Is the Focus of OB?

Organizational behavior focuses on three major areas. First, OB looks at *individual behavior.* Based predominantly on contributions from psychologists, this area includes such topics as

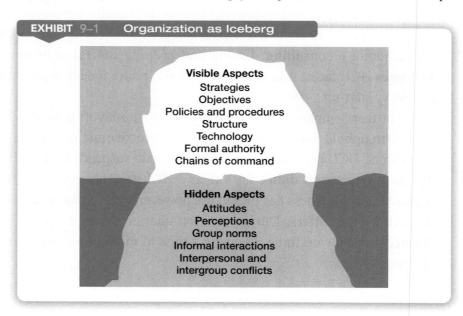

EXHIBIT 9–1   Organization as Iceberg

Visible Aspects
Strategies
Objectives
Policies and procedures
Structure
Technology
Formal authority
Chains of command

Hidden Aspects
Attitudes
Perceptions
Group norms
Informal interactions
Interpersonal and intergroup conflicts

attitudes, personality, perception, learning, and motivation. Second, OB is concerned with *group behavior*, which includes norms, roles, team building, leadership, and conflict. Our knowledge about groups comes basically from the work of sociologists and social psychologists. Finally, OB also looks at *organizational* aspects including structure, culture, and human resource policies and practices. We've addressed organizational aspects in previous chapters. In this chapter, we'll look at individual behavior and in the following chapter, at group behavior.

What Are the Goals of Organizational Behavior?

The goals of OB are to *explain, predict,* and *influence* behavior. Managers need to be able to *explain* why employees engage in some behaviors rather than others, *predict* how employees will respond to various actions and decisions, and *influence* how employees behave.

What employee behaviors are we specifically concerned with explaining, predicting, and influencing? Six important ones have been identified: employee productivity, absenteeism, turnover, organizational citizenship behavior (OCB), job satisfaction, and workplace misbehavior. **Employee productivity** is a performance measure of both work efficiency and effectiveness. Managers want to know what factors will influence the efficiency and effectiveness of employees. **Absenteeism** is the failure to show up for work. It's difficult for work to get done if employees don't show up. Studies have shown that the total costs of all major types of absences cost organizations an average 35 percent of payroll with unscheduled absences costing companies around $660 per employee per year.[2] Although absenteeism can't be totally eliminated, excessive levels have a direct and immediate impact on the organization's functioning. **Turnover** is the voluntary and involuntary permanent withdrawal from an organization. It can be a problem because of increased recruiting, selection, and training costs and work disruptions. Just like absenteeism, managers can never eliminate turnover, but it is something they want to minimize, especially among high-performing employees. **Organizational citizenship behavior** is discretionary behavior that's not part of an employee's formal job requirements, but which promotes the effective functioning of the organization.[3] Examples of good OCB include helping others on one's work team, volunteering for extended job activities, avoiding unnecessary conflicts, and making constructive statements about one's work group and the organization. Organizations need individuals who will do more than their usual job duties and the evidence indicates that organizations that have such employees outperform those that don't.[4] However, drawbacks to OCB arise if employees experience work overload, stress, and work-family conflicts.[5] *Job satisfaction* refers to an employee's general attitude toward his or her job. Although job satisfaction is an attitude rather than a behavior, it's an outcome that concerns many managers because satisfied employees are more likely to show up for work, have higher levels of performance, and stay with an organization. **Workplace misbehavior** is any intentional employee behavior that is potentially

Organizational behavior focuses on job satisfaction and how it influences employee productivity, absenteeism, and turnover. Job satisfaction is high at the Lexus of Westminster auto dealership where Trung Pham, shown here, works as a mechanic. Pham and the dealership's 125 other employees have a positive feeling about their jobs and the company they work for. They say their employer, a family-owned and operated business, values the contributions they make, treats them with respect and integrity, and entrusts them with great responsibility in providing customers with a world-class Lexus ownership experience. Satisfied employees help the dealership maintain low absenteeism and turnover rates and high worker productivity.

Newscom

---

behavior
The actions of people

organizational behavior
The study of the actions of people at work

employee productivity
A performance measure of both work efficiency and effectiveness

absenteeism
The failure to show up for work

turnover
Voluntary and involuntary permanent withdrawal from an organization

organizational citizenship behavior
Discretionary behavior that's not part of an employee's formal job requirements, but that promotes the effective functioning of the organization

workplace misbehavior
Any intentional employee behavior that is potentially harmful to the organization or individuals within the organization

harmful to the organization or individuals within the organization. Workplace misbehavior shows up in organizations in four ways: deviance, aggression, antisocial behavior, and violence.[6] Such behaviors can range from playing loud music just to irritate coworkers to verbal aggression to sabotaging work, all of which can create havoc in any organization. In the following pages, we'll address how an understanding of four psychological factors— employee attitudes, personality, perception, and learning—can help us predict and explain these employee behaviors.

WHAT ROLE DO ATTITUDES PLAY IN JOB PERFORMANCE?

9.2 Explain the role that attitudes play in job performance.

Attitudes are evaluative statements, either favorable or unfavorable, concerning objects, people, or events. They reflect how an individual feels about something. When a person says, "I like my job," he or she is expressing an attitude about work.

What Are the Three Components of an Attitude?

To better understand attitude, we need to look at its three components: cognition, affect, and behavior.[7] The **cognitive component** of an attitude is made up of the beliefs, opinions, knowledge, and information held by a person. For example, shortly after the September 11, 2001, attacks on the World Trade Center and the Pentagon, Congress debated for weeks as to whether airport baggage screeners should be federal employees. Some claimed the current private airport screeners were adequately doing their jobs, even though evidence presented during the debate showed that knives, pepper spray, and a loaded gun were missed by airport screeners.[8] The belief held by some congressional leaders that private screeners were effective is an example of cognition. The **affective component** is the emotional or feeling part of an attitude. This component would be reflected in the statement, "I don't like Erica because she smokes." Cognition and affect can lead to behavioral outcomes. The **behavioral component** of an attitude refers to an intention to behave in a certain way toward someone or something. So, to continue our example, I might choose to avoid Erica because of my feelings about her. Looking at attitudes as being made up of three components—cognition, affect, and behavior—helps to illustrate the complexity of attitudes. For the sake of clarity, keep in mind that the term usually refers only to the affective component.

What Attitudes Might Employees Hold?

Naturally, managers are not interested in every attitude an employee might hold. Rather, they're specifically interested in job-related attitudes, and the three most important and most studied are job satisfaction, job involvement, and organizational commitment.[9] **Job satisfaction** is an employee's general attitude toward his or her job. When people speak of employee attitudes, more often than not they mean job satisfaction. **Job involvement** is the degree to which an employee identifies with his or her job, actively participates in it, and considers his or her job performance important for self-worth. Finally, **organizational commitment** represents an employee's orientation toward the organization in terms of his or her loyalty to, identification with, and involvement in the organization.

A new concept associated with job attitudes that's generating widespread interest is **employee engagement**, which happens when employees are connected to, satisfied with, and enthusiastic about their jobs.[10] Highly engaged employees are passionate about and deeply connected to their work. Disengaged employees have essentially "checked out" and don't care. They show up for work, but have no energy or passion for it. A global study of more than 12,000 employees found that respect ranked as the number one factor contributing to employee engagement. In addition to respect, the top five engagement factors included type of work, work/life balance, providing good service to customers, and base pay.[11]

Having highly engaged employees produces both benefits and costs. Highly engaged employees are two-and-a-half times more likely to be top performers than their less-engaged coworkers. In addition, companies with highly engaged employees have higher retention rates, which help keep recruiting and training costs low. And both of these outcomes—higher performance and lower costs—contribute to superior financial performance.[12]

Do Individuals' Attitudes and Behaviors Need to Be Consistent?

Did you ever notice how people change what they say so that it doesn't contradict what they do? Perhaps a friend of yours had consistently argued that American-manufactured cars were poorly built and that he'd never own anything but a foreign import. Then his parents gave him a late model American-made car, and suddenly they weren't so bad. Or when going through sorority rush, a new freshman believes that sororities are good and that pledging a sorority is important. If she's not accepted by a sorority, however, she may say, "Sorority life isn't all it's cracked up to be anyway."

Research generally concludes that people seek consistency among their attitudes and between their attitudes and their behavior.[13] Individuals try to reconcile differing attitudes and align their attitudes and behavior so that they appear rational and consistent. They do so by altering either the attitudes or the behavior or by developing a rationalization for the discrepancy.

What Is Cognitive Dissonance Theory?

Can we assume from this consistency principle that an individual's behavior can always be predicted if we know his or her attitude on a subject? The answer isn't a simple "yes" or "no." Why? Cognitive dissonance theory.

Cognitive dissonance theory, proposed by Leon Festinger in the 1950s, sought to explain the relationship between attitudes and behavior.[14] **Cognitive dissonance** is any incompatibility or inconsistency between attitudes or between behavior and attitudes. The theory argued that inconsistency is uncomfortable and that individuals will try to reduce the discomfort and thus, the dissonance.

Of course, no one can avoid dissonance. You know you should floss your teeth every day, but don't do it. There's an inconsistency between attitude and behavior. How do people cope with cognitive dissonance? The theory proposed that how hard we try to reduce dissonance is determined by three things: (1) the *importance* of the factors creating the dissonance, (2) the degree of *influence* the individual believes he or she has over those factors, and (3) the *rewards* that may be involved in dissonance.

Cognitive dissonance refers to any incompatibility or inconsistency between attitudes and behaviors. For example, most people may believe that they are safe drivers, yet many may create potentially unsafe road conditions by driving and texting at the same time. To reduce the dissonance, these drivers may either stop their habit of driving and texting, or they may rationalize that driving and texting doesn't really pose any threat to others' safety, that they are in control of the situation, or that everyone else is doing the same thing.

Robert Crum/Shutterstock

---

attitudes
Evaluative statements, either favorable or unfavorable, concerning objects, people, or events

cognitive component
The part of an attitude made up of the beliefs, opinions, knowledge, and information held by a person

affective component
The part of an attitude that's the emotional or feeling part

behavioral component
The part of an attitude that refers to an intention to behave in a certain way toward someone or something

job satisfaction
An employee's general attitude toward his or her job

job involvement
The degree to which an employee identifies with his or her job, actively participates in it, and considers his or her job performance important for self-worth

organizational commitment
An employee's orientation toward the organization in terms of his or her loyalty to, identification with, and involvement in the organization

employee engagement
When employees are connected to, satisfied with, and enthusiastic about their jobs

cognitive dissonance
Any incompatibility or inconsistency between attitudes or between behavior and attitudes

If the factors creating the dissonance are relatively unimportant, the pressure to correct the inconsistency will be low. However, if those factors are important, individuals may change their behavior, conclude that the dissonant behavior isn't so important, change their attitude, or identify compatible factors that outweigh the dissonant ones.

How much influence individuals believe they have over the factors also affects their reaction to the dissonance. If they perceive the dissonance is something about which they have no choice, they won't be receptive to attitude change or feel a need to do so. If, for example, the dissonance-producing behavior was required as a result of a manager's order, the pressure to reduce dissonance would be less than if the behavior had been performed voluntarily. Although dissonance exists, it can be rationalized and justified by the need to follow the manager's orders—that is, the person had no choice or control.

Finally, rewards also influence the degree to which individuals are motivated to reduce dissonance. Coupling high dissonance with high rewards tends to reduce the discomfort by motivating the individual to believe that there is consistency.

Let's look at an example. Tracey Ford, a corporate manager, believes strongly that no company should lay off employees. Unfortunately, Tracey has to make decisions that trade off her company's strategic direction against her convictions on layoffs. She knows that organizational restructuring means some jobs may no longer be needed. She also knows layoffs are in the best economic interest of her firm. What will she do? Undoubtedly, Tracey is experiencing a high degree of cognitive dissonance. Because of the *importance* of the issues in this example, she can't ignore the inconsistency. To deal with her dilemma, she can follow several steps. She can change her behavior (lay off employees). Or she can reduce dissonance by concluding that the dissonant behavior is not so important after all ("I've got to make a living, and in my role as a decision maker, I often have to place the good of my company above that of individual organizational members"). She might also change her attitude ("There is nothing wrong in laying off employees"). Finally, another choice would be to seek out more consonant elements to outweigh the dissonant ones ("The long-term benefits to the surviving employees from our restructuring more than offset the associated costs"). Let's explain her behavior.

The *degree of influence* that Tracey believes she has also impacts how she reacts to the dissonance. If she perceives the dissonance to be uncontrollable—something about which she has no choice—she's less likely to feel she needs to change her attitude. If, for example, her boss told her that she had to lay off employees, the pressure to reduce dissonance would be less than if Tracey was performing the behavior voluntarily. Dissonance would exist but it could be rationalized and justified. This tendency illustrates why it's critical in today's organizations for leaders to establish an ethical culture. Without the leaders' influence and support, employees won't feel as much dissonance when faced with decisions of whether to act ethically or unethically.[15]

Finally, *rewards* also influence how likely Tracy is to reduce dissonance. High dissonance, when accompanied by high rewards, tends to reduce the tension inherent in the dissonance. The reward reduces dissonance by adding to the consistency side of the individual's balance sheet. Tracey might feel because she is well compensated in her job that she sometimes has to make hard decisions, such as laying off employees.

So what can we say about dissonance and employee behavior? These moderating factors suggest that although individuals experience dissonance, they won't necessarily move toward consistency, that is, toward reducing the dissonance. If the issues underlying the dissonance are of minimal importance, if an individual perceives that the dissonance is externally imposed and is substantially uncontrollable, or if rewards are significant enough to offset the dissonance, the individual will not be under great tension to reduce the dissonance.[16]

How Can an Understanding of Attitudes Help Managers Be More Effective?

Managers should be interested in their employees' attitudes because they influence behavior. Satisfied and committed employees, for instance, have lower rates of turnover and absenteeism. If managers want to keep resignations and absences down—especially

AND THE SURVEY SAYS... [17]

31 percent of employees worldwide are engaged with their job.

55 percent of adults surveyed say they "love" their job.

44 percent of employees say their top workplace break annoyance is someone making a mess for others to clean up.

43 percent of workers say they regularly wear casual business attire at the office.

45 percent of employers say they need workers with more or different skills.

99 percent of people polled say they have been bullied or witnessed bullying at work.

15 percent of millennials say that having a high-paying career is a top priority.

44 percent of Gen Yers rank job security as more important than personal job satisfaction.

among their more productive employees—they'll want to do things that generate positive job attitudes.

Whether satisfied workers are productive workers is a debate that's been going on for almost 80 years. After the Hawthorne Studies, managers believed that happy workers were productive workers. Because it's not easy to determine whether job satisfaction "caused" job productivity or vice versa, some management researchers felt that the belief was generally wrong. However, we can say with some certainty that the correlation between satisfaction and productivity is fairly strong.[18] Satisfied employees do perform better on the job. So managers should focus on those factors that have been shown to be conducive to high levels of employee job satisfaction: making work challenging and interesting, providing equitable rewards, and creating supportive working conditions and supportive colleagues.[19] These factors are likely to help employees be more productive.

Managers should also survey employees about their attitudes. As one study put it, "A sound measurement of overall job attitude is one of the most useful pieces of information an organization can have about its employees."[20] However, research has also shown that attitude surveys can be more effective at pinpointing employee dissatisfaction if done multiple times rather than just at one point in time.[21]

Finally, managers should know that employees will try to reduce dissonance. If employees are required to do things that appear inconsistent to them or that are at odds with their attitudes, managers should remember that pressure to reduce the dissonance is not as strong when the employee perceives that the dissonance is externally imposed and uncontrollable. It's also decreased if rewards are significant enough to offset the dissonance. So the manager might point to external forces such as competitors, customers, or other factors when explaining the need to perform some work that the individual may have some dissonance about. Or the manager can provide rewards that an individual desires.

WHAT DO MANAGERS NEED TO KNOW ABOUT PERSONALITY?

> Describe different personality theories.
>
> 9.3

"Incoming Bowling Green State University freshmen Erica Steele and Katelyn Devore had never met. But after they scored a 95 percent match on an online compatibility test, they signed up to room together."[22] If you've ever shared a living space with someone else (family or nonfamily), you know how important it can be for roommates to be compatible and to get along with each other. This compatibility is affected and influenced by our own and by other people's personalities.

Personality. We all have one. Some of us are quiet and passive; others are loud and aggressive. When we describe people using terms such as *quiet, passive, loud, aggressive, ambitious, extroverted, loyal, tense,* or *sociable*, we're describing their personalities. An individual's **personality** is a unique combination of emotional, thought, and behavioral patterns that affect how a person reacts to situations and interacts with others. Personality is most often described in terms of measurable traits that a person exhibits. We're interested in looking at personality because just like attitudes, it affects how and why people behave the way they do.

Can Personality Predict Behavior?

Literally dozens of behaviors are attributed to an individual's traits. So too are personality types influential in how people interact with one another and how they solve problems. Through the years, researchers attempted to focus specifically on which personality types

personality
A unique combination of emotional, thought, and behavioral patterns that affect how a person reacts to situations and interacts with others

and personality traits would identify information about the individual. Two of these efforts have been widely recognized: the Myers-Briggs Type Indicator® and the Big Five model of personality.

WHAT IS THE MYERS-BRIGGS TYPE INDICATOR?   One of the more widely used methods of identifying personalities is the Myers-Briggs Type Indicator (MBTI). The MBTI® assessment uses four dimensions of personality to identify 16 different personality types based on the responses to an approximately 100-item questionnaire. More than 2 million individuals take the MBTI assessment each year in the United States alone. It's used in such companies as Apple, Hallmark, AT&T, Exxon, 3M, as well as many hospitals, educational institutions, and the U.S. Armed Forces.

The 16 personality types are based on four dimensions: Extraversion versus Introversion (EI), Sensing versus Intuition (SN), Thinking versus Feeling (TF), and Judging versus Perceiving (JP). The EI dimension describes an individual's orientation toward the external world of the environment (E) or the inner world of ideas and experiences (I). The Sensing-Intuition dimension indicates an individual's preference for gathering data while focusing on a standard routine based on factual data (S) to focusing on the big picture and making connections among the facts (N). Thinking-Feeling reflects one's preference for making decisions in a logical and analytical manner (T) or on the basis of values and beliefs and the effects the decision will have on others (F). The Judging-Perceiving index reflects an attitude toward how one deals with the external world—either in a planned and orderly way (J) or preferring to remain flexible and spontaneous (P).[23]

Let's give you some examples. An ISTJ (Introversion - Sensing - Thinking - Judging) is quiet, serious, dependable, practical, and matter-of-fact. On the other hand, an ESFP (Extraversion - Sensing - Feeling - Perceiving) is outgoing, friendly, spontaneous, enjoys working with others, and learns best by trying a new skill with other people. An INFP (Introversion - Intuition - Feeling - Perceiving) is idealistic, loyal to personal values, and seeks to understand people and help them fulfill their potential. Finally, an ENTJ (Extraversion - Intuition - Thinking - Judging) is frank, decisive, and will assume leadership roles. This type also enjoys long-term planning and goal setting and is forceful in presenting ideas.[24]

How could the MBTI assessment help managers? Proponents of the instrument believe that it's important to know these personality types because they influence the way people interact and solve problems.[25] For example, if your boss prefers Intuition and you're a Sensing type, you'll deal with information in different ways. An Intuition preference indicates your boss is one who prefers gut reactions, whereas you, as a Sensing type, prefer to deal with the facts. To work well with your boss, you have to present more than just facts about a situation—you'll also have to discuss your gut feeling about the situation. The MBTI assessment has also been found to be useful in focusing on growth orientations for entrepreneurial types as well as profiles supporting emotional intelligence (something we'll look at shortly).[26]

WHAT IS THE BIG FIVE MODEL OF PERSONALITY?   Another way of viewing personality is through a five-factor model of personality—more typically called the Big Five model.[27] The Big Five factors are:

1 Extraversion	A personality dimension that describes the degree to which someone is sociable, talkative, and assertive.
2 Agreeableness	A personality dimension that describes the degree to which someone is good-natured, cooperative, and trusting.
3 Conscientiousness	A personality dimension that describes the degree to which someone is responsible, dependable, persistent, and achievement oriented.
4 Emotional stability	A personality dimension that describes the degree to which someone is calm, enthusiastic, and secure (positive) or tense, nervous, depressed, and insecure (negative).
5 Openness to experience	A personality dimension that describes the degree to which someone is imaginative, artistically sensitive, and intellectual.

The Big Five model provides more than just a personality framework. Research has shown that important relationships exist between these personality dimensions and job performance.[28] For example, one study reviewed five categories of occupations: professionals (e.g., engineers, architects, attorneys), police, managers, sales, and semiskilled and skilled employees. Job performance was defined in terms of employee performance ratings, training competency, and personnel data such as salary level. The results of the study showed that conscientiousness predicted job performance for all five occupational groups.[29] Predictions for the other personality dimensions depended on the situation and the occupational group. For example, extraversion predicted performance in managerial and sales positions, in which high social interaction is necessary.[30] Openness to experience was found to be important in predicting training competency. Ironically, emotional security was not positively related to job performance. Although it would seem logical that calm and secure workers would be better performers, that wasn't the case. Perhaps it's a function of the likelihood that emotionally stable workers often keep their jobs and emotionally unstable people may not. Given that all those participating in the study were employed, the variance on that dimension was probably small.

WHAT IS EMOTIONAL INTELLIGENCE?   People who understand their own emotions and are good at reading others' emotions may be more effective in their jobs. That, in essence, is the theme of the underlying research on emotional intelligence.[31]

Emotional intelligence (EI) refers to an assortment of noncognitive skills, capabilities, and competencies that influences a person's ability to cope with environmental demands and pressures.[32] It's composed of five dimensions:

- *Self-awareness*. Being aware of what you're feeling.
- *Self-management*. Managing your own emotions and impulses.
- *Self-motivation*. Persisting in the face of setbacks and failures.
- *Empathy*. Sensing how others are feeling.
- *Social skills*. Adapting to and handling the emotions of others.

Several studies suggest that EI may play an important role in job performance.[33] For instance, one study looked at the characteristics of Bell Lab engineers who were rated as stars by their peers. The scientists concluded that these stars were better at relating to others. That is, it was EI, not academic IQ, that characterized high performers. A second study of Air Force recruiters generated similar findings: Top-performing recruiters exhibited high levels of EI. Using these findings, the Air Force revamped its selection criteria. A follow-up investigation found that future hires who had high EI scores were 2.6 times more successful than those with low scores. Organizations such as American Express have found that implementing emotional intelligence programs has helped increase its effectiveness; other organizations also found similar results that emotional intelligence contributes to team effectiveness.[34] For instance, at Cooperative Printing in Minneapolis, a study of its 45 employees concluded that EI skills were twice as important in "contributing to excellence as intellect and expertise alone."[35] A poll of human resources managers asked this question: How important is it for your workers to demonstrate EI to move up the corporate ladder? Forty percent of the managers replied "very important." Another 16 percent said moderately important. Other studies also indicated that emotional intelligence can be beneficial to quality improvements in contemporary organizations.[36]

The implication is that employers should consider emotional intelligence as a criterion in their selection process—especially for those jobs that demand a high degree of social interaction.[37]

Myers-Briggs Type Indicator (MBTI)
A personality assessment that uses four dimensions of personality to identify different personality types

big five model
A personality trait model that examines five traits: extraversion, agreeableness, conscientiousness, emotional stability, and openness to experience

emotional intelligence (EI)
The ability to notice and to manage emotional cues and information

RIGHT ? WRONG
OR

It's been called the "desperation hustle."[38] Employees who are "anxious about layoffs want to look irreplaceable." So they clean up their act. Those who might not have paid much attention to their manner of dress now do. Those who were mouthy and argumentative are now quiet and compliant. Those who used to "watch the clock" are now the last to leave. The fear is there and it's noticeable. "Managing that fear can be challenging."

Think About:

• What ethical issues might arise for both employees and for managers?

• How could managers approach these circumstances ethically?

• What information in this chapter might help managers help employees?

Superstock

Can Personality Traits Predict Practical Work-Related Behaviors?

Five specific personality traits have proven most powerful in explaining individual behavior in organizations. These are locus of control, Machiavellianism, self-esteem, self-monitoring, and risk propensity.

Who has control over an individual's behavior? Some people believe that they control their own fate. Others see themselves as pawns of fate, believing that what happens to them in their lives is due to luck or chance. The **locus of control** in the first case is internal. In the second case, it is external; these people believe that their lives are controlled by outside forces.[39] A manager might also expect to find that externals blame a poor performance evaluation on their boss's prejudice, their coworkers, or other events outside their control, whereas "internals" explain the same evaluation in terms of their own actions.

The second characteristic is called **Machiavellianism ("Mach")** after Niccolo Machiavelli, who provided instruction in the sixteenth century on how to gain and manipulate power. An individual who is high in Machiavellianism is pragmatic, maintains emotional distance, believes that ends can justify the means,[40] and may have beliefs that are less ethical.[41] The philosophy "if it works, use it" is consistent with a high Mach perspective. Do high Machs make good employees? That answer depends on the type of job and whether you consider ethical implications in evaluating performance. In jobs that require bargaining skills (a labor negotiator) or that have substantial rewards for winning (a commissioned salesperson), high Machs are productive. In jobs in which ends do not justify the means or that lack absolute standards of performance, it's difficult to predict the performance of high Machs.

People differ in the degree to which they like or dislike themselves. This trait is called **self-esteem (SE)**.[42] The research on SE offers some interesting insights into organizational behavior. For example, SE is directly related to expectations for success. High SEs believe that they possess the ability to succeed at work. Individuals with high SE will take more risks in job selection and are more likely to choose unconventional jobs than are people with low SE.[43] The most common finding on self-esteem is that low SEs are more susceptible to external influence than are high SEs. Low SEs are dependent on positive evaluations from others. As a result, they're more likely to seek approval from others and more prone to conform to the beliefs and behaviors of those they respect than are high SEs. In managerial positions, low SEs will tend to be concerned with pleasing others and, therefore, will be less likely to take unpopular stands than will high SEs. Not surprisingly, self-esteem has also been found to be related to job satisfaction. A number of studies confirm that high SEs are more satisfied with their jobs than are low SEs.

Another personality trait researchers have identified is called **self-monitoring**.[44] Individuals high in self-monitoring can show considerable adaptability in adjusting their behavior to external, situational factors.[45] They're highly sensitive to external cues and can behave differently in different situations. High self-monitors are capable of presenting striking contradictions between their public persona and their private selves. Low self-monitors can't alter their behavior. They tend to display their true dispositions and attitudes in every situation; hence, they exhibit high behavioral consistency between who they are and what they do. Evidence suggests that high self-monitors tend to pay closer attention to the behavior of others and are more capable of conforming than are low self-monitors.[46] We might also hypothesize that high self-monitors will be more successful in managerial positions that require individuals to play multiple, and even contradicting, roles.

The final personality trait influencing worker behavior reflects the willingness to take chances—the propensity for *risk taking*. A preference to assume or avoid risk has been shown to have an impact on how long it takes individuals to make a decision and how much information they require before making their choice. For instance, in one classic study, 79 managers worked on a simulated human resources management exercise that required them to make hiring decisions.[47] High risk-taking managers made more rapid decisions and used less information in making their choices than did the low risk-taking managers. Interestingly, the decision accuracy was the same for both groups.

Although it's generally correct to conclude that managers in organizations are risk averse, especially in large companies and government bureaus,[48] individual differences are still found on this dimension.[49] As a result, it makes sense to recognize these differences and even to consider aligning risk-taking propensity with specific job demands. For instance, a high risk-taking propensity may lead to effective performance for a stock trader in a brokerage firm since this type of job demands rapid decision making. The same holds true for the entrepreneur.[50] On the other hand, this personality characteristic might prove a major obstacle to accountants performing auditing activities, which might be better done by someone with a low risk-taking propensity.

How Do We Match Personalities and Jobs?

"What if you're not happy in your job? Is it possible that you're in the wrong career entirely?"[51] As you do your job day-by-day, you may realize that your tasks don't mesh well with your personality or talents. Wouldn't it seem to make more sense to strive for a match between your personality and your chosen job or career path?

Obviously, individual personalities differ. So, too, do jobs. How do we match the two? The best-documented personality-job fit theory was developed by psychologist John Holland.[52] His theory states that an employee's satisfaction with his or her job, as well as his or her likelihood of leaving that job, depends on the degree to which the individual's personality matches the job environment. Holland identified six basic personality types as shown in Exhibit 9–2.

Holland's theory proposes that satisfaction is highest and turnover lowest when personality and occupation are compatible.[53] Social individuals should be in "people" type jobs, and so forth. The key points of this theory include the following: (1) there do appear to be intrinsic differences in personality among individuals; (2) there are different types of jobs; and (3) people in job environments compatible with their personality types should be more satisfied and less likely to resign voluntarily than people in incongruent jobs.

Do Personality Attributes Differ Across Cultures?

Do personality frameworks, like the Big Five model, transfer across cultures? Are dimensions like locus of control relevant in all cultures? Let's try to answer these questions.

locus of control
The degree to which people believe they control their own fate

machiavellianism ("Mach")
A measure of the degree to which people are pragmatic, maintain emotional distance, and believe that ends justify means

self-esteem (SE)
An individual's degree of like or dislike for himself or herself

self-monitoring
A personality trait that measures the ability to adjust behavior to external situational factors

---

EXHIBIT 9–2   Holland's Personality-Job Fit

PERSONALITY TYPE	CHARACTERISTICS	SAMPLE OCCUPATIONS
Realistic Prefers physical activities that require skill, strength, and coordination	Shy, genuine, persistent, stable, conforming, practical	Mechanic, drill-press operator, assembly-line worker, farmer
Investigative Prefers activities involving thinking, organizing, and understanding	Analytical, original, curious, independent	Biologist, economist, mathematician, reporter
Social Prefers activities that involve helping and developing others	Sociable, friendly, cooperative, understanding	Social worker, teacher, counselor, clinical psychologist
Conventional Prefers rule-regulated, orderly, and unambiguous activities	Conforming, efficient, practical, unimaginative, inflexible	Accountant, corporate manager, bank teller, file clerk
Enterprising Prefers verbal activities that include opportunities to influence others and attain power	Self-confident, ambitious, energetic, domineering	Lawyer, real estate agent, public relations specialist, small business manager
Artistic Prefers ambiguous and unsystematic activities that allow creative expression	Imaginative, disorderly, idealistic, emotional, impractical	Painter, musician, writer, interior decorator

Source: Reproduced by special permission of the publisher, Psychological Assessment Resources, Inc., *Making Vocational Choices*, 3rd ed., copyright 1973, 1985, 1992, 1997 by Psychological Assessment Resources, Inc. All rights reserved.

Even though personality attributes appear in most cross-cultural studies, differences exist in the emphasis countries place on personality dimensions. Chinese culture, for example, places a high premium on conscientiousness and self-monitoring. Chinese employees are hard-working, efficient, responsible, dependable, and achievement oriented. As high self-monitors, they show considerable adaptability in adjusting their behavior to external factors. In China, employee conscientiousness and ability to adapt are key factors that drive the country's competitiveness. These personality traits influence the behavior of Landsha Group employees, shown here, who work for China's leading producer of socks and stockings.

Zhang Jiancheng/Newscom

The five personality factors studied in the Big Five model appear in almost all cross-cultural studies.[54] A wide variety of diverse cultures, such as China, Israel, Germany, Japan, Spain, Nigeria, Norway, Pakistan, and the United States, have been the setting for these studies. Differences are found in the emphasis on dimensions. Chinese, for example, use the category of conscientiousness more often and use the category of agreeableness less often than do Americans. But a surprisingly high amount of agreement is found, especially among individuals from developed countries. As a case in point, a comprehensive review of studies covering people from the European Community found that conscientiousness was a valid predictor of performance across jobs and occupational groups.[55] U.S. studies found the same results.

We know that there are certainly no common personality types for a given country. You can, for instance, find high risk takers and low risk takers in almost any culture. Yet a country's culture influences the *dominant* personality characteristics of its people. We can see this effect of national culture by looking at one of the personality traits we just discussed: locus of control.

National cultures differ in terms of the degree to which people believe they control their environment. For instance, North Americans believe that they can dominate their environment; other societies, such as those in Middle Eastern countries, believe that life is essentially predetermined. Notice how closely this distinction parallels the concept of internal and external locus of control. On the basis of this particular cultural characteristic, we should expect a larger proportion of internals in the U.S. and Canadian workforces than in the workforces of Saudi Arabia or Iran.

As we have seen throughout this section, personality traits influence employees' behavior. For global managers, understanding how personality traits differ takes on added significance when looking at it from the perspective of national culture.

How Can an Understanding of Personality Help Managers Be More Effective?

Some 62 percent of companies are using personality tests when recruiting and hiring.[56] And that's where the major value in understanding personality differences probably lies. Managers are likely to have higher-performing and more-satisfied employees if consideration is given to matching personalities with jobs. In addition, compatibility leads to other benefits. By recognizing that people approach problem solving, decision making, and job interactions differently, a manager can better understand why, for instance, an employee is uncomfortable with making quick decisions or why an employee insists on gathering as much information as possible before addressing a problem. For instance, managers can expect that individuals with an external locus of control may be less satisfied with their jobs than those with an internal locus and also that they may be less willing to accept responsibility for their actions.

WHAT IS PERCEPTION AND WHAT INFLUENCES IT?

> Describe perception and the factors that influence it.
>
> 9.4

"L ke y ur b ain, the n w L nd Rov r autom tic lly adj sts to anyth ng."[57] This advertisement for a Land Rover SUV illustrates the perceptual process at work. You were likely able to read the sentence even with the missing letters because you recognized the word patterns and organized and interpreted them in a way that made sense.

Perception is a process by which we give meaning to our environment by organizing and interpreting sensory impressions. Research on perception consistently demonstrates that individuals may look at the same thing yet perceive it differently. One manager, for instance, can interpret the fact that her assistant regularly takes several days to make important decisions as evidence that the assistant is slow, disorganized, and afraid to make decisions. Another manager with the same assistant might interpret the same tendency as evidence that the assistant is thoughtful, thorough, and deliberate. The first manager would probably evaluate her assistant negatively; the second manager would probably evaluate the person positively. The point is that none of us see reality. We interpret what we see and call it reality. And, of course, as the example shows, we behave according to our perceptions.

What Influences Perception?

How do we explain the fact that Cathy, a marketing supervisor for a large commercial petroleum products organization, age 52, noticed Bill's nose ring during his employment interview, and Sean, a human resources recruiter, age 23, didn't? A number of factors operate to shape and sometimes distort perception. These factors can reside in the perceiver, in the object or target being perceived, or in the context of the situation in which the perception is made.

When an individual looks at a target and attempts to interpret what he or she sees, that individual's personal characteristics will heavily influence the interpretation. These personal characteristics include attitudes, personality, motives, interests, past experiences, and expectations. The characteristics of the target being observed can also affect what is perceived. Loud people are more likely than quiet people to be noticed in a group. So, too, are extremely attractive or unattractive individuals. Because targets

---

perception
A process by which we give meaning to our environment by organizing and interpreting sensory impressions

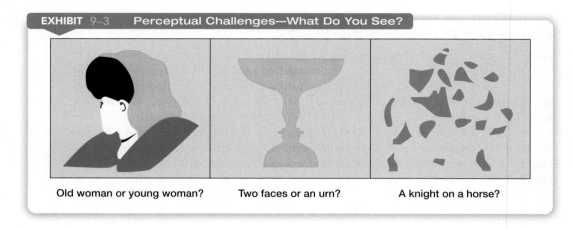

EXHIBIT 9–3   Perceptual Challenges—What Do You See?

Old woman or young woman?   Two faces or an urn?   A knight on a horse?

are not looked at in isolation, the relationship of a target to its background also influences perception (see Exhibit 9–3 for an example), as does our tendency to group close things and similar things together.

The context in which we see objects or events is also important. The time at which an object or event is seen can influence attention, as can location, lighting, temperature, and any number of other situational factors.

How Do Managers Judge Employees?

Much of the research on perception is directed at inanimate objects. Managers, though, are more concerned with human beings. Our perceptions of people differ from our perceptions of such inanimate objects as computers, robots, or buildings because we make inferences about the actions of people that we don't, of course, make about inanimate objects. When we observe people, we attempt to develop explanations of why they behave in certain ways. Our perception and judgment of a person's actions, therefore, will be significantly influenced by the assumptions we make about the person's internal state. Many of these assumptions have led researchers to develop attribution theory.

WHAT IS ATTRIBUTION THEORY?   **Attribution theory** has been proposed to explain how we judge people differently depending on what meaning we attribute to a given behavior.[58] Basically, the theory suggests that when we observe an individual's behavior, we attempt to determine whether it was internally or externally caused. Internally caused behavior is believed to be under the control of the individual. Externally caused behavior results from outside causes; that is, the person is seen as having been forced into the behavior by the situation. That determination, however, depends on three factors: distinctiveness, consensus, and consistency.

Distinctiveness refers to whether an individual displays a behavior in many situations or whether it is particular to one situation. Is the employee who arrived late to work today also the person coworkers see as a goof-off? What we want to know is whether this behavior is unusual. If it is, the observer is likely to give the behavior an external attribution. If this action is not unique, it will probably be judged as internal.

If everyone who is faced with a similar situation responds in the same way, we can say the behavior shows *consensus.* Our tardy employee's behavior would meet this criterion if all employees who took the same route to work today were also late. If consensus is high, you would be expected to give an external attribution to the employee's tardiness, whereas if other employees who took the same route made it to work on time, you would conclude the reason to be internal.

Finally, a manager looks for *consistency* in an employee's actions. Does the individual engage in the behaviors regularly and consistently? Does the employee respond the same way over time? Coming in 10 minutes late for work is not perceived in the same way if, for one employee, it represents an unusual case (she hasn't been late

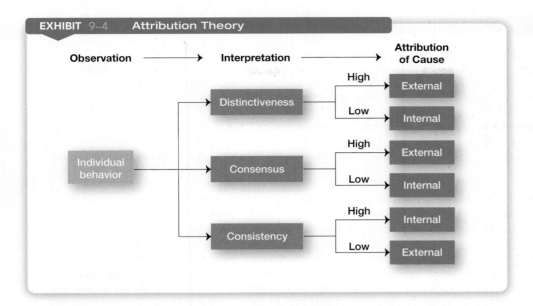

EXHIBIT 9–4   **Attribution Theory**

for several months), but for another it is part of a routine pattern (he is late two or three times a week). The more consistent the behavior, the more the observer is inclined to attribute it to internal causes.

Exhibit 9–4 summarizes the key elements in attribution theory. It would tell us, for instance, that if an employee, Mr. Flynn, generally performs at about the same level on other related tasks as he does on his current task (low distinctiveness), if other employees frequently perform differently—better or worse—than Mr. Flynn does on that current task (low consensus), and if Mr. Flynn's performance on this current task is consistent over time (high consistency), his manager or anyone else who is judging Mr. Flynn's work is likely to hold him primarily responsible for his task performance (internal attribution).

CAN ATTRIBUTIONS BE DISTORTED?   One of the more interesting findings drawn from attribution theory is that errors or biases distort attributions. For instance, substantial evidence supports the hypothesis that when we make judgments about the behavior of other people, we have a tendency to underestimate the influence of external factors and overestimate the influence of internal or personal factors.[59] This **fundamental attribution error** can explain why a sales manager may be prone to attribute the poor performance of her sales agents to laziness rather than to the innovative product line introduced by a competitor. Individuals also tend to attribute their own successes to internal factors such as ability or effort while putting the blame for failure on external factors such as luck. This **self-serving bias** suggests that feedback provided to employees in performance reviews will be predictably distorted by them, whether it is positive or negative.

WHAT PERCEPTUAL SHORTCUTS DO WE USE?   All of us, managers included, use a number of shortcuts to judge others. Perceiving and interpreting people's behavior is a lot of work, so we use shortcuts to make the task more manageable.[60] Such shortcuts can be

---

attribution theory
A theory used to explain how we judge people differently, based on what meaning we attribute to a given behavior

fundamental attribution error
The tendency to underestimate the influence of external factors and overestimate the influence of internal factors when making judgments about the behavior of others

self-serving bias
The tendency for individuals to attribute their successes to internal factors while putting the blame for failures on external factors

EXHIBIT 9–5	Perceptual Shortcuts	
SHORTCUT	**WHAT IT IS**	**DISTORTION**
Selectivity	People assimilate certain bits and pieces of what they observe depending on their interests, background, experience, and attitudes	"Speed reading" others may result in an inaccurate picture of them
Assumed similarity	People assume that others are like them	May fail to take into account individual differences, resulting in incorrect similarities
Stereotyping	People judge others on the basis of their perception of a group to which the others belong	May result in distorted judgments because many stereotypes have no factual foundation
Halo effect	People form an impression of others on the basis of a single trait	Fails to take into account the total picture of what an individual has done

valuable when they let us make accurate perceptions quickly and provide valid data for making predictions. However, they aren't perfect. They can and do get us into trouble. What are these perceptual shortcuts? (See Exhibit 9–5 for a summary.)

Individuals can't assimilate all they observe, so they're selective in their perception. They absorb bits and pieces. These bits and pieces are not chosen randomly; rather, they're selectively chosen depending on the interests, background, experience, and attitudes of the observer. **Selective perception** allows us to "speed read" others but not without the risk of drawing an inaccurate picture.

It's easy to judge others if we assume that they're similar to us. In **assumed similarity**, or the "like me" effect, the observer's perception of others is influenced more by the observer's own characteristics than by those of the person observed. For example, if you want challenges and responsibility in your job, you'll assume that others want the same. People who assume that others are like them can, of course, be right, but not always.

When we judge someone on the basis of our perception of a group he or she is part of, we're using the shortcut called **stereotyping**. For instance, "Married people are more stable employees than single persons" or "Older employees are absent more often from work" are examples of stereotyping. To the degree that a stereotype is based on fact, it may produce accurate judgments. However, many stereotypes aren't factual and distort our judgment.

When we form a general impression about a person on the basis of a single characteristic, such as intelligence, sociability, or appearance, we're being influenced by the **halo effect**. This effect frequently occurs when students evaluate their classroom instructor. Students may isolate a single trait such as enthusiasm and allow their entire evaluation to be slanted by the perception of this one trait. If an instructor who is quiet, assured, knowledgeable, and highly qualified has a classroom teaching style that lacks enthusiasm, that instructor might be rated lower on a number of other characteristics.

How Can an Understanding of Perception Help Managers Be More Effective?

Managers need to recognize that their employees react to perceptions, not to reality. So whether a manager's appraisal of an employee's performance is actually objective and unbiased or whether the organization's wage levels are among the highest in the community is less relevant than what employees perceive them to be. If individuals perceive appraisals to be biased or wage levels as low, they'll behave as if those conditions actually exist. Employees organize and interpret what they see, so there is always the potential for perceptual distortion. The message is clear: Pay close attention to how employees perceive both their jobs and management actions. Remember, the valuable employee who quits because of an inaccurate perception is just as great a loss to an organization as the valuable employee who quits for a valid reason.

HOW DO LEARNING THEORIES EXPLAIN BEHAVIOR?

Discuss learning theories and their relevance in shaping behavior.

9.5

When 20-year-old Elvis Andrus was signed by the Texas Rangers in 2009, he was excited to find out that the Rangers had signed another shortstop—11-time Gold Glove winner and fellow Venezuelan Omar Vizquel. Vizquel's role was clear: to be a mentor to the talented young player. Managers of major league baseball teams "regularly mix savvy veterans with talented young players, hoping tricks of the trade and advice on everything from how to turn a double play to how to avoid trouble in night spots on the road will rub off."[61]

Mentoring is a good example of the last individual behavior concept we're going to look at—learning. Learning is included in our discussion of individual behavior for the obvious reason that almost all behavior is learned. If we want to explain, predict, and influence behavior, we need to understand how people learn.

The psychologists' definition of learning is considerably broader than the average person's view that "it's what we do in school." Learning occurs all the time as we continuously learn from our experiences. A workable definition of **learning** is any relatively permanent change in behavior that occurs as a result of experience. Two learning theories help us understand how and why individual behavior occurs.

What Is Operant Conditioning?

Operant conditioning argues that behavior is a function of its consequences. People learn to behave to get something they want or to avoid something they don't want. Operant behavior is voluntary or learned behavior, not reflexive or unlearned behavior. The tendency to repeat learned behavior is influenced by reinforcement or lack of reinforcement that happens as a result of the behavior. Reinforcement strengthens a behavior and increases the likelihood that it will be repeated. Lack of reinforcement weakens a behavior and lessens the likelihood that it will be repeated.

B. F. Skinner's research widely expanded our knowledge of operant conditioning.[62] Behavior is assumed to be determined from without—that is, *learned*—rather than from within—reflexive or unlearned. Skinner argued that people will most likely engage in desired behaviors if they are positively reinforced for doing so, and rewards are most effective if they immediately follow the desired response. In addition, behavior that isn't rewarded or is punished, is less likely to be repeated. (For more information about Skinner's contributions, see the From the Past to the Present box.)

You see examples of operant conditioning everywhere. Any situation in which it's either explicitly stated or implicitly suggested that reinforcement (rewards) are contingent on some action on your part is an example of operant conditioning. Your instructor says that if you want a high grade in this course, you must perform well on tests by giving correct answers.

Small business owner Morgan Smith (left) applies social learning theory in teaching employees the skills they need to meet the firm's high standards of quality and efficiency. As owner and managing partner of Boneheads Restaurant, Smith serves as a trainer and role model in showing employees how to prepare food, use equipment, and serve customers. Under Smith's tutelage, employees learn through observation and direct experience and then practice what they learn. Smith is an important and influential model for employees. His goal for them is to reach their full potential, and he willingly invests time to achieve that goal. In this photo, Smith shows a chef at Boneheads how to adjust some equipment in the kitchen.

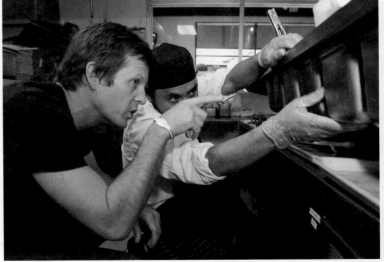

Newscom

---

selective perception
The tendency for people to only absorb parts of what they observe, which allows us to "speed read" others

assumed similarity
An observer's perception of others influenced more by the observer's own characteristics than by those of the person observed

stereotyping
When we judge someone on the basis of our perception of a group to which that person belongs

halo effect
When we form a general impression of a person on the basis of a single characteristic

learning
A relatively permanent change in behavior that occurs as a result of experience

operant conditioning
A theory of learning that says behavior is a function of its consequences

---

From the Past to the Present

Why does hearing Christmas carols evoke pleasant memories of childhood?[63] *Classical conditioning theory* would say it's because the songs are associated with a festive holiday spirit and make us remember all the fun and excitement. Classical conditioning can also explain why a scheduled visit by the "top brass" brings flurried activities of cleaning, straightening, and rearranging at a local outlet of a major retail company. However, classical conditioning is a passive theory. Something happens, and we react in a specific way. As such, it can explain simple reflexive behavior. But most behavior by people at work is voluntary rather than reflexive; that is, employees *choose* to arrive at work on time, ask their boss for help with some problem, or "goof off" when no one is watching. A better explanation for behavior is operant conditioning.

Operant conditioning says that people behave the way they do so they can get something they want or avoid something they don't want. It's voluntary or learned behavior, not reflexive or unlearned behavior. Harvard psychologist B. F. Skinner first identified the process of operant conditioning. He argued that creating pleasing consequences to follow specific forms of behavior would increase the frequency of that behavior. Skinner demonstrated that people will most likely engage in desired behaviors if they're

positively reinforced for doing so; that rewards are most effective if they immediately follow the desired response (behavior); and that behavior that is not rewarded or is punished is less likely to be repeated. For example, a professor places a mark by a student's name each time the student makes a contribution to class discussions. Operant conditioning would argue that this practice is motivating because it conditions a student to expect a reward (earning class credit) each time she demonstrates a specific behavior (speaking up in class). Operant conditioning can be seen in work settings as well. And smart managers quickly recognize that they can use operant conditioning to shape employees' behaviors to get work done in the most effective and efficient manner possible.

Think About:
- How do classical conditioning and operant conditioning differ?
- How could managers use operant conditioning?
- What's the connection between operant conditioning and shaping behavior?
- What ethical concerns might arise in "shaping" someone's behavior?

A salesperson working on commission knows that earning a sizeable income is contingent upon generating high sales in his or her territory. Of course, the linkage between behavior and reinforcement can also work to teach the individual to behave in ways that work against the best interests of the organization. Assume that your boss tells you that if you'll work overtime during the next three-week busy season, you'll be compensated for it at the next performance appraisal. Then, when performance appraisal time comes, you are given no positive reinforcements (such as being praised for pitching in and helping out when needed). What will you do the next time your boss asks you to work overtime? You'll probably refuse. Your behavior can be explained by operant conditioning: If a behavior isn't positively reinforced, the probability that the behavior will be repeated declines.

What Is Social Learning Theory?

Some 60 percent of the Radio City Rockettes have danced in prior seasons. The veterans help newcomers with "Rockette style"—where to place their hands, how to hold their hands, how to keep up stamina, and so forth.[64]

As the Rockettes are well aware, individuals can also learn by observing what happens to other people and just by being told about something as well as by direct experiences. Much of what we have learned comes from watching others (models)—parents, teachers, peers, television and movie actors, managers, and so forth. This view that we can learn both through observation and direct experience is called **social learning theory**.[65]

The influence of others is central to the social learning viewpoint. The amount of influence that these models have on an individual is determined by four processes:

1. *Attentional processes.* People learn from a model when they recognize and pay attention to its critical features. We're most influenced by models who are attractive, repeatedly available, thought to be important, or seen as similar to us.
2. *Retention processes.* A model's influence will depend on how well the individual remembers the model's action, even after the model is no longer readily available.

3. *Motor reproduction processes.* After a person has seen a new behavior by observing the model, the watching must become doing. This process then demonstrates that the individual can actually do the modeled activities.
4. *Reinforcement processes.* Individuals will be motivated to exhibit the modeled behavior if positive incentives or rewards are provided. Behaviors that are reinforced will be given more attention, learned better, and performed more often.

How Can Managers Shape Behavior?

Managers should be concerned with how they can teach employees to behave in ways that most benefit the organization.[66] Thus, managers will often attempt to mold individuals by guiding their learning in graduated steps. This process is called shaping behavior.

Consider the situation in which an employee's behavior is significantly different from that desired by management. If management reinforced the individual only when he or she showed desirable responses, little reinforcement might happen at all.

We shape behavior by systematically reinforcing each successive step that moves the individual closer to the desired response. If an employee who has continually been 30 minutes late for work arrives only 20 minutes late, we can reinforce this improvement. Reinforcement would increase as responses more closely approximate the desired behavior.

Four ways can be used to shape behavior: positive reinforcement, negative reinforcement, punishment, or extinction. When a response is followed with something pleasant, such as when a manager praises an employee for a job well done, it is called *positive reinforcement*. Rewarding a response with the termination or withdrawal of something pleasant is called *negative reinforcement*. Managers who habitually criticize their employees for taking extended coffee breaks are using negative reinforcement. The only way these employees can stop the criticism is to shorten their breaks. *Punishment* penalizes undesirable behavior. Suspending an employee for two days without pay for showing up drunk is an example of punishment. Eliminating any reinforcement that is maintaining a behavior is called *extinction*. When a behavior isn't reinforced, it gradually disappears. Managers who wish to discourage employees from continually asking distracting or irrelevant questions in meetings can eliminate that behavior by ignoring those employees when they raise their hands to speak. Soon, the behavior will be diminished.

Both positive and negative reinforcement result in learning. They strengthen a desired response and increase the probability of repetition. Both punishment and extinction also result in learning; however, they weaken behavior and tend to decrease its subsequent frequency.

How Can an Understanding of Learning Help Managers Be More Effective?

Employees are going to learn on the job. The only issue is whether managers are going to manage their learning through the rewards they allocate and the examples they set, or allow it to occur haphazardly. If marginal employees are rewarded with pay raises and promotions, they will have little reason to change their behavior. In fact, productive employees, who see marginal performance rewarded, might change their behavior. If managers want behavior A, but reward behavior B, they shouldn't be surprised to find employees' learning to engage in behavior B. Similarly, managers should expect that employees will look to them as models. Managers who are consistently late to work, or take two hours for lunch, or help themselves to company office supplies for personal use should expect employees to read the message they are sending and model their behavior accordingly.

social learning theory
A theory of learning that says people can learn through observation and direct experience

shaping behavior
The process of guiding learning in graduated steps, using reinforcement or lack of reinforcement

9.6 *Discuss* contemporary issues in OB.

WHAT CONTEMPORARY OB ISSUES FACE MANAGERS?

By this point, you're probably well aware of why managers need to understand how and why employees behave the way they do. We conclude this chapter by looking at two OB issues having a major influence on managers' jobs today.

How Do Generational Differences Affect the Workplace?

They're young, smart, brash. They wear flip-flops to the office or listen to iPods at their desk. They want to work, but don't want work to be their life. This is Generation Y, some 70 million of them, embarking on their careers, taking their place in an increasingly multigenerational workplace.[67]

JUST WHO IS GEN Y? There's no consensus about the exact time span that Gen Y comprises, but most definitions include those individuals born from about 1982 to 1997. One thing is for sure—they're bringing new attitudes with them to the workplace. Gen Ys have grown up with an amazing array of experiences and opportunities. And they want their work life to provide that as well, as shown in Exhibit 9–6. For instance, Stella Kenyi, who is passionately interested in international development, was sent by her employer, the National Rural Electric Cooperative Association, to Yai, Sudan, to survey energy use.[68] At Best Buy's corporate offices, Beth Trippie, a senior scheduling specialist, feels that as long as the results are there, why should it matter how it gets done. She says, "I'm constantly playing video games, on a call, doing work, and the thing is, all of it gets done, and it gets done well."[69] And Katie Patterson, an assistant account executive in Atlanta says, "We are willing and not afraid to challenge the status quo. An environment where creativity and independent thinking are looked upon as a positive is appealing to people my age. We're very independent and tech savvy."[70]

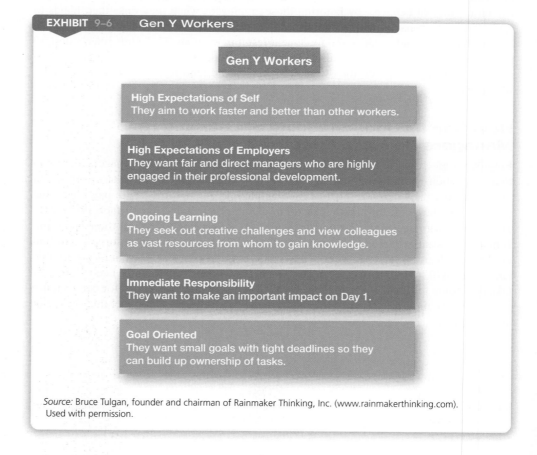

EXHIBIT 9–6   **Gen Y Workers**

Gen Y Workers

High Expectations of Self
They aim to work faster and better than other workers.

High Expectations of Employers
They want fair and direct managers who are highly engaged in their professional development.

Ongoing Learning
They seek out creative challenges and view colleagues as vast resources from whom to gain knowledge.

Immediate Responsibility
They want to make an important impact on Day 1.

Goal Oriented
They want small goals with tight deadlines so they can build up ownership of tasks.

Source: Bruce Tulgan, founder and chairman of Rainmaker Thinking, Inc. (www.rainmakerthinking.com). Used with permission.

DEALING WITH THE MANAGERIAL CHALLENGES.   Managing Gen Y workers presents some unique challenges. Conflicts and resentment can arise over issues such as appearance, technology, and management style.

How flexible must an organization be in terms of "appropriate" office attire? It may depend on the type of work being done and the size of the organization. There are many organizations where jeans, T-shirts, and flip-flops are acceptable. However, in other settings, employees are expected to dress more conventionally. But even in those more conservative organizations, one possible solution to accommodate the more casual attire preferred by Gen Y is to be more flexible in what's acceptable. For instance, the guideline might be that when the person is not interacting with someone outside the organization, more casual wear (with some restrictions) can be worn.

What about technology? This generation has lived much of their lives with ATMs, DVDs, cell phones, e-mail, texting, laptops, and the Internet. When they don't have information they need, they just simply enter a few keystrokes to get it. Having grown up with technology, Gen Ys tend to be totally comfortable with it. They're quite content to meet virtually to solve problems, while bewildered baby boomers expect important problems to be solved with an in-person meeting. Baby boomers complain about Gen Y's inability to focus on one task, while Gen Ys see nothing wrong with multitasking. Again, flexibility from both is the key.

Finally, what about managing Gen Ys? Like the old car advertisement that used to say, "This isn't your father's Oldsmobile," we can say that "this isn't your father's or mother's way of managing." Gen Y employees want bosses who are open minded; experts in their field, even if they aren't tech-savvy; organized; teachers, trainers, and mentors; not authoritarian or paternalistic; respectful of their generation; understanding of their need for work/life balance; providing constant feedback; communicating in vivid and compelling ways; and providing stimulating and novel learning experiences.[71]

Gen Y employees have a lot to offer organizations in terms of their knowledge, passion, and abilities. Managers, however, have to recognize and understand the behaviors of this group in order to create an environment in which work can be accomplished efficiently, effectively, and without disruptive conflict.

How Do Managers Deal with Negative Behavior in the Workplace?

Jerry notices the oil is low in his forklift but continues to drive it until it overheats and can't be used. After enduring 11 months of repeated insults and mistreatment from her supervisor, Maria quits her job. An office clerk slams her keyboard and then shouts profanity whenever her computer freezes up. Rudeness, hostility, aggression, and other forms of workplace negativity have become all too common in today's organizations. In a survey of U.S. employees, 10 percent said they witnessed rudeness daily within their workplaces and 20 percent said that they personally were direct targets of incivility at work at least once a week. In a survey of Canadian workers, 25 percent reported seeing incivility daily and 50 percent said they were the direct targets at least once per week.[72] And it's been estimated that negativity costs the U.S. economy some $300 billion a year.[73] What can managers do to manage negative behavior in the workplace?

The main thing is to recognize that it's there. Pretending that negative behavior doesn't exist or ignoring such misbehaviors will only confuse employees about what is expected and acceptable behavior. Although researchers continue to debate about the preventive or responsive actions to negative behaviors, in reality, both are needed.[74] Preventing negative behaviors by carefully screening potential employees for certain personality traits and responding immediately and decisively to unacceptable negative behaviors can go a long way toward managing negative workplace behaviors. But it's also important to pay attention to employee attitudes, since negativity will show up there as well. As we said earlier, when employees are dissatisfied with their jobs, they *will* respond somehow.

Newscom

Blizzard Entertainment understands the new attitudes of millennials and has created a casual and fun environment that appeals to employees like the Web software engineer shown here taking a lunch break with her dog. A developer of gaming software, Blizzard promises employees challenging work that stimulates personal and professional growth. Employees are encouraged to pursue what they are passionate about and to freely give ideas for developing new products. They can rely on supportive managers and peers to help them gain the knowledge and training they need. Blizzard values its tech-savvy employees and encourages them to "embrace your inner geek" in creating great games that contribute to the company's success.

9 Review

CHAPTER SUMMARY

9.1 Identify the focus and goals of organizational behavior (OB). OB focuses on three areas: individual behavior, group behavior, and organizational aspects. The goals of OB are to explain, predict, and influence employee behavior. Six important employee behaviors are as follows: Employee productivity is a performance measure of both efficiency and effectiveness. Absenteeism is the failure to report to work. Turnover is the voluntary and involuntary permanent withdrawal from an organization. Organizational citizenship behavior (OCB) is discretionary behavior that's not part of an employee's formal job requirements, but it promotes the effective functioning of an organization. Job satisfaction is an individual's general attitude toward his or her job. Workplace misbehavior is any intentional employee behavior that's potentially harmful to the organization or individuals within the organization.

9.2 Explain the role that attitudes play in job performance. Attitudes are evaluative statements concerning people, objects, or events. The cognitive component of an attitude refers to the beliefs, opinions, knowledge, or information held by a person. The affective component is the emotional or feeling part of an attitude. The behavioral component refers to an intention to behave in a certain way toward someone or something.

Four job-related attitudes include job satisfaction, job involvement, organizational commitment, and employee engagement. Job satisfaction refers to a person's general attitude toward his or her job. Job involvement is the degree to which an employee identifies with his or her job, actively participates in it, and considers his or her job performance to be important to his or her self-worth. Organizational commitment is the degree to which an employee identifies with a particular organization and its goals, and wishes to maintain membership in that organization. Employee engagement is when employees are connected to, satisfied with, and enthusiastic about their jobs.

According to cognitive dissonance theory, individuals try to reconcile attitude and behavior inconsistencies by altering their attitudes, altering their behavior, or rationalizing the inconsistency.

9.3 Describe different personality theories. The MBTI measures four dimensions: social interaction, preference for gathering data, preference for decision making, and style of making decisions. The Big Five Model consists of five personality traits: extraversion, agreeableness, conscientiousness, emotional stability, and openness to experience. Another way to view personality is through the five personality traits that help explain individual behavior in organizations: locus of control, Machiavellianism, self-esteem, self-monitoring, and risk taking.

Finally, how a person responds emotionally and how they deal with their emotions is a function of personality. A person who is emotionally intelligent has the ability to notice and to manage emotional cues and information.

9.4 Describe perception and the factors that influence it. Perception is how we give meaning to our environment by organizing and interpreting sensory impressions.

Attribution theory helps explain how we judge people differently. It depends on three factors. Distinctiveness is whether an individual displays different behaviors in different situations (that is, is the behavior unusual). Consensus is whether others facing a similar situation respond in the same way. Consistency is when a person engages in behaviors regularly and consistently. Whether these three factors are high or low helps managers determine whether employee behavior is attributed to external or internal causes.

The fundamental attribution error is the tendency to underestimate the influence of external factors and overestimate the influence of internal factors. The self-serving bias is the tendency to attribute our own successes to internal factors and to put the blame for personal failure on external factors. Shortcuts used in judging others are selective perception, assumed similarity, stereotyping, and the halo effect.

9.5 Discuss learning theories and their relevance in shaping behavior. Operant conditioning argues that behavior is a function of its consequences. Social learning theory says that individuals learn by observing what happens to other people and by directly experiencing something.

Managers can shape behavior by using positive reinforcement (reinforcing a desired behavior by giving something pleasant), negative reinforcement (reinforcing a desired response by withdrawing something unpleasant), punishment (eliminating undesirable behavior by applying penalties), or extinction (not reinforcing a behavior to eliminate it).

9.6 Discuss contemporary issues in OB. The challenge of managing Gen Y workers is that they bring new attitudes to the workplace. The main challenges are over issues such as appearance, technology, and management style.

Workplace misbehavior can be dealt with by recognizing that it's there; carefully screening potential employees for possible negative tendencies; and most importantly, by paying attention to employee attitudes through surveys about job satisfaction and dissatisfaction.

MyManagementLab   For more resources, please visit **www.mymanagementlab.com**

UNDERSTANDING THE CHAPTER

1. How is an organization like an iceberg? Use the iceberg metaphor to describe the field of organizational behavior.

2. Does the importance of knowledge of OB differ based on a manager's level in the organization? If so, how? If not, why not? Be specific.

3. Clarify how individuals reconcile inconsistencies between attitudes and behaviors.

4. Describe what is meant by the term *emotional intelligence.* Provide an example of how it's used in contemporary organizations.

5. "Instead of worrying about job satisfaction, companies should be trying to create environments where performance is enabled." What do you think this statement means? Explain. What's your reaction to this statement? Do you agree? Disagree? Why?

6. How might a manager use personality traits to improve employee selection in his or her department? Emotional intelligence? Discuss.

7. Describe the implications of social learning theory for managing people at work.

8. A Gallup Organization survey shows that most workers rate having a caring boss even higher than they value money or fringe benefits. How should managers interpret this information? What are the implications?

9. Write down three attitudes you have. Identify the cognitive, affective, and behavioral components of those attitudes.

10. Explain the challenges facing managers in managing generational differences and negative behavior in the workplace.

Go to p. 431
YOUR TURN TO BE **A MANAGER**   for Chapter 9.

Endnotes

1. R. Mobbs, "The Employee Is Always Right," *In the Black,* April 2011, pp. 12–15; V. Nayar, "Employee Happiness: Zappos vs. HCL," *Bloomberg BusinessWeek.com,* January 5, 2011; G. Hamel, "Extreme Makeover," *Leadership Excellence,* January 2011, pp. 3–4; V. Nayar, "The World in 2036: Vineet Nayar Envisages Bottom-Up Leadership," *Economist,* November 27, 2010, p. 114; V. Nayar, "Employees First, Customers Second," *Chief Learning Officer,* October 2010, pp. 20–23; V. Nayar, "Back to Front," *People Management,* August 12, 2010, pp. 26–29; V. Nayar, "A Maverick CEO Explains How He Persuaded His Team to Leap into the Future," *Harvard Business Review,* June 2010, pp. 110–113; B. Einhorn and K. Gokhale, "Bangalore's Paying Again to Keep the Talent," *Bloomberg BusinessWeek,* May 24, 2010, pp. 14–16; M. Srivastava and S. Hamm, "Using the Slump to Get Bigger in Bangalore," *BusinessWeek,* September 3, 2009, pp. 50–51; and S. Lauchlan, "HCL Embraces Slumdog Effect," *Computer Weekly,* June 23, 2009, p. 8.

2. "Survey on the Total Financial Impact of Employee Absences," *Medical Benefits,* November 30, 2010, p. 9; and K. M. Kroll, "Absence-Minded," *CFO Human Capital,* 2006, pp. 12–14.

3. D. W. Organ, *Organizational Citizenship Behavior: The Good Soldier Syndrome* (Lexington, MA: Lexington Books, 1988), p. 4. See also J. L. Lavell, D. E. Rupp, and J. Brockner, "Taking a Multifoci Approach to the Study of Justice, Social Exchange, and Citizenship Behavior: The Target Similarity Model," *Journal of Management* (December 2007), pp. 841–866; and J. A. LePine, A. Erez, and D. E. Johnson, "The Nature and Dimensionality of Organizational Citizenship Behavior: A Critical Review and Meta-Analysis," *Journal of Applied Psychology* (February 2002), pp. 52–65.

4. J. R. Spence, D. L. Ferris, D. J. Brown, and D. Heller, "Understanding Daily Citizenship Behaviors: A Social Comparison Approach," *Journal of Organizational Behavior* (May 2011), pp. 547–571; L. M. Little, D. L. Nelson, J. C. Wallace, and P. D. Johnson, "Integrating Attachment Style,

Vigor at Work, and Extra-Role Performance," *Journal of Organizational Behavior* (April 2011), pp. 464–484; N. P. Podsakoff, P. M. Podsakoff, S. W. Whiting, and P. Mishra, "Effects of Organizational Citizenship Behavior on Selection Decisions in Employment Interviews," *Journal of Applied Psychology* (March 2011), pp. 310–326; T. M. Glomb, D. P. Bhave, A. G. Miner, and M. Wall, "Doing Good, Feeling Good: Examining the Role of Organizational Citizenship Behaviors in Changing Mood," *Personnel Psychology,* Spring 2011, pp. 191–223; T. P. Munyon, W. A. Hochwarter, P. L. Perrewé, and G. R. Ferris, "Optimism and the Nonlinear Citizenship Behavior—Job Satisfaction Relationship in Three Studies," *Journal of Management* (November 2010), pp. 1505–1528; R. Ilies, B. A. Scott, and T. A. Judge, "The Interactive Effects of Personal Traits and Experienced States on Intraindividual Patterns of Citizenship Behavior," *Academy of Management Journal* (June 2006), pp. 561–575; P. Cardona, B. S. Lawrence, and P. M. Bentler, "The Influence of Social and Work Exchange Relationships on Organizational Citizenship Behavior," *Group & Organization Management,* April 2004, pp. 219–247; M. C. Bolino and W. H. Turnley, "Going the Extra Mile: Cultivating and Managing Employee Citizenship Behavior," *Academy of Management Executive,* August 2003, pp. 60–73; M. C. Bolino, W. H. Turnley, and J. J. Bloodgood, "Citizenship Behavior and the Creation of Social Capital in Organizations," *Academy of Management Review,* October 2002, pp. 505–522; and P. M. Podsakoff, S. B. MacKenzie, J. B. Paine, and D. G. Bachrach, "Organizational Citizenship Behaviors: A Critical Review of the Theoretical and Empirical Literature and Suggestions for Future Research," *Journal of Management,* 26, no. 3 (2000), pp. 543–548.

5. M. C. Bolino and W. H. Turnley, "The Personal Costs of Citizenship Behavior: The Relationship Between Individual Initiative and Role Overload, Job Stress, and Work-Family Conflict," *Journal of Applied Psychology* (July 2005), pp. 740–748.

6. This definition adapted from R. W. Griffin and Y. P. Lopez, "Bad Behavior in Organizations: A Review and Typology for Future Research," *Journal of Management* (December 2005), pp. 988–1005.

7. S. J. Becker, "Empirical Validation of Affect, Behavior, and Cognition as Distinct Components of Behavior," *Journal of Personality and Social Psychology* (May 1984), pp. 1191–1205.

8. "A Case of Cognitive Dissonance," *US News and World Report,* November 26, 2001, p. 10.

9. S. P. Robbins and T. A. Judge, *Essentials of Organizational Behavior,* 11th ed. (Upper Saddle River, NJ: Prentice Hall, 2010).

10. M. S. Christian, A. S. Garza, and J. E. Slaughter, "Work Engagement: A Quantitative Review and Test of Its Relations with Task and Contextual Performance," *Personnel Psychology,* Spring 2011, pp. 89–136; V. T. Ho, S-S Wong, and C. H. Lee, "A Tale of Passion: Linking Job Passion and Cognitive Engagement to Employee Work Performance," *Journal of Management Studies* (January 2011), pp. 26–47; D. R. May, R. L. Gilson, and L. M. Harter, "The Psychological Conditions of Meaningfulness, Safety and Availability and the Engagement of the Human Spirit at Work," *Journal of Occupational and Organizational Psychology* (March 2004), pp. 11–37; R. T. Keller, "Job Involvement and Organizational Commitment as Longitudinal Predictors of Job Performance: A Study of Scientists and Engineers," *Journal of Applied Psychology* (August 1997), pp. 539–545; W. Kahn, "Psychological Conditions

of Personal Engagement and Disengagement at Work," *Academy of Management Journal* (December 1990), pp. 692–794; and P. P. Brooke, Jr., D. W. Russell and J. L. Price, "Discriminant Validation of Measures of Job Satisfaction, Job Involvement, and Organizational Commitment," *Journal of Applied Psychology* (May 1988), pp. 139–145. Also, see, for example, J. Smythe, "Engaging Employees to Drive Performance," *Communication World,* May–June 2008, pp. 20–22; A. B. Bakker and W. B. Schaufeli, "Positive Organizational Behavior: Engaged Employees in Flourishing Organizations," *Journal of Organizational Behavior* (February 2008), pp. 147–154; U. Aggarwal, S. Datta, and S. Bhargava, "The Relationship Between Human Resource Practices, Psychological Contract, and Employee Engagement—Implications for Managing Talent," *IIMB Management Review,* September 2007, pp. 313–325; M. C. Christian and J. E. Slaughter, "Work Engagement: A Meta-Analytic Review and Directions for Research in an Emerging Area," *AOM Proceedings,* August 2007, pp. 1–6; C. H. Thomas, "A New Measurement Scale for Employee Engagement: Scale Development, Pilot Test, and Replication," *AOM Proceedings,* August 2007, pp. 1–6; A. M. Saks, "Antecedents and Consequences of Employee Engagement," *Journal of Managerial Psychology,* 21, no. 7 (2006), pp. 600–619; and A. Parsley, "Road Map for Employee Engagement," *Management Services,* Spring 2006, pp. 10–11.

11. Mercer, *IndustryWeek,* April 2008, p. 24.

12. J. M. George, "The Wider Context, Costs, and Benefits of Work Engagement," *European Journal of Work & Organizational Psychology* (February 2011), pp. 53–59; and "Employee Engagement Report 2011," *BlessingWhite Research,* http://www.blessingwhite.com/eee__report.asp (January 2011), pp. 7–8.

13. A. J. Elliott and P. G. Devine, "On the Motivational Nature of Cognitive Dissonance: Dissonance as Psychological Discomfort," *Journal of Personality and Social Psychology* (September 1994), pp. 382–394.

14. L. Festinger, *A Theory of Cognitive Dissonance* (Stanford, CA: Stanford University Press, 1957); C. Crossen, "Cognitive Dissonance Became a Milestone in 1950s Psychology," *Wall Street Journal,* December 4, 2006, p. B1; and Y. "Sally" Kim, "Application of the Cognitive Dissonance Theory to the Service Industry," *Services Marketing Quarterly,* April–June 2011, pp. 96–112.

15. H. C. Koh and E. H. Y. Boo, "The Link Between Organizational Ethics and Job Satisfaction: A Study of Managers in Singapore," *Journal of Business Ethics,* February 15, 2001, p. 309.

16. See, for example, W. D. Crano and R. Prislin, "Attitudes and Persuasion," *Annual Review of Psychology,* 2006, pp. 345–374; and J. Jermias, "Cognitive Dissonance and Resistance to Change: The Influence of Commitment Confirmation and Feedback on Judgment Usefulness of Accounting Systems." *Accounting, Organizations, and Society,* March 2001, p. 141.

17. And the Survey Says box based on "Employee Engagement Correlates to Career Advancement and Training," *T&D,* February 2011, p. 21; J. Yang and S. Ward, "My Feeling Toward My Job Is ..." *USA Today,* February 7, 2011, p. 1B; E. Spitznagel, "The Tragic Decline of Business Casual," *Bloomberg BusinessWeek,* October 11–17, 2010, pp. 94–95; B. M. Testa, "Multiskilled Employees Sought as Versatility Becomes a Workplace Virtue," *Workforce Management Online,* September 24, 2010; J. Yang and P. Trap, "Top Workplace Break Room Annoyances," *USA Today,* August 30, 2010, p. 1B; E. Frauenheim, "Recession Unleashes Boss Bullying," *Workforce*

Management Online, April 2010; S. Jayson, "A Detailed Look at Millennials," *USA Today,* February 24, 2010, p. 10B; and T. Janisch, "Digital Marketplace: Welcoming Gen Y to the Workforce," http://wisetechnology.com/articles (May 19, 2009).

18. T. A. Judge, C. J. Thoresen, J. E. Bono, and G. K. Patton, "The Job Satisfaction–Job Performance Relationship: A Qualitative and Quantitative Review," *Psychological Bulletin,* May 2001, pp. 376–407.

19. L. Saari and T. A. Judge, "Employee Attitudes and Job Satisfaction," *Human Resource Management,* Winter 2004, pp. 395–407; and T. A. Judge and A. H. Church, "Job Satisfaction: Research and Practice," in C. L. Cooper and E. A. Locke (eds.), *Industrial and Organizational Psychology: Linking Theory with Practice* (Oxford, UK: Blackwell, 2000).

20. D. A. Harrison, D. A. Newman, and P. L. Roth, "How Important Are Job Attitudes?: Meta-Analytic Comparisons of Integrative Behavioral Outcomes and Time Sequences," *Academy of Management Journal* (April 2006), pp. 305–325.

21. G. Chen, R. E. Ployhart, H. C. Thomas, N. Anderson, and P. D. Bliese, "The Power of Momentum: A New Model of Dynamic Relationships Between Job Satisfaction Change and Turnover Intentions," *Academy of Management Journal* (February 2011), pp. 159–181.

22. I. Arnsdorf, "No More New Kid on Campus," *Wall Street Journal,* August 5, 2010, pp. D1+.

23. CPP, Inc., Myers-Briggs Type Indicator® (MBTI®), http://www.cpp.com/products/mbti/index.asp (2011); and J. Llorens, "Taking Inventory of Myers-Briggs," *T&D,* April 2010, pp. 18–19.

24. Ibid.

25. See, for instance, J. Overbo, "Using Myers-Briggs Personality Type to Create a Culture Adapted to the New Century," *T&D,* February 2010, pp. 70–72; K. Garrety, R. Badham, V. Morrigan, W. Rifkin, and M. Zanko, "The Use of Personality Typing in Organizational Change: Discourse, Emotions, and the Reflective Subject," *Human Relations,* February 2003, pp. 211–235.

26. P. Moran, "Personality Characteristics and Growth-Orientation of the Small Business Owner Manager," *Journal of Managerial Psychology* (July 2000), p. 651; and M. Higgs, "Is There a Relationship Between the Myers-Briggs Type Indicator and Emotional Intelligence?" *Journal of Managerial Psychology* (September–October 2001), pp. 488–513.

27. J. M. Digman, "Personality Structure: Emergence of the Five Factor Model," in M. R. Rosenweig and L. W. Porter, eds., *Annual Review of Psychology,* vol. 41 (Palo Alto, CA: Annual Reviews, 1990), pp. 417–440; O. P. John, "The Big Five Factor Taxonomy: Dimensions of Personality in the Natural Language and in Questionnaires," in L. A. Pervin, ed., *Handbook of Personality Theory and Research* (New York: Guilford Press, 1990), pp. 66–100; and M. K. Mount, M. R. Barrick, and J. P. Strauss, "Validity of Observer Ratings of the Big Five Personality Factors," *Journal of Applied Psychology* (April 1996), pp. 272–280.

28. See, for example, T. W. Yiu and H. K. Lee, "How Do Personality Traits Affect Construction Dispute Negotiation: Study of Big Five Personality Model," *Journal of Construction Engineering & Management* (March 2011), pp. 169–178; H. J. Kell, A. D. Rittmayer, A. E. Crook, and S. J. Motowidlo, "Situational Content Moderates the Association Between the Big Five Personality Traits and Behavioral Effectiveness," *Human Performance,* February 2010, pp. 213–228; R. D. Meyer, R. S. Dalal, and S. Bonaccio, "A Meta-Analytic Investigation into the Moderating Effects of Situational Strength on the Conscientiousness–Performance Relationship," *Journal of Organizational Behavior* (November 2009), pp. 1077–1102; G. Vittorio, C. Barbaranelli, and G. Guido, "Brand Personality: How to Make the Metaphor Fit," *Journal of Economic Psychology* (June 2001), p. 377; G. M. Hurtz and J. J. Donovan, "Personality and Job Performance: The Big Five Revisited," *Journal of Applied Psychology* (December 2000), p. 869; W. A. Hochwarter, L. A. Witt, and K. M. Kacmar, "Perceptions of Organizational Politics as a Moderator of the Relationship Between Conscientiousness and Job Performance," *Journal of Applied Psychology* (June 2000), p. 472; and M. R. Barrick and M. K. Mount, "The Big Five Personality Dimensions and Job Performance: A Meta-Analytic Study," *Personnel Psychology* 44 (1991), pp. 1–26.

29. Barrick and Mount, "Autonomy as a Moderator of the Relationship Between the Big Five Personality Dimensions and Job Performance."

30. See also M. R. Furtner and J. F. Rauthmann, "Relations Between Self-Leadership and Scores on the Big Five," *Psychological Reports,* October 2010, pp. 339–353; R. Barrick, M. Piotrowski, and G. L. Stewart, "Personality and Job Performance: Test of the Mediating Effects of Motivation Among Sales Representatives," *Journal of Applied Psychology* (February 2002), pp. 43–52; and I. T. Robertson, H. Baron, P. Gibbons, R. MacIver, and G. Nyfield, "Conscientiousness and Managerial Performance," *Journal of Occupational and Organizational Psychology* (June 2000), pp. 171–78.

31. See, for example, J. L. Kisamore, I. M. Jawahar, E. W. Liguori, T. L. Mharapara, and T. H. Stone, "Conflict and Abusive Workplace Behaviors: The Moderating Effects of Social Competencies," *Career Development International,* October 2010, pp. 583–600; P. S. Mishra and A. K. Das Mohapatra, "Relevance of Emotional Intelligence for Effective Job Performance: An Empirical Study," *Vikalpa: The Journal for Decision Makers* (January–March 2010), pp. 53–61; T-Y. Kim, D. M. Cable, S-P. Kim, and J. Wang, "Emotional Competence and Work Performance: The Mediating Effect of Proactivity and the Moderating Effect of Job Autonomy," *Journal of Organizational Behavior* (October 2009), pp. 983–1000; J. M. Diefendorff and G. J. Greguras, "Contextualizing Emotional Display Rules: Examining the Roles of Targets and Discrete Emotions in Shaping Display Rule Perceptions," *Journal of Management* (August 2009), pp. 880–898; J. Gooty, M. Gavin, and N. M. Ashkanasy, "Emotions Research in OB: The Challenges That Lie Ahead," *Journal of Organizational Behavior* (August 2009), pp. 833–838; N. M. Ashkanasy and C. S. Daus, "Emotion in the Workplace: The New Challenge for Managers," *Academy of Management Executive,* February 2002, pp. 76–86; N. M. Ashkanasy, C. E. J. Hartel, and C. S. Daus, "Diversity and Emotions: The New Frontiers in Organizational Behavior Research," *Journal of Management,* 28, no. 3 (2002), pp. 307–338; S. Fox, "Promoting Emotional Intelligence in Organizations: Make Training in Emotional Intelligence Effective," *Personnel Psychology,* Spring 2002, pp. 236–240; B. E. Ashforth, "The Handbook of Emotional Intelligence: Theory, Development, Assessment, and Application at Home, School, and in the Work Place: A Review," *Personnel Psychology,* Autumn 2001, pp. 721–724; and R. Bar-On and J. D. A. Parker, *The Handbook of Emotional Intelligence: Theory, Development, Assessment, and Application at Home, School, and in the Work Place* (San Francisco, CA: Jossey-Bass, 2000).

32. See, for instance, C. S. P. Fernandez, "Emotional Intelligence in the Workplace," *Journal of Public Health Management and Practice* (February 2007), pp. 80–82.

33. R. Pearman, "The Leading Edge: Using Emotional Intelligence to Enhance Performance," *T&D,* March 2011, pp. 68–71; C. Prentice and B. King, "The Influence of Emotional Intelligence on the Service Performance of Casino Frontline Employees," *Tourism & Hospitality Research,* January 2011, pp. 49–66; E. H. O'Boyle, Jr., R. H. Humphrey, J. M. Pollack, T. H. Hawver, and P. A. Story, "The Relation Between Emotional Intelligence and Job Performance: A Meta-Analysis," *Journal of Organizational Behavior Online,* www.interscience.wiley. com, June 2010; and P. J. Jordan, N. M. Ashkanasy, and C. E. J. Hartel, "Emotional Intelligence as a Moderator of Emotional and Behavioral Reactions to Job Insecurity," *Academy of Management Review,* July 2002, pp. 361–372.

34. C. Cherniss and R. D. Caplan, "A Case Study of Implementing Emotional Intelligence Programs in Organizations," *Journal of Organizational Excellence* (Winter 2001), pp. 763–786; and S. B. Vanessa-Urch and W. Deuskat, "Building the Emotional Intelligence of Groups," *Harvard Business Review,* March 2001, pp. 81–91.

35. "Can't We All Just Get Along," *BusinessWeek,* October 9, 2000, p. 18.

36. C. Moller and S. Powell, "Emotional Intelligence and the Challenges of Quality Management," *Leadership and Organizational Development Journal* (July–August 2001), pp. 341–345.

37. See L.A. Downey, V. Papageorgiou, and C. Stough, "Examining the Relationship Between Leadership, Emotional Intelligence, and Intuition in Female Managers," *Leadership & Organization Development Journal* (April 2006), pp. 250–264.

38. Right or Wrong? box based on C. Mindrum, "The Twitching Organization," *Chief Learning Officer,* March 2011, pp. 20–25; M. Conlin, "Are People in Your Office Acting Oddly?" *BusinessWeek,* April 13, 2009, p. 54; and J. Hoffman, "Working Hard to Look Busy," *New York Times Online,* January 25, 2009.

39. See, for instance, J. Silvester, F. M. Anderson-Gough, N. R. Anderson, and A. R. Mohamed, "Locus of Control, Attributions and Impression Management in the Selection Interview," *Journal of Occupational and Organizational Psychology* (March 2002), pp. 59–77; D. W. Organ and C. N. Greene, "Role Ambiguity, Locus of Control, and Work Satisfaction," *Journal of Applied Psychology* (February 1974), pp. 101–102; and T. R. Mitchell, C. M. Smyser and S. E. Weed, "Locus of Control: Supervision and Work Satisfaction," *Academy of Management Journal* (September 1975), pp. 623–631.

40. I. Zettler, N. Friedrich, and B. E. Hilbig, "Dissecting Work Commitment: The Role of Machiavellianism," *Career Development International,* February 2011, pp. 20–35; S. R. Kessler, A. C. Bandelli, P. E. Spector, W. C. Borman, C. E. Nelson, and L. M. Penney, "Re-Examining Machiavelli: A Three-Dimensional Model of Machiavellianism in the Workplace," *Journal of Applied Social Psychology* (August 2010), pp. 1868–1896; W. Amelia, "Anatomy of a Classic: Machiavelli's Daring Gift," *Wall Street Journal,* August 30–31, 2008, p. W10; S. A. Snook, "Love and Fear and the Modern Boss, *Harvard Business Review,* January 2008, pp. 16–17; and R. G. Vleeming, "Machiavellianism: A Preliminary Review," *Psychology Reports,* February 1979, pp. 295–310.

41. P. Harris, "Machiavelli and the Global Compass: Ends and Means in Ethics and Leadership," *Journal of Business Ethics*

(June 2010), pp. 131–138; and P. Van Kenhove, I. Vermeir, and S. Verniers, "An Empirical Investigation of the Relationship Between Ethical Beliefs, Ethical Ideology, Political Preference and Need for Closure," *Journal of Business Ethics,* August 15, 2001, p. 347.

42. Based on J. Brockner, *Self-Esteem at Work: Research, Theory, and Practice* (Lexington, MA: Lexington Books, 1988), chs. 1–4.

43. See, for instance, R. Vermunt, D. van Knippenberg, B. van Knippenberg, and E. Blaauw, "Self-Esteem and Outcome Fairness: Differential Importance of Procedural and Outcome Considerations," *Journal of Applied Psychology* (August 2001), p. 621; T. A. Judge and J. E. Bono, "Relationship of Core Self-Evaluation Traits—Self-Esteem, Generalized Self Efficacy, Locus of Control, and Emotional Stability—With Job Satisfaction and Job Performance," *Journal of Applied Psychology* (February 2001), p. 80; and D. B. Fedor, J. M. Maslyn, W. D. Davis, and K. Mathieson, "Performance Improvement Efforts in Response to Negative Feedback: The Roles of Source Power and Recipient Self-Esteem," *Journal of Management* (January–February 2001), pp. 79–97.

44. M. Snyder, *Public Appearances, Private Realities: The Psychology of Self-Monitoring* (New York: W. H. Freeman, 1987).

45. See, for example, D. U. Bryant, M. Mitcham, A. R. Araiza, and W. M. Leung, "The Interaction of Self-Monitoring and Organizational Position on Perceived Effort," *Journal of Managerial Psychology,* 26, no. 2 (2011), pp. 138–154; B. B. Vilela and J. A. V. González, "Salespesons' Self-Monitoring: Direct, Indirect, and Moderating Effects on Salespersons' Organizational Citizenship Behavior," *Psychology & Marketing,* January 2010, pp. 71–89; and P. M. Fandt, "Managing Impressions with Information: A Field Study of Organizational Realities," *Journal of Applied Behavioral Science* (June 2001), pp. 180–205.

46. Ibid.

47. R. N. Taylor and M. D. Dunnette, "Influence of Dogmatism, Risk Taking Propensity, and Intelligence on Decision Making Strategies for a Sample of Industrial Managers," *Journal of Applied Psychology* (August 1974), pp. 420–423.

48. I. L. Janis and L. Mann, *Decision Making: A Psychological Analysis of Conflict, Choice, and Commitment* (New York: Free Press, 1977).

49. See, for instance, C. P. Cross, L. T. Copping, and A. Campbell, "Sex Differences in Impulsivity: A Meta-Analysis," *Psychological Bulletin,* January 2011, pp. 97–130; A. A. Schooler, K. Fujita, X. Zou, and S. J. Stroessner, "When Risk Seeking Becomes a Motivational Necessity," *Journal of Personality and Social Psychology* (August 2010), pp. 215–231; A. Chatterjee and D. C. Hambrick, "Executive Personality, Capability Cues, and Risk-Taking: How Narcissistic CEOs React to Their Successes and Stumbles," *Academy of Management Proceedings,* www.aomonline.org (2010); E. Soane, C. Dewberry, and S. Narendran, "The Role of Perceived Costs and Perceived Benefits in the Relationship Between Personality and Risk-Related Choices," *Journal of Risk Research* (April 2010), pp. 303–318; and N. Kogan and M. A. Wallach, "Group Risk Taking as a Function of Members' Anxiety and Defensiveness," *Journal of Personality* (March 1967), pp. 50–63.

50. H. Zhao, S. E. Seibert, and G. T. Lumpkin, "The Relationship of Personality to Entrepreneurial Intentions and Performance: A Meta-Analytic Review," *Journal of Management*

(March 2010), pp. 381–404; and K. Hyrshy, "Entrepreneurial Metaphors and Concepts: An Exploratory Study," *Journal of Managerial Psychology* (July 2000), p. 653; and B. McCarthy, "The Cult of Risk Taking and Social Learning: A Study of Irish Entrepreneurs," *Management Decision,* August 2000, pp. 563–575.

51. M. Goldman, "A Journey into Personality Self-Discovery, Vol. 2," *Bloomberg BusinessWeek Online,* March 22, 2011; M. Goldman, "A Journey into Personality Self-Discovery, Vol. 1," *Bloomberg BusinessWeek Online,* February 15, 2011; and P. Korkki, "The True Calling That Wasn't," *New York Times Online,* July 16, 2010.

52. J. L. Holland, *Making Vocational Choices: A Theory of Vocational Personalities and Work Environments* (Odessa, FL: Psychological Assessment Resources, 1997).

53. S. Bates, "Personality Counts: Psychological Tests Can Help Peg the Job Applicants Best Suited for Certain Jobs," *HR Magazine,* February 2002, pp. 28–38; and K. J. Jansen and A. K. Brown, "Toward a Multi-Level Theory of Person Environment Fit," *Academy of Management Proceedings from the Fifty-Eighth Annual Meeting of the Academy of Management,* San Diego, CA (August 7–12, 1998), pp. HR: FR1–FR8.

54. See, for instance, G. W. M. Ip and M. H. Bond, "Culture, Values, and the Spontaneous Self-Concept," *Asian Journal of Psychology,* vol. 1 (1995), pp. 30–36; J. E. Williams, J. L. Saiz, D. L. FormyDuval, M. L. Munick, E. E. Fogle, A. Adom, A. Haque, F. Neto, and J. Yu, "Cross-Cultural Variation in the Importance of Psychological Characteristics: A Seven-Year Country Study," *International Journal of Psychology* (October 1995), pp. 529–550; V. Benet and N. G. Walker, "The Big Seven Factor Model of Personality Description: Evidence for Its Cross-Cultural Generalizability in a Spanish Sample," *Journal of Personality and Social Psychology* (October 1995), pp. 701–718; R. R. McCrae and P. To. Costa Jr., "Personality Trait Structure as a Human Universal," *American Psychologist,* 1997, pp. 509–516; and M. J. Schmit, J. A. Kihm, and C. Robie, "Development of a Global Measure of Personality," *Personnel Psychology,* Spring 2000, pp. 153–193.

55. J. F. Salgado, "The Five Factor Model of Personality and Job Performance in the European Community," *Journal of Applied Psychology* (February 1997), pp. 30–43. Note: This study covered the 15-nation European community and did not include the 10 countries that joined in 2004.

56. G. Kranz, "Organizations Look to Get Personal in '07," *Workforce Management,* www.workforce.com (June 19, 2007).

57. H. H. Kelley, "Attribution in Social Interaction," in E. Jones et al. (eds.), *Behavior* (Morristown, NJ: General Learning Press, 1972).

58. Advertisement for Land Rover Discovery Series II.

59. G. Miller and T. Lawson, "The Effect of an Informational Option on the Fundamental Attribution Error," *Personality and Social Psychology Bulletin,* June 1989, pp. 194–204. See also G. Charness and E. Haruvy, "Self-Serving Bias: Evidence from a Simulated Labour Relationship," *Journal of Managerial Psychology* (July 2000), p. 655; and T. J. Elkins, J. S. Phillips, and R. Konopaske, "Gender-Related Biases in Evaluations of Sex Discrimination Allegations: Is Perceived Threat a Key?" *Journal of Applied Psychology* (April 2002), pp. 280–293.

60. S. T. Fiske, "Social Cognition and Social Perception," *Annual Review of Psychology*, 1993, pp. 155–194; G. N. Powell and Y. Kido, "Managerial Stereotypes in a Global Economy: A Comparative Study of Japanese and American Business Students' Perspectives," *Psychological Reports*, February 1994, pp. 219–26; and J. L. Hilton and W. von Hippel, "Stereotypes,"

in J. T. Spence, J. M. Darley, and D. J. Foss (eds.), *Annual Review of Psychology,* vol. 47 (Palo Alto, CA: Annual Reviews Inc., 1996), pp. 237–271.

61. P. White, "Baseball Elders Teach Lessons of the Game," *USA Today,* April 14, 2009, p. 1C+.

62. B. F. Skinner, *Contingencies of Reinforcement* (East Norwalk, CT: Appleton-Century-Crofts, 1971).

63. From the Past to the Present box based on B. F. Skinner, *Contingencies of Reinforcement;* and S. P. Robbins and T. A. Judge, *Organizational Behavior,* 14th ed. (Upper Saddle River, NJ: Pearson Prentice Hall, 2011).

64. A. Applebaum, "Linear Thinking," *Fast Company,* December 2004, p. 35.

65. A. Bandura, *Social Learning Theory* (Upper Saddle River, NJ: Prentice Hall, 1977).

66. For an interesting article on the subject, see D. Nitsch, M. Baetz, and J. C. Hughes, "Why Code of Conduct Violations Go Unreported: A Conceptual Framework to Guide Intervention and Future Research," *Journal of Business Ethics* (April 2005), pp. 327–341.

67. R. J. Alsop, "The Last Word: Youth and Consequences," *Workforce Management Online,* February 2011; M. Fertik, "Managing Employees in Their Twenties," *Bloomberg BusinessWeek Online,* January 19, 2011; M. Richtel, "Growing Up Digital: Wired for Distraction," *New York Times Online,* November 21, 2010; N. Lublin, "In Defense of Millennials," *Fast Company,* October 2010, pp. 72–74; A. D. Wright and T. D. Tapscott, "Millennials: Bathed in Bits," *HR Magazine,* July 2010, pp. 40–41; S. Jayson, "A Detailed Look at Millennials;" T. Janisch, "Digital Marketplace: Welcoming Gen Y to the Workforce"; and S. Armour, "Generation Y: They've Arrived at Work with a New Attitude," *USA Today,* November 6, 2005, pp. 1B+.

68. N. Ramachandran, "New Paths at Work," *US News & World Report,* March 20, 2006, p. 47.

69. D. Sacks, "Scenes from the Culture Clash," *Fast Company,* January–February 2006, p. 75.

70. S. Armour, "Generation Y: They've Arrived at Work with a New Attitude," p. 2B.

71. S. Armour, "Generation Y: They've Arrived at Work with a New Attitude"; B. Moses, "The Challenges of Managing Gen Y," *The Globe and Mail,* March 11, 2005, p. C1; and C. A. Martin, *Managing Generation Y* (Amherst, MA: HRD Press, 2001).

72. C. M. Pearson and C. L. Porath, "On the Nature, Consequences, and Remedies of Workplace Incivility: No Time for Nice? Think Again," *Academy of Management Executive,* February 2005, pp. 7–18.

73. J. Robison, "Be Nice: It's Good for Business," *Gallup Brain,* http://brain.gallup.com (August 12, 2004).

74. M. Sandy Hershcovis and J. Barling, "Towards a Multi-Foci Approach to Workplace Aggression: A Meta-Analytic Review of Outcomes from Different Perpetrators," *Journal of Organizational Behavior* (January 2010), pp. 24–44; R. E. Kidwell and S. R. Valentine, "Positive Group Context, Work Attitudes, and Organizational Behavior: The Case of Withholding Job Effort," *Journal of Business Ethics* (April 2009), pp. 15–28; P. Bordia and S. L. D . Resubog, "When Employees Strike Back: Investigating Mediating Mechanisms Between Psychological Contract Breach and Workplace Deviance," *Journal of Applied Psychology* (September 2008), pp. 1104–1117; and Y. Vardi and E. Weitz, *Misbehavior in Organizations* (Mahwah, NJ: Lawrence Erlbaum Associates, 2004), pp. 246–247.

Understanding Groups and Managing Work Teams

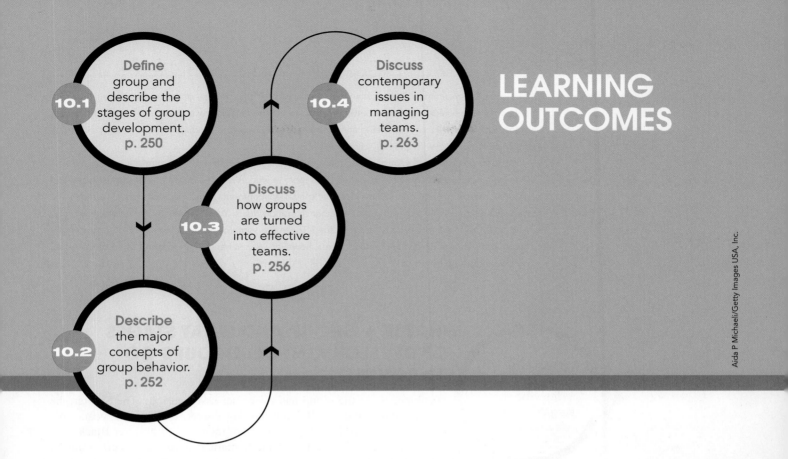

Aida P Michaeli/Getty Images USA, Inc.

Intel Inside…and Far Away

Located in Haifa on the Mediterranean coast, Intel's Israel Development Center was established in 1974 as the company's first development center outside the United States.[1] As the world's largest semiconductor manufacturer, Intel's components are used in more than 80 percent of the world's desktop and notebook computers and computer servers. Its technological capabilities are known the world over. For instance, a Russian bus manufacturer shortened vehicle development cycles and boosted product quality using Intel-based servers. Telecommunications provider Telefónica used Intel processors to launch its cloud services. And footwear company Adidas turned to Intel to help it create a virtual footwear wall. The Israeli team of engineers has been instrumental in developing many of the company's most successful innovations. The group has been described as having a "strong culture of debate and confrontation. Sometimes too much." However, a major challenge for this design group has been the geographical distance between it and other Intel design groups. Yet, Intel's managers have found ways to keep the teams connected and the innovations flowing.

Like company executives at Intel, managers today believe that the use of teams allows their organizations to increase sales or produce better products faster and at lower costs. Although the effort to create teams isn't always successful, well-planned teams can reinvigorate productivity and better position an organization to deal with a rapidly changing environment.

You've probably had a lot of experience working in groups—class project teams, maybe an athletic team, a fundraising committee, or even a sales team at work. Work teams are one of the realities—and challenges—of managing in today's dynamic global environment. Many organizations have made the move to restructure work around teams rather than individuals. Why? What do these teams look like? And how can managers build effective teams? These are some of the questions we'll be answering in this chapter. Before we can understand teams, however, we first need to understand some basics about groups and group behavior.

WHAT IS A GROUP AND WHAT STAGES OF DEVELOPMENT DO GROUPS GO THROUGH?

10.1

Define group and describe the stages of group development.

Each person in the group had his or her assigned role: The Spotter, the Back Spotter, the Gorilla, and the Big Player. For over 10 years, this group—former MIT students who were members of a secret Black Jack Club—used their extraordinary mathematical abilities, expert training, teamwork, and interpersonal skills to take millions of dollars from some of the major casinos in the United States.[2] Although most groups aren't formed for such dishonest purposes, the success of this group at its task was impressive. Managers would like their work groups to be successful at their tasks also. The first step is understanding what a group is and how groups develop.

What Is a Group?

A **group** is defined as two or more interacting and interdependent individuals who come together to achieve specific goals. *Formal groups* are work groups that are defined by the organization's structure and have designated work assignments and specific tasks directed at accomplishing organizational goals. Exhibit 10–1 provides some examples. *Informal groups* are social groups. These groups occur naturally in the workplace and tend to form around friendships and common interests. For example, five employees from different departments who regularly eat lunch together are an informal group.

EXHIBIT 10–1   Examples of Formal Work Groups

- **Command groups**—Groups that are determined by the organization chart and composed of individuals who report directly to a given manager.

- **Task groups**—Groups composed of individuals brought together to complete a specific job task; their existence is often temporary because when the task is completed, the group disbands.

- **Cross-functional teams**—Groups that bring together the knowledge and skills of individuals from various work areas or groups whose members have been trained to do each other's jobs.

- **Self-managed teams**—Groups that are essentially independent and that, in addition to their own tasks, take on traditional managerial responsibilities, such as hiring, planning and scheduling, and evaluating performance.

EXHIBIT 10–2   Stages of Group Development

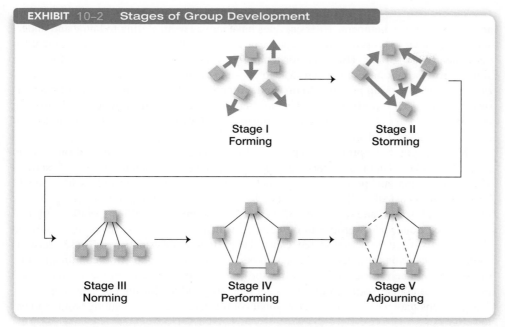

| Stage I Forming | Stage II Storming |

| Stage III Norming | Stage IV Performing | Stage V Adjourning |

What Are the Stages of Group Development?

Research shows that groups develop through five stages.[3] As shown in Exhibit 10–2, these five stages are: *forming, storming, norming, performing,* and *adjourning.*

The **forming stage** has two phases. The first occurs as people join the group. In a formal group, people join because of some work assignment. Once they've joined, the second phase begins: defining the group's purpose, structure, and leadership. This phase involves a great deal of uncertainty as members "test the waters" to determine what types of behavior are acceptable. This stage is complete when members begin to think of themselves as part of a group.

The **storming stage** is appropriately named because of the intragroup conflict. There's conflict over who will control the group and what the group needs to be doing. When this stage is complete, a relatively clear hierarchy of leadership and agreement on the group's direction will be evident.

The **norming stage** is one in which close relationships develop and the group becomes cohesive. The group now demonstrates a strong sense of group identity and camaraderie. This stage is complete when the group structure solidifies and the group has assimilated a common set of expectations (or norms) regarding member behavior.

These assembly-line workers at the Samsung Electronics Company's factory in Gumi, South Korea, proudly display the company's new Galaxy S2 mobile phones they produce. The figure of 1 million marks the number of units sold just one month after the phone's release. This group of young women is an example of the performing stage of group development. As they work together they have a strong sense of group identity and camaraderie and focus their energies on their task of assembling the smartphones to meet the demands of the marketplace. For permanent work groups such as these assembly-line employees, performing is the last stage in the group development process

Newscom

---

group
Two or more interacting and interdependent individuals who come together to achieve specific goals

forming stage
The first stage of group development in which people join the group and then define the group's purpose, structure, and leadership

storming stage
The second stage of group development, which is characterized by intragroup conflict

norming stage
The third stage of group development, which is characterized by close relationships and cohesiveness

The fourth stage is the **performing stage**. The group structure is in place and accepted by group members. Their energies have moved from getting to know and understand each other to working on the group's task. This is the last stage of development for permanent work groups. However, for temporary groups—project teams, task forces, or similar groups that have a limited task to do—the final stage is the **adjourning stage**. In this stage, the group prepares to disband. Attention is focused on wrapping up activities instead of task performance. Group members react in different ways. Some are upbeat, thrilled about the group's accomplishments. Others may be sad over the loss of camaraderie and friendships.

Many of you have probably experienced these stages as you've worked on a group project for a class. Group members are selected or assigned and then meet for the first time. There's a "feeling out" period to assess what the group is going to do and how it's going to be done. This is usually followed by a battle for control: Who's going to be in charge? Once this issue is resolved and a "hierarchy" agreed on, the group identifies specific work that needs to be done, who's going to do each part of the project, and dates by which the assigned work needs to be completed. General expectations are established. These decisions form the foundation for what you hope will be a coordinated group effort culminating in a project that's been done well. Once the project is complete and turned in, the group breaks up. Of course, some groups don't get much beyond the forming or storming stages. These groups may have serious interpersonal conflicts, turn in disappointing work, and get lower grades.

Does a group become more effective as it progresses through the first four stages? Some researchers say yes, but it's not that simple.[5] That assumption may be generally true, but what makes a group effective is a complex issue. Under some conditions, high levels of conflict are conducive to high levels of group performance. There might be situations in which groups in the storming stage outperform those in the norming or performing stages. Also, groups don't always proceed sequentially from one stage to the next. Sometimes, groups are storming and performing at the same time. Groups even occasionally regress to previous stages. Therefore, don't assume that all groups precisely follow this process or that performing is always the most preferable stage. Think of this model as a general framework that underscores the fact that groups are dynamic entities and managers need to know the stage a group is in so they can understand the problems and issues that are most likely to surface.

WHAT ARE THE MAJOR CONCEPTS OF GROUP BEHAVIOR?

10.2 Describe the major concepts of group behavior.

The basic foundation for understanding group behavior includes roles, norms and conformity, status systems, group size, and group cohesiveness. Let's take a closer look at each of those aspects.

What Are Roles?

We introduced the concept of roles in Chapter 1 when we discussed what managers do. Of course, managers aren't the only individuals in an organization who have roles. The concept of roles applies to all employees in organizations and to their lives outside the organization as well.

A **role** refers to behavior patterns expected of someone who occupies a given position in a social unit. Individuals play multiple roles, adjusting their roles to the group to which they belong at the time. In an organization, employees attempt to determine what behaviors are expected of them. They read their job descriptions, get suggestions from their bosses, and watch what their coworkers do. An individual who's confronted by divergent role expectations experiences role conflict. Employees in organizations often face such role conflicts. The credit manager expects her credit analysts to process a minimum of 30 applications a week, but the work group pressures members to restrict output to

20 applications a week so that everyone has work to do and no one gets laid off. A newly hired college instructor's colleagues want him to give out only a few high grades in order to maintain the department's reputation for high standards, whereas students want him to give out lots of high grades to enhance their grade point averages. To the degree that the instructor sincerely seeks to satisfy the expectations of both his colleagues and his students, he faces role conflict.

How Do Norms and Conformity Affect Group Behavior?

All groups have established **norms**, acceptable standards that are shared by the group's members. Norms dictate output levels, absenteeism rates, promptness or tardiness, the amount of socializing allowed on the job, and so on. Norms, for example, dictate the dress code of customer service representatives at a credit card processing company. Most workers who have little direct customer contact come to work dressed casually. However, on occasion, a newly hired employee will come to work dressed in a suit. Those who do are teased and pressured until their dress conforms to the group's standard.

Although each group has its own unique set of norms, common classes of norms appear in most organizations. These norms focus on effort and performance, dress, and loyalty. Probably the most widespread norms are related to levels of *effort and performance*. Work groups typically provide their members with explicit cues on how hard to work, what level of output to have, when to look busy, when it's acceptable to goof off, and the like. These norms are extremely powerful in affecting an individual employee's performance. They're so powerful that performance predictions based solely on an employee's ability and level of personal motivation often prove wrong.

Some organizations have formal *dress codes*—even describing what's considered acceptable for corporate casual dress. However, even in the absence of codes, norms frequently develop to dictate the kind of clothing that should be worn to work. College seniors, when interviewing for their first postgraduate job, pick up this norm quickly. Every spring, on college campuses around the country, students interviewing for jobs can be spotted; they're the ones walking around in the dark gray or blue pinstriped suits. They're enacting the dress norms they've learned are expected in professional positions. Of course, acceptable dress in one organization will be different from another's norms.

Few managers appreciate employees who ridicule the organization. Similarly, professional employees and those in the executive ranks recognize that most employers view persons who actively look for another job unfavorably. People who are unhappy know that they should keep their job searches secret. These examples demonstrate that *loyalty norms* are widespread in organizations. This concern for demonstrating loyalty, by the way, often explains why ambitious aspirants to top management positions

RIGHT ? OR WRONG

When coworkers work closely on a team project, is there such a thing as TMI (too much information)?[6] At one company, a team that had just finished a major project went out to lunch to celebrate. During lunch, one colleague mentioned that he was training for a 20-mile bike race. In addition to a discussion of his new helmet and Lycra shorts, the person also described shaving his whole body to reduce aerodynamic drag. Afterwards, another team member said, "Why, why, why do we need to go there? This is information about a coworker, not someone I really consider a friend, and now it's forever burned in my brain."

Think About:

- What do you think? Why are work colleagues sharing increasingly personal information?
- What benefits/drawbacks arise from sharing information like this?
- How have social media and technology contributed to this type of information disclosure?
- What are the ethical implications of sharing such personal information in the workplace?

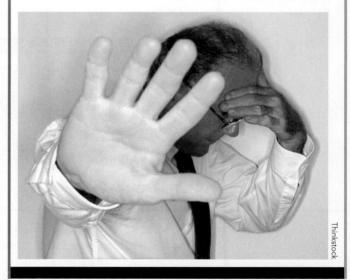

Thinkstock

performing stage
The fourth stage of group development, when the group is fully functional and works on the group task

adjourning stage
The final stage of group development for temporary groups, during which groups prepare to disband

role
Behavior patterns expected of someone who occupies a given position in a social unit

norms
Standards or expectations that are accepted and shared by a group's members

From the Past to the Present

Does the desire to be accepted as a part of a group leave one susceptible to conforming to the group's norms? Will the group exert pressure that's strong enough to change a member's attitude and behavior? According to the research by Solomon Asch, the answer appears to be yes.[7]

Asch's study involved groups of seven or eight people who sat in a classroom and were asked to compare two cards held by an investigator. One card had one line; the other had three lines of varying length. As shown in Exhibit 10–3, one of the lines on the three-line card was identical to the line on the one-line card. The difference in line length was quite obvious; under ordinary conditions, subjects made errors of less than 1 percent. The object was to announce aloud which of the three lines matched the single line. But what happens if all the members of the group begin to give incorrect answers? Will the pressure to conform cause the unsuspecting subject (USS) to alter his or her answers to align with those of the others? That's what Asch wanted to know. He arranged the group so that the USS was unaware that the experiment was fixed. The seating was prearranged so that the USS was the last to announce his or her decision.

The experiment began with two sets of matching exercises. All the subjects gave the right answers. On the third set, however, the first subject gave an obviously wrong answer—for example, saying C in Exhibit 10–3. The next subject gave the same wrong answer, and so did the others, until it was the unsuspecting subject's turn. He knew that "B" was the same as "X" but everyone else said "C."

The decision confronting the USS was this: Do you publicly state a perception that differs from the pre-announced position of the others? Or do you give an answer that you strongly believe to be incorrect in order to have your response agree with the other group members? Asch's subjects conformed in about 35 percent of many experiments and many trials. That is, the subjects gave answers that they knew were wrong but were consistent with the replies of other group members.

For managers, the Asch study provides considerable insight into group behaviors. The tendency, as Asch showed, is for individual members to go along with the pack. To diminish the negative aspects of conformity, managers should create a climate of openness in which employees are free to discuss problems without fear of retaliation.

Think About:

- DOES the desire to be accepted as a part of a group leave one susceptible to conforming to the group's norms? WILL a group exert pressure that's strong enough to change a member's attitude and behavior? What do YOU think?

- Think of groups that you've been part of (work or school). Were there times when you felt pressured to conform or when you pressured others to conform? What possible consequences (think in terms of people *and* outcomes) resulted or could have resulted?

- What can you use from this discussion to help you be a better manager?

EXHIBIT 10–3 **Examples of Cards Used in Asch's Study**

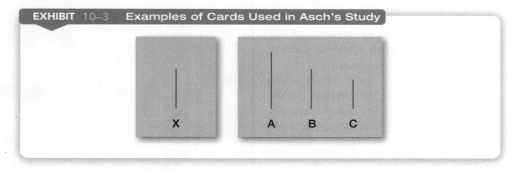

willingly take work home at night, come in on weekends, and accept transfers to cities in which they would otherwise prefer not to live. Because individuals desire acceptance by the groups to which they belong, they're susceptible to conformity pressures. The impact of group pressures for conformity on an individual member's judgment and attitudes was demonstrated in the classic studies by Solomon Asch.[8] Asch's results suggest that group norms press us toward conformity. We desire to be one of the group and to avoid being visibly different. We can generalize this finding to say that when an individual's opinion of objective data differs significantly from that of others in the group, he or she feels extensive pressure to align his or her opinion to conform with those of the others (see our previous discussion on groupthink, p. 85 found in Chapter 4). The From the Past to the Present, box has additional background information on Asch's contributions to group theory.

What Is Status and Why Is It Important?

Status is a prestige grading, position, or rank within a group. As far back as scientists have been able to trace human groupings, they've found status hierarchies: tribal chiefs and their followers, nobles and peasants, the haves and the have-nots. Status systems are important factors in understanding behavior. Status is a significant motivator that has behavioral consequences when individuals see a disparity between what they perceive their status to be and what others perceive it to be.

Status may be informally conferred by characteristics such as education, age, skill, or experience. However, anything can have status value if others in the group admire it. Of course, just because status is informal doesn't mean that it's unimportant or that there's disagreement on who has it or who doesn't. Members of groups have no problem placing people into status categories, and they usually agree about who's high, low, and in the middle.

It's important for employees to believe that the organization's formal status system is congruent. That is, there should be equity between the perceived ranking of an individual and the status symbols he or she is given by the organization. For instance, incongruence may occur when a supervisor earns less than his or her employees or when a desirable office is occupied by a lower-ranking individual. Employees may view such cases as a disruption to the general pattern of order and consistency in the organization.

Does Group Size Affect Group Behavior?

The size of a group affects that group's behavior. However, that effect depends on what criteria you're looking at.[9]

The evidence indicates, for instance, that small groups complete tasks faster than larger ones. However, if a group is engaged in problem solving, large groups consistently get better marks than their smaller counterparts. Translating these results into specific numbers is a bit trickier, but we can offer some parameters. Large groups—with a dozen or more members—are good for gaining diverse input. Thus, if the goal of the group is to find facts, larger groups should be more effective. On the other hand, smaller groups are better at doing something productive with those facts. Groups of approximately five to seven members tend to act more effectively.

One of the more disturbing findings is that, as groups get incrementally larger, the contribution of individual members often tends to lessen. That is, although the total productivity of a group of four is generally greater than that of a group of three, the individual productivity of each group member declines as the group expands. Thus, a group of four will tend to produce at a level of less than four times the average individual performance. The best explanation for this reduction of effort is that dispersion of responsibility encourages individuals to slack off; a behavior referred to as social loafing[10] When the results of the group can't be attributed to any single person, the relationship between an individual's input and the group's output is clouded. In such situations, individuals may be tempted to become "free riders" and coast on the group's efforts. In other words, efficiency is reduced when individuals think that their contributions cannot be measured. The obvious conclusion from this finding is that managers who use work groups should also provide a means by which individual efforts can be identified.

Are Cohesive Groups More Effective?

Intuitively, it makes sense that groups that experience a lot of internal disagreement and lack of cooperation are less effective than are groups in which individuals generally agree, cooperate, and like each other. Research has looked at group cohesiveness, the degree to which members are attracted to one another and share the

Group cohesiveness is high for the musical director and musicians of the Chicago Symphony Orchestra (CSO). Maestro Riccardo Muti (center) and the musicians of the orchestra share the group's goals of bringing unparalleled musical experiences to its audiences, preserving the legacy of symphonic music, and providing opportunities for everyone to have access to the art form. They also share the belief that the power of the music they perform can transform lives and communities, enact social change, and transcend cultural divides. As a highly cohesive group, the CSO is associated with excellent performances for audiences in Chicago and in musical venues around the world.

Todd Rosenberg/AP Images

---

status
A prestige grading, position, or rank within a group

social loafing
The tendency for individuals to expend less effort when working collectively than when working individually

group cohesiveness
The degree to which group members are attracted to one another and share the group's goals

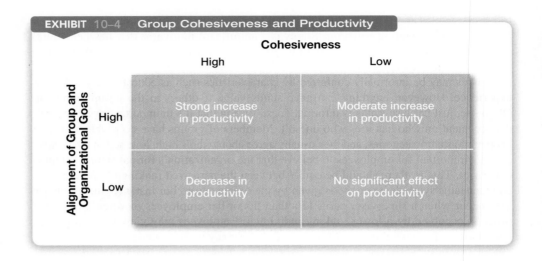

EXHIBIT 10–4　Group Cohesiveness and Productivity

Cohesiveness

	High	Low
High (Alignment of Group and Organizational Goals)	Strong increase in productivity	Moderate increase in productivity
Low (Alignment of Group and Organizational Goals)	Decrease in productivity	No significant effect on productivity

group's goals. The more that members are attracted to one another and the more that a group's goals align with each individual's goals, the greater the group's cohesiveness.

Previous research has generally shown that highly cohesive groups are more effective than are those with less cohesiveness, but the relationship between cohesiveness and effectiveness is more complex.[11] A key moderating variable is the degree to which the group's attitude aligns with its formal goals or those of the larger organization.[12] The more cohesive a group is, the more its members will follow its goals. If these goals are favorable (for instance, high output, quality work, cooperation with individuals outside the group), a cohesive group is more productive than a less cohesive group. But if cohesiveness is high and attitudes are unfavorable, productivity decreases. If cohesiveness is low and goals are supported, productivity increases, but not as much as when both cohesiveness and support are high. When cohesiveness is low and goals are not supported, cohesiveness has no significant effect on productivity. These conclusions are summarized in Exhibit 10–4.

HOW ARE GROUPS TURNED INTO EFFECTIVE TEAMS?

10.3 Discuss how groups are turned into effective teams.

When companies like W. L. Gore, Volvo, and Kraft Foods introduced teams into their production processes, it made news because no one else was doing it. Today, it's just the opposite—the organization that *doesn't* use teams would be newsworthy. It's estimated that some 80 percent of *Fortune* 500 companies have at least half of their employees on teams. In fact, more than 70 percent of U.S. manufacturers use work teams.[13] Teams are likely to continue to be popular. Why? Research suggests that teams typically outperform individuals when the tasks being done require multiple skills, judgment, and experience.[14] Organizations are using team-based structures because they've found that teams are more flexible and responsive to changing events than are traditional departments or other permanent work groups. Teams have the ability to quickly assemble, deploy, refocus, and disband. In this section, we'll discuss what a work team is, the different types of teams that organizations might use, and how to develop and manage work teams.

Are Work Groups and Work Teams the Same?

At this point, you may be asking yourself: Are teams and groups the same thing? No. In this section, we clarify the difference between a work group and a work team.[15]

Most of you are probably familiar with teams especially if you've watched or participated in organized sports events. Work *teams* do differ from work *groups* and have their own unique traits (see Exhibit 10–5). Work groups interact primarily to share information and to

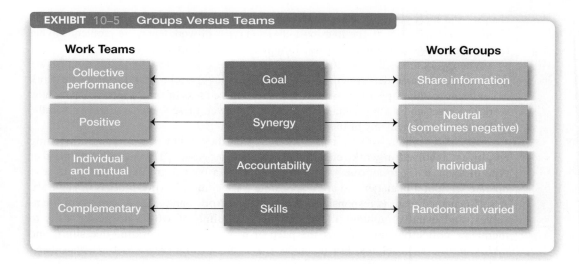

EXHIBIT 10–5   Groups Versus Teams

Work Teams		Work Groups
Collective performance	← Goal →	Share information
Positive	← Synergy →	Neutral (sometimes negative)
Individual and mutual	← Accountability →	Individual
Complementary	← Skills →	Random and varied

make decisions to help each member do his or her job more efficiently and effectively. There's no need or opportunity for work groups to engage in collective work that requires joint effort. On the other hand, **work teams** are groups whose members work intensely on a specific, common goal using their positive synergy, individual and mutual accountability, and complementary skills.

These descriptions should help clarify why so many organizations have restructured work processes around teams. Managers are looking for that positive synergy that will help the organization improve its performance.[16] The extensive use of teams creates the potential for an organization to generate greater outputs with no increase in (or even fewer) inputs. For example, until the economic downturn hit, investment teams at Wachovia's Asset Management Division (which is now a part of Wells Fargo & Company) were able to significantly improve investment performance. As a result, these teams helped the bank improve its Morningstar financial rating.[17]

Recognize, however, that such increases are simply "potential." Nothing inherently magical in the creation of work teams guarantees that this positive synergy and its accompanying productivity will occur. Accordingly, merely calling a group a team doesn't automatically increase its performance.[18] As we show later in this chapter, successful or high-performing work teams have certain common characteristics. If managers hope to gain increases in organizational performance, it will need to ensure that its teams possess those characteristics.

What Are the Different Types of Work Teams?

Teams can do a variety of things. They can design products, provide services, negotiate deals, coordinate projects, offer advice, and make decisions.[19] For instance, at Rockwell Automation's facility in North Carolina, teams are used in work process optimization projects. At Arkansas-based Acxiom Corporation, a team of human resource professionals planned and implemented a cultural

Team-based work is a key ingredient to the success of Facebook. Throughout the company, small work teams that require multiple skills, judgment, and experience work on a specific, common goal in creating new products and finding solutions for problems. For Facebook, work teams are more flexible and responsive to the company's dynamic business environment than are individuals, traditional departments, or other permanent work groups. Facebook's security team shown in this photo includes Max Kelly (standing in front), head of Internet security, and other team members whose task is to filter inappropriate content on the site. The team stands in front of the "Wall of Shame," a wall that highlights unusual correspondence and postings on the site.

David Butow/Redux Pictures

work teams
Groups whose members work intensely on specific, common goals using their positive synergy, individual and mutual accountability, and complementary skills

change. And every summer weekend at any NASCAR race, you can see work teams in action during drivers' pit stops.[20] The four most common types of work teams are problem-solving teams, self-managed work teams, cross-functional teams, and virtual teams.

When work teams first became popular, most were **problem-solving teams**, which are teams from the same department or functional area involved in efforts to improve work activities or to solve specific problems. Members share ideas or offer suggestions on how work processes and methods can be improved. However, these teams are rarely given the authority to implement any of their suggested actions.

Although problem-solving teams were helpful, they didn't go far enough in getting employees involved in work-related decisions and processes. This need led to another type of team, a **self-managed work team**, which is a formal group of employees who operate without a manager and are responsible for a complete work process or segment. A self-managed team is responsible for getting the work done *and* for managing themselves, and usually includes planning and scheduling of work, assigning tasks to members, collective control over the pace of work, making operating decisions, and taking action on problems. For instance, teams at Corning have no shift supervisors and work closely with other manufacturing divisions to solve production-line problems and coordinate deadlines and deliveries. The teams have the authority to make and implement decisions, finish projects, and address problems.[21] Other organizations such as Xerox, Boeing, PepsiCo, and Hewlett-Packard also use self-managed teams. It's estimated that about 30 percent of U.S. employers now use this form of team; and among large firms, the number is probably closer to 50 percent.[22] Most organizations that use self-managed teams find them to be effective.[23]

The third type of team is the **cross-functional team**, which we introduced in Chapter 5 and defined as a work team composed of individuals from various specialties. Many organizations use cross-functional teams. For example, ArcelorMittal, the world's largest steel company, uses cross-functional teams of scientists, plant managers, and salespeople to review and monitor product innovations.[24] The concept of cross-functional teams is even being applied in health care. For instance, at Suburban Hospital in Bethesda, Maryland, intensive care unit (ICU) teams composed of a doctor trained in intensive care medicine, a pharmacist, a social worker, a nutritionist, the chief ICU nurse, a respiratory therapist, and a chaplain meet daily with every patient's bedside nurse to discuss and debate the best course of treatment. The hospital credits this team care approach with reducing errors, shortening the amount of time patients spent in ICU, and improving communication between families and the medical staff.[25]

The final type of team is the **virtual team**, which is a team that uses technology to link physically dispersed members in order to achieve a common goal. For instance, a virtual team at Boeing-Rocketdyne played a pivotal role in developing a radically new product.[26] Another company, Decision Lens, uses a virtual team environment to generate and evaluate creative ideas.[27] In a virtual team, members collaborate online with tools such as wide-area

TECHNOLOGY AND THE MANAGER'S JOB   IT AND TEAMS

Work teams need information to do their work. With work teams often being not just steps away, but continents away from each other, it's important to have a way for team members to communicate and collaborate. That's where IT comes in. Technology has enabled greater online communication and collaboration within teams of all types.[28]

The idea of technologically aided collaboration actually originated with online search engines. The Internet itself was initially intended as a way for groups of scientists and researchers to share information. Then, as more and more information was put "on the Web," users relied on a variety of search engines to help them find that information. Now, we see many examples of collaborative technologies such as wiki pages, blogs, and even multiplayer virtual reality games.

Today, online collaborative tools have given work teams more efficient and effective ways to get work done. For instance, engineers at Toyota use collaborative communication tools to share process improvements and innovations. They have developed a "widely disseminated, collectively owned pool of common knowledge, which drives innovation at a speed few other corporate systems can match." And despite some recent "bumps," there's no disputing the successes Toyota has achieved. Managers everywhere should look to the power of IT to help work teams improve the way work gets done.

Think About:

· What challenges do managers face in managing teams that must rely on IT to communicate?

· Using, Exhibit 10–6, discuss how the four major components of team effectiveness would affect and be affected by a team's use of IT.

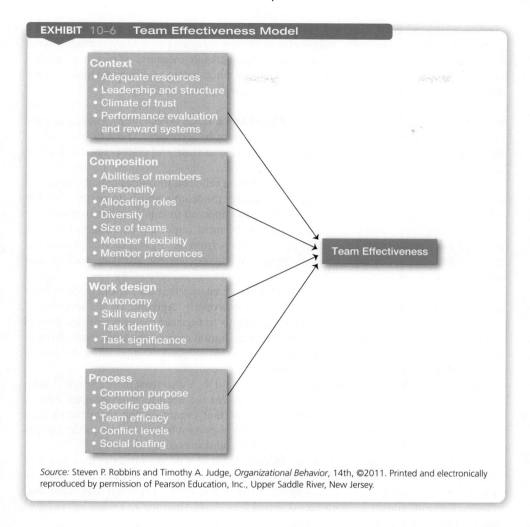

EXHIBIT 10–6 Team Effectiveness Model

Context
• Adequate resources
• Leadership and structure
• Climate of trust
• Performance evaluation
  and reward systems

Composition
• Abilities of members
• Personality
• Allocating roles
• Diversity
• Size of teams
• Member flexibility
• Member preferences

Work design
• Autonomy
• Skill variety
• Task identity
• Task significance

Process
• Common purpose
• Specific goals
• Team efficacy
• Conflict levels
• Social loafing

Team Effectiveness

Source: Steven P. Robbins and Timothy A. Judge, *Organizational Behavior*, 14th, ©2011. Printed and electronically reproduced by permission of Pearson Education, Inc., Upper Saddle River, New Jersey.

networks, videoconferencing, fax, e-mail, or Web sites where the team can hold online conferences.[29] Virtual teams can do all the things that other teams can—share information, make decisions, and complete tasks; however, they lack the normal give-and-take of face-to-face discussions. That's why virtual teams tend to be more task-oriented, especially if the team members have never personally met.

What Makes a Team Effective?

Much research has been done on what it is that makes a team effective.[30] Out of these efforts, we now have a fairly focused model identifying those characteristics.[31] Exhibit 10–6 summarizes what we currently know about what makes a team effective. As we look at this model, keep in mind two things. First, teams differ in form and structure. This model attempts to generalize across all teams, so you should only use it as a guide.[32] Secondly, the model assumes that managers have already determined that teamwork is preferable to individual work. Creating "effective" teams in situations in which individuals can do the job better would be wasted effort.

---

problem-solving teams
A team from the same department or functional area that's involved in efforts to improve work activities or to solve specific problems

self-managed work team
A type of work team that operates without a manager and is responsible for a complete work process or segment

cross-functional team
A work team composed of individuals from various specialties

virtual team
A type of work team that uses technology to link physically dispersed members in order to achieve a common goal

One thing we need to clarify first before looking at the model is what we mean by team effectiveness. Typically, it includes objective measures of a team's productivity, managers' ratings of the team's performance, and aggregate measures of member satisfaction. As you can see from the model, the four key components of effective teams include the context, the team's composition, work design, and process variables.

WHAT FACTORS IN THE CONTEXT APPEAR TO MAKE A TEAM EFFECTIVE? Four contextual factors appear to be most significantly related to team performance. These factors include adequate resources, leadership and structure, a climate of trust, and performance evaluation and reward systems.

As part of the larger organization system, a team relies on resources outside the group to sustain it. If it doesn't have *adequate resources*, the team's ability to perform its job effectively is reduced. This factor appears to be so important to team performance that one research study concluded that "perhaps one of the most important characteristics of an effective work group is the support the group receives from the organization."[33] Resources can include timely information, proper equipment, encouragement, adequate staffing, and administrative assistance.

If a team can't agree on who is to do what or ensure that all members contribute equally in sharing the work load, it won't function properly. Agreeing on the specifics of work and how all the team members' individual skills fit together requires *team leadership and structure*. This aspect can come from the organization or from the team itself. Even in self-managed teams, a manager's job is to be more of a coach by supporting the team's efforts and managing outside (rather than inside) the team.

Members of effective teams *trust* each other. And they also trust their leaders.[34] Why is trust important? It facilitates cooperation, reduces the need to monitor each other's behavior, and bonds members around the belief that others on the team won't take advantage of them. Trusting the team leader is also important because it means the team is willing to accept and commit to the leader's goals and decisions.

The final contextual factor of an effective team is a *performance evaluation and reward system*. Team members have to be accountable both individually and jointly. So, in addition to evaluating and rewarding employees for their individual contributions, managers should consider group-based appraisals, profit-sharing, and other approaches that reinforce team effort and commitment.

WHAT TEAM COMPOSITION FACTORS LEAD TO EFFECTIVENESS? Several team composition factors are important to a team's effectiveness. They include team member abilities, personality, role allocation, diversity, size of teams, member flexibility, and member preferences.

Part of a team's performance depends on its members' *knowledge, skills, and abilities*.[35] Research has shown that to perform effectively, a team needs three different types of skills. First, it needs people with technical expertise. Next, it needs members with problem-solving and decision-making skills. Finally, a team needs people with interpersonal skills. A team can't achieve its performance potential if it doesn't have or can't develop all these skills. And the right mix of these skills is also critical. Too much of one at the expense of another will lead to lower team performance. However, a team doesn't necessarily need all these skills immediately. It's not uncommon for team members to take responsibility for learning the skills in which the group is deficient. That way a team can achieve its full potential.

As we saw in the last chapter, *personality* significantly influences individual behavior. It's also true for team behavior. Research has shown that three of the Big Five dimensions are relevant to team effectiveness.[36] For instance, high levels of both conscientiousness and openness-to-experience tend to lead to higher team performance. Agreeableness also appears to matter. And teams that had one or more highly disagreeable members performed poorly. Maybe you've had that not-so-good experience in group projects that you've been part of!

Nine potential team *roles* have been identified. (See Exhibit 10–7.) High-performing work teams have people to fill all these roles who were selected to fulfill these roles based on their skills and preferences.[37] On many teams, individuals may play multiple roles.

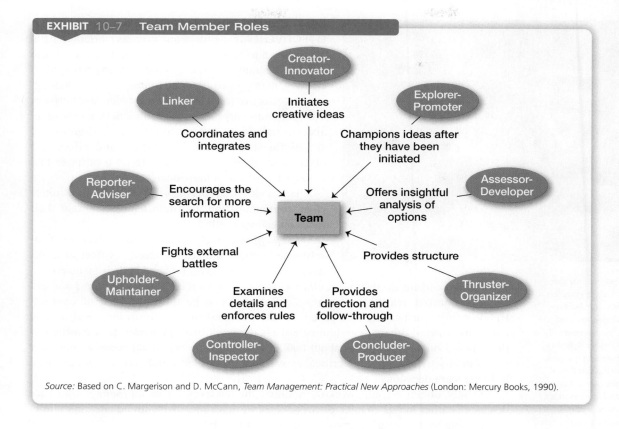

EXHIBIT 10–7   Team Member Roles

Source: Based on C. Margerison and D. McCann, *Team Management: Practical New Approaches* (London: Mercury Books, 1990).

It's important for managers to understand the individual strengths a person will bring to a team and select team members with those strengths in mind to ensure that these roles are filled.

Team *diversity* is another factor that can influence team effectiveness. Although many of us hold the optimistic view that diversity is desirable, research seems to show the opposite. One review found that "Studies on diversity in teams from the last 50 years have shown that surface-level social-category differences such as race/ethnicity, gender, and age tend to . . . have negative effects" on the performance of teams.[38] However, some evidence does show that the disruptive effects of diversity decline over time, but does not confirm that diverse teams perform better eventually.

What *size* should a work team be in order to be effective? At Amazon, work teams have considerable autonomy to innovate and to investigate ideas. Jeff Bezos, founder and CEO, uses a "two-pizza" philosophy; that is, a team should be small enough that it can be fed with two pizzas. This "two-pizza" philosophy usually limits groups to five to seven people, depending, of course, on team member appetites![39] Generally speaking, the most effective teams have five to nine members. And experts suggest using the smallest number of people who can do the task.

Team *member preferences* need to be considered. Why? Some people just prefer not to work on teams. Given the option, many employees will opt not to be part of a team. When people who would prefer to work alone are forced on a team, it creates a direct threat to the team's morale and to individual member satisfaction.[40]

HOW DOES WORK DESIGN AFFECT TEAM EFFECTIVENESS?   Effective teams need to work together and take collective responsibility for completing tasks. An effective team must be more than a "team in name only."[41] Important work design elements include *autonomy*, using a *variety of skills*, being able to complete a *whole and identifiable* task or product, and working on a task or project that has a *significant impact* on others. Research indicates that these characteristics enhance team member motivation and increase team effectiveness.[42]

Jim Dedmon/Newscom

Effective teams have a specific goal that facilitates communication and a common plan and purpose that provide direction, momentum, and commitment from team members. In this photo, the members of the pit crew team of NASCAR racer Kyle Busch work toward the goal of winning the race. While each crew member has a different job—such as jack man, tire carrier, fueler, and fire extinguisher—the team's plan is to function at top speed with no errors in checking the car, fixing parts, changing tires, and pumping gas. An effective pit crew can prevent problems and mean the difference between a victory and defeat. Here Busch's team is at work during a winning pit stop that qualified the racer for an all-star race.

WHAT TEAM PROCESSES ARE RELATED TO TEAM EFFECTIVENESS? Five team process variables have been shown to be related to team effectiveness. These include a common purpose, specific team goals, team efficacy, managed conflict, and minimal social loafing.

An effective team has a *common plan and purpose.* This common purpose provides direction, momentum, and commitment for team members.[43] Members of successful teams put a lot of time and effort into discussing, shaping, and agreeing on a purpose that belongs to them both individually and as a team.

Teams also need *specific goals.* Such goals facilitate clear communication and help teams maintain their focus on getting results.

Team efficacy emerges when teams believe in themselves and believe they can succeed.[44] Effective teams have confidence in themselves and in their members.

Effective teams need some *conflict.* Conflict on a team isn't necessarily bad and can actually improve team effectiveness.[45] But it has to be the right kind of conflict. Relationship conflicts—those based on interpersonal incompatibilities, tension, and autonomy toward others—are almost always dysfunctional. However, task conflicts—those based on disagreements about task content—can be beneficial because they may stimulate discussion, promote critical assessment of problems and options, and can lead to better team decisions.

Finally, effective teams work to minimize the tendency for *social loafing*, which we discussed earlier in this chapter. Successful teams make members individually and jointly accountable for the team's purpose, goals, and approach.[46]

How Can a Manager Shape Team Behavior?

A manager can do several things to shape a team's behavior including proper selection, employee training, and rewarding the appropriate team behaviors. Let's look at each.

WHAT ROLE DOES SELECTION PLAY? Some individuals already possess the interpersonal skills to be effective team players. When hiring team members, managers should check whether applicants have the technical skills required to successfully perform the job *and* whether they can fulfill team roles.

Some applicants may have been socialized around individual contributions and, consequently, lack team skills, which could also be true for some current employees being moved into teams due to organizational restructuring. When faced with this situation, a manager can do several things. First, and most obvious, if team skills are woefully lacking, don't hire the person. If successful performance is going to require interaction, not hiring the individual is appropriate. On the other hand, an applicant who has some basic skills can be hired on a probationary basis and required to undergo training to shape him or her into a team player. If the skills aren't learned or practiced, then the individual may have to be let go.

CAN INDIVIDUALS BE TRAINED TO BE TEAM PLAYERS? Performing well in a team involves a set of behaviors.[47] As we discussed in the preceding chapter, new behaviors *can* be learned. Even people who feel strongly about the importance of individual accomplishment can be trained to become team players. Training specialists can conduct exercises so employees can experience what teamwork is all about. The workshops can cover such topics as team problem solving, communications, negotiations, conflict resolution, and coaching skills. It's not unusual, too, for these individuals to be exposed to the five stages of team development that we discussed earlier.[48] At Verizon Communications, for example, trainers focus on how a team goes through various stages before it gels. And employees are reminded of the importance of patience, because teams take longer to do some things—such as make decisions—than do employees acting alone.[49]

WHAT ROLE DO REWARDS PLAY IN SHAPING TEAM PLAYERS? An organization's reward system needs to encourage cooperative efforts rather than competitive ones. For instance, Lockheed Martin's aeronautics division organized its some 20,000 employees into teams. Rewards are structured to return a percentage increase in the bottom line to the team members on the basis of achievements of the team's performance goals.

Promotions, pay raises, and other forms of recognition should be given to employees who are effective collaborative team members. Taking this approach doesn't mean that individual contribution is ignored, but rather that it's balanced with selfless contributions to the team. Examples of behaviors that should be rewarded include training new colleagues, sharing information with teammates, helping resolve team conflicts, and mastering new skills in which the team is deficient.[50] Finally, managers can't forget the inherent rewards that employees can receive from teamwork. Work teams provide camaraderie. It's exciting and satisfying to be an integral part of a successful team. The opportunity to engage in personal development and to help teammates grow can be a satisfying and rewarding experience for employees.[51]

WHAT CURRENT ISSUES DO MANAGERS FACE IN MANAGING TEAMS?

Few trends have influenced how work gets done in organizations as much as the use of work teams. The shift from working alone to working on teams requires employees to cooperate with others, share information, confront differences, and sublimate personal interests for the greater good of the team. Managers can build effective teams by understanding what influences performance and satisfaction. However, managers also face some current challenges in managing teams, including those associated with managing global teams and with understanding when teams aren't the answer.

> Discuss contemporary issues in managing teams.
>
> **10.4**

What's Involved with Managing Global Teams?

Two characteristics of today's organizations are obvious: they're global and work is increasingly done by teams. Because of those reasons, any manager is likely to have to manage a global team. What do we know about managing global teams? We know there are both drawbacks and benefits in using global teams (see Exhibit 10–8). What are some of the challenges associated with managing global teams?

HOW DO TEAM COMPOSITION FACTORS AFFECT MANAGING A GLOBAL TEAM? In global organizations, understanding the relationship between team effectiveness and team composition is more challenging because of the unique cultural characteristics represented

---

EXHIBIT 10–8   Global Teams

DRAWBACKS	BENEFITS
• Disliking team members	• Greater diversity of ideas
• Mistrusting team members	• Limited groupthink
• Stereotyping	• Increased attention on understanding others' ideas, perspectives, etc.
• Communication problems	
• Stress and tension	

Source: Based on N. Adler, *International Dimensions of Organizational Behavior*, 4th ed. (Cincinnati, OH: Southwestern Cengage Publishing, 2002), pp 141–147.

by members of a global team. In addition to recognizing team members' abilities, skills, knowledge, and personality, managers need to be familiar with and clearly understand the cultural characteristics of the groups and the group members they manage.[52] For instance, is the global team from a culture in which uncertainty avoidance is high? If so, members will not be comfortable dealing with unpredictable and ambiguous tasks. Also, as managers work with global teams, they need to be aware of the potential for stereotyping, which can lead to problems.

HOW DOES TEAM STRUCTURE AFFECT MANAGING A GLOBAL TEAM? Some of the structural areas where we see differences in managing global teams include conformity, status, social loafing, and cohesiveness.

Are conformity findings generalizable across cultures? Research suggests that Asch's findings are culture-bound.[53] For instance, as might be expected, conformity to social norms tends to be higher in collectivistic cultures than in individualistic cultures. However, groupthink tends to be less of a problem in global teams because members are less likely to feel pressured to conform to the ideas, conclusions, and decisions of the group.[54]

Also, the importance of status varies between cultures. The French, for example, are extremely status conscious. Also, countries differ on the criteria that confer status. For instance, in Latin America and Asia, status tends to come from family position and formal roles held in organizations. In contrast, while status is important in countries like the United States and Australia, it tends to be less "in your face." And it tends to be given based on accomplishments rather than on titles and family history. Managers must understand who and what holds status when interacting with people from a culture different from their own. An American manager who doesn't understand that office size isn't a measure of a Japanese executive's position or who fails to grasp the importance the British place on family genealogy and social class is likely to unintentionally offend others and lessen his or her interpersonal effectiveness.

Social loafing has a Western bias. It's consistent with individualistic cultures, like the United States and Canada, which are dominated by self-interest. It's not consistent with collectivistic societies, in which individuals are motivated by group goals. For instance, in studies comparing employees from the United States with employees from the People's Republic of China and Israel (both collectivistic societies), the Chinese and Israelis showed no propensity to engage in social loafing. In fact, they actually performed better in a group than when working alone.[55]

Cohesiveness is another group structural element that may create special challenges for managers. In a cohesive group, members are unified and "act as one." There's a great deal of camaraderie and group identity is high. In global teams, however, cohesiveness is often more difficult to achieve because of higher levels of "mistrust, miscommunication, and stress."[56]

HOW DO TEAM PROCESSES AFFECT MANAGING A GLOBAL TEAM? The processes that global teams use to do their work can be particularly challenging for managers. For one thing, communication issues often arise because not all team members may be fluent in the team's working language, which can lead to inaccuracies, misunderstandings, and inefficiencies.[57] However, research has also shown that a multicultural global team is better able to capitalize on the diversity of ideas represented if a wide range of information is used.[58]

Managing conflict in global teams isn't easy, especially when those teams are virtual teams. Conflict can interfere with how information is used by the team. However, research shows that in collectivistic cultures, a collaborative conflict management style can be most effective.[59]

The International Atomic Energy Agency and the government of Japan created an 18-member global team to study the Fukushima nuclear power station accident triggered by the 2011 earthquake in Japan. Comprised of experts with experience across a range of nuclear specialties, the team members came from 12 countries: Argentina, China, France, Hungary, India, Indonesia, Russia, South Korea, Spain, Turkey, the United Kingdom, and the United States. Using a global team brought a greater diversity of ideas to the team's mission of identifying lessons learned from the accident that can help improve nuclear safety around the world. In this photo the team begins its investigation by touring the crippled nuclear power plant.

TEPCO/Newscom

When Are Teams Not the Answer?

Teamwork takes more time and often more resources than does individual work.[60] Teams require managers to communicate more, manage conflicts, and run meetings. So, the benefits of using teams need to exceed the costs. And that's not always the case![61] In the rush to use teams, some managers have introduced them into situations in which it would have been better to have individuals do the work. So before implementing teams just because everyone's talking about their popularity, you should carefully evaluate whether the work requires or will benefit from a collective effort.

How do you know whether work is better done individually or by a group? Three "tests" have been suggested.[62] First, can the work be done better by more than one person? Task complexity would be a good indicator of a need for different perspectives. Simple tasks that don't require diverse input are probably better done by individuals. Second, does the work create a common purpose or set of goals for the people in the group that's more than the sum of individual goals? For instance, many car dealerships use teams to link customer-service personnel, mechanics, parts specialists, and sales representatives. Such teams can better meet the goal of outstanding customer satisfaction. The final test to assess whether teams or individuals are better suited for doing work is to look at the interdependence of the individuals. Using teams makes sense when there's interdependence between tasks; that is, when the success of everyone depends on the success of each person *and* the success of each person depends on the others. For example, soccer is an obvious team sport. Success requires a lot of coordination between interdependent players. On the other hand, swim teams aren't really teams, except on relays. They're groups of individuals, performing individually, whose total performance is merely the sum of their individual performances.

10 Review

CHAPTER SUMMARY

10.1 Define group and describe the stages of group development. A group is two or more interacting and interdependent individuals who come together to achieve specific goals. Formal groups are work groups that are defined by the organization's structure and have designated work assignments and specific tasks directed at accomplishing organizational goals. Informal groups are social groups.

The forming stage consists of two phases: joining the group and defining the group's purpose, structure, and leadership. The storming stage is one of intra-group conflict over who will control the group and what the group will be doing. The norming stage is when close relationships and cohesiveness develop as norms are determined. The performing stage is when group members work on the group's task. The adjourning stage happens when the group prepares to disband.

10.2 Describe the major concepts of group behavior. A role refers to a set of behavior patterns expected of someone occupying a given position in a social unit. At any given time, employees adjust their role behaviors to the group of which they are a part. Norms are standards shared by group members. They informally convey to employees which behaviors are acceptable and which are unacceptable. Status is another factor to know because it can be a significant motivator and it needs to be congruent. Also, group size affects group behavior in a number of ways. Smaller groups are generally faster at completing tasks than are larger ones. However, larger groups are frequently better at fact finding because of their diversified input. As a result, larger groups are generally better at problem solving. Finally, group cohesiveness is important because of its impact on a group's effectiveness at achieving its goals.

10.3 Discuss how groups are turned into effective teams. Effective teams have common characteristics. They have adequate resources, effective leadership, a climate of trust, and a performance evaluation and reward system that reflects team contributions. These teams have individuals with technical expertise as well as problem-solving, decision-making, and interpersonal skills and the right traits, especially conscientiousness and openness to new experiences. Effective teams also tend to be small, preferably of diverse backgrounds. They have members who fill role demands and who prefer to be part of a team. And the work that members do provides freedom and autonomy, the opportunity to use different skills and talents, the ability to complete a whole and identifiable task or product, and work that has a substantial impact on others. Finally, effective teams have members who believe in the team's capabilities and are committed to a common plan and purpose, specific team goals, a manageable level of conflict, and a minimal degree of social loafing.

10.4 Discuss contemporary issues in managing teams. The challenges of managing global teams can be seen in team composition factors, especially the diverse cultural characteristics; in team structure, especially conformity, status, social loafing, and cohesiveness; and in team processes, especially with communication and managing conflict; and in the manager's role in making it all work.

Managers also need to know when teams are not the answer. They can do this by assessing whether the work can be done better by more than one person; by whether the work creates a common purpose or set of goals for the members of the team; and by the amount of interdependence among team members.

MyManagementLab For more resources, please visit **www.mymanagementlab.com**

UNDERSTANDING THE CHAPTER

1. Think of a group to which you belong (or have belonged). Trace its development through the stages of group development as shown in Exhibit 10–2. How closely did its development parallel the group development model? How might the group development model be used to improve this group's effectiveness?

2. Contrast (a) self-managed and cross-functional teams, and (b) virtual and face-to-face teams.

3. How do you explain the popularity of work teams in countries such as the United States and Canada, whose national cultures place a high value on individualism?

4. "All work teams are work groups, but not all work groups are work teams." Do you agree or disagree with this statement? Discuss.

5. Would you prefer to work alone or as part of a team? Why?

6. "To have a successful team, first find a great leader." What do you think of this statement? Do you agree? Why or why not?

7. What traits do you think good team players have? Do some research to answer this question and write a short report detailing your findings using a bulleted list format.

8. Contrast the pros and cons of diverse teams.

9. How do you think scientific management theorists would react to the increased use of teams in organizations? How would behavioral science theorists react?

10. What challenges do managers face in managing global teams? How should those challenges be handled?

Go to p. 436

YOUR TURN TO BE **A MANAGER** for Chapter 10.

Endnotes

1. J. Terzakis, "Virtual Retrospectives for Geographically Dispersed Software Teams," *IEEE Computer Society,* May–June 2011, pp. 12–15; "Virtual Teams Must Function Correctly," *Strategic Direction,* April 2011, pp. 22–24; C. Scovotti and L. D. Spiller, "Cross-Border Student Collaborations: Opportunities for Videoconferencing," *Marketing Education Review,* Spring 2011, pp. 57–61; E. Markowitz, "Are the Best Leaders Revolutionaries?" *Inc. Online,* March 28, 2011; L. J. Gressgård, "Virtual Team Collaboration and Innovation in Organizations," *Team Performance Management,* March 2011, pp. 102–119; L. Tischler, "Intel's Virtual Footwear Wall for Adidas Turns Boutiques into Shoe-Topias," *Fast Company Online,* January 11, 2011; A. Gupta, S. Seshasai, R. Aron, and S. Pareek, "The 24-Hour Knowledge Factory: Work and Organizational Redesign and Associated Challenges," *Information Resources Management Journal* (October–December 2010), pp. 40–56; M. R. Haas, "The Double-Edged Swords of Autonomy and External Knowledge: Analyzing Team Effectiveness in a Multinational Organization," *Academy of Management Journal* (October 2010), pp. 989–1008; O. Coren, "Israel Offers Intel $110 Million for Commitment to Stay in the Country," *Haaretz.com,* August 26, 2010; M. B. O'Leary, "Go (Con)figure: Subgroups, Imbalance, and Isolates in Geographically Dispersed Teams," *Organization Science,* January–February 2010, pp. 115–131; and R. R. Nelson, "Project Retrospectives: Evaluating Project Success, Failure, and Everything In Between," *MIS Quarterly Executive,* September 2005, pp. 361–372.

2. B. Mezrich, *Bringing Down the House: The Inside Story of Six MIT Students Who Took Vegas for Millions* (New York: Free Press, 2002). The 2008 film *21* was a fictional work based loosely on the story.

3. B. W. Tuckman and M. C. Jensen, "Stages of Small-Group Development Revisited," *Group and Organizational Studies,* December 1977, pp. 419–427; and M. F. Maples, "Group Development: Extending Tuckman's Theory," *Journal for Specialists in Group Work* (Fall 1988), pp. 17–23.

4. And the Survey Says box based on J. Yang and P. Trap, "As a Manager, It's Most Challenging to . . . ," *USA Today,* April 19, 2011, p. 1B; J. Yang and K. Gelles, "Workplace Friendships," *USA Today,* April 13, 2010, p. 1B; K. Merriman, "Low-Trust Teams Prefer Individualized Pay," *Harvard Business Review,* November 2008, p. 32; B. J. West, J. L. Patera, and M. K. Carsten, "Team Level Positivity: Investigating Positive Psychological Capacities and Team Level Outcomes," *Journal of Organizational Behavior* (February 2009), p. 249; J. Yang and K. Simmons, "Traits of Good Team Players," *USA Today,* November 21, 2007, p. 1B; J. Yang and M. E. Mullins, "Workers More Productive in Small Groups," *USA Today,* January 10, 2007, p. 1B; and M. Weinstein, "Coming Up Short? Join the Club," *Training* (April 2006), p. 14.

5. L. N. Jewell and H. J. Reitz, *Group Effectiveness in Organizations* (Glenview, IL: Scott, Foresman, 1981); and M. Kaeter, "Repotting Mature Work Teams," *Training* (April 1994), pp. 54–56.

6. Right or Wrong box based on K. McCullum, "Hush, Hush," *OfficePro,* March–April 2011, pp. 18–22; and E. Bernstein, "You Did *What?* Spare the Office the Details," *Wall Street Journal*, April 6, 2010, pp. D1+.

7. From the Past to the Present box based on S. S. Wang, "Under the Influence: How the Group Changes What We Think," *Wall Street Journal*, May 3, 2011, pp. D1+; M. E. Shaw, *Group Dynamics: The Psychology of Small Group Behavior* (New York: McGraw-Hill, 1975); and E. J. Thomas and C. F. Fink, "Effects of Group Size," *Psychological Bulletin* (July 1963), pp. 371–384.

8. S. E. Asch, "Effects of Group Pressure upon the Modification and Distortion of Judgments," in H. Guetzkow (ed.), *Groups, Leadership, and Men* (Pittsburgh, PA: Carnegie Press, 1951), pp. 177–190.

9. Asch, "Effects of Group Pressure upon the Modification and Distortion of Judgments."

10. O. A. Alnuaimi, L. P. Robert Jr., and L. M. Maruping, "Team Size, Dispersion, and Social Loafing in Technology-Supported Teams: A Perspective on the Theory of Moral Disengagement," *Journal of Management Information Systems* (Summer 2010), pp. 203–230; C. Cheshire and J. Antin, "None of Us Is As Lazy As All of Us," *Information, Communication & Society,* June 2010, pp. 537–555; R. van Dick, J. Stellmacher, U. Wagner, G. Lemmer, and P. A. Tissington, "Group Membership Salience and Task Performance," *Journal of Managerial Psychology* 24, no. 7 (2009), pp. 609–626; A. Jassawalla, H. Sashittal, and A. Malshe, "Students' Perceptions of Social Loafing: Its Antecedents and Consequences in Undergraduate Business Classroom Teams," *Academy of Management Learning & Education,* March 2009, pp. 42–54; and R. Albanese and D. D. Van Fleet, "Rational Behavior in Groups: The Free Riding Tendency," *Academy of Management Review*, April 1985, pp. 244–255.

11. L. Berkowitz, "Group Standards, Cohesiveness, and Productivity," *Human Relations* November 1954, pp. 509–519.

12. See, for example, R. A. Henry, J. Kmet, and A. Landa, "Examining the Impact of Interpersonal Cohesiveness on Group Accuracy Interventions: the Importance of Matching Versus Buffering," *Organizational Behavior and Human Decision Processes* (January 2002), pp. 25–43.

13. Cited in T. Purdum, "Teaming, Take 2," *Industry Week,* May 2005, p. 43; and C. Joinson, "Teams at Work," *HR Magazine,* May 1999, p. 30.

14. See, for example, S. A. Mohrman, S. G. Cohen, and A. M. Mohrman, Jr., *Designing Team-Based Organizations* (San Francisco: Jossey-Bass, 1995); P. MacMillan, *The Performance Factor: Unlocking the Secrets of Teamwork* (Nashville, TN: Broadman & Holman, 2001); and E. Salas, C. A. Bowers, and E. Eden (eds.), *Improving Teamwork in Organizations: Applications of Resource Management Training* (Mahwah, NJ: Lawrence Erlbaum, 2002).

15. Information for this section is based on J. R. Katzenbach and D. K. Smith, *The Wisdom of Teams* (Boston: Harvard Business School Press, 1993), pp. 21, 45, 85; and D. C. Kinlaw, *Developing Superior Work Teams* (Lexington, MA: Lexington Books, 1991), pp. 3–21.

16. S. Adams and L. Kydoniefs, "Making Teams Work: Bureau of Labor Statistics Learns What Works and What Doesn't," *Quality Progress* (January 2000), pp. 43–49.

17. D. Hoffman, "At Wachovia, Fund Teams Work: Bank's Buddy System Improves Performance," *Investment News* (February 2001), p. 8.

18. T. Capozzoli, "How to Succeed with Self-Directed Work Teams," *Supervision* (February 2002), pp. 25–27.

19. See, for instance, E. Sunstrom, DeMeuse, and D. Futrell, "Work Teams: Applications and Effectiveness," *American Psychologist,* February 1990, pp. 120–133.

20. J. S. McClenahen, "Bearing Necessities," *Industry Week,* October 2004, pp. 63–65; P. J. Kiger, "Acxiom Rebuilds from Scratch," *Workforce,* December 2002, pp. 52–55; and T. Boles, "Viewpoint—Leadership Lessons from NASCAR," *Industry Week,* www.industryweek.com (May 21, 2002).

21. M. Cianni and D. Wanuck, "Individual Growth and Team Enhancement: Moving Toward a New Model of Career Development," *Academy of Management Executive*, February 1997, pp. 105–115.

22. C. Joinson, "Teams at Work," p. 30; and "Teams," *Training* (October 1996), p. 69.

23. J. P. Millikin, P. W. Hom, and C. C. Manz, "Self-Management Competencies in Self-Managing Teams: Their Impact on Multi-Team System Productivity," *Leadership Quarterly,* October 2010, pp. 687–702; O. Turel and Y. Zhang, "Does Virtual Team Composition Matter? Trait and Problem-Solving Configuration Effects on Team Performance," *Behavior & Information Technology,* July–August 2010, pp. 363–375; J. S. Bunderson and P. Boumgarden, "Structure and Learning in Self-Managed Teams: Why 'Bureaucratic' Teams Can Be Better Learners," *Organization Science,* May–June 2010, pp. 609–624; and G. M. Spreitzer, S. G. Cohen, and G. E. Ledford, Jr., "Developing Effective Self-Managing Work Teams in Service Organizations," *Group & Organization Management*, September 1999, pp. 340–366.

24. "Meet the New Steel," *Fortune,* October 1, 2007, pp. 68–71.

25. J. Appleby and R. Davis, "Teamwork Used to Save Money; Now It Saves Lives," *USA Today,* www.usatoday.com (March 1, 2001).

26. A. Malhotra, A. Majchrzak, R. Carman, and V. Lott, "Radical Innovation without Collocation: A Case Study at Boeing-Rocketdyne," *MIS Quarterly,* June 2001, pp. 229–249.

27. A. Stuart, "Virtual Agreement," *CFO,* November 2007, p. 24.

28. Technology and the Manager's Job box based on "Virtual Team Collaboration and Innovation in Organizations," *Team Performance Management*, March 2011, pp. 109–119; M. Flammia, Y. Cleary, and D. M. Slattery, "Leadership Roles, Socioemotional Strategies, and Technology Use of Irish and US Students in Virtual Teams," *IEEE Transactions on Professional Communication,* June 2010, pp. 89–101; P. Evans, "The Wiki Factor," *BizEd,* January–February 2006, pp. 28–32; and M. McCafferty, "A Human Inventory," *CFO,* April 2005, pp. 83–85.

29. "Virtual Team Collaboration and Innovation in Organizations"; M. Flammia, Y. Cleary, and D. M. Slattery, "Leadership Roles, Socioemotional Strategies, and Technology Use of Irish and U.S. Students in Virtual Teams"; A. Malhotra, A. Majchrzak, and B. Rosen, "Leading Virtual Teams," *Academy of Management Perspectives,* February 2007, pp. 60–70; B. L. Kirkman and J. E. Mathieu, "The Dimensions and Antecedents of Team Virtuality," *Journal of Management* (October 2005), pp. 700–718; J. Gordon, "Do Your Virtual Teams Deliver Only Virtual Performance?" *Training* (June 2005), pp. 20–25; L. L. Martins, L. L. Gilson, and M. T. Maynard, "Virtual Teams: What Do We Know and Where Do We Go from Here?" *Journal of Management* (December 2004), pp. 805–835; S. A. Furst, M. Reeves, B. Rosen, and R. S. Blackburn,

"Managing he Life Cycle of Virtual Teams," *Academy of Management Executive,* May 2004, pp. 6–20; B. L. Kirkman, B. Rosen, P. E. Tesluk, and C. B. Gibson, "The Impact of Team Empowerment on Virtual Team Performance: The Moderating Role of Face-to-Face Interaction," *Academy of Management Journal* (April 2004), pp. 175–192; F. Keenan and S. E. Ante, "The New Teamwork," *Business Week e.biz,* February 18, 2002, pp. EB12–EB16; and G. Imperato, "Real Tools for Virtual Teams," *Fast Company*, July 2000, pp. 378–387.

30. See, for instance, D. C. Jones and T. Kato, "The Impact of Teams on Output, Quality, and Downtime: An Empirical Analysis Using Individual Panel Data," *Industrial and Labor Relations Review,* January 2011, pp. 215–240; A. Gilley, J. W. Gilley, C. W. McConnell, and A. Veliquette, "The Competencies Used by Effective Managers to Build Teams: An Empirical Study," *Advances in Developing Human Resources,* February 2010, pp. 29–45; M. A. Campion, G. J. Medsker, and C. A. Higgs, "Relations Between Work Group Characteristics and Effectiveness: Implications for Designing Effective Work Groups," *Personnel Psychology,* Winter 1993, pp. 823–850; and J. R. Hackman, "The Design of Work Teams," in J. W. Lorsch (ed.), *Handbook of Organizational Behavior* (Upper Saddle River, NJ: Prentice Hall, 1987), pp. 315–342.

31. This model is based on M. A. Campion, E. M. Papper, and G. J. Medsker, "Relations Between Work Team Characteristics and Effectiveness: A Replication and Extension," *Personnel Psychology,* Summer 1996, pp. 429–452; D. E. Hyatt and T. M. Ruddy, "An Examination of the Relationship Between Work Group Characteristics and Performance: Once More into the Breech," *Personnel Psychology,* Autumn 1997, pp. 553–585; S. G. Cohen and D. E. Bailey, "What Makes Teams Work: Group Effectiveness Research from the Shop Floor to the Executive Suite," *Journal of Management* (September 1997), pp. 239–290; L. Thompson, *Making the Team* (Upper Saddle River, NJ: Prentice Hall, 2000), pp. 18–33; and J. R. Hackman, *Leading Teams: Setting the Stage for Great Performance* (Boston: Harvard Business School Press, 2002).

32. See M. Mattson, T. V. Mumford, and G. S. Sintay, "Taking Teams to Task: A Normative Model for Designing or Recalibrating Work Teams," paper presented at the National Academy of Management Conference, Chicago, August 1999; and G. L. Stewart and M. R. Barrick, "Team Structure and Performance: Assessing the Mediating Role of Intrateam Process and the Moderating Role of Task Type," *Academy of Management Journal* (April 2000), pp. 135–148.

33. R. I. Sutton, "The Boss as Human Shield," *Harvard Business Review,* September 2010, pp. 106–109; and Hyatt and Ruddy, "An Examination of the Relationship Between Work Group Characteristics and Performance," p. 577.

34. M. E. Palanski, S. S. Kahai, and F. J. Yammarino, "Team Virtues and Performance: An Examination of Transparency, Behavioral Integrity, and Trust," *Journal of Business Ethics* (March 2011), pp. 201–216; H. H. Chang, S. S. Chuang, and S. H. Chao, "Determinants of Cultural Adaptation, Communication Quality, and Trust in Virtual Teams' Performance," *Total Quality Management and Business Excellence,* March 2011, pp. 305–329; A. C. Costa and N. Anderson, "Measuring Trust in Teams: Development and Validation of a Multifaceted Measure of Formative and Reflective Indicators of Team Trust," *European Journal of Work & Organizational Psychology* (February 2011), pp. 119–154; M. Mach, S. Dolan, and S. Tzafrir,

"The Differential Effect of Team Members' Trust on Team Performance: The Mediation Role of Team Cohesion," *Journal of Occupational and Organizational Psychology* (September 2010), pp. 771–794; B. A. DeJong and T. Elfring, "How Does Trust Affect the Performance of Ongoing Teams? The Mediating Role of Reflexivity, Monitoring, and Effort," *Academy of Management Journal* (June 2010), pp. 535–549; M. Williams, "In Whom We Trust: Group Membership as an Affective Context for Trust Development," *Academy of Management Review,* July 2001, pp. 377–396; and K. T. Dirks, "Trust in Leadership and Team Performance: Evidence from NCAA Basketball," *Journal of Applied Psychology* (December 2000), pp. 1004–1012.

35. R. R. Hirschfeld, M. J. Jordan, H. S. Field, W. F. Giles, and A. A. Armenakis, "Becoming Team Players: Team Members' Mastery of Team Knowledge as a Predictor of Team Task Proficiency and Observed Teamwork Effectiveness," *Journal of Applied Psychology* 91, no. 2 (2006), pp. 467–474.

36. S. T. Bell, "Deep-Level Composition Variables as Predictors of Team Performance: A Meta-Analysis," *Journal of Applied Psychology* 92, no. 3 (2007), pp. 595–615; and M. R. Barrick, G. L. Stewart, M. J. Neubert, and M. K. Mount, "Relating Member Ability and Personality to Work-Team Processes and Team Effectiveness," *Journal of Applied Psychology* (June 1998), pp. 377–391.

37. M. Costello, "Team Weaver," *People Management*, January 2011, pp. 26–27; and C. Margerison and D. McCann, *Team Management: Practical New Approaches* (London: Mercury Books, 1990).

38. K. H. T. Yu and D. M. Cable, "Unpacking Cooperation in Diverse Teams," *Team Performance Management*, March 2011, pp. 63–82; A. Nederveen Pieterse, D. van Knippenberg, and W. P. van Ginkel, "Diversity in Goal Orientation, Team Reflexivity, and Team Performance," *Organizational Behavior and Human Performance,* March 2011, pp. 153–164; M.-E. Roberge and R. van Dick, "Recognizing the Benefits of Diversity: When and How Does Diversity Increase Group Performance," *Human Resource Management Review,* December 2010, pp. 295–208; and E. Mannix and M. A. Neale, "What Differences Make a Difference: The Promise and Reality of Diverse Teams in Organizations," *Psychological Science in the Public Interest,* October 2005, pp. 31–55.

39. A. Deutschman, "Inside the Mind of Jeff Bezos," *Fast Company,* August 2004, pp. 50–58.

40. Hyatt and Ruddy, "An Examination of the Relationship Between Work Group Characteristics and Performance"; J. D. Shaw, M. K. Duffy, and E. M. Stark, "Interdependence and Preference for Group Work: Main and Congruence Effects on the Satisfaction and Performance of Group Members," *Journal of Management* (June 2000), pp. 259–279; and S. A. Kiffin-Peterson and J. L. Cordery, "Trust, Individualism, and Job Characteristics of Employee Preference for Teamwork," *International Journal of Human Resource Management* (February 2003), pp. 93–116.

41. J. S. Bunderson and P. Boumgarden, "Structure and Learning in Self-Managed Teams: Why 'Bureaucratic' Teams Can Be Better Learners"; and R. Wageman, "Critical Success Factors for Creating Superb Self-Managing Teams," *Organizational Dynamics,* Summer 1997, p. 55.

42. Campion, Papper, and Medsker, "Relations Between Work Team Characteristics and Effectiveness," p. 430; B. L. Kirkman and B. Rosen, "Powering Up Teams," *Organizational Dynamics,* Winter 2000, pp. 48–66; and D. C. Man and S. S. K. Lam, "The

Effects of Job Complexity and Autonomy on Cohesiveness in Collectivist and Individualist Work Groups: A Cross-Cultural Analysis," *Journal of Organizational Behavior* (December 2003), pp. 979–1001.

43. A. Mehta, H. Feild, A. Armenakis, and N. Mehta, "Team Goal Orientation and Team Performance: The Mediating Role of Team Planning," *Journal of Management* (August 2009), pp. 1026–1046; K. Blanchard, D. Carew, and E. Parisi-Carew, "How to Get Your Group to Perform Like a Team," *Training and Development* (September 1996), pp. 34–37; K. D. Scott and A. Townsend, "Teams: Why Some Succeed and Others Fail," *HR Magazine,* August 1994, pp. 62–67; and K. Hess, *Creating the High-Performance Team* (New York: Wiley, 1987); Katzenbach and Smith, *The Wisdom of Teams,* pp. 43–64.

44. H. van Emmerik, I. M. Jawahar, B. Schreurs, and N. de Cuyper, "Social Capital, Team Efficacy and Team Potency: The Mediating Role of Team Learning Behaviors," *Career Development International* (February 2011), pp. 82–99; T. Lewis, "Assessing Social Identity and Collective Efficacy as Theories of Group Motivation at Work," *International Journal of Human Resource Management* (February 2011), pp. 963–980; K. Tasa, G. J. Sears, and A. C. H. Schat, "Personality and Teamwork Behavior in Context: The Cross-Level Moderating Role of Collective Efficacy," *Journal of Organizational Behavior* (January 2011), pp. 65–85; J. A. Goncalo, E. Polman, and C. Maslach, "Can Confidence Come Too Soon? Collective Efficacy, Conflict and Group Performance Over Time," *Organizational Behavior & Human Decision Processes,* September 2010, pp. 13–24; K. Tasa, S. Taggar, and G. H. Seijts, "The Development of Collective Efficacy in Teams: A Multilevel and Longitudinal Perspective," *Journal of Applied Psychology* (January 2007), pp. 17–27; C. B. Gibson, "The Efficacy Advantage: Factors Related to the Formation of Group Efficacy," *Journal of Applied Social Psychology* (October 2003), pp. 2153–2186; and D. I. Jung and J. J. Sosik, "Group Potency and Collective Efficacy: Examining Their Predictive Validity, Level of Analysis, and Effects of Performance Feedback on Future Group Performance," *Group & Organization Management,* September 2003, pp. 366–391.

45. K. C. Kostopoulos and N. Bozionelos, "Team Exploratory and Exploitative Learning: Psychological Safety, Task Conflict, and Team Performance," *Group & Organization Management,* June 2011, pp. 385–415; K. J. Behfar, E. A. Mannix, R. S. Peterson, and W. M. Trochim, "Conflict in Small Groups: The Meaning and Consequences of Process Conflict," *Small Group Research,* April 2011, pp. 127–176; R. S. Peterson and K. J. Behfar, "The Dynamic Relationship Between Performance Feedback, Trust, and Conflict in Groups: A Longitudinal Study," *Organizational Behavior and Human Decision Processes,"* September–November 2003, pp. 102–112; and K. A. Jehn, "A Qualitative Analysis of Conflict Types and Dimensions in Organizational Groups," *Administrative Science Quarterly,* September 1997, pp. 530–557.

46. O. A. Alnuaimi, L. P. Robert Jr., and L. M. Maruping, "Team Size, Dispersion, and Social Loafing in Technology-Supported Teams: A Perspective on the Theory of Moral Disengagement"; C. Cheshire and J. Antin, "None of Us Is As Lazy As All of Us"; R. van Dick, J. Stellmacher, U. Wagner, G. Lemmer, and P. A. Tissington, "Group Membership Salience and Task Performance"; A. Jassawalla, H. Sashittal, and A. Malshe, "Students' Perceptions of Social Loafing: Its Antecedents and Consequences in Undergraduate Business Classroom Teams";

K. H. Price, D. A. Harrison, and J. H. Gavin, "Withholding Inputs in Team Contexts: Member Composition, Interaction Processes, Evaluation Structure, and Social Loafing," *Journal of Applied Psychology* (December 2006), pp. 1375–1384; and R. Albanese and D. D. Van Fleet, "Rational Behavior in Groups: The Free Riding Tendency," *Academy of Management Review,* April 1985, pp. 244–255.

47. "Helping Hands," *HR Magazine,* May 2011, p. 18; M. O'Neil, "Leading the Team," *Supervision,* April 2011, pp. 8–10; J. Beeson, "Build a Strong Team," *Leadership Excellence,* February 2011, p. 15; S. Brutus and M. B. L. Donia, "Improving the Effectiveness of Students in Groups With a Centralized Peer Evaluation System," *Academy of Management Learning & Education,* December 2010, pp. 652–662; and N. H. Woodward, "Make the Most of Team Building," *HR Magazine,* September 2006, pp. 73–76.

48. R. M. Yandrick, "A Team Effort," *HR Magazine,* June 2001, pp. 136–141.

49. Ibid.

50. "How Should We Recognize Team Goals Over Individual?" *Workforce Management Online,* February 2011; S. J. Goerg, S. Kube, and R. Zultan, "Treating Equals Unequally: Incentives in Teams, Workers' Motivation, and Production Technology," *Journal of Labor Economics* (October 2010), pp. 747–772; T. Taylor, "The Challenge of Project Team Incentives," *Compensation & Benefits Review,* September–October 2010, pp. 411–419; M. J. Pearsall, M. S. Christian, and A. P. J. Ellis, "Motivating Interdependent Teams: Individual Rewards, Shared Rewards, or Something in Between?" *Journal of Applied Psychology* (January 2010), pp. 183–191; M. A. Marks, C. S. Burke, M. J. Sabella, and S. J. Zaccaro, "The Impact of Cross-Training on Team Effectiveness," *Journal of Applied Psychology* (February 2000), pp. 3–14; and M. A. Marks, S. J. Zaccaro, and J. E. Mathieu, "Performance Implications of Leader Briefings and Team Interaction for Team Adaptation to Novel Environments," *Journal of Applied Psychology* (December 2000), p. 971.

51. C. Garvey, "Steer Teams with the Right Pay: Team-Based Pay Is a Success When It Fits Corporate Goals and Culture, and Rewards the Right Behavior," *HR Magazine,* May 2002, pp. 71–77.

52. F. Niederman and F. B. Tan, "Emerging Markets Managing Global IT Teams: Considering Cultural Dynamics," *Communications of the ACM,* April 2011, pp. 24–27; R. M. B. Boyle and S. Nicholas, "Cross-Cultural Group Performance," *The Learning Organization,* March 2011, pp. 94–101; G. K. Stahl, M. L. Maznevski, A. Voigt, and K. Jonsen, "Unraveling the Effects of Cultural Diversity in Teams: A Meta-Analysis of Research on Multicultural Work Groups," *Journal of International Business Studies* (May 2010), pp. 690–709; and M. R. Haas, "The Double-Edged Sword of Autonomy and External Knowledge: Analyzing Team Effectiveness in a Multinational Organization."

53. R. Bond and P. B. Smith, "Culture and Conformity: A Meta-Analysis of Studies Using Asch's [1952, 1956] Line Judgment Task," *Psychological Bulletin,* January 1996, pp. 111–137.

54. I. L. Janis, *Groupthink,* 2nd ed. (New York: Houghton Mifflin Company, 1982), p. 175.

55. See P. C. Earley, "Social Loafing and Collectivism: A Comparison of the United States and the People's Republic of China," *Administrative Science Quarterly,* December 1989, pp. 565–581; and P. C. Earley, "East Meets West Meets

Mideast: Further Explorations of Collectivistic and Individualistic Work Groups," *Academy of Management Journal* (April 1993), pp. 319–348.

56. N. J. Adler, *International Dimensions of Organizational Behavior,* 4th ed. (Cincinnati, OH: Southwestern, 2002), p. 142.

57. K. B. Dahlin, L. R. Weingart, and P. J. Hinds, "Team Diversity and Information Use," *Academy of Management Journal* (December 2005), pp. 1107–1123.

58. Adler, *International Dimensions of Organizational Behavior,* p. 142.

59. S. Paul, I. M. Samarah, P. Seetharaman, and P. P. Mykytyn, "An Empirical Investigation of Collaborative Conflict Management Style in Group Support System-Based Global Virtual Teams," *Journal of Management Information Systems* (Winter 2005), pp. 185–222.

60. This section is based on S. P. Robbins and T. A. Judge, *Organizational Behavior,* 14th ed. (Upper Saddle River, NJ: Pearson Prentice Hall, 2011).

61. C. E. Naquin and R. O. Tynan, "The Team Halo Effect: Why Teams Are Not Blamed for Their Failures," *Journal of Applied Psychology* (April 2003), pp. 332–340.

62. A. B. Drexler and R. Forrester, "Teamwork—Not Necessarily the Answer," *HRMagazine,* January 1998, pp. 55–58. See also R. Saavedra, P. C. Earley, and L. Van Dyne, "Complex Interdependence in Task-Performing Groups," *Journal of Applied Psychology* (February 1993), pp. 61–72; and K. A. Jehn, G. B. Northcraft, and M. A. Neale, "Why Differences Make a Difference: A Field Study of Diversity, Conflict, and Performance in Work Groups," *Administrative Science Quarterly,* December 1999, pp. 741–763.

CHAPTER 11

Motivating and Rewarding Employees

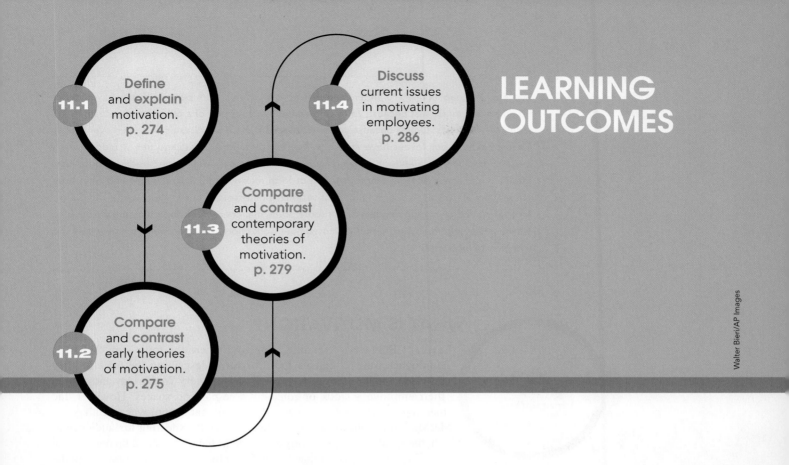

Walter Bieri/AP Images

Searching For?

Google gets more than 3,000 job applications a day.[1] And it's no wonder! With a massage every other week, onsite laundry, swimming pool and spa, free delicious all-you-can-eat gourmet meals, and fun diversions like a huge slide in the workplace, what more could an employee want? Sounds like an ideal job, doesn't it? However, many people are demonstrating by their decisions to leave the company that all those perks (and these are just a few) aren't enough to keep them there.

Google is number one on the list of "ideal" employers and has been in the top five of *Fortune*'s list of "best companies to work for" for five years running and was number one on the list for two of those years. But make no mistake, Google's executives offer these fabulous perks for several reasons: to attract the best knowledge workers it can in an intensely competitive, cutthroat market; to help employees work long hours and not have to deal with time-consuming personal chores; to show employees they're valued; and to have employees remain Googlers (the name used for employees) for many years. Yet, employees continue to jump ship. As one analyst said, "Yes, Google's making gobs of money. Yes, it's full of smart people. Yes, it's a wonderful place to work. So why are so many people leaving?"

Successful managers need to understand that what motivates them personally may have little or no effect on others. Just because you're motivated by being part of a cohesive work team, don't assume everyone is. Or just because you're motivated by your job doesn't mean that everyone is. Or just because employees have access to free food, free massages, and free laundry doesn't mean those extras are enough to keep them from looking elsewhere for career opportunities. Effective managers who get employees to put forth maximum effort know how and why those employees are motivated and tailor motivational practices to satisfy their needs and wants. Motivating and rewarding employees are some of the manager's most important and challenging activities. To get employees to put forth maximum work effort, managers need to know how and why they're motivated.

WHAT IS MOTIVATION?

11.1 Define and **explain** motivation.

Several CEOs were attending a meeting where the topic was "What do employees want?"[2] Each CEO took turns describing the benefits they provided and how they gave out free M&Ms every Wednesday and offered their employees stock options and free parking spaces. However, the meeting's main speaker made the point that "employees don't want M&Ms; they want to love what they do." Half expecting his audience to laugh, the speaker was pleasantly surprised as the CEOs stood up one-by-one to agree. They all recognized that "the value in their companies comes from the employees who are motivated to be there."

These CEOs understand how important employee motivation is. Like them, all managers need to be able to motivate their employees, which requires understanding what motivation is. Let's begin by pointing out what motivation is not. Why? Because many people incorrectly view motivation as a personal trait; that is, they think some people are motivated and others aren't. Our knowledge of motivation tells us that we can't label people that way because individuals differ in motivational drive and their overall motivation varies from situation to situation. For instance, you're probably more motivated to work hard and do well in some classes than in others.

Motivation refers to the process by which a person's efforts are energized, directed, and sustained toward attaining a goal.[3] This definition has three key elements: energy, direction, and persistence.[4]

The *energy* element is a measure of intensity or drive. A motivated person puts forth effort and works hard. However, the quality of the effort must be considered as well as its intensity. High levels of effort don't necessarily lead to favorable job performance unless the effort is channeled in a *direction* that benefits the organization. Effort that's directed toward, and consistent with, organizational goals is the kind of effort we want from employees. Finally, motivation includes a *persistence* dimension. We want employees to persist in putting forth effort to achieve those goals.

Motivating high levels of employee performance is an important organizational concern and managers keep looking for answers. For instance, a Gallup poll found that a large majority of U.S. employees—some 73 percent—are not excited about their work. As the researchers stated, "These employees are essentially 'checked out.' They're sleepwalking through their workday, putting time, but not energy or passion, into their work."[6] It's no wonder then that both managers and academics want to understand and explain employee motivation.

AND THE SURVEY SAYS...[5]

67 percent of employees say that their manager acknowledges and appreciates them at work.

21 percent of employees cite job security as the most important thing about their job.

54 percent of employees say that their colleagues are the ones who appreciate them the most at work.

70 percent of employees say that their relationship with their manager is important to how engaged they are with their work.

47 percent of employees say that their employer provides no forms of motivation.

50 percent of employees say that the perk they'd most like from their employer is free soda or water.

WHAT DO THE EARLY THEORIES OF MOTIVATION SAY?

Compare and **contrast** early theories of motivation.

11.2

The 1950s and 1960s were a fruitful time for the development of motivation concepts. Four specific theories formulated during this period are probably still the best-known explanations of employee motivation although they've been criticized and questioned. They include the hierarchy of needs theory, Theories X and Y, the two-factor theory, and three-needs theory. Although more valid explanations of motivation have been developed, you should know these early theories for at least two reasons. First, they represent the foundation from which contemporary theories grew. Second, practicing managers regularly use these theories and their terminology in explaining employee motivation. Let's take a look at them.

What Is Maslow's Hierarchy of Needs Theory?

Having a car to get to work is a necessity for many workers. When two crucial employees of Taleo/Vurv Technology in Jacksonville, Florida, had trouble getting to work, the owner decided to buy two inexpensive used cars for the employees. He said, "I felt that they were good employees and a valuable asset to the company." One of the employees who got one of the cars said, "It wasn't the nicest car. It wasn't the prettiest car. But boy did my overwhelming feeling of dread go from that to enlightenment. The 80-hour weeks we worked after that never meant anything. It was give and take. I was giving and the company was definitely giving back."[7] This manager understood employee needs (reliable transportation being an essential need for employees to be able to get to work) and their impact on motivation. The first motivation theory we're going to look at addresses employee needs.

The best-known motivation theory is probably Abraham Maslow's **hierarchy of needs theory**.[8] Maslow was a psychologist who proposed that within every person is a hierarchy of five needs:

1. **Physiological needs:** Food, drink, shelter, sex, and other physical requirements
2. **Safety needs:** Security and protection from physical and emotional harm, as well as assurance that physical needs will continue to be met
3. **Social needs:** Affection, belongingness, acceptance, and friendship
4. **Esteem needs:** Internal esteem factors such as self-respect, autonomy, and achievement and external esteem factors such as status, recognition, and attention
5. **Self-actualization needs:** Growth, achieving one's potential, and self-fulfillment; the drive to become what one is capable of becoming

Maslow argued that each level in the needs hierarchy must be substantially satisfied before the next need becomes dominant. An individual moves up the needs hierarchy from one level to the next. (See Exhibit 11–1.) In addition, Maslow separated the five needs into higher and lower levels. Physiological and safety needs were considered *lower-order needs*; social, esteem, and self-actualization needs were considered *higher-order needs*. Lower-order needs are predominantly satisfied externally while higher-order needs are satisfied internally.

How does Maslow's theory explain motivation? Managers using Maslow's hierarchy to motivate employees do things to satisfy employees' needs. But the theory also says that once a need is substantially satisfied, an individual isn't motivated to satisfy that need. Therefore, to motivate someone, you need to understand what need level that person is on in the hierarchy and focus on satisfying needs at or above that level.

motivation
The process by which a person's efforts are energized, directed, and sustained toward attaining a goal

hierarchy of needs theory
Maslow's theory that there is a hierarchy of five human needs: physiological, safety, social, esteem, and self-actualization

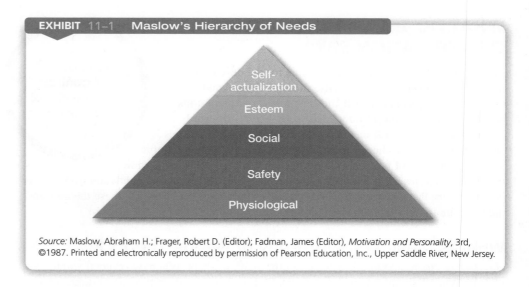

EXHIBIT 11-1   Maslow's Hierarchy of Needs

Self-actualization
Esteem
Social
Safety
Physiological

Source: Maslow, Abraham H.; Frager, Robert D. (Editor); Fadman, James (Editor), *Motivation and Personality*, 3rd, ©1987. Printed and electronically reproduced by permission of Pearson Education, Inc., Upper Saddle River, New Jersey.

Maslow's need theory is widely recognized, especially among practicing managers. Its popularity probably can be attributed to the theory's intuitive logic and ease of understanding.[9] But Maslow provided no empirical support for his theory, and several studies that sought to validate it could not.[10]

What Are McGregor's Theory X and Theory Y?

General Motors' new CEO has been described as brash, blunt, and demanding. Critics say that his approach may not go over well in a company that is "rebuilding itself from the brink of extinction." A manufacturing plant manager in another industry described his managerial style as: "If you're not a fan of in-your-face management, don't work here."[11] Both these managers are examples of what Douglas McGregor called a Theory X manager.

Douglas McGregor is best known for proposing two assumptions about human nature: Theory X and Theory Y.[12] Very simply, **Theory X** is a negative view of people that assumes workers have little ambition, dislike work, want to avoid responsibility, and need to be closely controlled to work effectively. **Theory Y** is a positive view that assumes employees enjoy work, seek out and accept responsibility, and exercise self-direction. McGregor believed that Theory Y assumptions should guide management practice and proposed that participation in decision making, responsible and challenging jobs, and good group relations would maximize employee motivation.

Unfortunately, no evidence confirms that either set of assumptions is valid or that being a Theory Y manager is the only way to motivate employees. For instance, Jen-Hsun Huang, founder of Nvidia Corporation, an innovative and successful microchip manufacturer, has been known to use both reassuring hugs and tough love in motivating employees. But he has little tolerance for screw-ups. "In one legendary meeting, he's said to have ripped into a project team for its tendency to repeat mistakes. 'Do you suck?' he asked the stunned employees. 'Because if you suck, just get up and say you suck.'"[13] His message, delivered in classic Theory X style, was that if you need help, ask for it. It's a harsh approach, but it has worked.

What Is Herzberg's Two-Factor Theory?

Frederick Herzberg's **two-factor theory** (also called motivation-hygiene theory) proposes that intrinsic factors are related to job satisfaction, while extrinsic factors are associated with job dissatisfaction.[14]

Berkshire Hathaway Chairman and CEO Warren Buffet is a Theory Y manager. He has a positive view of human nature and assumes that people enjoy work and accept responsibility. Buffet motivates employees by being approachable, trusting, and forgiving, by delegating decision-making authority, by giving them challenging work, and by making them feel valued. He constantly communicates that Berkshire Hathaway companies are well-managed, and he credits his managers for his success. Buffet is shown here playing the ukulele and singing with the Quebe Sisters band before participating in the company's annual shareholders' meeting.

Nati Harnick/AP Images

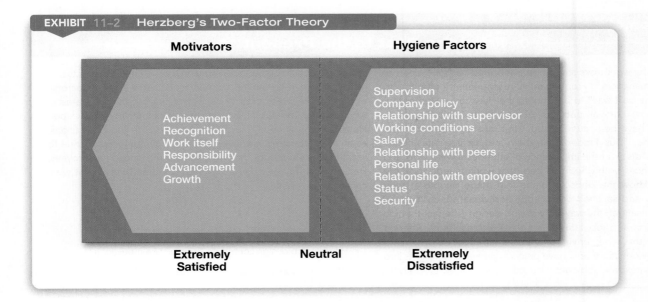

EXHIBIT 11-2   Herzberg's Two-Factor Theory

Motivators

Achievement
Recognition
Work itself
Responsibility
Advancement
Growth

Hygiene Factors

Supervision
Company policy
Relationship with supervisor
Working conditions
Salary
Relationship with peers
Personal life
Relationship with employees
Status
Security

**Extremely   Neutral   Extremely
Satisfied   Dissatisfied**

Herzberg wanted to know when people felt exceptionally good (satisfied) or bad (dissatisfied) about their jobs. (These findings are shown in Exhibit 11–2.) He concluded that the replies people gave when they felt good about their jobs were significantly different from the replies they gave when they felt badly. Certain characteristics were consistently related to job satisfaction (factors on the left side of the exhibit), and others to job dissatisfaction (factors on the right side). When people felt good about their work, they tended to cite intrinsic factors arising from the job itself such as achievement, recognition, and responsibility. On the other hand, when they were dissatisfied, they tended to cite extrinsic factors arising from the job context such as company policy and administration, supervision, interpersonal relationships, and working conditions.

In addition, Herzberg believed the data suggested that the opposite of satisfaction was not dissatisfaction, as traditionally had been believed. Removing dissatisfying characteristics from a job would not necessarily make that job more satisfying (or motivating). As shown in Exhibit 11–3, Herzberg proposed that a dual continuum existed: The opposite of "satisfaction" is "no satisfaction," and the opposite of "dissatisfaction" is "no dissatisfaction."

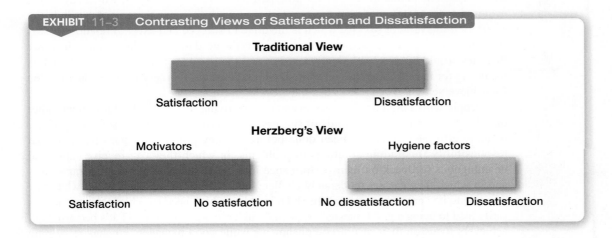

EXHIBIT 11-3   Contrasting Views of Satisfaction and Dissatisfaction

Traditional View

Satisfaction   Dissatisfaction

Herzberg's View

Motivators   Hygiene factors

Satisfaction   No satisfaction   No dissatisfaction   Dissatisfaction

theory X
The assumption that employees dislike work, are lazy, avoid responsibility, and must be coerced to work

theory Y
The assumption that employees are creative, enjoy work, seek responsibility, and can exercise self-direction

two-factor theory
Herzberg's motivation theory, which proposes that intrinsic factors are related to job satisfaction and motivation, whereas extrinsic factors are associated with job dissatisfaction

---

○ From the Past to the Present ○

Deciding how work tasks should be performed has long been of interest to managers.[15] From scientific management's attempts to find the "one best way" to do work to the Hawthorne Studies that attempted to unravel patterns of human behavior at work, researchers have been curious about the ideal approach to work design. In the 1950s, Frederick Herzberg and his associates began research to "discover the importance of attitudes toward work and the experiences both good and bad, that workers reported." He wanted to know the kinds of things that made people at their work happy and satisfied or unhappy and dissatisfied. What he discovered changed the way we view job design. The fact that job dissatisfaction and job satisfaction were the results of different aspects of the work environment was an important finding. Herzberg's two-factor theory gave practicing managers insights into both job context and job content. And if you wanted to motivate

employees, you'd better focus more on the job content aspects (the motivators) than on the job context aspects (the hygiene factors).

In addition, Herzberg's research stimulated additional interest in work design. The Job Characteristics model, for one, built upon Herzberg's findings in identifying the five core job dimensions, especially autonomy. As managers and organizations continue to search for work designs that will energize and engage employees, Herzberg's study of when people felt good and felt bad at work continues as a classic.

Think About:

• Why do you think jobs need to be "designed"?

• How can job design contribute to employee motivation?

• What would your "ideal" job look like?

Again, Herzberg believed that the factors that led to job satisfaction were separate and distinct from those that led to job dissatisfaction. Therefore, managers who sought to eliminate factors that created job dissatisfaction could keep people from being dissatisfied but not necessarily motivate them. The extrinsic factors that create job dissatisfaction were called **hygiene factors**. When these factors are adequate, people won't be dissatisfied, but they won't be satisfied (or motivated) either. To motivate people, Herzberg suggested emphasizing **motivators**, the intrinsic factors having to do with the job itself.

Herzberg's theory enjoyed wide popularity from the mid-1960s to the early 1980s, despite criticisms of his procedures and methodology. Although some critics said his theory was too simplistic, it has influenced how we currently design jobs. (See the From the Past to the Present box for additional information.)

What Is McClelland's Three-Needs Theory?

David McClelland and his associates proposed the **three-needs theory**, which says three acquired (not innate) needs are major motives in work.[16] These three needs include the **need for achievement (nAch)**, which is the drive to succeed and excel in relation to a set of standards; the **need for power (nPow)**, which is the need to make others behave in a way that they would not have behaved otherwise; and the **need for affiliation (nAff)**, which is the desire for friendly and close interpersonal relationships. Of these three needs, the need for achievement has been researched the most.

People with a high need for achievement are striving for personal achievement rather than for the trappings and rewards of success. They have a desire to do something better or more efficiently than it's been done before.[17] They prefer jobs that offer personal responsibility for finding solutions to problems, in which they can receive rapid and unambiguous feedback on their performance in order to tell whether they're improving, and in which they can set moderately challenging goals. High achievers avoid what they perceive to be very easy or very difficult tasks. Also, a high need to achieve doesn't necessarily lead to being a good manager, especially in large organizations. That's because high achievers focus on their *own* accomplishments while good managers emphasize helping *others* accomplish their goals.[18] McClelland showed that employees can be trained to stimulate their achievement need by being in situations where they have personal responsibility, feedback, and moderate risks.[19]

The other two needs in this theory haven't been researched as extensively as the need for achievement. However, we do know that the best managers tend to be high in the need for power and low in the need for affiliation.[20]

HOW DO THE CONTEMPORARY THEORIES EXPLAIN MOTIVATION?

Compare and **contrast** contemporary theories of motivation.

11.3

At Electronic Arts (EA), one of the world's largest video game designers, employees put in grueling hours developing games. However, EA takes care of its game developers by providing them with workday intramural sports leagues, pinball arcades, group fitness classes, and an open invite to pets at work.[21] With some 8,000 workers in more than 20 countries, EA's managers need to understand employee motivation.

The theories we look at in this section represent current explanations of employee motivation. Although these theories may not be as well known as those we just discussed, they are supported by research.[22] These contemporary motivation approaches include goal-setting theory, job design theory, equity theory, and expectancy theory.

What Is Goal-Setting Theory?

Before a big assignment or major class project presentation, has a teacher ever encouraged you to "Just do your best"? What does that vague statement, "do your best" mean? Would your performance on a class project have been higher had that teacher said you needed to score a 93 percent to keep your A in the class? Research on goal-setting theory addresses these issues, and the findings, as you'll see, are impressive in terms of the effect that goal specificity, challenge, and feedback have on performance.[23]

Substantial research support has been established for **goal-setting theory**, which says that specific goals increase performance and that difficult goals, when accepted, result in higher performance than do easy goals. What does goal-setting theory tell us?

First, working toward a goal is a major source of job motivation. Studies on goal setting have demonstrated that specific and challenging goals are superior motivating forces.[24] Such goals produce a higher output than does the generalized goal of "do your best." The specificity of the goal itself acts as an internal stimulus. For instance, when a sales rep commits to making eight sales calls daily, this intention gives him a specific goal to try to attain.

Next, will employees try harder if they have the opportunity to participate in the setting of goals? Not always. In some cases, participatively set goals elicit superior performance; in other cases, individuals performed best when their manager assigned goals. However, participation is probably preferable to assigning goals when employees might resist accepting difficult challenges.[25]

Finally, we know that people will do better if they get feedback on how well they're progressing toward their goals because feedback helps identify discrepancies between what they've done and what they want to do.

Working toward a goal is a major source of motivation for Mary Kay Cosmetics independent beauty consultants who receive generous recognition and rewards for their accomplishments. Consultants set their own specific sales goals for achieving different categories of rewards that range from jewelry to luxury trips to electronic equipment. Shown here is Mary Kay consultant Patricia Schneider, who has been setting and meeting her ambitious sales goals for 19 years and earning rewards that include jewelry and a pink bike. As the company's top sales producer in Orange County, California, Schneider has earned the use of her fourth pink Cadillac career car.

Newscom

---

hygiene factors
Factors that eliminate job dissatisfaction but don't motivate

motivators
Factors that increase job satisfaction and motivation

three-needs theory
McClelland's theory, which says that three acquired (not innate) needs—achievement, power, and affiliation—are major motives at work

need for achievement (nAch)
The drive to succeed and excel in relation to a set of standards

need for power (nPow)
The need to make others behave in a way that they would not have behaved otherwise

need for affiliation (nAff)
The desire for friendly and close interpersonal relationships

goal-setting theory
The proposition that specific goals increase performance and that difficult goals, when accepted, result in higher performance than do easy goals

But all feedback isn't equally effective. Self-generated feedback—where an employee monitors his or her own progress—has been shown to be a more powerful motivator than feedback coming from someone else.[26]

Three other contingencies besides feedback influence the goal-performance relationship: goal commitment, adequate self-efficacy, and national culture.

First, goal-setting theory assumes that an individual is committed to the goal. Commitment is most likely when goals are made public, when the individual has an internal locus of control, and when the goals are self-set rather than assigned.[27]

Next, **self-efficacy** refers to an individual's belief that he or she is capable of performing a task.[28] The higher your self-efficacy, the more confidence you have in your ability to succeed in a task. So, in difficult situations, we find that people with low self-efficacy are likely to reduce their effort or give up altogether, whereas those with high self-efficacy will try harder to master the challenge.[29] In addition, individuals with high self-efficacy seem to respond to negative feedback with increased effort and motivation, whereas those with low self-efficacy are likely to reduce their effort when given negative feedback.[30]

Finally, the value of goal-setting theory depends on the national culture. It's well adapted to North American countries because its main ideas align reasonably well with those cultures. It assumes that subordinates will be reasonably independent (not a high score on power distance), that people will seek challenging goals (low in uncertainty avoidance), and that performance is considered important by both managers and subordinates (high in assertiveness). Don't expect goal setting to lead to higher employee performance in countries where the cultural characteristics aren't like this.

Exhibit 11–4 summarizes the relationships among goals, motivation, and performance. Our overall conclusion is that the intention to work toward hard and specific goals is a powerful motivating force. Under the proper conditions, it can lead to higher performance. However, we have no evidence that such goals are associated with increased job satisfaction.[31]

How Does Job Design Influence Motivation?

Because managers want to motivate individuals on the job, we need to look at ways to design motivating jobs. If you look closely at what an organization is and how it works, you'll find that it's composed of thousands of tasks. These tasks are, in turn, aggregated into jobs. We use the term **job design** to refer to the way tasks are combined to form complete jobs. The jobs that people perform in an organization should not evolve by chance. Managers should design jobs deliberately and thoughtfully to reflect the demands of the changing environment, the organization's technology, and employees' skills,

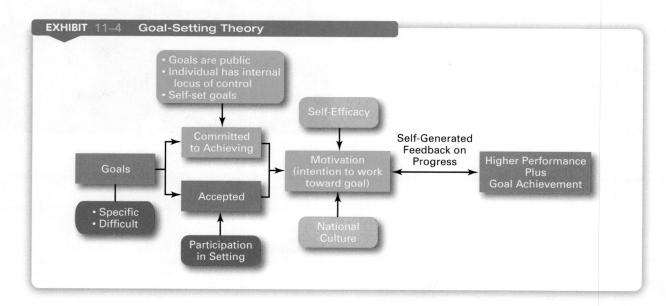

EXHIBIT 11–4 **Goal-Setting Theory**

abilities, and preferences.[32] When jobs are designed like that, employees are motivated to work hard. What are the ways that managers can design motivating jobs? We can answer that with the **job characteristics model (JCM)** developed by J. Richard Hackman and Greg R. Oldham.[33]

According to Hackman and Oldham, any job can be described in terms of the following five core job dimensions:

1. *Skill variety.* The degree to which the job requires a variety of activities so the worker can use a number of different skills and talents
2. *Task identity.* The degree to which the job requires completion of a whole and identifiable piece of work
3. *Task significance.* The degree to which the job affects the lives or work of other people
4. *Autonomy.* The degree to which the job provides freedom, independence, and discretion to the individual in scheduling the work and in determining the procedures to be used in carrying it out
5. *Feedback.* The degree to which carrying out the work activities required by the job results in the individual's obtaining direct and clear information about the effectiveness of his or her performance

Exhibit 11–5 presents the model. Notice how the first three dimensions—skill variety, task identity, and task significance—combine to create meaningful work. What we mean is that if these three characteristics exist in a job, we can predict that the person will view his or her job as being important, valuable, and worthwhile. Notice, too, that jobs that

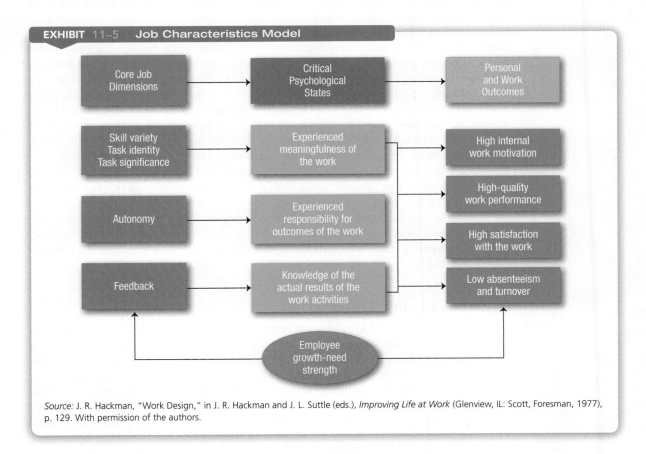

EXHIBIT 11–5   Job Characteristics Model

Source: J. R. Hackman, "Work Design," in J. R. Hackman and J. L. Suttle (eds.), *Improving Life at Work* (Glenview, IL: Scott, Foresman, 1977), p. 129. With permission of the authors.

self-efficacy
An individual's belief that he or she is capable of performing a task

job design
The way tasks are combined to form complete jobs

job characteristics model (JCM)
A framework for analyzing and designing jobs that identifies five primary core job dimensions, their interrelationships, and their impact on outcomes

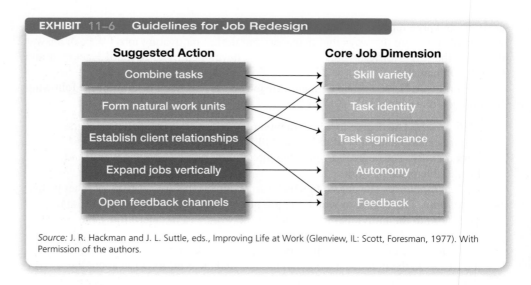

EXHIBIT 11–6   Guidelines for Job Redesign

Suggested Action	Core Job Dimension
Combine tasks	Skill variety
Form natural work units	Task identity
Establish client relationships	Task significance
Expand jobs vertically	Autonomy
Open feedback channels	Feedback

Source: J. R. Hackman and J. L. Suttle, eds., Improving Life at Work (Glenview, IL: Scott, Foresman, 1977). With Permission of the authors.

possess autonomy give the job incumbent a feeling of personal responsibility for the results and that, if a job provides feedback, the employee will know how effectively he or she is performing.

From a motivational point of view, the JCM suggests that internal rewards are obtained when an employee *learns* (knowledge of results through feedback) that he or she *personally* (experienced responsibility through autonomy of work) has performed well on a task that he or she *cares* about (experienced meaningfulness through skill variety, task identity, and/or task significance). The more these three conditions characterize a job, the greater the employee's motivation, performance, and satisfaction and the lower his or her absenteeism and the likelihood of resigning. As the model shows, the links between the job dimensions and the outcomes are moderated by the strength of the individual's growth need (the person's desire for self-esteem and self-actualization). Individuals are more likely to experience the critical psychological states and respond positively when their jobs include the core dimensions than are individuals with a low growth need. This distinction may explain the mixed results with **job enrichment** (vertical expansion of a job by adding planning and evaluation responsibilities): Individuals with low growth need don't tend to achieve high performance or satisfaction by having their jobs enriched.

The JCM provides significant guidance to managers for job design for both individuals and teams.[34] The suggestions shown in Exhibit 11–6, which are based on the JCM, specify the types of changes in jobs that are most likely to improve in each of the five core job dimensions.

What Is Equity Theory?

Do you ever wonder what kind of grade the person sitting next to you in class makes on a test or on a major class assignment? Most of us do! Being human, we tend to compare ourselves with others. If someone offered you $55,000 a year on your first job after graduating from college, you'd probably jump at the offer and report to work enthusiastic, ready to tackle whatever needed to be done, and certainly satisfied with your pay. How would you react, though, if you found out a month into the job that a coworker—another recent graduate, your age, with comparable grades from a comparable school, and with comparable work experience—was getting $60,000 a year? You'd probably be upset! Even though in absolute terms, $55,000 is a lot of money for a new graduate to make (and you know it!), that suddenly isn't the issue. Now you see the issue as what you believe is *fair*—what is *equitable*. The term *equity* is related to the concept of fairness and equitable treatment compared with others who behave in similar ways. There's considerable evidence that employees compare themselves to others and that inequities influence how much effort employees exert.[35]

Equity theory, developed by J. Stacey Adams, proposes that employees compare what they get from a job (outcomes) in relation to what they put into it (inputs) and then compare their inputs-outcomes ratio with the inputs-outcomes ratios of relevant others (Exhibit 11–7). If an employee perceives her ratio to be equitable in comparison to those of relevant others, there's no problem. However, if the ratio is inequitable, she views herself as underrewarded or overrewarded. When inequities occur, employees attempt to do something about it.[36] The result might be lower or higher productivity, improved or reduced quality of output, increased absenteeism, or voluntary resignation.

The **referent**—the other persons, systems, or selves individuals compare themselves against in order to assess equity—is an important variable in equity theory.[37] Each of the three referent categories is important. The "persons" category includes other individuals with similar jobs in the same organization but also includes friends, neighbors, or professional associates. Based on what they hear at work or read about in newspapers or trade journals, employees compare their pay with that of others. The "system" category includes organizational pay policies, procedures, and allocation. The "self" category refers to inputs-outcomes ratios that are unique to the individual. It reflects past personal experiences and contacts and is influenced by criteria such as past jobs or family commitments.

Originally, equity theory focused on **distributive justice**, which is the perceived fairness of the amount and allocation of rewards among individuals. More recent research has focused on looking at issues of **procedural justice**, which is the perceived fairness of the process used to determine the distribution of rewards. This research shows that distributive justice has a greater influence on employee satisfaction than procedural justice, while procedural justice tends to affect an employee's organizational commitment, trust in his or her boss, and intention to quit.[38] What are the implications for managers? They should consider openly sharing information on how allocation decisions are made, follow consistent and unbiased procedures, and engage in similar practices to increase the perception of procedural justice. By increasing the perception of procedural justice, employees are likely to view their bosses and the organization as positive even if they're dissatisfied with pay, promotions, and other personal outcomes.

RIGHT OR WRONG?

Book retailer Borders Group Inc. is in a mature and very competitive industry.[42] As a book seller, it's faced with the challenges of a product format that's evolved from physical to digital. Couple that with an economy in which consumers curtailed their spending and voila . . . you have a formula for financial failure, which is what happened. Borders filed for Chapter 11 bankruptcy protection in early 2011 and began immediately looking at ways to get lean, which included closing hundreds of stores, putting scores of employees out of work. Critics cried foul, however, when Borders continued with their plan to pay executives and other high-level employees $8.3 million in bonuses. A judge cleared an amended bonus pay plan that "ties the payments closer to the financial performance of Borders." Borders maintains that these bonuses were needed to "maintain its experienced work force" so that it could restructure and refocus for its eventual emergence from bankruptcy.

Think About:

- What do you think? Do you agree with Borders that this plan was needed, especially during this challenging period?

- What ethical issues do you see in this situation?

- What stakeholders might be impacted by this bonus plan? How might they be impacted?

- Could Borders have handled this differently? Discuss.

How Does Expectancy Theory Explain Motivation?

The most comprehensive explanation of how employees are motivated is Victor Vroom's **expectancy theory**.[39] Although the theory has its critics,[40] most research evidence supports it.[41]

---

job enrichment
The vertical expansion of a job by adding planning and evaluation responsibilities

equity theory
The theory that an employee compares his or her job's input-to-outcome ratio with that of relevant others and then corrects any inequity

referent
The persons, systems, or selves against which individuals compare themselves to assess equity

distributive justice
Perceived fairness of the amount and allocation of rewards among individuals

procedural justice
Perceived fairness of the process used to determine the distribution of rewards

expectancy theory
The theory that an individuals tends to act in a certain way, based on the expectation that the act will be followed by a given outcome and on the attractiveness of that outcome to the individual

EXHIBIT 11-7   Equity Theory Relationships

PERCEIVED RATIO COMPARISON*		EMPLOYEE'S ASSESSMENT
$\dfrac{\text{Outcomes A}}{\text{Inputs A}} <$	$\dfrac{\text{Outcomes B}}{\text{Inputs B}}$	Inequity (underrewarded)
$\dfrac{\text{Outcomes A}}{\text{Inputs A}} =$	$\dfrac{\text{Outcomes B}}{\text{Inputs B}}$	Equity
$\dfrac{\text{Outcomes A}}{\text{Inputs A}} >$	$\dfrac{\text{Outcomes B}}{\text{Inputs B}}$	Inequity (overrewarded)

*Person A is the employee, and Person B is a relevant other or referent.

Expectancy theory states that an individual tends to act in a certain way based on the expectation that the act will be followed by a given outcome and on the attractiveness of that outcome to the individual. It includes three variables or relationships (see Exhibit 11–8):

1. *Expectancy* or *effort-performance linkage* is the probability perceived by the individual that exerting a given amount of effort will lead to a certain level of performance.
2. *Instrumentality* or *performance-reward linkage* is the degree to which the individual believes that performing at a particular level is instrumental in attaining the desired outcome.
3. *Valence* or *attractiveness of reward* is the importance that the individual places on the potential outcome or reward that can be achieved on the job. Valence considers both the goals and needs of the individual.

This explanation of motivation might sound complicated, but it really isn't. It can be summed up in the questions: How hard do I have to work to achieve a certain level of performance, and can I actually achieve that level? What reward will performing at that level get me? How attractive is the reward to me, and does it help me achieve my own personal goals? Whether you are motivated to put forth effort (that is, to work hard) at any given time depends on your goals and your perception of whether a certain level of performance is necessary to attain those goals. Let's look at an example. Many years ago, when a woman went to work for IBM as a sales rep, her favorite work "reward" became having an IBM corporate jet fly to pick up her best customers and her and take them for a weekend of golfing at some fun location. But to get that particular "reward," she had to achieve at a certain level of performance, which involved exceeding her sales goals by a specified percentage. How hard she was willing to work (that is, how motivated she was to put forth effort) was dependent on the level of performance that had to be met and the likelihood that if she achieved at that level of performance she would receive that reward. Because she "valued" that reward, she always worked hard to exceed her sales goals. And the performance-reward linkage was clear because her hard work and performance achievements were always acknowledged by the company with the reward she valued (access to a corporate jet).

The key to expectancy theory is understanding an individual's goal and the linkage between effort and performance, between performance and rewards, and finally, between rewards and individual goal satisfaction. It emphasizes payoffs, or rewards. As a result, we

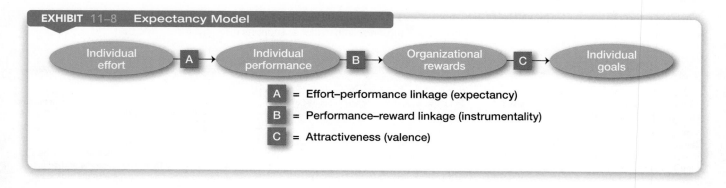

EXHIBIT 11-8   Expectancy Model

Individual effort → A → Individual performance → B → Organizational rewards → C → Individual goals

A = Effort–performance linkage (expectancy)
B = Performance–reward linkage (instrumentality)
C = Attractiveness (valence)

have to believe that the rewards an organization offers align with what the individual wants. Expectancy theory recognizes that no universal principle explains what motivates individuals and thus stresses that managers understand why employees view certain outcomes as attractive or unattractive. After all, we want to reward individuals with those things they value positively. Also, expectancy theory emphasizes expected behaviors. Do employees know what is expected of them and how they'll be evaluated? Finally, the theory is concerned with perceptions. Reality is irrelevant. An individual's own perceptions of performance, reward, and goal outcomes, not the outcomes themselves, will determine his or her motivation (level of effort).

How Can We Integrate Contemporary Motivation Theories?

Many of the ideas underlying the contemporary motivation theories are complementary, and you'll understand better how to motivate people if you see how the theories fit together.[43] Exhibit 11–9 presents a model that integrates much of what we know about motivation. Its basic foundation is the expectancy model. Let's work through the model, starting on the left.

The individual effort box has an arrow leading into it. This arrow flows from the individual's goals. Consistent with goal-setting theory, this goals-effort link is meant to illustrate that goals direct behavior. Expectancy theory predicts that an employee will exert a high level of effort if he or she perceives a strong relationship between effort and performance, performance and rewards, and rewards and satisfaction of personal goals. Each

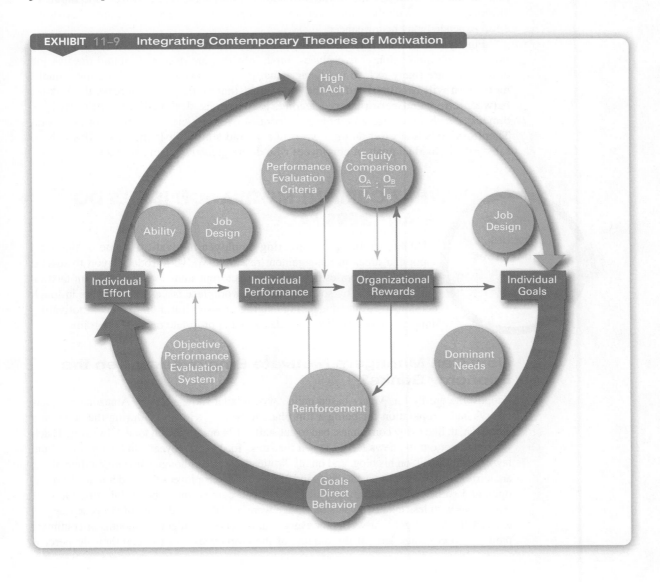

EXHIBIT 11–9 **Integrating Contemporary Theories of Motivation**

of these relationships is, in turn, influenced by certain factors. You can see from the model that the level of individual performance is determined not only by the level of individual effort but also by the individual's ability to perform and by whether the organization has a fair and objective performance evaluation system. The performance-reward relationship will be strong if the individual perceives that it is performance (rather than seniority, personal favorites, or some other criterion) that is rewarded. The final link in expectancy theory is the rewards-goal relationship. The traditional need theories come into play at this point. Motivation would be high to the degree that the rewards an individual received for his or her high performance satisfied the dominant needs consistent with his or her individual goals.

A closer look at the model also shows that it considers the achievement-need, reinforcement, equity, and JCM theories. The high achiever isn't motivated by the organization's assessment of his or her performance or organizational rewards, hence the jump from effort to individual goals for those with a high nAch. Remember that high achievers are internally driven as long as the jobs they're doing provide them with personal responsibility, feedback, and moderate risks. They're not concerned with the effort-performance, performance-reward, or rewards-goals linkages.

Reinforcement theory is seen in the model by recognizing that the organization's rewards reinforce the individual's performance. If managers have designed a reward system that is seen by employees as "paying off" for good performance, the rewards will reinforce and encourage continued good performance. Rewards also play a key part in equity theory. Individuals will compare the rewards (outcomes) they have received from the inputs or efforts they made with the inputs-outcomes ratio of relevant others. If inequities exist, the effort expended may be influenced.

Finally, the JCM is seen in this integrative model. Task characteristics (job design) influence job motivation at two places. First, jobs that are designed around the five job dimensions are likely to lead to higher actual job performance because the individual's motivation will be stimulated by the job itself—that is, they will increase the linkage between effort and performance. Second, jobs that are designed around the five job dimensions also increase an employee's control over key elements in his or her work. Therefore, jobs that offer autonomy, feedback, and similar task characteristics help to satisfy the individual goals of employees who desire greater control over their work.

WHAT CURRENT MOTIVATION ISSUES DO MANAGERS FACE?

11.4 Discuss current issues in motivating employees.

Understanding and predicting employee motivation is one of the most popular areas in management research. We've introduced you to several motivation theories. However, even current studies of employee motivation are influenced by some significant workplace issues—motivating in tough economic circumstances, managing cross-cultural challenges, motivating unique groups of workers, and designing appropriate rewards programs.

How Can Managers Motivate Employees When the Economy Stinks?

Zappos, the quirky Las Vegas–based online shoe retailer (now a part of Amazon.com), has always had a reputation for being a fun place to work.[44] However, during the economic recession, it, like many companies, had to cut staff—124 employees in total. CEO Tony Hsieh wanted to get out the news fast to lessen the stress for his employees. So he announced the layoff in an e-mail, on his blog, and on his Twitter account. Although some might think these are terrible ways to communicate that kind of news, most employees thanked him for being so open and so honest. The company also took good care of those being laid off. Laid-off employees with less than two years of service were paid through the end of the year. Longer-tenured employees got four weeks for every year of service. All got six months of continued paid health coverage and, at the request of the employees, got to keep their 40 percent merchandise discount through the Christmas season. Zappos had always been a model of how to nurture employees in good times, now it showed how to treat employees in bad times.

The economic recession of the last few years was difficult for many organizations, especially when it came to their employees. Layoffs, tight budgets, minimal or no pay raises, benefit cuts, no bonuses, long hours doing the work of those who had been laid off—this was the reality that many employees faced. As conditions deteriorated, employee confidence, optimism, and job engagement plummeted as well. As you can imagine, it wasn't an easy thing for managers to keep employees motivated under such challenging circumstances.

Managers came to realize that in an uncertain economy, they had to be creative in keeping their employees' efforts energized, directed, and sustained toward achieving goals. They were forced to look at ways to motivate employees that didn't involve money or that were relatively inexpensive.[45] So they relied on actions such as holding meetings with employees to keep the lines of communication open and to get their input on issues; establishing a common goal, such as maintaining excellent customer service, to keep everyone focused; creating a community feel so employees could see that managers cared about them and their work; and giving employees opportunities to continue to learn and grow. And, of course, an encouraging word always went a long way, as well.

How Does Country Culture Affect Motivation Efforts?

In today's global business environment, managers can't automatically assume that motivational programs that work in one geographic location are going to work in others. Most current motivation theories were developed in the United States by Americans and about Americans.[46] Maybe the most blatant pro-American characteristic in these theories is the strong emphasis on individualism and achievement. For instance, both goal-setting and expectancy theories emphasize goal accomplishment as well as rational and individual thought. Let's look at the cross-cultural transferability of the motivation theories.

Maslow's need hierarchy argues that people start at the physiological level and then move progressively up the hierarchy in order. This hierarchy, if it has any application at all, aligns with American culture. In countries such as Japan, Greece, and Mexico, where uncertainty avoidance characteristics are strong, security needs would be on top of the need hierarchy. Countries that score high on nurturing characteristics—Denmark, Sweden, Norway, the Netherlands, and Finland—would have social needs on top.[47] We would predict, for instance, that group work will be more motivating when the country's culture scores high on the nurturing criterion.

Another motivation concept that clearly has an American bias is the achievement need. The view that a high achievement need acts as an internal motivator presupposes two cultural characteristics—a willingness to accept a moderate degree of risk (which excludes countries with strong uncertainty avoidance characteristics) and a concern with performance (which applies almost singularly to countries with strong achievement characteristics). This combination is found in the Anglo-American countries of the United States, Canada, and Great Britain.[48] On the other hand, these characteristics are relatively absent in countries such as Chile and Portugal.

Equity theory has a relatively strong following in the United States, which is not surprising given that U.S.–style reward systems are based on the assumption that workers are highly sensitive to equity in reward allocations. In the United States, equity is meant to closely link pay to performance. However, recent evidence suggests that in collectivist cultures, especially in the former socialist countries of Central and Eastern Europe, employees expect rewards to reflect their individual needs as well as their performance.[49] Moreover, consistent with a legacy of communism and centrally planned economies, employees exhibited a greater "entitlement" attitude—that is, they expected outcomes to be greater than their inputs.[50] These findings suggest that U.S.–style pay practices may need to be modified in some countries in order to be perceived as fair by employees.

Despite these cross-cultural differences in motivation, a number of cross-cultural consistencies can be found. For instance, the desire for interesting work seems important to almost all workers, regardless of their national culture. In a study of seven countries, employees in Belgium, Britain, Israel, and the United States ranked "interesting work" number one among 11 work goals. It was ranked either second or third in Japan, the Netherlands, and Germany.[51] Similarly, in a study comparing job-preference outcomes among graduate students in the United States, Canada, Australia, and Singapore, growth, achievement, and responsibility were rated the top three and had identical rankings.[52] Both studies suggest some universality to the importance of intrinsic factors identified by Herzberg in his two-factor theory. Another recent study examining workplace motivation trends in Japan also seems to indicate that Herzberg's model is applicable to Japanese employees.[53]

How Can Managers Motivate Unique Groups of Workers?

Motivating employees has never been easy! Employees come into organizations with different needs, personalities, skills, abilities, interests, and aptitudes. They have different expectations of their employers and different views of what they think their employer has a right to expect of them. And they vary widely in what they want from their jobs. For instance, some employees get more satisfaction out of their personal interests and pursuits and only want a weekly paycheck—nothing more. They're not interested in making their work more challenging or interesting or in "winning" performance contests. Others derive a great deal of satisfaction in their jobs and are motivated to exert high levels of effort. Given these differences, how can managers do an effective job of motivating the unique groups of employees found in today's workforce? One thing is to understand the motivational requirements of these groups including diverse employees, professionals, and contingent workers.

MOTIVATING A DIVERSE WORKFORCE. To maximize motivation among today's workforce, managers need to think in terms of *flexibility*. For instance, studies tell us that men place more importance on having autonomy in their jobs than do women. In contrast, the opportunity to learn, convenient and flexible work hours, and good interpersonal relations are more important to women.[54] Having the opportunity to be independent and to be exposed to different experiences is important to Gen Y employees whereas older workers may be more interested in highly structured work opportunities.[55] Managers need to recognize that what motivates a single mother with two dependent children who's working full time to support her family may be very different from the needs of a single part-time employee or an older employee who is working only to supplement his or her retirement income. A diverse array of rewards is needed to motivate employees with such diverse needs. Many of the work/life balance programs (see Chapter 7) that organizations have implemented are a response to the varied needs of a diverse workforce. In addition, many organizations have developed flexible work arrangements (see Chapter 6) that recognize different needs. These types of programs (including telecommuting, compressed workweeks, flextime, and job sharing) may become even more popular as employers look for ways to help employees cope with high fuel prices.

Do flexible work arrangements motivate employees? Although such arrangements might seem highly motivational, both positive and negative relationships have been found. For instance, one study of the impact of telecommuting on job satisfaction found that job satisfaction initially increased as the extent of telecommuting increased, but as the number of hours spent telecommuting increased, job satisfaction started to level off, decreased slightly, and then stabilized.[56]

MOTIVATING PROFESSIONALS. In contrast to a generation ago, the typical employee today is more likely to be a professional with a college degree than a blue-collar factory worker. What special concerns should managers be aware of when trying to motivate a team of engineers at Intel's India Development

Motivating professional employees who have a strong and long-term commitment to their field of expertise is different from motivating other employees. Challenging work tends to be ranked high for financial services professionals such as Brenda Hung, the branch manager of TD Canada Trust, shown here cutting a ribbon to celebrate the opening of a renovated bank location. Hung and the other TD Canada Trust professionals enjoy tackling problems and finding solutions as they provide their customers with personal and commercial banking, wealth management, insurance, securities, and other financial products and services.

Jeff Vinnick/Newscom

Center, software designers at SAS Institute in North Carolina, or a group of consultants at Accenture in Singapore?

Professionals are different from nonprofessionals.[57] They have a strong and long-term commitment to their field of expertise. To keep current in their field, they need to regularly update their knowledge, and because of their commitment to their profession they rarely define their workweek as 8 A.M. to 5 P.M. five days a week.

What motivates professionals? Money and promotions typically are low on their priority list. Why? They tend to be well paid and enjoy what they do. In contrast, job challenge tends to be ranked high. They like to tackle problems and find solutions. Their chief reward is the work itself. Professionals also value support. They want others to think that what they're working on is important. That may be true for all employees, but professionals tend to be focused on their work as their central life interest, whereas nonprofessionals typically have other interests outside of work that can compensate for needs not met on the job.

MOTIVATING CONTINGENT WORKERS.   As full-time jobs have been eliminated through downsizing and other organizational restructurings, the number of openings for part-time, contract, and other forms of temporary work have increased. Contingent workers don't have the security or stability that permanent employees have, and they don't identify with the organization or display the commitment that other employees do. Temporary workers also typically get little or no benefits such as health care or pensions.[58]

There's no simple solution for motivating contingent employees. For that small set of individuals who prefer the freedom of their temporary status, the lack of stability may not be an issue. In addition, temporariness might be preferred by highly compensated physicians, engineers, accountants, or financial planners who don't want the demands of a full-time job. But these are the exceptions. For the most part, temporary employees are not temporary by choice.

What will motivate involuntarily temporary employees? An obvious answer is the opportunity to become a permanent employee. In cases in which permanent employees are selected from a pool of temps, the temps will often work hard in hopes of becoming permanent. A less obvious answer is the opportunity for training. The ability of a temporary employee to find a new job is largely dependent on his or her skills. If an employee sees that the job he or she is doing can help develop marketable skills, then motivation is increased. From an equity standpoint, when temps work alongside permanent employees who earn more and get benefits too for doing the same job, the performance of temps is likely to suffer. Separating such employees or perhaps minimizing interdependence between them might help managers counteract potential problems.[59]

How Can Managers Design Appropriate Rewards Programs?

Blue Cross of California, one of the nation's largest health insurers, pays bonuses to doctors serving its health maintenance organization members based on patient satisfaction and other quality standards. FedEx's drivers are motivated by a pay system that rewards them for timeliness and how much they deliver.[60] There's no doubt that employee rewards programs play a powerful role in motivating appropriate employee behavior. Some of the more popular rewards programs include open-book management, employee recognition, and pay-for-performance.

HOW CAN OPEN-BOOK MANAGEMENT PROGRAMS MOTIVATE EMPLOYEES?   Within 24 hours after managers of the Heavy Duty Division of Springfield Remanufacturing Company (SRC) gather to discuss a multipage financial document, every plant employee will have seen the same information. If the employees can meet shipment goals, they'll all share in a large year-end bonus.[61] Many organizations of various sizes involve their employees in workplace decisions by opening up the financial statements (the "books"). They share that information so that employees will be motivated to make better decisions about their work and better able to understand the implications of what they do, how they do it, and the ultimate impact on the bottom line. This approach is called

Each year Marriott International shines the spotlight on a select few employees by presenting them with the J. Willard Marriott Award of Excellence during a gala employee recognition celebration. Presented by J. W. Marriott (on the right), the hotelier's CEO and chairman, the award is Marriott's highest form of associate recognition. It honors employees who demonstrate achievement, character, dedication, effort, and perseverance in leading by example and exceeding expectations. Through many other awards and recognition programs, Marriott celebrates associates who exemplify the company's motto "Spirit to Serve" as they enhance the lives of customers, coworkers, and people in their communities.

open-book management and many organizations are using it.[62] At Best Buy, the "Donuts with Darren" sessions (held when Darren Jackson was the company's chief financial officer) were so popular that more than 600 employees regularly took part. His presentations covered the financials and the basics of finance.[63]

The goal of open-book management is to get employees to think like an owner by seeing the impact their decisions have on financial results. Because many employees don't have the knowledge or background to understand the financials, they have to be taught how to read and understand the organization's financial statements. Once employees have this knowledge, however, managers need to regularly share the numbers with them. By sharing this information, employees begin to see the link between their efforts, level of performance, and operational results.

HOW CAN MANAGERS USE EMPLOYEE RECOGNITION PROGRAMS? Employee recognition programs consist of personal attention and expressions of interest, approval, and appreciation for a job well done.[64] They can take numerous forms. For instance, Kelly Services, introduced a new version of its points-based incentive system to better promote productivity and retention among its employees. The program, called Kelly Kudos, gives employees more choices of awards and allows them to accumulate points over a longer time period. It's working. Participants generate three times more revenue and hours than employees not receiving points.[65] Most managers, however, use a far more informal approach. For example, when Julia Stewart—currently chairman and CEO of DineEquity, Inc.—was president of Applebee's Restaurants, she would frequently leave sealed notes on the chairs of employees after everyone had gone home.[66] These notes explained how important Stewart thought the person's work was or how much she appreciated the completion of a project. Stewart also relied heavily on voice mail messages left after office hours to tell employees how appreciative she was for a job well done. And recognition doesn't have to come only from managers. Some 35 percent of companies encourage coworkers to recognize peers for outstanding work efforts.[67] For instance, managers at Yum Brands Inc. (the Kentucky-based parent of food chains Taco Bell, KFC, and Pizza Hut) were looking for ways to reduce employee turnover. They found a successful customer-service program involving peer recognition at KFC restaurants in Australia. Workers there spontaneously rewarded fellow workers with "Champs cards, an acronym for attributes such as cleanliness, hospitality, and accuracy." Yum implemented the program in other restaurants around the world, and credits the peer recognition with reducing hourly employee turnover from 181 percent to 109 percent.[68]

A survey of organizations found that 84 percent had some type of program to recognize worker achievements.[69] And do employees think these programs are important? You bet! A survey of a wide range of employees asked them what they considered the most powerful workplace motivator. Their response? Recognition, recognition, and more recognition![70]

Consistent with reinforcement theory (see Chapter 9), rewarding a behavior with recognition immediately following that behavior is likely to encourage its repetition. And recognition can take many forms. You can personally congratulate an employee in private for a good job. You can send a handwritten note or e-mail message acknowledging something positive that the employee has done. For employees with a strong need for social acceptance, you can publicly recognize accomplishments. To enhance group cohesiveness and motivation, you can celebrate team successes. For instance, you can do something as simple as throw a pizza party to celebrate a team's accomplishments. Some of these things may seem simple, but they can go a long way in showing employees they're valued.

HOW CAN MANAGERS USE PAY-FOR-PERFORMANCE TO MOTIVATE EMPLOYEES? Here's a survey statistic that may surprise you: 40 percent of employees see no clear link between performance and pay.[71] You have to think: What are the companies where these employees work paying for? They're obviously not clearly communicating performance expectations.[72] Pay-for-performance programs are variable compensation plans that pay employees on the basis of some performance measure.[73] Piece-rate pay plans, wage incentive plans, profit-sharing, and lump-sum bonuses are examples. What differentiates these forms of pay from more traditional compensation plans is that instead of paying a person for time on the job, pay is adjusted to reflect some performance measure. These performance measures might include such things as individual productivity, team or work group productivity, departmental productivity, or the overall organization's profit performance.

Pay-for-performance is probably most compatible with expectancy theory. Individuals should perceive a strong relationship between their performance and the rewards they receive for motivation to be maximized. If rewards are allocated only on nonperformance factors—such as seniority, job title, or across-the-board pay raises—then employees are likely to reduce their efforts. From a motivation perspective, making some or all an employee's pay conditional on some performance measure focuses his or her attention and effort toward that measure, then reinforces the continuation of the effort with a reward. If the employee, team, or organization's performance declines, so does the reward. Thus, there's an incentive to keep efforts and motivation strong.

Pay-for-performance programs are popular. Some 80 percent of large U.S. companies have some form of variable pay plan.[74] These types of pay plans have also been tried in other countries such as Canada and Japan. About 30 percent of Canadian companies and 22 percent of Japanese companies have company-wide pay-for-performance plans.[75]

Do pay-for-performance programs work? For the most part, studies seem to indicate that they do. For instance, one study found that companies that used pay-for-performance programs performed better financially than those that did not.[76] Another study showed that pay-for-performance programs with outcome-based incentives had a positive impact on sales, customer satisfaction, and profits.[77] If an organization uses work teams, managers should consider group-based performance incentives that will reinforce team effort and commitment. But whether these programs are individual based or team based, managers need to ensure that they're specific about the relationship between an individual's pay and his or her expected level of appropriate performance. Employees must clearly understand exactly how performance—theirs and the organization's—translates into dollars on their paychecks.[78]

Trenise Duvernay teaches a fourth grade math class at a charter school in New Orleans. As a teacher, Duvernay wants to be rewarded for helping students succeed and supports the variable-pay initiative offered at her school. She is eligible for a merit bonus of $2,000 or more each year based on how well her students perform in classroom observations and on achievement tests. The pay plan motivates teachers by basing a portion of their pay on their performance in raising student achievement rather than on seniority or degrees. The move toward pay-for-performance plans to reward teachers for their individual efforts follows the widespread adoption of variable-pay plans in many businesses and government agencies.

A FINAL NOTE ON EMPLOYEE REWARDS PROGRAMS. During times of economic and financial uncertainty, managers' abilities to recognize and reward employees are often severely constrained. It's hard to keep employees productive during challenging times, even though it's especially critical. It's not surprising, then, that employees feel less connected to their work. In fact, a recent study by the Corporate Executive Board found that declining employee engagement has decreased overall productivity by 3 to 5 percent.[79] But there are actions managers can take to maintain and maybe even increase employees' motivation levels. One is to clarify each person's role in the organization. Show them how their efforts are contributing to improving the company's overall situation. It's also important to keep communication lines open and use two-way exchanges between top-level managers and employees to soothe fears and concerns. The key with taking any actions is continuing to show workers that the company cares about them. As we said at the beginning of the chapter, the value in companies comes from employees who are motivated to be there. Managers have to give employees a reason to want to be there.

open-book management
A motivational approach in which an organization's financial statements (the "books") are shared with all employees

employee recognition programs
Programs that consist of personal attention and expressions of interest, approval, and appreciation for a job well done

pay-for-performance programs
Variable compensation plans that pay employees on the basis of some performance measure

11 Review

CHAPTER SUMMARY

11.1 Define and explain motivation. Motivation is the process by which a person's efforts are energized, directed, and sustained toward attaining a goal.

The *energy* element is a measure of intensity or drive. The high level of effort needs to be *directed* in ways that help the organization achieve its goals. Employees must *persist* in putting forth effort to achieve those goals.

11.2 Compare and contrast early theories of motivation. Individuals move up the hierarchy of five needs (physiological, safety, social, esteem, and self-actualization) as needs are substantially satisfied. A need that's substantially satisfied no longer motivates.

A Theory X manager believes that people don't like to work, or won't seek out responsibility, so they have to be threatened and coerced to work. A Theory Y manager assumes that people like to work and seek out responsibility, so they will exercise self-motivation and self-direction.

Herzberg's theory proposed that intrinsic factors associated with job satisfaction were what motivated people. Extrinsic factors associated with job dissatisfaction simply kept people from being dissatisfied.

Three-needs theory proposed three acquired needs that are major motives in work: need for achievement, need for affiliation, and need for power.

11.3 Compare and contrast contemporary theories of motivation. Goal-setting theory says that specific goals increase performance, and difficult goals, when accepted, result in higher performance than do easy goals. Important points in goal-setting theory include intention to work toward a goal as a major source of job motivation; specific hard goals to produce higher levels of output than generalized goals; participation in setting goals as preferable to assigning goals, but not always; feedback to guide and motivate behavior, especially self-generated feedback; and contingencies that affect goal setting, such as goal commitment, self-efficacy, and national culture.

The job characteristics model is based on five core job dimensions (skill variety, task identity, task significance, autonomy, and feedback) that are used to design motivating jobs.

Equity theory focuses on how employees compare their inputs-outcomes ratios to relevant others' ratios. A perception of inequity will cause an employee to do something about it. Procedural justice has a greater influence on employee satisfaction than does distributive justice.

Expectancy theory says that an individual tends to act in a certain way based on the expectation that the act will be followed by a desired outcome. Expectancy is the effort-performance linkage (how much effort do I need to exert to achieve a certain level of performance); instrumentality is the performance-reward linkage (achieving at a certain level of performance will get me what reward); and valence is the attractiveness of the reward (is the reward what I want).

11.4 Discuss current issues in motivating employees. During rough economic conditions, managers must look for creative ways to keep employees' efforts energized, directed, and sustained toward achieving goals.

Most motivational theories were developed in the United States and have a North American bias. Some theories (Maslow's need hierarchy, achievement need, and equity theory) don't work well for other cultures. However, the desire for interesting work seems important to all workers and Herzberg's motivator (intrinsic) factors may be universal.

Managers face challenges in motivating unique groups of workers. A diverse workforce is looking for flexibility. Professionals want job challenge and support, and are motivated by the work itself. Contingent workers want the opportunity to become permanent or to receive skills training.

Open-book management is when financial statements (the books) are shared with employees who have been taught what that information means. Employee recognition programs consist of personal attention, approval, and appreciation for a job well done. Pay-for-performance programs are variable compensation plans that pay employees on the basis of some performance measure.

MyManagementLab   For more resources, please visit **www.mymanagementlab.com**

UNDERSTANDING THE CHAPTER

1. Most of us have to work for a living, and a job is a central part of our lives. So why do managers have to worry so much about employee motivation issues?

2. What is motivation? Explain the three key elements of motivation.

3. Contrast lower-order and higher-order needs in Maslow's needs hierarchy.

4. What role would money play in (a) the hierarchy of needs theory, (b) two-factor theory, (c) equity theory, (d) expectancy theory, and (e) motivating employees with a high nAch?

5. What are some of the possible consequences of employees perceiving an inequity between their inputs and outcomes and those of others?

6. What are some advantages of using pay-for-performance programs to motivate employee performance? Are there drawbacks? Explain.

7. Many job design experts who have studied the changing nature of work say that people do their best work when they're motivated by a sense of purpose rather than by the pursuit of money. Do you agree? Explain your position. What are the implications for managers?

8. Could managers use any of the motivation theories or approaches to encourage and support workforce diversity efforts? Explain.

9. Can an individual be too motivated? Discuss.

10. What challenges do managers face in motivating today's workforce?

Go to p. 441

YOUR TURN TO BE **A MANAGER** for Chapter 11.

Endnotes

1. S. Levy, "The Problem with Success," *Wall Street Journal*, April 7, 2011, p. A15; S. Levy, *In the Plex: How Google Thinks, Works, and Shapes Our Lives* (New York: Simon & Schuster), 2011; C. C. Miller and J. Wortham, "Silicon Valley Hiring Perks: Meals, iPads, and a Cubicle for Spot," *New York Times Online*, March 26, 2011; J. Light, "Google Is No. 1 on List of Desired Employers," *Wall Street Journal*, March 21, 2011, p. B8; M Moskowitz, R. Levering, and C. Tkaczyk, "100 Best Companies to Work For," *Fortune*, February 7, 2011, pp. 91+; C. C. Miller and M. Helft, "Google Shake-Up Is Effort to Revive Start-Up Spark," *New York Times Online*, January 20, 2011; C. C. Miller, "Google Grows and Works to Retain Nimble Minds," *New York Times Online*, November 28, 2010; A. Efrati and P-W. Tam, "Google Battles to Keep Talent," *Wall Street Journal*, November 11, 2010, pp. B1+; L. Petrecca, "With 3,000 Applications a Day, Google Can Be Picky," *USA Today*, May 19, 2010, p. 2B; S. E. Ante and K. Weisul, "And Google Begat . . . ," *Bloomberg BusinessWeek*, March 8, 2010, pp. 39–42; A. Lashinsky, "Where Does Google Go Next?" *CNNMoney.com*, May 12, 2008; and "Perk Place: The Benefits Offered by Google and Others May Be Grand, But They're All Business," *Knowledge @ Wharton*, http://knowledge.wharton.upenn.edu/ article (March 21, 2007).

2. P. Bronson, "What Should I Do with My Life Now?" *Fast Company*, April 2009, pp. 35–37.

3. R. M. Steers, R. T. Mowday, and D. L. Shapiro, "The Future of Work Motivation Theory," *Academy of Management Review*, July 2004, pp. 379–387.

4. N. Ellemers, D. De Gilder, and S. A. Haslam, "Motivating Individuals and Groups at Work: A Social Identity Perspective on Leadership and Group Performance," *Academy of Management Review*, July 2004, pp. 459–478.

5. And the Survey Says box based on J. Yang and P. Trap, "Does Your Manager Acknowledge and Appreciate You at Work?" *USA Today*, March 24, 2011, p. 1B; A. R. Carey and K. Gelles, "Which of These Is Most Important About Your Job?" *USA Today*, January 31, 2011, p. 1A; J. Yang and S. Ward, "Who Appreciates You the Most at Work?" *USA Today*, June 2, 2010, p. 1B; E. Frauenheim, "Bosses Don't Drive Workers Away, Poll Concludes," *Workforce Management Online*, April 2010; J. Yang and K. Simmons, "What Primary Motivation Does Your Employer Provide?" *USA Today*, February 22, 2010, p. 1B; and A. R. Carey and S. Ward, "What Small Perks Workers Want," *USA Today*, March 31, 2010, p. 1A.

6. J. Krueger and E. Killham, "At Work, Feeling Good Matters," *Gallup Management Journal*, http://gmj.gallup.com (December 8, 2005).

7. M. Meece, "Using the Human Touch to Solve Workplace Problems," *New York Times Online*, April 3, 2008.

8. "Maslow Motion," *New Statesman*, March 15, 2010, p. 37; "Dialogue," *Academy of Management Review*, October 2000, pp. 696–701; M. L. Ambrose and C. T. Kulik, "Old Friends, New Faces: Motivation Research in the 1990s," *Journal of Management*, 25, no. 3 (1999), pp. 231–292; A. Maslow, D. C. Stephens, and G. Heil, *Maslow on Management* (New York: John Wiley & Sons, 1998); and A. Maslow, *Motivation and Personality* (New York: McGraw-Hill, 1954).

9. R. Coutts, "A Pilot Study for the Analysis of Dream Reports Using Maslow's Need Categories: An Extension to the Emotional Selection Hypothesis," *Psychological Reports*,

October 2010, pp. 659–673; E. A. Fisher, "Motivation and Leadership in Social Work Management: A Review of Theories and Related Studies," *Administration in Social Work,* October–December 2009, pp. 347–367; and N. K. Austin, "The Power of the Pyramid: The Foundation of Human Psychology and, Thereby, of Motivation, Maslow's Hierarchy Is One Powerful Pyramid," *Incentive* (July 2002), p. 10.

10. See, for example, M. L. Ambrose and C. T. Kulik, "Old Friends, New Faces: Motivation Research in the 1990s"; J. Rowan, "Ascent and Descent in Maslow's Theory," *Journal of Humanistic Psychology* (Summer 1999), pp. 125–133; J. Rowan, "Maslow Amended," *Journal of Humanistic Psychology*, (Winter 1998), pp. 81–92; R. M. Creech, "Employee Motivation," *Management Quarterly*, Summer 1995, pp. 33–39; E. E. Lawler III and J. L. Suttle, "A Causal Correlational Test of the Need Hierarchy Concept," *Organizational Behavior and Human Performance*, April 1972, pp. 265–287; and D. T. Hall and K. E. Nongaim, "An Examination of Maslow's Need Hierarchy in an Organizational Setting," *Organizational Behavior and Human Performance*, February 1968, pp. 12–35.

11. S. Terlep and J. S. Lublin, "New GM CEO: Brash, Blunt, Demanding," *Wall Street Journal,* August 16, 2010, pp. B1+; and S. Fitch, "Zero Tolerance," *Forbes,* January 28, 2008, p. 52.

12. R. E. Kopelman, D. J. Prottas, and A. L. Davis, "Douglas McGregor's Theory X and Y: Toward a Construct-Valid Measure," *Journal of Managerial Issues* (Summer 2008), pp. 255–271; and D. McGregor, *The Human Side of Enterprise* (New York: McGraw-Hill, 1960). For an updated description of Theories X and Y, see an annotated edition with commentary of *The Human Side of Enterprise* (McGraw-Hill, 2006); and G. Heil, W. Bennis, and D. C. Stephens, *Douglas McGregor, Revisited: Managing the Human Side of Enterprise* (New York: Wiley, 2000).

13. R. Parloff, "Has Intel Finally Met Its Match?" *Fortune,* August 16, 2010, pp. 21–22; and J. M. O'Brien, "The Next Intel," *Wired,* July 2002, pp. 100–107.

14. F. Herzberg, B. Mausner, and B. Snyderman, *The Motivation to Work* (New York: John Wiley, 1959); F. Herzberg, *The Managerial Choice: To Be Effective or to Be Human*, rev. ed. (Salt Lake City: Olympus, 1982); R. M. Creech, "Employee Motivation"; and M. L. Ambrose and C. T. Kulik, "Old Friends, New Faces: Motivation Research in the 1990s."

15. From the Past to the Present box based on C. M. Christensen, "How Will You Measure Your Life?" *Harvard Business Review,* July–August 2010, pp. 46–51; D. A. Wren and A. G. Bedeian, *The Evolution of Management Thought* (New York: John Wiley & Sons, Inc., 2009); F. Herzberg, *One More Time: How Do You Motivate Employees?* (Boston, MA: Harvard Business School Press, 2008); and F. Herzberg, B. Mausner, and B. B. Snyderman, *The Motivation to Work.*

16. D. C. McClelland, *The Achieving Society* (New York: Van Nostrand Reinhold, 1961); J. W. Atkinson and J. O. Raynor, *Motivation and Achievement* (Washington, DC: Winston, 1974); D. C. McClelland, *Power: The Inner Experience* (New York: Irvington, 1975); and M. J. Stahl, *Managerial and Technical Motivation: Assessing Needs for Achievement, Power, and Affiliation* (New York: Praeger, 1986).

17. McClelland, *The Achieving Society.*

18. McClelland, *Power: The Inner Experience*; D. C. McClelland and D. H. Burnham, "Power Is the Great Motivator," *Harvard Business Review*, March–April 1976, pp. 100–110.

19. D. Miron and D. C. McClelland, "The Impact of Achievement Motivation Training on Small Businesses," *California Management Review*, Summer 1979, pp. 13–28.

20. "McClelland: An Advocate of Power," *International Management*, July 1975, pp. 27–29.

21. J. Flint, "How to Be a Player," *Bloomberg BusinessWeek,* January 24–January 30, 2011, pp. 108–109.

22. R. M. Steers, R. T. Mowday, and D. L. Shapiro, "The Future of Work Motivation Theory"; E. A. Locke and G. P. Latham, "What Should We Do About Motivation Theory? Six Recommendations for the Twenty-First Century," *Academy of Management Review,* July 2004, pp. 388–403; and M. L. Ambrose and C. T. Kulik, "Old Friends, New Faces: Motivation Research in the 1990s."

23. M. L. Ambrose and C. T. Kulik, "Old Friends, New Faces: Motivation Research in the 1990s."

24. J. C. Naylor and D. R. Ilgen, "Goal Setting: A Theoretical Analysis of a Motivational Technique," in B. M. Staw and L. L. Cummings (eds.), *Research in Organizational Behavior*, vol. 6 (Greenwich, CT: JAI Press, 1984), pp. 95–140; A. R. Pell, "Energize Your People," *Managers Magazine*, December 1992, pp. 28–29; E. A. Locke, "Facts and Fallacies About Goal Theory: Reply to Deci," *Psychological Science*, January 1993, pp. 63–64; M. E. Tubbs, "Commitment as a Moderator of the Goal-Performance Relation: A Case for Clearer Construct Definition," *Journal of Applied Psychology* (February 1993), pp. 86–97; M. P. Collingwood, "Why Don't You Use the Research?" *Management Decision*, May 1993, pp. 48–54; M. E. Tubbs, D. M. Boehne, and J. S. Dahl, "Expectancy, Valence, and Motivational Force Functions in Goal-Setting Research: An Empirical Test," *Journal of Applied Psychology* (June 1993), pp. 361–373; E. A. Locke, "Motivation Through Conscious Goal Setting," *Applied and Preventive Psychology,* vol. 5 (1996), pp. 117–124; M. L. Ambrose and C. T. Kulik, "Old Friends, New Faces: Motivation Research in the 1990s; E. A. Locke and G. P. Latham, "Building a Practically Useful Theory of Goal Setting and Task Motivation: A 35-Year Odyssey," *American Psychologist,* September 2002, pp. 705–717; Y. Fried and L. H. Slowik, "Enriching Goal-Setting Theory with Time: An Integrated Approach," *Academy of Management Review,* July 2004, pp. 404–422; G. P. Latham, "The Motivational Benefits of Goal-Setting," *Academy of Management Executive,* November 2004, pp. 126–129; and G. Yeo, S. Loft, T. Xiao, and C. Kiewitz, "Goal Orientation and Performance: Differential Relationships Across Levels of Analysis and as a Function of Task Demands," *Journal of Applied Psychology* (May 2009), pp. 710–726.

25. J. A. Wagner III, "Participation's Effects on Performance and Satisfaction: A Reconsideration of Research and Evidence," *Academy of Management Review*, April 1994, pp. 312–330; J. George-Falvey, "Effects of Task Complexity and Learning Stage on the Relationship Between Participation in Goal Setting and Task Performance," *Academy of Management Proceedings on Disk*, 1996; T. D. Ludwig and E. S. Geller, "Assigned Versus Participative Goal Setting and Response Generalization: Managing Injury Control Among Professional Pizza Deliverers," *Journal of Applied Psychology* (April 1997), pp. 253–261; and S. G. Harkins and M. D. Lowe, "The Effects of Self-Set Goals on Task Performance," *Journal of Applied Social Psychology* (January 2000), pp. 1–40.

26. J. M. Ivancevich and J. T. McMahon, "The Effects of Goal Setting, External Feedback, and Self-Generated Feedback on Outcome Variables: A Field Experiment," *Academy of*

Management Journal (June 1982), pp. 359–372; and E. A. Locke, "Motivation Through Conscious Goal Setting."

27. J. R. Hollenbeck, C. R. Williams, and H. J. Klein, "An Empirical Examination of the Antecedents of Commitment to Difficult Goals," *Journal of Applied Psychology* (February 1989), pp. 18–23; see, also, J. C. Wofford, V. L. Goodwin, and S. Premack, "Meta-Analysis of the Antecedents of Personal Goal Level and of the Antecedents and Consequences of Goal Commitment," *Journal of Management* (September 1992), pp. 595–615; Tubbs, "Commitment as a Moderator of the Goal-Performance Relation"; J. W. Smither, M. London, and R. R. Reilly, "Does Performance Improve Following Multisource Feedback? A Theoretical Model, Meta-Analysis, and Review of Empirical Findings," *Personnel Psychology,* Spring 2005, pp. 171–203.

28. M. E. Gist, "Self-Efficacy: Implications for Organizational Behavior and Human Resource Management," *Academy of Management Review*, July 1987, pp. 472–485; and A. Bandura, *Self-Efficacy: The Exercise of Control* (New York: Freeman, 1997).

29. E. A. Locke, E. Frederick, C. Lee, and P. Bobko, "Effect of Self-Efficacy, Goals, and Task Strategies on Task Performance," *Journal of Applied Psychology* (May 1984), pp. 241–251; M. E. Gist and T. R. Mitchell, "Self-Efficacy: A Theoretical Analysis of Its Determinants and Malleability," *Academy of Management Review*, April 1992, pp. 183–211; A. D. Stajkovic and F. Luthans, "Self-Efficacy and Work-Related Performance: A Meta-Analysis," *Psychological Bulletin,* September 1998, pp. 240–261; A. Bandura, "Cultivate Self-Efficacy for Personal and Organizational Effectiveness," in E. Locke (ed.), *Handbook of Principles of Organizational Behavior* (Malden, MA: Blackwell, 2004), pp. 120–136; and F. Q. Fu, K. A. Richards, and E. Jones, "The Motivation Hub: Effects of Goal Setting and Self-Efficacy on Effort and New Product Sales," *Journal of Personal Selling & Sales Management* (Summer 2009), pp. 277–292.

30. A. Bandura and D. Cervone, "Differential Engagement in Self-Reactive Influences in Cognitively Based Motivation," *Organizational Behavior and Human Decision Processes*, August 1986, pp. 92–113; and R. Ilies and T. A. Judge, "Goal Regulation Across Time: The Effects of Feedback and Affect," *Journal of Applied Psychology* (May 2005), pp. 453–467.

31. See J. C. Anderson and C. A. O'Reilly, "Effects of an Organizational Control System on Managerial Satisfaction and Performance," *Human Relations*, June 1981, pp. 491–501; and J. P. Meyer, B. Schacht-Cole, and I. R. Gellatly, "An Examination of the Cognitive Mechanisms by Which Assigned Goals Affect Task Performance and Reactions to Performance," *Journal of Applied Social Psychology* 18, no. 5 (1988), pp. 390–408.

32. See, for example, R. W. Griffin, "Toward an Integrated Theory of Task Design," in L. L. Cummings and B. M. Staw (eds.), *Research in Organizational Behavior*, vol. 9 (Greenwich, CT: JAI Press, 1987), pp. 79–120; and M. Campion, "Interdisciplinary Approaches to Job Design: A Constructive Replication with Extensions," *Journal of Applied Psychology* (August 1988), pp. 467–481.

33. See J. R. Hackman and G. R. Oldham, "Motivation Through the Design of Work: Test of a Theory," *Organizational Behavior and Human Performance,* August 1976, pp. 250–279; Y. Fried and G. R. Ferris, "The Validity of the Job Characteristics Model: A Review and Meta Analysis," *Personnel Psychology,* Summer 1987, pp. 287–322; S. J. Zaccaro and E. F. Stone, "Incremental

Validity of an Empirically Based Measure of Job Characteristics," *Journal of Applied Psychology* (May 1988), pp. 245–252; and R. W. Renn and R. J. Vandenberg, "The Critical Psychological States: An Underrepresented Component in Job Characteristics Model Research," *Journal of Management* (February 1995), pp. 279–303.

34. G. Van Der Vegt, B. Emans, and E. Van Der Vliert, "Motivating Effects of Task and Outcome Interdependence in Work Teams," *Journal of Managerial Psychology* (July 2000), p. 829; and B. Bemmels, "Local Union Leaders' Satisfaction with Grievance Procedures," *Journal of Labor Research* (Summer 2001), pp. 653–669.

35. J. S. Adams, "Inequity in Social Exchanges," in L. Berkowitz (ed.), *Advances in Experimental Social Psychology*, vol. 2 (New York: Academic Press, 1965), pp. 267–300; and M. L. Ambrose and C. T. Kulik, "Old Friends, New Faces: Motivation Research in the 1990s."

36. See, for example, R. L. Bell, "Addressing Employees' Feelings of Inequity," *Supervision,* May 2011, pp. 3–6; P. S. Goodman and A. Friedman, "An Examination of Adams' Theory of Inequity," *Administrative Science Quarterly*, September 1971, pp. 271–288; M. R. Carrell, "A Longitudinal Field Assessment of Employee Perceptions of Equitable Treatment," *Organizational Behavior and Human Performance*, February 1978, pp. 108–118; E. Walster, G. W. Walster, and W. G. Scott, *Equity: Theory and Research* (Boston: Allyn & Bacon, 1978); R. G. Lord and J. A. Hohenfeld, "Longitudinal Field Assessment of Equity Effects on the Performance of Major League Baseball Players," *Journal of Applied Psychology* (February 1979), pp. 19–26; J. E. Dittrich and M. R. Carrell, "Organizational Equity Perceptions, Employee Job Satisfaction, and Departmental Absence and Turnover Rates," *Organizational Behavior and Human Performance*, August 1979, pp. 29–40; and J. Greenberg, "Cognitive Reevaluation of Outcomes in Response to Underpayment Inequity," *Academy of Management Journal* (March 1989), pp. 174–184.

37. P. S. Goodman, "An Examination of Referents Used in the Evaluation of Pay," *Organizational Behavior and Human Performance*, October 1974, pp. 170–195; S. Ronen, "Equity Perception in Multiple Comparisons: A Field Study," *Human Relations*, April 1986, pp. 333–346; R. W. Scholl, E. A. Cooper, and J. F. McKenna, "Referent Selection in Determining Equity Perception: Differential Effects on Behavioral and Attitudinal Outcomes," *Personnel Psychology*, Spring 1987, pp. 113–127; and C. T. Kulik and M. L. Ambrose, "Personal and Situational Determinants of Referent Choice," *Academy of Management Review*, April 1992, pp. 212–237.

38. See, for example, R. C. Dailey and D. J. Kirk, "Distributive and Procedural Justice as Antecedents of Job Dissatisfaction and Intent to Turnover," *Human Relations,* March 1992, pp. 305–316; D. B. McFarlin and P. D. Sweeney, "Distributive and Procedural Justice as Predictors of Satisfaction with Personal and Organizational Outcomes," *Academy of Management Journal* (August 1992), pp. 626–637; M. A. Konovsky, "Understanding Procedural Justice and Its Impact on Business Organizations," *Journal of Management,* 26, no. 3 (2000), pp. 489–511; J. A. Colquitt, "Does the Justice of One Interact with the Justice of Many? Reactions to Procedural Justice in Teams," *Journal of Applied Psychology* (August 2004), pp. 633–646; J. Brockner, "Why It's So Hard to Be Fair," *Harvard Business Review,* March 2006, pp. 122–129; and B. M. Wiesenfeld, W. B. Swann, Jr., J. Brockner, and

C. A. Bartel, "Is More Fairness Always Preferred: Self-Esteem Moderates Reactions to Procedural Justice," *Academy of Management Journal* (October 2007), pp. 1235–1253.

39. V. H. Vroom, *Work and Motivation* (New York: John Wiley, 1964).

40. See, for example, H. G. Heneman III and D. P. Schwab, "Evaluation of Research on Expectancy Theory Prediction of Employee Performance," *Psychological Bulletin,* July 1972, pp. 1–9; L. Reinharth and M. Wahba, "Expectancy Theory as a Predictor of Work Motivation, Effort Expenditure, and Job Performance," *Academy of Management Journal* (September 1975), pp. 502–537; and K. T. Lambright, "An Update of a Classic: Applying Expectancy Theory to Understand Contracted Provider Motivation," *Administration & Society,* July 2010, pp. 375–403.

41. See, for example, V. H. Vroom, "Organizational Choice: A Study of Pre- and Postdecision Processes," *Organizational Behavior and Human Performance*, April 1966, pp. 212–225; L. W. Porter and E. E. Lawler III, *Managerial Attitudes and Performance* (Homewood, IL: Richard D. Irwin, 1968); W. Van Eerde and H. Thierry, "Vroom's Expectancy Models and Work-Related Criteria: A Meta-Analysis," *Journal of Applied Psychology* (October 1996), pp. 575–586; and M. L. Ambrose and C. T. Kulik, "Old Friends, New Faces: Motivation Research in the 1990s."

42. Right or Wrong box based on Borders Group, Inc., 2010 Form 10-K, www.borders.com (June 6, 2011); J. Checkler, "Judge Clears Bonuses at Borders," *Wall Street Journal,* April 23–24, 2011, p. B3; "News Briefs," *Publishers Weekly,* April 11, 2011, pp. 4+; P. Brickley, "Borders Seeks to Hand Out $8.3 Million in Bonuses," *Wall Street Journal,* March 26, 2011, p. B2; and J. A. Trachtenberg and M. Spector, "For Borders, A Scramble to Be Lean," *Wall Street Journal,* March 14, 2011, p. B1.

43. See, for instance, M. Siegall, "The Simplistic Five: An Integrative Framework for Teaching Motivation," *The Organizational Behavior Teaching Review* 12, no. 4 (1987–1988), pp. 141–143.

44. "100 Best Companies to Work For," *Fortune,* February 7, 2011, pp. 91+; V. Nayar, "Employee Happiness: Zappos vs. HCL," *Businessweek.com,* January 5, 2011; D. Richards, "At Zappos, Culture Pays," *Strategy+Business Online,* Autumn 2010; T. Hseih, "Zappos's CEO on Going to Extremes for Customers," *Harvard Business Review,* July–August 2010, pp. 41–45; A. Perschel, "Work-Life Flow: How Individuals, Zappos, and Other Innovative Companies Achieve High Engagement," *Global Business & Organizational Excellence,* July 2010, pp. 17–30; and J. M. O'Brien, "Zappos Know How to Kick It," *Fortune,* February 2, 2009, pp. 54–60.

45. T. Barber, "Inspire Your Employees Now," *Bloombeg BusinessWeek Online,* May 18, 2010; D. Mattioli, "CEOs Welcome Recovery to Look After Staff," *Wall Street Journal,* April 5, 2010, p. B5; J. Sullivan, "How Do We Keep People Motivated Following Layoffs?" *Workforce Management Online,* March 2010; S. Crabtree, "How to Bolster Employees' Confidence," *The Gallup Management Journal Online,* February 25, 2010; S. E. Needleman, "Business Owners Try to Motivate Employees," *Wall Street Journal,* January 14, 2010, p. B5; H. Mintzberg, "Rebuilding Companies as Communities," *Harvard Business Review,* July–August, 2009, pp. 140–143; and R. Luss, "Engaging Employees Through Periods of Layoffs," *Towers Watson,* www.towerswatson.com (March 3, 2009).

46. N. J. Adler with A. Gundersen, *International Dimensions of Organizational Behavior*, 5th ed. (Cincinnati, OH, 2008).

47. G. Hofstede, "Motivation, Leadership and Organization: Do American Theories Apply Abroad?" *Organizational Dynamics,* Summer 1980, p. 55.

48. Ibid.

49. J. K. Giacobbe-Miller, D. J. Miller, and V. I. Victorov, "A Comparison of Russian and U.S. Pay Allocation Decisions, Distributive Justice Judgments and Productivity Under Different Payment Conditions," *Personnel Psychology,* Spring 1998, pp. 137–163.

50. S. L. Mueller and L. D. Clarke, "Political-Economic Context and Sensitivity to Equity: Differences Between the United States and the Transition Economies of Central and Eastern Europe," *Academy of Management Journal* (June 1998), pp. 319–329.

51. I. Harpaz, "The Importance of Work Goals: An International Perspective," *Journal of International Business Studies* (First Quarter 1990), pp. 75–93.

52. G. E. Popp, H. J. Davis, and T. T. Herbert, "An International Study of Intrinsic Motivation Composition," *Management International Review,* January 1986, pp. 28–35.

53. R. W. Brislin, B. MacNab, R. Worthley, F. Kabigting Jr., and B. Zukis, "Evolving Perceptions of Japanese Workplace Motivation: An Employee-Manager Comparison," *International Journal of Cross-Cultural Management* (April 2005), pp. 87–104.

54. J. R. Billings and D. L. Sharpe, "Factors Influencing Flextime Usage Among Employed Married Women," *Consumer Interests Annual*, 1999, pp. 89–94; and I. Harpaz, "The Importance of Work Goals: An International Perspective," *Journal of International Business Studies* (First Quarter 1990), pp. 75–93.

55. N. Ramachandran, "New Paths At Work," *U.S. News & World Report,* March 20, 2006, p. 47; S. Armour, "Generation Y: They've Arrived at Work With a New Attitude," *USA Today,* November 6, 2005, pp. B1+; and R. Kanfer and P. L. Ackerman, "Aging, Adult Development, and Work Motivation," *Academy of Management Review,* July 2004, pp. 440–458.

56. T. D. Golden and J. F. Veiga, "The Impact of Extent of Telecommuting on Job Satisfaction: Resolving Inconsistent Findings," *Journal of Management* (April 2005), pp. 301–318.

57. See, for instance, M. Alpert, "The Care and Feeding of Engineers," *Fortune*, September 21, 1992, pp. 86–95; G. Poole, "How to Manage Your Nerds," *Forbes ASAP*, December 1994, pp. 132–136; T. J. Allen and R. Katz, "Managing Technical Professionals and Organizations: Improving and Sustaining the Performance of Organizations, Project Teams, and Individual Contributors," *Sloan Management Review,* Summer 2002, pp. S4–S5; and S. R. Barley and G. Kunda, "Contracting: A New Form of Professional Practice," *Academy of Management Perspectives,* February 2006, pp. 45–66.

58. K. Bennhold, "Working (Part-Time) in the 21st Century," *New York Times Online,* December 29, 2010; and J. Revell, C. Bigda, and D. Rosato, "The Rise of Freelance Nation," *CNNMoney,* cnnmoney.com (June 12, 2009); and R. J. Bohner, Jr. and E. R. Salasko, "Beware the Legal Risks of Hiring Temps," *Workforce,* October 2002, pp. 50–57.

59. H. G. Jackson, "Flexible Workplaces: The Next Imperative," *HR Magazine,* March 2011, p. 8; E. Frauenheim, "Companies Focus Their Attention on Flexibility," *Workforce Management Online,* February 2011; P. Davidson, "Companies Do More with Fewer Workers," *USA Today,* February 23, 2011, pp. 1B+; M. Rich, "Weighing Costs, Companies Favor Temporary Help," *New York Times Online,* December 19, 2010; P. Davidson, "Temporary Workers Reshape Companies, Jobs," *USA Today,* October 13, 2010, pp. 1B+; J. P. Broschak and A. Davis-Blake,

"Mixing Standard Work and Nonstandard Deals: The Consequences of Heterogeneity in Employment Arrangements," *Academy of Management Journal* (April 2006), pp. 371–393; M. L. Kraimer, S. J. Wayne, R. C. Liden, and R. T. Sparrowe, "The Role of Job Security in Understanding the Relationship Between Employees' Perceptions of Temporary Workers and Employees' Performance," *Journal of Applied Psychology* (March 2005), pp. 389–398; and C. E. Connelly and D. G. Gallagher, "Emerging Trends in Contingent Work Research," *Journal of Management* (November 2004), pp. 959–983.

60. C. Haddad, "FedEx: Gaining on the Ground," *BusinessWeek,* December 16, 2002, pp. 126–128; and L. Landro, "To Get Doctors to Do Better, Health Plans Try Cash Bonuses," *Wall Street Journal,* September 17, 2004, pp. A1+.

61. K. E. Culp, "Playing Field Widens for Stack's Great Game," *Springfield, Missouri, News-Leader,* January 9, 2005, pp. 1A+.

62. P. M. Buehler, "Opening Up Management Communication: Learning from Open Book Management," *Supervision,* August 2010, pp. 15–17; D. Drickhamer, "Open Books to Elevate Performance," *Industry Week,* November 2002, p. 16; J. Case, "Opening the Books," *Harvard Business Review*, March–April 1997, pp. 118–27; J. P. Schuster, J. Carpenter, and M. P. Kane, *The Power of Open-Book Management* (New York: John Wiley, 1996); and J. Case, "The Open-Book Revolution," *Inc.,* June 1995, pp. 26–50.

63. L. DeMars, "Glazed Over in a Good Way," *CFO,* July 2007, p. 80.

64. J. Singer, "Healing Your Workplace," *Supervision,* March 2011, pp. 11–13; P. Hart, "Benefits of Employee Recognition in the Workplace: Reduced Risk and Raised Revenues," *EHS Today,* February 2011, pp. 49–52; and F. Luthans and A. D. Stajkovic, "Provide Recognition for Performance Improvement," in E. A. Locke (ed.), *Principles of Organizational Behavior* (Oxford, England: Blackwell, 2000), pp. 166–180.

65. C. Huff, "Recognition That Resonates," *Workforce Management Online,* April 1, 2008.

66. J. Stewart, "I'm Standing Up for the Industry. Are You?" *Restaurant Business,* February 2011, pp. 36–37; and M. Littman, "Best Bosses Tell All," *Working Woman,* October 2000, p. 54.

67. E. White, "Praise from Peers Goes a Long Way," *Wall Street Journal,* December 19, 2005, p. B3.

68. Ibid.

69. K. J. Dunham, "Amid Sinking Workplace Morale, Employers Turn to Recognition," *Wall Street Journal,* November 19, 2002, p. B8.

70. See B. Nelson, "Try Praise," *Inc.,* September 1996, p. 115; and J. Wiscombe, "Rewards Get Results," *Workforce,* April 2002, pp. 42–48. Cited in S. Caudron, "The Top 20 Ways to Motivate Employees," *Industry Week,* April 3, 1995, pp. 15–16.

71. V. M. Barret, "Fight the Jerks," *Forbes,* July 2, 2007, pp. 52–54.

72. E. Krell, "All for Incentives, Incentives for All," *HR Magazine,* January 2011, pp. 35–38; and E. White, "The Best vs. the Rest," *Wall Street Journal,* January 30, 2006, pp. B1+.

73. R. K. Abbott, "Performance-Based Flex: A Tool for Managing Total Compensation Costs," *Compensation and Benefits Review*, March–April 1993, pp. 18–21; J. R. Schuster and P. K. Zingheim, "The New Variable Pay: Key Design Issues," *Compensation and Benefits Review*, March–April 1993, pp. 27–34; C. R. Williams and L. P. Livingstone, "Another Look at the Relationship Between Performance and Voluntary Turnover," *Academy of Management Journal* (April 1994), pp. 269–298; A. M. Dickinson and K. L. Gillette, "A Comparison of the Effects of Two Individual Monetary Incentive Systems on Productivity: Piece Rate Pay Versus Base Pay Plus Incentives," *Journal of Organizational Behavior Management* (Spring 1994), pp. 3–82; and C. B. Cadsby, F. Song, and F. Tapon, "Sorting and Incentive Effects of Pay for Performance: An Experimental Investigation," *Academy of Management Journal* (April 2007), pp. 387–405.

74. E. White, "Employers Increasingly Favor Bonuses to Raises," *Wall Street Journal,* August 28, 2006, p. B3.

75. "More Than 20 Percent of Japanese Firms Use Pay Systems Based on Performance," *Manpower Argus,* May 1998, p. 7; and E. Beauchesne, "Pay Bonuses Improve Productivity, Study Shows," *Vancouver Sun,* September 13, 2002, p. D5.

76. H. Rheem, "Performance Management Programs," *Harvard Business Review*, September–October 1996, pp. 8–9; G. Sprinkle, "The Effect of Incentive Contracts on Learning and Performance," *Accounting Review,* July 2000, pp. 299–326; and "Do Incentive Awards Work?" *HRFocus,* October 2000, pp. 1–3.

77. R.D. Banker, S.Y. Lee, G. Potter, and D. Srinivasan, "Contextual Analysis of Performance Impacts on Outcome-Based Incentive Compensation," *Academy of Management Journal* (August 1996), pp. 920–948.

78. S. A. Jeffrey and G. K. Adomza, "Incentive Salience and Improved Performance," *Human Performance,* 24, no. 1 (2011), pp. 47–59; T. Reason, "Why Bonus Plans Fail," *CFO,* January 2003, p. 53; and "Has Pay for Performance Had Its Day?" *McKinsey Quarterly,* no. 4 (2002), accessed at www.forbes.com.

79. E. Frauenheim, "Downturn Puts New Emphasis on Engagement," *Workforce Management Online,* July 21, 2009; S. D. Friedman, "Dial Down the Stress Level," *Harvard Business Review,* December 2008, pp. 28–29; and S. E. Needleman, "Allaying Workers' Fears During Uncertain Times," *Wall Street Journal,* October 6, 2008.

CHAPTER
12

Leadership
and
Trust

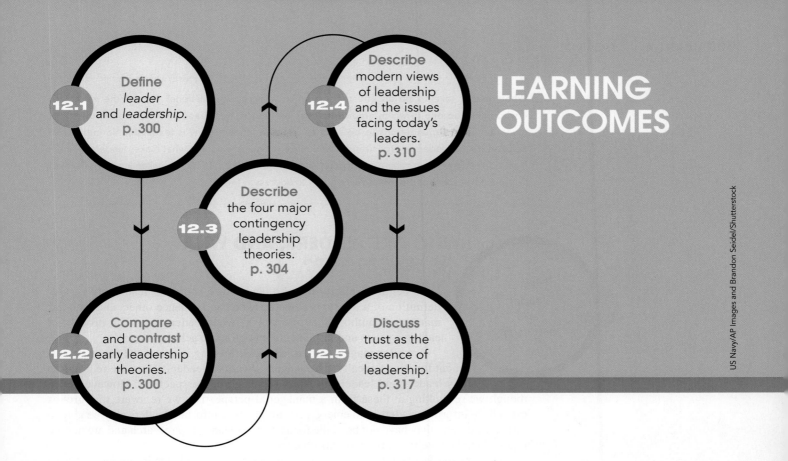

12.1 Define *leader* and *leadership*. p. 300

12.4 Describe modern views of leadership and the issues facing today's leaders. p. 310

12.3 Describe the four major contingency leadership theories. p. 304

12.2 Compare and **contrast** early leadership theories. p. 300

12.5 Discuss trust as the essence of leadership. p. 317

US Navy/AP Images and Brandon Seidel/Shutterstock

Master and Commander

With a father who was a Navy captain, Holly Graf, the first woman to command a Navy cruiser, had dreamed of doing just that since her high school days in Connecticut.[1] Upon graduation from the U.S. Naval Academy in 1985, colleagues sensed that she was on a fast track to leadership. Her assignments were well-rounded—from tours aboard a destroyer tender, a frigate, and a destroyer, to shore assignments at the Pentagon and as a Navy instructor at Villanova University. However, Graf's "darker side began to emerge when she was assigned to the destroyer U.S.S. *Curtis Wilbur* as the executive officer (XO) or second in command." One individual (now retired) says his tour on the *Curtis Wilbur* was "the worst time in my life." Graf's constant berating of the crew led him to complain to officials, but nothing was done. A few years later, Graf made U.S. Naval history by becoming the first female commander of a destroyer, the U.S.S. *Winston Churchill*. A Navy chaplain called his time aboard the *Churchill* as "the strangest of more than 200 such visits to ships in his career. Morale was the lowest he had ever encountered on any vessel." He tried to talk to Graf about what he was hearing from the crew and junior officers, but she cut him off and said she didn't want to talk to him about it. How effective do you think Graf could be with this kind of leader style?

What does it take to be an effective leader in today's organizations? Should the workplace environment be one in which employees feel like they're heard and trusted? It's important for managers in all organizations to be seen as effective leaders. Why is leadership so important? Because it's the leaders in organizations who make things happen. But what makes leaders different from nonleaders? What's the most appropriate style of leadership? What makes leaders effective? These are just some of the topics we're going to address in this chapter.

WHO ARE LEADERS, AND WHAT IS LEADERSHIP?

12.1 Define *leader* and *leadership*.

Let's begin by clarifying who leaders are and what leadership is. Our definition of a **leader** is someone who can influence others and who has managerial authority. **Leadership** is what leaders do. It's a process of leading a group and influencing that group to achieve its goals.

Are all managers leaders? Because leading is one of the four management functions, ideally all managers *should* be leaders. Thus, we're going to study leaders and leadership from a managerial perspective.[2] However, even though we're looking at these from a managerial perspective, we're aware that groups often have informal leaders who emerge. Although these informal leaders may be able to influence others, they have not been the focus of most leadership research and are not the types of leaders we're studying in this chapter.

Leaders and leadership, like motivation, are organizational behavior topics that have been researched a lot. Most of that research has been aimed at answering the question: "What is an effective leader?" We'll begin our study of leadership by looking at some early leadership theories that attempted to answer that question.

WHAT DO EARLY LEADERSHIP THEORIES TELL US ABOUT LEADERSHIP?

12.2 Compare and **contrast** early leadership theories.

People have been interested in leadership since they started coming together in groups to accomplish goals. However, it wasn't until the early part of the twentieth century that researchers actually began to study it. These early leadership theories focused on the *leader* (trait theories) and how the *leader interacted* with his or her group members (behavioral theories).

What Traits Do Leaders Have?

Ask the average person on the street what comes to mind when he or she thinks of leadership. You're likely to get a list of qualities such as intelligence, charisma, decisiveness, enthusiasm, strength, bravery, integrity, and self-confidence. These responses represent, in essence, **trait theories of leadership**. The search for traits or characteristics that differentiate leaders from nonleaders dominated early leadership research efforts. If the concept of traits were valid, all leaders would have to possess specific characteristics.

However, despite the best efforts of researchers, it proved impossible to identify a set of traits that would *always* differentiate a leader (the person) from a nonleader. Maybe it was a bit optimistic to think that there could be consistent and unique traits that would apply universally to all effective leaders, no matter whether they were in charge of Hyundai Motor Company, the Moscow Ballet, the country of Brazil, a local collegiate chapter of Alpha Chi Omega, or Ted's Malibu Surf Shop. However, later attempts to identify traits consistently associated with *leadership* (the process, not the person) were more successful. The seven traits shown to be associated with effective leadership are described briefly in Exhibit 12–1.[3]

EXHIBIT 12–1   Traits Associated with Leadership

1. *Drive.* Leaders exhibit a high effort level. They have a relatively high desire for achievement, they are ambitious, they have a lot of energy, they are tirelessly persistent in their activities, and they show initiative.

2. *Desire to lead.* Leaders have a strong desire to influence and lead others. They demonstrate the willingness to take responsibility.

3. *Honesty and integrity.* Leaders build trusting relationships with followers by being truthful, or nondeceitful, and by showing high consistency between word and deed.

4. *Self-confidence.* Followers look to leaders for an absence of self-doubt. Leaders, therefore, need to show self-confidence in order to convince followers of the rightness of their goals and decisions.

5. *Intelligence.* Leaders need to be intelligent enough to gather, synthesize, and interpret large amounts of information, and they need to be able to create visions, solve problems, and make correct decisions.

6. *Job-relevant knowledge.* Effective leaders have a high degree of knowledge about the company, industry, and technical matters. In-depth knowledge allows leaders to make well-informed decisions and to understand the implications of those decisions.

7. *Extraversion.* Leaders are energetic, lively people. They are sociable, assertive, and rarely silent or withdrawn.

Sources: Based on S. A. Kirkpatrick and E. A. Locke, "Leadership: Do Traits Really Matter?" *Academy of Management Executive,* May 1991, pp. 48–60; and T. A. Judge, J. E. Bono, R. Ilies, and M. W. Gerhardt, "Personality and Leadership: A Qualitative and Quantitative Review," *Journal of Applied Psychology* (August 2002), pp. 765–80.

Researchers eventually recognized that traits alone were not sufficient for identifying effective leaders because explanations based solely on traits ignored the interactions of leaders and their group members as well as situational factors. Possessing the appropriate traits only made it more likely that an individual would be an effective leader. Therefore, leadership research from the late 1940s to the mid-1960s concentrated on the preferred behavioral styles that leaders demonstrated. Researchers wondered whether there was something unique in what effective leaders *did*—in other words, in their *behavior*.

What Behaviors Do Leaders Exhibit?

It was hoped that the behavioral theories of leadership approach would provide more definitive answers about the nature of leadership and, if successful, also have practical implications quite different from those of the trait approach. If trait research had been successful, it would have provided a basis for selecting the right people to assume formal leadership positions in organizations. In contrast, if behavioral studies were to turn up critical behavioral determinants of leadership, people could be trained to be leaders, which is precisely the premise behind management development programs.

A number of studies looked at behavioral styles. We'll briefly review three of the most popular: Kurt Lewin's studies at the University of Iowa, the Ohio State studies, and the University of Michigan studies. Then we'll see how the concepts developed in those studies were used in a grid created for appraising leadership styles.

WHAT DID THE UNIVERSITY OF IOWA STUDIES TELL US ABOUT LEADERSHIP BEHAVIOR?

One of the first studies of leadership behavior was done by Kurt Lewin and his associates at the University of Iowa.[4] In their studies, the researchers explored three leadership

---

leader
Someone who can influence others and who has managerial authority

leadership
The process of leading a group and influencing that group to achieve its goals

trait theories of leadership
Theories that isolate characteristics (traits) that differentiate leaders from nonleaders

behavioral theories of leadership
Theories that isolate behaviors that differentiate effective leaders from ineffective leaders

Autocratic style describes the leadership of Martha Stewart, founder of Martha Stewart Living Omnimedia. In presiding over her many business ventures in publishing, broadcasting, and merchandising, Stewart's leadership behavior includes centralizing authority, dictating work methods, making unilateral decisions, and limiting employee participation. She is described as meticulous and highly demanding of her staff. Stewart is shown here shaking hands with the president of the Culinary Institute of America, where she delivered the commencement address and told graduates that she attributes her successful business career to passion, hard work, and generosity.

behaviors or styles: autocratic, democratic, and laissez-faire. An **autocratic style** is that of a leader who typically tends to centralize authority, dictate work methods, make unilateral decisions, and limit employee participation. A leader with a **democratic style** tends to involve employees in decision making, delegates authority, encourages participation in deciding work methods and goals, and uses feedback as an opportunity to coach employees. The democratic style can be further classified in two ways: consultative and participative. A *democratic-consultative leader* seeks input and hears the concerns and issues of employees but makes the final decision him- or herself. In this capacity, the democratic-consultative leader is using the input as an information-seeking exercise. A *democratic-participative leader* often allows employees to have a say in what's decided. Here, decisions are made by the group, with the leader providing one input to that group. Finally, the **laissez-faire** leader generally gives his or her employees complete freedom to make decisions and to complete their work in whatever way they see fit. A laissez-faire leader might simply provide necessary materials and answer questions.

Lewin and his associates wondered which one of the three leadership styles was most effective. On the basis of their studies of leaders from boys' clubs, they concluded that the laissez-faire style was ineffective on every performance criterion when compared with both democratic and autocratic styles. Quantity of work done was equal in groups with democratic and autocratic leaders, but work quality and group satisfaction were higher in democratic groups. The results suggest that a democratic leadership style could contribute to both good quantity and high quality of work.

Later studies of autocratic and democratic styles of leadership showed mixed results. For example, democratic leadership styles sometimes produced higher performance levels than autocratic styles, but at other times they produced group performance that was lower than or equal to that of autocratic styles. Nonetheless, more consistent results were generated when a measure of employee satisfaction was used.

Group members' satisfaction levels were generally higher under a democratic leader than under an autocratic one.[5] Did this finding mean that managers should always exhibit a democratic style of leadership? Two researchers, Robert Tannenbaum and Warren Schmidt, attempted to provide that answer.[6]

Tannenbaum and Schmidt developed a continuum of leader behaviors. The continuum illustrated that a range of leadership behaviors, from boss centered (autocratic) to employee centered (laissez-faire), is possible. In deciding which leader behavior from the continuum to use, Tannenbaum and Schmidt proposed that managers look at forces within themselves (such as comfort level with the chosen leadership style), forces within the employees (such as readiness to assume responsibility), and forces within the situation (such as time pressures). They suggested that managers should move toward more employee-centered styles in the long run because such behavior would increase employees' motivation, decision quality, teamwork, morale, and development.

This dual nature of leader behaviors—that is, focusing on the work to be done and focusing on the employees—is also a key characteristic of the Ohio State and University of Michigan studies.

WHAT DID THE OHIO STATE STUDIES SHOW?   The most comprehensive and replicated of the behavioral theories resulted from research that began at Ohio State University in the late 1940s.[7] These studies sought to identify independent dimensions of leader behavior. Beginning with more than 1,000 dimensions, the researchers eventually narrowed the list down to two categories that accounted for most of the leadership behavior described by employees. They called these two dimensions initiating structure and consideration.

Darryl Bautista/AP Images

Both the Ohio State and Michigan studies added a lot to our understanding of effective leadership.[9] Prior to the completion of these studies, it was widely thought by researchers and practicing managers that one style of leadership was good and another bad. However, as the research showed, both leader behavior dimensions—job-centered and employee-centered in the Michigan studies, and initiating structure and consideration in the Ohio State studies—are necessary for effective leadership. That dual focus of "what" a leader does still holds today. Leaders are expected to focus on both the task and on the people he or she is leading. Even the later contingency leadership theories used the people/task distinction to define a leader's style. Finally, these early behavioral studies were important for the "systematic methodology they introduced and the increased awareness they generated concerning the importance of leader behavior." Although the behavioral theories may not have been the final chapter in the book on leadership, they "served as a springboard for the leadership research that followed."

Think About:
- Is saying that the leader's "job" is to focus on the task and focus on the people too simplistic? Explain.
- How did the behavioral theories serve as a springboard for the leadership research that followed?

Initiating structure refers to the extent to which a leader is likely to define and structure his or her role and those of employees in the search for goal attainment. It includes behavior that attempts to organize work, work relationships, and goals. For example, the leader who is characterized as high in initiating structure assigns group members to particular tasks, expects workers to maintain definite standards of performance, and emphasizes meeting deadlines.

Consideration is defined as the extent to which a leader has job relationships characterized by mutual trust and respect for employees' ideas and feelings. A leader who is high in consideration helps employees with personal problems, is friendly and approachable, and treats all employees as equals. He or she shows concern for his or her followers' comfort, well-being, status, and satisfaction.

Extensive research based on these definitions found that a leader who is high in initiating structure and consideration (a high-high leader) achieved high employee performance and satisfaction more frequently than one who rated low on either consideration, initiating structure, or both. However, the high-high style did not always yield positive results. For example, leader behavior characterized as high on initiating structure led to greater rates of grievances, absenteeism, and turnover, and lower levels of job satisfaction for workers performing routine tasks. Other studies found that high consideration was negatively related to performance ratings of the leader by his or her manager. In conclusion, the Ohio State studies suggested that the high-high style generally produced positive outcomes, but enough exceptions were found to indicate that situational factors needed to be integrated into the theory.

HOW DID THE UNIVERSITY OF MICHIGAN STUDIES DIFFER? Leadership studies undertaken at the University of Michigan's Survey Research Center, at about the same time as those being done at Ohio State, had similar research objectives: to locate the behavioral characteristics of leaders that were related to performance effectiveness. The Michigan group also came up with two dimensions of leadership behavior, which they labeled employee oriented and production oriented.[8] Leaders who were **employee oriented** emphasized

autocratic style
A leader who centralizes authority, dictates work methods, makes unilateral decisions, and limits employee participation

democratic style
A leader who involves employees in decision making, delegates authority, encourages participation in deciding work methods, and uses feedback to coach employees

laissez-faire
A leader who generally gives employees complete freedom to make decisions and to complete their work however they see fit

initiating structure
The extent to which a leader defines and structures his or her role and the roles of employees to attain goals

consideration
The extent to which a leader has job relationships characterized by mutual trust, respect for employees' ideas, and regard for their feelings

employee oriented
A leader who emphasizes the people aspects

British entrepreneur Richard Branson, chairman and CEO of Virgin Group, is an employee-oriented leader who emphasizes interpersonal relations, takes a personal interest in the needs of employees, and accepts individual differences among workers. Described as fun-loving and sensitive to the needs of others, Branson has built one of the most recognized and respected brands in the world for products and services in the areas of travel, entertainment, and lifestyle. In this photo, Branson poses in front of the Eiffel Tower with some of Virgin's employees in Paris who joined him in a promotional tour to launch the French translation of his autobiography.

interpersonal relations; they took a personal interest in the needs of their employees and accepted individual differences among members. Leaders who were **production oriented**, in contrast, tended to emphasize the technical or task aspects of the job, were concerned mainly with accomplishing their group's tasks, and regarded group members as a means to that end.

The conclusions of the Michigan researchers strongly favored leaders who were employee oriented. Employee-oriented leaders were associated with higher group productivity and higher job satisfaction. Production-oriented leaders were associated with lower group productivity and lower worker satisfaction.

What Is the Managerial Grid?

The behavioral dimensions from these early leadership studies provided the basis for the development of a two-dimensional grid for appraising leadership styles. This **managerial grid** used the behavioral dimensions "concern for people" and "concern for production" and evaluated a leader's use of these behaviors, ranking them on a scale from 1 (low) to 9 (high).[10] Although the grid had 81 potential categories into which a leader's behavioral style might fall, only five styles were named: impoverished management (1,1), task management (9,1), middle-of-the-road management (5,5), country club management (1,9), and team management (9,9). Of these five styles, the researchers concluded that managers performed best when using a 9,9 style. Unfortunately, the grid offered no answers to the question of what made a manager an effective leader; it only provided a framework for conceptualizing leadership style. In fact, little substantive evidence supports the conclusion that a 9,9 style is most effective in all situations.[11]

Leadership researchers were discovering that predicting leadership success involved something more complex than isolating a few leader traits or preferable behaviors. They began looking at situational influences. Specifically, which leadership styles might be suitable in different situations and what were these different situations?

12.3 Describe the four major contingency leadership theories.

WHAT DO THE CONTINGENCY THEORIES OF LEADERSHIP TELL US?

"The corporate world is filled with stories of leaders who failed to achieve greatness because they failed to understand the context they were working in."[12] In this section we examine four contingency theories—Fiedler, Hersey-Blanchard, leader-participation, and path-goal. Each looks at defining leadership style and the situation, and attempts to answer the *if-then* contingencies (that is, *if* this is the context or situation, *then* this is the best leadership style to use).

What Was the First Comprehensive Contingency Model?

The first comprehensive contingency model for leadership was developed by Fred Fiedler.[13] The **Fiedler contingency model** proposed that effective group performance depended upon properly matching the leader's style and the amount of control and influence in the situation. The model was based on the premise that a certain leadership style would be most effective in different types of situations. The keys were (1) to define those leadership styles and the different types of situations, and then (2) identify the appropriate combinations of style and situation.

Fiedler proposed that a key factor in leadership success was an individual's basic leadership style, either task oriented or relationship oriented. To measure a leader's style, Fiedler developed the least-preferred co-worker (LPC) questionnaire. This questionnaire contained 18 pairs of contrasting adjectives—for example, pleasant–unpleasant, cold–warm, boring–interesting, or friendly–unfriendly. Respondents were asked to think of all the co-workers they had ever had and to describe that one person they *least enjoyed* working with by rating him or her on a scale of 1 to 8 for each of the sets of adjectives (the 8 always described the positive adjective out of the pair and the 1 always described the negative adjective out of the pair).

If the leader described the least preferred co-worker in relatively positive terms (in other words, a "high" LPC score—a score of 64 or above), then the respondent was primarily interested in good personal relations with co-workers and the style would be described as *relationship oriented*. In contrast, if you saw the least preferred co-worker in relatively unfavorable terms (a low LPC score—a score of 57 or below), you were primarily interested in productivity and getting the job done; thus, your style would be labeled as *task oriented*. Fiedler did acknowledge that a small number of people might fall in between these two extremes and not have a cut-and-dried leadership style. One other important point is that Fiedler assumed a person's leadership style was fixed regardless of the situation. In other words, if you were a relationship-oriented leader, you'd always be one, and the same for task-oriented.

After an individual's leadership style had been assessed through the LPC, it was time to evaluate the situation in order to be able to match the leader with the situation. Fiedler's research uncovered three contingency dimensions that defined the key situational factors in leader effectiveness. These were:

- *Leader-member relations:* the degree of confidence, trust, and respect employees had for their leader; rated as either good or poor.
- *Task structure:* the degree to which job assignments were formalized and structured; rated as either high or low.
- *Position power:* the degree of influence a leader had over activities such as hiring, firing, discipline, promotions, and salary increases; rated as either strong or weak.

Each leadership situation was evaluated in terms of these three contingency variables, which when combined produced eight possible situations that were either favorable or unfavorable for the leader. (See the bottom of the chart in Exhibit 12–2). Situations I, II, and III were classified as highly favorable for the leader. Situations IV, V, and VI were moderately favorable for the leader. And situations VII and VIII were described as highly unfavorable for the leader.

Once Fiedler had described the leader variables and the situational variables, he had everything he needed to define the specific contingencies for leadership effectiveness. To do so, he studied 1,200 groups where he compared relationship-oriented versus task-oriented leadership styles in each of the eight situational categories. He concluded that task-oriented leaders performed better in very favorable situations and in very unfavorable situations. (See the top of Exhibit 12–2 where performance is shown on the vertical axis and situation favorableness is shown on the horizontal axis.)

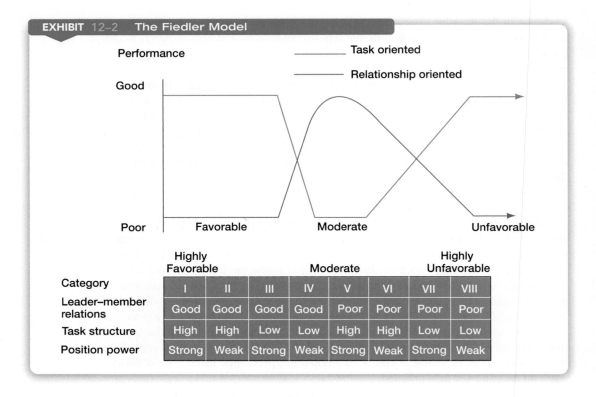

| **EXHIBIT** 12–2 The Fiedler Model |

Category	I	II	III	IV	V	VI	VII	VIII
Leader–member relations	Good	Good	Good	Good	Poor	Poor	Poor	Poor
Task structure	High	High	Low	Low	High	High	Low	Low
Position power	Strong	Weak	Strong	Weak	Strong	Weak	Strong	Weak

On the other hand, relationship-oriented leaders performed better in moderately favorable situations.

Because Fiedler treated an individual's leadership style as fixed, there were only two ways to improve leader effectiveness. First, you could bring in a new leader whose style better fit the situation. For instance, if the group situation was highly unfavorable but was led by a relationship-oriented leader, the group's performance could be improved by replacing that person with a task-oriented leader. The second alternative was to change the situation to fit the leader. This could be done by restructuring tasks; by increasing or decreasing the power that the leader had over factors such as salary increases, promotions, and disciplinary actions; or by improving the leader-member relations. Research testing the overall validity of Fiedler's model has shown considerable evidence to support the model.[14] However, his theory wasn't without criticisms. The major one is that it's probably unrealistic to assume that a person can't change his or her leadership style to fit the situation. Effective leaders can, and do, change their styles. Another is that the LPC wasn't very practical. Finally, the situation variables were difficult to assess.[15] Despite its shortcomings, the Fiedler model showed that effective leadership style needed to reflect situational factors.

How Do Followers' Willingness and Ability Influence Leaders?

Paul Hersey and Ken Blanchard developed a leadership theory that has had a strong following among management development specialists.[16] This model, called situational leadership theory (SLT), is a contingency theory that focuses on followers' readiness. Before we proceed, there are two points we need to clarify: Why a leadership theory focuses on the followers, and what is meant by the term *readiness*.

The emphasis on the followers in leadership effectiveness reflects the reality that it *is* the followers who accept or reject the leader. Regardless of what the leader does, the group's effectiveness depends on the actions of the followers. This is an important dimension that has been overlooked or underemphasized in most leadership theories.

And **readiness**, as defined by Hersey and Blanchard refers to the extent to which people have the ability and willingness to accomplish a specific task.

SLT uses the same two leadership dimensions that Fiedler identified: task and relationship behaviors. However, Hersey and Blanchard go a step further by considering each as either high or low and then combining them into four specific leadership styles described as follows:

- *Telling* (high task–low relationship): The leader defines roles and tells people what, how, when, and where to do various tasks.
- *Selling* (high task–high relationship): The leader provides both directive and supportive behavior.
- *Participating* (low task–high relationship): The leader and followers share in decision making; the main role of the leader is facilitating and communicating.
- *Delegating* (low task–low relationship): The leader provides little direction or support.

The final component in the model is the four stages of follower readiness:

- *R1:* People are both *unable and unwilling* to take responsibility for doing something. Followers aren't competent or confident.
- *R2:* People are *unable but willing* to do the necessary job tasks. Followers are motivated but lack the appropriate skills.
- *R3:* People are *able but unwilling* to do what the leader wants. Followers are competent, but don't want to do something.
- *R4:* People are both *able and willing* to do what is asked of them.

Software engineers and Web developers at YouTube work together in small teams to design, develop, and roll out key features and products in short time frames. Employees work in a fast-paced, creative, and intellectually challenging environment where they apply their problem-solving skills and technical knowledge in displaying a wide variety of video content for the second most visited site in the world. They have a high level of follower readiness. As well educated and responsible employees, they are willing and able to complete their tasks under leadership that gives them the freedom to make and implement decisions. This leader-follower relationship is consistent with Hersey and Blanchard's situational leadership theory.

SLT essentially views the leader-follower relationship as like that of a parent and a child. Just as a parent needs to relinquish control when a child becomes more mature and responsible, so, too, should leaders. As followers reach higher levels of readiness, the leader responds not only by decreasing control over their activities but also decreasing relationship behaviors. The SLT says if followers are at R1 (*unable* and *unwilling* to do a task), the leader needs to use the telling style and give clear and specific directions; if followers are at R2 (*unable* and *willing*), the leader needs to use the selling style and display high task orientation to compensate for the followers' lack of ability and high relationship orientation to get followers to "buy into" the leader's desires; if followers are at R3 (*able* and *unwilling*), the leader needs to use the participating style to gain their support; and if employees are at R4 (both *able* and *willing*), the leader doesn't need to do much and should use the delegating style.

SLT has intuitive appeal. It acknowledges the importance of followers and builds on the logic that leaders can compensate for ability and motivational limitations in their followers. However, research efforts to test and support the theory generally have been disappointing.[17] Possible explanations include internal inconsistencies in the model as well as problems with research methodology. Despite its appeal and wide popularity, we have to be cautious about any enthusiastic endorsement of SLT.

LiPo Ching/Newscom

How Participative Should a Leader Be?

Back in 1973, Victor Vroom and Phillip Yetton developed a **leader-participation model** that related leadership behavior and participation to decision making.[19] Recognizing that task structures have varying demands for routine and nonroutine activities, these researchers argued that leader behavior must adjust to reflect the task structure. Vroom and Yetton's model was normative. That is, it provided a sequential set of rules to be followed in determining the form and amount of participation in decision making in different types of situations. The model was a decision tree incorporating seven contingencies (whose relevance could be identified by making yes or no choices) and five alternative leadership styles.

More recent work by Vroom and Arthur Jago has revised that model.[20] The new model retains the same five alternative leadership styles but expands the contingency variables to twelve—from the leader's making the decision completely by himself or herself to sharing the problem with the group and developing a consensus decision. These variables are listed in Exhibit 12–3.

Research on the original leader-participation model was encouraging.[21] But unfortunately, the model is far too complex for the typical manager to use regularly. In fact, Vroom and Jago have developed a computer program to guide managers through all the decision branches in the revised model. Although we obviously can't do justice to this model's sophistication in this discussion, it has provided us with some solid, empirically supported insights into key contingency variables related to leadership effectiveness. Moreover, the leader-participation model confirms that leadership research should be directed at the situation rather than at the person. That is, it probably makes more sense to talk about autocratic and participative situations than autocratic and participative leaders. As House did in his path-goal theory, Vroom, Yetton, and Jago argue against the notion that leader behavior is inflexible. The leader-participation model assumes that the leader can adapt his or her style to different situations.[22]

How Do Leaders Help Followers?

Another approach to understanding leadership is **path-goal theory**, which states that the leader's job is to assist followers in attaining their goals and to provide direction or support needed to ensure that their goals are compatible with the goals of the group or organization. Developed by Robert House, path-goal theory takes key elements from the expectancy theory of motivation (see Chapter 11).[23] The term *path-goal* is derived from the belief that effective leaders clarify the path to help their followers get from where they are to the achievement of their work goals and make the journey along the path easier by reducing roadblocks and pitfalls.

EXHIBIT 12–3   Contingency Variables in the Revised Leader-Participation Model

1. Importance of the decision
2. Importance of obtaining follower commitment to the decision
3. Whether the leader has sufficient information to make a good decision
4. How well structured the problem is
5. Whether an autocratic decision would receive follower commitment
6. Whether followers "buy into" the organization's goals
7. Whether there is likely to be conflict among followers over solution alternatives
8. Whether followers have the necessary information to make a good decision
9. Time constraints on the leader that may limit follower involvement
10. Whether costs to bring geographically dispersed members together are justified
11. Importance to the leader of minimizing the time it takes to make the decision
12. Importance of using participation as a tool for developing follower decision skills

Source: Stephen P. Robbins and Timothy A. Judge, *Organizational Behavior*, 13th, ©2009. Printed and electronically reproduced by permission of Pearson Education, Inc., Upper Saddle River, New Jersey.

House identified four leadership behaviors:

◆ *Directive leader:* Lets subordinates know what's expected of them, schedules work to be done, and gives specific guidance on how to accomplish tasks.

◆ *Supportive leader:* Shows concern for the needs of followers and is friendly.

◆ *Participative leader:* Consults with group members and uses their suggestions before making a decision.

◆ *Achievement-oriented leader:* Sets challenging goals and expects followers to perform at their highest level.

In contrast to Fiedler's view that a leader couldn't change his or her behavior, House assumed that leaders are flexible and can display any or all of these leadership styles depending on the situation.

As Exhibit 12–4 illustrates, path-goal theory proposes two situational or contingency variables that moderate the leadership behavior-outcome relationship: those in the *environment* that are outside the control of the follower (factors including task structure, formal authority system, and the work group) and those that are part of the personal characteristics of the *follower* (including locus of control, experience, and perceived ability). Environmental factors determine the type of leader behavior required if subordinate outcomes are to be maximized; personal characteristics of the follower determine how the environment and leader behavior are interpreted. The theory proposes that a leader's behavior won't be

Chung Mong-Koo, chairman and CEO of South Korea's Hyundai-Kia Motor Group, is an achievement-oriented leader. Since assuming leadership of Hyundai Motor Company in 1999, Chung Mong-Koo has set difficult goals and has motivated his employees to achieve them. His achievements include elevating product quality from poor to world class, increasing sales volume, and improving brand image and customer satisfaction. Confident and aggressive, Chung Mong-Koo has transformed Hyundai into a top global competitor and the world's fastest-growing major car maker. Chung Mong-Koo (left) is shown here preparing to deliver his annual New Year's address to employees.

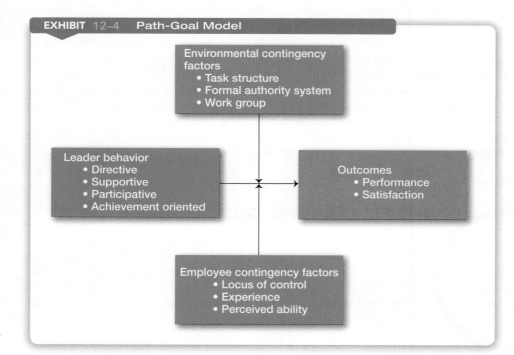

EXHIBIT 12–4   **Path-Goal Model**

Environmental contingency factors
• Task structure
• Formal authority system
• Work group

Leader behavior
• Directive
• Supportive
• Participative
• Achievement oriented

Outcomes
• Performance
• Satisfaction

Employee contingency factors
• Locus of control
• Experience
• Perceived ability

leader-participation model
A leadership contingency theory that's based on a sequential set of rules for determining how much participation a leader uses in decision making according to different types of situations

path-goal theory
A leadership theory that says the leader's job is to assist followers in attaining their goals and to provide direction or support needed to ensure that their goals are compatible with the organization's or group's goals

effective if it's redundant with what the environmental structure is providing or is incongruent with follower characteristics. For example, some predictions from path-goal theory are:

◆ Directive leadership leads to greater satisfaction when tasks are ambiguous or stressful than when they are highly structured and well laid out. The followers aren't sure what to do, so the leader needs to give them some direction.

◆ Supportive leadership results in high employee performance and satisfaction when subordinates are performing structured tasks. In this situation, the leader only needs to support followers, not tell them what to do.

◆ Directive leadership is likely to be perceived as redundant among subordinates with high perceived ability or with considerable experience. These followers are quite capable so they don't need a leader to tell them what to do.

◆ The clearer and more bureaucratic the formal authority relationships, the more leaders should exhibit supportive behavior and deemphasize directive behavior. The organizational situation has provided the structure as far as what is expected of followers, so the leader's role is simply to support.

◆ Directive leadership will lead to higher employee satisfaction when there is substantive conflict within a work group. In this situation, the followers need a leader who will take charge.

◆ Subordinates with an internal locus of control will be more satisfied with a participative style. Because these followers believe that they control what happens to them, they prefer to participate in decisions.

◆ Subordinates with an external locus of control will be more satisfied with a directive style. These followers believe that what happens to them is a result of the external environment so they would prefer a leader who tells them what to do.

◆ Achievement-oriented leadership will increase subordinates' expectancies that effort will lead to high performance when tasks are ambiguously structured. By setting challenging goals, followers know what the expectations are.

Research findings on the path-goal model have been mixed because the theory has so many variables to examine. Although not every study has found support, we can still say that evidence supports the logic underlying the theory.[24] That is, an employee's performance and satisfaction are likely to be positively influenced when the leader chooses a leadership style that compensates for shortcomings in either the employee or the work setting. However, if the leader spends time explaining tasks that are already clear or when the employee has the ability and experience to handle them without interference, the employee is likely to see such directive behavior as redundant or even insulting.

WHAT IS LEADERSHIP LIKE TODAY?

12.4 Describe modern views of leadership and the issues facing today's leaders.

What are the latest views of leadership, and what issues do today's leaders have to deal with? In this section, we're going to look at four contemporary views of leadership: leader-member exchange (LMX), transformational-transactional leadership, charismatic-visionary leadership, and team leadership. In addition, we'll discuss some issues that leaders have to face in leading effectively in today's environment.

What Do the Four Contemporary Views of Leadership Tell Us?

Remember our discussion at the beginning of this chapter where we said that leadership studies have long had the goal of describing what it takes to be an effective leader. That goal hasn't changed! Even the contemporary views of leadership are interested in answering that question. These views of leadership have a common theme: leaders who interact with, inspire, and support followers.

HOW DO LEADERS INTERACT WITH FOLLOWERS?   Have you ever been in a group in which the leader had "favorites" who made up his or her in-group? If so, that's the premise behind leader-member exchange (LMX) theory.[25] **Leader-member exchange (LMX) theory** says that leaders create in-groups and out-groups and those in the in-group will have higher performance ratings, less turnover, and greater job satisfaction.

LMX theory suggests that early on in the relationship between a leader and a given follower, a leader will implicitly categorize a follower as an "in" or as an "out." That relationship tends to remain fairly stable over time. Leaders also encourage LMX by rewarding those employees with whom they want a closer linkage and punishing those with whom they do not.[26] For the LMX relationship to remain intact, however, both the leader and the follower must "invest" in the relationship.

It's not exactly clear how a leader chooses who falls into each category, but evidence indicates that in-group members have demographic, attitude, personality, and even gender similarities with the leader or they have a higher level of competence than out-group members.[27] The leader does the choosing, but the follower's characteristics drive the decision.

Research on LMX has been generally supportive. It appears that leaders do differentiate among followers; that these disparities are not random; and followers with in-group status will have higher performance ratings, engage in more helping or "citizenship" behaviors at work, and report greater satisfaction with their boss.[28] These findings probably shouldn't be surprising when leaders are most likely to invest their time and other resources in those whom they expect to perform best.

HOW DO TRANSACTIONAL LEADERS DIFFER FROM TRANSFORMATIONAL LEADERS?
Many early leadership theories viewed leaders as **transactional leaders**; that is, leaders who lead primarily by using social exchanges (or transactions). Transactional leaders guide or motivate followers to work toward established goals by exchanging rewards for their productivity.[29] But another type of leader—a **transformational leader**—stimulates and inspires (transforms) followers to achieve extraordinary outcomes. Examples include Jim Goodnight of SAS Institute and Andrea Jung of Avon. They pay attention to the concerns and developmental needs of individual followers; they change followers' awareness of issues by helping those followers look at old problems in new ways; and they are able to excite, arouse, and inspire followers to exert extra effort to achieve group goals.

Transactional and transformational leadership shouldn't be viewed as opposing approaches to getting things done.[30] Transformational leadership develops from transactional leadership. Transformational leadership produces levels of employee effort and performance that go beyond what would occur with a transactional approach alone. Moreover, transformational leadership is more than charisma since the transformational leader attempts to instill in followers the ability to question not only established views but those views held by the leader.[31]

The evidence supporting the superiority of transformational leadership over transactional leadership is overwhelmingly impressive. For instance, studies that looked at managers in different settings, including the military and business, found that transformational leaders were evaluated as more effective, higher performers, more promotable than their transactional counterparts, and more interpersonally sensitive.[32] In addition, evidence indicates that transformational leadership is strongly correlated with lower turnover rates and higher levels of productivity, work engagement, employee satisfaction, creativity, goal attainment, and follower well-being.[33]

HOW DO CHARISMATIC LEADERSHIP AND VISIONARY LEADERSHIP DIFFER?   Jeff Bezos, founder and CEO of Amazon.com, is a person who exudes energy, enthusiasm, and drive.[34] He's fun-loving (his legendary laugh has been described as a flock

leader-member exchange (LMX) theory
A leadership theory that says leaders create in-groups and out-groups and those in the in-group will have higher performance ratings, less turnover, and greater job satisfaction

transactional leaders
Leaders who lead primarily by using social exchanges (or transactions)

transformational leaders
Leaders who stimulate and inspire (transform) followers to achieve extraordinary outcomes

Mark Richards/PhotoEdit

Amazon.com founder and chief executive Jeff Bezos is a charismatic leader. Described as energetic, enthusiastic, optimistic, and self-confident, Bezos has the drive to set and pursue goals for risky new ventures and to inspire his employees to work hard to achieve them. He started the company in 1994 with the vision of providing consumers with the service of an online bookstore, and he built it into the largest retailer on the Web. Bezos reinvented Amazon by introducing a product innovation, the Kindle electronic reader, that began with his long-term vision of "every book, ever printed, in any language, all available in less than 60 seconds." In this photo, Bezos uses his charisma to inspire employees working at an Amazon distribution center.

of Canadian geese on nitrous oxide), but has pursued his vision for Amazon with serious intensity and has demonstrated an ability to inspire his employees through the ups and downs of a rapidly growing company. Bezos is what we call a **charismatic leader**—that is, an enthusiastic, self-confident leader whose personality and actions influence people to behave in certain ways.

Several authors have attempted to identify personal characteristics of the charismatic leader.[35] The most comprehensive analysis identified five such characteristics: they have a vision, the ability to articulate that vision, willingness to take risks to achieve that vision, sensitivity to both environmental constraints and follower needs, and behaviors that are out of the ordinary.[36]

An increasing body of evidence shows impressive correlations between charismatic leadership and high performance and satisfaction among followers.[37] Although one study found that charismatic CEOs had no impact on subsequent organizational performance, charisma is still believed to be a desirable leadership quality.[38]

If charisma is desirable, can people learn to be charismatic leaders? Or are charismatic leaders born with their qualities? Although a small number of experts still think that charisma can't be learned, most believe that individuals can be trained to exhibit charismatic behaviors.[39] For example, researchers have succeeded in teaching undergraduate students to "be" charismatic. How? They were taught to articulate a far-reaching goal, communicate high performance expectations, exhibit confidence in the ability of subordinates to meet those expectations, and empathize with the needs of their subordinates; they learned to project a powerful, confident, and dynamic presence; and they practiced using a captivating and engaging voice tone. The researchers also trained the student leaders to use charismatic nonverbal behaviors including leaning toward the follower when communicating, maintaining direct eye contact, and having a relaxed posture and animated facial expressions. In groups with these "trained" charismatic leaders, members had higher task performance, higher task adjustment, and better adjustment to the leader and to the group than did group members who worked in groups led by noncharismatic leaders.

One last thing we should say about charismatic leadership is that it may not always be necessary to achieve high levels of employee performance. It may be most appropriate when the follower's task has an ideological purpose or when the environment involves a high degree of stress and uncertainty.[40] This aspect may explain why, when charismatic leaders surface, it's more likely to be in politics, religion, or wartime; or when a business firm is starting up or facing a survival crisis. For example, Martin Luther King Jr. used his charisma to bring about social equality through nonviolent means; and Steve Jobs achieved unwavering loyalty and commitment from Apple's technical staff in the early 1980s by articulating a vision of personal computers that would dramatically change the way people lived.

Although the term *vision* is often linked with charismatic leadership, **visionary leadership** is different: it's the ability to create and articulate a realistic, credible, and attractive vision of the future that improves upon the present situation.[41] This vision, if properly selected and implemented, is so energizing that it "in effect jump-starts the future by calling forth the skills, talents, and resources to make it happen."[42]

An organization's vision should offer clear and compelling imagery that taps into people's emotions and inspires enthusiasm to pursue the organization's goals. It should be able to generate possibilities that are inspirational and unique and offer new ways of doing things that are clearly better for the organization and its members. Visions that are clearly articulated and have powerful imagery are easily grasped and accepted. For instance, Michael Dell created a vision of a business that sells and delivers customized PCs directly to customers in less than a week. The late Mary Kay Ash's vision of women as entrepreneurs selling products that improved their self-image gave impetus to her cosmetics company, Mary Kay Cosmetics.

WHAT ABOUT LEADERS AND TEAMS?   Because leadership is increasingly taking place within a team context and more organizations are using work teams, the role of the leader in guiding team members has become increasingly important. The role of team leader *is* different from the traditional leadership role, as J. D. Bryant, a supervisor at Texas Instruments' Forest Lane plant in Dallas, discovered.[43] One day he was contentedly overseeing a staff of 15 circuit board assemblers. The next day he was told that the company was going to use employee teams and he was to become a "facilitator." He said, "I'm supposed to teach the teams everything I know and then let them make their own decisions." Confused about his new role, he admitted, "There was no clear plan on what I was supposed to do." What *is* involved in being a team leader?

Many leaders are not equipped to handle the change to employee teams. As one consultant noted, "Even the most capable managers have trouble making the transition because all the command-and-control type things they were encouraged to do before are no longer appropriate. There's no reason to have any skill or sense of this."[44] This same consultant estimated that "probably 15 percent of managers are natural team leaders; another 15 percent could never lead a team because it runs counter to their personality—that is, they're unable to sublimate their dominating style for the good of the team. Then there's that huge group in the middle: Team leadership doesn't come naturally to them, but they can learn it."[45]

The challenge for many managers is learning how to become an effective team leader. They have to learn skills such as patiently sharing information, being able to trust others and to give up authority, and understanding when to intervene. And effective team leaders have mastered the difficult balancing act of knowing when to leave their teams alone and when to get involved. New team leaders may try to retain too much control at a time when team members need more autonomy, or they may abandon their teams at times when the teams need support and help.[46]

One study looking at organizations that had reorganized themselves around employee teams found certain common responsibilities of all leaders. These responsibilities included coaching, facilitating, handling disciplinary problems, reviewing team and individual performance, training, and communication.[47] However, a more meaningful way to describe the team leader's job is to focus on two priorities: (1) managing the team's external boundary, and (2) facilitating the team process.[48] These priorities entail four specific leadership roles as shown in Exhibit 12–5.

RIGHT ? WRONG

The definition of "friend" on social networking sites such as Facebook and MySpace is so broad that even strangers may tag you. But it doesn't feel weird because nothing really changes when a stranger does this. However, what if your boss, who isn't much older than you are, asks you to be a friend on these sites? What then?

Think About:

- What are the implications if you refuse the offer?
- What are the implications if you accept?
- What ethical issues might arise because of this situation?
- What would you do?

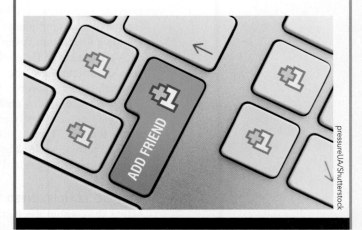

pressureUA/Shutterstock

charismatic leaders
Enthusiastic, self-confident leaders whose personalities and actions influence people to behave in certain ways

visionary leadership
The ability to create and articulate a realistic, credible, and attractive vision of the future that improves on the present situation

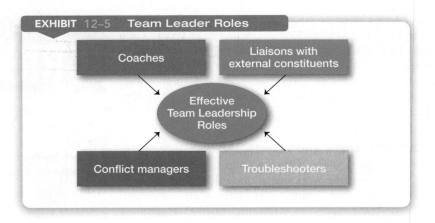

EXHIBIT 12–5   Team Leader Roles

What Issues Do Today's Leaders Face?

It's not easy being a chief information officer (CIO) today. A person responsible for managing a company's information technology activities faces a lot of external and internal pressures. Technology changes rapidly—almost daily, it sometimes seems. Business costs continue to rise. Competitors develop new strategies. Economic conditions continue to confound even the experts. Rob Carter, CIO of FedEx is on the hot seat facing such challenges.[49] He's responsible for all the computer and communication systems that provide around-the-clock and around-the-globe support for FedEx's products and services. If anything goes wrong, you know who takes the heat. However, Carter has been an effective leader in this seemingly chaotic environment.

Leading effectively in today's environment is likely to involve such challenges for many leaders. Twenty-first-century leaders face some important leadership issues. In this section, we look at these issues including empowering employees, cross-cultural leadership, and emotional intelligence and leadership.

WHY DO LEADERS NEED TO EMPOWER EMPLOYEES?   As we've described in different places throughout the text, managers are increasingly leading by not leading; that is, by empowering their employees. Empowerment involves increasing the decision-making discretion of workers. Millions of individual employees and employee teams are making the key operating decisions that directly affect their work. They're developing budgets, scheduling workloads, controlling inventories, solving quality problems, and engaging in similar activities that until very recently were viewed exclusively as part of the manager's job.[50] For instance, at The Container Store, any employee who gets a customer request has permission to take care of it. The company's chairman emeritus Garret Boone says, "Everybody we hire, we hire as a leader. Anybody in our store can take an action that you might think of typically being a manager's action."[51]

One reason more companies are empowering employees is the need for quick decisions by those people who are most knowledgeable about the issues—often those at lower organizational levels. If organizations want to successfully compete in a dynamic global economy, employees have to be able to make decisions and implement changes quickly. Another reason is that organizational downsizings left many managers with larger spans of control. In order to cope with the increased work demands, managers had to empower their people. Although empowerment is not a universal answer, it can be beneficial when employees have the knowledge, skills, and experience to do their jobs competently.

Technology also has contributed to the increases in employee empowerment. Managers face unique challenges in leading empowered employees who aren't physically present in the workplace as the Technology and the Manager's Job box discusses.

DOES NATIONAL CULTURE AFFECT LEADERSHIP?   One general conclusion that surfaces from leadership research is that effective leaders do not use a single style. They adjust their style to the situation. Although not mentioned explicitly, national culture is certainly

TECHNOLOGY AND THE MANAGER'S JOB — VIRTUAL LEADERSHIP

How do you lead people who are physically separated from you and with whom your interactions are primarily written digital communications?[52] That's the challenge of being a virtual leader. And unfortunately, leadership research has been directed mostly at face-to-face and verbal situations. But we can't ignore the reality that today's managers and their employees are increasingly being linked by technology rather than by geographic proximity. So what guidance would be helpful to leaders who must inspire and motivate dispersed employees?

It's easy to soften harsh words in face-to-face communication with nonverbal action. A smile or a comforting gesture can go a long way in lessening the blow behind strong words like *disappointed, unsatisfactory,*

inadequate, or *below expectations*. That nonverbal component doesn't exist in online interactions. The *structure* of words in a digital communication also has the power to motivate or demotivate the receiver. A manager who inadvertently sends a message in short phrases or in ALL CAPS may get a very different response than if the message had been sent in full sentences using appropriate punctuation.

To be an effective virtual leader, managers must recognize that they have choices in the words and structure of their digital communications. They also need to develop the skill of "reading between the lines" in the messages they receive. It's important to try and decipher the emotional content of a message as well as the written content. Also, virtual leaders need to think carefully about

what actions they want their digital messages to initiate. Be clear about what's expected and follow up on messages.

For an increasing number of managers, good interpersonal skills may include the abilities to communicate support and leadership through digital communication and to read emotions in others' messages. In this "new world" of communication, writing skills are likely to become an extension of interpersonal skills.

Think About:

- What challenges does a "virtual" leader face?
- Which is more important to a virtual leader: focusing on the task or focusing on the people? Explain your choice.
- How can virtual leaders use technology to help them be more effective leaders?

an important situational variable in determining which leadership style will be most effective. What works in China isn't likely to be effective in France or Canada. For instance, one study of Asian leadership styles revealed that Asian managers preferred leaders who were competent decision makers, effective communicators, and supportive of employees.[53] Another study of leadership in Sub-Saharan Africa found that charismatic leaders can help overcome cultural problems of corruption, poverty, tribalism, and violence.[54]

National culture affects leadership style because it influences how followers will respond. Leaders can't (and shouldn't) just choose their styles randomly. They're constrained by the cultural conditions their followers have come to expect. Exhibit 12–6 provides some

EXHIBIT 12–6 Cross-Cultural Leadership

- Korean leaders are expected to be paternalistic toward employees.
- Arab leaders who show kindness or generosity without being asked to do so are seen by other Arabs as weak.
- Japanese leaders are expected to be humble and speak frequently.
- Scandinavian and Dutch leaders who single out individuals with public praise are likely to embarrass, not energize, those individuals.
- Effective leaders in Malaysia are expected to show compassion while using more of an autocratic than a participative style.
- Effective German leaders are characterized by high performance orientation, low compassion, low self-protection, low team orientation, high autonomy, and high participation.

Sources: Based on J.-H. Shin, R. L. Heath, and J. Lee, "A Contingency Explanation of Public Relations Practitioner Leadership Styles: Situation and Culture," *Journal of Public Relations Research* (April 2011), pp. 167–190; J. C. Kennedy, "Leadership in Malaysia: Traditional Values, International Outlook," *Academy of Management Executive,* August 2002, pp. 15–17; F. C. Brodbeck, M. Frese, and M. Javidan, "Leadership Made in Germany: Low on Compassion, High on Performance," *Academy of Management Executive,* February 2002, pp. 16–29; M. F. Peterson and J. G. Hunt, "International Perspectives on International Leadership," *Leadership Quarterly,* Fall 1997, pp. 203–231; R. J. House and R. N. Aditya, "The Social Scientific Study of Leadership: Quo Vadis?" *Journal of Management* 23, no. 3 (1997), p. 463; and R. J. House, "Leadership in the Twenty-First Century," in A. Howard (ed.), *The Changing Nature of Work* (San Francisco: Jossey-Bass, 1995), p. 442.

empowerment
The act of increasing the decision-making discretion of workers

findings from selected examples of cross-cultural leadership studies. Because most leadership theories were developed in the United States, they have an American bias. They emphasize follower responsibilities rather than rights; assume self-gratification rather than commitment to duty or altruistic motivation; assume centrality of work and democratic value orientation; and stress rationality rather than spirituality, religion, or superstition.[55] However, the GLOBE research program, which we first introduced in Chapter 2, is the most extensive and comprehensive cross-cultural study of leadership ever undertaken. The GLOBE study has found that there are some universal aspects to leadership. Specifically, a number of elements of transformational leadership appear to be associated with effective leadership regardless of what country the leader is in.[56] These elements include vision, foresight, providing encouragement, trustworthiness, dynamism, positiveness, and proactiveness. The results led two members of the GLOBE team to conclude that "effective business leaders in any country are expected by their subordinates to provide a powerful and proactive vision to guide the company into the future, strong motivational skills to stimulate all employees to fulfill the vision, and excellent planning skills to assist in implementing the vision."[57] Some people suggest that the universal appeal of these transformational leader characteristics is due to the pressures toward common technologies and management practices, as a result of global competitiveness and multinational influences.

HOW DOES EMOTIONAL INTELLIGENCE AFFECT LEADERSHIP? We introduced emotional intelligence (EI) in our discussion of emotions in Chapter 9. We revisit the topic here because of recent studies indicating that EI—more than IQ, expertise, or any other single factor—is the best predictor of who will emerge as a leader.[58]

As we said in our earlier discussion of trait research, leaders need basic intelligence and job-relevant knowledge. But IQ and technical skills are "threshold capabilities." They're necessary but not sufficient requirements for leadership. It's the possession of the five components of emotional intelligence—self-awareness, self-management, self-motivation, empathy, and social skills—that allows an individual to become a star performer. Without EI, a person can have outstanding training, a highly analytical mind, a long-term vision, and an endless supply of terrific ideas but still not make a great leader, especially as individuals move up in an organization. The evidence indicates that the higher the rank of a person considered to be a star performer, the more that EI capabilities surface as the reason for his or her effectiveness. Specifically, when star performers were compared with average ones in senior management positions, nearly 90 percent of the difference in their effectiveness was attributable to EI factors rather than basic intelligence.

Interestingly, it's been pointed out that the maturing of Rudolph Giuliani's leadership effectiveness closely followed the development of his emotional intelligence. For the better part of the eight years he was mayor of New York, Giuliani ruled with an iron fist. He talked tough, picked fights, and demanded results. The result was a city that was cleaner, safer, and better governed—but also more polarized. Critics called Giuliani a tin-eared tyrant. In the eyes of many, something important was missing from his leadership. That something, his critics acknowledged, emerged as the World Trade Center collapsed. It was a newfound compassion to complement his command: a mix of resolve, empathy, and inspiration that brought comfort to millions.[59] It's likely that Giuliani's emotional capacities and compassion for others were stimulated by a series of personal hardships—including prostate cancer and the highly visible breakup of his marriage—both of which had taken place less than a year before the terrorist attacks on the World Trade Center.[60]

EI has been shown to be positively related to job performance at all levels. But it appears to be especially

Indra Nooyi, chief executive officer of PepsiCo, is a leader with high emotional intelligence. Nooyi possesses the five components of EI—self-awareness, self-management, self-motivation, empathy, and social skills—that have helped her emerge as a star performer in a job that demands a high degree of social interaction with employees, customers, and business and political leaders throughout the world. EI has contributed to Nooyi's high job performance and career success since she joined the company in 1994 as a senior vice president of strategy and development. Nooyi is shown here welcoming guests attending an annual PepsiCo shareholders meeting.

Newscom

relevant in jobs that demand a high degree of social interaction. And of course, that's what leadership is all about. Great leaders demonstrate their EI by exhibiting all five of its key components—self-awareness, self-management, self-motivation, empathy, and social skills (see p. 229).

Although there has been some controversy about the role of EI in leadership,[61] most of the research makes a case for concluding that EI is an essential element in leadership effectiveness.[62] As such, it could be added to the list of traits associated with leadership that we described earlier in the chapter.

WHY IS TRUST THE ESSENCE OF LEADERSHIP?

Discuss trust as the essence of leadership.

12.5

Trust, or lack of trust, is an increasingly important issue in today's organizations.[63] In today's uncertain environment, leaders need to build, or even rebuild, trust and credibility. Before we can discuss ways leaders can do that, we have to know what trust and credibility are and why they're so important.

The main component of credibility is honesty. Surveys show that honesty is consistently singled out as the number one characteristic of admired leaders. "Honesty is absolutely essential to leadership. If people are going to follow someone willingly, whether it be into battle or into the boardroom, they first want to assure themselves that the person is worthy of their trust."[64] In addition to being honest, credible leaders are competent and inspiring. They are personally able to effectively communicate their confidence and enthusiasm. Thus, followers judge a leader's **credibility** in terms of his or her honesty, competence, and ability to inspire.

Trust is closely entwined with the concept of credibility, and, in fact, the terms are often used interchangeably. **Trust** is defined as the belief in the integrity, character, and ability of a leader. Followers who trust a leader are willing to be vulnerable to the leader's actions because they are confident that their rights and interests will not be abused.[65] Research has identified five dimensions that make up the concept of trust:

- *Integrity:* honesty and truthfulness
- *Competence:* technical and interpersonal knowledge and skills
- *Consistency:* reliability, predictability, and good judgment in handling situations
- *Loyalty:* willingness to protect a person, physically and emotionally
- *Openness:* willingness to share ideas and information freely[66]

Of these five dimensions, integrity seems to be the most critical when someone assesses another's trustworthiness.[67] Both integrity and competence were seen in our earlier discussion of leadership traits found to be consistently associated with leadership.

Workplace changes have reinforced why such leadership qualities are important. For instance, trends of employee empowerment and self-managed work teams have reduced many of the traditional control mechanisms used to monitor employees. If a work team is free to schedule its own work, evaluate its own performance, and even make its own hiring decisions, trust becomes critical. Employees have to trust managers to treat them fairly, and managers have to trust employees to conscientiously fulfill their responsibilities.

Also, leaders have to increasingly lead others who may not be in their immediate work group or even may be physically separated—members of cross-functional or virtual teams, individuals who work for suppliers or customers, and perhaps even people who represent other organizations through strategic alliances. These situations don't allow leaders the luxury of falling back on their formal positions for influence. Many of these relationships,

credibility
The degree to which followers perceive someone as honest, competent, and able to inspire

trust
The belief in the integrity, character, and ability of a leader

EXHIBIT 12–7	Suggestions for Building Trust

1. **Practice openness.** Mistrust comes as much from what people don't know as from what they do know. Openness leads to confidence and trust. So keep people informed; make clear the criteria on how decisions are made; explain the rationale for your decisions; be candid about problems; and fully disclose relevant information.

2. **Be fair.** Before making decisions or taking actions, consider how others will perceive them in terms of objectivity and fairness. Give credit where credit is due; be objective and impartial in performance appraisals; and pay attention to equity perceptions in reward distributions.

3. **Speak your feelings.** Leaders who convey only hard facts come across as cold and distant. When you share your feelings, others will see you as real and human. They will know who you are and their respect for you will increase.

4. **Tell the truth.** If honesty is critical to credibility, you must be perceived as someone who tells the truth. Followers are more tolerant of being told something they "don't want to hear" than of finding out that their leader lied to them.

5. **Be consistent.** People want predictability. Mistrust comes from not knowing what to expect. Take the time to think about your values and beliefs. Then let them consistently guide your decisions. When you know your central purpose, your actions will follow accordingly, and you will project a consistency that earns trust.

6. **Fulfill your promises.** Trust requires that people believe that you're dependable. So you need to keep your word. Promises made must be promises kept.

7. **Maintain confidences.** You trust those whom you believe to be discrete and whom you can rely on. If people make themselves vulnerable by telling you something in confidence, they need to feel assured that you won't discuss it with others or betray that confidence. If people perceive you as someone who leaks personal confidences or someone who can't be depended on, you won't be perceived as trustworthy.

8. **Demonstrate confidence.** Develop the admiration and respect of others by demonstrating technical and professional ability. Pay particular attention to developing and displaying your communication, negotiating, and other interpersonal skills.

Sources: Based on P. S. Shockley-Zalabak and S. P Morreale, "Building High-Trust Organizations," *Leader to Leader*, Spring 2011, pp. 39–45; J. K. Butler Jr., "Toward Understanding and Measuring Conditions of Trust: Evolution of a Condition of Trust Inventory," *Journal of Management* (September 1991), pp. 643–663; and F. Bartolome, "Nobody Trusts the Boss Completely—Now What?" *Harvard Business Review*, March–April 1989, pp. 135–142.

in fact, are fluid and fleeting. So the ability to quickly develop trust and sustain that trust is crucial to the success of the relationship.

Why is it important that followers trust their leaders? Research has shown that trust in leadership is significantly related to positive job outcomes including job performance, organizational citizenship behavior, job satisfaction, and organizational commitment.[68] Given the importance of trust to effective leadership, leaders need to build trust with their followers. Some suggestions are shown in Exhibit 12–7.

Now, more than ever, managerial and leadership effectiveness depends on the ability to gain the trust of followers.[69] Downsizing, corporate financial misrepresentations, and the increased use of temporary employees have undermined employees' trust in their leaders and shaken the confidence of investors, suppliers, and customers. A survey found that only 39 percent of U.S. employees and 51 percent of Canadian employees trusted their executive leaders.[70] Today's leaders are faced with the challenge of rebuilding and restoring trust with employees and with other important organizational stakeholders.

A Final Thought Regarding Leadership

Despite the belief that some leadership style will always be effective regardless of the situation, leadership may not always be important! Research indicates that, in some situations, any behaviors a leader exhibits are irrelevant. In other words, certain individual, job, and organizational variables can act as "substitutes for leadership," negating the influence of the leader.[71]

For instance, follower characteristics such as experience, training, professional orientation, or need for independence can neutralize the effect of leadership. These characteristics can replace the employee's need for a leader's support or ability to create structure and reduce task ambiguity. Similarly, jobs that are inherently unambiguous and routine or that are intrinsically satisfying may place fewer demands on the leadership variable. Finally, such organizational characteristics as explicit formalized goals, rigid rules and procedures, or cohesive work groups can substitute for formal leadership.

12 Review

CHAPTER SUMMARY

12.1 Define *leader* and *leadership*. A leader is someone who can influence others and who has managerial authority. Leadership is a process of leading a group and influencing that group to achieve its goals. Managers should be leaders because leading is one of the four management functions.

12.2 Compare and contrast the early leadership theories. Early attempts to define leader traits were unsuccessful although later attempts found seven traits associated with leadership.

The University of Iowa studies explored three leadership styles. The only conclusion was that group members were more satisfied under a democratic leader than under an autocratic one. The Ohio State studies identified two dimensions of leader behavior—initiating structure and consideration. A leader high in both those dimensions at times achieved high group task performance and high group member satisfaction, but not always. The University of Michigan studies looked at employee-oriented leaders and production-oriented leaders. They concluded that leaders who were employee oriented could get high group productivity and high group member satisfaction. The Managerial Grid looked at leaders' concern for production and concern for people and identified five leader styles. Although it suggested that a leader who was high in concern for production and high in concern for people was the best, there was no substantive evidence for that conclusion.

As the behavioral studies showed, a leader's behavior has a dual nature: a focus on the task and a focus on the people.

12.3 Describe the four major contingency leadership theories. Fiedler's model attempted to define the best style to use in particular situations. He measured leader style—relationship oriented or task oriented—using the least-preferred co-worker questionnaire. Fiedler also assumed a leader's style was fixed. He measured three contingency dimensions: leader-member relations, task structure, and position power. The model suggests that task-oriented leaders performed best in very favorable and very unfavorable situations, and relationship-oriented leaders performed best in moderately favorable situations.

Hersey and Blanchard's situational leadership theory focused on followers' readiness. They identified four leadership styles: telling (high task–low relationship), selling (high task–high relationship),

participating (low task–high relationship), and delegating (low task–low relationship). They also identified four stages of readiness: unable and unwilling (use telling style); unable but willing (use selling style); able but unwilling (use participative style); and able and willing (use delegating style).

The leader-participation model relates leadership behavior and participation to decision making. It uses a decision tree format with seven contingencies and five alternative leadership styles.

The path-goal model developed by Robert House identified four leadership behaviors: directive, supportive, participative, and achievement-oriented. He assumes that a leader can and should be able to use any of these styles. The two situational contingency variables were found in the environment and in the follower. Essentially the path-goal model says that a leader should provide direction and support as needed; that is, structure the path so the followers can achieve goals.

12.4 Describe modern views of leadership and the issues facing today's leaders. Leader-member exchange (LMX) theory says that leaders create in-groups and out-groups and those in the in-group will have higher performance ratings, less turnover, and greater job satisfaction.

A transactional leader exchanges rewards for productivity where a transformational leader stimulates and inspires followers to achieve goals.

A charismatic leader is an enthusiastic and self-confident leader whose personality and actions influence people to behave in certain ways. People can learn to be charismatic. A visionary leader is able to create and articulate a realistic, credible, and attractive vision of the future.

A team leader has two priorities: manage the team's external boundary and facilitate the team process. Four leader roles are involved: liaison with external constituencies, troubleshooter, conflict manager, and coach.

The issues facing leaders today include employee empowerment, national culture, and emotional intelligence. As employees are empowered, the leader's role tends to be one of not leading. As leaders adjust their style to the situation, one of the most important situational characteristics is national culture. Finally, EI is proving to be an essential element in leadership effectiveness.

Discuss trust as the essence of leadership. The five dimensions of trust include integrity, competence, consistency, loyalty, and truthfulness. Integrity refers to one's honesty and truthfulness. Competence involves an individual's technical and interpersonal knowledge and skills. Consistency relates to an individual's reliability, predictability, and good judgment in handling situations. Loyalty is an individual's willingness to protect and save face for another person. Openness means that you can rely on the individual to give you the whole truth.

MyManagementLab For more resources, please visit **www.mymanagementlab.com**

UNDERSTANDING THE CHAPTER

1. Define *leader* and *leadership* and why managers should be leaders.

2. Discuss the strengths and weaknesses of the trait theory.

3. What does each of the behavioral leadership theories say about leadership?

4. What would a manager need to know to use Fiedler's contingency model? Be specific.

5. Do you think that most managers in real life use a contingency approach to increase their leadership effectiveness? Discuss.

6. "All managers should be leaders, but not all leaders should be managers." Do you agree or disagree with this statement? Support your position.

7. Do you think trust evolves out of an individual's personal characteristics or out of specific situations? Explain.

8. Do followers make a difference in whether a leader is effective? Discuss.

9. How can organizations develop effective leaders?

10. When might leaders be irrelevant?

Go to p. 445 — YOUR TURN TO BE A MANAGER for Chapter 12.

Endnotes

1. "Inbox," *Time,* April 5, 2010, p. 7; M. Thompson, "The Sea Witch," *Time,* March 22, 2010, pp. 30–33; B. H. Johnsen, J. Eid, S. Pallesen, P. T. Bartone, and O. A. Nissestad, "Predicting Transformational Leadership in Naval Cadets: Effects of Personality Hardiness and Training," *Journal of Applied Social Psychology* (September 2009), pp. 2213–2235; and P. Thunholm, "Military Leaders and Followers: Do They Have Different Decision Styles?" *Scandinavian Journal of Psychology* (August 2009), pp. 317–324.

2. Most leadership research has focused on the actions and responsibilities of managers and extrapolated the results to leaders and leadership in general.

3. See D. S. Derue, J. D. Nahrgang, N. Wellman, and S. E. Humphrey, "Trait and Behavioral Theories of Leadership: An Integration and Meta-Analytic Test of Their Relative Validity," *Personnel Psychology,* Spring 2011, pp. 7–52; T. A. Judge, J. E. Bono, R. Ilies, and M. W. Gerhardt, "Personality and Leadership: A Qualitative and Quantitative Review," *Journal of Applied Psychology* (August 2002), pp. 765–780; and S. A. Kirkpatrick and E. A. Locke, "Leadership: Do Traits Matter?" *Academy of Management Executive*, May 1991, pp. 48–60.

4. K. Lewin and R. Lippitt, "An Experimental Approach to the Study of Autocracy and Democracy: A Preliminary Note," *Sociometry* 1 (1938), pp. 292–300; K. Lewin, "Field Theory and Experiment in Social Psychology: Concepts and Methods," *American Journal of Sociology* 44 (1939), pp. 868–896; K. Lewin, R. Lippitt, and R. K. White, "Patterns of Aggressive Behavior in Experimentally Created Social Climates," *Journal of Social Psychology* 10 (1939), pp. 271–301; and R. Lippitt, "An Experimental Study of the Effect of Democratic and Authoritarian Group Atmospheres," *University of Iowa Studies in Child Welfare* 16 (1940), pp. 43–95.

5. B. M. Bass, *Stodgill's Handbook of Leadership* (New York: Free Press, 1981), pp. 298–299.

6. R. Tannenbaum and W. H. Schmidt, "How to Choose a Leadership Pattern," *Harvard Business Review,* May–June 1973, pp. 162–180.

7. R. M. Stodgill and A. E. Coons, eds., *Leader Behavior: Its Description and Measurement*, Research Monograph No. 88 (Columbus: Ohio State University, Bureau of Business Research, 1951). See also S. Kerr, C. A. Schriesheim, C. J. Murphy, and R. M. Stodgill, "Toward a Contingency

Theory of Leadership Based upon the Consideration and Initiating Structure Literature," *Organizational Behavior and Human Performance* (August 1974), pp. 62–82; and B. M. Fisher, "Consideration and Initiating Structure and Their Relationships with Leader Effectiveness: A Meta Analysis," in F. Hoy, ed., *Proceedings of the 48th Annual Academy of Management Conference* (Anaheim, CA, 1988), pp. 201–205.

8. R. Kahn and D. Katz, "Leadership Practices in Relation to Productivity and Morale," in D. Cartwright and A. Zander, eds., *Group Dynamics: Research and Theory*, 2nd ed. (Elmsford, NY: Pow, Paterson, 1960).

9. From the Past to the Present box based on D. S. Derue, J. D. Nahrgang, N. Wellman, and S. E. Humphrey, "Trait and Behavioral Theories of Leadership: An Integration and Meta-Analytic Test of Their Relative Validity," *Personnel Psychology,* Spring 2011, pp. 7–52; and D. A. Wren and A. G. Bedeian, *The Evolution of Management Thought*, 6th ed. (Hoboken, NJ: John Wiley & Sons, 2009), pp. 345–346.

10. R. R. Blake and J. S. Mouton, *The Managerial Grid III* (Houston: Gulf Publishing, 1984).

11. P. C. Nystrom, "Managers and the Hi-Hi Leader Myth," *Academy of Management Journal* (June 1978), pp. 325–331; and L. L. Larson, J. G. Hunt, and R. N. Osborn, "The Great Hi-Hi Leader Behavior Myth: A Lesson from Occam's Razor," *Academy of Management Journal* (December 1976), pp. 628–641.

12. W. G. Bennis, "The Seven Ages of the Leader," *Harvard Business Review,* January 2004, p. 52.

13. F. E. Fiedler, *A Theory of Leadership Effectiveness* (New York: McGraw-Hill, 1967).

14. R. Ayman, M. M. Chemers, and F. Fiedler, "The Contingency Model of Leadership Effectiveness: Its Levels of Analysis," *Leadership Quarterly,* Summer 1995, pp. 147–167; C. A. Schriesheim, B. J. Tepper, and L. A. Tetrault, "Lease Preferred Co-Worker Score, Situational Control, and Leadership Effectiveness: A Meta-Analysis of Contingency Model Performance Predictions," *Journal of Applied Psychology* (August 1994), pp. 561–573; and L. H. Peters, D. D. Hartke, and J. T. Pholmann, "Fiedler's Contingency Theory of Leadership: An Application of the Meta-Analysis Procedures of Schmidt and Hunter," *Psychological Bulletin*, March 1985, pp. 274–285.

15. See B. Kabanoff, "A Critique of Leader Match and Its Implications for Leadership Research," *Personnel Psychology*, Winter 1981, pp. 749–764; and E. H. Schein, *Organizational Psychology*, 3rd ed. (Upper Saddle River, NJ: Prentice Hall, 1980), pp. 116–117.

16. P. Hersey and K. H. Blanchard, *Management of Organizational Behavior: Leading Human Resources*, 8th ed. (Englewood Cliffs, NJ: Prentice Hall, 2001); and P. Hersey and K. Blanchard, "So You Want to Know Your Leadership Style?" *Training and Development Journal* (February 1974), pp. 1–15.

17. See, for instance, E. G. Ralph, "Developing Managers' Effectiveness: A Model with Potential," *Journal of Management Inquiry* (June 2004), pp. 152–163; C. L. Graeff, "Evolution of Situational Leadership Theory: A Critical Review," *Leadership Quarterly* 8, no. 2 (1997), pp. 153–170; and C. F. Fernandez and R. P. Vecchio, "Situational Leadership Theory Revisited: A Test of an Across-Jobs Perspective," *Leadership Quarterly* 8, no. 1 (1997), pp. 67–84.

18. And the Survey Says box based on J. Yang and P. Trap, "I'm Concerned Most About My Manager," *USA Today,* April 25, 2011, p. 1B; "The New Employment Deal: Insights from the

2010 Global Workforce Study," *Towers Watson,* 2010, p. 7; "Key Global Findings from the Hay Group 2010 Best Companies for Leadership Study," *Hay Group,* www.haygroup.com (2010); "Selected Results from Best Companies for Leadership Survey," *Bloomberg BusinessWeek Online,* February 16, 2010; and "Still Haven't Closed the Gap," *Training* (March–April 2009), p. 9.

19. V. H. Vroom and P. W. Yetton, *Leadership and Decision Making* (Pittsburgh: University of Pittsburgh Press, 1973).

20. V. H. Vroom and A. G. Jago, *The New Leadership: Managing Participation in Organizations* (Upper Saddle River, NJ: Prentice Hall, 1988). See especially Chapter 8.

21. See, for example, R. H. G. Field and R. J. House, "A Test of the Vroom Yetton Model Using Manager and Subordinate Reports," *Journal of Applied Psychology* (June 1990), pp. 362–366; J. T. Ettling and A. G. Jago, "Participation Under Conditions of Conflict: More on the Validity of the Vroom Yetton Model," *Journal of Management Studies* (January 1988), pp. 73–83; C. R. Leana, "Power Relinquishment versus Power Sharing: Theoretical Clarification and Empirical Comparison of Delegation and Participation," *Journal of Applied Psychology* (May 1987), pp. 228–233; and R. H. G. Field, "A Test of the Vroom Yetton Normative Model of Leadership," *Journal of Applied Psychology* (October 1982), pp. 523–532.

22. For additional information about the exchanges that occur between the leader and the follower, see A. S. Phillips and A. G. Bedeian, "Leader Follower Exchange Quality: The Role of Personal and Interpersonal Attributes," *Academy of Management Journal* 37, no. 4 (1994), pp. 990–1001; and T. A. Scandura and C. A. Schriesheim, "Leader Member Exchange and Supervisor Career Mentoring as Complementary Constructs in Leadership Research," *Academy of Management Journal* 37, no. 6 (1994), pp. 1588–1602.

23. R. J. House, "Path-Goal Theory of Leadership: Lessons, Legacy, and a Reformulated Theory," *Leadership Quarterly,* Fall 1996, pp. 323–352; R. J. House and T. R. Mitchell, "Path-Goal Theory of Leadership," *Journal of Contemporary Business* (Autumn 1974), p. 86; and R. J. House, "A Path-Goal Theory of Leader Effectiveness," *Administrative Science Quarterly*, September 1971, pp. 321–338.

24. A. Sagie and M. Koslowsky, "Organizational Attitudes and Behaviors as a Function of Participation in Strategic and Tactical Change Decisions: An Application of Path-Goal Theory," *Journal of Organizational Behavior* (January 1994), pp. 37–47; and J. C. Wofford and L. Z. Liska, "Path-Goal Theories of Leadership: A Meta-Analysis," *Journal of Management* (Winter 1993), pp. 857–876.

25. L. Ma and Q. Qu, "Differentiation in Leader-Member Exchange: A Hierarchical Linear Modeling Approach," *Leadership Quarterly,* October 2010, pp. 733–744; C. P. Schriesheim, S. L. Castro, X. Zhou, and F. J. Yamarinno, "The Folly of Theorizing 'A' but Testing 'B': A Selective Level-of-Analysis Review of the Field and a Detailed Leader-Member Exchange Illustration," *Leadership Quarterly,* Winter 2001, pp. 515–551; R. C. Liden, R. T. Sparrowe, and S. J. Wayne, "Leader-Member Exchange Theory: The Past and Potential for the Future," in G. R. Ferris (ed.), *Research in Personnel and Human Resource Management*, vol. 15 (Greenwich, CT: JAI Press, 1997), pp. 47–119; G. B. Graen and M. Uhl-Bien, "Relationship-Based Approach to Leadership: Development of Leader-Member Exchange (LMX) Theory of Leadership Over 25 Years: Applying a Multi-Domain Perspective," *Leadership Quarterly,* Summer 1995, pp. 219–247; and R. M. Dienesch and

R. C. Liden, "Leader-Member Exchange Model of Leadership: A Critique and Further Development," *Academy of Management Review,* July 1986, pp. 618–634.

26. J. B. Wu, A. S. Tsui, and A. J. Kinicki, "Consequences of Differentiated Leadership in Groups," *Academy of Management Journal* (February 2010), pp. 90–106; S. S. Masterson, K. Lewis, and B. M. Goldman, "Integrating Justice and Social Exchange: The Differing Effects of Fair Procedures and Treatment on Work Relationships," *Academy of Management Journal* (August 2000), pp. 738–748; S. J. Wayne, L. J. Shore, W. H. Bommer, and L. E. Tetrick, "The Role of Fair Treatment and Rewards in Perceptions of Organizational Support and Leader-Member Exchange," *Journal of Applied Psychology* (June 2002), pp. 590–598; R. C. Liden, S. J. Wayne, and D. Stilwell, "A Longitudinal Study of the Early Development of Leader-Member Exchanges," *Journal of Applied Psychology* (August 1993), pp. 662–674; and R. C. Liden and G. Graen, "Generalizability of the Vertical Dyad Linkage Model of Leadership," *Academy of Management Journal* (September 1980), pp. 451–465.

27. V. L. Goodwin, W. M. Bowler, and J. L. Whittington, "A Social Network Perspective on LMX Relationships: Accounting for the Instrumental Value of Leader and Follower Networks," *Journal of Management* (August 2009), pp. 954–980; R. Vecchio and D. M. Brazil, "Leadership and Sex-Similarity: A Comparison in a Military Setting," *Personnel Psychology,* vol. 60 (2007), pp. 303–335; M. Uhl-Bien, "Relationship Development as a Key Ingredient for Leadership Development," in S. E. Murphy and R. E. Riggio (eds.), *Future of Leadership Development* (Mahwah, NJ: Lawrence Erlbaum, 2003), pp. 129–147; R. C. Liden, S. J. Wayne, and D. Stilwell, "A Longitudinal Study of the Early Development of Leader-Member Exchanges"; and D. Duchon, S. G. Green, and T. D. Taber, "Vertical Dyad Linkage: A Longitudinal Assessment of Antecedents, Measures, and Consequences," *Journal of Applied Psychology* (February 1986), pp. 56–60.

28. See, for instance, F. O. Walumbwa, D. M. Mayer, P. Wang, H. Wang, K. Workman, and A. L. Christensen, "Linking Ethical Leadership to Employee Performance: The Roles of Leader-Member Exchange Theory, Self-Efficacy, and Organizational Identification," *Organizational Behavior & Human Decision Processes,* July 2011, pp. 204–213; K. J. Harris, A. R. Wheeler, and K. M. Kacmar, "The Mediating Role of Organizational Embeddedness in the LMX-Outcomes Relationship," *Leadership Quarterly,* April 2011, pp. 271–281; W. M. Bowler, J. R. B. Halbesleben, J. R. B. Paul, "If You're Close with the Leader, You Must Be a Brownnose: The Role of Leader-Member Relationships in Follower, Leader, and Coworker Attributions of Organizational Citizenship Behavior Motives," *Human Resource Management Review,* December 2010, pp. 309–316; G. Sears and C. Holmvall, "The Joint Influence of Supervisor and Subordinate Emotional Intelligence on Leader-Member Exchange," *Journal of Business & Psychology* (December 2010), pp. 593–605; V. Venkataramani, S. G. Green, and D. J. Schleicher, "Well-Connected Leaders' Social Network Ties on LMX and Members' Work Attitudes," *Journal of Applied Psychology* (November 2010), pp. 1071–1084; Z. Chen, W. Lam, and J. A. Zhong, "Leader-Member Exchange and Member Performance: A New Look at Individual-Level Negative Feedback-Seeking Behavior and Team-Level Empowerment Culture," *Journal of Applied Psychology* (January 2007), pp. 202–212; R. Ilies, J. D. Nahrgang, and F. P. Morgeson,

"Leader-Member Exchange and Citizenship Behaviors: A Meta-Analysis," *Journal of Applied Psychology* (January 2007), pp. 269–277; and C. R. Gerstner and D. V. Day, "Meta-analytic Review of Leader-Member Exchange Theory: Correlates and Construct Issues," *Journal of Applied Psychology* (December 1997), pp. 827–844.

29. B. M. Bass and R. E. Riggio, *Transformational Leadership,* 2d ed. (Mahwah, NJ: Lawrence Erlbaum Associates, Inc., 2006), p. 3.

30. J. Seltzer and B. M. Bass, "Transformational Leadership: Beyond Initiation and Consideration," *Journal of Management* (December 1990), pp. 693–703; and B. M. Bass, "Leadership: Good, Better, Best," *Organizational Dynamics*, Winter 1985, pp. 26–40.

31. B. J. Avolio and B. M. Bass, "Transformational Leadership, Charisma, and Beyond." Working paper, School of Management, State University of New York, Binghamton, 1985, p. 14.

32. R. S. Rubin, D. C. Munz, and W. H. Bommer, "Leading from Within: The Effects of Emotion Recognition and Personality on Transformational Leadership Behavior," *Academy of Management Journal* (October 2005), pp. 845–858; T. A. Judge and J. E. Bono, "Five-Factor Model of Personality and Transformational Leadership," *Journal of Applied Psychology* (October 2000), pp. 751–765; B. M. Bass and B. J. Avolio, "Developing Transformational Leadership: 1992 and Beyond," *Journal of European Industrial Training* (January 1990), p. 23; and J. J. Hater and B. M. Bass, "Supervisors' Evaluation and Subordinates' Perceptions of Transformational and Transactional Leadership," *Journal of Applied Psychology* (November 1988), pp. 695–702.

33. M. Tims, A. B. Bakker, and D. Xanthopoulou, "Do Transformational Leaders Enhance Their Followers' Daily Work Engagement?" *Leadership Quarterly,* February 2011, pp. 121–131; X.-H. (Frank) Wang, and J. M. Howell, "Exploring the Dual-Level Effects of Transformational Leadership on Followers," *Journal of Applied Psychology* (November 2010), pp. 1134–1144; A. E. Colbert, A. L. Kristof-Brown, B. H. Bradley, and M. R. Barrick, "CEO Transformational Leadership: The Role of Goal Importance Congruence in Top Management Teams," *Academy of Management Journal* (February 2008), pp. 81–96; R. F. Piccolo and J. A. Colquitt, "Transformational Leadership and Job Behaviors: The Mediating Role of Core Job Characteristics," *Academy of Management Journal* (April 2006), pp. 327–340; O. Epitropaki and R. Martin, "From Ideal to Real: A Longitudinal Study of the Role of Implicit Leadership Theories on Leader-Member Exchanges and Employee Outcomes," *Journal of Applied Psychology* (July 2005), pp. 659–676; J. E. Bono and T. A. Judge, "Self-Concordance at Work: Toward Understanding the Motivational Effects of Transformational Leaders," *Academy of Management Journal* (October 2003), pp. 554–571; T. Dvir, D. Eden, B. J. Avolio, and B. Shamir, "Impact of Transformational Leadership on Follower Development and Performance: A Field Experiment," *Academy of Management Journal* (August 2002), pp. 735–744; N. Sivasubramaniam, W. D. Murry, B. J. Avolio, and D. I. Jung, "A Longitudinal Model of the Effects of Team Leadership and Group Potency on Group Performance," *Group and Organization Management* (March 2002), pp. 66–96; J. M. Howell and B. J. Avolio, "Transformational Leadership, Transactional Leadership, Locus of Control, and Support for Innovation: Key Predictors of Consolidated-Business-Unit Performance," *Journal of Applied Psychology* (December 1993), pp. 891–911; R. T. Keller,

"Transformational Leadership and the Performance of Research and Development Project Groups," *Journal of Management* (September 1992), pp. 489–501; and Bass and Avolio, "Developing Transformational Leadership."

34. M. Thompson and B. Tracy, "Building a Great Organization," *Leader to Leader,* Fall 2010, pp. 45–49; and F. Vogelstein, "Mighty Amazon," *Fortune,* May 26, 2003, pp. 60–74.

35. J. M. Crant and T. S. Bateman, "Charismatic Leadership Viewed from Above: The Impact of Proactive Personality," *Journal of Organizational Behavior* (February 2000), pp. 63–75; G. Yukl and J. M. Howell, "Organizational and Contextual Influences on the Emergence and Effectiveness of Charismatic Leadership," *Leadership Quarterly*, Summer 1999, pp. 257–283; and J. A. Conger and R. N. Kanungo, "Behavioral Dimensions of Charismatic Leadership," in J. A. Conger, R. N. Kanungo and Associates, *Charismatic Leadership* (San Francisco: Jossey-Bass, 1988), pp. 78–97.

36. J. A. Conger and R. N. Kanungo, *Charismatic Leadership in Organizations* (Thousand Oaks, CA: Sage, 1998).

37. F. Walter and H. Bruch, "An Affective Events Model of Charismatic Leadership Behavior: A Review, Theoretical Investigation, and Research Agenda," *Journal of Management* (December 2009), pp. 1428–1452; K. S. Groves, "Linking Leader Skills, Follower Attitudes, and Contextual Variables via an Integrated Model of Charismatic Leadership," *Journal of Management* (April 2005), pp. 255–277; J. J. Sosik, "The Role of Personal Values in the Charismatic Leadership of Corporate Managers: A Model and Preliminary Field Study," *Leadership Quarterly,* April 2005, pp. 221–244; A. H. B. deHoogh, D. N. den Hartog, P. L. Koopman, H. Thierry, P. T. van den Berg, J. G. van der Weide, and C. P. M. Wilderom, "Leader Motives, Charismatic Leadership, and Subordinates' Work Attitudes in The Profit and Voluntary Sector," *Leadership Quarterly,* February 2005, pp. 17–38; J. M. Howell and B. Shamir, "The Role of Followers in the Charismatic Leadership Process: Relationships and Their Consequences," *Academy of Management Review,* January 2005, pp. 96–112; J. Paul, D. L. Costley, J. P. Howell, P. W. Dorfman, and D. Trafimow, "The Effects of Charismatic Leadership on Followers' Self-Concept Accessibility," *Journal of Applied Social Psychology* (September 2001), pp. 1821–1844; J. A. Conger, R. N. Kanungo, and S. T. Menon, "Charismatic Leadership and Follower Effects," *Journal of Organizational Behavior,* vol. 21 (2000), pp. 747–767; R. W. Rowden, "The Relationship Between Charismatic Leadership Behaviors and Organizational Commitment," *Leadership & Organization Development Journal* (January 2000), pp. 30–35; G. P. Shea and C. M. Howell, "Charismatic Leadership and Task Feedback: A Laboratory Study of Their Effects on Self-Efficacy," *Leadership Quarterly*, Fall 1999, pp. 375–396; S. A. Kirkpatrick and E. A. Locke, "Direct and Indirect Effects of Three Core Charismatic Leadership Components on Performance and Attitudes," *Journal of Applied Psychology* (February 1996), pp. 36–51; D. A. Waldman, B. M. Bass, and F. J. Yammarino, "Adding to Contingent-Reward Behavior: The Augmenting Effect of Charismatic Leadership," *Group & Organization Studies*, December 1990, pp. 381–394; and R. J. House, J. Woycke, and E. M. Fodor, "Charismatic and Noncharismatic Leaders: Differences in Behavior and Effectiveness," in Conger and Kanungo, *Charismatic Leadership*, pp. 103–104.

38. B. R. Agle, N J. Nagarajan, J. A. Sonnenfeld, and D. Srinivasan, "Does CEO Charisma Matter? An Empirical Analysis of the Relationships Among Organizational Performance, Environmental Uncertainty, and Top Management Team Perceptions of CEO Charisma," *Academy of Management Journal* (February 2006), pp. 161–174.

39. R. Birchfield, "Creating Charismatic Leaders," *Management*, June 2000, pp. 30–31; S. Caudron, "Growing Charisma," *Industry Week*, May 4, 1998, pp. 54–55; and J. A. Conger and R. N. Kanungo, "Training Charismatic Leadership: A Risky and Critical Task," in Conger and Kanungo, *Charismatic Leadership*, pp. 309–323.

40. J. G. Hunt, K. B. Boal, and G. E. Dodge, "The Effects of Visionary and Crisis-Responsive Charisma on Followers: An Experimental Examination," *Leadership Quarterly*, Fall 1999, pp. 423–448; R. J. House and R. N. Aditya, "The Social Scientific Study of Leadership: Quo Vadis?" *Journal of Management*, 23, no. 3 (1997), pp. 316–323; and R. J. House, "A 1976 Theory of Charismatic Leadership."

41. This definition is based on M. Sashkin, "The Visionary Leader," in Conger and Kanungo et al., *Charismatic Leadership*, pp. 124–125; B. Nanus, *Visionary Leadership* (New York: Free Press, 1992), p. 8; N.H. Snyder and M. Graves, "Leadership and Vision," *Business Horizons*, January–February 1994, p. 1; and J. R. Lucas, "Anatomy of a Vision Statement," *Management Review,* February 1998, pp. 22–26.

42. Nanus, *Visionary Leadership*, p. 8.

43. S. Caminiti, "What Team Leaders Need to Know," *Fortune*, February 20, 1995, pp. 93–100.

44. Ibid., p. 93.

45. Ibid., p. 100.

46. D. S. DeRue, C. M. Barnes, and F. M. Morgeson, "Understanding the Motivational Contingencies of Team Leadership," *Small Group Research,* October 2010, pp. 621–651; B. Meredith, "Leader Characteristics: Is There a Shift in Requirements?" *Leadership Excellence,* September 2010, p. 19; B. Neal, "Heroes and Sidekicks: Ensuring Proper Followership," *T&D,* September 2010, pp. 76–77; R. D. Ramsey, "Preparing to Be Tomorrow's Leader Today," *Supervision,* January 2010, p. 79; N. Steckler and N. Fondas, "Building Team Leader Effectiveness: A Diagnostic Tool," *Organizational Dynamics*, Winter 1995, p. 20.

47. R. S. Wellins, W. C. Byham, and G. R. Dixon, *Inside Teams* (San Francisco: Jossey-Bass, 1994), p. 318.

48. Steckler and Fondas, "Building Team Leader Effectiveness," p. 21.

49. "The 100 Most Creative People in Business 2010," *Fast Company,* June 2010, pp. 70–119; and G. Colvin, "The FedEx Edge," *Fortune,* April 3, 2006, pp. 77–84.

50. J. Fabre, "The Importance of Empowering Front-Line Staff," *Supervision,* December 2010, pp. 6–7; S. Raub and C. Robert, "Differential Effects of Empowering Leadership on In-Role and Extra-Role Employee Behaviors: Exploring the Role of Psychological Empowerment and Power Values," *Human Relations,* November 2010, pp. 1743–1770; N. D. Cakar and A. Erturk, "Comparing Innovation Capability of Small and Medium-Sized Enterprises: Examining the Effects of Organizational Culture and Empowerment," *Journal of Small Business Management* (July 2010), pp. 325–359; A. Srivastava, K. M. Bartol, and E. A. Locke, "Empowering Leadership in Management Teams: Effects on Knowledge Sharing, Efficacy, and Performance," *Academy of Management Journal* (December 2006), pp. 1239–1251; P. K. Mills and G. R. Ungson, "Reassessing the Limits of Structural Empowerment:

Organizational Constitution and Trust as Controls," *Academy of Management Review,* January 2003, pp. 143–153; W. A. Rudolph and M. Sashkin, "Can Organizational Empowerment Work in Multinational Settings?" *Academy of Management Executive,* February 2002, pp. 102–115; C. Gomez and B. Rosen, "The Leader-Member Link Between Managerial Trust and Employee Empowerment," *Group & Organization Management,* March 2001, pp. 53–69; C. Robert and T. M. Probst, "Empowerment and Continuous Improvement in the United States, Mexico, Poland, and India," *Journal of Applied Psychology* (October 2000), pp. 643–658; R. C. Herrenkohl, G. T. Judson, and J. A. Heffner, "Defining and Measuring Employee Empowerment," *Journal of Applied Behavioral Science* (September 1999), p. 373; R. C. Ford and M. D. Fottler, "Empowerment: A Matter of Degree," *Academy of Management Executive*, August 1995, pp. 21–31; and W. A. Rudolph, "Navigating the Journey to Empowerment," *Organizational Dynamics*, Spring 1995, pp. 19–32.

51. T. A. Stewart, "Just Think: No Permission Needed," *Fortune,* January 8, 2001, pp. 190–192.

52. Technology and the Manager's Job box based on K. D. Strang, "Leadership Substitutes and Personality Impact on Time and Quality in Virtual New Product Development Projects," *Project Management Journal* (February 2011), pp. 73–90; A. Rapp, M. Ahearne, J. Mathieu, and T. Rapp, "Managing Sales Teams in a Virtual Environment," *International Journal of Research in Marketing* (September 2010), pp. 213–224; M. Muethel and M. Hoegl, "Cultural and Societal Influences on Shared Leadership in Globally Dispersed Teams," *Journal of International Management* (September 2010), pp. 234–256; J. Grenny, "Virtual Teams," *Leadership Excellence,* May 2010, p. 20; L. A. Hambley, T. A. O'Neill, and T. J. B. Kline, "Virtual Team Leadership: The Effects of Leadership Style and Communication Medium on Team Interaction Styles and Outcomes," *Organizational Behavior and Human Decision Processes,* May 2007, pp. 1–20; and B. J. Avolio and S. S. Kahai, "Adding the 'E' to E-Leadership: How It May Impact Your Leadership," *Organizational Dynamics,* January 2003, pp. 325–338.

53. F. W. Swierczek, "Leadership and Culture: Comparing Asian Managers," *Leadership & Organization Development Journal* (December 1991), pp. 3–10.

54. I. Wanasika, J. P. Howell, R. Littrell, and P. Dorfman, "Managerial Leadership and Culture in Sub-Saharan Africa," *Journal of World Business* (April 2011), pp. 234–241.

55. House, "Leadership in the Twenty-First Century," p. 443; M. F. Peterson and J. G. Hunt, "International Perspectives on International Leadership," *Leadership Quarterly*, Fall 1997, pp. 203–231; and J. R. Schermerhorn and M. H. Bond, "Cross-Cultural Leadership in Collectivism and High Power Distance Settings," *Leadership & Organization Development Journal* 18, no. 4/5 (1997), pp. 187–193.

56. Wanasika, Howell, Littrell, and Dorfman, "Managerial Leadership and Culture in Sub-Saharan Africa"; R. J. House, P. J. Hanges, S. A. Ruiz-Quintanilla, P. W. Dorfman, and Associates, "Culture Specific and Cross-Culturally Generalizable Implicit Leadership Theories: Are the Attributes of Charismatic/Transformational Leadership Universally Endorsed?" *Leadership Quarterly,* Summer 1999, pp. 219–256; and D. E. Carl and M. Javidan, "Universality of Charismatic Leadership: A Multi-Nation Study," paper presented at the National Academy of Management Conference, Washington, DC, August 2001.

57. D. E. Carl and M. Javidan, "Universality of Charismatic Leadership," p. 29.

58. This section is based on D. Goleman, R. E. Boyatzis, and A. McKee, *Primal Leadership: Realizing the Power of Emotional Intelligence* (Boston: Harvard Business School Press, 2002); D. R. Caruso, J. D. Mayer, and P. Salovey, "Emotional Intelligence and Emotional Leadership," in R. E. Riggio, S. E. Murphy, and F. J. Pirozzolo (eds.), *Multiple Intelligences and Leadership* (Mahwah, NJ: Lawrence Erlbaum, 2002), pp. 55–74; J. M. George, "Emotions and Leadership: The Role of Emotional Intelligence," *Human Relations,* August 2000, pp. 1027–1055; D. Goleman, "What Makes a Leader?" *Harvard Business Review,* November–December 1998, pp. 93–102; and D. Goleman, *Working with Emotional Intelligence* (New York: Bantam, 1998).

59. "The Secret Skill of Leaders," *U.S. News & World Report* (January 14, 2002), p. 8. See, also, L. Gardner and C. Stough, "Examining the Relationship Between Leadership and Emotional Intelligence in Senior Level Managers," *Leadership and Organization Development Journal,* January–February 2002, pp. 68–79.

60. Ibid.

61. F. Walter, M. S. Cole, and R. H. Humphrey, "Emotional Intelligence: Sine Qua Non of Leadership or Folderol?" *Academy of Management Perspectives,* February 2011, pp. 45–59.

62. See Walter, Cole, and Humphrey, "Emotional Intelligence: Sine Qua Non of Leadership or Folderol"; L. A. Zampetakis and V. Moustakis, "Managers' Trait Emotional Intelligence and Group Outcomes: The Case of Group Job Satisfaction," *Small Group Research,* February 2011, pp. 77–102; H.-W. Vivian Tang, M.-S. Yin, and D. B. Nelson, "The Relationship Between Emotional Intelligence and Leadership Practices," *Journal of Managerial Psychology,* 25, no. 8 (2010), pp. 899–926; P. K. Chopra and G. K. Kanji, "Emotional Intelligence: A Catalyst for Inspirational Leadership and Management Excellence," *Total Quality Management & Business Excellence,* October 2010, pp. 971–1004; R. Boyatzis and A. McKee, "Intentional Change," *Journal of Organizational Excellence* (Summer 2006), pp. 49–60, and R. Kerr; J. Garvin, N. Heaton, and E. Boyle, "Emotional Intelligence and Leadership Effectiveness," *Leadership and Organizational Development Journal* (April 2006), pp. 265–279.

63. S. Simsarian, "Leadership and Trust Facilitating Cross-Functional Team Success," *Journal of Management Development* (March–April 2002), pp. 201–215.

64. J. M. Kouzes and B. Z. Posner, *Credibility: How Leaders Gain and Lose It, and Why People Demand It* (San Francisco: Jossey-Bass, 1993), p. 14.

65. Based on F. D. Schoorman, R. C. Mayer, and J. H. Davis, "An Integrative Model of Organizational Trust: Past, Present, and Future," *Academy of Management Review,* April 2007, pp. 344–354; G. M. Spreitzer and A. K. Mishra, "Giving Up Control Without Losing Control," *Group & Organization Management,* June 1999, pp. 155–187; R. C. Mayer, J. H. Davis, and F. D. Schoorman, "An Integrative Model of Organizational Trust," *Academy of Management Review*, July 1995, p. 712; and L. T. Hosmer, "Trust: The Connecting Link Between Organizational Theory and Philosophical Ethics," *Academy of Management Review*, April 1995, p. 393.

66. P. L. Schindler and C. C. Thomas, "The Structure of Interpersonal Trust in the Workplace," *Psychological Reports*, October 1993, pp. 563–573.

67. H. H. Tan and C. S. F. Tan, "Toward the Differentiation of Trust in Supervisor and Trust in Organization," *Genetic, Social, and General Psychology Monographs,* May 2000, pp. 241–260.

68. J. H. Cho and E. J. Ringquist, "Managerial Trustworthiness and Organizational Outcomes," *Journal of Public Administration Research and Theory* (January 2011), pp. 53–86; R. C. Mayer and M. B. Gavin, "Trust in Management and Performance: Who Minds the Shop While the Employees Watch the Boss?" *Academy of Management Journal* (October 2005), pp. 874–888; and K. T. Dirks and D. L. Ferrin, "Trust in Leadership: Meta-Analytic Findings and Implications for Research and Practice," *Journal of Applied Psychology* (August 2002), pp. 611–628.

69. R. Zemke, "The Confidence Crisis," *Training* (June 2004), pp. 22–30; J. A. Byrne, "Restoring Trust in Corporate America," *BusinessWeek,* June 24, 2002, pp. 30–35; S. Armour, "Employees' New Motto: Trust No One," *USA Today,* February 5, 2002, p. 1B; J. Scott, "Once Bitten, Twice Shy: A World of Eroding Trust," *New York Times,* April 21, 2002, p. WK5; J. Brockner, P. A. Siegel, J. P. Daly, T. Tyler, and C. Martin, "When Trust Matters: The Moderating Effect of Outcome Favorability," *Administrative Science Quarterly,* September 1997, p. 558; and J. Brockner, P. A. Siegel, J. P. Daly, T. Tyler, and C. Martin, "When Trust Matters: The Moderating Effect of Outcome Favorability," *Administrative Science Quarterly,* September 1997, p. 558.

70. "Weathering the Storm: A Study of Employee Attitudes and Opinions," *WorkUSA 2002 Study,* Watson Wyatt, www.watsonwyatt.com.

71. S. Kerr and J. M. Jermier, "Substitutes for Leadership: Their Meaning and Measurement," *Organizational Behavior and Human Performance*, December 1978, pp. 375–403; J. P. Howell, P. W. Dorfman, and S. Kerr, "Leadership and Substitutes for Leadership," *Journal of Applied Behavioral Science* 22, no. 1 (1986), pp. 29–246; J. P. Howell, D. E. Bowen, P. W. Dorfman, S. Kerr, and P. M. Podsakoff, "Substitutes for Leadership: Effective Alternatives to Ineffective Leadership," *Organizational Dynamics*, Summer 1990, pp. 21–38; and P. M. Podsakoff, B. P. Niehoff, S. B. MacKenzie, and M. L. Williams, "Do Substitutes for Leadership Really Substitute for Leadership? An Empirical Examination of Kerr and Jermier's Situational Leadership Model," *Organizational Behavior and Human Decision Processes*, February 1993, pp. 1–44.

CHAPTER 3

Managing Communication and Information

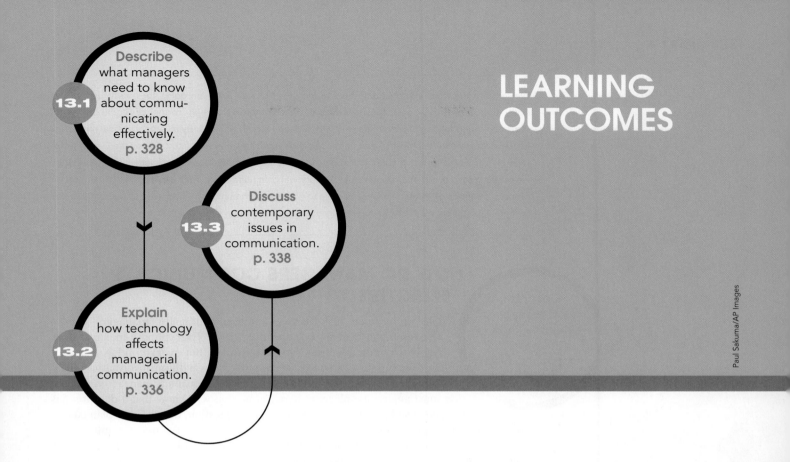

Paul Sakuma/AP Images

Social Benefit or Social Disaster?

Tweets. Twittering. Six years ago, the only definition we would have known for these words would have involved birds and the sounds they make.[1] Now, practically everyone knows that Twitter is also an Internet content service used by millions of people to trade short messages of 140 characters or less via the Web, cell phones, and other devices. And large companies are beginning to recognize the power of social media. At Best Buy, CEO Brian Dunn was encouraged by his chief marketing officer a few years ago to try out social media. With some 180,000 employees—and most of those 24 years old or younger and heavily involved with social media—Dunn realized that it would be a great way to engage them *and* customers. He was soon "talking" to employees and customers every night at 10 o'clock, tweeting on a variety of subjects including his experiences in Best Buy stores, his kids, and even the Minnesota Twins. However, at one point, Dunn's Twitter account was hacked and an offensive tweet put out there for everyone to see. Overseas on business at the time, Dunn first received a panicked call from his VP of operations at 4 A.M. and then many other calls. The entire executive team went into "crisis" mode to control the potential damage.

Welcome to the world of communication! In this "world," managers are going to have to understand both the importance and the drawbacks of communication—all forms of communication. Communication takes place every day in every organization. In all areas. By all organizational members. In many different forms. Most of that communication tends to be work-related. But as the Dunn Twitter story shows, sometimes that communication can cause some unintended consequences. In this chapter, we're going to look at basic concepts of interpersonal communication. We'll explain the communication process, methods of communicating, barriers to effective communication, and ways to overcome those barriers. In addition, we'll look at communication issues that today's managers face.

HOW DO MANAGERS COMMUNICATE EFFECTIVELY?

13.1 Describe what managers need to know about communicating effectively.

The importance of effective communication for managers cannot be overemphasized for one specific reason: Everything a manager does involves communicating. Not *some* things but *everything*! A manager can't formulate strategy or make a decision without information. That information has to be communicated. Once a decision is made, communication must again take place. Otherwise, no one will know that a decision has been made. The best idea, the most creative suggestion, or the finest plan cannot take form without communication. Managers, therefore, need effective communication skills. We're not suggesting, of course, that good communication skills alone make a successful manager. We can say, however, that ineffective communication skills can lead to a continuous stream of problems for a manager.

How Does the Communication Process Work?

Communication can be thought of as a process or flow. Communication problems occur when deviations or blockages disrupt that flow. Before communication can take place, a purpose, expressed as a message to be conveyed, is needed. It passes between a source (the sender) and a receiver. The message is encoded (converted to symbolic form) and is passed by way of some medium (channel) to the receiver, who retranslates (decodes) the message initiated by the sender. The result is **communication**, which is a transfer of understanding and meaning from one person to another.[2]

Exhibit 13–1 depicts the **communication process**. This model has seven parts: (1) the communication source or sender, (2) encoding, (3) the message, (4) the channel, (5) decoding, (6) the receiver, and (7) feedback.

EXHIBIT 13–1   **The Communication Process**

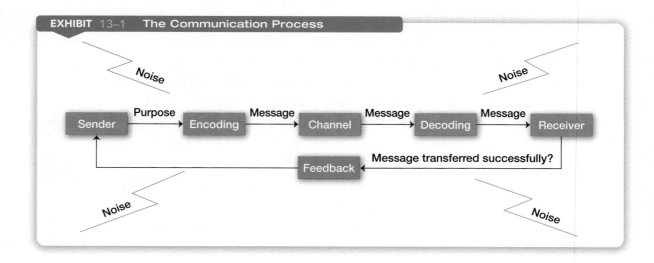

The source initiates a message by **encoding** a thought. Four conditions affect the encoded message: skill, attitudes, knowledge, and the social cultural system. Our message in our communication to you in this book depends on our writing *skills*; if we don't have the requisite writing skills, our message will not reach you in the form desired. Keep in mind that a person's total communicative success includes speaking, reading, listening, and reasoning skills as well. As we discussed in Chapter 9, our attitudes influence our behavior. We hold predisposed ideas on numerous topics, and our communications are affected by these *attitudes*. Furthermore, we're restricted in our communicative activity by the extent of our *knowledge* of the particular topic. We can't communicate what we don't know, and should our knowledge be too extensive, it's possible that our receiver will not understand our message. Clearly, the amount of knowledge the source holds about his or her subject will affect the message he or she seeks to transfer. And, finally, just as attitudes influence our behavior, so does our *position in the social cultural system* in which we exist. Your beliefs and values, all part of your culture, act to influence you as a communicative source.

The **message** is the actual physical product from the source that conveys some purpose. When we speak, the words spoken are the message. When we write, the writing is the message. When we paint, the picture is the message. When we gesture, the movements of our arms, the expressions on our faces are the message.[3] Our message is affected by the code or group of symbols we use to transfer meaning, the content of the message itself, and the decisions that we make in selecting and arranging both codes and content.[4]

The **channel** is the medium through which the message travels. It's selected by the source, who must determine whether to use a formal or an informal channel. Formal channels are established by the organization and transmit messages that pertain to the job-related activities of members. They traditionally follow the authority network within the organization. Other forms of messages, such as personal or social, follow the informal channels in the organization.

The receiver is the person to whom the message is directed. However, before the message can be received, the symbols in it must be translated into a form that can be understood by the receiver—the **decoding** of the message. Just as the encoder was limited by his or her skills, attitudes, knowledge, and social cultural system, the receiver is equally restricted. Accordingly, the source must be skillful in writing or speaking; the receiver must be skillful in reading or listening, and both must be able to reason. A person's knowledge, attitudes, and cultural background influence his or her ability to receive, just as they do the ability to send.

The final link in the communication process is a feedback loop. "If a communication source decodes the message that he encodes, if the message is put back into his system, we have feedback."[5] **Feedback** is the check on how successful we have been in transferring our messages as originally intended. It determines whether understanding has been achieved. Given the cultural diversity that exists in our workforce today, the importance of effective feedback to ensure proper communications cannot be overstated.[6]

Asako Hoshino, corporate vice president of Japan's Nissan Motor Company, chooses to use oral communication by holding a meeting in her Tokyo office with company managers and executives. For Hoshino, communicating verbally gives her and her coworkers the opportunity to share information, discuss what they hear, and ask questions and receive answers to ensure that what is said has been received and understood. In addition to a built-in feedback mechanism, oral communication has the advantage of conveying more information in less time than written communication.

Newscom

---

communication
A transfer of understanding and meaning from one person to another

communication process
The seven-part process of transferring and understanding of meaning

encoding
Converting a message into symbolic form

message
A purpose for communicating that's to be conveyed

channel
The medium by which a message travels

decoding
Translating a received message

feedback
Checking to see how successfully a message has been transferred

Are Written Communications More Effective Than Verbal Ones?

Written communications include memos, letters, e-mail and other forms of digital communication, organizational periodicals, bulletin boards, or any other device that transmits written words or symbols. Why would a sender choose to use written communications? Because they're tangible, verifiable, and more permanent than the oral variety. Typically, both sender and receiver have a record of the communication. The message can be stored for an indefinite period of time. If questions arise about the content of the message, it's physically available for later reference. This feature is particularly important for complex or lengthy communications. For example, the marketing plan for a new product is likely to contain a number of tasks spread out over several months. By putting it in writing, those who have to carry out the plan can readily refer to the document over the life of the plan. A final benefit of written communication comes from the process itself. Except in rare instances, such as when presenting a formal speech, more care is taken with the written word than with the spoken word. Having to put something in writing forces a person to think more carefully about what he or she wants to convey. Therefore, written communications are more likely to be well thought out, logical, and clear.

Of course, written messages have their drawbacks. Writing may be more precise, but it also consumes a great deal of time. You could convey far more information to your college instructor in a one-hour oral exam than in a one-hour written exam. In fact, you could probably say in 10 to 15 minutes what it takes you an hour to write. The other major disadvantage is feedback or, rather, lack of it. Oral communications allow receivers to respond rapidly to what they think they hear. However, written communications don't have a built-in feedback mechanism. Sending a memo is no assurance that it will be received and, if it is received, no guarantee that the recipient will interpret it as the sender meant. The latter point is also relevant in oral communication, but it's easier in such cases merely to ask the receiver to summarize what you have said. An accurate summary presents feedback evidence that the message has been received and understood.

Is the Grapevine an Effective Way to Communicate?

The **grapevine** is the unofficial way that communications take place in an organization. It's neither authorized nor supported by the organization. Rather, information is spread by word of mouth—and even through electronic means. Ironically, good information passes among us rapidly, but bad information travels even faster.[7] The grapevine gets information out to organizational members as quickly as possible.

The biggest question raised about grapevines, however, focuses on the accuracy of the rumors. Research on this topic has found somewhat mixed results. In an organization characterized by openness, the grapevine may be extremely accurate. In an authoritative culture, the rumor mill may not be accurate. But even then, although the information flowing is inaccurate, it still contains some element of truth. Rumors about major layoffs, plant closings, and the like may be filled with inaccurate information regarding who will be affected or when it may occur. Nonetheless, the reports that something is about to happen are probably on target.

How Do Nonverbal Cues Affect Communication?

Some of the most meaningful communications are neither spoken nor written. They are nonverbal communications. A loud siren or a red light at an intersection tells you something without words. A college instructor doesn't need words to know that students are bored; their eyes get glassy or they begin to read the school newspaper during class. Similarly, when papers start to rustle and notebooks begin to close, the message is clear: Class time is about over. The size of a person's office and desk or the clothes he or she wears also convey messages to others. However, the best-known areas of nonverbal communication are body language and verbal intonation.

Body language refers to gestures, facial configurations, and other movements of the body.[8] A snarl, for example, says something different from a smile. Hand motions, facial

---

From the Past to the Present

One of the most famous studies of the grapevine was conducted by management researcher Keith Davis who investigated the communication patterns among 67 managerial personnel.[9] The approach he used was to learn from each communication recipient how he or she first received a given piece of information and then trace it back to its source. It was found that, while the grapevine was an important source of information, only 10 percent of the executives acted as liaison individuals (that is, passed the information on to more than one other person). For example, when one executive decided to resign to enter the insurance business, 81 percent of the executives knew about it, but only 11 percent transmitted this information to others. At the time, this study was interesting both because of what it found, but more importantly because of what it showed about how the communication network worked.

Recent research by IBM and the Massachusetts Institute of Technology using a similar type of analysis focused more on people's social networks of contacts at work rather than on how information flowed through the organizational grapevine. However, what was noticeably interesting about this study was that it found that employees who have strong communication ties with their managers tend to bring in more money than those who steer clear of the boss.

What managers can learn from both these studies is that it's important to understand the social and communication networks that employees use as they do their work. Know who the key contact points are so that if you ever need to find out or relay information, you know who to go to.

Think About:

- Why is it important for managers to understand social and communication networks employees use?
- What have been your experiences with the "grapevine"?
- What did you learn from those experiences about dealing with the grapevine as a source of communication?

---

expressions, and other gestures can communicate emotions or temperaments such as aggression, fear, shyness, arrogance, joy, and anger.[10]

Verbal intonation refers to the emphasis someone gives to words or phrases. To illustrate how intonations can change the meaning of a message, consider the student who asks the instructor a question. The instructor replies, "What do you mean by that?" The student's reaction will vary, depending on the tone of the instructor's response. A soft, smooth tone creates a different meaning from one that is abrasive with a strong emphasis on the last word. Most of us would view the first intonation as coming from someone who sincerely sought clarification, whereas the second suggests that the person is aggressive or defensive. The adage, "it's not what you say but how you say it," is something managers should remember as they communicate.

The fact that every oral communication also has a nonverbal message cannot be overemphasized.[11] Why? Because the nonverbal component is likely to carry the greatest impact. Research indicates that from 65 to 90 percent of the message of every face-to-face conversation is interpreted through body language. Without complete agreement between the spoken words and the body language that accompanies it, receivers are more likely to react to body language as the "true meaning."[12]

What Barriers Keep Communication from Being Effective?

A number of interpersonal and intrapersonal barriers affect why the message decoded by a receiver is often different from what the sender intended. We summarize the more prominent barriers to effective communication in Exhibit 13–2 and briefly describe them here.

HOW DOES FILTERING AFFECT COMMUNICATION?   **Filtering** refers to the way that a sender manipulates information so that it will be seen more favorably by the receiver. For example, when a manager tells his boss what he feels that boss wants to hear, he is filtering

---

grapevine
An unofficial channel of communication

body language
Nonverbal communication cues such as facial expressions, gestures, and other body movements

verbal intonation
An emphasis given to words or phrases that conveys meaning

filtering
Deliberately manipulating information to make it appear more favorable to the receiver

EXHIBIT 13-2	Barriers to Effective Communication

BARRIER	DESCRIPTION
Filtering	The deliberate manipulation of information to make it appear more favorable to the receiver.
Selective Perception	Receiving communications on the basis of what one selectively sees and hears depending on his or her needs, motivation, experience, background, and other personal characteristics.
Information Overload	When the amount of information one has to work with exceeds one's processing capacity.
Emotions	How the receiver feels when a message is received.
Language	Words have different meanings to different people. Receivers will use their definition of words being communicated.
Gender	How males and females react to communication may be different, and they each have a different communication style.
National Culture	Communication differences arising from the different languages that individuals use to communicate and the national culture of which they are a part.

information. Does filtering happen much in organizations? Sure it does. As information is passed up to senior executives, it has to be condensed and synthesized by subordinates so upper management doesn't become overloaded with information. Those doing the condensing filter communications through their own personal interests and perceptions of what's important.

The extent of filtering tends to be the function of the organization's culture and number of vertical levels in the organization. More vertical levels in an organization mean more opportunities for filtering. As organizations become less dependent on strict hierarchical arrangements and instead use more collaborative, cooperative work arrangements, information filtering may become less of a problem. In addition, the ever-increasing use of e-mail to communicate in organizations reduces filtering because communication is more direct as intermediaries are bypassed. Finally, the organizational culture encourages or discourages filtering by the type of behavior it rewards. The more that organizational rewards emphasize style and appearance, the more managers will be motivated to filter communications in their favor.

HOW DOES SELECTIVE PERCEPTION AFFECT COMMUNICATION? The second barrier is **selective perception**. We've mentioned selective perception before in this book. We discuss it again here because the receivers in the communication process selectively see and hear based on their needs, motivations, experience, background, and other personal characteristics. Receivers also project their interests and expectations into communications as they decode them. The employment interviewer who expects a female job applicant to put her family ahead of her career is likely to see that tendency in female applicants, regardless of whether the applicants would do so or not. As we said in Chapter 9, we don't see reality; rather, we interpret what we see and call it reality.

HOW DOES INFORMATION OVERLOAD AFFECT COMMUNICATION? Individuals have a finite capacity for processing data. For instance, consider the international sales representative who returns home to find that she has more than 600 e-mails waiting for her. It's not possible to fully read and respond to each one of those messages without facing **information overload**. Today's typical executive frequently complains of information overload.[13] The demands of keeping up with e-mail, phone calls, faxes, meetings, and professional reading create an onslaught of data that is nearly impossible to process and assimilate. What happens when you have more information than you can sort out and use? You're likely to select out, ignore, pass over, or forget information. Or you may put off further processing until the overload situation is over. In any case, the result is lost information and less effective communication.

HOW DO EMOTIONS AFFECT COMMUNICATION?   How a receiver feels when a message is received influences how he or she interprets it. You'll often interpret the same message differently, depending on whether you're happy or distressed. Extreme emotions are most likely to hinder effective communications. In such instances, we often disregard our rational and objective thinking processes and substitute emotional judgments. It's best to avoid reacting to a message when you're upset because you're not likely to be thinking clearly.

HOW DOES LANGUAGE AFFECT COMMUNICATION?   Words mean different things to different people. "The meanings of words are not in the words; they are in us."[14] Age, education, and cultural background are three of the more obvious variables that influence the language a person uses and the definitions he or she applies to words. Columnist George F. Will and rapper Missy Elliott both speak English. But the language one uses is vastly different from how the other speaks.

   In an organization, employees usually come from diverse backgrounds and, therefore, have different patterns of speech. Additionally, the grouping of employees into departments creates specialists who develop their own **jargon** or technical language.[15] In large organizations, members are also frequently widely dispersed geographically—even operating in different countries—and individuals in each locale will use terms and phrases that are unique to their area.[16] And the existence of vertical levels can also cause language problems. The language of senior executives, for instance, can be mystifying to regular employees not familiar with management jargon. Keep in mind that while we may speak the same language, our use of that language is far from uniform. Senders tend to assume that the words and phrases they use mean the same to the receiver as they do to them. This assumption, of course, is incorrect and creates communication barriers. Knowing how each of us modifies the language would help minimize those barriers.

HOW DOES GENDER AFFECT COMMUNICATION?   Effective communication between the sexes is important in all organizations if they are to meet organizational goals. But how can we manage the various differences in communication styles? To keep gender differences from becoming persistent barriers to effective communication, individuals must strive for acceptance, understanding, and a commitment to communicate adaptively with each other. Both men and women need to acknowledge differences are present in communication styles, that one style isn't better than the other, and that it takes real effort to talk successfully with each other.[17]

HOW DOES NATIONAL CULTURE AFFECT COMMUNICATION?   Finally, communication differences can also arise from the different languages that individuals use to communicate and the national culture of which they're a part.[18] For example, let's compare countries that place a high value on individualism (such as the United States) with countries where the emphasis is on collectivism (such as Japan).[19]

   In the United States, communication patterns tend to be oriented to the individual and clearly spelled out. Managers in the United States rely heavily on memoranda, announcements, position papers, and other formal forms of communication to state their positions on issues. Supervisors here may hoard information in an attempt to make themselves look good (filtering) and as a way of persuading their employees to accept decisions and plans. And for their own protection, lower-level employees also engage in this practice.

Convergys Corporation provides customer service and sales support for clients in more than 70 countries speaking nearly 35 languages. Even though the call-center employees shown here at the company's facility in Gurgaon, India, and their clients speak the common language of English, communication barriers exist because of differences among country cultures, language accents, and different patterns of speech. To overcome these barriers, Convergys employees receive multicultural skills-based training and accent-neutralization training so they can be more easily understood by their calling clients.

Gurinder Osan/AP Images

selective perception
Selectively perceiving or hearing a communication based on your own needs, motivations, experiences, or other personal characteristics

information overload
What results when information exceeds processing capacity

jargon
Technical language, specific to a discipline or industry

In collectivist countries, such as Japan, there's more interaction for its own sake and a more informal manner of interpersonal contact. The Japanese manager, in contrast to the U.S. manager, engages in extensive verbal consultation with employees over an issue first and draws up a formal document later to outline the agreement that was made. The Japanese value decisions by consensus, and open communication is an inherent part of the work setting. Also, face-to-face communication is encouraged.[20]

Cultural differences can affect the way a manager chooses to communicate.[21] And these differences undoubtedly can be a barrier to effective communication if not recognized and taken into consideration.

How Can Managers Overcome Communication Barriers?

Given these barriers to communication, what can managers do to overcome them? The following suggestions should help make communication more effective (see also Exhibit 13–3).

WHY USE FEEDBACK? Many communication problems are directly attributed to misunderstanding and inaccuracies. These problems are less likely to occur if the manager gets feedback, both verbal and nonverbal.

A manager can ask questions about a message to determine whether it was received and understood as intended. Or the manager can ask the receiver to restate the message in his or her own words. If the manager hears what was intended, understanding and accuracy should improve. Feedback can also be more subtle as general comments can give a manager a sense of the receiver's reaction to a message.

Feedback doesn't have to be verbal. If a sales manager e-mails information about a new monthly sales report that all sales representatives will need to complete and some of them don't turn it in, the sales manager has received feedback. This feedback suggests that the sales manager needs to clarify the initial communication. Similarly, managers can look for nonverbal cues to tell whether someone's getting the message.

WHY SHOULD SIMPLIFIED LANGUAGE BE USED? Because language can be a barrier, managers should consider the audience to whom the message is directed and tailor the language to them. Remember, effective communication is achieved when a message is both received and *understood*. For example, a hospital administrator should always try to communicate in clear, easily understood terms and to use language tailored to different employee groups. Messages to the surgical staff should be purposefully different from those directed to the marketing team or office employees. Jargon can facilitate understanding if it's used within a group that knows what it means, but can cause problems when used outside that group.

WHY MUST WE LISTEN ACTIVELY? When someone talks, we hear. But too often we don't listen. Listening is an active search for meaning, whereas hearing is passive. In listening, the receiver is also putting effort into the communication.

EXHIBIT 13–3	Overcoming Barriers to Effective Communication
Use Feedback	Check the accuracy of what has been communicated—or what you think you heard.
Simplify Language	Use words that the intended audience understands.
Listen Actively	Listen for the full meaning of the message without making premature judgment or interpretation—or thinking about what you are going to say in response.
Constrain Emotions	Recognize when your emotions are running high. When they are, don't communicate until you have calmed down.
Watch Nonverbal Cues	Be aware that your actions speak louder than your words. Keep the two consistent.

Many of us are poor listeners. Why? Because it's difficult, and most of us would rather do the talking. Listening, in fact, is often more tiring than talking. Unlike hearing, **active listening**, which is listening for full meaning without making premature judgments or interpretations, demands total concentration. The average person normally speaks at a rate of about 125 to 200 words per minute. However, the average listener can comprehend up to 400 words per minute.[22] The difference leaves lots of idle brain time and opportunities for the mind to wander.

Active listening is enhanced by developing empathy with the sender—that is, by putting yourself in the sender's position. Because senders differ in attitudes, interests, needs, and expectations, empathy makes it easier to understand the actual content of a message. An empathetic listener reserves judgment on the message's content and carefully listens to what is being said. The goal is to improve one's ability to get the full meaning of a communication without distorting it by premature judgments or interpretations. Other specific behaviors that active listeners use include making eye contact, exhibiting affirmative nods and appropriate facial expressions, avoiding distracting actions or gestures that suggest boredom, asking questions, paraphrasing using your own words, avoiding interrupting the speaker, not talking too much, and making smooth transitions between being a speaker and a listener.

WHY MUST WE CONSTRAIN EMOTIONS? It would be naïve to assume that managers always communicate in a rational manner. We know that emotions can cloud and distort communication. A manager who's upset over an issue is more likely to misconstrue incoming messages and fail to communicate his or her outgoing messages clearly and accurately. What to do? The simplest answer is to calm down and get emotions under control before communicating. The following is a good example of why it's important to be aware of your emotions before communicating.

Neal L. Patterson, CEO of Cerner Corporation, a health care software development company based in Kansas City, was upset with the fact that employees didn't seem to be putting in enough hours. So he sent an angry and emotional e-mail to about 400 company managers that said, in part:

> We are getting less than 40 hours of work from a large number of our K.C.-based EMPLOYEES. The parking lot is sparsely used at 8 a.m.; likewise at 5 p.m. As managers, you either do not know what your EMPLOYEES are doing, or you do not CARE. You have created expectations on the work effort which allowed this to happen inside Cerner, creating a very unhealthy environment. In either case, you have a problem and you will fix it or I will replace you . . . I will hold you accountable. You have allowed things to get to this state. You have two weeks. Tick, tock."[23]

Although the e-mail was meant only for the company's managers, it was leaked and posted on an Internet discussion site. The tone of the e-mail surprised industry analysts, investors, and of course, Cerner's managers and employees. The company's stock price dropped 22 percent over the next three days. Patterson apologized to his employees and acknowledged, "I lit a match and started a firestorm."

RIGHT ? WRONG

Sixty percent. That's the percentage of respondents in an employee survey who said that gossip was their biggest pet peeve about their jobs.[24] Although office gossip can benefit individuals and organizations, it often consists of hearsay, half-truths, and innuendo. It also can absorb large amounts of employees' time.

Think About:

• What do you think? Is office gossip beneficial for individuals? Organizations?

• What ethical dilemmas might arise because of office gossip?

• As a manager, how will you handle office gossip?

Anna Bryukhanova/iStockphoto.com

active listening
Listening for full meaning without making premature judgments or interpretations

WHY THE EMPHASIS ON NONVERBAL CUES?   If actions speak louder than words, then it's important to make sure your actions align with and reinforce the words that go along with them. An effective communicator watches his or her nonverbal cues to ensure that they convey the desired message.

HOW IS TECHNOLOGY AFFECTING MANAGERIAL COMMUNICATION?

13.2 Explain how technology affects managerial communication.

Information technology has radically changed the way organizational members communicate. For example, it has significantly improved a manager's ability to monitor individual and team performance, it has allowed employees to have more complete information to make faster decisions, and it has provided employees more opportunities to collaborate and share information. In addition, information technology has made it possible for people in organizations to be fully accessible 24 hours a day, 7 days a week, regardless of where they are. Employees don't have to be at their desks with their computers on in order to communicate with others in the organization. Three developments in information technology appear to have had a significant effect on current managerial communication: networked computer systems, wireless capabilities, and knowledge management systems.

What Are Networked Communication Capabilities?

In a networked computer system, an organization links its computers together through compatible hardware and software, creating an integrated organizational network. Organization members can then communicate with each other and tap into information whether they're down the hall, across town, or anywhere on the globe. Although the mechanics of how networked systems work are beyond the scope of this book, we'll address some of the communication applications.

E-mail is the instantaneous transmission of messages on computers that are linked together. Messages wait at a receiver's computer and are read at the receiver's convenience. E-mail is fast and cheap and can be used to send the same message to many people at the same time. It's a quick and convenient way for organization members to share information and communicate. Files can also be attached to e-mail messages, which enables the receiver to print a hard copy of a document.

Some organization members who find e-mail slow and cumbersome are using *instant messaging (IM)*. This interactive, real-time communication takes place among computer users who are logged on to the computer network at the same time. Instant messaging was first popular among teens and preteens who wanted to communicate with their friends online. Now it's moved to the workplace. With IM, information that needs to be communicated can be done so instantaneously without waiting for colleagues to read e-mail messages. However, instant messaging is not without its drawbacks. It requires users to be logged on to the organization's computer network at the same time, which potentially leaves the network open to security breaches.

A *voice-mail* system digitizes a spoken message, transmits it over the network, and stores the message on a disk for the receiver to retrieve later.[25] This capability allows information to be transmitted even though a receiver may not be physically present to take the information. Receivers can choose to save the message for future use, delete it, or route it to other parties.

Fax machines can transmit documents containing both text and graphics over ordinary telephone lines. A sending fax machine scans and digitizes the document, and a receiving fax machine reads the scanned information and reproduces it in hard-copy form. Information that's best viewed in printed form can be easily and quickly shared by organization members.

Electronic data interchange (EDI) is a way for organizations to exchange business transaction documents such as invoices or purchase orders, using direct computer-to-computer networks. Organizations often use EDI with vendors, suppliers, and customers because it saves time and money. How? Information on transactions is transmitted from one organization's computer system to another through an interorganizational telecommunications network. The printing and handling of paper documents at one organization are eliminated as is the inputting of data at the other organization.

Meetings—one-on-one, team, divisional, or organization-wide—have always been one way to share information. The limitations of technology used to dictate that meetings take place among people in the same physical location. But that's no longer the case. Teleconferencing allows a group of people to confer simultaneously using telephone or e-mail group communications software. If meeting participants can see each other over video screens, the simultaneous conference is called videoconferencing. Work groups, large and small, which might be in different locations, can use these communication network tools to collaborate and share information. Doing so is often much less expensive than incurring travel costs for bringing members together from several locations.

Networked computer systems allow for organizational *intranets* and *extranets*. An intranet is an organizational communication network that uses Internet technology but is accessible only to organizational employees. Many organizations are using intranets as ways for employees to share information and collaborate on documents and projects—as well as access company policy manuals and employee-specific materials, such as employee benefits—from different locations.[26] An extranet is an organizational communication network that uses Internet technology and allows authorized users inside the organization to communicate with certain outsiders such as customers or vendors. Most of the large auto manufacturers, for example, have extranets that allow faster and more convenient communication with dealers.

Finally, organizations are using *Internet-based voice communication*. Popular Web sites such as Skype, Vonage, and Yahoo!, among others, let users chat with each other. A number of companies are making these services available for employees to use in conference calls or for instant messaging.

How Have Wireless Capabilities Affected Communication?

At Seattle-based Starbucks Corporation, district managers use mobile technology, giving them more time to spend in the company's stores. A company executive says, "These are the most important people in the company. Each has between 8 to 10 stores that he or she services. And while their primary job is outside of the office—and in those stores—they still need to be connected."[27] As this example shows, wireless communication technology has the ability to improve work for managers and employees.

TECHNOLOGY AND THE MANAGER'S JOB
FYEO: DECODING COMMUNICATION JARGON

Okay . . . how well do you know the Net lingo?[28] If you received an e-mail or text message with GFTD written in it, would you know what that meant? What about NSFW or BIL? When an employee received an e-mail at work from a friend with an attached slideshow entitled "Awkward Family Photos," she clicked through it and saw some pretty unusual—yes, awkward—photos. Looking back at the e-mail, that's when she also saw the abbreviation "NSFW" written at the bottom. Not knowing what that was, she looked the abbreviation up on netlingo.com (one of several Web sites that translate Internet and texting abbreviations). Come to find out, she should have paid more attention to the abbreviation: NSFW stands for "not safe for work."

As text-messaging shorthand becomes increasingly widespread in e-mails, text messages, and tweets, people need to be aware of what it means. At many workplaces, a working knowledge of Net lingo is becoming necessary. As employees use social media sites such as Twitter and Facebook and even text messaging to communicate with colleagues and customers, the shorthand abbreviations are often necessary to stay within message length limits. However, as the NSFW example showed, not knowing or even misunderstanding the lingo can lead to surprises, inappropriate responses, or miscommunications.

(BTW—which is Net lingo for "by the way": FYEO means "for your eyes only"; GFTD stands for "gone for the day"; and BIL is "boss is listening.")

Think About:

· What benefits does jargon or lingo have? What are the drawbacks?

· Go to www.netlingo.com and pick three phrases you were not familiar with. Were you surprised at the number of Net lingo phrases?

While networked computer systems require organizations and organizational members to be connected by wires, wireless communication doesn't. Smartphones, tablet computers, notebook computers, and mobile pocket communication devices have spawned a whole new way for managers to "keep in touch." Globally, millions of users use wireless technology to send and receive information from anywhere. One result: Employees no longer have to be at their desks with their computers plugged in and turned on in order to communicate with others in the organization. As technology continues to advance in this area, we'll see more and more organization members using wireless communication as a way to collaborate and share information.[29]

Steven Senne/AP Images

IBM cultivates a learning culture by using an internal social networking site called Beehive that enables employees to gather knowledge and share it with coworkers. Employees shown here with computer monitors displaying the Beehive portal can describe their expertise, promote their innovative ideas directly to other employees, generate feedback, and post pictures, videos, and updates about themselves. Beehive is helping to break down communication barriers by rank, location, and social groups within IBM and allowing employees to learn about projects and initiatives throughout the company. It also aids team building and trust among employees and allows IBM's management to get involved with employees and join their conversations.

How Does Knowledge Management Affect Communication?

Part of a manager's responsibility in fostering an environment conducive to learning and effective communications is to create learning capabilities throughout the organization. These opportunities should extend from the lowest to the highest levels in all areas. How can managers create such an environment? An important step is recognizing the value of knowledge as a major resource, just like cash, raw materials, or office equipment. To illustrate the value of knowledge, think about how you register for your college classes. Do you talk to others who have had a certain professor? Do you listen to their experiences with this individual and make your decision based on what they have to say (their knowledge about the situation)? If you do, you're tapping into the value of knowledge. But in an organization, just recognizing the value of accumulated knowledge or wisdom isn't enough. Managers must deliberately manage that base of knowledge. **Knowledge management** involves cultivating a learning culture in which organizational members systematically gather knowledge and share it with others in the organization so as to achieve better performance.[30] For instance, accountants and consultants at Ernst & Young document best practices that they've developed, unusual problems they've dealt with, and other work information. This "knowledge" is then shared with all employees through computer-based applications and through community of interest teams that meet regularly throughout the company. Many other organizations, including General Electric, Toyota, and Hewlett-Packard, have recognized the importance of knowledge management within a learning organization (see Chapter 6, pp. 150–151). Today's technologies are helping improve knowledge management and facilitating organizational communications and decision making.

WHAT COMMUNICATION ISSUES DO MANAGERS FACE TODAY?

13.3 Discuss contemporary issues in communication.

"Pulse lunches." That's what managers at Citibank's offices throughout Malaysia used to address pressing problems of declining customer loyalty and staff morale and increased employee turnover. By connecting with employees and listening to their concerns—that is, taking their "pulse"—during informal lunch settings, managers were able to make changes that boosted both customer loyalty and employee morale by more than 50 percent and reduced employee turnover to nearly zero.[31]

Being an effective communicator in today's organizations means being connected—most importantly to employees and customers, but in reality, to any of the organization's stakeholders. In this section, we examine five communication issues of particular significance to today's managers: managing communication in an Internet world, managing the organization's knowledge resources, communicating with customers, getting employee input, and communicating ethically.

Managing Communication in an Internet World

Lars Dalgaard, founder and chief executive of SuccessFactors, a human resource management software company, recently sent an e-mail to his employees banning in-house e-mail for a week. His goal? Getting employees to "authentically address issues amongst each other."[32] And he's not alone. Other companies have tried the same thing. As we discussed earlier, e-mail can consume employees, but it's not always easy for them to let go of it, even when they know it can be "intexticating." But e-mail is only one communication challenge in this Internet world. A recent survey found that 20 percent of employees at large companies say they contribute regularly to blogs, social networks, wikis, and other Web services.[33] Managers are learning, the hard way sometimes, that all this new technology has created special communication challenges. The two main ones are (1) legal and security issues, and (2) lack of personal interaction.

LEGAL AND SECURITY ISSUES. Chevron paid $2.2 million to settle a sexual harassment lawsuit stemming from inappropriate jokes being sent by employees over company e-mail. U.K. firm Norwich Union had to pay £450,000 in an out-of-court settlement after an employee sent an e-mail stating that its competitor, Western Provident Association, was in financial difficulties. Whole Foods Market was investigated by federal regulators and its board after CEO John P. Mackey used a pseudonym to post comments on a blog attacking the company's rival Wild Oats Markets.[34]

Although e-mail, blogs, tweets, and other forms of online communication are quick and easy ways to communicate, managers need to be aware of potential legal problems from inappropriate usage. Electronic information is potentially admissible in court. For instance, during the Enron trial, prosecutors entered into evidence e-mails and other documents they say showed that the defendants defrauded investors. Says one expert, "Today, e-mail and instant messaging are the electronic equivalent of DNA evidence."[35] But legal problems aren't the only issue, security concerns are as well.

A survey addressing outbound e-mail and content security found that 26 percent of the companies surveyed saw their businesses affected by the exposure of sensitive or embarrassing information.[36] Managers need to ensure that confidential information is kept confidential. Employee e-mails and blogs should not communicate—inadvertently or purposely—proprietary information. Corporate computer and e-mail systems should be protected against hackers (people who try to gain unauthorized access to computer systems) and spam (electronic junk mail). These serious issues must be addressed if the benefits of communication technology are to be realized.

PERSONAL INTERACTION. It may be called social media, but another communication challenge posed by the Internet age we live and work in is the lack of personal interaction.[37] Even when two people are communicating face-to-face, understanding is not always achieved. However, it can be especially challenging to achieve understanding and collaborate on getting work done when communication takes place in a virtual environment. In response, some companies have banned e-mail on certain days, as we saw earlier. Others have simply encouraged employees to collaborate more in-person. Yet, sometimes and in some situations, personal interaction isn't physically possible—your colleagues work

AND THE SURVEY SAYS...[38]

25 percent of employees say they withhold feedback on routine problems to avoid wasting their time.

47 percent of Wi-Fi users say they can wait one hour or less before getting "antsy" about checking e-mail, instant messaging, and social networking sites.

64 seconds is how long it takes to retrieve your train of thought after an e-mail interruption.

69 percent of executives say they're sending out more messages than ever to employees.

37 percent of employees say they're receiving more messages from executives.

54 percent of employees say their company prohibits employees from visiting social networking sites while at work.

42 percent of employees who have received employer-provided wireless devices feel they are expected to always be available.

28 percent of a day is how much the average worker loses to interruptions

knowledge management
Cultivating a learning culture in which organizational members systematically gather knowledge and share it with others

across the continent or even across the globe. In those instances, real-time collaboration software (such as private workplace wikis, blogs, instant messengers, and other types of groupware) may be a better communication choice than sending an e-mail and waiting for a response.[39] Instead of fighting it, some companies are encouraging employees to utilize the power of social networks to collaborate on work and to build strong connections. This trend is especially appealing to younger workers who are comfortable with this communication medium. Some companies have gone as far as to create their own in-house social networks. For instance, employees at Starcom MediaVest Group tap into SMG Connected to find colleague profiles that outline their jobs, list the brands they admire, and describe their values. A company vice president says, "Giving our employees a way to connect over the Internet around the world made sense because they were doing it anyway."[40]

Managing the Organization's Knowledge Resources

Kara Johnson is a materials expert at product design firm IDEO. To make finding the right materials easier, she built a master library of samples linked to a database that explains their properties and manufacturing processes.[41] What Johnson is doing is managing knowledge and making it easier for others at IDEO to learn and benefit from her knowledge. That's what today's managers need to do with the organization's knowledge resources—make it easy for employees to communicate and share their knowledge so they can learn from each other ways to do their jobs more effectively and efficiently. One way organizations can do this is to build online information databases that employees can access. For example, William Wrigley Jr. Co. launched an interactive Web site that allows sales agents to access marketing data and other product information. The sales agents can question company experts about products or search an online knowledge bank. In its first year, Wrigley estimates that the site cut research time of the sales force by 15,000 hours, making them more efficient and effective.[42] This one example, among many others, shows how managers can use communication tools to manage this valuable organizational resource called knowledge.

In addition to online information databases for sharing knowledge, companies can create **communities of practice**, which are groups of people who share a concern, a set of problems, or a passion about a topic, and who deepen their knowledge and expertise in that area by interacting on an ongoing basis. To make these communities of practice work, however, it's important to maintain strong human interactions through communication using such essential tools as interactive Web sites, e-mail, and videoconferencing. In addition, these groups face the same communication problems that individuals face—filtering, emotions, defensiveness, overdocumentation, and so forth. However, groups can resolve these issues by focusing on the same suggestions we discussed earlier.

The Role of Communication in Customer Service

You've been a customer many times; in fact, you probably find yourself in a customer service encounter several times a day. So what does a customer service encounter have to do with communication? As it turns out, a lot! *What* communication takes place and *how* it takes place can have a significant impact on a customer's satisfaction with the service and the likelihood of being a repeat customer. Managers in service organizations need to make sure that employees who interact with customers are communicating appropriately and effectively with those customers. How? By first recognizing the three components in any service delivery process: the customer, the service organization, and the individual service provider.[43] Each plays a role in whether communication is working. Obviously, managers don't have a lot of control over what or how the customer communicates, but they can influence the other two.

An organization with a strong service culture already values taking care of customers—finding out what their

Communication is an important part of the customer service strategy at the Four Seasons, a Toronto, Canada-based global luxury chain of hotels and resorts. Recognizing that *how* communication takes place has a significant impact on customer satisfaction, the company expects all employees to greet guests with a friendly hello and teaches them how to treat guests with warmth, courtesy, and respect. As front-line workers involved with critical service encounters, the concierge desk employees shown here are trained to listen actively and communicate efficiently and effectively in delivering exceptional service that sustains the Four Seasons' competitive advantage in service excellence.

Mark Peterson/Redux Pictures

needs are, meeting those needs, and following up to make sure that their needs were met satis-factorily. Each of these activities involves communication, whether face-to-face, by phone or e-mail, or through other channels. In addition, communication is part of the specific customer service strategies the organization pursues. One strategy that many service organizations use is personalization. For instance, at Ritz-Carlton Hotels, customers are provided with more than a clean bed and room. Customers who have stayed at a location previously and indicated that certain items are important to them—such as extra pillows, hot chocolate, or a certain brand of shampoo—will find those items waiting in their room at arrival. The hotel's database allows service to be personalized to customers' expectations. In addition, all employees are asked to communicate information related to service provision. For instance, if a room attendant overhears guests talking about celebrating an anniversary, he or she is supposed to relay the information so something special can be done.[44] Communication plays an important role in the hotel's customer personalization strategy.

Communication also is important to the individual service provider or contact employee. The quality of the interpersonal interaction between the customer and that contact employee does influence customer satisfaction, especially when the service encounter isn't up to expec-tations.[45] People on the front line involved with those "critical service encounters" are often the first to hear about or notice service failures or breakdowns. They must decide *how* and *what* to communicate during these instances. Their ability to listen actively and communicate appropriately with the customer goes a long way in whether the situation is resolved to the customer's satisfaction or spirals out of control. Another important communication concern for the individual service provider is making sure that he or she has the information needed to deal with customers efficiently and effectively. If the service provider doesn't personally have the information, there should be some way to get the information easily and promptly.[46]

Getting Employee Input

Nokia recently set up an intranet soapbox known as Blog-Hub, opening it up to employee bloggers around the world. There, employees have griped about their employer, but rather than shutting it down, Nokia managers want them to "fire away." They feel that Nokia's growth and success can be attributed to a "history of encouraging employees to say whatever's on their minds, with faith that smarter ideas will result."[47]

In today's challenging environment, companies need to get input from their employees. Have you ever worked somewhere that had an employee suggestion box? When an employee had an idea about a new way of doing something—such as reducing costs, improving delivery time, and so forth—it went into the suggestion box where it usually sat until someone decided to empty the box. Businesspeople frequently joked about the suggestion box and cartoonists lambasted the futility of putting ideas in the employee suggestion box. Unfortunately, this atti-tude about suggestion boxes still persists in many organizations, but it shouldn't. Managers do business in a world today where you can't afford to ignore such potentially valuable informa-tion. Exhibit 13–4 lists some suggestions for letting employees know that their opinions matter.

EXHIBIT 13–4   **How to Let Employees Know Their Input Matters**

- *Hold town-hall meetings* where information is shared and input solicited.
- *Provide information* about what's going on, good and bad.
- *Invest in training* so that employees see how they impact the customer experience.
- *Analyze problems together*—managers and employees.
- *Make it easy* for employees to give input by setting up different ways for them to do so (online, suggestion box, preprinted cards, and so forth).

---

communities of practice
Groups of people who share a concern, a set of problems, or a passion about a topic, and who deepen their knowledge and expertise in that area by interacting on an ongoing basis

Maurice Moreno/Newscom

Following the merger of United and Continental airlines, Jeff Smisek, CEO of the new airline, established clear guidelines for ethical communications. Smisek and his management team began building a culture for the new carrier based on being honest and direct with employees and customers. In holding CEO exchanges with employees throughout Europe, Asia, Latin America, and the United States, Smisek answered employee questions honestly. In response to the question "When are you going to snap me back to the wages I had in the year 2000?" Smisek truthfully answered, "Never. That was a different time. We are in a different business now." Smisek believes that people respect you when you give them honest answers, and he expects employees to communicate ethically with the new airline's customers.

Communicating Ethically

It's particularly important today that a company's communication efforts be ethical. **Ethical communication** "includes all relevant information, is true in every sense, and is not deceptive in any way."[48] On the other hand, unethical communication often distorts the truth or manipulates audiences. What are some ways that companies communicate unethically? It could be by omitting essential information. For instance, not telling employees that an impending merger is going to mean some of them will lose their jobs is unethical. It's also unethical to plagiarize, which is "presenting someone else's words or other creative product as your own."[49] It would also be unethical communication to selectively misquote, misrepresent numbers, distort visuals, and fail to respect privacy or information security needs. For instance, although British Petroleum attempted to communicate openly and truthfully about the Gulf Coast oil spill, the public felt that much of the company's communication had some unethical elements to it.

So how can managers encourage ethical communications? One thing is to "establish clear guidelines for ethical behavior, including ethical business communication."[50] In a global survey by the International Association of Business Communicators, 70 percent of communication professionals said their companies clearly define what is considered ethical and unethical behavior.[51] If no clear guidelines exist, it's important to answer the following questions:

- ◆ Has the situation been defined fairly and accurately?
- ◆ Why is the message being communicated?
- ◆ How will the people who may be affected by the message or who receive the message be impacted?
- ◆ Does the message help achieve the greatest possible good while minimizing possible harm?
- ◆ Will this decision that appears to be ethical now seem so in the future?
- ◆ How comfortable are you with your communication effort? What would a person you admire think of it?[52]

Remember that as a manager, you have a responsibility to think through your communication choices and the consequences of those choices. If you always remember that, you're likely to have ethical communication.

---

ethical communication
Presented material that contains all relevant information, is true in every sense, and is not deceptive in any way.

13 Review

CHAPTER SUMMARY

13.1 **Describe what managers need to know about communicating effectively.** Communication is the transfer and understanding of meaning. The communication process consists of seven elements: First, a *sender* or source has a message. A *message* is a purpose to be conveyed. *Encoding* converts a message into symbols. A *channel* provides the medium along which a message travels. *Decoding* happens when the *receiver* retranslates a sender's message. Finally, *feedback* lets the sender know whether the communication was successful. The barriers to effective communication include filtering, emotions, information overload, defensiveness, language, and national culture. Managers can overcome these barriers by using feedback, simplifying language, listening actively, constraining emotions, and watching for nonverbal clues.

13.2 **Explain how technology affects managerial communication.** Technology has radically changed the way organizational members communicate. It improves a manager's ability to monitor performance; it gives employees more complete information to make faster decisions; it provides employees more opportunities to collaborate and share information; and it makes it possible for people to be fully accessible, anytime anywhere. IT has affected managerial communication through the use of networked computer systems, wireless capabilities, and knowledge management systems.

13.3 **Discuss contemporary issues in communication.** The two main challenges of managing communication in an Internet world are the legal and security issues and the lack of personal interaction.

Organizations can manage knowledge by making it easy for employees to communicate and share their knowledge so they can learn from each other ways to do their jobs more effectively and efficiently. One way is through online information databases, and another way is through creating communities of practice.

Communicating with customers is an important managerial issue because *what* communication takes place and *how* it takes place can significantly affect a customer's satisfaction with the service and the likelihood of being a repeat customer.

It's important for organizations to get input from their employees. Such potentially valuable information should not be ignored.

Finally, it's important that a company's communication efforts be ethical. Ethical communication can be encouraged through clear guidelines and through answering questions that force a communicator to think through the communication choices made and the consequences of those choices.

MyManagementLab   For more resources, please visit www.mymanagementlab.com

UNDERSTANDING THE CHAPTER

1. Which type of communication do you think is most effective in a work setting? Why?

2. Why isn't effective communication synonymous with *agreement?*

3. Which do you think is more important for a manager: speaking accurately or listening actively? Why?

4. "Ineffective communication is the fault of the sender." Do you agree or disagree with this statement? Discuss.

5. Is information technology helping managers be more efficient and effective? Explain your answer.

6. How might a manager use the grapevine to his or her advantage? Support your response.

7. Research the characteristics of a good communicator. Write up your findings in a bulleted list report. Be sure to cite your sources.

8. Discuss the five contemporary communication issues facing managers.

9. For one day, track nonverbal communication that you notice in others. What types did you observe? Was the nonverbal communication always consistent with the verbal communication taking place? Describe.

Go to p. 449

YOUR TURN ᵀᴼ BE A MANAGER for Chapter 13.

Endnotes

1. B. J. Dunn, "Best Buy's CEO on Learning to Love Social Media," *Harvard Business Review,* December 2010, pp. 43–48; D. Brady, "Brian Dunn," *Bloomberg BusinessWeek,* December 6, 2010, p. 104; J. Castaldo, "Are You Sure You Really Want to Tweet That, Boss?" *Canadian Business,* November 22, 2010, p. 79; A. Scardillo, "Old Spice Guy's Lessons in Crisis Management," *Marketing Magazine,* August 30, 2010, p. 27; and J. Bernoff and T. Schadler, "Empowered," *Harvard Business Review,* July–August 2010, pp. 95–101.

2. D. K. Berlo, *The Process of Communication* (New York: Holt, Rinehart & Winston, 1960), pp. 30–32.

3. Ibid., p. 54.

4. See, for instance, "Get the Message: Communication Is Key in Managing Change Within Organizations—Yet Ensuring Its Effectiveness at Times of High Concerns Can Be Tricky," *Employee Benefits,* February 2002, pp. 58–60.

5. Ibid., p. 103.

6. L. R. Birkner and R. K. Birkner, "Communication Feedback: Putting It All Together," *Occupational Hazards,* August 2001, p. 9.

7. L. Hilton, "They Heard It Through the Grapevine," *South Florida Business Journal,* August 18, 2000, p. 53.

8. L. Talley, "Body Language: Read It or Weep," *HR Magazine,* July 2010, pp. 64–65; and M. Fulfer, "Nonverbal Communication: How to Read What's Plain as the Nose . . . Or Eyelid . . . Or Chin . . . On Their Faces," *Journal of Occupational Excellence* (Spring 2001), pp. 19–38.

9. From the Past to the Present box based on S. Baker, "Putting a Price on Social Connections," *BusinessWeek Online,* April 8, 2009; and K. Davis, "Management Communication and the Grapevine," *Harvard Business Review,* September–October 1953, pp. 43–49.

10. Ibid; and T. Fernsler, "The Secrets and Science of Body Language," *Nonprofit World,* p. 25.

11. P. Mornell, "The Sounds of Silence," *Inc.,* February 2001, p. 117.

12. A. Warfield, "Do You Speak Body Language?" *Training and Development* (April 2001), p. 60.

13. S. Begley, "I Can't Think," *Newsweek,* March 7, 2011, pp. 28–33; D. Dean and C. Webb, "Recovering from Information Overload," *McKinsey Quarterly,* Issue 1, 2011, pp. 80–88; and "Information Overload," *Australian Business Intelligence,* April 16, 2002.

14. S. I. Hayakawa, *Language in Thought and Action* (New York: Harcourt Brace Jovanovich, 1949), p. 292.

15. "Jargon Leaves Us Lost for Words," *Australian Business Intelligence,* August 23, 2002; and W. S. Mossberg, "A Guide to the Lingo You'll Want to Learn for Wireless Technology," *Wall Street Journal,* March 28, 2002, p. B1.

16. "Gobbledygook Begone," *Workforce,* February 2002, p. 12; and "Business-Speak," *Training and Development* (January 2002), pp. 50–52.

17. J. Langdon, "Differences Between Males and Females at Work," *USA Today,* www.usatoday.com (February 5, 2001); J. Manion, "He Said, She Said," *Materials Management in Health Care,* November 1998, pp. 52–62; G. Franzwa and C. Lockhart, "The Social Origins and Maintenance of Gender Communication Styles, Personality Types, and Grid-Group Theory," *Sociological Perspectives,* 41, no. 1 (1998), pp. 185–208; and D. Tannen, *Talking From 9 to 5: Women and Men in the Workplace* (New York: Avon Books, 1995).

18. See, for example, M. K. Kozan, "Subcultures and Conflict Management Styles," *Management International Review,* January 2002, pp. 89–106.

19. A. Mehrabian, "Communication Without Words," *Psychology Today,* September 1968, pp. 53–55.

20. See also W. L. Adair, T. Okumura, and J. M. Brett, "Negotiation Behavior when Cultures Collide: The United States and Japan," *Journal of Applied Psychology* (June 2001), p. 371.

21. C. H. Tinsley, "How Negotiators Get to Yes: Predicting the Constellation of Strategies Used Across Cultures to Negotiate Conflict," *Journal of Applied Psychology* (August 2001), p. 583.

22. See, for instance, S. P. Robbins and P. L. Hunsaker, *Training in Interpersonal Skills,* 4e (Upper Saddle River, NJ: Prentice Hall, 2006); M. Young and J. E. Post, "Managing to Communicate, Communicating to Manage: How Leading Companies Communicate with Employees," *Organizational Dynamics,* Summer 1993, pp. 31–43; J. A. DeVito, *The Interpersonal Communication Book,* 6th ed. (New York: HarperCollins, 1992); and A. G. Athos and J. J. Gabarro, *Interpersonal Behavior* (Upper Saddle River, NJ: Prentice Hall, 1978).

23. "Electronic Invective Backfires," *Workforce,* June 2001, p. 20; and E. Wong, "A Stinging Office Memo Boomerangs," *New York Times,* April 5, 2001, pp. C1+.

24. Right or Wrong box based on "Office Gossip Ban," *HR Professional,* November–December 2010, p. 15; "It's Not 'Unprofessional' to Gossip at Work," *Harvard Business Review,* September 2010, pp. 28–29; J. Grunert, "When Gossip Strikes," *OfficePro,* January–February 2010, pp. 16–18; B. Weissenberger, "Gossip in the Workplace," *Bloomberg BusinessWeek Online,* November 3, 2009; and B. Nefer, "Neutralizing the Power of Workplace Gossip," *Supervision,* April 2009, pp. 14–16.

25. See, for example, R. R. Panko, *Business Data Networks and Communications,* 4th ed. (Upper Saddle River, NJ: Prentice Hall, 2003).

26. "Virtual Paper Cuts," *Workforce,* July 2000, pp. 16–18.

27. J. Karaian, "Where Wireless Works," *CFO,* May 2003, pp. 81–83.

28. Technology and the Manager's Job box based on S. Raposo, "Quick! Tell Us What KUTGW Means," *Wall Street Journal,* August 5, 2009, pp. D1+; and C. Tuna, "Corporate Blogs and

Tweets Must Keep SEC in Mind," *Wall Street Journal,* April 27, 2009, p. B4.

29. See, for instance, A. Cohen, "Wireless Summer," *Time,* May 29, 2000, pp. 58–65; and K. Hafner, "For the Well Connected, All the World's an Office," *New York Times,* March 30, 2000, p. D1.

30. J. S. Brown and P. Duguid, "Balancing Act: How to Capture Knowledge Without Killing It," *Harvard Business Review,* May–June 2000, pp. 73–80; and J. Torsilieri and C. Lucier, "How to Change the World," *Strategy and Business,* October 2000, pp. 17–20.

31. S. Luh, "Pulse Lunches at Asian Citibanks Feed Workers' Morale, Lower Job Turnover," *Wall Street Journal,* May 22, 2001, p. B11.

32. S. Shellenbager, "Backlash Against Email Builds," *Wall Street Journal,* April 29, 2010, p. D6.

33. H. Green, "The Water Cooler Is Now on the Web," *BusinessWeek,* October 1, 2007, pp. 78–79.

34. The Associated Press, "Whole Foods Chief Apologizes for Posts," *New York Times Online,* July 18, 2007; E. White, J. S. Lublin, and D. Kesmodel, "Executives Get the Blogging Bug," *Wall Street Journal,* July 13, 2007, pp. B1+; C. Alldred, "U.K. Libel Case Slows E-Mail Delivery," *Business Insurance,* August 4, 1997, pp. 51–53; and T. Lewin, "Chevron Settles Sexual Harassment Charges," *New York Times Online,* February 22, 1995.

35. J. Eckberg, "E-mail: Messages Are Evidence," *Cincinnati Enquirer,* www.enquirer.com (July 27, 2004).

36. M. Scott, "Worker E-Mail and Blog Misuse Seen as Growing Risk for Companies," *Workforce Management,* www.workforce.com (July 20, 2007).

37. K. Byron, "Carrying Too Heavy a Load? The Communication and Miscommunication of Emotion by Email," *Academy of Management Review,* April 2008, pp. 309–327.

38. And the Survey Says box based on J. R. Detert, E. R. Burris, and D. A. Harrison, "Debunking Four Myths About Employee Silence," *Harvard Business Review,* June 2010, p. 26; A. R. Carey and S. Ward, "Are You Fretting About Messages?" *USA Today,* May 28, 2009, p. 1A; T. Jackson, "Did You Know?" *O Magazine,* December 2008, p. 172; J. Yang and A. Gonzalez, "Can You Hear Me Now?" *USA Today,* November 23, 2009,

p. 1B; J. Yang and J Snider, "No Facebooking for Me," *USA Today,* October 22, 2009, p. 1B; J. Marquez, "Employer-Provided Wireless Devices: Benefit of Electronic Leashes?" *Workforce Management Online,* April 8, 2009; and M. Jackson, "May We Have Your Attention Please?" *BusinessWeek,* June 23, 2008, p. 56.

39. J. Marquez, "Virtual Work Spaces Ease Collaboration, Debate Among Scattered Employees," *Workforce Management,* May 22, 2006, p. 38; and M. Conlin, "E-Mail Is So Five Minutes Ago," *BusinessWeek,* November 28, 2005, pp. 111–112.

40. H. Green, "The Water Cooler Is Now on the Web"; E. Frauenheim, "Starbucks Employees Carve Out Own 'Space,'" *Workforce Management,* October 22, 2007, p. 32; and S. H. Wildstrom, "Harnessing Social Networks," *BusinessWeek,* April 23, 2007, p. 20.

41. J. Scanlon, "Woman of Substance," *Wired,* July 2002, p. 027.

42. H. Dolezalek, "Collaborating in Cyberspace," *Training* (April 2003), p. 33.

43. B. A. Gutek, M. Groth, and B. Cherry, "Achieving Service Success Through Relationship and Enhanced Encounters," *Academy of Management Executive,* November 2002, pp. 132–144.

44. R. C. Ford and C. P. Heaton, "Lessons from Hospitality That Can Serve Anyone," *Organizational Dynamics,* Summer 2001, pp. 30–47.

45. M. J. Bitner, B. H. Booms, and L. A. Mohr, "Critical Service Encounters: The Employee's Viewpoint," *Journal of Marketing* (October 1994), pp. 95–106.

46. S. D. Pugh, J. Dietz, J. W. Wiley, and S. M. Brooks, "Driving Service Effectiveness Through Employee-Customer Linkages," *Academy of Management Executive,* November 2002, pp. 73–84.

47. J. Ewing, "Nokia: Bring on the Employee Rants," *BusinessWeek,* June 22, 2009, p. 50.

48. J. V. Thill and C. L. Bovee, *Excellence in Business Communication,* 9th ed. (Upper Saddle River, NJ: Prentice Hall, 2011), pp. 24–25.

49. Ibid.

50. Ibid.

51. Ibid.

52. Ibid.

CHAPTER 14

Foundations of Control

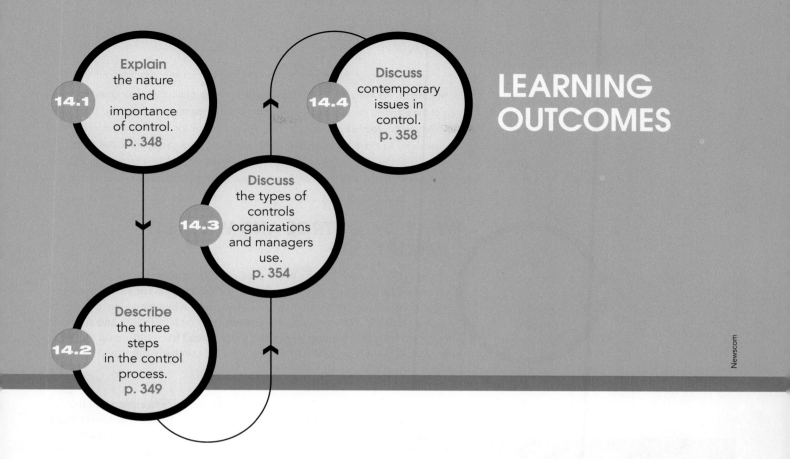

Deepwater in Deep Trouble

When all is said and done, which may not be for many years, it's likely to be one of the worst environmental disasters, if not the worst, in U.S. history.[1] British Petroleum's (BP) Deepwater Horizon offshore rig in the Gulf of Mexico exploded in a ball of flames on April 20, 2010, killing 11 employees. This initial tragedy set in motion frantic efforts to stop the flow of oil, followed by a long and arduous cleanup process. Although the impacts of the explosion and oil spill were felt most intensely by businesses and residents along the coast and by coastal wildlife, those of us inland who watched the disaster unfold were also stunned and dismayed by what we saw happening. What led to this disaster, and what should BP do to minimize the likelihood of it ever happening again?

Controlling is the final step in the management process. Managers must monitor whether goals that were established as part of the planning process are being accomplished efficiently and effectively. That's what they do when they control. Appropriate controls can help managers look for specific performance gaps and areas for improvement. As the BP story shows, things don't always go as planned. But that's why controlling is so important! In this chapter, we'll look at the fundamental elements of controlling, including the control process, the types of controls that managers can use, and contemporary issues in control.

14.1 Explain the nature and importance of control.

WHAT IS CONTROL AND WHY IS IT IMPORTANT?

"Bailout" was the magic word that cost Domino's Pizza 11,000 free pizzas. The company had prepared an Internet coupon for an ad campaign that was considered but not approved. However, when someone apparently typed "bailout" into a Domino's promotional code window and found it was good for a free medium pizza, the word spread like wildfire on the Web. Somewhere, somehow, a lack of control cost the company big time.[2]

What Is Control?

Control is the management function that involves monitoring activities to ensure that they're being accomplished as planned and correcting any significant deviations. Managers can't really know whether their units are performing properly until they've evaluated what activities have been done and have compared the actual performance with the desired standard. An effective control system ensures that activities are completed in ways that lead to the attainment of the organization's goals. The effectiveness of a control system is determined by how well it facilitates goal achievement. The more a control system helps managers achieve their organization's goals, the better it is.

Why Is Control Important?

A press operator at the Denver Mint noticed a flaw—an extra up leaf or an extra down leaf—on Wisconsin state quarters being pressed at one of his five press machines. He stopped the machine and left for a meal break. When he returned, he saw the machine running and assumed that someone had changed the die in the machine. However, after a routine inspection, the machine operator realized the die had not been changed. The faulty press had likely been running for over an hour and thousands of the flawed coins were now "co-mingled" with unblemished quarters. As many as 50,000 of the faulty coins entered circulation, setting off a coin collector buying frenzy.[4]

Can you see now why controlling is such an important managerial function? Planning can be done, an organizational structure created to facilitate efficient achievement of goals, and employees motivated through effective leadership. But there's no assurance that activities are going as planned and that the goals employees and managers are working toward are, in fact, being attained. Control is important, therefore, because it's the only way that managers know whether organizational goals are being met and if not, the reasons why. The value of the control function can be seen in three specific areas: planning, empowering employees, and protecting the workplace.

In Chapter 5, we described goals, which provide specific direction to employees and managers, as the foundation of

RIGHT OR WRONG?

The practice is called "sweethearting."[3] It's when cashiers use subtle tricks to pass free goods to friends, doing things such as concealing the bar code, slipping an item behind the scanner, passing two items at a time but only charging for one. It's impossible for even the most watchful human eyes to keep it from happening. So retailers are using technology to block it. Surveillance cameras are used to record and study cashiers staffing checkout lines.

Think About:

- What do you think? Is surveillance less invasive when it's a computer watching instead of a human?

- How could organizations make sure it's being ethical in monitoring employees?

Steve Krongard/Getty Images USA, Inc.

EXHIBIT 14–1   Planning–Controlling Link

planning. However, just stating goals or having employees accept goals doesn't guarantee that the necessary actions to accomplish those goals have been taken. As the old saying goes, "The best-laid plans often go awry." The effective manager follows up to ensure that what employees are supposed to do is, in fact, being done and goals are being achieved. As the final step in the management process, controlling provides the critical link back to planning. (See Exhibit 14–1.) If managers didn't control, they'd have no way of knowing whether their goals and plans were being achieved and what future actions to take.

The second reason controlling is important is because of employee empowerment. Many managers are reluctant to empower their employees because they fear something will go wrong for which they would be held responsible. But an effective control system can provide information and feedback on employee performance and minimize the chance of potential problems.

The final reason that managers control is to protect the organization and its assets.[5] Organizations face threats from natural disasters, financial pressures and scandals, workplace violence, supply chain disruptions, security breaches, and even possible terrorist attacks. Managers must protect organizational assets in the event that any of these should happen. Comprehensive controls and backup plans will help minimize work disruptions.

WHAT TAKES PLACE AS MANAGERS CONTROL?

When Maggine Fuentes joined Core Systems in Painesville, Ohio, as HR manager, she knew that her top priority was reducing employee injuries. The number of injuries was "through the roof; above the industry average." The high frequency and severity of the company's injury rates not only affected employee morale but also resulted in lost workdays and affected the bottom line.[6] Fuentes relied on the control process to turn this situation around.

Describe the three steps in the control process.

14.2

control
Management function that involves monitoring activities to ensure that they're being accomplished as planned and correcting any significant deviations

The **control process** is a three-step process of measuring actual performance, comparing actual performance against a standard, and taking managerial action to correct deviations or to address inadequate standards. (See Exhibit 14–2.) The control process assumes that performance standards already exist, and they do. They're the specific goals created during the planning process.

What Is Measuring?

To determine actual performance, a manager must first get information about it. Thus, the first step in control is measuring.

HOW DO MANAGERS MEASURE?   Four common sources of information frequently used to measure actual performance are personal observation, statistical reports, oral reports, and written reports. Each has particular strengths and weaknesses; however, use of a combination of them increases both the number of input sources and the probability of receiving reliable information.

Personal observation provides firsthand, intimate knowledge of the actual activity—information that is not filtered through others. It permits intensive coverage because minor as well as major performance activities can be observed, and it provides opportunities for the manager to read between the lines. **Management by walking around (MBWA)** is a phrase used to describe when a manager is out in the work area, interacting directly with employees, and exchanging information about what's going on. Management by walking around can pick up factual omissions, facial expressions, and tones of voice that may be missed by other sources. Unfortunately, in a time when quantitative information suggests objectivity, personal observation is often considered an inferior information source. It is subject to perceptual biases; what one manager sees, another might not. Personal

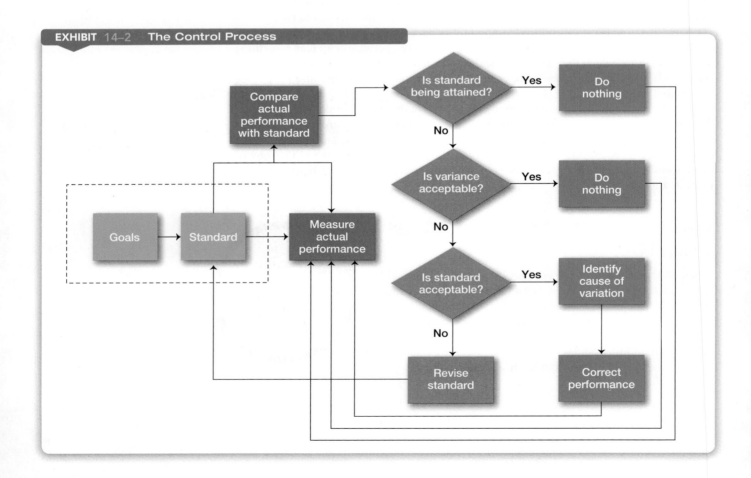

EXHIBIT 14–2   **The Control Process**

observation also consumes a good deal of time. Finally, this method suffers from obtrusiveness. Employees might interpret a manager's overt observation as a lack of confidence or a sign of mistrust.

The widespread use of computers has led managers to rely increasingly on *statistical reports* for measuring actual performance. This measuring device, however, isn't limited to computer outputs. It also includes graphs, bar charts, and numerical displays of any form that managers can use for assessing performance. Although statistical information is easy to visualize and effective for showing relationships, it provides limited information about an activity. Statistics report on only a few key areas and may often ignore other important, often subjective, factors.

Information can also be acquired through *oral reports*—that is, through conferences, meetings, one-to-one conversations, or telephone calls. In employee-oriented organizations where employees work closely together, this approach may be the best way to keep tabs on work performance. For instance, at the Ken Blanchard Companies in Escondido, California, managers are expected to hold one-on-one meetings with each of their employees at least once every two weeks.[7] The advantages and disadvantages of this method of measuring performance are similar to those of personal observation. Although the information is filtered, it is fast, allows for feedback, and permits expression and tone of voice as well as words themselves to convey meaning. Historically, one of the major drawbacks of oral reports has been the problem of documenting information for later reference. However, our technological capabilities have progressed in the past couple of decades to the point where oral reports can be efficiently taped and become as permanent as if they were written.

Actual performance may also be measured by *written reports*. Like statistical reports, they are slower yet more formal than firsthand or secondhand oral measures. This formality also often gives them greater comprehensiveness and conciseness than found in oral reports. In addition, written reports are usually easy to catalog and reference.

Given the varied advantages and disadvantages of each of these four measurement techniques, managers should use all four for comprehensive control efforts.

In controlling the quality and efficiency of its medical services, Mayo Clinic measures performance indicators that include outcomes achieved, such as readmission rates and safety records. The clinic also measures compliance with specific processes that enhance patient care, including giving the right consultations and therapies, the right medication at the right time, and the right diagnostic studies for specific problems. Through surveys, Mayo measures consumer satisfaction to ensure that every patient is treated with respect, dignity, and kindness by all members of the Mayo team, including the nurses and staff shown here working at Saint Marys Hospital, which is part of the clinic's medical center in Rochester, Minnesota.

WHAT DO MANAGERS MEASURE?   What managers measure is probably more critical to the control process than how they measure. Why? The selection of the wrong criteria can result in serious dysfunctional consequences. Besides, what we measure determines, to a great extent, what people in the organization will attempt to excel at.[8] For example, assume that your instructor has required a total of 10 writing assignments from the exercises at the end of each textbook chapter. But in the grade computation section of the syllabus, you notice that these assignments are not scored. In fact, when you ask your professor about this, she replies that these writing assignments are for your own enlightenment and do not affect your grade for the course; grades are solely a function of how well you perform on the three exams. We predict that you would, not surprisingly, exert most, if not all, of your effort toward doing well on the three exams.

Some control criteria are applicable to any management situation. For instance, because all managers, by definition, direct the activities of others, criteria such as employee satisfaction or turnover and absenteeism rates can be measured. Most managers have budgets for their area of responsibility set in monetary units (dollars, pounds, francs,

David Joles/Newscom

---

control process
A three-step process of measuring actual performance, comparing actual performance against a standard, and taking managerial action to correct deviations

management by walking around (MBWA)
When a manager is out in the work area interacting with employees

From the Past to the Present

We introduced benchmarking in the planning chapter (Chapter 5) as a way for organizations to promote quality.[9] Not surprisingly, since planning and controlling are so closely linked, it also has implications for control. Benchmarking has been a highly utilized management tool. Although Xerox is often credited with the first widespread benchmarking effort in the United States, the practice can actually be traced back much further.

The benefits of benchmarking have long been recognized in the manufacturing industry. At the Midvale Steel Company plant where he was employed, Frederick W. Taylor (of scientific management fame) used concepts of benchmarking to find the "one best way" to perform a job and to find the best worker to perform the job. Even Henry Ford recognized the benefits. Based on the techniques used at Chicago slaughterhouses where carcasses were hung from hooks mounted on a monorail, with each man performing his job and then pushing the carcass to the next work station, Ford's assembly line used the same concept for producing cars, beginning in 1913. "The idea that

revolutionized manufacturing was imported from another industry."

Today, managers in diverse industries such as health care, education, and financial services are discovering what manufacturers have long recognized—the benefits of benchmarking. For instance, the American Medical Association developed more than 100 standard measures of performance to improve medical care. Carlos Ghosn, CEO of Nissan, benchmarked Walmart's operations in purchasing, transportation, and logistics. At its most basic, benchmarking means learning from others. However, as a tool for monitoring and measuring organizational and work performance, benchmarking can be used to identify specific performance gaps and potential areas of improvement.

Think About:
- What are the benefits of benchmarking? The challenges in doing it?
- Could the concept of benchmarking apply in your personal life? Discuss.

lire, and so on). Keeping costs within budget is, therefore, a fairly common control measure. However, any comprehensive control system needs to recognize the diversity of activities among managers. For example, a production manager in a paper tablet manufacturing plant might use measures of the quantity of tablets produced per day, tablets produced per labor hour, scrap tablet rate, or percentage of rejects returned by customers. On the other hand, the manager of an administrative unit in a government agency might use number of document pages produced per day, number of orders processed per hour, or average time required to process service calls. Marketing managers often use measures such as percent of market held, number of customer visits per salesperson, or number of customer impressions per advertising medium.

As you might imagine, some activities are more difficult to measure in quantifiable terms. It is more difficult, for instance, for a manager to measure the performance of a medical researcher or a middle school counselor than of a person who sells life insurance. But most activities can be broken down into objective segments that allow for measurement. The manager needs to determine what value a person, department, or unit contributes to the organization and then convert the contribution into standards.

Most jobs and activities can be expressed in tangible and measurable terms. When a performance indicator cannot be stated in quantifiable terms, managers should look for and use subjective measures. Certainly, subjective measures have significant limitations. Still, they are better than having no standards at all and ignoring the control function. If an activity is important, the excuse that it's difficult to measure is inadequate. In such cases, managers should use subjective performance criteria. Of course, any analysis or decisions made on the basis of subjective criteria should recognize the limitations of the data.

How Do Managers Compare Actual Performance to Planned Goals?

The comparing step determines the variation between actual performance and the standard. Although some variation in performance can be expected in all activities, it's critical to determine an acceptable **range of variation** (see Exhibit 14–3). Deviations outside this range need attention. Let's work through an example.

Chris Tanner is a sales manager for Green Earth Gardening Supply, a distributor of specialty plants and seeds in the Pacific Northwest. Chris prepares a report during the first week of each month that describes sales for the previous month, classified by product line.

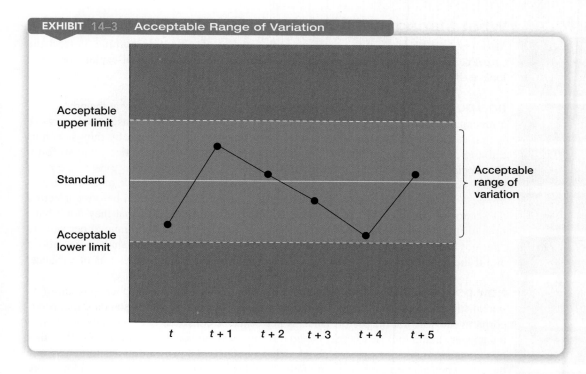

EXHIBIT 14–3 Acceptable Range of Variation

Exhibit 14–4 displays both the sales goals (standard) and actual sales figures for the month of June. After looking at the numbers, should Chris be concerned? Sales were a bit higher than originally targeted, but does that mean there were no significant deviations? That depends on what Chris thinks is *significant*; that is, outside the acceptable range of variation. Even though overall performance was generally quite favorable, some product lines need closer scrutiny. For instance, if sales of heirloom seeds, flowering bulbs, and annual flowers continue to be over what was expected, Chris might need to order more product from nurseries to meet customer demand. Because sales of vegetable plants were 15 percent below goal, Chris may need to run a special on them. As this example shows, both overvariance and undervariance may require managerial attention, which is the third step in the control process.

EXHIBIT 14–4 Example of Determining Significant Variation: Green Earth Gardening Supply—June Sales

PRODUCT	STANDARD	ACTUAL	OVER (UNDER)
Vegetable plants	1,075	913	(612)
Perennial flowers	630	634	4
Annual flowers	800	912	112
Herbs	160	140	(20)
Flowering bulbs	170	286	116
Flowering bushes	225	220	(5)
Heirloom seeds	540	672	132
Total	3,600	3,777	177

range of variation
The acceptable parameters of variance between actual performance and a standard

What Managerial Action Can Be Taken?

Managers can choose among three possible courses of action: do nothing, correct the actual performance, or revise the standards. Because "do nothing" is self-explanatory, let's look at the other two.

HOW DO YOU CORRECT ACTUAL PERFORMANCE? Depending on what the problem is, a manager could take different corrective actions. For instance, if unsatisfactory work is the reason for performance variations, the manager could correct it by things such as training programs, disciplinary action, changes in compensation practices, and so forth. One decision that a manager must make is whether to take immediate corrective action, which corrects problems at once to get performance back on track or to use basic corrective action, which looks at how and why performance deviated before correcting the source of deviation. It's not unusual for managers to rationalize that they don't have time to find the source of a problem (basic corrective action) and continue to perpetually "put out fires" with immediate corrective action. Effective managers analyze deviations and if the benefits justify it, take the time to pinpoint and correct the causes of variance.

HOW DO YOU REVISE THE STANDARD? It's possible that the variance was a result of an unrealistic standard—too low or too high a goal. In such cases, it's the standard that needs corrective action, not the performance. If performance consistently exceeds the goal, then a manager should look at whether the goal is too easy and needs to be raised. On the other hand, managers must be cautious about revising a standard downward. It's natural to blame the goal when an employee or a team falls short. For instance, students who get a low score on a test often attack the grade cutoff standards as too high. Rather than accept the fact that their performance was inadequate, they will argue that the standards are unreasonable. Likewise, salespeople who don't meet their monthly quota often want to blame what they think is an unrealistic quota. The point is that when performance isn't up to par, don't immediately blame the goal or standard. If you believe the standard is realistic, fair, and achievable, tell employees that you expect future work to improve, and then take the necessary corrective action to help make that happen.

WHAT SHOULD MANAGERS CONTROL?

14.3 Discuss the types of controls organizations and managers use.

Cost efficiency. The length of time customers are kept on hold. Customers being satisfied with the service provided. These are just a few of the important performance indicators that executives in the intensely competitive call-center service industry measure. To make good decisions, managers in this industry want and need this type of information so they can control work performance.

How do managers know what to control? In this section, we're first going to look at the decision of *what* to control in terms of when control takes place. Then, we're going to discuss some different areas in which managers might choose to establish controls.

When Does Control Take Place?

Management can implement controls before an activity commences, while the activity is going on, or after the activity has been completed. The first type is called feedforward control, the second is concurrent control, and the last is feedback control (see Exhibit 14–5).

WHAT IS FEEDFORWARD CONTROL? The most desirable type of control—feedforward control—prevents problems because it takes place before the actual activity.[11] For instance, when McDonald's opened its first restaurant in Moscow, it sent company quality control experts to help Russian farmers learn techniques for growing high-quality potatoes and to help bakers learn processes for baking high-quality breads. Why? McDonald's demands consistent product quality no matter the geographical location. They want french fries in Moscow to taste

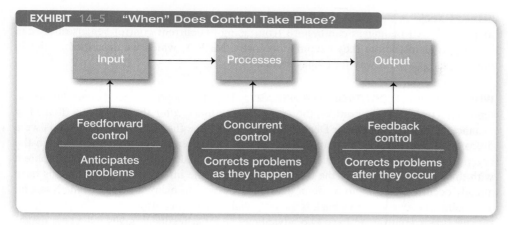

EXHIBIT 14–5   "When" Does Control Take Place?

Input → Processes → Output

Feedforward control — Anticipates problems

Concurrent control — Corrects problems as they happen

Feedback control — Corrects problems after they occur

Nissan North America used feedback control to correct defects in vehicles produced at its Canton, Mississippi, assembly plant. In this photo, a Nissan production technician at the plant explains how a defect-analysis and problem-solving team of technicians and engineers identified quality problems that occurred during vehicle design and production processes. Team members worked with suppliers to reengineer parts and formed cross-functional quality teams to correct problems reported on quality surveys or in warranty data. They studied each part of the assembly line to detect and fix problems that resulted in squeaks, rattles, and other defects. Feedback control gave Nissan managers information they needed to make new plans for preventing problems before the production phase.

like those in Omaha. Still another example of feedforward control is the scheduled preventive maintenance programs on aircraft done by the major airlines. These schedules are designed to detect and hopefully to prevent structural damage that might lead to an accident.

The key to feedforward controls is taking managerial action *before* a problem occurs. That way, problems can be prevented rather than having to correct them after any damage—poor-quality products, lost customers, lost revenue, etc.—has already been done. However, these controls require timely and accurate information that isn't always easy to get. Thus, managers frequently end up using the other two types of control.

WHEN IS CONCURRENT CONTROL USED?   Concurrent control, as its name implies, takes place while a work activity is in progress. For instance, the director of business product management at Google and his team keep a watchful eye on one of Google's most profitable businesses—online ads. They watch "the number of searches and clicks, the rate at which users click on ads, the revenue this generates—everything is tracked hour by hour, compared with the data from a week earlier and charted."[12] If they see something that's not working particularly well, they fine-tune it.

Technical equipment (such as computers and computerized machine controls) can be designed to include concurrent controls. For example, you've probably experienced this with word-processing software that alerts you to a misspelled word or incorrect grammatical usage. Also, many organizational quality programs rely on concurrent controls to inform workers whether their work output is of sufficient quality to meet standards.

The best-known form of concurrent control, however, is direct supervision. For example, Nvidia's CEO Jen-Hsun Huang had his office cubicle torn down and replaced with a conference table so he's now available to employees at all times to discuss what's going on.[13] Even GE's CEO Jeff Immelt spends 60 percent of

Rogelio Solis/AP Images

immediate corrective action
Corrective action that addresses problems at once to get performance back on track

basic corrective action
Corrective action that looks at how and why performance deviated before correcting the source of deviation

feedforward control
Control that takes place before a work activity is done

concurrent control
Control that takes place while a work activity is in progress

his workweek on the road talking to employees and visiting the company's numerous locations.[14] All managers can benefit from using concurrent control because they can correct problems before they become too costly. MBWA, which we described earlier in this chapter, is a great way for managers to do this.

WHY IS FEEDBACK CONTROL SO POPULAR?   The most popular type of control relies on feedback. In feedback control, the control takes place *after* the activity is done. For instance, remember our earlier Denver Mint example. The flawed Wisconsin quarters were discovered with feedback control. The damage had already occurred even though the organization corrected the problem once it was discovered. And that's the major problem with this type of control. By the time a manager has the information, the problems have already occurred, leading to waste or damage. However, in many work areas, the financial area being one example, feedback is the only viable type of control.

Feedback controls do have two advantages.[15] First, feedback gives managers meaningful information on how effective their planning efforts were. Feedback that shows little variance between standard and actual performance indicates that the planning was generally on target. If the deviation is significant, a manager can use that information to formulate new plans. Second, feedback can enhance motivation. People want to know how well they're doing, and feedback provides that information.

In What Areas Might Managers Need Controls?

Most organizations consist of countless activities taking place in different locations and functional areas of the organization. So *what* gets controlled? We need to look at some of the specific areas and control tools that managers can use.

HOW DO MANAGERS KEEP TRACK OF FINANCES?   Every business wants to earn a profit. To achieve this goal, managers need financial controls. For instance, they might analyze quarterly income statements for excessive expenses. They might calculate financial ratios to ensure that sufficient cash is available to pay ongoing expenses, that debt levels haven't become too high, or that assets are being used productively.

Traditional financial measures managers might use include ratio analysis and budget analysis. Exhibit 14–6 summarizes some of the most popular financial ratios that managers

EXHIBIT 14–6   **Popular Financial Ratios**

OBJECTIVE	RATIO	CALCULATION	MEANING
Liquidity	Current ratio	$\dfrac{\text{Current assets}}{\text{Current liabilities}}$	Tests the organization's ability to meet short-term obligations
	Acid test	$\dfrac{\text{Current assets} - \text{Inventories}}{\text{Current liabilities}}$	Tests liquidity more accurately when inventories turn over slowly or are difficult to sell
Leverage	Debt to assets	$\dfrac{\text{Total debt}}{\text{Total assets}}$	The higher the ratio, the more leveraged the organization
	Times interest earned	$\dfrac{\text{Profits before interest and taxes}}{\text{Total interest charges}}$	Measures how many times the organization is able to cover its interest expenses
Activity	Inventory turnover	$\dfrac{\text{Sales}}{\text{Inventory}}$	The higher the ratio, the more efficiently inventory assets are being used
	Total asset turnover	$\dfrac{\text{Sales}}{\text{Total assets}}$	The fewer assets used to achieve a given level of sales, the more efficiently management is using the organization's total assets
Profitability	Profit margin on sales	$\dfrac{\text{Net profit after taxes}}{\text{Total sales}}$	Identifies the profits that are being generated
	Return on investment	$\dfrac{\text{Net profit after taxes}}{\text{Total assets}}$	Measures the efficiency of assets to generate profits

will analyze. Liquidity ratios measure an organization's ability to meet its current debt obligations. Leverage ratios examine the organization's use of debt to finance its assets and whether it's able to meet the interest payments on the debt. Activity ratios assess how efficiently a company is using its assets. Finally, profitability ratios measure how efficiently and effectively the company is using its assets to generate profits. These ratios are calculated using selected information from the organization's two primary financial statements (the balance sheet and the income statement) and are sometimes expressed as a percentage. Because you've probably studied these ratios in other accounting or finance courses, or will in the near future, we won't elaborate on how they're calculated. We mention them here to remind you that managers use such ratios as internal control tools.

Budgets are another type of financial control tool that are used for planning and controlling. When a budget is formulated, it's a planning tool because it indicates which work activities are important and what and how much resources should be allocated to those activities. Budgets are also used for controlling because they provide managers with quantitative standards against which to measure and compare resource consumption. If deviations are significant enough to require action, the manager examines what has happened and tries to uncover why. With this information, necessary action can be taken. For example, if you use a personal budget for monitoring and controlling your monthly expenses, you might find that one month your miscellaneous expenses were higher than you had budgeted for. At that point, you might cut back spending in another area or work extra hours to get more income.

HOW IS AN ORGANIZATION'S INFORMATION CONTROLLED?   Some 77 million accounts on Sony's PlayStation network were hacked, exposing those users to years of identity-theft risk. A computer with personal information (Social Security numbers, birth dates, etc.) on some 26.5 million military veterans stored on it was stolen from the residence of a Department of Veteran Affairs employee who had taken the computer home without authorization. Although the computer was eventually recovered with no loss of personal information, the situation could have been damaging to a large number of people. And these are just a few of the attacks on companies' information resources.[16] Talk about the need for information controls! Managers deal with information controls in two ways: (1) as a tool to help them control other organizational activities, and (2) as an organizational area they need to control.

Managers need the right information at the right time and in the right amount to help them *monitor and measure organizational activities*. In measuring actual performance, managers need information about what is happening within their area of responsibility and about the standards in order to be able to compare actual performance with the standard. They also rely on information to help them determine if deviations are acceptable. Finally, they rely on information to help them develop appropriate courses of action. Information *is* important! Most of the information tools that managers use come from the organization's management information system.

A management information system (MIS) is a system used to provide managers with needed information on a regular basis. In theory, this system can be manual or computer-based, although most organizations have moved to computer-supported applications. The term *system* in MIS implies order, arrangement, and purpose. Further, an MIS focuses specifically on providing managers with *information* (processed and analyzed data), not merely *data* (raw, unanalyzed facts). A library provides a good analogy. Although it can contain millions of volumes, a library doesn't do you any good if you can't find what you want quickly. That's why librarians spend a great deal of time cataloging a library's collections and ensuring that materials are returned to their proper locations. Organizations today are like well-stocked libraries with an abundance of data. What is lacking, however, is an ability to process that data so that the right information is available to the right person when he or she

---

feedback control
Control that takes place after a work activity is done

management information system (MIS)
A system used to provide management with needed information on a regular basis

Valery Sharifulin/Newscom

Cisco Systems, the global leader in networking equipment, uses a Balanced Scorecard approach in evaluating its performance. In addition to measuring performance in the financial, internal processes, and people/innovation/growth areas, Cisco developed a scorecard to address its commitment to customer satisfaction, a core value that drives the company's success. Each year Cisco sets goals for customer satisfaction and uses a customer loyalty measurement system to track its success with customers, such as Russia's mobile operator SkyLink shown here. Managers use the information they receive from annual customer satisfaction surveys to establish goals for each of Cisco's functional areas and for hiring and resource allocation decisions.

needs it. An MIS collects data and turns them into relevant information for managers to use.

It seems that every week, there's another news story about information security breaches. A recent survey found that 85 percent of privacy and security professionals acknowledged a reportable data breach occurred within their organizations within the last year alone.[17] Because information is critically important to everything an organization does, managers must have comprehensive and secure controls in place to *protect that information.* Such controls can range from data encryption to system firewalls to data backups, and other techniques as well.[18] Problems can lurk in places that an organization might not even have considered, like search engines. Sensitive, defamatory, confidential, or embarrassing organizational information has found its way into search engine results. For instance, detailed monthly expenses and employee salaries on the National Speleological Society's Web site turned up in a Google search.[19] Equipment such as laptop computers and even RFID (radio-frequency identification) tags are vulnerable to viruses and hacking. Needless to say, information controls should be monitored regularly to ensure that all possible precautions are in place to protect important information.

WHAT IS THE BALANCED SCORECARD APPROACH TO CONTROL? The **balanced scorecard** approach is a way to evaluate organizational performance from more than just the financial perspective.[20] A balanced scorecard typically looks at four areas that contribute to a company's performance: financial, customer, internal processes, and people/innovation/growth assets. According to this approach, managers should develop goals in each of the four areas and then measure whether the goals are being met.

Although a balanced scorecard makes sense, managers will tend to focus on areas that drive their organization's success and use scorecards that reflect those strategies.[21] For example, if strategies are customer-centered, then the customer area is likely to get more attention than the other three areas. Yet, you can't focus on measuring only one performance area because others are affected as well. For instance, at IBM Global Services in Houston, managers developed a scorecard around an overriding strategy of customer satisfaction. However, the other areas (financial, internal processes, and people/innovation/growth) support that central strategy. The division manager described it as follows, "The internal processes part of our business is directly related to responding to our customers in a timely manner, and the learning and innovation aspect is critical for us since what we're selling our customers above all is our expertise. Of course, how successful we are with those things will affect our financial component."[22]

WHAT CONTEMPORARY CONTROL ISSUES DO MANAGERS CONFRONT?

14.4
Discuss contemporary issues in control.

The employees of Integrated Information Systems Inc. didn't think twice about exchanging digital music over a dedicated office server they had set up. Like office betting on college and pro sports, it was technically illegal, but harmless, or so they thought. But after the company had to pay a $1 million settlement to the Recording Industry Association of America, managers wished they had controlled the situation better.[23] Control is an important managerial function. We're going to look at two control issues that managers face today: cross-cultural differences and workplace concerns.

Do Controls Need to Be Adjusted for Cultural Differences?

The concepts of control that we've discussed are appropriate for organizational units that aren't geographically distant or culturally distinct. But what about global organizations? Would control systems be different, and what should managers know about adjusting controls for national differences?

Methods of controlling employee behavior and operations can be quite different in different countries. In fact, the differences in organizational control systems of global organizations are primarily in the measurement and corrective action steps of the control process. In a global corporation, for instance, managers of foreign operations tend not to be closely controlled by the home office if for no other reason than that distance keeps managers from being able to observe work directly. Because distance creates a tendency for formalized controls, the home office of a global company often relies on extensive, formal reports for control. The global company may also use information technology to control work activities. For instance, Seven and i Holdings (Japan's biggest retail conglomerate and parent company of the 7-Eleven convenience store chain in the United States) uses automated cash registers not only to record sales and monitor inventory but also to schedule tasks for store managers and to track their use of the built-in analytical graphs and forecasts. If managers don't use them enough, they're told to increase their activities.[24]

Technology's impact on control is most evident in comparisons of technologically advanced nations with more primitive countries. Organizations in technologically advanced nations such as the United States, Japan, Canada, Great Britain, Germany, and Australia use indirect control devices—particularly computer-related reports and analyses—in addition to standardized rules and direct supervision to ensure that activities are going as planned. In less technologically advanced countries, direct supervision and highly centralized decision making are the basic means of control.

TECHNOLOGY AND THE MANAGER'S JOB — MONITORING EMPLOYEES

Technological advances have made the process of managing an organization much easier.[25] But technological advancements have also provided employers a means of sophisticated employee monitoring. Although most of this monitoring is designed to enhance worker productivity, it could, and has been, a source of concern over worker privacy. These advantages bring with them difficult questions regarding what managers have the right to know about employees and how far they can go in controlling employee behavior, both on and off the job. Consider the following:

· The mayor of Colorado Springs, Colorado, reads the e-mail messages that city council members send to each other from their homes. He defended his actions by saying he was making sure that e-mails to each other were not being used to circumvent the state's "open meeting" law that requires most council business to be conducted publicly.

· The U.S. Internal Revenue Service's internal audit group monitors a computer log that shows employee access to taxpayers' accounts. This monitoring activity allows management to check and see what employees are doing on their computers.

· American Express has an elaborate system for monitoring telephone calls. Daily reports provided to supervisors detail the frequency and length of calls made by employees, as well as how quickly incoming calls are answered.

· Employers in several organizations require employees to wear badges at all times while on company premises. These badges contain a variety of data that allow employees to enter certain locations in the organization. Smart badges, too, can transmit where the employee is at all times!

Just how much control a company should have over the private lives of its employees also becomes an issue. Where should an employer's rules and controls end? Does the boss have the right to dictate what you do on your free time and in your own home? Could your boss keep you from engaging in riding a motorcycle, skydiving, smoking, drinking alcohol, or eating junk food? Again, the answers may surprise you. Today many organizations, in their quest to control safety and health insurance costs, are delving into their employees' private lives.

Although controlling employees' behaviors on and off the job may appear unjust or unfair, nothing in our legal system prevents employers from engaging in these practices. Rather, the law is based on the premise that if employees don't like the rules, they have the option of quitting. Managers, too, typically defend their actions in terms of ensuring quality, productivity, and proper employee behavior. For instance, an IRS audit of its southeastern regional offices found that 166 employees took unauthorized looks at the tax returns of friends, neighbors, and celebrities.

Think About:

· When does management's need for information about employee performance cross over the line and interfere with a worker's right to privacy?

· Is technology being misused?

· Is any action by management acceptable as long as employees are notified ahead of time that they will be monitored? What's your opinion?

---

balanced scorecard
A performance measurement tool that looks at more than just the financial perspective

Also, constraints on what corrective action managers can take may affect managers in foreign countries because laws in some countries do not allow managers the option of closing facilities, laying off employees, or bringing in a new management team from outside the country. Finally, another challenge for global companies in collecting data is comparability. For instance, a company's manufacturing facility in Mexico might produce the same products as a facility in Scotland. However, the Mexican facility might be much more labor intensive than its Scottish counterpart (to take advantage of lower labor costs in Mexico). If top-level executives were to control costs by, for example, calculating labor costs per unit or output per worker, the figures would not be comparable. Managers in global companies must address these types of global control challenges.

What Challenges Do Managers Face in Controlling the Workplace?

Today's workplaces present considerable control challenges for managers. From monitoring employees' computer usage at work to protecting the workplace against disgruntled employees intent on doing harm, managers need controls to ensure that work can be done efficiently and effectively as planned.

IS MY WORK COMPUTER REALLY MINE? If you work, do you think you have a right to privacy at your job? What can your employer find out about you and your work? You might be surprised at the answers! Employers can (and do), among other things, read your e-mail (even those marked "personal or confidential"), tap your telephone, monitor your work by computer, store and review computer files, monitor you in an employee bathroom or dressing room, and track your whereabouts in a company vehicle. And these actions aren't that uncommon. In fact, some 30 percent of companies have fired workers for misusing the Internet and another 28 percent have terminated workers for e-mail misuse.[26]

Why do managers feel they need to monitor what employees are doing? A big reason is that employees are hired to work, not to surf the Web checking stock prices, watching online videos, playing fantasy baseball, or shopping for presents for family or friends. Recreational on-the-job Web surfing is thought to cost billions of dollars in lost work productivity annually. In fact, a survey of U.S. employers said that 87 percent of employees look at non-work-related Web sites while at work and more than half engage in personal Web site surfing every day.[27] Watching online video has become an increasingly serious problem not only because of the time being wasted by employees but because it clogs already-strained corporate computer networks.[28] If you had to guess the video site viewed most often at work, what would you guess? If you said YouTube, you'd be absolutely correct![29] However, as innocent as it may seem (after all, it may be just a 30-second video), all this nonwork adds up to significant costs to businesses.

Another reason that managers monitor employee e-mail and computer usage is that they don't want to risk being sued for creating a hostile workplace environment because of offensive messages or an inappropriate image displayed on a coworker's computer screen. Concerns about racial or sexual harassment are one reason companies might want to monitor or keep backup copies of all e-mail. Electronic records can help establish what actually happened so managers can react quickly.[30]

Finally, managers want to ensure that company secrets aren't being leaked.[31] In addition to typical e-mail and computer usage, companies are monitoring instant messaging, blogs, and other social media outlets, and banning phone cameras in the office. Managers need to be certain that employees are not, even inadvertently, passing information on to others who could use that information to harm the company.

Because of the potentially serious costs and given the fact that many jobs now entail computers, many companies have workplace monitoring policies. Such policies should control employee behavior in a nondemeaning way and employees should be informed about those policies.

IS EMPLOYEE THEFT ON THE RISE? Would you be surprised to find that up to 85 percent of all organizational theft and fraud is committed by employees, not outsiders?[32] And it's a costly problem—estimated to be about $4,500 per worker per year.[33] In a recent survey of U.S. companies, 20 percent said that workplace theft has become a moderate to very big problem.[34]

Employee theft is defined as any unauthorized taking of company property by employees for their personal use.[35] It can range from embezzlement to fraudulent filing of expense reports to removing equipment, parts, software, or office supplies from company premises. Although retail businesses have long faced serious potential losses from employee theft, loose financial controls at start-ups and small companies and the ready availability of information technology have made employee stealing an escalating problem in all kinds and sizes of organizations. It's a control issue that managers need to educate themselves about and be prepared to deal with it.[36]

Why do employees steal? The answer depends on whom you ask.[37] Experts in various fields—industrial security, criminology, clinical psychology—have different perspectives. The industrial security people propose that people steal because the opportunity presents itself through lax controls and favorable circumstances. Criminologists say that it's because people have financial-based pressures (such as personal financial problems) or vice-based pressures (such as gambling debts). And the clinical psychologists suggest that people steal because they can rationalize whatever they're doing as being correct and appropriate behavior ("everyone does it," "they had it coming," "this company makes enough money and they'll never miss anything this small," "I deserve this for all that I put up with," and so forth).[38] Although each approach provides compelling insights into employee theft and has been instrumental in attempts to deter it, unfortunately, employees continue to steal. What can managers do?

The concept of feedforward, concurrent, and feedback control is useful for identifying measures to deter or reduce employee theft.[39] Exhibit 14–7 summarizes several possible managerial actions.

A growing number of employee thieves sell their stolen property on auction sites like eBay. For example, a former purchasing agent for California's state Department of Child Support Services was charged with embezzlement, grand theft, and possession of stolen property for stealing $320,000 in taxpayer money with a state-issued credit card that had no spending limit and no pre-approval required for purchases. The employee bought household items shown here for her own use or resold them on eBay and used the money to buy expensive items like the Lexus sports car. After filing an unusually large number of expenses, the employee's activity triggered a state audit that led to her arrest. To deter and reduce theft, the child services agency now requires pre-approval for employee purchases and has hired two internal auditors.

WHAT CAN MANAGERS DO ABOUT WORKPLACE VIOLENCE? A truck driver for a beer and wine distributor facing dismissal fatally shot eight coworkers outside Hartford, Connecticut, on August 3, 2010. On July 12, 2010, a man opened fire at his former company in Albuquerque, killing two people and wounding four others before fatally shooting himself. On November 5, 2009, at Fort Hood, Texas, an Army psychiatrist fatally shot 13 people and injured 32. On June 25, 2008, in Henderson, Kentucky, an employee at a plastics plant returned hours after arguing with his supervisor over his not wearing safety goggles and for using his cell phone while working on the assembly line. He shot and killed the supervisor, four other coworkers, and himself. In April 2007, the same month in which the Virginia Tech shootings occurred, a gunman at his former workplace in Troy, Michigan, and one at NASA in Houston shot and killed a person. On January 30, 2006, a former employee who was once removed from a Santa Barbara, California, postal facility because of "strange behavior" came back and shot five workers to death, critically wounded another, and killed herself. On January 26, 2005, an autoworker at a Jeep plant in Toledo, Ohio, who had met the day before with plant managers about a problem with his work, came in and killed a supervisor and wounded two other employees before killing himself.[40] Is workplace violence really an issue for managers? Yes. The latest data

employee theft
Any unauthorized taking of company property by
employees for their personal use

EXHIBIT 14-7 Controlling Employee Theft

FEEDFORWARD	CONCURRENT	FEEDBACK
Engage in careful prehiring screening.	Treat employees with respect and dignity.	Make sure employees know when theft or fraud has occurred—not naming names but letting people know that these incidents are not acceptable.
Establish specific policies defining theft, fraud, and discipline procedures.	Openly communicate the costs of stealing.	Use the services of professional investigators.
Involve employees in writing policies.	Let employees know on a regular basis about their successes in preventing theft and fraud.	Redesign control measures.
Educate and train employees about the policies.	Use video surveillance equipment if conditions warrant.	Evaluate your organization's culture and the relationships of managers and employees.
Have professionals review your internal security controls.	Install "lock out" options on computers, telephones, and e-mail.	
	Use corporate hotlines for reporting incidences.	
	Set a good example.	

Sources: Based on A. H. Bell and D. M. Smith, "Protecting the Company Against Theft and Fraud," *Workforce Online,* www.workforce.com (December 3, 2000); J. D. Hansen, "To Catch a Thief," *Journal of Accountancy* (March 2000), pp. 43–46; and J. Greenberg, "The Cognitive Geometry of Employee Theft," in *Dysfunctional Behavior in Organizations: Nonviolent and Deviant Behavior* (Stamford, CT: JAI Press, 1998), pp. 147–193.

available (2009) showed that 12 percent of work-related deaths in the United States were workplace homicides.[41] But workplace violence doesn't just include homicides. The U.S. National Institute of Occupational Safety and Health says that each year, some 2 million American workers are victims of some form of workplace violence such as verbal abuse, yelling at coworkers, purposeful damage of machines or furniture, or assaulting coworkers. In an average week, one employee is killed and at least 25 are seriously injured in violent assaults by current or former coworkers. According to a Department of Labor survey, 58 percent of firms reported that managers received verbal threats from workers.[42] Anger, rage, and violence in the workplace are intimidating to coworkers and adversely affect their productivity. The annual cost to U.S. businesses is estimated to be between $20 and $35 billion.[43] And office rage isn't a uniquely American problem. A survey of aggressive behaviors in Europe's workplaces found that between 5 percent and 20 percent of European workers are affected by workplace violence.[44]

What factors are believed to contribute to workplace violence? Undoubtedly, employee stress caused by job uncertainties, declining value of retirement accounts, long hours, information overload, other daily interruptions, unrealistic deadlines, and uncaring managers play a role. Even office layout designs with small cubicles where employees work amidst the noise and commotion from those around them have been cited as contributing to the problem.[45] Other experts have described dangerously dysfunctional work environments characterized by the following as primary contributors to the problem:[46]

- Employee work driven by TNC (time, numbers, and crises)
- Rapid and unpredictable change where instability and uncertainty plague employees
- Destructive communication style where managers communicate in excessively aggressive, condescending, explosive, or passive-aggressive styles; excessive workplace teasing or scapegoating
- Authoritarian leadership with a rigid, militaristic mind-set of managers versus employees; employees not allowed to challenge ideas, participate in decision making, or engage in team-building efforts

Swedish furniture retailer IKEA has raised its security level at all of its stores throughout Europe following explosions caused by bombs at stores in Germany, France, Belgium, and the Netherlands. Store managers evacuated the stores after the explosions, and bomb-sniffing dogs searched the stores. The explosions intimidated employees and customers, although they did not seriously injure anyone. As a safety precaution to make employees and shoppers feel safer, IKEA put extra security guards in its stores, established other security measures not divulged, and closely monitored police investigations to determine a motive for the violence.

Ilvy Njiokiktjien/Newscom

EXHIBIT 14–8	Controlling Workplace Violence	

FEEDFORWARD	CONCURRENT	FEEDBACK
Ensure management's commitment to functional, not dysfunctional, work environments.	Use MBWA (managing by walking around) to identify potential problems; observe how employees treat and interact with each other.	Communicate openly about violent incidents and what's being done.
Provide employee assistance programs (EAPs) to help employees with behavioral problems.	Allow employees or work groups to "grieve" during periods of major organizational change.	Investigate incidents and take appropriate action.
Enforce organizational policy that any workplace rage, aggression, or violence will not be tolerated.	Be a good role model in how you treat others. Use corporate hotlines or some other mechanism for reporting and investigating incidents.	Review company policies and change, if necessary.
Use careful prehiring screening.	Use quick and decisive intervention.	
Never ignore threats.	Get expert professional assistance if violence erupts.	
Train employees about how to avoid danger if a situation arises.	Provide necessary equipment or procedures for dealing with violent situations (cell phones, alarm system, code names or phrases, and so forth).	
Clearly communicate policies to employees.		

Sources: Based on M. Gorkin, "Five Strategies and Structures for Reducing Workplace Violence," *Workforce Management Online,* December 3, 2000; "Investigating Workplace Violence: Where Do You Start?" *Workforce Management Online,* December 3, 2000; "Ten Tips on Recognizing and Minimizing Violence," *Workforce Management Online,* December 3, 2000; and "Points to Cover in a Workplace Violence Policy," *Workforce Management Online,* December 3, 2000.

- Defensive attitude with little or no performance feedback given; only numbers count; and yelling, intimidation, or avoidance as the preferred ways of handling conflict
- Double standards in terms of policies, procedures, and training opportunities for managers and employees
- Unresolved grievances due to an absence of mechanisms or only adversarial ones in place for resolving them; dysfunctional individuals protected or ignored because of long-standing rules, union contract provisions, or reluctance to take care of problems
- Emotionally troubled employees and no attempt by managers to get help for these people
- Repetitive, boring work and little chance for doing something else or for new people coming in
- Faulty or unsafe equipment or deficient training, which keeps employees from being able to work efficiently or effectively
- Hazardous work environment in terms of temperature, air quality, repetitive motions, overcrowded spaces, noise levels, excessive overtime, and so forth; to minimize costs, a failure to hire additional employees when workload becomes excessive leading to potentially dangerous work expectations and conditions
- Culture of violence perpetuated by a history of individual violence or abuse, violent or explosive role models, or tolerance of on-the-job alcohol or drug abuse

Reading through this list, you surely hope that workplaces where you'll spend your professional life won't be like this. However, the competitive demands of succeeding in a 24/7 global economy put pressure on organizations and employees in many ways.

What can managers do to deter or reduce possible workplace violence? Once again, the concept of feedforward, concurrent, and feedback control can help identify actions that managers can take.[47] Exhibit 14–8 summarizes several suggestions.

14 Review

CHAPTER SUMMARY

14.1 Explain the nature and importance of control. Control is the management function that involves monitoring activities to ensure that they're being accomplished as planned and correcting any significant deviations.

As the final step in the management process, controlling provides the link back to planning. If managers didn't control, they'd have no way of knowing whether goals were being met.

Control is important because (1) it's the only way to know whether goals are being met and, if not, why; (2) it provides information and feedback so managers feel comfortable empowering employees; and (3) it helps protect an organization and its assets.

14.2 Describe the three steps in the control process. The three steps in the control process are measuring, comparing, and taking action. Measuring involves deciding how to measure actual performance and what to measure. Comparing involves looking at the variation between actual performance and the standard (goal). Deviations outside an acceptable range of variation need attention.

Taking action can involve doing nothing, correcting the actual performance, or revising the standards. Doing nothing is self-explanatory. Correcting the actual performance can involve different corrective actions, which can either be immediate or basic. Standards can be revised by either raising or lowering them.

14.3 Discuss the types of controls organizations and managers use. Feedforward controls take place before a work activity is done. Concurrent controls take place while a work activity is being done. Feedback controls take place after a work activity is done.

Financial controls that managers can use include financial ratios (liquidity, leverage, activity, and profitability) and budgets. One information control managers can use is an MIS, which provides managers with needed information on a regular basis. Others include comprehensive and secure controls, such as data encryption, system firewalls, data backups, and so forth, that protect the organization's information. Also, balanced scorecards provide a way to evaluate an organization's performance in four different areas rather than just from the financial perspective.

14.4 Discuss contemporary issues in control. Adjusting controls for cross-cultural differences may be needed primarily in the areas of measuring and taking corrective actions.

Workplace concerns include workplace privacy, employee theft, and workplace violence. For each of these, managers need to have policies in place to control inappropriate actions and ensure that work is getting done efficiently and effectively.

MyManagementLab For more resources, please visit **www.mymanagementlab.com**

UNDERSTANDING THE CHAPTER

1. What is the role of control in management?
2. Describe four methods managers can use to acquire information about actual work performance.
3. How are planning and control linked? Is the control function linked to the organizing and leading functions of management? Explain.
4. Contrast feedforward, concurrent, and feedback controls.
5. Why do you think feedback control is the most popular type of control? Justify your response.
6. In Chapter 8 we discussed the "white-water rapids" view of change. Do you think it's possible to establish and maintain effective standards and controls in this type of environment? Discuss.
7. Why is it that what is measured is more critical to the control process than how it is measured?
8. "Every individual employee in an organization plays a role in controlling work activities." Do you agree with this statement, or do you think control is something that only managers are responsible for? Explain.

9. What are some work activities in which the acceptable range of variation might be higher than average? What about lower than average? (Hint: Think in terms of the output from the work activities, who it might affect, and how it might affect them.)

10. How could you use the concept of control in your personal life? Be specific. (Think in terms of feedforward, concurrent, and feedback controls as well as specific controls for the different aspects of your life—school, work, family relationships, friends, hobbies, etc.)

Go to p. 452
YOUR TURN TO BE A MANAGER for Chapter 14.

Endnotes

1. P. Elkind and D. Whitford, "An Accident Waiting to Happen," *Fortune,* February 7, 2011, pp. 105–132; G. Chazan, "BP's Safety Drive Faces Rough Road," *Wall Street Journal,* February 1, 2011, pp. A1+; C. Hausman, "Report Says Lack of Oversight Contributed to the Gulf Spill Disaster," *Ethics Newsline Online,* January 11, 2011; B. Casselman, "Supervisor Says Flaw Was Found in Key Safety Device," *Wall Street Journal,* July 21, 2010, pp. A6; R. Gold, "Rig's Final Hours Probed," *Wall Street Journal,* July 19, 2010, pp. A1+; S. Lyall, "In BP's Record, a History of Boldness and Costly Blunders," *New York Times Online,* July 12, 2010; B. Casselman and R. Gold, "Unusual Decisions Set Stage for BP Disaster," *Wall Street Journal,* May 27, 2010, pp. A1+; H. Fountain and T. Zeller, Jr., "Panel Suggests Signs of Trouble Before Rig Explosion," *New York Times Online,* May 25, 2010; and R. Gold and N. King Jr., "The Gulf Oil Spill: Red Flags Were Ignored Aboard Doomed Rig," *Wall Street Journal,* May 13, 2010, p. A6.
2. "Domino's Delivered Free Pizzas," *Springfield, Missouri News-Leader,* April 3, 2009, p. 3B.
3. Right or Wrong box based on T. Harbert, "When IT Is Asked to Spy," *Computerworld,* October 11, 2010, pp. 14–20; D. M. Amato-McCoy, "The,'Not-So-Sweet' Side of Retail Loss," *Chain Store Age,* July 2009, pp. 38–39; A. Vanacore, "Cameras Scan Store Lines for 'Sweethearting,'" Associated Press, *Springfield, Missouri News-Leader,* May 11, 2009, p. 9A; L. Lewis, "Adios, Sweetheart," *Stores Magazine,* January 2009, pp. 72–74; and J. Tarnowski, "Good Night, Sweethearting," *Progressive Grocer,* May 1, 2008, p. 126.
4. B. Hagenbaugh, "State Quarter's Extra Leaf Grew Out of Lunch Break," *USA Today,* January 20, 2006, p. 1B.
5. J. F. Van Niekerk and R. Von Solms, "Information Security Culture: A Management Perspective," *Computers & Security,* June 2010, pp. 476–486; T. Vinas and J. Jusko "5 Threats That Could Sink Your Company," *Industry Week,* September 2004, pp. 52–61; "Workplace Security: How Vulnerable Are You?" Special section in *Wall Street Journal,* September 29, 2003, pp. R1–R8; P. Magnusson, "Your Jitters Are Their Lifeblood," *Business Week,* April 14, 2003, p. 41; and T. Purdum, "Preparing for the Worst," *Industry Week,* January 2003, pp. 53–55.
6. A. Dalton, "Rapid Recovery," *Industry Week,* March 2005, pp. 70–71.
7. B. Nelson, "Long-Distance Recognition," *Workforce,* August 2000, pp. 50–52.
8. S. Kerr, "On the Folly of Rewarding A, While Hoping for B," *Academy of Management Journal* (December 1975), pp. 769–783; and N. F. Piercy, D. W. Cravens, N. Lane, and D. W. Vorhies, "Driving Organizational Citizenship Behaviors and Salesperson In-Role Behavior Performance: The Role of Management Control and Perceived Organizational Support," *Journal of the Academy of Marketing Science* (Spring 2006), pp. 244–262.
9. From the Past to the Present box based on H. Min and H. Min, "Benchmarking the Service Quality of Fast-Food Restaurant Franchises in the USA," *Benchmarking: An International Journal* (April 2011), pp. 282–300; R. Pear, "A.M.A. to Develop Measure of Quality of Medical Care," *New York Times Online,* February 21, 2006; and A. Taylor III, "Double Duty," *Fortune,* March 7, 2005, pp. 104–110; C. Bogan and D. Callahan, "Benchmarking in Rapid Time," *Industrial Management,* March–April 2001, pp. 28–33; and L. D. McNary, "Thinking About Excellence and Benchmarking," *Journal for Quality and Participation* (July–August 1994).
10. And the Survey Says box based on J. Yang and P. Trap, "Participating in Office Pools," *USA Today,* April 5, 2010, p. 1B; J. Yang and S. Parker, "Unproductive Work Hours Cost Billions," *USA Today,* September 29, 2009, p. 1B; M. Leone, "Something Wicked This Way Comes," *CFO,* June 2010, pp. 14–15; "Light–Fingered Employees Lift Laptops, Hardware," *Workforce Management Online,* July 22, 2008; J. Casale, "Data Breach Threats from Within Growing," *Workforce Management Online,* April 2009; M. Conlin, "To Catch a Corporate Thief," *BusinessWeek,* February 16, 2009, p. 52; A. R. Carey and S. Ward, "Have a Boss Who Plays Games at Work?" *USA Today,* May 6, 2009, p. 1A; and S. L. Mintz, "The Gauge of Innocence," *CFO,* April 2009, pp. 52–57.
11. H. Koontz and R. W. Bradspies, "Managing Through Feedforward Control," *Business Horizons,* June 1972, pp. 25–36.
12. M. Helft, "The Human Hands Behind the Google Money Machine," *New York Times Online,* June 2, 2008.
13. B. Caulfield, "Shoot to Kill," *Forbes,* January 7, 2008, pp. 92–96.
14. T. Laseter and L. Laseter, "See for Yourself," *Strategy+Business,* www.strategy-business.com (November 29, 2007).
15. W. H. Newman, *Constructive Control: Design and Use of Control Systems* (Upper Saddle River, NJ: Prentice Hall, 1975), p. 33.

16. B. Molina and M. Snider, "PlayStation Breach Called One of the Largest Ever," *USA Today,* April 28, 2011, p. 2B; and D. Stout and T. Zeller Jr., "Vast Data Cache About Veterans Has Been Stolen," *New York Times Online,* May 23, 2006.

17. Deloitte & Touche and the Ponemon Institute, "Research Report: Reportable and Multiple Privacy Breaches Rising at Alarming Rate," *Ethics Newsline,* http://ethicsnewsline.wordpress.com (January 1, 2008).

18. B. Grow, K. Epstein, and C-C. Tschang, "The New E-Spionage Threat," *Business Week,* April 21, 2008, pp. 32–41; S. Leibs, "Firewall of Silence," *CFO,* April 2008, pp. 31–35; J. Pereira, "How Credit-Card Data Went Out Wireless Door," *Wall Street Journal,* May 4, 2007, pp. A1+; and B. Stone, "Firms Fret as Office E-Mail Jumps Security Walls," *New York Times Online,* January 11, 2007.

19. D. Whelan, "Google Me Not," *Forbes,* August 16, 2004, pp. 102–104.

20. E. R. Iselin, J. Sands, and L. Mia, "Multi-Perspective Performance Reporting Systems, Continuous Improvement Systems, and Organizational Performance," *Journal of General Management* (Spring 2011), pp. 19–36; L. Elmore, "The Balanced Business," *Women in Business,* Spring 2011, pp. 14–16; D. Agostino and M. Arnaboldi, "How the BSC Implementation Process Shapes Its Outcome," *International Journal of Productivity & Performance Management* (January 2011), pp. 99–114; R. S. Kaplan and D. P. Norton, "How to Implement a New Strategy Without Disrupting Your Organization," *Harvard Business Review,* March 2006, pp. 100–109; L. Bassi and D. McMurrer, "Developing Measurement Systems for Managers in the Knowledge Era," *Organizational Dynamics,* May 2005, pp. 185–196; G. M. J. DeKoning, "Making the Balanced Scorecard Work (Part 1)," *Gallup Brain,* www.brain.gallup.com (July 8, 2004); G. M. J. DeKoning, "Making the Balanced Scorecard Work (Part 2)," *Gallup Brain,* www.brain.gallup.com (August 12, 2004); K. Graham, "Balanced Scorecard," *New Zealand Management,* March 2003, pp. 32–34; K. Ellis, "A Ticket to Ride: Balanced Scorecard," *Training* (April 2001), p. 50; and T. Leahy, "Tailoring the Balanced Scorecard," *Business Finance,* August 2000, pp. 53–56.

21. J. B. Butler, S. C. Henderson, and C. Raiborn, "Sustainability and the Balanced Scorecard: Integrating Green Measures into Business Reporting," *Management Accounting Quarterly,* Winter 2011, pp. 1–10; T. L. Gonzalez-Padron, B. R. Chabowski, G. T. M. Hult, and D. J. Ketchen, "Knowledge Management and Balanced Scorecard Outcomes: Exploring the Importance of Interpretation, Learning, and Internationality," *British Journal of Management* (December 2010), pp. 967–982; and T. Leahy, "Tailoring the Balanced Scorecard."

22. T. Leahy, "Tailoring the Balanced Scorecard."

23. J. Yaukey and C. L. Romero, "Arizona Firm Pays Big for Workers' Digital Downloads," Associated Press, *Springfield, Missouri, News-Leader,* May 6, 2002, p. 6B.

24. Information on Hoovers Online, www.hoovers.com (June 17, 2011); and N. Shirouzu and J. Bigness, "7-Eleven Operators Resist System to Monitor Managers," *Wall Street Journal,* June 16, 1997, p. B1.

25. Technology and the Manager's Job box based on C. A. Ciocchetti, "The Eavesdropping Employer: A Twenty-First-Framework for Employee Monitoring," *American Business Law Journal* (Summer 2011), pp. 285–369;

G. M. Amsler, H. M. Findley, and E. Ingram, "Performance Monitoring: Guidance for the Modern Workplace," *Supervision,* January 2011, pp. 16–22; T. Harbert, "When IT Is Asked to Spy"; D. Searcey, "Employers Watching Workers Online Spurs Privacy Debate," *Wall Street Journal,* April 23, 2009, p. A13; D. Darlin, "Software That Monitors Your Work, Wherever You Are," *New York Times Online,* April 12, 2009; S. Boehle, "They're Watching You," *Training* (September 2008), pp. 23+; S. Shellenbarger, "Work at Home? Your Employer May Be Watching You," *Wall Street Journal,* July 30, 2008, p. D1+; J. Jusko, "A Watchful Eye," *Industry Week,* May 7, 2001, p. 9; "Big Brother Boss," *U.S. News and World Report,* April 30, 2001, p. 12; and L. Guernsey, "You've Got Inappropriate E-Mail," *New York Times,* April 5, 2000, pp. C1+.

26. "2007 Electronic Monitoring & Surveillance Survey," *American Management Association,* www.amanet.org.

27. S. Armour, "Companies Keep an Eye on Workers' Internet Use," *USA Today,* February 21, 2006, p. 2B.

28. B. White, "The New Workplace Rules: No Video-Watching," *Wall Street Journal,* March 4, 2008, pp. B1+.

29. Ibid.

30. N. Lugaresi, "Electronic Privacy in the Workplace: Transparency and Responsibility," *International Review of Law, Computers, & Technology,* July 2010, pp. 163–173; P-W Tam, E. White, N. Wingfield, and K. Maher, "Snooping E-Mail by Software Is Now a Workplace Norm," *Wall Street Journal,* March 9, 2005, pp. B1+; D. Hawkins, "Lawsuits Spur Rise in Employee Monitoring," *U.S. News & World Report,* August 13, 2001, p. 53; and L. Guernsey, "You've Got Inappropriate Mail," *New York Times,* April 5, 2000, pp. C1+.

31. S. Armour, "More Companies Keep Track of Workers' E-Mail," *USA Today,* June 13, 2005, p. 4B; and E. Bott, "Are You Safe? Privacy Special Report," *PC Computing,* March 2000, pp. 87–88.

32. A. M. Bell and D. M. Smith, "Theft and Fraud May Be an Inside Job," *Workforce Online,* www.workforce.com (December 3, 2000).

33. C. C. Verschoor, "New Evidence of Benefits from Effective Ethics Systems," *Strategic Finance,* May 2003, pp. 20–21; and E. Krell, "Will Forensic Accounting Go Mainstream?" *Business Finance,* October 2002, pp. 30–34.

34. B. Mirza, "Combat Costly Discrimination, Employee Fraud, Theft," *HR Magazine,* February 2011, p. 14; and S. E. Needleman, "Businesses Say Theft by Their Workers Is Up," *Wall Street Journal,* December 11, 2008, p. B8.

35. J. Greenberg, "The STEAL Motive: Managing the Social Determinants of Employee Theft," in R. Giacalone and J. Greenberg (eds.), *Antisocial Behavior in Organizations* (Newbury Park, CA: Sage, 1997), pp. 85–108.

36. M. S. Hershcovis, "Incivility, Social Undermining, Bullying . . . Oh My! A Call to Reconcile Constructs Within Workplace Aggression Research," *Journal of Organizational Behavior* (April 2011), pp. 499–519; B. E. Litzky, K. A. Eddleston, and D. L. Kidder, "The Good, the Bad, and the Misguided: How Managers Inadvertently Encourage Deviant Behaviors," *Academy of Management Perspective,* February 2006, pp. 91–103; "Crime Spree," *BusinessWeek,* September 9, 2002, p. 8; B. P. Niehoff and R. J. Paul, "Causes of Employee Theft and Strategies That HR Managers Can Use for Prevention," *Human Resource Management,* Spring 2000, pp. 51–64; and G. Winter, "Taking at the Office Reaches New Heights: Employee Larceny Is Bigger and Bolder," *New York Times,* July 12, 2000, pp. C1+.

37. This section is based on J. Greenberg, *Behavior in Organizations,* 10th ed. (Upper Saddle River, NJ: Prentice Hall, 2011).
38. A. H. Bell and D. M. Smith, "Why Some Employees Bite the Hand That Feeds Them," *Workforce Online,* www.workforce.com (December 3, 2000).
39. B. E. Litzky et al., "The Good, the Bad, and the Misguided"; A. H. Bell and D. M. Smith, "Protecting the Company Against Theft and Fraud"; J. D. Hansen, "To Catch a Thief," *Journal of Accountancy* (March 2000), pp. 43–46; and J. Greenberg, "The Cognitive Geometry of Employee Theft," in *Dysfunctional Behavior in Organizations: Nonviolent and Deviant Behavior* (Stamford, CT: JAI Press, 1998), pp. 147–193.
40. L. Waldman and T. El-Ghobashy, "Work Shooting Kills Nine," *Wall Street Journal,* August 4, 2010, p. A3; D. Leinwand, "Shooter Kills Two, Then Self at N.M. Plant," *USA Today,* July 13, 2010, p. 3A; R. Lenz, "Gunman Kills Five, Himself at Plant," *Associated Press, Springfield, Missouri, News-Leader,* June 26, 2008, p. 6A; S. Oppermann, "Violence in the Workplace: Is Your Agency Prepared?" *FedSmith,* www.fedsmith.com (May 30, 2007); CBS News, "Former Postal Worker Kills 5, Herself," www.cbsnews.com/stories (January 31, 2006); CBS News, and "Autoworker's Grudge Turns Deadly," www.cbsnews.com/stories (January 27, 2005).
41. L. D. Lieber, "HR's Role in Preventing Workplace Violence," *Employment Relations Today (Wiley),* Winter 2011, pp. 83–88.
42. J. McCafferty, "Verbal Chills," *CFO,* June 2005, p. 17; S. Armour, "Managers Not Prepared for Workplace Violence," July 15, 2004, pp. 1B+; and "Workplace Violence," OSHA Fact Sheet, U.S. Department of Labor, Occupational Safety and Health Administration, 2002.
43. "Ten Tips on Recognizing and Minimizing Violence," *Workforce Online,* www.workforce.com (December 3, 2000).
44. "Research News Round-Up," *Occupational Health,* April 2011, p. 12.
45. C. Cosh, "Keep a Close Eye Out for the Signs," *Macleans,* December 27, 2010, p. 24; and R. McNatt, "Desk Rage," *BusinessWeek,* November 27, 2000, p. 12.
46. M. Gorkin, "Key Components of a Dangerously Dysfunctional Work Environment," *Workforce Online,* www.workforce.com (December 3, 2000).
47. L. D. Lieber, "HR's Role in Preventing Workplace Violence"; C. Cosh, "Keep a Close Eye Out for the Signs"; "Ten Tips on Recognizing and Minimizing Violence"; A. C. Klotz and M. R. Buckley, "Where Everybody Knows Your Name: Lessons from Small Business About Preventing Workplace Violence," *Business Horizons,* November 2010, pp. 571–579; M. Gorkin, "Five Strategies and Structures for Reducing Workplace Violence"; "Investigating Workplace Violence: Where Do You Start?"; and "Points to Cover in a Workplace Violence Policy," all of these are articles from *Workforce Online,* www.workforce.com (December 3, 2000).

Operations Management

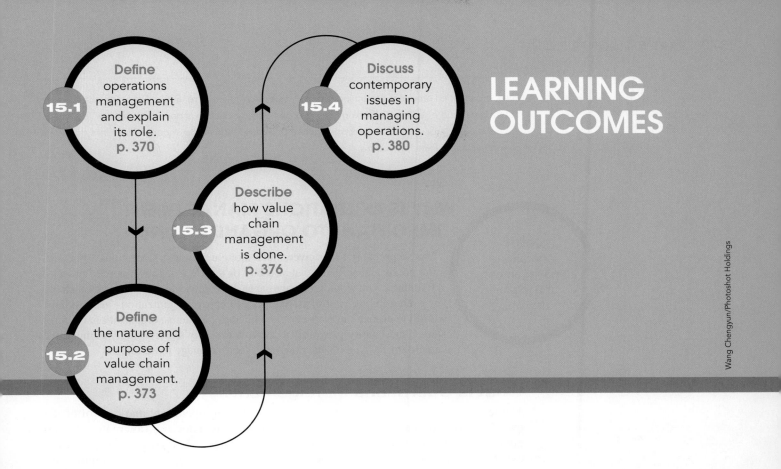

Wang Chengyun/Photoshot Holdings

Stirring Things Up

The steaming cup of coffee placed in a customer's hand at any Starbucks store location starts as coffee beans (berries) plucked from fields of coffee plants.[1] From harvest to storage to roasting to retail to cup, Starbucks understands the important role each value chain participant plays.

Starbucks offers a selection of coffees from around the world, and its coffee buyers personally travel to the coffee-growing regions of Latin America, Africa/Arabia, and Asia/Pacific to select and purchase the highest-quality *arabica* beans. Once the beans arrive at any one of its five roasting facilities (in Washington, Pennsylvania, Nevada, South Carolina, or Amsterdam), Starbucks' master professional roasters do their "magic" in creating the company's rich signature roast coffees, a process that's the "cumulative result of expert roasters knowing coffee and bringing balance to all of its flavor attributes." There are many potential challenges in "transforming" the raw material into the quality product and experience that customers expect at Starbucks—weather, shipping and logistics, technology, political instability, and so forth. All could potentially affect the company. Although those operations management challenges are significant, the most challenging issue facing Starbucks today is balancing its vision of the uniquely Starbucks' coffee experience with the realities of selling a $4 latte in today's world.

Every organization produces something, whether it's a good or a service. Some, like Starbucks, produce both a good and a service. Technology has changed how production is done. This chapter focuses on organizations' process of operations management. We also look at the important role that managers play in managing those operations.

15.1 Define operations management and explain its role.

WHY IS OPERATIONS MANAGEMENT IMPORTANT TO ORGANIZATIONS?

You've probably never given much thought to how organizations "produce" the goods and services that you buy or use. But it's an important process. Without it, you wouldn't have a car to drive or McDonald's fries to snack on, or even a hiking trail in a local park to enjoy. Organizations need to have well-thought-out and well-designed operating systems, organizational control systems, and quality programs to survive in today's increasingly competitive global environment. And it's the manager's job to manage those things.

What Is Operations Management?

The term operations management refers to the design, operation, and control of the transformation process that converts such resources as labor and raw materials into goods and services that are sold to customers. Exhibit 15–1 portrays a simplified overview of the transformation process of creating value by converting inputs into outputs. The system takes inputs—people, technology, capital, equipment, materials, and information—and transforms them through various processes, procedures, and work activities into finished goods and services. These processes, procedures, and work activities are found throughout the organization. For example, department members in marketing, finance, research and development, human resources, and accounting convert inputs into outputs such as sales, increased market share, high rates of return on investments, new and innovative products, motivated and committed employees, and accounting reports. As a manager, you'll need to be familiar with operations management concepts, regardless of the area in which you're managing, in order to achieve your goals more effectively and efficiently.

Why is operations management so important to organizations and managers? First, it encompasses processes in all organizations—services as well as manufacturing. Second, it's important in effectively and efficiently managing productivity. And third, it plays a strategic role in an organization's competitive success. Let's look more closely at each of these factors.

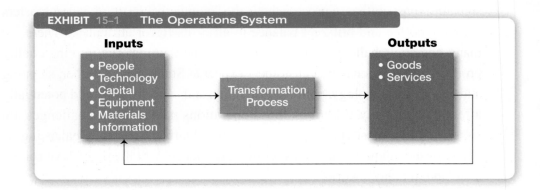

EXHIBIT 15–1   **The Operations System**

Inputs
- People
- Technology
- Capital
- Equipment
- Materials
- Information

Transformation Process

Outputs
- Goods
- Services

How Do Service and Manufacturing Firms Differ?

With a menu that offers more than 200 items made fresh each day, The Cheesecake Factory restaurants rely on a finely tuned production system. One food-service consultant says, "They've evolved with this highly complex menu combined with a highly efficient kitchen."[2]

All organizations produce goods or services through the **transformation process**. Simply stated, every organization has an operations system that creates value by transforming inputs into finished goods and services outputs. For manufacturers, the products are obvious: cars, cell phones, or food products. After all, **manufacturing organizations** produce physical goods. It's easy to see the operations management (transformation) process at work in these types of organizations because raw materials are turned into recognizable physical products. But that transformation process isn't as readily evident in **service organizations** because they produce nonphysical outputs in the form of services. For instance, hospitals provide medical and health care services that help people manage their personal health; taxi companies provide transportation services that move people from one location to another; cruise lines provide vacation and entertainment services; and residential plumbers and electricians ensure that we have electricity and running water where we live. All of these service organizations transform inputs into outputs. For example, look at your college. College administrators bring together inputs—instructors, books, academic journals, multimedia classrooms, and similar resources—to transform "unenlightened" students into educated and skilled individuals.

The reason we're making this point is that the U.S. economy, and to a large extent the global economy, is dominated by the creation and sale of services. Most of the world's developed countries are predominantly service economies. In the United States, for instance, almost 77 percent of all economic activity is services and in the European Union, it's nearly 73 percent.[3] In lesser-developed countries, the services sector is less important. For instance, in Nigeria, it accounts for only 33 percent of economic activity; in Laos, only 37 percent; and in Vietnam, 38 percent.[4]

Tyler Anderson/Newscom

The transformation process of creating value by converting inputs into outputs applies to both manufacturing and service organizations. While manufacturing firms produce physical goods, Netflix and other service organizations use inputs such as labor and technology to produce nonphysical outputs. Shown here is Netflix founder and CEO Reed Hastings, who created value for consumers by originally offering a DVD rental-by-mail service and then by introducing a streaming media service for viewing movies and television shows. After attempting to change what consumers valued about its service, Netflix had to do an about-face. As a result of the changes, Netflix saw its number of members drop significantly although it hopes to lure them back.

How Do Businesses Improve Productivity?

One jetliner has some 4 million parts. Efficiently assembling such a finely engineered product requires intense focus. Boeing and Airbus, the two major global manufacturers have copied techniques from Toyota. However, not every technique can be copied because airlines demand more customization than do car buyers and there are significantly more rigid safety regulations for jetliners than for cars.[5] At the Evans Findings Company in East Providence, Rhode Island, which makes the tiny cutting devices on dental-floss containers, one production shift each day is run without people.[6] The company's goal is to do as much as possible with no labor. And it's not because they don't care about their employees. Instead, like many U.S. manufacturers, Evans needed to improve productivity in order to survive, especially against low-cost competitors. So they turned to "lights-out" manufacturing where machines are designed to be so reliable that they make flawless parts on their own, without people operating them.

operations management
The study and application of the transformation process

transformation process
The process that converts resources into finished goods and services

manufacturing organizations
Organizations that produce physical goods

service organizations
Organizations that produce nonphysical products in the form of services

Although most organizations don't make products that have 4 million parts and most organizations can't function without people, improving productivity has become a major goal in virtually every organization. For countries, high productivity can lead to economic growth and development. Employees can receive higher wages and company profits can increase without causing inflation. For individual organizations, increased productivity gives them a more competitive cost structure and the ability to offer more competitive prices.

Over the past decade, U.S. businesses have made dramatic improvements to increase their efficiency. For example, at Latex Foam International's state-of-the-art digital facility in Shelton, Connecticut, engineers monitor all of the factory's operations. The facility boosted capacity by 50 percent in a smaller space and achieved a 30 percent efficiency gain.[7] And it's not just in manufacturing that companies are pursuing productivity gains. Pella Corporation's purchasing office improved productivity by reducing purchase order entry times anywhere from 50 percent to 86 percent, decreasing voucher processing by 27 percent, and eliminating 14 financial systems. Its information technology department slashed e-mail traffic in half and implemented work design improvements for heavy PC users such as call center users. The human resources department cut the time to process benefit enrollment by 156.5 days. And the finance department now takes 2 days, instead of 6 to do its end-of-month closeout.[8]

Organizations that hope to succeed globally are looking for ways to improve productivity. For example, McDonald's Corporation drastically reduced the time it takes to cook its french fries—65 seconds as compared to the 210 seconds it once took, saving time and other resources.[9] The Canadian Imperial Bank of Commerce, based in Toronto, automated its purchasing function, saving several million dollars annually.[10] And Skoda, the Czech car company owned by Germany's Volkswagen AG, improved its productivity through an intensive restructuring of its manufacturing process.[11]

From the Past to the Present

William Edwards Deming was an American statistician, professor, author, lecturer, and consultant.[12] He is widely credited with improving production in the United States during World War II, although he's probably best known for his work in Japan. From 1950 onward, he taught Japanese top managers how to improve product design and product quality, testing, and sales, primarily through applying statistical methods. His philosophy has been summarized as follows: "Dr. W. Edwards Deming taught that by adopting appropriate principles of management, organizations can increase quality and simultaneously reduce costs (by reducing waste, rework, staff attrition and litigation while increasing customer loyalty). The key is to practice continual improvement and think of manufacturing as a system, not as bits and pieces."

Putting that philosophy into practice required following Deming's 14 points for improving management's productivity. These suggestions are as follows:

- Plan for the long-term future.
- Never be complacent concerning the quality of your product.
- Establish statistical control over your production processes and require your suppliers to do so as well.
- Deal with the best and fewest number of suppliers.
- Find out whether your problems are confined to particular parts of the production process or stem from the overall process itself.

- Train workers for the job that you are asking them to perform.
- Raise the quality of your line supervisors.
- Drive out fear.
- Encourage departments to work closely together rather than to concentrate on departmental or divisional distinctions.
- Do not adopt strictly numerical goals.
- Require your workers to do quality work.
- Train your employees to understand statistical methods.
- Train your employees in new skills as the need arises.
- Make top managers responsible for implementing these principles.

These principles have withstood the test of time and are still applicable for managers looking to improve productivity.

Think About:

- Take each of Deming's 14 points for improving management's productivity and write a short explanation of what you think it means.
- Which one of these 14 points would you choose as the most important? Why?
- Given what you've learned in reading this textbook, do you think these principles are still appropriate today? Explain.

Productivity is a composite of people and operations variables. To improve productivity, managers must focus on both. The late W. Edwards Deming, a renowned quality expert, believed that managers, not workers, were the primary source of increased productivity. He outlined 14 points for improving management's productivity (see the From the Past to the Present box for more information). A close look at these suggestions reveals Deming's understanding of the interplay between people and operations. High productivity can't come solely from good "people management." The truly effective organization will maximize productivity by successfully integrating people into the overall operations system. For instance, at Simplex Nails Manufacturing in Americus, Georgia, employees were an integral part of the company's much-needed turnaround effort.[13] Some production workers were redeployed on a plantwide cleanup and organization effort, which freed up floor space. The company's sales force was retrained and refocused to sell what customers wanted rather than what was in inventory. The results were dramatic. Inventory was reduced by more than 50 percent, the plant had 20 percent more floor space, orders were more consistent, and employee morale improved. Here's a company that understood the important interplay between people and the operations system.

What Role Does Operations Management Play in a Company's Strategy?

Modern manufacturing originated more than 100 years ago in the United States, primarily in Detroit's automobile factories. The success that U.S. manufacturers experienced during World War II led manufacturing executives to believe that troublesome production problems had been conquered. These executives focused, instead, on improving other functional areas such as finance and marketing and paid little attention to manufacturing.

However, as U.S. executives neglected production, managers in Japan, Germany, and other countries took the opportunity to develop modern, technologically advanced facilities that fully integrated manufacturing operations into strategic planning decisions. The competition's success realigned world manufacturing leadership. U.S. manufacturers soon discovered that foreign goods were being made not only less expensively but also with better quality. Finally, by the late 1970s, U.S. executives recognized that they were facing a true crisis and responded. They invested heavily in improving manufacturing technology, increased the corporate authority and visibility of manufacturing executives, and began incorporating existing and future production requirements into the organization's overall strategic plan. Today, successful organizations recognize the crucial role that operations management plays as part of the overall organizational strategy to establish and maintain global leadership.[14]

The strategic role that operations management plays in successful organizational performance can be seen clearly as more organizations move toward managing their operations from a value chain perspective, which we're going to discuss next.

WHAT IS VALUE CHAIN MANAGEMENT AND WHY IS IT IMPORTANT?

15.2 Define the nature and purpose of value chain management.

It's 11 P.M., and you're reading a text message from your parents saying they want to buy you a laptop for your birthday this year and to order it. You log on to Dell's Web site and configure your dream machine. You hit the order button and within 3 or 4 days, your dream computer is delivered to your front door, built to your exact specifications, ready to set up and use immediately to type that management assignment due tomorrow. Or consider Siemens

AG's Computed Tomography manufacturing plant in Forchheim, Germany, which has established partnerships with about 30 suppliers. These suppliers are partners in the truest sense as they share responsibility with the plant for overall process performance. This arrangement has allowed Siemens to eliminate all inventory warehousing and streamlined the number of times paper changes hands to order parts from 18 to one. At the Timken's plant in Canton, Ohio, electronic purchase orders are sent across the street to an adjacent "Supplier City" where many of its key suppliers have set up shop. The process takes milliseconds and costs less than 50 cents per purchase order. And when Black & Decker extended its line of handheld tools to include a glue gun, it totally outsourced the entire design and production to the leading glue gun manufacturer. Why? Because they understood that glue guns don't require motors, which was what Black & Decker did best.[15]

As these examples show, closely integrated work activities among many different players are possible. How? The answer lies in value chain management. The concepts of value chain management have transformed operations management strategies and turned organizations around the world into finely tuned models of efficiency and effectiveness strategically positioned to exploit competitive opportunities.

What Is Value Chain Management?

Every organization needs customers if it's going to survive and prosper. Even a not-for-profit organization must have "customers" who use its services or purchase its products. Customers want some type of value from the goods and services they purchase or use, and these customers decide what has value. Organizations must provide that value to attract and keep customers. **Value** is defined as the performance characteristics, features and attributes, and any other aspects of goods and services for which customers are willing to give up resources (usually money). For example, when you download Katy Perry's new single on iTunes, buy a new pair of Australian sheepskin Ugg boots online at the company's Web site, purchase a Wendy's bacon cheeseburger at the drive-through location on campus, or get a haircut from your local hair salon, you're exchanging (giving up) money in return for the value you need or desire from these products— providing music during your evening study time, keeping your feet warm *and* fashionable during winter's cold weather, alleviating the lunchtime hunger pangs quickly since your next class starts in 15 minutes, or looking professionally groomed for the job interview you've got next week.

How *is* value provided to customers? Through transforming raw materials and other resources into some product or service that end users need or desire when, where, and how they want it. However, that seemingly simple act of turning varied resources into something that customers value and are willing to pay for involves a vast array of interrelated work activities performed by different participants (suppliers, manufacturers, and even customers)—that is, it involves the value chain. The **value chain** is the entire series of organizational work activities that add value at each step from raw materials to finished product. In its entirety, the value chain can encompass the supplier's suppliers to the customer's customer.[16]

Value chain management is the process of managing the sequence of activities and information along the entire value chain. In contrast to supply chain management, which is *internally* oriented and focuses on efficient flow of incoming materials (resources) to the organization, value chain management is *externally* oriented and focuses on both incoming materials and outgoing products and services. Although supply chain management is efficiency oriented (its goal is to reduce costs and make the organization more productive), value chain management is effectiveness oriented and aims to create the highest value for customers.[17]

At the BMW motorcycle plant in Berlin, Germany, production workers add value as they build motorcycles that are guided by a conveyor system through the entire assembly process according to individual orders. The flexibility, quality, and productivity of BMW's manufacturing plant are important aspects of the company's value chain. With state-of-the-art production technology, highly trained production workers, and process controls, BMW has mastered the complexity of tailoring products to individual customer specifications. By allowing every bike rider to order a custom-built motorcycle from anywhere in the world, BMW's production process provides value that attracts and keeps customers and differentiates the company from competitors.

Durand Florence/Newscom

What Are the Goals of Value Chain Management?

Who has the power in the value chain? Is it the supplier providing needed resources and materials? After all, suppliers have the ability to dictate prices and quality. Is it the manufacturer that assembles those resources into a valuable product or service? A manufacturer's contribution in creating a product or service is quite obvious. Is it the distributor that makes sure the product or service is available where and when the customer needs it? Actually, it's none of these. In value chain management, ultimately customers are the ones with the power.[18] They're the ones who define what value is and how it's created and provided. Using value chain management, managers seek to find that unique combination in which customers are offered solutions that truly meet their needs and at a price that can't be matched by competitors.[19] For example, in an effort to better anticipate customer demand and replenish customer stocks, Shell Chemical Company developed a supplier inventory management order network. The software used in this network allows managers to track shipment status, calculate safety stock levels, and prepare resupply schedules.[20] With this capability Shell Chemical enables its customers to purchase goods when desired and to receive them immediately.

A good value chain is one in which a sequence of participants works together as a team, each adding some component of value—such as faster assembly, more accurate information, or better customer response and service—to the overall process.[21] The better the collaboration among the various chain participants, the better the customer solutions. When value is created for customers and their needs and desires are satisfied, everyone along the chain benefits. For example, at Iomega Corporation, a manufacturer of personal computer storage devices, managing the value chain started first with improved relationships with internal suppliers, then expanded out to external suppliers and customers. As the company's experience with value chain management intensified and improved, so did its connection to customers, which ultimately paid off for all its value chain partners.[22]

How Does Value Chain Management Benefit Businesses?

Collaborating with external and internal partners in creating and managing a successful value chain strategy requires significant investments in time, energy, and other resources, and a serious commitment by all chain partners. Given this, why would managers ever choose to implement value chain management? A survey of manufacturers noted four primary benefits of value chain management: improved procurement, improved logistics, improved product development, and enhanced customer order management.[23]

RIGHT ?or WRONG

Okay...so here's an "unusual" ethics dilemma for you and it's a fitting conclusion in the last chapter of the textbook. Why? Because it illustrates that questions of ethics can pop up in the most ordinary of places. Suppose that you went to a popular shopping area where parking was extremely limited and the store owner had instituted "customers only" parking and you were lucky enough to find an open space. Then suppose that once you finished your business at that store—having spent a fair amount of money—you had other shopping to do in the same vicinity so you left your car in that same "customers only" parking space. You believed that what you did was okay since you "paid" for that spot with your purchase. But your significant other disagreed saying that since you had finished your business at that store, your car should be moved.[24]

Think About:

- What do you think? Is this ethical? Why or why not? *Does* the fact that you spent a fair amount of money at the store mean that you "paid" for that spot with your purchase? Did that give you the right to continue to use that parking space once your business was done at that store?

- What about the other stakeholders in this situation (for instance, the store where you shopped, other customers, other businesses in the area)? How might this one seemingly simple decision affect them?

rosesmith/Shutterstock.com

---

value
The performance characteristics, features, attributes, and other aspects of goods and services, for which customers are willing to give up resources

value chain
The entire series of work activities that add value at each step from raw materials to finished product

value chain management
The process of managing the sequence of activities and information along the entire value chain

15.3 Describe how value chain management is done.

HOW IS VALUE CHAIN MANAGEMENT DONE?

The dynamic, competitive environment facing contemporary global organizations demands new solutions.[25] Understanding how and why value is determined by the marketplace has led some organizations to experiment with a new **business model**—that is, a strategic design for how a company intends to profit from its broad array of strategies, processes, and activities. For example, IKEA, the home furnishings manufacturer, transformed itself from a small, Swedish mail-order furniture operation into the world's largest retailer of home furnishings by reinventing the value chain in the home furnishings industry. The company offers customers well-designed products at substantially lower prices in return for the customers' willingness to take on certain key tasks traditionally done by manufacturers and retailers—such as getting the furniture home and assembling it.[26] The company's adoption of a unique business model and willingness to abandon old methods and processes have worked well. It also helped that IKEA recognized the importance of managing its value chain.

What Are the Requirements for Successful Value Chain Management?

So what does successful value chain management require? Exhibit 15–2 summarizes the six main requirements: coordination and collaboration, technology investment, organizational processes, leadership, employees/human resources, and organizational culture and attitudes. Let's look at each of these elements more closely.

COORDINATION AND COLLABORATION. For the value chain to achieve its goal of meeting and exceeding customers' needs and desires, comprehensive and seamless integration among all members of the chain is absolutely necessary. All partners in the value chain must identify things that they may not value but that customers do. Sharing information and being flexible as far as who in the value chain does what are important steps in building coordination and collaboration. This sharing of information and analysis requires open communication among the various value chain partners. For example, Furon Company, a manufacturer of specialty polymer products, believes that better communication with customers and with suppliers has facilitated timely delivery of goods and services and opened up additional business opportunities for all its value chain partners.[27]

TECHNOLOGY INVESTMENT. Successful value chain management isn't possible without a significant investment in information technology. The payoff from this investment is that

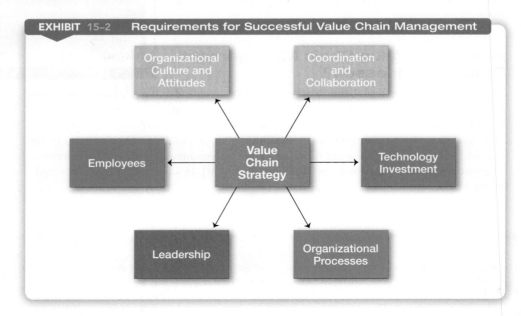

EXHIBIT 15–2   Requirements for Successful Value Chain Management

information technology can be used to restructure the value chain to better serve end users.[28] For example, Rollerblade, Inc., invested heavily in developing a Web site and used it to educate customers about its products. Although the company has chosen not to sell its products over the Web for fear of antagonizing its dealer network, managers remain flexible about the issue and would reconsider if they felt that value could be better delivered to customers by doing so.[29]

What types of technology are important? According to experts, the key tools include a supporting enterprise resource planning software (ERP) system that links all of an organization's activities, sophisticated work planning and scheduling software, customer relationship management systems, business intelligence capabilities, and e-business connections with trading network partners.[30] For instance, Dell Inc. manages its supplier relationships almost exclusively online. The company has one Web site for customers and one for suppliers. The supplier Web site is the primary mode of communication between Dell and 33 of its largest suppliers. The company's investment in this type of information technology allows it to meet customers' needs in a way that competitors haven't been able to match.[31]

ORGANIZATIONAL PROCESSES. Value chain management radically changes organizational processes—that is, the way organizational work is done.[32] Managers must critically evaluate all organizational processes from beginning to end by looking at core competencies—the organization's unique skills, capabilities, and resources—to determine where value is being added. Non-value-adding activities are eliminated. Questions such as "Where can internal knowledge be leveraged to improve flow of material and information?" "How can we better configure our product to satisfy both customers and suppliers?" "How can the flow of material and information be improved?" and "How can we improve customer service?" should be asked for each process. For example, when managers at Deere & Company implemented value chain management in its Worldwide Commercial and Consumer Equipment Division, a thorough process evaluation revealed that work activities needed to be better synchronized and interrelationships between multiple links in the value chain better managed. They changed numerous work processes division-wide in order to improve these relationships.[33]

Three important conclusions can be made about how organizational processes must change. First, better demand forecasting is necessary and possible because of closer ties with customers and suppliers. For example, in an effort to make sure that Listerine was on the store shelves when customers wanted it, Walmart collaborated with product manufacturer Pfizer Consumer Healthcare on improving product demand forecast information. Through their mutual efforts, the partners boosted Walmart's sales of Listerine by $6.5 million. Customers also benefited because they were able to purchase the product when and where they wanted it.

Second, selected functions may need to be done collaboratively with other partners in the value chain. This collaboration may even extend to sharing employees. For instance, Saint-Gobain Performance Plastics, headquartered in Northboro, Massachusetts, places its own employees in customer sites and brings employees of suppliers and customers to work on its premises. Saint-Gobain's CEO says this type of collaboration is essential if an organization wants to "go from being a mere component supplier to being a solutions provider."[34]

Finally, new measures are needed for evaluating the performance of various activities along the value chain. Because the goal in value chain management is meeting and exceeding customers' needs and desires, managers need a better picture of how well value is being created and delivered to customers. For instance, when Nestlé USA implemented a value chain management approach, it redesigned its measurement system to focus on one consistent set of factors, including accuracy of demand forecasts and production plans, on-time delivery, and customer service levels. This redesign allowed management to more quickly identify problems and take actions to resolve them.[35]

AND THE SURVEY SAYS...[36]

22 percent of manufacturers introduced product innovations during a recent three-year time span.

58 percent of companies are looking to connect better with their suppliers.

56 percent of those companies hope to reduce procurement costs.

16 percent of employers prefer using employee referrals to locate quality employees.

12 percent of companies say that sustainability is among their top three supply chain priorities.

63 percent of those companies see sustainability as an opportunity for revenue growth.

64 percent of manufacturers say that they currently have wireless networks or intend to have them.

---

business model
A strategic design for how a company intends to profit from its broad array of strategies, processes, and activities

organizational processes
The way organizational work is done

LEADERSHIP.   The importance of leadership to value chain management is plain and simple—successful value chain management isn't possible without strong and committed leadership.[37] From top organizational levels to lower levels, managers must support, facilitate, and promote the implementation and ongoing practice of value chain management. J. Michael Hagan, CEO of Furon Company, describes his role as follows: "Value is a mindset that not only has to be driven from the top down, but also from the bottom up. Everyone has to be asking whether a given task adds value, and if it doesn't, why do it."[38] Managers must make a serious commitment to identifying what value is, how that value can best be provided, and how successful those efforts have been. That type of organizational atmosphere or culture in which all efforts are focused on delivering superb customer value isn't possible without a serious commitment on the part of the organization's leaders.

Also, it's important that leaders outline expectations for what's involved in the organization's pursuit of value chain management. Ideally, articulating expectations should start with a vision or mission statement that expresses the organization's commitment to identifying, capturing, and providing the highest possible value to customers. For example, when American Standard Companies began its pursuit of value chain management, the CEO attended dozens of meetings across the country explaining the changing competitive environment and why the company needed to create better working relationships with its value chain partners.[39] Throughout the organization, then, managers should clarify expectations regarding each employee's role in the value chain. Being clear about expectations also extends to partners. For example, managers at American Standard identified clear requirements for suppliers and were prepared to drop any that couldn't meet them. The company was so serious about its expectations that it did cut hundreds of suppliers from air conditioning, bath and kitchen, and vehicle control systems businesses. The upside, though, was that those suppliers that met the expectations benefited from more business and American Standard had partners that could deliver better value to customers.

EMPLOYEES/HUMAN RESOURCES.   We know from our discussions of management theories and approaches throughout this textbook that employees are the organization's most important resource. So, not surprisingly, employees play an important part in value chain management. Three main human resources requirements for value chain management are flexible approaches to job design, an effective hiring process, and ongoing training.

Flexibility is the key description of job design in a value chain management organization. Traditional functional job roles—such as marketing, sales, accounts payable, customer service representative, and so forth—are inadequate in a value chain management environment. Instead, jobs need to be designed around work processes that link all functions involved in creating and providing value to customers. This type of flexible job design supports the company's commitment to providing superb customer value.[40] In designing jobs for a value chain approach, the focus needs to be on how each activity performed by an employee can best contribute to the creation and delivery of customer value, which requires flexibility in what employees do and how they do it.

The fact that jobs in a value chain management organization must be flexible contributes to the second requirement: Flexible jobs require employees who are flexible. In a value chain organization, employees may be assigned to work teams that tackle a given process and are often asked to do different things on different days, depending on need. In an environment focusing on collaborative relationships that may change as customer needs change, employees' ability to be flexible is critical. Accordingly, the organization's hiring process must be designed to identify those employees who have the ability to quickly learn and adapt.

Finally, the need for flexibility also requires a significant investment in ongoing employee training. Whether

Employees such as the team leaders of the Bing search engine shown here play a significant role in Microsoft's value chain. The software developer's mission is "to enable people and businesses throughout the world to realize their full potential." To achieve this mission, Microsoft needs people who are smart, creative, flexible, and energetic and who have a passion for customers, technology, and creating quality products. The company uses an unstructured interview approach during the hiring process to identify employees who will help customers, possess qualities such as the willingness to take on big challenges and see them through, and are hard-working, self-critical, questioning, and committed to personal excellence and self-improvement.

Stuart Isett/Newscom

the training involves learning how to use information technology software, how to improve the flow of materials throughout the chain, how to identify activities that add value, how to make better decisions faster, or how to improve any number of other potential work activities, managers must see to it that employees have the knowledge and tools they need to do their jobs. For example, at defense and electronics contractor Alenia Marconi Systems, based in Portsmouth, England, ongoing training is part of the company's commitment to efficiently and effectively meeting the needs of customers. Employees continually receive technical training as well as training in strategic issues including the importance of emphasizing people and customers, not just sales and profits.[41]

ORGANIZATIONAL CULTURE AND ATTITUDES.   The last requirement for value chain management is having a supportive organizational culture and attitudes. Those cultural attitudes include sharing, collaborating, openness, flexibility, mutual respect, and trust. And these attitudes encompass not only the internal partners in the value chain but external partners as well. For instance, American Standard has chosen to practice these attitudes the old-fashioned way—with lots of face time and telephone calls. One of the company's suppliers, St. Louis–based White Rogers, described their relationship as follows: "Their goals are our goals, because both companies focus on growth. The keys to the relationship are mutual respect and open communications at all levels. No one has to go through a liaison. If our engineers need to talk to theirs, we just go right to the source."[42] However, as we mentioned earlier, Dell has taken a completely different approach, as it works with its value chain partners almost exclusively through cyberspace.[43] Both approaches, however, reflect each company's commitment to developing long-lasting, mutually beneficial, and trusting relationships that best meet customers' needs.

What Are the Obstacles to Value Chain Management?

As desirable as value chain management may be, managers must tackle several obstacles in managing the value chain including organizational barriers, cultural attitudes, required capabilities, and people (see Exhibit 15–3).

ORGANIZATIONAL BARRIERS.   Organizational barriers are among the most difficult obstacles to handle. These barriers include refusal or reluctance to share information, reluctance to shake up the status quo, and security issues. Without shared information, close coordination and collaboration is impossible. And the reluctance or refusal of employees to shake up the status quo can impede efforts toward value chain management and prevent its successful implementation. Finally, because value chain management relies heavily on a substantial information technology infrastructure, system security and Internet security breaches are issues that need to be addressed.

EXHIBIT 15–3   Obstacles to Successful Value Chain Management

CULTURAL ATTITUDES.   Unsupportive cultural attitudes—especially trust and control—also can be obstacles to value chain management. The trust issue is a critical one, both lack of trust and too much trust. To be effective, partners in a value chain must trust each other. There must be a mutual respect for, and honesty about, each partner's activities all along the chain. When that trust doesn't exist, the partners will be reluctant to share information, capabilities, and processes. But too much trust also can be a problem. Just about any organization is vulnerable to theft of intellectual property—that is, proprietary information that's critical to an organization's efficient and effective functioning and competitiveness. You need to be able to trust your value chain partners so your organization's valuable assets aren't compromised.[44] Another cultural attitude that can be an obstacle is the belief that when an organization collaborates with external and internal partners, it no longer controls its own destiny. However, this just isn't the case. Even with the intense collaboration that's important to value chain management, organizations still control critical decisions such as what customers value, how much value they desire, and what distribution channels are important.[45]

REQUIRED CAPABILITIES.   We know from our earlier discussion of requirements for the successful implementation of value chain management that value chain partners need numerous capabilities. Several of these—coordination and collaboration, the ability to configure products to satisfy customers and suppliers, and the ability to educate internal and external partners—aren't easy. But they're essential to capturing and exploiting the value chain. Many of the companies we've described throughout this section endured critical, and oftentimes difficult, self-evaluations of their capabilities and processes in order to become more effective and efficient at managing their value chains.

PEOPLE.   The final obstacles to successful value chain management can be an organization's people. Without their unwavering commitment to do whatever it takes, value chain management won't be successful. If employees refuse to be flexible in their work—how and with whom they work—collaboration and cooperation throughout the value chain will be hard to achieve. In addition, value chain management takes an incredible amount of time and energy on the part of an organization's employees. Managers must motivate those high levels of effort from employees, which isn't an easy thing to do.

WHAT CONTEMPORARY ISSUES DO MANAGERS FACE IN MANAGING OPERATIONS?

15.4 Discuss contemporary issues in managing operations.

Redesigned milk jugs that have been adopted by Walmart and Costco are cheaper to ship, better for the environment, cost less, and keep the milk fresher. Experts say this type of redesign is "an example of the changes likely to play out in the American economy over the next two decades. In an era of soaring global demand and higher costs for energy and materials, virtually every aspect of the economy needs to be re-examined and many products must be redesigned for greater efficiency."[46]

If you somehow thought that managing operations didn't really matter in today's online 24/7 global economy, think again. It does matter . . . a lot. We're going to look at three contemporary issues that managers face in managing operations: technology's role in operations management, quality initiatives, and project management.

What Role Does Technology Play in Operations Management?

As we know from our previous discussion of value chain management, today's competitive marketplace has put tremendous pressure on organizations to deliver products and services that customers value in a timely manner. Smart companies are looking at ways to harness technology to improve operations management. Many fast-food companies are competing to see who can provide faster and better service to drive-through customers. With drive-through now representing a huge portion of sales, faster and better delivery can be a significant competitive edge. For instance, Wendy's added awnings to some of its menu boards and replaced some of the text with pictures. Others use confirmation screens, a technology that helped McDonald's boost accuracy by more than 11 percent. And technology used by two national chains tells managers how much food they need to prepare by counting vehicles in the drive-through line and factoring in demand for current promotional and popular staple items.[47]

Although an organization's production activities are driven by the recognition that the customer is king, managers still need to be more responsive. For instance, operations managers need systems that can reveal available capacity, status of orders, and product quality while products are in the process of being manufactured, not just after the fact. To connect more closely with customers, production must be synchronized across the enterprise. To avoid bottlenecks and slowdowns, the production function must be a full partner in the entire business system.

What's making such extensive collaboration possible is technology. Technology is also allowing organizations to control costs particularly in the areas of predictive maintenance, remote diagnostics, and utility cost savings. For instance, Internet-compatible equipment contains embedded Web servers that can communicate proactively—that is, if a piece of equipment breaks or reaches certain preset parameters indicating that it's about to break, it asks for help. But technology can do more than sound an alarm or light up an indicator button. For instance, some devices have the ability to initiate e-mail or signal a pager at a supplier, the maintenance department, or contractor describing the specific problem and requesting parts and service. How much is such e-enabled maintenance control worth? It can be worth quite a lot if it prevents equipment breakdowns and subsequent production downtime.

Managers who understand the power of technology to contribute to more effective and efficient performance know that managing operations is more than the traditional view of simply producing the product. Instead, the emphasis is on working together with all the organization's business functions to find solutions to customers' business problems. (See the Technology and the Manager's Job box for more information on technology's role in the factory of the future.)

Roland Weihrauch/Newscom

Amazon.com's fulfillment center shown here in Werne, Germany, is one of 40 the online retailer operates throughout the world. These centers stock millions of different items to meet Amazon's goal of carrying anything a customer wants to buy. To stock, retrieve, and ship its vast inventory, Amazon has developed sophisticated technology that tells the company what to order, where to store it, and what to charge for it. Amazon uses software and logistics technology to locate inventory and find the fastest way to get it to the customer. Technology increases Amazon's operating efficiency by reducing inventory costs and delivery times as well as providing online shoppers with the best customer service.

TECHNOLOGY AND THE MANAGER'S JOB — WELCOME TO THE FACTORY OF THE FUTURE!

What would the ideal factory of the future look like?[48] Experts at Georgia Tech's Manufacturing Research Center say that three important trends are driving what tomorrow's factories will look like. One trend is *globalization of the supply chain*. In the factories of the future, design and business processes will be performed where it's most efficient and effective to do so. For example, parts for Boeing's 787 Dreamliner are produced around the world and then come together in Boeing's U.S. facilities. The second trend is *technology that simultaneously dematerializes the product while vastly increasing complexity*. The challenge for managing operations is that despite simplicity in products, the production process is becoming more complex. The third trend is *demographics and the impact on demand patterns*. Products will have shorter life cycles and more variety and choices. "The challenge is for the future factory to be both adaptable over many different product life cycles and flexible with regard to the number of different products being produced in the same time frame." And it will be particularly important that these factories be efficient and effective.

Given these trends, it's clear that technology will continue to play a key role in transformation processes that need to be collaborative, adaptive, flexible, and responsive. But keep in mind that technology is simply a tool. Future factories will also require a talented and skilled workforce and a clear understanding of managing operations processes. Those are the challenges facing managers who want their organizations to survive and thrive.

Think About:

· How will technology contribute to the operations management process?

· What are the downsides to using technology in the operations management process?

· In the factory of the future, what role does a manager play?

How Do Managers Control Quality?

Quality problems are expensive. For example, even though Apple has had phenomenal success with its iPod, the batteries in the first three versions died after 4 hours instead of lasting up to 12 hours, as buyers expected. Apple's settlement with consumers cost close to $100 million. At Schering-Plough, problems with inhalers and other pharmaceuticals were traced to chronic quality control shortcomings, for which the company eventually paid a $500 million fine. And the auto industry paid $14.5 billion to cover the cost of warranty and repair work in one year.[49]

Many experts believe that organizations unable to produce high-quality products won't be able to compete successfully in the global marketplace. What is quality? When you consider a product or service to have quality, what does that mean? Does it mean that the product doesn't break or quit working—that is, is it reliable? Does it mean that the service is delivered in a way that you intended? Does it mean that the product does what it's supposed to do? Or does quality mean something else? Exhibit 15–4 provides a description of several quality dimensions. We're going to define quality as the ability of a product or service to reliably do what it's supposed to do and to satisfy customer expectations.

HOW IS QUALITY ACHIEVED? How quality is achieved is an issue managers must address. A good way to look at quality initiatives is with the management functions—planning, organizing and leading, and controlling—that need to take place.

When *planning for quality,* managers must have quality improvement goals and strategies and plans to achieve those goals. Goals can help focus everyone's attention toward some objective quality standard. For instance, Caterpillar's goal is to apply quality improvement techniques to help cut costs.[50] Although this goal is specific and challenging, managers and employees are partnering together to pursue well-designed strategies to achieve the goals, and are confident they can do so.

When *organizing and leading for quality,* it's important for managers to look to their employees. For instance, at the Moosejaw, Saskatchewan, plant of General Cable Corporation, every employee participates in continual quality assurance training. In

---

EXHIBIT 15–4   **What Is Quality?**

PRODUCT QUALITY DIMENSIONS

1. Performance—Operating characteristics
2. Features—Important special characteristics
3. Flexibility—Meeting operating specifications over some period of time
4. Durability—Amount of use before performance deteriorates
5. Conformance—Match with preestablished standards
6. Serviceability—Ease and speed of repair or normal service
7. Aesthetics—How a product looks and feels
8. Perceived quality—Subjective assessment of characteristics (product image)

SERVICE QUALITY DIMENSIONS

1. Timeliness—Performed in promised period of time
2. Courtesy—Performed cheerfully
3. Consistency—Giving all customers similar experiences each time
4. Convenience—Accessibility to customers
5. Completeness—Full service, as required
6. Accuracy—Performed correctly each time

Sources: Based on J. W. Dean and J. R. Evans, *Total Quality: Management, Organization, and Society* (St. Paul, MN: West Publishing Company, 1994); H. V. Roberts and B. F. Sergesketter, *Quality Is Personal* (New York: The Free Press, 1993); D. Garvin, *Managed Quality: The Strategic and Competitive Edge* (New York: The Free Press, 1988); and M. A. Hitt, R. D. Ireland, and R. E. Hoskisson, *Strategic Management,* 4th ed. (Cincinnati: South-Western Publishing, 2001), p. 121.

addition, the plant manager believes wholeheartedly in giving employees the information they need to do their jobs better. He says, "Giving people who are running the machines the information is just paramount. You can set up your cellular structure, you can cross-train your people, you can use lean tools, but if you don't give people information to drive improvement, there's no enthusiasm." Needless to say, this company shares production data and financial performance measures with all employees.[51]

Organizations with extensive and successful quality improvement programs tend to rely on two important people approaches: cross-functional work teams and self-directed or empowered work teams. Because achieving product quality is something that all employees from upper to lower levels must participate in, it's not surprising that quality-driven organizations rely on well-trained, flexible, and empowered employees.

Finally, managers must recognize when *controlling for quality* that quality improvement initiatives aren't possible without having some way to monitor and evaluate their progress. Whether it involves standards for inventory control, defect rate, raw materials procurement, or other operations management areas, controlling for quality is important. For instance, at the Northrup Grumman Corporation plant in Rolling Meadows, Illinois, several quality controls have been implemented, such as automated testing and IT that integrates product design and manufacturing and tracks process quality improvements. Also, employees are empowered to make accept/reject decisions about products throughout the manufacturing process. The plant manager explains, "This approach helps build quality into the product rather than trying to inspect quality into the product." But one of the most important things they do is "go to war" with their customers—soldiers preparing for war or live combat situations. Again, the plant manager says, "What discriminates us is that we believe if we can understand our customer's mission as well as they do, we can help them be more effective. We don't wait for our customer to ask us to do something. We find out what our customer is trying to do and then we develop solutions."[52]

Quality improvement success stories can be found globally. For example, at a Delphi assembly plant in Matamoros, Mexico, employees worked hard to improve quality and made significant strides. For instance, the customer reject rate on shipped products is now 10 ppm (parts per million), down from 3,000 ppm—an improvement of almost 300 percent.[53] Quality initiatives at several Australian companies including Alcoa of Australia, Wormald Security, and Carlton and United Breweries have led to significant quality improvements.[54] At Valeo Klimasystemme GmbH of Bad Rodach, Germany, assembly teams build different climate-control systems for high-end German cars including Mercedes and BMW. Quality initiatives by those teams have led to significant improvements.[55]

WHAT QUALITY GOALS MIGHT ORGANIZATIONS PURSUE? To publicly demonstrate their commitment to quality, many organizations worldwide have pursued challenging quality goals. The two best-known are ISO 9000 and Six Sigma.

ISO 9000 is a series of international quality management standards established by the International Organization for Standardization (www.iso.org), which set uniform guidelines for processes to ensure that products conform to customer requirements. These standards cover everything from contract review to product design to product delivery. The ISO 9000 standards have become the internationally recognized standard for evaluating and

In this photo, the hands of Portuguese football player Cristiano Ronaldo holds a Nike Mercurial Vapor Superfly II football boot during a Nike press conference in London. High-quality products like the Mercurial Vapor that are used and endorsed by world-class athletes have helped Nike earn the top spot as global designer, marketer, and distributor of athletic footwear, apparel, and equipment. For Nike, quality means designing and developing innovative products that help athletes of every level of ability reach their potential. The quality of Nike footwear products that satisfy customer expectations includes the dimensions of product performance, features, flexibility, durability, and aesthetics.

Ben Stansall/Newscom

ISO 9000
A series of international quality standards that set uniform guidelines for processes to ensure that products conform to customer requirements

comparing companies in the global marketplace. In fact, this type of certification can be a prerequisite for doing business globally. Achieving ISO 9000 certification provides proof that a quality operations system is in place. As of 2009, more than 1 million certifications had been awarded to organizations in 175 countries. Almost 40,000 U.S. businesses are ISO 9000 certified. More than 200,000 Chinese firms have received certification.[56]

More than 30 years ago, Motorola popularized the use of stringent quality standards more through a trademarked quality improvement program called **Six Sigma**.[57] Very simply, Six Sigma is a quality standard that establishes a goal of no more than 3.4 defects per million units or procedures. What does the name mean? Sigma is the Greek letter that statisticians use to define a standard deviation from a bell curve. The higher the sigma, the fewer the deviations from the norm—that is, the fewer the defects. At One Sigma, two-thirds of whatever is being measured falls within the curve. Two Sigma covers about 95 percent. At Six Sigma, you're about as close to defect-free as you can get.[58] It's an ambitious quality goal! Although it's an extremely high standard to achieve, many quality-driven businesses are using it and benefiting from it. For instance, General Electric estimates that it has saved billions since 1995, according to company executives.[59] Other examples of companies pursuing Six Sigma include ITT Industries, Dow Chemical, 3M Company, American Express, Sony Corporation, Nokia Corporation, and Johnson & Johnson. Although manufacturers seem to make up the bulk of Six Sigma users, service companies such as financial institutions, retailers, and health care organizations are beginning to apply it. What impact can Six Sigma have? Let's look at an example.

It used to take Wellmark Blue Cross and Blue Shield, a managed-care health care company, 65 days or more to add a new doctor to its medical plans. Now, thanks to Six Sigma, the company discovered that half the processes they used were redundant. With those unnecessary steps gone, the job now gets done in 30 days or less and with reduced staff. The company also has been able to reduce its administrative expenses by $3 million per year, an amount passed on to consumers through lower health premiums.[60]

Although it's important for managers to recognize that many positive benefits come from obtaining ISO 9000 certification or Six Sigma, the key benefit comes from the quality improvement journey itself. In other words, the goal of quality certification should be having work processes and an operations system in place that enable organizations to meet customers' needs and employees to perform their jobs in a consistently high-quality way.

How Are Projects Managed?

As we discussed in Chapter 6, many organizations are structured around projects. A **project** is a one-time-only set of activities with a definite beginning and ending point.[61] Projects vary in size and scope, from a NASA space shuttle launch to a wedding. **Project management** is the task of getting the activities done on time, within budget, and according to specifications.

Project management has actually been around for a long time in industries such as construction and movie making, but now it has expanded into almost every type of business. What explains the growing popularity of project management? It fits well with a dynamic environment and the need for flexibility and rapid response. Organizations are increasingly undertaking projects that are somewhat unusual or unique, have specific deadlines, contain complex interrelated tasks requiring specialized skills, and are temporary in nature. These types of projects don't lend themselves well to the standardized operating procedures that guide routine and continuous organizational activities.[62]

In the typical project, team members are temporarily assigned to and report to a project manager who coordinates the project's activities with other departments and reports directly to a senior executive. The project is temporary: It exists only long enough to complete its specific objectives. Then it's wound down and closed up; members move on to other projects, return to their permanent departments, or leave the organization.

If you were to observe a group of supervisors or department managers for a few days, you would see them regularly detailing what activities have to be done, the order in which they are to be done, who is to do each, and when they are to be completed. The managers are doing what we call scheduling. The following discussion reviews some useful scheduling devices.

HOW DO YOU USE A GANTT CHART? The Gantt chart is a planning tool developed around the turn of the century by Henry Gantt. The idea behind the Gantt chart is relatively simple. It's essentially a bar graph, with time on the horizontal axis and the activities to be scheduled on the vertical axis. The bars show output, both planned and actual, over a period of time. The Gantt chart visually shows when tasks are supposed to be done and compares the assigned date with the actual progress on each. This simple but important device allows managers to detail easily what has yet to be done to complete a job or project and to assess whether it's ahead of, behind, or on schedule.

Exhibit 15–5 shows a Gantt chart that was developed for book production by a manager in a publishing firm. Time is expressed in months across the top of the chart. Major activities are listed down the left side. The planning comes in deciding what activities need to be done to get the book finished, the order in which those activities need to be done, and the time that should be allocated to each activity. The blue shading represents actual progress made in completing each activity.

A Gantt chart, then, actually becomes a managerial control device as the manager looks for deviations from the plan. In this case, most activities were completed on time. However, if you look at the "review first pages" activity, you will notice that it's actually almost two and a half weeks behind schedule. Given this information, the manager might want to take some corrective action to make up the lost time and to ensure that no further delays will occur. At this point, the manager can expect that the book will be published at least two weeks late if no corrective action is taken.

A modified version of the Gantt chart is a load chart. Instead of listing activities on the vertical axis, load charts list either whole departments or specific resources. This information allows managers to plan and control for capacity utilization. In other words, load charts schedule capacity by workstations. For example, Exhibit 15–6 shows a load chart for six production editors at the same publishing firm. Each editor supervises the design and production of several books. By reviewing the load chart, the executive editor who supervises the six production editors can see who is free to take on a new book. If everyone is fully scheduled, the executive editor might decide not to accept any new projects, to accept some new projects and delay others, to ask the editors to work overtime, or to employ more production editors.

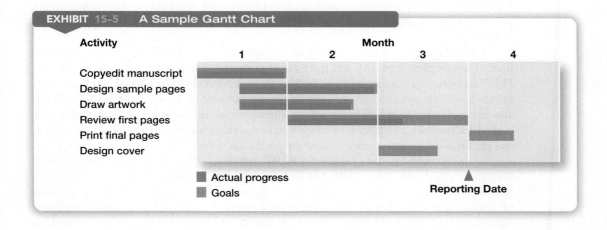

EXHIBIT 15–5 **A Sample Gantt Chart**

Activity	Month

Activity:
- Copyedit manuscript
- Design sample pages
- Draw artwork
- Review first pages
- Print final pages
- Design cover

Months: 1, 2, 3, 4

■ Actual progress
■ Goals

Reporting Date

Six Sigma
A quality standard that establishes a goal of no more than 3.4 defects per million units or procedures

project
A one-time-only set of activities with a definite beginning and ending point

project management
The task of getting project activities done on time, within budget, and according to specifications

gantt chart
A planning tool that shows in bar graph form when tasks are supposed to be done and compares that with the actual progress on each

load chart
A modified version of a Gantt chart that lists either whole departments or specific resources

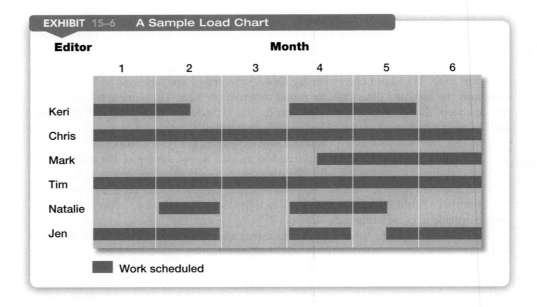

EXHIBIT 15-6   A Sample Load Chart

WHAT IS A PERT NETWORK ANALYSIS?   Gantt and load charts are helpful as long as the activities or projects being scheduled are few and independent of each other. But what if a manager had to plan a large project—such as a complex reorganization, the launching of a major cost-reduction campaign, or the development of a new product—that required coordinating inputs from marketing, production, and product design personnel? Such projects require coordinating hundreds or thousands of activities, some of which must be done simultaneously and some of which cannot begin until earlier activities have been completed. If you are constructing a shopping mall, you obviously cannot start erecting walls until the foundation has been laid. How, then, can you schedule such a complex project? You could use the program evaluation and review technique.

The program evaluation and review technique—usually just called PERT, or the **PERT network analysis**—was originally developed in the late 1950s for coordinating the more than 3,000 contractors and agencies working on the Polaris submarine weapon system. This project was incredibly complicated, with hundreds of thousands of activities that had to be coordinated. PERT is reported to have cut two years off the completion date for the Polaris project.

A PERT network is a flowchart-like diagram that depicts the sequence of activities needed to complete a project and the time or costs associated with each activity. With a PERT network, a project manager must think through what has to be done, determine which events depend on one another, and identify potential trouble spots (see Exhibit 15–7). PERT also makes it easy to compare the effects alternative actions will have on scheduling and costs. PERT allows managers to monitor a project's progress, identify possible bottlenecks, and shift resources as necessary to keep the project on schedule.

To understand how to construct a PERT network, you need to know three terms: *events, activities*, and *critical path*. Let us define these terms, outline the steps in the PERT process, and then develop an example. **Events** are end points that represent the completion of major activities. Sometimes called milestones, events indicate that something significant has happened (such as receipt of purchased items) or an important component is finished. In PERT, events represent a point in time. **Activities**, on the other hand, are the actions that take place. Each activity consumes time, as determined on the basis of the time or resources required to progress from one event to another. The **critical path** is the longest or most time-consuming sequence of events and activities required to complete the project in the shortest amount of time.[63] Let's apply PERT to a construction manager's task of building a 6,500-square-foot custom home.

As a construction manager, you recognize that time really is money in your business. Delays can turn a profitable job into a money loser. Accordingly, you must determine how long it will take to complete the house. You have carefully dissected the entire project into

---

EXHIBIT 15–7   Developing PERT Charts

Developing a PERT network requires the manager to identify all key activities needed to complete a project, rank them in order of dependence, and estimate each activity's completion time. This procedure can be translated into five specific steps:

1. Identify every significant activity that must be achieved for a project to be completed. The accomplishment of each activity results in a set of events or outcomes.

2. Ascertain the order in which these events must be completed.

3. Diagram the flow of activities from start to finish, identifying each activity and its relationship to all other activities. Use circles to indicate events and arrows to represent activities. The result is a flowchart diagram that we call the PERT network.

4. Compute a time estimate for completing each activity, using a weighted average that employs an optimistic time estimate (t_o) of how long the activity would take under ideal conditions, a most-likely estimate (t_m) of the time the activity normally should take, and a pessimistic estimate (t_p) that represents the time that an activity should take under the worst possible conditions. The formula for calculating the expected time (t_e) is then

$$t_e = \frac{t_o + 4t_m + t_p}{6}$$

5. Finally, using a network diagram that contains time estimates for each activity, the manager can determine a schedule for the start and finish dates of each activity and for the entire project. Any delays that occur along the critical path require the most attention because they delay the entire project. That is, the critical path has no slack in it; therefore, any delay along that path immediately translates into a delay in the final deadline for the completed project.

---

activities and events. Exhibit 15–8 outlines the major events in the construction project and your estimate of the expected time required to complete each activity. Exhibit 15–9 depicts the PERT network based on the data in Exhibit 15–8.

HOW DOES PERT OPERATE?   Your PERT network tells you that if everything goes as planned, it will take just over 32 weeks to build the house. This time is calculated by tracing the network's critical path: A B C D E I J K L M N P Q. Any delay in completing the events along this path will delay the completion of the entire project. For example, if it took six weeks instead of four to frame the house (event E), the entire project would be delayed by two weeks (or the time beyond that expected). But a one-week delay for installing the brick (event H) would have little effect because that event is not on the critical path. By using PERT, the construction manager would know that no corrective action would be needed. Further delays in installing the brick, however, could present problems—for such delays may, in actuality, result in a new critical path. Now back to our original critical path dilemma.

Notice that the critical path passes through N, P, and Q. Our PERT chart (Exhibit 15–9) tells us that these three activities take four weeks. Wouldn't path N O Q be faster? Yes. The PERT network shows that it takes only 3.5 weeks to complete that path. So why isn't N O Q on the critical path? Because activity Q cannot begin until both activities O and P are completed. Although activity O takes half a week, activity P takes one full week. So, the earliest we can begin Q is after one week. What happens to the difference between the critical activity (activity P) time and the noncritical activity (activity O) time? The difference, in this case half a week, becomes slack time. **Slack time** is the time difference between

---

PERT network analysis
A flowchart-like diagram that depicts the sequence of activities needed to complete a project and the time or costs associated with each activity

events
End points that represent the completion of major activities

activities
Actions that take place

critical path
The longest or most time-consuming sequence of events and activities required to complete a project in the shortest amount of time

slack time
The time difference between the critical path and all other paths

EXHIBIT 15-8   Major Activities in Building a Custom Home

EVENT	DESCRIPTION	TIME (WEEKS)	PRECEDING ACTIVITY
A	Approve design and get permits	3	None
B	Perform excavation/lot clearing	1	A
C	Pour footers	1	B
D	Erect foundation walls	2	C
E	Frame house	4	D
F	Install windows	0.5	E
G	Shingle roof	0.5	E
H	Install brick front and siding	4	F, G
I	Install electrical, plumbing, and heating and A/C rough-ins	6	E
J	Install insulation	0.25	I
K	Install sheetrock	2	J
L	Finish and sand sheetrock	7	K
M	Install interior trim	2	L
N	Paint house (interior and exterior)	2	H, M
O	Install all cabinets	0.5	N
P	Install flooring	1	N
Q	Final touch-up and turn over house to home owner	1	O, P

the critical path and all other paths. What use is there for slack? If the project manager notices some slippage on a critical activity, perhaps slack time from a noncritical activity can be borrowed and temporarily assigned to work on the critical one.

As you can see, PERT is both a planning and a control tool. Not only does PERT help us estimate the times associated with scheduling a project, but it also gives us clues about where our controls should be placed. Because any event on the critical path that is delayed will delay the overall project (making us not only late but also probably over budget), our attention needs to be focused on the critical activities at all times. For example, if activity F (installing windows) is delayed by a week because supplies have not arrived, that is not a major issue. It's not on the critical path. But if activity P (installing flooring) is delayed from one week to two weeks, the entire project will be delayed by one week. Consequently, anything that has the immediate potential for delaying a project (critical activities) must be monitored closely.

As we said in the beginning of this chapter, it's the manager's job to manage the organization's operating systems, organizational control systems, and quality programs. That's the only way organizations will survive in today's increasingly competitive global economy.

EXHIBIT 15-9   A PERT Network for Building a Custom Home

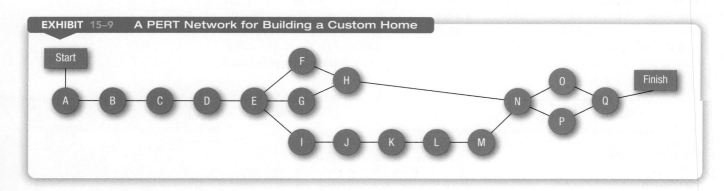

15 Review

CHAPTER SUMMARY

 15.1 Define operations management and explain its role. Operations management is the transformation process that converts resources into finished goods and services. Manufacturing organizations produce physical goods. Service organizations produce nonphysical outputs in the form of services. Productivity is a composite of people and operations variables. A manager should look for ways to successfully integrate people into the overall operations systems. Organizations must recognize the crucial role that operations management plays as part of their overall strategy in achieving successful performance.

15.2 Define the nature and purpose of value chain management. The value chain is the sequence of organizational work activities that add value at each step from raw materials to finished product. Value chain management is the process of managing the sequence of activities and information along the entire product chain.

The goal of value chain management is to create a value chain strategy that meets and exceeds customers' needs and desires and allows for full and seamless integration among all members of the chain.

Four benefits from value chain management include improved procurement, improved logistics, improved product development, and enhanced customer order management.

15.3 Describe how value chain management is done. The six main requirements for successful value chain management include coordination and collaboration, investment in technology, organizational processes, leadership, employees or human resources, and organizational culture and attitudes.

The obstacles to value chain management include organizational barriers (refusal to share information, reluctance to shake up the status quo, or security issues), unsupportive cultural attitudes, lack of required capabilities, and employees unwilling or unable to do it.

 15.4 Discuss contemporary issues in managing operations. Companies are looking at ways to harness technology to improve their operations management by extensive collaboration and cost control.

ISO 9000 is a series of international quality management standards that set uniform guidelines for processes to ensure that products conform to customer requirements. Six Sigma is a quality standard that establishes a goal of no more than 3.4 defects per million units or procedures.

Project management involves getting a project's activities done on time, within budget, and accomplished to specifications. A project is a one-time-only set of activities that has a definite beginning and ending point in time. Popular project scheduling tools include Gantt charts, load charts, and PERT network analysis.

MyManagementLab For more resources, please visit **www.mymanagementlab.com**

UNDERSTANDING THE CHAPTER

1. What is operations management and how is it used in both manufacturing and service organizations?

2. What strategic role does operations management play?

3. How might operations management apply to other managerial functions besides control?

4. Do you think that manufacturing or service organizations have greater need of operations management? Explain.

5. What is a value chain? What is value chain management? What is the goal of value chain management?

6. What types of organizational benefits does value chain management provide? What obstacles stand in the way of successful value chain management?

7. Explain why managing productivity is important in operations management.

8. Who has the power in the value chain? Explain your response.

9. Choose two tasks that you do every week (for example, shop for groceries, host a poker party, clean your house/apartment, do laundry). For each one, identify how you could (a) be more productive in doing that task, and (b) have higher-quality output from that task.

10. Select a company with which you're familiar. Describe its value chain. Be as specific as possible in your description. Evaluate how it "uses" the value chain to create value.

Go to p. 457

YOUR TURN ᵀᴼ/ᴮᴱ A MANAGER for Chapter 15.

Endnotes

1. "Starbucks' Quest for Healthy Growth: An Interview with Howard Schultz," *McKinsey Quarterly,* no. 2 (2001), pp. 34–43; "Return to Glory," *Retail Traffic,* May/June 2011, p. 38; J. Jannarone, "Grounds for Concern at Starbucks," *Wall Street Journal,* May 3, 2011, p. C10; M. Morrison, "Bang for Its Starbucks: Hits No. 3 Despite Limited Ad Spending," *Advertising Age,* May 2, 2011, pp. 1+; W. Kendall, "A Long, Hard Grind," *Management Today,* May 2011, p. 27; "Howard Schultz, On Getting a Second Shot," *Inc.,* April 2011, pp. 52–54; "Starbucks Corp. Plans Retail Push," *Nation's Restaurant News,* April 4, 2011, p. 6; "Starbucks Marks 40th Anniversary," *Beverage Industry,* April 2011, p. 8; R. Lowenstein, "When Latte Lost Its Luster," *Wall Street Journal,* March 29, 2011, p. A17; H. Schultz, "How Starbucks Got Its Mojo Back," *Newsweek,* March 21, 2011, pp. 50–55; G. Charles, "Change Brewing at Starbucks," *Marketing,* January 2011, pp. 14–15; "Starbucks Outlines Strategies for Growth," *Beverage Industry,* January 2011, p. 14; and H. Edwards, "Howard Schultz's Tall Order," *Marketing,* January 2011, p. 19; and S. Berfield, "Starbucks: Howard Schultz vs. Howard Schultz," *BusinessWeek Online,* August 6, 2009; J. Jargon, "Latest Starbucks Buzzword: 'Lean' Japanese Techniques," *Wall Street Journal,* August 4, 2009, p. A1.
2. D. Eng, "Cheesecake Factory's Winning Formula," *Fortune,* May 2, 2011, pp. 19–20; and D. McGinn, "Faster Food," *Newsweek,* April 19, 2004, pp. E20–E22.
3. *World Factbook 2011,* http://www.cia.gov/library/publications/the-world-factbook/.
4. Ibid.
5. D. Michaels and J. L. Lunsford, "Streamlined Plane Making," *Wall Street Journal,* April 1, 2005, pp. B1+.
6. T. Aeppel, "Workers Not Included," *Wall Street Journal,* November 19, 2002, pp. B1+.
7. A. Aston and M. Arndt, "The Flexible Factory," *BusinessWeek,* May 5, 2003, pp. 90–91.
8. P. Panchak, "Pella Drives Lean Throughout the Enterprise," *IndustryWeek,* June 2003, pp. 74–77.
9. J. Ordonez, "McDonald's to Cut the Cooking Time of Its French Fries," *Wall Street Journal,* May 19, 2000, p. B2.
10. C. Fredman, "The Devil in the Details," *Executive Edge,* April–May, 1999, pp. 36–39.
11. http://new.skoda-auto.com/Documents/AnnualReports/skoda_auto_annual_report_2007_%20EN_FINAL.pdf (July 8, 2008); and T. Mudd, "The Last Laugh," *IndustryWeek,* September 18, 2000, pp. 38–44.
12. From the Past to the Present box based on "Honorary Members Form Impressive Lineup of Quality Thinkers," *Quality Progress,* March 2011, p. 17; "W. Edwards Deming," *Quality Progress,* November 2010, p. 17; R. Aguayo, *Dr. Deming: The American Who Taught the Japanese About Quality* (New York: Fireside

Press, 1991); M. Walton, *The Deming Management Method* (New York: Penguin Group, 1986); and W. E. Deming, "Improvement of Quality and Productivity Through Action by Management," *National Productivity Review,* Winter 1981–1982, pp. 12–22.
13. T. Vinas, "Little Things Mean a Lot," *IndustryWeek,* November 2002, p. 55.
14. P. Panchak, "Shaping the Future of Manufacturing," *IndustryWeek,* January 2005, pp. 38–44; M. Hammer, "Deep Change: How Operational Innovation Can Transform Your Company," *Harvard Business Review,* April 2004, pp. 84–94; S. Levy, "The Connected Company," *Newsweek,* April 28, 2003, pp. 40–48; and J. Teresko, "Plant Floor Strategy," *IndustryWeek,* July 2002, pp. 26–32.
15. T. Laseter, K. Ramdas, and D. Swerdlow, "The Supply Side of Design and Development," *Strategy & Business,* Summer 2003, p. 23; J. Jusko, "Not All Dollars and Cents," *IndustryWeek,* April 2002, p. 58; and D. Drickhamer, "Medical Marvel," *IndustryWeek,* March 2002, pp. 47–49.
16. Q. H. Soon and Z. M. Udin, "Supply Chain Management from the Perspective of Value Chain Flexibility: An Exploratory Study," *Journal of Manufacturing Technology Management* (May 2011), pp. 506–526; G. Soni and R. Kodali, "A Critical Analysis of Supply Chain Management Content in Empirical Research," *Business Process Management,* April 2011, pp. 238–256; and J. H. Sheridan, "Managing the Value Chain," *IndustryWeek,* September 6, 1999, pp. 1–4, available online in archives at www.industryweek.com.
17. "Supply Chain Management: A New Narrative," *Strategic Direction,* March 2011, pp. 18–21; and J. H. Sheridan, "Managing the Value Chain."
18. S. Leibs, "Getting Ready: Your Suppliers," *IndustryWeek,* www. industryweek.com (September 6, 1999).
19. See, for example, J. Jusko, "Procurement—Not All Dollars and Cents," *IndustryWeek,* www.industryweek.com (April 4, 2002).
20. See "News Item Future Challenges for the Aromatics Supply Chain," speech given by Nancy Sullivan, Vice President Aromatics & Phenol, to the First European Aromatics and Derivatives Conference, London, UK (May 29, 2002). Available online at http://www.shellchemicals.com/newsroom/1,1098.71.00.html.
21. D. Bartholomew, "The Infrastructure," *IndustryWeek,* September 6, 1999, p. 1.
22. G. Taninecz, "Forging the Chain," *IndustryWeek,* May 15, 2000, pp. 40–46.
23. T. Vinas, "A Map of the World: IW Value-Chain Survey," *IndustryWeek,* September 2005, pp. 27–34.
24. Right or Wrong box based on C. Hausman, "Ethics of Using Store's Parking Lot Fuels Lively Debate in Newspaper Series,"

Ethics Newsline Online, April 25, 2011; J. Rose, "Ethics of Customer Parking in Portland: Circling the Block One More Time," *Oregonian Online,* April 21, 2011; and J. Rose, "The Ethics of 'Customer Only' Parking in the Pearl—and Beyond," *Oregonian Online,* April 16, 2011.

25. See J. H. Sheridan, "Now It's a Job for the CEO," *IndustryWeek,* March 20, 2000, pp. 22–30.
26. R. Norman and R. Ramirez, "From Value Chain to Value Constellation," *Harvard Business Review on Managing the Value Chain* (Boston: Harvard Business School Press, 2000), pp. 185–219.
27. S. Leibs, "Getting Ready: Your Customers," *IndustryWeek,* September 6, 1999, p. 4.
28. See, for example, C. Lunan, "Workers Doing More in Less Time," *Charlotte Observer,* June 1, 2002, p. D1.
29. S. Leibs, "Getting Ready: Your Customers," p. 3.
30. See, for instance, L. Harrington, "The Accelerated Value Chain: Supply Chain Management Just Got Smarter, Faster, and More Cost-Effective, Thanks to a Groundbreaking Alliance Between Intel and Technologies," *IndustryWeek,* April 2002, pp. 45–51.
31. Ibid.
32. Ibid.; and J. H. Sheridan, "Managing the Value Chain."
33. J. H. Sheriden, "Managing the Value Chain," p. 3.
34. S. Leibs, "Getting Ready: Your Customers," p. 4.
35. J. H. Sheriden, "Managing the Value Chain," pp. 2–3; S. Leibs, "Getting Ready: Your Customers," pp. 1, 4; and D. Bartholomew, "The Infrastructure," p. 6.
36. And the Survey Says box based on "Innovation Nation," *Industry Week,* November 2010, p. 15; "First-Hand Accounts," *Industry Week,* July 2008, p. 28; "State of the Workforce Report," *IndustryWeek,* November 2008, p. 18; "Sustainable Supply Chains," *IndustryWeek,* December 2008, p. 57; "Taking Charge of Mobile Workforce Costs," *IndustryWeek,* August 2009, p. 47; and "The Future of Manufacturing," *IndustryWeek,* November 2008, pp. 51–57.
37. G. Taninecz, "Forging the Chain."
38. S. Leibs, "Getting Ready: Your Customers," p. 1.
39. Ibid.
40. Ibid.
41. D. Drickhamer, "On Target," *IndustryWeek,* October 16, 2000, pp. 111–112.
42. S. Leibs, "Getting Ready: Your Customers," p. 2.
43. Ibid.
44. "Top Security Threats and Management Issues Facing Corporate America: 2003 Survey of *Fortune* 1000 Companies," ASIS International and Pinkerton, www.asisonline.org.
45. J. H. Sheridan, "Managing the Value Chain," p. 4.
46. S. Rosenbloom, "Solution, or Mess? A Milk Jug for a Green Earth," *New York Times Online,* June 30, 2008.
47. K. T. Greenfeld, "Taco Bell and the Golden Age of Drive-Thru," *Bloomberg BusinessWeek Online,* May 5, 2011;

and S. Anderson, Associated Press, "Restaurants Gear Up for Window Wars," *Springfield, Missouri, News-Leader,* January 27, 2006, p. 5B.
48. Technology and the Manager's Job box based on S. Minter, "What Is Advanced Manufacturing?" *IndustryWeek,* August 2009, p. 7; J. Bush, "Russia's Factories Shift Gears," *BusinessWeek,* May 18, 2009, pp. 50–51; D. Blanchard, "A Manufacturer for All Seasons," *IndustryWeek,* December 2008, p. 7; J. Teresko, "Planning the Factory of the Future," *IndustryWeek,* December 2008, pp. 22–24; and J. Teresko, "Winning with Digital Manufacturing," *IndustryWeek,* July 2008, pp. 45–47.
49. D. Bartholomew, "Quality Takes a Beating," *IndustryWeek,* March 2006, pp. 46–54; J. Carey and M. Arndt, "Making Pills the Smart Way," *BusinessWeek,* May 3, 2004, pp. 102–103; and A. Barrett, "Schering's Dr. Feelbetter?" *BusinessWeek,* June 23, 2003, pp. 55–56.
50. T. Vinas, "Six Sigma Rescue," *IndustryWeek,* March 2004, p. 12.
51. J. S. McClenahen, "Prairie Home Companion," *IndustryWeek,* October 2005, pp. 45–46.
52. T. Vinas, "Zeroing In on the Customer," *IndustryWeek,* October 2004, pp. 61–62.
53. W. Royal, "Spotlight Shines on Maquiladora," *IndustryWeek,* October 16, 2000, pp. 91–92.
54. See B. Whitford and R. Andrew (eds.), *The Pursuit of Quality* (Perth: Beaumont Publishing, 1994).
55. D. Drickhamer, "Road to Excellence," *IndustryWeek,* October 16, 2000, pp. 117–118.
56. J. Heizer and B. Render, *Operations Management,* 10th ed. (Upper Saddle River, NJ: Prentice Hall, 2011), p. 193.
57. G. Hasek, "Merger Marries Quality Efforts," *IndustryWeek,* August 21, 2000, pp. 89–92.
58. J. Jusko, "An Elite Crew," *IndustryWeek,* March 2011, pp. 17–18; and M. Arndt, "Quality Isn't Just for Widgets," *BusinessWeek,* July 22, 2002, pp. 72–73.
59. E. White, "Rethinking the Quality Improvement Program," *Wall Street Journal,* September 19, 2005, p. B3.
60. M. Arndt, "Quality Isn't Just for Widgets."
61. For a thorough overview of project management, see S. Berkun, *The Art of Project Management* (Upper Saddle River, NJ: Prentice Hall, 2005); or J. K. Pinto, *Project Management: Achieving Competitive Advantage and MS Project* (Upper Saddle River, NJ: Prentice Hall, 2007).
62. H. Maylor, "Beyond the Gantt Chart: Project Management Moving On," *European Management Journal* (February 2001), pp. 92–101.
63. For additional information on CPM, see W. A. Haga and K. A. Marold, "A Simulation Approach to the PERT/CPM Time-Cost Trade-Off Problem," *Project Management Journal* (June 2004), pp. 31–37.

MANAGING ENTREPRENEURIAL VENTURES

Russell Simmons is an entrepreneur. He cofounded Def Jam Records because the emerging group of New York hip-hop artists needed a record company, and the big record companies refused to take a chance on unknown artists. Def Jam was just one piece of Simmons's corporation, Rush Communications, which also included a management company; a clothing company called Phat Farm; a movie production house; television shows; a magazine; and an advertising agency. In 1999, Simmons sold his stake in Def Jam to Universal Music Group, and in 2004, he sold Phat Farm. Today, Simmons is involved in UniRush, a Cincinnati company that sells a prepaid Visa debit card and Russell Simmons'Argyle Culture, a clothing line aimed at older men. *USA Today* named Simmons one of the top 25 Influential People while *Inc.* magazine named him one of America's 25 Most Fascinating Entrepreneurs.

In this appendix, we're going to look at the activities engaged in by entrepreneurs like Russell Simmons. We'll start by looking at the context of entrepreneurship and then examining entrepreneurship from the perspective of the four managerial functions: planning, organizing, leading, and controlling.

What Is Entrepreneurship?

Entrepreneurship is the process of starting new businesses, generally in response to opportunities. For instance, Fred Carl, founder of the Viking Range Corporation, saw an opportunity to create an appliance that combined the best features of commercial and residential ranges.

Many people think that entrepreneurial ventures and small businesses are the same, but they're not. Entrepreneurs create **entrepreneurial ventures**—organizations that pursue opportunities, are characterized by innovative practices, and have growth and profitability as their main goals. On the other hand, a **small business** is an independent business having fewer than 500 employees that doesn't necessarily engage in any new or innovative practices and that has relatively little impact on its industry. A small business isn't necessarily entrepreneurial because it's small. To be entrepreneurial means that the business is innovative and seeking out new opportunities. Even though entrepreneurial ventures may start small, they pursue growth. Some new small firms may grow, but many remain small businesses, by choice or by default.

Who's Starting Entrepreneurial Ventures?

"Call them accidental entrepreneurs, unintended entrepreneurs, or forced entrepreneurs." As the unemployment rate hovers around double digits, many corporate "refugees" are becoming entrepreneurs. These individuals are looking to entrepreneurship, not because they sense some great opportunity, but because there are no jobs. The Index of Entrepreneurial Activity by the Kauffman Foundation showed the rate at which new businesses formed in 2010 remained high, representing the "highest level of entrepreneurship over the past decade and a half." The report found that "the patterns provided some early evidence that 'necessity' entrepreneurship is increasing and 'opportunity' entrepreneurship is decreasing." But "accidental or by design," entrepreneurship is on the rise again.

As many entrepreneurs (successful and not-so-successful) would attest, being an entrepreneur isn't easy. According to the Small Business Administration, only two-thirds of new businesses survive at least two years. The survival rate falls to 44 percent at four years, and to 31 percent at seven. But the interesting thing is that entrepreneurial venture survival rates are about the same in economic expansions and recessions.

What Do Entrepreneurs Do?

Describing what entrepreneurs do isn't an easy or simple task! No two entrepreneurs' work activities are exactly alike. In a general sense, entrepreneurs create something new, something different. They search for change, respond to it, and exploit it.

Initially, an entrepreneur is engaged in assessing the potential for the entrepreneurial venture and then dealing with start-up issues. In exploring the entrepreneurial context, entrepreneurs gather information, identify potential opportunities, and pinpoint possible competitive advantage(s). Then, armed with this information, an entrepreneur researches the venture's feasibility—uncovering business ideas, looking at competitors, and exploring financing options.

After looking at the potential of the proposed venture and assessing the likelihood of pursuing it successfully, an entrepreneur proceeds to plan the venture. This process includes such activities as developing a viable organizational mission, exploring organizational culture issues, and creating a well-thought-out business plan. Once these planning issues have been resolved, the entrepreneur must look at organizing the venture, which involves choosing a legal form of business organization, addressing other legal issues such as patent or copyright searches, and coming up with an appropriate organizational design for structuring how work is going to be done.

Only after these start-up activities have been completed is the entrepreneur ready to actually launch the venture. A launch involves setting goals and strategies, and establishing the technology-operations methods, marketing plans, information systems, financial-accounting systems, and cash flow management systems.

Once the entrepreneurial venture is up and running, the entrepreneur's attention switches to managing it. What's involved with actually managing the entrepreneurial venture? An important activity is managing the various processes that are part of every business: making decisions, establishing action plans, analyzing external and internal environments, measuring and evaluating performance, and making needed changes. Also, the entrepreneur must perform activities associated with managing people including selecting and hiring, appraising and training, motivating, managing conflict, delegating tasks, and being an effective leader. Finally, the entrepreneur must manage the venture's growth including such activities as developing and designing growth strategies, dealing with crises, exploring various avenues for financing growth, placing a value on the venture, and perhaps even eventually exiting the venture.

What Planning Do Entrepreneurs Need to Do?

Planning is important to entrepreneurial ventures. Once a venture's feasibility has been thoroughly researched, an entrepreneur then must look at planning the venture. The most important thing that an entrepreneur does in planning the venture is developing a **business plan**—a written document that summarizes a business opportunity and defines and articulates how the identified opportunity is to be seized and exploited. A written business plan can range from basic to thorough. The most basic type of business plan would simply include an *executive summary,* sort of a mini-business plan that's no

---

entrepreneurship
The process of starting new businesses, generally in response to opportunities

entrepreneurial ventures
Organizations that pursue opportunities, are characterized by innovative practices, and have growth and profitability as their main goals

small business
An independent business having fewer than 500 employees that doesn't necessarily engage in any new or innovative practices and that has relatively little impact on its industry

business plan
A written document that summarizes a business opportunity and defines and articulates how the identified opportunity is to be seized and exploited

longer than two pages. A *synopsis* type plan is a little more involved. It's been described as an "executive summary on steroids." In addition to the executive summary, it includes a business proposal that explains why the idea is relevant to potential investors. A *summary business plan* includes an executive summary and a page or so of explanation of each of the key components of a business plan. A *full business plan* is the traditional business plan, which we describe fully next. Finally, an *operational business plan* is the most detailed (50 or more pages) that is used by ventures already operating with an existing strategy. It's often used to "plan the business" but also can be used to raise additional money or to attract potential acquirers. It's important for entrepreneurs to know which type of business plan they need for their purposes.

What's in a Full Business Plan?

For many would-be entrepreneurs, developing and writing a business plan seems like a daunting task. However, a good business plan is valuable. It pulls together all of the elements of the entrepreneur's vision into a single coherent document. The business plan requires careful planning and creative thinking. But if done well, it can be a convincing document that serves many functions. It serves as a blueprint and road map for operating the business. And the business plan is a "living" document, guiding organizational decisions and actions throughout the life of the business, not just in the start-up stage.

If an entrepreneur has completed a feasibility study, much of the information included in it becomes the basis for the business plan. A good business plan covers six major areas: executive summary, analysis of opportunity, analysis of the context, description of the business, financial data and projections, and supporting documentation.

Executive summary. The executive summary summarizes the key points that the entrepreneur wants to make about the proposed entrepreneurial venture. These might include a brief mission statement; primary goals; brief history of the entrepreneurial venture, maybe in the form of a timeline; key people involved in the venture; nature of the business; concise product or service descriptions; brief explanations of market niche, competitors, and competitive advantage; proposed strategies; and selected key financial information.

Analysis of opportunity. In this section of the business plan, an entrepreneur presents the details of the perceived opportunity, which essentially includes (1) sizing up the market by describing the demographics of the target market; (2) describing and evaluating industry trends; and (3) identifying and evaluating competitors.

Analysis of the context. Whereas the opportunity analysis focuses on the opportunity in a specific industry and market, the context analysis takes a much broader perspective. Here, the entrepreneur describes the broad external changes and trends taking place in the economic, political-legal, technological, and global environments.

Description of the business. In this section, an entrepreneur describes how the entrepreneurial venture is going to be organized, launched, and managed. It includes a thorough description of the mission statement; a description of the desired organizational culture; marketing plans including overall marketing strategy, pricing, sales tactics, service-warranty policies, and advertising and promotion tactics; product development plans such as an explanation of development status, tasks, difficulties and risks, and anticipated costs; operational plans, including a description of proposed geographic location, facilities and needed improvements, equipment, and work flow; human resource plans, including a description of key management persons, composition of board of directors including their background experience and skills, current and future staffing needs, compensation and benefits, and training needs; and an overall schedule and timetable of events.

Financial data and projections. Every effective business plan contains financial data and projections. Although the calculations and interpretation may be difficult, they are absolutely critical. No business plan is complete without financial information. Financial plans should cover at least three years and contain projected income statements, pro forma cash flow analysis (monthly for the first year and quarterly for the next two), pro forma balance sheets, breakeven analysis, and cost controls. If major equipment or other capital purchases are expected, the items, costs, and available collateral should be listed. All financial projections and analyses should include explanatory notes, especially where the data seem contradictory or questionable.

Supporting documentation. This *is* an important component of an effective business plan. The entrepreneur should back up his or her descriptions with charts, graphs, tables, photographs, or other visual tools. In addition, it might be important to include information (personal and work-related) about the key participants in the entrepreneurial venture.

Just as the idea for an entrepreneurial venture takes time to germinate, so does the writing of a good business plan. It's important for an entrepreneur to put serious thought and consideration into the plan. It's not an easy thing to do. However, the resulting document should be valuable in current and future planning efforts.

What Issues Are Involved in Organizing an Entrepreneurial Venture?

Once the start-up and planning issues for the entrepreneurial venture have been addressed, the entrepreneur is ready to begin organizing the entrepreneurial venture. The main organizing issues an entrepreneur must address include the legal forms of organization, organizational design and structure, and human resource management.

What Are the Legal Forms of Organization for Entrepreneurial Ventures?

The first organizing decision that an entrepreneur must make is a critical one. It's the form of legal ownership for the venture. The two primary factors affecting this decision are taxes and legal liability. An entrepreneur wants to minimize the impact of both of these factors. The right choice can protect the entrepreneur from legal liability as well as save tax dollars, in both the short run and the long run.

The three basic ways to organize an entrepreneurial venture are sole proprietorship, partnership, and corporation. However, when you include the variations of these basic organizational alternatives, you end up with six possible choices, each with its own tax consequences, liability issues, and pros and cons. These six choices are sole proprietorship, general partnership, limited liability partnership (LLP), C corporation, S corporation, and limited liability company (LLC).

The decision regarding the legal form of organization is important because it has significant tax and liability consequences. Although the legal form of organization can be changed, it's not easy to do. An entrepreneur needs to think carefully about what's important, especially in the areas of flexibility, taxes, and amount of personal liability in choosing the best form of organization.

What Type of Organizational Structure Should Entrepreneurial Ventures Use?

The choice of an appropriate organizational structure is also an important decision when organizing an entrepreneurial venture. At some point, successful entrepreneurs find that they can't do everything. They need people. The entrepreneur must then decide on the most appropriate structural arrangement for effectively and efficiently carrying out the organization's activities. Without a suitable type of organizational structure, an entrepreneurial venture may soon find itself in a chaotic situation.

In many small firms, the organizational structure tends to evolve with very little intentional and deliberate planning by the entrepreneur. For the most part, the structure may be very simple—one person does whatever is needed. As an entrepreneurial venture grows and the entrepreneur finds it increasingly difficult to go it alone, employees are brought on board to perform certain functions or duties that the entrepreneur can't handle. As the company continues to grow, these individuals tend to perform those same functions. Soon, each functional area may require managers and employees.

As the venture evolves to a more deliberate structure, an entrepreneur faces a whole new set of challenges. All of a sudden, he or she must share decision making and operating responsibilities, which are typically the most difficult things for an entrepreneur to do—letting go and allowing someone else to make decisions. *After all*, he or she reasons, *how can anyone know this business as well as I do?* Also, what might have been a fairly informal, loose, and flexible atmosphere that worked well when the organization was small may no longer be effective. Many entrepreneurs are greatly concerned about keeping that "small company" atmosphere alive even as the venture grows and evolves into a more structured arrangement. But having a structured organization doesn't necessarily mean giving up flexibility, adaptability, and freedom. In fact, the structural design may be as fluid as the entrepreneur feels comfortable with and yet still have the rigidity it needs to operate efficiently.

Organizational design decisions in entrepreneurial ventures also revolve around the six elements of organizational structure discussed in Chapter 6: work specialization, departmentalization, chain of command, span of control, amount of centralization-decentralization, and amount of formalization. Decisions about these six elements will determine whether an entrepreneur designs a more mechanistic or organic organizational structure. When would each be preferable? A mechanistic structure would be preferable when cost efficiencies are critical to the venture's competitive advantage; when more control over employees' work activities is important; if the venture produces standardized products in a routine fashion; and when the external environment is relatively stable and certain. An organic structure would be most appropriate when innovation is critical to the organization's competitive advantage; for smaller organizations where rigid approaches to dividing and coordinating work aren't necessary; if the organization produces customized products in a flexible setting; and where the external environment is dynamic, complex, and uncertain.

What Human Resource Management (HRM) Issues Do Entrepreneurs Face?

As an entrepreneurial venture grows, additional employees must be hired to perform the increased workload. As employees are brought on board, two HRM issues of particular importance are employee recruitment and employee retention.

An entrepreneur wants to ensure that the venture has the people to do the required work. Recruiting new employees is one of the biggest challenges that entrepreneurs face. In fact, the ability of small firms to successfully recruit appropriate employees is consistently rated as one of the most important factors influencing organizational success.

Entrepreneurs, particularly, look for high-potential people who can perform multiple roles during various stages of venture growth. They look for individuals who "buy into" the venture's entrepreneurial culture—individuals who have a passion for the business. Unlike their corporate counterparts who often focus on filling a job by matching a person to the job requirements, entrepreneurs look to fill in critical skills gaps. They're looking for people who are exceptionally capable and self-motivated, flexible, multi-skilled, and who can help grow the entrepreneurial venture. While corporate managers tend to focus on using traditional HRM practices and techniques, entrepreneurs are more concerned with matching characteristics of the person to the values and culture of the organization; that is, they focus on matching the person to the organization.

Getting competent and qualified people into the venture is just the first step in effectively managing the human resources. An entrepreneur wants to keep the people he or she has hired and trained. A unique and important employee retention issue entrepreneurs must deal with is compensation. Whereas traditional organizations are more likely to view compensation from the perspective of monetary rewards (base pay, benefits, and incentives), smaller entrepreneurial firms are more likely to view compensation from a total rewards perspective. For these firms, compensation encompasses psychological rewards, learning opportunities, and recognition in addition to monetary rewards (base pay and incentives).

What Issues Do Entrepreneurs Face in Leading an Entrepreneurial Venture?

Leading is an important function of entrepreneurs. As an entrepreneurial venture grows and people are brought on board, an entrepreneur takes on a new role—that of a leader. In this section, we want to look at what's involved with that. First, we're going to look at the unique personality characteristics of entrepreneurs. Then we're going to discuss the important role entrepreneurs play in motivating employees through empowerment and leading the venture and employee teams.

What Type of Personality Do Entrepreneurs Have?

Think of someone you know who is an entrepreneur. Maybe it's someone you personally know or maybe it's someone you've read about, like Bill Gates of Microsoft. How would you describe this person's personality? One of the most researched areas of entrepreneurship has been the search to determine what—if any—psychological characteristics entrepreneurs have in common; what types of personality traits entrepreneurs have that might distinguish them from non-entrepreneurs; and what traits entrepreneurs have that might predict who will be a successful entrepreneur.

Is there a classic "entrepreneurial personality"? Although trying to pinpoint specific personality characteristics that all entrepreneurs share has the same problem as identifying the trait theories of leadership—that is, being able to identify specific personality traits that *all* entrepreneurs share—this hasn't stopped entrepreneurship researchers from listing common traits. For instance, one list of personality characteristics included the following: high level of motivation, abundance of self-confidence, ability to be involved for the long term, high energy level, persistent problem solver, high degree of initiative, ability to set goals, and moderate risk-taker. Another list of characteristics of "successful" entrepreneurs included high energy level, great persistence, resourcefulness, the desire and ability to be self-directed, and relatively high need for autonomy.

Another development in defining entrepreneurial personality characteristics was the proactive personality scale to predict an individual's likelihood of pursuing entrepreneurial ventures. The **proactive personality** is a personality trait describing those individuals who are more prone to take actions to influence their environment—that is, they're more proactive. Obviously, an entrepreneur is likely to exhibit proactivity as he or she searches for opportunities and acts to take advantage of those opportunities. Various items on the proactive personality scale were found to be good indicators of a person's likelihood of becoming an entrepreneur, including gender, education, having an entrepreneurial parent, and possessing a proactive personality. In addition, studies have shown that entrepreneurs have greater risk propensity than do managers. However, this propensity is moderated by the entrepreneur's primary goal. Risk propensity is greater for entrepreneurs whose primary goal is growth versus those whose focus is on producing family income.

proactive personality
A personality trait describing those individuals who are more prone to take actions to influence their environment

How Can Entrepreneurs Motivate Employees?

When you're motivated to do something, don't you find yourself energized and willing to work hard at doing whatever it is you're excited about? Wouldn't it be great if all of a venture's employees were energized, excited, and willing to work hard at their jobs? Having motivated employees is an important goal for any entrepreneur, and employee empowerment is an important motivational tool entrepreneurs can use.

Although it's not easy for entrepreneurs to do, employee empowerment—giving employees the power to make decisions and take actions on their own—is an important motivational approach. Why? Because successful entrepreneurial ventures must be quick and nimble, ready to pursue opportunities and go off in new directions. Empowered employees can provide that flexibility and speed. When employees are empowered, they often display stronger work motivation, better work quality, higher job satisfaction, and lower turnover.

Empowerment is a philosophical concept that entrepreneurs have to "buy into." It doesn't come easily. In fact, it's hard for many entrepreneurs to do. Their life is tied up in the business. They've built it from the ground up. But continuing to grow the entrepreneurial venture is eventually going to require handing over more responsibilities to employees. How can entrepreneurs empower employees? For many entrepreneurs, it's a gradual process.

Entrepreneurs can begin by using participative decision making in which employees provide input into decisions. Although getting employees to participate in decisions isn't quite taking the full plunge into employee empowerment, at least it's a way to begin tapping into the collective array of employees' talents, skills, knowledge, and abilities.

Another way to empower employees is through delegation—the process of assigning certain decisions or specific job duties to employees. By delegating decisions and duties, the entrepreneur is turning over the responsibility for carrying them out.

When an entrepreneur is finally comfortable with the idea of employee empowerment, fully empowering employees means redesigning their jobs so they have discretion over the way they do their work. It's allowing employees to do their work effectively and efficiently by using their creativity, imagination, knowledge, and skills.

If an entrepreneur implements employee empowerment properly—that is, with complete and total commitment to the program and with appropriate employee training—results can be impressive for the entrepreneurial venture and for the empowered employees. The business can enjoy significant productivity gains, quality improvements, more satisfied customers, increased employee motivation, and improved morale. Employees can enjoy the opportunities to do a greater variety of work that is more interesting and challenging.

How Can Entrepreneurs Be Leaders?

The last topic we want to discuss in this section is the role of an entrepreneur as a leader. In this role, the entrepreneur has certain leadership responsibilities in leading the venture and in leading employee work teams.

Today's successful entrepreneur must be like the leader of a jazz ensemble known for its improvisation, innovation, and creativity. Max DePree, former head of Herman Miller, Inc., a leading office furniture manufacturer known for its innovative leadership approaches, said it best in his book, *Leadership Jazz*, "Jazz band leaders must choose the music, find the right musicians, and perform—in public. But the effect of the performance depends on so many things—the environment, the volunteers playing the band, the need for everybody to perform as individuals and as a group, the absolute dependence of the leader on the members of the band, the need for the followers to play well. . . . The leader of the jazz band has the beautiful opportunity to draw the best out of the other musicians. We have much to learn from jazz band leaders, for jazz, like leadership, combines the unpredictability of the future with the gifts of individuals."

The way an entrepreneur leads the venture should be much like the jazz leader—drawing the best out of other individuals, even given the unpredictability of the situation. One way an entrepreneur does this is through the vision he or she creates for the organization.

In fact, the driving force through the early stages of the entrepreneurial venture is often the visionary leadership of the entrepreneur. The entrepreneur's ability to articulate a coherent, inspiring, and attractive vision of the future is a key test of his or her leadership. But if an entrepreneur can do this, the results can be worthwhile. A study contrasting visionary and nonvisionary companies showed that visionary companies outperformed the nonvisionary ones by six times on standard financial criteria, and their stocks outperformed the general market by 15 times.

As we know from Chapter 10, many organizations—entrepreneurial and otherwise—are using employee work teams to perform organizational tasks, create new ideas, and resolve problems. The three most common types of employee work teams in entrepreneurial ventures are empowered teams (teams that have the authority to plan and implement process improvements), self-directed teams (teams that are nearly autonomous and responsible for many managerial activities), and cross-functional teams (work teams composed of individuals from various specialties who work together on various tasks).

Developing and using teams is necessary because technology and market demands are forcing entrepreneurial ventures to make products faster, cheaper, and better. Tapping into the collective wisdom of a venture's employees and empowering them to make decisions just may be one of the best ways to adapt to change. In addition, a team culture can improve the overall workplace environment and morale. For team efforts to work, however, entrepreneurs must shift from the traditional command-and-control style to a coach-and-collaboration style.

What Controlling Issues Do Entrepreneurs Face?

Entrepreneurs must look at controlling their venture's operations in order to survive and prosper in both the short run and long run. The unique control issues that face entrepreneurs include managing growth, managing downturns, exiting the venture, and managing personal life choices and challenges.

How Is Growth Managed?

Growth is a natural and desirable outcome for entrepreneurial ventures. Growth is what distinguishes an entrepreneurial venture. Entrepreneurial ventures pursue growth. Growing slowly can be successful, but so can rapid growth.

Growing successfully doesn't occur randomly or by luck. Successfully pursuing growth typically requires an entrepreneur to manage all the challenges associated with growing, which entails planning, organizing, and controlling for growth.

How Are Downturns Managed?

Although organizational growth is a desirable and important goal for entrepreneurial ventures, what happens when things don't go as planned—when the growth strategies don't result in the intended outcomes and, in fact, result in a decline in performance? There are challenges, as well, in managing the downturns.

Nobody likes to fail, especially entrepreneurs. However, when an entrepreneurial venture faces times of trouble, what can be done? How can downturns be managed successfully? The first step is recognizing that a crisis is brewing. An entrepreneur should be alert to the warning signs of a business in trouble. Some signals of potential performance decline include inadequate or negative cash flow, excess number of employees, unnecessary and cumbersome administrative procedures, fear of conflict and taking risks, tolerance of work incompetence, lack of a clear mission or goals, and ineffective or poor communication within the organization.

Although an entrepreneur hopes to never have to deal with organizational downturns, declines, or crises, these situations do occur. After all, nobody likes to think about things going bad or taking a turn for the worse. But that's exactly what the entrepreneur should do—think about it *before* it happens (remember feedforward control from Chapter 14). It's important to have an up-to-date plan for covering crises. It's like mapping exit routes from your home in case of a fire. An entrepreneur wants to be prepared before an emergency hits. This plan should focus on providing specific details for controlling the most fundamental and critical aspects of running the venture—cash flow, accounts receivable, costs, and debt. Beyond having a plan for controlling the venture's critical inflows and outflows, other actions would involve identifying specific strategies for cutting costs and restructuring the venture.

What's Involved with Exiting the Venture?

Getting out of an entrepreneurial venture may seem to be a strange thing for entrepreneurs to do. However, the entrepreneur may come to a point at which he or she decides it's time to move on. That decision may be based on the fact that the entrepreneur hopes to capitalize financially on the investment in the venture—called **harvesting**—or that the entrepreneur is facing serious organizational performance problems and wants to get out, or even on the entrepreneur's desire to focus on other pursuits (personal or business). The issues involved with exiting the venture include choosing a proper business valuation method and knowing what's involved in the process of selling a business.

Although the hardest part of preparing to exit a venture may involve valuing it, other factors are also important. These include being prepared, deciding who will sell the business, considering the tax implications, screening potential buyers, and deciding whether to tell employees before or after the sale. The process of exiting the entrepreneurial venture should be approached as carefully as the process of launching it. If the entrepreneur is selling the venture on a positive note, he or she wants to realize the value built up in the business. If the venture is being exited because of declining performance, the entrepreneur wants to maximize the potential return.

Why Is It Important to Think About Managing Personal Challenges as an Entrepreneur?

Being an entrepreneur is extremely exciting and fulfilling, yet extremely demanding. It involves long hours, difficult demands, and high stress. Yet, many rewards can come with being an entrepreneur as well. In this section, we want to look at how entrepreneurs can make it work—that is, how can they be successful and effectively balance the demands of their work and personal lives?

Entrepreneurs are a special group. They're focused, persistent, hardworking, and intelligent. Because they put so much of themselves into launching and growing their entrepreneurial ventures, many may neglect their personal lives. Entrepreneurs often have to make sacrifices to pursue their entrepreneurial dreams. However, they can make it work. They can balance their work and personal lives. But how?

One of the most important things an entrepreneur can do is *become a good time manager*. Prioritize what needs to be done. Use a planner (daily, weekly, monthly) to help schedule priorities. Some entrepreneurs don't like taking the time to plan or prioritize, or they think it's a ridiculous waste of time. Yet identifying the important duties and distinguishing them from those that aren't so important actually makes an entrepreneur more efficient and effective. In addition, part of being a good time manager is delegating those decisions and actions the entrepreneur doesn't have to be personally involved in to trusted employees. Although it may be hard to let go of some of the things they've always done, entrepreneurs who delegate effectively will see their personal productivity levels rise.

Another suggestion for finding that balance is to *seek professional advice* in those areas of business where it's needed. Although entrepreneurs may be reluctant to spend scarce cash, the time, energy, and potential problems saved in the long run are well worth the investment. Competent professional advisers can provide entrepreneurs with information to make more intelligent decisions. Also, it's important to *deal with conflicts* as they arise—both workplace and family conflicts. If an entrepreneur doesn't deal with conflicts, negative feelings are likely to crop up and lead to communication breakdowns. When communication falls apart, vital information may get lost, and people (employees *and* family members) may start to assume the worst. It can turn into a nightmare situation that feeds upon itself. The best strategy is to deal with conflicts as they come up. Talk, discuss, argue (if you must), but an entrepreneur shouldn't avoid the conflict or pretend it doesn't exist.

Another suggestion for achieving that balance between work and personal life is to *develop a network of trusted friends and peers.* Having a group of people to talk with is a good way for an entrepreneur to think through problems and issues. The support and encouragement offered by these people can be an invaluable source of strength for an entrepreneur.

Finally, *recognize when your stress levels are too high.* Entrepreneurs *are* achievers. They like to make things happen. They thrive on working hard. Yet, too much stress can lead to significant physical and emotional problems (as we discussed in Chapter 8). Entrepreneurs have to learn when stress is overwhelming them and to do something about it. After all, what's the point of growing and building a thriving entrepreneurial venture if you're not around to enjoy it?

Sources: Entrepreneurship Module based on T. Padgett, "Russell Simmons: Getting Rich Is So Simple," *CNNMoney.com,* April 29, 2011; R. Schmidt and P. O'Connor, "Def Jam's Founder Out-Lobbies Big Banks," *Bloomberg BusinessWeek,* June 28, 2010, pp. 21–22; R. A. Smith, "From Phat to Skinny," *Wall Street Journal,* May 1, 2010, p. W7; J. Dean, "The Endless Flow of Russell Simmons," *Entrepreneur,* September 2009, pp. 24–28; S. Page, "Top 25 Influential People," *USA Today,* September 4, 2007, p. A10; S. Berfield, "Hip-Hop Nation," *BusinessWeek,* June 13, 2005, p. 12; R. Kurtz, "Russell Simmons, Rush Communications," *Inc.,* April 2004, p. 137; J. Reingold, "Rush Hour," *Fast Company,* November 2003, pp. 68–80; S. Berfield, "The CEO of Hip Hop," *BusinessWeek,* October 27, 2003, pp. 90–98; J. L. Roberts, "Beyond Definition," *Newsweek,* July 28, 2003, pp. 40–43; C. Dugas, "Hip-Hop Legend Far Surpassed Financial Goals," *USA Today,* May 15, 2003, p. 6B; "Jobless Entrepreneurship Tarnishes Steady Rate of U.S. Startup Activity, Kauffman Study Shows," www.kauffman.org/newsroom/ (March 7, 2011); "Frequently Asked Questions," *U.S. Small Business Administration,* www.sba.gov/advo (September 2008); D. E. Gumpert, "The Right Business Plan for the Job," *BusinessWeek Online,* January 7, 2008; W. H. Stewart, "Risk Propensity Differences Between Entrepreneurs and Managers: A Meta-Analytic Review," *Journal of Applied Psychology* (February 2001), pp. 145–153; I. O. Williamson, "Employer Legitimacy and Recruitment Success in Small Businesses," *Entrepreneurship Theory and Practice,* Fall 2000, pp. 27–42; R. L. Heneman, J. W. Tansky, and S. M. Camp, "Human Resource Management Practices in Small and Medium-Sized Enterprises: Unanswered Questions and Future Research Perspectives," *Entrepreneurship Theory and Practice,* Fall 2000, pp. 11–26; T. L. Hatten, *Small Business: Entrepreneurship and Beyond* (Upper Saddle River, NJ: Prentice Hall, 1997), p. 5; L. W. Busenitz, "Research on Entrepreneurial Alertness," *Journal of Small Business Management* (October 1996), pp. 35–44; J. M. Crant, "The Proactive Personality Scale as Predictor of Entrepreneurial Intentions," *Journal of Small Business Management* (July 1996), pp. 42–49; J. C. Collins and J. I. Porras, *Built to Last: Successful Habits of Visionary Companies* (New York: Harper Business, 1994); M. Depree, *Leadership Jazz* (New York: Currency Doubleday, 1992), pp. 8–9; P. B. Robinson, D. V. Simpson, J. C. Huefner, and H. K. Hunt, "An Attitude Approach to the Prediction of Entrepreneurship," *Entrepreneurship Theory and Practice,* Summer 1991, pp. 13–31; P. F. Drucker, *Innovation and Entrepreneurship: Practice and Principles* (New York: Harper & Row, 1985); and J. W. Carland, F. Hoy, W. R. Boulton, and J. C. Carland, "Differentiating Entrepreneurs from Small Business Owners: A Conceptualization," *Academy of Management Review,* 9, no. 2 (1984), pp. 354–359.

harvesting
Exiting a venture when an entrepreneur hopes to capitalize financially on the investment in the venture

CHAPTER 1

YOUR TURN
TO BE **A MANAGER**

Managers and **Management**

Skill Development: Becoming Politically Adept

Anyone who has had much work experience knows that politics exists in every organization. That is, people try to influence the distribution of advantages and disadvantages within the organization in their favor. Those who understand organizational politics typically thrive. Those who don't, regardless of how good their actual job skills are, often suffer by receiving less positive performance reviews, fewer promotions, and smaller salary increases. If you want to succeed as a manager, it helps to be politically adept.

Personal Insights: How Good Am I at Playing Politics?

Using the following 7-point scale, indicate the response that best describes how much you agree or disagree with each of the 18 statements.

1 = Strongly disagree
2 = Disagree
3 = Slightly disagree
4 = Neutral
5 = Slightly agree
6 = Agree
7 = Strongly agree

1. I spend a lot of time and effort making connections, working relationships, and networking with others. 1 2 3 4 5 6 7

2. I am able to make most people feel comfortable and at ease around me. 1 2 3 4 5 6 7

3. I am able to communicate easily and effectively with others. 1 2 3 4 5 6 7

4. It is easy for me to develop good rapport with most people. 1 2 3 4 5 6 7

5. I understand people very well. 1 2 3 4 5 6 7

6. I am good at building relationships with influential people at work. 1 2 3 4 5 6 7

7. I am particularly good at sensing the motivations and hidden agendas of others. 1 2 3 4 5 6 7

8. When communicating with others, it is important that they believe I am genuine and sincere in what I say and do. 1 2 3 4 5 6 7

9. I have developed a large network of colleagues and associates at work whom I can call on for support when I really need to get things done. 1 2 3 4 5 6 7

10. I know a lot of important people and am well connected at work. 1 2 3 4 5 6 7

11. I spend a lot of time at work developing connections and networking with others. 1 2 3 4 5 6 7

12. I am good at getting people to like me. 1 2 3 4 5 6 7

13. It is important that I make people believe I am genuine and sincere in what I say and do. 1 2 3 4 5 6 7

14. I try to show a genuine interest in other people. 1 2 3 4 5 6 7

15. I am good at using my connections and network to make things happen at work.   1 2 3 4 5 6 7

16. I have good intuition or "savvy" about how to present myself to others.   1 2 3 4 5 6 7

17. I always seem to instinctively know the right things to say or do to influence others.   1 2 3 4 5 6 7

18. I pay close attention to people's facial expressions.   1 2 3 4 5 6 7

Source: G. R. Ferris, R. W. Kolodinsky, R. W. Hochwarter, and D. D. Frink, "Conceptualization, Measurement, and Validation of the Political Skill Construct," paper presented at the 61st National Academy of Management Conference, Washington, DC, August 2001.

Analysis and Interpretation

The authors of this instrument define political skill as "an interpersonal style construct that combines social perceptiveness or astuteness with the capacity to adjust one's behavior to different and changing situational demands in a manner that inspires trust, confidence, and genuineness, and effectively influences and controls the responses of others." They have broken this down into four dimensions: *Self- and social astuteness* is the ability to astutely observe others and to be keenly attuned to diverse social situations. *Interpersonal influence/control* is the ability to exert a powerful influence on others. *Network building/social capital* means being adept at developing and using diverse networks of people. And *genuineness/sincerity* is the ability to appear to others as having high integrity, authenticity, and sincerity. The 18 items in this instrument tap into these four dimensions.

To calculate your score, add up your answers for the 18 items. Your score will range between 18 and 126. The higher your score, the better your political skills. That is, the better you are at not only knowing precisely what to do in different social situations at work but exactly how to do it in a sincere, engaging manner that disguises any ulterior, self-serving motives. The authors don't provide any specific cut-off scores, but we suggest that scores below 72 indicate that you are a bit politically naïve and may have difficulty furthering your self-interests in an organization. Scores above 100 suggest you are quite effective in gaining the support and trust of others and using that to advance your agenda.

Skill Basics

Forget, for a moment, the ethics of politicking and any negative impressions you might have of people who engage in organizational politics. If you want to be more politically adept in your organization, follow these eight suggestions:

1. *Frame arguments in terms of organizational goals.* Effective politicking requires camouflaging your self-interest. No matter that your objective is self-serving; all the arguments you marshal in support of it must be framed in terms of the benefits that will accrue to the organization. People whose actions appear to blatantly further their own interests at the expense of the organization are almost universally denounced, are likely to lose influence, and often suffer the ultimate penalty of being expelled from the organization.

2. *Develop the right image.* If you know your organization's culture, you understand what the organization wants and values from its employees—in terms of dress, associates to cultivate and those to avoid, whether to appear to be a risk taker or risk-aversive, the preferred leadership style, the importance placed on getting along well with others, and so forth. Then you are equipped to project the appropriate image. Because the assessment of your performance isn't always a fully objective process, you need to pay attention to style as well as substance. In addition, studies consistently show that people who can successfully project sincerity are perceived in a positive image.

3. *Gain control of organizational resources.* The control of organizational resources that are scarce and important is a source of power. Knowledge and expertise are particularly effective resources to control. They make you more valuable to the organization and, therefore, more likely to gain security, advancement, and a receptive audience for your ideas.

4. *Make yourself appear indispensable.* Because we're dealing with appearances rather than objective facts, you can enhance your power by appearing to be indispensable. You don't really have *to be* indispensable as long as key people in the organization believe that you are. If the organization's prime decision makers believe there is no ready substitute for what you are giving the organization, they are likely to go to great lengths to ensure that your desires are satisfied.

5. *Be visible.* If you have a job that brings your accomplishments to the attention of others, that's great. However, if you don't have such a job, you'll want to find ways to let others in the organization know what you're doing by highlighting successes in routine reports, having satisfied customers relay their appreciation to senior executives, being seen at social functions, being active in your professional associations, and developing powerful allies who speak positively about your accomplishments. Of course, the skilled politician actively and successfully lobbies to get the projects that will increase his or her visibility.

6. *Develop powerful allies.* It helps to have powerful people on your side. Network by cultivating contacts with potentially influential people above you, at your own level, and in the lower ranks. These allies often can provide you with information that's otherwise not readily available. In addition, decisions are sometimes made in favor of those with the greatest support. Having powerful allies can provide you with a coalition of support if and when you need it.

7. *Avoid "tainted" members.* In almost every organization, there are fringe members whose status is questionable. Their performance and/or loyalty is suspect. Keep your distance

from such individuals. Given the reality that effectiveness has a large subjective component, your own effectiveness might be called into question if you're perceived as being too closely associated with tainted members.

8. *Support your boss.* Your immediate future is in the hands of your current boss. Because that person evaluates your performance, you'll typically want to do whatever is necessary to have your boss on your side. You should make every effort to help your boss succeed, make her look good, support him if he is under siege, and spend the time to find out the criteria she will use to assess your effectiveness. Don't undermine your boss. And don't speak negatively of him to others.

Based on S. P. Robbins and P. L. Hunsaker, *Training in Interpersonal Skills: TIPS for Managing People at Work*, 6th ed. (Upper Saddle River, NJ: Prentice Hall, 2011), pp. 181–203; J. Marques, "Organizational Politics: Problem or Opportunity? Strategies for Success in the Workplace," *Human Resource Management International Digest*, 17, no. 6 (2009), pp. 38–41; and G. R. Ferris, S. L. Davidson, and P. L. Perrewe, *Political Skill at Work: Impact on Work Effectiveness* (Mountain View, CA: Davies-Black Publishing, 2005).

Skill Application

You used to be the star marketing manager for Hilton Electronics Corporation. But for the past year, you've been outpaced again and again by Jason, a new manager in the design department, who has been accomplishing everything expected of him and more. Meanwhile your best efforts to do your job well have been sabotaged and undercut by Maria—your and Jason's manager. For example, prior to last year's international consumer electronics show, Maria moved $60,000 from your budget to Jason's. Despite your best efforts, your marketing team couldn't complete all the marketing materials normally developed to showcase all of your organization's new products at this important industry show. And Maria has chipped away at your staff and budget ever since. Although you've been able to meet most of your goals with less staff and budget, Maria has continued to slice away resources from your group. Just last week, she eliminated two positions in your team of eight marketing specialists to make room for a new designer and some extra equipment for Jason. Maria is clearly taking away your resources while giving Jason whatever he wants and more. You think it's time to do something or soon you won't have any team or resources left.

Skill Practice

1. Make an appointment to interview a manager. Try to select someone who has at least three years of management experience. Ask this manager to describe a political situation he or she has confronted. How well-equipped was he or she to handle the situation? What was the outcome? What, if anything, would that person do differently today? What has that person learned about "organizational politics" since he or she left school?

2. Keep a one-week journal of your behavior and describe incidences of when you tried to influence others around you. Assess each incident by asking: Were you successful at these attempts to influence them? Why or why not? What could you have done differently?

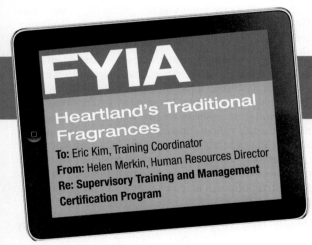

FYIA

Heartland's Traditional Fragrances

To: Eric Kim, Training Coordinator
From: Helen Merkin, Human Resources Director
Re: Supervisory Training and Management Certification Program

For Your Immediate Action

The good news: our sales numbers continue to grow. The bad news: it's putting a strain on our manufacturing supervisors. They're finding it difficult to keep our line employees motivated. We need to get some training in place to help them deal with this demanding pace or our line employees are likely to get even more stressed and we may see product quality go down.

I need you to look into two issues for me. One is a training program that focuses on important supervisory skills.

Do some research and put together a list of the skills you think are most important for our supervisors to have, together with a justification for why you think these skills are important.

The second issue is how we could help our supervisors achieve certification that verifies their skills, knowledge, and professionalism. Two certification programs that I'm aware of are the Certified Manager and the Certified Business Manager. Please research each of these programs and prepare a bulleted list of what each involves.

Keep your report to one page typed. Also, I'd like both sets of information as soon as possible. Thnx!

This fictionalized company and message were created for educational purposes only, and not meant to reflect positively or negatively on management practices by any company that may share this name.

Bringing the Real World to Life

Case Application: Saving the World: Part 2

Symantec, which designs content and network security software for both consumers and businesses, reflects the realities facing many organizations today: quickly shifting customer expectations and continuously emerging global competitors that have drastically shortened product life cycles. Managing talented people in such an environment can be quite challenging as well.

Symantec's virus hunters around the world deal with some 20,000 virus samples each month, not all of which are unique, stand-alone viruses. To make the hunters' jobs even more interesting is that computer attacks are increasingly being spread by criminals around the world wanting to steal information, whether corporate data or personal user account information that can be used in fraud. Dealing with these critical and time-sensitive issues requires special talents. The response-center team is a diverse group whose members weren't easy to find. "It's not as if colleges are creating thousands of anti-malware or security experts every year that we can hire. If you find them in any part of the world, you just go after them." The response center team's makeup reflects that. For instance, one senior researcher is from Hungary; another is from Iceland; and another works out of her home in Melbourne, Florida. But they all share something in common: They're all motivated by solving problems.

The launch of the Blaster-B worm, a particularly nasty virus, in late summer 2003 changed the company's approach to dealing with viruses. The domino effect of Blaster-B and other viruses spawned by it meant that frontline software analysts were working around the clock for almost two weeks. The "employee burnout" potential made the company realize that its virus-hunting team would now have to be much deeper talent-wise. Now, the response center's team numbers in the hundreds and managers can rotate people from the front lines, where they're responsible for responding to new security threats that crop up, into groups where they can help with new-product development. Others write internal research papers. Still others are assigned to develop new tools that will help their colleagues battle the next wave of threats. There's even an individual who tries to figure out what makes the virus writers tick—and the day never ends for these virus hunters. When Dublin's team finishes its day, colleagues in Santa Monica take over. When the U.S. team finishes its day, it hands off to the team in Tokyo, who then hands back to

Dublin for the new day. It's a frenetic, chaotic, challenging work environment that spans the entire globe. But the goals for managing the virus hunters are to "try to take the chaos out, to make the exciting boring," to have a predictable and well-defined process for dealing with the virus threats, and to spread work evenly to the company's facilities around the world. It's a managerial challenge that company managers have embraced.

DISCUSSION QUESTIONS

1. Keeping professionals excited about work that is routine and standardized *and* chaotic is a major challenge for Symantec's managers. How could they use technical, human, and conceptual skills to maintain an environment that encourages innovation and professionalism among the virus hunters? What managerial competencies might be important for these managers? Why?

2. What management roles would operations manager Patrick Fitzgerald be playing as he (a) had weekly security briefing conference calls with coworkers around the globe, (b) assessed the feasibility of adding a new network security consulting service, (c) kept employees focused on the company's commitments to customers?

3. Go to Symantec's Web site (www.symantec.com) and look up information about the company. What can you tell about its emphasis on customer service and innovation? In what ways does the organization support its employees in servicing customers and in being innovative?

4. What could other managers learn from Patrick Fitzgerald and Symantec's approach?

CHAPTER 2

YOUR TURN TO BE A MANAGER

The Management Environment

Skill Development: Reading an Organization's Culture

An organization's culture is a system of shared meaning. When you understand your organization's culture, you know whether it encourages teamwork, rewards innovation, or stifles initiative. When interviewing for a job, the more accurate a manager is at assessing the culture, the more likely he or she is to find a good person-organization fit. And once inside an organization, understanding the culture allows managers to know what behaviors are likely to be rewarded and which are likely to be punished.

Personal Insights: What's the Right Organizational Culture for Me?

For each of the seven statements, indicate your level of agreement or disagreement using the following scale:

1 = Strongly disagree
2 = Disagree
3 = Uncertain
4 = Agree
5 = Strongly agree

1. I like the thrill and excitement from taking risks.   1 2 3 4 5

2. I prefer managers who provide detailed and rational explanations for their decisions.   1 2 3 4 5

3. If a person's job performance is inadequate, it's irrelevant how much effort he or she made.   1 2 3 4 5

4. No person's needs should be compromised in order for a department to achieve its goals.   1 2 3 4 5

5. I like being part of a team and having my performance assessed in terms of my contribution to the team.   1 2 3 4 5

6. I like to work where there isn't a great deal of pressure and where people are essentially easygoing.   1 2 3 4 5

7. I like things to be stable and predictable.   1 2 3 4 5

Source: S.P. Robbins, *Organizational Behavior*, 8th ed. (Upper Saddle River, NJ: Prentice Hall, 1998), p. 617.

Analysis and Interpretation

This instrument taps the seven primary dimensions of an organization's culture: innovation and risk taking, attention to detail, outcome orientation, people orientation, team orientation, aggressiveness, and stability.

To calculate your score, add up your responses but reverse your scores for items 2 and 7. Your total score will range between 7 and 35. Scores of 21 or lower indicate that you're more comfortable in a formal, mechanistic, rule-oriented, and structured culture. This is often associated with large corporations and government agencies. The lower your number, the stronger your preference for this type of culture. Scores above 22 indicate a preference for informal, humanistic, flexible, and innovative cultures, which are more likely to be found in high-tech companies, small businesses, research units, or advertising agencies. The higher your score above 22, the stronger your preference for these humanistic cultures.

Organizational cultures differ. So do individuals. The better you're able to match your personal preferences to an organization's culture, the more likely you are to find satisfaction in your work, the less likely you are to leave, and the greater the probability that you'll receive positive performance evaluations.

Skill Basics

The ability to read an organization's culture can be a valuable skill. For instance, if you're looking for a job, you'll want to choose an employer whose culture is compatible with your values and in which you'll feel comfortable. If you can accurately assess a potential employer's culture before you make your job decision, you may be able to save yourself a lot of grief and reduce the likelihood of making a poor choice. Similarly, you'll undoubtedly have business transactions with numerous organizations during your professional career, such as selling a product or service, negotiating a contract, arranging a joint work project, or merely seeking out who controls certain decisions in an organization. The ability to assess another organization's culture can be a definite plus in successfully performing those pursuits.

You can be more effective at reading an organization's culture if you use the following behaviors. For the sake of simplicity, we're going to look at this skill from the perspective of a job applicant. We'll assume that you're interviewing for a job, although these skills are generalizable to many situations. Here's a list of things you can do to help learn about an organization's culture.

1. *Do background work.* Get the names of former employees from friends or acquaintances, and talk with them. Also talk with members of professional trade associations to which the organization's employees belong and executive recruiters who deal with the organization. Look for clues in stories told in annual reports and other organizational literature, and check out the organization's Web sites for evidence of high turnover or recent management shake-ups.

2. *Observe the physical surroundings.* Pay attention to signs, posters, pictures, photos, style of dress, length of hair, degree of openness between offices, and office furnishings and arrangements.

3. *Make note about those with whom you met.* Whom did you meet? How did they expect to be addressed?

4. *How would you characterize the style of the people you met?* Are they formal? Casual? Serious? Jovial? Open? Reticent about providing information?

5. *Look at the organization's human resources manual.* Are there formal rules and regulations printed there? If so, how detailed are they? What do they cover?

6. *Ask questions of the people with whom you meet.* The most valid and reliable information tends to come from asking the same questions of many people (to see how closely their responses align). Questions that will give you insights into organizational processes and practices might include: What's the background of the founders? What's the background of current senior managers? What are these managers' functional specialties, and were they

promoted from within or hired from outside? How does the organization integrate new employees? Is there a formal orientation program? Are there formal employee training programs and, if so, how are they structured? How does your boss define his or her job success? How would you define fairness in terms of reward allocations? Can you identify some people here who are on the "fast track"? What do you think has put them on the fast track? Can you identify someone in the organization who seems to be considered a deviant and how has the organization responded to this person? Can you describe a decision that someone made that was well received? Can you describe a decision that didn't work out well, and what were the consequences for that decision maker? Could you describe a crisis or critical event that has occurred recently in the organization and how did top management respond?

Based on A. L. Wilkins, "The Culture Audit: A Tool for Understanding Organizations," *Organizational Dynamics*, Autumn 1983, pp. 24–38; H. M. Trice and J. M. Beyer, *The Culture of Work Organizations* (Upper Saddle River, NJ: Prentice Hall, 1993), pp. 358–362; and D. M. Cable, L. Aiman-Smith, P. W. Mulvey, and J. R. Edwards, "The Sources and Accuracy of Job Applicants' Beliefs About Organizational Culture," *Academy of Management Journal* (December 2000), pp. 1076–1085.

Skill Application

After spending your first three years after college graduation as a freelance graphic designer, you're looking at pursuing a job as an account executive at a graphic design firm. You feel that the scope of assignments and potential for technical training far exceed what you'd be able to do on your own, and you're looking to expand your skills and meet a brand-new set of challenges. However, you want to make sure you "fit" into the organization where you're going to be spending more than eight hours every workday. What's the best way for you to find a place where you'll be happy and where your style and personality will be appreciated?

Skill Practice

1. If you're taking more than one course, assess the culture of the various classes in which you're enrolled. How do the classroom cultures differ?

2. Assume you're a newly hired CEO for a 30-person company that designs and makes computer games. Your past experience has been as a programmer, team leader, and operations vice president at a much larger gaming firm. In your new job, you will be replacing the founder who started the business in his garage. But the founder recently discovered he has a very serious illness and needs to give up active management of the firm. From your viewpoint, the company's current culture closely mirrors the characteristics of the founder: brash, risk-taking, assertive, and highly informal. You believe that future success requires the company to become more business-like: It needs more rules and regulations, more professionalism, less wild risk-taking, and more strategic planning. You realize that these changes will be difficult for many of the firm's employees. Nevertheless, they need to be implemented. How would you go about changing your firm's culture? Be specific.

For Your Immediate Action

Speedy Car Wash Services, Inc.

To: Michelle Bradley, Employee Care Manager
From: Alex Bilyeu, President
Re: Creating a Fun Workplace

Michelle, I saw an article the other day explaining the results of a survey that said only 8 percent of employers use fun to reduce employee stress at work. That same article said that research has shown that people who have fun at work are more creative, more productive, work better with others, and call in sick less often. I'm sold! So how and where do we start? Get me a bulleted list of ideas on how we can create a workplace here at Speedy that's both fun and yet still focused on work. I'm sure you'll have to do some research on this. And oh . . . have fun with it!

This fictionalized company and message were created for educational purposes only, and not meant to reflect positively or negatively on management practices by any company that may share this name.

Bringing the Real World to Life

Case Application:
Going to Extremes: Part 2

Not only is Zappos the number one e-retailer, but it also is ranked the sixth best company to work for in *Fortune* magazine's annual survey. Okay, so what is it really about Zappos that makes its culture so great? Let's take a closer look.

Zappos began selling shoes and other products online in 1999. Four years later, it was profitable, and it reached more than $1 billion in sales by 2009. Also, in 2009, Zappos was named *BusinessWeek*'s Customer Service Champ and was given an A+ rating by the Better Business Bureau. Also that year, Amazon (yeah . . . that Amazon) purchased Zappos for 10 million Amazon shares, worth almost $928 million at the time. Zappos' employees divided up $40 million in cash and restricted stock and were assured that Zappos management would remain in place.

The person who was determined to "build a culture that applauds such things as weirdness and humility" was Tony Hsieh (pronounced *Shay*) who became CEO of Zappos in 2000. And Tony is the epitome of weirdness and humility. For instance, on April Fools' Day 2010, he issued a press release announcing that "Zappos was suing Walt Disney Company in a class action suit claiming that Disney was misleading the public by saying that Disneyland is 'the happiest place on earth' because clearly" Hsieh argued, Zappos is.

Before joining Zappos, Hsieh had been cofounder of the Internet advertising network LinkExchange and had seen first-hand the "dysfunction that can arise from building a company in which technical skill is all that matters." He was determined to do it differently at Zappos. Hsieh first invited the 300 employees at Zappos to list the core values that the culture should be based upon. That process led to the 10 values that continue to drive the organization, which now employs about 1,400 people.

Another thing that distinguishes the Zappos culture is the recognition that organizational culture is more than a list of written values. The culture has to be "lived." And Zappos does this by maintaining a "complex web of human interactions." At Zappos, social media is used liberally to link employees with one another and with the company's customers. For instance, one recent tweet said, "Hey. Did anyone bring a hairdryer to the office today?" This kind of camaraderie can maintain and sustain employee commitment to the company.

Also, at Zappos, the company's "pulse" or "health" of the culture is surveyed monthly. In these happiness surveys, employees answer such "unlikely questions as whether they believe that the company has a higher purpose than profits, whether their own role has meaning, whether they feel in control of their career path, whether they consider their co-workers to be like family and friends, and whether they are happy in their jobs." Survey results are broken down by department and opportunities for "development" are identified and acted on. For example, when one month's survey showed that a particular department had "veered off course and felt isolated from the rest of the organization," actions were taken to show employees how integral their work was to the rest of the company.

And one other thing about Zappos: Every year, to celebrate its accomplishments, it publishes a *Culture Book,* a testimonial to the power of its culture. "Zappos has a belief that the right culture with the right values will always produce the best organizational performance, and this belief trumps everything else."

DISCUSSION QUESTIONS

1. Find a list of all 10 of Zappos' corporate values. Pick two of the values and explain how you think those values would influence the way employees do their work.

2. Using this list of corporate values and Exhibit 2–4, describe Zappos' organizational culture. In which areas would you say that Zappos' culture is very high (or typical)? Explain.

3. How did Zappos' corporate culture begin?

4. How is Zappos' corporate culture maintained?

5. "The right culture with the right values will always produce the best organizational performance." What do you think of this statement? Do you agree? Why or why not?

6. What could other companies learn from Tony Hsieh and Zappos' experiences?

YOUR TURN TO BE A MANAGER

Integrative **Managerial** Issues

Skill Development: Building High Ethical Standards

Ethics encompasses the rules and principles we use to define right and wrong conduct. Many organizations have formally written ethical codes to guide managers and employees in their decisions and actions. But individuals need to establish their own personal ethical standards. If managers are to successfully lead others, they need to be seen as trustworthy and ethical.

Personal Insights: How Do My Ethics Rate?

Indicate your level of agreement with these 15 statements using the following scale:

   1 = Strongly disagree
   2 = Disagree

3 = Neither agree or disagree

4 = Agree

5 = Strongly agree

1. The only moral of business is making money.	1 2 3 4 5
2. A person who is doing well in business does not have to worry about moral problems.	1 2 3 4 5
3. Act according to the law, and you can't go wrong morally.	1 2 3 4 5
4. Ethics in business is basically an adjustment between expectations and the ways people behave.	1 2 3 4 5
5. Business decisions involve a realistic economic attitude and not a moral philosophy.	1 2 3 4 5
6. "Business ethics" is a concept for public relations only.	1 2 3 4 5
7. Competitiveness and profitability are important values.	1 2 3 4 5
8. Conditions of a free economy will best serve the needs of society; limiting competition can only hurt society and actually violates basic natural laws.	1 2 3 4 5
9. As a consumer, when making an auto insurance claim, I try to get as much as possible regardless of the extent of the damage.	1 2 3 4 5
10. While shopping at the supermarket, it is appropriate to switch price tags on packages.	1 2 3 4 5
11. As an employee, I can take home office supplies; it doesn't hurt anyone.	1 2 3 4 5
12. I view sick days as vacation days that I deserve.	1 2 3 4 5
13. Employees' wages should be determined according to the laws of supply and demand.	1 2 3 4 5
14. The business world has its own rules.	1 2 3 4 5
15. A good businessperson is a successful businessperson.	1 2 3 4 5

Source: Adapted from A. Reichel and Y. Neumann, "Attitude Towards Business Ethics Questionnaire," *Journal of Instructional Psychology* (March 1988), pp. 25–53. With permission of the authors.

Analysis and Interpretation

No decision is completely value-free. It undoubtedly will have some ethical dimensions. This instrument presents philosophical positions and practical situations. Rather than specify "right" answers, this instrument works best when you compare your answers to those of others. With that in mind, here are mean responses from a group of 243 management students. How did your responses compare?

1. 3.09	6. 2.88	11. 1.58
2. 1.88	7. 3.62	12. 2.31
3. 2.54	8. 3.79	13. 3.36
4. 3.41	9. 3.44	14. 3.79
5. 3.88	10. 1.33	15. 3.38

Do you tend to be more or less ethical than the student norms presented above? On which items did you differ most? Your answers to these questions can provide insights into how well your ethical standards match other people with whom you will be working in the future. Large discrepancies might be a warning that others don't hold the same ethical values that you do.

Skill Basics

What You can do:

Know your values. What's important to you? Where do you draw the line?

Think before you act. Will your actions injure someone? What are your ulterior motives? Will your actions jeopardize your reputation?

Consider all consequences. If you make the wrong decision, what will happen? Every decision comes with consequences and you should be sure you've considered their implications.

Apply the "publicity test." What would your family and friends think if your actions were described in detail on the front page of your local newspaper or on the local TV news?

Seek opinions from others. Ask advice from others you respect. Use their experience and listen to their perspectives.

What Your Organization Can Do:

Create a formal ethics code. Organizations should set down their ethical standards and policies in a formal ethical code. The code should be widely distributed to all employees.

Set an ethical culture. Visibly reward employees who set a high ethical standard and visibly punish those who engage in unethical practices.

Ensure managers are role models. Employees look to their immediate superior and upper management for cues as to what is or is not acceptable behavior. Managers need to be positive ethical role models.

Offer ethics workshops. Employees should participate in regular ethics training to reinforce the importance of high ethical standards, to interpret the organization's ethical code, and to allow employees to clarify what they may see as "gray areas."

Appoint an ethics "advisor." A senior executive should be available for employees to meet and confer with to confidentially discuss ethical concerns.

Protect employees who report unethical practices. Mechanisms need to be put in place that protect employees from retributions or other negative consequences should they reveal unethical practices that are a threat to others.

Based on L. Nash, "Ethics Without the Sermon," *Harvard Business Review*, November–December 1981, pp. 78–92; W. D. Hall, *Making the Right Decision: Ethics for Managers* (New York: John Wiley, 1993); and L. K. Trevino and K. A. Nelson, *Managing Business Ethics: Straight Talk About How to Do It Right* (New York: John Wiley, 1995).

Skill Application

Form into teams of four or five people. Obtain a copy of your college's code of conduct. How many of the team members were aware of the code? How many had read it? Evaluate the code's provisions and policies. Are you uncomfortable with any of the code's provisions? Why? How effective do you think they have been in shaping student and faculty behavior? If they haven't been effective, what could be done to improve them?

Be prepared to present your team's findings to the class.

Skill Practice

1. On a scale of 1 to 10 (with 10 being high), how ethical would you describe yourself? What factors would you say have most shaped your views on ethics? Do you think your ethics have changed over time? If so, how and why? Do you think there is such a thing as "situational ethics"? If so, what situational factors would you consider relevant to your ethical behavior?

2. Research a recent highly publicized story of unethical behavior in business. What did this person or persons do? What do you think motivated the behavior? What could the organization have done better to have lessened the likelihood of such behavior? Had you been in the same situation, would you have acted similarly? Why or why not?

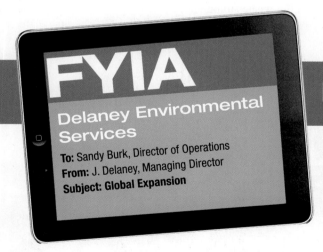

FYIA

Delaney Environmental Services

To: Sandy Burk, Director of Operations
From: J. Delaney, Managing Director
Subject: Global Expansion

For Your Immediate Action

Sandy, we need to start looking at expanding our global market opportunities. We've had a successful track record here in San Antonio providing environmental consulting and design services, and I believe that with our experience we have a lot to offer the Latin American market, particularly in Mexico.

Please research the potential problems we might face in moving into the Mexican market. Focus on: (1) cultural differences; (2) the current currency rate of exchange and how it's changed over the last three years; and (3) any legal or political situations we need to be aware of. Because this is just an initial analysis, please keep your report to one page or less.

This fictionalized company and message were created for educational purposes only, and not meant to reflect positively or negatively on management practices by any company that may share this name.

Bringing the Real World to Life

Case Application:
A Level Playing Field? Part 2

What is Deutsche Telekom doing to achieve its goal of bringing more women into management positions? One action the company is taking is to increase and improve recruiting of female university graduates. In fact, the company has committed to having at least 30 percent of the places in executive development programs held by women.

Other steps being taken by the company revolve around the work environment and work-family issues. The company plans to expand its parental-leave programs and introduce more flexible working hours for managers. Right now, fewer than 1 percent of the company's managers work part time. In addition, the company plans to double the number of available places in company child-care programs.

DISCUSSION QUESTIONS

1. What do you think of this "quota" approach that Deutsche Telekom is pursuing? What benefits and drawbacks does such an approach have?

2. What issues might Deutsche Telekom face in recruiting female university graduates? How could they address these issues?

3. What issues might the company face in introducing changes in work-family programs? Again, how could they address these issues?

4. Using the GLOBE highlights from the list within Chapter 3, find the dimensions where Germany is rated. How might those cultural realities affect actions that Deutsche Telekom wishes to pursue?

CHAPTER 4

YOUR TURN TO BE A MANAGER
Foundations of **Decision Making**

Skill Development: Using Your Creativity in Decision Making

Many decisions that managers make are routine, so they can fall back on experience and "what's worked in the past." But other decisions—especially those made by upper-level managers—are unique and haven't been confronted before. These are decisions that require creativity—the ability to produce novel and useful ideas. If managers are to successfully progress upward in an organization, they will find an increasing need to develop creative decisions.

Personal Insights: How Creative Am I?

Review the 30 adjectives listed here. Being honest and forthright with your answers, identify only those items that accurately describe you.

1. affected	11. honest	21. reflective
2. capable	12. humorous	22. resourceful
3. cautious	13. individualistic	23. self-confident
4. clever	14. informal	24. sexy
5. commonplace	15. insightful	25. sincere
6. confident	16. intelligent	26. snobbish
7. conservative	17. inventive	27. submissive
8. conventional	18. mannerly	28. suspicious
9. dissatisfied	19. narrow interests	29. unconventional
10. egotistical	20. original	30. wide interests

Source: H. G. Gough, "A Creative Personality Scale for the Adjective Check List," *Journal of Personality and Social Psychology* (August 1979), pp. 1398–1405.

Analysis and Interpretation

Creativity is the ability to combine ideas in a unique way or to make unusual associations between ideas. A creative person develops novel approaches to doing work or unique solutions to problems.

This questionnaire was developed to identify creative talent and potential. It has been widely used and replicated. It is composed of 30 items—18 of which have been found to be positively associated with creativity, and 12 that are negatively correlated.

To calculate your score, give yourself $+1$ if you described yourself using items 2, 4, 6, 10, 12, 13, 14, 15, 16, 17, 20, 21, 22, 23, 24, 26, 29, and 30. Give yourself a -1 for any of the remaining items you said accurately described you.

Your score will range between -12 and $+18$. The higher your positive score, the more you display characteristics associated with a creative personality.

For managers, creativity is useful in decision making. It helps them to see problems and alternatives that others might not. All jobs, of course, don't require high creativity. And highly creative individuals, when faced with routine and structured jobs, often become frustrated and dissatisfied.

Skill Basics

The uniqueness and variety of problems that managers face demand that they be able to solve problems creatively. Creativity is partly a frame of mind. You need to expand your mind's capabilities—that is, open yourself up to new ideas. Every individual has the ability to improve his or her creativity, but many people simply don't try to develop that ability.

You can be more effective at solving problems creatively if you use the following 10 suggestions.

1. *Think of yourself as creative.* Research shows that if you think you can't be creative, you won't be. Believing in your ability to be creative is the first step in becoming more creative.

2. *Pay attention to your intuition.* Every individual has a subconscious mind that works well. Sometimes answers will come to you when you least expect them. Listen to that "inner voice." In fact, most creative people will keep a notepad near their bed and write down ideas when the thoughts come to them.

3. *Move away from your comfort zone.* Every individual has a comfort zone in which certainty exists. But creativity and the known often do not mix. To be creative, you need to move away from the status quo and focus your mind on something new.

4. *Determine what you want to do.* This includes such things as taking time to understand a problem before beginning to try to resolve it, getting all the facts in mind, and trying to identify the most important facts.

5. *Think outside the box.* Use analogies whenever possible (for example, could you approach your problem like a fish out of water and look at what the fish does to cope? Or can you use the things you have to do to find your way when it's foggy to help you solve your problem?). Use different problem-solving strategies such as verbal, visual, mathematical, or theatrical. Look at your problem from a different perspective or ask yourself what someone else, like your grandmother, might do if faced with the same situation.

6. *Look for ways to do things better.* This may involve trying consciously to be original, not worrying about looking foolish, keeping an open mind, being alert to odd or puzzling facts, thinking of unconventional ways to use objects and the environment, discarding usual or habitual ways of doing things, and striving for objectivity by being as critical of your own ideas as you would those of someone else.

7. *Find several right answers.* Being creative means continuing to look for other solutions even when you think you have solved the problem. A better, more creative solution just might be found.

8. *Believe in finding a workable solution.* Like believing in yourself, you also need to believe in your ideas. If you don't think you can find a solution, you probably won't.

9. *Brainstorm with others.* Creativity is not an isolated activity. Bouncing ideas off of others creates a synergistic effect.

10. *Turn creative ideas into action.* Coming up with creative ideas is only part of the process. Once the ideas are generated, they must be implemented. Keeping great ideas in your mind, or on papers that no one will read, does little to expand your creative abilities.

Based on J. V. Anderson, "Mind Mapping: A Tool for Creative Thinking," *Business Horizons*, January–February 1993, pp. 42–46; and T. Proctor, *Creative Problem Solving for Managers* (New York: Routledge, 2005).

Skill Application

Every time the phone rings, your stomach clenches and your palms start to sweat. And it's no wonder! As sales manager for Brinkers, a machine tool parts manufacturer, you're besieged by calls from customers who are upset about late deliveries.

Your boss, Carter Hererra, acts as both production manager and scheduler. Every time your sales representatives negotiate a sale, it's up to Carter to determine whether production can actually meet the delivery date the customer specifies. And Carter invariably says, "No problem." The good thing about this is that you make a lot of initial sales. The bad news is that production hardly ever meets the shipment dates that Carter authorizes. And he doesn't seem to be all that concerned about the aftermath of late deliveries. He says, "Our customers know they're getting outstanding quality at a great price. Just let them try to match that anywhere. It can't be done. So even if they have to wait a couple of extra days or weeks, they're still getting the best deal they can." Somehow the customers don't see it that way. And they let you know about their unhappiness. Then it's up to you to try to soothe the relationship. You know this problem has to be taken care of, but what possible solutions are there? After all, how are you going to keep from making your manager mad or making the customers mad?

Break into groups of three. Assume you're the sales manager. What creative solutions can your group come up with to deal with this problem?

Skill Practice

1. How many words can you make using the letters in the word *brainstorm*? There are at least 95.

2. Take 20 minutes to list as many medical or health-related jobs as you can that begin with the letter *r* (for instance, radiologist, registered nurse). If you run out of listings before time is up, it's OK to quit early, but try to be as creative as you can.

FYIA

For Your Immediate Action

Magic Carpet Software

To: Rajiv Dutta, Research Manager
From: Amanda Schrenk, Vice President of Operations
Re: Software Design Decisions

Rajiv, we have a problem in our software design unit. Our diverse pool of extremely talented and skilled designers is, undoubtedly, one of our company's most important assets. However, I'm concerned that our designers' emotional attachment to the software they've created overshadows other important factors that should be considered in the decision whether to proceed with the new product design. At this point, I'm not sure how to approach this issue. The last thing I want to do is stifle their creativity. But I'm afraid if we don't come up with an action plan soon, the problem may get worse.

I need you to research the role of emotions in decision making. What do the "experts" say? Is it even an issue that we need to be concerned about? What's the best way to deal with it? Please provide me with a one-page bulleted list of the important points you find from your research. And be sure to cite your sources in case I need to do some follow-up.

This fictionalized company and message were created for educational purposes only, and not meant to reflect positively or negatively on management practices by any company that may share this name.

Bringing the Real World to Life

Case Application: Lift-Off: Part 2

NASA was established by the National Aeronautics and Space Act on July 29, 1958. Since that time, it has led U.S. efforts in space exploration including the Apollo lunar landing missions, the Skylab space station, the reusable manned spacecraft—which we know better as the Space Shuttle. As we stated in the chapter opener, NASA is facing uncertainty over its purpose and budget. "Implicitly acknowledging NASA's lack of direction, the White House has instructed the agency to take a deep breath, marshal resources, and chart a new course." Critics complain that the agency's space programs are too slow and too costly. A couple of possibilities being proposed are more international cooperation on space exploration and outsourcing certain tasks to private contractors. Although NASA's managers have important decisions to make about its future, we want to look at some past decisions where the outcomes were anything but what had been hoped for.

In an organization like NASA where equipment costs millions of dollars and where people's lives can be at stake, consistently making good decisions is not only expected, it's imperative. Over the years, NASA has had many successful endeavors. Getting men on the moon, not once, but six times, reflects outstanding technological prowess, far superior to any other country. Putting a rocket into space with a shuttle that then comes back to earth and lands on its own is a reflection of the incredible talent base that NASA has. Despite those successes, however, NASA has also had some spectacular disasters, which can be traced to errors in the decision-making process.

"Ever winter NASA revisits a week of tragedy during which the nation lost 17 astronauts and three space flight vehicles—*Apollo I* in 1967, space shuttle *Challenger* in 1986, and space shuttle *Columbia* in 2003. We are naturally drawn to ask why these accidents occurred—especially at such an accomplished organization working at the cutting edge of technology and exploration—and whether they could have been prevented."

The events leading up to the tragic end of the *Challenger* have been studied by many different people from many different perspectives—technological failures, poor decision-making practices, organizational culture, and so forth. That fateful launch day, January 28, 1986, was a sunny, but bitterly cold day in Florida. And the launch was

perfect . . . until 73 seconds into flight when *Challenger* exploded. During the resulting presidential commission investigation, engineers for Morton Thiokol, the contractor for NASA's failed rocket boosters, revealed that they had issued repeated warnings about launching in the bitterly cold conditions. They strongly believed that the joint design of the solid rocket booster seals was unsafe in those types of conditions. Furthermore, with management approval, the Morton Thiokol engineers had officially recommended against launching. When NASA's team refused to accept the conservative "unsafe to fly" recommendation, Thiokol's managers overruled the concerns of the engineers and reversed the earlier decision, giving NASA the green light to launch. Why did NASA officials not pass the Thiokol concerns to those higher up in the launch decision chain of command? Virtually all of them said that they responded identically because "ultimately all parties were in agreement that no launch commit criteria were violated," and "proper procedures were followed." As one Thiokol engineer later related, "There was no miscommunication that night. We clearly told NASA it would be unsafe to launch, but they wouldn't listen to us."

For space shuttle *Columbia,* a problem during launch—damage sustained when a piece of foam insulation the size of a small briefcase broke off from the external tank and damaged the shuttle's thermal protection system on its left wing—led to its demise on return. NASA's original shuttle specifications said that any debris (including foam) were safety issues that "needed to be resolved before a launch was cleared. However, over the years, launches were often given the go-ahead as engineers came to see that foam shedding and debris strikes were inevitable and unresolvable. Most shuttle launches have had such foam or debris strikes on the thermal tiles. And NASA's senior managers saw fit to overlook that risk, as it did at *Columbia's* launch. However, on February 1, 2003, as *Columbia* was on its return from its space mission, heat build-up destroyed the shuttle's wing structure and it disintegrated over Texas and Louisiana resulting in the deaths of all seven crew members. The investigative report concluded that "the beleaguered space agency, battling a declining budget, learned little from the 1986 *Challenger* explosion, which also killed seven astronauts, and that a sense of infallibility permeated its decision making." One investigator also wrote, "NASA had conflicting goals of cost, schedule, and safety. Unfortunately, safety lost out."

DISCUSSION QUESTIONS

1. In doing what the agency is in business to do, do you think NASA managers deal more with structured or unstructured problems? Explain.

2. Would NASA's decision-making conditions be considered certainty, risk, or uncertainty? Explain.

3. What evidences of groupthink and escalation of commitment do you see in the preceding story? How could these decision-making problems have been prevented? What could other organizations learn from NASA's decision-making mistakes?

4. How could NASA managers best utilize the decision-making process as they shape its post-shuttle future?

5. How might international cooperative space efforts and outsourcing certain tasks to private contractors affect the decision making done at NASA?

CHAPTER 5

YOUR TURN TO BE A MANAGER

Foundations of **Planning**

Skill Development: Goal Setting

It's been said that if you don't know where you're going, any road will get you there. It has also been said that the shortest distance between two points is a straight line. These two "adages" emphasize the importance of goals. Managers are typically judged on their ability to achieve goals. If individuals or units in the organization lack goals, there can be no direction or unity of effort. So successful managers are good at setting their own goals and helping others set goals.

Personal Insights: What's My Goal Orientation?

People have different views about how they approach work. Please read each of the following statements and select the response that reflects how much you agree or disagree with the statement.

      1 = Strongly disagree

      2 = Disagree

      3 = Sort of disagree

      4 = Neither

      5 = Sort of agree

      6 = Agree

      7 = Strongly agree

1. I am willing to select a challenging work assignment that I can learn a lot from.

2. I often look for opportunities to develop new skills and knowledge.

3. I enjoy challenging and difficult tasks at work where I'll learn new skills.

4. For me, further development of my work ability is important enough to take risks.

5. I like to show that I can perform better than my coworkers.

6. I try to figure out what it takes to prove my ability to others at work.

7. I enjoy it when others at work are aware of how well I am doing.

8. I prefer to work on projects where I can prove my ability to others.

9. I would avoid taking on a new task if there was a chance that I would appear rather incompetent to others.

10. Avoiding a show of low ability is more important to me than learning a new skill.

11. I'm concerned about taking on a task at work if my performance would reveal that I had low ability.

12. I prefer to avoid situations at work where I might perform poorly.

Source: D. VandeWalle, "Development and Validation of a Work Domain Goal Orientation Instrument," *Educational and Psychological Measurement*, December 1997, pp. 995–1015. With permission. Adaptations suggested in correspondence with the author. Sample comparative data was obtained from D. VandeWalle, W. L. Cron, and J. W. Slocum, Jr., "The Role of Goal Orientation Following Performance Feedback," *Journal of Applied Psychology* (August 2001), pp. 629–640.

Analysis and Interpretation

This questionnaire assesses your views toward developing or demonstrating ability in achievement situations. It breaks down goal orientations into three categories: (1) *learning orientation*—a desire to develop yourself by acquiring new skills, mastering new situations, and improving your competence (items 1–4); (2) *prove performance orientation*—the desire to prove your competence and to gain favorable judgments about it (items 5–8); and (3) *avoiding orientation*—the desire to avoid the disproving of your competence and to avoid negative judgments about it (items 9–12).

Add up your scores separately for the three categories and divide by 4. Your scores will range from 1 to 7 in each. The higher your score in a category, the greater your goal preferences in achievement situations. For instance, the higher your learning goal orientation, the more adaptive you are in demonstrating persistence, escalated effort, and engaging in solution-oriented self-instruction. No specific guidelines are offered for interpreting your score, but a sample of 102 undergraduate business students had mean scores of 5.12, 4.41, and 4.31 in the three respective categories.

Skill Basics

In addition to your own focus on goals, employees should also have a clear understanding of what they're attempting to accomplish. Managers have the responsibility to help employees with this understanding as they set work goals.

You can be more effective at setting goals if you use the following eight suggestions.

1. *Identify an employee's key job tasks.* Goal setting begins by defining what it is that you want your employees to accomplish. The best source for this information is each employee's job description.

2. *Establish measurable, specific, and challenging goals for each key task.* Identify the level of performance expected of each employee. Specify the target toward which the employee is working.

3. *Specify the deadlines for each goal.* Putting deadlines on each goal reduces ambiguity. Deadlines, however, should not be set arbitrarily. Rather, they need to be realistic given the tasks to be completed.

4. *Allow the employee to participate actively.* When employees participate in goal setting, they're more likely to accept the goals. However, it must be sincere participation. That is, employees must perceive that you are truly seeking their input, not just going through the motions.

5. *Prioritize goals.* When you give someone more than one goal, it's important to rank the goals in order of importance. The purpose of prioritizing is to encourage the employee to take action and expend effort on each goal in proportion to its importance.

6. *Rate goals for difficulty and importance.* Goal setting should not encourage people to choose easy goals. Instead, goals should be rated for their difficulty and importance. When goals are rated, individuals can be given credit for trying difficult goals, even if they don't fully achieve them.

7. *Build in feedback mechanisms to assess goal progress.* Feedback lets employees know whether their level of

effort is sufficient to attain the goal. Feedback should be both self-generated and supervisor-generated. Feedback should also be frequent and recurring.

8. *Link rewards to goal attainment.* It's natural for employees to ask, "What's in it for me?" Linking rewards to the achievement of goals will help answer that question.

Based on E. A. Locke and G. P. Latham, *Goal-Setting: A Motivational Technique That Works!* (Upper Saddle River, NJ: Prentice Hall, 1984); and E. A. Locke and G. P. Latham, "Building a Practically Useful Theory of Goal Setting and Task Motivation," *American Psychologist*, September 2002, pp. 705–717.

Skill Application

You worked your way through college while holding down a part-time job bagging groceries at the Food Town supermarket chain. You liked working in the food industry, and when you graduated, you accepted a position with Food Town as a management trainee. Three years have passed and you've gained experience in the grocery store industry and in operating a large supermarket. Several months ago, you received a promotion to store manager at one of the chain's locations. One of the things you've liked about Food Town is that it gives store managers a great deal of autonomy in running their stores. The company provides very general guidelines to its managers. Top management is concerned with the bottom line;

for the most part, how you get there is up to you. Now that you're finally a store manager, you want to establish an MBO-type program in your store. You like the idea that everyone should have clear goals to work toward and then be evaluated against those goals.

Your store employs 70 people, although except for the managers, most work only 20 to 30 hours per week. You have six people reporting to you: an assistant manager; a weekend manager; and grocery, produce, meat, and bakery managers. The only highly skilled jobs belong to the butchers who have strict training and regulatory guidelines. Other less-skilled jobs include cashier, shelf stocker, maintenance worker, and grocery bagger.

Specifically describe how you would go about setting goals in your new position. Include examples of goals for the jobs of butcher, cashier, and bakery manager.

Skill Practice

1. Set personal and academic goals you want to achieve by the end of this college term. Prioritize and rate them for difficulty.

2. Where do you want to be in five years? Do you have specific five-year goals? Establish three goals you want to achieve in five years. Make sure these goals are specific, challenging, and measurable.

FYIA

For Your Immediate Action

Winwood Performance Plus

To: Hannah Paul, Human Resources Manager
From: Eric Winwood, CEO
Subject: Environmental Issues

Hannah, as you know our entertainment consulting business has had a remarkable couple of years. The success we've achieved wouldn't be possible without the hard work our associates do, and I'm honored to be surrounded by such committed and talented individuals. I feel that our next push as

a company should be to become more environmentally responsible. All of us (me included) generate a lot of paper as we do our work, so I think our first step (and main focus right now) should be on controlling paper waste. I would like you to create a company-wide program for controlling paper waste. Before we get our associates involved, I'd like you to set some goals and develop some plans for this program. Get me your report (keep it to one page, please) outlining these goals and plans as soon as you can.

This fictionalized company and message were created for educational purposes only, and not meant to reflect positively or negatively on management practices by any company that may share this name.

Bringing the Real World to Life

Case Application: Flip Flop: Part 2

Four years. That's all it took for the Flip video camera, the most popular video camera in the United States, to go from hot start-up to obsolete. But even in the life cycle of tech products where things happen fast, this seemed to be in the blink of an eye—unusually fast, as one analyst said, especially for a "hot" product. What happened?

The Flip camera broke new ground when it was introduced. Customers loved that it was pocketable, inexpensive, and easy to use. Flip's name came from the arm that flips out of the camera body and lets the user connect it directly to a computer. The camera also had video-editing software that opened when it was connected to the computer. Although the actual video camera seemed tiny, it recorded remarkably good footage for a camera of its size. In addition, unlike other video cameras, the Flip could be held comfortably in front of you so you didn't feel "removed" from the event being recorded. The product was exactly what the founders envisioned—a practical pocket-sized, inexpensive, and easy-to-use video camera.

When Cisco Systems decided to acquire Flip, one of the hottest consumer products to hit store shelves in a while, many industry analysts questioned that decision, believing it was an "odd fit" for the company that's best known for its business enterprise networking services. The Flip camera was the first true consumer product under the Cisco umbrella. In its announcement, Cisco said that the acquisition was a key to its strategy to expand momentum in the media-enabled home. There was no doubt that Cisco was serious about the company's desire to expand its market from technical components into true consumer electronics. And there was another variable at work here, as well. The acquisition of Pure Digital Technologies (the actual company behind the Flip camera) was another sign that Cisco was making a statement by aggressively pushing into new markets when many of its competitors were floundering during the economic downturn.

Pure Digital became a part of Cisco's Consumer Business Group, which also included Linksys home networking, audio, and media-storage products. When Cisco acquired Pure Digital it also named Jonathan Kaplan, Pure Digital's CEO, as Cisco's senior vice president and general manager in charge of consumer products. Kaplan was to help set Cisco's strategy in this area. And Cisco did what it thought was necessary to compete in the consumer market using Flip as a key focus. It spent heavily on consumer branding, hiring celebrities such as Ellen Page to star in its television commercials and

paying for product placement in shows such as *24*. Even Cisco's CEO, John Chambers (who owned eight Flips), shot videos on a Flip and constantly had it in view during television interviews. It even had Sean "Diddy" Combs design a custom Flip camera. Flip sales during fiscal 2010 were $317 million. However, it must not have been enough. Cisco had suffered several quarters of disappointing financial results and challenges in its core businesses. Analysts said that the company had been trying to do too many different things and losing its focus on what made it great. In retrospect, it was easy to see that major strategic changes were looming.

First, Cisco announced in February that Jonathan Kaplan was leaving Cisco to pursue "other career opportunities." Then, CEO Chambers said in an interview that "revenue from consumer products over the holiday season fell short of the company's hopes." Then came the announcement in mid-April 2011 that Cisco was restructuring and shutting down its Flip video-camera unit. Chambers said, "We are making key, targeted moves as we align operations in support of our network-centric platform strategy." In addition, analysts pointed to the rapid innovation of smartphones as one of the most disruptive trends ever seen. As phones with built-in cameras and editing apps hit the market, it was only a matter of time until Flip became obsolete.

DISCUSSION QUESTIONS

1. "I don't think there's an analyst on the planet who thought that Flip was a good acquisition for Cisco." Why do you think these analysts felt that way?

2. Evaluate Cisco's consumer marketing efforts. Why might it be difficult for a company accustomed to selling to businesses to sell products to consumers?

3. Could Cisco have done anything else to build up its consumer products including the Flip? What were Flip's strengths? What external threats were happening during this time period?

4. Why do you think Cisco decided to shut down the Flip business rather than try to sell it?

5. What type of strategies do you see described in this case? Be specific.

6. What role would goal setting and planning have played in: (a) Flip's founding, (b) Cisco's acquisition of Flip, (c) Cisco's managing of the Flip business unit, and (d) Cisco's strategic decision to shut down the Flip business unit?

CHAPTER 6

YOUR TURN TO BE A MANAGER

Organization Structure and Design

Skill Development: Developing Your Power Base

Managerial jobs come with the power of authority. But sometimes that authority isn't enough to get things done. And other times you may not want to use your formal authority as a means of getting people to do what you want. You may, for instance, want to rely more on your persuasive skills than the power of your title. So effective managers increase their power by developing multiple sources of influence.

Personal Insights: How Power-Oriented Am I?

For each of statement, select the response that most closely resembles your attitude. Use the following ratings scale for your responses:

1 = Disagree a lot
2 = Disagree a little
3 = Neutral
4 = Agree a little
5 = Agree a lot

1. The best way to handle people is to tell them what they want to hear.   1 2 3 4 5

2. When you ask someone to do something for you, it is best to give the real reason for wanting it rather than giving reasons that might carry more weight.   1 2 3 4 5

3. Anyone who completely trusts anyone else is asking for trouble.   1 2 3 4 5

4. It is hard to get ahead without cutting corners here and there.   1 2 3 4 5

5. It is safest to assume that all people have a vicious streak, and it will come out when they are given a chance.   1 2 3 4 5

6. One should take action only when it is morally right.   1 2 3 4 5

7. Most people are basically good and kind.   1 2 3 4 5

8. There is no excuse for lying to someone else.   1   2   3   4   5

9. Most people more easily forget the death of their father than the loss of their property.   1   2   3   4   5

10. Generally speaking, people won't work hard unless they're forced to do so.   1   2   3   4   5

Source: R. Christie and F. L. Geis, *Studies in Machiavellianism.* ©Academic Press 1970. With permission.

Analysis and Interpretation

This instrument was designed to compute your Machiavellianism (Mach) score. Machiavelli wrote in the sixteenth century on how to gain and manipulate power. An individual with a high-Mach score is pragmatic, maintains emotional distance, and believes that ends can justify means.

To obtain your score, add your responses to questions 1, 3, 4, 5, 9, and 10. For the other four questions, reverse your scores (5 becomes 1, 4 becomes 2, and so on). The National Opinion Research Center, which used this instrument in a random sample of American adults, found that the national average was 25.

High-Machs are more likely to manipulate more, win more, are persuaded less, and persuade others more than do low-Machs. High-Machs are also more likely to shade the truth or act unethically in ambiguous situations where the outcome is important to them.

Skill Basics

You can increase the likelihood that you'll survive and thrive in your organization if you learn how to develop a power base. Remember, because you have power doesn't mean you have to use it. But it's nice to be able to call upon it when you do need it.

Four sources of power can be derived from your job. Another three sources are based on your personal unique characteristics.

All management jobs come with the power to coerce, reward, and impose authority. *Coercive power* is based on fear. If you can dismiss, suspend, demote, assign unpleasant work tasks, or write a negative performance review on someone, you hold coercive power over that person. Conversely, if you can give someone something of positive value or remove something of negative value—like control pay rates, raises, bonuses, promotions, or work assignments—you have *reward power*. And all managerial positions provide some degree—though within specific limitations—to exert authority over subordinates. If you can tell someone to do something and they see this request to be within your formal job description, you have *authority power* over them.

In addition to coercive, reward, and authoritative power, many managerial positions also possess *information power* that comes from access to and control over information. If you have data or knowledge that others need, and which only you have access to, it gives you power. Of course, you don't have to be a manager to have information power. Many employees are quite skilled at operating in secrecy, hiding technical short-cuts, or avoiding showing others exactly what they do—all with the intention of keeping important knowledge from getting into others' hands.

You don't have to be a manager or control information to have power in an organization. You can also exert influence based on your expertise, admiration that others might have for you, and through charismatic qualities. If you have a special skill or unique knowledge that others in the organization depend on, you hold *expert power*. In our current age of specialization, this source of power is increasingly potent. If others identify with you and look up to you to the extent that they want to please you, you have *referent power*. It develops out of admiration and the desire to be like someone else. The final source of influence is *charismatic power*, which is an extension of referent power. If others will follow you because they admire your heroic qualities, you have charismatic power over them.

Based on these sources of power, we can say that you can increase your power in organizations by taking on managerial responsibilities, gaining access to important information, developing an expertise that the organization needs, or displaying personal characteristics that others admire.

Based on J. R. P. French, Jr. and B. Raven, "The Bases of Social Power," in D. Cartwright (ed.), *Studies in Social Power* (Ann Arbor: University of Michigan Institute of Social Research, 1959), pp. 150–167; B. J. Raven, "The Bases of Power: Origin and Recent Developments," *Journal of Social Issues*, 49 (1993), pp. 227–251; E. A. Ward, "Social Power Bases of Managers: Emergence of a New Factor," *Journal of Social Psychology* (February 2001), pp. 144–147; and B. H. Raven, "The Bases of Power and the Power/Interaction Model of Interpersonal Influence," *Analyses of Social Issues and Public Policy*, December 2008, pp. 1–22.

Skill Application

Margaret is a supervisor in the online sales division of a large clothing retailer. She has let it be known that she is devoted to the firm and plans to build her career there. Margaret is hardworking and reliable, has volunteered for extra projects, has taken in-house development courses, and joined a committee dedicated to improving employee safety on the job. She undertook an assignment to research ergonomic office furniture for the head of the department and gave up several lunch hours to consult with the head of human resources about her report. Margaret filed the report late, but she explained the delay by saying that her assistant lost several pages that she had to redraft over the weekend. The report was well received, and several of Margaret's colleagues think she should be promoted when the next opening arises.

Evaluate Margaret's skill in building a power base. What actions has she taken that are helpful to her in reaching her goal? Is there anything she should have done differently?

Skill Practice

1. What can you do to improve your Mach score? Create a specific one-year plan to implement a program that will lead to an improved score.

2. Identify someone—a boss, coworker, friend, parent, sibling, significant other—with whom you would like to increase your power. Determine what tactic(s) might work, then cautiously practice your tactic(s).

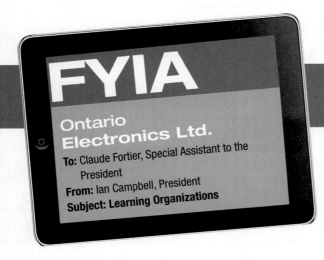

FYIA

Ontario Electronics Ltd.

To: Claude Fortier, Special Assistant to the President
From: Ian Campbell, President
Subject: Learning Organizations

For Your Immediate Action

First of all, thanks for keeping everything "going" while I attended the annual meeting of the Canadian Electronics Manufacturers Industry Association last week. Our luncheon speaker on the final day talked about how important it is for organizations to be responsive to customer and marketplace needs. One approach she discussed for doing this was becoming a learning organization. I'm now convinced that

our company's future may well depend on how well we're able to "learn."

I'd like you to find some current information on learning organizations. Although I'm sure you'll be able to find numerous articles about the topic, limit your report to five of what you consider to be the best sources of information on the topic. Write a one-paragraph summary for each of these five articles, being sure to note all the bibliographic information in case we need to find the article later. Since I'd like our executive team to move on this idea fairly quickly, please have your report back to me by the end of the week.

This fictionalized company and message were created for educational purposes only, and not meant to reflect positively or negatively on management practices by any company that may share this name.

Bringing the Real World to Life

Case Application: Volunteers Work: Part 2

Self check-outs. Self check-ins. Pumping your own gas (although most of you are probably too young to remember having an attendant that pumped your gas, checked your oil, and washed your windshield). Filling out online forms. Businesses have become very good at getting customers to do free work. Now, they're taking the concept even further, especially in customer service settings, by getting "volunteers" to perform specialized work tasks.

The role that these volunteer "enthusiasts" have played, especially in contributing innovations to research and development efforts, has been closely researched in recent years. For example, case studies highlight the product tweaks made by early skateboarders and mountain bikers to their gear. Researchers have

also studied the programmers behind open-source software like the Linux operating system. It seems that individuals who do this type of "volunteering" are motivated mainly by a payoff in enjoyment and respect among their peers and to some extent the skills they're able to develop. Now, as the concept of individuals volunteering for work tasks moves to the realm of customer service, can it work and what does it mean for managers?

For instance, at Verizon's high-speed fiber optic Internet, television, and telephone service, "volunteers" are answering customer questions about technical matters on a company-sponsored customer-service Web site for no pay. Mark Studness, director of Verizon's e-commerce unit was familiar with Web sites where users offered tips and answered questions. His challenge? Find a way to use that potential resource for customer service. His solution? "Super" or lead users—that is, users who provided the best answers and dialogue in Web forums.

The experiment at Verizon "suggests that company-sponsored online communities for customer service, if handled adeptly, hold considerable promise." Studness says that "you have to make an environment that attracts these super users of the world, because that's where the magic happens." A company that worked with Verizon to set up its structure said that "the mentality of super-users in online customer-service communities is similar to that of devout gamers." So they set up the structure with an elaborate rating system for contributors with ranks, badges, and "kudos counts." So far, Studness is happy with how it's gone. He says the company-sponsored customer-service site is "a very productive tool, partly because it absorbs many thousands of questions that would otherwise be expensive calls to a Verizon call center."

DISCUSSION QUESTIONS

1. What do you think about using "volunteers" to do work that other people get paid to do?

2. If you were in Mark Studness's position, what would you be most concerned about in this arrangement? How would you "manage" that concern?

3. How do these "volunteers" fit into an organization's structure? Take each of the six elements of organization design and discuss how each would affect this structural approach.

4. Do you think this approach could work for other types of work being done or in other types of organizations? Explain.

YOUR TURN TO BE A MANAGER

Managing **Human Resources**

CHAPTER 7

Skill Development: Developing Interviewing Skills

Managers, by definition, get things done through and with other people. Part of their job is selecting competent people who can fill key roles on their teams. A major element in this selection process is interviewing prospective candidates. The better managers are at developing their interviewing skills, the greater the chance that they'll select new employees who are competent and fit well into the organization.

Personal Insights: What Do You Know About Effective Interviewing?

Indicate the degree to which you agree or disagree with these 10 statements.

1 = Strongly disagree

2 = Disagree

3 = Neither agree or disagree

4 = Agree

5 = Strongly agree

1. Prior knowledge about the applicant will improve the accuracy of my evaluation.   1 2 3 4 5

2. Most interviewers favor applicants who share the interviewer's attitudes.   1 2 3 4 5

3. The best interviews are those where the interviewer prepares a set of specific questions ahead of time.   1 2 3 4 5

4. Insights into an applicant's skills and abilities are improved when the applicant feels uncomfortable and uncertain.   1 2 3 4 5

5. Most interviewers give equal weight to positive and negative information.   1 2 3 4 5

6. The best interview questions can be answered with a direct "yes" or "no."   1 2 3 4 5

7. A good interviewer takes detailed notes during or immediately after the interview.   1 2 3 4 5

8. The best predictor of what an applicant will do in the future is what he or she has done in the past.   1 2 3 4 5

9. Interviews are more effective for selecting managers than blue-collar workers.   1 2 3 4 5

10. End interviews by telling the applicant how well he or she performed in the interview.   1 2 3 4 5

Source: Developed by Stephen P. Robbins.

Analysis and Interpretation

Add up your score for items 2, 3, 7, 8, and 9. For the other five items, reverse the score. A 1 should be scored as 5, a 2 as 4, and so on. Your total score will range between 10 and 50. Scores of 40 or better indicate a fairly accurate understanding of effective interviewing.

Source: Developed by Stephen P. Robbins

Skill Basics

Every manager needs to develop his or her interviewing skills. The following highlights the key behaviors associated with effective interviewing.

1. *Review the job description and job specification.* What does the job look like that the applicant will be filling? And what qualifications does the ideal candidate possess? Reviewing pertinent information about the job provides valuable information about how to assess the candidate. And relevant job requirements help to reduce interview bias.

2. *Prepare a structured set of questions to ask all applicants for the job.* By having a set of prepared questions, you ensure that the information you wish to elicit is attained. Furthermore, if you ask all applicants similar questions, you'll have a common base against which to compare their answers.

3. *Before meeting an applicant, review his or her application form and résumé.* Doing so helps you to create a complete picture of the applicant in terms of what is represented on the résumé or application and what the job requires. You will also begin to identify areas to explore in the interview. That is, areas that are not clearly defined on the résumé or application but that are essential for the job will become a focal point of your discussion with the applicant.

4. *Open the interview by putting the applicant at ease and providing a brief preview of the topics to be* *discussed.* Interviews are stressful for job applicants. By opening with small talk (e.g., the weather), you give the person time to adjust to the interview setting. By providing a preview of topics to come, you're giving the applicant an agenda that helps the individual begin framing what he or she will say in response to your questions.

5. *Ask your questions and listen carefully to the applicant's answers.* Ask questions that can't be merely answered with only a *yes* or *no*. Inquiries that begin with *how* or *why* tend to stimulate extended answers. Avoid leading questions that telegraph the desired response (such as "Would you say you have good interpersonal skills?") and bipolar questions that require the applicant to select an answer from only two choices (such as "Do you prefer working with people or working alone?"). Since the best predictor of future behavior is past behavior, the best questions tend to be those that focus on previous experiences that are relevant to the current job.

6. *Closing the interview.* Wrap up the interview by telling the applicant what's going to happen next. Be honest with the applicant regarding others who will be interviewed and the remaining steps in the hiring process. Tell the applicant how and when you will let him or her know about your decision.

7. *Concluding.* Once the interview is over, write your evaluation while it is fresh in your mind. Ideally, you kept notes or recorded the applicant's answers to your questions and made comments of your impressions. Now that the applicant is gone, take the time to assess the applicant's responses.

Based on W. C. Donaghy, *The Interview: Skills and Applications* (Glenview, Il: Scott, Foresman, 1984), pp. 245–280; E. D. Pulakos and N. Schmitt, "Experience-Based and Situational Interview Questions: Studies of Validity," *Personnel Psychology*, Summer 1995, pp. 289–308; W. W. Larson, *Ten Minute Guide to Conducting Job Interviews* (New York: Alpha, 2001); and C. Sun, "10 Tips on Conducting Effective Interviews," *TechRepublic*, October 28, 2008.

Skill Application

Each class member should bring in a copy of his or her résumé. If they don't have one, this is a good time to create one.

The class members should pair off. Using their partner's résumé, each will conduct a job interview. Here's a brief background about the job: Your college's admissions office is looking to fill a position of recruitment officer. The job requires no specific previous admissions experience but does assume some familiarity with the college, the college community, and the type of student it attracts. There are typically three people doing this job at the college—which includes meeting prospective students and parents; representing the college at regional college fairs; interviewing students; and evaluating prospective applicants—but one has tendered her resignation. So there is now a vacancy.

Each "interviewer" has up to 15 minutes to conduct his or her interview. After the first is complete, roles are reversed. Upon completion, each "interviewee" should critique his or her interviewer against the skills identified in the previous section.

Skill Practice

1. Select a job vacancy listed in your newspaper or online. Have a friend or relative play the role of job applicants and practice your skill at interviewing to fill the job vacancy.

2. Review your personal experiences in job interviews. How would you rate your interviewers' general effectiveness? What did they do right? What did they do wrong?

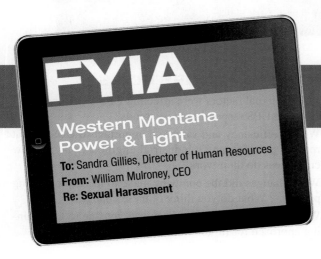

For Your Immediate Action

Western Montana Power & Light

To: Sandra Gillies, Director of Human Resources
From: William Mulroney, CEO
Re: Sexual Harassment

Sandra, I think we might have a problem. It appears that some of our employees aren't clear about the practices and actions that do or do not constitute sexual harassment. We can't have any ambiguity or uncertainty about this, as you know. We need to immediately develop a training program for all our employees and develop a workable procedure to handle any complaints that might arise.

I want this issue of sexual harassment to be the primary topic at next month's executive board meeting. To facilitate discussion, please give me a bulleted list describing the content of an initial two-hour employee workshop on sexual harassment.

This fictionalized company and message were created for educational purposes only, and not meant to reflect positively or negatively on management practices by any company that may share this name.

Bringing the Real World to Life

Case Application:
Thinking Outside the Box: Part 2

With more than 400,000 employees in 215 countries and territories, HRM is a significant and critical function for UPS. The company's top managers have recognized that if they want to position UPS to continue to grow in today's fast-changing global environment, they have to take a hard look at training policies and programs, especially in the way young workers are recruited, trained, and developed.

About five years ago, UPS began to notice a decline in the performance of young new drivers. "Previously, trainees needed 30 days to become proficient drivers. Younger drivers were now taking 90 to 180 days." These younger drivers were just as smart and had just as much potential, but the techniques that had been used for decades just were not clicking for these millennial trainees. In another sign that its traditional classroom driver training obviously wasn't working was that some 30 percent of its driver candidates didn't make it through the training period.

After much study (with the help of a $1.8 million grant from the Labor Department set up to look at the way millennials learn and with collaboration of higher education partners), the company was convinced that the twenty-somethings—the bulk of its driver recruits—responded best to high-tech instruction instead of books and lectures.

Thus, UPS invested in a "next-generation training facility called Integrad." Currently, UPS has two Integrad facilities—one outside of Baltimore and another outside of Chicago. There, trainees use video games, a "slip and fall simulator which combines a greased floor with slippery shoes," and an obstacle course around a mock village.

At the training center outside of Baltimore, applicants for a driver's job, which pays an average of $74,000 annually, spend one week practicing and training to be a driver. They move from one station to the next practicing the company's "340 Methods," which are techniques developed by industrial engineers "to save seconds and improve safety in every task from lifting and loading boxes to selecting a package from a shelf in the truck." Applicants play a video game where they're in the driver's seat and must identify obstacles. From computer simulations, they move to "Clarksville," a mock village with miniature houses and faux businesses. There, they drive a real truck and "must successfully execute five deliveries in 19 minutes." And, in the interest of safety and efficiency, trainees learn to carefully walk on ice with the slip and fall simulator.

How are the new training methods working? So far, so good. Of the 1,629 trainees who have completed it, "only 10 percent have failed the training program, which takes a total of six weeks overall including 30 days of driving a truck in the real world."

DISCUSSION QUESTIONS

1. What external factors were affecting UPS's HR practices? How did UPS respond to these trends?

2. Why is efficiency and safety so important to UPS? What role do the company's industrial engineers play in how employees do their work?

3. What changes did the company make to its driver training program? What do you think of these changes?

4. What advantages and drawbacks do you see to this training approach for (a) the trainee and (b) the company?

CHAPTER 8

YOUR TURN TO BE A MANAGER

Managing Change and Innovation

Skill Development: Reducing Workplace Stress

It's no secret that employees, in general, are more stressed out today than previous generations. Heavier workloads, longer hours, continual reorganizations, technology that breaks down traditional barriers between work and personal life, and reduced job security are among factors that have increased employee stress. This stress can lead to lower productivity, increased absenteeism, reduced job satisfaction, and higher quit rates. When stress is excessive, managers need to know how to reduce it.

Personal Insights: How Stressful Is My Life?

Review the following list of life events. Identify those that you have experienced in the last 12 months.

Life Event	Mean Value
1. Death of spouse	100
2. Divorce	73
3. Marital separation from mate	65
4. Detention in jail or other institution	63
5. Death of a close family member	63
6. Major personal injury or illness	53
7. Marriage	50
8. Being fired from job	47
9. Marital reconciliation with mate	45
10. Retirement from work	45
11. Major change in health or behavior of a family member	44
12. Pregnancy	40
13. Sexual difficulties	39
14. Gaining a new family member	39
15. Major business readjustment (merger, reorganization, bankruptcy, etc.)	39
16. Major change in financial state (positive or negative)	38
17. Death of a close friend	37
18. Changing to a different line of work	36
19. Major change in the number of arguments with spouse	35
20. Taking out a mortgage or loan for a major purchase (home, business, etc.)	31
21. Foreclosure on a mortgage or loan	30
22. Major change in responsibilities at work (promotion, demotion, transfer)	29
23. Son or daughter leaving home	29
24. In-law troubles	29
25. Outstanding personal achievement	28
26. Spouse beginning or ceasing work	26
27. Beginning or ceasing formal schooling	26
28. Major change in living conditions (building new house, remodeling, deterioration of neighborhood)	25
29. Revision of personal habits	24
30. Troubles with the boss	23
31. Major change in working hours or conditions	20
32. Change in residence	20
33. Changing to a new school	20
34. Major change in usual type and/or amount of recreation	19
35. Major change in church activities	19
36. Major change in social activities	18

(continued)

Life Event	Mean Value
37. Taking out a loan for a lesser purchase (car, TV, etc.)	17
38. Major change in sleeping habits.	16
39. Major change in number of family get-togethers	15
40. Major change in eating habits	15
41. Vacation	13
42. Christmas	12
43. Minor violation of the law (traffic tickets, disturbing the peace, etc.)	11

Source: T. H. Holmes and R. H. Rahe, "The Social Readjustment Rating Scale," *Journal of Psychometric Research* (1967), pp. 213–218.

Analysis and Interpretation

Life change events build up and create stress. This instrument weighs the events you've experienced in the past year in terms of their potential to create stress-induced illnesses or injuries during the next two-year period. Notice that positive events (marriage, a promotion, an inheritance) as well as negative ones can create stress.

Add up the mean values for the events that you've experienced in the past year. A cumulative score of 150 or less indicates a low susceptibility to stress-induced illnesses or injuries. A score of 151 to 300 indicates a 35 to 50 percent probability of stress-related health changes in the next two-year period. And scores of over 300 indicates an 80 percent chance of stress-induced health changes.

This instrument dramatizes that changes accumulate and, if they accumulate too much, they can overtake your body's ability to adjust. Of course, different personality types handle stress differently. Hardy types seem to do better at dealing with change and stress. These are people who believe they can control the events they encounter, are extremely committed to the activities in their lives, and who treat change in their lives as a challenge. If you're a hardy type, a high score on this instrument may not lead to negative health changes.

Skill Basics

Eliminating all stress at work isn't going to happen and it shouldn't. Stress is an unavoidable consequence of life. It also has a positive side—when it focuses concentration and creativity. But when it brings about anger, frustration, fear, sleeplessness, and the like, it needs to be addressed.

Many organizations have introduced stress-reduction interventions for employees. These include improved employee selection and placement, helping employees set realistic goals, training in time management, redesign of jobs, increased involvement of employees in decisions that affect them, expanded social support networks, improved organizational communications, and organizationally supported wellness programs. But what can *you* do, on your own, to reduce stress if your employer doesn't provide such programs or if you need to take additional action? The following individual interventions have been suggested:

Implement time-management techniques. Every person can improve his or her use of time. Time is a unique resource in that, if it's wasted, it can *never* be replaced. While people talk about *saving time*, it can never actually be saved. And if it's lost, it can't be retrieved. The good news is that it's a resource we all have in equal amounts. Everyone gets the same 24 hours a day, 7 days a week to use. When tasks seem to exceed the hours you have available, stress often results. But effective management of time can reduce stress. Time-management training can, for example, teach you how to prioritize tasks by importance and urgency, schedule activities according to those priorities, avoid confusing actions with accomplishments, and understand your productivity cycle so you can handle the most demanding tasks during the high part of your cycle when you are most alert and productive.

Create personal goals. Goal setting is designed to help you better prioritize your activities and better manage how you direct your efforts. Goals become, in effect, a personal planning tool. For instance, setting long-term goals provide general direction; while short-term goals—such as weekly or daily "to do" lists—reduce the likelihood that important activities will be overlooked and help you to maximize the use of your time.

Use physical exercise. A large body of evidence indicates that noncompetitive physical exercise can help you to release tension that builds up in stressful situations. These activities include aerobics, walking, jogging, swimming, and riding a bicycle. Physical exercise increases heart capacity, lowers the at-rest heart rate, provides a mental diversion from work pressures, and offers a means to "let off steam."

Practice relaxation training. You can teach yourself to reduce tension through meditation, deep-breathing exercises, and guided imaging. They work by taking your mind off the sources of stress, achieving a state of deep relaxation, and releasing body tension.

Expand your social support network. Having friends, family, or work colleagues to talk to provides an outlet when stress levels become excessive. Expanding your social support network, therefore, can be a means for tension reduction. It provides you with someone to hear your problems and to offer a more objective perspective on the situation.

Based on J. E. Newman and T. A. Beehr, "Personal and Organizational Strategies for Handling Job Stress," *Personnel Psychology*, Spring 1979, pp. 1–38; M. T. Matteson and J. M. Ivancevich, "Individual Stress Management Interventions: Evaluation of Techniques," *Journal of Management Psychology* (January 1987), pp. 24–30; and K. M. Richardson and H. R. Rothstein, "Effects of Occupational Stress Management Intervention Programs: A Meta-Analysis," *Journal of Occupational Health Psychology* (January 2008), pp. 69–93.

Skill Application

Dana had become frustrated in her job at Taylor Books—a chain of 22 bookstores in Georgia and Florida. After nearly 13 years as director of marketing, she felt she needed new challenges. When she was offered the job as senior account supervisor for Dancer Advertising in Tampa, she jumped at the opportunity. Now, after 4 months on the job, she's not so certain she made the right move.

At Taylor, she worked a basic 8-to-5 day. She was easily able to balance her work responsibilities with her personal responsibilities as a wife and mother of two children—ages 4 and 7. But her new job is very different. Clients call anytime—day, night, and weekends—with demands. People in Dancer's creative department are constantly asking for her input on projects. And Dana's boss expects her not only to keep her current clients happy, he also expects Dana to help secure new clients by preparing and participating in presentations and working up budgets. Last month, alone, Dana calculated that she spent 67 hours in the office plus another 12 at home working on Dancer projects. Short on sleep, frazzled by the hectic pace, having no time for her family or chores, she's lost five pounds and broken out in hives. Her doctor told her the hives were stress-induced and she needed to sort out her life.

Dana really likes her job as an account executive but feels the demands and pulls of the job are overwhelming. Yesterday she called her old boss at Taylor Books and inquired about coming back. His reply, "Dana, we'd love to have you back here but we filled your slot. We could find something for you in marketing but you wouldn't be director and the pay would be at least a third less."

If you were Dana, what would you do? Be specific.

Skill Practice

1. Think of a particularly stressful situation you had either at home or at work. What was the cause of the stress? How did you handle it? Was your approach effective? What might you have done differently to have obtained a better and/or faster result?

2. The next time you find yourself "stressed out," analyze the situation and apply one or more of the skill behaviors suggested earlier.

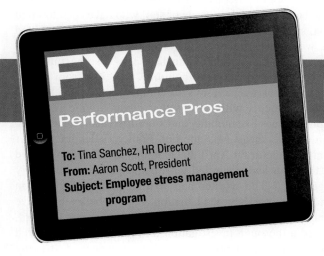

For Your Immediate Action

To: Tina Sanchez, HR Director
From: Aaron Scott, President
Subject: Employee stress management program

Well, Tina, we've made it through the initial phases of our restructuring efforts. The changes haven't been easy on any of us. But we've still got a long way to go, and that's where I need your assistance. To help minimize the pressures on our software developers and sales staff, I think we need to develop an employee stress management program that we could implement immediately. Due to finances, we don't have a lot of excess funds to spend on fitness equipment, so you're going to have to work within that constraint. Could you put together a brief (no more than one page) outline of what you think this program should include? Also, note the benefit(s) you think each suggestion would provide. I'd like some time to review your suggestions over the weekend, so please get me your report as soon as possible.

This fictionalized company and message were created for educational purposes only, and not meant to reflect positively or negatively on management practices by any company that may share this name.

Bringing the Real World to Life

Case Application: Stress Kills: Part 2

Here is what recent surveys are telling us about employee stress:

- 75 percent of Americans say their stress levels are high or moderate.
- 44 percent of Americans say their stress levels have gone up in the last five years.
- 81 percent of HR managers say that employee fatigue is a bigger problem than in past years.
- More than 50 percent of U.S. and Canadian workers say that they feel fatigued at the end of a workday. At least 40 percent of those workers say that their jobs made them depressed.
- 20 percent of U.K. workers say they have taken sick leave brought on by stress, but 90 percent have lied about the real reason for staying home.
- 30 percent of managers say they're more stressed at work today than a year ago.
- Reasons employees find work stressful: low pay, commuting, excessive workload, fear of being fired/laid off, annoying coworkers, and difficult bosses.

As you can see, stress and its effects on workers is (and should be) a serious concern for employers. When excessive pressure is placed on people from overwhelming demands or constraints they often feel they've got no choices or options. At France Télécom, the wave of employee suicides since 2008 was cause for concern. Trade union leaders "blame the allegedly brutal management culture of a company which has transformed itself over a decade from a ponderous state utility to a leading telecommunications company." However, for months, France Télécom management "dismissed the suicides as a contagious fad among its workforce." Unions then criticized the company for its poor choice of language.

The Paris prosecutor's office opened an investigation of the company over accusations of psychological harassment. The judicial inquiry stemmed from a complaint by the union Solidares Unitaires Démocratiques against France Télécom's former chief executive and two members of his top management team. The complaint accused management of conducting a "pathogenic restructuring." Excerpts of the inspector's report, although not made public, were published in the French media. It described a situation in which the company used various forms of psychological pressure in an effort to eliminate 22,000 jobs from 2006 to 2008. Company doctors alerted management about the possible psychological dangers of the stress that could accompany such drastic change. Despite these findings, a company lawyer denied that France Télécom had systematically pressured employees to leave.

Company executives realized that they needed to take drastic measures to address the issue. One of the first changes was a new CEO, Stéphane Richard, who said his priority "would be to rebuild the morale of staff who have been through trauma, suffering and much worse." The company also halted some workplace practices identified as being particularly disruptive, like involuntary transfers. It is also encouraging more supportive practices, including working from home. A company spokesperson says the company has completed two of six agreements with unions that cover a wide range of workplace issues like mobility and work/life balance and stress. Despite these measures, another France Télécom worker committed suicide in April 2011. A union official suggested that "the man had struggled with being made to frequently change jobs." The worker had written to management on several occasions about the situation and was believed to have had no reply. France Télécom's CEO, Stéphane Richard, promised a thorough investigation into the suicide. "We need to analyze in great depth and detail what happened. It is my intention that this investigation will be particularly painstaking and transparent."

DISCUSSION QUESTIONS

1. What is your reaction to the situation described in this case? What factors, both inside the company and externally, appear to have contributed to this situation?

2. What appeared to be happening in France Télécom's workplace? What stress symptoms might managers have looked for to be alerted to a problem?

3. Should managers be free to make decisions that are in the best interests of the company without worrying about employee reactions? Discuss. What are the implications for managing change?

4. What are France Télécom's executives doing to address the situation? Do you think it's enough? Are there other actions they might take? If so, describe those. If not, why not?

5. What could other companies and managers learn from this situation?

CHAPTER 9

Skill Development: Reading Emotions

Employees bring their emotions with them to work every day. Although managers would like to think that employees are always rational, they aren't. And any manager who deals with people by ignoring how emotions—such as fear, anger, love, hate, joy, and grief—shape employees' day-to-day behavior, isn't likely to be a very effective manager.

Personal Insights: What's My EI Score?

Indicate your level of agreement with these 10 statements using the following scale:

1 = Strongly disagree
2 = Disagree
3 = Neither agree or disagree
4 = Agree
5 = Strongly agree

1. I am usually aware—from moment to moment—of my feelings as they change.   1 2 3 4 5
2. I act before I think.   1 2 3 4 5
3. When I want something, I want it NOW!   1 2 3 4 5
4. I bounce back quickly from life's setbacks.   1 2 3 4 5
5. I can pick up subtle social cues that indicate others' needs or wants.   1 2 3 4 5
6. I'm very good at handling myself in social situations.   1 2 3 4 5
7. I'm persistent in going after the things I want.   1 2 3 4 5
8. When people share their problems with me, I'm good at putting myself in their shoes.   1 2 3 4 5
9. When I'm in a bad mood, I make a strong effort to get out of it.   1 2 3 4 5
10. I can find common ground and build rapport with people from all walks of life.   1 2 3 4 5

Source: Based on D. Goleman, *Emotional Intelligence: Why It Can Matter More Than IQ* (New York: Bantam Book, 1995).

Analysis and Interpretation

Emotional intelligence (EI) is an assortment of skills and competencies that have been shown to influence a person's ability to succeed in coping with environmental demands and pressures. People with high EI have the ability to accurately perceive, evaluate, express, and regulate emotions and feelings.

This questionnaire taps the five basic dimensions in EI: self-awareness (items 1 and 9), self-management (2, 4), self-motivation (3,7), empathy (5,8), and social skills (6,10). To calculate your EI score, add up your responses to the 10 items; however, reverse your scores for items 2 and 3.

Your score will fall between 10 and 50. Although no definite cutoff scores are available, scores of 40 or higher indicate a high EI. Scores of 20 or less suggest a relatively low EI.

EI may be most predictive of performance in jobs such as sales or management where success is as dependent on interpersonal skills as technical ability. EI should also be relevant in selecting members to teams. People with low EI are likely to have difficulty managing others, making effective sales presentations, and working on teams.

Skill Basics

Understanding another person's felt emotions is a difficult task. But we can learn to read others' display emotions. We do this by focusing on actual behavior as well as verbal, nonverbal, and paralinguistic cues.

1. *Assess others' emotional intelligence (EI).* Some people are more in touch with their emotions than others. Those who understand and can manage their emotions are said to be high in EI. When people exhibit the following behaviors, you should find that they have less variance in their emotions and are easier to read. People high in EI understand the way they feel (self-aware), are sensitive to the feelings of others (empathetic), voluntarily help others (socially responsible), see things the way they are rather than they way they wish them to be (reality-oriented), reach out to others and show concern for others' interests (sociable), and manage their frustrations and anger (impulse control).

2. *Ask about emotions.* The easiest way to find out what someone is feeling is to ask them. Saying something as simple as "Are you OK? What's the problem?" can frequently provide you with the information to assess an individual's emotional state. But relying on a verbal response has two drawbacks. First, almost all of us conceal our emotions to some extent for privacy and to reflect social expectations. So we might be unwilling to share our true feelings. Second, even if we want to convey our feelings verbally, we may be unable to do so. Some people have difficulty understanding their own emotions and, hence, are unable to express them verbally. So, at best, verbal responses provide only partial information.

3. *Look for nonverbal cues.* You're talking with a coworker. Does the fact that his back is rigid, his teeth clenched, and his facial muscles tight tell you something about his emotional state? It probably should. Facial expressions, gestures, body movements, and physical distance are nonverbal cues that can provide additional insights into what a person is feeling. Facial expressions, for instance, are a window into a person's feelings. Notice differences in facial features: the height of the cheeks, the raising or lowering of the brow, the turn of the mouth, the positioning of the lips, and the configuration of muscles around the eyes. Even something as subtle as the distance at which someone chooses to position him- or herself from you can convey their feelings, or lack, of intimacy, aggressiveness, repugnance, or withdrawal.

4. *Look for how things are said.* As Janet and I talked, I noticed a sharp change in the tone of her voice and the speed at which she spoke. I was tapping into the third source of information on a person's emotions—*paralanguage*. This is communication that goes beyond the specific spoken words. It includes pitch, amplitude, rate, and voice quality of speech. Paralanguage reminds us that people convey their feelings not only in *what* they say, but also in *how* they say it.

Based on V. P. Richmond, J. C. McCroskey, and S. K. Payne, *Nonverbal Behavior in Interpersonal Relations*, 2nd ed. (Englewood Cliffs, NJ: Prentice Hall, 1991), pp. 117–138; R. Bar-On, *The Emotional Intelligence Inventory (EQ-I): Technical Manual* (Toronto: Multi-Health Systems, 1997); L. A. King, "Ambivalence over Emotional Expression and Reading Emotions in Situations and Faces," *Journal of Personality and Social Psychology* (March 1998), pp. 753–762; and M. Lewis, J. M. Haviland-Jones, and L. F. Barrett (eds.), *Handbook of Emotions*, 3rd ed. (New York: Guilford Press, 2011).

Skill Application

Part A. Form groups of two. Each person is to spend a couple of minutes thinking (without sharing with the other person) of a time in the past when he or she was emotional about something. Examples might include being upset with a parent, sibling, or friend; being excited or disappointed about an academic or athletic achievement; being angry with someone over an insult or slight; being disgusted by something someone has said or done; or being happy because of something good that happened.

Part B. Now you'll conduct two role plays. Each will be an interview. In the first, one person will play the interviewer and the other will play the job applicant. The job is for a summer management internship with a large retail chain. Each role play will last no longer than 10 minutes. The interviewer is to conduct a normal job interview except you are to continually rethink the emotional episode you envisioned in Part A. Try hard to convey this emotion while, at the same time, being professional in interviewing the job applicant.

Part C. Now reverse positions for the second role play. The interviewer becomes the job applicant, and vice versa. The new interviewer will conduct a normal job interview except that he or she will continually rethink the emotional episode chosen in Part A.

Part D. Spend 10 minutes deconstructing the interview, with specific attention focused on what emotion(s) you think the other was conveying? What cues did you pick up? How accurate were you in reading those cues?

Skill Practice

1. Rent a video of an emotionally laden film such as *Death of a Salesman* or *Twelve Angry Men*. Carefully watch the actors for clues to the emotions they are exhibiting. Try to determine the various emotions projected and explain how you arrived at your conclusion.

2. If you're currently working, spend a day specifically looking for emotional cues in interactions with colleagues. How accurate do you think your assessments of those emotions were? What, if anything, did you see that you would normally miss?

Skill Development: Reading Personality

People are all different. And one way we differentiate people is by their personality traits. The more insight managers have to the personality of the people they need to work with—bosses, colleagues, subordinates, customers—the better job they can do. Why? Because they can adjust their behavior to reflect the characteristics of the person or persons with whom they have to work.

Personal Insights: What's My Basic Personality?

Listed here are 15 adjective pairs. For each, select the number along the scale (you must choose a whole number) that most closely describes you or your preferences.

1.	Quiet	1	2	3	4	5	Talkative
2.	Tolerant	1	2	3	4	5	Critical
3.	Disorganized	1	2	3	4	5	Organized
4.	Tense	1	2	3	4	5	Calm
5.	Imaginative	1	2	3	4	5	Conventional
6.	Reserved	1	2	3	4	5	Outgoing
7.	Uncooperative	1	2	3	4	5	Cooperative
8.	Unreliable	1	2	3	4	5	Dependable
9.	Insecure	1	2	3	4	5	Secure
10.	New	1	2	3	4	5	Familiar
11.	Sociable	1	2	3	4	5	Loner
12.	Suspicious	1	2	3	4	5	Trusting
13.	Undirected	1	2	3	4	5	Goal-oriented
14.	Enthusiastic	1	2	3	4	5	Depressed
15.	Change	1	2	3	4	5	Status quo

Source: Based on O. P. John, "The 'Big Five' Factor Taxonomy: Dimensions of Personality in the Natural Language and in Questionnaires," in L. A. Pervin (ed.), *Handbook of Personality Theory and Research* (New York: Guilford Press, 1990), pp. 66–100; and D. L. Formy-Duval, J. E. Williams, D. J. Patterson, and E. E. Fogle, "A 'Big Five' Scoring System for the Item Pool of the Adjective Check List," *Journal of Personality Assessment*, 65 (1995), pp. 59–76.

Analysis and Interpretation

The five-factor model of personality—often referred to as the Big Five—has an impressive body of research supporting that five basic personality dimensions underlie human behavior. These five dimensions are defined as follows:

Extraversion—Someone who is sociable, talkative, and assertive. High scores indicate you're an extravert; low scores indicate you're an introvert.

Agreeableness—Someone who is good-natured, cooperative, and trusting. It is a measure of your propensity to defer to others. High scores indicate you value harmony; low scores indicate you prefer having your say or way on issues.

Conscientiousness—Someone who is responsible, dependable, persistent, and achievement oriented. High scores indicate that you pursue fewer goals in a purposeful way; while low scores indicate that you're more easily distracted, pursue many goals, and are more hedonistic.

Emotional stability—Someone who is calm, enthusiastic, and secure. High scores indicate positive emotional stability, with low scores indicating negative emotional stability.

Openness to experience—Someone who is imaginative, artistically sensitive, and intellectual. High scores indicate you have a wide range of interests and a fascination with novelty and innovation; low scores indicate you're more conventional and find comfort in the familiar.

To calculate your personality score, add up your points as follows (reverse scoring those items marked with an asterisk):

Items 1, 6, and 11*. This is your extraversion score.

Items 2*, 7, and 12. This is your agreeableness score.

Items 3, 8, and 13. This is your conscientiousness score.

Items 4, 9, and 14*. This is your emotional stability score.

Items 5*, 10*, and 15*. This is your openness-to-experience score.

What defines a high or low score? No definite cutoffs are available. However, reasonable cutoffs for each dimension would be 12–15 points = high; 7–11 = moderate; and 3–6 = low.

The most impressive evidence relates to the conscientiousness dimension. Studies show that conscientiousness predicts job performance for all occupational groups. The preponderance of evidence indicates that individuals who are dependable, reliable, thorough, organized, able to plan, and persistent (that is, high on conscientiousness) tend to have higher job performance in most if not all occupations. In addition, individuals who score high in conscientiousness develop higher levels of job knowledge, probably because highly conscientious people exert greater levels of effort on their job. The higher levels of job knowledge then contribute to higher levels of job performance.

Other insights from your scores: High scores on extraversion indicate you may be suited to a managerial or sales position.

These occupations require high social interaction. And high scores on openness-to-experience is a good predictor of your ability to achieve significant benefits from training efforts.

Skill Basics

Ideally, it would be nice to know the personality characteristics of individuals we have to deal with in our jobs. It would allow us to better communicate and help us predict responses to our actions. Unfortunately, people don't come with ID tags identifying their personality traits. And we don't typically have the luxury of testing them to have a reliable measure of those traits. So we're usually forced to try to make sense of others' personality characteristics through observations. With the caveat that these observations are likely to be poor substitutes for a more objective, questionnaire-based assessment, the following should help you to gain insights into others' personality:

- Is the person more extroverted and enthusiastic or reserved and quiet? This question taps the dimension of extroversion.
- Is the person more critical and quarrelsome or sympathetic and warm? This question taps the dimension of agreeableness.
- Is the person dependable and self-disciplined or disorganized and careless? This question taps the dimension of conscientiousness.
- Is the person more anxious and easily upset or calm and emotionally stable? This question taps the dimension of emotional stability.
- Is the person more open to new experiences and complex or conventional and uncreative? This question taps the dimension of openness to experience.

Based on S. D. Gosling, P. J. Rentfrow, and W. B. Swann Jr., "A Very Brief Measure of the Big-Five Personality Domains," *Journal of Research in Personality* (December 2003), pp. 504–528; and P. Y. Herzberg and E. Brahler, "Assessing the Big-Five Personality Domains via Short Forms: A Cautionary Note and a Proposal," *European Journal of Psychological Assessment*, 23, no. 3 (2006), pp. 139–148.

Skill Application

Form into teams of three. Each team is to identify four well-known people (film stars, television personalities, business executives, local celebrities) with whom all members of the team feel familiar. The team will then analyze each of these people in terms of how they would describe his or her personality. Team members should be able to provide specific behavioral examples to support their personality assessment.

How much agreement was there among team members in assessing each personality? Where was there disagreement? To what degree did this exercise support the view that it's possible to read personality traits?

Skill Practice

1. Identify a person you know well and with whom you feel comfortable sharing intimate information. Assess that person's personality using the preceding questions. Now share that assessment with the individual. To what degree did the person agree or disagree with your assessment? "It's easier to accurately rate the traits of celebrities than your normal work colleagues, friends, or relatives because they tend toward extremes." Do you agree or disagree with this statement and why?

2. How would you rate yourself on the five personality traits? Ask four or five of your friends to also rate you. How closely did the ratings match? Based on your personality profile, what jobs do you think you're well suited for? What jobs do you think would be a poor fit with your personality traits?

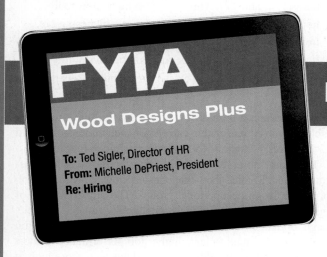

FYIA
Wood Designs Plus

To: Ted Sigler, Director of HR
From: Michelle DePriest, President
Re: Hiring

For Your Immediate Action

Ted, as we discussed last Friday, our manufacturing operations have grown to the point where we need to add a couple of people to our executive team; specifically, a corporate controller and a national sales director. The controller will be responsible for establishing operational and financial standards (in other words, a lot of number-crunching using financial and manufacturing statistics) for our various work units. The national sales director will be responsible for working closely with our sales staff to further develop long-lasting and mutually beneficial relationships with our customers.

I recall something from a management class I took in college that certain personality types fit best with certain types of jobs. Could you do some research on this topic for me? Write up a short report (no more than a page) describing the personality type that might be an appropriate match for each of these new positions. Get this to me by the end of the week.

This fictionalized company and message were created for educational purposes only, and not meant to reflect positively or negatively on management practices by any company that may share this name.

Bringing the Real World to Life

Case Application: Employees First: Part 2

HCL Technologies is headquartered in the world's largest democracy, so it's quite fitting that the New Delhi—based company is attempting a radical experiment in workplace democracy. CEO Vineet Nayar is committed to creating a company where the job of company leaders is to enable people to find their own destiny by gravitating to their strengths. As we discussed in the chapter opener, one thing that Nayar has done is to pioneer a culture in which employees are first. What has he done to put employees first? Part of the cultural initiative dealt with the organization's structure. HCL inverted its organizational structure and placed more power in the hands of frontline employees, especially those in direct contact with customers and clients. It increased its investment in employee development and improved communication through greater transparency. Employees were encouraged to communicate directly with Nayar. Through a forum called U&I (You and I), Nayar fielded more than a hundred questions from employees every week. "I threw open the door and invited criticism," he said. However, the signature piece of the company's cultural mission is probably what HCL called "trust pay." In contrast to the industry standard in which the average employee's pay is 30 percent variable, HCL decided to pay higher fixed salaries and reduce the variable component.

Does the unique "employees first" culture at HCL Technologies attract unique employees? Rajeev Sawhney, HCL's European president would say it does. He uses *Slumdog Millionaire,* the movie that won the Academy Award for Best Picture in 2009, as a parallel. "It (the movie) is a reflection of the Indian race. It shows the adversity that creates the desire in people to reach out and create. . . . With each adversity they face, there is a greater desire to reach out and do something more." Sawhney says that entrepreneurialism is a key value of the HCL culture. "You can still tell an HCL person from a mile off. I think there is a particular DNA for an HCL person.

It includes a very high need for achievement and very persuasive skills. HCL people are very energetic; they want to do lots of things and to take risks on behalf of the company."

DISCUSSION QUESTIONS

1. What is your impression of an "employees first" culture? Would this work in other organizations? Why or why not? What would it take to make it work?

2. How might an understanding of organizational behavior help CEO Vineet Nayar lead his company? Be specific. How about first-line company supervisors? Again, be specific.

3. What aspects of personality do you see in this story about HCL? How have the personality traits of HCL employees contributed to make HCL what it is?

4. Design an employee attitude survey for HCL's employees.

CHAPTER 10

YOUR TURN
TO BE **A MANAGER**

Understanding Groups and
Managing Work Teams

Skill Development: Working with Teams

Organizations have become increasingly designed around teams. Twenty years ago, the individual was the basic building block of an organization; today it's teams. And the manager who can't effectively be part of a team or lead a team is likely to have a short tenure in his or her management position.

Personal Insights: How Good Am I at Building and Leading a Team?

Use the following rating scale to respond to the 18 questions on building and leading an effective team:

  1 = Strongly disagree
  2 = Disagree
  3 = Slightly disagree
  4 = Slightly agree
  5 = Agree
  6 = Strongly agree

1. I am knowledgeable about the different stages of development that teams can go through in their life cycles.   1 2 3 4 5 6

2. When a team forms, I make certain that all team members are introduced to one another at the outset.   1 2 3 4 5 6

3. When the team first comes together, I provide directions, answer team members' questions, and clarify goals, expectations, and procedures.   1 2 3 4 5 6

4. I help team members establish a foundation of trust among one another and between themselves and me.   1 2 3 4 5 6

5. I ensure that standards of excellence—not mediocrity or mere acceptability—characterize the team's work.   1 2 3 4 5 6

6. I provide a great deal of feedback to team members regarding their performance.   1 2 3 4 5 6

7. I encourage team members to balance individual autonomy with interdependence among other team members.   1 2 3 4 5 6

8. I help team members become at least as committed to the success of the team as to their own personal success.   1 2 3 4 5 6

9. I help members learn to play roles that assist the team in accomplishing its tasks as well as building strong interpersonal relationships.   1 2 3 4 5 6

10. I articulate a clear, exciting, passionate vision of what the team can achieve.   1 2 3 4 5 6

11. I help team members become committed to the team vision.   1 2 3 4 5 6

12. I encourage a win/win philosophy in the team; that is, when one member wins, every member wins.   1 2 3 4 5 6

13. I help the team avoid "groupthink" or making the group's survival more important than accomplishing its goal.   1 2 3 4 5 6

14. I use formal process management procedures to help the group become faster, more efficient, and more productive, and to prevent errors.   1 2 3 4 5 6

15. I encourage team members to represent the team's vision, goals, and accomplishments to outsiders.   1 2 3 4 5 6

16. I diagnose and capitalize on the team's core competence.   1 2 3 4 5 6

17. I encourage the team to achieve dramatic breakthrough innovations as well as small continuous improvements.   1 2 3 4 5 6

18. I help the team work toward preventing mistakes, not just correcting them after-the-fact.   1 2 3 4 5 6

Source: Adapted from D. A. Whetten and K. S. Cameron, *Developing Management Skills*, 3rd ed. (New York: HarperCollins, 1995), pp. 534–535.

Analysis and Interpretation

The authors of this instrument propose that it assesses team development behaviors in five areas: diagnosing team development (items 1, 16); managing the forming stage (2–4); managing the conforming stage (6–9, 13); managing the storming stage (10–12, 14, 15), and managing the performing stage (5, 17, 18).

To calculate your total score, add up your scores on the 18 individual items. Your score will range between 18 and 108.

Based on a norm group of 500 business students, the following can help estimate where you are relative to others:

Total score of 95 or above = You're in the top quartile

72–94 = You're in the second quartile

60–71 = You're in the third quartile

Below 60 = You're in the bottom quartile

Skill Basics

Managers and team leaders need to be able to create effective teams. You can increase the effectiveness of your teams if you use the following nine behaviors.

1. *Establish a common purpose.* An effective team needs a common purpose to which all members aspire. This purpose is a vision. It's broader than any specific goals. This common purpose provides direction, momentum, and commitment for team members.

2. *Assess team strengths and weaknesses.* Team members will have different strengths and weaknesses. Knowing these strengths and weaknesses can help the team leader build on the strengths and compensate for the weaknesses.

3. *Develop specific individual goals.* Specific individual goals help lead team members to achieve higher performance. In addition, specific goals facilitate clear communication and help maintain the focus on getting results.

4. *Get agreement on a common approach for achieving goals.* Goals are the ends a team strives to attain. Defining and agreeing on a common approach ensures that the team is unified on the *means* for achieving those ends.

5. *Encourage acceptance of responsibility for both individual and team performance.* Successful teams make members individually and jointly accountable for the team's purpose, goals, and approach. Members understand what they are individually responsible for and what they are jointly responsible for.

6. *Build mutual trust among members.* When there is *trust,* team members believe in the integrity, character, and ability of each other. When trust is lacking, members are unable to depend on each other. Teams that lack trust tend to be short-lived.

7. *Maintain an appropriate mix of team member skills and personalities.* Team members come to the team with different skills and personalities. To perform effectively, teams need three types of skills. They need people with technical expertise, people with problem-solving and decision-making skills, and people with good interpersonal skills.

8. *Provide needed training and resources.* Team leaders need to make sure that their teams have both the training and the resources they need to accomplish their goals.

9. *Create opportunities for small achievements.* Building an effective team takes time. Team members have to learn to think and work as a team. New teams can't be expected to hit home runs every time they come to bat, especially at the beginning. Instead, team members should be encouraged to try for small achievements initially.

Based on J. R. Katzenback and D. K. Smith, *The Wisdom of Teams* (Boston: Harvard Business Press, 1993); M. Hanlan, *High Performance Teams: How to Make Them Work* (New York: Praeger, 2005); and L. Thompson, *Making the Team*, 3rd ed. (Upper Saddle River, NJ: Prentice Hall, 2008).

Skill Application

You're the leader of a five-member project team that's been assigned the task of moving your engineering firm into the growing area of high-speed intercity rail construction. You and your team members have been researching the field, identifying specific business opportunities, negotiating alliances with equipment vendors, and evaluating high-speed rail experts and consultants from around the world. Throughout the process, Tonya, a highly qualified and respected engineer, has challenged a number of things you've said during team meetings and in the workplace. For example, at a meeting two weeks ago, you presented the team with a list of 10 possible high-speed rail projects and started evaluating your organization's ability to compete for them. Tonya contradicted virtually all your comments, questioned your statistics, and was quite pessimistic about the possibility of getting contracts on these projects. After this latest display of displeasure, two other group members, Bryan and Maggie, came to you and complained that Tonya's actions were damaging the team's effectiveness. You originally put Tonya on the team for her unique expertise and insight. You'd like to find a way to reach her and get the team on the right track to its fullest potential.

Form three-member teams in class. Each team should analyze the leader's problem and suggest solutions. Each team should be prepared to present its conclusions to the class.

Skill Practice

1. Interview three managers at different organizations. Ask them about their experiences in managing teams. Have each describe teams that they thought were effective and why they succeeded. Have each also describe teams that they thought were ineffective and the reasons that might have caused this.

2. Think about teams of which you've been a member: Contrast a team in which members trusted each other with another team in which members lacked trust with each other. How did these conditions develop? What were the consequences in terms of interaction patterns and performance?

Skill Development: Resolving Conflicts

Studies have found that managing conflicts is one of the top activities consuming a manager's time. Therefore, how effective a manager is in handling conflicts will go a long way in determining how successful he or she will be on the job.

Personal Insights: What's My Preferred Conflict-Handling Style?

When you differ with someone, how do you respond? Use the following rating scale to record your answers:

1 = Practically never

2 = Once in a great while

3 = Sometimes

4 = Fairly often

5 = Very often

1. I work to come out victorious, no matter what.	1 2 3 4 5
2. I try to put the needs of others above my own.	1 2 3 4 5
3. I look for a mutually satisfactory solution.	1 2 3 4 5
4. I try not to get involved in conflicts.	1 2 3 4 5
5. I strive to investigate issues thoroughly and jointly.	1 2 3 4 5
6. I never back away from a good argument.	1 2 3 4 5
7. I strive to foster harmony.	1 2 3 4 5
8. I negotiate to get a portion of what I propose.	1 2 3 4 5
9. I avoid open discussions of controversial subjects.	1 2 3 4 5
10. I openly share information with others in resolving disagreements.	1 2 3 4 5
11. I would rather win than end up compromising.	1 2 3 4 5
12. I go along with suggestions of others.	1 2 3 4 5
13. I look for a middle ground to resolve disagreements.	1 2 3 4 5
14. I keep my true opinions to myself to avoid hard feelings.	1 2 3 4 5
15. I encourage the open sharing of concerns and issues.	1 2 3 4 5
16. I am reluctant to admit I am wrong.	1 2 3 4 5
17. I try to help others avoid losing face in a disagreement.	1 2 3 4 5
18. I stress the advantages of give-and-take.	1 2 3 4 5
19. I agree early on, rather than argue about a point.	1 2 3 4 5
20. I state my position as only one point of view.	1 2 3 4 5

Source: Based on conflict dimensions defined in K. W. Thomas, "Conflict and Conflict Management," in M. Dunnette (ed.), *Handbook of Industrial and Organizational Psychology* (Chicago: Rand McNally, 1976), pp. 889–935.

Analysis and Interpretation

Research has identified five conflict-handling styles. They are defined as follows:

Competing = A desire to satisfy one's interests, regardless of the impact on the other party to the conflict. Items 1, 6, 11, and 16 in this instrument tap this style.

Collaborating = Where the parties to a conflict each desire to satisfy fully the concerns of all parties. Items 5, 10, 15, and 20 in this instrument.

Avoiding = The desire to withdraw from or suppress the conflict. Items 4, 9, 14, and 19 in this instrument.

Accommodating = Willingness of one party in a conflict to place the opponent's interests above his or her own. Items 2, 7, 12, and 17 in this instrument.

Compromising = Where each party to a conflict is willing to give up something. Items 3, 8, 13, and 18 in this instrument.

To calculate your conflict-handling score, add up your totals for each of the five categories. Your score within each category will range from 4 to 20. The category you score highest in is your preferred conflict-handling style. Your next-highest total is your secondary style.

Ideally, we should adjust our conflict-handling style to the situation. For instance, avoidance works well when a conflict is trivial, when emotions are running high and time is needed to cool them down, or when the potential disruption from a more assertive action outweighs the benefits of a resolution. In contrast, competing works well when you need a quick resolution on important issues where unpopular actions must be taken, or when commitment by others to your solution is not critical. But the evidence indicates that we all have a preferred style for handling conflicts. When "push comes to shove," this is the style we tend to rely on.

Skill Basics

To manage conflict effectively, you need to know yourself, as well as the conflicting parties; to understand the situation that has created the conflict; and to be aware of your options.

What's your underlying conflict-handling style? Most of us have the ability to vary our conflict response according to the situation, but each of us has a preferred style for handling conflicts. These styles include *collaborating* (accommodating various points of view to seek a win-win solution); *compromising* (we both give up something so there is no clear winner or loser); *accommodating* (self-sacrificing by putting others' interests above your own); *forcing* (satisfying your own interest regardless of the impact on others); and *avoiding* (withdrawing from or suppressing differences).

Selectively choose the conflicts you want to handle. Not every conflict justifies your attention. Avoidance may appear to be a cop-out, but it can sometimes be the most appropriate response. Avoid trivial conflicts and save your efforts for the ones that count.

Evaluate the conflict parties. Who is involved in the conflict? What interests do you or they represent? What are each party's values, personality, feelings, and resources?

Assess the source of the conflict. The most common sources of interpersonal conflicts in organizations are communication differences, structural differences (i.e., rules, territorial battles, budget conflicts, questions of authority), and personality and value differences. Communication conflicts are typically the easiest to resolve, while personality and value differences the most difficult. Knowing the source of a conflict will narrow your choices of resolution techniques.

Select the best option. In addition to the five preferred-styles of handling conflict noted above, additional resolution techniques include expanding the scarce resource (such as a budget or promotion opportunities) that is causing the conflict; creating a shared goal that requires all parties to the conflict to cooperate on; behavioral-change intervention and counseling; and reorganizing jobs or departments.

Based on S. P. Robbins, *Managing Organizational Conflict* (Englewood Cliffs, NJ: Prentice Hall, 1974); K. W. Thomas, "Conflict and Conflict Management," in Marvin Dunnette (ed.), *Handbook of Industrial and Organizational Psychology* (Chicago: Rand McNally, 1976), pp. 889–935; and K. Cloke and J. Goldsmith, *Resolving Conflicts at Work: Eight Strategies for Everyone on the Job*, rev. ed. (San Francisco: Jossey-Bass, 2006).

Skill Application

Form teams of three. Analyze each of the following scenarios and formulate a conflict-handling strategy:

Situation 1. You are a staff specialist and have been assigned two projects: one by your immediate supervisor and one by the supervisor of another department. There is adequate time to complete both projects by the deadline date, however, neither project would be completed with the degree of excellence required by your organization. What would you do?

Situation 2. You are the moderator of a group session with five other people. The purpose of the session is to formulate a plan that requires consent from all participants. One of the participants is so involved with the important details of the plan that he is delaying the group from reaching agreement. As moderator, what would you do in this situation?

Situation 3. Your boss has called you into his office and you find that he wants your opinion about the performance of one of your coworkers. The coworker is your best friend and neighbor, but you are inclined to believe that his performance is substandard. What would you tell the boss?

Skill Practice

1.   Interview several managers to learn (a) what they think their basic conflict-handling style is; (b) how flexible they perceive themselves to be in adjusting their style to changing situations; (c) and how effective they have been in mastering the skills of conflict management.

2.   Think of three conflict situations you've faced in recent months. How did you handle the conflict? How effective was your approach? What could you have done differently to improve the outcome?

For Your Immediate Action

Colorado State High School Sports Association

To: Eric Gershman, Manager, Program Infractions Investigations

From: Audrey Costa, Director of Association Services

Subject: Conflicts on Investigation Teams

Eric, we've got a problem. I've been receiving complaints that the members of the five-person investigation teams we're sending out to high schools to investigate allegations of rules infractions are having conflicts. Because team members have to work closely together in interviewing people, interpreting the rules, and writing up reports, I'm worried that this conflict may be hurting the quality of the teams' investigation process. We've got to address this problem immediately in order to protect our reputation for being fair and reasonable in our rules enforcement. Please send me a bulleted list (no longer than a page) describing how you're going to address this problem and get it to me as soon as possible. Once I've had a chance to look it over, we'll get together to discuss it.

This fictionalized company and message were created for educational purposes only, and not meant to reflect positively or negatively on management practices by any company that may share this name.

Bringing the Real World to Life

Case Application: Intel Inside . . . and Far Away: Part 2

As one of Intel's premier research and development labs, the Israel Development Center (IDC) has employed engineers for almost 40 years. The technology behind the highly successful Centrino chips for laptops came out of this lab, as have processors for servers, PCs, and laptops. The group atmosphere at IDC, although quite confrontational, actually helped Centrino get off the ground and become a marketplace and financial success for Intel. Getting there, however, wasn't easy.

During the initial design stages of Centrino, the focus, as always, was on processor chip speed. But the reality is that fast

chips consume more power and shorten battery life. And when designing a product for use in wireless computers, that's not a good thing. An engineer at IDC came to the team leader and suggested that by giving up half the chip speed that power consumption could also be cut by half as well. Such a suggestion probably wouldn't have survived long at the home office because it involved challenging everything that the company stood for. However, here in a location where the group wasn't bound by such cultural constraints, it led to the development of a winning product.

Another benefit of having design groups thousands of miles away from headquarters in Santa Clara, California (some 28 percent of the company's R&D employees are located in more than 20 countries outside the United States), is that these off-site locations don't suffer from bureaucratic inertia associated with constant meetings and committees.

However, the challenge for Intel's geographically dispersed teams is that when team members live and work in different countries, time zones, diverse cultures, and dissimilar languages "add complexities to the difficult tasks associated with successful teamwork." One thing that has worked for Intel is the virtual retrospective.

A retrospective is "a formal method for evaluating project performance, extracting lessons learned, and making recommendations for the future." Because Intel's design teams are geographically dispersed, they collaborate virtually over an audio or video connection. Such retrospectives allow Intel's teams to connect and collaborate. The major problems, though, are simple things like finding a common time to meet. For instance, setting up a virtual retrospective between IDC and an

Intel team in Hillsboro, Oregon, involved a 10-hour time difference. However, they resolved it as the Israeli team members agreed to shift their work day and start the retrospective at 5 P.M. Haifa time, which was 7 A.M. Hillsboro time. Another challenge is that these virtual meetings usually last longer than normal simply because the teams usually have numerous issues to discuss. Also, team leaders need to take into account cultural differences (speaking styles, family commitments), safety (establishing an environment where all participants feel free to express observations and opinions), and fairness (locations with a large number of participants can dominate the discussion and limit input from sites with fewer participants).

Despite the challenges, Intel's project managers have found that having a way for their geographically dispersed teams to collaborate and connect is vital and valuable.

DISCUSSION QUESTIONS

1. What challenges have Intel's managers faced in connecting their geographically dispersed teams?

2. How have they dealt with these challenges?

3. Would a "confrontational" atmosphere be appropriate in all team situations? Explain.

4. Discuss how roles, norms, status, group size, and cohesiveness might affect these geographically dispersed teams.

5. Compare the team characteristics described here against the characteristics of effective teams as shown in Exhibit 10–6 (see p. 259). Which ones does the IDC team appear to have?

YOUR TURN TO BE A MANAGER
Motivating and Rewarding Employees

Skill Development: Applying Motivation Concepts

Great managers are great motivators. They're able to find the magic "potion" that stimulates employees to reach their full potential. The fact that there are hundreds of business books on motivation and dozens of experts who make a living by putting on motivation seminars only confirms the importance of this topic to managerial effectiveness.

Personal Insights: Do I Want an Enriched Job?

Listed here are 12 pairs of jobs. For each pair, indicate which job you would prefer—Job A or Job B. Assume that everything else about the jobs is the same. Use the following rating scale for your responses, and try to minimize your use of the "neutral" selection:

1 = Strongly prefer A
2 = Prefer A
3 = Slightly prefer A
4 = Neutral
5 = Slightly prefer B
6 = Prefer B
7 = Strongly prefer B

1. Job A   A job that offers little or no challenge.   1 2 3 4 5 6 7
   Job B   A job that requires you to be completely isolated from coworkers.

2. Job A   A job that pays very well.   1 2 3 4 5 6 7
   Job B   A job that allows considerable opportunity to be creative and innovative.

3. Job A   A job that often requires you to make important decisions.   1 2 3 4 5 6 7
   Job B   A job in which there are many pleasant people to work with.

4. Job A   A job with little security in a somewhat unstable organization.   1 2 3 4 5 6 7
   Job B   A job in which you have little or no opportunity to participate in decisions which affect your work.

5. Job A   A job in which greater responsibility is given to those who do the best work.   1 2 3 4 5 6 7
   Job B   A job in which great responsibility is given to loyal employees who have the most seniority.

6. Job A   A job with a supervisor who sometimes is highly critical.   1 2 3 4 5 6 7
   Job B   A job that does not require you to use much of your talent.

7. Job A   A very routine job.   1 2 3 4 5 6 7
   Job B   A job where your co-workers are not very friendly.

8. Job A   A job with a supervisor who respects you and treats you fairly.   1 2 3 4 5 6 7
   Job B   A job that provides constant opportunities for you to learn new and interesting things.

9. Job A   A job that gives you a real chance to develop yourself personally.   1 2 3 4 5 6 7
   Job B   A job with excellent vacations and fringe benefits.

10. Job A   A job where there is a real chance you could be laid off.   1 2 3 4 5 6 7
    Job B   A job with very little chance to do challenging work.

11. Job A   A job with little freedom and independence to do your work in the way you think best.   1 2 3 4 5 6 7
    Job B   A job with poor working conditions.

12. Job A   A job with very satisfying teamwork.   1 2 3 4 5 6 7
    Job B   A job that allows you to use your skills and abilities to the fullest extent.

Source: Adapted from J. R. Hackman and G. R. Oldham, *The Job Diagnostic Survey: An instrument for the Diagnosis of Jobs and the Evaluation of Job Redesign Projects.* Technical Report No. 4 (New Haven, CT: Yale University, Department of Administrative Sciences, 1974). With permission.

Analysis and Interpretation

This instrument is designed to assess the degree to which you desire complex, challenging work. A high need for growth suggests that you are more likely to experience the desired psychological states in the Job Characteristics Model when you have an enriched job.

This 12-item instrument taps the degree to which you have a strong versus weak desire to obtain growth satisfaction from your work. To calculate your growth need strength score, average the 12 items as follows:

1, 2, 7, 8, 11, and 12 (direct scoring)
3, 4, 5, 6, 9, and 10 (reverse scoring)

Average scores for typical respondents are close to the midpoint of 4.0. Research indicates that if you score high on this measure, you will respond positively to an enriched job.

Conversely, if you score low, you will tend *not* to find enriched jobs satisfying or motivating.

You should take away two insights from this exercise. First, it gives you an idea of your personal preference. Second, and more important in your role as a manager, it should remind you that everyone isn't like you. Some people have a greater need for growth and thus prefer characteristics like variety and autonomy in their jobs. But others prefer jobs that offer routine and standardized tasks. Don't automatically impose your needs onto others.

Skill Basics

Attempting to motivate others is a complex task. Unfortunately, no universal motivators are available that are guaranteed to work on anyone, anywhere. That said, we do know a lot about what works and doesn't work in terms of motivating others. The following suggestions summarize the essence of what we know is likely to be effective.

1. *Recognize individual differences.* People have different needs. Don't treat them all alike. Moreover, spend the time necessary to understand what's important to each person. This will allow you to individualize goals, level of involvement, and rewards to align with individual needs.

2. *Use goals and feedback.* People prefer to have goals. If you're in a position to assign or participate in setting goals for others, help them to set hard and specific goals. These are most likely to motivate. In addition, individuals are most likely to be motivated when they get feedback on how well they are faring in the pursuit of their goals.

3. *Allow people to participate in decisions that affect them.* If you are in a position to influence the level of participation, actively seek input from the person you seek to motivate. Employees are especially likely to respond positively when allowed to participate in setting work goals, choosing their benefit packages, solving productivity and quality problems, and the like.

4. *Link rewards to unsatisfied needs.* Recommendations #2 and #3 apply most directly to managers or team leaders trying to motivate their employees or team members. Effectively linking rewards to unsatisfied needs is a more generalizable action: It applies to motivating colleagues, friends, spouses, customers—as well as employees and team members. It builds on recommendation #1 and individual differences.

   Depending on your position in an organization and your resources, the rewards you control will vary. For example, senior-level executives typically can control pay increases, bonuses, promotion decisions, job assignments, and training decisions. They also can usually control job design such as allowing employees more freedom and control over their work, improving working conditions, increasing social interactions in the workplace, or modifying the workload. But everyone can offer others rewards such as recognition or providing sympathetic and sensitive help with problems. The key is identifying what needs are dominant and unsatisfied, then choosing rewards that will help satisfy those needs.

5. *Link rewards to performance.* The rewards you choose should be allocated so as to be contingent on performance. Importantly, the person you're trying to motivate must perceive a clear linkage. Regardless of how closely rewards are actually correlated to performance criteria, it's perception that counts. If individuals perceive this relationship to be low, motivation and performance will suffer.

6. *Maintain equity.* Rewards should be perceived by people in the organization as equating with the inputs they bring to their job. At a simplistic level, it means that experience, skills, abilities, effort, and other obvious inputs should explain differences in performance and, hence, pay, job assignments, and other obvious rewards.

Based on V. H. Vroom, *Work and Motivation* (New York: John Wiley, 1964); J. S. Adams, "Inequity in Social Exchanges," in L. Berkowitz (ed.), *Advances in Experimental Social Psychology* (New York: Academic Press, 1965),. pp. 267–300; and E. A. Locke and G. P. Latham, *A Theory of Goal Setting and Task Performance* (Upper Saddle River, NJ: Prentice Hall, 1990).

Skill Application

Sean's first job out of college is as a supervisor for Lyle's Catering Services. One of Lyle's main businesses is managing the food service operations at colleges and hospitals.

Sean has been given responsibility for the cafeteria at St. Paul College. He has a staff of approximately 12 full-time and 15 part-time workers. The cafeteria is open 7 days a week, from 6:30 A.M. until 8 P.M.

Sean has been in the job eight months and has become frustrated by the high employee turnover. Just since he's been on the job, 3 full-time and 6 part-time people have quit. Sean went back and looked at the personnel records for the past 5 years and this pattern has been a constant. He's frustrated by the cost and time involved in continually hiring and training new people. He's decided he needs to do something.

Sean has begun informally talking to employees. None seem particularly enthusiastic about their jobs. Even some of the "old timers"—who've worked in the cafeteria for six years or more—have little enthusiasm for their work. In fact, the part-timers seem more motivated than the full-timers even though the average part-timer makes only $11.50 an hour versus the full-timers' $15.00.

The class should form into small groups. Assume you are Sean. How can you improve the staff's motivation and reduce the turnover rate?

Skill Practice

1. Think of the worst job you've had. Was there anything management could have done to make the job better for you?

2. Interview a friend or family member who seems very satisfied in his or her job. What does this person like about his or job? What doesn't he or she like? What does he or she attribute this high job satisfaction to? How much of this person's high satisfaction do you think is attributable to the job and how much do you think is just inherent in the individual's personal outlook on life?

For Your Immediate Action

FYIA

La Mexican Kitchen

To: Linda Bustamante, Operations Manager
From: Matt Perkins, Shift Supervisor

Linda, HELP! We're having a difficult time keeping our food servers with us. It seems like I just get them trained and they leave. And we both know that our servers are key to our company's commitment to excellent customer service. We can

have the best food in town (and do!) but if our servers aren't motivated to provide excellent service, we won't have any customers.

Although these positions pay minimum wage, you and I both know a motivated server can make additional money from tips. But it seems that this isn't enough to motivate them to stay. So what would you recommend? Could you jot down some ideas about how to better motivate our food servers and send those to me? Thanks!

This fictionalized company and message were created for educational purposes only, and not meant to reflect positively or negatively on management practices by any company that may share this name.

Bringing the Real World to Life

Case Application:
Searching For?: Part 2

"For many people who work in the tech industry—fresh college grads and accomplished professionals alike—Google ranks near the top of lists of the most desirable employers." Yet, Google is now fighting off Facebook and other fast-growing Internet start-ups who want to poach its talented staff. It also has found itself losing employees who give up the fantastic benefits to go out on their own.

For instance, Sean Knapp and two colleagues, brothers Bismarck and Belsasar Lepe, came up with an idea on how to handle Web video. They left Google, or as one person put it, "expelled themselves from paradise to start their own company." When the threesome left the company, Google really wanted them and their project to stay. Google offered them a "blank check." But the trio realized they would do all the hard work and Google would own the product. So off they went, for the excitement of a start-up.

If this were an isolated occurrence, it would be easy to write off. But it's not. Other talented Google employees have done the same thing. In fact, there are so many of them who have left that they've formed an informal alumni club of ex-Googlers turned entrepreneurs.

Google is taking aggressive steps to retain its talent, especially those with start-up ambitions. One thing the company has done is give several engineers who said they wanted to leave to pursue their own ideas the opportunity to pursue those ideas within Google. These employees work independently and can recruit other engineers. In addition, Google's resources, such as its code base and computer servers, are available to them. In addition, from the very beginning, Google's founders (Larry Page and Sergey Brin) believed in giving everyone time—called 20 percent time—to work on their own projects.

Other Googlers have left because they felt Google had gotten too big and turned into a slow-moving bureaucratic company. Again, the company battled to keep the talent. For instance, when a Google product manager told his bosses that he was leaving to take a job at Facebook, they offered him a huge raise. But he told them it wasn't about the money. So they offered him a promotion, the opportunity to work in a different area, or even to start his own company inside Google. Yet, the former employee says that "At Facebook, I can see how quickly I could get things done compared to Google." However, there's one other thing that Facebook and other start-ups can offer experienced employees: They're still "private companies that haven't gone public and can lure workers with pre-IPO (initial public offering) stock."

DISCUSSION QUESTIONS

1. What's it like to work at Google? (Hint: Go to Google's Web site and find the section on Jobs at Google and go from there.) What's your assessment of the company's work environment?

2. Google is doing a lot for its employees, but obviously not enough to retain several of its talented employees. Using what you've learned from studying the various motivation theories, what does this situation tell you about employee motivation?

3. What do you think is Google's biggest challenge in keeping employees motivated?

4. If you were managing a team of Google employees, how would you keep them motivated?

5. Reread the chapter section on motivating professionals. Using this information, what would you tell managers at Google?

YOUR TURN TO BE A MANAGER

Leadership and Trust

Skill Development: Choosing a Leadership Style

The terms *management* and *leadership* are frequently used interchangeably. That's a misnomer. The two aren't the same but they are related. Although you don't need to hold a management position to be a leader, you're unlikely to be an effective manager if you can't be an effective leader.

Personal Insights: What Kind of Leader Am I?

The following items describe aspects of leadership behavior. Circle the number on the scale that best describes you. Use this scale for your responses:

   1 = Strongly disagree

   2 = Disagree

   3 = Neither agree or disagree

   4 = Agree

   5 = Strongly agree

1. I like to stand out from the crowd.   1 2 3 4 5

2. I feel proud and satisfied when I influence others to do things my way.   1 2 3 4 5

3. I enjoy doing things as part of a group rather than achieving results on my own.   1 2 3 4 5

4. I have a history of becoming an officer or captain in clubs and/or organized sports.   1 2 3 4 5

5. I try to be the one who is most influential in task groups at school or work.   1 2 3 4 5

6. In groups, I care most about good relationships.   1 2 3 4 5

7. In groups, I most want to achieve task goals.   1 2 3 4 5

8. In groups, I always show consideration for the feelings and needs of others.   1 2 3 4 5

9. In groups, I always structure activities and assignments to help get the job done.   1 2 3 4 5

Source: Based on S. P. Robbins and P. L. Hunsaker, *Training in Interpersonal Skills: TIPS for Managing People at Work*, 6th ed. (Upper Saddle River, NJ: Prentice Hall, 2011), pp. 220–221.

Analysis and Interpretation

This leadership instrument taps your readiness to be a leader and your leadership style. To calculate your readiness score, add the scale values you circled for items 1 through 5. Your leadership style score is composed of two subsets—a task-oriented score and a people-oriented score. Add your circled values for items 7 and 9; that's your task-oriented score. Add your circled values for items 6 and 8; that's your people-oriented score. Subtract your lower score from your higher score to calculate the difference and determine whether you are more task- or people-oriented.

If your readiness score is 20 or more, you are likely to enjoy being a leader. If your total score is 10 or less, at this time in your life, you are likely more interested in personal achievement than being a leader. If you score in the middle range, your leadership potential could go either direction, depending on events.

Your leadership style preference is indicated by whether your task-orientation or people-orientation score is higher. The difference between these scores indicates how strong this preference is.

The best leaders are ones who can balance their task/people orientation to various situations. If you're too task-oriented, you tend to be autocratic. You get the job done, but at a high emotional cost. If you're too people-oriented, your leadership style may be overly laissez-faire. People are likely to be happy in their work but sometimes at the expense of productivity.

Skill Basics

Simply put, leadership style can be categorized as task- or people-oriented. Neither one is right for all situations. Although a number of situational variables influence the choice of an effective leadership style, four variables seem most relevant:

1. *Task structure.* Structured tasks have procedures and rules that minimize ambiguity. The more structured a job is, the less need there is for a leader to provide task structure.

2. *Level of stress.* Situations differ in terms of time and performance stress. High-stress situations favor leaders with experience. Low stress favors a leader's intelligence.

3. *Level of group support.* Members of close-knit and supportive groups help each other out. They can provide both task support and relationship support. Supportive groups make fewer demands on a leader.

4. *Follower characteristics.* Personal characteristics of followers—such as experience, ability, and motivation—influence which leadership style will be most effective. Employees with extensive experience, strong abilities, and high motivation don't require much task behavior. They will be more effective with a people-oriented style. Conversely, employees with little experience, marginal abilities, and low motivation will perform better when leaders exhibit task-oriented behavior.

Based on R. J. House and R. N. Aditya, "The Social Scientific Study of Leadership: Quo Vadis?" *Journal of Management* (June 1997), pp. 409–473; and G. A. Yukl, *Leadership in Organizations*, 7th ed. (Upper Saddle River, NJ: Prentice Hall, 2010).

Skill Application

You recently graduated from college with your degree in business administration. You've spent the past two summers working at Connecticut Mutual Insurance (CMI), filling in as an intern on a number of different jobs while employees took their vacations. You have received and accepted an offer to join CMI full time as supervisor of the policy renewal department.

CMI is a large insurance company. In the headquarters office alone, where you'll be working, there are more than 1,500 employees. The company believes strongly in the personal development of its employees. This belief translates into a philosophy, emanating from the top executive offices, of trust and respect for all CMI employees. The company is also regularly atop most lists of "best companies to work for," largely due to its progressive work/life programs and strong commitment to minimizing layoffs.

In your new job, you'll direct the activities of 18 policy-renewal clerks. Their jobs require little training and are highly routine. A clerk's responsibility is to ensure that renewal notices are sent on current policies, to tabulate any changes in premiums, to advise the sales division if a policy is to be canceled as a result of nonresponse to renewal notices, and to answer questions and solve problems related to renewals.

The people in your work group range in age from 19 to 62, with a median age of 25. For the most part they are high school graduates with little prior working experience. They earn between $2,350 and $3,200 a month. You will be replacing a long-time CMI employee, Jan Allison. Jan is retiring after 37 years with CMI, the past 14 spent as a policy-renewal supervisor. Because you spent a few weeks in Jan's group last summer, you're familiar with Jan's style and are acquainted with most of the department members. But people don't know you very well and are suspicious of the fact that you're fresh out of college and have little experience in the department. The reality is that you got this job because management wanted someone with a college degree to oversee the department. Your most vocal critic is Lillian Lantz. Lillian is well into her 50s, has been a policy renewal clerk for over a dozen years, and—as the "grand old lady" of the department—carries a lot of weight with group members.

You know that it'll be very hard to lead this department without Lillian's support.

Using your knowledge of leadership concepts, which leadership style would you choose? And why?

Skill Practice

1. Think of a group or team to which you currently belong or of which you have been a part. What type of leadership style did the leader of this group appear to exhibit? Give some specific examples of the types of leadership behaviors he or she used. Evaluate the leadership style. Was it appropriate for the group? Why or why not? What would you have done differently? Why?

2. Observe two sports team (either college or professional—one that you consider successful and the other unsuccessful). What leadership styles appear to be used in these team situations? Give some specific examples of the types of leadership behaviors you observe. How would you evaluate the leadership style? Was it appropriate for the team? Why or why not? To what degree do you think leadership style influenced the team's outcomes?

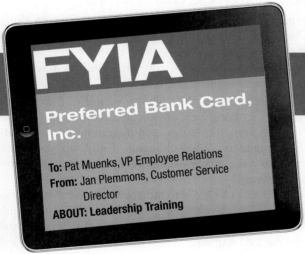

For Your Immediate Action

Preferred Bank Card, Inc.

To: Pat Muenks, VP Employee Relations
From: Jan Plemmons, Customer Service Director
ABOUT: Leadership Training

I agree completely with your recommendation that we need a leadership training program for our customer service team leaders. These leaders struggle with keeping our customer service reps focused on our goal of providing timely, accurate, and friendly service to our bank card holders who call in with questions or complaints.

Put together a one-page proposal that describes the leadership topics you think should be covered. Also, give me some suggestions for how we might present the information in a way that would be interesting. We need to get started on this immediately, so please get this report to me by early next week.

This fictionalized company and message were created for educational purposes only, and not meant to reflect positively or negatively on management practices by any company that may share this name.

Bringing the Real World to Life

Case Application: Master and Commander: Part 2

Go back and reread the chapter opener. As described there, it's easy to see that Commander Graf was quickly losing the trust of her crew and thus her ability to lead. Then, one eventful night began the unraveling of Graf's career.

On the eve of the Iraq war in 2003, the *Churchill* was steaming out of a Sicilian port when, without warning, all 9,000 tons of the vessel shuddered as it cleared the harbor's breakwater. It wasn't long before the 511-foot-long ship was adrift. "Commander Graf grabbed the cowering navigator and pulled him aside screaming, 'Did you run my #### ship aground?'" But amid all the chaos and shouting, the Navy chaplain aboard said that "the sound heard next was more startling. Sailors on the *Churchill's* stern, suspecting that their ship had run aground—meaning Graf's career would be instantly over—broke gleefully into song: "Ding Dong, the witch is dead!" He couldn't believe what he was hearing. Even today, the chaplain can't fathom which was worse, that U.S. sailors were openly berating a captain or that the captain seemed to deserve it. But that incident didn't end her career.

However, Graf's next command as captain of the guided missile-cruiser U.S.S. *Cowpens* would be her last. She was relieved of duty in January 2010, after nearly two years, for "cruelty and maltreatment" of her crew. The Navy Inspector General's report stated, "Persons in authority are forbidden to injure their subordinates by tyrannical or capricious conduct, or by abusive language." But Graf did so "by demeaning, humiliating, publicly belittling and verbally assaulting . . . subordinates while in command of *Cowpens* with harsh language and profanity . . . rarely followed by any instruction."

DISCUSSION QUESTIONS

1. What do you think of this description of Captain Holly Graf's leader style? Do you think that Captain Graf could even be called a leader? Discuss.

2. What kinds of power do you think Graf used as a ship commander? Explain your choices.

3. Not surprisingly, this whole scenario rocked the Navy to its core, because it reflected on the way the Navy chooses, promotes, and then monitors its hand-picked leaders. What changes, if any, do you think need to take place in its leadership training and development?

4. Some critics of Graf's treatment have said that institutional sexism played a role in her removal. Do you think that could be possible? Discuss. Would that "excuse" the way she led? Explain.

CHAPTER 13

YOUR TURN TO BE A MANAGER

Managing Communication and Information

Skill Development: Applying Listening Skills

Most of us like to talk more than we like to listen. In fact, it's been facetiously said that listening is just the price we have to pay to get people to allow us to talk. Managers must be effective communicators if they are to do their job well. Part of effective communication is conveying clear and understandable messages. But it's also using active listening skills to accurately decipher others' messages.

Personal Insights: How Good Are My Listening Skills?

Respond to each of the 15 statements using the following scale:

1 = Strongly agree
2 = Agree
3 = Neither agree or disagree
4 = Disagree
5 = Strongly disagree

1. I frequently attempt to listen to several conversations at the same time.	1 2 3 4 5
2. I like people to give me only the facts and then let me make my own interpretation.	1 2 3 4 5
3. I sometimes pretend to pay attention to people.	1 2 3 4 5
4. I consider myself a good judge of nonverbal communications.	1 2 3 4 5
5. I usually know what another person is going to say before he or she says it.	1 2 3 4 5
6. I usually end conversations that don't interest me by diverting my attention from the speaker.	1 2 3 4 5
7. I frequently nod, frown, or provide other nonverbal cues to let the speaker know how I feel about what he or she is saying.	1 2 3 4 5
8. I usually respond immediately when someone has finished talking.	1 2 3 4 5
9. I evaluate what is being said while it is being said.	1 2 3 4 5
10. I usually formulate a response while the other person is still talking.	1 2 3 4 5
11. The speaker's "delivery" style frequently keeps me from listening to content.	1 2 3 4 5
12. I usually ask people to clarify what they have said rather than guess at the meaning.	1 2 3 4 5
13. I make a concerted effort to understand other people's points of view.	1 2 3 4 5
14. I frequently hear what I expect to hear rather than what is said.	1 2 3 4 5
15. Most people feel that I have understood their point of view when we disagree.	1 2 3 4 5

Source: Adapted from E. C. Glenn and E. A. Pood, "Listening Self-Inventory," *Supervisory Management*, January 1989, pp. 12–15. Used with permission of publisher; ©1989 American Management Association, New York.

Analysis and Interpretation

Effective communicators have developed good listening skills. This instrument is designed to provide you with some insights into your listening skills.

To calculate your score, sum up your responses for all items; however, you need to reverse your scores (5 becomes 1, 4 becomes 2, etc.) for statements 4, 12, 13, and 15.

Scores range from 15 to 75. The higher your score, the better listener you are. Although any cutoffs are essentially arbitrary, if you score 60 or above, your listening skills are fairly well honed. Scores of 40 or less indicate you need to make a serious effort at improving your listening skills.

Skill Basics

Too many people take listening skills for granted. They confuse hearing with listening. Hearing is merely picking up sound vibrations. Listening is making sense out of what we hear; and it requires paying attention, interpreting, and remembering. Active listening is hard work and requires you to "get inside" the speaker's head in order to understand the communication from his or her point of view.

Eight specific behaviors are associated with active listening. You can be more effective at active listening if you use these behaviors.

1. *Make eye contact.* We may listen with our ears, but others tend to judge whether we're really listening by looking at our eyes.

2. *Exhibit affirmative nods and appropriate facial expressions.* The effective active listener shows interest in what's being said through nonverbal signals.

3. *Avoid distracting actions or gestures.* When listening, don't look at your watch, shuffle papers, play with your pencil, or engage in similar distractions. They make the speaker feel that you're bored or uninterested.

4. *Ask questions.* The critical listener analyzes what he or she hears and asks questions. This behavior provides clarification, ensures understanding, and assures the speaker that you're really listening.

5. *Paraphrase.* Restate *in your own words* what the speaker has said. The effective active listener uses phrases such as "What I hear you saying is . . ." or "Do you mean . . .?" Paraphrasing is an excellent control device to check whether you're listening carefully and is also a control for accuracy of understanding.

6. *Avoid interrupting the speaker.* Let the speaker complete his or her thoughts before you try to respond. Don't try to second-guess where the speaker's thoughts are going.

7. *Don't overtalk.* Most of us would rather speak our own ideas than listen to what others say. Although talking might be more fun and silence might be uncomfortable, you can't talk and listen at the same time. The good active listener recognizes this fact and doesn't overtalk.

8. *Make smooth transitions between the roles of speaker and listener.* In most work situations, you're continually shifting back and forth between the roles of speaker and listener. The effective active listener makes transitions smoothly from speaker to listener and back to speaker.

Based on K. J. Murphy, *Effective Listening* (New York: Bantam Books, 1987); and T. Drollinger, L. B. Comer, and P. T. Warrington, "Development and Validation of the Active Empathetic Listing Scale," *Psychology & Marketing*, February 2006, pp. 161–180.

Skill Application

Break into groups of two. This exercise is a debate. Person A can choose any contemporary issue. Some examples include business ethics, value of unions, stiffer college grading policies, gun control, and money as a motivator. Person B then selects a position on this issue. Person A must automatically take the counterposition. The debate is to proceed for 8–10 minutes, with only one catch. Before each speaks, he or she must first summarize, in his or her own words and without notes, what the other has said. If the summary doesn't satisfy the speaker, it must be corrected until it does.

Skill Practice

1. In another class—preferably one with a lecture format—practice active listening. Ask questions, paraphrase, exhibit affirming nonverbal behaviors. Then ask yourself: Was this harder for me than a normal lecture? Did it affect my note taking? Did I ask more questions? Did it improve my understanding of the lecture's content? What was the instructor's response?

2. Spend an entire day fighting your urge to talk. Listen as carefully as you can to everyone you interact with and respond as appropriately as possible to understand, not to make your own point. What, if anything, did you learn from this exercise?

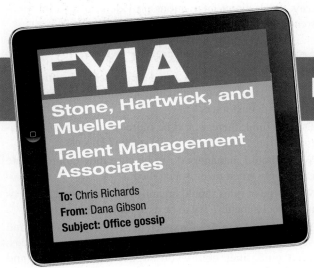

For Your Immediate Action

FYIA

Stone, Hartwick, and Mueller

Talent Management Associates

To: Chris Richards
From: Dana Gibson
Subject: Office gossip

I need some advice, Chris. As you know, my department and all its employees are being transferred from Los Angeles to Dallas. We've had to keep the information "under wraps" for competitive reasons. However, one of my employees asked me point blank yesterday about a rumor she's heard that this move is in the works. I didn't answer her question directly. But I'm afraid that the office grapevine is going to start spreading inaccurate information and then affect morale and productivity. What should I do now? Send me your written response soon (confidential, please!) about what you would do.

This fictionalized company and message were created for educational purposes only, and not meant to reflect positively or negatively on management practices by any company that may share this name.

Bringing the Real World to Life

Case Application:
Social Benefit or Social
Disaster? Part 2

As the biggest electronics consumer store in the United States, Best Buy sells a lot of electronic gadgets (and other merchandise, also). With selling all the latest gadgets and devices and with all their young employees, it's not surprising that the company has been an early user of social media. But as investor Warren Buffet once said, "It takes 20 years to build a reputation and five minutes to ruin it." That's something to think about (for all of us). When CEO Brian Dunn's Twitter account was hacked, he recalls that "it was embarrassing and irritating. I felt violated." So what happened next?

After the initial "shock" over what had happened, Best Buy's IT team advised Dunn to change his password. Like many of us are guilty of, Dunn had been using a password that was easy to remember because it was based on something in his life. Now he changes his password every three weeks and it's a "well-constructed, tortured password." For companies that want to use every communication tool available, being security-minded isn't a maybe, it's a

must. But the most important part of the company's response was that they continued doing what they had been doing . . . using social media. "Despite the headaches they can cause, sites like Twitter, Facebook, and YouTube are powerful tools for spotting trends and communicating with employees and customers."

One interesting and successful social media strategy that Best Buy developed is its "Twelpforce." It's a system in which employees see Best Buy–related problems that customers have aired on Twitter. More than 2,500 employees have signed up including customer service staff, in-store sales associates (the Blue Shirts), and the Geek Squad. Any of the Twelpforce can respond to a customer's complaint, concern, or comment. For example, when a customer recently tweeted about his dissatisfaction over how his iPhone problem was resolved, a customer service rep responded quickly on Twitter. She was able to take care of the problem and the customer then tweeted about how great Best Buy's service was. Funny thing . . . the customer's wife, who has more than 3,000 Twitter followers, also tweeted about the great service.

As far as CEO Dunn, he continues to be a heavy user of Twitter and Facebook. He also has a large monitor in his office that shows all the activity where Best Buy is mentioned. He says that he learns a lot from the time he spends on those platforms. Such direct interactions provide him with information, trends, and news he would probably miss otherwise.

DISCUSSION QUESTIONS

1. What are the advantages and drawbacks of companies using social media to communicate with employees? How about with customers?

2. Do you think there would be more or fewer communication barriers when using social media? Discuss.

3. What should managers do to be sure they communicate effectively when using social media?

4. What type of rules should organizations have for employees using social media? Try to be as specific as possible.

5. What have been your experiences—both positive and negative—with social media? From your experiences, what guidelines could you suggest for managers and organizations?

CHAPTER 14

YOUR TURN TO BE A MANAGER

Foundations of Control

Skill Development: Dealing with Difficult People

Almost all managers will, at one time or another, have to deal with people who are difficult. There is no shortage of characteristics that can make someone difficult to work with. Some examples include short-tempered, demanding, abusive, angry, defensive, complaining, intimidating, aggressive, narcissistic, arrogant, and rigid. Successful managers have learned how to cope with difficult people.

Personal Insights: How Good Am I at Disciplining Others?

This instrument contains eight disciplining practices. For each statement, select the answer that best describes you. Remember to respond as you *have* behaved or *would* behave, not as you think you *should* behave. If you have no managerial experience, answer the statements assuming you are a manager. Use the following scale to express your response:

1 = Usually
2 = Sometimes
3 = Seldom

When disciplining an employee:

1. I provide ample warning before taking formal action.   1 2 3
2. I wait for a pattern of infractions before calling it to the employee's attention.   1 2 3
3. Even after repeated offenses, I prefer informal discussion about correcting the problem rather than formal disciplinary action.   1 2 3
4. I delay confronting the employee about an infraction until his or her performance-appraisal review.   1 2 3
5. In discussing an infraction with the employee, my style and tone are serious.   1 2 3
6. I explicitly seek to allow the employee to explain his or her position.   1 2 3
7. I remain impartial in allocating punishment.   1 2 3
8. I allocate stronger penalties for repeated offenses.   1 2 3

Source: S. P. Robbins, *Training in Interpersonal Skills: TIPS for Managing People at Work* (Upper Saddle River, NJ: Prentice Hall, 1989), pp. 104–105.

Analysis and Interpretation

This instrument is based on the literature defining preferred discipline techniques. It is not a precise tool but it will give you some insights into how effective you might be in practicing discipline in the workplace.

To calculate your score, add up the points for questions 2, 3, and 4. For the other 5 questions (1, 5, 6, 7 and 8), reverse score them by giving a "1" response 3 points and a "3" response 1 point.

Your score on this test will range from 8 to 24. A score of 22 or higher indicates excellent skills at disciplining. You understand that effective discipline recognizes the need to provide ample warning, act in a timely fashion, use a calm and serious tone, be specific about the problem, keep the process impersonal, and that disciplinary action should be progressive and consider mitigating circumstances. Scores in the 19 to 21 range suggest some deficiencies. Scores below 19 indicate considerable room for improvement.

Skill Basics

No single approach is always effective in dealing with difficult people. However, we can offer several suggestions that are likely to lessen the angst these people create in your life and may have some influence in reducing their difficult behavior.

Don't let your emotions rule. Our first response to a difficult person is often emotional. We get angry. We show frustration. We want to lash out at them or "get even" when we think they've insulted or demeaned us. This response is not likely to reduce your angst and may escalate the other person's negative behavior. So fight your natural tendencies and keep your cool. Stay rational and thoughtful. At worst, while this approach may not improve the situation, it is also unlikely to encourage and escalate the undesirable behavior.

Attempt to limit contact. If possible, try to limit your contact with the difficult person. Avoid places where they hang out and limit nonrequired interactions. Also, use communication channels—like e-mail and text messaging—that minimize face-to-face contact and verbal intonations.

Try polite confrontation. If you can't avoid the difficult person, consider standing up to them in a civil but firm manner. Let them know that you're aware of their behavior, that you find it unacceptable, and that you won't tolerate it. For people who are unaware of the effect their actions have on you, confrontation might awaken them to altering their behavior. For those who are acting purposefully, taking a clear stand might make them think twice about the consequences of their actions.

Practice positive reinforcement. We know that positive reinforcement is a powerful tool for changing behavior. Rather than criticizing undesirable behavior, try reinforcing desirable behaviors with compliments or other positive comments. This focus will tend to weaken and reduce the exhibiting of the undesirable behaviors.

Recruit fellow victims and witnesses. Finally, we know strength lies in numbers. If you can get others who are also offended by the difficult person to support your case, several positive things can happen. First, it's likely to lessen your frustrations because others will be confirming your perception and can offer support. Second, people in the organization with authority to reprimand are more likely to act when complaints are coming from multiple sources. And third, the difficult person is more likely to feel pressure to change when a group is speaking out against his or her specific behaviors than if the complaint is coming from a single source.

Based on N. Pelusi, "Dealing with Difficult People," *Psychology Today*, September–October 2006, pp. 68–69; and R. I. Sutton, *The No Asshole Rule: Building a Civilized Workplace and Surviving One That Isn't* (New York: Business Plus, 2007).

Skill Application

Your career has progressed even faster than you thought possible. After graduating from college with an accounting degree, you passed your CPA exam and worked three years for a major accounting firm. Then you joined General Electric in their finance department. Two employers and four jobs later, you have just been hired by a *Fortune* 100 mining company as their vice president for finance. What you didn't expect in the new job was having to deal with Mark Hundley.

Mark is the vice president of company operations. He has been with the company for eight years. Your first impression of Mark was that he was a "know-it-all." He was quick to put you down and acted as if he was your superior rather than an equal. Based on comments you've heard around the offices, it seems you are not alone. Other executives all seemed to agree that Mark is a brilliant engineer and operations manager but very difficult to work with. Specific comments you've heard include "an abrasive attitude"; "talks down to people"; "arrogant"; "thinks everyone is stupid"; and "poor listener."

In your short time in the new job, you've already had several run-ins with Mark. You've even talked to your boss, the company president, about him. The president's response wasn't surprising: "Mark isn't easy to deal with. But no one knows this company's operations like he does. If he ever leaves, I don't know how we'd replace him. But, that said, he gives me a lot of grief. Sometimes he makes me feel like I work for him rather than the other way around."

What could you do to improve your ability to work with Mark?

Skill Practice

1. Talk with a manager at three different organizations. Ask each what guidance, if any, they've received from their organizations in terms of dealing with difficult colleagues. Have them describe specific problems they've faced and how they've handled them.

2. Think of a recent experience you've had with a person who is difficult to work or interact with. How did you handle the situation? How effective was your approach? What could you have done differently to improve the outcome?

Skill Development: Providing Feedback

A part of every manager's job is providing performance feedback. Although this often takes place once or twice a year, during an employee's performance review, good managers provide performance feedback to employees on a continuing basis.

Personal Insights: How Good Am I at Giving Performance Feedback?

For each of the following pairs, identify the statement that most closely matches what you *normally* do when you give feedback to someone else on their job performance.

1. a. Describe the behavior
   b. Evaluate the behavior

2. a. Focus on the feelings that the behavior evokes
   b. Tell the person what they should be doing differently

3. a. Give specific instances of the behavior
   b. Generalize

4. a. Deal only with behavior that the person can control
   b. Sometimes focus on something the person can do nothing about

5. a. Tell the person as soon as possible after the behavior
   b. Sometimes wait too long

6. a. Focus on the effect the behavior has on me
   b. Try to figure out why the individual did what he or she did

7. a. Balance negative feedback with positive feedback
   b. Sometimes focus only on the negative

8. a. Do some soul searching to make sure that the reason I am giving the feedback is to help the other person or to strengthen our relationship
   b. Sometimes give feedback to punish, win against, or dominate the other person

Source: Adapted from L. A. Mainiero and C. L. Tromley, *Developing Managerial Skills in Organizational Behavior*, 2nd ed. (Englewood Cliffs, NJ: Prentice Hall, 1994), pp. 125–126. With permission.

Analysis and Interpretation

This instrument is designed to assess how good you are at providing performance feedback. To calculate your score, add up how many "a" responses you totaled. Do the same for "b" responses.

The "a" responses are your self-perceived strengths and the "b" responses are your self-perceived weaknesses. By looking at the proportion of your "a" and "b" responses, you will be able to see how effective you feel you are when giving performance feedback and determine where your strengths and weaknesses lie. For instance, an a:b ratio of 8:0, 7:1, or 6:2 suggests relatively strong feedback skills. In contrast, ratios of 3:5, 2:6, 1:7, or 0:8 indicate significant self-perceived weaknesses that can be improved upon.

Skill Basics

Many managers are derelict in providing performance feedback, especially when it's negative. Like most of us, managers don't particularly enjoy communicating bad news. They fear offending the other person or having to deal with the recipient's defensiveness. Nevertheless, providing performance feedback is an important part of effective employee communication.

You can be more effective at providing feedback if you use the following six specific suggestions.

1. *Focus on specific behaviors.* Feedback should be specific rather than general. Avoid such statements as "You have a bad attitude" or "I'm really impressed with the good job you did." They're vague and although they provide information, they don't tell the recipient enough to correct the "bad attitude" or on what basis you concluded that a "good job" had been done so the person knows what behaviors to repeat or to avoid.

2. *Keep feedback impersonal.* Feedback, particularly the negative kind, should be descriptive rather than judgmental or evaluative. No matter how upset you are, keep the feedback focused on job-related behaviors and never criticize someone personally because of an inappropriate action.

3. *Keep feedback goal oriented.* Feedback should not be given primarily to "blow off steam" or "unload" on another person. If you have to say something negative, make sure it's directed toward the recipient's goals. Ask yourself whom the feedback is supposed to help. If the answer is *you*, bite your tongue and hold the comment. Such feedback undermines your credibility and lessens the meaning and influence of future feedback.

4. *Make feedback well timed.* Feedback is most meaningful to a recipient when there's a very short interval between his or her behavior and the receipt of feedback about that behavior. Moreover, if you're particularly concerned with changing behavior, delays in providing feedback on the undesirable actions lessen the likelihood that the feedback will be effective in bringing about the desired change. Of course, making feedback prompt merely for the sake of promptness can backfire if you have insufficient information, if you're angry, or if you're otherwise emotionally upset. In such instances, "well timed" could mean "somewhat delayed."

5. *Ensure understanding.* Make sure your feedback is concise and complete so that the recipient clearly and fully understands the communication. It may help to have the recipient rephrase the content of your feedback to find out whether it fully captured the meaning you intended.

6. *Direct negative feedback toward behavior that the recipient can control.* There's little value in reminding a person of some shortcoming over which he or she has no control. Negative feedback should be directed at behavior that the recipient can do something about. In addition, when negative feedback is given concerning something that the recipient can control, it might be a good idea to indicate specifically what can be done to improve the situation.

Based on C. R. Mill, "Feedback: The Art of Giving and Receiving Help," in L. Porter and C. R. Mill (eds.), *The Reading Book for Human Relations Training* (Bethel, ME: NTL Institute for Applied Behavioral Science, 1976), pp. 18–19; and S. Bishop, *The Complete Feedback Skills Training Book* (Aldershot, UK: Gower Publishing, 2000).

Skill Application

Craig is an excellent employee whose expertise and productivity have always met or exceeded your expectations. But recently he's been making work difficult for other members of your advertising team. Like his coworkers, Craig researches and computes the costs of media coverage for your advertising agency's clients. The work requires laboriously leafing through several large reference books to find the correct base price and add-on charges for each radio or television station and time slot, calculating each actual cost, and compiling the results in a computerized spreadsheet. To make things more efficient and convenient, you've always allowed your team members to bring the reference books they're using to their desks while they're using them. Lately, however, Craig has been piling books around him for days and sometimes weeks at a time. The books interfere with the flow of traffic past his desk and other people have to go out of their way to retrieve the books from Craig's pile. It's time for you to have a talk with Craig.

Skill Practice

1. Think of three things that a friend or family member did well recently. Did you praise the person at the time? If not, why? The next time someone close to you does something well, give him or her positive feedback.

2. You have a good friend who has a mannerism (for instance, speech, body movement, or style of dress) that you think is inappropriate and detracts from the overall impression that he or she makes. Come up with a plan for talking with this person. What will you say? How will you handle his or her reaction?

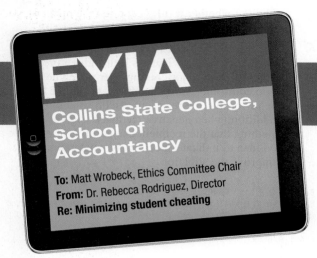

For Your Immediate Action

To: Matt Wrobeck, Ethics Committee Chair
From: Dr. Rebecca Rodriguez, Director
Re: Minimizing student cheating

Collins State College, School of Accountancy

Matt, you've probably heard that several of our faculty members want to develop some specific controls to minimize opportunities for our students to cheat on homework assignments and exams. As the ethics committee chair, I'd like you to work with them on developing some suggestions. As you look at this topic, please think in terms of ways to control cheating (1) before it happens, (2) while in-class exams or assignments are being completed, and (3) after it has happened.

Keep your list brief (around a page) and send it to me by the end of the week. I'd like to get this out to our entire faculty at our next scheduled monthly meeting.

This fictionalized company and message were created for educational purposes only, and not meant to reflect positively or negatively on management practices by any company that may share this name.

Bringing the Real World to Life

Case Application:
Deepwater in Deep Trouble: Part 2

One thing that has come to light in the disaster investigation is that it's no surprise that something like this happened. After Hurricane Dennis blew through in July 2005, a passing ship was shocked to see BP's new massive $1 billion Thunder Horse oil platform "listing precariously to one side, looking for all the world as if it were about to sink." Thunder Horse "was meant to be the company's crowning glory, the embodiment of its bold gamble to outpace its competitors in finding and exploiting the vast reserves of oil beneath the waters of the gulf." But the problems with this rig soon became evident. A valve installed backwards caused it to flood during the hurricane even before any oil had been pumped. Other problems included a welding job so shoddy that it left underwater pipelines brittle and full of cracks. "The problems at Thunder Horse were not an anomaly, but a warning that BP was taking too many risks and cutting corners in pursuit of growth and profits."

Then came the tragic explosion on the Deepwater Horizon. Before the rig exploded, there were strong warning signs that something was terribly wrong with the oil well. Among the red flags were several equipment readings suggesting that gas was bubbling into the well, a potential sign of an

impending blowout. Those red flags were ignored. Other decisions made in the 24 hours before the explosion included a critical decision to replace heavy mud in the pipe rising from the seabed with seawater, again possibly increasing the risk of an explosion. Internal BP documents also show evidence of serious problems and safety concerns with Deepwater. Those problems involved the well casing and blowout preventer. One BP senior drilling engineer warned, "This would certainly be a worst-case scenario."

The federal panel charged with investigating the spill examined 20 "anomalies in the well's behavior and the crew's response." The panel is also investigating in particular why "rig workers missed telltale signs that the well was close to an uncontrolled blowout." The panel's final report blamed both BP and its contractors for the failures that led to the explosion on the Deepwater Horizon. Many of those failings stemmed from shortcuts to save time and money. However, the report also faulted the government for lax oversight of the companies.

DISCUSSION QUESTIONS

1. What type(s) of control—feedforward, concurrent, or feedback—do you think would have been most useful in this situation? Explain your choice(s).

2. Using Exhibit 14–2, explain what BP could have done better.

3. Why do you think company employees ignored the red flags? How could such behavior be changed in the future?

4. What could other organizations learn from BP's mistakes?

YOUR TURN TO BE A MANAGER

Operations Management

CHAPTER 15

Skill Development: Project Management Skills

Managing any project will require good negotiation skills. You'll typically have to work across vertical and horizontal levels in the organization, deal with people over whom you have no formal authority, and have to negotiate schedules, deadlines, work assignments, and the like with people possibly both inside and outside the organization.

Personal Insights: What's My Negotiation Style?

Listed here are seven characteristics related to a person's negotiating style. Each characteristic demonstrates a range of variation. Indicate your own preference by selecting a point along the 1-to-5 continuum for each characteristic.

1. Approach	Confrontational	1	2	3	4	5	Collaborative
2. Personality	Emotional	1	2	3	4	5	Rational
3. Formality	High	1	2	3	4	5	Low
4. Communication	Indirect	1	2	3	4	5	Direct
5. Candidness	Closed	1	2	3	4	5	Open
6. Search for options	Limited	1	2	3	4	5	Many
7. Willingness to use power	Low	1	2	3	4	5	High

Source: Based on R. Fisher and W. Ury, *Getting to Yes* (New York: Penguin, 1981); and J. W. Salacuse, "Ten Ways That Culture Affects Negotiating Style: Some Survey Results," *Negotiation Journal* (July 1998), pp. 221–239.

Analysis and Interpretation

People differ in the way they handle negotiations. This instrument attempts to tap the key dimensions that differentiate preferences in negotiation style.

Add up the scores for the seven items. Your score on this test will range between 7 and 35. Research indicates that negotiation style is influenced by a number of factors—including the situation, your cultural background, and your work occupation. Nevertheless, experts in negotiation generally recommend individuals use a style that will result in a high score on this test. That is, they favor collaboration, rationality, a direct communication style, and so on. We think it best to consider your total score in a situational context. For instance, while a high total score may generally be favorable, the use of an informal style may be a handicap for North Americans or Europeans when negotiating with Nigerians, who favor high formality. Similarly, Latin Americans tend to show their emotions in negotiation. So if you're negotiating with Brazilians or Costa Ricans, a more emotional approach on your part may be appropriate or even expected.

Skill Basics

You can be more effective at negotiating if you use the following five recommended behaviors.

1. *Begin with a positive overture.* Studies on negotiation show that concessions tend to be reciprocated and lead to agreements. As a result, begin bargaining with a positive overture—perhaps a small concession—and then reciprocate the other party's concessions.

2. *Address problems, not personalities.* Concentrate on the negotiation issues, not on the personal characteristics of the individual with whom you're negotiating. When negotiations get tough, avoid the tendency to attack this person. Remember it's that person's ideas or position that you disagree with, not him or her personally. Separate the people from the problem, and don't personalize differences.

3. *Pay little attention to initial offers.* Treat an initial offer as merely a point of departure. Everyone must have an initial position. These initial offers tend to be extreme and idealistic. Treat them as such.

4. *Emphasize win–win solutions.* Inexperienced negotiators often assume that their gain must come at the expense of the other party. That needn't be the case. Assuming a zero-sum game means missed opportunities for trade-offs that could benefit both sides. So if conditions are supportive, look for an integrative solution. Frame options in terms of the other party's interests and look for solutions that can allow this person, as well as yourself, to declare a victory.

5. *Create an open and trusting climate.* Skilled negotiators are better listeners, ask more questions, focus their arguments more directly, are less defensive, and have learned to avoid words or phrases that can irritate the person with whom they're negotiating (such as "generous offer," "fair price," or "reasonable arrangement"). In other words, they're better at creating the open and trusting climate that is necessary for reaching a win–win settlement.

Based on R. Fisher and W. Ury, *Getting to Yes: Negotiating Agreement Without Giving In* (New York: Penguin Books, 1986); J. A. Wall, Jr. and M. W. Blum, "Negotiations," *Journal of Management* (June 1991), pp. 273–303; and M. E. Roloff, L. L. Putnam, and L. Anastasiou, "Negotiation Skills," in J. O. Greene and B. R. Burleson (eds.), *Handbook of Communication and Social Interaction Skills* (Mahwah, NJ: Lawrence Erlbaum, 2003), pp. 801–833.

Skill Application

As marketing director for Done Right, a regional home-repair chain, you've come up with a plan you believe has significant potential for future sales. Your plan involves a customer information service designed to help people make their homes more environmentally sensitive. Then based on homeowners' assessments of their homes' environmental impact, your firm will be prepared to help them deal with problems or concerns they may uncover. You're really excited about the competitive potential of this new service. You envision pamphlets, in-store appearances by environmental experts, as well as contests for consumers and school kids. After several weeks of preparations, you make your pitch to your boss, Nick Castro. You point out how the market for environmentally sensitive products is growing and how this growing demand represents the perfect opportunity for Done Right. Nick seems impressed by your presentation, but he's expressed one major concern. He thinks your workload is already too heavy. He doesn't see how you're going to have enough time to start this new service *and* still be able to look after all of your other assigned marketing duties.

People in the class should form pairs. One will play the marketing director; the other will play the role of Nick Castro. Nick seems convinced you can't handle your present responsibilities and start the new service. Negotiate a solution.

Skill Practice

1. Negotiate with a course instructor to raise the grade on an exam or paper on which you think you should have received a higher grade.

2. The next time you purchase a relatively expensive item (e.g., automobile, apartment lease, appliance, jewelry), negotiate a better price and gain some concessions such as an extended warranty, smaller down payment, maintenance services, or the like.

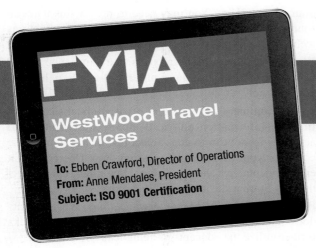

WestWood Travel Services

To: Ebben Crawford, Director of Operations
From: Anne Mendales, President
Subject: ISO 9001 Certification

I've been doing a lot of reading on total quality management and I think we need to look at using TQM principles. Since our business has grown from one office to five offices with nearly 50 employees, I want to ensure that we're doing everything we

can to meet our clients' needs, especially since we've lost some clients to competitors. Could you do an analysis describing how we might apply the concepts of customer focus, continuous process improvement, benchmarking, training, teamwork, and empowerment to our travel business to make us more competitive? Write up your analysis in a bulleted list format (no more than two pages please) and get it to me by the end of the week.

This fictionalized company and message were created for educational purposes only, and not meant to reflect positively or negatively on management practices by any company that may share this name.

Bringing the Real World to Life

Case Application: Stirring Things Up: Part 2

Starbucks products have become an unaffordable luxury for many. As revenues and profits declined during the economic downturn, CEO Howard Schultz realized that "the company needed to change almost everything about how it operates." Although it built its business as "the anti-fast-food joint," the recession and growing competition forced Starbucks to become more streamlined. Under one new initiative put into effect at its U.S. stores, employee time wasters such as bending over to scoop coffee from below the counter, idly standing by waiting for expired coffee to drain, or dawdling at the pastry case were discouraged. Instead, employees were to keep busy doing something, such as helping customers or cleaning. At one of the first stores to implement the "lean" techniques, the store manager looked for ways for her employees to be more efficient with simple things like keeping items in the same place, moving drink toppings closer to where drinks are handed to customers, and altering the order of assembly. After two months under the new

methods, her store experienced a 10 percent increase in transactions.

Another thing that Schultz did that was quite unprecedented was to close every one of its stores for three hours on one Tuesday evening to train ALL of their some 135,000 baristas (a barista is a person who prepares and serves espresso-based coffee drinks). During that training, baristas were reminded that "pouring espresso is an art. If poured too fast from the spout into a shot glass, the espresso's flavor will be weak and the body will be thin. A shot poured too slow means the grind is too fine, and the flavor will be bitter. The perfect shot looks like honey pouring from a spoon. It is dense and tastes caramely sweet." Despite warnings that closing the stores would be a public relations nightmare and a financial mistake, the decision seemed to be a sound one. In the weeks following the retraining, quality scores for the company's beverages went up and stayed there.

DISCUSSION QUESTIONS

1. Would you describe production/operations technology in Starbucks retail stores as unit, mass, or process? Explain

your choice. (Hint: You may need to review this material found in Chapter 6.) How does its production/operations technology approach affect the way products are produced?

2. What uncertainties does Starbucks face in its value chain? Can Starbucks manage those uncertainties? If so, how? If not, why not?

3. Go the company's Web site at www.starbucks.com and find the information on the company's environmental activities from bean to cup. Select one of the steps in the chain (or your professor may assign one). Describe what environmental actions it's taking. How might these affect the way Starbucks "produces" its products?

4. Research the concept of *lean organizations*. What benefits does "lean" offer? How might a business like Starbucks further utilize the concepts of being lean?

5. What lessons could other organizations learn from Starbucks' actions?

Glindex

A

Abilities/disability, workforce diversity and, 61–62

Absenteeism The failure to show up for work, 223

Achievement need, 287

Achievement oriented leader, 309

Achievement *vs.* nurturing, 52

Acid test ratios, 98

Active listening Listening for full meaning without making premature judgments or interpretations, 335, 334E13-3

Activities Actions that take place, 386

Activity ratios, 356E14-6, 357

Adjective rating scale, 176–177

Adjourning The final stage of group development for temporary groups during which group members are concerned with wrapping up activities rather than task performance, 252

Advertisements in recruiting, 168E7-3

Affective component That part of an attitude that's the emotional or feeling part, 224

Affirmative action programs Programs that ensure that decisions and practices enhance the employment, upgrading, and retention of members of protected groups, 165

Age, workforce diversity and, 61

Age Discrimination in Employment Act, 164E7-2

Agreeableness, in Big Five Model, 228

Ambiguous responsibility, 85

Americans with Disabilities Act, 61, 164E7-2

Analysis of opportunity in full business plan, 394

Anchoring effect, 76

Artifacts, 40

Artistic personality, 232

Asch study, 254, 254E10-3

Assertiveness, 53

Assessment centers, 171

Assumed similarity The assumption that others are like oneself, 236

Attentional processes, in social learning, 238

Attitudes Evaluative statements, either favorable or unfavorable, concerning objects, people, or events, 373, 374

  cognitive dissonance and, 225–226

  components of, 223

  consistency in, 225

  of employees, 224–225

  manager's understanding of, 226–227

  in value chain management, 379, 380

Attitude surveys, 227

Attractiveness, in expectancy theory, 284, 284E11-8

Attribution theory A theory used to explain how we judge people differently depending on what meaning we attribute to a given behavior, 234, 234–235, 235E9-4

  distorted attributions and, 235

Attrition as downsizing option, 169E7-4

Authority The rights inherent in a managerial position to give orders and expect the orders to be obeyed, 135

  chain of command in, 135, 136E6-3

  line *vs.* staff, 136, 137E6-4

  relationships, 136

  unity of command in, 136–137

  view of, today's *vs.* historical, 137

  vs. power, 137–139, 138E6-5

Autocratic style A leader who dictates work methods, makes unilateral decisions, and limits employee participation, 302

Autonomy, in job characteristics model, 281, 281E11-5

Availability bias, 76

B

Baby boomers, 34, 241

Balanced scorecard A performance measurement tool that looks at more than just the financial perspective, 358

Basic corrective action Corrective action that looks at how and why performance deviated before correcting the source of deviation, 354

Behavior The actions of people, 222

  personality predicted by, 227–233

    Big Five model, 228–229

    emotional intelligence, 229

    Myers-Briggs Type Indicator, 228

    work-related, 230–231

  in work teams, shaping, 262–263

    rewards used in, 263

    selection in, 262

    training individuals to be team players, 262

  See also Behavioral theories; Organizational behavior (OB)

Behavioral component That part of an attitude that refers to an intention to behave in a certain way toward someone or something, 224

Behaviorally anchored rating scales (BARS), 176E7-8, 177

Behavioral theories Leadership theories that identify behaviors that differentiated effective leaders from ineffective leaders, 301

  managerial grid and, 304

  Ohio State studies of, 302–303

  University of Iowa studies of, 301–302

  University of Michigan studies of, 303–304

Benchmarking The search for the best practices among competitors or noncompetitors that lead to their superior performance, 116, 352

Biases

  in decision-making process, 75–77

  in interviews, 171–172

Big Five Model Personality trait model that includes extraversion, agreeableness, conscientiousness, emotional stability, and openness to experience, 228–229

Blogs, 339, 340

Board representatives Employees who sit on a company's board of directors and represent the interest of employees, 166

Body language Gestures, facial configurations, and other body movements that convey meaning, 330–331

Boundaryless career When an individual takes personal responsibility for his or her own career, 193

Boundaryless organization An organization whose design is not defined by, or limited to, boundaries imposed by a predefined structure, 148, 146E6-10

Bounded rationality Making decisions that are rational within the limits of a manager's ability to process information, 79–80

Brainstorming An idea-generating process that encourages alternatives while withholding criticism, 86

Break-even analysis A technique for identifying the point at which total revenue is just sufficient to cover total costs, 97EQM-4, 96–97

Budgets in financial control, 357

Business description in full business plan, 394–395

Business plan A written document that summarizes a business opportunity and defines and articulates how the identified opportunity is to be seized and exploited, 394

  See also Full business plan

C

"Calm waters" metaphor A description of organizational change that likens that change to a large ship making a predictable trip across a calm sea and experiencing an occasional storm, 202, 203

Capabilities An organization's skills and abilities in doing the work activities needed in its business, 110

Career The sequence of work positions held by a person during his or her lifetime, 193

  development, then and now, 193–194

  successful, factors in, 194–196

C corporation, 395

Centralization The degree to which decision making takes place at upper levels of the organization, 140

Certainty A situation in which a decision maker can make accurate decisions because all outcomes are known, 83–84

Chain of command The line of authority extending from upper organizational levels to lower levels, which clarifies who reports to whom, 135, 136E6-3

  dual, 146

  line authority and, 136, 136E6-3

Change agents People who act as change catalysts and assume the responsibility for managing the change process, 202

Changing jobs, 196

Channel The medium a message travels along, 329

Charismatic leader An enthusiastic, self-confident leader whose personality and actions influence people to behave in certain ways, 312

Civil Rights Act, Title VII, 164E7-2

Classical conditioning, 238

Classroom lectures, 175E7-7

Code of ethics A formal document that states an organization's primary values and the ethical rules it expects managers and nonmanagerial employees to follow, 58

Process departmentalization Grouping activities on the basis of work or customer flow, 134–135

Process production Continuous flow of products being produced, 143

Product departmentalization Grouping activities by major product areas, 134

Production oriented leader A leader who emphasizes the technical or task aspects, 304

Product quality dimensions, 382E15-4

Profitability, 98EQM-5

Profitability ratios, 356E14-6, 357

Profit margin on revenues ratio, 99

Programmed decision A repetitive decision that can be handled using a routine approach, 81–82

policies in, 82

procedures in, 82

rules in, 82

vs. nonprogrammed decision, 82

Project A one-time-only set of activities with a definite beginning and ending point, 384

Project management The task of getting project activities done on time, within budget, and according to specifications, 384

Gantt chart in, 385–386E15-5–6

PERT network analysis in, 386–388, 387E15-7, 388E15-8–9

Project structure A structure in which employees continuously work on projects, 147, 147–148

Punishment, 239

Q

Quality, 382–384

achieving, 382–383

benchmarking used to promote, 116

dimensions of, 382E15-4

global, 383

goals, 383–384

as strategic weapon, 115–116

success stories in, 383

work teams and, 383

Quantitative approach The use of quantitative techniques to improve decision making, 24

Quantitative decision-making aids, 94–103

break-even analysis, 96–97, 97EQM-4

decision trees, 95–96, 96EQM-3

economic order quantity model, 101–103, 102EQM-8

linear programming, 99–100, 99–100EQM-6–7

payoff matrices, 94–95, 94–95EQM-1–2

queuing theory, 100–101

ratio analysis, 97–99, 98EQM-5

Queuing theory Also known as waiting line theory, it is a way of balancing the cost of having a waiting line versus the cost of maintaining the line. 100–101

R

Race The biological heritage (including physical characteristics, such as one's skin color and associated traits) that people use to identify themselves, 61

workforce diversity and, 61

Randomness bias, 76

Range of variation The acceptable parameters of variance between actual performance and the standard, 352, 352–353, 353E14-3–4

Ratio analysis, 97–99, 98EQM-5

Rational decision making Describes choices that are consistent and value-maximizing within specified constraints, 78

Readiness The extent to which people have the ability and willingness to accomplish a specific task, 307, 306–307

Real goals Those goals an organization actually pursues as shown by what the organization's members are doing, 117

Realistic job preview (RJP) A preview of a job that provides both positive and negative information about the job and the company, 172

Realistic personality, 232

Recruitment Locating, identifying, and attracting capable applicants, 159, 168

Reduced workweek as downsizing option, 169E7-4

Referent The persons, systems, or selves against which individuals compare themselves to assess equity, 283

Referent power, 139E6-6

Reinforcement processes, in social learning, 239

Reinforcement theory, 286, 290

Reliability The degree to which a selection device measures the same thing consistently, 170

Religion, workforce diversity and, 62

Renewal strategies A corporate strategy that addresses declining organizational performance, 113

Representation bias, 76

Resources An organization's assets that it uses to develop, manufacture, and deliver products to its customers, 110

Responsibility An obligation to perform assigned duties, 135

Retention processes, in social learning, 238

Retrenchment strategy, 113

Return on investment ratio, 99

Reward power, 139E6-6

Rewards programs, 289–291

economic and financial uncertainty and, 291

employee recognition programs and, 290

open-book management in, 289–290

pay-for-performance programs in, 290–291

RFID (radio-frequency identification) tags, 358

Rights view of ethics View that says ethical decisions are made in order to respect and protect individual liberties and privileges, 57

Ringisei Japanese consensus-forming group decisions, 88

Risk A situation in which a decision maker is able to estimate the likelihood of certain outcomes, 84, 196

Risk-taking, 231

Role Behavior patterns expected of someone who occupies a given position in a social unit, 252–253

of management, 9–10, 10E1-5

Rule An explicit statement that tells employees what can or cannot be done, 82

S

Safety needs, in hierarchy of needs theory, 275, 276E11-1

Satisfice Accepting solutions that are "good enough," 79

School placement in recruiting, 168E7-3

Scientific management The use of scientific methods to define the "one best way" for a job to be done, 7, 22

S corporation, 395

Selection process Screening job applicants to ensure that the most appropriate candidates are hired, 169

decision outcomes in, 169–170, 169E7-5

discrimination in, 170

realistic job preview used in, 172

reliability in, 170

tests and interviews used in, 170–172

validity in, 170

Selective perception Selectively perceiving or hearing a communication based on your own needs, motivations, experiences, or other personal characteristics, 236, 332, 332E13-2

Selective perception bias, 76

Self-actualization needs, in hierarchy of needs theory, 275, 276E11-1

Self-awareness, in emotional intelligence, 229

Self-efficacy An individual's belief that he or she is capable of performing a task, 280

Self-esteem (SE) An individual's degree of like or dislike for himself or herself, 230

Self-managed work team A type of work team that operates without a manager and is responsible for a complete work process or segment, 250E10-1, 258

Self-management, in emotional intelligence, 229

Self-monitoring A personality trait that measures the ability to adjust behavior to external situational factors, 230–231

Self-motivation, in emotional intelligence, 229

Self-serving bias The tendency for individuals to attribute their own successes to internal factors while putting the blame for failures on external factors, 235, 77

Selling, in situational leadership theory, 307

Sensing types, in MBTI, 228

Service quality dimensions, 382E15-4

Sexual harassment Any unwanted action or activity of a sexual nature that explicitly or implicitly affects an individual's employment, performance, or work environment, 183, 182–184

Sexual orientation, workforce diversity and, 62

Shaping behavior The process of guiding learning in graduated steps using reinforcement or lack of reinforcement, 239

Short-term plans Plans with a time frame of one year or less, 121

Simple structure An organizational design with low departmentalization, wide spans of control, authority centralized in a single person, and little formalization, 144–145, 144E6-9

Simulation exercises, 175E7-7

Single-use plan A one-time plan specifically designed to meet the needs of a unique situation, 121

Situational approach (or contingency approach) An approach to management that says that organizations, employees, and situations are different and require different ways of managing, 26

Situational leadership theory (SLT) A leadership contingency theory that focuses on followers' readiness, 306, 306–307

Six Sigma A quality standard that establishes a goal of no more than 3.4 defects per million units or procedures, 384

Skill-based pay A pay system that rewards employees for the job skills they demonstrate, 180

Skill variety, in job characteristics model, 281, 281E11-5

Slack time The time difference between the critical path and all other paths, 387–388

Small business An organization that is independently owned, operated, and financed; has fewer than 100 employees; doesn't necessarily engage in any new or innovative practices, and has relatively little impact on its industry, 13–14, 392

Social learning theory A theory of learning that says people can learn through observation and direct experience, 238–239